W9-BBL-467

# BUSINESS LAW AND THE REGULATORY ENVIRONMENT

## Concepts and Cases

# BUSINESS LAW AND THE REGULATORY ENVIRONMENT

## Concepts and Cases

## Lusk Series


**Michael B. Metzger,** J.D.
*Indiana University*

**Jane P. Mallor,** J.D.
*Indiana University*

**A. James Barnes,** J.D.
*Attorney at Law,*
*Washington, D.C.*

**Thomas Bowers,** J.D.
*Indiana University*

**Michael J. Phillips,** J.D., LL.M., S.J.D.
*Indiana University*



Sixth Edition 1986

Homewood, Illinois 60430

ISBN 0-256-03334-X

Library of Congress Catalog Card No. 85–80612

*Printed in the United States of America*

1 2 3 4 5 6 7 8 9 0 K 3 2 1 0 9 8 7 6

# Preface

When the first edition of this text appeared in 1935, Harold F. Lusk could not have foreseen either the far-reaching developments that would reshape almost every area of the law he described, or the tremendous success that his book would have in the marktplace. Yet Harold's approach, a painstaking attention to the details of the "black letter" law coupled with an emphasis on emerging trends that promised to transform existing legal rules, was admirably well-suited to the needs of business students in a dynamic legal environment.

When John D. Donnell, Charles M. Hewitt, and A. James Barnes assumed authorship of the text in the late 1960s, they continued to employ Harold's approach with notable success. One constant in the changing legal environment of business over the past five decades has been that the textbook bearing Harold Lusk's name has always been among the leading texts in the business law field. The book must surely rank as one of the all-time success stories in the history of business publishing.

This latest edition of the book combines the efforts of A. James Barnes with those of four new authors: Thomas Bowers, Jane Mallor, Michael Metzger, and Michael Phillips. John

Donnell and Charlie Hewitt, like Harold Lusk before them, have decided to "pass on the baton" and retire from the rigorous business of textbook writing. We, like John and Charlie, approached our task with some trepidation, mindful of the high standards set by our predecessors. Like them, however, we assumed the challenge with confidence in the viability of the approach pioneered by Harold Lusk and in our own ability to meet the challenge. All of the new authors are tenured professors in the Business Law Department at Indiana University. We have all developed an intimate familiarity with the book through years of using it as a teaching tool. In addition, all of us are actively engaged in researching many of the topics that we were called upon to discuss.

Current adopters of the book will immediately note that a majority of the chapters in the new edition have undergone major revision. Wherever possible, we have tried to make a complex subject more understandable to students by adopting a more relaxed, almost conversational writing style. We have included many new cases exemplifying the latest legal developments and containing fact situations sure to stimulate high student interest. These cases have been edited in a way that we hope will aid student understanding.

In many chapters, current adopters will also notice an increased emphasis on the social forces that shape legal rules. Wherever feasible, we have attempted to identify both the historical factors that contributed to the evolution of the legal rules under discussion and the social function performed by those rules. We have done this because we believe that a complete understanding of the law requires an understanding of the origins, as well as the content, of legal rules.

In addition to these changes in approach, this new edition has been reorganized in a variety of ways. The discussion of legal reasoning has been expanded and moved from Chapter 2 to Chapter 1 due to its obvious affinity with the opening chapter's expanded discussion of the nature of law. The chapters on agency law have been reorganized and reduced in number from three to two. The previously separate chapters on landlord-tenant and real property have been combined because of their common intellectual heritage and because many of the important legal trends relating to transactions for the sale of real property are having a similar impact on lease transactions. Finally, the material from the previously separate chapter on close corporations has been integrated into the other corporations chapters. Close corporations and publicly held corporations face many issues in common, and we believe that it is more efficient to confront those issues simultaneously. Also, we believe that an integrated treatment affords students a better understanding of both corporate forms.

Although it does not involve chapter consolidations, a similar integrative approach has been adopted in the contracts chapters of this edition. Rather than treating common law contract rules and their Uniform Commercial Code counterparts in separate sections of the chapters, we discuss these two converging bodies of law concurrently. In addition, we have incorporated many of the basic provisions of the *Restatement (Second) of Contracts* into the text because they exemplify the Code's strong impact on modern contract rules, and because, given the influential nature of the first *Restatement,* they may represent the future of contract law.

Readers also will find that many chapters have been substantially expanded to reflect the latest legal developments, or to facilitate the inclusion of essential new topics. For example, the chapter on crimes now includes a more expansive treatment of criminal procedure, corporate criminal liability, and the controversy surrounding the application of the RICO statute to corporate defendants. The chapter on employment law reflects a new emphasis on employment discrimination and the erosion of the employment "at will" doctrine. It also includes a topical discussion of current problem areas such as reverse discrimination, sexual harassment, and comparable worth. The contracts chapters now afford more expansive treatment to a variety of important topics, including promissory estoppel, unconscionability, liability for nondisclosure, and punitive damages as a remedy for breach of contract. The chapters on antitrust law now include a substantial discussion of the "Chicago School" challenge to traditional antitrust policy and its impact on recent antitrust enforcement. The corporations chapters also have been expanded to reflect the increasingly broad acceptance of the Revised Model Business Corporation Act. These examples are far from exhaustive.

In addition to expanding the substance and scope of a majority of the chapters carried over from the fifth edition, we have added two new chapters. A chapter on computer law dramatically highlights the legal dilemmas associated with this important technology and the ways in which the law is responding to these new challenges. Like the franchising chapter it replaces, the computer law chapter is an integrative effort, embracing the law of contract, product liability, intellectual property, privacy, and crimes. A new chapter on corporate social responsibility has also been incorporated into this revision. While prior editions included a treatment of corporate social responsibility issues scattered throughout the text, a practice that we have continued to follow in this revision, we saw the need for a specific chapter that would address the basic issues in the field in a more integrative fashion. In treating this controversial subject we have attempted to avoid the temptation to be judgmental. Instead, we have tried to delineate the basic issues and the major arguments of the parties on both sides of the debate, hoping to stimulate students to think independently about the subject after being properly informed of the complexity of the area and the trade-offs inherent in each of the contending policy positions.

This new edition also is accompanied by a variety of supplementary materials designed to enhance its effectiveness as a teaching tool. The teacher's manual includes suggestions for lecture preparation for each chapter and contains teaching hints, additional examples illustrating concepts introduced in the text and text cases, optional substantive material beyond that presented in the text, and suggestions for the discussion of text cases. A test manual containing multiple-choice, true-false, and essay questions is also available, and adopters are invited to use the Irwin Computerized Test Generator System. For students, a revised student workbook has been prepared by our colleague, Mary Jane Dundas, at Arizona State University.

As is usual with an effort of this magnitude, the final product reflects the contributions of a large number of people in addition to the named authors. Merritt Baker Fox of the Indiana University School of Law wrote the chapter on the international legal environment of business. Our other colleagues in the Business Law Department at Indiana University generously afforded us their counsel and guidance at various stages of the project. Our spouses tolerated the distraction, frequent absences, and irritability that inevitably accompany a project involving a year of night and weekend labor. We also had the assistance of able external reviewers, Mary Jane Dundas, Arizona State University; James E. Macdonald, Weber State College; Robert D. McNutt, California State University, Northridge; and Roscoe Shain, Austin Peay State University. These reviewers were drawn from the ranks of our colleagues in the business law field. In many cases we responded to their comments. In some cases, after due consideration, we elected not to respond. The responsibility for any mistakes or errors of judgment thus remains our own.

By its nature, a basic text of this sort presents its authors with a variety of often perplexing choices. Practical constraints place effective limits on the subjects that can be addressed and the detail in which these subjects can be presented. Virtually any chapter in this text could serve as the proper subject for a book in its own right. A comprehensive effort such as ours thus inevitably poses the risk of distortion through oversimplification. Reasonable persons can surely differ concerning the wisdom of many of the choices that we have made. We hope that knowledgeable readers will concur with our choices more often than not. As always, we solicit your comments and suggestions. Our goal is to make this text the best of its kind. With your help, we will be able to do so.

**Michael B. Metzger**
**Jane P. Mallor**
**A. James Barnes**
**Thomas Bowers**
**Michael J. Phillips**

# Contents

## PART I
## THE AMERICAN LEGAL SYSTEM

## PART VIII SALES



## PART IX COMMERCIAL PAPER

## APPENDIXES

# PART I

# THE AMERICAN LEGAL SYSTEM

# Chapter 1

# The Nature of Law

## INTRODUCTION

Today, people and businesses continually confront the legal system, and each reader of this text has encountered individual *laws.* But what is *law* in general? One way to answer this question is to list and describe the various types of rules that are regarded as law in the United States. We will call these rules **positive law.** Positive law can be defined as the rules that have been laid down (or posited) by some recognized political superior (a legislature, a court, and so forth). The first section of this chapter describes the various kinds of positive law.

However, this description gives us only a partial understanding of the nature of law. Thus, the next section of this chapter discusses the subject known as **jurisprudence** or legal philosophy. One concern of jurisprudence is to establish a general definition of law. Over time, different definitions of law have emerged, and these correspond to different "schools" of jurisprudence. The differences among these schools are not merely an academic matter. A person's position on many practical political and legal problems can be traced to his conscious or unconscious assumptions about the general nature of law.

The last section of the chapter explores the nature of law from a different angle. Even a person who rejects legal philosophy as impractical and merely learns the existing rules of positive law may be misled about their nature. People often think that legal rules are fairly definite, unchanging, and easy to apply, when in fact their meaning is frequently cloudy and subject to change. In order to suggest why this is so, the chapter concludes with a discussion of **legal reasoning:** the set of techniques that judges use in interpreting and applying legal rules.

## TYPES OF POSITIVE LAW

**Constitutions.** **Constitutions,** which exist at the state and federal levels, have two general functions. First, they establish the structure of government for the political unit they govern (a state or the federal government). This involves stating the branches and subdivisions of the government and the powers given and denied to each. The U.S. Constitution, for example, establishes a Congress and gives it power to legislate in certain areas, provides for a chief executive (the president), creates a Supreme Court and allows Congress to establish other federal courts, recognizes the states, and structures the relationship between the federal government and the states. Second, within their domain, constitutions forbid all units of government to take certain actions or pass certain laws. Most importantly, constitutions prohibit governmental action restricting certain individual rights. The Bill of Rights in the U.S. Constitution is an example, and state constitutions usually contain individual rights provisions as well.

**Statutes.** **Statutes** are laws created by Congress or a state legislature. They are stated in an authoritative form in statute books or "codes." As we will see later in this chapter, however, their interpretation and application are often difficult.

**Common Law.** The **common law** (also called "judge-made law" or "case law") is that law made and applied by judges as they decide cases not governed by statutes or other types of positive law. The common law originated in medieval England and has been continually evolving ever since. The English common law developed in the two or three centuries following the Norman conquest of England in 1066. Its name represents the Norman kings' desire to unite England under their rule. The common law developed from the decisions of judges in settling actual disputes. Over time, judges began to follow the decisions of other judges in similar cases. This practice became formalized in the doctrine of ***stare decisis*** (let the decision stand).

The common law was brought to America by the first English settlers, and its use was solidified during the colonial period.[1] After the American Revolution and the adoption of the U.S. Constitution, it continued to be used by American courts, and it is still applied in many cases today. The actual common law rules now in force, however, are often quite different from those applied by courts in the past. As you will see later in the chapter, the doctrine of *stare decisis* has enabled the common law to evolve to meet changing social conditions.

In theory, common law exists at the state level only. Many of the legal rules discussed in this text—for example, most of the contract law rules in Chapters 6–15—are common law rules. However, the states have codified (enacted into statute) many parts of the common law, particularly in the criminal law area.

---

[1] However, Louisiana adopted the *Code Napoléon,* which was based on Roman law. Its influence persists to this day in Louisiana.

Also, many states have passed statutes superseding judge-made law in certain situations. As you will see in Chapter 6, for example, the states have established special rules for contract cases involving the sale of goods by enacting Article 2 of the Uniform Commercial Code (UCC). These rules are usually uniform from state to state, and the tendencies toward codification and uniformity represented by the UCC typify many areas of 20th-century American law.

**The *Restatements.*** Despite the 20th-century movement toward codification, the common law continues to be important. The courts' frequent use of the ***Restatements*** illustrates this point. The *Restatements* are collections of common law (and sometimes statutory) rules promulgated by the American Law Institute, a body of distinguished legal scholars and practitioners. The *Restatements* cover many different areas of the law (for example, contracts, torts, and agency), and they usually present the rules followed by a majority of the states. The *Restatements* are not positive law, and they do not bind any court. However, state courts often find *Restatement* rules persuasive and make them binding within the state.

Because of their influence, the *Restatements* have attracted frequent—and conflicting—criticisms. Some critics have attacked the *Restatements* as misguided attempts to rigidly specify rules whose meaning and application inevitably change with circumstances. Other critics have contended that the *Restatements* often undermine settled common law rules by substituting rules based on their authors' personal preferences about the direction the law should take.

**Equity.** The body of positive law called **equity** has traditionally tried to do discretionary "rough justice" in situations where common law rules would produce unfair results. American equity law originated in medieval England. At that time, the existing common law rules were quite technical and rigid and the remedies available in common law courts were too few. This meant that some deserving plaintiffs could not obtain adequate relief in the common law courts. As a result, the chancellor, the king's most powerful executive officer, began to hear cases that the common law courts could not settle satisfactorily.

Eventually, separate equity courts emerged to handle the cases heard by the chancellor. These courts assumed control of a case only when there was no adequate remedy in a regular "law" court. In equity courts, procedures were more flexible than in the common law courts and rigid rules of law were de-emphasized in favor of generalized moral maxims. Equity courts also provided several unique remedies not available in the common law courts (which usually awarded only money damages or the recovery of property). Perhaps the most important of these *equitable remedies* is the **injunction,** a court order forbidding a party to do some act or commanding him to perform some act.

Like the common law, equity principles and practices were brought to the American colonies by the English settlers. They continued to be used after the Revolution and the adoption of the Constitution. Over time, however, the once-sharp line between law and equity has become somewhat blurred. Most states have abolished separate equity courts, now allowing one court to handle both "legal" and equitable claims. Also, equitable principles have tended to merge with common law rules, and some modern common law and statutory doctrines have equitable roots. An example is the doctrine of unconscionability discussed in Chapter 12. Finally, courts now may combine an award of money damages with an equitable remedy in certain cases.

**Administrative Regulations and Decisions.** During the 20th century, the **administrative agencies** established by Congress and the state legislatures have grown steadily in number and size. Today, their influence is felt throughout American life, and their power and importance cannot be overestimated. A major reason for the creation of administrative agencies was the myriad of social and economic problems created by the industrialization and continued economic expansion of the United States that began late in the 19th century. The creation of specialized agencies to deal with these problems was almost inevitable, because legislatures generally lacked the time and expertise to do so. The federal administrative agencies given detailed discussion in this text include the Securities and Exchange Commission (Chapter 26), the Federal Trade Commission (Chapter 46), and the Environmental Protection Agency (Chapter 48).

Where do administrative agencies get the power to make law? They can do so because of a **delegation** (or handing over) of power from the legislature. Agencies are normally created by statute. This legislation specifies the areas in which the agency may make law and the extent of its powers in each area. Often, the statutes delegating power to agencies are phrased in broad and general language. In such cases, the legislature basically points to a problem and gives the agency broad powers to deal with it. Also, legislative supervision of agency activities is often perfunctory. For these reasons, agencies are often relatively immune from popular control.

**Administrative regulations** (or administrative rules) are one form of law created by agencies. Like statutes, administrative regulations are stated in a precise form in one authoritative source. At the federal level, the sources are the *Federal Register* and the *Code of Federal Regulations* (C.F.R.). However, administrative regulations differ from statutes, because the body enacting them is an agency, not the legislature.

Some agencies have an internal court structure that enables them to hear cases arising under the statutes and regulations they enforce. The Federal Trade Commission procedures discussed in Chapter 46 are an example. Such **agency decisions** are another kind of positive law. As you will see in the next chapter, agency decisions may be appealed to regular state or federal courts. In practice, however, the agency's decision is often final.

**Treaties.** According to the U.S. Constitution, **treaties** made by the president with foreign governments and approved by two thirds of the U.S. Senate are "the supreme Law of the Land." As noted below, treaties can cause state (and occasionally federal) laws to become invalid.

**Ordinances.** State governments have subordinate units that exercise certain functions. Some of these units, such as school districts, have limited powers. Other units, such as counties, municipalities, and townships, exercise a number of governmental functions. The enactments of municipalities are called **ordinances;** zoning ordinances are an example. The enactments of other political subdivisions may also be referred to as ordinances.

**Executive Orders.** In theory, the president is a "chief executive" who effectuates the laws and secures their observance but has no lawmaking powers. The same is usually true of state governors and such local executives as the mayor of a municipality. However, these officers sometimes have the power to issue laws called **executive orders.** This power usually results from a legislative delegation, although some *presidential* executive orders may be justified on constitutional grounds.

The delegations of legislative power underlying executive orders are often imprecise and general. Thus, the executive's power to make law can be very broad. Chapter 47 provides an example of administrative action based on an executive order when it discusses the Labor Department regulations requiring affirmative action by federal contractors.

**Priority Rules.** Occasionally, different positive laws will conflict. Thus, rules for determining which law takes priority are necessary. The most important such rule is the principle of **federal supremacy,** which makes the U.S. Constitution, federal laws enacted pursuant to it, and treaties "the supreme Law of the Land." This means that federal law defeats conflicting state law. Also, a state constitution will defeat all other state laws inconsistent with it; the same is true for the U.S. Constitution and inconsistent federal laws. When a treaty conflicts with a federal statute, the measure that is latest in time will usually prevail. State statutes and any laws derived from them by delegation defeat inconsistent common law rules. Within either the state or the federal domain, finally, statutes take priority over other laws that depend on a delegation of power from the legislature for their validity.

**Classifications of Positive Law.** Cutting across the different types of positive law described above are three common classifications of positive law. These classifications involve distinction between: (1) civil law and criminal law, (2) substantive law and procedural law, and (3) public law and private law.

**Civil Law and Criminal Law.** **Criminal law** is the law applied when the government acts in a prosecutorial role by proceeding against someone for the commission of a crime. **Civil law** is the law applied when one party sues another because of the other's failure to meet some duty owed to the first party. Civil lawsuits usually involve private parties, but the government may be a party to a civil suit (as for instance where a city sues, or is sued by, a construction contractor).

Sometimes, the same behavior can violate both the civil law and the criminal law. For instance, a party whose careless driving causes the death of another may face both a criminal prosecution by the state and a civil suit for damages by the survivors of the deceased party. As this example may suggest, criminal penalties (e.g., imprisonment or fines) differ from civil remedies (e.g., money damages or equitable relief). Also, violations of the criminal law are often said to be wrongs against society as a whole, while violations of the civil law affect only specific injured parties. Most of the positive law rules discussed in this text are civil law rules. However, Chapter 3 deals specifically with the criminal law, and various criminal provisions are discussed in other chapters.

**Substantive Law and Procedural Law.** **Substantive law** sets out the rights and duties governing people as they act in society. **Procedural law** governs the behavior of governmental bodies (mainly courts) as they establish and enforce rules of substantive law. A statute making murder a crime, for example, is a rule of substantive law. But the rules describing the proper conduct of a criminal trial are procedural in nature. This text is mainly concerned with rules of substantive law. Chapters 2 and 3, however, examine some of the procedural rules governing civil and criminal cases respectively. Various procedural rules also appear in other chapters.

**Public Law and Private Law.** **Public law** concerns relations between the government and private individuals or groups. Examples include constitutional law and administrative law (the body of rules governing the behavior of administrative agencies). **Private law** establishes the rights and duties that exist among private parties of all sorts. The law of contract is one example. While private law is generally substantive law, not all substantive law is private. A rule of substantive criminal law like a burglary statute, for example, is ordinarily regarded as "public" because it establishes a duty that people owe to society (represented by the government), and not just to those individuals whose homes might be robbed. Procedural rules are probably best classed as public law, since they describe how courts and other governmental bodies must treat the private parties who come before them.

## JURISPRUDENCE

**Introduction.** Knowing the types of positive law is essential to understanding the American legal system and the business law topics discussed in this text. However, using the list just provided to define *law* is much like defining the word *automobile* by describing all the types of vehicles identified by that name. What is first needed is an abstract definition of law stating the important features common to all types of positive law. An obvious feature they all share is their issuance by a recognized political authority. But defining law in this way ignores certain realities. What public officials charged with enforcing the law *do*, for instance, may differ from what the positive law *says*. Also, the positive law influences, and is influenced by, the social order of which it is a part. Can any general definition of law ignore these realities? Finally, defining law by stating the features common to all types of positive law fails to confront a practical problem faced by citizens and public officials: whether there is an obligation to enforce or obey positive laws that are (or are thought to be) unjust.

The following discussion of the schools of jurisprudence reflects these considerations. Each school attempts to formulate a general definition of law. For some schools, practical consequences flow from the definition adopted. Thus, competing jurisprudential assumptions underlie many legal and political disputes. Whether the participants in these disputes know it or not, their positions often reflect such assumptions.

**Legal Positivism.** As you have just seen, one feature common to all types of positive law is their enactment by a recognized political authority—a legislature, a court, an administrative agency, and so forth. This common feature underlies the definition of law adopted by the school of jurisprudence called **legal positivism.**[2] Some legal positivists simply define law as the command of a recognized political authority. Others adopt a more general definition, stating that law is the command of a society's ultimate political authority (or sovereign). On this view, the different kinds of positive law are valid because the sovereign has delegated some of its ultimate lawmaking power to various subordinate political authorities (e.g., courts), thus giving them the power to make law. Locating the sovereign is easy in an absolute monarchy or a one-man dictatorship, but doing so in systems of divided powers, such as that of the United States, is a major problem for legal positivists.

Because legal positivists see law as a *command,* they usually treat law and morality as distinct. In their view, the sovereign does not tell citizens, "Obey because it's right," but rather says, "Obey or else." To positivists, therefore, legal validity and moral validity are different questions, and one's conclusion

[2] "Analytical positivism," "analytical jurisprudence," and the "will theory" are names for other jurisprudential approaches closely resembling legal positivism.

that a positive law is immoral does not affect its status as a law. Occasionally, this view is expressed in the slogan "Law is law, just or not."

Some positivists regard this separation of law and morality as a means for achieving order and definiteness in the statement of legal rules. Their goal is to express the law as an organized series of precise commands, all of which trace back to the sovereign. Other, more extreme positivists take the separation of law and morality further, urging that all duly enacted positive laws should be enforced and obeyed, whether right or wrong. This view has been criticized, since it seems to mean that *any* positive law (no matter how unjust) should be enforced and obeyed so long as some delegate of the sovereign (no matter how wicked) enacted it. In addition, this extreme positivist position may be self-contradictory. If law and morality are completely distinct, why is there a duty to enforce and obey positive law? Some positivists, however, argue that positive law should always be enforced and obeyed because doing so promotes the values of peace and order. Since this kind of legal positivism introduces a moral justification for positive law, it resembles the natural law school, which follows.

**Natural Law.** The basic idea behind most systems of **natural law** is that there is some higher law or set of absolute moral rules that binds all human beings in all times and places. This higher law may be discovered by divine revelation or, more often, by reason. Natural law thinkers view human law as flowing from or striving to approximate this higher law (which thus is a criterion for evaluating positive law). But just as a saw that becomes too dull no longer deserves to be called a saw, positive laws can depart so greatly from the ends set by the higher law that they no longer qualify as law. Such positive laws, natural law thinkers say, are not law and should not be enforced or obeyed. This view is sometimes expressed in the slogan "An unjust law is not law." St. Thomas Aquinas summed up the basic natural law position when he stated that "every human law has just so much of the nature of law, as it is derived from the law of nature. But if in any point it deflects from the law of nature, it is no longer law but a perversion of law."[3]

Natural law differs from legal positivism in some very fundamental ways. Natural law thinkers do not agree with those legal positivists who say that duly enacted positive laws should always be obeyed, whether just or not. In addition, natural law thinkers reject the legal positivists' separation of law and morality. To most legal positivists, law is simply a sovereign command and has no moral dimension. But the natural law definition of law has a moral component. Aquinas, for example, defined law as "an ordinance of reason for the common good, made by him who has care of the community, and promulgated." To natural law thinkers, in other words, positive law must possess some measure of moral goodness to be true law, or at least must not be bad.

Observing that different people, societies, and legal systems can have sharply conflicting moral views, critics often argue that natural law's conception of a universal, binding moral law is just an illusion. Natural law thinkers, these critics sometimes say, evade the problem of moral disagreement by phrasing the higher law in broad, empty platitudes that are consistent with almost any system of positive law. Natural law thinkers respond that no system of natural law could ever specify every detail of every society's positive law. Instead, they say, the higher law is a series of fundamental moral values that are widely held but that inevitably find different applica-

[3] This quotation and the one below are from Aquinas's *Summa Theologica*.

tion in different times and places. Critics of natural law also note that different natural law thinkers have espoused different values. In fact, there is an important division among natural law proponents: the conflict between the natural law ideas that characterized Western thought from the time of the ancient Greeks until about the 17th century and the natural law ideas that became dominant thereafter. In general, the earlier variety of natural law emphasized *personal virtue, duty,* and *the good of the community.* The later variety has stressed *individual rights,* especially rights of property and free economic activity.

Whatever their validity, the various criticisms of natural law are widely accepted today. In the 20th century, relatively few British or American philosophers have been clear and open natural law advocates. However, attitudes and positions resembling natural law have been fairly common. One example might be the tendency to make human rights (however defined) a criterion for judging all nations of the world. This suggests that, while it is easy to make skeptical attacks on natural law, it is difficult to ignore the moral concerns that natural law stresses. And the great virtue of natural law thought is its willingness to address perennial moral questions that are an inescapable part of human life.

**American Legal Realism.** Natural law thinkers regard most positive laws as sufficiently good to qualify as valid law, and legal positivists regard all duly enacted positive laws as valid. Our third school of jurisprudence, called **American legal realism,** differs from legal positivism and natural law by deemphasizing the rules of positive law. Recognizing that it is *people* who interpret and enforce positive law, American legal realists regard the positive "law in the books" as less important than the "law in action," the behavior of those who enforce and interpret that law. Thus, American legal realism defines law as what public decision makers (mainly judges) decide about matters before the legal system.

To bolster their distinction between the law in the books and the law in action, the realists point to the divergence between the two. For example, juries sometimes pay little attention to the rules of positive law that are supposed to guide their decisions and prosecutors often have discretion whether or not to enforce criminal statutes. Legal realists have been especially concerned with the behavior of judges, pointing out countless cases where the background, biases, or values of the judge (and not "the law") influenced particular decisions. Extreme legal realists, it has been jokingly said, believe that justice is what the judge ate for breakfast. Since it is the actions of such decision makers (and not the rules in the books) that really affect people's lives, the realists say, it is this behavior that is most important and that deserves to be called law.

American legal realism was mainly limited to elite American law schools of the 1920s, 1930s, and 1940s. It then died as a formal movement, but its influence has persisted. It is doubtful whether the legal realists ever developed a common position on the relation between law and morality or the duty to obey positive law. But legal realists were quick to give advice to judges, whom they regarded as important agents of legal and social change. The modern judge, they sometimes said, should be an enlightened "social engineer" who weighs all relevant social values and examines the latest social science discoveries before arriving at a decision and who makes the existing rules of positive law only one factor in that decision.[4] The realists seemed to feel that since judges inevitably base their decisions on personal values, they should do this intelligently. In order to facili-

[4] This is also true of some of the sociological approaches discussed below.

tate this kind of decision making, the realists sometimes favored statutes with fuzzy, discretionary standards that allow judges to decide individual cases according to their unique facts.[5]

**Sociological Jurisprudence.** The term **sociological jurisprudence** is a general label uniting a group of diverse jurisprudential approaches whose common aim is to examine law within its social context. There is no distinctive "sociological" definition of law. If one were attempted, it might go as follows: "Law is a process of social ordering reflecting society's dominant interests and values." By viewing law as a process of social ordering, sociological jurisprudence emphasizes the similarities between positive law and nonlegal ordering forces such as customs, common values, family ties, and the controls that organizations exert over their members. By stressing the importance of dominant social interests and values in shaping positive law, it criticizes the positivist view that law is merely the will of some sovereign.

Because sociological jurisprudence emphasizes social values, you might think that it resembles natural law. In fact, however, its treatment of morality differs greatly from the natural law approach. Most sociological thinkers are concerned only with the *fact* that certain moral values influence the law, and not with the goodness or badness of those values. A typical exponent of sociological jurisprudence might say: "Society X emphasizes values A, B, and C, and society X's legal system reflects these values. In my professional capacity, I cannot say whether this is right or wrong. Personally, though, I think that society X's laws are wonderful [or awful]." However, some sociological thinkers seem to go farther, arguing that the values which *in fact* shape the law also *should* shape it. This resembles the familiar view that "the law should keep up with the times." Some may hold this view even when society's values change for the worse. As Justice Oliver Wendell Holmes once wrote: "The first requirement of a sound body of law is, that it should correspond with the actual feelings and demands of the community, *whether right or wrong.*"[6]

To suggest the diversity of approaches to the study of law and society, a few well-known examples of "sociological" legal thinking are discussed below. Some of them illustrate the general points made above.

**The Historical School.** The historical approach, which is often treated as a separate school of jurisprudence, is identified with the 19th-century German legal philosopher Friedrich Karl von Savigny. Savigny's ideas were part of a reaction against earlier natural law thinking which claimed that reason could establish universal moral principles and that positive law should be consciously formulated to reflect those principles. Instead, Savigny saw law as an unplanned, almost unconscious, reflection of the collective spirit (*Volksgeist*) of a particular people. He felt that since each group or nation has its own distinct spirit, there is no universally valid law. To Savigny, legal change could only be explained historically: as a slow response to changing social conditions and values. And to those who share his views, any attempt to impose a law contrary to a people's collective values is likely to fail.

**The Living Law.** The writings of Eugen Ehrlich, an early 20th-century Austrian legal philosopher, followed Savigny in stressing the relationship between positive law and a na-

[5] An example is Article 2 of the Uniform Commercial Code. See Chapter 6.

[6] O.W. Holmes, *The Common Law* (1881) (italics added).

tion's social life. But Ehrlich went farther in de-emphasizing positive law. He distinguished between "state law" (positive law) and the "living law" (informal social controls). In doing so, he emphasized that positive law is merely one part of a spectrum of social controls. Thus, Ehrlich blurred the line between positive law and other forms of social ordering such as customs, family ties, and business practices.

**Pound and the Jurisprudence of Interests.** The term sociological jurisprudence is sometimes used to refer to the writings of Roscoe Pound, a very influential 20th-century American legal philosopher. Pound sought to identify the social interests that press upon government and the legal system, and thus shape positive law. He developed a detailed catalog of interests protected by the legal system, a catalog that changed with changes in American society during his life. His listing was intended to aid legislators and other legal decision makers in balancing those interests by making them explicit.

**Functionalism and the Limits of Law.** Functionalism expresses the idea that things are, or can be explained by, what they *do*. According to this view, law can best be described in terms of the social functions it performs: what it *does*.[7] Like Pound's interests, these functions are numerous. Today, for instance, positive law performs such traditional functions as keeping the peace, aiding orderly change, promoting compromise solutions, facilitating private planning, providing checks against arbitrary power, and influencing or enforcing standards of behavior. Also, American law has usually tried to advance economic growth. Throughout the 20th century, it has increasingly promoted social justice in its many forms, given greater protection to many personal rights, and attempted to protect the environment.

Clearly, many of these functions can conflict with one another. An example is the clash between economic growth and environmental protection. Rarely does the law achieve a particular end without sacrificing other ends to some degree. This means that lawmaking inevitably involves choices among competing values (or, in Pound's terms, the balancing of interests). For example, the recent increased emphasis on economic growth could occur at the expense of environmental protection.

Since almost every function that the law performs has associated costs, there are limits on its usefulness as a device for achieving social goals. Promoting one desirable end often involves sacrificing others. Another obstacle to the law's ability to advance chosen ends concerns the many inherent limits on its effectiveness as a control device. Since positive law usually reflects dominant social values, for example, it is doubtful whether laws conflicting with those values will ever be enacted, or, if enacted, will ever be enforced and obeyed. The fact that the law mainly controls individual and group behavior through penalties also puts limits on its effectiveness. One purpose behind the criminal law, for instance, is deterrence of undesirable behavior. However, this assumes rationality on the part of those to be influenced by the criminal law, and people sometimes behave irrationally. Finally, some matters are beyond the capacity of the law to handle satisfactorily, or are best left to the individuals involved. For example, there are relatively few legal rules telling people how to behave in intimate personal relationships.

**The Schools Compared—An Example.** As we have suggested, a person's conscious

[7] Note that the various social functions listed in this paragraph can be described as *values*. Thus, functionalism might resemble natural law.

or unconscious assumptions regarding jurisprudential questions often determine her response to practical political and legal problems. To illustrate the point, consider the many state statutes and local ordinances that forbid conducting business on Sunday. Today, these "Sunday closing laws" are often not enforced or obeyed. Despite this, *should* they be enforced and obeyed?

An extreme *legal positivist* would have little difficulty in answering this question. Law is one thing, he would say, and morality is another. Since Sunday closing laws are valid positive laws enacted by recognized political authorities, they should be enforced and obeyed—just or not.

The *natural law* position on these laws presents more difficulties. Natural law thinkers agree that positive laws which are sufficiently unjust or immoral should *not* be enforced and obeyed. Are Sunday closing laws unjust? Many natural law thinkers would probably say that the higher law is not (and should not be) sufficiently detailed to answer this question. Since Sunday closing laws are not plainly unjust, they might add, these laws should be enforced and obeyed. However, an extreme laissez-faire natural law thinker devoted to economic freedom might say that such laws *are* unjust because they restrict a businessperson's ability to conduct her business as she sees fit. Thus, he would say, Sunday closing laws should not be enforced and obeyed. A natural law exponent who is a Christian religious traditionalist, however, might take a contrary position. Such a person could conceivably regard Sunday closing laws as just and moral because they respect the Sabbath.

It is unclear whether *American legal realism* would take a definite position on the desirability of enforcing and obeying Sunday closing laws. But all American legal realists would be quick to observe that because Sunday closing laws are often not enforced and obeyed, they illustrate the gap between the "law in the books" and the "law in action." Since law is what decision makers such as police and prosecutors actually *do,* they might add, it is doubtful whether Sunday closing laws are genuine law in states and localities that do not enforce them.

Most adherents to *sociological jurisprudence* would probably refuse to comment on the duty to enforce and obey Sunday closing laws. But they could make innumerable observations about the social influences affecting these laws. For example, they could note the social factors that originally led to the enactment of Sunday closing laws (e.g., religious sentiment and the political power of organized religious groups). They could also note that the current failure to enforce Sunday closing laws reflects the growing secularization of American life, the prevalence of consumerist values, and the political influence of business. They could further suggest that a balancing of interests between these forces and the remaining religious influences explains why Sunday closing laws are still on the books despite their lack of enforcement. As suggested earlier, however, some sociological thinkers seem to feel that laws which are out of touch with current community needs, values, and desires are law in name only. Since most Americans now evidently want to be able to shop on Sunday, these thinkers could argue that Sunday closing laws should not be enforced and obeyed. This would be true regardless of whether such laws are intrinsically good or bad.

**The Approach of This Text.** The main objective of this text is to describe the most important legal rules affecting business. In the following chapters, jurisprudential matters will not be discussed. Yet jurisprudential assumptions underlie almost any examination of the law. For the most part, this text takes a legal positivist approach. That is, it expresses the legal rules affecting business as a series of commands issued by recognized political authorities, and does not label these rules right or wrong. However, this positivist approach sometimes fails to fully convey the importance and dynamic nature of the law. Thus, certain parts of this text adopt a functional outlook, viewing certain legal institutions and legal rules as attempts to advance social goals. Other parts of the text examine positive law rules from a more general sociological perspective, stressing the influence of social conditions, social values, and economic factors on the past and present development of the law.

## LEGAL REASONING

**Introduction.** Most business law texts (this one included) state positive law rules in what lawyers call "black letter" form, using precise sentences which say that certain legal consequences will occur if certain events happen. This way of expressing positive law can mislead you about the nature of law. It suggests a definiteness, certainty, permanence, and predictability that the law often lacks. To help dispel this impression, we will discuss the two most important kinds of legal reasoning: **case law reasoning** and **statutory interpretation.** However, it is first necessary to examine legal reasoning in general.

Legal reasoning is basically deductive, or syllogistic. That is, the legal rule is the major premise, the facts are the minor premise, and the result is the product of combining the two. Suppose a state statute says that those operating an automobile between 55 and 70 miles per hour must pay a $50 fine (the rule or major premise) and that Jim Smith is driving his car at 65 miles per hour (the facts or minor premise). If Jim is arrested, and if the necessary facts can be proven, he will be required to pay the $50 fine. Note that it is the relevant legal rule which makes certain facts significant; in this example, numerous things about Jim and his car were ignored. Legal reasoning is frequently more difficult than this example would suggest. The rules themselves may be inherently imprecise; ambiguities may appear as the rules are applied to new fact situations; and sometimes the rules may change as they are employed in new cases.

**Case Law Reasoning.** In cases governed by the common law, courts find the appropriate legal rules in prior cases or **precedents.** Such cases state the relevant facts and the applicable rules, and then combine the two to produce the result. The standard for choosing and applying prior cases to decide present cases is the doctrine of ***stare decisis,*** which states that like cases should be decided alike. That is, the present case should be decided in the same way as were prior cases presenting "like" facts and legal issues. If a court decides that the alleged precedent is not really "like" the present case and should not control the decision in that case, it will *distinguish* the prior case.

The doctrine of *stare decisis* presents a problem. Since every present case differs from the precedents in *some* respect, it is always possible to distinguish those precedents. For example, one *could* distinguish a prior case because the eyes of one of the parties to the present case are different in color from those of the parties to the past case. Of course, such distinctions are usually ridiculous, because the differences they identify are insignificant in moral or social policy terms. In other words, a good distinction of a prior case should involve a widely accepted policy reason for treating the present case differently from its predecessor. Since moral ideas, social policy, and their public acceptance are often subject to disagreement, and since each of these factors changes over time, judges will sometimes differ on the wisdom of distinguishing a prior case. This is a significant source of uncertainty in the common law. But it also gives the common law the flexibility to adapt to changing social conditions.

**An Example.** The above generalizations are illustrated by a famous series of New York defective goods[8] cases decided in the 19th and early 20th centuries. In these cases, the **plaintiff** (the party suing) argued that the **defendant** (the party being sued) was negligent[9] in the manufacture or preparation of some product, thus causing injury to the plaintiff, who had purchased the product. In the mid-19th century, such suits were often unsuccessful due to the general rule that a defendant manufacturer was not liable for its negligence unless there was **privity of contract** between the manufacturer and the plaintiff. Privity of contract is the existence of a direct contractual relationship between two parties. Thus, the effect of the "no liability outside privity" rule was to prevent the injured plaintiff from recovering against the manufacturer when the manufacturer sold a defective product to a "middleman" who resold it to the plaintiff. Over time, however, the New York courts began to allow injured plaintiffs who lacked privity of contract to recover damages from the manufacturer. These courts were recognizing *exceptions* to the general rule: that is, they were *distinguishing* prior cases announcing the rule and creating new rules in the process.

The first exception occurred in an 1852 case, *Thomas v. Winchester*,[10] which involved the sale of poisonous belladonna that had been mislabeled extract of dandelion. The main reason the court gave for allowing the plaintiff to recover and for distinguishing the prior cases following the no-liability-outside-privity rule was that "the death or great bodily harm of some person was the natural and almost inevitable consequence of the sale of belladonna by means of the false label." Eighteen years later, however, New York's highest court declined to follow the *Thomas v. Winchester* exception when it held for the manufacturer of a circular saw whose original defects caused it to fly apart and kill someone more than five years after it had been built.[11] The court might have distinguished *Thomas v. Winchester* by arguing that the saw was simply not as dangerous as a mislabeled bottle of belladonna. Instead, it distinguished *Thomas v. Winchester* on a different basis, arguing that *Thomas* was "unlike" the present case because it involved a product (poison) *intended by its nature to do harm.* Since a circular saw is not this kind of product, it concluded, the general no-liability-outside-privity rule, and not the *Thomas v. Winchester* exception, should control.

The court deciding the 1870 case was not troubled by an unfortunate fact: that the court deciding *Thomas v. Winchester* almost certainly did not want to limit its exception to products intended by their nature to do harm to others. Instead, the exception was aimed at *dangerous* products, no matter what their nature. The 1870 court's treatment of *Thomas v. Winchester* illustrates a technique that courts commonly use when confronted by a precedent they dislike: *limiting a prior case to its facts.* This means that they follow the prior case only in situations presenting very similar facts and that they reject the prior case in situations it was probably intended to cover.

After the 1870 decision, New York law on the no-liability-outside-privity rule went about as follows: (1) an injured plaintiff could

[8] The present law on this subject (the law of product liability) is discussed in Chapter 32.

[9] Negligence is discussed in Chapter 5.

[10] 6 N.Y. 397 (1852).

[11] *Loop v. Litchfield,* 42 N.Y. 351 (1870).

recover outside privity if the product causing the injury was one intended by its nature to do harm (e.g., poison, knives, and guns); but (2) the plaintiff could *not* recover in other cases where he lacked privity with the defendant. The second rule seemed to apply no matter how dangerous the product was. In 1873, for instance, the manufacturer of an exploding steam boiler escaped liability when sued by a party with whom he did not deal directly.[12]

This state of affairs, however, did not endure for very long.[13] In the late 19th and early 20th centuries, the New York courts allowed injured plaintiffs who lacked privity with the defendant to recover against the builder of a defective 90-foot scaffold, the manufacturer of an exploding coffee urn, and the filler of an exploding aerated water bottle.[14] These courts generally ignored the 1870s cases declaring that only manufacturers of products intended to harm others could be liable outside privity of contract. A major reason for ignoring these cases was that the rule they announced made little sense as a matter of public policy. If the point of the *Thomas v. Winchester* exception was to allow recovery against manufacturers of dangerous products, why limit it to products intended to harm others? As the above examples indicate, many products *not* intended to harm others can pose great risks if defectively manufactured.

These decisions set the stage for Justice Benjamin Cardozo's famous 1916 opinion in *MacPherson v. Buick Motor Co.*,[15] which allowed a person who had bought an automobile from an independent dealer to recover from the manufacturer for injuries caused when the car's wheel collapsed. Cardozo's opinion attempted to make a coherent whole of the conflicting New York precedents on the privity question. Cardozo read *Thomas v. Winchester* as declaring that an injured plaintiff could recover from a manufacturer with whom he lacked privity if the injury was a reasonably foreseeable consequence of the product's defective manufacture. He then tried to unite all of the other cases around this theme. Cardozo explained the 1870 case involving the circular saw as one where the risk of harm was insufficient to make the injury reasonably foreseeable, because the saw had functioned normally for five years. He also argued that the rule limiting recovery outside privity to products intended to do harm was no longer binding because subsequent cases had not followed it. After *MacPherson*, New York and the other states gradually abolished the no-liability-outside-privity rule. The rule's current status is discussed in Chapter 32.[16]

**Limits on Courts.** From the preceding example, you might think that "anything goes" in common law decision making. However, there are many factors that discourage judges from making radical changes in the common law (or other types of positive law). The first involves the mental makeup of most lawyers. Due to their training and the habits of the profession, lawyers believe in the doctrine of *stare decisis* and are wary of interpreting it too freely. Also, many courts require written opinions, which expose judges to academic and professional criticism. Another set of factors limiting judges concerns the structure and composition of courts.[17] Lower court judges who are too innovative

[12] *Losee v. Clute,* 51 N.Y. 494 (1873).

[13] Sociological jurisprudence helps explain why this change occurred. See the introduction to Chapter 32.

[14] The cases are: *Devlin v. Smith,* 89 N.Y. 470 (1882); *Torgeson v. Schultz,* 192 N.Y. 156, 84 N.E. 956 (1908); and *Statler v. Ray Mfg. Co.,* 195 N.Y. 478, 88 N.E. 1063 (1909).

[15] 217 N.Y. 382, 111 N.E. 1050 (1916).

[16] This illustrates another reason for the common law's ability to change over time. Although they exercise the power infrequently, courts may *overrule* their prior decisions.

[17] On the various types of courts, see Chapter 2.

may have their decisions reversed by higher courts. Also, disagreements among higher court judges tend to cancel each other out, or to be moderated in the search for compromise, because higher courts are typically composed of several judges. Finally, political factors inhibit judges. Some judges are elected, and even judges with lifetime tenure can sometimes be removed.

**Statutory Interpretation.** Because statutes are written in one authoritative form, their interpretation might seem less troublesome than case law reasoning. However, this is not the case. One explanation for the difficulties that courts face in interpreting statutes is the natural ambiguity of language. This is especially true where statutory words that appear to be clear are applied to situations that the legislature did not foresee. Also, legislators may deliberately use ambiguous language. This often occurs when the legislature is unwilling or unable to deal with all the situations that the statute was enacted to regulate. In such instances, the legislature will consciously employ vague language and have the courts fill in the details on a case-by-case basis. Other reasons for deliberate ambiguity include the need for legislative compromise and the desire of individual legislators to avoid taking controversial positions.

These problems, as well as the courts' occasional desire to rewrite statutes through "interpretation," are reflected in the statutory interpretation techniques listed below. Judges tend to use (or not use) the techniques as they see fit. To help illustrate these techniques, we will use a hypothetical air pollution statute requiring emission controls for "automobiles, trucks, buses, and other motorized passenger or cargo vehicles."

**Legislative Intent.** The polestar of statutory interpretation, it is often said, is the *intent* of the legislature. **Legislative intent** is a (sometimes fictional) legislative conclusion about the meaning of specific statutory language. One obvious source of legislative intent is the common and accepted meaning of the statute's words. For instance, there is no difficulty in concluding that the language quoted above includes a turbocharged 1983 Volvo. When the words of the statute have a clear, common, accepted meaning, courts sometimes employ the *plain meaning rule.* This rule states that in such cases the court should simply apply the statute according to the plain, accepted meaning of its words, and not concern itself with anything else.

Today, however, some courts refuse to follow the statute's plain meaning when the statute's **legislative history** provides evidence of a contrary legislative intent. Courts also resort to legislative history when the statutory language is ambiguous. A statute's legislative history includes the following sources: the reports of investigative committees or law revision commissions that led to the legislation, the hearings of the legislative committee(s) originally considering the legislation, any reports issued by such a committee after it approved the legislation, legislative debates, the report of a conference committee reconciling two houses' conflicting versions of the law, amendments or defeated amendments to the legislation, and other bills not passed by the legislature but proposing similar legislation. Suppose that it is unclear whether the "other motorized passenger or cargo vehicles" language in the hypothetical pollution statute applies to mopeds. In this case, courts would scan these sources for specific references to mopeds or other indications of what the legislature thought about including mopeds.

Often, however, the legislative history will provide no information (or conflicting information) about the meaning of statutory language. Also, some sources are more authoritative than others. The worth of debates, for instance, depends on which legislator (e.g., the sponsor of the bill) is being quoted. Some sources are useful only in particular situations; prior unpassed bills and amendments or defeated amendments are examples. Suppose, for example, that the original version of the pollution statute specifically included mopeds but that this reference was removed by amendment, or that six similar unpassed bills included mopeds, but the version that was eventually passed did not.

**Legislative Purpose.** **Legislative purpose** is often confused with legislative intent, and sometimes the two are difficult to distinguish. Legislative purpose refers to the overall aim, end, or object of the legislation, and not to a legislative conclusion about the meaning of statutory words. Courts making a "purpose" inquiry ask whether a particular interpretation of a statute is consistent with the statute's overall aims. Battery-powered automobiles, for instance, should come within the plain meaning of the pollution statute. But, since the purpose of such legislation is presumably to reduce air pollution from internal combustion engines, it can be argued that battery-powered vehicles should not be covered by the statute. Courts seeking to discover the legislative purpose usually examine the same legislative history sources that are used to find legislative intent.

**General Public Purpose.** Sometimes, courts construe statutory language in the light of various **general public purposes** that they identify. These purposes are *not* the purposes underlying the statute in question; rather, they are widely accepted general notions of public policy. In one recent case,[18] the U.S. Supreme Court used the general public policy against racial discrimination in education as one argument for denying tax-exempt status to a private university that discriminated on the basis of race.

[18] *Bob Jones University v. United States,* 461 U.S. 574 (1983).

**Prior Interpretations.** Sometimes, courts follow prior judicial (and even administrative) interpretations of statutory language regardless of the statute's plain meaning, intent, or purpose. One argument for following **prior interpretations** is that the legislature impliedly approved or enacted the prior interpretation by not amending the statute to eliminate it. Another is fear of the instability and uncertainty that might result if each successive court considering a statute were allowed to reconsider ambiguous legislative history. Whether courts will follow a prior interpretation depends on such factors as the number of past courts adopting the interpretation, the authoritativeness of those courts, and the number of years that the interpretation has been followed.

**Maxims.** Maxims are general rules of thumb employed in statutory interpretation. There are many maxims, quite a few of them stated in Latin. Two common maxims of statutory construction are *expressio unius est exclusio alterius* (the expression of one thing is the exclusion of another) and the *ejusdem generis* rule (when general words follow words of a specific, limited meaning, the general language should be limited to things of the same class as those specifically stated). Suppose that the pollution statute listed 32 types of gas-powered vehicles and ended with the words "and other motorized passenger or cargo vehicles." Here, the *ejusdem generis* maxim would probably dictate that battery-powered vehicles not be included.

## SUMMARY

There are at least two ways to answer the question "What is law?" One way is to list and describe all the types of rules typically referred to as "law" and enforced by sanctions in a particular society. In the United States, these rules of positive law are: constitutions, statutes, common law, equity, administrative regulations, administrative decisions, ordinances, treaties, and executive orders. Another way to answer this question is to attempt an abstract definition of law. The various efforts to provide such a definition are called schools of jurisprudence. The most important schools are *legal positivism* (which defines law as sovereign command and excludes morality from its definition), *natural law* (which regards morality as an essential component of law and often claims that bad positive laws are not law and should not be obeyed), *American legal realism* (which defines law as what public decision makers do), and *sociological jurisprudence* (a term uniting various approaches that view law in a broad social context).

This text mainly takes a legal positivist approach. It attempts to state the most important legal rules affecting business by describing them as a series of black-letter commands. However, this approach sometimes gives the law a false appearance of certainty, precision, stability, and predictability. Examining the reasoning processes that courts use in deciding common law cases and in interpreting statutes helps dispel this misleading impression. The doctrine of *stare decisis* used in deciding common law cases seems to compel the courts to follow the rules announced in similar prior cases. Because it allows judges to "distinguish" these cases and effectively create new rules of law to govern the present case, however, *stare decisis* actually permits flexibility and change.

Since they are rigidly stated in an authoritative fashion, statutes appear to have a certainty, precision, and stability lacking in judge-made law. For various reasons, however, legislation is often ambiguous as stated or applied. The different techniques of statutory interpretation enable courts to deal with such situations. Courts generally seek to determine the legislature's *intent* (its conclusion regarding the meaning of statutory language), and do so by examining the language itself and the statute's legislative history. In some cases, clear language or established intent will not be followed when these conflict with the statute's *purpose* or with some *general public purpose.* In other cases, the courts may follow *prior interpretations* giving statutory language a particular meaning.

## PROBLEM CASES

**1.** Suppose that Congress passes a federal statute that conflicts with a state constitutional provision. The state argues that the constitutional provision should prevail over the statute because constitutions are a higher, more authoritative kind of law than statutes. Is this argument correct? Why or why not?

**2.** Suppose that someone objects to the president's promulgation of an executive order by claiming that the U.S. Constitution gives the president only the power to *execute* the laws, not the power to make them. What concept explains the president's power to make law through executive orders? Explain its meaning.

**3.** Suppose that the president concludes a comprehensive trade treaty with a foreign nation. One portion of the treaty states that existing U.S. tariff laws will not apply to products made in that nation. What further action is required before the treaty will become valid law? Assuming that this action takes place, which law will control if there is a clash between the treaty and federal tariff statutes passed *before* the treaty became effective?

**4.** Nation X is a dictatorship in which one ruler has the ultimate lawmaking power. The ruler issues a statute declaring that certain religious minorities are to be exterminated. An international convocation of jurisprudential scholars meets to discuss the question "Is nation X's statute truly law?" What would be the typical natural law answer to this question? What would be the typical legal positivist response? Assume that all of those present at the convocation think that nation X's statute is morally wrong.

**5.** Nation Y has enacted positive laws forbidding all "abnormal" sexual relations between consenting adults. However, the police of nation Y rarely enforce these laws, and even when they do, prosecutors never bring charges against violators. What observation would American legal realists make about this situation? In order to determine what a believer in natural law would think about these laws, what additional thing would you have to know?

**6.** In 1885, Congress passed a statute stating that "it shall be unlawful for any . . . corporation . . . to . . . in any way assist or encourage the importation or migration of any alien or aliens, any foreigner or foreigners, into the United States . . . under contract or agreement . . . to perform labor or service of any kind in the United States." The legislative history of this statute revealed that it was passed because American businesses were contracting with foreigners to prepay their passage to the United States, in return for the immigrant's agreement to work for low wages for a fixed time period. This practice reduced the bargaining power and wages of American laborers. The Holy Trinity Church, a corporation, contracted with E. Walpole Warren, a U.S. alien residing in England, for Warren to travel to the United States and become Holy Trinity's rector and pastor. Pursuant to the contract, Warren did so. What technique of statutory interpretation would you use in arguing that this contract is covered by the statute? What technique would you use if you were arguing the contrary position?

**7.** Suppose that someone reads the discussion of case law reasoning and statutory interpretation in this chapter and remarks as follows: "It sure looks like anything goes when judges get hold of a case. With all the different techniques they have at their disposal, they can come up with almost any result they want and make it look 'legal.' I think this is a good thing, because it lets judges ignore rigid, outdated black-letter rules and make decisions that reflect modern ideas about enlightened social policy." This isn't an open-and-shut question, but which of the four schools of jurisprudence discussed in the chapter would be *least* likely to agree with these remarks? Which school would be *most* likely to agree with them?

# Chapter 2

# Court Structure, Jurisdiction, and Civil Procedure

## INTRODUCTION

The different types of positive law discussed in Chapter 1 are not self-executing, and they cannot perform their various functions unless they are enforced. In order to have an effective legal system, therefore, a society must do more than merely enact a body of rules to regulate private behavior. It must also establish procedures for determining whether these rules have been violated and what action should be taken once a violation has been proven. In the United States, the courts play a major role in the performance of these functions.

**The Functions Performed by Courts.** The courts' familiar role as an enforcer is discussed throughout this chapter. As enforcers, courts determine violations of the laws and order remedies or penalties for these violations. Less widely recognized, however, is the significant role that courts now play as lawmakers. The only type of positive law directly formulated by courts is the common law created by state courts. But the courts also have a voice in determining the content of other forms of positive law, for the power to decide that the laws have been violated includes the ability to determine what they mean. The courts' interpretation of statutes has already been discussed. Courts also determine the meaning of constitutional provisions when they decide cases involving a claim that government action is unconstitutional. Their power to declare the actions of the legislative and executive branches of government unconstitutional is called the power of **judicial review.** Although courts often defer to administrative agencies, they can determine the meaning of administrative regulations and decisions and can also declare them invalid on various grounds (including unconstitutionality). In appropriate situations, courts may also establish the meaning of the other kinds of positive law.

**Limits on Courts.** Despite the courts' law-making role, however, their power is still limited. Chapter 1 discussed some of the factors (for example, the mentality of lawyers and the political vulnerability of courts) that deter courts from taking a freewheeling approach when they formulate or interpret legal rules. In addition to these limitations on the courts' law-making function, the occasions when they can exercise this function are also limited. For one thing, courts cannot formulate new common law rules, interpret statutes, or exercise the power of judicial review whenever they desire. Ordinarily, they can do so only when a lawsuit raising the appropriate issues is initiated by some party. Further, the damages, penalties, or other relief that courts order when the law has been violated usually affect only the parties to the case (or, occasionally, similarly situated parties).

In addition, a number of general legal doctrines with constitutional dimensions limit the power of the courts. Although the matter is too complex for full discussion here, these doctrines might be summed up by the following proposition: courts only decide genuine, existing "cases or controversies" between real parties with tangible adverse interests in the resolution of the lawsuit. Thus, courts are usually reluctant to issue so-called *advisory opinions* on abstract legal questions that are not part of a real dispute. Similarly, the courts generally refuse to decide *feigned controversies,* which often involve collusive suits by parties seeking the resolution of some legal issue but lacking any tangible controversy regarding that issue. In much the same vein is the courts' frequent refusal to rule on disputes that are insufficiently *ripe* because future events may change their nature or eliminate them entirely, or disputes that are *moot* because events occurring after the beginning of the suit have made any decision beside the point. In one case,[1] for example, the U.S. Supreme Court refused to decide a white applicant's challenge to law school admissions policies favoring racial minorities, since by the time it heard the case the former applicant was in his last year of law school and the case was moot.

Expressing many of the same ideas, finally, is the doctrine of *standing to sue.* This doctrine, which is formulated in various ways and appears in a variety of legal contexts,[2] generally involves the idea that the party suing must have some fairly direct, tangible, and substantial stake in the outcome of the suit. Despite all these doctrines, however, state and federal statutes give the courts power to make a binding legal ruling called a *declaratory judgment* in certain cases where a full-fledged controversy might not exist. One example is a situation where there is a real legal dispute dividing the parties, but one or both fear that taking action to create a fully developed controversy might expose them to legal liability.

**The Objectives of This Chapter.** Because of the major role courts play in both the formulation and enforcement of the law, a stu-

[1] *DeFunis v. Odegaard,* 416 U.S. 312 (1974).

[2] See for example Chapter 44's discussion of standing in the antitrust context.

dent's understanding of business law is incomplete without some knowledge of the various kinds of courts, the cases each is empowered to decide, and the procedures under which they function. The United States has 52 separate court systems, one for each state and the District of Columbia, plus a federal court system. This chapter begins by describing the various kinds of state and federal courts. Included in this discussion is the topic of state and federal court **jurisdiction:** the power of a court to hear a case and to issue a decision binding on the parties. Then, the chapter examines the rules of procedure controlling courts that decide civil cases—lawsuits involving private parties (including, on occasion, the government).[3] Finally, since courts are not the only institutions with power to make legal determinations or decide disputes, the chapter concludes by discussing some other means of performing these functions.

## STATE COURTS AND THEIR JURISDICTION

**Inferior Courts.** Minor criminal matters and civil controversies involving small amounts of money are frequently decided in "inferior courts" or "courts of inferior jurisdiction." Such courts, which handle a large volume of cases, are sometimes called justice of the peace courts in rural areas and municipal courts in cities. Some cities also have a small claims court that handles civil matters involving a limited amount of money. In these courts, the procedures are often informal, the judicial officer may not be a lawyer, and the parties may argue their own cases. Also, inferior courts are usually not courts of record; that is, they ordinarily do not keep a transcript of the testimony and proceedings. For this reason, appeals from their decisions require a new trial (a trial *de novo*) in a court of record such as a trial court.

**Trial Courts.** Inferior courts perform the basic tasks involved in the resolution of any legal controversy: finding the relevant facts, identifying the appropriate rule(s) of law, and combining the facts and the law to reach a decision. State trial courts perform the same basic functions, but differ from inferior courts in at least three ways. First, they are not governed by the limits on civil damages awarded or criminal penalties imposed that apply to inferior courts. Thus, cases involving significant dollar amounts or major criminal penalties generally begin at the trial court level. Second, trial courts keep detailed records of their proceedings. Third, the trial court judge is almost always a lawyer. The trial court's fact-finding function may be handled by the judge or by a jury. Determination of the applicable law is always the judge's responsibility.

There is usually one trial court for each county. It may be called a "circuit," "superior," "district," "county," or "common pleas" court. Trial courts often have civil and criminal divisions. They may also contain divisions or special courts set up to hear particular matters—for example, domestic relations courts, probate courts, and juvenile courts.

**State Appeals Courts.** In general, state appeals (or appellate) courts only resolve legal questions and do not have a fact-finding function. While they can correct legal errors made by the trial judge, they usually must accept the trial court's findings of fact. These courts may also hear appeals from state administrative agency decisions. Some states have only one appeals court (usually called the "supreme court"), while others also have an intermediate appellate court (often called the "court of appeals") which sits between the

[3] On the distinctions between civil law and criminal law, and between procedural law and substantive law, see Chapter 1.

**An Illustrative State Court System**

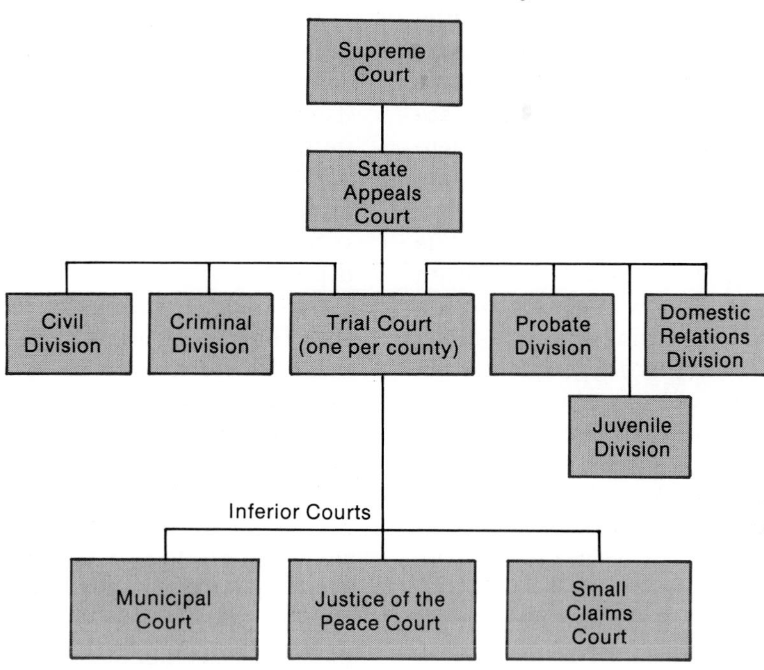


trial court and the supreme court. In states with two appellate courts, the court of appeals usually hears the appeal before the supreme court does, although appeals from a trial court to the supreme court are sometimes possible. Some state supreme court decisions may be appealed to the U.S. Supreme Court.

**State Court Jurisdiction.** The party suing in a civil case (the **plaintiff**) cannot bring suit in any court he chooses. The chosen court must have **jurisdiction** over the case: the power to hear a case and to issue a decision binding on the parties. For a state's courts to have jurisdiction in a civil case,[4] they must have *both* subject-matter jurisdiction *and* power over the parties or their property.

**Subject-Matter Jurisdiction. Subject-matter jurisdiction** involves the following question: Does the court have the power to decide the *type* of controversy involved in the case? Criminal courts, for example, cannot hear civil matters, and a suit for injuries caused by defective products cannot be brought in a domestic relations court. Also, a $500,000 suit for breach of contract cannot be pursued in a small claims court.

**Power over Person or Property.** Even if a court has subject-matter jurisdiction in a civil case, it cannot decide the case if it lacks legal power over the **defendant** (the party being sued) or over the property at issue in

[4] State *criminal* jurisdiction exists when the defendant has allegedly committed acts defined as criminal by state law and has done so within the state.

the case. There are two main types of jurisdiction that will satisfy this requirement; *either* will suffice. These are **in personam jurisdiction** and **in rem jurisdiction.** In personam jurisdiction is based on the residence, location, or activities of the defendant. A state court has in personam jurisdiction over defendants who are citizens or residents of the state (even if situated out-of-state), those who are within the state's borders when the suit is begun by serving process against them (even if nonresidents), or those who consent to the suit (for instance, by entering the state to defend against it).[5] Sometimes, in personam jurisdiction over out-of-state defendants is based on *implied consent.* Under nonresident motorist statutes, for example, driving on a state's highways generally subjects the nonresident motorist to the state's in personam jurisdiction if an accident occurs within the state and he is sued by a resident plaintiff.

When jurisdiction over an out-of-state defendant cannot be established in any of the ways just described, it may be based on the "long arm" statutes enacted by many states. These statutes subject out-of-state defendants to the state's in personam jurisdiction in specified situations, which vary among the states. Conduct that may subject nonresident individuals and businesses to long-arm jurisdiction includes doing business within the state, contracting to supply goods or services within the state, and committing a tort (a civil wrong) within the state.

In rem jurisdiction is based on the fact that property is located within the state. It gives state courts the power to determine rights to that property even if the persons whose rights are affected are outside the state's in personam jurisdiction. For example, a state court's decision regarding title to land within the state is said to "bind the world."[6]

[5] In some states, however, out-of-state defendants may make a *special appearance* to challenge the court's jurisdiction without consenting to that jurisdiction.

**Related Requirements.** Even if a state court has full jurisdiction over the defendant, it will not have the power to decide a case unless additional requirements are met. The state's exercise of jurisdiction must not violate the due process requirements set by the U.S. Constitution. Here, the most important aspect of due process is the requirement that the defendant receive adequate *notice* of the suit. The states attempt to satisfy this requirement by specifying the appropriate type of **service of process** for a particular case. In general, there are three types of service: (1) *actual* (involving hand delivery of the summons and the complaint), (2) *substituted* (embracing numerous means of notification other than hand delivery; for example, registered mail), and (3) *constructive* (by publication; for example, in newspapers). The means used to notify the defendant must comply both with state law and with federal due process requirements.

In addition, the plaintiff must file suit in a geographically convenient court within the state. This question of **venue** is regulated by state statute. Such a statute, for instance, might tell the plaintiff the county in which suit must be brought.

## FEDERAL COURTS AND THEIR JURISDICTION

**District Courts.** In the federal system, lawsuits usually begin in the federal district

[6] Another form of jurisdiction, *quasi–in rem jurisdiction,* is also based on the location of property within the state. Cases based on this kind of jurisdiction, unlike those based on in rem jurisdiction, do not necessarily determine rights in the property itself. Instead, the property is regarded as an extension of the out-of-state defendant, which enables the court to decide legal claims unrelated to the property.

courts, which are basically federal trial courts. Like state trial courts, the federal district courts have both fact-finding (by judge or jury) and law-finding (by the judge) functions. Each state has at least one district court, and each district court has at least one judge.

**District Court Jurisdiction.** There are many bases of federal district court civil jurisdiction.[7] The two most important are **diversity jurisdiction** and **federal question jurisdiction.** Diversity jurisdiction exists when: (1) the suit is between citizens of different states (or between citizens of a state and citizens or governments of foreign nations), and (2) the amount in controversy exceeds $10,000. Under diversity jurisdiction, a corporation is deemed to be a citizen of both the state where it has been incorporated and the state where it has its principal place of business. Federal question jurisdiction exists when the case arises under the Constitution, laws, or treaties of the United States. Generally, the "arises under" requirement is met when a right created by federal law is a basic part of the plaintiff's case. There is no "amount in controversy" requirement for federal question jurisdiction. Venue and service of process requirements also exist at the federal level; they are dealt with by statute and by various federal court rules.

**Concurrent Jurisdiction and Removal.** The federal district courts have exclusive jurisdiction over some matters: for example, patent and copyright cases. Often, however, they have *concurrent jurisdiction* with state courts; here, both state and federal courts have jurisdiction over the case. For example, a plaintiff may be able to assert state court in personam jurisdiction over an out-of-state defendant or may sue in a federal district court under that court's diversity jurisdiction. Also, a state court may decide a case involving a federal question if it has jurisdiction over that case. If concurrent jurisdiction is present and the plaintiff opts for a state court, the defendant (and only the defendant) may be able to *remove* the case to a federal district court. The case, of course, must be one over which the district court would have had jurisdiction if the plaintiff had sued there.

[7] Federal *criminal* jurisdiction is based on the alleged commission of acts defined as criminal by federal law.

**Specialized Courts.** The federal court system also includes certain specialized federal courts, including the Claims Court (which, concurrently with the district courts, hears claims against the United States), the Court of International Trade (which is concerned with tariff matters and related subjects), the Bankruptcy Courts (which operate as adjuncts of the district courts), and the Tax Court (which handles taxpayer petitions following IRS deficiency determinations). Usually, the decisions of these courts can be appealed to the federal courts of appeals.

**Courts of Appeals.** Like state intermediate appellate courts, the U.S. Courts of Appeals generally do not have a fact-finding function and only review the legal conclusions reached by lower federal courts. There are 13 federal courts of appeals: 11 organized territorially into "circuits" covering several states each, one for the District of Columbia, and the new Court of Appeals for the Federal Circuit. The courts of appeals use panels of three judges to hear most cases, but some matters may be heard *en banc* (by all the judges of the circuit).

Except for the Court of Appeals for the Federal Circuit, the main function of the U.S. Courts of Appeals is to hear appeals from the decisions of the federal district courts. Appeals from a district court are ordinarily taken to the court of appeals for the region in which the district court is located. (Since the Seventh Circuit comprises the states of Illinois, Indiana, and Wisconsin, for example, appeals from a district court in Indiana go to the Seventh Circuit Court of Appeals in Chicago.) The courts of appeals also hear appeals from many administrative agency decisions. The Court of Appeals for the Federal Circuit hears a wide variety of specialized appeals, including some patent, copyright, and trademark matters; Claims Court decisions; and decisions by the Court of International Trade.

**The U.S. Supreme Court.** The U.S. Supreme Court has original *and* exclusive jurisdiction over all controversies involving two or more states. It has original (but not exclusive) jurisdiction over cases involving foreign ambassadors and like parties, controversies between the United States and a state, and cases where a state proceeds against citizens of another nation. When the Supreme Court exercises its original jurisdiction, it acts as a trial court.

Cases involving the Supreme Court's original jurisdiction are relatively rare. Therefore, its main function is that of an appellate court. When acting as an appellate court, the Supreme Court has no fact-finding function and limits itself to questions of law. The main appellate function of the Supreme Court is to hear appeals from the federal courts of appeals and the state supreme courts. Appeals from these courts fall into two categories: the *appeal* jurisdiction (which is mandatory) and the *certiorari* jurisdiction (which is discretionary). Since most appeals to the Supreme Court involve its certiorari jurisdiction and relatively few of these are heard, the Court decides only a small percentage of the appeals directed to it.

Cases coming to the Supreme Court from the federal courts of appeals are within its appeal jurisdiction when the court of appeals has held a state statute invalid because it is inconsistent with federal law; other cases

A Simplified Model of the Federal and State Court Systems

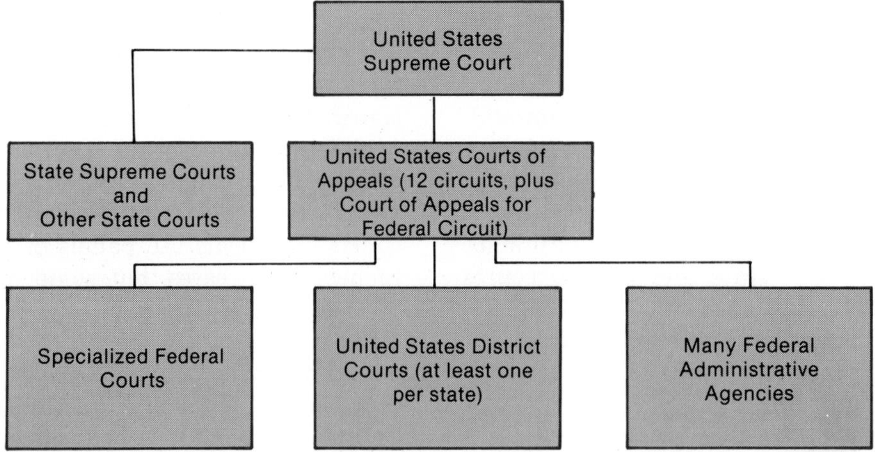

coming from the courts of appeals are within the Supreme Court's certiorari jurisdiction. Also, a court of appeals may certify a question of law to the Supreme Court when it desires instructions on the question. In such situations, the Supreme Court may give the requested instructions or decide the entire case. Appeals from the state supreme courts are within the U.S. Supreme Court's appeal jurisdiction when: (1) the state court has declared a federal statute or treaty invalid, or (2) a state statute is alleged to violate federal law and the state court finds the statute valid. Appeals from state supreme courts are within the U.S. Supreme Court's certiorari jurisdiction in a wide range of other cases presenting questions of federal law. The U.S. Supreme Court generally will not hear appeals from the state supreme courts if the case involves only questions of state law.

Sometimes, the U.S. Supreme Court will hear appeals directly from the federal district courts, thus bypassing the courts of appeals. This is allowed after the granting or denial of an injunction in a case required to be heard by a three-judge district court. (Various federal statutes specify when three-judge district courts are to be used; certain voting rights cases are one example.) Also, the Supreme Court may directly review decisions of *any* federal court holding a federal statute unconstitutional in a civil case to which the United States is a party.

## CIVIL PROCEDURE

**Introduction.** Procedural law is the body of legal rules governing the conduct of a case. These rules differ with each type of case involved. For example, the procedures used in a criminal proceeding differ from those governing civil suits, and courts that handle specialized matters may have their own procedural rules.[8] This discussion is concerned with *civil procedure:* the collection of rules governing the conduct of a trial court case between private parties. Much of this law is complex and technical, and it varies according to the jurisdiction[9] in question. Thus, the following presentation is only a generalized summary of the most widely accepted rules governing cases in state trial courts and the federal district courts. Knowledge of these basic procedural principles is important for two reasons. First, it is useful if you (or your employer) become involved in a civil controversy. In particular, it may help you to effectively cooperate with your attorney. Second, knowledge of these principles will help you to understand the cases that appear in subsequent chapters of this text.

**The Adversary System.** Civil procedure will be discussed by describing the most important steps in the typical civil case. In many of these steps, the *adversary system* is at work. That is, the parties (through their attorneys) are often presenting contrary positions of fact or law before a theoretically impartial judge and (if one is used) a jury. In a civil case, the lawyer for each party presents her client's version of the facts, tries to convince the judge or jury that this version is true, and attempts to undermine conflicting allegations by the other party.[10] Also, each attorney seeks to persuade the judge that her interpretation of the law is correct.

The adversary system reflects the familiar American idea that truth is best discovered through the presentation of competing ideas.

---

[8] Also, administrative agency decisions follow their own procedural rules. These are briefly discussed later in the chapter.

[9] In the discussion that follows, the term *jurisdiction* will be employed to refer to one of the 50 states or the federal government.

[10] Generally, the plaintiff must prove each element of his legal claim by a *preponderance of the evidence* in a civil case.

Those favoring the adversary system believe that allowing the parties to make competing arguments of fact and law gives the judge and jury the best chance of making accurate determinations because it enables both the presentation and the criticism of all relevant arguments. Critics of the adversary system contend that, rather than promoting the disinterested search for truth, it encourages the parties to employ incomplete, distorted, and even false arguments if such arguments will help them win the case. Defenders of the adversary system reply that it should "weed out" such arguments because they will be attacked by the other party and because an impartial judge is present. This weeding-out process, however, may not work if one or both parties lack competent counsel. Sometimes, for example, the adversary system's competition of ideas is unequal because one party has superior resources and thus can obtain better representation.

**The Summons.** The issuing and service of the **summons** is ordinarily the first step in a civil lawsuit.[11] The summons notifies the defendant that he is being sued. It usually describes the general nature of the suit, names the plaintiff, and states the time within which the defendant must enter an *appearance* in court. The appearance is ordinarily made by the defendant's attorney. As described earlier, the standards for proper service of the summons are set by statutes, court rules, and constitutional due process requirements.

**The Pleadings.** The term *pleadings* refers to the papers that the parties file with the court when they first state their cases. These include the **complaint,** the **answer,** and (in some jurisdictions) the **reply.** The complaint must fully state the plaintiff's claim in separate, numbered paragraphs. It must contain sufficient facts to show that the plaintiff is entitled to some legal relief and to give the defendant reasonable notice of the nature of the plaintiff's claim. The complaint must also state the remedy requested by the plaintiff (for example, money damages or an injunction).

Within a designated time after the complaint has been filed, the defendant must file an answer or else face a default judgment in favor of the plaintiff. As illustrated, the answer responds to the plaintiff's complaint paragraph by paragraph. Typically, the answer will admit or deny the allegations of each paragraph; depending on the jurisdiction, more precise responses may also be possible. The answer may also state an **affirmative defense** to the claim asserted in the complaint. An affirmative defense is a rule of law enabling the defendant to win the case even if all the allegations in the plaintiff's complaint are true and, by themselves, would entitle the plaintiff to recover. For example, suppose that the plaintiff bases her suit on a contract that she alleges the defendant has breached. The defendant's answer may admit or deny the existence of the contract or the assertion that the defendant breached it. In addition, the answer may present facts which, if proven, would show that the plaintiff's fraud induced the defendant to enter the contract.[12] In certain circumstances, the answer may also contain a **counterclaim.** A counterclaim is a new claim by the defendant arising from the matters stated in the complaint. Unlike an affirmative defense, it is not merely an attack on the plaintiff's claim, but the defendant's attempt to obtain legal relief. In addition to using fraud as an affirmative defense to the plaintiff's contract claim, for

---

[11] The summons should not be confused with the *subpoena,* which is an order, backed by judicial authority, compelling the production of a witness or of some tangible evidence at trial.

[12] On fraud in contract cases, see Chapter 9.

## Complaint

UNITED STATES DISTRICT COURT
SOUTHERN DISTRICT OF INDIANA
INDIANAPOLIS DIVISION

| | | |
|---|---|---|
| JOHN SMITH | ) | |
| | ) | |
| Plaintiff | ) | |
| | ) | |
| v. | ) | CIVIL ACTION NO. IP 79–53–C |
| | ) | |
| WORLD PRESS, INC. | ) | |
| and HERBERT MILLER | ) | |
| | ) | |
| Defendants | ) | |

PLAINTIFF'S COMPLAINT

Plaintiff, for his complaint, states:

1. Plaintiff is a citizen of the State of Indiana. Defendant World Press, Inc., is a Delaware corporation incorporated under the laws of the State of Delaware having its principal place of business in New York, N.Y. Defendant Herbert Miller is the author of the book *40 Seconds and Death* and is a citizen of the State of New York. The matter in controversy exceeds, exclusive of interests and costs, Ten Thousand Dollars ($10,000.00). Jurisdiction is based upon diversity of citizenship.
2. Defendant World Press, Inc., owns, operates, and publishes books under the name of World Press.
3. During 1979, defendant World Press, Inc. published without plaintiff's prior knowledge or consent, and expressly against plaintiff's permission, in excess of one million copies of the book *40 Seconds and Death,* authored by defendant Herbert Miller, which contained within Chapter Four (4) a section entitled "Weekend Tryst." This book unnecessarily exposed to the public the private affairs of the plaintiff, John Smith. A copy of said chapter is attached hereto as Exhibit One (1).
4. Said chapter disclosed private facts that would be offensive to a reasonable person and were not of legitimate public interest or concern. Defendant World Press, Inc. and defendant Herbert Miller knew that the plaintiff did not want the matters contained in the chapter to be exposed to the general public and published said chapter over the expressed warnings of the plaintiff.
5. Defendant Herbert Miller was personally told by the plaintiff that he did not want to be quoted by defendant Herbert Miller nor did plaintiff want any reference to plaintiff's family or relatives to appear in any publication. The matters published were

culled from a private conversation and amount to an unwarranted intrusion into the plaintiff's private life.

6. Defendant Herbert Miller misled the plaintiff to his detriment by publishing matters of a personal nature without securing the plaintiff's consent. The article exposed private matters concerning plaintiff's marital difficulties and his intimate relationships with family members.
7. The identity of the plaintiff was altered in the book, but the name used in the publication made the plaintiff's true identity readily apparent to neighbors, friends, relatives, business associates, and other members of the community who read the book.
8. As a direct and proximate result of the publication of said book the plaintiff has suffered great mental anguish and humiliation. Relatives of the plaintiff who had been purposely kept unaware of the marital difficulties existent between plaintiff and his wife were notified of same upon reading the book. The plaintiff has become the subject of public curiosity and gossip in his community, and his business affairs have been adversely affected. The plaintiff is a reasonable person of ordinary sensibilities who has been justifiably aggrieved by virtue of having his private life exposed by this publication in a manner constituting an actionable invasion of privacy.
9. Defendant World Press, Inc. and defendant Herbert Miller maliciously intended to injure and aggrieve the plaintiff by thrusting on him unwarranted and undesirable publicity and notoriety, knowing that the plaintiff did not wish the matters contained in the chapter to be published. The plaintiff seeks punitive damages of Five Hundred Thousand Dollars ($500,000.00).

WHEREFORE, plaintiff prays for judgment against the defendants World Press, Inc. and Herbert Miller as follows:

1. General damages of One Million Dollars ($1,000,000.00);
2. Special damages as may hereafter be ascertained;
3. Punitive damages of Five Hundred Thousand Dollars ($500,000.00);
4. Costs of this action;
5. Compensation for reasonable attorney's fees;
6. Such other and further relief as the Court may deem proper in the premises.

QUIK & BONO

By *John P. Quik*
Attorneys for Plaintiff,
John Smith

## Answer

UNITED STATES DISTRICT COURT
SOUTHERN DISTRICT OF INDIANA
INDIANAPOLIS DIVISION

| | | |
|---|---|---|
| JOHN SMITH | ) | |
| | ) | |
| Plaintiff | ) | |
| | ) | |
| v. | ) | CIVIL ACTION NO. IP 79–53–C |
| | ) | |
| WORLD PRESS, INC. | ) | |
| and HERBERT MILLER | ) | |
| | ) | |
| Defendants | ) | |

### DEFENDANTS' ANSWER

Defendants World Press, Inc. and Herbert Miller make the following answer to Complaint of plaintiff John Smith.

### First Defense

1. They admit the allegations of paragraph 1, except they deny that Herbert Miller is a citizen of New York. He is a citizen of Maine.
2. They admit that World Press, Inc. publishes books under the name World Press. They deny all other allegations of paragraph 2.
3. They admit that during 1979 World Press, Inc. published a book entitled *40 Seconds and Death* authored by Herbert Miller and that the book contained in its Chapter 4 a section entitled "Weekend Tryst." They admit that Exhibit One (attached to plaintiff's Complaint) is a copy of that section of the book. They deny all other allegations of paragraph 3.

4, 5, 6. They deny the allegations of paragraphs 4, 5, and 6.

7. They admit that plaintiff's real name was not used in the book. They are without knowledge or information sufficient to form a belief as to the truth of the remaining allegations of paragraph 7.

8, 9. They deny the allegations of paragraphs 8 and 9.

### Second Defense

Plaintiff John Smith consented to the publication of the information complained of.

Third Defense

The information published by defendants relates to an event and topic of general and public interest. Defendants' publication of the information complained of was privileged by the First and Fourteenth Amendments to the United States Constitution and by Article I, Section 9 of the Indiana Constitution.

Fourth Defense

The information published by defendants is true or substantially true in all relevant respects.

WHEREFORE, defendants World Press, Inc. and Herbert Miller pray that plaintiff John Smith take nothing by his complaint, for their costs, and for all other proper relief.

Roger P. Rogers
Roger P. Rogers
Attorney for Defendants
World Press, Inc. and Herbert Miller

example, the defendant might counterclaim for damages based on that fraud.

In some jurisdictions, the plaintiff is allowed or required to respond to an affirmative defense or a counterclaim by making a **reply.** The reply is the plaintiff's point-by-point "answer" to the new matters raised in the affirmative defense or counterclaim. Many jurisdictions, however, do not allow a reply to an affirmative defense; instead, the defendant's new allegations are automatically denied. Usually, though, a plaintiff who wishes to contest a counterclaim must reply to it.

Traditionally, the main function of the pleadings has been to define and limit the questions to be decided at later stages of the case. Only those issues raised in the pleadings have been considered part of the case; points omitted from the pleadings have been excluded from further consideration; and few, if any, amendments to the pleadings have been permitted. Also, the parties have usually been bound to allegations admitted in the pleadings, and only those allegations that have not been admitted have been regarded as in dispute between the parties. In addition, there have been many technical pleading rules whose violation could cause a party to lose a case before a decision on the merits. Many jurisdictions retain some of these rules. Over time, however, the main purpose behind pleading rules has shifted from defining and limiting the questions to be resolved in the case to affording the parties notice of each other's claims. Accompanying this shift have been a greater tendency to decide cases on their merits and a more relaxed attitude toward technical defects in the pleadings. Amendments to the pleadings, for example, are far more available today than they were in the past. Also, courts sometimes grant such amendments to allow issues not raised in the pleadings to be considered at trial.

**Motion to Dismiss.** Sometimes, it is evident from the pleadings that the plaintiff has no case. In such situations, it is wasteful for the case to proceed further and it is useful to have a procedural device for disposing of the case on the basis of the pleadings. This device has various names, but it is often called the **motion to dismiss.**

The motion to dismiss may be used for various purposes (for example, attacking the court's jurisdiction). The most important type of motion to dismiss, however, is the motion to dismiss for failure to state a claim upon which relief can be granted, sometimes called the **demurrer.** This motion basically says "So what?" to the factual allegations in the complaint. It asserts that the plaintiff cannot recover even if all of these allegations are true, because there is no rule of law entitling him to win on these facts. Suppose that Potter sues Davis on the theory that Davis's bad breath is a form of "olfactory pollution" entitling Potter to recover damages. Potter's complaint describes Davis's breath and the distress it causes Potter. Even if all of Potter's factual allegations are true, Davis's motion to dismiss will almost certainly be successful. Thus, Davis will win the case, for there is no rule of law allowing a civil recovery for bad breath. If the defendant's motion to dismiss fails, however, the case proceeds to the steps described below.

**Discovery.** In civil cases whose resolution depends on questions of fact, the parties often lack the information needed to prove their cases when the suit begins. To assist the parties in preparing their arguments and to narrow and clarify the issues to be resolved at trial, all jurisdictions permit extensive **discovery** of relevant information by the parties. The usual forms of discovery are: **depositions** (oral examinations of a party or a party's witness by the other party's attorney), **interrogatories** (written questions directed to a party, answered in writing, and signed under oath), **requests for documents and other evidence** (including examinations of the other party's files or records), **physical and mental examinations** (which are important in personal injury cases), and **requests for admissions** (one party's written requests that the other party agree to certain statements of fact or law). The limits of discovery are set by the trial judge, whose rulings are controlled by the procedural law of the jurisdiction. In an effort to make civil litigation less of a battle of wits or a sporting event and more of a disinterested search for the truth, many jurisdictions have liberalized their discovery rules to give parties freer access to all of the relevant facts.

Discovery findings are generally not admissible trial evidence; matters revealed through discovery must normally be proven at trial. However, some discovery findings may be employed at trial for certain purposes. Depositions, for instance, may sometimes be used as "paper testimony" from dead or distant witnesses, or to attack the credibility of a witness whose testimony differs from statements she made at an earlier deposition.

**Summary Judgment.** The court's resolution of a motion for **summary judgment** might be described as a "minitrial" or a "trial by affidavit." The summary judgment is a device for disposing of relatively clear cases without a formal trial. In order to prevail, the party moving for a summary judgment must show that: (1) there is no genuine issue of material (legally significant) fact, and (2) he is entitled to judgment as a matter of law. A summary judgment hearing differs from the judge's decision on a demurrer because it involves the resolution of factual issues. Here, the "evidence" includes the pleadings, discovery information, and affidavits (signed and sworn statements regarding matters of fact). The moving party will try to satisfy the first element of the test by using such evidence to convince the judge that there is no genuine question as to any significant fact. The other party, of course, will try to rebut these factual arguments. Even if the moving party's arguments are persuasive, he must meet the second element of the test. To do so, he must convince the court that, given the established facts, the applicable law directs that he must win.

Either or both parties may move for a summary judgment. If the court rules in favor of either party, that party wins the case. If no party's motion for summary judgment is granted, the case proceeds to trial. The judge may also grant a partial summary judgment, which settles some issues in the case but leaves the others to be decided at trial.

**The Pretrial Conference.** The **pretrial conference** is a fairly recent procedural device of considerable practical importance. During this conference, whose calling may be either mandatory or at the discretion of the trial judge, the judge meets informally with the attorneys for both parties. The judge may attempt to get the parties to *stipulate* (agree to) the resolution of certain issues in order to simplify the trial. He may also encourage them to *settle* the case by coming to an agreement that eliminates the need for a trial. Both efforts are intended to help clear the increasingly congested calendars of most civil courts. If the case is not settled, the judge will enter a pretrial order at the conclusion of the conference; this will include all the stipulations and other agreements made by the attorneys. Ordinarily, the terms of this order will bind the parties throughout the remainder of the case.

**The Trial.** Once the case has been through discovery and has survived any pretrial motions, it is set for trial. The trial may be before a judge alone, in which case the judge makes separate findings of fact and law and combines them to produce the court's judgment. But if the right to a jury trial exists and either party demands one, the jury will handle the fact-finding function, with the resolution of legal questions still entrusted to the judge.

The usual trial scenario is much the same whether the trial is before a judge alone or before both a judge and a jury. First, the attorneys for plaintiff and defendant make opening statements explaining what they intend to prove. After this, the plaintiff's witnesses and other evidence are introduced and the witnesses are cross-examined by the defendant's attorney. This may be followed by the plaintiff's "re-direct" examination of his witnesses, and perhaps by the defendant's "recross" examination of those same witnesses. Then, using the same procedures, the defendant's evidence is presented. Throughout each side's presentation, the opposing attorney may object to the presentation of certain evidence. The judge then decides whether the evidence is admissible. Such rulings are based on the law of evidence, which aims to ensure that the proof presented at trial is accurate, nonprejudicial, and legally relevant. After the plaintiff and defendant have completed their initial presentation of evidence, each is allowed to offer evidence rebutting the other's evidence. Once all of the evidence has been presented, each attorney will make a closing argument summarizing her position. In nonjury trials, the judge will then make findings of fact and law, render judgment, and state the relief to which the plaintiff is entitled if the plaintiff is victorious.

Jury trials, however, involve different procedures and present further problems. At the end of a jury trial, the judge issues a **charge** or **instruction** to the jury. The charge sets out the rules of law applicable to the case. The judge also summarizes the evidence for the jury; in most states, however, he may not interpret it by commenting on the weight of the evidence or the credibility of the witnesses. Then, the jury is supposed to make the necessary factual determinations, apply the law to these, and arrive at a **verdict** upon which the court's **judgment** is based. The most common type of verdict is the **general verdict,** which only requires that the jury declare which party wins and the relief (if any) to be awarded. The general verdict gives the jury much freedom to ignore the judge's charge and follow its own inclinations, for the jury need not state its factual findings or its application of the law to those findings. Defenders of the general verdict argue that it allows the jury to soften the rigors of the law by bringing common sense and community values to bear on the case. But it also weakens the "rule of law" and allows juries to commit injustices. The **special verdict** is a response to this problem. Here, the jury only makes specific findings of fact and the judge then applies the law to these findings. The decision to request a general or a special verdict is usually within the trial judge's discretion.

**The Directed Verdict.** The discretion that the general verdict gives the jury is a two-edged sword, and the American legal system is ambivalent about the jury. While granting the jury great power, the system also establishes devices for limiting that power. One of these devices, the motion for a **directed verdict,** basically takes the case away from the jury and gives a judgment to one party before the jury gets a chance to decide. The motion can be made by either party, and it usually occurs after the other (nonmoving) party has presented his evidence. The moving party basically asserts that, even when read most favorably to the other party, the evidence leads to only one result and need not be considered by the jury. Courts differ on the test governing a motion for a directed verdict: some will deny the motion if there is *any* evidence favoring the nonmoving party, while others will deny the motion only if there is *substantial* evidence favoring the nonmoving party.

**The Judgment notwithstanding the Verdict.** Sometimes, the case will be taken away from the jury and judgment entered for a party even *after* the jury has reached a verdict *against* that party. The device for doing so is the motion for **judgment notwithstanding the verdict** (also known as the judgment *non obstante veredicto* or the judgment n.o.v.). The standard used to decide this motion is the same standard that the jurisdiction uses to decide the motion for a directed verdict.

**Motion for New Trial.** In a wide range of situations that vary among jurisdictions, the losing party can successfully move for a new trial. Acceptable reasons for granting a new trial include jury or attorney misconduct, new evidence, and legal errors made by the judge at trial.

**Appeal.** In general, appellate courts consider only alleged errors of law at the trial court level. Trial court rulings on at least the following matters are considered "legal" and thus appealable: service of process, motion to dismiss, scope of discovery, summary judgment, admission of evidence, findings of law in a nonjury trial, jury instruction, directed verdict, judgment notwithstanding the verdict, and new trial. Also, appellate courts often review the damages or other relief awarded by a trial court. Most jurisdictions allow an appeal only when the trial court has issued a final judgment conclusively deciding the case. The appellate court may, among other things, *affirm* the lower court's decision, *reverse* it, or affirm one part of the decision and reverse another part. Some decisions that are reversed may be *remanded* (returned) to the trial court for proceedings not inconsistent with the appellate court's decision.

**Enforcing a Judgment.** The most common remedy in a civil case is an award of damages to the victorious plaintiff. In such cases, the defendant will often simply pay the judgment. Sometimes, however, the winning plaintiff must take steps to enforce the judgment. Ordinarily, the plaintiff will obtain a **writ of execution** enabling the sheriff to seize designated property of the defendant and sell it at a judicial sale to satisfy the judgment. A judgment winner may also use a procedure known as **garnishment** to seize property, money, or wages of the defendant that are in the hands of a third party. Where the property needed to satisfy the judgment is located in another state, the plaintiff must use the execution or garnishment procedures established by that state. Under the U.S. Constitution, the second state is required to give "full faith and credit" to the judgment of the state where the plaintiff originally sued. Where the court has awarded an equitable remedy such as an injunction, the defendant may be found in contempt of court and subjected to a fine or imprisonment if she fails to obey the court's order.

**Class Actions.** The preceding review of the stages of a civil case has proceeded as if the plaintiff and the defendant were each a single party. Actually, several plaintiffs and/or defendants can be parties to one lawsuit. Also, each jurisdiction has procedural rules stating when other parties can be *joined* to a suit that begins without them.

One special type of multiparty suit, the **class action,** allows one or more persons to sue on behalf of themselves and all others who have suffered similar harm from substantially the same wrong. For example, a woman who sues an employer for a pattern or practice of employment discrimination might sue on behalf of all similarly situated women. The usual justifications for the class action are that: (1) it allows legal wrongs causing relatively minor losses to a large number of widely dispersed parties to be fully compensated, and (2) it promotes economy of judicial effort by lumping similar claims into one suit. Class action suits by consumers, environmentalists, women, and minorities are now common events.

The requirements for a class action vary among jurisdictions. The issues addressed by class action statutes include the following: whether there are questions of law and fact common to all members of the alleged class, whether the class is small enough to allow all of its members to join the case as parties rather than use a class action, and whether the plaintiff(s) and their attorney(s) can competently represent the class without conflicts of interest or other forms of unfairness. To protect the individual class member's right to be heard, some jurisdictions have required that unnamed or absent class members be given notice of the suit if this is reasonably possible. The damages awarded in a successful class action are usually apportioned among the entire class. Establishing the total recovery and distributing it to the class, however, pose problems when the class is large, the class members' injuries are indefinite, or some members cannot be identified.

## PROCEDURE AT ADMINISTRATIVE AGENCY HEARINGS

Hearings before state or federal administrative agencies are quasi-criminal proceedings whose procedures are usually less formal than those followed by regular courts. The staff or field investigators employed by the agency investigate reported and suspected violations of the statutes and regulations that the agency enforces. If the agency's officials decide that there has been a violation, a hearing is held. The parties at the hearing are the agency and the alleged violator (the respondent). Presiding over the hearing is an administrative judge or hearing examiner who is independent of the agency personnel prosecuting the alleged violation. The respondent can usually be represented by an attorney, but trial by jury is not available. The agency will impose sanctions if the respondent is found guilty.

The respondent has the right to appeal an unfavorable agency decision to the courts, but she must first exhaust all of the agency's internal appeal procedures. Appellate courts are reluctant to overturn agency decisions. However, they will do so when the agency has acted without substantial evidence to support its decision; has been arbitrary, capricious, or discriminatory; has violated due process or other constitutional standards; or has taken actions that exceed its statutory authority.

## ARBITRATION AND OTHER DISPUTE SETTLEMENT MECHANISMS

The courts are not the only mechanisms for settling civil disputes. Nor are they always the most desirable means of doing so. Resolving every civil dispute through the courts would involve intolerable costs to individuals, businesses, and society. The advent of a "litigious society" and the increasing caseloads and delays that this has generated are already matters of public concern. Expanding the court system to decrease existing congestion would cost money; expanding it to provide a procedurally perfect trial for every civil dispute would require vastly greater expenditures. Much of the money diverted from other public concerns would go to the court system itself—to fund increased numbers of court buildings, judges, and other judicial personnel. But considerable sums would also be diverted to the legal profession because of the greater demand for representation that would accompany an increased use of the courts to resolve private disputes.

There are other reasons why the courts are imperfect devices for deciding all civil matters. The fact that success in court frequently depends on the wealth needed to purchase quality representation is just one factor making the justice dispensed by courts less than perfect. Juries, on the other hand, sometimes award very high damage recoveries to plaintiffs suing individuals or businesses with the perceived ability to pay. And quite often, the costs that this imposes on business are passed on to the public.

In light of these considerations, the fact that many civil cases are settled by the parties short of trial is generally regarded as desirable. But there are other alternative means of resolving disputes. One of these, **arbitration,** is discussed immediately below. Then, some other, more or less administrative, means for handling private disputes are discussed.

**Arbitration.** Arbitration is the submission (usually by prior agreement) of a dispute to a nonjudicial third party for decision. Often, the agreement to arbitrate is made before the dispute arises, but it can take place after the dispute begins. The third party hearing the dispute (the *arbitrator*) may or may not be a lawyer. The arbitrator is not required to follow the rules of evidence and procedure governing courts, and she has some freedom to follow rules of decision that differ from state or federal substantive law. The arbitrator's decision is called an *award,* and it ordinarily binds the parties. The award is filed with a court, which generally will enforce it if necessary. The losing party may object to the award after its filing, but courts will overturn the arbitrator's decision only on certain limited grounds such as bribery or other misconduct of the arbitrator.

The matters most frequently submitted to arbitration are disputes arising under labor contracts and commercial contracts. As compared with the court system, the main advantages claimed for arbitration are: (1) quicker resolution of disputes, (2) lower costs to the parties and less executive time in court, (3) the availability of professional arbitrators who are often expert in the subject matter of the dispute, and (4) the fact that attorneys are sometimes unnecessary.

**Other Methods.** In recent years, there has been increasing pressure to remove certain classes of disputes from the courts and to resolve them through some kind of administrative process. The situations in question generally involve fairly standardized injuries affecting a large number of people and resulting from a particular product or operation. Examples include injuries to consumers from defective products and injuries resulting from toxic materials used in the workplace. Suits for such injuries further burden an already overloaded court system. The across-the-board results in such cases tend to be less than satisfactory for plaintiffs, defendants, and society. Some claimants may receive excessively large awards or settlements, while others may get little or nothing. On the other hand, some businesses may face potentially crippling financial losses from the mass of suits directed against them.

The actual and proposed responses to such situations usually involve quasi-administrative procedures for compensating injured parties. Generally, these procedures increase the probability that the injured party will recover. But they also limit or standardize the amount of that recovery in the interests of achieving equality among claimants and avoiding massive financial losses to the firms responsible for their injuries. The workers' compensation systems discussed in Chapter 47 are traditional examples of this sort of arrangement. Schemes that are similar in some of their features have recently been proposed to handle product liability cases and certain workplace injuries caused by long-term exposure to toxic substances. Somewhat similar proposals have also been made for the handling of medical malpractice cases. Some of the "no fault" automobile insurance schemes enacted by several states contain similar features.

## SUMMARY

The typical state court system contains the following courts: (1) inferior courts (which handle various minor matters), (2) trial courts (which resolve questions of law and fact), (3) intermediate appellate courts (which handle appeals from the trial courts and are limited to questions of law), and (4) the supreme court (which handles appeals from lower courts and is the state's highest appellate court). For a state trial court to be able to decide a case, it must first have subject-matter jurisdiction: that is, it must be set up to handle disputes of the sort the case presents. In addition, the court must have either in personam jurisdiction (based on the residence, location, or activities of the defendant) or in rem jurisdiction (based on the presence of property within the state).

The most important federal courts are: (1) district courts (which are similar to state trial courts), (2) courts of appeals (which are similar to state intermediate appellate courts), and (3) the U.S. Supreme Court (whose main function is to handle appeals from the lower federal courts and the state supreme courts). The most important bases of district court jurisdiction are federal question jurisdiction (requiring an issue of federal law in the case) and diversity jurisdiction (requiring that the plaintiff and defendant be citizens of different states and that the amount in controversy exceed $10,000). There are also various specialized federal courts.

The typical procedural steps involved in a civil case before a trial court or a federal district court are: (1) the summons (whose function is to notify the defendant of the suit), (2) the complaint (which states the plaintiff's case), (3) the answer (which responds point by point to the complaint), (4) the reply (which "answers" an affirmative defense or a counterclaim in the answer), (5) the motion to dismiss (a device for disposing of the case on the basis of the pleadings), (6) discovery (a process of pretrial information gathering), (7) the summary judgment (another device for disposing of the case prior to trial), (8) the pretrial conference (where the judge may try to get the parties to settle the case or to stipulate how certain issues will be resolved), (9) the trial itself, (10) the directed verdict (a device for taking the case away from the jury before it decides), (11) the judgment notwithstanding the verdict (similar to a directed verdict but used after the jury has decided), and (12) the motion for a new trial. The class action, a procedural device of some importance in recent years, permits the consolidation of many similar claims into one suit, thus enabling a plaintiff to represent a larger group.

Administrative agency hearings are less formal than normal court trials. Agency decisions may be appealed to an appellate court, but the losing party must first have exhausted the agency's internal appeal procedures. Also, courts usually defer to the agency's presumed expertise when hearing such appeals.

The courts are not the only means for resolving civil matters. The parties may contract to have an arbitrator decide their dispute, and the courts will usually enforce an arbitrator's award. Also, there have been various actual and proposed steps to remove certain classes of cases from the courts' control and to use some kind of quasi-administrative procedure instead.

## PROBLEM CASES

**1.** Thomas sues James. At trial, Thomas's lawyer attempts to introduce certain evidence to help make his case. James's attorney objects, and the trial judge refuses to allow the evidence to be admitted. Thomas eventually loses the case at the trial court level. He appeals, his attorney arguing that the trial judge's decision not to admit the evidence was erroneous. James's attorney argues that the appellate court cannot consider this question, because appellate courts only review errors of *law* (not fact) at the trial court level. Is James's attorney correct? Why or why not?

**2.** Jackson sues Arthur for $500,000 in a state small claims court set up to handle cases where the amount in controversy does not exceed $5,000. The court clearly does not have jurisdiction over the case. What *kind* of jurisdiction is absent here?

**3.** Smith, an Indiana resident, travels to Ohio to watch the Indiana–Ohio State football game. Following Ohio State's 56-3 win, Smith attempts to drown his sorrows at a bar in Columbus, Ohio. After a few drinks, he gets into a fight with Johnson, an Ohio resident, and injures Johnson. Smith immediately flees to Indiana and remains there. Johnson, who has suffered $20,000 in personal injuries and has a respectable tort case against Smith, wants to sue Smith in either an Ohio trial court or in a federal district court. Will each court have jurisdiction over the case? Why or why not? Assume for purposes of this problem that: (a) subject-matter jurisdiction is present, (b) Smith has had no other contacts with Ohio, and (c) Ohio has a "long arm" statute like that described in the chapter.

**4.** State *two* differences between the motion to dismiss for failure to state a claim upon which relief can be granted (or demurrer) and the motion for summary judgment.

**5.** In a suit by Apple against Engle, the jury has rendered a verdict in favor of Engle. Apple and her attorney think that the evidence was overwhelmingly in Apple's favor. They also have some reason to believe that the jury was biased in Engle's favor because Engle's family is prominent and influential. What *two* motions can Apple's attorney make at this point in an attempt to overturn the jury's verdict?

**6.** While driving to work one day, Jones runs over Aaron, causing severe injuries. Aaron sues Jones in a state trial court. His complaint alleges that Jones's negligent driving caused his injuries. The law of the state declares that if the plaintiff's own negligence contributed to his injury, the defendant has a complete defense and the plaintiff cannot recover. Jones wants to argue that, whether he was negligent or not, Aaron's own negligence helped cause his injuries and that Aaron therefore has no case. In order to be *sure* of his ability to raise this argument at trial, what should Jones's attorney do in response to Aaron's complaint?

**7.** What is the main difference between a motion for a directed verdict and a motion for judgment notwithstanding the verdict?

**8.** A police officer stops Simpson for driving 75 miles per hour in a 45-mile-per-hour zone. A justice of the peace court finds Simpson guilty, imposing a heavy fine and suspending his license as required by state law. State law also declares that Simpson has the right to appeal this decision to a state trial court, and he wishes to do so. On appeal, Simpson wants to argue that he was actually driving within the speed limit. A friend tells Simpson that he has no grounds for appeal because this question of fact was resolved by the justice of the peace and such factual determinations cannot be reviewed on appeal. Is the friend correct?

**9.** Usually, it is difficult for a party who has suffered an unfavorable decision in an administrative agency hearing to have that decision overturned on appeal. State *two* reasons why this is so.

**10.** Jackson was born in Texas but has had no contact with that state for 20 years. Jackson's father dies, and a Texas court interprets his will so that Jackson receives none of his father's property, which is located in Texas. Jackson later decides to challenge this ruling. He argues that the Texas court had no jurisdiction over him and thus lacked the power to decide that he had no right to his father's property. Will this argument succeed? Why or why not? Assume that subject-matter jurisdiction existed and that Jackson received proper and timely notice of the court's proceedings.

# PART II

# CRIMES AND TORTS

# Chapter 3 Crimes

## INTRODUCTION

At first glance, a chapter on criminal law might seem out of place in a text devoted to the legal environment of business. Contracts, torts, agency, corporations, and the host of other legal topics covered in this text tend to come more readily to mind than crime when one thinks of legal subjects that are traditionally viewed as being important to people in business. However, a thorough understanding of the nature of the criminal law is also an essential component of a contemporary manager's education because people in business and their corporate employers are today more likely than ever before to have some unpleasant contact with the criminal justice system.

This century has witnessed a growing tendency on the part of our legal system to use the criminal law as a major device for controlling corporate behavior. Many modern regulatory statutes provide for criminal as well as civil penalties in the event of a statutory violation, and those criminal penalties frequently apply both to individual corporate employees and to their corporate employers.

Those who advocate using the criminal law

in this fashion commonly argue that the criminal law affords a level of deterrence superior to that produced by purely civil remedies such as damage awards. Corporations may be inclined to treat civil damage awards as a cost of doing business, and therefore may violate regulatory provisions when it is profitable to do so. Criminal prosecutions, on the other hand, threaten corporations with the stigma of a criminal conviction and, in some cases, may allow society to impose penalties on individual corporate employees who would not be directly affected by a civil judgment against their corporation. Moreover, by alerting private individuals to the existence of a violation that can serve as the basis for a civil damage suit, criminal prosecutions may also increase the likelihood that a corporation will be forced to bear the full costs of its actions.

Whatever the merit of these arguments, the threat of criminal prosecution is an inescapable part of the legal environment of business today. Accordingly, the remainder of this chapter focuses first on the nature of the criminal law in general and then proceeds with a discussion of many of the complex problems associated with the operation of the criminal sanction in the corporate context.

## THE CRIMINAL LAW

**Nature of Crime.** Crimes are *public wrongs*—acts prohibited by the *state*. Criminal prosecutions are initiated by an agent of the state (the prosecutor) in the name of the state. Persons convicted of committing criminal acts are exposed to the uniquely coercive force of *criminal sanctions:* the punishment society has provided for those who violate its most important rules. This punishment may take the form of a fine, imprisonment, or, in extreme cases, execution. In addition to such formal types of punishment, convicted criminals must bear the *stigma* associated with a criminal conviction: the social condemnation that results from being labeled a criminal offender. Our legal system also contains a wide variety of noncriminal forms of punishment. For example, the next two chapters deal with *torts,* private wrongs that are punished by awards of money damages. In some cases this "punishment" consists of forcing a person who commits a tort to compensate his victim for the damages resulting from the tort. In others, a court may also award punitive damages for the express purpose of punishing the wrongdoer. However, only the criminal sanction combines the threat to life or liberty with the stigma of conviction. This potent combination caused one authority to describe the criminal sanction as "the law's ultimate threat."[1]

Crimes are usually classified as felonies or misdemeanors, depending on the seriousness of the offense. A **felony** is a serious offense, such as murder, rape, or arson. Felonies generally involve serious moral culpability on the part of the offender and are punishable by confinement to a penitentiary for a substantial period of time. A person convicted of a felony may also suffer other serious consequences, such as *disenfranchisement* (loss of voting rights) and being barred from the practice of certain professions, such as law or medicine. A **misdemeanor** is a lesser offense, such as a minor traffic violation or disorderly conduct. Misdemeanors, which often do not involve significant moral culpability, are punishable by fines or limited confinement in a city or county jail.

Whether a given act is classed as criminal is a social question. As our social values have changed over time, so have our definitions of criminal conduct. Many observers have argued that the criminal sanction should be reserved for behavior involving serious moral culpability. As the rest of this chapter will indicate, however, we have criminalized a

[1] H. Packer, *The Limits of the Criminal Sanction,* 250 (Stanford, Calif.: Standford University Press, 1968).

wide variety of behavior that has very little moral content.

**Purpose of the Criminal Sanction.** Much of the disagreement about the circumstances in which the criminal sanction should be employed stems from a fundamental disagreement about the purpose of the criminal sanction. Persons who take a *utilitarian* view of the criminal sanction believe that the *prevention* of socially undesirable behavior is the only proper purpose for applying criminal penalties. The goal of prevention includes three major components: deterrence, rehabilitation, and incapacitation.

*Deterrence* theory holds that the threat or imposition of punishment will deter crime. Deterrence theorists focus on two types of deterrence: special deterrence and general deterrence. *Special deterrence* occurs when the punishment of a convicted offender deters him from committing further criminal offenses. *General deterrence* results when the punishment of a convicted wrongdoer deters others who might otherwise have been inclined to commit a similar offense. Several factors are generally considered to be influential in determining the effectiveness of deterrence. Among these are: the likelihood that the crime will be detected and that detection will be followed by prosecution, the probability that prosecution will result in a conviction, and the severity of the punishment that is likely to be imposed in the event of a conviction. Put in economic terms, effective deterrence requires that the penalty imposed for an offense, discounted by the likelihood of apprehension and conviction, must equal or exceed the gains to the offender from committing the offense.

The fundamental problem with deterrence theories is that we can never say with certainty whether deterrence "works" because we can never know what the crime rate would be in the absence of punishment. For example, unacceptably high levels of crime and *recidivism* (repeat offenses by previously punished offenders) may be the result of the failure to impose criminal sanctions of sufficient severity and with sufficient certainty to produce deterrence, rather than evidence that criminalizing the behavior in question cannot produce deterrence. Deterrence theory has one other fundamental problem: it tends to assume that potential offenders are rational beings who consciously weigh the threat of punishment against the benefits to be derived from an offense. However, the threat of punishment may not deter the commission of criminal offenses that are the product of irrational or unconscious drives.

The prevention of undesirable social behavior may also be achieved if we can successfully *rehabilitate* convicted offenders by changing their attitudes or values so that they will not be predisposed to commit future offenses. Critics of rehabilitation commonly point to high rates of recidivism as evidence of the general failure of our rehabilitation efforts to date. Even if rehabilitative strategies fail, however, the incarceration of convicted offenders contributes to the goal of prevention by *incapacitating* them: while they are imprisoned, their ability to commit other criminal offenses is drastically reduced.

Prevention is not the only goal advanced for the criminal sanction. Some persons see the central focus of criminal punishment as *retribution:* the infliction of deserved suffering on those who violate society's most fundamental rules. To a retributionist, punishment satisfies community and individual desires for revenge and vindicates and reinforces important social values. Thus, a retributionist is unlikely to see prevention as a sufficient justification for criminalizing behavior that is socially undesirable but morally neutral. On the other hand, when serious moral culpability is present, a retributionist would be likely to favor punishment even if convinced that it will not result in the prevention of future offenses.

**Essentials of Crime.** Before a person can be convicted of committing a crime, the state ordinarily must: (1) demonstrate that his alleged actions violated an existing criminal statute, (2) prove beyond a reasonable doubt that he did in fact commit the actions charged against him, and (3) prove that he had the legal capacity to form a criminal intent.

**Prior Statutory Prohibition.** Criminal offenses are *statutory* offenses. Only the legislature has the power to designate behavior as criminal. The U.S. Constitution prohibits ex post facto criminal laws. This means that a defendant's act must have been prohibited by statute at the time the act was committed and that the penalty imposed upon his conviction must be the one provided for at the time of his offense.

The Constitution also limits the power of Congress and the state legislatures to criminalize behavior in a variety of other ways. They cannot criminalize behavior that is constitutionally protected. For example, the First Amendment to the Constitution prohibits laws that unreasonably restrict the freedom of speech and expression. Similarly, in *Griswold v. Connecticut*[2] the Supreme Court struck down state statutes prohibiting the use of contraceptive devices and the counseling or assisting of others in the use of such devices, on the ground that the statutes violated a constitutionally protected *right of privacy* that was implicit in the Bill of Rights. This decision provided the constitutional basis for the Court's historic decision in *Roe v. Wade*,[3] which limited the states' power to criminalize abortions.

In addition to limiting the *kinds* of behavior which can be made criminal, the Constitution also limits the *manner* in which behavior may be criminalized. As the *Lawson* case which follows illustrates, the Due Process Clauses of the Fifth and Fourteenth Amendments[4] require that a criminal statute must clearly define the behavior prohibited so that an ordinary person would understand what behavior will violate the statute. Statutes that fail to provide such fair notice are stricken down as "void for vagueness." In addition, the Equal Protection Clause of the Fourteenth Amendment[5] prohibits criminal statutes that treat persons of the same class in a discriminatory fashion or that *arbitrarily* discriminate among different classes of persons.[6] As a general rule, legislatures have considerable latitude in making statutory classifications, so long as the classifications have some rational basis. "Suspect" classifications, such as those based on race, however, will be subjected to much closer judicial scrutiny.

Finally, the Constitution also limits the *type of punishment* that may be imposed on convicted offenders. The Eighth Amendment forbids the imposition of "cruel and unusual punishments" for criminal offenses. This has been interpreted as barring the imposition of sentences that are *disproportionate* to the defendant's offense. In making a disproportionality analysis, courts consider the harshness of the penalty imposed, other sentences imposed in the same jurisdiction for similar offenses, and the sentences imposed in other jurisdictions for the same offense. The Eighth Amendment provides the constitutional basis for those cases establishing constitutional limits on the circumstances in which the death penalty may be imposed.[7]

---

[2] 381 U.S. 479 (U.S. Sup. Ct. 1965).

[3] 410 U.S. 113 (U.S. Sup. Ct. 1973).

[4] Due process is discussed in greater detail in Chapter 42.

[5] Equal protection is discussed in greater detail in Chapter 42.

[6] For an example, see *McLaughlin v. Florida,* 379 U.S. 1984 (U.S. Sup. Ct. 1964), where the Court struck down a Florida statute forbidding cohabitation between black males and white females on the ground that no valid statutory purpose justified prohibiting only interracial cohabitation.

[7] See, for example, *Gregg v. Georgia,* 428 U.S. 153 (U.S. Sup. Ct. 1976); and *Furman v. Georgia,* 408 U.S. 238 (U.S. Sup. Ct. 1972).

## Kolender v. Lawson

### 461 U.S. 352 (U.S. Sup. Ct. 1983)

Edward Lawson was arrested for violating Section 647(e) of the California Penal Code, which made a person guilty of a misdemeanor who

> loiters or wanders upon the streets or from place to place without apparent reason or business and who refuses to identify himself and account for his presence when requested by any peace officer to do so, if the surrounding circumstances are such as to indicate to a reasonable man that the public safety demands such identification.

After being convicted, Lawson filed a civil suit in federal court seeking a declaratory judgment that the statute was unconstitutional, a mandatory injunction against further enforcement of the statute, and damages against the police officers who had detained him. The federal district court held that the statute was unconstitutional, and the Ninth Circuit Court of Appeals affirmed that judgment. The police officers appealed.

**WHITE, JUSTICE.** As construed by the California Court of Appeal, section 647(e) requires that an individual provide "credible and reliable" identification when requested by a police officer who has reasonable suspicion of criminal activity. "Credible and reliable" is defined by the Court as "identification carrying reasonable assurances that the identification in question is authentic and providing means for later getting in touch with the person who has identified himself." In addition, a suspect may be required to "*account for his presence* to the extent that it assists in producing credible and reliable identification."

Our Constitution is designed to maximize individual freedoms within a framework of ordered liberty. Statutory limitations on those freedoms are examined for substantive authority and content as well as for definiteness or certainty of expression. As generally stated, the void-for-vagueness doctrine requires that a penal statute define the criminal offense with sufficient definiteness that ordinary people can understand what conduct is prohibited and in a manner that does not encourage arbitrary and discriminatory enforcement. Although the doctrine focuses both on actual notice to citizens and on arbitrary enforcement, we have recognized recently that the more important aspect of vagueness doctrine "is not actual notice, but the other principal element of the doctrine—the requirement that a legislature establish minimal guidelines to govern law enforcement." Where the legislature fails to provide such minimal guidelines, a criminal statute may permit "a standardless sweep that allows policemen, prosecutors, and juries to pursue their personal predilections."

Section 647(e), as presently drafted and as construed by the state courts, contains no standard for determining what a suspect has to do in order to satisfy the requirement to provide a "credible and reliable" identification. As such, the statute vests virtually complete discretion in the hands of the police to determine whether the suspect has satisfied the statute and must be permitted to go on his way in the absence of probable cause to arrest. An individual, whom police may think is suspicious but do not have probable cause to believe has committed a crime, is entitled to continue to walk the public streets "only at the whim of any police officer" who happens to stop that individual under section

647(e). Our concern here is based upon the "potential for arbitrarily suppressing First Amendment liberties." In addition, section 647(e) implicates consideration of the constitutional right to freedom of movement. Section 647(e) is not simply a "stop-and-identify" statute. Rather, the statute requires that the individual provide a "credible and reliable" identification that carries a "reasonable assurance" of its authenticity, and that provides "means for later getting in touch with the person who has identified himself." In addition, the suspect may also have to account for his presence "to the extent that it assists in producing credible and reliable identification."

At oral argument, the police confirmed that a suspect violates section 647(e) unless "the officer is satisfied that the identification is reliable." In giving examples of how suspects would satisfy the requirement, appellants explained that a jogger, who was not carrying identification, could, depending on the particular officer, be required to answer a series of questions concerning the route that he followed to arrive at the place where the officers detained him, or could satisfy the identification requirement simply by reciting his name and address.

It is clear that the full discretion accorded to the police to determine whether the suspect has provided a "credible and reliable" identification necessarily "entrusts lawmaking 'to the moment-to-moment judgment of the policeman on his beat.' " Section 647(e) "furnishes a convenient tool for harsh and discriminatory enforcement by local prosecuting officials, against particular groups deemed to merit their displeasure," and "confers on police a virtually unrestrained power to arrest and charge persons with a violation."

We conclude section 647(e) is unconstitutionally vague on its face because it encourages arbitrary enforcement by failing to describe with sufficient particularity what a suspect must do in order to satisfy the statute.

Judgment for Lawson affirmed.

**Proof beyond a Reasonable Doubt.** Our legal system has long placed significant limits on the state's power to convict a person of a crime. These limits are thought to be essential due to the serious matters at stake in a criminal case: the life and liberty of the accused. One of the most fundamental safeguards that characterize the criminal justice system is the *presumption of innocence:* defendants in criminal cases are presumed to be innocent until proven guilty. The state must overcome this presumption by proving every element of the offense charged against the defendant *beyond a reasonable doubt.* Requiring the state to meet that severe burden of proof is the primary way in which the risk of erroneous criminal convictions is minimized. It also reflects a strong belief shared by all common law jurisdictions about the proper way in which laws should be enforced and justice administered.

**The Defendant's Capacity.** ***Mens rea*** (criminal intent) is an element of most serious crimes. The *level* of intent required for a criminal violation depends on the wording of the statute in question. Some criminal statutes require proof of intentional wrongdoing, while others impose liability for *reckless* or *negligent* conduct. In the criminal context, recklessness generally means that the defendant consciously disregarded a substantial risk that the harm prohibited by the statute would result from his actions. Negligence, in criminal cases, means that the defendant failed to perceive a substantial risk of harm that would have been perceived by a reasonable person. Criminal intent may be *inferred* from the nature of an accused's behavior, because a person is normally held to have intended the natural and probable consequences of his acts. The basic idea behind requiring intent for criminal responsibility is that the criminal law generally seeks to punish *conscious* wrongdoers. Accordingly, proof that the defendant had the *capacity* to form the required criminal intent is a traditional prerequisite of criminal responsibility. The criminal law recognizes three general types of incapacity: *intoxication, infancy,* and *insanity.*

Voluntary intoxication, while not a complete defense to criminal liability, can sometimes diminish the degree of a defendant's liability. This is so because a highly intoxicated person may be incapable of forming the *specific* criminal intent that is an element of some crimes. For example, many first-degree murder statutes require proof of *premeditation,* a conscious decision to kill. A person who kills while highly intoxicated may not be capable of premeditation and may therefore only be convicted of second-degree murder, which generally does not require proof of premeditation. Involuntary intoxication may be a complete defense to criminal liability.

At common law, a child under the age of seven was conclusively presumed to be incapable of forming a criminal intent. Children between the ages of 7 and 14 were presumed to be incapable of doing so, and those between the ages of 14 and 21 were presumed to be capable of doing so. These presumptions about a child's capacity, however, were rebuttable by specific evidence concerning the accused's moral and intellectual development. Most states today treat juvenile offenders below a certain statutory age (usually 16 or 17) differently from adult offenders, with special juvenile court systems and separate detention facilities. Juvenile law today tends to emphasize rehabilitation rather than capacity. Repeat offenders or offenders charged with very serious offenses may sometimes be treated as adults.

Insanity on a criminal defendant's part can affect a criminal prosecution in three ways. Insanity that renders a defendant incapable of assisting in the defense of his case can serve to delay his trial until he regains his sanity. Insanity that becomes manifest after conviction, but before sentencing, can serve to delay sentencing until sanity is regained. Finally, insanity at the time a criminal act was committed can serve as a complete defense to liability. It is this last type of insanity that has generated so much controversy in recent years.

This controversy stems from two major sources: significant disagreement concerning the proper test for insanity in criminal cases and public dissatisfaction with the insanity defense in general. The courts have adopted a variety of tests for criminal responsibility, all of which are designed to punish conscious wrongdoers. These tests are *legal* tests, not medical tests. A defendant who was medically insane at the time of the criminal act may still be legally responsible.

The primary common law test for insanity is the *M'Naghten*[8] rule: a criminal defendant is not responsible if, at the time of the offense, he did not know the nature and quality of his act, or if he did know it, he did not know that his act was wrong. Some states have replaced or supplemented this rule with the *irresistible impulse* rule. This rule absolves a defendant of responsibility if mental disease rendered him incapable of controlling his behavior and resisting the impulse to commit a crime. One modern insanity test that has been adopted by a large number of jurisdictions is the test proposed by the American

[8] This rule is derived from *Daniel M'Naghten's Case,* 8 Eng. Reprint 718 (House of Lords 1843).

Law Institute. This test provides that a defendant is not criminally responsible if at the time the act was committed, due to mental disease or defect, he lacked the substantial capacity to appreciate the wrongfulness of his act or to conform his conduct to the law's requirements. Public reaction to certain highly publicized cases in which insanity defenses were raised, however, has produced a noticeable tendency to return to the narrower *M'Naghten* standard. For example, the Comprehensive Crime Control Act of 1984, which governs the insanity standard applicable in federal criminal cases, provides that only defendants who are incapable of understanding the nature and wrongfulness of their acts are absolved from responsibility.

Public dissatisfaction with the insanity defense has also produced another noticeable trend in recent years: the creation of procedural rules that make it more difficult for defendants to raise an insanity defense successfully. Criminal defendants are presumed to be sane. Traditionally, once a defendant had introduced evidence tending to prove insanity, the state had the burden of proving his sanity beyond a reasonable doubt. Today, however, many states treat insanity as an *affirmative defense* and require the defendant to bear the burden of proving insanity. The Comprehensive Crime Control Act of 1984 adopts this approach. In addition, some states have instituted a "guilty, but mentally ill" verdict as an alternative to the traditional "not guilty by reason of insanity" verdict. This new alternative verdict allows jurors to convict rather than acquit mentally ill defendants, with the assurance that they will be given treatment after conviction.

## CRIMINAL PROCEDURE

**Criminal Prosecutions.** Persons who have been arrested for allegedly committing a crime are taken to the police station and "booked." Booking is an administrative procedure for recording the suspect's arrest and the offenses involved. Temporary release on bail may be available at this stage in some jurisdictions. After booking, the police file a report of the arrest with the prosecutor, who decides whether to charge the suspect with an offense. If the prosecutor decides in favor of prosecution, a complaint is prepared identifying the accused and detailing the charges against him.

Most states require that arrested suspects be promptly taken before a public official (a magistrate, commissioner, or justice of the peace) for an *initial appearance* at which the magistrate informs the accused of the charges against him and the nature of his constitutional rights. In misdemeanor cases, the accused may elect to plead guilty at this point and sentence may be imposed without further proceedings. If the accused pleads not guilty, the case is set for trial. In felony cases, or misdemeanor cases in which the accused pleads not guilty, the magistrate will set the amount of bail.

In many states, defendants in felony cases are protected against unjustified prosecutions by an additional procedural step: the *preliminary hearing.* The prosecutor must introduce enough evidence at this hearing to convince a magistrate that there is *probable cause* to believe that the accused committed a felony. If the magistrate is so convinced, he will "bind over" the defendant for trial in a criminal court.

After a bindover, the formal charge against the defendant is filed with a criminal court. This is accomplished in one of two ways: an *information* filed by the prosecutor or an *indictment* returned by a *grand jury.* About half of the states require that a grand jury approve the decision to prosecute a defendant accused of a felony. Grand juries are bodies of citizens who are selected in the same manner (often random drawings from a list of registered voters) as the members of a trial (petit) jury. Grand juries were originally composed of 23 members, a majority of whose votes were necessary to sustain an indictment. Today, many jurisdictions have reduced the size of the grand jury and there is significant variation in the number of votes required for an indictment. Indictment of a defendant prior to a preliminary hearing normally disposes of the need for a preliminary hearing, since the grand jury indictment serves essentially the same functions as a magistrate's "probable cause" determination.

The remainder of the states allow felony defendants to be charged by either indictment or information, at the discretion of the prosecutor. An *information* is a formal charge signed by the prosecutor that outlines the facts supporting the charges against the defendant. In states that allow felony prosecutions by information, the vast majority of felony cases are prosecuted in this fashion. Misdemeanor cases are almost exclusively prosecuted by information in virtually all jurisdictions.

Once an information or indictment has been filed with a trial court, the defendant is *arraigned:* brought before the court, informed of the charges against him, and asked to enter a plea. The defendant may plead guilty, not guilty, or nolo contendere to the charges against him. Nolo contendere pleas, although technically not an admission of guilt, are an indication that the defendant will not contest the charges. Nolo pleas are frequently attractive to corporate defendants who believe that their chances of mounting a successful defense are poor, because a nolo plea is inadmissible as evidence of guilt in a subsequent civil suit against the defendant based on the same statutory violation.

At the arraignment, the defendant also elects whether to be tried by a judge or a jury. Persons accused of a serious crime (those for which incarceration for more than six months is possible) have a constitutional right to be tried by a jury of their peers. The accused, however, generally has the power to waive this right.

**Procedural Safeguards.** In the preceding pages, you have already encountered several procedural devices designed to protect persons accused of crime. The Bill of Rights of the U.S. Constitution (the first 10 constitutional amendments) contains a number of additional provisions aimed at safeguarding the rights of criminal defendants. These procedural safeguards reflect two fundamental public policies. First, they are designed to protect against unjustified or erroneous criminal convictions. Second, and perhaps equally important, they reflect a conclusion about government's proper role in the administration of justice in a democratic society. Justice Oliver Wendell Holmes aptly addressed this latter point when he said, "I think it less evil that some criminals should escape than that the government should play an ignoble part." Although the specific language of the Bill of Rights applies only to the federal government, the U.S. Supreme Court has applied most of the Bill of Rights' most important guarantees to the states by "selectively incorporating" them into the 14th Amendment's Due Process Clause. Once a particular safeguard has been found to be "implicit in the concept of ordered liberty" or "fundamental to the American scheme of justice," it has been applied equally in state and federal criminal trials.

**The Fourth Amendment.** The Fourth Amendment provides:

> The right of the people to be secure in their persons, houses, papers, and effects, against unreasonable searches and seizures, shall not be violated, and no Warrants shall issue, but upon probable cause, supported by Oath or affirmation, and par-

ticularly describing the place to be searched, and the persons or things to be seized.

The basic purpose of the Fourth Amendment is to protect individual privacy rights against overzealous governmental intrusions. In *Mapp v. Ohio,*[9] the Supreme Court held that the only effective device for deterring unconstitutional searches and seizures was an **exclusionary rule** that prevented the state from using illegally seized evidence in a subsequent trial against an individual whose constitutional rights had been violated. This ruling generates enormous controversy because it often serves to prevent the state from introducing convincing evidence that a defendant committed a crime. In many criminal cases, the pivotal point in a criminal trial became the legality of the search in question. In many drug cases, for example, the defendant's possession of narcotics comprises the heart of the state's case. If evidence of possession is excluded because it is the product of an illegal search, the prosecution will fail.

Supporters of the rule argued that it was necessary to deter police from violating citizens' constitutional rights. Opponents of the rule argued that it would not deter police who believed they were acting lawfully and that since the exclusion of illegally seized evidence imposed no direct penalties on police officers who acted unlawfully, the rule was a poor device for achieving deterrence. A common complaint was that "because of a policeman's error, a criminal goes free."

In recent years, the Supreme Court has responded to these criticisms by narrowing the scope of the Fourth Amendment in a variety of ways. In a series of recent cases, the Court has: (1) upheld the legality of a warrantless "inventory" search of a man arrested for disturbing the peace (the search yielded a container of amphetamines);[10] (2) ruled that exposing an airline traveler's luggage to a narcotics detection dog in a public place was not a "search" within the meaning of the Fourth Amendment;[11] (3) reaffirmed the "open fields" doctrine, which holds that governmental intrusions on open fields are not an unreasonable search;[12] (4) adopted a broader "totality of the circumstances" test for the probable cause necessary to support the judicial issuance of search warrants;[13] (5) held that the warrantless use of an electronic "beeper" to monitor the movement over public highways of noncontraband items in an automobile did not constitute a "search" or a "seizure" within the meaning of the Fourth Amendment;[14] and (6) held that illegally obtained evidence may be introduced at a trial if the prosecution can convince the court that it would "inevitably" have been obtained by lawful means.[15]

Perhaps most importantly, as the *Leon* case, which follows, indicates, the Court has recently created a "good faith" exception to the exclusionary rule to allow the admission of evidence seized by police officers who reasonably believe that they are acting under a lawful search warrant. The Court has not as yet extended this exception to warrantless searches.

---

[9] 367 U.S. 643 (U.S. Sup. Ct. 1961).

[10] *Illinois v. Lafayette,* 462 U.S. 640 (U.S. Sup. Ct. 1983).

[11] *United States v. Place,* 426 U.S. 696 (U.S. Sup. Ct. 1983). In this case, however, the Court also held that the warrantless detention of the defendant's luggage for 90 minutes was unlawful, given the fact that the agents in question had several hours' advance notice of the defendant's arrival.

[12] *Oliver v. United States,* 52 U.S.L.W. 4425 (U.S. Sup. Ct. 1984). The "open fields" doctrine, first announced in *Hester v. United States,* 265 U.S. 57 (U.S. Sup. Ct. 1924), is based on the notion that the owner of open fields cannot have reasonable privacy expectations concerning property located in such fields or activities carried out in them.

[13] *Illinois v. Gates,* 462 U.S. 213 (U.S. Sup. Ct. 1983).

[14] *United States v. Knotts,* 460 U.S. 276 (U.S. Sup. Ct. 1983).

[15] *Nix v. Williams,* 104 S. Ct. 2501 (U.S. Sup. Ct. 1984).

## United States v. Leon

### 104 S. Ct. 3405 (U.S. Sup. Ct. 1984)

In August 1981, a confidential informant of unproven reliability told a Burbank, California, police officer that two persons named "Armando" and "Patsy" were selling large quantities of cocaine and methaqualone from their residence at 620 Price Drive in Burbank. The informant also said that he had witnessed a sale of methaqualone by "Patsy" at the residence approximately five months earlier. On the basis of this information, the police began an extensive investigation, focusing first on the Price Drive residence and later on two other residences as well. They determined that the cars parked at the Price Drive residence belonged to Armando Sanchez, who had previously been arrested for possession of marijuana, and Patsy Stewart, who had no criminal record.

While watching the Price Drive residence, the police saw a car belonging to Ricardo Del Castillo, a man with a previous arrest record for possession of 50 pounds of marijuana, arrive at the house. The driver entered the house and came out shortly thereafter carrying a small paper sack. A check of Del Castillo's probation records led police to Alberto Leon, whose telephone number Del Castillo had listed as his employer's. Leon had been arrested in 1980 on drug charges, and at that time a companion had informed police that Leon was heavily involved in drug importation. The police began to watch Leon's residence too, and during the investigation witnessed a variety of activities that were suggestive of drug dealings.

Based on these observations, in September 1981, Officer Cyril Rombach of the Burbank Police Department sought and obtained a search warrant from a state superior court judge covering Del Castillo's car and the residences and cars of Sanchez, Stewart, and Leon. The search yielded large quantities of drugs and other evidence. The defendants were indicted by a grand jury, and at trial they moved to suppress the evidence on the ground that Rombach's affidavit requesting the search warrant was insufficient to establish probable cause because it failed to establish the informant's credibility and because the information relating to the informant's knowledge of criminal activity was fatally stale. The district court agreed with the defendants, and the Ninth Circuit Court of Appeals affirmed the district court's ruling. The government appealed.

**White, Justice.** This case presents the question whether the Fourth Amendment exclusionary rule should be modified so as not to bar the use in the prosecution's case-in-chief of evidence obtained by officers acting in reasonable reliance on a search warrant issued by a detached and neutral magistrate but ultimately found to be unsupported by probable cause. To resolve this question, we must consider once again the tension between the sometimes competing goals of, on the one hand, deterring official misconduct and removing inducements to unreasonable invasions of privacy and, on the other, establishing procedures under which criminal defendants are "acquitted or convicted on the basis of all the evidence which exposes the truth."

The Fourth Amendment contains no provision expressly precluding the use of evidence obtained in violation of its commands, and an examination of its origin and purposes makes clear that the use of fruits of a past unlawful search or seizure "works no new

Fourth Amendment wrong." The wrong condemned by the Amendment is "fully accomplished" by the unlawful search or seizure itself, and the exclusionary rule is neither intended nor able to "cure the invasion of the defendant's rights which he has already suffered." The rule thus operates as "a judicially created remedy designed to safeguard Fourth Amendment rights generally through its deterrent effect, rather than a personal constitutional right of the person aggrieved."

Whether the exclusionary sanction is appropriately imposed in a particular case, our decisions make clear, is "an issue separate from the question whether the Fourth Amendment rights of the party seeking to invoke the rule were violated by police conduct." Only the former question is currently before us, and it must be resolved by weighing the costs and benefits of preventing the use in the prosecution's case-in-chief of inherently trustworthy tangible evidence obtained in reliance on a search warrant issued by a detached and neutral magistrate that ultimately is found to be defective.

The substantial social costs exacted by the exclusionary rule for the vindication of Fourth Amendment rights have long been a source of concern. "Our cases have consistently recognized that unbending application of the exclusionary sanction to enforce ideals of governmental rectitude would impede unacceptably the truth-finding functions of judge and jury." An objectionable collateral consequence of this interference with the criminal justice system's truth-finding function is that some guilty defendants may go free or receive reduced sentences as a result of favorable plea bargains. Particularly when law enforcement officers have acted in objective good faith or their transgressions have been minor, the magnitude of the benefit conferred on such guilty defendants offends basic concepts of the criminal justice system. Indiscriminate application of the exclusionary rule, therefore, may well "generate disrespect for the law and the administration of justice." Accordingly, "as with any remedial device, the application of the rule has been restricted to those areas where its remedial objectives are thought most efficaciously served."

Because a search warrant "provides the detached scrutiny of a neutral magistrate, which is a more reliable safeguard against improper searches than the hurried judgment of a law enforcement officer engaged in the often competitive enterprise of ferreting out crime," we have expressed a strong preference for warrants and declared that "in a doubtful or marginal case a search under a warrant may be sustainable where without one it would fail." Reasonable minds frequently may differ on the question whether a particular affidavit establishes probable cause, and we have thus concluded that the preference for warrants is most appropriately effectuated by according "great deference" to a magistrate's determination.

Deference to the magistrate, however, is not boundless. It is clear, first, that the deference accorded to a magistrate's finding of probable cause does not preclude inquiry into the knowing or reckless falsity of the affidavit on which that determination was based. Second, the courts must also insist that the magistrate purport to "perform his 'neutral and detached' function and not serve merely as a rubber stamp for the police." A magistrate failing to "manifest that neutrality and detachment demanded of a judicial officer when presented with a warrant application" and who acts instead as "an adjunct law enforcement officer" cannot provide valid authorization for an otherwise unconstitutional search.

Third, reviewing courts will not defer to a warrant based on an affidavit that does not "provide the magistrate with a substantial basis for determining the existence of probable cause." Sufficient information must be presented to the magistrate to allow that official to determine probable cause; his action cannot be a mere ratification of the bare conclusions of others. Even if the warrant application was supported by more than a "bare bones" affidavit, a reviewing court may properly conclude that, notwithstanding the deference that magistrates deserve, the warrant was invalid because the magistrate's probable-cause determination reflected an improper analysis of the totality of the circumstances or because the form of the warrant was improper in some respect.

Only in the first of these three situations, however, has the Court set forth a rationale for suppressing evidence obtained pursuant to a search warrant; in the other areas, it has simply excluded such evidence without considering whether Fourth Amendment interests will be advanced. To the extent that proponents of exclusion rely on its behavioral effects on judges and magistrates in these areas, their reliance is misplaced. First, the exclusionary rule is designed to deter police misconduct rather than to punish the errors of judges and magistrates. Second, there exists no evidence suggesting that judges and magistrates are inclined to ignore or subvert the Fourth Amendment or that lawlessness among these actors requires application of the extreme sanction of exclusion.

Third, and most important, we discern no basis, and are offered none, for believing that exclusion of evidence seized pursuant to a warrant will have a significant deterrent effect on the issuing judge or magistrate. Many of the factors that indicate that the exclusionary rule cannot provide an effective "special" or "general" deterrent for individual offending law enforcement officers apply as well to judges or magistrates. And, to the extent that the rule is thought to operate as a "systemic" deterrent on a wide audience, it clearly can have no such effect on individuals empowered to issue search warrants. Judges and magistrates are not adjuncts to the law enforcement team; as neutral judicial officers, they have no stake in the outcome of particular criminal prosecutions. The threat of exclusion thus cannot be expected significantly to deter them. Imposition of the exclusionary sanction is not necessary meaningfully to inform judicial officers of their errors, and we cannot conclude that admitting evidence obtained pursuant to a warrant while at the same time declaring that the warrant was somehow defective will in any way reduce judicial officers' professional incentives to comply with the Fourth Amendment, encourage them to repeat their mistakes, or lead to the granting of all colorable warrant requests.

If exclusion of evidence obtained pursuant to a subsequently invalidated warrant is to have any deterrent effect, therefore, it must alter the behavior of individual law enforcement officers or the policies of their departments. One could argue that applying the exclusionary rule in cases where the police failed to demonstrate probable cause in the warrant application deters future inadequate presentations or "magistrate shopping" and thus promotes the ends of the Fourth Amendment. Suppressing evidence obtained pursuant to a technically defective warrant supported by probable cause also might encourage officers to scrutinize more closely the form of the warrant and to point out suspected judicial errors. We find such arguments speculative and conclude that suppression of evidence obtained pursuant to a warrant should be ordered only on a case-by-case basis and only in those unusual cases in which exclusion will further the purposes of the exclusionary rule.

We have frequently questioned whether the exclusionary rule can have any deterrent effect when the offending officers acted in the objectively reasonable belief that their conduct did not violate the Fourth Amendment. But even assuming that the rule effectively deters some police misconduct and provides incentives for the law enforcement profession as a whole to conduct itself in accord with the Fourth Amendment, it cannot be expected, and should not be applied, to deter objectively reasonable law enforcement activity.

This is particularly true, we believe, when an officer acting with objective good faith has obtained a search warrant from a judge or magistrate and acted within its scope. In most such cases, there is no police illegality and thus nothing to deter. It is the magistrate's responsibility to determine whether the officer's allegations establish probable cause and, if so, to issue a warrant comporting in form with the requirements of the Fourth Amendment.

> In the ordinary case, an officer cannot be expected to question the magistrate's probable-cause determination or his judgment that the form of the warrant is technically sufficient. "Once the warrant issues, there is literally nothing more the policeman can do in seeking to comply with the law." Penalizing the officer for the magistrate's error, rather than his own, cannot logically contribute to the deterrence of Fourth Amendment violations.
>
> We conclude that the marginal or nonexistent benefits produced by suppressing evidence obtained in objectively reasonable reliance on a subsequently invalidated search warrant cannot justify the substantial costs of exclusion. We do not suggest, however, that exclusion is always inappropriate in cases where an officer has obtained a warrant and abided by its terms. The officer's reliance on the magistrate's probable-cause determination and on the technical sufficiency of the warrant he issues must be objectively reasonable, and it is clear that in some circumstances the officer will have no reasonable grounds for believing that the warrant was properly issued.
>
> Suppression therefore remains an appropriate remedy if the magistrate or judge in issuing a warrant was misled by information in an affidavit that the affiant knew was false or would have known was false except for his reckless disregard of the truth. The exception we recognize today will also not apply in cases where the issuing magistrate wholly abandoned his judicial role in the manner condemned in *Lo-Ji Sales, Inc. v. New York;* in such circumstances, no reasonably well-trained officer should rely on the warrant. Nor would an officer manifest objective good faith in relying on a warrant based on an affidavit "so lacking in indicia of probable cause as to render official belief in its existence entirely unreasonable."
>
> Judgment reversed in favor of the government.

**The Fifth Amendment.** In addition to the Due Process Clause, the Fifth Amendment contains two other provisions aimed at safeguarding the rights of criminal defendants. First, the Fifth Amendment protects against *compulsory testimonial self-incrimination* by providing that no "person . . . shall be compelled in any criminal case to be a witness against himself." This provision prevents the state from forcing a defendant to assist in his own prosecution by compelling him to make incriminating testimonial admissions. In *Miranda v. Arizona,*[16] the Supreme Court held that the Fifth Amendment required police to warn criminal suspects of their "right to remain silent" before commencing any custodial interrogation of them. The Court also required the police to inform suspects that any statements they make may be used as evidence against them, and that they have the right to the presence of an attorney, either retained or appointed. Any incriminating statements that the accused makes in the absence of a *Miranda* warning, or other evidence resulting from such statements, is inadmissible in a subsequent trial.

This "right to silence" has always been limited in a variety of ways. For example, the traditional limitation of the Fifth Amendment's scope to *testimonial* admissions has long been held to allow the police to compel an accused to furnish nontestimonial evidence such as fingerprints, samples of bodily fluids, and hair. In recent years, however, the Supreme Court has made a number of important decisions that many observers see as

[16] 384 U.S. 436 (U.S. Sup. Ct. 1966).

placing further significant limitations on the right to silence. For example, it was long believed that an implicit part of the right to silence was a corresponding limitation on any prosecutorial trial comments about the accused's failure to speak in his own defense. Initially, the Supreme Court appeared to agree with this belief. In *United States v. Hale,*[17] the Court held that evidence of an accused's postarrest silence was inadmissible as evidence of his guilt. This position was bolstered by the Court's subsequent conclusion in *Doyle v. Ohio*[18] that using an accused's silence after receiving a *Miranda* warning to impeach his credibility on the witness stand violated the Due Process Clause.

More recently, however, the Court has allowed prosecutors to use a defendant's pretrial silence to impeach his trial testimony in some circumstances. In *Jenkins v. Anderson,*[19] the Court held that the Fifth Amendment was not violated when a defendant's prearrest silence was used to discredit his trial testimony that he had killed his victim in self-defense. In *Fletcher v. Weir,*[20] a more recent case with facts similar to those of *Jenkins,* the defendant's silence after his arrest, but in advance of any *Miranda* warning, was held to be a proper basis for impeachment of his trial testimony on the self-defense issue.

Most recently, the Court in *New York v. Quarles*[21] narrowed the scope of the *Miranda* decision by recognizing a "public safety" exception to *Miranda.* In *Quarles,* a rape victim told police that her assailant had just entered a nearby supermarket and was carrying a gun. When the police apprehended the suspect and discovered that he was wearing an empty shoulder holster, he was asked where the gun was. He responded, "The gun is over there." The Supreme Court overruled the decisions of the New York trial and appellate courts that excluded the defendant's statement and gun from the evidence offered at trial because the police officer had failed to read him a *Miranda* warning before asking him about the gun. The Court held that the risk to public safety posed by the concealed gun justified the officer's decision to locate the gun before informing Quarles of his rights.

While the preceding discussion of the privilege against self-incrimination has focused on the rights of criminal defendants in general, the Fifth Amendment has long had particular relevance to persons in business who are charged with crimes. In 1886, the Supreme Court held that the Fourth and Fifth Amendments protected businesspersons against the compulsory production of their private papers as well as against compelled oral testimony.[22] Subsequent decisions, however, have drastically narrowed the scope of this "private papers" protection. First, a number of the Court's decisions have held that the private papers privilege is a *personal* privilege that cannot be asserted by a corporation, partnership, or unincorporated association or by an individual person acting as a representative of such an entity. Only sole proprietors and other individuals acting in their own behalf may assert the privilege. In addition, the Court has recently held that the Fifth Amendment does not bar an otherwise lawful search and seizure of a sole proprietor's business records by law enforcement officers, because in such a case the defendant is not compelled to aid in the production or authentication of incriminating evidence.[23]

Finally, the range of records that can effectively be characterized as "private papers"

---

[17] 422 U.S. 171 (U.S. Sup. Ct. 1975).

[18] 426 U.S. 610 (U.S. Sup. Ct. 1976).

[19] 447 U.S. 231 (U.S. Sup. Ct. 1980).

[20] 455 U.S. 603 (U.S. Sup. Ct. 1982).

[21] 52 U.S.L.W. 4790 (U.S. Sup. Ct. 1984).

[22] *Boyd v. United States,* 116 U.S. 616 (U.S. Sup. Ct. 1886).

[23] *Andresen v. Maryland,* 427 U.S. 463 (U.S. Sup. Ct. 1976).

has been considerably narrowed. It has long been held that the government has the power to require business proprietors to keep certain records relevant to transactions that are appropriate subjects for government regulations. Such "required records" may be subpoenaed and used against the record keeper in prosecutions for statutory violations. The Supreme Court's most recent statement on this subject, the *Doe* case, which follows, further narrows the protection that the Fifth Amendment affords to business records by holding that normal business records are outside the amendment's scope because they are voluntarily prepared, and therefore not the product of compulsion. Instead of focusing on the *content* of the records subpoenaed, the Court now appears to be focusing on the issue of whether the act of *producing* the records in response to a subpoena is sufficiently testimonial in nature to violate the privilege against self-incrimination.

One other Fifth Amendment provision worthy of note is the **Double Jeopardy Clause.** This provision protects criminal defendants from multiple prosecutions for the "same offense." It operates to prevent a defendant from being charged with more than one count of the same statutory violation for one offense (e.g., being charged with two robbery violations for a one-time robbery of one individual). It also prevents a second prosecution for the same offense after the defendant has been acquitted or convicted of that offense, and it bars the imposition of multiple punishments for the same offense.

The Double Jeopardy Clause does not, however, preclude the possibility that a single criminal act may result in several criminal prosecutions. For example, one criminal act may produce several statutory violations, all of which may be proper subjects for prosecution. A defendant who commits a rape may also be prosecuted for battery, assault with a deadly weapon, and kidnapping if the facts of the case indicate that several statutes were violated. Second, the Supreme Court has long used a "same evidence" test to determine what constitutes the "same offense."[24] This means that a single criminal act with multiple victims (e.g., a robbery of a restaurant where several patrons are robbed) could result in several prosecutions because the identity of each victim would be an additional fact of proof in each case. Finally, the Double Jeopardy Clause does not protect against multiple prosecutions by *different sovereigns.* A conviction or acquittal in a federal court will not prevent a subsequent prosecution in a state court for a state offense arising out of the same event, or vice versa.

[24] *Blockburger v. United States,* 284 U.S. 299 (U.S. Sup. Ct. 1932).

## United States v. Doe

### 52 U.S.L.W. 4296 (U.S. Sup. Ct. 1984)

During a federal grand jury investigation of alleged corruption in the awarding of county and municipal contracts, subpoenas were served on the owner of several sole proprietorships (named as John Doe in the Court's opinion to prevent disclosure of his identity) demanding that he produce certain of his business records. Doe filed a motion to quash the subpoenas on the ground that the records in question were protected by the Fifth Amendment. The district court granted Doe's motion except with respect to those records required by law to be kept or disclosed to a public agency. The Third Circuit Court of Appeals affirmed the district court's decision, and the government appealed.

**Powell, Justice.** The Court in *Fisher v. United States* (1976) expressly declined to reach the question whether the Fifth Amendment privilege protects the contents of an individual's tax records in his possession. The rationale underlying our holding in that case is, however, persuasive here. As we noted in *Fisher,* the Fifth Amendment only protects the person asserting the privilege from *compelled* self-incrimination. Where the preparation of business records is voluntary, no compulsion is present. A subpoena that demands production of documents "does not compel oral testimony; nor would it ordinarily compel the taxpayer to restate, repeat, or affirm the truth of the contents of the documents sought." Applying this reasoning in *Fisher,* we stated:

> The Fifth Amendment would not be violated by the fact alone that the papers on their face might incriminate the taxpayer, for the privilege protects a person only against being incriminated by his own compelled testimonial communications. The accountant's workpapers are not the taxpayer's. They were not prepared by the taxpayer, and they contain no testimonial declarations by him. Furthermore, as far as this record demonstrates, the preparation of all of the papers sought in these cases was wholly voluntary, and they cannot be said to contain compelled testimonial evidence, either of the taxpayer's or of anyone else. The taxpayer cannot avoid compliance with the subpoena merely by asserting that the item of evidence which he is required to produce contains incriminating writing, whether his own or that of someone else.

This reasoning applies with equal force here. Doe does not contend that he prepared the documents involuntarily or that the subpoena would force him to restate, repeat, or affirm the truth of their contents. The fact that the records are in Doe's possession is irrelevant to the determination of whether the creation of the records was compelled. We therefore hold that the contents of those records are not privileged.

Although the contents of a document may not be privileged, the act of producing the document may be. A government subpoena compels the holder of the document to perform an act that may have testimonial aspects and an incriminating effect. As we noted in *Fisher:*

> Compliance with the subpoena tacitly concedes the existence of the papers demanded and their possession or control by the taxpayer. It also would indicate the taxpayer's belief that the papers are those described in the subpoena. The elements of compulsion are clearly present, but the more difficult issues are whether the tacit averments of the taxpayer are both "testimonial" and "incriminating" for purposes of applying the Fifth Amendment. These questions perhaps do not lend themselves to categorical answers: their resolution may instead depend on the facts and circumstances of particular cases or classes thereof.

In *Fisher,* the Court explored the effect that the act of production would have on the taxpayer and determined that the act of production would have only minimal testimonial value and would not operate to incriminate the taxpayer. Unlike the Court in *Fisher,* we have the explicit finding of the District Court that the act of producing the documents would involve testimonial self-incrimination. The Court of Appeals agreed. The District Court's finding essentially rests on its determination of factual issues. Therefore, we will not overturn that finding unless it has no support in the record. Traditionally, we also have been reluctant to disturb findings of fact in which two courts below have concurred. We therefore decline to overturn the finding of the district court in this regard, where, as here, it has been affirmed by the Court of Appeals.

The Government, as it concedes, could have compelled Doe to produce the documents listed in the subpoena. Sections 6002 and 6003 of Title 18 provide for the granting of use immunity with respect to the potentially incriminating evidence.

The Government did state several times before the District Court that it would not use respondent's act of production against him in any way. But counsel for the Government never made a statutory request to the District Court to grant Doe use immunity. We are urged to adopt a doctrine of constructive use immunity. Under this doctrine, the courts would impose a requirement on the Government not to use the incriminatory aspects of the act of production against the person claiming the privilege even though the statutory procedures have not been followed.

We decline to extend the jurisdiction of courts to include prospective grants of use immunity in the absence of the formal request that the statute requires. As we stated in *Pillsbury Co. v. Conboy* (1983), in passing the use immunity statute, "Congress gave certain officials in the Department of Justice exclusive authority to grant immunities. Congress foresaw the courts as playing only a minor role in the immunizing process."

The decision to seek use immunity necessarily involves a balancing of the Government's interest in obtaining information against the risk that immunity will frustrate the Government's attempts to prosecute the subject of the investigation. Congress expressly left this decision exclusively to the Justice Department. If, on remand, the appropriate official concludes that it is desirable to compel Doe to produce his business records, the statutory procedure for requesting use immunity will be available.

We conclude that the Court of Appeals erred in holding that the contents of the subpoenaed documents were privileged under the Fifth Amendment. The act of producing the documents at issue in this case is privileged and cannot be compelled without a statutory grant of use immunity pursuant to 18 U.S.C. Sections 6002 and 6003.

Judgment affirmed in part, and reversed in part. Case remanded to the District Court for further proceedings.

**The Sixth Amendment.** The Sixth Amendment contains a number of provisions aimed at safeguarding the rights of criminal defendants. It provides that defendants in criminal cases are entitled to a speedy trial by an impartial jury, at which they are entitled to confront and cross-examine the witnesses against them. It also provides that the accused in a criminal case enjoys the right "to have the assistance of counsel" in his or her defense. This provision has been interpreted to mean not only that the defendant has the right to employ his own attorney to represent him but that indigent defendants charged with a crime are entitled to court-appointed counsel.[25] An accused must be informed of his *right to counsel* once he has been taken into custody,[26] and once the accused has requested the assistance of counsel, no further interrogation of him is allowed unless he voluntarily initiates further conversations with the authorities.[27] Finally, an accused is entitled to *effective* assistance by his counsel. This means that he is entitled to counsel at a point in the proceedings when counsel can effectively assist him[28] and that

[25] *Gideon v. Wainwright,* 372 U.S. 335 (U.S. Sup. Ct. 1963).

[26] *Miranda v. Arizona,* 384 U.S. 436 (U.S. Sup. Ct. 1966).

[27] *Edwards v. Arizona,* 451 U.S. 477 (U.S. Sup. Ct. 1981).

[28] *Powell v. Alabama,* 287 U.S. 45 (U.S. Sup. Ct. 1932).

inadequate assistance by counsel can be a proper basis for setting aside a conviction and ordering a new trial.[29]

## WHITE-COLLAR CRIMES AND THE DILEMMAS OF CORPORATE CONTROL

**Introduction.** "White-collar crime" is the term broadly used to describe a wide variety of nonviolent criminal offenses committed by persons in business and by business organizations. Although this term is often used to include offenses committed by corporate employees against the interests of their corporate employers (e.g., theft, embezzlement, accepting a bribe), our discussions in this part of the text will focus on criminal offenses committed by corporate employers and their employees against society as a whole. Each year, corporate crime costs consumers billions of dollars. It may take a variety of forms, from consumer fraud, securities fraud, and tax evasion to price-fixing, environmental pollution, and other regulatory violations. Corporate crime confronts our legal system with a variety of problems—problems that to date we have failed to resolve satisfactorily.

Corporations form the backbone of the most successful economic system in history. They dominate the international economic scene, and they have provided us with incalculable benefits in the form of efficiently produced goods and services. Yet these same corporations may pollute the environment, swindle their customers, produce dangerously defective products, and conspire with others to injure or destroy competition. How are we to gain effective control over these large organizations that are so important to our existence? Increasingly, we have come to rely on the criminal law as a major instrument of corporate control.

But the criminal law was developed with individual wrongdoers in mind. Who is "at fault" when a large organization causes some social harm? Corporate crime is *organizational* crime: any given corporate action may be the product of the combined actions of a number of individuals acting within the corporate hierarchy, none of whom had sufficient knowledge to possess individually the *mens rea* necessary for criminal responsibility under traditional criminal law principles. And how are we to apply such criminal sanctions as imprisonment or death to a "legal" person like a corporation?

**Evolution of Corporate Criminal Liability.** The common law initially rejected the notion that corporations could be criminally responsible for the actions of their employees. Early corporations were small in size and number and had little impact on public life. Their small size meant that it was relatively easy to pinpoint individual wrongdoers within the corporation and thereby avoid the difficult conceptual problems associated with corporate criminal liability. After all, corporations were legal entities; they lacked a "mind," and it was therefore hard to conceive of them as having the criminal intent necessary for common law crimes. They also lacked a physical body, and therefore were immune to imprisonment, the basic common law criminal sanction.

As corporations grew in size and power, however, and the social need to control their activities grew accordingly, the common law rules on corporate criminal liability began to change. The first cases in which criminal liability was imposed on corporations involved suits against public corporations such as municipalities (then the most common type of corporation) for the failure to perform such

[29] In *Strickland v. Washington,* 104 S. Ct. 2052 (U.S. Sup. Ct. 1984), the Court held that a defendant's conviction would not be set aside unless his attorney's performance fell below an objective standard of reasonableness and so prejudiced him as to result in the denial of a fair trial.

public duties as road and bridge repair. As commercial corporations grew in size and number, similar liability was imposed on them by statutes creating *public welfare offenses,* regulatory offenses for which no proof of *mens rea* was required.

By the turn of this century, American courts had begun to impose criminal liability on corporations for general criminal offenses that required proof of *mens rea.* This expansion of corporate criminal liability was achieved by *imputing* the criminal intent of its employees to the corporation in a fashion similar to the imposition of tort or contract liability on corporations under the doctrine of *respondeat superior.*[30] Today, it is generally thought that a corporation can be criminally liable for almost any criminal offense if the statute in question indicates a legislative intent to hold corporations liable. This legislative intent requirement can sometimes be problematic, because many state criminal statutes are derived from common law crimes and may contain language that suggests an intent to hold only humans liable. For example, many state manslaughter statutes define the offense as "the killing of one human being by the act of another." However, where statutes are framed in more general terms, referring to "persons" for example, the courts are generally willing to apply them to corporate defendants.

**Corporate Criminal Liability Today.** The modern rule on corporate criminal liability is that a corporation can be held liable for criminal offenses committed by its employees *acting within the scope of their employment* and *for the benefit of the corporation.* A major current issue in corporate criminal liability concerns which corporate employees' intent will be imputed to the corporation. Some commentators have argued that a corporation should be criminally responsible only for offenses that were committed by high corporate officials or that can be "linked" to them by their authorization or acquiescence. (Virtually all courts will impose criminal liability on a corporation under such circumstances.) Such arguments are based on notions of fairness: if any group of corporate employees can fairly be said to constitute a corporation's "mind," that group is its top officers and directors.

The problem with imposing corporate liability only on the basis of the actions or knowledge of top corporate officers is that such a strategy will often insulate the corporation from liability because many corporate offenses may be directly traceable only to middle managers or more subordinate corporate employees. It may be impossible to demonstrate that any higher level corporate official had sufficient knowledge to constitute *mens rea.* The federal courts have recognized this fact by adopting a general rule that a corporation can be criminally liable for the actions of any of its agents regardless of whether any "link" between such agents and higher level corporate officials can be demonstrated.

Another significant current controversy regarding the nature of corporate criminal responsibility concerns whether a *due diligence* defense to corporate criminal liability should be recognized. Those who advocate such a defense argue that it is unfair to impute the intent of some employees to their corporate employer without also considering good faith corporate efforts to prevent statutory violations. They also point out that the major justification advanced for corporate criminal liability is deterrence: the hope that the threat or imposition of criminal penalties will encourage corporate efforts aimed at complying with legal rules. Thus, they argue that recognizing a "due diligence" defense would en-

---

[30] *Respondeat superior* is discussed in detail in Chapter 17. For an early landmark case on this subject, see *New York Central & Hudson River R.R. v. United States,* 212 U.S. 481 (U.S. Sup. Ct. 1909).

courage corporate compliance efforts, while imposing liability regardless of such efforts undermines deterrence by discouraging them. Most courts have found these arguments unconvincing and have generally rejected the idea of a due diligence defense. As the *Basic Construction* case, which follows, indicates, however, some courts are willing to admit evidence of corporate compliance efforts to determine whether corporate employees were acting to benefit the corporation.

## United States v. Basic Construction Co.

**711 F.2d 570 (4th Cir. 1983)**

Basic Construction Company, Henry S. Branscome, Inc., and its owner, Henry Branscome, were convicted of violating Section 1 of the Sherman Act by conspiring to rig the bidding for state road paving contracts. At their trial, the court gave the jury the following instruction on corporate liability:

> A corporation is legally bound by the acts or statements of its agents done or made within the scope of their employment, and within their apparent authority, acts done within the scope of employment and acts done on behalf of or to the benefit of a corporation, and directly related to the performance of the type [*sic*] duties the employee has general authority to perform.
>
> When the act of an agent is within the scope of his employment or within the scope of his apparent authority, the corporation is held legally responsible for it. This is true even though the agent's acts may be unlawful, and contrary to the corporation's actual instructions.
>
> A corporation may be responsible for the action of its agents done or made within the scope of their authority, even though the conduct of the agents may be contrary to the corporation's actual instructions, or contrary to the corporation's stated position.
>
> However, the existence of such instructions and policies, if any be shown, may be considered by you in determining whether the agents, in fact, were acting to benefit the corporation.

At trial, Basic introduced evidence that would have tended to prove that it had a longstanding, well-known, and strictly enforced policy against bid rigging. Such evidence tended to show that the bid-rigging activities with which it was charged were perpetrated by two relatively minor officials and without the knowledge of high-level corporate officers. On appeal, Basic argued that, in light of this evidence, the district court should have instructed the jury that it could consider the evidence of Basic's antitrust compliance policy in deciding whether the company had the requisite intent to violate the Sherman Act.

**PER CURIAM.** Basic rests its argument primarily on *United States v. United States Gypsum Co.* (1978). *Gypsum* involved a criminal antitrust prosecution in which the district court had instructed the jury that, if it found that the practice of competing producers giving to other producers on request, the price of gypsum board that was currently offered to a specific customer had the effect of fixing or raising prices, then they should presume as a matter of law that the parties intended such a result. The Supreme Court held that these instructions were erroneous. The Court said that intent is an element that must be proved, and cannot be presumed, in a criminal antitrust prosecution. Basic argues that the instructions given by the district court in the instant case run counter to the holding in *Gypsum* because they fix absolute criminal liability on a corporation for acts done by its employees, although such acts may have been in violation of corporate policies and express instructions. *Gypsum,* Basic argues, requires that the government prove that the corporation, presumably as represented by its upper level officers and managers, had an intent separate from that of its lower level employees to violate the antitrust laws. Consequently, Basic asserts that the jury should have been instructed to consider corporate antitrust compliance policies in determining whether Basic had the requisite intent.

We do not think that *Gypsum* requires so much. Rather, the case, on the point at issue, holds that intent to violate the antitrust laws must be proved in a criminal antitrust prosecution, and it defines the required intent. The Court there was not confronted with, and did not decide, the issue of corporate liability for the acts of employees. The instructions given by the district court in the instant case are amply supported by case law. These cases hold that a corporation may be held criminally responsible for antitrust violations committed by its employees if they were acting within the scope of their authority, or apparent authority, and for the benefit of the corporation, even if such acts were against corporate policy or express instructions. In *United States v. Koppers Co.* (1981), the Second Circuit rejected the argument, as do we, that *Gypsum* changes the law on corporate criminal antitrust liability for the acts of its employees.

In the instant case, the district court properly allowed the jury to consider Basic's alleged antitrust compliance policy in determining whether the employees were acting for the benefit of the corporation. It also properly instructed on the issue of intent in an antitrust prosecution, i.e., that corporate intent is shown by the actions and statements of the officers, directors, and employees who are in positions of authority or have apparent authority to make policy for the corporation.

Judgment for the government affirmed.

**Problems with Corporate Criminal Liability.** Despite the legal theories that justify corporate criminal liability, the punishment of corporations still remains a highly problematic subject. Does a corporate criminal conviction "stigmatize" a corporation in the same way that being branded a criminal stigmatizes an individual? The idea of viewing a corporation as a "criminal" may be difficult for most people to embrace. Perhaps the only stigmatization resulting from a corporate criminal conviction will be that felt by corporate employees, many of whom will be entirely innocent of any wrongdoing. Is it just to punish the innocent in an attempt to punish the guilty?

And what of the cash fine, the primary punishment imposed on corporations convicted of criminal violations? Most critics of contemporary corporate control strategies argue that the fines imposed on convicted corporations tend to be too small to provide effective deterrence. What is needed, they argue, are fines that are keyed in some fashion to the corporate defendant's wealth (e.g., a percentage of the defendant's income or total capital). But such large fines present a variety of practical and conceptual difficulties. Where market conditions permit, criminal fines are likely to be "passed on" to consumers in the form of higher prices, and where a "pass on" is impossible, corporate shareholders are likely to absorb the loss. Fines large enough to threaten corporate solvency may cause injury to corporate employees and others who are economically dependent on the corporation's economic well-being. Yet most of these individuals will neither have had the power to prevent the violation in question nor have derived any benefit from it. On the other hand, fines imposed on a corporation may place no direct burden on the managers who are responsible for a violation. Given the element of randomness inherent in criminal fines, legislatures may be unwilling to authorize, and courts reluctant to impose, fines that are large enough to produce deterrence.

Aside from such problems of practicality and fairness, fines suffer from other deficiencies that make them less than adequate corporate control devices. Fine strategies tend to assume that all corporations are rationally acting profit maximizers: fines of sufficient size, it is argued, will erode the profit drive that underlies most corporate violations. But many studies of actual corporate behavior indicate that many corporations are neither profit maximizers nor rational actors. Mature firms with well-established market shares may embrace goals other than profit maximization (e.g., technological prominence, increased market share, higher employee salaries). In addition, the interests of the managers who make corporate decisions and establish corporate policies may not be synonymous with the long-range economic interests of their corporate employers. The fact that their employers may at some future point have to pay a sizable fine may not make much of an impression on top managers who tend to have relatively short terms in office and who are often compensated in part by large bonuses keyed to year-end profitability.

Even if corporate managers were otherwise motivated to avoid corporate violations, there are reasons to doubt whether they would always be capable of doing so. Most organization theorists acknowledge that large organizations tend to suffer from problems of control. Many corporate wrongs may result from internal bureaucratic malfunctions rather than the conscious actions of any intracorporate individual or group. Fines are as unlikely to deter such "structural" violations as they are to encourage internal reform efforts in response to a fine imposed after a violation has occurred.

**Individual Liability for Corporate Crime.** Individuals who commit criminal offenses while acting in their corporate capacities have always been personally exposed to criminal liability. In fact, most European nations reject corporate criminal liability in favor of exclusive reliance on individual criminal responsibility. Certainly, individual liability has many attractive features, particularly in view of the problems connected with imposing criminal liability on corporations. Individual liability is more consistent with traditional criminal law notions about the personal nature of guilt. Individual liability may provide better deterrence than corporate liability if it enables society to bring the threat of criminal punishment to bear against the individual corporate officers who make important corporate decisions. The possibility of personal liability may induce individuals to resist corporate pressures to violate the law and may prevent corporations from treating financial penalties merely as a cost of doing business. And to the extent that guilty individuals can be identified and punished, the ends of the criminal law may be achieved without unfairly stigmatizing innocent corporate employees or punishing innocent shareholders or consumers.

**Problems with Individual Liability.** Attractive as individual liability may sound, it too poses some significant problems when applied in the corporate context. Identifying responsible individuals within the corporate hierarchy is a difficult and often impossible task if we adhere to traditional notions of criminal responsibility and insist on proof of some criminal intent as a precondition of liability. The division of authority that typifies large corporations produces a diffusion of responsibility that often makes assigning individual responsibility exceedingly difficult. Corporate decisions are often *collective* decisions, the products of the combined actions of numerous individuals within the corporate hierarchy, none of whom may have had complete knowledge or any specific intent.

It may be particularly difficult to prove knowledge on the part of high-level executives, because "bad news" may not reach them or because they may consciously try to avoid such knowledge. It may therefore only be possible to demonstrate culpability on the part of middle-level managers. But juries may be unwilling to convict such individuals if they are seen as scapegoats for their unindicted superiors. Finally, some corporate crimes may be "structural" in the sense that they are the products of internal bureaucratic failures rather than the conscious actions of any individual or group.

Even when a culpable individual can be identified, significant problems remain in effectively applying the criminal sanction to him. The individual in question may have died, retired, or been transferred to another post outside the jurisdiction where the offense occurred. White-collar defendants are rarely imprisoned after conviction, and when imprisonment does result, it is commonly in the form of a short sentence to a "country club" institution, with early parole a high possibility. The reluctance to imprison white-collar offenders is generally attributed to the positive image that such offenders normally possess (i.e., they tend to be well-educated, well-spoken community leaders) and to public doubts about the moral culpability involved in most white-collar offenses. Thus, most convicted white-collar offenders merely receive a fine, which is often small in comparison to their wealth and is frequently indemnified by their corporate employers.[31]

These difficulties in imposing criminal penalties on individual corporate employees have led to the creation of regulatory offenses imposing *strict* or *vicarious* liability on corporate officers. **Strict liability offenses** dispense with the requirement of proof of any criminal intent on the part of the defendant, but ordinarily require proof that the defendant committed some wrongful act. **Vicarious liability offenses** impose criminal liability on a defendant for the acts of third parties (normally employees under the defendant's personal supervision), but may require proof of some form of *mens rea* on the defendant's part (e.g., a negligent or reckless failure to supervise). Some regulatory statutes have adopted these approaches, and it is not uncommon to encounter a statute that embodies elements of both (i.e., imposes liability on a corporate executive for the acts or omissions of other corporate employees without requiring proof of criminal intent on the part of any corporate employee). The *Park* case, which follows, is probably the most famous recent example of such a prosecution.

Strict liability offenses have been widely criticized on a variety of grounds. First, it is often argued that the idea of *mens rea* is a basic principle in our legal system and that it is unjust to stigmatize with a criminal conviction persons who are not morally culpable. Second, the critics commonly express doubts about whether strict liability offenses will produce the deterrence that their proponents seek. They may reduce the moral impact of the criminal sanction by applying it to relatively trivial offenses. And they may not result in enough convictions or severe enough penalties to produce deterrence because juries and judges may be unwilling to convict or

---

[31] Indemnification is discussed in detail in Chapter 24.

punish defendants who are not viewed as morally culpable. While the courts have generally upheld the constitutionality of strict liability offenses, they are generally disfavored, with most courts requiring a clear indication of a legislative intent to dispense with the element of *mens rea.*[32]

Finally, even if prosecutors were generally able to identify and convict responsible individuals within the corporation and judges and juries were willing to impose significant penalties on such individuals, there are several reasons why individual liability in the absence of corporate liability would probably fail to achieve effective corporate control. If corporations were immune from criminal liability, they might stand to benefit financially from law violations by their employees. Individual liability, unlike corporate fines, does not force a corporation to give up the profits flowing from a violation. Thus, corporations would have no incentive to avoid future violations and incarcerated offenders would merely be replaced by others who might eventually yield to the pressures that produced the violations in the first place. Also, corporate liability may, in some cases, encourage corporate efforts aimed at preventing future violations. And it is uniquely appropriate when an offense has occurred but no identifiable individual is sufficiently culpable to justify an individual prosecution.

[32] See, for example, *United States v. U.S. Gypsum Co.,* 425 U.S. 422 (U.S. Sup. Ct. 1978).

## United States v. Park

**421 U.S. 658 (U.S. Sup. Ct. 1975)**

John R. Park was the chief executive officer of Acme Markets, Inc., a national retail food chain with approximately 36,000 employees, 874 retail outlets, and 16 warehouses. Acme and Park were charged with five counts of violating the Federal Food, Drug, and Cosmetic Act by storing food shipped in interstate commerce in warehouses where it was exposed to rodent contamination.

The violations were detected during Food and Drug Administration (FDA) inspections of Acme's Baltimore warehouse. A 12-day inspection during November and December 1971 disclosed evidence of rodent infestation and unsanitary conditions at the warehouse. Among other things, mouse pellets were found on the floor of the hanging meat room and beside bales of lime Jell-O, and one bale of Jell-O was found to contain a chewed rodent hole. The FDA notified Park by letter of these findings. After receiving the letter, Park conferred with Acme's vice president for legal affairs, who told him that the Baltimore division vice president "was investigating the situation immediately and would be taking corrective action." When a subsequent FDA investigation, in March 1972, disclosed continued rodent contamination at the Baltimore warehouse despite improved sanitation there, the charges were filed against Acme and Park. Acme pleaded guilty to the charges, but Park refused to do so. Park was convicted on each count and fined $50 per count.

Park appealed his conviction, arguing that the trial court's instructions to the jury were defective because they could have been interpreted as justifying a conviction based solely on his corporate position. He also argued that the trial court erred in allowing the government to introduce evidence of a 1970 FDA letter that informed him of similar problems at Acme's Philadelphia warehouse. The Fourth Circuit Court of Appeals agreed, reversing Park's conviction. The government appealed.

**Burger, Chief Justice.** In *United States v. Dotterweich* (1943), this Court looked to the purposes of the Act and noted that they "touch phases of the lives and health of people which, in the circumstances of modern industrialism, are largely beyond self-protection." It observed that the Act is of "a now familiar type" which "dispenses with the conventional requirement for criminal conduct—awareness of some wrongdoing. In the interest of the larger good it puts the burden of acting at hazard upon a person otherwise innocent but standing in reponsible relation to a public danger."

Central to the Court's conclusion that individuals other than proprietors are subject to the criminal provisions of the Act was the reality that "the only way in which a corporation can act is through the individuals who act on its behalf."

At the same time, however, the Court was aware of the concern that literal enforcement "might operate too harshly by sweeping within its condemnation any person however remotely entangled in the proscribed shipment." A limiting principle, in the form of "settled doctrines of criminal law" defining those who "are responsible for the commission of a misdemeanor," was available. In this context, the Court concluded, those doctrines dictated that the offense was committed "by all who have a responsible share in the furtherance of the transaction which the statute outlaws."

The rationale of the interpretation given the Act in *Dotterweich,* as holding criminally accountable the persons whose failure to exercise the authority and supervisory responsibility reposed in them by the business organization resulted in the violation complained of, has been confirmed in our subsequent cases. Thus, the Court has reaffirmed the proposition that "the public interest in the purity of its food is so great as to warrant the imposition of the highest standard of care on distributors."

Thus *Dotterweich* and the cases which have followed reveal that in providing sanctions which reach and touch the individuals who execute the corporate mission—and this is by no means necessarily confined to a single corporate agent or employee—the Act imposes not only a positive duty to seek out and remedy violations when they occur but also, and primarily, a duty to implement measures that will insure that violations will not occur. The duty imposed by Congress on responsible corporate agents is, we emphasize, one that requires the highest standard of foresight and vigilance, but the Act, in its criminal aspect, does not require that which is objectively impossible. The theory upon which responsible corporate agents are held criminally accountable for "causing" violations of the Act permits a claim that a defendant was "powerless" to prevent or correct the violation to "be raised defensively at a trial on the merits." If such a claim is made, the defendant has the burden of coming forward with evidence, but this does not alter the Government's ultimate burden of proving beyond a reasonable doubt the defendant's guilt, including his power, in light of the duty imposed by the Act, to prevent or correct the prohibited condition.

Turning to the jury charge in this case, it is of course arguable that isolated parts can be read as intimating that a finding of guilt could be predicated solely on Park's corporate position. Viewed as a whole, the charge did not permit the jury to find guilt solely on the basis of Park's position in the corporation; rather, it fairly advised the jury that to find guilt it must find Park "had a responsible relation to the situation," and "by virtue of his position . . . had authority and responsibility" to deal with the situation.

Our conclusion that the Court of Appeals erred in its reading of the jury charge suggests as well our disagreement with that court concerning the admissibility of evidence demonstrating that Park was advised by FDA in 1970 of insanitary conditions in Acme's Philadelphia warehouse. Park testified in his defense that he had employed a system in which he relied upon his subordinates, and that he was ultimately responsible for this system. He testified further that he had found these subordinates to be "dependable" and had "great confidence" in them. By this and other testimony Park evidently sought to persuade the jury that, as the president of a large corporation, he had no choice but to delegate duties to those in whom he reposed confidence, that he had no reason to suspect his subordinates were failing to insure compliance with the Act, and that, once violations were unearthed, acting through those subordinates he did everything possible to correct them.

Although we need not decide whether this testimony would have entitled Park to an instruction as to his lack of power, had he requested it, the testimony clearly created the "need" for rebuttal evidence. That evidence was not offered to show that Park had a propensity to commit criminal acts, that the crime charged had been committed; its purpose was to demonstrate that Park was on notice that he could not rely on his system of delegation to subordinates to prevent or correct insanitary conditions at Acme's warehouses, and that he must have been aware of the deficiencies of this system before the Baltimore violations were discovered. The evidence was therefore relevant since it served to rebut Park's defense that he had justifiably relied upon subordinates to handle sanitation matters. And, particularly in light of the difficult task of juries in prosecutions under the Act, we conclude that its relevance and persuasiveness outweighed any prejudicial effect.

Judgment of the Court of Appeals reversed; Park's conviction sustained.

**New Directions.** The preceding discussion suggests that future efforts at corporate control are likely to include both corporate and individual criminal liability. It also suggests, however, that new approaches are necessary if society is to gain more effective control over corporate activities. New remedies are needed that reflect both our historical experience with attempts to apply the criminal sanction in the corporate context and our knowledge of the nature of corporate behavior.

In the area of individual liability, a variety of novel criminal penalties have been suggested. For example, white-collar offenders could be deprived of their leisure time or sentenced to render public service rather than being incarcerated or fined. Some have even suggested licensing managers, with license suspensions as a penalty for offenders. The common thread in all these approaches is an attempt to create penalties that will be meaningful to the defendant, yet not so severe that judges and juries will be unwilling to impose them with sufficient certainty to produce deterrence.

In the area of corporate liability, one of the most novel and promising recent suggestions involves more imaginative judicial use of corporate probation for convicted corporate offenders.[33] The court could require convicted corporations to do, or hire independent consultants to do, self-studies aimed at identifying the source of a violation and proposing appropriate steps to prevent future violations. If bureaucratic failures caused the violation, the court could order a limited restructuring of the corporation's internal decision-making

[33] See Note, "Structural Crime and Institutional Rehabilitation: A New Approach to Corporate Sentencing," 89 *Yale L. J.* 353 (1979).

processes as a condition of obtaining probation or avoiding a penalty. Possible orders might include requiring the collection and monitoring of the data necessary to discover or prevent future violations and the creation of new executive positions charged with the duty to monitor such data. Restructuring would tend to minimize the harm to innocent persons inherent in corporate financial penalties, but it might also be a more effective way of achieving corporate rehabilitation than relying exclusively on a corporation's desire to avoid future fines as an incentive for it to police itself. Since restructuring would also represent a new form of governmental intrusion into the private sector, it should be applied sparingly and with discretion.

## IMPORTANT WHITE-COLLAR CRIMES

**Regulatory Offenses.** A wide range of federal and state regulatory statutes provide for criminal as well as civil liability in the event of a violation. Several major federal regulatory offenses are discussed in detail in later chapters in this text, including violations of the Sherman Antitrust Act, the Securities Act of 1933 and the Securities Exchange Act of 1934, the Clean Waters Act of 1972, the Resource Conservation and Recovery Act, and the Electronic Funds Transfer Act. The federal Food, Drug, and Cosmetic Act, at issue in the *Park* case, makes it a federal offense to mislabel or adulterate food, drugs, or cosmetic products in interstate commerce.

**Fraudulent Acts.** Many business crimes involve some form of *fraudulent* conduct. In most states, it is a crime to obtain money or property by fraudulent pretenses, to issue fraudulent checks, to make false credit or advertising statements, or to give short weights or measures. Various forms of fraud in bankruptcy proceedings (e.g., fraudulent concealment or transfer of a debtor's assets or false claims by creditors) are federal criminal offenses.[34] In addition, the federal Mail Fraud and Wire Fraud acts make it a federal offense to use the mail or telephone or telegrams to accomplish a fraudulent scheme and the Travel Act of 1961 makes it a federal offense to travel or use facilities in interstate commerce to commit a variety of criminal acts.

**Bribery.** Offering gifts, favors, or anything of value to *public officials* in order to influence their official decisions to the benefit of private interests has long been a criminal offense under state and federal law. In 1977, Congress passed the Foreign Corrupt Practices Act, making it a federal offense to give anything of value to officials of foreign governments in an attempt to influence their official actions.[35] In addition, most states have enacted *commercial bribery statutes* making it illegal to offer kickbacks and payoffs to private individuals in order to secure some commercial advantage.

**RICO.** When Congress passed the Racketeer Influenced and Corrupt Organizations Act (RICO)[36] as part of the Organized Crime Control Act of 1970, it was concerned about organized crime's increasing entry into legitimate business enterprises. The broad language of the RICO statute, however, has resulted in its application in a wide variety of cases having nothing to do with organized crime. This development has made RICO one of the most controversial pieces of legislation affecting business in our legal history. The supporters of RICO argue that it has become an effective and much-needed tool for attacking a wide range of unethical business prac-

---

[34] Bankruptcy is discussed in detail in Chapter 41.

[35] The Foreign Corrupt Practices Act is discussed in detail in Chapter 26.

[36] 18 U.S.C. 1961–1968 (1976).

tices. Its critics assert, however, that RICO is an overbroad statute that needlessly taints business reputations. They also argue that it has operated unduly to favor plaintiffs in commercial litigation rather than serving as an aid to law enforcement. The lower federal courts disagree on many important points about the meaning of this controversial statute. As a result, many significant issues concerning RICO's scope await ultimate judicial or legislative resolution.

**Criminal RICO.** The criminal sections of the RICO statute make it a federal crime to: (1) use income derived from a "pattern of racketeering activity" to acquire an interest in an "enterprise," (2) acquire or maintain an interest in an enterprise through a pattern of racketeering activity, (3) conduct or participate in the affairs of an enterprise through a pattern of racketeering activity, or (4) conspire to do any of the preceding acts. RICO is a *compound* criminal statute because it requires both the proof of a "predicate" criminal offense and a "pattern of racketeering activity." *Racketeering activity* includes the commission of one of over 30 state or federal criminal offenses. Most of the offenses that qualify have no relation to normal business transactions (e.g., arson, gambling, extortion), but mail and wire fraud, securities fraud, and bribery are also included. Thus, almost any business fraud may be alleged to be a "racketeering activity." In order to show a *pattern* of such activity, the prosecution must prove the commission of two predicate offenses within a 10-year period. Most courts have interpreted the statutory term *enterprise* broadly to include partnerships and unincorporated associations as well as corporations.

Individuals found guilty of RICO violations are subject to a fine of up to $25,000 per violation and imprisonment for up to 20 years. In addition, they risk the forfeiture of any interest gained in any enterprise as a result of a violation.

**Civil RICO.** The RICO statute also allows the government to seek numerous civil penalties in the event of a violation. These include *divestiture* of a defendant's interest in an enterprise, the *dissolution* or *reorganization* of the enterprise, and *injunctions* against future racketeering activities by the defendant.

The most controversial sections of RICO, however, are those that allow private individuals to recover *treble damages* (three times their actual loss) plus attorney's fees for injuries caused by a statutory violation. This highly attractive remedy has led in recent years to the frequent use of RICO by plaintiffs in commercial fraud cases. Stockbrokers, banks, insurance companies, and employment agencies have been typical targets of recent civil RICO suits. To qualify for recovery under RICO, a plaintiff must allege that the defendant has violated RICO's provisions and that, as a result, the plaintiff was "injured in his business or property."

In the *Sedima* case, which follows, the Supreme Court recently resolved two major issues concerning RICO's scope in an expansive fashion. First, the Court rejected the requirement imposed by some lower federal courts that civil RICO plaintiffs prove a "distinct racketeering injury" as a precondition of recovery. In another part of its opinion, which is not reproduced below, the Court rejected the idea that civil RICO plaintiffs must prove that the defendant has been convicted of a predicate offense in order to recover. Although other issues concerning RICO's scope remain unresolved, the tenor of the Court's decision in *Sedima* suggests that Congress must be the source of the relief sought by RICO's critics.

## Sedima, S.P.R.L. v. Imrex Co., Inc.

### 84–648 (U.S. Sup. Ct. 1985)

In 1979, Sedima, a Belgian corporation, entered into a joint venture with Imrex Company calling for Imrex to provide electronic components to another Belgian firm. The buyer was to order parts through Sedima; Imrex was to obtain the parts in the United States and ship them to Europe. The agreement called for Sedima and Imrex to split the net proceeds, and Imrex filled roughly $8 million in orders placed with it through Sedima. Sedima became convinced, however, that Imrex was presenting inflated bills, cheating Sedima out of a portion of its proceeds by collecting for bogus expenses. Sedima filed suit against Imrex on several theories, including three federal RICO counts. Two of those counts were based on predicate acts of mail fraud and wire fraud. The third count alleged a conspiracy to violate section 1962(c) of the RICO statute. Claiming an injury of at least $175,000, the amount of the alleged overbilling, Sedima sought treble damages and attorney's fees.

The district court dismissed Sedima's RICO claims due to Sedima's failure to allege that it suffered a "racketeering injury" distinct from the injury resulting from the alleged predicate acts of mail fraud and wire fraud. When the Second Circuit Court of Appeals affirmed, Sedima appealed.

**White, Justice.** The decision below was one episode in a recent proliferation of civil RICO litigation within the Second Circuit and in other Courts of Appeals. In light of the variety of approaches taken by the lower courts and the importance of the issues, we granted certiorari.

In considering the Court of Appeals' prerequisite for a private civil RICO action—"injury . . . caused by an activity which RICO was designed to deter"—we are somewhat hampered by the vagueness of that concept. Apart from reliance on the general purposes of RICO and a reference to "mobsters," the court provided scant indication of what the requirement of racketeering injury means. It emphasized Congress's undeniable desire to strike at organized crime, but acknowledged and did not purport to overrule Second Circuit precedent rejecting a requirement of an organized crime nexus. The court also stopped short of adopting a "competitive injury" requirement; while insisting that the plaintiff show "the kind of economic injury which has an effect on competition," it did not require "actual anticompetitive effect."

The court's statement that the plaintiff must seek redress for an injury caused by conduct that RICO was designed to deter is unhelpfully tautological. Nor is clarity furnished by a negative statement of its rule: standing is not provided by the injury resulting from the predicate acts themselves. That statement is itself apparently inaccurate when applied to those predicate acts that unmistakably constitute the kind of conduct Congress sought to deter. The opinion does not explain how to distinguish such crimes from the other predicate acts Congress has lumped together in section 1961(l). The court below is not alone in struggling to define "racketeering injury," and the difficulty of that task itself cautions against imposing such a requirement.

We need not pinpoint the Second Circuit's precise holding, for we perceive no distinct "racketeering injury" requirement. Given that "racketeering activity" consists of no more and no less than commission of a predicate act, we are initially doubtful about a requirement of a "racketeering injury" separate from the harm from the predicate acts. A reading of the statute belies any such requirement. Section 1964(c) authorizes a private suit by "any person injured in his business or property by reason of a violation of section 1962." Section 1962 in turn makes it unlawful for "any person"—not just mobsters—to use money derived from a pattern of racketeering activity to invest in an enterprise, to acquire control of an enterprise through a pattern of racketeering activity, or to conduct an enterprise through a pattern of racketeering activity. If the defendant engages in a pattern of racketeering activity in a manner forbidden by these provisions, and the racketeering activities injure the plaintiff in his business or property, the plaintiff has a claim under section 1964(c). There is no room in the statutory language for an additional amorphous "racketeering injury" requirement.

A violation of section 1962(c), the section on which Sedima relies, requires (1) conduct (2) of an enterprise (3) through a pattern (4) of racketeering activity. The plaintiff must, of course, allege each of these elements to state a claim. Conducting an enterprise that affects interstate commerce is obviously not in itself a violation of section 1962, nor is mere commission of the predicate offenses. In addition, the plaintiff only has standing if, and can only recover to the extent that, he has been injured in his business or property by the conduct constituting the violation. As the Seventh Circuit has stated, "a defendant who violates section 1962 is not liable for treble damages to everyone he might have injured by other conduct, nor is the defendant liable to those who have not been injured." *Haroco, Inc. v. American National Bank & Trust Co. of Chicago* (1984).

But the statute requires no more than this. Where the plaintiff alleges each element of the violation, the compensable injury necessarily is the harm caused by predicate acts sufficiently related to constitute a pattern, for the essence of the violation is the commission of those acts in connection with the conduct of an enterprise. Those acts are, when committed in the circumstances delineated in section 1962(c), "an activity which RICO was designed to deter." Any recoverable damages occurring by reason of a violation of section 1962(c) will flow from the commission of the predicate acts.

This less restrictive reading is amply supported by our prior cases and the general principles surrounding this statute. RICO is to be read broadly. This is the lesson not only of Congress's self-consciously expansive language and overall approach, but also of its express admonition that RICO is to "be liberally construed to effectuate its remedial purposes." The statute's "remedial purposes" are nowhere more evident than in the provision of a private action for those injured by racketeering activity. Far from effectuating these purposes, the narrow readings offered by the dissenters and the court below would in effect eliminate section 1964(c) from the statute.

RICO was an aggressive initiative to supplement old remedies and develop new methods for fighting crime. While few of the legislative statements about novel remedies and attacking crime on all fronts were made with direct reference to section 1964(c), it is in this spirit that all of the Act's provisions should be read. The specific references to section 1964(c) are consistent with this overall approach. Those supporting section 1964(c) hoped it would "enhance the effectiveness of Title IX's prohibitions" and provide "a major new tool." Its opponents, also recognizing the provision's scope, complained that it provided too easy a weapon against "innocent businessmen," and would be prone to abuse.

Underlying the Court of Appeals' holding was its distress at the "extraordinary, if not outrageous," uses to which civil RICO has been put. Instead of being used against mobsters and organized criminals, it has become a tool for everyday fraud cases brought against "respected and legitimate 'enterprises.' " Yet Congress wanted to reach both "legitimate" and "illegitimate" enterprises. The former enjoy neither an inherent incapacity for criminal activity nor immunity from its consequences. The fact that section 1964(c) is used against respected businesses allegedly engaged in a pattern of specifically identified criminal conduct is hardly a sufficient reason for assuming that the provision is being misconstrued.

It is true that private civil actions under the statute are being brought almost solely against such defendants, rather than against the archetypal, intimidating mobster. Yet this defect—if defect it is—is inherent in the statute as written, and its correction must lie with Congress. It is not for the judiciary to eliminate the private action in situations where Congress has provided it simply because the plaintiffs are not taking advantage of it in its more difficult applications.

Judgment reversed in favor of Sedima.

## SUMMARY

A thorough knowledge of the criminal law is an important component of a contemporary businessperson's education because in recent years the criminal sanction has been increasingly used as a major device for controlling business behavior. In major part, this trend reflects the belief that the criminal law provides a greater degree of deterrence than that afforded by civil remedies.

Crimes are public wrongs: offenses against the state that are prosecuted by the state. The criminal sanction is the law's ultimate threat because it combines a threat to life or liberty with the stigma of a criminal conviction. Crimes are classified as felonies or misdemeanors, depending on the seriousness of the offense involved. Conviction of a felony, a serious criminal offense, entails far more serious consequences than does conviction of a misdemeanor.

Significant social disagreement exists concerning the kinds of behavior that should be made criminal and the underlying purpose of the criminal sanction. Utilitarians view the prevention of socially undesirable behavior as the only proper justification of criminal penalties. Retributionists see criminal punishment as the infliction of deserved suffering on those who violate fundamental social rules.

Given the powerful nature of the criminal sanction, several important restrictions operate to limit the state's power to convict a person of a crime. All crimes are statutory in the United States. Criminal responsibility requires the violation of an existing statute that does not criminalize consitutionally protected behavior and that is worded clearly enough to give an ordinary person notice of the conduct prohibited. The state must prove each element of a criminal offense beyond a reasonable doubt and within an extensive framework of procedural restraints aimed at safeguarding the rights of the accused.

The state must also prove that the defendant had the capacity to entertain the criminal intent required for all serious criminal offenses. Three kinds of incapacity have been traditionally recognized: infancy, insanity, and intoxication.

The common law initially refused to hold corporations responsible for criminal offenses. Over time, however, this rule changed to the point where today a corporation can be found to have committed almost any criminal offense that has been given proper statutory wording. Corporate criminal intent is normally derived by imputing the intent of corporate agents to the corporation. Significant disagreement exists, however, about whether a corporation should be criminally responsible for the actions of any of its employees or only for the actions of its higher officials. Disagreement also exists concerning whether good faith corporate efforts to avoid violations should be a defense to liability.

Individual corporate employees who commit crimes in the course of their employment are personally criminally responsible. Due to the nature of corporate decision making, however, it is often difficult to pinpoint the individuals responsible for corporate crimes. This has led to regulatory statutes that impose strict or vicarious criminal responsibility on corporate officers.

For a variety of reasons, neither corporate nor individual liability has proven to be a very effective means of controlling corporate crime. New approaches that seek to learn from this lack of success and to employ our knowledge about the true nature of corporate behavior are needed if society is to achieve a greater level of control.

## PROBLEM CASES

**1.** Margaret Papachristou and Betty Calloway, two white females, and Eugene Melton and Leonard Johnson, two black males, were convicted of violating a Jacksonville, Florida, vagrancy ordinance. At the time of the arrest, they were riding in Calloway's car on the main thoroughfare in Jacksonville. The arresting officers denied that the racial mixture in the car played any part in their decision to make the arrest. They argued that the arrest was made because the defendants had stopped near a used-car lot that had been burglarized several times. The ordinance in question provided, among other things, that "rogues and vagabonds, or dissolute persons who go about begging, common gamblers, persons who use juggling or unlawful games or plays, common drunkards, common night walkers, . . . [or] persons wandering or strolling around from place to place without any lawful purpose or object, . . . shall be deemed vagrants" and be guilty of a misdemeanor. The defendants appealed their conviction, arguing that the ordinance was unconstitutional. Are they right?

**2.** Michael M., a 17½-year-old male, was charged with violating California's "statutory rape" statute by having sexual intercourse with Sharon, a 16½-year-old female. The statute in question defined unlawful sexual intercourse as "an act of sexual intercourse accomplished with a female not the wife of the perpetrator where the female is under the age of 18 years." Prior to the trial, Michael filed a motion to set aside the information charging him with the offense, arguing that the statute was unconstitutional because it discriminated on the basis of gender in violation of the Equal Protection Clause. The California courts denied his request on the ground that the legislative purpose of preventing teenage pregnancies justified treating males differently from females under the statute. Since only females could suffer the harm that the statute sought to avoid, and only males could cause it, the fact that only females could be victims and only males could violate the statute did not offend the Constitution. Were the California courts correct in reaching this conclusion?

**3.** In 1979, Jerry Helm was convicted in a South Dakota state court of issuing a $100 "no account" check. The normal maximum penalty for such a violation was five years' imprisonment and a $5,000 fine. Helm, however, was sentenced to life imprisonment without possibility of parole under a South Dakota recidivist statute because he had six prior felony convictions—three for third-degree burglary, one for obtaining money under false pretenses, one for grand larceny, and one for third-offense driving while intoxicated. Helm sought to have his sentence set aside on the ground that it constituted cruel and unusual punishment under the 8th and 14th Amendments. Should his sentence be set aside?

**4.** The Internal Revenue Service (IRS) levied assessments on GM Leasing Corporation for nonpayment of taxes and seized certain automobiles that belonged to GM and were parked in front of the building out of which GM operated. The IRS also made a warrantless forced entry into the building and seized certain of GM's books and records, none of which qualified as "required records." GM then sued the IRS, seeking return of the automobiles and suppression of the seized evidence on the ground that the IRS had violated GM's Fourth Amendment rights. Is GM correct?

**5.** During the investigation of the death of a minor whose body had been found in his wrecked pickup truck, James Bradshaw was questioned at the police station, where he was advised of his *Miranda* rights, arrested for furnishing liquor to the victim, and again advised of his rights. Bradshaw denied any involvement and asked for an attorney. Later, while being transferred from the police station to a jail, Bradshaw asked a police officer, "Well, what is going to happen to me now?" The officer answered that Bradshaw did not have to talk to him, and Bradshaw said he understood. A discussion followed between Bradshaw and the officer during which the officer suggested that Bradshaw take a polygraph (lie detector) examination, which he did after again being informed of his rights. After failing the examination, Bradshaw admitted that he had been driving the truck in question, had consumed a considerable amount of alcohol, and had passed out at the wheel before the truck left the highway. He was subsequently charged with first-degree manslaughter, driving while under the influence of intoxicants, and driving while his license was revoked. At trial, he moved to suppress his confession, on the ground that his Fifth Amendment rights had been violated. Should evidence of his confession be excluded?

**6.** Harrison Cronic and two associates were indicted on mail fraud charges involving a "check kiting" scheme whereby checks were transferred between a Florida bank and an Oklahoma bank. When Cronic's retained counsel withdrew shortly before the scheduled trial date, the district court appointed a young lawyer to represent him. The lawyer in question had a real estate practice and had never participated in a jury trial. The court allowed him only 25 days to prepare his case, although the government had taken over 4½ years and reviewed thousands of documents in the investigation. Cronic was convicted, but the court of appeals reversed his conviction because it inferred that he had been denied the effective assistance of counsel required by the Sixth Amendment. The court of appeals did not examine the trial performance of Cronic's lawyer. Instead, it based its inference on the short time that had been afforded Cronic's counsel for investigation and preparation, the seriousness of the charge, the complexity of the possible defenses, and the lawyer's inexperience. Was the court of appeals correct in reversing Cronic's conviction?

**7.** Federal agents observed employees of Johnson & Towers, Inc., a truck repair company, pumping toxic chemicals from a tank into a trench that flowed into navigable waters. The company and two of its employees were subsequently indicted for violating the Resource Conservation and Recovery Act (RCRA), which requires generators of toxic wastes to obtain disposal permits from the Environmental Protection Agency. Johnson & Towers had neither applied for nor obtained such a permit. The company pleaded guilty to the charges, but the employees moved to dismiss the charges against them, arguing that the RCRA criminal provision only applied to "owners and operators," who were obligated by statute to obtain a permit. The RCRA's criminal provisions applied to "any person who . . . knowingly treats, stores, or disposes of any hazardous waste" without having acquired a permit or in knowing violation of a permit. Since neither of the indicted employees was an owner or operator of the company, the district court granted their motion to dismiss the charges against them. Was dismissal proper?

**8.** During an investigation of certain bank loan officers and loan recipients, a federal grand jury issued a subpoena directing a sole proprietor's bookkeeper to produce all the proprietorship records in her custody. The evidence indicated that the bookkeeper actively prepared and maintained the records and that the sole proprietor had never asked to see them or to review them with her. He was rarely in the office in which the records were kept, and his infrequent visits there were unrelated to the records. Nonetheless, he sought to quash the subpoena on the ground that it violated his Fifth Amendment privilege against self-incrimination. Should the subpoena be enforced?

**9.** Gary Lewellyn, a Des Moines stockbroker, was convicted of embezzlement, making false statements, and mail fraud in connection with converting over $17 million in money and securities from two Iowa banks. In response to a pretrial government motion, the trial court ruled that Lewellyn could not rely on a defense of insanity by reason of pathological gambling and excluded evidence related to that defense. The court applied the American Law Institute insanity test and concluded that a defense of insanity based on impulse control in the form of pathological gambling was not available to a defendant charged with embezzlement even if there was evidence to support a finding that he lacked substantial capacity to conform his conduct to the law's requirements. Was the court's exclusion of Lewellyn's evidence of insanity proper?

**10.** Willie Cruso Free, a prisoner in a federal correctional institution, was convicted of second-degree murder for killing another prisoner who allegedly refused to engage in homosexual relations with him. He was also charged with violating a federal statute prohibiting the conveyance from place to place in a federal correctional institution of any weapon designed to kill, injure, or disable another person. This second charge involved the weapon used in the murder and was later dismissed by the trial court at the time of sentencing. Free argued that the separate charges were multiple charges for the same offense and thus violated the Double Jeopardy Clause. Was his argument correct?

Chapter

4

# Intentional Torts

## INTRODUCTION

**Nature and Function of Tort Law.** **Torts** are *private (civil) wrongs* against persons or their property. The basis of tort liability is a breach of a legal duty owed to another person that results in some legally recognizable harm to that person. The primary aim of tort law is to compensate injured persons for such harms. Thus, persons injured by the tortious act of another may file a civil suit for the *actual (compensatory) damages* that they have suffered as a result of a tort. Depending on the facts of the particular case, these damages may be for direct and immediate harms, such as physical injuries, medical expenses, and lost pay and benefits, or for harms as intangible as loss of privacy, injury to reputation, or emotional distress.

In cases in which the behavior of the person committing a tort is particularly reprehensible, injured victims may also be able to recover an award of *punitive damages*. Punitive damages are designed to punish flagrant wrongdoers and to deter them and others from engaging in similar conduct in the future. This punishment element of punitive damage awards performs a function similar to the deterrent function performed by the criminal law, and some kinds of behavior can give rise to both criminal and tort liability. For example, a rapist may be criminally liable for rape and also liable for the torts of assault, battery, false imprisonment, and intentional infliction of mental distress. However, since tort suits are civil rather than criminal, the plaintiff's burden of proof in a tort case is the *preponderance of the evidence,* rather than the more stringent "beyond a reasonable doubt" standard that applies to criminal cases. This means that the greater weight of the evidence introduced at the trial must support the plaintiff's position on every element of the case.

In tort law, society is engaged in a constant balancing of competing social interests. Excessive protection of some people's physical integrity, for example, may unduly impair other people's freedom of movement. Likewise, undue protection of peace of mind, privacy, and personal reputation may inordinately restrict constitutionally protected freedoms such as freedom of speech and freedom of the press. Over time, our tort law has demonstrated a tendency to afford protection to an increasingly broad range of personal interests. Some commentators have explained this tendency by saying that it demonstrates the courts' growing sensitivity to the nature of life in an increasingly interdependent urban industrialized society. Whatever its origins, this and the next chapter will demonstrate that, although the range of the human interests that tort law seeks to protect is expanding, the courts have remained mindful of the fact that the protection of any given interest necessarily involves a trade-off in the form of limitations placed on other competing social interests.

Torts are generally classified according to the level of fault exhibited by the wrongdoer's behavior. This chapter deals with **intentional torts:** types of behavior that indicate either the wrongdoer's conscious desire to cause harm to a legally protected interest or the wrongdoer's knowledge that such harm is substantially certain to result from his actions. Chapter 5 discusses tort liability founded on principles of *negligence* and *strict liability.*

## INTERFERENCE WITH PERSONAL RIGHTS

**Battery.** The tort of **battery** protects a fundamental personal interest: the right to be free from harmful or offensive bodily contacts. Battery is the *intentional, harmful,* or *offensive touching of another without* his *consent.* A contact is *harmful* if it produces any bodily injury. Even nonharmful contacts may be considered battery if they are *offensive:* calculated to offend a reasonable sense of personal dignity. Direct contact between a wrongdoer's body and the body of another is not necessary for a battery to result. For example, if Delano throws a rock at Stevens or places a harmful or offensive substance in his food, Delano has committed a battery if Stevens is hit by the rock or if he eats the food.

Also, the person who suffers the harmful or offensive touching does not have to be the person whom the wrongdoer intended to injure for liability for battery to occur: under a general intentional tort concept called the doctrine of *transferred intent,* a wrongdoer who intends to injure one person, but injures another, is nonetheless liable to the person injured, despite the absence of any specific intent to injure him. So, if Walters is hit by the rock thrown at Stevens, or if he eats Stevens' food, Delano would be liable to Walters for battery. Finally, touching anything connected with a person's body in a harmful or offensive manner can also create liability for battery. So, if Johnson snatches Martin's purse, or kicks her dog while she is walking her dog on a leash, he may be liable for battery even though he has not touched her body.

Some of the most interesting battery cases involve the nature of the *consent* that is necessary to avoid liability for battery. As a general rule, consent must be *freely* and *intelligently* given to be a defense to battery. In some cases, consent may be inferred from a person's voluntary participation in an activity. Such consent is ordinarily limited, however, to contacts that are considered a normal consequence of the activity in question. For example, Joe Frazier would be unable to win a battery suit against Muhammad Ali for injuries he suffered during their famous "Thrilla in Manila" title fight. However, the quarterback who is knifed on the 50-yard line has a valid battery claim.

**Assault.** The tort of **assault** protects the personal interest in freedom from the *apprehension* of battery. Any *attempt* to cause a harmful or offensive contact with another, or any *offer* to cause such a contact, is an assault if it causes a *well-grounded apprehension of imminent (immediate) battery* in the mind of the person threatened with contact. Whether or not the threatened contact actually occurs is irrelevant.

Since assault is limited to threats of *imminent* battery, threats of *future* battery will not create liability for assault. Likewise, since assault focuses on the apprehension in the mind of the victim, the threats in question must create a reasonable apprehension of battery in the victim's mind. Therefore, threatening words, unaccompanied by any other acts or circumstances indicating an intent to carry out the threat, will not amount to an assault. Finally, the elements of assault require that the victim actually experience an apprehension of imminent battery before liability will result. Therefore, if Markham fires a rifle at Thomas from a great distance and misses him, and Thomas learns of the attempt on his life only at a later date, Markham is not liable to Thomas for the tort of assault.

**False Imprisonment.** The tort of **false imprisonment** protects the personal interest in freedom from *confinement.* False imprisonment is the intentional *confinement of another* for an *appreciable time* (a few minutes is enough) *without his consent.* Confinement may result from physical barriers to the plaintiff's freedom of movement (e.g., locking a person in a room that has no other doors or windows), the use of physical force or the threat to use physical force against the plaintiff, the assertion of legal authority to detain the plaintiff, or the detention of the plaintiff's property (e.g., a purse containing a large sum of money). Likewise, a threat to harm another (e.g., the plaintiff's spouse or child) can also be confinement if it is used to prevent the plaintiff from moving.

The confinement required for false imprisonment must be *complete.* Partial confinement of another, by blocking his path or by depriving him of one means of escape where other reasonable means of escape exist (e.g., locking one door of a building with other, unlocked doors), will not amount to false imprisonment. The fact that a means of escape exists, however, will not render a confinement partial if the plaintiff cannot reasonably be expected to know of its existence or if it involves some unreasonable risk of harm to the plaintiff (e.g., he would have to walk a tightrope or climb out of a second-story window) or some affront to his sense of personal dignity (e.g., Jones steals Smith's clothes while Smith is swimming in the nude).

Since the personal interest in freedom from confinement protected by false imprisonment involves a mental element (knowledge of confinement) as well as a physical element (freedom of movement), it has generally been held that the plaintiff must have *knowledge* of his confinement before liability for false imprisonment will arise. Similarly, liability for false imprisonment will not arise in cases where the person has *consented* to his confinement. Such consent, however, must be freely given, and consent in the face of an implied or actual threat of force or an assertion of legal authority by the confiner is not freely given.

Many contemporary false imprisonment cases involve shoplifting. The common law held storeowners liable for any torts committed in the process of detaining a suspected shoplifter if subsequent investigation revealed that the person detained was innocent of any wrongdoing. Most states, in an attempt to accommodate the legitimate interests of storeowners in preventing theft of their property, have passed statutes giving storeowners a *conditional privilege* to stop persons who they reasonably believe are shoplifting, as long as the owner acts in a reasonable manner and only detains the suspect for a reasonable length of time. Storeowners who act within the scope of such a statute are not liable for any torts committed in the process of detaining a suspected shoplifter.

## Manning v. Grimsley

**643 F.2d 20 (1st Cir. 1981)**

On September 16, 1975, David Manning, Jr., was a spectator at Fenway Park in Boston for a baseball game between the Baltimore Orioles and the Boston Red Sox. Ross Grimsley was a pitcher for Baltimore. During the first three innings, Grimsley was warming up by throwing a ball from a pitcher's mound to a plate in the bull pen located near the right field bleachers. The spectators in the bleachers continuously heckled Grimsley. On several occasions immediately following the heckling, Grimsley looked directly at the hecklers, not just into the stands. At the end of the third inning, Grimsley, after his catcher had left his catching position and was walking over to the bench, faced the bleachers and wound up or stretched as though to pitch in the direction of the plate. Instead, the ball traveled from Grimsley's hand at more than 80 miles per hour at an angle of 90 degrees to the path from the pitcher's mound to the plate and directly toward the hecklers in the bleachers. The ball passed through the wire mesh fence in front of the bleachers and struck Manning. Manning filed a battery action against Grimsley. When the trial judge directed a verdict for Grimsley, Manning appealed.

**Wyzansky, Senior District Judge.** We, unlike the district judge, are of the view that from the evidence that Grimsley was an expert pitcher, that on several occasions immediately following heckling he looked directly at the hecklers, not just into the stands, and that the ball traveled at a right angle to the direction in which he had been pitching and in the direction of the hecklers, the jury could reasonably have inferred that Grimsley intended (1) to throw the ball in the direction of the hecklers, (2) to cause them imminent apprehension of being hit, and (3) to respond to conduct presently affecting his ability to warm up and, if the opportunity came, to play in the game itself.

The foregoing evidence and inferences would have permitted a jury to conclude that Grimsley committed a battery against Manning. This case falls within the scope of *Restatement (Second) of Torts* section 13 (1965), which provides:

(1) An actor is subject to liability to another for battery if
(a) he acts intending to cause a harmful or offensive contact with the person of the other or a third person, *or an imminent apprehension of such a contact,* and
(2) a harmful contact with the person of the other directly or indirectly results.

Although we have not found any Massachusetts case which directly supports that aspect of section 13 at issue in this case, we have no doubt that it would be followed by the Massachusetts Supreme Judicial Court. Section 13 has common law roots that precede the American Revolution. The whole rule and especially that aspect of the rule which permits recovery by a person who was not a target of the wrongdoer embody a strong social policy including obedience to the criminal law by imposing an absolute civil liability to anyone who is physically injured as a result of an intentional harmful contact or a threat thereof directed either at him or a third person.

Judgment reversed in favor of Manning.

---

## Peterson v. Sorlien

**299 N.W. 2d 123 (Minn. Sup. Ct. 1980)**

Susan Peterson, a college student, became involved with an organization called The Way Ministry. Her parents, alarmed at personality changes they saw in her, hired a professional "deprogrammer" to break the hold that The Way had on her. When her father picked her up at the end of the term, instead of taking her home, he took her to the home of a friend, where she was met by the deprogrammer. For the first three days, she lay curled in a fetal position, plugged her ears, and refused to listen to her father or the deprogrammer. Later, however, her behavior changed, and she spoke with her father, went roller skating, went on a picnic, and spent several days out of town with a former cult member. At the end of 16 days, she left the residence where she had been staying and returned to The Way. Later, she filed a false imprisonment suit against her parents. The trial court ruled in her parents' favor, and Susan appealed.

**Sheran, Chief Justice.** This case marks the emergence of a new cultural phenomenon: youth-oriented religious or pseudo-religious groups which utilize the techniques of what has been termed "coercive persuasion" or "mind control" to cultivate an uncritical and devoted following. Coercive persuasion is fostered through the creation of a controlled environment that heightens the susceptibility of a subject to suggestion and manipulation through sensory deprivation, physiological depletion, cognitive dissonance, peer pressure, and a clear assertion of authority and dominion. The aftermath of indoctrination is a severe impairment of autonomy and the ability to think independently, which induces a subject's unyielding compliance and the rupture of past connections, affiliations, and associations.

One psychologist characterized the process of cult indoctrination as "psychological kidnapping."

The period in question began on Monday, May 24, 1976, and ceased on Wednesday, June 9, 1976, a period of 16 days. The record clearly demonstrates that Susan willingly remained in the company of her friend and the programmer for at least 13 of those days. Had Susan desired, manifold opportunities existed for her to alert the authorities of her allegedly unlawful detention. If one is aware of a reasonable means of escape that does not present a danger of bodily or material harm, a restriction is not total and complete and does not constitute unlawful imprisonment.

Susan's behavior during the initial three days at issue must be considered in the light of her actions in the remainder of the period. Because the cult conditioning process induces dramatic and non-consensual change giving rise to a new temporary identity on the part of the individual whose consent is under examination, Susan's volitional capacity prior to treatment may well have been impaired. Following her readjustment, the evidence suggests that Susan was a different person, "like her old self." As such, the question of Susan's consent becomes a function of time.

The facts in this case support the conclusion that Susan only regained her volitional capacity to consent after engaging in the first three days of the deprogramming process. We hold that when parents, or their agents, acting under the conviction that the judgmental capacity of their adult child is impaired, seek to extricate that child from what they reasonably believe to be a religious or pseudo-religious cult, and the child at some juncture assents to the actions in question, limitations upon the child's mobility do not constitute meaningful deprivations of personal liberty sufficient to support a judgment for false imprisonment.

Judgment for Susan's parents affirmed.

**Defamation.** The tort of **defamation** protects the individual's interest in his *reputation.* It recognizes the value that society places on reputation, not only in terms of the individual's personal dignity, but also in terms of the value that a good reputation has in the individual's business dealings with others. Defamation is ordinarily defined as the unprivileged *publication of false and defamatory statements* concerning another. A defamatory statement is one that harms the reputation of another by injuring his community's estimation of him or by deterring others from associating or dealing with him. Whether a given statement is defamatory is ordinarily decided by a jury.

Since the primary focus of defamation is to protect the *individual's* right to reputation, an essential element of defamation is that the alleged defamatory statement must be "of and concerning" the plaintiff: that is, the statement must harm the particular plaintiff's reputation. This causes several problems. First, can allegedly fictional accounts (e.g., in novels and short stories) amount to defamation if the fictional characters bear a substantial resemblance to real persons? Most courts that have dealt with the issue say they can, if a "reasonable reader" would identify the plaintiff as the subject of the story. Similarly, humorous or satirical accounts will ordinarily not amount to defamation unless a reasonable reader would believe that they purport to describe real events.

Likewise, statements of personal opinion are ordinarily not the proper subjects of defamation since they are not statements of fact concerning the plaintiff, unless such statements imply the existence of undisclosed facts that are false and defamatory. Thus, the statement that "Smedley is a lousy governor" would probably not be actionable. However, the statement "I think Irving must be a homosexual" may be defamatory, since a jury may believe that the statement implies that its maker knows facts that justify this opinion.

What about defamatory statements concerning particular groups of persons? The courts generally hold that an individual member of a defamed group cannot recover for damage to his personal reputation unless the group is so small that the statement can reasonably be understood as referring to specific members or unless the circumstances in which the statement is made are such that it is reasonable to conclude that a particular group member is being referred to. So, the statement that "all Germans are thieves," standing alone, would not provide the basis for a defamation suit by any person of German descent. However, if Schmidt, a person of German origin, is being considered for a controller's position in her employer's company and a fellow employee makes the same statement in response to a question concerning Schmidt's qualifications for the job, the statement would probably be a proper basis for a defamation suit.

Finally, the courts have placed some limits on the kinds of persons or entities that can suffer injury to reputation. For example, it is generally held that no liability attaches to defamatory statements concerning the dead. Corporations and other business entities have a limited right to reputation and can file suit for defamatory statements that harm them in conducting their business or deter others from dealing with them. As a general rule, statements about a corporation's officers, employees, or shareholders will not amount to defamation of the corporation unless such statements also reflect upon the manner in which the corporation conducts its business. Statements concerning the quality of a corporation's products or the quality of its title to land or other property may be the basis of a *disparagement* suit.[1]

**Publication.** The elements of the tort of defamation require *publication* of a defamatory statement before liability for defamation will arise. This requirement can be misleading because, as a general rule, no widespread communication of a defamatory statement is required for publication. Communication of the defamatory statement to *one person* other than the person defamed is ordinarily sufficient for publication. Making a defamatory statement about a person in a personal conversation with him or in a private letter sent to him will not, therefore, satisfy the publication requirement. In addition, the courts generally hold that one who repeats or republishes a defamatory statement is liable for defamation, regardless of whether he identifies the source of the statement.

**Libel and Slander.** The courts have divided the tort of defamation into two categories, libel and slander, depending on the medium used to communicate the defamatory statement. **Libel** refers to written or printed defamations or to those that have a physical form (e.g., a defamatory picture or statue). **Slander** refers to oral defamation. The advent of radio and television initially resulted in some judicial confusion concerning the proper classification of defamatory statements communicated by these new media. Today, the great majority of courts treat broadcast defamations as libel. The distinction

[1] Disparagement is discussed in detail in Chapter 43.

between libel and slander is important because the courts have traditionally held that libel, due to its more permanent nature and the seriousness that we tend to attach to the written word, is actionable without any proof of special damage (the loss of anything of monetary value) to the plaintiff. Slander, however, is generally not actionable without proof of special damage, unless the nature of the slanderous statement is so serious that it can be classified as slander per se. In slander per se, injury to the plaintiff's reputation is presumed. Four kinds of defamatory statements ordinarily qualify for per se treatment: allegations that the plaintiff has committed a crime involving moral turpitude or potential imprisonment, that he has a "loathsome" disease (usually a venereal disease or leprosy), that he is professionally incompetent or guilty of professional misconduct, or that he is guilty of serious sexual misconduct.

**Defamation and the Constitution.** Nowhere is the social balancing task of tort law more obvious than in cases of defamation. Overzealous protection of individual reputation could result in an infringement of constitutionally protected rights such as freedom of speech and freedom of the press, and thereby inhibit the free flow of information necessary to a free society. In recent years, the Supreme Court has sought to balance these conflicting social interests in a series of important cases that seek to define the amount of protection that the Constitution affords to otherwise defamatory statements. In *New York Times v. Sullivan,*[2] the Court held that *public officials* seeking to recover for defamatory statements relating to performance of their official duties must prove *actual malice* (knowledge of falsity or reckless disregard for the truth) on the part of a media defendant in order to recover any damages. This significant limitation on public officials' right to reputation was justified largely by the public interest in "free and unfettered debate" on important social issues.

For similar reasons, the Court subsequently[3] extended the "actual malice" test to *public figures* (persons in the public eye because of their celebrity status or because they have voluntarily involved themselves in matters of public controversy). More recently, in *Gertz v. Robert Welch, Inc.,*[4] the Court refused to extend the "actual malice" test to media defamation of private citizens who involuntarily become involved in matters of public concern. Instead, the Court held that to recover compensatory damages such persons must prove some degree of fault at least amounting to negligence on the part of the defendant and that to recover punitive damages they must prove "actual malice." The Court has yet to speak definitively on the question of the constitutional standards that apply to defamatory statements about private persons made by other private persons, but it would not be too surprising if the *Gertz* test were applied to such cases at some point in the future.

**Defenses to Defamation.** *Truth* is an absolute defense to defamation. The tort of defamation requires that a statement serving as the basis of a defamation suit be *false* as well as defamatory.

Even where defamatory statements are false, a defense of *privilege* may serve to prevent liability in some cases. The idea of privilege recognizes the fact that, in some circumstances, other social interests may be more important than an individual's right to reputation. Privileges are either *absolute* or *condi-*

[2] 376 U.S. 254 (U.S. Sup. Ct. 1964).

[3] *Curtis Publishing Co. v. Butts,* 388 U.S. 130 (U.S. Sup. Ct. 1967).

[4] 418 U.S. 323 (U.S. Sup. Ct. 1974).

*tional. Absolute* privileges shield the author of a defamatory statement regardless of his knowledge, motive, or intent. Absolutely privileged statements include statements made by participants in judicial proceedings, statements made by legislators or witnesses in the course of legislative proceedings, statements made by certain executive officials in the course of their official duties, and statements made between spouses in private. *Conditional privileges* are conditioned upon their proper use. One who *abuses* a conditional privilege by making a defamatory statement with the knowledge that it is false, or in reckless disregard of the truth, loses the protection afforded by the privilege. Conditional privileges can also be abused when the author of a defamatory statement acts with an improper motive (e.g., for a purpose other than protecting the interests justifying the privilege) or exceeds the scope of the privilege (e.g., by communicating the defamation unnecessarily to third persons who do not share his interests). Conditional privileges are often recognized when the author of a defamatory statement acts to protect legitimate interests of her own or the legitimate interests of a third person with whom she shares some interest or to whom she owes some duty.

In recent years, the courts have also begun to recognize a conditional privilege of "fair comment." This privilege protects fair and accurate media reports of defamatory matter that is contained in reports of official action or proceedings or originates from public meetings. The privilege is justified by the public's right to know what occurs in such proceedings and meetings.

## Barger v. Playboy Enterprises, Inc.

**564 F. Supp. 1151 (N.D. Cal. 1983)**

*Playboy* magazine published "Undercover Angel," an article by Laurence Linderman. The article purported to describe the experiences of Dan Black, an undercover narcotics agent who infiltrated the Hell's Angels motorcycle gang. Among other things, the article described an "Angel's wedding" at Clear Lake, California, as followed the next morning by assorted sexual activities between the bride and gang members other than her husband and stated that Angels beat up their "mommas" unless they agreed to perform unusual sexual acts. Several wives of members of the Oakland and Richmond Hell's Angels chapters filed suit against *Playboy,* alleging that the article defamed them and the wives of other gang members. The trial court dismissed their complaint for failure to adequately allege that the article referred to them personally. They amended their complaint, and *Playboy* again moved to dismiss it on the same ground.

**Patel, District Judge.** Plaintiffs who sue for defamation must show that the allegedly libelous statements were made "of and concerning" them, i.e., referred to them personally. When an article names specific individuals, this is easily done. However, when the statements concern groups, as here, plaintiffs face a more difficult and sometimes insurmountable task. If the group is small and its members easily ascertainable, plaintiffs may succeed. But where the group is large—in general, any group numbering over 25 members—the courts in California and other states have consistently held that plaintiffs cannot show that the statements were "of and concerning them."

This rule embodies two important public policies. First, where the group referred to is large, the courts presume that no reasonable reader would take the statements as literally applying to each individual member. Second, and most importantly, this limitation on liability safeguards freedom of speech by effecting a sound compromise between the conflicting interests involved in libel cases. On the one hand is the societal interest in free press discussions of matters of general concern, and on the other is the individual interest in reputation. The courts have chosen not to limit freedom of public discussion except to prevent harm occasioned by defamatory statements *reasonably susceptible* of special application to a given individual.

Accordingly, the court must determine whether the terms "brides" and "mommas" would reasonably refer to groups small enough to meet the "of and concerning" requirement. Abandoning their prior interpretation of the article as defaming Hell's Angels wives by its statements about brides, plaintiffs now contend that not all wives are or ever have been "Hell's Angels brides." Thus, although they admit that wives number approximately 100 to 125 nationwide—well above the threshold for showing "of and concerning"—they claim that "brides" number only about 15 to 20. This alchemy is accomplished by plaintiffs' imaginative interpretation of the term "Hell's Angels bride" as "those females who were married to Hell's Angels members at a wedding ceremony followed by a wedding party of some sort, attended by at least some members of the Hell's Angels Motorcycle Club." They cannot, however, plead libel by imputing an esoteric meaning to the term "bride" which has no reasonable basis in the article and is inaccessible to the ordinary reader. Nowhere does the article state or imply that it uses "bride" to mean anything different than a woman newly married to a member of the Hell's Angels.

The only other group plaintiffs claim has been defamed by the article is "Hell's Angels mommas," which plaintiffs define as women involved in extra-marital sexual relationships with Hell's Angels members. Plaintiffs admit that this group numbers "at least 500" nationwide. Thus, it is far too numerous to show "of and concerning." Moreover, since "brides" and "mommas" as defined in the complaint are mutually exclusive groups, and plaintiffs claim to belong to the former group only, plaintiffs have not pleaded that the statements about mommas refer to them at all.

Complaint dismissed in favor of *Playboy.*

---

**Invasion of Privacy.** The recognition of a personal *right of privacy* is a relatively recent development in tort law. At present, four distinct kinds of behavior have been recognized as providing a proper basis for an invasion of privacy suit: (1) intrusion upon a person's solitude or seclusion, (2) public disclosure of private facts concerning a person, (3) publicity placing a person in a false light in the public eye, and (4) appropriation of a person's name or likeness for commercial purposes. The thread tying these different kinds of behavior together is that they all infringe upon a person's "right to be let alone."

**Intrusion upon Solitude.** Any intentional intrusion upon the solitude or seclusion of another constitutes invasion of privacy if that intrusion would be highly offensive to a reasonable individual. The intrusion in question may be physical, such as illegal searches of a person's home or body or the opening of his mail. It may also be a nonphysical intrusion such as tapping his telephone, examining his bank account, or subjecting him to harassing telephone calls. As a general rule, no liability attaches to examining public records concerning a person, or observing or photographing him in a public place, since a person does not have a reasonable expectation of privacy in these instances.

**Publicity concerning Private Facts.** Publicizing facts concerning a person's private life can amount to invasion of privacy if the publicized facts are such that publicity concerning them would be highly offensive to a reasonable person. The idea is that the public has no legitimate right to know certain aspects of a person's private life. Thus, publicity concerning a person's failure to pay his debts, humiliating illnesses that he has suffered, and details concerning his sex life constitute an invasion of privacy. It is important to note that truth is *not* a defense to this type of invasion of privacy, since the essence of the tort is giving unjustified publicity to purely private matters. It is also important to note that "publicity" in this context means a widespread dissemination of private details.

This variant of invasion of privacy, like the tort of defamation, represents a potential source of conflict with the constitutionally protected values of freedom of the press and freedom of speech. The courts have attempted to accommodate these conflicting social interests in several ways. First, no liability ordinarily attaches to publicity concerning matters of public record or of legitimate public interest. Also, public figures and public officials have no right of privacy concerning information that is reasonably related to their public lives.

**False Light.** Publicity that places a person in a *false light* in the public eye can amount to invasion of privacy if the false light in which the person is placed would be highly offensive to a reasonable person. This variant of invasion of privacy may in some cases also involve defamation, and, as in defamation cases, truth is an absolute defense to liability. For liability for invasion of privacy to arise, however, it is not necessary that a person be defamed by the false light in which he is placed. All that is required is unreasonable and highly objectionable publicity attributing to a person characteristics that he does not possess or beliefs that he does not hold. Signing a person's name to a public telegram or letter without her consent or attributing authorship of an inferior scholarly or artistic work to her are examples of this form of invasion of privacy.

**Appropriation of Name or Likeness.** Some of the earliest invasion of privacy cases involved the appropriation of a person's name or likeness for commercial purposes without his consent. Liability for invasion of privacy can be created by using a person's name or image in an advertisement to imply his endorsement of a product or service or a nonexistent connection with the person or business placing the ad. This variant of invasion of privacy differs markedly from the other variants previously discussed in that it recognizes the existence of a personal property right connected with a person's identity that he has the exclusive right to control.

The potential for conflict between this property right and the freedoms of speech and of the press has been illustrated in recent years by cases involving public figures' "right of publicity." To what extent do public persons have the right to control the use of their names, likenesses, or other matters associated with their identities? For example, should a well-known movie star have the right to prevent the writing of a book about her life or the televising of a "docudrama" about her? At this point, the scope of a public person's right of publicity varies greatly from state to state and considerable disagreement exists concerning such issues as its duration and inheritability.

**Other Limitations.** In addition to the various limitations on the right of privacy discussed above, the student should be aware of two further limits applicable to invasion of privacy actions. First, with the exception in some states of cases involving the appropriation of a person's name or likeness, the right of privacy is a purely *personal* right. This means that only living individuals whose personal privacy has been invaded can bring suit for invasion of privacy. Therefore, family members of a person exposed to publicity ordinarily cannot maintain an invasion of privacy action unless their personal privacy has also been violated. Also, corporations and other business organizations generally have no personal right of privacy. They do, however, have limited rights associated with the use of their names and identities. These rights are protected by the law of unfair competition.[5]

[5] This subject is discussed in detail in Chapter 43.

## Bilney v. Evening Star Newspaper Co.

**406 A.2d 652 (Md. Ct. App. 1979)**

John Bilney and five other members of the University of Maryland's varsity basketball team were the subjects of articles appearing in the *Washington Star* and the *Diamondback,* a student newspaper. The articles indicated that Bilney, Larry Gibson, Jo Jo Hunter, and Billy Bryant were on academic probation and that the two other players had been reinstated after having been on probation. The players filed suit against the publishers of the newspaper, alleging invasion of privacy. The trial court ruled in favor of the newspapers, and the players appealed.

**Wilner, Judge.** Conceding that they were public figures—and that the information printed was true—the players maintain that their scholastic status was a purely private matter unaffected by any public interest or concern.

The *Restatement (Second) of Torts,* Sec. 652A describes four ways in which one may tortiously invade the privacy of another. At issue here is the third of these methods—Sec. 652A(2)(c)—"unreasonable publicity given to the other's private life, as stated in Sec. 652D." Section 652D provides:

> One who gives publicity to a matter concerning the private life of another is subject to liability to the other for invasion of his privacy, if the matter publicized is of a kind that
> (a) would be highly offensive to a reasonable person, and
> (b) is not of legitimate concern to the public.

Comment *e* to Sec. 652D deals with "voluntary public figures." Not all of it is relevant here, but this much, we think, is:

> One who voluntarily places himself in the public eye, by engaging in public activities, or by assuming a prominent role in institutions or activities having general economic, cultural, social or similar public interest, or by submitting himself or his work for public judgment, cannot complain when he is given publicity that he has sought, even though it may be unfavorable to him. In such cases, however, the legitimate interest of the public in the individual may extend beyond these matters which are themselves made public, and to some reasonable extent may include information as to matters that would otherwise be private.

The concept described in the emphasized portion of comment *e* is touched on in greater detail in comment *h.* That says, in relevant part:

> Permissible publicity to information concerning either voluntary or involuntary public figures is not limited to the particular events that arouse the interest of the public. That interest, once aroused by the event, may legitimately extend, to some reasonable degree, to further information concerning the individual and to facts about him, which are not public and which, in the case of one who had not become a public figure, would be regarded as an invasion of his purely private life.
>
> The extent of the authority to make public private facts is not, however, unlimited. In determining what is a matter of legitimate public interest, account must be taken of the customs and conventions of the community; and in the last analysis what is proper becomes a matter of the community mores. The line is to be drawn when the publicity ceases to be the giving of information to which the public is entitled, and becomes a morbid and sensational prying into private lives for its own sake, with which a reasonable member of the public, with decent standards, would say that he had no concern.

These players achieved the status of public figures solely by virtue of their membership on the University Basketball Team. Their possible exclusion from the team—whether for academic or any other reason—was therefore a matter of legitimate public interest. Publication of that eligibility-threatening status was not unreasonable and did not trample upon community mores. Having sought and basked in the limelight, by virtue of their membership on the team, the players will not be heard to complain when the light focuses on their potentially imminent withdrawal from the team.

Judgment for the newspapers affirmed.

---

## Carson v. Here's Johnny Portable Toilets, Inc.

**698 F.2d 831 (6th Cir. 1983)**

John W. Carson, host and star of "The Tonight Show," has used the phrase "Here's Johnny" as a method of introduction since he hosted a daily television program for ABC in 1957. In 1967, Carson had authorized the use of the phrase by a chain of restaurants called Here's Johnny Restaurants. With Carson's consent, Johnny Carson Apparel, Inc., a menswear manufacturer in which Carson owned stock and held the office of president, had used the phrase "Here's Johnny" on clothing labels and in advertising campaigns. In 1977, Johnny Carson Apparel had licensed Marcy Laboratories to use "Here's Johnny" as the name of a line of men's toiletries. However, neither Carson nor Johnny Carson Apparel had ever registered the phrase "Here's Johnny" as a trademark or service mark.

In 1976, a Michigan corporation, Here's Johnny Portable Toilets, Inc., began renting and selling Here's Johnny portable toilets. The founder of the corporation admitted that at the time he founded it he had been aware of identification of the phrase "Here's Johnny" with Carson. He also said that he coupled the phrase with a second one, "The World's Foremost Commodian," to make "a good play on a phrase." Carson filed suit for invasion of his privacy and publicity rights. The trial court dismissed his suit, and Carson appealed.

**BROWN, SENIOR CIRCUIT JUDGE.** In an influential article, Dean Prosser delineated four distinct types of the right of privacy: (1) intrusion upon one's seclusion or solitude, (2) public disclosure of embarrassing private facts, (3) publicity which places one in a false light, and (4) appropriation of one's name or likeness for the defendant's advantage. This fourth type has become known as the "right of publicity." Prosser's first three types of the right of privacy generally protect the right "to be let alone," while the right of publicity protects the celebrity's pecuniary interest in the commercial exploitation of his identity. The theory of the right is that a celebrity's identity can be valuable in the promotion of products, and the celebrity has an interest that may be protected from the unauthorized commercial exploitation of that identity.

The district court dismissed Carson's claim because Here's Johnny Portable Toilets, Inc., did not use Carson's name or likeness. It held that "it would not be prudent to allow recovery for a right of publicity claim which does not more specifically identify Johnny Carson." We believe that, on the contrary, the district court's conception of the right of publicity is too narrow. If the celebrity's identity is commercially exploited, there has been an invasion of his right whether or not his "name or likeness" is used. Carson's identity may be exploited even if his name, John W. Carson, or his picture is not used.

In *Motschenbacher v. R. J. Reynolds Tobacco Co.* (1974), the court held that the unauthorized use of a distinctive race car of a well known professional driver, whose name or likeness was not used, violated his right of publicity. In *Hirsch v. S. C. Johnson & Son, Inc.* (1979), the court held that Johnson's use of the name "Crazylegs" on a shaving gel for women violated Elroy Hirsch's right of publicity. Hirsch, a famous football player, had been known by this nickname.

In this case, Earl Braxton, president and owner of Here's Johnny Portable Toilets, Inc., admitted that he knew that the phrase "Here's Johnny" had been used for years to introduce Carson. That the "Here's Johnny" name was selected by Braxton because of its identification with Carson was the clear inference from Braxton's testimony. We therefore conclude that, applying correct legal standards, Carson is entitled to judgment. The proof showed without question that the corporation had appropriated Carson's identity in connection with its corporate name and its product.

Judgment reversed in favor of Carson.

**Infliction of Emotional Distress.** For many years, the courts refused to allow recovery for purely emotional injuries in the absence of some other tort. Thus, victims of such torts as assault, battery, and false imprisonment could recover for the emotional injuries resulting from these torts, but the courts were unwilling to recognize an independent tort of infliction of emotional distress. The reasons for this judicial reluctance included a fear of spurious or trivial claims, concerns about the difficulty in proving purely emotional harms, and uncertainty concerning the proper boundaries of an independent tort of intentional infliction of emotional distress. Recent advances in medical knowledge concerning emotional injuries, however, have helped to overcome some of these judicial impediments. Today, most courts will allow recovery for *severe* emotional distress regardless of whether the elements of any other tort are proven.

The courts are not, however, in complete agreement on the elements of this new tort. All courts require that a wrongdoer's conduct must be *outrageous* before liability for emotional distress will arise. The *Restatement (Second) of Torts* speaks of conduct "so outrageous in character, and so extreme in degree as to go beyond all possible bounds of decency, and to be regarded as atrocious and utterly intolerable in a civilized community."[6] Some courts, however, still fear fictitious claims and require proof of some bodily harm resulting from the victim's emotional distress. The courts also differ in the extent to which they will allow recovery for emotional distress suffered as a result of witnessing outrageous conduct directed at persons other than the plaintiff. The *Restatement (Second) of Torts* suggests that persons be allowed to recover for severe emotional distress resulting from witnessing outrageous behavior toward a member of their immediate family.[7] Where the third person is not a member of the plaintiff's immediate family, the *Restatement (Second)* restricts liability to severe emotional distress that results in some bodily harm.[8]

**Misuse of Legal Proceedings.** Three intentional tort theories protect persons against the harm that can result from wrongfully instituted legal proceedings. **Malicious prosecution** affords a remedy for the financial and emotional harm, and the injury to reputation, that can result when *criminal* proceedings are wrongfully brought against a person. Since this tort balances society's interest in efficient enforcement of the criminal law against the individual's interest in freedom from unjustified criminal prosecutions, a plaintiff seeking to recover for malicious prosecution must prove *both* that the defendant *acted "maliciously"* (without probable cause to believe that an offense had been committed and for an improper purpose) and that the criminal proceedings were *terminated in the plaintiff's favor.* As a general rule, proof that the defendant acted in good faith on the advice of legal counsel, after fully disclosing the relevant facts, conclusively establishes probable cause. Also, proof of the plaintiff's guilt is generally held to be a complete defense to liability, and the issue of his guilt can be retried in the malicious prosecution suit, despite his acquittal in the criminal proceedings. Proof of the plaintiff's innocence, however, will not support a malicious prosecution action if the criminal proceedings were not terminated in his favor.

The tort of **wrongful use of civil proceedings** is similar to that of malicious prosecution, but is designed to protect persons from wrongfully instituted *civil* suits. Its elements are very similar to those of malicious prosecution: it requires proof that the civil proceedings were initiated without probable cause and for an improper purpose and proof that the suit was terminated in favor of the person sued.

The tort of **abuse of process** imposes liability on those who initiate legal proceedings for a primary purpose other than the one for which such proceedings are designed. Abuse of process cases normally involve situations in which the legal proceedings are used in an attempt to compel the other person to take

[6] *Restatement (Second) of Torts* § 46, comment *d* (1965).

[7] *Restatement (Second) of Torts* § 46(2)(a) (1965).

[8] *Restatement (Second) of Torts* § 46(2)(b) (1965).

some action unrelated to the subject of the suit. For example, Rogers wishes to buy Herbert's property, but Herbert refuses to sell. In order to pressure him into selling, Rogers files a nuisance suit against Herbert contending that Herbert's activities on his land interfere with Rogers' use and enjoyment of his adjoining property. Rogers may be liable to Herbert for abuse of process despite the fact that he had probable cause to file the suit and regardless of whether he wins the suit.

**Evolving Concepts of Tort Liability.** Recent developments indicate a continuing tendency to expand the scope of tort law as society recognizes an increasing range of personal interests that deserve legal protection. For example, some recent cases have recognized a right of fired employees to recover against their employers for a new tort of *wrongful or abusive discharge*.[9] Also, some courts have allowed plaintiffs to recover punitive damages in tort suits arising out of a defendant's bad faith breach of contract.[10] Finally, plaintiffs in so-called toxic tort suits, mass actions seeking to recover for a variety of injuries resulting from exposure to toxic substances, are currently attempting to employ a variety of novel tort theories to support their claims. All of these examples illustrate the dynamic nature of our legal system in general and of tort law in particular. Given the historical development of tort law, one can reasonably expect that as growing technical knowledge or changing social circumstances create the need to protect new personal interests, tort law will evolve to satisfy that need.

[9] This subject is discussed in detail in Chapter 47.

[10] This subject is discussed in detail in Chapter 15.

## Chuy v. Philadelphia Eagles Football Club

**431 F. Supp. 254 (E.D. Pa. 1977)**

Donald Chuy was a lineman for the Philadelphia Eagles. In a game against the New York Giants, Chuy suffered a serious injury to his left shoulder while executing a downfield block. As a result, he also developed an acute coronary embolism. The embolism was later dissolved, but Chuy's football career was over. Dr. James Nixon, the team physician, allegedly told Hugh Brown, a sportswriter, that Chuy was suffering from a rare terminal blood disease called polycythemia vera. This resulted in a newspaper story that the wire services distributed nationwide. Chuy read the story, became panic-stricken, and underwent a long period of depression, anticipating his death. When tests indicated that he did not have the disease, Chuy concluded that Dr. Nixon's statements were part of a conspiracy by the Eagles to deny him payment under the remaining years of his contracts with the Eagles. Chuy's contracts provided for continued payment only for disabilities caused by football injuries, not unrelated diseases. Chuy filed suit for intentional infliction of emotional distress. The jury ruled in Chuy's favor, awarding him $10,000 in compensatory damages and $60,500 in punitive damages. The Eagles appealed.

**Becker, District Judge.** The legal theory upon which Chuy rested this claim derives from the *Restatement (Second) of Torts* section 46 (1965), which provides as follows:

(1) One who by extreme and outrageous conduct intentionally or recklessly causes severe emotional distress to another is subject to liability for such emotional distress.

The Eagles' argument has several facets. First, the Eagles assert that there is insufficient evidence to sustain a finding of intent or recklessness on the part of Dr. Nixon. Second, the Eagles contend that Chuy failed to prove that his distress in response to the alleged statement was "reasonable" in accordance with the directive of comment *j* to section 46 (comment *j*, among other things, requires that the victim's distress "must be reasonable and justified under the circumstances").

Viewed as a whole, Chuy produced sufficient evidence from which the jury could, if it wished, draw the inference that Dr. Nixon intentionally or recklessly inflicted mental distress upon him and that such conduct was outrageous. It was Dr. Nixon's testimony that he never said to Hugh Brown that Chuy had polycythemia vera, and that he knew quite well what that disease was, so that there was no inadvertent diagnosis. We reject the Eagles' argument that the statement by Dr. Nixon was not so outrageous as to create liability. Announcing to the press that an unsuspecting young athlete has a serious disease when there was no basis for such a conclusion does not comport with any tolerable standard of decency, and is plainly within the scope of section 46.

We also cannot agree that the effect of comment *j* is to set up a reasonableness standard by which the victims of outrageous conduct must be judged at the risk of losing their cause of action. One who has been subject to mental stress will not lose his action because his subsequent conduct may not in the cool ambience of hindsight appear to satisfy ordinary expectations of reasonableness. What comment *j* suggests, we think, is that one who brings suit asserting the intentional infliction of mental distress may be barred if the *mental distress itself* was an unreasonable or peculiar reaction, and not because the victim of truly outrageous conduct who is in fact distressed did not act as would a reasonably prudent man to mitigate his hardship.

Judgment for Chuy affirmed.

## INTERFERENCE WITH PROPERTY RIGHTS

**Nature of Property Rights.** The rights associated with the acquisition and use of property have traditionally occupied an important position in our legal system. Tortious interference with property rights is generally treated as an offense against the right to *possession.* Therefore, in cases where the party entitled to possession is not the same as the owner of the property in question (e.g., a tenant leasing property from its owner), the party entitled to possession is ordinarily the proper person to file suit for interference with his possessory rights. However, if the interference also results in lasting damage to the property, its owner may also have a right to recover for such damage.

**Trespass to Land.** A person is liable for **trespass** if he: (1) intentionally and unlawfully enters land in the possession of another, (2) unlawfully remains on such land after entering lawfully (e.g., a tenant who refuses to move at the end of the lease), (3) unlawfully causes anything to enter such land, or (4) fails to remove anything that he has a duty to remove from such land. No actual harm to the land is required for liability for intentional trespasses, but actual harm is required for liability for reckless or negligent trespasses. In addition, a person can be liable for trespass even though the trespass resulted from his mistaken belief that his entry was legally justified because he had a right to possess the land, had the consent of the party entitled to possession, or had some other legal right or privilege entitling him to enter.

**Nuisance.** Unlawful and unreasonable interferences with another person's right to the use or enjoyment of his land are called **nuisances.** Nuisance suits, unlike trespass actions, do not necessarily involve any physical invasion of a person's property. Noise, vibration, and unpleasant odors are all examples of things that could amount to nuisances but that would not justify a trespass action. In nuisance suits, the courts attempt to balance the competing interests of landowners to use their land as they see fit. Nuisance law recognizes an unfortunate fact of life: to preserve freedom, it must be limited. Put another way, my free use of my property may destroy your enjoyment of yours. For example, should I be able to open a solid waste disposal plant next to your restaurant? The law of nuisance attempts to resolve such perplexing issues.[11]

**Trespass to Personal Property.** Any intentional intermeddling with personal property in the possession of another is a trespass if it: (1) results in harm to that property (e.g., Franks strikes Goode's dog or throws paint on his car) or (2) deprives the party entitled to possession of its use for an appreciable time (e.g., Franks hides Goode's car, and Goode cannot find it for several hours).

**Conversion. Conversion** is the intentional exercise of dominion or control over another's property. To amount to conversion, the defendant's actions must be such a serious interference with another's right to control the property that they justify requiring the defendant to pay damages for the full value of the property. The difference between conversion and trespass to personal property is based on the *degree* of interference with another's property rights. In considering whether an interference with another's property amounts to its conversion, the courts consider such factors as the extent of the harm done to the property, the extent and duration of the interference with the other's right to control the property, and whether the defendant acted in good faith. For example, Sharp goes to Friendly Motors and asks to test-drive a new Ford Thunderbird Turbo. If Sharp wrecks the car, causing major damage, or if he drives it across the United States, Sharp is probably liable for conversion and obligated to pay Friendly Motors the reasonable value of the car. On the other hand, if Sharp is merely involved in a "fender bender," or if he keeps the car for eight hours, he is probably liable only for trespass, and therefore only obligated to pay damages to compensate Friendly for the loss in value of the car or for its loss of use of the car.

**Business Torts.** Today, courts also recognize a variety of tort actions designed to protect various types of economic interests. These torts are discussed in detail in Chapter 43.

[11] Nuisances are discussed in detail in Chapter 29.

## Dial v. City of O'Fallon

**411 N.E. 2d 217 (Ill. Sup. Ct. 1980)**

The city of O'Fallon built a sewer system in 1926, but due to backups into homes served by the system, an overflow outlet was constructed in 1961. During heavy rains, however, the overflow outlet discharged raw sewage into an open ditch that flowed into a neighboring pond. This later became illegal under state environmental regulations, and in 1974 the city closed the overflow outlet as part of the settlement of a nuisance suit against the city. In early 1975, after a period of heavy rainfall, sewage backed up into Geraldine Dial's finished basement to a height of 25½ inches. This and subsequent backups caused serious damage to Dial's home and personal possessions. Dial filed suit against the city on trespass to land and negligence theories. She later settled her negligence claim with the city's liability insurance carrier, but proceeded on her trespass claim because the city's liability policy did not cover intentional wrongdoing. The trial court ruled in Dial's favor, and the city appealed.

**Ryan, Justice.** On appeal, the city contends that although it was negligent in maintaining the sewer system, its conduct does not give use to liability on the theory of trespass to land. We may summarize the *Restatement (Second) of Torts* on this subject as follows: (1) One is subject to liability for an intentional intrusion on land irrespective of whether he causes harm to a legally protected interest. (2) One is liable for negligent or reckless intrusion on land if he thereby causes harm to a legally protected interest. (3) And one is not liable for an unintentional nonnegligent intrusion on land even though the entry causes harm to a legally protected interest. Under section 158 of the *Restatement* (intentional intrusion), or section 165 (negligent or reckless intrusion), a person is liable not only for his own entry but also if he causes a thing or third person to enter the land of another.

It is clear that the backup in the sewers resulted from the intentional closing of the overflow. The city engineer testified that, when the overflow was closed, it was assumed there was going to be some backup but they were not aware it was going to be as severe as it was. He also testified that the overflow originally had been installed as a result of some extremely heavy rainfall in 1961. An employee of the city's sewer department testified that he knew that when the overflow was closed there would be some backup into some homes "if we got a heavy enough rain."

Judgment for Dial affirmed.

## SUMMARY

The basis of tort liability is a breach of a legal duty owed to another person that results in a legally recognizable harm to that person. Tort law seeks to compensate injured persons by allowing them to recover money damages for any harm they have suffered. In some cases, tort law also allows injured persons to recover punitive damages in excess of their actual losses. Punitive damages are designed to punish flagrant wrongdoers and to deter them and others from engaging in similar conduct in the future.

Tort law involves a constant attempt to balance conflicting social rights and duties. Over time, the law of torts has recognized an expanding number of personal interests that are deserving of protection. At present, tort law protects a wide variety of personal interests: the right to be free from harmful or offensive bodily contacts (battery), the right to be free from the apprehension of such contacts (assault), the right to reputation (defamation), the right to privacy (invasion of privacy), the right to be free from disagreeable emotions (intentional infliction of emotional distress), and the right to be free from improperly instituted criminal or civil proceedings (malicious prosecution, wrongful use of civil proceedings, and abuse of process).

Intentionally causing a harmful or offensive contact with another can give rise to liability for battery. Causing another to have a reasonable apprehension of an imminent battery constitutes assault. Confining another against his will for an appreciable time can create liability for false imprisonment.

The publication of false and defamatory statements about another can result in liability for defamation. Defamation is divided into two categories: slander (verbal defamation) and libel (written defamation). Broadcast defamations, whether by radio or television, are normally treated as libels. In order to balance the individual's right to reputation against the constitutionally protected rights of freedom of speech and the press, public officials and "public figures" face higher burdens of proof in defamation suits than do private persons. Also, the law recognizes several other defenses to defamation. Truth is an absolute defense to defamation, and some defamatory statements, though untrue, may be privileged.

The tort of invasion of privacy protects the individual's "right to be let alone" by imposing liability for four kinds of behavior: intruding on a person's physical solitude or seclusion, publicizing private facts about a person, casting a person in a false light in the public eye, and appropriating a person's name or likeness for commercial purposes. As in the case of defamation, public officials and "public figures" enjoy narrower privacy rights than do private persons.

Although the courts disagree on the elements of the tort, most courts now recognize an independent tort of intentional infliction of emotional distress. The courts do agree, however, that only "outrageous" conduct will create liability and that the resulting emotional distress must be severe. Some courts also require some significant bodily harm to the plaintiff as a result of the emotional distress he suffered, but there is a discernible trend in favor of allowing recovery for severe emotional distress standing alone.

The tort of malicious prosecution protects against wrongful initiation of criminal proceedings. Both it and the tort of wrongful use of civil proceedings require that the proceedings in question be initiated without probable cause and that they be terminated in favor of the person wrongfully subjected to them. The tort of abuse of process imposes liability on those who employ legal proceedings for wrongful purposes. Unlike liability for either malicious prosecution or wrongful use of civil proceedings, liability for abuse of process is possible even if the defendant had probable cause to initiate legal proceedings and in spite of the fact that the proceedings were ultimately resolved against the person wrongfully subjected to them.

Tort law also protects personal rights in property. The torts of trespass and nuisance protect an individual's right to possess and enjoy the use of his land. The torts of trespass and conversion protect the individual's rights in the possession and enjoyment of his personal property. The basic distinction between trespass and conversion is that conversion deals with interferences that are so serious as to justify forcing the defendant to pay the full value of the property in question, rather than requiring him merely to pay for the loss of value or use of the property.

## PROBLEM CASES

1. Patsy Mink and several other women were given diethylstilbestrol (DES) as part of a medical experiment conducted by the University of Chicago and Eli Lilly & Co. between September 1950 and November 1952. The drug was administered during prenatal care at the University Hospital as part of a double-blind study to determine the value of DES in preventing miscarriages. The women were told neither that they were part of an experiment nor that they were being given DES. Later, DES was found to cause reproductive tract disorders in some children of women who took the drug. The plaintiffs filed a class action suit for battery on behalf of the 1,000 women who were given DES in the study. The defendants moved to dismiss the suit, arguing that the plaintiffs had failed to state a claim. Could the defendants be liable for battery?

2. Mrs. Garner was shopping in the Southwest drugstore in Laurel, Mississippi. While she was at the cosmetic counter looking for soap, she was approached by Ratliff, the store manager, who asked if he could help her. She told him what she wanted, and he had a salesperson wait on her. The salesperson helped her find the soap and went with her to the cashier, where she paid for it. When she left the store, Ratliff followed her and, in the presence of a number of people, said to her in a rude and loud manner, "Hey, wait there. . . . You stop there. I want to see what you got in that little bag. You stole a bar of soap." She said: "You mean you're accusing me of stealing this soap?" He replied: "Yes, you stole the soap, and let's prove it, let's go back." Garner said that the incident made her sick and that she had to visit her doctor twice thereafter. She sued Southwest for slander and false imprisonment. Southwest relied on a conditional privilege statute as a defense. Was Ratliff's behavior privileged?

3. In 1978, under the headline "Buddy, We Hardly Know Ya," *New Times* magazine published a story about the mayor of Providence, Rhode Island, who was then a candidate for reelection. The article concerned a woman's claim that the mayor had raped her in 1966. The article noted that the mayor had made a $3,000 settlement with the woman, and it strongly implied that the settlement was made prior to, and was the primary reason for, the decision not to prosecute the mayor. The evidence indicated that the magazine knew that the decision not to prosecute was made prior to the settlement and was independent of it. The magazine defended against the mayor's libel suit by arguing that the article was a statement of opinion and was also protected by the constitutional privilege of neutral reportage. Was the magazine right?

4. William Proxmire was a U.S. senator from Wisconsin. In March 1975, he created a "Golden Fleece of the Month Award" to publicize wasteful government spending. In April 1975, the second Golden Fleece Award went to the National Science Foundation, the National Aeronautics and Space Administration, and the Office of Naval Research for spending almost half a million dollars over a seven-year period to fund research by Ronald Hutchinson, a behavioral scientist. Hutchinson's research sought an objective measure of aggression by concentrating on patterns of animal behavior, such as jaw clenching. Proxmire made the award in a speech before the Senate.

The speech was the subject of an advance press release prepared by his office and was referred to in a newsletter sent to his constituents. In the speech Proxmire said: "Dr. Hutchinson's studies should make the taxpayers as well as his monkeys grind their teeth. In fact, the good doctor has made a fortune from his monkeys and in the process made a monkey out of the American taxpayer." Hutchinson sued Proxmire for defamation, and Proxmire defended by arguing that his speech was protected under the Speech and Debate Clause of the Constitution and that Hutchinson was a public figure. The Speech and Debate Clause provides that senators and representatives "for any speech or Debate in either House . . . shall not be questioned in any other place." Were Proxmire's statements constitutionally privileged?

**5.** As part of its regular "Page from Our Past" feature, the *Iberville South,* a local weekly newspaper, reproduced the original front page of a randomly selected 25-year-old edition of the paper. The reproduced front page carried the details of the criminal convictions of three brothers for cattle theft. The brothers, who were still local residents, filed suit for invasion of privacy. They argued that the 25-year-old matter was no longer a subject of public concern and that they had served their term of imprisonment, had become law-abiding and hardworking citizens, and had ultimately received full pardons. Are they entitled to recover for invasion of privacy?

**6.** Actress Ann-Margret appeared nude from the waist up in the movie *Magic.* The magazine *High Society Celebrity Skin,* which specialized in printing photographs of well-known women in revealing situations and positions, published photographs taken from the movie without her consent. Ann-Margret filed suit for invasion of privacy. Should she win?

**7.** William Harris, a General Motors employee, had a speech impediment that caused him to stutter. During part of 1975, Harris worked under Robert Jones's supervision at a GM assembly plant. Over a five-month period, Jones approached Harris more than 30 times at work and verbally and physically mimicked his stuttering disability. In addition, two or three times a week during this period, Jones approached Harris and told him, in a "smart" manner, not to get nervous. Harris said that as a result of Jones's conduct he was "shaken up" and felt "like going into a hole" and hiding. Harris had been under the care of a physician for a nervous condition for six years prior to the commencement of Jones's harassment. He admitted that many things made him nervous, including "bosses." He testified that Jones's conduct heightened his nervousness and worsened his speech impediment. He saw his physician on one occasion during the five-month period that Jones was mistreating him and received a prescription for nerve pills, which he had received periodically for six years prior to being mistreated by Jones. Harris filed suit against Jones and GM for intentional infliction of mental distress. The trial court ruled against him on the ground that his emotional distress as a result of Jones's actions was not sufficiently severe to justify recovery. Was the trial court right?

**8.** John Dickens, a 31-year-old man, had sexual relations with and gave alcohol and marijuana to Earl Puryear's daughter, a 17-year-old high school student. On April 2, 1975, Puryear lured Dickens onto his property and pointed a gun at him while four masked men beat Dickens with nightsticks until he was semiconscious. They then handcuffed him to a piece of farm machinery and resumed striking him with nightsticks. Puryear, while brandishing a knife and cutting Dickens's hair, threatened him with castration. After two hours, Dickens was released and told by Puryear to go home, pull his telephone off the wall, pack his clothes, and leave North Carolina; otherwise, he would be killed. On

March 31, 1978, Dickens filed suit against Puryear for intentional infliction of emotional distress. He alleged that as a result of Puryear's actions he was unable to sleep, afraid to leave his home at night, afraid to meet strangers, and afraid he might be killed; suffered from chronic diarrhea and a gum disorder; and was unable to effectively perform his job. The trial court granted Puryear's motion for summary judgment on the ground that Dickens's claim was barred by the state's one-year statute of limitations for assault and battery claims because it amounted to an attempt to recover for mental injuries resulting from those torts. Dickens argued that he had asserted a valid intentional infliction of mental distress claim and that his suit was therefore within the three-year statute of limitations applicable to that tort. Was the trial court correct in granting Puryear summary judgment?

**9.** Mr. and Mrs. Bhattal checked in at the Grand Hyatt–New York, sent their luggage to their room, and, after stopping briefly at their room, locked the door and went to lunch with friends. When they returned, their luggage was gone. As a result of a computer error, hotel employees had transported their luggage to John F. Kennedy International Airport along with the luggage of members of a Saudi Arabian flight crew who had previously occupied the Bhattals' room. Their luggage apparently departed for Saudi Arabia and was never recovered. The Bhattals filed a conversion suit against the hotel. Are they entitled to recover?

**10.** James Shelton was a lifelong friend of Robert and Jessie Evans. Robert Evans died in 1946, and Jessie Evans died in 1967, naming Shelton as her sole heir. The executor of Evans's estate asked Shelton to collect the rents on the properties in the estate. Shelton deposited the rents he collected in a special account. The executor also transferred an automobile from the estate to Shelton. Benjamin Amos, a District of Columbia attorney representing, on a contingent fee basis, several relatives of Robert Evans who were pressing claims against the estate, hired Robert Truel, a Pittsburgh attorney, to take depositions from Shelton concerning his involvement with the estate. Amos induced Ethel Evans, an elderly relative of Robert Evans, to sign four criminal complaints against Shelton, charging that he had wrongfully converted assets of the estate, among which was the automobile that Shelton had received from the executor. Two hearings were held before a magistrate. Ethel Evans appeared at the first hearing, but she offered no evidence to support the complaints. Amos asked for and was granted a postponement, but at the second hearing he asked that all the charges be withdrawn. Truel testified that Ethel Evans did not understand either the contents of the complaints or the nature of the criminal process she had invoked. Shelton filed a malicious prosecution suit against Amos, and a jury awarded him $20,000 in compensatory damages and $30,000 in punitive damages. Was the jury's decision correct?

Chapter 5

# Negligence and Strict Liability

## NEGLIGENCE

**Origins and Elements.** The industrial revolution that changed the face of 19th-century America created serious problems for the law of torts. Railroads, machinery, and other newly developing technologies were contributing to a growing number of injuries to persons and their property that did not fit within the intentional torts framework because most of them were unintended. Some of these injuries were simply the unavoidable consequences of life in a high-speed, technologically advanced, modern society. Holding infant industries totally responsible for all of the harms they caused could have seriously impeded the process of industrial development. To avoid such a result, new tort rules were needed. In response to these growing social pressures, the courts created the law of negligence.

Negligence focuses on conduct that falls below the legal standards that the law has established to protect members of society against unreasonable risks of harm. Negligence essentially involves an unintentional breach of a legal duty owed to another that results in some legally recognizable injury to the other's person or property. A plaintiff in a negligence suit must prove several things in order to recover: (1) that the defendant had a *duty* not to injure him, (2) that the defendant *breached* that duty, and (3) that the defendant's breach of duty was the *actual* and *legal (proximate) cause* of his *injury.* To be successful, a plaintiff must also overcome any *defenses* to negligence liability that are raised by the defendant. Most of these defenses involve behavior by the plaintiff that may have originally contributed to his injury.

**Duty.** The basic idea of negligence is that each member of society has a duty to conduct his or her affairs in a way that avoids an unreasonable risk of harm to others. The law of negligence holds each of us up to an *objective,* yet *flexible,* standard of conduct: that of a "reasonable man of ordinary prudence in similar circumstances." This standard is objective because the "reasonable man" is a hypothetical person who is always thoughtful and cautious and never unreasonably endangers others. It is flexible because it allows consideration of all the circumstances surrounding a particular injury. For example, the law does not require the same level of caution and deliberation of a person confronted with an emergency requiring rapid decisions and action as it does of a person in circumstances allowing for calm reflection and deliberate action. Likewise, to a limited extent, the law considers the personal characteristics of the particular defendant whose conduct is being judged. For example, children are generally required to act as a reasonable person of similar age, intelligence, and experience would act under similar circumstances. Persons with physical disabilities are required to act as would a reasonable person with the same disability. Mental deficiencies, however, will ordinarily not relieve a person from the duty to conform to the "reasonable man" standard.

**Special Duties.** The question of whether a particular duty exists is entirely a question of law. Does the law recognize a duty of the defendant to protect the interests of this particular plaintiff from harm? Legal duties can originate from a variety of sources. A *contractual relationship* between the plaintiff and the defendant can give rise to a variety of duties that might not exist otherwise. For example, most professional malpractice cases are based on claims that professionals negligently breached professional duties owed to their clients or to third persons who rely on their competent performance of professional tasks.[1]

Other *special relationships* between the parties have long been recognized as the source of special legal duties. For example, common carriers and innkeepers have long been held virtually strictly liable for damaging or losing the property of their customers. In recent years, many courts have extended this duty to include an affirmative duty to protect passengers or guests against the foreseeable wrongful acts of third persons. This has happened despite the fact that the law has long refused to recognize any general duty to aid and protect others from third-party wrongdoing unless a defendant's actions foreseeably increased the risk of such wrongdoing. Some recent decisions have imposed a similar duty upon landlords to protect their tenants against the foreseeable criminal acts of others.

The relationship between the parties can also affect the *level* of duty that one person owes to another. For example, the common law has long held that the level of duty that

[1] This subject is discussed in detail in Chapter 27.

a person in possession of land owes to other persons who enter upon the land depends on whether such persons were invitees, licensees, or trespassers. **Invitees** are members of the public who are lawfully on land open to the public (e.g., a park, swimming pool, or government office), or persons who are on private premises for a purpose connected with the business interests of the possessor of the land (e.g., customers, deliverymen, or paying boarders). **Licensees** are those whose privilege to enter upon the land depends entirely on the possessor's consent. Licensees include persons who are on the land solely for their own purposes (e.g., someone soliciting money for charity), members of the possessor's household, and social guests. **Trespassers** are persons who enter or remain upon another's land without any legal right or privilege to do so.

At common law, a possessor of land owed invitees a duty to exercise reasonable care to keep the premises in reasonably safe condition for their use. He also had a duty to protect invitees against dangerous conditions on the premises that he knew about, or reasonably should have discovered, and that they were unlikely to discover. He only owed licensees a duty to warn them of known dangerous conditions that they were unlikely to discover. The possessor of land owed no duty to trespassers to maintain his premises in a safe condition, and only a duty not to willfully and wantonly injure them once their presence was known. In recent years, however, there has been a marked tendency to erode these common law distinctions. Many courts today, for example, no longer distinguish between licensees and invitees, holding that the possessor of land owes the same duties to licensees that he owes to invitees. Also, numerous exceptions have been made to the minimal duties that possessors of land owe to trespassers. For example, a higher level of duty is ordinarily owed to trespassers who the possessor of land knows are constantly entering the land (e.g., using a well-worn path across the land) and greater duties are ordinarily owed to protect children if the possessor of land knows that they are likely to trespass.

Finally, *statutes* can create legal duties that can be the source of a negligence action. The doctrine of **negligence per se** provides that one who violates a statute is guilty of negligent conduct if a harm that the statute was designed to protect against results to a person whom the statute was designed to protect. The defendant who has violated a statute may still seek to avoid liability by arguing that his violation was not the legal cause of the plaintiff's injury or by asserting some other general defense to liability, but the statutory violation is generally held to be conclusive evidence of breach of duty.

**Breach.** A person is guilty of breach of duty if he or she exposes another to an *unreasonable, foreseeable* risk of harm. Negligence consists of doing something that a reasonable person would not have done under the circumstances, or failing to do something that a reasonable person would have done under the same circumstances. If a person guards against all foreseeable risks and exercises reasonable care, but harm to others nonetheless occurs, no liability for negligence will ordinarily result. For example, if Wilson is carefully driving his car within the speed limit and has a heart attack that causes him to lose control and crash into a car driven by Thomas, Wilson would ordinarily not be liable to Thomas for his injuries. He owed Thomas, as another member of the public using the highways, a duty to exercise reasonable care while driving. However, the accident was not the result of any breach of that duty since the manner in which it occurred was unforeseeable. If, on the other hand, Wilson's doctor had advised him that he had a heart condition which made driving dangerous, his failure to heed his doctor's warning would probably amount to a breach of duty because he was plainly exposing others to a foreseeable risk of harm by driving.

Of course, many types of behavior involve some risk of harm to others, but the risk must be an *unreasonable* one before the behavior will amount to a breach of duty. In deciding the reasonableness of the risk, the courts balance the social utility of a person's conduct and the ease of avoiding or minimizing the risk against the likelihood that harm will result and the probable seriousness of that harm. As the risk of serious harm to others increases, so does the duty to take steps to avoid that harm.

## Hresil v. Sears, Roebuck & Co.

**403 N.E.3d 678 (Ill. Ct. App. 1980)**

On September 14, 1972, at about 5:30 P.M., Ludmila Hresil and her niece walked into the Sears retail store located near Cicero, Illinois. There were few shoppers in the store at the time.

Hresil and her niece first visited the children's department. They remained there approximately half an hour, during which time the niece purchased some merchandise. As they prepared to leave the department, the niece stopped to make an additional purchase. At this time, Hresil was observing the women's department, where she saw no other shoppers for over 10 minutes.

After the niece completed her purchase, the two women walked through the women's department. Hresil, who was pushing a shopping cart, suddenly lost her balance and struggled to avoid a fall. Although she managed to regain her balance, her right leg struck the shopping cart and began to swell.

While her niece went for assistance, Hresil observed the floor area upon which she had slipped. She saw a "gob" on the floor with her heel mark clearly imprinted in it. An employee who came with her niece to assist Hresil commented that "it looked like someone spit on the floor, like it was phlegm."

Hresil went to a hospital emergency room that evening and to her doctor the following day. She was forced to undergo two subsequent operations on her leg, and she suffered permanent injury. Hresil filed suit for damages against Sears. The trial court ruled in Sears's favor, and Hresil appealed.

**McGillicuddy, Presiding Judge.** Although a store owner is not the insurer of his customer's safety, he does owe the customer the duty of exercising ordinary care in maintaining the premises in a reasonably safe condition. If the customer is injured by an accident involving a foreign substance on the premises and there is no evidence explaining the origin of the foreign substance, liability may be imposed on the store owner if the substance was present for a sufficient period of time so that the owner or operator of the premises should have discovered its presence.

In the instant case Hresil refers to her testimony that for 10 minutes prior to her fall no other customer was present in the women's department. From this evidence she infers that the foreign substance was present in the store at least 10 minutes prior to her fall. She asserts that it is a question of fact for the jury whether 10 minutes is sufficient time to give Sears constructive notice of the presence of the foreign substance.

Viewing the evidence most favorably to Hresil, we can assume that the foreign substance was present on the floor of the store for at least 10 minutes prior to her fall. However, we conclude, as a matter of law, that 10 minutes was an insufficient period of time to give constructive notice to the operator of this self-service store of the presence of the foreign substance. The accident occurred at a time when few shoppers were present in the store, and the evidence reveals that the salespersons were located at the store exit. To charge the store with constructive notice of the presence of the substance would place upon the store the unfair requirement of the constant patrolling of its aisles.

In *Saviola v. Sears, Roebuck & Co.,* the plaintiff was injured when a pin became embedded in her ankle as she was walking near a counter containing men's white shirts. No sales personnel or customers were in the area. Although there was no evidence of the length of time 8 or 10 pins, supposedly from packages of men's shirts, had been on the floor, the court found that the bent condition of some of the pins might indicate that they had been on the floor long enough to have been walked on. The court further found that Sears had ample time to discover the presence of the pins before the accident and, therefore, had constructive notice of the unsafe condition of the premises. In the instant case there is no evidence that any other customer or store employee had discovered or walked through the foreign substance.

Judgment for Sears affirmed.

---

## Duarte v. State of California

**148 Cal. Rptr. 804 (Cal. Ct. App. 1978)**

Tanya Gardini was a freshman at the California State University in San Diego. She was raped and murdered in her dorm room by Lee Ellis Handy, Jr., a navy seaman. Her mother, Yvonne Duarte, filed suit against the university, arguing that before Tanya's murder there had been a chronic pattern of attacks on female students and that the university had failed to take reasonable steps to protect or warn students. She also alleged that the university "covered up" such incidents so that the true extent of the danger was not generally known. The trial court ruled in the state's favor, and Duarte appealed.

**Staniforth, Associate Justice.** Under the common law, as a general rule one person owed no duty to control the conduct of another or to warn those endangered by such conduct. The courts have carved out exceptions (which may well have swallowed the rule) in cases where the defendant stands in some special relationship to either the person whose conduct needs to be controlled or in a relationship to the foreseeable victim of that conduct. At section 315 of the *Restatement (Second) of Torts,* a duty of care may arise from either "(a) a special relation . . . between the actor and the third person which imposes a duty upon the actor to control the third person's conduct, or (b) a special relation . . . between the actor and the other which gives to the other right of protection."

The legal responsibility for the protection of another person from the criminal misconduct of a third party (absent a specific contractual undertaking) has been historically founded on some recognized relationship existing between the parties such as carrier and passenger, innkeeper and guest, invitor and business guest, school district and pupil, employer and employee, landlord and tenant. The list and the concept has a general elasticity, characteristic of tort law principles.

*Kline v. 1500 Massachusetts Avenue Corp.,* the landmark case, holds a landlord liable both on negligence and contract principles in failing to protect a tenant against criminal conduct of third parties. The *Kline* court based liability, found "duty" on these premises. First the court found the "logic of the situation" required the imposition of a duty of protection upon the landlord.

> The landlord is no insurer of his tenants' safety, but he certainly is no bystander. And where, as here, the landlord has notice of repeated criminal assaults and robberies, has notice that these crimes occurred in the portion of the premises exclusively within his control, has every reason to expect like crimes to happen again, and has the exclusive power to take preventive action, it does not seem unfair to place upon the landlord a duty to take those steps which are within his power to minimize the predictable risk to his tenants.

Tanya was not the victim of a sudden unexpected outburst. She had a landlord-tenant relationship-plus with the university. Tanya had in many substantial respects surrendered the control of her person, control of her own security to the university. The university, it is charged, failed to warn and concealed the true state of affairs concerning rapes and assaults upon students. The charge here is that no security devices were instituted, let alone minimal safety precautions such as warning of the degree of danger. The university allegedly has superior knowledge and also the means of instituting some reasonable protective measures. The university not only had control over the campus areas and the residential facilities, but also many aspects of Tanya's personal activities. Tanya herself could not purchase and install security devices or hire a private police force. She could not possess a dog or a firearm.

Further the pleadings here allege the most important factor of liability—foreseeability. It is asserted the university knew of past assaults and of the conditions inviting further assaults. By failure to institute reasonable means within their power of accomplishment the likelihood of Tanya becoming a rape victim was increased.

We conclude that the duty of care here arose not only from the factual situation in which the university was on notice of potential harm to a person or class of persons. But in addition the duty here rests upon, arose out of that special landlord-tenant relationship here alleged. Tanya was not only entitled to a safe roof and adequate walls, but to an essentially safe place of residence. The contract between the university and Tanya was more than leasing of space in a student dormitory. She submitted her security to control by the university. In this fact matrix an obligation arose to provide such protective measures which were within the university's reasonable capacity to thwart or diminish the possibility of a foreseeable assault.

Judgment reversed in favor of Duarte.

## Walz v. City of Hudson

**327 N.W.2d 120 (S.D. Sup. Ct. 1982)**

The city of Hudson, South Dakota, operated the Hudson Municipal Liquor Store. Larry Van Egdom bought liquor at the store and immediately thereafter, while driving his car, ran into Guy Ludwig, who had stopped on his motorcycle at a stop sign. Ludwig died, and Lela Walz, the administrator of his estate, filed suit against the city. Walz argued that Van Egdom was obviously intoxicated at the time the liquor was sold and that since the sale to Van Egdom violated SDCL 35–4–78(2), a state criminal statute prohibiting the sale of alcoholic beverages to intoxicated persons, the sale to him amounted to negligence per se. When the trial court dismissed her suit for failure to state a claim, Walz appealed.

**Fosheim, Chief Justice.** Walz urges that we overrule our decision in *Griffin v. Sebek* (1976), thus affording her a cause of action against the city. In *Griffin* the plaintiffs brought a negligence action against defendants, licensed tavernkeepers, seeking damages for personal injury resulting from defendants' unlawful sale of alcoholic beverages. Our decision, affirming the trial court's order granting defendants' motion to dismiss for failure to state a claim, said the issue was whether, in the absence of a dram shop act, "the common law now authorizes or should be liberalized to afford a remedy." We determined that no such cause of action exists in South Dakota and declined to expand the common law to afford a remedy. We also did not extend SDCL 35–4–78(2) to impose a civil liability duty. We take judicial notice that since *Griffin* was decided, alcohol has been involved in 50.8 percent of this state's traffic fatalities from 1976 to 1981; in 1981 alone, 62 percent of South Dakota's traffic fatalities were alcohol related. This tragic waste of life prompts us to review our conclusions in *Griffin.* If the Legislature does not concur with our application of SDCL 35–4–78(2), as now announced, it is the prerogative of the Legislature to so assert. We fully realize this decision, while hopefully helpful, certainly cannot resolve the problems of alcohol-related deaths or injuries.

Negligence is the breach of a legal duty imposed by statute or common law. *Griffin* recognized that a liquor licensee is not liable at common law for damages resulting from a patron's intoxication. The common law is in force in South Dakota except where it conflicts with federal or state constitutions and laws. SDCL 35–4–78(2) makes it a crime to sell intoxicating beverages to one in Mr. Van Egdom's inebriated state and violation of a statute is negligence as a matter of law if the statute "was intended to protect the class of persons in which plaintiffs are included against risk of the type of harm which has in fact occurred." The reason for this rule is that the statute or ordinance becomes the standard of care or conduct to which the reasonably prudent person is held. Failure to follow the statute involved constitutes a breach of the legal duty imposed and fixed by such statute. Since negligence is a breach of a legal duty, the violator of a statute is then negligent as a matter of law.

Justice Dunn dissented in *Griffin.* He argued that SDCL 35–4–78(2) was passed for the protection of the plaintiffs. Since *Griffin* essentially turned on a reluctance to impose a common law duty in the absence of express civil liability legislation, we did not fully reach Justice Dunn's interpretation of SDCL 35-4-78(2). We do now. We believe that statute was enacted to include the protection of the class of people in Mr. Ludwig's position from the risk of being killed or injured "as a result of the drunkenness to which the particular sale of alcoholic liquor contributes."

We conclude that SDCL 35-4-78(2) establishes a standard of care or conduct, a breach of which is negligence as a matter of law. It follows that such negligence must be a proximate cause of any resulting injury and defenses, such as contributory negligence, are available when appropriate.

Judgment reversed in favor of Walz.

---

**Causation.** Even if a person breaches a duty that he or she owes to another person, no liability for negligence will result unless the breach of duty was the *actual cause* (cause in fact) of injury to the other person. In order to determine the existence of actual cause, many courts employ a *"but for"* test: a defendant's conduct is the actual cause of a plaintiff's injury if that injury would not have occurred *but for* the defendant's breach of duty. In some cases, however, a person's negligent conduct may combine with the negligent conduct of another to cause a plaintiff's injury. For example, on a windy day Allen negligently starts a fire by trying to use gasoline to start his charcoal grill. The fire started by Allen spreads and joins forces with another fire started by Baker, who was burning brush on his property but who failed to take any precautions to prevent the fire from spreading. The combined fires burn Clark's home to the ground. Clark sues both Allen and Baker for negligence. In such a case, the court would ask whether each defendant's conduct was a *substantial factor* in bringing about Clark's loss. If the evidence indicates that Clark's house would have been destroyed by either fire in the absence of the other, both Allen and Baker are liable for Clark's loss.

**Proximate Cause.** Holding persons guilty of negligent conduct responsible for all of the harms that actually result from their negligence could, in some cases, expose them to potentially catastrophic liability. Although the law has long tended to say that those who are guilty of intentional wrongdoing are liable for all of the direct consequences of their acts, however bizarre or unforeseeable, the courts have also recognized that a person who was merely negligent should not necessarily be responsible for every injury actually caused by her negligence. This idea of placing some legal limit on a negligent defendant's liability for the consequences of her actions is called **proximate cause,** and courts often say that a negligent defendant is liable only for the *proximate* results of her conduct. Thus, although a defendant's conduct may have been the *actual cause* of a particular plaintiff's injury, she is liable only if her conduct was also the *proximate (legal) cause* of that injury.

The courts have not, however, reached any substantial agreement on the test that should be employed for proximate cause. In reality, the proximate cause question is a question of social policy. In deciding which test to adopt, a court must weigh the possibility that negligent persons will be exposed to catastrophic liability by a lenient test for proximate cause against the fact that a restrictive test will inevitably prevent some innocent victims from recovering any compensation for their losses. It is not surprising that the courts have responded in a variety of ways to this difficult choice.

Some courts have said that a negligent person is liable only for the "natural and probable consequences" of his actions. Others have limited a negligent person's liability for unforeseeable injuries by saying that he is liable only to plaintiffs who are within the "scope of the foreseeable risk." Thus, such courts hold that if the defendant could not have reasonably foreseen *some* injury to the plaintiff as a result of his actions, he is not liable to the plaintiff for any injury that in fact results from his negligence. Although this rule is often characterized as a rule of causation, in reality it is a rule limiting the defendant's *duty,* because courts adopting the rule hold that a defendant owes *no duty* to those to whom he cannot foresee any injury. On the other hand, such courts commonly hold that a defendant may be liable even for unforeseeable injuries to persons whom he has exposed to a foreseeable risk of harm.[2] The *Restatement (Second) of Torts* suggests that a defendant's negligence is not the legal cause of a plaintiff's injury if, looking back after the harm, it appears "highly extraordinary" to the court that the defendant's negligence should have brought about the plaintiff's injury.[3]

**Superseding Causes.** In some cases, an *intervening force* occurring after a defendant's negligence may play a significant role in bringing about a particular plaintiff's injury. For example, a high wind may spring up that causes a fire set by Davis to spread and damage Parker's property, or after Davis negligently runs Parker down with his car, a thief may steal Parker's wallet while he is lying unconscious in the street. Such cases present difficult problems for the courts, which must decide when an intervening force should relieve a negligent defendant from liability. As a general rule, if the intervening force is a *foreseeable* one, either because it frequently occurs in the ordinary course of human events or because the defendant's negligence substantially increases the risk of its occurrence, it will *not* operate to relieve the defendant from liability. So, in the first example given above, if high winds are a reasonably common occurrence in the locality in question, Davis may be liable for the damage to Parker's property even though his fire would not have spread that far under the wind conditions that existed when he started it. Likewise, in our second example, Davis may be responsible for the theft of Parker's wallet if the theft is foreseeable, given the time and location of the accident.

If, on the other hand, the intervening force that contributes to the plaintiff's injury is an unforeseeable one, most courts will hold that it is a **superseding** or **intervening cause** which absolves the defendant of any liability for his negligence. For example, Dalton negligently starts a fire that causes injury to several persons. The driver of an ambulance summoned to the scene to aid the injured has been drinking on duty and, as a result, loses control of his ambulance and runs up onto a sidewalk, injuring several pedestrians. Most courts would not hold Dalton responsible for the pedestrians' injuries. One important exception to this general rule, however, concerns intervening forces that produce a harm identical to the harm risked by the defendant's negligence. For example, the owners of a concert hall fail to install the number of emergency exits required by law for the protection of patrons. A negligently operated aircraft crashes into the hall during a concert, and a large number of patrons are burned to death in the ensuing fire because the few available exits are jammed by panicked patrons trying to es-

---

[2] The most famous case adopting this approach is *Palsgraf v. Long Island Railroad Co.,* 12 N.E. 99 (N.Y. Ct. App. 1928).

[3] *Restatement (Second) of Torts* § 435(2) (1965).

cape. Most courts would probably find that the owners of the hall were liable for the patrons' deaths.

**Generally Accepted Causation Rules.** Whatever test for proximate cause a court says it adopts, most courts generally agree on certain basic principles of causation. One such basic principle is that persons guilty of negligence "take their victims as they find them." This means that a negligent defendant is liable for the full extent of his victim's injuries even if those injuries are aggravated by some preexisting physical characteristic of the victim. Similarly, negligent defendants are normally held liable for diseases contracted by their victims while in a weakened state caused by their injuries, and *jointly* liable (along with the attending physician) for negligent medical care that their victims receive for their injuries.

Negligent defendants are also commonly held responsible for injuries sustained by persons seeking to avoid being injured by the defendant's negligence. For example, Peters swerves to avoid being hit by Denning's negligently driven car and in the process loses control of her own car and is injured. Denning is liable for Peters's injuries. Finally, it is commonly said that "negligence invites rescue." This means that negligent persons are liable to those who are injured in attempting to rescue the victims of their negligence. One corollary of this "rescue" rule is that the claim of a would-be rescuer will ordinarily not be defeated by contributory fault on the part of the rescuer so long as he is not reckless in making the rescue attempt.

***Res Ipsa Loquitur.*** In some cases, negligence may be difficult to prove because the defendant has superior knowledge of the circumstances surrounding the plaintiff's injury and it may not be in the defendant's best interests to disclose those circumstances if they point to liability on his part. Consider, for example, the position of a person who goes into the hospital for an appendectomy and awakens after the operation to find that both of his legs have been amputated. Since he was anesthetized during the operation, he has no way of knowing what caused his loss. The only persons who do know are the hospital personnel who performed the operation, but the odds are that they are the ones responsible for the tragedy. The doctrine of ***res ipsa loquitur*** ("the thing speaks for itself") can aid such a plaintiff in proving his case. *Res ipsa* applies when: (1) the defendant has *exclusive control* of the instrumentality of harm (and therefore probable knowledge of, and responsibility for, the cause of the harm), and (2) the harm that occurred *would not ordinarily occur* in the absence of negligence. When both of these elements are present, most states hold that an *inference* arises that the defendant was negligent and that his negligence was the cause of the plaintiff's injury. The burden is then on the defendant to rebut the inference that he is responsible. If he fails to introduce evidence that does so, a court or jury *may* choose to impose liability on him. Some courts, however, allow *res ipsa* to create a *presumption* of negligence that requires a directed verdict for the plaintiff in the absence of proof by the defendant rebutting the presumption.

## Brown v. Tinneny

### 421 A.2d 839 (Pa. Super. Ct. 1980)

On October 14, 1976, Molly Brown, age 13, was walking home from school. Behind her were several boys, including John Tinneny and Timothy Labos, who were also walking home from school. (Tinneny and Labos were both 16 years old.) The boys were horseplaying and tossing stones at each other. When one of the stones struck Molly, she increased her pace and crossed the street. The boys, however, also crossed the street. About this time, Tinneny saw near the curb a small glass vial, approximately 2 inches high and ½ inch wide, with a hard, black cap. The vial contained a colorless liquid. Tinneny picked up the vial and tossed it at Labos. The vial missed Labos and landed in the grass. As Labos began to pick up the vial, Tinneny came forward and grabbed him. The impact of Tinneny's grip dislodged the cap on the vial and caused the liquid inside to splash on Molly's back. At the time, Molly was on the sidewalk approximately 10 to 15 feet from Tinneny and Labos. It so happened that the liquid in the vial was nitric acid, and Molly sustained burns where the acid splashed her body.

Molly's parents, as her guardians and in their own right, sued Tinneny and Labos for Molly's injuries. The jury ruled in favor of Tinneny and Labos, and Molly's parents appealed.

**Spaeth, Judge.** Molly's parents contend that the trial court committed reversible error when it instructed the jury on the *Restatement (Second) of Torts* section 435(2) (1965). This provision states:

> The actor's [defendant's] conduct may be held not to be a legal cause of harm to another where after the event and looking back from the harm to the actor's negligent conduct, it appears to the court highly extraordinary that it should have brought about the harm.

Except for its deletion of the phrase "to the court," the trial court, over appellants' objection, read this section verbatim to the jury. The Browns assert that this was error because section 435(2) explicitly places upon the court the responsibility of determining whether an actor is to be relieved, as a matter of law, from the consequences of his negligent conduct because of the extraordinariness of his conduct having caused the harm suffered. In their view, by charging on section 435(2), the court confused its functions with the jury's. The Browns further assert that looking back from Molly's harm to Tinneny's and Labos's negligent conduct, it cannot be said as a matter of law that it was highly extraordinary that the conduct should have brought about the harm.

We agree with the Browns that section 435(2) describes a function of the court, not the jury. The section states that it must appear "to the court" that it is highly extraordinary that the actor's negligent conduct should have brought about the harm in question, if the actor is to be held not to have been the legal cause of the harm. Comments c, d, and e to section 435(2) similarly refer to determinations by the court in the application of the section. Moreover, the *Restatement (Second) of Torts* section 453 (1965) provides:

> It is the exclusive function of the court to declare the existence or non-existence of rules which restrict the actor's responsibility short of making him liable for harm which his negligent conduct is

a substantial factor in bringing about, and to determine the circumstances to which such rules are applicable.

We also agree with the Browns that looking back from Molly's harm to Tinneny's and Labos's negligent conduct, it cannot be said as a matter of law that it was highly extraordinary that their conduct should have brought about the harm. It was certainly not highly extraordinary that Molly was burned when the nitric acid splashed on her—indeed the burns were inevitable. Nor was it highly extraordinary that the cap to the vial containing the acid was dislodged during Tinneny's and Labos's horseplay and the acid thrown a distance of 10 to 15 feet. That the vial contained nitric acid was somewhat unusual, but we cannot say as a matter of law that it was highly extraordinary that liquid in a small, unmarked vial lying by the roadway should prove to be corrosive or otherwise capable of causing physical injury.

In holding that section 435(2) sets forth a function of the court, and that Tinneny and Labos were not entitled to relief from liability under that provision, we realize that "analytically, the highly extraordinary nature of the result which has followed from the actor's conduct . . . indicates that the hazard which brought about or assisted in bringing about that result was not among the hazards with respect to which the conduct was negligent." *Restatement (Second) of Torts* section 435, Comment c.

We also realize that whether a victim's harm proceeded from a hazard the foreseeability of which rendered the actor's conduct negligent is a question for the jury in a case where different conclusions may be reached on the issue. Further, we realize that in the present case the foreseeability of the hazard to Molly created by Tinneny's and Labos's horseplay was a question legitimately before the jury, and that it was within the jury's prerogative to conclude that because a reasonable person would not have foreseen the hazard that caused Molly's injuries, Tinneny and Labos had not breached their duty towards her and were not liable for her injuries. Nevertheless, we believe that the trial court erred in charging on section 435(2).

Our cases hold that "foreseeability is not an element to be considered in determining whether negligent conduct was the proximate cause of an accident, [although] it is an element to be considered in determining the existence of negligent conduct." We have further held that "once the actor's conduct has been found to constitute negligence, the actor is responsible for all the unforeseen consequences thereof no matter how remote, which follow in a natural sequence of events," and accordingly have reversed a jury verdict where the trial court erroneously charged that foreseeability was a consideration to be taken into account in determining legal cause.

Given the charge, it is entirely possible that the jury believed that a reasonable person should have recognized the risk of harm to Molly created by Tinneny's and Labos's horseplay with the vial, but nevertheless exonerated them because they believed that it was highly extraordinary that the harm that occurred in fact occurred.

Judgment reversed in favor of the Browns; case remanded for new trial.

## The Concord Florida, Inc. v. Lewin

### 341 So.2d 242 (Fla. Ct. App. 1977)

On February 2, 1973, a madman ran in the front door of the crowded Concord Cafeteria in Miami Beach, threw a five-gallon container of gasoline on the floor, lit a match to the gasoline, and then ran away. In the fire that ensued, many patrons were burned and/or suffered smoke inhalation, while others were injured in their chaotic attempts to flee the burning building.

As a result of this incident, over 70 individuals filed suit against Concord Florida, Inc., the owner of the cafeteria, alleging injuries suffered as a result of Concord's failure to provide ample emergency fire exits, to clearly designate the location of the present fire exits, and to provide a reasonably safe place for its patrons—all in violation of the Metropolitan Dade County Fire Prevention and Safety Code.

The trial court refused to allow Concord to argue that the madman's behavior was an "intervening cause" which relieved Concord of liability and instructed the jury that violations of the fire code would amount to negligence per se. The jury found in favor of the fire victims, and Concord appealed.

**Hendry, Judge.** Concord first contends that negligence includes the element of foreseeable risk. As such, Concord argues that it was entitled to present to the jury the question of whether or not the possibility of a gasoline throwing maniac was so foreseeable that Concord was negligent in not guarding against such an occurrence. Concord argues that by prohibiting it from presenting its defense of intervening cause to the jury, during the negligence portion of the trial, the trial judge effectively conceded the issue of negligence to the fire victims.

Inherent in Concord's contention is the idea that the act in question was an intervening cause which would insulate Concord from liability. The fire victims, however, rely upon the case of *Mozer v. Semenza* in support of their contention that such an act does not in fact constitute an intervening cause.

The facts of that case are very similar to those of this case. There, an arsonist set fire to a hotel, injuring patrons who attempted to flee over a negligently maintained open stairwell. The defendants in that trial attempted to defend on the ground of intervening cause (the arsonist). In rejecting that claim, we held that:

> [T]he act of the arsonist was not an "independent intervening cause." The scope of defendant's duty to maintain reasonably safe premises does not include a duty to foresee a *particular fire* but it does include a duty to reasonably guard against *the risk of fire.* Viewed from this standpoint it is not important to the liability of the defendant whether the fire started in one way or another. It was reasonably foreseeable that there would, even under modern conditions, be a likelihood of fire and it was the duty of the defendant to provide a reasonably safe place in anticipation of that danger.

The above analysis is consistent with Section 442 B of the *Restatement (Second) of Torts,* which provides that:

> Where the negligent conduct of the actor creates or increases the risk of a *particular harm* and is a substantial factor in causing that harm, the fact that the harm is brought about through the

interaction of another force does not relieve the actor of liability, except where the harm is intentionally caused by a third person and is *not within the scope of the risk created by the actor's conduct.*

The emphasized portion of the above appears to be the crux of the matter and, though not specifically cited, determinative in the *Mozer* case. The scope of the risk created there and scope of the risk created here was not that of an arsonist or madman *setting fire* to a building, per se, but rather the risk of *fire,* itself. In failing to adequately protect its patrons from fire by providing proper safety measures such as emergency exits and signs indicating the location of said exits, Concord assumed the foreseeable risk that fire might someday trap its patrons leaving them without an escape route.

We therefore hold that the act of the madman, in and of itself, was not an intervening cause, cutting off the liability of Concord.

Judgment for the fire victims affirmed.

---

**Injury.** The plaintiff in a negligence case must prove not only that the defendant breached a duty owed to the plaintiff and that the breach of duty was the legal cause of her injury, but also that the resulting injury was to an interest that the law seeks to protect. Ordinarily, purely physical injuries to a person or her property present no problem in this respect, since the law has long protected such interests. Serious problems arise, however, when injuries are purely *emotional* in nature. As you learned in Chapter 4, the law has long demonstrated a considerable reluctance to afford recovery for purely emotional harms, due, among other things, to the danger of spurious claims and the difficulty inherent in placing a monetary value on emotional injuries. Given our great reluctance to impose liability for purely emotional harms caused by intentional wrongs, one might correctly assume that an even greater reluctance would exist when the conduct producing an emotional injury was merely negligent.

**Negligent Infliction of Emotional Distress.** Until fairly recently, most courts would not allow a plaintiff to recover for emotional injuries resulting from a defendant's negligent behavior in the absence of some "impact" or contact with the plaintiff's person. Today, many courts have abandoned the impact rule and will allow recovery for foreseeable emotional injuries standing alone. A large number of such courts, however, still require, as a precondition of recovery, proof that some serious physical "injury" or symptoms resulted from the plaintiff's emotional distress. Nonetheless, a growing number of courts have dispensed with the injury requirement where the plaintiff has suffered serious emotional distress as a foreseeable consequence of the defendant's negligent conduct.

**Third-Party Emotional Distress.** In recent years, a growing number of negligence cases have involved claims by third persons for emotional injuries that they suffered by witnessing a negligently caused harm to another person, usually a spouse or child. For example, Mr. Porter has a heart attack after seeing Mrs. Porter run down by a car negligently driven by Denton. Is Denton liable for Mr. Porter's injury? Until fairly recently, most courts would have denied Mr. Porter any recovery on the ground that he had suffered no "impact" as a result of Denton's negligence. In recent years, however, many courts have abandoned the impact rule in third-party cases in favor of the "zone of danger" test, which allows third parties who are themselves in the zone of danger created by a defendant's negligence to recover for emotional injuries resulting from the threat of harm to them, regardless of whether any impact ever occurred. Courts following this rule would therefore allow Mr. Porter to recover if he was close enough to his wife to be in danger of being hit by Denton's car. Some courts would insist, in addition, that Mr. Porter prove that he suffered some physical "injury" as a result of his emotional distress.

Today, some courts have abandoned the zone of danger requirement entirely and will allow recovery for emotional injuries suffered by third parties, regardless of whether there was any threat of injury to them. Most courts that have taken this step still attempt to limit recovery in a variety of ways. For example, such courts commonly require that a close personal relationship exist between the third-party plaintiff and the direct victim of the defendant's negligence and that the third party's emotional distress result from actually witnessing the injury to the direct victim. Also, a requirement that the third party demonstrate some physical "injury" resulting from his or her emotional distress is commonly imposed. This area of the law is undergoing rapid development, however, and some recent cases may be found dispensing with the injury requirement or allowing recovery for emotional distress suffered as a result of seeing the direct victim in an injured state shortly after the injury occurred.

## Sinn v. Burd

**404 A.2d 672 (Pa. Sup. Ct. 1979)**

JoAnne Marie Sinn lived with her husband and two minor children in Elizabeth Township, Allegheny County. On June 12, 1975, at approximately 5:53 P.M., the deceased, Lisa Sinn, and her sister, Deborah, were standing by the Sinns' mailbox, which was located alongside the Greenock–Buena Vista Road, approximately 36 feet from the nearest intersection. An automobile operated by Brad Burd struck Lisa and hurled her through the air, causing injuries that resulted in her death. Deborah was not struck by the vehicle, although it narrowly missed her. Mrs. Sinn witnessed the accident from a position near the front door of her home. She filed suit for the physical and mental injuries that she suffered as a result of witnessing Lisa's death. The trial court dismissed her complaint on the ground that she had not been within the zone of danger created by Burd's negligence, and Mrs. Sinn appealed.

**Nix, Justice.** Prior to the beginning of this decade, this state was a firm adherent to the "impact rule" regulating recovery for damages in tort. This rule prevented the complaining party from recovering damages for injuries resulting from fright, nervous shock, or mental or emotional disturbances, unless this distress was accompanied by physical impact—*i.e.,* physical injury—upon the person of the complaining party. Our cases applied this rule with obstinate rigidity in that recovery was denied not only when the complaining party was a nearby witness, but also to the actual victim of the tortfeasor's negligent or frightening conduct.

In the first month of this decade, this Court joined the ranks of forward-looking jurisdictions and abandoned the impact rule in *Niederman v. Brodsky.* In *Niederman,* an automobile skidded onto a sidewalk, narrowly missed the plaintiff, but struck his son who was standing beside him. The plaintiff, although untouched by the automobile, suffered a heart attack which required hospitalization. The trial court dismissed plaintiff's complaint for its failure to allege any physical impact. In an opinion by Mr. Justice Roberts, this Court reversed the dismissal, abandoned the impact rule, and adopted the zone of danger theory. That is, "where the plaintiff was in personal danger of physical impact because of the direction of a negligent force against him and where plaintiff actually did fear the physical impact," he could recover for the shock, mental pain, and physical injuries attendant to the negligent incident even though he was not struck by the negligent force.

Since the *Niederman* decision, experience has taught us that the zone of danger requirement can be unnecessarily restrictive and prevent recovery in instances where there is no sound policy basis supporting such a result. The restrictiveness of the zone of danger test is glaringly apparent where it is allowed to deny recovery to a parent who has suffered emotional harm from witnessing a tortious assault upon the person of his or her minor child. A majority of the commentators and a growing number of jurisdictions have considered this problem in recent years and have concluded that it is unreasonable for the zone of danger requirement to exclude recovery in such cases.

This new awareness of the unfairness of the zone of danger requirement in these cases is based upon the implicit acceptance that the emotional impact upon a parent witnessing the killing of a minor child is at least as great and as legitimate as the apprehension that is inspired by a person being personally within the zone of danger.

Our cases have recognized five policy arguments relevant to bystander recovery. They are medical science's supposed difficulty in proving causation between the claimed damages and the alleged fright, the fear of fraudulent or exaggerated claims, the concern that to allow such a recovery will precipitate a veritable flood of litigation, the problem of unlimited and unduly burdensome liability, and the difficulty of reasonably circumscribing the area of liability.

It has long been assumed that medical science is unable to establish that the alleged psychic injuries in fact resulted from seeing a gruesome accident. Advancements in medical and psychiatric science throughout this century have discredited these hoary beliefs. Advancements in modern science lead us to further conclude that psychic injury is capable of being proven despite the absence of a physical manifestation of such injury. Some courts in abandoning the impact rule permit recovery for emotional distress only where the plaintiff can prove that the psychic injury caused her to suffer physical damage as well. This requirement of resulting physical injury is another synthetic device to guarantee the genuineness of the claim.

Courts upholding and those courts denying bystander recovery agree that concern over fraud is without justification. The commentators are in accord with the judicial rejection of this argument. One medicolegal expert takes the view that with the development of medical and psychiatric understanding of methods of ascertaining psychic injury, "[v]ery rarely, today, can a malingerer recover damages."

The fear of a flood of litigation is an insufficient reason to deny bystander recovery. Again, commentators and courts on both sides of the recovery issue agree that this fear is specious. We obviously do not accept the "too much work to do" rationale. We place the responsibility exactly where it should be: not in denying relief to those who have been injured, *but* on the judicial machinery of the Commonwealth to fulfill its obligation to make itself available to litigants. Who is to say which class of aggrieved plaintiffs should be denied access to our courts because of speculation that the workload will be a burden?

Bystander recovery would not present a problem of unlimited or unduly burdensome liability. The more complex and interwoven societal relations become, the greater the responsibility one must accept for his or her conduct. The conduct which is offered as supporting the liability—*i.e.,* in this case the negligent operation of the vehicle—is of the kind which has traditionally been held to have been actionable by plaintiffs who had sustained probable damages. The departure that is being urged is as to *the scope of damages that will be recognized as flowing from that conduct.* In this context, we are satisfied that the developments in the fields of medical science and psychiatry provide the impetus for expanding our legal recognition of the consequences of the negligent act. To arbitrarily refuse to recognize a now demonstrable injury flowing from a negligent act would be wholly indefensible.

In an attempt to still the concerns of those troubled by "the fear of unlimited liability" the Supreme Court of Hawaii suggested the limiting of recovery "to claims of serious mental distress." We believe this is a reasonable response to the concern. We agree that it would be unreasonable to hold the defendant responsible for the mental distress that may be experienced by the most timid or sensitive members of the community.

We are confident that the application of the traditional tort concept of foreseeability will reasonably circumscribe the tortfeasor's liability in such cases. Foreseeability enters into the determination of liability in determining whether the emotional injuries sustained by the plaintiff were reasonably foreseeable to the defendant. In the seminal *Dillon* case, the California Supreme Court identified three factors determinative of whether the injury to the plaintiff was reasonably foreseeable:

> (1) Whether plaintiff was located near the scene of the accident as contrasted with one who was a distance away from it. (2) Whether the shock resulted from a direct emotional impact upon plaintiff from the sensory and contemporaneous observance of the accident, as contrasted with learning of the accident from others after its occurrence. (3) Whether plaintiff and the victim were closely related, as contrasted with an absence of any relationship or the presence of only a distant relationship.

It is clear that Mrs. Sinn's injuries were of a nature reasonably foreseeable under the circumstances alleged. Where the bystander is a mother who witnessed the violent death of her small child and the emotional shock emanated directly from personal observation of the event, we hold as a matter of law that the mental distress and its effects are foreseeable injuries.

Judgment reversed in favor of Sinn.

**Defenses to Negligence.** The common law traditionally recognized two defenses to negligence: **contributory negligence** and **assumption of risk.** Both of these defenses are based on the idea of *contributory fault:* if a plaintiff's own behavior contributed in some way to his injury, this fact should relieve the defendant from liability. As the following paragraphs indicate, however, the contributory fault idea often produced harsh results, and recent years have witnessed a significant erosion of its impact in negligence cases.

**Contributory Negligence.** The doctrine of **contributory negligence** provides that plaintiffs who *fail to exercise reasonable care for their own safety* are totally barred from any recovery if their contributory negligence is a *substantial factor* in producing their injury. So, if Parker steps into the path of Dworkin's speeding car without first checking to see whether any cars are coming, Parker would be denied any recovery against Dworkin because of the clear causal relationship between his injury and his failure to exercise reasonable care for his own safety. On the other hand, if Parker is injured one night when his speeding car crashes into a large, unmarked hole in the street caused by a city street repair project, and the facts indicate that the accident would have occurred even if Parker had been driving at a legal speed, he will not be barred from recovering damages from the city for its negligence.

In some cases, a contributorily negligent plaintiff may be able to overcome an otherwise valid contributory negligence defense by arguing that the defendant had the **last clear chance** to avoid harm. The doctrine of last clear chance focuses on who was *last* at fault *in time*. Therefore, if despite the plaintiff's contributory negligence, the harm could have been avoided if the defendant had exercised reasonable care, the defendant's *superior opportunity* to avoid the accident makes him more at fault. For example, Durban pulls into the path of Preston's speeding car without looking, causing an accident. When Preston files suit to recover for the damage, Durban argues that the fact that Preston was speeding amounts to contributory negligence. If Preston can convince the court that the accident could have been avoided if Durban had looked before pulling onto the highway, he has a good chance of overcoming Durban's contributory negligence defense.

**Comparative Negligence.** Contributory negligence can sometimes produce harsh results because it may operate to prevent slightly negligent persons from recovering any compensation for their losses. In reaction to this potential unfairness, a growing majority of the states have adopted **comparative negligence** systems either by statute or by judicial decision. The details of these systems vary by state, but the principle underlying them is essentially the same: courts seek to determine the *relative fault* of the parties to a negligence action, and award damages in proportion to the degree of fault determined. For a simple example, assume that Dunne negligently injures Porter and Porter suffers $10,000 in damages. A jury, however, determines that Porter was 20 percent at fault. Under a comparative negligence system, Porter could recover only $8,000 from Dunne. But what if Porter is determined to be 60 percent at fault? Here, the results will vary depending on whether the state in question has adopted a *pure* or a *mixed* comparative fault system. Under a "pure" comparative fault system, plaintiffs are allowed to recover a portion of their damages even if they are more at fault than the defendant, so Porter could recover $4,000. Under a "mixed" system, plaintiffs who are as much at fault as, or, in some states, more at fault than, the defendant are denied any recovery. In such a state, Porter would be denied any recovery, just as though contributory negligence principles still applied.

**Assumption of Risk.** In some cases, a plaintiff has *voluntarily* exposed herself to a *known danger* created by the defendant's negligence. Such plaintiffs are said to have *assumed the risk* of their injury and ordinarily are denied any recovery for it. For example,

Stevens voluntarily goes for a ride in Markley's car, even though Markley has told him that her brakes are not working properly. Stevens has assumed the risk of injury as a result of the car's defective brakes. A person must fully understand the nature and extent of the risk, however, to be held to have assumed it. Some states that have adopted comparative negligence systems have done away with the assumption of risk defense in negligence cases and treat all forms of contributory fault under their comparative negligence scheme.

## Goetzman v. Wichern

### 327 N.W.2d 742 (Iowa Sup. Ct. 1983)

Mary Goetzman filed a medical malpractice action against her doctor, Homer Wichern, arguing that he was negligent in the diagnosis and treatment of her breast cancer over a period from 1974 to 1978. She alleged that his negligence made it necessary for her to have a mastectomy and to undergo radiation therapy and chemotherapy, proximately causing substantial damages. Wichern argued that Goetzman had been contributorily negligent in failing to follow his advice and cooperate with his diagnostic and treatment recommendations. Goetzman urged the trial court to apply comparative negligence principles to the case. The trial court refused to do so, and when the jury entered a verdict against her, Goetzman appealed.

**McCormick, Justice.** In *Rusch v. City of Davenport* (1858), this court adopted the common law contributory negligence rule. The court said that in order to recover for injuries sustained in an accident caused by a defendant's negligence the plaintiff had the burden to prove "that the accident happened without any want of reasonable care on his part." Subsequently it was held that an injured party was barred from recovery if guilty of negligence that "contributed in any way, or in any degree directly" to his injury. The main reason for changing the doctrine of contributory negligence as a complete bar to recovery to one of comparative negligence is fairness:

> The predominant argument for its abandonment rests, of course, upon the undeniable inequity and injustice in casting an entire accidental loss upon a plaintiff whose negligence combined with another's negligence in causing the loss suffered, no matter how trifling plaintiff's negligence might be. Liability based on fault is the cornerstone of tort law, and a system such as contributory negligence which permits one of the contributing wrongdoers to avoid all liability simply does not serve any principle of fault liability. *Scott v. Rizzo* (Sup. Ct. N.M. 1981).

In its pure form, the doctrine of comparative negligence assigns responsibility for damages in proportion to a party's fault in proximately causing them. The rule thus operates to reduce rather than bar recovery. The main alternative comparative negligence systems apportion damages on the basis of fault either up to the point at which a plaintiff's negligence equals defendant's negligence or exceeds it. When that point is reached, plaintiff is barred from recovery. These systems thus lower, but do not eliminate, the bar of contributory negligence.

We have experienced more than 100 years of judicial and legislative efforts to ameliorate the harshness of the contributory negligence doctrine in Iowa. The doctrine of last clear chance, the rescue doctrine, and several rules against imputed negligence exemplify the judicial effort.

Moreover, *stare decisis* does not preclude the change. That principle does not require blind imitation of the past or adherence to a rule merely because "it was laid down in the time of Henry IV." We must reform common law doctrines that are unsound and unsuited to present conditions. Most of the major civil and common law nations in the world, including England, now have comparative negligence systems. Since the Supreme Court's decision in *United States v. Reliable Transfer Co.* (1975), all major maritime nations apply the principle in admiralty cases. Thirty-eight states in this country now have comparative negligence by statute or judicial decision.

We are convinced that comparative negligence is a fairer system. It diminishes but does not defeat the right to recover damages caused by another party's fault. We are also convinced that the pure form of comparative negligence should be adopted in Iowa. It gives full rather than partial effect to the principle of comparative fault by reducing a person's recovery based on another party's fault by the percentage of the person's own fault in the occurrence. Of the eight other states that adopted comparative negligence by judicial decision, only West Virginia adopted a modified version. In doing so, the West Virginia court asserted that the practical result of a pure comparative negligence system "is that it favors the party who has incurred the most damages regardless of his amount of fault or negligence."

Examples can be conceived of a seriously negligent plaintiff who is seriously injured suing a slightly negligent defendant who is slightly injured, and who counterclaims. The result may be that the seriously negligent plaintiff will achieve a substantial net recovery from the slightly negligent defendant. In responding to a contention that this result is unfair, the New Mexico court said:

> How can it be argued that such a result would be unfair, when each party would be held responsible to the other person for harm caused to that other person by his proportionate fault? It surely is a fairer allocation of liability than the "modified" forms which require plaintiff to have been less negligent than or not more than equally as negligent as defendant. Those formulae punish either the plaintiff or counter-plaintiff who is but slightly more negligent with bearing his own loss and about one-half of the losses of the other party as well.

We agree with this response. Under a system of comparative negligence, the keystone to fairness is proportionate responsibility for fault, not the relative severity of injuries. Each party's recovery of damages is reduced in proportion to that party's responsibility for them. As a result, no one is unjustly enriched.

Only the pure form of comparative negligence proportions a reduction of recovery to a person's fault in all cases and prevents a party at fault from escaping liability in any case. As demonstrated in the reasoning of the courts that have adopted the pure form, it is the fairest, most logical and simplest to administer of all available systems.

We hold that in all cases in which contributory negligence has previously been a complete defense, it is supplanted by the doctrine of comparative negligence. In such cases contributory negligence will not bar recovery but shall reduce it in the proportion that the contributory negligence bears to the total negligence that proximately caused the damages.

Judgment reversed in favor of Goetzman.

## McPherson v. Sunset Speedway, Inc.

**594 F.2d 711 (8th Cir. 1979)**

On October 4, 1975, Robert McPherson and his wife attended a dirt track stock car race at the Sunset Speedway. Instead of sitting in the grandstand, which was adequately protected from the racing cars by a wall and a fence, McPherson and his wife bought more expensive tickets entitling them to admission into the infield pit area, which was unprotected. While they were there, a racing car went out of control, entered the area, and struck one of the two cars between which McPherson was standing, knocking it into the other car and leaving McPherson trapped between them. McPherson, who had been seriously injured, filed a suit against the Speedway's owners, arguing that they were negligent in failing to protect infield spectators from such injuries. The trial court granted a motion for a directed verdict on behalf of the Speedway's owners on the ground that McPherson had assumed the risk of injury. McPherson appealed.

**HENLEY, CIRCUIT JUDGE.** We agree with Judge Robinson that the Nebraska law with regard to the common law doctrine of assumption of risk was stated authoritatively in *Hollamon v. Eagle Raceways, Inc.,* a case not unlike this one. It was there said:

> [W]here one, knowing and comprehending the danger, voluntarily exposes himself to it, although not [negligent] in so doing, he is deemed to have assumed the risk and is precluded from a recovery for an injury resulting therefrom.

In appraising the conduct of McPherson the trial judge said:

> The question remains whether, as a matter of law [McPherson] knew and understood the risk to be incurred by [his action]. In this regard, the evidence shows that Mr. McPherson had been a stock car owner and racer since at least 1970. He testified that he had entered similar infield areas on various tracks in Iowa over 100 times and that he knew before entering the infield at Sunset Speedway on October 4, 1975 that there was no protective barrier between the infield and the track itself. He also testified that he had not considered stock car racing dangerous before entering the infield in question. The court can lend no credence to this latter testimony since the plaintiff will not be heard to say that he did not comprehend a risk which must have been quite clear and obvious to him.

From our consideration, we are satisfied that the trial judge made a correct appraisal of the Nebraska law with respect to assumption of risk as a complete defense in a negligence action and did not err in his application of the law to the established facts of the case.

Judgment for Sunset affirmed.

## RECKLESSNESS

Behavior that indicates a conscious disregard for a known high risk of probable harm to others amounts to **recklessness.** In terms of the moral culpability of the defendant, recklessness lies midway between intentional wrongdoing and negligence. Recklessness involves conduct posing a foreseeable risk of harm to others, but that risk of harm must be significantly greater than the degree of risk necessary to make conduct negligent. In recklessness, as in negligence, the objective "reasonable man" test is applied to the defendant. Would a reasonable person, knowing all the facts at the defendant's disposal, have perceived the aggravated risk of harm to others that resulted from his or her conduct?

Proof of reckless behavior offers a plaintiff several significant advantages over proof of mere negligence. First, as a general rule, mere contributory negligence on the part of the plaintiff will *not* prevent recovery for recklessly caused injuries. Only proof that the plaintiff acted in reckless disregard for his own safety or assumed the risk of injury created by the defendant's recklessness will operate as a defense to recklessness. For example, Roberts bets his friends that he can drive down a busy street blindfolded. In doing so, he runs down Mann. Since Roberts's conduct amounted to recklessness, the fact that Mann stepped into the path of Roberts's car without looking would *not* bar Mann's recovery. However, if Mann saw Roberts's car weaving down the road and still attempted to cross the street in front of it, or if Mann had bet Roberts's friends that he could run in front of the car without being hit, Mann *would* be denied any recovery. Also, as a general rule, courts are more willing to find that a reckless defendant's conduct was the legal cause of a plaintiff's injuries than they would be if the defendant's conduct was merely negligent. Finally, since recklessness involves a higher degree of fault than negligence, a plaintiff who can prove recklessness on the defendant's part stands a good chance of recovering punitive as well as compensatory damages (which are ordinarily the only form of damages recoverable for mere negligence).

## STRICT LIABILITY

**Introduction.** The third fundamental basis of tort liability, in addition to intentional wrongdoing and negligence, is **strict liability.** Strict liability means that defendants who participate in certain types of harm-producing activities may be held *strictly liable* for any harm that results to others, even though they did not intend to cause the harm and did everything in their power to prevent it. Also, defendants in strict liability cases have fewer defenses to liability than do defendants in negligence cases because most courts hold that contributory negligence is *not* a defense to strict liability, although assumption of risk is a good defense. The imposition of strict liability basically represents a social policy decision that the risk associated with an activity should be borne by those who pursue it, rather than by wholly innocent persons who are exposed to that risk. Today, the two most important types of activities that are subject to strict liability are *abnormally dangerous (or ultrahazardous) activities* and the *manufacture or sale of defective and unreasonably dangerous products.* The product liability dimension of strict liability is discussed in detail in Chapter 32.

**Abnormally Dangerous Activities.** Abnormally dangerous activities are those which *necessarily involve a risk of harm to others that cannot be eliminated by the exercise of reasonable care.* Activities that have been classed as abnormally dangerous include blasting, crop dusting, stunt flying, and, in one recent case, the transportation of large quantities of gasoline by truck. The *Richman* case, which follows, discusses the numerous factors that courts must consider before deciding whether a particular activity should be classified as abnormally dangerous. It also illustrates the fact that the greater the social utility attached to an activity and the greater the costs of minimizing the risk associated with that activity, the less likely a court will be to label the activity as an abnormally dangerous one.

## Richman v. Charter Arms Corp.

**571 F. Supp. 192 (E.D. La. 1983)**

Early in the afternoon of April 4, 1981, Willie Watson obtained a handgun manufactured by Charter Arms Corporation from an acquaintance. That evening, Watson used the gun, allegedly a "snub-nosed .38," to kidnap, rob, rape, and murder Kathy Newman, a third-year medical student at Tulane University. Watson was convicted of these crimes and sentenced to death. Newman's mother, Julie Richman, filed suit against Charter Arms under a strict liability theory, arguing that the marketing of handguns was an ultrahazardous activity. Charter Arms moved for a summary judgment on the ground that strict liability principles should not apply to the marketing of handguns.

**Mentz, Justice.** In the past, Louisiana courts have found a number of activities to be ultrahazardous. [Here, the court cited cases involving the storage of toxic gas, pile driving, crop dusting, blasting, and the demolition of buildings.] No Louisiana court has held, however, that the marketing of handguns for sale to the general public is an ultrahazardous activity. Still, this is not dispositive. For no Louisiana court has held to the contrary, either.

An ultrahazardous activity is not an unreasonably dangerous activity. It is an activity "in which the risk may be altogether reasonable and still high enough that the party ought not undertake the activity without assuming the consequences."

The relevant sections in the *Restatement* are sections 519 and 520. Section 519 reads as follows:

> (1) One who carries on an abnormally dangerous [or ultrahazardous] activity is subject to liability for harm to the person, land or chattels of another resulting from the activity, although he has exercised the utmost care to prevent the harm.
>
> (2) This strict liability is limited to the kind of harm, the possibility of which makes the activity abnormally dangerous.

Section 520 contains a list of "the factors to be considered in determining whether an activity is abnormally dangerous." Those factors are:

> (a) existence of a high degree of risk of some harm to the person, land or chattels of others;
> (b) likelihood that the harm that results from it will be great;
> (c) inability to eliminate the risk by the exercise of reasonable care;
> (d) extent to which the activity is not a matter of common usage;

(e) inappropriateness of the activity to the place where it is carried on; and
(f) extent to which its value to the community is outweighed by its dangerous attributes.

Richman argues, in effect, that the harm threatened by Charter's marketing practices—namely, serious physical injuries and deaths—is "major in degree" and "sufficiently great." She also argues that the likelihood of such harms occurring is far from "relatively slight." The ultimate validity of these arguments depends on whether she can establish a causal connection between the harms threatened and the injury sustained. That issue is for a jury to decide. At this point, however, the Court cannot find as a matter of law that her arguments are without merit.

Factor (c) concerns whether the party engaging in the allegedly ultrahazardous or abnormally dangerous activity can eliminate the risk of serious harm by exercising reasonable care. According to Mrs. Richman, marketing handguns for sale to the general public is not an activity that "can be made entirely safe by the taking of all reasonable precautions." In saying this, she is not suggesting that no way exists for Charter to reduce the risk of harm. She readily acknowledges that Charter could reduce the risk by altering its current marketing practices—by restricting sales to, say, law enforcement agencies and sporting clubs. But, this, she says, is beside the point. For what is ultrahazardous or abnormally dangerous, in her view, is not the marketing of handguns per se but the marketing of handguns to the general public. Her point is that, so long as Charter continues its current marketing practices, no amount of due care will significantly reduce the risk of harm. This argument, like her arguments in connection with factors (a) and (b), is not without legal merit.

The fourth factor, (d), is "common usage." In the context of this case, the paramount question regarding this factor is whether handgun use is an activity that "is customarily carried on by the great mass of mankind or by many people in the community." Operating an automobile is just one potentially dangerous activity that is also a common activity. Consuming liquor is another: it, too, "is customarily carried on by the great mass of mankind or by many people in the community." The same holds true for the use of knives; many people use them every evening at the dinner table. Handgun use, on the other hand, appears to fit into a different category. Handguns are not an item of "general use"; they are an item of extraordinary or abnormal use. Many people in the community are likely on an average day to operate an automobile, to consume a drink, or to use a knife. Few people, however, are likely to use a handgun except in highly unusual circumstances—when attacked by a criminal assailant, for example, or when acting as a criminal assailant. Thus, the Court cannot conclude that the operation of handguns is "a matter of common usage."

The final factor, (f), concerns the value of the activity to the community. Richman argues that marketing handguns for sale to the general public has no utility at all. Quite clearly, this is an exaggeration. For the social utility of an activity that produces jobs and enables some people to defend themselves cannot be denied. Furthermore, the legislature, by not banning handgun sales to the general public, either by statute or by constitutional amendments, has indicated that it thinks the social utility of the marketing practices is at least as great as the social disutility of those practices. Still, none of these factors about the value of the marketing practices leads to the conclusion that "the community is largely devoted to the [defendant's] dangerous enterprise and [that the community's] prosperity largely depends upon it."

Charter maintains that, if liability is imposed in this case, no company that markets handguns for sale to the general public will be able in the future to obtain insurance.

The result, according to Charter, will be catastrophic for handgun manufacturers: all such companies will be forced either to alter their marketing practices radically or to go out of business. This argument has a ring of plausibility to it. At the same time, however, it is highly speculative. One problem is that Charter has introduced no evidence to support the argument.

Perhaps the most significant fact Charter ignores is that increased insurance costs can be passed on to consumers in the form of higher prices for handguns. The people who benefit most from marketing practices like Charter's are handgun manufacturers and handgun purchasers. Innocent victims rarely, if ever, are beneficiaries. Consequently, it hardly seems unfair to require manufacturers and purchasers, rather than innocent victims, to pay for the risks those practices entail. Thus, both fairness and economic efficiency suggest that the community would be better off if Charter's marketing practices were classified as ultrahazardous. The Court, though, cannot reach that conclusion on this motion. All the Court can conclude here is that Charter's marketing practices are not so valuable to the community that they should automatically be exempt from the ultrahazardous classification.

Charter's motion for summary judgment denied.

## SUMMARY

Negligence is the unintentional breach of a duty owed to another person that results in some legally recognizable injury to that person or her property. Each member of society has a general duty to conduct himself as would a reasonable person of ordinary prudence in similar circumstances. Other sources of duty include statutes and contractual or other special relationships between the parties. Statutory violations amount to negligence per se (a presumption of negligence) if they result in the suffering of a harm that the statute was designed to prevent by a person whom the statute was designed to protect.

Breach of duty results when a defendant exposes a person to whom the duty is owed to an unreasonable, foreseeable risk of harm. To determine whether a particular risk of harm is an unreasonable one, the courts balance the social utility of the defendant's conduct and the ease of reducing or eliminating the risk against the likelihood that harm will occur and the seriousness of the probable harm.

Breach of duty standing alone, however, will not produce negligence liability. The plaintiff in a negligence suit must also prove that the defendant's breach of duty was the actual and proximate (legal) cause of his injury. To determine the existence of actual cause, courts employ a "but for" or a "substantial factor" test. The courts have employed a variety of tests for proximate cause. The *Restatement (Second) of Torts* suggests that negligent defendants should not be held responsible for "highly extraordinary" consequences of their negligence. In some cases, intervening forces may combine with a negligent defendant's conduct to produce a particular plaintiff's injury. Whether such intervening forces will amount to an intervening or superseding cause that absolves the defendant of liability depends on several factors, the most prominent of which are the foreseeability of the intervening force, whether the defendant's act increased the risk that the intervening force would come into play, and whether the resulting harm is similar in nature to the harm risked by the defendant's conduct.

In some cases, negligence may be difficult to prove because the person or persons who are most likely to be responsible for the plaintiff's injury have superior knowledge about the causes of the injury and a strong disincentive to share that knowledge with the plaintiff if it points to their liability. The doctrine of *res ipsa loquitur* aids plaintiffs in such cases by creating an inference of negligence when the harm that occurred would not ordinarily occur in the absence of negligence and the defendant had exclusive control of the instrumentality of harm. Where *res ipsa* applies, a defendant must come forward with evidence to rebut the inference that he was negligent and that his negligence caused the plaintiff's injury, or risk being found liable by a court or jury.

In recent years, a trend has emerged to broaden the types of injuries for which negligent defendants may be held responsible. The courts, fearing spurious claims and concerned about the difficulties in evaluating purely emotional injuries, long refused to allow persons who had suffered negligently inflicted emotional distress to recover for their injuries in the absence of some "impact" or physical contact with the victim. Recently, many courts have dispensed with the impact requirement, but many still require some physical injury or symptoms as a result of the victim's emotional distress before they will allow recovery. Similarly, the courts traditionally refused to allow recovery for emotional distress caused by witnessing negligently inflicted harms to third persons in the absence of some impact with the person suffering the emotional injury. Today, many courts will allow third parties who were themselves within the "zone of danger" created by the defendant's negligence to recover for their emotional injuries. Some courts have gone even farther and dispensed with the zone of danger requirement where the person injured was a close relative of the third party suffering emotional distress and the distress was the product of the third party's witnessing of the harm to the person injured. However, many courts taking this more liberal position still insist on proof of some physical injury or symptoms resulting from the third party's emotional distress.

Even if a defendant's breach of duty was the actual and proximate cause of a plaintiff's injury, contributory fault on the plaintiff's part can operate to bar or diminish the plaintiff's right to recover. The doctrine of contributory negligence bars any recovery by plaintiffs whose failure to exercise reasonable care for their own safety was a substantial factor in producing their injury. In some cases, however, contributorily negligent plaintiffs can still recover if they can prove that the defendant had the "last clear chance" to avoid the harm. A growing majority of the states have reacted to the potential harshness of contributory negligence by adopting comparative negligence systems. The details of these systems vary by state, but the essential idea of comparative negligence involves weighing the relative fault of the parties and diminishing a plaintiff's recovery in proportion to his fault.

Plaintiffs who voluntarily expose themselves to a known risk of harm created by a defendant's negligence are held to have assumed the risk of injury and are barred from any recovery. Some states that have adopted comparative negligence systems have dispensed with both assumption of risk and contributory negligence, treating all issues of contributory fault in negligence cases under their comparative negligence system.

Conduct that demonstrates a conscious disregard for a known high degree of probable harm to others constitutes recklessness. In terms of moral culpability, recklessness lies midway between negligence and intentional wrongdoing. Mere contributory negligence by the plaintiff is not a good defense to recklessness, and reckless defendants are more likely to be found legally responsible for the consequences of their actions and to be subjected to punitive damages than are defendants who were merely negligent.

In some instances, the law imposes strict liability on defendants for injuries produced by their activities, even though the defendants did not intend any harm and may have done everything possible to avoid harm. Strict liability represents a social policy decision that those who participate in certain kinds of activities must shoulder all of the risks associated with them. The two most important types of conduct that are subjected to strict liability are the manufacture or sale of defective and unreasonably dangerous products and participation in "ultrahazardous" or "abnormally dangerous" activities. The product liability dimension of strict liability is discussed later in the text. Abnormally dangerous activities are those necessarily involving a significant risk of harm to others that cannot be eliminated by the exercise of reasonable care. The decision to classify a particular activity as abnormally dangerous involves judicial consideration of a wide variety of factors in addition to the risk associated with the activity, including the social utility of the activity, the costs associated with minimizing or eliminating the risk, and whether the activity is one commonly pursued in the area in which the injury occurred. Finally, as a general rule, mere contributory negligence by a plaintiff will not prevent her recovery on a strict liability theory, but assumption of risk by the plaintiff will operate as a bar to recovery.

## PROBLEM CASES

**1.** Gene Adkins was shopping in a store owned by Ashland Supermarkets, when the store was robbed at gunpoint. The operators of the store, Mr. and Mrs. Craycraft, obstructed the robbery by disobeying the robber's instructions, telling their employees to disobey his orders, and arguing with the robber. The robber became angry and started shooting. Mr. Craycraft was killed, and his wife and Adkins were wounded. Adkins filed suit against Ashland, claiming that the Craycrafts were negligent in resisting the robber's demands. Were the Craycrafts negligent?

**2.** On February 25, 1976, Lloyd Fullman, Jr., bought a .22-caliber rifle and rifle cartridges from a Sears store in Delaware. Delaware law required sellers of "deadly weapons" to receive a positive identification of any purchaser of such a weapon from two freeholders prior to the sale. Fullman merely produced a driver's license and was allowed to purchase the rifle and ammunition. Fullman had three prior felony convictions and, as a convicted felon, was prohibited by Delaware law from purchasing the rifle and cartridges. Six weeks after the purchase, Fullman attempted to rob a Wilmington restaurant and shot James Hetherton, an off-duty police officer employed as a guard, in the head. Hetherton sued Sears, arguing that Sears was negligent because it failed to require two freeholders to identify Fullman and because it failed to determine whether Delaware law prohibited Fullman from possessing the rifle and cartridges. Was Sears's conduct negligent?

**3.** Two Stratford, Connecticut, police officers observed a green Chevrolet parked in a shopping center parking lot. They thought that the car might have been stolen, because the boys in it looked too young to have valid driver's licenses. When they approached the car, the boys drove off, and the police officers pursued them. A high-speed chase ensued, and while the car was fleeing the wrong way down a one-way street, it had a head-on collision with a car driven by Joseph Tetro, seriously injuring him. Tetro filed a negligence suit against the police officers and the town and won a jury verdict of $59,000. The defendants appealed, arguing that their negligence was not the proximate cause of Tetro's injuries. Was the jury correct in imposing liability?

**4.** Stephen and Valerie Molien were members of the Kaiser Health Plan. A Kaiser staff doctor, while giving Mrs. Molien a routine physical examination, negligently concluded that she had syphilis. She was told to tell her husband of the diagnosis, and he was required to undergo testing to see whether he was the source of her infection. Tests revealed that he did not have the disease. As a result of the incorrect diagnosis, Mrs. Molien came to suspect that Mr. Molien had engaged in extramarital sexual activities and filed for divorce. Mr. Molien sued Kaiser for negligent infliction of emotional distress. Kaiser moved to dismiss his claim, arguing that some physical injury was required for a valid emotional distress claim. Is physical harm necessary for a valid emotional distress claim?

**5.** A fire of unknown origin erupted in Cherokee Nitrogen Company's bulk storage warehouse, and high winds carried burning debris onto National Gypsum's property. Collins and other employees of National Gypsum came outside in order to fight the spreading grass fires. Sometime after the fire erupted, the Cherokee warehouse exploded with tremendous force, resulting in injuries to Collins, who was approximately 300 yards away. Collins and a number of other National Gypsum and Cherokee employees were taken to the hospital for treatment. As a result of his injuries, which included partial hearing loss, Collins brought suit against Cherokee, seeking damages under the doctrine of *res ipsa loquitur.* The trial court refused to allow Collins to invoke *res ipsa.* Was the trial court correct in doing so?

**6.** Scott was working for a contractor in the construction of a regional library. He noticed that a steel cable with a piece of chain attached in order to lengthen it was being used as a choker in the unloading of steel from a truck with a crane. Concerned, he came down from the building to warn nearby workmen of the dangerous situation. When the supervisor was informed that it was dangerous to use the chain to unload steel and that someone was likely to get hurt, the supervisor and crew ignored the warning. As the steel was moved ahead, the chain broke and struck Scott on his head and about his body while he was standing about 20 feet away. Hampshire Company, the roofing contractor, owned the steel. When Hampshire moved for a directed verdict at the close of Scott's case, the trial judge, assuming the existence of primary negligence, ruled that Scott had assumed the risk and was therefore guilty of contributing to the accident. Was the trial judge correct?

**7.** Tanya House joined the European Health Spa in May 1974. On June 30, 1974, she slipped on a foreign substance and fell while entering a shower at the spa. House testified that she had used the spa's facilities on several occasions prior to her fall and that on each occasion the showers had been slippery, filthy, and dirty. Further, she stated that she had slipped on some of these occasions due to these conditions. She admitted that on the day of the accident she did not look down at the condition of the shower step or floor, but simply took a step and fell. The trial court entered a judgment for House, and the spa appealed, arguing that her contributory negligence should prevent any recovery by House. Is the spa's argument correct?

**8.** Dale Hatley, age nine, was injured when a teenager collided with him during a "boys only" skating period at Skateland. During this period, high-speed skating and other maneuvers generally prohibited at other times were permitted. The boy who collided with Dale was "Shooting the Duck"—squatting down and skating on one foot, with his free leg extended in front. Dale was standing by the railing talking to two family members when he was hit. At the time of the accident, three attendants were stationed around the rink to supervise the activities. Dale had been to Skateland on several previous occasions. He had fallen twice before the accident occurred, and he admitted that he had seen other people fall and collide with each other while skating and that he had had others run over him after he had fallen. He sued Skateland, arguing that it had negligently failed to supervise the activities at the rink. Skateland argued that Dale had assumed the risk of injury. Did Dale assume the risk of his injury?

**9.** Chris Ewing went to the Cloverleaf Bowl on his 21st birthday. In the cocktail lounge of the bowling alley, Chris was given a free vodka collins when the bartender discovered that it was his birthday. In the next hour and a half, despite the fact that he was becoming obviously intoxicated, Chris was served 10 straight shots of 151-proof rum and two beer chasers. He died of acute alcohol poisoning the following day. His two small sons filed suit against the Cloverleaf Bowl. The trial court granted Cloverleaf's motion for a nonsuit, finding as a matter of law that Chris was guilty of contributory negligence and that the bartender was not reckless. Should the trial court have allowed the jury to hear the case?

**10.** Early in the evening of May 15, 1975, Wilfredo Dominguez, age 11, and two other youths hitched a ride on the outside of a bus operated by the Manhattan and Bronx Surface Transit Operating Authority. They first jumped onto the bus as it began to pull away from a bus stop. While the bus driver was making a right-hand turn at the next corner, he was cut off by a taxicab and turned too sharply, causing the bus to go over the curb and strike an elevated subway support column. Wilfredo was knocked off the bus and seriously injured. His mother filed suit on his behalf, and the trial court judge charged the jury that, although Wilfredo had been contributorily negligent, it could award him recovery if it found that the bus driver had the last clear chance to avoid the accident. Was the trial court judge correct?

**11.** Carol J. House, age 17, was driving home from an after-school job on the evening of November 22, 1967, along Capitol Lake Drive in Olympia, Washington. Her car struck a pool of several thousand gallons of gasoline that were spilling from an overturned gasoline tank trailer. An explosion occurred, and flames engulfed her car, incinerating her. The driver of the truck testified that before leaving the Texaco plant where he picked up the gasoline, he had thoroughly inspected the trailer. While entering an off ramp, he felt a jerk and realized that the trailer had come loose. It ran down a hill, crashed through a chain link fence, and came to rest upside down on Capital Lake Drive. The cause of the accident was unknown. Carol's estate sued the operator of the truck on a negligence theory, seeking to use *res ipsa loquitur* to help prove negligence on the operator's part. The operator tried to rebut any inference of negligence by proving reasonable care in the inspection, operation, and maintenance of the truck. The operator also introduced evidence that Carol had been exceeding the speed limit by 10 miles per hour at the time the accident occurred. The jury found no negligence on the operator's part. Should the operator of the truck be liable on the basis of strict liability?

# PART III

# CONTRACTS

# Chapter 6 Introduction to Contracts

## THE NATURE OF CONTRACTS

**Definition.** Scholars and courts have formulated numerous definitions of the term *contract*. The *Restatement (Second) of Contracts* defines a **contract** as "a promise or set of promises for the breach of which the law gives a remedy, or the performance of which the law in some way recognizes as a duty."[1] The essence of this definition for our purposes is that a contract is a *legally enforceable promise or set of promises*. Not all of the promises that people make attain the status of contracts. We have all made and broken numerous promises without fear of being sued by those to whom our promises were made. What separates such "social" promises from legally enforceable contracts?

**Elements.** Over the years, the common law courts have developed several basic tests that a promise must meet before it will be treated as a contract. These tests comprise the basic elements of contract. Contracts are *agreements* (an agreement is an *offer* that is made and *accepted*) that are *voluntarily* created by

[1] *Restatement (Second) of Contracts* § 1 (1979).

persons with the *capacity* to contract. The objectives of the agreement must be *legal* and, in most cases, the agreement must be supported by some *consideration* (a bargained-for exchange of legal value). Finally, the law requires *written* evidence of the existence of some kinds of agreements before it will enforce them. The following chapters will discuss each of these elements and other points that are necessary to enable you to distinguish contracts from unenforceable, "social" promises.

## THE SOCIAL UTILITY OF CONTRACT

Contracts enable persons acting in their own interests to enlist the support of the law in furthering their personal objectives. Contracts enable us to enter into agreements with others with the confidence that we may call on the law, and not merely the good faith of the other party, to ensure that those agreements will be honored. Within broad limits defined by contract doctrine and public policy, the contract device enables us to create the private "law" that will govern our relations with others: the terms of the agreements we make.

Contracts facilitate the kind of private planning that is necessary in a modern, industrialized society. Few people would invest in a business enterprise if they could not rely on the fact that the builders and suppliers of their facilities and equipment, the suppliers of the raw materials necessary to manufacture products, and the customers who agree to purchase those products will all honor their commitments. How could we make loans, sell goods on credit, or rent property unless loan agreements, conditional sales agreements, and leases were backed by the force of the law? Contract, then, is an inescapable and valuable part of the world as we know it. Like that world, its particulars tend to change over time, while its general characteristics remain largely stable.

## THE EVOLUTION OF CONTRACT LAW

**Classical Contract Law.** The contract idea is ancient. Thousands of years before Christ, Egyptians and Mesopotamians recognized devices like contracts, and by the 15th century the common law courts of England had developed a variety of theories to justify enforcing certain types of promises. Contract law did not, however, assume major importance in our legal system until the 19th century, when numerous social factors combined to shape the common law of contract. Laissez-faire (free market) economic ideas had a profound influence on public policy thinking during this period, and the Industrial Revolution created a perceived need for private planning and certainty in commercial transactions. The typical contract situation in the early decades of the 19th century involved face-to-face transactions between parties with relatively equal bargaining power who dealt with relatively simple kinds of goods.

The contract law that emerged from this period was strongly influenced by these factors. Its central tenet was "freedom of contract": contracts should be enforced because they are the products of the free wills of their creators, who should, within broad limits, be free to determine the extent of their obligations. The proper role of the courts in such a system of contract was to enforce these freely made bargains, but otherwise to adopt a "hands-off" stance. Contractual liability should not be imposed unless the parties clearly agreed to assume it, but once an agreement had been made, liability was near absolute. The fact that the items exchanged were of unequal value was usually legally irrelevant. The freedom to make good deals carried with it the risk of making bad deals. As long as a person voluntarily entered a contract, it would generally be enforced against him, even if the result was grossly unfair. And since equal bargaining power tended to be assumed, the courts were generally unwilling to hear defenses based on unequal bargaining power. This judicial posture allowed the courts to formulate a "pure" contract law consisting of precise, clear, and technical rules that were capable of general, almost mechanical, application. Such a law of contract was seen as meeting the needs of the marketplace by affording the predictable and consistent results necessary to facilitate private planning.

**Modern Contract Law Development.** As long as most contracts resembled the typical transaction envisioned by 19th-century contract law, such rules made perfect sense. If the parties dealt face-to-face, they were likely to know each other personally or at least to know each other's reputation for fair dealing. Face-to-face deals enabled the parties to inspect the goods in advance of the sale, and since the subject matter of most contracts was relatively simple, the odds were great that the parties had relatively equal knowledge about the items they bought and sold. If the parties also had equal bargaining power, it was probably fair to assume that they were capable of protecting themselves and negotiating an agreement that seemed fair at the time. Given the truth of these assumptions, there was arguably no good reason for judicial interference with private contracts.

The Industrial Revolution, however, undermined many of these assumptions. Regional, and later national, markets produced longer chains of distribution. This fact, combined with more efficient means of communication, meant that people often contracted with persons whom they did not know for goods that they had never seen. And rapidly developing technology meant that those goods were becoming increasingly complex. Thus, sellers often knew far more about their products than did the buyers with whom they dealt. Finally, the emergence of large business organizations after the Civil War produced obvious disparities of bargaining power in many contract situations. These large organizations found it more efficient to standardize their numerous transactions by employing standard form contracts, which also could be used to exploit disproportionate bargaining power by dictating the terms of their agreements.

The upshot of all this is that many contracts today no longer resemble the stereotypical agreements envisioned by the common law of contract. It has been estimated that over 90 percent of all contracts today are form contracts.[2] Any student who has signed a lease, taken out a loan, or bought a car on time has had experience with form contracts. Contract law is changing to reflect these changes in social reality. The 20th century has witnessed a dramatic increase in public intervention into private contractual relationships. Think of all the statutes governing the terms of what were once purely private contractual relationships. Legislatures commonly dictate many of the basic terms of insurance contracts. Employment contracts are governed by a host of laws concerning maximum hours worked, minimum wages paid, employer liability for on-the-job injuries, unemployment compensation, and retirement benefits. In some circumstances, product liability statutes impose liability on the manufacturers and sellers of products regardless of the terms of their sales contracts. The avowed purpose of much of this public intervention has been to protect persons who lack sufficient bargaining power to protect themselves.

Nor have the legislatures been the only

[2] Slawson, "Standard Form Contracts and Democratic Control of Lawmaking Power," 84 *Harv. L. Rev.* 529 (1971).

source of public supervision of private agreements. Twentieth-century courts have been increasingly concerned with creating contract rules that produce "just" results. The result of this concern has been an increasingly "hands-on" posture by courts that often feel compelled to intervene in private contractual relationships to protect weaker parties. In the name of avoiding injustice, some modern contract doctrines impose contractual liability, or something quite like it, in situations where traditional contract rules would have denied liability. Similarly, other modern contract doctrines allow parties to avoid contract liability in cases where traditional common law rules would have recognized a binding agreement and imposed liability.

In the process of evolving to accommodate changing social circumstances, the basic nature of the contract rules themselves is changing. The precise, technical rules that characterized traditional common law contract are giving way to broader, imprecise standards such as "good faith," "injustice," "reasonableness," and "unconscionability." The reason for such standards is clear. If courts are increasingly called upon to intervene in private contracts in the name of fairness, it is necessary to fashion "rules" that afford the degree of judicial discretion required to reach "just" decisions in the increasingly complex and varied situations where intervention is needed.

This heightened emphasis on fairness, like every other choice made by law, carries with it some cost. Imprecise, discretionary modern contract rules do not produce the same measure of certainty and predictability that their precise and abstract predecessors afforded. And since modern contract rules often impose liability in the absence of the clear consent required by traditional common law contract rules, one price of increased fairness in contract cases has been a diminished ability of private parties to control the nature and extent of their contractual obligations.

This change in the nature of contract law is far from complete, however. The idea that a contract is an agreement freely entered into by the parties still lies at the heart of contract law today, and contract cases may be found that differ very little in their spirit or ultimate resolution from their 19th-century predecessors. However, it is probably fair to say that these are most likely to be cases where 19th-century assumptions about the nature of contracts are still largely valid: that is, cases involving contracts between parties with relatively equal bargaining power and relatively equal knowledge about the subject of the contract. Despite the existence of such cases, however, it is evident that contract law is in the process of significant change. Subsequent chapters highlighting the differences between modern contract rules and their traditional common law forebears will render this conclusion inescapable. Before discussing particular examples of this new thrust in contract law, however, we should familiarize ourselves with some basic contract terminology that will be used throughout the text.

## BASIC CONTRACT CONCEPTS AND TYPES

**Bilateral and Unilateral Contracts.** Contracts have traditionally been classified as **bilateral** or **unilateral,** depending on whether one or both of the parties have made a promise. In unilateral contracts, only one party makes a promise. For example, if a homeowner says to a painter, "I will pay you $1,000 if you paint my house," the homeowner has made an offer for a unilateral contract, a contract that will be created only if and when the painter paints the house. If the homeowner instead says to the painter, "If you promise to paint my house, I will promise to pay you $1,000," he has asked the painter to commit to painting the house rather than just to perform the act of painting. This offer contemplates the formation of a bilateral contract. If the painter makes the requested promise to paint the house, a bilateral contract is created at that point.

In succeeding chapters, you will learn that unilateral contracts cause some particular problems related to offer and acceptance and to mutuality of obligation. These problems have caused many commentators to argue that the unilateral-bilateral contract distinction should be abandoned. The *Restatement (Second) of Contracts* and the Uniform Commercial Code, both of which are discussed later in this chapter, do not expressly use unilateral-bilateral terminology, but both of these important sources of modern contract principles contain provisions aimed at dealing with typical unilateral contract problems. Despite this evidence of disfavor, the courts continue to use unilateral contract terminology, in part because it enables them to do justice in some cases by imposing contractual liability on one party without the necessity of finding a return promise of the other party. For example, many recent employment cases have used unilateral contract analyses to hold employers liable for promises relating to pension rights, bonuses or incentive pay, profit-sharing benefits, and so forth, even though the employees in question did not make any clear return promise to continue their employment for any specified time or to do anything else in exchange for the employer's promise.[3]

**Valid, Unenforceable, Voidable, and Void Contracts.** A **valid contract** is one that meets all of the legal requirements for a binding contract. Valid contracts are therefore enforceable in court.

An **unenforceable contract** is one that meets the basic legal requirements for a contract but may not be enforceable due to the operation of some other legal rule. In Chapter 13, you will learn that the statute of frauds requires written evidence of certain kinds of contracts. An otherwise valid oral contract of a type that the statute of frauds requires to be in writing may be unenforceable due to the parties' failure to reduce the contract to written form. Another example of an unenforceable contract is an otherwise valid contract whose enforcement is barred by the applicable contract statute of limitations.

**Voidable contracts** are those in which one or more of the parties have the legal right to cancel their obligations under the contract. They are enforceable against both parties unless a party with the power to void the contract has exercised that power. In Chapter 9, for example, you will learn that contracts induced by misrepresentation, fraud, duress, or undue influence are voidable at the election of the injured party.

**Void contracts** are agreements that create no legal obligations because they fail to contain one or more of the basic elements required for enforceability. A void contract is, in a sense, a contradiction in terms. It would be more accurate to say that no contract was created in such cases. In Chapter 12, for example, you will learn that a contract to commit a crime, such as an agreement for the sale of cocaine, does not create binding legal obligation. Nonetheless, practical constraints may sometimes encourage a party to such a contract to perform his agreement rather than raise an illegality defense.

**Express and Implied Contracts.** In an **express contract,** the parties have directly stated the terms of their contract orally or in writing at the time the contract was formed. The mutual agreement necessary to create a contract may also, however, be demonstrated by the conduct of the parties. When the surrounding facts and circumstances indicate that an agreement has in fact been

[3] See Petit, "Modern Unilateral Contracts," 63 *B.U.L. Rev.* 551 (1983).

reached, an **implied contract** has been created. When you go to a doctor for treatment, for example, you do not ordinarily state the terms of your agreement in advance, although it is clear that you do, in fact, have an agreement. A court would infer a promise by your doctor to use reasonable care and skill in treating you and a return promise on your part to pay a reasonable fee for her services.

**Executed and Executory Contracts.** A contract is **executed** when all of the parties have fully performed their contractual duties, and it is **executory** until such duties have been fully performed.

Any contract may be described using one or more of the above terms. For example, Eurocars, Inc. orders five new Mercedes-Benz 500 SLs from Mercedes. Mercedes sends Eurocars its standard acknowledgment form accepting the order. The parties have a *valid, express, bilateral* contract that will be *executory* until Mercedes delivers the cars and Eurocars pays for them.

## Faris v. Enberg

**158 Cal. Rptr. 704 (Cal. Ct. App. 1979)**

Edgar C. Faris conceived the idea for a sports quiz show. He contacted television sports announcer Dick Enberg to see whether Enberg would be willing to participate in the show as its master of ceremonies. He also offered Enberg the opportunity of becoming a coproducer and part owner of the show. Enberg met with Faris, expressed interest in his proposal, and asked for and was given a copy of the format for the show. Later, the "Sports Challenge" show appeared on television with a different producer and with Enberg as master of ceremonies. There were certain differences and similarities between the show and Faris's idea. Faris filed suit against Enberg for breach of implied contract. The trial court ruled in Enberg's favor and Faris appealed.

**ROTHMAN, ASSOCIATE JUSTICE.** In *Desny v. Wilder,* the California Supreme Court said that:

> The idea man who blurts out his idea without having first made his bargain has no one but himself to blame for the loss of his bargaining power. The law will not in any event, from demand stated subsequent to the unconditional disclosure of an abstract idea, imply a promise to pay for the idea, for its use, or for its previous disclosure. The law will not imply a promise to pay for an idea from the mere facts that the idea has been conveyed, is valuable, and has been used for profit; this is true even though the conveyance has been made with the hope or expectation that some obligation will ensue.

Accordingly, for an implied-in-fact contract one must show: that he or she prepared the work; that he or she disclosed the work to the offeree for sale; under all circumstances attending disclosure it can be concluded that the offeree voluntarily accepted the disclosure knowing the conditions on which it was tendered (i.e., the offeree must have the opportunity to reject the attempted disclosure if the conditions were unacceptable); and the reasonable value of the work.

Applying these elements to the instant case, we find that the trial court correctly determined that there was no triable issue of fact on a cause of action for an implied-in-fact contract. So far as the record before us reveals, Faris never thought of selling his sports quiz show idea to anyone—including Enberg. He appears at all times to have intended to produce it himself, and sought out Enberg, as master of ceremonies. He obviously hoped to make his idea more marketable by hiring a gifted sports announcer as his master of ceremonies. Not only did Faris seek to induce Enberg to join him by showing him the product, but also sought to entice him by promises of a "piece" of the enterprise for his involvement. Faris never intended to submit the property for sale and did not tell Enberg that he was submitting it for sale. There is no reason to think that Enberg, or anyone else with whom Enberg spoke, would have believed that Faris's submission was an offer to sell something, which if used would oblige the user to pay.

Judgment for Enberg affirmed.

## QUASI CONTRACT

The traditional common law insistence on the presence of all the elements required for a binding contract before contractual obligation will be imposed can cause injustice in some cases. One person may have provided goods or services to another person who benefited from them but has no contractual obligation to pay for them, because no facts exist that would justify a court in implying a promise to pay for them. Such a situation can also arise in cases where the parties contemplated entering into a binding contract but some legal defense exists that prevents the enforcement of the agreement. Consider the following examples:

1. Jones paints Smith's house by mistake, thinking it belongs to Reed. Smith knows that Jones is painting his house but does not inform him of his error. There are no facts from which a court can infer that Jones and Smith have a contract, because the parties have had no prior discussions or dealings.

2. Thomas Products fraudulently induces Perkins to buy a household products franchise by grossly misstating the average revenues of its franchisees. Perkins discovers the misrepresentation after he has resold some products that he has received but before he has paid Thomas for them. Perkins elects to rescind (cancel) the franchise contract on the basis of the fraud.

In the above examples, both Smith and Perkins have good defenses to contract liability, but enabling Smith to get a free paint job and Perkins to avoid paying for the goods he resold would *unjustly enrich* them at the expense of Jones and Thomas. To deal with such cases and to prevent such unjust enrichment, the courts imply *as a matter of law* a promise by the benefited party to pay the *reasonable value* of the benefits he received. This idea is called **quasi contract** because it represents an obligation imposed by law to avoid injustice, not a contractual obligation created by voluntary consent. Quasi contract liability has been imposed in a wide variety of situations too numerous and varied to detail. In general, however, quasi contract liability is imposed when one party *confers a benefit* on another who *knowingly accepts it* and *retains it* under circumstances that make it *unjust* to do so without paying for it. So, if Jones painted Smith's house while Smith was away on vacation, Smith would probably not be liable for the reasonable value of the paint job because he did *not* knowingly accept it and because he has no way to return it to Jones.

### CBS Surgical Group, Inc. v. Holt

**426 A.2d 819 (Conn. Super. Ct. 1981)**

A surgeon employed by CBS Surgical Group amputated Marion Holt's leg, which necessitated her confinement to a nursing home until her death. Alfred Maringola, a friend of Holt's, cashed her checks, handled her financial affairs, and ran errands for her after her confinement. CBS was not paid for the surgery, but it later discovered that Holt had received a $2,000 medicare check to cover the costs of the operation. Maringola admitted that Holt had given him the check with instructions to cash it and return the proceeds to her. Maringola cashed the check, but the evidence indicated that Holt never received the proceeds. CBS filed suit against Maringola on a quasi-contract theory, seeking to recover the $2,000. Although Holt's name appears in the case, she was never actually a party to the suit. The trial court ruled in favor of CBS, and Maringola appealed.

**Daly, Judge.** Three essential elements must be established in order that a plaintiff may establish a claim based on unjust enrichment. These elements are: 1. A benefit conferred upon the defendant by the plaintiff; 2. An appreciation or knowledge by the defendant of the benefit; and 3. The acceptance or retention by the defendant of the benefit under such circumstances as to make it inequitable for the defendant to retain the benefit without payment of its value.

There is neither a finding nor evidence to support a finding that the first element has been met in this case. The surgery on Holt's leg performed by CBS's surgeon did not confer any benefit upon Maringola. The only person who benefited from the surgery was Holt. CBS's performance of its contractual obligation to provide medical services to Holt did not work any advantage to Maringola sufficient for equity to demand that he pay for those services.

It is true that Maringola was unjustly enriched by the proceeds from the check earmarked to compensate CBS for its services. Maringola, however, was obligated to return the proceeds to Holt, not CBS. It appears that Holt's estate, and not CBS, is the proper party to bring an action based on unjust enrichment.

Judgment reversed in favor of Maringola.

## PROMISSORY ESTOPPEL

Another very important idea that 20th-century courts have developed to deal with the unfairness that would sometimes result from the strict application of traditional contract principles is the doctrine of **promissory estoppel.** There are numerous situations in which a person may rely on a promise made by another even though the promise and the circumstances surrounding it are not sufficient to justify the conclusion that a contract has been created, because one or more of the elements required for a binding contract are missing. To allow the person who made such a promise (the promisor) to argue that no contract was created would sometimes work an injustice on the person who relied on the promise (the promisee). For example, John's parents told him that they would give him the family farm when they died. Relying on this promise, John stayed at home and worked on the farm for several years. However, when John's parents died, they left the farm to his sister Martha. Should Martha and the parents' estate be allowed to defeat John's claim to the farm by arguing that the parents' promise was unenforceable because John gave no consideration for the promise (since the parents did not request that he stay home and work on the farm in exchange for their promise)?

In the early decades of this century, many courts began to protect the reliance of promisees like John by saying that persons who made promises that produced such reliance were *estopped* (equitably prevented) from raising any defense they had to the enforcement of their promise. Out of such cases grew the doctrine of promissory estoppel. Section 90 of the *Restatement (Second) of Contracts* says:

> A promise which the promisor should reasonably expect to induce action or forbearance on the part of the promisee or a third person and which does induce such action or forbearance is binding if injustice can be avoided only by enforcement of the promise. The remedy granted for breach may be limited as justice requires.

Thus, the elements of promissory estoppel are: a *promise* that the *promisor should foresee is likely to induce reliance,* significant *reliance* on the promise by the promisee, and *injustice* as a result of that reliance. When you consider these elements, it is obvious that promissory estoppel is fundamentally different from traditional contract principles. Contract is traditionally thought of as protecting *agreements* or bargains. Promissory estoppel, on the other hand, protects *reliance.* Early promissory estoppel cases applied the doctrine only to donative (gift) promises like the one made by John's parents in the example above. As subsequent chapters will demonstrate, however, promissory estoppel is now being used by the courts to prevent offerors from revoking their offers, to enforce indefinite or illusory promises, and to enforce oral promises that would ordinarily have to be in writing. Given the basic conceptual differences between estoppel and contract, and the judicial tendency to use promissory estoppel to compensate for the absence of more and more of the traditional elements of contract, some commentators have been led to suggest that promissory estoppel may be emerging as a theory of obligation independent of contract rather than as simply an ever-expanding exception to contract principles.[4] Whether or not promissory estoppel ever gains independent theory status, however, its growth as a new device for enforcing promises is one of the most important developments in modern contract law.

## THE UNIFORM COMMERCIAL CODE

**Origins and Purposes of the Code.** The Uniform Commercial Code was created by the American Law Institute and the National Conference of Commissioners on Uniform State Laws. All of the states except Louisiana (which has adopted only part of the Code) have adopted it. The drafters of the Code had several purposes in mind, the most obvious of which was to establish a uniform set of rules to govern commercial transactions, which are often conducted across state lines in today's national markets. Despite the Code's almost universal adoption, however, complete uniformity has not been achieved.

---

[4] Metzger and Phillips, "The Emergence of Promissory Estoppel as an Independent Theory of Recovery," 35 *Rutgers L. Rev.* 472 (1983).

Many states have varied or amended the Code's language in specific instances, and some Code provisions were drafted in alternative ways, giving the states more than one version of particular Code provisions to choose from. Also, the various state courts have reached different conclusions about the meaning of particular Code sections.

In addition to promoting uniformity, the drafters of the Code sought to create a body of rules that would deal realistically and fairly with common problems that occur in everyday commercial transactions. Finally, the drafters tried to formulate rules that would promote fair dealing and higher standards of dealing in the marketplace.

**Scope of the Code.** The Code contains nine substantive articles, most of which are discussed in detail in Parts VIII, IX, and X of this book. The most important Code article for our present purposes is Article 2, the Sales article of the Code.

**Nature of Article 2.** Many of the provisions of Article 2 exhibit the basic tendencies of "modern" contract law that were discussed earlier in this chapter. Accordingly, they differ from traditional contract law rules in a variety of important ways. The Code is more concerned with rewarding people's legitimate expectations than with technical rules, so it is generally more flexible than contract law. A court that applies the Code is more likely to find that the parties had a contract than is a court that applies contract law [2–204] (the numbers in brackets refer to specific Code sections). In some cases, the Code gives less weight than does contract law to technical requirements such as consideration [2–205 and 2–209].

The drafters of the Code sought to create practical rules to deal with what people actually do in today's marketplace. We live in the day of the form contract, so some of the Code's rules try to deal fairly with that fact [2–205, 2–207, 2–209(2), and 2–302]. The words *reasonable, commercially reasonable,* and *seasonably* (within a reasonable time) are found throughout the Code. This reasonableness standard is different in kind from the hypothetical "reasonable man" standard that you encountered in tort law. A court that tries to decide what is "reasonable" under the Code is more likely to be concerned with what people really do in the marketplace than with what a nonexistent "reasonable man" would do.

The drafters of the Code wanted to promote fair dealing and higher standards in the marketplace, so they imposed a **duty of good faith** [1–203] in the performance and enforcement of every contract under the Code. "Good faith" means "honesty in fact" and "the observance of reasonable commercial standards of fair dealing" [2–103(1)(b)]. The parties cannot alter this duty of good faith by agreement [1–102(3)]. The Code also expressly recognizes the concept of an **unconscionable contract,** one that is grossly unfair or one-sided, and it gives the courts broad discretionary powers to deal fairly with such contracts [2–302].

The Code also recognizes that buyers tend to place more reliance on professional sellers and that professionals are generally more knowledgeable and better able to protect themselves than nonprofessionals. So, the Code distinguishes between *merchants* and nonmerchants by holding merchants to a higher standard in some cases [2–201(2), 2–205, and 2–207(2)]. The Code defines the term *merchant* [2–104(1)] on a case-by-case basis. If a person regularly deals in the kind of goods being sold, or pretends to have some special knowledge about the goods, or employed an agent in the sale who fits either of these two descriptions, that person is a "merchant" for the purposes of the contract in question. So, if you buy a used car from a used-car dealer, the dealer is a merchant for the purposes of your contract. But, if you buy a refrigerator from a used-car dealer, the dealer is probably not a merchant.

**Application of the Code.** Article 2 expressly applies only to *contracts for the sale of goods* [2–102]. The Code contains a somewhat complicated definition of *goods* [2–105], but the essence of the definition is that *goods* are *tangible, movable, personal property.* So, contracts for the sale of such items as motor vehicles, books, appliances, and clothing are covered by Article 2. But Article 2 does *not* apply to contracts for the sale of real estate, stocks and bonds, or other intangibles.

Article 2 also does not apply to *service* contracts. This can cause confusion because, while contracts of employment or other personal services are clearly not covered by Article 2, many contracts involve elements of both goods and services. The test that the courts most frequently use to determine whether Article 2 applies to such a contract is to ask which element, goods or services, *predominates* in the contract. Is the major purpose or thrust of the agreement the rendering of a service, or is it the sale of goods, with any services involved being merely incidental to that sale? This means that contracts calling for services that involve significant elements of personal skill or judgment in addition to goods will probably not be governed by Article 2. Construction contracts, remodeling contracts, and auto repair contracts are all examples of mixed goods and services contracts that may be considered outside the scope of the Code.

Two other important qualifications must be made concerning the application of Code contract principles. First, the Code does not change *all* of the traditional contract rules. Where no specific Code rule exists, traditional contract law rules apply to contracts for the sale of goods. Second, and ultimately far more important, the courts have demonstrated a significant tendency to apply Code contract concepts by analogy to contracts not specifically covered by Article 2. For example, the Code concepts of good faith dealing and unconscionability have enjoyed wide application in cases that are technically outside the scope of Article 2. Thus, the Code is an important influence shaping the evolution of contract law in general, and if this trend toward broader application of Code principles continues, the time may come when the dichotomy between Code principles and traditional contract rules is a thing of the past.

---

## Consolidated Edison Co. of New York, Inc. v. Westinghouse Electric Corp.

**567 F. Supp. 358 (S.D.N.Y. 1983)**

In 1971, Westinghouse and Consolidated Edison (Con Ed) entered into a contract calling for Westinghouse to "furnish and construct a complete and operable nuclear power plant" for Con Ed. The plant, known as Indian Point Power Plant Unit Number 2 (IP 2), was subsequently built in Buchanan, New York, and Con Ed accepted the completed plant on May 22, 1974. In 1975, defects that required extensive monitoring, repairs, and modifications and prevented Con Ed from obtaining maximum output from the plant allegedly began to appear in the plant's steam generators and steam turbines. Con Ed and Westinghouse negotiated over the plant's alleged defects for several years and entered into agreements tolling any statutes of limitations that would otherwise apply to Con Ed's potential claims against Westinghouse. A tolling agreement covering the steam generators was entered on May 12, 1978, within four years of Con Ed's acceptance of the plant. The agreement covering the steam turbines was not, however, executed until two years later. Con Ed filed suit against Westinghouse on various theories, including breach of contract and breach of warranty. Westinghouse filed a motion to dismiss Con Ed's claims, arguing, among other things, that they were barred by the applicable statutes of limitations.

**Lasker, District Judge.** Under New York law, a four-year statute of limitations applies to causes of action based on contracts for the sale of goods, which are governed by the Uniform Commercial Code [2–725], while a six-year statute of limitations applies to causes of action based on service or construction contracts, which are governed by the common law. Thus, although Con Ed's contract claims with respect to the steam generators are timely under either measure, the timeliness of its contract claims with respect to the steam turbines and other equipment depends upon whether the IP 2 Agreement is "in essence" a contract for the sale of goods under the UCC, or whether instead it is a service contract—a "work, labor and materials contract."

Westinghouse argues, in favor of the applicability of the UCC, that the primary object of the Agreement was the purchase by Con Ed of Westinghouse-manufactured and -designed component parts—the steam generators, turbines, and other components of the IP 2 Plant.

In answer Con Ed points out that the IP 2 Agreement is a contract not simply for the sale of specific items of power plant equipment, but for the construction of a complete nuclear power plant. The Agreement, Con Ed argues, not only required Westinghouse to provide all architectural and engineering services necessary to the construction of the plant, along with the labor required for its construction, but also provided that Westinghouse would take all necessary steps to assure that the plant would be granted an operating license under the requirements established by the United States Atomic Energy Commission. Con Ed contends that the scope of Westinghouse's responsibilities under the Agreement, which continued throughout several years of design, construction, testing and licensing, differentiates the Agreement from typical "goods" contracts involving the one-time installation of a specific item of equipment.

The New York cases exploring the distinction between sales and services contracts provide no clear answer to the proper classification of the IP 2 Agreement. In several instances New York courts have held that contracts as to which "service predominates and the transfer of title to personal property is an incidental feature of the transaction" are outside the scope of the UCC. In the present case, however, on the record as it stands, neither the goods nor the services aspect of the Agreement can reasonably be characterized as "incidental." Just as Con Ed plainly could not have considered the power generating equipment to be an incidental feature of its contract with Westinghouse, so also the architectural, engineering and testing services provided by Westinghouse, and the labor necessary to carry them out, were crucial to the Agreement's objective.

Where, as here, the question is closely balanced, factual development is necessary before the issue is resolved. The pleadings do not reveal the allocation of contract price as between construction and equipment costs, the precise nature and scope of the services undertaken by Westinghouse, or other matters that may contribute to a proper resolution of the question. It may be, as Westinghouse argues, that the "essential" nature of the contract will not be significantly clearer following development of the record, but the accuracy of this prediction cannot be determined in advance of obtaining the facts.

Westinghouse motion to dismiss denied.

## RESTATEMENT (SECOND) OF CONTRACTS

**Nature and Origins.** In 1932, the American Law Institute published the first *Restatement of Contracts,*[5] an attempt to codify and systematize the soundest principles of contract law gleaned from thousands of often conflicting judicial decisions. As the product of a private organization, the *Restatement* did not have the force of law, but as the considered judgment of some of the leading scholars of the legal profession, it was highly influential in shaping the evolution of contract law. The *Restatement (Second) of Contracts,* issued in 1979, is an attempt to reflect the significant changes that have occurred in contract law in the years following the birth of the first *Restatement.* The tone of the *Restatement Second* differs dramatically from that of the first *Restatement,* which is often characterized as a positivist attempt to formulate a system of "black letter" rules of contract law. The *Restatement Second,* in contrast, reflects the "shift from rules to standards"[6] that has occurred in modern contract law: the shift from precise, technical rules to broader, discretionary principles aimed at producing just results. The *Restatement Second* plainly bears the mark of the legal "realists," discussed in Chapter 1, and has been heavily influenced by the Uniform Commercial Code. In fact, many *Restatement Second* provisions are virtually identical to their Code analogues. For example, the *Restatement Second* has explicitly embraced the Code concepts of *good faith*[7] and *unconscionability.*[8]

**Impact.** The *Restatement Second,* like its predecessor, does not have the force of law, and its relative newness prevents any accurate assessment of its impact on contemporary contract cases. Nonetheless, given the influential role played by the first *Restatement* and the previously mentioned tendency of the courts to employ Code principles by analogy in contract cases, it seems fair to assume that the *Restatement Second* will serve as a major inspiration for contract developments in the decades to come. For this reason, significant attention is given to the *Restatement Second* in the following chapters.

[5] See Chapter 1 for a general discussion of the *Restatement* phenomenon.

[6] Speidel, "Restatement Second: Omitted Terms and Contract Method," 67 *Cornell L. Rev.* 785, 786 (1982).

[7] *Restatement (Second) of Contracts* § 205 (1979).

[8] *Restatement (Second) of Contracts* § 208 (1979).

## SUMMARY

Contracts are legally enforceable promises or sets of promises. To attain contract status, promises must conform to certain legal requirements prescribed by contract law. Contract law, like other bodies of law, is constantly changing in response to changing social needs and values. Modern contract law, in a quest for "just" results, is evolving in the direction of increased public supervision of private contracts and broad, discretionary rules. The basic essence of contract law, however, still derives from the idea that contracts are consensual, private agreements.

In their search for justice, the courts have developed doctrines that can operate to impose obligations on people in the absence of the agreement required by traditional contract law. *Quasi-contract* doctrine is used by the courts to prevent persons who have received goods or services from others from being unjustly enriched, by implying a promise to pay for those goods or services as a matter of law. *Promissory estoppel* protects persons who rely on the promises of others by preventing promisors from raising legal defenses to the enforcement of their promises that they might otherwise have. In recent years, promissory estoppel principles have been applied to an increasing range of contract problems, leading some scholars to conclude that contract is in danger of being eclipsed by promissory estoppel.

Article 2 of the Uniform Commercial Code is an important source of modern contract principles. Technically, it applies only to contracts for the sale of *goods,* and it dramatically changes some of the basic rules governing such contracts. The Code, however, has had significant influence on the rules governing other kinds of contracts because the courts often apply Code principles to such contracts by analogy.

The *Restatement (Second) of Contracts* clearly reflects the influence of the Code. Many *Restatement Second* provisions were obviously inspired by their Code counterparts. The *Restatement Second* is also similar to the Code in its tendency to employ broad discretionary standards that facilitate judicial supervision of contracts in the name of fairness. Although the *Restatement Second* does not have the force of law, the influence formerly enjoyed by the first *Restatement* and the existing tendency of many courts to employ Code principles like those adopted by the *Restatement Second* suggest that it will also be a significant source of inspiration for future contract developments.

## QUESTIONS AND PROBLEM CASES

1. What distinguishes contracts from unenforceable, "social" promises?
2. What assumptions did the common law make concerning the characteristics of typical contracts?
3. How do modern contract rules tend to differ from the classical common law contract rules?
4. Why do some scholars suggest that promissory estoppel may be evolving into a separate theory of recovery independent of contract?
5. Michelle Triola Marvin lived with actor Lee Marvin for almost six years. Michelle called herself Mrs. Marvin, and Lee occasionally introduced her as Mrs. Marvin. The couple had no joint bank accounts and held no property jointly, however. Lee repeatedly told Michelle that he did not believe in marriage because of the property rights that a wife acquires by it. While Michelle lived with Marvin, she had the use of a Mercedes-Benz, stayed at his beach house, received numerous expensive gifts, and often traveled with him abroad at his expense. When the couple separated, she claimed that she was entitled to half of his property in exchange for giving up a singing career and providing him with homemaking services and companionship. Did Michelle have any contractual or quasi-contractual right to half of Lee Marvin's property?
6. Glick was a subcontractor on a construction project on a nursing home being built by Seufert, a general contractor and owner of the real estate. Glick was hired by another subcontractor, Patoka Valley Plumbing and Heating Company, to complete the plumbing work on the project. When Patoka did part of the work incorrectly and lagged behind in completing the project, Seufert urged Glick to make corrections and finish the job. Glick refused to continue until he knew who would pay him. Seufert's construction superintendent told Glick to go ahead and that he would "try to help him get his money." Glick finished the work and sent Patoka a bill for $5,528.14, which was never paid. He then sent a bill to Seufert. Seufert told Glick that since Glick had failed to promptly notify him of Patoka's nonpayment, he had already paid Patoka in full and was powerless to help Glick get his money by withholding payments. Glick sued Seufert under a quasi contract theory. Was Seufert liable to Glick in quasi contract?
7. Helen Preston consulted Dr. Benjamin

Thompson, a specialist in fitting and preparing dentures, about obtaining a new set of dentures. She paid him $750, and after numerous appointments where measurements were taken, she received her dentures. She experienced some pain and had trouble eating with the lower set. Dr. Thompson made numerous adjustments to the lower set and indicated a willingness to continue working with her until the fit was satisfactory. She refused to continue, however, and filed suit against Dr. Thompson for breach of the Code's implied warranty of merchantability. Was Preston's agreement with Dr. Thompson a sale of "goods" under the Code?

8. Prince lived in a mobile home next to a children's home he was constructing in Freestone County, Texas. While he was adjusting a television antenna beside the mobile home and underneath a high-voltage electric transmission line maintained by the Navarro County Electric Cooperative, he was injured when electric current allegedly jumped from the transmission line to the aerial. He filed suit against the cooperative for breach of the Code's implied warranty of merchantability. The cooperative argued that electricity was not "goods" for the purposes of the Code. Should the Code apply to this case?

# Chapter 7 The Agreement: Offer

## INTRODUCTION

The concept of mutual agreement lies at the heart of traditional contract law. Courts faced with deciding whether two or more persons entered into a contract look first for an *agreement*, or a "meeting of the minds" between the parties. Did the parties arrive at an understanding on terms that each party found acceptable, or did their negotiations falter before a true agreement was reached? Courts seeking to answer such questions concern themselves with the *objective* intent of the parties. That is, they do not ask whether the parties *subjectively* (consciously) intended to contract. Instead, they ask whether a reasonable person familiar with the circumstances surrounding the parties' negotiations would conclude that the parties reached an agreement by which they intended to be bound.

## WHAT IS AN OFFER?

**Definition.** Section 24 of the *Restatement (Second) of Contracts* defines an offer as "the manifestation of willingness to enter into a bargain, so made as to justify another person in understanding that his assent to that bargain is invited and will conclude it." In other words, when we consider all that the parties said and did, did one of the parties ever, in effect, say to the other: "This is it—if you agree to these terms, we have a contract." The question of whether an offer was ever made is a critically important first step in the contract formation process. A person who makes an offer (the **offeror**) gives the person to whom she makes the offer (the **offeree**) the power to bind her to a contract by accepting the offer. But, if no offer was ever made, there was nothing to accept and no contract will result.

Traditional contract law rules on contract formation are designed to assure that persons are never bound to contracts unless they clearly intend to be bound. Therefore, the basic thing that the courts require for the creation of an offer is some objective indication of a *present intent to contract* on the part of the offeror. The two main things from which the courts infer an intent to contract are the *definiteness* of the alleged offer and the fact that it has been *communicated to the offeree.*

**Definiteness.** If an alleged offer fails to state specifically what the offeror is willing to do and what he asks in return for his performance, there is a good chance that the parties are still in the process of negotiation. If Smith says to Ford, "I'd like to buy your house," and Ford responds, "You've got a deal," do we have a contract? Obviously not. Smith's statement is merely an "invitation to offer" or an "invitation to negotiate." It does not indicate a present intent to contract on Smith's part. It merely indicates a willingness to contract in the future if the parties can reach agreement on mutually acceptable terms. However, if Smith sends Ford a detailed and specific written document stating all of the material terms and conditions on which he is willing to buy the house and Ford writes back agreeing to Smith's terms, a contract has probably been created.

Definiteness and specificity in offers are also important in contract law because the offer will often contain all the terms of the parties' contract. This is so because all that offerees are allowed to do in most cases is to accept or reject the terms of the offer. Agreements that are incomplete or indefinite because they omit material terms or imprecisely state such terms pose several problems for courts applying traditional contract principles. The fact that the parties' agreement is indefinite on some points or lacks certain terms that such contracts normally address may, of course, indicate that the parties never, in fact, reached agreement on the omitted or indefinite terms. Even if the parties apparently intended to create a binding contract, however, how can a court that takes the traditional "hands-off" approach justify imposing contractual liability when the parties have failed to clearly indicate their intent on a particular issue? Classical contract principles see courts as contract enforcers, not as contract makers. Therefore, agreements that are too indefinite are generally unenforceable at common law.

**Definiteness and Modern Contract Law.** The traditional contract law insistence on definiteness can serve useful ends by preventing a person from being held to an agreement when no "meeting of the minds" ever occurred or from being bound by a contract term to which he never assented. But it can often operate to frustrate the expectations of parties who intend to contract but, for whatever reason, fail to procure an agreement that is sufficiently definite. Modern contract principles, with their increased emphasis on furthering people's justifiable expectations and their encouragement of a "hands-on" approach by the courts, will often create contractual liability in situations where no contract would have resulted at common law. Perhaps no part of the Code better illustrates this basic difference between modern contract principles and their classical counterparts than does the basic Code section on contract formation [2–204]. Sales contracts under Article 2 can be created "in any manner sufficient to show agreement, including conduct which recognizes the existence of a contract" [2–204(1)]. So, if the parties are acting as though they have a contract (by delivering or accepting goods or payment, for example), this may be enough to create a binding contract, even if it is impossible to point to a particular moment in time when the contract was created [2–204(2)].

Nor will the fact that the parties left open one or more terms of their agreement necessarily mean that their agreement is too indefinite to enforce. A sales contract will be created if the court finds that the parties "*intended* to make a contract" and that their agreement is complete enough to allow the court to reach a fair settlement of their dispute ("a reasonably certain basis for giving an appropriate remedy" [2–204(3)]). The Code contains a series of "gap filling" rules to enable courts to "fill in the blanks" on matters of price [2–305], quantity [2–306], delivery [2–307, 2–308, and 2–309(1)], and time for payment [2–310] when such terms have been left open by the parties.[1] Of course, if a term was left out because the parties were *unable* to reach agreement about it, this would indicate that the intent to contract was absent and no contract would result, even under the Code's more liberal rules. Intention is still at the heart of these modern contract rules; the difference is that courts applying Code principles will seek to further the parties' *underlying* intent to contract even though the parties have failed to express their intention about specific aspects of their agreement.

The *Restatement (Second) of Contracts* takes an approach to the definiteness question that is quite similar to the Code approach. The terms of an alleged offer must be "reasonably certain" before it can form the basis of a contract,[2] but reasonable certainty merely means that those terms "provide a basis for determining the existence of a breach and for giving an appropriate remedy."[3] The basic thrust of the *Restatement Second,* however, is still to further the intent of the parties, and it expressly recognizes the fact that open or uncertain terms may indicate the absence of an intent to contract.[4] Where an agreement is sufficiently definite to be a contract, but essential terms are left open, the *Restatement Second* provides that "a term which is reasonable in the circumstances is supplied by the court."[5] Like the Code, the *Restatement Second* specifically indicates that where the parties' conduct indicates an intent to contract, a contract may result "even though neither offer nor acceptance can be identified and even though the moment of formation cannot be determined."[6]

Unlike the Code, the *Restatement Second* also indicates that "action in reliance" on an indefinite agreement may justify its full or partial enforcement.[7] This provision highlights one of the most intriguing recent developments in contract law—the use of **promissory estoppel** to enforce indefinite agreements.[8] It has long been the rule that promissory estoppel could not be used to enforce indefinite agreements because their indefiniteness meant that the court was left with no promise capable of being enforced. People sometimes do, however, act in reliance

[1] These Code provisions are discussed in detail in Chapter 31.

[2] *Restatement (Second) of Contracts* § 33(1) (1979).

[3] *Restatement (Second) of Contracts* § 33(2) (1979).

[4] *Restatement (Second) of Contracts* § 33(3) (1979).

[5] *Restatement (Second) of Contracts* § 204 (1979).

[6] *Restatement (Second) of Contracts* § 22(2) (1979).

[7] *Restatement (Second) of Contracts* § 34(3) (1979).

[8] See the general discussion of promissory estoppel in Chapter 6.

on indefinite agreements, and to protect that reliance a few courts have deviated from the general rule. In such cases, it is common for courts to overcome the indefiniteness problem by awarding damages based on the promisee's losses due to reliance rather than by attempting to enforce the indefinite agreement.

*Hoffman v. Red Owl Stores, Inc.,*[9] is probably the most famous case of this type. Hoffman wanted to acquire a Red Owl franchised convenience store and, in reliance on Red Owl's promises during their negotiations, sold his bakery at a loss, bought a small grocery to gain experience, moved his family, and bought an option on a proposed site for the franchised store. The negotiations fell through, and when Hoffman sued, Red Owl argued that no contract resulted, because the parties had never reached agreement on the essential terms governing their relationship. The Supreme Court of Wisconsin agreed, but nonetheless allowed Hoffman to recover his reliance losses on the basis of promissory estoppel. In doing so, the court noted that nothing in the language of section 90 of the *Restatement* required that a promise serving as the basis of promissory estoppel be "so comprehensive in scope as to meet the requirements of an offer." The court also observed that "it would be a mistake to regard an action grounded on promissory estoppel as the equivalent of a breach of contract action." This language suggests that promissory estoppel may be an independent theory of recovery apart from contract.

At least one observer, however, has characterized *Hoffman* as representing an extension of the "good faith" idea into the area of contract negotiations.[10] Or *Hoffman* may simply be viewed as allowing reliance to "substitute for" the offer and acceptance required by classical contract theory. However it is viewed, when one considers cases like *Hoffman* and the way in which the definiteness problem is handled by both the Code and the *Restatement Second,* it seems safe to say that indefiniteness is no longer the obstacle to the creation of contractual liability that it once was. As the *Savoca* case, which follows, indicates, however, many courts still take a more traditional approach to indefinite contracts.

**Communication to Offeree.** When an offeror communicates the terms of an offer to an offeree, he objectively indicates an intent to be bound by these terms. An uncommunicated offer, on the other hand, may be evidence that the offeror has not yet decided to enter into a binding agreement. For example, assume that Stevens and Meyer have been negotiating over the sale of Meyer's restaurant. Reilly, a mutual friend, tells Meyer that Stevens has decided to offer him $150,000 for the restaurant and has drawn up a written offer to that effect. After learning the details of the offer from Reilly, Meyer telephones Stevens and says, "I accept your offer." Is Stevens now contractually obligated to buy the restaurant? No. Since Stevens did not communicate the proposal to Meyer, there was no offer for Meyer to accept.

[9] 26 Wis.2d 683, 133 N.W.2d 267 (Wis. Sup. Ct. 1965).

[10] Summers, "'Good Faith' in General Contract Law and the Sales Provisions of the Uniform Commercial Code," 54 *U. Va. L. Rev.* 195, 223 (1968).

## Savoca Masonry Co., Inc. v. Homes & Son Constr. Co., Inc.

**542 P.2d 817 (Ariz. Sup. Ct. 1975)**

Homes, a general contractor, accepted Savoca's oral bid to operate as the masonry subcontractor for a construction project. Three days later, however, Homes contracted to have a third party do the masonry work in order to comply with the project architect's desire to save money on it. Homes informed Savoca that it had no binding contract because its oral bid did not cover all of the essential elements involved in the project. Savoca sued for breach of contract. The trial court ruled in Homes's favor, and Savoca appealed.

**Struckmeyer, Judge.** Homes argues that there is such a lack of specified material terms that the parties cannot be said to have shown a mutual assent to incur contractual obligations and cites *Plumbing Shop, Inc. v. Pitts* (1965). There, a subcontractor submitted an oral bid to a general contractor who was bidding on a government construction project. The general contractor was awarded the contract and informed the subcontractor of that fact. Discussions were had with the subcontractor on procedures for completing the work and, among other things, the subcontractor submitted a cost breakdown for the work proposed. The general contractor, however, refused to enter into written contract with the subcontractor. On appeal after the suit, the Washington court said:

> More importantly, the record before us is devoid of any evidence of agreement, express or otherwise, to any term of the alleged contract other than the price. Such essentials, as manner of payment, time for completion of the mechanical portion of the work, penalty provisions, bonding, etc., are normally critical to any construction contract. The plaintiff argues that substantial agreement had been reached on the essential terms and with respect to such "housekeeping" items, as time of performance, the law will imply a reasonable time. . . . But our role is not that of contract maker; we merely give legal effect to bargained-for contractual relations. Any prudent general contractor, with the attendant responsibility for coordinating all aspects of a project in order to meet the quality and time requirements of the general contract, probably would require a substantial degree of specificity with respect to time of completion of various portions of the mechanical work in order to insure the overall progress of the project.

This is precisely the case here. Only the price and work involved were agreed upon; other provisions which might in the end have proven critical were not. We think important mutual obligations of the parties were still to be agreed upon at the time of the asserted oral acceptance.

Judgment for Homes affirmed.

## Allied Disposal v. Bob's Home Service

### 595 S.W.2d 417 (Mo. Ct. App. 1980)

Allied, a disposer of chemical wastes, contracted with Bob's, the owner of a disposal site, as follows:

> Allied will be the exclusive user of the site except for the use of Bob's to service its current customers. No use of the site could be made by any other person or business without Allied's written consent.
>
> Allied will use only Bob's site for disposal of chemical waste it hauls and will not use any other site without the written permission of Bob's.
>
> The parties will use their best efforts to obtain necessary state permits for each type of waste to be disposed of on the site and will use the same efforts to obtain federal permits if necessary.
>
> The price that Allied will pay Bob's for the use of the site will be mutually agreed upon by the parties for each contract of hauling that Allied has.

Several months later, Bob's entered a contract giving Chem-Dyne, a competitor of Allied, exclusive control of the disposal site. Allied filed suit for breach of contract. The trial court dismissed the suit on the ground that Allied's agreement with Bob's was too indefinite to be a contract, due to the open price term. Allied appealed.

**SMITH, PRESIDING JUDGE.** Section 2–304(3) of the Uniform Commercial Code provides: "Even though one or more terms are left open a contract for sale does not fail for indefiniteness if the parties have intended to make a contract." Section 2–305 deals even more specifically with contracts in which the price is not settled. In such a case the contract is valid if the parties intended to contract. The price is a "reasonable price at the time of delivery if . . . (b) the price is left to be agreed by the parties and they fail to agree. . . ." Although these provisions do not apply specifically to contracts for services they do reflect a legislative policy of the state to obviate the prior doctrine invalidating contracts where the price was left to further agreement.

We conclude, therefore, that the present state of the law recognizes that an "agreement to agree" on price does not preclude, in and of itself, the validity of a contract.

Here it is apparent from the allegations that the parties intended to contract. They operated under that contract for several months and the petition does not reflect that the allegedly vague term has been a subject of controversy. The nature of the business is unusual and is subject to extensive state regulation. It is at least to be inferred that each type of waste to be disposed of under the contract required different handling because of state (and possibly federal) regulation and that establishing a price in advance for each type was difficult or impossible. The contract so reflects. Allied has a cause of action under the rationale of the Uniform Commercial Code.

Judgment reversed in favor of Allied.

## SPECIAL OFFER PROBLEM AREAS

**Advertisements.** The courts have generally held that advertisements for the sale of goods at specified prices are *not* offers; instead, they are treated as invitations to offer or negotiate. The same rule is generally applied to signs, handbills, displayed goods, catalogs, price lists, and price quotations. This rule probably fairly reflects the intentions of the sellers involved, who probably only have a limited number of items to sell and do not intend to give every person who sees their ad (sign, catalog, etc.) the power to bind them to a contract. Thus, would-be buyers are, in legal effect, making offers to purchase the goods, which the seller is free to accept or reject. This is so because the buyer is manifesting a present intent to contract on definite terms (the terms of the ad, etc.) and there is no offer for him to accept.

In some cases, however, particular ads have been held to amount to offers. Such ads are usually highly specific about the nature and number of items offered for sale and what is requested in return. This specificity precludes the possibility that the offeror will be contractually bound to an infinite number of offerees. In addition, many of the ads that have been treated as offers have required some special kinds of performance by would-be buyers or have in some other way clearly indicated that immediate buyer action will create a binding agreement. The potential for unfairness to those who attempt to accept such ads and their fundamental difference from ordinary ads probably justify treating them as offers. So, if Monarch Motors runs a special 10th anniversary advertisement that says, "Our 10th customer on Saturday, March 25, 1984, will be entitled to purchase a new Rolls-Royce Silver Shadow with every available option for 10 percent under dealer cost," most courts would probably hold that this ad was an offer and that the 10th customer was entitled to purchase the car as advertised.

**Rewards.** Advertisements offering rewards for lost property, for information, or for the capture of criminals are generally treated as offers for unilateral contracts. In order to accept the offer and be entitled to the stated reward, offerees must perform the requested act—return the lost property, supply the requested information, or capture the wanted criminal. Some courts have held that only offerees who started performance with knowledge of the offer are entitled to the reward. Other courts, however, have indicated that all that is required is that the offeree know of the reward before completing performance. In reality, the result in most such cases will probably reflect the court's perception of the equities of the particular case at hand.

**Auctions.** Sellers at auctions are generally treated as making an invitation to offer. Those who bid on offered goods are therefore treated as making offers that the owner of the goods may accept or reject. Acceptance occurs only when the auctioneer strikes the goods off to the highest bidder, and the auctioneer may withdraw the goods at any time before acceptance. However, when an auction is advertised as being "without reserve," the seller is treated as having made an offer to sell the goods to the highest bidder and the goods cannot be withdrawn after a call for bids has been made unless no bids are made within a reasonable time.[11]

**Bids.** The bidding process is a fertile source of contract disputes. Advertisements for bids are generally treated as invitations to offer. Those who submit bids are treated as offerors. According to general contract principles, bid-

[11] These rules and others concerned with the sale of goods by auction are contained in section 2–328 of the U.C.C.

ders can withdraw their bids at any time prior to acceptance by the person inviting the bids (the offeree) and the offeree is free to accept or reject any bid. The previously announced terms of the bidding may alter these rules, however. For example, if the advertisement for bids unconditionally states that the contract will be awarded to the lowest responsible bidder, this will be treated as an offer that is accepted by the lowest bidder. Only proof by the offeror that the lowest bidder is not responsible will prevent the formation of a contract. Also, under some circumstances discussed later in this chapter, promissory estoppel may operate to prevent bidders from withdrawing their bids.

Bids for governmental contracts are generally covered by specific statutes rather than by general contract principles. Such statutes ordinarily establish the rules governing the bidding process, often require that the contract be awarded to the lowest bidder, and frequently establish special rules or penalties governing the withdrawal of bids.

## Southworth v. Oliver

**587 P.2d 994 (Or. Sup. Ct. 1978)**

J. W. Southworth and Joseph Oliver were ranchers in Grant County, Oregon. Oliver and his wife decided to sell over 2,900 acres of land in Bear Valley and asked Southworth, who owned land adjoining the sale tract, whether he would be interested in buying. Southworth said he was "very interested" in the land and would attempt to arrange financing for the purchase, and he asked Oliver to let him know the price as soon as Oliver decided on it. Several weeks later, Oliver sent Southworth and three other ranchers a letter briefly describing the land and stating a price of $324,419 and other specific terms of sale. Four days later, Southworth wrote, stating: "I accept your offer." Oliver refused to sell, arguing that his letter was not an offer but merely an invitation to negotiate. Southworth filed suit for specific performance of the alleged contract. The trial court issued a specific performance decree, and Oliver appealed.

**Tongue, Justice.** Although a price quotation, standing alone, is not an offer, there may be circumstances under which a price quotation, when considered together with the facts and circumstances, may constitute an offer which, if accepted, will result in a binding contract. We believe that the "surrounding circumstances" under which this letter was prepared by the Olivers and sent by them to Southworth were such as to have led a reasonable person to believe that the Olivers were making an offer to sell to Southworth the lands described upon the terms stated.

That letter did not come to Southworth "out of the blue" as in some of the cases involving advertisements or price quotations. Neither was this a price quotation resulting from an inquiry by Southworth. According to what we believe to be the most credible testimony, the Olivers decided to sell the lands in question and Joseph Oliver then sought out Southworth. Under these facts and circumstances we agree with the conclusion by the trial court that when Southworth received the letter, a reasonable person in his position would have believed that the Olivers were making an offer to sell those lands to him.

This conclusion is strengthened by the definiteness of the proposal, not only with respect to price, but terms, and the fact that the addressee was not an indefinite group. The Olivers contend that they "obviously did not intend [the letter] as an offer." While it may be proper to consider evidence of the Olivers' subjective intent under the "objective test" to which the court is committed, it is the manifestation of a previous intention that is controlling, rather than a person's actual intent.

Judgment for Southworth affirmed.

## WHAT TERMS ARE INCLUDED IN OFFERS?

After making a determination that an offer existed, a court must decide what terms were included in the offer so that it can determine the terms of the parties' contract. Put another way, what terms of the offer are binding on the offeree who accepts it? Should offerees, for example, be bound by fine print clauses or by clauses located on the back of the contract? Originally, the courts tended to hold that offerees were bound by all the terms of the offer on the theory that every person had a duty to protect himself by reading agreements carefully before signing them.

In today's world of lengthy, complex form contracts, however, people often sign agreements that they have not fully read or do not fully understand. Modern courts tend to recognize this fact by saying that offerees are bound only by terms of which they had *actual* or *reasonable notice*. If the offeree actually read the term in question, or if a reasonable person should have been aware of it, it will probably become part of the parties' contract. So, a fine print provision on the back of a theater ticket would probably not be binding on a theater patron, because a reasonable person would not expect such a ticket to contain contractual terms. However, the terms printed on a multipage airline or steamship ticket might well be considered binding on the purchaser.

This modern approach to deciding the terms of a contract gives courts an indirect, but effective, way of promoting fair dealing by refusing to enforce unfair contract terms on the ground that the offeree lacked reasonable notice of them. Disclaimers and exculpatory clauses (contract provisions that seek to relieve offerors of some legal duty that they would otherwise owe to offerees) are particularly likely to be subjected to close judicial scrutiny. Many courts insist on proof that the offeree had actual notice of such terms before they will be considered a part of the contract. Also, as you will learn in greater detail in Chapter 12, even terms that would otherwise clearly be part of the parties' contract may be inoperative if they are unconscionable or contrary to public policy.

## Belger Cartage Service, Inc. v. Holland Constr. Co.

**582 P.2d 1111 (Kan. Sup. Ct. 1978)**

Holland needed a crane to move some heavy equipment. Holland contacted Belger, and Belger sent a crane, a boom, and two employees to the job site. A work order was signed (whether it was signed before or after the accident is disputed). In small print on the reverse of the work order were the following provisions:

> It is further agreed and understood that any work performed on such premises is performed at the sole risk of the lessee. With regard to such equipment or deliveries or work performed, Belger Cartage Service, Inc. is hereby relieved from any and all responsibility regardless of its own fault or negligence.

The two employees sent by Belger with the crane and boom operated the equipment at all times, with employees of Holland on the ground operating tag lines. When a conveyor was being lifted, the cable on the boom broke and the conveyor fell. The conveyor as well as the crane and boom were damaged. The only evidence as to the precise cause of the accident was that the conveyor was lifted at an improper angle in relation to the boom. As a result, the cable rubbed the side of the pulley, frayed, and broke.

Belger contended that its employees became Holland's employees by virtue of the circumstances and the quoted provisions of the work order and that Holland was therefore responsible for their negligence. Holland contended that the terms were never communicated as a part of the contract and that Belger was liable for the damage to Holland's conveyor. The trial court ruled in Holland's favor, and Belger appealed.

**McFarland, Justice.** The exculpatory clause was in small print on the reverse side of the form. Everything on the reverse side was printed. All signatures and "personalized" data were on the front of the order. There was no evidence that the clauses were discussed or that Holland had actual knowledge thereof. The evidence was disputed as to whether or not the work order was signed before or after the accident.

In determining the enforceability of exculpatory clauses purportedly transferring employees to another and relieving the transferring employer from all responsibility for harm they might cause, such clauses are to be strictly construed against the transferring employer. The trial court may consider the totality of the circumstances surrounding the execution and performance of the contract, including, but not limited to, whether the employer to whom the employees were purportedly transferred had knowledge of the clauses by having them pointed out to him or the clauses themselves being conspicuous in the contract; the nature of the work to be performed, including the degree of skill required and the degree of risk of harm involved; and the actual performance of the parties.

There was substantial evidence to support all of the trial court's findings [that the disclaimer provisions were not an enforceable part of the contract].

Judgment for Holland affirmed.

## TERMINATION OF OFFERS

After a court has determined the existence and content of an offer, it must determine the *duration* of the offer. Was the offer still in existence when the offeree attempted to accept it? If not, no contract was created and the offeree is himself treated as having made an offer that the original offeror is free to accept or reject. This is so because, by attempting to accept an offer that has terminated, the offeree has indicated a present intent to contract on the terms of the original offer even though he lacks the power to bind the offeror to a contract, due to the original offer's termination.

**Terms of the Offer.** The offeror is often said to be "the master of his offer." This means that offerors have the power to determine the terms and conditions under which they will be bound to a contract. An offeror may include terms in the offer that limit its effective life. These may be specific terms, such as "you must accept by December 5, 1986" or "this offer good for five days," or more general terms, such as "for immediate acceptance," "prompt wire acceptance," or "by return mail." General time limitation language in an offer can raise difficult problems of interpretation for courts trying to decide whether an offeree accepted before the offer terminated. Even more specific language, such as "this offer good for five days," can cause problems if the offer does not specify whether the five-day period begins when the offer is sent or when the offeree receives it. Not all courts agree on such questions, so wise offerors should be as specific as possible in stating when their offers terminate.

**Lapse of Time.** Offers that fail to provide a specific time for acceptance are valid for a *reasonable time.* What constitutes a reasonable time depends on the circumstances surrounding the offer. How long would a reasonable person in the offeree's position believe she had to accept the offer? Offers involving things subject to rapid fluctuations in value, such as stocks, bonds, or commodities futures, will have a very brief duration. The same is true for offers involving goods that may spoil, such as produce.

The nature of the parties' negotiations is another factor that is relevant to determining the duration of an offer. Most courts hold that when parties bargain face-to-face or over the telephone, the normal time for acceptance does not extend past the conclusion of their conversation unless the offeror indicates a contrary intention. Where negotiations are carried out by mail or telegram, the time for acceptance would ordinarily include at least the normal time for communicating the offer and a prompt response by the offeree. It is often said, for example, that a mailed offer is promptly accepted by an acceptance mailed at any time on the day the offer was received. However, the absence of any rapid fluctuations in the value of the items offered could operate to extend the time for acceptance. Finally, in cases where the parties have dealt with each other on a regular basis in the past, the timing of their prior transactions would be highly relevant in measuring the reasonable time for acceptance.

**Revocation.** As the master of his offer, an offeror can give an offeree the power to bind him to a contract by making an offer: he can also terminate that power by *revoking* his offer. The general common law rule on revocations is that offerors may revoke their offers *at any time prior to acceptance,* even if they have promised to hold the offer open for a stated period of time. However, there are several *exceptions* to this general rule that can operate to prevent an offeror from revoking.

**Options.** An **option** is a separate contract in which an offeror agrees not to revoke her offer for a stated time in exchange for some valuable consideration.[12] The offeree who enters an option contract has no obligation to accept the offeror's offer; in effect, she has merely purchased the right to consider the offer for the stated time without fear that the offeror will be allowed to revoke. The traditional common law rule on options requires the actual payment of the agreed-upon consideration before an option contract will become enforceable. Therefore, if, "in exchange for $100," Martin gave Berry a 30-day option to purchase his house for $150,000 and Berry never, in fact, paid the $100, no option was created and Martin could revoke his offer at any time prior to its acceptance by Berry.

**Firm Offers.** The Code makes a major change in the common law rules governing the revocability of offers by recognizing the concept of a **firm offer** [2–205]. A firm offer is irrevocable for the *time stated in the offer.* If no time is stated, it is irrevocable for a *reasonable time.* Regardless of the terms of the offer, the outer limit on a firm offer's irrevocability is *three months.* Not all offers for the sale of goods qualify as firm offers, however. To be a firm offer, an offer must be made by a *merchant* in a *signed writing* which contains *assurances* that the offer will be held open (some indication that it will not be revoked). An offer for the sale of goods that fails to satisfy these three requirements is governed by the general common law rule and revocable at any time prior to acceptance.

Indicating that an offer will be held open for a particular time can sometimes serve an offeror's interests because it may increase the likelihood of ultimate acceptance by an offeree who is given assurance that sufficient time will be available to investigate the merits of the offer. The receipt of such an offer creates obvious expectations about the duration of the offer in the minds of offerees, and it is these expectations that the Code's firm offer provision is designed to protect. In some cases, however, *offerees* are the true originators of an "assurance" term in an offer. When offerees have effective control of the terms of the offer by providing their customers with preprinted purchase order forms or order blanks, they may be tempted to take advantage of their merchant customers by placing an assurance term in their order forms. This would allow offerees to await market developments before deciding whether to fill the order, while their merchant customers, who may have signed the order without reading all of its terms, would be powerless to revoke. To prevent such unfairness, the Code requires that assurance terms on forms provided by offerees be *separately signed* by the offeror before a firm offer will result.

**Offers for Unilateral Contracts.** The general rule that an offeror can revoke at any time prior to acceptance causes special problems when applied to offers for unilateral contracts. Since the offeree in a unilateral contract must fully perform the requested act in order to accept, the application of the general rule would allow an offeror to revoke after the offeree had begun performance but before he had had a chance to complete it. To prevent injustice to offerees who rely on such offers by beginning performance, two basic approaches are available to modern courts. Some courts have held that once the offeree has begun to perform, the offeror's power to revoke is suspended for the amount of time reasonably necessary for the offeree to complete performance. Section 45 of the *Restatement Second* takes a similar approach for offers that unequivocally require acceptance by performance by saying that once the offeree begins performance, an "option contract" is created. The offeror's duty to perform his side of the bargain is conditional on full perfor-

[12] Consideration is discussed in detail in Chapter 10.

mance by the offeree. This approach clearly protects the offeree, but from an offeror's standpoint it is less than desirable because the offeree has no duty to complete the requested performance.

Another approach to the unilateral contract dilemma is to hold that a bilateral contract is created once the offeree begins performance. This is essentially the position taken by section 62 of the *Restatement Second,* which says that when the offer invites acceptance either by a return promise or performance, the beginning of performance operates as an acceptance and a promise by the offeree to render complete performance. This approach protects both the offeror and the offeree, but may be contrary to the actual intent of the parties, neither of whom may wish to be bound to a contract until complete performance is achieved.

**Promissory Estoppel.** In some cases, the doctrine of promissory estoppel can operate to prevent offerors from revoking their offers prior to acceptance. Section 87(2) of the *Restatement Second* says:

> An offer which the offeror should reasonably expect to induce action or forbearance of a substantial character on the part of the offeree before acceptance and which does induce such action or forbearance is binding as an option contract to the extent necessary to avoid injustice.

Promissory estoppel has often been used to prevent revocation in the bidding context. For example, Ace Construction Company, a general contractor, is bidding for the contract to build a new business school for Gigantic State University (GSU). Prime Plumbing, Inc., a plumbing subcontractor, submits a bid of $150,000 to Ace for the plumbing work on the GSU project. Prime's bid is the lowest bid that Ace receives, and since Prime has a good reputation, Ace uses Prime's figure in computing the bid it submits to GSU. Ace's bid is accepted by GSU, but before Ace can notify Prime and accept Prime's bid, Prime attempts to revoke the bid, citing rising labor and materials costs. The next lowest bid that Ace received for the plumbing work was for $200,000. Given these facts, many modern courts would hold that Prime is estopped from revoking. Prime has made a *promise* (its bid) that, given the nature of the bidding process, it should reasonably expect to induce reliance by Ace. Ace has, in fact, *relied* on Prime's bid by basing its offer to perform, in part, on Prime's bid. And Ace will now suffer injustice (the loss of $50,000 in profit) if Prime is allowed to revoke.

**Effectiveness of Revocations.** The question of when a revocation is effective to terminate an offer is often a critical issue in the contract formation process. For example, Davis offers to landscape Winter's property for $1,500. Two days after making the offer, Davis changes his mind and mails Winter a letter revoking the offer. The next day, Winter, who has not received Davis' letter, telephones Davis and attempts to accept. Contract? Yes, because the general rule on this point is that revocations are effective only when they are *actually received* by the offeree. The basic idea behind this rule is that the offeree is justified in relying on the intent to contract manifested by the offeror's offer until he actually knows that the offeror has changed his mind. This explains why many courts have also held that if the offeree receives reliable information indicating that the offeror has taken action inconsistent with an intent to enter the contract proposed by the offer (e.g., selling the property that was the subject of the offer to someone else), this will terminate the offer. In such circumstances, the offeree would be unjustified in believing that the offer could still be accepted.

The only major exception to the general rule on effectiveness of revocations concerns offers to the general public. Since it would be impossible in most cases to reach every offeree with a revocation, it is generally held that a revocation made in the same manner as the offer is effective when published, without proof of communication to the offeree.

**Rejection.** An offeree may *expressly reject* an offer by indicating that he is unwilling to accept it. He may also *impliedly reject* it by making a **counteroffer,** an offer to contract on terms materially different from the terms of the offer.[13] As a general rule, either form of rejection by the offeree terminates his power to accept the offer. This is so because an offeror who receives a rejection may rely on the offeree's expressed desire not to accept the offer by making another offer to a different offeree. Therefore, if either party manifests an intent to keep the offer open despite a rejection, many courts will hold that no termination has occurred. If the offeror indicates in the offer that it will continue in effect despite a rejection, there is no need to fear that he will rely on rejection terminating the offer. Likewise, if the offeree indicates that she rejects the offer at the present time but will take it under advisement in the future, there is no basis for reliance by the offeror. One further exception to the general rule that rejections terminate offers concerns offers that are the subject of an option contract. Some courts hold that a rejection does not terminate an option contract and that the offeree who rejects still has the power to accept the offer later, so long as the acceptance is effective within the option period.[14]

**Effectiveness of Rejections.** As a general rule, rejections, like revocations, are effective only when *actually received* by the offeror. This is because there is no probability that the offeror will rely on a rejection by making another offer to a different offeree until she actually has notice of the rejection. Therefore, an offeree who has mailed a rejection could still change her mind and accept if she communicates the acceptance before the offeror receives the rejection.[15]

**Death or Insanity of Either Party.** The death or insanity of either party to an offer automatically (without notice) terminates the offer. A "meeting of the minds" is obviously impossible when one of the parties has died or become insane.

**Destruction of Subject Matter.** If, prior to an acceptance of an offer, the subject matter of a proposed contract is destroyed without the knowledge or fault of either party, the offer is terminated.[16] So, if Marks offers to sell Wiggins his lakeside cottage and the cottage is destroyed by fire before Wiggins accepts, the offer was terminated upon the destruction of the cottage and a subsequent acceptance by Wiggins would not create a contract.

**Intervening Illegality.** An offer is terminated if the performance of the contract it proposes becomes illegal before the offer is accepted. So, if a grain elevator has offered to sell wheat to a representative of the Soviet Union, but two days later, before the offer has been accepted, Congress places an embargo on all grain sales to the Soviet Union to protest the invasion of Afghanistan, the offer is terminated by the embargo.[17]

[13] Counteroffers are discussed in detail in Chapter 8.

[14] Section 37 of the *Restatement Second* adopts this rule.

[15] This subject is discussed in detail in Chapter 8.

[16] In some circumstances, destruction of subject matter can also serve as a legal excuse for a party's failure to perform his obligations under an existing contract. This subject is discussed in Chapter 15.

[17] In some circumstances, intervening illegality can also serve as a legal excuse for a party's failure to perform his obligations under an existing contract. This subject is discussed in Chapter 15.

## Berryman v. Kmoch

### 559 P.2d 790 (Kan. Sup. Ct. 1977)

On June 19, 1973, Wade Berryman signed an option agreement giving Norbert Kmoch, a real estate broker, a 120-day option to purchase 960 acres of Berryman's land in exchange for "$10.00 and other valuable consideration." Berryman, however, never received any payment for the option. Kmoch hired two agricultural consultants to produce a farm report that he intended to use to interest other investors in joining him to exercise the option. In the latter part of July 1973, Berryman telephoned Kmoch and asked to be released from the option agreement. Nothing definite was agreed to, and Berryman later sold the land to another person. In August, Kmoch decided to exercise the option and contacted the Federal Land Bank representative in Garden City, Kansas, to make arrangements to buy the land. After being told by the bank representative that Berryman had sold the property, Kmoch sent Berryman a letter attempting to exercise the option. Berryman filed a declaratory judgment suit to have the option declared null and void. The trial court ruled in favor of Berryman, and Kmoch appealed.

**Fromme, Justice.** An option contract to purchase land must be supported by consideration the same as any other contract. An option contract which is not supported by consideration is a mere offer to sell which may be withdrawn at any time prior to acceptance. Kmoch contends that the option contract should have been enforceable under the doctrine of promissory estoppel.

In order for the doctrine of promissory estoppel to be invoked as a substitute for consideration the evidence must show (1) the promise was made under such circumstances that the promisor reasonably expected the promisee to act in reliance on the promise, (2) the promisee acted as could reasonably be expected in relying on the promise, and (3) a refusal by the court to enforce the promise must be virtually to sanction the perpetration of fraud or must result in other injustice.

The requirements are not met here. This was an option contract promising to sell the land to Kmoch. It was not a contract listing the real estate with Kmoch for sale to others. Kmoch was familiar with real estate contracts and personally drew up the present option. He knew no consideration was paid for it and that it had the effect of a continuing offer subject to withdrawal at any time before acceptance. The evidence which Kmoch desires to introduce in support of promissory estoppel does not relate to acts which could reasonably be expected as a result of extending the option promise. It relates to time, effort, and expense incurred in an attempt to interest other investors in this particular land.

Now we turn to the question of revocation or withdrawal of the option-promise before acceptance. Where an offer is for the sale of an interest in land or in other things, if the offeror, after making the offer, sells or contracts to sell the interest to another person, and the offeree acquires reliable information of that fact, before he has exercised his power of creating a contract by acceptance of that offer, the offer is revoked.

Kmoch admitted that Berryman told him over the telephone that he no longer wanted to be obligated by the option. He further admitted being advised by a representative of the bank that Berryman had disposed of his land. Kmoch's power of acceptance was thereby terminated and his attempted exercise of the option later came too late.

Judgment for Berryman affirmed.

## Chaplin v. Consolidated Edison Co. of New York

**537 F. Supp. 1224 (S.D.N.Y. 1982)**

Phyllis Chaplin and the Epilepsy Foundation of America filed a class action suit against Consolidated Edison (Con Ed) alleging that Con Ed discriminated against epileptics in violation of Sections 503 and 504 of the Rehabilitation Act of 1973. In August 1981, Con Ed's lawyer sent Chaplin's lawyer a settlement proposal approved by Con Ed. Chaplin's lawyer wrote back, stating that Chaplin and the Foundation had "a series of objections to the proposed settlement." On September 16, 1981, Con Ed's lawyer sent a letter in reply, which said:

> We are still willing to finalize the agreement as it presently stands, thereby resolving this matter. Any further negotiation is an impossibility; and if this agreement is not satisfactory to your client in its present form, then I must withdraw all offers of settlement.

Chaplin's lawyer answered in a letter dated September 17, 1981, which said:

> Based on my previous communications with my clients, I believed that I could convince them to accept the proffered terms. Unfortunately, that was not the case. After careful consideration they presented objections which have substantial merit.

The settlement climate changed dramatically that same day, when the Second Circuit Court of Appeals held in *Davis v. United Air Lines* that Section 503 of the Rehabilitation Act did not create a private cause of action. On September 30, 1981, Chaplin's lawyer informed Con Ed's lawyer that Chaplin and the Foundation had had "a change of heart" and decided to accept the settlement offer. Con Ed's lawyer replied by telephone that the settlement was no longer acceptable. Chaplin and the Foundation filed a motion for an injunction ordering Con Ed to execute the settlement proposal, arguing that they had accepted it by their "change of heart" letter.

**Lasker, District Judge.** The inquiry turns upon a careful reading of the letters of September 16th and 17th. In her letter of September 16th, Con Ed's lawyer stated that the offer was still open. However, she emphatically limited the offer:
"If this agreement is not satisfactory to your client in its present form, then I must withdraw all offers of settlement." Con Ed's position was explicit: take it or leave it. Plaintiffs' counsel wrote in reply that he could not convince his clients "to acccept the proffered terms." While it is true that the letter does not reject the possibility of arriving at *some* settlement, it does reject the settlement proposed by Con Ed. The offer, as noted above, had been limited to the precise terms proffered and a rejection of those terms could only be a rejection of the offer. Reading the two letters together, we can only conclude that the September 17th letter was a rejection of Con Ed's offer.

An offer is extinguished upon rejection. Thus, at the time of plaintiff's purported acceptance, no offer existed.

Motion by Chaplin denied.

## SUMMARY

Courts seeking to determine the existence of a contract look for evidence of a "meeting of the minds" of the parties. The first step in this process is to determine whether an offer existed that, when accepted by the offeree, resulted in the formation of a contract. An offer is a combination of facts and circumstances that objectively indicate a present intent to contract on the part of the offeror. Traditional contract law principles require that an alleged offer be definite and specific and be communicated to the offeree by the offeror. Modern contract principles embodied in the UCC and the *Restatement (Second) of Contracts,* however, require a significantly lesser degree of definiteness in offers, with the result that courts applying these principles are more likely to recognize the existence of a contract and, in some cases, to supply contract terms omitted or left indefinite by the parties.

Several kinds of common business situations involve questions concerning the existence of offers. Advertisements, price quotes, catalogs, signs, and so forth are generally treated as invitations to offer. As a result, would-be buyers in such cases are normally treated as offerors, not offerees. Under some extraordinary circumstances, however, an advertisement or a price quote can amount to an offer. Offers of rewards are generally treated as offers for unilateral contracts that can only be accepted by performance of the act that the reward requests. Bids are generally treated as offers that the bidder may revoke at any time prior to acceptance and that the offeree is free to accept or reject. In some circumstances, an offeree's reliance on a bid may operate to estop the offeror from revoking it. Bidders at auctions are normally treated as making offers unless the auction is "without reserve," in which case the seller is treated as having made an offer to sell to the highest bidder that cannot be revoked once bidding starts.

Modern courts hold that offerees are bound by all the terms in the offer that they have "reasonable notice" of. In some cases, this means that fine print terms or terms on the back of the contract will not become part of the parties' contract. Disclaimers and exculpatory clauses are particularly likely to be excluded from a contract on this basis.

The duration of offers is limited. Offerees who attempt to accept terminated offers are treated as having made an offer that the original offeror is free to accept or reject. An offer may expire by its own terms or, if no terms are stated, after the passage of a reasonable time. As a general rule, offerors can revoke their offers at any time prior to acceptance. There are several limitations on this rule, however. Offerors who enter option contracts, agreeing not to revoke in exchange for some valuable consideration, cannot revoke for the option period. The Code recognizes the concept of an irrevocable "firm offer" which applies to offers for the sale of goods that meet certain other qualifications. Promissory estoppel may also operate to prevent revocation in some circumstances. Finally, once an offeree attempts to accept an offer for a unilateral contract by beginning performance of the acts requested by the offer, modern courts employ a variety of theories to prevent the offeror from revoking prior to the offeree's completion of performance.

Rejection of an offer by the offeree, whether express or implied, will also terminate the offer. Both revocations and rejections are effective only when actually communicated to the other party. The death or insanity of either party automatically terminates an offer. Likewise, destruction of the subject matter of an offer or the subsequent illegality of the performance called for by an offer will also cause termination.

## PROBLEM CASES

1. Treece was a vice president of Vend-A-Win, Inc., a manufacturer of punchboards. While testifying before the Washington State Game Commission, he said, "I'll put up $100,000 to anyone who can find a crooked board. If they find it, I'll pay it." The statement evoked laughter from the audience. Barnes heard Treece's statement repeated on a TV newscast and then read a report of the hearings. He had two fraudulent punchboards that he had purchased a few years earlier while working as a bartender. He later traveled to Seattle, met Treece and Vend-A-Win's secretary-treasurer, and turned over a punchboard, receiving a signed receipt in return. Both Treece and Vend-A-Win refused to pay the $100,000. Is Barnes entitled to the money?

2. On July 31, 1966, Calan Imports advertised a 1964 Volvo station wagon for sale in the *Chicago Sun-Times.* Calan had instructed the newspaper to advertise the price of the automobile at $1,795. However, through an error of the newspaper and without fault on Calan's part, the price given was $1,095. O'Brian visited Calan's place of business, examined the automobile, and stated that he wished to purchase it for $1,095. One of Calan's salesmen at first agreed, but then refused, to sell the car for the erroneous price listed in the advertisement. O'Brian brought suit against Calan for an alleged breach of contract. Was O'Brian entitled to the car?

3. Korea Tungsten Mining Company (KTM) owned a parcel of real estate in Manhattan. KTM placed newspaper ads indicating that it would accept "sealed written bids" for the property and that the property would be sold to the highest bidder. When the bids were opened, Nova-Park New York, Inc. (Nova), had bid $750,000. S.S.I. Investors Limited (S.S.I.) had submitted an "alternative" bid, which read: "The total price of Five Hundred and Fifty-six Thousand dollars ($556,000) and/or one dollar ($1.00) more than the highest bidding price you have received for the above property." Counsel for KTM was initially unsure as to who had submitted the highest bid. KTM's counsel rejected S.S.I.'s bid a few days later, and afterward sold the land to Nova. S.S.I. then sued for specific performance, claiming it had a contract with KTM. Did KTM enter a contract to sell the land to S.S.I.?

4. Gust Paloukos visited the showrooms of Glen's Chevrolet and agreed to purchase a 1974 ¾-ton Chevrolet pickup from George Rowe, one of Glen's salesmen. Rowe filled out a form headed "WORK SHEET—This is NOT a Purchase Order" in bold print. The form indicated Paloukos's name and address and described the truck as a new yellow or green 1974 ¾-ton, four-wheel-drive vehicle with a radio, V–8 engine, and automatic transmission at a purchase price of $3,650. Rowe printed his name in a space provided for the salesman's name, and Paloukos signed at the bottom of the form (no signature line was provided). Glen's sales manager approved the sale, and Paloukos paid a $120 deposit and was told that the truck would be ordered. Five months later, Glen's sent Paloukos a letter stating that, due to "a product shortage," Glen's would be unable to deliver the truck

and returned his deposit. Paloukos filed suit for breach of contract. Glen's argued that the worksheet was too indefinite to create a contract. Did Paloukos have a contract with Glen's?

**5.** Stanley A. Klopp, Inc. had been an authorized John Deere dealer since 1936 and had entered into annual dealer franchise agreements. In 1965, the contract for the first time contained a clause that barred dealers from recovering lost future profits if John Deere decided not to renew the franchise. In May 1978, Deere notified Klopp that it would not offer Klopp a new contract in October 1979. Klopp filed suit for lost future profits, claiming that the future profits clause was invalid because its president had not read the agreements he signed, believing them to be substantially similar to earlier dealership agreements that he had signed with Deere. Was the future profits clause enforceable against Klopp?

**6.** Nicholas Hermes owned 20 percent of the outstanding shares of the William F. Meyer Company. Hermes entered an option agreement with Melvin Meyer, a director of the company, giving Meyer the right to buy his stock for $60,000 at any time between March 1, 1975, and September 1, 1977. The option said that $1 and other valuable consideration had been given to support it. No consideration was ever actually given to Hermes. On June 8, 1977, Hermes sent Meyer a letter attempting to withdraw the option. On August 6, 1977, Meyer sent Hermes a letter and a certified check for $60,000, attempting to accept the option. Hermes later sued the William F. Meyer Company to compel its liquidation and the distribution of its assets to shareholders. The company argued that Hermes no longer had an interest in the company since Meyer had exercised the option. Was Hermes's offer to sell an enforceable option?

**7.** Century 21 operated a racetrack and sent a letter to numerous race drivers stating that the point leader in the Figure 8 division at the end of the season would receive a $2,000 bonus. David Sigrist raced in all of the Figure 8 races held at Century's track and was the point leader when Century cut the season short on the ground that there were not enough entries to put on a good show for spectators. Century refused to pay Sigrist the bonus, claiming that it had revoked its offer before acceptance by Sigrist and that, since the season ended early, Sigrist had not completed the performance requested by the offer. Had Sigrist accepted Century's offer before revocation?

**8.** James Lowenstern observed that Bradlees, a store operated by Stop & Shop Companies, often priced popular records substantially below the average retail market price. He decided to go into a wholesale record business, buying records from Bradlees and reselling them to other retail stores at a profit. Bradlees had a policy of offering "rain checks" to customers when its supply of an advertised item ran out. The rain check included the customer's name, the item, and its price, and was signed by a store employee. On April 4, 1979, Lowenstern appeared at Bradlees with several rain checks, some dated in 1978 and four dated February 19, 1979. Lowenstern attempted to use the rain checks to buy all the sale records that Bradlees had in stock. Bradlees refused to sell, and Lowenstern filed suit. The evidence indicated that on February 19, 1979, Bradlees's manager had told Lowenstern that rain checks would not be honored for more than 20 copies of any record. Were the rain checks enforceable firm offers under the Code?

**9.** De Santis Construction Company submitted a $275,000 bid over the telephone to James King & Son, Inc. for the concrete work on a new Macy's store to be built in the Sunrise Mall at Massapequa, Long Island. After confirming De Santis's bid, King, a general contractor, submitted a $3,917,000 bid to

Macy's for the complete project. King's bid included De Santis's $275,000 figure for the concrete work. King was ultimately awarded the contract with Macy's and advised De Santis that it was awarding De Santis the concrete subcontract. King asked De Santis to execute a written subcontract on a standard form that King regularly used with its subcontractors. De Santis refused to sign the agreement, arguing that its bid was too indefinite to amount to an offer and that therefore no contract had resulted between the parties. King had to hire another subcontractor to do the concrete work for $44,000 more than De Santis's bid. Is King entitled to recover the $44,000 as damages for breach of contract?

**10.** Harley McKibben and Adolph and Randolph Vetter owned a mining claim near Fairbanks, Alaska. They entered a mining lease agreement with Mohawk Oil and Gas, Inc. that gave them the right to 45 percent of the value of all ores and minerals extracted from the claim after the deduction of mining and smelting costs. On October 9, 1979, their attorney, Richard Savell, sent Mohawk a letter disputing the meaning of certain lease provisions and accusing Mohawk of diluting the ore and removing precious metals from the mine without reporting this to his clients. The letter demanded an accounting and stated that "lessors hereby declare that they are immediately entitled to 45 percent of the ore presently stockpiled" and that "in order to reach an understanding short of civil litigation, please contact this office within 20 days of the date of this letter." On October 31, 1979, Mohawk's attorney wrote to Savell denying his allegations but accepting his offer to settle the dispute. Savell later advised Mohawk that his letter was not an offer to settle his clients' claim, and on March 21, 1980, he filed suit against Mohawk. Mohawk moved for a summary judgment, arguing that the parties had reached a binding settlement of their dispute. Is Mohawk's argument correct?

# Chapter 8

# The Agreement: Acceptance

## WHAT IS AN ACCEPTANCE?

Since the idea of *mutual agreement* lies at the heart of traditional contract law, a court that has determined that one of the parties to a dispute made an *offer* next seeks to determine whether the offeree *accepted* that offer. In this inquiry, the court is looking for the same *present intent to contract* on the part of the offeree that it found on the part of the offeror. The difference is that the offeree must objectively indicate a present intent to contract *on the terms of the offer* before a contract will result. The offeror, as the "master of his offer," may specify in detail what behavior is required of the offeree in order to bind him to a contract. If the offeror does so, the offeree must ordinarily comply with all the terms of the offer before a contract will result. These requirements for acceptance are evident in the *Restatement (Second) of Contracts* definition of an **acceptance** as "a manifestation of assent to the terms [of the offer] made by the offeree in the manner invited or required by the offer."[1]

[1] *Restatement (Second) of Contracts* § 50(1) (1979).

**Intention to Accept: Counteroffers.** The traditional contract law rule is that an acceptance must be the "mirror image" of the offer. Attempts by offerees to change the terms of the offer or to add new terms to it are treated as **counteroffers** because they impliedly indicate an intent by the offeree to reject the offer instead of being bound by its terms. However, if an offeree merely asks about the terms of the offer without indicating its rejection (an *inquiry regarding terms*), or accepts the offer's terms while complaining about them (a *grumbling acceptance*), no rejection will be implied. Also, recent years have witnessed a judicial tendency to apply the "mirror image" rule in a more liberal fashion by holding that only "material" variances between an offer and a purported acceptance will result in an implied rejection of the offer. Distinguishing among a counteroffer, an inquiry regarding terms, and a grumbling acceptance is often a difficult task. The fundamental issue, however, remains the same: Did the offeree objectively indicate a present intent to be bound by the terms of the offer?

**The "Battle of the Forms."** Strictly applying the mirror image rule to modern commercial transactions, most of which are carried out by using preprinted form contracts, would often result in frustrating the parties' true intent. Offerors use standard order forms prepared by their lawyers, and offerees use standard acceptance or acknowledgment forms drafted by their counsel. The odds that these forms will agree in every detail are slight, as are the odds that the parties will read each other's forms in their entirety. Instead, the parties to such transactions are likely to read only crucial provisions concerning the kinds of goods ordered, their price, and the delivery date called for, and if these terms are agreeable, believe that they have a contract. If a dispute arose before the parties started to perform, however, a court strictly applying the mirror-image rule would hold that no contract resulted, due to the variance in their forms. If a dispute arose after performance had commenced, the court would probably hold that the offeror had impliedly accepted the offeree's counteroffer and was bound by its terms.

Since neither of these results is very satisfactory, the Code, in a very controversial provision often called the "Battle of the Forms" section [2–207], has changed the common law mirror-image rule for contracts involving the sale of goods. The Code provides that a definite and timely *expression of acceptance* creates a contract, even if it includes terms that are *different* from those stated in the offer or even if it states *additional* terms on points that the offer did not address [2–207(1)]. The only exception to this rule occurs when the attempted acceptance is *expressly conditional* on the offeror's agreement to the terms of the acceptance [2–207(1)]. In such a case, no contract is created.

What are the terms of a contract created in this fashion? This has been the subject of considerable disagreement among the courts and legal scholars. The Code clearly says that if the parties are both *merchants*, the *additional* terms become part of the contract unless: (1) the offer *expressly* limited acceptance to its own terms; (2) the new terms would *materially alter* the nature of the offer; or (3) the offeror gives *notice of objection* to the new terms within a reasonable time after receiving the acceptance [2–207(2)].

The major disagreement centers on what happens to any *different* terms (those contradicting a term in the offer) contained in the acceptance. The Code is silent on this point. The language of the statute suggests that such terms do not become part of the contract, but is the offeree bound by terms in the offer that the acceptance indicates he or she objects to? Some commentators say yes, but others argue that the different terms should cancel out conflicting terms in the offer. This is clearly what happens when the offeree has made his acceptance expressly conditional on the offeror's agreement to the new terms or when the offeree's response to the offer is clearly not "an expression of acceptance" (e.g., an express rejection). In such cases, the Code provides that conduct by the parties that "recognizes the existence of a contract" (e.g., an exchange of performance) creates a contract. The terms of this contract are those on which the parties' writings *agree,* supplemented by appropriate gap-filling provisions from the Code [2–207(3)].

**Acceptance in Unilateral Contracts.** A unilateral contract involves the exchange of a promise for an act. To accept an offer to enter such a contract, the offeree must *perform the requested act.* As you learned in the last chapter, however, courts applying modern contract rules may prevent an offeror from revoking such an offer once the offeree has begun performance. This is achieved by holding either that a bilateral contract is created by the beginning of performance or that the offeror's power to revoke is suspended for the period of time reasonably necessary for the offeree to complete performance.

**Acceptance in Bilateral Contracts.** A bilateral contract involves the exchange of a promise for a promise. As a general rule, to accept an offer to enter such a contract, an offeree must *make the promise requested by the offer.* This may be done in a variety of ways. For example, Wallace sends Stevens a detailed offer for the purchase of Stevens's business. Within the time period prescribed by the offer, Stevens sends Wallace a letter that says, "I accept your offer." Stevens has *expressly* accepted Wallace's offer, creating a contract on the terms of the offer. Acceptance, however, can be *implied* as well as *express.* Offerees who take action that objectively indicates agreement risk the formation of a contract. For example, offerees who act in a manner that is inconsistent with an offeror's ownership of offered property are commonly held to have accepted the offeror's terms. So, if Arnold, a farmer, leaves 10 bushels of corn with Porter, the owner of a grocery store, saying, "Look this corn over. If you want it, it's $5 a bushel," and Porter sells the corn, he has impliedly accepted Arnold's offer. But what if Porter just let the corn sit and when Arnold returned a week later, Porter told Arnold that he did not want it? Could Porter's failure to act ever amount to an acceptance?

**Silence as Acceptance.** Since contract law generally requires some objective indication that an offeree intends to contract, the general rule is that an offeree's silence, without more, is *not* an acceptance. In addition, it is generally held that an offeror cannot impose on the offeree a duty to respond to the offer. So, even if Arnold had said to Porter, "If I don't hear from you in three days, I'll assume you're buying the corn," Porter's silence would still not amount to acceptance.

On the other hand, the circumstances of a case sometimes impose a duty on the offeree to reject the offer affirmatively or be bound by its terms. These are cases in which the offeree's silence objectively indicates an intent to accept. Customary trade practice or prior dealings between the parties may indicate that silence signals acceptance. So, if Arnold and Porter had dealt with each other on numerous prior occasions and Porter had always promptly returned items that he did not want, Porter's silent retention of the goods for a week would probably constitute an acceptance. Likewise, an offeree's silence can also operate as an acceptance if the offeree has indicated that it will (e.g., Porter tells Arnold, "If you don't hear from me in three days, I accept").

Finally, it is generally held that offerees who accept an offeror's performance knowing what the offeror expects in return for his performance have impliedly accepted the offeror's terms. So, if Apex Paving Corporation offers to do the paving work on a new subdivision being developed by Majestic Homes Corporation, and Majestic fails to respond to Apex's offer but allows Apex to do the work, most courts would hold that Majestic is bound by the terms of Apex's offer.

**Acceptance When a Writing Is Anticipated.** Frequently, the parties to a contract intend to prepare a written draft of their agreement for both parties to sign. This is a good idea not only because the law requires written evidence of some kinds of contracts,[2] but also because it provides written evidence of the terms of the agreement if a dispute arises at a later date. If a dispute arises before such a writing has been prepared or signed, however, a question may arise concerning whether the signing of the agreement was a necessary condition to the creation of a contract. A party to the agreement who now wants out of the deal may argue that the parties did not intend to be bound until both parties signed the writing. A clear expression of such an intent by the parties during the negotiation process will prevent the formation of a contract until both parties have signed. However, in the absence of such a clear expression of intent, the courts will ask whether a reasonable person familiar with all the circumstances of the parties' negotiations would conclude that the parties intended to be bound only when a formal agreement was signed. If it appears that the parties had concluded their negotiations and reached agreement on all the essential aspects of the transaction, most courts would probably find a contract at the time agreement was reached, even though no formal agreement had been signed.

**Acceptance of Ambiguous Offers.** Although offerors have the power to specify the manner in which their offer can be accepted by requiring that the offeree make a return promise (a bilateral contract) or perform a specific act (a unilateral contract), often an offer is unclear about which form of acceptance is necessary to create a contract. In such a case, both the Code [2–206(1)(a)] and the *Restatement Second*[3] suggest that the offer may be accepted in any manner that is *reasonable* in light of the circumstances surrounding the offer. Thus, either a promise to perform or performance, if reasonable, will create a contract.

**Acceptance by Shipment.** The Code specifically elaborates on the rule stated in the preceding section by stating that an order requesting "prompt" or "current" shipment of goods may be accepted either by a *prompt promise to ship* or by a *prompt* or *current shipment* of the goods [2–206(1)(b)]. So, if Ampex Corporation orders 500 IBM typewriters from Marks Office Supply, to be shipped "immediately," Marks could accept either by promptly promising to ship the goods or by promptly shipping them. If Marks decided to accept by shipping, any subsequent attempt by Ampex to revoke the order would be ineffective.

But what if Marks did not have 500 IBMs in stock and Marks knew that Ampex desperately needed the goods? Marks might be tempted to ship another brand of typewriters, hoping that Ampex would be forced by its circumstances to accept them because by the time they arrived, it would be too late to get the correct goods elsewhere. Marks would argue that by shipping the wrong goods it had made a counteroffer because it had not performed the act requested by Ampex's order. If Ampex accepts the goods, Marks could argue that Ampex has impliedly accepted the

[2] This subject is discussed in detail in Chapter 13.

[3] *Restatement (Second) of Contracts* § 30(2)(1979).

counteroffer. If Ampex rejects the goods, Marks would arguably have no liability since it did not accept the order. The Code prevents such a result by providing that prompt shipment of either *conforming* goods (what the order asked for) or *nonconforming* goods (something else) will operate as an acceptance of the order [2–206(1)(b)]. This protects such buyers as Ampex because sellers who ship the wrong goods have simultaneously *accepted* their offers and *breached* the contract by sending the wrong merchandise.

But what if Marks is an honest seller that is merely trying to help out a customer that has placed a "rush" order? Must it expose itself to liability for breach of contract in the process? The Code prevents such a result by providing that no contract is created if the seller notifies the buyer within a reasonable time that the shipment of nonconforming goods is intended as an "accommodation" [2–206(1)(b)]. In this case, the shipment is merely a counteroffer that the buyer is free to accept or reject and the seller's notification gives the buyer the opportunity to seek the goods he needs elsewhere.

**Who Can Accept an Offer?** The only person with the legal power to accept an offer and create a contract is the *original offeree.* An attempt to accept by anyone other than the offeree is treated as an offer, since the party attempting to accept is indicating a present intent to contract on the original offer's terms. For example, Price offers to sell his car to Waterhouse for $5,000. Anderson learns of the offer, calls Price, and attempts to accept. Anderson has made an offer that Price is free to accept or reject.

## Rybin Investment Co. v. Wade

**316 N.W.2d 744 (Neb. Sup. Ct. 1982)**

Howard Wade and Robert Dalton submitted a signed written offer to purchase the Cottonwood Marina to Rybin Investment Company, the marina's owner. The offer included the following statement:

> Seller agrees that no verbal agreements exist that could restrict purchasers in future operations.

George Rybin, the president of Rybin Investment, signed the offer after adding the following language to the front of the document:

> It is understood and agreed that the present tenant, Robert Tank, has first right of refusal on this offer.

When Rybin's agent returned the offer to Wade and Dalton, he put two circles next to the altered portion of the document and asked them to initial it. They refused to do so, and after showing it to their financial backers, they told Rybin's agent that they would not approve the contract. Subsequent negotiations over the purchase of the marina fell through, and Rybin filed suit for specific performance of the agreement. The trial court ordered specific performance, and Wade and Dalton appealed.

**WHITE, JUSTICE.** The acceptance of the offer must be an unconditional acceptance of the offer as made, otherwise no contract is formed. There must be no substantial variation between the offer and the acceptance. If the acceptance differs from the offer or is coupled with any condition that varies or adds to the offer, it is not an acceptance, but it is a counterproposition. The basic question is whether the language added by Rybin constitutes a counteroffer.

We believe that the language Rybin added to the document substantially alters the offer so as to constitute a counteroffer. Wade and Dalton testified that the statement concerning existing verbal agreements was put in the offer because they knew that Mr. Tank had requested a right of first refusal from Rybin. The language that Rybin added to the document substantially alters the purpose for which Wade and Dalton had their particular statements put into the offer.

Our past decisions have been in accord with the view taken by the *Restatement Second:* "Where one to whom an offer is made makes a counter-proposition of different terms and new conditions, such counter-proposition amounts to a rejection of the offer." *Farmers Union Fidelity Ins. Co. v. Farmers Union Co-op Ins. Co.* (1947). Rybin's power to accept the offer was thereby terminated and no contract exists.

Judgment reversed in favor of Wade and Dalton.

## CBS, Inc. v. Auburn Plastics, Inc.

**413 N.Y.S.2d 50 (N.Y. Sup. Ct. 1979)**

In September 1973, Auburn Plastics submitted price quotations to CBS for the manufacture of eight cavity molds to be used in making CBS's toys. The quotations were based on drawings and samples that CBS had previously submitted to Auburn. Each quotation was headed by the word "PROPOSAL" and contained numerous terms regarding the proposed agreement between the parties. Among other things, the quotations included a term requiring acceptance by CBS within 15 days of the date of the quotation and an underlined sentence stating that the conditions on the reverse side of the proposal were part of the proposal and all subsequent orders. One condition stated on the reverse side gave Auburn the right to an additional 30 percent withdrawal charge above the quoted price of molds and tools if CBS demanded delivery of the molds.

In December 1973 and January 1974, CBS sent Auburn detailed purchase orders for eight molds. The orders all contained a provision stating that Auburn's acceptance of the orders meant that Auburn understood and accepted all of the terms included in the orders. The orders gave CBS the right to remove the molds from Auburn at any time without an additional withdrawal charge and provided that no modification of the terms of the orders would be binding on CBS unless it was agreed to in writing by CBS.

Auburn responded to the purchase orders by sending acknowledgment forms which stated that the sale was subject to the terms and conditions of its price quotations. CBS paid for the molds and ordered toy parts from Auburn that were made from the molds. In May 1978, Auburn announced a price increase, and CBS then requested delivery of the molds. Auburn refused to deliver unless CBS paid the 30 percent withdrawal charge. CBS filed suit to recover the molds. The trial court ruled in CBS's favor and Auburn appealed.

**CARDAMONE, JUSTICE.** The earliest communications between the parties are Auburn's price quotations. While it appears that the quotations were sufficiently detailed and specific to constitute offers, CBS did not respond to them until months after 15 days had passed. Thus, the purchase orders submitted by CBS did not create enforceable contracts since they had no binding effect on Auburn.

In our view, CBS's purchase orders constituted offers to buy the molds, and Auburn's acknowledgements of those orders represented its acceptance of the offers. While the acknowledgements incorporate the conditions contained in the price quotations and therefore conflict with the terms of the offer on the matter of the mold withdrawal charge, they are nonetheless operable as acceptances since they are not expressly made conditional on CBS's consent to the different terms [U.C.C. § 2–207(1)].

Whether the condition in Auburn's acknowledgements calling for the additional withdrawal charge become a part of the contracts requires the application of subsection 2–207(2) of the Code. The parties are clearly merchants and, therefore, since the purchase orders expressly limited acceptance to their terms [2–207(2)(a)] and also because notification of objection to a withdrawal charge was implicitly given by CBS [2–207(2)(c)], the provision for such a charge did not become part of the contracts.

Judgment for CBS affirmed.

## Barton Chemical Corp. v. Pennwalt Corp.

**399 N.E.2d 288 (Ill. Ct. App. 1979)**

After protracted negotiations, Barton reached an oral understanding with Pennwalt concerning the third in a series of two-year chemical requirements contracts entered by the parties. The parties' prior contracts had required approval by Pennwalt's home office before any negotiated agreement was binding on Pennwalt. Pennwalt sent a letter to Barton confirming the terms of the oral agreement and stating that it would forward a contract as soon as its new contract forms were printed. This was never done, but the purchase of the chemicals went forward during the first year of the alleged contract period. When Pennwalt asked for a price increase, Barton filed suit, arguing that a contract existed under the terms of Pennwalt's letter. Pennwalt argued that the letter required the signing of a formal document before a contract existed. The trial court ruled in Pennwalt's favor, and Barton appealed.

**MCGLOON, JUSTICE.** In Illinois, whether a binding contract exists only after formal documents are executed is a question of intent. The mere reference to the execution of a formal, written contract does not necessarily end the inquiry as to what the parties intended. As noted in *Lambert Corp. v. Evans* (1978),

> Even if the parties agree, point by point, on all the terms of a contract, if they understand that the execution of a formal document shall be a prerequisite to their being bound, there is no contract until the document is executed. On the other hand, if it is agreed that a formal document will be prepared to memorialize a bargain the parties have already made, the bargain is enforceable even though the document has not been executed.

In the present case, prior dealings between Barton and Pennwalt would indicate that a formal contract approved by Pennwalt's home office was a condition precedent to a binding contract and that the confirmation letter was only provisional. Yet, the fact remains that while no formal, written contract was ever executed, effective November 1, 1974, the parties began complying with the new price and quantity terms set forth in Pennwalt's confirmation letter. Their conduct thus indicates that both parties intended to be bound even in the absence of a formal contract. Though Pennwalt now challenges the validity of the agreement, it is doing so only after reaping the benefits of the terms it sought, namely, increases in the price and quantity of chlorine and caustic soda to be sold to Barton. Consequently, we find little merit to Pennwalt's contention that a binding contract did not exist. We conclude that the conduct of the parties and the clear language of the letter firmly establishes that the parties renegotiated the price and quantity terms of the contract.

Judgment reversed in favor of Barton.

## COMMUNICATION OF ACCEPTANCE

**Necessity of Communication.** To accept an offer for a *bilateral contract,* the offeree must make the *promise* requested by the offer. In Chapter 7, you learned that an offeror must communicate the terms of his proposal to the offeree before an offer will result. This was so because communication is a necessary component of the present intent to contract required for the creation of an offer. For similar reasons, it is generally held that an offeree must communicate his intent to be bound by the offer before a contract will be created. To accept an offer for a *unilateral contract,* however, the offeree must *perform the requested act.* The traditional contract law rule on this point assumes that the offeror will learn of the offeree's performance and holds that no further notice from the offeree is necessary to create a contract unless the offeror specifically requests notice. Because this rule can sometimes cause hardship to offerors who may not, in fact, know that the offeree has commenced performance, the Code and the *Restatement Second* have modified the traditional rule. If the offeree has reason to know that the offeror has no way of learning of his performance with reasonable promptness and certainty, the *Restatement Second*[4] provides that the offeror is discharged from any contractual obligation unless the offeree takes reasonable steps to notify him of performance, the offeror learns of performance within a reasonable time, or the offer indicates that notification of acceptance is not required.

The Code takes a different approach by saying that in cases where the *beginning of performance* operates as an acceptance, an offeror who is not notified of acceptance within a reasonable time may treat the offer as having "lapsed" before acceptance [2–206(2)]. The full meaning of this provision is unclear. It apparently does not require notice when the offeree accepts by *performing* (e.g., shipping the goods). In such a case, it is apparently assumed that the offeror will learn of performance within a reasonable time. It expressly applies only when acceptance is accomplished by *beginning performance.* Whether loading goods on a truck for shipment is enough to constitute beginning performance, or whether the statute is intended to apply only to more specific kinds of offeree behavior (e.g., begin-

[4] *Restatement (Second) of Contracts* § 54(2)(1979).

ning to manufacture specially ordered goods) is not apparent from the language of the statute.

**Manner of Communication.** The offeror, as the "master of his offer," has the power to specify the precise time, place, and manner in which acceptance must be communicated. If the offeror does so, and the offeree deviates from the offer's instructions in any significant way, no contract will result unless the offeror indicates that he is willing to be bound by the deviating acceptance. If the offer merely suggests a method or place of communication, or is silent on such matters, the offeree may accept within a reasonable time by any reasonable means of communication.

**When Is Acceptance Communicated?** The question of when an acceptance has been effectively communicated is often a critically important issue in contract cases. The offeror may be trying to revoke an offer that the offeree is desperately trying to accept. A mailed or telegraphed acceptance may get lost and never be received by the offeror. The time limit for accepting the offer may be rapidly approaching. Was the offer accepted before a revocation was received or before the offer expired? Does a lost acceptance create a contract when it is dispatched, or is it totally ineffective?

When the parties are dealing face-to-face or the offeree is accepting by telephone, these problems are minimized. As soon as the offeree says, "I accept," or words to that effect, a contract is created (assuming that the offer is still in existence). Problems with the timing of acceptances multiply, however, when the offeree is using a means of communication that creates a time lag between the dispatching of the acceptance and its actual receipt by the offeror. Offerors have the power to minimize these problems by requiring in their offer that they must *actually receive* the acceptance for it to be effective. Offerors who do this maximize the time that they have to revoke their offers and ensure that they will never be bound by an acceptance that they have not received.

Offerors who fail to require actual receipt of an acceptance may find to their dismay that the law has developed rules that make some acceptances effective the moment they are dispatched, regardless of whether the offeror ever receives them. These rules generally apply when the offeror has made the offer under circumstances that might reasonably lead the offeree to believe that acceptance by some means other than telephone or face-to-face communication is acceptable. They are designed to protect the offeree's reasonable belief that a binding contract was created when the acceptance was dispatched.

**Authorized Means of Communication.** As a general rule, an acceptance is effective *when dispatched* (delivered to the agency of communication) if the offeree accepts by the **authorized means** of communication. This is so even if the acceptance is never received by the offeror. An offeror may *expressly* authorize acceptance by a particular means of communication by saying, in effect: "You *may* accept by mail (telegram, etc.)." If the offeror does so, the offeree's acceptance is effective when mailed (or telegraphed, as the case may be). Any attempt by the offeror to revoke thereafter (e.g., by a letter of revocation mailed before the acceptance was mailed but received after it was mailed) would be ineffective.

A means of communication may also be *impliedly* authorized by the offeror. Under traditional contract principles, if the offer or circumstances do not indicate otherwise, the offeror impliedly authorizes the offeree to accept by the *same means* that the offeror used to communicate the offer. So, mailed offers impliedly invite mailed acceptances, telegraphed offers impliedly invite acceptance by telegram, and so forth. In addition, *trade usage* can impliedly authorize a given means of acceptance. Thus, if the parties are both members of a particular trade and the trade custom is to offer by mail and accept by telegram, a telegram would be the impliedly authorized means of accepting such an offer unless the offer indicates to the contrary.

In recent years, the authorized means concept has been broadened considerably by numerous cases holding that offerors who remain silent impliedly authorize acceptance by *any reasonable means.* What is "reasonable" depends on the circumstances in which the offer was made. These include the speed and reliability of the means used by the offeree, the nature of the transaction (e.g., does the agreement involve goods subject to rapid price fluctuations?), the existence of any trade usage governing the transaction, and the existence of prior dealings between the parties (e.g., has the offeree previously used the mail to accept telegraphed offers from the offeror?). So, under proper circumstances, a mailed response to a telegraphed offer or a telegraphed response to a mailed offer might be considered "reasonable," and therefore effective upon dispatch. The Code expressly adopts the "reasonable means" test for offers involving the sale of goods [2–206(1)(a)], and the *Restatement Second*[5] suggests that it be used in all contract cases.

**Acceptance by Nonauthorized Means.** What if an offeree attempts to accept the offer by mail when the authorized means for acceptance was clearly by telegram? The traditional rule in such cases is that an acceptance by a nonauthorized means is effective only when it is *actually received* by the offeror, provided that it is received within the time that an acceptance by the authorized means would have been received. This rule seems somewhat artificial, however, because once an acceptance reaches the offeror, she has actual notice that a contract has been created and is not in any danger of acting in reliance (e.g., by selling offered goods to a third party) on the impression that she is not bound by a contract. At this point, the means that the offeree used to communicate acceptance would logically seem to be irrelevant because the end result from the offeror's standpoint is the same, regardless of the means used by the offeree. Why, then, should we allow the offeror to revoke prior to timely receipt of an acceptance by a nonauthorized means but deny her the power to revoke after the dispatch of an acceptance by the authorized means? The Code has accepted this reasoning by providing that in all contracts for the sale of goods an acceptance by a nonauthorized means is effective *upon dispatch* if it is received within the time that an acceptance by the authorized means would normally have arrived [1–201(38)]. Section 67 of the *Restatement Second* adopts the Code rule for all contracts.

**Contradictory Offeree Responses.** Consider this example: White mails Case an offer to sell his house for $75,000. Case mails White a counteroffer, offering to pay $70,000 for the house. In the last chapter, you learned that Case's counteroffer would be effective to terminate White's offer only when White actually receives it. Therefore, if Case changed his mind and communicated an acceptance of the offer to White before White received his counteroffer, a contract would result. But what if Case mails an acceptance to White four hours after mailing the counteroffer? If we applied the normal rules of offer and acceptance to these facts, we might conclude that the parties had a contract because Case's acceptance was by the authorized means (mail), was effective upon dispatch, and was probably dispatched before White received Case's coun-

[5] *Restatement (Second) of Contracts* § 30(2), 63, 65 (1979).

teroffer. White, however, may receive Case's counteroffer and sell the house to a third party before he receives Case's acceptance. To prevent such an unfair result, most courts hold that when an offeree dispatches an acceptance after first dispatching a rejection, the acceptance will not create a contract unless it is received before the rejection. Therefore, if White receives the counteroffer before he receives the acceptance, no contract will result. If, on the other hand, he receives the acceptance before receiving the counteroffer, a contract will result.

However, what if Case mailed White an acceptance, changed his mind, and shortly thereafter mailed White a rejection? Applying normal offer and acceptance rules to these facts, we would conclude that Case's acceptance was effective upon dispatch and that Case no longer had the power to reject the offer. But what if White received Case's rejection first and relied on it by selling to someone else? In such a situation, Case would be *estopped* from enforcing the contract due to White's reliance.

**Stipulated Means of Communication.** An offer may *stipulate* the means of communication that the offeree must use to accept the offer by saying, in effect: "You *must* accept by mail (telegram, etc.)." An acceptance by the **stipulated means** of communication is effective upon dispatch, just like an acceptance by an authorized means of communication. The difference is that an acceptance by other than the stipulated means will not create a contract because it is an acceptance at variance with the terms of the offer.

## Southwestern Stationery, Inc. v. Harris Corp.

**624 F.2d 168 (10th Cir. 1980)**

Southwestern wished to purchase a used printing press from Harris. Following negotiations, Harris sent Southwestern several copies of a Harris purchase order for the press and also supplied instructions for submitting the order. On April 29, 1976, Southwestern completed the purchase order and forwarded four copies with both a down-payment check and an irrevocable letter of credit for the balance of the purchase price. About two weeks later, Harris notified Southwestern that the deal was off because the third party that owned the press had refused to sell it to Harris. Harris returned the uncashed check, the letter of credit, and three copies of the purchase order, none of which had any Harris notations of acceptance. Southwestern then purchased a comparable new press and sued for damages for breach of contract. The trial court ruled in Harris's favor, and Southwestern appealed.

**McKay, Circuit Judge.** The primary dispute centers on the meaning of the acceptance clause language found on the back of the Harris purchase order. That clause reads:

> This order is subject to acceptance by Seller at its home office written herein. Thereupon, Seller shall mail to Purchaser a signed duplicate copy hereof, and the same shall constitute the entire contract between the parties. The contract and the notes given hereunder shall be governed by the laws of the State of Ohio. Purchaser has retained a copy of this order as signed by it. The banking by Seller or other disposition of funds paid by Purchaser to Seller or the disposition by

Seller of any trade-in equipment offered by Purchaser to Seller hereunder shall not constitute an acceptance of this order by Seller.

In addition, the purchase order includes on its face the following signature block:

This order is hereby accepted and dated at Seller's Cleveland, Ohio, Office on ______________________HARRIS CORPORATION, a Delaware Corporation

Sheet Fed Press Division, Seller

By ________________________________________

Southwestern argues that the method of acceptance is not made explicit by the document and therefore, under the governing Uniform Commercial Code, any reasonable means of acceptance will suffice.

Southwestern focuses on the initial sentence of the acceptance clause. That sentence requires Harris's acceptance but specifies no method. Under the Southwestern theory, the second sentence, requiring the mailing to Southwestern of a signed duplicate copy, delineates a procedure to be followed after acceptance has otherwise been effected. The introductory word "thereupon" merely orders the steps in the transaction.

Read out of context, the two sentences may suggest ambiguity. However, read in conjunction with the remainder of the purchase order, the particular terms are not lacking in clarity. The signature block clearly requires a Harris signature for the contract to be "hereby accepted." That language is subject to only one reasonable interpretation.

It is true that the Uniform Commercial Code was designed to substitute standards of reasonableness for the overly formalistic rules of commercial common law. Nevertheless, parties retain their power to require specific methods of acceptance. Any other "reasonable manner of acceptance" is sufficient only if the parties have not "otherwise unambiguously indicated [the means of acceptance] by the language or circumstances [2–206(1)(a)]."

Judgment for Harris affirmed.

## Cushing v. Thomson

**386 A.2d 805 (N.H. Sup. Ct. 1978)**

On March 30, 1978, R. R. Cushing, Jr., a member of an antinuclear protest group called the Portsmouth Area Clamshell Alliance, submitted an application to the New Hampshire adjutant general's office seeking permission to hold a dance in the Portsmouth armory. On March 31, 1978, the adjutant general mailed a signed contract offer agreeing to rent the armory to the Alliance for the evening of April 29, 1978. The agreement required the renter to accept by signing a copy of the agreement and returning it to the adjutant general within five days after its receipt.

On Monday, April 3, Cushing received the offer and signed it on behalf of the Alliance. At 6:30 on the evening of Tuesday, April 4, Cushing received a telephone call from the adjutant general advising him that Meldrim Thomson, Jr., the governor of New Hampshire, had ordered withdrawal of the rental offer. Cushing told the adjutant general that he had already signed the contract. On April 6, the adjutant general's office received the signed contract in the mail, dated April 3, and postmarked April 5. Cushing sued for specific performance of the rental agreement. The trial court ruled in his favor, and the state appealed.

**Per Curiam.** To establish a contract of this character there must be an offer and an acceptance thereof in accordance with its terms. When the parties to such a contract are at a distance from one another and the offer is sent by mail, the reply accepting the offer may be sent by the same medium, and the contract will be complete when the acceptance is mailed, properly addressed to the party making the offer and beyond the acceptor's control. Withdrawal of the offer is ineffectual once the offer has been accepted by posting in the mail.

The state argues, however, that there is no evidence to sustain a finding that Cushing had accepted the adjutant general's offer before it was withdrawn. Such a finding is necessarily implied in the court's ruling that there was a binding contract. Mr. Cushing introduced a sworn affidavit in which he stated that on April 3, he executed the contract and placed it in the outbox for mailing. Moreover, Cushing's counsel represented to the court that it was customary office practice for outgoing letters to be picked up from the outbox daily and put in the U.S. mail.

Thus the representation that it was customary office procedure for the letters to be sent out the same day that they are placed in the office outbox, together with the affidavit, supported the implied finding that the completed contract was mailed before the attempted revocation. Because there is evidence to support it, this court cannot say as a matter of law that the trial court's finding that there was a binding contract is clearly erroneous, and therefore it must stand.

Judgment for Cushing affirmed.

## SUMMARY

In determining whether an offer was accepted to create a binding contract, the courts look for behavior by an offeree that objectively indicates a present intent to contract on the terms of the offer. This behavior may be in the form of words or action by the offeree. Also, in some limited cases, silence or inaction by the offeree may signal his assent to the terms of the offer. Acceptance of offers for unilateral contracts requires that the offeree perform the act requested by the offer. In bilateral contract cases, the offeree must make the promise requested by the offer. In some cases, the offer is unclear about whether acceptance may be accomplished by performing an act or making a promise. In such cases, both the Code and the *Restatement Second* provide that an offeree can accept either by performing or promising to perform.

Traditional contract principles require the offeree's acceptance to be the "mirror image" of the offer and treat acceptances that attempt to vary the terms of an offer as counteroffers. Recent years, however, have witnessed a judicial tendency to relax the strict application of this rule by treating only acceptances containing "material" variances as counteroffers. The Code, in its controversial "Battle of the Forms" section [2–207], expressly changes the "mirror image" rule by allowing acceptances stating additional or different terms to operate as acceptances. Between merchants, these new terms become part of the contract unless the offer limits acceptance to its own terms, the new terms would materially alter the offer, or the offeree objects to the new terms within a reasonable time after he has notice of them.

As a general rule, acceptances, like offers, must be communicated to the other party to the agreement before they will become effective. In the case of offers for unilateral contracts, however, the traditional rule is that the offeree's performance of the act requested by the offer is all that is required for acceptance. To prevent unfairness to offerors who may assume that no acceptance has occurred because they have not, in fact, learned of the offeree's performance, the Code and the *Restatement Second* require in some cases that the offeree give notice of performance to the offeror.

The offeror, as the "master of the offer," can specify the exact means that the offeror may use to accept the offer. Attempts by offerees to accept in any other way will not create a contract. If the offeror fails to specify exact means of acceptance, the offeree may accept by any reasonable means.

When the parties are dealing face-to-face or over the telephone, an acceptance is effective the instant that it is communicated to the other party. When the offeree uses some delayed means of communication, such as mail or telegram, critical timing questions can arise about when an acceptance is effective. Offerors can specify that they will be bound to a contract only when they actually receive an acceptance. In the absence of such a statement by the offeror, an acceptance is effective when dispatched by the offeree if the offeree uses the *authorized means* of communication. A means of communication may be expressly or impliedly authorized. Traditional contract law rules provide that the offeror who does not indicate a contrary intent impliedly authorizes the offeree to accept by the same means of communication that has been used to communicate the offer. Trade usage can also operate to authorize a particular means of communication. Many contemporary courts have broadened these rules by holding that the offeror who remains silent impliedly authorizes acceptance by any reasonable means. The Code and the *Restatement Second* adopt this position.

Under traditional contract principles, an acceptance by a nonauthorized means is effective only when it is received by the offeror, and then only if it is received within the time in which a properly dispatched acceptance would have been received. The Code and the *Restatement Second* change this rule by providing that an acceptance by a nonauthorized means is effective upon dispatch if it reaches the offeror within the same time in which a properly dispatched acceptance would have been received.

An offeror may also *stipulate* that the offeree must accept by a particular means of communication. Acceptances by a stipulated means, like those by an authorized means, are effective upon dispatch, even if never received by the offeror. Acceptances by a nonstipulated means, however, are never effective to create a contract.

## PROBLEM CASES

1. A building owned by James Kuehn was damaged by fire. An insurance adjuster from Kuehn's insurance company contacted George Moore and requested that Moore submit a written estimate for the necessary repair work. Moore submitted a written proposal to Kuehn, who said he wanted to look it over more carefully before signing it. Kuehn did, however, tell Moore, "The roof ought to be fixed, so get on it." Moore did

all of the repairs called for by his written proposal. He also, at Kuehn's request, did some additional work not covered by the proposal. Kuehn never signed the proposal and paid Moore for only part of the work. When Moore filed suit for breach of contract, Kuehn argued that he had never entered a binding contract with Moore. Did Kuehn accept Moore's written proposal?

**2.** The *New York Daily News* ran a Super Zingo Sweepstakes contest. Players were required to submit entry ballots resembling bingo cards. The correctly marked entries went into a pool from which winners were drawn at random. The advertisements for the contest stressed the amount of the top prize ($50,000) in bold 1⅜-inch print. The contest rules were in tiny 1⁄16-inch lettering and included a provision restricting entry to persons over 18. Dorothy Johnson submitted an entry and listed her grandson Shawn's name on the entry blank. Her entry was selected for the top prize, but the *News* later refused to pay, arguing that by listing Shawn's name, she had violated the contest rules. Is Dorothy entitled to the prize?

**3.** Panhandle Eastern Pipe Line Company fired Nowlin Smith in October 1979. Smith filed a grievance under the company's collective bargaining agreement with his union. On December 13, 1979, after several intracompany proceedings, Panhandle sent Smith a letter offering to withdraw the discharge if Smith would agree to certain terms and conditions. Smith signed the letter under the typewritten words "Understood, Agreed to and Accepted," added some handwritten notations, and again signed his name. The union representative also signed the letter and returned it to the company. The notations that Smith wrote on the letter asked to see his personnel file and contest any mistakes he found there (a right all company employees had), stated that his file contained mistakes, and asserted that he was having financial problems as a result of Panhandle's actions. Panhandle argued that by writing on the letter, Smith had failed to use the required mode of acceptance and had made a counteroffer. Is Panhandle right?

**4.** Kodiak Island Borough offered to sell 4 acres of land to Royal Large for $10,500 on September 15, 1975. The letter containing the offer required Large to accept within 10 days. On September 24, 1975, Large sent a letter of acceptance proposing a 10 percent down payment, with the balance of the price to be paid over 10 years at 6 percent interest. These were the standard contract terms used by the borough. On December 23, 1975, Large submitted a check for $1,550 to the borough as a down payment. The next day, his check was returned and he was told that it would not be accepted until a written contract was executed. Later, the newly elected borough assembly decided not to sell the land. Large filed suit for breach of contract. Is he entitled to the land?

**5.** Golden Dipt requested bids from several manufacturers for the construction of a pneumatic bulk flour handling system in its plant at Millstadt, Illinois. Systems Engineering and Manufacturing Company (SEMCO) submitted a bid for $198,564. SEMCO's bid provided that its price was firm for 30 days, required any order to be accompanied with a 25 percent down payment, and provided that the bid was not binding until it had been delivered to and accepted by SEMCO. The president of Golden Dipt phoned SEMCO and told SEMCO's marketing manager that the SEMCO proposal had been approved and that the paperwork would follow. A few days later, SEMCO notified Golden Dipt that a mistake had been made in the calculation of its bid and that the price for the system was $31,795 more than the price originally quoted. Golden Dipt hired another company to install the system and sued SEMCO for breach of contract. Did Golden Dipt accept SEMCO's bid?

**6.** Brack Barker was shopping in a self-service food store owned by Allied. He took a carton of Dr Pepper off a shelf and attempted to place it in his shopping cart. One of the bottles exploded, and pieces of it struck him in the right eye, causing a permanent 90 percent loss of vision. Barker filed suit for breach of the Code's implied warranty of merchantability. Allied argued that no contract for the sale of goods had been created under the Code. Did Barker's actions create a contract for the sale of the soft drinks?

**7.** Chase Manhattan Bank issued several credit cards to Hobbs. Each card was accompanied by a "retail installment credit agreement" executed by the bank which stated that the agreement would become effective when the cardholder signed a sales slip evidencing a purchase and that the cardholder was liable for attorney's fees of up to 20 percent of any past-due amount referred to any attorney for collection. Hobbs used the cards to make $1,861.74 in purchases that he never paid for. The bank sued for that amount, plus $372.34 in attorney's fees. Hobbs argued that he had no agreement with the bank obligating him to pay attorney's fees. Is Hobbs liable for attorney's fees?

**8.** On April 2, 1976, Lawrence Pribil made a written offer to purchase Bertha Ruther's land. Bertha and her husband signed the owners' acceptance blanks in the offer and handed it to their real estate broker, John Thor. Thor asked his secretary to send a copy of the agreement to Pribil, which she did by a letter dated April 14, 1976, and postmarked "April 15, 1970, p.m." Pribil received the letter on April 16, 1976. Bertha Ruther became dissatisfied with the transaction the day after she signed the acceptance when she found out that a test well had been drilled on the property at Pribil's request. She also learned that the driller had estimated that the well would produce 500 to 800 gallons of water a minute. She testified that on April 13, 1976, she called Pribil's home and told his wife she would not sell the property. Pribil's wife said that the conversation did not occur until 10 days later. Ruther also testified that she called Thor on April 14, 1976, and told him she was going to "terminate the contract." Thor said that this took place on the morning of April 15, 1976, and that he immediately called Pribil and told him the deal was off. Pribil sued for breach of contract. Did Ruther effectively reject Pribil's offer before her acceptance was communicated to him?

**9.** Tunis sent Allen a "piece goods purchase order" which included a provision that any disputes between the parties would be resolved by arbitration or in the New York courts "as the buyer shall elect." The purchase order also included language stating that it represented the only agreement between the parties and that no terms in any document sent by Allen would be binding unless these were consented to in writing by Tunis. Allen confirmed Tunis' order by sending a "finished goods contract order" which provided that all disputes were subject to arbitration. Allen's form also provided that Tunis' failure to object within five days or its acceptance of a payment for the goods constituted an acceptance of Allen's terms and that Allen would not be bound by any other terms unless it agreed to them in writing. Tunis returned a copy of Allen's form stamped with the legend "THIS FORM RETURNED AND REJECTED. OUR ORDER IS ONLY AGREEMENT IN EFFECT." After Tunis had accepted delivery of some of the ordered goods, a dispute arose over whether all the goods had been shipped and over the timeliness of the shipment. Allen argued that the dispute should be arbitrated, but Tunis asserted that the case should go to court. Should the dispute be arbitrated?

**10.** Reliance Steel Products sent a purchase order for certain steel products to Kentucky Electric Steel. Reliance's purchase order contained a clause stating that Reliance would not be bound by any terms other than those in its purchase order unless it agreed in writing to a change of terms. Kentucky responded with its standard order acknowledgment form, which contained a "Limitation of Liability" clause that limited Kentucky's liability for defective goods to replacing the goods or allowing the buyer a credit for them. Reliance later filed a breach of contract suit against Kentucky, arguing that some of the goods it received did not conform to contract specifications. Reliance asked for a damage award based on damage to its fabricating machinery and lost profits that it claimed resulted from Kentucky's breach. Kentucky argued that such damages were barred by its "Limitation of Liability" clause. Is Kentucky right?

# Chapter 9

# Reality of Consent

## INTRODUCTION

Reliable enforcement of contractual obligations is necessary in a complex economy that depends on planning for the future. In some situations, however, there are compelling reasons for permitting people to escape their contracts. Sometimes, a person is "robbed" of his ability to protect his own interests, such as when his agreement is induced by force, trickery, or unfair persuasion. Sometimes, a person agrees to a contract with a basic misunderstanding about what he is contracting for. In such situations, the normal assumption that a contract is the product of mutual and voluntary consent is untenable. A person who has made an agreement under these circumstances should not be held to it, because his consent is not *real.* Another reason for refusing to hold such a person to his contract is that courts want to discourage unscrupulous bargaining behavior. It would be inconsistent for a legal system committed to honesty and fair dealing to lend the power of the law to a contract created by dishonest means.

This chapter discusses four doctrines that permit people to escape or *avoid* their obligations under a contract when their consent cannot be considered to have been real: misrepresentation, duress, undue influence, and mistake. Two doctrines that involve similar considerations, capacity and unconscionability, will be discussed in Chapters 11 and 12.

Contracts that involve the circumstances discussed in this chapter are generally considered to be **voidable;** that is, the injured person has the option of rescinding (canceling) such contracts. This remedy protects people who would not have entered a contract but for misrepresentation, duress, undue influence, or mistake. It also prevents people who have engaged in unscrupulous conduct from benefiting from the conduct.

A person who wants to rescind a contract for one of the reasons discussed above must act promptly in order to preserve her remedy. She must object and signify her intent to cancel the contract promptly upon learning the facts that give her the right to rescind. Otherwise, she will be considered to have **ratified,** or affirmed, the contract.

## MISREPRESENTATION

**Nature of Misrepresentation.** According to the *Restatement (Second) of Contracts,* a misrepresentation is "an assertion that is not in accord with the facts."[1] When a false assertion about an important fact is justifiably relied on by the promisee and plays a significant role in inducing him to enter the contract, the resulting contract is voidable on the ground of **misrepresentation.**

Misrepresentation does not have to be intentionally deceptive. The person making the misrepresentation may believe in good faith that what she says is true. While people often use the terms *fraud* and *misrepresentation* interchangeably, there is an important difference between these terms. Fraud is a type of misrepresentation that is *knowingly made* with *intent to deceive,* while misrepresentation, a broader concept, does not have to be intentional. Either fraud or misrepresentation gives the complaining party the right to rescind a contract. As will be discussed later, a person who commits fraud may be liable in tort for damages.

[1] Restatement (Second) of Contracts § 159.

**Elements of Misrepresentation.** A mere untrue assertion does not in itself establish misrepresentation. Courts do not want to permit people who have exercised poor business judgment or poor common sense to avoid their contractual obligations, nor do they want to grant rescission of a contract when there have been only minor misstatements of relatively unimportant details. A drastic remedy such as rescission should be used only when a person has been seriously misled about a fact important to the contract by someone he had the right to rely on. A person seeking to rescind a contract on grounds of misrepresentation must be able to establish each of the following requirements.

**Assertion of Fact.** To have misrepresentation, one of the parties must have made an assertion of fact or engaged in some conduct that is the equivalent of an assertion of fact. The assertion must relate to some *past or existing fact,* as distinguished from a promise or a prediction about some future happening. However, a car salesman's statement that "this car will get gas mileage of at least 30 miles per gallon" could be an assertion of present fact because it implies that the car is at present designed to achieve the promised performance.

Statements about the value or quality of items being sold are difficult to corroborate. Moreover, people discount such statements as "sales talk" or "puffing." For these reasons, a statement of opinion that purports to reflect a person's judgment rather than his knowledge is not the type of assertion that will be sufficient for misrepresentation. Thus, a seller's statement that "this is a great deal for you" would not be an assertion of fact, while her statement that "this car has never been in a collision" would be.

The **concealment** of a fact through some active conduct intended to prevent the other party from discovering the fact is considered to be the equivalent of an assertion. Like a false statement of fact, concealment can be the basis for a claim of misrepresentation or fraud. For example, if Smith is offering his house for sale and paints the ceilings to conceal the fact that the roof leaks, his active concealment constitutes an assertion of fact. Concealment is distinguished from nondisclosure in that concealment involves the active hiding of a fact, while nondisclosure is the failure to offer information. The circumstances under which nondisclosure can be misrepresentation are discussed later in this chapter.

**Materiality.** To rescind a contract on the ground of misrepresentation, the fact asserted or concealed must be **material.** This means that it must be important enough to play a significant role in inducing a reasonable person to enter the contract. What is material depends on the parties' individual situation and motivations. For example, the Johnsons, who live in Ohio, contract by mail through a real estate broker to buy a house in Florida. The description of the house contained in the literature sent to the Johnsons states that the house is "within easy walking distance to schools, churches, and shopping centers." When the Johnsons move into their new house, they discover that the nearest school is 5 miles away. Has there been a misrepresentation of a material fact? To answer that question, one would need to know more about the Johnsons. If they are a young couple with school-age children, the description of the house would probably be material. If they are an elderly couple whose children are grown, the distance of the nearest school might be unimportant.

**Actual Reliance.** Reliance means that a person pursues some course of action because of his faith in an assertion made to him. For misrepresentation to exist, there must have been a causal connection between the assertion and the complaining party's decision to enter the contract. If the complaining party knew that the assertion was false or was not aware that an assertion had been made, there has been no reliance.

**Justifiable Reliance.** Courts also scrutinize the reasonableness of the behavior of the complaining party by requiring that her reliance be *justifiable.* A person does not act justifiably if she relies on an assertion that is obviously false or not to be taken seriously. Also, people are expected to take reasonable steps to discover facts relevant to the contracts they enter. Classical contract law held that a person who did not attempt to discover readily discoverable facts was generally not justified in relying on the other party's statements about them. For example, a person would not be entitled to rely on the other party's assertions about facts that are a matter of public record or that could be discovered through reasonable inspection of available documents or records.

However, the extent of the responsibility placed on a relying party to conduct an independent investigation is unclear in modern contract law. For example, section 172 of the *Restatement (Second) of Contracts* states that the complaining party's fault in not knowing or discovering facts before entering the contract does not make his reliance unjustifiable unless the degree of his fault was so extreme as to amount to a failure to act in good faith and in accordance with reasonable standards of fair dealing. Recognizing that the traditional rule operated to encourage misrepresentation, courts in recent years have tended to decrease the responsibility of the relying party and to place a greater degree of accountability on the person who makes the assertion. The case of *Cousineau v. Walker,* which follows, is an excellent example of this trend.

## Cousineau v. Walker

### 613 P.2d 608 (Alaska Sup. Ct. 1980)

Devin and Joan Walker owned property in Eagle River, Alaska. In 1976, they listed the property for sale with a real estate broker. They signed a multiple listing agreement, which described the property as having 580 feet of highway frontage and stated, "ENGINEER REPORT SAYS OVER 1 MILLION IN GRAVEL ON PROP." This listing contract expired without the property having been sold. The Walkers then signed a new listing contract with the same broker. The new listing described the property as having 580 feet of highway frontage, but the gravel content was listed as "minimum 80,000 cubic yds of gravel." An appraisal was prepared to determine the property's value. Mr. Walker specifically instructed the appraiser not to include the value of gravel in the appraisal. Although the appraisal stated that it did not take any gravel into account, the ground was described as "all good gravel base."

Wayne Cousineau, a contractor who was also in the gravel extraction business, became aware of the property when he saw the multiple listing. After visiting the property with his real estate broker and discussing gravel extraction with Mr. Walker, Cousineau offered to purchase the property. He then attempted to determine the lot's road frontage, but was unsuccessful because the property was covered with snow. He was also unsuccessful in obtaining the engineer's report allegedly showing "over 1 million in gravel." Walker admitted at trial that he had never seen a copy of the report either. Nevertheless, the parties signed and consummated a contract of sale for the purchase price of $385,000. There was no reference to the amount of highway frontage in the purchase agreement.

After the sale was completed, Cousineau began developing the property and removing gravel. Cousineau learned that the description of highway frontage contained in the real estate listing was incorrect when a neighbor threatened to sue him for removing gravel from the neighbor's adjacent lot. A subsequent survey revealed that the highway frontage was 410 feet—not 580 feet, as advertised. At about the same time, the gravel ran out after Cousineau had removed only 6,000 cubic yards.

Cousineau stopped making payments and informed the Walkers of his intention to rescind the contract. The property was sold at a foreclosure sale and reacquired by Walker. Cousineau brought an action against the Walkers, seeking the return of his money. The trial court found for the Walkers, and Cousineau appealed.

**Boochever, Justice.** An innocent misrepresentation may be the basis for rescinding a contract. There is no question that the statements made by Walker and his real estate agent in the multiple listing were false. Three questions must be resolved, however, to determine whether Cousineau is entitled to rescission and restitution on the basis of the misrepresentation. First, it must be determined whether Cousineau in fact relied on the statements. Second, it must be determined whether the statements were material to the transaction. Finally, assuming that Cousineau relied on the statements and that they were material, it must be determined whether his reliance was justified.

Even if the sale was based on the appraisal rather than the listings, the appraisal does not disclaim the earlier statements regarding the amount of highway frontage and the existence of gravel. In fact, the appraisal might well reaffirm a buyer's belief that gravel existed, since it stated there was a good gravel base. All the documents prepared regarding the sale make provisions for the transfer of gravel rights. Cousineau's first act upon acquiring the property was to contract for gravel removal. We conclude that the court erred in finding that Cousineau did not rely on Walker's statement that there was gravel on the property. We are also convinced that the trial court's finding that Cousineau did not rely on Walker's statement regarding the amount of highway frontage was clearly erroneous. Cousineau was experienced and knowledgeable in real estate matters. In determining whether to purchase the property, he would certainly have considered the amount of highway frontage to be of importance.

A material fact is one to which a reasonable man might be expected to attach importance in making his choice of action. The reason behind the rule requiring proof of materiality is to encourage stability in contractual relations. The rule prevents parties who later become disappointed at the outcome of their bargain from capitalizing on any insignificant discrepancy to void the contract.

We conclude that the statements regarding highway frontage and gravel content were material. A reasonable person would be likely to consider the existence of gravel deposits an important consideration in developing a piece of property. Walker's real estate agent testified that the statements regarding gravel were placed in the listings because gravel would be among the property's "best points" and a "selling point." The buyers received less than three-fourths of the highway frontage described in the listings. Certainly the amount of highway frontage on a commercial tract would be considered important.

The bulk of the Walkers' brief is devoted to the argument that Cousineau's unquestioning reliance on Walker and his real estate agent was imprudent and unreasonable. Cousineau failed to obtain and review the engineer's report. He failed to obtain a survey or examine the plat available at the recorder's office. He failed to make calculations that would have revealed the true frontage of the lot. Although the property was covered with snow, the buyer, according to Walker, had ample time to inspect it. The buyer was an experienced businessman who frequently bought and sold real estate. Discrepancies existed in the various property descriptions which should have alerted Cousineau to potential problems. In short, the Walkers urge that the doctrine of *caveat emptor* precludes recovery.

There is a split of authority regarding a buyer's duty to investigate a vendor's fraudulent statements, but the prevailing trend is toward placing a minimal duty on a buyer. The recent draft of the Restatement of Contracts allows rescission for an innocent material misrepresentation unless a buyer's fault was so negligent as to amount to "a failure to act in good faith and in accordance with reasonable standards of fair dealing." We conclude that a purchaser of land may rely on material representations made by the seller and is not obligated to ascertain whether such representations are truthful. A buyer of land, relying on an innocent misrepresentation, is barred from recovery only if the buyer's acts in failing to discover defects were wholly irrational, preposterous, or in bad faith.

Although Cousineau's actions may well have exhibited poor judgment for an experienced businessman, they were not so unreasonable or preposterous in view of Walker's description of the property that recovery should be denied.

Judgment reversed in favor of Cousineau.

## FRAUD

**Nature of Fraud.** Fraud has all the elements of misrepresentation discussed above plus the element of **scienter.** This means that the misrepresentation must have been made knowingly with intent to deceive. A misrepresentation is "knowingly made" if the defendant knew the truth, made the statement without sufficient information to have known the truth, or possessed enough information to have known the truth. The intent to deceive can be inferred from the fact that the defendant knowingly made a misstatement of fact to a person who was likely to rely on it. A person who seeks to recover damages for fraud must be able to prove that he suffered economic injury.

**Contents of Contract.** As the use of form contracts (preprinted contracts) has proliferated, courts have been presented with an increasing number of claims of fraud involving misrepresentation of the contents or legal effect of documents. Should a person who believes the other party's statement about what a contract states and does not read the contract be permitted to rescind the contract later? Common sense dictates that people should be expected to use whatever means are at their disposal to protect themselves. Thus, the traditional rule has been that false representations as to the legal effect or contents of a document do not constitute fraud, because the signer of the document could easily read the contract himself and was not justified in relying on the representation.

However, if the signer is prevented from reading the contract or if there is a relationship of trust and confidence between the parties to the contract (also called a fiduciary relationship), false representations about the provisions or effect of a contract can be fraud. This type of fraud, called fraud in the execution or fraud **in factum,** generally prevents a contract from being created. The case of *Lyle v. Moore,* which follows, takes this principle one step further. It states that when there is a relationship of trust and confidence between the parties, fraud may be found in the failure to call the relying party's attention to important terms of a written contract about which he might not be aware.

**Remedies for Fraud.** As is true for unintentional misrepresentation, the contract remedy for fraud is rescission of the contract. Because fraud may also constitute the tort of deceit, however, a person who commits fraud may be liable for tort damages, including punitive damages. In a number of states, a person injured by fraud must elect between rescinding the contract and suing for deceit. In other states, an injured party may rescind *and* sue for damages in tort. Section 2–721 of the Uniform Commercial Code specifically states that no election of remedies is required in contracts for the sale of goods.

## NONDISCLOSURE

Suppose two businesspeople, Smith and Jones, are negotiating for the sale of Smith's business. As in most contracting situations, each person has more information about his bargaining position than does the other person. Jones may have a distorted impression about the profitability of the business, for example, that results from his lack of information rather than from any concealment by Smith or from any misinformation provided by Smith. When, if ever, does Smith have a duty to tell Jones of facts relevant to the contract so that Smith's failure to do so is the equivalent of misrepresentation? This question involves the more basic question of how much honesty the law should require of people in commercial transactions, given that candor will often harm a person's bargaining position.

Reflecting the 19th-century ideal that each party was capable of driving his own bargain and the philosophy that courts should not intervene in the parties' relationship unless extreme wrongdoing was involved, traditional contract law held that mere silence generally was *not* misrepresentation. A person had no duty to disclose facts relevant to the contract except in rare situations, such as when the parties stood in a fiduciary relationship. Even under the traditional approach, a distinction was made between nondisclosure, a failure to state facts, which generally was not considered to be misrepresentation, and active concealment, which could be fraud or misrepresentation.

In recent years, the circumstances under which a person has the duty to take affirmative steps to disclose relevant information have been expanded. Some duties of disclosure are created by statutes, such as the Interstate Land Sales Full Disclosure Act, discussed in Chapter 29. Others have been created by the courts. As under traditional contract law, a person who stands in a relationship of trust and confidence has the responsibility to disclose important facts to the other party. This makes sense, because a person who has good reason to believe that the other party is looking out for his welfare will not approach the contract with the same degree of vigilance as the person who is dealing with a stranger. Courts have also held that people have the duty to disclose material facts when one person knows of problems that the other person will be unable to discover or when disclosure is necessary to correct a half-truth or a previous assertion that has become untrue. Section 161 of the *Restatement (Second) of Contracts* states that nondisclosure is misrepresentation where it would amount to a failure to act in good faith. This suggests the development of a broad duty to disclose in an increasingly wide range of contracting situations.

## Lyle v. Moore

**599 P.2d 336 (Mont. Sup. Ct. 1979)**

Lyle, a real estate broker, was at one time a good friend of Max and Pearl Moore. The Moores owned a farm, part of which lay in Montana and part of which extended into the province of Saskatchewan, Canada. The Moores were considering selling the portion of the farm that lay in Canada. Lyle learned of this through a third party and approached the Moores, telling them that he knew a prospective buyer who would pay more for the farm than they had planned to ask.

On March 3, 1975, Lyle met with the Moores to obtain a real estate broker's listing contract for the sale of the farm. The contract was a one-page document that was to expire on April 1, 1975. It contained the following language:

> You hereby are granted the absolute, sole and exclusive right to sell or exchange the said described property. In the event of any sale, by me or any other person . . . . during the term of your exclusive employment, or in case I withdraw the authority hereby given prior to said expiration date, I agree to pay you the said commission just the same as if a sale had actually been consummated by you.

The contract also provided that Lyle would receive 6 percent of the $220,000 selling price, or $13,200, if he were successful in selling the property for that price. Mr. and Mrs. Moore signed the contract without reading it.

Lyle introduced the Moores to a prospective buyer from Kansas, who indicated interest in the property. While negotiations were under way for the possible sale of the farm to this buyer, the Moores met with their accountant to discuss the tax consequences of such a sale. The accountant suggested that the Moores sell the property to their sons. On March 10, 1975, the Moores withdrew Lyle's authority to sell the property. Later, they sold the property to their sons. Lyle sued the Moores to recover the commission provided for in the listing contract. The trial court found for Lyle, and the Moores appealed.

**HASWELL, CHIEF JUSTICE.** One issue presented by defendants is whether the listing agreement signed by defendants was invalid because Lyle used it to take advantage of the Moores without their consent or knowledge. The District Court found that "no fraud, misrepresentation or undue influence on the part of plaintiff induced the execution of the employment contract by defendants." It is this finding with which we take issue.

In *Carnell v. Watson,* we recognized a fiduciary relationship between a real estate broker and his client. This fiduciary relationship has been found to encompass a "duty of full disclosure" by a number of courts. The duty includes the duty to reveal the nature and extent of the broker's fees to the client. Furthermore, because of the fiduciary relationship between a broker and his client, the broker must make a full and understandable explanation to the client before having him sign any contracts, particularly when the contracts are with the broker himself.

Lyle's own testimony indicates that he did not fully disclose to the Moores the fact that he would be entitled to his commission if they withdrew his authority to sell prior to the April 1st deadline. That this might seem like a small oversight is not borne out by the amount of the judgment in this case. It was a significant part of the contract which the Moores signed and should not have been overlooked. There is further testimony that Lyle hurried the Moores' signing and even encouraged them not to read the contract before signing it.

Moore testified on direct examination as follows:

**Q.** Did you and your wife and Mr. Lyle discuss whether that agreement should be read by you and your wife? **A.** Well, I didn't, and—but my wife asked Mr. Lyle, she said at that time, she said, after I had already signed it, that maybe she should read the fine print before she signed her name to something and that's, Mr. Lyle kind of laughed and he said that wasn't necessary. He said, I just want this to show the Kansas man. So then she signed it. But she didn't read anything.

**Q.** Did Mr. Lyle at that time review the listing agreement with you? **A.** No. The only thing he reviewed was the writing he put on it. He never did review any of the fine print typed on it. Just what he wrote there, himself.

**Q.** Were you given an opportunity to read the contract at that time? **A.** No.

**Q.** Why not? **A.** Well, he was in, seemed to be in a hurry. Wanted to get it signed and then, of course, I didn't ask him to read it but my wife had mentioned it and he said it was, there was no reason to read it.

As we have noted, there are times when the law imposes a duty upon a party to speak rather than to remain silent and thereby to disclose information to place the person with whom he is dealing on an equal footing with him. The failure to speak in such a case amounts to the suppression of a fact which should have been disclosed and constitutes fraud.

Here the fiduciary relationship which exists between a broker and his client imposed upon Lyle a duty to disclose a number of facts. These included the fact that the Moores could not withdraw his authority under the agreement without forfeiting a sizeable commission, nor could they sell the property on their own during the term of the agreement. The District Court erred in finding there was no fraud involved in the execution of the employment contract.

Judgment reversed in favor of the Moores.

## DURESS

**Nature of Duress.** Duress is wrongful coercion that induces a person to enter a contract. One kind of duress is physical compulsion to enter a contract. For example, Smith overpowers Jones, grasps his hand, and forces him to sign a contract. This kind of duress is rare, but when it occurs, a court would find that the contract was **void.** A far more common type of duress occurs when a person is induced to enter a contract by a *threat* of physical, emotional, or economic harm. In these cases, the contract is considered **voidable** at the option of the victimized person.

**Elements of Duress.** The doctrine of duress has undergone dramatic changes. Classical contract law took a very narrow view of the type of coercion that constituted duress, limiting duress to threats of physical harm. Because courts today place an increasing emphasis on fair results, they have taken a much broader view of the types of coercion that will constitute duress. Courts are now willing to find duress in threats to economic interests, not just in threats of physical harm. Still, two elements must exist before a threat will be found to constitute duress.

**Threat Must Be Wrongful.** Every contract negotiation involves the implied threat that a person will not enter the contract unless his demands are met. This is not the type of threat that is considered to be duress. The threat must be one that the law would consider *wrongful.* A threat to commit a crime or a tort would clearly be wrongful, but it is not necessary that the threat be of this nature.

A threat to breach a contract can be considered duress if it appears that the person making the threat is attempting to extort additional payments when he has no reasonable justification for breaching the contract. Generally, however, hard bargaining that merely takes advantage of a difficult financial position that the bargainer did not create is not considered to be duress. This principle is illustrated by the case of *Selmer Co. v. Blakeslee-Midwest Co.,* which follows.

Threats to institute legal actions can also be considered sufficiently wrongful to constitute duress. A threat to file either a civil or a criminal suit that has no reasonable basis would clearly be considered wrongful. What of a threat to file a well-founded lawsuit or prosecution? Generally, if there is a reasonable basis for the action, a person's threat to file a civil lawsuit is not considered to be wrongful. Otherwise, every person who settled a suit out of court could later claim duress. However, if the threat to sue is made in bad faith for an ulterior motive, duress may exist even if the person who makes the threat has a reasonable basis for bringing the suit. In one case, for example, duress was found when a husband who was in the process of divorcing his wife threatened to sue for custody of their children—something he had the right to do—unless the wife transferred to him stock that she owned in his company.[2] Section 176 of the *Restatement (Second) of Contracts* takes the position that a threat to institute a criminal prosecution is always impermissible pressure to enter a contract, even if the person making the threat has good reason to believe that the other person has committed a crime.

**Coercion.** The person complaining of duress must be able to establish that the wrongful threat was sufficiently coercive to have deprived him of his ability to resist entering the agreement. Classical contract law applied an objective standard which required that the degree of coercion exercised had to be sufficient to overcome the will of a person of ordinary courage. In recent years, courts have tended to examine the alternatives open to the coerced individual. Section 175 of the *Restatement* provides that to constitute duress the wrongful act or threat must be such that it leaves a person "no reasonable alternative" but to enter the contract.

[2] *Link v. Link,* 179 S.E.2d 697 (N.C. 1971).

## Selmer Co. v. Blakeslee-Midwest Co.

**704 F.2d 924 (7th Cir. 1983)**

Blakeslee-Midwest was a general contractor that had a contract to build a prestressed concrete structure. Selmer agreed to act as a subcontractor on this project. The contract between Blakeslee-Midwest and Selmer provided that Blakeslee-Midwest would provide Selmer with prestressed concrete materials and that Selmer would erect them for $210,000. Blakeslee-Midwest breached its obligations under the contract in several ways. Among other things, Blakeslee-Midwest was late in supplying Selmer with the needed materials. Rather than canceling the contract, Selmer orally agreed to complete the work on the condition that Blakeslee-Midwest would pay it for the extra costs of completion that were caused by Blakeslee's defaults. When the job was completed, Selmer demanded payment of $120,000 for extras. Blakeslee offered $67,000 and refused to budge from that offer. Because Selmer was in desperate financial straits, it accepted this offer.

Several years later, Selmer sued Blakeslee for the additional extra costs that it had incurred because of Blakeslee's breaches. Selmer claimed that the settlement agreement was invalid because it was procured by economic duress. The trial court found for Blakeslee-Midwest, and Selmer appealed.

**POSNER, CIRCUIT JUDGE.** If you extract a promise by means of a threat, the promise is unenforceable. Such promises are made unenforceable in order to discourage threats by making them less profitable. The fundamental issue in a duress case is therefore not the victim's state of mind but whether the statement that induced the promise is the kind of offer to deal that we want to discourage, and hence that we call a "threat." Selmer argues that Blakeslee-Midwest said to it in effect, "give up $53,000 of your claim for extras ($120,000 minus $67,000), or you will get nothing." This has the verbal form of a threat but is easily recast as a promise innocuous on its face—"I promise to pay you $67,000 for a release of your claim." There is a practical argument against treating such a statement as a threat: it will make an inference of duress inescapable in any negotiation where one party makes an offer from which it refuses to budge, for the other party will always be able to argue that he settled only because there was a (figurative) gun at his head. It would not matter whether the party refusing to budge was the payor like Blakeslee-Midwest or the promisor like Selmer. If Selmer had refused to complete the job without being paid exorbitantly for the extras and Blakeslee-Midwest had complied with this demand because financial catastrophe would have loomed if Selmer had walked off the job, we would have the same case. A vast number of contract settlements would be subject to being ripped open upon an allegation of duress if Selmer's argument were accepted.

The question is starkly posed whether financial difficulty can by itself justify setting aside a settlement on grounds of duress. It cannot. The adverse effect on the finality of settlements and hence on the willingness of parties to settle their contract disputes without litigation would be great if the cash needs of one party were alone enough to entitle him to a trial on the validity of the settlement.

Matters stand differently when the complaining party's financial distress is due to the other party's conduct. Although Selmer claims that it was the extra expense caused by Blakeslee-Midwest's breaches of the original contract that put it in a financial vise, it could have walked away from the contract without loss or penalty when Blakeslee-Midwest broke the contract. It was not forced by its contract to remain on the job; it stayed on the job for extra pay. We do not know why Selmer was unable to weather the crisis that arose when Blakeslee-Midwest refused to pay $120,000 for Selmer's extra expenses—whether Selmer was undercapitalized or overborrowed or what—but Blakeslee-Midwest cannot be held responsible for whatever it was that made Selmer so necessitous, when, as we have said, Selmer need not have embarked on the extended contract.

Judgment for Blakeslee-Midwest affirmed.

## UNDUE INFLUENCE

**Nature of Undue Influence.** Undue influence is unfair persuasion. Like duress, undue influence involves wrongful pressure exerted on a person during the bargaining process. In undue influence, however, the pressure is exerted through *persuasion* rather than through coercion. The doctrine of undue influence was developed to give relief to persons who are unfairly persuaded to enter a contract while in a position of mental or physical weakness that makes them particularly vulnerable to being preyed upon by dominant parties.

All contracts are based on persuasion. There is no precise dividing line between permissible persuasion and impermissible persuasion. Nevertheless, several hallmarks of undue influence cases can be identified.

Undue influence cases involve people who, though they have capacity to enter a contract, are in a position of vulnerability. There must be a relationship between the parties to the contract that makes the weaker party more susceptible to persuasion than he might otherwise be. This relationship is often one of trust and confidence, such as the relationship between husband and wife or between lawyer and client. However, as demonstrated by *Odorizzi v. Bloomfield School District,* which appears below, the relationship can be one in which one of the parties holds dominant psychological power that is not derived from a confidential relationship.

The mere existence of a close relationship between the parties that results in economic advantage to one of them is not sufficient for undue influence. It must also appear that the weaker person entered the contract because he was subjected to unfair methods of persuasion. In determining this, a court will look at all of the surrounding facts and circumstances. Was the person isolated and hurried into the contract, or did he have access to outsiders for advice and time to consider his alternatives? Was the contract he entered a reasonably fair one that he might have entered voluntarily, or was it so lopsided and unfair that one could infer that the person would probably not have entered it unless he had been under the domination of another?

Since undue influence is not a tort, the only remedy is rescission of the contract. A large proportion of undue influence cases arise after the death of the person who has been the subject of undue influence, when his relatives seek to set aside that person's contracts or wills.

## Odorizzi v. Bloomfield School District

**54 Cal. Rptr. 533 (Cal. Dist. Ct. 1966)**

Donald Odorizzi was an elementary school teacher employed by the Bloomfield School District. He was arrested on criminal charges of homosexual activity. After having been arrested, questioned by police, booked, and released on bail, and after having gone 40 hours without sleep, he was visited in his home by the superintendent of the district and the principal of his school. They told him that they were trying to help him and that they had his best interests at heart. They advised him to resign immediately, stating that there was no time to consult an attorney. They said that if he did not resign immediately, the district would dismiss him and publicize the proceedings, but that if he resigned at once, the incident would not be publicized and would not jeopardize his chances of securing employment as a teacher elsewhere. Odorizzi gave them a written letter of resignation, which they accepted. The criminal charges against Odorizzi were later dismissed, and he sought to resume his employment with the district. When the district refused to reinstate him, he filed this action to rescind his letter of resignation on grounds that his consent had been obtained through duress, fraud, undue influence, or mistake. His complaint was dismissed, and he appealed. For various reasons, the appellate court found that Odorizzi had not stated a cause of action for duress, fraud, or mistake. It then considered Odorizzi's claim of undue influence.

**Fleming, Justice.** Undue influence is a shorthand legal phrase used to describe persuasion which overcomes the will without convincing the judgment. The hallmark of such persuasion is high pressure, a pressure which works on mental, moral, or emotional weakness to such an extent that it approaches the boundaries of coercion. In this sense, undue influence has been called overpersuasion. While most reported cases of undue influence involve persons who bear a confidential relationship to one another, a confidential or authoritative relationship between the parties need not be present when the undue influence involves unfair advantage taken of another's weakness or distress.

In essence, undue influence involves the use of excessive pressure applied by a dominant subject to a servient object. In combination, the elements of undue susceptibility in the servient person and excessive pressure by the dominating person make the latter's influence undue. Undue susceptibility may consist of weakness which need not be longlasting nor wholly incapacitating, but may be merely a lack of full vigor due to age, physical condition, emotional anguish, or a combination of such factors. In the present case, Odorizzi has pleaded that such weakness at the time he signed his resignation prevented him from freely and competently applying his judgment to the problem before him. He declares he was under severe mental and emotional strain at the time. It is possible that exhaustion and emotional turmoil may incapacitate a person from exercising his judgment.

The difficulty, of course, lies in determining when the forces of persuasion have overflowed their normal banks and become oppressive flood waters. There are second thoughts to every bargain. Undue influence cannot be used as a pretext to avoid bad bargains. If we are temporarily persuaded against our better judgment to do something about which we later have second thoughts, we must abide the consequences of the risks inherent in managing our own affairs.

However, overpersuasion is generally accompanied by certain characteristics which tend to create a pattern. The pattern usually involves several of the following elements: (1) discussion of the transaction at an unusual or inappropriate time, (2) consummation of the transaction in an unusual place, (3) insistent demand that the business be finished at once, (4) extreme emphasis on untoward consequences of delay, (5) the use of multiple persuaders by the dominant side against a single servient party, (6) absence of third-party advisers to the servient party, (7) statements that there is no time to consult financial advisers or attorneys.

The difference between legitimate persuasion and excessive pressure rests to a considerable extent in the manner in which the parties go about their business. For example, if a day or two after Odorizzi's release on bail the superintendent of the school district had called him into his office during business hours and directed his attention to those provisions of the Education Code compelling his leave of absence and authorizing his suspension on the filing of written charges, had told him that the district contemplated filing written charges against him, had pointed out the alternative of resignation available to him, had informed him he was free to consult counsel or any adviser he wished and to consider the matter overnight and return with his decision the next day, it is extremely unlikely that any complaint about the use of excessive pressure could ever have been made against the school district. Rather, the representatives of the school board undertook to achieve their objective by overpersuasion and imposition to secure Odorizzi's signature but not his consent to his resignation through a high-pressure carrot-and-stick technique. Odorizzi has stated sufficient facts to put in issue the question whether his free will had been overborne by the district at a time when he was unable to function in a normal manner.

Judgment reversed in favor of Odorizzi.

## MISTAKE

**Nature of Mistake.** A mistake, as the term is used in contract law, is an erroneous belief about a matter material to a contract. As in misrepresentation cases, the complaining party in a mistake case has entered the contract because of a belief that is at variance with the actual facts. Mistake is unlike misrepresentation, however, in that the erroneous belief is not the result of the other party's misstatements. The doctrine of mistake stands apart from the other doctrines discussed in this chapter because it is not concerned with policing dishonest or unscrupulous conduct. Rather, it is concerned with achieving just results by releasing people from their contracts when a basic misunderstanding about a key fact prevents a "meeting of the minds" between the parties.

To justify relief, the mistake must be an erroneous belief about some *past or existing fact* that is *material* to the contract. The mistake must be one that concerns the subject matter of the contract, not merely a collateral matter. Often, the mistake involves the nature or quality of the subject matter of the contract. *Beachcomber Coins, Inc. v. Boskett,* which follows, is a good example of the type of mistake that can justify relief. Ignorance or poor judgment will not justify relief, because when a person enters a contract despite his awareness of his ignorance or limited knowledge, he bears the risk of mistake. Suppose someone gives you an old, locked file cabinet. Without opening the file cabinet, you sell it and "whatever is inside" to one of your friends for $25. When your friend succeeds in opening the cabinet, he finds $10,000 in cash. In this case, you would not be able to rescind the contract because, in essence, you gambled on your limited knowledge . . . and lost.

A number of the older mistake cases state that mistake about a principle of law will not justify rescission. The rationale for this view was that everyone was presumed to know the law. More modern cases, however, have granted relief even when the mistake is an erroneous belief about some aspect of law.

Mistake cases are generally classified as *mutual* or *unilateral,* depending on whether both or only one of the parties was acting on an erroneous belief. In determining whether to grant relief, courts frequently distinguish between mutual and unilateral mistake.

**Mutual Mistake.** Assuming that the other requirements of the doctrine of mistake are met, mutual mistake is always a basis for rescission at the request of either party to the contract. Common types of mutual mistakes include situations in which both parties have a common erroneous belief about some fact important to the transaction and situations in which an ambiguous term of an agreement was interpreted differently by the parties. In such cases, no true contract was ever formed because there was no "meeting of the minds" between the parties.

**Unilateral Mistake.** Courts are less willing to grant relief when the mistake is in the mind of only one of the parties. The basic rule is that unilateral mistake is not a basis for rescission. The reasoning behind this rule is that the law does not want to give people an easy exit from their contracts. Courts also want to encourage people to exercise reasonable care to find out all the facts when entering their agreements. There are, however, important exceptions to this basic rule. Traditionally, courts have permitted rescission if the nonmistaken party knew of the mistake or if the mistake was so obvious that the nonmistaken party should have realized that a mistake had been made. This is so because the nonmistaken person could have prevented the loss by acting in good faith and informing the person in error that he had made a mistake. It also reflects the moral judgment that people should not take advantage of the mistakes of others. In addition to this exception, section 153 of the *Restatement (Second) of Contracts* permits relief from unilateral mistake where the adverse consequences of the mistake would be so serious that the enforcement of the contract would be unconscionable.

**Mistake Caused by a Person's Negligence.** Courts sometimes state that relief will not be granted when a person's mistake was caused by her own negligence. However, a review of mistake cases reveals that courts have often granted rescission even when the mistaken party was somewhat negligent. Section 157 of the *Restatement (Second) of Contracts* focuses on the *degree* of the mistaken party's negligence in making the mistake. Like the *Restatement* section that deals with justifiable reliance in misrepresentation law, it states that a mistaken party's fault in failing to know or discover facts before entering the contract does not bar relief unless his fault amounts to a failure to act in good faith and in accordance with reasonable standards of fair dealing.

**Mistakes in Drafting Writings.** Sometimes, the parties' mistake takes the form of erroneous *expression* of an agreement, frequently caused by a clerical error in drafting or typing a contract, deed, or other document. Suppose Arnold agrees to sell Barber a vacant lot next to Arnold's home. The vacant lot is "Lot 3, block 1"; Arnold's home is on "Lot 2, block 1." The person typing the contract strikes the wrong key, and the contract reads, "Lot 2, block 1." Neither Arnold nor Barber notices this error when they read and sign the contract, yet clearly they did not intend to have Arnold sell the lot on which his house stands. In such a case, a court will *reform* the contract. That is, it will modify the written instrument to express the agreement that Arnold and Barber really made but failed to express correctly.

## Beachcomber Coins, Inc. v. Boskett

**400 A.2d 78 (N.J. Super. Ct. 1979)**

Boskett, a part-time coin dealer, paid $450 for a dime purportedly minted in 1916 at Denver and two additional coins of relatively small value. After carefully examining this dime, Beachcomber Coins, a retail coin dealer, bought the coin from Boskett for $500. Beachcomber then received an offer from a third party to purchase the dime for $700, subject to certification of its genuineness from the American Numismatic Society. That organization labeled the coin a counterfeit. Beachcomber then brought this action against Boskett for rescission. The trial court held for Boskett, and Beachcomber appealed.

**CONFORD, JUDGE.** The evidence and trial judge's findings establish this as a classic case of rescission for mutual mistake of fact. It is undisputed that both parties believed that the coin was a genuine Denver-minted one. The mistake was mutual in that both parties were laboring under the same misapprehension as to this particular, essential fact. The price asked and paid was directly based on that assumption. That Beachcomber may have been negligent in its inspection of the coin does not bar its claim for rescission.

Boskett's contention that Beachcomber assumed the risk that the coin might be of greater or lesser value than that paid is not supported by the evidence. In this case both parties were certain that the coin was genuine. Beachcomber thought so after its inspection, and Boskett would not have paid nearly $450 for it otherwise.

Judgment reversed in favor of Beachcomber.

## Foster & Marshall, Inc. v. Pfister

**674 P.2d 1215 (Or. Ct. App. 1984)**

Robert and Wendy Pfister asked Foster & Marshall, a stock brokerage firm, to evaluate some stocks that they owned. One of these stocks was 100 shares of "Tracor Computing Corp." The stock was no longer traded on the New York Stock Exchange. The Pfisters did not know the value of the stock, but they believed it to be of little value. They were surprised when Foster & Marshall told them that the stock was trading at $49.50 under its new name, "Continuum Co., Inc.," so that the value of the Pfisters' stock was $4,950. They asked Foster & Marshall to recheck the figures and brought their stock certificates in for verification. On Foster & Marshall's reassurances that they owned 100 shares of Continuum and that these were worth $4,950, Mr. and Mrs. Pfister sold the stock to Foster & Marshall. A year after the transaction, Foster & Marshall discovered that the Tracor Computing stock had been exchanged for Continuum stock at a 10-to-1 ratio and that the Pfisters had owned only 10 shares of Continuum. Consequently, Foster & Marshall had overpaid them by $4,466.25. It then sued the Pfisters for overpayment. The trial court granted a summary judgment to Foster & Marshall, and the Pfisters appealed.

**Warren, Judge.** A party making a unilateral mistake of fact is not entitled to restitution unless the mistake is basic to the contract and known to the other party, or circumstances are such that the other party, as a reasonable person, should have known of the mistake. There is no evidence that the Pfisters had actual knowledge of Foster & Marshall's mistake in valuation of the stock. Therefore, the question is whether the Pfisters, as reasonable persons, should have known of the mistake.

Foster & Marshall argues that, because Mr. Pfister stated that he was "suspicious" (when told of the value of the stock), he knew or should have known that the valuation was mistaken. However, Pfister then insisted that Foster & Marshall recheck the value with the actual stock certificate. Foster & Marshall consulted its Seattle research department and reaffirmed its valuation. Pfister, relying on Foster & Marshall's expertise, then sold the stock to Foster & Marshall. After repeated assurances from an expert in the field as to the value of stock, a reasonable person would not be negligent in relying on that valuation.

It is not inequitable as a matter of law to hold Foster & Marshall to the bad bargain it made as a result of its own negligent research. The Pfisters contend that they have changed their position in reliance on the payment. As a result of the payment to them of $4,962.50, they made a commitment to build a new home which before the payment, had been a "borderline decision."

Judgment reversed and remanded in favor of the Pfisters.

## SUMMARY

The doctrines discussed in this chapter involve situations in which people have the ability to escape contractual obligations because their consent was either based on a distorted impression of the relevant facts or extorted through unscrupulous means. Generally, contracts induced by misrepresentation, fraud, duress, undue influence, or mistake are voidable. To take advantage of this right to avoid a contract, the complaining party must disaffirm the contract promptly.

Misrepresentation is an assertion about a fact material to a contract which is not in accordance with the truth and upon which the other party justifiably relies. Fraud is misrepresentation knowingly made with intent to deceive. "Sales talk," or "puffing," is not a ground for a claim of fraud or misrepresentation. Active concealment of a material fact can be fraud. Although traditional law normally held that a person's mere silence was not misrepresentation, modern law has created duties of disclosure in a broadening range of situations. The contract remedy for misrepresentation or fraud is rescission. Fraud may lead to tort liability for the tort of deceit.

Duress is the exertion of wrongful coercion that induces another person to enter a contract. To constitute duress, the threat must be one that the law considers wrongful. Threats to commit a tort or a crime, file an unfounded criminal or civil lawsuit, or breach a contract without justification are all considered to be wrongful and can be the basis for a claim of duress. Sometimes, threatening to do an act that one has the right to do can be considered wrongful if the threat is made in bad faith, for an ulterior motive. The degree of coercion must have been such that it left the wronged party no choice but to consent to the contract. In recent decades, courts have been much more willing to recognize threats to economic interests as coercive.

Undue influence is unfair persuasion of a person who is in a weak mental or physical state by one who stands in a confidential relationship with that person or holds psychological power over him. If such a relationship exists between the parties and the stronger one has used his position to effect a transaction by which he benefits at the expense of the weaker one, the courts will hold the transaction voidable on the ground of undue influence.

Mistake is an erroneous belief about some matter material to the contract. Mistake must be distinguished from ignorance, limited knowledge, or poor judgment. One who enters a contract knowing that he is ignorant or has limited knowledge about a material fact relating to the contract cannot later escape the contract by claiming mistake. However, there are circumstances under which the courts will relieve a party of a contractual obligation on the ground of mistake. In determining whether to grant relief in the form of rescission or reformation, courts often distinguish between mutual mistakes and unilateral mistakes. If both parties are mistaken about a material fact (mutual mistake), courts will grant relief. If only one of the parties is mistaken (unilateral mistake), courts will generally decline to grant relief unless the nonmistaken party knew or should have known that a mistake had been made. The *Restatement* would grant relief in unilateral mistake cases if the mistake would lead to such serious adverse consequences for the mistaken party that enforcement of the contract would be unconscionable.

Though courts have often said that no relief will be granted where the mistake flows from a party's own negligence, in practice they have granted rescission or reformation in some cases involving slight negligence on the part of mistaken parties. The *Restatement* takes the position that a mistaken person's fault in failing to discover or know facts before entering a contract will not bar relief unless the fault amounted to a failure to act in good faith or to meet reasonable standards of fair dealing. Mistakes in drafting documents will be corrected through the remedy of reformation.

## PROBLEM CASES

**1.** Dr. Sharp was interested in buying stock in Idaho Investment Corporation. Before buying the stock, he asked officers of another corporation for their opinion of Idaho. They gave Idaho a favorable review, so Sharp bought the stock. After having done so, Sharp read some Idaho sales material and a prospectus, which reported Idaho's prospects optimistically. In fact, Idaho's performance fell far short of the predictions made in these materials. Sharp brought an action for damages for fraud based on the statements made in Idaho's sales material and prospectus. Does he have a good case?

**2.** Reed wanted to order 4,000 labels from Monarch. Instead of writing 4,000 on the purchase order form, he used the Roman numeral for 1,000, M, which was commonly used in the label industry. Unfortunately, Reed wrote "4MM," which means 4 million rather than 4,000. Reed and Monarch had dealt together for several years, and Reed had never before ordered more than 4,000 of any type of label at any given time. The price of 4 million labels was $2,680; the price of 4,000 was $13. When transferring Reed's purchase order to the Monarch order form, Monarch's salesman changed the shipping instructions from "parcel post" and "ship at once" to "best way" and "as soon as possible." Monarch sues Reed for the price of the 4 million labels. Should Reed be allowed to rescind the contract?

**3.** Tarrant delivered a diamond engagement ring to Monson, a jeweler, for repairs. Monson stated that the ring would be fixed in two weeks. Tarrant returned to the store several times, but Monson was unable to deliver the ring. After several months, Monson admitted that he could not find the ring and told Tarrant that she could have the ring set of her choice as a replacement. Tarrant chose a replacement set that was worth approximately $450 more than her original ring. Six months later, Monson found Tarrant's ring in his safe. He discovered that he had mislabeled the envelope in which the ring had been stored. Upon making this discovery, Monson informed Tarrant and offered to exchange the rings. Tarrant replied that she would do so if Monson gave her a pair of diamond earrings in addition. Monson refused and brought suit to recover the repair expenses and to rescind the replacement agreement on the ground of mutual mistake of fact. Should he win?

**4.** Heintz was employed as a farmhand by Ollie May Vestal and her late husband from 1959 until Mrs. Vestal's death at the age of 85, in 1977. Mrs. Vestal lived alone on the farm, and Heintz was in charge of all her affairs. She relied on him to perform all of the physical work necessary in running a farm. In 1974, Mrs. Vestal signed a promissory note for more than $26,000, payable to Heintz. The consideration for this note was the use of certain vehicles, trailer rent, and percentage bonuses for Heinz. The amount of the note was quite large in relation to the alleged consideration. Can the validity of the promissory note be attacked on the basis of one of the doctrines you have learned about in this chapter?

**5.** Parham went to East Bay Raceway, where he had never been before, to watch an auto race. After paying admission and receiving a ticket, he was admitted to the grandstand area. He then went to a ticket shack leading to Raceway's restricted areas and told Raceway's employee on duty that he wanted to enter the pit area. The employee told him that he must pay a dollar for "insurance," sign his name on a form for "insurance," and get his hand stamped if he wanted to enter the pit area. Parham paid his dollar and signed a form that was attached to a clipboard with the upper half of the form covered by a folded-up piece of paper. Unknown to Parham, the hidden upper portion of the form he signed contained a release from liability. After entering the pit area, Parham was hit by a racecar and suffered personal injuries. He sued Raceway for these injuries. Raceway defended on the ground that Parham had signed a release. Parham argues that the release is invalid because it was induced by fraud. What result? Why?

**6.** Kory worked for the city of Miami. Under the city's civil service rules, she was to be a probationary employee for six months, during which time she could be discharged without cause. On the last working day of Kory's probationary period, her supervisor handed her a memo which stated that she was discharged. She asked whether she might resign instead, as she was seeking another position with the city. The supervisor stated that he had no objection to this but that the decision was up to her. Shortly thereafter, she returned with a handwritten letter of resignation, which was accepted. When her attempts to find other employment were unsuccessful, Kory visited a lawyer from whom she learned that the supervisor who attempted to discharge her technically did not have the right to do so because he was an assistant director of a department rather than a director, as required by the civil service rules. Kory seeks to set aside her letter of resignation, arguing that it was procured by duress. Should she prevail?

**7.** The Isaacs bought Lot 31, a parcel of undeveloped real estate located on a hillside, from Bokor, a real estate developer. Because of the rugged terrain of the property, only one point on the lot was appropriate for a building site. Dense foliage made it difficult for a person to see from one corner to any other corner or for a person standing in the center portion of the lot to see the lot lines and corners. Although Bokor denied it, the Isaacs claimed that he had walked some of the lot lines with them and had accompanied them to the very attractive building site. The Isaacs contracted with Bokor to build a house for them at that point, which all the parties believed was located within the borders of Lot 31. After construction was substantially under way, a neighbor informed Bokor that he had discovered that the house was being built on the neighbor's property. This was verified by a surveyor. The Isaacs disaffirmed the contract and demanded the return of all the money they had paid. Bokor denied any misrepresentation and sued for the unpaid balance of the building contract. What should the result be? Why?

**8.** The Sontags and the Eatons had been good friends for 15 years. The Eatons decided to sell the campground they owned in Maine. When the Sontags visited the Eatons in their Connecticut home at Christmastime, the campground became a recurrent topic of conversation. The Eatons sent the Sontags plans of the campground project and information about the complete investment costs to date. The Eatons allegedly stated that the campground was a "gold mine." The Sontags bought the campground for $80,000. Their first summer operation was a complete disappointment, as they grossed slightly over $400. The Sontags complained that the Eatons had overcharged them and asked the Eatons to repurchase the property. The Eatons refused; the Sontags ceased making payments; and the Eatons sued them. The Sontags claim that the transaction should be rescinded on the ground of undue influence and fraud. What result? Why?

**9.** Vilanor induced Upledger to purchase an apartment building, making false statements regarding the amount of rents and the duration of leases. Upledger admitted that he had not investigated these claims by consulting the tenants or inspecting the leases. The trial court ruled for the defendant on the ground that Upledger had a duty to protect himself by making reasonable inquiry. Should this ruling be reversed on appeal?

**10.** Wurtz was the owner of a hotel, and Fleishman sought to purchase the property. For tax reasons, Wurtz wanted to exchange the property for real estate rather than cash. After protracted negotiations, it was agreed that Fleishman would acquire a McDonald's restaurant in New Mexico and a warehouse in Wisconsin to exchange for Wurtz's property. Fleishman made commitments on these properties and spent substantial sums for architectural studies, title investigation, and legal fees related to the hotel. The closing date originally agreed upon passed, but the parties were in continual contact and negotiation. The night before the actual closing, Wurtz threatened to back out of the deal unless Fleishman agreed to pay $50,000 additional consideration. Fleishman, who had committed large sums to the purchase of the exchange properties, feared bankruptcy if the deal fell through and offered Wurtz stock worth $47,000. After the closing, Fleishman refused to transfer the promised shares, claiming economic duress. Wurtz sued to get the shares. Will Wurtz win?

# Chapter 10

## THE IDEA OF CONSIDERATION

One of the things that separates a contract from an unenforceable social promise is that a contract requires *voluntary agreement* by two or more parties. Not all agreements, however, will amount to an enforceable contract. At a fairly early point in the development of classical contract law, the common law courts decided not to enforce "gratuitous" (free) promises. Instead, it was decided that only promises *supported by consideration* would be enforceable in a court of law. This was consistent with the notion that the purpose of contract law was to enforce freely made *bargains.* As one 19th-century work on contract put it: "The common law . . . gives effect only to contracts that are founded on the mutual exigencies of men, and does not compel the performance of any merely gratuitous agreements."[1] A common definition of **consideration** is *legal value, bargained for and given in exchange for an act or a promise.*

Thus, a promise generally will not be enforced against the person who made it (the *promisor*) unless the person to whom the

[1] T. Metcalf, *Principles of the Law of Contracts,* p. 161 (1874).

promise was made (the *promisee*) has given up something of legal value in exchange for the promise. In effect, the requirement of consideration means that a promisee must pay the "price" that the promisor asked for in order to gain the right to enforce the promisor's promise. So, if the promisor did not ask for anything in exchange for making her promise or if what the promisor asked for did not have legal value (e.g., because it was something that she was already entitled to), her promise will not be enforceable against her because it is not supported by consideration.

Consider the early case of *Thorne v. Deas,*[2] in which the part owner of a sailing vessel named the *Sea Nymph* promised his co-owners that he would insure the ship for an upcoming voyage. He failed to do so, and when the ship was lost at sea, the court found that he was not liable to his co-owners for breaching his promise to insure the ship. Why? Because his promise was purely gratuitous: he had neither asked for nor received anything in exchange for making it. Therefore, it was unenforceable because it was not supported by consideration. This early example illustrates two important aspects of the consideration requirement. First, the requirement tended to limit the scope of a promisor's liability for his promises by insulating him from liability for gratuitous promises and by protecting him against liability for reliance on such promises. Second, the mechanical application of the requirement often produced unfair results. This potential for unfairness has produced considerable dissatisfaction with the consideration concept. As the rest of this chapter will indicate, the relative importance of consideration in modern contract law has been somewhat eroded by numerous exceptions to the consideration requirement and by judicial applications of consideration principles in a manner aimed at producing fair results.

## LEGAL VALUE

Consideration can be an *act* (as in the case of a unilateral contract) or a *promise* (as in the case of a bilateral contract). An act or a promise can have *legal value* in one of two ways. If, in exchange for the promisor's promise, the promisee does, or agrees to do, something he had no prior legal duty to do, that provides legal value. If, in exchange for the promisor's promise, the promisee refrains from doing, or agrees not to do, something he has a legal right to do, that also provides legal value. Note that this definition does not require that an act or a promise have *monetary* (economic) value to amount to consideration. Thus, in a famous 19th-century case, *Hamer v. Sidway,*[3] an uncle's promise to pay his nephew $5,000 if he refrained from using tobacco, drinking, swearing, and playing cards or billiards for money until his 21st birthday was held to be supported by consideration when the nephew refrained from doing any of these acts, even though the nephew may have benefited from refraining to do so. He had a legal right to indulge in such activities, and he had refrained from doing so at his uncle's request and in exchange for his uncle's promise. This was all that was required for consideration.

**Adequacy of Consideration.** The point that the legal value requirement is not concerned with actual value is further borne out by the fact that the courts generally will *not* concern themselves with questions regarding the *adequacy* of the consideration that the promisee gave. This means that as long as the promisee's act or promise satisfies the le-

[2] 4 Johns. 84 (N.Y. 1809).

[3] 27 N.E. 256 (N.Y. Ct. App. 1891).

gal value test, the courts will not ask whether that act or promise was worth what the promisor gave, or promised to give, in return for it. This rule on adequacy of consideration reflects the laissez-faire assumptions underlying classical contract law. Freedom of contract includes the freedom to make bad bargains as well as good ones, so promisors' promises are enforceable if they "got what they asked for" in exchange for making their promises, even if "what they asked for" was not nearly so valuable in worldly terms as what they promised in return. Also, a court taking a "hands-off" stance concerning private contracts would be reluctant to step in and "second-guess" the parties by setting aside a transaction that both parties at one time considered satisfactory. Finally, the rule against considering the adequacy of consideration can promote certainty and predictability in commercial transactions by denying legal effect to what would otherwise be a possible basis for challenging the enforceability of a contract: the inequality of the exchange.

Several qualifications must be made concerning the general rule on adequacy of consideration. First, if the inadequacy of consideration is apparent *on the face of the agreement,* most courts will conclude that the agreement was a disguised gift rather than an enforceable bargain. Thus, an agreement calling for an unequal exchange of money (e.g., $500 for $1,000) or identical goods (20 business law textbooks for 40 identical business law textbooks) and containing no other terms would probably be unenforceable.

Gross inadequacy of consideration may also give rise to an inference of fraud, duress, lack of capacity, or some other independent basis for setting aside a contract. However, inadequacy of consideration, standing alone, is never sufficient to prove lack of true consent or contractual capacity.

It should also be noted that although gross inadequacy of consideration is not, by itself, ordinarily a sufficient reason to set aside a contract, the courts may refuse to grant specific performance or other equitable remedies to persons seeking to enforce unfair bargains.

Finally, some agreements recite "$1," or "$1 and other valuable consideration," or some other small amount as consideration for a promise. If no other consideration is actually exchanged, this is called *nominal consideration.* Often, such agreements are attempts to make gratuitous promises look like true bargains by reciting a nonexistent consideration. Most courts will refuse to enforce such agreements unless they find that the stated consideration was truly bargained for. Similar reasoning (holding that an agreement is not a true bargain) has been employed by a few courts to strike down agreements where the alleged consideration was so inadequate that it "shocks the conscience of the court."

**Adequacy and Unconscionability.** The advent of the Uniform Commercial Code has given modern courts a potentially powerful tool for policing unfair agreements: the Code's broad section on "unconscionable" contracts [2–302].[4] In recent years, a few courts have used this section to strike down contracts involving grossly unfair price provisions. These cases normally involve situations where a consumer has agreed to pay a merchant two or three times the market price for the goods. They also commonly involve other factors frequently encountered in unconscionability cases, such as complex, well-hidden, or deceptive contract terms and high-pressure sales tactics. While such cases are still fairly rare, they may represent the seeds of a significant new direction in the evolution of contract law.

**Illusory Promises.** For a promise to serve as consideration in a bilateral contract, the promisee must have promised to do, or to re-

[4] Unconscionability is discussed in detail in Chapter 12.

frain from doing, something at the promisor's request. It seems obvious, therefore, that if the promisee's promise is *illusory* because it really does not bind the promisee to do or refrain from doing anything, such a promise could not serve as consideration. Agreements of this kind are often said to lack the *mutuality of obligation* that is required for an agreement to be enforceable. So, a promisee's promise to "buy all the sugar that I want" or to "paint your house if I feel like it" would not be sufficient consideration for a promisor's return promise to sell sugar or hire a painter. In neither case has the promisee given the promisor anything of legal value in exchange for the promisor's promise.

**Cancellation or Termination Clauses.** The fact that an agreement allows one or both of the parties to cancel or terminate their contractual obligations does not necessarily mean that the party or parties with the power to cancel have given an illusory promise. Such provisions are a common and necessary part of many business relationships. The central issue in such cases concerns whether a promise subject to cancellation or termination actually represents a binding obligation. A right to cancel or terminate at any time, for any reason, and without any notice would clearly render illusory any other promise by the party possessing such a right. However, limits on the circumstances (e.g., a dealer's failure to live up to dealership obligations) or the time (e.g., no cancellations for the first 90 days) in which cancellation may occur or a requirement of advance notice of cancellation (e.g., a 30-day notice requirement) would all effectively remove a promise from the illusory category. This is so because in each case the party making such a promise has bound himself to do *something* in exchange for the other party's promise.

Of course, some parties to agreements may not want their agreements to amount to binding contracts. For example, a manufacturer selling through a system of independent retail dealers may want to retain maximum flexibility by giving itself a unilateral right to terminate a dealer at any time, for any reason, without notice. Such an "intentional no contract" strategy relies on the fact that the manufacturer's greater bargaining power may allow it to impose such terms on its dealers. This kind of business strategy is very difficult, if not impossible, to pursue today, however, given the numerous "dealer day in court" statutes that past abuses have produced and the fact that many courts have stricken down unilateral cancellation clauses as unconscionable.

**Output and Requirements Contracts.** Contracts in which one party to the agreement agrees to buy all of the other party's production of a particular commodity (*output* contracts) or to supply all of another party's needs for a particular commodity (*requirements* contracts) are common types of business transactions that can serve legitimate business purposes. They can reduce a seller's selling costs and provide buyers with a secure source of supply. Nonetheless, many common law courts refused to enforce such agreements on the ground that their failure to specify the quantity of goods to be produced or purchased rendered them illusory. The courts also feared that a party to such an agreement might be tempted to exploit the other party if subsequent market conditions made it profitable for the seller in an output contract or the buyer in a requirements contract to demand that the other party buy or provide more of the particular commodity than the other party had actually intended to buy or sell. The Code legitimizes such contracts by limiting a party's demands to those quantity needs that occur in good faith and are not unreasonably disproportionate to any quantity estimate contained in the contract, or to any normal prior output or requirements if no estimate is stated [2–306(1)]. This subject is discussed in greater detail in Chapter 31.

**Exclusive Dealing Contracts.** When a manufacturer of goods enters an agreement giving a distributor the exclusive right to sell the manufacturer's products in a particular territory, does such an agreement impose sufficient obligations on both parties to meet the "legal value" test? Put another way, does the distributor have any duty to sell the manufacturer's products and does the manufacturer have any duty to supply any particular number of products? Such agreements are commonly encountered in today's business world, and they can serve the legitimate interests of both parties. The Code recognizes this fact by providing that, unless the parties agree to the contrary, an exclusive dealing contract imposes a duty on the distributor to use his best efforts to sell the goods and imposes a reciprocal duty on the manufacturer to use his best efforts to supply the goods [2–306(2)].

## Bonner v. Westbound Records, Inc.

**394 N.E. 2d 1303 (Ill. Ct. App. 1979)**

On March 24, 1972, Leroy Bonner and four other members of a rock group called The Ohio Players signed contracts with Westbound Records and Bridgeport Music, Inc. The contract with Westbound required the group to record exclusively for Westbound for five years. Under the contract with Bridgeport, Bridgeport was to employ the group as authors and arrangers of musical compositions for the duration of the recording contract with Westbound. Both contracts gave Westbound and Bridgeport the discretionary power to decide whether to market any records or music produced under the agreement. Upon signing the contracts, the group was given a $4,000 "advance against royalties" by Westbound and Bridgeport.

In the 21 months immediately following the execution of the contracts, the group recorded four single records and two albums for Westbound. These were successfully distributed on a national basis, and one of the records, "Funky Worm," was the recipient of a gold record, which in the record industry symbolizes sales in excess of $1 million. During the months in which these recordings were being made, Westbound advanced $59,390 for the costs of recording session wages for the group. In addition, Westbound and Bridgeport advanced $22,509 to the group to enable them to pay taxes they owed and to settle litigation against them. The group had no personal obligation to repay any of these advances. Westbound and Bridgeport could recoup the advances only out of royalties payable to the group.

In January 1974, the group repudiated the recording agreement with Westbound and signed an exclusive recording contract with Mercury Records. They filed suit seeking a judgment that the recording contract was unenforceable due to lack of consideration. The trial court ruled in the group's favor, and Westbound appealed.

**Simon, Presiding Justice.** The group argues that the recording agreement lacked mutuality because even though The Ohio Players were obligated to make a minimum number of recordings, Westbound was not required to make even a single recording using The Ohio

Players. It is our view that consideration passed to The Ohio Players when they accepted $4,000 to enter the agreements. The fact that this payment was made by Westbound and Bridgeport by a check containing the notation that it was "an advance against royalties" does not disqualify the payment from being regarded as consideration. If sufficient royalties were not earned to repay Westbound the $4,000, The Ohio Players would not have been obligated to return it. By making the $4,000 advance, Westbound suffered a legal detriment and The Ohio Players received a legal advantage.

It is not the function of either the circuit court or this court to review the amount of the consideration which passed to decide whether either party made a bad bargain unless the amount is so grossly inadequate as to shock the conscience of the court.

The advance The Ohio Players received, taken together with their expectation of what Westbound would accomplish in their behalf, does not shock our conscience. On the contrary, to a performing group which had never been successful in making records, Westbound offered an attractive proposal. The adequacy of consideration must be determined as of the time a contract is agreed upon, not from the hindsight of how the parties fare under it.

Even had Westbound and Bridgeport not made the $4,000 advance, the group could not prevail. During the first 21 months of the agreement, Westbound expended in excess of $80,000 to promote the group and pay their taxes and compromise litigation against them, and during this period the group recorded four single records and two albums. The consistent pattern of good faith efforts by both parties demonstrates that they intended to be bound and to bind each other. Disregarding the performance under the agreements, the law implies mutual promises to use good faith in interpreting an agreement and good faith and fair dealing in carrying out its purposes.

The provisions in the contract reserve to Westbound and Bridgeport the discretion to control the content of recordings and the timing and number of releases. Flexibility of this type was essential in order to achieve the greatest success for the group as well as for Westbound and Bridgeport. Nothing in either agreement or in the conduct of the parties demonstrates that Westbound or Bridgeport could or did use this discretion arbitrarily or in bad faith.

Judgment reversed in favor of Westbound.

**Preexisting Duties.** The legal value component of our consideration definition not only requires that a promisee do or promise to do *something* in exchange for a promisor's promise; it also requires that the promisee do, or promise to do, something that he or she had *no prior legal duty to do.* Thus, as a general rule, performing or agreeing to perform a preexisting duty will *not* be consideration. This seems fair because the promisor in such a case has effectively made a gratuitous promise, since she was already entitled to the promisee's performance.

**Preexisting Public Duties.** Every member of society has a duty to obey the law and refrain from committing crimes or torts. Therefore, a promisee's promise not to commit such an act can never be consideration. So, Thomas's promise to pay Brown $100 a year in exchange for Brown's promise not to burn Thomas's barn would not be enforceable against Thomas. Since Brown has a preexisting duty not to burn Thomas's barn, his promise lacks legal value.

Similarly, public officials, by virtue of their public offices, have a preexisting legal duty to perform their public responsibilities. For example, Smith, the owner of a liquor store, promises to pay Fawcett, a police officer whose "beat" includes Smith's store, $50 a week to "keep an eye on the store" while walking her beat. Smith's promise is unenforceable because Fawcett has agreed to do something that she already has a duty to do.

**Preexisting Contractual Duties.** The most important preexisting duty cases are those that involve preexisting *contractual* duties. These cases generally occur when the parties to an existing contract agree to *modify* that contract. The general common law rule on contract modification holds that an agreement to modify an existing contract requires some *new consideration* to be binding.

For example, Turner enters into a contract with Acme Construction Company for the construction of a new office building for $350,000. When the construction is partially completed, Acme tells Turner that due to rising labor and materials costs it will stop construction unless Turner agrees to pay an extra $50,000. Turner, having already entered into contracts to lease office space in the new building, promises to pay the extra amount. When the construction is finished, Turner refuses to pay more than $350,000. Is Turner's promise to pay the extra $50,000 enforceable against him? No. All Acme has done in exchange for Turner's promise to pay more is build the building, something that Acme had a preexisting contractual duty to do. Therefore, Acme's performance is not consideration for Turner's promise to pay more.

While the result in the preceding example seems fair (why should Turner have to pay $400,000 for something he had a right to receive for $350,000?) and is consistent with consideration theory, the application of the preexisting duty rule to contract modifications has been the focus of a great deal of criticism. Plainly, the rule can protect a party to a contract such as Turner from being pressured into paying more because the other party to the contract is trying to take advantage of his situation by demanding an additional amount for performance. However, mechanical application of the rule could also produce unfair results when the parties have freely agreed to a fair modification of their contract. Some critics argue that the purpose of contract modification law should be to enforce freely made modifications of existing contracts and to deny enforcement to coerced modifications. Such critics commonly suggest that general principles such as good faith and unconscionability, rather than technical consideration rules, should be used to police contract modifications.

Other observers argue that most courts in fact apply the preexisting duty rule in a manner calculated to reach fair results, because there are several exceptions to the rule that can be used to enforce a fair modification agreement. For example, any new consideration furnished by the promisee will provide sufficient consideration to support a promise to modify an existing contract. So, if Acme had promised to finish construction a week before the completion date called for in the original contract, or had promised to make some change in the original contract specifications (e.g., install a better grade of carpet), Acme would have done something that it had no legal duty to do in exchange for Turner's new promise. Turner's promise to pay more would then be enforceable because it would be supported by new consideration.

Many courts will also enforce an agreement to modify an existing contract if the modification resulted from *unforeseen circumstances* that made one party's performance far more difficult than the parties originally anticipated. For example, if Acme had requested the extra payment because abnormal subsurface rock formations made excavation on the construction site far more costly and time consuming than could have been reasonably expected, many courts would enforce Turner's promise to pay more.

Courts can also enforce fair modification agreements by holding that the parties mutually agreed to terminate their original contract and then entered a new one. Because contracts are created by the will of the parties, they can be terminated in the same fashion. Each party agrees to release the other party from his contractual obligations in exchange for the other party's promise to do the same. Since such a mutual agreement terminates all duties owed under the original agreement, any subsequent agreement by the parties would not be subject to the preexisting duty rule. A court is likely to take this approach, however, only when it is convinced that the modification agreement was fair and free from coercion.

**Code Contract Modification.** The drafters of the Code sought to avoid many of the problems caused by the consideration requirement by dispensing with it in two important situations. As you learned in Chapter 6, the Code does not require consideration for firm offers [2–205]. The Code also provides that an agreement to modify a contract for the sale of goods needs *no consideration* to be binding [2–209(1)].

For example, Video World orders 500 RCA videodisc players at $150 per unit in response to an RCA promotional campaign heralding the introduction of this new home entertainment device. Initial sales figures indicate, however, that the consuming public is unimpressed with videodisc technology. Video World seeks to cancel its order, but RCA refuses to agree to cancellation. Instead, RCA seeks to mollify a valued customer by offering to reduce the price to $100 per unit. Video World agrees, but when the players arrive, RCA bills Video World for $150 per unit. Under classical contract principles, RCA's promise to reduce the price of the goods would not be enforceable because Video World has furnished no new consideration in exchange for RCA's promise. Under the Code, no new consideration is necessary and the agreement to modify the contract is enforceable.

Several things should be made clear about the operation of this Code rule. First, RCA had no duty to agree to a modification and could have insisted on payment of $150 per unit. Second, modification agreements under the Code are still subject to scrutiny under the general Code principles of good faith and unconscionability, so unfair agreements or agreements that are the product of coercion are unlikely to be enforced. Finally, the Code contains two provisions to protect people from fictitious claims that an agreement has been modified. If the original agreement requires any modification to be in writing, an oral modification is unenforceable [2–209(2)]. Regardless of what the original agreement says, if the price of the goods in the modified contract is $500 or more, the modification is unenforceable unless the requirements of the Code's statute of frauds section [2–201][5] are satisfied [2–209(3)].

[5] Section 2–201 of the Code is discussed in detail in Chapter 13.

## Carroccia v. Todd

**615 P.2d 225 (Mont. Sup. Ct. 1980)**

William and Michelle Carroccia contracted to have Charles Todd build them a log home on their ranch near Big Timber, Montana. Todd built the home, but it had numerous structural problems resulting from the inadequate construction techniques he used. After a windstorm had damaged the house, the Carroccias hired Todd to replace tie-rods in the walls of the house in an attempt to correct the structural problems. The tie-rods themselves were improperly installed, and the structural problems persisted, necessitating further repairs by the Carroccias. They never paid Todd for installing the tie-rods, and they filed suit against him for negligence in constructing the house. Todd counterclaimed for payment for installing the tie-rods. The trial court ruled in the Carroccias' favor, and Todd appealed.

**Sheehy, Justice.** Todd had a common law duty to construct the house in a workmanlike manner. Here the duty of construction included proper installation of log doors and windows in such a manner as to assure stability. The tie rods were installed only after the original construction had proven inadequate. The instability persisted after the installation of the rods.

A promise to do what a person is already obligated by law or contract to do is not sufficient consideration for a promise made in return. Todd's duty as a contractor was not fulfilled by him at any time before or after the installation of the tie rods. Consideration was therefore lacking in the claimed supplemental agreement.

Judgment for the Carroccias affirmed.

## Ruble Forest Products, Inc. v. Lancer Mobile Homes

**524 P.2d 1204 (Or. Sup. Ct. 1974)**

Between August 10 and September 18, 1971, Ruble, a lumber broker, sold 11 truckloads of lumber to Lancer for $31,091.24. Lancer paid $9,695.42 on the account but failed to pay the balance due. On October 15, Ruble telephoned Lancer requesting payment and Lancer stated that it had received "about $5,000" worth of defective lumber from Ruble since 1969 and that there would have to be a "compromise" deal before it made any further payments. Ruble then offered to extend Lancer a "credit" of $2,500 on the account, and a schedule for payment of the balance was agreed upon. Lancer made the last of the scheduled payments on January 24, 1972. On March 22, 1972, Ruble filed this suit for the $2,500 balance. The trial court ruled in Lancer's favor, and Ruble appealed.

**TONGUE, JUSTICE.** Ruble relies upon the rule that an agreement to take less than the whole amount of a liquidated claim is without consideration and unenforceable. It is true that this is the rule at common law, as recognized in Oregon and in most jurisdictions, unless changed by statute.

Even at common law, however, it is also the established rule, that:

> A compromise and settlement of a bona fide controversy between the parties, where each having equal knowledge or equal means of knowledge of the facts in good faith claims a right in himself against the other, and which claim the parties consider good or doubtful, constitutes a valid binding agreement and is a sufficient consideration to support a new contract, even though the law and facts were such that a court would not have adjudged such an adjustment.

In addition, as contended by Lancer, this sale of lumber was subject to the provisions of the Uniform Commercial Code, including the following provision, as stated in ORS 72.2090(1) and (3):

> (1) An agreement modifying a contract within ORS 72.1010 to 72.7250 needs no consideration to be binding. It is still required, however, that in order for an agreement modifying a contract to be valid, the agreement must have been made in good faith.

Thus, as stated in Comment 2 to ORS 72.2090:

> [M]odifications made thereunder must meet the test of good faith imposed by the Uniform Commercial Code. The effective use of bad faith to escape performance on the original contract terms is barred, and the extortion of a "modification" without legitimate commercial reason is ineffective as a violation of the duty of good faith. Nor can a mere technical consideration support a modification made in bad faith.

The test of good faith between merchants or as against merchants includes observance of reasonable commercial standards of fair dealing in the trade, and may in some situations require an objectively demonstrable reason for seeking a modification.

Ruble vigorously contends that "it [was] not in good faith for Lancer to thus coerce Ruble by withholding payment of any part of the debt" and that Lancer "completely failed to carry its burden of proof as to a bona fide dispute and a bona fide compromise of that dispute."

We find that Lancer offered evidence which was sufficient to support a finding by the trial court that Lancer did not act in bad faith with an intent to coerce Ruble, but acted in good faith, and that there was a bona fide controversy between these parties.

Judgment for Lancer affirmed.

---

**Debt Settlement Agreements.** One special variant of the preexisting duty rule that causes considerable confusion occurs when a debtor offers to pay a creditor a sum less than the creditor is demanding, in exchange for the creditor's promise to accept the part payment as full payment of the debt. If the creditor later sues for the balance of the debt, is the creditor's promise to take less enforceable? The answer depends on the nature of the debt and on the circumstances of the debtor's payment.

**Liquidated Debts.** A promise to discharge a **liquidated debt** for part payment of the debt *at or after* its due date is *unenforceable* for lack of consideration. Liquidated debts are both *due and certain:* there is no bona fide dispute about the *existence* or the *amount* of the debt. If a debtor does nothing more than pay less than an amount he clearly owes, how could that be consideration for a creditor's promise to take less? Such a debtor has actually done less than he had a preexisting legal duty to do, namely, to pay the full amount of the debt.

For example, Connor borrows $10,000 from Friendly Finance Company, payable in one year. On the day payment is due, Connor sends Friendly a check for $9,000 marked: "Payment in full for all claims Friendly Finance has against me." Friendly cashes Connor's check (impliedly promising to accept it as full payment by cashing it) and later sues Connor for $1,000. Friendly is entitled to the $1,000 because Connor has given no consideration to support Friendly's implied promise to accept $9,000 as full payment.

However, had Connor done something he had no preexisting duty to do in exchange for Friendly's promise to settle for part payment, he could enforce Friendly's promise and avoid paying the $1,000. For example, if Connor had *paid early* (before the loan contract called for payment), or in a *different medium of exchange* than that called for in the loan contract (e.g., $4,000 in cash and a car worth $5,000), he would have given consideration for Friendly's promise.

**Unliquidated Debts.** A bona fide (good faith) dispute about either the existence or the amount of a debt makes the debt an **unliquidated debt.** For example, Computer Corner, a retailer, orders 50 personal computers and associated software packages from Computech for $75,000. After receiving the goods, Computer Corner refuses to pay Computech the full $75,000, arguing that some of the computers were defective and that some of the software it received did not conform to its order. Computer Corner sends Computech a check for $60,000 marked: "Payment in full for all goods received from Computech." A creditor in Computech's position obviously faces a real dilemma. If Computech cashes Computer Corner's check, it will be held to have impliedly promised to accept $60,000 as full payment. This promise would be enforceable against Computech if it later sought to collect the remaining $15,000, because by agreeing to settle a disputed claim, Computech has entered a binding **accord and satisfaction.** Computech's promise to accept part payment as full payment would be enforceable because Computer Corner has given consideration to support it: Computer Corner has given up its right to have a court determine the amount it owes Computech. Since this is something that Computer Corner had no duty to do, and it and the $60,000 are what was given in exchange for Computech's implied promise, the consideration requirement is satisfied. The result in this case is supported not only by consideration theory but also by a strong public policy in favor of encouraging parties to settle their disputes out of court. Who would bother to settle disputed claims out of court if settlement agreements were unenforceable?

Computech could refuse to accept Computer Corner's settlement offer and sue for the full $75,000, but doing so involves several risks. A court may decide that Computer Corner's arguments are valid and award Computech less than $60,000. Even if Computech is successful, it may take years to resolve the case in the courts through the expensive and time-consuming litigation process, and there is always the chance that Computer Corner may file for bankruptcy before any judgment can be collected. Faced with such risks, Computech may feel that it has no practical alternative other than to cash Computer Corner's check.

In some states, a creditor such as Computech has a third, and much more desirable, alternative course of action to either returning the debtor's "full payment" check or cashing it and entering an accord and satisfaction. Some state courts have held that the Code has changed the common law accord and satisfaction rule by allowing a creditor to accept a full-payment check "under protest" or "without prejudice" without giving up any rights to sue for the balance due under the contract [1–207]. Whether section 1–207 was ever intended to have this effect is a matter that is subject to considerable dispute, and some courts have rejected such an interpretation of the Code. However, in states where the courts have applied section 1–207 to accord and satisfaction cases, a creditor can now accept part payment under protest and still seek to collect the remainder of the debt.

**Composition Agreements.** Composition agreements are agreements between a debtor and two or more creditors who agree to accept as full payment a stated percentage of their liquidated claims against the debtor at or after the date on which those claims are payable. Composition agreements are generally enforced by the courts despite the fact that enforcement appears to be contrary to the general rule on part payment of liquidated debts. Many courts have justified enforcing composition agreements on the ground that the creditors' mutual agreement to accept less than the amount due them provides the necessary consideration. The main reason why creditors agree to compositions is that they fear that their failure to do so may force the debtor into bankruptcy proceedings, in which case they might ultimately recover a smaller percentage of their claims than that agreed to in the composition.

**Forbearance to Sue.** An agreement by a promisee to refrain (or forbear) from pursuing a legal claim against a promisor can be valid consideration to support a return promise (usually to pay a sum of money) by a promisor. The promisee has agreed not to do something that she has a legal right to do (file suit) in exchange for the promisor's promise. The courts do not wish to sanction extortion by allowing people to threaten to file spurious claims against others in the hope that those threatened will agree to some payment to avoid the expense or embarrassment associated with defending a lawsuit. On the other hand, we have a strong public policy favoring private settlement of disputes and we do not want to require people to "second-guess" the courts. Therefore, it is generally said that the promisee must have a *good faith* belief in the validity of his or her claim before forbearance will amount to consideration.

## Flambeau Prods. Corp. v. Honeywell Information Sys., Inc.

**330 N.W. 2d 228 (Wis. Ct. App. 1983)**

Flambeau contracted to purchase computer equipment and key tapes from Honeywell's Wisconsin office. The purchase contracts provided that Flambeau was to pay the purchase price in monthly installments. Honeywell granted Flambeau the option of prepaying its obligations under the contract at any time and established a $14,000 credit for computer programming services that Flambeau could use until October 1, 1976. Flambeau utilized part of this credit prior to its expiration.

Flambeau requested a prepayment quotation from Honeywell for payment as of January 31, 1977. Honeywell quoted $109,412 as the amount of principal and accrued interest due, which Flambeau did not dispute. After receiving this quotation, Flambeau sent a check for $95,412 and a letter addressed to Honeywell to a post office box in Chicago, Illinois, which was a lockbox that Honeywell had established with the Northern Trust Company. The check was marked as payment in full of Flambeau's obligations under the purchase contracts. The accompanying letter also stated that the check was in full settlement of Flambeau's contractual obligations, and it indicated that a $14,000 deducation for unused programming had been taken from the figure Honeywell had quoted. Although Northern Trust was not authorized to cash checks bearing qualifying notations, it cashed Flambeau's check and deposited the proceeds in Honeywell's account on February 4, 1977.

Honeywell's Wisconsin office did not learn until March 11, 1977, that the check had been tendered and cashed and that Flambeau had sent an accompanying letter. On the next business day, Honeywell's Wisconsin office notified Flambeau via letter that the check did not constitute full payment of Flambeau's contractual obligations and that Honeywell did not accept it as such. Honeywell also requested that Flambeau remit the remaining balance plus accrued interest. Honeywell did not return any of the proceeds from the cashed check to Flambeau.

Flambeau sought a declaratory judgment against Honeywell to the effect that Flambeau had no additional obligations to Honeywell and that Honeywell had no security interest in Flambeau's computer equipment. The trial court ruled in Flambeau's favor, and Honeywell appealed.

**Cane, Justice.** Flambeau argues that its assertion of a claimed offset in the letter accompanying the check rendered Honeywell's claim disputed and unliquidated, and that its payment of an amount it concedes it owed to Honeywell and Honeywell's retention of the proceeds after Honeywell learned of Flambeau's claim constituted an accord and satisfaction.

It is undisputed that Northern Trust, as agent for Honeywell, had no authority to cash a check marked as payment in full. There is no evidence that Northern Trust had any knowledge of a possible dispute between Flambeau and Honeywell that could be imputed to Honeywell, or that it was authorized to settle an account on Honeywell's behalf. There is also no evidence that Flambeau disputed the amount Honeywell quoted until it sent the check and letter in which it claimed an offset.

Even if Honeywell's retention of the check proceeds for its use after it learned of and disputed Flambeau's right to an offset constituted an accord and satisfaction under common law principles, we conclude that an accord and satisfaction was not effected because Honeywell reserved its right to full performance from Flambeau under section 1–207 of the UCC. Because the controversy between Flambeau and Honeywell involves a commercial transaction for the sale of goods, that transaction is governed by the provisions of the code.

Section 1–207 provides:

> Performance or acceptance under reservation of rights. A party who with explicit reservation of rights performs or promises performance or assents to performance in a manner demanded or offered by the other party does not thereby prejudice the rights reserved. Such words as "without prejudice," "under protest" or the like are sufficient.

Wisconsin has not addressed the applicability of section 1–207 to the cashing of a check marked "payment in full" whereby the creditor attempts to reserve his right to recover the balance of his claim not covered by the check. Some jurisdictions have either held or stated by way of dicta that section 1–207 allows a payee in a Code-covered transaction to cash a conditional check, retain the proceeds, and avoid the operation of an accord and satisfaction if he explicitly reserves his right to full performance from the payor. Other jurisdictions have reached the opposite conclusion. At least one commentator on the Uniform Commercial Code has questioned the applicability of section 1–207 to the conditional check and has relied on the official comment section to 1–207, which states in part: "This section provides machinery for the continuation of performance along the lines contemplated by the contract despite a pending dispute." Because an accord and satisfaction involves a new contract, it is argued that this is inconsistent with a "performance along the lines contemplated by the contract." Others have recognized, however, that offering a reasonable payment in full satisfaction of an obligation inflicts "commercial torture" on the payee and have concluded that where the payee has explicitly reserved his rights, section 1–207 applies to the conditional check situation. Although some have criticized this interpretation on the ground that it may discourage settlements and unfairly favor creditors, it is also recognized that the common law doctrine of accord and satisfaction often gives debtors an unfair advantage over creditors, and that section 1–207 may be an effort to balance the scales.

The Wisconsin Legislative Council's report concerning section 1–207 supports a conclusion that the statute applies to the acceptance under protest of a conditional check tendered in a Code-covered transaction. The annotation states in part: "Provides a method of procedure whereby one party claiming a right which the other party feels to be unwarranted can make certain that the fact that he proceeds with or promises or assents to performance will not operate as a waiver of his claim to such right." This conclusion is also bolstered by the 1961 Report of the Commission on Uniform State Laws, which interpreted section 1–207 as follows: "The Code rule would permit, in Code-covered transactions, the acceptance of a part . . . payment tendered in full settlement without requiring the acceptor to gamble with his legal right to demand the balance of the . . . payment." It is clear that this interpretation deals with the situation of an offered compromise of a disputed or unliquidated claim and not a liquidated claim, since there never was a risk of losing the right to recover the balance of a liquidated claim by agreeing to accept partial payment.

Flambeau argues that even if section 1–207 applies in this case, Honeywell failed to reserve its rights under the statute. We disagree. Although Honeywell retained the proceeds after the check was cashed, it sent a letter to Flambeau immediately after it learned of the check and accompanying letter in which Flambeau claimed an offset. In that letter, Honeywell responded to Flambeau's contention that Flambeau had paid off its obligations to Honeywell by stating, "this is not the case." The letter also indicated that Honeywell did not consider the check to be in full payment of the account. The wording was sufficient to put Flambeau on notice that Honeywell protested the amount of the check, and the letter was a proper and explicit reservation of rights under section 1–207. Honeywell therefore explicitly reserved its rights under section 1–207, and its retention of the check proceeds did not effect an accord and satisfaction.

Judgment reversed in favor of Honeywell.

## BARGAINED FOR EXCHANGE

Up to this point, we have focused on the legal value component of our consideration definition. But the fact that a promisee's act or promise provides legal value is not, in itself, a sufficient basis for finding that it amounted to consideration. In addition, the promisee's act or promise must have been *bargained for* and *given in exchange* for the promisor's promise. In effect, it must be the "price" that the promisor asked for in exchange for making his promise. Over a hundred years ago, Oliver Wendell Holmes, one of our most renowned jurists, expressed this idea when he said, "It is the essence of a consideration that, by the terms of the agreement, it is given and accepted as the motive or inducement of the promise."[6]

**Past Consideration.** It is generally said that *past consideration is no consideration.* To understand the meaning of this statement, consider once again the famous case of *Hamer v. Sidway,* discussed earlier in this chapter. There, an uncle's promise to pay his nephew $5,000 for refraining from smoking, drinking, swearing, and other delightful pastimes until his 21st birthday was supported by consideration because the nephew had given legal value by refraining from participating in the prohibited activities. However, what if the uncle had said to his nephew on the eve of his 21st birthday: "Your mother tells me you've been a good lad and abstained from tobacco, hard drink, foul language, and gambling. Such goodness should be rewarded. Tomorrow, I'll give you a check for $5,000." Should the uncle's promise be enforceable against him? Clearly not, because although his nephew's behavior still passes the legal value test, in this case it was not bargained for and given in exchange for the uncle's promise.

**Moral Obligation.** As a general rule, promises made to satisfy a preexisting moral obligation are unenforceable for lack of consideration. The fact that a promisor or some member of the promisor's family, for example, has received some benefit from the promisee in the past (e.g., food and lodging, or emergency care) would not constitute consideration for a promisor's promise to pay for that benefit, due to the absence of the bargain element. Some courts find this result distressing and will enforce such promises despite the absence of consideration. In addition, a few states have passed statutes making promises to pay for past benefits enforceable if such a promise is contained in a writing that clearly expresses the promisor's intent to be bound.

[6] O. W. Holmes, *The Common Law,* p. 230 (1881).

### Sigler v. Mariotte

**619 P.2d 1068 (Ariz. Ct. App. 1980)**

Virginia Sigler lived in Helen Mariotte's home and paid rent to Mariotte from 1949 until 1977. During this period, Sigler and Mariotte were close companions and shared food expenses. In 1976, Mariotte was hospitalized and went from the hospital to a nursing home. Sigler was anxious to have Mariotte return home and told Mariotte's son and his wife that if Mariotte were released from the nursing home, she would take care of her at no charge. The son and his wife felt that more than one person was needed to care for Mariotte, and they hired another woman to care for Mariotte on a full-time basis after she came home for $85 a week plus room and board. Sigler assisted the woman in taking care of Mariotte.

On December 21, 1977, Sigler told Mariotte's son and his wife that she wanted compensation for taking care of Mariotte. They agreed to pay for her room and board. On June 15, 1979, Mariotte signed a document prepared by Sigler directing the administrator of her estate to pay Sigler $85 per week, plus room and board, from August 1, 1976, for as long as Sigler continued to live with her and care for her. The payment was to be deferred until after Mariotte's death. About one month later, Mariotte's daughter-in-law filed a petition for appointment as guardian and conservator of Mariotte's estate, arguing that Mariotte was senile and incapable of managing her own affairs. Sigler filed a claim for compensation under the 1979 agreement, which the daughter-in-law denied after her appointment. Sigler filed suit to enforce the agreement. The trial court ruled against Sigler, and she appealed.

**Howard, Justice.** There is substantial evidence that from August 1976 to December 21, 1977, Virginia agreed to perform services free of charge. The rule is that past benefits do not constitute sufficient consideration for a promise conferred under such circumstances as to raise no moral obligation, for example, where services were intended to be rendered gratuitously.

The offer of room and board by Helen's son was accepted by Virginia when she continued staying with Helen and caring for her. Acceptance of an offer may be implied from acts or conduct. Therefore, Virginia's contract with Helen lacked consideration. As to services rendered prior to June 15, 1979, they were intended to be gratuitous until December 21, 1977, and as to those rendered from December 21, 1977 to June 15, 1979, they had already been paid for pursuant to the agreement between Virginia and Helen's son and daughter-in-law.

There was also a failure of consideration to support the agreement to care for Helen from June 15, 1979, in exchange for room and board and $85 per week because Virginia was already under a contractual obligation to do so for room and board only. Virginia never rescinded her contract with the son and daughter-in-law.

Judgment for Mariotte affirmed.

## EXCEPTIONS TO THE CONSIDERATION REQUIREMENT

The consideration requirement is a classic example of a traditional contract law rule. It is precise, abstract, and capable of almost mechanical application. It can also, in some instances, result in significant injustice. Modern courts and legislatures have responded to this potential for injustice by carving out numerous exceptions to the requirement of consideration. Some of these exceptions (for example, the Code firm offer and contract modification rules) have already been discussed in this and preceding chapters. In the remaining portion of this chapter, we will focus on several other important exceptions to the consideration requirement.

**Promissory Estoppel.** As you learned in Chapter 6, the doctrine of **promissory estoppel** first emerged from attempts by courts around the turn of this century to reach just results in donative (gift) promise cases. Classical contract consideration principles did not recognize a promisee's reliance on a donative promise as a sufficient basis for enforcing the promise against the promisor. Instead, donative promises were unenforceable because they were not supported by consideration. In fact, the essence of a donative promise is that it does not seek or require any bargained-for exchange. Yet people continued to act in reliance on donative promises, often to their considerable disadvantage.

Refer to the facts in *Thorne v. Deas,* discussed earlier in this chapter. The co-owners of the *Sea Nymph* clearly relied to their injury on their fellow co-owner's promise to get insurance for the ship. Some courts in the early years of this century began to protect such relying promisees by *estopping* promisors from raising the defense that their promises were not supported by consideration. In a wide variety of cases involving gratuitous agency promises (like *Thorne v. Deas*), promises of bonuses or pensions made to employees, and promises of gifts of land, courts began to use a promisee's detrimental (harmful) reliance on a donative promise as, in effect, a *substitute for* consideration.

In 1932, the first *Restatement of Contracts* legitimized these cases by expressly recognizing promissory estoppel in section 90. The elements of promissory estoppel were then essentially the same as they are today: a *promise* that the promisor should reasonably expect to induce reliance, *reliance* on the promise by the promisee, and *injustice* to the promisee as a result of that reliance. Promissory estoppel is now widely used as a "consideration substitute," not only in donative promise cases, but also in cases involving "commercial" promises (those contemplating a bargained-for exchange). The construction contract bid cases discussed in Chapter 7 are an example of this expansion of promissory estoppel's reach. In fact, although promissory estoppel has expanded far beyond its initial role as a consideration substitute into other areas of contract law, it is probably fair to say that it is still most widely accepted in the consideration context.

**Debts Barred by Statutes of Limitations.** *Statutes of limitations* set an express statutory time limit on a person's ability to pursue any legal claim. A creditor who fails to file suit to collect a debt within the time prescribed by the appropriate statute of limitations loses the right to collect it. Many states, however, will enforce a *new promise* by a debtor to pay such a debt, even though technically such promises are not supported by consideration, because the creditor has given nothing in exchange for the new promise. Most states afford debtors some protection in such cases, however, by requiring that the new promise be in writing to be enforceable.

**Debts Barred by Bankruptcy Discharge.** Once a bankrupt debtor is granted a discharge,[7] creditors no longer have the legal right to collect discharged debts. Most states will enforce a new promise by the debtor to pay (reaffirm) the debt regardless of whether the creditor has given any consideration to support it. The Bankruptcy Reform Act of 1978, however, has made it much more difficult for debtors to reaffirm debts discharged in bankruptcy proceedings. The Act requires a reaffirmation promise to be made prior to the date of the discharge, gives the debtor the right to revoke his promise within 30 days after it becomes enforceable, requires the Bankruptcy Court to counsel individual (as opposed to corporate) debtors about the legal effects of reaffirmation, and requires Bankruptcy Court approval of reaffirmations by individual debtors. In addition, a few states require reaffirmation promises to be in writing to be enforceable.

[7] Bankruptcy is discussed in detail in Chapter 41.

**Charitable Subscriptions.** Promises to make gifts for charitable or educational purposes are often enforced, despite the absence of consideration, when the institution or organization to which the promise was made has acted in reliance on the promised gift. This result is usually justified on the basis of either promissory estoppel or public policy.

## Sanders v. Arkansas-Missouri Power Co.

### 593 S.W.2d 56 (Ark. Ct. App. 1980)

Sanders, a lineman for the Arkansas-Missouri Power Company, was seriously injured when he came into contact with a "hot" electric line in the course of his employment. In a suit against his employer, brought several years after the accident, Sanders alleged that in exchange for his promise to return to work for the Power Company when he was able to do so, the Power Company promised him that he would receive full pay and benefits until he was able to return to work and that the Power Company made such payments for 18 months. He further alleged that in reliance on the Power Company's promise and its performance for 18 months, he built a house with special wheelchair accommodations. Sanders was totally and permanently disabled, and sought to recover a sum equal to the total value of the promised payments, reduced to their present value, for the remainder of his working life. Sanders's theories were breach of contract and, in the alternative, promissory estoppel. The Power Company's defense was lack of consideration. The trial court dismissed Sanders's complaint, and he appealed.

**Newbern, Judge.** We must assume, as alleged by Sanders, that agents of the Power Company promised Sanders that he would be paid his full salary and company benefits until he was medically able to return to work. In exchange for that promise, Sanders alleges he promised to resume "a position of employment as soon as medically possible." We recognize that a promise to hold oneself available to resume work has been held sufficient to constitute consideration for an agreement to pay a monthly salary for life.

In the case before us, Sanders has pleaded total and permanent disability, and it becomes obvious he has made a promise it is impossible for him to perform. We cannot say this complaint states a cause of action for breach of contract based on mutual promises where it alleges one of the promises is impossible of performance. We cannot countenance Sanders's statement he is "holding himself ready" to perform when in the next breath he alleges his inability to do so. These statements cancel each other and make Sanders's alleged promise illusory at best.

Perhaps the broadest statement of the doctrine of detrimental reliance or promissory estoppel is that found in 1 *Corbin, Contracts* section 119, p. 515 (1963):

> [I]f a promisee acts in such reasonable reliance upon a promise, that promise may be held enforceable even though the promisor did not in fact know of such action and so did not regard it as consideration or as anything else. Even the promisee who acts in reliance may not regard his action as any reason for enforcing the promise; he may perform the action because he believes the promise will be kept without the necessity of any enforcement.

We hold the complaint before us stated facts sufficient to state a cause of action in that Sanders alleged he had built a new home especially equipped for a wheelchair user in reliance on the promise of Power Company. Of course, Sanders will have to prove to the trier of fact that his action was indeed based upon that reliance and that it was reasonable, but we find it sufficiently stated.

Judgment reversed in favor of Sanders.

## SUMMARY

As a general rule, only promises that are supported by consideration are enforceable as contracts. Consideration is defined as legal value, bargained for and given in exchange for an act or a promise. Legal value means that, in exchange for the promisor's promise, a promisee must have done, or agreed to do, something that he had no duty to do, or that a promisee refrained from doing, or agreed not to do, something that he had a right to do. Illusory promises—those that do not really obligate a promisee to do anything—cannot serve as consideration.

Likewise, performing or agreeing to perform an act that the promisee had a preexisting duty to perform will not amount to consideration. This is true whether the preexisting duty is public or contractual in nature. At common law, an agreement to modify an existing contract must be supported by new consideration to be enforceable. Some commentators have argued that this rule, while it properly prevents the enforcement of coerced modifications, can also prevent the enforcement of voluntary and equitable modification agreements. There are many ways, however, in which a court can enforce a fair modification agreement. Any new consideration furnished by the promisee, however slight, can support a modification agreement. Modification agreements made in the face of unforeseeable circumstances that make performance of the contract unduly burdensome are also commonly enforced by the courts. Also, a court may find that the parties mutually agreed to terminate their original agreement and their duties to each other under that agreement. In such circumstances, a subsequent agreement entered into by the parties would be supported by consideration even though one of the parties has not agreed to do anything more than he was obligated to do under the original contract, because the termination of the original contract relieved him of any duty to perform.

The Code simplifies the contract modification process by providing that agreements to modify contracts for the sale of goods do not need to be supported by consideration [2–209(1)]. Such agreements must meet the Code good faith requirements, however, and unconscionable modification agreements will not be enforced. In some circumstances, oral modification agreements may be unenforceable under the Code [2–209(2) and (3)].

Agreements to settle debts for part payment may or may not be enforceable, depending on the nature of the debt and on the circumstances of the part payment. An agreement to settle a liquidated debt for part payment received at or after the due date of the debt is unenforceable for lack of consideration. An agreement to settle an unliquidated debt, however, creates a binding accord and satisfaction. Some state courts have interpreted section 1–207 of the Code in a way that would allow a creditor to accept a partial payment of an unliquidated debt without entering an accord and satisfaction, even though the debtor clearly intends the part payment to operate as full satisfaction of the debt. Other courts have rejected this interpretation of the Code. Also, composition agreements are ordinarily enforced on public policy grounds despite the fact that they involve the settlement of liquidated claims by part payment.

Forbearing or agreeing to forbear from asserting a legal right can amount to consideration. As a general rule, the courts do not require that a forbearing promisee have a legally valid claim, but do require that the promisee have a good faith belief in the validity of his claim.

To say that a promisee's act or promise must have legal value, however, does not mean that it must have any actual value or that its value must in any way equal the value of the promisor's promise. As a general rule, the courts will not inquire into the adequacy of consideration. However, grossly inadequate consideration may be evidence of fraud, duress, or contractual incapacity, and many courts will refuse to grant equitable remedies such as specific performance to promisees who have driven too hard a bargain. Grossly inadequate consideration may also support the conclusion that the agreement in question is a disguised gift rather than an enforceable bargain. Finally, a few courts have refused to enforce contracts for the sale of goods at prices far in excess of the value of the goods on the ground that such contracts are unconscionable.

In addition to having legal value, a promisee's act or promise must be bargained for if it is to serve as consideration. This means that it must be the "price" that the promisor asked for in exchange for making his promise. Thus, past performances by a promisee cannot serve as consideration for a present promise by a promisor, because performance rendered in advance of a promise is, by definition, unbargained for. The common law courts adhered to the rule that "past consideration is no consideration" even in cases where the promisee's prior performance could be viewed as creating a moral duty on the part of the promisor to pay for that performance. Some modern courts, however, will enforce promises based on moral obligations and a few states have passed statutes making such promises enforceable if they are made in writing.

In recent years, the courts have made a number of exceptions to the requirement of consideration. The most important of these is the doctrine of promissory estoppel, which originated in cases where courts sought to protect reliance on gratuitous promises. Promises to pay debts barred by bankruptcy discharge or by the applicable statute of limitations are enforced by many courts despite the absence of consideration. Promises of charitable subscriptions are also commonly enforced when the institution or organization to which the promise was made has acted in reliance on the promised gift.

## PROBLEM CASES

1. The Reillys intended to purchase real estate from the Bisluks. The Reillys applied for a first-mortgage loan from Rogers Park, filling out Rogers Park's printed loan application form. The form provided, among other things, that a service charge of $2,310 would be due if Rogers Park gave the Reillys a loan commitment and the Reillys did not complete the loan within 30 days. The sale of the real estate was never completed. The Reillys sued Rogers Park for the return of a $500 loan standby fee, minus any actual expenses that Rogers Park had incurred. Rogers Park counterclaimed, arguing that it was entitled to the $2,310 service charge less the $500 it had received from the Reillys. Is Rogers Park entitled to the service charge?

2. In 1966, Agnes Maszewski left her apartment to live with John Piskadlo in a house he owned. The following year, John deeded the house to Agnes, reserving a life

estate for himself. They continued to live together until 1970, when their relationship began to sour. Agnes attempted to leave, but John requested that she stay. They then signed a reconciliation agreement in which they mutually agreed that neither would have the right to evict the other from the house, although either had the right to leave voluntarily at any time. In 1973, when John was 77 years of age and Agnes 81, John changed the locks on the house and evicted Agnes. Agnes filed suit to enforce the reconciliation agreement, and John argued that her promise not to evict him was illusory because, as holder of a life estate in the property, he was entitled to possession for the rest of his life. Assuming that John is correct about the nature of a life estate, was the reconcilation agreement enforceable?

**3.** Carl Jessee, a carpenter, orally agreed to do the interior finish work on a store owned by Dana Smith. The price of his services was agreed to be "cost plus 25 percent." Jessee finished the work and submitted a labor bill for 125 percent of the cost of materials. He claimed that he had told Smith's store manager that Smith would have to pay for the materials used and, in addition, that amount plus 25 percent for his labor. Smith refused to pay the bill and offered instead to pay Jessee 25 percent of the cost of the materials, $400 for gas, and two stuffed animals worth $90. Witnesses knowledgeable in the customs of the building trade testified that a "cost plus 10 percent" contract meant a labor charge of 110 percent of the materials cost and that a "cost plus 25 percent" contract for interior finish work was reasonable. The trial court ruled that the contract was unenforceable because the labor charge was "exorbitant." Jessee appealed. Was the trial court's holding correct?

**4.** Eugene Leitner and his law partners considered purchasing certain property in Peoria and constructing an office building on it that would house their law offices and contain additional space for rental to other tenants. On April 27, 1972, the partners agreed to make an offer of $125,000 for the property and entered into negotiations with the owner of the property. Several months later, before any agreement between the owner and the partners had been reached, Leitner, his son, and an architect bought the land themselves. Leitner's partners felt that by buying the land, he had breached a fiduciary duty owed to them. After a lengthy period of negotiations, Leitner promised to pay the partners $13,500 within the next five years. The building was built, but the venture was not as profitable as the parties had anticipated. Leitner died, and his estate refused to pay the partners the amount agreed upon, arguing that the agreement was not supported by consideration. Was Leitner's promise supported by consideration?

**5.** In 1964, while married to Lula Velma Kennard McCray, Thomas Kennard entered into a licensing agreement with International Tool Company giving International the right to market certain of Kennard's inventions in return for the periodic payment of royalties. Kennard and McCray were divorced in 1965, and the divorce decree ordered him to pay her certain sums for the support of their two children. As part of the property settlement incorporated into the decree, McCray was awarded one half of Kennard's royalties. Later in 1965, Kennard married Eula Fay Pope Kennard. In 1967, the court found Kennard in contempt for failure to pay child support. McCray, however, never attempted to enforce the contempt order against him. In 1969, Kennard agreed to assign his remaining half of the royalties to McCray in exchange for release from his duty to pay child support. Kennard died in 1975, and Eula Fay was named executrix in his will, which also named her as his sole beneficiary. She filed suit against International and McCray, arguing that the agreement assigning Kennard's remaining royalties to McCray was not supported by consideration, since state public policy denied parents the right to modify child support agreements without court approval. McCray argued that by not enforcing Kennard's child support obligations against him, she had given valid consideration. Was McCray entitled to the royalties?

6. White Sands had purchased equipment from Clark Leasing under an installment contract that gave Clark the right to repossess and resell the equipment in the event of default. White Sands defaulted on its obligations under the agreement, and agreed to turn over the equipment to Clark, provided Clark would accept it in full settlement of White Sands's indebtedness. Clark accepted delivery and resold the equipment, but the resale did not bring in enough to cover the balance due. Clark then brought suit for the deficiency, and White Sands set up accord and satisfaction as a defense. Was Clark entitled to the deficiency?

7. George Slattery was a licensed independent polygraph (lie detector) operator. While employed by the Dade County Public Safety Department, he administered a polygraph examination to a man suspected of a crime. During the examination the suspect confessed to shooting and killing a Wells Fargo guard in an unrelated robbery. Slattery learned that Wells Fargo had offered a $25,000 reward for information leading to the arrest and conviction of the person who shot the guard. After informing the authorities of the confession, Slattery sought to claim the reward. When Wells Fargo refused to pay, he filed suit. Was Slattery entitled to the reward?

8. Brian Construction Company contracted to build a post office building in Bristol, Connecticut. It entered a subcontract with John Brighenti that called for Brighenti to do all excavation, grading, site work, asphalt paving, landscaping, and concrete work on the job. When Brighenti began excavating, he discovered considerable debris below the suface, apparently from an old factory that had previously stood on the site. Test borings taken from the site by Brian and given to Brighenti before the execution of the subcontract had failed to indicate the presence of the debris, which included concrete foundation walls, slab floors, underground tanks, twisted metal, and various combustible material. Removal of the debris was necessary for completion of the project, but its presence meant that the excavation work would be much more difficult and time consuming than either party had originally contemplated. After initially refusing to pay any additional amount for removal, Brian finally agreed to pay Brighenti his costs plus 10 percent to remove the debris. Brighenti returned to work, but later he walked off the job. When Brian sued him for damages, he argued that he had no duty to remove the debris under the original contract and that the oral agreement modifying the original contract was unenforceable for lack of consideration. Was the modification binding?

9. Chesapeake Shoe Company, a shoe wholesaler, ordered basketball shoes from Brooks Shoe Company, an athletic shoe manufacturer. The contract called for delivery of the shoes in April 1981. Due to late shipment of the shoes by Brooks's suppliers, the shoes did not arrive in the United States until July 1981. Benowitz, Brooks's vice president of sales, called Goldfein, Chesapeake's president, after Brooks received the shoes and asked whether Chesapeake still wanted them. Goldfein said that it did, and the shoes were shipped to Chesapeake. Chesapeake failed to pay for the shoes, and when Brooks sued for the purchase price, Chesapeake argued that due to the late delivery it was entitled to a credit of $20,760 against the $109,511.06 purchase price. Is Chesapeake entitled to the credit?

**10.** Northwestern Bank lent money to Lionel Birkeland, who assigned to Northwestern a life insurance policy issued by Employers' Life Insurance Company as collateral for the loan. In September 1969, Northwestern sent Employers' a "Life Insurance Assignment Questionnaire" asking whether Birkeland had paid the annual premium on the policy and whether Employers' would notify Northwestern of any premium default by Birkeland in time for Northwestern to protect its collateral. Employers' answered that the premium had been paid and that it would give notice of default. In October 1972, Northwestern again wrote Employers' about the status of the policy and was told that the policy was still assigned to Northwestern and that it had a face value of $109,381. In fact, the policy had lapsed in August 1972 because of Birkeland's failure to pay the premium payment due the preceding June. Northwestern did not learn of the lapse until Birkeland's death, in September 1975. It then filed suit against Employers' for the $15,791 that Birkeland owed the bank. Is Northwestern entitled to recover its loss from Employers'?

# Chapter 11

# Capacity of Parties

## INTRODUCTION

As you have read in preceding chapters, a person's voluntary consent to enter an agreement provides a basis for imposing legal obligations on that person. It follows, then, that a person must have the *ability* to give consent before he can be legally bound to an agreement. To give rise to truly voluntary agreements of the sort that the law should enforce, this ability to give consent must involve more than the mere physical ability to say yes or shake hands or sign one's name. Rather, the person's maturity and mental ability must be such that he can fairly be presumed capable of representing his own interests effectively. This concept is embodied in the legal term **capacity.**

Capacity means the ability to incur legal obligations and acquire legal rights. The primary classes of people who are considered to lack capacity are minors (infants), persons suffering from mental illnesses or defects, and intoxicated persons. Contract law gives them the right to *avoid* (escape) contracts that they enter during incapacity. This rule provides a means of protecting people who, because of mental impairment, intoxication, or youth and inexperience, are disadvantaged in the normal give-and-take of the bargaining process.

Lack of capacity to contract comes up in court in one of two ways. In some cases, it is asserted by a plaintiff as the basis of a lawsuit for the return of benefits given pursuant to a contract. In others, it arises as a defense to the enforcement of a contract when the defendant is the party who lacked capacity. The responsibility for alleging and proving incapacity is placed on the person who bases his claim or defense on his lack of capacity.

## MINORS' CONTRACTS

**Minor's Right to Disaffirm.** Courts have long recognized that, because of the lack of judgment and experience that often attends youth, minors (who in legal terms are also known as **infants**) are in a vulnerable position in their dealings with adults. Thus, courts granted the minor the right to avoid her contracts as a means of protecting her against her own improvidence and against overreaching by adults. The exercise of this right to avoid a contract is called **disaffirmance.** The right to disaffirm is personal to the minor. That is, only the minor or her guardian or the administrator of her estate may disaffirm the contract. No formal act or written statement is required to make a valid disaffirmance. Any words or acts that effectively communicate the minor's desire to cancel the contract can constitute disaffirmance. State law often creates statutory exceptions to the minor's right to disaffirm, however. These statutes prevent minors from disaffirming such transactions as marriage, agreements to support their children, and educational loans.

The minor's contract is **voidable** at the option of the minor, not void.[1] If the minor wishes to enforce the contract instead of disaffirming it, the adult party must perform. Thus, any adult contracting with a minor finds himself in the undesirable legal position of being bound on the contract unless it is to the minor's advantage to disaffirm the contract. The minor's right to disaffirm has the effect of discouraging adults from dealing with minors.

**Period of Minority.** At common law, the age of majority was 21 years. However, the ratification in 1971 of the 26th amendment to the Constitution giving 18-year-olds the right to vote stimulated a trend toward reducing the age of majority. The age of majority has been lowered by 49 states. In almost all of these states, the new age of majority for contracting purposes is 18.

**Emancipation.** As a general rule, parents have the right to receive services from their child and to collect their child's wages until the child reaches majority. **Emancipation** is the surrender of the parents' right to receive the child's wages. There are no formal requirements for emancipation. The parent merely has to consent, expressly or impliedly, to the minor's entering into a contract of employment in which the minor will have the right to retain his wages. Marriage also constitutes emancipation. Emancipation has limited significance in modern times, however. In almost all states, the mere fact that a minor is emancipated does not give him capacity to contract. As you will see in *Kiefer v. Fred Howe Motors, Inc.*, a person younger than the legal age of majority is generally held to lack capacity to enter a contract, even if he is married and employed full-time.

**Time of Disaffirmance.** Contracts entered during minority that affect title to *real estate* cannot be disaffirmed until majority. This rule is apparently based on the special impor-

[1] See Chapter 6 for a discussion of the distinction between void and voidable contracts.

tance of real estate and on the need to protect a minor from improvidently disaffirming a transaction (such as a mortgage or conveyance) involving real estate. All other contracts entered during minority may be disaffirmed at any time between the time when the contract is formed and a reasonable time *after* the person reaches majority. Thus, a person may in some situations disaffirm a contract after—even several years after—she attains legal adulthood.

What is a "reasonable time" for purposes of determining the period of time after majority during which a person retains the right to disaffirm? A few states have statutes that prescribe a definite time limit on the power of avoidance. In Oklahoma, for example, a person who wishes to disaffirm a contract must do so within one year after reaching majority.[2] In most states, however, there is no set limit on the time during which a person may disaffirm after reaching majority. What is a reasonable time will depend on the facts of each particular case. One factor that courts may consider in determining whether the person disaffirmed in a reasonable time is the degree to which the adult party's interests would be harmed by delay. If the contract is completely executory—that is, no performance has been rendered by either party—the former minor is likely to be accorded a longer period of time in which to disaffirm. But if the adult has given something of value to the minor that deteriorates or depreciates over time, the period of time in which it is reasonable to permit the former minor to disaffirm is likely to be shorter. You will see this approach in the case of *Bobby Floars Toyota, Inc. v. Smith.*

**Return of Consideration on Disaffirmance.** If neither party has performed his part of the contract, the parties' relationship will simply be canceled by the disaffirmance. Since neither party has given anything to the other party, no further adjustments are necessary. But what about the situation where, as is often the case, the minor has paid money to the adult and the adult has given property to the minor? Minors who disaffirm are entitled to the return of any consideration that they have given the adult party. In return, minors are obligated to return any consideration given by the adult that they still have in their possession.

A disaffirming minor can recover property that she has parted with, even in some situations in which the property has been transferred to innocent third parties. Under the Uniform Commercial Code, however, a minor cannot recover *goods* that have been sold to a good faith purchaser.[3]

**Obligation to Pay Reasonable Value of Necessaries.** Though the law regarding minors' contracts is designed to discourage adults from dealing with (and possibly taking advantage of) minors, it would be undesirable for the law to discourage adults from selling minors the items that they need for basic survival. For this reason, disaffirming minors are required to pay the reasonable value of items that have been furnished to them that are classified as "necessaries." A necessary is something that is essential for the minor's continued existence and general welfare. Examples of necessaries include food, clothing, shelter, medical care, tools of the minor's trade, and basic educational or vocational training. Whether a given item is considered a necessary depends on the facts of a particular case. The minor's age, station in life, and personal circumstances are all relevant to this issue. The range of items that will be considered necessaries is broader for married minors and other emancipated minors than

[2] Okla. Stat. Ann. tit. 15 § 18 (1983).

[3] UCC § 2–403.

it is for unemancipated minors. Furthermore, an item sold to a minor is not considered a necessary if the minor's parent or guardian has already supplied him with similar items.

A minor's liability for necessaries supplied to him is **quasi contractual**. That is, the minor is liable for the *reasonable value* of the necessaries that she actually receives. She is not liable for the entire price agreed upon if that price exceeds the actual value of the necessaries, and she is not liable for necessaries that she contracted for but did not receive. For example, Joy Jones, a minor, signed a one-year lease for an apartment in Mountain Park at a rent of $300 per month. After living in the apartment for three months, Joy broke her lease and moved out. Because she is a minor, Joy has the right to disaffirm the lease. Because shelter is a necessary, however, she must pay the reasonable value of what she has actually received—three months' rent. If she can establish that the actual value of what she has received is less than $300 per month, she will be bound to pay only that lesser amount. Furthermore, she will not be obligated to pay for the remaining nine months' rent, because she has not received any benefits from the remainder of the lease.

**Claims for Loss or Depreciation of Nonnecessaries.** A difficult problem arises when the item furnished to the minor was *not* a necessary and the minor cannot fully return it upon disaffirmance because it has been consumed, lost, damaged or because it has depreciated in value. Most states will permit the minor to disaffirm even if he is unable to return the consideration. But must the minor pay the adult for the damage to or depreciation of the consideration?

The traditional rule is that the minor who cannot fully return the consideration that was given to him is *not* obligated to pay the adult for the benefits he has received or to compensate the adult for loss or depreciation of the consideration given by the adult. This rule, which is illustrated in the case of *Halbman v. Lemke,* is designed to protect minors by discouraging adults from dealing with them. After all, if an adult knew that he might be able to demand the return of anything that he transferred to a minor, he would have little incentive to refrain from entering into contracts with minors. However, the rule can work harsh results for innocent adults who have dealt fairly with minors. For this reason, the traditional rule that minors have no duty to reimburse the adult for loss or depreciation of consideration that they have received has struck a discordant note with many modern courts and is not uniformly followed. The courts and legislatures of some states have adopted rules that require disaffirming minors to pay the adult the sum that would be necessary to place him in *statu quo* (the position he would have been in if the contract had never come into existence). The reason for the lack of uniformity regarding minors' obligations upon disaffirmance is that a powerful conflict exists between the policy favoring just results and the policy favoring protection of minors; different states have resolved this conflict in different ways.

**Misrepresentation of Age.** Another troubling situation in which there is little consensus among American jurisdictions occurs when a minor misrepresents himself as being of legal age. The significance of a minor's misrepresentation of his age differs from state to state. Some states will permit the minor to disaffirm but will require him to place in *statu quo* the adult party who relied on the misrepresentation. Other states follow the common law rule, which provides that misrepresentation of age does not affect a minor's right to disaffirm and does not create any obligation to pay for benefits received. The theory behind this rule, which can create severe hardship for innocent adults who rely on minors' misrepresentations of age, is that one who lacks capacity cannot acquire it merely by claiming to be of legal age. Other states hold that the minor is precluded from asserting the defense or claim of minority and that he is therefore bound by the terms of the agreement. A fourth approach, used in still other states, is to permit the minor to disaffirm but to hold him liable to the adult in tort for *deceit.* As you will see in the *Kiefer* case, the elements of deceit must be present for the minor to be liable in tort.

**Ratification.** Though a person has the right to disaffirm contracts made during minority, this right can be given up after the person reaches legal age. When a person who has reached majority indicates that he intends to be bound by a contract that he made while still a minor, he surrenders his right to disaffirm. This act of affirming the contract and surrendering the right to avoid the contract is known as **ratification.** Ratification makes a contract valid from its inception. Because ratification represents the former minor's election to be bound by the contract, he cannot later disaffirm. Ratification can be done effectively only after the minor reaches majority. Otherwise, it would be as voidable as the initial contract.

There are no formal requirements for ratification. Any of the former minor's words or acts after reaching majority that indicate with reasonable clarity his intent to be bound by the contract are sufficient. Ratification can be *expressed* in an oral or written statement, or, as is more often the case, it can be *implied* by conduct on the part of the former minor.

Naturally, ratification is clearest when the former minor has made some express statement of his intent to be bound. Predicting whether a court will determine that a contract has been ratified is a bit more difficult when the only evidence of the alleged ratification is the conduct of the minor. As shown by the section of the *Bobby Floars Toyota* case that deals with ratification, a former minor's acceptance or retention of benefits given by the other party for an unreasonable time after he has reached majority can constitute ratification. Also, a former minor's continued performance of his part of the contract after reaching majority has been held to imply his intent to ratify the contract. The most difficult situation in which to determine whether ratification has occurred involves an executory contract in which the former minor simply takes no action—neither performing the contract nor accepting benefits nor disaffirming the contract—after reaching majority. Some courts have held that a person's mere inaction after reaching majority does not amount to a ratification. Others have held that a person's failure to disaffirm within a reasonable time after reaching majority amounts to a waiver of the right to disaffirm and *is* a ratification.

## Halbman v. Lemke

**298 N.W.2d 562 (Wis. Sup. Ct. 1980)**

James Halbman was a minor employed at a gas station managed by Michael Lemke. Lemke agreed to sell a 1968 Oldsmobile to Halbman for $1,250. Halbman paid $1,000 cash and took possession of the car. He agreed to pay $25 per week until the balance was paid, at which time title would be transferred. About five weeks later, after Halbman had paid $1,100 of the purchase price, a connecting rod in the car's engine broke. Halbman took the car to a garage, where it was repaired at a cost of $637.40. Halbman did not pay the repair bill. The next month, Lemke endorsed the title of the car over to Halbman—even though Halbman had not paid the entire purchase price—in an effort to avoid liability for the car. Halbman returned the title to Lemke along with a letter that disaffirmed the contract and demanded the return of Halbman's money. Lemke refused to return the money and did not pay for the repair bill or remove the car. After the repair bill had remained unpaid for several months, the garage removed the car's engine and transmission in satisfaction of the debt and had the rest of the car towed to the house of Halbman's father. During this time, the car was vandalized, making it unsalvageable. Halbman brought this suit seeking the return of the $1,100 he had paid toward the contract. The trial court granted judgment for Halbman, and Lemke appealed.

**Callow, Justice.** Lemke argues that he should be entitled to recover for the damage to the vehicle up to the time of disaffirmance, which he claims equals the repair bill.

Neither party challenges the absolute right of a minor to disaffirm a contract for the purchase of items which are not necessities. That right, known as the doctrine of incapacity or the infancy doctrine, is one of the oldest and most venerable of our common law traditions. Although the origins of the doctrine are somewhat obscure, it is generally recognized that its purpose is the protection of minors from foolishly squandering their wealth through improvident contracts with crafty adults who would take advantage of them in the marketplace.

Once there has been a disaffirmance, however, as in this case between a minor buyer and an adult seller, unresolved problems arise regarding the rights and responsibilities of the parties relative to the disposition of the consideration exchanged on the contract. The law regarding the rights and responsibilities of the parties relative to the consideration exchanged on a disaffirmed contract is characterized by confusion, inconsistency, and a general lack of uniformity as jurisdictions attempt to reach a fair application of the infancy doctrine in today's marketplace. The cases upon which Lemke relies for the proposition that a disaffirming minor must make restitution for loss and depreciation serve to illustrate some of the ways other jurisdictions have approached this problem of balancing the needs of minors against the rights of innocent merchants. Because these cases would at some point force the minor to bear the cost of the very improvidence from which the infancy doctrine is supposed to protect him, we cannot follow them. We hold that, absent misrepresentation or tortious damage to the property, a minor who disaffirms a contract for the purchase of an item which is not a necessity may recover his purchase price without liability for use, depreciation, damage, or other diminution in value.

Judgment for Halbman affirmed.

## Kiefer v. Fred Howe Motors, Inc.

**158 N.W.2d 288 (Wis. Sup. Ct. 1968)**

Kiefer, a 20-year-old minor who was married and had a child, bought a 1960 Willys Station Wagon from Fred Howe Motors, Inc. Kiefer signed a "motor vehicle purchase contract," which contained the following language just above the signature line:

> I represent that I am 21 years of age or over and recognize that the dealer sells the above vehicle upon this representation.

Kiefer paid the contract price of $412 and took the car home. He later had trouble with the car. After requesting that the dealer take the car back and having his attorney write the dealer a letter declaring the contract void, Kiefer filed suit for the return of his money. The trial court ruled in favor of Kiefer, and Howe appealed.

**Wilkie, Justice.** Howe urges that this court adopt a rule that an emancipated minor over 18 years of age be made legally responsible for his contracts. The underpinnings of the general rule allowing the minor to disaffirm his contracts were undoubtedly the protection of the minor. It was thought that the minor was immature in both mind and experience and that, therefore, he should be protected from his own bad judgments as well as from adults who would take advantage of him. The doctrine often seems commendable and just. However, in today's modern and sophisticated society the infancy doctrine seems to lose some of its gloss. Paradoxically, we declare the infant mature enough to shoulder arms in the military, but not mature enough to vote; mature enough to marry and be responsible for his torts and crimes, but not mature enough to assume the burden of his own contractual indiscretions. In Wisconsin, the infant is deemed mature enough to use a dangerous instrumentality—a motor vehicle—at 16, but not mature enough to purchase it without protection until he is 21.

No one really questions that a line as to age must be drawn somewhere below which a legally defined minor must be able to disaffirm his contracts for non-necessaries. The law over the centuries has considered this age to be 21. Legislatures in other states have lowered the age. We suggest that Howe might better seek the change it proposes in the legislative halls rather than in this court.

Undoubtedly, the infancy doctrine is an obstacle when a major purchase is involved. However, we believe that the reasons for allowing that obstacle to remain viable outweigh those for casting it aside. Minors require some protection from the pitfalls of the marketplace. Reasonable minds will always differ on the extent of the protection that should be afforded. For this court to remove the contractual disabilities from a minor simply because he becomes emancipated, which in most cases would be the result of marriage, would be to suggest that the married minor is somehow vested with more wisdom and maturity than his single counterpart. However, logic would not seem to dictate this result, especially when today a youthful marriage is oftentimes indicative of a lack of wisdom and maturity.

Howe's last argument is that Kiefer should be liable in tort for damages because he misrepresented his age. Howe would use these damages as a set-off against the contract price sought to be reclaimed by Kiefer. The question becomes whether the requisites for a tort action in misrepresentation are present in this case. No evidence was adduced to show that Kiefer had an intent to defraud the dealer. Without the element of scienter being satisfied, Kiefer is not susceptible to an action in misrepresentation. Furthermore, we fail to see how the dealer could be justified in the mere reliance on the fact that Kiefer signed a contract containing a sentence that said he was 21 or over. The trial court observed that Kiefer was sufficiently immature looking to arouse suspicion. The dealer never took any affirmative steps to determine whether Kiefer was in fact over 21. It never asked to see a draft card or the most logical indicium of age under the circumstances, a driver's license. Therefore, because there was no intent to deceive, and no justifiable reliance, Howe's action for misrepresentation must fail.

Judgment for Kiefer affirmed.

## Bobby Floars Toyota, Inc. v. Smith

**269 S.E.2d 320 (N.C. Ct. App. 1980)**

Charles Smith, age 17, purchased a car from Bobby Floars Toyota, signing an agreement to pay the balance of the purchase price in 30 monthly installments. Ten months after he reached majority, Smith voluntarily returned the car to Floars and stopped making payments. At this point, he had made 11 monthly payments, 10 of which were made after his 18th birthday. Floars sold the car at public auction and sued Smith for the remaining debt. The trial court dismissed Floars's case, and Floars appealed.

**Morris, Chief Judge.** The only question is whether Smith's voluntarily relinquishing the automobile 10 months after attaining the age of majority constitutes a timely disaffirmance of his contract with Floars. The rule is that the contracts of an infant may be disaffirmed by the infant during minority or within a reasonable time after reaching majority. What is a reasonable time depends on the circumstances of each case. In the instant case, we believe that 10 months is an unreasonable time within which to elect between disaffirmance and ratification, in that this case involves an automobile, an item of personal property which is constantly depreciating in value. Modern commercial transactions require that both buyers and sellers be responsible and prompt.

We are of the further opinion that Smith waived his right to avoid the contract. The privilege of disaffirmance may be lost where the infant affirms or ratifies the contract after reaching majority. Certain affirmations or conduct evidencing ratification is sufficient to bind the infant, regardless of whether a reasonable time for disaffirmance had passed. In the present case, it is clear that Smith recognized as binding the installment note evidencing the debt owed from his purchase of an automobile. He continued to possess and operate the automobile after his 18th birthday, and he continued to make monthly installments as required by the note for 10 months after becoming 18. We hold, therefore, that Smith's acceptance of the benefits and continuance of payments under the contract constituted a ratification of the contract, precluding subsequent disaffirmance.

Judgment reversed and remanded in favor of Floars.

## CAPACITY OF MENTALLY IMPAIRED PERSONS AND INTOXICATED PERSONS

**Theory of Incapacity.** Like minors, people who suffer from a mental illness or defect are at a disadvantage in their ability to protect their own interests in the bargaining process. Contract law makes their contracts either void or voidable to protect them from the results of their own impaired perceptions and judgment and from others who might take advantage of them.

**Test for Mental Incapacity.** Incapacity on grounds of mental illness or defect, which is often referred to in cases and texts as "insanity," encompasses a broad range of causes for impaired mental functioning, such as mental illness, brain damage, mental retardation, or senility. Even a person who suffers from some form of mental defect or illness could still have full capacity unless the defect or illness has affected the particular transaction in question. For example, a person could have periodic psychotic episodes, yet enter a binding contract during a lucid period.

The usual test for mental incapacity is a *cognitive* one; that is, courts will ask whether the person had sufficient mental capacity to understand the nature and effect of the contract. Some courts, such as the court in the *Ortolere* case, below, have criticized the traditional test as unscientific because it does not take into account the fact that a person suffering from a mental illness or defect might be unable to *control* his conduct. The *Restatement (Second) of Contracts* provides that a person's contracts are voidable if he is unable to *act* in a reasonable manner in relation to the transaction and the other party has reason to know of his condition.[4] Where the other party has reason to know of the condition of the mentally impaired person, the *Restatement* standard would provide protection to people who understood the transaction but, because of some mental defect or illness, were unable to exercise appropriate judgment or to control their conduct effectively.

Many states treat intoxicated persons like they treat mentally impaired persons. As a general rule, the fact that one or both of the parties to a contract had been drinking when the contract was formed would *not* affect their capacity to enter a contract. However, if a person is so intoxicated at the time he enters a contract that he is unable to understand the nature of the business at hand, he may be held to lack capacity. The *Restatement (Second) of Contracts* provides that a party's intoxication is a ground for lack of capacity if the other party has reason to know that, because of intoxication, the affected person cannot understand or act reasonably in relation to the transaction.[5]

**The Effect of Mental Incapacity.** If a person is under guardianship at the time the contract is formed—that is, if a court has found a person mentally incompetent after holding a hearing on his mental competency and has appointed a guardian of his estate—the contract is considered **void.** Contract law makes a distinction between a contract involving a person who has been **adjudicated** (judged by a court) incompetent at the time the contract was made and a contract involving a person who was suffering from some mental impairment at the time the contract was entered but whose incompetency was not established until *after* the contract was formed. If, after a contract has been formed, a court finds that a person lacked capacity on grounds of mental illness or defect, the contract is **voidable** at the election of the party who lacked capacity (or his guardian or personal representative).

In states in which intoxication is a ground for a claim or defense of lack of capacity, the contracts of a person who was intoxicated at

[4] *Restatement (Second) of Contracts* § 15 (1979).

[5] *Restatement (Second) of Contracts* § 16 (1979).

the time the contracts were formed are considered voidable, not void.

**The Right to Disaffirm.** If a contract is found to be voidable on the ground of mental impairment, the person who lacked mental capacity at the time the contract was made has the right to disaffirm the contract. As in the case of a disaffirming minor, he must return any consideration given by the other party that remains in his possession. Must the incapacitated party pay the other party the additional sum that would be necessary to reimburse him for loss, damage, or depreciation of the consideration given to him? This is generally said to depend on whether the contract was basically fair and on whether the other party had reason to be aware of his impairment. If the contract is fair, bargained for in good faith, and the other party had no reasonable cause to know of the mental incapacity, the contract cannot be disaffirmed unless the other party is placed in *statu quo.* However, if the other party had reason to know of the mental illness or defect, the incapacitated party is allowed to disaffirm without placing the other party in *statu quo.* This distinction discourages people from attempting to take advantage of mentally impaired people, but it spares those who are dealing in good faith and have no such intent.

A person under mental incapacity is liable for the reasonable value of **necessaries** in the same manner as are minors. Similarly, it is possible for a person who was under a mental incapacity at the time the contract was made to **ratify** the contract if he regains mental capacity.

---

## Ortolere v. Teachers' Retirement Board of the City of New York

**303 N.Y.S.2d 362 (N.Y. Ct. App. 1969)**

Grace Ortolere had been an elementary school teacher for 40 years. In March 1964, she suffered a "nervous breakdown" and went on a leave of absence, which was to expire in February 1965. She was under the care of a psychiatrist, who diagnosed her illness as involutional psychosis, melancholia type, and cerebral arteriosclerosis.

Ortolere was a member of the Teachers' Retirement System of the city of New York, which entitled her to certain retirement payments and benefits in case she died before retirement. She was permitted to choose among various options concerning the payment of her retirement allowance. Some years before, Ortolere had executed a selection of "Option One" benefits, which entitled her to periodic retirement allowances and provided that if she died before her full retirement benefits had been paid, the reserve would be payable to her husband. When her leave of absence expired, Ortolere was still not well enough to return to teaching. The Board of Education requested that she report to its panel psychiatrist for evaluation. In February 1965, while still under psychiatric treatment, Ortolere wrote a letter to the Retirement Board stating that she intended to retire and listing eight detailed questions that reflected great understanding of the retirement system and the various alternatives available. Several days later, she changed her election of benefits, selecting the option that gave her the maximum retirement allowance payable during her lifetime, with nothing payable on or after her death. She also borrowed from the system the maximum cash withdrawal permitted. Within two months, she died of cerebral thrombosis.

Her husband and executor brought this action to disaffirm her second selection of retirement benefits. The trial court decided in favor of Ortolere. The decision was appealed, and the first appellate court reversed in favor of the Retirement Board. Ortolere appealed from this decision.

**Breitel, Judge.** The well-established rule is that contracts of a mentally incompetent person who has not been adjudicated insane are voidable. Traditionally, contractual mental capacity has been measured by what is largely a cognitive test. Under this standard the inquiry is whether the mind was so affected as to render a person wholly and absolutely incompetent to comprehend and understand the nature of the transaction.

These traditional standards governing competency to contract were formulated when psychiatric knowledge was quite primitive. They fail to account for one who by reason of mental illness is unable to control his conduct even though his cognitive ability seems unimpaired. Because the cognitive rules are, for the most part, too restrictive and rest on a false factual basis, they must be re-examined.

It is quite significant that Restatement, 2d, Contracts, states the modern rule on competency to contract. The new Restatement section reads: "A person incurs only voidable contractual duties by entering into a transaction if by reason of mental illness or defect . . . he is unable to act in a reasonable manner in relation to the transaction and the other party has reason to know of his condition."

The avoidance of duties under an agreement entered into by those who have done so by reason of mental illness, but who have understanding, depends on balancing competing policy considerations. There must be stability in contractual relations and protection of the expectations of parties who bargain in good faith. On the other hand, it is also desirable to protect persons who may understand the nature of the transaction but who, due to mental illness, cannot control their conduct. Hence, there should be relief only if the other party knew or was put on notice as to the contractor's mental illness.

The Retirement Board was, or should have been, fully aware of Mrs. Ortolere's condition. They, or the Board of Education, knew of her leave of absence for medical reasons and the resort to staff psychiatrists by the Board of Education. It is not a sound scheme which would permit 40 years of contribution to be nullified by a one-instant act committed by one known to be mentally ill. Her selection of a "no option" retirement while under psychiatric care, ill with cerebral arteriosclerosis, aged 60, and with a family in which she had always manifested concern, was so unwise and foolhardy that a factfinder might conclude that it was explainable only as a product of psychosis.

Judgment reversed and remanded in favor of Ortolere.

## SUMMARY

Minors, people suffering from mental illnesses or defects, and intoxicated persons are considered to lack capacity to enter a contract because they are at an inherent disadvantage in their dealings with others.

The age of majority in almost all states is 18. A contract formed when a party is younger than the age of majority is **voidable** at the option of the minor. The minor has the right to avoid his obligations under a contract by disaffirming the contract. He may do so at any time between the time the contract was formed and a reasonable time *after* reaching majority. If he disaffirms, he must return any consideration given him by the other party that remains in his possession. If what he has purchased from the other party is considered to be a **necessary,** he must pay the reasonable value of what he has actually received. If what he has purchased is *not* a necessary, the common law rule is that he is entitled to the return of anything he has given the other party and that he does not have to pay the other party for loss or depreciation in value of the consideration given to him by that party. Some states have declined to follow this rule, however, and have designed other rules to promote the fair treatment of innocent adults who have dealt fairly with minors.

A minor's misrepresentation of his age has different results in different states. In some states, misrepresentation of age makes no difference in the minor's rights and obligations. In others, it places an obligation on the minor to put the adult in *statu quo,* makes him liable in tort for deceit, or precludes him from asserting his minority as a claim or defense. Once a minor reaches majority, he can **ratify** a contract in any way that shows his intent to be bound by the contract. Ratification operates as a surrender of the right to avoid the contract. It can be made expressly, in specific words, or impliedly, through conduct of the former minor. When a contract has been ratified, it is treated as valid from its inception and cannot later be disaffirmed.

A contract entered into by a person who lacks capacity because of a mental illness or defect is voidable, unless the person was under guardianship at the time the contract was formed. In that case, the contract would be considered void. In determining mental capacity, courts generally ask whether the person was capable of understanding the nature and consequences of the contract. The *Restatement* and some courts permit disaffirmance if a person is unable to act reasonably because of a mental defect or illness and the other party has reason to know of his impairment. Upon disaffirmance, the incapacitated person must return any consideration that remains in his possession. He may be obligated to place the other party in *statu quo* if the contract was fair and the other party had no reason to know of his mental impairment. Like the minor, the mentally incapacitated person must pay the reasonable value of necessaries that he has actually received and can, upon obtaining full mental capacity, bind himself to a contract made during incapacity by ratifying it.

Persons who are so intoxicated at the time they enter a contract that they do not understand the nature and consequences of a contract are often treated as lacking capacity to contract. The *Restatement* provides that a contract formed at a time when one of the parties was intoxicated to this extent would be voidable if the other person had reason to know that he was unable to understand the contract or act in a reasonable way in relation to it because of his intoxication.

## PROBLEM CASES

1. Jones entered into a contract for skydiving lessons with Free Flight when he was 17. The contract expressly disclaimed Free Flight's liability for any injuries Jones might suffer. Ten months after Jones's 18th birthday, a plane furnished by Free Flight crashed while carrying him. Jones sued for injuries, and Free Flight asserted as a defense the disclaimer that was contained in the contract. Does Jones's lack of capacity when the contract was formed permit him to avoid the disclaimer?

2. Robertson, while a minor, contracted to borrow money from his father for a college education. His father mortgaged his home and took out loans against his life insurance policies to get some of the money he lent to Robertson, who ultimately graduated from

dental school. Two years after Robertson's graduation, his father aked him to begin paying back the amount of $30,000 at $400 per month. Robertson agreed to pay $24,000 at $100 per month. He did this for three years before stopping the payments. His father sued for the balance of the debt. Could Robertson disaffirm the contract?

**3.** Rogers, a married minor, contracted for the services of Gastonia Personnel Corporation, an employment agency. He agreed to pay Gastonia a specified fee if he accepted employment as a result of a "lead" supplied to him by Gastonia. Gastonia referred Rogers to an employer and Rogers accepted the job. He then refused to pay Gastonia the fee agreed upon. Is Rogers obligated to pay the fee?

**4.** Parrent, age 15, injured his back while working for Midway Toyota, Inc. He claimed workers' compensation benefits from Midway. After receiving partial benefits, Parrent entered into a final settlement agreement with Midway regarding the remainder of the claim. Parrent's mother was present when he signed the agreement and did not object to the signing, but she did not cosign it. Later, Parrent sought to disaffirm the settlement on the ground of his minority. What result?

**5.** Lee bought a car from Haydocy Pontiac, representing herself to be 18 when she was in fact only 17. She lent the car to a friend, who sold it to another car dealer. Lee made no payments on the car, and when Haydocy filed suit, she sought to disaffirm the contract on the ground of minority. Neither Lee nor Haydocy was able to recover the car. How should the case be resolved?

**6.** Wilson bought 60 acres of land from Williams for $3,000. In the course of evaluating the title to the land, Wilson's attorney advised him that he had discovered that two years earlier Williams had been committed to the Mississippi State Hospital for several months. Less than a month after the sale, Williams began a long series of treatments for mental illness. A member of Williams' family began an action to rescind the sale of the property, claiming that the land was worth $6,500 and that Williams had been incompetent to execute the deed. Can the deed be disaffirmed?

**7.** White, a 19-year-old minor, ordered contact lenses from Cidis, an optometrist, advising Cidis that she wanted them as soon as possible. She agreed to pay $225 for the lenses and gave Cidis her personal check for $100. Accordingly, Cidis examined her and ordered the lenses from his laboratory, incurring an indebtedness of $110. Several days later, White called and disaffirmed the contract on the advice of her father. She stopped payment on her check. At the time of disaffirmance, White was working and, though living at home, paid for her room and board. Cidis sues White for the loss he sustained. What result?

Chapter 12

# Illegality

## INTRODUCTION

The law enforces voluntary agreements between private individuals because it is normally in the public interest to do so. Sometimes, however, the interests that usually favor the enforcement of an agreement are subordinated to conflicting social concerns. As you read in Chapters 9 (Reality of Consent) and 11 (Capacity of Parties), for example, persons who did not truly consent to a contract or who lacked the capacity to contract have the power to cancel their contracts. In these situations, concerns about protecting disadvantaged persons and preserving the integrity of the bargaining process are considered to outweigh the public interest in enforcing private agreements. Similarly, when an agreement involves the commission of an act or the making of a promise that violates some legislative or court-made rule, the public interests threatened by the agreement outweigh the interests that favor its enforcement. Such an agreement will be denied enforcement on grounds of **illegality,** even if there is voluntary consent between two parties who have capacity to contract.

**Meaning of Illegality.** When a court says that an agreement is illegal, it does not necessarily mean that the agreement violates a criminal law—although an agreement to commit a crime is one type of illegal agreement. Rather, an agreement is illegal either because the legislature has declared that particular type of contract to be unenforceable or "void" or because the agreement violates a **public policy** that has been developed by courts or that has been manifested in constitutions, statutes, administrative regulations, or other sources of law. Public policy is a broad concept that is impossible to define precisely, but it is generally taken to mean a lawmaker's view of what is in the best interests of the public. Public policy may be based on a prevailing moral code, on an economic philosophy, or on the need to protect a valued social institution such as the family or the judicial system. Public policies—the judges' or legislators' perceptions of what objectives promote public welfare—guide their decisions about the resolution of cases or the enactment of statutes or rules. If the enforcement of an agreement would create a threat to a public policy, a court may determine that it is illegal, even if no statute specifically states that that particular type of agreement is unenforceable.

**Determining whether an Agreement Is Illegal.** If a statute states that a particular type of agreement is unenforceable or void, courts will apply the statute and refuse to enforce the agreement. However, relatively few such statutes exist. More frequently, a legislature will forbid specified conduct but will not address the enforceability of contracts that involve the forbidden conduct. In such cases, courts must determine whether the importance of the public policy that underlies the statute in question and the degree of interference with that policy are sufficiently great to outweigh any interests that favor enforcement of the agreement.

In some cases, it is relatively easy to predict that an agreement will be held to be illegal. For example, an agreement to commit a serious crime is certain to be illegal. However, the many laws enacted by legislatures are of differing degrees of importance to the public welfare. The determination of illegality would not be so clear if the agreement violated a statute that was of relatively small importance to the public welfare.

Similarly, the public policies developed by courts are rarely absolute; they, too, depend on a balancing of several factors. In determining whether to hold an agreement illegal, a court will consider the importance of the public policy involved and the extent to which enforcement of the agreement would interfere with that policy. They will also consider the seriousness of any wrongdoing involved in the agreement and how directly that wrongdoing was connected with the agreement.

For purposes of our discussion, illegal agreements will be classified into four categories: (1) agreements that are declared by statute to be unenforceable, (2) agreements that violate public policy as manifested in legislation, (3) agreements that violate public policy developed by courts, and (4) agreements that violate the judicial and legislative public policy against **unconscionability.**

## AGREEMENTS DECLARED VOID BY STATUTE

State legislatures have enacted statutes that declare certain types of agreements unenforceable, void, or voidable. These statutes differ from state to state, but three of the most common statutes of this kind are *usury statutes, Sunday laws,* and *wagering statutes.*

**Usury Statutes.** Usury statutes prohibit charging more than a stated rate of interest for the use of money. Such statutes are not uniform in their prohibitions or their penalties. In several states, for example, usury laws do not apply to loans to corporations. In many states, a higher price can be charged for credit sales than for cash sales without the price differential being considered to be interest. When the rate of interest charged for the use of money exceeds the statutory limit for the particular type of transaction in question, however, the lender will be subject to a penalty. Some statutes provide for complete forfeiture of all interest and principal. Other statutes provide for forfeiture of all interest. Still others provide for forfeiture only of interest in excess of the legal rate.

**Sunday Laws.** Sunday laws prohibit the transaction of certain business and the performance of certain types of work on Sunday. Like usury laws, Sunday laws vary substantially from state to state. The more common form prohibits and invalidates contracts and sales made on Sunday that are not the result of necessity or charity. Exceptions are often made for certain businesses, such as hotels and newspapers.

**Wagering Statutes.** All states either prohibit or regulate wagering, or gambling. There is a thin line separating wagering, which is illegal, from well-accepted, lawful transactions in which a person will profit from the happening of an uncertain event. How is illegal wagering distinguished from insurance contracts and stock and commodity transactions, for example? The hallmark of a wager is that neither party has any financial stake or interest in the uncertain event except for the stake that he has created by making the bet. The person making a wager *creates* the risk that he may lose the money or property wagered upon the happening of an uncertain event. Suppose Smith bets Jones $20 that the Cubs will win the pennant in 1984. Smith has no financial interest in a Cubs victory other than that which he has created through his bet. Rather, he has created the risk of losing $20 for the sole purpose of bearing that risk.

If, however, people make an agreement about who shall bear an existing risk in which one of them has an actual stake or interest, that is a legal risk-shifting agreement. Property insurance contracts are classic examples of risk-shifting agreements. The owner of the property pays the insurance company a fee (premium) in return for the company's agreement to bear the risk of the uncertain event that the property will be damaged or destroyed. If, however, the person who takes out the policy had no legitimate economic interest in the insured property (called an **insurable interest** in insurance law), the agreement is an illegal wager.

Stock and commodity market transactions are good examples of speculative bargains that are legal. In both cases, the purchasers are obviously hoping that their purchases will increase in value and the sellers believe that they will not. The difference between these transactions and wagers lies in the fact that the parties to stock and commodities transactions are legally bound to the purchase agreement, even though the purchaser may never intend to take delivery of the stock or commodity. In an illegal wager—such as a bet on the performance of certain stock—no purchase or ownership is involved. Nothing is at stake except the risk that the parties have created by their bet.

## AGREEMENTS IN VIOLATION OF PUBLIC POLICY MANIFESTED IN LEGISLATION

**Agreements to Commit Illegal Acts.** Few criminal statutes specifically state that contracts involving the commission of a certain criminal act should be denied enforcement. However, the enforcement of such agreements would threaten the public interest in protecting life, health, and property. It would also promote disobedience of the criminal code and disrespect for the courts. For these reasons, agreements that require the commission of a crime are illegal. Thus, if Smith pays Jones $5,000 to set fire to Smith's warehouse, the agreement is illegal. Sometimes, the very formation of a certain type of contract is a crime, even if the acts agreed upon are never carried out. An example of this is an agreement to murder another person. Naturally, such agreements are considered illegal under contract law as well as under criminal law. Contracts that require the commission of a tort are also illegal. If Smith pays Jones $5,000 to publish a defamatory statement about Johnson, the agreement would be denied enforcement on the ground of illegality.

**Agreements That Promote Illegal Acts.** Sometimes, a contract will appear to be perfectly legal and in fact can be performed without the commission of an illegal act, yet it aids the commission of an illegal act. Suppose Smith sells Jones a gun on credit, and the gun is later used in the commission of a crime. Can Smith recover the price of the gun from Jones? The answer depends on whether Smith knew of the illegal purpose and whether the sale was intended to further that illegal purpose. The outcome of cases in which an agreement has aided the commission of illegal acts is somewhat difficult to predict. Generally speaking, such agreements will be held illegal only if there is a direct connection between the illegal conduct and the agreement in the form of active, intentional participation in or facilitation of a serious crime. Knowledge of the other party's illegal purpose, standing alone, generally is not sufficient to render such an agreement illegal.

The *Hendrix* case, which follows, is an example of a case in which the court found the connection between the agreement and criminal activity sufficiently close for the public interest to be harmed by enforcement of the agreement. Note that in *Hendrix* there was a combination of two important factors: Hendrix's knowledge of the illegal purpose of the agreement and his active participation in that purpose.

## Hendrix v. McKee

**575 P.2d 134 (Or. Sup. Ct. 1978)**

James Hendrix was an electrical engineer who designed gambling devices and was the president of a corporation that specialized in designing gambling devices used in Nevada. In 1974, Hendrix met and visited Harold McKee in Oregon. McKee showed Hendrix the upright electromechanical "amusement devices" that he had placed in the Bend-Redmond area. During this visit, Hendrix entered into an employment contract to work for McKee for two years. Initially, Hendrix was employed to design a "pull tab" gambling machine that he knew was illegal in Oregon. Later, at McKee's request, Hendrix moved to Oregon and began working on new upright devices similar to the ones he had been shown in 1974. He was paid $2,500 per month—$1,500 by check and $1,000 in cash. Hendrix did not report the cash payments on his state or federal income tax returns. During this period of time, McKee was charged with and pleaded guilty to the felony of promoting gambling in the first degree, which stemmed from his involvement with upright electronic machines. In June 1975, after he had been employed by McKee for almost a year, Hendrix was notified of his immediate termination. Hendrix brought suit against McKee for breach of the employment contract. When the trial court ruled in McKee's favor, Hendrix appealed.

**Lent, Justice.** It is often stated that courts will not enforce "illegal" contracts. This is an oversimplification of a legal principle, the application of which often involves construction of statutes and contractual provisions, delineation and balancing of public policies, and a difficult sorting and sifting process.

It is elementary that public policy requires that men of full age and competent understanding shall have the utmost liberty of contracting, and that their contracts, when entered into freely and voluntarily, shall be enforced by courts. It is only when some other overpowering rule of public policy intervenes, rendering such agreement illegal, that it will not be enforced.

The contract in question, while illegal in result, was capable of being performed in a legal manner. Where an agreement is capable of being performed in a legal manner, the mere fact that one of the parties intended to perform it in an illegal manner will not preclude its enforcement. The illegal intent that defeats a contract must be the common intent of both parties. If the purpose of either in making it is lawful, and if he supposes the other's to be, his right to recover upon the contract after performance is clear.

The key to this "common intent" was Hendrix's knowledge at the time he entered the contract. There were abundant facts in evidence which would justify the trial court in drawing an inference of such knowledge. Hendrix's whole career had been inextricably involved with the gambling business. Before accepting employment, he was taken on a tour of McKee's upright device placements. He knew at the time of contracting that the "pull tab" machine was illegal in Oregon. In addition, the manner in which he received his monthly salary is a fertile source of inference. The $1,000 cash payment "under the table" was suspicious and yields an inference that Hendrix had knowledge that something was not quite legitimate about the transaction. There was sufficient evidence to support the trial court's finding of fact.

Judgment for McKee affirmed.

**Agreement to Perform an Act for Which a Party Is Not Properly Licensed.** Congress and the state legislatures have enacted a variety of statutes that regulate professions and businesses. A common type of regulatory statute is one that requires a person to obtain a license or registration before engaging in a certain business or profession. For example, state statutes require lawyers, physicians, dentists, teachers, and other professionals to be licensed to practice their professions. In order to obtain the required license, they must meet specified requirements such as attaining a certain educational degree and passing an examination. Real estate brokers, stockbrokers, insurance agents, sellers of liquor and tobacco, pawnbrokers, electricians, barbers, and others too numerous to mention are also often required by state statute to meet licensing requirements to perform services or sell regulated commodities to members of the public.

What is the status of an agreement in which

one of the parties agrees to perform an act regulated by state law for which she is not properly licensed? Once again, the answer to this question depends on a balancing of the public interest that would be harmed by enforcement against the public and individual interests that favor enforcement. In determining whether to enforce the agreement, a court will consider the purpose of the legislation that has been offended by the agreement. If the statute is **regulatory**—that is, the purpose of the legislation is to protect the public against dishonest or incompetent practitioners—an agreement by an unlicensed person is generally held to be unenforceable. For example, if Jones, a first-year law student, agrees to draft a will for Smith for a fee of $150, Jones could not enforce the agreement and collect a fee from Smith for drafting the will, because she is not licensed to practice law. This result makes sense, even though it imposes a hardship on Jones. The public interest in assuring that people on whose legal advice others rely have an appropriate educational background and proficiency in the subject matter outweighs any interest in seeing that Jones receives what she bargained for.

On the other hand, where the licensing statute was intended primarily as a **revenue raising** measure—that is, as a means of collecting money rather than as a means of protecting the public—an agreement to pay a person for performing an act for which she is not licensed will generally be enforced. For example, suppose that in the example used above, Jones is a lawyer who is licensed to practice law in her state and who has met all of her state's educational, testing, and character requirements but has neglected to pay her annual registration fee. In this situation, there is no compelling public interest that would justify the harsh measure of refusing enforcement and possibly inflicting forfeiture on the unlicensed person.

Whether a statute is a regulatory statute or a revenue-raising statute depends on the intent of the legislature, which may not always be expressed clearly. Generally, statutes that require proof of character and skill and impose penalties for violation are considered to be regulatory in nature. Those that impose a significant license fee and allow anyone who pays the fee to obtain a license are usually classified as revenue raising.

It would be misleading to imply that cases involving unlicensed parties always follow such a mechanical test. In some cases, courts may grant recovery to an unlicensed party even where a regulatory statute is violated. If the public policy promoted by the statute is relatively trivial in relation to the amount that would be forfeited by the unlicensed person and the unlicensed person is neither dishonest nor incompetent, a court may conclude that the statutory penalty for violation of the regulatory statute is sufficient to protect the public interest and that enforcement of the agreement is appropriate. Under section 181 of the *Restatement (Second) of Contracts,* an agreement to pay an unlicensed person for doing an act for which a license is required is unenforceable only if the licensing statute has a regulatory purpose *and* if the interest in enforcement of the promise is clearly outweighed by the public policy behind the statute. The *Wilson* case, which follows, is a good example of the method by which courts analyze cases involving unlicensed parties.

## Wilson v. Kealakekua Ranch, Ltd.

**551 P.2d 525 (Hawaii Sup. Ct. 1976)**

Ben Lee Wilson had been licensed to practice architecture in the state of Hawaii, but his license lapsed in 1971 because he failed to pay a required $15 renewal fee. A Hawaii statute provides that any person who practices architecture without having been registered and "without having a valid unexpired certificate of registration . . . shall be fined not more than $500 or imprisoned not more than one year, or both." In 1972, Wilson performed architectural and engineering services for Kealakekua Ranch for which he billed the Ranch $33,994.36. When the Ranch failed to pay Wilson's fee, he brought this action for breach of contract. The trial court found for the Ranch on the ground that the agreement was illegal, and Wilson appealed.

**Richardson, Chief Justice.** Where, as here, the statute provides a criminal sanction but is silent as to whether its violation will deprive the parties of their right to sue on the contract, the courts have distinguished between statutes for revenue and statutes for protection of the public against incompetence and fraud. If the purpose of the statute is for the protection of the public against fraud and incompetence, it is more likely that the statute breaker will be denied the enforcement of his bargain. However, even in these cases enforcement of the wrongdoer's bargains is not always denied him. In very many cases the statute breaker is neither fraudulent nor incompetent. He may have rendered excellent service or delivered goods of the highest quality, his non-compliance with the statute seems nearly harmless, and the real defrauder seems to be the defendant who is enriching himself at the plaintiff's expense. Although many courts yearn for a mechanically applicable rule, they have not made one in the present instance. Justice requires that the penalty should fit the crime; and justice and sound policy do not always require the enforcement of licensing statutes by large forfeitures going not to the state but to repudiating defendants. It must be remembered that in most cases the statute itself does not require these forfeitures. It fixes its own penalties, usually fine or imprisonment of minor character with a degree of discretion in the court. The added penalty of non-enforceability of bargains is a judicial creation. In most cases it is wise to apply it; but when it causes great and disproportionate hardship, its application may be avoided.

It is not disputed that Wilson was first registered in accordance with the statute in 1967. At that time, the Board of Registration determined that Wilson was of sufficient knowledge, skill, competence, character, and reputation to practice architecture in this State. While the provisions of the statute requiring initial registration are clearly designed to protect the public from unfit and incompetent practitioners of architecture, we think that the provision requiring renewal, with which Wilson failed to comply, is purely for the purposes of raising revenues. Renewal involves nothing more than the remittance of the annual $15.00 fee. Reexamination and reinvestigation play no part in the renewal process. Once registered, the statute prescribes scrutiny by the Board only when a charge has been filed with the Board that an architect is guilty of negligence, incompetence, misconduct, or violation of the statute or rules. We see no relationship between the payment of annual fees and the competence or character of an architect. We conclude, therefore, that the provision requiring renewal by way of payment of a $15.00 fee was not for public protection, but for revenue.

We do not believe that the legislature intended unenforceability in addition to penal sanctions, since unenforceability would result in a forfeiture wholly out of proportion to the requirements of public policy or appropriate individual punishment. Wilson's failure to remit the $15.00 already renders him liable to a fine of up to $500 and/or imprisonment for up to a year. Finding the contract unenforceable, null and void, would impose an additional punishment of up to $34,000, redounding to the benefit of the Ranch. While the public has a legitimate interest in assuming the collection of revenues, we think that the penal sanctions in the instant case are more than adequate to secure that interest. Additional punishment, especially a disproportionate forfeiture, is not justified and could not have been intended by the legislature.

Judgment reversed in favor of Wilson.

## AGREEMENTS IN VIOLATION OF PUBLIC POLICY ARTICULATED BY COURTS

Legislative bodies manifest public policy by the laws they enact, which contain rules that lawmakers consider necessary for the public welfare. Courts, too, have broad discretion to articulate public policy and to decline to lend their powers of enforcement to an agreement that would contravene what they deem to be in the best interests of society. There is no simple rule for determining when a particular agreement is contrary to public policy. Public policy may change with the times; changing social and economic conditions may make behavior that was acceptable in an earlier time unacceptable today, or vice versa. The following are examples of agreements that are frequently considered vulnerable to attack on public policy grounds.

**Agreements in Restraint of Competition.** The policy against restrictions on competition is one of the oldest public policies declared by the common law. This same policy is also the basis of the federal and state antitrust statutes, which you will study in Chapters 44 and 45. The policy against restraints on competition is based on the economic judgment that the public interest is best served by free competition. Nevertheless, courts have long recognized that some contractual restrictions on competition serve legitimate business interests and should be enforced. Therefore, agreements that limit competition are scrutinized very closely by the courts to determine whether the restraint imposed is in violation of public policy.

If the *sole* purpose of an agreement is to restrain competition, it violates the public policy and is illegal. For example, if Smith and Jones own competing businesses and they enter an agreement whereby each agrees not to solicit or sell to the other's customers, such an agreement would be unenforceable. If, however, the restraint on competition is part of (*ancillary* to) a legitimate transaction, the result may be different because there are strong interests that counterbalance the public policy against such restraints.

A very common ancillary restraint on competition is an agreement by a person to refrain from practicing his trade or profession in competition with the other party. Such promises are called **ancillary covenants not to compete.** They are often included in *contracts for the sale of a business, partnership agreements,* and *employment contracts.* In these transactions, the promisee has a legitimate business interest to be protected. In the sale of a business, part of what the buyer is paying for is the goodwill of the business. The buyer wants to make sure that the seller does not open a competing business soon after the sale and attract away the very customers whose goodwill the buyer has just paid for. In an employment contract, the employer wants to assure itself that it will not disclose trade secrets, confidential information, and customer lists to an employee only to have the employee quit and enter a competing business.

To protect himself, the buyer or the employer in the above examples might bargain for a contractual clause which would provide that the seller or employee agrees not to engage in a particular competing activity in a specified *geographic area* for a specified *time* after the sale of the business or the termination of employment. If the seller or employee, as the case may be, violates the covenant, the buyer or employer may seek damages or an injunction (a court order preventing the promisor from violating the covenant).

Though covenants not to compete are scrutinized on a case-by-case basis, there are several basic standards that such a covenant must satisfy to be enforced. First, the covenant must be *ancillary* to or part of an otherwise valid contract. For example, if an employee quit his job and, after quitting, promised not to compete with his former employer, such a promise would not be enforced, because it was formed after the contract of employment was terminated. Thus, it was not ancillary to any valid transaction. Second, the restriction on competition must be *reasonable.* Another way of stating this is that the restrictions must not be any greater than necessary to protect a legitimate interest. It would be unreasonable for a person to restrain the other party from engaging in some activity that is not a competing activity, because this would not threaten his legitimate interests. This point is made in the *Ellis* case, which follows. Time and geographic area restrictions must also be reasonable. Of course, what is reasonable depends on the facts of the case. In the sale of a business conducted throughout a three-state area, a restriction on the seller's engaging in the same business in those three states would probably be reasonable. If the company sold engages in business only within a 30-mile radius of the capital city of one of those states, however, the three-state restriction would be unreasonable.

In determining whether a covenant not to compete is against public policy, courts often will also consider the degree of hardship that the covenant would place on the public and on the party whose ability to compete would be restrained. The hardship to the public was a factor considered by the court in the *Ellis* case, for example. Restrictions on competition work a greater hardship on an employee than on a person who has sold a business. For this reason, courts often state that covenants not to compete contained in employment contracts are judged by a stricter standard than are similar covenants contained in contracts for the sale of a business.

The courts of different states treat unreasonably broad covenants not to compete in different ways. Some courts will strike the entire restriction if they find it to be unreasonable, and will refuse to grant the buyer or employer any protection. Others will refuse to enforce the restraint as written, but will adjust the covenant and impose such restraints as would be reasonable. This approach is taken in *Ellis.*

## Ellis v. McDaniel

**596 P.2d 222 (Nev. Sup. Ct. 1979)**

Charles Ellis, an orthopedic surgeon, entered into a contract of employment with the Elko Clinic. Among other provisions, the contract of employment provided:

> In the event that Dr. Ellis's employment by the Elko Clinic terminates for any reason, Dr. Ellis shall not undertake to practice medicine within a distance of five miles from the city limits of Elko, Nevada for a period of two years from the termination date of his employment.

During Dr. Ellis's employment, he treated patients who would otherwise have had to travel to Reno, Salt Lake City, or elsewhere to seek the services of an orthopedic surgeon. At the expiration of his employment contract, Dr. Ellis gave notice to the Clinic that he intended to establish his own office in Elko for the practice of his specialty. The Clinic filed this action to prevent his proposed breach of the contract. The trial court granted a preliminary injunction against Dr. Ellis, and Dr. Ellis appealed.

**Manoukian, Justice.** There is no inflexible formula for deciding the question of reasonableness. However, because the loss of a person's livelihood is a very serious matter, post employment anti-competitive covenants are scrutinized with greater care than are similar covenants incident to the sale of a business.

Here, as the covenant is territorially limited to the geographic area serviced by the Clinic, and durationally limited to a reasonable length of time, the preliminary considerations of reasonableness are satisfied. Recognizing that the good will and reputation of the Clinic are valuable assets and that certain of its orthopedic patients are likely to follow Dr. Ellis on his departure, we are nonetheless constrained to agree with Dr. Ellis that since none of the doctors at the Elko Clinic are orthopedic specialists, a restraint on Dr. Ellis's practice of his specialty in the Elko area is unreasonable and beyond the scope of any legitimate protectible interest of the Clinic. Although an injunction against Dr. Ellis's practice as a general practitioner is a reasonable restraint in order to protect the good will of the Elko Clinic, a prohibition against his practice as an orthopedic surgeon is not.

Moreover, Elko General Hospital is the only hospital between Reno and Salt Lake City equipped to perform major surgical procedures. If Dr. Ellis is not permitted to practice his specialty there, patients in need of orthopedic services will be forced to travel great distances at considerable risk and expense in order to avail themselves of such services. Thus, in this case, the public interest in retaining the services of the specialist is greater than the interest in protecting the integrity of the contract provision to its outer limits.

Finally, assessing the relative hardships, we conclude that the loss to Dr. Ellis and the public by enforcing the covenant is far in excess of the threatened danger to the Clinic. We therefore deny enforcement of the covenant to the extent that it purports to prohibit Dr. Ellis from practicing orthopedic surgery. We will enforce the covenant by prohibiting Dr. Ellis from engaging in the *general practice* of medicine within the time and space limitations set out in the contract.

Order modified in favor of Dr. Ellis.

**Exculpatory Clauses.** An **exculpatory clause** is a provision in a contract that purports to relieve a person from tort liability. Exculpatory clauses are suspect on public policy grounds for two reasons. First, courts are concerned that a party who can contract away his liability for negligence will not have the incentive to use care to avoid injury to others. Second, courts are concerned that an agreement that accords one party such a powerful advantage might have been the result of abuse of superior bargaining power rather than truly voluntary choice. Though exculpatory agreements are often said to be "disfavored" in the law, courts do not wish to prohibit parties who are truly dealing on a fair and voluntary basis from ordering the manner in which the risks of a transaction shall be borne when such an agreement does not threaten public health or safety.

In determining whether an exculpatory clause should be enforced, then, a court is balancing its concerns about public welfare against the interest in allowing competent parties to agree about their own affairs. Several limitations on the enforceability of exculpatory clauses have been developed. An exculpatory clause that purports to relieve a person from liability for fraud or other willful torts will be considered to be against public policy. Also against public policy are exculpatory clauses that relieve a party that owes a duty to the public (such as an airline) from liability.

Another possible limitation on the enforceability of exculpatory clauses arises from the increasing array of statutes and common law rules that impose certain obligations on one party to a contract for the benefit of the other party to the contract. Workers' compensation statutes and laws requiring landlords to maintain leased property in a habitable condition are examples of such laws. Sometimes, the person on whom such an obligation is placed will attempt to escape it by inserting an exculpatory or waiver provision in a contract. Such clauses are often—though not always—found to be against public policy because, if enforceable, they would frustrate the very purpose of imposing the duty in question. For example, an employee's agreement to relieve her employer from workers' compensation liability is likely to be held illegal as a violation of public policy. A court may also refuse to enforce an exculpatory clause if it finds that the clause is **unconscionable** or the product of abuse of superior bargaining power. (Unconscionability is discussed later in this chapter.)

Though there are many limitations on the enforceability of exculpatory clauses, *Jones v. Dressel,* which follows, shows that it is still possible to enforce a specifically expressed exculpatory clause that is agreed to by parties with equal bargaining power, so long as no duty to the public is involved and the clause does not purport to relieve a party from liability for willful torts. In light of the difficulty in predicting whether an exculpatory clause will be enforced, it goes without saying that such clauses are no substitute for careful conduct.

**Agreements Injurious to Public Service.** Because the public interest is best served by public officials who fully and faithfully perform their duties, agreements that induce public servants to deviate from their public duties are illegal. For example, an agreement to pay a public employee more or less than her lawful salary would be illegal. Agreements that create a conflict between a public employee's personal interests and her public duties are also illegal. Although everyone is entitled to make his views or desires regarding legislation known to members of Congress or state legislatures, it is illegal to offer elected officials presents or personal favors to influence their decisions on legislative matters. Obviously, an agreement to bribe a public servant is illegal.

**Agreements to Influence Fiduciaries.** A **fiduciary** is a person in a position of trust or confidence, such as a trustee, agent, or partner. An agreement that tends to induce a fiduciary to breach his or her fiduciary duties to a principal or beneficiary is illegal. This is so because such an agreement is basically a fraud on the beneficiary or principal, who is entitled to the fiduciary's loyalty. As a general rule, the fiduciary is not allowed to enter any transaction whereby his personal interests will be in conflict with his fiduciary duties, unless he makes full disclosure of the conflicting interests and the beneficiary or principal effectively consents.

**Agreements That Impair Family Relationships.** In view of the central position of the family as a valued social institution, it is not surprising that an agreement that unreasonably tends to interfere with family relationships will be considered illegal. Examples of this type of contract include agreements whereby one of the parties agrees to divorce a spouse or agrees not to marry. In recent years, courts have been presented with an increasing number of agreements between unmarried cohabitants that purport to agree upon the manner in which the parties' property will be shared or divided upon separation. The earlier cases refused to enforce such agreements on the ground that they were based on an illegal consideration—illegal sexual relations. Though the cases are by no means uniform, more recent cases have been more hospitable to the claims of unmarried cohabitants and have enforced their agreements.

## Jones v. Dressel

**623 P.2d 370 (Colo. Sup. Ct. 1981)**

William Michael Jones signed a contract with Free Flight Sport Aviation, Inc. that gave him the right to use Free Flight's recreational skydiving facilities, including an airplane that ferried skydivers to the parachute jumping site. An exculpatory clause exempting Free Flight from liability for negligence was included in the contract.

Approximately one year later, Jones was injured while riding in a Free Flight airplane that crashed shortly after takeoff. He sued Free Flight for negligence, and Free Flight asserted the exculpatory clause as a defense. The trial court found for Free Flight, and Jones appealed.

**Erickson, Justice.** Jones asserts that the exculpatory agreement is void as a matter of public policy. An exculpatory agreement, which attempts to insulate a party from liability from his own negligence, must be closely scrutinized, and in no event will such an agreement provide a shield against a claim for willful and wanton negligence. In determining whether an exculpatory agreement is valid, there are four factors which a court must consider: (1) the existence of a duty to the public; (2) the nature of the service performed; (3) whether the contract was fairly entered into; and (4) whether the intention of the parties is expressed in clear and unambiguous language.

Measured against these four factors, we conclude that the trial court correctly held that the exculpatory agreement was valid. The duty to the public factor is not present in this case. The service provided by Free Flight was not a matter of practical necessity for even some members of the public; because the service provided by Free Flight was not an essential service, it did not possess a decisive advantage of bargaining strength over Jones. There was no disagreement between the parties that the contract was fairly entered into. Likewise, the agreement expressed the parties' intention in clear and unambiguous language. We conclude that the exculpatory agreement was not void as a matter of public policy.

Judgment for Free Flight affirmed.

## AGREEMENTS IN VIOLATION OF LEGISLATIVE AND JUDICIAL PUBLIC POLICY AGAINST UNCONSCIONABILITY

**Development of the Doctrine of Unconscionability.** Under classical contract law, courts were reluctant to inquire into the fairness of an agreement. Because prevailing social attitudes and economic philosophy strongly favored freedom of contract, American courts took the position that so long as there had been no fraud, duress, misrepresentation, mistake, or undue influence in the bargaining process, unfairness in an agreement entered into by competent adults—who were presumed to be capable of protecting their own interests—did not render the agreement unenforceable.

As the changing nature of our society produced many contract situations in which the bargaining positions of the parties were grossly unequal, the classical contract assumption that each party was capable of protecting himself was no longer persuasive. Legislatures responded to this problem by enacting a variety of statutory measures to protect individuals against the abuse of superior bargaining power in specific situations. Examples of such legislation include minimum wage laws and rent control ordinances. Courts responded to the problem of abuse of superior bargaining power by declaring **contracts of adhesion** (contracts in which a stronger party is able to dictate unfair terms to a weaker party, leaving the weaker party no practical choice but to "adhere" to the terms) to be against public policy. Some courts also borrowed a doctrine that had been developed and used for a long time in courts of equity,[1] whereby they would refuse to enforce an oppressively unfair contract on the ground that it was **unconscionable.** One of the most far-reaching efforts to correct abuses of superior bargaining power was the enactment of section 2–302 of the Uniform Commercial Code, which gives courts the power to refuse to enforce all or part of a contract or to modify a contract if it is found to be unconscionable.

**Meaning of Unconscionability.** The UCC does not define unconscionability, leaving it instead for the courts to define. Though the concept is impossible to define with precision, unconscionability is generally taken to mean the *absence of meaningful choice* together with *terms unreasonably advantageous* to one of the parties.

Some indicators of unconscionability are found in the process by which the agreement is reached. This is sometimes referred to by courts and writers as *procedural unconscionability.* Lack of knowledge and understanding on the part of a party that is caused by the presence of fine print or inconspicuously placed terms, the use of complex, legalistic

[1] Courts of equity are discussed in Chapter 1.

language, and the use of high-pressure sales tactics are among the factors that are considered in determining whether a contract is unconscionable. A major indicator that is considered is the lack of voluntariness as shown by a marked imbalance in the parties' bargaining positions, particularly where the weaker party is unable to negotiate more favorable terms because of economic need, lack of time, or market factors. In fact, in most contracts that have been found to be unconscionable, there has been a serious inequality of bargaining power between the parties. Unequal bargaining power does not, in and of itself, make a contract unconscionable. If it did, every consumer's contract with the telephone company or the electric company would be unenforceable.

Rather, in an unconscionable contract, the party with the stronger bargaining power *exploits* that power by driving a bargain containing a term or terms that are so unfair that they "shock the conscience of the court." Thus, another major indicator of unconscionability is the presence of contract terms that are oppressive or unreasonably one-sided. This aspect of unconscionability is often referred to as *substantive unconscionability.* Examples include situations in which a party to the contract bears a disproportionate amount of the risk or negative aspects of the transaction and situations in which a party is deprived of a remedy for the other party's breach. In a few cases, unconscionability has been found in situations in which one party is able to extract a price far in excess of the usual market price.

There is no mechanical test for determining whether a clause is unconscionable. Generally, in cases in which courts have found a contract term to be unconscionable, there are elements of *both* procedural and substantive unconscionability. The *Holyfield* case, which follows, presents an example of a court's analysis of whether a contract term was unconscionable. Though courts have broad discretion to determine what contracts will be deemed to be unconscionable, it must be remembered that the doctrine of unconscionability is designed to prevent oppression and unfair surprise—not to relieve people of the effects of bad bargains.

The cases concerning unconscionability are quite diverse. Some courts, such as the court in *Murphy v. McNamara,* have found unconscionability in contracts involving grossly unfair sales prices. Although the doctrine of unconscionability has been raised primarily by victimized consumers, there have been cases in which businesspeople in an inherently weak bargaining position have been successful in asserting unconscionability.

**Procedure for Determining Unconscionability.** Section 2–302 states that when a claim of unconscionability is asserted or when it appears to the court that a term may be unconscionable, the court must afford the parties the opportunity to present evidence about the setting, purpose, and effect of the contract. This apparently means that the court must hold a hearing on the issue of unconscionability. The purpose of such a hearing is to enable the court to make a determination of whether the term is unconscionable. Section 2–302 specifically states that unconscionability is a *matter of law.* That is, only the judge can decide whether a clause is unconscionable; it is not a matter for consideration by the jury.

**Applicability of the Concept of Unconscionability.** By virtue of its inclusion in Article 2 of the Uniform Commercial Code, the prohibition against unconscionable terms applies to every contract for the sale of goods. The concept of unconscionability is not confined to contracts for the sale of goods, however. Section 208 of the *Restatement (Second) of Contracts,* which closely resembles the unconscionability section of the UCC, provides that courts may decline to enforce unconscionable terms or contracts. The prohibition of unconscionability has been adopted as part of the public policy of many states by courts in cases that did not involve the sale of goods, such as contracts for the sale or rental of real estate. It is therefore fair to state that the concept of unconscionability has become part of the general body of contract law.

**Consequences of Unconscionability.** The UCC and the *Restatement* sections on unconscionability give courts the power to manipulate a contract containing an unconscionable provision so as to reach a just result. If a court finds that a contract or a term in a contract is unconscionable, it can do one of three things: it can refuse to enforce the entire agreement; it can refuse to enforce the unconscionable provision but enforce the rest of the contract; or it can "limit the application of the unconscionable clause so as to avoid any unconscionable result." This last alternative has been taken by courts to mean that they can make adjustments in the terms of the contract as a means of avoiding the unconscionability.

## Murphy v. McNamara

**416 A.2d 170 (Conn. Super. Ct. 1979)**

Carolyn Murphy, a welfare recipient with four minor children, saw an advertisement in the local newspaper that had been placed by Brian McNamara, a television and stereo dealer. It stated the following:

> Why buy when you can rent? Color TV and stereos. *Rent to own!* Use our Rent-to-own plan and let TV Rentals deliver either of these models to your home. *We feature*—Never a repair bill—No deposit—No credit needed—No long term obligation—Weekly or monthly rates available—Order by phone—Call today—Watch color TV tonight.

As a result of this advertisement, Murphy leased a 25-inch Philco color console television set from McNamara under the "Rent to Own" plan. The lease agreement provided that Murphy would pay a $20 delivery charge and 78 weekly payments of $16. At the end of this period, Murphy would own the set. The agreement also provided that the customer could return the set at any time and terminate the lease as long as all rental payments had been made up to the return date. Murphy entered the lease because she believed that she could acquire ownership of a television set without first establishing credit, as was stressed in McNamara's ads. At no time did McNamara inform Murphy that the terms of the lease required her to pay a total of $1,268 for the set. The retail sales price for the same set was $499.

After making $436 in payments over a period of about six months, Murphy read a newspaper article criticizing the lease plan and realized the amount that the agreement required her to pay. She stopped making payments, and McNamara sought to repossess the set, threatening to file a criminal complaint against her if she failed to return it. Murphy, claiming that the agreement was unconscionable, filed suit for an injunction barring McNamara from repossessing the TV set or filing charges against her.

**Berdon, Judge.** An excessive price charged a consumer with unequal bargaining power can constitute a violation of 2–302 of the Uniform Commercial Code. In the case of *Jones v. Star Credit Corp.,* the plaintiffs, welfare recipients, purchased a home freezer unit for $900.00. The freezer had a retail value of approximately $300.00. The court held the contract was unconscionable under 2–302 of the Uniform Commercial Code and reformed the contract by excusing further payments over the $600.00 already paid by the plaintiffs. There have been similar holdings by other courts. The failure on the part of McNamara to advise Murphy of the total price she would be required to pay under the terms of the contract further compounded the unfairness of his trade practices.

In sum, an agreement for the sale of consumer goods entered into with a consumer having unequal bargaining power and which calls for an unconscionable purchase price, constitutes an unfair trade practice. By unequal bargaining power, the court means that at the time the contract was made there was such an inequality of bargaining power (for example, because of the consumer's need for credit) that the merchant could insist on the inclusion of unconscionable terms in the contract which were not justifiable on the grounds of commercial necessity. The intent of this rule is not to erase the doctrine of freedom of contract, but to make realistic the assumption of the law that the agreement has resulted from real bargaining between parties who had freedom of choice and understanding and ability to negotiate in a meaningful fashion. Viewed in that sense, freedom to contract survives but the marketers of consumer goods are brought to an awareness that the restraint of unconscionability is always hovering over their operations and that courts will employ it to balance the interests of the consumer public and those of the seller.

Injunction granted, prohibiting McNamara from repossessing the TV set, using harassing collection techniques, or filing criminal charges against Murphy, but permitting McNamara to file suit for the difference between the amount Murphy paid and the value of the set.

---

## Bank of Indiana, National Association v. Holyfield

**476 F. Supp. 104 (D. Miss. 1979)**

Mr. and Mrs. Holyfield owned a 700-acre dairy farm and had been in the dairy business in Simpson County, Mississippi, for many years. The Holyfields were in a relatively poor financial condition and, desiring to increase their milk production, they began to make inquiries about leasing additional cows. After a lengthy process in which the Holyfields were required to establish their credit rating, Goodwin Brothers Leasing agreed to lease the Holyfields 115 cows at a total cost of $127,692.60, paid in monthly installments of $1,978.21, plus a security deposit.

The Holyfields were presented with a lengthy and complicated lease agreement. Mr. Holyfield signed this document, without reading it, while standing in his front yard. The lease provided that the Holyfields would be required to continue making their lease payments even if the cows were destroyed without any fault on their part. The Holyfields were told that Goodwin Brothers would carry insurance on the cows, but in fact, the amount of insurance purchased by Goodwin Brothers was inadequate to cover even the cost of the cows. After the Holyfields had made lease payments for over 1½ years, a tornado struck their farm, killing at least 30 of the leased cows and totally destroying their barn, fences, and milking equipment. This made it impossible for them to milk the surviving cows, which stopped producing milk as a result. With Goodwin Brothers's consent, the surviving cows were sold as beef cattle at auction. The total payments made by the Holyfields plus the insurance and auction proceeds amounted to more than $82,000 on Goodwin Brothers's original investment of $70,000. The Bank of Indiana, which had merged with Goodwin Brothers, brought suit against the Holyfields for the remaining debt. The Holyfields asserted the doctrine of unconscionability.

**Nixon, District Judge.** Unconscionability has generally been recognized to include an absence of meaningful choice on the part of one of the parties together with contract terms which are unreasonably favorable to the other party. Whether a meaningful choice is present in a particular case can only be determined by consideration of all the circumstances surrounding the transaction. In many cases, the meaningfulness of the choice is negated by a gross inequality of bargaining power. The manner in which the contract was entered is also relevant to this consideration. Did the party to the contract, considering his obvious education or lack of it, have a reasonable opportunity to understand the terms of the contract, or were the important terms hidden in a maze of fine print and minimized by deceptive sales practices? Ordinarily, one who signs an agreement without full knowledge of its terms might be held to assume the risk that he has entered a one-sided bargain. But when a party of little bargaining power, and hence little real choice, signs a commercially unreasonable contract with little or no knowledge of the terms, it is hardly likely that his consent was ever given to all the terms. In such a case, the usual rule that the terms of the agreement are not to be questioned should be abandoned and the court should consider whether the terms of the contract are so unfair that enforcement should be withheld.

This is exactly the situation in the case at bar. It is hard to conceive of a "tougher" agreement than the Holyfields signed. If all of the cows were killed the day after the Holyfields got them, through no fault of theirs, they would have been liable for the entire lease amount. The tremendous return the Bank received on its investment, the lengthy and complex form of the lease, the disproportionate risk borne by the Holyfields—all combine to make this lease too hard a bargain for a court of conscience to assist.

Mr. and Mrs. Holyfield have limited business education, especially when compared with that of the Bank. Mr. Holyfield did not read the lease before he signed it, and in fact there was no opportunity to do so at the time it was presented. The clauses in the lease were never explained to him prior to the time that he signed it. Unquestionably, the Bank is in a superior bargaining position than the Holyfields, especially in light of the unstable financial position the Holyfields were in when they executed this lease, and the lease was not presented to them as being negotiable in any of its terms, but rather on a "take-it-or-leave-it" basis. Finally, the court is influenced by the Bank's failure to obtain adequate insurance for the cows. This court refuses to enforce the remainder of this contract, and the Bank will recover nothing from the Holyfields.

Judgment for the Holyfields.

## EFFECT OF ILLEGALITY

**General Rule.** As a general rule, courts will refuse to give any remedy for the breach of an illegal agreement. A court will refuse to enforce an illegal agreement and will also refuse to permit a party who has fully or partially performed her part of the agreement to recover what she has parted with. This "hands off illegal agreements" approach is reflected in *State v. Strickland,* which follows. The reason for this rule is to serve the public interest, not to punish the parties.

In some cases, the public interest is best served by allowing some recovery to one or both of the parties. Such cases constitute exceptions to the "hands off" rule. The following discussion concerns the most common situations in which courts will grant some remedy even though they find the agreement to be illegal.

**Excusable Ignorance of Facts or Legislation.** Though it is often said that ignorance of the law is no excuse, courts will, under certain circumstances, permit a party to an illegal agreement who was excusably ignorant of facts or legislation that rendered the agreement illegal to recover damages for breach of the agreement. This exception is used where only *one* of the parties acted in ignorance of the illegality of the agreement and the other party was aware that the agreement was illegal. For this exception to apply, the facts or legislation of which the person claiming damages was ignorant must be of a relatively minor character—that is, it must not involve an immoral act or a serious threat to the public welfare. Finally, the person who is claiming damages cannot recover damages for anything that he does after learning of the illegality. For example, Jones enters a contract to perform in a play at Smith's theater. Jones does not know that Smith does not have the license to operate a theater as required by statute. Jones can recover the wages agreed upon in the parties' contract for work that he performed before learning of the illegality.

When *both* of the parties are ignorant of facts or legislation of a relatively minor character, courts will not permit them to enforce the agreement and receive what they had bargained for, but they will permit the parties to recover what they have parted with.

**Rights of Parties Not Equally in the Wrong.** The courts will often permit a party who is not equally in the wrong (in technical legal terms, not *in pari delicto*) to recover what she has parted with under an illegal agreement. One of the most common situations in which this exception is used involves the rights of "protected parties"—people who were intended to be protected by a regulatory statute—who contract with parties who are not properly licensed under that statute. Most regulatory statutes are intended to protect the public. As a general rule, if a person guilty of violating a regulatory statute enters into an agreement with another person for whose protection the statute was adopted, the agreement will be enforceable by the party whom the legislature intended to protect. For example, most states require foreign corporations—that is, those incorporated outside the state—to get a license before doing business in the state. These statutes often specifically provide that an unlicensed corporation cannot enforce contracts that it enters into with citizens of the state. Citizens of the licensing state, however, are generally allowed to enforce their contracts with the foreign corporation.

Another common situation in which courts will grant a remedy to a party who is not equally in the wrong is one in which the less guilty party has been induced to enter the agreement by misrepresentation, fraud, duress, or undue influence.

**Rescission before Performance of Illegal Act.** Obviously, public policy is best served by any rule that encourages people not to commit illegal acts. People who have fully or partially performed their part of an illegal contract have little incentive to raise the question of illegality if they know that they will be unable to recover what they have given because of the courts' hands off approach to illegal agreements. To encourage people to cancel illegal contracts, courts will allow a person who rescinds such a contract before any illegal act has been performed to recover any consideration that he has given. For example, Jones, the owner of a restaurant, offers Smith, an employee of a competitor's restaurant, $1,000 for some of the competitor's recipes. If Jones has second thoughts and tells Smith the deal is off before receiving any recipes, he can recover the $1,000.

**Divisible Contracts.** If part of an agreement is legal and part is illegal, the courts will enforce the legal part so long as it is possible to separate the two parts. A contract is said to be *divisible*—that is, the legal part can be separated from the illegal part—if the contract consists of several promises or acts by one party, each of which corresponds with an act or a promise by the other party. In other words, there must be a separate consideration for each promise or act for a contract to be considered divisible.

Where no separate consideration is exchanged for the legal and illegal parts of an agreement, the agreement is said to be *indivisible*. As a general rule, an indivisible contract that contains an illegal part will be entirely unenforceable unless it comes within one of the exceptions discussed above. However, if the major portion of a contract is legal, but the contract contains an illegal provision that does not affect the primary, legal portion, courts will often enforce the legal part of the agreement and simply decline to enforce the illegal part. For example, suppose Alberts sells his barbershop to Bates. The contract of sale provides that Alberts will not engage in barbering anywhere in the world for the rest of his life. The major portion of the contract—the sale of the business—is perfectly legal. A provision of the contract—the ancillary covenant not to compete—is overly restrictive, and thus illegal. A court would enforce the sale of the business but modify or refuse to enforce the restraint provision.

## State v. Strickland

### 400 A.2d 451 (Md. Ct. Spec. App. 1979)

James Strickland attempted to bribe Judge Sylvania Woods to show leniency toward one of Strickland's friends who had a case pending before the judge. Judge Woods immediately reported this to the state's attorney, and was asked to play along with Strickland until the actual payment of money occurred. Strickland gave $2,500 to the judge, who promptly turned it over to the state's attorney's office. Strickland was indicted for bribery, pled guilty, and was sentenced to a four-year prison term. Three months after the criminal trial, Strickland filed a motion for the return of his $2,500. The trial judge ordered that the money be returned to Strickland. The state appealed.

**GILBERT, CHIEF JUDGE.** Strickland, for whatever else he may lack, suffers not for want of *chutzpah.* A basic principle of contract law is that agreements to commit a crime are illegal, void. Without question, courts will not order damages for breach of such a contract. Parties of that ilk are left where they are found, to stew in their own juice. So that, even if it be postulated that Judge Woods breached a contract with Strickland, or that there was a complete failure of consideration between the parties, Strickland would be devoid of legal means of recovering whatever money he paid for the sought performance of an illegal act.

The public expects that the courts will administer justice both fairly and impartially. Any attempt to bribe a member of the judiciary is a reprehensible, odious act striking at the heart of the judicial system. For the bribe then to be repaid to the briber, on order of a court, erodes the public's confidence in the court's common sense and judgment. We hold that public policy forbids the return of the money to the briber, whether his efforts be a success or a failure.

Judgment reversed in favor of the State.

## SUMMARY

An illegal agreement is one that involves a violation of some *public policy* (public interest recognized by a court, legislature, or other lawmaker) and threatens the public welfare to the extent that the normal interests favoring enforcement of contracts are outweighed by the need to avoid the danger to the public. Deciding whether to hold an agreement illegal requires courts to balance a number of factors. They must consider how important the public policy is and how much the agreement in question would interfere with that policy. They must also consider whether any serious wrongdoing was involved in the agreement and how directly the agreement was connected with any wrongdoing.

If the formation or performance of an agreement requires the commission of a serious crime or a tort, the agreement will be considered illegal. Similarly, an agreement that promotes the commission of a crime or a tort can be illegal. Sometimes, a legislature, in a statute prohibiting a certain act, will expressly provide that a contract that involves the performance of that act is void. Examples of such statutes include statutes prohibiting usury, wagering, and certain transactions on Sunday. An agreement in violation of such a statute is illegal.

State and local legislation also require persons who practice a variety of trades, businesses, and professions to be licensed as a condition of doing business. When a person enters into an agreement to perform a regulated act for which she is not properly licensed, the agreement would be considered illegal if the violated licensing statute was *regulatory,* that is, designed for the protection of the public. If the purpose of the licensing statute was *revenue raising,* or if the purpose of the statute is relatively unimportant compared to the forfeiture that would result from a denial of enforcement, the agreement is not illegal.

Courts have broad discretion to articulate public policies and to refuse to enforce agreements that present a serious threat to those policies. One such policy is the public policy against restrictions on competition. If the sole purpose of an agreement is to restrain competition, it is illegal. If an agreement that restrains competition is part of an otherwise legal contract, the agreement is called an *an-*

*cillary covenant not to compete.* Such covenants are legal so long as the restriction is no greater than is needed to protect a valid business interest. The ancillary covenant not to compete will be scrutinized to determine whether the nature of the restriction and the time and geographic area of the restriction are reasonable. If a court finds that the restriction is too broad, it may refuse to enforce it completely or it may enforce the restriction to the extent that is reasonable under the circumstances.

Exculpatory agreements (agreements to relieve a party of tort liability) are held to be illegal if the exculpated party owes a duty to the public or if such an agreement purports to excuse a person from liability for fraud or other willful torts. Such agreements are often held to be ineffective in relieving a party to a contract from a statutory or common law duty to act for the benefit of the other party to the contract. An exculpatory clause relieving a person who owes no duty to the public from negligence liability might still be found to be against public policy if the parties to the agreement were not dealing on a fair and equal bargaining basis. In such a situation, the exculpatory agreement might be found to be a *contract of adhesion* (a contract in which one of the parties has no choice but to agree to the terms dictated by the other party) or an *unconscionable contract.* Under other public policies created by courts, agreements that impair family relationships, agreements to influence fiduciaries, and agreements injurious to public service are made illegal.

A very important development in contract law regarding the protection of public policy is the enactment of section 2–302 of the Uniform Commercial Code, which gives courts the power to refuse to enforce *unconscionable* provisions in contracts. An unconscionable provision is a term which is unreasonably favorable to one of the parties and about which the other party had no meaningful choice. If a court finds, after holding a hearing at which evidence about unconscionability is presented, that a provision in a contract is unconscionable, the court can refuse to enforce the entire contract, refuse to enforce the unconscionable provision, or make adjustments in the contract so as to avoid the unconscionable result. The doctrine of unconscionability has been adopted widely as part of the common law of many states, so that it is frequently applied even in cases that do not involve the sale of goods.

When an agreement is held to be illegal, it is generally unenforceable. Furthermore, a party who has partially or fully performed his part of an illegal agreement generally will not be able to recover what he has parted with. Courts make exceptions to this rule when it is in the public interest to do so. When one of the parties to an illegal agreement was excusably ignorant of the facts or laws that made the agreement illegal, courts will permit him to enforce the agreement as to any performance rendered before he learned of the illegality, provided that the law involved is of a relatively minor character. If both parties are ignorant of a fact or law under conditions similar to those stated above, either will be able to recover for consideration given.

Another exception is that a party who is not equally in the wrong with the other party to an illegal agreement may have a remedy. A party protected by a regulatory statute may recover for breach of an agreement entered into with a person who has not complied with the provisions of the statute. A person who has been induced to enter an illegal agreement by fraud, misrepresentation, duress, or undue influence may recover any consideration he has parted with.

Another exception to the rule that courts will give no remedy to parties to an illegal agreement is that a person who withdraws from an illegal agreement by rescinding it before the illegal act has been committed will be permitted to recover any consideration given. An additional exception is that if an agreement is *divisible,* courts will enforce the legal portion and refuse enforcement to the illegal portion. If an agreement that contains an illegal portion is indivisible, courts will normally refuse enforcement to the entire agreement unless the illegal part is a relatively minor provision of the agreement that does not affect the major, legal portion.

## PROBLEM CASES

**1.** Wassermann was a stockholder in the Alaska Commercial Company, and Sloss was the president of the company. Certain leases that the company held from the government of the United States and the government of the USSR were about to expire. Sloss told Wassermann that it would be necessary to give stock in the Alaska Commercial Company to high officials of both governments in order to obtain renewal of the leases. Wassermann transferred 400 shares of the stock to Sloss for this purpose. However, Sloss did not use the stock for this purpose and refused to return it to Wassermann. Wassermann brought suit to recover the stock, and Sloss asserted illegality as a defense. Is this a good defense?

**2.** Discount Fabric House, Inc. had placed an ad in the Yellow Pages every year since 1975. Each year, it signed an advertising contract with Wisconsin Telephone Company for the Yellow Pages ad. The contract was a printed form used by all subscribers who desired to place such an ad. No subscriber could bargain for or change any terms. One of the terms of the contract was that the subscriber agreed to relieve the telephone company of liability for any negligent act. In 1978, the telephone company omitted important trade identification from Discount Fabric House's ad. Discount Fabric House sued the telephone company for business losses resulting from this omission. As a defense, the telephone company set up the exculpatory clause contained in the advertising contract. Will the exculpatory clause be enforced?

**3.** Carroll owned real estate known as the Hillside Ranch, on which she operated a house of prostitution in violation of Montana law. Carroll conveyed the property to Beardon, knowing that Beardon also planned to operate a house of prostitution on the property. Beardon made a down payment and signed a mortgage and note in which she agreed to pay Carroll the balance of the sales price at monthly intervals. After occupying the property for some time (and using it for the intended purpose), Beardon failed to make several payments, and Carroll brought suit to foreclose the mortgage. Beardon asserted illegality as a defense. What result?

**4.** Lachman had an oil and gas lease on a tract of land in Oklahoma, on which an oil and gas well had been drilled. He contracted with Sperry to perform a directional survey of the well. The contract between Lachman and Sperry provided that Sperry could not communicate information about the survey or the well to any third person. In the survey, Sperry found that the well deviated from the vertical so that it bottomed on an adjoining tract of land, whose oil and gas rights belonged to someone else. Lachman's well was producing oil and gas from the adjoining tract. Sperry communicated this fact to Lachman, and some time later employees of Sperry told the owners of the oil and gas rights of the adjoining tract about the deviation. The owners of the adjoining tract brought suit against Lachman and won a judgment that established their right to the proceeds of all oil and gas produced by the well. Lachman then sued Sperry, arguing that its disclosure of the survey results was a breach of contract. Is the contract legal?

**5.** In 1976, Porubiansky became a patient at the Emory University School of Dentistry Clinic, a training facility for dental students that offered dental services to the public at a reduced price. At that time, she was required to sign an "Information-Consent" form. A provision of this form stated that she would agree to waive and relinquish any claim that might arise from any dental treatment performed at the Clinic. In 1977, Porubiansky had an impacted tooth removed by a dentist employed by the Clinic. Her jaw was broken during this procedure. Alleging negligence, she sued Emory University. The university asserts that the Information-Consent form is a complete bar to the suit. Will the Information-Consent form be enforced?

**6.** In 1963, the Interstate Commerce Commission issued an order that, if allowed to stand, would have resulted in a loss of $13 million to Southern Railway Company. An officer of Southern turned to an attorney named Troutman, who was inexperienced in ICC work but was a very close friend of the president of the United States. Southern asked Troutman to try to persuade the president to "ditch" the ICC and to lend his support to a case that Southern had in court against the ICC. The government backed Southern in the ICC case, and Southern won. Troutman later sued Southern to recover $200,000 as the reasonable value of legal services rendered. Southern argued that Troutman had been hired to use his personal influence with a public official and that such contracts were against public policy and thus unenforceable. May Troutman recover his fee?

**7.** Mrs. Wynn, a compulsive gambler, was $1,750 in debt to the owners of the Rainbow Club and the Monterey Club, card clubs licensed by the city in which they were located. These clubs offered check-cashing services and charged members rental fees based on the amount of money being wagered in a particular card game held on their premises. The owners were familiar with Mrs. Wynn and knew of her compulsive gambling. Mr. Wynn telephoned the owners of the clubs and offered to repay his wife's debts (for which he would otherwise not have been liable under state law) if the owners agreed to bar her from their clubs in the future. The owners agreed, and they sent a letter to Mr. Wynn confirming this agreement. Mr. Wynn repaid the debt. Several years later, Mrs. Wynn returned to the clubs and began gambling again, running up debts of more than $30,000. Mr. Wynn sued the clubs' owners. They asserted that their agreement with Mr. Wynn was illegal, because it would have required them to violate the California Civil Rights Law, which provides that all persons are entitled to the full and equal accommodations or services of all business establishments, regardless of sex, race, color, religion, ancestry, or national origin. What should the result be?

**8.** For 10 years, Plunkett had owned a drugstore in Arcadia, Louisiana, a small town in which only three physicians practiced. He sold the drugstore to Reeves for $60,000. The inventory of the store amounted to $20,000 of the sales price, and the only other property included in the sale was the fixtures in the store, which were worth a minimal amount of money. Most of the sales price, then, was for goodwill. The contract of sale provided that Plunkett would neither operate a drugstore nor be employed as a pharmacist in Arcadia after the sale of the business. Plunkett repeatedly assured Reeves during the negotiations that he would not be returning to the drug business in Arcadia. Four years later, Plunkett returned and attempted to repurchase the drugstore. When Reeves refused to sell it, Plunkett brought suit to have the restriction on competition declared illegal. Plunkett argues that the restriction is illegal because there is no time limit on it. What result?

**9.** Hiram Ricker & Sons contracted with

the Students International Meditation Society (SIDS) to furnish lodging and food to approximately 1,000 SIDS students at a one-month teacher training course to be held on Ricker's property in Poland Springs, Maine. At the end of the month, SIDS paid $185,000 to Ricker. Alleging that SIDS owed an additional $65,780, Ricker filed suit against SIDS for breach of contract. SIDS defended on the ground that the contract was illegal because Ricker's victualer's license, which was required by state law, had expired and because Ricker did not have sanitation permits for all of its premises during the entire period of the contract. SIDS demands the return of the $185,000 it paid. What should the result be?

**10.** Frostifresh Corporation sold a refrigerator-freezer to Reynoso. The contract was negotiated entirely in Spanish by Reynoso and a Spanish-speaking salesman employed by Frostifresh. During the conversation between the two, Reynoso told the salesman that he had but one week left on his job and could not afford to buy the appliance. The salesman told Reynoso that the appliance would cost him nothing because he would be paid bonuses or commissions of $25 each on the numerous sales that would be made to his neighbors and friends. The installment contract that was presented to Reynoso was written entirely in English and was not explained or translated to him. In the contract, there was a cash sales price of $900, to which was added a credit charge of $245.88, making a total of $1,145.88 to be paid for the appliance. The cost of the appliance to Frostifresh was $348. Reynoso paid $32 and failed to make further payments. Frostifresh sued him for the remaining debt plus late charges and attorney's fees. Reynoso defends on grounds of unconscionability. Will the contract be enforced?

**11.** Flynn entered an employment agreement to work for Eastern Distributing Company. The contract contained a covenant whereby Flynn agreed not to disclose the list of Eastern's customers and further agreed not to go to work for any competitor of Eastern within a 50-mile radius for one year after leaving Eastern's employment. Flynn left his job with Eastern and immediately went to work for a competitor, servicing the same customers that he had handled for Eastern. Eastern sues to enforce the covenant. What result?

**12.** Victoria lived with Robert for 15 years in a family-like setting, during which time she bore him three children. Though Victoria and Robert were never legally married, he promised her that he would "share his life, his future, his earnings, and his property" with her. Victoria participated in earning money for the family and in helping Robert to attain his education and progress in his career. When the two separated, Victoria sued Robert for an equal share of the profits and properties accumulated by the parties during the time they lived together. Assuming that such a contract was made, is it legal?

## INTRODUCTION

Your study of contract law so far has focused on the requirements for the formation of a valid contract. You should be aware, however, that even when all the elements of a valid contract exist, the enforceability of the contract and the nature of the parties' obligations can be greatly affected by the *form* in which the contract is set out and by the *language* that is used to express the agreement. An otherwise valid contract can become unenforceable if it does not comply with the formalities required by state law. A person may be unable to offer evidence about promises and agreements made in preliminary negotiations, because the parties later adopted a written contract that did not contain those terms. And, of course, the legal effect of any contract is determined in large part by the way in which a court interprets the language it contains. This chapter discusses the ways in which the enforceability of a contract and the scope of contractual obligations can be affected by the manner in which people express their agreements.

## THE STATUTE OF FRAUDS

Many people mistakenly believe that oral contracts are never enforceable. Generally speaking, an oral contract that can be proven is binding and enforceable. A policy requiring all contracts to be in writing would probably not be workable because the cost of such a policy in terms of time, expense, and the frustration of people's bargained-for expectations would be too great. Nevertheless, oral contracts are less desirable in many ways than written contracts. They are more easily misunderstood or forgotten than written contracts. They are also more subject to the danger that a person might fabricate terms or fraudulently claim to have made an oral contract where none exists.

In 17th-century England, the dangers inherent in oral contracts were exacerbated by a legal rule that prohibited parties to a lawsuit from testifying in their own cases. Since the parties to an oral contract could not give testimony, the only way they could prove the existence of the contract was through the testimony of third parties. As you might expect, third parties were sometimes persuaded to offer false testimony about the existence of contracts. In an attempt to stop the widespread fraud and perjury that resulted, Parliament enacted the Statute of Frauds in 1677. It required written evidence before certain classes of contracts would be enforced. Although the possibility of fraud exists in every contract, the statute focused on contracts in which the potential for fraud was great or the consequences of fraud were especially serious.

The legislatures of American states adopted very similar statutes, also known as statutes of frauds. These statutes have produced a great deal of litigation, due in part to the public's ignorance of their provisions. It is difficult to imagine an aspect of contract law that is more practical for businesspeople to know about than the circumstances under which an oral contract will not suffice. Almost all states require written evidence of the following types of contracts: (1) collateral contracts in which a person promises to perform the obligation of another person, (2) contracts for the sale of an interest in real estate, (3) bilateral contracts that cannot be performed within a year from the date of their formation, (4) contracts for the sale of goods for $500 or more, (5) contracts in which an executor or administrator promises to be personally liable for the debt of the estate he is handling, and (6) contracts in which marriage is the consideration. Of this list, the first four have the greatest significance in modern commercial transactions. The statutes of frauds of the various states are not uniform, however. Some states require written evidence of types of contracts in addition to those listed above. For example, a number of states require written evidence of contracts to pay a commission for the sale of real estate. Others require written evidence of contracts to pay debts that have been barred by the statute of limitations or discharged in bankruptcy.

The following discussion examines in greater detail the most significant types of contracts that are "within" (that is, covered by the requirements of) most statutes of frauds.

## CONTRACTS WITHIN THE STATUTE OF FRAUDS

**Collateral Contracts.** A collateral contract is one in which one person (the *guarantor*) agrees to pay the debt or obligation that a second person (the *principal debtor*) owes to a third person (the *obligee*) if the principal debtor fails to perform. For example, Jones, who wants to help Smith establish a business, promises First Bank that he will repay the loan that First Bank makes to Smith if Smith fails to pay it. Here, Jones is the guarantor,

Smith is the principal debtor, and First Bank is the obligee. Jones's promise to First Bank must be in writing to be enforceable.

A collateral contract involves at least three parties and at least *two* promises to perform (a promise by the principal debtor to pay the obligee and a promise by the guarantor to pay the obligee). In a collateral contract, the guarantor promises to pay *only if the principal debtor fails to do so.* The essence of the collateral contract is that the debt or obligation is owed primarily by the principal debtor and the guarantor's debt is *secondary.* Thus, not all three party transactions are collateral contracts. The contracts described below are common three-party situations that are *not* within the statute of frauds.

**Original Contracts.** When a person undertakes an obligation that is not conditioned on the default of another person, and the debt is his own rather than that of another person, his obligation is said to be *original,* not collateral. For example, when Jones calls Johnson Florist Company and says, "Send flowers to Smith," Jones is undertaking an obligation to pay his *own*—not someone else's—debt. This is not changed by the fact that Smith is benefited by the contract between Jones and Johnson Florist. The contract between Jones and Johnson Florist is an original contract and would not have to be in writing.

The same result is reached when a creditor agrees to accept a contract with a new debtor in satisfaction of a debt previously owed by another debtor. Such transactions are called **novations.** In a novation, a creditor releases the original debtor and permits a new debtor to take his place. For example, Smith owes $300 to First Bank. First Bank accepts Jones's promise to pay Smith's debt as satisfaction of that debt. This is a type of original contract, because Smith has been released from liability for the debt and Jones is now the only debtor.

Another common three-party transaction that is outside the statute of frauds occurs when two people are *jointly liable* on a debt to a third person. For example, if Smith and Jones together borrow money from First Bank to buy inventory for their joint business, they are *both* personally liable for the loan. Both of their promises are original, and no writing is required.

**Main Purpose Exception.** There are some situations in which a contract that is technically collateral is treated like an original contract because the person promising to pay the debt of another does so for the primary purpose of securing some personal benefit. Under the **main purpose** or **leading object** exception, no writing is required where the guarantor makes a collateral promise for the main purpose of obtaining some personal economic advantage. In such cases, the contract is outside the statute of frauds and does not have to be in writing. The *White Stag* case, which follows, is a good example of the operation of this exception.

## White Stag Mfg. Co. v. Wind Surfing, Inc.

### 679 P.2d 312 (Or. Ct. App. 1984)

Kenneth Gross was the primary creditor of Wind Surfing, a manufacturer of ski apparel. Wind Surfing also owed money to White Stag. In June 1979, Gross telephoned White Stag to inquire whether it would extend credit to Wind Surfing for the upcoming ski season. White Stag was not willing to talk about new orders until Wind Surfing's past-due balance was paid. Gross told a White Stag employee that he would be willing to give White Stag a letter of credit or his personal guaranty to secure payment. At White Stag's request, Gross sent his personal financial statement. After several telephone conversations, White Stag agreed to allow Wind Surfing an open line of credit for $25,000 if Gross would extend his guaranty or provide a bank letter of credit. This was confirmed by a letter, in which White Stag enclosed a personal guaranty form for Gross to sign. The personal guaranty form was never signed and returned, although Gross told a White Stag employee that he had signed the form and that it was in the mail. During this general time period, Gross personally wired money to cover part of the past-due account. White Stag released Wind Surfing's order and made shipments of goods over the next months until Wind Surfing's outstanding balance was $49,637.87. Gross's guaranty never arrived, and Wind Surfing never paid its accounts. White Stag sued Wind Surfing as principal debtor and Gross as guarantor. The trial court entered judgment for White Stag against Gross, and Gross appealed.

**Warren, Judge.** Gross claims that the trial court erred in holding that the Statute of Frauds did not bar White Stag's recovery. The "main purpose" doctrine excuses the requirement that a promise to answer for the debt of another be in writing when the consideration for the promise is in fact or apparently desired by the promisor mainly for his or her own advantage, rather than to benefit the third person. The doctrine is applied when the pecuniary interests of a promisor in a commercial context replace the gratuitous elements often present in collateral contracts. It eliminates the need for the evidentiary safeguards provided by the writing requirement of the Statute of Frauds. The decisive factor is whether the promise is such that the promisor became, within the intention of the parties, a primarily liable debtor. The trial court found that Gross's main purpose, as a substantial general creditor, in guaranteeing the account of Wind Surfing, was to see the business of his debtor continue and prosper so that he could be repaid the substantial funds he had advanced to Wind Surfing.

There is evidence in this case that Gross had a substantial, personal, immediate and pecuniary interest in Wind Surfing's continued existence. He had lent it $47,000. As a general creditor with no secured interest, his only realistic hope of recovering that money was the continued existence of and prosperity of Wind Surfing. Gross actively pursued the White Stag credit department. He testified that his actions to further the success of Wind Surfing were in the hope of getting back all of the money he had loaned it and eventually acquiring a one-third interest in Wind Surfing. Under these circumstances, we accept the trial court's finding that Gross was motivated by personal benefit to guarantee the account. It was correct in holding that the main purpose exception to the Statute of Frauds is applicable and that White Stag is entitled to full recovery.

Judgment for White Stag affirmed.

---

**Interest in Land.** Any contract that transfers an interest in real estate is within the statute of frauds. The inclusion of real estate contracts in the statute of frauds reflects the values of an earlier, agrarian society in which land was the primary basis of wealth. Our legal system historically has treated land as being more important than other forms of property. Courts have interpreted the real estate provision of the statute of frauds to require written evidence of any transaction that will affect *ownership* rights in real estate. Thus, a contract to sell or mortgage real estate must be evidenced by a writing, as must an option to purchase real estate or a contract to grant an easement or permit the mining and removal of minerals on land. Leases are also transfers of an interest in land, but most states' statutes of frauds do not require leases to be in writing unless they are long-term leases, usually those for one year or more. On the other hand, a contract to erect a building or to insure a building would not be within the real estate provision of the statute of frauds, because such contracts do not involve the transfer of ownership rights.

**Part Performance Exception.** The purpose of the real estate provision of the statute of frauds is, of course, to provide evidence that a contract was made. The normal way of satisfying the requirements of this provision is to introduce written evidence of an agreement. Sometimes, however, the parties' conduct can "speak louder than words" and provide good evidence of the existence of a contract. For example, Smith and Jones orally enter into a contract for the sale of Jones's land. If Smith pays Jones a substantial part of the purchase price and either takes possession of the land or begins to make improvements on it, Smith's conduct tends to prove that he and Jones had a contract. Under the **part performance exception,** Smith's conduct would be sufficient to meet the requirements of the statute of frauds, and the contract would not have to be in writing. The part performance exception is based not only on the evidentiary value of performance but also on the desire to avoid injustice that would otherwise result from the performing party's reliance.

To constitute part performance, a party's conduct must clearly imply the existence of a contract and must not be consistent with any other interpretation. This requirement is demonstrated in *Martin v. Scholl,* which follows. Although a person's reliance on an oral contract could be shown in many ways, part performance ordinarily requires that the buyer pay part or all of the purchase price and either make substantial improvements on the property or take possession of it. Generally, payment of all or part of the purchase price, standing alone, has been held not to constitute part performance.

## Martin v. Scholl

**678 P.2d 274 (Utah Sup. Ct. 1983)**

Rodney Martin began working as a ranch laborer for George Chaffin in 1936. He became foreman over all of Chaffin's farm and ranch properties in 1947, and continued in that capacity until 1976. In 1947, Chaffin orally agreed to convey to Martin 120 acres of land referred to as "the home place" if Martin would continue working as his foreman. Martin remained, working 8 to 16 hours a day, seven days a week, and working around-the-clock when necessary. Martin's wife and son also performed labor and personal services on Chaffin's farms and ranches. For this work, Martin's salary ranged from $75 per month in 1947 to $375 per month in 1975. From 1960 to 1969, Martin received $369 per month without a single raise.

In 1968, Chaffin formed a limited partnership called the George C. Chaffin Investment Company, to which he conveyed certain real estate, including the home place. Martin was unaware of this conveyance. Chaffin died in 1975 without conveying the home place to Martin. Martin sued to enforce the oral contract he made with Chaffin. The trial court ordered specific performance for Martin, and the Investment Company appealed.

**Howe, Justice.** Ordinarily a verbal gift of land or an oral agreement to convey land is within the statute of frauds. However, the doctrine of part performance allows a court to enforce an oral agreement if it has been partially performed, notwithstanding the statute.

The oral contract and its terms must be clear and definite. The acts done in performance of the contract must be equally clear and definite. The acts must be in reliance on the contract. Such acts in reliance must be such that (a) they would not have been performed had the contract not existed, and (b) the failure to perform on the part of the promisor would result in fraud on the performer who relied, since damages would be inadequate. Reliance may be made in innumerable ways, all of which could refer exclusively to the contract. Professor Corbin states that the performance must be one that is in some degree evidential of the existence of a contract and not readily explainable on any other ground.

The critical observation to make in reading these delineations of what constitutes sufficient part performance is that it must be proved by strong evidence. The greatest value of exclusively referable acts of reliance is their evidentiary significance. Acts of part performance must be exclusively referable to the contract in that the possession of the party seeking specific performance and the improvements made by him must be reasonably explicable only on the postulate that a contract exists. Where the contract is admitted or strong evidence of independent acts which prove the contract exists, the requirement of exclusively referable acts has been relaxed.

We conclude that the trial court erred in holding that there was sufficient part performance. The trial court drew one conclusion from Martin's services but that is legally insufficient since they admit of another equally valid conclusion. The fact that Martin worked for Chaffin as his foreman is not an exclusively referable act of reliance on the alleged oral agreement since it was consonant with Martin's employment. Martin's long hours, not atypical of a ranch foreman's life, were remunerated by salary. Martin's wife's driving Chaffin to various locations on occasion and asking him to stay for dinner when he was at the Martin house during mealtime were not inconsistent with good relations between an employer and an employee and his family. Further, Martin's son was compensated for his labors from the time he reached the age of 14.

The fact that Martin continued to work long, hard hours for his employer might be viewed as sufficient reliance had there been an admission of an oral agreement or independent acts pointing to such an agreement. However, the evidence of the oral contract in this case required the judge to weigh the credibility of Martin's witnesses against the witnesses for the Investment Company who vigorously disputed the existence of an oral contract. Thus, the necessity of showing acts of part performance which are exclusively referable to the claimed agreement remains vital. Martin's acts of claimed part performance of a vigorously disputed contract are so equivocal that they do not meet high evidentiary standards.

As unfortunate as it would be to deprive a man who had worked his life in reliance upon the expectation of receiving property, it would be equally serious to take property from an owner after his death (when he cannot be heard) on the strength of a questionable oral agreement supposedly made many years prior. If the statute of frauds is to be given any force, we cannot affirm the trial court.

Decree reversed in favor of the Investment Company.

**Contracts That Cannot Be Performed within One Year.** A bilateral, executory contract that cannot be performed within one year from the day on which it comes into existence is within the statute of frauds and must be evidenced by a writing. This provision has been repealed in the English statute of frauds, but it has been retained in American statutes. The apparent purpose of this provision is to guard against the risk of faulty or willfully inaccurate recollection of long-term contracts. Courts have tended to construe it very narrowly.

One aspect of this narrow construction is that the provision has been held to apply only to *executory* contracts, not to contracts that have already been completely performed by one or both parties. If Smith and Jones have already performed a contract under which Smith worked for Jones for five years at a stated salary, the statute of frauds would not invalidate the contract or change the parties' rights in any way. Similarly, the one-year provision applies only to *bilateral* contracts. Thus, a contract in which Smith lends Jones $100 and Jones orally promises to repay the loan in two years would not be within the statute of frauds, because it is a unilateral contract.

In addition, this provision of the statute has been held to apply only when the *terms* of the contract make it impossible for the contract to be completed within one year. If the contract is for an indefinite period of time, it is not within the statute of frauds. Thus, Smith's agreement to work for Jones for an indefinite period of time would not have to be evidenced by a writing, even if Smith eventually works for Jones for many years. As demonstrated by *Augusta Bank & Trust v. Broomfield,* which follows, the mere fact that performance is unlikely to be completed in one year does not bring the contract within the statute of frauds. In most states, a contract "for life" is not within the statute of frauds, because it is possible—since death is an uncertain event—for the contract to be performed within a year. In a few states, such as New York, contracts for life are within the statute of frauds.

**Computing Time.** In determining whether a contract is within the one-year provision, courts begin counting time on the date on which the contract comes into existence. If, under the terms of the contract, it is possible to perform it within one year from this date, the contract does not fall within the statute of frauds, and does not have to be in writing. If, however, the terms dictate that performance *cannot* be completed until more than one year from the date on which the contract came into existence, the contract falls within the statute and must meet its requirements to be enforceable. Thus, if Smith and Jones agree on August 1, 1986, that Smith will work for Jones for one year, beginning October 1, 1986, the terms of the contract dictate that it is not possible to complete performance until October 1, 1987. Because that date is more than one year from the date on which the contract came into existence, the contract falls within the statute of frauds and must be evidenced by a writing to be enforceable.

**Contracts to Extend Time of Performance.** If Smith contracts on August 1, 1986, to work for Jones for six months, beginning August 2, 1986, the contract does not fall within the statute of frauds because it can be performed in less than one year. But suppose that the parties later agree to *extend* their contract and that on October 1, 1986, Smith and Jones agree that Smith will work for Jones for an additional 11 months after the performance of the existing contract. Would the contract to extend the time of performance fall within the statute? In making this determination, courts compute time from the day on which the contract to extend the time for performance came into existence until the day on which performance is to be completed. In the hypothetical situation posed above, the contract to extend the time for performance could not be performed within a year from the time when the agreement to extend came into existence. Thus, the contract to extend is within the statute of frauds and must be evidenced by a writing.

## Augusta Bank & Trust v. Broomfield

**643 P.2d 100 (Kan. Sup. Ct. 1982)**

Don Broomfield, a contractor, entered into an oral contract with the owners of the Robbins Trust land (Owners) to level that 4,000-acre tract of land for irrigation purposes. Broomfield leveled approximately 2,000 acres. Though the Owners initially paid on time, their payments became more erratic as the work proceeded. This caused Broomfield to fall behind in loan payments that he owed to Augusta Bank & Trust (Bank). The Bank sued Broomfield, and Broomfield, in turn, sued the Bank and the Owners on several counts, including a suit against the Owners for breach of the contract to level the 4,000 acres. Though the jury awarded Broomfield damages in this suit, the trial judge set aside this verdict because enforcement of the leveling contract was barred by the one-year provision of the statute of frauds. Broomfield appealed.

**Herd, Justice.** When a defendant asserts the statute of frauds as an affirmative defense, the burden of proof is on him. In this case, the Owners must show the contract to level the Robbins Trust land could not have been performed within one year. They offered statements by Broomfield to the effect that, with the same equipment, it would have taken him approximately one year to level the other 2,000 acres. Broomfield based this estimate on the fact it took him a year to complete the first 2,000 acres. Thus, it is argued that the oral agreement could not have been performed within one year and as such is unenforceable. We do not agree.

Under the prevailing interpretation, the enforceability of a contract under the one-year provision does not turn on the actual course of subsequent events, nor on the expectations of the parties as to the probabilities. Contracts of uncertain duration are simply excluded; the provision covers only those contracts whose performance cannot possibly be completed within a year.

Here, with more equipment and more personnel, the contract to level the Robbins Trust land could have been performed within one year. There was no evidence offered to show performance could not *possibly* have been completed within a year. Thus, the contract does not fall within the terms of the Kansas statute of frauds.

Judgment reversed and remanded in favor of Broomfield.

**Sale of Goods for $500 or More.** The original English Statute of Frauds required a writing for contracts for the sale of goods for a price of 10 pounds sterling or more. In the United States today, the writing requirement for the sale of goods is governed by section 2–201 of the Uniform Commercial Code. This section provides that contracts for the sale of goods for the price of $500 or more are not enforceable without a writing or other specified evidence that a contract was made. There are a number of alternative ways of satisfying the requirements of section 2–201. These will be explained later, in the section on meeting the requirements of the statute of frauds.

**Modifications of Existing Sales Contracts.** Just as some contracts to extend the time for performance fall within the one-year provision of the statute of frauds, contracts to modify existing sales contracts can fall within the statute of frauds if the contract as modified is for a price of $500 or more.[1] Section 2–209(3) provides that the requirements of the statute of frauds must be satisfied if the contract as modified is within its provisions. For example, if Smith and Jones enter into a contract for the sale of goods at a price of $490, the original contract does *not* fall within the statute of frauds. However, if they later modify the contract by increasing the contract price to $510, the modification falls within the statute of frauds and must meet its requirements to be enforceable.

[1] Modifications of sales contracts are discussed in greater detail in Chapter 10.

## MEETING THE REQUIREMENTS OF THE STATUTE OF FRAUDS

**Nature of the Writing Required.** The statutes of frauds of the various states are not uniform in their formal requirements. However, most states require only a *memorandum* of the parties' agreement; they do not require that the entire contract be in writing. The memorandum must provide written evidence that a contract was made, but—as you will learn in *Farrow v. Cahill*—it need not have been created with the intent that the memorandum itself would be binding. In fact, in some cases, written offers that were accepted orally have been held sufficient to satisfy the writing requirement. A memorandum may be in any form, including letters, telegrams, receipts, or any other writing indicating that the parties had a contract. It may be made at any time before suit is filed. If a memorandum of the parties' agreement is lost, its loss and its contents may be proven by oral testimony.

**Contents of the Memorandum.** Although there is a general trend away from requiring complete writings to satisfy the statute of frauds, an adequate memorandum must still contain several things. Generally, the essential terms of the contract must be indicated in the memorandum, although states differ in their requirements concerning how specifically the terms must be stated. The identity of the parties must be indicated in some way, and the subject matter of the contract must be identified with reasonable certainty. This last requirement causes particular problems in contracts for the sale of land, since many statutes require a detailed description of the property to be sold.

**Contents of Memorandum under UCC.** The standard for determining the sufficiency of the contents of a memorandum is more flexible in cases concerning contracts for the sale of goods. This looser standard is created by the language of UCC section 2–201, which states that the writing must be sufficient to indicate that a contract for sale has been made between the parties but that a writing can be sufficient even if it omits or incorrectly states a term agreed upon. However, the memorandum is not enforceable for more than the *quantity* of goods stated in the memorandum. Thus, a writing that includes no quantity term would not satisfy the Code's writing requirement.

**Signature Requirement.** The memorandum must be signed by the *party to be charged* or his authorized agent. (The party to be charged is the person using the statute of frauds as a defense—generally the *defendant* unless the statute of frauds is asserted as a defense to a counterclaim). This means that it is not necessary for purposes of meeting the statute of frauds for *both* parties' signatures to appear on the document. It is, however, in the best interests of both parties for both signatures to appear on the writing; otherwise, the contract evidenced by the writing is enforceable only against the signing party. Unless the statute expressly provides that the memorandum or contract must be signed at the end, the signature may appear anyplace on the memorandum. Any writing, mark, initials, stamp, engraving, or other symbol placed or printed on a memorandum will suffice as a signature, as long as the party to be charged intended it to authenticate (indicate the genuineness of) the writing.

**Memorandum Consisting of Several Writings.** In many situations, the elements required for a memorandum are divided among several documents. For example, suppose that Smith and Jones enter into a contract for the sale of real estate, intending to memorialize their agreement in a formal written document later. While final drafts of a written contract are being prepared, Jones repudiates the contract. Smith has a copy of an unsigned preliminary draft of the contract that identifies the parties and contains all of the material terms of the parties' agreement, an unsigned note written by Jones that contains the legal description of the property, and a letter signed by Jones that refers to the contract and to the other two documents. None of these documents, standing alone, would be sufficient to satisfy the statute of frauds. However, Jones can combine them to meet the requirements of the statute, provided that they all relate to the same agreement. This can be shown by physical attachment, as where the documents are stapled or bound together, or by references in the documents themselves that indicate that they all apply to the same transaction. In some cases, it has also been shown by the fact that the various documents were executed at the same time.

## Farrow v. Cahill

### 663 F.2d 201 (D.C. Cir. 1980)

In 1971, Harold Farrow, who owned a law firm in Oakland, California, hired Robert Cahill and Joel Kaswell to open a Washington, D.C. branch office of the firm. Cahill and Kaswell operated the Washington branch for several years, then decided to buy the branch office, break away from the Farrow firm, and form their own partnership. In 1974, they met with Farrow and another member of the firm and, after working out an agreement, drafted a handwritten "Memorandum Agreement." This memorandum specified that, among other obligations, Cahill and Kaswell would pay the Farrow firm a percentage of their gross receipts until at least December 31, 1980, and that Farrow would indemnify Cahill and Kaswell for certain debts and liabilities. The memorandum also stated that its effectiveness depended on the "consent of all present members of the firm." The memorandum was signed by Kaswell, Farrow, and another member of the Farrow firm. Although Cahill accepted the agreement by his conduct, he never signed it. Cahill and Kaswell made an initial payment to Farrow as required by the agreement, but made no further payments. Farrow brought suit to enforce the agreement. The trial court decided in Farrow's favor, and Cahill and Kaswell appealed.

**WILKEY, CIRCUIT JUDGE.** The most meritorious claim Cahill and Kaswell put before us is that enforcement of their agreement with Farrow is barred by the District of Columbia Statute of Frauds, which provides that:

> An action may not be brought . . . upon an agreement that is not to be performed within one year from the making thereof, unless the agreement upon which the action is brought, or a memorandum or note thereof, is in writing . . . and signed by the party to be charged therewith or a person authorized by him.

Cahill and Kaswell argue that the Statute bars enforcement against Cahill, who did not sign the "Memorandum Agreement," and contend that the contract could not be performed in one year.

We hold that even if the Statute does apply, the "Memorandum Agreement" satisfies it. It is undisputed that it embodies the terms of the contract and, as such, constitutes a suitable "memorandum or note thereof." Furthermore, it is also "signed by the party to be charged therewith or a person authorized by him," because Kaswell, who signed the document, was a partner in the new firm of Cahill and Kaswell and therefore an agent both of the partnership and of his partner. There is no dispute that Kaswell had authority to negotiate and to authenticate the terms of the agreement. Nonetheless, it is worth noting that possible confusion might arise because Kaswell signed the document *before* the contract came into being—before the "consent of all the present members of the firm" had been obtained. Effective assent required the consent not only of Kaswell but also of Cahill.

Neither of these observations affect the result that the Statute of Frauds has been satisfied, however. The Statute does not require that the contract itself be in writing *or* that the signature of the party to be charged be affixed to the writing as the operative, legally effective act of assent. The Statute attempts to provide a measure of protection against fraud but it stops well short of requiring that the contract itself be in writing. For this reason, the "memorandum or note" required by the Statute need not be made by the parties as an expression of the contract or signed with the intention of assenting to the contract's terms in order to satisfy the Statute. Generally, the purpose for which a memorandum was prepared and the intent with which it was signed are simply immaterial to determining whether the Statute has been satisfied.

Thus, the fact that Kaswell did not and could not by his act of signing the "Memorandum Agreement" give his partnership's assent to the contract does not decide the sufficiency of the document in satisfying the Statute. Nor does it matter that the document was prepared and signed prior to the time at which the contract became effective—the moment at which the consent of all the present members of the firm was obtained. It is well settled that a memorandum satisfying the Statute may be made before the contract is concluded. Farrow, suing on his contract with Kaswell and Cahill and offering the written "Memorandum Agreement" in satisfaction of the Statute, bore the burden of independently proving the existence of a contract on the terms of the written document. The fact that the document offered in satisfaction of the Statute was created and signed prior to the time the contract was concluded does not affect its use in compliance with the Statute.

Judgment for Farrow affirmed.

## ALTERNATIVE MEANS OF SATISFYING THE STATUTE OF FRAUDS IN SALE OF GOODS CONTRACTS

As you have learned, the basic requirement of the UCC statute of frauds [2–201] is that a contract for $500 or more be evidenced by a written memorandum that indicates the existence of the contract, states the quantity of goods to be sold, and is signed by the party to be charged. Recognizing that the underlying purpose of the statute of frauds is to provide more evidence of the existence of a contract than the mere oral testimony of one of the parties, however, the Code permits the statute of frauds to be satisfied by any of four alternative types of evidence. Under the UCC, then, a contract for the sale of goods for more than $500 for which there is no written memorandum signed by the party to be charged can meet the requirements of the statute of frauds in any of the ways discussed below.

**Confirmatory Memo between Merchants.** Suppose Smith and Jones enter into a contract over the telephone for the sale of goods at a price of $5,000. Smith then sends a memorandum to Jones confirming the deal they made orally. If Smith receives and does not object to the memo, it would be fair to say that the parties' conduct provides some evidence that a contract exists. Under some circumstances, the UCC permits such confirmatory memoranda to satisfy the statute of frauds even though the writing is signed by the party who is seeking to enforce the contract rather than the party against whom enforcement is sought [2–201(2)]. This exception applies only when *both* of the parties to a contract are *merchants.* Furthermore, the memo must be sent within a reasonable time after the contract is made and must be sufficient to bind the person who sent it if enforcement were sought against him (that is, it must indicate that a contract was made, state a quantity, and be signed by the sender). If the party against whom enforcement is sought receives the memo, has reason to know its contents, and yet fails to give written notice of objection to the contents of the memo within 10 days after receiving it, the memo can be introduced to meet the requirements of the statute of frauds. The *Thomson Printing Co.* case, which follows, presents a good example of the operation of the "confirmatory memo" exception.

**Part Payment or Part Delivery.** Suppose Smith and Jones enter a contract for the sale of 1,000 units of goods at $1 each. After Smith has paid $600, Jones refuses to deliver the goods and asserts the statute of frauds as a defense to enforcement of the contract. The Code permits part payment or part delivery to satisfy the statute of frauds, but *only for the quantity of goods that have been delivered or paid for* [2–201(3)(c)]. Thus, Jones would be required to deliver only 600 units rather than the 1,000 units Smith alleges that Jones agreed to sell.

**Admission in Pleadings or Court.** Another situation in which the UCC statute of frauds can be satisfied without a writing occurs when the party being sued admits the existence of the oral contract in his trial testimony or in any document that he files with the court. For example, Jones refuses to perform an oral contract he made with Smith for the sale of $2,000 worth of goods, and Smith sues him. If Jones admits the existence of the oral contract in pleadings or in court proceedings, his admission is sufficient to meet the statute of frauds. This exception is justified by the strong evidence that such an admission provides. After all, what better evidence of a contract can there be than is provided when the party being sued admits under penalty of perjury that a contract exists? When such an admission is made, the statute of frauds is satisfied as to *the quantity of goods admitted* [2–201(3)(b)]. For example, if Jones only admits contracting for $1,000 worth of goods, the contract is enforceable only to that extent.

**Specially Manufactured Goods.** Finally, an oral contract within the UCC statute of frauds can be enforced without a writing in some situations involving the sale of *specially manufactured goods.* This exception to the writing requirement will apply only if the nature of the specially manufactured goods is such that they are not suitable for sale in the ordinary course of the seller's business. Completely executory oral contracts are not enforceable under this exception. The seller must have made a substantial beginning in manufacturing the goods for the buyer, or must have made commitments for their procurement, before receiving notice that the buyer was repudiating the sale [2–201(3)(a)]. For example, Smith has an oral contract with Jones for the sale of $2,500 worth of calendars imprinted with Smith's name and address. If Smith repudiates the contract *before* Jones has made a substantial beginning in manufacturing the calendars, the contract will be unenforceable under the statute of frauds. If, however, Smith repudiated the contract *after* Jones had made a substantial beginning, the oral contract would be enforceable.

The specially manufactured goods provision is based both on the evidentiary value of the seller's conduct and on the need to avoid the injustice that would otherwise result from the seller's reliance. The prerequisites for this exception are discussed in greater detail in the *Colorado Carpet* case, which follows.

## Thomson Printing Machinery Co. v. B. F. Goodrich Co.

**714 F.2d 744 (7th Cir. 1983)**

James Thomson was the president of Thomson Printing, a buyer and seller of used printing machinery. On April 10, 1979, Thomson went to B. F. Goodrich's surplus machinery department in Akron, Ohio, to look at some machinery that was for sale. Thomson discussed the sale terms, including a price of $9,000, with Goodrich's surplus equipment manager, Ingram Meyers. Four days later, Thomson sent a purchase order for the equipment and a check for $1,000 in part payment to the Goodrich office in Akron. The purchase order and check specified the parties' names and many details about the sale. Thomson did not, however, specifically address the envelope, check, or order to Ingram Meyers or the surplus equipment department. Meyers did not learn of the purchase order until weeks later, when Thomson called to arrange for removal of the machines. By then, the machines had been sold to another purchaser. Thomson Printing brought suit against Goodrich for breach of contract. The jury rendered a verdict for Thomson Printing, but the trial judge overruled the verdict and entered judgment for Goodrich on the ground that enforcement of the contract was barred by the statute of frauds. Thomson Printing appealed.

**Cudahy, Circuit Judge.** A modern exception to the usual writing requirement is the "merchants" exception to the Uniform Commercial Code section 2–201, which provides:

> Between merchants if within a reasonable time a writing in confirmation of the contract and sufficient against the sender is received and the party receiving it has reason to know its contents, it satisfies the [writing requirement] against such party unless written notice of objection to its contents is given within 10 days after it is received.

We must emphasize that the only effect of this exception is to take away from a merchant who receives a writing in confirmation of a contract the Statute of Frauds defense if the merchant does not object. The sender must still persuade the trier of fact that a contract was in fact made.

In the instant case, James Thomson sent a "writing in confirmation" to Goodrich four days after his meeting with Ingram Meyers, a Goodrich employee and agent. Goodrich argues, however, that Thomson's writing in confirmation cannot qualify for the section 2–201(2) exception because it was not received by anyone at Goodrich who had reason to know its contents. Goodrich claims that Thomson erred in not specifically designating on the envelope, check or purchase order that the items were intended for Ingram Meyers or the surplus equipment department. Consequently, Goodrich contends, it was unable to "find a home" for the check and purchase order despite attempts to do so, in accordance with its regular procedures, by sending copies of the documents to several of its divisions.

Goodrich misreads the requirements of 2–201. First, the literal requirements of 2–201(2) are that a writing "is received" and that Goodrich "has reason to know its contents." There is no dispute that the purchase order and check were received by Goodrich, and there is at least no specific or express requirement that the receipt referred to be by any Goodrich agent in particular.

As for the "reason to know its contents" requirement, this element is best understood to mean that the confirmation was an instrument which should have been anticipated and therefore should have received the attention of appropriate parties. In the case before us there is no doubt that the confirmatory writings were based on actual negotiations and therefore could have been anticipated and appropriately handled. Notice received by an organization is effective from the time when it would have been brought to [the attention of the individual conducting that transaction] if the organization had executed *due diligence.*

Thus, the question comes down to whether Goodrich's mailroom, given the information it had, should have notified the surplus equipment manager, Ingram Meyers, of Thomson's confirmatory writing. At whatever point Meyers should have been so notified, then at that point Thomson's writing was effective even though Meyers did not see it. One cannot say that Goodrich's mailroom procedures were reasonable as a matter of law; if Goodrich had exercised due diligence in handling Thomson Printing's purchase order and check, these items would have reasonably promptly come to Ingram Meyers's attention. First, the purchase order on its face should have alerted the mailroom that the documents referred to a purchase of used printing equipment. Since Goodrich had only one surplus machinery department, the documents' "home" should not have been difficult to find. Second, even if the mailroom would have had difficulty in immediately identifying the kind of transaction involved, the purchase order had Thomson Printing's phone number printed on it and we think a reasonable routine in these particular circumstances would have involved at some point in the process a simple phone call to Thomson Printing. Thus, we think Goodrich's mailroom mishandled the confirmatory writings. This failure should not permit Goodrich to escape liability by pleading nonreceipt.

Judgment reversed in favor of Thomson Printing.

## Colorado Carpet Installation, Inc. v. Palermo

**668 P.2d 1384 (Colo. Sup. Ct. 1983)**

Colorado Carpet sells and installs carpeting and other flooring materials. Fred and Zuma Palermo orally ordered carpeting, padding, and ceramic tile from Colorado Carpet for a total price of more than $4,000. Colorado Carpet ordered the carpeting from manufacturers, who filled the orders and delivered the carpeting to a Denver warehouse. Colorado Carpet also purchased and delivered tile to the Palermos, but Mrs. Palermo had a disagreement with Colorado Carpet's tile man and arranged with another contractor to supply and install other tile. Colorado Carpet removed its tile from the Palermo home, returned half of it to the supplier for a refund and sold the other half. It also shipped part of the carpeting back to its manufacturer for some credit and sold the rest to a local purchaser. Colorado Carpet then sued the Palermos for its lost profits, labor, and storage and shipping costs. The Palermos asserted the statute of frauds as a defense. The trial court awarded damages to Colorado Carpet. The Palermos appealed, and the Colorado Court of Appeals reversed the judgment in favor of the Palermos. Colorado Carpet appealed.

**Quinn, Justice.** Four distinct criteria are necessary to satisfy the "specially manufactured goods" exception to the statute of frauds: (1) the goods must be specially made for the buyer; (2) the goods must be unsuitable for sale to others in the ordinary course of the seller's business; (3) the seller must have substantially begun to have manufactured the goods or to have made a commitment for their procurement; and (4) the manufacture or commitment must have been commenced under circumstances reasonably indicating that the goods are for the buyer and prior to the seller's receipt of notification of contractual repudiation. In this case there is no dispute that the third and fourth statutory criteria have been established. There being no controversy about these matters, we confine our consideration to the statutory provisions requiring the goods to be "specially manufactured for the buyer" and "not suitable for sale to others in the ordinary course of the seller's business."

The specially manufactured goods exception is premised on notions of both evidentiary reliability and fairness. Certain marketing practices provide sufficiently reliable evidence on the matter of a contractual relationship as to dispense with the written requirements of the statute of frauds. It is a reasonable assumption, for example, that a seller will not make or procure goods not suitable for sale to others in the normal course of the seller's business unless a purchaser has contracted with the seller to purchase these goods. Denying enforcement of the contract under such circumstances can result in unfairness to the seller by encumbering him with unsalable goods. There is no unfairness in nonenforcement, however, when the goods are of a class customarily sold by the seller and are readily marketable to others in the ordinary course of the seller's business.

The term "specially manufactured goods" refers to the character of the goods as specially made *for a particular buyer,* and not to whether they were "specially made" in the usual course of the seller's business. There is no evidence from which one may reasonably conclude that the carpets were "specially made." These styles of carpets had been observed by Mrs. Palermo in retail carpeting outlets in the Denver area, and both carpets were ordered by Colorado Carpet as stock items from carpet manufacturers in California and Georgia. No special dying, weaving or other treatment was required to fill the orders. The carpeting was not cut to any unusual shape nor even to the precise dimensions of the rooms where they were to be installed, but rather was cut in a rectangular shape with footage adequate for the entire project. In short, there is no showing of any unusual or special features of the carpeting that might attest to its character as specially made for a particular buyer.

The record is similarly deficient in establishing that the carpeting satisfied the other statutory requirement of "not suitable for sale to others in the ordinary course of the seller's business." The business of Colorado Carpet was to purchase carpeting from wholesalers or manufacturers and then to resell the carpeting to retail purchasers at a price inclusive of a labor charge for installation. As a dealer in carpeting and other flooring materials, Colorado Carpet continually dealt with goods of this nature and reasonably could be expected to find a buyer for them. There certainly was nothing in the character of the carpeting that required basic or essential changes to be made in order to render them marketable to other purchasers. Indeed, Colorado Carpet received credit from the manufacturer upon its return of the upstairs carpet and had little difficulty in selling the downstairs carpet to a local purchaser. The record is manifestly insufficient to support the trial court's determination that the carpeting qualified for the specially manufactured goods exception to the statute of frauds. As the court of appeals correctly ruled, the trial court erred in enforcing the contract.

Judgment for the Palermos affirmed.

## PROMISSORY ESTOPPEL AND THE STATUTE OF FRAUDS

The statute of frauds, which was created to prevent fraud and perjury, has often been criticized because it can create unjust results. One of the troubling features of the statute is that it can as easily be used to defeat a contract that was actually made as it can to defeat a fictitious agreement. As you have seen, courts and legislatures have created several exceptions to the statute of frauds that reduce the statute's potential for creating unfair results. In recent years, courts in some states have begun to use the doctrine of **promissory estoppel**[2] to allow some parties to recover under oral contracts that the statute of frauds would ordinarily render unenforceable.

Courts in these states hold that when one of the parties would suffer serious losses because of his reliance on an oral contract, the other party is estopped from raising the statute of frauds as a defense. This position has been approved in the *Restatement (Second) of Contracts.* Section 139 of the *Restatement* provides that a promise that induces action or forbearance can be enforceable notwithstanding the statute of frauds if the reliance was foreseeable to the person making the promise and if injustice can be avoided only by enforcing the promise. The idea behind this section and the cases employing promissory estoppel is that the statute of frauds, which is designed to prevent injustice, should not be allowed to work an injustice. Section 139 and these cases also impliedly recognize the fact that the reliance required by promissory estoppel to some extent provides evidence of the existence of a contract between the parties, since it is unlikely that a person would materially rely on a nonexistent promise.

[2] The doctrine of promissory estoppel is discussed in Chapter 10.

The use of promissory estoppel as a means of circumventing the statute of frauds is still controversial, however. Many courts fear that enforcing oral contracts on the basis of a party's reliance will essentially negate the statute. In cases involving the UCC statute of frauds, an additional source of concern involves the interpretation of section 2–201. Some courts have construed the provisions listing specific alternative methods of satisfying 2–201's formal requirements to be *exclusive,* precluding the creation of any further exceptions by courts. The *Allen Campbell* case is an example of a case adopting and employing the theory of promissory estoppel to enforce a contract notwithstanding the statute of frauds.

## EFFECT OF FAILURE TO COMPLY WITH THE STATUTE OF FRAUDS

Under the typical statute of frauds, an oral contract within the statute that does not comply with its formal requirements is not treated as an illegal contract. Most statutes of frauds state that contracts which do not comply are *unenforceable* rather than void or voidable. One significant aspect of this treatment is that if both parties to such an oral contract have fully performed their obligations, neither party is allowed to rescind the contract. The mutual performance of the parties is ample evidence that a contract existed. Even if the contract is executory, it will be enforced if the party against whom enforcement of the contract is sought does not raise the statute of frauds as a defense. Finally, if one of the parties has rendered some performance under the contract, conferring benefits on the other party short of what would be necessary for part performance, he can recover the reasonable value of the performance in an action based in *quasi contract.*

## Allen M. Campbell Co. v. Virginia Metal Industries, Inc.

**708 F.2d 930 (4th Cir. 1983)**

Allen Campbell Company intended to bid on a Department of the Navy contract to construct housing for enlisted personnel at Camp LeJeune, North Carolina. Virginia Metal telephoned Campbell approximately one-half hour before the deadline for the submission of bids. In this conversation, Virginia Metal quoted a price to supply all hollow metal doors and frames required by the plans and specifications in Campbell's bid. The price promised was $193,121 plus tax. Campbell based the computation of its bid on Virginia Metal's quoted price. Campbell was the successful bidder and was awarded the contract. Virginia Metal later backed out, and Campbell had to obtain the metal doors and frames from another supplier. This cost Campbell $45,562 more than it had been led to expect that Virginia Metal would charge. Campbell then filed suit against Virginia Metal in federal court. Applying North Carolina law, the trial court dismissed the suit. Campbell appealed.

**MURNAGHAN, CIRCUIT JUDGE.** The law has developed the concept of promissory estoppel, which allows recovery even in the absence of consideration where reliance and change of position to the detriment of the promisee make it unconscionable not to enforce the promise. At the present stage of the case, action in reliance on the promise to sell doors and frames cannot be disputed. Campbell submitted its bid for the entire project to the Government in reliance upon Virginia Metal's quoted price. In the case as pleaded by Campbell, the elements of promissory estoppel are clearly present. Even in the absence of consideration, there was a sufficiently binding promise by Virginia Metal. We must next deal with the contention of Virginia Metal that it cannot be held liable since its promise was not in writing. The Uniform Commercial Code requires that a contract for the sale of goods involving more than $500 must be in writing. The question becomes whether North Carolina's doctrine of promissory estoppel creates an exception to or is displaced by the statute of frauds. There is a split of authority in decisions from states other than North Carolina on the question of whether promissory estoppel is to be deemed an exception to the statute of frauds. While North Carolina has not explicitly committed itself as to the availability of promissory estoppel as a means for overcoming the UCC statute of frauds, it has expressed approval of the position taken in *Restatement (Second) of Contracts* section 139, the cornerstone of the rationale adopted by the courts which have held that promissory estoppel will, in circumstances like those here presented, render inapplicable the UCC statute of frauds. In light of what we perceive to be the law that North Carolina courts would apply to the facts of this case, the fact that the promise was entirely oral would not bar recovery.

Reversed and remanded in favor of Campbell.

## THE PAROL EVIDENCE RULE

**Explanation of the Rule.** In many situations, contracting parties prefer to express their agreements in writing even when they are not required to do so by the statute of frauds. Written contracts rarely come into being without some prior discussions or negotiations between the parties, however. Various promises, proposals, or representations are usually made by one or both of the parties before the execution of a written contract. What happens when one of those prior promises, proposals, or representations is not included in the terms of the written contract? For example, suppose that Jones wants to buy Smith's house. During the course of negotiations, Smith states that he will pay for any major repairs that the house needs for the first year that Jones owns it. The written contract that the parties ultimately sign, however, does not say anything about Smith paying for repairs, and, in fact, states that Jones will take the house "as is." The furnace breaks down three months after the sale, and Smith refuses to pay for its repair. What is the status of Smith's promise to pay for repairs? The basic problem is one of defining the boundaries of the parties' agreement. Are all the promises made in the process of negotiation part of the contract, or do the terms of the written document that the parties signed supersede any preliminary agreements?

The **parol evidence rule** provides the answer to this question. The term *parol evidence* means written or spoken statements that are *not contained in the written contract.* The parol evidence rule provides that when parties enter a *written contract* that they intend as a complete *integration* (a complete and final statement of their agreement), a court will not permit the use of evidence of prior or contemporaneous statements to add to, alter, or contradict the terms of the written contract. This rule is based on the presumption that when people enter into a written contract, the best evidence of their agreement is the written contract itself. It also reflects the idea that later expressions of intent are presumed to prevail over earlier expressions of intent. In the hypothetical case involving Smith and Jones, assuming that they intended the written contract to be the final integration of their agreement, Jones would not be able to introduce evidence of Smith's promise to pay for repairs. The effect of excluding preliminary promises or statements from consideration is, of course, to confine the parties' contract to the terms of the written agreement. The lesson to be learned from this example is that people who put their agreements in writing should make sure that all the terms of their agreement are included in the writing.

**Scope of the Parol Evidence Rule.** The parol evidence rule is relevant only in cases in which the parties have expressed their agreement in a *written* contract. Thus, it would *not* apply to a case involving an oral contract or to a case in which writings existed that were not intended to embody the final statement of at least part of the parties' contract. The parol evidence rule has been made a part of the law of sales in the Uniform Commercial Code [2–202], so it is applicable to contracts for the sale of goods as well as to contracts governed by the common law of contracts. Furthermore, the rule excludes only evidence of statements made *prior to* or *during* the signing of the written contract. It does not apply to statements made *after* the signing of the contract. Thus, evidence of *subsequent statements* is freely admissible.

**Admissible Parol Evidence.** In some situations, evidence of statements made outside the written contract is admissible notwithstanding the parol evidence rule. Parol evidence is permitted in the following situations either because the writing is not the best evidence of the contract or because the evidence is offered, not to contradict the terms of the writing, but to explain the writing or to challenge the underlying contractual obligation that the writing represents.

**Additional Terms in Partially Integrated Contracts.** In many instances, parties will desire to introduce evidence of statements or agreements that would *supplement* rather than contradict the written contract. Whether they can do this depends on whether the written contract is characterized as *completely integrated* or *partially integrated.* A completely integrated contract is one that the parties intend as a *complete and exclusive* statement of their entire agreement. As illustrated by the *Walt Bennett Ford* case, the parol evidence rule forbids the use of parol evidence to add to or supplement the terms of a completely integrated contract.

A partially integrated contract is one that expresses the parties' final agreement as to some but not all of the terms of their contract. When a contract is only partially integrated, the parties are permitted to use parol evidence to prove the *additional* terms of their agreement. Such evidence cannot, however, be used to contradict, alter, or vary the written terms of the contract. To determine whether a contract is completely or partially integrated, a court must determine the parties' intent as indicated by the writing and by all the surrounding circumstances. Sometimes, the parties will expressly agree that their contract is completely integrated. Form contracts and commercial contracts frequently contain provisions known as *merger clauses* or *integration clauses,* which provide that the written contract is the complete integration of the parties' agreement.[3] You can see an example of a merger clause in the *Walt Bennett Ford* case. Such clauses are designed to prevent a party from enforcing prior statements or agreements. Courts generally uphold merger clauses and refuse to admit evidence of additional terms in contracts that contain such clauses.

[3] The use of merger clauses in computer contracts is discussed in Chapter 50.

**Explaining Ambiguities.** Parol evidence can be offered to *explain an ambiguity* in the written contract. Suppose a written contract between Jones and Smith provides that Jones will buy "Smith's truck," but Smith has two trucks. The parties could offer evidence of negotiations, statements, and other circumstances preceding the creation of the written contract to identify the truck to which the writing refers. Used in this way, parol evidence helps the court interpret the contract. It does not contradict the written contract.

**Circumstances Invalidating Contract.** Any circumstances that would be relevant to show that a contract is not valid can be proven by parol evidence. For example, evidence that Smith pointed a gun at Jones and said, "Sign this contract, or I'll kill you," would be admissible to show that the contract was voidable because of duress. Likewise, parol evidence would be admissible to show that a contract was illegal or was induced by fraud, misrepresentation, undue influence, or mistake. This is true even if the written contract contains a merger clause.

**Existence of Condition.** It is also permissible to use parol evidence to show that a writing was executed with the understanding that it was *not to take effect until the occurrence of a condition (a future, uncertain event that creates a duty to perform).*[4] Suppose Smith signs a contract to purchase a car with

[4] Conditions are discussed in greater detail in Chapter 15.

the agreement that the contract is not to be effective unless and until Smith gets a new job. If the written contract is silent about any conditions that must occur before it becomes effective, Smith could introduce parol evidence to prove the existence of the condition. Such proof merely elaborates on, but does not contradict, the terms of the writing.

**Subsequent Agreements.** As you read earlier, parties can always introduce proof of *subsequent agreements.* This is true even if the terms of the later agreement cancel, subtract from, or add to the obligations stated in the written contract. The idea here is that when a writing is followed by a later statement or agreement, the writing is no longer the best evidence of the agreement. You should be aware, however, that subsequent modifications of contracts may sometimes be unenforceable due to lack of consideration or failure to comply with the statute of frauds.

## Walt Bennett Ford, Inc. v. Dyer

**631 So.2d 312 (Ark. Ct. App. 1982)**

Everlener Dyer purchased a used Ford from Walt Bennett Ford (Bennett) for $5,895. She signed a written contract, which showed that no taxes were included in the sales price. Dyer contended, however, that the salesman who negotiated the purchase with her told her both before and after her signing of the contract that the sales tax on the automobile had been paid.

The contract Dyer signed contained the following language:

> The above comprises the entire agreement pertaining to this purchase and no other agreement of any kind, verbal understanding, representation, or promise whatsoever will be recognized.

It also stated:

> This contract constitutes the entire agreement between the parties and no modification hereof shall be valid in any event and Buyer expressly waives the right to rely thereon, unless made in writing, signed by Seller.

Later, when Dyer attempted to license the automobile, she discovered that the Arkansas sales tax had not been paid on it. She paid the sales tax and sued Bennett for breach of contract. The trial court entered judgment for Dyer, and Bennett appealed.

**COOPER, JUDGE.** Bennett argues that the trial court was in error in allowing testimony which violated the parol evidence rule. We agree.

The Uniform Commercial Code contains a codification of the parol evidence rule. The parol evidence rule requires, in the absence of fraud, duress, mutual mistake, or something of the kind, the exclusion of all prior or contemporaneous oral or written evidence that would add to or vary the parties' integrated written contract.

In *Green Chevrolet Company v. Kemp,* the Arkansas Supreme Court dealt with a case in which the buyer bought a used vehicle. The buyer alleged breach of an express and implied warranty of all mechanical parts for one year. The trial court allowed the buyer and his wife to testify that the seller's agent had made oral guarantees of the mechanical parts for one year. The written contracts provided that the buyer accepts the car "as is," and that the contract covers all conditions and agreements between the parties. The Arkansas Supreme Court ruled that the trial court erred in admitting the testimony of the buyer and his wife with reference to representations made by the seller's agent. The Court held that their testimony contradicted the terms of the conditional sales contract, and that it was therefore a violation of the parol evidence rule.

In the case at bar, the retail purchase order contained [a merger clause and a clause requiring all modifications to be in writing]. We find the case at bar to be indistinguishable from *Kemp,* and therefore, we hold that the trial court erred in allowing the admission of parol evidence to vary the terms of the written contract.

Judgment reversed in favor of Bennett.

## INTERPRETATION OF CONTRACTS

Once a court has decided what promises are included in a contract, it is faced with *interpreting* the contract to determine the *meaning* and *legal effect* of the terms used by the parties. Courts have adopted broad, basic standards of interpretation that guide them in the interpretation process.

The court will first attempt to determine the parties' *principal objective.* Every clause will then be determined in the light of this principal objective. Ordinary words will be given their usual meaning and technical words (such as those which have a special meaning in the parties' trade or business) will be given their technical meaning, unless a different meaning was clearly intended.

Guidelines grounded in common sense are also used to determine the relationship of the various terms of the contract. Specific terms that follow general terms are presumed to qualify those general terms. Suppose that a provision which states that the subject of the contract is "guaranteed for one year" is followed by a provision describing the "one-year guarantee against defects in workmanship." Here, it is fair to conclude that the more specific term qualifies the more general term and that the guarantee described in the contract is a guarantee of workmanship only, and not of parts and materials.

Sometimes, there is internal conflict in the terms of an agreement and courts must determine which term should prevail. When the parties use a form contract or some other type of contract that is partially printed and partially handwritten, the handwritten provisions will prevail. If the contract was drafted by one of the parties, any ambiguities will be resolved *against* the party who drafted the contract. This principle is illustrated by *Grove v. Charbonneau Buick-Pontiac, Inc.,* which follows.

If both parties to the contract are members of a trade, profession, or community in which certain words are commonly given a particular meaning (this is called a *usage*), the courts will presume that the parties intended the meaning that the usage gives to the terms they use. For example, if the word *dozen* in the bakery business means 13 rather than 12, a contract between two bakers for the purchase of 10 dozen loaves of bread will be presumed to mean 130 loaves of bread rather than 120. Usages can also add provisions to the parties' agreement. If the court finds that a certain practice is a matter of common usage in the parties' trade, it will assume that the parties intended to include that practice in their agreement. If contracting parties are members of the same trade, business, or community but do not intend to be bound by usage, they should specifically say so in their agreement.

## Grove v. Charbonneau Buick-Pontiac, Inc.

**240 N.W.2d 853 (N.D. Sup. Ct. 1976)**

On Labor Day weekend in 1974, Lloyd Grove participated in the Dickinson Elks Club's annual Labor Day Golf Tournament. He had learned of the tournament and the prizes to be awarded from a poster that was placed at a golf course. Included in the poster was an offer by Charbonneau Buick-Pontiac of a 1974 automobile "to the first entry who shoots a hole-in-one on Hole No. 8." This offer was also placed on a sign on the automobile at the tournament.

The Dickinson golf course at which the tournament was played had only 9 holes, but there were 18 separately located and marked tee areas, so that the course could be played as an 18-hole course by going around the 9-hole course twice. The first nine tees were marked with blue markers and tee numbers. The second nine tees were marked with red markers and tee numbers. Because of this layout of the course, the tee area marked "8" and the tee area marked "17" were both played to the eighth hole. The tee area marked "17" lay to one side of the tee area marked "8" and was approximately 60 yards farther from the hole.

Grove scored his hole-in-one on hole No. 8 on the first day of the tournament while playing from the 17th tee in an 18-hole match. Grove claimed the prize, but Charbonneau refused to award it, insisting that Grove had not scored his hole-in-one on the 8th hole, as required, but had scored it on the 17th hole. Grove brought suit against Charbonneau for breach of contract. The trial court awarded damages for Grove, and Charbonneau appealed.

**Sand, Judge.** The sole dispute between Grove and Charbonneau relates to the interpretation of the words and phrases used in the offer. When good arguments can be made for either of two contrary positions as to the meaning of a term in a document, an ambiguity exists. Where a contract contains ambiguous terms which are in dispute, it is the duty of the court to construe them. The ambiguous terms of a contract will be interpreted most strongly against the party who caused the ambiguity.

In *Schreiner v. Weil Furniture Co.,* the court stated that a document must be interpreted against the one who has prepared it, and applied such a rule to an offer of a prize made to the public. The court held that it was the duty of the defendant to explain the contest so that the public would not be misled. We believe the rule on ambiguous contracts applies to this case, and therefore, any language of this contract which is not clear must be interpreted most strongly against Charbonneau. The offer does not contain any qualifications or limitations as to what is meant by the phrase "on hole No. 8." Neither does the award or offer make any statement restricting or qualifying that the hole-in-one on hole No. 8 may be accomplished only from tee No. 8. If Charbonneau had in mind to impose limitations, he could have made this in the offer so that a person of ordinary intelligence would have been fully apprised of the offer in every respect.

If this rule of law on ambiguous contracts were not applied, it would permit the promoter who is so inclined to keep adding requirements or conditions which were not stated in the offer. By interpreting and construing the ambiguous provisions of the offer most strongly against the party who caused them, we construe [the contract] to mean that an entrant in the tournament who drives the ball in one stroke into hole No. 8 from either the 8th or the 17th tee has met the conditions of the offer and is entitled to the award.

Judgment for Grove affirmed.

## SUMMARY

All states have enacted statutes patterned after the English Statute of Frauds. These statutes state that certain types of contracts must be evidenced by a writing to be enforceable. Although the statutes are not uniform, generally included in the class of contracts for which a writing is required are: collateral contracts; contracts for the sale of an interest in land; bilateral, executory contracts that cannot be performed within a year from the date on which the contract came into existence; and contracts for the sale of goods for $500 or more.

A collateral contract is a contract in which one person promises to pay the debt or obligation of another person. A collateral contract must be distinguished from an original contract (in which a person obligates herself to perform an obligation in all events rather than merely to pay if another person fails to do so). No writing is required for an original contract unless it falls within some other provision of the statute of frauds. If a person's primary purpose in promising to pay the debt of another is to benefit himself, the *leading object* or *main purpose* exception to the statute of frauds provides that the promise does not have to be evidenced by a writing.

A contract for the sale of any ownership interest in land is within the statute of frauds. This includes ownership interests less than full ownership, such as easements, long-term leases, options, and mortgages. If a person has relied on an oral contract for the sale of land by doing acts that are *exclusively referable* to the contract, his conduct satisfies the statute of frauds under the *part performance exception*. Generally, part performance requires the payment of a substantial portion of the purchase price and either taking possession of the land or making improvements on it.

Bilateral, executory contracts that cannot be performed within a year from the date on which the contract came into existence are also within the statute of frauds. To determine whether a contract comes within the one-year provision, the amount of time between the date on which the contract came into being and the date on which the terms provide that performance will be completed must be calculated. Contracts for an indefinite period of time, even those "for life," are not within the statute of frauds of most states, because they *can* be performed within a year.

Under UCC section 2-201, contracts for the sale of goods for a price of $500 or more are within the statute of frauds and must be evidenced by a writing or come within an exception to the writing requirement specified in the UCC. Modifications of sale of goods contracts are within the statute of frauds if the sales price of the contract as modified exceeds $500.

If a contract is within the statute of frauds

and none of the exceptions to the statute of frauds are applicable, the contract must be evidenced by a memorandum indicating the existence of the contract. The memorandum does not have to *be* the contract, or even be intended by the parties as binding, but it must provide written evidence tending to prove that a contract exists. The memorandum must be signed by the party who is using the statute of frauds as a defense ("the party to be charged"). It must identify the parties and the subject matter and, to varying degrees controlled by state law, describe the important terms of the agreement. In sale of goods contracts, the UCC states that it does not matter whether the memorandum states all of the important terms, or even states some of them incorrectly, but the contract cannot be enforced for more than the quantity stated in the memorandum.

The UCC provides for four additional alternative ways of satisfying the statute of frauds in sale of goods contracts for $500 or more. Parties can use these ways to satisfy the statute when they do not have a writing or when they have a writing, but it is not signed by the party to be charged. First, if both parties are merchants and one of them sends a *confirmatory memorandum* signed by him, stating a quantity and indicating that a contract has been made, the memo will be sufficient to meet the statute of frauds if the other party receives it, has reason to know of its contents, and does not object in writing within 10 days. Second, an oral contract for the sale of more than $500 worth of *specially manufactured goods* is enforceable if the specially manufactured goods are of a type that cannot be resold in the ordinary course of the seller's business and if the seller has already made a substantial beginning in manufacturing the goods or has made commitments to procure the goods. Third, an oral contract for more than $500 worth of goods can be enforced up to the quantity paid for or delivered if there has been *part payment or part delivery.* Fourth, an oral sale of goods contract for more than $500 can be enforced up to the quantity admitted if the party against whom enforcement is sought admits the existence of the contract in court proceedings or pleadings.

A contract within the statute of frauds that does not comply with the statute's requirements is considered to be *unenforceable,* not void or voidable. Violation of the statute of frauds will not be a ground for invalidating a contract that has already been performed. A person who has conferred benefits pursuant to a contract that is unenforceable because of the statute of frauds can recover what he has parted with under the doctrine of quasi contract.

In some states, the doctrine of promissory estoppel has been applied to estop a party from asserting the statute of frauds when the other party has relied materially on an oral contract and would suffer serious losses if the contract were not enforced.

The parol evidence rule provides that evidence of statements made prior to or during the signing of a written contract cannot be admitted to add to, alter, or vary the terms of the written contract. The parol evidence rule is part of the UCC as well as the common law of contracts. There are a variety of purposes for which parol evidence (evidence of statements not contained in the written contract) can be used, however. First, the parol evidence rule applies to prevent the use of evidence of prior or contemporaneous statements only. Evidence of *subsequent agreements* is admissible. Second, parol evidence can be used to add to or supplement a written contract if the contract is only *partially integrated.* Third, parol evidence can be used to demonstrate *circumstances invalidating the contract;* for example, to show that the contract was unenforceable due to illegality or voidable due to duress, undue influence, mistake, fraud, or misrepresentation. Fourth, parol evidence can be used to *explain ambiguous terms* in the contract. Fifth, parol evidence is admissible to show that *the contract was not to be effective until the occurrence of a condition.*

Courts have developed guidelines to help them interpret the meaning and legal effect of language in a contract. They attempt to understand the parties' principal objective and to interpret the individual provisions of the contract so as to further that objective. Courts use specific rules to resolve situations in which ambiguity exists or there is an internal inconsistency in the terms used in the contract. Usages of a trade or industry are also helpful in determining the meaning and effect of contract terms.

## PROBLEM CASES

1. Cagle went to Roy Buckner Chevrolet to buy a limited edition sports car known as an "Indy Vette." After agreeing to sell the car to Cagle at list price, Roy Buckner's sales manager, Kelly, partially completed the "buyer's order," writing "list price" on the form and signing his name in the middle of the page rather than in the space provided for the signature of an officer of Roy Buckner Chevrolet. Cagle signed his name, too, and gave Kelly a $500 deposit. Later, when Roy Buckner received the Indy Vette, it notified Cagle that it would not sell it to him and attempted to return his deposit. Cagle brought suit, and Roy Buckner asserted the statute of frauds as a defense, claiming that the buyer's order was insufficient because it was only partially completed and because it was not signed in the proper space by Kelly. Is this a good defense?

2. Wood, a certified public accountant, worked for Dan P. Holl & Co. from 1974 to 1982 under an oral employment agreement of indefinite duration. During the later years of this employment, a profit-sharing plan was instituted and Holl made contributions on Wood's behalf, which were deducted from her salary. The profit-sharing plan provided for a 10-year vesting period; that is, an employee who served less than 10 years would receive no part of his or her account under the plan. Wood and Holl had numerous conversations about this aspect of the plan, and Holl repeatedly assured her that if she "was to leave, those funds would be paid even if he had to pay them from monies from other sources." Wood resigned in 1982. Wood attempted to enforce Holl's promise to pay her profit-sharing account, but Holl asserted that enforcement of Wood's employment contract was barred by the one-year provision of the statute of frauds. What result?

3. Buker wanted to lease commercial space for the operation of a restaurant in a building owned by National Management Company. During one of the meetings that Buker had with Young, National's chief executive, Young stated that the building was old but had been repaired recently and was in operable condition so far as he knew. Young also remarked that although National's lessees were obligated to make minor repairs, Buker had nothing to worry about. Buker later signed a written lease for an eight-year term. In this lease, Buker acknowledged that the premises were in good repair and undertook the responsibility for keeping them in that condition during the term of the lease. Buker experienced trouble with the building almost from the beginning of the lease. The boilers worked erratically; the roof leaked; and the sewage system frequently became inoperable. Buker sued National for breach of warranty. Can Buker offer evidence of the statements that Young made at the meeting?

4. In August 1979, Jellibeans, Inc. entered into an agreement to purchase from Baker three adjacent lots known as Lots 3833, 3847, and 3861. The agreement was contained in

three separate documents that were all executed at the same time: a purchase agreement for Lots 3833 and 3847, a three-year option to purchase Lot 3861, and a lease for a term ending at the exercise of the option on a part of Lot 3861 that was to be used for parking for the other two lots. Within the period of the option, Jellibeans wrote a letter to Baker stating its intention to exercise the option and purchase Lot 3861. When Jellibeans learned that Baker was attempting to sell Lot 3861 to someone else, it brought suit for specific performance. Baker asserted the statute of frauds as a defense, arguing that the terms stated in the written option were too indefinite to satisfy the statute. The missing terms were described in greater detail in the other two documents executed by the parties, but none of the three documents expressly mentioned any of the other documents. Can the three documents be considered together to meet the requirements of the statute of frauds?

**5.** In June 1976, Moore went to First National Bank and requested the president of the bank to allow his sons, Rocky and Mike, to open an account in the name of Texas Continental Express, Inc. Moore promised to bring his own business to the bank and orally agreed to make good any losses that the bank might incur from receiving dishonored checks from Texas Continental. The bank then furnished regular checking account and bank draft services to Texas Continental. Several years later, Texas Continental wrote checks totaling $448,942.05, that were returned for insufficient funds. Texas Continental did not cover the checks, and the bank turned to Moore for payment. When Moore refused to pay, the bank sued him. Does Moore have a good statute of frauds defense?

**6.** In January 1980, Mayer entered into an oral contract of employment with King Cola for a three-year term. Mayer moved from Chattanooga to St. Louis and began working. King Cola paid his moving expenses. In accordance with the parties' negotiations, Mayer awaited a written contract, but none was ever executed. The employment relationship soon began to deteriorate, and after several months King Cola's president told Mayer that he was not going to be given a contract. In May 1980, King Cola discharged Mayer. In a state that does not recognize the doctrine of promissory estoppel as an exception to the statute of frauds, will Mayer be able to enforce the contract?

**7.** On June 30, 1981, Wilda Fannin attended the auction of a house owned by the Crattys and outbid all the other entrants. The property was "knocked down" to her at $45,500. She immediately posted a 10 percent down payment in accordance with the terms of the sale. Several days later, Fannin toured the house again and discovered a deteriorating basement wall. She demanded the return of her down payment, and when the Crattys refused to refund it, she brought suit. The Crattys counterclaimed for $6,500, which represented the difference between the price at which the house was sold to Fannin and the price subsequently offered to them by a third party. Assuming that the contract between Fannin and the Crattys was oral and has not yet been fully performed, can Fannin get a refund of her down payment? Can the Crattys recover damages for breach of the contract?

**8.** Twin City Foods, a food processor, entered a contract with Stender, a grower, obligating Twin City to harvest and vine Stender's pea crop at maturity and to pay Stender a specified price. The contract gave Twin City the right to divert some of Stender's crop for seed or feed purposes at a lower price. It specified that Twin City could divert as much of Stender's crop as quality "of salvage might dictate in the event of *adverse weather conditions that might delay harvest of pea crop beyond optimum maturity for processing.*" Weather conditions resulted in an early maturation of Stender's entire crop. Twin City claimed the right to divert Stender's crop under the adverse weather clause, arguing that the custom in the pea industry was to plant peas in a staggered manner to avoid having the entire crop mature at once. Did the adverse weather clause give Twin City the right to divert Stender's crop?

**9.** Wilson entered into an oral contract over the telephone to sell Cargill 28,000 bushels of ordinary winter wheat at $1.48 per bushel and 6,000 bushels of higher protein wheat at $1.63 per bushel. Both parties were merchants. Following the telephone call, Cargill's manager completed two standard grain purchase contracts, signed them as Cargill's agent, signed Wilson's name to them, and sent them to Wilson. Wilson received the contracts and made no objection to their contents or to the fact that Cargill's manager had signed Wilson's name to them. Wilson began delivering wheat, but several months later Cargill discovered that Wilson did not intend to deliver the rest of the wheat. It sued Wilson for breach of contract. Wilson asserted the statute of frauds as a defense. Will Cargill prevail?

**10.** Hancock Construction Company entered into an oral contract with Kempton & Snedigar Dairy for the sale of certain real estate. Hancock specifically asked Snedigar whether the contract was considered to be binding and whether he could rely on it. Snedigar replied that it was, and shook hands with Hancock. In reliance on this oral contract, Hancock immediately had engineering studies of the property made and arranged to obtain a loan of $292,830. Hancock brought suit for breach of contract when the dairy refused to go through with the deal. The dairy raised the statute of frauds as a defense. Can Hancock defeat this statute of frauds defense?

**11.** Vanguard Machinery produced printhead assemblies for IBM Corporation. During 1979 and 1980, Vanguard produced more than 7,000 assemblies to IBM's specifications. IBM rejected more than 3,000 of these because they did not meet the specifications. It did not purchase any more parts from Vanguard. Vanguard brought suit against IBM, claiming that it had made an oral contract with IBM for the sale of 50,000 printhead assemblies, the contract price for which would be greatly in excess of $500. The only writings between the parties were the written purchase orders for the 7,000 assemblies. Vanguard counters IBM's statute of frauds defense with the argument that the specially manufactured goods exception applies here. Will Vanguard prevail?

**12.** McDaniel was a tenant of Silvernail. Silvernail signed the following document, agreeing to sell McDaniel part of her property:

> I agree to sell to George McDaniel the house on R.R.2, in which he now lives, plus two acres for $6,000 to be agreed.
>
> (s)Alfreda Silvernail

Silvernail later refused to convey a deed, and McDaniel filed suit to enforce the contract. Does the statute of frauds bar enforcement of this contract?

**13.** Gardner testified that City Dodge's salesman had represented to him that the car he purchased had never been wrecked. City Dodge denied that such a representation had been made and pointed to the sales agreement that Gardner had signed, which provided that "no other agreement, promise, or understanding of any kind pertaining to this purchase will be recognized." When Gardner discovered that the vehicle had been wrecked, he returned it to City Dodge, unilaterally rescinded the contract, and sued on a theory of fraud and deceit. City Dodge contends that because of the words quoted above and the parol evidence rule, no evidence can be introduced concerning oral representations made by City Dodge at the time of sale. Is City Dodge correct?

# Chapter 14

# Rights of Third Parties

## INTRODUCTION

In preceding chapters, we have emphasized the way in which a private agreement between two or more people creates legal rights and duties *on the part of the contracting parties.* Since a contract is founded upon the voluntary and mutual consent of the contracting parties, it might seem to follow that they are the only ones who have rights and duties under the contract. Although this is generally true, there are two situations in which people who were not parties to a contract have legally enforceable interests under the contract: when a contract has been assigned to a third party and when a contract is intended to benefit a third person (**third party beneficiary).** This chapter discusses the circumstances in which third parties have rights under a contract.

## ASSIGNMENTS OF CONTRACTS

A contract consists of both rights and duties. A party to a contract has the right to receive the promised performance from the other party as well as the duty to perform his own promise. These rights and duties can, in most situations, be transferred to a third person. The transfer of a *right* under a contract is called an **assignment.** The appointment of another person *to perform a duty* under a contract is called a **delegation.**

Contract rights have not always been transferable. Early common law refused to permit assignment or delegation because debts were considered to be too personal to transfer. A debtor who failed to pay an honest debt was subject to severe penalties, including imprisonment, because such a failure to pay was viewed as the equivalent of theft. The identity of the creditor was of great importance to the debtor, since one creditor might be more lenient than another. Courts also feared that the assignment of debts would stir up unwanted litigation. In an economy that was primarily land-based, the extension of credit was of relatively small importance. As trade increased and became more complex, however, the practice of extending credit became more common. The needs of an increasingly commercial society demanded that people be able to trade freely in intangible assets such as debts. Consequently, the rules of law regarding the assignment of contracts gradually became more liberal. Today, public policy favors free assignability of contracts.

**Nature of Assignment of Rights.** A person who owes a duty to perform under a contract is called an **obligor.** The person to whom he owes the duty is called the **obligee.** An assignment occurs when the obligee indicates the intent to transfer his right to receive the obligor's performance to a third person. When there has been an assignment, the person making the assignment—the original obligee—is called the **assignor.** The person to whom the right has been transferred is called the **assignee.** For example, Smith borrows $500 from Jones, promising to repay Jones in six months. Needing cash immediately, Jones assigns his right to receive Smith's repayment to Kelly for $400. In this case, Smith is the obligor, Jones is the assignor, and Kelly is the assignee. The effect of the assignment is to extinguish the assignor's right to receive performance and to transfer that right to the assignee. In the above example, Kelly now

**Assignment**

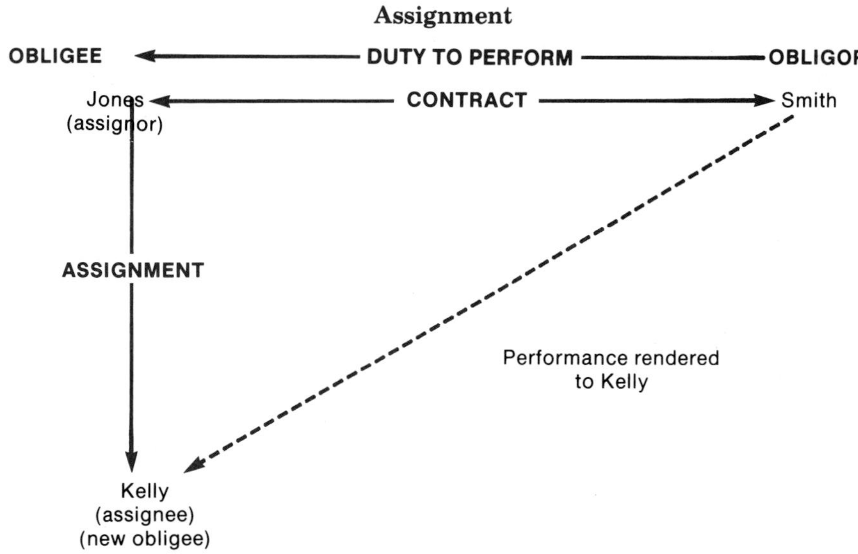

owns the right to collect payment from Smith. If Smith fails to pay, Kelly can file suit against Smith to collect the debt.

An assignment can be made in any way that is sufficient to show the assignor's intent to assign. No formal language is required, and unless the case falls within some provision of the statute of frauds, no writing is required. An assignment can be given away as well as sold, so consideration is not required for an effective assignment.

**Assignability of Rights.** Most, but not all, contract rights are assignable. Although the free assignability of contract rights performs a valuable function in our modern credit-based economy, assignment is undesirable if it would adversely affect some important public policy or if it would materially vary the bargained-for expectations of the parties. There are three basic limitations on the assignability of contract rights.

First, an assignment will not be effective if it is *contrary to public policy.* For example, most states have enacted statutes that prohibit or regulate a wage earner's assignment of future wages. These statutes are designed to protect people against unwisely impoverishing themselves by signing away their future incomes.

Second, an assignment will not be effective if it *adversely affects the obligor in some significant way.* An assignment is ineffective if it materially changes the obligor's duty or increases the burden or risk on the obligor. Naturally, any assignment will change an obligor's duty to some extent. The obligor will have to pay money or deliver goods or render some other performance to X instead of to Y. These changes are not considered to be sufficiently material to render an assignment ineffective. Thus, a right to receive money or goods or land is generally assignable. In addition, covenants not to compete are generally considered to be assignable to buyers of businesses. For example, if Jones sells RX Drugstore to Smith, including in the contract of sale a covenant whereby Jones promises not to operate a competing drugstore within a 30-mile radius of RX for 10 years after the sale, and Smith later sells RX to Kelly, Kelly could enforce the covenant not to compete against Jones. The reason for permitting assignment of covenants not to compete is that the purpose of such covenants is to protect an asset of the business—goodwill—for which the buyer has paid.

An assignment could be ineffective because of its variation of the obligor's duty, however, if the contract right involved a *personal relationship* or an element of *personal skill, judgment, or character.* For this reason, contracts of employment in which an employee works under the direct and personal supervision of an employer cannot be assigned to a new employer. As you will see in *The Evening News Association* case, however, contracts of employment that do not involve personal supervision by an individual employer can be assigned.

A purported assignment would be ineffective if it significantly increased the burden of the obligor's performance. For example, if Smith contracts to sell Jones all of Jones's requirements of wheat, a purported assignment of Jones's rights to a corporation that has much greater requirements of wheat would probably be ineffective because it would significantly increase the burden on Smith.

A contract right may also be nonassignable because *the original contract expressly forbids assignment.* Anti-assignment clauses in contracts are not always enforced, however. Because of the strong public policy favoring assignability, anti-assignment clauses are viewed with disfavor and are interpreted narrowly. For example, a court might interpret a contractual ban on assignment as prohibiting only the delegation of duties. It might view an assignment made in violation of an anti-assignment clause as a breach of contract for which damages may be recovered, but not as an invalidation of the assignment. The UCC provides that unless a contrary intent is shown, an anti-assignment clause that purports to forbid assignment of the contract should be interpreted as forbidding only the delegation of duties [2–210(3)]. In addition, a right to damages for breach of a sales contract may be assigned despite an agreement prohibiting assignment.

## The Evening News Association v. Peterson

**477 F. Supp. 77 (D.D.C. 1979)**

Gordon Peterson was employed by Post-Newsweek as a newscaster-anchorman on station WTOP–TV (Channel 9) under a three-year employment contract that was to end June 30, 1980, and could be extended for two additional one-year terms at the option of Post-Newsweek. In June 1978, Post-Newsweek sold its operating license to the Evening News Association (Evening News), and Channel 9 was then designated as WDVM–TV. The contract of sale between Post-Newsweek and Evening News provided for the assignment of all contracts, including Peterson's employment contract. Peterson continued working for the station for more than a year after the change of ownership and received all of the compensation and benefits provided by his contract with Post-Newsweek. In early August 1979, he negotiated a new contract with a competing television station and tendered his resignation to Evening News. Evening News sued Peterson. Peterson defended on the ground that his employment contract was not assignable.

**Parker, District Judge.** Contract rights as a general rule are assignable. This rule, however, is subject to exception where the assignment would vary materially the duty of the obligor, increase materially the burden or risk imposed by the contract, or impair materially the obligor's chance of obtaining return performance. There has been no showing, however, that the services required of Peterson by the Post-Newsweek contract have changed in any material way since Evening News entered the picture. Both before and after, he anchored the same news programs. Similarly he has had essentially the same number of special assignments since the transfer as before.

The general rule of assignability is also subject to exception where the contract calls for the rendition of personal services based on a relationship of confidence between the parties. In *Munchak Corp. v. Cunningham,* the court concluded that a basketball player's personal services contract could be assigned by the owner of the club to a new owner, despite a contractual prohibition on assignment to another club, on the basis that the services were to the club. The court found it inconceivable that the player's services could be affected by the personalities of successive corporate owners. The policy against the assignment of personal services contracts is to prohibit an assignment of a contract in which the obligor undertakes to serve only the original obligee.

Given the silence of the contract on assignability, this court cannot but conclude on the facts of this case that Peterson's contract was assignable. Peterson's contract with Post-Newsweek gives no hint that he was to perform as other than a newscaster-anchorman for their stations. Nor is there any hint that he was to work with particular Post-

Newsweek employees or was assured a policy-making role in concert with any given employees. Peterson's employer was a corporation, and it was for Post-Newsweek that he contracted to perform. The corporation's duties under the contract did not involve the rendition of personal services to Peterson; essentially they were to compensate him. Nor does the contract give any suggestion of a relation of special confidence between the two or that Peterson was expected to serve the Post-Newsweek stations only so long as the latter had the license for them.

Judgment for Evening News.

**Limitations on Assignee's Right to Receive Performance.** When an assignment occurs, the assignee is said to "step into the shoes of his assignor." This means that the assignee acquires all of the rights that his assignor had under the contract. The assignee has the right to receive the obligor's performance, and if performance is not forthcoming, the assignee has the right to sue in his own name for breach of the obligation. By the same token, the assignee acquires no greater rights than those possessed by the assignor. As the case of *Bruder v. State* demonstrates, the assignee is subject to any claims or defenses that the obligor could have asserted against the assignor. For example, if Smith induces Jones's consent to a contract by duress and subsequently assigns his rights under the contract to Kelly, Jones can assert the doctrine of duress against Kelly as a ground for avoiding the contract.

**Necessity for Notifying Obligor of Assignment.** Assignees should promptly notify the obligor of the assignment. This is necessary because if the obligor does not have reason to know of the assignment, she could render performance to the assignor and claim that her obligation had been discharged by performance. An obligor who renders performance to the assignor without notice of the assignment has no further liability under the contract. However, once the obligor has been given notice of the assignment, she remains liable to the assignee even if she later renders performance to the assignor. For example, Smith borrows $500 from Jones, promising to repay the debt by June 1. Jones assigns the debt to Kelly, but no one informs Smith of the assignment, and Smith pays the $500 to the original obligee, Jones. In this case, Smith is not liable for any further payment. But if Kelly had immediately notified Smith of the assignment and, after receiving notice, Smith had mistakenly paid the debt to Jones, Smith would still have the legal obligation to pay $500 to Kelly.

An assignor who accepts performance from the obligor after the assignment holds any benefits that he receives as a trustee for the assignee. If the assignor fails to pay those benefits to the assignee, however, an obligor who has notice of the assignment and renders performance to the wrong person may have to pay the same debt twice.

**Successive Assignments.** Notice to the obligor may be important in one other situation. If an assignor assigns the same right to two assignees in succession, both of whom pay for the assignment, a question of priority results. An assignor who assigns the same right to different people will be held liable to the assignee who acquires no rights against the obligor, but which assignee is entitled to the obligor's performance? Which assignee will have recourse only against the assignor? There are several views on this point.

In states that follow the "American rule," the first assignee has the better right. This view is based on the rule of property law that a person cannot transfer greater rights in property that he owns. In states that follow the "English rule," however, the assignee who first gives notice of the assignment to the obligor, without knowledge of the other assignee's claim, has the better right. The *Restatement (Second) of Contracts* takes a third position. Section 342 of the *Restatement* provides that the first assignee has priority unless the subsequent assignee gives value (pays for the assignment) and, without having reason to know of the other assignee's claim, does one of the following: obtains payment of the obligation, gets a judgment against the obligor, obtains a new contract with the obligor by novation, or possesses a writing of a type customarily accepted as a symbol or evidence of the right assigned (such as a passbook for a savings account).

**Assignor's Warranty Liability to Assignee.** Suppose that Smith, a 16-year-old boy, contracts to buy a used car for $2,000 from Jones. Smith pays Jones $500 as a down payment and agrees to pay the balance in equal monthly installments. Jones assigns his right to receive the balance of the purchase price to Kelly, who pays $1,000 in cash for the assignment. Later, when Kelly attempts to enforce the contract, however, Smith disaffirms the contract on grounds of lack of capacity. Thus, Kelly has paid $1,000 for a worthless claim. Does Kelly have any recourse against Jones? When an assignor is *paid* for making an assignment, the assignor is held to have made certain *implied warranties* about the claim assigned.

The assignor impliedly warrants that the claim assigned is *valid.* This means that the obligor has capacity to contract, the contract is not illegal, the contract is not voidable for any other reason known to the assignor (such as fraud or duress), and the contract has not been discharged prior to assignment. The assignor also warrants that she has *good title* to the rights assigned and that any written instrument representing the assigned claim is *genuine.* In addition, the assignor impliedly agrees that she *will not do anything to impair the value of the assignment.* These guarantees are imposed by law unless the assignment agreement clearly indicates to the contrary. One important aspect of the assigned right that the assignor does *not* impliedly warrant, however, is that the obligor is *solvent.*

## Bruder v. State

**601 S.W.2d 102 (Tex. Civ. App. 1980)**

John Handy Jones paid Richard Sullivan, the chief of the Addison Police Department, $6,400 in exchange for Sullivan's cooperation in allowing Jones and others to bring marijuana by airplane into the Addison airport without police intervention. Instead of performing the requested service, Sullivan arrested Jones. The $6,400 was turned over to the district attorney's office and was introduced into evidence in the subsequent trial, in which Jones was tried for and convicted of bribery. After his conviction, Jones assigned his alleged claim to the $6,400 to Melvyn Bruder. Based on the assignment, Bruder brought suit against the state of Texas to obtain possession of the money. The trial court rendered judgment for the state, and Bruder appealed.

**CARVER, JUSTICE.** The law is well settled that no legal right arises out of an unlawful act; and no action can be maintained upon a claim arising out of or based upon an illegal act. Because Jones could assert no claim to the bribe money itself, we hold that Bruder, as Jones's assignee, can make no better claim than his assignor.

Judgment for the state affirmed.

## DELEGATION OF DUTIES

**Nature of Delegation.** A delegation of duties occurs when an obligor indicates his intent to appoint another person to perform his duties under a contract. For example, Smith buys Jones's retail furniture business. The business has several existing contracts to deliver furniture to customers. As a part of the sale of the business, Jones assigns the rights in the existing contracts to Smith and delegates to him the performance of those contracts. Regarding the delegation of duties involved in this transaction, Jones is the *delegating party,* Smith is the *delegate,* and the customers to whom performance is due are the obligees.

In contrast to an assignment of a *right,* which extinguishes the assignor's right and transfers it to the assignee, the delegation of a *duty* does *not* extinguish the duty owed by the delegating party. The delegating party remains liable to the obligee unless the obligee agrees to substitute the delegate's promise for that of the delegating party (this is called a **novation,** and will be discussed in greater detail below). This makes sense, because if it were possible for a person to escape his duties under a contract by merely delegating them to another, any party to a contract could avoid liability by delegating duties to an insolvent acquaintance.

The significance of an effective delegation is that *performance* by the delegate will dis-

**Delegation**

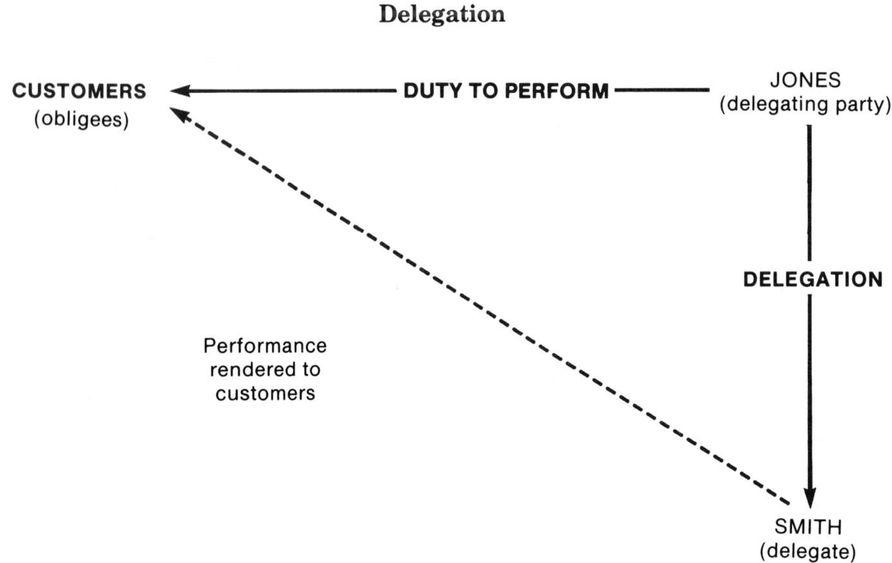

charge the delegating party. In addition, if the duty is a delegable one, the obligee cannot insist on performance by the delegating party; he must accept the performance of the delegate.

**Delegable Duties.** A duty that can be performed fully by a number of different persons is delegable. Not all duties are delegable, however. The grounds for finding a duty to be nondelegable resemble closely the grounds for finding a right to be nonassignable. Both the UCC [2–210(1)] and section 318(2) of the *Restatement (Second) of Contracts* take the position that a party to a contract may delegate his duty to perform to another person unless the parties have agreed to the contrary or unless the other party has a "substantial interest" in having the original obligor perform the acts required by the contract. The key factor used in determining whether the obligee has such a substantial interest is the degree to which performance is dependent on the individual traits, skill, or judgment of the person who owes the duty to perform. For example, if Jones hires Smith, a lawyer, to perform certain specialized legal services, Smith could not effectively delegate her duty to perform to another lawyer over Jones's objections. Similarly, an employee could not delegate her performance under a contract of employment to another person. A duty is also nondelegable if delegation would violate public policy or if the original contract between the parties forbids delegation.

**Language Creating a Delegation.** No special, formal language is necessary to create an effective delegation of duties. In fact, since parties frequently confuse the terms *assignment* and *delegation,* one of the problems frequently presented to courts is determining whether the parties intended an assignment only or both an assignment and a delegation. Unless the agreement indicates a contrary intent, courts tend to interpret assignments as *including* a delegation of the assignor's duties. Both the UCC [2–210(4)] and section 328 of the *Restatement (Second) of Contracts* provide that unless the language or the circumstances indicate to the contrary, general language of assignment such as an assignment of "the contract" or of "all my rights under the contract" is to be interpreted as creating *both* an assignment and a delegation. Such an interpretation is not justifiable in all circumstances, however. The *Newton* case, which follows, presents a situation in which the circumstances surrounding the assignment indicated that the parties did not intend a delegation.

**Assumption of Duties by Delegate.** A delegation gives the delegate the right to perform the duties of the delegating party. The mere fact that duties have been delegated does not, however, place legal responsibility on the delegate to perform. The delegate who fails to perform will not be liable to either the delegating party or the obligee unless the delegate has *assumed* the duty by expressly or impliedly undertaking the obligation to perform. Frequently, a term of the contract between the delegating party and the delegate provides that the delegate assumes responsibility for performance. A common example of this is the *assumption* of an existing mortgage debt by a purchaser of real estate. Suppose Smith buys a house from Jones, agreeing to assume the outstanding mortgage on the property held by First Bank. By this assumption, Smith undertakes personal liability to both Jones and First Bank. If Smith fails to make the mortgage payments, First Bank has a cause of action against Smith personally. An assumption does *not* release the delegating party from liability, however. Rather, it creates a situation in which both the delegating party and the assuming delegate owe duties to the obligee. If the assuming delegate fails to pay, the delegating party can be held liable. Thus, in the example described above, if Smith fails to make mortgage payments and First Bank is unable to collect the debt from Smith, it can sue Jones. Jones, of course, would have an action against Smith for breach of their contract.

**Discharge of Delegating Party by Novation.** As you have seen, the mere delegation of duties—even when the delegate assumes those duties—does not release the delegating party from her legal obligation to the obligee. A delegating party can, however, be discharged from performance by **novation.** A novation occurs when the obligee agrees to release the delegating party in exchange for the delegate's promise to perform. A novation requires more than the obligee's consent to having the delegate perform the duties. In the example used above, the mere fact that First Bank accepted mortgage payments from Smith would not create a novation. Rather, the language used by the parties or the circumstances of the case must show that the obligee consents to the *substitution* of one obligor for another.

---

## Newton v. Merchants & Farmers Bank of Dumas

**668 S.W.2d 51 (Ark. Ct. App. 1984)**

Wayne Newton, a general contractor, had a contract with Aubrey Mitcherson to construct an addition to the Delta Motor Lodge. Newton subcontracted the plumbing work for the project to Kenneth Rogers. Rogers agreed to do the plumbing work for $22,100, to be paid in three installments. To have cash ready to meet expenses before the first installment was paid, Rogers borrowed $15,500 from the Merchants & Farmers Bank. In return for the money, Rogers signed a consumer note and security agreement in which he assigned his subcontract for the Delta job to the bank. On November 11, the bank sent Newton a letter giving him notice of the assignment. The letter requested Newton to make all checks payable to Rogers *and* the bank. Newton responded by sending a letter to the bank acknowledging the assignment and promising to issue payments jointly to Rogers and the bank. On March 12, Newton wrote a check for $7,085 to Rogers alone, not naming the bank as copayee.

Rogers paid his general operating expenses for the Delta job, but failed to pay one of his suppliers, Southern Pipe and Supply Company, which had supplied Rogers with plumbing fixtures for the job. Rogers completed the job, but Newton never paid him the balance due on the subcontract. Rogers defaulted on the loan to the bank, and the bank filed suit against Newton to enforce the assigned subcontract. Newton argued that the assignment of Rogers's subcontract also delegated to the bank the duty to pay Southern Pipe. The trial court awarded judgment for the bank, and Newton appealed.

**Glaze, Judge.** The only argument we need address is Newton's contention that Rogers delegated to the Bank his duty to pay Southern Pipe for the plumbing fixtures as well as his right to receive payments under the subcontract. The *Restatement (Second) of Contracts* section 328(1) states:

> Unless the language or the circumstances indicate to the contrary, as in an assignment for security, an assignment of "the contract" or of "all my rights under the contract" or an assignment in similar general terms is an assignment of the assignor's rights and a delegation of his unperformed duties under the contract.

In applying the foregoing rule to the facts at bar, we observe that the language of the consumer note and security agreement Rogers signed to get the loan from the Bank describes the assignment as a "security interest" to secure the $15,500 loan. In addition, the Bank's letter of February 11 to Newton formally notified Newton that the assignment of Rogers's subcontract was to secure the loan. Newton was well aware that Rogers assigned his right to payments for the plumbing work to the Bank to obtain the capital necessary to start the job. There is no evidence showing the Bank intended to perform Rogers's duties under the contract.

In fact, the most convincing evidence of Rogers's *non-delegation* of his duty to pay Southern Pipe is Newton's omission of the Bank as payee on the initial check to Rogers for $7,085. In brief, if Newton had believed then, as he asserts now, that the Bank was responsible for paying Southern Pipe, he surely would have included the Bank as payee on the check.

We conclude that Rogers assigned his right to payments on his subcontract with Newton, and such assignment did not delegate to the Bank his duty to pay Southern Pipe.

Judgment for the Bank affirmed.

## THIRD PARTY BENEFICIARIES

There are many situations in which the performance of a contract would constitute some benefit to a person who was not a party to the contract. Despite the fact that a nonparty may expect to derive advantage from the performance of a contract, the general rule is that no one but the parties to a contract or their assignees can enforce it. In some situations, however, parties contract for the purpose of benefiting some third person. In such cases, the benefit to the third person is an essential part of the contract, not just an incidental result of a contract that was really designed to benefit the parties. Where the parties to a contract *intended* to benefit a third party, courts will give effect to their intent and permit the third party to enforce the contract. Such third parties are called **third party beneficiaries.**

**Intended Beneficiaries versus Incidental Beneficiaries.** For a third person (other than an assignee) to have the right to enforce a contract, she must be able to establish that the contract was made with the *intent* to benefit her. A few courts have required that *both* parties must have intended to benefit the third party. Most courts, however, have found it to be sufficient if the person to whom the promise to perform was made (the *promisee*) intended to benefit the third party. In ascertaining intent to benefit the third party, a court will look at the language used by the parties and all the surrounding circumstances. One factor that is frequently important in determining intent to benefit is whether the party making the promise to perform (the *promisor*) was to render performance directly to the third party. For example, if Smith contracts with Jones Florist to deliver flowers to Kelly, the fact that performance was to be rendered to Kelly would be good evidence that the parties intended to benefit Kelly. This factor is not conclusive, however. There are some cases in which intent to benefit a third party has been found even though performance was to be rendered to the promisee rather than to the third party. Intended beneficiaries are often classified as either *donee* or *creditor* beneficiaries. These classifications are discussed in greater detail below.

A third party who is unable to establish that the contract was made with the intent to benefit her is called an *incidental beneficiary.* A third party is classified as an incidental beneficiary when the benefit derived by that third party was merely an unintended by-product of a contract that was created for the benefit of those who were parties to it. As you will see in the *David v. J. Elrod Realtors* case, incidental beneficiaries acquire no rights under a contract. For example, Smith contracts with Jones Construction Company to build a valuable structure on Smith's land. The performance of the contract would constitute a benefit to Kelly, Smith's next-door neighbor, by increasing the value of Kelly's land. The contract between Smith and Jones was made for the purpose of benefiting them, however. Any advantage derived by Kelly is purely incidental to their primary purpose. Thus, Kelly could not sue and recover damages if either Smith or Jones breaches the contract.

As a general rule, members of the public are held to be incidental beneficiaries of contracts entered into by their municipalities or other governmental units in the regular course of carrying on governmental functions. A member of the public cannot recover a judgment in a suit against a promisor of such a contract, even though all taxpayers will suffer some injury from nonperformance. A different result may be reached, however, if a party contracting with a governmental unit agrees to reimburse members of the public for damages or if the party undertakes to perform some duty for individual members of the public.

**Donee Beneficiaries.** If the promisee's primary purpose in contracting is to make a *gift* of the agreed-upon performance to a third party, that third party is classified as a *donee beneficiary.* If the contract is breached, the donee beneficiary will have a cause of action against the promisor, but not against the promisee (donor). For example, Smith contracts with Perpetual Life Insurance Company, agreeing to pay premiums in return for which Perpetual agrees to pay $100,000 to Smith's husband when Smith dies. Smith's husband is a donee beneficiary, and can bring suit and recover judgment against Perpetual if Smith dies and Perpetual does not pay.

**Creditor Beneficiaries.** If the promisor's performance is intended to *satisfy a legal duty* that the promisee owes to a third party, the third party is a *creditor beneficiary.* The creditor beneficiary has rights against *both* the promisee (because of the original obligation) and the promisor. For example, Smith buys a car on credit from Jones Auto Sales. Smith later sells the car to Kelly, who agrees to pay the balance due on the car to Jones. In this case, Jones is a creditor beneficiary and can sue both Kelly and Smith if Kelly does not perform.

**Defenses against Beneficiary.** The promisor who breaches a contract that was intended to benefit a third party is subject to suit by both the promisee and the third party beneficiary. Since the rights of the third party beneficiary derive from the original contract between the promisor and the promisee, any circumstances that make that contract unenforceable or voidable can defeat the claim of the third party beneficiary. In a suit brought by the third party beneficiary against the promisor, the promisor can assert any defenses against the third party beneficiary that he could assert against the promisee (such as fraud and lack of consideration).

**Vesting of Beneficiary's Rights.** Another possible threat to the interests of the third party beneficiary is that the promisor and the promisee might modify or discharge their contract so as to extinguish or alter the beneficiary's rights. For example, Jones, who owes $500 to Smith, enters into a contract with Kelly whereby Kelly agrees to pay the $500 to Smith. What happens if, before Smith is paid, Kelly pays the money to Jones and Jones accepts it or Kelly and Jones otherwise modify the contract? Courts have held that there is a point at which the rights of the beneficiary *vest,* and the beneficiary is no longer subject to loss of his claim by modification or discharge. A modification or discharge that occurs after the beneficiary's rights have vested cannot be asserted as a defense to a suit brought by the beneficiary. The exact time at which the beneficiary's rights vest differs from jurisdiction to jurisdiction. Some courts have held that vesting occurs when the contract is formed. A second view is that vesting occurs when the beneficiary learns of the contract and consents to it. A third view is that vesting does not occur until the beneficiary does some act in reliance on the promise that was made for his benefit.

The contracting parties' ability to vary the rights of the third party beneficiary can also be affected by the terms of their agreement. A provision of the contract between the promisor and the promisee stating that the duty to the beneficiary cannot be modified would be effective to prevent modification. Likewise, a contract provision in which the parties specifically reserved the right to change beneficiaries or modify the duty to the beneficiary would be enforced. Provisions reserving the right to change beneficiaries are very common in insurance contracts.

## David v. J. Elrod Realtors on Devon, Inc.

**394 N.E.2d 583 (Ill. Ct. App. 1979)**

Robert and Lorraine Alawerdy employed J. Elrod Realtors to find a buyer for real estate that they owned in Chicago. Under the agreement, the Alawerdys promised to pay Elrod a 6 percent broker's commission. In April 1976, Ted and Fe David entered into a sales contract with the Alawerdys to buy the property. The sales contract, which empowered Elrod to act as broker and escrowee, was executed on a form provided by Elrod. It required the Davids to obtain a commitment for a mortgage loan within 21 days. Pursuant to the contract, the Davids deposited $3,600 in escrow with Elrod. The Davids made their best efforts to secure a mortgage loan but were unable to do so. Since the 21 days had elapsed, the Alawerdys notified the Davids that the contract was canceled and directed Elrod to return the $3,600 that the Davids had paid. Elrod returned $1,450 of the money but kept the remaining $2,150, which represented the commission it would have earned had the sale been consummated. The Davids brought suit for the return of their money. The trial court entered judgment for Elrod, and the Davids appealed.

**CAMPBELL, JUSTICE.** As a general rule only a party to a contract or those in privity with him may enforce the contract, except that a third party beneficiary may sue for a breach of a contract made for his benefit. For a person to assert the rights of a third party beneficiary the contract must clearly show that the benefit was not solely incidental but that the contract was made for his direct benefit. The mere fact that a person relied upon a contract or was injured by a breach of contract does not create a right to pursue a claim for breach of contract which he otherwise would not have had. An examination of the agreement indicates that only the Alawerdys and the Davids were parties to this contract. Elrod did not sign this contract, nor has Elrod claimed any assignment by the Alawerdys of any of the Alawerdys' rights under the sales agreement. There is no provision in the contract authorizing Elrod to unilaterally determine that there was a default or breach by the Davids or to determine that Elrod was entitled to and earned a brokers commission. Elrod has offered no legal theory to justify the retention of any portion of the earnest money deposit after having been directed by the sellers to return said deposit. We find that there is no support in the record entitling Elrod to any rights under the contract either express or implied except as mere custodians of funds.

Judgment reversed in favor of the Davids.

## SUMMARY

There are two situations in which people who were not parties to a contract can claim rights under the contract. The first is where there has been an **assignment** of a contract right. An assignment occurs when a person (the assignor) who has a right to receive the performance of an obligor transfers that right to a third person (the assignee). An assignment extinguishes the rights of the assignor and gives the assignee the right to enforce the contract. Most contract rights can be assigned. There are, however, three limitations on assignability. First, an assignment that would materially change the obligor's duty or increase the risk or burden on the obligor will be held ineffective. Second, an assignment that would violate public policy will be held ineffective. Third, an agreement between the assignor and the obligor specifically prohibiting assignment of rights will prevent effective assignment if the agreement is held to be enforceable. Courts tend to interpret such agreements narrowly, however.

The assignee is subject to any claims or defenses that the obligor could have asserted against the assignor. The obligor must be notified of the assignment, or his rendering of performance to the assignor will be a discharge of the claim. In making an assignment, the assignor impliedly warrants that he has title to the claim, that any writings on which the claim is based are genuine, that the claim is valid, and that he will not do anything to defeat or impair the value of the claim. Thus, the assignee will be able to recover damages from the assignor if the assignee's rights are defeated by a defense asserted by the obligor. The assignor is also subject to liability to the assignee if he collects the assigned claim or if he causes the assignee to lose his right to the performance by making successive assignments of the same claim. The assignor does not, however, impliedly warrant the obligor's solvency.

The appointment of another person (the delegate) to perform the duties of the obligor (delegating party) under a contract is called a **delegation.** Duties are delegable unless the obligee has a substantial interest in having the delegating party perform or supervise the performance of the contract (as where performance depends on the personal skill, discretion, or character of the delegating party), or public policy would be violated by a delegation, or the parties have agreed in their contract that delegation will not be permitted. Unless the language of the contract or the surrounding circumstances indicate to the contrary, general language of assignment is held to constitute a delegation of duties as well as an assignment of rights. An effective delegation only means that performance by the delegate will discharge the duty. It does *not* release the delegating party from his duty to the obligee.

The delegate is not under a legal duty to perform unless he has expressly or impliedly *assumed* the duty of performance. When the delegate assumes the duty, he undertakes a legal duty to both the delegating party and the obligee. Assumption does not discharge the delegating party. When assumption occurs, both the delegating party and the delegate are under a duty to the obligee. The delegating party remains liable for the performance of the duty unless the obligee has released him by **novation.** A novation occurs when the obligee agrees to release the delegating party in return for the delegate's promise to perform. The obligee's mere acceptance of performance from the delegate—even when there has been an assumption—is not sufficient to constitute a novation. Some further consent to substitute the delegate's duty to perform for that of the delegating party is necessary for a novation.

A second situation in which a third party can claim rights under a contract occurs when the contracting parties made the contract with the intent to benefit a third person. Such third persons are called **third party beneficiaries.** In order to claim rights as a third party beneficiary, the third party must prove that she was an *intended beneficiary.* This means that she must prove that the promisee intended to benefit her. Intended beneficiaries are generally classified as either *donee beneficiaries* or *creditor beneficiaries.* When the promisee intended to bestow the promised performance as a gift, the beneficiary is called a donee beneficiary. When the promisee intended the performance to satisfy a legal duty to the third party, the beneficiary is called a creditor beneficiary. If a person can prove that she was an intended beneficiary, either donee or creditor, she can bring suit to enforce the contract. The creditor beneficiary will also have rights against the promisee under the original obligation. When the benefit to a third person is merely incidental, and the contracting parties formed the contract primarily for their own benefit, the third person is classified as an *incidental beneficiary.* An incidental beneficiary has no rights under a contract, and cannot sue for its nonperformance.

Although intended beneficiaries can sue to enforce a contract, they are subject to any defenses that the promisor could assert against the promisee. Unless the contracting parties have agreed not to modify the rights of the third party beneficiary, those rights are subject to modification or discharge by the original contracting parties if the modification or discharge occurs before the rights of the third party beneficiary have *vested.* There are several views about the time at which the rights of a third party beneficiary vest (become invulnerable to modification or discharge). The variation of the rights of a third party beneficiary can be affected by an agreement between the contracting parties forbidding modification or reserving the right to modify.

## PROBLEM CASES

1. Davis owned a tract of land whose mineral deposits he sold to Basalt Rock Company. As part of the consideration for the conveyance of the land, Basalt agreed that over a period of 60 years it would sell Davis, "as he

may require, such amount of basalt of any size for plastering purposes" at an agreed price. The contract further provided that "the price is based on a blend of basalt in accordance with the formula attached." The contract gave Davis the right to change the formula and provided for price adjustments to compensate for the changes. Davis assigned the contract to Soule. Basalt refused to recognize the assignment and refused to make deliveries to Soule. Soule sued Basalt for breach of contract, and Basalt asserted that the contract was not assignable. Was it?

**2.** Southern Sports Corporation owned a professional basketball club, the Cougars. Cunningham contracted with Southern to play basketball for the Cougars. His contract prohibited its assignment to another "club" without Cunningham's consent. Southern assigned the club and Cunningham's contract to Munchak Corporation. Cunningham then refused to play for the Cougars, contending that the contract had been illegally assigned to Munchak. Was Cunningham's contract assignable?

**3.** Milford sold a registered quarter horse, Hired Chico, to Stewart. The parties signed a written contract in which Milford reserved the right to two breedings each year on Hired Chico, "regardless to whom the horse may be sold to." Stewart later sold the horse to McKinnie, who knew of and had read the contract between Milford and Stewart. After McKinnie purchased the horse, he refused to permit Milford any of the breedings provided for in the original agreement. Was McKinnie obligated by the terms of the contract?

**4.** In July 1977, there was a massive power failure in New York City. Strauss, a tenant in a building owned by Belle Realty Corporation, was injured during the blackout when he descended an unlighted stairway in the basement of his apartment building to search for running water. Strauss brought suit against the utility company, Consolidated Edison, which was under contract with Belle to provide electricity to the building. Can Strauss claim rights as a third party beneficiary?

**5.** Goodell was a stockholder of Better Baked Foods, Inc. and served as a director and attorney for Better Baked. Goodell entered into a contract with K.T. Enterprises whereby K.T. agreed to build a continuous belt conveyor system in accordance with certain specifications and to ship the unit to Better Baked and install it there according to its direction. Although all of the parties knew that the conveyor was for Better Baked's pizza-freezing business, the contract provided that Goodell would take title to the system. The conveyor that K.T. produced did not meet specifications, and ultimately a substitute system had to be procured from another company at a cost of $12,820 more than Goodell's contract price. Better Baked sued K.T. for breach of the contract. Can Better Baked enforce the contract?

**6.** By a contract with the New York State Thruway Authority, Ettinger was given the exclusive franchise to operate a towing service along a certain stretch of the Thruway. The contract provided that Ettinger would respond to service calls within 30 minutes. Ettinger failed to respond at all to a call for assistance made by Kornblut, who died of a heart attack while attempting to repair his car himself. Kornblut's widow sued Ettinger for breach of contract, claiming that Kornblut was a third party beneficiary of the franchise contract. Can Mrs. Kornblut recover damages?

# Chapter 15

# Performance and Remedies

## INTRODUCTION

Contracts are often formed before either of the parties renders any actual performance to the other. A person may be content to bargain for and receive the other person's promise at the formation stage of a contract, because this permits him to plan for the future. Ultimately, however, all parties bargain for the *performance* of the promises that have been made to them.

In most contracts, each party carries out his promise and is *discharged* from further obligation under the contract when his performance is complete. Sometimes, however, a person fails to perform or performs in a manner that is unsatisfactory to the other party. In such cases, courts are often called upon to determine the respective rights and duties of the parties. This frequently involves deciding such questions as whether performance was due, whether the contract was breached, to what extent it was breached, and what the consequences of the breach should be. This task is made more difficult by the fact that contracts often fail to specify the consequences of nonperformance or defective performance. In deciding questions involving the performance of contracts and remedies for breach of contract, courts draw upon a variety of legal principles that attempt to do justice, prevent forfeiture and unjust enrichment, and effectuate the parties' presumed intent.

This chapter presents an overview of the legal concepts that are used to resolve disputes arising in the performance stage of contracting. It includes a discussion of the remedies that are used when a court determines that a contract has been breached.

## CONDITIONS

**Nature of Conditions.** One issue that frequently arises in the performance stage of a contract is whether performance is due. Some duties are *unconditional* or *absolute*—that is, the duty to perform does not depend on the occurrence of any further event other than the passage of time. For example, if Jones promises to pay Smith $100, Jones's duty is unconditional. When a party's duty is unconditional, it is clear that he has the duty to perform unless his performance is *excused.* The various excuses for nonperformance will be discussed later in this chapter. When a duty is unconditional, the promisor's failure to perform constitutes a *breach of contract.*

In many situations, however, a promisor's duty to perform depends on the occurrence of some event that is called a **condition.** A condition is an uncertain, future event that affects a party's duty to perform. For example, if Jones contracts to buy Smith's house on condition that First Bank approve Jones's application for a mortgage loan by January 10, Jones's duty to buy Smith's house is *conditioned* on the bank's approving his loan application by January 10. When a promisor's duty is conditional, his duty to perform is affected by the occurrence of the condition. In this case, if the condition does not occur, Jones has no duty to buy the house. Thus, his failure to buy it because of the nonoccurrence of the condition will *not* constitute a breach of contract.

Almost any event can be a condition. Some conditions are beyond the control of either party, such as when Smith promises to buy Jones's business if the prime rate drops by a specified amount. Others are within the control of a party, such as when one party's performance of a duty under the contract is a condition of the other party's duty to perform.

**Types of Conditions.** There are several different ways of classifying conditions. One way of classifying conditions focuses on the time at which the duty of performance arises. When the duty to perform does not arise until the happening of an event, the condition is called a **condition precedent.** In the hypothetical case described above in which Jones's duty to buy Smith's house was conditioned on the bank's approving Jones's loan application, Jones's duty was subject to a condition precedent.

When each party's duty to perform arises at the same time, each person's performance is conditioned on the performance or **tender** of performance (offer of performance) by the other. Such conditions are called **concurrent conditions.** For example, if Smith promises to buy Jones's car for $5,000, the parties' respective duties to perform are subject to a concurrent condition. Smith does not have the duty to perform unless Jones tenders his performance, and vice versa.

In some situations, the parties may agree that the duty to perform may be discharged by the occurrence of some future, uncertain event. Such conditions are called **conditions subsequent.** For example, Smith and Jones agree that Smith will begin paying Jones $2,000 per month but that if XYZ Corporation dissolves, Smith's obligation to pay will cease. In this case, Smith's duty to pay is subject to being discharged by a condition subsequent. The major significance of the distinction between conditions precedent and conditions subsequent is that the plaintiff bears the burden of proving the occurrence of a condition precedent, while the defendant bears the burden of proving the occurrence of a condition subsequent.

Another way of classifying conditions is to focus on the means by which the condition is imposed. A condition that is specified in the language of the parties' contract is called an **express condition.** For example, if Smith promises to sell his regular season football tickets to Jones *on condition that* Indiana University wins the Rose Bowl, Indiana's winning the Rose Bowl is an express condition of Smith's duty to sell the tickets.

A condition that is not specifically stated by the parties but is *implied* by the nature of the parties' promises is called an **implied-in-fact** condition. For example, if Smith promises to unload cargo from Jones's ship, the ship's arrival in port would be an implied-in-fact condition of Smith's duty to unload the cargo. Express conditions and implied-in-fact conditions must be strictly complied with to give rise to the duty of performance.

Sometimes, conditions are imposed by law rather than by the agreement of the parties. Such conditions are called **constructive conditions** or **implied-in-law conditions.** Courts impose constructive conditions to do justice between the parties. In bilateral contracts that do not state the date for performance or that call for an exchange of performances, the law normally infers that each party's performance is a constructive condition of the other party's duty to perform. For example, if Smith promises to buy Jones's motorcycle for $900, Smith will have the duty to pay only if Jones tenders the motorcycle and Jones will have the duty to tender the motorcycle only if Smith tenders the money. (This would also be an example of a concurrent condition.) Without such a constructive condition, a person who did not receive the performance promised him would still have to render his own performance.

**Creation of Express Conditions.** Although no particular language is required to create an express condition, the conditional nature of promises is usually indicated by such words as *provided that, on condition that, if, when, while, after,* and *as soon as*. *Norton v. Herron,* which follows, involves the question whether a contract provision is to be interpreted as a condition. The following discussion explores two common types of express conditions.

**Satisfaction of Third Parties.** It is common for building and construction contracts to provide that the property owner's duty to pay is conditioned on the builder's production of certificates to be issued by a specific architect or engineer. These certificates indicate the satisfaction of the architect or engineer with the builder's work. They often are issued at each stage of completion, after the architect or engineer has inspected the work done.

The standard usually used to determine whether the condition has occurred is a *good faith* standard. As a general rule, if the architect or engineer is acting honestly and has some good faith reason for withholding a certificate, the builder cannot recover payments due. In legal terms, the condition that will create the owner's duty to pay has not occurred. The rationale for this is that the court will not substitute its judgment for that of the architect or engineer for whose expert judgment the parties freely contracted.

If the builder can prove that the withholding of the certificate was fraudulent or done in bad faith (as a result of collusion with the owner, for example), the court may order that payment be made despite the absence of the certificate. In addition, production of the certificate may be excused by the death, insanity, or incapacitating illness of the named architect or engineer.

**Personal Satisfaction.** Sometimes, a contract will provide that a party's duty to perform is conditioned on his *personal satisfaction* with the other party's performance. For example, Smith commissions Jones to paint a portrait of Smith's wife, but makes his duty to pay conditional on his personal satisfaction with the portrait. How will a court determine whether the condition of personal satisfaction has occurred? If the court applies a standard of actual, subjective satisfaction, and Smith asserts that he is not satisfied, it would be very difficult for Jones to prove that the condition has occurred. If, on the other hand, the court applies an objective, "reasonable man" standard of satisfaction, Jones stands a better chance of proving that the condition has occurred.

In determining which standard of satisfaction to apply, courts distinguish between cases in which the performance bargained for involves personal taste and comfort and cases that involve mechanical fitness or suitability for a particular purpose. If personal taste and comfort are involved, as they would be in the hypothetical case described above, a promisee who is honestly dissatisfied with the other party's performance has the right to reject the performance without being liable to the promisor. If, however, the performance involves mechanical fitness or suitability, the court will apply a "reasonable man" test. If the court finds that a reasonable man would be satisfied with the performance, the condition of personal satisfaction has been met and the promisee must accept the performance and pay the contract price. For example, if Smith Manufacturing Company hires Jones to design a conveyor belt system for use in its factory, conditioning its duty to pay on its personal satisfaction with the system, a court would be likely to find that this is a contract involving mechanical fitness and suitability, for which an objective test of satisfaction could be used.

Because the "honest satisfaction" standard involves a danger of forfeiture by the party performing, courts prefer the objective test of satisfaction when objective evaluation is feasible. *Forman v. Benson,* which follows, presents a good discussion of the choice of standards problem in contracts conditioned on personal satisfaction.

**Excuse of Conditions.** In most situations involving conditional duties, the promisor does not have the duty to perform unless and until the condition occurs. There are, however, a variety of situations in which the occurrence of a condition will be *excused.* In such a case, the person whose duty is conditional will have to perform even though the condition has not occurred. One ground for excusing a condition is that the occurrence of the condition has been *prevented* or *hindered* by the party who is benefited by the condition. For example, Smith hires Jones to construct a garage on Smith's land, but when Jones attempts to begin construction, Smith refuses to allow Jones access to the land. In this case, Smith's duty to pay would normally be subject to a constructive condition that Jones build the garage. However, since Smith prevented the occurrence of the condition, the condition will be excused, and Jones can sue Smith for damages for breach of contract even though the condition has not occurred.

Other grounds for excuse of a condition include **waiver** and **estoppel.** When a person whose duty is conditional voluntarily gives up his right to the occurrence of the condition (waiver), the condition will be excused. Suppose that Smith contracts to sell his car to Jones on condition that Jones pay him $2,000 by June 14. Jones fails to pay on June 14, but when he tenders payment on June 20, Smith accepts and cashes the check without reservation. Smith has thereby *waived* the condition of payment by June 14.

When a person whose duty is conditional leads the other party to rely on his noninsistence on the condition, the condition will be excused because of estoppel. For example, Jones agrees to sell his business to Smith on condition that Smith provide a credit report and personal financial statement by July 17. On July 5, Jones tells Smith that he can have until the end of the month to provide the necessary documents. Relying on Jones's assurances, Smith does not provide the credit report and financial statement until July 29. In this case, Jones would be *estopped* (precluded) from claiming that the condition did not occur.

A condition may also be excused when performance of the act that constitutes the condition becomes *impossible.* For example, if a building contract provides that the owner's duty to pay is conditioned on the production of a certificate from a named architect, the condition would be excused if the named architect died or became incapacitated before issuing the certificate.

In all of these situations, the significance of excuse of a condition is that the person whose duty would otherwise not arise until the occurrence of the condition will have the duty to perform even though the condition has not occurred.

## Norton v. Herron

**677 P.2d 877 (Alaska Sup. Ct. 1984)**

Carol Herron met with Donald Norton in April 1980 regarding her interest in buying his house. At this meeting, she indicated that she owned property in Montana that was on the market. She told Norton that she expected the proceeds from the sale of the Montana property to generate some $17,000 cash. The parties later agreed on a purchase price and arranged to have Transamerica Title Company draw up the agreement and act as escrow agent. The written contract signed by the parties provided for Herron to buy the house for a total price of $87,000, approximately $17,000 of which was to be paid at the date of closing. The terms of the agreement pertaining to the cash at closing stated:

> [C]ash down at closing (approximately $17,000.00) is to come from the proceeds of the buyer's property in Montana which is on the market to be sold at this time. It is agreed that the closing of this escrow shall be within 30 days after the closing of the Montana transaction, but no later than May 15, 1981.

In August 1980, Herron's Montana property was sold, but the sale failed to raise $17,000 and Herron did not notify Norton of the Montana sale at that time. On May 14, 1981, Herron tendered $17,000 into the escrow established at Transamerica. Norton refused to go forward with the closing, arguing that Herron was in default. Herron filed suit to enforce the agreement. The trial court found for Herron, and Norton appealed.

**Compton, Justice.** Norton contends that the agreement made it a condition precedent for Herron to sell her Montana property and forward proceeds of the sale into the escrow established at Transamerica. Herron argues that there was no such intention; rather, she claims that the source of the funds was immaterial provided she perform by tendering $17,000.

We have recognized that the primary underlying purpose of the law of contracts is the attempted realization of reasonable expectations that have been induced by the making of a promise. In order to give legal effect to the parties' reasonable expectations, the court must look first to the written agreement itself and also to evidence regarding the parties' intent at the time the contract was made.

In our opinion, the evidence cited by the parties shows that the transfer of the proceeds from the Montana sale to the Transamerica escrow was not intended as a condition precedent. The primary purpose of the agreement was to sell Norton's house. Norton was concerned with selling to a qualified buyer who could provide him with a sizeable cash payment by a stated date to allow him to invest in other land. The buyer tendered the agreed upon payment of $17,000 on May 14, 1981, one day prior to the final closing date of May 15, 1981. It would be unreasonable to void the agreement on the ground of Norton's refusal to accept the agreed upon sum simply because it came from a different source. Arguably, Norton was concerned with Herron being able to make the monthly mortgage payments. However, in light of Norton's failure to inquire in any manner as to the probability of a sale or Herron's credit as a whole, we are unconvinced that the parties intended that the contract made the forwarding of the proceeds of the Montana sale a condition precedent to the sale of the house.

In reaching this conclusion we also note the genuine reluctance of courts to give effect to conditions precedent, and the accepted requirement that such conditions be expressed in plain, unambiguous language or arise by clear implication. Such an interpretation protects both parties to the transaction and also does not involve the consequences that a slight failure to perform wholly destroys all rights under the contract. Well established authority holds that the existence of the word "only," or words of similar clarity, will determine whether the agreement is one with a condition precedent.

The provision in this case refers to the probable source of the down payment, or possibly, to the time by which closing must be accomplished, but it does not clearly express an intent that it is the only means by which Norton could be paid.

Judgment for Herron affirmed.

---

## Forman v. Benson

**446 N.E.2d 535 (Ill. Ct. App. 1983)**

In late March 1981, Eric Forman made a written offer to buy real estate owned by Art Benson. The offer was communicated to Benson at a conference at which both Forman's and Benson's real estate agents were present. The offer proposed that Forman would buy the property on contract, taking possession of it in September 1981 and paying the purchase price of $125,000 to Benson over a 10-year period. Because Benson did not know Forman and was concerned about Forman's creditworthiness, at the suggestion of Forman's agent a clause stating that the contract was "subject to seller's approving buyer's credit report" was inserted in the contract before Benson signed it.

Forman furnished Benson with a credit report and a personal financial statement. Benson told Forman's real estate agent that the report "looks real good" and that he would have his attorney review it and begin the title work on the property. During the next six weeks, Benson met with Forman three times to discuss the pending sale. During these meetings, Benson requested additional financial information. Benson also attempted to negotiate for a higher interest rate and purchase price. In May 1981, Benson informed Forman that he rejected Forman's credit rating. Forman later brought suit to enforce the contract. The trial court held for Forman, and Benson appealed.

**Hopf, Justice.** The trial court found that Benson was held to a standard of reasonableness in his rejection of the contract on the basis of Forman's credit report, and found that Benson's rejection was unreasonable. Benson argues that approval of the buyer's credit worthiness was intended to be a matter of personal satisfaction on the part of the seller and was not subject to a standard of reasonableness.

Satisfaction clauses generally fall into one of two classes. In one class, the decision as to whether a party is satisfied is completely reserved to the party for whose benefit the clause is inserted, and the reasons for his decision may not be inquired into and overhauled by either the other party or the courts. Cases falling into this class generally involve matters which are dependent upon the feelings, taste, or judgment of the party making the decision. The second class of cases are those in which the party to be satisfied is to base his determination on grounds which are just and reasonable. These cases generally involve matters which are capable of objective evaluation, or which involve considerations of operative fitness or mechanical utility. Matters of financial concern generally fall into this second category of cases. The adequacy of the grounds of a determination in this class are open to judicial scrutiny and are judged by a reasonable man standard.

However, the parties may agree to a reservation in one party of the absolute and unqualified freedom of choice on a matter not involving fancy, taste, or whim. The fact that the clause was added as a concession or inducement to one of the parties is significant in determining whether the reasonableness standard should be applied. A reasonableness standard is favored by the law when the contract concerns matters capable of objective evaluation. However, where the circumstances are such that it is clear the provision was added as a personal concession to one of the contracting parties, the subjective, rather than the objective standard, should be applied.

In the present case, it is uncontroverted that the clause in question was inserted as a concession to Benson and as an inducement to him to sign the contract, which he subsequently did. In light of the fact that the relationship between the parties was to endure over a 10-year period of time, we think it is a reasonable construction of the provision that it was intended to allow Benson the freedom of making a personal and subjective evaluation of Forman's credit worthiness. We, therefore, conclude that the trial court erred in applying a reasonableness standard to the instant case.

The personal judgment standard, however, does not allow Benson to exercise unbridled discretion in rejecting Forman's credit, but rather is subject to the requirement of good faith. We hold that while Benson may have had a basis in his personal judgment for rejecting Forman's credit, his attempted renegotiation demonstrates that his rejection was based on reasons other than Forman's credit rating and was, therefore, in bad faith. This conduct, in addition to demonstrating bad faith, also constitutes a waiver of Benson's right to reject the credit information. A waiver is an intentional relinquishment of a known right. To constitute a waiver the words or conduct of a party must be inconsistent with his intention to rely on the requirements of the contract. Here, Benson's attempt to renegotiate the purchase price and interest rate were logically inconsistent with any alleged disapproval of Forman's credit rating.

Judgment for Forman affirmed.

## PERFORMANCE AND BREACH

When a person's performance is due, any failure to perform that is not excused is a breach of contract. The consequences of a given breach of contract depend on the degree of performance that was expected of a party and on the magnitude of the breach.

**Degrees of Performance.** You have already learned that when a party's duty is subject to an express condition, that condition must be strictly and completely complied with to give rise to a duty of performance. Thus, when a person's performance is an express condition of the other party's duty to perform, that performance must *strictly* and *completely* comply with the contract in order to give rise to the other party's duty to perform. For example, if Smith agrees to pay Jones $500 for painting his house "on condition that" Jones finish the job no later than June 1, 1986, a standard of strict or complete performance would be applied to Jones's performance. If Jones does not finish the job by June 1, his breach will have several consequences. First, Smith can sue him for breach of contract. Second, since the condition precedent to Smith's duty to pay has not occurred, Smith does not have a duty to pay the contract price. Third, since it is now too late for the condition to occur, Smith can cancel or terminate the contract.

The **strict performance** standard is also applied to contractual obligations that can be performed either exactly or to a high degree of perfection. Examples of this type of obligation include promises to pay money, to deliver deeds, and, generally, promises to deliver goods. A promisor who performs such promises completely and in strict compliance with the contract is entitled to receive the entire contract price. The promisor whose performance deviates from perfection is not entitled to receive the contract price if he does not render perfect performance within an appropriate time. He may, however, be able to recover in quasi contract for any benefits that he has conferred on the other party.

The application of a strict performance standard can lead to a substantial forfeiture by the performing party. The performing party may have given the promisee most of what he is entitled to receive, but still be unable to recover the contract price because his performance deviated in some minor respect from the terms of the contract. The law's commitment to freedom of contract justifies such results in cases in which the parties have expressly bargained for strict compliance with the terms of the contract. This justification would *not,* however, support the application of a strict compliance standard to a party whose performance was merely a *constructive* condition of the other party's duty to perform.

Thus, a lower standard of performance is applied to duties that are difficult to perform without some deviation from perfection if performance of those duties is *not* an express condition. A common example of this type of obligation is a promise to erect a building. Other examples include promises to construct roads, to cultivate crops, and to render some types of personal or professional services. The standard of performance applied to these types of duties is called **substantial performance.** Substantial performance is performance that falls short of complete performance in minor respects but does not deprive the promisee of a material part of the consideration she bargained for. When a substantial performance standard is applied, the person who has substantially performed may recover the contract price less any damages resulting from the defects in his performance. The obvious purpose behind the doctrine of substantial performance is to prevent forfeiture by a party who has given the injured party most of what she bargained for. One limitation on the doctrine of substantial performance is that the doctrine is generally held to be inapplicable to a situation in which the breach of contract has been *willful.* The *Warren* case, which follows, presents an example of the operation of the doctrine of substantial performance.

## Warren v. Denison

**563 S.W.2d 299 (Tex. Ct. App. 1978)**

The Warrens hired Denison, a building contractor, to construct a house on their property. The parties executed a written contract in which the Warrens agreed to pay the principal sum of $73,400 for the construction. Other signed documents gave Denison the right to foreclose on the house if the Warrens defaulted in their payments. Denison constructed the house, but the Warrens failed to pay $48,400 due on the construction contract, alleging that Denison had used poor workmanship in constructing the house. Denison attempted to foreclose on the house, and the Warrens brought suit, seeking damages and a judgment that they were under no obligation to perform further duties under the construction contract. The trial court found for Denison, and the Warrens appealed.

**Dodson, Justice.** The Texas courts have applied the doctrine of substantial performance to construction contracts. This doctrine recognizes that literal performance of each and every particular of such contracts is virtually impossible. Rather than require perfect performance of every particular, substantial performance is regarded as full performance in allowing the builder to recover on the contract. However, in such instances, the measure of recovery is the contract price *less* the cost of completing or repairing the building to contract specifications.

It is apparent that a finding that the builder did not complete the contract in a good workmanlike manner does not necessarily mean that he has not substantially performed the contract. The instances of failure to perform in a workmanlike manner are often no more than deviations from perfect compliance, which reduce the recovery on a contract otherwise substantially performed. A job can be substantially performed with some breaches of workmanlike construction preventing perfect performance.

The jury found that at the time the Warrens took possession of the dwelling in question it was fit for the ordinary purposes for which such dwelling was to be used. The jury found that the dwelling as constructed had a market value of $5,718.50 greater than it would have had if it had been built according to the plans and specifications. The jury found that the dwelling in question was not free from defects in workmanship at the time the Warrens took possession. However, the jury did find that any defects in the dwelling could be reasonably repaired for $1,961.50 and that $200 was a reasonable and necessary cost for the Warrens to obtain inspections and estimates for repairs of the defects. Thus, the Warrens were entitled to have this total of $2,161.50 deducted from the contract balance.

Judgment for Denison affirmed.

**Material Breach.** The consequences of a breach of contract are determined by the *materiality* of the breach. When a promisor's performance fails to reach the degree of perfection that the promisee is justified in expecting under the circumstances, the promisor is guilty of a **material breach** of contract. (This is another way of saying that the performing party failed to give substantial performance.) The party who is injured by a material breach has the right to withhold his own performance. If the breach is not remedied within an appropriate time, the injured party is justified in canceling the contract and suing for damages for total breach of contract. The promisor who materially breaches a contract has no right of action on the contract, although he may be able to recover under a quasi-contract theory for any benefits that he has conferred on the other party.

The standard for determining materiality is a flexible one that must take into account the facts of each individual case. One of the most important factors to be considered is whether the breach deprives the injured party of the benefits that he reasonably expected. Courts will also take into account the extent to which the breaching party will suffer forfeiture if the breach is held to be material, the magnitude and timing of the breach, the degree of good faith exercised by the breaching party, and the extent to which the injured party can be adequately compensated by the payment of damages.

**Anticipatory Repudiation.** One type of breach of contract occurs when the promisor indicates *before the time for performance* that he is unwilling or unable to carry out the contract. This is called **anticipatory repudiation** or **anticipatory breach.** When anticipatory repudiation occurs, the party who is notified of the repudiation may treat the contract as breached. He may withhold his own performance and sue for damages immediately, without having to wait for the time for performance to arrive.

Anticipatory repudiation may take the form of an express statement by the promisor, or it may be implied from actions of the promisor that indicate an intent not to perform. For example, if Smith, who is obligated to convey real estate to Jones, conveys the property to some third person instead, Smith has repudiated the contract.

**Time for Performance.** A party's failure to perform on time is a breach of contract. In some cases, delay may be serious enough to constitute a *material* breach.

At the outset, it is necessary to determine when performance is "due." Some contracts specifically state the time for performance. In some contracts that do not specifically state the time for performance, such a time can be inferred from the circumstances surrounding the contract. For example, in a contract in which Jones promised to deliver Easter baskets to Smith for $100, the nature of the contract would imply that Jones's performance was due by Easter. In still other contracts, no time for performance is either stated or implied. When no time for performance is stated or implied, performance must be completed within a "reasonable time," as judged by the circumstances of each case.

After a court determines when performance was due, it must determine the *consequences* of late performance. In some contracts, the parties expressly state that *time is of the essence.* This means that a party's timely performance by a specific date is an *express condition* of the other party's duty to perform. Thus, in a contract that contains a time is of the essence provision, any delay constitutes a *material* breach. Sometimes, courts will imply such a term even when the language of the contract does not state that time is of the essence. A court would be likely to do this if late performance is of little or no value to the promisee. For example, Smith contracts with the local newspaper to run an advertisement for Christmas trees from December 15, 1985, to December 24, 1985, but the newspaper does not run the ad until December 26, 1985. In this case, the time for performance is an essential part of the contract and the newspaper has committed a material breach.

When a contract does not contain language indicating that time is of the essence and a court determines that the time for performance is not a particularly important part of the contract, the promisee must accept late performance rendered within a reasonable time of when performance was due. The promisee is then entitled to deduct or set off from the contract price any losses caused by the delay.

**Good Faith Performance.** Section 1–203 of the UCC provides that every contract or duty within the Code's provisions imposes an obligation of **good faith** in its performance or enforcement. The duty of good faith is a broad and flexible one that is generally taken to mean that neither party to a contract will do anything to prevent the other from obtaining the benefits of the contract.

The duty of good faith has also been applied in many cases not governed by the UCC. It has been imposed by law in insurance contracts in a number of states and provides grounds for a lawsuit against an insurance company that, in bad faith, fails to pay claims or otherwise fails to perform its duties to an insured. The duty of good faith has also been held applicable to contracts of employment in at least five states. In these states, an employer who discharges an employee in bad faith can be held liable for damages.[1]

[1] This theory of liability is discussed in greater detail in Chapter 47.

## EXCUSES FOR NONPERFORMANCE

Although nonperformance of a duty that has become due will ordinarily constitute a breach of contract, there are some situations in which nonperformance is excused because of factors that arise after the formation of the contract. The following discussion concerns the most common grounds for excuse of nonperformance.

**Impossibility.** When performance of a contractual duty becomes impossible after the formation of the contract, the duty will be discharged on grounds of **impossibility.** This does not mean that a person can be discharged merely because he has contracted to do something that he is simply unable to do or that causes him hardship or difficulty. Impossibility in the legal sense of the word means "it cannot be done" rather than "I cannot do it." Thus, promisors who find that they have agreed to perform duties that are beyond their capabilities or that turn out to be unprofitable or burdensome are generally not excused from performance of their duties. Impossibility will provide an excuse for nonperformance, however, when some event arises after the formation of the contract that renders performance objectively impossible.

There are a variety of situations in which a person's duty to perform may be discharged on grounds of impossibility. The three most common situations involve illness or death of the promisor, supervening illegality, and destruction of the subject matter of the contract. Some courts recognize a less rigorous standard of impossibility that can be used under a wide variety of circumstances: **commercial impracticability.** The impracticability standard has been adopted by the UCC for sale of goods contracts and by the *Restatement (Second) of Contracts* as well.

**Illness or Death of Promisor.** Incapacitating illness or death of the promisor excuses nonperformance when the promisor has contracted to perform personal services. For example, if Smith, a college professor who has a contract with State University to teach for an academic year, dies before the completion of the contract, her estate will not be liable for breach of contract. The promisor's death or illness does *not,* however, excuse the nonperformance of duties that can be delegated to another, such as the duty to deliver goods, pay money, or convey real estate. For example, if Smith had contracted to convey real estate to Jones and died before the closing date, Jones could enforce the contract against Smith's estate.

**Supervening Illegality.** If a statute or governmental regulation enacted after the creation of a contract makes performance of a party's duties illegal, the promisor is excused from performing. Statutes or regulations that merely make performance more difficult or less profitable do not, however, excuse nonperformance.

**Destruction of the Subject Matter of the Contract.** If something that is essential to the promisor's performance is destroyed after the formation of the contract through no fault of the promisor, the promisor is excused from performing. For example, Smith, the owner of a concert hall, hires Jones, a concert pianist, to give a concert at the hall. If the hall is destroyed by fire before the date of the concert, Smith's nonperformance will be excused. The destruction of items that the promisor intended to use in performing does not excuse nonperformance if substitutes are available, even though securing them makes performance more difficult or less profitable. For example, Smith contracts to erect a building for Jones, planning to use certain equipment in the construction process. Destruction of the equipment before the contract is performed would *not* give Smith an excuse for failing to perform.

**Commercial Impracticability.** Section 2–615 of the Uniform Commercial Code has extended the scope of the common law doctrine of impossibility to cases in which unforeseen developments make performance by the promisor highly impracticable, unreasonably expensive, or of little value to the promisee. Rather than using a standard of impossibility, then, the Code uses the more relaxed standard of **impracticability.** Despite the less stringent standard applied, cases actually excusing nonperformance on grounds of impracticability are relatively rare. To be successful in claiming excuse based on impracticability, a promisor must be able to establish that the event which makes performance impracticable occurred without his fault and that the nonoccurrence of the event was a basic assumption on which the contract was made. This basically means that the event was unforeseeable at the time of contracting and that the promisor did not expressly or impliedly assume the risk that the event would occur.

Case law and official comments to section 2–615 indicate that neither increased cost nor collapse of a market for particular goods is sufficient to excuse nonperformance, because those are the types of business risks that every promisor assumes. However, drastic price increases or severe shortages of goods resulting from unforeseen circumstances such as wars and crop failures can give rise to impracticability. The *Asphalt International* case, which follows, presents an example of a case in which an event that occurred after the formation of the contract was held to constitute an excuse for nonperformance.

If the event causing impracticability affects only a part of the seller's capacity to perform, the seller must allocate production and deliveries among customers in a "fair and reasonable" manner and must notify them of any delay or any limited allocation of the goods. You can read more about commercial impracticability in Chapter 33 (Performance of Sales Contracts).

The impracticability standard has been adopted in section 261 of the *Restatement (Second) of Contracts,* which closely resembles the provisions of section 2–615 of the UCC. States that follow the *Restatement* approach apply the impracticability standard to all types of contracts, not just those for the sale of goods.

**Frustration of Venture.** Closely associated with impossibility and impracticability is the doctrine of **frustration of venture** or **commercial frustration.** This doctrine provides an excuse for nonperformance when events that occur after the formation of the contract would deprive the promisor of the benefit of return performance. Frustration can be distinguished from impossibility and impracticability by the fact that the promisor in a frustration case is not necessarily prevented from performing. Rather, in frustration cases, the promisor is excused because the return performance by the other party has become worthless to him. The doctrine of frustration is discussed in greater detail in the case of *Downing v. Stiles,* which follows.

## Asphalt International, Inc. v. Enterprise Shipping Corp., S.A.

**667 F.2d 261 (2d Cir. 1981)**

Asphalt International chartered the tanker *Oswego Tarmac* from its owner, Enterprise Shipping Corporation. The contract provided that Enterprise was to maintain the vessel in good order but that it was absolved of responsibility for any loss or damage resulting from a collision and that if the vessel should be lost, the contract would cease. While loading asphalt cargo alongside a pier in Curaçao, the vessel was rammed four times amidships by the bow of the motor vessel *Elektra* with such heavy impact that four of its tanks ruptured and heated asphalt spewed across the harbor. Expert appraisers hired by the owners of both ships to assess the damage submitted a joint field survey in which they estimated the cost of repair at not less than $1.5 million. The fair market value of the *Oswego Tarmac* prior to the collision was $750,000. Enterprise advised Asphalt that it considered the *Oswego Tarmac* a complete loss. It refused Asphalt's request that Enterprise repair the vessel. Instead, Enterprise sold it as scrap for $157,500. It then collected insurance proceeds in an amount that exceeded the vessel's fair market value. Asphalt brought suit against Enterprise for breach of contract. The trial court found for Enterprise, and Asphalt appealed.

**KAUFMAN, CIRCUIT JUDGE.** A basic tenet of commercial law, now embodied in the Uniform Commercial Code for cases involving the sale of goods, is that a party's duty to perform pursuant to a contract may be excused on the grounds of commercial impracticability. We must determine whether the collision of the vessels rendered performance of a duty to repair possible only at excessive and unreasonable cost or whether the collision altered the essential nature of the agreement.

We are of the view that the trial court's finding of fact that the *Oswego Tarmac* could only be repaired at "excessive and unreasonable" cost is not clearly erroneous. Surely, imposing the repair obligation on Enterprise sought by Asphalt would require a type of performance essentially different from that for which Asphalt contracted. Indeed, Asphalt's repair request, which would, in effect, require Enterprise to rebuild its virtually demolished vessel, would alter the essential nature of the contract. The contract merely provided for leasing of the vessel to transport asphalt.

We cannot agree with the argument advanced by Asphalt that Enterprise may not enjoy the defense of impracticability because it suffered no financial hardship, but rather received a windfall profit of $961,000 by virtue of the insurance proceeds it collected. The doctrine of commercial impracticability focuses on the reasonableness of the expenditures at issue, not upon the ability of a party to pay the commercially unreasonable expense. The existence of insurance coverage in excess of the fair market value of the ship bears no relationship to the controlling issue—the reasonableness of the requested repairs.

Judgment for Enterprise affirmed.

## Downing v. Stiles

**635 P.2d 808 (Wyo. Sup. Ct. 1981)**

Charles and Christine Downing operated the Rustler Bar, a retail liquor business, in a building that they owned in Basin, Wyoming. They were also partners with Janice Stiles in the operation of the Maverick Recreation Center, a restaurant located in the basement of the same building. Much of Maverick's business came from patronage by Rustler Bar customers. The Downings sold the Rustler Bar and their building to Dennis Morris. Later, they sold their share in the Maverick to Stiles for $25,000, which was to be paid in semiannual installments.

The Rustler Bar went out of business in June 1978. Stiles stopped making payments to the Downings in December 1978. In January 1979, a fire destroyed the building and its contents. The Downings brought suit against Stiles. The trial court found that Stiles was excused from further performance, and the Downings appealed.

**Rooney, Justice.** The trial court found that the Maverick Recreation Center was dependent on the business with Rustler Bar, and that without it, the center was not a viable operation. The value of performance was destroyed by the frustrating event, which was the failure of the Rustler Bar. The doctrine of "commercial frustration" or "frustration of venture" grew out of the so-called coronation cases initiated in *Krell v. Henry,* wherein a defendant was excused from payment for use of an apartment from which to view the coronation proceedings of King Edward VII because the proceedings were cancelled when the king became ill.

An event which substantially frustrates the objects contemplated by the parties when they made the contract excuses nonperformance of the contract. In such case it is sometimes said that the foundation of the contract is gone.

The court should apply the doctrine of commercial frustration to relieve a party to a contract from further performance thereunder only if:

1. The contract is at least partially executory.
2. A supervening event occurred after the contract was made.
3. The non-occurrence of such event was a basic assumption on which the contract was made.
4. Such occurrence frustrated the party's principal purpose for the contract.
5. The frustration was substantial, and
6. The party has not agreed, expressly or impliedly, to perform in spite of the occurrence of the event.

In this case, Stiles did not contend that the supervening event was the fire. The discontinuance of the Rustler Bar business was the event designated as supervening. The contract was partly executory, the event occurred subsequent to the making of the contract, and Stiles had not agreed, expressly or impliedly, to perform in spite of the occurrence of the event. Although subject to considerable dispute, it may even be said that the non-occurrence of the event was a basic assumption on which the contract was made. But the evidence does not establish the continuation of Rustler Bar's business as the principal purpose for which the contract was made, and, therefore, that the frustration was substantial. Certainly, the frustration was not "total or nearly total."

The principal purpose of the purchase was to carry on a restaurant business. The fact is that such restaurant business was carried on for six or seven months after the Rustler Bar ceased doing business. It was not until just prior to the fire that Stiles refused to make payment under the contract. This fact reflects the recognition that one of the risks assumed by Stiles under the contract was the decrease and discontinuance of Rustler Bar's business. Stiles had not sought any provision in the agreement whereby Rustler Bar was bound to use Stiles for its food service. If such were the principal purpose of the purchase agreement between Stiles and the Downings, assurance of such should have been secured along with the lease.

Such assurance should designate the extent of such service. For otherwise, where is the line drawn? Can Stiles be discharged from performance of her contract with appellants when service to Rustler Bar's customers falls off 10 percent? or 25 percent? or 90 percent? In the language of Comment a to section 265, *Restatement, Contracts 2d:*

> It is not enough that the transaction has become less profitable for the affected party or even that he will sustain a loss. The frustration must be so severe that it is not fairly to be regarded as within the risks that he assumed under the contract.

Accordingly, it was error to apply the doctrine of commercial frustration to the circumstances of this case.

Judgment reversed in favor of the Downings.

## DISCHARGE

**Nature of Discharge.** Parties who have been released from their obligations under a contract are said to be **discharged.** Normally, both parties to a contract are discharged when they have completely performed their contractual duties. There are, however, several other circumstances that can operate to discharge a party's duty of performance.

Earlier in this chapter, you learned about several situations in which a party's duty to perform could be discharged even though that party had not himself performed. These include the nonoccurrence of a condition precedent, the occurrence of a condition subsequent, material breach by the other party, and circumstances under which a party is excused from performance by impossibility, impracticability, or frustration. The following discussion deals with additional ways in which a discharge can occur.

**Discharge by Mutual Agreement.** Just as contracts are created by mutual agreement, they can also be discharged by *mutual agreement*. An agreement to discharge a contract must be supported by consideration to be enforceable.

**Discharge by Waiver.** A party to a contract may voluntarily relinquish any right he has under a contract, including the right to receive return performance. Such a relinquishment of rights is known as a **waiver.** If one party tenders an incomplete or defective performance and the other party accepts that performance without objection, knowing that the defects will not be remedied, the party to whom performance was due will have discharged the other party from his duty of performance. The Uniform Commercial Code provides in section 1–107 that "any claim or right arising out of an alleged breach can be discharged in whole or in part without consideration by a written waiver or renunciation signed and delivered by the aggrieved party."

To avoid waiving rights, a person who has received defective performance should give the other party prompt notice that she expects complete performance and will seek damages if the defects are not corrected.

**Discharge by Alteration.** If the contract is represented by a *written* instrument, and one of the parties intentionally makes a material alteration in the instrument without the other's consent, the alteration acts as a discharge of the other party. If the other party consents to the alteration or does not object to it when she learns of it, she is not discharged. Alteration by a third party without the knowledge or consent of the contracting parties does not affect the parties' rights.

**Discharge by Statute of Limitations.** Courts have long refused to grant a remedy to a person who delays bringing a lawsuit for an unreasonable time. All of the states have enacted statutes known as **statutes of limitation,** which specify the period of time in which a person can bring a lawsuit.

The time period for bringing a contract action varies from state to state, and many states prescribe time periods for cases concerning oral contracts that are different from those for cases concerning written contracts. Section 2–725 of the Uniform Commercial Code provides for a four-year statute of limitations for contracts involving the sale of goods.

The statutory period ordinarily begins to run from the date of the breach. It may be delayed if the party who has the right to sue is under some incapacity at that time (such as minority or insanity) or is beyond the jurisdiction of the state. A person who has breached a contractual duty is discharged from liability for breach if no lawsuit is brought before the statutory period elapses.

## REMEDIES FOR BREACH OF CONTRACT

**The Theory of Remedies.** Our discussion of the performance stage of contracts so far has focused on the circumstances under which a party has the duty to perform or is excused from performing. In situations in which a person is injured by a breach of contract and is unable to obtain compensation by settlement out of court, a further important issue remains: What remedy will a court fashion to compensate for breach of contract?

Contract law seeks to encourage people to rely on the promises made to them by others.

The objective of granting a remedy in a case of breach of contract is not to punish the breaching party but to compensate the injured party. Ordinarily, this is done by awarding the injured person a judgment for money damages. However, when money damages would not constitute an adequate remedy, the court may employ one of the equitable remedies that will be discussed later.

**Limitations of Recovery of Damages in Contract Cases.** An injured party's ability to recovery damages in a contract action is limited by three principles. First, a party can only recover damages for losses that can be proved with reasonable certainty. Losses that are purely speculative are not recoverable. Thus, if Jones Publishing Company breaches a contract to publish Smith's memoirs, Smith may not be able to recover damages for lost royalties, since he may be unable to establish, beyond speculation, how much money he would have earned in royalties if the book had been published.

Second, a breaching party is responsible for paying only those losses that were foreseeable to him at the time of contracting. A loss is foreseeable if it would ordinarily be expected to result from a breach or if the breaching party had reason to know of particular circumstances that would make the loss likely. For example, if Jones Manufacturing Company renders late performance in a contract to deliver parts to Smith Motors without knowing that Smith is shut down waiting for the parts, Jones will not have to pay the business losses that result from Smith's having to close its operation.

Third, plaintiffs injured by a breach of contract have the duty to **mitigate** (avoid or minimize) damages. A party cannot recover for losses that he could have avoided without undue risk, burden, or humiliation. For example, an employee who has been wrongfully fired would be entitled to damages equal to his wages for the remainder of the employment period. The employee, however, has the duty to minimize the damages by making reasonable efforts to seek a similar job elsewhere. The *Parker* case involves the question of whether an injured party carried out her duty to mitigate.

**Compensatory Damages.** Subject to the limitations discussed above, a person who has been injured by a breach of contract is entitled to recover **compensatory damages.** In calculating the compensatory remedy, a court will attempt to give the injured party the "benefit of his bargain" by placing him in the position he would have been in had the contract *been performed as promised.* The interest protected by the compensatory remedy is called the *expectation interest* because the injured party is to be compensated for the value of the contract that he "expected" to receive.

The starting point in calculating compensatory damages is to determine the *loss in value* of the performance that the plaintiff had the right to expect. Loss in value is the difference between the value of the performance that was promised and the value of any performance that the injured party actually received.

If the breaching party rendered defective or incomplete performance, the loss in value is the difference between the value of the performance had it been rendered as the breaching party promised and the value of the performance actually rendered. For example, if Landlord leases a defective apartment to Tenant, warranting it to be fit for residential purposes, the loss in value would be the rental value that the apartment would have had if it had been in the condition that was warranted and the rental value that the apartment actually had. If the breaching party rendered no performance at all, the loss in value is simply the value of the promised performance. For example, if Smith repudiates a contract to sell his house, which has a market value of $100,000, to Jones for $90,000, the loss in value experienced by Jones is $100,000.

In addition to loss in value, compensatory damages include additional losses in the form of **consequential damages** and **incidental damages** that have been caused by the breach of contract. Consequential damages compensate for losses that result because of some special or unusual circumstances of the particular contractual relationship of the parties. For example, Apex Trucking Company buys a computer system from ABC Computers. The system fails to operate properly, and Apex is forced to pay its employees to perform the tasks manually, spending $10,000 in overtime pay. In this situation, Apex might seek to recover the $10,000 in overtime pay in addition to the loss of value that it has experienced. It is important to remember, however, that the recovery of consequential damages is subject to the limitations on damage recovery discussed earlier. Foreseeability of the damages is of particular concern in cases in which consequential damages are sought. Incidental damages compensate for reasonable costs that the injured party incurs after the breach in an effort to avoid further loss. For example, if Smith Construction Company breaches an employment contract with Jones, Jones's reasonable expenses in attempting to procure substitute employment can be recovered as incidental damages.

After determining the sum allowable for loss of value and additional loss, a court will subtract from that sum any cost or loss that the plaintiff has been able to avoid by not having to perform his own promise. When Smith breaches his promise to sell his $100,000 house to Jones for $90,000, for example, Jones saves $90,000 by not buying the house. Thus, his compensatory remedy (assuming that he suffered no allowable consequential or incidental loss) would be $10,000.

The usual measure of compensatory damages, then, is:

Loss in value
+ Other loss (consequential and incidental damages)
− Cost or loss avoided by the injured party

Our discussion has focused on the most common formulation of damage remedies in contracts cases. The normal measure of compensatory damages is not appropriate in every case, however. When it is not appropriate, a court may use an alternative measure of damages. For example, we said earlier that Smith, whose publisher breaches a contract to publish his memoirs, might not be able to establish the loss in value that he suffered because of his inability to prove how much money he would have earned in royalties. In cases such as this, in which an injured party's expectation interest is speculative, a court might protect his *reliance interest* and permit him to recover his expenditures in performing or preparing to render his own performance.

**Nominal Damages.** **Nominal damages** are very small damage awards that are given when a technical breach of contract has occurred without causing any actual or provable loss. The sums awarded as nominal damages typically vary from two cents to a dollar.

**Liquidated Damages.** The parties to a contract may expressly provide in their contract that a specific sum shall be recoverable if the contract is breached. Such provisions are called **liquidated damages** provisions. For example, Smith rents space in a shopping mall in which she plans to operate a retail clothing store. She must make improvements in the space before opening the store, and it is very important to her to have the store opened for the Christmas shopping season.

She hires Jones Construction Company to construct the improvements. The parties agree to include in the contract a liquidated damages provision stating that if Jones is late in completing the construction, Smith will be able to recover a specified sum for each day of delay. Such a provision is highly desirable from Smith's point of view because, without a liquidated damages provision, Smith would have a difficult time in establishing the precise losses that would result from delay.

If the amount specified in a liquidated damages provision is reasonable and if the nature of the contract is such that actual damages would be difficult to determine, courts will enforce the provision. When liquidated damages provisions are enforced, the amount of damages agreed upon will be the injured party's exclusive damage remedy. If the amount specified is unreasonably great in relation to the probable loss or injury, however, or if the amount of damages could be readily determined in the event of breach, the courts will declare the provision to be a *penalty* and will refuse to enforce it.

**Punitive Damages.** **Punitive damages** are damages awarded in addition to the compensatory remedy that are designed to punish a defendant for particularly reprehensible behavior and to deter the defendant and others from committing similar behavior in the future. Generally, punitive damages are *not* recoverable in contracts cases. However, punitive damages may be awarded when they are allowed by a specific statutory provision (such as some consumer protection statutes) or when the defendant has committed *fraud* or some other *independent tort.* A number of cases exist in which punitive damages have been imposed on insurance companies for breaches of their duty of good faith. In such cases, courts usually circumvent the traditional rule against awarding punitive damages in contracts cases by holding that breach of the duty of good faith is an independent tort.

A small minority of states will permit the use of punitive damages in contracts cases in which the defendant's conduct, though not technically a tort, was malicious, oppressive, or tortious in nature. The *Vernon Fire and Casualty* case, which follows, is one of the relatively unusual cases in which punitive damages were imposed for breach of contract.

**Enforcement of Damage Awards.** If a judgment for damages has been rendered, the creditor is entitled to the court's aid in the enforcement of the judgment if the debtor does not pay it. To enforce the judgment, the court can issue either a **writ of execution** or a **writ of garnishment.** A writ of execution orders the sheriff to seize and sell enough of the defendant's property to satisfy the judgment. All of the states have **exemption laws** that exempt certain classes and amounts of a debtor's property from execution. A writ of garnishment is designed to reach things belonging to the debtor that are in the hands of third parties, such as wages, bank accounts, and accounts receivable. Garnishment proceedings, like execution sales, are highly regulated by state statute.

## Vernon Fire and Casualty Insurance v. Sharp

### 349 N.E.2d 173 (Ind. Sup. Ct. 1976)

A. W. Sharp owned a creosote plant. Vernon Fire and Casualty and Great American Insurance Company issued casualty insurance policies on the plant that provided for scheduled coverage for the various structures and contents of the plant. On June 7, 1971, a fire destroyed most of the plant. It also destroyed some property owned by the plant's manager, John Easter.

Sharp claimed benefits under the policies by filing a formal proof of loss. Easter also filed a claim with Vernon and Great American, although his property was not scheduled in Sharp's policies. Easter later filed a separate action against Vernon and Great American and one of their agents, alleging that they had negligently failed to procure insurance on his personal property. A dispute arose between Sharp, Vernon, and Great American about the portion of the face value of the policies to which Sharp was entitled. The insurance companies knew that Sharp was in desperate need of funds in order to rebuild the business, but they would not pay him even the portion of the value of the policies that they admitted he was entitled to unless he procured a release of Easter's lawsuit against the insurance companies. Sharp brought suit against Vernon and Great American. The trial court awarded Sharp compensatory damages and $17,000 in punitive damages. Vernon and Great American appealed.

**Hunter, Justice.** The general rule is that punitive damages are not recoverable in contract actions. In most contract situations, the rule is a fair one, considering the nature of the interest to be protected. As Dean Prosser notes:

> Contract actions are created to protect the interest in having promises performed. Contract obligations are imposed because of conduct of the parties manifesting consent, and are owed only to the specific individuals named in the contract. Even as to these individuals, the damages recoverable for a breach of the contract duty are limited to those reasonably within the contemplation of the defendant when the contract was made, while in a tort action a much broader measure of damages is applied.

Compensatory and consequential damages which may be assessed against a promisor who decides not to live up to his bargain lend a needed measure of stability and predictability to the free enterprise system.

The general rule is not ironclad. Exceptions have developed where the conduct of the breaching party not only amounts to a breach of the contract, but also *independently* establishes the elements of a common-law tort such as fraud. The requirement that an independent tort be found serves several purposes. First, it maintains the general rule of not allowing punitive damages in contract actions, because the punitive damages are awarded for the *tort,* not on the contract. Secondly, the independent tort requirement facilitates judicial review of the evidence by limiting review to a search for the elements of the tort.

Neither of these functions of the independence requirement is very compelling when it appears from the evidence that a serious wrong, tortious in nature, has been committed, but the wrong does not conveniently fit the confines of a predetermined tort. The foregoing circumstances alone, however, will not sustain the award of punitive damages. It must also appear that the public interest will be served by the deterrent effect punitive damages will have upon future conduct of the wrongdoer and parties similarly situated. Only when these factors coalesce will the independent tort requirement be abrogated, and the allowance of punitive damages be sustained.

Vernon and Great American maintain that their conduct in dealing with their insured reflects nothing more than a legitimate exercise of an insurer's "right to disagree" as to the amount of recovery. It is evident that the insurer is permitted to dispute its liability in good faith because of the prohibitive social costs of a rule which would make claims nondisputable. Insurance companies burdened with such liability would either close their doors or increase premium rates to the point where only the rich could afford insurance.

The jury had before it evidence that the insurance companies sought to use their knowledge of Sharp's desperate need for funds for reconstruction to require Sharp to procure a settlement of a separate lawsuit brought by Easter. The jury could reasonably conclude that Vernon and Great American acted in an intentional and wanton manner in dealing with Sharp in regard to securing a settlement of Easter's claim, and since this conduct did not relate solely to the insurance companies' actions in paying the proceeds, it was not privileged. We believe such conduct might also have been characterized as oppressive. Sharp's evidence showed that Vernon and Great American dealt with his claim with an "interested motive" and wrongfully attempted by virtue of their superior position to exact additional consideration from Sharp before performing their obligations under the contract. This evidence was sufficient to establish a serious intentional wrong. We conclude that the public policy of this state permits the recovery of punitive damages under the circumstances of this case.

Award of punitive damages in favor of Sharp affirmed.

---

## Parker v. Twentieth Century-Fox Film Corporation

**474 P.2d 689 (Cal. Sup. Ct. 1970)**

Shirley MacLaine Parker entered into a contract with Twentieth Century-Fox to play the female lead in Fox's contemplated production of a movie entitled *Bloomer Girl.* The contract provided that Fox would pay Parker a minimum "guaranteed compensation" of $53,571.42 per week for 14 weeks, beginning May 23, 1966, for a total of $750,000. Fox decided not to produce the movie, and in a letter dated April 4, 1966, it notified Parker that it would not "comply with our obligations to you under" the written contract. In the same letter, with the professed purpose "to avoid any damage to you," Fox instead offered to employ Parker as the leading actress in another movie, tentatively entitled *Big Country, Big Man.* The compensation offered was identical. Unlike *Bloomer Girl,* however, which was to have been a musical production, *Big Country* was to be a dramatic "western type" movie. *Bloomer Girl* was to have been filmed in California; *Big Country* was to be produced in Australia. Certain other terms of the substitute contract varied from those of the original. Parker was given one week within which to accept. She did not, and the offer lapsed. Parker then filed suit against Fox for recovery of the agreed upon guaranteed compensation. The trial court held for Parker, and Fox appealed.

**BURKE, JUSTICE.** The general rule is that the measure of recovery by a wrongfully discharged employee is the amount of salary agreed upon for the period of service, less the amount which the employer affirmatively proves the employee has earned or with reasonable effort might have earned from other employment. However, before projected earnings from other employment opportunities not sought or accepted by the discharged employee can be applied in mitigation, the employer must show that the other employment was comparable, or substantially similar, to that of which the employee has been deprived; the employee's rejection of or failure to seek other available employment of a different or inferior kind may not be resorted to in order to mitigate damages.

In the present case, the sole issue is whether Parker's refusal of Fox's substitute offer of "Big Country" may be used in mitigation. Nor, if the "Big Country" offer was of employment different or inferior when compared with the original "Bloomer Girl" employment, is there an issue as to whether Parker acted reasonably in refusing the substitute offer.

It is clear that the trial court correctly ruled that Parker's failure to accept Fox's tendered substitute employment could not be applied in mitigation of damages because the offer of the "Big Country" lead was of employment both different and inferior. The mere circumstance that "Bloomer Girl" was to be a musical review calling upon Parker's talents as a dancer as well as an actress, and was to be produced in the City of Los Angeles, whereas "Big Country" was a straight dramatic role in a "western type" story taking place in an opal mine in Australia, demonstrates the difference in kind between the two employments; the female lead in a western style motion picture can by no stretch of the imagination be considered the equivalent of or substantially similar to the lead in a song-and-dance production.

Judgment for Parker affirmed.

**Equitable Remedies.** If the legal remedies for breach of contract are not adequate to fully compensate for a party's injuries, a court may grant an **equitable remedy.** Whether equitable relief is granted depends on the circumstances of a particular case. Courts grant equitable relief only when justice is served by doing so.[2] The two most common equitable remedies are **specific performance** and **injunction.**

**Specific Performance.** If the subject matter of the contract is *unique,* so that a money damage award will not adequately compensate an injured party, a court may order the breaching party to **specifically perform** the contract. Real estate has traditionally been treated as being unique and is the most common subject of specific performance decrees. For example, Jones enters into a contract to sell her house to Smith for $75,000. Jones later learns that the market value of the house is $80,000 and refuses to go through with the sale. Smith sues Jones for breach of contract. Smith's normal compensatory remedy would be the value of the unfulfilled promise less the cost to him of performing his part of the bargain (the market price less the contract price; in this example, $5,000). However, because real estate is generally

[2] The nature of equitable remedies is discussed in Chapter 1.

viewed as being unique, the court could order Jones to specifically perform her duties under the contract by giving Smith a deed to the property.

Personal property is not generally considered to be unique, but antiques, heirlooms, works of art, and objects of purely sentimental value may be sufficiently unique to merit a decree of specific performance. In general, specific performance is not decreed for promises to perform personal services. A decree requiring a person to specifically perform personal services would probably be ineffective in giving the injured party what he bargained for. In addition, it would involve a type of involuntary servitude.

**Injunctions.** An **injunction** is a court order prohibiting a person from doing certain acts. Injunctions are available when a breach of contract threatens to produce an *irreparable injury*. For example, Smith hires Jones to work as a salesperson in Smith's insurance agency. A term of the employment contract provides that Jones agrees not to work as an insurance salesperson for any of Smith's competitors within a specified geographic area for a period of two years after terminating his employment with Smith. If Jones quits his job with Smith and attempts to take a job with a competing insurance agency within the specified geographic area, Smith may file suit for breach of contract and may be able to persuade the court to *enjoin* Jones from working for a competing agency in violation of the contract provision.

## SUMMARY

A problem arising in the performance stage of contracts that is frequently presented to courts is determining when performance is due. A party's duty to perform is absolute unless it is subject to some condition. A condition is an uncertain event, other than the passage of time, that affects a party's duty to perform. An event that must occur before performance is due is called a condition precedent. An event that discharges a party from his duty to perform is called a condition subsequent. A condition that requires simultaneous performance of duties by the parties is called a concurrent condition.

Conditions may be created in several ways. They may be created by the express language of a contract (express conditions) or implied by the circumstances surrounding the contract or by the nature of the contract (implied-in-fact conditions). Although no particular language is necessary to create an express condition, such conditions are usually created by such language as "on condition that," "so long as," and "provided that."

A type of express condition that is common in building contracts is a contractual provision stating that one party's duty to perform is conditioned on a third party's satisfaction with the promisor's performance. The third person is held to a standard of honest satisfaction. Another type of express condition exists when a contract provides that a party's duty to pay is conditioned on his personal satisfaction with the other party's performance. In such cases, the standard for determining whether the condition has occurred will depend on whether the subject of the contract involves a matter of personal taste or convenience or whether it involves mechanical suitability or use. In the former type of case, a standard of honest or good faith satisfaction is applied. In the latter type of case, an objective, "reasonable man" standard is used to determine whether the condition has occurred.

Sometimes, conditions are imposed by courts even when the parties' contract does not state or imply a condition. This type of condition is called a constructive condition or an implied-in-law condition. It is imposed to do justice between the parties.

Although a party whose duty is conditional normally has no obligation to perform unless a condition occurs, there are some circumstances under which the occurrence of a condition may be excused. When a condition is excused, a party whose duty is conditional will have the obligation to perform notwithstanding the nonoccurrence of the condition.

When a promisor's performance is an express or implied-in-fact condition of the promisee's duty to render return performance and when a contract is capable of perfect performance, the promisor will be held to a standard of strict compliance with the contract. However, when performance is only a constructive condition and the nature of the contract is such that the promised performance is very difficult to render perfectly, the promisor will be held to the lower standard of substantial performance. Substantial performance falls somewhat short of complete performance, but does not deprive the promisee of a material part of the consideration for which he bargained. If the promisor substantially performs his obligations, he will be entitled to receive the other party's promised performance. Any recovery that he might receive is decreased by the amount of damages that his imperfect performance has caused. If the promisor's performance is defective in some major respect, he is guilty of material breach. When material breach occurs, the promisee is entitled to withhold his own performance and sue for damages for total breach.

In some exceptional circumstances in which unforeseen events occur after the formation of a contract, a promisor will be excused from performing. That is, even though the promisor had the legal duty to perform, his nonperformance will not be considered a breach of contract and he will be discharged from his obligations. A major basis for excusing nonperformance is impossibility. When an event occurs after the formation of the contract that renders performance impossible to carry out, the promisor will be excused. Impossibility means that the act cannot be done, not that the promisor is personally unable to do it. The mere fact that the promisor contracted to do something that he was incapable of doing or has suffered insolvency does not render the performance impossible. Impossibility generally arises in one of three situations: incapacitating illness or death of the promisor in contracts that require the promisor to perform personal services, supervening illegality caused by the enactment of statutes or governmental regulations that make performance illegal, and destruction of subject matter essential to the performance of the contract.

The UCC adopted a somewhat lower standard for excuse based on unforeseen events. It provides that performance is excused if performance is made *commercially impracticable* by a contingency occurring after the formation of the contract, the nonoccurrence of which was a basic assumption of the contract. The *Restatement (Second) of Contracts* contains a similar provision. A basis for excuse that is closely related to impossibility and impracticability is the doctrine of commercial frustration or frustration of venture. When a promisor has contracted to obtain a specific objective, his performance can be excused if an event that occurs subsequent to the formation of the contract would cause that objective to be frustrated.

When a party is released from further duties under a contract, it is said that his duties are *discharged.* Contracts are generally discharged by performance. Duties are also discharged by the other party's material breach, nonoccurrence of a condition precedent (unless such a condition has been excused), occurrence of a condition subsequent, and impossibility or the related doctrines of impracticability or frustration. Discharge can also occur by mutual agreement, waiver, or the promisee's failure to comply with the statute of limitations.

A variety of remedies are available for compensating parties who have been injured by a breach of contract. To recover damages in a contract case, the plaintiff must be able to prove his loss with reasonable certainty, and the loss must be one that was foreseeable to the breaching party at the time of contracting. The objective in granting a remedy is to place the injured party in the position in which he would have been if the contract had been performed as promised. Compensatory damages for breach of contract consist of the value of the unfulfilled promise plus allowable consequential and incidental damages less the cost to the promisee of performing his promise. Consequential damages are those that result from special circumstances of the injured party that are a direct result of the breach of contract. Incidental damages compensate for reasonable costs incurred by the plaintiff in attempting to avoid further loss. Courts sometimes use alternative damage remedies, such as permitting an injured party to recover money spent in reliance on the contract, when the normal measure of damages is inappropriate. Nominal damages are damages in a very small amount that are awarded in cases in which there has been a technical breach of contract that has caused no actual loss. Sometimes, parties will include a term in their contract whereby they agree that damages in a specified sum will be due upon breach of contract. These provisions are called liquidated damages provisions. Courts will enforce liquidated damages provisions where the amount of damages specified is reasonable in light of the injured party's probable losses and where it would be difficult to assess the amount of damages. Where the amount of damages specified is unreasonably great in relation to probable losses or where damages would be easy to calculate, courts will refuse to enforce the liquidated damages provision on the ground that it constitutes a penalty. Punitive damages generally are not awarded in contracts cases unless the breaching party is guilty of fraud or some other independent tort. A few states will, however, impose punitive damages in contracts cases in which the breaching party has been guilty of oppressive or malicious conduct.

When a contract has been breached, the injured party has the duty to take actions to mitigate, or decrease, the amount of damages that he might suffer.

When damages remedies appear to be inadequate to fully compensate the injured party, courts will sometimes grant an equitable remedy. The two most common equitable remedies are specific performance and injunction. When specific performance is decreed, the breaching party is ordered to perform his duties under the contract. Specific performance is used only when the subject of the contract is unique. Land is generally considered to be unique. Specific performance is not given in cases concerning contracts for personal property unless the property is of a special, unique nature, such as antiques or works of art. Specific performance is not granted in contracts for the performance of personal services. Injunctions are orders to people to refrain from doing specific acts. They are decreed only when an act threatens to do irreparable harm to an injured party.

## PROBLEM CASES

1. Weiss paid Nurse Midwifery Associates $750 to perform a "package" of midwifery services to his wife before, during, and after the birth of their child. Nurse Midwifery rendered prenatal and postnatal services to Weiss's wife on approximately 12 occasions, but because it did not have adequate advance notice of the birth of the child, it failed to

provide services during delivery. Weiss sued for the return of his $750. Should he win?

**2.** Wegematic contracted to provide the Federal Reserve Board with a digital computing system, which it represented as a "truly revolutionary system utilizing all of the latest technological advances." The contract specified the date on which performance was due, and provided that in the event that Wegematic failed to comply with any provision of the contract, the board could procure substitute performance from another source and hold Wegematic liable for the difference in cost. Wegematic failed to deliver the system on time, notifying the board that the delay was due to the necessity for redesigning the system and that the delivery of the system might be delayed for two more years. The board procured a substitute system from another supplier and sued Wegematic for the difference in cost. Wegematic claimed that engineering difficulties made its timely performance commercially impracticable. Does the doctrine of commercial impracticability provide an excuse in this case?

**3.** Light contracted to build a house for the Mullers. After the job was completed, the Mullers refused to pay Light the balance they owed him under the contract, claiming that he had done some of the work in an unworkmanlike manner. When Light sued for the money, the Mullers counterclaimed for $5,700 damages for delay under a liquidated damages clause in the contract. The clause provided that Light must pay $100 per day for every day of delay in completion of the construction. The evidence indicated that the rental value of the home was between $400 and $415 per month. Should the liquidated damages provision be enforced?

**4.** Cramer contracted to remodel a house for Essivein. In performing the contract, Cramer installed only seven radiators instead of eight as specified in the contract, leaving the bathroom without a radiator. He also installed a used bathtub and a used washbasin in the bathroom, although the contract required that both be new. Essivein refused to pay Cramer, who brought suit on the contract to recover the contract price for work and material. Is Cramer entitled to a judgment under the doctrine of substantial performance?

**5.** Merritt Hill Vineyards entered into a written agreement with Windy Heights Vineyards and its sole stockholder, Taylor, to buy a majority stock interest in Windy Heights's Yates County vineyard. As the contract required, Merritt paid a $15,000 deposit. The contract provided that if the sale did not close, Taylor would be able to keep the deposit as liquidated damages if certain conditions precedent specified in Section 3 of the contract were met. Among those conditions were the requirement that Windy Heights or Taylor obtain a satisfactory title insurance policy and confirmation of certain mortgages. At the closing, Merritt Hill discovered that neither the title policy nor the mortgage confirmation had been procured. It refused to close and demanded the return of its deposit. When Windy Heights and Taylor did not return the money, Merritt Hill brought suit. Is it entitled to the return of its deposit?

**6.** Prill Manufacturing Company entered into a contract making Colorado Coal Furnace Distributors the exclusive distributor of Prill's new model coal furnace. Although most metropolitan area building codes require International Congress of Building Officials (ICBO) approval of furnaces before an installation permit will be issued, the distributorship agreement did not mention Prill's obtaining ICBO approval for the new design. Only a manufacturer can apply for and receive ICBO approval. When Prill delayed in getting ICBO approval, Colorado withheld payment for inventory from Prill, claiming that such approval was necessary and that Prill had a duty to obtain it. Prill canceled the distributorship, and Colorado sued for damages. Did Prill have the duty to obtain ICBO approval?

**7.** Columbia Christian College decided to sell a 268-acre tract of land it owned. It gave Commonwealth Properties a 180-day option to purchase the land in exchange for $10,000. The option provided in part that Commonwealth had to attempt to secure certain zoning approval of the site and that if the zoning application was still pending at the expiration of the 180-day option, the option would be extended. It further provided that if the option were extended, Commonwealth would be obligated to purchase the property, subject only to "satisfactory decisions" regarding the outcome of the zoning approval. The parties later agreed to extend the option by six months. During the extension period, the Planning Commission recommended zoning approval on condition that certain changes be made in the final plan. Commonwealth notified the college that it would not buy the land because it did not consider the zoning approved by the Planning Commission to be satisfactory, since the research necessary to answer the commission's concerns would cost $100,000 and take six months to complete. The college brought suit against Commonwealth. What result?

**8.** Handicapped Children's Education Board hired Lukaszewski to serve as a speech and language therapist for the spring term. Lukaszewski was assigned to the Lightfoot School in Sheboygan Falls, which was approximately 45 miles from her home. Rather than move, she commuted to work. The board then offered Lukaszewski the same position for the next school year, and she accepted. Before school started, she was offered a higher paying position at another school that was nearer to her home. She attempted to resign from her job at the Lightfoot School, but the board refused to release her from her contract, threatening legal action if she breached it. Lukaszewski returned to the Lightfoot School, but was quite upset about the situation. She was examined by a physician, who discovered that she had high blood pressure. The physician advised her that driving long distances was dangerous for her and that her medical condition would not improve unless she changed her situation. Lukaszewski then tendered her resignation on health grounds and went to work for the school that had previously offered her a job. The board hired a replacement for Lukaszewski, but had to pay the replacement a higher salary. It sued Lukaszewski for breach of contract. Did Lukaszewski's medical condition excuse her nonperformance?

# PART IV

# AGENCY LAW

# Chapter 16

# The Agency Relationship

## INTRODUCTION

**The Significance of Agency Law.** Agency is a two-party relationship in which one party (the **agent**) is authorized to act on behalf of, and under the control of, the other party (the **principal**). Examples of the agency relationship are innumerable. They include hiring a salesperson to sell goods, retaining an attorney, engaging a real estate broker to sell a house, and hiring a corporate officer.

Agency law arose from the desire of people to extend their activities beyond the limits of their own bodies. It reflects the old Latin maxim *Qui facit per alium facit per se* (He who acts for another, himself acts). The main economic significance of the agency relationship is the agent's ability to make contracts for the principal and to bind the principal to those contracts. In fact, it is difficult to imagine how modern commercial relations could continue without the legal institution of agency. If agency law did not exist, an individual proprietor's ability to engage in trade would be restricted by the need to make each contract for purchase or sale in person. Because they are artificial persons that can act only through their agents, corporations could not function without agency law. Agency makes it possible for such actors to expand the range of their economic activities by increasing the number of transactions that they can complete within a given time.

**Topic Coverage and Organization.** Given the need for the agency relationship and its widespread use, certain legal problems inevitably arise. Obviously, it is necessary to know when an agency is created and how it will terminate. Since agency is a relationship of trust and confidence, the principal has a clear interest in the agent's faithful, capable, and conscientious performance of his duties. Thus, in addition to the obligations that the agent expressly agrees to assume, agency law imposes a number of special duties on the agent. For the agent's protection, it also imposes certain duties on the principal. These matters, which largely involve relations between the principal and the agent, are the concern of this chapter.

In addition, agency law governs the relations of third parties with the principal and the agent. The main function of agency is to increase the number of transactions in which persons can engage, and thus to promote commercial activity. For this to be done predictably and without unfairly binding principals, agents, or third parties, rules for determining the contractual liability of principal and agent are required. Also, since agents may injure third parties in the course of their duties, rules governing the tort liability of principal and agent are necessary. These and other topics are discussed in the next chapter.

## CREATION OF THE AGENCY RELATIONSHIP AND RELATED MATTERS

**Formation.** The agency relationship is based on the mutual consent of the parties. An agency is created by the manifested agreement of two persons that one person (the agent) shall act for the benefit of the other (the principal) under the principal's direction. As the term *manifested* suggests, the test for the existence of an agency is *objective.* If the parties' behavior and the surrounding facts and circumstances indicate an agreement that one person is to act for the benefit and under the control of another, courts will hold that the relationship exists. If the facts establish an agency, it is immaterial whether either party is aware of the existence of the relationship or subjectively desires that it exist. In fact, an agency may be present even where the parties have expressly stated that they do not intend to create it, or intend to create some other legal relationship instead. Once an agency relationship has been found to exist, agency law usually determines the rights and liabilities of the parties with respect to each other and to third persons.[1]

Although the agency relationship is consensual and typically involves a contract, it need not be contractual. Thus, consideration is not essential and a writing is required in only a few instances.[2] (In most states, for example, contracts in which an agent is to sell real estate require a writing.) Of course, it is often desirable that the terms of the agency agreement be spelled out in a written contract. Such a writing is sometimes called a *power of attorney.*

**Capacity.** The incapacity of either the principal or the agent will usually make the agency agreement voidable at the option of the party lacking capacity. Subject to the exceptions discussed in Chapter 11, an agency

[1] Under agency law, there are also situations where the principal is liable for the acts of a party who is not an agent at the time the acts occur. See the discussions of the "apparent agent" and ratification in the following chapter.

[2] Also, it is sometimes said that if the contract the agent forms is in writing, the agency agreement must likewise be written. However, it is doubtful whether this "equal dignity rule" enjoys widespread acceptance.

in which either party is a minor or an insane person at the time of its formation will be voidable. As you will see, an agency may be terminated if the principal or the agent loses capacity after it has been created. Also, the principal's or agent's incapacity may affect the liability of either to third parties.

Business organizations such as corporations can appoint agents. (In fact, the artificial corporate person only can act through its agents.) In a partnership, each partner generally acts as the agent of the other partners in transacting partnership business,[3] and partnerships can appoint nonpartner agents as well. In addition, corporations, partnerships, and other business organizations can act as agents. A husband or wife may act as agent for the other spouse, but there is no agency merely by virtue of marriage.

**Nondelegable Obligations.** Certain duties or actions cannot be delegated by a principal to an agent. For example, making statements under oath, voting in public elections, and signing wills must be done personally. Contracts for personal services where personal performance is crucial often cannot be delegated to an agent. Contracts by lawyers, doctors, artists, and entertainers are examples. Sometimes, obligations arising from relationships of trust and confidence and requiring personal judgment or discretion cannot be delegated to an agent.

[3] See Chapter 19 for a discussion of how agency law operates in the partnership context.

**Agency Terminology.** In its development, agency law has generated a number of technical definitions and distinctions. Usually, these are relevant only for certain purposes, and we will discuss them where they assume importance. When we consider the principal's contract liability in the next chapter, for example, we will distinguish the agent's *express, implied,* and *apparent* authority and we will examine the difference between *general* and *special* agents. The contract liability of the agent depends on whether the principal is *disclosed, partially disclosed,* or *undisclosed.* Also, determining the tort liability of the principal for acts of the agent often involves distinguishing *employees* from *independent contractors.*

## Warren v. United States

**613 F.2d 591 (5th Cir. 1980)**

Bobby and Modell Warren were cotton growers. For two years, they took their cotton crops to certain cotton gins that ginned and baled the cotton. Then, after being instructed to do so by the Warrens, the gins obtained bids for the cotton from prospective buyers and the Warrens told the gins which bids to accept. The gins sold the cotton to the designated buyers, collecting the proceeds. At the Warrens' instruction, the gins deferred payment of the proceeds to the Warrens until the year after the one in which each sale was made.

The Warrens did not report the proceeds as taxable income for the year when the gins received the proceeds, instead including the proceeds in the return for the following year. After an IRS audit, the Warrens were compelled to treat the proceeds as taxable income for the year when the proceeds were received, and to pay accordingly. The Warrens eventually won a refund action in federal district court. The government appealed. Its position was that: (1) the gins were agents of the Warrens; and (2) because of the established rule that receipt of proceeds by an agent is receipt by the principal, the proceeds were taxable income for the year in which they were received by the gins.

**Johnson, Circuit Judge.** The relationship between the Warrens and the gins for the purpose of selling the cotton was indisputably that of principal and agent. The Warrens instructed the gins to solicit bids, the Warrens decided whether to accept the highest price offered, and the Warrens determined whether or not to instruct the gins to hold the proceeds from the sale until the following year. The gins' role in the sale of the cotton was to adhere to the Warrens' instructions. The Warrens were the owners of the cotton held for sale; the Warrens were in complete control of its disposition.

This case is distinguishable from those cases where it was recognized that proceeds from the sale of a crop by a farmer, pursuant to a bona fide arm's-length contract between the buyer and seller calling for payment in the taxable year following delivery, are includable in gross income for the taxable year in which payment is received. In the case at bar the bona fide arm's-length agreement was not between the buyer and seller but rather between the seller and his agent. The Warrens' decision to have the gins hold the sales proceeds until the following year was a self-imposed limitation, not a part of the sales transaction between the buyer and seller. Such a self-imposed limitation does not change the general rule that receipt by an agent is receipt by the principal. The income was received by the Warrens' agents in the year of the sale. The fact that the Warrens restricted their access to the sales proceeds does not change the tax status of the money received.

Judgment reversed in favor of the government.

## DUTIES OF AGENT TO PRINCIPAL

**Introduction.** Most agencies are created by contract. Where this is so, the agent must perform according to the terms of the agreement and normal contract rules regarding interpretation, performance, and remedies apply. Regardless of whether the relationship is contractual, agency law also establishes certain *fiduciary duties* owed by the agent to the principal. These duties exist because agency is a relationship of trust and confidence. They supplement the duties created by a contract of agency. Often, however, the parties may eliminate or modify the fiduciary duties by agreement if they so desire.

A *gratuitous agent* (one who serves without compensation) has much the same fiduciary duties as an agent who receives compensation. Ordinarily, however, the gratuitous agent is not obligated to perform for the principal. Nonetheless, a gratuitous agent *will* be liable for her failure to perform when she causes the principal to reasonably rely on her to undertake certain acts, and the principal thus refrains from performing those acts himself. Suppose that, as a favor to her friend Porter, Astor agrees to submit a written bid for certain real estate on Porter's behalf but then neglects to submit the bid, which would have been successful. Porter does not learn of Astor's failure to act until it is too late to submit another bid. Astor is liable for the losses that Porter has suffered because of her failure to act.

**Agent's Duty of Loyalty.** The agency relationship exists for the principal's benefit.

Thus, the agent is obliged to recognize a **duty of loyalty** to the principal. The agent must use his best efforts to advance the principal's interests, must do nothing to frustrate those interests, must subordinate personal concerns by avoiding conflicts of interest with the principal, and must not disclose confidential information received from the principal.

**Conflicts of Interest.** If the agent has interests that conflict with the interests of the principal, the agent's ability to serve the principal is likely to suffer. Thus, when conducting the principal's business, the agent is generally forbidden to *deal with himself.* For example, an agent authorized to sell property cannot sell that property to himself. This rule often extends to transactions with the agent's relatives or business associates, or with business organizations in which the agent has an interest. However, the agent may enter into such transactions if the principal consents to his doing so. For this consent to be effective, the agent must disclose all of the relevant facts to the principal before dealing with the principal on his own behalf.

Unless the principal agrees otherwise, the agent is also forbidden to *compete with the principal* with regard to the business of the agency so long as he remains an agent. Thus, an agent employed to purchase specific property may not buy it himself if the principal still desires it. Moreover, as you will learn from the *New World* case, an agent may not solicit the principal's customers for a planned competing business while he is still employed by the principal.

Finally, as illustrated by the *Adams* case, an agent who is authorized to make a certain transaction cannot *act on behalf of the other party* to the transaction unless the principal knowingly consents to this. Thus, one ordinarily cannot act as agent for both parties to a transaction without first disclosing the double role to, and obtaining the consent of, both principals. In this case, the agent is under a duty to disclose to each principal all of the factors reasonably affecting each principal's decision. Sometimes, though, an agent who acts as a middleman may serve both parties to a transaction without notifying either. For instance, an agent may be simultaneously employed as a "finder" by a firm seeking suitable businesses to acquire and a firm looking for prospective buyers, so long as neither principal expects the agent to advise it or negotiate for it.

**Confidential Information.** Another facet of the agent's duty of loyalty is the obligation to ensure that the agency relation is one of **confidentiality.** Unless otherwise agreed, an agent has a duty not to *use* or *disclose* confidential information acquired through the agency. "Confidential information" means facts that have value because they are not widely known or that would harm the principal's business if they became widely known. Examples of such information include the principal's business plans, financial condition, contract bids, technological discoveries, manufacturing methods, customer files, and other trade secrets.[4] Although (absent an agreement to the contrary)[5] the agent is free to compete with the principal after termination of the agency, the duty not to use or disclose confidential information still remains.[6] However, the former agent may utilize general knowledge and skills acquired during the agency.

**Agent's Duty to Obey Instructions.** Because the agent acts under the principal's control and for the principal's benefit, she has

[4] Trade secrets law is discussed in Chapter 43.

[5] Covenants not to compete are discussed in Chapter 12.

[6] For a discussion of the patent and trade secrets problems created when an employee or a former employee tries to utilize ideas, discoveries, or inventions found or created during the course of her employment, see Chapter 43.

a duty to **obey all reasonable instructions** given by the principal for carrying out the agency business. However, an agent has no duty to obey an order to behave illegally or unethically. Thus, a sales agent need not follow directions to misrepresent the quality of the principal's goods and professionals such as attorneys and accountants are not obligated to obey directions that conflict with accepted ethical rules governing their professions.

Where the principal's directions are unclear or materially changed circumstances create reasonable doubt about the principal's wishes, it is up to the agent to ask questions. If this is impossible, the agent will not violate the duty of obedience if she acts reasonably on the basis of known facts. In emergencies where the principal cannot be reached for directions, agents may be justified in using their own reasonable judgment, even if this contradicts the principal's instructions. This is especially true when following instructions would clearly cause injury to the principal. Suppose that the manager of a retail store is told to make no expenditures while its owner is on an African safari. If a storm damages the store's roof and threatens further water damage to the store's interior and the merchandise, the manager would not violate the duty of obedience by paying for temporary repairs.

**Agent's Duty to Act with Care and Skill.** As the *Myers* case at the end of this section illustrates, a paid agent has the duty to possess and exercise the degree of **care and skill** that is standard in the locality for the kind of work that the agent is employed to perform. A gratuitous agent is subject to a lower standard of care. Paid agents who represent that they possess a higher-than-customary level of skill may be held to a correspondingly higher standard of performance. Similarly, the agent's duty may change if the principal and the agent agree that the agent will be required to possess and exercise a greater- or lesser-than-customary degree of care and skill. The agent may also warrant (guarantee) that he will be successful in his efforts or that his performance will be satisfactory to the principal. Absent such a warranty, though, the agent does not assume the risk of failure.

**Agent's Duty to Notify the Principal.** The principal has an interest in being informed of matters that are important to the agency business. Also, as discussed in Chapter 17, knowledge possessed by the agent is sometimes imputed to the principal, and this may affect the principal's rights with respect to third parties. Therefore, the agent is under a duty to promptly communicate to the principal matters within his knowledge that are reasonably relevant to the subject matter of the agency and that he knows or should know are of concern to the principal. However, there is no such **duty to notify** where the agent receives information that is privileged or confidential. For example, an attorney may acquire confidential information from a client and thus be obligated not to disclose it to a second client. If the attorney cannot properly represent the second client without revealing this information, he should refuse to represent that client.

**Agent's Duty to Account.** The agent's duties of loyalty and care require that the agent give the principal any money or property received in the course of the agency business. As the *New World* case makes clear, this includes profits resulting from the agent's breach of the duty of loyalty (or other duties). It also includes incidental benefits received as a result of the agency business. Examples of such incidental benefits are bribes, kickbacks, and gifts from third parties with whom the agent deals on the principal's behalf. However, the parties may agree that the agent can retain certain benefits received during the agency, such as tips from customers and entertainment provided by third parties with whom the agent does business.

Another type of **duty to account** concerns agents whose business involves collections, receipts, or expenditures. Here, the agent must keep accurate records and accounts of all transactions, and disclose these to the principal once the principal makes a reasonable demand for them. Also, an agent who obtains or holds property for the principal usually may not commingle that property with her own property. For example, the agent ordinarily cannot deposit the principal's funds in her own name or in her own bank account.

**Remedies of the Principal.** The principal has a wide choice of actions and remedies when the agent breaches a duty. The following examples are not an exhaustive list. If the agency relation was created by contract, the agent's wrongdoing should be a breach of that contract and the principal should get the various kinds of contract damages where appropriate. Also, the principal may obtain injunctive relief where the agent discloses or threatens to disclose confidential information, or appropriates or threatens to appropriate the principal's property. In addition, the principal may rescind contracts entered into by an agent who has represented two principals without the knowledge of one or both, has dealt with himself, or has failed to disclose relevant facts to the principal. Agents who retain money or property due the principal (including bribes or gifts), or who profit from the breach of duty, may also be liable for the amount of their unjust enrichment.

Also tort actions are possible when the agent has misbehaved. The principal may recover for losses caused by the agent's negligent failure to follow instructions, to notify, or to perform with appropriate skill and care. The tort of conversion is available where the agent has unjustifiably retained, stolen, transferred, destroyed, failed to separate, or otherwise misappropriated the principal's property.

## New World Fashions, Inc. v. Lieberman

### 429 So. 2d 1276 (Fla. Dist. Ct. App. 1983)

New World Fashions, Inc., a corporation in the business of assisting persons interested in entering the retail clothing business, employed Abbott Lieberman as a sales representative on August 8, 1978. Lieberman was fired on March 30, 1979 for stealing New World's clients for a similar business that he was about to start. While working for New World, Lieberman told one potential client, a Mrs. Kight, that he would soon go into business himself in competition with New World and that he could offer her either New World's contract or his own. Later, he made a contract to set up a retail store for Kight, a service that New World would otherwise have provided. New World's claims for compensatory damages, punitive damages, injunctive relief, and an accounting were denied by the trial court, and New World appealed.

**Nimmons, Judge.** Under the evidence presented, New World was entitled to an accounting for loss of profits as a consequence of Lieberman's breach of his duty to New World. An agent may not, without the principal's knowledge and consent, enter into any business in competition with his principal and keep for himself any profit accruing from such transaction. Of course, a principal and agent may have the kind of relationship which would contemplate the agent being authorized to engage in activities in competition with the principal's business. As stated in *Restatement (Second) of Agency* § 393, Comment a:

> There is no violation of the agent's duty if the principal understands that the agent is to compete; a course of dealing between the parties may indicate that this is understood. Likewise, an agent can properly act freely on his own account in matters not within the field of his agency and in matters in which his interests are not antagonistic to those of the principal.

However, there was no understanding that Lieberman would be competing with New World; nor was there any course of dealing between the parties which would suggest acquiescence by New World in any competitive dealings by Lieberman.

Of course, absent agreement to the contrary, there is nothing to preclude an agent from competing with his principal after the termination of their relationship. In fact, the agent is entitled to make arrangements to compete prior to the agency's termination and the agent has no duty to disclose such plans. However, he is not entitled to solicit customers for such rival business before the termination of the agency; nor can he properly do other similar acts in direct competition with the principal's business.

We hold that New World was entitled to an accounting in equity for the profits realized by Lieberman from his transaction with Kight. Inasmuch as Lieberman, at the time of trial, was no longer engaged in a business competitive with New World, the trial judge correctly denied the prayer for a permanent injunction. We have examined the remaining claims asserted by New World and find them to be without merit.

Judgment reversed in favor of New World.

## Adams v. Kerr

**655 S.W.2d 49 (Mo. Ct. App. 1983)**

On March 4, 1980, the Kerrs, an elderly couple, entered into a real estate listing contract with Red Carpet Mehler Company, a real estate broker, for the sale of their four-family flat. The listing price was $118,000. Red Carpet then persuaded the Kerrs to accept $110,000 if offered and to consider accepting a cash down payment plus a secured note for the balance. On March 23, Robert Adams, a partner in a real estate partnership named A&E Associates, offered to purchase the Kerrs' property for $110,000. The payment terms were $22,000 cash down along with a secured note for $88,000. Red Carpet submitted Adams's offer to the Kerrs, who accepted it. At the time they accepted, the Kerrs were unaware that Red Carpet was managing property for A&E Associates and had been representing A&E for several years.

Adams's offer set the terms for the sale. It was signed by Adams individually as purchaser and did not mention A&E. It also stated that the ultimate grantee of the Kerrs' property was to be "as directed" by Adams. The contract further provided that it was not binding unless Adams submitted a credit report satisfactory to the Kerrs. On March 29, Adams gave the Kerrs a one-page net worth analysis for A&E Associates. This document gave no phone number for A&E Associates, provided little detail about A&E's business operations, and applied only to the period ending August 1, 1979. The Kerrs were unable to locate or identify A&E and could not uncover any further information about its operations. They also requested, but never received, a certified credit report on A&E. It was only at this time that the Kerrs learned that Red Carpet was managing property for A&E.

On April 9, the Kerrs informed Red Carpet that they would not go through with the sale. Later, the Kerrs received a letter from Red Carpet's attorney threatening suit on behalf of Red Carpet and Adams if the Kerrs did not sell. At the April 18 closing, the Kerrs discovered that the ultimate grantees of their property were to be Adams, his partner Donald Ehrhardt, and their wives. The Kerrs again asked for a credit report, but were refused. Red Carpet repeated its threat to sue if the Kerrs did not go through with the deal, but the Kerrs refused to sell. They also refused to pay Red Carpet's commission on the aborted sale.

Adams sued the Kerrs for specific performance of the sale contract, and Red Carpet sued for its commission. The Kerrs counterclaimed against Red Carpet for, among other things, breach of its fiduciary duties to them. The trial court directed a verdict for Red Carpet on the Kerrs' counterclaim, and the Kerrs appealed.

**Karohl, Judge.** The Kerrs' counterclaim alleged that Red Carpet breached its fiduciary duty by: (1) divulging confidential information as to price and terms of sale to prospective purchasers; and (2) representing both parties without full disclosure or consent to their dual capacity.

We conclude that the Kerrs made a submissible case of breach of fiduciary duty against Red Carpet. The broker is the agent of the seller who lists the property with him unless it is otherwise understood and provided, and therefore owes the seller its undivided loyalty and is required to exercise the utmost fidelity and good faith. It is the broker's duty to keep the principal fully informed, to make full disclosure of all facts, and to exercise reasonable care and diligence in the performance of his duty. The broker must not do anything which makes the transaction more difficult or burdensome for his principal or which endangers the transaction. Moreover, there is scarcely a rule of law which has received more uniform approval than that an agent cannot serve the opposing party without the knowledge and consent of his principal. A broker that represents both seller and purchaser without disclosing forfeits his commission. Further, after the broker finds a buyer, he must not take any action that improperly hinders or prejudices his principal.

Although Red Carpet advised Mrs. Kerr that it managed property for Adams and A&E Associates, this was not until after the Kerrs had signed the sale contract. Thus, the Kerrs were not informed of the dual representation before they signed the contract. Thereafter, Red Carpet failed to pursue and furnish a credit report from the true purchasers, Mr. and Mrs. Adams and Mr. and Mrs. Ehrhardt. In effect, they ordered the Kerrs to close and take back a purchase money note from the four individual purchasers without the benefit of the credit report called for in the contract, or be sued. Red Carpet caused its attorney to send a letter threatening suit to one principal, the Kerrs, when their other principal, Adams, had not complied with the terms of the contract. It clearly breached its duty of undivided loyalty to the Kerrs.

Judgment in favor of Red Carpet on the Kerrs' counterclaim for breach of fiduciary duty reversed. (*Note:* In another portion of its opinion, the court also denied Red Carpet's claim for a commission and Adams's specific performance claim. The principal's duty to compensate the agent is discussed below.)

## F. W. Myers & Co. v. Hunter Farms

### 319 N.W.2d 186 (Iowa Sup. Ct. 1982)

Hunter Farms was seeking to obtain a supply of a farm herbicide called Sencor. It received an offer to sell from the Petrolia Grain & Feed Company of Petrolia, Canada. A representative of Petrolia's supplier contacted an "import specialist" with the U.S. Customs Service to determine the import duty on the shipment of Sencor. The specialist stated that the rate would probably be 5 percent but that the final rate could be determined only by examining the shipment at the time of importation. This information was forwarded to Hunter Farms, which eventually ordered the Sencor. In the meantime, Hunter had employed F. W. Myers & Co., an import broker, to assist in moving the Sencor through customs and Myers had performed as agreed. Unfortunately, the actual import duty imposed on the shipment of Sencor turned out to be much higher than the 5 percent suggested by the import specialist. Because the Sencor contained chemicals not listed on its label, the duty was increased from about $30,000 to over $128,000. Myers paid the additional amount under protest and requested that Hunter compensate it for this additional expense. Hunter refused to do so.

Myers then sued Hunter to get Hunter to reimburse it for the additional expense. (The principal's duty to reimburse is discussed in the next section.) Myers was successful at the trial court level. Hunter appealed, arguing that it was not obligated to reimburse Myers, because Myers had breached the agent's duties of care and notification by failing to inform Hunter that the 5 percent figure was only advisory.

**Larson, Justice.** An agent is required to exercise such skill as is required to accomplish the object of his employment. If he fails to exercise reasonable care, diligence, and judgment under the circumstances, he is liable to his principal for any loss or damage resulting. Thus:

> Unless otherwise agreed, a paid agent is subject to a duty to the principal to act with standard care and with the skill which is standard in the locality for the kind of work which he is employed to perform and, in addition, to exercise any special skill that he has. *Restatement* (*Second*) *of Agency* § 379(1).

We believe that there was substantial evidence to support the trial court's finding that there was no breach of duty by Myers. Evidence was presented that the standard of care for import brokers did not include a special duty to render advice to the importer unless requested to do so. Expert testimony showed such brokers are basically involved in drafting the necessary papers, arranging for the necessary bonds, and actual forwarding of the duty payment. There was no evidence of a request to advise Hunter on import law, nor was there any evidence that Myers was advised that Hunter was new in the import business.

Hunter contends, however, that Myers had a special duty of disclosure to advise Hunter that the five-percent figure was advisory or only an estimate. It claims the trial court erred in failing to recognize and apply this duty of care. The scope of an agent's duty to disclose is explained by the *Restatement* in this manner:

Unless otherwise agreed, an agent is subject to a duty to use reasonable efforts to give his principal information which is relevant to affairs entrusted to him and which, as the agent has notice, the principal would desire to have and which can be communicated without violating a superior duty to a third person. *Restatement* (*Second*) *of Agency* § 381.

This standard requires that the agent have notice that the principal would desire to have the relevant information. In this case, there was evidence that the open-ended nature of an initial duty assessment was widely known and understood by importers. Myers was never informed of the need to convey this information to Hunter, which, it could reasonably presume, possessed the fundamental knowledge of an importer. Myers was never advised of Hunter's lack of experience in the business, nor was it aware of the problem in labelling the herbicide which caused the increase in the duty charged. Absent knowledge of Hunter's special need for advice and of the circumstances which might give rise to the additional importation fees, there was no special duty on Myers to advise Hunter of the special nature of the assessment.

Judgment for Myers affirmed.

## DUTIES OF PRINCIPAL TO AGENT

**Introduction.** If an agency is formed by contract, the agency contract should set out the duties of the principal to the agent. In addition, the law implies certain duties from the existence of the agency relationship, however formed. The most important[7] such duties are the principal's obligations to **compensate** the agent, to **reimburse** the agent for money spent in the principal's service, and to **indemnify** the agent for losses suffered in conducting the principal's business. Generally, these duties can be eliminated or modified by agreement between the parties. There is obviously no duty to compensate a gratuitous agent, but the other two duties still exist absent an agreement to the contrary.

**Duty to Compensate Agent.** Where an agency contract states the compensation that the agent is to receive, disputes about the compensation due the agent are settled by applying the rules of contract interpretation. In other cases, the relationship of the parties and the surrounding circumstances determine whether and to what extent the agent is to be compensated. In the absence of a contract provision on compensation, for example, the principal may not be required to pay for undertakings that she did not request, services to which she did not consent, or tasks that are typically undertaken without pay. Also, the principal usually will not be obliged to compensate an agent who has *materially* breached the agency contract or has committed a *serious* breach of a fiduciary duty. Where compensation is due, but its amount is not expressly stated, the amount will be the market price or the customary price for the agent's services, or, if neither is available, their reasonable value.

Sometimes, the agent's compensation is contingent on the accomplishment of a specific result. For instance, a plaintiff's attorney may be retained on a contingent fee basis (being paid a certain percentage of the recovery

[7] The principal may also have other duties, including the duties to: provide the agent with an opportunity for service, not interfere with the agent's work, keep accounts, act in a manner not harmful to the agent's reputation or self-esteem, and (in the case of employees) maintain a safe workplace. The last duty has been greatly affected by the workers' compensation systems and the Occupational Safety and Health Act, discussed in Chapter 47.

if the suit succeeds or is settled), or a real estate broker may be entitled to a fee only if a suitable buyer is found. In such cases, the agent is not entitled to compensation unless he achieves the result within the time stated or (if no time is stated) a reasonable time. This is true regardless of how much effort or money the agent expends. However, the principal must cooperate with the agent in the achievement of the result and must not do anything to frustrate the agent's efforts. Otherwise, the agent will be entitled to compensation despite the failure to perform as specified. Also, an agent who achieves the stipulated result must be compensated even though the principal is not benefited by his performance.

To illustrate these points, consider a manufacturer who agrees to pay a sales agent a certain commission on all orders that the principal accepts and approves. The principal will be obligated to pay the commission once it accepts and approves an order, even if later developments make it impossible to ship the goods specified in the order. But no matter how hard the agent works, the commission will not be payable if her efforts fail to produce suitable orders—unless the principal's failure to accept and approve is so arbitrary that it amounts to a failure to cooperate.

**Duties of Reimbursement and Indemnity.** If, while acting on the principal's behalf, the agent has made expenditures directly requested by the principal or reasonably to be inferred from services that the principal has directly requested, the agent is entitled to **reimbursement** for those expenditures absent an agreement to the contrary. Unless otherwise agreed, for example, an agent requested to make overnight trips as part of his agency duties can recover reasonable transportation and hotel expenses.

The principal's duty of reimbursement overlaps with her duty of **indemnity.** Agency law implies a promise by the principal to indemnify the agent for losses (usually legal liabilities) suffered while engaging in activities that the principal has authorized the agent to undertake. For example, an agent who as part of his duties becomes liable on a contract[8] is entitled to indemnification for amounts that he is required to pay as a result. However, the duty of indemnity (and the duty of reimbursement) do not exist where the liability, loss, or expenditure results from actions that the agent knew or should have known were illegal.

**Remedies of the Agent.** The agent's claim for breach of the duties just discussed is usually contractual, and normal contract remedies (except specific performance) are available. In some cases, the principal's failure to pay, indemnify, or reimburse the agent will enable the agent to acquire a lien on property or funds of the principal that are in the agent's possession. This usually allows the agent to hold the property or funds until the principal's obligation has been paid. Also, an agent whose principal violates the duties to pay, indemnify, or reimburse can refuse to render further services to the principal.

Of course, the agent's *own* breach of duty may defeat his claim against the principal. Where the breach is not serious enough to give the principal a complete defense, the principal may still set off losses caused by the breach against the agent's recovery.

## TERMINATION OF THE AGENCY RELATIONSHIP

An agency may be terminated in a variety of ways. These can be grouped under two general headings: (1) **termination by acts of the**

[8] The agent's liability to third parties on contracts made for the principal is discussed in the next chapter.

**parties** and (2) **termination by operation of law.**

**Termination by Acts of the Parties.** The parties can control the termination of their agency through either the provisions they put in the agency agreement or their actions after concluding the agreement. First, an agency will terminate at a time or upon the happening of an event stated in the agreement. If no such time or event is stipulated, the agency terminates after a reasonable time. Second, an agency created to accomplish a specified result terminates when that result has been accomplished. For example, if the only objective of an agency is to sell certain property, the agency will terminate when the property is sold. Third, an agency may be terminated at any time by mutual agreement of the parties.

Finally, an agency will terminate if the principal revokes it or the agent renounces it. Generally, revocation or renunciation occurs when either party manifests to the other that he does not wish the agency to continue. Conduct inconsistent with the continuance of the agency can constitute such a manifestation. For example, the agent may learn that the principal has hired another agent to perform the same job. A party can revoke or renounce even if this violates the agency agreement. However, while either party has the *power* to terminate in such cases, there is no *right* to do so. This means that where one party terminates in violation of the contract, he will not be bound to perform any further, but may be liable for damages to the other party.[9] However, the terminating party will *not* be liable where the revocation or renunciation is justified by the other party's serious breach of a fiduciary duty.

**Termination by Operation of Law.** Numerous other events may terminate the agency relation. These events generally do not involve the parties' willful choices. Instead, they usually involve situations where it is reasonable to believe that the principal would not wish the agent to act further or where accomplishment of the agency objectives has become impossible or illegal. Although courts may recognize exceptions in certain cases, an agency relationship will usually be terminated by:

1. **The death of the principal or the agent.** Here, the agent's notice of the principal's death is usually not required.
2. **The principal's permanent loss of capacity.** This is a *permanent* loss of capacity occurring *after* creation of the agency. The usual cause is the principal's insanity. A brief period of insanity may sometimes cause a temporary suspension of the agency relation during the time that the principal is insane.
3. **The agent's loss of capacity to perform the agency business.** The scope of this basis for termination is unclear. As you will see in the next chapter, an agent who becomes insane or otherwise personally incapacitated can still bind the principal to contracts with third parties. Thus, it probably makes little sense to regard the agency relationship as terminated in such cases. As a result, termination under this heading may be limited to such situations as the loss of a license needed to perform agency duties (for example, a license needed to sell certain goods).

[9] In the case of agents who are *employees*, the traditional "employment at will" doctrine states that either the employer or the employee could terminate at will and without liability where the employment was not for a fixed time. Chapter 47 discusses the doctrine and the exceptions that are increasingly eroding it. The term *employee* is defined in the next chapter.

4. **Changes in the value of the agency property or subject matter** (for example, a significant decline in the value of land to be sold by an agent).
5. **Changes in business conditions** (for example, a markedly lower supply and a greatly increased price for goods to be purchased by an agent).
6. **The loss or destruction of the agency property or subject matter or the termination of the principal's interest therein** (for example, a situation in which a house to be sold by a real estate broker burns down or is taken by a mortgage holder to satisfy a debt owed by the principal).
7. **Changes in the law that make the agency business illegal** (for example, a situation in which drugs to be sold by an agent are banned by the government).
8. **The bankruptcy of the principal**—as to transactions that the agent should realize are no longer desired by the principal. Consider, for example, the likely effect of the principal's bankruptcy on an agency to purchase antiques for the principal's home, as opposed to its likely effect on an agency to purchase necessities of life for the principal.
9. **The bankruptcy of the agent**—where the agent's financial condition affects his ability to serve the principal. This could occur where the agent is employed to purchase goods on his own credit for the principal.
10. **Impossibility of performance by the agent.** This covers a wide range of circumstances, some of which fall within the categories just stated.
11. **A serious breach of the agent's duty of loyalty.**
12. **The outbreak of war**—where this leads the agent to the reasonable belief that his services are no longer desired. One example might be the outbreak of war between the principal's country and the agent's country.

**Termination of Agency Powers Given as Security.** An agency power given as security for a duty owed by the principal, sometimes called an "agency coupled with an interest," is an exception to some of the termination rules just discussed. In this case, the agent has an interest in the subject matter of the agency that is distinct from the principal's interest and is not exercised for the principal's benefit. This interest exists to benefit the agent or a third person (and not the principal) by securing performance of an obligation owed by the principal. A common example is a secured loan agreement authorizing the lender (the agent) to sell property used as security if the debtor (the principal) defaults. For example, suppose that Allen lends Peters $100,000 and Peters gives Allen a lien or security interest on Peters's land to secure the loan. Such an agreement typically would authorize Allen to act as Peters's "agent" to sell the land if Peters fails to repay the loan.

Because the power given the "agent" in such cases is not for the principal's benefit, it is sometimes said that an agency coupled with an interest is not a true agency relationship. In any event, courts distinguish it from situations where the agent only has an interest in being compensated from the profits or proceeds of property held for the principal's benefit. For example, if an agent is promised a commission for selling the principal's property, the relationship is not an agency coupled with an interest. In this case, the power exercised by the agent (selling the principal's property) benefits the principal.

The main significance of the agency coupled with an interest is that the principal cannot revoke it. Also, it will not be terminated by either the principal's or the agent's loss of capacity. In addition, the death of the agent will not terminate this relationship and the death of the principal will do so only when the obligation owed by the principal ends with the principal's death. However, unless the agency coupled with an interest is held for the benefit of a third party, the agent can voluntarily surrender it. Of course, the agency coupled with an interest will terminate when the principal performs her obligation as promised.

## SUMMARY

Because the agency relationship enables individuals and businesses to multiply their transactions, it is vital to a commercial economy. Courts will hold that an agency exists if the facts indicate an agreement that one person will act for the benefit and under the control of another. However, while the agency relationship is based on mutual consent, it need not be contractual. In a few cases, however, a writing is necessary to create an agency. The incapacity of either the principal or the agent at the time an agency is formed will render the agency voidable at the option of the party lacking capacity. Also, there are certain duties that cannot be delegated to an agent.

Since the agency relationship is for the benefit of the principal, agency law imposes a number of duties on the agent. These supplement the duties expressly created by an agency agreement. The agent's duties are: (1) loyalty to the principal; (2) obedience to the principal's reasonable, lawful, and ethical instructions; (3) care and skill in performing agency duties; (4) notification of matters affecting the principal's interest in the agency business; (5) the return of profits and other things of value received in the course of the agency business; and (6) an accounting of the agency's financial operations generally.

The agency relation also imposes certain duties on the principal. The most important such duties are: (1) to compensate the agent, (2) to reimburse the agent for expenditures connected with the agency business, and (3) to indemnify the agent for losses suffered in the course of the agency business.

An agency can be terminated by the acts of the parties or by operation of law. Termination by acts of the parties includes: (1) the occurrence of an event or the passage of a time period stated in the agency agreement, (2) the passage of a reasonable time (if no termination date has been set by agreement), (3) accomplishment of the results for which the agency was established, (4) mutual agreement of the parties, (5) the principal's revocation, and (6) the agent's renunciation. If the revocation or renunciation violates the agency contract, however, the terminating party may be liable for damages.

Termination by operation of law includes: (1) the death of the principal or the agent, (2) the principal's permanent loss of capacity, (3) the agent's loss of capacity (but the scope of this basis for termination is unclear), (4) changes in the value of the agency property or subject matter, (5) changes in business conditions, (6) loss or destruction of the agency property or termination of the principal's interest therein, (7) changes in the law that make the agency business illegal, (8) the principal's or the agent's bankruptcy (in certain cases), (9) impossibility of performance, (10) a serious breach of the agent's duty of loyalty, and (11) the outbreak of war (in certain cases). An agency coupled with an interest, however, cannot be terminated by the principal's revocation, the principal's or the agent's incapacity, the agent's death, or (sometimes) the principal's death.

## PROBLEM CASES

**1.** Joan Marie Ottensmeyer was a contestant for the title of Miss Hawaii–USA 1974.

The pageant was run by Richard You as a franchisee of Miss Universe, Inc. After finishing as first runner-up, Ottensmeyer sued Miss Universe, Inc., arguing that as its agent You had prevented her from winning a title to which she was rightfully entitled and from obtaining the benefits thereof. The franchise agreement between Miss Universe and You contained language explicitly stating that You was not Miss Universe's agent. By itself, is this language sufficient to prevent the formation of an agency relationship between Miss Universe and You?

**2.** Melabs of California manufactured a portable electric telephone that was designed to fit inside an attaché case and to operate on the same airwaves as fixed telephone installations in vehicles. Melabs and Marlin American Corporation entered into a contract giving Marlin the right to distribute the phone. The contract gave Marlin the exclusive right to establish a sales and marketing program and to develop all brochures, sales aids, forms, advertising materials, and other marketing aids. On the other hand, it gave Melabs the right to approve all contract forms. It also established that uniform terms, conditions, and prices would be offered to the ultimate distributors of the phones. In addition, it transferred ownership of subsequent distributorships established by Marlin to Melabs in the event that Marlin went bankrupt. Finally, there was evidence that, in practice, Melabs exercised approval rights over the use of its trademark in advertising matters. On these facts, did Melabs possess sufficient control over Marlin to create an agency relationship between Melabs and Marlin?

**3.** Cloyd was employed by Wormhoudt Lumber Company to find construction jobs that would use Wormhoudt's materials. He did this by locating property owners who wanted to build and bringing them together with contractors. Cloyd also computed costs for materials and labor, including a profit for the contractor. If the contractor and owner were satisfied, they would make a contract between themselves. A contractor who paid Wormhoudt for the materials within 30 days of the billing was entitled to a 10 percent discount. Cloyd persuaded several contractors to split the 10 percent discount with him in return for being recommended by him. Later, he got some contractors to commit themselves to a price for the labor on a job, to which he added the retail price of the materials plus a profit for the contractor. Then, he split both the profit and the discount with the contractor. Shortly after Cloyd left his employment with Wormhoudt, one of the contractors reported Cloyd's dealings to Wormhoudt. Can Wormhoudt recover Cloyd's secret profits?

**4.** Simmerson contracted to sell certain real and personal property to Spillman. According to the contract, Spillman was to pay Simmerson's legal fees in connection with the transaction. After the transaction was closed, Blanks, Spillman's attorney, volunteered to file the financing statement giving Simmerson a security interest in the personal property sold to Spillman. He failed to do this, resulting in loss to Simmerson. Simmerson sued Blanks for his negligence, and the court found that there was no attorney-client contract between Blanks and Simmerson. Can Blanks be liable to Simmerson on his gratuitous promise?

**5.** David Lerner wanted to arrange a ski vacation for his wife and son. He phoned United Airlines to book a complete ski trip package from January 9 to January 15. This included airline tickets, hotel vouchers, and ski lift tickets. It did not include ground transportation from the Salt Lake City Airport to the lodge in Alta, Utah, where the Lerners were to stay—a distance of 25 miles.

When Mrs. Lerner arrived in Salt Lake City on January 9, she learned that the only road to Alta had been closed because of the danger of avalanches. She was told that the road might be opened the next day, but this did not occur until the afternoon of January 12.

Mrs. Lerner was able to ski at Alta for only 2½ days, and she said that her vacation had been totally ruined. United refused to give the Lerners credit for the extra expenses in Salt Lake City and sued Mr. Lerner for the balance of his United credit card account. Lerner argued that United had a duty as his agent to warn him that the danger of avalanches might frustrate his wife's vacation and that he thus was not obligated to pay United for the ski trip package. Did United breach a duty to Lerner?

**6.** Sears, Roebuck contracted with Heidt's Protective Services to provide security personnel in a Sears store. Art Keolian was a Heidt's employee assigned to work as a uniformed guard in the Sears store pursuant to the contract. Keolian confronted a woman who had been identified by a salesclerk as a shoplifter. When she refused to return to the store with him, Keolian shoved her to the ground, straddled her body, and pinned her arms above her head. Then, the police arrived and took both Keolian and the woman to the station. A subsequent investigation proved that the shoplifting charges were without foundation.

The woman sued Sears and Heidt's, and Sears filed a claim against Heidt's for indemnification for any liability that it was found to have. The trial judge's instruction to the jury made Heidt's liability to Sears depend *only* on whether Heidt's had expressly promised to provide a qualified guard. Is this instruction legally correct?

**7.** Richard Larsen, a North Dakota farmer, phoned the North Dakota Agricultural Marketing Association (NDAMA) in order to find a buyer for 12,000 bushels of durum wheat. NDAMA called back the following day, quoting a price for delivery in Superior, Wisconsin, available from the Minnesota Farm Bureau Marketing Association (MFBMA). Larsen accepted, and he was sent a written confirmation stating: "We confirm your sale of durum today to Minnesota Farm Bureau Mkt." He arranged to ship six loads of durum. The trucker making the deliveries experienced delays in unloading the grain in Superior and demanded a higher rate for hauling the remaining 7,300 bushels. Larsen then refused to deliver the remainder of the grain due on the contract. NDAMA was forced to pay damages to MFBMA because of Larsen's breach and sued Larsen for indemnification. Will NDAMA win?

**8.** In March of 1976, Marie Price Reel appointed her nephew as agent to purchase "flower bonds" on her behalf. Flower bonds were U.S. government securities that sold at a substantial discount, paid a low rate of interest, and could be redeemed at par value for the payment of estate taxes upon the death of their owner. Reel was in a coma from the time she suffered a massive stroke on April 24, 1976, until her death on May 4, 1976. After her stroke but before her death, the nephew purchased flower bonds with a face value of $225,000 on Reel's behalf. The government refused to accept the bonds in payment of estate taxes, claiming that Reel did not own them at the time of her death because her incapacity had terminated the agency. Medical testimony established that, although Reel's recovery from the stroke was unlikely, she had *some* chance of recovering and regaining her faculties. Did Reel's stroke completely terminate the agency? Do *not* consider whether the stroke may have caused a *temporary* suspension of the relationship.

# Chapter 17

# Third-Party Relations of the Principal and the Agent

## INTRODUCTION

In an agency, the agent is an extension or alter ego of the principal. Thus, the agency relationship enables people to increase the number of transactions in which they can engage, and thereby stimulates commercial activity. The agent's dealings and interactions with third parties, however, create numerous legal problems that agency law must confront if it is to achieve its aims.

Suppose that the Porter Corporation appoints Arthur as a sales agent. Arthur's duty is to travel from place to place by automobile, selling Porter's products. Porter has a clear interest in being able to predict and control its liability on contracts made by Arthur. Similarly, the buyers with whom Arthur deals need to know when Arthur can legally bind Porter to the sales contracts that he makes. Thus, rules for determining when the principal will be liable on contracts made by the agent are crucial to the successful operation of the agency relationship.

Also, both Arthur and the buyers should be interested in knowing when *Arthur* will be liable on his contracts. Thus, rules for determining the *agent's* contractual liability are also important to the effective functioning of the agency relationship. Moreover, since the agent is the principal's alter ego, notifications that Arthur dispatches or receives may be treated as if they had been sent or received by Porter. Similarly, information coming Arthur's way may be treated as information known to Porter.

Agents can cause various injuries to third parties while acting for the principal. Suppose that Arthur makes false representations about Porter's goods, or runs down a pedestrian while pursuing Porter's business affairs. Typically, Arthur should (and will) be liable in such cases, but the desirability of requiring Porter to compensate injured parties may vary with the circumstances. Thus, determining the principal's tort liability for the agent's acts is a major concern of agency law. The principal's liability for crimes committed in the course of the agency business is also a matter of concern.

Finally, the agent's ability to pursue the principal's interests may depend on his ability to appoint his own agents. Arthur, for example, may need someone to keep records or to represent him in remote areas. Thus, agency law sometimes permits agents to appoint *subagents.* The subagent's ability to bind the principal and the agent in contract and tort is another preoccupation of agency law.

## CONTRACT LIABILITY OF THE PRINCIPAL

**Introduction.** The principal is liable to third parties for the contracts of an agent having **actual authority** or **apparent authority** to make such contracts.[1] Both sorts of authority are based on the principal's manifested consent that the agent may act for the principal. In the case of actual authority, this assent is communicated to the *agent,* while for apparent authority it is communicated to the *third party.* There are two kinds of actual authority: **express authority** and **implied authority.** Thus, the principal can be bound on the basis of the agent's express, implied, or apparent authority to make contracts for the principal.

**Express Authority.** Express authority is created by words of the principal that completely and precisely state what the agent has the power to do. The language creating express authority can be written or oral. In either case, it must be communicated to the agent. Thus, for express authority to bind the principal to the agent's contract, the principal must have explicitly informed the agent that he could make the contract in question. For example, suppose that Payne orally instructs her agent, Andrews, to purchase a certain antique chair owned by Tucker for $800 or less, to draw up a contract to that effect, and to sign the contract for Payne. If Andrews agrees to buy the chair for $800, completes an appropriate contract, gets Tucker to sign it, and signs it himself, Payne will be contractually liable to Tucker on the basis of Andrews's express authority. However, Andrews would not have express authority to buy the chair for $900 or to buy a different chair.

**Implied Authority.** Implied (or incidental) authority exists because it is often impossible or impractical for the principal to specify the agent's authority fully, especially where the agent's duties are extensive. In general, courts attempting to ascertain the agent's implied authority will weigh the principal's express statements (if any), the nature of the agency, usages of trade, the relations between the principal and the agent, and other relevant facts and circumstances. Then, as the

[1] The agent's actual or apparent authority can bind the principal in other ways, too. See, for example, the rules regarding notification discussed later in the chapter. Also, the agent's authority can help define some of the fiduciary duties discussed in the last chapter—for example, the agent's duty of obedience.

*Kanavos* case below states, they will ask what the agent could reasonably assume that the principal wanted him to do in light of all the factors known to him.

Implied authority may derive directly from a grant of express authority. For example, an agency expressly set up to conduct certain business will ordinarily give the agent implied authority to perform two overlapping kinds of acts: (1) those customarily done in conducting that business and (2) those reasonably necessary for conducting that business. Implied authority may also exist where there is no relevant grant of express authority. Here, courts determine implied authority from the facts and circumstances (often, a course of dealing between principal and agent).

Implied authority cannot conflict with express authority. Similarly, there will be no implied authority to perform a certain act where the principal has limited the agent's authority by express statement or by clear implication and the act would conflict with that limitation.

**General and Special Agents.** The rather blurred distinction between a **general agent** and a **special agent** may be important in determining the scope of an agent's implied (and apparent) authority. A general agent is authorized to conduct a series of transactions involving continuity of service; a special agent is authorized to conduct a single transaction or a series of transactions not involving continuity of service. In extreme cases, it is easy to distinguish general and special agents. For instance, a continuously employed general manager or purchasing agent is a general agent, while a person employed to buy or sell a single object is a special agent. In borderline cases, the greater the number of acts to be performed and parties to be dealt with and the longer the time needed to finish the agency business, the likelier it is that the agency will be regarded as general. Also, general agents tend to serve in a more continuous (uninterrupted) fashion than special agents. The degree of discretion or bargaining freedom given to the agent, however, is usually not a test for distinguishing the two kinds of agents.

**Examples of Implied Authority.** The courts have created a number of general rules or presumptions for determining the implied authority of certain agents in certain situations. Of course, the principal's *express* instructions or limitations may enlarge or diminish the agent's authority in each of these situations.

An agent hired to manage a business usually has implied authority to make contracts reasonably related to the operation of the business or customary in that type of business. These include contracts for obtaining equipment and supplies, making repairs, employing employees, and selling goods or services. However, a manager generally has no power to borrow money or issue negotiable instruments in the principal's name unless the principal is in business to do either of these things. An agent given full control of real property has implied authority to contract for repairs and insurance, and may rent the property for certain periods if this is customary. But the agent may not sell the property or allow any third-party liens or other interests to be taken on it. Agents appointed to sell the principal's goods may have implied authority to make warranties that are customary for the goods sold in the market where they are sold, and to bind the principal to these warranties. The general agent has this power, but the special agent may not have it.

**Apparent Authority.** Apparent authority arises when the principal's behavior, as reasonably interpreted by a third party, causes that party to believe that the agent is authorized to perform an act or make a contract.[2] Like actual authority, apparent authority depends on the principal's manifested consent to the agent's actions. But in apparent authority cases, the main concern is what the principal communicates to the *third party,* either directly or through the agent. Communications to the *agent* are irrelevant except as they become known to the third party or affect the agent's outward behavior. The principal's communications, finally, must cause the third party to form a *reasonable* belief that the agent has authority.

**Examples of Apparent Authority.** A principal may clothe an agent with apparent authority by making direct statements to a third party, telling the agent to do so, or giving the agent permission to behave in such a way as to create an appearance of authority. Trade customs and established business practices often assist in creating apparent authority. For instance, if the principal appoints his agent to a formal position such as "general manager" that involves certain widely recognized powers, the agent will have apparent authority to bind the principal when he exercises those powers. Here, the principal's behavior (appointing the agent to the position), as reasonably interpreted in light of business practices, has created apparent authority in the agent. (This is true even though the principal obviously did not create the business practices that were one of the factors underlying the agent's apparent authority.) However, agents cannot give themselves apparent authority, and there is no apparent authority where the agent creates an appearance of authority without the principal's consent. In the example above, apparent authority would not exist if the agent, without the principal's knowledge or permission, falsely told third parties that he had been promoted to general manager.

Established business customs can help create apparent authority in other ways as well. An agent may have apparent authority to bind the principal by the agent's statements if such statements are customary in the kind of business that the agent transacts. This is true even where the principal has forbidden the agent to make the statements, as long as the prohibition remains unknown to third parties. The general agent, for instance, can subject his principal to liability on forbidden contractual promises that customarily accompany transactions that the agent *is* authorized to complete. Warranties made by a general agent empowered to sell goods are an example. Special agents, however, usually do not have apparent authority to bind the principal in this way.

Suppose that Perry employs Arthur as general sales agent for his manufacturing business. Certain warranties are customary for Perry's products in the markets where they are sold, and agents like Arthur are ordinarily empowered to give these warranties. However, Perry tells Arthur not to make any such warranties to buyers of his products, thus cutting off Arthur's express and implied authority. Despite Perry's orders, Arthur makes the usual warranties in a sale to Thomas, who is familiar with customs in the trade. If Thomas did not know of the limitation on Arthur's authority, the warranties will be binding on Perry.

Finally, apparent authority is often found where the principal has, to the knowledge of a third person, permitted the agent to exercise a power that the agent has been expressly forbidden to exercise. Suppose Potter has told Abram, the manager of his wholesale busi-

[2] Apparent authority is sometimes explained through a concept known as *agency by estoppel.* According to this doctrine, the principal is "estopped" to deny the agency's existence or the agent's authority when: (1) his actions create an appearance of authority in the agent, (2) a third party relies to his detriment on this appearance of authority, and (3) the third party relies reasonably and in good faith.

ness, to hire loaders for his trucks but to hire them for no more than one day at a time. No one else has been informed of this limitation on Abram's actual authority. With Potter's knowledge and without his objection, however, Abram has frequently employed loaders by the week. Then, Abram agrees to employ Towell as a loader for a week, but Potter intervenes and fires Towell after one day. If Towell knew about the earlier employment by the week, Potter would be bound to the one-week employment contract with him on the basis of Abram's apparent authority.

Note that in neither of the two preceding examples did the agent give himself apparent authority without the principal's consent. Arthur's apparent authority to make warranties derived from his appointment as a general sales agent and customs in the trade, not from his own behavior. And Potter had acquiesced in Abram's practice of hiring loaders by the week.

**The Apparent Agent.** A person may have apparent authority to bind the principal even though he has never been appointed as agent. The usual tests for determining apparent authority apply in this case. Assume that Pringle is in the business of selling fresh fruit and produce, and does so from a panel truck bearing his name and occupation. Sometimes, Pringle contracts to supply customers with foodstuffs not then in his possession. One day, Pringle lends the truck to his friend Abbott, who uses it for personal business. While in possession of the truck, Abbott represents himself as Pringle's assistant and contracts with some of Pringle's regular customers to deliver certain food and produce the next day. Pringle may well be liable to the buyers on the basis of apparent authority, even though Abbott had never been employed by Pringle.

**Liability for Agent's Misrepresentations.** The principal's liability for the agent's misrepresentations is a topic that straddles contract and tort,[3] but usually depends on the authority possessed by the agent. The principal is directly liable for misrepresentations made by the agent during actually or apparently authorized transactions if she *intended* that the agent make the misrepresentations. Some courts may extend this liability to situations where the principal negligently allows the agent to make misrepresentations.

Even if the principal is not directly at fault, she may be liable for an agent's misrepresentations if the agent had express, implied, or apparent authority to make true statements on the subject. Suppose that an agent to sell farmland falsely states that a spring on the land never runs dry, when in fact it does so almost every summer, and that this statement induces a third party to buy the land. The principal obviously will be liable if she intended that the agent make the false statement. Even if the principal is blameless, she will be liable if the agent had actual or apparent authority to make true statements about the spring.

If the misrepresentation was intended by the agent, or if the principal intended that the agent make it, the third party can recover in tort for losses that result. In some states, the third party may recover for misrepresentations that were caused by the negligence of the principal or the agent. In either case, the third party can elect to rescind the transaction instead of pursuing a tort suit.

**Exculpatory Clauses.** Both honest and dishonest principals may attempt to protect themselves from liability for an agent's misrepresentations by including so-called exculpatory clauses in contracts that the agent makes with third parties. Typically, such

[3] On the elements of fraud and misrepresentation and their tort and contract applications, see Chapters 4 and 9.

clauses state that the agent lacks authority to make representations not contained in the written contract and that only the representations stated in the contract will be binding. Exculpatory clauses will not protect a principal who knows of past misrepresentations or expects future misrepresentations by the agent, or who desires that the agent make false statements. Where the principal is innocent of such knowledge or motives, exculpatory clauses will typically protect him from *tort* liability if the agent misrepresents. But the third party may still rescind the transaction, because it would be unjust to permit the principal to benefit from the misrepresentation while disclaiming responsibility for it.

**Incapacity of Principal or Agent.** A person of limited legal capacity, such as a minor or an insane person, cannot enlarge his capacity by acting through an agent. Thus, subject to the exceptions in Chapter 11, the incapacity of the principal will render the agent's contracts with third parties voidable at the principal's option. This follows from the agent's role as alter ego of the principal. For the same reason, the *agent's* incapacity usually will *not* affect the contract liability of a principal who has capacity. However, the principal may escape liability where the agent's incapacity is so extreme that the agent cannot receive or convey ideas, or cannot follow the principal's instructions.

**Effect of Termination of Agency.** Once an agency relation has been terminated by any of the means described in the previous chapter, the agent's *express* authority and *implied* authority end. However, *apparent* authority may persist after termination unless third parties receive *notice* of the termination. This usually protects third parties who deal with the ex-agent on the basis of his apparent authority. Facts known to the third party that reasonably indicate the termination of the agency will constitute notice and end the ex-agent's apparent authority.

The two general ways in which an agency will terminate are *termination by act of the parties* and *termination by operation of law.* Termination by act of the parties will *not* automatically end the agent's apparent authority, because the necessary notice to third parties will normally be absent. Termination by operation of law *may or may not* cause apparent authority to cease. Apparent authority *will* end when the principal dies or loses capacity or when performance of the agency business becomes impossible.[4] This is true even where there is no notice. Other bases for termination by operation of law do not automatically end the agent's apparent authority; here, notice is usually necessary. However, some of these bases for termination (for example, destruction of the agency subject matter) may fit within the heading of impossibility, and others (for example, changed values or business conditions) may be sufficiently "public" to give third parties notice.

Thus, even though the agency has ended, there are situations where the agent's apparent authority persists. In order to protect themselves against liability on contracts by ex-agents with apparent authority, principals should take care that third parties are notified of the termination. For third parties who have previously dealt with the agent, a direct, personal communication is needed to terminate the agent's apparent authority. For third parties who were aware of the agency but did no business with the agent, constructive notice (often by newspaper advertisement) will ordinarily suffice.

**Ratification.** Ratification is a process whereby the principal binds himself to an unauthorized act done by an agent or by a

[4] *Restatement (Second) of Agency* § 124A, comment a; and § 133 (1958).

person purporting to act as an agent. Ratification relates back to the time when the act was performed. For contracts, its effect is to bind the principal as if the agent had possessed authority at the time the contract was made. The principal can also ratify the torts of an agent.

**Conduct Amounting to Ratification.** For ratification to occur, the principal's words or other behavior must indicate an intent to treat the agent's unauthorized act(s) as authorized. Ratification can be *express* or *implied.* An express ratification occurs when the principal communicates his intent to ratify by written or oral words to that effect. Implied ratification arises when the principal's behavior evidences an intent to ratify. Part performance of the agent's contract by the principal or the principal's acceptance of benefits under the contract may work an implied ratification. As the *Bradshaw* case below states, even the principal's silence, acquiescence, or failure to repudiate the transaction can sometimes constitute ratification.

**Additional Requirements.** Even if the principal's behavior indicates an intent to ratify, there are other requirements that must be met before ratification will occur. These requirements have been variously stated; the following list is typical.

1. The act ratified must be one that would have been *valid* at the time it was performed. For example, an agent's illegal contract cannot be made binding by the principal's subsequent ratification. However, a contract that was voidable when made due to the principal's incapacity may be ratified by a principal who has later attained or regained capacity.

2. The principal must have been *in existence* at the time the agent acted. However, as discussed in Chapter 23, after a corporation comes into existence, it may often adopt prior contracts made by its promoters.

3. At the time the act to be ratified occurred, the agent must have indicated to the third party that she was acting for *a* principal, and not for herself. It is not necessary that the agent have disclosed the identity of the principal.

4. The principal must be *legally competent* at the time of ratification. For instance, an insane principal cannot ratify.

5. The principal must have *knowledge* of all the material facts regarding the prior act or transaction at the time it is ratified.

6. The principal must ratify the *entire* act or contract. The principal cannot ratify the beneficial parts of a contract and reject those that are detrimental.

7. In ratifying, the principal must use the *same formalities* that are required to give the agent authority to execute the transaction. For example, as the *Bradshaw* case illustrates, an agency in which the agent is to sell real estate typically must be in writing. Thus, the ratification of such a sale must also be in writing. In most cases, however, few formalities are needed to give the agent authority.

**Intervening Events.** Certain events occurring after the agent's contract but before the principal's ratification may cut off the principal's power to ratify. These include: (1) the third party's withdrawal from the contract, (2) the third party's death or loss of capacity, (3) the principal's failure to ratify within a reasonable time,[5] and (4) changed circumstances. In the last case, the power to ratify is especially likely to end where the change in circumstances places a greater burden on the third party than that party assumed when the contract was made.

[5] Note, however, that the principal's silence or acquiescence may also constitute ratification. Whether the principal's failure to act will amount to ratification or will cut off the power to ratify depends on the facts of the case.

## Kanavos v. Hancock Bank & Trust Co.

**439 N.E.2d 311 (Mass. App. Ct. 1982)**

Since about 1965, the Kanavos brothers (Kanavos) had been borrowing substantial sums from the Hancock Bank and Trust Company (Hancock). They always dealt with James M. Brown, who eventually became Hancock's executive vice president and chief loan officer. Brown's office was located in Hancock's central office building and was opposite the office of the president, Kelly. Brown often checked loan details with Kelly, but Kelly invariably deferred to Brown's judgment.

In 1974, Kanavos suffered financial reverses and was unable to repay $300,000 in unsecured loans from Hancock. Brown then cooked up a complex deal to liquidate these loans. In essence, Kanavos gave Hancock all the stock of one of Kanavos's holdings, a corporation called 1025 Hancock Street, Inc. (1025, Inc.), in return for discharge of the $300,000 debt. However, Kanavos retained the option to buy back the 1025, Inc. shares at a stated price. Brown negotiated all the details of this transaction, although it had to be approved by Hancock's board of directors. Kelly was present at the execution of this contract, signing all of the relevant papers for Hancock. Shortly thereafter, the agreement was amended to raise Hancock's purchase price for the shares and also Kanavos's repurchase price. Brown handled all aspects of this amendment.

1025, Inc.'s main asset was an apartment building called Executive House. After the deal was completed, Brown became president and treasurer of 1025, Inc., with broad authority to run Executive House. Kanavos, who hoped to repurchase the 1025, Inc. shares, continually pressed Kelly and Brown on a variety of matters pertaining to the corporation's operations and his attempts to get financing for the repurchase. Kelly always told Kanavos to deal with Brown. Finally, Brown told Kanavos that he wished Kanavos would not exercise the repurchase option and made Kanavos an offer to amend the earlier agreement. The offer was as follows: in exchange for Kanavos's agreement not to exercise the option, Hancock would give Kanavos a 60-day option to match the highest bidder on any sale of 1025, Inc.'s property, or would pay Kanavos $40,000 if the property were sold to someone else. The offer was contained in a letter signed by Brown; no one else at Hancock was involved with this offer.

Kanavos accepted the offer, but Hancock backed out of this new agreement. Kanavos sued to enforce the agreement. The trial court directed a verdict for Hancock, holding that Brown lacked authority to bind Hancock to the agreement.

**Kass, Justice.** Among the exhibits introduced was a document which Brown identified as his job description. In broad terms he was to manage the commercial and consumer loan division. In furtherance of a duty to develop and maintain a profitable loan portfolio, he, personally or through subordinates, was to direct the resolution of particularly complex and/or unusual credit, lending, or collection problems related to important customers. He was also to maintain a continuous review of the loan portfolio and oversee the resolution of significant delinquent and workout loans. That description sketches an authority to alter a subsidiary aspect of a loan or workout agreement. *Restatement (Second) of Agency* § 33 ("An agent is authorized to do, and to do only, what it is reasonable for him to infer that the principal desires him to do in the light of the principal's manifestations and the facts as he knows or should know them at the time he acts"). The jury could have believed that the sale of stock with a repurchase option was a furtherance of a workout arrangement, and Brown's job description would have supported a jury finding that he had authority to amend the repurchase option in a manner that did not fundamentally alter the agreement, that is, to substitute for the price certain in the agreement, as amended, a right of last refusal or a cash payment should the property be sold to someone else. It was a revision which did not commit the Bank to any step which, in the business context, was so major or unusual that a businessman in Brown's position would reasonably expect to require a vote of the board of directors.

Whether Brown's job description impliedly authorized the right of last refusal or cash payment modification is a question of how, in the circumstances, a person in Brown's position could reasonably interpret his authority. Whether Brown had *apparent authority* to make the modification is a question of how, in the circumstances, a third person, e.g., a customer of the Bank such as Kanavos, would reasonably interpret Brown's authority in light of the manifestations of his principal, the Bank.

Apparent authority is drawn from a variety of circumstances. In the instant case there was evidence of the following variety of circumstances: Brown's title of executive vice-president; the location of his office opposite the president; his frequent communications with the president; the long course of dealing and negotiations; the encouragement of Kanavos by the president to deal with Brown; the earlier amendment of the agreement by Brown on behalf of the Bank on material points; the size of the Bank; the secondary, rather than fundamental, nature of the change in the terms of the agreement now repudiated by the Bank; and Brown's broad operating authority over the Executive House—all these added together would support a finding of apparent authority. This reasoning would not apply, of course, where in the business context, the requirement of specific authority is presumed, e.g., the sale of a major asset by a corporation or a transaction which by its nature commits the corporation to an obligation outside the scope of its usual activity.

Judgment reversed in favor of Kanavos.

---

## Bradshaw v. McBride

### 649 P.2d 74 (Utah Sup. Ct. 1982)

Aretta Parkinson originally owned some real property called the Parkinson Farm. Before her death, she willed the farm to her eight children. Shortly after Aretta's death, Roma Funk, one of her children, visited Barbara Bradshaw, a co-owner of land adjoining the Parkinson Farm. The two women concluded an oral contract for the sale of the farm to Bradshaw and her family. There was conflicting testimony as to what Funk told Bradshaw about her authority to represent her brothers and sisters. Funk later employed Bryant Hansen, a real estate broker, to help her complete the details of the transaction. Hansen prepared an earnest money agreement, which the Bradshaws signed but which was not signed by any of the Parkinson children. Hansen also prepared warranty deeds, which were signed by three of the Parkinson children but never delivered to the Bradshaws.

Despite the absence of a written agreement, the Bradshaws took possession of the farm after the oral agreement and made certain improvements. Other relevant facts appear in the opinion below.

The Parkinson children eventually refused to go through with the deal, and the Bradshaws sued them for specific performance. The trial court held for the Bradshaws, and the Parkinson children appealed.

**STEWART, JUSTICE.** The Parkinson children contend that Funk was not authorized to act as agent for her brothers and sisters. The general rule is that one who deals with an agent has the responsibility to ascertain the agent's authority despite the agent's representations. The Bradshaws concede this point, but argue that the Parkinsons subsequently ratified the oral contract. The trial court found ratification in their failure to come forward and repudiate or disaffirm Mrs. Funk's agreement to sell the property or her authority to act for them.

A principal may impliedly or expressly ratify an agreement made by an unauthorized agent. Ratification of an agent's acts relates back to the time the unauthorized act occurred and is sufficient to create the relationship of principal and agent. A deliberate and valid ratification with full knowledge of all the material facts is binding and cannot afterward be revoked or recalled. However, a ratification requires the principal to have knowledge of all material facts and an intent to ratify. Under some circumstances failure to disaffirm may constitute ratification of the agent's acts. In quoting *Williston on Contracts,* this Court stated:

> Ratification, like original authority, need not be express. Any conduct which indicates assent by the purported principal to become a party to the transaction or which is justifiable only if there is ratification is sufficient. Even silence with full knowledge of the facts may manifest affirmance and thus operate as a ratification. The person with whom the agent dealt will so obviously be deceived by assuming the professed agent was authorized to act as such, that the principal is under a duty to undeceive him. . . . So a purported principal may not be willfully ignorant, nor may he purposely shut his eyes to means of information within his possession and control and thereby escape ratification if the circumstances are such that he could reasonably have been expected to dissent unless he were willing to be a party to the transaction.

The trial court found that the Parkinson children other than Funk had ratified the Funk-Bradshaw agreement, in part, by their knowledge and acceptance of the agreement. This finding, however, is clearly not supported by the evidence in the record as to two Parkinson children who were not notified of the agreement until receipt of the warranty deeds prepared by Hansen. Funk testified that she did not contact her brother Foch or John Lister [the administrator of one of the Parkinson children's estate]. At trial, Foch testified that when he first learned of the agreement he was opposed to it, but was willing to go along only if the court found it enforceable. He continually stated his objection to the agreement, and his actions cannot be interpreted as ratification. John Lister testified that he did not become aware of the agreement until he received the real estate documents from Hansen. Lister did not sign the documents and did nothing to ratify the agreement between Funk and Bradshaw. When presented with a writing to convey ownership in property, Lister had no duty to disavow any putative agreement. On the contrary, his failure to sign is evidence of rejection. It is clear that neither Foch nor Lister in fact ratified the agreement.

Furthermore, as to all the Parkinson children, there was no ratification as a matter of law because the Utah statute of frauds requires that any agent executing an agreement conveying an interest in land on behalf of his principal must be authorized in writing. In order to enforce an oral agreement, the same kind of authorization that is required to clothe an agent initially with authority to contract must be given by the principal to constitute a ratification of an unauthorized act. Where the law requires the authority to be given in writing, the ratification must also generally be in writing. There was, therefore, no ratification in this case.

Judgment reversed in favor of the Parkinson children. (*Note:* the court also concluded that the case did not fit within the statute of frauds' part performance exception for contracts for the sale of an interest in land.)

## NOTICE TO OR FROM AGENT

A person has notice of a fact if he has actual conscious knowledge of it or has been given notification of it. The notice that an agent gives to, or receives from, third parties may affect the principal's legal rights and powers. However, somewhat different rules apply depending on whether the case involves a *notification* to or from the agent or a situation where the agent simply has *knowledge* of certain facts.

**Notification.** Notification is a more or less formal act that communicates information to others and that the notifier uses to affect legal rights. Examples include the revocation, rejection, or acceptance of an offer to contract. Generally, if a third party gives notification to an agent having express, implied, or apparent authority to receive it, the principal is bound as if the notification had been given directly to him. For example, assume that Thomas enters into a sales contract with Phillips through Anderson, Phillips's salesman. The contract gives Thomas the privilege of canceling a shipment if he notifies Phillips. If Thomas informs Anderson of her desire to cancel, she is not liable for the shipment if (as is likely) Anderson has actual or apparent authority to receive the notification. This is true even if Anderson never communicates this information to Phillips. The same general rule applies where the agent gives notification to the third party: if the agent has actual or apparent authority to give the notification, the principal will be bound by it. These rules do not apply where, in giving or receiving the notification, the agent is acting adversely to the principal's interests and the third party knows this.

**Knowledge.** In certain circumstances that are not precisely defined, the agent's knowledge of certain facts will be imputed to the principal. This means that the principal's rights and liabilities are what they would have been if the principal had actually known what the agent knew. Generally, the agent's knowledge will be imputed to the principal when it is relevant to the activities that the agent is authorized to undertake or when the agent is under a duty to disclose it to the principal. Suppose that Phillips asks Anderson to purchase a tract of real estate on his behalf. Anderson knows that Tarr has a valid but unrecorded interest in the land. Anderson fails to inform Phillips of Tarr's interest, and Phillips purchases the land through Anderson. Phillips will take the land subject to Tarr's interest to the same extent as if he had actually known of the interest himself.

Usually, the time, place, or manner of the agent's acquisition of knowledge is irrelevant in determining whether that knowledge will be imputed to the principal. However, the principal is not affected by privileged information known to the agent. A common example is information relevant to the interests of a client that an attorney has acquired on a confidential basis from a previous client. Also, knowledge possessed by an agent who is acting adversely to the principal's interests will usually not be imputed to the principal.

## CONTRACT LIABILITY OF THE AGENT

**Introduction.** The agent as well as the principal may be liable on contracts that the agent makes for the principal. The agent's liability depends on whether he acts for a **disclosed principal,** a **partially disclosed principal,** or an **undisclosed principal.** In general, the agent is *not* liable for contracts made on behalf of a disclosed principal, but *is* bound to contracts made for partially disclosed and undisclosed principals. This section considers each of these situations in turn, and then examines the liability of agents who act for legally nonexistent principals and principals who lack capacity.

**Disclosed Principal.** A principal is disclosed if the third party knows or has reason to know: (1) that the agent is acting for a principal and (2) the principal's identity. The agent for a disclosed principal is usually *not bound* to contracts made on behalf of such a principal. For example, if Adkins calls on Thompson, a retailer, and presents a business card identifying her as a sales agent for Parker Manufacturing Company, Parker is a disclosed principal. Assuming that Adkins has authority to make such transactions, an order by Thompson will create a contract between Parker and Thompson. Adkins will not be liable on the contract. This rule is usually consistent with the third party's intentions. Here, Thompson probably intended to contract only with Parker.

**Liability of Agent by Agreement.** An agent acting for a disclosed principal may become contractually liable by *expressly agreeing* to become liable. The agent may do so by: (1) making the contract in his own name rather than in the principal's name, (2) joining the principal as an obligor on the contract, or (3) acting as surety or guarantor for the principal. Where the contract is written, it may be worded in such a way that it is unclear whether the agent is bound. Here, the form in which the principal's promise (if present) is expressed, the nature of the agent's promise, and the precise form in which the agent signs are frequently critical. Normal rules of contract interpretation apply in such cases.[6] Except where prohibited by the parol evidence rule, oral evidence or other extrinsic evidence is usually admissible to ascertain the parties' intentions.

The agent can usually avoid liability by naming the principal as the party to be bound in the body of the agreement and by signing in such a way that his representative capacity is clearly indicated. For example, the body of a contract in which Adkins acts for the Parker Manufacturing Company should read: "The Parker Manufacturing Company agrees . . ." And signature forms such as the following will reinforce the inference that Parker, and not the agent Adkins, is to be bound: "Parker Manufacturing Company, by Adkins"; "Parker Manufacturing Company—Adkins, Agent"; or "Adkins, for Parker Manufacturing Company." Where the signature form does not include the principal's name, an agent who merely adds the term *agent* to her signature (for example, "Adkins, Agent") or who simply signs without any indication of her status ("Adkins") will find it more difficult to avoid liability. Still, the way the agreement is written or extrinsic evidence of the parties' understanding may sometimes relieve the agent of liability even in these cases.

**Agent's Liability on Unauthorized Contracts.** An agent who contracts for a disclosed

[6] On rules of contract interpretation and the parol evidence rule, see Chapter 13.

principal can also become liable to the third party if he lacks the power to bind the principal. Here, the principal will not be liable and, if the agent is not bound, a third party who relied on the agent's authority may suffer losses. Thus, the agent is deemed to make an *implied warranty* that he possesses authority to contract. This warranty applies both to parties who purport to be agents for a designated person but in fact are not and to actual agents who lack authority to make the contract in question. Suppose that Aikens is a traveling salesman for Pittman, a seller of widgets. Aikens has actual authority to receive offers for the sale of widgets, but not to make actual contracts of sale. Representing himself as Pittman's agent but saying nothing about his specific powers, Aikens contracts with Troutman to sell and deliver a certain quantity of Pittman's widgets. Troutman does not know Aikens, and while it is customary in the widget trade for the principal to approve all sales, Troutman honestly but unreasonably believes that Aikens has authority to contract for Pittman. Pittman will not be liable on the contract, because Aikens lacked actual or apparent authority to bind him. But Aikens will be liable to Troutman under the implied warranty of authority.[7]

There are three situations where the above rules will not apply and the real or alleged agent will not be liable on an unauthorized contract. First, where the third party knows that the agent lacks authority, neither the principal nor the agent will be bound. However, the agent will still be bound where the third party had *reason to know* that authority was lacking but failed to realize this. Second, if the principal subsequently ratifies the contract, the principal will be bound and the agent will be discharged. Since ratification relates back to the time the transaction was completed, the relation of the parties is the same as it would have been had the agent possessed authority in the first place.

Finally, the agent will usually escape liability if he notifies the third party that he does not warrant his authority to contract. The agent may do so by giving direct notice that the existence of authority is not warranted. Also, if he is honestly uncertain about the existence or scope of his authority, he may disclaim any warranty of authority by fully disclosing the sources of his possible authority to the third party, thus putting the risk of error on that party. For instance, if the agent shows his contract of employment or power of attorney to the third party and the third party decides that the agent has authority to bind the principal, the agent is not liable even if he actually lacks authority.

**Partially Disclosed Principal.** A principal is partially disclosed if the third party: (1) knows or has reason to know that the agent is acting for *a* principal but (2) does *not* know or have reason to know the principal's identity. A typical example is the situation where an agent to buy or sell property states that she represents a party who does not desire his name to be known.

Where the principal is partially disclosed, the third party must rely on the agent's integrity. Thus, the agent is liable on contracts made for a partially disclosed principal. Where the agent has the authority to bind the partially disclosed principal, both are liable. In this case, the third party is not required to elect whether to proceed against the principal or the agent.[8] That is, he may sue and obtain a judgment against either without forfeiting his claim against the other. However, once the principal satisfies the third party's claim, the agent is discharged. If the third

[7] Also, a person who intentionally misrepresents that he has authority to contract will be liable to the third party in tort, and some states may allow tort liability for negligent misrepresentations. Where the third party can sue in tort, he may elect to recover damages or to rescind the contract.

[8] The same rule applies where the *disclosed principal* and his agent are both liable on the contract.

party collects from the agent, the principal should be required to indemnify the agent. Also, the agent may be relieved from liability if the parties so agree. For example, the agent and the third party may agree that the agent will remain liable only until the principal's identity is disclosed.

**Undisclosed Principal.** A principal is undisclosed where the third party lacks knowledge or reason to know: (1) the principal's existence and (2) the principal's identity. For example, if a large corporation wishes to buy farmland for a factory near a small city, it may get the land more cheaply if it employs a local real estate agent to make the purchase without disclosing that she is acting for anyone.

When the principal is undisclosed, the third party must assume that the agent is acting as a principal. For this reason, the agent is liable on contracts with the third party. Where the agent has authority to bind the undisclosed principal, the principal will also be liable on the contract. If the third party discovers that an agency exists and learns the identity of the principal, the third party may either recognize the agency and hold the principal liable, or proceed against the agent. This means that: (1) the third party can join the principal and the agent in one action, but if either objects, the third party must elect which party to pursue; (2) the principal is discharged once a third party who knows the principal's identity obtains a judgment against the agent; and (3) the agent is discharged once the third party obtains a judgment against the principal.[9] However, the principal is not discharged if the third party obtains a judgment against the agent before learning the principal's identity. As before, the principal may be required to indemnify the agent if the agent is held liable.

[9] *Restatement (Second) of Agency* §§ 210, 210A, 337 (1958).

**Nonexistent Principal.** An agent who purports to act for a legally nonexistent principal such as an unincorporated association will be personally liable. Courts usually base this rule on the theory that one purporting to act as an agent impliedly represents that he has an existing principal. The rule applies even where the third party is aware that the principal is nonexistent.[10] However, this liability can be avoided if the parties so agree.

**Principal Lacking Capacity.** An agent who contracts for a *wholly incompetent* person, such as one who has been adjudicated insane, is liable on the contract. This is usually true even where the third party knows of the principal's status. However, the agent may be relieved of liability if the parties so agree. On the other hand, an agent contracting for a disclosed principal who merely *lacks capacity to contract* (for example, a minor) is generally not liable to the third party. This is true despite the principal's ability to avoid the contract. However, the agent will be liable if: (1) she misrepresents the capacity of her principal, or (2) she has reason to believe that the third party is unaware of the principal's incapacity and fails to disclose this.

[10] For a closely analogous situation, see Chapter 23's discussion of the promoter's liability on contracts made for a corporation before it comes into existence.

## Wired Music, Inc. v. Great River Steamboat Co.

**554 S.W.2d 466 (Mo. Ct. App. 1977)**

A sales representative of Wired Music, Inc. sold Frank Pierson, president of the Great River Steamboat Company, on purchasing a Muzak Program Service for Great River's riverboat and restaurant, the *Becky Thatcher.* Pierson signed a form contract drafted by Wired Music in the following manner:

By /s/ Frank C. Pierson, Pres.<br>
Title

The Great River Steamboat Co.<br>
Port of St. Louis Investments, Inc.<br>
For the Corporation

In signing, Pierson crossed out "Port of St. Louis Investments, Inc.," which had been incorrectly listed as the name of the corporation, and inserted the proper name. The contract was for a five-year period at a monthly rate of $58.50. It included the following clause arguably making Pierson a surety or guarantor for Great River: "The individual signing this agreement for the subscriber guarantees that all of the above provisions shall be complied with."

Great River made payments under the contract totaling $234.15 and then discontinued them. Wired Music brought an action for $3,500 damages against Pierson personally. The trial court ruled in Pierson's favor, and Wired Music appealed.

**Gunn, Judge.** The general rule regarding liability incurred by an individual who signs an instrument on behalf of another party is: where the principal is disclosed and the capacity in which the individual signs is evident, e.g., president, secretary, agent, the liability is the principal's and not that of the individual signing for the principal. Of course, where the circumstances surrounding the transaction disclose a mutual intention to impose personal responsibility on the individual executing the agreement, the individual may be personally liable even though the form of the signature is that of the agent.

The determinative issue here is whether, in view of the form of the signature to the agreement, the language of the so-called guaranty clause is sufficient to manifest a clear and explicit intent by Pierson to assume a personal guaranty contract. We hold that standing alone it does not. Furthermore, the contract language imposing a personal obligation is inconsistent with the form of execution, which positively limited Pierson's participation to his official corporate capacity and not as an individual. Such inconsistency creates at least a latent ambiguity which permits the admission of parol evidence to explain the true intent of the parties.

Pierson has stressed that he neglected to read the contract prior to its signing. The law is settled that one who signs a contract is presumed to have known its contents and accepted its terms. Thus, Pierson's failure to examine the terms of the instrument would afford no defense to the corporation regarding its obligations under the contract, as his signature was sufficient to bind the corporation. Such neglect is a relevant circumstance, however, in ascertaining Pierson's intent to assume personal liability, as his personal signature appeared nowhere on the instrument. Without knowledge of the guaranty clause he could not have possessed the requisite intent to assume obligations under it. The record is destitute of any indication that Pierson was ever made aware of potential personal liability under the guaranty clause, and he steadfastly denied any such knowledge. Wired Music, Inc. drafted the contract, and its agents procured Pierson's corporate signature without explanation of or bargaining over its terms. Under these circumstances we find that there was an absence of the meeting of the minds as to the nature and the extent of the personal obligations imposed, essential to the formation of a binding guaranty.

Judgment for Pierson affirmed.

---

## Van D. Costas, Inc. v. Rosenberg

**432 So.2d 656 (Fla. Dist. Ct. App. 1983)**

Seascape Restaurants, Inc. operated a restaurant called The Magic Moment. Jeff Rosenberg was one-third owner and president of Seascape. Van D. Costas, the president of Van D. Costas, Inc., contracted to construct a "magical entrance" to the Magic Moment. Jeff Rosenberg signed the contract on a line under which appeared the words "Jeff Rosenberg, the Magic Moment." The contract did not refer to Seascape, and Costas knew nothing of Seascape's existence. After a dispute over performance of the contract, Costas sued Rosenberg for breach of contract. The suit failed at the trial court level and Costas appealed.

**Grimes, Judge.** Section 321 of the *Restatement (Second) of Agency* discusses the liability of the agent under circumstances in which it appears that he is acting for someone else but the identity of his principal is unknown to the other party.

> Unless otherwise agreed, a person purporting to make a contract with another for a partially disclosed principal is a party to the contract. *Comment: a.* A principal is a partially disclosed principal when, at the time of making the contract in question, the other party thereto has notice that the agent is acting for a principal but has no notice of the principal's identity. The fact that, to the knowledge of the agent, the other party does not know the identity of the principal is of great weight in ascribing to the other party the intention to hold the agent liable either solely, or as a surety or co-promisor with the principal. The inference of an understanding that the agent is a party to the contract exists unless the agent gives such complete information concerning his principal's identity that he can be readily distinguished. If the other party has no reasonable means of ascertaining the principal, the inference is almost irresistible and prevails in the absence of an agreement to the contrary.

In view of the contractual reference to the Magic Moment trade name, the annotation at 150 A.L.R. 1303 (1944) entitled "Use of trade name in connection with contract executed by agent as sufficient disclosure of agency or principal to protect agent against personal liability" is directly on point. The annotator points out that with the possible exception of a single decision, all of the prior cases on the subject have held that the use of a trade name is not a sufficient disclosure of the identity of the principal to eliminate the liability of the agent.

Of course, if the contracting party knows the identity of the principal for whom the agent purports to act, the principal is deemed to be disclosed. A dispute concerning such knowledge presents an issue of fact. Here, however, nothing indicates that Costas had ever heard of Seascape at the time the contract was signed. Subsequent knowledge of the true principal is irrelevant where performance of an indivisible contract has commenced. The trial court emphasized that Costas drafted the contract. However, it was not incumbent upon him to ferret out the record ownership of the Magic Moment when he had every reason to believe that one of the owners was signing the contract. Jeff knew that the owner was Seascape, and he had it within his power to avoid personal liability by properly disclosing his principal. Since there is no evidence that Costas knew or should have known the true principal, the law holds Jeff legally responsible.

Judgment reversed in favor of Costas.

## James G. Smith & Associates v. Everett

**439 N.E.2d 932 (Ohio Ct. App. 1981)**

Dale Everett did business as the Dale F. Everett Company, Inc. (the Company). He also formed a retail business known as "The Clubhouse," which had no legal status aside from its registration with the secretary of state as a trade name of the Company. Everett arranged with James G. Smith, doing business as James G. Smith & Associates (Smith), for radio advertising. In doing so, Everett signed a "Space Estimate and Authorization" allowing Smith to purchase $8,424 of advertising time. Everett signed as follows: "THE CLUBHOUSE, Client, By Dale F. Everett." Smith later sent billing statements for the ads to "The Clubhouse, Inc." Everett never paid Smith for the ads because a bank had taken possession of all the Company's assets to satisfy a loan. Smith sued the Company and Everett personally for the $8,424. He recovered against the Company (which admitted liability), but failed to recover against Everett personally. Unable to satisfy his judgment against the Company, Smith appealed. Everett's position all along was that, because of the signing and billing described above, Smith knew that Everett was acting as an agent for a disclosed principal.

**Norris, Judge.** The circumstances presented by this case are not unlike those which give rise to frequent litigation—a person incorporates his business, incurs indebtedness in running the business which subsequently fails, and then is confronted by claims of creditors who do not wish to be limited in their recovery to inadequate or nonexistent corporate assets.

It is true that by incorporating his business, a person may escape liability for debts of the business, under certain circumstances. Whether he will escape personal liability for debts of the business is most often a question for the law of agency. A corporation can act only through agents. When a person incorporates his business and proceeds to conduct business on behalf of the corporation, he is acting as an agent for the corporation. But, like any other agent, he may still incur personal liabilities. Thus, he will avoid personal liability for debts of the corporation only if he complies with the rules which apply in all agency relationships—he must so conduct himself in dealing on behalf of the corporation with third persons that those persons are aware that he is an agent of the corporation and it is the corporation (principal) with which they are dealing, not the agent individually.

Because the authorities are sometimes confusing or incomplete in their treatment of the subject, it would be well to summarize the situations under which the Ohio cases hold that an agent may or may not be held personally liable to the persons with whom he deals:

(1) *Where the agent is acting for a disclosed principal,* i.e., where both the existence of the agency and the identity of the principal are known to the person with whom the agent deals. An agent who acts for a disclosed principal and who acts within the scope of his authority and in the name of the principal is ordinarily not liable on the contracts he makes. The rationale for this rule is that in this situation the third party intends to deal with the principal, not his agent.

(2) *Where the principal is only partially disclosed,* i.e., where the existence of an agency is known to the third person, but the identity of the principal is not known. Here, the agent is held to be a party to the transaction and is liable to the third party, as is the agent's principal. The reason for the rule is that since the identity of the principal is not known to the third party, he ordinarily will not be willing to rely wholly upon the credit and integrity of an unknown party.

(3) *Where the principal is undisclosed,* i.e., where neither the existence of an agency nor the identity of the principal is known to the third party. Here, the dealing is held to be between the agent and the third party, and the agent is liable. Should the identity of the principal be discovered, he may be held liable by the third party, who must elect to pursue either the principal or the agent. The rationale for the agent's liability is that, since the third party was unaware of the agency, he intended to deal with the agent as an individual, not as an agent.

(4) *Where there is a fictitious or nonexistent principal, or the principal is without legal capacity or status.* If an agent purports to act on behalf of such a "principal," the agent will be liable to the third party. One cannot be an agent for a nonexistent principal; there is no agency. This situation frequently arises where a corporate promoter enters into contracts prior to the time the corporation is actually incorporated.

In the case before us, there is no evidence that Smith knew Everett was acting on behalf of Dale F. Everett Company, Inc. Clearly, Dale F. Everett Company, Inc. was not a disclosed principal. Construing the evidence most favorably to Everett, Smith knew that an agency existed, but did not know the identity of the principal, Dale F. Everett Company, Inc. The only "principal" identified by Everett was The Clubhouse, which was without legal capacity or status. At best, then, Everett was dealing on behalf of a partially disclosed principal [the Company], or a principal without legal capacity or status [The Clubhouse]. In either event, he was a party to the contract with Smith and was personally liable on that contract.

Judgment reversed in favor of Smith.

## TORT LIABILITY OF THE PRINCIPAL

**Introduction.** The principal's tort liability to third parties depends on factors different from those already discussed.[11] This liability may be either *direct* or *imputed* (vicarious). **Direct liability** expresses the simple idea that the principal is responsible for his *own* torts, including those committed through an agent. In cases of **imputed liability,** the principal is responsible for the torts of the agent because of the relationship between them. As you will see, the principal's imputed tort liability depends heavily on whether the agent is classed as an *employee* or as an *independent contractor*.

**Direct Liability.** The principal is liable to third parties for the agent's tortious conduct if the principal *directed* the conduct and *intended* that it occur. For instance, suppose that Pellier instructs Able, his agent, to beat up Tabler. If Able follows Pellier's instructions and beats up Tabler, Pellier will be liable for the intentional torts of assault and battery. This rule also includes situations where the principal intentionally directs the agent to behave negligently or recklessly or to engage in an ultrahazardous activity. For example, the principal will be liable where he instructs an agent to do construction work in a negligent, substandard manner, or (regardless of the care employed) directs an agent to engage in an ultrahazardous activity such as crop-dusting.

The principal may also be directly liable to third parties for her own *negligence* regarding the agent. Examples include: (1) improper or unclear instructions; (2) the failure to make appropriate regulations governing the agent's conduct; (3) the employment of unsuitable persons; (4) the furnishing of improper tools, instruments, or materials; and (5) careless supervision. For example, suppose that Presser employs Allen to collect a debt from Thorson. Allen is a thug with violent propensities and Presser knows or should know this. Even if Presser instructs Allen not to use force, he will probably be liable for negligent selection of an agent if Allen beats up Thorson. The *Becker* case later in the chapter goes beyond these typical instances of negligence liability to make the principal liable for its failure to require a solvent or suitably insured subcontractor.

**Employees versus Independent Contractors.** The principal's imputed liability to third parties is largely determined by the employee–independent contractor distinction.[12] An **employee** (or servant) is an agent hired by a principal (the employer or master) who controls, or has the right to control, the physical performance of the work. An **independent contractor** is a person who contracts with the principal to accomplish some task but who is neither controlled by the principal nor subject to the principal's right of control in the physical performance of that task. There is no sharp line between employees and independent contractors; the *Massey* case below lists the factors typically considered in such determinations. Sometimes it is said that employees are part of the principal's personal or business household, while independent contractors are not. The key point, though, is usually the principal's control over the physical details of the work. If the agent merely agrees to produce a specified result and determines for herself how that result is to be achieved, she is probably an independent contractor. Employees are not limited to those who work

[11] However, this is generally not true for the principal's imputed liability for the agent's fraud, which, as described above, depends on the agent's authority.

[12] This text follows the *Restatement* conventions regarding the "agent" status of employees and independent contractors. According to *Restatement (Second) of Agency* § 2, employees are always agents, while independent contractors may or may not be agents.

for hourly wages or in menial jobs; high corporate officers, for instance, are usually classed as employees. Professionals such as brokers, accountants, and attorneys are often independent contractors, although they may sometimes be employees. Consider the distinction between a principal represented by an attorney engaged in his own independent practice and a principal who maintains a permanent staff of salaried in-house attorneys. Finally, franchisees are usually regarded as independent contractors.

**Employer Liability for Torts of Employees.** The well-known doctrine of *respondeat superior* (let the master answer) states that an employer is liable for torts of employees committed while acting within the scope of their employment. This doctrine applies both to employee negligence and to the intentional torts of employees. *Respondeat superior* is a rule of imputed liability; the employer is liable, not through any fault of his own, but because of his relationship with the employee. The rule rests on the following assumptions and policy choices: (1) torts by employees and resulting injuries to third parties are an inevitable part of doing business, and the only real question is where financial responsibility for these will lie; (2) the employer is in the best position to assume this responsibility and absorb the resulting losses through insurance or financial reserves; (3) the economic burden that this creates can often be shifted to the general public through higher prices, thus "socializing" the risk; and (4) the rule gives employers some incentive to select reliable employees and to take care in their training and supervision. However, since the principal is usually not liable for the torts of independent contractors, *respondeat superior* falls well short of making principals insurers of all the activities that they pursue through agents.

**Scope of Employment.** The *respondeat superior* doctrine's **scope of employment** requirement is a notoriously flexible and ambiguous test. It forces courts to consider a range of factors whose applications vary from situation to situation. Generally, an employee's conduct is within the scope of his employment if it: (1) is of the *kind* that he was employed to perform, (2) occurs substantially within the *time period* authorized by the employer, (3) occurs substantially within the *location* authorized by the employer, and (4) is motivated at least in part by the *purpose of serving the employer.*

To be conduct of the same *kind* that the employee is employed to perform, the act need only be of the same general nature as behavior expressly authorized, or be incidental to its performance. For instance, the *Gatzke* case below treats on-the-job smoking as an act incidental to employment. The fact that an employer has forbidden a certain act does not automatically remove that act from the scope of employment; otherwise, employers could eliminate *respondeat superior* liability by issuing blanket commands not to commit torts. Even criminal conduct may be within the scope of employment. Here, the test seems to be whether the employer could reasonably anticipate the criminal behavior in question. Thus, a delivery driver who exceeds the speed limit while on a "rush job" is probably within the scope of employment, but a driver who shoots another driver after a traffic altercation probably is not.

The authorized *time* of employment is the time during which the employer has the right to control the details of the employee's work. Ordinarily, this is simply the employee's assigned time of work. Beyond this, there is an extra period of time during which the employment may continue. For instance, a security guard whose regular quitting time is 5:00 will probably meet the "time" test if he unjustifiably injures an intruder at 5:15. Doing the same thing three hours later, however, would put the guard outside the scope of employment.

The employee's conduct is within the scope of employment only if it occurs in a *location* authorized by the employer or in a location not unreasonably distant from it. This is generally a question of degree. For example, a saleswoman told to limit her activities to New York City would probably satisfy the "location" requirement while pursuing the employer's business in suburbs just outside the city limits, but not while pursuing the same business in Philadelphia. Generally, the smaller the authorized area of activity, the smaller the departure from that area needed to put the employee outside the scope of employment. For example, consider the different physical distance limitations that should apply to a factory worker as opposed to a traveling salesman.

Finally, to be within the scope of employment, the employee's acts must be performed with the *purpose* of advancing the employer's interests. As the *Gatzke* case suggests, this test is met where the employee's actions are motivated *to any appreciable extent* by the desire to serve the employer. Motives that are partially personal will not, by themselves, place an act outside the scope of employment.

**The Loaned Employee.** Sometimes, an employer may order an employee to work for a second employer. If this "loaned employee" commits a tort while doing so, the presumption is that the employee remains under the control of the first employer and that the first employer will be liable. But if primary control over the employee's conduct has been shifted to the second employer, that employer will be responsible for the employee's wrongdoing. This is most likely to be true where the employee is unskilled, is paid by the hour, gets needed tools from the second employer, and serves the second employer for a substantial length of time.

**Liability for Torts of Independent Contractors.** Generally, the principal is *not* liable for torts committed by independent contractors. But, as the *Becker* case illustrates, the principal can be *directly* liable for tortious behavior connected with the retention of an independent contractor. Also, the principal may be vicariously liable where an independent contractor fails to perform a *nondelegable duty*—a duty whose proper performance is so important to the community that the principal cannot avoid liability by contracting it away to another party. There are many such duties. Examples include a carrier's duty to transport its passengers safely, a municipality's duty to keep its streets in repair, and a railroad's duty to maintain safe crossings. In addition, one who operates under a license is liable for the negligence of a person to whom he delegates duties covered by the license.

Moreover, the principal will be liable for an independent contractor's negligent failure to take the special precautions needed to conduct certain *highly dangerous* or *inherently dangerous* activities.[13] Examples of such activities include excavations in publicly traveled areas, the clearing of land by fire, and the destruction of buildings. For example, a contractor engaged in demolishing a building presumably has duties to warn pedestrians and to keep them at a safe distance. If the independent contractor fails to meet these duties and injury results, the principal will be liable.

[13] This is not the same as the principal's direct liability for intentionally authorizing an agent to undertake an "ultrahazardous" activity. Here, the liability is imputed and it is based on the contractor's negligence. Also, there are probably more "inherently dangerous" activities than "ultrahazardous" activities.

**Ratification.** Even where the principal would not otherwise be liable for an agent's torts, she can become liable by ratifying them. The usual tests for ratification apply in this case.

## Becker v. Interstate Properties

### 569 F.2d 1203 (3d Cir. 1977)

Gary Becker was severely injured while working at a shopping center project being developed by IP Construction Corporation. The injury was caused by the negligent acts of an employee of Windsor Contracting Corporation, a subcontractor of Becker's employer, Wood-Pine Corporation. Windsor's insurance policy provided liability coverage of only $10,000 per accident, compared to the typical construction policy of $250,000 per accident. Windsor had only a negligible equity in its equipment and a net worth of only a few thousand dollars. IP knew or should have known that Wood-Pine would hire a subcontractor. In fact, its contract with Wood-Pine required IP to approve any subcontract let by Wood-Pine. Also, IP had required such subcontractors to have adequate insurance on some previous occasions. [For purposes of this case, treat Windsor as if it were an independent contractor of IP.]

Becker sued Windsor and its employee for negligence in federal district court. Because of the limited recovery possible from these parties, he also sued IP. IP won at the district court level, the court holding that under New Jersey law IP could not be held liable for the torts of an independent contractor. Becker appealed.

**Adams, Circuit Judge.** The immunity of the employer of an independent contractor is in tension with the more general tort doctrine of *respondeat superior,* and the former represents a judicial gloss on the latter. Indeed, some authorities have advocated the all-out abolition of the independent contractor immunity, and one noted commentator has espoused the view that the proliferation of exceptions to the immunity precept is "sufficient to cast doubt on the validity of the rule." Nonetheless, we discern no indication that the New Jersey courts are prepared to abandon on a wholesale basis the rule of an employer's immunity for the acts of his independent contractors and to adopt a pure theory of "enterprise liability."

This case brings before us a young construction worker whose body has in all probability been ruined for life. Yet, he is denied all but nominal recovery against the subcontractor who is responsible for his injury because that subcontractor is effectively judgment-proof and was not required by the developer to carry standard insurance. In such a situation, we believe that the failure to engage a properly solvent or adequately insured subcontractor is a violation of the duty to obtain a competent independent contractor.

First, [we seek] to ensure that the burden of accidental loss be shifted to those best able to bear and distribute that loss, rather than having it imposed on the hapless victim. In this case, as in any case in which a financially-irresponsible contractor is hired, the choice of the party to bear the loss falls between the developer and the victim. Where, as here, the developer is a substantial entrepreneur and a member of an industry that carries large liability insurance policies as a matter of course, there is little question that he is in the better position to bear the loss of such an accident. Moreover, the developer can spread the increased costs of insurance or liability to ultimate users of the project. It is only in rare circumstances that a victim will have a similar option.

Second, where feasible, liability for an accident should be allocated to those in the best position to control the factors leading to such accidents. Indeed, this is said to be the basis for the independent contractor exception to *respondeat superior*—the independent contractor is in a better position to control the work of his employees than is the employer. In the situation contemplated by the financial-irresponsibility exception, however, the loss must fall either upon the developer or upon the victim, for the subcontractor is by definition incapable of bearing it. In general, the developer has more control than the victim.

Third, the costs of accidents should be borne by those who secure the benefit of the activities that engender the mishaps. Where only one party is involved, a decision declining to insure carries with it an automatic penalty: unshielded liability to tort judgments. By hiring an independent contractor, however, the developer could obtain the advantage of lowered operating costs (passed on to him by his contractor in the form of reduced prices) without liability for the decision to expose third parties to the risk of uncompensated losses.

Judgment reversed in favor of Becker.

**Hunter, Circuit Judge, Dissenting.** The majority has formulated a new duty in the law of torts, which until now has not been part of the law of any jurisdiction in this country. This concept imposes liability upon a contractor for selecting a subcontractor who, though mechanically competent, is not sufficiently responsible financially.

To my knowledge, New Jersey courts have never defined the scope of a tort duty on the basis of an individual's financial capabilities. The majority's decision will cause uncertainty and doubt for every financial stratum and every court, as well as hinder the employment opportunities of an independent contractor trying to enter the marketplace but lacking much in the way of start-up capital.

Behind this "duty" that the majority imposes lie significant policy questions relating to economic and social costs and benefits. It appears to me that the New Jersey courts would look to the legislature for the determination of whether to adopt this novel aspect of tort law.

---

## Massey v. Tube Art Display, Inc.

**551 P.2d 1387 (Wash. Ct. App. 1976)**

Redford had been a backhoe operator for five years. Although he had worked for other sign companies, he had spent 90 percent of his time during the past three years working for Tube Art Display, Inc. He had no employees, was not registered as a contractor or subcontractor, was not bonded, and did not obtain the permits required for the jobs he did. He dug holes exactly as directed by the sign company employing him. He did, however, pay his own business taxes, and he did not participate in any of the fringe benefits available to Tube Art employees.

Tube Art obtained a permit from the city of Seattle to install a sign in the parking lot of a combination commercial and apartment building in which Massey carried on a business. Telling Redford how to proceed, Tube Art's service manager laid out the exact location of a 4 x 4-foot square on the asphalt surface with yellow paint and directed that the hole be 6 feet deep. Redford started working that evening. At 9:30 P.M., he struck a small natural gas pipeline with the backhoe. He examined the pipe and, finding no indication of a leak or break, concluded that the line was not in use and left the worksite. About 2 A.M., an explosion and fire occurred in the building serviced by the line. Two people were killed, and most of the building's contents were destroyed.

Massey, a tenant in the building, sued Tube Art for the destruction of his business and inventory. He alleged that Redford was negligent in not making an inspection before digging and in not notifying the gas company that he had struck the line, and, further, that Redford was operating under the control of Tube Art as its employee. The trial court decided in Massey's favor, and Tube Art appealed.

**Swanson, Judge.** Traditionally, servants have been looked upon as persons employed to perform services in the affairs of others under an express or implied agreement, and who, with respect to physical conduct in the performance of those services, are subject to the other's control or right of control. An independent contractor, on the other hand, is generally defined as one who contracts to perform services for another, but who is not controlled by the other nor subject to the other's right to control with respect to his physical conduct in performing the services.

In determining whether one acting for another is a servant or independent contractor, several factors must be taken into consideration. These are listed in *Restatement (Second) of Agency* § 220(2) as follows:

a. the extent of control which, by the agreement, the master may exercise over the details of the work;
b. whether or not the one employed is engaged in a distinct occupation or business;
c. the kind of occupation, with reference to whether, in the locality, the work is usually done under the direction of the employer or by a specialist without supervision;
d. the skill required in the particular occupation;
e. whether the employer or the workman supplies the instrumentalities, tools, and the place of work for the person doing the work;
f. the length of time for which the person is employed;
g. the method of payment, whether by the time or by the job;
h. whether or not the work is a part of the regular business of the employer;
i. whether or not the parties believe they are creating the relation of master and servant; and
j. whether the principal is or is not in business.

All of these factors are of varying importance in determining the type of relationship involved, and, with the exception of the element of control, not all the elements need be present. It is the right to control another's physical conduct that is the essential and oftentimes decisive factor in establishing vicarious liability.

We find no disputed evidence of the essential factor—the right to control. Nor is there any dispute that control was exercised over the most significant decisions—the size and location of the hole. [Therefore, Redford is an employee of Tube Art and Tube Art is liable for Redford's negligence under the doctrine of *respondeat superior.*]

Judgment for Massey affirmed.

## Edgewater Motels, Inc. v. Gatzke

**277 N.W.2d 11 (Minn. Sup. Ct. 1979)**

A. J. Gatzke, a district manager for the Walgreen Company, spent several weeks in Duluth, Minnesota, supervising the opening of a new Walgreen restaurant there. He remained at the restaurant approximately 17 hours a day, and he was on call 24 hours a day to handle problems arising in other Walgreen restaurants in the district. While in Duluth, he lived at the Edgewater Motel at Walgreen's expense. After some heavy drinking late one night, Gatzke returned to his motel room and spent some time at a desk filling out an expense account required by his employer. Gatzke was a heavy smoker, and he testified that he probably smoked a cigarette while completing the expense account. Shortly after Gatzke went to bed, a fire broke out in his motel room. Gatzke escaped, but fire damage to the motel totaled over $330,000. An expert witness testified that the fire was caused by a burning cigarette or a match and that it started in or near a wastebasket located beside the desk at which Gatzke worked.

Edgewater sued Walgreen for Gatzke's negligence. The jury found for Edgewater, in the process concluding that Gatzke acted within the scope of his employment when he filled out the form and disposed of the cigarette. The trial court, however, granted Walgreen's motion for judgment notwithstanding the verdict. Edgewater appealed. The question for the appellate court was whether the trial judge erred in setting aside the jury's finding that Gatzke's negligent conduct occurred within the scope of his employment.

**Scott, Justice.** It is reasonably inferable from the evidence that Gatzke's negligent smoking of a cigarette was a direct cause of the damages sustained by Edgewater. The question is whether the facts reasonably support the imposition of vicarious liability on Walgreen's for the conceded negligent act of its employee.

For an employer to be held vicariously liable for an employee's negligent conduct, the employee's wrongful act must be committed within the scope of his employment. To support a finding that an employee's negligent act occurred within his scope of employment, it must be shown that his conduct was, to some degree, in furtherance of the interests of his employer. This principle is recognized by *Restatement (Second) of Agency* § 235, which states: "An act of a servant is not within the scope of employment if it is done with no intention to perform it as a part of or incident to a service on account of which he is employed." Other factors to be considered in the scope of employment determination are whether the conduct is of the kind that the employee is authorized to perform and whether the act occurs substantially within authorized time and space restrictions. No hard and fast rule can be applied to resolve the "scope of employment" inquiry. Rather, each case must be decided on its own individual facts.

The initial question is whether an employee's smoking of a cigarette can constitute conduct within his scope of employment. This issue has not been dealt with by this court. The courts which have considered the question have not agreed on its resolution. A number of courts have ruled that the act of smoking, even when done simultaneously with work-related activity, is not within the employee's scope of employment because it is a matter personal to the employee which is not done in furtherance of the employer's interest. Other courts have reasoned that the smoking of a cigarette, if done while engaged in the business of the employer, is within an employee's scope of employment because it is a minor deviation from the employee's work-related activities, and thus merely an act done incidental to general employment. We agree with this analysis and hereby hold that an employer can be vicariously liable for an employee's negligent smoking of a cigarette if he was otherwise acting in the scope of his employment at the time of the negligent act.

Thus, we must next determine whether Gatzke was otherwise in the scope of his employment at the time of his negligent act. Even assuming that Gatzke was outside the scope of his employment while he was at the bar, there is evidence from which a jury could reasonably find that Gatzke resumed his employment activities after he returned to his motel room and filled out his expense account. The expense account was, of course, completed so that Gatzke could be reimbursed by Walgreen's for his work-related expenses. In this sense, Gatzke is performing an act for his own personal benefit. However, the completion of the expense account also furthers the employer's business in that it provides detailed documentation of business expenses so that they are properly deductible for tax purposes. In this light, the filling out of the expense form can be viewed as serving a dual purpose: that of furthering Gatzke's personal interests and promoting his employer's business purposes. Accordingly, it is reasonable for the jury to find that the completion of the expense account is an act done in furtherance of the employer's business purposes.

Additionally, the record indicates that Gatzke was an executive type of employee who had no set working hours. He considered himself a 24-hour-a-day man; his room at the Edgewater Motel was his "office away from home." It was therefore also reasonable for the jury to determine that the filling out of his expense account was done within authorized time and space limits of his employment.

Judgment reversed in favor of Edgewater.

## TORT LIABILITY OF THE AGENT

Generally, an agent is liable for his own torts.[14] The fact that the agent has acted at the principal's command will not absolve the agent from liability. For example, if under Parkham's orders Adams enters Tingle's land without Tingle's consent, Adams cannot escape liability for trespass by asserting that he acted as agent for Parkham.

**Exceptions.** However, there are certain situations where the agent can avoid tort liability. First, an agent can escape liability if she was exercising a privilege of the principal. Suppose that in the above example Tingle had granted Parkham a valid easement or right-of-way to transport his farm products over a private road crossing Tingle's land. Here, Adams would not be liable to Tingle for driving across Tingle's land to transport farm products. However, the agent must not exceed the scope of the privilege and must act for the purpose for which the privilege was given. Thus, Adams would not be protected if he took his Jeep on a midnight joyride across Tingle's land. Also, the privilege given the agent must be delegable in the first place. If Tingle had given the easement to Parkham exclusively, Adams would not be privileged to drive across Tingle's land.

Moreover, a principal who is privileged to take certain actions in defense of his person

[14] The liability of certain professional agents is discussed in Chapter 27.

or property may often authorize an agent to do the same. In such cases, the agent will escape liability if the principal could have done so. For example, if properly authorized, an agent may be able to use force to protect the life or property of the principal.

In addition, an agent who makes misrepresentations in the conduct of the principal's business will not be liable in tort unless he either knew or had reason to know of their falsity. Suppose Parker authorizes Arnold to sell his house, falsely telling Arnold that the house is fully insulated. Arnold does not know that the statement is false, and could not discover its falsity through an ordinary, reasonable inspection. If Arnold tells Thomas that the house is fully insulated and Thomas relies on this statement in purchasing the house, Parker will be directly liable to Thomas, but Arnold will not be liable. Finally, the agent will not be liable for injuries to third persons caused by defective tools or instrumentalities furnished by the principal unless the agent had actual knowledge or reason to know of the defect.

**Actions against Principal and Agent.** In many cases, both the principal and the agent will be liable for the torts of the agent. Here, the principal and the agent are *jointly and severally* liable. This means that the third party may join the principal and the agent in one action and get a judgment against each, or may sue either or both individually and get a judgment against either or both. However, the third party is entitled to only one satisfaction for his claim. Once actual recovery is obtained from either the principal or the agent, no further recovery is possible. In cases where one party has had to satisfy the judgment alone despite the other party's joint liability, the various duties discussed in the previous chapter may come into play. Depending on the facts, the agent may be liable to the principal for liabilities incurred due to the agent's breach of duty or the principal may be required to indemnify the agent for a judgment satisfied against the agent.

## CRIMINAL LIABILITY

Generally, a principal is not liable for the crime of an agent or an employee unless the principal directed, approved, or participated in the crime. Under certain statutes, however, an otherwise innocent employer may be liable for conduct of an employee within the scope of his employment. Examples include statutes forbidding the sale of alcoholic beverages and impure food. Also, there is a growing tendency to hold an employer liable for the crimes of advisory, decision-making, or managerial employees.[15] Finally, agents are generally liable for their own crimes, and their status as agents or the fact that they acted at the principal's direction has no effect on their criminal liability.

## SUBAGENTS

**Agent's Authority to Appoint Subagents.** A **subagent** is basically the agent of an agent. More precisely, a subagent is a person appointed to undertake the principal's business by an agent with authority to make the appointment. Ordinarily, a corporation, partnership, or other organization acting as an agent will have implied authority to appoint subagents. Unless otherwise agreed, however, an agent employed to conduct a transaction does not have authority to delegate acts that involve discretion or special skills possessed by the agent. Such an agent, though, can appoint a subagent to perform mechanical or *ministerial* tasks not involving judgment or

[15] The criminal liability of corporations and their employees is discussed in Chapters 3 and 24.

discretion. For instance, if the Providence Company makes Allgood its general purchasing agent, Allgood can appoint Sampson his subagent to type contracts, answer the telephone, and perform other routine tasks, but not to make decisions regarding needed purchases. Also, the authority to appoint a subagent may sometimes be implied where the agent cannot complete the agency business within a reasonable time or without the help of others or where an emergency makes the hiring of a subagent necessary.

In some cases, however, a party appointed by an agent will not be a subagent. This happens when the agent is given authority to appoint agents *for the principal.* In such cases, the appointed party is simply an agent for the principal and not an agent of the appointing agent. When the appointing agent will possess this sort of authority depends on the facts and circumstances of the individual case. For example, the sales manager of a corporation would probably have authority to hire sales agents, but these would most likely be agents of the corporation and not agents of the sales manager.

**Liability to Third Parties for Acts of Subagents.** When an agent appoints a subagent, the agent becomes a principal with respect to the subagent. Thus, the *agent's* tort liability and contract liability for acts of the subagent are determined by the usual rules governing the principal's liability for acts of the agent. However, note that where an agent is appointed *for the principal,* the appointing agent will ordinarily escape liability for the appointed agent's acts. The main exception is the situation where the appointing agent is *directly* liable (e.g., by negligently selecting an agent for the principal).

The subagent is also the *principal's* agent. Thus, the subagent can subject the principal to tort and contract liability under the usual rules discussed earlier. The principal is liable on contracts made by a subagent if: (1) these contracts are within actual or apparent authority granted by the agent; and (2) this grant of authority to the subagent was actually or apparently authorized by the principal. Suppose that Peters employs the Ajax Realty Company to sell his house, and Ajax assigns one of its employees to handle the matter. If the employee contracts to sell Peters's home, Peters is bound on the contract. Usually, however, the principal will not be liable for the subagent's torts. Although the subagent may be the *agent's* employee, only rarely will there be an employer-employee relationship between the principal and the subagent. Thus, the principal is generally not subject to *respondeat superior* liability for the torts of a subagent. Some courts, however, have held the principal liable for the subagent's misrepresentations. In the above example, for instance, Peters could be liable for misrepresentations made by Ajax's employee in the course of selling Peters's house.

**Fiduciary Duties.** The agent and the subagent owe each other all the normal duties that the principal (here, the agent) owes the agent (here, the subagent), and vice versa. A subagent who is aware of the original principal's existence owes that principal all of the normal duties an agent owes to a principal, except those imposed by contract. The principal, in turn, is not contractually liable to the subagent; for example, she normally is under no duty to compensate him. But the principal will be required to indemnify the subagent as she would agents generally. Finally, the agent is responsible to the principal for the conduct of the subagent, and will be required to compensate or indemnify the principal if the subagent's actions cause direct harm to the principal or make the principal liable to third parties.

## SUMMARY

A principal is liable on contracts made by the agent if the agent has express, implied, or apparent authority to make the contracts in question. *Express authority* is present when the principal employs explicit language authorizing the agent to perform certain acts and communicates this to the agent. *Implied authority* derives from express authority and from all of the facts and circumstances surrounding the agency. It is based on what the agent could reasonably assume that the principal wanted the agent to do, given a certain grant of express authority and given the surrounding circumstances. *Apparent authority* is based on what the principal communicates to the third party. It arises when the principal's words and/or actions create a reasonable belief by the third party that the agent is authorized to perform certain acts. Even if the agent's contract was unauthorized, the principal may become bound to the contract by *ratifying* it.

The *agent's* contractual liability depends on a different set of factors. Generally, an agent who contracts for a *disclosed principal* will not be liable on contracts made for the principal. The principal is disclosed when the third party has knowledge or reason to know of both the principal's existence and his identity. However, the agent for a disclosed principal may bind himself to the contract by expressly so agreeing. And an agent who acts in excess of her authority may be liable to the third party under an implied warranty of authority. The agent who contracts for a *partially disclosed* or an *undisclosed* principal will typically be bound to the contract. The principal is partially disclosed when the third party has knowledge or reason to know that the agent is acting for a principal but lacks knowledge or reason to know of the principal's identity. The principal is undisclosed when the third party lacks knowledge or reason to know of both the principal's existence and his identity. Usually, agents who contract for legally nonexistent principals will be liable. Agents who contract for principals who lack capacity may or may not be liable.

Generally, a *notification* received or given by an agent with express, implied, or apparent authority to do so is notification to or from the principal. Also, there are many situations where the agent's *knowledge* of certain facts will be imputed to the principal.

The principal's tort liability for acts of the agent may be *direct* or *imputed.* Direct liability occurs when the principal commands or authorizes the agent to engage in tortious behavior or is negligent in hiring, instructing, directing, or equipping the agent. The principal's imputed liability for the torts of agents depends on whether the agent is classed as an *employee* or as an *independent contractor.* The agent is an employee where the principal has the right to control the physical details of the agent's work. Principals (employers) are liable for all torts of their employees committed within the *scope of their employment.* To be within the scope of employment, the employee's act usually must: (1) be of the kind that he was employed to perform, (2) occur substantially within the time and space limits of the employment, and (3) be motivated at least in part by the purpose of serving the employer. Subject to certain exceptions, the principal will *not* be liable for the torts of independent contractors.

Agents are generally liable for their own torts, and, with a few exceptions, the fact that they acted for a principal will not relieve them of liability. Agents are likewise generally liable for their own crimes. A principal is usually not liable for crimes committed by an agent unlesss he directed, approved, or participated in their commission.

A *subagent* is an agent appointed by an

agent with authority to do so. Subagents must be distinguished from agents who are appointed by an agent, but only to serve the principal. Generally, the subagent's ability to make the principal liable in contract or in tort is governed by the same tests establishing the agent's ability to do so. The same is true regarding the liability of the agent (here, a principal) for the subagent's acts. The fiduciary duties between agent and subagent, and between principal and subagent, are generally the same as those existing between principal and agent. However, the principal is not contractually liable to the subagent and the subagent's duties to the principal depend on the subagent's knowledge of the principal's existence.

## PROBLEM CASES

**1.** Barton was sales manager for Bonanni, who manufactured hosiery and sold it using door-to-door salespeople. Barton was expressly authorized to hire and supervise the sales staff employed by Bonanni. Barton contracted with Hinkson to employ him as a salesperson for Bonanni. Barton, as agent for Bonanni, agreed to pay Hinkson a 5 percent commission on all orders taken and submitted to Bonanni. Barton took Hinkson on a sales demonstration trip that lasted four days. During this time, Hinkson was paid $10 per day. Hinkson took orders and submitted them to Bonanni, but due to a shortage of materials Bonanni was unable to fill a substantial percentage of the orders submitted by Hinkson. Bonanni paid Hinkson the agreed commission on orders filled, but refused to pay commissions on orders submitted but not filled. Hinkson sued Bonanni to recover a judgment for such commissions. Bonanni's defense was that Barton had no authority to contract to pay a commission on orders submitted but not filled. Did Barton have authority to contract to pay a commission on such orders?

**2.** Kjome, a sales agent for Arntson, sold 200 gallons of Shell Oil Company's Weed Killer No. 20 to Start, a commercial grower of lily bulbs. At the time of the transaction, Start had told Kjome that he wanted a weed killer for use on a field in which he had planted lily bulblets. Kjome expressly warranted that the weed killer could be used safely on the field. When applied, however, the weed killer destroyed most of the bulblets. When sued for damages on a breach of warranty theory, Arntson's defense was that Kjome had no authority to warrant the product. Is Arntson liable on the warranty? Assume that Kjome is a general agent and that Arntson never told him not to make the warranty in question.

**3.** Letbetter purchased merchandise from a salesperson representing United Laboratories. The contract of sale expressly provided that no representations of the salesperson would be binding upon the seller unless they were written into the order. It also contained a recital that the seller expressly denied liability and assumed no responsibility for the application or resale of the materials purchased on the order. The salesperson made representations about the suitability of the materials for certain uses, but the representations were not included in the sales orders. The materials were not suitable for the purposes represented. Is United Laboratories liable *in tort* for the salesperson's representations? Assume that United Laboratories did not intend that the saleperson make the representations and that it had no reason to think that they would be made.

**4.** Bikos was employed by the partnership owning Sagewood Apartments in El Paso, Texas to manage the apartments. Bikos had recently moved to El Paso from Indiana, where he owed $18,000 in gambling debts. Bikos had authority to collect rents from tenants, but he was not empowered to write checks on the account in which the rents were deposited. In order to raise money to pay his gambling debts, meet living expenses, and engage in new gambling operations, Bikos permitted some tenants to pay a year's rent in advance in exchange for a small discount on their monthly rent. From the sums thus received, he deposited one month's rent for each participating tenant and used the rest for his own purposes. Soon, Bikos needed more funds to make upcoming monthly deposits for the tenants who had already paid in advance. He therefore sold some of the tenants short-term savings certificates paying a very high rate of interest. The certificates were issued in the name of Sagewood Apartments, showing Bikos's name as manager and a fictitious name signed by Bikos as treasurer. Bikos's employers had not authorized him to issue savings certificates to tenants and knew nothing of Bikos's dealings with his tenants. Eventually, Biko was arrested for felony theft. Then, tenants who had paid Bikos for the worthless certificates sued the apartments' owners for the amounts they had paid. Did Bikos have implied or apparent authority to issue the certificates?

**5.** Hall moved to Florida in 1976, employing McCormick to manage an apartment building in Illinois that he owned. In 1978, McCormick told Hall that he had a buyer for the building. The deal fell through, for McCormick told Hall on September 10 that he had contracted to list the property with Kennedy, a real estate broker, on September 2. Hall told McCormick that he was "terribly upset" about the listing with Kennedy and that he and McCormick had agreed that he would find his own real estate broker if the buyer backed out. However, Hall never told McCormick to cancel the agreement with Kennedy and never tried to do so himself. Three weeks later, when Kennedy found a new buyer for the building, Hall at first accepted the buyer's offer but then tried to rescind the deal. About 10 days after this, Hall wrote Kennedy to tell him to continue his efforts to sell the building.

The September 2 listing agreement with Kennedy stated that Kennedy was entitled to a commission once he found a ready, willing, and able purchaser (which he had). Nonetheless, Hall refused to pay the commission. Kennedy sued Hall to recover the commission. Assuming for the sake of argument that Kennedy originally lacked authority to act as broker for Hall, did Hall later ratify the listing agreement?

**6.** McDowell owned land adjacent to the tracks of the Peoria & Eastern Railroad. He allowed Kenworthy to park a truck trailer on the land in such a way that the trailer extended approximately 4 feet into the railroad's right-of-way. This obstructed the view from a nearby road crossing, and as a result a motorist was struck by a Peoria & Eastern locomotive. The railroad settled with the motorist for $25,000 and then sought indemnity from McDowell and Kenworthy. They defended on the ground that a conductor, two brakemen, and two engineers employed by the railroad had seen the trailer on various occasions. None of these men had reported the trailer's position to superiors. Each testified that he did not know the exact location of the railroad's right-of-way. Can the knowledge of these employees be imputed to the railroad?

**7.** Olive and James Dean were the sole officers and shareholders of the Dean-King Corporation. The corporation owned a restaurant called Harry's Steak House, which was managed by the Deans. Charles Masinton had sold grocery products to the restaurant for some time, dealing with one or both of the Deans on all occasions. These products were paid for by checks signed by one or both of the Deans. The checks were imprinted with "Dean-King Corporation d/b/a Harry's Steak House, Inc." in the upper left corner. Sometime after this course of dealing began, James Dean became ill and amounts owing to Masinton were not paid. Eventually, Masinton sued Olive Dean to collect $10,880.03 in unpaid bills, arguing that he had had no knowledge that he was dealing with a corporation. Will Olive Dean be personally liable to Masinton?

**8.** Twelve individuals agreed to sponsor and promote a group of Little League baseball teams called the Golden Spike Little League. The league was a loosely formed voluntary association without any legal identity. The 12 individuals arranged with Smith & Edwards to furnish the needed uniforms and equipment, signed for them, picked them up, and distributed them to the teams. No one ever paid Smith & Edwards the $3,900 bill for the uniforms and equipment. Smith & Edwards sued the 12 individuals in their personal capacities for the amount due. If they defend by saying that they acted as agents for a disclosed principal (the league), will the defense be successful? Why or why not?

**9.** Western Stock Center, Inc. contracted with S.T.O.P. Corporation to remove the ammonia piping system from one of its buildings. Western knew that the walls of the building were made of wood and cork, that they were permeated with grease, and that an electric cutting torch would be used in the salvage operations. Western did not dictate how S.T.O.P. was to perform the job or supervise S.T.O.P. during the job. Also, it made no inquiry as to S.T.O.P.'s experience in doing this type of work.

S.T.O.P. had no such experience, and the building was destroyed by a fire started by a torch used by one of S.T.O.P.'s employees. Sevit, Inc. was a tenant in the building. It brought an action for approximately $35,000 against Western, the owner, for property damage and lost profits due to the loss of its lease. Sevit's suit was based on three theories: (1) that Western was negligent in selecting S.T.O.P. to do the salvage work; (2) that Western was negligent in failing to supervise S.T.O.P.'s work; and (3) that Western was liable because the work was "inherently dangerous." Should Western's motion for a directed verdict in its favor be granted?

**10.** While on duty one evening within the confines of the base, Johnny Lee Thornton, a military policeman at Fort Leonard Wood, Missouri, stopped a vehicle containing two male and two female teenagers. After falsely telling the occupants that their car matched the description of a car that had taken part in a service station robbery, Thornton handcuffed the two young men and placed them in the back seat of his jeep. Then, he shot them both with his military-issue .45-caliber pistol. After that, Thornton ordered the two women into the jeep, took them to a cabin in a remote part of the base, forced them to have various forms of sexual relations with him and with each other, and shot them both. Thornton buried all of the victims in the snow. However, one of the women survived. Thornton was eventually convicted on various criminal charges.

The survivor of the incident and the representatives of the deceased parties sued the United States for Thornton's various torts under the Federal Tort Claims Act. The suit was based on *respondeat superior,* and not on the government's direct liability. Did Thornton act within the scope of his employment? Assume that Thornton did act within the time and space limits of his employment.

**11.** Agnes Greening, a Montana resident, sued the Mutual Life Insurance Company of New York (MONY) and Al Pontrelli, an insurance agent, in a Montana trial court. She entered a contract claim for accidental death benefits under her husband's life insurance policies with MONY and a tort claim for punitive damages for Pontrelli's and MONY's bad faith in connection with the insurance contract. The defendants tried to remove the case to federal district court. Under federal law, however, they could not do so unless complete diversity of citizenship was present. Since Pontrelli was a Montana resident, this meant that the defendants had to argue that Greening had no basis for suing Pontrelli in either contract or tort. Assuming that Greening's contract and tort claims were justified, could Pontrelli be liable on either basis? Assume that Pontrelli sold Greening the policies in question, that he acted as a MONY agent in doing so, and that Greening knew this. Also assume that while representing MONY, Pontrelli acted with tortious bad faith.

# PART V

# PARTNERSHIP LAW

# Chapter 18

# Introduction to Sole Proprietorship, Partnership, and Related Forms

## INTRODUCTION

In this chapter, you begin your study of business organizations. One of the most important decisions made by a person beginning a business is choosing a *form* of business. This decision is important because, among other reasons, the business owner's liability and her control of the business vary greatly among the many forms of business. In addition, some business forms offer significant tax advantages to their owners.

In the next eight chapters, you will study six forms of business:

1. Sole proprietorship.
2. Partnership (sometimes called general partnership).
3. Joint venture.
4. Mining partnership.
5. Limited partnership.
6. Corporation.

Early in this chapter, you will study the sole proprietorship briefly. Next you will begin your three-chapter study of partnerships, joint ventures, and mining partnerships, learning in this chapter their characteristics and the formalities for their creation. You will study limited partnerships in Chapter 21. Corporations will be discussed in Chapters 22 to 25.

## SOLE PROPRIETORSHIP

A **sole proprietorship,** as its name states, has only one owner. The sole proprietorship is merely an extension of its owner: a *sole proprietor* owns his own business, and no one else owns any part of it.

As the sole owner of a business, the sole proprietor has the right to make all the management decisions of the business. In addition, all the profits of the business are his. In return for his complete managerial control and sole ownership of profits, he assumes great liability: he is *personally liable* for all the obligations of the business. All the debts of the business, including debts on contracts signed only in the name of the business, are his debts. If the assets of the business are insufficient to pay the claims of its creditors, the creditors may require the sole proprietor to pay the claims from his individual, nonbusiness assets, such as his house and automobile. A sole proprietor may lose everything if his business becomes insolvent. Hence, the sole proprietorship is a risky form of business for its owner.

In light of this risk, you may ask why any person would organize a business as a sole proprietorship. There are two reasons. First, few people carefully consider the business-form decision. They merely begin their businesses. Second, the sole proprietorship is formed very easily. A person need merely set up her business to establish a sole proprietorship. No formalities are necessary. She may have a sole proprietorship even though she does not intend to create one. These two reasons explain why the sole proprietorship is the most common form of business in the United States.

Since the sole proprietorship is merely an extension of its owner, it has no life apart from its owner. It is not a legal entity. It cannot sue or be sued. Instead, creditors must sue the owner, and the owner in his own name must sue those who harm the business. In addition, a sole proprietorship is easily transferred, because only the sole proprietor need consent to its sale or other transfer.

A sole proprietor may hire employees for the business, but they are employees of the sole proprietor. Under the law of agency, he is responsible for his employees' authorized contracts and for the torts they commit in the course of their employment.[1] Also, a sole proprietorship is not an income tax–paying entity for federal income tax purposes. All of the income of a sole proprietorship is income to its owner and must be reported on the sole proprietor's individual federal income tax return.

Many sole proprietorships have trade names. For example, Caryl Stanley may operate her bagel shop under the name Caryl's Bagel Shop. Caryl would be required to file the trade name under a state statute requiring the registration of fictitious business names. If she were sued by a creditor, the creditor would address his complaint to "Caryl Stanley, doing business as Caryl's Bagel Shop."

## INTRODUCTION TO PARTNERSHIPS

**History of Partnerships.** The basic concept of partnership, two or more people joining forces to attain benefits for their common welfare, is as ancient as the history of collective human endeavor. Partnerships were known in ancient Babylonia, ancient Greece, and the Roman Empire. The Babylonians, a commercial and agricultural people, in their Code of Hammurabi—2300 B.C.—included

[1] The law of agency is covered in Chapters 16 and 17.

provisions regulating partnerships. Under Hebrew law, the Jews, who were originally a pastoral people, held land jointly from the earliest time in a crude form of partnership. Later, when they engaged in commerce that was carried on by caravan, men would join their capital and labor, organize the caravans, and share the profits and losses of such undertakings. These early partnerships were organized to undertake a single venture and were in many respects similar to our modern joint venture.

The definition of a partnership in the sixth-century Justinian Code of the Roman Empire does not differ materially from that in our laws today. The partnership was likewise known in Asian countries, including China. During the Middle Ages, much trade between nations was carried on by partnerships.

Since trade in England during its earlier period was carried on at merchants' fairs, and controversies arising out of trade were settled in the merchants' courts, English partnership cases were not heard and determined in the common law courts. By the close of the 17th century, however, the partnership was recognized in the English common law. When the United States became an independent nation, it adopted the English common law insofar as that law was suitable to social and economic conditions in this country; consequently, the United States, in effect, adopted the English law of partnerships. In the early part of the 19th century, the partnership became the most important form of association.

**Modern Partnership Law.** Today, the common law of partnership has been largely supplanted by statutory law. Every state has a statute on partnership law. The Uniform Partnership Act (UPA) has been adopted by nearly every state. It is the product of the National Conference of Commissioners on Uniform State Laws, a group of practicing lawyers, judges, and law professors who have drafted proposed statutes in a number of important areas of law. The UPA, drafted in 1914, was one of its earliest efforts. The aims of the UPA are to codify partnership law in one document, to make that law more nearly consistent with itself, and to attain uniformity throughout the country. It has been adopted in 48 states (Georgia and Louisiana are the exceptions), in the District of Columbia, and in several territories, including Guam and the Virgin Islands. Because of its nearly total adoption in the United States, the UPA is the framework of your study of partnerships. It is reproduced in an appendix to this book.

The UPA does not anticipate every partnership problem. In Section 5, it states that the common law, the law of equity, and the law of merchants will apply in the absence of an applicable UPA provision.

**Principal Characteristics of Partnerships.** For most of its basic characteristics, a partnership is similar to a sole proprietorship; yet in other respects it is similar to a corporation. Under the UPA and federal tax law, a partnership will have the following characteristics:

1. A partnership may be created with *no formalities,* much like a sole proprietorship. Essentially, two people merely need to agree to own and conduct a business together in order to create a partnership. (Aggregate theory.)[2]

2. Each partner has a *right to manage* the business. A partner is both an owner and a manager. He may not be excluded from management without his consent. Each partner is an agent of the other partners. Each partner may hire agents, and every partner is lia-

[2] The parenthetic words *aggregate theory* and *entity theory* in this section refer to the aggregate and entity theories of partnership law and identify for which theory the listed partnership characteristics are examples. The aggregate and entity theories are defined in the following section.

ble for the agents' authorized contracts and for torts that the agents commit in the course of their employments. (Aggregate theory.)

3. A partnership is *not an employer of the partners,* for most purposes. As a result, for example, a partner who leaves a partnership is not entitled to unemployment benefits. (Aggregate theory.)

4. Partners are *fiduciaries* of each other. They must act in the best interests of the partnership, not in their individual best interests. (Aggregate theory.)

5. Partners have *unlimited liability* for the obligations of the business. If the business becomes insolvent, business creditors may require a partner to pay a partnership liability from her individual assets, such as her house and her bank accounts. (Aggregate theory.)

6. The *profits or losses* of the business are *shared* by the partners, who report their shares of the profits or losses on their individual federal income tax returns, since the partnership does not pay federal income taxes. (Aggregate theory.) Nevertheless, a partnership does keep its own financial records and must file an information return with the Internal Revenue Service. (Entity theory.)[3]

7. A partnership *may own property* in its own name. (Entity theory.)

8. A partnership *may not sue or be sued* in its own name. The partners must sue or be sued. (Aggregate theory.)

9. A partner *may not sue her partners.* Her sole remedy is to seek an accounting between the partners. (Aggregate theory.)[4]

10. A partner's ownership interest in a partnership is *not freely transferable.* A purchaser of his interest will not be a partner, but will be entitled to receive only his share of the partnership's profits. (Aggregate theory.)

11. Generally, a partnership has *no life apart from its owners.* If a partner dies, the partnership dissolves and may be terminated. (Aggregate theory.) Under certain circumstances, however, the UPA allows the partnership to continue after the death of a partner. (Entity theory.)

**Entity and Aggregate Theories.** Studying the list above, you may perceive that in some respects the partnership is treated as an **entity,** that is, as a person separate and distinct from its partners. In other respects, the partnership is viewed as an **aggregate** of the partners, with no life or powers apart from them. This distinction must be addressed in some detail.

The history of partnership law reveals the lengthy competition between the entity and aggregate theories of partnership. Merchants tended to adopt the entity theory. For example, a partnership may own property in its own name. This is the view of the partnership in France and other civil law countries and in Louisiana, whose law is based on the civil law. The English common law courts, however, tended to adopt the aggregate theory. Under this view, for example, partners may not sue the partnership, for they are not considered persons distinct from their partnership. Allowing a partner to sue the partnership would be like allowing the partner to sue himself. Although American courts generally followed the aggregate theory, occasionally they gave recognition to the entity theory.

**Effect of the UPA.** The entity/aggregate confusion stimulated the development of the UPA. The original draft of the UPA clearly adopted the entity theory, but the final form is more of a hybrid. As the above list of partnership characteristics indicates, the UPA

[3] The federal income tax return filed by a partnership is merely an information return, in which the partnership indicates its gross income and deductions and the names and addresses of its partners. I.R.C. § 6031. The information return allows the Internal Revenue Service to determine whether the partners accurately report partnership income on their individual returns.

[4] Partners' actions for an accounting are covered in Chapter 19.

recognizes the partnership primarily as an aggregate of the partners. In a few situations, the UPA confers entity status on a partnership, such as by permitting ownership of property in the firm name. In addition, the UPA stipulates that accounting is between the firm and the partners rather than merely between the partners, and it gives creditors of the firm priority in partnership assets over creditors of the individual partners. It also permits the firm to continue its business in situations where the aggregate theory would suggest immediate dissolution and discontinuance.

Many states have modified the UPA to create entity status for partnerships or to expand the number of situations in which the partnership is an entity. Several other states permit suits by and against partnerships in the name of the partnership. Some states qualify the partnership as an employer of the partners for purposes of workers' compensation benefits. The *Restatement (Second) of Agency* indicates, in the comments to Section 14A, that a managing partner should be considered an employee of the partnership. Nebraska goes the farthest, defining a partnership as an entity.[5] Even in Nebraska, however, a partnership is not an entity for all purposes; for example, partners are still liable for partnership obligations.

## CREATION OF PARTNERSHIP

**Introduction.** The most important issue in partnership law is whether two people who have associated in an enterprise have created a partnership. If they are partners, then the law of partnership applies to their disputes with each other and with persons with whom they have dealt.

**Consequences of Being a Partner.** As a prelude to examining the factors that determine whether a partnership has been created, you should know the consequences of being held to be another person's partner. The following are the five most important consequences:

1. You *share ownership* of the business. For example, you want to bring an employee into your business, which is worth $250,000. If you and the employee conduct your affairs like partners, your employee will own half of your business.
2. You *share the profits* of the business.
3. You *share management* of the business. Your partner must be allowed to participate in management decisions.
4. Your partner is your *agent.* You are liable for your partner's torts and contracts made in the ordinary course of business. For example, suppose that you merely wanted to be a businessman's lender or employee, but instead the two of you inadvertently arranged your affairs like partners. Rather than being a lender or employee and having no liability for the actions of the businessman, as his partner you are liable for the torts and contracts that he makes in the course of business.
5. You owe *fiduciary duties* to your partner, such as the duties to devote full-time to the business, not to compete with the business, not to self-deal, and not to disclose confidential matters.

**No Formalities for Creation.** No formalities are necessary to create a partnership. Two persons may become partners in accordance with a written partnership contract (articles of partnership); they may agree orally to be partners; or they may become partners merely by arranging their affairs as if they were partners. If partners conduct business under a trade name, they must file the name with the secretary of state in compliance with state statutes requiring the registration of fictitious business names.

**Articles of Partnership.** When people decide to become partners, they *should* employ

[5] Neb. Rev. Stat. § 67–306(1) (1981).

a lawyer to prepare a written partnership agreement. Although such **articles of partnership** are not required to form a partnership, they are highly desirable for the same reasons that written contracts are generally preferred. In addition, the Statute of Frauds makes unenforceable an agreement to form a partnership having a term exceeding one year.[6]

**Advantages of Written Articles.** Careful preparation of the articles of partnership permits the parties to consider and provide for many contingencies, such as business losses and the death of one or more partners. A written partnership agreement may eliminate disagreements arising from misunderstandings or bad memory. Even the most carefully drawn articles of partnership, however, will fail to anticipate all contingencies. As to these, partnership law applies.

**Absence of Articles of Partnership.** When there is no written partnership agreement, a dispute may arise over whether persons who are associated in some enterprise are partners. For example, someone may claim that she is a partner in order to share in the property of a successful business. More frequently, an unpaid creditor may seek to hold a person liable for a debt incurred by another person in the same enterprise.

**UPA Definition of Partnership.** UPA Section 6 defines a partnership as an "association of two or more persons to carry on a business for profit as co-owners." There are four distinct elements to the UPA definition: (1) an association of two or more persons, (2) carrying on a business, (3) as co-owners of the business, and (4) for profit. If the definition is satisfied, then the courts will treat those involved as partners.

A partnership may be created even when a person does not believe he is a partner, and occasionally, even if the parties agree that they are not partners. The burden of proving that a partnership exists falls on the party alleging the partnership.

**Association of Two or More Persons.** As an association, a partnership is a *voluntary and consensual relationship.* It cannot be imposed upon a person; a person must agree expressly or impliedly to have a person associate with him. For example, a partner cannot force her partners to accept her daughter into the partnership.

No person can be a partner with himself: a partnership must have *at least two partners.* A person may be a partner with his spouse.

**Who Is a Person?** Not everyone or everything may be a partner. UPA Section 2 defines a person as an individual, partnership, corporation, or other association. A limited partnership may be a partner. Most states do not permit a trust to be a partner, but they allow the trustee to be a partner for the benefit of the trust.

**Minors.** A minor may become a member of a partnership. Since, as a general rule, minors' contracts are voidable, a minor has a right to disaffirm the partnership agreement and withdraw at any time.[7] The courts are divided over whether the minor, upon disaffirmance, can recover from her adult partners the full amount of her investment or must bear a proportionate share of losses up to, but not exceeding, the amount of her investment. A minor is *not* permitted to recover capital contributions unless creditors' claims can be satisfied. The existence of a minor partner does not permit the other partners to disaffirm the contracts of the partnership.

**Insane Persons.** The contracts of a person officially adjudged insane are void, and

[6] The Statute of Frauds is discussed in Chapter 13.

[7] The contractual capacity of minors is covered in Chapter 11.

such a person cannot become a member of a partnership.[8] Insanity after entering a partnership is grounds for judicial dissolution. UPA Section 32 provides that a partner may ask a court to order the dissolution of a partnership if a partner has been *adjudged insane* or shown to be of *unsound mind.* An insane person not officially adjudged insane is usually treated similar to a minor: his contracts are voidable at his election.

**Carrying On a Business.** Any trade, occupation, or profession may qualify as a business. In *Neild v. Wolfe,* which follows, the court refused to find that two lovers who merely coinhabited an apartment carried on a business.

The carrying on of a business is usually considered to require a *series of transactions* conducted over a period of time. For example, a group of farmers buying supplies in order to get lower prices is not carrying on a business, but only part of one. If the group buys harvesting equipment with which it intends to harvest crops for others for a fee for many years, it is carrying on a business.

Likewise, if Richard and Jessica together own and manage an apartment house for 10 years, they are carrying on a business. If they jointly own only one single-family home and plan to sell it for a profit within a year, they are not carrying on a business, and therefore the operation is not a partnership. Engaging in a single venture, such as constructing buildings on several lots of land, is not carrying on a business even though the venture involves several transactions.[9] Usually, however, courts will treat a short-term project as a joint venture and will apply partnership law to the joint venture, as discussed later in this chapter.

[8] The contractual capacity of insane persons is covered in Chapter 11.

[9] *Walker, Mosby & Calvert, Inc. v. Burgess,* 151 S.E. 165 (Va. 1930).

**Co-ownership.** Partners must *co-own the business* in which they associate. There is no requirement that the capital contribution or the assets of the business be co-owned. Also, by itself co-ownership of assets does not establish a partnership. For example, two persons who own a building as joint tenants are not necessarily partners. To be partners, they also must co-own a business.

The two most important factors in establishing co-ownership of the business are the *sharing of profits* and the *sharing of management* of the business.

**Sharing Profits.** UPA Section 7(4) declares that the receipt by a person of a share of the profits of a business is prima facie evidence that she is a partner in the business. The rationale for this rule is that a person would not be sharing the profits of a business unless she were a co-owner. This rule brings under partnership law many persons who fail to realize that they are partners. For example, two college students who decide to purchase basketball tickets, resell them, and split the profits are partners.

Sharing the gross revenues of a business does not create a presumption of partnership. The profits, not the gross receipts, must be shared. For example, brokers who split a commission on the sale of land are not partners.

Section 7(4) provides that *no* presumption of partnership may be made when a share of profits is received (1) by a creditor as payment on a debt; (2) by an employee as wages; (3) by a landlord as rent; (4) by a widow, widower, or representative of a deceased partner; (5) by a creditor as interest on a loan; or (6) as consideration to the transferor of a business or other property for his sale of the goodwill of the business or other property. These exceptions reflect the normal expectations of the parties that no partnership exists in such situations. In the *Holler* case, which follows, the court used these exceptions to find that no partnership existed.

Despite these exceptions, if the parties arrange their affairs in a manner that otherwise establishes an *objective intent* to create a partnership, the courts will find that a partnership exists. For example, if an employee not only shares profits but also exercises managerial control of the business, a partnership may exist.

A clearly expressed intent not to share *losses* is evidence inconsistent with the partnership relation but is not conclusive. A failure to provide for the sharing of losses has no effect since the possibility of losses is seldom anticipated by the parties when they form a business. In the absence of an agreement to the contrary, partners share losses as they share profits.

**Sharing Management.** A voice in management by itself is not conclusive proof of the existence of a partnership. For example, a creditor may be granted considerable control in a business, such as a veto power over partnership decisions and the right of consultation, without becoming a partner.

Although either sharing profits or sharing management is by itself not *conclusive* proof of a partnership, when people share both profits and management, a court is almost certain to hold that they are a partnership. For example, an owner of a farm and her tenant who own livestock and equipment together and who divide income and expenses are not deemed to be partners. This is a very common method of farm tenancy, and a partnership is seldom intended by the owner and the tenant. On the other hand, if the owner and tenant participate regularly in determining what crops are to be planted or when the livestock is to be sold, they may be held to be partners and, therefore, be bound by each other's acts and contracts, such as contracts to purchase seed corn.

Even if the parties claim that they share profits for one of the five reasons listed in UPA Section 7(4), the sharing of management may overcome the presumption that they are not partners. As stated earlier, managerial control by an employee who is sharing profits may prove partnership. Landlords who, for example, are empowered to determine what crops a tenant may grow on farmland are often treated as partners by the courts.

Creditors, however, occupy a privileged position. Many cases have permitted creditors to share profits and to exercise considerable control over a business without becoming partners. Creditor control is often justified on the grounds that it is merely reasonable protection for the creditor's risk. If, however, a creditor has an unlimited claim against the profits of the business and the debt has no set repayment date, the creditor is more nearly like a partner than like a creditor and will be treated as a partner.

**For Profit.** If an endeavor is carried on by several people for charitable or other nonprofit objectives, it is not a partnership, since the objective is not to make a profit. If Alex, Tina, and Geri operate a restaurant booth at a county fair each year to raise money for a Boy Scout troop, their relationship is not a partnership, but merely an association. (Nevertheless, like partners, they may be individually liable for the debts of the enterprise.)

**Intent.** Frequently, courts say that there must be *intent* to form a partnership. This rule is more correctly stated as follows: *the parties must intend to create a relationship that the law recognizes as a partnership.* A partnership may exist even if the parties entered it inadvertently, without considering whether they had created a partnership. A written agreement to the effect that the parties do not intend to form a partnership is not conclusive if their actions provide evidence of their intent to form a relationship that meets the UPA partnership test. Intent is determined by the words and acts of the parties, interpreted in light of the circumstances.

## CREATION OF JOINT VENTURE AND MINING PARTNERSHIP

**Joint Ventures.** Courts frequently distinguish **joint ventures** (sometimes called joint adventures, joint enterprises, or syndicates) from partnerships. A joint venture may be found when a court is reluctant to call an arrangement a partnership because the purpose of the arrangement is not to establish an ongoing business involving many transactions; instead it is limited to a single project. For example, an agreement to buy and resell for profit a particular piece of real estate, perhaps after development, is likely to be viewed as a joint venture rather than a partnership. In all other respects, joint ventures are created just as partnerships are created. The joint venturers may have a formal written agreement. In its absence, a court will apply UPA Sections 6 and 7—modified so as not to require the carrying on of a business—to determine whether a joint venture has been created. The *Holler* case, which follows, illustrates the application of UPA Section 7 to determine whether a joint venture has been created.

The legal implications of the distinction between a partnership and a joint venture are not entirely clear. Generally, partnership law applies to joint ventures. For example, all of the participants in a joint venture are personally liable for debts, and joint venturers owe each other the fiduciary duties imposed upon partners. Joint ventures are treated as partnerships for federal income tax purposes. A joint venturer, like a partner, is entitled to an accounting in equity. The most significant difference between joint venturers and partners is that joint venturers are usually held to have *less implied and apparent authority* than partners, due to the limited scope of the enterprise.[10]

Two or more corporations frequently join together to form another corporation to conduct some business in which they all are interested. This jointly owned corporation is frequently referred to as a joint venture, but it is not a joint venture; it is a corporation, and it falls under the rules of corporation law rather than those of partnership law. It is, in essence, a close corporation.[11]

**Mining Partnerships.** Although similar to an ordinary partnership or a joint venture, a mining partnership is recognized as a distinct relationship in a number of states. Persons who cooperate in the working of either a mine or an oil or gas well are treated as mining partners if there is (1) *joint ownership* of a mineral interest, (2) *joint operation* of the property, and (3) *sharing* of profits and losses. Joint operation requires more than merely financing the development of a mineral interest, but it does not require active physical participation in operations; it may be proved by furnishing labor, supplies, services, or advice. The delegation of sole operating responsibility to one of the participants does not bar treatment as a mining partnership.

The relationship of mining partners is identical to that of ordinary partners, with two exceptions. First, a mining partner does *not* need the approval of the other mining partners to transfer her interest to another person, who thereby becomes a mining partner. Second, the bankruptcy or death of a partner does not *not* dissolve a mining partnership.

[10] Authority of partners and joint venturers is discussed in Chapter 19.

[11] The close corporation is defined in Chapter 22.

## Neild v. Wolfe

**445 N.Y.S.2d 934 (N.Y. Sup. Ct. 1981)**

Gail Neild and Charles Wolfe were former lovers who once thought that they would marry. On May 1, 1974, they moved into an apartment at 235 East 87th Street in Manhattan, New York. The lease was executed in Charles's name. Gail and Charles agreed that since Charles's salary was twice Gail's salary, Charles would pay two thirds of the rent and Gail would pay one third. In addition, Charles paid for all of the furnishings in the apartment.

In the spring of 1979, their relationship deteriorated. They began to sleep in different rooms, agreed to separate, and started to search for another apartment for Gail. In late summer of 1980, an apartment for Gail still not having been found, she went to England for four months to visit her family. Upon her return, Charles refused to let her into the apartment. Subsequently, she found another place to live.

On February 13, 1981, the tenants of 235 East 87th Street received a notice indicating the landlord's intent to convert the building to a cooperative, whose tenants would own their apartments. The notice offered each tenant the opportunity to purchase his apartment. The offering price was a bargain, being below the fair market value of the apartment and allowing the tenant to profit by accepting the offer.

Charles purchased the apartment he and Gail occupied. On May 19, 1981, Gail sued Charles, seeking one third of the difference between Charles's purchase price of the apartment and its fair market value. She alleged that when they lived together, she and Charles had formed a partnership or joint venture, giving her a one-third interest in the apartment.

**Lehner, Judge.** The essence of a partnership or joint venture is an association to carry on a business for profit.

This is a classic case of two people who fall in love and decide to live together. Surely, the apartment in which they resided was not thought of as a business investment. This court is well aware of the housing situation in Manhattan, but it is far reaching to presume that Gail and Charles rented an apartment in 1974 and lived together in order to derive profits from a conversion that conceivably would occur in the future. People live together for many reasons, including the fact that "two can live cheaper than one." Gail acknowledged that the apartment only constituted "a roof over their heads." The court finds the allegation that Gail and Charles created a partnership or joint venture in the apartment insufficient as a matter of law.

Judgment for Charles Wolfe.

## P & M Cattle Co. v. Holler

### 559 P.2d 1019 (Wyo. Sup. Ct. 1977)

In 1971, Rusty Holler, a rancher, offered to pasture cattle on his land at $3 per head per month. P & M Cattle Company, a partnership owned by Bill Poage and L. W. Maxfield, expressed an interest in pasturing its cattle on Holler's land. After negotiations, the following contract was made:

> 2-23-1971
>
> Contract—Rusty Holler (60 Bar Ranch)—L. W. Maxfield and Bill Poage
>
> Rusty to furnish grass for 1000 steers and 21 heifers. Maxfield & Poage to furnish money for cattle plus trucking & salt and max of $300.00 per month to Rusty for labor.
>
> Rusty to take cattle around May 1st. Cattle to be sold at a time this fall agreed upon by all parties involved.
>
> Cost of Cattle plus freight—salt and labor to be first cost. Net money from sale of cattle less first cost to be split 50–50 between Rusty (½) and Maxfield and Poage (½) (death loss to be part of first cost).

The contract was signed by Holler, Maxfield, and Poage. It was renewed orally for the years 1972, 1973, and 1974.

Substantial profits were made and shared in the first three years of the relationship. In 1974, however, P & M sold the cattle pastured on Holler's land at an $89,000 loss. P & M claimed that it was involved with Holler in a joint venture, obligating Holler to undertake his share of any loss. P & M sued Holler, asking him to pay $44,500, half of the loss.

The trial court held that Holler was not liable for the losses, because he was not a partner or a joint venturer of P & M. P & M appealed.

**Raper, Judge.** Since joint ventures are a species of and governed by the law of partnerships, we must go to the Uniform Partnership Act. Section 7(4) lays out the criteria for resolving the question as to whether a partnership exists:

> The receipt by a person of a share of the profits of a business is prima facie evidence that he is a partner in the business, but no such inference shall be drawn if such profits were received in payment:
>
> (a) As a *debt* by installments or otherwise,
> (b) As *wages* of an employee or rent to a landlord,
> (c) As an annuity to a widow or representative of a deceased partner,
> (d) As interest on a loan, though the amount of payment vary with the profits of the business,
> (e) As the *consideration* for the sale of the good-will of a business or other property by installments or otherwise. [Emphasis added.]

As can be seen from Section 7(4), an agreement to share profits is far from decisive that a partnership is intended. As in any contractual relationship, the intent of the parties is controlling. The parties must intend to create the relationship of joint venture or partnership.

In the case before us there was no express agreement to form a partnership. True, there was an agreement, but nowhere in that document is there mentioned the term partnership. Nowhere is mentioned any sharing of losses, which is normally concomitant with a sharing of profits in a partnership. While Section 7(4) creates an inference, that inference is not conclusive.

Since we cannot look at the face of the instrument here and determine whether there is a partnership, it is necessary that we examine the complete relationship between P & M and Holler. We can in such a circumstance go outside the four corners of the contract to test the claim of a would-be partner and look at what the parties did and how they treated the arrangement between them. The contemporary construction of a contract by acts of the parties is entitled to serious consideration by the court whose duty it becomes to determine its meaning.

In the first place, the agreement is not labeled a partnership agreement, and the term partnership is nowhere mentioned within its terms. From the inception of the relationship, then, none of the parties ever identified it as a partnership.

The pact was conceived in an atmosphere created by Holler's desire to sell grass. The division of losses was never discussed between the parties until P & M delivered the bad news to Holler following the fall 1974 cattle sales. No partnership federal income tax information return for any of the years 1971–74 was prepared and submitted to the Internal Revenue Service of the United States. On the income tax returns made by P & M during the period in question, the part of profits paid to Holler was carried as a business expense listed as "contract feeding." Holler included such payments on his individual income tax return as sale of "crops"; none of the cattle grazed by Holler were carried on his income tax return as livestock inventory. The livestock were carried on P & M's partnership income tax returns. On the check given by P & M to Holler in 1973, for Holler's share of the profits at the end of the season, it was shown as being paid for "pasture."

Within the framework of the Uniform Partnership Act, there was no partnership. The division of profits was only a measure—a standard of payment by P & M to Holler in discharge of a debt for services and grass under Section 7(4)(a), or in payment to Holler for wages of an employee in caring for the cattle while on his ranch and rent to him as landlord for his pasture under Section 7(4)(b) or sale of grass as personal property under Section 7(4)(e), or through a combination of those lettered subsections for wages and rent or sale of property. We need not determine precisely what it was as long as it was outside the pale of partnership.

Judgment for Holler affirmed.

## PARTNERSHIP BY ESTOPPEL

**Introduction.** Two persons may not be partners, yet in the eyes of a third person, they may *appear* to be partners. If the third person deals with one of the alleged partners, he may suffer a detriment. For example, John thinks that Hannah, a wealthy person, is a partner of Diana, a poor person. John decides to do business with Diana on the grounds that if Diana does not perform as agreed, he will be able to recover damages from Hannah. If

John is wrong and Hannah is not Diana's partner, John ordinarily has no recourse against Hannah. UPA Section 7(1) states that "persons who are not partners as to each other are not partners as to third persons." However, if John can prove that Hannah misled him to believe that she and Diana were partners, he may sue Hannah for Diana's failure to perform as agreed. This is an application of the doctrine of **partnership by estoppel.**

Partnership by estoppel is similar to two concepts that you have already studied: promissory estoppel[12] and apparent authority of agents.[13] It is based on a person's substantial, detrimental reliance on another person's representations.

**Elements.** UPA Section 16 deals with partnership by estoppel. Essentially, Section 16 states that to recover against a party as if she were a partner, a person must prove (1) that the party *held herself out or permitted herself to be held out as a partner,* (2) that the person dealt with the party's purported partner in *justifiable reliance* on the holding out, and (3) that the person was *injured* as a result.

**Holding Out.** Few problems arise in determining whether a person holds himself out as a partner. For example, he might refer to himself as another person's partner. Or he might, as did the person in the *Volkman* case, which follows, appear frequently in the office of a purported partner and confer with him. Perhaps he and another person will share office space, have one door to an office with both of their names on it, have one telephone number, and share a secretary who answers the phone giving the names of both persons.

[12] See Chapter 10.

[13] See Chapter 17.

**Consenting to Holding Out.** The cases are not in accord as to what acts constitute consent to a holding out. Some of the earlier cases took the view that a person consents if she is aware of the holding out and fails to take affirmative actions to stop it and to notify the public. The later cases and the UPA reject that view and instead take the view that to be held liable as a partner, one must *consent* to the holding out. Under this view, mere knowledge that one is being held out as a partner will *not* amount to consent. For example, suppose Joan tells Eric that Gus is a partner in Bob's new retail shoe business. In fact, Gus owns the building but is not a partner. Later, Gus learns of the conversation between Joan and Eric. Gus does not have to seek out Joan and Eric to tell them that he is not Bob's partner in order to avoid being held liable as a partner for Bob's debts. Had Joan made the statement to Eric in Gus's presence, however, Gus must deny the partnership relation, or he will be held liable for Eric's subsequent reliance on Gus's silence.

**Reasonable Reliance and Injury.** A partner by estoppel is *not* liable to everyone who deals with the purported partnership. He is liable only to those persons who *reasonably rely* on the holding out and *suffer injury* thereby. This means that partnership by estoppel, like any estoppel concept, is determined on a case-by-case basis. For example, Joan tells Sam that she is Tim's partner, but she does not tell this to Carl. Sam can prove partnership by estoppel, but Carl cannot. If Sam tells Carl what Joan told him, then Carl can prove partnership by estoppel.

A third person's reliance upon the appearance of a partnership must be *reasonable.* If a reasonable person has information that would prevent her from relying upon the holding out of a person as a partner, no partnership by estoppel may result. For example, Linda knows that Fred and Shelley are employer and employee. Fred calls Shelley "my partner" in the presence of Shelley and Linda. Fred and Shelley are not partners by estoppel. Linda should be required to make inquiries before she may rely upon Fred's calling Shelley "my partner."

The injury suffered by the third person must be the result of his reliance. If the third person would have done business with another person whether or not that person was a partner of someone held out as a partner, there is no injury as a result of reliance. Hence, there is no partnership by estoppel.

**Effect of Partnership by Estoppel.** Once partnership by estoppel has been proved, the person who held himself out or who consented to being held out is liable as though he were a partner. He is liable on contracts entered into by third persons upon their belief that he was a partner. He is liable for torts committed during the course of relationships entered by third persons who believed he was a partner.

**Not a Partner in Fact.** Although a party is a partner by estoppel to a person who knows of the holding out and who justifiably relies on it to his injury, the partner by estoppel is not a partner in fact and may not share in the profits, management, or value of the purported partnership. Partnership by estoppel is merely a device to allow creditors to sue parties who mislead them into believing that a partnership exists.

**Ostensible Partnership.** Some of the earlier cases held that a person could become a member of a partnership by being held out as a partner, even though he never consented to becoming a partner and never participated in the affairs of the partnership. This theory of *ostensible partnership* has been abandoned.

## Volkman v. DP Associates

### 268 S.E.2d 265 (N.C. Ct. App. 1980)

Alvin and Carol Volkman decided to build a house, and they contacted David McNamee for construction advice. McNamee informed the Volkmans that he either had just commenced business or was going into business with Phillip Carroll. Subsequently, the Volkmans received correspondence from McNamee on DP Associates stationery. They assumed that the DP was derived from the first names of McNamee and Carroll: David and Phillip. Prior to the signing of the contract, McNamee introduced Carroll to Mr. Volkman at the DP Associates office, where Carroll said, "I hope we'll be working together." Carroll stated that McNamee would be the person at DP Associates primarily doing business with the Volkmans, but indicated that he also would be available for consultation.

The Volkmans reviewed the written contract in the DP Associates office with McNamee. McNamee suggested that they use a straight contractor's form to identify DP Associates as acting as a general contractor. He then left the room, saying, "I will ask Phil." When he returned, he said that they would use the form.

After the contract was signed but before construction of the house began, Mr. Volkman visited the office of DP Associates. He again saw and spoke with Carroll, who said to him, "I am happy that we will be working with you." During construction, Mr. Volkman visited the office of DP Associates several times and saw Carroll there. During one visit, he expressed to Carroll his concern about construction delays, but Carroll told him not to worry, because McNamee would take care of it.

DP Associates failed to perform the contract as agreed. The Volkmans sued DP Associates, McNamee, and Carroll. Carroll asked the trial court to dismiss the suit against him. He argued that the Volkmans produced no documents tending to show a partnership existed between McNamee and Carroll, that all money was paid to DP Associates, that the Volkmans never saw Carroll on the construction site, and that they knew of no other construction project supervised by Carroll. Carroll also argued that the Volkmans understood that they were purchasing his services and construction expertise through DP Associates.

The trial court dismissed the Volkmans' suit against Carroll, on the grounds that Carroll was not a partner in DP Associates. The Volkmans appealed.

**VAUGHN, JUDGE.** If the Volkmans are unable to prove a partnership in fact, they may be able to show that Carroll should be held as a partner by estoppel or under the agency theory of apparent authority. The Uniform Partnership Act as adopted in this State provides that "the law of estoppel shall apply." The essentials of equitable estoppel are a representation, either by words or conduct, made to another, who reasonably believing the representation to be true, relies upon it, with the result that he changes his position to his detriment. It is essential that the party estopped shall have made a representation by words or acts and that someone shall have acted on the faith of this representation in such a way that he cannot without damage withdraw from the transaction.

As well as making the law of estoppel expressly applicable to partnerships, Uniform Partnership Act Section 16 as adopted in this State sets forth in more detail the conditions for liability as a partner by estoppel:

> Partner by estoppel—(a) When a person, by words spoken or written, by conduct, or by contract, represents himself, or consents to another representing him to anyone, as a partner in an existing partnership or with one or more persons not actual partners, he is liable to any such person to whom such representation has been made, who has, on faith of such representation, given credit to the actual or apparent partnership, and if he has made such representation or consented to its being made in a public manner, he is liable to such person, whether the representation has or has not been made or communicated to such person so giving credit by or with the knowledge of the apparent partner making the representation or consenting to its being made.
>
> (1) When a partnership liability results, he is liable as though he were an actual member of the partnership.
>
> (2) When no partnership liability results, he is liable jointly with the other persons, if any, so consenting to the contract or representation as to incur liability, otherwise separately.

Liability by estoppel may result either from Carroll's representation of himself as a partner "by words spoken or written" or "by conduct" or Carroll's "consent" to such a representation by another. The Volkmans indicated they may be able to show that Carroll by his oral statements to them and conduct in their presence and by his consent to the representations of McNamee to the Volkmans, some of which were in the presence of Carroll, represented himself as a partner and should be estopped to deny such association. They may be able to show further they relied upon these representations not knowing them to be false and that based upon the representations of Carroll and McNamee, the Volkmans changed their position and were thereby damaged.

In addition to an estoppel theory of liability, Carroll may be liable under apparent authority, a theory of agency law applicable to partnerships. There is virtually no difference between estoppel and apparent authority. Both depend on reliance by a third person on a communication from the principal to the extent that the difference may be merely semantic. Despite its title, "Partner by Estoppel," the statutory section provides for a form of liability more akin to that of apparent authority than to estoppel.

If this view is taken, the liability of the person seeking to deny partner status is not based on estoppel to deny agency or authority but on the objective theory of contract law, *i.e.,* a person should be bound by his words and conduct. Thus, when Carroll told Mr. Volkman, "I am happy that we will be working with you," and conducted himself as he did in the DP Associates office in the presence of Mr. Volkman, the jury may find that Carroll was indicating a willingness to be bound by the statements and acts of McNamee, that Carroll held himself out as a partner of McNamee in DP Associates, that McNamee had apparent authority to act for Carroll, and that the Volkmans reasonably relied upon this holding out. If so, Carroll is bound as if he directly dealt with the Volkmans.

Judgment reversed in favor of the Volkmans.

## PARTNERSHIP CAPITAL, PARTNERSHIP PROPERTY, AND PARTNERS' PROPERTY RIGHTS

**Partnership Capital.** When a partnership is formed, partners contribute at least some property to the partnership. The contribution may be cash or other property, and it is called *partnership capital.* To supplement beginning capital, other property may be contributed to the partnership as needed, such as by the partners permitting the partnership to retain some of its profits. Partnership capital is the equity of the business.

Loans made by partners to a partnership are not partnership capital, but instead are debts of the business. Partners who make loans to a partnership are both owners and creditors.

**Partnership Property.** The partnership may own all or only a part of the property it uses. For example, it may own the business and perhaps a small amount of working capital in the form of cash or a checking account, yet own no other assets. All other tangible and intangible property used by the partnership may be individually or jointly owned by one or more of the partners or rented by the partnership from third parties. A determination of what is partnership property becomes essential not only when the partnership is dissolved and the assets are being distributed[14] but also when creditors of either the partnership or one of the partners are seeking assets to satisfy a debt.

For example, Sarah enters a partnership with Gary. They agree to share profits equally. She allows the partnership to use her building, which is worth $25,000. Now suppose the value of the building increases to $50,000. If the building is Sarah's, all of the $25,000 increase in value is hers. If it is partnership property, Sarah shares only half of the increase.

**UPA Rule.** Section 8 of the UPA provides that (1) all property originally brought into the partnership or subsequently acquired by purchase or otherwise, on account of the partnership, is partnership property, and (2) un-

[14] Dissolution and the distribution of assets are discussed in Chapter 20.

less the contrary intention appears, property acquired with partnership funds is partnership property.

**Intent.** Fundamentally, the *intent* of the partners controls. It is best to have a written record of the partners' intent as to ownership of all property used by the partnership, such as in the articles of partnership. Other writings, such as accounting records, will show the partnership assets; assets appearing in the partnership's books will be presumed to belong to the partnership.

It is also presumed that money used by a partnership as working capital is partnership property in the absence of clear evidence that it was intended to be merely a loan. In addition, the presumption is very strong that property purchased with partnership funds and used in the partnership is partnership property, even when the property is not necessary to the partnership business.

**Title to Partnership Property.** Under the common law, partnerships could hold title to personal property; however, title to real estate could not be carried in the firm name. Today, under UPA Section 8(3), a partnership may hold title to real property. Nevertheless, it is not uncommon today for individual partners to take or retain title in partnership property, because they believe this to be more convenient.

If title is taken in the partnership name, it will be presumed that the property is partnership property. However, because of the common law rule, the presumption is not as strong that real property held in the name of a partner is individual property. Other indicia may overcome the presumption.

**Other Indicia.** The payment of property taxes or insurance premiums, the maintainance, repair, and improvement of property by the partnership, and the deduction of these expenses on the partnership income tax return will be used as indications of the intent of the parties with respect to property not held in the name of the partnership. Listing the property on a partnership financial statement given to a prospective lender may be treated as an admission of the partners that it is partnership property. It must be noted, however, that mere use of the property by the partnership creates no presumption that it is partnership property. This applies equally to personal and real property.

**Priority of Indicia.** Frequently, the indicia of ownership are in conflict, complicating a determination of ownership. The agreement of the partners is the most important factor considered by the courts, followed by possession of title. As stated above, however, title is merely presumptive proof, not conclusive proof, especially with real property held in a partner's name. When all other indicia point against the partner with title, the property will belong to the partnership.

**Partners' Property Rights.** Under UPA Section 24, a partner has three property rights: (1) her *rights in specific partnership property,* (2) her *partnership interest,* and (3) her *right to participate in the management* of the business. The first two rights are discussed here. The management right will be discussed in Chapter 19.

**Rights in Partnership Property.** A partnership owns partnership property *as a unit;* the partners as individuals do not own proportionate interests in separate items of partnership property. Instead, according to UPA Section 25, partnership property is co-owned by the partners as **tenants in partnership.**

As a tenant in partnership, each partner has the right to possess partnership property for partnership purposes. A partner has no individual right to use or possess partnership property for her own purposes, such as paying a personal debt, unless she has the consent of the other partners. Likewise, a partner's personal creditor may not make a claim against partnership assets.

If a partner misuses partnership assets, the partner will have violated her duties as a partner. Such wrongful acts may be grounds for the dissolution of the partnership. Although a partner has wrongfully deprived the partnership and her partners of the possession of partnership property, the other partners cannot sue the partner to recover possession. Generally, the only remedy available to partners for breach of partnership duties is the remedy of dissolution and accounting, as discussed in the following chapter.

Upon the death of a partner, his rights in partnership property pass to the surviving partners. This is called the **right of survivorship.**

**Partnership Interest.** Although a partner does not own partnership property, he does co-own the partnership. His ownership interest is called a **partnership interest** and is part of his personal property.

A partner may not give his personal creditors any interest in separate items of partnership property, but Section 27 of the UPA permits a partner to **assign his partnership interest** to a creditor. And although a partner's personal creditors may not obtain an execution of judgment against separate items of partnership property, a creditor may obtain execution against a partner's partnership interest by obtaining a **charging order** against that interest.

**Assignment.** The **assignment of a partnership interest** is a voluntary act of a partner. It entitles the assignee to receive the assigning partner's share of the profits, but it does not give the assignee the right to inspect the partnership's books and records or to manage the partnership.

A partner's assignment of his partnership interest does not dissolve the partnership or terminate the assigning partner's participation in it. An assignee for value, including a creditor, may ask a court to dissolve a partnership at will.[15] Seeking dissolution will allow the creditor to get to the partnership's assets by receiving his debtor's share of the liquidation proceeds.[16]

The nonassigning partners may not exclude the assigning partner from the partnership. They may, however, dissolve the partnership by their *unanimous* agreement, even if the term or objective of the partnership has not been met. They have such a right because the assignment indicates that the assigning partner has personal financial troubles and may not be able to undertake his share of future partnership liabilities.

**Charging Order.** Under UPA Section 28, a partner's personal creditor with a judgment against the partner may ask a court to issue a **charging order,** that is, an order charging the partner's partnership interest with payment of the unsatisfied amount of the judgment. Unlike assignment, a charging order is obtained without the partner's consent. As with assignment, however, the partner may continue to participate in management, and the creditor is entitled to receive only the partner's share of the profits. The court may appoint a receiver to receive the profits for the creditor and to look after the creditor's interest. If the profits are insufficient to pay the debt, the court may order foreclosure and sell the partner's interest to satisfy the charging order.

Neither the issuance of a charging order

[15] A partnership at will is a partnership with no term, which may rightfully be dissolved by any partner at any time.

[16] The priority of claims against partnership assets is discussed in Chapter 20.

nor the purchase of a partnership interest at a foreclosure sale causes a dissolution. But the purchaser of a partnership interest, like the assignee for value, may ask a court to dissolve a partnership at will. The other partners may eliminate this potential threat to the continuation of the partnership. Under Section 28 of the UPA, the partnership itself or one or more of the partners, with the consent of all partners not subject to the charging order, may *redeem* the charging order by paying the amount due on the judgment. If the other partners so choose, however, they may dissolve the partnership by their unanimous agreement, just as nonassigning partners may do.

**Joint Venturers.** Transfers of interests in joint ventures are treated in the same way as transfers of partnership interests.

**Mining Partners.** A mining partner's interest is *freely transferable.* The transferee becomes a partner with all the rights of ownership and management, and the transferor loses all of his partnership rights. The other mining partners cannot object to the transfer, and their consent to a transfer is not required.

## Gauldin v. Corn

**595 S.W.2d 329 (Mo. Ct. App. 1980)**

In 1966, Claude Gauldin and Joe Corn agreed orally to form a 50–50 partnership to raise cattle and hogs. The business was conducted on 25 acres of an 83-acre tract of land owned at the beginning of the partnership by Corn's parents and later by Corn and his wife.

Partnership funds were used to bulldoze the land, to build ponds and fences, and to seed and fertilize the land. Partnership funds were also used to build a barn in 1970 and to construct a hog-raising building in 1975. The buildings were constructed for and used by the partnership. Gauldin and Corn did not discuss who owned the buildings or the other improvements. Gauldin knew when the buildings were constructed that they would be permanent improvements to the land and would become part of it. No rent was paid for the land, and there was no agreement to consider the use of the land as a contribution by Corn. The taxes on the land were paid by Corn's parents and by Corn and his wife, as was the cost of upkeep.

Corn's health deteriorated, and his doctor advised him to stop raising hogs and cattle. In March 1977, Gauldin paid Corn $7,500 and paid off a $1,500 partnership debt in return for the removable assets and the right to remain on the land through May. Corn gave Gauldin a receipt, which indicated that Gauldin was purchasing the removable assets only.

In June 1977, Gauldin took the animals and other removable assets from the land. In addition, he claimed that the buildings were partnership assets and that he was entitled to half of their fair market value. When Corn refused to pay him, Gauldin sued Corn for a dissolution of the partnership and an accounting, asking the court to order Corn to pay him $5,750, half the value of the buildings. Corn answered that he and Gauldin had already dissolved the partnership and divided its assets. The trial court found that the land was not partnership property and held for Corn. Gauldin appealed.

**Greene, Judge.** The rule is well established that improvements made upon lands owned by one partner, if made with partnership funds for purposes of partnership business, are the personal property of the partnership, and the non-landowning partner is entitled to his proportionate share of their value. This is a fair and equitable rule which is consistent with the language contained in Missouri's Uniform Partnership Law. Section 8 states in part:

> 1. *All property* originally brought into the partnership stock or *subsequently acquired by purchase or otherwise, on account of the partnership, is partnership property.*
> 2. *Unless the contrary intention appears,* property acquired with partnership funds is partnership property. (Emphasis added.)

The general rule governing the disposition of improvements upon dissolution of a partnership is activated only where, as here, there is no agreement between the partners that controls such disposition. It matters not that the landowning partner contributed the use of his land to the partnership, that the non-landowning partner knew that the improvements, when made, could not be removed from the land, or that a joint owner with the landowning partner was not joined in the suit for dissolution and accounting of the partnership. The trial court, after finding that the partners had no agreement regarding the disposition of fixed assets upon dissolution of the partnership, should have awarded Gauldin his proportionate share of the value of the improvements.

Judgment reversed in favor of Gauldin.

## SUMMARY

The Uniform Partnership Act is in effect in almost all states. In some respects it treats the partnership as an entity separate from its members, but in other respects it adopts the common law aggregate theory.

No formalities are required to create a partnership. It is a voluntary association of two or more people to carry on a business as co-owners for profit. Any person with legal capacity may become a partner, including partnerships and corporations. Minors and insane persons may be partners, but are permitted to withdraw with few penalties.

An association to conduct a single transaction is not a partnership, but it is probably a joint venture, to which partnership law applies.

One who receives a share of the profits of a business will be viewed as a partner unless it can be shown that the sharing was for certain specified purposes. The co-ownership requirement applies to the business; it is not necessary that all partners co-own the property used in the business. Generally, a sharing of the profits and the management of a business is sufficient evidence of the existence of a partnership.

People who hold themselves out, or who permit others to hold them out, as partners will be held liable as partners to persons who rely on these statements, under the doctrine of partnership by estoppel. Mere knowledge that one has been held out as a partner does not require one to correct the misstatement.

Whether property used by a partnership is partnership property is fundamentally a question of determining the intent of the parties. An agreement is the best evidence, but title and the source of funds to purchase the property are also important. Who maintains, repairs, and improves the property also may affect the ownership decision.

Each partner has the right to use partnership property for partnership purposes. The property is owned by the partners as tenants in partnership. A partner may not use partnership assets to pay his personal creditors, and a partner's personal creditor may not satisfy his claim against partnership property. A partner may assign his partnership interest to creditors, who then receive the partner's share of the profits. Creditors may obtain charging orders against the interest of a partner; these orders entitle them to the debtor's share of the profits.

## PROBLEM CASES

**1.** Hamel, Lamb, and Adams were partners in the operation of the Breakers Hotel. Tamir paid Lamb and Adams $15,000 for a 10 percent share of their portion of the hotel business and the profits. Lamb and Adams agreed that he would become a partner. Hamel had no knowledge of the agreement, and he had not given Lamb and Adams authority to make such an agreement. Is Tamir a partner in the business?

**2.** Herbst owned a farm. He did not farm it, but instead agreed to have Parzych farm it for him. Parzych and Herbst were to share equally in the net profits and losses, but the farming operation was to be "under the full control of Parzych." The agreement further stated: "The parties do not intend by this agreement to establish a partnership of any kind or type, but rather a relationship of Debtor and Creditor and Landlord and Tenant." Parzych told Clover Leaf Mill that he and Herbst were partners. Parzych purchased farm supplies from Clover Leaf and failed to pay for them. Is Herbst liable to Clover Leaf for the cost of the supplies?

**3.** Jaworsky, a veterinarian, entered into an agreement with LeBlanc, a lumberyard operator and racehorse owner who was not a veterinarian, to sell veterinary medicines and supplies that could be purchased only by a veterinarian. The agreement provided that (1) LeBlanc would provide office space for Jaworsky in one of his lumberyard buildings, (2) Jaworsky would provide furniture and surgical equipment, (3) Jaworsky would purchase $1,000 worth of medicines and supplies in his own name, (4) LeBlanc would advance the money for their purchase and for additional inventory as needed, (5) LeBlanc would sell them at prices set by Jaworsky, (6) LeBlanc would retain all of the profits derived from sales until his $1,000 had been returned plus $350 interest, (7) thereafter profits would be divided equally, and (8) LeBlanc would pay only cost for medicines and supplies used on his own horses, and they would receive Jaworsky's veterinary services at reduced rates. Was this arrangement a partnership?

**4.** John Williams was hired as assistant manager of a restaurant in Chapel Hill, North Carolina, operated by Pizzaville, Inc. Six months later, he was promoted to manager. About two years afterward, he was designated as managing partner and supplied with business cards so describing him. A few years later, he was discharged, at which time he was receiving a salary of $270 per week plus a share of the profits. The profit-sharing formula allocated 70 percent of gross sales to Williams, from which he was required to pay for the cost of the food purchases and employees' wages. He could retain whatever was left. After his discharge, he sued to obtain a share of the value of the business, claiming that he was a partner. Was Williams a partner?

**5.** Ann and Harley Eggers were married in 1967 and divorced in 1970. In 1973, Harley asked Ann to move back into his home. She agreed, provided that Harley would divorce the woman he had married in the interim, would agree to pay her for the work she did, and would give her an independent bank account and some interest in some property as security. Ann and Harley lived together for five years, holding themselves out as husband and wife. Ann worked for Harley's businesses during this time, pursuant to an express oral contract obligating Harley to employ her in his businesses for 20 hours per week at $2.50 per hour. Ann did not contribute any money toward the purchase of any property of the businesses. She did not contribute her earnings to the businesses, and she did not share in the decision making.

Ann and Harley separated on July 7, 1978. Shortly thereafter, Ann sought an equitable division of property, including the businesses and Harley's other assets. Ann argued that there was a partnership or joint venture between Harley and her, which would allow the court to award her a share in the property acquired in Harley's name while they lived together. Was Ann correct?

**6.** Three physicians formed a partnership to operate the Overland Medical Center and signed a partnership agreement. Later, they agreed with a Dr. Stuart that he would affiliate with the Center and operate its dermatology department. They agreed that the Center would receive 10 percent of Dr. Stuart's gross receipts for a five-year period and 8 percent of his outstanding accounts receivable at the end of that period. No partnership agreement was signed. Dr. Stuart was listed as a partner in the financial statements of the Center after the five-year period, with his equity interest indicated as 4 percent. Dr. Stuart left after eight years at the Center. In making a settlement with the Center, he claimed to be a partner entitled to a portion of the value of the partnership. Was he a partner?

**7.** Filip was the owner of Trans Texas Properties. One of his employees, Tracey Peoples, in placing advertising in the *Austin American-Statesman,* stated on a credit application that Elliott was a partner with Filip in Trans Texas Properties. Elliott did not authorize Peoples to represent that Filip and Elliott were partners and was unaware that Peoples had used his name on the credit application. However, Elliott had made no effort to discover whether Peoples had so used his name. Is Elliott liable for the cost of the advertising?

**8.** Maxine Krone bought land from Rex McCann. She wanted to build a house on the land. McCann recommended that Neal Warnes build the house and introduced Warnes to Krone. Krone, McCann, and Warnes discussed how much of a down payment Krone should receive on the sale of her present home in order to pay McCann the down payment on the land and to pay Warnes his initial money to build the house. Krone decided to hire Warnes only after McCann had told her that Warnes was reliable. Krone paid Warnes $3,450 in advance. Warnes did not begin work on the house, so Krone called McCann several times about this. He assured her that Warnes would begin work on the house. Warnes disappeared and never built the house. Krone sued McCann for the amount she had paid to Warnes, claiming that Warnes and McCann were partners by estoppel. Is she correct?

**9.** Ben and Arthur Schaefer went into partnership in an auto dealership in 1933. Between 1944 and 1967, they acquired considerable real estate. Their real estate business was kept separate from the auto dealership, and all payments for real estate purchased, proceeds from real estate sold, income from leases, and expenses were paid from or deposited in a checking account titled "Ben G. Schaefer and Arthur E. Schaefer, Real Estate Trust Account, Partnership." When purchasing 13 parcels of real estate, the Schaefers took nine deeds in which the grantees appeared merely as the two Schaefers, three deeds which indicated that they were tenants in common, and one deed which referred to them as partners. Some leases were signed by one partner alone, some by both partners, and some by both partners and their wives. Some deeds on realty sold were signed by both partners and their wives. The partnership tax returns uniformly reported these transactions.

Ben died. His wife, Marilynn, was heir to his estate. She claimed a half interest in the parcels of real estate. Arthur claimed that the parcels were partnership property and subject to the claims of partnership creditors before being distributed to her. Is the real estate partnership property?

**10.** Carolyn Putnam, a 50 percent partner in a partnership operating Frog Jump Inn, withdrew from the partnership. She sold her partnership interest to John Shoaf. A year later, it was discovered that during the time Putnam was a partner, the partnership's bookkeeper had embezzled money from the partnership. The partnership recovered $68,000. Putnam claims that she is entitled to half of the $68,000. Is she correct?

Chapter 19

# Operation of Partnership and Related Forms

## INTRODUCTION

Having learned how to create a partnership, you will now learn the rules of its operation. Two relationships are important during the operation of a partnership business:

1. The relation of the partners to each other.
2. The relation of the partners to third parties who are affected by the business of the partnership.

In most respects, these two relationships are identical to the relationship of agent and principal, the relationship of principal and third party, and the relationship of agent and third party. For example, a partner owes fiduciary duties to his partners, as does an agent to her principal. A partner may be liable for his partners' torts, just as a principal may be liable for his agent's torts. And like an agent, a partner may make contracts on behalf of his partners.

In this chapter, you should keep the two partnership relations in mind as you study partners' duties to each other, partners' management rights, and partners' liability for partnership contracts and torts. You begin your study with a brief look at these two relations.[1]

**Relations between Partners.** A partnership relation is a fiduciary relation of the highest order. It is one of mutual *trust, confidence, and honesty.* The partners may, within certain limits, define the rights and duties owed to each other. In the absence of an agreement, the rights and duties of the parties will be determined by the application of the rules and principles of partnership law and agency law.[2]

**Articles of Partnership.** Although not required, a written partnership agreement (usually a formal document known as the **articles of partnership**) is used by many partnerships. The major purpose of the partnership agreement is to state expressly the relations between the partners in carrying on and terminating the business. Generally, partners are free to make whatever contract they wish between themselves. They may, for example, provide by agreement for unequal sharing of profits and losses, for the payment of salary to some of the partners, and for unequal shares of management. They may also establish different classes of partners, such as junior and senior partners, with different rights. They may not, however, remove the duty of trust that partners owe each other.

Like any contract, a partnership agreement may be modified by agreement of the partners. An inconsistent course of action followed by the partners may also cause a change in the agreement. Unless another rule for amendment is provided in the agreement, a partnership agreement may be amended only by the unanimous consent of the partners.

[1] Unless otherwise stated, all the law of partnership discussed in this chapter also applies to joint ventures and mining partnerships. Only the rules that uniquely affect joint ventures or mining partnerships will be pointed out as such.

[2] The law of agency is covered in Chapters 16 and 17.

**Relations of Partners to Third Persons.** When a partnership is formed, the relationship between the partners and third parties is defined by partnership law and agency law. Hence, partners are liable for each other's authorized contracts and torts committed in the course and scope of business. The partners and a third party may agree, by contract, to alter the relationship between the partners and the third party as determined by partnership law and agency law. The modification would be binding only upon the third party and the partners who agreed to it. The partners cannot, merely by agreement between themselves, diminish the duties and liabilities that they have to third persons with whom they deal on behalf of the partnership.

## DUTIES OF PARTNERS TO EACH OTHER

**Duty of Loyalty and Good Faith.** Since each partner is an agent of the other partners, the partners' relation is one of trust and confidence. Therefore, partners owe each other the highest degree of *loyalty and good faith* in all partnership matters. This fiduciary duty is imposed by law and need not be provided for in the partnership agreement. Partners may not agree to relieve each other of the duty of loyalty and good faith. Several duties are encompassed by the duty of loyalty and good faith: (1) not to self-deal; (2) not to compete; (3) to serve; (4) to maintain confidentiality; (5) not to make a secret profit.

**Self-Dealing.** A partner has a duty *not to self-deal.* When a partner deals with her partnership, there is a risk that she will prefer her own interests over those of the partnership. Therefore, a partner may contract with her partnership only if she deals in *good faith* and makes a *full disclosure* of all material facts affecting the transaction that she should know are not known to the partnership. In addition, a partner may not acquire property prior to becoming a partner in anticipation of selling the property at a profit to the partnership after it has been organized, unless she discloses her profit and all the material facts. The remedy for a breach of this duty not to self-deal is a *return of the profit* that she made in the transaction with the partnership.

The duty not to self-deal also exists when the assets of the partnership are being liquidated. A partner may purchase partnership assets during liquidation under the same rules as have been stated above. Even at a public sale of partnership property, a partner may not purchase such property if he fails to disclose information that materially affects the value of the property.

Partners may expressly or impliedly approve a self-dealing transaction. In *Covalt v. High,* which appears later in this chapter, the court found that the partners' knowledge of each other's conflicts of interest prevented a breach of their fiduciary duties.

**Competing.** A partner may *not compete* with his partnership unless he obtains consent from the other partners. For example, a partner of a retail clothing store may not open a clothing store nearby. However, he may open a grocery store and not breach his fiduciary duty. In *Veale v. Rose,* which follows, the court found that an accountant breached the duty not to compete by providing his own clients with the same types of accounting services that his accounting partnership could have provided.

**Duty to Serve.** Each partner has a duty to *serve the partnership* unless the partners agree otherwise. The basis of this duty is the expectation that all partners will work. Sometimes, this duty is termed the duty to *devote full time* to the partnership.

Partners may agree to relieve a partner of the duty to serve, as was done in *Altman v. Altman,* which appears later in this chapter. Often, so-called *silent partners* will merely contribute capital to the partnership. They do not have the duty to serve; however, a silent partner has the same liability for partnership debts as any other partner.

The remedies for breach of the duty to serve include assessing the partner for the cost of hiring a person to do his work, paying the other partners additional compensation, or dissolving the partnership.

**Other Duties.** A partner owes the other duties of loyalty and good faith that an agent owes his principal. A partner must maintain the *confidentiality* of partnership information, such as a trade secret or a customer list. A partner may not use partnership property for his individual purposes (as did one partner in *Veale v. Rose*) or make a *secret profit* or commission out of the transaction of partnership business (for example, by receiving an undisclosed kickback from a supplier).

**Duty to Act within Authority.** A partner has the duty *not to exceed the authority* granted him by the partnership agreement or, if there is no agreement, the authority normally held by partners in his circumstances. Like an agent, he is responsible to the other partners for losses resulting from unauthorized transactions negotiated in the name of the partnership. For example, suppose Amy, Bess, and Cliff are partners and the partnership agreement provides that no partner shall purchase supplies from Joe. Suppose Amy purchases supplies from Joe, who is unaware of the limitation on the partners' authority, and the partnership suffers a loss because the supplies are of low quality. Amy will have to bear the loss because of her breach of the partnership agreement.

**Duty of Care.** In transacting partnership business, each partner owes a duty to use *reasonable care and skill.* A partner is not liable to her partners for losses resulting from honest errors in judgment, but a partner is liable for losses resulting from her negligence or lack of care and skill in the transaction of partnership business. She must make a *reasonable investigation* before making a decision, so that she has an adequate basis for making the decision. The decision she makes must be that of an *ordinarily prudent business manager* in her position in light of the same circumstances.

For example, a grocery store has stocked avocados for three years and has always sold them. If Fred, one of the partners, orders the same amount of avocados as usual, but they do not sell, Fred is not liable for the loss to the partnership. His decision appears reasonable as of the time he made it. If prior to the time he made the decision, however, sales of avocados have fallen and trade magazines that Fred should read have published customer surveys showing lower expected sales of avocados, Fred would be liable.

**Duty to Inform.** Under UPA Section 20, each partner owes a duty to *disclose* to the other partners all *information* material to the partnership business. She owes a duty to inform the partners of notices she has received that affect the rights of the partnership. Since partners are presumed to have knowledge of matters appearing on the books of the partnership, failure to inform a partner of such matters is not a breach of this duty.

The extensive nature of the partners' relation of trust is exhibited by the rules regarding disclosure when one partner sells his partnership interest to another partner. The selling partner owes a duty to disclose to the buying partner all the facts having a bearing on the value of the partnership interest that are not open to the buying partner. Likewise, the buying partner owes the same duty of full disclosure to the selling partner. In other words, the ordinary rule of contract law that parties deal with each other at arm's length is suspended when partners transfer partnership interests to each other.

**Duty to Account.** Like agents, partners have a duty *to account* for their use or disposal of partnership funds and partnership property, as well as their receipt of any benefit or profit without the consent of the other partners. Partnership property should be used for partnership purposes, not for a partner's personal use.

**Books of the Partnership.** UPA Section 19 requires a partnership to keep financial records of business transactions. Which books are kept and which of the basic accounting principles are followed may be determined by agreement of the partners.

Each partner owes a duty to keep a reasonable record of all business transacted by him for the partnership and to make such records available to the person keeping the partnership books. UPA Section 19 further provides that (1) such books shall be kept at the principal place of business and (2) every partner shall at all times have access to them and may inspect and copy them.

It is desirable for partnerships to close the books and render an account to all partners annually. If the accounts as stated are agreed to, expressly or impliedly, then an action can be maintained to enforce payment of the amounts shown to be due to a partner.

**Right to an Accounting.** In addition to a right to inspect the books of the partnership, a partner has a right to a formal **accounting** of the partnership affairs. It is generally by an accounting that a partner can recover from his partners for their breaches of their fiduciary duties.

An accounting is an extreme action and is ordinarily taken only after dissolution of a partnership. An accounting is not merely a presentation of financial statements. It is a judicial review of all partnership and partners' transactions to determine whether partners have properly used partnership assets and to award each partner his rightful share of partnership assets. The court will take into consideration breaches of fiduciary duties and will adjust appropriately the amounts payable to the partners.

At common law, a partner could bring a court action seeking an accounting only by dissolving the partnership or by waiting until it had been dissolved. It is still the general rule that lawsuits between partners alleging a breach of a partnership duty, such as self-dealing or competing, are not permitted during the life of the partnership. UPA Section 22, however, specifically permits an accounting, ordered by a court if necessary, under several conditions, such as when a partner is wrongfully excluded from management or a partner has not received his share of the profits.

**Right of Indemnification.** Closely related to the duty to account is the right of a partner to be *indemnified* for expenditures made from personal funds and liabilities incurred during the ordinary conduct of the business. For example, a partner uses her own truck to pick up some partnership supplies, which she pays for with her personal check. The partner is entitled to be reimbursed for the cost of the supplies and for her cost of picking up the supplies, including fuel.

**Joint Ventures and Mining Partnerships.** The fiduciary duties of partners also exist in joint ventures and mining partnerships, although in such organizations there are a few special rules regarding their enforcement. For example, a joint venturer may seek an accounting to settle claims between the joint venturers, or he may sue his joint venturers to recover joint property or to be indemnified for expenditures that he has made on behalf of the joint venture. A mining partner's remedy against his partners is an accounting; however, a mining partner has a lien against his partners' shares in the mining partnership for his expenditures on behalf of the mining partnership. The lien can be enforced against purchasers of his partners' shares.

## Veale v. Rose

**657 S.W.2d 834 (Tex. Ct. App. 1983)**

Larry Rose, Paul G. Veale, Sr., Paul G. Veale, Jr., Gary W. Gibson, and James H. Parker were certified public accountants who rendered professional accounting services as partners under the firm name Paul G. Veale and Company. Their written partnership agreement expressed the general duties of the partners. In addition, the agreement expressly recognized that Veale, Sr., and Rose had outside investments and a number of other business commitments. All of the partners were allowed to pursue other business activities and to receive compensation therefor, so long as the activities did not conflict with the partnership practice of public accounting or materially interfere with the partners' duties to the partnership. The partnership agreement provided, in part:

> Except with the expressed approval of the other partners as to each specific instance, no partner shall perform any public accounting services or engage in the practice of public accounting other than for and on behalf of this partnership.

While a partner of Paul G. Veale and Company, Larry Rose performed accounting services for Right Away Foods and Ed Payne. He was paid personally by those clients. Rose was an officer and shareholder of Right Away. In addition, Rose failed to bill Tex-Pack Express for Veale and Company employee time and computer time used to render services to Tex-Pack Express. Rose was an owner of Tex-Pack.

When the other partners discovered these actions, they refused to pay Rose his share of the partnership profits. Rose sued for an accounting and for the money due to him. The other partners counterclaimed for the amount of money due to them from Rose's competing with the partnership when rendering services to Right Away and Payne and for the fees due from his failing to bill Tex-Pack. The jury found that the other partners owed Rose his share of the profits and that Rose had not competed with the partnership or failed to bill clients. It awarded Rose $177,670.34. Rose's partners appealed.

**Nye, Chief Justice.** Partners may be said to occupy a fiduciary relationship toward one another which requires of them the utmost degree of good faith and honesty in dealing with one another. Breaches of a partner's duty not to compete with the partnership are compensable at law by awarding to the injured partners their proportionate shares of the profits wrongfully acquired by the offending partner.

While a partner of Veale and Company, Rose rendered accounting services for Right Away Foods for which he billed and received payment personally. The partnership did not share in the proceeds of these private billings. Rose himself admitted that he billed Right Away Foods for the services of a CPA. He also admitted that there was no reason why he could not have rendered the same services to Right Away Foods as a partner in the accounting firm. One of the other partners, Parker, testified that he knew of other public accounting firms that performed the types of services in question. He indicated that he was unaware of any required forms that are not prepared by public accounting firms. The preponderance of all of the evidence clearly establishes that Rose performed accounting services for Right Away Foods while a partner of Paul G. Veale and Company, in competition with the partnership. The jury's answer in this respect was in error.

Rose also admitted that he performed accounting services for various enterprises owned by Mr. Payne during his tenure as a partner at Veale, for which he billed and received payment personally. His later testimony that he performed these services, in effect, after hours, or in addition to his duties to the partnership, is of no value in light of the obligations imposed by the partnership agreement and by the common understanding of the term "competition."

Next we turn to Rose's failure to bill Tex-Pack. The misappropriation by one partner, to his own use, of property of the partnership is considered in law as constructive, if not actual, fraud on the partnership, and is actionable.

Again, the record is replete with Rose's admissions that he had used employee and computer time and had not billed Tex-Pack Express for their services. His explanations and assertions that his action in not billing Tex-Pack Express was done with the knowledge and consent of Paul G. Veale, Sr., are also of no effect, as far as this issue is concerned.

Our determination that the jury's responses were against the great weight and preponderance of the evidence, and indeed in some respects completely contrary to the evidence, necessitates that we reverse the trial court's judgment.

There were fact issues existing as to whether Rose's partners waived their rights to complain about such matters. Rose has referred us to the record of considerable evidence that his former partners knew of his involvement with Right Away Foods and Ed Payne, as well as his use of partnership assets on behalf of Tex-Pack Express, and that they never complained about them. According to Rose, there was at least tacit agreement or acquiescence by all the partners to his actions in these matters. He also cited evidence of personal use of partnership assets by other partners which, if believed by the jury, could support an issue of estoppel.

However, these defenses were not considered by the jury, but were reserved because the jury found no wrongdoing by Rose. Because no answers have been provided by the jury or by the trial court on the issues of waiver and estoppel, we must remand this aspect of the case for a new trial.

Judgment reversed in favor of Rose's partners. Remanded for a new trial.

## COMPENSATION OF PARTNERS

**Partners' Salaries.** A partner's compensation is a share of the profits of the business. Ordinarily, a partner is not entitled to salary or wages, even if he spends a disproportionate amount of time conducting the business of the partnership, as is illustrated in *Altman v. Altman,* which follows. Likewise, a partner is not entitled to receive rent for the use by the partnership of property belonging to him. UPA Section 18(f) specifies, however, that a surviving partner is entitled to reasonable compensation for winding up partnership affairs.[3]

A partner may enforce her right to receive her share of the profits and other compensation by seeking an accounting.

**Profits and Losses.** Pursuant to UPA Section 18(a), absent an agreement to the contrary, partners share partnership profits equally, according to the number of partners, and not according to their capital contributions or to the amount of time that each devotes to the partnership. For example, a partnership has two partners, John, who contributes $85,000 of capital to the partnership and does 35 percent of the work, and Emma, who contributes $15,000 and does 65 percent of the work. When the partnership makes a $50,000 profit in the first year, each partner receives $25,000, half of the profits.

**Losses.** Absent an agreement to the contrary, losses are shared in the same way as profits. If there is no agreement regarding how profits or losses are shared, losses are shared equally.

**Effect of Partnership Agreement.** The partners may agree to alter the above compensation, profit-sharing, and loss-sharing rules. For example, two partners may agree that one partner will receive a salary of $15,000 and 35 percent of all the profits beyond that salary and will assume 20 percent of the losses and that the other partner will receive 65 percent of the profits beyond her salary and assume 80 percent of the losses. For a partner who has no other source of income, a salary agreement is especially important if the partnership is not expected to be profitable during its first few years of operation.

Partners may agree to split profits on one basis and losses on another basis, perhaps be-

[3] The winding up of partnerships is discussed in Chapter 20.

cause of different capital and personal service contributions or because one partner has higher outside income than the other partners and can make better use of a loss as a tax deduction. If there is an agreement on how to share profits, losses are shared in the same way, even if there is no provision for sharing losses. The basis of this rule is the presumption that partners want to share benefits and detriments in the same proportions. Nevertheless, the presumption does not work in reverse. If the partnership agreement specifies how losses are shared but does not specify how profits are shared, profits are shared equally by the partners, not as losses are shared.

**Effect of Agreement on Creditors' Rights.** Each partner has *unlimited* personal liability to partnership creditors. Loss-sharing agreements between partners *do not* bind partnership creditors, unless the creditors agree to be bound. For example, two partners agree to share losses 60–40, the same proportion in which they contributed capital to the partnership. After the partnership assets have been distributed to the creditors, $50,000 is still owed to them. The creditors may collect the entire $50,000 from the partner who agreed to assume only 60 percent of the losses. That partner may, however, collect $20,000—40 percent of the amount—from the other partner.

## Altman v. Altman

**653 F.2d 755 (3d Cir. 1981)**

From 1952 to 1973, two brothers, Sydney Altman and Ashley Altman, operated several partnerships engaged in real estate construction and management in southeastern Pennsylvania. They shared equally in the management and control of the partnerships, and through their joint efforts, their businesses became very profitable and substantial enterprises. They received identical salaries, and each brother was permitted to charge certain personal expenses to the partnerships. The brothers agreed that the amount of such expenses would be equal. Therefore, if one brother charged more personal expenses to the partnerships than did the other brother, he would pay the other brother one half of the amount by which his personal expenses exceeded those of his brother.

In January 1973, Sydney moved to Florida to establish residency in that state for the purpose of obtaining a divorce. The brothers agreed that Sydney would return to Pennsylvania after his divorce and resume full-time duties with the partnerships. During the first six months after he moved to Florida, Sydney commuted to Pennsylvania every week to work for two to three days. In July 1973, Ashley suggested that Sydney need only return to Pennsylvania once a month until his divorce became final.

Sydney told Ashley in November 1973 that he was considering retiring and remaining in Florida permanently. They tried to reach an agreement on the sale of Sydney's partnership interests but were unable to do so. In September 1975, Sydney sued for a judicial dissolution of the partnerships. He alleged that Ashley had violated the partnership agreements and misappropriated partnership assets by paying himself compensation beyond his share of the profits of the businesses.

Ashley continued to manage the businesses by himself until the district court handed down its decision in June 1977. By that time, he had managed the partnerships by himself for nearly four years. The district court granted Sydney a judicial dissolution of the partnerships because it found that Ashley had breached the partnership agreements from 1973 through 1977 by unilaterally paying himself salaries and charging personal expenses in excess of what the brothers had agreed upon. Ashley was directed to pay Sydney $153,750.67 to equalize partnership distributions, salaries, and reimbursed personal expenses. Ashley appealed.

**Seitz, Chief Judge.** Ashley challenges the district court's holding that he is not entitled to compensation beyond his share of the partnership profits for managing the partnerships between August 1973 and June 1977. In the absence of an agreement to the contrary, a partner is not entitled to compensation beyond his share of the profits for services rendered by him in performing partnership matters. A right to compensation arises only where the services rendered extend beyond normal partnership functions. Ashley, however, does not expressly contend that the services he performed went beyond normal partnership functions. Instead, he relies on *Greenan v. Ernst* (1962), in which the Pennsylvania Supreme Court concluded that it would be "highly inequitable" to deny compensation to an active partner who had assumed sole responsibility for the management of a partnership when the inactive partners either "could not or would not" assume any responsibility. The court noted that the "skill and efforts" of the active partner produced large profits for the partnership and therefore benefited the other partners.

Ashley emphasizes that after August 1973, the entire management and supervision of the partnerships were left to him. He asserts that he not only preserved the partnerships' properties, but also maximized profits during this period. In addition, he points out the high caliber of his management of the partnerships.

Ashley apparently is contending that compensation is awarded under Pennsylvania law whenever it would be highly inequitable not to do so. However, *Greenan* does not support this contention. Thus, Ashley must show more than the fact that a failure to award compensation would be highly inequitable; he must also show that his services extended beyond normal partnership functions.

The district court found that the services performed by Ashley did not extend beyond normal partnership functions. In *Greenan,* the Pennsylvania Supreme Court appeared to relax the definition of "beyond normal partnership functions" by allowing compensation to a partner who had assumed responsibility for the continued operation of an existing partnership. However, the critical factor in *Greenan* was that the active partner had taken an existing partnership and expanded it substantially beyond its previous size and scope. In contrast, the services rendered by Ashley maintained the operation of existing businesses in the same manner as they had been operated before Sydney's departure. In addition, unlike the situation in *Greenan,* the lack of participation in the partnerships by Sydney was with the consent of Ashley.

We uphold the district court's finding that Ashley is not entitled to compensation beyond his share of the partnership profits for managing the partnerships.

Judgment for Sydney Altman affirmed.

## COLLECTIVE MANAGEMENT POWERS OF PARTNERS

**Introduction.** Most of the business decisions of a partnership may be made by a single partner, yet bind the partnership and the other partners. Other decisions require the collective action of the partners. In this section, you will study the actions that must or may be taken by collective action of the partners and the right of a partner to participate in such actions. In the next section, you will study the individual powers of the partners to bind the partnership and each other.

**Management Powers.** In the absence of an agreement to the contrary, each partner is a general manager of the partnership business with the power to make independent decisions in the normal business of the partnership. For example, a partner in a sporting goods shop could order merchandise, hire an additional employee, borrow needed money from a bank, and mark down some merchandise for sale.

Usually, partners will discuss management decisions among themselves before taking action, even if doing so is not required by a partnership agreement. If they discuss a matter of this kind, they will usually vote, formally or informally, on what action to take. Each partner has one vote, regardless of the relative sizes of their partnership interests or their shares of the profits. The vote of a majority of the partners controls such ordinary business decisions. If there is an equal split of the partners on whether to take a *new* course of action, then that course may not be taken. Such a split prevented partnership action in *Covalt v. High,* which follows.

**Right and Duty to Manage.** Each partner has a right to participate in management, and no partner may be excluded from management. In addition, as you learned earlier, a partner has a duty to serve the partnership, a duty based on the normal expectations of partners.

**Effect of Partnership Agreement.** The partners may modify the rules of management by unanimous agreement. They may agree that a partner, such as a silent partner, will relinquish his management right. They may grant authority to manage the business to one or more partners. Such a delegation of management powers will not, however, release a partner from liability to creditors, as is shown in *Nuttall v. Dowell*, which appears after the next section.

A partnership agreement may create classes of partners, some of which will have veto power, as was done in the *Westland Towers* case, which follows the next section. Some classes of partners may be given greater voting rights. Unequal voting rights are found often in very large partnerships, such as an accounting firm with several hundred partners. Such partnerships have three classes of partners: junior partners, who have few management rights; senior partners, who have more management rights; and managing partners, to whom most management functions have been delegated.

**Major Business Decisions.** Even if the management of a partnership is in the hands of only some of the partners, any major change in the nature of the partnership's business or in the partnership's location that would materially alter the risks of the partnership must be approved by all the partners. For example, a decision to merge a large accounting partnership with another partnership would have to be approved not only by managing partners but also by junior partners and senior partners. Similarly, the decision of a grocery store partnership to move the business to another city would need unanimous partner approval. However, a grocery chain with 33 stores would need only majority approval to open a new store in another town, since the effect of this decision on the business is far less significant.

**Unanimous Partners' Agreement Required.** In addition to major business decisions, other actions are so important that one partner should not be able to do them by himself. To make clear that no one partner may do certain acts, in the absence of a contrary agreement, UPA Section 9(3) requires unanimity for five listed actions. These actions are: (1) an *assignment of partnership property* for the benefit of creditors, (2) *disposal of the goodwill* of the business, (3) an act making it *impossible to carry on the ordinary business of the partnership* (such as the sale of the entire inventory of a retailing partnership), (4) *a confession of a judgment against the partnership,* and (5) a submission of a partnership claim or liability to *arbitration.*

In addition, Section 9(2) of the UPA requires unanimous approval of acts "not apparently for the carrying on of business of the partnership in the usual way." Such acts include an agreement for the partnership to serve as a *surety or guarantor* of the debt of another, to pay or to assume an *individual debt of a partner,* and at least under old precedents, to make *charitable gifts* or to provide *gratuitous services.*

## INDIVIDUAL AUTHORITY OF PARTNERS

**Types of Authority.** In conducting the business of a partnership, a partner will have contacts with customers, suppliers, and lenders. Whether the partnership and the other partners will have *liability for the contracts* that a partner makes with these persons is essentially determined by the rules of agency authority. Like agents, partners may have **express, implied,** and **apparent** authority to act for the partnership. In addition, partners may **ratify** the unauthorized contracts of a partner.

**Express and Implied Authority.** As you learned in the last section, every partner is a general manager of the business of the partnership. This power is expressed in UPA Section 9(1), which states that a partnership is bound by the act of every partner for apparently carrying on *in the usual way* the business of the partnership. Such authority is *implied* from the nature of the business. It permits a partner to bind the partnership and his partners for acts within the *ordinary affairs* of the business. The scope of this **implied authority** is determined with reference to what is usual business for partnerships of the same general type in the locality. In *Hodge v. Garrett,* which follows, the court used this test to determine that a partner in a drive-in theater had no implied authority to sell partnership land.

Implied authority of a partner may not contradict a partner's **express authority,** which is created by agreement of the partners. An agreement among the partners can expand, restrict, or even completely eliminate the implied authority of a partner. For example, the partners in a newspaper publishing business may agree that one partner shall have the authority to purchase a magazine business for the partnership and that another partner shall not have the authority to sell advertising space in the newspaper. The partners' implied authority to be general managers is modified in accordance with these *express* agreements.

Express authority may be stated orally or in writing, or it may be obtained by acquiescence. For example, if one partner exceeds his authority and the other partners know of it and do not complain, that partner may have express authority to do such acts in the future. Regardless of the method of agreement, all of the partners must agree to the modification of implied authority. Together, a partner's express and implied authority constitute her *actual* authority.

**Apparent Authority.** When implied authority is restricted or eliminated, the partnership risks the possibility that **apparent authority** to do a denied act will remain. To prevent apparent authority from arising despite a limitation on a partner's implied authority, UPA Section 9(1) requires that third persons with whom the partner deals have *knowledge* of the limitation on his authority. Just as a principal must notify third persons of limitations on an agent's authority, so must a partnership notify its customers, suppliers, and others of express limitations on the implied authority of partners. A third party's knowledge of a limitation on a partner's implied authority was found in the *Westland Towers* case, which follows.

Suppose that Caren, Mel, and Rex are partners and that they agree that Caren will be the only purchasing agent for the partnership. This agreement must be communicated to third parties selling goods to the partnership, or the other partners will have apparent authority to bind the partnership on purchase contracts.

**Ratification.** The agency rules of ratification apply with equal force to unauthorized acts of partners. Ratification is discussed in detail in Chapter 17.

**Special Transactions.** Usually, the application of these types of authority is no more difficult in partnership law than in agency law. Nevertheless, the validity of some partner's actions are affected by special partnership rules that reflect a concern for protecting important property and the credit standing of partners. This concern is especially evident in the rules for conveying real property and for borrowing money.

**Power to Convey Partnership Real Property.** Each state requires that a conveyance of real property located in the state be made only in compliance with certain formalities, such as the execution of a deed signed by the owners of the real property.[4] At a minimum, any individual partner's conveyance of partnership property must meet these formalities. In addition, to bind the partnership, an individual partner's conveyance of real property must be expressly, impliedly, or apparently authorized or be ratified. For example, the partners may expressly agree that a partner may sell the partnership's real property.

The more difficult determination is whether a partner has *implied* authority to convey real property. A partner has implied authority to sell real property if a partnership sells real property in the usual course of the partnership business. Such would be the case with the partner of a real estate partnership that frequently buys and sells land. By contrast, a partner has no implied authority to sell the building in which the partnership's retail business is conducted. Here, unanimous agreement of the partners is required, since the sale of the building may affect the ability of the firm to continue. In addition, a partner has no implied authority to sell land held for investment not in the usual course of business. A sale of such investment land would be authorized only if the partners concurred, as was held in *Hodge v. Garrett,* which follows.

**Formalities of Conveyance.** *In addition* to being authorized to convey real property, a partner must follow the formalities for conveyance required by state law. If real property is *held in the partnership name,* any

[4] The formalities of conveying interests in real property are discussed in Chapter 29.

partner authorized to convey the property need merely execute a deed in the name of the partnership. If the partner signs his own name instead of the partnership name, only an *equitable title* (a right to require a proper conveyance) passes to the transferee. The partner in *Hodge v. Garrett* obeyed the proper formalities by signing a deed in the partnership's name; however, the court held that he had no authority to convey the land.

When the title to the real property is in the name of one or more, but not all, of the partners, and the real property record does not disclose the partnership's rights in the property, a conveyance signed by the partners in whose name the property is recorded will pass good title to an innocent purchaser for value. The purchaser's notice or knowledge of the partnership's interest in the property, however, will cause him to take the property subject to the partnership's interest. If the title to the real property is held in the name of all the partners and the conveyance is executed by all the partners, the conveyance passes all of their and the partnership's rights in the property.

**Borrowing Money and Issuing Negotiable Instruments.** One of the most significant powers that an agent may possess is the power *to borrow money* and *to issue negotiable instruments* in the name of her principal. In agency law, an agent ordinarily has no such implied authority. This rule is grounded in the fear that an agent might impose extensive liability on a principal. This rationale fails somewhat in the area of partnerships, because a partner binds herself when she binds the partnership on loans and negotiable instruments; therefore, some restraint exists on her willingness to borrow excessive amounts.

Nevertheless, partnership law restricts the ability of a partner to borrow and to issue negotiable instruments in the name of a partnership. Essentially, a partner must possess express, implied, or apparent authority. Express authority gives a court few problems. Finding implied and apparent authority to borrow is more difficult, and doing so has not always been aided by the courts' adoption of terminology that hides these bases of authority—trading partnerships and nontrading partnerships.

**Trading and Nontrading Partnerships.** Although the UPA does not explicitly recognize the distinction, a number of courts have distinguished between trading and nontrading partnerships. A **trading partnership** has an inventory; that is, its regular business is buying and selling merchandise, such as retailing, wholesaling, importing, or exporting. For example, a toy store and a clothing store are trading partnerships. Since most of their inventory is financed, these firms need to borrow to stay in business. A **nontrading partnership** has no significant inventory, but is engaged in providing services, such as accounting services or real estate brokerage. Such partnerships have no normal borrowing needs.

The distinction between trading and nontrading partnerships is not always clear. Businesses such as general contracting, manufacturing, and dairy farming, although not exclusively devoted to buying and selling inventory, have been held to be trading partnerships. The rationale for their inclusion in this category is that borrowing is necessary in the ordinary course of business to augment their working capital.

This suggests why the distinction between trading partnerships and nontrading partnerships is useless or misleading. There is no necessary connection between borrowing money and buying and selling. The more important inquiry should be whether a partner has the implied authority—in the usual course of business—or the apparent authority to borrow money. By eliminating the use of the terms *trading partnership* and *nontrading partnership,* you can focus on the essential question: Was the partner's borrowing in the ordinary course of business?

Asking this question allows you to determine that a partner of a trading partnership that has never borrowed money has no authority, except perhaps apparent authority, to borrow money. Such a partner may have apparent authority if: (1) it appears that this type of business needs to borrow in the ordinary course of business; and (2) the lender does not know of the partnership's history of not borrowing.

**Borrowing Money.** If a court finds that a partner has authority to borrow money, the partnership is liable for his borrowings on behalf of the partnership. There is a limit, however, to a partner's capacity to borrow. A partner may have authority to borrow, yet borrow beyond the *ordinary needs* of the business. A partnership will not be liable for any loan whose amount exceeds the ordinary needs of the business, unless otherwise agreed by the partners.

A partnership is liable for a partner's authorized borrowings in its name even if the partner steals the proceeds of the loan. On the other hand, if money is borrowed in a partner's own name, the fact that it is used for partnership purposes does not create partnership liability to the lender. Such a loan is a loan to the partner, who then makes a contribution or a different loan to the partnership.

The power to borrow money on the firm's credit will ordinarily carry with it the power to grant the lender a *lien* or *security interest* in firm assets to secure the repayment of the borrowed money.[5] Security interests are a normal part of business loan transactions.

[5] Security interests in personal property are discussed in Chapter 40. Mortgages and other liens against real property are covered in Chapter 39.

**Issuing Instruments.** A partner who has the power to borrow money also has the authority to issue negotiable instruments, such as promissory notes,[6] for that purpose. If it is customary to give collateral for such instruments, he also has the power to grant security interests in the firm's assets.

When a partnership has a checking account, a partner has express authority to *draw checks* if his name appears on the signature card filed with the bank. A partner whose name is not on the signature card filed with the bank may bind the partnership on a check drawn by that partner in the partnership name, if the check is issued to a third person who has no knowledge of the limitations on the partner's authority. This liability is based on apparent authority, since drawing checks is an ordinary matter for a partnership.

**Negotiating Instruments.** A partnership receives many negotiable instruments during the course of its business. For example, an accounting firm's clients often pay fees by check. Even though a partner may *not* have authority to *issue* negotiable instruments, he often *has* implied authority to *negotiate*[7] instruments on behalf of the partnership.

If a partnership has a bank account, a partner will have implied authority to *indorse and deposit* in the account checks drawn payable to the partnership. As a general rule, a partner will also have implied authority to *indorse and cash* checks drawn payable to the order of the partnership. Likewise, partners have implied authority to *indorse* drafts and notes payable to the order of the partnership and to *sell* them at a discount.[8]

**Admissions and Notice.** Other rules governing the authority of partners are identical

[6] Negotiable instruments are defined in Chapter 35.

[7] Negotiation is the transfer of an instrument to another person such that he becomes a holder of it. Negotiation is discussed in detail in Chapter 36.

[8] The issuance, indorsement, and negotiation of negotiable instruments are discussed in Chapters 35 and 36.

to those governing the authority of agents. Under UPA Section 11, a partnership is bound by *admissions* or *representations* made by a partner concerning partnership affairs that are within the scope of her authority. Likewise, pursuant to Section 12, *notice* to or the knowledge of a partner relating to partnership affairs is **imputed** to the partnership. These rules reflect the reality that a partnership *speaks, sees, and hears* through its partners.

**Joint Ventures and Mining Partnerships.** Most of the authority rules of partnerships apply to joint ventures and mining partnerships. These business organizations are in essence partnerships with limited purposes. Therefore, their members have less implied and apparent authority than do partners. Joint venturers, however, have considerable apparent authority if third persons are unaware of the limited scope of the joint venture. A mining partner has no implied authority to borrow money or issue negotiable instruments. As with partners, joint venturers and mining partners may by agreement expand or restrict each other's agency powers.

## Covalt v. High

**675 P.2d 999 (N.M. Ct. App. 1983)**

Louis Covalt and William High were corporate officers and shareholders in Concrete Systems, Inc. (CSI). Covalt owned 25 percent of CSI, and High owned the remaining 75 percent. Both men received salaries and bonuses from CSI. In late 1971, after both High and Covalt had become corporate officers, they orally agreed to form a partnership, with High as managing partner. The partnership bought land and constructed a building on it. In February 1973, CSI leased the building from the partnership for a five-year term. Following the expiration of the initial term of the lease, CSI remained a tenant of the building. Periodically, CSI and the partnership orally agreed to certain rental increases.

In December 1978, Covalt resigned his corporate position with CSI and was employed by a competitor of CSI. However, he remained a partner with High in the ownership of the land and the building. On January 9, 1979, Covalt wrote to High demanding that the monthly rent for the building leased to CSI be increased from $1,850 to $2,850. High said that he would determine whether the rent could be increased. Thereafter, however, High did not agree to the rent increase and took no action to renegotiate the amount of the monthly rent.

Covalt sued for a judicial dissolution and an accounting. He alleged that High breached a fiduciary duty as a partner by failing to negotiate and obtain an increase in the rent charged CSI. The trial court found that CSI could afford the requested rental increase and that High's failure to assent to Covalt's demand was a breach of his fiduciary duty. The trial court ordered High to pay Covalt $9,500 plus interest. High appealed.

**DONNELLY, JUDGE.** The status resulting from the formation of a partnership creates a fiduciary relationship between partners. The status of partnership requires of each member an obligation of good faith and fairness in their dealings with one another, and a duty to act in furtherance of the common benefit of all partners in transactions conducted within the ambit of partnership affairs.

The problems that have arisen between the partners here emphasize the importance of formulating written partnership agreements detailing the rights and obligations of the partners. Except where the partners expressly agree to the contrary, it is a fundamental principle of law of partnership that all partners have equal rights in the management and conduct of the business of the partnership.

Under UPA Section 18(e), Covalt was legally invested with an equal voice in the management of the partnership affairs. Assuming, but not deciding, that High's status as a managing partner is not to be considered, neither partner had the right to impose his will or decision concerning the operation of the partnership business upon the other. The fact that a proposal may benefit the partnership does not mandate acceptance by all the partners. As specified in UPA Section 18(h), "any difference arising as to ordinary matters connected with the partnership business may be decided by a majority of the partners."

If the partners are equally divided, those who forbid a change must have their way. For example, one partner cannot either engage a new or dismiss an old employee against the will of his copartner, nor, if the lease of the partnership place of business expires, insist on renewing the lease and continuing the business at the old place.

In the absence of an agreement of a majority of the partners, an act involving the partnership business may not be compelled by the copartner. If the parties are evenly divided as to a business decision affecting the partnership, and in the absence of a written provision in the partnership agreement providing for such contingency, then, as between the partners, the power to exercise discretion on behalf of the partners is suspended so long as the division continues.

At the time of the formation of the partnership, both Covalt and High were officers and shareholders of CSI. Each was aware of the potential for conflict between their duties as corporate officers to further the business of the corporation, and that of their role as partners in leasing realty to their corporation for the benefit of the partnership business. In the posture of being both a landlord and representatives of the tenant (CSI), they had conflicting loyalties and fiduciary duties. After Covalt's resignation as an officer of the corporation, he continued to remain a shareholder of the corporation. Each partner's conflict of interest was known to the other and was acquiesced in when the partnership was formed.

Thus, there was no breach of a fiduciary duty. In the absence of a mutual agreement, or a written instrument detailing the rights of the parties, the remedy for such an impasse is a dissolution of the partnership.

Judgment reversed in favor of High.

## Hodge v. Garrett

**614 P.2d 420 (Idaho Sup. Ct. 1980)**

Louise Garrett, Rex Voeller, and others owned Pay-Ont Drive-in Theatre, a partnership. Voeller, the managing partner of Pay-Ont, signed a contract to sell Bill Hodge a small parcel of land belonging to the partnership. The contract stated that the title to the land was in the name of the partnership, and Voeller signed in the name of the partnership. This land was adjacent to the theater. The contract reserved an easement for use as a driveway into the theater. When the partnership refused to deliver possession of the land to Hodge, he sued Garrett and the other partners. The partners argued that Voeller had no authority to sell the property. The trial court held that Voeller had such authority and ordered the partnership and the partners to convey the land to Hodge. Garrett and the other partners appealed.

**Bistline, Justice.** At common law, one partner could not, without the concurrence of his copartners, convey away the real estate of the partnership, bind his partners by a deed, or transfer the title and interest of his copartners in the firm real estate. This rule was changed by the adoption of the Uniform Partnership Act.

The meaning of UPA Sections 9 and 10(1) was stated by Crane & Bromberg, *Law of Partnership,* as follows:

> If record title is in the partnership and a partner conveys in the partnership name, legal title passes. But the partnership may recover the property if it can show (A) that the conveying partner was not apparently carrying on business in the usual way or (B) that he had in fact no authority and the purchaser had knowledge of that fact.

Thus, this contract is enforceable if Voeller had the actual authority to sell the property, or, even if Voeller did not have such authority, the contract is still enforceable if the sale was in the usual way of carrying on the business and Hodge did not know that Voeller did not have this authority.

Although actual authority to sell the property may be implied from the nature of the business, or from similar past transactions, nothing in the record in this case indicates that Voeller had express or implied authority to sell real property belonging to the partnership. There is no evidence that Voeller had sold property belonging to the partnership in the past, and obviously the partnership was not engaged in the business of buying and selling real estate.

The next question, since actual authority has not been shown, is whether Voeller was conducting the partnership business in the usual way in selling this parcel of land such that Voeller had apparent authority. The trial court made no finding that it was customary for Voeller to sell real property, or even personal property, belonging to the partnership. Nor was there any evidence to this effect. Nor did the court discuss whether it was in the usual course of business for the managing partner of a theater to sell real property. Yet the trial court found that Voeller had apparent authority to sell the property. From this it must be inferred that the trial court believed it to be in the usual course of business for a partner who has exclusive control of the partnership business to sell real property belonging to the partnership, where that property is not being used in the partnership business. We cannot agree with this conclusion. For a theater, "carrying on in the usual way the business of the partnership" means running the operations of the theater; it does not mean selling a parcel of property adjacent to the theater.

Here the contract of sale stated that the land belonged to the partnership, and, even if Hodge believed that Voeller as the exclusive manager had authority to transact all business for the firm, Voeller still could not bind the partnership through a unilateral act that was not in the usual business of the partnership.

Judgment reversed in favor of Garrett and the other partners.

## City National Bank of Detroit v. Westland Towers Apartments

**309 N.W.2d 209 (Mich. Ct. App. 1981)**

William Risman, Robert Risman, Don Horace, Charles Granader, and Harry Granader were partners of Westland Towers Apartments. City National Bank of Detroit (CNB) issued a letter of credit for $250,947 to Westland Towers. The letter of credit served as collateral for a mortgage to finance Westland Towers' construction of a low- and moderate-income housing project. Construction of the project was delayed due to cost overruns and disputes between the partners. William Risman requested that CNB extend the expiration date of the letter of credit, and CNB agreed to the extension. Approval of the extension by Westland Towers was required to avoid releasing it from liability to CNB for the amount of the letter of credit. The partners met to approve the extension, but could not come to an agreement.

The partnership agreement provided rules for partner approval of contracts:

EXECUTION OF PARTNERSHIP CONTRACT

Paragraph 10. All contracts, agreements, and other instruments to which the partnership may be a party shall be signed in the partnership name by any two of the following: WILLIAM RISMAN, ROBERT RISMAN or DON HORACE, and CHARLES GRANADER or HARRY GRANADER.

In addition, the partnership agreement gave certain management power to William and Robert Risman:

MANAGING PARTNERS

Paragraph 11. WILLIAM RISMAN and ROBERT RISMAN are hereby designated as the managing PARTNERS in whom the parties hereto vest the direct responsibility for the management of the partnership business, including the right and power in their sole and uncontrolled discretion to:
(b) borrow money for the partnership.

Any action by the managing PARTNERS may be taken by the consent of a majority of the managing PARTNERS, and any checks, contracts or other instruments may be executed by the managing PARTNERS on behalf of this partnership only when signed in the manner heretofore provided.

The Rismans agreed to an extension of the letter of credit, but the Granaders did not. CNB attempted to acquire the signature of either of the Granaders, but both Granaders refused to sign. Upon CNB's request, the partnership's attorney gave his opinion that the Rismans, as managing partners, were authorized to approve the extension of the expiration date of the letter of credit. William Risman for himself and by power of attorney for Robert Risman extended the expiration date.

On the new expiration date, the partnership refused to pay CNB the amount of the letter of credit. CNB sued the partnership and the partners for that amount. The trial court held that neither the partnership nor the partners were liable. CNB appealed.

**Bronson, Judge.** CNB first argues that William Risman had the authority to unilaterally enter into a binding agreement with it with respect to the extension of the expiration date of the letter of credit. The question is whether the customer consented to the extension of the expiration date. The customer here was not Risman, but the Westland Towers partnership.

CNB relies on Section 9(1) of the Uniform Partnership Act for the proposition that irrespective of Risman's actual authority, his acts were nonetheless binding on the partnership:

> Every partner is an agent of the partnership for the purpose of its business, and the act of every partner, including the execution in the partnership name of any instrument, for apparently carrying on in the usual way the business of the partnership of which he is a member binds the partnership, unless the partner so acting has in fact no authority to act for the partnership in the particular matter, and the person with whom he is dealing has knowledge of the fact that he has no such authority.

Initially, we note our disagreement with the lower court on the issue of whether obtaining the extension was within the usual course of business. We hold that it was. The more difficult problem with allowing CNB to rely on Section 9(1) is caused by the last clause of this provision which would divest CNB of the right to rely on Risman's acts if it had knowledge of the fact that he had no authority to unilaterally agree to the extension of the letter of credit. This "knowledge" proviso requires an examination of the pertinent portions of the partnership agreement of which CNB concededly was aware.

We have no quarrel with the lower court's conclusion that paragraph 10 of the partnership agreement is properly interpreted as requiring one signature from William or Robert Risman or Don Horace and a second signature from Charles or Harry Granader to result in a valid execution of a contract on behalf of the partnership. However, when paragraph 10 is construed with paragraph 11, an ambiguity is apparent. Paragraph 11 provides in part that William and Robert Risman have "sole and uncontrolled" discretion to borrow money for the partnership and to execute instruments evincing any indebtedness on behalf of the partnership. Paragraph 11 of the partnership agreement then goes on to state that any instruments executed by the managing partners must be "signed in the manner heretofore provided." This is ostensibly a reference to the signing requirement imposed by paragraph 10. However, the signature requirement is seemingly in conflict with the "sole and uncontrolled" discretion language of paragraph 11.

The seemingly conflicting portions of paragraphs 10 and 11 can be construed consistent with each other. That is, while the partnership agreement requires one signature from each of two groups of partners, if the managing partners determine that a particular contract shall be entered into, the two general partners have no discretion to refuse to sign the applicable instrument, assuming the instrument represents a legal obligation under the law and partnership agreement. The contractual provisions in issue evince an intent on the part of the partnership: (1) to give operating control to the Rismans and (2) to make certain that the Granaders were kept fully informed of all material transactions involving partnership business.

In the instant case, obtaining an extension of the letter of credit was undoubtedly within the scope of the authority of the managing partners pursuant to paragraph 11(b) of the partnership agreement. As such, the Granaders had no legal right to refuse to sign the consent to extend the letter of credit's expiration date. This does not necessarily mean, however, that CNB could extend the expiration date of the letter of credit on the authority of the managing partners alone. Indeed, we hold that this avenue of operation was not open to CNB if it had knowledge of the managing partners' disability to execute an instrument on their own signatures. The Granaders' wrongful refusal to sign the agreement would merely have given the Rismans a cause of action to compel the signature of one or the other of them or to obtain a court order allowing the transaction to proceed on the authority of the managing partners alone. If they were unsuccessful in obtaining an expedited review of their cause so that the benefits of the project were lost, they would have had a cause of action against the Granaders for breach of the partnership agreement.

We now turn to a discussion of whether CNB had knowledge of William Risman's lack of authority to execute the contract extending the time the letter of credit expired. It is clear that CNB did not possess knowlege of Risman's lack of authority as the term knowledge is generally used. That is, from the bank's perspective, William Risman's authority was unclear. However, the term knowledge as used in UPA Section 3 has a special meaning:

> (1) A person has knowledge of a fact within the meaning of this act not only when he has actual knowledge thereof, but also when he has knowledge of such other facts as in the circumstances shows bad faith.

Under the definitions of knowledge appearing above, we agree with the trial court that CNB did have sufficient knowledge of Robert Risman's lack of authority so that it may not claim the benefits of UPA Section 9(1). CNB engaged in a course of conduct tending to show that it at least doubted William Risman's authority. CNB had a copy of the partnership agreement, and its own actions clearly reveal that it doubted Risman's authority under this contract. More importantly, CNB was aware that the Granaders considered one of their signatures imperative for the execution of any valid instrument on behalf of the partnership.

We conclude that the partnership agreement did not allow any instrument or contract to be entered into without one signature from the Risman group and one signature from a Granader, and we conclude that CNB had knowledge of this requirement so that CNB cannot recover on the letter of credit.

Judgment for the partnership and the partners affirmed.

---

## Nuttall v. Dowell

**639 P.2d 832 (Wash. Ct. App. 1982)**

Charles Nuttall bought a 10-acre plot of land, part of a 40-acre parcel of undeveloped land known as the "Holly 40." The land was burdened with a 15-foot easement along the western boundary. This easement and a similar one along his western neighbor's eastern boundary were combined to provide for access to otherwise landlocked property.

After taking possession of the land, Nuttall first cleared some land and built a small log cabin as a temporary residence. Nuttall also dug a well by hand, cleared the proposed site for his permanent home, and cleared and constructed a road leading into the homesite.

After these events occurred, Nuttall's neighbors to the west conducted an accurate survey of the western boundary line. As a result, Nuttall's proper western boundary moved 130 feet east of where it was originally represented to be, thus placing Nuttall's well and proposed homesite on neighboring land to the west. The ripple effect of this dislocation caused the easement road to lie entirely on Nuttall's land, thereby isolating one-half acre of Nuttall's property from the rest of the property. The proper relocation of the boundary line also reduced Nuttall's acreage to 9 instead of the 10 acres that he had contracted to purchase. In addition, the boundary relocation caused disputes between Nuttall and his neighbors to the east and west.

Nuttall bought the land from a partnership of Harold Schwartz, a licensed real estate broker, Gerald Dowell, an accountant, and Lester Dowell, an airline pilot. The partnership had purchased the Holly 40 with the intention of dividing it into smaller parcels for resale. The Dowells gave Schwartz complete responsibility to sell the land. Although Schwartz and the Dowells knew that the Holly 40 had not previously been surveyed or subdivided, they conducted no survey prior to their resale efforts because of the high cost that this would entail. Instead, Schwartz gathered some boundary information from a survey map of the county road that ran through the northern portion of the Holly 40, from land to the east that had been surveyed, and from boundary stakes placed by previous owners. By a process of elimination, Schwartz determined what he thought to be fairly accurate boundaries. In preparation for sale, Schwartz marked the boundaries with stakes and surveyor's ribbons.

After Nuttall became interested in the property through advertisements by Schwartz, he viewed the 10-acre parcel that he was to buy. He saw the stakes and flags placed by Schwartz and was told that they were "accurate within a couple of feet at the most."

Nuttall sued the Dowells and Schwartz for the damages he suffered due to Schwartz's misrepresentation of the boundaries. The trial court found that Schwartz acted negligently and incompetently in attempting to locate the boundary for the easement and awarded Nuttall damages of $1,900, representing the cost of having the easement road properly relocated. The court refused to find the Dowells liable to Nuttall, and Nuttall appealed.

**Pearson, Judge.** The trial court found Schwartz and the Dowells to be joint owners of the Holly 40. The trial court held that Schwartz acted as an agent in all the boundary and acreage representations, but concluded that since the Dowells did not actively participate in the location of the easement road, the liability for the breach of one partner could not be imputed to the entire partnership. We disagree.

Our disagreement rests upon Schwartz's status as a joint adventurer engaged in the enterprise of buying, dividing, and reselling land. All three defendants recognized and characterized their relationship as one of "partnership which had as its business the purchase and sale of real estate." No evidence was offered at trial to negate the inference that Schwartz had the authority to make each and every representation presented to Nuttall during this entire land transaction. In fact, Lester Dowell conceded at trial that he and his brother left all the details to Schwartz. It is apparent that the Dowells, one an airline pilot and the other an accountant, considered Schwartz as a real estate expert who possessed the relevant knowledge, resources, and expertise needed to implement this partnership venture.

Under UPA Section 13, a partner is bound by the wrongful act or omission of any partner acting in the ordinary course of business. This vicarious liability applies to contractual liability.

At the time of Schwartz's misconduct, he was engaged in furtherance of the partnership business and was acting pursuant to the agreement between Nuttall and the partnership, which had been agreed to by all the partners. Furthermore, the partners testified that they never had any intention of conducting a survey on the Holly 40. The clear inference is that the Dowells were fully aware of the situation and assumed, as they had in the entire transaction, that Schwartz, with his superior expertise, would locate the easement road, just as he had done with the boundaries. Hence, the Dowells are vicariously liable to Nuttall for Schwartz's attempted performance of a contractual obligation.

Judgment reversed in favor of Nuttall.

## LIABILITY FOR TORTS AND CRIMES

**Torts.** The standards and principles of agency law's **respondeat superior** are applied in determining the liability of the partnership and of the other partners for the torts of a partner.[9] Under Section 13 of the UPA, the other partners are liable for torts of a partner committed *within the ordinary course* of partnership business or *within the ordinary authority* of that partner. In addition, if a partner commits a *breach of trust,* all of the partners are liable under UPA Section 14. For example, all of the partners in a stock brokerage firm are liable for a partner's embezzlement of a customer's securities and funds.

**Intentional Torts.** While partners are usually liable for their partner's *negligence,* they are not usually liable for their partner's *intentional* torts, as is illustrated by *Vrabel v. Acri,* which follows. The reason for this rule is that intentional torts are not usually within the ordinary course of business or within the ordinary authority of a partner.

A few intentional torts may create liability for all partners. For example, a partner who repossesses consumer goods from debtors of the partnership may trespass on consumer property or batter a consumer. Such activities have been held to be in the ordinary course of business. Also, partners who authorize a partner to commit intentional torts are liable for such torts.

**Partners' Remedies.** If the partnership and the other partners are held liable for a partner's tort, they may, during an accounting, recover the amount of their vicarious liability from the wrongdoing partner. This rule places ultimate liability on the wrongdoing partner without affecting the ability of tort victims to obtain recovery from the partnership or the other partners.

**Crimes.** When a partner commits a crime in the course and scope of transacting partnership business, his partners usually are **not** criminally liable. If the partners have *participated* in the criminal act or *authorized* its commission, then they are liable. They may also be liable, if they know of a partner's criminal tendencies, yet place him in a position in which he may commit a crime.

Until recent times, a partnership could not be held liable for a crime in most states, because it was not viewed as a legal entity. However, modern criminal codes usually define partnerships as "persons" that may commit crimes. If a crime is committed by a partner acting within the course and scope of his authority, the partnership may be indicted and convicted.

[9] The doctrine of *respondeat superior* is discussed in detail in Chapter 17.

## Vrabel v. Acri

**103 N.E.2d 564 (Ohio Sup. Ct. 1952)**

On February 17, 1947, Stephen Vrabel and a companion went into the Acri Cafe in Youngstown, Ohio, to buy alcoholic drinks. While Vrabel and his companion were sitting at the bar drinking, Michael Acri, without provocation, drew a .38-caliber gun, shot and killed Vrabel's companion, and shot and seriously injured Vrabel. Michael was convicted of murder and sentenced to a life term in the state prison.

Since 1933, Florence and Michael Acri, as partners, had owned and operated the Acri Cafe. From the time of his marriage to Florence in 1931 until 1946, Michael had been in and out of hospitals, clinics, and sanitariums for the treatment of mental disorders and nervousness. Although Michael beat Florence when they had marital difficulties, he had not attacked, abused, or mistreated anyone else. Florence and Michael separated in September 1946, and Florence sued Michael for divorce soon afterward. Before their separation, Florence had operated and managed the café primarily only when Michael was ill. Following the marital separation and up until the time he shot Vrabel, Michael was in exclusive control of the management of the café.

Vrabel brought suit against Florence Acri to recover damages for his injuries on the ground that, as Michael's partner, she was liable for his tort. The trial court ordered Florence to pay Vrabel damages of $7,500. Florence appealed.

**Zimmerman, Judge.** The authorities are in agreement that whether a tort is committed by a partner or a joint adventurer, the principles of law governing the situation are the same. So, where a partnership or a joint enterprise is shown to exist, each member of such project acts both as principal and agent of the others as to those things done within the apparent scope of the business of the project and for its benefit.

Section 13 of the Uniform Partnership Act provides: "Where, by any wrongful act or omission of any partner acting in the ordinary course of business of the partnership or with the authority of his copartners, loss or injury is caused to any person, not being a partner in the partnership, or any penalty is incurred, the partnership is liable therefor to the same extent as the partner so acting or omitting to act."

However, it is equally true that where one member of a partnership or joint enterprise commits a wrongful and malicious tort not within the actual or apparent scope of the agency or the common business of the particular venture, to which the other members have not assented, and which has not been concurred in or ratified by them, they are not liable for the harm thereby caused.

Because at the time of Vrabel's injuries and for a long time prior thereto Florence had been excluded from the Acri Cafe and had no voice or control in its management, and because Florence did not know or have good reason to know that Michael was a dangerous individual prone to assault cafe patrons, the theory of negligence urged by Vrabel is hardly tenable.

We cannot escape the conclusion, therefore, that the above rules, relating to the nonliability of a partner or joint adventurer for wrongful and malicious torts committed by an associate outside the purpose and scope of the business, must be applied in the instant case. The willful and malicious attack by Michael Acri upon Vrabel in the Acri Cafe cannot reasonably be said to have come within the scope of the business of operating the cafe, so as to have rendered the absent Florence accountable.

Since the liability of a partner for the acts of his associates is founded upon the principles of agency, the statement is in point that an intentional and willful attack committed by an agent or employee, to vent his own spleen or malevolence against the injured person, is a clear departure from his employment and his principal or employer is not reponsible therefor.

Judgment reversed in favor of Florence Acri.

## LAWSUITS BY AND AGAINST PARTNERSHIPS AND PARTNERS

**Suits by the Partnership and the Partners.** Since a partnership was not considered a legal entity at common law, a partnership could not sue in its own name; instead, all of the partners had to join in the suit. This meant that if the partnership wanted to sue someone for breaching a contract or defaming the partnership business, *all* of the partners had to agree to bring the suit. Especially for large partnerships, this requirement was cumbersome. Today, many statutes (but not the UPA) permit a partnership to sue in its own name through the action of one or more partners with authority to bring suits.

**Suits against the Partners.** Section 15 of the UPA imposes upon partners a different type of liability for torts than it does for contracts.

**Joint and Several Liability for Torts.** Partners are **jointly** and **severally** liable for partnership torts. This means that a tort victim may sue all of the partners (jointly) or sue fewer than all of the partners (severally). If a tort victim sues all of the partners jointly, the judgment may be satisfied against assets of the partnership and assets of the individual partners. If fewer than all of the partners are sued severally, the judgment may generally be satisfied from the individual assets of the partners sued.

If fewer than all of the partners are sued and made to pay the entire amount of the tort victim's damages, those partners may seek **indemnification** or **contribution** from the other partners for their shares of the liability.

**Joint Liability for Contracts.** Partners are **jointly** liable for contractual obligations of the partnership. This means that all of the partners must be sued if the partnership has breached a contract. Otherwise, no individual partner may be required to pay a judgment and the assets of the partnership cannot be used to satisfy the contract creditor's judgment.

Courts and legislatures have fashioned many modifications to this requirement of joining all the partners. Some states make partners jointly and severally liable for contracts. Others have *joint debtor* statutes that permit creditors—both contract and tort claimants—to sue fewer than all of the partners and yet collect from partnership property.

**Creditor's Release of a Partner.** Under the common law, when a person releases one partner from joint liability, all of the partners are released. Section 294(1) of the *Restatement (Second) of Contracts* adopts the view that the release of one partner discharges only the partners' joint liability. If the partners had several liability also, it would remain.

**Suits against the Partnership.** The common law and the UPA do not permit a partnership to be sued in its own name. This prohibition is especially cumbersome for a party suing for breach of contract. Since the UPA imposes joint liability on partners for partnership contracts, it is necessary to sue each of the joint obligors, which is especially difficult when the partners live in a number of states. As noted above, many states have responded to this difficulty by enacting statutes that make all joint obligations joint and several. In addition, *common-name statutes* permit suits against the partnership even if fewer than all of the partners are notified of the suit. Pursuant to such statutes, a judgment against the partnership is enforceable against the assets of the partnership and against the individual assets of those partners who have been served with process.

## SUMMARY

Partners have great freedom to determine by agreement their relationships to each other. Partnership law provides rules that apply when no agreement is applicable. However, partners may not by agreement eliminate their fiduciary duties to the partnership and to each other, and they may not, by agreement among themselves, diminish the duties they owe to third persons.

Partners are fiduciaries of each other, and they owe each other many of the same duties that agents owe their principals. Under partnership law, partners may not self-deal, they may not compete with the partnership, and they must devote full time to the partnership business, unless otherwise agreed. Partners owe a duty to exercise due care in making business decisions and to account for their business transactions.

All of the partners are entitled to free access to the records of the partnership, and under certain circumstances a partner may ask a court to order and supervise an accounting.

A partner's compensation is her share of the profits of the business, unless otherwise agreed. Usually, profits and losses are shared equally. If the partners agree to share profits on some other basis, then losses will also be shared on that basis, unless the partners agree to share losses differently from the way in which they share profits.

Each partner has an equal voice in the management of the partnership. When there are differences of opinion, the majority rules, except that unanimity is required for major changes, as in the nature or location of the business. Each partner is ordinarily a general manager of the partnership. Therefore, a partner has broad implied and apparent authority to act for the partnership and may, despite a restrictive agreement among the partners, impose contractual liability on it. Partners in a trading partnership have authority to borrow money in the partnership name. A partner's power to convey real property depends on how title to the property is held.

The principles of agency law apply in determining when a partner's tort imposes liability on the other partners and the partnership. Under modern criminal statutes, partnerships may be held liable for crimes committed by partners acting within the scope of their authority.

Partners are jointly liable on contracts of the partnership, and they are jointly and severally liable for torts. Today, most states permit partnerships to sue and be sued in their own names. In many states, it is not necessary to sue all of the partners to recover a judgment against partnership assets.

## PROBLEM CASES

1. Lehman, a machinist, and Alford, a physician, formed a partnership to manufacture a small tractor using certain parts on which Lehman was to obtain a patent. Alford contributed $20,000 to the venture. Lehman was to contribute the patent and the use of his machine shop, equipment, and tools. Lehman was to have complete management of the business and was to devote full time to it. The written partnership agreement provided that Lehman "shall be allowed an annual salary in an amount or amounts to be agreed upon by the parties hereto."

The venture was a complete failure, and the $20,000 was gone. Lehman never devoted full-time to the business, but continued to do other work. Upon dissolution, Lehman claimed that he was entitled to $17,500 as salary, although Alford and Lehman had never agreed what Lehman's salary would be. Alford claimed that Lehman was to have no salary unless the business made a profit. Is Lehman entitled to a salary for his services?

2. Raymond Hurley and several others formed a partnership to invest in real estate. Hurley was the managing partner. He made a contract to purchase a piece of property on behalf of the partnership. The contract did not disclose, and Hurley did not disclose to the other partners, that $35,000 of the partnership's funds was to be used to pay off a prior debt that Hurley owed to the seller. The seller had refused to conclude the purchase unless the debt was paid. Later, Hurley sold a portion of the partnership property to a corporation in which he and his wife were the major shareholders. No appraisal of the current value of the property was obtained prior to this sale.

The other partners sued Hurley. They sought for the partnership the $35,000 plus the difference between the purchase price and the market value of the partnership property sold by Hurley to the corporation. Is Hurley liable?

3. Mary Truman and Claude Joe Martin were unmarried but living together. They agreed orally to a joint venture or partnership arrangement to operate "Pete's Truck Stop." Subsequent to opening this restaurant business, Claude Joe also operated a bar, a tree trimming business, and an irrigation supply business. When Mary and Claude Joe broke up, Mary sued Claude Joe for half of the profits that he had made from his other activities during the term of the joint venture or partnership. Is Mary entitled to a share of the profits?

4. J. R. Cude and Nathan Couch paid $7,000 for a laundromat that had been operating in Couch's building. They put new washers and dryers in the building. After their business had operated for about 7½ years, Couch sued for a dissolution and liquidation of the assets. At the public sale of the assets, prospective bidders were informed that Couch would not lease the building for a continuation of the business and that the equipment would have to be removed. Cude was one of the bidders, but the highest bidder was a stranger who bid $800. Later, Cude learned that the stranger was Platkin, the father-in-law of Couch's son, and that Platkin was acting as agent for Couch. Couch and his son then operated the laundromat in the same building. Cude sued Couch for damages for breach of fiduciary duties. Will Cude win?

5. Wallace Woodruff, Howard Barth, and Lillie Bryant were partners in the Flour Bluff Finance Company, which engaged in the business of making loans of from $50 to $100. After a dispute, Bryant resigned as manager. She continued to receive her share of the profits after leaving the firm. About eight months later, a partnership composed of Lillie Bryant, her husband, and two others opened a business called Pay Day Loans about 100 feet from Flour Bluff Finance Company. It

made the same kinds of loans as Flour Bluff. Woodruff and Barth then sued Lillie Bryant for breach of a partner's fiduciary duty and for a temporary injunction to prevent her from working for Pay Day Loans. Has Bryant breached a fiduciary duty?

**6.** Joseph Schuler, Robert Hurlbut, and Bernard Birnbaum formed a partnership for the purpose of constructing and operating a nursing home in Corning, New York. They retained an architectural firm to prepare preliminary plans for submission to the appropriate state agency. The state did not grant a license, and the partnership was dissolved. The architectural firm sued Schuler for its services. Hurlbut approved the settlement and paid his share, but Birnbaum refused to do so. Schuler then sued Birnbaum to recover one third of the settlement and legal expenses. Birnbaum's defense was that a partner may not be sued by another partner prior to an accounting. Should Schuler be permitted to sue Birnbaum?

**7.** Doug Conners and David Inmon formed a partnership, Commercial Truck Refinishing. They agreed that Conners would manage the business. Both the partnership and Conners, as an individual, owed money to Southwest Auto Supply, Inc. Conners wrote a $3,500 check on the partnership checking account payable to Southwest and instructed the manager of Southwest to apply the check to his personal debt to Southwest. Three months later, the partnership went out of business. Southwest then sued Inmon on the debt owed by the partnership. Inmon claimed that Conners had acted without authority in making the $3,500 payment on his personal account with partnership funds. Inmon argued that the payment should be credited to the partnership account. Is Inmon correct?

**8.** Holland loaned Dalton Waldrop $12,500 to buy certain well-drilling equipment that was described in the loan agreement between Holland and Waldrop. A year later, Dalton Waldrop formed a partnership for the drilling of wells with his brother, Thomas Waldrop. They used the equipment that Dalton had purchased with the borrowed money. When Dalton failed to repay the loan, Holland claimed that the partnership, and hence Thomas Waldrop personally, was liable to repay the loan because the proceeds of the loan were used by the partnership. Is Holland correct?

**9.** Warren Ten Brook, Milton Smith, and Maude Smith agreed to form a partnership to operate an automobile dealership. The partnership agreement stated that the initial capital would be $25,800, to be contributed in equal shares by the partners; that the Smiths would advance $2,600 to Ten Brook; and that Ten Brook would pay his portion of the capital from his share of the profits of the business. Ten Brook was made general manager, but the signature of either Maude or Milton Smith was required on all partnership checks. Maude Smith kept the books and handled the money of the partnership.

The business needed working capital and had to sell some used cars at a loss in order to continue operations. Holloway, an acquaintance of Ten Brook, agreed to lend the business $6,000, giving him her check payable to the partnership. The check was deposited by one of the Smiths in the partnership bank account, and the amount of the check was later withdrawn for use in buying and selling automobiles. Ten Brook gave Holloway a note for $6,000 plus 5 percent interest, which he signed in the name of the partnership.

When the note was not paid, Holloway sued Ten Brook and the Smiths. The Smiths argued that they were not liable on the loan, because the loan was made to Ten Brook personally rather than to the partnership and because the amount of the loan was part of Ten Brook's capital contribution to the partnership. Are the Smiths correct?

**10.** Smithtown General Hospital, a partnership, permitted a prosthetic device salesman to participate in surgery on a patient at the hospital. The unauthorized practice of medicine is a technical assault under the New York criminal code. The state of New York prosecuted the hospital for assault. The criminal code imposed liability only upon persons, and defined a person to include "a partnership, where appropriate." The hospital asked the court to rule that as a partnership, it was not a person and, therefore, could not commit assault. Is the hospital correct?

# Chapter 20

# Dissolution, Winding Up, and Termination of Partnerships

## INTRODUCTION

This chapter is about the death of partnerships. Three terms are important in this connection: dissolution, winding up, and termination. Essentially, **dissolution** is a change in the relation of the partners, as when a partner dies. Here, the partners' relations change because there is one fewer partner who can act for them and affect their liability. **Winding up,** which follows dissolution, is the orderly liquidation of the partnership assets and the distribution of the proceeds to those having claims against the partnership. **Termination,** the end of the partnership's existence, automatically follows winding up.

In this chapter, you will learn to distinguish these three concepts. You will learn what changes in partners' relations cause dissolution. You will study the process of winding up, especially the powers of the partner who winds up. And you will learn how a partnership can avoid the harmful effects of dissolution and winding up.

## DISSOLUTION

**Dissolution Defined.** **Dissolution** is defined in Section 29 of the Uniform Partnership Act (UPA) as

> the change in the relation of the partners caused by any partner ceasing to be associated in the carrying on as distinguished from the winding up of the business.

A dissolution may be caused by a partner's retirement, death, or bankruptcy, among other things. Whatever the cause of dissolution, however, it is characterized by a *partner's ceasing to carry on the business.*

**Importance of Dissolution.** Dissolution is the starting place for the winding up (liquidation) and termination of a partnership. Although winding up does not always follow dissolution, it often does. Winding up usually has a severe effect on a business: it usually causes the death of the business, because the assets of the business are sold and the proceeds of the sale are distributed to creditors and partners. Hence, for a profitable business, winding up should be avoided. By preventing dissolution, winding up is avoided.

A dissolution and a winding up are followed by termination of the partnership. But termination of the *partnership* does not automatically terminate the *business.* Indeed, during winding up, the business may be sold as a whole and carried on without any interruption by the remaining partners, by one of the partners as a sole proprietorship, by a purchaser, or by a corporation formed by all or some of the partners.

**Power and Right to Dissolve.** Under UPA Section 31(2), a partner always has the *power* to dissolve the partnership at any time, such as by withdrawing from the partnership. A partner does not, however, always have the *right* to dissolve a partnership. For example, a partner has no right to withdraw from a partnership before its 20-year term expires.

There are many causes of dissolution. Some are *wrongful,* and others are *nonwrongful.* If a partner dissolves a partnership in a way in which he has the *right to dissolve* the partnership, the dissolution is nonwrongful. If a partner dissolves a partnership in a way in which he has the *power, but not the right, to dissolve* the partnership, the dissolution is wrongful. Since the consequences that follow a nonwrongful dissolution differ from those that follow a wrongful dissolution, it is necessary to distinguish between wrongful and nonwrongful dissolutions.

**Nonwrongful Dissolution.** A partner has the power and the right to dissolve the partnership provided that she does *not violate the partnership agreement* in dissolving the partnership. Such dissolutions are nonwrongful. UPA Section 31(1) lists the following as nonwrongful dissolutions:

1. Automatic dissolution at the end of the term stated in the partnership agreement. For example, a partnership with a 20-year term is automatically dissolved at the expiration of that term.

2. Automatic dissolution upon the partnership's accomplishment of its objective, if the partnership agreement provides for dissolution at that point. For example, a partnership organized to build 15 condominiums dissolves when it completes their construction.

3. Withdrawal of a partner at any time from a partnership at will. A partnership at will is a partnership whose partnership agreement does not specify any specific term or objective. The partnerships in the *Paciaroni v. Crane* and *Wester & Co. v. Nestle* cases, which appear later in this chapter, were partnerships at will that were dissolved by the withdrawal of partners.

4. Unanimous agreement of the partners who have not assigned their partnership in-

terests or suffered charging orders against their partnership interests.[1]

5. Expulsion of a partner in accordance with the partnership agreement. For example, the removal of a partner who has stolen partnership property dissolves the partnership if the partnership agreement allows removal on such grounds.

In addition, UPA Section 31 lists three other nonwrongful causes of dissolution:

1. The illegality of the partnership business.

2. The death of a partner. The partnership in the *Mahan v. Mahan* case, which appears later in the chapter, was dissolved in this way.

3. The bankruptcy of a partner. The partner must be *adjudicated a bankrupt.* Mere insolvency does not effect a dissolution. Bankruptcy causes dissolution because the bankrupt partner will probably not be able to undertake his share of partnership losses.

Finally, Section 32 of the UPA permits a court to *order* a dissolution in several situations. Four of these causes of *judicial dissolutions* are nonwrongful:

1. The *adjudicated* insanity of a partner.

2. The inability of a partner to perform the partnership contract. For example, a two-man partnership that remodels kitchens is dissolved when one of the partners becomes paralyzed in an automobile accident.

3. The inability of the partnership to conduct business except at a loss. This recognizes the partnership's profit-making objective. Often, a partnership is not making a profit because of irreconcilable differences among the partners that prevent the business from being conducted beneficially. The court in *Saballus v. Timke,* which follows, ordered dissolution on this ground.

4. At the request of a purchaser of a partnership interest in a partnership at will. This allows the creditor to whom a partner has assigned his partnership interest to obtain a dissolution and then to seek a winding up that will allow him to be paid his claim against the partner.

[1] Assignment of partnership interests and charging orders against partnership interests are covered in Chapter 18.

**Consequences of Nonwrongful Dissolution.** If a dissolution is nonwrongful, then *each* partner, including the dissolving partner, has three rights: (1) to demand that the business of the partnership be wound up, (2) to participate in the winding-up process (except for a bankrupt partner), and (3) to share in whatever goodwill value the business has. In addition, a partner who has dissolved a partnership nonwrongfully is *not* liable to her partners for any damages that may be caused by the dissolution.

The right to *demand a winding up* is the most important of the three rights. It permits other partners to escape from a partnership that may have changed drastically because one partner is no longer associated with it. This escape is accomplished by seeking a winding up, a liquidation of the assets of the partnership.

**Right to Continue.** The partnership need not be liquidated after a nonwrongful dissolution. The partners may *unanimously* agree to continue the business. If any one partner demands winding up, however, the partnership assets must be liquidated.

**Wrongful Dissolution.** Under UPA Section 31(2), a partner has the power to dissolve a partnership at any time. If a dissolution is *contrary to the partnership agreement,* it is wrongful. For example, a partner may retire before the end of the 15-year term of a partnership or before the partnership accomplishes its stated objective of inventing a process to make rubber from banana peels.

In addition, some judicial dissolutions may be wrongful. Under UPA Section 32, a court may order a dissolution when: (1) a partner's conduct prejudicially affects the business, or (2) a partner willfully and persistently breaches the partnership agreement or her fiduciary duties. For example, a partner may continually insult customers, causing a loss of business; or a partner may persistently and substantially use partnership property for his own benefit; or three partners may refuse to allow a fourth partner to enter the partnership's place of business. In all of these situations, the *aggrieved* partners could seek judicial dissolution. As to the aggrieved partners, the dissolution would be *nonwrongful.* As to the wrongdoing partners, the dissolution would be *wrongful.*[2] In *Saballus v. Timke,* the court found breaches of fiduciary duties by both partners and granted a dissolution. It was unnecessary in that case to determine whether the dissolution was wrongful, since both partners were wrongdoers.

**Consequences of Wrongful Dissolution.** The partner who wrongfully dissolves a partnership (1) has no right to demand that the business be wound up, (2) has no right to participate in the winding up if the business is wound up, (3) has no right to have the goodwill of the business taken into account in valuing his interest, and (4) is liable for damages for breach of the partnership agreement. Such damages would include the cost of seeking judicial dissolution, the expense of finding a substitute partner, and the legal fees for drafting new partnership agreements.

**Right to Continue.** In the event of a wrongful dissolution, UPA Section 38(2) gives the innocent partners the right to continue the business themselves or with new partners. This right prevents a wrongdoing partner from forcing a liquidation of the partnership.

In addition, each of the innocent partners has all of the rights, discussed above, that are possessed by partners when there is a nonwrongful dissolution. This means that if there is a wrongful dissolution, any innocent partner may force a winding up. This is not normally the case, however. Usually, innocent partners choose to continue the business.

**Acts Not Causing Dissolution.** As you learned in Chapter 18, a partner's assignment of his partnership interest does not dissolve a partnership, and neither does a creditor obtaining a charging order. In *Wester & Co. v. Nestle,* an assignment of a partnership interest caused no dissolution, but the assigning partner's simultaneous withdrawal from the partnership did dissolve the partnership.

In addition, there are many acts that may appear to cause dissolution, but in fact do not, including the following:

1. *Addition* of a partner. Since no one *disassociates* from the partnership when a partner is added, there is no dissolution. Also, the addition of a partner must be by unanimous partner agreement or in accordance with the partnership agreement.

2. *Disagreement among the partners.* Disagreements, even irreconcilable differences, are expectable, but they are not grounds for dissolution. If the disagreements threaten partnership assets or profitability, then a court may order dissolution, as was the case in *Saballus v. Timke.*

3. *Death of a partner,* if the partnership agreement states that death shall not cause a dissolution. Although death clearly disassociates a partner from the carrying on of the business, the statutes or judicial decisions of several states permit the partners to vary the definition of dissolution by their agreement. Even those states that do not permit partners to exclude death from the definition of dissolution permit the partners to eliminate the

[2] J. Crane and A. Bromberg, *Law of Partnership* §§ 75(d) and 78(a) (1968).

right to demand a winding up after the death of a partner. Hence, in any state, the partners can by agreement avoid the harmful effects of a winding up either by redefining dissolution or by eliminating the right to demand winding up.

**Additional Effects of Dissolution.** There are several other effects of dissolution besides those discussed above. As you will see in the next section, dissolution terminates most of the express and implied authority of partners. In addition, if dissolution is by the death of a partner, title to all of the partnership property vests in the surviving partner or partners. This is the **right of survivorship** discussed in Chapter 18. Also, as a later section of this chapter indicates, a few fiduciary duties terminate upon dissolution.

As stated earlier, however, a dissolution does *not* terminate the partnership. It continues until the business is wound up. Most importantly, dissolution does not release the partnership or the partners from tort or contract liability.

**Joint Ventures and Mining Partnerships.** Essentially, the partnership rules of dissolution apply to joint ventures. It is more likely in a joint venture than in a partnership that a member's death will either *not dissolve* the joint venture or *not permit a demand to wind up,* since courts find an implied agreement among joint venturers that the limited objective of the joint venture will be carried out.

Mining partnerships are more difficult to dissolve than general partnerships, due to the free transferability of mining partnership interests. The death or bankruptcy of a mining partner will not effect a dissolution. In addition, a mining partner may sell his interest to another person and disassociate himself from the carrying on of the mining partnership's business without causing a dissolution. The other rules of partnership dissolution apply to mining partnerships.

## Saballus v. Timke

**460 N.E.2d 755 (Ill. Ct. App. 1983)**

Ronald Saballus and Vernon Timke formed a partnership to acquire and improve Midwest Plaza North, a three-story office building in Oak Brook, Illinois. Midwest Plaza North was one of two parcels of real estate owned by Saballus. Saballus transferred these two parcels to the partnership at what he represented to be his cost, $288,000. In fact, that was his purchase cost for four parcels of real estate, two of which he did not transfer to the partnership.

The partners executed a partnership agreement that obligated each partner to undertake 50 percent of the expense of operating the business. The agreement provided that if a partner failed to perform his obligations under the agreement, the other partner could terminate the interest of the breaching partner without terminating the business. The nonbreaching partner would be obligated to pay the breaching partner the value of his partnership interest as determined by a formula in the partnership agreement. Saballus managed the partnership, and Timke provided the necessary capital. Timke maintained the financial record books of the partnership.

To finance the improvement of Midwest Plaza North, the partnership applied for a

$1,825,000 loan. The lender required the partnership to deposit $275,000 with it as security for the loan. Since this amount exceeded the partnership's assets, it was necessary for each partner to contribute additional money to the partnership. It was not clear, however, by what amount the security deposit exceeded the assets of the partnership. Saballus attempted to find out from Timke what assets the partnership had, but Timke was evasive and refused to allow Saballus to see the partnership's books. Saballus then refused to pay his share of the $275,000 security deposit, so Timke deposited all of that amount with the lender. Within two months, Saballus withdrew $187,000 of the $275,000 and deposited it in a bank account over which he had exclusive control. From this account, Saballus paid his wife a $14,800 real estate commission, and he paid $25,195 to his own corporation for services rendered by it to the partnership.

Timke notified Saballus that he was terminating Saballus' partnership interest because Saballus had failed to pay his share of the security deposit. Saballus then sued Timke for an accounting and a dissolution. Timke counterclaimed, asking the court to order Saballus to surrender his partnership interest to Timke.

The trial court held that Saballus had breached the partnership agreement, and it ordered his partnership interest terminated in accordance with the partnership agreement. Timke was ordered to pay Saballus $53,682.66, the value of Saballus' partnership interest, less the payment to Saballus' wife and a payment to Saballus' corporation after his partnership interest was terminated by Timke. Both partners were displeased with the decision, and both appealed.

**Lorenz, Justice.** We first consider Timke's argument that we should hold, as a matter of law, that the following actions by Saballus constituted a repudiation of the partnership agreement and termination of his interest: (1) Saballus' failure to contribute his pro rata share for the loan security; (2) Saballus' establishment of a partnership bank account under his sole control with $187,000 in deposits into and withdrawals from the account without Timke's consent; (3) the payment of $14,800 to Saballus' wife as a real estate commission; and (4) Saballus' failure to disclose to Timke that the purchase cost of $288,000 originally included two parcels of land in addition to those conveyed to the partnership.

While Timke persistently argues on appeal that Saballus breached their contractual agreement by failing to provide a pro rata share of the security requirement and must suffer the consequences of having his 50 percent partnership interest terminated, the circumstances surrounding the loan indicate that Timke himself breached his fiduciary duty by failing to render information on demand and to render an accounting to his partner. Timke, as financial captain of the venture, retained possession and control of the partnership books. As a general rule, one of the ordinary duties of partners is to keep true and correct books showing the firm accounts, such books being at all times open to inspection by all members of the firm. Partners also must render on demand true and full information of all things affecting the partnership to any partner.

Under the UPA Section 22, any partner has the right to a formal accounting as to partnership affairs if he is wrongfully excluded from the partnership business or possession of its property by his co-partners, or *"whenever other circumstances render it just and reasonable."* Thus, a wrongful exclusion, or "freeze-out," of one partner by a co-partner from participation in the conduct of the business or from the management of the partnership business, will be grounds for judicial dissolution. In *Heyman v. Heyman* (1904), our supreme court stated that among the acts and circumstances, which had been deemed sufficient to justify a decree of dissolution, are the following: "Excluding a partner from any voice in the management of the business, and disregard of his advice and wishes; irreconcilable differences and personal ill-will between the partners, rendering co-operation in the business impossible; refusal to keep accounts open to the co-partners, to account at reasonable times, and to pay over profits as agreed."

It is apparent that certain partnership funds entrusted to Timke were available as security for the loan, but were not utilized as security for the loan. Also Saballus, who repeatedly requested access to the partnership books kept by Timke in order to determine the accuracy or source of these figures on partnership funds available to be used as security for the loan, was both "put-off" and denied access to the partnership books by Timke prior to the loan closing.

It is also clear that Saballus did not disclose to Timke that four lots were included in the original purchase price of $288,000, and although he did pay partnership obligations out of the bank account, Saballus did not obtain Timke's consent in order to establish the account.

Thus, although it would be difficult to decide which of the parties is most in the wrong, we believe that equity demands a decree of dissolution in this case, where, as here, the relations existing between the partners render it impracticable for them to conduct business beneficially. We determine that a dissolution, and not a termination of Saballus' partnership interest, is proper.

Judgment reversed in favor of Saballus. Remanded to the trial court.

## WINDING UP THE PARTNERSHIP BUSINESS

**The Process.** If a partnership is to be terminated, the next step after the dissolution is the **winding up** of the partnership's affairs. This involves the orderly liquidation—or sale—of the assets of the business. Liquidation may be accomplished asset by asset; that is, each asset may be sold separately. It may also be accomplished by a sale of the business as a whole, including all tangible assets and goodwill. Or it may be accomplished by a means somewhere between these two extremes. The partnership continues to exist until the liquidation has been completed and the proceeds have been distributed to creditors and partners.

**Distributions in Kind.** Winding up does not always require the sale of the assets or the business. If the partnership has valuable assets, the partners may wish to receive the assets rather than the proceeds from their sale. Such *distributions in kind* are rarely permitted. They are allowed if there are no creditors' claims against the partnership and if the in-kind distribution is fair to the partners; that is, the value of the assets can be ascertained, and the assets can be distributed in a manner that satisfies the claims of each partner.

**Fiduciary Duties.** In winding up the partnership, the partners continue as fiduciaries to each other, especially in negotiating sales or making distributions of partnership assets to members of the partnership. Nevertheless, there is a termination of the fiduciary duties unrelated to winding up. For example, a partner who is not winding up the business is free to compete with his partnership during winding up.

**Who May Demand Winding Up?** A partner who has not wrongfully dissolved the partnership, or his legal representative, may demand winding up. Thus, if a partnership has been dissolved nonwrongfully, any partner, even the dissolving partner, may demand winding up. If the partnership has been wrongfully dissolved, only the innocent partners may demand winding up.

**Who May Wind Up?** Not every partner has the right to perform the actual liquidation of the partnership's assets. Under UPA Section 37, any *surviving, nonbankrupt* partner who has not wrongfully dissolved the partnership may wind up. A partner who wrongfully dissolved the partnership has no right to wind up the business. If a dissolution is due to the death or bankruptcy of a partner, the surviving partners and the nonbankrupt partners have the right to wind up the business.

If the dissolution is by court decree, usually no partner will wind up. Instead, a *receiver* is appointed by the court to wind up the business. Under Section 37, *any* partner may ask the court to wind up the partnership's affairs.

**Compensation during Winding Up.** Normal compensation rules continue during winding up. Partners share profits and losses equally, absent an agreement to the contrary, as is illustrated in *Mahan v. Mahan,* which appears later in this chapter. Ordinarily, the compensation of a winding-up partner is his share of the profits. Nevertheless, if the partners agree to give special compensation to the winding-up partner, he is entitled to the agreed-upon compensation. In addition, when the winding-up partner provides *extraordinary* services or is the sole survivor after dissolution by death, he is entitled to the reasonable value of his winding-up services.

**Partner's Authority in Winding Up.** Dissolution terminates most of the express and implied authority of the partners. A winding-up partner usually will not have the authority to conduct the ordinary business of the partnership. The purpose of winding up is liquidation, *not continuation* of the business. Even though most express and implied authority terminates upon dissolution, apparent authority will remain if proper notice of the dissolution is not given to creditors and other persons.

**Express and Implied Authority.** During winding up, a partner has the implied authority to do those acts that are *reasonably necessary to the winding up* of the partnership affairs; that is, he has the power to bind the partnership in any transaction necessary to the liquidation of the assets. He may collect money due, sell partnership property, prepare assets for sale, sue to enforce partnership rights, and do whatever else is appropriate under the circumstances. He may maintain and preserve assets or enhance them for sale, for example, by painting a building or by paying a debt to prevent foreclosure on partnership land. In *Paciaroni v. Crane,* which follows, the winding-up partners were permitted to continue to race a horse, because the horse's value would be enhanced by racing.

In addition, a partner may have the express authority that the partners agree he may exercise during winding up. For example, the partners may agree that the winding-up partner may continue to operate the business as before dissolution.

Although these rules generally describe the authority of a partner during winding up, some transactions are affected by special rules for determining the existence of implied authority. These transactions are completing executory contracts and borrowing money.

**Completing Executory Contracts.** Since partnerships remain liable on contracts made before dissolution, a partner has the implied authority *to complete contracts made before dissolution.* A partner may not enter into *new* contracts unless the contracts aid the liquidation of the partnership's assets. For example, a partner may fulfill an existing contract to deliver coal. She may not make a new contract to deliver coal, unless doing so aids the liquidation of coal that the partnership owns or has contracted to purchase. The rationale for this rule is that since the partnership is liable on executory contracts before dissolution and remains liable for such contracts after dissolution, it will be liable for breach of contract if it fails to perform them. Hence, performance of a contract already begun but not finished serves to preserve partnership assets that would otherwise be lost in a lawsuit for breach of contract.

**Borrowing Money.** As a general rule, a partner who is winding up a partnership business has no implied authority to borrow money in the name of the partnership. Nevertheless, if a partner can preserve the assets of the partnership or enhance them for sale by borrowing money and using it to pay partnership obligations, he has implied authority to engage in *new* borrowing and to issue the necessary negotiable instruments. For example, a partnership will have a valuable machine repossessed and sold far below its value at a foreclosure sale unless it can refinance a loan. A partner may borrow the money needed to refinance the loan, thereby preserving the asset.

**Apparent Authority.** If notice is not given of the dissolution, persons who are aware of the partnership's existence may reasonably believe that each partner has the authority to conduct the business in the usual way. Such *apparent* authority will make the partnership liable for contracts for which it may not wish to be liable.

Section 35 of the UPA specifies certain steps that the partnership may take to cut off this apparent authority. *Prior creditors* of the partnership must have knowledge or notice of the dissolution. This can be a personal notification, such as by telephone, or a written notice delivered to the creditor's residence or place of business. For third persons who were *not creditors* but had merely done business with the partnership *without extending credit* or were merely *aware of the existence* of the partnership, notice published in newspapers of general circulation in the places where the partnership did business will terminate apparent authority. *No notice* need be given to persons who were previously unaware of the partnership's existence.

**Disputes among Winding-Up Partners.** If more than one partner has the right to wind up the partnership, the partners may disagree concerning what steps should be taken during winding up. For decisions in the ordinary course of winding up, the decision of *a majority* of the partners will control, unless the partnership agreement specifies otherwise. If the decision is an extraordinary one, such as continuing the business for an extended period of time, *unanimous* partner approval is required. In *Paciaroni v. Crane,* the court found that the decision concerning who should train and race a horse during winding up was not an ordinary decision that could be made by less than all the partners.

## Paciaroni v. Crane

### 408 A.2d 946 (Del. Ct. Ch. 1979)

Black Ace, a harness racehorse of exceptional speed, was the fourth best pacer in the United States in 1979. He was owned by a partnership of Richard Paciaroni, James Cassidy, and James Crane. Paciaroni owned 50 percent of the partnership; Cassidy, 25 percent; and Crane, 25 percent. The partnership had no written agreement and had no term specified for its duration. Crane, a professional trainer, was in charge of the daily supervision of Black Ace, including the selection of equipment, rigging, and training. It was understood that all of the partners would be consulted on the races in which Black Ace would be entered, the selection of drivers, and other major decisions; however, the recommendations of Crane were always followed by the other partners because of his superior knowledge of harness racing.

In 1978, as a two-year-old, Black Ace won three of his nine starts. In 1979, he raced primarily in three-year-old stake races, and he had won $96,969 through mid-August. Seven other races remained in 1979, including the prestigious Little Brown Jug in Delaware, Ohio, and the Messenger at Roosevelt Raceway on Long Island, New York. The purse money for these races was $600,000.

A disagreement among the partners arose when Black Ace developed a ringbone condition and Crane failed to follow the advice of a veterinarian selected by Paciaroni and Cassidy and instead followed the advice of another veterinarian. Black Ace became uncontrollable by his driver, and in a subsequent race he fell and failed to finish the race. Soon thereafter, Paciaroni and Cassidy sent a telegram to Crane dissolving the partnership and directing him to deliver Black Ace to another trainer whom they had selected. Crane refused to relinquish control of Black Ace, so Paciaroni and Cassidy sued him in August 1979, asking the court to appoint a receiver who would race Black Ace in the remaining 1979 stake races and then sell the horse. Crane objected to allowing anyone other than himself to race the horse. Before the trial court issued the following decision, Black Ace had raced in three additional races and won $40,000.

**Brown, Vice Chancellor.** All three partners agree that the horse must be sold in order to wind up partnership affairs. The only dispute is as to when he must be sold and what is to be done with him in the meantime.

Paciaroni and Cassidy take the position that since the partnership relation continues until the time of termination and distribution of assets, then as a consequence the will of the majority of the partnership interests should control the manner of winding up. From this they rely on the following provisions of the Uniform Partnership Act, Section 18:

> (e) All partners have equal rights in the management and conduct of the partnership business.
>
> (h) Any difference arising as to ordinary matters connected with the partnership business may be decided by a majority of the partners; but no act in contravention of any agreement between the partners may be done rightfully without the consent of all the partners.

In particular, they rely on the first portion of Section 18(h) as giving them, as the majority, the right to have the horse finish the stakes racing season under the guidance of their new trainer and over the objection of Crane.

It is the latter portion of Section 18(h) on which Crane relies. It is his argument that there is a prevailing custom in the harness racing business that a trainer who also owns an interest in a horse, even though it be less than a majority interest, has the right to train and control the racing of the horse so long as his ownership interest continues. He says that this custom forms a part of the oral agreement between him, Paciaroni, and Cassidy, and that consequently any attempt by the latter to take charge of the horse by majority vote would be in contravention of the partnership agreement. In other words, he says that under the latter portion of Section 18(h), he cannot be removed as trainer and the horse given to another trainer without the consent of all three partners—and Crane does not give his consent.

To prove his point Crane has offered the testimony of several trainers and persons close to the harness racing business to establish that such a custom does exist. Included was the testimony of Herve Filion, the leading trainer-driver in total races won and purse winnings for the past eight years.

However, when the basis for the testimony offered by all of these witnesses is examined closely, it reveals a common flaw. All state, in one form or another, that such an industry custom exists because they can recall of no situation where the majority owners have taken a horse away from a trainer–minority owner and given it to another trainer without the trainer-owner's consent. While this may be completely accurate as a matter of fact, it does not necessarily establish a custom or usage that the majority owners could not make such a change over the trainer-owners's objection should they want to do so. I find on the evidence that Crane has not established an industry custom to the extent that it would permit the Court to make it a part of the partnership agreement between the parties.

I turn to the argument of Paciaroni and Cassidy that they have a similar right under Section 18(h) by virtue of constituting the majority interests. This argument I also reject. I do so because Section 18(h) permits a majority vote to decide any "difference arising as to ordinary matters connected with the partnership business." Under the exceptional circumstances of this case, I do not view the difference between the parties to be one which has arisen in the ordinary course of partnership business. Quite the contrary. The partnership is dissolved. Crane is fearful that if the horse is allowed to continue racing with the changes made by the new trainer as authorized by Paciaroni and Cassidy, he may well suffer injury and decline from his present value before he can be sold, thus jeopardizing Crane's one-fourth interest. Crane is also fearful that his professional reputation will suffer if it becomes general knowledge that the horse he has developed has been taken from him by legal process and is being raced by another. Paciaroni and Cassidy, on the other hand, say that the horse should be raced because his value may well be increased thereby. They say that they have the once-in-a-lifetime opportunity to be the owners of a champion caliber racehorse. They say that they also have the right to seek to obtain the highest possible price for him when he is sold, something that can only be done if he finishes out his stake race season. This difference between the partners is hardly one which has arisen in the ordinary course of partnership business. Accordingly, I conclude that Paciaroni and Cassidy have no statutory right to wind up affairs simply because they can outvote Crane.

In my view, it throws matters into Section 37. That statute reads as follows:

> Unless otherwise agreed the partners who have not wrongfully dissolved the partnership or the legal representative of the last surviving partner, not bankrupt, has the right to wind up the partnership affairs; provided, however, that any partner, his legal representative or his assignee, *upon cause shown, may obtain winding up by the court.* (Emphasis added)

Since I have found that the partnership was a partnership at will, it follows that the partnership was not wrongfully dissolved. I conclude that both sides to this controversy have sought a winding up of partnership affairs by the Court.

It is generally accepted that once dissolution occurs, the partnership continues only to the extent necessary to close out affairs and complete transactions begun but not then finished. It is not generally contemplated that new business will be generated or that new contractual commitments will be made. This, in principle, would work against permitting Black Ace to participate in the remaining few races for which he is eligible.

However, in Delaware, there have been exceptions to this. Where, because of the nature of the partnership business, a better price upon final liquidation is likely to be obtained by the temporary continuation of the business, it is permissible, during the winding up process, to have the business continue to the degree necessary to preserve or enhance its value upon liquidation, provided that such continuation is done in good faith with the intent to bring affairs to a conclusion as soon as reasonably possible. And one way to accomplish this is through an application to the Court for a winding up under UPA Section 37, which carries with it the power of the Court to appoint a receiver for that purpose.

The business purpose of the partnership was to own and race Black Ace for profit. The horse was bred to race. He has the ability to be competitive with the top pacers in the country. He is currently "racing fit" according to the evidence. He has at best only seven more races to go over a period of the next six weeks, after which time there are established horse sales at which he can be disposed of to the highest bidder. The purse money for these remaining stake races is substantial. The fact that he could possibly sustain a disabling injury during this six-week period appears to be no greater than it was when the season commenced. Admittedly, an injury could occur at any time. But this is a fact of racing life which all owners and trainers are forced to accept. And the remaining stake races are races in which all three partners originally intended that he would compete, if able.

The alternative to racing on through the remaining stakes would be to turn Black Ace out to pasture until he can be placed in a suitable sale. The balance of his three-year-old racing season would be lost and his true potential might never be realized while he is owned by the partnership. While this might go to preserve whatever present value he now has, it would not seem to be the most plausible thing to do when the reason for which the horse exists is measured against the unique opportunities remaining available to him.

Under these circumstances, I conclude that the winding up of the partnership affairs should include the right to race Black Ace in some or all of the remaining 1979 stake races for which he is now eligible. The final question, then, is who shall be in charge of racing him.

On this point, I rule in favor of Paciaroni and Cassidy. They may, on behalf of the partnership, continue to race the horse through their new trainer, subject, however, to the conditions hereafter set forth. In reaching this decision, I must confess that I have a great deal of sympathy for James Crane. Nonetheless, when such an impasse occurs, someone must come up short regardless of the good intentions that brought it about in the first place. On the facts of this case, it must be Crane. At the same time, he does have a monetary interest in the partnership assets which must be protected if Paciaroni and Cassidy are to be permitted to test the whims of providence in the name of the partnership during the next six weeks. Accordingly, I make the following ruling.

(1) Paciaroni and Cassidy shall first post security in the sum of $100,000 so as to secure to Crane his share of the value of Black Ace. It is simply to protect Crane against the possibility that during the winding up process that much of his present interest in the value of Black Ace may be lost or diminished by destruction or injury to the horse prior to final liquidation as a result of continuing to race him.

(2) If Paciaroni and Cassidy are unable or unwilling to meet this condition, then they shall forego the right to act as liquidating partners. In that event, each party, within seven days, shall submit to the Court the names of two persons who they feel qualified, and who they know to be willing, to act as receiver for the winding up of partnership affairs, including the supervision and control of the horse for the remainder of this racing season. I shall then consider designating one such person as receiver.

(3) In the event that no suitable person can be found to act as receiver, or in the event that the Court should deem it unwise to appoint any person from the names so submitted, then the Court reserves the power to terminate any further racing by Black Ace and to require that he simply be maintained and cared for until such time as he can be sold as a part of the final liquidation of the partnership.

Judgment for Paciaroni and Crane.

## WHEN THE BUSINESS IS CONTINUED

Cessation of business need not follow dissolution of a partnership. The remaining partners could purchase the business during winding up; someone else could purchase the business; or the partnership agreement could provide that there will be no winding up and that the business may be carried on by the remaining partners. And as stated earlier, partners who have not wrongfully dissolved the partnership may agree to continue the partnership and its business.

When there is no winding up and the business is continued, the claims of creditors are affected, since old partners are no longer with the business and new partners may enter the business. Before studying the rules for liability of the various partners to creditors, you should first consider the advantages of continuing the partnership business.

**Advantages of Continuing.** When a partner dies, desires to retire, or is forced to withdraw from a partnership, all of the parties involved usually find it advantageous to continue the partnership and its business rather than to seek a winding up. This choice is made because a partnership's going-concern value is normally greater than its liquidated value. The UPA recognizes the greater going-concern value of the partnership, giving innocent partners the right to continue the partnership after a wrongful dissolution.

It is not always sufficient for partners to rely on this right to continue the business, since the exercise of this right requires the unanimous agreement of the partners who have not wrongfully dissolved the partnership. Thus, one partner's insistence on seeking a winding up would be sufficient to destroy a profitable business. Therefore, it is important for the partners to provide that certain events will not dissolve the partnership or that certain types of dissolution will give no partner the right to demand a winding up.

Such an agreement is especially necessary for large partnerships, some of which may have more than 100 partners. In the absence of such an agreement, the necessity of going through a winding up whenever a partner dies or retires would make such partnerships completely impracticable.

**Successor's Liability for Prior Obligations.** Under Section 41 of the UPA, when the business of a partnership is continued after dissolution, creditors of the old partnership are creditors of the person or partnership continuing the business, giving these creditors equal status with the other creditors of such person or partnership. In addition, the original partners remain liable for obligations incurred prior to dissolution unless there is agreement with the creditors to the contrary. Thus, for example, partners may not escape liability by forming a new partnership or a corporation to carry on the old business of the partnership unless there is a *novation.* Novation is discussed below.

**Outgoing Partner's Liability for Prior Obligations.** Under UPA Section 36(1), outgoing partners remain liable to their former partners and to partnership creditors for partnership losses and liabilities. UPA Section 41(8) further protects creditors of the original partnership by giving them priority over personal creditors of a retired or deceased partner with respect to the consideration due or paid to her for the value of her partnership interest.

Usually, when the business is being continued, the continuing or new partners agree expressly to relieve the outgoing partner from liability for the obligations of the dissolved partnership. Such an agreement may also be implied, as when the assets are retained in the continuing business.

Nevertheless, even an express agreement to hold the outgoing partner harmless is not binding on a creditor unless the creditor joins in the agreement and thereby creates a *novation.* A novation may be express, or it may be *implied* pursuant to UPA Section 36(2) by such actions as a creditor's knowledge of a partner's withdrawal and his continued extension of credit to the partnership. A creditor's acceptance of a negotiable instrument in full settlement of a claim has also been held to be an implied novation; however, a creditor's mere receipt of partial payment from a partnership does not release the outgoing partner.

In addition, under Section 36(3) a *material modification* of an obligation will release an outgoing partner from that obligation, when the creditor has knowledge that the continuing partners have released the outgoing partner from liability. In *Wester & Co. v. Nestle,* which follows, the court found both an implied novation and a material alteration. Consequently, the court relieved an outgoing partner from liability to a landlord.

If former partners release an outgoing partner from liability but there is no novation, the outgoing partner may be made to pay a partnership creditor. However, the outgoing partner may recover the amount paid from his former partners.

**Outgoing Partner's Liability for Obligations Incurred after Dissolution.** Ordinarily, an outgoing partner has no liability on partnership obligations incurred after he leaves the partnership, because he no longer controls the partnership or shares as a co-owner in its profits. Nevertheless, outgoing partners may be liable for obligations incurred by a person or partnership continuing the business after their departure, under the theory of *partnership by estoppel.*[3] There is no such liability to creditors who are aware of the change in partners. Also, the risk of estoppel liability can be eliminated by giving the notice prescribed by Section 35 of the UPA.

---

[3] Partnership by estoppel is discussed in Chapter 18.

Section 35 requires actual—or personal—notice to those who extended credit to the partnership prior to dissolution. Such notice may be either oral or written and must be actually delivered. Constructive notice—notice published several times in a newspaper of general circulation—is sufficient for those who knew of the partnership but were not prior creditors. No notice need be given to persons who were not previously aware of the partnership's existence or who knew of the dissolution.

**Liability of Incoming Partners.** Pursuant to UPA Sections 17 and 41(7), a person joining an existing partnership becomes liable for all *prior* obligations of the partnership as if she had been a partner when the obligations were incurred; however, her liability is limited to the partnership's assets. In effect, this limits her liability for past obligations to her capital contribution to the partnership. For partnership obligations incurred *after* she becomes a partner, she is fully liable.

**Rights of Outgoing Partners.** An outgoing partner is entitled to receive the value of his partnership interest. He becomes a creditor of the new partnership for the value of his partnership interest, but his claim is subordinate to the claims of other creditors.

**Valuation of the Outgoing Partner's Interest.** The value of an outgoing partner's interest in the partnership is determined at the time of the dissolution. Often, the partnership agreement will state a method for calculating the value of a partnership interest. Usually, courts will accept such an agreed-upon valuation method. If, however, the agreed-upon method results in an inequitable valuation, such as paying a partner $\frac{1}{50}$th of the value of her interest, the partners' agreement will be disregarded. This point was made in *Mahan v. Mahan,* which follows the next section.

In the absence of a contrary agreement, if dissolution results from death or retirement, UPA Section 42 permits the outgoing partner to choose between two valuation methods: (1) taking the value of his partnership interest at the time of dissolution plus interest or (2) taking the value of his partnership interest at the time of dissolution plus a share of subsequent profits based on the proportion of that value to the total value of the partnership at the time of dissolution. The election need not be made until there is an accounting. This option provides some incentive for the continuing partners to settle with an outgoing partner promptly to avoid winding up. The outgoing partner in *Smith v. Kennebeck,* which follows, had this choice.

If there is no agreement and dissolution does not result from death or retirement (as with dissolutions caused by bankruptcy or by willful, persistent breaches of the partnership agreement), the partner will receive the value of her interest at the time of dissolution.

**Valuing Goodwill.** When a partnership business is continued after dissolution, it is frequently difficult to determine the value of the partnership, especially the goodwill that is transferred to the continuing partners. Consequently, the value of the outgoing partner's interest in the dissolved partnership is difficult to determine. Goodwill is the well-founded expectation of continued public patronage of a business. Part of goodwill represents the difference between the going-concern value of a business and the liquidation value of its assets.

In service partnerships, the goodwill may be so closely tied to the individual partners that no goodwill remains with the business when valuable partners withdraw from the partnership. These difficulties and uncertainties make it advisable to include an agreement on valuing goodwill in the original articles of partnership. Too frequently, courts conclude that goodwill should be ignored unless there is such an agreement or unless goodwill appears in the partnership accounts.

**Valuation of Interest of Wrongfully Dissolving Partner.** A wrongfully dissolving partner must be paid the value of his partnership interest in cash by the continuing partners, or the partners must post a bond in order to have the privilege of continuing the business. In addition, they must indemnify him against all present and future partnership liabilities. However, as you learned earlier, under UPA Section 38(2)(c)(II), goodwill is excluded from the valuation of the partnership interest of a partner who has wrongfully caused dissolution, and the valuation of that interest is further reduced by the damages that he has caused his partners due to his dissolution.

## Wester & Co. v. Nestle

**669 P.2d 1046 (Colo. Ct. App. 1983)**

Junior Nestle and Eric Ellis were the owners of Red Rocks Meat and Deli, a partnership. They had no partnership agreement and no specified term for the partnership. They operated the partnership in a building that they leased from Wester & Co. In October 1978, Nestle left the business. John Herline purchased Nestle's partnership interest, including Nestle's entire interest in partnership equipment, leases, and other assets. In return, a new partnership of Ellis and Herline agreed to assume all the liabilities of the former partnership and to release Nestle from liability.

Soon after, Herline left the partnership, and Ellis operated the business as a sole proprietorship. In January 1980, Wester & Co. and Ellis modified the original lease to include adjacent space and to increase the rent. In May 1980, Ellis failed to pay the rent. Wester & Co. sued Nestle for the rent.

At the trial, Ellis testified that the assignment and release agreement had been mailed to Wester & Co. in October 1978, thereby giving notice that Nestle was no longer liable on the lease; that he introduced Herline to Wester & Co. as his new partner; that Wester & Co. did not object to a change in partners or request that Nestle remain liable; and that when the lease was modified, it was clear to Wester & Co. that Ellis was then operating as a sole proprietor. As supporting evidence, Nestle submitted the affidavit of the president of Wester & Co., in which he acknowledged being told when the lease was modified that Nestle was no longer a partner.

Wester & Co. argued that the partnership between Ellis and Nestle had not been dissolved by Nestle's sale or assignment of his partnership interest to Herline, so that Nestle was liable as a current partner. In addition, Wester & Co. denied receiving notice prior to January 1980 that Nestle had withdrawn from the partnership, and it maintained that it had not agreed to look to the remaining partners and the new partnership to satisfy its debts.

The court found that there had been a dissolution in October 1978 and that due to Wester & Co.'s knowledge of the situation and the parties' course of dealings, it had consented to Nestle's discharge from liability. The court also concluded that the modified lease materially altered Nestle's liability on the underlying lease, thereby discharging Nestle from liability. Wester & Co. appealed.

**STEINBERG, JUDGE.** Wester & Co.'s reliance on UPA Section 27 is misplaced. That section states that a:

> conveyance by a partner of his interest in the partnership does not of itself dissolve the partnership, nor, as against the other partners in the absence of agreement, entitle the assignee . . . to interfere in the management or administration of the partnership business or affairs . . . but it merely entitles the assignee to receive in accordance with his contract the profits to which the assigning partner would otherwise be entitled.

When a partner assigns his rights to profits to an assignee, but the remaining partners have not agreed to admit the assignee as a partner, this section assures that the assignee does not become a partner without the consent of the remaining partners. By distinguishing between assignees of a partnership interest and the admission into the partnership of new partners, Section 27 operates to allow conveyance of a right to receive profits without giving the assignee an interest in the firm's assets. Hence, the provision that the partnership is not dissolved merely protects the original parties from an unwanted partner or from a finding of partnership from the fact of the assignee's receipt of a share of the profits.

In contrast, Section 29, upon which Nestle relies, is consistent with the concept expressed in Section 31(1)(b), that dissolution is caused by "the express will of any partner when no definite term or particular undertaking is specified." Section 29 provides that dissolution of a partnership is the change in relation of the partners caused by any partner ceasing to be associated in the carrying on of the business. Thus, no party is compelled to continue as a partner when, by his express will, he chooses to withdraw.

By the plain meaning of Section 29, when one partner withdraws from the business, the partnership is dissolved as to that party, though the remaining partners may elect to continue operating as a partnership. We follow that construction and thus agree with the trial court that the partnership between Ellis and Nestle was dissolved in October 1978.

The dissolution of a partnership does not of itself discharge the existing liability of any partner, pursuant to UPA Section 36(1). Under Section 36(2), a partner is discharged from existing liability by an agreement to that effect between the withdrawing partner, the remaining partners, and the partnership creditor, and "such agreement may be inferred from the course of dealing between the creditor and the person or partnership continuing the business." Under Section 36(3), a material alteration in an existing liability will discharge from liability a partner whose obligations have been assumed.

The trial court found, on conflicting testimony, that the conditions for discharge from liability under both of these subsections existed, and such factual findings, supported by evidence in the record, may not be disturbed upon appeal.

Judgment for Nestle affirmed.

## Smith v. Kennebeck

**502 S.W.2d 290 (Mo. Sup. Ct. 1973)**

Charles Smith and his brother Thomas Smith entered into a partnership with Jack Kennebeck in October 1963. On November 10, 1964, Thomas Smith and Kennebeck informed Charles Smith by letter that they were dissolving the partnership and forming a corporation to operate the business. He was offered the same 25 percent share in the corporation that he had in the partnership. Charles Smith did not want to incorporate, so he refused the offer. The other two partners continued the business as partners, completing work in process for previous orders, until the corporation was incorporated on December 24. The assets of the partnership then passed to the corporation.

Charles Smith sued Thomas Smith and Jack Kennebeck, asking for an accounting and damages of $75,000. The trial court determined that Charles was entitled to $2,621.67, the value that his interest would have had if he had become an owner of the corporation. The court based its valuation on asset value computations by Bo-Tax Company, the accountants for the former partnership. Many of the Bo-Tax valuations were far below current asset value. Charles appealed on the grounds that the court should have considered the current value of the assets of the business.

**Hyde, Special Commissioner.** The Bo-Tax Co. computation does not appear to be a proper basis for determining Charles's interest. The Bo-Tax agent who made it was not a certified public accountant. It was reviewed by Ernst & Ernst, who did not examine the books of the partnership, and their report shows that the Bo-Tax accountant had not seen a copy of the partnership agreement which stated the value of Charles's capital interest as $5,000. Moreover, it states profits only through November 10, 1964, and does not consider profits on uncompleted work on contracts on hand at that time or all profits on completed contracts. The trial court apparently considered the Bo-Tax statement to be a "winding up" account as it found that Charles was only "entitled to the value of his share as computed on November 10, 1964." We cannot hold that was a valid winding up of the partnership and that Charles was only entitled to the amount shown by it. It is insufficient not only because it did not take into consideration the work on then existing contracts, but also because the individual defendants continued the business as partners until its incorporation and then had the corporation continue it without any other offers or effort to settle Charles's claim for his interest.

Since our view is that the evidence fails to show there ever was a valid winding up of the partnership, but instead shows a continuation of the business without Charles's consent, Charles's rights were as stated in Crane and Bromberg, *Law of Partnership* Section 86:

> The situation changes if the business is not wound up, but continued, whether with or without agreement. In either case, the noncontinuing partner (or his representative) has a first election between two basic alternatives, either of which can be enforced in an action for an accounting. He can force a liquidation, taking his part of the proceeds and thus sharing in profits and losses after dissolution. Alternatively, he can permit the business to continue (or accept the fact that it has continued) and claim as a creditor (though subordinate to outside creditors) the value of his interest at dissolution.

This gives him a participation in all values at dissolution, including asset appreciation and good will, and means he is unaffected by later changes in those values. If he takes the latter route, he has a second election to receive in addition either interest (presumably at the local legal rate) or profits from date of dissolution.

Judgment reversed in favor of Charles Smith and remanded for a redetermination of the value of his interest.

## DISTRIBUTION OF ASSETS

After the partnership's assets have been liquidated, the proceeds will be distributed to those persons who have claims against the partnership. Both creditors and partners will have claims. As you might expect, the claims of creditors must be satisfied before the claims of partners may be paid.

**Order of Distribution.** Section 40 of the UPA states the order of distribution of the assets of a partnership:

1. Those owing to creditors other than partners.
2. Those owing to partners other than for capital and profits.
3. Those owing to partners in respect of capital.
4. Those owing to partners in respect of profits.

As you can see, partners who are also creditors of the partnership are subordinated to other creditors. This is done to prevent partners from underfunding a partnership to the detriment of creditors. The subordination of partner-creditors also emphasizes that the partners are liable for all the partnership's liabilities. Note, however, that a partner who is also a creditor of the partnership is paid his claim as a creditor before any partner receives any return of his capital contribution. Thus, for example, a partner's loan to the partnership will be repaid before any partner has his capital returned. Under some circumstances, a partner may be allowed interest on such a loan. Interest is not payable, however, on the capital contributions of partners unless the partners unanimously agree to the contrary.

If the partnership has not suffered losses that impair its capital, few problems are presented in the distribution of its assets. Everyone having an interest in the partnership will be paid in full. If there is a disagreement as to the amount due to a claimant, the dispute will usually be resolved by an accounting ordered by the court.

**Distribution of Assets of Insolvent Partnership.** If the partnership has suffered losses, the order of distribution set out above will be followed, but problems will frequently be encountered. For example, partnership creditors and the creditors of individual partners may compete for partnership assets and the assets of individual partners, and the partnership losses must be allocated among partners. In adjusting the rights of partnership creditors and the creditors of individual partners, the rule that partnership creditors have first claim on partnership assets and that individual creditors have first claim on individual assets is usually followed. This is an example of **marshaling of assets.** Under Section 723(c) of the federal Bankruptcy Code, however, the trustee in bankruptcy of a partnership is entitled to share pro rata with unsecured creditors of a partner. To this extent, federal law preempts Section 40(h) of the UPA.[4]

**Example.** Suppose that Alden, Bass, and Casey form a partnership and that Alden contributes $25,000, Bass contributes $15,000, and Casey contributes $10,000. After operating for several years, the firm suffers losses and becomes insolvent. When the partnership is liquidated, its assets total $30,000 in cash. It owes $40,000 to partnership creditors. Therefore, the capital balance of the partnership is a negative $10,000. This results from partnership losses totaling $60,000 ($50,000 of capital already contributed and lost plus the $10,000 negative net worth). The situation could be represented by the following equation:

Loss = Ending owners' capital
 − Beginning owners' capital

($60,000) = ($10,000) − $50,000

In the absence of a provision in the partnership agreement concerning the distribution of profits and losses, they are distributed equally. Therefore, each partner would be liable for $20,000, or one third of the loss. Their shares of the loss reduce the partners' capital claims against partnership assets, as shown in the following table.

| | *Capital Contributed at Beginning* | *Share of Loss* | *Capital Claim at Liquidation* |
|---|---|---|---|
| Alden | $25,000 | − $20,000 = | $5,000 |
| Bass | 15,000 | − 20,000 = | (5,000) |
| Casey | 10,000 | − 20,000 = | (10,000) |
| Totals | $50,000 | − $60,000 = | (10,000) |

Suppose the personal assets and liabilities of the individual partners at the date of liquidation are as follows:

| | *Individual Assets* | *Individual Liabilities* |
|---|---|---|
| Alden | $75,000 | $5,000 |
| Bass | 10,000 | 2,000 |
| Casey | 2,000 | 6,000 |

Now we shall distribute partnership assets and pay the claims against the partnership. Following the order of distribution in UPA Section 40, the $30,000 in cash from the liquidation will be distributed pro rata to pay the nonpartner creditors of the partnership. Since the creditors are owed $40,000, the $30,000 payment leaves $10,000 of partnership debts to outsiders unpaid.

Before partnership creditors are paid from partners' individual assets, the claims of the individual partners' creditors must be paid from such assets. Alden's individual creditors will be paid in full, leaving a $70,000 balance in Alden's individual estate. The individual creditors of Bass will be paid in full, leaving an $8,000 balance in his individual estate. Casey is insolvent; his individual creditors will receive one third of their claims, since he has only $2,000 of individual assets to cover $6,000 of individual liabilities.

So far, partnership liabilities of $30,000 have been paid, leaving $10,000 unpaid, and individual liabilities have been satisfied except for those of Casey. Casey's creditors will not be able to collect anything more.

The remaining $10,000 of partnership liabilities must now be satisfied to the extent that *any* partner has assets sufficient to pay the claim. To undertake their shares of the partnership loss, Bass is legally liable to contribute $5,000 and Casey $10,000 to the partnership, the negative amounts in the "Capital Claim at Liquidation" column in the table above. This would permit completion of the payment of the partnership creditors ($10,000) and the return of Alden's capital to the extent that it exceeded his share of the partnership loss (the $5,000 figure in the

[4] Bankruptcy law is covered in Chapter 41.

"Capital Claim at Liquidation" column above).

However, Casey has no assets and can contribute nothing. Therefore, his share of the partnership loss in excess of his capital investment will be redistributed between the solvent partners. Bass has only $3,000 left in his estate after paying off his individual creditors ($2,000) and his remaining share ($5,000) of the partnership loss. Thus, Bass will be able to pay only $3,000 of Casey's loss and Alden must pay the remainder, $7,000.

Since Alden and Bass have paid part of Casey's share of the partnership loss, they will have claims against Casey that they may pursue in the future, unless he goes through bankruptcy. Casey owes Alden $7,000 and Bass $3,000.

Unpaid partnership creditors have a right to sue and collect from any solvent partner. Had they chosen to sue Alden and collect the entire amount from him, he would then have had to proceed against Bass if Bass did not come forward with the $3,000 of his personal assets available to pay the claims of creditors.

*Mahan v. Mahan,* which follows, is another example of the distribution of partnership assets.

**Termination.** After the assets of a partnership have been distributed, the partnership automatically terminates.

## Mahan v. Mahan

### 489 P.2d 1197 (Ariz. Sup. Ct. 1971)

Helen Mahan's deceased husband, Terrell Mahan, and his brother, Gordon Mahan, were partners in an agricultural and construction partnership. In 1964, the partnership traded one of the partnership properties for a home that Terrell and Helen later occupied. Accordingly, Terrell's capital account was reduced by $23,000, leaving a balance of $4,005.45, which was one eighth of the total partnership capital account of $31,308.06. The partnership became inactive soon thereafter, and it remained so until Terrell's death in 1966. In 1969, Helen Mahan sued Gordon for an accounting and a sale of the property of the partnership.

There was disagreement at the trial about the market value of the partnership assets, which were carried on the books as follows:

| | |
|---|---|
| Red Lake Ranch | $15,622.61* |
| Investment | 9,150.00† |
| Oil lease | 4,000.00‡ |
| Miscellaneous | 4,502,00§ |
| | $33,274.61 |

* Sold in 1961 for $284,200 but sale not completed; appraised for $43,868.44 in 1963; the $15,622.61 was a figure allowed by the IRS for tax purposes after the aborted sale.

† Represents 7,500 shares of Unita Finance Company, which Helen Mahan's and the partnership's accountant testified was worthless, and 180 shares of Arizona Livestock Production Credit Association, which the accountant testified was worth $5 per share, or $900.

‡ Valueless, according to the accountant.

§ Subject to extreme disagreement on several items.

Helen introduced evidence that these book values did not represent the current value of the assets. Nevertheless, the court accepted them. The court also held that the partners shared profits according to their capital contribution. The court then ordered Gordon to pay Helen one-eighth of the partnership assets of $33,274.61 or $4,159.29. Helen appealed.

**CAMERON, JUSTICE.** Helen contends that after payment of the partnership debts, she should share with Gordon on a 50-50 basis. We agree with Helen as long as it is understood that the capital account represents a debt of the partnership.

Upon liquidation, the rules of payment are governed by UPA Section 40, which decrees that the liabilities of the partnership shall rank in the following order of payment:

a. Those owing to creditors other than partners.
b. Those owing to partners other than for capital and profits.
c. Those owing to partners in respect of capital.
d. Those owing to partners in respect of profits.

The capital of the partnership is the amount specified in the agreement of the partners, which is to be contributed by the partners for the purpose of initiating and operating the partnership business. Thus, ordinarily we look to the initial contributions for a determination of the amounts "owing to partners in respect of capital." While the general rule is that the amount of capital may not be changed absent consent of all the partners, the partners in this case have apparently consented to adjustments in their capital accounts. Thus, we accept, for purposes of this case, adjustments in Helen's and Gordon's capital accounts to $4,005.45 and $27,302.61 respectively.

Therefore, whether the money left after satisfaction of creditors' claims and recoupment of partnership capital is termed profits or surplus, the clear mandate of the authorities is that, absent agreement to the contrary, it is divided equally as profits.

Gordon has placed reliance on UPA Section 42, relating to continuation of the business when a partner dies. In the instant case, the business was not continued by the surviving partner. Quite the contrary. The partnership remained dormant, and nothing was done until suit was brought by Helen to compel an accounting. Where the efforts of one partner in the production of profits in an active partnership cease, it is apparent that he no longer bears full entitlement to his respective share of the profits. In this case, however, where the partnership has been and continues to be inactive, any appreciation of worth is due to the nature of the partnership property rather than the effort of the surviving partner. Thus, we hold that any profit or surplus resulting shall be shared equally.

This conclusion is buttressed by the situation confronting Helen and her husband Terrell when they gave up $23,000 of their capital account for a $23,000 home. They knew that the partnership had few or no debts and owned a piece of property that had sold for $284,200 a few years previous. If the value of the land had stayed reasonably constant in the interim, the partnership would have been worth over $300,000. It is highly unlikely that Helen and her husband intended, when they gave up $23,000 of their capital account for a $23,000 house, that they were actually giving up not $23,000 but well over $100,000.

Whether the court erred in accepting the book value of the assets can be answered by looking at the figures we have reconstructed. Every single component of the $33,274.61 book value has been strongly contested. The Red Lake Ranch, for example, was sold in 1961 for over $280,000, but has an arbitrary book value of $15,622.61. An "investment" valued at $9,150 is made of two investments, one worthless and the other worth only $900. In short, the book values are completely arbitrary and should not have been used.

Our determination that the trial court erred in accepting book value is in accord with general principles of partnership accounting. The normal rule is that book value is only used in ascertaining the respective share when there is an explicit contractual provision to that effect, and even then it is not used where the facts of the case make it inequitable to do so. Here there was no contractual provision mandating the use of book value, and even if there were, the facts show book value in this case to be so disproportionate to possible real values that it would be inequitable for it to be used anyway.

Having decided that book value should not be used in valuing the partnership assets, we are forced to conclude that the trial court should have granted Helen's wish to have the assets liquidated.

We hold that partnership assets must be liquidated, and that the general creditors be paid first. If the assets are insufficient for this purpose, the estate and Gordon should be charged equally for the losses. If the assets are more than sufficient, then Gordon should be paid first up to the amount of $23,297.16 to set off the withdrawal from the capital account by Terrell. Any amount left over should be equally divided between Terrell's estate and the surviving partner, Gordon Mahan.

Judgment reversed in favor of Helen Mahan.

## SUMMARY

A dissolution is a change in the relation of the partners caused by one or more partners disassociating from the carrying on of the business. Dissolution does not terminate the partnership or always lead to winding up.

Dissolution may be wrongful or nonwrongful. A wrongful dissolution is one in violation of the partnership agreement, such as the retirement of a partner prior to the end of the term of the partnership. Some judicial dissolutions may be wrongful, such as dissolution ordered due to a partner's willful, persistent breach of his fiduciary duties.

Nonwrongful dissolution is dissolution that is not in contravention of the partnership agreement. Causes of nonwrongful dissolution include the death, bankruptcy, or retirement of a partner at an age permitted by the partnership agreement.

A wrongfully dissolving partner may not demand or perform winding up. In addition, she may not share in the goodwill of the business, and she must pay damages to the other partners for breaching the partnership agreement. Partners who have not wrongfully dissolved the partnership may agree unanimously to continue it.

Winding up is the orderly liquidation of the assets of the partnership. The partnership relationship continues during winding up. The surviving, nonbankrupt partners who have not wrongfully dissolved the partnership have the right to wind up the partnership business. The winding-up partners have the implied authority to do whatever is reasonably necessary to accomplish the winding up. They do not have actual authority to engage in new business. The partners still have apparent authority to bind the partnership to third parties who are unaware of the dissolution. This apparent authority may be cut off by actual notice to those who have extended credit to the partnership and by constructive notice to others.

If the partnership business is continued, the original partners remain liable on the debts of the former partnership unless there is a novation. Also, unless there is a contrary agreement, the creditors of the previous partnership remain creditors of the continuing business. A person joining an existing partnership assumes liability for its previous obligations, but only to the extent of the partnership assets.

In winding up a partnership, first, there is a marshaling of assets, whereby partnership creditors have first claim on partnership assets and creditors of individual partners have first claim on the individual assets of their debtors. After partnership creditors have been paid, partners are repaid their loans to the partnership. If assets remain, partners are entitled first to the return of their capital and then to shares in any undistributed profits.

## PROBLEM CASES

1. Horton, Davis & McCaleb was a partnership organized to practice law. The partnership had been dissolved, and it was in the process of winding up. By the action of McCaleb, the partnership filed a claim against the assets of Earl Howe, who had died. Earl Howe's estate argued that the partnership was no longer in existence and therefore could not make a claim. Is this correct?

2. Cooper and Isaacs were partners in the sale of janitorial supplies, doing business as Lesco Associates. Their partnership agreement listed the grounds for dissolution, which did not include irreconcilable differences between the partners. In 1970, after eight years of operation, Cooper sued for a judicial dissolution and winding up because of irreconcilable differences between the partners on matters of policy. Isaacs filed a counterclaim charging that Cooper's suit constituted a wrongful dissolution that did not permit Cooper to seek a winding up. Isaacs wanted to continue the business. Should the court dissolve the partnership and order winding up?

3. Mr. and Mrs. Ben-Dashan and George Plitt formed a partnership to breed standardbred horses. The partnership business was conducted on Plitt's farm. Plitt fed and cared for the animals and was reimbursed by the partnership for his expenses. The partners dissolved the partnership in March 1973, but could not agree what to do with the remaining 16 horses. The Ben-Dashans sued to force a winding up. The court ordered the sale of the horses, which occurred in May 1974. Plitt had fed and cared for the horses at his own expense from March 1973 to May 1974. He asked the Ben-Dashans to pay their share of the expenses. They refused to pay, claiming that Plitt was responsible for not selling the horses at some earlier time. Are the Ben-Dashans liable for a part of the feeding and caring expenses?

4. Ed Cox and Son, a partnership consisting of Ed Cox and William B. Cox, entered into a contract with the state of South Dakota for the construction of a section of highway. Ed Cox and Son borrowed money from Farmers State Bank. On June 1, 1956, they dissolved the partnership, but did not tell the bank, and the bank was unaware of the dissolution. After June 1, Ed Cox borrowed more money from the bank. The money was used to pay for labor and materials necessary to complete the construction contract. When the loan was not repaid, the partnership was sued on the loan. The partnership argued that it was not liable for amounts borrowed after June 1. Is this correct?

5. Forrest Meuret and Richard Meuret were a father and a son who had entered a partnership to purchase and repair agricultural equipment. After Richard misappropriated partnership funds, the partnership was dissolved. By court order, it was not wound up immediately but was continued for one year to allow a more advantageous liquidation of the assets. This required that Forrest operate the business by fulfilling old customer or-

ders and any new orders obtained during the winding up. At that time, Forrest borrowed $20,000 from a bank. He used the loan proceeds to pay current liabilities incurred after the dissolution. Richard claims that he is not liable for any of the $20,000 loan. Is he correct?

**6.** The partnership agreement of the Lebanon Trotting Association (LTA) established LTA for a term of 20 years from January 1, 1952. The purpose of the partnership was to engage in the business of harness racing. The main asset of the partnership was a lease for a fairground racetrack owned by the Warren County Agricultural Society (WCAS). The lease extended beyond December 31, 1971, and gave LTA an option to renew it. In addition, the lease prohibited LTA from assigning the lease without the consent of WCAS. When LTA dissolved upon the expiration of its term, it asked the court for a declaratory judgment that it could sell or terminate the lease. Peter Battista, one of the partners, contested the action, arguing that LTA should be permitted to fulfill the lease and operate the racetrack. Should LTA be permitted to fulfill the lease and operate the racetrack?

**7.** Daniel Wierzbinski was injured in 1975, while operating a machine as an employee of an upholstery business. He alleged that the injury was caused by the negligent manufacture and design of the machine, which was produced in 1941 by Lochner Manufacturing Company, a partnership. The people who were partners in 1941 had since died. The sons of one of the original partners had continued the business as a partnership. Wierzbinski sued the partnership, alleging that it was liable for the tort of its predecessor because it had continued its predecessor's business. The current partners moved to dismiss the action. Is the partnership liable?

**8.** Dawson Little was a partner in Ordway-Saunders Company, a partnership engaged in a general insurance and mortgage banking business in Amarillo, Texas. The articles of partnership stated that the books of the partnership would be kept on an accrual basis and declared that "the assets and liabilities of the partnership and the capital accounts are shown on the books of the partnership and made a part hereof for all purposes." Little withdrew from the partnership. He was paid his share of the capital account as shown on the partnership books. However, he claimed that he was entitled to an additional amount for these reasons: some real estate owned by the partnership was carried on the books at cost rather than at its current market value; the retained earnings of a corporation owned by the partnership were not included on the partnership books; and no value had been assigned to goodwill. Goodwill had never been carried as an asset on the books of the partnership, nor had any of the real estate or retained earnings of the corporate shares been carried on the books when other partners had withdrawn. An expert witness at the trial estimated the goodwill to be worth $1.3 million. Is Little entitled to a share of the market appreciation of the real estate, the retained earnings of the corporation, and the goodwill of the partnership business?

**9.** Cletus, Roy, and Claude Dreifuerst were brothers. They formed a partnership that operated two feed mills, one located at St. Cloud and the other at Elkhart Lake, Wisconsin. They had no written articles of partnership. Cletus and Roy gave Claude notice of dissolution. When the three brothers were unable to agree on how to wind up the partnership, Cletus and Roy brought suit. Claude wanted the partnership assets sold, arguing that Cletus and Roy could buy them at a public sale. Cletus and Roy argued that the assets should be divided in kind, giving them the assets from the Elkhart Lake mill and Claude the assets from the St. Cloud mill. The value of each mill was not clearly determinable, and there were some creditors' claims against the partnership. Will the court order the mills sold?

**10.** Donne Seguin and Betty Boyd were partners for the purpose of buying and selling real estate. Seguin contributed $112,800 to the partnership; Boyd contributed $900. Their agreement provided for equal sharing of profits and losses. After the partnership was dissolved, a court ordered the partnership property sold. The court directed that the proceeds be used to pay creditors first and then to pay Seguin the amount by which Seguin's contribution exceeded Boyd's. Boyd argued that the proceeds after payment of creditors should be split evenly, since she did not guarantee the return of Seguin's investment in the partnership. How will the proceeds be distributed?

**11.** Carl Sundstrom and Roy Sundstrom operated, as partners, the *Custer County Chronicle*, a newspaper. Carl alone contributed to the partnership the physical assets used by the partners. Roy contributed no capital to the partnership venture. Carl received 55 percent of the profits of the business, and Roy received 45 percent. The partnership was dissolved by Roy's death. In winding up the affairs of the partnership, Carl contended that he was entitled to compensation for the depreciation of the physical assets that he had contributed to the partnership. The partnership agreement was silent on the matter of compensation for depreciation of the physical assets, and there was no evidence that the matter of depreciation had ever been considered by the partners. Is Carl entitled to compensation for depreciation of the physical assets?

# Chapter 21 Limited Partnerships

## INTRODUCTION

**History.** The partnership form—with managerial control and unlimited liability for all partners—is not acceptable for all business arrangements. Often, business managers want an infusion of capital into a business, yet are reluctant to surrender managerial control to those contributing capital. Investors wish to contribute capital to a business, share in its profits, and yet limit their liability to the amount of their investment. A need, therefore, exists for a business form that has two types of owners: one type of owner who contributes capital to the business, manages it, shares in its profits, and possesses *unlimited* liability for its obligations; and a second type of owner who contributes capital and shares profits, but possesses no management powers and has liability *limited* to her investment in the business.

In continental Europe during the Middle Ages, the *commenda* or *société en commandite* met this need for a new business form. Under this contractual arrangement, an investor, called a *commendator,* provided capital to a business manager, called a *commendatarius.* The *commendator* received most of the profits, but his liability for losses was limited to his capital contribution. France sanctioned the *commenda* by statute in 1807. In 1822, New York and Connecticut were the first states to recognize this form—the **limited partnership.** Today, every state has a statute permitting the creation of limited partnerships, although Louisiana calls them partnerships *in commendam.*

**The Uniform Limited Partnership Act.** The adoption of uniform limited partnership statutes has created substantial similarity in the laws that the states apply to limited partnerships. The National Conference of Commissioners on Uniform State Laws, a body of lawyers, judges, and legal scholars, drafted the Uniform Limited Partnership Act (ULPA) in 1916. In 1976, the commissioners drafted the Revised Uniform Limited Partnership Act (RULPA), which more clearly and comprehensively states the law of limited partnership. As of October 1985, 41 states have adopted the RULPA; 8 states follow the ULPA. (Louisiana has not adopted either one.) Since the RULPA will soon be adopted by nearly every state in the United States, it forms the foundation of the discussion in this chapter. The ULPA's provisions are discussed when they vary significantly from the RULPA's provisions and when they help to explain the evolution of limited partnership law. In addition, reference will be made to the Uniform Partnership Act (UPA), which applies to limited partnerships in the absence of an applicable provision in the RULPA or the ULPA. Most of the cases in this chapter were decided under the ULPA, since there has been relatively little litigation under the RULPA.

**Principal Characteristics of Limited Partnerships.** Many characteristics of a limited partnership are similar to those of a partnership, yet some of its features are like those of a corporation. Under the uniform acts and federal tax law, a limited partnership will have the following characteristics:

1. A limited partnership may be *created only in accordance with a statute.* It does not exist in the common law. If the statute is not followed, unlimited liability may be imposed upon all the partners.

2. A limited partnership has two types of partners: *general partners* and *limited partners.* It must have one or more of each of these types of partners.

3. All partners, limited and general, *share the profits* of the business.

4. Each general partner has *unlimited liability* for the obligations of the business. Each limited partner has liability *limited to his capital contribution* to the business.

5. Each general partner has a *right to manage* the business, and she is an agent of the limited partnership. A limited partner has *no right to manage* the business or to act as its agent, but he does have the right to vote on several important matters, such as admitting new partners. If a limited partner does manage the business, he may incur unlimited liability for partnership obligations.

6. General partners are *fiduciaries* of the business. Limited partners are *not fiduciaries.*

7. A partner's interest in a limited partnership is *not freely transferable.* An assignee of a general or limited partnership interest is not a partner, but is entitled only to the assigning partner's share of capital and profits, absent a contrary agreement.

8. The withdrawal of a limited partner does *not automatically dissolve* a limited partnership. Withdrawal of a general partner *dissolves* a limited partnership, absent a contrary agreement of the partners.

9. A limited partnership *pays no federal income taxes.* Its partners report their shares of the profits and losses on their individual federal income tax returns. A limited partnership files an *information return* with the Internal Revenue Service, notifying the IRS of

each partner's share of the year's profit or loss.

**Use of Limited Partnerships.** The limited partnership form is used primarily in real estate investment activities, oil and gas drilling, and other *tax shelter* ventures. Losses of the business are deductible on the individual income tax returns of the partners, offsetting income from other sources. That is, the losses "shelter" income from other sources. The limited partnership has an advantage over the partnership, since limited partners have limited liability. It has an advantage over the S Corporation, whose owners may deduct its losses and have limited liability, because an S Corporation is limited to 35 owners, while a limited partnership may have an unlimited number of owners.[1]

## CREATION OF LIMITED PARTNERSHIP

**Certificate of Limited Partnership.** A limited partnership may be created only by complying with the applicable state statute. RULPA Section 201 requires that two or more persons execute a *certificate of limited partnership* and that the certificate be filed with the secretary of state. The certificate must include, among other things, the following information:

1. The name of the limited partnership, which must contain the words *limited partnership.* (The ULPA does not require the words *limited partnership* to appear in the name.) The name may not include the surname of a limited partner unless it is the same as the surname of a general partner.
2. The general character of its business.
3. The names and addresses of all partners, listing separately the limited and general partners. In addition, each partner must sign the certificate.
4. The capital contribution of each partner. If property other than cash is contributed, a description and a statement of the value of the property must be included.
5. The events permitting a partner to withdraw from the limited partnership.
6. Any power of a limited partner to make his assignee a limited partner.
7. The events causing the dissolution of the limited partnership.
8. Any right of partners to receive distributions of limited partnership property.
9. The name and address of an agent for service of process. Designating an agent in the certificate eases a creditor's obligation to notify a limited partnership that it is being sued by the creditor.

The purpose of drafting and filing the certificate of limited partnership is to put creditors on notice of the various partners' contributions and the extent of partners' liabilities. To ensure easy access by creditors, most states adopting the ULPA require a filing with the *recorder's office* in the county where the limited partnership does business.

For many limited partnerships, the certificate serves as the articles of limited partnership. Often, however, the partners enter into a more detailed written limited partnership agreement.

Under RULPA Section 201(b), a limited partnership begins its existence at the time the certificate is filed with the office of the secretary of state.

**Who May Be a Partner?** Any *person* may be a general or limited partner. RULPA

[1] S Corporations are discussed in Chapter 22.

Section 101(11) defines person to mean a natural person, partnership, limited partnership, trust, estate, association, or corporation. Hence, as commonly occurs, a corporation may be the sole general partner of a limited partnership, as was the situation in the *Frigidaire* case, which appears after the next section. Since all the owners of a corporation have limited liability, there is often no natural person who has unlimited liability for a limited partnership's obligations. Courts, including the *Frigidaire* court, recognize the harm to creditors that may result if a corporate general partner is undercapitalized, and they will therefore *pierce the corporate veil* and impose unlimited liability upon the owners of an undercapitalized corporate general partner.[2]

**Types of Capital Contributions.** RULPA Section 101(2) permits partners to make capital contributions of cash, property, services or a promise to contribute cash, property, or services. ULPA Section 3 does not permit limited partners to provide services as their capital contributions, although it does permit general partners to do so.

**Defective Compliance with Limited Partnership Statute.** During the early history of limited partnerships, courts were averse to limiting the liability of limited partners, and even today, courts are largely averse to doing so. Hence, many courts hold that a failure to comply with any of the requirements of the limited partnership act results in the imposition of unlimited liability on purported limited partners. Defective compliance might result from failing to file a certificate of limited partnership or from filing a defective certificate. A defective certificate might, for example, list those intending to be limited partners without specifying their status as limited partners.

RULPA Section 201(b) requires at least *substantial compliance* with the requirements listed above before a limited partner will have limited liability. Absent substantial compliance with the law, a limited partner will usually be liable as a general partner.

RULPA Section 304 permits a person who erroneously, but *in good faith,* believes that she is a limited partner to escape the liability of a general partner either: (1) by causing a proper certificate of limited partnership (or an amendment thereto) to be filed with the secretary of state or (2) by withdrawing from *future equity participation* in the firm. However, such a person remains liable as a general partner to third parties who, prior to such person's withdrawal or filing of an appropriate certificate, believed *in good faith* that such person was a general partner.

ULPA Section 11 contains only a part of the RULPA rule. It allows a person who erroneously believes that he is a limited partner to escape liability as a general partner by renouncing any interest in profits *upon discovering the error. Blow v. Shaughnessy,* which follows, applies Section 11 of the ULPA.

Generally, defects in compliance will not affect the *relations between the partners.* Even when a court finds that no limited partnership has been created, an ordinary partnership will be found if the relation of the partners satisfies the partnership definition that you studied in Chapter 18. In such a situation, the rights of the partners between themselves are determined by their defective or defectively filed certificate of limited partnership or other limited partnership agreement. In *Blow v. Shaughnessy,* the court found that no partnership of any kind resulted, because the general partner failed to comply with the ULPA requirements and the purported lim-

[2] Undercapitalized corporations and piercing the corporate veil are discussed in Chapter 22.

ited partners had not signed a partnership agreement.

**Amendments to Certificate.** RULPA Section 202 requires that a limited partnership keep its filed certificate current. Current filings allow creditors to discover current facts, not merely those facts that existed when the original certificate was filed. Under RULPA Section 202(b), an amendment reflecting any of the following facts *must* be filed within 30 days of its occurrence: (1) a change in a partner's contribution; (2) the admission of a new partner; (3) the withdrawal of a partner; or (4) the continuation of the business after a judicial dissolution due to the withdrawal of the last general partner.

A general partner aware of a falsity in a certificate must file *promptly* an amendment to correct the falsity. An amendment to change the address of a limited partner must be filed only once a year. Other amendments to a limited partnership certificate may be filed at any time.

The ULPA amendment requirements are substantially different from those of the RULPA. Under ULPA Section 24, the certificate must be amended whenever the business is continued after the death, retirement, or insanity of a general partner. The admission of a new partner also requires an amendment. Amendment is not necessary upon the death or withdrawal of a limited partner. Amendment is required when there is a change in the nature of the partnership's business, in the time stated in the certificate for dissolution, or in other statements made in the certificate.

**Failure to File Amendments.** Essentially, failing to file necessary amendments to the certificate imposes the same liability upon limited partners as does a defective attempt to create a limited partnership. Both RULPA Section 304 and ULPA Section 11 protect a limited partner who erroneously believed that he was a limited partner, despite the partnership's failure to file an amendment indicating his status. In addition, RULPA Section 202(e) provides a *safe harbor* for a limited partner when a filing is made within 30 days of the occurrence of any of the four events listed in RULPA Section 202(b), above.

**Foreign Limited Partnerships.** A limited partnership is *domestic* in the state in which it is organized; it is *foreign* in every other state. Under the ULPA, confusion exists whether the limited partners of a foreign limited partnership are entitled to limited liability for the limited partnership's transactions occurring in a foreign state. RULPA Section 901 makes it clear that the laws of the domestic state apply to the internal affairs of the limited partnership, allowing a limited partner protection regardless where business is conducted.

Nevertheless, to be privileged to do business in a foreign state, a limited partnership must *register* to do business in that state. To register, a limited partnership must file an *application for registration* with the secretary of state of the foreign state. The application must include the name and address of the limited partnership, the names and addresses of the partners, and the name and address of an agent for service of process. The application must be accompanied by the payment of a fee. The secretary of state reviews the application and, if all requirements are met, issues a *certificate of registration.*

**Failure to Register as Foreign Limited Partnership.** There are few penalties for failing to register as a foreign limited partnership. The RULPA does not impose fines for a failure to register, but a few states have amended it to do so. Massachusetts imposes a $500 per year fine for a failure to register.

In addition, a foreign limited partnership may not use the foreign state's courts to sue to enforce any right or contract. Once it registers, a limited partnership may use the state courts, even if it sues to enforce a contract that was made before it registered.

Failure to register does not invalidate any contracts made in the foreign state or prevent a limited partnership from defending itself in a suit brought in the state's courts.

**Application of Securities Laws.** A limited partnership interest is a security under both federal and state securities laws, which are designed to protect investors in securities. Therefore, before a general partner offers or sells limited partnership interests, she must comply with any applicable federal and state laws requiring a disclosure of important information to prospective purchasers of securities. The federal and state securities laws are discussed in detail in Chapter 26.

## Blow v. Shaughnessy

**313 S.E.2d 868 (N.C. Ct. App. 1984)**

In a six-month period, Elizabeth Blow and her fellow limited partners watched the value of their investment in a limited partnership fall from $500,000 to $25,000. They sued the general partner and his advisers for fraud and breach of fiduciary duty.

Beginning in 1979, Blow and others purchased limited partnership interests in Capital City Investments (CCI). CCI was organized in 1979 by Jeffrey Shaughnessy to invest and trade in securities, commodities, and other items. The limited partnership agreement listed Shaughnessy as the sole general partner. Shaughnessy signed the agreement. The limited partners were listed, but none signed the agreement. No certificate of limited partnership was filed in the county recorder's office, where recording was required.

On behalf of CCI, Shaughnessy entered into a contract with Merrill Lynch, Pierce, Fenner and Smith, Inc., the securities brokerage firm, under which Merrill Lynch was to provide investment services to CCI. The contract also provided that any controversy arising out of CCI's dealing with Merrill Lynch must be submitted to arbitration, rather than litigated in the courts.

After the value of their investment declined from $500,000 to $25,000, Blow and the other limited partners sued Shaughnessy and Merrill Lynch for engaging in highly speculative and reckless investment strategies. Merrill Lynch asked the court to dismiss the suit on the grounds that arbitration was required under the contract with the limited partnership. Blow contended that there was no valid agreement binding her. She argued that Shaughnessy had no authority to act for her, because there was no limited partnership. The trial court agreed with Blow and held that she was not required to submit the claim to arbitration. Merrill Lynch appealed.

**Eagles, Judge.** The essence of Merrill Lynch's argument is that the customer agreements, with their arbitration clauses executed by Shaughnessy, are valid as to Blow and therefore binding on her. We have carefully considered the argument, but are not persuaded by it.

No certificate of limited partnership was filed with the county recorder. ULPA Section 2, governing the formation of limited partnerships, provides in pertinent part:

> (a) Two or more persons desiring to form a limited partnership shall
>
> (1) Sign and swear to a certificate.
>
> (2) File for record the certificate in the office of the recorder of the county where the principal place of business is located.
>
> (b) A limited partnership is formed if there has been substantial compliance in good faith with the requirements of subsection (a).

It is generally held that a failure to file a certificate of limited partnership is a failure of "substantial compliance" such that any assertion of limited partnership is negated. Here, not only has no certificate ever been filed, but there is nothing in the record that suggests that the required certificate was ever prepared. Thus, notwithstanding the existence of a Limited Partnership Agreement, we hold that no limited partnership existed here.

Merrill Lynch contends that there was nevertheless some relationship between Blow and Shaughnessy. Merrill Lynch argues that the relationship was that of a general partnership, relying on the theory that a general partnership is formed by operation of law where, as here, there has not been substantial compliance with the statutory requirements for the formation of a limited partnership. The usual situation in which the law implies a general partnership is that in which a party is claiming limited partnership status in order to avoid the great liability that attaches to status as a general partner or where the evidence shows that the parties intended the existence of a partnership for some agreed upon function.

Our research discloses, however, that a *de facto* general partnership is not the necessary result of a failure to comply with the statutory requirements of limited partnership formation. ULPA Section 11 provides as follows:

> A person who has contributed to the capital of a business conducted by a person or partnership erroneously believing that he has become a limited partner in a limited partnership, is not, by reason of his exercise of the rights of a limited partner, a general partner with the person or in the partnership carrying on the business, or bound by the obligations of such person or partnership; provided that on ascertaining the mistake he promptly renounces his interest in the profits of the business, or other compensation by way of income.

Section 11 of the ULPA is broad and highly remedial. The existence of a partnership—limited or general—is not essential in order that it shall apply. The language is comprehensive and covers all cases where one has contributed to the capital of a business conducted by a partnership or person, erroneously believing that he is a limited partner. It ought to be construed liberally, and with appropriate regard for the legislative purpose to relieve limited partners from the strictness of the earlier statutes and decisions.

Thus, where a limited partnership is found not to exist, it is the intent of the parties and not the operation of law, as defendants contend, that determines whether or not a general partnership results.

While a limited partnership agreement did exist, there was no evidence that Blow or any other purchaser ever signed it.

The evidence further shows that CCI was established and promoted as a limited partnership with Shaughnessy as the general partner. However, there is no evidence that any steps were ever taken to comply with ULPA Section 2, regarding limited partnership formation. Applying the principles set forth above to these facts, it is clear that, under ULPA

Section 11, no partnership relationship would be formed. CCI had no income, so there was no interest in such income for Blow to renounce, as called for under the statute. Further, there is no indication that Blow acted as a principal or in any way behaved as other than the limited partner that she erroneously thought herself to be. The nature of CCI's business was such that there was no intention on the part of Blow to continue in the operation of CCI as a general partner.

The trial court therefore correctly failed to make findings or conclusions to the effect that any partnership—general or limited—existed. The narrow question before the trial court was whether there was a valid agreement between Blow and Merrill Lynch such that Blow was bound by the arbitration provisions therein. We believe that the court correctly answered that question in the negative.

Judgment for Blow affirmed.

## RIGHTS AND LIABILITIES OF PARTNERS IN LIMITED PARTNERSHIPS

The partners of a limited partnership have many rights and liabilities. Some are identical to those of partners in an ordinary partnership, but others are special to limited partnerships. Some are common to both general and limited partners, while others are not shared.

**Common Rights and Liabilities.** The duty to *contribute capital as promised* is one of the most important liabilities of a partner. The most important right of a partner is to *share in the profits* of the business. There are many other rights and liabilities.

**Capital Contributions.** A partner is obligated to contribute as capital the cash, property, or other services that he promised to contribute. Under RULPA Section 502, this obligation may be enforced by the limited partnership or by one of its creditors.

**Share of Profits.** Under RULPA Section 503, profits are shared on the basis of the *value of each partner's capital contribution* unless there is an agreement to the contrary. For example, if two general partners contribute $1,000 each and 20 limited partners contribute $20,000 each, and the profit is $40,200, each general partner's share of the profits is $100 and each limited partner's share is $2,000.

This is different from the ULPA, which does not specify how profits are shared. Therefore, in states that follow the ULPA, the Uniform Partnership Act applies, and profits are shared equally, unless otherwise provided.

**Share of Losses.** Losses are shared in the same manner as profits are shared, absent an agreement to the contrary. Since most limited partnerships are tax shelters, partnership agreements often provide for limited partners to take all the losses of the business, up to the limit of their capital contributions. This loss allocation maximizes the tax benefit from limited partnership losses.

**Share of Distributions.** Under RULPA Section 504, partners share distributions of a limited partnership's cash or other assets in relation to the amounts of their capital contributions, absent an agreement to the contrary. If a partner is not paid a distribution to which he is entitled, he may sue the limited partnership as if he were a creditor.

A partner may not receive a distribution that impairs the limited partnership's ability to pay its creditors. Under RULPA Section 607, after a distribution, the fair value of partnership assets must at least equal the limited partnership's liabilities to creditors (excluding liabilities to partners for the return of their capital contributions).

Consider this example. Grant and Ginny are general partners and Linda and Lyle are limited partners in a retail business called Universal Recordings, Ltd. Linda and Lyle each contribute $25,000 to the capital of the partnership. Grant and Ginny make no capital contribution. Linda later lends the firm another $10,000. The firm has $20,000 in assets, but it has debts of $15,000, including Linda's loan. The firm has net income of $9,000 for the year. It can distribute only $5,000 of the earnings to the partners, because its assets exceed its liabilities by only that amount ($20,000 − $15,000). Note that if Linda were owed the $10,000 as a return of her capital contribution, however, the full $9,000 in profits for the year could legally be distributed, since the assets of $20,000 would exceed the liabilities of $5,000 by $15,000. In fact, the firm could distribute $15,000, even though profits were only $9,000.

**Voting Rights.** RULPA Sections 302 and 405 permit the partners to establish the *voting rights* that partners have on partnership matters. The partnership agreement may require that certain transactions be approved by general partners, by limited partners, or by all the partners. The agreement may give each general partner more votes than it grants limited partners, or vice versa. These sections make it clear that limited partners have *no right* to vote on any matter *as a class.* This is not clear under the ULPA.

**Admission of New Partners.** Like an ordinary partnership, a limited partnership is a *voluntary association.* Therefore, no new partner may be admitted unless each partner has consented to the admission. Under RULPA Section 301, new *limited* partners may be admitted by unanimous consent of the partners *or* in accordance with the limited partnership agreement. There is a different rule for the admission of additional general partners, however, since general partners can manage the limited partnership and affect its profitability. Under RULPA Section 401, new *general* partners may be admitted only with the *specific written consent* of *each* partner. The limited partnership agreement *cannot* remove the right of each partner to approve the admission of a new general partner.

**Partnership Interest.** Like a partner in an ordinary partnership, each partner in a limited partnership owns a *partnership interest.* It is his personal property. Under RULPA Section 702, it may be sold or *assigned* to others, such as creditors; under Section 703, a creditor may obtain a *charging order* against it. An assignee or a creditor with a charging order does *not* become a limited or general partner, but is entitled to receive only the partner's *share of distributions.* Nevertheless, if the limited partnership agreement so provides, an *assignee* of a *limited* or a *general* partner may become a *limited partner.* The new limited partner will then assume all the rights and liabilities of a limited partner, except for liabilities *unknown* to her and *not ascertainable* from the limited partnership certificate.

A partner's assignment of his partnership interest *terminates* his status as a partner. Contrary to this rule, a partner remains a partner despite a court's grant of a charging order.

A limited partnership agreement may *restrict,* but *not prohibit,* the assignment of a partnership interest. For example, a restriction may require limited partners to offer to sell their interests to the limited partnership before selling them to anyone else. Such restrictions are binding upon assignees with *notice* of the restrictions.

**Right to Withdraw.** Like partners in an ordinary partnership, partners in a limited partnership have the power to withdraw from the partnership and receive the value of their partnership interests, even though there is a return of capital contributions. Under RULPA Section 602, a general partner may withdraw from a limited partnership *at any time;* if the withdrawal breaches the limited partnership agreement, the value of her interest is reduced by the damages suffered by the limited partnership.

RULPA Section 603 permits a limited partner to withdraw in accordance with the limited partnership agreement. Absent a contrary provision in the agreement, a limited partner may withdraw after giving *six months' prior notice* to each general partner.

RULPA Section 607, discussed above, which limits the amount of assets that may be distributed to partners, applies equally to the payment of the value of a partner's interest. In addition, under RULPA Section 608(a), a partner who lawfully receives a return of capital is liable to the limited partnership to the extent necessary to pay those who were creditors before the withdrawal.

**False Statements in Filings.** Partners may be liable to persons suffering losses from their reliance on *false statements* in a certificate of limited partnership or a certificate of amendment. For example, assume that a limited partnership certificate obligates a limited partner to contribute $200,000 to the limited partnership. The partners agree to permit that limited partner to reduce his contribution to only $10,000, but no amendment is filed. A bank deciding whether to make a loan to the limited partnership reads the filed certificate, sees the obligation to contribute $200,000, and decides to lend $150,000 to the limited partnership. If the bank is not repaid, it may be able to collect its damages from the partners, including the limited partners.

Each limited partner is liable only if she *knows* of a false statement in the certificate *when it was executed.* A general partner is liable if he *knows or should know* of a false statement in the certificate when it was executed. In addition, a general partner is liable if he knows or should know that a statement in a filed certificate *has become false* and he has not amended the certificate within a reasonable time.

**Other Rights of General Partners.** RULPA Section 403 provides that general partners have the rights of partners in an ordinary partnership, except as modified by the RULPA. Therefore, a general partner has the same *right to manage* and the same *agency powers* as a partner in an ordinary partnership. Likewise, he has no right to compensation beyond his share of the profits, absent an agreement to the contrary. Since most limited partnerships are tax shelters that are designed to lose money during their early years of operation, most limited partnership agreements provide for the payment of salaries to general partners.

A general partner may also be a limited partner, and thereby increase her share of the profits of the limited partnership. Of course, becoming a limited partner does not reduce her unlimited liability for obligations of the business.

**Other Liabilities of General Partners.** RULPA Section 403 makes it clear that a general partner has the same *unlimited liability* for the obligations of a limited partnership as does a partner for the obligations of an ordinary partnership. In addition, a general partner is in a position of *trust* when he manages the business, and therefore owes *fiduciary duties* to the limited partnership. All of the fiduciary duties that you studied in Chapter 19 (*e.g., not to self-deal or to compete*) apply with equal force to general partners.

**Other Rights of Limited Partners.** Limited partners have the right to be *informed* about partnership affairs. RULPA Section 305 obligates the general partners to provide financial information and tax returns to the limited partners on demand. In addition, a limited partner may *inspect and copy* a list of the partners, the certificate of limited partnership and amendments, tax returns, and partnership agreements.

**Derivative Suits.** RULPA Section 1001 permits a limited partner to sue to enforce a limited partnership right of action against a person who has harmed the limited partnership. This right of action is called a *derivative suit* or a derivative action because it derives from the limited partnership. Any recovery obtained by the limited partner goes to the limited partnership, since it is the person that was harmed.

The limited partner who initiates a derivative action must have been a partner at the time the wrong occurred and must have asked the general partners to sue, unless it is obvious that the general partners will not sue. Most derivative suits are brought against general partners who have breached the fiduciary duties that they owe to the limited partnership. If a majority of the general partners have breached their fiduciary duties, a limited partner need not ask the general partners to sue, since it is obvious that they will not sue themselves.

Since a limited partner will incur legal expenses if he brings a derivative suit, he may be paid for his expenses out of any judgment or settlement obtained for the limited partnership. If the limited partner loses the suit, he gets nothing.

ULPA Section 26 appears to prevent limited partners from bringing derivative actions. Many courts have held, however, that a limited partner, like a beneficiary of a trust, may sue on behalf of the partnership to recover against a general partner who has breached a fiduciary duty owed to the limited partnership.

**Other Liabilities of Limited Partners.** A limited partner's chief liability is for losses of the limited partnership, but *only to the extent of her contribution.* In return for limited liability, a limited partner gives up the right to participate in the management of a limited partnership. Conversely, if a limited partner engages in management activities, she may *lose her limited liability.* The RULPA and the ULPA have different rules on what activities will cause a limited partner to have the liability of a general partner.

**ULPA Section 7.** Section 7 of the ULPA states that a limited partner who "in addition to the exercise of his rights and powers as a limited partner . . . takes part in the control of the business" becomes liable to creditors as a general partner. Although there have been relatively few cases interpreting this provision, "control" may be viewed as participation in the firm's *day-to-day management decisions* as contrasted with isolated involvement with major decisions. For example, a limited partner of a real estate investment limited partnership would be liable as a general partner if he regularly aided the general partners in determining what real estate to purchase. A limited partner who only once vetoed a loan agreement with a bank, however, would retain his limited liability.

Some uncertainty exists concerning how far a limited partner may go in making suggestions, voting on certain major partnership issues, or exercising a veto power. As a result, some states have provisions that grant limited partners voting rights on certain matters. In addition, some courts have imposed a *reliance* or *estoppel* test, holding that limited liability is not lost if the creditor did not know that the limited partner was participating in control or if the creditor knew that the limited partner was only a limited partner.

**RULPA Section 303.** The RULPA has two tests for determining whether a limited partner engaging in control is liable beyond his contribution to creditors. If a limited partner is acting *substantially like a general partner,* then he has the liability of a general partner to *all* creditors of the limited partnership. If he *takes part in control of the business,* but does *not* act substantially like a general partner, he is liable only to those persons who deal with the limited partnership with *actual knowledge* of his participation in control.

In addition, the RULPA clarifies the kinds of management activities that limited partners may perform without becoming personally liable for partnership debts. The following are among the acts that RULPA Section 303(b) declares do not, individually, amount to participation in control, and are therefore, acts that a limited partner may perform, yet retain his limited liability:

1. Being an *agent, an employee, or a contractor* for the limited partnership or a general partner.
2. Being a *consultant* or *adviser* to a general partner.
3. Acting as a *surety* for the partnership.
4. Approving or disapproving an amendment to the partnership agreement.
5. Voting on such partnership matters as dissolution, sale of substantially all the assets, changes in the nature of the business, and removals of general partners.

In the *Frigidaire* case, which follows, although the limited partners actively managed the limited partnership, they did not lose their limited liability, because they acted as agents of the general partner and did not mislead anyone to believe that they were general partners.

**Limited Partner's Name in Firm Name.** Including a limited partner's *surname* in the name of a limited partnership may mislead a creditor to believe that a limited partner is a general partner. Under RULPA Section 304(d), a limited partner who *knowingly* permits her name to be included in the firm name is liable to creditors who have *no actual knowledge* that she is a limited partner, *unless* a general partner has the same surname as that of the limited partner.

## Frigidaire Sales Corp. v. Union Properties, Inc.

**562 P.2d 244 (Wash. Sup. Ct. 1977)**

Leonard Mannon and Raleigh Baxter formed Union Properties, Inc., a corporation, to develop commercial real estate. When Union found a real estate opportunity, it would create a limited partnership to own and to develop the property, with Union as the sole general partner. Mannon and Baxter were the sole shareholders, directors, and officers of Union. They managed Union on a day-to-day basis.

Commercial Investors, Ltd., was one of the limited partnerships that Union created. As usual, Union was the sole general partner in Commercial. In addition, Mannon and Baxter were the only limited partners.

Commercial made a contract with Frigidaire Sales Corporation. Mannon and Baxter, as president and secretary-treasurer of Union, signed the contract on behalf of Commercial. Frigidaire knew that Union was the only general partner in Commercial. When acting for Commercial, Mannon and Baxter were always careful to indicate that they were acting as agents of Union.

When Commercial breached the contract with Frigidaire, Frigidaire sued Union. In addition, Frigidaire sued Mannon and Baxter personally on the ground that they were liable as general partners because they had day-to-day control of Commercial. The trial court held that Mannon and Baxter were not liable to Frigidaire. Frigidaire appealed.

**Hamilton, Associate Judge.** Frigidaire does not contend that Mannon and Baxter acted improperly by setting up the limited partnership with a corporation as the sole general partner. Limited partnerships are a statutory form of business organization, and parties creating a limited partnership must follow the statutory requirements. In Washington, parties may form a limited partnership with a corporation as the sole general partner. Frigidaire's sole contention is that Mannon and Baxter should incur general liability for the limited partnership's obligations, because they exercised the day-to-day control and management of Commercial.

Frigidaire cites *Delaney v. Fidelity Lease Ltd.* (1975) as support for its contention that Mannon and Baxter should incur general liability under ULPA Section 7 for the limited partnership's obligations. That case also involved the issue of liability for limited partners who controlled the limited partnership as officers, directors, and shareholders of the corporate general partner. The Texas Supreme Court found that the limited partners had incurred general liability because of their control of the limited partnership.

We find the Texas Supreme Court's decision distinguishable from the present case. In *Delaney,* the corporation and the limited partnership were set up contemporaneously, and the sole purpose of the corporation was to operate the limited partnership. The Texas Supreme Court found that the limited partners who controlled the corporation were obligated to their other limited partners to operate the corporation for the benefit of the partnership. This is not the case here. The pattern of operation of Union Properties was to investigate and conceive of real estate investment opportunities and, when it found such opportunities, to cause the creation of limited partnerships with Union Properties acting as the general partner. Commercial was only one of several limited partnerships so conceived and created. Mannon and Baxter did not form Union Properties for the sole purpose of operating Commercial. Hence, their acts on behalf of Union Properties were not performed merely for the benefit of Commercial.

Further, the Texas Supreme Court was concerned with the possibility that limited partners might form the corporate general partner with minimum capitalization. However, we agree with our Court of Appeals' analysis that this concern with minimum capitalization is not peculiar to limited partnerships with corporate general partners, but may arise anytime a creditor deals with a corporation. Because our limited partnership statutes permit parties to form a limited partnership with a corporation as the sole general partner, this concern about minimal capitalization, standing by itself, does not justify a finding that the limited partners incur general liability for their control of the corporate general partner. If a corporate general partner is inadequately capitalized, the rights of a creditor are adequately protected under the "piercing-the-corporate-veil" doctrine of corporation law.

In addition, Frigidaire was never led to believe that Mannon and Baxter were acting in any capacity other than in their corporate capacities. Mannon and Baxter scrupulously separated their actions on behalf of the corporation from their personal actions. Frigidaire never mistakenly assumed that Mannon and Baxter were general partners with general liability. Frigidaire knew Union was the sole general partner and did not rely on Mannon and Baxter's control by assuming that they were also general partners. If Frigidaire had not wished to rely on the solvency of Union as the only general partner, it could have insisted that Mannon and Baxter personally guarantee contractual performance.

Judgment for Mannon and Baxter affirmed.

## DISSOLUTION AND WINDING UP OF A LIMITED PARTNERSHIP

**Dissolution.** Like an ordinary partnership, a limited partnership may be dissolved and its affairs wound up. Because a limited partnership has limited partners—who are not involved in carrying on the business—some events that cause a dissolution of an ordinary partnership do not cause the dissolution of a limited partnership.

**Causes of Dissolution.** Under RULPA Section 801, there are four causes of dissolution:

1. At the time or upon the occurrence of an event specified in the certificate of limited partnership. For example, the certificate may specify that a limited partnership is to have a 20-year term. Or the certificate may provide for dissolution of a limited partnership after it has accomplished its objective of building a shopping mall.
2. By the written consent of all the partners.
3. By court order, under Section 802, when it is *not reasonably practicable* to carry on the business in conformity with the limited partnership agreement.
4. Upon the withdrawal of a *general* partner. Such a withdrawal includes retirement, death, bankruptcy, assignment of a general partnership interest, removal by the other partners, and adjudicated insanity. For a general partner that is not a natural person, such as a partnership or a corporation, its *own* dissolution is a withdrawal causing a dissolution of the limited partnership.

The RULPA specifically permits a limited partnership to *avoid dissolution* after the withdrawal of a general partner if the limited partnership certificate permits the business to be conducted by the remaining general partners or if all of the partners agree to continue the business.

ULPA Section 20 provides simply for dissolution upon the retirement, death, or insanity of a general partner, unless the right to continue is granted in the certificate or unless all other general and limited partners agree to continue the business. The ULPA has no section on judicial dissolution, so Section 32 of the UPA applies.[3] In the *Mandell* case, which follows, judicial dissolution was obtained because the partners' deadlock caused the limited partnership to incur large losses.

**Events Not Causing Dissolution.** The death, bankruptcy, insanity, or withdrawal of a *limited* partner does not result in dissolution, unless the certificate of limited partnership compels dissolution. The addition of a partner, general or limited, does not cause a

[3] The grounds for judicial dissolution under the UPA are discussed in Chapter 20.

dissolution, since no one has ceased to be associated with the carrying on of the business.

**Certificate of Cancellation.** RULPA Section 203 requires a limited partnership to file a *certificate of cancellation* upon its dissolution and the commencement of winding up. The certificate of cancellation cancels the certificate of limited partnership.

**Winding Up.** Nearly all of the winding-up rules that apply to ordinary partnerships also apply to limited partnerships.

**When Winding Up Is Required.** Pursuant to RULPA Section 801, dissolution *requires* the winding up of a limited partnership's affairs. The only way to prevent winding up is to prevent dissolution, such as by an agreement of the partners that an event shall not cause a dissolution.

**Who May Wind Up.** RULPA Section 803 permits general partners who have *not wrongfully dissolved* a limited partnership to perform the winding up. Wrongful dissolution is defined by ordinary partnership law. It includes dissolution in violation of the limited partnership agreement or wrongful conduct that leads to a judicial dissolution, such as a general partner's breach of his fiduciary duties.

Limited partners may wind up if there are no surviving general partners. In addition, any partner may *ask a court* to perform a winding up, as was done in the *Mandell* case.

**Powers during Winding Up.** The winding-up partner has the same powers that a partner in an ordinary partnership has during winding up. He has the implied authority to do those acts that are reasonably necessary to liquidate the assets. He possesses the apparent authority to do all of the acts that he was able to do before dissolution, unless appropriate notice is given to persons who dealt with the partnership or knew of its existence.

**Distribution of Assets.** After the assets have been liquidated during winding up, the proceeds are distributed to those persons having claims against the limited partnership. Under RULPA Section 804, the proceeds are distributed as follows:

1. To firm *creditors,* including partners, except for unpaid distributions to partners.
2. To partners for *unpaid distributions,* including the return of capital to withdrawing partners.
3. To partners to the extent of their *capital contributions.*
4. To partners in the proportion in which they share distributions. Hence, the partners share the proceeds that remain after all other claimants have been paid.

Between partners, the order of distribution may be changed by a partnership agreement. For example, a limited partnership agreement may combine priorities 2 and 3 above, providing that unpaid distributions to partners shall be paid at the same time as capital contributions are returned. However, the priority of creditors may not be harmed by a partners' agreement, such as an agreement to pay creditors *after* partners have received the return of their capital.

Under ULPA Section 23, the order in which the claims against the limited partnership are to be paid after dissolution is different from the RULPA's order:

1. Firm creditors other than general partners.
2. Limited partners as to their share of profits.

3. Limited partners as to their capital contributions.
4. General partners to the extent that they are creditors of the firm.
5. General partners as to profits.
6. General partners as to capital contributions.

The distribution of assets under the RULPA or the ULPA is subject to a state's fraudulent conveyance statute and to federal bankruptcy law on preferences.[4]

[4] Fraudulent conveyances, preferences, and other aspects of bankruptcy law are covered in Chapter 41.

## Mandell v. Centrum Frontier Corporation

**407 N.E.2d 821 (Ill. Ct. App. 1980)**

Frontier Investment Associates, a limited partnership, was formed in 1976 to purchase, develop, lease, manage, and sell Park Place, a 56-story apartment building in Chicago. Sheldon Mandell, Howard Mandell, Jerome Mandell, and Norman Mandell were the limited partners. Centrum Frontier Corporation and William Thompson were the general partners. Thompson was the only shareholder of Centrum.

The partnership agreement provided that neither Thompson, Centrum, nor the Mandells could sell Park Place without one another's approval. In addition, when the limited partnership obtained a $22 million loan from Continental Illinois Bank, the Mandells insisted upon an agreement that Thompson would not convert the apartments to condominiums without the consent of a majority of the Mandells. The $22 million loan was secured by assets of the Mandells.

Thompson's cash flow projections for Park Place forecast substantial positive cash flows for the years 1978 to 1985. The cash flow projections were rarely met. For the first 17 months of operation, the partnership suffered a negative cash flow of $2,123,825; the cash flow projections were met in only 2 of these months. The partnership's average *daily* cash loss was $4,100. Interest on the loan was unpaid. By the summer of 1979, it was clear that Continental Illinois Bank would soon sell the Mandells' assets to pay the interest on the loan.

The Mandells and Thompson made separate efforts to sell Park Place. The Mandells rejected a sale negotiated by Thompson. Sheldon Mandell negotiated a profitable sale of Park Place, but Thompson refused to agree to that sale. Thompson also refused the Mandells' offer to buy his interest in the limited partnership. The Mandells then sued Centrum and Thompson, asking the court to dissolve the limited partnership and order the sale of Park Place. Thompson contested the action by introducing evidence that Park Place could be developed at a $48 million profit if the Mandells would consent to its conversion to condominiums. Thompson argued that the Mandells had breached the partnership agreement by not consenting to a condominium conversion.

The trial court ordered a dissolution and sale of Park Place on the grounds that there was a deadlock of the partners such that the business could not be carried on at a profit. Thompson and Centrum appealed. Before the court of appeals heard the case, Park Place was sold to the Mandells for $30 million at a public sale. Thompson and Centrum alleged that the Mandells' purchase was a breach of their fiduciary duty.

**O'Connor, Justice.** Thompson and Centrum first contend that the trial court erred in ordering the partnership dissolved because (1) it was not proved at trial that the partnership can only be carried on at a loss, and (2) deadlock was improperly relied upon in decreeing the dissolution.

Section 32(1)(e) of the Illinois Uniform Partnership Act, which applies to limited partnerships, provides:

> (1) On application by or for a partner the court shall order a dissolution whenever:
> (e) The business of the partnership can only be carried on at a loss.

A court will dissolve a partnership when it is reasonably certain that the business of the partnership cannot be carried on at a profit. A history of past losses is an indication that future profits are not to be expected.

It is clear that the partnership suffered losses during all but 2 months of the 17-month period prior to the filing of this suit. An analysis of the cash flow of the partnership reflects an aggregate cash loss of $2,123,825 during that 17-month period, an average of $4,100 per day. The losses were increasing at the time of the hearing.

Because the partnership had a negative cash flow during 15 months of the 17 months prior to filing this suit and the losses continued even after the trial court had ordered Park Place sold, we find that the trial court properly decreed dissolution of the partnership on the ground that Frontier could only be carried on at a loss.

Thompson and Centrum argue further that the trial court erred when it refused to consider the tax benefits the Mandells received by virtue of their participation in the partnership. The substance of this argument is that because the partnership never operated at a real economic loss as to the Mandells, the partnership should not have been dissolved. We disagree. The focus is to be placed on the losses of the partnership as an entity and not the losses of the individual partners. We find that the trial court did not err in refusing to consider any tax benefits received by the Mandells personally because of their participation in the partnership.

Thompson and Centrum also argue that because the ultimate purpose of the partnership included the future development and sale of Park Place, the trial court erred when it failed to consider that the partnership would be enormously profitable if Park Place were sold as condominiums. We disagree. Even assuming that the business of the partnership was to sell Park Place and that such a sale would be enormously profitable, under the existing circumstances conversion was not possible. The partnership agreement prohibited Thompson and Centrum from converting without the approval of the Mandells; the Mandells refused to agree to Thompson's conversion proposal. Because conversion was not possible under the existing circumstances, we find that the trial court did not err in refusing to consider whether or not the partnership would be profitable if Park Place were converted to condominiums.

Thompson and Centrum's final contention is that the trial court was misused as an instrumentality of a freeze-out. It is well-established law in Illinois that a fiduciary relationship exists between partners. Partners owe each other the duty to exercise the highest degree of honesty and good faith in their dealings and in the handling of partnership assets. A partnership is not terminated upon dissolution, but continues until the winding up of the partnership affairs is completed.

There is no allegation that the Mandells breached any fiduciary duty owed Thompson and Centrum when they filed their complaint requesting dissolution and a judicial sale of Park Place or when they bought Park Place at the subsequent judicial sale. Because daily losses were being incurred by the partnership, the Mandells sought dissolution. After ordering the partnership dissolved, the trial court also ordered a judicial sale of the property, which was subsequently conducted according to procedures that would insure fairness. Notice of the judicial sale appeared in five major newspapers for six consecutive weeks, as well as being posted at the Daley Center and the State of Illinois Building in Chicago. Although only two prospective bidders attended the sale and only one of the two made a bid, the $30 million price paid to purchase Park Place cannot be said to be below its market value in view of the fact that one of Thompson's own experts testified that a developer would pay $29 million to purchase the property.

The mere fact that the Mandells were the purchasers at the sale does not indicate that the dissolution and subsequent sale were merely a device to exclude Thompson and Centrum from the business. In addition, we again note that Thompson and Centrum had an opportunity equal to that of the Mandells to purchase Park Place at the sale. In every dissolution of a partnership where a judicial sale follows, there is a possibility that one or more of the partners may buy at the sale. However, this is not wrongful so long as grounds exist for the dissolution of the partnership, the judicial sale is conducted properly, and the partner-purchaser is not guilty of any breach of the fiduciary duty owed to his partners. All three conditions were met here.

Thompson and Centrum were not excluded from their interest in the partnership. They are entitled to their proportionate share of the proceeds of the sale.

Judgment for the Mandells affirmed.

## SUMMARY

A limited partnership is a statutory form of business organization composed of one or more general partners and one or more limited partners. Statutory formalities must be followed to create a limited partnership, including the filing of a certificate of limited partnership. Limited partnerships are used mostly as tax shelters, by passing the tax consequences of partnership transactions directly through to the partners.

Generally, the rights and liabilities of general partners in limited partnerships are similar to the rights of partners in ordinary partnerships. A partner's right to withdraw funds or property is usually determined by the limited partnership agreement. However, this right is subject to the rights of creditors.

Limited partners are generally not liable for partnership debts in excess of their capital contributions. A limited partner who participates in "control" of the partnership loses limited liability, although the definition of control is not clear. The RULPA expressly permits certain types of management activities by limited partners.

Limited partnerships are dissolved and wound up in much the same way as ordinary partnerships, except that the death, bankruptcy, or withdrawal of a limited partner does not cause a dissolution. Also, partners who are creditors share the same priority during distribution as do the other creditors of the limited partnership.

## PROBLEM CASES

**1.** Chena Hot Springs Group was formed to be a limited partnership, but it never filed a limited partnership certificate. Betz was one of the general partners. Pursuant to the limited partnership agreement, Betz was removed as a general partner and paid the value of his interest as determined by a formula in the partnership agreement, which Betz had signed. Betz sued the other partners to invalidate his retirement or to force a dissolution. He argued that no limited partnership was formed and that he was therefore not bound by the limited partnership agreement. Is Betz bound by the agreement?

**2.** John Fulton and Victoria Rinaldi entered into a contract to purchase bay-front property for $450,000. They signed the contract and mortgage agreements as general partners of Seventh-Sixth Street Limited Partnership, although no such partnership was then in existence. The amount of the mortgages was $265,000. They intended to create a limited partnership with themselves as general partners. The limited partnership agreement obligated limited partners to pay $10,400 if mortgage payments could not be met.

Only seven limited partnership units were sold. As a result, Fulton and Rinaldi could not meet a mortgage payment. They then restructured the debts, signing an agreement that increased the amount of the mortgages to $450,000. The partnership agreement and other documents were redrafted to increase the limited partners' obligation to $18,000. The revised certificate of limited partnership was filed immediately; however, the investors were not notified of the changes.

The limited partnership defaulted on the mortgages. The receiver of the partnership, acting for the creditors, sued the limited partners for their share of the mortgage debt. The limited partners claimed that the limited partnership never came into existence. They therefore argued that they had no liability, because Fulton and Rinaldi had no authority to act for them. Did a limited partnership come into existence?

**3.** Florida limited partnership law requires that two or more persons sign a limited partnership certificate in order to create a limited partnership. Allen Peele executed a power of attorney authorizing Robert Menke to sign, swear, and file a certificate of limited partnership on his behalf. The next day, Robert Menke executed and signed a certificate of limited partnership for Camp Carson Mines, Ltd., signing both his own name and that of Allen Peele. The agreement was filed with the secretary of state, who issued a certificate of limited partnership nine days later.

Camp Carson failed to pay its debts, and a creditor brought an involuntary bankruptcy case against it. One of the limited partners opposed the petition on the grounds that since only Menke had signed the certificate of limited partnership, Camp Carson had not been validly created and therefore was not a person. Bankruptcy law defines person as including partnerships. Was Camp Carson validly created, and did the bankruptcy law therefore apply to it?

**4.** Lowe was a limited partner of Blomquist Electric Company, a limited partnership. A general partner left the limited partnership, and an amended certificate of limited partnership was filed, but Lowe was not designated therein as a limited partner. Lowe signed the amended certificate. Arizona Power and Light Company extended credit to Blomquist after the amendment was filed, but was unaware of the defective filing. When Blomquist failed to pay Arizona Power and Light, it sued Lowe. Is Lowe liable?

**5.** Harry Whitley contracted with Black Watch Farms, a limited partnership, to receive a finder's fee if he negotiated a sale of the partnership interests to a third person. He did so but was not paid, because after the sale of the partnership interests, the purchaser took all the assets of the limited partnership. He sued the limited partners, claiming that the purchase of their interests by a person outside the limited partnership was a return of capital at a time when the debt to him was outstanding. Are the limited partners liable to Whitley?

6. North Olathe Warehouse Associates (NOWA), a Missouri limited partnership, conducted business in Kansas. On January 30, 1976, it filed an application to register to do business in Kansas with the Kansas secretary of state. On the same day, it assumed a $25,000 liability to North Olathe Industrial Park (NOIP). The assumption of liability occurred in Johnson County, Kansas. Four days later, NOWA filed its articles of limited partnership with the county recorder of Johnson County.

NOWA failed to pay the debt, and NOIP sued NOWA's limited partners. NOIP argued that the limited partners were liable as general partners because NOWA failed to register as a foreign limited partnership by not making a timely filing with the Johnson County recorder. Are the limited partners liable as general partners?

7. Horne-Long Associates was a limited partnership with 1 general partner and 18 limited partners. Horne-Long breached a contract with Northampton Valley Construction, owing over $186,000. Northampton sued the limited partners of Horne-Long because the limited partnership certificate stated that the general partner could require the limited partners to make additional contributions to meet the obligations of the partnership. Northampton claimed that this provision made the limited partners de facto general partners, since the general partner should have called on the limited partners to pay the debt. Is Northampton correct?

8. Seven Hills Associates, a limited partnership, was formed in Ohio to own and operate a two-story commercial office building. The only general partner was Raphael Silver. The building obtained its heat and utilities from equipment located in an adjacent building owned by a corporation in which Silver had the controlling interest.

James Strain, one of the limited partners in Seven Hills Associates, brought a derivative action against Silver. He alleged that Silver had breached his fiduciary duty to Seven Hills Associates by operating the two buildings as if they were commonly owned. As a result, the expenses of the partnership's building had been higher and its income lower than they would otherwise have been. The mortgage payments on the partnership's building could not be made. Consequently, the lender had foreclosed on the building and the limited partners had lost their investments. Silver's defense is that a derivative action cannot be maintained by a limited partner under the ULPA. Is this a good defense?

9. Hacienda Farms, Ltd. was organized as a limited partnership. De Escamilla was the general partner, and Russell and Andrews were the limited partners. Any two of the partners could sign checks drawn on the partnership's bank account. Russell and Andrews visited the farm about twice a week and discussed what crops should be raised. They insisted that peppers, eggplant, and watermelons be planted, although de Escamilla thought the soil unsuitable. The partnership went into bankruptcy. The trustee in bankruptcy asked the court to rule that Russell and Andrews were liable as general partners to creditors of the partnership. Are they liable as general partners?

# PART VI

# CORPORATIONS

# Chapter 22

# History and Nature of Corporations

## INTRODUCTION

The modern corporation is the most important form of business in the history of the world. It has facilitated the rapid economic development of the last 150 years by permitting businesses to attain economies of scale. Businesses organized as corporations can attain such economies because they have a greater capacity to raise capital, a capacity created by corporation law. Corporation law allows a person to invest his money in a corporation and become an owner without imposing unlimited liability or management responsibilities on him. Many people are willing to invest their savings in a large, risky business if they have limited liability and no management responsibilities. Far fewer people are willing to invest in a partnership or other business form in which owners have unlimited liability and management duties.

The purpose of the next few chapters is to study the corporation as a business form, especially to understand the rights and responsibilities of persons affiliated with, doing business with, and affected by corporations. In this chapter, you begin your study of corporations by examining the history and nature of corporations and the history and nature of government regulation of corporations.

## HISTORY OF CORPORATIONS

Although modern corporation law emerged in only the last 150 years, ancestors of the modern corporation existed in the times of Hammurabi, ancient Greece, and the Roman Empire. As early as 1248 in France, privileges of incorporation were given to mercantile ventures to encourage investment for the benefit of society. In England, the corporate form was used extensively before the 16th century. Merchants conducted their business affairs as corporations as a matter of contract and without approval of the Crown, that is, the government. Gradually, the Crown asserted control over these corporations. By the middle of the 18th century, a corporation could be created *only* by an act of the Crown.

The British Crown sparingly granted corporate status. Merchant and craft guilds were among the first to receive corporate charters from the Crown. Guilds sought corporate charters because such charters gave them monopolies in a trade or profession. The guilds' members were protected by the corporations' enforcement of the monopolies granted by the Crown. But the guilds' members were independent businesses: they did not share one another's profits. Not until 1555, when Queen Mary chartered the Russia Company, did there exist joint trading companies—corporations whose owners shared in the profits of the venture.

**British Trading Companies.** The famous British trading companies, such as the Russia Company and the Massachusetts Bay Company, were the forerunners of the modern corporation. These companies were given monopolies in trade and granted powers to govern in the areas they colonized. They were permitted to operate as corporations due to the benefits that they would confer on the British Empire, such as the exploitation of natural resources. Although these trading companies were among the few corporations of the time whose owners were granted limited liability, they rarely sought corporate status to confer limited liability on their owners or even to obtain perpetual life. Instead, they sought corporate charters primarily because the Crown granted them *monopolies and governmental powers.*

In the beginning, these trading companies obtained new capital for each voyage, whether to the New World, India, or elsewhere. At the end of each voyage, the owners' capital was returned and the profits were divided. The East India Company, in 1657, was the first company to receive permanent capital from its owners.

**Early American Corporation Law.** Beginning in 1776, corporation law in the United States evolved independently of English corporation law. Early American corporations received *special charters* from state legislatures. These charters were granted one at a time by special action of the legislatures. Few special charters were granted. To obtain such charters, persons sometimes paid bribes to legislators.

**Emergence of General Incorporation Statutes.** In the late 18th century, general incorporation statutes emerged in the United States. North Carolina in 1795, Massachusetts in 1799, and other states in later years passed statutes permitting incorporation by *any* group of persons meeting the requirements of the statutes. Initially, these statutes permitted incorporation only for limited purposes beneficial to the public, such as operating toll bridges and water systems. Incorporation was still viewed as a privilege, and many restrictions were placed on corporations. Incorporation was permitted for only short periods of time. Maximum limits on capitalization were low. Ownership of real and personal property was often restricted.

During the last 150 years, these restrictive provisions have disappeared in most states. In 1837, Connecticut became the first state to permit the formation of corporations for "any lawful purpose." Today, modern incorporation statutes are mostly enabling, granting the persons who control a corporation great flexibility in establishing, financing, and operating it.

**Emergence of Limited Liability of Owners.** Limited liability for owners of *nontrading* companies was recognized in the 15th century. Crown charters in England were always accompanied by limited liability on the theory that the Crown had created a separate person. This limited liability, however, was recognized mainly to prevent a member's creditors from seizing corporate assets. Many corporate charters expressly granted a corporation the power to assess its owners for money to pay its debts, and in 1671 the House of Lords held that this power could be asserted by creditors. In response, ingenious lawyers drafted corporate charters that eliminated such assessment power, thereby creating by contract limited liability for the owners. By the end of the 17th century, individual owners of a *trading* company were recognized as not being liable for its debts.

**American Corporation Law.** The American incorporation statutes of the late 18th and early 19th centuries whittled away at the English development of limited liability. Some states provided for limited liability; others had double liability; and Massachusetts, for example, had unlimited liability for owners of manufacturing corporations. By 1830, when Massachusetts accepted limited liability, the general principle of limited liability of owners for corporate debts was well established. Today, modern statutes grant limited liability to the owners of corporations, with few exceptions.

## PRINCIPAL CHARACTERISTICS OF CORPORATIONS

The essential features of the modern corporation have changed little in the last 150 years. These features are:

1. A corporation may be *created only by permission of a government.*

2. A corporation is a legal *person* and a legal *entity* independent of its owners (called shareholders) and its managers (called directors and officers). Its life is unaffected by the retirement or death of its shareholders, officers, and directors.

A corporation may *acquire, hold, and convey property* in its own name. A corporation may *sue and be sued* in its own name. Harm to a corporation is not harm to the shareholders; therefore, with few exceptions, a shareholder may not sue to enforce a claim of the corporation.

Generally, *shareholders owe no fiduciary duties* to the corporation. A shareholder who is not an officer or a director may deal with the corporation as may any other person. A shareholder may be a creditor of the corporation. *Directors and officers are fiduciaries* of the corporation, restricted in their dealings with the corporation, much like agents who deal with their principals.

A corporation is a person under the Constitution of the United States. Like natural persons, it is protected from unreasonable searches and seizures and is guaranteed due process and equal protection under the law. It also has free speech rights.[1] It has its own

[1] See Chapter 42 for a discussion of the constitutional rights of corporations.

*domicile* and its own place of *residence,* whose locations determine in part whether a state may constitutionally impose its laws on the corporation.

3. There is no necessary identity of ownership and management of a corporation. A shareholder has *no right or duty to manage* the business of a corporation. The directors and officers need not be shareholders.

4. Generally, the ownership interest in a corporation is *freely transferable.* A shareholder may sell her shares to whomever she wants whenever she wants. The purchaser becomes a shareholder with the same rights that her seller had.

5. The shareholders have *limited liability.* With few exceptions, they are not liable for the debts of a corporation beyond their capital contributions to the corporation.

6. A corporation *pays federal income taxes* on its income. Shareholders have personal income from the corporation only if the corporation makes a distribution of its assets to them. For example, a shareholder would have personal income from the corporation if the corporation paid him a dividend.

## CLASSIFICATIONS OF CORPORATIONS

Corporations may be divided into three classes: (1) corporations *for profit,* (2) corporations *not for profit,* and (3) *government-owned* corporations. State corporation statutes establish procedures for the incorporation of each of these classes and for their operation. In addition, a large body of common law applies to all corporations.

**For-Profit Corporations.** Most business corporations are for-profit corporations. Their shareholders expect a return on investment in the form of dividends paid by the corporation and increased market value of their shares. Nearly all for-profit corporations are incorporated under the *general incorporation law* of a state. All of the states require professionals, such as physicians, dentists, lawyers, and accountants, to incorporate under *professional corporation acts.* In addition, for-profit corporations that especially affect the public interest, such as banks, insurance companies, and savings and loan associations, are usually required to incorporate under special statutes.

**Close Corporations and Publicly Held Corporations.** For-profit corporations range from small, one-person businesses to huge international organizations such as General Motors Corporation. Corporations with few shareholders are usually called *close corporations;* General Motors is an example of a *publicly held* corporation because its shares are available to public investors.

Generally, close corporations and publicly held corporations are subject to the same rules under state corporation law. Many states, however, allow close corporations greater latitude in the regulation of their internal affairs than is granted to public corporations. For example, the shareholders may be permitted to manage the close corporation as if it were a partnership and may be able to place severe restrictions on the transfer of its shares. A close corporation, however, may be required to meet special requirements of the state incorporation statute.[2]

A Subchapter S corporation, or *S Corporation,* is a special type of close corporation. It is treated nearly like a partnership for federal tax purposes. Its shareholders report the earnings or losses of the business on their individual federal income tax returns. An S Corporation election is made by complying with Internal Revenue Code requirements, including the requirement that they have no more than 35 shareholders.

[2] The formalities for electing close corporation status are discussed in Chapter 23.

**Not-for-Profit Corporations.** Some corporations that appear to be little different from other businesses are actually classified as nonprofit corporations. Charities, churches, fraternal organizations, mutual insurance companies, some savings and loan associations, and such businesses as the Blue Cross and Blue Shield companies are incorporated as nonprofit corporations. These corporations have *members* rather than shareholders, and none of the surplus revenue from their operations may be distributed to their members. Since they generally pay no income tax, nonprofit corporations can reinvest a larger share of their incomes in the business than can for-profit corporations. Another type of nonprofit business, the cooperative, is usually incorporated under a special statute, but it too has this reinvestment advantage. As a result, some of the largest agribusiness organizations are cooperatives.

**Government-Owned Corporations.** Many American corporations are owned by governments and perform governmental and business functions. A municipality (city) is one type of government-owned corporation. Other types are created to furnish more specific services: for example, school corporations, water companies, and irrigation districts. Still others, such as the Tennessee Valley Authority and the Federal Deposit Insurance Corporation, have no taxing powers and operate much like for-profit corporations, except that at least some of their directors are appointed by governmental officials, and some or all of their financing frequently comes from government. The TVA and the FDIC are chartered by Congress, but government-owned corporations may also be authorized by states. Government-operated businesses seek corporate status to free themselves from governmental operating procedures, which are more cumbersome than business operating procedures.

## REGULATION OF CORPORATIONS

**Federal versus State Incorporation.** The framers of the U.S. Constitution decided not to provide for the incorporation (or chartering) of general business corporations by the federal government. Therefore, such corporations are incorporated by the individual states. The early corporate charters were grants of privilege and included numerous restrictions on the corporations. Even after states began to adopt general incorporation statutes, these tended to be restrictive, as indicated at the beginning of this chapter. Today, few restrictions remain in corporation statutes, and those that remain are designed to provide only a minimum level of protections for shareholders and creditors. These protections will be discussed in Chapters 24 and 25.

The freedom that the states give to corporations has been condemned by legal scholars and critics of business. Several bills have been introduced in Congress that would require the largest corporations to incorporate under federal law instead of, or in addition to, state law. The critics argue that leaving incorporation to the states has resulted in competition for incorporation fees and a "race for the bottom," which has been won by Delaware. Delaware owes its victory to the fact that historically its legislature and its courts have been attentive to business interests and have given corporate management much freedom from shareholder and creditor intervention.[3]

At various times in the past, proposals for federal incorporation have dropped from public view in favor of passage of major federal regulatory statutes dealing with the primary concerns of those times. Such statutes include the Interstate Commerce Act in 1887, the Sherman Act in 1890, the Clayton Act and the Federal Trade Commission Act in 1914,

[3] As you will see in Chapters 24 and 25, however, in recent years the Delaware courts have pioneered in expanding the rights of shareholders.

the Securities Act of 1933, and the Securities Exchange Act of 1934.[4] Much controversy exists concerning whether dealing with the social problems posed by large corporations through a federal incorporation act, coupled with a superagency to administer it, would be more successful than our present patchwork of statutes and numerous administrative agencies. There appears to be nothing inherent in the incorporation process that would make regulation through that means superior to the present pattern of regulation. Lack of social responsibility is not a problem limited to 500 or more of the largest corporations. Therefore, regulation through federal chartering is not a substitute for specific regulatory statutes applicable to a much greater number of corporations.

**State Incorporation Statutes.** State incorporation statutes set out the basic rules that a corporation, its shareholders, and its managers must follow in organizing, financing, operating, and dissolving a corporation. The statutes vary greatly, but this variety causes few problems to interstate businesses. A business may incorporate in only one state, yet do business in all the others. Mostly, the corporation law of the state of incorporation applies to a corporation.

**Model Business Corporation Act.** Although there is no need for a *uniform* state incorporation statute, the American Bar Association's Committee on Corporate Laws has prepared a *model* statute for adoption by state legislatures. The purpose of the model statute is to improve the rationality of corporation law. It is called the *Model Business Corporation Act* (MBCA). The MBCA has been amended many times, and it was completely revised in 1984.

The revised MBCA is the basis of a recent revision of the Virginia corporation law and is under consideration in about another one-third of the states. Most of its provisions already represent the majority rule in the United States. Other MBCA provisions may become majority rules in the near future. Therefore, your study of statutory corporation law in this book will concentrate on the revised MBCA. Most of the revised MBCA is reprinted in an appendix.

The old MBCA is the basis for the statutes of a majority of the states. In addition, many other states have adopted selected sections. Nevertheless, Delaware and several other major commercial and industrial states, such as New York and California, do not follow the old MBCA. The old MBCA provisions will be addressed when these differ greatly from the provisions of the revised MBCA, represent the majority rule, or provide an historical context for the present state of the law. Provisions of the Delaware and California acts will be mentioned when important.

**Close Corporation Statutes.** Several states have special provisions or statutes that are applicable only to close corporations. In 1982, the ABA's Committee on Corporate Laws adopted the *Statutory Close Corporation Supplement to the Model Business Corporation Act.* The Supplement is designed to provide a rational, statutory solution to the special problems facing close corporations.

**State Common Law of Corporations.** Although nearly all of corporation law is statutory law, including the courts' interpretation of the statutes, there is a substantial body of common law of corporations. Most of this common law deals with creditor and shareholder rights. For example, the law of piercing the corporate veil, which you will study later in this chapter, is common law protecting creditors of corporations. Also, in recent years

[4] See Chapter 44 for a discussion of the Sherman Act, Chapter 45 for the Clayton Act, Chapter 46 for the Federal Trade Commission Act, and Chapter 26 for the securities acts.

the Delaware courts have created important new common law rights protecting shareholders.

The common law provides a fertile ground for judicial experiments with new solutions to intracorporate conflicts. Often, legislatures study the development of the common law and enact statutes that in part reflect the common law thinking of judges. For example, statutory close corporation statutes have evolved from the common law of close corporations.

## REGULATION OF FOREIGN CORPORATIONS

A corporation may be incorporated in one state, yet do business in many other states in which it is not incorporated. The corporation's contacts with those states may permit them, among other things, to regulate the corporation's transactions with their citizens, to subject the corporation to suits in their courts, or to tax the corporation. Under what circumstances a state may impose its laws on a business incorporated in another state is the issue presented in the area of foreign corporations.

**Definitions.** A corporation is a *domestic corporation* in the state that has granted its charter; it is a *foreign corporation* in all the other states in which it does business. For example, a corporation organized in Delaware and doing business in Florida is domestic in Delaware and foreign in Florida. Note that a corporation domiciled in one country is an *alien corporation* in other countries in which it does business.

**State Jurisdiction over Foreign Corporations.** Generally, a state may impose its laws on a foreign corporation if such imposition does not violate the Constitution of the United States, notably the Commerce Clause and the Due Process Clause of the 14th Amendment.[5]

**Commerce Clause.** Under the Commerce Clause, the power to regulate interstate commerce is given to the federal government. The states have no power to exclude or to discriminate against foreign corporations that are engaged solely in *interstate* commerce. Nevertheless, a state may require a foreign corporation doing interstate business in the state to comply with its laws if the application of these laws does not unduly burden interstate commerce. A state statute does not unduly burden interstate commerce if (1) the statute serves a *legitimate state interest,* (2) the state has chosen the *least burdensome means* of promoting that interest, and (3) that legitimate state interest *outweighs the statute's burden* on interstate commerce. Examples of these tests appear later in the chapter.

When a foreign corporation does *intrastate* business in a state, the state may regulate the corporation's activities, provided again that the regulation does not unduly burden interstate commerce. Since conducting intrastate business increases a corporation's contact with a state, it is easier to prove that there is no undue burden.

**Due Process Clause.** The Due Process Clause requires that a foreign corporation have sufficient contacts with a state before a state may exercise jurisdiction over the corporation. The leading case in this area is the *International Shoe* case.[6] In that case, the Supreme Court ruled that a foreign corporation must have "certain minimum contacts" with the state such that asserting jurisdiction over

[5] The Commerce Clause and the Due Process Clause are discussed in detail in Chapter 42.

[6] *International Shoe Co. v. State of Washington,* 326 U.S. 310 (1945).

the corporation does not offend "traditional notions of fair play and substantial justice." The Supreme Court justified its holding with a "benefit theory": when a foreign corporation avails itself of the protection of a state's laws, it should suffer any reasonable burden that the state imposes as a consequence of such benefit. In other words, a foreign corporation should be required to "pay" for the benefits that it receives from the state.

**Doing Business.** To aid their determination of whether a state may constitutionally impose its laws on a foreign corporation, courts have traditionally used the concept of *doing business.* Courts have generally held that a foreign corporation is subject to the laws of a state when it is doing business in the state. The activities that constitute doing business differ, however, depending on the purpose of the determination. There are five such purposes: (1) to determine whether a corporation is *subject to a lawsuit* in a state's courts, (2) to determine whether the corporation's activities are *subject to taxation,* (3) to determine whether the corporation's activities are *subject to health and safety regulation* by the state, (4) to determine whether the corporation must *qualify* to carry on its activities in the state, and (5) to determine whether the state may *regulate the internal affairs* of the corporation.

Interpreting the Constitution, courts have held that fewer contacts with a state are necessary to subject a foreign corporation to a lawsuit in the state than are necessary to permit its activities within the state to be taxed or regulated. Before a state can require a foreign corporation to qualify to do intrastate business, the corporation must be carrying on activities within the state beyond those required for taxation. To allow a state to regulate the internal affairs of a foreign corporation, the foreign corporation must have even greater contacts with the state.

**Subjecting Foreign Corporations to Suit.** The Supreme Court of the United States has held that a foreign corporation may be brought into a state's court in connection with its activities within the state, provided that the state does not violate the corporation's due process rights under the 14th Amendment of the Constitution and its rights under the Commerce Clause.

**Minimum Contacts Test.** The *International Shoe* minimum contacts test must be met. Subjecting the corporation to suit cannot offend "traditional notions of fair play and substantial justice." A court must weigh the corporation's contacts within the state against the inconvenience to the corporation of requiring it to defend a suit within the state. The burden on the corporation must be reasonable in relation to the benefit that it receives from conducting activities in the state. Stated this way, a state's compliance with the minimum contacts test ensures that subjecting the foreign corporation to suit in the state will violate neither the Commerce Clause nor the Due Process Clause.

Under the minimum contacts test, even an isolated event may be sufficient to confer jurisdiction on a state's courts. For example, driving a truck from Arizona through New Mexico toward a final destination in Florida provides sufficient contacts with New Mexico to permit a suit in New Mexico's courts against the foreign corporation for its driver's negligently causing an accident within New Mexico.

**Long-Arm Statutes.** Since the decision in the *International Shoe* case was reached, most of the states have passed *long-arm statutes* to permit their courts to exercise jurisdiction under that decision. These statutes frequently specify several kinds of corporate activities that make foreign corporations subject to suit within the state, such as the commission of a tort, the making of a contract, or the ownership of property. Most of the long-arm statutes grant jurisdiction over causes of action growing out of any transaction within the state.

Some long-arm statutes give a state's courts jurisdiction in product liability cases if the foreign corporation should have expected use of the product in the state. The constitutionality of such a provision is doubtful, since in a recent case the Supreme Court held that the mere foreseeability of a product's use in a state does not permit a state's courts to exercise jurisdiction over the seller of the product.[7] In that case, New York residents bought a car in New York from a New York corporation. They were injured while driving the car in Oklahoma and sued the New York corporation in an Oklahoma court. The Supreme Court held that Oklahoma's courts had no jurisdiction over the New York corporation.

Many long-arm statutes have a catchall provision that subjects to jurisdiction any nonresident who has "the necessary minimum contacts with the state." Application of a catchall provision turns each case into an exercise in interpretation of the Due Process and Commerce Clauses.

*Hervish v. Growables, Inc.*, which follows, is an example of the application of a long-arm statute.

**Taxation.** A state may tax a foreign corporation if such taxation does *not discriminate* against interstate commerce, otherwise unduly *burden interstate commerce,* or violate the corporation's *due process* rights. Generally, a state's imposition of a tax must serve a legitimate state interest and be reasonable in relation to a foreign corporation's contacts with the state.

For example, a North Carolina corporation's *property* located in Pennsylvania is subject to property tax in Pennsylvania. The corporation receives the benefit of state protection of private property. It may be required to pay its share of the cost of such protection.

Oklahoma may require a Kansas corporation whose trucks use its roads to pay a road use tax. The tax serves a legitimate state interest of financing the construction and maintenance of Oklahoma roads, which the Kansas corporation uses. Nevertheless, Oklahoma may not impose a more onerous tax on Kansas corporations than it imposes on its own corporations. Such a tax discriminates against interstate commerce.

**Federal Interstate Income Tax Act.** Greater contacts are needed to subject a corporation to *income taxation* in a state than are needed to subject it to property or road use taxation. Under the Federal Interstate Income Tax Act, using an independent agent, such as a manufacturer's representative, to sell goods that are prepared and shipped from outside the state does not subject the manufacturer to income taxation. Nevertheless, a truck line that regularly carries goods into a state in interstate commerce has been held subject to income taxation. Also, a manufacturer with a sales office in a state is subject to state corporate income taxation, even if the goods sold are prepared and shipped from outside the state.

**Health and Safety Regulations.** A state may subject foreign corporations to its health and safety regulations if the application of such regulations, as a reasonable exercise of the state's *police power,* does not violate the Constitution, principally the Commerce Clause and the Due Process Clause. The 10th Amendment of the Constitution permits a state to regulate the health, safety, and welfare of its citizens. This police power allows

[7] *World-Wide Volkswagen Corp. v. Woodson,* 444 U.S. 286 (1980).

a state to regulate highway speeds and the quality of merchandise sold in the state, among other things. For example, New York may require a Wisconsin dairy corporation that is selling in New York to comply with New York laws imposing sanitary standards for dairy products. Such laws protect state citizens from harmful food, a legitimate state interest that outweighs the small burden imposed on interstate commerce.

**Qualifying to Do Business.** A state may require that foreign corporations *qualify* to conduct *intrastate* business in the state. The level of doing business that constitutes intrastate business, and thereby justifies state jurisdiction, has been difficult to define. To help clarify the confusion in this area, MBCA Section 15.01 lists several activities that do *not* constitute doing business. For example, soliciting, by mail or through employees, orders that require acceptance outside the state is not doing business. Selling through independent contractors or owning real or personal property is not doing business.

**Isolated Transaction.** Also classified as not doing business is conducting an isolated transaction that is completed within 30 days and is not one in the course of repeated transactions of a like nature. This *isolated transaction* safe harbor allows a tree grower to bring Christmas trees into a state in order to sell them to one retailer. However, a Christmas tree retailer who comes into a state for 29 days before Christmas and sells to consumers from a street corner is required to qualify. Although both merchants have consummated their transactions within 30 days, the grower has engaged in only one transaction, but the retailer has engaged in a series of transactions. In addition, other one time transactions, such as the sale of a building or an entire stock of goods, are not doing business, coming within the isolated transaction exception. The court in the *National Steeplechase* case, which follows, applied the isolated transaction safe harbor.

**Examples.** The MBCA, in the comments to Section 15.01, indicates that maintaining an office to conduct intrastate business, selling personal property not in interstate commerce, entering into contracts relating to local business or sales, or owning or using real estate for general corporate purposes does constitute doing business. Passive ownership of real estate for investment, however, is not doing business.

Under the MBCA, maintaining a stock of goods within a state from which to fill orders, even if the orders are taken or accepted outside the state, is doing business. Peddling goods from a truck sent in from outside the state has been held to require qualification. Even performing service activities, such as machinery repair and construction work, may be doing business. Note, however, that the *National Steeplechase* case holds that providing services for four days annually to an independent in-state business is not doing business requiring qualification.

**Qualification Requirements.** A state's qualification (or admission) requirements must not violate a foreign corporation's constitutional rights, especially its rights under the Commerce Clause. Any requirement must be reasonable in relation to the state's interests and the corporation's contacts with the state.

Constitutional problems are rare in this area, since all states permit foreign corporations to qualify to do business in their states by complying with a few simple statutory provisions. MBCA Section 15.01 provides that a foreign corporation must apply for a *certificate of authority* from the secretary of state, pay an application fee, maintain a registered office and a registered agent in the state, file an annual report with the secretary of state, and pay an annual fee. The registered agent is frequently a corporation that makes a business of providing such representation to many foreign corporations.

Three states require or permit *domestication* as an alternative to qualification. Essentially, domesticated corporations must comply with the corporation law that applies to domestic corporations of the state. For most purposes, domesticated corporations are identical to domestic corporations.

**Penalties for Failure to Qualify.** Doing intrastate business without qualifying usually subjects the foreign corporation to a fine, in some states as much as $10,000. MBCA Section 15.02 subjects the corporation to daily fines. It also disables the corporation to use the state's courts to bring a lawsuit until it obtains a certificate of authority. The corporation may defend itself in the state's courts, however, even if it has no certificate of authority.

**Regulation of Internal Affairs.** A corporation may incorporate in one state, yet do most of its business in another state. Such a corporation is called a *pseudoforeign corporation* in the state in which it conducts most of its business. Only a few states subject pseudo foreign corporations to extensive regulation of their internal affairs, regulation similar to that imposed on their domestic corporations. California's statute requires corporations that have more than 50 percent of their business and shares in California to elect directors by cumulative voting,[8] to hold annual directors' elections, and to comply with California's dividend payment restrictions, among other requirements. *Wilson v. Louisiana-Pacific Resources, Inc.,* which follows, considers whether the Constitution permits application of the California statute to pseudoforeign corporations. Foreign corporations raise many constitutional objections to the California statute, including the Full Faith and Credit Clause, the Commerce Clause, and the Due Process Clause.

The California statute's regulation of the internal affairs of pseudoforeign corporations is a positive development in corporate governance. As more states subject foreign corporations and domestic corporations to the same corporate governance provisions, the advantage of shopping for the state with the most lenient incorporation law may nearly disappear. Statutes such as California's may reduce the need for federal incorporation and federal corporate governance standards.

[8] Cumulative voting is discussed in Chapter 25.

## Hervish v. Growables, Inc.

**449 So.2d 684 (La. Ct. App. 1984)**

Growables, Inc., a manufacturer of furniture, was incorporated in St. Petersburg, Florida. In July 1982, Debra Hervish, a resident of Florida, obtained from her mother a brochure about Growables' line of children's furniture. She went to Growables' offices in Florida to place an order for 14 pieces of furniture. While at Growables' office, she deposited $2,000 toward the total purchase price of $2,662. She told Growables that she would soon be moving to Louisiana, and she asked that the furniture be shipped there. Growables agreed to do so.

In early August 1982, Mrs. Hervish moved to Kenner, Louisiana, and informed Growables of her new address. Thereafter, she contacted Growables three or four times to find out why shipment of the furniture had been delayed beyond the eight weeks estimated by Growables.

On November 2, 1982, the furniture was delivered to Mrs. Hervish by Ryder Truck Lines. At the time of delivery, she paid the Ryder driver the balance of the purchase price plus the shipping charges, a total of $877. Upon opening the cardboard cartons in which the furniture had been shipped, Mrs. Hervish discovered that every piece of furniture was damaged. After making futile demands for recovery from Ryder and Growables, she sued Growables in a Louisiana trial court.

Growables asked the trial court to dismiss the suit on the ground that the Louisiana courts could not take long-arm jurisdiction over Growables. The trial court agreed with Growables and dismissed Hervish's suit. Hervish appealed.

**Chehardy, Judge.** The Louisiana long-arm statute provides, in pertinent part,

> A court may exercise personal jurisdiction over a nonresident, who acts directly or by an agent, as to a cause of action arising from the nonresident's:
> (a) transacting any business in this state;
> (b) contracting to supply services or things in this state;
> (c) causing injury or damage by an offense or quasi-offense committed through an act or omission in this state;
> (d) causing injury or damage in this state by an offense or quasi-offense committed through an act or omission outside of this state, if he regularly does or solicits business, or engages in any other persistent course of conduct, or derives substantial revenue from goods used or consumed or services rendered, in this state.

This statute was intended by the Legislature to extend the personal jurisdiction of Louisiana courts over nonresidents to the full limits of due process under the Fourteenth Amendment.

In order for the proper exercise of jurisdiction over a nonresident, there must be sufficient minimum contacts between the nonresident defendant and the forum state to satisfy due process and traditional notions of fair play and substantial justice. Whether or not a particular defendant has sufficient minimum contracts with a state is to be determined from the facts and circumstances peculiar to each case.

It is essential in each case that there be some act by which the defendant purposefully avails itself of the privilege of conducting activities within the forum state, thus invoking the benefits and protections of its law. It appears that knowledge alone or foreseeability that a chattel will come to rest in a particular state is insufficient to subject a defendant to jurisdiction, unless the facts and circumstances lead to a conclusion that the defendant purposefully availed itself of the privilege of conducting activities within the forum state in such a manner that the defendant has clear notice that it would be subject to suit there.

Applying these standards to the case before us, we must examine the contacts between Growables, Inc., and Louisiana to determine whether the relationship is sufficient to satisfy due process requirements. At the time Mrs. Hervish ordered the furniture, she was a Florida resident. She obtained the brochure advertising the furniture in Florida; she went personally to the Growables office in Florida to place the order. The only incidents that took place in Louisiana are Mrs. Hervish's calls to Growables to question the delay in shipment, the delivery—through a third-party truck—of the furniture into this state, and

Mrs. Hervish's payment of the balance of the purchase price to the truck driver upon delivery.

There is no evidence that Growables transacts any business in Louisiana, that its representatives or agents travel to Louisiana for business purposes, or that it advertises or otherwise solicits business in Louisiana or from Louisiana residents, either directly or by mail. There is no evidence that Growables derives any substantial revenue from business in Louisiana, or "engages in any persistent course of conduct" in this state.

In fact, the only classification of the long-arm statute Growables will fit into is subparagraph (b), "contracting to supply services or things in this state." We can, however, find no other case in which a Louisiana court has found an isolated incident of delivery, without other affiliating circumstances, sufficient to apply long-arm jurisdiction to a foreign defendant. This single transaction would not justify our concluding that the defendant purposefully availed itself of the privilege of conducting activities within Louisiana in such a manner that the defendant had clear notice it would be subject to suit here.

Accordingly, we conclude the district court properly found a lack of personal jurisdiction over Growables.

Judgment for Growables affirmed.

---

## Commonwealth of Kentucky v. National Steeplechase and Hunt Ass'n, Inc.

**612 S.W.2d 347 (Ky. Ct. App. 1981)**

The National Steeplechase and Hunt Association (NSHA) is a New York corporation that sanctions, regulates, and supervises steeplechase races. Its first sanctioned race was the Oxmoor Steeplechase, near Louisville, Kentucky, in 1948. It has supervised the High Hope Steeplechase in Fayette County, Kentucky, since 1967 and the Hard Scuffle Steeplechase in Oldham County, near Louisville, since 1975. Each of the sanctioned events lasts no more than three to four days every year.

The NSHA has never obtained from the Kentucky secretary of state a certificate to do business in Kentucky as a foreign corporation. No annual reports have been filed, and no registration fees have been paid. The NSHA does not maintain a registered office or a registered agent in the state.

In 1975, the Commonwealth of Kentucky sued the NSHA to collect all of the fees and penalties due to the Commonwealth as a result of the failure of the NSHA to qualify to do business in Kentucky. The Commonwealth also sought to enjoin the NSHA from transacting further business until it complied with the statute. The trial court held that the NSHA was not doing business in Kentucky and therefore did not need to qualify. The Commonwealth appealed.

**Wintersheimer, Judge.** The sanctioning of steeplechase meetings does not constitute the transaction of business in Kentucky. The NSHA promulgates rules; approves the racecourses, race officials and the financial responsibility of the sponsoring organization; receives entries for each meeting by telephone or mail; assembles the information on the meetings; and prepares a booklet and identification badges for each meet. All of these functions are performed in the New York office. The NSHA maintains no offices or employees in Kentucky. All communications are conducted by mail or telephone. The NSHA provides a service and information to the local sponsoring organization. We cannot say that the attendance by NSHA employees at the meetings constitutes the transaction of business in Kentucky.

The leasing of fences and jumps by the NSHA to the local organizations in Kentucky is within the exception provided for interstate commerce in the Kentucky statute. The NSHA driver transporting the jumps to Kentucky does not assist the local agency in setting up the equipment. It is uncontroverted that the employee does not continue to deal with the equipment after it is delivered.

The isolated transaction section applies to the activities of the NSHA employees in Kentucky. The statute makes an exception for isolated transactions completed within 30 days and not in the course of a number of repeated transactions of a like nature. Here, the meetings generally last no more than three to four days. Three different locations are now used annually. We cannot say that the presence of the NSHA's employees at these meetings and the occasional utilization of them as stewards fall outside the isolated transaction section.

The statutes authorizing the collection of delinquent fees for failure to qualify as a foreign corporation are penal in nature and must be strictly construed against the state and liberally interpreted in favor of the foreign corporation. Because the NSHA is not doing business in Kentucky, it is not subject to the imposition of any penalties.

Judgment for the NSHA affirmed.

## Wilson v. Louisiana-Pacific Resources, Inc.

**187 Cal. Rptr. 852 (Cal. Ct. App. 1982)**

Section 2115 of the California General Corporation Law requires that a foreign corporation doing a majority of its business in California (on the basis of a three-factor formula that includes property, payroll, and sales) and having a majority of its outstanding voting securities owned by persons with addresses in California comply with certain internal governance provisions of the California corporation law. Among the provisions are parts of section 708, which provide for the cumulative voting of shares for the election of directors.

Ross A. Wilson, a shareholder of Louisiana-Pacific Resources, Inc., a Utah corporation, brought suit against Louisiana-Pacific seeking a declaratory judgment that Louisiana-Pacific met the tests of section 2115 and that he was therefore entitled to vote his shares cumulatively in accordance with section 708. In the years preceding Wilson's suit, the average of Louisiana-Pacific's property, payroll, and sales in California exceeded 50 percent, and more than 50 percent of its shareholders entitled to vote resided in California. Except for being domiciled in Utah and having a transfer agent there, Louisiana-Pacific had virtually no business connections with Utah. Its principal place of business had been in California since at least 1971; its meetings of shareholders and directors were held in California; and all of its employees and bank accounts were in California.

Louisiana-Pacific argued that section 2115 violated several provisions of the Constitution of the United States. The trial court concluded that there existed no constitutional obstacle to the application of the cumulative voting requirement to Louisiana-Pacific. Louisiana-Pacific appealed.

**GRODIN, JUDGE.** The law of the State of Utah provides for straight voting in an election of directors, but permits cumulative voting, if the articles of incorporation so provide. Neither the articles of incorporation nor the bylaws of Louisiana-Pacific provide for cumulative voting. Louisiana-Pacific contends that for California to require cumulative voting under these circumstances would violate the full faith and credit clause and the commerce clause of the Constitution.

### I. Full Faith and Credit

The full faith and credit clause of the Constitution requires that "Full Faith and Credit . . . be given in each State to the public Acts, Records, and Judicial Proceedings of every other State." The Supreme Court has recognized that a rigid and literal enforcement of the full faith and credit clause would lead to the absurd result that, wherever a conflict arises, a state's statute must be enforced in another state's courts, but cannot be enforced in its own courts.

For a state's substantive law to be selected in a constitutionally permissible manner, the state must have a significant contact or significant aggregation of contacts, creating state interests, such that choosing its law is neither arbitrary nor fundamentally unfair. We find that such contacts exist here; the criteria that a foreign corporation must meet in order to be subject to section 2115 assure the existence of a significant aggregation of contacts. And the state interests created by those contacts are indeed substantial. The right of cumulative voting is a substantial right. A contrary holding would enable a foreign corporation to destroy the rights which the State of California has deemed worthy of protection.

Utah, on the other hand, has no interests which are offended by cumulative voting; whatever interest it might have in maintaining a *laissez faire* policy on that score would seem to be clearly outweighed by the interests of California, in which a majority of shareholders and the corporation's business activity are located.

### II. Commerce Clause

Although the federal Constitution grants Congress power "[t]o regulate commerce . . . among the several States," Congress has not chosen to regulate the subject of this litigation nor has it undertaken to establish guidelines for regulation by the states. Louisiana-Pacific's commerce clause argument is based, therefore, upon the negative implications of dormant congressional authority.

The United States Supreme Court in *Pike v. Bruce Church, Inc.* (1970) has established the standard for determining the validity of state statutes in such situations:

> Where the statute regulates even-handedly to effectuate a legitimate local public interest, and its effects on interstate commerce are only incidental, it will be upheld unless the burden imposed on such commerce is clearly excessive in relation to the putative local benefits. If a legitimate local purpose is found, then the question becomes one of degree. And the extent of the burden that will be tolerated will of course depend on the nature of the local interest involved, and on whether it could be promoted as well with a lesser impact on interstate activities.

We observe, initially, that the challenged statute regulates even-handedly within the meaning of the *Pike* guidelines; it applies to covered foreign corporations the same rules which are applied to corporations domiciled within the state. The statute thus imposes no special or distinct burden upon out-of-state interests.

The nature, strength, and duration of California's interest in the cumulative voting principle, and in the application of that principle to pseudo-foreign corporations, have previously been considered in this opinion. There remains to be considered the effects of that application upon interstate activities.

One effect of section 2115 may well be to deter corporations from making their legal homes elsewhere for the purpose of avoiding California's protective corporate legislation, and thus to diminish the practice of "charter-mongering" among states; but that, presumably, is not an effect which would offend the policies of the commerce clause, and Louisiana-Pacific does not so contend. Rather, Louisiana-Pacific contends that the application of cumulative voting requirements to pseudo-foreign corporations as provided by section 2115 will have the effect of causing it and other foreign corporations already operating in California to reduce their property, payroll, and sales in this state below the 50 percent level, and will deter foreign corporations contemplating the transaction of business in this state from increasing their business activities above that level.

There is no suggestion, or evidence, that section 2115 was adopted for the purpose of deterring foreign corporations from doing business in this state; also, there is no direct evidence that it has had or will have such an effect. On the contrary, what evidence there is on this point consists of testimony by Louisiana-Pacific's president that he knew of no adverse effect on Louisiana-Pacific's business that would be caused by cumulative voting.

Louisiana-Pacific argues that adverse consequences are predictable from potentially conflicting claims of shareholders as to which state law governs the method of voting by shareholders.

The potential for conflict and resulting uncertainty from California's statute is substantially minimized by the nature of the criteria specified in section 2115. A corporation can do a majority of its business in only one state at a time; and it can have a majority of its shareholders resident in only one state at a time. If a corporation meets those requirements in this state, no other state is in a position to regulate the method of voting by shareholders on the basis of the same or similar criteria. If California's statute were replicated in all states, no conflict would result. The potential for conflict is speculative and without substance.

We conclude that to the extent that the cumulative voting requirement imposed by section 2115 upon pseudo-foreign corporations is shown to have any effect upon interstate commerce, the effect is incidental and minimal in relation to the purpose that requirement is designed to achieve.

Judgment for Wilson affirmed.

## PIERCING THE CORPORATE VEIL

A corporation is a legal entity separate from its shareholders, even if there is only one shareholder. Nevertheless, in order *to promote justice and to prevent inequity,* courts will sometimes ignore the separateness of a corporation and its shareholders by *piercing the corporate veil.* The primary consequence of piercing the corporate veil is that a corporation's shareholders may lose their limited liability.

Two requirements must exist for a court to pierce the corporate veil: (1) *domination* of a corporation by its shareholders; and (2) use of that domination for an *improper purpose.*

**Domination.** As an entity separate from its shareholders, a corporation should act for itself, not for its shareholders. If the shareholders make the corporation act to its detriment and to the benefit of shareholders, domination is proved. For example, shareholders' directing a corporation to pay a shareholder's personal expenses is domination. Domination is also proved if the shareholders cause the corporation to fail to observe corporate formalities (such as failing to hold shareholder and director meetings or to maintain separate accounting records). Some courts say that shareholder domination makes the corporation the *alter ego* (other self) of the shareholders. Other courts say that domination makes the corporation an *instrumentality* of the shareholders. Alter ego satisfied the domination requirement in *Valley Finance, Inc. v. United States,* which follows.

To prove domination, it is not sufficient, or even necessary, to show that there is only one shareholder. Many one-shareholder corporations will never have their veils pierced.

However, nearly all corporations whose veils are pierced are close corporations, since domination is more easily accomplished in a close corporation than in a publicly held corporation. Close corporation statutes, however, make it clear that mere shareholder domination of the corporation is not sufficient grounds for piercing the veil. Section 17 of the Statutory Close Corporation Supplement to the Model Business Corporation Act states that the shareholders of a close corporation may operate the corporation as a partnership, have no annual meeting of shareholders, have no board of directors, and yet retain limited liability. The purpose of Section 17 is to prevent a court from piercing the veil of a corporation merely because it is a close corporation dominated by its shareholders. If in addition, however, a close corporation is used for an improper purpose, a court may be justified in piercing the veil.

**Improper Use.** The improper use of a corporation may be any of three types: *defrauding creditors, circumventing a statute, or evading an existing obligation.*

**Defrauding Creditors.** Creditors reasonably expect that shareholder-managers will adequately finance their corporations and will not transfer corporate assets to themselves or to affiliated corporations other than for adequate consideration. If these expectations are not met, a court will find an improper use of the corporation.

**Thin Capitalization.** Severe undercapitalization, called *thin capitalization* or *thin incorporation,* is often found to defraud creditors of a corporation. An example of thin capitalization is forming a business with a high debt-to-equity ratio, such as a $10 million asset business with only $1,000 of equity capital, with the shareholders contributing the remainder of the needed capital as secured creditors. By doing so, the shareholders elevate their bankruptcy repayment priority to a level above that of general creditors, thereby reducing the shareholders' risk. The high debt-to-equity ratio harms creditors by failing to provide an equity cushion sufficient to protect their claims. In such a situation, either the shareholders will be liable for the corporation's debts or the shareholders' loans to the corporation will be subordinated to the claims of other creditors.

Note that shareholders do not defraud creditors merely by forming a corpoation to limit their liability, provided that the corporation is adequately capitalized. For example, it would be proper to incorporate a high-risk venture, such as hazardous waste disposal, to reduce the owners' liability for injuries caused by the hazardous waste. If the corporation were thinly capitalized, however, a court would pierce the veil to hold the shareholders liable to those harmed by the corporation's disposal practices.

**Looting.** In addition, transfers of corporate assets to shareholders in less-than-arm's-length transactions (called *looting*) defraud creditors. For example, shareholder-managers loot a corporation by paying themselves excessively high salaries or by having the corporation pay their personal credit card bills, leaving insufficient assets in the corporation to pay creditors' claims. A court will hold the shareholders liable to the creditors.

In some situations, a court may find that less-than-arm's-length transactions between corporations of common ownership justify piercing the veils of these corporations, making each corporation liable to the creditors of the other corporation. For example, a shareholder-manager operates two corporations from the same office. Corporation One transfers inventory to Corporation Two, but it receives less than full value for the inventory. Also, both corporations employ the same workers, but all of the wages and fringe benefits are paid by Corporation One. In such a situation, the veils of the corporations will be pierced, allowing the creditors of Corporation One to satisfy their claims against the assets of Corporation Two.

**Circumventing a Statute.** A corporation should not be used to engage in a course of conduct that is prohibited by a statute. For example, a city ordinance prohibits retail businesses from being open on consecutive Sundays. To avoid the statute, a retail corporation forms a subsidiary owned entirely by the retail corporation; on alternate weeks it leases its building and inventory to the subsidiary. A court will pierce the veil because the purpose of creating the subsidiary corporation is to circumvent the statutory prohibition.[9]

**Evading an Existing Obligation.** Sometimes, a corporation will attempt to escape liability on a contract by reincorporating or by forming a subsidiary corporation. The new corporation will claim that it is not bound by the contract, even though it is doing the same business as was done by the old corporation. In such a situation, courts pierce the corporate veil and hold the new corporation liable on the contract.

For example, to avoid an onerous labor union contract, a corporation creates a wholly owned subsidiary and sells its entire business to the subsidiary. The subsidiary will claim that it is not a party to the labor contract and may hire nonunion labor. A court will pierce the veil between the two corporations because the subsidiary was created only to avoid the union contract. If a subsidiary is formed for an otherwise proper purpose, such as to have it engage in an extremely risky venture, the subsidiary may be permitted to hire nonunion labor for that venture. In such a situation, it appears that the subsidiary was formed, not to evade the contract, but to reduce the parent corporation's exposure to tort liability, which is a legitimate use of a subsidiary corporation. The subsidiary must be adequately capitalized, however, or a court will pierce its veil on the grounds of thin capitalization.

---

[9] *Sundaco, Inc. v. State of Texas,* 463 S.W.2d 528 (Tex. Ct. Civ. App. 1970).

## Valley Finance, Inc. v. United States

**629 F.2d 162 (D.C. Cir. 1980)**

Pacific Development, Inc., was incorporated in the District of Columbia in 1968 to engage in the business of international brokerage and consulting. Tongsun Park, a South Korean with close ties to President Park Chung Hee, was Pacific's founder, president, and sole shareholder. It was doubtful whether Pacific had a board of directors prior to December 1974. The directors met infrequently after 1974. When they did meet, they approved without discussion or question corporate decisions made by Park.

Park wrote checks on Pacific's bank accounts to cover his unrelated personal and business expenses. Pacific employees served as Park's household servants. Park made loans with Pacific funds to politically influential people and then forgave the loans. Pacific personnel provided administrative and managerial services for Park's other business ventures, and Pacific's profits were assigned to Park or to his other companies.

In 1977, the Internal Revenue Service assessed $4.5 million in back income taxes against Park. To collect the taxes, the IRS seized some of Pacific's assets, claiming that the company was a mere alter ego of Park. Valley Finance, Inc., another corporation wholly owned by Park, had loaned money to Pacific. The Pacific real property that had been seized by the IRS was collateral for Valley's loan to Pacific. Pacific and Valley sought the return of the Pacific assets that had been seized, claiming that it was improper to pierce the corporate veil of Pacific.

The trial court found that Pacific was merely the alter ego of Park and ruled that the IRS properly seized Pacific's assets. Pacific and Valley appealed.

**Gesell, District Judge.** The concept of a distinct corporate entity has long served useful business purposes, encouraging risk-taking by individual investors as well as overall convenience of financial administration. Ordinarily, such considerations justify treating the corporation as a separate entity, independent of its owner. On occasion, however, this concept is abused; it yields results contrary to the interests of equity or justice. Courts have not hesitated to ignore the fiction of separateness and approve a piercing of the corporate veil when the corporate device frustrates the clear intention of the law. The Government's inability otherwise to satisfy legitimate tax debts may form a sound basis for such disregard of corporate form.

Given the diversity of corporate structures and the range of factual settings in which unjust or inequitable results are alleged, it is not surprising that no uniform standard exists for determining whether a corporation is simply the alter ego of its owners. The fact of sole ownership is not by itself sufficient, although it is certainly not irrelevant. Evidence of plain fraud is similarly of probative value, though not a prerequisite. We have previously suggested that the court may ignore existence of the corporate form whenever an individual so dominates his organization as in reality to negate its separate personality. Obviously, control by the individual must be active and substantial, but it need not be exclusive in a hypertechnical or day-to-day sense. The test is a practical one, based largely on a reading of the particular factual circumstances.

Park founded Pacific in 1968, and was its president and sole shareholder on a continuous basis thereafter. Despite protestations in the record, there is no evidence that a major corporate decision was ever made by anyone other than Park. The board of directors played no meaningful role.

It is equally apparent that Park used corporate funds and staff for his own private purposes on a regular basis. The record sufficiently establishes that the corporation operated primarily, if not exclusively, to perform staff functions for its founder and sole shareholder.

This conclusion is further supported by substantial evidence that Park manipulated the few ventures in which Pacific was involved in order to advance his own distinct business or financial interests. By persistently exercising control over the assignment of profits and payments, Park effectively used Pacific as an incorporated pocketbook. In short, the record is replete with evidence that the corporation was fundamentally an extension of its taxpayer-owner.

Judgment for the Internal Revenue Service affirmed.

## SUMMARY

Corporations have existed for thousands of years. The modern corporation, characterized by limited liability for its shareholders, has emerged in only the last 150 years. Early modern corporate charters were special, restrictive grants of the Crown in England and of state legislatures in the United States. Today, general incorporation statutes impose few limitations on persons organizing, financing, operating, and dissolving corporations.

A corporation is a legal entity separate and distinct from its shareholders. A corporation can hold property and sue and be sued in its own name. The members of a corporation are not personally liable for its debts, and its existence is not affected by the death of its members. The shareholders ordinarily have no fiduciary duties to the corporation. Corporations pay federal income taxes, unless the shareholders elect S Corporation status.

Corporations may be classified into several types. The principal ones are for-profit corporations, not-for-profit corporations, and governmental corporations. For-profit corporations include close and public-issue corporations.

Critics have from time to time proposed requiring some of the largest businesses to incorporate under a federal statute. Instead, corporations have been regulated primarily by the general incorporation statutes of the states.

A corporation is a domestic corporation in the state of its incorporation and a foreign corporation elsewhere. A state may impose its laws on a foreign corporation, provided that the application of its laws does not violate the federal Constitution, especially the Commerce Clause and the Due Process Clause.

A foreign corporation must be doing business in a state to be subject to its laws. The courts define doing business for five purposes: (1) for lawsuits in the state's courts, (2) for taxation by the state, (3) for regulation of health and safety, (4) for qualification, and (5) for regulation of a pseudoforeign corporation's internal affairs.

The courts of a state may exercise jurisdiction over a foreign corporation if that corporation's contacts with the state and its citizens are sufficient to make it fair to subject the corporation to suit in the state. The taxing power of a state over business activities within the state is also very broad, but it has been restricted by the Federal Interstate Income Tax Act. A state may, within its police power, require a foreign corporation to comply with regulations that protect the health, safety, and welfare of its citizens. A corporation must be doing intrastate business in a state to be required to qualify to do business within the state. A pseudoforeign corporation may be required to comply with shareholder protection provisions that are applicable to domestic corporations.

Shareholders normally have no individual liability for the debts of the corporation, so their risk of loss is limited to their investment. However, courts may pierce the corporate veil when incorporation is for the purpose of defrauding creditors, circumventing a law, or evading an obligation.

## PROBLEM CASES

**1.** Golden Dawn Foods was a wholesale grocery firm incorporated in Pennsylvania. All of its warehouses were in Pennsylvania. It neither owned nor leased any real property in Ohio. Sales representatives dispatched from its Pennsylvania office sold to approximately 50 independent retail stores in Ohio and 100 stores in Pennsylvania. Golden Dawn did not provide merchandising or other services to its customers in Ohio. One of its Ohio customers defaulted on a promissory note, and Golden Dawn sued the customer in an Ohio court. The customer argued that Golden Dawn had no right to maintain an action in Ohio since it was an unqualified foreign corporation doing business in Ohio. Was Golden Dawn doing business in Ohio so as to be required to qualify?

**2.** Julia Cosmetics, Inc., a Louisiana corporation, designed and intended to market a line of cosmetics associated with the character Julia, portrayed by Diahann Carroll. "Julia" was a television show owned by the National Broadcasting Company. NBC, a Delaware corporation, held trademark rights to "Julia"; therefore, Julia Cosmetics entered into a licensing contract with NBC to use the name and to associate its product with the show. NBC was to receive 5 percent of Julia Cosmetics' gross sales. NBC reserved the right to approve Julia Cosmetics' products and marketing procedures.

Julia Cosmetics found it extremely difficult and frustrating to get approval from NBC, failing to receive approval from NBC for a period of almost one year. Julia Cosmetics then filed an action in federal court in Louisiana against NBC for breach of the licensing contract. NBC moved to quash service of process for lack of jurisdiction. NBC claimed that it did not have sufficient contacts with Louisiana to fall under its long-arm statute. NBC had entered into contracts with six independent television and seven independent radio stations located in Louisiana to broadcast NBC network programs, but it owned no property, had no office or agent, and did not advertise or solicit advertising in Louisiana. Since the licensing contract was negotiated and completed in New York, NBC claimed that the contract had no connection with Louisiana.

Louisiana law provided for jurisdiction over a cause of action arising from a nonresident "causing injury or damage in this state by an offense or quasi-offense committed through an act or omission outside of this state, if he regularly does or solicits business, or engages in any other persistent course of conduct, or derives substantial revenue from this state." Does the Louisiana court have jurisdiction over NBC?

**3.** Delta Molded Products, Inc., an Alabama corporation, purchased several plastic molding machines and auxiliary equipment from IMPCO on an installment purchase contract made in Alabama. The contract provided for installation services by IMPCO. Delta went into bankruptcy. IMPCO filed a petition with the bankruptcy court seeking recovery of the machines and equipment, which Delta had not fully paid for. Other creditors alleged that IMPCO was doing business in Alabama without having qualified to do so, and therefore, under an Alabama statute, could not bring suit in Alabama's courts. IMPCO argued that it was merely seeking to recover possession of machinery wrongly held by the bankruptcy trustee and that for this purpose it was entitled to pursue its action. Is IMPCO's argument valid?

**4.** The Florida Department of Commerce invited printing companies to bid on a proposed printing project. Universal Printing, a Missouri corporation, was the lowest bidder and was awarded the contract. Graphic Productions, the second lowest bidder, contested the award of the contract to Universal, on the grounds that Universal had not qualified to do business in Florida at the time its bid was submitted to the Department of Commerce. Is submitting a bid for a contract the equivalent of doing business, requiring qualification?

**5.** In 1978, ECA Environmental Management Services, Inc., made a contract with Terra-Spread, a fertilizer-spreading business. The contract obligated ECA to order at least 4,000 tons of fertilizer from Terra-Spread. To help Terra-Spread perform the contract, Montana Merchandising, Inc. (MMI), loaned Terra-Spread $7,000.

ECA failed to perform the contract as agreed, ordering only 1,000 tons of fertilizer. Consequently, Terra-Spread repaid MMI only $5,000 of the $7,000 loan. MMI sued Terra-Spread for the balance of the loan. Terra-Spread counterclaimed against MMI, arguing that ECA was the alter ego of MMI and that MMI was therefore liable for ECA's breach of the fertilizer contract.

MMI was the sole shareholder of ECA. ECA had no minutes of shareholder or director meetings since August 1977. Each ECA director was also a director of MMI. The Terra-Spread contract was proposed by MMI at a meeting of its directors. MMI routinely transferred ECA funds into MMI's accounts, and ECA's bank accounts were managed by MMI. At the time of the contract, ECA owed MMI almost $1.5 million, a debt secured by all of ECA's assets. Is MMI liable for ECA's breach of the Terra-Spread contract?

**6.** New York law required that every taxicab company carry $10,000 of accident liability insurance for each cab in its fleet. The purpose of the law was to ensure that passengers and pedestrians injured by cabs operated by these companies would be adequately compensated for their injuries. Carlton organized 10 corporations, each owning and operating two taxicabs in New York City. Each of these corporations carried $20,000 of liability insurance, and Carlton was the principal shareholder of each corporation. The vehicles, the only freely transferable assets of these corporations, were collateral for claims of secured creditors. The 10 corporations were operated more or less as a unit with respect to supplies, repairs, and employees. Walkovszky was severely injured when he was run down by one of the taxicabs. He sued Carlton personally, alleging that the multiple corporate structure amounted to fraud upon those who might be injured by the taxicabs. Should the court pierce the corporate veil to reach Carlton individually?

**7.** Jerome Glazer is a member of the Louisiana State Mineral Board, which has the authority to lease any lands belonging to the state for the development and production of minerals, oil, and gas. Glazer is also the sole shareholder, chief administrative officer, president, and chairman of the board of directors of Glazer Steel Corporation.

Louisiana has a Code of Ethics for Government Employees. The code prohibits public servants from becoming involved in conflicts of interests. It prohibits a public servant from receiving payment for the performance of services for any person who is known by the public servant to have contractual or business relationships with the public servant's agency.

Exxon, Texaco, and Shell Oil Company have mineral leases awarded by the Mineral Board. From April 1980 to March 1981, Glazer Steel Corporation sells steel to these three oil companies. Jerome Glazer knows that the three oil companies hold leases awarded by the Mineral Board.

A disciplinary action is brought against Glazer on the grounds that he has violated the Code of Ethics. Glazer argues that the activities of Glazer Steel cannot be attributed to him personally. Has he violated the Code of Ethics?

**8.** J. P. Mascaro and Sons, Inc., had a contract to haul rubbish for a county. The corporation claimed to have hauled more rubbish than it actually carried. Two of its officers, Michael Mascaro and J. P. Mascaro, Jr., were found guilty of the crimes of theft by deception and unsworn falsification to authorities. Michael was fined $5,000, and J. P., Jr., was fined $1,000. Both were placed on probation for five years. Later, the corporation was convicted of the same crimes. It appealed the conviction on the grounds that the conviction was barred by the earlier convictions of its two officers, who were also substantial shareholders. Should the corporation's conviction be upheld?

# Chapter 23

# Organization, Dissolution, and Financial Structure of Corporations

## INTRODUCTION

A person desiring to incorporate a business must comply with the applicable state corporation law, which sets forth several requirements. In this chapter, you will learn that failing to comply with these requirements can create various problems. For example, a person may make a contract on behalf of the corporation before it is incorporated. Should the corporation be liable on this contract? Should the person who made the contract on behalf of the prospective corporation be liable on the contract? Should the people who thought that they were shareholders have limited liability, or should they be liable as partners?

Also in this chapter, you will study the many types of dissolution. It is easier to dissolve a corporation than it is to organize one. Dissolution ends the normal conduct of the corporation's business and precedes the winding up and the termination of the corporation.

Any corporation needs money to begin and to continue its operation. In this chapter, you will study the types of securities that a corporation may issue to finance its business and the rules that affect the issuance of corporate securities.

Corporate shares are usually freely transferable by their owners, yet there is no ready market for the shares of some corporations. This paradox of transferability can cause problems, especially for close corporations. Many of these problems are resolved by using share transfer restrictions. In this chapter, you will study the uses and the legality of restrictions on share transfer.

## PROMOTERS

**Role of Promoter.** A **promoter** incorporates a business, organizes its initial management, and raises its initial capital. Typically, a promoter discovers a business or an idea that needs to be developed, finds people who are willing to invest in the business, negotiates the contracts necessary for the initial operation of the proposed venture, incorporates the business, and helps management start the operation of the business.

In its broadest sense, the term *promoter* applies to anyone who organizes and starts a corporation. Thus, the term may be applied to a partner who forms a corporation that assumes the business of the partnership. It is usually applied, however, only to a person who forms a corporation to carry on a new business.

**Relation of Promoter and Corporation.** The relation of a promoter to the corporation and the persons who invest in it is unique. A promoter is not an agent of the corporation, but he owes fiduciary duties to it.

**No Agency Relationship.** A promoter is *not an agent* of the proposed corporation, since he is self-appointed and the corporation is not yet in existence. A promoter is not an agent of prospective investors in the business, since they did not appoint him and they have no power to control him.

**Fiduciary Relationship.** Although not an agent of the proposed corporation, a promoter owes a *fiduciary duty* to the corporation and to its prospective investors, including shareholders and possibly creditors. A promoter owes such parties a duty of full disclosure and honesty. For example, a promoter breaches this duty when she diverts money received from prospective shareholders to pay her expenses, unless the shareholders agree to such payment. Taking a secret profit at the expense of the corporation or the prospective shareholders is also a breach the promoter's fiduciary duty.

For example, a promoter purchases land that he knows the business needs, intending to sell it to the business after its incorporation. The promoter's failure to disclose his profit to the corporation permits the corporation to rescind the transaction or to recover the promoter's secret profit. On the other hand, the promoter's full disclosure of his interest in the land and his profit to an independent board of directors, which approves the corporation's purchase of the land at the increased price, prevents the corporation from recovering the promoter's profit. Note, however, that if the board of directors is controlled or manipulated by the promoter, the corporation may recover against the promoter despite board approval, because corporate assent has not been given freely.

**Promoter's Receipt of Watered Shares.** A more confusing fiduciary duty problem is the *watered shares* problem, in which the promoter conveys property to the corporation at a greatly inflated value in payment for shares of the corporation. If this occurs with the knowledge and consent of all the persons interested in the corporation, and no additional shareholders are contemplated as part of the promotional scheme at the time that consent is obtained, there is no wrongdoing. A problem arises, however, when future shareholders are contemplated. There is a split of authority, but the trend is to allow recovery of the promoter's profits when the corporation sells additional shares to the public at a price that is more than the promoter paid and that is substantially in excess of the fair market value of the shares.

**Effect of Securities Statutes.** The opportunities for a promoter to cause a corporation to sell shares at inflated prices were greatly lessened by the enactment of the Securities Act of 1933 and the Securities Exchange Act of 1934, as well as state securities laws.[1] These laws require disclosure of material information to prospective shareholders, including the price that the promoters paid for their shares and details on the promoters' dealings with the company. Many state statutes forbid corporations to sell securities to the public at a higher price than the promoters paid, unless the new business proves that the higher public price is justified, for example, by its profitability.

**Promoter's Preincorporation Contracts.** A promoter may purport to make contracts for the corporation before it comes into existence. Such contracts are called *preincorporation contracts.* Three parties may have liability on such contracts: (1) the corporation, (2) the promoter, and (3) the third party with whom the promoter made the contract.

**Corporation's Liability on Promoter's Contracts.** When a corporation comes into existence, it does *not* automatically become liable on the *preincorporation* contracts made in its behalf by the promoter. It cannot be held liable as a principal whose agent made the contracts, since the promoter was not its agent and the corporation was not in existence when the contracts were made.

After incorporation, however, a corporation may agree to become bound on a promoter's preincorporation contracts. An agreement may be found from a corporation's **ratification** or **adoption** of the promoter's contracts.

**Ratification.** Ratification is based on the agency concept that permits a principal to ratify the unauthorized acts of an agent.[2] The corporation's liability relates back to the time when the promoter made the contract, and the promoter is released from liability. Ratification has dubious applicability in the promoter context, however, because no principal was in existence when the act was done. In addition, the theory is unfair to the third party, because it releases the promoter from liability on the contract without the third party's consent. This unfairness is obvious when the corporation fails to perform the contract and the third party cannot sue the promoter.

**Adoption.** Adoption is identical to ratification, except that it does not relate back to the time when the promoter made the contract and it *does not automatically release the promoter* from liability. The basis of adoption is that the contract between the promoter and the other party contains an implied continuing offer to the corporation. The corporation accepts this offer when it acknowledges the contract as a binding obligation. Adoption is the theory that is *most commonly used* by courts to bind corporations to preincorporation contracts.

**How to Ratify or Adopt.** For the corporation to ratify or adopt a promoter's contract,

[1] The federal and state securities statutes are discussed in Chapter 26.

[2] Ratification is discussed in Chapter 17.

the corporation must *accept* the contract *with knowledge of all its material facts.* In addition, the contract must be *within the powers* of the corporation.[3]

*Acceptance* may be express or implied. Formal action is not required. The corporation's knowing receipt of the benefits of the contract is sufficient for acceptance. For example, a promoter makes a preincorporation contract with a genetic engineer, requiring the engineer to work for a prospective corporation for 10 years. After incorporation, the promoter presents the contract to the board of directors, but the board takes no formal action to accept the contract. Nevertheless, the board allows the engineer to work for the corporation as the contract provides and pays him the salary required by the contract. The board's actions constitute an acceptance of the contract, binding the corporation to the contract for its 10-year term.

**Promoter's Liability on Preincorporation Contracts.** A promoter is liable on preincorporation contracts she negotiates, even if the promoter's name does not appear on the contract. If there are two or more promoters, they are considered partners or joint venturers, and they are jointly liable for each other's preincorporation contracts.

If the corporation is *not formed,* a promoter remains liable on a preincorporation contract. Also, the *mere formation* of the corporation does *not* release a promoter from liability.

**Effect of Adoption.** Generally, the promoter remains liable on a preincorporation contract even after the corporation's acceptance of the contract, since *adoption* does not automatically release the promoter. Under the adoption theory, the corporation cannot by itself relieve the promoter of liability to the third party. The third party must agree, expressly or impliedly, to release the promoter from liability.

**Novation.** The promoter, the corporation, and the third party may agree to release the promoter from liability and to make the corporation liable on the contract. This is called a **novation.** Usually, novation will occur by express or implied agreement of all the parties. However, the *ratification* theory includes an automatic novation. The adoption theory does not.

**Intent of Third Party and Promoter.** A few courts have held that a promoter is not liable on preincorporation contracts if the third party *knew of the nonexistence* of the corporation, yet insisted that the promoter sign the contract in behalf of the nonexistent corporation. Other courts have found that the promoter is not liable if the third party clearly stated that he would *look only to the corporation* for performance. While such court decisions protect promoters from liability, they also eliminate mutuality of obligation during the preincorporation period. They allow the third party to escape liability until the corporation becomes liable on the contract.

**Liability of Third Party.** If the promoter is liable on the preincorporation contract, the third party also is liable. The promoter can enforce the contract against the third party. After accepting the contract, the corporation can enforce the contract against the third party.

**Reducing Promoter's Risk of Liability.** Since the liability of promoters on preincorporation contracts may be substantial, many promoters take steps to reduce their risk of liability. The best way is to *incorporate the business* before making any contracts. If this is done, the corporation, which is now in existence, is liable on any contracts that the pro-

[3] The powers of a corporation are discussed in Chapter 24.

moter is authorized to make in its behalf. The promoter, now an agent, has no contractual liability. There is one risk in incorporating before making contracts. The corporation may be inadequately capitalized, giving a court grounds to pierce the corporate veil and to hold the promoter liable for the corporation's obligations, including contracts.[4]

Some promoters put *automatic-novation clauses* in preincorporation contracts. Such clauses *automatically release* the promoter from liability upon the occurrence of a specified subsequent event, for example, incorporation, acceptance of the contract by the corporation, or nonacceptance of the contract through no fault of the promoter. *RKO-Stanley Warner Theatres, Inc. v. Graziano,* which follows, shows that promoters who desire to escape liability should state clearly in the preincorporation contract when their liability ceases.

**Liability of Corporation to Promoter.** Valuable as the services of a promoter may be to a prospective corporation and to society, a corporation generally is *not required* to compensate a promoter for his promotional services, or even his expenses, unless the corporation has agreed expressly to compensate the promoter. The justification for this rule is that the promoter is self-appointed and acts for a corporation that is not in existence.

Nevertheless, a corporation *may choose* to reimburse the promoter for her reasonable expenses and to pay her the value of her services to the corporation. Corporations often compensate their promoters with shares. In most states, however, promotional services are *not* valid consideration for shares, because the corporation is not in existence when the services are rendered. The trend in the law, however, is to permit the issuance of shares in return for a promoter's services. Model Business Corporation Act (MBCA) Section 6.21(c) permits the issuance of shares for a promoter's services.[5]

**Preincorporation Share Subscriptions.** Promoters sometimes use *preincorporation share subscriptions* to ensure that the corporation will have adequate capital when it begins its business. Under the terms of a share subscription, a prospective shareholder *offers* to buy a specific number of the corporation's shares at a stated price. Generally, corporate acceptance of preincorporation subscriptions occurs by action of the board of directors after incorporation.

In most states, preincorporation subscriptions are irrevocable for a stated period of time, in the absence of a contrary provision in the subscription. This gives the corporation time to come into existence. MBCA Section 6.20(a) provides for a six-month period, unless this term is modified by the subscription. In addition, unanimous agreement of the subscribers will effect a revocation.

Promoters have no liability on preincorporation share subscriptions. They have a duty, however, to make a good faith effort to bring the corporation into existence. However, when a corporation fails to accept a preincorporation subscription or becomes insolvent, the promoter is not liable to the disappointed subscriber, absent fraud or other wrongdoing by the promoter.

Preincorporation subscriptions are rarely used today. Instead, the business is incorporated first, and then the promoter obtains from prospective investors either *postincorporation subscriptions* or *executory contracts* to purchase shares. Postincorporation subscriptions and executory contracts to purchase shares are discussed later in this chapter.

[4] Piercing the corporate veil is discussed in Chapter 22.

[5] Proper types of consideration for shares are discussed later in this chapter.

## RKO-Stanley Warner Theatres, Inc. v. Graziano

**355 A.2d 830 (Pa. Sup. Ct. 1976)**

In April 1970, RKO-Stanley Warner Theatres, Inc., contracted to sell the Kent Theatre in Philadelphia for $70,000 to Jack Jenofsky and Ralph Graziano, who were in the process of forming a corporation that was to be known as Kent Enterprises, Inc. The contract included Paragraph 19, added by Jenofsky and Graziano's lawyer, which stated the following:

> It is understood by the parties hereto that it is the intention of the Purchaser to incorporate. Upon condition that such incorporation be completed by the closing date, all agreements, covenants, and warranties contained herein shall be construed to have been made between Seller and the resultant corporation, and all documents shall reflect same.

The original closing date was September 30, but the closing date was twice postponed at the request of Jenofsky and Graziano. Kent Enterprises, Inc. was incorporated on October 9, 1970. A final closing date of October 21, 1970, was set, but Jenofsky and Graziano failed to complete the sale on that date.

RKO sued Jenofsky and Graziano on the contract. Jenofsky claimed that the quoted provision in the contract released him from any personal liability. The trial court held that Jenofsky and Graziano were liable on the contract. Jenofsky appealed.

**Eagan, Justice.** The legal relationship of Jenofsky to Kent Enterprises, Inc., at the date of the execution of the agreement of sale was that of promoter. As such, he is subject to the general rule that a promoter, although he may assume to act on behalf of a projected corporation and not for himself, will be held personally liable on contracts made by him for the benefit of a corporation he intends to organize. This personal liability will continue even after the contemplated corporation is formed and has received the benefits of the contract, unless there is a novation or other agreement to release liability.

The imposition of personal liability upon a promoter where that promoter has contracted on behalf of a corporation is based upon the principle that one who assumes to act for a nonexistent principal is himself liable on the contract in the absence of an agreement to the contrary. Nevertheless, even though a contract is executed by a promoter on behalf of a proposed corporation, where the person with whom the contract is made agrees to look to the corporation alone for responsibility, the promoter incurs no personal liability with respect to the contract.

There are three possible understandings that parties may have when an agreement is executed by a promoter on behalf of a proposed corporation. He may (1) take on its behalf an offer from the other which, being accepted after the formation of the company, becomes a contract, (2) make a contract at the time binding himself, with the understanding that if a company is formed, it will take his place and that then he shall be relieved of responsibility, or (3) bind himself personally and look to the proposed company, when formed, for indemnity.

Jenofsky contends that the parties, by their inclusion of Paragraph 19 in the agreement, manifested an intention to release him from personal responsibility upon the mere formation of the proposed corporation, provided the incorporation was consummated prior to the scheduled closing date.

While Paragraph 19 does make provision for recognition of the resultant corporation as to the closing documents, it makes no mention of any release of personal liability of Jenofsky and Graziano. Because the agreement fails to provide expressly for the release of personal liability, it is subject to more than one possible construction.

Where an agreement is ambiguous and reasonably susceptible of two interpretations, it must be construed most strongly against those who drew it. Also the construction that makes the contract rational and probable must be preferred. The trial court determined that the intent of the parties was to hold Jenofsky personally responsible until such time as the corporation was formed and it adopted the agreement. We believe this construction represents the only rational and prudent interpretation of the parties' intent.

This agreement was entered into on the financial strength of Jenofsky and Graziano alone as individuals. Therefore, it would have been illogical for RKO to have consented to the release of their personal liability upon the mere formation of a corporation prior to closing, for it is a well-settled rule that a contract made by a promoter, even though made for and in the name of a proposed corporation, in the absence of a subsequent adoption by the corporation, will not be binding upon the corporation. If as Jenofsky contends, the intent was to release the promoters from personal responsibility upon the mere incorporation prior to closing, the effect of the agreement would have been to create the possibility that RKO, in the event of nonperformance, would be able to hold no party accountable, there being no guarantee that the resultant corporation would ratify the agreement. Without express language in the agreement indicating that such was the intention of the parties, we may not attribute this intention to them.

Therefore, we hold that the intent of the parties was to have Jenofsky and Graziano personally liable, until the intended corporation was formed and it ratified the agreement.

Judgment for RKO affirmed.

## INCORPORATION

**Determining Where to Incorporate.** A promoter must decide where to incorporate a business. If the business of a proposed corporation is to be primarily *intrastate,* it is usually cheaper to incorporate in the state where the corporation's business is to be conducted. For the business that is primarily *interstate,* however, the business may benefit by incorporating in a state different from the state in which it has its principal place of business.

Two factors affect the decision where to incorporate: (1) the cost of organizing and maintaining the corporation in the state and (2) the freedom from shareholder and creditor intervention that the state's corporation statute grants to the corporation's management.

**Fees and Taxes.** Incorporation fees and taxes, annual fees, and other fees, such as those on the transfer of shares or the dissolution of the corporation, vary considerably from state to state. Delaware has been a popular state in which to incorporate because its fees tend to be low.

**Management Freedom.** Promoters frequently choose to incorporate in a state whose corporation statute and court decisions grant managers broad management discretion. For example, it is easier to pay a large dividend and to effect a merger in Delaware than in many other states. Nearly 40 percent of the corporations listed on the New York Stock Exchange are incorporated in Delaware. Ohio has become a popular incorporation state in recent years because the Ohio legislature has been willing to protect the managements of Ohio corporations from hostile takeovers by passing protective antitakeover legislation.

**Steps in Incorporation.** The steps prescribed by the incorporation statutes of the different states vary, but they generally include the following, which appear in the MBCA:

1. Preparation of articles of incorporation.
2. Signing and authenticating of the articles by one or more incorporators.
3. Filing of the articles with the secretary of state, accompanied by the payment of specified fees.
4. Issuance of a certificate of incorporation by the secretary of state.
5. Holding an organization meeting for the purpose of adopting bylaws, electing officers, and transacting other business.

In addition, many states require that some *minimum capitalization* (typically $1,000) be contributed to the corporation. Also, some states require the filing of a copy of the articles of incorporation with an official of the county where the corporation has its principal place of business.

**Incorporators.** Many states require that three natural adult persons serve as **incorporators.** The MBCA specifies that one or more persons, including corporations, partnerships, and unincorporated associations, may act as the incorporators. Incorporators have no function beyond lending their names and signatures to the process of bringing the corporation into existence. No special liability attaches to a person merely because she serves as an incorporator.

**Articles of Incorporation.** The basic governing document of the corporation is the **articles of incorporation.** The articles are similar to a constitution. They state many of the rights and responsibilities of the corporation, its management, and its shareholders.

The content of the articles of incorporation is dictated by the state corporation statute. The articles may not contain any provision that conflicts with that law. The MBCA lists the matters that *must* be included in the articles and matters that *may* be included. The following *must* be included:

1. The name of the corporation.
2. The number of shares that the corporation has authority to issue.
3. The address of the initial registered office of the corporation and the name of its registered agent.
4. The name and address of each incorporator.

These few requirements make it clear that it is very easy to draft articles of incorporation.

In addition, under the MBCA the articles *may* include the following:

1. The names and addresses of the individuals who are to serve as the initial directors.
2. The purpose of the corporation.
3. The duration of the corporation.
4. The par value of shares of the corporation.
5. Additional provisions not inconsistent with law for managing the corporation, regulating the internal affairs of the corporation, and establishing the powers of the corporation and its directors and shareholders. For example, these

additional provisions may contain the procedures for electing directors, the quorum requirements for shareholder and board of directors meetings, and the dividend rights of shareholders.

**Name.** The incorporators must give the corporation a name, which, under MBCA Section 4.01(b), must be *distinguishable from the name of any other corporation* incorporated or qualified to do business in the state. The name must include the word *corporation, incorporated, company,* or *limited,* or the abbreviation *corp., inc., co.,* or *ltd.*

To aid in the selection of a name unlike those of preexisting corporations, MBCA Section 4.02 provides for advance application to the secretary of state for a desired name. If the name is available, it may be reserved for a period of 120 days while the corporation is being formed. For example, when it became apparent that the Baltimore Colts professional football team would be moved to Indianapolis, the promoters reserved the names Indiana Colts and Indianapolis Colts, choosing the latter name when they subsequently incorporated the team in Indiana.

**Purpose.** Although the MBCA does not require the inclusion of a statement of purpose in the articles, the majority rule is that the corporate *purpose* must be included in them. Generally, it is sufficient to state, alone or together with specific purposes, that the corporation may engage in "any lawful activity." Therefore, the limitations on the scope of a corporation's business are almost entirely self-imposed. The limitations are stated in the articles for the protection of management, the shareholders, and those who deal with the corporation.

**Duration.** Most of the state corporation statutes permit corporations to have perpetual existence. If desired, the articles of incorporation may provide for a shorter duration even when the applicable statute permits perpetual life.

**Initial Capitalization.** Most of the state corporation statutes require the articles to recite the initial capitalization of the business. Usually, the statutes require that there be a minimum amount of initial capital, such as $1,000.

**Filing of Articles of Incorporation.** The articles of incorporation must be filed with the office of the secretary of state, and a filing fee must be paid. The *existence* of the corporation begins when the articles are properly filed.

Some states require a *duplicate filing* of the articles with an office, usually the county recorder's office, in the county in which the corporation has its principal place of business. The purpose of a duplicate filing is to ease creditors' access to the articles.

**Issuance of Certificate of Incorporation.** The office of the secretary of state reviews the articles of incorporation that are filed with it. If the articles contain everything that is required, the secretary of state issues a *certificate of incorporation,* which certifies that the corporation has met the requirements of the incorporation statute and that it is in existence.

**The Organization Meeting.** After the articles of incorporation have been approved by the secretary of state, an organization meeting is held. Usually, it is the first formal meeting of the directors, but some statutes allow the organization meeting to be held by the incorporators.

The subject matter of the meeting differs from state to state. The MBCA specifies only that *bylaws shall be adopted* and *officers elected.* If the meeting is the first meeting of the board of directors, other matters may be considered: adopting a corporate seal, approving the form of share certificates, accepting share subscriptions, authorizing the issuance of shares, adopting preincorporation agreements, authorizing reimbursement for promoters' expenses, and fixing the salaries of officers. The board may also take action on matters appropriate to begin the operation of the corporation, such as authorizing applications for qualification to do business in other states as a foreign corporation. In addition, the board may transact any other business within its powers, such as ordering inventory and hiring employees.

**Seal.** A corporation should adopt a *seal,* a design impressed on documents or affixed to them as proof of authenticity. Many states require that any corporate signing of documents pertaining to real estate (e.g., deeds and mortgages) be authenticated by a seal. If the corporation does not adopt a seal, it may be asked to certify that it has no seal when it executes such documents. Customarily, the seal is held by the corporate secretary and affixed to documents by him.

**Bylaws of the Corporation.** The function of the bylaws is to supplement the articles of incorporation by defining more precisely the powers, rights, and responsibilities of the corporation, its managers, and its shareholders and by stating other rules under which the corporation and its activities will be governed. The bylaws are more detailed than the articles. If the articles of incorporation are analogous to a constitution, the bylaws are analogous to statutes.

The bylaws usually state the authority of the officers and the directors, specifying what they may do and may not do; the time and place at which the annual shareholders' meetings will be held; the procedure for calling special meetings of shareholders; and the procedures for shareholder and director meetings, including whether more than a majority is required for approval of specified actions. The bylaws may make provision for special committees of the board, defining their membership and the scope of their activities. They set up the machinery for the transfer of shares, the maintenance of share records, and for the declaration and payment of dividends.

**Adoption and Amendment of Bylaws.** MBCA Section 2.06 gives the incorporators or the initial directors the *power to adopt* the initial bylaws. The board of directors holds the power *to repeal and to amend* the bylaws, unless the articles reserve this power to the shareholders. Under MBCA Section 10.20, the shareholders, as the ultimate owners of the corporation, always retain the power to amend the bylaws, even if the directors also have such power.

**Validity of Bylaws.** To be valid, bylaws must be *consistent with the law and with the articles of incorporation.* In *Quinn v. Stuart Lakes Club, Inc.,* which follows, a bylaw was invalidated because it violated a state law prohibiting most forms of the tontine, a type of gambling in which a piece of property is won by the person who lives the longest. It should be noted, however, that state corporation law sometimes expressly permits the bylaws to contradict the articles. For example, MBCA Section 8.03(a) allows a bylaw concerning the number of directors to take priority over a conflicting provision in the articles.

**Persons Bound by Bylaws.** Officers, directors, and shareholders of the corporation are bound by the bylaws. Officers and directors can be held liable to the corporation for damaging the corporation by exceeding the authority granted them in the bylaws. Corporate employees and others who deal with the corporation, however, have been held not to be bound by the bylaws unless they have knowledge of their content. Hence, a bylaw limiting an agent's actual authority may fail to destroy the agent's apparent authority, if the third party with whom the agent deals does not know of the limitation.

## Quinn v. Stuart Lakes Club, Inc.

**439 N.Y.S.2d 30 (N.Y. App. Div. 1981)**

Stuart Lakes Club, Inc., was organized in New York in 1928. Its purposes were to purchase land; to foster, protect, and propagate fish and game; and to promote legitimate fishing and hunting. In 1935, the club purchased 75 acres of land. The land had two lakes and a clubhouse.

The club was used by business executives and professionals as a retreat from the tensions of daily life. Each member of the club owned one common share of the corporation. At its height, the club had 40 to 45 members, but its membership gradually dwindled. At a meeting on October 27, 1952, the board of directors amended the bylaws to include a new Article 9, which stated, "When any member ceases to be a member of the Club, either by death, resignation, or otherwise, his share shall be considered void and the certificate returned to the Treasurer for cancellation."

The purpose of Article 9 was to make the last surviving member of the club its sole owner, and therefore the beneficial owner of the club's valuable land and clubhouse.

As of October 22, 1969, the club had three members: James Crawford, John Quinn, and Charles Treacy. On October 23, 1969, Quinn died in an automobile accident. Treacy died in 1971, leaving Crawford as the sole surviving member.

Amy Quinn, the daughter of John Quinn and the sole beneficiary under his will, was asked by the club to surrender the share held by John, but Amy refused to do so. In 1973, she sued Crawford and the club, asking the court to declare Article 9 of the bylaws ineffective, void, against public policy, and unenforceable. She asked the court to hold that as owner of the share, she was a member of the club. The trial court held for Amy Quinn, declaring her to be a member of the club. Crawford and the club appealed.

**Bloom, Justice.** When the last survivors of the Club, in practical effect, closed the membership rolls to new members and adopted Article 9 of the bylaws, they created a survivorship lottery. It is a form of tontine. Seemingly, the very purpose of precluding expanded membership was to insure that the last survivor would inherit the house, the land, and all the other assets of the Club. This form of death gamble, bottomed on the principle that the last survivor shall fall heir to the corporation, ought not to be encouraged or expanded beyond the limits of tontine insurance that have previously been recognized by law. Accordingly, we hold that Article 9 of the bylaws of the Club is not to be given effect.

Judgment for Quinn affirmed.

## DEFECTIVE ATTEMPTS TO INCORPORATE

Promoters and business managers sometimes make representations to others that they are acting for a corporation, although *fewer than all of the conditions for incorporation* have been met. For example, the corporation may not have filed its articles of incorporation or may not have held an organization meeting. These are examples of *defective attempts to incorporate.*

**Consequences.** One possible consequence of defective incorporation is to make the promoters, the managers, and the purported shareholders *personally liable* for the obligations of the defectively formed corporation. This may include both *contract* and *tort* liability. For example, an employee of an insolvent corporation drives the corporation's truck over a pedestrian. If the pedestrian proves that the corporation was defectively formed, he may be able to recover damages for his injuries from the promoters, the managers, and the shareholders.

A second possible consequence of defective incorporation is that a party to a contract involving the purported corporation may claim nonexistence of the corporation in order to avoid a contract made in the name of the corporation. For example, a person makes an ill-advised contract with the corporation. If the person proves that the corporation was defectively formed, he will escape liability on the contract because he made a contract with a nonexistent person, the defectively formed corporation.

The courts have tried to determine when these two consequences should arise by making a distinction between de jure corporations, de facto corporations, corporations by estoppel, and corporations so defectively formed that they are treated as being nonexistent.

**De Jure Corporation.** A de jure corporation is formed when the promoters substantially comply with each of the *mandatory conditions precedent* to the incorporation of the business. They need not have complied with *directory provisions.*

**Mandatory versus Directory Provisions.** *Mandatory* provisions are distinguished from *directory* provisions by statutory language and the purpose of the provision. Mandatory provisions are those that the corporation statute states "shall" or "must" be done or those that are necessary to protect the public interest. Directory provisions are those that "may" be done and that are unnecessary to protect the public interest.

For example, statutes provide that the incorporators shall file the articles of incorporation with the secretary of state. This is a mandatory provision, due not only to the use of the word *shall* but also to the importance of the filing in protecting the public interest. The filing notifies the public of the existence of a business whose owners have limited liability. Other mandatory provisions include drafting the articles of incorporation. Directory provisions include minor matters, such as the adoption of a seal and the inclusion of the incorporators' addresses in the articles of incorporation.

**Effect of De Jure Status.** If a corporation has complied with each mandatory provision, it is a de jure corporation and is treated as a corporation for *all purposes.* The validity of a de jure corporation cannot be attacked, except in a few states in which the state in a *quo warranto* proceeding may attack the corporation for noncompliance with a *condition subsequent to incorporation,* such as a failure to file an annual corporation report.

**De Facto Corporation.** A de facto corporation exists when the promoters fail in some material respect to comply with all of the mandatory provisions of the incorporation statute, yet comply with most such provisions.

There are three requirements for a de facto corporation:

1. There is a *valid statute* under which the corporation could be organized.
2. The promoters or managers make an *honest attempt* to organize under the statute.
3. The promoters or managers *exercise corporate powers*. That is, they act as if they were acting for a corporation.

Generally, failing to file the articles of incorporation with the secretary of state will prevent the creation of a de facto corporation. However, a de facto corporation will exist despite the lack of an organization meeting or the failure to make a *duplicate* filing of the articles with a county recorder.

**Effect of De Facto Status.** A de facto corporation is treated as a corporation against either an attack by a third party or an attempt of the business itself to deny that it is a corporation. The state, however, may attack the claimed corporate status of the business in a *quo warranto* action.

**Corporation by Estoppel.** When people *hold themselves out* as representing a corporation or *believe themselves to be dealing with* a corporation, a court will *estop* these people from denying the existence of a corporation. This is called *corporation by estoppel.* For example, a manager states that a business has been incorporated and induces a third person to contract with the purported corporation. The manager will not be permitted to use a failure to incorporate as a defense to the contract, because he has misled others to *believe reasonably* that a corporation exists. Also, a third party that contracts with a group of managers who purport to be acting on behalf of a corporation will not be permitted to escape liability by proving a failure of the group to incorporate the business, if the third party *intended to deal* with the corporation.

Under the doctrine of estoppel, each contract must be considered individually to determine whether either party to the contract is estopped from denying the corporation's existence. The application of corporation by estoppel in tort suits is rare, since tort victims are seldom given an opportunity to form a belief that their tortfeasor is a corporation.

**Liability for Defective Incorporation.** If people attempt to organize a corporation, but their efforts are so defective that not even a corporation by estoppel is found to exist, the courts have generally held such persons to be partners with unlimited liability for the contracts and torts of the business. However, most courts impose the unlimited *contractual* liability of a partner only on those who are *actively engaged in the management* of the business or who are responsible for the defects in its organization. *Tort* liability, however, is generally imposed on everyone—the promoters, the managers, and the purported shareholders of the defectively formed corporation.

**Modern Approaches to the Defective Incorporation Problem.** As you can see, the law of defective incorporation is confusing. It becomes even more confusing when you consider that many of the defective incorporation cases look like promoter liability cases, and vice versa. A court may have difficulty in deciding whether to apply the law of promoter liability or the law of defective incorporation to preincorporation contracts. It is not surprising, therefore, that modern corporation statutes have attempted to eliminate this confusion by adopting simple rules for determining the existence of a corporation and the liability of its promoters, managers, and shareholders.

**Existence of Corporation under the MBCA.** Most states have a provision similar to Section 56 of the *old MBCA*. It states that the *issuance of a certificate of incorporation* by the secretary of state is *conclusive* proof of incorporation, except against the state, which is permitted to bring a *quo warranto* action challenging corporate status. Consequently, the promoters may omit even a mandatory provision, yet create a corporation, provided that the secretary of state has issued a certificate of incorporation. Some courts have held that a failure to obtain issuance of a certificate is conclusive proof of the *nonexistence* of the corporation. Some courts, including the court in *Robertson v. Levy,* which follows, have held that the old MBCA eliminates the concepts of de facto corporation and corporation by estoppel.

Revised MBCA Section 2.03 adopts essentially the same rule as old Section 56. It states that incorporation occurs when the articles are filed. The *filing* of the articles, as evidenced by the return of a copy of the articles stamped by the secretary of state, is *conclusive* proof of the existence of the corporation, except in a proceeding brought by the state.

**Liability for Defective Incorporation under the MBCA.** Most of the state corporation statutes have sections similar to Section 146 of the old MBCA. That section imposes joint and several liability on those persons "who assume to act as a corporation without authority to do so," such as when a certificate of incorporation has not been issued. *Robertson v. Levy* illustrates the thinking of the courts that have held that the *only* way for promoters and managers to escape personal liability is not to transact business until the secretary of state issues the certificate of incorporation. It is not clear, however, that the rule of *Robertson v. Levy* should be read to impose liability on shareholders who assume no role in the incorporation or management of the business.

Revised MBCA Section 2.04 clarifies the liability of shareholders when there is a defective attempt to incorporate. It imposes joint and several liability on those persons who *purport to act on behalf of a corporation* if they *know* that there has been no incorporation. Section 2.04 would impose liability on promoters, managers, and shareholders who both (1) *participate* in the policy and operational decisions of the business *and* (2) *know* that the articles have not been filed. Section 2.04 would, however, release from liability *innocent* shareholders and others who either (1) *take no part in the formation or the management* of the defectively formed corporation *or* (2) mistakenly *believe that the articles have been filed.*

## Robertson v. Levy

**197 A.2d 443 (D.C. Ct. App. 1964)**

Eugene Levy agreed to form a corporation, Penn Ave. Record Shack, Inc., that would purchase a business from Martin Robertson. On December 27, 1961, Levy filed articles of incorporation for Record Shack with the superintendent of corporations of the District of Columbia, but the superintendent issued no certificate of incorporation. On December 31, 1961, Robertson assigned a lease to Levy, who was acting as president of Record Shack. On January 2, 1962, the superintendent of corporations rejected the articles of incorporation of Record Shack. On the same day, Levy began to operate the business as Penn Ave. Record Shack, Inc. On January 8, Robertson sold the assets of the business to the Record Shack and received a promissory note for the purchase price signed "Penn Ave. Record Shack, Inc., by Eugene M. Levy, President." Levy refiled the articles, and on January 17, 1962, a certificate of incorporation of Penn Ave. Record Shack, Inc., was issued by the superintendent of corporations.

Robertson accepted one payment on the promissory note from the corporation. In June 1962, Record Shack ceased doing business; no assets remained. Robertson sued Levy for the balance of the promissory note. The trial court found no liability for Levy, holding that Robertson was estopped to deny the existence of the corporation because he had accepted one payment from Record Shack. Robertson appealed.

**Hood, Chief Judge.** In early common law times, private corporations were looked upon with distrust and disfavor. This distrust of the corporate form for private enterprise was eventually overcome by the enactment of statutes that set forth certain prerequisites before the status was achieved, and by court decisions that eliminated other stumbling blocks. Problems soon arose, however, where there was substantial compliance with the prerequisites of the statute, but not complete formal compliance. Thus the concepts of de jure corporations, de facto corporations, and corporations by estoppel came into being.

One of the reasons for enacting modern corporation statutes was to eliminate problems inherent in the de jure, de facto, and estoppel concepts. Thus sections 56 and 146 of the MBCA were enacted as follows:

> Section 56. Effect of Issuance of Certificate of Incorporation.
> Upon the issuance of the certificate of incorporation, the corporate existence shall begin, and such certificate of incorporation shall be conclusive evidence that all conditions precedent required to be performed by the incorporators have been complied with and that the corporation has been incorporated under this chapter.
> Section 146. Unauthorized Assumption of Corporate Powers.
> All persons who assume to act as a corporation without authority so to do shall be jointly and severally liable for all debts and liabilities incurred or arising as a result thereof.

No longer must the courts inquire into the equities of a case to determine whether there has been good faith compliance with the statute. The corporation comes into existence only when the certificate has been issued. Before the certificate issues, there is no corporation de jure, de facto, or by estoppel.

The authorities that have considered the problem are unanimous in their belief that section 56 and section 146 have put to rest de facto corporations and corporations by estoppel. Thus the Comment to section 56 of the MBCA, after noting that de jure incorporation is complete when the certificate is issued, states that: "Since it is unlikely that any steps short of securing a certificate of incorporation would be held to constitute apparent compliance, the possibility that a de facto corporation could exist under such a provision is remote."

The portion of section 56 stating that the certificate of incorporation will be "conclusive evidence" that all conditions precedent have been performed eliminates the problems of estoppel and de facto corporations once the certificate has been issued. The existence of the corporation is conclusive evidence against all who deal with it. Under section 146, if an individual or group of individuals assumes to act as a corporation before the certificate of incorporation has been issued, joint and several liability attaches. We hold, therefore, that the impact of these sections, when considered together, is to eliminate the concepts of estoppel and de facto corporateness under the Business Corporation Act of the District of Columbia. It is immaterial whether the third person believed he was dealing with a corporation or whether he intended to deal with a corporation. The certificate of incorporation provides the cutoff point; before it is issued, the individuals, and not the corporation, are liable.

Turning to the facts of this case, Record Shack was not a corporation when the original agreement was entered into, when the lease was assigned, when Levy took over Robertson's business, when operations began under the Penn Ave. Record Shack, Inc., name, or when the bill of sale was executed. Only on January 17 did Record Shack become a corporation. Levy is subject to personal liability because, before this date, he assumed to act as a corporation without any authority so to do. Robertson is not estopped from denying the existence of the corporation because after the certificate was issued he accepted one payment on the note. An individual who incurs statutory liability on an obligation under section 146, is not relieved of liability at a later time by complying with section 56. Subsequent partial payment by the corporation does not remove this liability.

Judgment reversed in favor of Robertson.

## CLOSE CORPORATION ELECTION

Close corporations[6] face problems that normally do not affect publicly held corporations. In recognition of these problems, nearly half of the states have statutes that attend to the special needs of close corporations. For example, some corporation statutes allow a close corporation to be managed by its shareholders. Other statutes allow one shareholder to effect a dissolution of a close corporation.

To take advantage of these close corporation statutes, most statutes require that a corporation make an *election* to be treated as a close corporation. Usually, the election is made when the corporation is organized. Section 3 of the Statutory Close Corporation Supplement to the MBCA permits a corporation with *fewer than 50 shareholders* to elect to become a close corporation. The Close Corporation Supplement requires the articles of incorporation to state that the corporation is a statutory close corporation. Other provisions of the Close Corporation Supplement will be discussed later in this chapter and in Chapters 24 and 25.

[6] Close corporations are defined in Chapter 22.

Since close corporation status is elective, there is no penalty for a corporation's failure to meet the election requirements for such status. The only consequence of a failure to meet the requirements of a close corporation is that the close corporation statutory provisions are inapplicable. Instead, statutory corporation law will treat the corporation as it treats any other general corporation.

Note, however, that a court may decide to apply special *common law* rules applicable only to close corporations even when a corporation fails to meet the statutory requirements for treatment as a close corporation. These special common law rules for close corporations will be discussed later in this chapter and in Chapters 24 and 25.

## DISSOLUTION AND TERMINATION OF CORPORATIONS

Just as there are requirements that must be met in order to create a corporation, so, too, certain requirements must be met in order to dissolve a corporation. A *dissolution* does not terminate a corporation. Instead, a dissolution requires a corporation to cease its business, to wind up its affairs, and to liquidate its assets. *Termination* occurs after the corporation's assets have been liquidated and the proceeds distributed.

Historically, a corporation could not be dissolved without the permission of the state that created it. Today, corporation statutes permit a corporation to *dissolve itself.* No consent of the state is required.

The MBCA permits voluntary and involuntary dissolutions. A voluntary dissolution may be accomplished only with the consent of the corporation. An involuntary dissolution may be accomplished without the corporation's consent and despite its opposition.

**Voluntary Dissolution.** The MBCA allows a voluntary dissolution *before a corporation commences business* and *after a corporation commences business.*

**Before Business Commenced.** Under MBCA Section 14.01, a corporation that has not issued shares or commenced business may be dissolved by the *vote of a majority of its incorporators or initial directors.*

**After Business Commenced.** MBCA Section 14.02 provides that a corporation *doing business* may be dissolved by *action of its directors and shareholders.* The section requires that the *directors adopt a dissolution resolution.* A *majority of the shares outstanding* must be cast in favor of dissolution at a shareholders' meeting.

**Articles of Dissolution.** For a voluntary dissolution to be effective, the corporation must file *articles of dissolution* with the secretary of state. The articles of dissolution state the name of the corporation, the date dissolution was approved, and the votes cast for and against dissolution. A dissolution is effective when the articles are filed.

**Involuntary Dissolution.** A corporation may be dissolved without its consent by *administrative action* of the secretary of state or by *judicial action* of a court.

**Administrative Dissolution.** MBCA Section 14.20 permits the secretary of state to commence an administrative proceeding to dissolve a corporation that has not filed its annual report, paid its franchise tax, or appointed or maintained a registered office or agent in the state. In addition, the secretary of state may administratively dissolve a corporation whose period of duration as stated in its articles has expired.

Administrative dissolution is a simple process. The secretary of state must give written notice to the corporation of the grounds for dissolution. If within 60 days the corporation does not correct the default cited by the secretary or demonstrate that the default does not exist, the secretary dissolves the corporation by signing a certificate of dissolution.

**Judicial Dissolution.** The secretary of state, the shareholders, or the creditors may petition a court to order the involuntary dissolution of a corporation. The *secretary of state,* under MBCA Section 14.20, may obtain judicial dissolution if it is proved that a corporation obtained its articles of incorporation by fraud or exceeded or abused its legal authority.

Under Section 14.30, *any shareholder* may obtain judicial dissolution when there is a *deadlock of the directors that is harmful to the corporation,* when the *shareholders are deadlocked and cannot elect directors,* or when the *directors are acting contrary to the best interests of the corporation.*

The MBCA also permits certain *creditors* to request dissolution if the corporation is *insolvent.*

**Dissolution of Close Corporations.** Many close corporations are nothing more than incorporated partnerships, in which all the shareholders are managers and friends or relatives. Recently, corporation law has reflected the special needs of those shareholders of close corporations who want to arrange their affairs to make the close corporation more like a partnership.

In partnership law, any partner has the power to dissolve the partnership at any time. This is an important power, for it allows a partner to leave a partnership in which, for example, he is continually outvoted by the other partners and to obtain the value of his interest in the partnership.

In Section 15(a), the Close Corporation Supplement to the MBCA recognizes that a close corporation shareholder should have the same dissolution power as a partner. This section, and similar provisions in many states, permits the articles of incorporation to empower any shareholder to dissolve the corporation at will or upon the occurrence of a specified event, such as the death of a shareholder.

**Winding Up and Termination.** *Winding up* (liquidation) must follow dissolution. Winding up is the orderly collection and disposal of the corporation's assets and the distribution of the proceeds of the sale of assets. From these proceeds, the claims of creditors will be paid first. Next, the liquidation preferences of preferred shareholders will be paid. Then, common shareholders share any proceeds that remain.

After winding up has been completed, the corporation's existence *terminates.*

## FINANCING THE CORPORATION

**Sources of Funds.** Any business needs money to operate and to grow. One advantage of incorporation is the large number of sources of funds that are available to businesses that incorporate. One such source is the sale of corporate **securities,** including shares, debentures, bonds, and long-term notes payable.

Besides obtaining funds from the sale of securities, a corporation may be financed by other sources. A bank may lend money to the corporation in exchange for the corporation's short-term promissory notes, called *commercial paper.* Retained earnings provide a source of funds once the corporation is operating profitably. In addition, the corporation may use normal short-term financing, such as accounts receivable financing and inventory financing.

In this chapter, you will study only one source of corporate funds: a corporation's sale of securities. A corporate **security** may be either a share in the corporation or an obligation of the corporation. These two kinds of securities are called *equity securities* and *debt securities.*

**Equity Securities.** Every business corporation issues equity securities, which are commonly called stock or **shares.** The issuance of shares creates an ownership relationship, the holders of the shares—called stockholders or **shareholders**—being the owners of the corporation.

Modern statutes permit corporations to issue several classes of shares and to vary the rights of the various classes. Subject to minimum guarantees contained in the state business corporation law, the shareholders' rights are a *matter of contract* and appear in the articles of incorporation, in the bylaws, and on the share certificates.

There are two main types of equity securities: *common shares* and *preferred shares.*

**Common Shares.** *Common shares* (or common stock) are a type of equity security. Ordinarily, the owners of common shares—*common shareholders*—have the exclusive right to *elect the directors,* who manage the corporation.

Common shareholders usually enjoy no preferences. Instead, the common shareholders often occupy a position inferior to that of other investors, notably creditors and preferred shareholders. The claims of common shareholders are *subordinate* to the claims of creditors and other classes of shareholders when dividends are paid and when assets are distributed upon liquidation.

In return for this subordination, however, the common shareholders have an exclusive claim to the corporate earnings and assets that exceed the claims of creditors and other shareholders. Therefore, the common shareholders bear the major risks of the corporate venture, yet stand to profit the most if it is successful. They may receive the *residual (leftover) earnings and assets* after the dividend and liquidation preferences of other classes of shares have been satisfied.

**Preferred Shares.** Shares that have *preferences with regard to assets or dividends* over other classes of shares are called *preferred shares* (or preferred stock). *Preferred shareholders* are customarily given liquidation and dividend preferences over common shareholders. A corporation may have several classes of preferred shares. In such a situation, one class of preferred shares may be given preferences over another class of preferred shares. Under the MBCA, the preferences of preferred shareholders must be set out in the articles of incorporation, the basic contract between shareholders and the corporation.

**Liquidation Preference.** The liquidation preference of preferred shares is usually for a stated dollar amount. During a liquidation, this amount must be paid to each preferred shareholder before any common shareholder or other shareholder subordinated to the preferred class may receive his share of the corporation's assets.

**Dividend Preference.** Dividend preferences may vary greatly. For example, the dividends may be cumulative or noncumulative. Dividends on *cumulative* preferred shares, if not paid in any year, accumulate until paid. The entire accumulation must be paid before any dividends may be distributed to common shareholders. Dividends on *noncumulative* preferred shares do not accumulate if unpaid. For such shares, only the current year's dividends must be paid to preferred shareholders prior to the payment of dividends to common shareholders.

*Participating* preferred shares have priority as to a stated amount or percentage of the dividends to be paid by the corporation. Then, the preferred shareholders participate with the common shareholders in additional dividends paid.

Some close corporations attempt to create preferred shares with a *mandatory dividend* right. These mandatory dividend provisions have generally been held illegal as unduly restricting the powers of the board of directors. Today, a few courts and some special close corporation statutes legitimize mandatory dividends.[7]

**Redemption.** Preferred shares may be made *redeemable* if the articles allow redemption. Redeemable preferred shares may be purchased by the *corporation at its option* at a price stated in the articles, despite the shareholders' unwillingness to sell. Some statutes permit the articles to give the *shareholders* the right to force the corporation to redeem preferred shares.[8]

[7] The legality of mandatory dividends is discussed in Chapter 25.

[8] Redemption is discussed in greater detail in Chapter 25.

**Conversion.** Preferred shares may be *convertible* into another class of shares, usually common shares. A conversion right allows a shareholder to *exchange* one class of shares for another class of shares. The conversion rate or price is stated in the articles.

**Voting Rights.** Preferred shares have voting rights unless the articles provide otherwise. Usually, most voting rights are taken from preferred shares, except important rights such as voting for a dissolution or a merger. Often, preferred shareholders are given the right to vote for directors in the event of the corporation's default in the payment of dividends.

**Authorized, Issued, and Outstanding Shares.** There are three terms, among others, that describe a corporation's common and preferred shares: authorized, issued, and outstanding. *Authorized* shares are shares that a corporation is permitted to issue by its articles of incorporation. A corporation may not issue more shares than are authorized. *Issued* shares are shares that have been sold to shareholders. *Outstanding* shares are shares that are currently held by shareholders. The distinctions between these terms are important. For example, a corporation pays cash and property dividends only on outstanding shares. All shares are affected by a share split. Only outstanding shares may be voted at a shareholders' meeting.

**Canceled Shares.** Sometimes, a corporation will purchase its own shares. A corporation may *cancel* repurchased shares. Canceled shares do not exist: they are neither authorized, issued, nor outstanding. Since canceled shares do not exist, they cannot be reissued.

**Shares Restored to Unissued Status.** Repurchased shares may be *restored to unissued status* instead of being canceled. If this is done, the shares are merely authorized and they may be reissued at a later time.

**Treasury Shares.** If repurchased shares are neither canceled nor restored to unissued status, they are called *treasury shares.* Such shares are authorized and issued, but not outstanding. They may be sold by the corporation at a later time. The corporation may *not vote them* at shareholders' meetings, and it may *not pay a cash or property dividend on them.*

The MBCA *abolishes* the concept of treasury shares. It provides that repurchased shares are *restored to unissued status* and may be reissued, unless the articles of incorporation require cancellation.

**Options, Warrants, and Rights.** Equity securities include options to purchase common shares and preferred shares. The MBCA expressly permits the board of directors to issue *options* for the purchase of the corporation's shares. Share options are often issued to top-level managers as an incentive to increase the profitability of the corporation. An increase in profitability should increase the market value of the corporation's shares, resulting in increased compensation to the employees who own and exercise share options.

*Warrants* are options evidenced by *certificates*. They are sometimes part of a package of securities sold as a unit. For example, they may be sold along with notes, bonds, or even shares. Underwriters may receive warrants as part of their compensation for aiding a corporation in selling its shares to the public.

*Rights* are short-term certificated options that are usually transferable. Rights are used to give present security holders an option to subscribe to a proportional quantity of the same or a different security of the corporation. They are most often issued in connection with a *preemptive right* requirement, which obligates a corporation to offer each existing shareholder the opportunity to buy the corporation's newly issued shares in the same proportion as the shareholder's current ownership of the corporation's shares.[9]

**Debt Securities.** Corporations have the power to borrow money necessary for their operations by issuing *debt securities.* Such power is inherent. The articles of incorporation do not have to authorize the corporation to issue debt securities.

Debt securities create a *debtor-creditor relationship* between the corporation and the security holder. With the typical debt security, the corporation is obligated to pay *interest* periodically and to pay the amount of the debt (the *principal*) on the maturity date.

Debt securities include notes payable, debentures, and bonds.

**Notes.** Generally, *notes* have a shorter term than debentures or bonds. They seldom have terms exceeding five years. Notes may be secured or unsecured. For *secured notes,* property of some kind serves as *collateral* for the payment of the debt. If the debt is not paid, the noteholders may force the sale of the collateral and take the proceeds of the sale.[10]

**Debentures.** *Debentures* are long-term, unsecured debt securities. A debenture may have a term of 30 years or more. Debentures usually have *indentures.* An indenture is a contract that protects the rights of the debenture holders. For example, an indenture defines what acts constitute default by the corporation and what rights the debenture holders have upon default. It may place restrictions on the corporation's right to issue other debt securities.

[9] The preemptive right is discussed in greater detail in Chapter 25.

[10] Rights of secured creditors are covered in detail in Chapters 39 and 40.

**Bonds.** *Bonds* are long-term, secured debt securities that usually have indentures. They are identical to debentures, except that bonds are *secured.* The collateral for bonds may be real property, such as a building, or personal property, such as an airplane or a railroad car.

**Importance of Security for a Debt.** In the event of liquidation, secured noteholders and bondholders have priority as to the assets that secure their debts. Therefore, they are likely to receive greater portions of their claims than are unsecured noteholders and debenture holders. The claims of unsecured noteholders and debenture holders are paid at the same time as the claims of general creditors.

**Convertible Debt Securities.** It is not uncommon for notes or debentures to be *convertible* into other securities, usually preferred or common shares. The right to convert belongs to the owner *(holder)* of the convertible note or debenture. This conversion right permits an investor to receive interest as a debt holder and, after conversion, to share in the increased value of the corporation as a shareholder.

## CONSIDERATION FOR SHARES

The board of directors has the power to issue shares on behalf of the corporation. The board must decide at what *price* and for what *type of consideration* it will issue the shares. Corporation statutes restrict the discretion of the board in accepting specified kinds of consideration and in determining the value of the shares it issues.

**Quality of Consideration for Shares.** Not all kinds of consideration in *contract law* are acceptable as legal consideration for shares in *corporation law.*[11] To protect creditors and other shareholders, the statutes require legal consideration to have *real value.*

**Proper Consideration.** Most corporation statutes, including old MBCA Section 19, permit shares to be issued for *money,* for *tangible or intangible property,* and for *labor actually performed or services rendered to the corporation.* Therefore, cash, land, buildings, trademarks, patents, and 10 years of *past work* by the corporation's president would be acceptable consideration for shares. Note that *past consideration* is proper for shares, although it is not consideration in contract law. In most states, preincorporation promoter's services are not proper consideration for shares, because the services were not rendered *to the corporation.* The corporation was not in existence when the services were rendered.

In *Kaiser v. Moulton*, which follows, the court approved the issuance of shares for a check or for the finding of development land for the corporation. Finding the land was a service performed for the corporation.

**Improper Consideration.** In most states, and under old MBCA Section 19, promissory notes or future services are *not* acceptable kinds of consideration for shares. A president's promise to work for the next 10 years or to pay for the shares in 10 years would *not* be acceptable. The reason for excluding *executory promises* from the list of valid consideration is that the promised acts may never be performed.

**Revised MBCA Approach.** Revised MBCA Section 6.21(b) rejects the old MBCA's restrictions and permits shares to be issued in return for any tangible or intangible property or *benefit to the corporation,* including *promissory notes* and *contracts* for services to be performed. The rationale for the revised MBCA rule is a recognition that future services and promises of future services have value that is as real as that of tangible property.

In addition, the revised MBCA permits corporations to issue shares to their promoters in consideration for their promoters' preincorporation services. This rule acknowledges that a corporation benefits from a promoter's preincorporation services, since the corporation would not exist without the work of the promoter.

**Value of Consideration Received.** Disputes may arise concerning the value of property that the corporation receives for its shares. For example, the value of a building may be difficult to determine. In all states, the *board of directors* has the authority to *value the consideration received* for shares. The board's valuation of the consideration is conclusive if it acts as *prudent directors* would act, if it has *reasonable basis* for the valuation, and if it acts in the *best interests of the corporation. Kaiser v. Moulton* illustrates the courts' deference to the board's judgment in valuing consideration.

**Quantity of Consideration for Shares.** The board is required to issue shares for an adequate dollar amount of consideration. Whether shares have been issued for an adequate amount of consideration depends in part on the *par value* or *stated value* of the shares.

**Par Value or Stated Value.** *Par value* is an *arbitrary* dollar amount that is assigned to the shares by the *articles of incorporation.* When shares have no par value (so-called *no-par shares*), they may have a *stated value*. Stated value is an arbitrary dollar amount

[11] The definition of consideration in contract law is in Chapter 10.

that is assigned to shares by the *board of directors,* usually at the time they are issued. Neither par value nor stated value reflects the fair market value of the shares, but par value or stated value is the *minimum* amount of consideration for which the shares may be issued.

**Shares Issued for Less than Par or Stated Value.** Shares issued for less than par value or stated value are called *discount shares.* The board of directors is liable to the corporation for issuing shares for less than par or stated value. A shareholder who purchases shares from the corporation for less than par or stated value is liable to the corporation for the difference between the par or stated value and the amount she paid.

**Shares Issued for More than Par or Stated Value.** It is not always enough, however, for the board to issue shares for their par or stated value. Many times, shares are worth more than their par or stated value. The board must exercise care to ensure that the corporation receives the *fair value* of the shares it issues.

When the board decides to issue shares for more than their par or stated value, its judgment as to the amount of consideration that is received for the shares is conclusive. In setting the amount of consideration for the shares, the board must act in good faith, exercise the care of ordinarily prudent directors, and act in the best interests of the corporation.

**Treasury Shares and Par or Stated Value.** The par or stated value of shares is important *only when the shares are issued* by the corporation. Since treasury shares are issued, but not outstanding, the corporation does not issue treasury shares when it resells them. Therefore, the board may issue treasury shares *for less than par or stated value,* provided that it sells the shares for an amount equal to their *fair value.*

**Shareholder Resale of Discount Shares.** Since par or stated value is designed only to ensure that the corporation receives adequate consideration for its shares, a shareholder may buy shares from another shareholder for less than par or stated value and incur no liability. However, if the purchasing shareholder *knows* that the selling shareholder bought the shares from the corporation for less than par or stated value, the purchasing shareholder *is* liable to the corporation for the difference between the par or stated value and the amount paid by the selling shareholder.

**Par or Stated Value and the MBCA.** The MBCA eliminates the concept of par or stated value as applied to the discount share problem. The board need merely issue shares for their fair value. Its judgment as to the fair value of the shares is conclusive, if it acts in good faith, with the care of ordinarily prudent directors, and in the best interests of the corporation.

**Accounting for Consideration Received.** The consideration received by a corporation for its equity securities appears in the *equity* or *capital* accounts in the shareholders' equity section of the corporation's balance sheet. The terms *stated capital* and *capital surplus* indicate the equity accounts created and increased by the contributions of shareholders.

**Stated Capital and Capital Surplus.** The *stated capital* account includes the product of the number of shares outstanding multiplied by the par value of each share or, in the case of no-par shares, by the stated value of each share. If the shares are sold for more than the par or stated value, the *excess,* or surplus, is *capital surplus.* If the directors issue no-par shares but *fail to indicate a stated value* for the shares, *all* of the consideration received for the shares is *stated capital.*

Changes in the value of the corporation's assets or in the market price of its shares will not affect the amounts in the stated capital and capital surplus accounts on the books of the corporation, since those accounts reflect only the shareholders' contributions, not the value of the corporation.

In 1980, the MBCA discontinued its use of the terms *stated capital* and *capital surplus* and abolished the concept of par or stated value for most purposes. Under the MBCA, all consideration received for shares is lumped under one accounting entry: *capital.* Most states, however, recognize par value and stated value. Therefore, the traditional distinction between stated capital and capital surplus is still in effect in most states.

## Kaiser v. Moulton

**631 S.W.2d 44 (Mo. Ct. App. 1981)**

In 1955, Arthur Kaiser joined his cousin, Jerry Kaiser, in the business of real estate development. Generally, they used separate corporations for each development. In April 1962, Jerry Kaiser & Associates, Inc., was incorporated as a real estate development company. It had authority to issue 3,000 common shares having a par value of $10 per share. The articles of incorporation provided that 50 shares were to be issued before the corporation commenced business and that the capital with which the corporation would commence business was $500.

David Moulton entered the corporation in 1963 and worked on various deals with Jerry Kaiser. In June 1963, Arthur Kaiser met a real estate agent who informed him of the availability of some unimproved land. Arthur told Jerry and David about this opportunity. The land, along with an adjoining tract, was subsequently acquired by Jerry Kaiser & Associates, Inc., and developed as Sherwood Manor Apartments.

A special meeting of the shareholders of the corporation was held on November 1, 1963. At the meeting, the shareholders voted to amend the articles of incorporation to authorize the issuance of 1,000 shares of $10 par value Class A nonvoting common stock. A meeting of the directors of the corporation was held immediately after the shareholders' meeting. At that meeting, Jerry Kaiser, as the chairman of the board, announced that Arthur Kaiser had rendered services to the corporation. The board then approved the issuance to Arthur of 25 shares of the $10 par value Class A common stock. The corporation issued to Arthur share certificate number 1 for 25 shares "of the $10 par value Class A nonvoting stock of Jerry Kaiser & Associates, Inc., fully paid and non-assessable."

In 1980, Arthur sued the corporation and the other shareholders to inspect the books of the corporation and to obtain other relief. The corporation refused to allow him to inspect the books of the corporation on the ground that he was not a shareholder, because he had not paid for the shares with a proper type of consideration, and because he had paid too little for the shares. After the trial court held that Arthur was a shareholder, the corporation and the other shareholders appealed.

**STEWART, JUDGE.** The corporation contends that the issuance of 25 shares to Arthur Kaiser was void because it violated the Missouri Constitution, which states, "No corporation shall issue stock, except for money paid, labor done, or property actually received." Arthur testified that he paid for the shares by check, but because of the length of time that had passed, he had destroyed all of his cancelled checks that he had written in 1963. Arthur's attorney testified that in 1964, Arthur had told him that he had received the shares for services rendered to the corporation. Moulton, the chief officer of the corporation, testified that he did not recall Arthur presenting a check to the corporation. Although the corporation had records that would show whether Arthur had paid by check, it did not produce such records.

When we consider Arthur's testimony along with the inference that the trial court could reasonably draw from the corporation's failure to produce the corporate records that would reflect the capital accounts of the corporation, we conclude that the court could reasonably have found that Arthur paid for the shares by check. We are also of the opinion that the trial court could have found that Arthur's shares were issued for "labor done." At the meeting of the board of directors, on November 1, 1963, Jerry Kaiser as chairman announced that Arthur had rendered services to the corporation, and the members of the board unanimously authorized the issuance of 25 shares of $10 par value Class A common stock. The stock as issued stated that it was fully paid and non-assessable. It is conceded that Arthur is the person who learned of the availability of the initial tract of land that was developed into Sherwood Manor. He brought the matter to the attention of Jerry Kaiser and David Moulton.

As set out in the Missouri corporation statute, "In the absence of actual fraud in the transaction, the judgment of the board of directors or the shareholders, as the case may be, as to the value of the consideration received for shares shall be conclusive." When we consider that the par value of the shares issued to Arthur Kaiser amounted to only $250, it would not be unreasonable for the trial court to conclude that Arthur's efforts in finding a major portion of the property used in developing Sherwood Manor were sufficient consideration for the issuance of the 25 shares. The trial court did not err in declaring Arthur the owner of the shares.

Judgment for Arthur Kaiser affirmed.

## SHARE SUBSCRIPTIONS

**Nature of Share Subscriptions.** Under the terms of a *share subscription,* a prospective shareholder promises to buy a specific number of the shares of a corporation at a stated price. If the subscription is accepted by the corporation, its *subscriber* is a *shareholder* of the corporation, even if the shares have not been issued.

**Distinguished from Executory Contracts.** Subscriptions should not be confused with *executory contracts* to purchase shares. A prospective shareholder who merely has an executory contract to purchase shares is not a shareholder until the share certificate has been delivered. Subscriptions are distinguished from executory contracts by the *intent of the parties.* If a corporation and an investor intended that the investor have the rights of a shareholder immediately upon the creation of a contract, the contract is a subscription.

**Writing Requirement.** Under the MBCA, subscriptions need not be in writing to be enforceable. Usually, however, subscriptions are written.

Under UCC section 8–319, which has been adopted by all of the states, an executory contract to purchase shares must be in writing to be enforceable.

**Uses of Subscriptions.** Promoters use written share subscriptions in the course of selling shares of a proposed corporation to ensure that equity capital will be provided once the corporation comes into existence. These are called *preincorporation subscriptions.* You studied preincorporation subscriptions in this chapter's discussion of promoters.

Close corporations may use share subscriptions when they seek to sell additional shares after incorporation. These are examples of *postincorporation subscriptions,* subscription agreements made *after* incorporation. A postincorporation subscription is a *contract* between the corporation and the subscriber at the time the subscription agreement is made.

**Payment of Subscription Price.** A subscription, whether preincorporation or postincorporation, may provide for payment of the price of the shares on a specified day, in installments, or upon the demand of the board of directors. The board may not discriminate when it demands payment. It must demand payment from all the subscribers of a class of shares or from none of them.

A share certificate may not be issued to a share subscriber until the price of the shares has been fully paid. If the subscriber fails to pay as agreed, the corporation *may sue the subscriber* for the amount owed.

## ISSUANCE OF SHARES

**Function of Share Certificates.** A *share certificate* is *evidence* that a person has been issued shares, owns the shares, and is a shareholder. The certificate states the corporation's name, the shareholder's name, and the number and class of shares. The certificate, however, is not the shares. A person can be a shareholder without receiving a share certificate, as is a holder of a share subscription.

**Uncertificated Shares.** Under MBCA Section 6.25, share certificates are not required. An increased use of computers may result in electronic, rather than paper, transfers of share ownership. The use of computers may also eliminate the paperwork crises that have been serious problems for brokerage firms, which currently handle huge quantities of share certificates.

**Liability for Overissuance under UCC.** UCC Article 8 regulates, among other things, the issuance of securities. Under Article 8, a corporation has a duty to issue only the number of shares authorized by its articles. Overissued shares are void.

When a person is entitled to overissued shares, the corporation may not issue the shares. Under UCC section 8–104, however, the person has two remedies. The corporation must obtain identical shares, if such shares are reasonably available, and deliver them to the person entitled to issuance. If identical shares are unavailable, the corporation must reimburse the person for the value paid for the shares plus interest.

**Director Liability.** The directors may incur liability, including criminal liability, for an overissuance of shares. To prevent overissuance through error in the issuance or transfer of their shares, corporations often employ a bank or a trust company as a *registrar.*

## TRANSFER OF SECURITIES

**Function of Securities Certificates.** Securities certificates are evidence of the ownership of securities. Therefore, their transfer is *evidence of the transfer* of the ownership of securities. UCC Article 8 covers the registration and transfer of investment securities, as represented by certificates.

**Shares.** *Share certificates* are issued in *registered* form; that is, they are registered with the corporation in the name of a specific person. The indorsement of a share certificate on its back by its registered owner and the delivery of the certificate to another person transfers ownership of the shares to the other person. Alternatively, a separate document, often referred to as a *stock power,* may be used for transfer purposes. The transfer of a share certificate without naming a transferee creates a *street certificate*. The transfer of a street certificate may be made by delivery without indorsement. Any holder of a street certificate is presumed to be the owner of the shares it represents.

**Debt Securities.** Bonds, debentures, and notes, as investment securities, are also covered by Article 8. They may be *registered* (payable to a specified person in whose name the certificate is registered with the corporation) or *bearer* (payable to whoever holds the certificate). A registered debt security certificate is transferred in the same manner as a share certificate, while a bearer debt security certificate is transferred by delivery alone.

**Restrictions on Transferability of Shares.** Historically, a shareholder has been *free to sell* her shares to whomever she wants whenever she wants. Since shares are the property of the shareholder, the courts have been reluctant to allow *restrictions upon the free transferability* of shares, even if the shareholder agreed to a restriction on the transfer of her shares.

Gradually, the courts and the legislatures have recognized that shares are also contracts. Under the rubric of freedom of contract, they have permitted the use of some restrictions on the transfer of shares to which shareholders agree. Today, modern corporation statutes legitimize most transfer restrictions, especially when used by close corporations. Transfer restrictions are especially important to shareholders of close corporations.

**Uses of Transfer Restrictions.** A corporation and its shareholders have a number of reasons to use transfer restrictions: (1) to maintain the balance of power, (2) to guarantee a market for the shares, (3) to prevent unwanted persons from becoming shareholders, (4) to preserve a close corporation or Subchapter S election, and (5) to preserve an exemption from registration of a securities offering.

**To Maintain the Balance of Power.** For example, four persons may each own 25 shares each in a corporation. No single person can control such a corporation. If one of the four can buy 26 additional shares from the other shareholders, he will acquire control. The shareholders may therefore agree that each shareholder is entitled to buy an equal amount of any shares sold by any selling shareholders.

**To Guarantee a Market for the Shares.** In a close corporation, there may be no ready market for the shares of the corporation. To ensure that a shareholder can obtain the value of her investment upon her retirement or death, the shareholders and the corporation may be required to buy a shareholder's shares upon the occurrence of a specific event, such as death or retirement.

**To Prevent Unwanted Persons from Becoming Shareholders.** In a close corporation, the shareholders may want only themselves or other approved persons as shareholders. The shareholders may therefore agree that no shareholder will sell shares to someone who is not approved by the other shareholders.

**To Preserve a Close Corporation or Subchapter S Election.** Close corporation statutes and Subchapter S limit the number of shareholders that a close corporation or a Subchapter S corporation may have. A transfer restriction may prohibit the shareholders from selling shares such that there are too many shareholders to preserve a close corporation or Subchapter S election.

**To Preserve an Exemption from Registration of a Securities Offering.** Under the Securities Act of 1933 and the state securities acts, an offering of securities is exempt from registration if the offering is to a limited number of investors, usually 35.[12] A transfer restriction may require a selling shareholder to obtain permission from the corporation's legal counsel, which permission will be granted upon proof that the shareholder's sale of the shares does not cause the corporation to lose its exemption.

### Types of Restrictions on Transfer.

There are four types of restrictions on transfer: (1) rights of first refusal and option agreements, (2) buy-and-sell agreements, (3) consent restraints, and (4) provisions disqualifying purchasers.

**Rights of First Refusal and Option Agreements.** A *right of first refusal* grants to the corporation and the other shareholders the right to *match the offer* that a selling shareholder receives for her shares. An *option agreement* grants the corporation and the other shareholders *an option* to buy the selling shareholder's shares at a price determined by the agreement. A right of first refusal or an option agreement is used primarily to maintain the corporate balance of power and to prevent unwanted persons from becoming shareholders.

Instead of stating a share price, an option agreement usually has a formula for calculating the value of the shares. For example, the earnings may be capitalized or the gross revenue multiplied by a factor to determine the value of the business, which value is then divided by the number of shares to calculate the value of each share. Ordinarily, as in *St. Louis Union Trust Co. v. Merrill Lynch,* which follows, the courts will permit or require purchase of the shares at the agreement price even when the fair value of the shares is much lower or much higher than the agreement price.

**Buy-and-Sell Agreements.** A *buy-and-sell agreement* compels a shareholder to sell his shares to the corporation or to the other shareholders at the price stated in the agreement. It also obligates the corporation or the other shareholders to buy the selling shareholder's shares at that price. The agreement is called a *cross-purchase agreement* when the shareholders are obligated to buy and sell. It is called a *redemption agreement* when the corporation is the person that is obligated to buy. As with option agreements, the price of the shares is usually determined by a stated formula. This type of agreement is used primarily to ensure a market for the shares upon the death or retirement of a shareholder.

Funding of the purchase price is important, since those persons having the option or obligation to buy will need to have funds with which to purchase the shares. Commonly, the

[12] Exemptions from registration under the federal and state securities acts are discussed in Chapter 26.

purchase of the shares of a deceased shareholder is funded by an annuity contract or a life insurance policy that is purchased at the time the agreement is made.

**Consent Restraints.** A *consent restraint* requires a selling shareholder to obtain the consent of the corporation or the other shareholders before she may sell her shares. Consent restraints may be used to preserve close corporation and Subchapter S elections, to maintain securities act exemptions, and to prevent unwanted persons from becoming shareholders.

**Provisions Disqualifying Purchasers.** A *provision disqualifying purchasers* is used to exclude unwanted persons from the corporation. For example, a transfer restriction may prohibit the shareholders from selling to a competitor of the business.

**Legality of Transfer Restrictions.** At first, courts upheld restrictions on transfer by finding them to be *reasonable* restraints on the alienation of property. The reasonableness of the restraint was judged in light of the character and needs of the corporation. Initially, only rights of first refusals, option agreements, and buy-and-sell agreements used by close corporations met the reasonableness test.

**MBCA Approach.** Today, modern statutes and the MBCA legitimize most transfer restrictions. MBCA Section 6.27(c) makes per se reasonable any restriction that maintains a corporation's status when that status is dependent on the *number or identity of shareholders,* as with a close corporation or Subchapter S status. The MBCA also makes per se reasonable any restriction that preserves exemptions under the Securities Act of 1933 and state securities laws. In addition, the MBCA has a catchall provision that authorizes transfer restrictions for any other reasonable purpose.

MBCA Section 6.27(d) describes the types of restrictions that may be imposed. Option agreements, rights of first refusal, and buy-and-sell agreements are permitted. Consent restraints and provisions disqualifying purchasers are permitted, if these restraints and provisions are not *manifestly unreasonable.* The corporation statutes of states such as Delaware and California have provisions similar to those of the MBCA. *St. Louis Union Trust Co. v. Merrill Lynch,* which follows, considers the Delaware statutory provision validating option agreements.

A transfer restriction may be contained in the articles of incorporation, the bylaws, an agreement among the shareholders, or an agreement between the corporation and the shareholders.

**Enforceability.** For a restriction to be *enforceable* against a shareholder, the *shareholder must agree* to the restriction or purchase the shares with *notice* of the restriction. Under MBCA Section 6.27(b), a *purchaser* of the shares has *notice* of a restriction if it is noted *conspicuously* on the face or the back of a share certificate or if it is a restriction of which he has *knowledge.* UCC section 8–204 requires that an enforceable restriction be noted *conspicuously* on the certificate or that the transferee have *actual knowledge* of the restriction. *Ling and Co. v. Trinity Savings and Loan Ass'n,* which follows, addresses the issue of whether a restriction is reasonable and whether it is conspicuously noted on the certificate.

**Effect of Statutory Close Corporation Supplement.** Although transfer restrictions are important to close corporations, many close corporations fail to address the share transferability problem. Therefore, a few states provide statutory resolution of the close corporation transferability problem. In these states, statutes offer solutions to the transferability problem that are similar to the solutions that the shareholders would have provided *had they thought about the problem.*

For example, Section 4 of the Close Corporation Supplement prohibits the transfer of close corporation shares except to certain persons, including shareholders and family members. This is a *statutory disqualification of specified purchasers.* The section permits, however, a close corporation shareholder to accept a cash offer for her shares from a person to whom she may not otherwise transfer her shares, if the corporation and the other shareholders do not match the offer within 75 days. This is a *statutory right of first refusal.* If the shareholders have solved the transferability problem differently in the articles, Section 4 of the Close Corporation Supplement does not apply.

Not all transferability problems are settled by the Close Corporation Supplement. There is no statutory buy-and-sell provision, although under Section 14 the articles may require the corporation to purchase the shares of a deceased shareholder at the request of his estate, thereby guaranteeing a market for the deceased shareholder's shares.

**Corporation's Duty to Transfer Shares.** Under UCC section 8–401, a corporation owes a duty to register the transfer of any registered shares presented to it for registration, provided that the shares have been properly indorsed and their transfer is not restricted. If the corporation refuses to make the transfer, it is liable to the transferee for either conversion or specific performance.

A corporation has the right to make a reasonable inquiry and investigation before it transfers shares. It will not be liable for any delay that is reasonably necessary to make an investigation warranted by the circumstances of the case.

When an owner of shares claims that his shares have been lost, destroyed, or stolen, the corporation must issue new shares to the owner unless the corporation has notice that the shares have been acquired by a bona fide purchaser. A bona fide purchaser is a purchaser of the shares for value in good faith with no notice of any adverse claim against the shares. If after the issuance of the new shares, a bona fide purchaser of the original shares presents them for registration, the corporation must register the transfer, unless overissuance would result. The corporation's liability for overissuance was discussed above.

## Ling and Co. v. Trinity Savings and Loan Ass'n

**482 S.W.2d 841 (Tex. Sup. Ct. 1972)**

Bruce Bowman borrowed some money from Trinity Savings and Loan Association. He pledged 1,500 shares of Ling and Company Class A common stock as collateral for the loan. Bowman failed to repay Trinity. Trinity sued Bowman on the loan and asked the court to order the sale of the shares pledged as collateral. Ling and Company objected to the sale of the shares on the ground that Ling's articles of incorporation restricted transfer of its shares. Trinity sued Ling also, asking the court to invalidate the restrictions on transfer.

The restrictions appeared in Article 4 of Ling's articles of incorporation. One restriction was an option agreement that granted to the corporation and the other shareholders the option to buy the shares before the shares might be sold to any other person.

On the front side of the share certificate, in small print, it was stated that the shares were subject to the provisions of the articles of incorporation, that a copy of the articles could be obtained from the secretary of the corporation or the secretary of state, and that specific references to provisions setting forth restrictions were on the back of the certificate. On the backside, also in small type, the reference to the articles was repeated and specific mention was made of Article 4. Here, the option agreement was referred to but not stated fully.

The trial court held that the restrictions were invalid and ordered the sale of the shares. After the court of appeals affirmed the trial court's decision, Ling appealed to the Supreme Court of Texas.

**Reavley, Justice.** The court of civil appeals struck down the restrictions for three reasons: the lack of conspicuous notice thereof on the share certificate, the unreasonableness of the restrictions, and the statutory prohibition against an option in favor of other shareholders whenever they number more than 20.

### Conspicuousness

The Texas Business Corporation Act provides that a corporation may impose restrictions on the transfer of its shares, if they are "expressly set forth in the articles of incorporation and copied at length or in summary form on the face or so copied on the back and referred to on the face of each certificate." The Legislature, at the same time, permitted an incorporation by reference on the face or back of a certificate of a provision in the articles of incorporation that restricts the transfer of the shares. The court of appeals objected to the general reference to the articles of incorporation and the failure to print the full conditions imposed upon the transfer of the shares. Nevertheless, reference is made on the face of the certificate to the restrictions described on the reverse side; the notice on the reverse side refers to the particular article of the articles of incorporation as restricting the transfer or encumbrance of the shares and requiring "the holder thereof to grant options to purchase the shares represented hereby first to the Corporation and then pro rata to the other holders of the Class A Common Stock." We hold that the content of the certificate complies with the requirements of the Texas Business Corporation Act.

There remains the requirement that the restriction or reference on transferability be "noted conspicuously on the security." UCC section 1–201(10) defines "conspicuous" and makes the determination a question of law for the court to decide. The UCC provides that a conspicuous term is so written as to be noticed by a reasonable person. Examples of conspicuous matter are given there as a "printed heading in capitals or larger or other contrasting type or color." This means that something must appear on the face of the certificate to attract the attention of a reasonable person when he looks at it. The line of print on the face of the Ling certificate does not stand out and cannot be considered conspicuous.

Our holding that the restriction is not noted conspicuously on the certificate does not entitle Trinity to a judgment under this record. The restriction is effective against a person with actual knowledge of it. The record does not establish conclusively that Trinity lacked knowledge of the restriction when Bowman executed an assignment of these shares to Trinity Savings and Loan.

### Reasonableness

A corporation may impose restrictions on the disposition of its shares, if the restrictions "do not unreasonably restrain or prohibit transferability." The court of appeals held that it is unreasonable to require a shareholder to notify all other record holders of Class A Common Stock of his intent to sell and give the other holders a 10-day option to buy. The record does not reveal the number of holders of this class of shares; we only know that there are more than 20. We find nothing unusual or oppressive in these first option provisions. Conceivably the number of shareholders might be so great as to make the burden too heavy upon the shareholder who wishes to sell and, at the same time, dispel any justification for contending that there exists a reasonable corporate purpose in restricting the ownership. There is, however, no proof of that.

### Statutory Limit on Optionees

The Texas Business Corporation Act provides that any of the following restrictions may be imposed upon the transfer of corporate shares:

(1) Restrictions reasonably defining pre-emptive or prior rights of the corporation or its shareholders of record, to purchase any of its shares offered for transfer.
(2) Restrictions in connection with buy and sell agreements binding on all holders of shares of that class, so long as there are no more than 20 holders of such class.
(3) Restrictions reasonably defining rights of the corporation or of any other person or persons, granted as an option or options or refusal or refusals on any shares.

The court of appeals regarded subsection (2) as being applicable to this case. Since it was stipulated that there were more then 20 holders of record of Class A stock, the court of appeals held that the restriction fails for this reason. We disagree. Subsection (2) is not applicable to the Ling restriction. There is no obligation to purchase these shares placed upon anyone, and these restrictions can only be considered as options covered by subsections (1) and (3) and not as buy and sell agreements covered by subsection (2).

Judgment reversed in favor of Ling. Case remanded to the trial court.

---

## St. Louis Union Trust Co. v. Merrill Lynch, Pierce, Fenner & Smith, Inc.

**562 F.2d 1040 (8th Cir. 1977)**

In 1947, Kenneth Bitting operated a stock brokerage partnership known as Bitting, Jones & Company in St. Louis, Missouri. In that year, the Bitting partnership merged into Merrill Lynch, a national stock brokerage partnership. The former Bitting partnership became the St. Louis office of Merrill Lynch. Between 1947 and 1951, Bitting was an employee of the Merrill Lynch partnership. In 1951, he became a general partner of the firm.

In 1959, the Merrill Lynch partnership was dissolved, and its business was incorporated.

In return for their interests in the partnership, the partners, including Kenneth Bitting, received common shares of Merrill Lynch.

Under Merrill Lynch's original articles of incorporation, all common shares, including those issued to Kenneth Bitting, were restricted against transfer. Under the terms of the articles, Merrill Lynch was granted an option to purchase the holder's shares at an adjusted net book value price upon the occurrence of several specified contingencies, including the death of the holder. This transfer restriction was conspicuously noted on each share certificate. Likewise, the shareholder or his executors were given a right to offer the shares to Merrill Lynch, which was then required to purchase those shares at book value.

On October 8, 1970, Kenneth Bitting died. Pursuant to its articles, Merrill Lynch exercised its option to purchase his 40,000 shares at a price of $26.597 per share, the net book value as of October 30, 1970. The option was exercised by the company on November 18, 1970.

Between 1959 and 1971, Merrill Lynch was a privately held company. On April 12, 1971, the company announced that it was going public; that is, it was going to issue its common shares to the public. On June 23, 1971, following registration with the U.S. Securities and Exchange Commission and a 3-for-1 share split, 4 million Merrill Lynch common shares were offered to the public at a price of $28 per share. Because of the share split, the offering price per share was approximately three times the price that was paid to Bitting's executors in accordance with the terms of the share restriction contained in Merrill Lynch's articles of incorporation.

Bitting's executors, including St. Louis Union Trust Company, sued Merrill Lynch and its directors, alleging that the decision to go public in the spring of 1971 was made by a tightly knit group of insiders within the company's management hierarchy before the company purchased Bitting's shares. The executors argued that Bitting's shares were purchased in furtherance of a fraudulent scheme on the part of these insiders to enhance the price at which the company's shares were to be offered to the public and to maintain their control of the company after it went public.

After a nonjury trial, the federal district court found for the executors and held that the option was unenforceable under Delaware law. Merrill Lynch appealed.

**Ross, Circuit Judge.** We first address the issue of whether the share restriction was enforceable under Delaware law when the share option was exercised in November, 1970. We hold that the restriction was enforceable under Section 202(c)(1) of the Delaware General Corporation Law.

Article VI, Section 1(a) of the Merrill Lynch articles of incorporation, the provision under which Kenneth Bitting's shares were called, provides in pertinent part as follows:

> In the event of the death of any holder of common shares of the Corporation, the Corporation shall have the right and option, which shall be prior to any other right and option, to purchase the common shares of the Corporation held by the deceased for a period of 90 days from the earlier of (i) the date the Corporation receives from the legal representative of such holder written notice of the death of such holder, or (ii) the date the Corporation mails written notice that the Corporation is on notice of such death.

This restriction was noted conspicuously on each Merrill Lynch share certificate and was indisputably assented to by Bitting when the shares were issued to him.

The enforceability of the restriction rests on our construction of section 202 of the Delaware General Corporation Law, which was in existence in November, 1970, when the restriction was enforced. Section 202(a) carries the label "Restriction on transfer of securities" and reads as follows:

A written restriction on the transfer or registration of transfer of a security of a corporation, if permitted by this section and noted conspicuously on the security, may be enforced against the holder of the restricted security or any successor or transferee of the holder including an executor, administrator, trustee, guardian, or other fiduciary entrusted with like responsibility for the person or estate of the holder.

Section 202(c) declares four types of restrictions valid without inquiry into the existence of a lawful or reasonable purpose. Section 202(c)(1) provides as follows:

(c) A restriction on the transfer of securities of a corporation is permitted by this section if it:

(1) Obligates the holder of the restricted securities to offer to the corporation or to any other holders of securities of the corporation or to any other person or to any combination of the foregoing, a prior opportunity, to be exercised within a reasonable time, to acquire the restricted securities.

This statute on its face validates the share restriction at issue. The statute declares the enforceability of any restriction that "obligates the holder of the restricted securities to offer to the corporation a prior opportunity to acquire the restricted securities." That is precisely what Merrill Lynch's articles required of Kenneth Bitting's estate in this case.

The executors advance the argument that section 202(c)(1) was intended to permit only the exercise of a right of first refusal and not the exercise of an automatic option to purchase triggered by the contingency of death or other circumstance. The construction urged by the executors would amount to nothing less than a judicial rewriting of the statute, and we reject it. Professor Folk, the reporter for the Delaware revision commission that prepared the law for adoption, has stated that section 202(c)(1) was intended to validate options to purchase as well as mere rights of first refusal.

The executors' construction would also violate the purpose of section 202(c)(1). That purpose was to broaden, not limit, the circumstances in which such restrictions would be enforced in order to clear up the preexisting uncertain contours of the common law. Before section 202(c) was adopted in 1967, the Delaware courts required that a share restriction be supported by specific justification, e.g., a reasonable or lawful purpose, to be enforceable. What specific justification was sufficient to sustain a restriction under the common law was the subject of much uncertainty. It was the purpose of section 202(c) to eliminate this uncertainty by substantively validating a wide variety of commonly accepted share restrictions, such as the provision before us. Accordingly, we hold that the share restriction is enforceable under Delaware law.

Having determined that the share restriction was enforceable, we now consider the merits of the claim that the directors breached their fiduciary duty of good faith in enforcing the share restriction. Although directors generally do not occupy a fiduciary position with respect to shareholders in face-to-face dealings, Delaware creates such a duty in special circumstances where advantage is taken of inside information by a corporate insider who deliberately misleads an ignorant shareholder. Implicit in this formulation of the rule is the element of causation: the shareholder must rely on the misleading representation or omission in order to establish a cause of action for breach of fiduciary duty.

Any information concerning the public offering could not have subjectively influenced the executors to act differently than they did in selling the shares to the corporation pursuant to the terms of the share restriction. The parties were influenced only by 1) the lawful execution of the share restriction, which contractually bound them to sell the stock on the contingency of death, and 2) the death of Kenneth Bitting. The directors had no duty to disclose any information concerning the public offering, since such information was irrelevant to the executors' investment decision.

The executors cite several cases holding that even valid corporate machinery cannot be used for any improper motive to injure minority shareholders. We have no quarrel with this proposition; however, none of the cases cited involved share restrictions. None of these cases even remotely impugns the corporation's right to exercise a repurchase option that was specifically assented to by the shareholder, exercised consistently by the corporation, and supported by lawful business purposes.

Judgment reversed in favor of Merrill Lynch.

## SUMMARY

The promoter brings the corporation into existence and begins its operation. Promoters are not agents, but they are fiduciaries of the corporation and of the investors. The corporation is not liable on the promoter's preincorporation contracts until the board of directors accepts the contracts. The promoter normally remains liable on preincorporation contracts, unless there is a novation.

The corporation law of the state of incorporation states what steps must be followed to incorporate. When a corporation is formed defectively, the promoter, the managers, and the shareholders may be liable for the debts of the business, unless the court finds that there is a corporation de jure, a corporation de facto, or a corporation by estoppel. Modern statutes make issuance of the certificate of incorporation conclusive proof of the existence of the corporation.

Dissolution ends the business of the corporation, except the business necessary for winding up. A corporation may be dissolved voluntarily or involuntarily. Involuntary dissolutions include administrative dissolution by the secretary of state and judicial dissolution at the request of the attorney general, a shareholder, or a creditor.

Corporations are financed in part by the issuance of equity and debt securities. Corporations may issue two or more classes of shares with different preferences, limitations, and rights. If there is only one class of shares, these will be common shares. If both common and preferred shares are issued, common shareholders are generally given the right to elect directors, and preferred shareholders have priority over common shareholders on dividends and on the assets distributed upon liquidation. Corporations may issue debt securities, including notes, debentures, and bonds. The claims of the holders of such securities are prior to the claims of shareholders.

A preincorporation share subscription is treated as an offer. A contract results when the offer is accepted by the corporation. Under the MBCA, acceptance occurs by act of the directors after incorporation. A postincorporation subscription is a contract when it is accepted by the corporation.

Article 8 of the UCC applies to investment securities and gives them characteristics of negotiable instruments. It establishes the duties and liabilities of corporations as issuers of shares and debt securities.

A corporation may restrict the transfer of its shares. To be enforceable against a shareholder, a restriction must be agreed to by the shareholder, noted conspicuously on the share certificate, or known to the shareholder prior to purchase. In addition, the restriction must be one authorized by statute, such as a buy-and-sell agreement, a right of first refusal, a consent restraint, or a provision disqualifying specified purchasers.

## PROBLEM CASES

1. Productora e Importadora de Papel (PIPSA) was a paper producer and importer with headquarters in Mexico City. It negoti-

ated a newsprint supply contract with George Dietrich, who signed the contract as president of Trans-Milpak, Inc. (TM), a corporation not yet in existence. When the contract was breached by TM, PIPSA sought damages of more than $800,000 from James Fleming. Fleming and Dietrich were the promoters of TM. TM argued that Fleming was liable as a copromoter even though he had not participated in the negotiations. Is Fleming liable?

2. In August 1969, K&E Company contracted to sell real estate in Hoboken, New Jersey, to K&J Holding Corporation for $750,000. K&J Holding gave K&E a check for $10,000 as a down payment. Cohen signed as president of K&J Holding, a corporation not yet in existence. The agreement provided for closing the transaction on November 3, 1969. On October 31, K&J Holding was incorporated. On November 3, however, the president of K&E wrote to the attorney for K&J Holding, enclosing a check for the amount of the down payment. The K&E president stated that he had discovered that incorporation papers for K&J Holding had not been filed at the time the contract was made. He asserted that the real estate contract was void.

K&J Holding sued K&E for specific performance. K&E defended on the grounds that since K&J Holding was not in existence at the time of the contract, K&E could not enforce the contract against K&J Holding and that K&E was therefore not bound to the contract due to lack of mutuality of obligation. Is this a good defense?

3. Susan Stap, a professional tennis player, contracted to play tennis for the Chicago Aces Tennis Team of the World Team Tennis League. The contract, obligating the Chicago Aces to pay Stap a base salary and certain bonuses, was made on January 24, 1974. The contract stated that the "Chicago Aces Tennis Team, Inc. (Club), employs Sue Stap (Player) to perform in or on behalf of the Club's participation in World Team Tennis." Throughout the remainder of the contract, the designations "Club" and "Player" were used in provisions concerning compensation, benefits, and employment duties. The contract was signed by Stap and by the "Chicago Aces Tennis Team, Inc., by Jordan H. Kaiser, Pres." The Chicago Aces were not incorporated until May 1974. On June 1, 1974, an amendment to the contract changed Stap's bonuses. The amendment was signed by Stap and by "Jock A. Miller, General Manager, Chicago Aces."

The Chicago Aces folded, failing to pay Stap the required salary and bonuses. Stap sued Jordan Kaiser on the contract. Is Kaiser liable on the contract with Stap?

4. Donald Emmick approached J. B. Morris with a plan to incorporate Morris' farm under the name Oahe Enterprises, Inc., with Emmick as the manager. Morris agreed to the plan. At the Oahe organization meeting, the board of directors, whose members were Emmick, Morris, and Morris's son, issued $50 par value shares to Morris and his wife and to Emmick. Emmick's contribution for his 120,000 shares of Oahe was 6,315 common shares of Colonial Manors, Inc. Emmick represented to the board of Oahe that the Colonial Manors shares were worth $19 per share. In reality, the Colonial Manors shares were worth only 47 cents per share.

Eventually, Emmick had a falling out with the other shareholders, including Warren Golden. Golden sued for a dissolution and liquidation of Oahe. Golden asked that the court reduce the number of shares held by Emmick to reflect the true value of the Colonial Manors shares contributed by Emmick. The result of the reduction would be to decrease the amount of assets that would be paid to Emmick and to increase the amount that would be received by Golden. Emmick responded that the judgment of the Oahe board of directors as to the value of the consideration received for its shares should be conclusive.

Will the court reduce the number of shares held by Emmick to reflect the true value of the consideration that he contributed?

5. Milton Bradley Company was a corporation organized in Massachusetts. The Massachusetts corporation statute gave the power to make bylaws to the shareholders. In 1977, the directors of Milton Bradley voted unanimously to submit to the shareholders a proposed bylaw. The proposed bylaw required an affirmative vote of 75 percent of the shareholders of each class of common shares for a merger of the corporation with any other corporation, unless an exception applied. According to the bylaw, an exception applied: (1) if the other corporation held 90 percent or more of Milton Bradley's common shares or (2) if the proposal to merge had first been approved by an affirmative vote of two thirds of the board of directors. If an exception applied, only a majority of the shares needed to be cast in favor of the merger.

Two days prior to the annual shareholders' meeting at which the proposed bylaw was to be considered for adoption, Jo Seibert filed suit claiming that the bylaw violated the Massachusetts corporation statute. The Massachusetts statute permitted a corporation to adopt bylaws to require a vote greater than a majority to approve a merger. Seibert argued that the statute did not permit a shifting percentage requirement, but allowed only one fixed proportion. The meeting was held, and the bylaw was adopted by a vote of over 70 percent of the outstanding shares and over 85 percent of the shares voted.

Is the bylaw valid?

6. AC&C Wreckers, Inc., a building demolition business, had filed its articles of incorporation on August 30, 1968, but it had neglected to file a certified copy of the articles with the county recorder and to publish them in a newspaper, as required by statute. Nevertheless, AC&C conducted its business as a corporation, kept corporate minutes, and had assets of its own. Collins, a lawyer who was not in charge of the corporation's business, was the major shareholder.

Terrel was injured on February 25, 1969, while employed at AC&C. Terrel sought to hold Collins personally liable for his injuries, because of AC&C's failure to complete the required steps in incorporation. Is Collins personally liable?

7. Albert Jordan was a master dental mechanic whose work included the molding of dental devices by the lost wax process. He conceived the idea that this process could be adapted to produce precision castings of shapes that had previously required machining. For the process to be practical commercially, however, some way had to be found to control furnace temperatures precisely during several hours of the production cycle. Jordan claimed to know how to do this.

Metamold Corporation was formed to exploit Jordan's idea. Jordan received 300 common shares of Metamold, valued at $30,000 by the board of directors. In payment for the shares, Jordan gave Metamold "all inventions and processes, whether now, or later to be, copyrighted or patented, that I have appertaining to casting by plastic mold processes. I agree to disclose fully all my knowledge, skill, and ideas with respect to casting by way of plastic mold processes."

Jordan's process was not new or original. Other companies used essentially the same process. Although an important part of the process was Jordan's idea of using a furnace to burn out the molds, Jordan did not consider that idea patentable. Jordan promised to write out his process, but died before he had finished. What he had disclosed by the time of his death had been copied from standard trade journals. Jordan did not produce any castings in quantity or a single casting that was satisfactory. He later admitted that he did not know how the problem of plastic castings could ever be solved.

A share certificate for his 300 shares was never issued to Jordan. Metamold refused to issue him a certificate, arguing that Jordan had not paid "cash or property" for the shares, as required by the general corporation statute. Had Jordan contributed property for the shares?

**8.** C. C. Morris, Brown Morris, and Bill Hoover were owners and operators of two radio stations in Ada, Oklahoma. In 1953, they organized a corporation to operate KTEN, a new television station in Ada. They obtained a channel from the Federal Communications Commission, pledged their radio stations as collateral for the new corporation's obligations, personally guaranteed the debt of the new corporation to Radio Corporation of America in the amount of $240,000 for equipment, designed the facilities, planned the operations, and hired and trained personnel. They also became the directors of the corporation.

The articles of incorporation authorized 650 Class A voting shares and 650 Class B nonvoting shares, both classes having a par value of $500 per share. The Class A shares were issued to the directors by a resolution of the directors, which stated that the consideration was their experience in broadcasting, their standing with the FCC, and their personal guarantee of the debt to RCA for equipment.

When the corporation faced financial difficulties, it sued Bill Hoover, claiming that he had not paid proper consideration for his shares. Was his consideration proper for the issuance of shares?

**9.** While a managerial employee of Levi Strauss & Co., Arthur Chow acquired 11,295 of Levi Strauss's common shares under its employee share purchase plan. The plan allowed key employees to purchase the shares on favorable terms, while granting the corporation a repurchase option in the event of termination of employment. This provision entitled the corporation to repurchase Chow's shares at book value for a period of 30 days after his death.

When Chow died in 1970, the corporation exercised its option to repurchase 75 percent of the shares, permitting Mrs. Chow to retain 25 percent. The repurchase was made at the book value of $16.16 per share. Later that year, the board of directors decided to make a public offering. This was made in March 1971, and for some time thereafter the shares traded at above $50 per share.

In her suit, Mrs. Chow claimed that the repurchase option was invalid because it was an unreasonable restraint on the owner's right to sell. Was Mrs. Chow correct?

**10.** Marvin Liliedahl borrowed $34,500 from the Avoyelles Trust & Savings Bank and secured the loan with the pledge of 5,000 shares of Liliedahl & Mitchel, Inc. The corporation's articles of incorporation included a restriction on the transfer of its shares. The restriction gave a right of first refusal to the corporation and then to the shareholders. Reference to this restriction was imprinted on the share certificate pledged to the bank.

Liliedahl defaulted on the loan. The bank sued, and the court ordered the sheriff to seize the share certificate and to advertise and sell the shares. Mitchel, as an individual and as president of the corporation, then sought to enjoin the sale, claiming that the restriction barred a judicial sale free of the restriction. Is the restriction binding when the shares are pledged?

# Chapter 24

# Managing the Corporation

## INTRODUCTION

Shareholders have no right to manage the business of the corporation merely because of their status as shareholders. Instead, shareholders elect individuals to a *board of directors,* to which management is entrusted. Often, the board delegates much of its management responsibilities to officers.

In publicly held corporations, shareholders have no power or right to interfere with the legitimate managerial discretion of the board or the officers. In close corporations, however, some courts have granted shareholders limited authority to interfere with decisions of the board. Modern close corporation statutes have gone so far as to grant the shareholders of a close corporation the option of dispensing with a board of directors and managing the corporation as if it were a partnership.

This chapter explains the legal aspects of the board's and officers' management of the corporation. You will learn that while the board and officers have management authority, they do not possess unlimited management discretion. Their management of the corporation must be *consistent with the objectives and powers of the corporation,* and they owe duties to the corporation to manage it *prudently* and in the *best interests of the corporation* and the shareholders as a whole. You will also learn that under tort and criminal law management owes duties to the persons with whom it deals. In addition, you will study the special rules that permit close corporation shareholders to manage their corporations.

## OBJECTIVES OF THE CORPORATION

**Profit Objective.** The management of the corporation must be *consistent with the objectives* of business corporations as stated by the courts and the legislatures. The traditional objective of the business corporation has been to *enhance corporate profit and shareholder gain.* According to this objective, the managers of a corporation must seek the accomplishment of the profit objective to the exclusion of all others. As was made clear in *Ford v. Dodge,*[1] which appears in the next chapter, such other interests as employee and customer welfare must be subordinated to the interest of corporate profits. Interests other than profit maximization may be considered, provided that they do not hinder the ultimate profit objective.

**Other Objectives.** Courts before and after *Ford v. Dodge* permitted corporations to take *socially responsible actions* that were *beyond the profit-maximization requirement.*[2] In addition, every state recognizes corporate powers that are not economically inspired.[3] Corporations may make contributions to colleges, political campaigns, child abuse prevention centers, literary associations, and employee benefit plans, regardless of economic benefit to the corporations. Every state expressly recognizes the right of shareholders to choose freely the extent to which profit maximization captures all of their interests and all of their sense of responsibility.[4]

> Presently management can freely choose to act socially responsible, even if there exists no likelihood of resulting profits. At the same time the corporation may choose to be strictly profit oriented.[5]

**The ALI Corporate Governance Project.** Since 1978, the American Law Institute has sponsored a project to study the governance of corporations and to recommend changes in corporate governance. The project—the joint effort of lawyers, judges, and legal scholars—has produced several drafts of the ALI's *Principles of Corporate Governance: Analysis and Recommendations.* (For convenience, this text book will refer to the project as the ALI Corporate Governance Project.)

One portion of the project is concerned with the objectives of corporations. Section 2.01 of the ALI Corporate Governance Project recommends that during the conduct of its business a corporation may take *ethical considerations* into account and may devote resources to public welfare, humanitarian, educational, and philanthropic purposes, whether or not corporate profit and shareholder gain are thereby enhanced. The ethical considerations taken into account must be reasonably regarded as *appropriate to the responsible conduct of business* by a *significant portion of the community.* Not every ethical consideration will meet this standard. Excluded are ethical considerations that are likely to violate the *fair expectations of the shareholders* as a whole.

For example, a corporation may choose to perform a contract for which it has a defense to performance if that choice is based on the ethical consideration that seriously made business promises should normally be kept.

[1] 170 N.W.2d 668 (Mich. Sup. Ct. 1919).

[2] Mangrum, "In Search of a Paradigm of Corporate Social Responsibility," 17 *Creighton L. Rev.* 21, at 55–65 (1983).

[3] Id. at 66.

[4] Id. at 68.

[5] Id. at 65.

Suppose, however, that the management of a chain of restaurants decides to convert the restaurants to strictly vegetarian menus because eating meat violates a personal belief of the management. If management knows that the decision will reduce both the long-run and short-run profits of the corporation, this management belief is not an ethical consideration that is regarded as appropriate to the responsible conduct of business.

The ALI recommendation does not impose a legal obligation on corporate managers to consider ethical matters. The approach recommended by the ALI is not the law anywhere currently.

## CORPORATE POWERS

The actions of management are limited not only by the objectives of business corporations but also by the *powers* granted to business corporations. Such limitations may appear in the state statute, the articles of incorporation, and the bylaws.

**State Statutes.** The primary source of a corporation's powers is the corporation statute of the state in which it is incorporated. To avoid the confusion caused by common law decisions that limited the powers of corporations, many of the state corporation statutes expressly specify the powers of corporations. These powers include making gifts for charitable and educational purposes, entering a partnership, lending money to corporate officers and directors, and purchasing and disposing of their own shares—powers often denied to corporations under the common law.

In fact, modern statutes attempt to authorize corporations to engage in *any* activity. Model Business Corporation Act (MBCA) Section 3.02 contains an extensive list of corporate powers, but the preamble to that list makes it clear that a corporation has the power to do *anything that an individual may do.*

**Limitations.** Few state corporation statutes impose limits on the powers of corporations. For example, some states limit or prohibit the acquisition of agricultural land by corporations. Most other limitations have been abolished. For example, in the last half of this century, corporations have been empowered to make charitable contributions. Business corporations at one time were not permitted to enter the professions, such as medicine and accounting. Today, every state has a special statute that allows professionals to incorporate.

**Articles of Incorporation.** Most corporation statutes require the corporation to *state its purpose* in its *articles of incorporation.* The purpose is usually phrased in broad terms, even if the corporation has been formed with only one type of business in mind. For example, a corporation formed to mine coal may have a purpose clause stating that it has been formed "to mine coal and to engage in any other lawful business." Such a corporation would not be limited by its articles of incorporation. Most corporations have purpose clauses stating that they may engage in any lawful business.

Nevertheless, the promoters or the shareholders may desire to use the statement of purpose as a *self-imposed limitation.* In such instances, the purpose clause states the express powers of the corporation and becomes a *promise of the corporation to its shareholders* that it will confine its business to those express powers and the powers that may be implied therefrom. In the *Marsili* case, which follows, the court held that making a political contribution was among the implied powers of a public utility corporation.

Under MBCA Section 2.02, the inclusion of a purpose clause in the articles is optional.

Also, any corporation incorporated under the MBCA has the purpose of engaging in any lawful business, unless the articles state a narrower purpose. Hence, under the MBCA, a corporation with no purpose clause in its articles may engage in any lawful business, thereby being able to do what any individual may do.

**The *Ultra Vires* Doctrine.** At one time, ascertaining the powers of a corporation was vitally important. The original conception of the corporation was that it was an artificial person created and given limited powers by the state. An act of a corporation beyond its powers was a nullity because it was *ultra vires,* which is Latin for *beyond the powers.* Therefore, any act not permitted by the corporation statute or by the corporation's articles of incorporation was void due to lack of capacity.

This lack of capacity or power of the corporation was a *defense to a contract* assertable either by the corporation or by the other party that dealt with the corporation. Often, *ultra vires* was merely a *convenient justification for reneging* on an agreement that was no longer considered desirable. This misuse of the doctrine has led to its near abandonment.

**The *Ultra Vires* Doctrine Today.** Today, the *ultra vires* doctrine is of *small importance.* Modern statutes and well-drafted articles of incorporation nearly eliminate the potential for *ultra vires* problems. MBCA Section 3.04 and most other statutes do not permit the corporation or the other party to an agreement to avoid an obligation on the ground that the corporate action is *ultra vires.* In addition, MBCA Section 3.02 and other modern business corporation statutes grant corporations broad powers and nearly all drafters of articles of incorporation use broad purpose clauses.

The *ultra vires* doctrine survives only to a small extent under modern statutes. Under MBCA Section 3.04, *ultra vires* may be asserted in three situations: (1) by a shareholder, (2) by the corporation suing its management for exceeding the corporation's powers, and (3) by the state's attorney general.

**Shareholder Suit.** A shareholder may seek an *injunction* to restrain the corporation from carrying out a *proposed* action that is *ultra vires.* A shareholder may sue to rescind a contract that has not yet been performed (an *executory contract*) but not a contract that has been performed (an *executed contract*). This right of action allows a shareholder to enforce the articles of incorporation, which include the purpose clause.

The grant of the injunction must be *equitable.* In this context, equitable means that the *third party* dealing with the corporation *knew* that the corporation's action was *ultra vires.* When enforcement of the *ultra vires* act is enjoined, the *third party may recover damages* from the corporation. These damages, however, may *not include lost profits* from the transaction; they may encompass only costs associated with transacting with the corporation, such as attorney's fees for drafting contracts and agent's commissions.

**Suit against Management.** The corporation may claim that a corporate act is *ultra vires* in an action *against its officers or directors.* Section 3.04 does not state whether the directors and officers are *liable for damages* to the corporation resulting from their *ultra vires* action. Courts are likely to find such liability, however, unless the officer or director proves that she *reasonably believed* she *acted within the powers* of the corporation and that she exercised *reasonable care to ascertain those powers.*

**Action by Attorney General.** A state's *attorney general* may challenge a corporation's lack of power. The MBCA does not make clear, however, whether the attorney general is empowered to *dissolve* a corporation that has committed an *ultra vires* act or to *enjoin* it from committing such an act. Many states grant their attorneys general the power to dissolve the corporation or to enjoin it from committing an *ultra vires* act.

## Marsili v. Pacific Gas and Electric Co.

**124 Cal. Rptr. 313 (Cal. Ct. App. 1975)**

In 1971, the ballot in the San Francisco city election included Proposition T, which would prohibit the construction of any building more than 72 feet high unless plans for the proposed building were approved in advance by the voters. A group called Citizens for San Francisco opposed Proposition T. It asked Pacific Gas and Electric Company (PG&E) to contribute $10,000 to its campaign. PG&E's management reviewed the potential effect of Proposition T on the corporation. PG&E's management concluded that the proposition would raise its property taxes in San Francisco by an estimated $380,000 in the first year and by as much as $1,135,000 per year in 10 years and that the proposition would also require redesigning and obtaining additional land for an already planned electric power substation. The executive committee of the board of directors approved the contribution, which was reported to the California Public Utilities Commission. The contribution was not treated as an operating expense for rate-making purposes or claimed as an income tax deduction.

Three PG&E shareholders, including Mr. and Mrs. Marsili, sued PG&E and its directors, arguing that the contribution was *ultra vires* on the grounds that neither PG&E's articles of incorporation nor the laws of California permitted PG&E to make political donations. The shareholders asked that the contribution be returned to PG&E. The trial court held that PG&E had the power to make the contribution, and it therefore refused to require the return of the contribution. The shareholders appealed.

**Kane, Associate Judge.** *Ultra vires* refers to an act that is beyond the powers conferred upon a corporation by its charter or by the laws of the state of incorporation. The powers conferred upon a corporation include both express powers, granted by charter or statute, and implied powers to do acts reasonably necessary to carry out the express powers. In California, the express powers that a corporation enjoys include the power to "do any acts incidental to the transaction of its business . . . or expedient for the attainment of its corporate purposes."

The articles of PG&E are manifestly consistent with this statutory imprimatur. For example, they authorize all activities incidental or useful to the manufacturing, buying, selling, and distributing of gas and electric power, including the construction of buildings and other facilities convenient to the achievement of its corporate purposes, and the performance of "all things whatsoever that shall be necessary or proper for the full and complete execution of the purposes for which the corporation is formed."

In addition to the exercise of such express powers, the generally recognized rule is that the management of a corporation, in the absence of express restrictions, has discretionary authority to enter into contracts and transactions that are reasonably incidental to its business purposes.

No restriction appears in the articles of PG&E which would limit the authority of its board of directors to act upon initiative or referendum proposals affecting the affairs of the company or to engage in activities related to any other legislative or political matter in which the corporation has a legitimate concern. Furthermore, there are no statutory prohibitions in California which preclude a corporation from participating in any type of political activity. In these circumstances, the contribution by PG&E to Citizens for San Francisco was proper if it can fairly be said to fall within the express or implied powers of the corporation.

The crux of the controversy is whether a contribution toward the defeat of a local ballot proposition can ever be said to be convenient or expedient to the achievement of legitimate corporate purposes. The shareholders take the flat position that in the absence of express statutory authority corporate political contributions are illegal. This contention cannot be sustained. We believe that where, as here, the board of directors reasonably concludes that the adoption of a ballot proposition would have a direct, adverse effect upon the business of the corporation, the board of directors has abundant statutory and charter authority to oppose it.

Judgment for PG&E affirmed.

## THE BOARD OF DIRECTORS

**Introduction.** Traditionally, the board of directors has had *the power and the duty* to *manage or direct* the corporation. In a large publicly held corporation, it is impossible for the board to manage the corporation on a day-to-day basis, since many of the directors devote most of their time to their other business interests. Modern statutes, including MBCA Section 8.01, permit a corporation to be managed *under the direction of* the board of directors. Consequently, the board of directors *delegates* major responsibility for management to committees of the board such as an executive committee, to individual board members such as the chairman of the board, and to the officers of the corporation, especially the chief executive officer (CEO). In theory, the board *supervises* the actions of its committees, the chairman, and the officers to ensure that the board's policies are being carried out and that the delegatees are managing the corporation prudently.

**Major Functions of Modern Boards of Directors.** Since few boards of directors manage their corporations, you may ask what functions modern boards perform. Several studies have identified the functions of the boards of directors in large corporations. In a study published in 1975 by the Conference Board, four broad, overriding duties of boards were found:

1. To protect the assets and other interests of the shareholders of the corporation.
2. To ensure the continuity of the corporation by enforcing the articles and bylaws and by seeing that a sound board of directors is maintained.
3. To see that the company is well managed.
4. To make decisions that are not delegable, such as the payment of dividends.

The ALI Corporate Governance Project, in Section 3.02, recommends that a board:

1. Elect and evaluate high-level corporate executives.
2. Oversee the conduct of business with a view to evaluating whether the corporation's resources are being managed consistently with the objectives of the corporation.
3. Review and approve corporate plans and actions that management considers major and changes in accounting principles and practices that management considers material. This function includes board approval of broad corporate policies, such as defining the business of the corporation in terms of products and markets and establishing guidelines for product pricing and labor relations.

**Board Powers under Corporation Statutes.** By statute, the board of directors may take several corporate actions *by itself.* These powers are in addition to the board's general *power to manage or direct* the corporation. For example, the board may *issue shares* of stock and *set the price of shares.* It may *repurchase shares* and *declare dividends.* It may *adopt and amend bylaws.* It may *elect and remove officers* and *fill vacancies on the board.* This is only a partial list of the board's powers.

**Matters Requiring Board Initiative.** Some corporate actions require *board initiative.* That is, board approval is necessary to *propose such actions to the shareholders* who then must approve the action. Board initiative is required for important changes in the corporation, such as *amendment of the articles* of incorporation; *merger* of the corporation; the *sale of all or substantially all of the corporation's assets;* and *voluntary dissolution.*[6]

[6] The procedures for voluntary dissolution are covered in Chapter 23. The other actions requiring board initiative are covered in Chapter 25.

**Committees of the Board.** Most publicly held corporations have committees of the board of directors. These committees, which have fewer members than the board has, can more efficiently handle management decisions and exercise board powers than can a large board. Only directors may serve on board committees. The committees may exercise all the authority of the board within the limits specified by the articles, the bylaws, and resolutions of the board of directors.

**Limitations on Delegation.** Although many board powers may be delegated to committees of the board, some decisions are so important that corporation statutes require their *approval by the board as a whole.* Under MBCA Section 8.25(e), the powers that may not be delegated concern important corporate actions, such as *declaring dividends, filling vacancies* on the board or its committees, *adopting and amending bylaws,* approving *issuances of shares,* and approving *repurchases of the corporation's shares.*

**Executive Committee.** The most common board committee is the *executive committee.* It is usually given authority to act for the board on most matters when the board is not in session. Generally, it consists of the inside directors and perhaps one or two outside directors[7] who can attend a meeting on short notice.

The executive committee has been the most important committee of the board. Often, it has acted as a screening committee for preliminary consideration of complicated or weighty matters prior to their presentation to the full board for ratification.

Although an executive committee still exists in most corporations, its importance has

[7] The term *inside director* is applied to one who is an officer of a corporation or its affiliated corporation and devotes substantially full time to it. The term is also often applied to controlling shareholders who are not officers and to former officers. *Outside directors* have no such affiliations with the corporation.

diminished. Today, it is likely to be used for routine matters, such as approval of a contract that has already been accepted in principle at a regular board meeting.

**Other Committees.** Other common board committees are audit, nominating, compensation, and shareholder litigation committees. The New York Stock Exchange requires firms whose securities are listed for trading to establish *audit committees* composed entirely of outside directors. The Securities and Exchange Commission (SEC) strongly encourages all publicly held firms to have audit committees, and the ALI Corporate Governance Project Sections 3.03 and 3.05 recommend the use of audit committees by publicly held corporations. Most public-issue firms now have audit committees, which recommend independent public accountants and supervise the public accountants' audit of the corporate financial records.

The SEC and ALI Corporate Governance Project Section 3.06 have encouraged corporations to form *nominating committees* that are wholly or largely composed of outside directors. The purpose of such committees is to choose the management slate of directors that is to be submitted to shareholders at the annual election of directors. Nominating committees also often plan generally for management succession. The number of these committees has grown rapidly in recent years, but they are not required by present law.

*Compensation committees* review and approve the salaries, bonuses, stock options, and other benefits of high-level corporate executives. Although present law does not require that such committees be used, their use is encouraged by the SEC and ALI Corporate Governance Project Section 3.07. Nearly all large publicly held corporations have a compensation committee, usually composed solely or primarily of directors who have no affiliation with the executives whose compensation is being approved.

Since 1976, the use of *special litigation committees* or *shareholder litigation committees* has proliferated. Such a committee is given the task of determining whether a corporation should sue someone who has allegedly harmed the corporation. Usually, the committee is formed when a shareholder asks the board of directors to cause the corporation to sue some or all of the directors for mismanaging the corporation. Not surprisingly, a shareholder litigation committee rarely recommends that the corporation sue its directors and officers.

**Powers and Rights of Directors as Individuals.** A director is *not an agent* of the corporation merely by virtue of having been elected as a director. The directors may manage the corporation only when they act as a board, unless the articles, bylaws, or a resolution of the board of directors grants agency powers to the directors individually.

A director has the *right to inspect* corporate books and records that contain corporate information essential to the director's performance of her duties. The director's right of inspection is denied when the director has an interest adverse to the corporation, as would hold true for a director who plans to sell a corporation's trade secrets to a competitor.

**Compensation of Directors.** MBCA Section 8.11 and other modern statutes permit the directors to *fix their own compensation.* Outside directors of most large publicly held firms are compensated by an *annual retainer fee* plus an *attendance fee* for each board or committee meeting attended. A recent survey of 1,000 of the largest corporations found that, based on 1980 data, the average annual retainer fee was $12,000. Generally, attendance fees ranged from $400 to $600 per meeting.[8]

---

[8] *Board of Directors: Eighth Annual Study* (New York: Korn/Ferry, International, 1981), pp. 13–17.

## ELECTION AND REMOVAL OF DIRECTORS

**Qualifications of Directors.** Generally, anyone may serve as a director of a corporation. MBCA Section 8.02 states *no qualifications* for directors. A director need not even be a shareholder. Nevertheless, a corporation is permitted to specify qualifications for directors in the articles of incorporation.

**Number of Directors.** A board of directors may not act unless it has the *number* of directors required by the state corporation law. MBCA Section 8.03 and several state corporation statutes require *only one director,* recognizing that in close corporations with a single shareholder-manager, additional board members are superfluous. Several statutes, including the New York statute and the old MBCA, require three directors, unless there are fewer than three shareholders, in which case the corporation may have no fewer directors than it has shareholders. The board of directors of the New York corporation in *Lehman v. Piontkowski,* which follows the next section, was unable to act when the corporation had two shareholders but only one director.

Most statutes, including MBCA Section 8.03(a), provide that the number of directors may be *fixed by either the articles or the bylaws.* Section 8.03 permits the *board to fix and to change the number* of directors, subject to a few limitations that protect the shareholders' right to set the number of directors.

Most large publicly held corporations have boards with more than 10 members. For example, General Motors has 25, IBM has 24, and ITT has 13.

**Election of Directors.** Directors are *elected by the shareholders* at the *annual shareholder meeting.* Usually, each shareholder is permitted to vote for as many nominees as there are directors to be elected. The shareholder may cast as many votes for each nominee as he has shares. The top votegetters among the nominees are elected as directors. This voting process, called *straight voting,* permits a holder of more than 50 percent of the shares of a corporation to dominate the corporation by electing a board of directors that will manage the corporation as he wants it to be managed.

**Class Voting and Cumulative Voting.** To avoid domination by a large shareholder, among other reasons, some corporations allow class voting or cumulative voting. *Class voting* may give certain classes of shareholders the right to elect a specified number of directors. *Cumulative voting* permits shareholders to multiply the number of their shares by the number of directors to be elected and to cast the resulting total of votes for one or more directors. As a result, cumulative voting may permit minority shareholders to obtain representation on the board of directors. Class voting, cumulative voting, and other shareholder voting rights are discussed in detail in Chapter 25.

**The Proxy Solicitation Process.** Most individual investors purchase corporate shares in the public market to increase their wealth, not to elect or to influence the directors of corporations. Nearly all institutional investors—such as pension funds, mutual funds, and bank trust departments—have the same profit motive. Individuals and institutional investors are generally passive investors with little interest in exercising their shareholder right to elect directors by attending shareholder meetings.

Once public ownership of the corporation's shares exceeds 50 percent, the corporation cannot conduct any business at its shareholder meetings unless some of the shares of these passive investors is voted. This is because the corporation will have a shareholder *quorum* requirement, which may require that 50 percent or more of the shares be voted for a shareholder vote to be valid. Since passive investors rarely attend shareholder meetings, the management of the corporation must solicit **proxies,**[9] if it wishes to have a valid shareholder vote. Shareholders who will not attend a shareholder meeting must be asked to appoint someone else to vote their shares for them. This is done by furnishing each such shareholder with a proxy to sign. The proxy designates a person who may vote the shares for the shareholder.

**Management Solicitation of Proxies.** To ensure its *perpetuation in office* and the *approval of other matters* submitted for a shareholder vote, the corporation's management solicits proxies from shareholders for directors' elections and other important matters on which shareholders vote, such as mergers. The management designates an officer, a director, or some other person to vote the proxy. The person who is designated to vote for the shareholder is also called a **proxy.** Typically, the chief executive officer (CEO) of the corporation, the president, or the chairman of the board of directors names the person who serves as the proxy.

Usually, the proxies are merely signed and returned by the public shareholders, including the institutional shareholders. (Institutional investors own about a third of the total outstanding shares of publicly held corporations.) Passive investors follow the *Wall Street rule:* either support management or sell the shares. As a result, management almost always receives enough votes from its proxy solicitation to ensure the reelection of directors and the approval of other matters submitted to the shareholders, even when other parties solicit proxies in opposition to management.

[9] A proxy is usually a preprinted data processing form (computer card) with spaces for voting on matters submitted for a shareholder vote. See Chapter 26 for a discussion of the proxy requirements of the U.S. Securities and Exchange Commission.

**Effect on Corporate Governance.** Management's solicitation of proxies produces a result that is quite different from the theory of corporate management that directors serve as representatives of the shareholders. The *CEO can nominate directors* of his choice, and they will almost *certainly be elected.* The directors will appoint *officers chosen by the CEO.* The CEO's nominees for director will probably not be unduly critical of his programs or of his methods for carrying them out. This is particularly true if a large proportion of the directors are officers of the company and thus are more likely to be dominated by the CEO.

In such situations, the *CEO,* not the shareholders, selects the directors, and the *CEO,* not the board of directors, manages the corporation. Furthermore, the board of directors does not even function effectively as a representative of the shareholders in supervising and evaluating the CEO and the other officers of the corporation. The board members and the other officers, who are generally chosen by the CEO, are in effect *subordinates of the CEO,* even though, as is true in most publicly held corporations, the CEO is not a major shareholder of the corporation.

Although many boards of directors of publicly held corporations have tended to be dominated by the chief executive, exceptions occur. For example, a CEO only recently selected by the board might not have an opportunity to name her own board members. An exception might also occur when one or more of the directors own or represent owners of a large block of the corporation's stock.

**Term of Office.** Directors usually hold office for *only one year,* but they may have longer terms. Most statutes, including MBCA Section 8.06, permit *staggered terms* for directors. Under the MBCA, a corporation having a board of nine or more members may establish either two or three approximately equal classes of directors, with only one class of directors coming up for election at each annual shareholders' meeting. If there are two classes of directors, the directors serve *two-year terms;* if there are three classes, they serve *three-year terms.*

The original purpose of staggered terms was to permit continuity in management. Today, staggered terms are frequently used to make it difficult to remove existing directors. Someone who wants to replace management must mount successful proxy solicitation fights several years in a row.

**Vacancies on the Board.** Most statutes permit the directors to fill *vacancies on the board.* MBCA Section 8.10 provides that a majority vote of the remaining directors is sufficient to select persons to serve out unexpired terms, even though the remaining directors are less than a quorum.[10] Section 8.10 also permits the directors to fill a *vacancy created by a board-approved increase* in the size of the board. Apparently, the newly appointed director will serve a full term, even if the term exceeds a year.

**Removal of Directors.** Although the common law permitted shareholders to remove directors only for cause, modern corporation statutes permit *shareholders* to remove directors *with or without cause,* unless the articles provide that directors may be removed only for cause. The rationale for the modern rule is that the shareholders should have the power to *judge the fitness of directors at any time.*

Most corporations have *provisions in their articles* authorizing the shareholders to remove directors *only for cause.* Cause for removal would include *mismanagement* or *conflicts of interest.* Before removal for cause, the director must be given notice and an opportunity for a hearing.

[10] A quorum of directors is usually a majority of directors. Quorum requirements are discussed later in this chapter.

**Shareholder Vote.** MBCA Section 8.08(d) permits shareholders to remove a director only at a *shareholder meeting called for that purpose.* The director may be removed only if the number of votes cast to remove him would be sufficient to elect him. Usually, this means that a director may be removed by a majority vote of the shares voted at the shareholder meeting.

If a director has been *elected by a class* of shareholders or *through cumulative voting,* different rules apply. A director elected by a separate class of shareholders may be *removed only by that class* of shareholders, thereby protecting the voting rights of the class. A director elected by cumulative voting may not be removed if the *votes cast against her removal* would have been *sufficient to elect her* to the board, thereby protecting the voting rights of minority shareholders. In *Lehman v. Piontkowski,* which follows the next section, the minority shareholder-director could not have been removed as a director if the corporation had had cumulative voting of shares.

## DIRECTORS' MEETINGS

**Formal Meetings.** Traditionally, directors could act only when they were properly convened as a board. They could not vote by proxy or informally, as by a telephone poll. This rule was based on a belief in the value of consultation and collective judgment.

**Actions without Meetings.** Today, the corporation laws of a majority of the states and MBCA Section 8.21 specifically permit action by the directors *without a meeting* if *all of the directors consent in writing to the action taken.* Such authorization is useful for dealing with routine matters or for formally approving an action based on an earlier policy decision made after full discussion. Close corporations are more likely to take advantage of this method of action than are large public corporations holding monthly meetings of the board.

**Meetings by Telephone.** MBCA Section 8.20 permits a board to meet by *telephone or television* hookup. This section permits a meeting of directors who may otherwise be unable to convene. The only requirement is that the directors be able to *hear one another simultaneously.*

**Notice of Meetings.** Directors are entitled to *reasonable notice* of all *special* meetings, but not of regularly scheduled meetings. Most of the corporation statutes require that the notice for a special meeting state the *purpose* of the meeting, allowing the directors to prepare for it. MBCA Section 8.22, however, does not require inclusion of the purpose unless this is required by the articles or bylaws.

**Waiver of Notice.** A director's *attendance* at a meeting *waives* any required notice, unless at the beginning of the meeting the director *objects* to the lack of notice. The normal practice is for the corporate secretary to obtain signed waivers when notice is defective. Under MBCA Section 8.23(a), written waivers of notice are effective whether these are signed *before or after* the meeting.

**Quorum Requirement.** For the directors to act, a *quorum* of the directors must be present. The quorum requirement ensures that the decision of the board will represent the views of a significant portion of the directors. MBCA Section 8.24 provides that a quorum shall be a *majority* of the number of directors. The MBCA permits the corporation to require a *greater number* for a quorum by a provision in the articles or the bylaws. As an alternative, the MBCA permits the articles to set the board's quorum *below a majority* of the directors, provided that the quorum is *no fewer than one third* of the number of directors.

**Voting.** Each director has *one vote.* If a quorum is present, a vote of a *majority of the directors present* is an act of the board, unless the articles or the bylaws require the vote of a greater number of directors. Such *supermajority voting provisions* are common in close corporations but not in publicly held corporations. The use of supermajority voting provisions by close corporations is covered later in this chapter.

## Lehman v. Piontkowski

**460 N.Y.S.2d 817 (N.Y. App. Div. 1983)**

Jacob Lehman and Shlomo Piontkowski were orthopedic surgeons who practiced together in a professional corporation that had originally been organized by Lehman. They were the only shareholders and the only directors of the corporation.

Each was an employee of the corporation. Piontkowski's employment contract granted to the board of directors of the corporation the power to terminate his employment for personal misconduct of such a material nature as to be professionally detrimental to the corporation. Piontkowski could terminate the contract on any grounds after 90 days' notice to the corporation. The employment contract also contained a restrictive covenant, which prevented Piontkowski from competing with the corporation within a 10-mile radius of the corporation's place of business for two years following the termination of his employment. The restrictive covenant provided that in the event of its breach Piontkowski would be liable for liquidated damages equal to half of the corporation's annual gross income.

From 1977 to 1979, Lehman and Piontkowski disagreed on the allocation of the corporation's income. Dissatisfied with Lehman's refusal to allocate him a greater share of the income, Piontkowski canceled scheduled elective surgery of his patients, informed his patients that he was on vacation, and asked another corporate employee to work for him in a new office that he planned to open. Piontkowski's new office was within 10 miles of the corporation's office. Piontkowski sent a letter to the corporation proposing that his employment be terminated immediately and that the restrictive covenant not be enforced.

Lehman, acting as president of the corporation, sent Piontkowski a letter rejecting this proposal. The letter stated that Piontkowski had violated his employment obligations by canceling surgery and scheduling a vacation without permission of the president and the board of directors. As president, Lehman stated that he deemed these actions to be personal misconduct so material as to be professionally detrimental to the corporation. With the letter, Lehman sent a notice calling a special shareholder meeting and a special directors' meeting.

At the shareholder meeting, Lehman proposed that Piontkowski be removed as a director and voted his six shares to oust Piontkowski. Piontkowski did not vote his four shares. Lehman then nominated himself as sole director, voted his shares to elect himself sole director, and moved to adjourn the shareholder meeting.

Lehman then called the special directors' meeting to order and, as the sole director, dismissed Piontkowski as an employee. He informed Piontkowski that his contract was terminated as of 7:30 that night.

Afterward, Lehman and the corporation sued Piontkowski, seeking to recover damages of $500,000 for Piontkowski's breach of the restrictive convenant and asking for an injunction preventing Piontkowski from competing with the corporation in violation of the restrictive covenant. The trial court denied both parties' motions for summary judgment, and both parties appealed.

**Memorandum by the Court.** The record reveals serious doubts whether Piontkowski's expulsion as director and the termination of his employment were proper and lawful. We hold that these proceedings were improper as a matter of law.

By letter, Piontkowski was informed that Lehman, as president, deemed Piontkowski's actions to be personal misconduct that was so material as to be professionally detrimental to the corporation. This opinion was not stated to be that of the board of directors, as was required by the employment contract, but rather was that of Lehman individually and as president of the corporation. The board had not formally met to make a determination that Piontkowski had committed detrimental misconduct as a material breach of the contract. Therefore, the letter was of no legal effect.

At the special shareholder meeting, Lehman's first order of business was to vote his majority of the shares to dismiss Piontkowski as a director. Although such an act was specified as a purpose of the meeting and is one that may ordinarily be undertaken (the corporation's by-laws specifically permit the removal of a director by the vote of a majority of the outstanding shares), it was of no effect in the present matter. The New York Business Corporation Law provides that "the number of directors constituting the entire board shall not be less than three, except that where all the shares of a corporation are owned . . . by less than three shareholders, the number of directors may be less than three but not less than the number of shareholders."

Here there is no question that there were two shareholders at the commencement of the special shareholder meeting. Piontkowski's expulsion as a director and the election of Lehman as the sole director were therefore improper as a matter of law. The removal of Piontkowski as a director left the corporation with only one director and, concomitantly, without a validly constituted board of directors. The New York statute prohibits such an occurrence. The subsequent act of an illegally constituted one-man board of directors in terminating Piontkowski's employment was invalid.

As the proceedings that effected Piontkowski's unilateral expulsion from the corporation were illegal and invalid, the corporation is not entitled to enforce the restrictive covenants in Piontkowski's employment contract.

Judgment reversed in favor of Piontkowski.

## CORPORATE GOVERNANCE PROPOSALS

**Traditional Corporate Governance Model.** The traditional *corporate governance* model depicts the shareholders as delegating management duties to a board of directors. As the owners of the corporation, the shareholders have the power and the right to elect the directors of the corporation at annual shareholder meetings. The board of directors is entrusted with the power and the right to manage the corporation. The board either manages the corporation or delegates its duties to officers and supervises them for the shareholders.

**Corporate Governance in Practice.** *In theory,* this management model exists today, except for some close corporations that may be managed by their owners much as if they were partnerships. *In practice,* however, most public-issue corporations do not operate according to this model. As you have already learned in this chapter, the board of directors performs few management functions and *shareholders seldom voice effectively their preference for directors.* Instead, the board delegates most management decisions to the chairman of the board and the officers, exercising little supervision over them. In addition, the directors and officers of publicly held corporations perpetuate themselves as managers by dominating director elections. This domination is accomplished by means of the proxy solicitation process in nearly all publicly held corporations.

**Improving Corporate Governance.** Proposals for improving corporate governance in public-issue corporations have been made by people of widely varying backgrounds and viewpoints. All of the proposals seek to develop a board that is capable of functioning *independently of the CEO* by changing the *composition* or the *operation* of the board of directors. A number of the proposals are discussed in the following paragraphs.

**Independent Directors.** Some corporate governance critics propose that a federal agency, such as the SEC, *appoint one or more directors.*[11] These *public directors* would spend as much as half of their time on their

[11] E.g., Christopher D. Stone, *Where the Law Ends* (New York: Harper & Row, 1975).

directorial duties and would serve as *watchdogs of the public interest.* Other critics would require that shareholders elect at least a majority of directors *without prior ties* to the corporation, thus excluding shareholders, suppliers, and customers from the board.[12]

Section 3.04 of the ALI Corporate Governance Project recommends that the board of every large publicly held corporation have a majority of directors free of any significant relationship with the corporation's high-level executives. The New York Stock Exchange requires a minimum of two directors independent of management for its listed companies. The purpose of these proposals is to create a board that can objectively analyze managerial performance.

**Exclude Insiders from the Board.** Harold Williams, a former SEC chairman, has been the most visible advocate of *excluding all corporate officers and other insiders* from the boards of directors of large publicly held corporations. Such exclusion, he argues, would increase confidence of the public and the shareholders that the board acts *independently of the CEO* and in the *long-term best interests* of the corporation. The major criticism of this proposal is that the excluded persons—officers—are best equipped to help outside directors make decisions. Excluding officers from the board may prevent knowledgeable and detailed board discussion about the business, and it may discourage management from taking important issues to a board that cannot understand them.

**Codetermination.** *Codetermination* requires the larger corporations to have one third (in some instances one half) of the board consist of *employee representatives.* Where codetermination is in effect, the corporation has two boards: a *supervisory board* on which the employee representatives sit with the shareholder representatives and a *managing board* composed solely of corporate officers. Codetermination developed in post–World War II Germany, and it has spread through several of the European Common Market countries.

Recently, several American corporations, of which Chrysler is the best known, have put one or more *labor union representatives* on their boards. These companies were in poor financial condition, and their unions granted major concessions to them. In return for those concessions, management agreed to place union representatives on its slate of director nominees.

**Director Nominations.** Two proposals recommend changing the method by which directors are nominated for election. One proposal would *encourage shareholders to make nominations* for directors.[13] Supporters of this proposal argue that in addition to reducing the influence of the CEO, it would also broaden the range of backgrounds represented on the board.

SEC personnel, the ALI Corporate Governance Project, and others recommend that publicly held corporations establish a *nominating committee composed of outside directors.* This committee would have responsibility for selecting the management nominees for directors. This proposal has broad support, and many publicly held corporations have already adopted it.[14]

**Board Staff.** In 1972, Arthur Goldberg, a former U.S. Supreme Court justice, resigned from the Trans World Airlines board, declar-

[12] E.g., Ralph Nader, Mark Green, and Joel Seligman, *Taming the Giant Corporation* (New York: W. W. Norton, 1976).

[13] *The Role and Composition of the Board of Directors of the Large Publicly Owned Corporation* (New York: Business Roundtable, 1978), p. 5.

[14] According to an SEC study, about 30 percent of all publicly held corporations and 38 percent of those listed on the New York Stock Exchange have nominating committees. *SEC Staff Report on Corporate Accountability,* p. 606.

ing that it was impossible for a board to exercise independence from the CEO unless it had a *small staff of its own.*[15] Section 3.09 of the ALI Corporate Governance Project recommends that nonmanagement directors be empowered to hire, at the corporation's expense, *lawyers, accountants, and other experts to advise them* on extraordinary problems arising in the exercise of their oversight function. Critics of these proposals say that a staff for the directors would needlessly duplicate existing personnel, promote undesirable competition between the directors' staff and the corporate staff, and create an adversary relationship between outside directors and the corporation's officers.

**Specialist Directors.** Ralph Nader and his associates propose that each board member be assigned to, if not especially chosen for, a *special area of oversight responsibility,* such as employee welfare, consumer protection, and environmental protection.[16] There has been a general consensus that assignment of specific responsibilities to board committees would make the board of directors function more effectively.

**Impact of Corporate Governance Proposals.** Mostly due to SEC and public pressures for changes in corporate governance, the boards of directors of the 1980s operate significantly differently from the boards of the 1960s and the early 1970s. Boards supervise officers more closely. More directors are outside rather than inside directors. Boards meet more frequently, and more important, they have working committees that assume specific responsibilities. In addition, today's directors perceive themselves as being more nearly independent of the CEO. As a consequence, they act more nearly independently of the CEO.

[15] Arthur J. Goldberg, "Debate on Outside Directors," *New York Times,* October 29, 1972, p. 12.

[16] Nader, Green, and Seligman, *Taming the Giant Corporation,* p. 125.

## OFFICERS OF THE CORPORATION

**Appointment of Officers.** The *board of directors* has the authority to *appoint the officers* of the corporation. Most of the corporation statutes provide that the officers of a corporation shall be the *president,* one or more *vice presidents,* a *secretary,* and a *treasurer.* Some of the statutes permit fewer than four officers, and most allow more than four. Usually, any two or more offices may be held by the same person, *except for the offices of president and secretary.* Since some corporate documents must be signed by both the president and the secretary, the prohibition against having one person hold both offices provides a measure of safety by ensuring that no single individual can execute such documents.

**MBCA Approach.** MBCA Section 8.40 grants the corporation great flexibility in determining the number of its officers. The section requires only that there be an officer performing the duties normally granted to a corporate secretary. Under the MBCA, one person may hold several offices, including the offices of president and secretary. If a corporation desires the protection of dual signatures as a safety measure, it must create positions for two officers whose signatures are required on corporate documents.

**Authority of Officers.** The officers are agents of the corporation. As agents, officers have *express authority* conferred on them by the bylaws or the board of directors. In addition, officers have *implied authority* to do the things that are reasonably necessary to accomplish their express duties. Also, officers have *apparent authority* when the corporation leads third parties to believe reasonably that the officers have authority to act for the corporation. Like any principal, the corporation may *ratify* the unauthorized acts of its officers. This may be done expressly by a resolution of the board of directors or impliedly by the board's acceptance of the benefits of the officer's acts.[17]

**Inherent Authority.** The most perplexing issue with regard to the authority of officers is whether an officer has *inherent authority* merely by virtue of the title of his office. Courts have held that certain *official titles confer authority* on officers, but such powers are much more restricted than you might expect.

Traditionally, a *president* possessed no power to bind the corporation by virtue of the office. Instead, she served merely as the presiding officer at shareholder meetings and directors' meetings. The modern trend, however, empowers the president to bind the corporation on *transactions in the ordinary course of the corporation's business.*

Few problems arise in assessing the authority of a president with an additional title such as *general manager* or *chief executive officer.* Titles of this kind give the officer broad implied authority to make contracts and to do other acts in the ordinary business of the corporation.

A *vice president* has no authority by virtue of that office. An executive who is vice president of a specified department, however, such as a vice president of sales, will have the authority to transact the normal corporate business falling within the function of the department.

The *secretary* usually keeps the minutes of directors' meetings and shareholder meetings, maintains other corporate records, retains custody of the corporate seal, and certifies corporate records as being authentic. The secretary has no authority to make contracts for the corporation by virtue of that office. Nevertheless, the corporation is bound by documents certified by the secretary. For example, a corporation is bound by a board resolution certified by the secretary stating the president's authority to contract for the corporation even if the resolution was not properly adopted by the board.

The *treasurer* has custody of the corporation's funds. He is the proper officer to receive payments to the corporation and to disburse corporate funds for authorized purposes. The treasurer binds the corporation by his receipts, checks, and indorsements, but he does not by virtue of that office alone have authority to borrow money, to issue negotiable instruments, or to make other contracts on behalf of the corporation.

**Officer Liability.** Like any agent, a corporate officer ordinarily has *no liability on contracts* that she makes on behalf of her principal, the corporation. To avoid personal liability on corporate contracts, an officer should make clear that she signs for the corporation and not in her individual capacity, as was discussed in Chapter 17.

However, an officer who acts within her apparent authority, but beyond her actual authority, will be liable to the corporation for resulting losses. To avoid liability for *exceeding her actual authority,* an officer may request that her authority for conducting out-of-the-ordinary transactions be stated in writing, for example, in a bylaw or a specific resolution of the board of directors.

**Employees of the Corporation.** Employees of the corporation who are not officers may also be empowered to act as agents for the corporation. The usual rules of agency apply to their relationships with the corporation and with third parties.

[17] Ratification is discussed in Chapter 17.

## MANAGING CLOSE CORPORATIONS

Many of the management formalities that you have studied in this chapter are appropriate for publicly held corporations, yet inappropriate for close corporations.[18] Close corporations tend to be *more loosely managed* than public corporations. For example, they may have few board meetings. Frequently, each shareholder wants to be *involved in management* of the close corporation, or if he is not involved in management, he wants to protect his interests by placing *restrictions on the managerial discretion* of those who do manage the corporation.

Initially, courts struggled with the management problems of close corporations, attempting to solve those problems by applying traditional corporation law, which was designed with the publicly held corporation in mind. In recent years, however, courts and legislatures have adopted rules that respond to the special management problems of close corporations. These rules are designed to *reduce management formalities* and to *prevent the domination of shareholders.*

**Fewer Management Formalities.** Modern close corporation statutes permit close corporations to dispense with most, if not all, management formalities. Section 10 of the Statutory Close Corporation Supplement to the MBCA permits the close corporation to *dispense with the board of directors* and to be *managed by the shareholders.* California General Corporation Law Section 300 permits the close corporation to be managed *as if it were a partnership.*

**Preventing Domination.** A shareholder of a close corporation may be dominated by the shareholders who control the board of directors. These shareholders may show domination by dismissing the dominated shareholder as an employee or by paying him a lower salary than is paid to the dominating shareholder-employees. To prevent such domination, close corporation shareholders have resorted to two devices: *restrictions on the managerial discretion* of the board of directors and *supermajority voting requirements* for board actions.

[18] The definition of a close corporation is in Chapter 22.

**Restrictions on Board Discretion.** Traditionally, shareholders could not restrict the managerial discretion of directors. This rule recognized the traditional role of the board as manager and of the shareholders as passive owners. By the mid-1930s, however, the courts had recognized some power of the shareholders of close corporations to restrict board discretion.

In 1936, the highest court in New York upheld a management agreement among all the shareholders who were also the sole directors on the ground that the invasion of the board's powers was so slight as to be negligible.[19] The court's characterization of the invasion of board power as negligible may be suspect, since the shareholder agreement obligated the board to hire a shareholder for life and to pay him one fourth of the corporation's profits. But the court apparently had some limits in mind, because a few years later the same court invalidated a unanimous shareholder agreement that granted one shareholder-manager full management power.[20]

Modern close corporation statutes eliminate the need for courts to decide whether shareholders have intruded impermissibly into the sanctity of the boardroom. In Section 11, the Statutory Close Corporation Supplement grants the shareholders *unlimited power to restrict the discretion* of the board

[19] *Clark v. Dodge,* 199 N.E. 641 (N.Y. Ct. App. 1936).

[20] *Long Park, Inc. v. Trenton–New Brunswick Theatres Co.,* 77 N.E.2d 633 (N.Y. Ct. App. 1948).

of directors. And, as was stated above, close corporation statutes even permit the shareholders to dispense with a board of directors altogether and to manage the close corporation as if it were a partnership.

**Supermajority Director Voting.** Any corporation may require that board action be possible only with the *approval of more than a majority* of the directors, such as three fourths or unanimous approval. *Supermajority voting* requirements are uncommon in publicly held corporations, but their ability to protect valuable interests of minority shareholders makes their use in close corporations almost mandatory. A supermajority vote is often required to *dismiss an employee-shareholder,* to *reduce the level of dividends,* and to *change the corporation's line of business.* Supermajority votes are rarely required for ordinary business matters, such as deciding with which suppliers the corporation should deal.

## DIRECTORS' AND OFFICERS' DUTIES TO THE CORPORATION

**Introduction.** Directors and officers are in positions of trust and therefore owe *fiduciary duties* to the corporation. These duties are similar to the duties that an agent owes his principal. They are as follows:

1. To act within the authority of the position and within the objectives and powers of the corporation.
2. To act with due care in conducting the affairs of the corporation.
3. To act with loyalty to the corporation.

**Acting within Authority.** Like any agent, an officer has a duty to act *within the authority* conferred on her by the articles of incorporation, the bylaws, and the board of directors. As discussed above in the section on corporate objectives, ordinarily the directors and officers must manage the corporation to enhance corporate profits. In addition, as discussed in the section on the *ultra vires* doctrine, the directors and officers must act within the scope of the powers of the corporation. An officer or a director may be liable to the corporation if it is damaged by an act exceeding that person's or the corporation's authority. For additional material on the liability of officers and directors for exceeding their authority, see the discussion of agents' liability for exceeding their authority in Chapter 16 and the discussion of directors' liability for *ultra vires* acts, which appears earlier in this chapter.

**Duty of Care.** Directors and officers are liable for losses to the corporation resulting from their lack of *care or diligence.* MBCA Sections 8.30 and 8.42 are typical of modern statutes, which expressly state the standard of care that must be exercised by directors and officers. These sections provide that a director or officer shall discharge his duties

(1) in good faith;
(2) with the care an ordinarily prudent person in a like position would exercise under similar circumstances; and
(3) when exercising his business judgment, with the belief, premised upon a rational basis, that his decision is in the best interests of the corporation.[21]

**Prudent Person Standard.** The duty of care does *not* hold directors and officers to the standard of a prudent businessperson, a person of some undefined level of business skill. Instead, managers need merely meet the standard of the ordinarily prudent *person* in the same circumstances, a standard focusing on the basic manager attributes of *common*

[21] The ALI Corporate Governance Project, in § 4.01, recommends a similar standard of care.

*sense, practical wisdom,* and *informed judgment.*

The special background, qualifications, or management responsibilities of a manager may increase the level of care required of that manager. For example, the chief financial officer with 30 years of experience is held to a higher level of care than is expected from an assistant financial officer who just graduated from MBA school. Nevertheless, a director or officer *lacking business expertise or experience* is *not excused* from exercising the common sense, practical wisdom, and informed judgment of an *ordinarily prudent person.* Therefore, an officer or director cannot escape liability merely by proving that he did his best.

The phrase "in a like position" recognizes that the care to be exercised is determined with reference to the particular corporation. The phrase "under similar circumstances" limits the evaluation of the director's or officer's performance to the time of the decision, thereby *preventing the application of hindsight* in judging her performance. The phrase does not require a director or officer to anticipate all the problems that the corporation may face unless some event makes it obvious that the corporation should address a particular problem.

**Good Faith and Rational Basis.** The *good faith* and the *rational basis* elements of the MBCA duty of care test combine to require that a director or officer, after making a *reasonable investigation,* honestly believe that her decision is in the best interests of the corporation. For example, the board of directors decides to purchase an existing manufacturing business for $1.5 million without inquiring into the value of the business or examining its past financial performance. Although the directors may believe that they made a prudent decision, they have no reasonable basis for that belief. Therefore, if the plant is worth only $500,000, the directors will be liable to the corporation for its damages, $1 million, for breaching the duty of care.

**Reliance on Others.** Since it is impossible for directors and officers to investigate every fact that may affect a business decision, they are permitted to *rely on other persons* who gather and present such material to them. MBCA Sections 8.30(b) and 8.42(b) state that a director or officer may rely on information, opinions, reports, and statements *prepared by officers, employees, and outside consultants.* A director may also rely on such data if it is provided by board committees of which he is not a member. The ALI Corporate Governance Project, in Sections 4.02 and 4.03, also permits directors and officers to rely on others.

A director or officer may rely on officers and employees whom she *reasonably believes* to be *competent and reliable.* She may rely on outside consultants as to matters that she reasonably believes fall within the *consultants' professional or expert competence.* For example, the board may rely on financial statements certified by independent auditors when deciding whether to sell an unprofitable line of business. It may not rely on the auditors' advice with regard to bringing a lawsuit against someone, since such matters fall within the expertise of lawyers, not auditors.

**Duties of Loyalty.** Directors and officers owe a duty of *utmost loyalty and fidelity* to the corporation. Judge Benjamin Cardozo stated this duty of trust in a much-quoted opinion. He declared that a director

> owes loyalty and allegiance to the corporation—a loyalty that is undivided and an allegiance that is influenced by no consideration other than the welfare of the corporation. Any adverse interest of a director will be subjected to a scrutiny rigid and uncompromising. He may not profit at the ex-

pense of his corporation and in conflict with its rights; he may not for personal gain divert unto himself the opportunities which in equity and fairness belong to his corporation.[22]

Directors and officers owe the corporation the same duties of loyalty that agents owe their principals, though many of these duties have special names in corporation law.[23] The most important of these duties of loyalty are the duties not to *self-deal,* not to *usurp a corporate opportunity,* not to *oppress minority shareholders,* and not to *trade on inside information.*

**Self-Dealing with the Corporation.** When a director or officer *self-deals* with his corporation, the director or officer may *prefer his own interests* over those of the corporation. The director's or officer's interest may be *direct,* such as his interest in selling his land to the corporation, or it may be *indirect,* such as his interest in having a business of which he is an owner, director, or officer supply goods to the corporation.

Originally, courts held that any transaction with a corporation in which a director or an officer was interested was voidable at the election of the corporation. This rule created some unfortunate results because some of the transactions in which a director or an officer was interested clearly benefited the corporation. More recently, therefore, the majority of courts have held that a self-dealing transaction is *voidable only if it is unfair* to the corporation.

**Intrinsic Fairness Standard.** Modern corporation statutes deal expressly with the self-dealing issue. Under MBCA Section 8.31, a self-dealing transaction is *not voidable* if the transaction is *fair* to the corporation. In addition, if the transaction is fair, the self-dealing (*interested*) director or officer is excused from liability to the corporation. A transaction is fair if reasonable persons in an *arm's-length bargain* would have bound the corporation to it. This standard is often called the *intrinsic fairness standard.*

**Approval of the Board or Shareholders.** Under the MBCA, the *burden of proving fairness* lies initially on the *interested director or officer.* The burden of proof *shifts* to the corporation that is suing the officer or director for self-dealing if the transaction was *approved by the board of directors or the shareholders.*

Under the MBCA, approval must be given by an *informed, disinterested board* or by *informed, disinterested shareholders.* The interested director or officer must *disclose* to the board or the shareholders the *material facts* of the transaction and also his *interest* in it. For board approval, a majority of the *disinterested* directors must approve the transaction. Such a majority is considered a quorum of the board, even if the number of disinterested directors is fewer than half the number of directors. For shareholder approval, a majority of the shares held by disinterested shareholders must be cast in favor of the transaction. Such a majority is a quorum of the shares.

**Effect of Board or Shareholder Approval.** Board or shareholder approval of a self-dealing transaction does not by itself relieve an interested director or officer of liability to the corporation. Such approval merely *shifts* to the corporation the *burden of proving the unfairness* of the transaction. The interested director or officer will be liable if the corporation can prove that the transaction was unfair to it.

**Effect of Unanimous Shareholder Approval.** Generally, *unanimous* approval of

[22] *Meinhard v. Salmon,* 164 N.E.2d 545, 546 (N.Y. Ct. App. 1928).

[23] An agent's duties of loyalty are covered in Chapter 16.

a self-dealing transaction by *informed* shareholders *conclusively* releases an interested director or officer from liability for self-dealing even if the transaction is unfair to the corporation. The rationale for this rule is that fully informed shareholders should know what is best for themselves and their corporation.

**Loans to Directors.** Early corporation law made illegal any *loans* by the corporation *to directors or officers* on the ground that such loans might result in the looting of corporate assets. Modern corporation statutes, for example, MBCA Section 8.32, allow loans to directors only after certain procedures have been followed. Either the *shareholders* must approve the loan, or the *directors, after finding that the loan benefits the corporation,* must approve it.

**Parent-Subsidiary Transactions.** Self-dealing is a concern when a parent corporation *dominates* a subsidiary corporation. Often, the subsidiary's directors will be directors or officers of the parent also. When persons with dual directorships approve transactions between the parent and the subsidiary, the opportunity for *overreaching* arises. There may be *no arm's-length bargaining* between the two corporations. Hence, such transactions must meet the intrinsic fairness test. *Sinclair v. Levien,* which follows, addresses self-dealing between a parent and its subsidiary.

**Usurpation of a Corporate Opportunity.** Directors and officers may steal not only assets of their corporations (such as computer hardware and software) but also *opportunities* that their corporations could have exploited. Both types of theft are equally wrongful. As fiduciaries, directors and officers are liable to their corporation for *usurping corporate opportunities.* Such usurpation has three elements: (1) the opportunity comes to the director or officer in *his corporate capacity;* (2) the opportunity is *related to the corporation's business;* and (3) the corporation is *able to take advantage of the opportunity.* If any of the elements is not met, the director or officer may take the opportunity *for himself.*

**Director's or Officer's Corporate Capacity.** The opportunity must come to the director or officer *in her corporate capacity.* Clearly, opportunities received at the corporate offices are received by the manager in her corporate capacity. In addition, courts hold that CEOs and other high-level officers are nearly always acting in their corporate capacities, even when they are away from their corporate offices.

**Relation to Corporate Business.** The opportunity must have a *relation or connection* to an *existing or prospective* corporate activity. Some courts apply the *line of business test,* considering how closely related the opportunity is to the lines of business in which the corporation is engaged. Other courts use the *interest or expectancy test,* requiring the opportunity to relate to property in which the corporation has an existing interest or in which it has an expectancy growing out of an existing right. In *Guth v. Loft,* which follows, the court used both tests to find that an opportunity to become the manufacturer of Pepsi-Cola syrup was usurped by the president of a corporation that was in the beverage syrup manufacturing, retail candy, and soda fountain businesses.

**Corporation Able to Take Advantage of Opportunity.** The corporation must be able *financially* to take advantage of the opportunity. Managers are required to make a good faith effort to obtain *external financing* for the corporation, but they are *not required to* *use their personal funds* to enable the corporation to take advantage of the opportunity.

**Effect of Rejection by Corporation.** A director or officer is free to exploit an opportunity that has been *rejected* by the corporation. Generally, an *informed, disinterested* majority of the *directors* may reject an opportunity unless rejection by the board is manifestly unreasonable. *Informed, disinterested shareholders* may also reject an opportunity.

**Oppression of Minority Shareholders.** Directors and officers owe a duty to manage the corporation in the *best interests of the corporation and the shareholders as a whole.* Consequently, when the management of a corporation takes an action that benefits the corporation and the shareholders as a whole, an individual shareholder will not usually be permitted to complain that the action harmed him. If, however, a group of shareholders has been isolated for beneficial treatment to the detriment of another isolated group of shareholders, the disadvantaged group may complain of *oppression.*

Most of the suits claiming oppression of minority shareholders involve close corporations. The oppression may occur when directors representing the majority shareholders fail to pay dividends and refuse to hire minority shareholders as employees of the corporation. Since there is no market for the shares of a close corporation (apart from selling to the other shareholders), these oppressed minority shareholders have investments that provide them no return. They receive no dividends or salaries, and they can sell their shares only to the other shareholders, who are usually unwilling to pay the true value of the shares. Such oppression is usually not actionable, because courts hold that a situation of this kind is a normal expectation of minority ownership in a close corporation.

Other conduct, however, has been held wrongful. For example, in *Donahue v. Rodd Electrotype Co.,*[24] the directors caused the corporation to buy back shares of the majority shareholder's father at a favorable price. The offer was not available to minority shareholders. The court held that the same offer should have been made to all minority shareholders. In *Zahn v. Transamerica Corp.,*[25] the board of directors failed to disclose to preferred shareholders information that would have revealed that these shareholders should have converted their shares to common shares rather than allowing the corporation to redeem the shares. The court held that the board violated a duty to treat each class of shareholders fairly and not to prefer one class of shareholders over another.

**Freeze-Outs.** Since the late 1960s, a special form of oppression, the *freeze-out,* has proliferated. A freeze-out is usually accomplished by merging the corporation with a newly formed corporation under terms by which the minority shareholders do not receive shares of the new corporation, but instead receive only cash or other securities. The minority shareholders are thereby *frozen out as shareholders.*

**Going Private.** *Going private* is a special term for a freeze-out of shareholders of *publicly owned corporations.* Some public corporations discover that the burdens of public ownership, such as the periodic disclosure requirements of the SEC, exceed the benefits of being public. Many of these publicly owned companies choose to freeze out their minority shareholders to avoid such burdens. Often, going private transactions appear abusive because the corporation goes public at a high price and goes private at a much lower price.

[24] 328 N.E.2d 505 (Mass. Sup. Jud. Ct. 1975).

[25] 162 F.2d 36 (3d Cir. 1947).

**Business Purpose Test.** In 1977, the Supreme Court of Delaware, in *Singer v. Magnavox*,[26] adopted a *business purpose* test for freeze-outs. The court held that the use of corporate power *solely* to eliminate the minority shareholders violated the directors' fiduciary duty to the minority shareholders. Later in 1977, the same court, in *Tanzer v. Int'l Gen. Indus., Inc.*,[27] held that *facilitating the long-term debt financing* of the corporation was a proper business purpose justifying a freeze-out of minority shareholders.

**Intrinsic Fairness Test.** In 1983, however, Delaware abandoned the business purpose test as unworkable. In *Weinberger v. UOP*,[28] the supreme court of Delaware held that a freeze-out between a parent corporation and a subsidiary that was dominated by the parent had to meet the intrinsic fairness test applied to self-dealing transactions. The court held that in the freeze-out context, fairness had two basic aspects: *fair dealing* and *fair price*. Fair dealing requires the board of directors to obtain any required approval of the minority shareholders only after *disclosing all of the information* material to their decision regarding whether to approve the transaction. A determination of fair value requires the consideration of all *the factors relevant to the value* of the shares, except speculative projections.

**SEC Rules.** In 1979, the SEC promulgated Rules 13e–3 and 13e–4 under the Securities Exchange Act of 1934, requiring a *publicly held* company to make a statement on the fairness of its proposed going private transaction and to disclose the material facts on which the statement is based. SEC attempts to require going private transactions to meet standards of fairness were abandoned on the ground that such attempts were beyond the powers of the SEC.

**Trading on Inside Information.** Officers and directors have *confidential access* to nonpublic information about the corporation. Often, disclosure of nonpublic, *inside information* affects the value of the corporation's securities. Sometimes, directors and officers purchase their corporation's securities with knowledge of inside information. They may make a profit when the prices of the securities increase after the inside information has been disclosed publicly.

**Early Court Decisions.** In the early insider trading cases, courts concluded that directors and officers owed a fiduciary duty to the corporation, but not to existing or potential shareholders. Therefore, the directors and officers were entitled to make a profit from their knowledge of nonpublic, inside information by buying and selling the corporation's securities without disclosing that information to the other party to the transaction. As a result, the directors and officers were accountable for their trading profits neither to the corporation, which suffered no loss, nor to the individuals from whom they bought or to whom they sold securities, to whom they owed no duty of disclosure.

**Current Judicial Trend.** In this century, however, there has been a judicial trend toward finding a duty of directors and officers, and even employees and controlling shareholders, to *disclose* information that they have received confidentially from inside the corporation *before they buy or sell* the corporation's securities. As will be discussed in Chapter 26, the illegality of insider trading is already the law under the Securities Exchange Act; however, it remains only a minority rule under state corporation law.

[26] 380 A.2d 969 (Del. Sup. Ct. 1977).

[27] 379 A.2d 1121 (Del. Sup. Ct. 1977).

[28] 457 A.2d 701 (Del. Sup. Ct. 1983).

**Federal Securities Law.** The federal securities laws have imposed new duties on directors and officers. These laws and their effect on the duties of directors, officers, and others who are considered insiders are discussed in Chapter 26.

**Director Right to Dissent.** A director who *assents* to an action of the board of directors may be held liable for the board's exceeding its authority or its failing to meet its duty of due care or loyalty. A director who *attends a board meeting* is deemed to have assented to any action taken at the meeting, *unless he dissents.*

**How to Dissent.** Under MBCA Section 8.24(d), to register his dissent to a board action, and thereby to protect himself from liability, the director must *not vote in favor* of the action *and* must *make his position clear* to the other board members. His position is made clear either by requesting that his *dissent appear in the minutes* or by giving *written notice of his dissent* to the chairman of the board *at the meeting* or to the secretary *immediately after the meeting.* These procedures ensure that the dissenting director will attempt to *dissuade* the board from approving an imprudent action.

**Failure to Attend Board Meetings.** Generally, directors are not liable for failing to attend meetings. A few courts, however, have held a director liable for *continually failing* to attend meetings, with the result that the director was unable to prevent the board from harming the corporation by its self-dealing.

## Guth v. Loft, Inc.

**5 A.2d 503 (Del. Sup. Ct. 1939)**

Loft, Inc. manufactured and sold candies, syrups, and beverages and operated 115 retail candy and soda fountain stores. Loft sold Coca-Cola at all of its stores, but it did not manufacture Coca-Cola syrup. Instead, it purchased its 30,000-gallon annual requirement of syrup and mixed it with carbonated water at its various soda fountains.

In May 1931, Charles Guth, the president and general manager of Loft, became dissatisfied with the price of Coca-Cola syrup and suggested to Loft's vice president that Loft buy Pepsi-Cola syrup from National Pepsi-Cola Company, the owner of the secret formula and trademark for Pepsi-Cola. The vice president responded that he was investigating the purchase of Pepsi syrup.

Before being employed by Loft, Guth had been asked by the controlling shareholder of National Pepsi, Megargel, to acquire the assets of National Pepsi. Guth refused at that time. However, a few months after Guth had suggested that Loft purchase Pepsi syrup, Megargel again contacted Guth about buying National Pepsi's secret formula and trademark for only $10,000. This time, Guth agreed to the purchase, and Guth and Megargel organized a new corporation, Pepsi-Cola Company, to acquire the Pepsi-Cola secret formula and trademark from National Pepsi. Eventually, Guth and his family's corporation owned a majority of the shares of Pepsi-Cola Company.

Very little of Megargel's or Guth's funds were used to develop the business of Pepsi-Cola. Instead, from 1931 to 1935, without the knowledge or consent of the Loft board of directors, Guth used Loft's working capital, its credit, its plant and equipment, and its executives and employees to produce Pepsi-Cola syrup. In addition, Guth's domination of Loft's board of directors ensured that Loft would become Pepsi-Cola's chief customer.

By 1935, the value of Pepsi-Cola's business was several million dollars. Loft sued Guth asking for the court to order Guth to transfer to Loft his shares of Pepsi-Cola Company and to pay Loft the dividends he had received from Pepsi-Cola Company. The trial court found that Guth had usurped a corporate opportunity and ordered Guth to transfer the shares and to pay Loft the dividends. Guth appealed.

**Layton, Chief Justice.** Corporate officers and directors are not permitted to use their position of trust and confidence to further their private interests. While technically not trustees, they stand in a fiduciary relation to the corporation and its stockholders. A public policy, existing through the years, and derived from a profound knowledge of human characteristics and motives, has established a rule that demands of a corporate officer or director the most scrupulous observance of his duty, not only affirmatively to protect the interests of the corporation committed to his charge, but also to refrain from doing anything that would work injury to the corporation, or to deprive it of profit or advantage which his skill and ability might properly bring to it, or to enable it to make in the reasonable and lawful exercise of its powers. The rule that requires an undivided and unselfish loyalty to the corporation demands that there shall be no conflict between duty and self-interest.

If an officer or director of a corporation, in violation of his duty, acquires gain or advantage for himself, the law denies to the betrayer all benefit and profit. The rule does not rest upon the narrow ground of injury to the corporation resulting from a betrayal of confidence, but upon a broader foundation of a wise public policy that, for the purpose of removing all temptation, extinguishes all possibility of profit flowing from a breach of the confidence imposed by the fiduciary relation.

The rule, referred to briefly as the rule of corporate opportunity, is merely one of the manifestations of the general rule that demands of an officer or director the utmost good faith in his relation to the corporation which he represents.

It is true that when a business opportunity comes to a corporate officer or director in his individual capacity rather than his official capacity, and the opportunity is one which, because of the nature of the enterprise, is not essential to his corporation, and is one in which it has no interest or expectancy, the officer or director is entitled to treat the opportunity as his own. The corporation has no interest in it, if the officer or director has not wrongfully embarked the corporation's resources therein.

On the other hand, it is equally true that, if there is presented to a corporate officer or director a business opportunity which the corporation is financially able to undertake, is in the line of the corporation's business and is of practical advantage to it, is one in which the corporation has an interest or a reasonable expectancy, and by embracing the opportunity, the self-interest of the officer or director will be brought into conflict with that of his corporation, the law will not permit him to seize the opportunity for himself. And if in such circumstances the interests of the corporation are betrayed, the corporation may elect to claim all of the benefits of the transaction for itself.

The real issue is whether the opportunity to secure a very substantial stock interest in a corporation to be formed for the purpose of exploiting a cola beverage on a wholesale scale was so closely associated with the existing business activities of Loft, and so essential thereto, as to bring the transaction within that class of cases where the acquisition of the property would throw the corporate officer purchasing it into competition with his company.

Guth suggests a doubt whether Loft would have been able to finance the project along the lines contemplated by Megargel, viewing the situation as of 1931. The answer to this suggestion is two-fold. The trial court found that Loft's net asset position at that time was amply sufficient to finance the enterprise, and that its plant, equipment, executives, personnel and facilities, supplemented by such expansion for the necessary development of the business as it was well able to provide, were in all respects adequate. The second answer is that Loft's resources were found to be sufficient, for Guth made use of no other resources to any important extent.

Guth asserts that, no matter how diversified the scope of Loft's activities, its primary business was the manufacturing and selling of candy in its own chain of retail stores, and that it never had the idea of turning a subsidiary product into a highly advertised, nation-wide specialty. It is contended that the Pepsi-Cola opportunity was not in the line of Loft's activities, which essentially were of a retail nature. It is pointed out that, in 1931, Loft's manufacturing operations were centered in its New York factory and that it was a definitely localized business, not operated on a national scale. The Megargel proposition envisaged annual sales of syrup of at least a million gallons, which could be accomplished only by a wholesale distribution.

Loft, however, had many wholesale activities. Its wholesale business in 1931 amounted to over $800,000. It was a large company by any standard, with assets exceeding $9 million, excluding goodwill. It had an enormous plant. It paid enormous rentals. Guth, himself, said that Loft's success depended upon the fullest utilization of its large plant facilities. Moreover, it was a manufacturer of syrups and, with the exception of cola syrup, it supplied its own extensive needs. Guth, president of Loft, was an able and experienced man in that field. Loft, then, through its own personnel, possessed the technical knowledge, the practical business experience, and the resources necessary for the development of the Pepsi-Cola enterprise.

Guth says that the expression, "in the line" of a business, is a phrase so elastic as to furnish no basis for a useful inference. The phrase is not within the field of precise definition, nor is it one that can be bounded by a set formula. It has a flexible meaning, which is to be applied reasonably and sensibly to the facts and circumstances of the particular case. Where a corporation is engaged in a certain business, and an opportunity is presented to it embracing an activity as to which it has fundamental knowledge, practical experience and ability to pursue, which, logically and naturally, is adaptable to its business having regard for its financial position, and is one that is consonant with its reasonable needs and aspirations for expansion, it may be properly said that the opportunity is in the line of the corporation's business.

The manufacture of syrup was the core of the Pepsi-Cola opportunity. The manufacture of syrups was one of Loft's not unimportant activities. It had the necessary resources, facilities, equipment, technical and practical knowledge and experience. The tie was close between the business of Loft and the Pepsi-Cola enterprise. Conceding that the essential of an opportunity is reasonably within the scope of a corporation's activities, latitude should be allowed for development and expansion. To deny this would be to deny the history of industrial development.

It is urged that Loft had no interest or expectancy in the Pepsi-Cola opportunity. That it had no existing property right therein is manifest; but we cannot agree that it had no concern or expectancy in the opportunity within the protection of remedial equity. Loft had a practical and essential concern with respect to some cola syrup with an established formula and trademark. A cola beverage has come to be a business necessity for soft drink establishments; and it was essential to the success of Loft to serve at its soda fountains an acceptable five-cent cola drink in order to attract into its stores the great multitude of people who have formed the habit of drinking cola beverages.

When Guth determined to discontinue the sale of Coca-Cola in the Loft stores, it became, by his own act, a matter of urgent necessity for Loft to acquire a constant supply of some satisfactory cola syrup, secure against probable attack, as a replacement; and when the Pepsi-Cola opportunity presented itself, Guth having already considered the availability of the syrup, it became impressed with a Loft interest and expectancy arising out of the circumstances and the urgent and practical need created by him as the directing head of Loft.

Guth's appropriation of the Pepsi-Cola opportunity to himself placed hirn in a competitive position with Loft with respect to a commodity essential to it, thereby rendering his personal interests incompatible with the superior interests of his corporation; and this situation was accomplished, not openly and with his own resources, but secretly and with the money and facilities of the corporation which was committed to his protection.

The fiduciary relation demands something more than the morals of the marketplace. Guth did not offer the Pepsi-Cola opportunity to Loft, but captured it for himself. He invested little or no money of his own in the venture, but commandeered for his own benefit and advantage the money, resources, and facilities of his corporation and the services of his officials. He thrust upon Loft the hazard, while he reaped the benefit. His time was paid for by Loft. In such a manner he acquired for himself 91 percent of the capital stock of Pepsi-Cola, now worth many millions. A genius in his line he may be, but the law makes no distinction between the wrongdoing genius and the one less endowed. Guth had no right to appropriate the opportunity to acquire the Pepsi-Cola trademark and formula to himself.

Judgment for Loft affirmed.

## Sinclair Oil Corp. v. Levien

**280 A.2d 717 (Del. Sup. Ct. 1971)**

Sinclair Oil Corporation (Sinclair) was in the business of exploring for oil and producing and marketing crude oil and oil products. It owned about 97 percent of the shares of Sinclair Venezuelan Oil Company (Sinven), a subsidiary organized by Sinclair to operate in Venezuela. Sinclair nominated all the members of Sinven's board of directors. Almost without exception, Sinven's directors were officers, directors, or employees of corporations owned by Sinclair.

From 1960 through 1966, Sinclair caused Sinven to pay out \$108 million in dividends, \$38 million in excess of Sinven's earnings during the same period. Sinclair received 97 percent of these dividends. Although the dividends paid exceeded earnings, the payments were made in compliance with the Delaware General Corporation Law, which authorized the payment of dividends to the extent of surplus.

In 1961, Sinclair created Sinclair International Oil Company (International), a wholly owned subsidiary used for the purpose of coordinating all of Sinclair's foreign operations. Sinclair caused Sinven to make a contract with International that obligated Sinven to sell all of its crude oil and refined oil products to International. Sinclair caused International to breach this contract by allowing it to delay payments and to fail to comply with minimum purchase requirements under the contract.

Francis Levien, a shareholder of Sinven, sued Sinclair on behalf of Sinven, alleging that Sinclair caused Sinven to pay out such excessive dividends that the industrial development of Sinven was effectively prevented. Levien attacked the dividends on the ground that they resulted from an improper motive—Sinclair's need for cash. The trial court held that Sinclair caused these dividends to be paid during a period when it needed large amounts of cash. Applying the intrinsic fairness standard, the trial court held that Sinclair did not sustain its burden of proving that these dividends were intrinsically fair to the minority stockholders of Sinven.

Levien also contended that Sinclair harmed Sinven by not causing Sinven to sue International to enforce their contract. The trial court held that Sinclair had failed to prove that its decision not to enforce the contract was intrinsically fair. The trial court entered judgment for Levien as a representative of Sinven, and Sinclair appealed.

**Wolcott, Chief Judge.** By reason of Sinclair's domination, it is clear that Sinclair owed Sinven a fiduciary duty. The trial court held that because of Sinclair's fiduciary duty and its control over Sinven, its relationship with Sinven must meet the test of intrinsic fairness. The standard of intrinsic fairness involves both a high degree of fairness and a shift in the burden of proof. Under this standard the burden is on Sinclair to prove, subject to careful judicial scrutiny, that its transactions with Sinven were objectively fair.

A parent does indeed owe a fiduciary duty to its subsidiary when there are parent-subsidiary dealings. However, this alone will not evoke the intrinsic fairness standard. This standard will be applied only when the fiduciary duty is accompanied by self-dealing—the situation when a parent is on both sides of a transaction with its subsidiary. Self-dealing occurs when the parent, by virtue of its domination of the subsidiary, causes the subsidiary to act in such a way that the parent receives something from the subsidiary to the exclusion of, and detriment to, the minority stockholders of the subsidiary.

Consequently it must be determined whether the dividend payments by Sinven were, in essence, self-dealing by Sinclair. The dividends resulted in great sums of money being transferred from Sinven to Sinclair. However, a proportionate share of this money was received by the minority shareholders of Sinven. Sinclair received nothing from Sinven to the exclusion of its minority stockholders. As such, these dividends were not self-dealing. We hold therefore that the trial court erred in applying the intrinsic fairness test as to these dividend payments.

Next, Sinclair argues that the trial judge committed error when he held it liable to Sinven for breach of contract. Clearly, Sinclair's act of contracting with its dominated subsidiary was self-dealing. Under the contract Sinclair received the products produced by Sinven, and of course the minority shareholders of Sinven were not able to share in the receipt of these products. If the contract was breached, then Sinclair received these products to the detriment of Sinven's minority shareholders. We agree with the trial court's finding that the contract was breached by Sinclair, both as to the time of payments and the amounts purchased.

As Sinclair has received the benefits of this contract, so must it comply with the contractual duties. Under the intrinsic fairness standard, Sinclair must prove that its causing Sinven not to enforce the contract was intrinsically fair to the minority shareholders of Sinven. Sinclair has failed to meet this burden. Late payments were clearly breaches for which Sinven should have sought and received adequate damages. As to the quantities purchased, Sinclair argues that it purchased all the products produced by Sinven. This, however, does not satisfy the standard of intrinsic fairness. Sinclair has failed to prove that Sinven could not possibly have produced or in some way have obtained the contract minimums.

Judgment reversed in part in favor of Levien and affirmed in part in favor of Sinclair.

## THE BUSINESS JUDGMENT RULE

Absent bad faith, fraud, or breach of fiduciary duty, the judgment of the board of directors is conclusive. This is the *business judgment rule.* This rule means that when directors and officers have complied with their duty of care and their fiduciary duties, they are protected from liability to the corporation for their unwise decisions. In addition, the *courts are precluded from substituting their business judgment* for that of the corporation's managers. The business judgment rule recognizes that the directors and officers—not the shareholders and the courts—are best able to make business judgments and should not ordinarily be vulnerable to second-guessing. Shareholders and the courts are ill-equipped to make better business decisions than those made by the officers and directors of a corporation, who have more business experience and are more familiar with the needs, strengths, and limitations of the corporation.

**Elements of the Business Judgment Rule.** The comments to MBCA Section 8.30 list three requirements for the business judgment rule to apply to a management decision:[29] (1) an *informed decision,* (2) *no conflicts of interest,* and (3) a *rational basis.*

**Informed Decision.** Managers must make an *informed decision.* They must take the steps necessary to become informed about the relevant facts before making a decision. These steps may include merely listening to a proposal, reviewing written materials, or making inquiries. As stated earlier in this chapter, managers may rely on information collected and presented by other persons.

**No Conflicts of Interest.** Managers must be *free from conflicts of interest.* There must be *no self-dealing.* In *Sinclair Oil Corp. v. Levien,* the court refused to apply the business judgment rule to the breach of contract decision, because it found that there had been self-dealing. However, the court found no self-dealing in the dividend payment decision and applied the business judgment rule to it.

**Rational Basis.** Managers must have a *rational basis* for believing that the decision is in the best interests of the corporation. This is the most difficult element to understand, for it seemingly contradicts the most fundamental aspect of the business judgment rule, namely, that the courts may not judge the correctness, wisdom, or reasonableness of the managers' decision.

The comments to MBCA Section 8.30 and to Section 4.01(d) of the ALI Corporate Governance Project provide little guidance in understanding this contradiction. Nevertheless, based on courts' statements of the business judgment rule, it appears that the rational basis element requires that the managers' decision *not be manifestly unreasonable.* Some courts have held that the directors' wrongdoing must amount to *gross negligence* for the business judgment rule not to apply. In es-

[29] The ALI Corporate Governance Project, in § 4.01(d), has a nearly identical definition of the business judgment rule.

sence, this element allows the courts to make a low-level review of the reasonableness of the managers' decision in order to determine whether the business judgment rule should protect that decision.

**Purpose of Business Judgment Rule.** The business judgment rule is designed to *encourage persons to become corporate managers* and to encourage them to *make difficult business decisions.* Boards of directors and officers continually make decisions involving the balancing of risks and benefits to the corporation. With the advantage of hindsight, some of these decisions may appear unwise. Such a result, however, should not, and does not, by itself provide the basis for imposing personal liability on directors and officers.

**If Business Judgment Rule Is Inapplicable.** If the business judgment rule *does not apply* because one or more of its elements are missing, a court may *substitute its judgment* for that of the managers. If the court finds that the managers made an unwise decision that harmed the corporation, it may impose liability on the managers and order them to pay damages to the corporation. In addition, the court may award equitable relief, such as an injunction or rescission of the wrongful action.

Nevertheless, courts rarely refuse to apply the business judgment rule. As a result, the rule has been criticized frequently as providing too much protection for the managers of corporations. In *Shlensky v. Wrigley,* which follows, the court applied the business judgment rule to protect a decision made by the board of directors of the Chicago Cubs not to install lights and not to hold night baseball games at Wrigley Field.

**Smith v. Van Gorkom.** An important recent case, *Smith v. Van Gorkom,*[30] limited the scope of application of the business judgment rule. In that case, the Supreme Court of Delaware found that the business judgment rule did not apply to the board's approval of a merger. The board approved the merger after only two hours' consideration, even though there was no need to decide so quickly. The board relied solely on the market price of the shares and on an *oral* report of the chairman of the board. The directors were given no information concerning the intrinsic value of the corporation. The directors failed to obtain an investment banker's report, prepared after careful consideration, that the merger price was fair. In addition, they received no written summary of the merger terms. The court held that the board could not rely blindly on the report of the chairman. It found that the directors, at a minimum, had been grossly negligent.

A surprise decision, *Smith v. Van Gorkom* has been heralded as restricting the application of the business judgment rule and imposing higher standards on directors. Some commentators have attacked the case as wrongly decided.[31]

**Opposition to Acquisition of Control of the Corporation.** In the last 20 years, many outsiders have attempted to acquire control of publicly held corporations. Typically, these outsiders will make a tender offer for the shares of a corporation. A tender offer is an offer to the shareholders to buy their shares at a price above the current market price. The tender offeror hopes to acquire a majority of the shares, which will give him control of the corporation.[32]

**Defense Tactics.** Most tender offers are opposed by the corporation's management.

[30] 488 A.2d 858 (Del. Sup. Ct. 1985).

[31] Herzel, Davis, & Colling, "'Smith' Brings Down Whip on Directors' Backs," *Legal Times,* May 13, 1985, p. 14.

[32] Tender offer regulation is covered in the securities regulation chapter, Chapter 26.

The defenses to tender offers are many and varied, and they carry interesting names, such as the "Pac-Man defense" and the "white knight."[33] Defense tactics are successful about three fourths of the time.

**Suits against Directors.** Frequently, shareholders sue directors who oppose an outsider's tender offer. Shareholders contend that directors oppose the tender offer only to preserve their corporate positions. Shareholders also argue that the corporation's interests are better served if the tender offer succeeds.

**Application of Business Judgment Rule.** The business judgment rule applies to a board's decision to oppose a tender offer, provided that the elements of the rule are met: informed decision, no conflicts of interest, and rational basis. Courts have held that directors are able to *separate their interest in remaining directors* from the *best interests of the corporation.* Therefore, no conflict of interest automatically arises when directors oppose a tender offer.

Generally, courts have refused to find directors liable for opposing a tender offer. Nevertheless, the business judgment rule will not apply if the directors make a decision to oppose the tender offer before they have carefully studied it. The directors may be held liable for damages suffered by the corporation. In addition, if the directors' actions indicate that they are opposing the tender offer in order to preserve their jobs, they will be liable to the corporation.

A May 1985 decision of the Delaware Supreme Court, *Unocal Corp. v. Mesa Petroleum Co.,*[34] upheld the application of the business judgment rule to a board's decision to block a hostile tender offer. The court held that the board does not have "unbridled discretion to defeat any perceived threat by any Draconian means available," but may use those defense tactics that are reasonable compared to the takeover threat. The board may consider a variety of concerns, including the "inadequacy of the price offered, nature and timing of the offer, questions of illegality, the impact on 'constituencies' other than shareholders (i.e., creditors, customers, employees, and perhaps even the community generally), the risk of nonconsummation, and the quality of securities being offered in the exchange."[35]

**Shareholder Derivative Suits.** A special application of the business judgment rule is made in the context of directors terminating a derivative suit by a shareholder of a corporation. Such a use of the business judgment rule is discussed in the shareholders' rights portion of Chapter 25.

---

[33] With the Pac-Man defense, the corporation turns the tables on the tender offeror (which is usually another publicly held corporation) by making a tender offer for the tender offeror's shares. As a result, two tender offerors are trying to buy each other's shares. This is similar to the Pac-Man video game, in which Pac-Man and his enemies chase each other.

The white knight is a tender offeror whom management prefers over the original tender offeror—called a black knight. The white knight rescues the corporation from the black knight by offering more money for the corporation's shares.

[34] 493 A.2d 946 (Del. Sup. Ct. 1985).

[35] *Id.* at 955.

## Shlensky v. Wrigley

### 237 N.E.2d 776 (Ill. Ct. App. 1968)

The Chicago National League Ball Club, Inc., a Delaware corporation with its principal place of business in Chicago, owned and operated the Chicago Cubs major league baseball team. It also operated Wrigley Field, the Cubs' home park. Through the 1965 baseball season, the Cubs were the only major league baseball team that played no home games at night, because Wrigley Field had no lights for nighttime baseball.

Eighty percent of the shares of the corporation were owned by Philip K. Wrigley, who was also the president and a director of the corporation. Wrigley refused to install lights because of his personal opinion that baseball was a daytime sport and that installing lights and scheduling night baseball games would result in the deterioration of the surrounding neighborhood. The other directors assented to the policy laid down by Wrigley in matters involving the installation of lights and the scheduling of night games.

In the years 1961–65, the Cubs had operating losses from their baseball operations. Except for the year 1963, attendance at the Cubs' home games was substantially below that at their road games, many of which were played at night. Comparing attendance at the Cubs' games with that at the games played by the Chicago White Sox, whose weekday games were generally played at night, the weekend attendance figures for the two teams were similar, but the weeknight games of the White Sox drew many more fans than did the Cubs' weekday games.

William Shlensky, a minority shareholder of the corporation, sued Wrigley and the other directors on behalf of the corporation. He asked the court to force the board of directors to install lights at Wrigley Field and to schedule night games. He requested damages for lost profits. He alleged that the profitability of the corporation was harmed by the board's refusal to install lights at Wrigley Field. Shlensky charged that the directors acted for reasons contrary and wholly unrelated to the business interests of the corporation and that the directors were negligent in failing to exercise reasonable care and prudence in the management of the corporation's affairs. The trial court dismissed Shlensky's complaint and entered a judgment for Wrigley and the other directors. Shlensky appealed.

**SULLIVAN, JUSTICE.** It is Shlensky's position that fraud, illegality, and conflict of interest are not the only bases for a stockholder's action against the directors. Contrariwise, the directors argue that the courts will not step in and interfere with an honest business judgment of the directors unless there is a showing of fraud, illegality, or conflict of interest.

It is fundamental in the law of corporations that the majority of a corporation's stockholders shall control the policy of the corporation and shall regulate and govern the lawful exercise of its business. Everyone purchasing or subscribing for shares in a corporation impliedly agrees that he will be bound by the acts and proceedings done or sanctioned by a majority of the shareholders, or by the agents of the corporation duly chosen by such majority, within the scope of the powers conferred by the articles of incorporation. Courts will not undertake to control the policy or business methods of a corporation, although it may be seen that a wiser policy might be adopted and the business more successful if other methods were pursued.

It is not the function of courts to resolve for corporations questions of policy and business management. The directors are chosen to pass upon such questions. Their judgment, unless shown to be tainted with fraud, is accepted as final. The judgment of the directors of corporations enjoys the benefit of a presumption that it was formed in good faith and was designed to promote the best interests of the corporation they serve.

Shlensky argues that the directors are acting for reasons unrelated to the financial interest and welfare of the Cubs. However, we are not satisfied that the motives assigned to Philip K. Wrigley, and through him to the other directors, are contrary to the best interests of the corporation and the stockholders. For example, it appears to us that the effect on the surrounding neighborhood might well be considered by a director who was considering the patrons who would or would not attend the games if the park were in a poor neighborhood. Furthermore, the long run interest of the corporation in its property value at Wrigley Field might demand all efforts to keep the neighborhood from deteriorating.

By these thoughts we do not mean to say that we have decided that the decision of the directors was a correct one. That is beyond our jurisdiction and ability. We are merely saying that the decision is one properly before directors and the motives alleged in the amended complaint show no fraud, illegality, or conflict of interest in their making of that decision.

Finally, we do not agree with Shlensky's contention that a failure to follow the example of the other major league clubs in scheduling night games constituted negligence. Shlensky made no allegation that these teams' night schedules were profitable or that the purpose for which night baseball had been undertaken was fulfilled. Furthermore, it cannot be said that directors, even those of corporations that are losing money, must follow the lead of the other corporations in the field. Directors are elected for their business capabilities and judgment, and the courts cannot require them to forego their judgment because of the decisions of directors of other companies. Courts may not decide these questions in the absence of a clear showing of dereliction of duty on the part of the specific directors, and mere failure to "follow the crowd" is not such a dereliction.

Judgment for Wrigley affirmed.

## LIABILITY FOR TORTS AND CRIMES

**Liability of the Corporation.** Directors, officers, and other employees of the corporation may commit torts and crimes while conducting corporate affairs. For many years, courts struggled to find a theory for corporate tort and criminal liability. Today, special statutes and the law of agency provide bases for finding a corporation liable for its agents' torts and crimes.

**Torts.** Early cases held that torts committed by a corporation's employees were *ultra vires.* Therefore, the courts refused to find a corporation liable for its employee's torts. Today, the vicarious liability rule of *respondeat superior* applies to corporations. The only issue is whether the employee acted within the scope of her authority, which, as was discussed in Chapter 17, may encompass acts that the employee was expressly instructed to avoid.

**Crimes.** The traditional view was that a corporation could not be guilty of a crime, because criminal guilt required intent and a corporation, not having a mind, could form no intent. In addition, a corporation had no body that could be imprisoned. In essence, courts refused to find corporate criminal liability for violations of statutes that set standards for persons by holding that a corporation was not a person for purposes of criminal liability.

Today, few courts have difficulty holding corporations liable for crimes.[36] Modern criminal statutes, such as the Model Penal Code, either expressly provide that corporations may commit crimes or define the term *person* to include corporations. The *Fortner* case, which follows, interprets such a criminal statute. In addition, some criminal statutes designed to protect the public welfare do not require intent as an element of some crimes, thereby removing the grounds used by early courts to justify relieving corporations of criminal liability.

Courts are especially likely to impose criminal liability on a corporation when the criminal act is *requested, authorized, or performed* by the *board of directors,* an *officer,* another person having responsibility for *formulating company policy,* or a *high-level administrator* having supervisory responsibility over the subject matter of the offense and acting within the scope of his employment. The Model Penal Code, which is similar to the Kentucky Penal Code cited in the *Fortner* case, expressly *imputes* to a corporation the *criminal mind of such high-level managers.* The Model Penal Code distinguishes between a *mere agent* and a *high managerial agent* of a corporation, making corporations more easily liable for the crimes of the latter.

**Directors' and Officers' Liability.** A person is always *liable for his torts and crimes,* even when these are committed on behalf of his principal. Therefore, directors and officers are personally liable when they commit torts or crimes during the performance of their corporate duties.

**Torts of Subordinates.** A director or officer is usually *not liable* for the torts of employees of the corporation, since the corporation, not the director or the officer, is the principal. He will be liable, however, if he *authorizes* the tort or *participates* in its commission.

**Crimes of Subordinates.** A director or officer has *criminal liability* if she *requests, authorizes, conspires,* or *aids and abets* the commission of a crime by an employee. In *United States v. Park,* which appears in Chapter 3, the president of a corporation was held criminally liable for unsanitary conditions in a food warehouse because he was not justified in relying on the employees to whom he had delegated the sanitation duties. In the past, the penalties imposed by courts on white-collar criminals, especially corporate executives, have been little more than slaps on the wrist. Such leniency is disappearing in response to the publicity that has been given to widespread corporate wrongdoing and to public awareness of past judicial leniency.

**Violations of Corporation Statutes.** MBCA Section 1.29 imposes criminal liability on corporate officers and directors who sign a report or application filed with the secretary of state that they *know* to be false. Several state statutes impose civil or criminal liability on officers and directors for failure to perform other statutory duties, such as filing proper annual reports for the corporation or granting shareholders access to the corporate books and records. Similar liabilities exist under federal statutes requiring corporate reports, such as the federal securities acts, which are discussed in Chapter 26. In addition, civil and criminal liability may attach to the directors' paying an illegal dividend, especially if creditors are defrauded thereby.

[36] See Chapter 3.

## Commonwealth v. Fortner LP Gas Co.

**610 S.W.2d 941 (Ky. Ct. App. 1981)**

On March 13, 1979, a school bus was returning children to their homes in Livingston County, Kentucky. Phillip Kirkham, age 10, and his sister, Windy Kirkham, age 6, left the bus and attempted to cross the highway when a truck came upon the scene. The truck was owned by Fortner LP Gas Company, Inc., a corporation. The driver of the truck observed the bus about 400 feet ahead, geared down, applied the brakes, but failed to stop. The truck struck both children, injuring Phillip and killing Windy instantly.

A subsequent inspection of the truck revealed grossly defective brakes. The Commonwealth of Kentucky prosecuted the corporation for causing Windy's death. A grand jury indicted the corporation for manslaughter in the second degree, a felony punishable by a $20,000 fine. The corporation moved to dismiss the indictment on the ground that it could not commit the crime of manslaughter. The lower court sustained the corporation's motion, dismissing the indictment. The Commonwealth appealed.

**Gant, Judge.** For many years *Commonwealth v. Illinois Central Railway* (1913) has been the definitive case on corporate responsibility for criminal conduct, but that case must be considered in light of its date, the statutory changes since that date, and its total holding. Basically, the holding of that court that "corporations cannot be indicted for offenses that derive their criminality from evil intention or which consist in a violation of those social duties which appertain to man" was predicated on two things. First, in 1913 there was no separate punishment for corporations provided by statute, and second, the court was unwilling, in a criminal prosecution, to extend the definition of the word "person" to include corporations. But the court warned that "as to lesser degrees, for which the penalty prescribed may be a fine, it would seem that an indictment might be made to lie, if authorized by a statute including corporations."

The present case is clearly distinguishable from the *Illinois Central* case, and all the more, Kentucky statutes clearly authorize indictments against a corporation. The Kentucky Penal Code contains the following definition:

> "Person" means human being, and where appropriate, a public or private corporation, an unincorporated association, a partnership, a government, or a governmental authority.

But we are not limited to this one indicia within the Code. There is a specific section, as follows:

> Corporate liability.
>
> (1) A corporation is guilty of an offense when:
> (a) The conduct constituting the offense consists of a failure to discharge a specific duty imposed upon corporations by law; or
> (b) The conduct constituting the offense is engaged in, authorized, commanded, or wantonly tolerated by the board of directors or by a high managerial agent acting within the scope of his employment in behalf of the corporation; or

(c) The conduct constituting the offense is engaged in by an agent of the corporation acting within the scope of his employment and in behalf of the corporation and:
1. The offense is a misdemeanor or violation; or
2. The offense is one defined by a statute which clearly indicates a legislative intent to impose such criminal liability on a corporation.

Of further persuasion of legislative intent to impose corporate criminal liability is Kentucky Revised Statutes Section 534.050, which provides for corporate fines for the commission of any class of crime, including a $20,000 fine for the commission of any felony, such as manslaughter.

As pointed out in the Commentaries to the Penal Code:

> The major difficulty with corporate responsibility under the criminal law has been the obvious fact that corporations cannot be imprisoned for commission of crimes. This difficulty should be eliminated through the creation in Section 534.050 of a penalty structure that provides corporate fines for commission of all classes of crimes.

Taken collectively, these statutes are clearly the type envisioned by the court in *Commonwealth v. Illinois Central Railway* when it said that an indictment might lie if authorized by statute.

Judgment reversed in favor of the Commonwealth of Kentucky.

## INSURANCE AND INDEMNIFICATION

The extensive potential liability of directors deters many persons from becoming directors. They fear that their liability for their actions as directors may far exceed their fees as directors. To encourage persons to become directors, corporations *indemnify* them for their outlays associated with defending lawsuits brought against them and paying judgments and settlement amounts. In addition, or as an alternative, corporations purchase *insurance* that will make such payments for the directors. Indemnification and insurance are provided for officers also.

**Indemnification of Directors.** Today, all of the corporation statutes limit the ability of corporations to indemnify directors in order to preserve the deterrence function of tort and criminal law. Nevertheless, the ability of a director to obtain indemnification is quite extensive.

**Mandatory Indemnification.** Under MBCA Section 8.52, a director is entitled to *mandatory indemnification* of her reasonable litigation expenses when she is sued and *wins completely* (is *wholly successful*). The greatest part of such expenses is attorney's fees. If the corporation refuses to indemnify a director in such a situation, she may ask a court to order the corporation to indemnify her.

**Voluntary Indemnification.** Under MBCA Section 8.51, a director who *loses* a lawsuit *may* be indemnified by the corporation. This is called *voluntary indemnification,* because the corporation voluntarily indemnifies the director.

The corporation must establish that the director acted in *good faith* and reasonably believed that she acted in the *best interests* of the corporation. In addition, such indemnification must be approved by someone independent of the director, for example, a *disinterested board* of directors or *disinterested shareholders.* Voluntary indemnification may cover not only the director's reasonable expenses but also fines and damages that the director has been ordered to pay.

A corporation may not elect to indemnify a director who was held *liable to the corporation* or who was found to have received a *personal benefit.* Such a rule tends to prevent indemnification of directors who have wronged the corporation by failing to exercise due care or by breaching a fiduciary duty. However, if the director paid an amount *to the corporation* as part of a *settlement,* the director may be indemnified for his reasonable expenses, but *not for the amount that he paid to the corporation.* The purpose of these rules is to avoid the circularity of having the director pay damages to the corporation and then having the corporation indemnify the director for the same amount of money.

**Court-Ordered Indemnification.** A court may order a corporation to indemnify a director, if it determines that the director meets the standards for mandatory or voluntary indemnification. When a director fails to meet those standards, a court may order indemnification to a director who is *fairly and reasonably* entitled to indemnification in view of all the relevant circumstances. The MBCA does not suggest what such relevant circumstances may be.

**Indemnification of Nondirectors.** Under the MBCA, officers and employees who are not directors are entitled to the *same mandatory indemnification rights* as directors. The corporation may, however, *expand nondirectors' indemnification rights* beyond the limits imposed on directors' indemnification rights.

**Insurance.** The MBCA does not limit the ability of a corporation to purchase *insurance* on behalf of its directors, officers, and employees. Insurance companies, however, are unwilling to insure all risks. In addition, some risks are *legally uninsurable as against public policy.* Therefore, liability for misconduct such as self-dealing, usurpation, and securities fraud is uninsurable.

## SUMMARY

The objectives and powers of a corporation are determined by the state corporation statute, the articles of incorporation, and the bylaws. Corporate actions beyond the powers of the corporation are *ultra vires.* Modern statutes do not permit the corporation and the other party to a contract to use *ultra vires* as a defense. Shareholders may sue to enjoin an *ultra vires* act.

A corporation is managed under the direction of the board of directors. The board delegates many of its duties to committees of the board and to officers, but some board functions may not be delegated. Generally, directors may take action only at a properly convened meeting, but many statutes permit action without a meeting if all of the directors consent in writing.

The directors are elected by the shareholders and may be removed by them. In publicly held corporations, the proxy solicitation process frequently permits the chief executive officer to cause the election of his nominees and to dominate the board of directors. Recently, board members have assumed more independence. Directors normally hold office until the next annual meeting, but most of the corporation statutes also permit staggered terms. Some states require a minimum of three directors; the MBCA requires only one.

Numerous proposals for changing the composition and functions of the board have been made. Audit, nominating, and compensation committees, when composed entirely or predominantly of outside directors, tend to strengthen the independence of the board.

Officers are agents of the corporation, and like all agents, they have express, implied, and apparent authority. Some officers, such as the president and the treasurer, also have inherent authority, which arises from the titles of the offices they hold.

Special rules apply to the management of close corporations. Modern statutes permit close corporations to dispense with a board of directors and to be managed like partnerships. Restrictions on the management discretion of the directors are permitted in close corporations.

Directors and officers must act within their authority and within the powers given to the corporation. They also have the duty to act with due care. Their duty of loyalty requires them to act in the best interests of the corporation as a whole. Most management actions are protected from judicial scrutiny by the business judgment rule: absent bad faith, fraud, or breach of a fiduciary duty, the judgment of the managers of a corporation is conclusive.

The general agency rules concerning torts apply to corporations. Corporations may also be found guilty of crimes, including those requiring intent, if the offenses are authorized or performed by policymaking managers or high-level administrators acting within the scope and in the course of their employments.

Corporations are permitted to purchase insurance policies that will pay for a director's or officer's legal costs and judgments. Within certain constraints, a corporation may also indemnify a director or an officer.

## PROBLEM CASES

**1.** 711 Kings Highway Corporation leased a building to F.I.M.'s Marine Repair Service, Inc. Under the terms of the lease, the building was to be used as a motion-picture theater. F.I.M.'s articles of incorporation stated F.I.M.'s purpose as marine activities, including marine repairing and the building and equipping of boats and vessels. 711 Kings Highway wanted to avoid liability on the lease. It sued F.I.M., asking the court to declare the lease invalid and to enjoin F.I.M. from enforcing any rights under the lease, on the grounds that the lease was *ultra vires*. Did the court void the lease on the grounds that it was *ultra vires*?

**2.** Venture Capital Corporation, a loan company, was organized and promoted by Maurice Shear, who became the majority shareholder, president, chief executive officer, treasurer, and one of the three directors. The other directors were Shear's lawyer and his secretary. Walter Juergens, induced by a prospective public stock offering, bought 35,000 common shares of Venture for $26,000. When Venture failed to make a public offering, Juergens demanded that Venture buy back his shares. Shear promised Juergens that his $26,000 would be refunded. Venture paid Juergens only $10,000, but Shear promised to pay the remaining $16,000 within a month.

Venture's bylaws provided that the president, "subject to the direction of the board of directors, shall have general charge of the business, affairs, and property of the Corporation and general supervision of its officers and agents." Shear actively managed all of the corporation's business, and the other directors permitted him to exercise complete control over the management of all corporate affairs. He was also given exclusive authority by the board of directors to sell and issue the corporate shares. During the period of time that Juergens attempted to receive a refund for his shares, Shear caused Venture to make refunds to 13 other shareholders. At a shareholder meeting attended by all of the directors, Shear gave an annual report to the directors, that included Venture's balance sheet. The balance sheet carried a $16,000 liability,

Common Stock Refunds Payable, reflecting the obligation to Juergens.

Juergens sued Venture for the remaining $16,000. Venture defended on the grounds that Shear had no express or implied authority to enter into any refund agreement and that the board of directors never ratified the agreement. Is Juergens entitled to the refund?

**3.** The board of directors of Pine Belt Producers Co-operative, Inc., authorized its president, Claude O'Bryan, to sign a $35,000 note payable to the First National Bank of Ruston, Louisiana, and to deposit the proceeds in an account in the bank. The resolution also authorized any two of three named officers to withdraw funds from the account on behalf of the corporation. Later, the board, at O'Bryan's request, authorized him to arrange an additional loan to cover up to $80,000 in unusual expenses incurred due to a national trucking strike. Shortly afterward, he signed a note for $57,000 on behalf of the corporation. The bank gave O'Bryan a check for $57,000, payable to Pine Belt. O'Bryan indorsed the check in the name of Pine Belt and gave it back to the bank. By agreement with O'Bryan, the bank used the check to pay a personal debt of a vice president of Pine Belt.

When Pine Belt refused to pay the bank on the $57,000 note, the bank sued. Pine Belt defended on the grounds that O'Bryan had no authority to indorse its checks or to use corporate funds to pay noncorporate debts. Were these good defenses?

**4.** Lillian Pritchard was a director of Pritchard & Baird Corporation, a business founded by her husband. After the death of her husband, her sons took control of the corporation. For two years, they looted the assets of the corporation through theft and improper payments. The corporation's financial statements revealed the improper payments to the sons, but Mrs. Pritchard did not read the financial statements. She did not know what her sons were doing to the corporation or that what they were doing was unlawful.

On behalf of creditors of the corporation, a bankruptcy trustee sued Mrs. Pritchard, claiming that as a director, she had failed to discharge her duty to protect the assets of the corporation. Mrs. Pritchard argued that she was a figurehead director, a simple housewife who served as a director as an accommodation to her husband and sons. Was Mrs. Pritchard held liable to the creditors?

**5.** Elton Risley, the president, director, and majority shareholder of Dredging Corporation, purchased from Dredging 365 common shares of Margate Bridge Company. The price of the shares was $100 per share, well under their actual value. Without giving prior notice, Elton Risley called a meeting of the Dredging directors to approve the sale. One of the three directors, Harry Kaupp, was in Florida on corporate business and did not attend. Carl Risley and Elton Risley attended, both signing a waiver of notice and a statement approving the transaction. Carl Risley did not favor the sale, but when asked at the meeting how he voted, he merely replied, "What can I do?" The minutes, signed by Carl Risley as corporate secretary, showed a unanimous vote in favor of the sale.

Dredging sued Elton Risley to rescind the sale of the Margate shares to him, claiming that the directors' meeting was not valid and that the sale had therefore not been approved by the board. Will Dredging be successful?

**6.** Weiss Medical Complex, Ltd., (WMC) included restrictive covenants in its employment contracts with many of its physicians. The restrictive covenants prohibited the physicians from performing medical services within a 10-mile radius of the clinic for one year after leaving its employment. A meeting of the WMC board of directors was held to act on a proposal to revoke the clinic's policy of requiring the restrictive covenants. The bylaws called for 13 directors, but only 7 had been elected. All seven attended the meeting. Four of them had signed employment contracts containing the restrictive covenants. By unanimous vote, the policy was changed and all existing restrictive covenants were terminated. Later, a shareholder meeting was called to ratify the action of the directors. Ratification was not obtained, because a majority of the shareholders voted against ratification.

Two years later, Drs. Kim and Ladpli terminated their employment with the clinic and established an office within 10 miles of the clinic. The clinic brought suit against them for violating their restrictive covenants. Their defense was that the action of the board of directors rescinded the effectiveness of the covenants. Who won?

**7.** At an annual shareholder meeting of Fleetwood Corporation, the shareholders adopted a resolution that declared, "The officers of the corporation are granted authority to sell the net fixed assets of the Fleetwood Corporation for a price that will yield to the shareholders an amount not less than $500 per share." Five months later, Reginald Brown, president of Fleetwood, met individually with four shareholders and told them that the shareholder resolution obligated them to sell their shares for $500 per share. He told three of them that an investors' syndicate was the purchaser, and he told one of them that he (Brown) was also selling his shares. Each shareholder signed a written purchase agreement obligating him to offer his shares for sale at $500 per share. The written purchase agreements contradicted Brown's earlier statements by specifying that Brown would purchase the shares, would not sell his own shares, and would become the controlling shareholder after the repurchases. In addition, Fleetwood's assets had been appraised recently, but Brown did not inform the selling shareholders of this appraisal, which increased the fair market value of Fleetwood shares to $775 per share. A few weeks later, Fleetwood's board of directors assumed Brown's option rights and bought the shares for $500 per share.

The selling shareholders sued Brown for fraud and breach of fiduciary duty. Has Brown breached a fiduciary duty to the selling shareholders?

**8.** Care Corporation, a company operating health care centers and bowling alleys, was interested in acquiring other companies in the bowling industry. Over a period of a year, Care bought 26 percent of the common shares of Treadway Companies, Inc., which operated motels and bowling alleys. The management of Treadway feared that Care would eventually become the controlling shareholder of Treadway and cause Treadway to be merged into Care. Treadway's management believed that a merger with Care would not be in the best interests of Treadway's shareholders.

Daniel Lieblich, Treadway's chairman of the board and president, consulted a firm of investment bankers, Swordco, to determine whether there were any potential merger candidates other than Care. Initially, Swordco did not report on any merger candidates, but it did report that a Treadway-Care merger would not be in Treadway's best interests. Lieblich also contacted Sidney Friedberg, chairman of Fair Lanes, Inc.

After several weeks of negotiations, Fair Lanes bought 230,000 Treadway shares from Treadway as the first step toward a possible merger. The sale was approved by Treadway's board of directors after the directors had discussed the negotiations with Swordco, had sent Swordco to Fair Lanes armed with questions that they wished answered, had asked Swordco for pro forma balance sheets for the proposed combined company, and had adjourned their deliberations for a week while they reflected on the information that they had received. The sales agreement permitted Fair Lanes to name a majority of the nominees to the Treadway board of directors, but it also provided that Lieblich would retain a position in the merged entity.

The sale reduced Care's interest in Treadway, which had grown to 34 percent, to only 28 percent, thereby preventing Care from being able to stop a Treadway merger with Fair Lanes, for which a two-thirds vote of the outstanding shares of Treadway was required. As a further obstacle in Care's path, Treadway filed a suit against Care, alleging that Care had illegally attempted to acquire control of Treadway. Care counterclaimed against Treadway and its board of directors, alleging that the sale of 230,000 shares to Fair Lanes had been for the improper purpose of preserving the board's control of Treadway. The Treadway board claimed that the business judgment rule protected its decision to sell the shares to Fair Lanes. Does the business judgment rule apply?

**9.** Vicksburg Furniture Manufacturing, Ltd., owned a factory. The managment of Vicksburg was dominated by Gangwer, who ran the corporation and exerted exclusive control over it. The factory, insured against fire by the Aetna Casualty and Surety Company, was destroyed by a fire that started at about 5 P.M. Employees had been dismissed about an hour and a half earlier, and the factory was locked. Only three people, including Gangwer, held keys to the factory. The building showed no signs of forced entry and could not have been entered without a key. A witness said that he saw Gangwer appear at the factory about a half hour after everyone had left and that Gangwer had remained in the building for 30 minutes. About 45 minutes later, the fire was discovered.

Aetna refused to pay Vicksburg under the fire insurance policy on the ground that Vicksburg had committed corporate arson. Vicksburg denied that it was responsible for Gangwer's acts. Must Aetna pay Vicksburg under the policy?

**10.** Sol Price was the president and chief executive officer of Fed-Mart Corporation, a chain of discount department stores. When Fed-Mart sued one of its franchisees, the franchisee counterclaimed against Fed-Mart and Price, alleging that Price had violated the antitrust laws on behalf of Fed-Mart.

The Fed-Mart board of directors authorized indemnification of Price's prospective legal expenses. The next year, however, Price was dismissed as president and chief executive. When the corporation refused further defense of Price in the antitrust suit, Price employed his own attorney.

The trial court dismissed the suit against Price on the ground that the franchisee had not proved that he suffered damages. The trial court stated that the franchisee had presented evidence from which the court could conclude that Price had caused Fed-Mart to commit several per se violations of the antitrust laws, but the court did not decide whether such violations had occurred.

Fed-Mart asked the trial court to declare that it was not required to indemnify Price for his attorney's fees. The trial court held that Price had met the good faith standard of the California statute and was therefore entitled to indemnification. Fed-Mart appealed. Was the trial court correct in ruling that Price was entitled to indemnification for his attorney's fees?

Chapter 25

# Shareholders' Rights and Liabilities

## INTRODUCTION

The shareholders are the ultimate owners of a corporation, but as you learned in Chapter 24, a shareholder has *no right to manage* the corporation. Instead, a corporation is managed by its board of directors and its officers for the benefit of its shareholders.

The shareholders' role in a corporation is limited to electing and removing directors, approving certain important matters, and ensuring that the actions of the corporation's managers are consistent with the applicable state corporation statute, the articles of incorporation, and the bylaws. In playing this role, however, shareholders possess a *wide range of powers and rights.* For example, shareholders have the power and the right to vote on many corporate transactions, such as a merger. Shareholders who oppose certain fundamental corporate actions may require the corporation to buy their shares. In addition, shareholders, on behalf of the corporation, may sue managers who breach their duties of care or loyalty.

Shareholders also assume a few responsibilities. For example, all shareholders are required to pay the promised consideration for shares. Shareholders are liable for receiving dividends beyond the lawful amount. Some of the states make shareholders liable for specified corporate debts beyond the shareholders' capital contributions. In addition, controlling shareholders may owe special duties to minority shareholders.

Close corporation shareholders enjoy rights and perform duties in addition to the rights and duties held by shareholders of publicly owned corporations. As you learned in Chapter 24, close corporation shareholders may agree to grant themselves the right of management. In addition, some courts have found close corporation shareholders to be fiduciaries of each other.

This chapter's study of the rights and responsibilities of shareholders begins with an examination of shareholder voting rights.

## SHAREHOLDERS' MEETINGS

Collective action of the shareholders is ordinarily taken at annual or special shareholders' meetings. Most of the states also permit shareholder action without a meeting.

**Annual Meeting.** The purpose of an *annual shareholders' meeting* is to elect new directors and to conduct whatever other business is necessary. Often, the shareholders are asked to approve the corporation's independent auditors, to ratify stock option plans for management, and to vote on shareholders' proposals.

**Annual Meeting Required.** The general corporation statutes of most states and Model Business Corporation Act (MBCA) Section 7.01 provide that an annual meeting of shareholders *shall* be held at the *time specified in the bylaws.* MBCA Section 7.03 specifies that any shareholder may petition a court to order an annual meeting if none has been held.

**Location of Meeting.** Most states permit the shareholder meeting to be held *anywhere.* Many publicly held corporations encourage shareholder attendance by renting large halls in convenient locations. A few corporations rotate shareholder meetings among the major cities of the country for the convenience of their shareholders. Other corporations hold their shareholder meetings at inconvenient locations to discourage shareholder attendance.

**Special Meetings.** Special shareholders' meetings may be held whenever a corporate matter arises that requires shareholders' action, such as the approval of a merger or a dissolution of the corporation, and the *matter cannot wait until the next annual shareholders' meeting.* Under MBCA Section 7.02, a special shareholders' meeting may be called by the board of directors or by a person authorized to do so by the bylaws, usually the president or the chairman of the board. In addition, the holders of at least 10 percent of the shares entitled to vote at the meeting may call a special meeting. One of the more common reasons why shareholders call a special meeting is to remove a director.

**Notice of Meetings.** To permit shareholders to arrange their schedules for attendance at shareholders' meetings, MBCA Section 7.05 and most of the state corporation statutes require that an officer of the corporation give shareholders *notice* of annual and special meetings of shareholders. Notice need be given only to shareholders entitled to vote who are *shareholders of record* on the day before the notice is mailed. Shareholders of record are those whose names appear on the share-transfer book of the corporation.

**Content of Notice.** Notice of a *special* meeting must list the *purpose* of the meeting. Under the MBCA, notice of an *annual* meeting need not include the purpose of the meeting unless shareholders will be asked to approve extraordinary corporate changes: amendments of the articles of incorporation (Section 10.03),[1] mergers (Section 11.03), sales of all or substantially all the assets other than in the regular course of business (Section 12.02), and dissolution (Section 14.02).

**Defective Notice.** *Lack* of notice or *defective* notice *voids* any action taken at the shareholders' meeting. A shareholder may *waive* her objection to notice defects in much the same way as a director may waive such objection to the defects in a board meeting's notice. Under MBCA Section 7.06, a shareholder's *attendance without objection* to the notice is a waiver. In addition, a shareholder may waive objection by *signing a written waiver* that is delivered to the corporation for inclusion in the minutes of the shareholders' meeting.

**Conduct of the Meeting.** The president or the chairman of the board usually presides at shareholders' meetings. Minutes of shareholders' meetings are usually kept by the secretary. When matters are submitted to shareholders for their action, *election inspectors* are used. Election inspectors determine whether a quorum of shareholders is present and who may vote, and they receive and count the votes.

**Quorum.** To conduct business at a shareholders' meeting, a **quorum** of the *outstanding shares* must be represented in person or by proxy. If the approval of more than one class of shares is required, a quorum of each class of shares must be present. Most of the state corporation statutes and MBCA Sections 7.25 and 7.27 define a quorum as the majority of shares outstanding, yet permit a greater percentage to be established in the articles (or the bylaws in some states). Delaware sets one third of the shares as a minimum for a quorum. Once a quorum is present, a later withdrawal by a shareholder will not affect the validity of an action taken by the remaining shareholders.

**Voting Requirements.** Ordinarily, a majority of the votes *cast* at the shareholders' meeting will decide issues that are put to a vote. If the approval of more than one class of shares is required, a majority of the votes cast by each class must favor the issue. MBCA Section 7.27 permits the articles to require a greater than majority vote. Such *supermajority voting requirements* are frequently used in close corporations to give minority shareholders veto power and, thereby, to prevent oppression of minority shareholders.

**Action without a Meeting.** Generally, shareholders can act only at a properly called meeting. However, MBCA Section 7.04 and the corporation statutes of many states permit shareholders to act without a meeting if *all of the shareholders consent in writing* to the action. Delaware General Corporation Law Section 228 requires merely the written consent of those shareholders having at least the minimum number of shares necessary to take an action at a shareholders' meeting at which all of the shares entitled to vote were present and voted.

## ELECTION OF DIRECTORS AND SHAREHOLDER CONTROL DEVICES

Very few matters require shareholder action. For the most part, a corporation's management may manage the corporation *free from interference by shareholders.* Some matters, however, require shareholder approval be-

[1] The numbers in parentheses refer to the sections of the Model Business Corporation Act, which appears in an Appendix.

cause they involve extremely important changes in the corporation. In these instances, shareholder approval is required to ensure that management does not prefer its own interests over the best interests of the corporation and the shareholders. And, of course, shareholders possess the important right to elect directors to the board.

**Election of Directors.** The most important shareholder voting right is the right to *elect the directors.*

**Straight Voting.** Normally, directors are elected by a single class of shareholders in *straight voting,* in which each share has one vote for each new director to be elected and the nominees with the most votes are elected. Straight voting allows a majority shareholder, such as Henry Ford in *Dodge v. Ford,* which appears later in this chapter, to elect the entire board of directors. Thus, minority shareholders are unable to elect any representatives to the board without the cooperation of the majority shareholder.

Straight voting is also a problem in close corporations in which a few shareholders own equal numbers of shares. In such corporations, no shareholder controls the corporation, yet if the holders of a majority of the shares act in concert, those holders will elect all of the directors and control the corporation. Such control may be exercised to the detriment of the other shareholders.

Two alternatives to straight voting aid minority shareholders' attempts to gain representation on the board and prevent harmful coalitions in close corporations. These alternatives are *cumulative voting* and *class voting.*

**Cumulative Voting.** Many corporations allow a shareholder to *cumulate her votes* by multiplying the number of directors to be elected by the shareholder's number of shares. A shareholder may then allocate her votes among the nominees as she chooses. She may choose to cast all of her votes for only one nominee. Cumulative voting is required by constitutions or statutes in almost half of the states. Most of the other states *permit* corporations to provide for cumulative voting in their articles.

The formula for determining the minimum number of shares required to elect a desired number of directors under cumulative voting is:

$$X = \frac{S \times R}{D + 1} + 1$$

where $X$ is the number of shares needed to elect a desired number of directors, $S$ is the total number of shares voting at the shareholders' meeting, $R$ is the number of director representatives desired, and $D$ is the total number of directors to be elected at the meeting.

The lower the number of directors to be elected, the greater is the number of shares needed to enable a shareholder to elect a director. Hence, having *classes of directors* will reduce a minority shareholder's ability to elect directors by cumulating his votes.[2] For example, if nine directors are elected each year, a shareholder needs just over 10 percent of the shares to elect one director by cumulating his votes. Suppose, however, that there are three classes of directors. The directors will serve three-year terms and only three directors will be elected each year. Under these conditions, a shareholder must own over 25 percent of the shares to elect one director.

Although the purpose of cumulative voting is to give minority shareholders an opportunity to elect representatives to the board of directors, it has been debated whether minority representation on the board is desirable. Not surprisingly, few large publicly held cor-

[2] Classes of directors are discussed in Chapter 24.

porations are domiciled in states with mandatory cumulative voting.

Sometimes, cumulative voting is used in close corporations to ensure a balance of power. For example, a close corporation has four directors and four shareholders, each of whom owns 25 shares. With straight voting, no shareholder is able to elect himself as a director. With cumulative voting, each shareholder is able to elect himself to the board.

**Classes of Shares.** As you learned in Chapter 23, a corporation may have several *classes of shares.* The two most common classes are *common shares* and *preferred shares,* but a corporation may have several classes of common shares and several classes of preferred shares. MBCA Section 7.21 provides that *each share,* whether denoted common or preferred, is *entitled to one vote* on each of the matters voted on at a shareholders' meeting, including the election of directors, *unless* the articles provide otherwise. Usually, preferred shares do not have the right to vote for directors, though some articles confer such a right if the corporation fails to pay a preferred dividend.

MBCA Section 6.01 permits a corporation to designate the voting rights of each class of shares. Many close corporations have two or more classes of common shares with *different voting rights.* Each class may be entitled to elect one or more directors, in order to balance power in a corporation. For example, a corporation has four shareholders, who own 25 shares each, and four directors. With straight voting and no classes of shares, no shareholder can elect himself as a director. Suppose, however, that the corporation has four classes of shares, each with the right to elect one of the directors. If each shareholder owns all the shares of one of the classes, each shareholder can elect himself to the board.

MBCA Section 6.01 permits the articles of incorporation to provide that some shares shall have more than one vote per share or less than one vote per share. Using classes with unequal voting rights permits shareholders to share dividends in a different proportion than the proportion in which they share voting power. For example, two people enter a business together. One of them wants to receive 75 percent of any dividends. The other shareholder agrees to that, but she wants to elect two of the five directors. The corporation could have two classes of common shares. Class A common shares would receive 75 percent of all dividends and elect three directors. Class B common shares would receive 25 percent of all dividends and elect two directors. One shareholder would be issued all of the Class A shares, and the other would receive all of the Class B shares.

**Other Shareholder Control Devices.** While cumulative voting and class voting are two useful methods by which shareholders can allocate or acquire voting control of a corporation, there are three other devices that may also be used for these purposes: *voting trusts; shareholder voting agreements;* and proxies, especially *irrevocable proxies.*

**Voting Trusts.** MBCA Section 7.30 and other statutes permit shareholders to establish **voting trusts.** The shareholders transfer their shares to one or more voting trustees and receive voting trust certificates in exchange. The shareholders retain many of their rights, including the right to receive dividends, but the *voting trustees* elect directors and vote on other matters submitted to shareholders. The voting trustees may be subject to strict limitations on how to vote the shares. For example, they may be required to vote them for director nominees agreed to by the participating shareholders.

**Purpose of Voting Trust.** The purpose of a voting trust is to *control the corporation* through the concentration of shareholder voting power in the voting trustees, who often are participating shareholders. If several minority shareholders collectively own a majority of the shares of a corporation, they may create a voting trust. They will be able to control the corporation through the voting trustees.

You may ask why shareholders need a voting trust when they are in apparent agreement on how to vote their shares. The reason is that they may have disputes in the future. Such disputes, many of which may be based on petty differences, could prevent the shareholders from agreeing on how to vote. The voting trust ensures that the shareholder group will control the corporation despite the emergence of differences.

**Formalities.** Courts were originally hostile to voting trusts, since voting trusts separated the ownership of shares from the right to vote and were often unknown to the other shareholders. Modern statutes, such as the MBCA, recognize the legitimate function of voting trusts and authorize their use under strict constraints. MBCA Section 7.30 limits the duration of voting trusts to *10 years,* though the participating shareholders may agree to extend the term for another 10 years. Also, a voting trust must be made *public,* with copies of the voting trust document available for inspection at the corporation's offices.

**Shareholder Voting Agreements.** As an alternative to a voting trust, shareholders may merely make a contract as to how they will vote their shares. Such *shareholder voting agreements* (or stock pooling agreements) have two advantages over voting trusts. First, their duration may be *perpetual.* Second, they may be kept *secret* from the other shareholders.

Historically, these two advantages were offset by two major disadvantages growing out of the courts' hostility toward such agreements. First, courts held many shareholder voting agreements illegal as attempts to circumvent the restrictions on voting trusts. Second, many courts, such as the court in the *Ringling* case, which follows, refused to grant specific enforcement of such agreements when a shareholder refused to vote as agreed. Shareholders could avoid these problems by expressly providing for specific performance or by using irrevocable proxies. Today, however, modern statutes, such as MBCA Section 7.31, specifically validate shareholder voting agreements, exclude them from the requirements imposed on voting trusts, and make them specifically enforceable.

**Proxies.** As you learned in Chapter 24, a shareholder may appoint a **proxy** to vote his shares. If several minority shareholders collectively own a majority of the shares of a corporation, they may appoint a proxy to vote their shares and thereby control the corporation.

There are several problems with using proxies to exercise control over a corporation. First, the ordinary proxy has only a *limited duration*—11 months under MBCA Section 7.22—unless a longer term is specified. Second, the ordinary proxy is *revocable* at any time. As a result, unless there is careful planning, there is no guarantee that control agreements accomplished through the use of proxies will survive future shareholder disputes.

**Irrevocable Proxies.** Modern corporation statutes, such as MBCA Section 7.22, allow proxies to be valid for longer than 11 months and permit *irrevocable proxies.* A proxy is irrevocable only if it so states and if it is *coupled with an interest.* Courts have struggled with the definition of *coupled with an interest,* so modern statutes specifically define when a proxy may be irrevocable. MBCA Section 7.22 provides that a proxy is coupled with an interest when, among other things, the person holding the proxy is a party to a shareholder voting agreement or has agreed to purchase the shareholder's shares (as under a *buy-and-sell agreement,* which was discussed in Chapter 23). The principal use of irrevocable proxies is in conjunction with shareholder voting agreements.

## Ringling Bros.–Barnum & Bailey Combined Shows v. Ringling

**53 A.2d 441 (Del. Sup. Ct. 1947)**

Ringling Bros.–Barnum & Bailey Combined Shows, a corporation primarily in the circus business, had 1,000 common shares outstanding. All of the shares were owned by members of the Ringling family: 315 shares were held by Edith Conway Ringling, 315 by Aubrey B. Ringling Haley, and 370 by John Ringling North. The shares could be voted cumulatively in an election of directors. The corporation had seven directors.

Mrs. Ringling and Mrs. Haley each had sufficient votes, independently of the other, to elect two of the seven directors. By voting for the same additional candidate, they could be sure of his election regardless of how Mr. North, the remaining stockholder, might vote. In 1941, Mrs. Ringling and Mrs. Haley entered into a shareholder voting agreement for the purpose of ensuring that together they would elect five directors. It provided that they would agree on how to vote their shares on any matter put to shareholders. In the event of their failure to agree, an arbitrator, Karl Loos, would determine how the shares might be voted. The term of the agreement was 10 years.

At the annual shareholders' meetings in 1943, 1944, and 1945, Mrs. Ringling and Mrs. Haley reached agreement on how to vote their shares. In each of these years, they elected five of the seven directors.

Before the 1946 meeting, Mrs. Ringling and Mrs. Haley discussed with Loos the matter of voting for directors. They agreed that Mrs. Ringling should cast sufficient votes to elect herself and her son and that Mrs. Haley should elect herself and her husband, but they did not agree upon a fifth director.

Although attempts were made to postpone the shareholders' meeting until Mrs. Ringling and Mrs. Haley could reach agreement, the meeting was held. At the shareholders' meeting, Mrs. Ringling objected to the holding of the meeting and refused to vote her shares. Loos directed Mrs. Ringling to cast 882 votes for Mrs. Ringling, 882 for her son, Robert, and 441 for a Mr. Dunn, who had been a member of the board for several years. Mrs. Ringling complied with Loos's directions.

Loos next directed that Mrs. Haley cast 882 votes for Mrs. Haley, 882 for her husband, and 441 for Dunn. Instead of complying, Mr. Haley, who was acting as his wife's proxy, attempted to cast 1,103 votes for Mrs. Haley and 1,102 for Mr. Haley.

Mr. North cast 864 votes for a Mr. Woods, 863 for a Mr. Griffin, and 863 for himself.

The chairman of the board ruled that the five candidates proposed by Loos, together with Woods and North, had been elected. The Haley-North group disputed this ruling and argued that Griffin had been elected instead of Dunn. At the directors' meeting that followed the shareholders' meeting, both Dunn and Griffin attempted to vote as directors. After the board meeting, Mrs. Ringling sued Mrs. Haley, asking the court to enforce the shareholder agreement between her and Mrs. Haley and to order a new election of directors.

The trial judge held that the agreement to vote in accordance with the direction of Loos was valid as a shareholder voting agreement. He held that Mrs. Haley's refusal to comply with Loos's instruction authorized Mrs. Ringling to vote Mrs. Haley's shares as her proxy. The judge ordered a new election of directors. Mrs. Haley appealed.

**PEARSON, JUDGE.** Before taking up Mrs. Haley's objections to the agreement, let us analyze particularly what it attempts to provide with respect to voting, including what functions and powers it attempts to repose in Mr. Loos, the arbitrator. The agreement recites that the parties desire "to continue to act jointly in all matters relating to their stock ownership or interest in" the corporation. The parties agreed to consult and confer with each other in exercising their voting rights and to act jointly—that is, concertedly; unitedly; towards unified courses of action—in accordance with such agreement as they might reach. Thus, so long as the parties agree for whom or for what their shares shall be voted, the agreement provides no function for the arbitrator. His role is limited to situations where the parties fail to agree upon a course of action. In such cases, the agreement directs that the question in disagreement shall be submitted for arbitration to Mr. Loos and his decision thereon shall be binding upon the parties. These provisions are designed to operate in aid of what appears to be a primary purpose of the parties, to act jointly in exercising their voting rights, by providing a means for fixing a course of action whenever they themselves might reach a stalemate.

Should the agreement be interpreted as attempting to empower the arbitrator to carry his directions into effect? Certainly there is no express delegation or grant of power to do so, either by authorizing him to vote the shares or to compel either party to vote them in accordance with his directions. The agreement expresses no other function of the arbitrator than that of deciding questions in disagreement which prevent the effectuation of the purpose to act jointly. The power to enforce a decision does not seem a necessary or usual incident of such a function. Mr. Loos is not a party to the agreement. What he does is for the benefit of the parties, not for his own benefit. Whether the parties accept or reject his decision is no concern of his, so far as the agreement or the surrounding circumstances reveal. We think the parties sought to bind each other, but to be bound only to each other, and not to empower the arbitrator to enforce decisions he might make.

From this conclusion, it follows necessarily that no decision of the arbitrator could ever be enforced if both parties to the agreement were unwilling that it be enforced, for the obvious reason that there would be no one to enforce it. Under the agreement, something more is required after the arbitrator has given his decision in order that it should become compulsory: at least one of the parties must determine that such decision shall be carried into effect.

The agreement does not describe the undertaking of each party with respect to a decision of the arbitrator other than to provide that it "shall be binding upon the parties." It seems to us that this language, considered with relation to its context and the situations to which it is applicable, means that each party promised the other to exercise her own voting rights in accordance with the arbitrator's decision. The agreement is silent about any exercise of the voting rights of one party by the other.

Having examined what the parties sought to provide by the agreement, we come now to the Haleys' contention that the voting provisions are illegal and revocable. They say that the courts of this state have definitely established the doctrine that there can be no agreement by which the voting power of stock of a Delaware corporation may be irrevocably separated from the ownership of the stock, except a voting trust.

In our view, neither the cases nor the statute sustain the rule for which the Haleys contend. Their sweeping formulation would impugn well-recognized means by which a shareholder may effectively confer his voting rights upon others while retaining various other rights. For example, the Haleys' rule would apparently not permit holders of voting stock to confer upon stockholders of another class, by the device of an amendment of the certificate of incorporation, the exclusive right to vote during periods when dividends are not paid on stock of the latter class. The broad prohibition seems inconsistent with their concession that proxies coupled with an interest may be irrevocable. The Delaware statute authorizes voting trusts and prescribes numerous requirements to their validity.

But the statute does not purport to deal with agreements whereby shareholders attempt to bind each other as to how they shall vote their shares. Various forms of such voting agreements have been held valid and have been distinguished from voting trusts. We think the particular agreement before us does not violate the Delaware voting trust requirements or constitute an attempted evasion of those requirements, and is not illegal for any other reason.

Generally speaking, a shareholder may exercise wide liberality of judgment in the matter of voting, and it is not objectionable that his motives may be for personal profit, or determined by whims or caprice, so long as he violates no duty owed his fellow shareholders. The ownership of voting stock imposes no legal duty to vote at all. A group of shareholders may, without impropriety, vote their respective shares so as to obtain advantages of concerted action. They may lawfully contract with each other to vote in the future in such way as they, or a majority of their group, from time to time determine. Reasonable provisions for cases of failure of the group to reach a determination because of an even division in their ranks seem unobjectionable. The provision here for submission to the arbitrator is plainly designed as a deadlock-breaking measure, and the arbitrator's decision cannot be enforced unless at least one of the parties (entitled to cast one-half of their combined votes) is willing that it be enforced. We find the provision reasonable. It does not appear that the agreement enables the parties to take any unlawful advantage of the outside shareholder, or of any other person. It offends no rule of law or public policy of this state of which we are aware.

Accordingly, the failure of Mrs. Haley to exercise her voting rights in accordance with his decision was a breach of her contract. The votes representing Mrs. Haley's shares should not be counted.

Since no infirmity in Mr. North's voting has been demonstrated, his right to recognition of what he did at the meeting should be considered in granting any relief to Mrs. Ringling, for her rights arose under a contract to which Mr. North was not a party. With this in mind, we have concluded that the election should not be declared invalid, but that effect should be given to a rejection of the votes representing Mrs. Haley's shares. No other relief seems appropriate in this proceeding. With respect to the election of directors, the return of the election inspectors should be corrected to show a rejection of Mrs. Haley's votes, and to declare the election of the six persons for whom Mr. North and Mrs. Ringling voted.

Judgment for Mrs. Ringling affirmed as modified.

## OTHER MATTERS SUBMITTED TO SHAREHOLDERS

Other matters besides the election of directors require shareholder action, some because they make fundamental changes in the structure or business of the corporation. These fundamental corporate changes are *amendments of the articles, mergers* and *consolidations, share exchanges, sales of all or substantially all the assets* other than in the ordinary course of business, and *dissolutions.*

**Amendment of the Articles.** At common law, the corporate charter was considered a contract between the state and the corporation, between the corporation and the shareholders, and among the shareholders. It could not be changed without the consent of all the parties, including the unanimous consent of the shareholders. Modern corporation statutes, such as MBCA Section 1.02, reserve to the legislature the right to change the statutes and regulations, thus changing the corporate charter. And modern statutes, such as MBCA Sections 10.01 and 10.03, also permit the corporation itself to amend its articles without the unanimous approval of the shareholders.

**Procedure for Amending Articles.** Amendment of the articles of incorporation requires compliance with the procedure set out by the statute of the state of incorporation. MBCA Section 10.03 requires that a written notice setting forth the proposed amendment or a summary of the changes to be effected by it must be given to all of the shareholders who are entitled to vote. The directors must also recommend the amendment to the shareholders, unless the board has a conflict of interest.

The amendment must be approved by a majority of the votes *present* at the meeting. Some states require approval by a majority of the *outstanding votes,* but the MBCA imposes this requirement only if the amendment gives rise to a *right of appraisal,* which is discussed later in the chapter. The articles may alter the approval percentage, requiring supermajority approval.

MBCA Section 10.04 further provides that the holders of any class of shares are entitled to vote as a class on certain amendments that would affect the value or rights of that class of shares. Such amendments include changing the number of authorized shares of the class, changing the dividend or liquidation preference of preferred shares, creating a new class with a dividend or liquidation preference superior to that of existing preferred shares, limiting or denying existing preemptive rights, and canceling accrued dividends on preferred shares.

Two other procedures for amending the articles exist. The shareholders may amend the articles by their *unanimous written consent,* under MBCA Section 7.04. In addition, Section 10.02 permits the directors to make minor amendments, such as changing the name of the corporation's registered agent. In addition, the articles may authorize the directors to make any amendment without shareholder approval.

**Other Fundamental Transactions.** The following fundamental transactions require shareholder approval because they instantly or significantly change the character of the shareholders' investments.

**Merger and Consolidation.** A **merger** is a transaction in which one corporation merges into a second corporation. The first corporation disappears; the second corporation takes all the business and assets of both corporations and becomes liable for the debts of both corporations. Usually, the shareholders of the disappearing corporation become shareholders of the surviving corporation. Ordinarily, the approval of the shareholders of both corporations is required.

A **consolidation** is similar to a merger, except that both old corporations go out of existence and a new corporation takes the business, assets, and liabilities of the old corporations. Both corporations' shareholders must approve the consolidation. Modern corporate practice makes consolidations obsolete, since it is usually desirable to have one of the old corporations survive. The MBCA does not recognize consolidations. However, the effect of a consolidation can be achieved by creating a new corporation and merging the two old corporations into it.

**Share Exchange.** A **share exchange** is a transaction by which one corporation becomes the owner of all of the outstanding shares of a second corporation through a *compulsory* exchange of shares. The shareholders of the second corporation are compelled to exchange their shares for shares of the first corporation. The second corporation remains in existence and becomes a wholly owned subsidiary of the first corporation. Only the selling shareholders must approve the share exchange.

The share exchange, which is compulsory, must be distinguished from a shareholder's *voluntary* sale of his shares of the second corporation. A voluntary sale does not require an approval of the shareholders as a body. Instead, a shareholder may exercise his independent judgment regarding whether to sell his shares.

**Sale of Assets.** A *sale of all or substantially all of the assets of the business other than in the regular course of business* is self-defining. This transaction must be approved by the shareholders of the selling corporation, since it drastically changes the shareholders' investment. The "substantially all" language is included in the definition of the transaction in order to prevent corporations from avoiding a shareholder vote by retaining a small residue of assets. Substantially all means nearly all, however. A corporation, therefore, that sells its building, but retains its machinery with the intent of continuing operations at another location, has not sold all or substantially all of its assets.

**Dissolution.** A **dissolution** is the first step in the termination of the corporation's business. The usual dissolution requires shareholder approval. Dissolution was discussed in detail in Chapter 23.

**Procedures Required.** Most statutes establish similar procedures to effect all of the above fundamental transactions. Under the MBCA, the procedure includes approval of the board of directors, notice to all of the shareholders whether or not they are entitled to vote, and a majority vote of shareholders entitled to vote under the statute, articles, or bylaws. A majority vote will be insufficient if a corporation has a supermajority shareholder voting requirement.

**Class Voting.** If there is more than one class of shares, the articles may provide that matters voted on by shareholders must be approved by each class. For example, a merger may have to be approved by a majority of the preferred shareholders and a majority of the common shareholders. As an alternative, the articles may require only the approval of the shareholders as a whole.

Under MBCA Section 11.03, voting by classes is required for mergers and share exchanges if these would substantially affect the rights of the classes. For example, the approval of preferred shareholders is required if a merger would change the liquidation preference of preferred shareholders.

**When Shareholder Approval Not Required.** In many states, no approval of shareholders of the *surviving corporation* is required for a merger *if* the merger does not fundamentally alter the character of the business or substantially reduce the shareholders' voting or dividend rights. For example, in Delaware and under MBCA Section 11.03, the shareholders of the surviving corporation have no right to vote on a merger if the *number of voting shares* and the *number of shares with unlimited dividend rights* are not increased by more than 20 percent. The rationale for this rule is that such a merger does not alter a shareholder's prospects any more than do many other management decisions that do not require shareholder approval. Approval of the shareholders of the disappearing corporation is required, however, since their rights are changed substantially.

**Short-Form Merger.** Many statutes, including MBCA Section 11.04, permit a merger between a parent corporation and its subsidiary without the approval of the shareholders of either corporation. Instead, the board of directors of the parent approves the merger and sends a copy of the merger plan to the subsidiary's shareholders. This simplified merger is called a **short-form merger.** It is available only if the parent owns a high percentage of the subsidiary's shares—90 percent under the MBCA and the Delaware statute.

There are two reasons for this simpler procedure for effecting short-form mergers. One is that the parent's high ownership makes obvious the outcome of any vote of the subsidiary's shareholders. The other is that the rights of the parent's shareholders are not materially changed, since the parent's ownership of the subsidiary's business has changed only from an indirect 90 percent ownership to a direct 100 percent ownership.

**Shareholder Control Agreements.** The shareholder control agreements that you studied above—voting trusts, shareholder voting agreements, and irrevocable proxies—may be used by a group of shareholders owning a majority of the shares to ensure that they will not only be able to elect directors but also to dictate the outcome of a shareholder vote on the above transactions.

**Other Matters Submitted to Shareholders.** The articles of incorporation and the bylaws may require that other matters be submitted for shareholder approval. For example, shareholders may be given the right to amend the bylaws and to set the consideration received for newly issued shares. In addition, state corporation statutes permit certain corporate actions to be authorized after shareholder approval. For example, loans to officers, self-dealing transactions, and indemnifications of managers for litigation expenses may be approved by shareholders. Also, many of the states require shareholder approval of share option plans for high-level executive officers, but the MBCA (Section 6.24) does not. The Securities and Exchange Commission requires shareholder approval of the independent auditors of a corporation subject to the reporting requirements of the Securities Exchange Act of 1934.

Usually, the approval of a majority of the outstanding votes will suffice, unless the articles or bylaws require class voting or a supermajority vote. In some cases, however, unanimous shareholder approval is required. For example, if an officer has engaged in a *waste of corporate assets,* such as paying corporate funds to a relative who does no work for the corporation, approval of all the shareholders is required. If even one shareholder fails to approve the transaction, that shareholder may sue on behalf of the corporation to recover the funds wrongfully paid.

## SHAREHOLDER PROPOSALS AND RIGHT TO SPEAK

Among the rights of shareholders is *full participation* in shareholders' meetings. This includes the right to offer resolutions,[3] to speak for or against such resolutions as are proposed, and to ask questions of the officers of the corporation.

In recent years, these rights have been rather systematically pursued by certain shareholders who might be said to fall into two classes. One class is typified by Lewis D. Gilbert, who has made an occupation of attending the shareholders' meetings of large corporations and proposing resolutions aimed at protecting or enhancing the interests of minority shareholders. The proposals have included amending the corporate articles to permit cumulative voting for directors, setting ceilings on top-executive pay, and limiting corporate charitable contributions. In addition, groups seeking social or political changes, such as restrictions on the production of nuclear power and the provision of greater opportunities for minority groups, have introduced resolutions at shareholders' meetings that would, for example, prohibit trade with South Africa or ban the production of weapons. Shareholders have also questioned and criticized management in regard to these issues. None of these proposals has drawn more than a few percent of shareholders' votes. In most cases, calling attention to the issue seems to have been the proposers' primary motivation.

**Corporate Governance Proposals.** Several critics of corporate activities have proposed changes in the law to strengthen the participation of small shareholders in publicly held corporations. These proposals have included providing shareholders with more information about corporate operations, making shareholder nomination of directors practicable, making it easier for shareholders to place resolutions before the entire body of shareholders, and allowing the beneficiaries of institutional investors, such as pension fund beneficiaries, to vote the shares held by the institutional investors.[4]

There is considerable doubt, however, that the great majority of the shareholders would take advantage of the proposed devices, or even favor their being made available if the cost is to be borne by the company. As you learned in Chapter 24, most shareholders subscribe to the *Wall Street rule:* sell the shares if you do not like what management is doing with the corporation. Of the relatively few shareholders who have offered shareholder resolutions in publicly held corporations, nearly all seem to have done so in order to further a special interest that goes beyond the corporation, such as fighting apartheid in South Africa, rather than to advance their investment interest in the corporation.[5]

## SHAREHOLDERS' RIGHT OF APPRAISAL

**Introduction.** Many times, shareholders will approve an action by less than a unanimous vote, indicating that some shareholders opposed the action. For the most part, the dissenting shareholders have no recourse. Their choice is to remain shareholders or to

[3] See Chapter 26 for a discussion of SEC rules on shareholders' proposals.

[4] See Ralph Nader, Mark Green, and Joel Seligman, *Taming the Giant Corporation* (New York: W. W. Norton, 1976), especially chap. 4.

[5] David Vogel, *Lobbying the Corporation* (New York: Basic Books, 1978).

sell their shares. For close corporation shareholders, there is no choice. The dissenting shareholder in a close corporation has no ready market for her shares, so she will remain a shareholder.

Some corporate transactions, as you have seen above, so materially change a shareholder's investment in the corporation or have such an adverse effect on the value of a shareholder's shares that it has been deemed unfair to require the dissenting shareholder either to remain a shareholder merely because there is no fair market for the shares or to suffer a loss in value when he sell his shares. Corporate law has therefore responded by creating a **right of appraisal** or **dissenters' rights** for shareholders who disagree with specified fundamental corporation transactions. This right of appraisal requires the corporation to pay dissenting shareholders the *fair value* of their shares.

Not all corporate transactions and not all shareholders are covered by the right of appraisal. Corporation statutes have complex provisions that state when the right of appraisal arises and what procedures a shareholder must follow to assert that right.

**Actions Covered.** Most of the appraisal statutes cover mergers, short-form mergers, and sales of all or substantially all the assets other than in the ordinary course of business. MBCA Section 13.02 covers these transactions plus share exchanges and amendments of the articles of incorporation that materially and adversely affect liquidation, dividend, redemption, preemptive, or voting rights. Some of the appraisal statutes cover consolidations also.

**Shareholders Covered.** Most of the corporation statutes, including MBCA Section 13.02, require that a shareholder have the *right to vote* on the action to which he objects, though a shareholder of a subsidiary in a short-form merger has the right of appraisal despite his lack of voting power. In addition, most corporation statutes, including MBCA Section 13.21, require that the shareholder *not vote in favor* of the transaction. The shareholder may either vote against the action or abstain from voting. Some states require that the shareholder vote against the action. Under all of the corporation statutes, a shareholder may not vote in favor of the transaction and later change his mind and seek appraisal.

**Shares Covered.** Most of the corporation statutes exclude from the appraisal remedy shares that are traded on a recognized securities exchange, such as the New York Stock Exchange. Instead, the shareholder should sell his shares on the stock exchange if he dissents to the corporate action. This exclusion reflects the rationale that a liquid securities market is the best determinant of the value of shares.

The MBCA has no such exclusion, on the ground that the market price may be *adversely affected by the news* of the proposed or consummated corporate action to which the shareholder objects. The shareholder is entitled to the fair value of his shares unaffected by the action that he deems harmful.

**Procedure to Exercise Right.** Generally, corporation statutes require that the shareholder notify the corporation of his intent to seek appraisal before the shareholders have voted on the protested action. Next, the corporation must notify dissenting shareholders entitled to the right of appraisal and tell them where they may demand payment and what form they must submit. The dissenting shareholders must then demand payment. Upon receipt of the demand for payment, the corporation must pay the dissenting shareholders the fair value of the shares. If a dissenting shareholder disagrees with the corporation's valuation of the shares or if the corporation fails to pay the dissenting shareholder, he may demand the payment of his estimate of the fair value of the shares. If the shareholder and the corporation cannot agree on the fair value of the shares, then a court will determine their fair value.

**Determination of Fair Value.** Under the MBCA, *fair value* means the value of the shares immediately before the corporate action is effected, excluding any increase or decrease in value due to the anticipated effects of the action. Such a valuation allows the shareholder to receive an amount that would have been the value of the shares if the corporation had not even considered taking the objectionable action. Most judges use a combination of valuation techniques—such as market value, capitalization of earnings, and book value—to appraise the shares.

**Exclusivity of Remedy.** Most of the corporation statutes make the appraisal remedy the sole remedy for a shareholder who objects to the action, unless the shareholder can prove that the transaction is unlawful or fraudulent. In addition, a shareholder who has sought appraisal may not refuse the court-ordered amount and decide to remain a shareholder.

**Criticisms of the Appraisal Remedy.** Both promanagement and proshareholder rights groups have criticized the appraisal remedy. Management criticizes it as a nuisance that can severely affect the cash position of the corporation. Shareholders criticize it because the procedures and other technicalities make its use expensive, difficult, and risky. In addition, most judges are ill-equipped to value corporate shares, with the result that archaic valuation methods are often used to value the shares.

The MBCA has attempted to reconcile these viewpoints by removing some of the technicalities and by motivating the corporation and the shareholders to resolve the issue out of court. In addition, the Supreme Court of Delaware recently recognized the need for courts to value shares by methods generally considered acceptable in the financial community.[6]

On the other hand, the right of appraisal has proven an effective way for minority shareholders to force the directors to reconsider a proposed action. For example, the directors may submit to shareholders a merger with terms that are slightly unfavorable to some classes of shareholders. If large numbers of shareholders seek the appraisal remedy, the directors may be forced to change the merger terms before seeking shareholder approval, in order to avoid a disastrous cash drain on the corporation. Used in such a manner, the right of appraisal operates as an effective check on management's discretion.

## DISTRIBUTIONS TO SHAREHOLDERS: DIVIDENDS

**Introduction.** During the life of a corporation, shareholders may receive distributions of the corporation's assets. Most people are familiar with one type of distribution, dividends, but there are other important types of distributions to shareholders, including payments to shareholders upon the corporation's repurchase of its shares.

There is one crucial similarity among all the types of distributions to shareholders: corporate assets are transferred to shareholders. An asset transfer to shareholders may harm the corporation's creditors. In addition, a distribution to one class of shareholders may harm another class of shareholders who have a liquidation priority over that of the shareholders who have received the distribution.

[6] *Weinberger v. U.O.P., Inc.,* 457 A.2d 701 (Del. Sup. Ct. 1983).

The existence of these potential harms compels corporation law to restrict the ability of corporations to make distributions to shareholders. In this part of the study of law, you will learn about the different types of distributions to shareholders and about the legal rules affecting the amounts that may be distributed. Your study begins with dividends.

**Types of Dividends.** One important objective of a business corporation is to make a profit. Shareholders usually invest in a corporation primarily to share in the expected profit either through appreciation of the value of their shares or through dividends. There are two types of dividends: *cash or property dividends* and *share dividends.* Only cash or property dividends are distributions of the corporation's assets. Share dividends are not distributions, but in some circumstances they may adversely affect the rights of some shareholders.

**Cash or Property Dividends.** Dividends are usually paid in cash. However, other assets of the corporation—such as airline discount coupons or shares of another corporation—may also be distributed as dividends. Cash or property dividends on common shares are declared by the board of directors and paid by the corporation on the date stated by the directors. Once declared, dividends are *debts* of the corporation and shareholders may sue to force payment of the dividends.

**Board Discretion.** The board's dividend declaration, including the amount of dividend and whether to declare a dividend, is protected by the business judgment rule. Nevertheless, there are limits to the board's discretion. For example, the board may not refuse to declare dividends when such refusal results in the oppression of minority shareholders, especially in a close corporation. In *Dodge v. Ford,* which follows, one of the few cases in which a court ordered the payment of a dividend, the court found that Henry Ford had the wrong motives for refusing to pay a dividend. In addition, federal tax law imposes a limitation on the board's discretion by imposing a tax on a corporation's excessive retained earnings. Also, some loan agreements and bond and debenture indentures prohibit or limit the ability of a corporation to pay dividends.

**Preferred Dividends.** Preferred shares nearly always have a set dividend rate stated in the articles of incorporation. Even so, unless the preferred dividend is mandatory, which is rare, the board has discretion to determine whether to pay a preferred dividend and what amount to pay. Most preferred shares are *cumulative preferred shares,* on which unpaid dividends cumulate. The entire accumulation must be paid before common shareholders may receive any dividend. Some preferred shares are *cumulative-to-the-extent-earned,* entitling preferred shareholders to receive unpaid dividends for all prior periods in which funds were legally available for payment, before any dividend may be paid to common shareholders. Even when preferred shares are noncumulative, the current dividend must be paid to preferred shareholders before any dividend may be paid to common shareholders.

**Legal Capital Rules.** To protect the claims of the corporation's creditors, all of the corporation statutes specify the sources from which dividends may be paid. Nearly all of the statutes make a dividend payment illegal if it would render the corporation **insolvent,** that is, unable to pay its currently maturing obligations. In addition, most of the statutes permit a dividend only to the extent of **earned surplus** (retained earnings). However, states such as Delaware permit a solvent corporation to pay a dividend to the extent of surplus, which includes retained earnings and capital surplus.

While these limitations may seem restrictive, other provisions in most of the statutes permit the directors to increase the amount of dividends that may be paid by transferring amounts between the capital accounts of the corporation and by increasing the valuations of corporate assets. In addition, Delaware permits what is called a *nimble dividend,* allowing a corporation to pay a dividend out of current net profits even when the corporation has a negative surplus, but only if its capital equals the liquidation preferences of all shares.

**MBCA Approach.** The existence of these statutes, which create the false impression that shareholder capital may not be distributed to shareholders, has led to simpler dividend payment rules. MBCA Section 6.40, for example, has two requirements: (1) the *solvency test* and (2) the *balance sheet test.*

1. *The solvency test:* The dividend may not make the corporation insolvent, that is, unable to pay its debts as they come due in the usual course of business. This requirement protects creditors, who are concerned primarily with the corporation's ability to pay debts as they mature.
2. *The balance sheet test:* After the dividend has been paid, the corporation's assets must be sufficient to cover its liabilities and the liquidation preference of shareholders having a priority in liquidation over the shareholders receiving the dividend. This requirement protects not only creditors but also preferred shareholders. It prevents a corporation from paying to common shareholders a dividend that will impair the liquidation rights of preferred shareholders. In valuing the assets, directors are permitted to use any reasonable valuation method rather than merely historical cost.

**Person Entitled to Dividend.** A problem may arise when a shareholder sells his shares after the dividend declaration but before the dividend has been paid. The corporation may treat the *shareholder of record* as the person who is entitled to receive the dividend. The directors set the record date at the time the dividend is declared.

As between the seller and the buyer of the shares, the right to a dividend is determined by their agreement. Absent an agreement, the seller is entitled to the dividend if the sale was made after the record date. If the sale was made on a stock exchange, the transferee is entitled to the dividend unless she bought the stock after it was declared ex dividend, which is five business days before the record date for the dividend.

**Share Dividends and Share Splits.** Corporations sometimes distribute additional shares of the corporation to their shareholders. Often, this is done in order to give shareholders something instead of a cash dividend so that the cash can be retained and reinvested in the business. Another common objective is to adjust the market price of the shares so that it falls within the popular $20–40 per share range. Such an action may be called either a **share dividend** or a **share split.**

**Share Dividend.** Traditionally, a share dividend of a *specified percentage of outstanding shares* is declared by the board of directors. For example, the board may declare a 10 percent share dividend. Then, each shareholder will receive 10 percent more shares than she currently owns. A share dividend is paid on outstanding shares only. Unlike a cash or property dividend, a share dividend may be revoked by the board after it has been declared.

Usually, share dividends are paid in shares of the same class. However, a *share dividend of a different class* may be made. For example, preferred shareholders may receive a share dividend paid in common shares.

**Share Split.** Traditionally, a share split results in shareholders receiving a specified number of shares in exchange for each share that they currently own. For example, shares may be split 2 for 1. Each shareholder will now have two shares for each share that he previously owned. A holder of 50 shares will now have 100 shares instead of 50. A share split affects all *authorized* shares, not merely outstanding shares.

**Legal and Accounting Rules.** The distinction between a share dividend and a share split is important due to their different legal and accounting treatment. Most of the corporation statutes require that the *par or stated value* of share dividend shares be *transferred from a surplus account to stated capital.* The transfer is necessary to maintain a fictional adherence to the requirement that shares be issued for at least par or stated value. If the shares distributed are treasury shares, no transfer is necessary.[7] For share splits, most of the statutes require that the articles be amended by shareholder action to *reduce the par value* of the shares and to *increase the number of authorized shares.*

Deciding which procedure to follow may be difficult because the distinction between share dividends and share splits may be blurred, as when a board declares a 100 percent share dividend or when there is a 21-for-20 share split. The Financial Accounting Standards Board (FASB) takes the position that a distribution of a relatively small number of shares is likely to be viewed by shareholders as a dividend because it does not appreciably reduce the market value of the stock. Such a distribution should be treated as a share dividend, and there should be a transfer from retained earnings to the stated capital account.[8] If the purpose of the distribution is to reduce the market price of the stock so as to gain wider distribution, then the transaction is a share split and no capital transfer is necessary. The crossover point between a share dividend and a share split, according to the FASB, is a distribution of about 20–25 percent of the outstanding shares of the issue.

**MBCA Approach.** The MBCA recognizes that a share split or a share dividend in the same class of shares does not affect the value of the corporation or the shareholder's wealth. The effect is like that produced by taking a pie with four pieces and dividing each piece in half. Each person may receive twice as many pieces of the pie, but each piece is worth only half as much. The total amount received by each person is unchanged. Therefore, MBCA Section 6.23 permits share splits and share dividends of the same class of shares to be made *without transferring amounts among the capital accounts.*

If shares of one class are distributed to shareholders of another class, however, the distribution must be authorized by the articles or approved by the shareholders of the class whose shares are distributed. Such a share distribution reduces the wealth of the shareholders of the class whose shares are distributed, and it increases the wealth of the shareholders of the class that receives the shares.

**Reverse Share Split.** A *reverse share split* is a decrease in the number of shares of a

[7] Treasury shares are defined in Chapter 23.

[8] ARB no. 43, chap. 7, § B10–16.

class such that, for example, two shares become one share. For par value shares, a reverse share split increases the par value per share by the same factor by which the number of shares are reduced. Most of the state corporation statutes require shareholder action to amend the articles to effect a reverse share split, because the number of authorized shares is reduced and the par value per share is increased. The purpose of a reverse share split is usually to increase the market price of the shares. Sometimes, it is used in freeze-out transactions, which are discussed later in this chapter.

## Dodge v. Ford Motor Co.

**170 N.W. 668 (Mich. Sup. Ct. 1919)**

In 1916, brothers John and Horace Dodge owned 10 percent of the common shares of the Ford Motor Company. At that time, Henry Ford owned 58 percent of the outstanding common shares and controlled the corporation and its board of directors. From its beginning in 1903, Ford Motor Company had been profitable. Starting in 1911, the corporation paid a regular annual dividend of $1.2 million, which was 60 percent of its capital stock of $2 million but only about 1 percent of its total equity of $114 million. In addition, from 1911 to 1915, the corporation paid special dividends totaling $41 million.

The policy of the corporation for some time had been to reduce the selling price of its cars each year, while maintaining or improving quality. In June 1915, the board and officers agreed to take various steps to expand productive capacity, including the construction of new plants for $10 million, the acquisition of land for $3 million, and the erection of an $11 million smelter. Not all the details of the planned expansion were settled, and the board had not formally approved the plan. To finance the planned expansion, the board decided not to reduce the selling price of cars beginning in August 1915 and to accumulate a large surplus.

A year later, the board reduced the selling price of cars by $80 per car. The corporation was able to produce 600,000 cars annually, all of which, and more, could have sold for $440 instead of the new $360 price, a forgone revenue of $48 million. At the same time, the corporation announced a new dividend policy of paying no special dividend. Instead, it would reinvest all earnings except the regular dividend. The directors then declared the regular dividend of $1.2 million.

Henry Ford announced his justification for the new dividend policy in a press release: "My ambition is to employ still more men, to spread the benefits of this industrial system to the greatest possible number, to help them build up their lives and their homes." At the time the new dividend policy was announced, the corporation had a $112 million surplus, expected profits of $60 million, total liabilities of $18 million, $52.5 million in cash on hand, and municipal bonds worth $1.3 million.

The Dodge brothers sued the corporation and the directors to force them to declare a special dividend. The trial court ordered the corporation to declare a dividend of $19.3 million. Ford Motor Company appealed.

**Ostrander, Chief Justice.** It is a well-recognized principle of law that the directors of a corporation, and they alone, have the power to declare a dividend of the earnings of the corporation, and to determine its amount. Courts will not interfere in the management of the directors unless it is clearly made to appear that they are guilty of fraud or misappropriation of the corporate funds, or they refuse to declare a dividend when the corporation has a surplus of net profits which it can, without detriment to the business, divide among its stockholders, and when a refusal to do so would amount to such an abuse of discretion as would constitute a fraud, or breach of that good faith which they are bound to exercise towards the stockholders.

The record, and especially the testimony of Mr. Ford, convinces this court that he has to some extent the attitude towards shareholders of one who has dispensed and distributed to them large gains and that they should be content to take what he chooses to give. His testimony creates the impression, also, that he thinks the Ford Motor Company has made too much money, has had too large profits, and that, although large profits might be still earned, a sharing of them with the public, by reducing the price of the output of the company, ought to be undertaken. We have no doubt that certain sentiments, philanthropic and altruistic, creditable to Mr. Ford, had large influence in determining the policy to be pursued by the Ford Motor Company.

The difference between an incidental humanitarian expenditure of corporate funds for the benefit of the employees, like the building of a hospital for their use and the employment of agencies for the betterment of their condition, and a general purpose and plan to benefit mankind at the expense of others, is obvious. There should be no confusion (of which there is evidence) of the duties which Mr. Ford conceives that he and the stockholders owe to the general public and the duties which in law he and his co-directors owe to protesting, minority stockholders. A business corporation is organized and carried on primarily for the profit of the stockholders. The powers of the directors are to be employed for that end. The discretion of directors is to be exercised in the choice of means to attain that end and does not extend to a change in the end itself, such as the reduction of profits or the nondistribution of profits among stockholders in order to devote them to other purposes.

It is not within the lawful powers of a board of directors to shape and conduct the affairs of a corporation for the merely incidental benefit of shareholders and for the primary purpose of benefiting others, and no one will contend that if the avowed purpose of the directors was to sacrifice the interests of shareholders, it would not be the duty of the courts to interfere.

We are not, however, persuaded that we should interfere with the proposed expansion of the Ford Motor Company. In view of the fact that the selling price of products may be increased at any time, the ultimate results of the larger business cannot be certainly estimated. The judges are not business experts. It is recognized that plans must often be made for a long future, for expected competition, for a continuing as well as an immediately profitable venture. It may be noticed incidentally, that the corporation took from the public the money required for the execution of its plan, and that the very considerable salaries paid to Mr. Ford and to certain executive officers and employees were not diminished. We are not satisfied that the alleged motives of the directors, in so far as they are reflected in the conduct of the business, menace the interests of shareholders.

Assuming the general plan and policy of expansion were for the best ultimate interest of the company and therefore of its shareholders, what does it amount to in justification of a refusal to declare and pay a special dividend? The Ford Motor Company was able to estimate with nicety its income and profit. It could sell more cars than it could make. The profit upon each car depended upon the selling price. That being fixed, the yearly income and profit was determinable, and, within slight variations, was certain.

There was appropriated for the smelter $11 million. Assuming that the plans required an expenditure sooner or later of $10 million for duplication of the plant, and for land $3 million, the total is $24 million. The company was a continuing business, at a profit—a cash business. If the total cost of proposed expenditures had been withdrawn in cash from the cash surplus (money and bonds) on hand August 1, 1916, there would have remained $30 million.

The directors of Ford Motor Company say, and it is true, that a considerable cash balance must be at all times carried by such a concern. But there was a large daily, weekly, monthly receipt of cash. The output was practically continuous and was continuously, and within a few days, turned into cash. Moreover, the contemplated expenditures were not to be immediately made. The large sum appropriated for the smelter plant was payable over a considerable period of time. So that, without going further, it would appear that, accepting and approving the plan of the directors, it was their duty to distribute on and near the 1st of August 1916, a very large sum of money to stockholders.

Judgment for the Dodge brothers affirmed.

## OTHER CORPORATE DISTRIBUTIONS

Declaring a dividend is only one of the ways in which a corporation may distribute its assets. A corporation may also distribute its assets by repurchasing its shares from its shareholders. Like a dividend, such a repurchase may harm creditors and other shareholders. In addition, a corporation may distribute its assets in a partial liquidation.

**Share Repurchases.** All of the corporation statutes, including MBCA Section 6.31, permit a corporation to repurchase its shares. Such a repurchase may be either a *redemption* or an *open-market repurchase*.

**Redemptions.** The right of redemption (or call) is usually a right of the corporation to force an *involuntary* sale by the shareholder at a fixed price. The shareholder must sell the shares to the corporation at the corporation's request; however, the shareholder cannot force the corporation to redeem the shares. Some states, such as New York, permit the right of redemption to be held by a shareholder; that is, the corporation may be forced to repurchase shares at a shareholder's request or upon the occurrence of an event, such as a shareholder's death.

Under MBCA Section 6.01, the right of redemption must appear in the articles of incorporation. It is common for a corporation to issue preferred shares subject to redemption at the corporation's option. Usually, common shares are *not* redeemable. However, common shares may be redeemable, if the corporation has a nonredeemable class or classes of shares that possess all of the rights normally held by common shareholders.

**Uses of Redemption.** The right of redemption has many uses. First, it allows a corporation to reacquire preferred shares whose dividend rate is higher than the present market dividend rate. Second, when used with convertible preferred shares, it permits a corporation to force the conversion of the preferred shares into common shares, thereby eliminating a high dividend requirement without reducing the corporation's cash or capital. For example, a corporation has preferred shares, each of which may be converted into four common shares. The redemption price is $110 per preferred share, and the market value of the common shares is $30 per share. If the corporation calls the shares for redemption, rational shareholders will maximize their wealth by converting their preferred shares into common shares worth $120, which is $10 more than the redemption price. Third, when shareholders hold the right to redeem, redemption may be used to guarantee a market for the shares of a close corporation.

**Legal Capital Rules.** Most of the corporation statutes treat redemptions differently from dividends, imposing fewer restrictions on redemptions. Generally, the statutes impose the same limitations on redemptions as does MBCA Section 6.40:

1. *The solvency test:* The redemption may not render the corporation insolvent (unable to pay its obligations as they come due in the usual course of business).
2. *The balance sheet test:* After the redemption, the corporation's assets must be sufficient to cover the corporation's liabilities and the liquidation preference of shareholders having a priority in liquidation over the shareholders whose shares were redeemed.

MBCA Section 6.40 adopts these tests, which are the same as its dividend rules, recognizing that a redemption is no different from a dividend or any other distribution of assets to shareholders.

**Open-Market Purchases.** A corporation is empowered to purchase its shares from any shareholder who is willing to sell them, despite the absence of such power in the articles. Such repurchases are *voluntary* on the shareholder's part, requiring the corporation to pay current market prices to entice the shareholder to sell.

**Uses.** A corporation may repurchase its shares when the market price is low and may resell the shares when the market price increases. The corporation may repurchase its shares for resale to executives who are participants in corporate share option plans. In addition, the repurchase of shares can be an effective device to fight a takeover of the company by reducing the number of shares in the hands of people who would be willing to sell them to investors who are attempting to take over the corporation.

**Legal Capital Rules.** Most of the corporation statutes treat open-market repurchases of shares in the same way as dividends are treated, requiring that the corporation be solvent and that the repurchase be only to the extent of retained earnings (and sometimes capital surplus also). MBCA Section 6.40 treats such repurchases in the same way as any other distribution is treated, imposing the *solvency test* and the *balance sheet test.*

**Distributions from Capital Surplus.** Several of the corporation statutes, including *former* MBCA Section 46, permit a corporation to distribute its assets to the extent of capital surplus. Some of the statutes treat such distributions as dividends are treated, but other statutes require that such distributions be authorized by the articles of incorporation or by a vote of the shareholders.

**Partial Liquidations.** A *partial liquidation* of a corporation's capital, either in money or property, is also called a distribution. Some of the corporation statutes treat partial liquidations as dividends are treated, and others treat them as they treat distributions from capital surplus that require approval of the shareholders or authorization in the articles.

The MBCA treats partial liquidations in the same way as it treats any other distribution of assets.

## SHAREHOLDERS' INSPECTION AND INFORMATION RIGHTS

**Inspection Right.** Inspecting a corporation's books and records is sometimes essential to the exercise of a shareholder's rights. For example, a shareholder may be able to decide how to vote in a director election only after examining corporate financial records that reveal whether the present directors are managing the corporation profitably. Also, a close corporation shareholder may need to look at the books to determine the value of his shares.

Many corporate managers are resistant to shareholders' inspecting the corporation's books and records, charging that shareholders are nuisances or that shareholders often have improper purposes for making such an inspection. Sometimes, management objects solely on the ground that it desires secrecy. As a result, disputes are frequent between corporations and shareholders who seek to examine corporate records.

**Common Law.** At common law, shareholders had the right to inspect corporate books and records, including shareholders' lists, books of account, minute books, and the properties of the corporation, so long as the right was exercised for a *proper purpose.* Nevertheless, even if the shareholder's purpose was proper, he or she might suffer much delay and find it very expensive to obtain a remedy (usually a *writ of mandamus* ordering the corporation to open its books and records to the shareholder).

The line between proper and improper purposes is not always clear, and in earlier cases the courts put the heavy burden of proving a proper purpose on the shareholder. Requests to inspect the books of account so as to determine the value of shares or the propriety of dividends and to inspect the stock ledger so as to identify fellow shareholders in order to communicate with them concerning corporate affairs—including an effort to replace management—are clearly proper purposes.

On the other hand, learning business secrets, aiding a competitor, getting the names of shareholders for a mailing list, and obtaining prospects for a personal business are clearly improper purposes. Even so, mere ownership of stock in a competing corporation is not, in itself, a sufficient ground for denying access to the records. Simple curiosity or even a desire to be informed about corporate affairs has been held to be an insufficient purpose, especially where other means of gaining information, such as attendance at shareholders' meetings, have not been fully utilized. In addition, the advancement of political views is not a proper purpose, as is illustrated in the *Pillsbury* case, which follows.

**Statutory Inspection Rights.** Most of the state corporation statutes specifically grant shareholders inspection rights. The purpose of these statutes is to facilitate the shareholder's inspection of the books and records of corporations whose managements resist or delay proper requests by shareholders. The statutes permit shareholders to employ a lawyer or an accountant to exercise their inspection right and allow them to photocopy the records.

**Absolute Right of Inspection.** MBCA Section 7.20 gives shareholders an *absolute right* of inspection of an alphabetical listing of the shareholders entitled to notice of a meeting, including the number of shares owned. This record must be made available to shareholders for a specified period of time before the meeting and must also be available at the meeting. Access to a *shareholder list* allows a shareholder to contact other shareholders about important matters, such as shareholder proposals.

MBCA Section 16.02 also grants an absolute right of inspection of, among other things, the articles, bylaws, and minutes of shareholder meetings within the past three years, after five days' notice by the shareholder.

**Qualified Right of Inspection.** The shareholder's right to inspect other records, however, is *qualified* (restricted) by MBCA Section 16.02. To inspect accounting records, board and committee minutes, and shareholder minutes more than three years old, a shareholder must give five days' notice and have a *proper purpose.*

In addition, a shareholder must describe with *particularity* his purpose and the records that he wishes to inspect. He must show that the records are directly connected to his purpose. The MBCA does not indicate what is needed to meet the particularity requirement. It is probably not enough for a shareholder merely to state that he wants to determine the value of his shares. The *Pillsbury* case, which follows, deals briefly with the particularity and direct-connection requirements of Minnesota law.

**Eligible Shareholders.** Many statutes, including *former* MBCA Section 52, require the shareholder to own a specified number of shares (for example, 5 percent of the outstanding shares) or to have been a shareholder for a specified period of time (for example, six months). These eligibility requirements are intended to prevent a person from buying a few shares merely to look at the corporation's records.

**Revised MBCA Rule.** The MBCA eliminated these eligibility requirements, on the grounds that the good faith and proper purpose requirements would prevent such an action. The MBCA allows *any shareholder* to assert the right to inspect. Some courts, such as the Minnesota Supreme Court in the *Pillsbury* case, consider the amount of shareholdings and the timing of purchases in determining whether a shareholder has acted in good faith.

**Information Rights.** MBCA Section 16.20 requires the corporation to furnish its shareholders *annual financial statements,* including a balance sheet, an income statement, and a statement of changes in shareholders' equity. The Securities Exchange Act of 1934 also requires *publicly held* corporations to furnish such statements, as well as other information, to their shareholders.[9]

[9] Financial reporting requirements of the Securities and Exchange Commission are discussed in Chapter 26.

## State ex rel. Pillsbury v. Honeywell, Inc.

**191 N.W.2d 406 (Minn. Sup. Ct. 1971)**

On July 3, 1969, Charles Pillsbury attended a meeting of the Honeywell Project, a group opposed to American involvement in Vietnam. The group believed that a substantial part of the production of Honeywell, Inc., consisted of munitions used in the Vietnam War and that Honeywell should stop its munitions production. Pillsbury had long opposed the Vietnam War, but it was at this meeting that he first learned of Honeywell's production of antipersonnel fragmentation bombs. He was upset to learn that such bombs were produced in his own community by a company that he had known and respected.

On July 14, he directed his agent to purchase 100 shares of Honeywell stock. The agent purchased the shares in the name of a Pillsbury family nominee, Quad & Co. The sole purpose of Pillsbury's purchase was to permit him to communicate with other Honeywell shareholders in the hope of persuading Honeywell's board of directors to cease producing munitions. Later in July, he learned that he was a contingent beneficiary of 242 shares of Honeywell under the terms of a trust formed for his benefit by his grandmother. On August 11, having discovered that the 100 shares were purchased in the name of a family nominee, Pillsbury purchased one share of Honeywell in his own name.

Pillsbury next made two formal demands on Honeywell requesting that he be permitted to inspect its original shareholder ledger, its current shareholder ledger, and all corporate records dealing with weapons and munitions manufacture. Honeywell refused the request, and Pillsbury sued, asking the court to order Honeywell to produce the records. The trial court ordered judgment for Honeywell, ruling that Pillsbury had not demonstrated a proper purpose germane to his interest as a stockholder. Pillsbury appealed.

**Kelly, Justice.** Under the law of Delaware, the shareholder must prove a proper purpose to inspect corporate records other than shareholder lists. Pillsbury contends that a stockholder who disagrees with management has an absolute right to inspect corporate records for purposes of soliciting proxies. He would have this court rule that such solicitation is *per se* a proper purpose. Honeywell argues that a proper purpose contemplates concern with investment return. We agree with Honeywell.

While inspection will not be permitted for purposes of curiosity, speculation, or vexation, adverseness to management and a desire to gain control of the corporation for economic benefit does not indicate an improper purpose. Several courts would confer an almost absolute right to inspection. We believe that a better rule would allow inspections only if the shareholder has a proper purpose for such communication. This rule was applied in a case where inspection was denied because the shareholder's objective was to discredit politically the president of the company, who was also the New Jersey secretary of state.

In terms of the corporate norm, inspection is merely the act of the concerned owner checking on what is in part his property. In the context of the large firm, inspection can be more akin to a weapon in corporate warfare. Considering the huge size of many modern corporations and the necessarily complicated nature of their bookkeeping, it is plain that to permit their thousands of stockholders to roam at will through their records would render impossible not only any attempt to keep their records efficiently, but also the proper carrying on of their businesses. Because the power to inspect may be the power to destroy, it is important that only those with a bona fide interest in the corporation enjoy that power.

Courts have also balked at compelling inspection by a shareholder holding an insignificant amount of stock in the corporation. Pillsbury's standing as a shareholder is quite tenuous. He owns only one share in his own name, bought for the purposes of this suit. He had previously ordered his broker to buy 100 shares, but there is no showing of investment intent. He had a contingent beneficial interest in 242 shares. Courts are split on the question of whether an equitable interest entitles one to inspection. Indicative of Pillsbury's concern regarding his equitable holdings is the fact that he was unaware of them until he had decided to bring this suit.

Pillsbury had utterly no interest in the affairs of Honeywell before he learned of Honeywell's production of fragmentation bombs. Where it is shown that such shareholding is only colorable, or solely for the purpose of maintaining proceedings of this kind, we fail to see how the shareholder can be a person interested, entitled to a right to inspect. But for his opposition to Honeywell's policy, Pillsbury probably would not have bought Honeywell shares, would not be interested in Honeywell's profits, and would not desire to communicate with Honeywell's shareholders. His avowed purpose in buying Honeywell shares was to place himself in a position to try to impress his opinions favoring a reordering of priorities upon Honeywell management and its other shareholders. Such a motivation can hardly be deemed a proper purpose germane to his economic interest as a shareholder.

Pillsbury had already formed strong opinions on the immorality and the social and economic wastefulness of war long before he bought stock in Honeywell. His sole motivation was to change Honeywell's course of business because that course was incompatible with his political views. If unsuccessful, Pillsbury indicated that he would sell the Honeywell stock.

We do not mean to imply that a shareholder with a bona fide investment interest could not bring this suit if motivated by concern with the long- or short-term economic effects on Honeywell resulting from the production of war munitions. Similarly, this suit might be appropriate when a shareholder has a bona fide concern about the adverse effects of abstention from profitable war contracts on his investment in Honeywell.

In this case, however, Pillsbury was not interested in even the long-term well-being of Honeywell or the enhancement of the value of his shares. His sole purpose was to persuade the company to adopt his social and political concerns, irrespective of any economic benefit to himself or Honeywell. This purpose on the part of one buying into the corporation does not entitle Pillsbury to inspect Honeywell's books and records.

Pillsbury argues that he wishes to inspect the stockholder ledger in order that he may correspond with other shareholders with the hope of electing to the board one or more directors who represent his particular viewpoint. This court has said that a shareholder's motives or good faith are not a test of his right of inspection, except as bad faith actually manifests some recognized improper purpose—such as vexation of the corporation, or purely destructive plans, or *nothing specific,* just pure idle curiosity, or necessarily illegal ends, or *nothing germane to his interests.*

While a plan to elect one or more directors is specific and the election of directors normally would be a proper purpose, here the purpose was not germane to Pillsbury's or Honeywell's economic interest. Instead, the plan was designed to further his political and social beliefs. Since the requisite propriety of purpose germane to his or Honeywell's economic interest is not present, the allegation that Pillsbury seeks to elect a new board of directors is insufficient to compel inspection.

Judgment for Honeywell affirmed.

## PREEMPTIVE RIGHT

**Introduction.** The market price of a shareholder's shares will be reduced if a corporation issues additional shares at a price less than the market price. In addition, a shareholder's proportionate voting, dividend, and liquidation rights may be adversely affected by the issuance of additional shares. For example, if a corporation's only four shareholders each own 100 shares worth $10 per share, then each shareholder has shares worth $1,000, a 25 percent interest in any dividends declared, 25 percent of the voting power, and a claim against 25 percent of the assets after creditors' claims have been satisfied. If the corporation subsequently issues 100 shares to another person for only $5 per share, the value of each shareholder's shares falls to $900 and his dividend, voting, and liquidation rights are reduced to 20 percent. In a worse scenario, the corporation issues 201 shares to one of the existing shareholders, giving that shareholder majority control of the corporation and reducing the other shareholders' interests to under 16⅔ percent each. As a result, the minority shareholders will be dominated by the majority shareholder and will receive a greatly reduced share of the corporation's dividends.

Such harmful effects of an issuance could have been prevented if the corporation had been required to offer each existing shareholder a percentage of the new shares equal to her current proportionate ownership. If, for example, in the latter situation described above, the corporation had offered 50 shares to each shareholder, each shareholder could have remained a 25 percent owner of the corporation; her interests in the corporation would not have been reduced, and her total wealth would not have been decreased.

Corporation law recognizes the importance of giving a shareholder the option of maintaining the value of his shares and retaining his proportionate interest in the corporation. This is the shareholder's **preemptive right,** an option to subscribe to a new issuance of shares in proportion to the shareholder's present interest in the corporation.

**Scope of Preemptive Rights.** The preemptive rights doctrine evolved in the courts. Today, nearly every state corporation law has a provision dealing with preemptive rights.

**Common Law.** Generally, the preemptive right applies to any *issuance* of shares, especially if the shares are newly authorized. There is a conflict of authority with respect to the subsequent issuance of shares that were authorized when the corporation was organized. The rationale of courts holding that the preemptive right does not apply to such an issuance is that there was an implied agreement with the original shareholders that these shares would be sold to raise capital for the business. If the sale of these shares is long postponed, however, the rationale breaks down and they are probably subject to the preemptive right.

A resale of treasury shares is *not* subject

to the preemptive right. Treasury shares are already issued, although not outstanding.[10] In addition, courts have held that the preemptive right does not apply to shares issued in connection with a merger or a consolidation, or shares issued for a noncash consideration.

**Statutes.** Some of the states merely codify the common law, and others provide that the preemptive right exists unless it has been denied in the articles of incorporation. Most of the states, however, provide that there is no preemptive right unless the articles create such a right.

MBCA Section 6.30 is representative of the most modern statutory provisions that adopt a comprehensive scheme for determining preemptive rights. It provides that the preemptive right does not exist except to the extent provided by the articles. The MBCA permits the corporation to state expressly when the preemptive right arises.

In addition, the MBCA defines preemptive rights when the corporation merely states in its articles that "the corporation elects to have preemptive rights." In such a situation, the preemptive right exists for all issuances of shares except for several types of issuances and two classes of holders. The *excluded issuances* are issuances to managers and employees as compensation, issuances of shares within six months of incorporation, and issuances of shares for noncash consideration. The two *excluded classes of holders* are (1) common shareholders for an issuance of nonconvertible preferred shares and (2) nonvoting preferred shareholders for all issuances, including issuances of the same class of preferred shares that they currently own.

**Mechanics.** When the preemptive right exists, the corporation must notify a shareholder of her option to buy shares, the number of shares that she is entitled to buy, the price of the shares, and when the option must be exercised. Usually, the shareholder is issued a **right,** a written option that she may exercise herself or sell to a person who wishes to buy the shares. Often, rights of publicly held corporations are traded on the national stock exchanges. Finance principles instruct shareholders that they should either exercise their right to purchase additional shares or sell the right. Allowing the right to expire will decrease the shareholder's total wealth.

**Criticisms of Preemptive Rights.** The preemptive right has been criticized as an inefficient method of protecting shareholders from directors who issue shares for too little consideration. The critics of preemptive rights point out that the directors' general duty of care and loyalty adequately protect shareholders. In addition, they note that the mechanics of a preemptive rights offering are burdensome and time consuming. A corporation may have to wait many months to make a stock issuance because it may take that long to determine how many shareholders will exercise their preemptive right. Lastly, these critics maintain that most shareholders are unconcerned about a reduction in their proportionate voting, dividend, and liquidation interests. They contend that the sole concerns of most shareholders are that the market price of their shares should not fall and that the dividend they receive should remain unchanged. If directors act prudently by issuing shares for adequate consideration and by wisely investing the proceeds of the issuance, those concerns should be satisfied.

Modern corporation statutes, such as MBCA Section 6.30, reflect these criticisms by severely limiting shareholders' preemptive rights, unless the articles provide otherwise. Today, almost no publicly held corporations grant preemptive rights to shareholders. The preemptive right is important only in close

[10] Treasury shares are defined in Chapter 23.

corporations, in which shareholders are concerned about balances of power.

## SHAREHOLDERS' LAWSUITS

**Shareholders' Individual Lawsuits.** A shareholder has the right to sue in his own name to prevent or to redress a breach of the shareholder's contract. For example, a shareholder may sue to recover dividends declared but not paid (as did the Dodge brothers in *Dodge v. Ford*), to enjoin the corporation from committing an *ultra vires* act, to enforce the shareholder's right of inspection (as Pillsbury tried to do in *Pillsbury v. Honeywell, Inc.*), to ask a court to dissolve the corporation (as was discussed in Chapter 23), and to enforce preemptive rights.

On the other hand, when a corporation has been harmed by the actions of another person, the right to sue belongs to the corporation and any damages awarded by a court belong to the corporation. Hence, as a general rule, a shareholder has no right to sue in his own name someone who has harmed the corporation, and he may not recover for himself damages from that person. This is the rule even when the tortfeasor's actions impair the value of the shareholder's investment in the corporation. If individual shareholders were permitted to sue for their proportionate shares of a wrong to the corporation, there might be a multiplicity of suits and the individual shareholders might benefit to the detriment of corporate creditors.

A few exceptions to this rule exist under circumstances in which although the wrong is to the corporation, the injury is primarily to the shareholders, and the rights of creditors are not affected. For instance, where nearly all of the shareholders have participated in a misappropriation of funds, the nonparticipating shareholders may be allowed to recover a judgment sufficient to place them on a par with the participating shareholders. A few courts justify individual shareholder recovery on the ground that permitting only the corporation to recover would allow the wrongdoing shareholders to share indirectly in the damages awarded to the corporation.

**Shareholder Class Action Suits.** When several people have been injured similarly by the same persons in similar situations, one of the injured people may sue for the benefit of all the people injured. Likewise, if several shareholders have been similarly affected by a wrongful act of another, one of these shareholders may bring a **class action** on behalf of all the affected shareholders.

Most shareholder class actions have been brought under the federal securities laws, which are discussed in Chapter 26. An appropriate class action under state corporation law would be an action seeking a dividend payment that has been brought by a preferred shareholder for all of the preferred shareholders. Any recovery, such as the special dividend in *Dodge v. Ford,* is prorated to all members of the class.

To certify a shareholder as a representative of the shareholders, the court must find that the number of shareholders is *so large* that it is impracticable for all of them to be plaintiffs, that the shareholder's interest is *substantially the same* as that of the other shareholders, and that the shareholder will *fairly and adequately protect* the interests of the other shareholders. A shareholder bringing a class action need not seek the cooperation of other shareholders, but he must give notice of the class action to all the shareholders. Such notice must be by the best notice practicable under the circumstances, including personal notice to shareholders who can be identified through a reasonable effort.

**Reimbursement of Litigation Expenses.** A shareholder who successfully brings a class action is entitled to be reimbursed from the award amount for his *reasonable expenses,* including attorney's fees. Otherwise, few rational shareholders would sue, since ordinarily the cost of the suit will far exceed the direct benefit to the shareholder. If the class action suit is unsuccessful and has no reasonable foundation, the court may order the suing shareholder to pay the defendants' reasonable litigation expenses, including attorney's fees.

**Shareholders' Derivative Suits.** One or more shareholders are also permitted under certain circumstances to bring an action for the benefit of the corporation when the directors have failed to pursue a corporate cause of action. For example, if the corporation has a claim against its chief executive for wrongfully diverting corporate assets to her personal use, the corporation is unlikely to sue the chief executive, because she controls the board of directors. Clearly, the CEO should not go unpunished. Consequently, corporation law authorizes a shareholder to bring a **derivative suit** (or derivative action) against the CEO on behalf of the corporation and for its benefit. Such a suit may also be used to bring a corporate claim against an outsider. If the derivative suit succeeds and damages are awarded, the damages ordinarily go to the corporate treasury for the benefit of the corporation. Most of the lawsuits against officers and directors in the cases in Chapter 24 were derivative actions.

**Eligible Shareholders.** Although allowing shareholders to bring derivative suits creates a viable procedure for suing wrongdoing officers and directors, this procedure is also susceptible to abuse. **Strike suits** (law suits brought to gain out-of-court settlements for the complaining shareholders personally or to earn large attorney's fees, rather than to obtain a recovery for the corporation) have not been uncommon. To discourage abuse, the Federal Rules of Civil Procedure and similar state rules and statutes require that the person bringing the action be a *current shareholder.* In addition, that person must have held his shares *at the time the alleged wrong occurred* or must have acquired them by operation of law (such as inheritance) from someone who held them at that time. This rule prevents someone from buying shares merely to bring a suit based on a wrong that occurred before he bought them.

Many statutes, including former MBCA Section 49, provide that the corporation may require the shareholders initiating a derivative suit to *post a security bond.* No security bond is needed if these shareholders own a specified percentage or dollar amount of the corporation's shares.

**Revised MBCA Approach.** These eligibility requirements are designed to deter strike suits, but their effect has been to discriminate against small shareholders. Consequently, the revised MBCA has eliminated the security requirement. *Any* shareholder, regardless of his holdings, may commence a derivative suit without posting a bond.

**Demand on Directors.** Since the decision to sue someone is ordinarily made by corporate managers, the Federal Rules of Civil Procedure and state statutes or rules require that a shareholder first *demand* that the board of directors bring the suit. A demand informs the board that the corporation may have a right of action against someone that the board, in its business judgment, may decide to pursue. Therefore, if a demand is made and the board decides to bring the suit, the shareholder may not institute a derivative suit.

Problems arise, however, when a shareholder fails to make a demand or when a demand is made but the board refuses to sue.

**Demand Excused.** Ordinarily, a shareholder's failure to make a demand on the board prevents her from bringing a derivative suit. Nevertheless, the shareholder may initiate the suit if she proves that a demand on the board would have been useless or *futile.* Demand is futile, and therefore *excused,* if the board is unable to make a disinterested decision regarding whether to sue. Futility may be proved where all or a majority of the directors are interested in the challenged transaction, such as in a suit alleging that the directors issued shares to themselves at below-market prices.

In a recent case, *Aronson v. Lewis,* the Supreme Court of Delaware said that futility would exist when there was a *reasonable doubt that the business judgment rule would apply.* This reasonable doubt may be due to many things, including the *directors' interest* in the challenged transaction, their *lack of independence* from the alleged wrongdoers, or their acting *contrary to the best interests* of the corporation.[11]

The Delaware court refused to find futility in the case before it, however. The directors had approved an employment agreement between the corporation and one of the directors. That director owned 47 percent of the shares and nominated all of the directors. The court found that the shareholder had not proved that the directors lacked independence from the controlling director or that they were "beholden" to him. And the court found no proof that the agreement was a waste of corporate assets. The court ruled that approving the agreement was a valid exercise of business judgment.

**Demand Refused.** If a shareholder makes a demand on the board and it *refuses* the shareholder's demand to bring a suit, the question arises whether the shareholder should be permitted to bring the suit. Whether a corporation should bring a lawsuit is an ordinary business decision appropriate for a board of directors to make. The business judgment rule, therefore, is available to insulate from court review a board's decision not to bring a suit. Accordingly, for most lawsuits, a board decision not to sue is binding on the shareholders. The shareholders will not be able to bring a derivative suit after a board's refusal to sue.

Of course, if a shareholder derivative suit accuses the board of harming the corporation, such as by misappropriating the corporation's assets, the board's refusal will not be protected by the business judgment rule, because the board is interested in its decision to sue. In such a situation, the shareholder may sue the directors despite the board's refusal.

**Shareholder Litigation Committees.** To ensure the application of the business judgment rule in demand refusal situations, boards have attempted to isolate themselves from the decision regarding whether to sue by creating a special committee of the board, called a *shareholder litigation committee* (SLC) or an independent investigation committee, whose purpose is to decide whether to sue. The SLC should consist of directors who are not defendants in the derivative suit, who are not interested in the challenged action, who are independent of the defendant directors, and if possible, who were not directors at the time the wrong occurred. Usually, the SLC has independent legal counsel that assists its determination regarding whether to sue.

Not surprisingly, SLCs rarely decide that the corporation should sue the directors, citing such reasons as that the litigation is not in the best interests of the corporation and is likely to disrupt management and harm employee morale, and that the cost of the liti-

[11] *Aronson v. Lewis,* 473 A.2d 805, 814–15, 818 (Del. Sup. Ct. 1984).

gation will outweigh the expected benefit to the corporation in light of the probable outcome of the lawsuit. Since the SLC is a committee of the board, its decision is protected by the business judgment rule. Therefore, an SLC's decision not to sue prevents a shareholder from suing.

**Judicial Reaction to the Use of SLCs.** Since 1976, however, several shareholder derivative suits have challenged the application of the business judgment rule to an SLC's decision to dismiss a shareholder derivative suit against some of the directors. The suing shareholders argue that it is improper for an SLC to dismiss a shareholder derivative suit, because there is a *structural bias*. That is, the SLC members are motivated by a desire to avoid hurting their fellow directors and adversely affecting future working relationships within the board.

Most of the courts that have been faced with this question have upheld, under the business judgment rule, the decisions of special litigation committees. Consistent with the business judgment rule, the courts have required at a minimum that the SLC members be *independent* of the defendant directors, be *disinterested* with regard to the subject matter of the suit, make a *reasonable investigation* into whether to dismiss the suit, and act in *good faith*.

In the *Zapata* case, which follows, however, the influential Delaware Supreme Court adopted a test that permits a court to second-guess an SLC and use its independent judgment to determine whether a derivative suit is in the best interests of the corporation. The court held that in *demand futility* situations, a trial court must apply a *two-step test* to determine whether the decision of an SLC to dismiss a suit should be respected by the trial court. The *Zapata* two-step test has been followed in some states and rejected in others. In most of the states, the courts have yet to rule on this issue.

Most courts that have ruled on the issue have held that the *Zapata* two-step test does not apply in a *demand refused* case.

**Demand on Shareholders.** The Federal Rules of Civil Procedure and many state laws also require that a shareholder exhaust intracorporate remedies by making a demand on the shareholders. The reason for requiring a demand on the shareholders is that the shareholders, if asked, may vote to ratify the wrongful action or to waive the corporation's right to sue the person who has harmed the corporation. Such a demand is excused if the class of shareholders is so large that a demand would be impracticable or expensive or if a demand would be futile, as where the wrongdoers own a majority of the shares. The MBCA recognizes the absurdity of requiring a demand on the shareholders and therefore does not require one.

**Settlements.** Rules and statutes in several states, the Federal Rules of Civil Procedure, and MBCA Section 7.40(c) require the trial court's approval of any derivative suit settlement. The intent of this rule is to deter strike suits and to encourage settlements that benefit all of the shareholders, not just the shareholder who brought the derivative suit.

**Litigation Expenses.** If a shareholder is *successful* in a derivative suit, she is entitled to a *reimbursement of her reasonable litigation expenses* out of the corporation's damage award. On the other hand, if the suit is *unsuccessful* and has been brought *without reasonable cause,* most of the corporation statutes, including MBCA Section 7.40(d), authorize the court to require the shareholder to *pay the defendants' expenses,* including attorney's fees. The purpose of this rule is to deter strike suits by punishing shareholders who litigate in bad faith.

**Defense of Corporation by Shareholder.** Occasionally, the officers or managers will refuse to defend a suit brought against a corporation. If a shareholder shows that the corporation has a valid defense to the suit and that the refusal or failure of the directors to defend is a breach of their fiduciary duty to the corporation, the courts will permit the shareholder to *defend* for the benefit of the corporation, its shareholders, and its creditors.

## Zapata Corp. v. Maldonado

**430 A.2d 779 (Del. Sup. Ct. 1981)**

In 1974, the board of directors of Zapata Corporation authorized Zapata's repurchase of some of its shares at a price above their current market price. The repurchase was expected to increase the market price of the shares.

Zapata had a share option plan that permitted its executives to purchase Zapata shares at a below-market price. Most of the directors participated in the share option plan. The exercise date of the share options was *after* the date of the planned share repurchase. After the repurchase had been approved by the board, the directors moved the share option exercise date to a date *before* the date of the repurchase. The effect of the advancement of the option exercise date was to reduce the federal income tax liability of the executives, including the directors, and to increase the corporation's federal tax liability.

William Maldonado, a Zapata shareholder, believed that the board action was a breach of a fiduciary duty and that it harmed the corporation. In 1975, he instituted a derivative suit on behalf of Zapata against all of the directors. He failed to make a demand upon the directors to sue themselves, alleging that this would be futile since they were all defendants.

The derivative suit was still pending in 1979, when four of the defendants were no longer directors. The remaining directors then appointed two new outside directors to the board and created an Independent Investigation Committee consisting solely of the two new directors. It was instructed to investigate Maldonado's claims and the expected effect of the lawsuit on the corporation. The board authorized the committee to make a final and binding decision regarding whether the derivative suit should be brought on behalf of the corporation. Following a three-month investigation, the committee concluded that Maldonado's derivative suit should be dismissed as against Zapata's best interests.

Soon after, Zapata asked the court of chancery (the trial court where Maldonado brought the suit) to dismiss the derivative suit on the ground that the business judgment rule gave the committee the authority to terminate shareholder derivative suits. The vice chancellor (the equivalent of a judge in the court of chancery) refused to dismiss the suit, holding that Maldonado possessed an individual right to maintain the derivative action and that the business judgment rule did not apply. Zapata appealed.

**QUILLEN, JUSTICE.** We turn first to the Court of Chancery's conclusions concerning the right of a shareholder in a derivative action. We find that its determination that a shareholder, once demand is made and refused, possesses an independent, individual right to continue a derivative suit for breaches of fiduciary duty over objection by the corporation, as an absolute rule, is erroneous. Consistent with the purpose of requiring demand, a board decision to cause a derivative suit to be dismissed, after demand has been made and refused, will be respected unless it is wrongful. In other words, when shareholders, after making demand and having their suit rejected, attack the board's decision as improper, the board's decision falls under the business judgment rule and will be respected if the requirements of the rule are met. That situation should be distinguished from the instant case, where demand was not made, and the power of the board to seek dismissal due to disqualification presents a threshold issue.

A claim of a wrongful decision not to sue is thus the first exception and first context of dispute. Absent a wrongful refusal, the shareholder simply lacks legal managerial power.

But it cannot be implied that, absent a wrongful board refusal, a shareholder can never have an individual right to initiate an action. A shareholder may sue in his derivative right to assert a cause of action in behalf of the corporation, *without prior demand* on the directors to sue, when it is apparent that a demand would be futile, that the officers are under an influence that sterilizes discretion and could not be proper persons to conduct the litigation.

These conclusions, however, do not determine the question before us. They merely bring us to the question to be decided.

Derivative suits enforce corporate rights, and any recovery obtained goes to the corporation. We see no inherent reason why the two phases of a derivative suit—the shareholder's suit to compel the corporation to sue and the corporation's suit—should automatically place in the hands of the litigating shareholder sole control of the corporate right throughout the litigation. Such an inflexible rule would recognize the interest of one person or group to the exclusion of all others within the corporate entity. Thus, we reject the view of the Vice Chancellor as to the first aspect of the issue on appeal.

The question to be decided becomes: When, if at all, should an authorized board committee be permitted to cause litigation, properly initiated by a derivative stockholder in his own right, to be dismissed? A board has the power to choose not to pursue litigation when demand is made upon it, so long as the decision is not wrongful. If the board determines that a suit would be detrimental to the company, the board's determination prevails. Even when demand is excusable, circumstances may arise when continuation of the litigation would not be in the corporation's best interests. Our inquiry is whether, under such circumstances, there is a permissible procedure under Delaware General Corporation Law Section 141(a) by which a corporation can rid itself of detrimental litigation. If there is not, a single stockholder in an extreme case might control the destiny of the entire corporation. To allow one shareholder to incapacitate an entire board of directors merely by leveling charges against them gives too much leverage to dissident shareholders. But potentials for abuse by the directors must be recognized.

Section 141(c) allows a board to delegate all of its authority to a committee. Accordingly, a committee with properly delegated authority would have the power to move for dismissal of a derivative suit if the entire board did.

The corporate power inquiry then focuses on whether the board, tainted by self-interest of a majority of its members, can legally delegate its authority to a committee of two disinterested directors. We do not think that the interest taint of the board's majority is per se a legal bar to the delegation of the board's power to an independent committee composed of disinterested board members. The committee can properly act for the corporation to move to dismiss derivative litigation that is believed to be detrimental to the corporation's best interest.

Our focus now switches to the Court of Chancery that is faced with a shareholder assertion that a derivative suit should continue for the benefit of the corporation and with an assertion made by a board committee that the same derivative suit should be dismissed.

At the risk of stating the obvious, the problem is relatively simple. If, on the one hand, corporations can consistently wrest bona fide derivative actions away from well-meaning derivative plaintiffs through the use of the committee mechanism, the derivative suit will lose much, if not all, of its effectiveness as an intracorporate means of policing boards of directors. If, on the other hand, corporations are unable to rid themselves of meritless or harmful litigation and strike suits, the derivative action, created to benefit the corporation, will produce the opposite, unintended result. It thus appears desirable to us to find a balancing point where bona fide shareholder power to bring corporate causes of action cannot be unfairly trampled on by the board of directors, but the corporation can rid itself of detrimental litigation.

The question has been treated by other courts as one of the business judgment of the board committee. These courts have held that if a committee, composed of independent and disinterested directors, conducted a proper review of the matters before it, considered a variety of factors, and reached, in good faith, a business judgment that the action was not in the best interest of the corporation, the action must be dismissed. The issues become solely independence, good faith and reasonable investigation. The ultimate conclusion of the committee, under that view, is not subject to judicial review.

We are not satisfied, however, that acceptance of the business judgment rationale at this stage of derivative litigation is a proper balancing point. There is sufficient risk in the realities of a situation like this one to justify caution beyond adherence to the theory of business judgment.

We must be mindful that directors are passing judgment on fellow directors in the same corporation and fellow directors, in this instance, who designated them to serve both as directors and committee members. The question naturally arises whether a "there but for the grace of God go I" empathy might not play a role. And the further question arises whether inquiry as to independence, good faith and reasonable investigation is sufficient safeguard against abuse, perhaps subconscious abuse.

Whether the Court of Chancery will be persuaded by the exercise of a committee power resulting in a motion for dismissal of a derivative action, where demand has not been made, should rest in the independent discretion of the Court of Chancery. We thus steer a middle course between those cases that yield to the independent business judgment of a board committee and this case as determined below, which would yield to unbridled plaintiff stockholder control.

We recognize that the final substantive judgment whether a particular lawsuit should be maintained requires a balance of many factors—ethical, commercial, promotional, public relations, employee relations, fiscal, as well as legal. We recognize the danger of judicial overreaching but the alternatives seem to us to be outweighed by the fresh view of a judicial outsider. Moreover, if we failed to balance all the interests involved, we would in the name of practicality and judicial economy foreclose a judicial decision on the merits. At this point, we are not convinced that is necessary or desirable.

After an objective and thorough investigation of a derivative suit, an independent committee may cause its corporation to file a motion to dismiss the derivative suit. The Court of Chancery should apply a two-step test to the motion.

First, the Court should inquire into the independence and good faith of the committee and the bases supporting its conclusions. The corporation should have the burden of proving independence, good faith and reasonable investigation, rather than presuming independence, good faith and reasonableness. If the Court determines either that the committee is not independent or has not shown reasonable bases for its conclusions, or if the Court is not satisfied for other reasons relating to the process, including but not limited to the good faith of the committee, the Court shall deny the corporation's motion to dismiss the derivative suit. If, however, the Court is satisfied that there is no genuine issue whether the committee was independent and showed reasonable bases for good faith findings and recommendations, the Court may proceed, in its discretion, to the next step.

The second step provides, we believe, the essential key in striking the balance between legitimate corporate claims as expressed in a derivative stockholder suit and a corporation's best interests as expressed by an independent investigating committee. The Court should determine, applying its own independent business judgment, whether the motion should be granted. The second step is intended to thwart instances where corporate actions meet the criteria of step one, but the result does not appear to satisfy its spirit, or where corporate actions would simply prematurely terminate a stockholder grievance deserving of further consideration in the corporation's interest. The Court of Chancery of course must carefully consider and weigh how compelling the corporate interest in dismissal is when faced with a non-frivolous lawsuit. The Court of Chancery should, when appropriate, give special consideration to matters of law and public policy in addition to the corporation's best interests.

This second step shares some of the same spirit and philosophy of the statement of the Vice Chancellor: "Under our system of law, courts and not litigants should decide the merits of litigation."

Judgment reversed in favor of Zapata. Case remanded to Court of Chancery for further proceedings in accordance with this opinion.

## SHAREHOLDER LIABILITY

**Introduction.** Shareholders have many responsibilities and liabilities in addition to their many rights. You have already studied some of the liabilities, such as the liability for paying too little consideration for shares and the liability for not fulfilling a subscription for shares, which were discussed in Chapter 23. Also in Chapter 23, you studied shareholder liability for corporate obligations when there is a defective attempt to incorporate. And in Chapter 22, you learned that shareholders are liable for a corporation's debts if the corporate veil is pierced. In this section, other grounds for shareholder liability are discussed.

**Shareholder Liability on Illegal Distributions.** Dividends and other distributions of a corporation's assets received by a shareholder with *knowledge of their illegality* may be recovered on behalf of the corporation. Furthermore, if the corporation was *insolvent* at the time an illegal distribution was made, the shareholder is liable for the amount of the distribution despite his lack of knowledge of the illegality.

Under MBCA Section 8.33(b), primary liability is placed on the directors who authorized the unlawful distribution. Any director against whom a claim is asserted for the wrongful distribution is entitled to contribution from shareholders who received a dividend or other distribution knowing that it was illegally declared. These liability rules enforce the asset-distribution legal capital rules that were discussed earlier in the chapter.

**Shareholder Liability for Corporate Debts.** One of the chief attributes of a shareholder is his *limited liability:* ordinarily, he has no liability for corporate obligations beyond his capital contribution. As mentioned above, however, defective incorporation and piercing the corporate veil are grounds on which a shareholder may be held liable for corporate debts beyond his capital contribution.

**Liability for Employee Wages.** In addition, a number of states at one time imposed personal liability on shareholders for *wages owed to corporate employees,* even if the shareholders had fully paid for their shares. New York and Wisconsin still impose this liability, though the liability is extremely limited. The New York corporation statute, for example, imposes liability on only the 10 largest shareholders of corporations with no publicly traded shares. Essentially, the New York statute applies only to close corporations. The purpose of the statute is to protect employees by making the social judgment that small business owners should not be able to escape liability to their employees merely by incorporating. The statute reflects the reality that the relation between the owners and the employees of a close corporation is more nearly like the relationship between a sole proprietor and his employees than like the relation between the owners and the employees of a publicly held corporation.

**Sale of a Control Block of Shares.** The per share value of the shares of a majority shareholder of a corporation is greater than the per share value of the shares of a minority shareholder. This difference in value is due to the majority shareholder's ability to control the corporation and pay herself a high salary and high dividends. Therefore, a majority shareholder can sell her shares for a *premium* over the fair market value of minority shares.

Majority ownership is not always required for control of a corporation. In a close corporation it is required, but in a publicly held corporation with a widely dispersed, hard-to-mobilize shareholder group, minority ownership of from 5 to 30 percent may be enough to obtain control. Therefore, a holder of minority control in such a corporation will also be able to receive a premium.

Noncontrolling shareholders often object when a controlling shareholder sells his shares for more money per share than the noncontrolling shareholders can obtain for their shares. Their objections may result in a suit against the controlling shareholder, asking the court to require him to share his premium with the other shareholders or to relinquish the premium to the corporation.

**Divergence of Views.** Legal scholars are divided over whether a controlling shareholder should be required to relinquish his premium merely because it was paid for a controlling block of shares. On the one hand, it is argued that shareholders are *not fiduciaries of each other.* In addition, it is said that the noncontrolling shareholders *knew* that their *shares would not be worth as much as control shares* when they became shareholders. And it is argued that *control is an inseparable element* of the ownership of a majority or large block of shares.

On the other hand, it is maintained that the value of control arises out of the *ability to dominate property* (the corporation) that *in part belongs to others.* It is also said that the premium is a *bribe* paid to the controlling shareholder to entice the controlling shareholder to sell—in effect—the corporation cheaply.

**Legality of the Premium.** Current corporation law imposes no liability on any shareholder, whether or not the shareholder is a controlling shareholder, *merely* because she is able to sell her shares for a premium. Nevertheless, if the premium is accompanied by wrongdoing, controlling shareholders have been held liable either for the amount of the premium or for the damages suffered by the corporation. There are four grounds on which the courts have found liability.

**Selling to Persons Who Will Harm the Corporation.** A seller of control shares is liable for selling to a purchaser who harms the corporation if the seller had or should have had a *reasonable suspicion* that the purchaser would mismanage or loot the corporation. The seller is liable to the corporation for the harm caused.

In one case, for example, the sellers' knowledge of facts indicating the purchasers' *history of mismanagement and personal use of corporate assets* obligated them not to sell to the purchasers.[12] A seller may also be placed on notice of a purchaser's bad motives by other factors, such as the purchaser's *lack of interest in the physical facilities* of the corporation and the purchaser's great *interest in the liquid assets* of the corporation. These factors tend to indicate that the purchaser has a short-term interest in the corporation.

The mere payment of a premium is not enough to put the seller on notice. If the *premium is unduly high,* however, such as a $43.75 offer for shares traded in the $7–10 range, a seller must doubt whether the purchaser will be able to recoup his investment without looting the corporation.[13]

When a seller has, or should have, a reasonable suspicion that a purchaser will mismanage or loot the corporation, he must make a *reasonable investigation* prior to selling to the purchaser. Unless a reasonably adequate investigation discloses such facts as would convince a reasonable person that no wrongdoing is intended or likely to result, he may not sell to the purchaser. If the selling shareholder has no suspicion, and should not have any suspicion, he has no duty to investigate the purchaser and may sell to the purchaser.

**Resignations of Directors.** Sometimes, a contract for the sale of control will obligate the seller to *replace the present directors* with nominees of the purchaser. It is illegal to sell a corporate office or directorship. Some courts have held that the premium for control shares was paid for directorships and required the seller to return the premium to the corporation.[14] Other courts have recognized the inevitability of the purchaser's electing his own directors and allow the seller to retain the premium.[15]

---

[12] *DeBaun v. First Western Bank & Trust Co.,* 120 Cal. Rptr. 354 (Cal. Ct. App. 1975).

[13] *Clagett v. Hutchinson,* 583 F.2d 1259 (4th Cir. 1978).

[14] E.g., *In re Caplan,* 246 N.Y.S.2d 913 (N.Y. App. Div. 1964). The court could find no proof that the amount of shares sold—3 percent of the outstanding shares—was enough to give the purchaser the ability to effect a change in the directors in the absence of the resignation agreement.

[15] E.g., *Essex Universal Corp. v. Yates,* 305 F.2d 572 (2d Cir. 1962).

**Sale of Corporate Asset.** Borrowing from the principles that apply to the usurpation of a corporate opportunity, a few courts have found liability when the selling shareholder takes or sells a *corporate asset.* For example, if the purchaser wants to buy the corporation's assets and the controlling shareholder proposes that the purchaser buy her shares instead, the controlling shareholder is liable for usurping a corporate opportunity.

A more unusual situation existed in *Perlman v. Feldman.*[16] In that case, Newport Steel Corporation had excess demand for its steel production, due to the Korean War. Another corporation, in order to guarantee a steady supply of steel, bought at a premium a minority, yet controlling, block of shares of Newport from Feldman, its chairman and president. The court ruled that Feldman was required to share the premium with the other shareholders because he had sold a corporate asset—the excess demand for steel. The court reasoned that Newport could have exploited that asset to its advantage.

The case is unusual for at least two reasons. First, the court intentionally left unclear whether Feldman would have been liable if he had been only the controlling shareholder and not the chairman or president. Hence, it is impossible to determine whether the duty here is a manager's or a shareholder's duty. Second, although the suit was a derivative suit, the court awarded the premium not to the corporation, but to the minority shareholders. The court rationalized this holding on the ground that it did not want the purchasing corporation, which was now a shareholder of Newport, to share indirectly in the premium. The case has been heavily criticized, but it remains the law in its jurisdiction.

[16] 219 F.2d 173 (2d Cir. 1955).

**Oppression of Minority Shareholders.** A few courts have recognized the duty of controlling shareholders, especially in a close corporation, to use their ability to control the corporation in a fair, just, and equitable manner that benefits all of the shareholders proportionately. This is in part a duty to be impartial, that is, not to prefer themselves over the minority shareholders. For example, controlling shareholders have an obligation not to cause the corporation to buy their shares at a price that is not made available to minority shareholders.

This duty of controlling shareholders is similar to the duty of managers not to oppress minority shareholders, which was discussed in Chapter 24. Often, it is difficult to determine in a particular case whether the court is imposing a duty on the managers or on the controlling shareholders, since both are nearly always the same people. Some carefully written court opinions, however, such as *Jones v. H. F. Ahmanson & Co.,* which follows, clearly indicate that the duty belongs to the controlling shareholders.[17]

**Close Corporation Statutes.** Some statutes, such as Section 11 of the Statutory Close Corporation Supplement to the MBCA, permit close corporation shareholders to dispense with a board of directors or to arrange corporate affairs as if the corporation were a partnership. The effect of these statutes is to impose management responsibilities, including the fiduciary duties of directors, on the shareholders. In essence, the shareholders are partners and owe each other fiduciary duties similar to those owed between partners.

[17] Some scholars classify *Jones v. H. F. Ahmanson & Co.* as a sale of control case that grounds liability on the controlling shareholders' failure to be impartial. Since partiality is one manifestation of oppression, the case is included here under the heading of oppression of minority shareholders.

## Jones v. H. F. Ahmanson & Co.

**460 P.2d 464 (Cal. Sup. Ct. 1969)**

United Savings and Loan Association of California (the Association) converted from a depositor-owned to a stockholder-owned savings institution in 1956. Of the 6,568 shares issued, 987 (14.8 percent) were purchased by depositors, including June Jones. After the conversion, H. F. Ahmanson & Co. became the controlling shareholder. The Association retained most of its earnings in reserves, so that the book value of the shares increased to several times their 1956 value. Because the shares had a high book value and were closely held, there was little buying and selling of shares. The few sales made were mostly among existing shareholders.

In 1958, due to great investor demand, publicly traded savings and loan shares were enjoying a steady increase in market price. To take advantage of this opportunity for profit, Ahmanson and a few other shareholders of the Association incorporated United Financial Corporation of California in 1959 and exchanged each of their Association shares for a "derived block" of 250 shares in United. United then owned more than 85 percent of the shares of the Association. The minority shareholders of the Association, including June Jones, were not given an opportunity to exchange their shares.

In 1960 and 1961, United made two public offerings of its shares. Part of the proceeds of one offering was distributed to the original United shareholders, that is, the former majority shareholders of the Association, resulting in a return of capital of $927.50 for each "derived block."

By mid-1961, trading in United shares was very active, while sales of Association shares decreased to half of the formerly low level, with United as virtually the only purchaser. In 1960, United had offered to purchase Association shares from the minority shareholders for $1,100 per share. Some of the minority shareholders accepted this offer. At that time, each "derived block" held by the majority shareholders was worth $3,700.

The Association had paid extra dividends of $75 and $57 per share in 1959 and 1960, but in 1961 United caused the Association president to announce to the minority shareholders that in the near future only the $4 regular dividend would be paid. Later that year, United proposed to exchange 51 United shares for each Association share. Each block of 51 United shares had a market value of $2,400, a book value of $210, and earnings of $134. Each Association share had a book value of over $1,700 per share and earnings of $651 per share. At this time, each "derived block" held by former majority shareholders in the Association had a market value of $8,800.

June Jones sued the former majority shareholders, including Ahmanson, claiming that they had breached the fiduciary duty owed to the minority shareholders. The majority shareholders argued that they owed no fiduciary duty to the minority shareholders. The trial court agreed that no duty was owed and held for the majority shareholders. Jones appealed.

**Traynor, Chief Justice.** Defendants take the position that as shareholders they owe no fiduciary obligation to other shareholders, absent reliance on inside information, use of corporate assets, or fraud. This view has long been repudiated in California. The Courts of Appeal have often recognized that majority shareholders, either singly or acting in concert to accomplish a joint purpose, have a fiduciary responsibility to the minority and to the corporation to use their ability to control the corporation in a fair, just, and equitable manner. Majority shareholders may not use their power to control corporate activities to benefit themselves alone or in a manner detrimental to the minority. Any use to which they put the corporation or their power to control the corporation must benefit all shareholders proportionately and must not conflict with the proper conduct of the corporation's business.

The majority shareholders maintain that they made full disclosure of the circumstances surrounding the formation of United, that the creation of United and its share offers in no way affected the control of the Association, that the minority shareholders' proportionate interest in the Association was not affected, that the Association was not harmed, and that the market for Association shares was not affected. Therefore, they conclude, they have breached no fiduciary duty to Jones and the other minority shareholders.

The majority shareholders would have us retreat from a position demanding equitable treatment of all shareholders by those exercising control over a corporation. The rule that has developed in California is a comprehensive rule of "inherent fairness from the viewpoint of the corporation and those interested therein." The rule applies alike to officers, directors, and controlling shareholders in the exercise of powers that are theirs by virtue of their position and to transactions wherein controlling shareholders seek to gain an advantage in the sale or transfer of use of their controlling block of shares.

Thus, we have held that majority shareholders do not have an absolute right to dissolve a corporation, although ostensibly permitted to do so by the California General Corporation Law, because their statutory power is subject to equitable limitations in favor of the minority. We recognized that the majority had the right to dissolve a corporation to protect their investment *if* no alternative means were available *and* no advantage was secured over other shareholders, and noted that there is nothing sacred in the life of a corporation that transcends the interests of its shareholders, but because dissolution falls with such finality on those interests, above all corporate powers it is subject to equitable limitations.

The increasingly complex transactions of the business and financial communities demonstrate the inadequacy of the traditional theories of fiduciary obligation as tests of majority shareholder responsibility to the minority. These theories have failed to afford adequate protection to minority shareholders and particularly to those in close corporations whose disadvantageous and often precarious position renders them particularly vulnerable to the vagaries of the majority. Although the courts have recognized the potential for abuse or unfair advantage when a shareholder sells his shares at a premium over investment value [citing *Perlman v. Feldman* (1955)] or in a controlling shareholder's use of control to avoid equitable distribution of corporate assets [citing *Zahn v. Transamerica Corp.* (1947)], no comprehensive rule has emerged outside California. Nor have most commentators approached the problem from a perspective other than that of the advantage gained in the sale of control.

The case before us, in which no sale or transfer of actual control is directly involved, demonstrates that injury can be inflicted with impunity under the traditional rules and supports our conclusion that the comprehensive rule of good faith and inherent fairness to the minority in any transaction where control of the corporation is material properly governs controlling shareholders in this state.

The majority shareholders created United during a period of unusual investor interest in the shares of savings and loan associations. Two courses were available to the majority in their effort to exploit the bull market in savings and loan shares. The first was either to cause the Association to effect a stock split and create a market for the Association shares or to create a holding company for Association shares and permit all shareholders to exchange their shares before offering holding company shares to the public. All shareholders would have benefited alike had this been done. The second course was taken by the majority shareholders. It appears that the market created for United was a market that would have been available for Association shares had the majority taken the first course of action.

After United shares became available to the public, it became a virtual certainty that no equivalent market could or would be created for Association shares. Thus, the majority shareholders chose a course of action in which they used their control of the Association to obtain an advantage not made available to all shareholders. They did so without regard to the resulting detriment to the minority shareholders and in the absence of any compelling business purpose.

Had defendants afforded the minority an opportunity to exchange their shares on the same basis or offered to purchase them at a price arrived at by independent appraisal, their burden of establishing good faith and inherent fairness would have been much less. At the trial, they may present evidence tending to show such good faith or compelling business purpose that would render their action fair under the circumstances. On appeal, we decide only that the majority shareholders owed a duty to the minority. We do not decide whether the duty was breached.

In so holding, we do not suggest that the duties of corporate fiduciaries include in all cases an obligation to make a market for and to facilitate public trading in the stock of the corporation. But when, as here, no market exists, the controlling shareholders may not use their power to control the corporation for the purpose of promoting a marketing scheme that benefits themselves alone to the detriment of the minority. Nor do we suggest that a control block of shares may not be sold or transferred to a holding company. We decide only that the circumstances of any transfer of controlling shares will be subject to judicial scrutiny when it appears that the controlling shareholders may have breached their fiduciary obligation to the corporation or the remaining shareholders.

If, after trial, Jones proves the majority has breached its duty to the minority shareholders, she will be entitled to receive at her election either the appraised value of her shares on the date the majority shareholders exchanged their shares for the United shares with interest, or a sum equivalent to the fair market value of a "derived block" of United shares on the date she brought this suit with interest and the sum of $927.50 (the public issue proceeds distributed to the majority shareholders) with interest, for each Association share.

Judgment reversed in favor of Jones.

## SUMMARY

Shareholders have a number of rights but few responsibilities. Shareholders have a right to attend annual and special shareholders' meetings. Most of the corporation statutes establish a majority of the shares as the quorum for a meeting. Who is to preside at the meeting is usually established by the bylaws.

At meetings, all shareholders have the right to vote, unless the articles of incorporation remove that right. Shareholders elect and remove directors, amend the articles of incorporation, and vote on mergers, share exchanges, sales of all or substantially all the assets, and dissolutions. Shareholders have the right to offer resolutions and to comment and ask questions at shareholders' meetings. A shareholder who dissents to certain matters approved by the shareholders may seek appraisal of her shares.

Many of the states require corporations to permit cumulative voting for the election of directors. Most of the other states permit cumulative voting if it is provided for in the articles. Class voting is also permitted. Cumulative voting and class voting are two means by which shareholders may allocate control of a corporation. In addition, shareholders may use voting trusts, shareholder voting agreements, and irrevocable proxies to obtain control of a corporation.

Corporation statutes usually specify the sources from which cash or property dividends may be paid to shareholders and the rules for share repurchases, share dividends, and share splits. The MBCA requires that a dividend payment not make the corporation insolvent or reduce the assets of a corporation below the corporation's liabilities and liquidation preferences. The declaration of dividends is the responsibility of the directors and is protected by the business judgment rule.

Corporate repurchases of shares are also distributions of assets to shareholders. The MBCA treats repurchases in the same way as it treats dividends. A share dividend is a distribution of additional shares in the corporation. Under the MBCA, only director action is necessary to make a share dividend of the same class of shares. The MBCA treats a share split in the same way as it treats a share dividend.

The right of a shareholder to inspect the records of the corporation depends on the corporation statute. The MBCA gives the shareholder an absolute right to inspect the shareholder list and the right to inspect other records for a proper purpose.

The common law gave shareholders a preemptive right to buy a proportionate share of additional shares that the corporation planned to sell. Today, many states permit corporations to avoid the preemptive right.

There are three types of shareholder lawsuits. Shareholders may bring actions in their own names to redress or to prevent a breach of their shareholder contract. They may bring a class action representing themselves and other shareholders who are similarly harmed as individual shareholders. They may also bring derivative suits on behalf of the corporation if the directors fail to sue. However, the board's decision not to sue is protected by the business judgment rule. Any judgment awarded in a derivative suit goes to the corporation, not to the complaining shareholder.

A shareholder is liable for an illegally paid dividend if the shareholder knows of the illegality or if the corporation is insolvent. In a very few states, shareholders may be liable for employees' wages. Under certain circumstances, controlling shareholders will be liable to the corporation or to minority shareholders for selling their shares at a premium above the market price of the shares. Controlling shareholders may be liable for oppressing minority shareholders.

## PROBLEM CASES

1. Quigley owned 1,750 of the 3,705 outstanding shares of stock in Levisa Oil Corporation. At the annual shareholders' meeting, the management proposed increasing the number of directors from four to five. Quigley and another shareholder, who together owned more than 50 percent of the shares, considered the proposal contrary to their interests. When Quigley was ruled out of order by the

chairman of the meeting, she and the other shareholder walked out. After they left, the remaining shareholders elected a five-member board. The new board then voted to issue 250 additional shares. These were sold to the wife of a shareholder who, like Quigley, owned 1,750 shares. This gave the shareholder and his wife control of the corporation.

Quigley sued, claiming that all actions taken after she left the meeting, including the election of the directors, were invalid for lack of a quorum. Is her position correct?

**2.** Musselman and Hall Contractors, Inc., was a Missouri corporation whose shares were owned in equal proportions by Edward and Harry Hall. They were the only directors. Edward died, and his shares went to his widow, Margaret Hall. However, Harry Hall filled the vacancy on the board by appointing his wife, Florence Hall. As directors, they then elected Harry president and Florence vice president—the only corporate officers.

Harry and Florence did not call an annual shareholders' meeting for the date specified in the bylaws, so Margaret did. Margaret appeared at the scheduled time at the registered office of the corporation, but Harry did not. Since a quorum was not present, directors could not be elected and Harry and Florence continued in office. Margaret then brought an action seeking to enjoin Harry from refusing to attend shareholders' meetings. Should the court require Harry to attend?

**3.** Giant Foods, Inc., a supermarket operator, was incorporated by N. M. Cohen and Samuel Lehrman in 1935. It was controlled by the Cohen and Lehrman families. Each family owned an equal number of voting shares and elected two directors. The Cohens held Class AC shares, and the Lehrmans held Class AL shares. Following Samuel's death, in 1949, a third class of voting shares, Class AD common, was created with power to elect the fifth director but with no right to dividends or to a share in the assets upon liquidation. This class of shares was redeemable by the corporation upon payment of the par value. It was created solely to prevent a deadlock of the directors. Only one Class AD share was authorized, and it was issued to Joseph Danzansky, who had served as legal counsel to the firm since 1944. He was elected the fifth director and regularly participated in corporate meetings.

No deadlock arose until 1964. Then, a resolution, passed with the votes of the AC and AD shares, gave Danzansky a 15-year employment contract with the corporation and options for 25,000 nonvoting common shares. The two Lehrman directors voted against this resolution. When Danzansky was then elected president, Jacob Lehrman sued, claiming that the issuance and voting of the one share of Class AD stock was a voting trust and illegal because it was not limited to 10 years as required by Delaware's voting trust statute. Was the arrangement an illegal voting trust?

**4.** Autohaus on Edens, Inc., was incorporated in 1972 in Illinois to sell and service new and used automobiles. Joseph and Ralph Rosengarden each purchased 40 percent of its shares, and Leonard Wasserman bought 20 percent.

The shareholders made an oral agreement that they would vote for each other as directors and officers and that they would receive equal salaries and any distributed profits as long as they remained shareholders. Wasserman was elected vice president and general manager.

After five years, the Rosengardens informed Wasserman that he was being ousted from the corporation and would not receive any future salaries or distributed profits. He was denied access to the premises of the corporation. He then sued for remuneration under the shareholders' agreement, for an accounting, and for dissolution of the corporation. The

Rosengardens' defense was that the agreement was void as a shareholders' agreement and was merely an employment contract of unspecified duration that they could terminate without liability at any time. Is Wasserman entitled to continue to receive one third of the salaries and distributed profits?

**5.** Golden agreed in January with the president of Oahe Enterprises, Inc., to transfer farming and ranching equipment to Oahe in exchange for shares. As part of the transaction, he became a director and secretary-treasurer of the corporation. A certificate for 387 shares was executed but not delivered to Golden. In July, Golden tendered his resignation as an officer and director and expressed his desire to withdraw as a shareholder and to receive cash for his equipment. After negotiations, a value for the equipment and its use was set at $16,922.32, and then Golden agreed to accept 338.64 shares as an alternative. A certificate for shares in that amount was executed in December but retained by the corporation.

Later, the corporation sued Golden for fraud in the farm equipment transaction. Golden cross-claimed with a demand for stock of a value of $16,922.32. In the meantime, the president of Oahe Enterprises sold all of the corporation's assets without notice to Golden or shareholder approval. When Golden learned of the sale a year later, he sued to obtain possession of the stock certificate and to have the sale of the corporate assets set aside. The corporation's defense was that Golden was not a shareholder. It argued that even if he were a shareholder, his only remedy was to petition for appraisal of his shares, which he had failed to do within the statutory period. Is Golden a shareholder? If so, should the sale of the corporate assets be set aside?

**6.** A Plan and Agreement of Reorganization between Rath Packing Company, an Iowa corporation, and Needham Packing Company, a Delaware corporation, called for a transfer of all of Needham's assets to Rath. In addition, Rath would issue 5.5 Rath common shares and two newly created Rath preferred shares in exchange for each five Needham shares. Lastly, Rath would change its name to Rath-Needham Corporation. Upon execution of the plan, Needham shareholders would control 54 percent of the common shares of the Rath-Needham Corporation if the preferred shares were converted. The book value of Rath common shares would be reduced from $27.99 to $15.93, while Needham shareholders would have the book value of their holdings, assuming conversion of preferred shares, increased to $23.90 from $6.61.

The Iowa corporation statute required an affirmative vote of two thirds of the shares to accomplish a merger, but only a majority for an amendment to the articles, which could include a change of corporate name and the establishment of new classes of securities. The plan involved several amendments to Rath's articles, but it was not designated a merger and it did not follow the statutory procedure for a merger. Of the outstanding Rath shares, 61 percent were voted in favor of the plan (77 percent of the shares voted). If the plan was a merger, the number of votes was insufficient for shareholder approval. If the plan merely required an amendment of the articles, the number of votes was sufficient. Was the plan a merger, and did it therefore have to be approved by two thirds of the Rath shares?

**7.** Certain shareholders of Endicott Johnson Corporation dissented from the merger of Endicott into McDonough Corporation and sought court appraisal of their shares. In determining the fair value of the shares, the trial court relied on an appraiser who eliminated market value as a meaningful factor, on the grounds that earnings before 1969 were not helpful due to a radical management change that year, while earnings after 1969 were nearly meaningless due to McDonough's ownership of a significant number of Endicott shares. The trial court accepted the appraiser's valuation of $45.75 per share.

Endicott Johnson appealed, arguing that market value should have been given substantial weight. The average market price in public trading had been $26.25 per share for the six months immediately prior to the merger; McDonough had owned only 31.8 percent of the shares during some of that period; and there were more than 2,000 other shareholders. The dissenting shareholders, on the other hand, proved that the Endicott shares had been delisted by the NYSE and were traded only over-the-counter and that prior to the merger McDonough had acquired 70 percent of the shares. Should the court's determination of fair value be affirmed on appeal?

8. Raymond Miller and Don Law were the founders of Magline, Inc. John Thorpe joined the corporation as an officer and director shortly thereafter. In 1962, Miller was injured seriously and stopped his active participation in the company. Thorpe resigned as an officer in the same year. Both Miller and Thorpe, however, continued to be shareholders and directors. Law, who had served as president from the beginning, and four other officers and directors owned 59 percent of Magline's shares. Miller and Thorpe owned 41 percent of the shares.

In 1950, Law, Miller, and Thorpe had established a policy of paying the Magline officers low salaries supplemented by bonuses based on a percentage of the company's earnings and retaining the other profits in the company. In 1962, the directors set the total bonuses for the officers at 23 percent of the corporation's profits. The next directors' meeting was not held until 1966. During the intervening period, the corporation's profits had increased dramatically. Magline's profits from 1964 through 1969 were the highest in its history. As a result, the base salaries of officers were increased in 1966 and the bonus percentage was reduced to 14½ percent of company earnings. At a second board meeting in 1966, this bonus percentage was continued for 1967, with Miller and Thorpe abstaining from the vote. Their motions to declare a $10 per share dividend were defeated in 1966, 1967, and 1968.

Law's total compensation as president was $10,016 in 1962. It reached $137,558 in 1965, then dropped to $75,402 after the bonus percentages were reduced in 1966. It was $120,183 in 1967, and $107,887 in 1968. From 1963 to 1968, Magline's earned surplus account increased from $459,710 to $2,492,156. At the end of the 1968–69 fiscal year, Magline had current assets totaling $2,959,732, including $343,980 in cash. Miller and Thorpe sued Magline and the other directors to force the payment of dividends. Should the court order the payment of dividends?

9. Ormand Industries, Inc., a Delaware corporation operating in California, had a division in the outdoor advertising business. Ormand Industries was controlled by Jarrell Ormand, the chairman of the board and chief executive officer, who together with his family owned 20 percent of the stock.

H. P. Skoglund had bought and sold several outdoor advertising companies. He was a major shareholder in such a company operated by Barry Ackerley in Seattle, Washington. Skoglund began to buy Ormand Industries shares in 1972, and Ackerley began to do so in 1975. They acquired approximately 4.7 percent of the shares. Based on their experience in the industry and an analysis of Ormand Industries' annual reports, Skoglund and Ackerley believed that Ormand Industries was being mismanaged or perhaps looted by its management. They met with Jarrell Ormand and told him that they intended to remove him and his family from the management.

They demanded the right to inspect the corporate books and financial records. They based their demand on several grounds. First, they believed that the net profits were unreasonably low and that the cost of advertising space to Ormand Industries was far out of line with the industry averages. Second, they alleged that the corporation had purchased another business from Jarrell Ormand and had later resold it at a loss of $500,000 to Ormand Industries. Another ground for their demand was that Jarrell Ormand had purchased additional stock in the corporation at a very low price. In addition, they had been told by Robert Brunson, the former president of Ormand Industries' outdoor advertising division, that corporate funds and employees were used for the personal benefit of Jarrell Ormand and his family. Moreover, seven members of the Ormand family were on the corporate payroll, some of whom Skoglund and Ackerley believed contributed little in the way of services.

Ormand Industries denied the demand for inspection on the ground that Skoglund and Ackerley were competitors. It alleged that the demand was made in bad faith as a device to obtain control of the company. It also argued that the demand was too broad. Must Skoglund and Ackerley be permitted to inspect Ormand Industries' books and records?

**10.** In 1976, Control Data Corporation (CDC) voluntarily disclosed to its shareholders and the Securities and Exchange Commission, after conducting its own internal investigation, that the company had made illegal payments to foreign governments during an earlier period. The Justice Department then filed criminal charges against the corporation. CDC pleaded guilty and paid $1,381,000 in civil and criminal penalties.

Abbey, a shareholder of CDC, sued the directors of CDC, alleging mismanagement and waste of corporate assets. As a result of the lawsuit, the board of directors created a Special Litigation Committee to investigate the charges. It consisted of CDC's seven nonofficer directors, all of whom held responsible positions in business or government. None of them had been named as a defendant in the suit, and there was no indication that any of them had had knowledge of the illegal foreign payments when these were made. The committee retained a law firm that had not previously served CDC, and it conducted an investigation of the charges.

The committee concluded that legal action against the defendants could significantly impair their ability to manage corporate affairs and that the illegal foreign payments were a customary business practice at the time they were made and were intended to serve the business interests of CDC. For these and other reasons, it decided to dismiss the suit. Is the committee's decision protected by the business judgment rule?

# Chapter 26

# Securities Regulation

## INTRODUCTION

**Background.** Modern securities regulation arose from the rubble of the great stock market crash of October 1929. After the crash, Congress studied its causes and discovered that several abuses were prevalent in securities transactions, the most important ones being:

1. Investors lacked the necessary information to make intelligent decisions on whether to buy, sell, or hold securities.
2. Disreputable sellers of securities made outlandish claims about the expected performance of securities and sold securities in nonexistent companies.

Faced with these perceived abuses, Congress was presented with a choice of regulatory schemes: (1) require securities sellers to obtain federal administrative agency approval of the securities that are to be sold, or (2) require securities sellers to disclose the information that investors need in order to make intelligent investment decisions.

The first scheme, called *merit registration,* had been chosen by most of the states that had specifically regulated transactions in securities. The basis of merit registration is the belief that investors cannot distinguish between good and bad investments. On the other hand, the second scheme is based on the *disclosure of relevant information.* It assumes that investors are able to make intelligent investment decisions if they are given sufficient information about the company whose securities they are to buy. The disclosure scheme assumes that investors need assistance from government in acquiring information but that they need no help in evaluating information.

**Disclosure Scheme.** Congress rejected merit registration and chose the disclosure scheme. In the early 1930s, Congress passed two major statutes, which remain essentially unchanged and are the hub of federal securities regulation in the United States today. These two statutes, the *Securities Act of 1933* and the *Securities Exchange Act of 1934,* have three basic purposes:

1. To require the disclosure of meaningful information about a security and its issuer[1] so as to allow investors to make intelligent investment decisions.
2. To establish liability for those who make inadequate and erroneous disclosures of information.
3. To require the registration of issuers, insiders, professional sellers of securities, securities exchanges, and other self-regulatory securities organizations.

The most important of these purposes is the first. The crux of the securities acts is to impose upon issuers of securities, other sellers of securities, and selected buyers of securities the *affirmative duty* to disclose important information, even if they are not asked by investors to make the disclosures. This is a dramatic departure from the law of contracts and torts that was applied to securities transactions before 1933. Contract law and tort law essentially require only that sellers or buyers of securities not defraud investors (1) by materially misstating facts or (2) by failing to disclose material facts when a fiduciary or other duty runs from the seller or the buyer to the investor with whom she is transacting.

**Function of Disclosure.** Why require affirmative disclosure in securities transactions when our laws rarely require such disclosure in other contexts? There are three reasons. First, unlike a tangible good such as an automobile, a security is intangible. Its characteristics and quality can not be ascertained by an examination of the physical evidence of the security, the security certificate. A car buyer can look under the hood of a car or kick its tires, but no similar physical examination of a security is possible. Second, while investors can ask questions of issuers and sellers of securities, few do so or are able to do so, either because they have no access to the issuers or because they do not know what questions to ask. Third and most important, Congress wanted to restore investor confidence in the securities markets. By requiring disclosure, Congress hoped to bolster investor confidence in the honesty of the stock market and thus to encourage more investors to invest in securities. Building investor confidence would increase capital formation and, it was hoped, stimulate the depressed American economy.

**Securities Act of 1933.** The Securities Act of 1933 (1933 Act) is concerned primarily with *public distributions* of securities. That is, the 1933 Act regulates the sale of securities while they are passing from the *hands of the issuer into the hands of the public investors.* An is-

[1] An issuer is the person whose obligation is represented by the security. For example, General Motors is the issuer of its common stock.

suer selling securities publicly must make necessary disclosures at the time the issuer sells the securities to the public. The 1933 Act is chiefly a *onetime disclosure* statute. Although some of the 1933 Act liability provisions cover all fraudulent sales of securities, the mandatory disclosure provisions apply *only during a public distribution* of securities by the issuer and those assisting the issuer.

**Securities Exchange Act of 1934.** By contrast, the mandatory disclosure provisions of the Securities Exchange Act of 1934 (1934 Act) require *periodic disclosures* by issuers of securities. An *issuer with publicly traded equity securities* must report annually and quarterly to its shareholders. Any other material information about the issuer must be disclosed as the issuer obtains it, unless the issuer has a valid business purpose for withholding disclosure.

**Securities and Exchange Commission.** The Securities and Exchange Commission (SEC) was created by the 1934 Act. Its responsibility is to administer the 1933 and 1934 acts and five other securities statutes. Like other federal administrative agencies, the SEC has legislative, executive, and judicial functions. Its legislative branch promulgates rules and regulations; its executive branch brings enforcement actions against alleged violators of the securities statutes and their rules and regulations; its judicial branch decides whether a person has violated the securities statutes.

## WHAT IS A SECURITY?

The first question to consider is the definition of a security. If a transaction involves no security, then the law of securities regulation does not apply. The 1933 Act defines the term *security* broadly:

> Unless the context otherwise requires . . . the term "security" means any note, stock, . . . bond, debenture, evidence of indebtedness, certificate of interest of participation in any profit-sharing agreement, . . . preorganization certificate or subscription, . . . investment contract, voting trust certificate, . . . fractional undivided interest in oil, gas, or mineral rights, . . . or, in general, any interest or instrument commonly known as a "security". . . .

The 1934 Act definition excludes notes and drafts that mature not more than nine months from the date of issuance.

**Investment Contract.** These definitions of a security include many contracts that the general public may believe are not securities. This is because the term *investment contract* is broadly defined by the courts. The Supreme Court's three-part test for an investment contract, called the *Howey* test,[2] has been the guiding beacon in the area for the past 40 years. The test states that an investment contact is an *investment of money* in a *common enterprise* with an *expectation of profits solely from the efforts of others.*

**An Investment of Money.** The purchaser must have an *investment motive,* not a consumption motive (as with the purchase of a membership in a country club) or a commercial motive (as with a bank lending money to a corporate creditor).

**A Common Enterprise.** The fortunes of the investors must be *similarly affected* by the efforts of the investment promoters or managers.

**An Expectation of Profits from the Efforts of Others.** The undeniably *significant efforts* that determine the success or failure of the venture must be those of the investment

[2] *SEC v. W. J. Howey Co.,* 328 U.S. 293 (U.S. Sup. Ct. 1946).

promoters or managers, not those of the investors.

**Examples.** In the *Howey* case, the sales of plots in an orange grove along with a management contract were held to be sales of securities. The purchasers had investment motives (they did not consume the oranges produced by the trees). They were similarly affected by the efforts of the sellers who grew and sold the oranges. The sellers, not the buyers, did all of the work needed to make the plots profitable. In other cases, sales of limited partnerships, Scotch whisky receipts, livestock with agreements to care for them, and restaurant franchises have been held to constitute investment contracts and therefore securities.

**Economic Realities Test.** In recent years, the courts have used the *Howey* test to hold that contracts with typical security names are not securities. Using an *economic realities test,* the courts point out that these contracts possess few of the typical characteristics of a security. For example, in the *Forman* case, which follows, the Supreme Court held that although the interest of a cooperative apartment tenant was denoted as stock, it was not a security, because the economic realities of the transaction bore few similarities to those of the typical stock sale and the *Howey* test was not met.

**Sale-of-Business Doctrine.** A few federal courts of appeals have held that the sale of 100 percent of the shares of a corporation is not the sale of securities. Examining the economic realities, these courts have ruled that in such a transaction the transfer of securities certificates is a mere formality and that the substance of the transaction is the sale of a business. In addition, these courts have held that the *Howey* test is not met, because the buyer, not the seller, is expected to manage the business. Therefore, the securities laws are not needed to protect the buyer.

**Rejection by Supreme Court.** In May 1985, however, the Supreme Court of the United States rejected the sale-of-business doctrine in two cases, one case involving the privately negotiated sale of 50 percent of the shares of a corporation[3] and the other case involving the privately negotiated sale of 100 percent of a corporation's shares.[4] The Court found that the shares bore all the characteristics of common stock. It therefore refused to apply the *Howie* test. On policy grounds, the court justified its decisions by pointing out the difficulty of determining what percentage sale of shares is needed to invoke the sale-of-business doctrine.

[3] *Gould v. Ruefenacht,* 53 U.S.L.W. 4607 (May 28, 1985).

[4] *Landreth Timber Co. v. Landreth,* 53 U.S.L.W. 4602 (May 28, 1985).

## United Housing Foundation, Inc. v. Forman

**421 U.S. 837 (U.S. Sup. Ct. 1975)**

Co-op City is a massive, state-subsidized housing cooperative in the Bronx, New York. To acquire an apartment in Co-op City, a tenant must buy 18 shares of stock in Riverbay Corporation, a nonprofit cooperative housing corporation, for each room desired. The sole purpose of acquiring these shares is to enable the tenant to occupy an apartment in Co-op City. The shares cannot be transferred to a nontenant or used as collateral for debts. They can be willed only to a surviving spouse. No voting rights attach to the shares, since the tenant of each apartment is entitled to only one vote regardless of the number of shares he owns. Any tenant who moves out must sell his stock to Riverbay at its initial purchase price. If Riverbay is unable to repurchase the shares, the tenant may sell the shares only to a prospective tenant at no profit.

In May 1965, Riverbay circulated an Information Bulletin in an effort to attract tenants. The Bulletin stated that Riverbay's mortgage payments and current operating expenses would be met by monthly rental charges paid by the tenants. The Bulletin estimated the average monthly cost at $23 per room.

Due to increased construction costs, Riverbay was required to secure larger mortgage loans. As a result, the average monthly rental charges increased periodically, reaching an amount of $40 a room by July 1974.

Forman and other Co-op City tenants sued Riverbay and others under two securities antifraud provisions, Section 10(b) of the Securities Exchange Act of 1934 and Section 17(a) of the Securities Act of 1933, asking for $30 million in damages and other remedies. The tenants claimed that the Information Bulletin falsely represented that a Riverbay subsidiary would bear all cost increases arising from such factors as inflation. The tenants alleged that they were misled in their purchases of shares, since the Bulletin failed to disclose several important facts.

Riverbay claimed that the securities laws did not apply, because there was no purchase or sale of a security. The district court held in favor of Riverbay, finding that no security was involved in the transactions. The court of appeals reversed this decision, ruling in favor of the tenants and holding that the stock was a security. Riverbay appealed.

**POWELL, JUSTICE.** As we conclude that the disputed transactions are not purchases of securities within the contemplation of the federal statutes, we reverse.

We reject at the outset any suggestion that the present transaction must be considered a security transaction simply because the statutory definition of a security includes the words "any stock." In searching for the meaning and scope of the word security in the Acts, form should be disregarded for substance and the emphasis should be on economic reality. Congress intended the application of these statutes to turn on the economic realities underlying a transaction, and not on the name appended thereto.

In holding that the name given to an instrument is not dispositive, we do not suggest that the name is wholly irrelevant to the decision whether it is a security. There may be occasions when the use of a traditional name such as stocks or bonds will lead a purchaser justifiably to assume that the federal securities laws apply. This would clearly be the case when the underlying transaction embodies some of the significant characteristics typically associated with the named instrument.

In the present case, the tenants do not contend that they were misled by the use of the word stock into believing that the federal securities laws governed their purchase. Common sense suggests that people who intend to acquire only a residential apartment in a state-subsidized cooperative, for their personal use, are not likely to believe that in reality they are purchasing investment securities simply because the transaction is evidenced by something called a share of stock. These shares have none of the characteristics that in our commercial world fall within the ordinary concept of a security. They lack the most common feature of stock: the right to receive dividends contingent upon an apportionment of profits. Nor do they possess the other characteristics traditionally associated with stock: they are not negotiable; they cannot be pledged or hypothecated; they confer no voting rights in proportion to the number of shares owned; and they cannot appreciate in value. In short, the inducement to purchase was solely to acquire subsidized low-cost living space; it was not to invest for profit.

The Court of Appeals concluded that a share in Riverbay was also an investment contract as defined by the Securities Acts. The tenants argue that what they agreed to purchase is commonly known as a security within the meaning of these laws. In either case, the basic test for distinguishing the transaction from other commercial dealings is whether the scheme involves an investment of money in a common enterprise with profits to come solely from the efforts of others.[5] The touchstone is the presence of an investment in a common venture premised on a reasonable expectation of profits to be derived from the entrepreneurial or managerial efforts of others. The investor is attracted solely by the prospects of a return on his investment. By contrast, when a purchaser is motivated by a desire to use or consume the item purchased—to occupy the land or to develop it themselves—the securities laws do not apply.

In the present case there can be no doubt that investors were attracted solely by the prospect of acquiring a place to live. The Information Bulletin emphasized the fundamental nature and purpose of the undertaking.

Nowhere does the Bulletin seek to attract investors by the prospect of profits resulting from the efforts of the promoters or third parties. On the contrary, the Bulletin repeatedly emphasizes the nonprofit nature of the endeavor.

The possibility of net income derived from the leasing by Co-op City of commercial facilities, professional offices and parking spaces, and its operation of community washing machines, if any, is to be used to reduce tenant rental costs. Conceptually, one might readily agree that net income from the leasing of commercial and professional facilities is the kind of profit traditionally associated with a security investment. But in the present case this income—if indeed there is any—is far too speculative and insubstantial to bring the entire transaction within the Securities Acts.

The prospect of such income is never mentioned in the Information Bulletin. Thus it is clear that investors were not attracted to Co-op City by the offer of these potential rental reductions. The stores and services in question were established not as a means of returning profits to tenants, but for the purpose of making essential services available for the residents of this enormous complex. By statute these facilities can only be incidental and appurtenant to the housing project.

We do not address the tenants' allegation of fraud. We decide only that the type of transaction before us, in which the purchasers were interested in acquiring housing rather than making an investment for profit, is not within the scope of the federal securities laws.

Judgment reversed in favor of Riverbay.

---

[5] [Footnote 16 by the Court.] This test speaks in terms of profits to come *solely* from the efforts of others. We note that the Court of Appeals for the Ninth Circuit has held that the word solely should not be read as a strict or literal limitation on the definition of an investment contract, but rather must be construed realistically, so as to include within the definition those schemes which involve in substance, if not in form, securities. *SEC v. Glenn W. Turner Enterprises,* 474 F.2d 476, 482, *cert. denied*, 414 U.S. 821 (U.S. Sup. Ct. 1973). We express no view as to the holding of that case.

## SECURITIES ACT OF 1933

**Introduction.** The 1933 Act has two principal regulatory components: (1) *registration* provisions and (2) *antifraud* provisions. The registration requirements of the 1933 Act are designed to give investors the information they need to make intelligent decisions about whether to purchase securities. The issuer of the securities is required to file a *registration statement* with the Securities and Exchange Commission and to make a *prospectus* available to prospective purchasers. The various antifraud provisions in the 1933 Act impose liability on sellers of securities for misstating or omitting facts of material significance to investors.

**Registration of Securities under the 1933 Act.** The 1933 Act requires the issuer of securities to *register the securities* with the SEC prior to the offer or sale of the securities.

**Registration Statement.** *Historical and current data* about the issuer and its business (including certified financial statements), full details about the *securities to be offered,* and the *use of the proceeds* of the issuance, among other information, must be included in a *registration statement* prepared by the issuer of the securities. The *issuer* must *file* the registration statement with the SEC.

**Signing of Registration Statement.** The registration statement must be signed by the issuer, its chief executive officer, its chief financial officer, its chief accounting officer, and at least a majority of its board of directors. Signing a registration statement is an important event, for it makes a person potentially liable for errors in the statement.

**Effective Date of Registration Statement.** The registration statement becomes *effective* after it has been reviewed by the SEC. The SEC review involves only the *completeness* of the registration statement and whether it contains *per se fraudulent* statements. Examples of per se fraudulent statements are statements that tout the securities ("These are the best securities you can buy") and forecasts that are not reasonably based (a new company promising a 35 percent annual return on investment on its common stock).

The 1933 Act provides that the registration statement becomes effective on the *20th day after its filing,* but the SEC may advance the date or it may require an amendment that will restart the 20-day period. The effective date is usually later than 20 days after the original filing date.

**Prospectus.** Most of the information in the registration statement must be included in the prospectus. The prospectus is the basic *selling document* of an offering registered under the 1933 Act. It must be furnished to every purchaser of the registered security prior to or concurrently with the delivery of the security to the purchaser. The prospectus enables an investor to base his investment decision on *all of the relevant data* concerning the issuer, not merely on the favorable information that the issuer would be inclined to disclose voluntarily.

**Section 5: Timing, Manner, and Content of Offers and Sales.** The 1933 Act restricts the issuer's ability to communicate with prospective purchasers of the securities. Section 5 of the 1933 Act states the basic rules regarding the timing, manner, and content of offers and sales. It creates three important periods of time in the life of a security offering: (1) the *pre-filing* period, (2) the *waiting* period, and (3) the *post-effective* period.

**The Pre-filing Period.** Prior to the filing of the registration statement (the pre-filing period), the issuer and *any other person* may *not offer or sell* the securities to be registered.

**Example of Tombstone Ad**

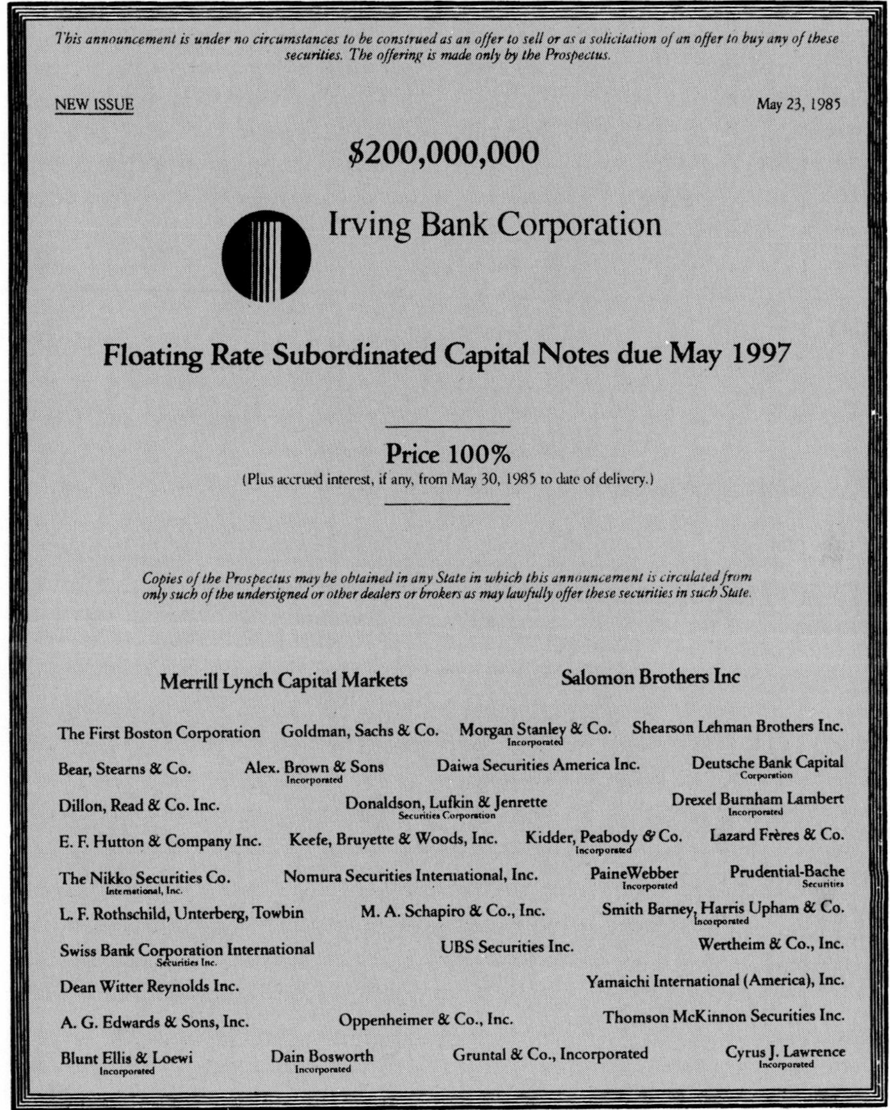


A prospective issuer, its directors and officers, and its underwriters must avoid publicity about the issuer and the prospective issuance of securities during the pre-filing period. Press releases, advertisements, speeches, and press conferences may be deemed offers if their intent or effect is to *condition the market* to receive the securities.

SEC Rule 135 permits the issuer to publish a *notice* about a prospective offering during the pre-filing period. The notice may contain only the name of the issuer and a basic description of the securities and the offering.

**The Waiting Period.** The *waiting period* is the time between the filing date and the effective date, when the issuer is *waiting* for the SEC to declare the registration statement effective. Usually, the waiting period will last at least 20 days. During the waiting period, Section 5 permits the securities to be *offered but not sold.* However, not all kinds of offers are permitted. Face-to-face *oral* offers (including personal phone calls) are allowed during the waiting period. However, *written* offers may be made only by a statutory prospectus, usually a *preliminary prospectus* that omits the price of the securities.

The preliminary prospectus is also called a *red herring prospectus,* because a legend in red ink appears on the front cover of the prospectus. The legend warns that the document is incomplete and that the securities may not be sold until the registration statement be-

**Communications with Investors by or on Behalf of Issuer Permitted by Section 5 during a 1933 Act Registration**

*Filing date of registration statement* | *Effective date of registration statement*

| *Type of Communication* | *Pre-filing Period* | *Waiting Period* | *Post-effective Period* |
|---|---|---|---|
| Annual reports, press releases, and quarterly reports | Yes; unless designed to assist the placement of securities or arouse interest in a prospective sale of securities | Yes; unless designed to assist the placement of securities or arouse interest in a prospective sale of securities | Yes; without restriction if used contemporaneously with or after delivery of Final Prospectus |
| Notice of proposed offering (Rule 135) | Yes | Yes | Yes |
| Tombstone ad (Rule 134) | No | Yes | Yes |
| Offer by formal prospectus | No | Yes | Yes |
| Oral face-to-face offers (including telephone calls) | No | Yes | Yes |
| Oral offers at sales meeting | No | Yes, if each investor has an opportunity to ask unlimited questions | Yes, if each investor has an opportunity to ask unlimited questions, or if each investor has received a Final Prospectus |
| Offer by free-writing | No | No | Yes, contemporaneously with of after delivery of Final Prospectus |
| Sale | No | No | Yes, contemporaneously with or after delivery of Final Prospectus |

comes effective. (A *final prospectus* will be available after the registration statement becomes effective. It will contain the price of the securities.)

**Tombstone Ad.** As during the pre-filing period, general publicity during the waiting period may be construed as an illegal offer because it conditions the market to receive the securities. One type of general advertisement, called the *tombstone ad,* is permitted during the waiting period and thereafter. The tombstone ad, which appears in financial publications, is permitted by SEC Rule 134, which allows disclosure of the same information as is allowed by Rule 135 plus the price of the securities and the names of the underwriters who are helping the issuer to sell the securities. In addition, Rule 134 requires the tombstone ad to state that it is *not an offer.*

**Purpose of Waiting Period.** The waiting period is an important part of the regulatory scheme of the 1933 Act. It provides an investor with adequate time (at least 20 days) to judge the wisdom of buying the security during a period when he cannot be pressured to buy it. Not even a contract to buy the security may be made during the waiting period.

**The Post-effective Period.** After the effective date (the date on which the SEC declares the registration effective), Section 5 permits the security not only to be offered but also to be sold, provided that the buyer has received a final prospectus. (A preliminary prospectus is not adequate for this purpose.) Any written offer not previously allowed is permitted during the post-effective period, if each offeree has received a final prospectus.

## EXEMPTIONS FROM THE REGISTRATION REQUIREMENTS OF THE 1933 ACT

Complying with the registration requirements of the 1933 Act is a burdensome, time-consuming, and expensive process. An issuer's first public offering may consume six months and cost in excess of $1 million. It is understandable why some issuers prefer to avoid registration when they sell securities. Fortunately for them, several *exemptions from registration* are available to issuers.

Although it is true that the registration provisions apply primarily to issuers and those who help issuers sell their securities publicly, the 1933 Act states that *every person* who sells a security is potentially subject to the restrictions on the timing of offers and sales. Few students learn the most important rule of the 1933 Act: **Every transaction in securities must be registered with the SEC or be exempt from registration.**

This rule applies to every person, including the small investor who through the New York Stock Exchange sells securities that may have been registered by the issuer 15 years earlier. That small investor must either have the issuer *register* her sale of securities (only an issuer may register securities, although others may sell pursuant to the issuer's registration) or find an exemption from registration that applies to her situation. Fortunately, most small investors who resell securities will have an exemption from the registration requirements of the 1933 Act.[6] The most important exemptions, however, are those available to issuers.

**Types of Exemptions.** There are two types of exemptions from the registration requirements of the 1933 Act: securities exemptions and transaction exemptions. *Exempt securities* never need to be registered, regardless of who sells the securities, how they are sold, or to whom they are sold. Securities sold in *exempt transactions* are exempt from the registration requirements for those transactions only. Each transaction stands by itself. A se-

[6] The transaction exemption ordinarily used by these resellers is for *transactions not involving an issuer, underwriter, or dealer.* This exemption is discussed later in the chapter.

curity may be exempt today because it is sold pursuant to a transaction exemption. Yet the same security may have to be registered tomorrow when it is offered or sold again in a transaction for which there is no exemption.

**Exempt Securities.** Some securities are exempted from the registration provisions of the 1933 Act, including Section 5, because (1) the character of the issuer makes registration unnecessary, (2) the issuance of such securities is subject to regulation under another statutory scheme, or (3) the purchasers of the securities can adequately protect themselves. The following are the most important securities exemptions.

(Excluded from the list of securities exemptions are the intrastate offering and small offering exemptions. Although the 1933 Act denotes them (except for the Section 4(6) exemption) as *securities* exemptions, they are in practice *transaction* exemptions. An exempt security is exempt from registration *forever*. But when securities originally sold pursuant to an intrastate or small offering exemption are resold at a later date, the subsequent sales may have to be registered. The exemption of the earlier offering does not exempt a future offering. The Proposed Federal Securities Code treats these two exemptions as transaction exemptions.)

**Government-Issued or -Guaranteed Securities.** Securities issued or guaranteed by any *government* in the United States and its territories are exempt securities. For example, municipal bonds, issued by city governments, are exempt securities. A debenture issued by a corporation and guaranteed by the federal government is also exempt.

**Short-Term Notes and Drafts.** A note or draft[7] that has a maturity date *not more than nine months* after its date of issuance is exempt from registration. For example, commercial paper issued by General Motors and due in three months is exempt. The reasons for the exemption are that such commercial paper is used primarily in lending transactions, not investment transactions, and that the lender and the borrower have nearly equal bargaining power. The lender should be able to protect itself without the benefit of a securities registration.

**Securities of Nonprofit Issuers.** A security issued by a nonprofit religious, charitable, educational, benevolent, or fraternal organization is exempt. For example, bonds issued by a nonprofit university or by a church would be exempt from registration under the 1933 Act.

**Securities of Financial Institutions.** Securities issued by banks and by savings and loan associations are exempt. The issuance of these securities is subject to regulation by other administrative agencies.

**ICC-Regulated Issuers.** Securities issued by railroads and trucking companies regulated by the Interstate Commerce Commission are exempt. The ICC regulates the issuance of such securities.

**Insurance Policies and Annuity Contracts.** An insurance policy or an annuity contract is exempt from registration. For example, a life insurance contract is exempt from 1933 Act registration. Such contracts are regulated by the various state insurance departments.

**Not Antifraud Exemptions.** Although the types of securities listed above are *exempt from the registration* provisions of the 1933 Act, they are *not* exempt from the *antifraud* provisions of the act. Therefore, any fraud

[7] Notes and drafts are defined in Chapter 35.

committed in the course of selling such securities can be attacked by the SEC and by the persons who were defrauded.

**Transaction Exemptions.** The most important 1933 Act exemptions are the *transaction exemptions.* If a security is sold pursuant to a transaction exemption, that sale is exempt. Subsequent sales, however, are not automatically exempt. Future sales must be made pursuant to a registration or another exemption. Hence, *every transaction in securities must be registered or be exempt from registration.*

As with the securities exemptions, the transaction exemptions are exemptions from the registration provisions only. The antifraud provisions of the 1933 Act apply equally to exempted and nonexempted transactions.

**Transaction Exemptions for Issuers.** The most important transaction exemptions are those available to issuers. These exemptions are the private offering exemption, the intrastate offering exemption, and the small offering exemptions.

**Private Offering Exemption.** Section 4(2) of the 1933 Act provides that the registration requirements of the 1933 Act "shall not apply to . . . transactions by an issuer not involving any public offering." The rationale for the *private offering exemption* is that the purchasers in a private placement of securities do not need the registration protections of the 1933 Act. Such purchasers can protect themselves because they are wealthy or because they are sophisticated in investment matters and have access to the information that they need to make intelligent investment decisions.

**SEC Rule 506.** Under its authority to promulgate rules and regulations, the SEC has established Rule 506, which states the requirements that the issuer must meet to take advantage of the private offering exemption. Rule 506, which is part of SEC Regulation D,[8] requires that there be *no more than 35 purchasers* of the securities, that each purchaser be *sophisticated in investment matters,* and that each investor be given or have access to the *information she needs* to make an informed investment decision.

Under Rule 506, the issuer must reasonably believe that each purchaser is either (a) an *accredited investor* or (b) "has such knowledge and experience in business and financial matters that he is capable of evaluating the risks and merits of the prospective investment." Accredited investors include institutional investors (such as banks and mutual funds), wealthy investors, and high-level insiders of the issuer (such as executive officers, directors, and partners). An investor who is not sophisticated himself may qualify by using a *purchaser representative* to assist him in evaluating the investment.

Rule 506 prohibits the issuer from making any general public selling effort. This prevents the issuer from using the radio, newspapers, and television. In addition, the issuer must take reasonable steps to ensure that the purchasers do not resell the securities in a manner that makes the issuance a public distribution rather than a private one. The rule requires the issuer to inquire for whom the purchaser is buying the securities. Usually, an *investment letter* is used to provide this information. In such a letter, the investor states that she is purchasing the securities for investment and not for resale within two years. The issuer must also put a legend on the securities certificate that resale is restricted unless the securities are subsequently registered or are sold pursuant to a new ex-

[8] SEC Regulation D was promulgated in 1982 to make the private offering and small offering exemptions more easily available for small issuers. The purpose of Regulation D is to promote capital formation for small issuers. Regulation D includes the small offering exemption Rules 504 and 505, which are discussed below, in addition to Rule 506.

emption from registration. Finally, the issuer must file a notice (Form D) with the SEC.

**Intrastate Offering Exemption.** Under Section 3(a)(11) of the 1933 Act, an offering of securities solely to investors in one state by an issuer resident and doing business in that state is exempt from the registration requirements. The reason for the exemption is clear. There is little federal government interest in an offering that occurs in only one state. Note also that the issuer may not be totally exempt from registration. *State* securities law may require a registration.[9]

**Rule 147.** The SEC has defined the intrastate offering exemption more precisely in Rule 147. An issuer must have *80 percent* of its *gross revenues* and 80 percent of its *assets* in the state and use 80 percent of the *proceeds* of the offering in the state. *Resale* of the securities is limited to persons within the state for *nine months.* Issuers usually obtain investment letters from purchasers.

**Small Offering Exemptions.** Sections 3(b) and 4(6) of the 1933 Act permit the SEC to exempt from registration offerings by issuers not exceeding $5 million. Several SEC rules and regulations permit an issuer to sell small amounts of securities and avoid registration. The rationale for these exemptions is that the dollar amount of the securities or the number of purchasers is too small for the federal government to be concerned with registration. State securities law may require registration, however.

**Rule 504.** SEC Rule 504 of Regulation D allows the issuer to sell up to *$500,000* of securities in a *12-month period* and avoid registration. As with Rule 506, no general selling efforts are allowed, resale is restricted, and a notice (Form D) must be filed with the SEC. Rule 504 sets no limits on the number of offerees or purchasers. The purchasers need not be sophisticated in investment matters, and the issuer need not make any disclosures to the investors.

**Rule 505.** Rule 505 of Regulation D allows the issuer to sell up to *$5 million* of securities in a *12-month period* and avoid registration. As with Rules 504 and 506, no general selling efforts are allowed, resale is restricted, and a notice (Form D) must be filed with the SEC. As with Rule 506, there may be *no more than 35 purchasers*—excluding accredited investors—and investors must be given or have access to necessary information. As with Rule 504, the purchasers need not be sophisticated in investment matters.

**Regulation A.** Regulation A permits an issuer to sell up to *$1.5 million* of securities in a *one-year* period. There is no limit on the number of purchasers, no purchaser sophistication requirement, and no resale restrictions. No disclosure need be made if the amount of the offering does not exceed $100,000.

For offerings that *exceed $100,000,* Regulation A requires disclosure and regulates the manner and timing of offers and sales much as a registered offering is regulated. In fact, Regulation A is more nearly a *low-level registration* than an exemption from registration. The Regulation A disclosure document is the *offering circular,* which must be filed with the SEC. There is a 10-day waiting period after the filing of the offering circular, during which no offers or sales may be made. Ten days after the filing date, oral offers are permitted, as are written offers accompanied or preceded by an offering circular. Sales are permitted after the waiting period.

[9] State securities law is covered at the end of this chapter.

**Integration of Offerings.** It might seem possible to avoid registration by separating one offering into several smaller offerings and finding an exemption for each of the smaller offerings. Not surprisingly, the SEC has acted to stop such a circumvention of the disclosure provisions of the 1933 Act by requiring the *integration* of offerings that are essentially only one offering. If the offerings are integrated, it is likely that the SEC will be able to prove that the issuer has offered or sold securities in violation of Section 5 of the 1933 Act. The following factors are used to determine whether two or more offerings should be integrated:

1. Whether there is a single plan of financing.
2. Whether the same classes of securities are issued.
3. Whether the sales are made at about the same time.
4. Whether the same type of consideration is received.
5. Whether the sales are made for the same general purpose.

**Transaction Exemptions for Nonissuers.** There are several exemptions that allow *nonissuers*—average investors, usually—to offer and sell the securities they own, yet avoid the need to have the issuer register the securities. The most frequently used nonissuer exemption is Section 4(1) of the 1933 Act. It provides an exemption for "transactions by any person other than an issuer, underwriter, or dealer."

This exemption is used by most investors when they sell securities. For example, if you buy General Motors common shares on the New York Stock Exchange, you may freely resell them without a registration. You are not an issuer (General Motors is). You are not a dealer (because you are not in the *business* of selling securities). And you are not an underwriter (because you are not helping General Motors distribute the shares to the public).

It is more difficult to determine whether an investor can use this exemption when the investor sells *restricted securities.*

**Sale of Restricted Securities.** *Restricted securities* are securities issued pursuant to a Rule 504, 505, or 506 exemption. Restricted securities are supposed to be held for two years. If they are sold earlier, the investor may be deemed an *underwriter.*

For example, an investor may buy 10,000 shares of common stock issued by Arcom Corporation pursuant to a Rule 506 private offering exemption. One month later, the investor sells the securities to 40 other investors. The original investor is an *underwriter* because he has helped Arcom distribute the shares to the public. The original investor may not use the issuer's private offering exemption, because it exempted only the issuer's sale to him. Here is seen the importance of knowing the rule discussed earlier: every transaction in securities must be registered with the SEC or be exempt from registration.

**SEC Rule 144.** SEC Rule 144 allows purchasers of restricted securities to resell the securities and not be deemed underwriters. The resellers must hold the securities for at least *two years.* Investment information concerning the issuer of the securities must be publicly available. In any *three-month period,* the reseller may *sell only a limited amount* of securities: the greater of 1 percent of the outstanding securities or the average weekly volume of trading. And the reseller must file a notice (Form 144) with the SEC.

If a purchaser who is *not an insider of the issuer* has held the restricted securities for at least three years, Rule 144 permits her to sell *unlimited* amounts of the securities. In

## Securities and Transaction Exemptions from the Securities Act of 1933

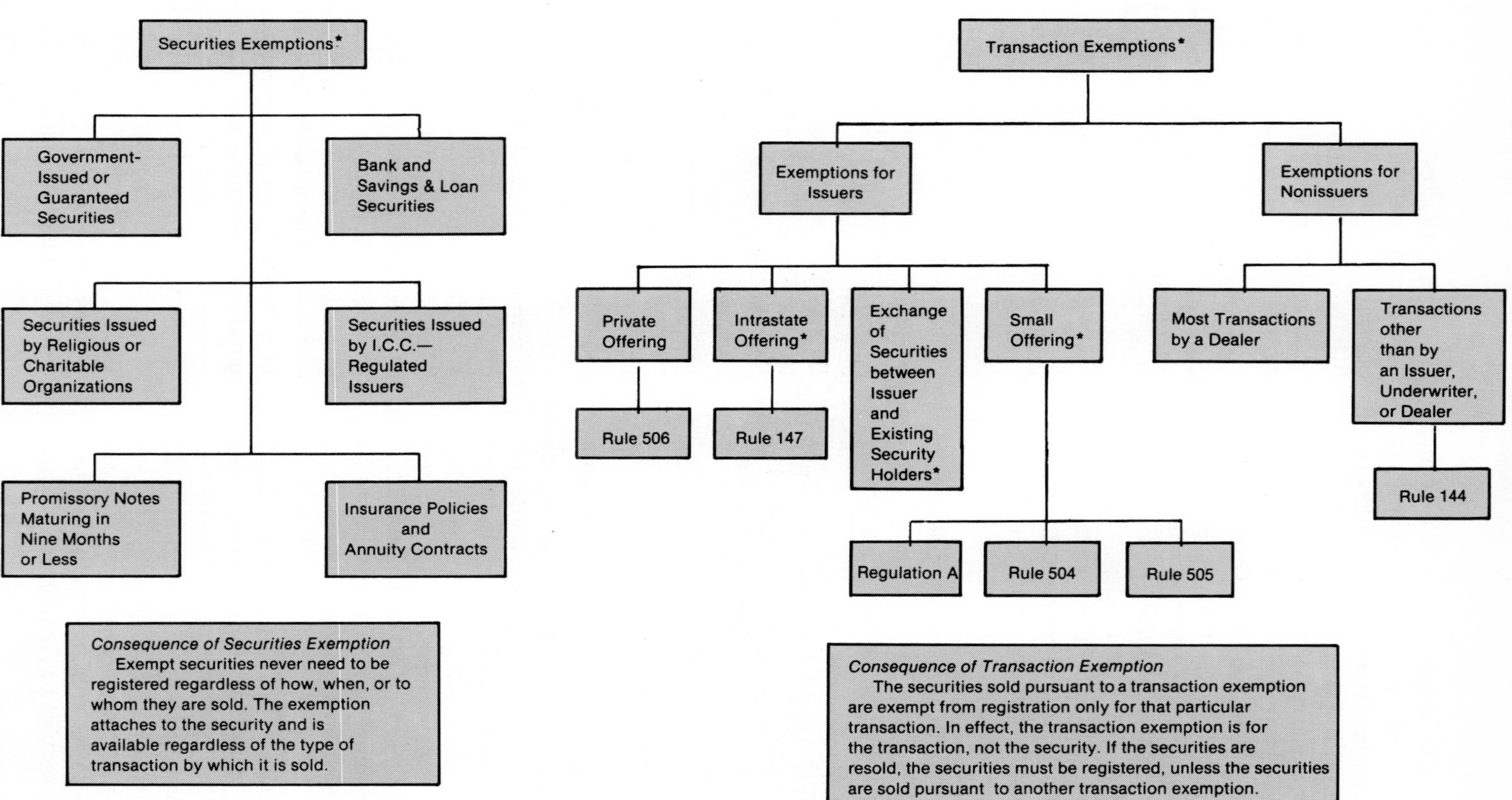


Note: These are exemptions from the *registration* provisions of the 1933 Act. The 1933 Act *antifraud* provisions apply to these transactions and these securities.

* The Securities Act of 1933 lists the small offering, intrastate offering, and exchange of securities between issuers and existing securities holders as *securities* exemption, yet they are *in effect transaction* exemptions, because the exemptions apply only when the securities are sold in these types of transactions. The exemptions do not attach to the securities. If the securities are resold, the securities must be registered, unless the securities are sold pursuant to another transaction exemption.

addition, investment information concerning the issuer need not be publicly available.

Rule 144 has two purposes: (1) to prevent an issuer of securities from circumventing the registration provisions of the 1933 Act and (2) to permit bona fide investors to sell their securities without obtaining a registration.

## LIABILITY PROVISIONS OF THE 1933 ACT

**Introduction.** To accomplish its objectives of preventing fraud, deception, and manipulation and providing remedies to the victims of such practices, Congress included a number of liability provisions in the Securities Act of 1933.

**Liability for Improper Offers and Sales.** Section 12(1) of the 1933 Act imposes liability on any person who violates the provisions of Section 5. As you learned above, Section 5 states when sales may be made and what types of offers may be made at what times during the registration process. The purchaser's remedy is rescission or damages. Usually, Section 5 is violated by sellers who have failed to register securities for which there is no exemption from registration. If securities are offered and sold in compliance with an exemption, Sections 5 and 12(1) do not apply.

**Liability for Defective Registration Statements.** Section 11 of the 1933 Act provides civil liabilities for damages when a *registration statement* on its effective date *misstates or omits a material fact.* A *purchaser* of securities issued pursuant to the defective registration statement may sue certain classes of persons that are listed in Section 11: the issuer, its chief executive officer, its chief accounting officer, its chief financial officer, the directors, other signers of the registration statement, the underwriter, and experts who contributed to the registration statement (such as auditors who certified the financial statements or lawyers who issued an opinion concerning the tax aspects of a limited partnership). The purchaser's remedy under Section 11 is for damages caused by the misstatement or omission.

Section 11 was a *radical* liability section when it was enacted, and it remains so today. It is radical for three reasons. First, *reliance is usually not required.* The purchaser need not show that she relied on the misstatement or omission in the registration. In fact, the purchaser need not have read the registration statement or even seen it. Second, *privity is not required.* The purchaser need not prove that she purchased the securities from the defendant. All that she has to prove is that the defendant is in one of the classes of persons liable under Section 11. Third, the purchaser need not prove that the defendant negligently or intentionally misstated or omitted a material fact. Instead, the *defendant* has the burden of *proving that he exercised due diligence.*

**Section 11 Defenses.** A defendant can escape liability under Section 11 by proving that the *purchaser knew* of the misstatement or omission when she purchased the security. The defendant's other defense is the *due diligence defense.* It is the more important of the two defenses.

**The Due Diligence Defense.** Any defendant except the issuer may escape liability under Section 11 by proving that he acted with due diligence in determining the accuracy of the registration statement. An issuer has no due diligence defense, because an issuer should not be entitled to retain proceeds from a sale of securities procured by fraud or deception.

The due diligence defense basically requires the defendant to prove that he was not negligent. The exact defense varies, however, according to the class of defendant and the portion of the registration statement that is defective. Most defendants must prove that after a *reasonable investigation* they had *reasonable grounds to believe* and *did believe* that the registration statement was true and contained no omission of material fact.

*Experts* need to prove due diligence only in respect to the parts that they have contributed. They are not liable for other parts of the registration statement. For example, independent auditors must prove due diligence in ascertaining the accuracy of certified financial statements. As the *BarChris* case, which follows, indicates, due diligence requires that an auditor at least comply with generally accepted auditing standards.

*Nonexperts* (the directors, officers, partners, and underwriters) are liable for the entire registration statement. However, they generally have no duty of investigation in respect to the parts of the registration statement contributed by experts (*expertised portions*). The nonexperts merely need to show that they had *no reason to believe* and did *not believe* that the *expertised portions* of the registration statement contained any misstatement or omission of material fact.

The *BarChris* case is the leading case on the due diligence defense. It establishes that due diligence depends on several factors, including the level of the defendant's competence and the defendant's relationship with the issuer.

**Other Liability Provisions.** Section 12(2) prohibits misstatements or omissions of material fact in any written or oral communication in connection with the offer or sale of any security (except government-issued or -guaranteed securities). *Privity* is required, but it has been defined broadly to permit a purchaser to sue any person whose actions *directly and proximately cause* the purchaser's loss.[10] She must show that she *relied* on the misstatement or omission and that she did not know of the untruth or omission. The defendant may escape liability by proving that he did not know and could not reasonably have known of the untruth or omission. The purchaser's remedy is rescission or damages, as is her remedy under Section 12(1).

Section 17(a) broadly prohibits the use of any device or artifice to defraud, or the use of any untrue or misleading statement, in connection with the offer or sale of *any* security. Two of the subsections of Section 17(a) require that the defendant merely act negligently, while the third subsection requires proof of scienter. Scienter is the intent to deceive, manipulate, or defraud the purchaser. Some courts have held that scienter also includes recklessness. The Supreme Court has not decided whether a buyer has a private right of action for damages under Section 17(a), and the courts of appeals are split on the issue.

**Jurisdictional Requirement.** Since these liability sections are part of federal law, there must be some connection between the illegal activity and interstate commerce for liability to exist. Section 11 merely requires the filing of a registration statement with the SEC. Sections 12(1), 12(2), and 17(a) require the use of the mails or other instrumentality or means of interstate communication or transportation. This has been interpreted to include the use of the telephone even when both the buyer and the seller are in the same city. It is generally assumed by securities lawyers, however, that an intrastate offer by phone before the filing date of a registration statement does not violate Section 12(1).

**SEC Actions.** The SEC is empowered to investigate violations of the 1933 Act and to

[10] *Avco Financial Services, Inc. v. Davis* 739 F.2d 1057 (6th Cir. 1984), *cert. denied,* 53 U.S.L.W. 3867 (June 10, 1985).

hold hearings to determine whether the act has been violated. Such hearings are held before an administrative law judge, who is an employee of the SEC. The administrative law judge is a finder of both fact and law. Decisions of the ALJ are reviewed by the commissioners of the SEC. Decisions of the commissioners are appealed to the U.S. courts of appeals.

Most SEC actions are not litigated. Instead, the SEC issues consent orders, by which the defendant promises not to violate the securities laws in the future but does not admit to having violated them in the past.

The SEC does not have the power to issue injunctions; only courts may issue injunctions. Section 20 of the 1933 Act empowers the SEC to ask federal district courts for injunctions against persons who have violated or are about to violate the Act. The SEC may also ask the courts to grant *ancillary relief,* a remedy in addition to an injunction. Ancillary relief includes the disgorgement of profits that a defendant has made in a fraudulent sale.

**Criminal Liability.** Section 24 of the 1933 Act provides for criminal liability for any person who willfully violates the Act or its rules and regulations. The maximum penalty is a $10,000 fine and five years' imprisonment. Criminal actions under the 1933 Act are brought by the attorney general of the United States, not by the SEC.

## Escott v. BarChris Construction Corp.

**283 F. Supp. 643 (S.D.N.Y. 1968)**

BarChris Construction Corporation was in the business of constructing bowling centers. With the introduction of automatic pinsetters in 1952, there was a rapid growth in the popularity of bowling, and BarChris's sales increased from $800,000 in 1956 to over $9 million in 1960. By 1960, it was building about 3 percent of the lanes constructed, while Brunswick Corporation and AMF were building 97 percent. BarChris contracted with customers to construct and equip bowling alleys for them. Under the contracts, the customer was required to make a relatively small down payment in cash. After the alleys were constructed, BarChris took the balance of the purchase price in notes that it discounted with a factor. The factor kept part of the face value of the notes as a reserve until the customer paid the notes. The factor could call on BarChris to repurchase the notes if the customer defaulted.

In 1960, BarChris began to offer its customers an alternative method of financing. This involved selling the *interior* of a bowling alley to a factor, James Talcott, Inc. Talcott then leased the alley either to a BarChris customer (Type A financing) or to a BarChris subsidiary that then subleased to the customer (Type B financing). Under Type A financing, BarChris guaranteed 25 percent of the customer's obligation under the lease. With Type B financing, BarChris was liable for 100 percent of its subsidiaries' lease obligations. Under either financing method, BarChris made substantial expenditures before receiving reimbursement and therefore experienced a constant need of cash, a need that grew as its operations expanded.

In early 1961, BarChris decided to issue debentures and to use part of the proceeds to help its cash position. In March 1961, BarChris filed with the SEC a registration statement covering the debentures. The statement became effective on May 16. The proceeds of the offering were received by BarChris on May 24, 1961. By that time, BarChris was experiencing difficulties in collecting the amounts due it from some of its customers, and other customers were in arrears on their payments to the factors of the discounted notes. Due to overexpansion in the bowling alley industry, many operators failed. On October 29, 1962, BarChris filed a petition under the Bankruptcy Act. On November 1, it defaulted on the payment of interest on the debentures.

Escott and other purchasers of the debentures sued BarChris and its officers, directors, and auditors, among others, under Section 11 of the Securities Act of 1933. BarChris's registration statement contained material misstatements and omitted material facts. It misstated current assets by $609,689 (15.6 percent) in the 1960 balance sheet certified by its auditors, Peat, Marwick. It understated BarChris's contingent liabilities by $618,853 (42.8 percent) as of April 30, 1961. It overstated gross profit for the first quarter of 1961 by $230,755 (92 percent), and sales for the first quarter of 1961 by $519,810 (32.1 percent). The March 31, 1961, backlog was overstated by $4,490,000 (186 percent).

In addition, the registration statement reported that prior loans from officers had been repaid, but failed to disclose that officers had made new loans to BarChris totaling $386,615. BarChris had used $1,160,000 of the proceeds of the debentures to pay old debts, a use not disclosed in the registration statement. BarChris's potential liability of $1,350,000 to factors due to customer delinquencies on factored notes was not disclosed. The registration statement represented BarChris's contingent liability on Type B financings as 25 percent instead of 100 percent. It misrepresented the nature of BarChris's business by failing to disclose that BarChris was already engaged and was about to become more heavily engaged in the operation of bowling alleys, including one called Capitol Lanes, as a way of minimizing its losses from customer defaults.

Trilling, BarChris's controller, signed the registration statement. Auslander, a director, signed the registration statement. Peat, Marwick consented to being named as an expert in the registration statement. All three, therefore, would be liable to Escott unless they could meet the due diligence defense of Section 11.

**McLean, District Judge.** I turn now to the question of whether Trilling, Auslander, and Peat, Marwick have proved their due diligence defenses. The position of each defendant will be separately considered.

### Trilling

Trilling was BarChris's controller. He signed the registration statement in that capacity, although he was not a director. Trilling entered BarChris's employ in October 1960. He was Kircher's [BarChris's treasurer] subordinate. When Kircher asked him for information, he furnished it.

Trilling was not a member of the executive committee. He was a comparatively minor figure in BarChris. The description of BarChris's management on page 9 of the prospectus does not mention him. He was not considered to be an executive officer.

Trilling may well have been unaware of several of the inaccuracies in the prospectus. But he must have known of some of them. As a financial officer, he was familiar with BarChris's finances and with its books of account. He knew that part of the cash on deposit on December 31, 1960, had been procured temporarily by Russo [BarChris's executive vice president] for window-dressing purposes. He knew that BarChris was operating Capitol Lanes in 1960. He should have known, although perhaps through carelessness he did not know at the time, that BarChris's contingent liability on Type B lease transactions was greater than the prospectus stated. In the light of these facts, I cannot find that Trilling believed the entire prospectus to be true.

But even if he did, he still did not establish his due diligence defenses. He did not prove that as to the parts of the prospectus expertised by Peat, Marwick he had no reasonable ground to believe that it was untrue. He also failed to prove, as to the parts of the prospectus not expertised by Peat, Marwick, that he made a reasonable investigation which afforded him a reasonable ground to believe that it was true. As far as appears, he made no investigation. He did what was asked of him and assumed that others would properly take care of supplying accurate data as to the other aspects of the company's business. This would have been well enough but for the fact that he signed the registration statement. As a signer, he could not avoid responsibility by leaving it up to others to make it accurate. Trilling did not sustain the burden of proving his due diligence defenses.

**Auslander**

Auslander was an outside director, i.e., one who was not an officer of BarChris. He was chairman of the board of Valley Stream National Bank in Valley Stream, Long Island. In February 1961, Vitolo [BarChris's president] asked him to become a director of BarChris. In February and early March 1961, before accepting Vitolo's invitation, Auslander made some investigation of BarChris. He obtained Dun & Bradstreet reports which contained sales and earnings figures for periods earlier than December 31, 1960. He caused inquiry to be made of certain of BarChris's banks and was advised that they regarded BarChris favorably. He was informed that inquiry of Talcott had also produced a favorable response.

On March 3, 1961, Auslander indicated his willingness to accept a place on the board. Shortly thereafter, on March 14, Kircher sent him a copy of BarChris's annual report for 1960. Auslander observed that BarChris's auditors were Peat, Marwick. They were also the auditors for the Valley Stream National Bank. He thought well of them.

Auslander was elected a director on April 17, 1961. The registration statement in its original form had already been filed, of course without his signature. On May 10, 1961, he signed a signature page for the first amendment to the registration statement which was filed on May 11, 1961. This was a separate sheet without any document attached. Auslander did not know that it was a signature page for a registration statement. He vaguely understood that it was something "for the SEC."

At the May 15 directors' meeting, however, Auslander did realize that what he was signing was a signature sheet to a registration statement. This was the first time that he had appreciated the fact. A copy of the registration statement in its earlier form as amended on May 11, 1961, was passed around at the meeting. Auslander glanced at it briefly. He did not read it thoroughly. At the May 15 meeting, Russo and Vitolo stated that everything was in order and that the prospectus was correct. Auslander believed this statement.

Auslander knew that Peat, Marwick had audited the 1960 figures. He believed them to be correct because he had confidence in Peat, Marwick. He had no reasonable ground to believe otherwise.

As to the nonexpertised portions, however, Auslander is in a different position. He seems to have been under the impression that Peat, Marwick was responsible for all the figures. This impression was not correct, as he would have realized if he had read the prospectus carefully. Auslander made no investigation of the accuracy of the prospectus. He relied on the assurance of Vitolo and Russo, and upon the information he had received in answer to his inquiries back in February and early March. These inquiries were general ones, in the nature of a credit check. The information which he received in answer to them was also general, without specific reference to the statements in the prospectus, which was not prepared until some time thereafter.

It is true that Auslander became a director on the eve of the financing. He had little opportunity to familiarize himself with the company's affairs. The question is whether, under such circumstances, Auslander did enough to establish his due diligence.

Section 11 imposes liability in the first instance upon a director, no matter how new he is. He is presumed to know his responsibility when he becomes a director. He can escape liability only by using that reasonable care to investigate the facts which a prudent man would employ in the management of his own property. In my opinion, a prudent man would not act in an important matter without any knowledge of the relevant facts, in sole reliance upon general information which does not purport to cover the particular case. To say that such minimal conduct measures up to the statutory standard would, to all intents and purposes, absolve new directors from responsibility merely because they are new. This is not a sensible construction of Section 11, when one bears in mind its fundamental purpose of requiring full and truthful disclosure for the protection of investors.

Auslander has not established his due diligence defense with respect to the misstatements and omissions in those portions of the prospectus other than the audited 1960 figures.

### Peat, Marwick

The part of the registration statement purporting to be made upon the authority of Peat, Marwick as an expert was the 1960 figures. But because the statute requires the court to determine Peat, Marwick's belief, and the grounds thereof, "at the time such part of the registration statement became effective," for the purposes of this affirmative defense, the matter must be viewed as of May 16, 1961, and the question is whether at that time Peat, Marwick, after reasonable investigation, had reasonable ground to believe and did believe that the 1960 figures were true and that no material fact had been omitted from the registration statement which should have been included in order to make the 1960 figures not misleading. In deciding this issue, the court must consider not only what Peat, Marwick did in its 1960 audit, but also what it did in its subsequent S–1 review. The proper scope of that review must also be determined.

### The 1960 Audit

Peat, Marwick's work was in general charge of a member of the firm, Cummings, and more immediately in charge of Peat, Marwick's manager, Logan. Most of the actual work was performed by a senior accountant, Berardi, who had junior assistants, one of whom was Kennedy.

Berardi was then about 30 years old. He was not yet a CPA. He had had no previous experience with the bowling industry. This was his first job as a senior accountant. He could hardly have been given a more difficult assignment.

It is unnecessary to recount everything that Berardi did in the course of the audit. We are concerned only with the evidence relating to what Berardi did or did not do with respect to those items which I have found to have been incorrectly reported in the 1960 figures in the prospectus. More narrowly, we are directly concerned only with such of those items as I have found to be material.

First and foremost is Berardi's failure to discover that Capitol Lanes had not been sold. This error affected both the sales figure and the liability side of the balance sheet. Fundamentally, the error stemmed from the fact that Berardi never realized that Heavenly Lanes and Capitol were two different names for the same alley. Berardi assumed that Heavenly was to be treated like any other completed job.

Berardi read the minutes of the board of directors meeting of November 22, 1960, which recited that "the Chairman recommended that the Corporation operate Capitol Lanes." Berardi knew from various BarChris records that Capitol Lanes, Inc., was paying rentals to Talcott. Also, a Peat, Marwick work paper bearing Kennedy's initials recorded that Capitol Lanes, Inc., held certain insurance policies.

Berardi testified that he inquired of Russo about Capitol Lanes and that Russo told him that Capitol Lanes, Inc., was going to operate an alley someday but as yet it had no alley. Berardi testified that he understood that the alley had not been built and that he believed that the rental payments were on vacant land.

I am not satified with this testimony. If Berardi did hold this belief, he should not have held it. The entries as to insurance and as to "operation of alley" should have alerted him to the fact that an alley existed. He should have made further inquiry on the subject. It is apparent that Berardi did not understand this transaction.

He never identified this mysterious Capitol with the Heavenly Lanes which he had included in his sales and profit figures. The vital question is whether he failed to make a reasonable investigation which, if he had made it, would have revealed the truth.

Certain accounting records of BarChris, which Berardi testified he did not see, would have put him on inquiry. One was a job cost ledger card for job no. 6036, the job number which Berardi put on his own sheet for Heavenly Lanes. This card read "Capitol Theatre (Heavenly)." In addition, two accounts receivable cards each showed both names on the same card, Capitol and Heavenly. Berardi testified that he looked at the accounts receivable records but that he did not see these particular cards. He testified that he did not look on the job cost ledger cards because he took the costs from another record, the costs register.

The burden of proof on this issue is on Peat, Marwick. Although the question is a rather close one, I find that Peat, Marwick has not sustained that burden. Peat, Marwick has not proved that Berardi made a reasonable investigation as far as Capitol Lanes was concerned and that his ignorance of the true facts was justified.

This disposes of the inaccuracies in the 1960 figures. I turn now to the errors in the current assets. As to cash, Berardi properly obtained a confirmation from the bank as to BarChris's cash balance on December 31, 1960. He did not know that part of this balance had been temporarily increased by the deposit of reserves returned by Talcott to BarChris conditionally for a limited time. I do not believe that Berardi reasonably should have known this. It would not be reasonable to require Berardi to examine all of BarChris's correspondence files [which contained correspondence indicating that BarChris was to return the cash to Talcott] when he had no reason to suspect any irregularity.

### The S–1 Review

The purpose of reviewing events subsequent to the date of a certified balance sheet (referred to as an S–1 review when made with reference to a registration statement) is to ascertain whether any material change has occurred in the company's financial position which should be disclosed in order to prevent the balance sheet figures from being misleading. The scope of such a review, under generally accepted auditing standards, is limited. It does not amount to a complete audit.

Berardi made the S–1 review in May 1961. He devoted a little over two days to it, a total of 20½ hours. He did not discover any of the errors or omissions pertaining to the state of affairs in 1961 which I have previously discussed at length, all of which were material. The question is whether, despite his failure to find out anything, his investigation was reasonable within the meaning of the statute.

What Berardi did was to look at a consolidating trial balance as of March 31, 1961, which had been prepared by BarChris, compare it with the audited December 31, 1960 figures, discuss with Trilling certain unfavorable developments which the comparison disclosed, and read certain minutes. He did not examine any important financial records other than the trial balance.

In substance, Berardi asked questions, he got answers which he considered satisfactory, and he did nothing to verify them. Since he never read the prospectus, he was not even aware that there had ever been any problem about loans from officers. He made no inquiry of factors about delinquent notes in his S–1 review. Since he knew nothing about Kircher's notes of the executive committee meetings, he did not learn that the delinquency situation had grown worse. He was content with Trilling's assurance that no liability theretofore contingent had become direct. Apparently the only BarChris officer with whom Berardi communicated was Trilling. He could not recall making any inquiries of Russo, Vitolo, or Pugliese [a BarChris vice-president].

There had been a material change for the worse in BarChris's financial position. That change was sufficiently serious so that the failure to disclose it made the 1960 figures misleading. Berardi did not discover it. As far as results were concerned, his S–1 review was useless.

Accountants should not be held to a standard higher than that recognized in their profession. I do not do so here. Berardi's review did not come up to that standard. He did not take some of the steps which Peat, Marwick's written program prescribed. He did not spend an adequate amount of time on a task of this magnitude. Most important of all, he was too easily satisfied with glib answers to his inquiries.

This is not to say that he should have made a complete audit. But there were enough danger signals in the materials which he did examine to require some further investigation on his part. Generally accepted accounting standards require such further investigation under these circumstances. It is not always sufficient merely to ask questions.

Here again, the burden of proof is on Peat, Marwick. I find that burden has not been satisfied. I conclude that Peat, Marwick has not established its due diligence defense.

Judgment for Escott and the other purchasers.

## SECURITIES EXCHANGE ACT OF 1934

**Introduction.** The Securities Exchange Act of 1934 is chiefly concerned with disclosing material information to investors. Unlike the 1933 Act, which is primarily a one-time disclosure statute, the 1934 Act requires *periodic disclosure* by issuers with publicly held equity securities. In addition, the 1934 Act regulates insiders' transactions in securities, proxy solicitations, tender offers, brokers and dealers, and securities exchanges. The 1934 Act also has several sections prohibiting fraud and manipulation in securities transactions.

**Registration of Securities under the 1934 Act.** Under the 1934 Act, issuers must register *classes of securities.* This is different from the 1933 Act, which requires issuers to register issuances of securities. Under the 1934 Act, registered classes of securities remain registered until the issuer takes steps to deregister the securities. Under the 1933 Act, securities are registered only for the term of an issuance.

Issuers with securities registered under the 1934 Act become subject to certain further requirements that will be discussed later in this chapter, such as the rules pertaining to the solicitation of proxies and the filing of certain periodic reports. In addition, insiders of issuers with registered securities may be subject to the recapture of short-swing profits and may be required to report their transactions in the stock of the company.

**Securities Covered.** Two types of *securities* must be *registered* under the 1934 Act. First, an issuer whose *total assets exceed $3 million* must register a class of equity securities with at least *500 shareholders.* The securities must be traded in interstate commerce. Second, an issuer must register any security traded on a *national security exchange,* such as common shares traded on the American Stock Exchange. The information required in the 1934 Act *registration statement* is similar to that required under the 1933 Act.

**Termination of Registration.** An issuer may avoid the expense and burden of complying with the periodic disclosure and other requirements of the 1934 Act if the issuer *terminates* its registration. A 1934 Act registration may be *terminated* if the issuer has fewer than 300 shareholders. In addition, such a registration may be terminated if the issuer has fewer than 500 shareholders of any class of equity securities and assets of no more than $3 million. However, an issuer with securities traded on a national securities exchange would not be able to terminate a registration of those securities.

**Periodic Reports.** To maintain a steady flow of material information to investors, the 1934 Act requires public issuers to file *periodic reports* with the SEC. Three types of issuers must file such reports:

1. An issuer with *assets of more than $3 million* and at least *500 holders* of any class of equity securities traded in interstate commerce.
2. An issuer whose equity securities are traded on a *national securities exchange.*
3. An issuer who has made a *registered offering* under the 1933 Act.

These types of issuers must file several periodic reports, including an annual report (Form 10-K) and a quarterly report (Form 10-Q). They must file a monthly report (Form 8-K) when material events occur. Comparable reports must also be sent or made to their shareholders. The most important are the annual and quarterly reports.

**10-K.** The 10-K annual report must include audited financial statements for the fiscal year plus current information about the conduct of the business, its management, and the status of its securities. In effect, the 10-K report is intended to update the information required in the 1934 Act registration statement. This report must be signed by a majority of the board of directors.

**10-Q and 8-K.** The quarterly report, the 10-Q, requires only a summarized, unaudited operating statement and unaudited figures on capitalization and shareholders' equity. The 8-K monthly report is required within 10 days of the end of any month in which any specified event occurs, such as a change in the amount of securities, a default under the terms of an issue of securities, an acquisition or disposition of assets, a change in control of the company, a revaluation of assets, or "any materially important event."

**EDGAR.** Most securities issuers file *paper* reports with the SEC. Since September 1984, however, a few issuers have filed computerized reports, transmitting them by telephone or by sending computer tapes or disks to the SEC. These computerized filings are made with the SEC's Electronic Data Gathering, Analysis, and Retrieval system—*EDGAR*. The purpose of EDGAR is to ease the issuer's burden of filing reports and to facilitate access to filed reports. Currently, EDGAR is financed by the federal government. It is hoped that by 1987 EDGAR will be funded through subscription fees paid by users of its data.

**Suspension of Duty to File Reports.** An issuer's duty to file periodic reports is *suspended* if the issuer has fewer than 300 shareholders. In addition, a suspension occurs if the issuer has fewer than 500 shareholders of any class of equity securities and assets of no more than $3 million. However, an issuer with securities traded on a national securities exchange would remain obligated to file periodic reports.

**Short-Swing Trading by Insiders.** Section 16(a) of the 1934 Act requires that *statutory insiders* individually file a statement *disclosing their holdings* of any class of the issuer's equity securities. A statutory insider is a person who falls into any of the following categories:

1. An *officer* of a corporation with equity securities registered under the 1934 Act.
2. A *director* of such a corporation.
3. An *owner of 10 percent* or more of a class of equity securities registered under the 1934 Act.

In addition, statutory insiders must *report any transaction* in such securities within 10 days following the end of the month in which the transaction occurs. They must also report purchases and sales made up to six months before and up to six months after becoming an officer, director, or a 10 percent holder.

**Short-Swing Profits.** Section 16(b) of the 1934 Act provides that any profit made by a statutory insider is recoverable by the issuer if the profit resulted from the purchase and sale (or the sale and purchase) within less than a *six-month* period of *any* class of the issuer's equity securities. This provision was designed to stop speculative insider trading on the basis of information that "*may* have been obtained by such owner, director, or officer by reason of his relationship to the issuer." The application of the provision is without regard to intent to use or actual use of inside information. A few cases have held that forced sales made by a person without access to inside information do not violate Section 16(b).

## PROXY SOLICITATION REGULATION

**Introduction.** One of the most important regulatory provisions of the 1934 Act is Section 14, which regulates the *solicitation of proxies* by *any* person. In the public corporation, shareholders rarely attend and vote at shareholder meetings. Many shareholders are able to vote at shareholder meetings only by **proxy,** by which these shareholders direct other persons to vote their shares. Just as investors need information to be able to make intelligent investment decisions, so too do such shareholders need information to determine whether to give a proxy to another person and how to direct that person to vote.

**Proxy Statement.** SEC Regulation 14A requires any person soliciting proxies from holders of securities registered under the 1934 Act to furnish each holder with a *proxy statement* containing certain information. Usually, the only party soliciting proxies is the corporation's management, which is seeking proxies from common shareholders to enable it to reelect itself to the board of directors.

If the management of the corporation does not solicit proxies, it must nevertheless inform the shareholders of material information affecting matters that are to be put to a vote of the shareholders. This *information statement,* which contains about the same information as a proxy statement, must be sent to all shareholders that are entitled to vote at the meeting. The proxy statement or information statement must be filed with the SEC at least 10 days before it is mailed to the shareholders. If the proxy or information statement is issued in connection with an annual meeting of shareholders at which directors are to be elected, the shareholders must also receive a current annual report of the corporation.

**Content of Proxy Statement.** The primary purpose of the SEC rules concerning information that must be included in the proxy statement is to permit shareholders to make informed decisions in voting for directors and on any resolutions proposed by the management or shareholders. Information on each director nominee must include the candidate's principal occupation, his share holdings in the corporation, his previous service as a director of the corporation, his material transactions with the corporation (such as goods or services provided), and his directorships in other corporations. The total remuneration of the five directors or officers who are highest paid, including bonuses, fringe benefits and other perquisites, and grants under stock option plans, must also be included in the proxy statement.

**Proxy.** The rules regarding the content of the **proxy** ensure that the shareholder understands how the proxy will be voted. The proxy form must indicate in boldface type on whose behalf it is being solicited—for example, the corporation's management. Generally, the proxy must permit the shareholder to vote for or against the proposal or to abstain from voting on any resolutions on the meeting agenda. The proxy form may ask for discretionary voting authority if the proxy indicates in bold print how the shares will be voted. For directors' elections, the shareholders must be provided with a means for withholding approval from each nominee.

**False Statements.** Rule 14a–9 prohibits misstatements or omissions of material fact in the course of a proxy solicitation. If a violation is proved, a court may enjoin the holding of the shareholders' meeting, void the proxies that were illegally obtained, or rescind the action taken at the shareholders' meeting.

**Proxy Contests.** A shareholder may decide to solicit proxies in competition with management. Such a competition is called a *proxy contest,* and a solicitation of this kind is also subject to SEC rules. To facilitate proxy contests, the SEC requires the corporation either to furnish a shareholder list to shareholders who desire to wage a proxy contest or to mail the competing proxy material for them.

**Shareholder Proposals.** In a large public corporation, it is very expensive for a shareholder to solicit proxies in support of a proposal for corporate action that she will offer at a shareholders' meeting. Therefore, she usually asks the management to include her proposal in its proxy statement. SEC Rule 14a–8 covers proposals by shareholders.

Under Rule 14a–8, the corporation must include a shareholder's proposal in its proxy statement if, among other things, the shareholder owns at least *1 percent or $1,000* of the securities to be voted at the shareholders' meeting. A shareholder may submit only *one* proposal per meeting. The proposal and its supporting statement may not exceed 500 words.

**Excludable Proposals.** Under Rule 14a–8, a corporation's management may exclude many types of shareholder proposals from its proxy statement. For example, the following are excludable:

1. A proposal that is *not a proper matter for a shareholder vote.* According to SEC No-Action Letters,[11] improper matters include a proposal to *require* that management nominate union representatives to the board of directors. Such a requirement would intrude on the discretion of the board. Note, however, that a proposal *requesting* that management nominate union representatives is not excludable.

2. A proposal that would require the issuer to *violate a state or federal law.* For example, one shareholder asked North American Bank to put a lesbian on the board of directors. The SEC staff advised North American Bank that the proposal was excludable because it may have required the corporation to violate anti-discrimination laws.

3. The proposal relates to a *personal grievance.* A proposal that the corporation pay the shareholder $1 million for damages that she suffered from using one of the corporation's products would be excludable.

4. The proposal deals with the *ordinary business operations* of the corporation. Few well-drafted proposals are excluded on this basis. For example, the SEC staff advised one corporation that a proposal to require the board of directors to develop procedures for dealing with its lettuce suppliers who committed unfair labor practices was *not* excludable.

In addition, one part of Rule 14a–8 prevents a shareholder from submitting a proposal similar to recent proposals that have been overwhelmingly rejected by shareholders. SEC No-Action Letters indicate that slight differences between proposals may be sufficient to require a proposal's inclusion in management's proxy statement. For example, the SEC staff stated that a proposal that the corporation *terminate* its contracts with South African companies and remove its personnel from South Africa did not duplicate an earlier proposal that required the board not to do any *more* business with South Africa than it was doing currently.

[11] No-Action Letters are defined at the end of this section.

**No-Action Letters.** A company that wishes to exclude a submitted shareholder proposal from its proxy statement usually seeks a *No-Action Letter* from the SEC. Although not legally binding, such a letter indicates the position of the SEC staff. If the SEC agrees with the company, it is unlikely to take action against the company for excluding the proposal.

**Effectiveness of Shareholder Proposals.** Very few shareholder proposals receive more than a few percent of the votes cast by shareholders. Nevertheless, many such proposals have a significant effect on management actions. Some shareholder proposals are highly publicized, such as proposals that a corporation stop doing business in South Africa. To avoid embarrassing publicity, management will often effect a shareholder proposal even though the shareholders have not approved the proposal. In this respect, the threat of an embarrassing shareholder proposal places great political leverage in the hands of shareholders.

## LIABILITY PROVISIONS OF THE 1934 ACT

To prevent fraudulent, deceptive, or manipulative practices and provide remedies to the victims of such practices, Congress included a number of liability provisions in the 1934 Act.

**Manipulation of a Security's Price.** Section 9 specifically prohibits a number of deceptive practices that may be used to cause security prices to rise or fall by *fraudulently stimulating market activity.* The prohibited practices include simultaneous purchases and sales of securities (called *wash sales*).

**Liability for False Statements in Filed Documents.** Section 18 is the 1934 Act counterpart to Section 11 of the 1933 Act. Section 18 imposes liability on any person responsible for a false or misleading statement of material fact in *any document filed* with the SEC pursuant to the 1934 Act. (Filed documents include the 10-K report and proxy statements.) Any person who *relies* on a false or misleading statement may sue for damages. As with Section 11, the purchaser need not prove that the defendant was negligent or acted with scienter. Instead, the defendant has a defense that he acted in *good faith* and had *no knowledge* that the statement was false or misleading. This defense is easier to meet than the Section 11 due diligence defense, requiring only that the defendant prove that he did not act with scienter. Partly for this reason, Section 18 is rarely used.

**Section 10(b) and Rule 10b–5.** The most important liability section in the 1934 Act is Section 10(b). Section 10(b) is an extremely broad provision prohibiting the use of any manipulative or deceptive device in contravention of any rules that the SEC prescribe as "necessary or appropriate in the public interest or for the protection of investors." Rule 10b–5 was adopted by the SEC under Section 10(b). The rule states:

It shall be unlawful for any person, directly or indirectly, by use of any means or instrumentality of interstate commerce or of the mails, or of any facility of any national securities exchange,

(a) to employ any device, scheme, or artifice to defraud,

(b) to make any untrue statement of a material fact or to omit to state a material fact necessary in order to make the statements made, in the light of the circumstances under which they were made, not misleading, or

(c) to engage in any act, practice, or course of business which operates or would operate as a fraud or deceit upon any person,

in connection with the purchase or sale of any security.

Rule 10b–5 applies to *all* transactions in *all* securities. Securities need not be registered under the 1933 Act or the 1934 Act for Rule 10b–5 to apply. The rule applies to transactions executed on a securities exchange as well as face-to-face transactions.

**Elements of a Rule 10b–5 Violation.** The most important elements of a Rule 10b–5 violation are a misstatement or omission of material fact, scienter, and reliance. In addition, private persons suing under the rule must be purchasers or sellers.

**Misstatement or Omission of Material Fact.** The essence of fraud, deception, and manipulation is falsity or nondisclosure when there is a duty to speak. Rule 10b–5 imposes liability on persons who *misstate* material facts. For example, if a manager of an unprofitable business induces shareholders to sell their stock to him by representing that the business will fail, although he knows that the business has become potentially profitable, he violates Rule 10b–5.

In addition, a person is liable under Rule 10b–5 if he *omits* material facts when he has a *duty to disclose.* For a person to be liable for an *omission,* there must be a duty of *trust or confidence* breached either by a nondisclosure or by the selective disclosure of confidential information, as was held in the *Dirks* case, which follows. For example, a securities broker is liable to his customer for not disclosing that he owns the shares that he recommends to the customer. As an agent of the customer, he owes a fiduciary duty to his customer to disclose his conflict of interest. In addition, a person is liable for omitting to tell all of the material facts after he has chosen to disclose some of them. His selective disclosure created the duty to disclose all of the material facts.

A manipulation of securities prices not involving false statements, such as engaging in wash sales, is also a violation of Rule 10b–5. There is an omission to disclose the manipulation, which misleads investors to believe that the market price reflects the true value of a security.

However, in *Santa Fe Industries, Inc. v. Green,*[12] the Supreme Court held that a mere *breach of a fiduciary duty,* such as mismanagement of the company by the directors, creates no Rule 10b–5 liability. In addition to a breach of a fiduciary duty, there must be deception or manipulation. Deception may be proved if the fiduciary duty breached is a duty of confidentiality or a duty of disclosure.

**Materiality.** The misstated or omitted fact must be *material.* In essence, material information is any information that is likely to have an impact on the price of a security in the market. The *Texas Gulf Sulphur* case, which follows, states one definition of materiality. The latest Supreme Court pronouncement on materiality is *TSC Industries, Inc. v. Northway,*[13] a Rule 14a–9 case. It states:

> An omitted fact is material if there is a substantial likelihood that a reasonable shareholder would consider it important to his decision. The standard contemplates a showing of a substantial likelihood that the omitted fact would have assumed actual significance in the deliberations of the reasonable shareholder. There must be a substantial likelihood that the disclosure of the omitted fact would have been viewed by the reasonable investor as having significantly altered the total mix of information made available.

It is generally believed that the *Northway* materiality standard applies to all of the liability sections of the securities acts. Such matters as proposed mergers, tender offers for the corporation's stock, plans to introduce an important new product, or indications of an abrupt change in the expectations of the company are examples of what would be considered material facts.

**Scienter.** For fraud, deception, or manipulation to exist, the defendant must have acted with *scienter.* Mere negligence is not enough under Rule 10b–5. Scienter is an intent to deceive, manipulate, or defraud. The Supreme Court has not decided whether recklessness is sufficient for the scienter requirement, though many lower courts have held that reckless conduct violates Rule 10b–5.

**Purchaser or Seller.** The Supreme Court has held that Rule 10b–5 requires that private plaintiffs seeking damages be actual purchasers or sellers of securities.[14] Persons who were deterred from purchasing securities by fraudulent statements may *not* recover lost profits under Rule 10b–5.

**Reliance.** Under Rule 10b–5, private plaintiffs alleging misstatements must prove that they *relied* on the misstatement of material fact. *Reliance* is not usually required in *omission* cases; the investor need merely

[12] 430 U.S. 462 (U.S. Sup. Ct. 1977).

[13] 426 U.S. 438 (U.S. Sup. Ct. 1976).

[14] *Blue Chip Stamps v. Manor Drug Stores,* 421 U.S. 723 (U.S. Sup. Ct. 1975).

prove that the omitted fact was material. In *Shores v. Sklar,* which follows, the court held that an investor's reliance on the availability of the securities on the market satisfied the reliance requirement of Rule 10b–5. This *market reliance* existed even though the sellers had never communicated with the purchaser. The SEC as plaintiff need *not* prove reliance.

**Jurisdictional Requirement.** The wrongful action must be accomplished *by the mails, an instrumentality of interstate commerce, or a national securities exchange.* This element satisfies the federal jurisdiction requirement. Use of the mails or a telephone within one state has been held to meet this element.

**Conduct Covered by Rule 10b–5.** The scope of activities proscribed by Rule 10b–5 is not immediately obvious. While it is easy to understand that actual fraud and price manipulation are covered by the rule, two other areas are less easily mastered: the corporation's continuous disclosure obligation and insider trading.

**Continuous Disclosure of Material Information.** The purpose of the securities acts is to ensure that investors have the information they need in order to make intelligent investment decisions at all times. The periodic reporting requirements of the 1934 Act are designed to accomplish this result. If important developments arise between the disclosure dates of reports, however, investors will not have all of the information they need to make intelligent decisions unless the corporation discloses the material information immediately. Rule 10b–5, as interpreted in the *Texas Gulf Sulphur* case, which follows, may be read to require a corporation to disclose material information *immediately,* unless the corporation has a valid business purpose for withholding disclosure. In addition, *Texas Gulf Sulphur* held that when the corporation does choose to disclose information, it must do so accurately.

In a recent case, a federal court of appeals held that Rule 10b–5 did not require disclosure of merger negotiations, because the boards of directors of the two corporations had not yet agreed in principal to merge.[15] In that case, Heublein, Inc., was negotiating a merger with R. J. Reynolds in an attempt to defeat a hostile tender offer. When the price of Heublein shares spurted for no apparent reason, the New York Stock Exchange asked Heublein to explain the price increase. Heublein responded that no corporate development could explain the spurt, although the merger negotiations had already begun. The court of appeals held that the "no corporate development" statement was not a violation of Rule 10b–5, because the directors had not agreed in principle to merge and Heublein had no reason to believe that news of the negotiations had been leaked to investors.

**Trading on Inside Information.** Many interesting Rule 10b–5 cases involve the failure to disclose nonpublic, corporate information known to an insider. Some of these cases involve face-to-face transactions between an insider and another shareholder. For example, a corporation's president acquires all of the corporation's outstanding shares at a low price. His failure to tell the sellers about contracts that would increase the value of the shares violates Rule 10b–5. In other cases, the buyer and seller have not met face-to-face. Instead, the transaction has been executed on a stock exchange. Trading on an exchange by a person in possession of confidential corporate information has been held to violate Rule 10b–5, even though the buyer and seller never met.

[15] *Greenfield v. Heublein, Inc.,* 742 F.2d 751 (3d Cir. 1984), *cert. denied,* 53 U.S.L.W. 3594 (U.S. Sup. Ct. Feb. 19, 1985).

**Disclose or Refrain from Trading.** The essential rule that exists in all of the inside trading cases is that a person with nonpublic, inside information must *either disclose the information before trading or refrain from trading.* The difficult task in the insider trading area is determining when a person is subject to this *disclose-or-refrain rule.*

**Insider Liability.** In *United States v. Chiarella,*[16] the Supreme Court laid down the test for determining an insider's liability for trading on nonpublic, corporate information:

> The duty to disclose arises when one party has information that the other party is entitled to know because of a fiduciary or similar relation of trust and confidence between them. A relationship of trust and confidence exists between the shareholders of a corporation and those insiders who have obtained confidential information by reason of their position with that corporation. This relationship gives rise to a duty to disclose because of the necessity of preventing a corporate insider from taking unfair advantage of the uninformed stockholders.

Under this test, insiders include not only officers and directors of the corporation, but also *anyone who is entrusted with corporate information for a corporate purpose.* Insiders include outside consultants, lawyers, engineers, investment bankers, public relations advisers, news reporters, and personnel of government agencies *who are given confidential corporate information for a corporate purpose.*

**Tippee Liability.** Furthermore, *tippees* of insiders, such as relatives and friends of insiders, stockbrokers, and security analysts, are forbidden to trade on inside information and are subject to recovery of their profits if they do. In the *Dirks* case, the Supreme Court stated the applicability of Rule 10b–5 to tippees. A tippee has liability if (1) an insider has breached a fiduciary duty of trust and confidence to the shareholders by disclosing to the tippee and (2) the tippee knows or should know of the insider's breach. The insider has not breached her fiduciary duty to the shareholders unless she has received a personal benefit by disclosing to the tippee.

**Breach of Fiduciary Duty.** In *Dirks,* the Supreme Court held that liability for inside trading is premised upon an insider's breach of a fiduciary duty owed to the shareholders. The courts have considered whether a breach of a fiduciary duty owed to *someone other than the shareholders* of the corporation whose shares the tippee is buying or selling can create Rule 10b–5 liability. In *United States v. Newman,*[17] the Second Circuit Court of Appeals held that criminal liability might attach to a person who had breached a duty of confidence owed to his employer, even though no duty was owed to the shareholders on the other side of the securities transaction. In *Moss v. Morgan Stanley,*[18] a case with the same facts as *Newman,* the same court held that the shareholders could not bring a suit for damages against the person who breached a fiduciary duty to his employer but breached no duty owed to the shareholders. The court refused to expand the holding of *Newman* to create a duty of disclosure to the general public.

**Extent of Liability for Insider Trading.** There is much confusion about the extent of a defendant's liability when she has traded on inside information or has passed such information to someone who trades on the information. At the very least, a defendant has been required to give up the profits

[16] 445 U.S. 222 (U.S. Sup. Ct. 1980).

[17] 664 F.2d 12 (2d Cir. 1981), *aff'd after remand,* 722 F.2d 729 (2d Cir. 1983), *cert. denied,* 104 S. Ct. 193 (1983).

[18] 719 F.2d 5 (2d Cir. 1983).

that she made by trading on inside information. A few courts have imposed liability to the extent of the losses of the persons who were defrauded, a level of liability that has been labeled "draconian" because it may far exceed any benefit that the defendant received from using the information. Yet mere disgorgement of profits has been assailed as not adequately deterring insider trading, because the defendant may realize an enormous profit if her trading is not discovered and loses nothing beyond her profits if it is. In response to this issue of liability, in 1984 Congress passed an amendment to Section 21(d) of the 1934 Act permitting the SEC to seek a civil penalty of *three times* the profit gained or the loss avoided by trading on inside information. This treble penalty is paid to the Treasury of the United States. The penalty applies only to SEC actions; it does not affect the amount of damages that may be recovered by private plaintiffs.

**Criminal Liability.** Like the 1933 Act, the 1934 Act provides for liability for criminal violations of the Act. Section 32 provides for a fine of up to $100,000 and imprisonment of up to five years for willful violations of the 1934 Act or the related SEC rules. Criminal penalties were imposed for a violation of the 1934 Act in *United States v. Natelli,* which appears in Chapter 27.

## Shores v. Sklar

**647 F.2d 462 (5th Cir. 1981)**

Alabama law permits a municipality to create an industrial development board. Such a board has the power to induce industry to settle in Alabama by issuing tax-exempt bonds. It uses the proceeds of an issuance of tax-exempt bonds to build an industrial building, which it leases to a manufacturing business, usually at below-market rates. The lease payments made by the manufacturing business are the sole revenue source for the payment of interest and principal on the bonds. If the business fails, the bonds are not repaid.

J. C. Harrelson, the president and chief shareholder of Alabama Supply and Equipment Company (ASECo), and Clarence Hamilton conspired to defraud investors. They induced Frisco City, Alabama, to create the Industrial Development Board of Frisco City to issue tax-exempt bonds to investors. Harrelson and Hamilton promised the Board that ASECo would lease the building constructed with the proceeds. They also promised that ASECo would manufacture mobile homes in the building.

The Board offered and sold bonds pursuant to an Offering Circular prepared by Jerald Sklar, an attorney. The Offering Circular misstated or omitted several material facts.

The Board used the proceeds of the bond issuance to build a manufacturing plant. The plant was built in part by Coliseum Properties. Coliseum Properties, however, merely served as a vehicle by which substantial parts of the proceeds of the issuance were diverted and used for the benefit of others. The controlling persons of Coliseum Properties made improper payments to ASECo and to Harrelson in exchange for the construction contract.

After the ASECo plant was constructed, ASECo ceased all operations and defaulted on its rental payments to the Board, causing the value of the bonds to drop precipitously.

The building was sold in an attempt to pay the principal on the bonds. After the sale of the industrial facility, the bondholders received only $373.33 for each $1,000 bond.

Clarence Bishop purchased four of the bonds for $4,096. He never saw the Offering Circular or knew that one existed. He bought the bonds solely on his broker's oral representations that they were a good investment and that others in the community had purchased them.

Bishop, through his executor, James Shore, sued Sklar and others for fraud under Rule 10b–5. Sklar argued that since Bishop had not read the Offering Circular, he could not prove reliance, a necessary element of a Rule 10b–5 violation. The district court ruled in favor of Sklar and against Bishop because Bishop failed to read or even to seek to read the Offering Circular. Bishop appealed.

**Clark, Circuit Judge.** The requisite element of causation in fact [reliance] would be established if Bishop proved the scheme was intended to and did bring the bonds onto the market fraudulently and proved he relied on the integrity of the offerings of the securities market. His lack of reliance on the Offering Circular, only one component of the overall scheme, is not determinative. Bishop has alleged the necessary elements of an action under 10b–5. Bishop's burden of proof will be to show that (1) the defendants knowingly conspired to bring securities onto the market which were not entitled to be marketed, intending to defraud purchasers, (2) Bishop reasonably relied on the bonds' availability on the market as an indication of their apparent genuineness, and (3) as a result of the scheme to defraud, he suffered a loss.

It is asserted that allowing recovery to one who has never read the Offering Circular minimizes the importance of such documents and discourages investors from reading them. We disagree. First, the purposes of the securities acts and Rule 10b–5 are far broader than merely providing full disclosure or fostering informed investment decisions. The Supreme Court has held that the acts were designed "to protect investors against fraud and to promote ethical standards of honesty and fair dealing." The central purpose of the acts is the protection of investors and the promotion of free and honest securities markets. Second, if Bishop proves no more than that the bonds would have been offered at a lower price or higher interest rate, rather than that they would never have been issued or marketed, he cannot recover. Thus, a purchaser of securities will still have the strongest incentive to read the disclosure statement if he wants to ensure he gets full value for his securities purchases.

Under Bishop's theory, it would have availed him nothing to have read the Offering Circular. The theory is not that he bought inferior bonds, but that the bonds he bought were fraudulently marketed. The securities laws allow an investor to rely on the integrity of the market to the extent that the securities it offers to him for purchase are entitled to be in the market place.

Judgment reversed in favor of Bishop.

## SEC v. Texas Gulf Sulphur Co.

### 401 F.2d 833 (2d Cir. 1968)

Texas Gulf Sulphur (TGS) had for several years made aerial geophysical surveys in eastern Canada, followed by drilling exploratory cores into geologic formations that looked promising. On November 12, 1963, the core from the first drilling on a parcel of land near Timmins, Ontario, was fabulously high in copper content as well as in zinc and silver. Diversionary holes were then drilled elsewhere until the balance of the land covered by the formation could be acquired by TGS. By March 31, 1964, the land-acquisition program had progressed far enough for TGS to resume drilling in the area. The next two cores also showed substantial quantities of the same minerals, and additional rigs were constructed to drill more holes, beginning on April 8. Meanwhile, rumors of a major ore strike were circulating in Canada, and on Saturday, April 11, two major New York newspapers printed reports of TGS's activity and inferred a rich strike from the fact that the drill cores were being flown to the United States.

Also on Saturday, Stephens, the president of TGS, and Fogarty, the executive vice president, concerned by the publicized rumors, talked with Mollison, the TGS vice president who was in charge of the operations near Timmins. Mollison had left the drilling on Friday and was at his home near New York City for the weekend. As a result, on Sunday a news release was distributed for use on Monday, April 13. The release stated that most of the drilling in eastern Canada had shown nothing of value, with a few holes indicating small or marginal ore bodies. It said that shipment of the cores to the United States was routine. It then added:

> Recent drilling on one property near Timmins has led to preliminary indications that more drilling would be required for proper evaluation of this prospect. The drilling done to date has not been conclusive, but the statements made by many outside quarters are unreliable and include information and figures that are not available to TGS.
>
> The work done to date has not been sufficient to reach definite conclusions and any statement as to size and grade of ore would be premature and possibly misleading. When we have progressed to the point where reasonable and logical conclusions can be made, TGS will issue a definitive statement to its stockholders and to the public in order to clarify the Timmins project.

Three days later, on April 16 at 10 A.M., TGS held a conference for the financial press and disclosed that the ore body would run to at least 25 million tons of ore.

The price of TGS common stock began to rise immediately. The price rose from approximately $18 per share on November 12, 1963, to $58 on May 15, 1964. Many shareholders of TGS had sold their shares after the ore find but before its public disclosure. The SEC claimed that the first press release of TGS, issued on April 12, was deceptive and misleading in violation of the 1934 Act. The district court held for TGS. The SEC appealed.

**WATERMAN, CIRCUIT JUDGE.** The basic test of materiality is whether a *reasonable* man would attach importance in determining his choice of action in the transaction in question. This, of course, encompasses any fact which in reasonable and objective contemplation *might* affect the value of the corporation's stock or securities. Thus, material facts include not only information disclosing the earnings and distributions of a company, but also those facts which affect the probable future of the company and those which may affect the desire of investors to buy, sell, or hold the company's securities.

In each case, then, whether facts are material within Rule 10b–5 when the facts relate to a particular event and are undisclosed by those persons who are knowledgeable thereof will depend at any given time upon a balancing of both the indicated probability that the event will occur and the anticipated magnitude of the event in light of the totality of the company activity. Here, knowledge of the possibility of the existence of a mine of the vast magnitude indicated by the remarkably rich drill core located rather close to the surface within the confines of a large anomaly (suggesting an extensive region of mineralization) might well have affected the price of TGS stock and would certainly have been an important fact to a reasonable, if speculative, investor in deciding whether he should buy, sell, or hold.

Our survey of the facts conclusively establishes that knowledge of the results of the discovery hole would have been important to a reasonable investor and might have affected the price of the stock.[19]

Finally, a major factor in determining whether the discovery was material fact is the importance attached to the drilling results by those who knew about it. The timing of stock purchases by those who knew of the discovery virtually compels the inference that the insiders were influenced by the drilling results. No reason appears why outside investors, perhaps better acquainted with speculative modes of investment and with, in many cases, perhaps more capital at their disposal for intelligent speculation, would have been less influenced, and would not have been similarly motivated to invest if they had known what the insider investors knew of the discovery.

### The Corporate Defendant

The investing public is hurt by exposure to false or deceptive statements irrespective of the purpose underlying their issuance. It does not appear to be unfair to impose upon corporate management a duty to ascertain the truth of any statements the corporation releases to its shareholders or to the investing public at large.

Accordingly, we hold that Rule 10b–5 is violated whenever assertions are made, as here, in a manner reasonably calculated to influence the investing public, for example, by means of the financial media, if such assertions are false or misleading or are so incomplete as to mislead irrespective of whether the issuance of the release was motivated by corporate officials for ulterior purposes. It seems clear, however, that if corporate management demonstrates that it was diligent in ascertaining that the information it published was the whole truth and that such diligently obtained information was disseminated in good faith, Rule 10b–5 would not have been violated.

The only remedy the Commission seeks against the corporation is an injunction, and therefore we do not find it necessary to decide whether a lack of due diligence on the part of TGS alone, absent a showing of bad faith, would subject the corporation to any liability for damages.[20] We hold only that, in an action for injunctive relief, the district

---

[19] [Footnote 11 by the Court.] We do not suggest that material facts must be disclosed immediately; the timing of disclosure is a matter for the business judgment of the corporate officers entrusted with the management of the corporation within the affirmative disclosure requirements promulgated by the exchanges and by the SEC. Here a valuable corporate purpose was served by delaying the publication of the discovery.

[20] [Editor's note.] The Supreme Court in *Ernst & Ernst v. Hochfelder,* 425 U.S. 185 (U.S. Sup. Ct. 1976), held that scienter was required in a private right of action for damages.

court has the discretionary power under Rule 10b–5 and Section 10(b) to issue an injunction, if the misleading statement resulted from a lack of due diligence on the part of TGS.[21]

It is not altogether certain from the present record that the draftsmen could, as the SEC suggests, have readily obtained current reports of the drilling progress over the weekend of April 10–12, but they certainly should have obtained them if at all possible for them to do so.

However, even if it were not possible to evaluate and transmit current data in time to prepare the release on April 12, it would seem that TGS could have delayed the preparation a bit until an accurate report of a rapidly changing situation was possible.

At the very least, if TGS felt compelled to respond to the spreading rumors of a spectacular discovery, it would have been more accurate to have stated that the situation was in flux and that the release was prepared as of April 10 information rather than purporting to report the progress to date. Moreover, it would have obviously been better to have specifically described the known drilling progress as of April 10 by stating the basic facts. Such an explicit disclosure would have permitted the investing public to evaluate the prospect of a mine at Timmins without having to read between the lines to understand that preliminary indications were favorable—in itself an understatement.

The choice of an ambiguous general statement rather than a summary of the specific facts cannot reasonably be justified by any claimed urgency. The avoidance of liability for misrepresentation in the event that the Timmins project failed, a highly unlikely event as of April 12 or April 13, did not forbid the accurate and truthful divulgence of detailed results which need not, of course, have been accompanied by conclusory assertions of success.

Judgment for the SEC. Remanded to the trial court to determine whether TGS has violated the 1934 Act.

---

[21] [Editor's note.] The Supreme Court in *Aaron v. SEC,* 446 U.S. 680 (U.S. Sup. Ct. 1980), held that scienter was required in SEC injunctive actions, not merely a lack of due diligence.

## SEC v. Dirks

**103 S. Ct. 3255 (U.S. Sup. Ct. 1983)**

Raymond Dirks was a security analyst in a New York brokerage firm. On March 6, 1973, Dirks received information from Ronald Secrist, a former officer of Equity Funding of America, a seller of life insurance and mutual funds. Secrist alleged that the assets of Equity Funding were vastly overstated as the result of fraudulent corporate practices. He also stated that the SEC and state insurance departments had failed to act on similar charges of fraud made by Equity Funding employees. Secrist urged Dirks to verify the fraud and to disclose it publicly.

Dirks visited Equity Funding's headquarters in Los Angeles and interviewed several officers and employees of the corporation. The senior management denied any wrongdoing, but certain employees corroborated the charges of fraud. Dirks openly discussed the information he had obtained with a number of clients and investors. Some of these persons sold their holdings of Equity Funding securities.

Dirks urged a *Wall Street Journal* reporter to write a story on the fraud allegations. The reporter, fearing libel, declined to write the story.

During the two-week period in which Dirks investigated the fraud and spread the word of Secrist's charges, the price of Equity Funding stock fell from $26 per share to less than $15 per share. The New York Stock Exchange halted trading in Equity Funding stock on March 27. On that date, Dirks voluntarily presented his information on the fraud to the SEC. Only then did the SEC institute an action for fraud against Equity Funding. Shortly thereafter, California insurance authorities impounded Equity Funding's records and uncovered evidence of the fraud. On April 2, *The Wall Street Journal* published a front-page story based largely on information assembled by Dirks. Equity Funding immediately went into receivership.

The SEC brought an administrative proceeding against Dirks for violating Rule 10b–5 by passing along confidential inside information. The SEC found that he had violated Rule 10b–5, but it merely censured him, since he had played an important role in bringing the fraud to light. Dirks appealed to the Court of Appeals for the District of Columbia Circuit. The court of appeals affirmed the judgment. Dirks then appealed to the Supreme Court.

**POWELL, JUSTICE.** In the seminal case of *In re Cady, Roberts & Co.* (1961), the SEC recognized that the common law in some jurisdictions imposes on corporate insiders an affirmative duty of disclosure when dealing in securities. The SEC found that not only did breach of this common-law duty establish the elements of a Rule 10b–5 violation, but also that individuals other than corporate insiders could be obligated either to disclose material nonpublic information before trading or to abstain from trading altogether.

In *U.S. v. Chiarella* (1980), we accepted the two elements set out in *Cady, Roberts* for establishing a Rule 10b–5 violation: (i) the existence of a relationship affording access to inside information intended to be available only for a corporate purpose, and (ii) the unfairness of allowing a corporate insider to take advantage of that information by trading without disclosure. In examining whether Chiarella had an obligation to disclose or abstain, the Court found that there is no general duty to disclose before trading on material nonpublic information, and held that a duty to disclose under Section 10(b) does not arise from the mere possession of nonpublic market information. Such a duty arises from the existence of a fiduciary relationship.

Not all breaches of fiduciary duty in connection with a securities transaction, however, come within the ambit of Rule 10b–5. There must also be manipulation or deception. In an inside-trading case, this fraud derives from the inherent unfairness involved where one takes advantage of information intended to be available only for a corporate purpose and not for the personal benefit of anyone.

There can be no duty to disclose when the person who has traded on inside information was not the corporation's agent, was not a fiduciary, or was not a person in whom the sellers of the securities had placed their trust and confidence. Not to require such a fiduciary relationship would depart radically from the established doctrine that duty arises from a specific relationship between two parties and would amount to recognizing a general duty between all participants in market transactions to forego actions based on material, nonpublic information. This requirement of a specific relationship between the shareholders and the individual trading on inside information has created analytical difficulties for the

SEC and courts in policing tippees who trade on inside information. Unlike insiders who have independent fiduciary duties to both the corporation and its shareholders, the typical tippee has no such relationship.[22] In view of this absence, it has been unclear how a tippee acquires the *Cady, Roberts* duty to refrain from trading on inside information.

The SEC's theory of tippee liability appears rooted in the idea that the antifraud provisions require equal information among all traders. This conflicts with the principle set forth in *Chiarella* that only some persons, under some circumstances, will be barred from trading while in possession of material nonpublic information. We affirm today that a duty to disclose arises from the relationship between the parties and not merely from one's ability to acquire information because of his position in the market.

The conclusion that recipients of inside information do not invariably acquire a duty to disclose or abstain does not mean that such tippees always are free to trade on the information. Not only are insiders forbidden by their fiduciary relationship from personally using undisclosed corporate information to their advantage, but also they may not give such information to an outsider for the same improper purpose of exploiting the information for their personal gain. The transactions of those who knowingly participate with the fiduciary in such a breach are as forbidden as transactions on behalf on the trustee himself. A contrary rule would open up opportunities for devious dealings in the name of the others that the trustee could not conduct in his own. Thus, the tippee's duty to disclose or abstain is derivative from that of the insider's duty. As we noted in *Chiarella,* the tippee's obligation has been viewed as arising from his role as a participant after the fact in the insider's breach of a fiduciary duty.

Thus, a tippee assumes a fiduciary duty to the shareholders of a corporation not to trade on material nonpublic information only when the insider has breached his fiduciary duty to the shareholders by disclosing the information to the tippee and the tippee knows or should know that there has been a breach.

In determining whether a tippee is under an obligation to disclose or abstain, it thus is necessary to determine whether the insider's tip constituted a breach of the insider's fiduciary duty. Whether disclosure is a breach of duty therefore depends in large part on the purpose of the disclosure. Thus, the test is whether the insider personally will benefit, directly or indirectly, from his disclosure. Absent some personal gain, there has been no breach of duty to stockholders. And absent a breach by the insider, there is no derivative breach.

This requires courts to focus on objective criteria, *i.e.,* whether the insider receives a direct or indirect personal benefit from the disclosure, such as a pecuniary gain or a reputational benefit that will translate into future earnings. For example, there may be a relationship between the insider and the recipient that suggests a *quid pro quo* from the latter, or an intention to benefit the particular recipient. The elements of fiduciary duty and exploitation of nonpublic information also exist when an insider makes a gift of confidential information to a relative or friend who trades. The tip and trade resemble trading by the insider himself followed by a gift of the profits to the recipient.

---

[22] [Footnote 14 by the Court.] Under certain circumstances, such as where corporate information is revealed legitimately to an underwriter, accountant, lawyer, or consultant working for the corporation, these outsiders may become fiduciaries of the shareholders. The basis for recognizing this fiduciary duty is not simply that such persons acquired nonpublic corporate information, but rather that they have entered into a special confidential relationship in the conduct of the business of the enterprise and are given access to information solely for corporate purposes. When such a person breaches his fiduciary relationship, he may be treated more properly as a tipper than a tippee. For such a duty to be imposed, however, the corporation must expect the outsider to keep the disclosed nonpublic information confidential, and the relationship at least must imply such a duty.

Under the inside-trading and tipping rules set forth above, we find that there was no actionable violation by Dirks. Dirks was a stranger to Equity Funding, with no pre-existing fiduciary duty to its shareholders. He took no action, directly or indirectly, that induced the shareholders or officers of Equity Funding to repose trust or confidence in him. There was no expectation by Dirks' sources that he would keep their information in confidence. Nor did Dirks misappropriate or illegally obtain the information about Equity Funding. Unless the insiders breached their *Cady, Roberts* duty to shareholders in disclosing the nonpublic information to Dirks, he breached no duty when he passed it on to investors as well as to *The Wall Street Journal.*

It is clear that neither Secrist nor the other Equity Funding employees violated their *Cady, Roberts* duty to the corporation's shareholders by providing information to Dirks. Secrist intended to convey relevant information that management was unlawfully concealing, and he believed that persuading Dirks to investigate was the best way to disclose the fraud. The tippers received no monetary or personal benefit for revealing Equity Funding's secrets, nor was their purpose to make a gift of valuable information to Dirks. The tippers were motivated by a desire to expose the fraud. In the absence of a breach of duty to shareholders by the insiders, there was no derivative breach by Dirks. Dirks therefore could not have been a participant after the fact in an insider's breach of a fiduciary duty.

Judgment reversed in favor of Dirks.

## TENDER OFFER REGULATION

**History.** Until the early 1960s, the predominant procedure by which one corporation acquired another was the merger, a transaction requiring the cooperation of the acquired corporation's management. Since the 1960s, the *tender offer* has become an often used acquisition device. A tender offer is a public offer by a *bidder* to purchase a *subject company's* equity securities directly from its shareholders at a specified price for a fixed period of time. The offering price is usually well above the market price of the shares. Such offers are often made even though there is opposition from the subject company's management. Opposed offers are called *hostile tender offers.*

**The Williams Act.** In 1968, the Williams Act amendments to the 1934 Act were passed to provide investors with more information on which to base tender offer decisions. The aim of the amendments is to give the bidder (usually a corporation) and the subject company equal opportunities to present their cases to the shareholders. Strict reporting and procedural requirements are established for both parties. The Williams Act applies only when the subject company's equity securities are registered under the 1934 Act.

**Definition of Tender Offer.** The Williams Act does not define a tender offer. The courts look at several factors to determine whether a person has made a tender offer. The *greater the number of people solicited* and the *lower their investment sophistication,* the more likely it is that the bidder will be held to have made a tender offer. Also, the *shorter the offering period,* the *more rigid the price,* and the *greater the publicity* concerning the offer, the more likely it is that the purchase efforts of the bidder will be treated as a tender offer. Given these factors, a person who purchases shares directly from several shareholders risks having a court treat the purchases like a tender offer. The Williams Act clearly states, however, that there is no tender offer unless the bidder intends to become a holder of at least 5 percent of the subject company's shares.

**Regulation of Tender Offers.** A bidder making a tender offer must file a tender offer statement, Schedule 14D–1, with the SEC before the offer is made. The information in this schedule includes the terms of the offer (for example, the price), the background of the bidder, and the purpose of the tender offer (including whether the bidder intends to control the subject company).

**Minimum Offering Period.** An SEC rule requires the bidder to keep the tender offer open for at least *20 business days* and prohibits any purchase of shares during that time. The purpose of this rule is to give shareholders adequate time to make informed decisions regarding whether to tender their shares. Tendering shareholders must be permitted to *withdraw* their shares during the first 15 days of the tender offer. An additional 10 days must be allowed for withdrawal if a competing tender offer is made. These rules allow the highest bidder to buy the shares, as in an auction.

**Price Increases.** If the bidder increases the offering price during the term of the tender offer, all of the shareholders must be paid the higher price even if they tendered their shares at a lower price. If more shares are tendered than the bidder offered to buy, the bidder must *prorate* purchases among all of the shares tendered. This proration rule is designed to foster careful shareholder decisions about whether to sell shares. Shareholders might rush to tender their shares if the bidder could accept shares on a first come, first served basis.

**Subject Company's Response.** The management of the subject company is required to inform the shareholders of its position on the tender offer, with its reasons, within 10 days after the offer has been made. It must also provide the bidder with a list of the holders of the equity securities that the bidder seeks to acquire.

**Tender Offer Advisory Committee.** In 1983, an SEC advisory committee studied tender offers and made several recommendations, which have not yet become law. These recommendations deal in part with the defense tactics used by the managements of subject companies. The advisory committee recommended that restrictions be imposed on the use of the most abusive defense tactics, such as golden parachutes.[23] It also made other recommendations that would protect shareholders, such as preserving the tender offer's usefulness in facilitating the ouster of entrenched, inefficient subject company management.

**Tender Offers versus Private Acquisitions of Shares.** The Williams Act regulates private acquisitions of shares differently from tender offers. When the bidder privately seeks a controlling block of the subject company's shares on a stock exchange or in face-to-face transactions with only a few shareholders, no advance notice to the SEC or disclosure to shareholders is required. A person making a *private acquisition* is required to file a state-

[23] A "golden parachute" is a special employment contract between a subject company and its officer. Under such a contract, the subject company is required to pay the officer a substantial sum of money—sometimes in the millions of dollars—if the officer is removed. A golden parachute is supposed to deter bidders from making a tender offer for the subject company because it increases their cost of removing the subject company's management. In reality, golden parachutes rarely deter bidders. Instead, they merely compensate—sometimes excessively—the terminated officers of the subject company.

ment (Schedule 13D) with the SEC and to send a copy to the subject company within 10 days after he becomes a holder of 5 percent of its shares. No filing is required if he has purchased no more than 2 percent of the shares within the past 12 months.

**State Regulation of Tender Offers.** Statutes that apply to tender offers have been enacted by 33 states. A number of these statutes have been held unconstitutional as being preempted by the Williams Act or as violating the Commerce Clause of the U.S. Constitution.[24] Most of the state corporation statutes favor subject companies by requiring long periods of *advance notice* to the subject company and *long minimum offering periods.* Some statutes give the state securities commissioner authority to determine whether the offer is "fair, just, and equitable" and permit the subject company to delay the tender offer until such a ruling has been made.

## THE FOREIGN CORRUPT PRACTICES ACT

**Background.** The Foreign Corrupt Practices Act (FCPA) was passed by Congress in 1977 as an amendment to the Securities Exchange Act of 1934. Its passage followed discoveries that more than 400 American corporations had given bribes or made other improper or questionable payments in connection with business abroad and within the United States. Many of these payments were bribes to high-level officials of foreign governments for the purpose of obtaining contracts for the sale of goods or services. In some instances, publicity and even rumors concerning such payments had strained relations between the United States and foreign countries.

Officers of the companies that had made the payments, even when admitting that the payments were bribes, argued that such payments were customary and necessary in business transactions in many countries. This argument was pressed forcefully with regard to *facilitating* payments. Such payments, sometimes called *grease,* were said to be essential to get lower-level government officials in a number of countries to perform their nondiscretionary or ministerial tasks, such as preparing or approving necessary import or export documents.

In a significant number of cases, bribes had been accounted for as commission payments, as normal transactions with foreign subsidiaries, or as payments for services rendered by professionals or other firms or had in other ways been made to appear as normal business expenses. These bribes were then illegally deducted as normal business expenses in income tax returns filed with the Internal Revenue Service.

**Firms Covered.** Under the FCPA, it is a crime for *any American firm*—whether or not it has securities registered under the 1934 Act—to offer, promise, or make payments or gifts of anything of value to foreign officials and certain others. The FCPA also establishes record-keeping and internal control requirements for firms subject to the Securities Exchange Act of 1934.

**The Payments Prohibition.** Payments are prohibited if the person making the payment *knows or should know* that some or all of it will be used for the purpose of *influencing a governmental decision.* An offer to make a prohibited payment or a promise to do so is

[24] E.g., *Edgar v. MITE Corp.,* 102 S. Ct. 2629 (U.S. Sup. Ct. 1982). Preemption and the Commerce Clause are discussed in Chapter 42.

a violation even if the offer is not accepted or the promise is not carried out. The FCPA prohibits offers or payments to foreign political parties and candidates for office as well as offers and payments to government officials. Payments of kickbacks to foreign businesses and their officials are not prohibited unless it is known or should be known that these payments will be passed on to government officials or other illegal recipients. The payments prohibition applies to all American firms, whether or not they are required to file reports with the SEC under the 1934 Act.

**Grease Payments.** *Grease* payments are *not* prohibited by the FCPA. Payments are not illegal so long as the recipient has *no discretion* in carrying out a governmental function. For example, suppose a corporation applies for a radio license in Italy and makes a payment to the government official who issues the licenses. If the official grants licenses to every applicant and the payment merely speeds up the processing of the application, the FCPA is not violated. On the other hand, if only a few applicants are granted licenses and the payment is made to ensure that the corporation will obtain a license, the payment is illegal.

**Penalties.** Substantial penalties for violations may be imposed. A company may be fined up to $1 million. Directors, officers, employees, or agents participating in violations are liable for fines of up to $10,000 and prison terms of up to five years.

**Record-Keeping and Internal Controls Requirements.** The FCPA added Section 13(b)(2) to the 1934 Act. It imposes record-keeping and internal controls requirements on firms that are subject to the 1934 Act. The purpose of such controls is to prevent unauthorized payments and transactions and unauthorized access to company assets.

The new section requires the making and keeping of records and accounts "which, in reasonable detail, accurately, and fairly reflect the transactions and dispositions of the assets of the issuer" of securities. It also requires the establishment and maintenance of a system of internal accounting controls. This system must provide "reasonable assurances" that the firm's transactions are executed in accordance with management's authorization and that the firm's assets are used or disposed of only as authorized by management. In addition, the recording of transactions must permit the preparation of financial statements that conform to generally accepted accounting principles. Furthermore, at reasonable intervals management must see that the records are compared with the actual assets available, and if they do not agree, it must determine the reason for the discrepancy.

The record-keeping provisions are written in general terms. As a result, there has been some confusion among accountants and executives about what kinds of records and what steps by management will assure compliance. There is agreement that a top-management review to determine the adequacy of internal controls and record-keeping practices is required and that the board of directors should exercise some oversight. Communications to employees clarifying the need for accountability for firm assets and prohibiting payments or other uses of firm assets without proper authorization are recommended.

These requirements apply not only to transactions and records relating to business with foreign governments or conducted in foreign countries but also to purely domestic business activities. The payment of a bribe is not essential to a violation of this part of the act. No specific penalties are provided; the general penalties of the 1934 Act apply.

## STATE SECURITIES LEGISLATION

**Purpose and History.** State securities laws are frequently referred to as *blue-sky laws,* since the early state securities statutes were designed to protect investors from promoters and security salespersons who would "sell building lots in the blue sky," according to one state legislator. The first state to enact a securities law was Kansas, in 1911. All of the states now have such legislation.

**Uniform Securities Act.** In August 1985, the National Conference of Commissioners on Uniform State Laws adopted a new Uniform Securities Act. The new act replaced the Uniform Securities Act of 1956. Both acts contain *antifraud provisions,* require the *registration of securities,* and demand *broker-dealer registration.* Thirty-five states have adopted the 1956 Act, but none has adopted the 1985 Act at this time. Many states that have adopted the Uniform Securities Act of 1956 have made significant changes in it. In recent years, states have amended their acts to create exemptions similar to those in Regulation D of the 1933 Act.

**Registration by Coordination.** Both Uniform Securities Acts permit an issuer to register its securities by *coordination.* Instead of filing a registration statement under the Securities Act of 1933 and a different one as required by state law, registration by coordination allows the issuer to file the 1933 Act registration statement with the state securities administrator. Registration by coordination decreases the issuer's expense of complying with state law when making an interstate offering of its securities.

**Securities Fraud.** All of the state securities statutes provide penalties for fraudulent sales and permit the issuance of injunctions to protect investors from additional or anticipated fraudulent acts. Most of the statutes grant broad power to investigate fraud to some state official—usually the attorney general or his appointee as securities administrator. All of the statutes provide criminal penalties for selling fraudulent securities and conducting fraudulent transactions.

**Disclosure and Merit Registration.** Most of the state securities statutes adopt the philosophy of the 1933 Act that informed investors can make intelligent investment decisions. The states with such statutes have a registration scheme much like the 1933 Act, with required *disclosures* for public offerings and exemptions from registration for small and private offerings. Other states reject the contention that investors with full information can make intelligent investment decisions. The securities statutes in these states give a securities administrator power to deny registration on the *merits* of the security. Only securities that are not unduly risky and promise an adequate return to investors may receive administrator approval.

**Broker-Dealer Registration.** Most of the state securities statutes regulate professional sellers of securities, notably securities brokers and dealers. These statutes register securities brokers and require proof of the financial responsibility of dealers. Dealers must disclose pertinent facts about the securities they are selling and avoid sales of fraudulent securities.

## SUMMARY

The federal securities acts passed in 1933 and 1934 require that investors be given accurate and adequate information concerning security issues. They also prohibit fraudulent, deceptive, and manipulative practices. A security is broadly defined to include any investment in a common enterprise with an expectation of profits from the efforts of others.

The Securities Act of 1933 requires issuers of securities to file a registration statement with the SEC. There are two exemptions from this requirement: securities exemptions, such as government-guaranteed securities; and transaction exemptions, such as the small offering exemptions, the private offering exemption, and the intrastate offering exemption.

The most important liability provision of the 1933 Act is Section 11, which imposes liability on certain defendants for material defects in the registration statement, unless they can prove their due diligence defenses.

Issuers register classes of securities under the 1934 Act, rather than issuances of securities. Companies of a certain size must register, whether or not their securities are traded on a stock exchange. The 1934 Act also imposes periodic reporting requirements on issuers and regulates proxy solicitations and tender offers.

Directors, officers, and 10 percent holders of registered shares must file reports of their shareholdings and transactions in the shares of an issuer with securities registered under the 1934 Act. Their short-swing profits in the issuer's shares may be recovered by the corporation.

The most often used liability provision of the 1934 Act is Section 10(b), under which SEC Rule 10b–5 has been issued. The rule has been used extensively to impose liabilities for failure to provide an investor with adequate information, for deceptive practices, and especially for insider trading.

The Foreign Corrupt Practices Act was passed in 1977. It prohibits payments or gifts to officials and political parties in foreign governments. Grease payments, however, are not prohibited. The FCPA also requires all issuers of registered securities to maintain accurate accounting records.

Both civil and criminal penalties may be imposed for violating the federal securities acts. All of the states have enacted blue-sky laws in order to protect investors. Some of these laws are quite similar in approach to the federal securities legislation. Others give the administrator authority to bar the sale of unduly risky securities.

## PROBLEM CASES

1. Dare To Be Great, Inc., offered courses designed to improve an individual's self-motivation and sales ability. The basic course, called Adventure I, provided the purchaser with a portable tape recorder, 12 tape-recorded lessons, and certain printed material presented in notebook form. The purchaser was also entitled to attend a 12–16-hour series of group meetings. The cost was $300. For an additional $700, the purchaser also received Adventure II, which included 12 more tape recordings and permitted him to attend 80 hours of group sessions. For $2,000, the purchaser also received Adventure III, which gave him six more tape recordings, a notebook of written material called "The Fun of Selling" as well as other written instructions, and 30 more hours of group sessions. In addition, after fulfilling a few nominal requirements, the Adventure III purchaser became an "independent sales trainee" empowered to sell the Adventures. For each Adventure I that he sold, he received $100; for each Adventure II, $300; for each Adventure III, $900.

For $5,000, a purchaser received Adventure IV as well as Adventures I through III. Besides receiving additional tapes, he had the opportunity to attend two week-long courses in Florida and to sell Adventure IV, for which he received $2,500. An alternative Plan selling for $1,000 resembled Adventure II but permitted the purchaser to sell the Plan to others if he first brought two purchasers to the person who sold him the Plan. After that, he would receive $400 for each additional sale he made. If he brought three purchasers into the Plan, he might sell the $1,000 Plan without buying it himself.

The SEC sued Dare for securities fraud. Dare argued that no security was involved. Are the Adventures or Plans securities?

**2.** Allen Gross was engaged in raising earthworms in the Phoenix, Arizona, area. He distributed a newsletter as part of his marketing efforts. In it, he solicited others to buy breeder earthworm farm franchises from him. He projected very large profits for the franchisees. He stated that earthworms multiplied 60 times per year. He promised to buy back at $2.25 per pound all worms suitable for fish bait. This promise was important, because Gross was the only wholesaler of earthworms in the state. The newsletter also said that little work was required and that success was assured because Gross would dispose of the worms in the large fishers' market of the Phoenix area.

Gerald and Mary Smith purchased an earthworm franchise from Gross. Subsequently, they discovered that they had paid 10 times the true market value of the worms they received and that the worms would multiply at a maximum of 8 times per year. They learned that there was little demand for worms in Phoenix and that Gross could pay $2.25 per pound only by selling the worms to new franchisees at inflated prices. They sued Gross for fraud under the federal securities law, alleging that they had purchased an investment contract. Was the franchise a security?

**3.** Arthur Vining Davis, a noted industrialist and philanthropist, transferred all of his real estate holdings on Florida's Gold Coast to the Arvida Corporation. The transfer was announced by Arvida in a press release distributed in New York and to the principal wire services. The press release stated that $25–$30 million of additional capital would be raised through an offering of stock to the public and that a public offering was scheduled to be made within 60 days through a nationwide investment banking group headed by Loeb, Rhoades and Dominick & Dominick. It also stated that the corporation proposed to undertake a comprehensive program of orderly development of the real estate on the Gold Coast. The release attracted such buying interest from securities dealers that over 100 firms contacted the proposed underwriters for inclusion in the underwriting syndicate. The SEC brought suit seeking an injunction to prevent Arvida from offering to sell securities before filing a registration statement, a violation of Section 5 of the 1933 Act. Should the injunction be issued?

**4.** McDonald Investment Company was a Minnesota corporation. Its principal and only business office was in Minnesota, where all books, correspondence, and other records were kept. To raise capital to lend to land developers throughout the United States, especially Arizona, McDonald proposed to offer installment notes solely to Minnesota residents. McDonald's income-producing operations would consist entirely of earning interest on its loans and receivables invested outside Minnesota. McDonald claims that the offering is exempt from registration under the Securities Act of 1933 as an intrastate offering. Is McDonald correct?

**5.** Charles Timm was a real estate broker in Minneapolis. He participated in oil ventures on a limited scale. Thompson, an acquaintance of Timm who made his living from investments, advised Timm that he was interested in buying an oil lease and asked Timm to let him know if he learned of one that seemed attractive. While in Oklahoma, Timm learned that Pierce owned a 1/16th interest in an oil and gas lease on land known as Tract 1, which Pierce offered to sell for $19,000. Timm obtained more information by letter, which he passed on to Thompson and to Collier, a friend of Thompson. Timm insisted that Thompson and Collier make their own independent investigation and decision. Timm drove with them to Oklahoma to see the property and to check the drilling and production records, at which time they bought the 1/16th interest and Timm received a 5 percent commission.

Shortly thereafter, Anderson, a friend of Timm, inquired about oil leases and Timm told him that while in Oklahoma with Thompson and Collier, he had learned of another 1/16th interest in Tract 1 being available from a different owner. In a similar fashion, Timm served as intermediary in the sale of three more fractional interests in the lease on Tract 1. In two of these cases, Timm's acquaintances did not visit the leased property but relied on the judgment of a friend who had been an earlier purchaser. Several months later, Timm arranged similar sales in two other tracts to Thompson, Collier, and Anderson. In all, there were five different buyers and four different sellers through Timm.

Operation and development expenses on the leases exceeded income. Thompson, Collier, and Anderson brought suit against Timm to recover their investments and the amounts by which expenses exceeded income, alleging that the leases were unregistered securities sold in violation of the Securities Act of 1933. Timm argued that the sales were exempt as private offerings. Was Timm correct?

**6.** Shirley Woolf, a lawyer and businesswoman, and Robert Milberg, a securities broker, purchased $10,000 in subordinated convertible debentures in Fiberglass Resources Corporation through S. D. Cohn, a securities broker-dealer. Fiberglass was to be formed by taking over a plant and a line of business that had been owned by Koppers Company. Cohn's plan of financing involved an issue of $600,000 in debentures through a private offering. Woolf and Milberg had been involved in previous business relations with Cohn. All contact had been by phone.

Fiberglass was unsuccessful. Woolf and Milberg sued Cohn to recover their losses, alleging misrepresentation and nonqualification of the offering as a private offering. Cohn testified that he had sold the debentures to only 10 investors. He also stated that Woolf and Milberg were equally at fault, because they signed a letter that they were buying the securities for investment and for no other person, although they were representing five other investors besides themselves.

Was the trial court correct in holding that the offer was a private offering and that Woolf and Milberg could not win because of the misrepresentation in the letter?

**7.** Occidental Petroleum Corporation made a hostile tender offer for the shares of Kern County Land Company. Between May 8 and June 8, 1967, it purchased more than 10 percent of Kern's stock, which was registered under the 1934 Act. Kern found a friendly company, Tenneco Corporation, with which to merge and thereby defeat the attempt of Occidental to take over Kern. Under the terms of the merger, one share of Kern was to be exchanged for securities of Tenneco worth $105.

Occidental did not want to become a minority shareholder of Tenneco. On June 2, 1967, Occidental granted Tenneco an option to purchase the Tenneco shares that Occidental would receive in the merger for its Kern shares at a price of $105 per Kern share. Tenneco paid $10 per share for this option, which was to be credited against the purchase price of the shares if Tenneco exercised the option. The option was exercisable after December 9, 1967, which was six months and one day after Occidental's last purchase of Kern stock. The merger was approved by Kern's shareholders in July 1967. Occidental did not vote its shares, but it did not oppose the merger. The merger became effective on August 30,

1967, but Occidental did not submit its Kern shares for exchange. On December 11, 1967, Tenneco exercised its option, and as a result Occidental earned a profit of $19.5 million.

Kern brought suit against Occidental under Section 16(b) of the 1934 Act. It alleged that the August 30 merger and the grant of the option were sales within six months of the purchases of Kern stock during the tender offer. Were the merger and the option grant sales for purposes of Section 16(b)?

**8.** Under an antitrust reorganization plan, Blue Chip Stamps Company (Old Blue Chip) was to merge into a newly formed corporation, New Blue Chip. Under the terms of the plan, New Blue Chip was required to offer a substantial number of its common shares to retailers that had bought stamps from Old Blue Chip in the past but were not shareholders of Old Blue Chip. The reorganization plan was executed and the offering registered under the 1933 Act. Somewhat more than 50 percent of the offered units were purchased. Subsequently, the purchased shares rose greatly in value.

Manor Drug Stores was one of the retailers to which the plan required that the shares be offered. Manor Drug, however, did not buy the shares. Manor Drug alleged that it would have bought the shares had not New Blue Chip used a prospectus that was materially misleading in its overly pessimistic appraisal of New Blue Chip's status and future prospects. Manor Drug claimed that New Blue Chip intentionally made the prospectus overly pessimistic to discourage some of the retailers from exercising their rights to buy the shares so that the shares could be offered to the public at a higher price. Manor Drug sued New Blue Chip, alleging a violation of Rule 10b–5. Will the court find a right of action for Manor Drug under Rule 10b–5?

**9.** Alex Campbell was a financial columnist for the *Los Angeles Herald-Examiner.* In 1969, he interviewed officers of American Systems, Inc. (ASI), and his highly favorable description of ASI was published in the *Herald-Examiner* on June 4. It was based solely on misleading information, given to Campbell by ASI officers, that made no mention of the problems confronting ASI. As he did frequently before writing a favorable column, Campbell purchased ASI stock. He bought 5,000 shares directly from the corporation at $2 per share. The market price at that time was $3.625.

Following publication of the column, the market price of ASI stock rose to $4.35 per share, and Campbell sold 2,000 of his shares, recouping his entire investment. Several months earlier, ASI had entered into a merger agreement with Reading Guidance Center, Inc. (RGC). The merger agreement provided that the RGC shareholders would receive ASI stock with a market value of $1.8 million as determined by the average closing bid for ASI stock for the five market days preceding the closing date, June 10, 1969. As a result of the increase in the market price of ASI stock, the owners of RGC came to hold 45 percent of the shares of the merged corporation instead of the 52 percent that they would have held without the effect of Campbell's article.

Campbell was aware of the projected merger, but not of ASI's problems. The RGC shareholders sued Campbell under SEC Rule 10b–5 for purposely using his column to increase the price of ASI stock for his own benefit. They alleged that his failure to state in his column that he stood to gain financially from an increase in the price of the stock was a material omission violating Rule 10b–5. Did Campbell have such a duty of disclosure?

**10.** Douglas Aircraft filed a registration statement for a $75 million issue of debentures with the SEC on June 7, 1966. Merrill Lynch was the managing underwriter. Also on June 7, Douglas released a statement showing earnings of 85 cents per share for the first five months of its fiscal year. Later in June, certain Merrill Lynch personnel learned, because of the underwriting relationship, that Douglas would report substantially less earnings for the first six months of the year than it had reported for the first five months.

Within a few days and before any public announcement, Merrill Lynch personnel disclosed this information to several Merrill Lynch customers that were institutional investors and that knew the loss had not been announced. These investors sold 165,000 shares of Douglas common on the New York Stock Exchange before and during a rapid drop in its price.

Several individual investors who were unaware of the unfavorable information bought shares on the New York Stock Exchange during this period. They brought an action under Rule 10b–5 against Merrill Lynch and the customers that had received the tip and sold Douglas stock. Have Merrill Lynch and the customers violated Rule 10b–5?

Chapter 27

# Legal Responsibilities of Accountants and Other Professionals

## INTRODUCTION

In recent years, there has been a great increase in the number of lawsuits brought against professionals. Everyone has read about lawsuits against physicians for medical malpractice, but other professionals, such as accountants, management consultants, financial advisers, and securities brokers, have also become increasingly vulnerable to professional liability suits.

In part, this increased litigation may be additional proof that we are a litigious society whose members are quick to sue when they suffer harm. In part, it is due to an increased awareness of the poor quality of the services provided by some professionals. And in part, it is the result of an increased willingness of courts to fashion remedies for persons harmed by the wrongful conduct of professionals.

This chapter covers principally the legal responsibilities of *accountants.* It does not discuss the requirements for admission to the accounting profession, but rather considers the professional relationships of accountants with their clients and others who rely on their work. As you read the chapter, you will be able to trace the evolution of the law of accountants' liability and to discern that accountants are being held liable to more classes of persons for more types of wrongs. This chapter also covers the criminal and administrative sanctions for wrongful professional conduct.

**Bases of Professional Liability.** You have studied elsewhere in this book many of the legal theories that justify imposing liability on professionals. For example, you studied criminal liability in Chapter 3, liability for breach of contract in Chapter 15, liability for fraud in Chapter 9, liability for negligence in Chapter 5, liability of an agent for breach of trust and failure to exercise ordinary skill and care in Chapter 16, and liability for violations of the securities laws in Chapter 26. These bases of liability will be reviewed in this chapter. The main basis of liability, and the basis that will be emphasized in this chapter, is the duty of professionals to exercise ordinary skill and care.

**General Standard of Performance.** The general duty that accountants and other professionals owe to their clients and to other persons who are affected by their actions is *to exercise the skill and care of the ordinarily prudent professional in the same circumstances.* Hence, accountants are not insurers or guarantors of the accuracy of their work. For example, an accountant who is performing an audit of a client's financial records has no duty to discover every incorrect accounting treatment or to detect every embezzlement that the client's employees may have perpetrated. The accountant is required only to exercise reasonable care. This standard is a subset of the *negligence* standard that you studied in Chapter 5.

There are two elements to the general duty of performance: skill and care. An accountant must have the *skill* of the ordinarily prudent accountant. This element focuses on the education or knowledge of the accountant, whether acquired formally at school or by self-instruction. For example, to prepare tax returns, she must *know* the tax laws as well as the ordinarily prudent accountant does. To audit financial records, she must be trained in auditing techniques and the rules of financial accounting.

The *care* element requires an accountant to be as careful or diligent as the ordinarily prudent accountant. For example, in preparing a tax return, he must discover the income exclusions, the deductions, and the tax credits that the reasonably careful accountant would find. In auditing financial statements, he must at least follow generally accepted auditing standards (GAAS) and value assets and liabilities in accordance with generally accepted accounting principles (GAAP). GAAS and GAAP are standards and principles embodied in the rules, releases, and pronouncements of the Securities and Exchange Commission, the American Institute of Certified Public Accountants (AICPA), and the Financial Accounting Standards Board (FASB).

**Deference to Professional Standards.** Courts and legislatures usually defer to the members of each profession in determining what the ordinarily prudent professional would do. Such deference recognizes the lawmakers' lack of understanding of the nuances of each profession's practices. This lack of understanding means that courts must rely on members of a profession to give expert testimony as to the professional standards of conduct. For example, in a trial against an accountant for malpractice, other accountants will appear as witnesses to aid the court's determination of what the ordinarily prudent accountant would have done in the same circumstances.

In the past, this reliance on professional witnesses was a major obstacle to a patient or client seeking to prove a professional's lack of care, because professionals were reluctant to testify against each other. In recent years, as the number of lawsuits against professionals has increased as have the fees paid to professional witnesses, a class of readily available witnesses has developed in many professions, easing the patient's or client's burden of proving a professional's lack of care.

Courts will not always defer to the standards of conduct set by a profession. A profession will not be permitted to establish a standard of conduct that is harmful to the interests of clients, patients, or other members of society. For example, a court would not defer to an FASB pronouncement that states that the cost of a building with a 40-year life may be expensed entirely in the year of acquisition.

Until about a decade ago, some courts found accountants liable despite their claims that they had followed GAAS and GAAP in good faith.[1] These courts insisted that attention be focused on substance rather than form: the financial statements must as a whole fairly present the financial condition of a client company and the results of its operations. These decisions are contradictory, because GAAP requires that financial statements fairly present the financial condition of the company and the results of its operations.[2] In recent decisions, courts have regularly held that compliance with GAAP and GAAS in good faith discharges an auditor's professional obligations.

**Local versus National Standard.** Originally, professionals were held to the standard of the ordinarily prudent person in his locality. This local standard has given way to a *national standard* in recent years. Due to improved means of communication in the modern world, few professionals today can argue that they are unaware of modern professional techniques.

## ACCOUNTANTS' LIABILITY TO CLIENTS

The great increase in litigation against accountants in the last 20 years has been almost entirely in third-party suits, that is, suits by persons who are not in privity of contract with the accountant. Even so, accountants are frequently sued by their clients. For example, an accountant may wrongfully claim deductions on an individual's tax return. When the IRS discovers the wrongful deduction, the individual will have to pay the extra tax, interest, and perhaps a penalty. The individual may sue his accountant to recover the amount of the penalty. Or an accountant may prepare an income statement that understates a client's income. The client uses the income statement to apply for a loan, but is denied the loan because her stated net income is inadequate. The client may sue her accountant for damages caused by the erroneous income statement.

There are two principal bases of liability of an accountant to his client: contract and tort.

**Contractual Liability.** As a party to a *contract,* an accountant has the duty to perform as he has agreed to perform. This includes an *implied duty* to perform the contract as the *ordinarily prudent accountant* would perform it. If the accountant fails to perform as agreed, all of the remedies discussed in Chapter 15 are available to the client. Ordinarily, an accountant is liable only for those damages that are reasonably contemplated by the accountant. For example, an accountant would be liable for a client's tax penalties if she completely failed to prepare the client's tax return.

[1] E.g., *United States v. Simon,* 425 F.2d 796 (2d Cir. 1969). Contra *SEC v. Arthur Young & Co.,* 590 F.2d 785 (9th Cir. 1979).

[2] *AICPA SAS No. 5,* § 3 (1975).

An accountant would not be liable for breach of contract if the client obstructed the accountant's performance of the contract. For example, an accounting firm would not be liable for failing to complete an audit on time if the client refused to give the firm access to needed records and property.

**Delegation of Contractual Duty.** An accountant may not delegate his duty to perform a contract without the consent of the client. Delegation is denied because performance depends on the skill, training, and character of the accountant. As a result, for example, Price Waterhouse, a public accounting firm, may not delegate to Arthur Andersen, another public accounting firm, the contractual duty to audit the financial statements of General Motors.[3]

**Tort Liability.** Accountants' tort liability may be based upon the common law concepts of negligence, fraud, and breach of trust or upon the violation of a statute, principally the federal and state securities laws.

**Negligence.** As stated earlier, the duty of an accountant to exercise the skill and care of the ordinarily prudent accountant is grounded in *negligence*. Hence, an accountant is liable to a client for her negligence. A client who *suffers a loss* that is *proximately caused* by an accountant's failure to exercise the skill and care of the *ordinarily prudent accountant* may sue the accountant to recover his damages. For example, a client may recover excess taxes that he paid because of his accountant's lack of due care in claiming allowable deductions on a tax return. In addition, an accountant would be liable for negligently giving tax advice, such as telling a client to reduce her tax liability by establishing a certain type of trust fund for her children. When the Internal Revenue Service rules that the trust's income is income to the client, the accountant may be liable to the client.

Often, an accountant will audit a company, yet fail to uncover an embezzlement or other intentional wrongdoing or fraud by an employee of the company. Ordinarily, an accountant has no specific duty to uncover employee *embezzlement or fraud*. Nevertheless, an accountant must uncover employee fraud or embezzlement if an ordinarily prudent accountant would have discovered it. In addition, an accountant owes a duty to investigate suspicious circumstances that tend to indicate fraud, regardless of how he became aware of those circumstances. Also, an accountant has a duty to inform a proper party of his suspicions. It is not enough to inform or confront the person suspected of fraud. For example, in the *1136 Tenants' Corporation* case, which follows, the accounting firm was held liable because it found evidence that should have created suspicion that an embezzlement had occurred. The accounting firm should have notified its client of its suspicions.

If an accountant is hired to perform a *fraud audit* to investigate suspected fraud or embezzlement, she has a greater duty to investigate. She must be as skillful and careful as the ordinarily prudent auditor performing a fraud audit.

An accountant is liable to his client only for the embezzlement that occurs *after* she should have discovered the embezzlement, as in the *1136 Tenants' Corporation* case.

**Contributory and Comparative Negligence.** Courts are reluctant to permit an accountant to escape liability to a client merely because the client was *contributorily negligent*. Since the accountant has skills superior to those of the client, courts generally allow clients to rely on the accountant's duty to discover employee fraud, available tax deduc-

[3] Delegation of contractual duties is covered in detail in Chapter 14.

tions, and other matters for which the accountant is hired. The client is not required to exercise reasonable care to discover these things himself.

Nevertheless, some courts have allowed the defense of *contributory negligence* or the defense of *comparative negligence* when clients negligently fail to follow an accountant's advice or when clients possess information that makes their reliance on the accountant unwarranted.[4]

**Fraud.** An accountant is liable to his client for *fraud* when he *misrepresents* facts to his client and acts with *scienter.* Scienter is knowledge of the untruth or reckless disregard for the truth. Thus, accountants are liable in fraud for their intentional or reckless disregard for accuracy in their work. Recklessness has been defined as "the pretense of knowledge when knowledge there is none."[5]

For example, an accountant chooses not to examine the current figures in a client's books of account, but relies on last year's figures because he is behind in his work for other clients. As a result, the accountant understates the client's income on an income statement that the client uses to apply for a loan. The client obtains a loan, but he has to pay a higher interest rate because his low stated income makes the loan a higher risk for the bank. Such misconduct by the accountant is *fraud.*

The chief advantage of establishing fraud is that the client may get a higher damage award if this is done. Usually, a client may receive only compensatory damages for a breach of contract or negligence. By proving fraud, a client may be awarded punitive damages as well.

**Breach of Trust.** The accountant-client relation is a confidential, fiduciary relation. Information and assets that are entrusted to an accountant may be used only to benefit the client. Therefore, an accountant may not disclose sensitive matters, such as a client's income and wealth. In addition, an accountant may not use the assets of his client for his own benefit.

**Securities Law.** As you learned in Chapter 26, federal and state securities law creates several rights of action for persons harmed in connection with the purchase or sale of securities. These rights of action are based in tort, usually fraud. Although available to clients of an accountant, they are rarely used for that purpose. Usually, third parties (nonclients) sue under the securities law. Therefore, the securities law sections that apply to accountants are discussed in greater detail in the next section of this chapter.

---

[4] Contributory negligence and comparative negligence are covered in detail in Chapter 5.

[5] *Ultramares Corp. v. Touche,* 174 N.E. 441, 444 (N.Y. Ct. App. 1931).

## 1136 Tenants' Corp. v. Max Rothenberg & Co.

**319 N.Y.S.2d 1007 (N.Y. App. Div. 1971)**

1136 Tenants' Corporation, a cooperative apartment house, employed Jerome Riker as manager of the apartment house. In 1963, Riker hired Max Rothenberg & Co., a firm of certified public accountants, to perform write-up services, including the maintenance of ledgers and journals and the preparation of financial reports. The apartment house claimed that audit services were included in the work, for which Rothenberg received a $600 fee.

A Rothenberg employee performed both write-up and audit services and discovered that several invoices were missing from the financial records of the apartment house. He noted the missing invoices on his worksheet. These invoices were needed to prove that payments of $44,000 had been made to creditors of the apartment house and were not embezzled by someone with authority to make payments for the apartment house. Nevertheless, Rothenberg's employee failed to notify the apartment house that there were missing invoices. In fact, there were no invoices. Riker had embezzled the $44,000 from the apartment house by ordering it to make unauthorized payments to him. Riker embezzled more money after the audit was completed. The apartment house sued Rothenberg for $174,000 for negligently failing to inform it of Riker's embezzlement. The trial court held Rothenberg liable to the apartment, and Rothenberg appealed.

**Per Curiam.** Utilization of the simplest audit procedures would have revealed Riker's defalcations. Moreover, *even if* Rothenberg were hired to perform only write-up services, it is clear, beyond dispute, that it did become aware that material invoices purportedly paid by Riker were missing, and accordingly, had a duty to at least inform Tenants' Corporation of this fact. But even this it failed to do. Rothenberg was not free to consider these and other suspicious circumstances as being of no significance and prepare its financial reports as if same did not exist.

Judgment for 1136 Tenants' Corporation affirmed.

## ACCOUNTANTS' LIABILITY TO THIRD PERSONS: COMMON LAW

**Introduction.** Other people besides an accountant's clients may use her work product. Banks may use financial statements prepared by a loan applicant's accountant in deciding whether to make a loan. Investors may use financial statements certified by a company's auditors in deciding whether to buy or sell the company's securities.

As with clients, nonclients may sue accountants for common law negligence, common law fraud, and violations of the securities laws. In this section, common law negligence and fraud are discussed.

**Negligence.** When an accountant fails to perform as the ordinarily prudent accountant would perform, she risks having liability for negligence. Nevertheless, many courts have restricted the ability of nonclients to sue an accountant for negligence. Since nonclient users of an accountant's work product have not contracted with the accountant, they are not in *privity of contract* with the accountant. Many courts have used *lack of privity* to prevent *third parties*—creditors, shareholders, and other investors of an accountant's client—from obtaining damages caused by the accountant's negligence. Essentially, these courts hold that an accountant owes no duty to nonclients to exercise ordinary skill and care.

This judicial stance conflicts with the usual principles of negligence law under which a negligent person is liable to all persons who are reasonably foreseeably damaged by his negligence. Courts have generally refused to make accountants liable to all foreseeable users.

The rationale for this judicial stance was expressed in the *Ultramares* case,[6] a decision of the highest court in New York. In that case, Judge Benjamin Cardozo declared that an auditor had a duty to all, including third parties, to certify financial statements *without fraud.* However, he refused to hold the auditor liable when no fraud was proved. His rationale was stated as follows: "If liability for negligence exists, a thoughtless slip or blunder, the failure to detect a theft or forgery beneath the cover of deceptive entries, may expose accountants to a liability in an indeterminate amount for an indeterminate time to an indeterminate class."

*Ultramares* dominated the thinking of judges for many years, and its impact is still felt today. However, many courts understand that many nonclients use and reasonably rely on the work product of accountants. These courts have expanded the class of persons who may sue an accountant for negligence.

Today, a court adopts one of the following three tests to determine whether a nonclient may sue an accountant for negligence.

**Primary Benefit Test.** The *Ultramares* court adopted a *primary benefit test* for imposing liability for negligence. Under this test, an accountant has liability for negligence only to those persons for whose primary benefit the accountant prepares financial reports and other documents. It is not enough that the accountant be able to foresee use by a nonclient. The accountant must prepare the document primarily for use by a specified nonclient. Only the specified nonclient may sue for negligence, even if other persons use the document. Courts applying this test have been reluctant to find that nonclients are primary beneficiaries of reports prepared by an accountant.

Recently, New York's highest court, following the rule of *Ultramares,* listed three requirements for nonclients to hold accountants liable for negligence:

(1) The accountants must have been aware that their work product was to be used for a particular purpose; (2) in the furtherance of which a known party was intended to rely; and (3) some conduct on the part of the accountants linking them to that party must evince the accountants' understanding of that party's reliance.[7]

**Foreseen Users and Foreseen Class of Users Test.** By 1965, a draft of the *Restatement (Second) of Torts* interpreted the law of professional negligence to expand the class of protected persons beyond merely primary

[6] *Ultramares Corp. v. Touche,* 174 N.E. 441, 444 (N.Y. Ct. App. 1931).

[7] *Credit Alliance Corp. v. Arthur Andersen & Co.,* No. 218, 219, slip op. (N.Y. Ct. App. July 2, 1985).

beneficiaries to *foreseen users* and to users within a *foreseen class of users* of reports. The protected persons are those to whom the accountant intends to give reports and those to whom he knows a client will give reports. Merely foreseeable users are not protected persons under this doctrine.

For example, an accountant prepares an income statement that he knows his client will use to obtain a loan at Bank X. *Any* bank to which the client supplies the statement to obtain a loan, including Bank Y, may sue the accountant for a negligently prepared income statement. Bank X is a foreseen user, and Bank Y is in a class of foreseen users. On the other hand, if an accountant prepares an income statement for a tax return, and the client, without the accountant's knowledge, uses the income statement to apply for a loan, the bank is not among the protected class of persons. Even though it was foreseeable that the client would so use the income statement, such use was not foreseen.

Some courts accept the foreseen user part of this test but reject the foreseen class component.

**Foreseeable Users Test.** In the last 20 years, a few courts have applied traditional negligence causation principles to accountants' negligence. They have extended liability to *foreseeable users* of accountants' reports. One court viewed reliance by potential creditors as foreseeable, but not reliance by a prospective purchaser of the corporation's shares.[8] *Citizens State Bank v. Timm, Schmidt & Co.,* which follows, held that accountants might be liable to creditors foreseeably using financial statements, on the ground that accountants should be liable for the foreseeable consequences of their negligent actions.

**Current Status of Tests.** The foreseen users and class of users test is the predominant test used by courts today. Especially in recent years, courts have tended to refuse to follow the *Ultramares* primary benefit test. In New York, however, the highest court recently reaffirmed its adherence to *Ultramares* and its rejection of the foreseen class of users and foreseeable users tests.[9]

Although few courts have adopted the foreseeable users test, there is a clear trend toward expanding the class of persons to whom accountants owe a duty of ordinary skill and care. The *Timm* case, which follows, expresses some of the reasons for this trend, including the desire of courts to deter accountants' negligence and to reduce the cost of credit.

**Fraud.** Fraud is such reprehensible conduct that the courts have extended an accountant's liability for fraud to all foreseeable users of his work product. As you learned in the last section, to prove fraud a nonclient must establish that an accountant acted with scienter. Scienter includes intentional and reckless disregard of the truth.

**Correcting Erroneous Reports.** An accountant's duty to nonclients includes the duty to correct his report when he subsequently discovers that the report is false or misleading. In such a situation, the accountant has a duty to *disclose the new information* to anyone who he knows is relying on the earlier report.[10] Liability for a failure to correct erroneous reports may be based on negligence or fraud. Of course, as is shown in the *Timm* case, disclosure of the correct facts *after* a person's reliance will not relieve an accountant from liability for damages caused by the earlier reliance.

---

[8] *Milliner v. Elmer Fox & Co.,* 529 P.2d 806 (Utah Sup. Ct. 1974).

[9] *Credit Alliance Corp. v. Arthur Andersen & Co.,* No. 218, 219, slip op. (N.Y. Ct. App. July 2, 1985).

[10] *Fisher v. Kletz,* 266 F. Supp. 180 (S.D.N.Y. 1967).

## Citizens State Bank v. Timm, Schmidt & Co.

**335 N.W.2d 361 (Wis. Sup. Ct. 1983)**

Timm, Schmidt & Co. was an accounting firm in Stevens Point, Wisconsin. For the years 1973–76, Timm prepared financial statements for Clintonville Fire Apparatus, Inc. (CFA). For every year except 1973, Timm sent an opinion letter to CFA which stated that the financial statements fairly presented the financial condition of CFA and that the statements were prepared in accordance with generally accepted accounting principles.

In November 1975, CFA obtained a $300,000 loan from Citizens State Bank. Citizens made the loan to CFA after reviewing the financial statements that Timm had prepared. Citizens made additional loans to CFA in 1976. By the end of 1976, CFA owed Citizens $380,000.

In early 1977, while preparing CFA's financial statement for 1976, Timm employees discovered that the 1974 and 1975 financial statements contained a number of material errors totaling over $400,000. These errors were corrected. When Timm informed Citizens of the errors, Citizens called all of CFA's loans due. As a result, CFA was ultimately liquidated and dissolved. CFA's assets were insufficient to pay the loans from Citizens. Citizens sued Timm seeking to recover $152,000, the amount due on its loans to CFA. At the trial, there was evidence that Timm had failed to comply with generally accepted auditing standards (GAAS) when it first audited the 1974 and 1975 financial statements. In addition, there was evidence that Timm would have discovered the errors earlier had GAAS been followed. There was conflicting evidence regarding whether Timm knew that CFA would use the financial statements to obtain loans from Citizens.

The trial court held that Citizens was not within the class of persons to whom Timm could be held liable for its negligent acts. Citizens appealed to the court of appeals, which affirmed the trial court's decision. Citizens next appealed to the Supreme Court of Wisconsin.

**Day, Justice.** The question is whether accountants may be held liable for the negligent preparation of audited financial statements to a third party not in privity who relies on the financial statements.

Accountants have long been held not liable for their negligence to relying third parties not in privity under an application of Judge Cardozo's decision in *Ultramares v. Touche* (1931). In recent years, *Ultramares* has received new attention and courts have started to find accountants liable to third parties.

In *Rusch Factors, Inc. v. Levin* (1968), the court, citing section 552 of the Restatement (Second) of Torts, imposed liability on an accountant to a relying third party not in privity. In *Rusch Factors,* the accountant knew the statements he prepared were to be used by his client for the purpose of obtaining credit from a third party even though he did not know of the specific relying third party. Nevertheless, the court allowed liability to be imposed.

In this state, this Court concluded that an attorney may be held liable to a will beneficiary not in privity for the attorney's negligence in supervising the execution of a will. Part of the rationale for this decision was that the imposition of liability would make attorneys more careful in the execution of their responsibilities to their clients.

That rationale is applicable here. Unless liability is imposed, third parties who rely upon the accuracy of the financial statements will not be protected. Unless an accountant can be held liable to a relying third party, this negligence will go undeterred.

There are additional policy reasons to allow the imposition of liability. If relying third parties, such as creditors, are not allowed to recover, the cost of credit to the general public will increase because creditors will either have to absorb the costs of bad loans made in reliance on faulty information or hire independent accountants to verify the information received. Accountants may spread the risk through the use of liability insurance.

We conclude that the absence of privity alone should not bar negligence actions by relying third parties against accountants. Although the absence of privity does not bar this action, the question remains as to the extent of an accountant's liability to injured third parties. Courts that have examined this question have generally relied upon section 552 of the Restatement to restrict the class of third persons who could sue accountants for their negligent acts. Under section 552(2)(a) and (b), liability is limited to loss suffered:

> (a) By the person or one of a limited group of persons for whose benefit and guidance he [the accountant] intends to supply the information or knows the recipient [the client] intends to supply it and
>
> (b) Through reliance upon it in a transaction that he [the accountant] intends the information to influence or knows the recipient [the client] so intends or in a substantially similar transaction.

Under section 552, liability is not extended to all parties whom the accountant might reasonably foresee as using the information. Rather, the Restatement's formulation of a limited group of persons extends causes of action to a limited number of third parties who are expected to gain access to the financial statement information in an expected transaction. This limitation is stressed in comment h. to section 552 where it is noted that:

> It is not required that the person who is to become the plaintiff be identified or known to the defendant as an individual when the information is supplied. It is enough that the maker of the representation intends it to reach and influence either a particular person or persons, known to him, or a group or class of persons, distinct from the much larger class who might reasonably be expected sooner or later to have access to the information and foreseeably to take some action in reliance upon it.

The fundamental principle of Wisconsin negligence law is that a tortfeasor is fully liable for all foreseeable consequences of his act except as those consequences are limited by policy factors. The Restatement's statement of limiting liability to certain third parties is too restrictive a statement of policy factors for this Court to adopt.

We conclude that accountants' liability to third parties should be determined under the accepted principles of Wisconsin negligence law. According to these principles, a finding of non-liability will be made only if there is a strong public policy requiring such a finding. Liability will be imposed on Timm for the foreseeable injuries resulting from its negligent acts unless recovery is denied on grounds of public policy.

This Court has set out a number of public policy reasons for not imposing liability despite a finding of negligence causing injury:

> (1) The injury is too remote from the negligence; or (2) the injury is too wholly out of proportion to the culpability of the negligent tortfeasor; or (3) in retrospect it appears too highly extraordinary that the negligence should have brought about the harm; or (4) because allowance of recovery

would place too unreasonable a burden on the negligent tortfeasor; or (5) because allowance of recovery would be too likely to open the way for fraudulent claims; or (6) allowance of recovery would enter a field that has no sensible or just stopping point.

The question of Timm's liability to Citizens cannot be determined upon the information contained in the record. A full factual resolution is necessary before it can be said that public policy precludes Timm's liability for its allegedly negligent conduct.

Under the accepted principles of Wisconsin negligence law, Timm could be liable to Citizens if Timm's actions were the cause of Citizens' injuries and if the injuries were reasonably foreseeable unless public policy precluded recovery.

Timm's affidavits do not dispute that Citizens' reliance upon the financial statements led to the making of the loans and ultimately to the losses which were incurred. Each affidavit recites that Timm employees had no knowledge that the financial statements would actually be used by CFA to apply for a new bank loan or to increase existing loan indebtedness. However, the affidavit of Elmer Timm stated that "as a certified public accountant, I know that audited statements are used for many purposes and that it is common for them to be supplied to lenders and creditors, and other persons."

These affidavits and other information contained in the record do not dispose of the issue of whether it was foreseeable that a negligently prepared financial statement could cause harm to Citizens. Therefore, we conclude that the trial judge erred in granting judgment for Timm.

Judgment reversed in favor of Citizens State Bank. Remanded for trial.

## ACCOUNTANTS' LIABILITY TO THIRD PARTIES: SECURITIES LAW

The slow reaction of the common law in creating a negligence remedy for third parties led to an increased use of securities law, especially the federal securities acts, by persons who were not in privity with an accountant. Many liability sections in these statutes either eliminate the privity requirement or expansively define privity. As a result, in recent years, most of the investors who have sued accountants for damages caused by defective financial statements have alleged violations of the federal securities acts.

**Securities Act of 1933.** There are several liability sections under the Securities Act of 1933 (1933 Act). The 1933 Act is discussed in detail in Chapter 26. The most important liability section of the Securities Act of 1933 is Section 11, which imposes liability for errors in registration statements.

**Errors in 1933 Act Registration Statements.** Section 11 specifically imposes on auditors and other experts liability for *misstatements or omissions of material fact* in information that they provide for Securities Act *registration statements.* An auditor is liable to any *purchaser* of securities issued pursuant to a defective registration statement. *Material facts* are those that an investor would consider important. For example, a 1 percent error in the sales of a business is not material. A 25 percent error in sales would be material. Materiality is discussed in detail in Chapter 26, including the *Texas Gulf Sulphur* case.

**Due Diligence Defense.** Under Section 11, as interpreted by *Escott v. BarChris,* which appears in Chapter 26, auditors may escape liability by proving that they exercised due diligence. This *due diligence defense* requires that an auditor of certified financial statements prove that he made a *reasonable investigation* and that he *reasonably believed* that the certified financial statements were accurate *at the time the registration statement became effective.* Since the effective date is often several months after an audit has been completed, an auditor must perform an additional review of the audited statements to ensure that the statements are accurate as of the effective date. In the *BarChris* case in Chapter 26, the auditor failed to exercise due diligence during its *postaudit review* of the financial statements. In essence, due diligence means that an auditor was not negligent, which is proved usually by showing that he complied with GAAS and GAAP.

**Amount of Liability.** Under Section 11, an auditor is potentially liable to a purchaser of registered securities for the purchaser's entire loss. However, if an auditor proves that a purchaser's loss was caused in full or in part by another's misstatements or omissions or by a general decline in the price of all securities, the auditor's liability is reduced accordingly.

**Advantages of Section 11.** Section 11 substantially aids a third party's ability to sue an auditor successfully. Essentially, the third party needs to prove only that he purchased a security issued pursuant to a registration statement that contained a materially defective certified financial statement furnished by the auditor. He need not prove negligence; the auditor must prove due diligence. Usually, he need not prove reliance; he need not even have read or seen the defective financial statement. And he need not establish privity of contract with the auditor; he need merely prove that the auditor is a person who furnished the certified financial statements for inclusion in the registration statement.

**Statute of Limitations.** Under Section 11, an auditor has liability for only a limited period of time, pursuant to the *statute of limitations* in Section 13. A purchaser must sue the auditor *within one year after the misstatement or omission was or should have been discovered.* In addition, a purchaser may sue the auditor *no more than three years after the securities were offered* to the public. Although the word *offered* is used, this three-year period usually does not begin until after the registered securities are *first delivered* to a purchaser.

**Other 1933 Act Liability Sections.** Sections 12(2) and 17(a) of the 1933 Act have also been used against accountants.

**Section 12(2).** Section 12(2) requires a showing of *privity* and *reliance* on a *material misstatement or omission* by an accountant in connection with the offer or sale of a security. Under Section 12(2), privity has been interpreted to require only that the accountant's actions directly and proximately cause a security purchaser's loss.[11] The accountant may escape liability by proving that she *did not know and could not reasonably have known* of the untruth or omission; that is, she must prove that she was not negligent. Section 12 has a *one-year/three-year statute of limitations* similar to the one for Section 11. However, the three-year period begins when the security is *sold.*

**Section 17(a).** Under Section 17(a), a purchaser of a security must prove his *reliance* on a *misstatement or omission of material fact* for which an accountant is responsible. Under

[11] *Avco Financial Services, Inc. v. Davis,* 739 F.2d 1057 (6th Cir. 1984), *cert. denied,* 53 U.S.L.W. 3867 (June 10, 1985).

two of the subsections of Section 17(a), the investor need prove only negligence. Under the third, the investor must prove *scienter.* The Supreme Court has not decided whether a private right of action exists under Section 17(a), and the courts of appeal are divided on the issue.

**Securities Exchange Act of 1934.** Two sections of the 1934 Act—Section 18(a) and Section 10(b)— especially affect the liability of accountants to nonclients. These sections are discussed in detail in Chapter 26.

**Errors in Filed Reports.** Section 18(a) of the 1934 Act imposes liability on accountants who furnish *misleading and false statements of material fact* in any *report or document filed* with the Securities and Exchange Commission under the 1934 Act. Such reports or documents include the annual 10-K report, which includes certified financial statements; the monthly 8-K report; and proxy statements. The quarterly 10-Q report, which includes unaudited financial statements, is excluded from Section 18(a) coverage by SEC Rule 15d–13(d). Annual reports sent to shareholders are not covered by Section 18(a), since they are filed with the SEC only for "information purposes."

Under Section 18(a), a purchaser or seller of a security must have actually known of and *relied* on the defective statement. This is sometimes called eye-ball reliance. In addition, he must prove that the misleading and false information *caused* his damages. Lastly, he must show that the security's purchase or sales *price* was affected by the false and misleading statement.

**Defense.** An accountant may escape from Section 18(a) liability by proving that she acted in *good faith and had no knowledge* that the information was misleading. That is, she must show that she acted *without scienter.* Negligence is not enough to impose liability under Section 18(a).

**Advantage and Disadvantage.** The only significant advantage that Section 18(a) has over the common law of fraud is that the purchaser or seller need *not prove privity.* Its biggest disadvantage is that investors seldom see and rely on many documents filed with the SEC (such as the 10-K and 8-K).

**Statute of Limitations.** In addition, Section 18(a) has a statute of limitations. An auditor must be sued *within one year after discovery of the facts* constituting a violation and *within three years after the violation occurred.* One court has required investors to exercise reasonable diligence to discover the facts constituting a violation.[12]

**Section 10(b) and Rule 10b–5.** Securities Exchange Act Rule 10b–5, pursuant to Section 10(b), has been the basis for most of the recent suits investors have brought against accountants. Rule 10b–5 prohibits any person from making a *misstatement or omission of material fact* in connection with the purchase or sale of any security. A purchaser or seller of a security may sue an accountant who has misstated or omitted a material fact. The purchaser or seller must *rely* on the misstatement or omission. In omission cases, reliance may be inferred from materiality. In addition, the accountant must act with *scienter.* Privity is *not* required.

**Scienter.** Scienter is an *intent* to deceive, manipulate, or defraud. Negligence is not enough. Although the Supreme Court of the United States has not ruled whether scienter encompasses gross recklessness or recklessness, some courts have held that it does, especially when a fiduciary duty is owed by the

[12] *Goldenberg v. Bache & Co.,* 270 F.2d 675 (5th Cir. 1959).

accountant to the plaintiff. *Oleck v. Fischer,* which follows, is a Rule 10b–5 case in which the court considered whether auditors were reckless. Generally, gross negligence does not satisfy the scienter requirement. A few courts have held gross negligence to be sufficient when a fiduciary duty is present. Ordinarily, only a client, not a third party, will be able to prove the existence of a fiduciary duty.

**Statute of Limitations.** No 1934 Act section expressly places a statute of limitations on suits brought under Rule 10b–5. However, the courts have applied state statutes of limitations to Rule 10b–5 actions. Early cases adopted the statute of limitations for general fraud actions, but recent cases favor the statute of limitations in the state securities statutes. The Supreme Court has not ruled on the issue. When it does rule, it is likely to hold that the Section 18(a) statute of limitations should apply to Rule 10b–5, on the ground that Rule 10b–5 is better analogized to a 1934 Act liability section than to state statutes.[13]

[13] L. Loss, *Fundamentals of Securities Regulation,* pp. 1169–70 (1983).

**Aiding and Abetting.** Many suits brought against accountants under the federal securities acts allege the accountant's direct participation in a wrongful action, such as in Section 11 suits. Accountants may also be held liable for assisting others, that is, *aiding and abetting* violations of the securities acts by others. For example, accountants who wrongfully overlook misrepresentations by others or encourage the dissemination of misleading information prepared by others may be held liable as aiders and abetters. Aiding and abetting liability is one way to circumvent the privity requirement of Securities Act Section 12(2).

**State Securities Law.** All of the states have securities statutes with liability sections. Most of the states have a liability section similar to Section 12(2) of the Securities Act. Accountants are rarely sued under state securities statutes, but the use of state remedies should increase as litigants recognize the difficulty of proving scienter under Rule 10b–5 and other federal liability sections.

## Oleck v. Fischer

**623 F.2d 791 (2d Cir. 1980)**

In March 1971, Lawrence and Theodore Oleck sold their shares in Blue Circle Telephone Answering Service, Inc., to Sherwood Diversified Services, Inc., in exchange for cash and promissory notes of Sherwood. In negotiating and concluding the transaction, the Olecks were given and relied on Sherwood's 1970 financial statements that had been audited and certified by Arthur Andersen & Co. Before the notes were paid in full, Sherwood became insolvent. The Olecks sued Andersen and various officers of Sherwood, including Alan Fischer, under Section 10(b) of the Securities Exchange Act of 1934 and Rule 10b–5 thereunder. The Olecks alleged that Andersen failed to disclose adequately (1) the high probability that Sherwood would not be able to collect on $2.5 million of notes issued by U.S. New Media International Corporation and (2) that Sherwood would have to pay an additional $2 million as a guarantor of New Media's bank loan. Sherwood's risk in these transactions depended on New Media's ability to collect its accounts receivable. The Olecks alleged that Andersen failed to explore adequately New Media's ability to collect its accounts receivable.

The district court found that the Olecks had not proved that Andersen had acted with *scienter* in examining New Media's ability to collect its accounts receivable. Therefore, it held that Andersen was not liable under Section 10(b) and Rule 10b–5. The Olecks appealed.

**LEVAL, JUDGE.** In seeking to interpret the kind and quality of scienter necessary to establish liability after *Ernst & Ernst v. Hochfelder* (1976), this court has adhered to the proposition that reckless conduct will generally satisfy the scienter requirement. Certain cases have suggested that the sufficiency of reckless conduct may turn on the existence of a fiduciary duty or duty to disclose, and that, absent any such duty, no liability may be found without a conscious intention to defraud.

The district judge concluded that recklessness would satisfy the scienter requirement in this case by reason of the foreseeability to the accountant that the certification would be relied on by third parties. He found no reckless disregard for the truth. He concluded that Andersen's failures were at worst "judgmental," not rising "above the level of negligence," and thus non-actionable under *Hochfelder*. These findings were reasonably supported by the evidence.

The district judge found that Andersen's audit team had perceived the collectibility of the New Media notes as an important focus of inquiry which in turn depended for security on the extent and collectibility of New Media's receivables. Accordingly they devised a 10-step program to evaluate New Media in these respects.

Based on figures and projections furnished primarily by New Media, Andersen concluded that New Media had growing sales proceeding for the current year at a rate exceeding $17,800,000, with booked orders totaling $5,900,000 for the next four months. It observed that New Media's accounts were "mostly major firms."

A summary prepared by Andersen concluded that New Media's "cash projections were reasonable and attainable and that the cash flow shows the ability to pay principal and interest on the Sherwood notes without any detriment to its cash position." Andersen interviewed New Media's bankers and found "no plans to request payment against their $2 million loan." The New Media receivables were found to be more than adequate security to cover the bank debt and the Sherwood notes. Andersen also obtained and relied on an opinion of Sherwood's counsel to the effect that Sherwood's lien on the Media receivables was enforceable. Based on these investigations, Andersen concluded that "a reserve for collectibility of $500,000 would be sufficient."

The district judge was convinced that Andersen made those investigations and observations in good faith and was justified in issuing a clean opinion.

The Olecks argued that Andersen could not reasonably have accepted and relied on the information furnished by New Media's executives. This contention was fully considered by the district judge, who was not persuaded by it. His findings depended in significant part on his assessment of the credibility of Andersen's witnesses. Those findings were adequately supported by the evidence and may not be disturbed on appeal.

Judgment for Arthur Andersen affirmed.

## QUALIFIED OPINIONS AND DISCLAIMERS OF OPINION

After performing an audit of financial statements, an independent auditor *certifies* the financial statements by issuing an *opinion letter.* The opinion letter expresses whether the audit has been performed in compliance with GAAS and whether, in the auditor's opinion, the financial statements fairly present the client's financial position and results of operations in conformity with GAAP. Usually, an auditor issues an *unqualified opinion*—that is, an opinion that there has been compliance with GAAS and GAAP. Sometimes, an auditor issues a *qualified opinion,* a *disclaimer of opinion,* or an *adverse opinion.* Up to this point, you have studied the liability of an auditor who has issued unqualified opinions, yet has not complied with GAAS and GAAP. What liability should be imposed on an auditor who discloses that he has not complied with GAAS and GAAP?

An auditor is relieved of responsibility *only to the extent that a qualification or disclaimer is expressed* in the opinion letter. Therefore, general letters that purport to totally disclaim liability for false and misleading financial statements will not completely excuse an accountant from exercising ordinary skill and care.

**Qualified Opinion.** For example, an auditor who *qualifies* his opinion of the ability of the financial statements to present the financial position of a company by indicating that there is uncertainty about how a massive antitrust suit against the company may be decided, would not be held liable for damages resulting from an unfavorable verdict in the antitrust suit. He would remain liable, however, for failing to make an examination in compliance with GAAS that would have revealed other serious problems.

**Disclaimer.** For another example, consider an auditor who, due to the limited scope of the audit, disclaims *any* opinion on the ability of the financial statements to present the financial position of the company. She would nevertheless be liable for the nondiscovery of problems that the limited audit should have revealed.

**Adverse Opinion.** Likewise, an accountant who issued the *adverse* opinion that depreciation had not been calculated according to GAAP would not be liable for damages resulting from the wrongful accounting treatment of depreciation, but he would be liable for damages resulting from the wrongful treatment of receivables.

**Unaudited Financial Statements.** Merely issuing *unaudited* statements does not create a disclaimer as to their accuracy. The mere fact that the statements are unaudited only permits an accountant to exercise a lower level of inquiry. Even so, an accountant must act as the ordinarily prudent accountant would act in preparing unaudited financial statements under the same circumstances.

## CRIMINAL, INJUNCTIVE, AND ADMINISTRATIVE PROCEEDINGS

In addition to being held liable for damages to clients and third parties, an accountant may be found criminally liable for his violations of securities, tax, and other laws. For criminal violations, he may be fined and imprisoned. His wrongful conduct may also result in the issuance of an injunction, which bars him from doing the same acts in the future. In addition, his wrongful conduct may be the subject of administrative proceedings by the Securities and Exchange Commission and state licensing boards. An administrative proceeding may result in the revocation of an accountant's license to practice or her suspension from practice. Finally, disciplinary proceedings may be brought against an accountant by professional societies, such as the AICPA.

**Criminal Liability.** Both the Securities Act of 1933 and the Securities Exchange Act of 1934 have criminal provisions that can be applied to accountants. Section 24 of the 1933 Act imposes criminal liability for *willful* violations of any section of the 1933 Act, including Sections 11, 12(2), and 17(a), or any SEC rule or regulation. Also, willfully making an untrue statement or omitting any material fact in a 1933 Act registration statement imposes criminal liability on an accountant. An accountant who knows that financial statements are false and misleading, yet certifies them for inclusion in a registration statement, will be criminally liable under Section 24. The maximum penalty for a criminal violation of the 1933 Act is a $10,000 fine and five years' imprisonment.

Section 32(a) of the 1934 Act imposes criminal penalties for willful violations of any section of the 1934 Act, such as Sections 10(b) and 18(a), and any SEC rule or regulation, such as Rule 10b–5. In addition, willfully making false or misleading statements in reports that are required to be filed under the 1934 Act incurs criminal liability. Such filings include 10-Ks, 10-Qs, 8-Ks, and proxy statements. In the *Natelli* case, which follows, permitting the booking of unbilled sales after the close of the fiscal period in an unaudited statement supplied by auditors for inclusion in a proxy statement was held to come within the reach of Section 32(a). An accountant may be fined up to $100,000 and imprisoned for up to five years for a criminal violation of the 1934 Act. However, an accountant who proves that he had *no knowledge* of an *SEC rule or regulation* may not be imprisoned for violating that rule or regulation.

Most of the states have statutes imposing criminal penalties on accountants who willfully falsify financial statements or other reports in filings under the state securities laws and who willfully violate the state securities laws or aid and abet criminal violations of these laws by others.

**Tax Law.** Federal tax law imposes on accountants a wide range of penalties for a wide range of wrongful conduct. Most of the violations occur when accountants prepare clients' tax returns. At one end of the penalty spectrum is a $25 fine for failing to furnish a client with a copy of his income tax return or failing to sign a client's return. At the other end is a fine of $100,000 and imprisonment of three years for tax fraud. In between is the penalty for promoting abusive tax shelters. The fine is $1,000, or 10 percent of the accountant's income from her participation in the tax shelter, whichever is greater. In addition, all of the states impose criminal penalties for specified violations of their tax laws.

**Other Crimes.** Several other federal statutes also impose criminal liability on accountants. The most notable of these statutes is the general *mail fraud statute,* which prohibits the use of the mails to commit fraud. To be held liable, an accountant must *know or foresee* that the mails will be used to transmit materials containing fraudulent statements provided by her.

In addition, the general *false-statement-to-government-personnel statute* prohibits fraudulent statements to government personnel. The *false-statement-to-bank statute* proscribes fraudulent statements on a loan application to a bank or other financial institution.

**Injunctions.** Adminstrative agencies, such as the SEC and the Internal Revenue Service, may bring injunctive actions against an accountant in a federal district court. The purpose of such an injunction is to prevent an accountant from committing a future violation of the securities or tax laws. Hence, the mere existence of a past violation will not be sufficient grounds for the SEC or the IRS to obtain an injunction. There must be proof of the likelihood of a future violation.

After an injunction has been issued, violating the injunction may result in serious sanctions. Not only may penalties be imposed for contempt, but a criminal violation may also be more easily proven.

**Administrative Proceedings.** The SEC has the authority to bring administrative proceedings against persons who violate the provisions of the securities acts. In recent years, the SEC has stepped up enforcement of SEC Rule of Practice 2(e). Rule 2(e) permits the SEC to bar temporarily or permanently from practicing before the SEC an accountant who does not possess the qualifications required to practice before it. Rule 2(e) also permits the SEC to take action against an accountant who has willfully violated or aided and abetted another's violation of the securities acts. An SEC administrative law judge hears the case and makes an initial determination. The SEC commissioners then issue a final order, which may be appealed to a federal court of appeals.

Rule 2(e) administrative proceedings can impose severe penalties on an accountant, as is illustrated by *In the Matter of Bruce R. Ashton,* which follows. By suspending an accountant from practicing before it, the SEC may take away a substantial part of an accountant's practice.

In addition, state licensing boards may suspend or revoke an accountant's license to practice if she engages in illegal or unethical conduct. If such action is taken, an accountant may lose her entire ability to practice accounting.

## United States v. Natelli

**527 F.2d 311 (2d Cir. 1975)**

Anthony Natelli was the partner in charge of the Washington, D.C., office of Peat, Marwick, Mitchell & Co., a large CPA firm. He was the engagement partner for the audit of National Student Marketing Corporation. Joseph Scansaroli was Peat, Marwick's audit supervisor on that engagement. Peat, Marwick became the independent public auditor of Student Marketing in August 1968.

Student Marketing provided its corporate clients with a wide range of marketing services to help them reach the lucrative youth market. In its financial statements for the nine months ended May 31, 1968, Student Marketing had counted as income the entire amount of oral customer commitments to pay fees in Student Marketing's "fixed-fee marketing programs." Those fees had not yet been paid. They were to be paid for services that Student Marketing would provide over a period of several years. Standard accounting practice required that part of the unpaid fees be considered income in the present year but that part be deferred as income until the years when Student Marketing actually performed the services for which the fees were paid. Therefore, in making the year-end audit, Natelli concluded that he would use a percentage-of-completion approach on these commitments, taking as income in the present year only those fees that were to be paid for services in that year.

However, the customer fee commitments were oral only, making it difficult to verify whether they really existed. In addition, Student Marketing had not even recorded the fee commitments in its financial records during the 1968 fiscal year.

The decision regarding whether to include the fee commitments as income was critical. Excluding them would result in showing a large loss—$232,000—for the fiscal year at a time when Student Marketing's stock was selling for $80, an increase of $74 in the five months since Student Marketing had first sold its shares publicly.

Natelli directed Scansaroli to try to verify the fee commitments by telephoning the customers, but not by seeking written verification. However, Scansaroli never called Student Marketing's clients. Instead, Scansaroli accepted a schedule prepared by Student Marketing showing estimates of the percentage of completion of services for each corporate client and the amount of the fee commitment from each client. This resulted in an adjustment of $1.7 million for "unbilled accounts receivable." The adjustment turned a loss for the year into a profit twice that of the year before.

Soon after, Natelli informed Student Marketing that Peat, Marwick thereafter would allow income to be recorded only on written commitments supported by contemporaneous logs kept by account executives.

By May 1969, a total of $1 million of the customer fee commitments had been written off as uncollectible, three quarters of which was attributable to purported sales made by an account executive who had been fired for taking kickbacks. The effect of the write-off was to reduce 1968 income by $209,750. However, Scansaroli, with Natelli's approval, offset this by reversing a deferred tax item of approximately the same amount.

Student Marketing issued a proxy statement in September 1969, in connection with a shareholders' meeting to consider merging six companies into Student Marketing. The proxy statement was filed with the Securities and Exchange Commission. It contained several financial statements, some of which had been audited by Peat, Marwick. Others had not been audited, but Peat, Marwick had aided in their preparation. In the proxy statement, a footnote to the financial statements failed to show that the write-off of customer fee commitments had affected Student Marketing's fiscal 1968 income.

The proxy statement required an unaudited statement of nine months' earnings through May 31, 1969. This statement was prepared by Student Marketing with Peat, Marwick's assistance. A commitment for $1.2 million from the Pontiac Division of GM was produced two months after the end of May, but it was dated April 28, 1969. At 3 A.M. on the day the proxy statement was to be printed, Natelli informed Randall, the chief executive and founder of Student Marketing, that this commitment could not be included, because it was not a legally binding contract. Randall responded at once that he had "a commitment from Eastern Airlines" for a somewhat comparable amount attributable to the same period. Such a letter was produced at the printing plant a few hours later, and the Eastern commitment was substituted for the Pontiac sale in the proxy. Shortly thereafter, another Peat, Marwick accountant, Oberlander, discovered $177,547 in "bad" commitments from 1968. These were known to Scansaroli in May 1969 as being doubtful, but they had not been written off. Oberlander suggested to the company that these commitments plus others, for a total of $320,000, be written off, but Scansaroli, after consulting with Natelli, decided against the suggested write-off.

There was no disclosure in the proxy statement that Student Marketing had written off $1 million (20 percent) of its 1968 sales and over $2 million of the $3.3 million of unbilled sales booked in 1968 and 1969. A true disclosure would have shown that Student Marketing had made no profit for the first nine months of 1969.

Subsequently, it was revealed that many of Student Marketing's fee commitments were fictitious. The attorney general of the United States brought a criminal action against Natelli and Scansaroli for violating Section 32(a) of the Securities Exchange Act of 1934 by willfully and knowingly making false and misleading statements in a proxy statement. The district court jury convicted both Natelli and Scansaroli, and they appealed.

**Gurfein, Circuit Judge.** Natelli argues that there is insufficient evidence to establish that he knowingly assisted in filing a proxy statement that was materially false. We are constrained to find that there was sufficient evidence for his conviction.

The original action of Natelli in permitting the booking of unbilled sales after the close of the fiscal period in an amount sufficient to convert a loss into a profit was contrary to sound accounting practice, particularly when the cost of sales based on time spent by account executives in the fiscal period was a mere guess. When the uncollectibility, and indeed, the non-existence of these large receivables was established in 1969, the revelation stood to cause Natelli severe criticism and possible liability. He had a motive, therefore, intentionally to conceal the write-offs that had to be made.

With this background of motive, the jury could assess what Natelli did with regard to (1) the footnote and (2) the Eastern commitment and the Oberlander "bad" contracts.

Honesty should have impelled Natelli and Scansaroli to disclose in the footnote that annotated their own audited statement for fiscal 1968 that substantial write-offs had been taken, after year-end, to reflect a loss for the year. A simple desire to right the wrong that had been perpetrated on the stockholders and others by the false audited financial statement should have dictated that course.

The accountant owes a duty to the public not to assert a privilege of silence until the next audited annual statement comes around in due time. Since companies were being acquired by Marketing for its shares in this period, Natelli had to know that the 1968 audited statement was being used continuously. Natelli contends that he had no duty to verify the Eastern commitment because the earnings statement within which it was included was unaudited.

This raises the issue of the duty of the CPA in relation to an unaudited financial statement contained within a proxy statement where the figures are reviewed and to some extent supplied by the auditors. The auditors were associated with the statement and were required to object to anything they actually knew to be materially false. In the ordinary case involving an unaudited statement, the auditor would not be chargeable simply because he failed to discover the invalidity of booked accounts receivable, inasmuch as he had not undertaken an audit with verification. In this case, however, Natelli knew the history of post-period bookings and the dismal consequences later discovered.

We do not think this means, in terms of professional standards, that the accountant may shut his eyes in reckless disregard of his knowledge that highly suspicious figures, known to him to be suspicious, were being included in the unaudited earnings figures in the proxy statement with which he was associated.

There is some merit to Scansaroli's point that he was simply carrying out the judgments of his superior, Natelli. The defense of obedience to higher authority has always been troublesome. There is no sure yardstick to measure criminal responsibility except by measurement of the degree of awareness on the part of a defendant that he is participating in a criminal act, in the absence of physical coercion such as a soldier might face. Here the motivation to conceal undermines Scansaroli's argument that he was merely implementing Natelli's instructions, at least with respect to concealment of matters that were within his own ken. We think the jury could properly have found him guilty on the specification relating to the footnote.

With respect to the Eastern commitment, we think Scansaroli stands in a position different from that of Natelli. Natelli was his superior. He was the man to make the judgment whether or not to object to the last-minute inclusion of a new commitment in the nine-months statement. There is insufficient evidence that Scansaroli engaged in any conversations about the Eastern commitment or that he was a participant with Natelli in any check on its authenticity. Since in the hierarchy of the accounting firm it was not his responsibility to decide whether to book the Eastern contract, his mere adjustment of the figures to reflect it under orders was not a matter for his discretion.

Conviction of Natelli affirmed. Conviction of Scansaroli reversed.

## In the Matter of Bruce R. Ashton

### SEC Release No. AAER–15 (October 27, 1983)

Bruce R. Ashton was a certified public accountant who had appeared and practiced before the Securities and Exchange Commission. For 1978 and 1979, Consolidated Publishing Company filed with the SEC materially false and misleading financial statements containing audit reports issued by Ashton. In those reports, Ashton represented that he had examined the financial statements in accordance with generally accepted auditing standards and that the financial statements had been prepared in accordance with generally accepted accounting principles. In fact, there had been no compliance with GAAS and GAAP.

Pursuant to Rule 2(e) of the SEC's Rules of Practice, the SEC initiated an administrative proceeding against Ashton. Ashton consented to the issuance of the following order.

**By the Commission.** The Commission finds that it is in the public interest to impose a remedial sanction.

Accordingly, it is hereby ordered:

(1) Bruce R. Ashton, CPA, is hereby suspended from appearing or practicing before the Commission;

(2) Two years from June 23, 1983, the date of the order temporarily suspending Mr. Ashton from practice, Mr. Ashton may appear and practice before the Commission if he first demonstrates that the following conditions have been met:

(a) He has completed at least 50 hours of professional seminars or college courses in any one year prior to his again commencing practice before the Commission, approved by either the American Institute of Certified Public Accountants or the California Society of Certified Public Accountants, including at least 20 hours relating to auditing standards or securities; and

(b) He has tendered to the Commission the name of a certified public accountant not unacceptable to the Commission (the Commission will not unreasonably object) who will review each audit report issued by Mr. Ashton which is to be filed with the Commission or which he knows or should know (i.e. does not recklessly disregard the facts available to him) will be used in connection with the purchase or sale of any security, prior to such filing or use, for a period of 1½ years from the date Mr. Ashton commences practice before the Commission.

(3) Upon commencing practice before the Commission, Bruce R. Ashton shall:

(a) Comply with generally accepted accounting principles, generally accepted auditing standards, and all accounting and auditing standards of the Commission; and

(b) Have each audit report he issues which is to be filed with the Commission or used in connection with the purchase or sale of any security reviewed for a period of 1½ years by the certified public accountant referred to in Section 2(b) of this Order prior to such filing or use.

## OWNERSHIP OF WORKING PAPERS AND ACCOUNTANT-CLIENT PRIVILEGE

**Working Papers.** The personal records that a client entrusts to an accountant remain the property of the client. An accountant returns these records to his client. Nevertheless, the *working papers* produced by independent auditors belong to the accountant, not the client. Working papers are the records made during an audit. They include such items as work programs or plans for the audit, evidence of the testing of accounts, explanations of the handling of unusual matters, data reconciling the accountant's report with the client's records, and comments about the client's internal controls and other matters of significance. The client has a *right of access* to the working papers. The accountant must obtain the client's permission before the working papers can be transferred to another accountant.

**Accountant-Client Privilege.** A lawyer-client privilege has long been recognized by the common law. This privilege protects most of the communications between lawyers and their clients. In addition, it protects a lawyer's working papers from the discovery procedures available in a lawsuit.

The common law does not recognize such a privilege between accountants and their clients. However, a large minority of the states have granted such a privilege by statute. The provisions of the statutes vary, and under some of the statutes it is not clear whether it is the client or the accountant who can claim the privilege. Usually, the privilege belongs to the client, and an accountant may not refuse to disclose the privileged material if the client consents to its disclosure.

Generally, the state privileges are recognized in both state and federal courts *deciding questions of state law.* Nevertheless, federal courts do not recognize the privilege in matters *involving federal questions,* including antitrust and criminal matters. In federal tax matters, for example, no privilege of confidentiality is recognized, as was held by the Supreme Court of the United States in *United States v. Arthur Young & Co.,* which follows. An accountant can be required to bring his working papers into court and to testify as to matters involving the client's records and discussions with the client. In addition, an accountant may be required by subpoena to make available his working papers involving a client who is being investigated by the IRS or who has been charged with tax irregularities. The same holds true for SEC investigations.

## United States v. Arthur Young & Co.

### 104 S. Ct. 1495 (U.S. Sup. Ct. 1984)

In 1975, while performing a routine audit of the tax returns of Amerada Hess Corporation, the Internal Revenue Service discovered questionable payments of $7,830. The IRS issued a summons to Arthur Young & Co., the accounting firm that had prepared the tax accrual workpapers that might reveal the nature of the payments. The workpapers had been prepared in the process of Arthur Young's review of Amerada Hess's financial statements, as required by federal securities law. In the summons, the IRS ordered Arthur Young to make available to the IRS all of its Amerada Hess files, including its tax accrual workpapers. Amerada Hess directed Arthur Young not to comply with the summons.

The IRS asked the district court to order Arthur Young to comply with the summons. The district court found the tax accrual workpapers relevant to the IRS investigation and held that there was no accountant-client privilege that would protect the workpapers. Arthur Young appealed. The court of appeals created a work-product immunity doctrine for tax accrual workpapers prepared by independent auditors in the course of compliance with federal securities laws. It refused to enforce the summons insofar as the summons sought the tax accrual papers. The IRS appealed to the Supreme Court of the United States.

**Burger, Chief Judge.** Our complex and comprehensive system of federal taxation, relying as it does upon self-assessment and reporting, demands that all taxpayers be forthright in the disclosure of relevant information to the taxing authorities. Without such disclosure, and the concomitant power of the Government to compel disclosure, our national tax burden would not be fairly and equitably distributed. In order to encourage effective tax investigations, Congress has endowed the IRS with expansive information-gathering authority.

While this authority of the IRS is subject to traditional privileges and limitations, any other restrictions upon the IRS summons power should be avoided absent unambiguous directions from Congress. We are unable to discern the sort of unambiguous directions from Congress that would justify a judicially created work-product immunity for tax accrual workpapers summoned by the IRS. Indeed, there is a congressional policy choice in favor of disclosure of all information relevant to a legitimate IRS inquiry. In light of this explicit statement by the Legislative Branch, courts should be chary in recognizing exceptions to the broad summons authority of the IRS or in fashioning new privileges that would curtail disclosure.

We do not find persuasive the argument that a work-product immunity for accountants' tax accrual workpapers is a fitting analogue to the attorney work-product doctrine. The work-product doctrine was founded upon the private attorney's role as the client's confidential advisor and advocate, a loyal representative whose duty it is to present the client's case in the most favorable possible light. An independent certified public accountant performs a different role. By certifying the public reports that collectively depict a corporation's financial status, the independent auditor assumes a *public* responsibility transcending any employment relationship with the client. The independent public accountant performing this special function owes ultimate allegiance to the corporation's creditors and stockholders, as well as to the investing public. This "public watchdog" function demands that the accountant maintain total independence from the client at all times and requires complete fidelity to the public trust. To insulate from disclosure a certified public accountant's interpretations of the client's financial statements would be to ignore the significance of the accountant's role as a disinterested analyst charged with public obligations.

We cannot accept the view that the integrity of the securities markets will suffer absent some protection for accountants' tax accrual workpapers. The Court of Appeals apparently feared that, were the IRS to have access to tax accrual workpapers, a corporation might be tempted to withhold from its auditor certain information relevant and material to a proper evaluation of its financial statements. But the independent certified public accountant cannot be content with the corporation's representations that its tax accrual reserves are adequate; the auditor is ethically and professionally obligated to ascertain for himself as far as possible whether the corporation's contingent tax liabilities have been accurately stated. If the auditor were convinced that the scope of the examination had been limited by management's reluctance to disclose matters relating to the tax accrual reserves, the auditor would be unable to issue an unqualified opinion as to the accuracy of the corporation's financial statements. Instead, the auditor would be required to issue a qualified opinion, an adverse opinion, or a disclaimer of opinion, thereby notifying the investing public of possible potential problems inherent in the corporation's financial reports. Responsible corporate management would not risk a qualified evaluation of a corporate taxpayer's financial posture to afford cover for questionable positions reflected in a prior tax return. Thus, the independent auditor's obligation to serve the public interest assures that the integrity of the securities markets will be preserved, without the need for a work-product immunity for accountants' tax accrual workpapers.

We also reject Arthur Young's position that fundamental fairness precluded IRS access to accountants' tax accrual workpapers. Arthur Young urges that the enforcement of an IRS summons for accountants' tax accrual workpapers permits the Government to probe the thought processes of its taxpayer citizens, thereby giving the IRS an unfair advantage in negotiating and litigating tax controversies. But if the SEC itself, or a private plaintiff in securities litigation, sought to obtain the tax accrual workpapers at issue in this case, they would surely be entitled to do so. No sound reason exists for conferring lesser authority upon the IRS than upon a private litigant suing with regard to transactions concerning which the public has no interest.

Beyond question it is desirable and in the public interest to encourage full disclosures by corporate clients to their independent accountants; if it is necessary to balance competing interests, however, the need of the Government for full disclosure of all information relevant to tax liability must also weigh in that balance. This kind of policy choice is best left to the Legislative Branch.

Judgment reversed in favor of the Internal Revenue Service.

## SUMMARY

Recently, accountants, as well as other professionals, have been frequent targets of lawsuits. These suits may be brought by clients against accountants under the common law for breach of contract, for negligence, and for fraud. In addition, clients may sue under state and federal securities laws.

An accountant is generally held to the standard of the ordinarily prudent accountant. If she meets this standard, few courts will hold her liable. If the standard is breached, clients may sue the accountant for damages caused thereby.

Courts have different rules on whether a nonclient may sue an accountant for negligence. Some require the nonclient to be the primary beneficiary of the accountant's work. Others require that the nonclient be a foreseen user or within a foreseen class of users. A few courts impose liability for negligence if the use of the accountant's work by a nonclient is foreseeable. If an accountant has committed fraud, she is liable to foreseeable third parties.

Mostly, nonclients sue accountants under the federal securities laws. Accountants may be held liable for incomplete and incorrect information that they furnish for use in a Securities Act registration statement, unless they can prove that they have exercised due diligence. Section 10(b) and Rule 10b–5 of the Securities Exchange Act are frequently used by nonclients. Accountants are liable under those provisions for misstatements or omissions of material fact in connection with the purchase or sale of a security. The accountant must have acted with scienter to be found liable. In addition, an accountant may be held liable for aiding and abetting violations of the securities acts by others.

Accountants have been found criminally liable under the federal securities acts, tax laws, and mail fraud laws. The SEC and the IRS may obtain injunctions against accountants to prevent future violations. The SEC may suspend from practicing before it an accountant who has violated the securities laws.

The working papers of accountants belong to them rather than to their clients, but the client has a right of access to the papers. Accountants may be required to produce in court their records concerning a client. Some states recognize a privilege of confidentiality in such records, but this privilege is not recognized by federal courts for federal questions.

## PROBLEM CASES

**1.** Devco Premium Finance Company hired Miller & Holley, a public accounting firm, to devise a test to determine the number and size of Devco's accounts receivables that might be uncollectible. Miller & Holley negligently failed to follow up on indications that many of Devco's accounts receivable were not collectible and negligently failed to alert Devco's management that Devco's internal accounting controls were so weak that they did not reveal the full extent of Devco's receivable collection problem. For its part, Devco was negligent in failing to demand reports from its employees on the age of its accounts receivable. Subsequently, Devco lost a substantial amount of money because it could not collect on many of its receivables. Devco sued Miller & Holley for damages. Miller & Holley argued that its liability should be reduced by Devco's negligence. Is Miller & Holley correct?

**2.** Coopers & Lybrand was the independent accountant for two limited partnerships. The limited partnerships became insolvent, and the limited partners lost their investments. The limited partners sued Coopers & Lybrand for negligently performing accounting work for the limited partnerships, resulting in the loss of the limited partners' investments. Coopers & Lybrand argued that the case should be dismissed because there was no privity. Is Coopers & Lybrand correct?

**3.** Robert Brumley purchased two thirds of the shares of KPK Corporation after relying on materially misleading financial statements that had been negligently audited by Touche Ross & Co. The financial statements were prepared for KPK. Touche Ross did not know that the statements would be given to Brumley. Brumley lost $2.5 million when the value of the shares declined due to the disclosure of the true condition of KPK. Brumley sued Touche Ross for negligence. He argued that Touche Ross knew and foresaw that the audited statements would be circulated by KPK and that it was foreseeable that KPK would give the audited statements to potential purchasers of its shares. Is Brumley within the class of persons to whom Touche Ross can be liable for negligence?

**4.** A Rhode Island corporation sought a loan from Rusch Factors, Inc. Rusch Factors requested certified financial statements to determine the financial condition of the company. The company employed Leonard Levin, a CPA, to prepare the statements. Levin was told that the statements would be used by Rusch Factors. Due to Levin's negligence, the financial statements represented the company to be in good financial condition. In fact, it was insolvent. Rusch Factors relied on the financial statements and loaned the company $337,000. The company was unable to repay $121,000 of the loan, so Rusch Factors sued Levin for that amount. Is Levin liable to Rusch Factors?

**5.** Yale Express System, Inc., was a nationwide trucking business. Peat, Marwick, Mitchell & Co. (PMM) was employed in early 1964 to audit Yale's financial statements for inclusion in Yale's 1963 annual report to shareholders. Shortly after the audit was completed, Yale employed PMM for an assignment involving special studies of current income and expenses. Before the end of 1964, PMM discovered that the figures in the 1963 annual report were materially false and misleading. In May 1965, when the results from the special studies were released, Yale disclosed publicly that the earlier information was misleading.

Yale Express later became bankrupt. Stephen Fischer, a shareholder, brought a common law action for fraud against PMM based on PMM's failure to notify investors promptly when it discovered that Yale's certified statements were misleading. Is PMM liable to Fischer for fraud?

**6.** Seedkem, Inc., extended $700,000 in credit to Agri-Products, Inc. after Agri-Products had furnished Seedkem with a copy of its current financial statements. The statements had been prepared by Paul Safranek, a certified public accountant. The financial statements were marked as "unaudited." In addition, Safranek expressly disclaimed making any opinion as to the accuracy of the statements.

When Agri-Products failed, Seedkem sought damages from Safranek. It alleged that Safranek had been negligent in preparing the financial statements, because he knew that they did not conform to generally accepted accounting principles. Safranek argued that he could not be held liable, for these reasons: the financial statements were marked unaudited; he had expressly disclaimed reliability of the statements; and there was no privity. Is Safranek correct?

**7.** International Trading Corporation, an importer of cement, had unloading facilities at several eastern seaports. It was permitted by Rhode Island Hospital Trust National Bank to exceed an agreed-upon line of credit because it represented to National Bank that it had spent $212,000 to improve its facilities with its own labor and that this would substantially reduce its operating expenses. In fact, the improvements were fictitious.

In permitting International to exceed its line of credit, National Bank had relied on financial statements examined by Swartz, Bresenoff, Yavner & Jacobs, a CPA firm, during an audit of International. In a letter that accompanied the statements, the firm expressed certain reservations concerning the financial statements. With regard to the alleged improvements, the firm stated: "Practically all of this work was done by company employees, and materials and overhead were borne by the company. Unfortunately, fully complete detailed cost records were not kept and no exact determination could be made as to the actual cost of said improvements."

The letter concluded: "Because of the limitations upon our examination and the material nature of the items not confirmed by us, we are unable to express an opinion as to the fairness of the accompanying statements."

The firm knew that National Bank would be given a copy of the financial statements and the letter. National Bank was unable to collect its loan and sued the firm for negligence in failing to verify the existence of the improvements and their value when they found no records of expenditures for materials. The firm relied on the disclaimer as a defense. Is this a good defense?

**8.** Gerald Herzfeld invested in Firestone Group, Ltd. (FGL) after receiving unaudited FGL financial statements showing assets of over $20 million, net worth of nearly $1 million, and after-tax income of $315,000, or approximately $2 per share. After Herzfeld had made this investment, FGL had its financial statements audited by Laventhol, Krekstein, Horwath & Horwath. During the audit, Laventhol was given two contracts for transactions that did not appear in the minutes of directors' meetings or in FGL's financial records. One was a purported FGL purchase of 23 nursing homes for $13,362,500 from Monterey Nursing Inns, Inc., with a down payment of $5,000 by FGL. The other was for the sale of these nursing homes to Continental Recreation, Inc., for $15,393,000, with a $25,000 down payment. No other payment was due for two months, which was after the end of the period covered by the financial statements. Recognizing the $2,030,500 anticipated profit in the year ended November 30 would have converted a $772,108 loss into a profit of over $1.25 million.

Laventhol learned that the transaction had not been entered in FGL's books or in the minutes of the directors' meetings. FGL wanted all of the profit to be included in the period ended November 30 and threatened to withdraw its account if Laventhol did not approve. Laventhol insisted, however, that only $235,000 (the down payment plus the amount provided in the contract for liquidated damages) be recognized as income currently and that the rest be treated as "deferred gross profit." A note to the income statement prepared by Laventhol declared that the remainder of the profit would be recognized when the January 30 payment was received. In its opinion letter, Laventhol said that the statement was "subject to the collectibility of the balance receivable on the contract." The financial statements and the opinion letter were sent to FGL's investors. Subsequently, neither the nursing home purchase contract nor the sales contract was consummated. FGL went into bankruptcy about a year later.

Herzfeld sued Laventhol under Rule 10b–5. Is Laventhol liable to Herzfeld?

**9.** Louis Sternbach & Co., the independent auditor for Solitron Corporation, certified financial statements of Solitron in which consignments were treated as sales. For other sales, Solitron could produce no purchase orders from customers. To confirm these sales, Sternbach had contacted Solitron customers, but it had received no confirmations.

When many of the sales proved to be fictitious, Solitron shareholders sued Sternbach for aiding and abetting Solitron's violation of Rule 10b–5. Was Sternbach held liable?

**10.** The Internal Revenue Service audited the 1977–79 federal income tax returns of Trio Manufacturing Company, a close corporation. The IRS issued a summons to George Pennington, the certified public accountant who prepared the corporate income tax returns of Trio and who conducted audits of Trio for the years 1977–79. The summons sought information regarding Trio's tax liability, including any and all workpapers, analyses, and computations prepared in the course of Pennington's annual audits of Trio. Trio directed Pennington to refuse to comply with the summons. The IRS asked the district court to order Pennington to comply with the summons. Trio objected on the grounds that the summons sought documents that were not relevant to the IRS's audit and that were protected by an accountant work product privilege. Should an accountant-work product privilege be found here?

# PART VII

# PROPERTY

# Chapter 28

# Personal Property and Bailments

## INTRODUCTION

The concept of property has special importance to the organization of society. The essential nature of a particular society is often reflected in the way it views property, including the degree to which property ownership is concentrated in the state, the extent it permits individual ownership of property, and the rules that govern such ownership. History is replete with wars and revolutions that arose out of conflicting claims to, or views concerning, property. And significant documents in our own Anglo-American legal tradition, such as the Magna Carta and the Constitution, deal explicitly with property rights.

This chapter will discuss the nature and classification of property. It will also examine the various ways that interests in personal property can be obtained and transferred, such as by production, purchase, or gift. The last half of the chapter explores the law of bailments. A bailment is involved, for example, when you check your coat in a coatroom at a restaurant or when you park your car in a public parking garage and leave your keys with the attendant.

## NATURE AND CLASSIFICATION

**Property.** The word **property** has a variety of meanings. It may refer to an object, such as a building, or it may refer to legal rights connected with an object, such as the lease of a building, which gives the tenant the right to occupy and use the building. However, the word *property* may also refer to legal rights that have economic value but are not connected with an object. A patent is an example of this kind of property.

When we talk about ownership of property, we are talking about a *bundle of legal rights* that are recognized and enforced by society. For example, ownership of a building includes the exclusive right to use, enjoy, sell, mortgage, or rent the building. If someone else tries to use the property without the owner's consent, the owner can use the courts and legal procedures to eject that person. Ownership of a patent includes the right to sell it, to license others to use it, or to produce the patented article personally.

In the United States, private ownership of property is protected by the Constitution. It provides that no person shall be deprived by the state of "*life, liberty or property without due process of law.*" We recognize and encourage the rights of individuals to acquire, enjoy, and use property. These rights, however, are not unlimited. For example, a person cannot use property in an unreasonable manner to the injury of others. Also, the state has the "*police power*" to impose reasonable regulations on the use of property, to tax it, and to take it for public use by paying the owner compensation for it.

**Possession.** The importance of **possession** in the law of property is indicated in the old saying "Possession is nine points of the law." In any primitive society, possession is the equivalent of ownership. In the early development of our law, the courts held that in a case of violation of property rights, the right violated was the right of peaceful possession. As can be seen in the case that follows, *Justice v. Fabey,* a presumption of entitlement may be accorded to the person in possession of property and he may be entitled to certain due process procedures, such as a hearing, before he can be deprived of that property.

In our modern society, the word *possession* is used with such a variety of meanings that it is futile to attempt to define it in precise terms. In its simplest sense, possession signifies that a person has manual control over a physical object; in law, however, this simple concept is inadequate. In connection with possession of personal property, two elements are of general importance: (1) *manual control* and (2) *intent* to claim property rights. The courts recognize legal possession, which is the legal right to control the physical object; manual control is not an essential element of legal possession. If a woman is wearing her watch, she has both legal and manual control of the watch. She has possession of the watch in the popular sense of the word, and she also has legal possession. If she leaves her watch in her house while she is on vacation, she does not have manual control of the watch, but she does have legal control. She has legal possession, and anyone taking the watch from her house without her consent has invaded her right of possession.

Employees of agents may have manual control of their employer's or principal's property, but do not have legal possession of the property. The employee or agent has only *custody* of the property; the employer or principal has legal possession. For example, if a storekeeper gives a clerk the day's receipts to count in the storekeeper's presence, the clerk has custody of the receipts, but the storekeeper has legal possession.

**Real and Personal Property.** Property can be divided into different classes based on its characteristics. The same piece of property may fall into more than one class. The most important classification is that of **real property** and **personal property.** Real property is the earth's crust and all things firmly attached to it. Personal property includes all other objects and rights that can be owned.

Real property can be turned into personal property if it is detached from the earth. Similarly, personal property can be attached to the earth and become real property. For example, marble in the ground is real property. When the marble is quarried, it becomes personal property, but if it is used in constructing a building, it becomes real property again. Perennial vegetation that does not have to be seeded every year, such as trees, shrubs, and grass, is usually treated as part of the real property on which they are growing. When trees and shrubs are severed from the land, they become personal property. Crops that must be planted each year, such as corn, oats, and potatoes, are usually treated as personal property. However, if the real property on which they are growing is sold, the new owner of the real property also becomes the owner of the crops.

**Tangible and Intangible Property.** **Tangible property** has a physical existence; land, buildings, and furniture are examples. Property that has no physical existence is called **intangible property;** patent rights, easements, and bonds are intangible property.

The distinction between tangible and intangible property is important primarily for tax and estate planning purposes. Generally, tangible property is subject to tax in the state in which it is located, whereas intangible property is usually taxable in the state where its owner lives.

**Public and Private Property.** Property is also classified as public or private based on the ownership of the property. If the property is owned by the government or a government unit, it is classified as **public property;** but if it is owned by an individual, a group of individuals, a corporation, or some other business organization, it is **private property.**

## Justice v. Fabey

**34 UCC Rep. 515 (E.D.Pa. 1982)**

The Philadelphia Police Department obtained a truck in a raid, seizing it as stolen property. Sometime later, Zappone Brothers purchased the truck from the police pound without obtaining a certificate of title. Milton Justice purchased the truck from Zappone in May 1976 and remained in possession of it until April 1981. At that time, the police ascertained the original owner of the stolen truck, seized it from Justice, and returned it to its owner. Justice brought suit against Joseph Fabey, the police officer who seized the truck from him, and the police department, contending that he had been deprived of his property without a hearing and hence without due process of law.

**POLLACK, DISTRICT JUDGE.** The central question in this case is whether at the point of seizure, Justice's possession of the truck established, under Pennsylvania law, some presumptive entitlement to the truck so that the police were required by the due process clause to provide a hearing before an impartial official to determine who had proper title to the truck. If, as it appears from the pleadings, that determination was open to dispute at the time of the seizure by virtue of Justice's possession, then due process may require the police to provide Justice with some opportunity to demonstrate his claim of ownership.

Justice alleges a deprivation of property without due process. Whether Justice has stated a cause of action turns on whether he had a constitutionally cognizable property interest in the truck. Because property interests do not stem from the Constitution itself, but are created and defined by an independent source such as state law, it becomes necessary to look to the law of Pennsylvania to determine the nature of Justice's interest in the truck.

Section 2–403 of the Uniform Commercial Code provides that "a purchaser of goods acquires all title which his transferor had or had power to transfer." Further, a person with voidable title—that is, one who has obtained goods through the assent of the original owner but who may not have acquired good title—"has power to transfer a good title to a good faith purchaser for value." One who has acquired goods by theft, however, cannot confer title by sale, even to a bona fide purchaser. Assuming that Justice was a bona fide purchaser for value from Zappone Brothers, who in turn purchased in good faith from the Philadelphia Police Department, the threshold question with respect to Justice's acquisition of some significant property interest is whether either transferor had power to convey at least a voidable title to the truck. Under Pennsylvania property law, it appears that since both Zappone Brothers' and the City's possession of the truck are ultimately traceable to the initial theft, neither had power to transfer good title to Justice.

However, while Justice may not be able ultimately to establish good title to the seized truck under Pennsylvania law, this does not conclusively determine whether the police were required under the due process clause to afford him some kind of hearing when they sought to take possession of the truck. It is clear that the Fourteenth Amendment not only safeguards rights of undisputed ownership, but also extends to any other significant property interest. The fact that a processor's claim of ownership may be disputed does not negate the existence of a property interest or his right to procedural safeguards mandated by the Fourteenth Amendment. As the Supreme Court has stated, "It is a purpose of the ancient institution of property to protect those claims upon which people rely in their daily lives, reliance that must not be arbitrarily undermined."

In Pennsylvania possession of a chattel is deemed to be prima facie evidence of ownership. Thus, any person claiming ownership of property which is in the possession of another bears the burden of proving facts essential to his claim of ownership. And while there appears to be no clear Pennsylvania authority on the matter, it would seem that one's earlier possession of property, which has subsequently been seized, is prima facie evidence of one's entitlement to the property.

Justice alleges that, at the time Officer Fabey seized his truck, he had enjoyed undisturbed possession of the truck for almost five years. He further alleges that during this time he expended a considerable amount of money to maintain and virtually reconstruct the vehicle.

Therefore, in light of Pennsylvania law, which attaches a presumption of entitlement to one in possession, and the broad protection afforded by the Fourteenth Amendment, I find that Justice's complaint alleges facts constituting a property interest in the truck sufficient to impose upon government officials a due process obligation not to terminate Justice's possession of the truck without according him a hearing to adjudicate his claim of ownership.

Judgment for Justice.

## ACQUIRING OWNERSHIP OF PERSONAL PROPERTY

**Possession.** In very early times, the most common way of obtaining ownership of personal property was simply by *taking possession* of unowned property. For example, the first person to take possession of a wild animal became its owner. Today, we still recognize the right to ownership of unowned property by taking possession of it. Wildlife and abandoned property are classified as unowned property. The first person to take possession of wildlife or abandoned property becomes the owner.

To acquire ownership of a wild animal by taking possession, a person must obtain enough control over it to deprive it of its freedom. If a person fatally wounds a wild animal, the person becomes the owner. Wild animals caught in a trap or fish caught in a net are usually considered to be the property of the person who set the trap or net. If a captured wild animal escapes and is caught by another person, that person generally becomes the owner. However, if the person knows that the animal is an escaped animal and that the prior owner is chasing it to recapture it, then the person does not become the owner.

If property is abandoned by the owner, it becomes unowned property. If a television set is taken to the city dump and left there, the first person who takes possession of it with the intention of claiming ownership becomes the new owner.

**Production or Purchase.** The most common ways of obtaining ownership of property are by *producing* it and by *purchasing* it. A person owns the property that he makes unless the person has agreed to do the work for someone else. In that case, the employer is the owner of the product of the work. For example, a person who creates a painting or knits a sweater is the owner unless he has been hired by someone to do the painting or knit the sweater.

Another major way of acquiring property is by purchase. The law of sale of goods is discussed in Chapters 31–34.

**Lost and Mislaid Property.** Suppose Barber's camera falls out of her handbag while she is walking down the street. Lawrence later finds the camera in the grass where it fell. Jones then steals the camera from Lawrence's house. What rights to the camera do Barber, Lawrence, and Jones have? Barber is still the owner of the camera. She has the right to have it returned to her if she discovers where it is—or if Lawrence knows that it belongs to Barber. As the finder of lost property, Lawrence has a better right to the camera than anyone else except its true owner (Barber). This means that she has the right to require Jones to return it to her if she finds out that Jones has it.

If the finder of **lost property** knows who the owner is and refuses to return it, the finder is guilty of larceny. If the finder does not know who the true owner is or cannot easily find out, the finder must still return the property if the real owner shows up and asks for the property. If the finder does not return it, he is liable for *conversion* and must pay the owner the fair value of the property.

Some states have a statute that allows finders of property to clear their title to the property. The statutes generally provide that the person must give public notice of the fact that the property has been found, perhaps by putting an ad in a local newspaper. All states have **statutes of limitations** that require the true owner of property to claim it or bring a legal action to recover possession of it within a certain number of years. A person who keeps possession of lost or unclaimed property for longer than that period of time will become its owner.

The courts have made a distinction between

**lost property** and **mislaid property.** If Hall, while shopping in Frederick's store, drops her wallet in the aisle, the wallet is generally considered lost property; but if she lays it on the counter and, forgetting it, leaves the store, it is considered mislaid property. If the wallet is mislaid, Frederick becomes the bailee of it. If Wilson finds the wallet in the aisle, he has the right to take possession of it. If Wilson discovers the wallet on the counter, Frederick has the right to take possession of it. The *Dolitsky v. Dollar Savings Bank* case, which follows, illustrates the distinction courts have made between lost and mislaid property.

The distinction between lost and mislaid property was developed to increase the chances that the property would be returned to its real owner who knowingly placed it down but forgot to pick it up. In that case, the owner might well be expected to remember later where the property had been left and return for it. Sometimes, it is very difficult to distinguish between lost property and misplaced property. As a result, the courts are not always consistent in the way they make the distinction.

**Gifts.** Title to personal property can be obtained by **gift.** A gift is a voluntary transfer of property for which the donor gets no consideration in return. To have a valid gift, (1) the **donor** must *intend* to make a gift, (2) the donor must make *delivery* of the gift, and (3) the **donee** must *accept* the gift. The most critical requirement is delivery. The person who makes the gift must actually give up possession and control of the property either to the donee (the person who receives the gift) or to a third person to hold it for the donee. Delivery is important because it makes clear to the donor that he is voluntarily giving up ownership without getting something in exchange. A promise to make a gift is usually not enforceable; the person must actually part with the property. In some cases, the delivery may be *symbolic.* For example, handing over the key to a strongbox can be symbolic delivery of the property in the strongbox.

There are two kinds of gifts: gifts *inter vivos* and gifts *causa mortis.* A gift *inter vivos* is a gift between two living persons; a gift *causa mortis* is a gift made in *contemplation of death.* For example, an uncle is about to undergo a serious heart operation. He gives his watch to his nephew and tells the nephew that he wants him to have it if he does not survive the operation. A gift *causa mortis* is a *conditional gift.* It is not effective if (1) the donor recovers from the peril or sickness under fear of which the gift was made, (2) the donor revokes or withdraws the gift before he dies, or (3) the donee dies before the donor. If one of these events takes place, ownership of the property goes back to the donor.

The elements of a valid gift, as well as the difference between an *inter vivos* gift and a gift *causa mortis,* are discussed in the *Welton v. Gallagher* case which follows.

Ownership can also be transferred when the owner dies. The property may pass under the terms of a **will** if the will was validly executed. If there is no valid will, the property is transferred to the **heirs** of the owner according to state laws. Transfer of property at the death of the owner will be discussed in Chapter 30.

**Conditional Gifts.** Sometimes, a gift is made on condition that the donee comply with certain restrictions or perform certain actions. A conditional gift is not a completed gift, and it may be revoked by the donor before the donee complies with the conditions. However, if the donee has partially complied with the conditions, the donor cannot withdraw the gift without giving the donee an opportunity to comply fully.

Gifts in contemplation of marriage, such as engagement rings, have given rise to much litigation. Generally, gifts of this kind are considered to have been made on an implied condition that they are to be returned if the donee breaks the engagement without legal justification or if it is broken by mutual consent. However, if the engagement is unjustifiably broken by the donor, he or she is generally not entitled to recover gifts made in contemplation of marriage. Some states have enacted legislation prescribing the rules applicable to the return of engagement presents.

**Uniform Gifts to Minors Act.** The Uniform Gifts to Minors Act provides a fairly simple and flexible method for making gifts of money and securities to minors. The act has been adopted in one form or another in every state. Under it, an adult can make a gift of money to a minor by depositing it with a broker or bank in an account in the donor's name, or with another adult or a bank with trust powers, as "custodian" for the minor "under the Uniform Gifts to Minors Act." Similarly, a gift of registered securities can be made by registering the securities in the name of another adult, a bank trustee, or a broker as custodian for the minor. A gift of unregistered securities can be made by delivering the securities to another adult or a bank trustee along with a statement that he or it is to hold the securities as custodian and then obtaining a written acknowledgment from the custodian. The custodian is given fairly broad discretion to use the gift for the minor's benefit but may not use it for the personal benefit of the custodian. If the donor fully complies with the Uniform Gifts to Minors Act, the gift is considered to be irrevocable.

**Confusion.** Title to personal property can be obtained by **confusion.** Confusion is the intermixing of goods that belong to different owners in such a way that they cannot later be separated. For example, suppose wheat belonging to several different people is mixed in a grain elevator. If the mixing was by agreement or if it resulted from an accident without negligence on anyone's part, then each person owns his proportionate share of the entire quantity of wheat.

However, a different result would be reached if the wheat was wrongfully or negligently mixed. Suppose a thief steals a truckload of Grade #1 wheat worth $4.50 a bushel from a farmer. The thief dumps the wheat into his storage bin, which contains a lower-grade wheat worth $2.50 a bushel with the result that the mixture is worth only $2.50 a bushel. The farmer has first claim against the entire mixture to recover the value of his wheat that was mixed in. The thief, or any other person whose intentional or negligent act results in confusion of goods, must bear any loss caused by the confusion.

**Accession.** Title to personal property can also be obtained by **accession.** Accession means increasing the value of property by adding materials and/or labor. As a general rule, the owner of the original property becomes the owner of the improvements. For example, Hudson takes his automobile to a shop that replaces the engine with a larger engine and puts in a new four-speed transmission. Hudson is still the owner of the automobile as well as the owner of the parts added by the auto shop.

Problems can arise if materials are added or work is performed on personal property without the consent of the owner. If property is stolen from one person and improved by the thief, the original owner can get it back and does not have to reimburse the thief for the work done or the materials used in improving it. For example, a thief steals Rourke's used car, puts a new engine in it, replaces the tires, and repairs the muffler. Rourke is entitled to get his car back from the thief and does not have to pay him for the engine, tires, or muffler.

The problem is more difficult if property is mistakenly improved in good faith by someone who believes that he is the owner of the property. Then, two innocent parties—the original owner and the person who improved the property—are involved. Usually, the person who improved the property in good faith is entitled to recover the cost of the improvement made to the property. Alternatively, the improver can keep the property and pay the original owner the value of the property as of the time he obtained it. Whether the original owner has the right to recover the property after paying for the improvements depends on several factors. First, what is the relative increase in value? Second, has the form or identity of the property been changed? Third, can the improvements be separated from the original property?

## Dolitsky v. Dollar Savings Bank

**118 N.Y.S.2d 65 (N.Y.C. Mun. Ct. 1952)**

Betty Dolitsky rented a safe-deposit box from Dollar Savings Bank. The safe-deposit vault of the bank was in the basement, and the vault area was walled off from all other parts of the bank. Only box renters and officers and employees of the bank were admitted to this area. To gain access to the area, a box renter had to obtain an admission slip, fill in the box number and sign the slip, have the box number and signature checked by an employee against the records of the bank, and then present the slip to a guard who admitted the renter to the vault area.

On November 7, 1951, Dolitsky requested access to her box. While Dolitsky was in the booth, she was looking through an advertising folder that the bank had placed there and found a $100 bill, which she turned over to the attendant. Dolitsky waited one year, and during that time the rightful owner of the $100 bill made no claim for it. Dolitsky then demanded that the bank surrender the bill to her, claiming that she was entitled to the bill as finder. The bank claimed that the bill was mislaid property and that it owed a duty to keep the bill for the rightful owner. Dolitsky then brought an action against the bank.

**Trimarco, Justice.** At common law property was lost when possession had been casually and involuntarily parted with, so that the mind had no impress of and could have no knowledge of the parting. Mislaid property was that which the owner had voluntarily and intentionally placed and then forgotten.

Property in someone's possession cannot be found in the sense of common-law lost property. If the article is in the custody of the owner of the place when it is discovered it is not lost in the legal sense; instead it is mislaid. Thus, if a chattel is discovered anywhere in a private place where only a limited class of people have a right to be and they are customers of the owner of the premises, who has the duty of preserving the property of his customers, it is in the possession of the owner of the premises.

In the case of mislaid property discovered on the premises of another, the common-law rule is that the proprietor of the premises is held to have the better right to hold the same for the owner, or the proprietor has custody for the benefit of the owner, or the proprietor is the gratuitous bailee of the owner. The effect of the cases, despite their different description of the relationship, is that the proprietor is the bailee of the owner. Thus, the discoverer of mislaid property has the duty to leave it with the proprietor of the premises, and the latter has the duty to hold it for the owner.

The Dollar Savings Bank is a gratuitous bailee of mislaid property once it has knowledge of the property. As such the bank has the duty to exercise ordinary care in the custody of the articles with a duty to redeliver to the owner.

The recent case of *Manufacturers Savings Deposit Co. v. Cohen,* which held that property found on the floor of a booth located in an outer room used by a safe-deposit company in conjunction with a bank, access thereto not being limited to box holders or officials of the safe-deposit company, was lost property and as such should have been turned over to the property clerk of the police. The court found that the booth on the floor of which the money was found was not located within the safe-deposit vault but rather in an outer room adjoining said vault and in a part of the bank which was accessible to the ordinary customer of the bank for the purchase of bonds and the opening of new accounts; as such the court considers the room in which the booth was located a public place which was not restricted to safe-deposit officials and persons having safe-deposit boxes in the vault. The case is further distinguished from the present case since its facts disclose that the money was found on the floor of the booth, which indicated to the court that the money was not mislaid. The court points out that the testimony shows the money to have been found on the floor of the booth and not on any table or other normal resting place.

Judgment for Dollar Savings Bank.

---

## Welton v. Gallagher

**630 P.2d 1077 (Hawaii Ct. App. 1981)**

In October 1973, Richard Welton, a businessman in his late 60s, met Florence Gallagher, a widow in her late 40s. Welton subsequently underwent several operations for cancer. After he was released from the hospital, Gallagher devoted much time and attention to him. In 1975, she helped him operate an ice-cream business that he had purchased. Shortly thereafter, he moved into her house and spent considerable money fixing it up. Welton subsequently moved out to live with Gallagher's niece, Sandra Kwock, a woman in her 20s, who agreed to take care of him for the rest of his life in return for his giving her $25,000 in bearer bonds. Kwock left town with the bonds, much to Welton's dismay. In April 1976, Welton moved back in with Gallagher, gave her $20,000 in bearer bonds, and told her to place them in her safe-deposit box. Gallagher said that he told her he wanted her to have them as a gift because she was much more deserving than her niece. Later in 1976, Welton and Gallagher ended their relationship and he moved out of her house. He also demanded that she return the bonds, but she refused.

Welton filed suit against Gallagher seeking return of the bonds. The trial court held that Welton had made a completed *inter vivos* gift of the bonds. Welton appealed.

**Burns, Judge.** Mr. Welton asserts that Mrs. Gallagher has failed to prove the elements of gift. For a transaction to amount to a gift, it must appear that there was a sufficient delivery of the property, an acceptance of the property, and an intention to make a gift.

Delivery is not a complex matter. As the Hawaii Supreme Court stated in *Siko v. Sequirant,* "A donor must divest himself of control of the gift for delivery to be complete." In other words, the donor must do acts sufficient to strip himself of dominion and control over the property. Here, Mr. Welton gave Mrs. Gallagher bearer bonds, bonds which by definition are redeemable by whosoever holds them. She testified that he told her he was giving her the bonds with no strings attached and that she should place the bonds in her own safe deposit box, a box to which he had no rights of entry. Clearly he ceased to have any control over the bonds and can be deemed therefore to have delivered them to Mrs. Gallagher.

The matter of acceptance is likewise fairly straightforward. The exercise by the donee of dominion over the subject of the gift or an assertion of a right thereto is generally held to be evidence of acceptance; and where the gift is beneficial to the donee and imposes no burdens upon her, acceptance is presumed. Here, Mrs. Gallagher exercised dominion over the bonds by placing them in her safe deposit box. She has always maintained they belong to her; certainly they benefit and do not burden her. Therefore, acceptance is presumed.

The final element necessary for a finding of a valid gift is donative intent.

The most difficult element to establish a completed gift is the donative intent of the donor. Whether such an intent exists is addressed to the perception of the trial court. The existence or absence of intent to make a gift is an evidentiary issue to be resolved by the finder of fact. His resolution of that issue will not be overturned on appeal if his finding is supported by substantial evidence.

The trial court did base its finding of donative intent on substantial evidence: Mr. Welton was very fond of Mrs. Gallagher; he had made substantial gifts to her in the past. He was particularly grateful to her for taking him back after his misadventure with Sandra Kwock. He was an experienced businessman and was fully aware of the consequences of relinquishing all control over bearer bonds. He did not demand that the bonds be placed in a joint account or depository; he did not convey any written instructions or reservation of authority when he gave the bonds to Mrs. Gallagher.

Because all the elements of a valid gift are present, we hold that there was no error in the finding of the lower court that such a gift was made.

Mr. Welton's alternative theory on this appeal is that even though a valid gift was made, it was a gift *causa mortis* and, therefore, revocable. The elements of a gift *causa mortis* are these:

(1) The gift must be made in view of approaching death from some existing sickness or peril; (2) the donor must die from such sickness or peril without having revoked the gift; (3) there must be a delivery of the subject of the gift to the donee, subject, however, to revocation in the event of recovery from the pending sickness. The vital, although not the only difference between a gift *causa mortis* and one *inter vivos* is that the former may be revoked by the donor if he survives the pending sickness or peril, and does not pass an irrevocable title until the death of the donor, while a gift *inter vivos* is irrevocable and vests an immediate title.

In this case, although Mr. Welton had undergone cancer surgery in 1973, there is no indication in the testimony that in April of 1976 he felt himself to be in immediate peril. Indeed his own statements regarding starting a new business and his active social life strongly indicate that he was not preeminently occupied in contemplating the transience of life and the prospect of his own imminent departure therefrom. The trial court was correct in finding that the gift was *inter vivos.*

Judgment for Gallagher affirmed.

## BAILMENTS

**Nature of Bailments.** A car is taken to a parking garage where the attendant gives its owner a claim check and then drives the car down the ramp to park it. Charles borrows his neighbor's lawn mower to cut his grass. Axe asks Carne, who lives in the next apartment, to take care of her cat while she goes on a vacation. These are everyday situations that involve **bailments.** This chapter will focus on the legal aspects of bailments. For example, what are the owner's rights if his car is damaged while it is parked in a public parking garage? How effective are the signs near checkrooms that say, "Not responsible for loss of or damage to checked property"?

**Elements of a Bailment.** A bailment is the delivery of personal property by one person (the **bailor**) to another person (the **bailee**) who accepts it and is under an express or implied agreement to return it to the bailor or to someone designated by the bailor. The essential elements are: (1) the bailor has *title* to or the *right to possess* the item or property; (2) *possession* and *temporary control* of the property is given to the bailee; and (3) the bailee owes a *duty to return* the property as directed by the bailor.

**Creation of Bailment Relation.** A bailment is created by an express or implied contract. Whether or not a bailment exists must be determined from all the facts and circumstances of the particular situation. For example, a patron goes into a restaurant and hangs her hat and coat on an unattended rack. It is unlikely that this created a bailment, because the restaurant owner never assumed control over the hat and coat. However, if there is a checkroom and the hat and coat are checked with the attendant, a bailment will arise.

If a customer parks his car in a parking lot, keeps the keys, and can drive the car out himself whenever he wishes, a bailment has not been created. The courts treat this situation as a lease of space. Suppose he takes his car to a parking garage where an attendant gives him a claim check and then the attendant parks the car. There is a bailment of the car because the parking garage has accepted delivery and possession of the car. However, a distinction is made between the car and some packages locked in the trunk. If the parking garage was not aware of the packages, it would probably not be a bailee of them as it did not knowingly accept possession of them.

The *Hallman v. Federal Parking Services* case, which follows, involves damage to and loss of an automobile and its contents that had been entrusted to a hotel.

**Custody.** A distinction is made between delivering *possession* of goods and merely giving *custody* of goods. If a shopkeeper entrusts goods to a clerk in the store, the shopkeeper is considered to have given the clerk custody of the goods but the shopkeeper has retained legal possession. Because the shopkeeper has retained legal possession, there has not been a bailment of goods to the clerk.

**Types of Bailments.** Bailments are commonly divided into three different classes: (1) bailments for the *sole benefit of the bailor,* (2) bailments for the *sole benefit of the bailee,* and (3) *mutual benefit bailments.* The type of bailment may be important in determining the liability of the bailee for loss of or damages to the property. However, some courts no longer rely on these distinctions for this purpose.

**Bailments for Benefit of Bailor.** A bailment for the sole benefit of the bailor is one in which the bailee renders some service but does not receive a benefit in return. For example, Brown allows a neighbor to park her car in his garage while she is on vacation and she does not pay Brown anything for the privilege. The neighbor (bailor) has received a benefit from Brown (bailee), but Brown has not received a benefit in return.

**Bailments for Benefit of Bailee.** A bailment for the sole benefit of the bailee is one in which the owner of the goods allows someone else to use them free of charge. For example, Anderson lends a lawn mower to her neighbor so he can cut his grass.

**Mutual Benefit Bailments.** If both the bailee and the bailor receive benefits from the bailment, it is a mutual benefit bailment. For example, Sutton rents a U-Haul trailer from a store. Sutton, the bailee, benefits by being able to use the trailer, while the store benefits from his payment of the rental charge. Similarly, if furniture is stored at a commercial warehouse, it is a mutual benefit bailment. The customer gets the benefit of having his goods cared for, while the storage company benefits from the storage charge paid. On some occasions, the benefit to the bailee is less tangible. For example, a customer checks a coat at an attended coatroom at a restaurant. Even if no charge is made for the service, it is likely to be treated as a mutual benefit bailment because the restaurant is benefitting from the customer's patronage.

**Special Bailments.** Certain kinds of professional bailees, such as innkeepers and common carriers, are treated somewhat differently by the law and are held to a higher level of responsibility than is the ordinary bailee. The rules applicable to common carriers and innkeepers are detailed later in this chapter.

**Duties of the Bailee.** The bailee has two basic duties: (1) to take *reasonable care* of the property that has been entrusted to him and (2) to *return* the property at the termination of the bailment.

**Bailee's Duty of Care.** The bailee is responsible for using reasonable care to protect the property during the time he has possession of it. If the bailee does not exercise reasonable care and the property is lost or damaged, the bailee is liable for negligence. Thus, the bailee would have to reimburse the bailor for the amount of loss or damage. If the property is lost or damaged without the fault or negligence of the bailee, the bailee is not liable to the bailor.

Whether the care exercised by the bailee in a particular case was reasonable depends in part on who is benefiting from the bailment. If it is a mutual benefit bailment, then the bailee must use ordinary care, which is the same kind of care a reasonable person would use to protect his own property in that situation. If the bailee is a professional that holds itself out as a professional bailee—such as a warehouse—it must use the degree of care a person in that profession would use. This is likely to be more care than the ordinary person would use. In addition, there is usually a duty on a professional bailee to explain any loss or damage to property, that is, to show it was not negligent. If it cannot do so, it will be liable to the bailor.

If the bailment is solely for the benefit of the bailor, then the bailee may be held to a somewhat lower degree of care. If the bailee is doing the bailor a favor, it is not reasonable to expect him to be as careful as when the bailor is paying the bailee for keeping the goods. On the other hand, if the bailment is for the sole benefit of the bailee, it is reasonable to expect that the bailee will use a higher degree of care. A person who lends a sailboat to a neighbor would probably expect the neighbor to be even more careful with it than he would be.

Who benefits from the bailment is one consideration in determining what is reasonable care. Other factors include: the nature and value of the property, how easily the property can be damaged or stolen, whether the bailment was paid for or free, and the experience of the bailee. Using reasonable care includes using the property only as was agreed between the parties. For example, a neighbor borrows a lawn mower to cut his lawn. However, if he uses it to cut the weeds on a trash-filled vacant lot and the mower is damaged, he would be liable because he was exceeding the agreed purpose of the bailment—that is, to cut his lawn.

**Bailee's Duty to Return the Property.** One of the essential elements for a bailment is the duty of the bailee to return the property at the termination of the bailment. The bailee must return the goods in an undamaged condition to the bailor or to someone designated by the bailor. If the goods have been damaged or lost, the bailee may excuse the failure to return undamaged goods by showing that the goods were lost or damaged without negligence on his part. If the bailed property is taken from the bailee by legal process, the bailee should notify the bailor and must take whatever action is necessary to protect the bailor's interest.

In most instances, the bailee must return the identical property that was bailed. A person who lends a 1985 Volkswagen Rabbit to a friend expects to have that particular car returned. In some cases, the bailor does not expect the identical goods back. For example, a farmer who stores 1,500 bushels of Grade #1 wheat at a local grain elevator expects to get back 1,500 bushels of Grade #1 wheat when the bailment is terminated.

The bailee is also liable to the bailor if he misdelivers the bailed property at the termination of the bailment. The property must be returned to the bailor or to someone specified by the bailor.

If a third person claims to have rights in the bailed property that are superior to the rights of the bailor and demands possession of the bailed property, the bailee is in a dilemma. If the bailee refuses to deliver the bailed property to the third-person claimant and the third-person claimant is entitled to its possession, the bailee is liable to the claimant. If the bailee delivers the bailed property to the third-party claimant and the third-party claimant is not entitled to possession, the bailee is liable to the bailor. The circumstances may be such that the conflicting claims of the bailor and the third-person claimant can be determined only by judicial decision. In some cases, the bailee may protect himself by bringing the third-party claimant into a lawsuit along with the bailor so that all the competing claims can be adjudicated by the court before the bailee releases the property, but this remedy is not always available. The bailee cannot set up a claim to the bailed property that is adverse to the rights of the bailor if the claim is based on a right that existed at the time the property was bailed. By accepting the property as bailee, the bailee is estopped from denying the bailor's title to the bailed property.

**Limits on Liability.** Bailees may try to limit or relieve themselves of liability for the bailed property. Common examples include the signs near checkrooms, "Not responsible for loss of or damage to checked property," and disclaimers on claim checks, "Goods left at owner's risk." Any attempt by the bailee to be relieved of *liability for intentional wrongful acts* is *against public policy* and will not be enforced.

A bailee's ability to be relieved of liability for *negligence* is also limited. The courts look to see whether the disclaimer or limitation of liability was *communicated* to the bailor. Did the attendant point out the sign near the checkroom to the person when the coat was checked? Did the parking lot attendant call the person's attention to the disclaimer on the back of the claim check? If not, the court may hold that the disclaimer was not communicated to the bailee and did not become part of the bailment contract. Even if the bailee was aware of the disclaimer, it still may not be enforced on the ground that it is contrary to public policy.

Courts do not look with favor on efforts by a person to be relieved of liability for negligence. People are expected to use reasonable care and to be liable if they do not and if someone or something is injured as a result. If the disclaimer was offered on a take-it-or-leave-it basis and was not the subject of arm's-length bargaining, it is not likely to be enforced. A bailee may be able to limit liability to a certain amount or to relieve himself of liability for certain perils. Ideally, the bailee will give the bailor a chance to declare a higher value and to pay an additional charge to be protected up to the declared value of the goods. Common carriers, such as railroads and trucking companies, often take this approach.

In the *Carter v. Reichlin Furriers* case which follows, the court refused to enforce a limitation on liability on the grounds that the bailor had never agreed to it.

The bailor's knowledge of the bailee's facilities or of his method of doing business or the nature of prior dealings may give rise to an implied agreement as to the bailee's duties. The bailee may, if he wishes, assume all the risks incident to the bailment and contract to return the bailed property undamaged or to pay any damage to or loss of the property.

**Right to Compensation.** Whether or not the bailee gets paid for keeping the property or must pay for having the right to use it depends on the bailment contract or the understanding of the parties. If the bailment is made as a favor, then the bailee is not entitled to compensation even though the bailment is for the sole benefit of the bailor. If the bailment is the rental of property, then the bailee must pay the agreed-upon rental rate. If the bailment is for the storage or repair of property, then the bailee is entitled to the contract price for the storage or repair services. If no specific price was agreed upon, yet compensation was contemplated by the parties, then the bailee gets the reasonable value of the services provided.

In many instances, the bailee will have a lien on the bailed property for the reasonable value of the services. For example, a chair is taken to an upholsterer to have it recovered. When the chair has been recovered, the upholsterer has the right to keep it until the agreed price or—if no price was set—the reasonable value of the work is paid. Artisan's liens are discussed in Chapter 39.

**Bailor's Liability for Defects in the Bailed Property.** When personal property is rented or loaned, the bailor makes an implied warranty that the property has no hidden defects that make it unsafe for use. If the bailment is for the sole benefit of the bailee, then the bailor is liable for injuries that result from defects in the bailed property only if the bailor knew about the defects and did not tell the bailee. For example, Price lends his car, which has bad brakes, to Sloan. If Price does not tell Sloan about the bad brakes and if Sloan is injured in an accident because the brakes fail, Price is liable for Sloan's injuries.

If the bailment is a mutual benefit bailment, then the bailor has a larger obligation. The bailor must use *reasonable care* in *inspecting* the property and seeing that it is safe for the purpose for which it is rented. The bailor is liable for injuries suffered by the bailee because of defects that the bailor either knew about or should have discovered by reasonable inspection. For example, Friedman's Rent-All rents trailers. Suppose Friedman's does not inspect the trailers after they are returned. A wheel has come loose on a trailer that Friedman's rents to Hirsch. If the wheel comes off while Hirsch is using the trailer and the goods Hirsch is carrying in it are damaged, Friedman's is liable to Hirsch.

In addition, if goods are rented to someone (mutual benefit bailment) for his personal use, there may be an *implied warranty* that the goods are *fit for the purpose for which they are rented.* Liability does not depend on whether the bailor knew about or should have discovered the defect. The only question is whether the property was fit for the purpose for which it was rented. Some courts have also imposed *strict liability* on lessors/bailors of goods that turn out to be more dangerous than the lessee/bailee would have expected. This liability is imposed regardless of whether the lessor was negligent or at fault. Courts sometimes apply the Uniform Commercial Code's implied warranties of merchantability and fitness for a particular purpose to bailment situations. Implied warranties and strict liability are discussed in detail in Chapter 32.

## Hallman v. Federal Parking Services

**134 A.2d 382 (D.C. Ct. App. 1957)**

Ward Hallman and his family were taking an automobile trip to Florida. They stopped at the New Colonial Hotel to spend the night. Hallman asked the registration clerk whether the hotel had parking facilities. He was told that the bellboy would take care of the car. The bellboy took the luggage needed by the Hallmans from the car and put it in their room. Then he took the car to a nearby parking lot that was not owned by the hotel. The bellboy left the car with the attendant, who locked it and kept the keys. When the bellboy took the car to the lot, it still contained some luggage on the floor and rear seat and several garments hung on racks. When he returned to the hotel, he gave Hallman a claim check bearing the name of the parking lot and the stamped name New Colonial. The next morning, Hallman went to pick up his car and discovered that the side window was broken. Personal property worth $567 had been stolen from the car.

Hailman then brought an action against the New Colonial Hotel and the owner of the parking lot, Federal Parking Services, Inc., to recover for the loss of personal property and damage to his automobile.

**ROVER, CHIEF JUDGE.** Hallman argues that once the property of a guest is taken into the custody and control of the innkeeper the goods are considered *infra hospitium* and the liability for loss or destruction of the goods imposed is that of an insurer, unless the property is lost or destroyed by an act of God, the public enemy, or by fault of the guest. This is undoubtedly the rule of common law having its source in the ancient case of

*Calye* which dealt with the innkeeper's liability for the loss of a guest's horse put to pasture. The common-law rule is of force in this jurisdiction. The doctrine of *infra hospitium* has been applied in cases where a car or its contents are lost while in the exclusive care and custody of a hotel. However, where the hotel takes custody of the vehicle, as here, and delivers it to a lot or garage not an integral part of the hotel and thereafter a loss of property occurs, the better rule imposes the liability of a bailee for hire on the hotel. As such it is required to exercise an ordinary degree of care to protect and return the property of which it assumes custody.

We conclude that when the bellboy, with actual authority of the New Colonial Hotel to deliver automobiles to the lot, took possession of the keys and the vehicle, both the vehicle and the contents of the automobile were accepted by the hotel into its custody. It had physical control and the intent to control the property; a bailment relationship was therefore created. That payment for parking was made to the lot and not the New Colonial Hotel is immaterial, for the service was incident to this type of business and a hotel, particularly in a metropolitan area, derives indirect benefits and profits by providing such facilities.

Turning to the New Colonial Hotel's acceptance of the property in the vehicle, Hallman and his family were in transit stopping only for the night. They could reasonably be expected to leave luggage, wearing apparel, and other personal belongings in the car not necessary for their night's lodging. Courts have uniformly held that the liability of a bailee for hire for the loss of property in an automobile depends on notice or knowledge of the contents. The notice need not be actual or express; constructive or implied notice may be inferred. Clearly the hotel was put on notice that Hallman was a traveler and the apparel hanging from racks was in plain view. Upon entering the car, the luggage on the floor and rear seat could easily be seen, and common knowledge and experience could anticipate that the car might contain in its interior other articles normally carried by travelers.

Judgment for Hallman for the reasonable value of the lost property and for the cost of repairs to Hallman's automobile.

---

## Carter v. Reichlin Furriers

**386 A.2d 648 (Conn. Super. Ct. 1977)**

On April 18, 1973, Mrs. Carter brought her fur coat to Reichlin Furriers for cleaning, glazing, and storage until the next winter season. She was given a printed form of receipt, upon the front of which an employee of Reichlin had written $100 as the valuation of the coat. There was no discussion of the value of the coat, and Carter did not realize that such a value had been written on the receipt, which she did not read at the time. A space for the customer's signature on the front of the receipt was left blank. Below this space in prominent type appeared a notice to "see reverse side for terms and conditions." The other side of the receipt stated that it was a storage contract and that by its acceptance the customer would be deemed to have agreed to its terms unless notice to the contrary were given within 10 days. Fifteen conditions were listed. One of the conditions was as follows: "Storage charges are based upon valuation herein declared by the depositor, and amount recoverable for loss or damage to the article shall not exceed its actual value or the cost of repair or replacement with materials of like kind and quality or the depositor's valuation appearing in this receipt, whichever is less."

In the fall of 1973, after Carter had paid the bill for storage and other services on the coat, Reichlin informed her that the coat was lost. At that time, the fair market value of the coat was $450. Carter sued Reichlin for loss of the coat and sought $450 damages. Reichlin claimed that its liability was limited to $100. The trial court awarded $450 damages to Mrs. Carter and Reichlin appealed.

**SHEA, JUDGE.** In this appeal the only issue is whether the provision in the receipt limiting any damages for loss of the coat to a maximum of $100 must be given effect despite the finding of the trial court that Mrs. Carter never agreed to that provision and had no actual knowledge of it. Reichlin Furriers claims that that result is required by a section of the Uniform Commercial Code, §7–204(2), which provides, in part, that "damages may be limited by a term in the warehouse receipt or storage agreement limiting the amount of liability in case of loss or damage, and setting forth a specific liability per article or item, or value per unit of weight, beyond which the warehouseman shall not be liable."

The commentary on that section of the Code indicates that it was enacted in order to resolve a controversy as to whether a limitation of the liability of a bailee in a receipt or contract impaired the obligation of reasonable care required of a bailee. It has been the law of this state that a provision in a receipt wholly relieving a bailee from liability for the loss of property is contrary to public policy and invalid. On the other hand, a limitation placed by the parties on the extent of the bailee's liability for loss of the goods has been expressly sanctioned. We conclude that the provision for such a limitation in § 7–204(2) is merely declaratory of the common law of this state. We cannot perceive in that enactment any intention to allow such a limitation to become effective apart from an agreement of the parties found to have been made under ordinary principles of contract law. There is no reason to suppose that the statute intended to differentiate a "warehouse receipt" from a "storage agreement" in that respect.

Whether or not a particular provision forms part of a contract is ordinarily a factual question for the trial court. The finding that Mrs. Carter was unaware of the valuation of her coat marked upon her receipt would not be conclusive. An actual "meeting of the minds" would not be required if, under all the circumstances, Mrs. Carter's conduct would warrant a reasonable belief that she had assented to the terms of the receipt which she received and held for approximately six months. The modern tendency is to draw a distinction between the bailor who is a businessman and one who is a member of the public. In Connecticut, provisions exculpating a bailee or limiting his liability are not necessarily a part of the bailment contract in the absence of actual knowledge of them. The mere handing of a receipt containing such a limitation to a bailor has been held insufficient to require a finding of constructive notice. In the present case the trial court found that Mrs. Carter never read the receipt and that the valuation inserted was never discussed with her. It was not the "depositor's valuation" referred to in the limitation provision, but, rather, that of the Reichlin's employee. The receipt was not signed by either party although spaces were provided for that purpose by the draftsman of the document. Nothing in the evidence would compel a conclusion that Mrs. Carter's conduct justified a reasonable person in assuming that she had consented to the limitation of damages contained in the receipt.

Judgment for Mrs. Carter affirmed.

## SPECIAL BAILMENTS

**Common Carriers.** Bailees that are **common carriers** are held to a higher level of responsibility than that to which bailees that are private carriers are held. Common carriers are licensed by governmental agencies to carry the property of anyone who requests the service. Airlines licensed by the Department of Transportation (DOT) and trucks and buses licensed by the Interstate Commerce Commission (ICC) are examples of common carriers. *Private contract carriers* carry goods only for persons selected by the carrier.

Both common carriers and private contract carriers are bailees. However, the law makes the common carrier an *absolute insurer* of the goods it carries. The common carrier is responsible for any loss of or damage to goods entrusted to it. The common carrier can avoid responsibility only if it can show that the loss or damage was caused by: (1) an act of God, (2) an act of a public enemy, (3) an act or order of the government, (4) an act of the person who shipped the goods, or (5) the nature of the goods themselves.

The common carrier is liable if goods entrusted to it are stolen by some unknown person but not if the goods are destroyed when a tornado hits the warehouse. If goods are damaged because the shipper improperly packages or crates them, then the carrier is not liable. Similarly, if perishable goods are not in suitable condition to be shipped and deteriorate in the course of shipment, the carrier is not liable so long as it used reasonable care in handling them.

Common carriers are usually permitted to limit their liability to a stated value unless the bailor declares a higher value for the property and pays an additional fee.

**Hotelkeepers.** Hotelkeepers are engaged in the business of offering food and/or lodging to transient persons. They hold themselves out to serve the public and are obligated to do so. Like the common carrier, the hotelkeeper is held to a higher standard of care than that of the ordinary bailee.

The hotelkeeper is not a bailee in the strict sense of the word. The guest does not usually surrender the exclusive possession of his property to the hotelkeeper. However, the hotelkeeper is treated as the virtual insurer of the guest's property. The hotelkeeper is not liable for loss of or damage to property if he can show that it was caused by: (1) an act of God, (2) an act of a public enemy, (3) an act of a governmental authority, (4) the fault of a member of the guest's party, or (5) the nature of the goods.

Most states have passed laws that limit the hotelkeeper's liability. Commonly, the law requires the hotel owner to post a notice advising guests that any valuables should be checked into the hotel vault. The hotelkeeper's liability is then limited, usually to a fixed amount, for valuables that are not so checked.

**Safe-Deposit Boxes.** If a person rents a safe-deposit box at a local bank and places some property in the box, the box and the property are in the manual possession of the bank. However, it takes both the renter's key and the key held by the bank to open the box, and in most cases the bank does not know the nature, amount, or value of the goods in the box. Although a few courts have held the rental of a safe-deposit box not to be a bailment, most courts have found that the renter of the box is a bailor and the bank is a bailee. As such, the bank is not an insurer of the contents of the box. However, it is obligated to use due care and to come forward and explain loss of or damage to the property entrusted to it.

**Involuntary Bailments.** Suppose a person owns a cottage on a beach. After a violent storm, a sailboat washed up on his beach. As the finder of lost or misplaced property, he may be considered the *involuntary bailee* of the sailboat. This relationship may arise when a person finds himself in possession of property that belongs to someone else without having agreed to accept possession.

The duties of the involuntary bailee are not well defined. The bailee does not have the right to destroy the property or to use it. If the true owner shows up, the property must be returned to him. Under some circumstances, the involuntary bailee may be under an obligation to assume control of the property and/or to take some minimal steps to ascertain who the owner is.

In the case which follows, *Capezzaro v. Winfrey,* a constructive and involuntary bailee was held liable for disposing of the bailed property because it had knowledge of an adverse claim to the property.

## Capezzaro v. Winfrey

**379 A.2d 493 (N.J. Super. Ct. 1977)**

Michael Capezzaro reported to the police that he had been robbed of $7,500 at gunpoint by a woman. The following day, Henrietta Winfrey was arrested with a total of $2,480.66 in her possession. Capezzaro positively identified her as the woman who had robbed him and claimed that the money found on her was part of the money that she had taken from him. Winfrey was jailed, and the money was impounded by the police as evidence of the crime. Several months later, Winfrey was indicted for the armed robbery of Capezzaro. Approximately two years afterward, this and other indictments against Winfrey were dismissed by the prosecutor based on medical opinion that she was unable to know right from wrong at the time she allegedly committed the crimes with which she had been charged.

When the warden of the county jail notified the police officers in charge of the police department's property room that the indictment against Winfrey had been dismissed, the police officers released the $2,408.66 claimed by Capezzaro to Winfrey. Eventually, Capezzaro found out about the dismissal of the indictment and the release of the money. He then instituted a lawsuit against Winfrey and the city of Newark, claiming that the released money was his.

**Per Curiam.** A constructive bailment or a bailment by operation of law may be created when a person comes into possession of personal property of another, receives nothing from the owner of the property, and has no right to recover from the owner for what he does in caring for the property. Such person is ordinarily considered to be a gratuitous bailee, liable only to the bailor for bad faith or gross negligence. *Zuppa v. Hertz Corp.* states:

> It is the element of lawful possession, however created, and the duty to account for the thing as the property of another, that creates the bailment, regardless of whether such possession is based upon contract in the ordinary sense or not.
>
> Where possession has been acquired accidentally, fortuitously, through mistake or by an agreement for some other purpose since terminated, the possessor, "upon principles of justice," should keep it safely and restore or deliver it to its owner. Under such circumstances, the courts have considered the possession *quasi*-contracts of bailment or constructive and involuntary bailments.

Here the police seized and obtained custody of the money which was found in Winfrey's girdle during a search in her cell after her arrest on the robbery charge and after Capezzaro claimed Winfrey had stolen it from him. It is undisputed that the money was being kept by the police as evidence for use in Winfrey's prosecution. It follows, then, that the City of Newark, through its police department, was holding the money for its own benefit as well as for the benefit of its rightful owner.

Ordinarily, a person who has possession of property may be presumed by another to be the rightful owner thereof in the absence of any knowledge to the contrary. However, here the police were fully aware of Capezzaro's adverse claim, but notwithstanding such knowledge and without notice to Capezzaro turned the money over to Winfrey.

The city contends that when the indictment was dismissed, any claim by Capezzaro lost its validity and it was obligated to return the monies in question to Winfrey as bailor. We disagree. A bailee with knowledge of an adverse claim makes delivery to the bailor at his peril, and only if he is ignorant of such a claim will he be protected against a subsequent claim by the rightful owner. The position of a bailee in such situation and his possible courses of action are set forth in *Williston on Contracts* (3d ed. 1967).

> If a bailee knows goods are stolen, or that the bailor is acting adversely to a clearly valid right, even though the true owner has as yet made no demand for them, the bailee will be liable to him for conversion if delivery is made to the bailor. In case, therefore, the bailee knows or has been notified of an adverse claim, he will deliver to the bailor at his peril. The bailee must, for his own protection, choose one of two courses:
>
> First, he may satisfy himself of the validity of one of the two claims and obtain authority from the owner of the claim to refuse delivery to all other claimants. In such a case he may plead at law to an action by any but the rightful owner the title of the latter, or the right of one having a superior right to possession. If this title or right can be proved, a perfect defense is established. Second, if no actual adverse claim has been made, but the bailee knows of the existence of an adverse right, or if the bailee cannot determine which of two claimants has the better title, and neither claimant will give a bond indemnifying the bailee from all damage caused by delivery to him, the only course open to the bailee is to file a bill of interpleader against the several possible owners, praying a temporary injunction against actions against himself until the true ownership of the goods is determined.
>
> And it should be added that a bailee who redelivers the goods to the bailor, or upon his order, in ignorance of his lack of title, is fully protected against subsequent claims of the rightful owner.

The police returned the money to Winfrey after being informed by the warden of the county jail that the indictments had been dismissed. They did not contact Capezzaro before doing so, even though they were on notice of his adverse claim. The dismissal of the indictment for the reasons here present did not vitiate Capezzaro's adverse claim to the money. Inherent in the jury's verdict is a finding that the city was negligent in releasing the money without a determination of the validity of the adverse claim. This finding and the verdict are amply supported by the evidence.

Judgment for Capezzaro affirmed.

## SUMMARY

Ownership of property is the exclusive right to possess, enjoy, and dispose of objects or rights having economic value. In law, property is a bundle of legal rights to things having economic value, which rights are recognized and protected by society. Property is classified according to its various characteristics. The earth's crust and all things firmly attached to it are classified as real property; all other objects and rights subject to ownership are classified as personal property. Things that have a physical existence are classified as tangible property. Rights that have economic value but are not related to things having a physical existence are classified as intangible property. Property owned by the government or a governmental unit is classified as public property. Property owned by any person or association, even though used exclusively for public purposes, is classified as private property.

Ownership of personal property may be acquired by (1) production, (2) purchase, (3) taking possession, (4) gift, (5) finding, (6) confusion, and (7) accession. A person owns property produced by his own labor or by the labor of persons whom he hires to work for him. The owner of personal property may sell or barter his property to another, and the purchaser then becomes the owner of the property. The person who first reduces unowned property—wildlife or abandoned property—to possession with the intent of claiming ownership of the property acquires ownership.

A gift is the transfer of the ownership of property from the donor to the donee without any consideration being given by the donee. To have a valid gift, the donor must deliver the possession of the property to the donee or to some third person with the intent of vesting ownership in the donee.

The finder of lost property acquires ownership of the property against everyone except the original owner. A distinction, which is not clear-cut, is made between lost property and mislaid property. If a person confuses his property with that of another person, the other person may acquire ownership of the entire mass through the doctrine of confusion. If property is improved by the labor and addition of materials by another without the owner's consent, the owner of the original property becomes the owner of the property in its improved state. This is known as obtaining title by accession.

A bailment is created when an owner of personal property, the bailor, delivers the possession of the property to another, the bailee, who intends to take control of it and who is obligated to return the property to the bailor or to dispose of it as directed by the bailor. A bailment is created by an express or implied agreement.

The bailee owes a duty of due care to prevent loss of or damage to the bailed property. In determining whether or not due care has been exercised by the bailee, the nature of the bailment is of considerable importance, as is the type of property and the bailee's skill. Within the limits of the legality of their contract, the parties may, by agreement, increase or decrease the scope of the bailee's liability.

When the bailment terminates, the bailee must return the bailed property to the bailor or dispose of it according to the bailor's direction. If a third person having a right of possession superior to that of the bailor demands the surrender of the property, the bailee is obligated to deliver the property to that person.

The bailee is entitled to reasonable compensation for services rendered in the care of the property. If the bailment contract stipulates the compensation, the bailee is entitled to the stipulated compensation.

If the bailor rents property to the bailee, the bailor owes a duty to inspect the property to see that it is free from dangerous defects.

A common carrier is the insurer of the goods it carries against loss or damage, unless such loss or damage is caused by an act of God, an act of a public enemy, an act of the state, an act of the shipper, or the nature of the goods. A hotelkeeper is an insurer of the goods of his guests. Many states have statutes permitting hotelkeepers to limit their liability.

A person may become an involuntary bailee if the goods of another are deposited on his land by storm or flood or by the acts of third persons or if the domestic animals of another stray onto his land. Such a bailee owes a minimum duty of care. He cannot willfully destroy the property or convert it to his own use.

## PROBLEM CASES

**1.** Liesner shot and mortally wounded a previously unowned wolf. Before Liesner could reach the wolf, Warnie, with his gun pointed within 3 feet of the wolf, fired the finishing shot. Liesner had the wolf in such condition that escape was improbable, if not impossible. Who owned the wolf, Liesner or Warnie?

**2.** In 1945, Liesner was serving in the U.S. Army. He was one of the first soldiers to occupy Munich, Germany. He and some other soldiers entered Adolf Hitler's apartment and removed various items of his personal belongings. Liesner brought his share to his home in Louisiana. It included Hitler's uniform jacket and cap and some of his decorations and personal jewelry. Liesner's possession of these items was well known. They had been featured in a number of magazine articles, and they were occasionally displayed to the public. In 1968, Liesner's chauffeur stole the collection and sold it to a dealer in historical materials in New York. The dealer sold the collection to the Mohawk Arms Company, which had no knowledge that it had been stolen. Liesner learned that Mohawk Arms had the collection and demanded that it be returned. Mohawk Arms claimed that it did not have to return the collection to Liesner because the collection properly belonged to the occupational military authority or to the Bavarian government and not to Liesner. Was Liesner entitled to the return of the collection that had been stolen from him?

**3.** While the *Olympia,* a passenger ship, was moored at a pier in New York City and receiving passengers for an imminent sailing, Kalyvakis, a steward on the ship, found \$2,010 in U.S. currency on the floor of a public men's room on the upper deck. The room was accessible to all passengers, their guests, and the ship's personnel; the money was found shortly before visitors and guests were required to leave the ship. Kalyvakis deposited the money with the chief steward to be held for the true owner should he make any claim for it. No claim has been made for the money for three years, and Kalyvakis asks that the money be returned to him. His employer contends that the money belongs to it, the owner of the ship. Which of the parties is entitled to the money?

**4.** Henry Blandy desired to make some provisions for the support of his daughter, Amanda. He purchased and set apart as a "gift" to her \$2,000 worth of U.S. bonds. Blandy never delivered the bonds to Amanda, who lived some distance away, and she never had manual possession of them. Rather, by her request and assent they were left under the dominion and control of her father for safekeeping. Each year, he collected and sent to her the interest that had accrued on the bonds. Blandy then decided that an investment in the cashmere goat business would be more profitable to his daughter, so he sold the bonds and invested money in that business. Afterward, he wrote Amanda, telling her that if she did not accept the new investment, he would pay her \$2,000 plus interest in place of the bonds. Blandy died, and Amanda claimed that she was entitled to \$2,000 because her father had made her a valid gift of the bonds. Did Blandy make a valid gift?

**5.** Ochoa's Studebaker automobile was stolen. Eleven months later, the automobile somehow found its way into the hands of the U.S. government, which sold it at a "junk" auction for $85 to Rogers. At the time it was purchased by Rogers, no part of the car was intact. It had no top except a part of the frame; it had no steering wheel, tires, rims, cushions, or battery; the motor, radiator, and gears were out of the car; one wheel was gone, as was one axle; the fenders were partly gone; and the frame was broken. It was no longer an automobile but a pile of broken and dismantled parts of what was once Ochoa's car. Having purchased these parts, Rogers used them in the construction of a delivery truck at an expense of approximately $800. When the truck was completed, he put it to use in his furniture business. Several months later, Ochoa was passing Rogers' place of business and recognized the vehicle from a mark on the hood and another on the radiator. He discovered that the serial and engine numbers matched those on the car he had owned. Ochoa demanded the vehicle from Rogers, who refused to surrender it. Ochoa brought suit to recover possession of the property. In the alternative, he asked for the value of the vehicle at the time of the suit, which he alleged to be $1,000, and for the value of the use of the car from the time Rogers purchased it from the government. Was Ochoa entitled to recover possession of his property, which Rogers had substantially improved?

**6.** R. B. Bewley and his family drove to Kansas City to attend a week-long church convention. When they arrived at the hotel where they had reservations, they were unable to park their car and unload their luggage because of a long line of cars. They then drove to a nearby parking lot, where they took a ticket, causing the gate arm to open, and drove in 15 or 20 feet. A parking attendant told them that the lot was full, that they should leave the keys with him, and that he would park the car. They told the attendant that they had reservations at the nearby hotel and that after they checked in, they would come back for their luggage. Subsequently, someone broke into the Bewleys' car and stole their personal property from it. Was the parking lot a bailee of the property?

**7.** George Pringle, the head of the drapery department at Wardrobe Cleaners, went to the home of Dr. Arthur Axelrod to inspect some dining room draperies for dry-cleaning purposes. He spent about 30 minutes looking at the drapes and inspected both the drapes and the lining. He pointed out some roach spots on the lining that could not be removed by cleaning, but this was not of concern to the Axelrods. He did not indicate to them that the fabric had deteriorated from sunburn, age, dust, or air conditioning so as to make it unsuitable for dry cleaning. He took the drapes and had them dry-cleaned. When the drapes were returned, they were unfit for use. The fabric had been a gold floral design on an eggshell-white background. When returned, it was a blotchy gold. Wardrobe Cleaners stated that it was difficult to predict how imported fabrics would respond to the dry-cleaning process and that the company was not equipped to pretest the fabric to see whether it was colorfast. The Axelrods sued Wardrobe Cleaners for $1,000, the replacement value of the drapes. Was Wardrobe cleaners liable for the damage caused to the drapes during the dry-cleaning process?

**8.** Mrs. Olson asked Security Van Lines to store a Persian rug for her while Security was in the process of moving the Olsons to a smaller home. She signed a document authorizing Security to prepare the rug for storage and to store it for her. The document had no clauses relating to Security's liability. Some 10 days after leaving the rug with Security, Mrs. Olson was sent a warehouse receipt that limited Security's liability for damage to $50 and excluded liability for moth damage. The rug was extensively damaged by moths, and Mrs. Olson sued to recover its value, $3,053. Security claimed that its liability was limited to $50. Is this claim correct?

**9.** Hertz Truck Leasing & Rental Service leased a truck to Contract Packers. Francisco Cintrone was a driver-helper for Contract Packers. While Cintrone was on a delivery, the brakes on the truck failed. He was injured when, as a result, the truck hit a trestle bridge. He sued Hertz to recover for his injuries. Is Hertz liable for injuries suffered by a third person because of the defect in the bailed property?

**10.** While a guest at the Diplomat Hotel, Lauren Coppedge hid her jewelry box behind two telephone books on a nightstand in her hotel room. She later checked out without retrieving her valuables. The jewelry box was discovered by a maid who turned it over to the housekeeping department, which in turn delivered it to the director of hotel security. It subsequently disappeared, and it was never returned to Coppedge. Under state law, a hotelkeeper that provides a place for the safekeeping of its guests' valuables and provides appropriate notice to the guests has its liability limited to $500. The Diplomat had safe-deposit facilities, and it provided notice to its guests. Coppedge claimed that the limitation should not apply (1) because the loss occurred after she had checked out or (2) because the hotel did not follow the proper procedure and give her a receipt for the property. Should the hotel's liability for the loss of Coppedge's jewelry be limited to $500?

# Chapter 29

# Real Property

## INTRODUCTION

Land has always occupied a position of special importance in the law. In the agrarian society of previous eras, land was the basic measure and source of wealth. In an industrialized society, land is not only a source of food, clothing, and shelter but also an instrument of commercial and industrial development. It is not surprising, then, that a complex body of law exists regarding the ownership, acquisition, and use of land. This body of law is known as the law of **real property.**

This chapter presents a survey of the law of real property. It will discuss the scope of real property, the various ownership interests in real property, the ways in which real property is transferred, and the controls that society places on an owner's use of real property. The last part of the chapter explores the legal doctrines that govern the relationship between landlords and tenants.

## SCOPE OF REAL PROPERTY

**Real property** includes not only land but also things that are firmly attached to the land or embedded in the land. Thus, buildings and other permanent structures, coal, oil, and minerals in the earth are considered part of real property. Real property is distinguished from personal property by the fact that real property is *immovable* or attached to something immovable, while personal property is not. The distinction is important because the rules of law governing real property transactions such as sale, taxation, and inheritance are frequently different from those applied to personal property transactions.

It is possible for an item of personal property to be attached to or used in conjunction with real property in such a way that it is treated as being part of the real property. This type of personal property is called a **fixture.**

**Fixtures.** A fixture is a type of property that bridges the gap between real and personal property. When an item is found to be a fixture, it ceases to be personal property and becomes part of the real property to which it is attached. A conveyance (transfer of ownership) of the real property will also convey the fixtures on that property, even if the fixtures are not specifically mentioned.

It is very common for people to install items of personal property on the real property that they own or rent. A variety of disputes can arise regarding rights to such property. Suppose that Smith buys a chandelier and installs it in his home. When he sells the house to Jones, can Smith remove the chandelier, or is it part of the house that Jones has bought? Suppose Kelly, a commercial tenant, installs showcases and tracklights in the store that he leases from Johnson. When Kelly's lease expires, can he remove the showcases and the lights, or do they now belong to Johnson? If the parties' contract is silent on these matters, a court will resolve the case by referring to the law of fixtures. There is no mechanical formula for determining whether an item has become a fixture, but courts will consider the following factors.

**Factors Determining whether an Item Is a Fixture.** One of the factors that helps to determine whether an item is a fixture is the degree to which the item is *attached* or *annexed* to the real property. If the item is firmly attached to the real property and cannot be removed without damaging the property, it is likely to be considered a fixture. An item of personal property that can be removed with little or no injury to the property is less likely to be considered a fixture.

Actual physical attachment to real property is not necessary, however. A close physical connection between the item of personal property and the real property may be sufficient for a court to conclude that the item is *constructively annexed.* For example, heavy machinery or automatic garage door openers can be considered fixtures even though they are not physically attached to real property.

Another factor to be considered is the degree to which the use of the item is necessary or beneficial to the use of the real property. This factor is called *adaptation.* It is particularly relevant in cases in which the item is either not physically attached to the real property at all or the physical attachment is slight. When an item would be of little value except for use with a particular piece of property, it is likely to be considered a fixture even though it is unattached or could easily be removed. For example, keys and custom-sized window screens and storm windows have been held to be fixtures.

The third factor to be considered is the *intent* of the person who installed the item. Intent is judged not by what that person subjectively intended, but by what the circumstances indicate that he intended. To a great extent, intent is indicated by the first two factors, annexation and adaptation. There is a presumption that an owner of real property who improves it by attaching items of personal property intended those items to become part of the real estate. Thus, if the owner does *not* want an item to be considered a fixture, he must specifically reserve the right to keep the attached property. A seller of a house who wants to keep an antique chandelier that has been installed in the house should either replace the chandelier before the house is shown to prospective purchasers or make it clear in the contract of sale that the chandelier will be excluded from the sale.

The *Kerman* case, which follows, presents a typical example of a court's analysis of whether an item of personal property is a fixture.

**Express Agreement.** If the parties have formed an express agreement that clearly states their intent about whether a particular item is to be considered a fixture, a court will generally enforce that agreement. For example, the buyer and seller of a house might agree to permit the seller to remove a fence or shrubbery that would otherwise be considered a fixture. The parties' right to dictate the classification of property is not unlimited, however. A court would not enforce an agreement that provided that a piece of land was to be treated as personal property, for example.

**Tenants' Fixtures.** An exception to the normal rules about fixtures is made when a *tenant* attaches personal property to leased premises for the purpose of carrying on his trade or business. Such fixtures are called **trade fixtures.** Trade fixtures remain the personal property of the tenant, and can be removed at the termination of the lease. The purpose of making an exception for trade fixtures is to encourage trade and industry.

There are two limitations on the tenant's right to remove trade fixtures. First, the tenant cannot remove the fixtures if doing so would cause substantial damage to the landlord's realty. Second, the tenant must remove the fixtures by the end of the lease if the lease is for a definite period; if the lease is for an indefinite period, the tenant may be given a reasonable time after the expiration of the lease to remove the fixtures. If she does not remove the fixtures within the appropriate time, they become the property of the landlord.

Leases may contain terms that expressly address the parties' rights in any fixtures. A lease might give the tenant the right to attach items or make other improvements and to remove them later. The reverse may also be true. The lease might state that any improvements made or fixtures attached will become the property of the landlord at the termination of the lease. Courts will generally enforce the parties' agreement about the ownership of fixtures.

**Security Interests in Fixtures.** Special rules apply to personal property that is subject to a lien or security interest[1] at the time it is attached to real property. For example, a person buys a dishwasher on a time-payment plan from an appliance store and has it installed in his kitchen. To protect itself, the appliance store must take a security interest in the dishwasher and perfect that interest by filing a financing statement in the local real estate records within a period of time specified by the Uniform Commercial Code. The appliance store would then be able to remove the dishwasher if the buyer defaulted in his payments. It could, however, be liable to third parties, such as prior real estate mortgagees, for any damage to the real estate caused by the removal of the dishwasher. The rules concerning security interests in personal property that will become fixtures are covered in Chapter 40.

[1] Liens and security interests are discussed in Chapter 40.

## Kerman v. Swafford

### 680 P.2d 622 (N.M. Ct. App. 1984)

In 1971, Ralph Swafford bought three metal buildings and installed them on his ranch. The buildings included (1) a horse barn with a dirt floor middle; (2) an office, a trophy room, and a tack room; and (3) an open-air hay shed with no siding. The buildings were prefabricated at a factory and were assembled at the ranch by Swafford's agent and bolted to concrete slabs. They were never moved after their assembly and installation.

In 1973, Swafford mortgaged the property to Edward Kerman. Swafford later defaulted on the debt, and Kerman instituted foreclosure proceedings. Kerman bought the ranch at the foreclosure sale. He allowed Swafford to remain on the ranch for a time, but later sued to recover possession. Swafford counterclaimed, alleging that the portable buildings were his. The trial court held for Kerman, and Swafford appealed.

**Minzner, Judge.** Intent, adaptation, and annexation are the three relevant factors which determine whether an article is a fixture to be treated as part of the realty. Adaptation and annexation are principally relevant as indicators of intent, which our courts have recognized as the controlling consideration and the chief fixture test. Although the question of intent is typically a fact question for the jury, intent regarding fixture determination is a different question. Where a court finds sufficient objectively manifested intent, a fixture may be presumed or inferred from the circumstances.

Here, the nature of the property, the manner of its construction, and its intended use all go to show that Swafford intended to make permanent additions to the land. The buildings here are substantial. They were attached with bolts to concrete slabs, and they are necessary and useful to the operation of the ranch. Therefore, in 1971, when Swafford installed the buildings, they were presumptively part of the real estate.

Objects which are attached to the realty at the time a mortgage is granted and which are, from all outward manifestations, intended for permanent use and enjoyment in connection with the realty, pass under a mortgage. Swafford gave Kerman an interest in the nature of a mortgage on the land. At that time the buildings were attached and appeared to be intended for permanent use and enjoyment. These facts justify a presumption that the lien on the land included a lien on the buildings.

Swafford relies on the portable nature of the buildings to argue that Kerman failed to establish either annexation or intent. Property is annexed when it is actually or constructively affixed to the realty. A building need not be permanently or physically anchored to the land to be characterized as a fixture. Although there was evidence that the buildings can be disassembled without damage to the realty, that fact does not indicate a lack of annexation.

Judgment for Kerman affirmed.

## RIGHTS AND INTERESTS IN REAL PROPERTY

**Estates in Land.** When we think of ownership of real property, we normally think of one person owning all of the rights in a particular piece of land. There are, however, a variety of types of interests in real property that can be shared by a number of people. The term *estate* is used to describe the nature of a person's ownership interests in real property. Estates in land can be classified as being either **freehold estates** or **nonfreehold estates.** Nonfreehold (or leasehold) estates are those held by persons who lease real property. They will be discussed in the part of the chapter that deals with landlord-tenant law. Freehold estates are ownership interests in real property that are of uncertain duration. The most common types of freehold estates are fee simple absolute and life estates.

**Fee Simple Absolute.** The **fee simple absolute** is the highest form of land ownership in the United States. What we normally think of as "full ownership" of land is the fee simple absolute. A person who owns real property in fee simple absolute has the right to possess and use the property for an unlimited period of time, subject only to governmental regulations or private restrictions. He also has the unconditional power to dispose of the property during his lifetime or upon his death. A person who owns land in fee simple absolute may grant many rights to others without giving up the ownership of his fee simple. For example, he may lease the property to a tenant or grant mineral rights, easements, or mortgages to another.

**Life Estate.** A **life estate** is a property interest that gives a person the right to possess and use property for a time that is measured by his lifetime or that of another person. For example, if Smith has a life estate in Blackacre (a hypothetical tract of land) that is measured by his life, he has the right to use Blackacre during his life. At his death, the property will revert to the person who conveyed the estate to him or it will pass to some other designated person. While a life tenant such as Smith has the right to use the property, he has the obligation not to do acts that will result in permanent injury to the property.

**Co-Ownership of Real Property.** Co-ownership of real property exists when two or more persons share the same estate (the same type of ownership interest) in the same property. The co-owners do not have separate rights to any portion of the real property; each has a share in the whole property. Seven types of co-ownership are recognized in the United States.

**Tenancy in Common.** People who own property under a **tenancy in common** have undivided interests in the property and equal rights to possess the property. When property is transferred to two or more people without a specification about their form of co-ownership, there is a presumption that they will take the property as tenants in common. The ownership interests of the tenants in common do not have to be equal. Thus, one tenant could have a two-thirds ownership interest in the property and the other tenant could have a one-third interest.

Each tenant in common has the right to possess and use the property. However, she cannot exclude the other tenants in common from also possessing and using the property. If the property is rented or otherwise produces income, each tenant has the right to share in the income in proportion to her share of ownership. Similarly, each must pay her proportionate share of the cost of taxes and necessary repairs.

A tenant in common can dispose of her interest in the property during life and at death. When one tenant dies, her share passes to her heirs or, if she has made a will, to the person or persons specified in her will. Suppose Smith and Jones own Blackacre as tenants in common. Smith dies, having executed a valid will in which she leaves her share to Kelly. In this situation, Jones and Kelly become tenants in common.

Tenants in common can sever the cotenancy by agreeing to divide up the property or, if they are unable to agree, by petitioning a court for **partition** of the property. The court will physically divide the property if that is feasible, so that each tenant will get her proportionate share. If physical division is not appropriate, the court will order the property sold and divide the proceeds.

**Joint Tenancy.** A **joint tenancy** is created when *equal* interests in real property are conveyed to two or more people by a single document that specifies that they are to own the property as joint tenants. The rights of use, possession, contribution, and partition are the same for a joint tenancy as for a tenancy in common. The distinguishing feature of a joint tenancy is that it gives the owners the **right of survivorship.** This means that upon the death of one of the joint tenants, that person's interest automatically passes to the surviving joint tenant(s). This feature makes it easy for a person to transfer property at death without making a will. For example, Smith buys property with his grandson, the two of them taking title to the property as joint tenants. At Smith's death, his interest will pass to his grandson without even going through the normal probate process.[2] By the same token, a provision in a joint tenant's will that purports to devise (transfer by will) his interest to someone other than his surviving joint tenants is ineffective.

[2] The probate process is discussed in Chapter 30.

A joint tenant may mortgage, sell, or give away his interest in the property during his lifetime. For that reason, a joint tenant's interest in property is subject to the claims of his creditors. When a joint tenant transfers his interest, the joint tenancy is *severed* and a tenancy in common is created as to the share affected by the transaction. When a joint tenant sells his interest to a third person, the third person becomes a tenant in common with the remaining joint tenant(s). As you will see in *Yannopoulos v. Sophos,* making a contract to sell property can constitute a severance of the joint tenancy.

**Tenancy by the Entirety.** Approximately half of the states permit married couples to own real property as **tenants by the entirety.** A tenancy by the entirety is basically a type of joint tenancy with the added requirement that the owners be married. Like the joint tenancy, the tenancy by the entirety involves the right of survivorship. Neither spouse can transfer the property by will if the other is still living. Upon the death of the husband or wife, the property passes automatically to the surviving spouse.

This tenancy cannot be severed by the act of only one of the parties. Neither spouse can transfer the property unless the other one also signs the deed. Thus, a creditor of one tenant cannot claim an interest in that person's share of the property held in tenancy by the entirety. Divorce, however, will sever a tenancy by the entirety and transform it into a tenancy in common.

**Community Property.** A number of western and southern states recognize a system of co-ownership of property by married couples that is known as **community property.** This type of co-ownership is based on the theory that marriage is a partnership in which each spouse contributes to the property base of the family. Property that is acquired during the marriage through a spouse's industry or efforts is classified as *community* property, in which each spouse has an equal interest. This is true regardless of who produced or earned the property. Since each spouse has an equal share in the community property, neither can convey the property without the other's joining in the transaction. A number of community property states permit the parties to dispose of their interests in community property at death.

Not all property owned by a married person is community property, however. Property that a spouse owned before marriage or acquired during marriage by gift or inheritance is *separate property.* Property exchanged for separate property also remains separately owned. The details of each state's community property system vary, depending on the specific provisions of that state's community property statutes.

**Tenancy in Partnership.** When a partnership takes title to property in the name of the partnership, its form of co-ownership is called **tenancy in partnership.** The incidents of tenancy in partnership are set out in Section 25 of the Uniform Partnership Act. You can read more about this form of co-ownership in Chapter 18.

**Condominium Ownership.** Condominiums are an ancient form of co-ownership that has become very common in the United States in recent years, even in locations outside urban and resort areas. In a condominium, a purchaser takes title to her individual unit and also becomes a tenant in common with other unit owners in facilities that are shared, such as hallways, elevators, swimming pools, and parking areas. The condominium owner pays property taxes on her individual unit. She can generally mortgage or sell her individual unit without the approval of the other unit owners. She also makes a monthly payment for the maintenance of the common areas. For federal income tax purposes, she is treated in the same way as the owner of a single-family home, and is allowed to deduct her property taxes and mortgage interest expenses.

**Cooperative Ownership.** In a cooperative, an entire building is owned by a corporation or by a group of people. A person who wants to buy a unit buys stock in the corporation and holds his apartment under a long-term lease (called a **proprietary lease**), which he can renew. Frequently, the cooperative owner must obtain the approval of the other owners to sell or sublease his unit.

## Yannopoulos v. Sophos

### 365 A.2d 1312 (Pa. Super. Ct. 1976)

Harry Sophos and his sister, Flora Sophos Towry, owned real estate as joint tenants with the right of survivorship. On November 12, 1973, Sophos executed a contract to sell the property. The following day, Towry sent a telegram indicating her approval of the sale. On November 16, 1973, Sophos died. Towry and her husband executed the sales contract and went through with the sale and kept the proceeds. Later, Yannopoulos, the representative of Sophos's estate, filed suit against Towry (suing her under the name of "Flora Sophos") and the purchaser, claiming that the estate should get half the proceeds of the sale on the ground that the execution of the contract before Harry Sophos's death transformed the joint tenancy into a tenancy in common. The trial court found for Yannopoulos, and Towry appealed.

**WATKINS, PRESIDENT JUDGE.** The question involved is whether the execution of the agreement of sale by Harry Sophos, and later joined in by the other parties, severed the joint tenancy, converting the estate into a tenancy in common. Towry's position is that since the property was held as a joint tenancy with the right of survivorship and not as a tenancy in common, the death of Sophos resulted in the termination of his interest in the premises and therefore Towry possessed the sole interest in the proceeds of the sale as the surviving owner.

A joint tenancy in real estate with the right of survivorship is severable by the act, voluntary or involuntary, of either of the parties. Upon this occurrence the realty becomes a tenancy in common. The issue in the instant case is whether the execution of the sales agreement by Sophos was sufficient to terminate the joint tenancy, resulting in Sophos's estate having a one-half interest in the proceeds of the sale.

This seems to have occurred in this case. The moment an agreement of sale is executed and delivered it vests equitable title to the realty in the purchaser. The sellers are then relegated to the position of trustees of the real estate, holding the bare legal title for the purchasers who become trustees for the balance of the purchase money for the sellers.

The action of the parties, therefore, destroyed the joint tenancy, since neither joint tenant possessed the equitable interest in it.

Decree for Yannopoulos affirmed.

**Interests in Real Property Owned by Others.** In a variety of situations, a person may hold a legally protected interest in real property that is owned by someone else. Such interests are not *possessory*—that is, they do not give their holder the right to complete dominion over the land. Rather, they give him the right to *use* another person's property or to limit the way in which the other person uses his own property. The following discussion explores the nature of these types of interests.

**Easements.** An **easement** is the right to make certain uses of another person's property (*affirmative easement*) or the right to prevent another person from making certain uses of his own property (*negative easement*). The right to run a sewer line across another person's property is an example of an affirmative easement. An easement that prevents a neighbor from erecting a structure on his land that would block your solar collector is an example of a negative easement.

The duration and transferability of an easement depend on whether it is classified as an **easement appurtenant** or an **easement in gross.** An easement appurtenant is an easement that is primarily designed to benefit a certain tract of land. The land benefited by the easement is called the *dominant tenement.* The land on which the easement exists is called the *servient tenement.* Easements appurtenant pass with the land. If the dominant owner sells his tract, the new owner will also get the easement. If the servient owner sells his tract, the land will still be burdened by the easement. For example, Smith and Jones are next door neighbors. They share a common driveway that runs along the borderline of their property. Each has an easement in the part of the driveway that lies on the other's property. If Smith sells his property to Kelly, Kelly will also get the easement in the part of the driveway that is on Jones's land. By the same token, Jones still has an easement in the part of the driveway that lies on Kelly's land.

An easement that is merely a personal right of the easement holder rather than a right that is designed to benefit the use of a certain tract of land is called an **easement in gross.** Since an easement in gross is a personal right, it has no dominant tenement. For example, if a farmer gave a friend an easement permitting him to hunt quail on the farmer's land for the rest of his life, this personal right would be classified as an easement in gross. Easements held by utility companies (permitting them to run and repair utility lines, for example) are usually easements in gross. Ordinarily, easements in gross are not assignable, transferable, or inheritable unless they are commercial easements (easements used for commercial purposes). The *Nelson* case, which follows, involves the question whether an easement is an easement appurtenant or an easement in gross.

Easements can be acquired in a number of different ways:

1. *By grant.* When an owner of property expressly gives an easement in his property to another while retaining his ownership of the property, he is said to **grant** an easement. For example, Smith may sell or give Jones, the owner of adjoining property, the right to cross Blackacre to get to an alley behind Blackacre.

2. *By reservation.* When a person transfers ownership of his land but retains the right to use the transferred land for some specified purpose, he is said to **reserve** an easement in the land that was once his. For example, Smith sells Blackacre to Jones, reserving the mineral rights to the property and also reserving an easement to enter Blackacre to remove the minerals. The *Nelson* case involves the reservation of an easement.

3. *By implication.* Sometimes, easements are *implied* from the nature of the transaction rather than created by express agreement of the parties. Such easements are called **easements by implication.** There are two types of easements by implication: **easements by prior use** and **easements by necessity.**

An easement by prior use is created when land is subdivided and a path, road, or other apparent and beneficial use exists at the time that part of the land is conveyed to another person. In this situation, the new owner will have an easement to continue using the path, road, or other prior use that runs across the other person's land. The creation of this easement is based on the presumption that since the prior use of the property was apparent and continuous at the time the property was subdivided, the parties intended that the new owner would have the right to continue using it. Suppose that a private road running through Blackacre from north to south links the house located on the northern portion of Blackacre to the highway that lies beyond Blackacre to the south. Smith, the owner of Blackacre, sells the northern portion of Blackacre to Jones. Jones would have an easement by implication to continue making use of the private road running across the portion of the land that has been retained by Smith. To prevent this type of easement from arising, the parties must specify in their contract that such an easement will not exist.

An easement by necessity is created when real property once held in common ownership is subdivided in such a way that the only way the new owner can gain access to his land is through passage over the land of another that was once part of the same tract. An easement by necessity does not depend on the existence of any prior use; rather, it is based on the *necessity* of obtaining access to property. For example, Smith owns 80 acres fronting on a road and bounded on the other three sides by the land of adjacent landowners. If Smith conveys the back 40 acres to Jones, Jones will have an easement by necessity across Smith's remaining property because that is Jones's only means of access to his property.

4. *By prescription.* An **easement by prescription** is created when one person uses another person's land openly, continuously, and in a manner adverse to the owner's rights for a period of time specified by state statute. The property owner should thus be on notice that someone else is acting as if he has certain rights to use the property. If the property owner does not take action to assert his rights during the statutory period, he may lose his right to stop the other person from making use of his property. Suppose State X provides that easements by prescription can be obtained through 15 years of prescriptive use. Smith, who lives in State X, uses the driveway of his next-door neighbor, Jones, for 20 years. He does this openly, on a daily basis, and without Jones's permission. If Jones does not take action to stop Smith within the 15-year period provided by statute, Smith will have obtained an easement by prescription. This means that Smith not only has the right to use the driveway while Jones owns the property but also that if Jones sells his property to Kelly, Smith will still be entitled to use the driveway. The *Nelson* case also involves an easement by prescription. This type of easement is based on the concept of *adverse possession,* which will be discussed later in the chapter.

Because an easement is a type of interest in land, it is within the coverage of the statute of frauds. An express agreement granting or reserving an easement must be in writing to be enforceable. Under the statutes of most states, the grant of an easement must be executed with the same formalities as are observed in executing the grant of a fee simple interest in real property. However, easements not granted expressly, such as easements by prior use, necessity, or prescription, are enforceable even though they are not in writing.

## Nelson v. Johnson

### 679 P.2d 662 (Idaho Sup. Ct. 1984)

In 1956, Robert and Marjorie Wake owned land in Cassia County, Idaho. They operated a farm on part of the property and used the rest as a cattle ranch. As part of the ranching operation, the Wakes drove their cattle from the ranch each spring and autumn down a county road that bounded the farmland, then eastward over an access road on the farm to Butler Springs, which was also located on the farm. From Butler Springs, they ranged the cattle further eastward onto adjacent Bureau of Land Management property and U.S. Forest Service land, where they would use their grazing rights. At the onset of winter, they drove the cattle back through Butler Springs, across the access road, and down the county road to the ranch.

In December 1956, the Wakes sold the farm portion of the land on contract to Jesse and Maud Hess. The contract of sale between the Wakes and the Hesses contained a clause expressly reserving an easement in the Wakes to use the Butler Springs water and the right-of-way from Butler Springs across the property to the federal reserve land. The contract described the Butler Springs area, but it did not describe the access road leading to Butler Springs from the county road.

In 1963, the Hesses sold the farm to Raymond and Wilma Johnson. The contract between the Hesses and the Johnsons referred to the easement held by the Wakes. The Wakes continued to use the access road and Butler Springs until 1964, when they sold their ranch. The sale of the ranch specifically granted the Butler Springs easement to the purchasers. The ranch then changed hands several times, but all of the owners continued to use the access road and Butler Springs. In 1978, Lyle and Lola Nelson bought the ranch. Shortly after the Nelsons took possession of the ranch, the Johnsons sent a letter to them "revoking permission" for the use of the access road. In 1979, the Johnsons placed locks on the gates across the access road. The Nelsons filed an action alleging that they had easement rights in both the Butler Springs area and the access road leading to it. The trial court ruled that the Nelsons had an easement, and the Johnsons appealed.

**Huntley, Justice.** In construing an easement in a particular case, the instrument granting the easement is to be interpreted in connection with the intention of the parties and the circumstances in existence at the time the easement was granted and utilized. The trial court in this case determined that the easement reserved in the 1956 Wake-Hess contract was appurtenant in nature, with a dominant estate in the cattle ranch and a servient estate in the farm, and that the easement had consequently passed with the dominant estate upon each transfer of title. The evidence fully supports that interpretation. The language of the reservation clause in the contract, as well as the established pattern of use of the Butler Springs area, indicate a clear intention by the parties that the easement be for the benefit of the cattle ranch. There is no showing that the parties intended it to be a mere personal right.

The definitions of "appurtenant" and "in gross" further make it clear that the easement is appurtenant. The primary distinction between an easement in gross and an easement appurtenant is that in the latter there is, and in the former there is not, a dominant estate to which the easement is attached. An easement in gross is merely a personal interest in the land of another, whereas an easement appurtenant is an interest which is annexed to the possession of the dominant tenement and passes with it. An appurtenant easement must bear some relation to the use of the dominant estate and is incapable of existence separate from it; any attempted severance from the dominant estate must fail. The easement in the Butler Springs area is a beneficial and useful adjunct of the cattle ranch, and it would be of little use apart from the operations of the ranch. Moreover, in case of doubt, the weight of authority holds that the easement should be presumed appurtenant. Accordingly, the decision of the trial court is affirmed as to the reserved easement in the Butler Springs area.

A prescriptive easement must be established by open, notorious use of the servient property with the actual or imputed knowledge thereof by the owner of the servient tenement. The use must be continuous for a prescriptive period of five years and must be done under a claim of right.

The use of the access road was open and known to both the Hesses and the Johnsons. The Nelsons and their predecessors in interest claimed a right of way in the access road, and no permission was given for such use until Johnson purported to do so in 1978. In fact, Mr. Johnson testified at trial that he believed the ranch owners had driven the cattle over the road by right. These facts established a prescriptive use of the road for the period between 1956 and 1978, at a minimum, which clearly meets the five year requirement. The finding of the trial court that a prescriptive easement in the access road had been established is affirmed.

Judgment for the Nelsons affirmed.

**License.** A **license** is a temporary right to enter the land of another for a specific purpose. A license is generally much more informal than an easement, and may be created orally or in any other manner that shows the landowner's permission for the licensee to enter the property. Licenses are generally considered to be personal rights that are not really interests in land. For example, if Smith invites Jones to his house for dinner, he has given Jones a license to enter his land. This gives Jones the right to enter Smith's land for a specified purpose without being liable for trespass. A license can generally be revoked at the will of the licensor unless the license is coupled with an interest, such as ownership of personal property that exists on the licensor's property, or unless the licensee has paid money or something else of value for the license or in reliance on the license. For example, Smith pays Jones $600 for trees on Jones's land, which are to be cut and hauled away. Smith has an irrevocable license to enter Jones's land to cut and haul away the trees.

**Restrictive Covenants.** Within certain limitations, owners of real estate can create private and enforceable agreements that restrict the use of real property. Such private agreements are called **restrictive covenants.** For example, Smith owns two adjacent lots. He sells one to Jones with the express agreement that Jones promises not to operate on the property any business involving the sale of liquor. This commitment is included in the deed that Smith gives to Jones. Similarly, a developer sells lots in a subdivision, placing a restriction in each deed concerning the minimum size of houses that can be built on the property.

The validity and enforceability of such private restrictions on the use of real property depend on the purpose, nature, and scope of the restriction. A restraint that violates public policy will not be enforced. For example, a restraint that prohibits the future sale of the property to a non-Caucasian violates public policy and is unenforceable. Similarly, if a restraint is so great that it effectively prevents the sale or transfer of the property, it is unenforceable as a violation of the public policy that favors free alienation (transfer) of land. Since public policy favors the unlimited use and transfer of land, ambiguous language in a restrictive covenant is construed in favor of the less restrictive interpretation. You will see the interplay of public policy and interpretation in the *Crane Neck* case, which follows.

However, a restraint that is clearly expressed and that does not unduly restrict the use and transfer of the property or otherwise violate public policy will be enforced. For example, restrictions that relate to the minimum size of lots, maintenance of the area as a residential community, or the cost, size, and design of buildings are usually enforceable.

An important question that frequently arises regarding restrictive covenants is whether subsequent owners of the property are bound by the restriction even though they were not parties to the original agreement. Under certain circumstances, the covenant is said to "run with the land" so as to bind subsequent owners of the restricted land. For a covenant to run with the land, four requirements must be met:

1. The covenant must have been *binding* on the people who were originally parties to it. That is, it must be a valid covenant under the guidelines discussed above and, since restrictive covenants are within the statute of frauds, it must have been in writing.

2. The covenant must show that the original parties *intended* the covenant to bind their successors.

3. The covenant must *"touch and concern"* the restricted land. This means that it must involve the use, value, or character of the land in question and not just a personal obligation of one of the original parties. A covenant that restricts the use of Smith's land to single-family residential purposes involves the use and character of Smith's land, and thus would be considered to touch and concern the land.

4. The original parties must have been in a relationship called *"privity of estate."* This means that at the time the covenant was established, the original parties must have been buyer and seller, landlord and tenant, or testator (a person who makes a will) and devisee (a person who receives land under a will).

Restrictive covenants can be enforced by the parties to the agreement, by persons who were intended to benefit from the covenant, and—if the covenant runs with the land—by the successors of the original parties. If the restriction is contained in a subdivision plat (recorded description of a subdivision) in the form of a general building scheme, other property owners in the subdivision may be able to enforce it.

Restrictive covenants can be terminated in a variety of ways. They can be voluntarily relinquished, or *waived.* They can also be terminated *by their own terms* (such as when the covenant specifies that it is to endure for a certain length of time) or by *dramatically changed circumstances.* For example, if Smith's property is subject to a restrictive covenant that restricts it to residential use, the covenant may be terminated by the fact that all of the surrounding property has come to be used for industrial purposes. When a restriction has been held invalid or has been terminated, the basic deed remains valid but is treated as if the restriction had been stricken from it.

---

## Crane Neck Association, Inc. v. NYC/Long Island County Services Group

**460 N.Y.S.2d 69 (N.Y. Sup. Ct., App. Div. 1983)**

Acting under the authority of the New York Mental Hygiene Law, New York City/Long Island County Services Group (County Services) leased property in the hamlet of Crane Neck, New York, for the establishment of a community residence for eight mentally disabled adults. The leased property and a number of neighboring properties had once been part of a 500-acre estate owned by Eversly Childs during the early part of the century. When Childs developed the land, he imposed identical deed restrictions on all of the parcels conveyed. The covenant, which was expressly declared to be a covenant running with the land and binding on the successors of all the parties, prohibited the construction or maintenance of *"any building other than single family dwellings."* Crane Neck Association (Crane Neck), an association of homeowners whose property was also subject to the deed restriction, filed an action seeking to bar County Services from operating the community residence, on the ground that doing so would violate the terms of the restrictive covenant. The trial court decided in favor of Crane Neck, and County Services appealed.

**Brown, Justice.** Crane Neck, in arguing for a narrow construction of the term "single family dwelling," asserts that the group of persons residing in the community residence is significantly distinct from the traditional concept of "family" (i.e., a group of persons united by blood, marriage, historical and legal bonds) as was envisioned at the time the covenant was created.

While this traditional concept of family is the one which is most immediately recognizable, there is a significant body of law which holds that the term "family" may be construed to extend beyond this traditional, biological concept to encompass other groupings of individuals. In *City of White Plains v. Ferraioli,* the court was called upon to decide whether a group consisting of a married couple, their 2 children, and 10 foster children qualified as a single family dwelling in accordance with a local zoning ordinance. In upholding the establishment of the group home, the court reasoned that it was necessary to look to the character of the grouping to see whether in theory, size, appearance and structure the group residence emulated the traditional family unit. "So long as the group home bears the generic character of a family unit as a relatively permanent household and is not a framework for transients or transient living, it conforms to the purpose of the ordinance. Moreover, in no sense is the group home an institutional arrangement. Indeed, the purpose of the group home is to be quite the contrary of an institution and to be a home like other homes."

There are also a number of decisions from sister states in which the courts have construed the term "family" in a restrictive covenant to encompass a group residence for mentally disabled individuals. It should be noted that the courts in these cases took cognizance of the strong public policy considerations in favor of establishing such group residences in reaching the conclusion that the groupings in question were families within the terms of the restrictive covenants.

In New York, case law, insofar as it concerns the establishment of community residences for the mentally disabled in areas zoned for single family dwellings, is now reflected in the provisions of the Mental Hygiene Law. It is specifically provided therein that a community residence established pursuant to the statute "shall be deemed a family unit for purposes of local laws and ordinances." Crane Neck argued, however, that these statutory and case law expansions of the term "family" in relation to zoning ordinances and local laws should not apply to the use of that term in the instant private restrictive covenant.

In reviewing the scope of restrictive covenants, it must be recognized that covenants restricting the use of land are contrary to the general policy in favor of the free and unobstructed use of real property, and, to that end, are to be strictly construed against those seeking enforcement. If a covenant is found to be susceptible to two constructions, then the less restrictive construction will be adopted, with all doubts and ambiguities being resolved in favor of such less restrictive construction.

A fundamental purpose of group residences such as the one at bar is to move the care of mentally disabled persons away from institutional settings and toward less restrictive environments whenever that possibility exists. The residence here is intended to create "a small family type living experience" for those residents. The goal is to establish a relatively permanent, stable environment, operating as a single household unit under a set of houseparents, which as much as possible bears the generic characteristics of the traditional family.

It is the emulation of the traditional family unit which, in our opinion, satisfies the terms of the restrictive covenant, notwithstanding the lack of a biological or legal relationship among residents. The primary purpose of that covenant, preservation of the quality of life and character of the neighborhood, will not be contravened by the presence of this group residence.

It is our opinion that as a matter of public policy the restrictive covenant in question may not be enforced so as to bar the establishment of this residence. Actions seeking to enforce restrictive covenants are equitable in nature and enforcement will not be had where it would contravene public policy. In recent years, on both the State and Federal level, great emphasis has been focused upon efforts to maximize treatment services and habilitation programs for persons with developmental disabilities, while at the same time steps have been taken to assure that such services are provided in a fashion that is least restrictive to personal liberty. In particular, these efforts have been characterized by the deinstitutionalization of the mentally retarded and their placement in less restrictive environments in the community at large. Implementation of this policy of establishing community residences for the mentally disabled has been greatly aided by the passage of the Mental Hygiene Law, which sets forth guidelines for site selection for such facilities.

We view this expressed policy as being broad enough to overcome not only challenges to group residences which are based upon local zoning ordinances, but also those based upon private restrictive covenants. Communities and residents should not be permitted to decide unilaterally by means of restrictive covenants, possibly employing language more specific than that at bar, that they will not permit the establishment of group residences in their area.

Accordingly, we declare that the use in question is not violative of the terms of the restrictive covenant and as a matter of public policy, such a private restrictive covenant may not be enforced so as to prevent the establishment of community residences under the Mental Hygiene Law.

Judgment reversed in favor of County Services.

## ACQUISITION OF RIGHTS IN REAL PROPERTY

Title to real property can be obtained in a number of ways, including purchase, gift, will or inheritance, tax sale, and adverse possession. Original title to land in the United States was acquired either from the federal government or from a country that held the land prior to its acquisition by the United States. The land in the 13 original colonies had been granted by the king of England either to the colonies or to certain individuals. The land in the Northwest Territory was ceded by the states to the federal government, which in turn issued grants or patents of land. Original ownership of much of the land in Florida and the Southwest came by grants from the rulers of Spain.

**Acquisition by Purchase.** The right to sell real property is a basic ownership right. In fact, unreasonable restrictions on the right of an owner to sell her property are considered to be unenforceable as against public policy. Most people who own real property acquired title by buying it from someone else. Each state sets the requirements for the conveyance of real property located within that state. The various elements of selling and buying real property, including brokerage agreements, contracts to buy real estate, and deeds, will be discussed later in this chapter.

**Acquisition by Gift.** Ownership of real property may be acquired by gift. For such a gift to be valid, the donor must deliver a properly executed deed to the property to the donee or to some third person who is to hold it for the donee. It is not necessary that the donee or the third person actually take possession of the property. The essential element of the gift is the *delivery* of the deed. Suppose Smith makes out a deed to the family farm and leaves it in a safe-deposit box for delivery to her son when she dies. The attempted gift will not be valid, because Smith did not deliver the gift during her lifetime.

**Acquisition by Will or Inheritance.** The owner of real property generally has the right to dispose of that property by will. The requirements for making a valid will are discussed in Chapter 30. If the owner of real property dies without leaving a valid will, the property will go to his heirs as determined under the laws of the state in which the real property is located.

**Acquisition by Tax Sale.** If the taxes assessed on real property are not paid, they become a *lien* on the property. This lien has priority over all other claims to the land. If the taxes remain unpaid for a period of time, the government can sell the land at a tax sale, and the purchaser at the tax sale acquires title to the property. However, some states have statutes that give the original owner a limited time (perhaps a year) in which to buy the property back from the tax sale purchaser for his cost plus interest.

**Acquisition by Adverse Possession.** Each state has a statute of limitations that gives an owner of land a specific number of years in which to bring a lawsuit to regain possession of his land from someone who is trespassing on it. This period generally ranges from 5 to 20 years, depending on the state. If someone wrongfully possesses land and acts as if he were the owner, the real owner must take steps to have the person ejected from the land. If this is not done within the statutory period, the right to eject the possessor will be lost. The person who stayed in possession of the property for the statutory period will acquire title to the land by **adverse possession.**

To acquire title to land by adverse possession, a person must possess land in a manner that puts the true owner on notice that he has a cause of action against that person. The adverse possessor's possession must be *open, actual, continuous, exclusive, and hostile (or adverse)* to the owner's rights. The hostility element does not mean that the adverse possessor must act in a malicious or hostile way. Rather, it means that the adverse possessor's possession must be inconsistent with the owner's rights. If a person is in possession of another's property under a lease, as a cotenant, or with the permission of the owner, his possession is not hostile. In some states, the person in possession of land must also pay the taxes on the land in order to gain title by adverse possession.

It is not necessary that the same person occupy the land for the statutory period. The periods of possession of several adverse possessors can be "tacked" together for purposes of calculating the period of possession if each possessor claims rights from the other. The possession must, however, be continuous for the necessary time.

Adverse possession can occur in some fairly common situations. *Ford v. Eckert,* which follows, presents a good example of a boundary dispute between neighboring landowners in which one of them ultimately gains ownership of disputed border property through adverse possession.

## Ford v. Eckert

**406 N.E.2d 1209 (Ind. Ct. App. 1980)**

The Grant family owned property in Birdseye, Indiana, from 1938 to 1946. The property was separated from neighboring property by a fence attached to a hickory tree. In 1946, the Grants sold the property to Ada Ford. The fence was still standing at this time. Sometime prior to 1960, the fence was removed. Ford, however, continued to mow and take care of what she believed to be her property up to where the fence had been located. In 1960, after the fence had been removed, the lot on the other side of where the fence had been was sold to Hilda Eckert. Eckert did not object to Ford's mowing on what Eckert believed to be her side of the line, but she did not acquiesce in any other ownership activity beyond where she thought the line should be. The problem arose when a survey was performed by the town of Birdseye to put in a new water system. The survey disclosed that the true boundary line was not the line assumed by Ford and that the strip she had been mowing was in fact located on Eckert's side of the line. Ford brought suit, claiming adverse possession. The trial court found no adverse possession and held for Eckert. Ford appealed.

**Robertson, Presiding Judge.** In order to establish title by adverse possession, Ford has to show her possession to be actual, visible, open and notorious, exclusive, under claim of ownership, hostile and continuous for the statutory period.

Prior to 1951, the applicable statute of limitations for adverse possession was 20 years. Since Eckert bought the property in 1960, and testified that she never acquiesced in ownership actions by Ford, Ford must show that the land was adversely possessed prior to Eckert's purchase of the property. It is clear that the statutory period need not be maintained by one person, but that successive periods may be tacked together to attain the necessary period. Here, Ford purchased the property in 1946. To prevail, she must present evidence as to the adverse possession of the same property by a prior owner. This is accomplished by tacking the eight years that the Grants were in possession, 1938–1946. From Grant's testimony, it is apparent that the Grants exercised the same control and ownership over the disputed area as did Ford.

A mere mistake in fact does not render the possession any less adverse. Here, Ford and her predecessors clearly intended to claim all the land up to the fence. They acted as if they were the sole owners of the property by maintaining it and using the land for its normal purpose. These facts evidence Ford and her predecessors' intent to claim title to the land. The fact that they believed the land to actually be theirs does not negate a conclusion that the possession was adverse. Consequently, we find the statutory requirements to be met.

We hold, therefore, that the facts presented show title to the land had passed to Ford prior to the acquisition of the property by Eckert.

Judgment reversed in favor of Ford.

## TRANSFER BY SALE

**Steps in a Sale.** The major steps normally involved in the sale of real property are: (1) contracting with a real estate broker to locate a buyer for the property; (2) negotiating and signing a contract to sell the property; (3) arranging for the financing of the purchase and the satisfaction of other requirements, such as arranging for a survey or for the acquisition of title insurance; (4) closing the sale, at which time the sale is consummated, usually by payment of the purchase price and transfer of the deed; and (5) recording the deed.

**Real Estate Brokerage.** Although engaging a real estate broker is not a legal requirement for the sale of real property, it is common for a person who wants to sell his property to "list" the property with a broker. A listing contract empowers the seller's broker to act as his agent in procuring a ready, willing, and able buyer on the seller's terms and managing the details of the transfer of the property. A number of states require listing contracts to be in writing. The listing contract should specify the duration of the listing period, the terms on which the seller will sell, and the amount or percentage of the commission that will be due to the broker if he brings about the sale. There are several types of listing contracts. If the listing contract provides that the broker has the *exclusive right to sell* the property, the owner will have to pay the broker's commission if the property is sold within the listing period, even if the owner himself procures the buyer.

The traditional rule has been that the broker has the right to obtain a commission if the seller and prospective buyer enter into a contract for the sale of the property during the listing period, even if the deal later falls through for some reason (failure to locate financing, for example). Influenced by a New Jersey case, *Ellsworth Dobbs, Inc. v. Johnson*,[3] however, a growing number of states have held that the broker will not be able to recover a commission when, through no fault of the seller's, the deal is not consummated. *Tristram's Landing*, below, is an example of such a case.

Real estate brokerage is regulated by state statutes that require people to meet specified qualifications to be licensed as brokers. A person who practices real estate brokerage without a license will not be able to collect a commission and may be subject to criminal sanctions or administrative penalties as well. A broker owes a fiduciary duty (a duty of high trust) to his client, and can be liable for damages for breaching that duty.

[3] 236 A.2d 843 (N.J. Sup. Ct. 1967).

### Tristram's Landing, Inc. v. Wait

**327 N.E.2d 727 (Mass. Sup. Ct. 1975)**

Linda Wait owned real estate in Nantucket that she wanted to sell. Van der Wolk, a real estate broker for Tristram's Landing, called Wait and asked for authority to show the property. Wait agreed that Tristram's Landing could act as the broker, though not as the exclusive broker, and that the price for the property was $110,000. During this conversation, there was no mention of a commission, but Wait knew that the normal commission in Nantucket was 5 percent. Early in 1973, Van der Wolk located a prospective purchaser, Louise Cashman. Wait and Cashman executed a contract to sell the property for $105,000. Cashman paid $10,500 as a down payment. The contract called for an October 1, 1973 closing date. It also contained this provision: "It is understood that a broker's commission of five (5) percent on the said sale is to be paid to the broker by the seller." On October 1, Wait appeared at the registry of deeds with a deed to the property. Cashman did not appear for the closing, and thereafter refused to go through with the purchase. Wait did not take any action against Cashman to enforce the agreement or to recover damages for its breach, but she kept the $10,500 down payment.

Van der Wolk presented Wait with a bill for a commission in the amount of $5,250 (5 percent of the agreed sales price). Wait refused to pay a commission, taking the position that Tristram's Landing was not entitled to a commission because there had been no sale. Tristram's Landing then filed suit to recover the commission. The trial court held in favor of Tristram's Landing, and Wait appealed.

**Tauro, Chief Justice.** The general rule regarding whether a broker is entitled to a commission from one attempting to sell real estate is that, absent special circumstances, the broker is entitled to a commission if he produces a customer ready, able, and willing to buy upon the terms and for the price given the broker by the owner. In the past, this rule has been construed to mean that once a customer is produced by the broker and accepted by the seller, the commission is earned, whether or not the sale is actually consummated. Furthermore, execution of a purchase and sale agreement is usually seen as conclusive evidence of the seller's acceptance of the buyer.

We believe, however, that it is both appropriate and necessary at this time to clarify the law, and we now join the growing minority of States who have adopted the rule of *Ellsworth Dobbs, Inc. v. Johnson.*

In the *Ellsworth* case, the New Jersey court noted that ordinarily when an owner of property lists it with a broker for sale, his expectation is that the money for the payment of commission will come out of the proceeds of the sale. The court went on to say that the principle binding the seller to pay commission if he signs a contract of sale with the broker's customer, regardless of the customer's financial ability, puts the burden on the wrong shoulders. Since the broker's duty to the owner is to produce a prospective buyer who is financially able to pay the purchase price and take title, a right in the owner to assume such capacity when the broker presents his purchaser ought to be recognized. Reason and justice dictate that it should be the broker who bears the burden of producing a purchaser who is not only ready, willing and able at the time of the negotiations, but who also consummates the sale at the time of closing.

Thus, we adopt the following rules: when a broker is engaged by an owner of property to find a purchaser for it, the broker earns his commission when (a) he produces a purchaser ready, willing and able to buy on the terms fixed by the owner, (b) the purchaser enters into a binding contract with the owner to do so, and (c) the purchaser completes the transaction by closing the title in accordance with the provisions of the contract. If the contract is not consummated because of lack of financial ability of the buyer to perform or because of any other default of his, there is no right to commission against the seller. On the other hand, if the failure of completion of the contract results from the wrongful act or interference of the seller, the broker's claim is valid and must be paid.

Judgment reversed in favor of Wait.

**Contract for Sale.** The principles regarding contract formation, performance, assignment, and remedies that you learned in earlier chapters are applicable to contracts for the sale of real estate. The contract for the sale of real estate should provide for such matters as the purchase price, the type of deed the purchaser will get, the items of personal property that are included in the sale, and any other aspect of the transaction that is important to the parties. The contract may make the "closing" of the sale contingent on the buyer's finding financing at a specified rate of interest and the seller's procurement of a survey, title insurance, and termite insurance. Because the contract is within the statute of frauds, it must be evidenced by a writing to be enforceable.

**Financing the Purchase.** The various arrangements for financing the purchase of real property, such as mortgages, land contracts, and deeds of trust, are discussed in Chapter 39.

**Federal Disclosure Laws.** Congress has enacted several statutes designed to protect purchasers of real estate. One important piece of protective legislation is the federal Real Estate Settlement Procedures Act (RESPA).[4] For any real estate transaction involving federally related loans (such as VA and FHA loans), RESPA requires that the buyer be given advance disclosure of the costs that will be incurred in settlement (closing) of the transaction and that a record be kept of the actual settlement charges. The required Settlement/Disclosure Statement itemizes each settlement cost charged to the buyer and each charged to the seller. These settlement charges commonly include such items as real estate brokers' commissions, appraisal fees, and insurance premiums. Among the purposes of the Settlement Statement are to give the buyer notice of the cash that she will need to have at settlement as well as an opportunity to engage in "comparison shopping" of settlement terms so that she can arrange the most favorable terms. RESPA also prohibits a number of practices, such as kickbacks or payments for referral of business to title companies.

Another important piece of legislation is the Interstate Land Sales Full Disclosure Act,[5] which Congress passed in response to fraud and misrepresentation committed by some sellers of land, particularly retirement and vacation properties. The act generally applies to developers who subdivide property into 50 or more lots and who use interstate means, such as the mail and telephone, to sell the property. The act requires that a "property report" disclose certain kinds of information about the property and the developer's plans regarding it. The report is filed with the U.S. Department of Housing and Urban Development, and it must be made available to prospective purchasers. A developer who violates the act is subject to civil and criminal penalties.

**Deeds.** Each state has statutes that set out the formalities necessary to accomplish a valid conveyance of land. As a general rule, a valid conveyance is accomplished by the execution and delivery of a **deed.** A deed is a written instrument that conveys title from one person (*the grantor*) to another person (*the grantee*.) There are two basic types of deeds in general use in the United States: **quitclaim deeds** and **warranty deeds.** The precise rights conveyed by a deed depend on the type of deed that the parties use.

**Quitclaim Deeds.** A **quitclaim deed** conveys whatever title the grantor has at the time he executes the deed. It does not, however, contain any warranties of title. The grantor who executes a quitclaim deed does not claim to have good title, or in fact, any

[4] 12 U.S.C. §§ 1730f, 1831b, 2601 et seq.

[5] 17 U.S.C. § 1701 et seq.

title at all. The grantee has no action against the grantor under a quitclaim deed if the title proves to be defective. Quitclaim deeds are frequently used to cure a technical defect in the chain of title to property.

**Warranty Deeds.** A **warranty deed,** unlike a quitclaim deed, contains covenants of warranty. In addition to conveying title to the property, the grantor who executes a warranty deed guarantees the title that she has conveyed. There are two types of warranty deeds. In a **general warranty deed,** the grantor warrants against all defects in the title and all encumbrances (such as liens and easements), even those that arose before the grantor received her title. In a **special warranty deed,** the grantor warrants against only those defects in the title or those encumbrances that arose after she acquired the property. If the property conveyed is subject to some encumbrance such as a mortgage, a long-term lease, or an easement, it is a common practice for the grantor to give a special warranty deed that contains a provision excepting those specific encumbrances from the warranty.

**Form and Execution of Deed.** Some states have enacted statutes setting out a suggested form for deeds. The statutory requirements of the different states for the execution of deeds are not uniform, but they do follow a similar pattern. As a general rule, a deed states the *name of the grantee,* contains a *recitation of consideration* and a *description of the property conveyed,* and is *signed by the grantor.* In most states, the deed must be notarized (acknowledged by the grantor before a notary public or other authorized officer) to be eligible for recording in public records.

No technical words of conveyance are necessary for a valid deed. Any language is sufficient if it indicates with reasonable certainty the intent to transfer the ownership of property. The phrases "grant, bargain, and sell" and "convey and warrant" are commonly used. Deeds contain recitations of consideration primarily for historical reasons. The consideration recited is not necessarily the purchase price of the real property. Sometimes, deeds state that the consideration for the conveyance is "one dollar and other valuable consideration."

The property conveyed must be described in such a manner that it can be identified. Generally, this means that the *legal description* of the property must be used. Several methods of legal description are used in the United States. In urban areas, descriptions are usually by lot, block, and plat. In rural areas in which the land has been surveyed by the government, property is usually described by reference to the government survey. It may also be described by a metes and bounds description that specifies the boundaries of the tract of land.

**Recording Deeds.** The delivery of a valid deed conveys title from a grantor to a grantee. Nevertheless, in order to prevent his interest from being defeated by third parties who may claim an interest in the same property, the grantee should immediately **record** the deed. When a deed is recorded, it is deposited and indexed in a systematic way in a public office, where it operates to give notice of the grantee's interest to the rest of the world.

Each state has a *recording statute* that establishes a system for the recording of all transactions that affect the ownership of real property. The statutes are not uniform in their provisions. In general, they provide for the recording of all deeds, mortgages, land contracts, and similar documents. They also commonly declare that an unrecorded transfer is void as against an innocent purchaser or mortgagee who has paid value. Many states will not invalidate such an unrecorded transfer unless the subsequent purchaser or mortgagee recorded his interest first. Suppose that on May 1, 1984, Smith sells Blackacre to Jones for $50,000, deeding the property to Jones by a special warranty deed. Jones does not record the deed. On June 1, 1984, Smith sells Blackacre to Kelly for $75,000, giving Kelly a special warranty deed to the same property. Kelly, not knowing about the prior deed to Jones, records his deed immediately. In this case, Kelly would prevail over Jones even though his deed was obtained after Jones's deed.

**Methods of Assuring Title.** One of the things that a person must be concerned about in buying real property is whether the seller of the property has *good title* to it. In buying property, a buyer is really buying the seller's ownership interests. Because the buyer does not want to pay a large sum of money for something that turns out to be worthless, it is important for him to obtain some assurance that the seller has good title to the property. This is commonly done in one of three ways.

In some locations, it is customary to have an **abstract of title** examined by an attorney. An abstract of title is a history of the passage of title of a piece of real property according to the public records. It is *not* a guarantee of good title. After examining the abstract, an attorney will render an opinion about whether the grantor has **marketable title** to the property. Marketable title is title that is free from defects or reasonable doubt about its validity. If the title is defective, the nature of the defects will be stated in the title opinion.

A method of title assurance that is possible in a few states is the **Torrens system** of title registration. Under this system, a person who owns land in fee simple obtains a certificate of title. When the property is sold, the grantor delivers a deed and a certificate of title to the grantee. The grantee then gives the deed and certificate of title to the designated government official and receives a new certificate of title. All liens and encumbrances against the title are noted on the certificate, so that the purchaser is assured that the title is good except as to the liens and encumbrances noted on the certificate. However, some claims or encumbrances, such as adverse possession and easements by prescription, do not appear on the records and must be discovered by making an inspection of the property. In some Torrens states, certain encumbrances, such as tax liens, short-term leases, and highway rights, are valid against the purchaser even though they do not appear on the certificate.

The preferred and most common means of protecting title to real property is to purchase a policy of **title insurance.** Title insurance is designed to reimburse the insured for loss if the title turns out to be defective. Title insurance not only compensates for loss of the title; it also pays litigation costs if the insured must go to court to defend the title. Lenders commonly require that a separate policy of title insurance be obtained for the lender's protection. Title insurance may be obtained in combination with the other methods of assuring title that were discussed earlier.

**Warranties of Quality in the Sale of Houses.** Another concern of people who buy improved real estate is the condition of structures on the property. Traditionally, the rule of **caveat emptor** ("let the buyer beware") applied to the sale of real property unless the seller committed fraud or misrepresentation or made *express warranties* about the condition of the property. Thus, the seller made no *implied warranties* that the property was habitable or suitable for the buyer's use. The sale of land was considered an arm's-length transaction in which the buyer had the opportunity to become acquainted with the property and discover any defects in its condition before the sale. The buyer had two choices: either to obtain an express warranty from the seller or to take the property at her own risk.

The law's attitude toward the relationship

of buyer and seller in the sale of residential property began to change in the late 1960s. Courts began to see that the same policies that favored the creation of implied warranties in the sale of goods applied with equal force to the sale of residential real estate.[6] Like goods, housing is frequently mass-produced. As in the sale of goods, there is often a disparity of knowledge and bargaining power between the builder-vendor and the buyer of a house. Many defects in houses are of a type that evades discovery during a buyer's inspection. This creates the possibility of serious loss, since the purchase of a home is often the largest single investment that a person ever makes. For these reasons, courts in the majority of states now hold that builders, builder-vendors (persons who build and sell houses), and developers make an **implied warranty of habitability** when they build or sell real property for residential purposes. The *Tyus* case, which follows, discusses in more detail the rationales supporting the implied warranty of habitability.

The implied warranty of habitability is basically a guarantee that the house is free of *latent* (that is, hidden) defects that would render it unsafe or unsuitable for human habitation. A breach of the warranty will subject the defendant to liability for damages, measured by either the cost of repairs or the loss in value of the house. If the breach is so serious that it constitutes a material breach,[7] it can even lead to rescission of the sale. The application of the warranty has been limited to builders, builder-vendors, and developers. That is, an ordinary seller of a house who is not the builder or developer does not make a warranty of habitability.

One further issue that has caused a great deal of litigation is whether the warranty extends to subsequent purchasers of the house. For example, XYZ Development Company builds a house and sells it to Smith. If Smith later sells the house to Jones, can Jones sue XYZ for breach of warranty if a serious defect renders the house uninhabitable? The earlier cases limited the warranty to *new* houses and held that subsequent purchasers had no cause of action for breach of warranty against the original builder. A considerable number of more recent cases, however, have extended the implied warranty to subsequent purchasers for a reasonable time. This appears to be the trend. The decisions in these cases recognize that the purchase of a house is one of the largest investments a buyer will ever make and that buyers have justifiable expectations about the durability of a house. Naturally, the extension of the warranty to subsequent purchasers greatly increases the legal vulnerability of builders and developers.

Another issue that has arisen regarding the implied warranty of habitability is whether the warranty can be *disclaimed* or *limited* in the contract of sale. Subject to the doctrine of unconscionability, concerns about public policy,[8] and legal rules of interpretation and construction,[9] it appears that the warranty can be validly disclaimed or at least limited by appropriate provisions in a contract. As you will see in the *Tyus* case, however, such clauses are strictly construed against the builder-vendor.

**Duty to Disclose Latent Defects.** Another basis for liability on the part of sellers of real estate is the *duty to disclose hidden defects.* If the seller (including ordinary sellers of real estate) knows of a material defect in the property that is *latent* or hidden (not reasonably discoverable by the buyer), he has the duty to disclose it. If he fails to do so, his silence

[6] See Chapter 32 for discussion of the development of similar doctrines in the law of products liability.

[7] Material breach is discussed in Chapter 15.

[8] See Chapter 12 for further discussion of these doctrines.

[9] The interpretation of contracts is discussed in Chapter 13.

may be held to constitute misrepresentation.[10] For example, Jones knows that the basement of his house floods during heavy rainfalls. Assuming that a prospective purchaser would not be able to discover this through a reasonable inspection, Jones would have the duty to inform a prospective purchaser of the defect. In a few states, courts have gone even further and protected buyers even when the seller was not aware of the hidden defect.

[10] The circumstances under which nondisclosure constitutes misrepresentation are discussed in Chapter 9.

## Tyus v. Resta

**476 A.2d 427 (Pa. Super. Ct. 1984)**

Richard and Patricia Resta built a house and offered it for sale. On August 23, 1976, they entered into a contract to sell the house to Nelson and Frances Tyus. Paragraph 13 of the contract stated:

> Buyer has inspected the property or hereby waives the right to do so and he has agreed to purchase it as a result of such inspection and not because of or in reliance upon any representation made by the Seller . . . and that he has agreed to purchase it in its present condition unless otherwise specified herein. It is further understood that his agreement contains the whole agreement between the Seller and the Buyer and there are no other terms, obligations, covenants, representations, statements or conditions, oral or otherwise of any kind whatsoever concerning this sale.

After living in the house, the Tyuses noticed a pervasive dampness in it, which produced mold, mildew, and a constant bad odor. The dampness resulted from an improper crawl space drainage system underneath the house. In May 1978, the Tyuses filed suit against the Restas for breach of the implied warranty of habitability. The trial court awarded damages to the Tyuses, and the Restas appealed.

**Beck, Judge.** In 1972, Pennsylvania numbered among the first jurisdictions acknowledging an implied warranty of habitability in contracts whereby builder-vendor sold newly constructed houses. We are now asked to decide whether in selling new homes builder-vendors can limit or disclaim the implied warranties.

Compared to the ordinary home purchaser, the builder-vendor possesses superior knowledge and expertise in all aspects of building. In the vast majority of cases the vendor enjoys superior bargaining position. Standard form contracts are generally utilized and express warranties are rarely given, expensive, and impractical for most buyers to negotiate. Inevitably the buyer is forced to rely on the skills of the seller.

The Pennsylvania Supreme Court recognized that the implied warranties of habitability and reasonable workmanship were necessary to equalize the disparate positions of the builder-vendor and the average home purchaser by safeguarding the reasonable expectations of the purchaser compelled to depend upon the builder-vendor's greater manufacturing and marketing expertise. One who purchases a development home justifiably relies on the skill of the developer that the house will be a suitable living unit. Not only does a housing developer hold himself out as having the necessary expertise with which to produce an adequate dwelling, but he has by far the better opportunity to examine the suitability of the home site and to determine what measures should be taken to provide a home fit for habitation. As between the builder-vendor and the vendee, the position of the former, even though he exercises reasonable care, dictates that he bear the risk that a home which he has built will be functional and habitable in accordance with contemporary community standards.

Thus, given the important consumer protection afforded by the implied warranties, we hold that such warranties may be limited or disclaimed only by clear and unambiguous language in a written contract between the builder-vendor and the home purchaser. Furthermore, since the language of a contract must be construed strictly against the party responsible for it and since this general principle is even more forcefully applied when the contract is reduced to writing by a party possessing special knowledge with respect to the subject matter, we additionally hold that the contractual language purportedly creating an express restriction or exclusion of an implied warranty must be strictly construed against the builder-vendor.

To create clear and unambiguous language of disclaimer, the parties' contract must contain language which is both understandable and sufficiently particular to provide the new home purchaser adequate notice of the implied warranty protections that he is waiving by signing the contract. To supply proper notice, language of disclaimer must refer to its effect on specifically designated, potential latent defects. Evidence that the purchaser and the builder-vendor actually negotiated the waiver language in the contract will tend to indicate that the purchaser was aware of the waiver language and its import and accordingly, will tend to substantiate a valid waiver.

The Restas argue that paragraph 13 of the contract negates any and all warranties. The inspection clause introducing paragraph 13 refutes the existence of representations as to defects which would be apparent to the Tyuses upon a reasonable inspection. However, the warranties of habitability and reasonable workmanship are not created by representations of a builder-vendor but rather are implied in law. Moreover, the implied warranties of a builder-vendor do not extend to defects of which the purchaser had actual notice or which are or should be visible to a reasonably prudent man. A reasonable pre-purchase inspection requires examination of the premises by the intended purchaser—not by an expert. Defects which would not be apparent to an ordinary purchaser constitute latent defects covered by the implied warranties. Furthermore, a reasonable inspection does not necessitate a minute inspection of every nook and cranny.

Our inquiry becomes whether a reasonable pre-purchase inspection of the house by the Tyuses should have included the exploration of the crawl space under the house. At trial, the Tyuses' expert gave the following description of the crawl space: "It is about between 30 and 36 inches high. You drop through a little opening about three by four onto a little landing area; then you go underneath the foundation, and it is basically leveled gravel." Based upon the physical impediments to investigating the crawl space, we conclude that a reasonable pre-purchase house inspection did not require the Tyuses to examine the crawl space. Therefore, the crawl space drainage system remained a latent defect encompassed by the implied warranties. Consequently, the inspection clause in paragraph 13 does not effectively disclaim the warranties of habitability and reasonable workmanship.

The "present condition" provision of paragraph 13 fails to refer specifically to its potential impact on the implied warranties. Accordingly, while the "present condition" language alerts the buyers to observe patent defects, the language does not adequately apprise the buyers of their duty to ascertain latent defects normally covered by the implied warranties.

The final segment of paragraph 13 consists of an integration clause which declares that the parties' written contract embodies "the whole agreement between the Seller and the Buyer." The integration clause may be sufficient to exclude a matter which one of the parties might contend was *in fact* agreed prior to the signing of the contract. Standing alone, these words are not sufficient to exclude an *implied warranty,* which is applicable only by operation of law.

Therefore, we hold that when the alleged disclaimer of implied warranties in paragraph 13 is construed strictly against the Restas, the disclaimer fails because it does not refer to its impact on specific, potential latent defects and so does not notify the buyers of the implied warranty protection they are waiving by signing the contract supplied by the Restas.

Judgment for the Tyuses affirmed.

## LAND USE CONTROL

**Introduction.** While an owner of real property generally has the right to make such use of his property as he desires, society has placed a number of limitations on this right. This is one example of the principle that to protect freedom, it is sometimes necessary to limit it. A property owner's unrestrained use of his property may destroy the value of his neighbor's property. One such limitation on the use of property is found in nuisance law, which permits public and private actions against landowners who use their property in a way that causes injury to others. Other limitations are created by zoning and subdivision ordinances, which contain specific requirements and prohibitions about the use of real property. Finally, the government, through its power of eminent domain, can deprive a person of his ownership of land. The following discussion explores these controls on land use in greater detail.

**Nuisance Law.** A person's enjoyment of his own land depends to a great extent on the uses that his neighbors make of their land. When the uses of neighboring landowners conflict, the aggrieved party frequently resorts to a court for resolution of the conflict. A person who unreasonably interferes with another person's interest in the use or enjoyment of his property is subject to an action for **nuisance.**

The term *nuisance* has no set definition. It may be conceived of as any use or activity that unreasonably interferes with the rights of others. It can be either intentional or negligent. Property uses that are inappropriate to the neighborhood (such as operating a funeral parlor in a single-family residential neighborhood), bothersome to neighbors (such as keeping a pack of barking dogs in one's backyard), dangerous to others (such as storing large quantities of gasoline in 50-gallon drums in one's garage), or immoral (such as operating a house of prostitution) can all be held to be nuisances. To amount to a nuisance, a use does not have to be illegal. The mere fact that a use is permitted under relevant zoning laws does not mean that it cannot be a nuisance. Furthermore, the fact that a use was in existence before neighboring landowners acquired their property does not mean that it cannot be a nuisance.

The test for determining whether conduct will be considered a nuisance is necessarily flexible and highly dependent on the facts of the individual case. A court will balance a number of factors, such as the social importance of the parties' respective uses, the extent and duration of the aggrieved party's loss, and the feasibility of abating (stopping) the nuisance. A plaintiff who puts his land to an unusually sensitive or "delicate" use cannot enjoin the activities of others that interfere with the delicate use. The *Page County Appliance Center* case, which follows, discusses in greater detail the standards for determining the existence of a nuisance.

Nuisances may be *private* or *public.* To bring a *private nuisance* action, the plaintiff must be a landowner or occupier whose enjoyment of his own land is substantially lessened because of a nuisance. The remedies for private nuisance include damages and injunctive relief. A *public nuisance* occurs when a nuisance causes harm to members of the public, who need not necessarily be injured in their use of property. For example, if a power plant creates noise and emissions that constitute a health hazard to pedestrians and workers in nearby buildings, a public nuisance may exist even though the nature of the injury is something other than the loss of enjoyment of the injured persons' property. Public nuisances involve a broader class of affected parties than do private nuisances. The action to abate the nuisance must usually be brought by the government in the name of the public. Remedies generally include criminal-type fines and injunctive relief. Private parties can sue for the abatement of a public nuisance or for damages caused by a public nuisance only when they can show that they have suffered a unique harm different from that suffered by the general public.

## Page County Appliance Center, Inc. v. Honeywell, Inc.

**347 N.E.2d 171 (Iowa Sup. Ct. 1984)**

Since 1953, Page County Appliance Center (Appliance Center) had owned and operated a store that sold television sets, stereos, and a variety of appliances. Before 1980, Appliance Center had no trouble with the reception for its display TVs. In early January of 1980, however, ITT Electronic Travel Services (ITT) leased a computer to Central Travel Service as part of a nationwide plan to lease computers to travel agents. Central Travel was located two doors away from Appliance Center. The computer was manufactured, installed, and maintained by Honeywell. After this installation, many of Appliance Center's customers began to complain that its display television pictures were bad. Appliance Center was finally able to trace the problem to interference caused by the operation of Central Travel's computer. The interference resulted from radiation leaking from the computer. As a result, Appliance Center's income fell significantly in 1980 and 1981. The sale of color television sets, which had constituted 60 percent of its gross sales, dropped drastically.

Central Travel notified ITT and Honeywell of the problem. After many unsuccessful attempts to alleviate the problem and several instances of delay by Honeywell, Appliance Center filed suit against ITT, Honeywell, and Central Travel in December 1980. In May 1982, while the suit was pending, Honeywell modified the computer to resolve Appliance Center's problems. Because Appliance Center had sought only injunctive relief from Central Travel, the court rendered judgment for Central Travel. In the action against Honeywell and ITT, however, the trial court awarded Appliance Center $71,000 in compensatory damages and $150,000 in punitive damages. Honeywell and ITT appealed.

**Reynoldson, Chief Justice.** We note that Appliance Center is alleging a private nuisance, that is, an actionable interference with a person's interest in the private use and enjoyment of his property. Principles governing our consideration of nuisance claims are well established. One's use of property should not unreasonably interfere with or disturb a neighbor's comfortable and reasonable use and enjoyment of his or her estate. A fair test of whether the operation of a lawful trade or industry constitutes a nuisance is the reasonableness of conducting it in the manner, at the place, and under the circumstances shown by the evidence. Each case turns on its own facts and ordinarily the ultimate issue is one of fact, not law. The existence of a nuisance is not affected by the intention of its creator not to injure anyone. Priority of occupation—"who was there first"—is a circumstance of considerable weight.

When the alleged nuisance is claimed to be offensive to the person, courts apply the standard of "normal persons in a particular locality" to measure the existence of a nuisance. This normalcy standard also is applied where the use of property is claimed to be affected. The plaintiff cannot, by devoting his own land to an unusually sensitive use, make a nuisance out of conduct of the adjoining defendant which would otherwise be harmless.

One is subject to liability for a nuisance not only when he carries on the activity but also when he participates to a substantial extent in carrying it on. Even one who contracts out nuisance-causing work to independent contractors may have the duty to take reasonably prompt and efficient means to suppress the nuisance. A failure to act under circumstances in which one is under a duty to take positive action to prevent or abate the invasion of a private interest may make one liable.

The trial court's instructions required Appliance Center to prove Honeywell and ITT "unreasonably" interfered with the Center's use and enjoyment of its property. Honeywell and ITT objected that the instructions made no attempt to define the unreasonableness concept. Because reasonableness is a question for the jury, the court on retrial should provide more guidance for the jury. Reasonableness is a function of the manner in which, and the place where, defendant's business is conducted, and the circumstances under which defendant operates. Additional factors include priority of location, character of the neighborhood, and the nature of the alleged wrong. The character and gravity of the resulting injury is, in fact, a major factor in determining reasonableness. Balanced against the gravity of the wrong is the utility and meritoriousness of the defendant's conduct.

Another instruction given in this case stated that "one who contributes to the creation or continuance of a nuisance may be liable." ITT objected that neither this instruction nor any other informed the jury that a defendant's conduct must be a "substantial factor" in bringing about the alleged harm. Upon retrial, the instructions should incorporate this requirement. Both Honeywell and ITT objected because the court did not submit to the jury the issue whether Appliance Center was devoting its premises to an unusually sensitive use. We hold Honeywell and ITT were entitled to have this question resolved by the jury. Honeywell and ITT shall be granted a new trial in conformance with this opinion.

Judgment reversed and remanded in favor of Honeywell and ITT.

**Zoning and Subdivision Ordinances.** State legislatures commonly delegate to cities and other political subdivisions the *police power* to impose reasonable regulations designed to promote the public health, safety, and morals and the general welfare of the community. **Zoning ordinances,** which regulate the use of real property, are created in the exercise of this police power. Normally, zoning ordinances divide a city or town into a number of districts and specify or limit the use to which property in those districts can be put. They also prescribe and restrict the improvements that are built on the land.

Zoning ordinances restrict the use of property in a number of ways. One common type of restriction is a *control of uses* on the land, such as restriction of an area to single-family or high-density residential uses or commercial, light industry, or heavy industry uses. Another type of restriction is *control of height and bulk,* which prescribe the height of buildings; the setback from front, side, and rear lot lines; and the portion of a lot that can be covered by a building. *Control of population density* is another common type of restriction. Such restrictions specify the amount of living space that must be provided for each person and specify the maximum number of persons who can be housed in a given area. Zoning ordinances also commonly contain *controls of aesthetics,* whereby the use of land is restricted to maintain or create a certain aesthetic character of the community. Restrictions on the architectural style of buildings, the use of billboards and other signs, and the creation of special zones for historical buildings are examples of this type of restriction.

Many local governments also have ordinances dealing with proposed subdivisions. These ordinances often require that the developer meet certain requirements as to lot size, street and sidewalk layout, and sanitary facilities. They also require that the city or town approve the proposed development. In addition, they often require developers to dedicate a portion of the land to the city for streets, parks, and schools. The purpose of such ordinances is to protect the prospective purchasers of property in the subdivision and the community as a whole, by ensuring that minimum standards are met by the developer.

**Recent Zoning Developments.** Some urban planners believe that it is undesirable to segregate totally the living, working, shopping, and entertainment areas of a community, as is commonly done in zoning schemes. They argue that a more livable environment is one that mixes these uses in a way that ensures the vitality of an area for the major part of each day. In response to this philosophy, cities and counties are allowing "planned unit developments" and "new towns," which mix these uses. Local governments establish guidelines for such developments, and require that plans be submitted to and approved by zoning authorities pursuant to the guidelines.

People are becoming more aware of the shortcomings of making our land use decisions on a piecemeal basis at the local level. Airports, major shopping centers, highways, and new towns require a regional, rather than a local, planning focus. Moreover, sensitive ecological areas, such as marshes, can easily be destroyed if these are not protected by regional zoning. Accordingly, a number of states and the federal government have enacted, or are considering, legislation to put some land use planning on a regional or statewide basis.

**Nonconforming Uses.** A zoning ordinance has prospective effect. That is, the uses and buildings that already exist at the time the ordinance is passed (*nonconforming uses*) are permitted to continue. However, the ordinance may provide for the gradual phasing out (*amortization*) of nonconforming uses and buildings that do not conform to the general zoning plan.

**Relief from Zoning Ordinances.** A property owner who wants to initiate some use of his property that is not permitted by the existing zoning ordinance can try several avenues of relief from that ordinance. He can try to have the zoning law *amended* on the ground that the proposed amendments are in accordance with the overall zoning plan. He can also try to obtain a *variance* from the zoning law on the ground that the ordinance works an undue hardship on him by depriving him of opportunity to make reasonable use of his land. Attempts to obtain amendments or variances often produce heated battles before the zoning authorities because they often conflict with the interests of nearby property owners who have a vested interest in maintaining the status quo.

**Challenges to the Validity of the Zoning Ordinance.** A disgruntled property owner might also attack the constitutionality of the zoning ordinance. Zoning ordinances have produced a great deal of litigation in recent years, as cities and towns have used their zoning power as a means of social control. For example, a city might create a special zone for adult bookstores or other uses that are considered moral threats to the community. This has given rise to challenges that such ordinances unconstitutionally restrict freedom of speech.

Another type of litigation has involved ordinances designed to restrict single-family residential zones to living units of traditional families related by blood or marriage or to no more than two unrelated adults. Many cities and towns have attempted to "zone out" such other living groups as groups of unrelated students, communes, religious cults, and group homes like the one you read about in the *Crane Neck* case by specifically defining the term *family* in a way that excludes these groups. In the case of *Belle Terre v. Boraas,*[11] the Supreme Court upheld such an ordinance as applied to a group of unrelated students. It subsequently held, however, that an ordinance that defined "family" in such a way as to prohibit a grandmother from living with her grandsons was an unconstitutional intrusion on personal freedom regarding marriage and family life.[12] In some cases, restrictive definitions of the term *family* have been held unconstitutional under *state constitutions.* In others, such definitions have been narrowly construed by the courts.

An additional type of litigation has involved zoning laws that restrict the use of land in a way that makes it less profitable for development. Affected property owners have challenged the application of such zoning ordinances on the ground that they constitute an unconstitutional "taking" of property without just compensation.[13] So long as the property owner retains some reasonable use of the property, the exercise of police power over the use of the property has generally been held *not* to constitute a taking.

**Eminent Domain.** The Constitution provides that private property shall not be taken for public use without just compensation. Implicit in this provision is the principle that the state has the power to take property for public use by paying "just compensation" to the owner of the property. This power, which is called the power of **eminent domain,** makes it possible for the government to acquire private property for highways, water control projects, municipal and civic centers, public housing, urban renewal, and other public uses. Governmental units can delegate their power of eminent domain to private corporations such as railroads and public utilities.

Although the eminent domain power is probably necessary to efficient government, there are several major problems inherent in its use. One of them is determining when the

[11] 416 U.S. 1 (U.S. Sup. Ct. 1974).

[12] *Moore v. City of East Cleveland,* 431 U.S. 494 (U.S. Sup. Ct. 1977).

[13] This issue is discussed in Chapter 42.

power can be properly exercised. When the governmental unit itself uses the property taken, as would be the case in property acquired for the use of a municipal building or a public highway, the exercise of the power is proper. The exercise of the power is not so clearly justified, however, when the government acquires the property and resells it to a private developer. Although such acquisitions may be more vulnerable to challenge, recent cases have applied a very lenient standard in determining what constitutes a public use.[14]

Another problem with regard to the eminent domain power is determining what is meant by "just compensation." A property owner is entitled to receive the "fair market value" of his property, but some people believe that this measure of compensation falls short of reimbursing the owner for what he has lost, since it does not cover the lost goodwill of a business or the emotional attachment a person may have to his home.

A third problem is determining when a "taking" has occurred. The answer to this is easy when the government institutes a legal action to condemn property or when the government completely dispossesses the owner. It is much more difficult to determine whether a taking has occurred when zoning power has been used to restrict the permissible use of a given piece of property to a narrow and publicly beneficial use,[15] or when the government uses nearby land in such a way as to almost completely destroy the usefulness of adjoining, privately owned land, as sometimes occurs in the operation of municipal airports. When the government effectively takes land without having paid for it, the owner of the land can bring an **inverse condemnation** action to obtain compensation for the taking.

[14] This and other issues relating to eminent domain are discussed further in Chapter 42.

[15] See Chapter 42 for further discussion.

## LANDLORD AND TENANT

**Introduction.** In recent years, there has been considerable change in the law of landlord and tenant. In England and in early America, farms were the most common subjects of leases. The tenant's primary object was to lease land on which crops could be grown or cattle grazed. Accordingly, traditional landlord-tenant law viewed the lease as primarily a conveyance of land and paid relatively little attention to its contractual aspects.

In our industrialized society, however, the relationship and objectives of the landlord and tenant have changed dramatically. The landlord-tenant relationship today is typified by the lease of property for residential or commercial purposes. The tenant occupies only a small portion of the total property. He bargains primarily for the use of structures on the land rather than for the land itself. He is likely to have signed a form lease provided by the landlord, the terms of which he may have had little opportunity to negotiate. In areas where there is a shortage of affordable housing, a tenant's ability to bargain for favorable lease provisions is further hampered. Thus, tenants no longer can be presumed to be capable of negotiating to protect their own interests, because the typical landlord-tenant relationship can no longer fairly be characterized as one in which the parties have equal knowledge and bargaining power.

The law was slow to recognize the changing nature of the landlord-tenant relationship, but its view of the lease as being primarily a conveyance of property has gradually given way to a view of the lease as primarily a contract. The significance of this new view of the lease is that modern contract doctrines, such as unconscionability, constructive conditions, the duty to mitigate damages, and implied warranties, can be applied to leases. Such doctrines can operate to compensate for tenants' lack of bargaining power. In addition, state legislatures and city councils have enacted statutes and ordinances that protect both landlords and tenants.

Our discussion of the law of landlord and tenant will focus on the nature of leasehold interests, the traditional rights and duties of both landlord and tenant, and recent statutory and judicial developments that affect those rights and duties.

**Types of Leases.** A **lease** is a contract by which an owner of property conveys to another the right to possess the leased premises exclusively for a period of time. The interest conveyed to the tenant (lessee) is a **leasehold estate.** There are four different kinds of leases, each of which differs in the duration of the tenants' right to possess the property and in the manner in which that right terminates.

A **tenancy for a term** results when the landlord and tenant agree on a specific duration of the lease and fix the date on which the tenancy will terminate. For example, if Smith, a college student, leases an apartment for the academic year ending May 30, 1986, a tenancy for a term will have been created. The tenant's right to possess the property ends on the date agreed upon without any further notice, unless the lease contains a provision that permits extension.

A **periodic tenancy** is created when the parties agree that rent will be paid in successive intervals until notice to terminate is given, but do not agree on a specific duration of the lease. If the tenant pays monthly, the tenancy is from month-to-month; if the tenant pays yearly, as is sometimes done in agricultural leases, the tenancy is from year-to-year. To terminate a periodic tenancy, either party must give advance notice to the other. The precise amount of notice required is defined by state statutes. To terminate a tenancy from month-to-month, for example, most states require that the notice be given at least one month in advance.

A **tenancy at will** occurs when property is leased for an indefinite period of time and is terminable at the will of either party. Generally, tenancies at will involve situations in which the tenant does not pay rent or does not pay it in any certain intervals. For example, Smith allows his friend Jones to live in the apartment over his garage. Although the tenancy at will is terminable by either party "at will," most states require that the landlord give advance notice to the tenant before terminating the tenancy.

The last type of tenancy is the **tenancy at sufferance.** This tenancy occurs when a tenant remains in possession of the property after the expiration of a lease. The landlord has the option of treating the tenant as a trespasser, and bringing an action to eject him, or of continuing to treat him as a tenant and collecting rent from him. Until the landlord makes his election, the tenant is a tenant at sufferance. Suppose that Jones has leased an apartment for one year from Smith. At the end of the year, Jones "holds over" and does not move out. Jones is a tenant at sufferance. The landlord may eject him as a trespasser or continue treating him as a tenant. If the landlord elects the latter alternative, a new tenancy will be created. The new tenancy will be either a tenancy for a term or a periodic tenancy, depending on the facts of the case and any presumptions that are made by state law. Thus, a tenant who holds over for even a few days runs the risk of creating a new tenancy that he might not want.

**Execution of a Lease.** As a sale of an interest in land, a lease may be covered by the statute of frauds. In most states, a lease for a term of more than one year from the date it is made must be evidenced by a writing to be enforceable. In a few states, however, only leases for a term of more than three years have to be evidenced by a writing.

Good business practice demands that leases be carefully drafted to define clearly the parties' respective rights and obligations. The need to use care in drafting leases is especially great in the case of long-term and commercial leases. Leases normally contain provisions covering such essential matters as the uses that the tenant can make of the property, the circumstances under which the landlord has the right to enter the property, the rent to be paid, the duty to repair, any warranties regarding the quality of the property, any limitations on the parties' right to assign the lease or sublet the property, the term of the lease, and the possible extension of the term. Permissible lease terms are often regulated by state or local law. For example, approximately 15 states have enacted the Uniform Residential Landlord and Tenant Act, which prohibits the inclusion of certain lease provisions, such as an agreement by the tenant to pay the landlord's attorney's fees in an action to enforce the lease.

## RIGHTS, DUTIES, AND LIABILITIES OF THE LANDLORD

**Landlord's Rights.** The landlord is entitled to receive the agreed rent for the term of the lease. At the expiration of the lease, the landlord has the right to the return of the property in as good a condition as it was when leased, except for normal wear and tear and any destruction by an act of God.

**Traditional Duties of a Landlord.** Landlords have certain traditional obligations that are imposed by law whenever a landlord leases property. One of these obligations is the landlord's **implied warranty of possession.** This means that the tenant will have the right to possess the property for the term of the lease. Suppose Smith rents an apartment from Jones for a term to begin on January 2, 1986, and to end on January 1, 1987. When Smith attempts to move in on January 2, 1986, he finds that Kelly, the previous tenant, is still in possession of the property. In this case, Jones has breached the implied warranty of possession.

By leasing property, the landlord also makes an **implied warranty of quiet enjoyment.** This is a guarantee that the tenant's possession will not be interfered with as a result of any act or omission on the landlord's part. In the absence of a provision in the lease to the contrary, the landlord may not enter the leased property during the term of the lease. If he does, he will be liable for trespass. *Gottdiener v. Mailhot,* a case that appears later in this chapter, presents a situation in which the warranty of quiet enjoyment was breached by the landlord's failure to protect tenants from excessively noisy neighbors.

**Landlord's Responsibility for the Quality of Leased Property.** At common law, a landlord made no implied warranties about the *condition* or *quality* of leased premises. In fact, as an adjunct to the landlord's right to receive the leased property in good condition at the termination of the lease, the *tenant* had the duty to make repairs. Even in situations in which the lease contained an express warranty or an express duty to repair on the landlord's part, a tenant was not entitled to withhold rent if the landlord failed to carry out his obligations. This was because the contract principle that one party is not obligated to perform if the other party fails to perform was not considered to be applicable to leases. In recent years, however, changing concepts of the landlord-tenant relationship have resulted in dramatically increased legal responsibility on the part of landlords for the condition of property leased for residential purposes.

**Constructive Eviction.** One doctrine that courts developed to give relief to a tenant who had lost the value of the leasehold because of the defective condition of leased property was the doctrine of **constructive eviction.** Under this doctrine, if leased property becomes uninhabitable during the term of the lease, the tenant may terminate the lease because the defective condition of the property has effectively evicted him. Constructive eviction gives a tenant the right to vacate the property without obligation to pay further rent if he does so *promptly* after giving the landlord reasonable notice and opportunity to correct the defect. The *Gottdiener* case presents an example of the operation of constructive eviction. Because constructive eviction requires the tenant to move out of the leased premises, it is an unattractive doctrine for tenants who cannot afford to move or who live in an area where there is an acute housing shortage.

**The Implied Warranty of Habitability.** The legal principle that landlords made no implied warranty about the quality of leased property was developed in an era in which tenants bargained primarily for the use of land for agricultural purposes. Any buildings that existed on the property were frequently of secondary importance. Buildings were rather simple structures, lacking modern conveniences such as plumbing and wiring. They were also more easily inspected and repaired by the tenant, who was generally more self-sufficient than the typical tenant is today. Because of the relative simplicity of the structures, the landlord and tenant were considered to have equal knowledge of the condition of the property at the time the property was leased. Thus, a rule requiring the tenant to make repairs was considered reasonable.

The position of modern residential tenants differs greatly from that of the typical agricultural tenant of an earlier era. The typical modern tenant bargains not for the use of the land itself, but rather for the use of a building on the land for dwelling purposes. The structures on land today are much more complex, frequently involving systems (such as plumbing and electrical systems) to which the tenant does not have physical access. This complexity makes it difficult for the tenant to perceive defects during inspection, and even more difficult for the tenant to make repairs, especially since the typical tenant today is far less adept at making repairs than his grandparents might have been. Likewise, placing a duty on tenants to negotiate for express warranties and duties to repair is no longer feasible, because residential leases are frequently executed on standard forms provided by landlords.

For these reasons, statutes or judicial decisions in most states now impose an **implied warranty of habitability** in the lease of property for residential purposes. According to the vast majority of cases, this warranty is applicable only to *residential* property, and not to property leased for commercial uses. The content of the implied warranty of habitability is basically the same in lease situations as it is in sales: the property must be safe and suitable for human habitation. In lease situations, however, the landlord must not only deliver a habitable dwelling at the beginning of the lease but must also *maintain* the property in a habitable condition during the term of the lease. A number of statutes and judicial decisions provide that the warranty requires that leased property comply with any applicable housing codes. From a tenant's point of view, the implied warranty of habitability is superior to constructive eviction, because a tenant does not have to vacate leased premises in order to seek a remedy for breach of warranty. The *Breezewood Management* case, which appears below, is a good example of the implied warranty of habitability.

The precise nature of the remedies for breach of the implied warranty of habitability differs from state to state. Breach of the implied warranty of habitability can render the landlord liable for damages, generally measured by the decrease in the value of the leasehold. It can also be asserted as a defense to nonpayment of rent if the landlord files an action to evict the tenant or sues the tenant for nonpayment of rent. Some states have statutes that permit several types of self-help on the part of tenants, such as the right to have the defect repaired and deduct the cost of repairs from the rent, the right to withhold rent, or the right to pay a reduced rent reflecting the decreased value of the property until it has been placed in habitable condition. An unremedied breach of the implied warranty of habitability that is serious enough to constitute a material breach of the lease can entitle the tenant to cancel the lease.

**Housing Codes.** Many cities and states have enacted housing codes that impose duties on a property owner with respect to the condition of property leased to others. Typical of these provisions is Section 2304 of the District of Columbia Housing Code, which provides: "No person shall rent or offer to rent any habitation or the furnishing thereof unless such habitation and its furnishings are in a clean, safe and sanitary condition, in repair and free from rodents or vermin." Such codes also commonly call for the provision or maintenance of specified minimum space per tenant and specified minimum temperatures in the building, ceiling heights, bathroom and kitchen facilities, and heat, water, and other services. They also usually require that windows, doors, floors, and screens be kept in repair, that keys and locks meet certain specifications, that the property be painted and free of lead paint, and that the landlord issue written receipts for rent payments. A landlord's failure to conform to the housing code may result in the imposition of a fine or liability for injuries that result from disrepair. It may also result in the landlord's losing part or all of his claim to the agreed-upon rent. As you will see in the *Breezewood* case, the violation of an applicable housing code can give rise to or strengthen a tenant's claim that there has been a breach of the implied warranty of habitability. Some housing codes provide that a tenant has the right to withhold rent until the repairs have been made and that the tenant may have the right to move out.

**Security Deposits.** Landlords commonly require their tenants to make security deposits or advance payments of rent. Such deposits operate to protect the landlord's legal right to the reversion of the property in good condition and his right to receive rent. In recent years, many cities and states have enacted statutes or ordinances designed to prevent abuse of security deposits. Some of these laws limit the amount that a landlord can demand and may also require that the landlord place the funds in interest-bearing accounts in leases for more than a minimal amount of time. Such laws also commonly require landlords to account to tenants for such deposits within a specified period of time (30 days, for example) after the termination of the lease. The landlord's failure to comply with these laws may result in the imposition of a penalty prescribed by law.

## Gottdiener v. Mailhot

### 431 A.2d 851 (N.J. Super. Ct. 1981)

In December 1975, Paul and Janet Mailhot leased an apartment in Oakwood Village, a 516-unit apartment complex, from Alexander and Ernest Gottdiener. They later renewed their tenancy through January 31, 1980. The Mailhots experienced no problems with their apartment until the fall of 1978, when new tenants moved into the apartment immediately beneath theirs. On several occasions in December 1978 and January 1979, the Mailhots complained to the Gottdieners of "intolerable noise" coming from the downstairs apartment, such as slamming doors, yelling and screaming children, and excessive volume from the television and radio after 10 P.M. The Gottdieners made some efforts to resolve the conflict, but these efforts were not successful. According to Mr. Mailhot, the neighbors began a campaign of harassment and retaliation. He claimed that someone from the apartment below had maliciously damaged his vehicle. The Mailhots again requested that the Gottdieners take some measures to resolve the situation, but a subsequent meeting proved fruitless. The Mailhots began to look for another place to live. They notified the Gottdieners that they intended to terminate their tenancy as of August 31, 1979. The Gottdieners procured another tenant, effective in December 1979. They then sued the Mailhots for rent for the months of September, October, and November. The trial court found that the Mailhots did not have to pay the rent. The Gottdieners appealed.

**COLE, J.A.D.** The law of landlord and tenant, including that related to constructive eviction, has undergone considerable change in recent years. Where there is a covenant of quiet enjoyment which is breached substantially by a landlord, the doctrine of constructive eviction is available as a remedy for the tenant; and any act or omission of the landlord which renders the premises substantially unsuitable for the purpose for which they are leased, or which seriously interferes with the beneficial enjoyment of the premises, is a breach of that covenant and constitutes a constructive eviction of the tenant.

In *Millbridge Apartments v. Linden,* the court held that constructive eviction could be applied to a situation similar to that before us. There, tenants frequently complained to their landlord that their neighbors were extremely loud. Judge Weinberg stated that:

> Residential tenants expect to live within reasonable boundaries of quiet. Continual noise of a loud nature infringes upon those expectations and makes one's premises substantially unsuitable for the purposes for which they are leased. Accordingly, this court holds that noise may constitute a constructive eviction and legally justify a tenant's vacating.

We agree. We hold that in order to justify early termination of the lease, or for that matter an abatement of rent, the tenant must show that the noise or conduct of a cotenant made the premises substantially unsuitable for ordinary residential living and that it was within the landlord's power to abate the nuisance. The test is objective; the noise or disruptive conduct must be such as truly to render the premises uninhabitable in the eyes of a reasonable person.

Unquestionably, the Gottdieners had the power to correct the problem. A good cause for evicting a residential tenant is that the person has continued to be, after written notice to cease, so disorderly as to destroy the peace and quiet of other tenants.

The Gottdieners further contend that even assuming that they breached the covenant of quiet enjoyment by not abating the noise, the Mailhots waived their right to terminate the lease because they failed to take such action within a reasonable time. What constitutes a reasonable time depends upon the circumstances of each case. In considering the problem, courts must be sympathetic toward the tenant's plight. Adequate evidence supports the conclusion that the Mailhots waited a reasonable time in order to determine whether the Gottdieners would solve the problem, and left only after it was apparent that the Gottdieners would not take any further measures. There was thus no waiver of their right to terminate the lease.

Judgment for the Mailhots affirmed.

## Breezewood Management Company v. Maltbie

**411 N.E.2d 670 (Ind. Ct. App. 1980)**

On August 2, 1978, Dan Maltbie and John Burke, students at Indiana University, entered into a one-year written lease with Breezewood Management Company for the rental of an apartment in an older house in Bloomington, Indiana. The agreed rent was $235 per month. When Burke and Maltbie moved in, they discovered numerous defects: rotting porch floorboards, broken and loose windows, an inoperable front door lock, leaks in the plumbing, a back door that would not close, a missing bathroom door, inadequate water pressure, falling plaster, exposed wiring over the bathtub, and a malfunctioning toilet. Later, they discovered a leaking roof, cockroach infestation, the absence of heat and hot water, more leaks in the plumbing, and pigeons in the attic.

The city of Bloomington had a minimum housing code in effect at that time. Code enforcement officers inspected the apartment and found over 50 violations, 11 of which were "life-safety" violations, defined as conditions that might be severely "hazardous to health of the occupant." These conditions remained largely uncorrected after notice by the code officers and further complaints by Burke and Maltbie.

On May 3, 1979, Maltbie vacated the apartment, notified Breezewood, and refused to pay any further rent. Breezewood agreed to let Burke remain and pay $112.50 per month. Breezewood then filed suit against Burke and Maltbie for $610.75, which was the balance due under the written rental contract plus certain charges. Burke and Maltbie each filed counterclaims against Breezewood, claiming damages and abatement of the rent for breach of the implied warranty of habitability. At trial, Burke and Maltbie presented evidence showing that the reasonable rental value of the apartment in its defective condition was only $50 per month during colder weather and $75 per month during warmer weather. The trial court entered judgment against Breezewood on its claim and awarded Burke and Maltbie a total of $1,030 in damages on their counterclaims. Breezewood appealed.

**ROBERTSON, PRESIDING JUDGE.** Over time, many exceptions have eroded the common law doctrine of *caveat lessee*. In most circumstances, the modern tenant lacks the skill and "know-how" to inspect and repair housing to determine if it is fit for its particular purpose. In *Boston Housing Authority v. Hemingway,* the court treated the lease agreement as a contract in which the landlord promised to deliver premises suitable to the tenant's purpose in return for the tenant's promise to pay rent. In *Javins v. First National Realty Corporation,* the United States Court of Appeals for the District of Columbia found an implied warranty of habitability in the lease agreement, the minimum habitability standards being established by the Housing Regulations for the District of Columbia. The court stated that landlord tenant law should be governed by the same implied warranty of fitness which covers a sale of goods under the Uniform Commercial Code. The court said:

> In the case of the modern apartment dweller, the value of the lease is that it gives him a place to live. The city dweller who seeks to lease an apartment on the third floor of a tenement has little interest in the land 30 or 40 feet below, or even in the bare right to possession within the four walls of his apartment. When American city dwellers seek shelter today, they seek a well known package of goods and services—a package which includes not merely walls and ceilings, but also adequate heat, light, and ventilation, serviceable plumbing facilities, secure windows and doors, proper sanitation, and proper maintenance.

In the case at bar, the Bloomington Housing Code was in effect at the time of the lease agreement, and, by law, was incorporated into it. Burke and Maltbie had a reasonable expectation that their basic housing needs would be met: heating, plumbing, electricity, and structural integrity of the premises. For the reasons that a housing code was in effect and the premises violated many of its provisions, we hold that Breezewood breached an implied warranty of habitability.

Judgment for Burke and Maltbie affirmed.

---

**Landlord's Tort Liability.** The traditional rule that a landlord had no legal responsibility for the condition of leased property had two effects. The first has already been discussed: the uninhabitability of the premises traditionally did not give a tenant the right to withhold rent, assert a defense to nonpayment, or terminate a lease. The second effect was that, subject to a few exceptions, a landlord was not liable in tort for injuries suffered on leased property. This rule was based on the idea that the tenant had the ability and responsibility to inspect the property for defects before leasing it. By leasing the property, the tenant was presumed to take it as it was, with any existing defects. As to any defects that might arise during the term of the lease, the landlord's immunity was justified by the fact that he had no control over the leased property, because he had surrendered it to the tenant.

Courts have created a number of exceptions to this no-liability rule, however. One of those exceptions is that the landlord has a duty to use reasonable care to *maintain the common areas* (such as stairways, parking lots, and elevators) of which the landlord retains control. If a tenant or a tenant's guest is injured by the landlord's negligent maintenance of a common area, the landlord can be held liable. A second exception is that landlords have the duty to *disclose hidden defects that they know about if the defects are not reasonably discoverable by the tenant.* A third exception is that if a landlord repairs leased property, he has the duty to *exercise reasonable care in making the repairs.* The landlord can be liable for the consequences of negligently made repairs, even though he was not obligated to make them. A fourth exception is that the landlord has a duty to maintain property that is leased for *admission to the public.* A final exception is that the landlord who rents a *fully furnished dwelling for a short time* impliedly warrants that the premises are safe and habitable. Except for these circumstances, the landlord was not liable for injuries suffered by the tenant on leased property. Note that none of these exceptions would apply to what is one of the most common occasions for injury: when the tenant is injured by a defect in his own apartment and the defect is caused by the landlord's failure to repair rather than by negligently done repairs.

Currently, there is a strong trend toward abolishing the traditional rule of landlord tort immunity. The proliferation of housing codes and the development of the implied warranty of habitability have persuaded a sizable number of courts to impose on landlords the duty to use *reasonable care* in their maintenance of the leased property. As we have discussed, a landlord's duty to keep the property in repair may be based on an express clause in the lease, the implied warranty of habitability, or provisions of a housing code or statute. Given the duty to make repairs, the landlord can be liable if injury results from his negligent failure to carry out his duty regarding the condition of the property. As a general rule, a landlord will not be liable unless he had *notice* of the defect and a reasonable opportunity to repair it. *Stephens v. Stearns,* which follows, is an example of a case that adopts the modern trend in landlord tort liability.

**Protection of Tenants against Criminal Conduct.** One aspect of the overall trend toward increasing the legal accountability of landlords is that courts have imposed on landlords the duty to protect tenants from foreseeable criminal conduct. Landlords have been found liable for injuries sustained by tenants when the landlords failed to maintain sufficient security control over access to an apartment building or failed to provide sufficient lighting outside a building in a high-crime area. Some states have held that the implied warranty of habitability includes the obligation to provide reasonable security. While the landlord is not an insurer of tenants' safety, he must take reasonable precautions to provide proper locks and lighting. For larger buildings or buildings in high-crime areas, security guards or alarm systems may be required.

## Stephens v. Stearns

### 678 P.2d 41 (Idaho Sup. Ct. 1984)

Mildred Stephens leased a town house in a Boise apartment complex from Thornton Stearns. The town house had two separate floors connected by an internal stairway. One night, Stephens was descending the internal stairway in her town house when she slipped or fell forward at the top of the stairs. She "grabbed" in order to catch herself, but was unable to do so, and fell down the stairs. She suffered serious injury. The stairway was not equipped with a handrail, although handrails were required by a Boise ordinance. Stephens filed suit against Stearns. The trial court directed a verdict for Stearns, and Stephens appealed.

**Donaldson, Chief Justice.** Under the common-law rule, a landlord is generally not liable to the tenant for any damage resulting from dangerous conditions existing at the time of the leasing. However, there are a number of exceptions to the general rule. Rather than attempt to squeeze the facts of this case into one of the common-law exceptions, Stephens has brought to our attention the modern trend of the law in this area. Under the modern trend, landlords are simply under a duty to exercise reasonable care under the circumstances. The Tennessee Supreme Court had the foresight to grasp this concept many years ago when it stated: "The ground of liability upon the part of a landlord when he demises dangerous property has nothing to do with the relation of landlord and tenant. It is the ordinary case of liability for personal misfeasance, which runs through all the relations of individuals to each other." Seventy-five years later, the Supreme Court of New Hampshire followed in *Sargent v. Ross*. The *Sargent* court abrogated the common-law rule and its exceptions, and adopted the reasonable care standard by stating:

> Henceforth, landlords as other persons must exercise reasonable care not to subject others to an unreasonable risk of harm. . . . A landlord must act as a reasonable person under all of the circumstances including the likelihood of injury to others, the probable seriousness of such injuries, and the burden of reducing or avoiding the risk.

Tennessee and New Hampshire are not alone in adopting this rule. As of this date, several other states have also judicially adopted a reasonable care standard for landlords. After examining both the common-law rule and the modern trend, we today decide to leave the common-law rule and its exceptions behind, and we adopt the rule that a landlord is under a duty to exercise reasonable care in light of all the circumstances.

We stress that adoption of this rule is not tantamount to making the landlord an insurer for all injury occurring on the premises, but merely constitutes our removal of the landlord's common-law cloak of immunity. Those questions of hidden danger, public use, control, and duty to repair, which under the common law were prerequisites to the consideration of the landlord's negligence, will now be relevant only inasmuch as they pertain to the elements of negligence, such as foreseeability and unreasonableness of the risk. We hold that Stearns did owe a duty to Stephens to exercise reasonable care in light of all the circumstances, and that it is for a jury to decide whether that duty was breached. Therefore, we reverse the directed verdict in favor of Stearns and remand for a new trial.

Judgment reversed in favor of Stephens.

## RIGHTS, DUTIES, AND LIABILITIES OF THE TENANT

**Rights of the Tenant.** The tenant has the right to *exclusive possession* and *quiet enjoyment* of the property during the term of the lease. The landlord does not have the right to enter the leased property without the tenant's consent, unless he is acting under an express provision of the lease that gives him the right to enter. The tenant may use the leased property for any lawful purpose that is reasonable and appropriate, unless the purpose for which it may be used is expressly limited in the lease. Furthermore, the tenant now has the right to receive leased residential property in a habitable condition at the beginning of the lease and the right to have it maintained in a habitable condition throughout the lease.

**Duties of the Tenant.** The tenant has the duty to *pay rent* in the agreed amount and at the agreed times. The tenant also has the duty not to commit **waste** on the property. This means that the tenant is responsible for the care and upkeep of the property and that he has the duty not to do any act that would harm the property. In the past, the fulfillment of this duty required that the tenant perform ordinary repairs. Today, the duty to make repairs has generally been shifted to the landlord by court ruling, statute, or lease provision. The tenant now has no duty to make major repairs unless the damage has been caused by his own negligence. When damage exists through no fault of the tenant, the tenant still has the duty to take steps to prevent further damage from the elements, as when a window breaks or a roof leaks.

**Assignment and Subleasing.** As is true of most other types of contracts, the rights and duties under a lease can generally be assigned and delegated to third parties. **Assignment** occurs when the landlord or the tenant transfers all of his remaining rights under the lease to another person. For example, a landlord may sell an apartment building to another person and assign the leases to the buyer, who will then become the new landlord. A tenant may assign the remainder of his lease to someone else, who then acquires whatever rights the tenant had under the lease (including, of course, the right to exclusive possession of the leased premises). **Subleasing** occurs when the tenant transfers to a third person some but not all of his remaining right to possess the property under the lease. The relationship of tenant to sublessee becomes that of landlord and tenant. For example, Smith, a college student whose two-year lease on an apartment is to terminate on May 1, 1986, sublets his apartment to Jones for the summer months of 1985. This is a sublease because Smith has not transferred all of his remaining rights under the lease.

The significance of the distinction between an assignment and a sublease is that a sublessee does not acquire rights or duties under the lease between the landlord and tenant, whereas an assignee does. An assignee steps into the shoes of the original tenant and acquires any rights that he had under the lease. For example, if the lease contained an option to renew, the assignee tenant would have the right to exercise this option if he desired to do so. The assignee is also personally liable to the landlord for the payment of rent.

In both an assignment and a sublease, the tenant remains liable to the landlord for the commitments made in the lease. If the assignee or sublessee fails to pay rent, for example, the tenant has the legal obligation to pay it.

Leases commonly contain limitations on assignment and subleasing. Leases often require the landlord's consent to any assignment, and provide that such consent shall not be withheld unreasonably. Total prohibitions against assignment are disfavored in the law and are either construed narrowly or considered void as against public policy.

**Tenant's Liability for Injuries to Third Persons.** The tenant is normally liable to persons who suffer physical injury or property damage on the part of the property over which the tenant has control, if the injuries are caused by his negligence.

## TERMINATION OF THE LEASEHOLD

Normally, a leasehold is terminated by the expiration of the term, at which time the tenant *surrenders* the property and the landlord accepts it back. Sometimes, however, the lease terminates early because of a breach of the lease by one of the parties.

**Eviction.** If a tenant breaches the lease (most commonly, by nonpayment of rent), the landlord may take action to *evict* the tenant. State statutes usually provide for a relatively speedy procedure for eviction. The landlord who desires to evict a tenant must be careful to comply with any applicable state or city regulations governing evictions. Such regulations may forbid forcible entry to change locks or other self-help measures taken by the landlord. At common law, a landlord had a lien on the tenant's personal property, which entitled him to remove and hold such property as security for the rent. This lien has been abolished in many states. Where the lien still exists, it is subject to constitutional limitations that require that the tenant be given notice of the lien and an opportunity to defend and protect his belongings before they can be sold to satisfy it.

**Abandonment.** If a tenant abandons the leased property before the expiration of the lease, he is making an offer to surrender the leasehold. If the landlord accepts this surrender, he relieves the tenant of the obligation to pay rent for the remaining period of the lease. If the landlord does not accept the surrender, he can sue the tenant for the rent due until such time as he rerents the property, or if he cannot find a new tenant, for the rent due for the remainder of the term.

At common law, the landlord had no obligation to mitigate (decrease) the damages caused by the abandonment by attempting to rerent the leased property. In fact, taking possession of the property for the purpose of trying to rent it to someone else was a risky move for the landlord: his retaking of possession might be construed as acceptance of the surrender. Many states now place the duty on the landlord to attempt to mitigate damages by making a reasonable effort to rerent the property. These states also hold that the landlord's retaking of possession for the purpose of rerenting does not constitute a waiver of his right to pursue an action to collect unpaid rent.

## SUMMARY

Real property includes not only land but also things that are firmly attached to it or embedded under it. Fixtures are personal property that, by its attachment or association with land, is regarded as real property. In determining whether articles shall be considered fixtures, courts consider the intent of the party who annexed the articles, the manner in which the articles are annexed or attached to the property, and the degree to which the articles are necessary or beneficial to the use of the property. Fixtures become part of real property and are conveyed along with a conveyance of the property to which they are attached. An exception to this rule is made in the case of fixtures attached by a tenant for the purpose of carrying on a trade or business. Trade fixtures can be removed by the tenant, provided that she does so by the time the lease expires and provided that removal does not cause substantial harm to the leased property.

There are a variety of ownership interests in real property. The basic form of ownership is fee simple absolute. Another common form of ownership is the life estate. Seven types of co-ownership of real property are recognized: (1) tenancy in common, (2) joint tenancy, (3) tenancy by the entirety, (4) community property, (5) tenancy in partnership, (6) condominiums, and (7) cooperatives. Interests in land owned by others include easements, licenses, and restrictive covenants.

Real property may be acquired in a number of ways. The formal requirements for the transfer of real property are determined by the statutes of the state in which it is located. The most common way of acquiring real property is by purchase. Real property may also be acquired by gift. To have a valid gift, the donor must deliver to the donee or to some third person for the benefit of the donee, a deed that complies with the statutory requirements of the given state. A person may also acquire real property through adverse possession. Adverse possession requires that a person possess property openly, exclusively, continuously, and adversely for the statutory period. In addition, some states require that the adverse possessor pay taxes on the property. Real property may also be acquired at a tax sale. Under the laws of most states, the government can have property sold to collect unpaid taxes. The purchaser at the tax sale will be given a tax deed that, if valid, cuts off prior claims to the real property.

Any agreement affecting an interest in land and a conveyance of real property is required to be in writing. Two forms of deeds are in general use in the United States: the quitclaim deed and the warranty deed. In a quitclaim deed, the grantor conveys his interest in the property, whatever that interest may be. The quitclaim deed does not represent that the grantor has good title, or any title at all. In the warranty deed, on the other hand, the grantor conveys his interest and, in addition, warrants the title to be free from all defects except those stated in the deed. To be valid, a deed must comply with certain formal requirements. These requirements are not uniform, but as a general rule the deed must name the grantee, contain words of conveyance, describe the property, and be executed by the grantor.

In recent years, most states have imposed on builder-vendors of residential property an implied warranty of habitability, which is an implied guarantee that the property will be safe and suitable for human habitation. A number of courts have extended this warranty to subsequent purchasers of residential property.

There are three means by which a buyer of real property can attempt to get assurance of the seller's title: have a lawyer examine an abstract of title and render a title opinion; register the property and obtain a certificate of title through the Torrens system (which is in use in some states); or purchase a title insurance policy.

Society places a number of restraints on the ownership of real property. First, a person may not create or contribute to a nuisance on property that unreasonably interferes with another person's enjoyment of his own land. Second, legislative bodies have the police power to regulate health, safety, and welfare, which they may use to impose reasonable restrictions on the use of real property, as is done in zoning ordinances. Third, the government may acquire ownership of property for public use through the power of eminent domain. This requires that the government pay the owner just compensation for the property.

The law regarding the relationship of landlord and tenant has changed dramatically in recent years. A lease is a contract whereby an owner of property conveys to a tenant the exclusive right to possess the leased property for a period of time. There are four types of tenancies or leasehold interests: tenancy for a term, periodic tenancy, tenancy at will, and tenancy at sufferance. A lease must be evidenced by a writing under the statute of frauds of most states if it is for a term of one year or more; in a few states, only leases for three years or more are within the statute of frauds. The particular rights, duties, and liabilities of landlords and tenants are determined by express provisions of the lease, common law, and statute or ordinance.

The landlord is entitled to receive the agreed rent and has the right to have the premises returned to him at the end of the lease in as good condition as they were in when leased, except for normal wear and tear. When leasing property, the landlord makes an implied warranty that the tenant will be put in possession at the beginning of the lease and an implied warranty of quiet enjoyment, which guarantees that the landlord will not do anything to interfere with the tenant's possession during the term of the lease.

While under traditional law the landlord did not warrant the condition of the premises, there is now a strong trend toward increasing the legal responsibility of landlords for the quality of leased residential property. If an act or omission of the landlord causes a substantial defect in leased property that renders it uninhabitable, the doctrine of constructive eviction gives the tenant the right to vacate the property without liability for further rent if he does so promptly after giving the landlord reasonable notice and opportunity to repair the defect.

The law of most states now provides that the landlord makes an implied warranty of habitability whenever he leases property for residential use. This warranty guarantees that the property will be safe and suitable for human habitation. In many states, it guarantees that the property will comply with any applicable housing code. Housing codes are prevalent now. They commonly impose duties to repair on landlords and set out various requirements concerning the condition of leased property and such rental practices as the handling of security deposits.

Traditionally, landlords were not liable for injuries suffered by tenants or their visitors on leased property unless the case fell within a number of exceptions that had been created by courts. Now, however, there is a trend toward abolishing the tort immunity of landlords and holding them to a duty of reasonable care toward tenants and others who are lawfully on leased property.

The tenant has the right to quiet possession of the leased property and the right to use it for any lawful purpose, unless the lease limits the purposes for which the property may be used. The tenant has the obligation to pay the agreed rent and to refrain from committing acts that would damage the property. The tenant can be liable if his negligence causes damage to leased property or damage to third persons on the leased property under his control.

Leases can generally be assigned or subleased unless some provision of the lease limits those rights. Total prohibitions of assignments are disfavored and are construed narrowly or considered to be against public policy. When a tenant assigns or subleases property, he remains liable for all of his obligations under the lease, including the obligation to pay rent if the assignee or sublessee fails to pay.

Normally, a lease is terminated by the tenant's surrender of the leased premises at the end of the agreed lease term. The landlord may terminate the lease early by evicting the tenant if the tenant defaults in some obligation under the lease. If a tenant abandons the property prior to the end of the lease, he may be subject to liability for unpaid rent. Many states now place the duty on the landlord to make a reasonable effort to rerent the property in order to mitigate damages caused by a tenant's default.

## PROBLEM CASES

**1.** Kelm leased his building to Timper. The first floor of the building had always been used as a tavern. When Timper originally leased the building, an old-fashioned bar was situated against one of the walls. Without Kelm's knowledge or consent, Timper removed this old bar and installed a new 60-foot circular bar in the center of the tavern. The bar, which was worth about $2,000, was installed in such a way that its removal would leave 12 holes in the floor, varying in diameter from 1 to 6 inches. The holes were made so that the bar could have the necessary electrical, water, and sewage facilities and so that beer could be piped from the basement. A bottle chute had also been installed. Is Kelm entitled to keep the bar?

**2.** Strickland bought a 30,000-gallon aeration sewage treatment plant for his restaurant. To finance the purchase of the sewage treatment plant, he entered into a security agreement with Kingsley Bank, designating the plant as collateral. The plant was installed on a lot across from the restaurant in a concrete trench approximately 4 feet deep. It was connected to the restaurant by a series of pipes. Nevertheless, there was evidence that the plant was relatively portable. When Strickland failed to make several payments, the bank sought to repossess the plant. Strickland argued that the bank could not repossess the plant, because it had become a fixture on the property. Should the bank be able to repossess the sewage treatment plant?

**3.** Yancy rented a building to Roberts, who operated a restaurant on the first floor and converted the second floor into apartments. The lease contained a provision permitting Roberts to remove from the second floor any fixtures he attached, provided that such removal did not injure the real estate. Shortly before the lease was to expire, Roberts began to remove property from the building and to move it to a new location. He removed booths, stools, sinks, dishwashers, refrigerators, and other items of equipment used in his restaurant business. He also took various lighting fixtures, paneling, and Sheetrock from the walls and canopies and false ceilings from over the booths. The lighting fixtures were replacements for the ones in the premises when Roberts took possession. The paneling was nailed to wooden strips nailed to Sheetrock and in turn to the wooden walls. The false ceilings were made of two-by-fours nailed to the walls and covered by paneling and Celotex. On the second floor, Roberts was preparing to take plumbing fixtures, hot water heaters, shower stalls, commodes, lighting fixtures, the heating system, and other items that he had installed, when Yancy filed a lawsuit seeking damages for injury to the property and an injunction preventing Roberts from removing "permanent improvements" from the property. Which of these items of property was Roberts entitled to take, and which did he have to leave when he vacated the property?

**4.** The Carters purchased two lots in a subdivision. Each lot in the subdivision had a restriction in the deed that prohibited the use of house trailers on the lots, except for a period of up to 90 days during the time that a house was being constructed on a lot. The Carters moved a trailer onto one of the lots. They removed the tongue and wheels and set the trailer up on concrete blocks. They also connected the trailer to a septic tank and attached power and water lines. A number of the neighbors brought suit to enforce the deed restriction. The Carters claimed that the restriction did not apply, because their home was no longer a trailer. What should the result be?

**5.** Kourlias, age 75, offered his home for sale. The asking price was $15,000. Hawkins offered Kourlias $10,000 plus the use of an upstairs room and kitchen privileges in the property "free of charge for as long as Kourlias lives or cares to stay there." Kourlias accepted the offer. Hawkins was given a deed granting him a fee simple interest but reserving Kourlias' continued interest in the property. What kind of legal interest does Kourlias have in the property?

**6.** Wornom owned a tract of land. In 1928, Wornom subdivided the tract. In 1934, Wornom graded and opened an alleyway extending along the southern and eastern boundaries of the tract. The alley runs behind Lot 3 and across Lots 1 and 2. Wornom conveyed Lot 3 to his daughter, Marion Proctor. In his will, Wornom left Lot 2 to his son Percy. In 1978, after Percy's death, Martin acquired Lot 2 from Percy's widow. Wornom used the alley for 21 years prior to his death. Wornom, Percy, and Marion's husband (Proctor) maintained the roadbed for their own use and that of visiting family members. The alley was also used for vehicular and pedestrian travel. Proctor had used the alley daily since its creation in 1934. Although he had not received express permission to do so, he had never encountered hindrance from his father-in-law or any of the owners of Lot 2 until 1978, when Martin erected a fence across the alley, where he planned to install a swimming pool. Has Proctor acquired an easement by prescription that entitles him to use the alleyway across Lot 2?

**7.** Sewell and Reilly owned adjoining lots. They entered into a written agreement whereby each agreed to allow the other to use the south 10 feet of his lot for alley purposes "for so long as the alley" over the other party's lot remained open. What interest did this agreement create?

**8.** Major developed a subdivision in which he built a number of houses and offered them for sale. The Rozells bought a house from Major. Upon the first rain, water entered under the crawl space of the house and accumulated to a depth of 17½ inches in a room in which the furnace and hot water heater were located, frequently putting out the hot water heater. Major's attempts to keep the water out were unsuccessful. Water continued to accumulate in the room every time there was a rainfall of any consequence. As a result, the house was damp and had a peculiar odor and things mildewed. Do the Rozells have a cause of action against Major?

**9.** The opening and a considerable portion of the cavity of Marengo Cave were located on land owned by the Marengo Cave Company. From 1883, when the cave was discovered, until 1932, the Cave Company and its predecessors in title exercised complete control over the entire cave, charging a fee for admission to others who wished to view it and making improvements in the cave. In 1908, Ross bought land adjoining the Marengo Cave Company land. In 1932, a survey showed that part of the cave lay under Ross's land. Marengo Cave Company claims adverse possession of the part of the cave that extends under Ross's land. Are the elements of adverse possession met here?

**10.** In 1956, the predecessor of Spur Industries began operating a small cattle-feeding operation of 6,000–7,000 head of cattle in an area that included about 25 cattle pens in a 7-mile radius. The feedlot was located about 1½ miles from Youngstown, Arizona, a retirement community. In 1959, Del Webb Development Company acquired 20,000 acres nearby, about half of which was located between Youngstown and the feedlot, and began to build Sun City, a retirement community. In 1960, Spur Industries acquired the feedlot and began expanding the acreage and the number of cattle served. By 1967, it was feeding 20,000–30,000 cattle. Sun City residents were bothered by the bad odor and flies that resulted from the operation of the feedlot. There was considerable sales resistance to the 1,300 apartments in the area closest to the feedlot. Del Webb brought suit against Spur, seeking an injunction on the ground of nuisance. Should its action be successful?

**11.** Garwacki and Mastello shared a second-story apartment, which Garwacki rented from LaFraneire. Mastello invited Young to attend a dinner party at the apartment. Young went to the porch of the apartment to call down to Mastello, who was in the driveway below. As she placed her hands on the porch railing and leaned forward, the railing gave way. Young fell to the ground and was injured. The porch is accessible only from the living room of the apartment, and it is not a common area shared with other tenants. Should LaFraneire be liable for Young's injuries?

**12.** Coombs rented an apartment from Birkenhead. Prior to the tenancy, Birkenhead promised to provide heat and all necessary repairs. When Coombs moved into the apartment, she discovered that the toilet and shower were not working properly. She requested that Birkenhead repair the toilet, but Birkenhead did not respond to her request, leaving Coombs with the task of manually emptying the toilet after each use. The situation persisted for a month, until Coombs hired a local plumber to fix the toilet and shower. With Birkenhead's permission, she paid the bill herself and deducted the amount from her next month's rent. Thereafter, the relationship between Coombs and Birkenhead began to deteriorate. On separate occasions, Birkenhead disconnected Coombs's heat, hot water, and electricity. They removed her kitchen stove and repeatedly threatened to board up the premises and kick out Coombs and her child. Coombs continued to pay the rent, less the cost of repairing and restoring the disrupted services. After Coombs had lived in the apartment for approximately four months, Birkenhead brought suit to eject her for failing to pay all of the agreed rent. Coombs counterclaimed for damages for breach of the implied warranty of habitability and intentional infliction of emotional distress. What are the parties' respective rights and liabilities?

**13.** Cain rented an apartment from Vontz. There had been a break-in at Cain's apartment, which resulted in the destruction of the locking devices on her door. Vontz agreed to repair the door and replace the locks, but failed to do so. One night, while Cain slept, someone entered her apartment and shot her twice in the head, killing her. Her mother brought suit against Vontz. Should he be held liable for damages caused by the criminal conduct of some unknown third person?

**14.** On October 1, Zankman entered into a two-year lease with Landlord for the rental of an apartment that he intended to use not only as a residence but also as a place to make and receive business calls and to conduct business correspondence. The lease was executed both in Zankman's name and in the name of New Jersey Steel Products. Zankman paid his October and November rent, but he notified the landlord on December 1 that he would be late with his December payment. On December 29, he received a telegram advising him that unless his rent were paid by 11 A.M. his apartment would be padlocked the next day. On December 30, Zankman left his apartment briefly. When he returned, he found that his apartment had been padlocked. He was not allowed to remove his belongings until January 8. A New Jersey statute provides that "with regard to any property occupied solely as a residence by the party in possession, entry shall not be made in any manner without the consent of the party in possession unless the entry and detention is made pursuant to legal process." Zankman claims that the entry to his apartment to padlock it was unlawful. What conclusion would a court reach?

**15.** Landlord leased a supper club known as Mr. Porterhouse to Sabella for a term of 36 months. The lease obligated Landlord to provide heating and cooling. The heating and cooling system in the lounge and bar portion of the supper club did not work adequately. Despite notice and opportunity to correct it, the problem was never corrected. Nine months into the lease, Sabella moved out, claiming constructive eviction. Is Sabella entitled to terminate the lease under these circumstances?

**16.** Kridel entered into a lease with Sommer, owner of the Pierre Apartments, to lease apartment 6–L for two years. Kridel, who was to be married in June, planned to move into the apartment in May. His parents and future parents-in-law had agreed to assume responsibility for the rent, since Kridel was a full-time student who had no funds of his own. Shortly before Kridel was to have moved in, his engagement was broken. He wrote Sommer a letter explaining his situation and stating that he could not take the apartment. Sommer did not answer the letter, and when a third person inquired about renting apartment 6–L, the person in charge told her that the apartment was already rented to Kridel. Sommer did not enter the apartment or show it to anyone until he rented apartment 6–L to someone else when there were approximately eight months left on Kridel's lease. He sued Kridel for the full rent for the period of approximately 16 months before the new tenant's lease took effect. Kridel argued that Sommer should not be able to collect rent for the first 16 months of the lease, because he did not take reasonable steps to rerent the apartment. Should Sommer be able to collect the 16 months' rent?

# Chapter 30 Estates and Trusts

## INTRODUCTION

One of the basic features of the ownership of property is the right to dispose of the property during life and at death. You have already learned about the ways in which property is transferred during the owner's life. The owner's death is another major event for the transfer of property. Most people want to be able to choose who will get their property when they die. There are a variety of ways in which a person may control the ultimate disposition of his property. He may take title to the property in a form of joint ownership that gives his co-owner a right of survivorship. He may create a trust and transfer property to it to be used for the benefit of a spouse, child, elderly parent, or other beneficiary. He may execute a will in which he directs that his real and personal property be distributed to persons named in the will. If, however, a person makes no provision for the disposition of his property at his death, his property will be distributed to his heirs as defined by state law. This chapter focuses on the transfer of property at death and on the use of trusts for the transfer and management of property, both during life and at death.

## WILLS

**Right of Disposition by Will.** The right to control the disposition of property at death has not always existed. In the English feudal system, the king owned all land. The lords and knights had only the right to use land for their lifetime. A landholder's rights in land terminated upon his death, and no rights descended to his heirs. In 1215, the king granted the nobility the right to pass their interest in the land they held to their heirs. Later, that right was extended to all property owners. In the United States, each state has enacted statutes that establish the requirements for a valid will, including the formalities that must be met to pass property by will.

**Nature of a Will.** A **will** is a document executed with specific legal formalities by a **testator** (person making a will) that contains his instructions about the way his property will be disposed of at his death. A will can dispose only of property belonging to the testator at the time of his death. Furthermore, wills do not control property that goes to others through other planning devices (such as life insurance policies) or by operation of law (such as by right of survivorship). For example, property held in joint tenancy or tenancy by the entirety is not controlled by a will, because the property passes automatically to the surviving cotenant by right of survivorship. In addition, life insurance proceeds are controlled by the insured's designation of beneficiaries, not by any provision of a will. (Because joint tenancy and life insurance are ways of directing the disposition of property, they are sometimes referred to as "will substitutes.")

**Testamentary Capacity.** The capacity to make a valid will is called **testamentary capacity.** To have testamentary capacity, a person must be *of sound mind* and *of legal age.* This does not mean that a person must be in perfect mental health to have testamentary capacity. Because people often delay executing wills until they are weak and in ill health, the standard for mental capacity to make a will is fairly low. To be of "sound mind," a person need only be sufficiently rational to be capable of understanding the nature and character of his property, of realizing that he is making a will, and of knowing the persons who would normally be the beneficiaries of his affection.

Lack of testamentary capacity is a common ground upon which wills are challenged by persons who were excluded from a will. Fraud and undue influence are also common grounds for challenging the validity of a will. The *Prigge* case, which follows, is a good example of a will contest based on lack of testamentary capacity and undue influence.

**Execution of a Will.** Unless a will is executed with the formalities required by state law, it is *void.* The courts are strict in interpreting statutes concerning the execution of wills. If a will is declared void, the property of the deceased person will be distributed according to the provisions of state laws that will be discussed later.

The formalities required for a valid will differ from state to state. For that reason, an individual should consult the laws of his state before making a will. If he should move to another state after having executed a will, he should consult a lawyer in his new state to determine whether a new will needs to be executed. Most states require that a will be *in writing,* that it be *witnessed* by two or three *disinterested* witnesses (persons who do not stand to inherit any property under the will), and that it be *signed* by the testator or by someone else at the testator's direction. Most states also require that the testator *publish* the will, that is, declare or indicate at the time of signing that the instrument is his will.

Another formality required by most states is that the testator sign the will in the presence and the sight of the witnesses and that the witnesses sign in the presence and the sight of each other. As a general rule, an **attestation clause,** which states the formalities that have been followed in the execution of the will, is written following the testator's signature. These detailed formalities are designed to prevent fraud. The *Hall* case, which follows, involves an analysis of the sufficiency of the execution of a will.

Some states recognize certain types of wills that are not executed with these formalities. These informal wills are discussed below.

**Holographic Wills.** **Holographic wills** are wills that are entirely written and signed in the testator's handwriting. They are recognized in about half of the states, even though they are not executed with the formalities usually required of valid wills. For a holographic will to be valid in the states that recognize them, it must evidence testamentary intent and must be actually *handwritten* by the testator. A typed holographic will would be invalid. Some states also require that the will be dated.

**Nuncupative Wills.** A **nuncupative** will is an oral will. Such wills are recognized as valid in some states, but only under limited circumstances and to a limited extent. In a number of states, for example, nuncupative wills are valid only when made by soldiers in military service and sailors at sea, and even then they will be effective only to dispose of personal property that was in the actual possession of the person at the time the oral will was made. Other states place low dollar limits on the amount of property that can be passed by a nuncupative will.

**Limitations on Disposition by Will.** A person who takes property by will takes it subject to all outstanding claims against the property. For example, if real property is subject to a mortgage or other lien, the beneficiary who takes the property gets it subject to the mortgage or lien. In addition, the rights of the testator's creditors are superior to the rights of beneficiaries under his will. Thus, if the testator was insolvent (his debts exceeded his assets), persons named as beneficiaries do not receive any property by virtue of the will.

Under the laws of most states, the surviving spouse of the testator has statutory rights in property owned solely by the testator that cannot be defeated by a contrary will provision. This means that a husband cannot effectively disinherit his wife, and vice versa. As a general rule, a surviving spouse is given the right to claim certain personal property of the deceased spouse. She is also given the right to use the family home for a stated period, usually a year, as well as a portion of the deceased spouse's real estate or a life estate in a portion of his real estate. At common law, a widow had the right to a life estate in one third of the lands owned by her husband during their marriage. This was known as a widow's **dower right.** A similar right for a widower was known as **curtesy.** A number of states have changed the right by statute to give a surviving spouse a one-third interest in fee simple in the real and personal property owned by the deceased spouse at the time of his or her death. Naturally, a testator can leave his spouse more than this if he desires. In community property states, each spouse has a one-half interest in community property that cannot be defeated by a contrary will provision. (Note that the surviving spouse will obtain *full* ownership of any property owned by the testator and the surviving spouse as joint tenants or tenants by the entirety.)

**Revocation of Wills.** One important feature of a will is that it is *revocable* until the moment of the testator's death. For this reason, a will confers *no present interest* in the testator's property.

A person is free to revoke a prior will and, if she wishes, to make a new will. Wills can be revoked in a variety of ways. Physical destruction and mutilation done with intent to revoke a will constitute revocation, as do other acts such as crossing out the will or creating a writing that expressly cancels the will. In addition, a will is revoked if the testator later executes a valid will that expressly revokes the earlier will. A later will that does not *expressly* revoke an earlier will operates to revoke only those portions of the earlier will that are inconsistent with the later will.

State statutes provide that certain changes in relationships operate as revocations of a will. In some states, marriage will operate to revoke a will that was made when the testator was single. Similarly, a divorce may revoke provisions in a will made during marriage that leave property to the divorced spouse. Under the laws of some states, the birth of a child after the execution of a will may operate as a partial revocation of the will.

**Codicils.** A **codicil** is an amendment of a will. If a person wants to change a provision of a will without making an entirely new will, she may amend the will by executing a codicil. One may *not* amend a will by merely striking out objectionable provisions and inserting new provisions. The same formalities are required for the creation of a valid codicil as for the creation of a valid will.

## In the Matter of Estate of Prigge

**352 N.W.2d 443 (Minn. Ct. App. 1984)**

John Prigge died in 1982, survived by two sisters, Marian and Jean; one brother, Louis; and some nephews and nieces. John had never married and had been a farmer all his life. In 1980, he sold his farm and moved in with his sister Marian. While John was living with her, Marian, at John's request, prepared a handwritten document expressing his testamentary intent. John took the document to a lawyer, who prepared a will based on the contents of the document. John executed the will in 1981. In the will, John devised his entire estate to Marian and her six children in equal shares and specifically excluded Louis and Jean. John died in 1982. Louis and Jean contested the will on grounds of lack of testamentary capacity and undue influence. The trial court found that the will was valid. Louis and Jean appealed.

**NIERENGARTEN, JUDGE.** Louis and Jean initially contend that John did not possess the capacity to make a will. A testator will be found to have testamentary capacity if, when making the will, he understands the nature, situation, and extent of his property and the claims of others on his bounty or his remembrance, and he is able to hold these things in his mind long enough to form a rational judgment concerning them. Less mental capacity is required to make a will than to conduct regular business affairs.

It is undisputed that John was a man of average or below average intelligence who sometimes needed direction. His mother would have to balance his checkbook and take care of his bookwork. He had to be constantly reminded to do things around the house.

He failed to do his tax returns in 1978 and 1979 and did not keep good track of his bills. Following the death of his mother and uncle, who helped him farm, the family operation declined in quality. These are the characteristics that Louis and Jean claim evidenced John's lack of testamentary capacity.

To rebut this, the attorney who drafted John's will testified that John was of sound mind, had testamentary capacity, knew the natural heirs of his bounty, knew the extent of his property, and was under no restraint when he made his will. The attorney also testified that John did not appear to have any doubts as to what he wanted in his will and had no difficulty arriving at the decisions on the various questions asked of him. There was additional testimony that John had, over the years, signed many documents, such as security agreements, mortgages, and contracts, without anyone's aid. In 1980, John held an auction in which he sold most of his farming equipment. The sale required execution of an auction sale agreement with the Lake City Bank. The Vice-President of the bank testified he had no doubt that John had the ability to understand the agreement. A first cousin of John testified that John mentioned to her he had made out a will and that "some of them aren't going to like it." The circumstances here are not so unusual as to disturb the trial court's findings of testamentary capacity.

Louis and Jean also argue that John was unduly influenced and susceptible to suggestion. To show undue influence, the evidence must show not only that the influence was exerted, but that it was so dominant and controlling of the testator's mind that he ceased to act of his own free volition and became a mere puppet of the wielder of that influence. Among the factors important as bearing upon undue influence are the opportunity to exercise it, active participation in the preparation of the will by the party exercising it, a confidential relationship between the person making the will and the party exercising the influence, disinheritance of those whom the decedent probably would have remembered in his will, singularity of the provisions of the will, and the exercise of influence or persuasion to induce him to make the will.

Louis and Jean's undue influence claim centers around the handwritten will drafted by John's sister, Marian, while he lived with her. That act, in itself, creates a situation where close scrutiny of possible undue influence is required. Where the beneficiary sustains confidential relations and drafts the will, or controls its drafting, a presumption of undue influence arises or an inference to that effect may be drawn.

John requested Marian to write down what he wanted in his will and to make sure the spelling of the names was correct. But it didn't end there. John then took the draft into an attorney's office where he received advice and assistance. As the attorney testified, John knew what he wanted and what he was doing. The relationship between John and his brothers and sisters negated undue influence. Whereas Marian and her husband had helped John on many occasions for at least eight years before he sold the family farm, John had an estranged relationship with Louis and Jean and had not associated with them except on a very limited basis. The record supports a finding of no undue influence.

Judgment upholding the validity of the will affirmed.

## In re Estate of Hall

### 328 F. Supp. 1305 (D.C. Dist. Ct. 1971)

In 1932, Francesca Hall wrote on the front and back of a single sheet of paper a document that she entitled "Last Will and Testament." The document purported to give all of her estate coming from her grandfather Clapp (approximately 70 percent of her estate at that time) to "whatever organization cares for the disabled sailors and seamen of the United States Navy and their families." The last line on the back side of the paper was an incomplete sentence stating, "All personal effects to be left to . . ." Hall did not sign the writing at the bottom of the back side, but her name did appear in her own writing in the body of the document, at the top of the first page. The signatures of two witnesses, Cousins and Lockner, appeared at the top of the first page. Cousins (the only surviving witness) later testified that Hall wrote another two pages and that she signed the last page at the bottom. He also testified that Lockner was not present when Hall signed her name or when any part of the document was written. The remaining pages of the document were detached and destroyed, and it was not possible to learn who had detached them or what dispositions of property had been made in them. Later in 1932, Hall was declared incompetent. She spent the last 30 years of her life in a hospital for the mentally ill. She died in 1968.

In the course of administering Hall's estate, the handwritten document was discovered in a safety-deposit box at a bank. Upon learning of the existence of the document, the Navy Relief Society brought an action to have the document admitted to probate as a holographic will.

**PRATT, DISTRICT JUDGE.** The court is presented with an incomplete document which does not effect a total disposition of all of Hall's estate. The administrators urge that the writing in question is not a valid will, challenging the document on three grounds: (1) Hall's name, which appears only in the first line of the text of the writing, is not a valid testamentary signature; (2) said writing is not a complete statement of Hall's final intentions; and (3) Lockner's signature was not duly subscribed according to statute.

The District has no special statute dealing with holographic wills. Section 103 of Title 18 of the Code provides that:

> A will is void unless it is:
>
> (1) in writing and signed by the testator, or by another person in his presence and by his express direction; and
>
> (2) attested and subscribed in the presence of the testator, by at least two credible witnesses.

The burden of proving formal execution of a will rests on the party wishing to have the document admitted to probate, in this case the Navy Relief Society. Where a will appears regular on its face, the normal presumption of regularity would lighten the burden on the moving party. The document before the court, however, is not regular on its face. The last two pages of the original document, including the page with Hall's signature, and that of Cousins, are missing under unknown circumstances. It is uncertain whether Lockner ever attested the original complete document on the last page. It is certain that

Lockner did not see Hall sign her name or write any part of the paper. The writing does not effect a complete disposition of Hall's assets. These facts, coupled with Hall's admitted mental problems, place a heavy burden on the Navy Relief Society in its efforts to show due execution.

District law requires that even holographic wills be attested and subscribed in the presence of the testator by two witnesses. Because it is manifestly incomplete and because the testator's signature on the first page cannot be viewed as carrying with it any testamentary intent, the court cannot accept the paper before it as a complete, duly executed document, entitled to be admitted to probate.

Will held not to be properly admissible.

## INTESTACY

If a person dies without making a will, or if he makes a will that is declared invalid, he is said to have died **intestate.** When that occurs, his property will be distributed to the persons designated as the intestate's heirs under the appropriate state's **intestacy** or **intestate succession** statute. The intestate's real property will be distributed according to the intestacy statute of the state in which the property is located. His personal property will be distributed according to the intestacy statute of the state in which he was **domiciled** at the time of his death. A domicile is a person's permanent home. A person can have only one domicile at a time. When a person resides and owns property in only one state, it is easy to apply the concept of domicile. As you will see in the *Elson* case, however, the application of the concept is more difficult when a person resides in more than one state or when he has recently moved to a new state.

**Characteristics of Intestacy Statutes.** The provisions of intestacy statutes are not uniform. Their purpose, however, is to distribute property in a way that reflects the *presumed intent* of the deceased, that is, to distribute it to the persons most closely related to him. In general, such statutes first provide for the distribution of most or all of a person's estate to his surviving spouse, children, or grandchildren. If no such survivors exist, the statutes typically provide for the distribution of the estate to parents, siblings, or nieces and nephews. If no relatives at this level are living, the property may be distributed to surviving grandparents, uncles, aunts, or cousins. Generally, persons with the same degree of relationship to the deceased person take equal shares. If the deceased had no surviving relatives, the property **escheats** (goes) to the state.

**Example of Intestacy Statute.** A good example of an intestacy statute is the one in effect in the District of Columbia. It provides for the following distributions:

(1) If the deceased person left a surviving spouse, then:
  (a) the spouse takes a one-third interest if the deceased person was also survived by children or their descendants;
  (b) the spouse takes a one-half interest if the deceased was not survived by children or their descendants but was survived by a father, mother, brother, sister, niece, or nephew;
  (c) the surviving spouse takes everything if the deceased is not survived by children, grand-

children, father, mother, brother, sister, niece, or nephew;

(2) Any surplus left beyond the share of the surviving spouse, or the entire surplus where there is no surviving spouse, is distributed as follows:
   (a) If there are children, the children take equal shares ("per capita") and children of any deceased children share equally the share their parent would have taken had he or she been alive ("per stirpes");
   (b) If there are no children or their descendants, then the mother and father, or the survivor, take the surplus;
   (c) If there are no children, descendants of children, mother or father surviving, then the surplus is divided equally among the surviving brothers and sisters (per capita) with descendants of brothers and sisters splitting equally the share their parent would have taken had he or she been alive;

(3) If none of the previously mentioned persons are alive, then the surplus is distributed equally among the collateral relatives (relatives such as cousins who share a common ancestor with the decedent but are not in his direct bloodline) who are the nearest and same degree removed from the deceased. If there are no collateral relatives, the grandparents or the survivor, take equal shares.

Suppose that Smith, who is domiciled in the District of Columbia, dies leaving a wife and two children. Under the intestacy statute described above, his wife is entitled to one third of his estate and the two children are entitled to split the remaining two thirds. If Smith were survived by a wife, a mother, and a father, but not by any children, then his wife would get half of his estate and his parents would split the other half. If Smith died leaving only two brothers and a sister, each of them would get one third of his estate. While the exact portion of the estate to which a surviving spouse, child, or other relative is entitled varies somewhat from state to state, the basic scheme of distribution is similar in most states.

**Special Rules.** Under intestacy statutes, a person must have a relationship to the deceased person through blood or marriage in order to inherit any part of his property. State law generally includes adopted children within the definition of "children," and treats adopted children in the same way as it treats natural children. (An adopted child would inherit from his adoptive parents, not from his biological parents.) Half brothers and half sisters are usually treated in the same way as brothers and sisters related by whole blood. An illegitimate child may inherit from his mother, the same as a legitimate child. As a general rule, illegitimate children do not inherit from their fathers unless paternity has been either acknowledged or established in a legal proceeding.

A person must be alive at the time the decedent dies to claim a share of the decedent's estate. An exception may be made for children or other descendants who are born *after* the decedent's death. If a person who is entitled to a share of the decedent's estate survives the decedent but dies before receiving his share, his share in the decedent's estate becomes part of his own estate.

**Murder Disqualification.** Many states provide that a person who is convicted of the homicide (murder or manslaughter) of another person may not inherit any of the victim's property. Similarly, a person usually cannot share in the proceeds of life insurance on the life of a person he has murdered.

**Simultaneous Death.** A statute known as the Uniform Simultaneous Death Act provides that where two persons who would inherit from each other (such as husband and wife) die under circumstances that make it difficult or impossible to determine who died first, each person's property is to be distributed as though he or she survived. This means, for example, that the husband's property will go to his relatives and the wife's property to her relatives.

## In re Estate of Elson

**458 N.E.2d 637 (Ill. Ct. App. 1983)**

Natalie Elson died in an automobile accident in Pennsylvania on November 14, 1981. She was 27 at the time of her death. She had lived her entire life in Illinois. Her primary interest in life was horses, and she studied recreation and equine sciences while attending Southern Illinois University. After graduating from Southern Illinois and receiving further training in horsemanship, she decided to move to Pennsylvania to study dressage. She hoped to compete in the 1984 Olympics as a rider. Five or six days before her death, she moved to Pennsylania. She told several friends that she intended to return to Illinois after a year. Natalie's stepmother found an unmailed letter that Natalie had written to her sister the day before she died. It stated that she had "moved to Pennsylvania!" When Natalie left for Pennsylvania, she took her horse and a carload of her belongings with her. She left some items in storage in Illinois, and she left her jewelry in a safe-deposit box in Illinois. Upon arriving in Pennsylvania, she opened new bank accounts in Delaware (she lived near the Delaware border) and also established a safe-deposit box there. She retained her Illinois driver's license.

After Natalie's death, her father was appointed administrator of her estate by a Pennsylvania court. He distributed all of the property that Natalie owned in Illinois. Margo Elson, Natalie's sister, filed a petition in Illinois, contending that Natalie had not abandoned Illinois as her domicile. The trial court held that Natalie was domiciled in Pennsylvania. Margo appealed.

**Nash, Justice.** An Illinois court may exercise jurisdiction over the estate of a decedent either when the deceased was domiciled in Illinois or at the time of her death owned property in this State. "Domicile" has been defined as the place where a person has her true, permanent home to which she intends to return whenever she is absent. Domicile is a continuing thing, and from the moment a person is born she must, at all times, have a domicile. A person can have only one domicile; once a domicile is established, it continues until a new one is actually acquired. To effect a change of domicile there must be an actual abandonment of the first domicile, coupled with an intent not to return to it; also, physical presence must be established in another place with the intention of making the last-acquired residence her permanent home.

The question of domicile, as it relates to a decedent, is one of the most difficult in the law because it turns on the proof of the intent of a deceased person. The matter of domicile is largely one of intention and, hence, is primarily a question of fact. Very slight circumstances often decide the question of domicile.

The trial judge, as the trier of fact, is in a superior position to hear and weigh the evidence and to determine the credibility and demeanor of the witnesses. Accordingly, a reviewing court may not overturn a judgment merely because it might disagree with it or might have come to a different conclusion. Given the particular facts of this case, we cannot say that the trial court's findings were against the manifest weight of the evidence. We conclude there is sufficient evidence to establish that Natalie intended to abandon her Illinois domicile permanently and acquire a permanent domicile in Pennsylvania.

Judgment holding that domicile was in Pennsylvania affirmed.

## ADMINISTRATION OF ESTATES

When a person dies, an orderly procedure is needed to collect his property, settle his debts, and distribute any remaining property to those who will inherit it under his will or by intestate succession. This process occurs under the supervision of a probate court and is known as the **administration process** or the **probate process.** Assets that pass by operation of law (such as assets owned jointly with right of survivorship) and assets that are transferred by other devices such as trusts or life insurance policies do not pass through probate.

Summary (simple) procedures are sometimes available when an estate is relatively small—for example, when it has assets of less than $7,500.

**Determining the Existence of a Will.** The first step in the probate process is to determine whether the deceased left a will. This may require a search of the deceased person's personal papers and safe-deposit box. If a will is found, it must be *proved* to be admitted to probate. This involves the testimony of the persons who witnessed the will, if they are still alive. If the witnesses are no longer alive, the signatures of the witnesses and the testator will have to be established in some other way. In many states, a will may be proved by an affidavit (declaration under oath) sworn to and signed by the testators and the witnesses at the time the will was executed. This is called a **self-proving affidavit.** If a will is located and proved, it will be admitted to probate and govern many of the decisions that must be made in the administration of the estate.

**Selecting a Personal Representative.** Another early step in the administration of an estate is to select a **personal representative** to administer the estate. If the deceased left a will, it is likely that he designated his personal representative in the will. The personal representative under a will is also known as an **executor.** Almost anyone could serve as an executor. The testator may have chosen, for example, his spouse, a grown child, a close friend, an attorney, or the trust department of a bank.

If the decedent died intestate, or if the personal representative named in a will is unable to serve, the probate court will name a personal representative to administer the estate. In the case of an intestate estate, the personal representative is called an **administrator.** A preference is usually accorded to a surviving spouse, child, or other close relative. If no relative is available and qualified to serve, a creditor, bank, or other person may be appointed by the court.

Most states require that the personal representative *post a bond* in an amount in excess of the estimated value of the estate to ensure that her duties will be properly and faithfully performed. A person making a will may direct that his executor may serve without posting a bond. Courts may accept such an exemption.

**Responsibilities of the Personal Representative.** The personal representative has a number of important tasks in the administration of the estate. She must see that an inventory is taken of the estate's assets and that the assets are appraised. Notice must then be given to creditors or potential claimants against the estate so that they can file and prove their claims within a specified time, normally five months. As a general rule, the surviving spouse of the deceased person is entitled to be paid an allowance during the time the estate is being settled. This allowance has priority over other debts of the estate. The personal representative must see that any properly payable funeral or burial expenses are paid and that the creditors' claims are satisfied.

Both the federal and state governments impose estate or inheritance taxes on estates of a certain size. The personal representative is responsible for filing estate tax returns. The federal tax is a tax on the deceased's estate, with provisions for deducting items such as debts, expenses of administration, and charitable gifts. In addition, an amount equal to the amount left to the surviving spouse may be deducted from the gross estate before the tax is computed. State inheritance taxes are imposed on the person who receives a gift or statutory share from an estate. It is common, however, for wills to provide that the estate will pay all taxes, including inheritance taxes, so that the beneficiaries will not have to do so. The personal representative must also make provisions for filing an income tax return and for paying any income tax due for the partial year prior to the decedent's death.

When the debts, expenses, and taxes have been taken care of, the remaining assets of the estate are distributed to the decedent's heirs (if there was no will) or to the beneficiaries of the decedent's will. Special rules apply when the estate is too small to satisfy all of the bequests made in a will or when some or all of the designated beneficiaries are no longer living.

When the personal representative has completed all of these duties, the probate court will close the estate and discharge the personal representative.

## TRUSTS

**Nature of a Trust.** A **trust** is a legal relationship in which a person who has legal title to property has the duty to hold it for the use or benefit of another person. The person benefited by a trust is considered to have **equitable title** to the property, because it is being maintained for his benefit. A trust can be created in a number of ways. An owner of property may *declare* that he is holding certain property in trust. For example, a mother might state that she is holding 100 shares of General Motors stock in trust for her daughter. A trust may also arise *by operation of law.* For example, when a lawyer representing a client who has been injured in an automobile accident receives a settlement payment from an insurance company, the lawyer holds the settlement payment as trustee for the client. Most commonly, however, trusts are created through *express instruments* whereby an owner of property transfers title to the property to a trustee who is to hold, manage, and invest the property for the benefit of either the original owner or a third person. For example, Smith transfers certain stock to First Trust Bank with instructions to pay the income to his daughter during her lifetime and to distribute the stock to her children after her death.

**Trust Terminology.** A person who creates a trust is known as a **settlor** or **trustor.** The person who holds the property for the benefit of another person is called the **trustee.** The person for whose benefit the property is held in trust is the **beneficiary.** A single person may occupy more than one of these positions; however, if there is only one beneficiary, he cannot be the sole trustee. The property held in trust is called the **corpus.** A distinction is made between the property in trust, which is the principal, and the income that is produced by the principal.

A trust that is established and effective during the settlor's lifetime is known as an **inter vivos trust.** A trust can also be established in a person's will. Such trusts take effect only at the death of the settlor. They are called **testamentary trusts.**

**Why People Create Trusts.** Smith owns a portfolio of valuable stock. She has two young children and an elderly father whom she would like to provide for. Why might it be advantageous to Smith to transfer the stock to a trust for the benefit of the members of her family?

First, there may be income tax or estate tax advantages in doing so, depending on the type of trust she establishes and the provisions of that trust. The tax implications of a trust are very complicated. A person who is interested in setting up a trust to obtain tax advantages should seek the advice of a competent attorney experienced in estate planning. In addition, the trust property can be used for the benefit of others and may even pass to others after the settlor's death without the necessity of having a will. Many people prefer to pass their property by trust rather than by will because trusts afford more privacy: unlike a probated will, they do not become an item of public record. Trusts also afford greater opportunity for postgift management than do outright gifts and bequests. If Smith wants her children to enjoy the income of the trust property during their young adulthood without distributing unfettered ownership of the property to them before she considers them able to manage it properly, she can accomplish this through a trust provision. A trust can prevent the property from being squandered or spent too quickly. Trusts can be set up so that a beneficiary's interest cannot be reached by his creditors in many situations. Such trusts, called **spendthrift trusts,** will be discussed later.

Placing property in trust can operate to increase the amount of property held for the beneficiaries if the trustee makes good investment decisions. Another important consideration is that a trust can be used to provide for the needs of disabled beneficiaries who are not capable of managing funds.

**Creation of Express Trusts.** There are five basic requirements for the creation of a valid express trust. Special and somewhat less restrictive rules govern the establishment of charitable trusts.

**Capacity.** The settlor must have had the *legal capacity* to convey the property to the trust. This means that the settlor must have had the capacity needed to make a valid contract if the trust is an *inter vivos* trust or the capacity to make a will if the trust is a testamentary trust. For example, a trust would fail under this requirement if at the time the trust was created, the settlor had not attained the age required by state law for the creation of valid wills and contracts.

**Intent and Formalities.** The settlor must *intend* to create a trust at the present time. To impose enforceable duties on the trustee, the settlor must meet certain formalities. Under the laws of most states, for example, the trustee must accept the trust by signing the trust instrument. In the case of a trust of land, the trust must be in writing so as to meet the statute of frauds. If the trust is a testamentary trust, it must satisfy the formal requirements for wills.

**Conveyance of Specific Property.** The settlor must convey *specific property* to the trust. The property conveyed must be property that the settlor has the *right to convey.*

**Identity of Beneficiaries.** The *beneficiaries* of the trust must be described clearly enough so that their identities can be ascertained. Sometimes, beneficiaries may be members of a specific class, such as "my children."

**Proper Purpose.** The trust must be created for a *proper purpose.* It cannot be created for a reason that is contrary to public policy, such as the commission of a crime.

**Charitable Trusts.** A distinction is made between private trusts and trusts created for charitable purposes. In a private trust property is devoted to the benefit of specified persons, whereas in a charitable trust property is devoted to a charitable organization or to other purposes beneficial to society. While some of the rules governing private and charitable trusts are the same, a number of these rules are different. For example, when a private trust is created, the beneficiary must be known at the time or ascertainable within a certain time (established by a legal rule known as the **rule against perpetuities**). However, a charitable trust is valid even though no definitely ascertainable beneficiary is named and even though it is to continue for an indefinite or unlimited period.

A special doctrine known as **cy pres** is applicable to charitable trusts when property is given in trust to be applied to a particular charitable purpose that becomes impossible, impracticable, or illegal to carry out. If the settlor indicated a general intention to devote the property to charitable purposes, the trust will not fail. The court will direct the application of the property to some charitable purpose that falls within the settlor's general charitable intention.

**Powers and Duties of the Trustee.** In most express trusts, the settlor names a specific person to act as trustee. If the settlor does not name a trustee, the court will appoint one. Similarly, a court will replace a trustee who resigns, is incompetent, or refuses to act.

The trust codes of most states contain provisions giving trustees broad management powers over trust property. These provisions can be limited or expanded by express provisions in the trust instrument. The trustee must use a *reasonable degree of skill, judgment, and care* in the exercise of his duties unless he holds himself out as having a greater degree of skill, in which case he will be held to a higher standard. He *may not commingle* the property he holds in trust with his own property or with that of another trust.

A trustee owes a *duty of loyalty* (fiduciary duty) to the beneficiaries. This means that he must administer the trust for the benefit of the beneficiaries and avoid any conflict between his personal interests and the interest of the trust. For example, a trustee cannot do business with a trust that he administers without express permission in the trust agreement. He must not prefer one beneficiary's interest to another's, and he must account to the beneficiaries for all transactions. Unless the trust agreement provides otherwise, the trustee must make the trust productive. He may not delegate the performance of discretionary duties (such as the duty to select investments) to another, but he may delegate the performance of ministerial duties (such as the preparation of statements of account).

**Transfer of the Beneficiary's Interest.** Generally, the beneficiary of a trust may voluntarily assign his rights to the principal or income of the trust to another person. In addition, any distributions to the beneficiary are subject to the claims of his creditors. Sometimes, however, trusts contain provisions known as **spendthrift clauses,** which restrict the voluntary or involuntary transfer of a beneficiary's interest. Such clauses are generally enforced, and they preclude assignees or creditors from compelling a trustee to recognize their claims to the trust. The enforceability of such clauses is subject to four exceptions, however: (1) a person cannot put his own property beyond the claims of his own creditors, and thus a spendthrift clause is not effective in a trust when the settlor makes himself a beneficiary; (2) divorced spouses and minor children of the beneficiary can compel payment for alimony and child support; (3) creditors of the beneficiary who have furnished necessaries can compel payment; and (4) once the trustee distributes property to a beneficiary, it can be subject to valid claims of others. The *American Security and Trust* case, which follows, presents an example of the operation of a spendthrift clause.

A trust may give the trustee discretion as to the amount of principal or income paid to a beneficiary. In such a case, the beneficiary cannot require the trustee to exercise his discretion in the manner desired by the beneficiary.

**Termination and Modifications of a Trust.** Normally, a settlor cannot revoke or modify a trust unless he reserves the power to do so at the time he establishes the trust. However, a trust may be modified or terminated with the consent of the settlor and all of the beneficiaries. When the settlor is dead or otherwise unable to consent, a trust can be modified or terminated by consent of all the persons with a beneficial interest, but only when this would not frustrate a material purpose of the trust. Because trusts are under the supervisory jurisdiction of a court, the court can permit a deviation from the terms of a trust when unanticipated changes in circumstances threaten accomplishment of the settlor's purpose.

**Implied and Constructive Trusts.** Under exceptional circumstances in which the creation of a trust is necessary to effectuate a settlor's intent or avoid unjust enrichment, the law *implies* or imposes a trust even though no express trust exists or an express trust exists but has failed. One trust of this type is a **resulting trust,** which arises when there has been an incomplete disposition of trust property. For example, if Smith transfers property to Jones as trustee to provide for the needs of Smith's grandfather and the grandfather dies before the trust funds are exhausted, Jones will be deemed to hold the property in a resulting trust for Smith or Smith's heirs. Similarly, if Smith transfers the property to Jones as trustee and the trust fails because Smith did not meet one of the requirements of a valid trust, Jones will not be permitted to keep the trust property as his own. A resulting trust will be implied.

A **constructive trust** is a trust created by operation of law to avoid fraud, injustice, or unjust enrichment. This type of trust imposes on the constructive trustee a duty to convey property he holds to another person on the ground that the constructive trustee would be unjustly enriched if he were allowed to retain it. For example, when a person procures the transfer of property by means of fraud or duress, he becomes a constructive trustee and is under an obligation to return the property to its original owner.

## American Security and Trust Co. v. Utley

### 382 F.2d 451 (D.C. Cir. 1967)

Sidney Graves was the beneficiary of a testamentary trust contained in the will of his wife, who died in 1962. The trust contained a spendthrift clause. In 1963, Graves signed a promissory note for $4,500, payable to Fred Utley. When Graves failed to make full payment by the due date on the note, Utley brought suit against Graves and obtained a default judgment. He then sought to attach the accrued trust income held by the trustee of the trust, American Security. The trial court held for Utley, and American Security appealed.

**Burger, Circuit Judge.** This appeal presents the question whether the income provided for the beneficiary of a spendthrift trust is subject to the claim of a creditor, and if so, to what extent. The District Court determined that because the beneficiary was the settlor's spouse, who elected to take under the will creating the trust rather than under the provisions of statute, the income was subject to claims of creditors.

The District Court applied the well-known rule that where the settlor of the trust is also the beneficiary, the interest in the trust can be invaded. We have no quarrel with the rule that one may not create a trust for his own benefit and place the income beyond reach of his creditors. However, the view adopted by the District Court is contrary to the weight of authority and not warranted as a matter of sound policy.

We have long recognized the validity of the so-called spendthrift trust, but not without limitation. The historical purpose of a settlor in creating a trust, the income of which was protected from invasion, was to protect the interests of the beneficiary. This purpose has been held to render the income totally immune from claims. We see no reason for an absolutist "all or nothing" approach. It does not follow from the general validity of spendthrift trusts that trust income is protected from all obligations. We view the primary purpose of such a trust to assure that the beneficiary will be provided for, independent of his own improvidence. To accomplish this, the income need not be immune from debts incurred for the necessities of life; indeed to allow such claims is entirely compatible with the purpose of the trust. This result has been reached in other areas of the law, such as infants' contracts.

The immunity of an infant from liability on his contracts has much in common with the historic basis for the immunity of a spendthrift trust. In each situation, the beneficiary of the rule receives sufficient protection if the immunity does not include debts for the necessities of life. What are "necessaries" will obviously vary with the circumstances, income, and background of the beneficiary. We think the law governing contracts of infants will afford adequate guidelines; housing, food, and medical care are examples of the obvious basic necessities of life.

The District Court had no occasion to inquire into the circumstances which gave rise to the indebtedness, and we therefore remand for a determination of the basis of the debt incurred and the purposes to which the proceeds of the loan were devoted. If the District Court finds the debt to have been incurred for necessaries such as those for which an infant would be liable in contract in otherwise comparable circumstances, the claim may be allowed against the income of the trust; if not, judgment must be for American Security.

Reversed and remanded in favor of American Security.

## SUMMARY

A person may dispose of his property by will if he has testamentary capacity and executes a will in compliance with the formalities required by state statute. State statutes normally require that the will be in writing, that it be witnessed by a specified number of disinterested persons, and that it be published and signed by the testator in the presence of witnesses. A will procured by fraud or undue influence will not be accepted as a valid will. Property that passes to another by operation of law or by a contract such as a life insurance contract is not controlled by the provisions of a will. Surviving spouses have statutory rights to receive a share of the estate of their deceased spouses. A will transfers no interest in property until the death of the testator. The testator can revoke the will at any time before his death.

The property of a person who dies intestate (without leaving a valid will) will be distributed to the persons who are his heirs under state intestacy laws, or laws of intestate succession. Real property will descend according to the laws of the state in which it is located; personal property will descend according to the laws of the state in which the intestate had his permanent home or domicile.

Estates are administered under the supervision of a probate court. If a will exists, the testator may have named a personal representative called an executor to administer his estate. The personal representative for an intestate estate is called an administrator. If there is no will or the named executor cannot serve, the court will select a personal representative. The personal representative has a number of important duties, including the duty to prepare estate and income tax returns. The steps in the administration of an estate include taking an inventory of the assets, having them appraised, determining the creditors and the persons to whom the estate is to be distributed, paying all proper debts and expenses, and distributing the remainder to those who are entitled to it.

A trust arises when one person who has legal rights to certain property also has the duty to hold it for the use or benefit of another person. *Inter vivos* trusts are those that are established during the lifetime of the person who created the trust (the settlor). Testamentary trusts are those that are created in a will and take effect at death. Trusts may be expressly created, or they may arise by implication or the operation of law.

Generally, the beneficiary of a trust has the right to assign the principal or interest in his share of the trust and his rights are subject to the claims of his creditors. Normally, the creator of a trust may not revoke or modify the trust unless he reserves the right to do so at the time he establishes it; however, there are some exceptions. The trustee owes a duty to use reasonable skill, judgment, and care in the exercise of his duties. He also owes the beneficiaries a duty of loyalty.

## PROBLEM CASES

1. In 1978, Robinson executed a will in which he left his entire estate to his wife, Edith, who suffered from Alzheimer's disease

and was unable to care for herself. On March 4, 1980, 32 minutes before Robinson was pronounced dead, he allegedly executed a new will by making his mark on the last page of the will. At the time of the alleged execution, Robinson had no palpable pulse. His temperature of at least 104 degrees, his blood pressure of 50 over 20, and the absence of urine in his bladder, indicated that he was in shock. He was unable to respond to verbal stimuli, and there was no indication that he had read the will. The new will, which was signed by two witnesses, named Miller as executor and created two trusts for the benefit of Edith. Upon her death, the trustees were directed to distribute the trusts' assets to Edith's brother and several charitable organizations. Miller offered the will into probate. Was it a valid will?

**2.** Pfifer executed a formal, typed, and witnessed will in 1981. On May 3, 1981, he attempted to change the will by crossing out certain names and numerical figures and substituting new names and figures for them. He dated and initialed these interlineations and additions. On May 4, he was found dead in a motel room in California. His death was attributed to suicide. A California statute recognizes the validity of unwitnessed holographic wills that are entirely written, dated, and signed by the testator. California law also provides that the presence of nonhandwritten material on a holograph does not defeat its validity so long as the printed words are not essential to the substance of the holograph or essential to its validity as a will. Should the will be admitted as a valid holographic will or codicil?

**3.** Jansa executed a will in which she left all of her property to her two sons. The will was found in her safe-deposit box after her death. Also discovered in the box were two additional instruments containing language identical to that of the will, except that they purported to leave Jansa's home to her grandson if he survived her, with the remainder to her two sons. One of the instruments was written entirely in Jansa's handwriting but was not signed by her, and the other was signed by her but, except for the signature, was entirely typewritten. Neither was attested to by witnesses. The grandson alleges that the two instruments found with the will were valid holographic codicils to the will and that he is entitled to inherit the house. Texas law recognizes holographic wills if they are entirely handwritten and signed by the testator. It does not require that holographic wills be witnessed. Are the two instruments valid codicils?

**4.** Floyd, age 84, was suffering from an incurable cancer and was confined to his bed at the time he executed his will. He conversed for about one half hour with the two men who witnessed the will, talking about their families and other matters. The will was read to him topic by topic, and he approved each item as read and said at the conclusion of the reading that that was the way he wanted his property distributed. He had left a life estate in all of his property to his wife and the remainder to his grandson and his wife. They had cared for Floyd during his last illness. Objections were filed to the probate of the will on the ground of lack of testamentary capacity. Should the will be admitted to probate?

**5.** Rudolph died on August 16, 1978, leaving wills dated in 1956 and 1960 as well as a handwritten instrument that purported to be his last will and testament. That instrument was dated "Monday 26, 1978." The probate court took judicial notice of the fact that in the year 1978 the 26th of the month occurred on Monday only once—in June. A California statute provides that "a holographic will is one that is entirely written, dated and signed by the hand of the testator himself. It is subject to no other form and need not be witnessed." Objection is made to admitting the document to probate as a holographic will on the ground that it is not properly dated. Should the will be admitted to probate?

**6.** Bauert and Lightfoot operated a business partnership. Each took out a policy of life insurance in the amount of $200,000 and named the other as beneficiary. The premiums on the insurance were paid from the partnership bank account. The two men orally agreed that if either of them died, the survivor would use the life insurance proceeds to pay any partnership indebtedness and would pay the remaining proceeds to the widow and heirs of the deceased partner. Bauert died. At the time, the partnership owed a debt of $48,000 to First National Bank. Lightfoot assigned the proceeds of the insurance policy to the bank to partially cover a debt of $400,000 that he personally owed to the bank. Bauert's widow then brought an action against the bank, claiming that she was entitled to the insurance proceeds that exceeded the $48,000 debt. Should the court impose a constructive trust for the benefit of Mrs. Bauert?

# PART VIII

# SALES

Chapter 31

# Formation and Terms of Sales Contracts

## INTRODUCTION

In Chapters 6–15 you studied the common law rules that govern the creation and performance of contracts generally. Throughout much of recorded history, special rules—the law merchant—were developed to control mercantile transactions in goods. Because transactions in goods commonly involve buyers and sellers located in different states—and even different countries—a common body of law to control those transactions can greatly facilitate the smooth flow of commerce. To address this need, a Uniform Sales Act was drafted in the early 1900s, and adopted by about two-thirds of the states. Subsequently, the Uniform Commercial Code was prepared to simplify and modernize the rules of law governing commercial transactions.

This chapter briefly reviews some of the Code rules that govern the formation of sales contracts that were discussed in Chapters 6–15. It also covers a number of key terms in sales contracts, such as delivery terms, title, and risk of loss. Finally, it discusses the rules governing sales on trial, such as sales on approval and consignments.

**Sale of Goods.** A **sale of goods** is the transfer of ownership to tangible personal property in exchange for money, other goods, or the performance of services. The law of sales of goods is codified in Article 2 of the Uniform Commercial Code. While the law of sales is based on the fundamental principles of contract and personal property, it has been modified to accommodate current practices of merchants. In large measure, the Code has discarded many technical requirements of earlier law that did not serve any useful purpose in the marketplace and has replaced them with rules that assure merchants and consumers the most just and equitable results that are in keeping with commercial expectations.

Article 2 of the Code applies only to *transactions in goods.* Thus, it does not cover contracts to provide services or contracts to sell real property. However, some courts have applied the principles set out in the Code to such transactions. When a contract appears to call for the furnishing of both goods and services, a question may arise as to whether the Code applies. For example, the operator of a beauty parlor may use a commercial permanent solution intended to be used safely on humans that causes injury to a person's head. The injured person might then bring a lawsuit claiming that there was a breach of the Code's warranty of the suitability of the permanent solution. In such cases, the courts commonly look to see whether the sale of goods is the *predominant* part of the transaction or merely an *incidental* part; where the sale of goods predominates, the Code will normally be applied.

The *Colorado Carpet Installation v. Palermo* case, which follows, illustrates the type of analysis courts go through to determine whether a particular contract should be considered as one for the sale of goods governed by the Code.

**Merchants.** Many of the Code's provisions apply only to **merchants** or to transactions between merchants.[1] In addition, the Code sets a higher standard of conduct for merchants because persons who regularly deal in goods should be expected to be familiar with the practices of that trade and with commercial law. Ordinary consumers and nonmerchants, on the other hand, frequently have little knowledge of or experience in these matters.

**Code Requirements.** The Code requires that parties to sales contracts act in *good faith* and in a *commercially reasonable* manner. Further, when a contract contains an unfair or unconscionable clause, or the contract as a whole is unconscionable, the courts have the right to refuse to enforce the unconscionable clause or contract [2–302].[2] The Code's treatment of unconscionability is discussed in detail in Chapter 12.

A number of the Code provisions concerning the sale of goods were discussed in the chapters on contracts. The following is a list of some of the important provisions discussed earlier, together with the section of the Code and the pages in the text where the discussion can be found.

1. *Firm offers.* Under the Code, an offer in writing by a merchant that gives assurance that the offer will be held open is not revocable for lack of consideration during the time stated, or for a reasonable time if no time is stated, up to a period of three months [2–205]. (See page 156.)

2. *Statute of frauds.* The **statute of frauds** in the Code applies to the sale of goods at a price of $500 or more. The Code makes special exceptions for written confirmations between

[1] Under the Code, a "merchant" is defined to mean "a person who deals in goods of the kind or otherwise by his occupation holds himself out as having knowledge or skill peculiar to the practices or goods involved in the transaction or to whom such knowledge or skill may be attributed by his employment of an agent or broker or other intermediary who by his occupation holds himself out as having such knowledge or skill" [§ 2–104(1)].

[2] The numbers in brackets refer to the sections of the Uniform Commercial Code.

merchants, part payment or part delivery, admissions in legal proceedings, and specially manufactured goods [2–201]. (See pages 270, 273–75.)

3. *Formation.* Under the Code, a contract for the sale of goods may be made in any manner that shows that the parties reached agreement, even though no particular moment can be pointed to as the time when the contract was made. Where the parties intended to make a contract but left one or more terms open, the contract is valid despite the lack of definiteness so long as the court has a basis for giving a remedy [2–204]. (See pages 146–47.)

4. *Additional terms in acceptances.* The Code states that an expression of acceptance or written confirmation sent within a reasonable time operates as an acceptance even if it states terms additional to or different from those offered, unless acceptance is expressly made conditional on assent to the additional or different terms [2–207]. (See page 166.)

## Colorado Carpet Installation, Inc. v. Palermo

**668 P.2d 1384 (Colo. Sup. Ct. 1983)**

At the request of Fred and Zuma Palermo, Colorado Carpet submitted a written proposal to provide and install carpeting and tile in their home. The prices quoted were on the basis of a price per square foot of material that expressly included all labor. Much of the carpeting and tile had to be specially ordered by Colorado Carpet. The Palermos never accepted the proposal in writing, and there was a disagreement as to how much of the proposal had been agreed to orally. After Colorado Carpet obtained the material and began installation of the tile, Mrs. Palermo became dissatisfied and asked another contractor to supply and install the tile.

Colorado Carpet, after unsuccessfully negotiating with the Palermos, removed its material from their home. It then brought suit against the Palermos for breach of the oral contract. The trial court held that the contract was one for the sale of services. The court of appeals reversed, holding that the contract was one for the sale of goods under the UCC but that it was unenforceable because it did not come within the "specially manufactured goods" exception to the statute of frauds. Colorado Carpet appealed.

**Quinn, Justice.** We first address the court of appeals' determination that the contract was one for the sale of goods, rather than for the performance of labor or services. We conclude that the agreement in question involved a contract for the sale of goods as contemplated by § 2–201(1).

This section prohibits the enforcement of contracts "for the sale of goods for the price of $500 or more . . . unless there is some writing sufficient to indicate that a contract for sale has been made between the parties and signed by the party against whom enforcement is sought." By its terms, the statute applies only to contracts for the sale of goods, and not to contracts for labor or services.

In this case the subject of the contract involved "goods" because the carpeting and other materials were movable at the time that Colorado Carpet procured them for installation pursuant to the agreement. Since the agreement contemplated that title to the carpeting and other materials would pass to the Palermos, it constituted a "contract for sale." The scope of the contract, however, included not only the sale of goods but also the performance of labor or service. Thus, we must determine whether such a mixed contract qualified as a contract for the sale of goods or, instead, constituted a contract for labor or service outside the scope of § 2–201(1).

The performance of some labor or service frequently plays a role in sales transactions. "Goods," however, are not the less "goods" merely because labor or services may be essential to their ultimate use by the purchaser. The mere furnishing of some labor or service, in our view, should not determine the ultimate character of a contract for purposes of § 2–201(1) of the Uniform Commercial Code. Rather, the controlling criterion should be the primary purpose of the contract—that is, whether the circumstances underlying the formation of the agreement and the performance reasonably expected of the parties demonstrate the primary purpose of the contract as the sale of goods or, in contrast, the sale of labor or service. We agree in this respect with the following statement in *Bonebrake v. Cox:*

> The test for inclusion is not whether goods or services are mixed, but, granting that they are mixed, whether their predominant factor, their thrust, their purpose, reasonably stated, is the rendition of service, with goods incidentally involved (e.g., contract with artist for painting), or is a transaction of sale, with labor incidentally involved (e.g., insulation of a water heater in a bathroom).

This "primary purpose" test, we believe, is designed to promote one of the expressed statutory policies of the Uniform Commercial Code—"to simplify, clarify, and modernize the law governing commercial transactions." Useful factors to consider in determining whether "goods" or "service" predominates include the following: the contractual language used by the parties; whether the agreement involves one overall price that includes both goods and labor or, instead, calls for separate and discrete billings for goods on the one hand and labor on the other; the ratio that the cost of goods bears to the overall contract price; and the nature and reasonableness of the purchaser's contractual expectations of acquiring a property interest in goods (goods being defined as things that are movable at the time of identification to the contract).

Considering the contract under these guidelines, we are satisfied that, as a matter of law, its primary purpose was the sale of goods and not the sale of labor or service. The language in Colorado Carpet's proposal referred to the parties as "seller" and "customer." In addition, the agreement called for an overall contract price that included both the cost of goods and labor, and the charge for labor was slight in relation to the total contractual price. Finally, the carpeting and other materials were movable when Colorado Carpet procured them for the purpose of selling them to the Palermos. The fact that these materials might later be installed in the Palermo home and assume the character of fixture does not undermine the primary purpose of the contract as one for a sale of goods. We therefore agree with the court of appeals that the agreement between Colorado Carpet and the Palermos constituted a contract for the sale of goods, with labor or service only incidentally involved, and thus was within the statute of frauds provisions of the Uniform Commercial Code.[3]

Judgment for the Palermos affirmed.

---

[3] See page 276 for the portion of the opinion that discusses the application of the Code's Statute of frauds to the facts of this case.

## TERMS OF THE CONTRACT

**General Terms.** Within broad limits, the parties to a contract to sell goods may include any terms upon which they agree. Many practices have become common in the everyday transactions of business, and under the Code, if a particular matter is not specifically covered in a contract or is unclear, common trade practices are used to fill out the terms of the contract.

The Code sets out in some detail the rights of the parties when they use certain terms, and those meanings apply unless the parties agree otherwise. For example, if a contract includes an open-price clause where the price is to be determined later, or if a contract is silent about price, the price is what would be considered reasonable at the time of delivery. If the price is to be fixed by either the buyer or the seller, that person must act in good faith in setting the price. However, if it is clear from their negotiations that the parties do not intend to be bound unless they agree on a price, and the price is not agreed on or fixed, no contract results [2–305].

**Output and Needs Contracts.** In an "output" contract, one party is bound to sell its entire output of particular goods and the other party is bound to buy that output. In a "needs" or "requirements" contract, the quantity of goods is based on the needs of the buyer. In determining the quantity of goods to be produced or taken pursuant to an output or needs contract, the rule of good faith applies. Thus, no quantity can be demanded or taken that is unreasonably disproportionate to any estimate that was given or to the quantity that would normally be expected.

For example, Farmer contracts to supply Sam's Grocery with all of the apples it requires for sale to customers. If Sam's has sold between 500 and 700 bushels of apples a year over the past 10 years, Farmer could not be required to deliver 5,000 bushels of apples to Sam's one year because Sam had an unusual demand for them. Similarly, if the parties entered into an exclusive dealing contract for certain goods, the seller is obligated to use his best efforts to supply the goods to the buyer and the buyer is obligated to use his best efforts to promote their sale [2–306].

**Time for Performance.** If no time for performance is stated in the sales contract, a reasonable time for performance is implied. If a contract requires successive performances over an indefinite period of time, the contract is valid for a reasonable time; however, either party can terminate it at any time upon the giving of reasonable notice unless the parties have agreed otherwise as to termination [2–309]. For example, Farmer Jack agrees to sell his entire output of apples each fall to a cannery at the then current market price. If the contract does not contain a provision spelling out how and when the contract can be terminated, Farmer Jack can terminate it if he gives the cannery a reasonable time to make arrangements to acquire apples from someone else.

**Delivery Terms.** Standardized shipping terms that through commercial practice have come to have a specific meaning are customarily used in sales contracts. The terms **FOB (free on board)** and **FAS (free alongside ship)** are basic delivery terms. If the delivery term of the contract is FOB or FAS the place at which the goods originate, the seller is obligated to deliver to the carrier goods that *conform to the contract* and are *properly prepared for shipment* to the buyer, and the seller must make a *reasonable contract for transportation* of the goods on behalf of the buyer. Under such delivery terms, the goods are at the risk of the buyer during transit and he must pay the shipping charges. If the term is "FOB destination," the seller must deliver the goods to the designated destination and they are at the seller's risk and expense during transit. These terms will be discussed in more detail later in this chapter.

## TITLE

**Passage of Title.** **Title** to goods cannot pass from the seller to the buyer until the goods are identified to the contract [2–401(1)]. For example, if Seller agrees to sell Buyer 50 chairs and Seller has 500 chairs in his warehouse, title to 50 chairs will not pass from Seller to Buyer until the 50 chairs that Buyer has purchased are selected and identified as the chairs sold to Buyer.

The parties may agree between themselves when title to the goods will pass from the seller to the buyer. If there is no agreement, then the *general rule* is that the *title to goods passes to the buyer when the seller completes his obligations as to delivery* of the goods:

1. If the contract requires the seller to "ship" the goods to the buyer, then title passes to the buyer when the seller delivers conforming goods to the carrier.

2. If the contract requires the seller to "deliver" the goods to the buyer, title does not pass to the buyer until the goods are delivered to the buyer and tendered to him.

3. If delivery is to be made without moving the goods, then title passes at the time and place of contracting. An exception is made if title to the goods is represented by a document of title such as a warehouse receipt; then, title passes when the document of title is delivered to the buyer.

If the buyer rejects goods tendered to him, title reverts to the seller [2–401(4)].

**Importance of Title.** At common law, most of the problems relating to risks, insurable interests in goods, remedies, and similar rights and liabilities were determined on the basis of who was the technical title owner at the particular moment the right or liability arose. Under the Code, however, the rights of the seller and buyer and of third persons are determined irrespective of the technicality of who has the title, unless the provision of the Code expressly refers to title. Determination of who has title to the goods is important in instances in which the rights of the seller's or the buyer's creditors in the goods are an issue. The *Russell v. Transamerica Insurance Co.* case, which appears later in this chapter, illustrates another instance in which determination of the title holder may be important: whether the seller's insurance policy covers a particular loss.

## TITLE AND THIRD PARTIES

**Obtaining Good Title.** A fundamental rule of property law is that a buyer cannot receive better title to goods than the seller had. If Thief steals a television set from Adler and sells it to Brown, Brown does not get good title to the set, because Thief had no title to it. Adler would have the right to recover the set from Brown. Similarly, if Brown sold the set to Carroll, Carroll could get no better title to it than Brown had. Adler would have the right to recover the set from Carroll.

Under the Code, however, there are several exceptions to the general rule that a buyer cannot get better title to goods than his seller had. The most important exceptions include the following: (1) a person who has a **voidable title** to goods can pass good title to a bona fide purchaser for value; (2) a person who buys goods in the regular course of a retailer's business takes free of any interests in the goods that the retailer has given to others; and (3) a person who buys goods in the ordinary course of a dealer's business takes free of any claim of a person who entrusted those goods to the dealer.

**Transfers of Voidable Title.** A seller who has a *voidable title* has the power to pass good title to a *good faith purchaser for value* [2–403(1)]. A seller has a voidable title to goods if he has obtained his title through fraudulent representations. For example, a person would have a voidable title if he obtained goods by impersonating another person or by paying for them with a bad check or if he obtained goods without paying the agreed purchase price when it was agreed that the transaction was to be a cash sale. Under the Code, **good faith** means "honesty in fact in the conduct or transaction concerned" [1–201(19)] and a buyer has given **value** if he has given any consideration sufficient to support a simple contract [1–201(44)].

For example, Jones goes to the ABC Appliance Store, convinces the clerk that he is really Clark, who is a good customer of ABC, and leaves with a stereo charged to Clark's account. If Jones sells the stereo to Davis, who gives Jones value for it and has no knowledge of the fraud that Jones perpetrated on ABC, Davis gets good title to the stereo. ABC cannot recover the stereo from Davis; instead, it must look for Jones, the person who deceived it. In this situation, both ABC and Davis were innocent of wrongdoing, but the law considers Davis to be the more worthy of its protection because ABC was in a better position to have prevented the wrongdoing by Jones and because Davis bought the goods in good faith and for value. The same result would be reached if Jones had given ABC a check that later bounced and then sold the stereo to Davis, who was a good faith purchaser for value. Davis would have good title to the stereo, and ABC would have to pursue its right against Jones on the bounced check.

The *R. H. Macy's New York, Inc. v. Equitable Diamond Corp.* case, which follows, illustrates the difficulty of trying to determine whether a subsequent buyer can qualify as a good faith purchaser for value and thus get good title from a seller with a voidable title.

**Buyers in the Ordinary Course of Business.** A person who buys goods in the ordinary course of business from a person dealing in goods of that type takes free of any security interest in the goods given by his seller to another person [9–307(1)]. A **buyer in ordinary course** is a person who in *good faith* and *without knowledge* that the sale to him is in violation of the ownership rights of a third party buys goods in the *ordinary course of business* of a *person selling goods of that kind,* other than a pawnbroker [1–201(9)].

For example, Brown Buick may borrow money from Bank in order to finance its inventory of new Buicks; in turn, Bank may take a security interest in the inventory to secure repayment of the loan. If Carter buys a new Buick from Brown Buick, he gets good title to the Buick free and clear of the Bank's security interest if he is a buyer in the ordinary course of business. The basic purpose of this exception is to protect those who innocently buy from merchants and thereby to promote confidence in such commercial transactions. The exception also reflects the fact that the bank is more interested in the proceeds from the sale than in the inventory. Security interests and the rights of buyers in the ordinary course of business are discussed in more detail in Chapter 40.

**Entrusting of Goods.** A third exception to the general rule is that if goods are *entrusted* to a *merchant who deals in goods of that kind,* the merchant has the *power* to transfer all rights of the entruster to a *buyer in the ordinary course of business* [2–403(12)]. For example, Gail takes her watch to Jeweler, a retail jeweler, to have it repaired, and Jeweler sells the watch to Mary. Mary would acquire good title to the watch, and Gail would have to proceed against Jeweler for conversion of her watch. The purpose behind this rule is to protect commerce by giving confidence to buyers that they will get good title to the goods they buy from merchants in the ordinary course of business. However, a merchant-seller cannot pass good title to stolen goods even if the buyer is a buyer in the ordinary course of business. This is because the original owner did nothing to facilitate the transfer.

As you will see in the *Porter v. Wertz* case below, not only should the owner of property be careful as to whom he entrusts the property, but also a buyer must exercise some caution to be sure he will get a good title.

## R. H. Macy's New York, Inc. v. Equitable Diamond Corp.

**34 UCC Rep. 896 (N.Y. Civ. Ct. 1982)**

Macy's, a retail department store chain, sold a 2.25-carat diamond solitaire ring to Marie Draper for $9,742.50. Draper paid for the ring with a check that was subsequently dishonored for insufficient funds. On November 18, 1981, Equitable Diamond Corporation, a diamond dealer in a building that housed numerous diamond dealers purchased the ring from Draper for $2,500. On December 7, 1981, Equitable sold the ring for $4,000 to Ideal Cut Diamonds, another diamond dealer who occupied a counter adjoining the one occupied by Equitable. The following day, Ideal sold the ring to a customer for $4,900.

Macy's brought suit against Equitable and Ideal to recover the value of the diamond ring. Equitable and Ideal moved to have the case dismissed on the ground that Macy's had not stated a cause of action against them.

**Tomkins, Judge.** Macy's argues that Equitable never acquired title to the ring since as a "thief," Ms. Draper had no title to transfer. Equitable and Ideal on the other hand counter that Draper had voidable title to the ring and that as good faith purchasers for value they acquired full title to the ring notwithstanding the defects in Ms. Draper's title [§ 2–403(1)].

Macy's contends that the exceptionally low price asked by Draper should have alerted Equitable to the defects in title. Macy's asserts that the excellent condition of the ring made it obvious to Equitable that the ring was worth much more than the price Equitable paid. As further evidence is the low price at which Equitable sold the ring within a short period of time at a substantial profit to a fellow dealer. Accordingly, Macy's urges that Equitable was not a good faith purchaser for value.

The Uniform Commercial Code provides that if passage of title is conditioned upon the performance of an act, then title is voidable and full title can be transferred to a third party if that third party was a "good faith purchaser for value" [§ 2–403(1)]. In the instant case, passage of title from Macy's to Ms. Draper was conditioned upon the payment of her check. Therefore, she had voidable title to the ring and could only transfer full title to the ring to a third party who qualified as a good faith purchaser for value under the Code.

Equitable and Ideal assert that they acted in good faith in the purchase of the ring and that they did all they were required to do under the circumstances including the filing of a notice of purchase with the Police Department and requiring Ms. Draper to represent in writing to them that the property sold was her personal property and she was the sole owner thereof.

Equitable and Ideal also point out that in the diamond industry, dealers purchase diamonds for prices far below those charged to retail customers by stores such as Macy's. According to them, Macy's allegedly marks up items such as jewelry substantially over the wholesale price which the item could be obtained for in the diamond district. Mr. Friedman, principal of Equitable, stated in his affidavit that in the diamond market $2,500 for the ring in question was entirely fair and reasonable.

"Good faith" has been defined in this context as "honesty in fact and the observance of reasonable commercial standards of fair dealing."

The question of whether the price at which Equitable purchased the ring was so low as to put it on notice that title to the ring may be defective is an issue to be resolved at trial and may be determinative of the good faith issue.

If a merchant chooses to take advantage of the low price at which an item is being offered for sale and purchases, when the unusually low price puts the merchant on notice of possible defective title, he does so at his peril and without the protection of the Uniform Commercial Code § 2–403(1).

It appears to the court that where a diamond dealer purchases a ring for $2,500, sells it to a fellow dealer for $4,000, who in turn sells the ring to another dealer for $4,900, the good faith requirements of Uniform Commercial Code § 2–403(1) become an issue of fact to be resolved at trial. It cannot be said as a matter of law that honesty in fact and the observance of reasonable commercial standards of fair dealing are present.

Based upon the foregoing, the court finds that Equitable and Ideal have not established to the satisfaction of this court that Equitable acted as a good faith purchaser for value. A determination on this issue can only be made after a trial at which time the credibility of all witnesses will be judged.

The motion to dismiss denied and case set for trial.

---

## Porter v. Wertz

**416 N.Y.S.2d (N.Y. Sup. Ct. 1979) aff'd 439 N.Y.S.2d 105 (N.Y. Ct. App. 1981)**

Samuel Porter, a collector of artworks, was the owner of a painting by Maurice Utrillo entitled *Château de Lion-sur-Mer.* In 1972–73, he entered into a number of transactions with a Harold Von Maker, who was using the name Peter Wertz—a real person who was an acquaintance of Von Maker. Von Maker bought one painting from Porter, paying $50,000 cash and giving him a series of 10 promissory notes for $10,000 each. Von Maker also convinced Porter to let him hang the Utrillo in his home while he decided whether or not to buy it.

When payment on the first of the $10,000 notes was not made on the due date, Porter investigated and found that he was dealing, not with Peter Wertz, but with Von Maker, a man with a history of fraudulent dealings. A letter that Porter had obtained from Von Maker, which was signed with the name Peter Wertz, acknowledged receipt of the Utrillo.

The letter also stated that the painting was on consignment with a client of Von Maker and that within 30 days Von Maker would either return the painting or pay Porter $30,000. However, at the time Von Maker had given this assurance to Porter, he had already disposed of the Utrillo by using the real Peter Wertz to sell it to the Richard Feigen gallery for $20,000. Wertz delivered the painting to a Ms. Drew-Bear at the Feigen gallery after being introduced to Feigen by an art associate of Von Maker.

Porter then brought an action against Peter Wertz and Richard Feigen to recover either possession of the painting or its equivalent value. Feigen claimed to have obtained good title to the painting as a buyer in the ordinary course of business.

**Birns, Judge.** The provisions of statutory estoppel are found in section 2–403 of the Uniform Commercial Code. Subsection 2 provides that "any entrusting of possession of goods to a merchant who deals in goods of that kind gives him power to transfer all rights of the entruster to a buyer in the ordinary course of business." Uniform Commercial Code, section 1–201, subdivision 9, defines a "buyer in the ordinary course of business" as "a person who in good faith and without knowledge that the sale to him is in violation of the ownership rights or security interest of a third party in the goods buys in ordinary course from a person in the business of selling goods of that kind."

In order to determine whether the defense of statutory estoppel is available to Feigen, we must begin by ascertaining whether Feigen fits the definition of "buyer in the ordinary course of business." [UCC, § 1–201(9).] Feigen does not fit that definition, for two reasons. First, Wertz, from whom Feigen bought the Utrillo, was not an art dealer—he was not "a person in the business of selling goods of that kind" [UCC, § 1–201(9)] in the transaction with Wertz. Uniform Commercial Code, § 2–103, subdivision (1)(b), defines "good faith" in the case of a merchant as "honesty in fact and the observance of reasonable commercial standards of fair dealing in the trade." Although this definition by its terms embraces the "reasonable commercial standards of fair dealing in the trade," it should not—and cannot—be interpreted to permit, countenance or condone commercial standards of sharp trade practice or indifference as to the "provenance," i.e., history of ownership or the right to possess or sell an objet d'art, such as is present in the case before us.

We note that neither Ms. Drew-Bear nor her employer Feigen made any investigation to determine the status of Wertz, i.e., whether he was an art merchant, "a person in the business of selling goods of that kind" [UCC, § 1–201(9)]. Had Ms. Drew-Bear done so much as call either of the telephone numbers Wertz had left, she would have learned that Wertz was employed by a delicatessen and was not an art dealer. Nor did Ms. Drew-Bear or Feigen make any effort to verify whether Wertz was the owner or authorized by the owner to sell the painting he was offering. Ms. Drew-Bear had available to her the Petrides volume on Utrillo which included *Château de Lion-sur-Mer* in its catalogue of the master's works. Although this knowledge alone might not have been enough to put Feigen on notice that Wertz was not the true owner at the time of the transaction, it should have raised a doubt as to Wertz's right of possession, calling for further verification before the purchase by Feigen was consummated. Thus, it appears that statutory estoppel provided by Uniform Commercial code, § 2–403(2), was not available as a defense to Feigen.

Judgment for Porter.

## RISK OF LOSS

The transportation of goods from sellers to buyers can be a risky business. The carrier of the goods may lose, damage, or destroy them; floods, tornadoes, and other natural catastrophes may take their toll; thieves may steal all or part of the goods. If neither party is at fault for the loss, who should bear the risk? If the buyer has the risk when the goods are damaged or lost, the buyer is liable for the contract price. If the seller has the risk, he is liable for damages unless substitute performance can be tendered.

The common law placed the risk on the party who had technical title at the time of the loss. The Code rejects this approach and provides specific rules governing risk of loss that are designed to provide certainty and to place the risk on the party best able to protect against loss and most likely to be insured against it. Risk of loss under the Code depends on the terms of the parties' agreement, on the moment the loss occurs, and on whether one of the parties was in breach of contract when the loss occurred.

**The Terms of the Agreement.** The contracting parties, subject to the rule of good faith, may specify who has the risk of loss in their agreement [2–509(4)]. This they may do directly or by using certain commonly accepted shipping terms in their contract. In addition, the Code has certain general rules on risk of loss that amplify specific shipping terms and control risk of loss in cases where specific terms are not used [2–509].

**Shipment Contracts.** If the contract requires the seller to ship the goods by carrier but does not require their delivery to a specific destination, the risk passes to the buyer when the seller delivers the goods to the carrier [2–509(1)(a)]. The following are commonly used shipping terms that create *shipment contracts:*

1. *FOB (free on board) point of origin.* This term calls for the seller to deliver the goods free of expense and at the seller's risk at the place designated. For example, a contract between a seller located in Chicago and a buyer in New York calls for delivery FOB Chicago. The seller must deliver the goods at his expense and at his risk to a carrier in the place designated in the contract, namely Chicago, and arrange for their carriage. Because the shipment term in this example is FOB Chicago, the seller bears the risk and expense of delivering the goods to the carrier, but the seller is not responsible for delivering the goods to a specific destination. If the term is "FOB vessel, car, or other vehicle," the seller must load the goods on board at his own risk and expense [2–319(1)].
2. *FAS (free alongside ship).* This term is commonly used in maritime contracts and is normally accompanied by the name of a specific vessel and port, for example, "FAS (the ship) *Calgary,* Chicago Port Authority." The seller must deliver the goods alongside the vessel Calgary at the Chicago Port Authority at his own risk and expense [2–319(2)].
3. *CIF (cost, insurance, and freight).* This term means that the price of the goods includes the cost of shipping and insuring them. The seller bears this expense and the risk of loading the goods [2–320].
4. *C&F.* This term is the same as CIF, except that the seller is not obligated to insure the goods [2–320].

The *Morauer v. Deak & Co., Inc.* case, which follows, provides an example of the risk borne by a buyer in a shipment contract.

**Destination Contracts.** If the contract requires the seller to deliver the goods to a specific destination, the seller bears the risk and expense of delivery to that destination [2–509(1)(b)]. The following are commonly used shipping terms that create *destination contracts:*

1. *FOB destination.* An FOB term coupled with the place of destination of the goods puts the expense and risk of delivering the goods to that destination on the seller [2– 319(1)(b)]. For example, a contract between a seller in Chicago and a buyer in Phoenix might call for shipment FOB Phoenix. The seller must ship the goods to Phoenix at her own expense, and she also retains the risk of delivery of the goods to Phoenix.

2. *Ex-Ship.* This term does not specify a particular ship, but it places the expense and risk on the seller until the goods are unloaded from whatever ship is used [2–322].

3. *No arrival, no sale.* This term places the expense and risk during shipment on the seller. If the goods fail to arrive through no fault of the seller, the seller has no further liability to the buyer [2–324].

For example, a Chicago-based seller contracts to sell a quantity of shirts to a buyer FOB Phoenix, the buyer's place of business. The shirts are destroyed en route when the truck carrying the shirts is involved in an accident. The risk of the loss of the shirts is on the seller, and the buyer is not obligated to pay for them. The seller may have the right to recover from the trucking company, but between the seller and the buyer, the seller has the risk of loss. If the contract had called for delivery FOB the seller's manufacturing plant, then the risk of loss would have been on the buyer. The buyer would have had to pay for the shirts and then pursue any claims that he had against the trucking company.

**Goods in the Possession of Third Parties.** If the goods are in the possession of a bailee and are to be delivered without being moved, the risk of loss passes to the buyer upon delivery to him of a negotiable document of title for the goods; if no negotiable document of title has been used, the risk of loss passes when the bailee indicates to the buyer that the buyer has the right to the possession of the goods [2–509(2)]. For example, if Farmer sells Miller a quantity of grain currently stored at Grain Elevator, the risk of loss of the grain will shift from Farmer to Miller (1) when a negotiable warehouse receipt for the grain is delivered to Miller or (2) when Grain Elevator notifies Miller that it is holding the grain for Miller.

**Risk Generally.** If the transaction does not fall within the situations discussed above, the risk of loss passes to the buyer upon receipt of the goods if the seller is a merchant; if the seller is not a merchant, then the risk of loss passes to the buyer upon the tender of delivery of the goods to the buyer [2–509(3)]. If Jones bought a television set from ABC Appliance on Monday, intending to pick it up on Thursday, and the set was stolen on Wednesday, the risk of loss remained with ABC. However, if Jones had purchased the set from his next-door neighbor and could have taken delivery of the set on Monday (i.e., delivery was tendered then), the risk of loss was Jones's.

**Effect of Breach on Risk of Loss.** When a seller tenders goods that do not conform to the contract and the buyer has the right to reject the goods, the risk of loss remains with the seller until any defect is cured or until the buyer accepts the goods [2–510(1)]. Where the buyer rightfully revokes his acceptance of goods, the risk of loss is with the seller to the extent that any loss is not covered by the buyer's insurance [2–510(2)]. This rule gives the seller the benefit of any insurance carried by the buyer.

For example, if Adler bought a new Buick from Brown Buick that he later returned to Brown because of serious defects in it and if through no fault of Adler's the automobile was damaged while in his possession, then the risk of loss would be with Brown. However, if Adler had insurance on the automobile covering damage to it and recovered from the insurance company, Adler would have to turn the insurance proceeds over to Brown or use them to fix the car before returning it to Brown.

When a buyer repudiates a contract for goods and those goods have already been set aside by the seller, the risk of loss stays with the buyer for a commercially reasonable time after the repudiation [2–510(3)]. Suppose Cannery contracts to buy Farmer's entire crop of peaches. Farmer picks the peaches, crates them, tenders delivery to Cannery, and stores them in his barn for Cannery. Cannery then tells Farmer that it does not intend to honor the contract. Shortly thereafter, but before Farmer has a chance to find another buyer, the peaches are spoiled by a fire. If Farmer's insurance covers only part of the loss, Cannery must bear the rest of the loss.

**Insurable Interest.** The general practice of insuring risks is recognized and provided for under the Code. A buyer may protect his interest in goods that are the subject matter of a sales contract before he actually obtains title. The buyer obtains an insurable interest in existing goods when they are identified as the goods covered by the contract even though they are in fact nonconforming. The seller retains an insurable interest in goods so long as he has either title or a security interest in them [2–501(2)]. The importance of the seller's retention of an insurable interest in goods he has sold is illustrated in the *Russell v. Transamerican Insurance Co.* case below.

## Morauer v. Deak & Co., Inc.

**26 UCC Rep. 1142 (D.C. Super. Ct. 1979)**

On March 12, 1975, Raymond Morauer contracted with Deak & Co., a dealer in foreign currency, to purchase for investment purposes several bags of silver coins and a quantity of gold coins. He paid for his purchase with personal checks totaling $35,000. After his checks had cleared, he came to Deak's place of business to take delivery. Morauer had a discussion with Deak's assistant manager about the District of Columbia tax on the sale of gold. Both parties agreed that in order to avoid the tax, an admittedly legal endeavor, Deak would ship all of Morauer's gold coins to his residence in suburban Maryland. There was no District of Columbia tax on silver coins, so Morauer took possession of them.

Deak placed the gold coins in two packages and, as authorized by Morauer, sent the packages to his house by registered mail, return receipt requested. Deak did not insure the packages with the U.S. Postal Service but instead, in accordance with its custom, relied on its own insurance contract with its insurer to cover any risk of loss. Only one package was received by Morauer; however, he did not open it and thus did not realize at the time that he had received only a portion of his gold coins. More than two years later, while making an inventory of his collection, Morauer discovered the problem and notified Deak. By that time, the Post Office had destroyed its records of the shipment and Deak's insurance coverage for that shipment had expired. Morauer then brought a lawsuit asking the value at their time of purchase of the gold coins that he had not received.

**Smith, Judge.** The court must determine whether the risk of loss of the gold coins in question passed from the defendant Deak to Morauer upon Deak's delivery of the coins to the Post Office for shipment to Morauer. If so, then Deak is not liable to Morauer for the value of the lost shipment. If the risk of loss did not pass, however, then Deak is liable for the full value of the coins at time of purchase.

The case is governed by § 2–509(1) of the UCC, and the court must determine whether paragraph (a) or paragraph (b) of subsection (1) controls. If the contract was a so-called "shipment" contract, then the risk of loss passed to Morauer, the buyer, on Deak's delivery to the carrier, § 2–509(1)(a), provided, however, that Deak also satisfied the UCC's requirements for a valid "shipment" contract, § 2–504. If, on the other hand, the contract called for delivery at a particular destination, then the risk of loss never passed to Morauer, because the goods were never delivered, and Morauer must prevail, § 2–509(1)(b).

The fact that the parties had agreed that Deak would ship the coins to Morauer's residence in Maryland is not dispositive of this controversy. A "ship to" term in a sales contract has no significance in determining whether the agreement is a "shipment" or "destination" contract. Moreover, there is a preference in the UCC for "shipment" contracts. The drafters of the UCC state the preference and give the reasons for it in the following manner:

> For the purposes of subsections (2) and (3) there is omitted from this Article the rule under prior uniform legislation that a term requiring the seller to pay the freight or cost of transportation to the buyer is equivalent to an agreement by the seller to deliver to the buyer or at an agreed destination. This omission is with the specific intention of negating the rule, for *under this Article the "shipment" contract is regarded as the normal one and the "destination" contract as the variant type. The seller is not obligated to deliver at a named destination and bear the concurrent risk of loss until arrival, unless he has specifically agreed so to deliver or the commercial understanding of the terms used by the parties contemplates such delivery.* Uniform Code Comment No. 5; § 2–503 (emphasis added).

Here we have an order and payment by Morauer in person to Deak with receipts signed by Kirsch, Deak's agent, indicating Morauer's home address and, in one instance, including the further instruction, "c/o Mrs. Geraldine Morauer." Morauer and Kirsch discussed delivery of the coins, and Morauer decided that to avoid payment of the District of Columbia sales tax, he would have them shipped to his residence. Deak mailed the gold coins in two packages, both of which were properly addressed, stamped and deposited at the United States Post Office. Deak also included the cost of postage as part of Morauer's total bill. Therefore, we hold that Deak was authorized by the contract to ship the gold coins to Morauer by carrier, and that the risk of loss passed from Deak to Morauer on delivery of the packages of coins to the Post Office.

Although the court's finding that the parties were operating under a "shipment" contract puts the risk of loss on Morauer from the time of Deak's delivery to the authorized carrier, there remains the question whether defendant Deak met all the statutory requirements of "shipment" contracts under the applicable UCC section 2–504. That section states:

> Where the seller is required or authorized to send the goods to the buyer and the contract does not require him to deliver them at a particular destination, then unless otherwise agreed he must
>
> (a) put the goods in the possession of such a carrier and make such a contract for their transportation as may be reasonable having regard to the nature of the goods and other circumstances of the case; and
>
> (b) obtain and promptly deliver or tender in due form any document necessary to enable the buyer to obtain possession of the goods or otherwise required by the agreement or by usage of trade; and

(c) promptly notify the buyer of the shipment.

Failure to notify the buyer under paragraph (c) or to make a proper contract under paragraph (a) is a ground for rejection only if material delay or loss ensues.

In the case now before this court Deak followed its regular practice of insuring the shipments with its own insurance company, properly addressed each package and sent both by first-class, registered mail, with a return receipt requested. Deak therefore made all arrangements with the carrier, the United States Postal Service, as were "reasonable having regard to the nature of the goods and other circumstances of the case." § 2–504(a). Deak had no obligation under paragraph (b) of § 2–504, insofar as there were no documents necessary to enable Morauer to obtain possession of the goods, and none "otherwise required by the agreement or by usage of trade." And finally, Deak was in compliance with § 2–504(c) in that Kirsch notified Morauer of the mailing of the gold coins when Morauer went to Deak's office to take delivery personally of the silver coins he had also purchased.

Judgment in favor of Deak.

---

## Russell v. Transamerica Insurance Co.

### 322 N.W.2d 178 (Mich. Ct. App. 1982)

Russell, a full-service boat dealer and marine equipment service company, entered into an agreement to sell a 19-foot Kinsvater boat to Robert Clouser for $8,500. Pursuant to the agreement, Clouser made a down payment of $1,700, with the balance of the purchase price to be paid when he took possession of the boat. Under the agreement, Russell was to retain possession of the boat in order to transfer an engine and drive train from another boat. Upon the completion of these alterations, Clouser was to take delivery of the boat at Russell's marina.

While the boat was being tested by employees of Russell, prior to delivery to Clouser, it hit a seawall and was completely destroyed. Russell was insured by Transamerica Insurance under a policy that excluded watercraft hazards, except for damage to any watercraft under 26 feet in length *not* owned by Russell. Transamerica refused to honor a claim from Russell for the damage to Clouser's boat, contending that the damage was excluded because Russell owned the boat at the time of the accident. Russell then brought suit against Transamerica Insurance. The trial court ruled in favor of Transamerica Insurance, and Russell appealed.

**Lambros, Judge.** The trial court, granting summary judgment in favor of Transamerica, stated:

The facts reflect that the boat was in possession of Russell on August 4, 1977. Robert Clouser could not have taken delivery of the boat on the day in question. Under § 2–401(2), therefore, title had not passed to Clouser. . . . Effectively speaking, the risk of loss was, on August 4, 1977, on Russell's shoulders.

Under subsection (3)(b) of § 2–401, if delivery is to be made without moving the goods and no documents of title are involved, title passes at the time of contracting if the goods are already identified at the time of contracting. We note that goods need not be in a deliverable state to be identified to the contract.

In the instant case, because the 19-foot Kinsvater boat had been identified at the time the parties contracted for sale, because no documents of title were to be delivered by the sellers, there being no Michigan requirement for documents of title for boats at that time, and because delivery of the boat was to be effected without its being moved, title passed to the buyer at the time of contracting under 2–401 (3)(b). The fact that the boat was not outfitted with all the equipment specified in the contract did not prevent its identification to the contract nor did it prevent title from passing at that time.

In addition, we find that the trial court erred in its decision in equating risk of loss with title. Under § 2–509, risk of loss passes to the buyer on his receipt of the goods or on tender of delivery by the seller. Risk of loss, then, does not necessarily follow title. In the instant case, because Russell retained possession of the boat after title passed, he bore the risk of loss. Title in the buyer, however, triggered the policy exception to the watercraft hazard exclusion regardless of where risk of loss lay.

We hold that the trial court erred in granting summary judgment in favor of Transamerica because title in the boat at the time of the accident was in one other than Russell and the boat was, thus, covered under Russell's policy.

Judgment reversed in favor of Russell.

## SALES ON TRIAL

A common commercial practice is for a seller of goods to entrust possession of goods to a buyer to either give the buyer an opportunity to decide whether or not to buy them or to try to resell them to a third person. The entrusting may be known as a **sale on approval,** a **sale or return** or a **consignment,** depending on the terms of the entrusting. Occasionally, the goods may be damaged, destroyed, or stolen, or the creditors of the buyer may try to claim them; on such occasions, the form of the entrusting will determine whether the buyer or the seller had the risk of loss and whether the buyer's creditors can successfully claim the goods.

**Sale on Approval.** In a sale on approval, the goods are delivered to the buyer with an understanding that he may use or test them for the purpose of determining whether he wishes to buy them [2–326(1)(a)]. In a sale on approval, neither the risk of loss nor title to the goods passes to the buyer until he accepts the goods. The buyer has the right to use the goods in any manner consistent with the purpose of the trial, but any unwarranted exercise of ownership over the goods is considered to be an acceptance of the goods. Similarly, if the buyer fails to notify the seller of his election to return the goods, he is considered to have accepted them [2–327]. For example, if Dealer agrees to let Hughes take a new automobile home to drive for a day to see whether she wants to buy it and Hughes takes the car on a two-week vacation trip, Hughes will be considered to have accepted the automobile because she used it in a manner beyond that contemplated by the trial and as if she were its owner. If Hughes had driven the automobile for a day, decided not to buy it, and parked it in her driveway for two weeks without telling Dealer of her intention to return it, Hughes would also be deemed to have accepted the automobile.

Once the buyer has notified the seller of his election to return the goods, the return of the goods is at the seller's expense and risk. Because the title and risk of loss of goods delivered on a sale on approval remain with the seller, goods held on approval are not subject to the claims of the buyer's creditors until the buyer accepts them [2–326].

**Sale or Return.** In a "sale or return," goods are delivered to a buyer for resale with the understanding that the buyer has the right to return them [2–326(1)(b)]. Under a sale or return, the title and risk of loss are with the buyer. While the goods are in the buyer's possession, they are subject to the claims of his creditors [2–326 and 2–327]. For example, if Publisher delivers some paperbacks to Bookstore on the understanding that Bookstore may return any of the paperbacks that remain unsold at the end of six months, the transaction is a sale or return. If Bookstore is destroyed by a fire, the risk of loss of the paperbacks was Bookstore's and it is responsible to Publisher for the purchase price. Similarly, if Bookstore becomes insolvent and is declared a bankrupt, the paperbacks will be considered part of the bankruptcy estate. If the buyer elects to return goods held on a sale or return basis, the return is at the buyer's risk and expense.

The case which follows, *In re Monahan & Co., Ltd.*, illustrates the risks borne by a person who makes goods available on a "sale or return" basis.

**Sale on Consignment.** Sometimes, goods are delivered to a merchant "on consignment." If the merchant to whom goods are consigned maintains a place of business dealing in goods of that kind under a name other than that of the person consigning the goods, then the consignor must take certain steps to protect his interest in the goods or they will be subject to the claims of the merchant's creditors. The consignor must (1) make sure that a sign indicating the consignor's interest is prominently posted at the place of business, or (2) make sure that the merchant's creditors know that he is generally in the business of selling goods owned by others, or (3) comply with the filing provisions of Article 9 of the Code—Secured Transactions.[3]

For example, Jones operates a retail music store under the name of City Music Store. Baldwin Piano Company delivers some pianos to Jones on consignment. If no notices are posted indicating Baldwin's interest in the pianos, if Jones is not generally known to be selling from a consigned inventory, and if Baldwin does not file its interest with the recording office pursuant to Article 9 of the Code, then the goods are subject to the claims of Jones's creditors. This is crucial to Baldwin because it may have intended to retain title. However, the Code treats a "consignment" to a person doing business under a name other than that of the consignor as a "sale or return" [2– 326(3)]. If Jones did business as the Baldwin Piano Company, Baldwin's interest would be protected from the claims of Jones's creditors without the need for Baldwin to post a sign or to file under Article 9.

[3] These provisions are discussed in detail in Chapter 40.

## In re Monahan & Co., Ltd.

### 36 UCC Rep. 121 (Bankr. D. Mass. 1983)

W. N. Provenzano was a manufacturer and wholesaler of jewelry located in New York City. On November 3, 1980, Arthur Jervis, its representative, left two rings with Monahan & Co., a retail jewelry business. At that time, a memorandum agreement was signed by Jervis and an employee of Monahan. The agreement stated:

> The goods described and valued as below are delivered to you for EXAMINATION AND INSPECTION ONLY and remain our property subject to our order and shall be returned to us on demand. Such merchandise, until returned to us and actually received, are at your risk from all hazards. NO RIGHT OR POWER IS GIVEN TO YOU TO SELL, PLEDGE, HYPOTHECATE OR OTHERWISE DISPOSE of this merchandise regardless of prior transactions. A sale of this merchandise can only be effected and title will pass only if, as and when we the said owner shall agree to such sale and a bill of sale rendered therefor.

The agreement also had the address of Provenzano printed on it. Filled in on the agreement was a description of the two rings in question. Jervis also wrote by hand on the agreement "To work with Customer."

In January and February 1981, Provenzano made several demands for the return of the two rings. The rings were not returned. On February 2, 1981, Monahan filed a voluntary Chapter 11 bankruptcy petition. Sometime thereafter, Monahan sold the two rings, one for $4,250 and the other to an unknown purchaser for an unknown amount.

Provenzano brought suit, claiming that the goods were delivered to Monahan on a bailment and not for resale and that Monahan, as bailee, had therefore unlawfully converted the goods. Provenzano claimed that it was entitled to $15,000, the asserted fair market value of the rings.

**Glennon, Bankruptcy Judge.** The issue presented to this court is whether the adoption of the Uniform Commercial Code in Massachusetts changes what would have been a bailment relationship. I find that it does.

UCC § 2–326(3) states that even if title is reserved, the transaction will be considered a "sale or return" if the goods are delivered to a person for sale and such person maintains a place of business at which he deals in goods of the kind involved and under a name other than the name of the person making delivery. Clearly in the instant case, Monahan dealt in retail jewelry and was selling jewelry other than under the name of Provenzano. The issue disputed by Provenzano is whether the goods were delivered to Monahan for sale. Both Mr. Jervis, the salesman, and Monahan had potential customers to whom they wanted to sell the rings. Clearly, the rings were left with Monahan so that they could be sold. Provenzano's argument that the rings were left only to be shown to a customer and could only be sold after Provenzano agreed they could be sold does not negate the fact that the rings were left for the purpose of being sold. While the agreement initially states that the goods were delivered "for examination and inspection only," it further states that "a sale can only be effected . . . when we the said owner shall agree to such sale and a bill of sale rendered therefor." Thus, the agreement does provide for a sale, albeit the right to sell is subject to certain terms. I find that the goods were delivered to Monahan for sale and thus the transaction is within UCC § 2–326 and is not controlled by the common law of bailment.

Since the transaction is within UCC § 2–236, the issue becomes what is the status of Provenzano's claim as to the two rings. Subsection (2) of § 2–326 provides that goods held on sale or return are subject to the claims of the buyer's creditors while in the buyer's possession. Since the rings were in the possession of Monahan on the day the Chapter 11 bankruptcy petition was filed, Provenzano would have a general unsecured claim against the debtor's estate.

Although the result may seem unfair, Provenzano was not without protection. Subsection (3) of § 2–326 provides three ways for the consignor to protect its title and interest. The consignor can protect its interest by posting a sign in compliance with local law protecting its rights as a consignor; the interest will be protected if it can be established that the person to whom the goods were delivered is generally known by its creditors to be engaged in selling goods of others; or the consignor can comply with the filing provisions of Article 9. The official comment to this section makes it clear that the purpose of this section is to protect the debtor's creditors who may be misled by the secret reservation of title to the consigned goods. The evidence indicates that none of the above three conditions existed; therefore Provenzano cannot escape the rule of § 2–326(2).

I find that the two rings which were in Monahan's possession on the day of the filing are subject to the claims of all of Monahan's creditors in bankruptcy court. Provenzano has a general unsecured claim for the price it would have charged Monahan for the two rings as stated in the memorandum, i.e., $3,250 and $3,400.

Provenzano allowed an unsecured claim for $6,650 against the bankruptcy estate.

## SUMMARY

Article 2 of the Uniform Commercial Code codifies the law of the sale of goods. Although the Uniform Commercial Code does not apply to contracts to provide services or contracts to sell real property, some courts have applied Code principles by analogy to such contracts. The Code permits parties considerable flexibility to form a contract to sell goods. It sets out the rights of the parties when certain terms are used, and it contains certain other provisions that are to be used if the parties do not specifically agree to the contrary.

Unless otherwise agreed, title passes when the seller has completed his performance. If he is to ship goods, title passes upon delivery to the carrier; if he is to deliver goods, title passes upon delivery and tender. If the goods are in the possession of a bailee and a document of title has been issued, title passes at the place and time of the making of the contract. Rejection of the goods by the buyer reverts title in the seller.

A fundamental rule of property law is that a seller cannot pass better title to goods than he has. Among the exceptions to this general rule are: (1) a person who has voidable title to goods can pass good title to a bona fide purchaser for value; (2) a buyer in the ordinary course of a retailer's business takes free of any interests in the goods that the retailer has given to others; and (3) a person who buys goods in the ordinary course of a dealer's business takes free of any claims of a person who entrusted those goods to the dealer.

The parties to the sales contract may by explicit agreement designate who shall bear the risk of loss or how the risk of loss shall be divided. The inclusion in the sales contract of delivery terms will indicate which of the parties shall bear the risk of loss during transit. If the delivery term is FOB point of origin, the risk of loss passes to the buyer when goods are delivered to the carrier and a reasonable contract for their carriage is made. If the delivery term is FOB destination, the risk of loss passes upon tender of delivery to the buyer. If goods are in the possession of a bailee and are not to be moved, the risk of loss passes to the buyer upon delivery of a negotiable document of title. If there is no negotiable document of title, the risk of loss passes when the bailee acknowledges the buyer's rights.

In a sale on approval, the goods are delivered to the buyer for use or trial and the risk of loss and title remain in the seller. The goods are not subject to claims of the buyer's creditors, and any return of the goods is at the seller's risk and expense. In a sale or return, the goods are sold to the buyer for resale but may be retained at the buyer's option. The risk of loss and title is in the buyer, and the goods are subject to the claims of the buyer's creditors. The return of the goods is at the buyer's risk and expense.

## PROBLEM CASES

1. Hoffman Fuel Company agreed to supply heating fuel oil to Levin's residence in Carmel, New York, on an automatic delivery basis. In December 1975, the oil supply ran out because Hoffman failed to deliver oil. As a result, the water in Levin's heating system froze, causing substantial damage to the heating system and additional damage to the house. In 1981, Levin brought suit against Hoffman seeking to recover for the damage. Hoffman argued that the agreement was essentially one for the sale of goods, so that the four-year statute of frauds in the UCC was applicable. Levin claimed that the agreement was for the sale of a service, so that the New York general six-year statute of limitations was applicable. Should this be considered a contract for the sale of goods governed by the UCC?

2. On February 21, 1974 Lawrence Harbach, a farmer, entered into an oral contract to sell 25,000 bushels of soybeans at $3.81 per bushel to Continental Grain Company, with delivery in October, November, and December. Continental mailed a written confirmation to Harbach to which Harbach never made any written objection. Continental claimed that this satisfied the "merchant" exception to the statute of frauds. Harbach refused to honor the contract, and Continental brought suit for breach of contract. At the trial, one issue was whether Harbach should be considered a "merchant" within the meaning of the Uniform Commercial Code. For several years, Harbach had raised and sold grain as a sole proprietor and as president of a farming corporation; he had sold soybeans for only a few months prior to the alleged sale to Continental. However, his sales of corn had exceeded $100,000 per year from 1970 to 1973. He had also owned or operated three chemical and fertilizer businesses over the past 15 years. Should Harbach be considered a "merchant" for the purpose of applying the Code?

3. Samuel Higgonbottom sold his Mercedes-Benz to Katrina Walters in exchange for a check for $13,500 made out to Walters. He gave her the title to the vehicle indorsed over to her. Walters transferred ownership of the vehicle, together with the ownership papers, to Benzel-Busch, which in turn sold it to A-Leet. Higgonbottom discovered that the check given to him was originally issued in the sum of $13.50 and had been fraudulently raised by Walters. Neither Benzel-Busch nor A-Leet was aware of the fraud.

Higgonbottom then sued A-Leet to recover possession of the vehicle. Is Higgonbottom entitled to recover the vehicle from A-Leet?

**4.** SST Grain Company hired William McColery to haul a quantity of soybeans from Falls City, Nebraska, to the Far-Mar-Co grain elevator in St. Joseph, Missouri. Although McColery's primary business was as a trucker, he also had a reputation in the Fall City area as a sometime "merchant" who bought and sold grain. McColery had previously dealt with Far-Mar-Co both as a trucker and as a seller of grain purportedly belonging to himself. When McColery arrived at Far-Mar-Co's elevator with SST's soybeans, he represented that they were his and received payment. He then absconded with the money. SST brought suit against Far-Mar-Co, claiming that Far-Mar-Co had converted SST's soybeans by paying McColery rather than SST. Far-Mar-Co contends that it got good title to the beans from McColery and that SST's remedy is to go against McColery. Which is correct?

**5.** Eberhard Manufacturing Company entered into a contract to sell certain truck parts to Brown, with the parts to be "shipped to" Brown's place of business in Birmingham, Alabama. Eberhard packaged the parts and placed them on board a common carrier with instructions to deliver the goods to Brown. The parts were lost while in transit. The parties did not expressly agree as to which of them had the risk of loss, and the contract did not contain an FOB term. Which party had the risk of loss, Eberhard or Brown?

**6.** Halstead Hospital was planning new facilities to be financed through the issuance of industrial revenue bonds. A New York City law firm that had been retained by Halstead to serve as its counsel and agent for the bonds closing placed an order to print the bonds with Northern Bank Note Company in Chicago. The law firm confirmed the verbal order by letter and stated that the bond closing was set for December 18. Northern accepted the order, promising that the work would be completed for shipment by December 16 and that the bonds would be at the Signature Company in New York on December 17 so that they could be inspected and signed prior to the formal closing on the following day. Northern printed the bonds and boxed them in four separate cartons. It arranged to have a courier pick up the cartons on December 16 and deliver them to New York on the following morning. However, one of the boxes did not arrive in New York until after December 18. This necessitated cancellation of the December 18 closing. Halstead then brought suit against Northern for breach of contract because of the untimely delivery. One of the issues was whether the contract should be considered a shipment contract or a destination contract. How should the court decide this issue?

**7.** White Motor Company, a manufacturer of trucks, delivered to Bronx Trucks an autocar truck pursuant to an order placed by Bronx Trucks. White Motor received a signed receipt from the manager of Bronx Trucks for the delivery and invoiced Bronx Trucks for the agreed purchase price. After the truck had been delivered and invoiced, it was stolen from Bronx Truck's garage. The title papers to the truck were not delivered to Bronx Truck until after the truck had been stolen. White Motor sued Bronx Truck for the purchase price of the truck, and Bronx Truck defended on the grounds that it did not have title to the truck when it was stolen and thus White Motor was still the owner of it and had the risk of loss. Is Bronx Truck responsible for paying the purchase price to White Motor?

**8.** The Cedar Rapids YMCA bought a large number of cases of candy from Seaway Candy under an agreement by which any unused portion could be returned. The YMCA was to sell the candy to raise money to send boys to camp. The campaign was less than successful, and 688 cases remained unsold. They were returned to Seaway Candy by truck. When delivered to the common carrier, the candy was in good condition. When it arrived at Seaway four days later, it had melted and was completely worthless. Seaway then brought suit against the YMCA to recover the purchase price of the candy spoiled in transit. Between Seaway and the YMCA, which had the risk of loss?

**9.** General Electric Company delivered a stock of large lamps to Pettingell Supply Company "as agent to sell or distribute such lamps." Under the agency contract, Pettingell could sell the lamps directly to certain customers for their own use or resale; it was also authorized to make deliveries of lamps under contracts of sale entered into by General Electric and the purchasers as well as to make deliveries to other retail agents of General Electric. About 20 percent of Pettingell's sales of GE lamps were direct sales to its own customers. Pettingell was also a wholesaler of other electrical supplies, hardware, and housewares. The lamps were its only consignment business. Pettingell had financial difficulties and entered into an assignment for the benefit of creditors. Those creditors claimed the stock of GE lamps, while GE claimed that the lamps were its property because it had a principal-agency relationship with Pettingell. Who is entitled to the lamps?

Chapter 32

# Product Liability

## INTRODUCTION

Product liability law is the body of legal rules dealing with civil suits for losses and injuries resulting from the sale of defective goods.[1] This body of rules is of considerable practical importance to businesspeople. Imagine that you are a manager of a firm manufacturing goods for sale to the public or selling goods produced by other firms. Some of the products that your firm sells will be defective, and various parties may sue your employer as a result. Thus, the legal rules governing such suits should be of concern to you. In your role as a consumer of goods, however, you would obviously view these rules in a quite different light. Finally, like an ordinary consumer, your firm will purchase products made or sold by other firms. If these products turn out to be defective, your employer may want to sue the seller or manufacturer. The rules of product liability law also govern such suits.

[1] This chapter does not discuss the various "consumer protection" measures that involve the payment and credit aspects of consumer transactions. Nor does it discuss product safety regulation. For discussions of these matters, see Chapter 46. Also, some of the product liability implications of the sale of computers are discussed in Chapter 50.

## THE EVOLUTION OF PRODUCT LIABILITY LAW

**The 19th Century.** In the 19th century, the rules governing suits for defective goods were very much to the seller's or manufacturer's advantage. This was the era of *caveat emptor* (let the buyer beware). In contract cases, there was usually no liability unless the seller had made an express promise to the buyer and the goods failed to conform to this promise. Some courts went further, requiring that the words *warrant* or *guarantee* accompany the promise before liability would exist. In negligence suits, the maxim of "no liability without fault" was in full force, and plaintiffs frequently faced problems in proving the defendant's fault because the evidence needed to do so was within the defendant's control. In both contract and negligence cases, finally, the doctrine of "no liability outside privity of contract" often prevented plaintiffs from suing a party with whom they had not dealt directly.[2]

The social and economic conditions that prevailed for much of the 19th century go some way toward explaining these legal rules. At that time, laissez-faire values strongly influenced public policy. One expression of these values was the idea that sellers and manufacturers should be contractually bound only where they had made an actual promise to a party with whom they had dealt directly. Another factor that contributed to the creation of rules limiting manufacturers' liability for defective products was the desire to promote industrialization by preventing potentially crippling liabilities to infant industries. Certain features of the 19th-century economy, however, made the prodefendant rules discussed above less burdensome to plaintiffs than would otherwise have been the case. Chains of distribution tended to be short, so the "no liability outside privity" defense could not always be used. Goods tended to be simple, thus enabling buyers to inspect them for defects. Before the rise of the large corporation late in the 19th century, sellers and buyers were often of relatively equal size, sophistication, and bargaining power. This permitted a certain amount of genuine "sharp trading" between them.

**The 20th Century.** Today, many of the social and economic tendencies typifying the 19th century are conspicuous by their absence. Despite their recent revival, laissez-faire values do not exercise the influence that they did a century ago. Instead, a somewhat more protective, interdependent climate has emerged. With the development of a viable industrial economy, there has been less need to protect manufacturers from liability for defective goods. The emergence of long chains of distribution has meant that consumers frequently do not deal directly with the party ultimately responsible for the defective condition of their goods. With the development of a corporate-based economy, consumers have been less able to bargain on equal terms with such parties in any event. The growing complexity of goods has made buyer inspections more difficult. Finally, the emergence of a full-fledged "consumer society" has meant that product-related losses are more frequent and that the quality of consumer goods looms larger in the array of national concerns.

As a result of all these developments, product liability law has shifted from its earlier *caveat emptor* emphasis to a stance of *caveat venditor* (let the seller beware). This has been particularly true since the 1960s, the decade marking the beginning of the "product liability explosion." Now, courts and legislatures are quite likely to intervene in private contracts for the sale of goods in order to protect

---

[2] Privity of contract is the existence of a direct contractual relationship between two parties. The gradual demise of the "no liability outside privity" rule in New York in the late 19th and early 20th centuries is discussed in Chapter 1.

the consumer. The net result of this intervention and of related legal developments has been greater liability for sellers and manufacturers of defective goods and higher dollar recoveries against such parties. Underlying this shift toward *caveat venditor* is the perception that sellers and manufacturers are best able to bear the economic costs that product defects create for consumers and that such parties are often equipped to "pass on" these costs in the form of higher prices. Thus, the economic risk associated with defective products has been effectively spread throughout society, or *socialized.*

**The Current "Crisis" in Product Liability Law.** The "socialization of risk" policy underlying much of modern product liability law has come under increasing pressure in recent years. Partly in response to the explosion in liability, the product liability insurance premiums paid by sellers and manufacturers have increased considerably. Since such increased costs are more difficult to "pass on," some firms have been put in an economic bind. Businesses unwilling or unable to secure product liability insurance, on the other hand, run the risk of crippling damage awards. It has also been argued that the fear of increased liability has deterred product innovation. These developments have created increased pressure to limit seller and manufacturer liability for defective goods. Generally, this pressure has made itself felt in two ways: (1) actual and proposed moves toward limiting plaintiffs' *ability to recover* for defective goods and (2) actual and proposed moves aimed at preserving plaintiffs' ability to recover, while limiting the *amount* of such recoveries.

## THE ORGANIZATION OF THIS CHAPTER

Imagine that you are the buyer of a new automobile from a local car dealer. If you are a typical consumer, you might well expect that: (1) "sales talk" aside, the car will perform as well as the salesperson said it would perform; (2) the car will also perform as well as its manufacturer has claimed in its advertisements; (3) the car will conform to any written guarantees that were made by the manufacturer or the dealer; (4) the car will be suitable for the ordinary purposes for which such vehicles are used; (5) the car will be suitable for any *special* purposes that you relied on the dealer to consider when it advised you on model, engine, options, and so forth; (6) the car has been properly manufactured and designed; (7) the car is free of significant defects or unusual problems of which you have not been warned; and (8) the car is free of any defects that would make it unreasonably dangerous to drive.

The first half of this chapter discusses certain *theories of product liability recovery* that provide legal protection for the expectations just described. These theories are rules of law stating that plaintiffs can recover for defective goods once certain facts have been proven. The second half of the chapter discusses certain legal problems that are common to all the theories of recovery and whose resolution may vary from theory to theory. For example, what happens if the seller or manufacturer includes contract language that attempts to disclaim liability for defects in the goods? What types of damages can be obtained under each theory? When, if ever, is the absence of privity still a defense for the seller or manufacturer? What happens when the plaintiff's carelessness, misuse of the product, or voluntary acceptance of the risk created by a known product hazard contributes to her losses?

The many conflicting (yet overlapping) theories of product liability recovery and the many legal problems "cutting across" each theory make modern product liability law very complex, detailed, and confusing. These problems are aggravated because the rules discussed in this chapter are largely state law, and the 50 states sometimes differ on key points. Such state-by-state differences create obvious planning and risk management problems for business. Partly in response to this confusion and partly as a reaction to the product liability explosion, a federal product liability act has recently been proposed. The chapter concludes with a brief discussion of one version of this proposed act.

## EXPRESS WARRANTY

**Warranties in General.** A product **warranty** is a contractual promise regarding the nature of the product sold. In a product liability suit based on breach of warranty, the plaintiff is asserting that the goods failed to live up to the seller's promise. Product liability warranties may be express or implied. **Express warranties** are based on the seller's words or on some other voluntary behavior from which a promise regarding the goods can be readily inferred. **Implied warranties** are created by *operation of law.* In an implied warranty case, the promise arises automatically once certain tests have been met. The law implies the promise in order to protect the buyer; whether the seller has freely assented to this implied promise is of no concern.

**Creating an Express Warranty.** UCC section 2–313(1) states that an express warranty can be created in any of three ways. First, any *affirmation of fact or promise* relating to the goods creates an express warranty that the goods will conform to that affirmation of fact or promise. For instance, a statement that an insecticide will kill certain insects creates an express warranty to that effect. Second, any *description* of the goods creates an express warranty that the goods will conform to that description. Although this type of express warranty might overlap with the type just described, it mainly applies where the seller uses descriptive adjectives to characterize the product. Statements that glass is "shatterproof" or that a container is "biodegradable" are examples. Finally, a *sample* or *model* of the goods to be sold creates an express warranty that the rest of the goods will conform to the sample or model. A "sample" is an object actually drawn from the bulk of the goods to be sold, while a "model" is an object offered for the buyer's inspection when the goods themselves are unavailable. Whatever the category in which they fit, pictures, drawings, blueprints, and technical specifications can also create express warranties.

In all of the situations just discussed, no formal words such as "warrant" or "guarantee" are needed to create an express warranty. Nor is it necessary that the seller have a specific intention to make a warranty. How *definite* must a statement be before it can qualify as an express warranty? The *Ewers* case which follows deals with this problem.

**Value, Opinion, and Sales Talk.** Statements of *value* ("This chair would bring you $2,000 at an auction") or *opinion* ("I think this is a good car") do not create express warranties. Statements that amount to "sales talk" or "puffing" also do not create express warranties. Examples include such statements as "This is a good buy," "These are quality goods," or "You'll be happy with this." Of course, there is no clear line between statements of value or opinion and sales talk, on the one hand, and an express warranty, on the other. In close cases, courts consider a number of factors. The more *specific* the statement, the more likely it is that the statement will be considered a warranty. Written statements that appear in the parties' contract of sale are more apt to be deemed warranties than are written statements that appear elsewhere.[3] The *relative knowledge* possessed by the buyer and the seller is another relevant factor. A car salesman's statements about a used car, for instance, stand a greater chance of being express warranties where the buyer knows little about cars than where the buyer is another car dealer. Also, the seller's statements are less likely to be treated as warranties where they are *hedged* or *qualified,* rather than unequivocal.

**The "Basis of the Bargain" Problem.** Under pre-Code law, there could be no recovery for breach of an express warranty unless the buyer *relied* on that warranty in making the purchase. The UCC has abandoned this test, instead requiring that the warranty be "part of the basis of the bargain." The meaning of this basis of the bargain standard is unclear. Some courts say that reliance is still required, while others, such as the *Ewers* court, state that the seller's affirmation must have been only a *contributing factor* in the buyer's decision to purchase. Generally, however, the buyer must at least have had *knowledge* of the warranty for the basis of the bargain test to be met.

**Advertisements.** Statements made in advertisements, catalogs, or brochures may be express warranties. Such sources, however, are frequently filled with sales talk. Also, basis of the bargain problems may arise where the source's role in inducing the sale is uncertain because the buyer heard or read this source well before the sale occurred.

[3] Where the warranty is made orally and the contract of sale is expressed in a writing, parol evidence rule problems may arise. On the parol evidence rule, see Chapter 13.

## Ewers v. Eisenzopf

**276 N.W.2d 802 (Wis. Sup. Ct. 1979)**

Ewers, who owned a saltwater aquarium with tropical fish, purchased several seashells, a piece of coral, and a driftwood branch from the Verona Rock Shop. The shop sold an assortment of rocks, jewelry, novelties, and seashells, but it did not specialize in aquariums or water life. Just before the purchase, Ewers asked the salesclerk whether the items he bought were suitable for placement in a saltwater aquarium. The clerk, a part-time employee with three years' experience at the shop, replied that the items were "suitable for saltwater aquariums, if they were rinsed."

Ewers then made the purchase, took the items home, rinsed them for 20 minutes in a saltwater solution, and placed them in his aquarium. Within one week, 17 of Ewers's tropical fish died. The cause of death was pollution from toxic matter released into the water by the decay of once-living creatures contained in the shells and the coral. Preventing such pollution required a week-long cleansing process that involved soaking the shells and the coral in boiling water.

Ewers sued Eisenzopf, the owner of the shop, for breach of express warranty. The state small claims court, trial court, and circuit court found for Eisenzopf. The circuit court concluded (1) that the clerk's statement was too indefinite to constitute an express warranty and (2) that even if such a warranty existed, it was not breached, since the proper method for cleaning the purchased items was "little more than an extended rinsing or soaking." Ewers appealed to the Wisconsin Supreme Court.

**COFFEY, JUSTICE.** Although section 2–313(2) does not require the magic words of "warrant" or "guarantee" to establish an express warranty, a buyer has the burden of proving the purchase was consummated on the basis of factual representations regarding the title, character, quantity, quality, identity, or condition of the goods. In the present case, the circuit court found that an express warranty was not made, as Ewers's question and the sales clerk's answer were not "so clear and definite as to constitute a warranty." However, section 2–313(1) does not require a warranty to be stated with any degree of preciseness. No technical or particular words need be used to constitute an express warranty, yet whatever words are used must substantially mean the seller promises or undertakes to insure that certain facts are, or shall be, as he represents them. In the case before us, the statement by the sales clerk that the shells, coral, and branch were "suitable for salt water aquariums, if they were rinsed" is an affirmation of fact regarding the quality and condition of the goods sold.

The second element required to establish an express warranty is that the affirmation of fact pertaining to the goods must become "a basis of the bargain." The statutory language does not require the affirmation to be the sole basis for the sale, only that it is *a factor* in the purchase. The seller's intent to establish a warranty and the buyer's reliance on the affirmation are not determinative. Certainly, the sales clerk's representations regarding the suitability of the goods induced Ewers to purchase the shells, coral, and branch, for if these items were not suitable for the fish tank, Ewers would not have consummated the transaction.

Additionally, we cannot agree with the circuit court that the curing or cleansing process to make the shells satisfactory for use is the same as the colloquial meaning of the word "rinsed." Had the seller more thoroughly described the required cleansing process of submerging the items in boiling water for a period of a week, we would be reaching a different result. But the goods did not and could not conform to the seller's affirmation of suitability for their intended use.

We hold that the seller's statements constituted an express warranty when the seller specifically stated that the merchandise would be suitable for use in the aquarium after rinsing. Therefore, the buyer is entitled to recover, as the terms of the warranty were not fulfilled. The fact that Eisenzopf's shop does not primarily cater to buyers of aquarium equipment and that the shop owner is relatively inexperienced in the field does not relieve him of liability.

Judicial decisions must not inhibit the free flow of relevant information between the buyer and the seller. Nevertheless, a merchant must be cautious in going beyond "puffing" in making claims and representations about its product. Further, the seller must give specific directions when he claims the goods are suitable for an intended and limited use. A merchant's vague or incomplete directions will induce the purchase of merchandise, and often these directions are as misleading as when erroneous affirmations of fact are given. A merchant who knows the limitations of his product will bear no liability as long as he is truthful and accurate in his representations to the customer.

Judgment reversed in favor of Ewers.

## IMPLIED WARRANTY OF MERCHANTABILITY

UCC section 2–314(1) states that "a warranty that the goods shall be merchantable is implied in a contract for their sale if the seller is a merchant with respect to goods of that kind." A plaintiff suing for breach of this **implied warranty of merchantability** must show that: (1) a merchant sold goods; (2) the goods were not merchantable at the time of the sale; (3) he was injured by the goods; and (4) the injury was proximately caused by the goods' failure to meet the merchantability standard.[4] Note that the seller must be a merchant with respect to goods of *the kind sold.* A hardware store owner's sale of a used car to a friend, for example, will not trigger the implied warranty of merchantability.

**The Merchantability Standard.** UCC section 2–314(2) states that, to be merchantable, goods must at least: (1) pass without objection in the trade; (2) be fit for the ordinary purposes for which such goods are used; (3) be of even kind, quality, and quantity within each unit (case, package, or carton); (4) be adequately contained, packaged, and labeled; (5) conform to any promises or statements of fact made on the container or label; and (6) in the case of fungible goods, be of fair average quality for the kind of goods described in the contract. The most important of these requirements is that the goods must be *fit for the ordinary purposes for which such goods are used.* As the *Taterka* case indicates, the goods need not be perfect to be so regarded; rather, they must meet the reasonable expectations of the average consumer. This "reasonable consumer expectations" test is a flexible general standard whose application requires courts to exercise case-by-case discretion. A test of this kind is almost inevitable, given the wide range of products sold in the United States today and the varied defects that such products can present.

**Application of the Standard.** Where the goods fail to function properly or have harmful side effects, it is easy to conclude that they are not merchantable. A crop herbicide that fails to kill weeds or damages the crop, for example, will not be merchantable. Section 2–314(1) expressly states that the implied warranty of merchantability applies to sales of food and drink, but the courts disagree on the standard to be applied in contaminated food cases. Under the "foreign-natural" test used by some courts, the warranty is breached if the contamination is "foreign" to the food product, but not if it is "natural" to that product. Under this test, a plaintiff who cracks her tooth on a rock contained in a cherry pie could recover, while a plaintiff whose tooth is cracked by a cherry pit could not. Other courts, however, ask whether the food met the consumer's reasonable expectations; this test is probably easier on the plaintiff in most situations. In cases involving allergic reactions to drugs or other products, courts frequently inquire whether an "appreciable" number of buyers will suffer the reaction. Finally, the failure to provide an adequate warning of hazards associated with the product is sometimes regarded as a breach of the implied warranty of merchantability.

Courts attempting to inject some content into section 2–314(2)'s flexible merchantability standard often consider certain factors that apply in a wide range of product liability situations. They may compare the defendant's product with similar products in the trade. They may also consider state and federal product safety regulations when attempting to define the merchantability standard.

[4] The term *merchant* is defined in Chapter 6. Chapter 5's discussion of proximate cause in the negligence setting is probably relevant here also. The types of "injury" for which the plaintiff can recover in implied warranty cases are discussed later in this chapter. Finally, as noted later in the chapter, the plaintiff is required to give the defendant notice in warranty cases.

## Taterka v. Ford Motor Company

**271 N.W.2d 653 (Wis. Sup. Ct. 1978)**

Steven Taterka purchased a 1972 Ford Mustang from a Milwaukee Ford dealer on January 14, 1972. In October of 1974, after Taterka had put 75,000 miles on the car and Ford's 12-month/12,000-mile express warranty had expired, Taterka discovered that the taillight assembly gaskets on his Mustang had been installed in such a way that water was permitted to enter the taillight assembly, thus causing rust to form. On November 7, 1974, Taterka called Ford's Boston District Office and notified it of the problem. However, Ford did nothing for Taterka, even though the problem was a recurrent one of which Ford was aware.

Taterka then sued Ford for breach of the implied warranty of merchantability in a Wisconsin trial court on July 28, 1975. Finding that the car was merchantable, the trial court granted Ford's motion for summary judgment. Taterka appealed.

**Hansen, Judge.** Taterka contends that the trial court abused its discretion in granting summary judgment because a material issue of fact existed regarding the auto's merchantability. A finding of merchantability requires an examination of the defects alleged to exist in the particular product in light of the standard of quality expected for that product. The issue of merchantability presents a question of fact. The question to be answered [on appeal of the trial court's granting of Ford's motion for summary judgment] is whether conflicting inferences can be drawn from the undisputed facts.

Taterka alleged manufacturing defects, including improper corrosion treatment and installation of taillight assembly gaskets. This allegation was supported by a newspaper article on the Ford rust problem, an affidavit from a body shop owner, and Ford's own research reports on the rusting. Ford argues that the automobile's merchantability and fitness were demonstrated by the fact that it was driven as a personal vehicle in excess of 75,000 miles.

Where automobiles are concerned, the term "unmerchantable" has only been applied where a single defect poses a substantial safety hazard or numerous defects classify the car as a "lemon." The ordinary purpose for which a car is intended is to provide transportation. Where a car can provide safe, reliable transportation, it is generally considered merchantable.

The automobile here involved had been driven for 33 months and in excess of 75,000 miles without a serious misadventure. In fact, it had been driven 90,000 miles at the time of the hearing on the motion for summary judgment in 1976. The only inference that can reasonably be drawn from the undisputed facts is that the rust problem did not render the car unfit for the purpose of driving and therefore unmerchantable. Since conflicting interences did not arise from the undisputed facts, summary judgment was appropriate.

Judgment for Ford affirmed.

## IMPLIED WARRANTY OF FITNESS

The **implied warranty of fitness for a particular purpose** created by UCC section 2–315 arises where: (1) the seller has reason to know a particular purpose for which the buyer requires the goods; (2) the seller has reason to know that the buyer is relying on the seller's skill or judgment to select suitable goods; and (3) the buyer in fact relies on the seller's skill or judgment in purchasing the goods. In many implied warranty of fitness cases, the buyer will make his purposes known to the seller and will make it clear that he is relying on the seller to select goods suitable for his needs. But the test of section 2–315 is the seller's *reason to know* of the buyer's purpose and the buyer's reliance, not the seller's actual knowledge. Thus, the seller will also be liable where the circumstances reasonably indicate to her that the buyer has a particular purpose and is relying on the seller to satisfy that purpose, even though the buyer fails to make either explicit. Where these first two elements of a section 2–315 claim are satisfied, there will usually be little difficulty in concluding that the buyer has in fact relied on the seller's skill or judgment. However, recovery is less likely where the buyer is more expert than the seller, has submitted technical specifications for the goods she wishes to buy, actually selects the goods purchased, or insists on a particular brand.

The implied warranty of fitness is quite different from the implied warranty of merchantability. For the fitness warranty, there is no requirement that the seller be a merchant, and the conditions giving rise to this warranty plainly differ from those set out by section 2–314. Also, the seller who gives a fitness warranty impliedly promises that the goods will be fit for the buyer's *particular* purposes, not the ordinary purposes for which such goods are used. If a 400-pound man asks a department store for a hammock that will support his weight but is sold a hammock that can support only normally sized people, there is a breach of the implied warranty of fitness but no breach of the implied warranty of merchantability. If the hammock is incapable of supporting *anyone's* weight, however, both warranties are breached.

### Dempsey v. Rosenthal

**468 N.Y.S.2d 441 (N.Y. Civ. Ct. 1983)**

Ruby Dempsey purchased a nine-week-old pedigreed male poodle from the American Kennels Pet Stores. She named the poodle Mr. Dunphy. Dempsey later testified that before making the purchase, she told the salesperson that she wanted a dog suitable for breeding purposes. Five days after the sale, she had Mr. Dunphy examined by a veterinarian, who discovered that the poodle had one undescended testicle. This condition did not seriously affect Mr. Dunphy's fertility, but it was a genetic defect that would probably be passed on to any offspring sired. Also, a dog with this condition could not be used as a show dog.

Dempsey demanded a refund from American Kennels, but her demand was denied. She then sued in small claims court, alleging that American Kennels had breached the implied warranty of fitness.

**Saxe, Judge.** UCC sections 2–314 and 2–315 make it clear that the warranty of fitness for a particular purpose is narrow, more specific, and more precise than the warranty of merchantability, which involves fitness for the *ordinary* purposes for which goods are used. The following are the conditions that are not required by the implied warranty of merchantability, but that must be present if a plaintiff is to recover on the basis of the implied warranty of fitness: (1) the seller must have reason to know the buyer's particular purpose, (2) the seller must have reason to know that the buyer is relying on the seller's skill or judgment to furnish appropriate goods, and (3) the buyer must, in fact, rely upon the seller's skill or judgment.

I find that the warranty of fitness for a particular purpose has been breached. Ms. Dempsey testified that she specified to the salesperson that she wanted a dog that was suitable for breeding purposes. Although this is disputed by the defendant, the credible testimony supports Ms. Dempsey's version of the event. Further, it is reasonable for the seller of a pedigree dog to assume that the buyer intends to breed it. But it is undisputed by the experts here (for both sides) that Mr. Dunphy was as capable of siring a litter as a male dog with two viable and descended testicles. This, the defendant contends, compels a finding in its favor. I disagree. While it is true that Mr. Dunphy's fertility level may be unaffected, his stud value, because of this hereditary condition (which is likely to be passed on to future generations), is severely diminished.

Judgment for Dempsey.

## NEGLIGENCE

Product liability suits based on a seller's or manufacturer's **negligence**[5] usually allege one or more of the following: (1) improper manufacture of the goods (including selection of materials), (2) improper packaging, (3) improper inspection, (4) failure to provide adequate warnings or instructions regarding hazards or defects, or (5) defective design. Claims based on negligence per se are also possible; examples include situations where the defendant's product violates some product safety or pure food regulation.

**Improper Manufacture or Inspection.** Negligence suits based on the manufacturer's improper materials, assembly, handling, or inspection often encounter problems because the evidence needed to prove a breach of duty is under the defendant's control. However, modern liberal discovery rules and the doctrine of *res ipsa loquitur* can help plaintiffs establish a breach of duty in such situations.[6]

**The Middleman's Duty to Inspect.** Unless they have knowledge of a defect or reason to know of its existence, "middlemen" such as retailers, distributors, and wholesalers are usually under no duty to inspect *new* goods that they receive from the manufacturer or other parties in the chain of distribution. This is particularly true when the goods are shipped to them in sealed containers and are to be resold in these containers. The *Durnin* case, which follows, presents a situation

[5] Negligence is discussed in Chapter 5. The product liability applications of the two major negligence defenses—contributory negligence and assumption of risk—are discussed later in this chapter.

[6] Discovery is discussed in Chapter 2, and *res ipsa loquitur* is discussed in Chapter 5.

where the dealer had reason to know of a possible hidden defect, and thus was under a duty to inspect after the sale. Sellers of new goods also have a duty to inspect where they are engaged in the preparation or installation of the goods. Such sellers will be negligent if they fail to discover defects that are reasonably apparent given the preparation or inspection work they do. A new-car dealer, for instance, is liable for the failure to identify automobile defects reasonably discoverable through a routine "dealer prep," but not hidden or latent defects. Middlemen who sell *used* goods (especially used-car dealers) will be liable in negligence if they fail to discover reasonably apparent defects in their goods.

**Failure to Warn.** Sellers and manufacturers are under a general duty to give an appropriate warning when their products pose a reasonably foreseeable risk of harm and there is reason to believe that users of these products will not realize their dangerous condition. But, in determining whether there is a duty to warn and the nature of any duty that might exist, courts consider other factors besides the reasonable foreseeability of the risk. These include: the severity of the likely harm, the ability of a particular warning to reduce the risk of harm, the burden that giving a warning imposes on the seller or manufacturer, and the feasibility of designing a safer product rather than providing a warning. However, there is sometimes no duty to warn where the risk posed by the product is *obvious*. The manufacturer or seller of an ax, for instance, is not required to warn buyers that its careless use can cause dismemberment.

**Design Defects.** Manufacturers will be liable in negligence where the *design* of their products fails to meet a judicially determined standard of reasonableness and causes injury as a result. The most important factor in determining the reasonableness of a product's design is the reasonable foreseeability that harm will result from the design. But, like failure to warn cases, design defect cases involve additional factors besides the reasonable foreseeability of harm. In determining the design standard to which the defendant is subject, courts also examine the *magnitude* of the foreseeable harm, *industry practices* at the time the product was manufactured, the *state of the art* (the condition of existing scientific and technical knowledge) at that time, the product's compliance with *government safety regulations,* and the *social utility* of the product. As the *Hagans* case in the next section illustrates, courts may employ some sort of *risk-benefit analysis* in weighing these factors. Common reasons for deciding that a product's design is *not* defective include the conclusions that there is no way to design it more safely, that the cost of doing so would be prohibitive, or that the product's existing design has considerable social value. In some cases of this sort, however, courts will impose a duty to provide a suitable warning.

## Thomasson v. A. K. Durnin Chrysler-Plymouth, Inc.

**399 So. 2d 1205 (La. Ct. App. 1981)**

Henry and Peggy Thomasson purchased a new 1974 Plymouth Fury manufactured by the Chrysler Corporation from A. K. Durnin Chrysler-Plymouth, Inc. Their car was one of a group of Chrysler automobiles containing a defect in the lower control arm assembly of the front suspension. This defect was potentially quite dangerous, but it could not be discovered without disassembling the front suspension. Due to a Chrysler recall campaign regarding this defect, Durnin received notice of the types of vehicles subject to the defect and the times when they were manufactured. Durnin also received a list of the serial numbers of the affected vehicles. Similar past lists sent to Durnin had been incomplete, and the Thomassons' car did not appear on the current list from Chrysler. Also, Chrysler never notified the Thomassons of the problem. In its recall efforts, Durnin attempted to locate only those vehicles appearing on Chrysler's list. It made no effort to screen vehicles in the affected category when they were brought in for repairs or servicing.

On several occasions, the Thomassons experienced steering difficulties with their Plymouth, and they brought these difficulties to Durnin's attention when the car was brought in for repairs. Durnin, however, never discovered the defect in the front suspension of their Plymouth. Later, the Thomassons were involved in an accident that occurred when the lower front suspension of their Fury collapsed, causing Mr. Thomasson to lose control of the car. The accident was caused by the suspension defect that Durnin had failed to discover.

The Thomassons sued Durnin in a Louisiana trial court. The trial court held in their favor, and Durnin appealed.

**COVINGTON, JUDGE.** A seller of a dangerously defective product ordinarily is not required to search for latent, nonapparent defects. However, under certain peculiar circumstances, his duty may be more exacting. Where a manufacturing defect causes an accident and the dealer has prior notice of difficulties relating to the defect with an opportunity to discover and correct the defect, in order to avoid liability the dealer has the burden of showing that he made reasonable and adequate efforts to discover the source of the difficulties and that the defect could not be discovered in spite of such efforts.

In this case, the dealer was apprised of problems related to the steering of the vehicle by the Thomassons, which put it on notice that the vehicle had difficulties. Although the defect could not have been discovered without disassembly of the defective parts, Durnin had been put on notice by Chrysler's recall campaign literature that the type of vehicle sold to the Thomassons was suspect. A simple inspection of the date plate on the inside door frame would have shown the date of manufacture. The dealer could thereby easily ascertain that this vehicle was the subject of the recall, even without specific notice of the serial number. Furthermore, Durnin was aware, or should have been aware, of the magnitude of the danger created by the defective lower control arm assembly.

The combination of those factors—the notice from the manufacturer, the specific complaints from the owner, the ease of discovery, the opportunity to correct, and the magnitude of the risk—should have incited Durnin to proceed beyond a routine inspection or repair in the case of the Thomasson vehicle. Under those circumstances, it was not sufficient for Durnin to simply follow the procedure outlined in the recall literature, especially when the accompanying lists of vehicles were known by it to have been incomplete in the past. Hence, because of its negligent breach of duty, Durnin is liable for the damages caused by the failure of the front suspension lower control arm.

Judgment for the Thomassons affirmed.

## STRICT LIABILITY

**Introduction.** Parties seeking to recover under the product liability theories discussed above sometimes face significant difficulties. Sellers do not always give express warranties. As you will see later in the chapter, the traditional "no privity" defense is occasionally a problem in express and implied warranty cases. As you will also see, sellers can frequently disclaim (contract away) implied warranty liability. These problems are much less severe when the plaintiff sues in negligence. Here, however, there must be a breach of duty on the defendant's part, and this must be *proven* by the plaintiff.

Beginning in the early 1960s, the limitations inherent in the existing theories of recovery and the growing desire to compensate those injured by defective products led increasing numbers of courts to impose strict liability (liability irrespective of fault)[7] on the sellers and manufacturers of such products. By doing so, these courts effectively adopted the "socialization of risk" policy discussed at the beginning of the chapter. A major force behind this movement was the American Law Institute's promulgation of section 402A of the *Restatement (Second) of Torts* in 1965. By now, section 402A has been adopted by the courts of most states. More than any other legal rule discussed in this chapter, section 402A symbolizes the "product liability explosion."

[7] Strict liability is discussed in Chapter 5.

**Requirements of Section 402A.** Section 402A basically provides that a "seller engaged in the business of selling" a particular product is liable for physical injury or property damage suffered by the ultimate user or consumer of that product, if the product was "in a defective condition unreasonably dangerous to the user or consumer or to his property." Section 402A removes many of the difficulties that plaintiffs face under the other theories of recovery. The section states a rule of strict liability that eliminates the need to establish a breach of duty by the defendant, because its provisions apply even though "the seller has exercised all possible care in the preparation and sale of his product." As you will see later in the chapter, the absence of privity between plaintiff and defendant is rarely a problem in 402A cases and disclaimers are usually ineffective in such cases. As you will also see, however, the types of damages obtainable under section 402A are somewhat limited.

The strict liability rule announced by section 402A applies only in certain circumstances. First, the defendant must be "engaged in the business" of selling the product that harmed the plaintiff. Thus, section 402A imposes liability only on parties that resemble the UCC merchant. It does not apply, for instance, to a college professor who sells his car, or to a housewife who occasionally sells her homemade preserves to neighbors. Second, the defendant may be able to avoid liability where the product is substantially modified by another party after its sale and the modification contributes to the plaintiff's injury or other loss.

More importantly, section 402A liability requires that the product be in a "defective condition" when it leaves the seller, and also that it be "unreasonably dangerous" as a result of this condition. The usual test for "defectiveness" is the product's failure to meet the reasonable expectations of the average consumer. An "unreasonably dangerous" product is one that is dangerous to an extent beyond the reasonable contemplation of the ordinary consumer. Although good whiskey can cause harm in certain circumstances, it is not unreasonably dangerous for 402A purposes; whiskey contaminated with a poisonous substance, however, would meet this test. Due to section 402A's unreasonably dangerous requirement, it probably covers a smaller range of product defects than does the implied warranty of merchantability. A power mower that simply fails to operate, for instance, is not unreasonably dangerous, although it would violate the merchantability standard. Many courts, however, blur the defective condition and unreasonably dangerous requirements, and a few have done away with the latter test.

**Applications of Section 402A.** As the *Hagans* case, which follows, illustrates, design defect and failure-to-warn suits can be brought under section 402A. Despite section 402A's status as a strict liability provision, the standards applied in such cases resemble those applied in similar cases that proceed in negligence. By its terms, section 402A should apply to retailers and other middlemen who market goods containing defects that they did not create and could not reasonably have discovered. Negligence liability is unlikely in these situations, but courts in some states have employed the strict liability rule of section 402A to hold such middlemen liable. In other courts, however, the middleman receives some protection against such 402A liability. These courts may require that the manufacturer be joined to the plaintiff's suit if possible, or may refuse recovery against the middleman if the manufacturer can be sued. Finally, as the *SAS* case at the end of this section reveals, some courts have concluded that section 402A should not apply to commercial contracts between business entities of equal economic power that have negotiated the specifications of the product and the risk of loss from product defects.

## Hagans v. Oliver Machinery Co.

**576 F.2d 97 (5th Cir. 1978)**

Curtis Hagans lost the ring finger of his left hand while operating an industrial table saw manufactured by the Oliver Machinery Company. The accident occurred while he was feeding a board into the saw by pushing the board forward with his right hand and placing his left hand atop the board to steady it. The saw's circular blade hit a knot in the board, causing the board to jerk up abruptly. Then, as the board rapidly moved forward and descended, Hagans's left hand fell onto the circular blade. There was no claim that Hagans's own carelessness contributed to his injury.

When manufactured by Oliver, the saw was equipped with a blade guard assembly and an "antikickback" device that would have prevented Hagans's injuries. These safety devices, however, were designed to be removable because they prevented the saw from performing many common woodworking functions. For reasons that are unclear, they were not attached to the saw when Hagans was injured.

Hagans sued Oliver in federal district court under section 402A, alleging Oliver's defective design of the saw and its failure to warn of the risks posed by its defective design. The jury returned a verdict in his favor. Oliver appealed the trial judge's denial of its motions for a directed verdict and for judgment notwithstanding the verdict.

**RONEY, CIRCUIT JUDGE.** Because many products have both utility and danger, the alleged defect is required to render the offending product "unreasonably dangerous" before strict liability is imposed under section 402A. A product is unreasonably dangerous if its utility does not outweigh the magnitude of the danger inhering in its introduction into commerce.

In balancing utility against danger, the court must not view the scales from the standpoint of either the user or the manufacturer. Rather, the court is required to consider the legitimate interests of both sides, cognizant that the user is entitled to expect that the product has been properly designed to meet the demands of its proper usage without deficiencies rendering it unreasonably dangerous, but also cognizant that the manufacturer is not charged to design every part to be the best that science can produce or to guarantee that no harm will come to the user. The standard can thus be expressed from the perspectives of both seller and user: a product is defective and unreasonably dangerous if a reasonable seller aware of the dangers involved would not sell the product or if the risk of injury exceeds that contemplated by an ordinary and reasonable consumer.

Hagans argued that the removable blade guard assembly should have been designed into the saw as an unremovable safety feature through welding, rivets, or other means of permanent attachment. He produced evidence that Oliver had known that commercial table saws annually accounted for a large number of industrial accidents, that technology was available to permanently attach the blade guard to the saw, and that his injury would have been avoided had the saw been equipped with the blade guard.

Oliver introduced evidence that the saw exceeded industry safety practices and national and associational safety standards, that few competing manufacturers included blade guards as standard equipment, and that no competitor manufactured an industrial table saw with a permanently affixed blade guard. More importantly, it was undisputed that permanent attachment of the blade guard assembly would substantially limit the saw's usefulness. Common woodworking functions could not be performed with the guard in position. Hagans offered no evidence that a permanent guard assembly could have been devised which would protect the operator during every woodworking operation performable on the saw.

When designing the saw, Oliver was faced with the difficult task of reconciling its safety concerns with the realities of a competitive marketplace. Recognizing that potential customers expect industrial table saws to perform a wide range of woodworking operations, and that some of those operations cannot be performed with a blade guard assembly on the saw, Oliver elected to equip the saw with a removable blade guard assembly. So equipped, the saw is capable of performing the wide range of woodworking operations expected of it, while at the same time providing the blade guard's protection for those operations which can be performed with a blade guard in place. [Thus,] Oliver struck a compromise that maximized the product's utility and safety.

Industrial woodcutting tools are essential to many American industries. Unless civilization is to grind to a halt, these tools, including industrial table saws, must continue to be marketed despite their inherent dangers. Texas law does not require a manufacturer to destroy the utility of his product in order to make it safe.

Hagans also argues that Oliver's failure to warn users of the risks involved in operating the saw without the blade guard rendered the saw unreasonably dangerous. A conspicuous warning plate permanently attached to the machine would have sufficed, according to Hagans. The rule requiring manufacturers to inform users of the risks inhering in their products is based on the sound policy that the user is entitled to the information necessary to make an intelligent choice whether the product's utility or benefits justify exposing himself to the risk of harm. Implicit, therefore, in the duty to warn is the requirement that the user be ignorant of the dangers warned against. Thus, it is generally held that there is no duty to warn when the danger is obvious or was actually known to the injured person. One can imagine no more obvious danger than that posed by the jagged edge of a circular saw blade spinning at 3,600 revolutions per minute. Moreover, Hagans admitted that he was aware of the dangers involved in cutting knotted wood on the saw.

Hagans also contends that Oliver should have provided a warning informing users of the existence of the removable blade guard assembly. But it seems superfluous to require a manufacturer to warn a user of the danger of using a machine without a safety device where the user is fully conscious of such danger in the absence of the safety device.

Judgment reversed in favor of Oliver.

## Scandinavian Airline Sys. v. United Aircraft Corp.

### 601 F.2d 425 (9th Cir. 1979)

Scandinavian Airline System (SAS) is a large international air carrier with a fleet of jet aircraft. Part of that fleet consists of McDonnell Douglas DC-9 jets with engines manufactured by the United Aircraft Corporation. Two of these engines malfunctioned, causing damage to the engines themselves and to the DC-9s on which they were installed. SAS had purchased one of the engines from McDonnell Douglas as part of the purchase of a DC-9; the other was purchased directly from United. In each case, extensive bargaining regarding engine specifications and the risk of loss for defects in the engines took place among United, SAS, and McDonnell Douglas.

SAS sued both United and McDonnell Douglas in federal district court, using a variety of product liability theories. SAS appealed from the portion of a partial summary judgment for United that held section 402A inapplicable to its claim against United. The district court had decided that the policy justifications for using section 402A did not apply to SAS's suit against United.

**Hug, Circuit Judge.** A number of policies underlie the strict liability doctrine. The first California case to adopt strict tort liability was *Greenman v. Yuba Power Products, Inc.* (1962). There the court stated: "The purpose of such liability is to insure that the costs of injuries resulting from defective products are borne by the manufacturers that put such products on the market rather than by the injured persons who are powerless to protect themselves." The risk distribution principle was again relied upon in *Seely v. White Motors Co.* (1965), where the court stated that the doctrine "rests on the proposition that the cost of an injury and the loss of time or health may be an overwhelming misfortune to the person injured, and a needless one, for the risk of injury can be insured by the manufacturer and distributed among the public as a cost of doing business." In *Price v. Shell Oil Co.* (1970), the court concluded that: "the paramount policy to be promoted by the rule is the protection of otherwise defenseless victims of manufacturing defects and the spreading throughout society of the cost of compensating them."

The trial judge's decision does not conflict with the risk distribution rationale. SAS and United are financial equals. Further, both are business entities who sell a product or perform a service which is ultimately paid for by SAS's customers. Whether the loss is thrust initially upon the manufacturer (United) or consumer (SAS), it is ultimately passed on as a cost of doing business included in the price of the products of one or the other. Unlike the consumers in *Greenman, Seely,* and *Price,* SAS can allocate its risk of loss equally as well as United. Therefore, the societal interest in loss shifting present in those cases is absent here.

Several other policies have been identified as underlying the doctrine of strict products liability. The consumer's difficulty in inspecting for defects has been stated as a reason for its application. Another policy concerns the difficulty a consumer faces in trying to prove negligence. Finally, the rule is further rationalized as an inducement to manufacturers to design and produce a safe product, and as a means to avoid the artificial conditions to recovery in warranty created by the rules of privity.

Here, SAS had the expertise and personnel to inspect the engines for defects. SAS does not have the lack of technical knowledge and expertise which would burden members of the general public in proving negligence in designing or manufacturing the engines. SAS does not face problems of privity which the doctrine of strict liability seeks to avoid. Finally, the fact that United will still be liable to airline passengers for any injuries they receive as a result of defective United products will serve as a significant deterrent from manufacturing unsafe products.

The trial judge's decision finds strong support in *Kaiser Steel Corp. v. Westinghouse Elec. Corp.* There the California Court of Appeal stated: "The doctrine of strict products liability does not apply as between parties who: (1) deal in a commercial setting; (2) deal from positions of relatively equal economic strength; (3) bargain the specifications of the product; and (4) negotiate concerning the risk of loss from defects in it." SAS, United, and McDonnell Douglas dealt in a commercial setting from positions of relatively equal economic strength. The specifications of the engines were negotiated by the parties. Finally, McDonnell Douglas, United, and SAS all negotiated the risk of loss for defects in the engines.

Judgment for United affirmed.

## OTHER THEORIES OF RECOVERY

**The Magnuson-Moss Act.** The portions of the federal Magnuson-Moss Warranty Act that are relevant here[8] apply to sales of *consumer products* that cost more than *$10 per item* and that are made to a *consumer.* The act defines a "consumer product" as tangible personal property normally used for personal, family, or household purposes. If the seller gives a *written warranty* in connection with the sale of such a product to a *consumer,* the warranty must be designated "Full" or "Lim-

[8] Other aspects of the Magnuson-Moss Act, including some additional rules triggered by the giving of a full or limited warranty, are discussed later in this chapter and in Chapter 46.

ited." If the seller elects to give a full warranty, it must promise to (1) *remedy* any defects in the product and (2) *replace* the product or *refund* its purchase price if, after a reasonable number of attempts, it cannot be repaired. These terms are not imposed where the seller chooses to give a limited warranty; rather, the seller is bound to whatever promises it actually makes. Remember, however, that neither warranty applies if the seller simply declines to give a written warranty.

**Section 402B.** Section 402B of the *Restatement (Second) of Torts* allows *consumers* to recover for *personal injury* resulting from certain *misrepresentations* regarding goods they have purchased. For the consumer to recover, the misrepresentation must have: (1) been made by one engaged in the business of selling goods of the kind purchased; (2) been made to the public by advertising, labels, or similar means; (3) concerned a fact *material* to the goods purchased; and (4) been *actually* and *justifiably* relied on by the consumer. Suppose that the manufacturer of a laxative states in its advertising that the laxative will produce no adverse side effects if used as directed. Smith, who has been influenced by the advertisements and has no reason to doubt their accuracy, buys a bottle of the laxative from a drugstore. If after using it according to directions, Smith suffers injury to his digestive system, he will be able to recover from the manufacturer for that injury.

**Industry-Wide Liability.** The recent development that we term "industry-wide liability" is not a "theory of recovery" in the same sense as the theories just described. Instead, it is a way for plaintiffs to bypass problems of *causation* that exist where several firms within an industry have manufactured a standardized product that later causes harm and it is impossible for the plaintiff to prove *which* firm produced the product causing his injury. For example, there have been several cases of this sort involving "DES," a generic drug originally administered to women to prevent miscarriages, and much later causing various ailments in their daughters. Using a variety of doctrinal approaches, the courts considering such cases have recently tended to *apportion* liability among the firms in the industry that might have produced the product that harmed the plaintiff. Typically, the apportionment is on the basis of market share at some relevant time. This approach has also been employed in a few cases involving injuries resulting from long-term exposure to asbestos. Not all courts have chosen to impose industry-wide liability, however, and among those that have, there is still disagreement on many legal questions.

## DISCLAIMERS

**Introduction.** At this point in the chapter, we turn from the basic theories of product liability recovery to consider several problems common to each theory.[9] The first of these problems is the impact of liability disclaimers. A product liability **disclaimer** is the seller's attempt to avoid liability for defective goods by including a term to that effect in the sales contract. The basic argument for enforcing disclaimers and allowing the seller to escape liability is a simple one: freedom of contract. For many purchases by ordinary consumers, however, this freedom is illusory. In such situations, the disclaimer appears on a standard form and is offered along with the product on a "take it or leave it" basis by the seller or manufacturer. In addition, it is doubtful that many consumers read disclaimers at or before the time of purchase. As a result, there

[9] Below, we will not discuss how these problems are resolved when the plaintiff sues under section 402B or the Magnuson-Moss Act.

is frequently little genuine bargaining over product liability disclaimers. Often, they are effectively dictated by a seller or manufacturer with superior size and organization. Because the realities surrounding the sale differ from situation to situation, and because some theories of recovery are more hospitable to contractual restrictions of liability than others, the law regarding product liability disclaimers is fairly involved. Our discussion begins with implied warranty disclaimers, which are most likely to meet with success, but which also present the most intricate body of legal rules.

**Implied Warranty Disclaimers.** The basic tests established by UCC section 2–316(2) seemingly make it easy for sellers to disclaim the implied warranties of merchantability and fitness for a particular purpose. Section 2–316(2) states that to exclude or modify the implied warranty of *merchantability,* the seller must: (1) use the word *merchantability,* and (2) make the disclaimer *conspicuous* if it is in writing. To exclude or modify the implied warranty of *fitness,* the seller must: (1) use a writing, and (2) make the disclaimer *conspicuous.* The disclaimer is conspicuous if it is so written that a reasonable person ought to have noticed it. Capital letters, larger type, contrasting type, and contrasting colors usually satisfy this test. The *FMC* case below elaborates on the conspicuousness requirement. It suggests that some courts may impose fairly stringent tests of conspicuousness on sellers in order to protect consumers.

Note that, unlike the fitness warranty disclaimer, a disclaimer of the implied warranty of merchantability can be oral. Note also that, while disclaimers of the latter warranty must always use the word *merchantability,* no special words are needed to disclaim the implied warranty of fitness. For example, a conspicuous written statement that "ALL IMPLIED WARRANTIES ARE HEREBY DISCLAIMED" would disclaim the implied warranty of fitness but not the implied warranty of merchantability.

**Other Ways to Disclaim Implied Warranties.** According to UCC section 2–316 (3)(a), the seller can also disclaim either implied warranty by using such terms as "with all faults," "as is," and "as they stand." Many courts have held that these terms must be conspicuous in order to be effective as disclaimers. Also, since they are commercial terms of art that ordinarily refer to used goods, these terms may be ineffective as disclaimers both where *new* products are sold and where products of any sort are sold to an *ordinary consumer.*

UCC section 2–316(3)(b) describes two situations where the buyer's *inspection* of the goods or her *refusal to inspect* can have the same practical effect as a disclaimer. If the buyer examines the goods before the sale and fails to discover a defect that should have been reasonably apparent to her, there can be no implied warranty suit based on that defect. Also, if the seller requests that the buyer examine the goods and the buyer refuses to do so, the buyer will not be allowed to base an implied warranty suit on a defect that would have been reasonably apparent had she made the inspection. The definition of a "reasonably apparent" defect will vary with the buyer's expertise. Unless the defect is blatant, ordinary consumers may often have little to fear from section 2–316(3)(b).

Finally, UCC section 2–316(3)(c) declares that an implied warranty can be excluded or modified by *course of dealing* (the parties' previous conduct), *course of performance* (the parties' previous conduct under the same contract), or *usage of trade* (any practice regularly observed in the trade). For example, if it is accepted in the trade that farmers who buy seed cannot sue for defects in the seed after the seed is planted, courts may conclude that there is a disclaimer through usage of trade covering seed whose defects are discovered only after planting.

**Unconscionable Disclaimers.** As the *FMC* case suggests, courts may find a disclaimer *unconscionable* under UCC section 2–302 even if it meets the tests of section 2–316. A court's decision in this regard depends on: (1) whether, as a matter of statutory interpretation, section 2–302 should override section 2–316; and (2) the facts of the case, viewed in light of the many factors relevant to unconscionability determinations under section 2–302.[10] As *FMC* also illustrates, freely bargained disclaimers between business professionals are unlikely to be held unconscionable. A personal injury suit by a poor, uneducated consumer against a large corporate defendant, however, is generally a different matter.

**The Impact of the Magnuson-Moss Act.** As we saw earlier, the Magnuson-Moss Act requires that the sale of consumer goods to a consumer by a seller giving a written warranty obligates the seller to designate the warranty "Full" or "Limited" if the price of the goods exceeds $10 per item. If a full warranty is given, the seller may not disclaim, modify, or limit the duration of any implied warranty. If a limited warranty is given, the seller may not disclaim or modify any implied warranty but may limit its duration to the duration of the limited warranty if this is done conspicuously and if the limitation is not unconscionable. These provisions significantly restrict a seller's ability to avoid implied warranty liability to consumer purchasers to whom the seller has given a written warranty. However, a seller can still disclaim by refusing to give a written warranty while placing the disclaimer on some other writing.

[10] Section 2–302 is discussed in Chapter 12.

**Express Warranty, Negligence, and 402A Disclaimers.** Liability under the other theories of product liability recovery is less easily disclaimed than implied warranty liability. UCC section 2–316(1) states that an express warranty and contract language seeming to disclaim it should be read consistently if possible, but that the disclaimer must give way if such a reading is unreasonable. Since it is generally unreasonable for a seller to exclude with one hand what he has freely and openly promised with the other, it is very difficult to disclaim an express warranty.

In cases involving ordinary consumers, disclaimers of negligence liability and section 402A liability are usually ineffective. However, such disclaimers are often effective in commercial transactions between sophisticated parties of equal bargaining power if the disclaimer is clearly stated in their contract.

**Limitation of Remedies.** Along with their efforts to disclaim *liability* for defects in their goods, sellers often try to limit the *remedies* available to buyers. As the *FMC* case explains, a disclaimer attacks the *theory of recovery* on which the plaintiff's suit is based; if the disclaimer is effective, there can be no damage recovery of any sort under that theory. A successful remedy limitation, on the other hand, only prevents the plaintiff from recovering certain *types of damages* and does not attack the theory of recovery itself. Damages not excluded may still be recovered, because the theory is left intact. Due to the expense they create for sellers and manufacturers, consequential damages are the usual target of remedy limitations.

**When Remedy Limitations Are Effective.** The effectiveness of consequential damage limitations depends to a great degree on the theory of recovery employed by the plaintiff. In *negligence* and *402A* cases, remedy limitations should be effective only in situations where disclaimers would be allowed to operate. Thus, attempts to limit consequential damages should almost never work in consumer cases, but usually should be effective if they are clearly stated in freely negotiated commercial contracts between sophisticated parties with equal bargaining power.

UCC section 2–719(3) allows the exclusion or limitation of consequential damages in *express and implied warranty* cases, but also provides that this may be unconscionable. Where the sale is for *consumer goods* and the plaintiff has suffered *personal injury,* a consequential damages limitation is quite likely to be unconscionable. Where the plaintiff has suffered loss of a "commercial" nature, however, the limitation may or may not be unconscionable. This means that all of the factors relevant to unconscionability determinations under UCC section 2–302 should come into play where the plaintiff tries to recover for property damage or indirect economic loss and the seller argues that the section's limitation of consequential damages blocks such recoveries.

## FMC Finance Corp. v. Murphree

**632 F.2d 413 (5th Cir. 1980)**

FMC Finance Corporation leased six buses to Perimeter Express, Inc. The lease contract between FMC and Perimeter expressly disclaimed all implied warranties, specifically referring to the implied warranties of merchantability and fitness. Alfred and Dorothy Murphree, stockholders of Perimeter, were guarantors under the lease. They agreed to pay Perimeter's obligations as determined by the lease agreement if Perimeter were to default.

One year later, after claiming dissatisfaction with the performance of the buses, Perimeter defaulted on the lease and returned the buses to FMC, which subsequently sold the buses. After Perimeter went bankrupt, FMC sued the Murphrees in federal district court on their guaranty contract. It sought the difference between the amount due on the lease and the amount realized from the sale of the buses. The Murphrees argued that they were not obligated to pay, because FMC had sold Perimeter defective buses, thus breaching the implied warranties of merchantability and fitness. FMC argued that these warranties had been disclaimed in its lease contract with Perimeter. The district court directed a verdict for FMC, holding the disclaimers valid. The Murphrees appealed.

**Johnson, Circuit Judge.** The issues presented on appeal are governed by Illinois law. Illinois has adopted the Uniform Commercial Code and applies selected provisions of the UCC to equipment leases.

Section 2–316(2) provides that for a written disclaimer of the implied warranties to be valid, the disclaimer language must be "conspicuous." Section 1–201(10) defines a conspicuous writing as one that a reasonable person against whom it is to operate ought to have noticed. It further provides that a printed heading in capitals is conspicuous, and that language in the body of a form is conspicuous if it is in larger or other contrasting type or color.

Disclaimers of implied warranties are not favored by Illinois courts and are strictly construed against sellers. Therefore, a writing is not conspicuous if it is only in slight contrast with the rest of the instrument. Since the concept of conspicuousness is one of reasonableness and notice, the circumstances play a crucial role in whether language is conspicuous. Where the disclaimer is in a commercial transaction involving experienced businesspersons rather than a consumer transaction involving ordinary purchasers, the concept of reasonableness under the circumstances depends on what a reasonable businessperson is expected to notice.

Section 4 of the lease agreement is the warranty disclaimer. That clause has a boldface heading "Warranties," and that boldface heading is larger than the boldface heading of the earlier and some of the later lease clause headings. The disclaimer language itself is in capital letters, though they are not boldface. No other lease clause has language that is in capitals.

Because of this contrast, the early positioning of the clause in the lease, and the business experience of Alfred Murphree, the disclaimer is so written and positioned that in examining the lease contract a reasonable businessperson such as Murphree ought to have noticed its provisions. That Murphree did not actually read the lease does not detract from the validity of the disclaimer. The concept of conspicuousness is what a reasonable person ought to have noticed, and, as an experienced businessman, Murphree is expected to have read the instrument that creates the obligation on which he gave his personal guaranty.

The Murphrees also contend that the disclaimer provision is unconscionable. Illinois applies UCC section 2–302, the unconscionability provision, to equipment leases. The test is whether, in light of the general commercial background and commercial needs of the particular trade or case, the clause is so one-sided that it is unconscionable under the circumstances. The principle is one of preventing oppression and unfair surprise, and not the disturbance of the allocation of risks merely because of superior bargaining power.

FMC contends that a warranty disclaimer that meets the requirements of section 2–316 cannot be unconscionable under section 2–302. There is some merit to this argument: the 2–316 requirements protect the buyer from unexpected and unbargained for disclaimer language because the conspicuousness provides reasonable notice. On the other hand, section 2–302 expressly applies to "any clause of the contract," and section 2–316 does not expressly state that all disclaimers meeting its requirements are immune from section 2–302. Furthermore, though the disclaimer may be conspicuous, unconscionability may still exist if the disclaimer is oppressive. For example, the seller may refuse to bargain over the clause, not from mere superior bargaining power, but from grossly disparate bargaining power and lack of seller competition on warranties.

Although section 2–302 could apply to a warranty disclaimer meeting the requirements of section 2–316, cases finding warranty disclaimers unconscionable are often the result of a misapplication of UCC section 2–719(3). That provision authorizes courts to strike down a clause that limits or excludes consequential damages if it is unconscionable, and states that limitations on consequential damages for personal injury are prima facie unconscionable. The misapplication flows from a misunderstanding of the difference between a warranty disclaimer and a limitation on consequential damage remedies. Warranty disclaimer is a defense to the *existence of a cause of action,* while the consequential damage limitation merely restricts *remedies* once the breach has been established. If there is no warranty because of a valid disclaimer, there is no problem of limiting warranty breach remedies.

While Illinois courts will readily apply the unconscionability doctrine to contracts between consumers and skilled corporate sellers, they are reluctant to rewrite the terms of a negotiated contract between businessmen. Because this case involves a commercial transaction that was a product of extensive negotiation, and because there does not appear to be any grossly disparate bargaining power or lack of competition among sellers on warranties, this court holds that the otherwise valid warranty disclaimer is not unconscionable.

Judgment for FMC affirmed.

## DAMAGES IN PRODUCT LIABILITY SUITS

**The Types of Damages.** The kind of damages that the plaintiff seeks to recover is one of the most important factors influencing his choice of theories in a product liability suit. Where goods are defective, the buyer has not received full value for the purchase price and has suffered economic loss as a result. This category of harm, usually called **basis of the bargain damages** or **direct economic loss,** is measured by the value of the goods as promised under the contract, less their value as received. Product defects may cause other, less direct, forms of loss as well. Such losses, which go under the general heading of **consequential damages,** include *personal injury, property damage* (damage to the plaintiff's other property), and *indirect economic loss* (for example, lost profits or lost business reputation). One lawsuit can involve all these types of damages. Suppose that the owner of a small business buys some chemicals for use in that business. Due to a defect in the chemicals, they explode, rendering them valueless, causing physical injury to the buyer, damaging some of his personal property, and temporarily shutting down his business (which causes him to lose sales). Plaintiffs in product liability suits may also recover **punitive damages** in certain cases. These damages are intended to punish defendants who engage in especially outrageous forms of behavior and to deter them and others from so behaving in the future.

**Negligence and 402A Cases.** Plaintiffs who sue in negligence or under section 402A can usually recover only for their *personal injury* and *property damage.* Basis of the bargain damages are rarely available, though recoveries for foreseeable indirect economic loss are sometimes allowed. Punitive damages are recoverable where the defendant has acted with a conscious or reckless disregard for the safety of those likely to be affected by the goods it sells. Examples of such behavior include concealment of known product dangers, knowing violation of government or industry product safety standards, failure to correct known dangerous defects, and grossly inadequate product testing or quality control procedures.

**Express and Implied Warranty Cases.**[11] Because of the traditional rule that punitive damages are not available in contract cases, such damages are rarely awarded in express and implied warranty suits. Whether the other types of damages will be recoverable in a breach of warranty case depends heavily on whether there was **privity of contract** (a direct contractual relationship) between the plaintiff and the defendant.[12] Where the plaintiff and the defendant dealt directly, the plaintiff can recover: (1) basis of the bargain damages (the value of the goods as warranted minus their value as received), (2) personal

[11] Chapter 34 contains a general discussion of the buyer's remedies under Article 2 of the UCC.

[12] The "no liability outside privity" defense is discussed in the next section.

injury and property damage (if proximately resulting from the breach of warranty), and (3) indirect economic loss (if the defendant had reason to know that this was likely).[13]

As you will see in the next section, a plaintiff who sues for breach of warranty and who lacks privity with the defendant may not be able to recover at all. In warranty cases where the plaintiff *can* successfully sue outside privity, the most common recoveries are for personal injury and property damage, in that order. In *implied* warranty cases, basis of the bargain recoveries are fairly infrequent and indirect economic loss recoveries very rare. In *express warranty* cases, however, courts frequently allow the plaintiff to recover basis of the bargain damages and indirect economic loss despite the absence of privity.

## THE "NO PRIVITY" DEFENSE

**Introduction.** Today, products often move through long chains of distribution before reaching the final purchaser. This means that the plaintiff in a product liability suit often did not deal directly with the party who was ultimately responsible for his losses. Imagine a hypothetical chain of distribution in which goods defectively built by a manufacturer of component parts move "vertically" through the manufacturer of a product in which those parts are used, a wholesaler, and a retailer, ultimately reaching the buyer. Depending on the nature of the defect, its consequences may move "horizontally" as well, affecting members of the buyer's family, guests in his home, and even bystanders. Assume that the buyer, his family and guests, and the bystander suffer losses of various sorts because of the defect in the component parts. Can they sue the component parts manufacturer or any other party in the vertical chain of distribution?

As you saw at the beginning of the chapter, the ability to mount such suits was severely limited under 19th-century law. This was due to the general rule that there could be no recovery for losses caused by defective goods unless there was **privity of contract** between the plaintiff and the defendant. In the example above, for instance, the buyer would have been required to sue his dealer. If the buyer was successful, the retailer might have sued the wholesaler, and so on "up the chain." For a variety of reasons (including the middleman's limited negligence liability for failure to inspect), the party ultimately responsible for the defect often escaped liability in such situations.

**In Negligence and 402A Cases.** By now, the old "no liability outside privity" rule has been severely eroded. It has little, if any, effect in *402A* cases, where even bystanders frequently recover against remote manufacturers. In *negligence* cases, the plaintiff is able to sue a remote defendant if the plaintiff's injury was a reasonably foreseeable consequence of the defect. Thus, depending on the circumstances, bystanders and other distant parties might recover against a manufacturer in negligence as well.

**Privity under the UCC.** The "no privity" defense still retains some vitality in cases brought under the UCC. Here, the privity question is supposedly governed by section 2–318, which comes in three alternative versions from which the states can choose. Alternative A declares that a seller's express or implied warranty runs to persons in the family or household of *his* buyer and to guests in the buyer's home, if they suffer personal injury and if it is reasonable to expect that these persons may use, consume, or be af-

[13] The general considerations governing recovery for consequential damages such as personal injury, property damage, and indirect economic loss are briefly discussed in Chapter 15. Chapter 5's discussion of the negligence doctrine of proximate cause may shed some light on the meaning of the word *proximately*.

fected by the goods sold. With a little reflection, you will see that Alternative A does little to undermine the traditional "no privity" defense. In the hypothetical chain of distribution above, Alternative A would allow the buyer, his family, and guests in his home to sue the *retailer* for their personal injuries, but that is all. Alternatives B and C go much further. Alternative B lets the seller's express or implied warranty extend to any person who has suffered personal injury, if it was reasonable to expect that this person would use, consume, or be affected by the goods sold. Alternative C is much the same, but it also extends the warranty to those suffering property damage. If the "reasonable to expect" test is met, these two provisions should extend to most remote parties, including bystanders.

However, it is questionable whether the language of section 2–318 is much of a guide to the courts' decisions in UCC privity cases. For one thing, some states have adopted their own provisions on the privity question and do not follow any version of section 2–318. A majority of the states, though, have probably enacted Alternative A or something quite like it. But one of the comments to section 2–318 says that Alternative A should not restrict courts that wish to extend liability farther than the section expressly permits. The courts in Alternative A states have generally taken this hint, allowing recoveries by plaintiffs who would not be able to win if Alternative A were read literally. As a result of these developments, the plaintiff's ability to recover outside privity in UCC cases varies quite a bit from state to state and situation to situation. Here, we will merely indicate some of the more important factors affecting the courts' decisions on this question.

In *implied warranty* cases, at least three factors significantly affect the plaintiff's ability to recover outside privity. The first of these, a factor suggested by section 2–318's language, is the *reasonable foreseeability* that a party like the plaintiff would be harmed by the product defect in question. The second factor is the *status of the plaintiff*. Ordinary consumers and other relatively powerless, isolated individuals have a better chance of recovering outside privity than corporations and other business concerns. The third factor, the *type of damages* that the plaintiff seeks to recover, was discussed above. To review, plaintiffs outside privity are most likely to recover for personal injury, somewhat less likely to recover for property damage, occasionally able to recover basis of the bargain damages, and rarely able to obtain indirect economic loss. In *express warranty* cases, finally, plaintiffs will usually recover despite the absence of privity if the party giving the warranty could reasonably have expected that they would rely on it.

## TIMING PROBLEMS

**Statute of Limitations.** In cases brought under the UCC, the plaintiff must usually sue within four years after the time the seller offers the defective goods to the buyer (effectively, the time of the sale). If the defect manifests itself after that time, the plaintiff normally has no claim. Where "a warranty explicitly extends to future performance of the goods and discovery of the breach must await the time of such performance," however, the four-year period is dated from the time the defect was discovered or should have been discovered [UCC section 2–725(2)]. Just when this exception applies is unclear; the giving of a "lifetime" warranty might be an example. In negligence and 402A cases, the state's tort statute of limitations applies. Usually, this is two years or less. Here, however, the period runs from the time the defect was, or should have been, discovered (usually the time of the injury). This often makes the tort statute of limitations more advantageous to the plaintiff. For this reason, courts occasionally use the tort limitation in UCC suits, especially those involving personal injury.

**Statutes of Repose.** In addition to statutes of limitations, a number of states have enacted *statutes of repose.* The time period for these statutes varies from 5 to 12 years; 10 years is typical. This period begins to run when the product is sold to the last person in the chain of distribution not buying for resale (typically, an ordinary consumer). Thus, a consumer injured by a product more than 10 years after its date of purchase would be unable to sue the manufacturer for the defect in a state with a 10-year statute of repose. This is true even though the suit is begun soon enough to satisfy the applicable statute of limitations. As this example suggests, the aim behind statutes of repose is to limit manufacturer liability for goods that have been in use for extended time periods. Some of these statutes have been struck down on state constitutional grounds.

**Notice.** In express and implied warranty cases, the buyer must notify the seller of its breach within a reasonable time after the buyer discovers or should have discovered the breach. The "reasonable time" varies with the circumstances of the case. Almost any form of notice will suffice. Failure to give notice means that the buyer is barred from any recovery. There is no notice requirement for negligence and 402A suits.

## DEFENSES

Some of the factors discussed above—for example, the absence of privity or a valid disclaimer—can be considered "defenses" to a product liability suit. Here, however, we are concerned with defenses that involve the plaintiff's behavior. These defenses overlap to some degree. Also, the states differ both in the defenses they recognize and in the theories to which each defense applies.

**Product Misuse. Product misuse** (or **abnormal use**) occurs when the plaintiff has used the product in some unusual, unforeseeable way and this causes the injury or other loss for which she sues. Examples of product misuse include ignoring the manufacturer's instructions, mishandling the product, and materially altering the product. The *Mulherin* case, which follows, provides another example. However, if the defendant had reason to foresee the misuse and failed to take reasonable precautions to protect against it, there will be no defense. Product misuse is usually available to the defendant in warranty, negligence, and 402A cases.

**Assumption of Risk. Assumption of risk** is the plaintiff's voluntary consent to a known danger.[14] Among the numerous examples of assumption of risk in the product liability context are knowingly consuming adulterated food and taking a long automobile trip on tires known to be defective. Like product misuse, assumption of risk is ordinarily available as a defense in warranty, negligence, and 402A cases.

**Contributory Negligence. Contributory negligence** is the plaintiff's failure to act with reasonable, prudent self-protectiveness. In the product liability context, it can appear in a wide variety of forms. Perhaps the most common of these is the simple failure to notice an obvious defect. Contributory negligence is clearly a defense in a negligence suit, but it is usually not a defense in a 402A case. The

[14] Assumption of risk and contributory negligence are discussed in Chapter 5. Some states have eliminated the traditional assumption of risk defense by effectively combining it with contributory negligence. The "unreasonable use of the product despite knowledge of the defect and awareness of the danger" test in the *Mulherin* case is an example.

courts are divided regarding the availability of contributory negligence in warranty cases.

**Comparative Fault.** Where they operate, the three defenses just discussed will *completely* absolve the defendant from liability. The "all or nothing" situation this creates has recently provoked a response in several states. In these states, courts now apportion liability on the basis of relative fault, merely *reducing the plaintiff's recovery* in proportion to her percentage share of the responsibility for the harm she has suffered. Sometimes, this doctrine of **comparative fault** is based on an existing comparative negligence[15] statute. Sometimes, as in the *Mulherin* case, courts create the defense themselves. The states adopting comparative fault generally require the fact finder to establish the plaintiff's and the defendant's percentage shares of the total fault for the injury. The plaintiff's "fault" can be based on negligence, assumption of risk, product misuse, or some combination of the three. In such states, the plaintiff's recovery will typically equal the plaintiff's damages times the defendant's percentage share of the fault. This is an example of a recent tendency suggested at the beginning of the chapter: preserving the plaintiff's right to recover but limiting the amount of that recovery.

Many of the states adopting comparative fault have made it applicable to 402A suits. In such states, the defense should apply to the other theories of recovery as well, but this is not yet completely clear. As the *Mulherin* case suggests, a state's adoption of comparative fault should prevent the traditional forms of product misuse, assumption of risk, and contributory negligence from operating as complete defenses.

[15] Comparative negligence is discussed in Chapter 5.

## Mulherin v. Ingersoll-Rand Co.

### 628 P.2d 1301 (Utah Sup. Ct. 1981)

Wesley Mulherin stood on a winch manufactured by the Ingersoll-Rand Company in order to reach some chains that were securing drainage hoses used in mining operations. His object was to detach the chains from the hoses. While he did so, one of the hoses broke free. It came into contact with the winch's throttle control handle. This started the winch, whose unexpected operation severed Mulherin's left leg above the knee.

Mulherin sued Ingersoll-Rand in a Utah trial court under section 402A. The trial court found that the winch was defective and unreasonably dangerous due to its design. But the trial court held for Ingersoll-Rand because it found that Mulherin's behavior in standing on the winch was product misuse and that product misuse was a complete defense in a 402A case. Mulherin appealed to the Utah Supreme Court.

**Oaks, Justice.** The circumstances constituting strict liability under section 402A were present in this case. But Ingersoll-Rand can still urge at least two affirmative defenses: (1) misuse of the product, and (2) unreasonable use of the product despite knowledge of the defect and awareness of the danger. The legislative enactment of comparative negligence does not control this case since the statute only applies to the defense of contributory negligence in an action to recover damages for negligence or gross negligence.

We must decide whether comparative principles shall also be applied to actions based on strict liability. We do so in the context of concurrent proximate causes of the injury: the defective condition of the winch, and Mulherin's misuse of the winch. Both parties can therefore be said to be at fault in contributing to Mulherin's injuries. (As used in this context, the word "fault" is not synonymous with "negligence," but instead connotes responsibility.) Ingersoll-Rand is legally deficient for placing an unreasonably defective product in the stream of commerce, and Mulherin is legally blameworthy for misusing it. The latter fault should not blot out the consequences of the former, when both were concurrent causes of the accident.

We hold that both faults should be considered by the trier of fact in determining the relative burden each party should bear for the injury. The defense of misuse is therefore not a complete bar to recovery from Ingersoll-Rand, but should be applied according to comparative principles. Specifically, we adopt this rule: where both defense and misuse contribute to cause the damaging event, the plaintiff's recovery [will be limited] to that portion of his damages equal to the percentage of the cause contributed by the product defect.

In contrast to the statutory limitation governing comparative principles in the case of negligence and contributory negligence, the rule we adopt for strict liability will not altogether bar recovery where plaintiff's relative fault and causation exceed that of defendant. We decline to express any opinion on other questions that may arise in the application of comparative principles to claims based on strict liability. For example, there is no occasion to determine whether some kinds of misuse are so foreseeable that the manufacturer or seller is bound to anticipate and protect against them, so that they are not a defense to strict liability. At the opposite extreme, there is no occasion to express any opinion on the possibility that some kinds of misuse are so extraordinary or unforeseeable that they entirely override the causative effect of a possible defect.

Reversed in favor of Mulherin.

## FEDERAL LEGISLATION?

With the exception of the Magnuson-Moss Act and the Risk Retention Act of 1981,[16] Congress has left the formulation of product liability law to the states. The current "crisis" in product liability, however, has led Congress to consider a takeover and substantial revamping of the area. Below, we discuss one version of the proposed federal Product Liability Act.[17] Any legislation that Congress eventually passes may differ in some respects from this version of the act.

**Relation to State Law.** The Product Liability Act governs only suits for property damage, personal injury, and emotional distress resulting from defective goods. For such suits, it displaces state law. State courts, however, may still enforce the act. The act does not apply to claims for basis of the bargain damages and "commercial loss" (mainly indirect

[16] This legislation, which was a response to soaring product liability insurance rates, makes it easier for firms to: (1) set up "captive insurers" (insurers created by a company or group of companies) to provide them with insurance, and (2) group together when purchasing product liability insurance from a certain carrier or carriers.

[17] The following discussion is taken from the version of S. 44, 98th Cong., 1st Sess. (1983) reprinted in *Prod. Safety & Liab. Rep. (BNA)* 253 (March 30, 1984).

economic loss). Here, state law (largely the UCC) still controls.

**Liability of Manufacturers.** Under the Product Liability Act, a manufacturer is liable to a claimant if the product was *unreasonably dangerous* and this was a *proximate cause* of the injury sustained by the claimant. A product can be "unreasonably dangerous" in: (1) construction, (2) design, (3) its failure to include adequate warnings or instructions, or (4) its failure to conform to an express warranty. A product is unreasonably dangerous in *construction* if it materially deviates from the manufacturer's design specifications, formulas, or performance standards or from otherwise identical units built by the manufacturer. This is a strict liability test, but one that probably makes life a bit easier for manufacturers. Since they are not held to some kind of "consumer expectation" test, they can to some degree dictate the standards to which their goods will be subject by their choice of product specifications.

Strict liability does not carry over to *design defects,* where the manufacturer's liability is tested by negligence standards ("reasonable prudence"). The reasonable prudence standard also applies in *failure to warn* suits. For both design defect and failure to warn cases, the act states additional specific rules elaborating the reasonable prudence standard. Given the many factors that courts now consider in each situation, it is unclear how much the act's treatment of these areas departs from current law. *Express warranty* suits under the act resemble those now brought under the UCC.

**Liability of Sellers.** A product *seller* other than a manufacturer (for example, a wholesaler or retailer) is liable on the bases of *negligence* and *express warranty* for harm caused by the defective goods it sells. This would eliminate the possibility, discussed earlier in the chapter, that such middlemen might be strictly liable under section 402A. Here, negligence is again determined by a "reasonable prudence" standard. There are several ways in which the seller can fail to observe such prudence; examples include negligent inspection of the product and the negligent failure to give adequate warnings or instructions. In certain situations, however, the seller will be liable under *the standards applied to manufacturers.* This occurs where the manufacturer is not subject to service of process in the state in which the suit is brought or where the claimant cannot enforce a judgment against the manufacturer.

**Defenses and Damages.** Although the act says nothing on the subject, it is unlikely that the absence of privity or the existence of a disclaimer will be a defense for the seller or manufacturer. The act has a 10-year statute of limitations that begins to run at the time the plaintiff discovered or should have discovered the harm and its cause. There is also a 25-year statute of repose in design defect and failure to warn cases involving "capital goods." In addition, the act establishes a "comparative responsibility" defense that resembles the comparative fault rule described earlier.

As we have seen, the act governs only suits for property damage, personal injury, and emotional distress. In addition, punitive damages may be assessed against the seller or manufacturer where the harm suffered was the result of its reckless disregard for the safety of those who might be harmed by the product. The trier of fact (judge or jury) determines whether punitive damages are to be awarded, but the *judge* determines the amount. Only *one* punitive damage award may be made for each instance of reckless manufacturer behavior.

Clearly, the act's provisions on comparative responsibility and punitive damages would considerably reduce the size of product liability recoveries in many cases. This again displays the recent tendency toward maintaining fairly extensive liability for sellers and manufacturers, while reducing the amounts that they will be required to pay.

## SUMMARY

The most important theories of product liability recovery are: (1) express warranty, (2) implied warranty of merchantability, (3) implied warranty of fitness for a particular purpose, (4) negligence, and (5) strict liability under section 402A. An *express warranty* is created by: (1) any affirmation of fact or promise relating to the goods, (2) any description of the goods, or (3) a sample of a model of the goods. Statements of value or opinion regarding the goods, including "sales talk," do not create an express warranty.

The *implied warranty of merchantability* is created when goods are sold by a person who is a merchant with respect to goods of that kind. The most important aspect of merchantability is that the goods must be fit for the ordinary purposes for which such goods are used. The *implied warranty of fitness* arises when: (1) the seller has reason to know any particular purpose for which the buyer requires the goods; (2) the seller has reason to know that the buyer is relying on the seller's skill or judgment to select suitable goods; and (3) the buyer actually relies on the seller's skill or judgment. Here, the seller impliedly warrants that the goods are fit for the buyer's *particular* purposes.

In product liability cases, *negligence* most commonly arises from: (1) careless manufacture of the goods, (2) careless inspection, (3) careless packaging, (4) failure to provide suitable warnings, and (5) design defects. Under *section 402A,* a seller engaged in the business of selling a particular product is *strictly liable* for defects in that product if it is defective and unreasonably dangerous. The product is defective if it fails to meet the reasonable expectations of the average consumer. It is unreasonably dangerous if it is dangerous to an extent beyond that contemplated by the ordinary consumer. Design defect and failure to warn cases can be brought under section 402A as well as in negligence.

*Disclaimers* of liability by the seller or manufacturer will rarely be effective in express warranty cases and in negligence or 402A cases involving ordinary consumers. However, disclaimers may work in negligence and 402A cases involving freely bargained commercial contracts between sophisticated parties with equal bargaining power. To disclaim the implied warranty of merchantability, the seller must use the word *merchantability* and must make the disclaimer conspicuous if it is written. To disclaim the implied warranty of fitness, the seller must use a writing and must make the disclaimer conspicuous. Sometimes, the seller can also disclaim either implied warranty by using such terms as "with all faults" and "as is." The buyer's failure to discover reasonably apparent defects has the same effect as a disclaimer if the buyer has: (1) actually inspected the goods or (2) refused to inspect after the seller has requested this. Implied warranties can also be disclaimed by trade usage, course of dealing, or course of performance. The federal Magnuson-Moss Act imposes severe limitations on the seller's ability to disclaim where it applies.

The only *damages* ordinarily recoverable in negligence and 402A cases are personal injury and property damage. In express and implied warranty cases, the plaintiff who has dealt directly with the defendant may recover for basis of the bargain damages, personal injury, property damage, and indirect economic loss. In such cases, the plaintiff who lacks privity with the defendant can generally obtain only a personal injury recovery, and perhaps a property damage recovery. Punitive damages are sometimes available in negligence and 402A cases, but only rarely in cases brought under the UCC.

In negligence and 402A cases, the absence of *privity of contract* is rarely a defense. Occasionally, however, the "no privity" defense may be effective in cases brought under the UCC. In implied warranty cases, the defense is *least* likely to work where: (1) the plaintiff's loss or injury was a foreseeable consequence of the product defect; (2) the plaintiff is an ordinary consumer; and/or (3) the case involves personal injury or property damage.

The failure to sue within the time limit set by an applicable *statute of limitations* or *statute of repose* will defeat the plaintiff's product liability case. The time from which a statute of limitations is dated varies from theory to theory, as does the time period for which it runs. Statutes of repose usually run for a longer period than statutes of limitations; they date from the time the product is sold to the last party in the chain of distribution not buying for resale. In UCC cases, the plaintiff must also give the defendant *notice* of the defect within a reasonable time after it was discovered or should have been discovered.

The defendant may have a complete *defense* where the plaintiff's injury is caused by his own contributory negligence, assumption of risk, or product misuse. Assumption of risk and product misuse are defenses for all the product liability theories discussed here; the application of contributory negligence varies from theory to theory. Some states have recently begun to employ a *comparative fault* defense in product liability cases. Here, the plaintiff's recovery is reduced in proportion to her percentage share of the responsibility for the harm she suffered.

## PROBLEM CASES

**1.** Carpenter went to the City Drug Store to buy some hair dye. While looking over the products that the store carried, she was offered assistance by a salesclerk. The clerk stated that she and several of her friends used a particular brand and that their hair had come out "very nice" and "very natural." The clerk also told Carpenter that "she would get very fine results." Carpenter bought the recommended product, and after using it, she developed a severe skin reaction. She then sued the drugstore, arguing that the salesclerk's statements were express warranties. Were these statements express warranties?

**2.** Jones, an amusement ride operator, bought a "pony cart" ride from the manufacturer of the ride. Later, Jones sold the ride to Nicole, another ride operator. Jones's dealings in amusement rides were limited to purchases direct from the manufacturer and a few trades of equipment with other operators and manufacturers. During the period that the ride was owned by Nicole, Allen was injured while exiting from it. Allen then sued Nicole and Jones. Among his theories of recovery was breach of the implied warranty of merchantability. Assuming that there is no privity problem here, can Allen recover against *Jones* under the implied warranty of merchantability?

**3.** Gail Battiste contracted ciguatera fish poisoning from eating a fish dinner at the Villa Olga Restaurant. Ciguatera fish poisoning does not depend on the existence of a foreign object in fish; rather, it is a natural, latent condition in fish. Battiste sued the owner of the restaurant for breach of the implied warranty of merchantability. What would be the likely result if the court adopts the "foreign-natural" test? What would be the likely result under the "reasonable expectations" test?

**4.** Reid purchased a can of aerosol deodorant from Eckerds Drugs. The can, whose contents were 92% alcohol, had a warning on its exterior telling the user never to use the product near fire or flame, and not to expose or store it at temperatures exceeding 120 degrees Farenheit. While getting ready for work one morning, Reid liberally applied the deodorant to his underarms and neck. He then put the can of deodorant down, walked across the room, picked up a cigarette, and lit it with a match. When Reid struck the match, he heard a loud report and burst into blue flame as the deodorant on his body ignited. He was severely burned as a result.

Reid sued Eckerds under the implied warranty of merchantability, arguing that the can of deodorant was not merchantable because it failed to warn him of the possibility of the precise injury he suffered. Can Reid mount a "failure to warn" claim under the implied warranty of merchantability? Will Eckerds be able to defend against Reid's suit by arguing that it was not responsible for the allegedly inadequate warning?

**5.** Wilson, a farmer engaged in raising squash, asked an agent of the E-Z Flo Chemical Company about preemergent herbicides for use on his crops. The agent recommended a new product, Alanap, distributed by E-Z Flo and manufactured by Uniroyal Chemical. Relying on the agent's recommendation, Wilson bought a supply of Alanap. E-Z Flo had received a manual from Uniroyal along with the Alanap; the manual stated that the product should not be applied in cold, wet weather. E-Z Flo did not alert Wilson to this warning when he bought the Alanap. Wilson applied the Alanap to his land on the last day of winter, using it on all but four rows of his crop. Except for these four rows, the crop turned out to be a total loss. Wilson sued E-Z Flo for breach of the implied warranty of fitness for a particular purpose. Will he succeed?

**6.** Hanlon was employed by the Wayne Iron Works to operate a press brake built by the Cyril Bath Company. A press brake is a machine used to bend, form, or punch metal; its force comes from a powered ram that moves vertically. As originally manufactured, the press brake had a starting device that consisted of a treadle attached to the front of the machine at a point 8 inches above the floor. It required an operator to lift his foot a considerable distance and then exert 65 pounds of downward pressure. For this device, Wayne Iron Works substituted a small, portable, electrical starting switch that was connected with the press brake by a flexible cable. This switch could be laid on the floor and required little pressure to activate the ram. While operating the press brake one day, Hanlon attempted to remove a piece of metal from the machine with his left hand. While doing so, he accidentally moved his foot so that it pressed down on the electrical foot switch lying on the floor. This activated the ram and caused it to descend upon his fingers, severing them. Hanlon sued Cyril Bath under section 402A, alleging defective design. Can he recover under section 402A? Do not consider such defenses as contributory negligence, assumption of risk, or product misuse.

**7.** Williams bought a used car from College Dodge, Inc. As part of the sale, he was required to fill out a "vehicle buyer's order" form. This was used to apply for a change of title to the car and required a considerable amount of information. On the back of this form, together with more printing, but set in larger type, was this sentence: "No implied warranties are made, either of merchantability or fitness for a particular purpose." After buying the car, Williams began to have serious problems with the engine. Eventually, he tried to rescind the contract with College Dodge, claiming a breach of the implied warranty of merchantability. College Dodge defended on the basis of the disclaimer. If you were an attorney for College Dodge, what would be your argument on this point? If you were arguing for Williams, what would you contend in return?

**8.** Coombes was a member of a golf course maintenance crew. The golf course purchased a "three-wheel utility vehicle" manufactured by the Toro Company from Turf Products Corporation. While Coombes was operating the vehicle, the engine stalled and the brakes failed. As a result, the vehicle rolled backward down an incline and Coombes was thrown to the ground and injured when it overturned on him. Coombes sued both Toro and Turf Products for breach of warranty. Can he sue either under a *literal* reading of Alternative A of UCC section 2–318?

**9.** Moulton purchased a 1969 Ford LTD from Hull-Dobbs, a Ford dealer. His sales contracts with Ford and Hull-Dobbs contained perfectly valid disclaimers of the implied warranty of merchantability that satisfied the requirements of UCC section 2–316(2). One year later, while Moulton was driving his car along an interstate highway, the Ford suddenly veered to the right, jumped the guardrail, and fell 26 feet to the street below. The accident was caused by a defect in the car's steering mechanism, and Moulton was seriously injured. Moulton sued Ford under the implied warranty of merchantability. Ford defended on the basis of its disclaimer. Moulton argued that the disclaimer was invalid in a personal injury case under UCC section 2–719(3), which makes the exclusion of consequential damages unconscionable in a case involving consumer goods and personal injury. Will Moulton's argument be successful?

**10.** The Keystone Aeronautics Corporation purchased some used helicopters from the R. J. Enstrom Corporation. Both corporations were of some size and business sophistication, and the terms of their contracts were the result of extensive bargaining. The contracts of sale contained various provisions by which Enstrom attempted to remove all liability due to defects in the helicopters. One of the helicopters later crashed due to a possible defect, causing property damage to the helicopter. Keystone sued Enstrom in negligence and under section 402A, among other theories. Enstrom defended on the basis of its disclaimers. Keystone argued in return that disclaimers of liability could not be effective in a 402A case or a negligence case. Will this argument work?

# Chapter 33

# Performance of Sales Contracts

## INTRODUCTION

In the two previous chapters, we have discussed the formation and terms of sales contracts, including those terms concerning express and implied warranties. In this chapter, we present the legal rules that govern the performance of contracts. Among the topics covered are the basic obligations of the buyer and seller with respect to delivery and payment, the rights of the parties when the goods delivered do not conform to the contract, and the circumstances under which the performance of a party's contractual obligations are excused.

## GENERAL RULES

The parties to a contract for the sale of goods are obligated to perform the contract according to its terms. The Uniform Commercial Code gives the parties great flexibility in deciding between themselves how a contract will be performed. The practices in the trade or business as well as any past dealings between the parties are used to supplement or explain the contract. The Code gives both the buyer and the seller certain rights, and it also sets out what is expected of them on points that they did not deal with in their contract. It should be kept in mind that the Code changes basic contract law in a number of respects.

**Good Faith.** The buyer and seller must act in **good faith** in the performance of a sales contract [1–203].[1] Good faith is defined to mean "honesty in fact" in performing the duties assumed in the contract or in carrying out the transaction [1–201(19)]. Thus, if the seller is required by the contract to select an assortment of goods for the buyer, the selection must be made in good faith; the seller should pick out a reasonable assortment [2–311]. It would not, for example, be good faith to include only unusual sizes or colors.

**Course of Dealing.** The terms in the contract between the parties are the primary means for determining the obligations of the buyer and seller. The meaning of those terms may be explained by looking at any performance that has already taken place. For example, a contract may call for periodic deliveries of goods. If a number of deliveries have been made by the buyer without objection by the seller, the way the deliveries were made shows how the parties intended them to be made. Similarly, if there were any past contracts between the parties, the way the parties interpreted those contracts is relevant to the interpretation of the present contract. If there is a conflict between the express terms of the contract and the past *course of dealing* between the parties, the express terms of the contract prevail [2–208(2)].

**Usage of Trade.** Terms in a contract may also be supplemented by **usage of trade** [2–202; 1–205]. The *Heggblade-Marguleas-Tenneco, Inc. v. Sunshine Biscuit, Inc.* case, which follows, illustrates how important trade usage can be in determining the interpretation of a contract between merchants.

**Modification.** Under the Code, consideration is not required to support a *modification* or *rescission* of a contract for the sale of goods. However, the parties may specify in their agreement that modification or rescission must be in writing, in which case a signed writing is necessary for enforcement of any modification to the contract or its rescission [2–209].

**Waiver.** In a contract that entails a number of instances of partial performance (such as deliveries or payments) by one party, the other party must be careful to object to any late deliveries or payments. If the other party does not object, it may be waiving its rights to cancel the contract if other deliveries or payments are late [2–208(3), 2–209(4)].

For example, a contract calls for a fish market to deliver fish to a supermarket every Thursday and for the supermarket to pay on delivery. If the fish market regularly delivers the fish on Friday and the supermarket does not object, it will be unable to cancel the contract for that reason. Similarly, if the supermarket does not pay cash but sends a check the following week, then unless the fish market objects, it will not be able to assert the late payments as grounds for later canceling the contract.

A party that has waived rights to a portion of the contract not yet performed may retract the waiver by giving reasonable notice to the other party that strict performance will be required. The retraction of the waiver is effective unless it would be unjust because of a material change of position by the other party in reliance on the waiver [2–209(5)].

**Assignment.** Under the Code, the duties of either the buyer or the seller may generally be *delegated* to someone else. If there is a

[1] The numbers in brackets refer to the sections of the Uniform Commercial Code.

strong reason for having the original party perform the duties, perhaps because the quality of the performance might differ otherwise, the duties cannot be delegated. Also, duties cannot be delegated if the parties agree in the contract that there is to be no assignment of duties. However, rights to receive performance—for example, the right to receive goods or payment—can be assigned [2–210].

## Heggblade-Marguleas-Tenneco, Inc. v. Sunshine Biscuit, Inc.

**131 Cal. Rptr. 183 (Cal. Ct. App. 1976)**

On October 15, 1970, Bell Brand Foods, a subsidiary of Sunshine Biscuit, entered into one contract with Heggblade-Marguleas-Tenneco, Inc. (HMT), under which HMT was to deliver 5,000 hundredweight (cwt.) sacks of Kennebec potatoes between May 15 and July 15, 1971, at $2.60 per sack, and another contract under which HMT was to deliver 95,000 cwt. sacks of Kennebec potatoes between May 15 and July 15, 1971, at $2.35 per sack. HMT was a company that had been formed through the merger of a potato grower and a company that marketed agricultural products and had had no prior experience in marketing processing potatoes.

Because processing potato contracts are executed eight or nine months before the harvest season, the custom in the processing potato industry is to treat the quantity solely as a reasonable estimate of the buyers' needs based on their customers' demands and of the growers' ability to supply based on the anticipated yield for the delivery period. As a result of a decline in demand for Bell Brand products from May through July 1971, Bell Brand's sales for the late spring and summer of 1971 decreased substantially. Consequently, Bell Brand's need for potatoes from its suppliers was severely reduced and it prorated the reduced demand among its suppliers, including HMT, as fairly as possible. By the end of the harvest season, Bell Brand was able to take only 60,105 cwt. sacks from HMT on the two contracts. HMT claimed to have sustained damages of $87,000 because it overplanted and brought a lawsuit against Bell Brand seeking damages for breach of contract. The trial court held for Bell Brand, and HMT appealed.

**Franson, Acting Presiding Judge.** HMT contends that the quantity terms in the contracts are definite and unambiguous, hence it was error to admit into evidence the custom of the processing potato industry that the amounts specified are reasonable estimates. HMT's contention is without merit.

California Uniform Commercial Code § 2–202 states the parol evidence rule applicable to the sale of personal property:

> Terms with respect to which the confirmatory memoranda of the parties agree or which are otherwise set forth in a writing intended by the parties as a final expression of their agreement with respect to such terms as are included therein may not be contradicted by evidence of any prior agreement or of a contemporaneous oral agreement but may be supplemented
>
> (a) By course of dealing or usage of trade [Section 1–205].

California Uniform Commercial Code § 2–202, subdivision (a), permits a trade usage to be put in evidence "as an instrument of interpretation." The Uniform Commercial Code comment to subdivision (a) of § 2–202 states that evidence of trade usage is admissible "in order that the true understanding of the parties as to the agreement may be reached. Such writings are to be read on the assumption that . . . the usages of trade were taken for granted when the document was phrased. Unless carefully negated, they have become an element of the meaning of the words used. Similarly, the course of actual performance by the parties is considered the best indication of what they intended the writing to mean."

A case factually similar to the instant case is *Columbia Nitrogen v. Royster Co.* (4th Cir. 1971). There the seller sued the buyer for breach of contract for the purchase of a specified quantity of phosphate. The buyer's defense was a trade usage which imposed no duty to accept at the quoted prices the minimum quantity stated in the contract. The trial court had excluded this evidence because " custom and usage are not admissible to contradict the express, plain, unambiguous language of a valid written contract, which by virtue of its detail negates the proposition that the contract is open to variances in its terms." The Court of Appeals interpreted Uniform Commercial Code § 2–202(a) as meaning that where the contract does not expressly state that trade usage cannot be used to explain or supplement the written terms, the evidence of trade usage should be admitted to interpret the contract.

We find *Columbia Nitrogen Corp. v. Royster* persuasive. Under subdivision (a) of § 2–202, established trade usage and custom are a part of the contract unless the parties agree otherwise. Since the contracts in question are silent about the applicability of the usage and custom, evidence of such usage and custom was admissible to explain the meaning of the quantity figures.

Persons carrying on a particular trade are deemed to be aware of prominent trade customs applicable to their industry. The knowledge may be actual or constructive, and it is constructive if the custom is of such general and universal application that the party must be presumed to know of it.

Judgment for Bell Brand affirmed.

## DELIVERY

**Basic Obligation.** The basic duty of the seller is to *deliver* the goods called for by the contract. The basic duty of the buyer is to *accept and pay for* the goods if they conform to the contract [2–301]. The buyer and seller may agree that the goods are to be delivered in several lots or installments. If there is no such agreement, then a single delivery of all the goods must be made. Where delivery is to be made in lots, the seller may demand the price of each lot upon delivery unless there has been an agreement for the extension of credit [2–307].

**Place of Delivery.** The buyer and seller may agree on the place where the goods will be delivered. If no such agreement is made, then the goods are to be delivered at the seller's place of business. If the seller does not have a place of business, then delivery is to be made at his home. If the goods are located elsewhere than the seller's place of business or home, the place of delivery is the place where the goods are located [2–308].

**Seller's Duty of Delivery.** The seller's basic obligation is to tender delivery of goods that conform to the contract with the buyer. **Tender of delivery** means that the seller must make the goods available to the buyer. This must be done during reasonable hours and for a reasonable period of time, so that the buyer can take possession of the goods [2–503].

The contract of sale may require the seller merely to ship the goods to the buyer but not to deliver the goods to the buyer's place of business. If this is the case, the seller must put the goods into the possession of a carrier, such as a trucking company or a railroad. The seller must also make a *reasonable contract* with the carrier to take the goods to the buyer. Then, the seller is required to notify the buyer that the goods have been shipped [2–504]. Shipment terms were discussed in Chapter 31.

If the seller does not make a reasonable contract for delivery or notify the buyer and a material delay or loss results, the buyer has the right to reject the shipment. For example, suppose the goods are perishable, such as fresh produce, and the seller does not have them shipped in a refrigerated truck or railroad car. If the produce deteriorates in transit, the buyer can reject the produce on the ground that the seller did not make a reasonable contract for shipping it.

In some situations, the goods sold may be in the possession of a bailee, such as a warehouse. If the goods are covered by a negotiable warehouse receipt, the seller must indorse the receipt and give it to the buyer [2–503(4)(a)]. This enables the buyer to obtain the goods from the warehouse. Such a situation exists when grain being sold is stored at a grain elevator. The law of negotiable documents of title, including warehouse receipts, is discussed in Chapter 38.

If the goods in the possession of a bailee are not covered by a negotiable warehouse receipt, then the seller must notify the bailee that the goods have been sold to the buyer and must obtain the bailee's consent to hold the goods for delivery to the buyer or release of the goods to the buyer. The risk of loss as to the goods remains with the seller until the bailee agrees to hold them for the buyer [2–503(4)(b)].

## INSPECTION AND PAYMENT

**Buyer's Right of Inspection.** Normally, the buyer has the *right to inspect* the goods before he accepts or pays for them. The buyer and seller may agree on the time, place, and manner in which the inspection will be made. If no agreement is made, then the buyer may inspect the goods at any reasonable time and place and in any reasonable manner [2–513(1)].

If the shipping terms are **cash on delivery (COD),** then the buyer must pay for the goods before inspecting them unless they are marked "Inspection Allowed." However, if it is obvious even without inspection that the goods do not conform to the contract, the buyer may reject them without paying for them first [2–512(1)(a)]. For example, if a farmer contracted to buy a bull and the seller delivered a cow, the farmer would not have to pay for it. The fact that a buyer may have to pay for goods before inspecting them does not deprive the buyer of remedies against the seller if the goods do not conform to the contract [2–512(2)].

If the goods conform to the contract, the buyer must pay the expenses of inspection. However, if the goods are nonconforming, he may recover his inspection expenses from the seller [2–513(2)].

**Payment.** The buyer and seller may agree in their contract that the price of the goods is to be paid in money or in other goods, services, or real property. If all or part of the price of goods is payable in real property, then only the transfer of goods is covered by the law of sales of goods. The transfer of the real property is covered by the law of real property [2–304].

The contract may provide that the goods are sold on credit to the buyer and that the buyer has a period of time to pay for them. If there is no agreement for extending credit to the buyer, the buyer must pay for them upon delivery. The buyer can usually inspect goods before payment except where the goods are shipped COD, in which case the buyer must pay for them before inspecting them.

Unless the seller demands cash, the buyer may pay for the goods by personal check or by any other method used in the ordinary course of business. If the seller demands cash, the seller must give the buyer a reasonable amount of time to obtain it. If payment is made by check, the payment is conditional on the check being honored by the bank when it is presented for payment [2–511(3)]. If the bank refuses to pay the check, the buyer has not satisfied the duty to pay for the goods. In that case, the buyer does not have the right to retain the goods and must give them back to the seller.

## ACCEPTANCE, REVOCATION, AND REJECTION

**Acceptance.** **Acceptance** of goods occurs when a buyer, after having a reasonable opportunity to inspect them, either indicates that he will take them or fails to reject them. To **reject** goods, the buyer must notify the seller of the rejection and specify the defect or nonconformity. If a buyer treats the goods as if he owns them, the buyer is considered to have accepted them [2–606].

For example, Ace Appliance delivers a new color television set to Baldwin. Baldwin has accepted the set if, after trying it and finding it to be in working order, she says nothing to Ace or tells Ace that she will keep it. Even if the set is defective, Baldwin is considered to have accepted it if she does not give Ace timely notice that she does not want to keep it because it is not in working order. If she takes the set on a vacation trip even though she knows that it does not work properly, this is also an acceptance. In the latter case, her use of the television set would be inconsistent with its rejection and the return of ownership to the seller.

If a buyer accepts any part of a **commercial unit** of goods, he is considered to have accepted the whole unit [2– 606(2)]. A commercial unit is any unit of goods that is treated by commercial usage as a single whole. It can be a single article (such as a machine), a set or quantity of articles (such as a dozen, bale, gross, or carload), or any other unit treated as a single whole [2–105(6)]. Thus, if a bushel of apples is a commercial unit, then a buyer purchasing 10 bushels of apples who accepts 8½ bushels is considered to have accepted 9 bushels.

The *Salinas Lettuce Farmers Cooperative v. Larry Ober Co., Inc.* case, which follows, discusses the concept of a commercial unit in the context of a truckload of produce.

**Effect of Acceptance.** Once a buyer has accepted goods, he cannot later reject them unless at the time they were accepted, the buyer had reason to believe that the nonconformity would be cured. By accepting goods, the buyer does not forfeit or waive remedies against the seller for any nonconformities in the goods. However, if the buyer wishes to hold the seller responsible, he must give the seller timely notice that the goods are nonconforming.

The buyer is obligated to pay for goods that are accepted. If the buyer accepts all of the goods sold, he is, of course, responsible for the full purchase price. If the buyer accepts only part of the goods, he must pay for that part at the contract rate [2–607(1)].

**Revocation of Acceptance.** Under certain circumstances, a buyer is permitted to **revoke** or undo the acceptance. A buyer may revoke acceptance of nonconforming goods where: (1) the nonconformity *substantially impairs* the *value* of the goods; and (2) the buyer accepted them *without knowledge* of the nonconformity because of the difficulty of discovering the nonconformity, or the buyer accepted the goods because of the seller's *assurances* that the defect would be cured [2–608(1)].

The right to revoke acceptance must be exercised within a reasonable time after the buyer discovers or should have discovered the nonconformity. Revocation is not effective until the buyer notifies the seller of the intention to revoke acceptance. After a buyer revokes acceptance, his rights are the same as they would have been if the goods had been rejected when delivery was offered [2–608].

The right to revoke acceptance could arise, for example, where Arnold buys a new car from Dealer. While driving the car home, Arnold discovers that it has a seriously defective transmission. When she returns the car to Dealer, Dealer promises to repair it, so Arnold decides to keep the car. If the dealer does not fix the transmission after repeated efforts to fix it, Arnold could revoke her acceptance on the grounds that the nonconformity substantially impairs the value of the car, that she took delivery of the car without knowledge of the nonconformity, and that her acceptance was based on Dealer's assurances that he would fix the car. Similarly, revocation of acceptance might be involved where a serious problem with the car not discoverable by inspection shows up in the first month's use.

Revocation must be invoked prior to any *substantial change* in the goods, however, such as serious damage in an accident or wear and tear from using them for a period of time. What constitutes a "substantial impairment in value" and when there has been a "substantial change in the goods" are questions that courts frequently have to decide when an attempted revocation of acceptance results in a lawsuit. The case below of *McCullough v. Bill Swad Chrysler-Plymouth, Inc.* contains an excellent discussion of many of these issues.

**Buyer's Rights on Improper Delivery.** If the goods delivered by the seller do not conform to the contract, the buyer has several options. The buyer can (1) reject all of the goods, (2) accept all of them, or (3) accept any commercial units and reject the rest [2–601]. The buyer, however, cannot accept only part of a commercial unit and reject the rest. The buyer must pay for the units accepted at the price per unit provided in the contract.

Where the contract calls for delivery of the goods in separate installments, the buyer's options are more limited. The buyer may reject an *installment delivery* only if the nonconformity *substantially affects the value* of that delivery and *cannot be corrected* by the seller in a timely fashion. If the nonconformity is relatively minor, the buyer must accept the installment. The seller may offer to replace the defective goods or give the buyer an allowance in the price to make up for the nonconformity [2–612].

Where the nonconformity or defect in one installment impairs the value of the whole contract, the buyer may treat it as a breach of the whole contract but must proceed carefully so as not to reinstate the remainder of the contract [2–612(3)].

**Rejection.** If a buyer has a basis for rejecting a delivery of goods, the buyer must act within a reasonable time after delivery. The buyer must also give the seller *notice* of the rejection, preferably in writing [2–602]. The buyer should be careful to state all of the defects on which he is basing the rejection, including all of the defects that a reasonable inspection would disclose. This is particularly important if these are defects that the seller might **cure** (remedy) and the time for delivery has not expired. In that case, the seller may notify the buyer that he intends to redeliver conforming goods.

If the buyer fails to state in connection with his rejection a particular defect that is ascertainable by reasonable inspection, he will not be permitted to use the defect to justify his rejection if the seller could have cured the defect had he been given reasonable notice of it. In a transaction taking place between merchants, the seller has, after rejection, a right to a written statement of all the defects in the goods on which the buyer bases his right to reject and the buyer may not later assert defects not listed in justification of his rejection [2–605].

**Right to Cure.** If the seller has some reason to believe that the buyer would accept nonconforming goods, then the seller can take a reasonable time to reship conforming goods. The seller has this opportunity even if the original time for delivery has expired. For example, Ace Manufacturing contracts to sell 200 red baseball hats to Sam's Sporting Goods, with delivery to be made by April 1. On March 1, Sam's receives a package from Ace containing 200 blue baseball hats and refuses to accept them. Ace can notify Sam's that it intends to cure the improper delivery by supplying 200 red hats, and it has until April 1 to deliver the red hats to Sam's. If Ace thought that Sam's would accept the blue hats because on past shipments Sam's did not object to the substitution of blue hats for red, then Ace has a reasonable time even after April 1 to deliver the red hats [2–508].

If the buyer wrongfully rejects goods, he is liable to the seller for breach of the sales contract [2–602(3)].

**Buyer's Duties after Rejection.** If the buyer is a merchant, then the buyer owes certain duties concerning the goods that he rejects. First, the buyer must follow any reasonable instructions that the seller gives concerning disposition of the goods. The seller, for example, might request that the rejected goods be shipped back to the seller. However, if the goods are perishable or may deteriorate rapidly, then the buyer must make a reasonable effort to sell the goods. The seller must reimburse the buyer for any expenses that the buyer incurs in carrying out the seller's instructions or in trying to resell perishable goods. In reselling goods, the buyer must act reasonably and in good faith [2–603(2)]. The *Traynor v. Walters* case, below, illustrates the decisions that a buyer who receives nonconforming, perishable goods must make and some of the possible consequences of those decisions.

If the rejected goods are not perishable or if the seller does not give the buyer instructions, then the buyer has several options. First, the buyer can *store* the goods for the seller. Second, the buyer can *reship* them to the seller. Third, the buyer can *resell* them for the seller's benefit. If the buyer resells the goods, the buyer may keep his expenses and a reasonable commission on the sale. If the buyer stores the goods, the buyer should exercise care in handling them. The buyer must also give the seller a reasonable time to remove the goods [2–604].

If the buyer is not a merchant, then his obligation after rejection is to hold the goods with reasonable care for a sufficient time to give the seller an opportunity to remove them. The buyer is not obligated to ship the goods back to the seller [2–602].

## Salinas Lettuce Farmers Cooperative v. Larry Ober Co., Inc.

**28 UCC Rep. 684 (U.S. Dept. Ag. 1980)**

The Salinas Lettuce Farmers Cooperative (located in Salinas, California) sold a quantity of mixed vegetables to H. M. Shield, a produce broker located in Pompano Beach, Florida, at an agreed price of $2,490.25 FOB loading points in California. Among the vegetables were 115 cartons of green cabbage (which were federally inspected at the loading point and certified as U.S. No. 1 Grade with no decay at that time), 4 cartons of broccoli, and 10 cartons of romaine. When the vegetables arrived at Pompano Beach, the cabbage and broccoli were badly discolored and the romaine was decaying. Shield accepted the vegetables in the load, though he tried to reject the cabbage, broccoli, and romaine by sending a telegram.

Farmers Cooperative then brought a proceeding under the Perishable Agricultural Commodities Act to recover the balance due on the purchase price of the vegetables. This was an administrative action conducted by an administrative law judge in the U.S. Department of Agriculture.

**Campbell, Judicial Officer.** The Uniform Commercial Code, § 2–601, which was in effect in both California and Florida at the time of this transaction, provides in relevant part that:

> if the goods or tender of delivery fail in any respect to conform to the contract, the buyer may
> (a) reject the whole; or
> (b) accept the whole; or
> (c) accept any commercial unit or units and reject the rest.

Section 2–105(6) of the UCC provides that:

> "commercial unit" means such a unit of goods as by commercial usage is a single whole for purposes of sale and division of which materially impairs its character or value on the market or in use. A commercial unit may be a single article (as a machine) or a set of articles (as a suite of furniture or an assortment of sizes) or a quantity (as a bale, gross or carload) or any other unit treated in use or in the relevant market as a single whole.

It is obvious that under this definition, in order for a unit of goods to be a "commercial unit" such as would be qualified for a partial rejection as allowed by UCC § 2–601, the unit of goods must meet both of two requirements. The first requirement is that the unit of goods must by commercial usage be a single whole for purposes of sale. We take the term commercial usage to refer to the normal practices and expectations prevailing between the parties to a contract and others in similar situations within the same market relative to a given type of transaction. It is recognized that within the same market with which we are concerned in this case the common commercial unit is often either a carlot or trucklot of a specific commodity. However, here, the parties were dealing in less than trucklot quantities, and in fact were dealing with several lots of different perishable agricultural commodities. Thus, the question that is raised is the treatment of a mixed load of vegetables in the perishable agricultural commodities industry: i.e., does the industry consider each lot of distinct vegetables to be a commercial unit, or does it consider the entire shipment to constitute a commercial unit?

Because of the extreme perishability of agricultural commodities, the viability of severing one commodity in a shipment from others, and treating it as a separate commercial unit from those others, is very doubtful. The seller is frequently many miles from the buyer's place of business, which is the point at which rejection of a commodity occurs. Such seller lacks the ability to control what happens to his goods if they are rejected, and particularly so when a portion is accepted while another portion is not. Thus, there has arisen in the industry the practice, after rejection, of having the buyer dispose of goods for the account of the seller. However, such practice has never been construed to permit a buyer to accept what he wants out of a shipment of one commodity, and to handle the rest for the account of the seller. We find on balance that the practice of the industry is the same whether the trucklot (or carload) contains a single commodity or several commodities. The industry traditionally treats the entire trucklot as a commercial unit, with receivers accepting or rejecting such unit, and seeking damages for goods which do not meet contract specifications.

We find that the second requirement set forth in UCC § 2–105(6) also dictates that a truckload of mixed vegetables be treated as a single commercial unit. Section 2–105(6) states that if division of commodities would materially impair their value on the market, the entire shipment must be considered a commercial unit. While with respect to individual shipments the acceptance of such commodities and the rejection of others might not always impair the value of the rejected goods, the value most often would be impaired because of the difficulty of disposing of small quantities of perishable agricultural commodities which have already been determined to be inferior by the original buyer.

For the above reasons, we conclude that whenever there is a shipment of several perishable agricultural commodities, the entire truckload (or carload) is the commercial unit. A buyer may not accept some commodities and reject others. Rather, its appropriate course of action if it accepts some goods, is to accept the entire shipment, and seek damages for breach of warranty on the inferior goods.

Since we have determined that Shield's attempted rejection of the 115 cartons of cabbage, 4 cartons of broccoli, and 10 cartons of romaine was ineffective as an attempt to reject part of a commercial unit, we must assume that those commodities were accepted, along with the rest of the truckload. This is in accord with § 2–606 of the UCC, which states: "(1) Acceptance of goods occurs when the buyer . . . (b) fails to make an effective rejection." That section states further that: "(2) Acceptance of a part of any commercial unit is acceptance of that entire unit."

Shield, having accepted the truckload, became liable for the entire contract price, less damages resulting from any breach of warranty. The burden is on Shield to prove the breach and resulting damages by a preponderance of the evidence. A warranty was given in this case, to the effect that the produce in this F.O.B. sale was in suitable shipping condition when placed with the agency of transportation at the shipping point. Suitable shipping condition means that the commodity, at the time of billing, is in a condition which if the shipment is handled under normal transportation service and conditions, will assure delivery without abnormal deterioration at the contract destination.

Judgment against Shield for the balance due on the purchase price.

## Traynor v. Walters

### 10 UCC Rep. 965 (Pa. Dist. Ct. 1972)

David Traynor was a wholesaler of Christmas trees who had supplied New York City florists for several years. George and Ruth Walters were growers of Christmas trees in central Pennsylvania. During the fall of 1967, Traynor and the Walters entered into a contract for the sale of 1,680 Christmas trees of "top quality." Traynor refused to accept a number of the trees shipped by the Walters and brought suit to recover damages for breach of contract.

**Muir, District Judge.** Of the first delivery, a total of 185 trees were accepted by Traynor as conforming to the contract and 440 trees were of very poor quality which did not conform to the contract because they were dry, poorly colored, unsheared and poorly shaped and because they had large patches of few needles, especially on the lower branches. Each of the 625 trees of the December 7 delivery was baled prior to being loaded into the buyer's truck for shipment to New York City. The truck arrived in New York City early on December 8, and the trees were unbaled and inspected the same day. Because the trees were baled before delivery, it was impossible for Traynor or his agents to ascertain whether the trees conformed to the contract until the shipment arrived at its destination and the trees could be unbaled. On the same day, Traynor telephoned the Walters from New York to inform them that 440 of the trees of the December 7 delivery did not conform to the contract.

In order to recover damages for nonconformity of delivered goods, a buyer under these circumstances must effectively reject the tendered goods. Rejection must be within a reasonable time after delivery or tender of delivery and is ineffective unless the buyer seasonably notifies the seller. § 2–602(1). Here, notification within 24 hours of delivery was within a reasonable time under the circumstances. The 440 trees were rightfully rejected, and the rejection was effective. With respect to the nonconforming trees in the December 7 delivery, therefore, Traynor is entitled to recover damages.

Christmas trees which have been cut for marketing during the Christmas season are goods which are "perishable or threaten to decline in value speedily." § 2–603(1). Therefore, since the Walters had no agent or place of business in New York City, Traynor, a "merchant" within the scope of § 2–104, was under a duty after rejection of the goods in his possession to follow any reasonable instructions from the Walters with respect to the goods and in the absence of such instructions to make reasonable efforts to sell them for the Walters', account. Here, Traynor incurred expenses in connection with caring for and selling the nonconforming trees, including rental of a site from which to sell the trees, and wages for salesmen and a night watchman. In addition to incidental and consequential damages, Traynor is entitled to recover his expenses incurred in disposing of the nonconforming trees for the Walters' account. § 2–603(2).

As to the trees accepted, Traynor must pay at the contract rate. § 2–607(1).

On December 13, 1967, the Walters tendered a second delivery, consisting of 200 Scotch Pine and 71 Douglas Fir. The 200 Scotch Pine did not conform to the contract because they were poorly shaped and had no needles on the lower branches. The 71

Douglas Fir conformed to the contract, and no claim for damages is made with respect to them. On December 14, Traynor advised the Walters by telephone that the 200 Scotch Pine trees did not conform to the contract and refused the Walters' offer for a further delivery of 600 more Scotch Pine trees. This was reasonable notice of rejection of the 200 nonconforming trees, and Traynor is entitled to damages and expenses incurred in selling them for the Walters' account.

On December 14, the Walters by telephone tendered delivery of an additional 600 Scotch Pine trees, allegedly of different origin from the nonconforming Scotch Pine trees sent in the first two deliveries. Traynor refused to accept any further shipment of Scotch Pine trees at that time, but renewed his demands for other types of trees yet undelivered under the contract. We come now to the question whether Traynor was within his rights in refusing to accept any future shipment of Scotch Pine trees. The starting point is the Walters' right to cure. Section 2–508(1) provides:

> (1) Where any tender or delivery by the seller is rejected because nonconforming and the time for performance has not yet expired, the seller may seasonably notify the buyer of his intention to cure and may then within the contract time make a conforming delivery.

The sellers' right to cure under § 2–508(1) ceases to exist upon expiration of the "time for performance" and the intention to cure. In the instant case, when the Walters notified the buyer that they had an additional 600 Scotch Pine trees available for delivery, this statement was notice to Traynor of their intention to cure the prior nonconforming deliveries of Scotch Pine. Therefore, whether the Walters could cure by a delivery on December 14 depends upon (1) whether or not the Walters' time for performance had expired and (2) whether the Walters' notice of intention to cure was seasonable.

While Friday, December 8, 1967, was the original last date for the Walters' performance of the contract, the time for performance was written on Exhibit A, a purchase order, as "Pickup December 8 and 9." This date was later extended to December 10 at the latest, and the purchase order bears the writing "6–10," which reflects this change in the Walters' date of performance. Traynor later informed the Walters that his buyers in New York would have to have the trees by the weekend of December 16, and that after that date Traynor would have no wholesale market for the trees. The tender of the additional 600 trees was made on December 14. This was within the Walters' time for delivery. This conclusion is bolstered by the fact that the Traynor renewed his demands for trees of varieties other than Scotch Pine trees on the same date. In my opinion, the tender of the delivery of the 600 additional Scotch Pine trees was within the modified time for the Walters' performance, even if the contract were construed to provide that time was of the essence. The Walters' notification of their intention to cure the earlier nonconforming deliveries of Scotch Pine trees was seasonable under all circumstances. Therefore, tested by the criteria of § 2–508(1), the Walters had a valid right to cure by the tender of the 600 Scotch Pine trees on December 14.

Section 2–612, relating to breach of installment contracts, outlines a buyer's correlative right to cancel the contract for nonconformity of previous installments. Section 2–612(1) defines an "installment contract" as "one which requires or authorizes the delivery of goods in separate lots to be separately accepted." This definition includes installment deliveries tacitly authorized by the circumstances or by the option of either party. The instant contract tacitly authorized installment deliveries at the option of the parties and is therefore within the class of sales contracts governed by § 2–612(3), which provides as follows:

(3) Whenever nonconformity or default with respect to one or more installments substantially impairs the value of the whole contract there is a breach of the whole. But the aggrieved party reinstates the contract if he accepts a nonconforming installment without seasonably notifying of cancellation or if he brings an action with respect only to past installments or demands performance as to future installments.

Assuming, without deciding, that the nonconforming parts of the first two deliveries impaired the value of the whole contract and gave Traynor the right to treat the earlier nonconforming deliveries as a breach of the whole contract, Traynor reinstated the contract on December 14 by demanding delivery in future installments of yet undelivered Douglas Fir and Colorado Blue Spruce.

Since Traynor's rejection of the 600 Scotch Pine trees tendered on December 14 was wrongful, he is not entitled to recover damages with respect to these trees. For purposes of the computation of damages, the 600 trees Traynor refused to accept are, therefore, treated as conforming deliveries.

Judgment for Traynor for $4,778.45.

---

## McCullough v. Bill Swad Chrysler-Plymouth, Inc.

**449 N.E.2d 1289 (Ohio Sup. Ct. 1983)**

On May 23, 1978, Deborah McCullough purchased a 1978 Chrysler LeBaron from Bill Swad Chrysler-Plymouth. The automobile was covered by both a limited warranty and a vehicle service contract (extended warranty). Following delivery, McCullough advised the salesman that she had noted problems with the brakes, transmission, air conditioning, paint job, and seat panels and the absence of rustproofing. The next day, the brakes failed and the car was returned to the dealer for the necessary repairs. When the car was returned, McCullough discovered that the brakes had not been properly repaired and that none of the cosmetic work had been done. The car was returned several times to the dealer to correct these problems and others that developed subsequently. On June 26, the car was again returned to the dealer, who kept it for three weeks. Many of the defects were not corrected, however, and new problems with the horn and brakes arose. While McCullough was on a shopping trip, the engine abruptly shut off and the car had to be towed to the dealer. Then, while she was on her honeymoon, the brakes again failed. The car was taken back to the dealer with a list of 32 defects that needed correction.

After repeated efforts to repair it were unsuccessful, McCullough sent a letter to the dealer calling for recision of the purchase, requesting return of the purchase price, and offering to return the car upon receipt of shipping instructions. She received no answer and continued to drive it. McCullough then filed suit. In May 1979, the dealer refused to do any further work on the car, claiming that it was in satisfactory condition. By the time of the trial, in June 1980, it had been driven 35,000 miles, approximately 23,000 of which had been logged after McCullough mailed her notice of revocation.

**Locher, Justice.** The case essentially poses but a single question: Whether McCullough, by continuing to operate the vehicle she had purchased from Swad Chrysler-Plymouth after notifying the latter of her intent to rescind the purchase agreement, waived her right to revoke her initial acceptance. After having thoroughly reviewed both the relevant facts in the present cause and the applicable law, we find that McCullough, despite her extensive use of the car following her revocation, in no way forfeited such right.

The ultimate disposition of the instant action is governed primarily by UCC § 2–608, which provides, in pertinent part:

> (A) The buyer may revoke his acceptance of a lot or commercial unit whose nonconformity substantially impairs its value to him if he has accepted it:
>
> (1) on the reasonable assumption that its nonconformity would be cured and it has not been seasonably cured;
>
> (B) Revocation of acceptance must occur within a reasonable time after the buyer discovers or should have discovered the ground for it and before any substantial change in condition of the goods which is not caused by their own defects. It is not effective until the buyer notifies the seller of it.
>
> (C) A buyer who so revokes has the same rights and duties with regard to the goods involved as if he had rejected them.

Swad Chrysler-Plymouth essentially argues that McCullough's revocation of her initial acceptance of the automobile was ineffective as it did not comply with the mode prescribed for revocation in § 2–608. Specifically, Swad Chrysler-Plymouth asserts that McCullough's continued operation of the vehicle after advising Swad of her revocation was inconsistent with her having relinquished ownership of the car, that the value of the automobile to McCullough was not substantially impaired by its alleged nonconformities, and that the warranties furnished by Swad Chrysler-Plymouth provided the sole legal remedy for alleviating the automobile's defects. Each of these contentions must be rejected.

Although the legal question presented in Swad Chrysler-Plymouth's first objection is a novel one for the bench, other state courts which have addressed the issue have held that whether continued use of goods after notification of revocation of their acceptance vitiates such revocation is solely dependent upon whether such use was reasonable.

In ascertaining whether a buyer's continued use of an item after revocation of its acceptance was reasonable, the trier of fact should pose and divine the answers to the following queries: (1) Upon being apprised of the buyer's revocation of his acceptance, what instructions, if any, did the seller tender the buyer concerning return of the now rejected goods? (2) Did the buyer's business needs or personal circumstances compel the continued use? (3) During the period of such use, did the seller persist in assuring the buyer that all nonconformities would be cured or that provisions would otherwise be made to recompense the latter for the dissatisfaction and inconvenience which the defects caused him? (4) Did the seller act in good faith? (5) Was the seller unduly prejudiced by the buyer's continued use?

It is manifest that, upon consideration of the aforementioned criteria, McCullough acted reasonably in continuing to operate her motor vehicle even after revocation of acceptance. First, the failure of the seller to advise the buyer, after the latter has revoked his acceptance of the goods, how the goods were to be returned entitles the buyer to retain possession of them. Swad, in the case at bar, did not respond to McCullough's request for instructions regarding the disposition of the vehicle. Failing to have done so, Swad can hardly be heard now to complain of McCullough's continued use of the automobile.

Secondly, McCullough, a young clerical secretary of limited financial resources, was scarcely in a position to return the defective automobile and obtain a second in order to meet her business and personal needs. A most unreasonable obligation would be imposed upon McCullough were she to be required, in effect, to secure a loan to purchase a second car while remaining liable for repayment of the first car loan.

Additionally, Swad Chrysler-Plymouth, by attempting to repair McCullough's vehicle even after she tendered her notice of revocation, provided both express and tacit assurances that the automobile's defects were remediable, thereby inducing her to retain possession. Moreover, whether Swad Chrysler-Plymouth acted in good faith through this episode is highly problematic, especially given the fact that whenever repair of the car was undertaken, new defects often miraculously arose while previous ones frequently were uncorrected. Swad's refusal to honor the warranties before their expiration also evidences less than fair dealing.

Finally, it is apparent that Swad was not prejudiced by McCullough's continued operation of the automobile. Had Swad retaken possession of the vehicle pursuant to McCullough's notice of revocation, the automobile, which at the time had been driven only 12,000 miles, could easily have been resold. Indeed, the car was still marketable at the time of trial, as even then the odometer registered less than 35,000 miles. In any event, having failed to reassume ownership of the automobile when requested to do so, Swad alone must bear the loss for any diminution of the vehicle's resale value occurring between the two dates.

Swad maintains, however, that even if McCullough's continued operation of the automobile after revocation was reasonable, such use is "prima facie evidence" that the vehicle's nonconformities did not substantially impair its value to McCullough, thus precluding availability of the remedy of revocation. Such an inference, though, may not be drawn. As stated earlier, external conditions beyond the buyer's immediate control often mandate continued use of an item even after revocation of its acceptance. Thus, it cannot seriously be contended that McCullough, by continuing to operate the defective vehicle, intimated that its nonconformities did not substantially diminish its worth in her eyes.

We must similarly dismiss Swad's assertion that, as McCullough's complaints primarily concerned cosmetic flaws, the defects were trivial. First, the chronic steering, transmission, and brake problems which McCullough experienced in operating the vehicle could hardly be deemed inconsequential. Moreover, even purely cosmetic defects, under the proper set of circumstances, can significantly affect the buyer's valuation of the good.

Whether a complained-of nonconformity substantially impairs an item's worth to the buyer is a determination exclusively within the purview of the fact finder and must be based on objective evidence of the buyer's idiosyncratic tastes and needs. Any defect that shakes the buyer's faith or undermines his confidence in the reliability and integrity of the purchased item is deemed to work a substantial impairment of the item's value and to provide a basis for revocation of the underlying sales agreement.

Judgment for McCullough.

## ASSURANCE, REPUDIATION, AND EXCUSE

**Assurance.** The buyer or seller may become concerned that the other party may not be able to perform his contract obligations. If there is a reasonable basis for that concern, the buyer or seller can demand **assurance** from the other party that the contract will be performed. If such assurances are not given within a reasonable time not exceeding 30 days, the party is considered to have repudiated the contract [2–609].

For example, a farmer contracts to sell 1,000 bushels of apples to a canner, with delivery to be made in September. In March, the canner learns that a severe frost has damaged many of the apple blossoms in the farmer's area and that 50 percent of the crop has been lost. The canner has the right to demand assurances in writing from the farmer that he will be able to fulfill his obligations in light of the frost. The farmer must provide those assurances within 30 days. Thus, he might advise the canner that his crop sustained only relatively light damage or that he had made commitments to sell only a small percentage of his total crop and expects to be able to fulfill his obligations. If the farmer does not provide such assurances in a timely manner, he is considered to have repudiated the contract. The canner then has certain remedies against the farmer for breach of contract. These remedies are discussed in the next chapter.

The *Creusot-Loire International, Inc. v. Coppus Engineering Corp.* case, which follows, illustrates a situation where a buyer became concerned about the seller's ability to perform and demanded assurances from the seller.

**Anticipatory Repudiation.** Sometimes, one of the parties to a contract *repudiates* the contract by advising the other party that he does not intend to perform his obligations. When one party repudiates the contract, the other party may suspend his performance. In addition, he may either await performance for a reasonable time or use the remedies for breach of contract that are discussed in the next chapter [2–610].

Suppose the party who repudiated the contract changes his mind. Repudiation can be withdrawn by clearly indicating that the person intends to perform his obligations. The repudiating party must do this before the other party has canceled the contract or has materially changed position by, for example, buying the goods elsewhere [2–611].

**Excuse.** Unforeseen events may make it difficult or impossible for a person to perform his contractual obligations. The Code rules for determining when a person is excused from performing are similar to the general contract rules. General contract law uses the test of **impossibility.** In most situations, however, the Code uses the test of **commercial impracticability.**

The Code attempts to differentiate events that are unforeseeable or uncontrollable from events that were part of the risk borne by a party. If the goods required for the performance of a contract are destroyed without fault of either party prior to the time that the risk of loss passed to the buyer, the contract is voided [2–613]. Suppose Jones agrees to sell and deliver an antique table to Brown. The table is damaged when Jones's antique store is struck by lightning and catches fire. The specific table covered by the contract was damaged without fault of either party prior to the time that the risk of loss was to pass to Brown. Under the Code, Brown has the option of either canceling the contract or accepting the table with an allowance in the purchase price to compensate for the damaged condition [2–613].

If unforeseen conditions cause a delay or the inability to make delivery of the goods, and thus make performance *impracticable,* the seller is excused from making delivery. However, if a seller's capacity to deliver is only partially affected, the seller must allocate production in any fair and reasonable manner among his customers. The seller has the option of including any regular customer not then under contract in his allocation scheme. When the seller allocates production, he must notify the buyers [2–615]. When a buyer receives this notice, the buyer may either terminate the contract or agree to accept the allocation [2–616].

For example, United Nuclear contracts to sell certain quantities of fuel rods for nuclear power plants to a number of electric utilities. If the federal government limits the amount of uranium that United has access to, so that United is unable to fill all of its contracts, United is excused from full performance on the grounds of commercial impracticability. However, United may allocate its production of fuel rods among its customers by reducing each customer's share by a certain percentage and giving the customers notice of the allocation. Then, each utility can decide whether to cancel the contract or accept the partial allocation of fuel rods.

In the absence of compelling circumstances, courts do not readily excuse parties from their contractual obligations, particularly where it is clear that the parties anticipated a problem and sought to provide for it in the contract. The unsuccessful effort of a seller to excuse its non-performance of a contract to supply coal because of an increase in the cost of production is illustrated by *Missouri Public Service Co. v. Peabody Coal Co.*, which follows.

## Creusot-Loire International, Inc. v. Coppus Engineering Corp.

**535 F. Supp. 45 (S.D.N.Y. 1983)**

Creusot-Loire, a French manufacturing and engineering concern, was the project engineer to construct ammonia plants in Yugoslavia and Syria. The design process engineer for the two plants—as well as a plant being constructed in Sri Lanka— specified burners manufactured by Coppus Engineering Corporation. After the burner specifications were provided to Coppus, it sent technical and service information to Creusot-Loire. Coppus expressly warranted that the burners were capable of continuous operation using heavy fuel oil with combustion air preheated to 260° C. The warranty extended for one year from the start-up of the plant but not exceeding three years from the date of shipment.

In January 1979, Creusot-Loire ordered the burners for the Yugoslavia plant and paid for them; in November 1979, the burners were shipped to Yugoslavia. Due to construction delays, the plant was not to become operational until the end of 1983. In 1981, however, Creusot-Loire became aware that there had been operational difficulties with the Coppus burners at the Sri Lanka and Syria plants and that efforts to modify the burners had been futile. Creusot-Loire wrote to Coppus expressing concern that the burners purchased for the Yugoslavia plant, like those in the other plants, would prove unsatisfactory and asking for proof that the burners would meet contract specifications. When subsequent discussions failed to satisfy Creusot-Loire, it requested that Coppus take back the burners and refund the purchase price. Coppus refused. Finally, Creusot-Loire indicated that it would accept the burners only if Coppus extended its contractual guarantee to cover the delay in the start-up of the Yugoslavia plant and if Coppus posted an irrevocable letter of credit for the purchase price of the burners. When Coppus refused, Creusot-Loire brought an action for breach of contract, seeking a return of the purchase price.

**CANNELLA, DISTRICT JUDGE.** Turning to Coppus's claim that Creusot-Loire's request for assurance was unreasonable, the court notes that Coppus promised to do more than just deliver the burners. The contract plainly states that Coppus was obligated to provide burners which would operate under certain conditions. The present record establishes that Creusot-Loire was justified in seeking assurances that the burners were able to meet the Yugoslavian operating specifications. As the Official Comment to § 2–609 recognizes, a buyer of precision parts has reasonable grounds for insecurity "if he discovers that his seller is making defective deliveries of such parts to other buyers with similar needs." Coppus's own documents indicate that the burners delivered to Sri Lanka did not conform to specifications; thus Creusot-Loire was justified in seeking assurances from Coppus.

With respect to Coppus's claim that the assurances sought by Creusot-Loire were unreasonable, the court initially observes that after being asked for technical assurances in February, Coppus did not respond until September, thereby heightening Creusot-Loire's suspicions. Further, the court finds that the assurances later sought by Creusot-Loire—an extension of contractual guarantee and the posting of a letter of credit—were not unreasonable in light of the circumstances. First, Creusot-Loire's contention that its demand for a letter of credit comported with accepted international business practice is not seriously contested. Second, the record demonstrates that Coppus's stalling and lack of candor forced Creusot-Loire to request security in the form of a letter of credit and an extension of the warranty. Third, while it understands that Coppus bargained for a contract that included a limited warranty, in view of the strategy adopted to meet Creusot-Loire's demand for assurances, the court concludes that Creusot-Loire's request to extend its warranty also was reasonable. Thus, Coppus's failure to provide any assurances, save its statement that the burners would work if installed, constitutes a repudiation of the contract.

Coppus's claim that Creusot-Loire did not timely revoke its acceptance is also without merit. What constitutes a reasonable time for Creusot-Loire to revoke its acceptance depends upon the nature, purpose and circumstances of the case. UCC § 1–204(2). While case law indicates that as a matter of law revocation within the warranty period, which occurred in this case, is timely, the evidence establishes that Creusot-Loire timely revoked its acceptance. After Creusot-Loire sought assurances in February 1981, it did not receive an answer until September. Moreover, Coppus's September response indicates that further assurances were forthcoming. Thus, it was not until November that Creusot-Loire learned that Coppus had no experience with burners operating under "Yugoslavian-like" conditions and that it was unlikely that the burners could satisfy the contract specifications. Accordingly, the court concludes that any delay in revoking acceptance occurred because Creusot-Loire reasonably relied on Coppus's assurances that the burners would work. Moreover, it is clear that after it learned that Coppus had been less than candid with its assurances, Creusot-Loire revoked its acceptance within a reasonable time. Finally, as Creusot-Loire correctly observes, Coppus has not shown that it was prejudiced by this alleged delay.

Judgment for Creusot-Loire.

## Missouri Public Service Co. v. Peabody Coal Co.

**583 S.W.2d 721 (Mo. Ct. App. 1979)**

In 1967, Peabody Coal Company made an offer to supply the coal needs of one of Missouri Public Service Company's electric generating plants for 10 years at a base price of $5.40 per net ton, subject to certain price adjustments from time to time relating to the cost of labor, taxes, compliance with government regulations, and increases in transportation costs as reflected in railroad tariffs. Peabody's offer also included an inflation cost escalator based on the Department of Labor's Industrial Commodities Index. The parties signed an agreement on December 22, 1967.

Performance of the contract was profitable for Peabody for two years, but then production cost increases outpaced the price adjustment features of the contract. In 1974, Peabody requested a number of modifications in the price adjustment mechanisms. Public Service rejected this request, but did offer a $1 a ton increase in the original cost per net ton. Following further discussions between the parties, on May 6, 1975, Peabody notified Public Service by letter that all coal shipments would cease in 60 days unless the modifications it sought were immediately agreed to by Public Service. Public Service treated the letter as an anticipatory repudiation and brought suit against Peabody for specific performance.

At the trial, Peabody introduced evidence that its losses under the contract were $3.4 million. It also claimed that the Industrial Commodities Index, which prior to the execution of the contract had been an accurate measure of inflation, had ceased to be an effective measure because of the 1973 oil embargo, runaway inflation, and the enactment of new mine safety regulations. The trial court ruled in favor of Missouri Public Service, and Peabody appealed.

**Swofford, Chief Judge.** Peabody's final allegation of error is that the trial court erred in refusing to relieve or excuse it from its obligations under the contract upon the basis of "commercial impracticability" under Section 2–615 (UCC), which section reads, in part:

> Excuse by failure of presupposed conditions
>
> Except so far as a seller may have assumed a greater obligation and subject to the preceding section on substituted performance:
>
> (a) Delay in delivery or nondelivery in whole or in part by a seller who complies with paragraphs (b) and (c) is not a breach of his duty under a contract for sale *if performance as agreed has been made impracticable by the occurrence of a contingency the nonoccurrence of which was a basic assumption on which the contract was made or by* compliance in good faith with any applicable foreign or domestic governmental regulation or order whether or not it later proves to be invalid. (Emphasis supplied.)

The comments accompanying this section treat it as dealing with the doctrine of "commercial impracticability," and central to this concept is that the doctrine may be applicable upon the occurrence of a supervening, unforeseen event not within the reasonable contemplation of the parties at the time the contract was made. Such occurrence must go to the heart of the contract.

Further light is shed upon the provisions of Section 2–615, in Comment No. 4 accompanying that section, which states:

> 4. *Increased cost alone does not excuse performance* unless the rise in cost is due to some unforeseen contingency which alters *the essential nature of the performance.* Neither is a rise or a collapse in the market in itself a justification, *for that is exactly the type of business risk which business contracts made at fixed prices are intended to cover.* But a severe shortage of raw materials or of supplies due to a contingency such as war, embargo, local crop failure, unforeseen shutdown of major sources of supply or the like, which either causes a marked increase in cost or altogether prevents the seller from securing supplies necessary to his performance, is within the contemplation of this section. (Emphasis added.)

It should again be emphasized that in the negotiations leading to the contract now before this court an escalator clause was agreed upon to cover the contingencies of increase in Peabody's costs due to wages reflected by labor contracts; payments for unemployment, social security taxes and Workers' Compensation insurance premiums; costs of compliance with federal, state and local laws, regulations or orders; railroad tariffs; and increase in the costs of material and supplies, explosives, electric power and administrative and supervisory expense based upon the Industrial Commodities Index of the Department of Labor. There is no evidence nor, indeed, serious claim that Public Service did not abide by the letter of these provisions, and in addition, prior to suit, agreed to a further price increase of $1 per net ton, which Peabody rejected.

The facts as shown by the record lead to the conclusion that at least some of the loss resulted from the fact that for some unexplained reason the Industrial Commodities Index lagged behind the Consumer Price Index, the measuring factor first proposed by Peabody, in reflecting inflationary cost increases. That such indexes were based upon different commercial and economic factors was presumably known by both parties since each was skilled and experienced in those areas and the divergence between the indexes could not be said to be unforeseeable. Be that as it may, Peabody agreed to the use of the Industrial Commodities Index factor.

The other claim made by Peabody, alleged to bring it within the doctrine of "commercial impracticability," is the Arab oil embargo. Such a possibility was common knowledge and had been thoroughly discussed and recognized for many years by our government, media economists and business, and the fact that the embargo was imposed during the term of the contract here involved was foreseeable. Peabody failed to demonstrate that this embargo affected its ability to secure oil or petroleum products necessary to its mining production, albeit at inflated cost. In fact, as previously stated, this embargo can reasonably be said to have, at least indirectly, contributed to the marked appreciation to the value of Peabody's coal reserves by forcing the market value of that alternative source of energy upward in this country.

It is apparent that Peabody did make a bad bargain and an unprofitable one under its contract with Public Service, resulting in a loss, the cause and size of which is disputed. But this fact alone does not deal with either the "basic assumption" on which the contract was negotiated or alter the "essential nature of the performance" thereunder so as to constitute "commercial impracticability." The court below properly decreed specific performance.

Judgment for Public Service affirmed.

## SUMMARY

The basic rules of contract law regarding the performance of contracts apply to sales contracts. Granting options as to performance to the buyer and seller does not affect the validity of a sales contract that is otherwise valid. Each party must act in good faith and within the scope of what is commercially reasonable in exercising his options and must cooperate in a reasonable manner in the performance of the contract.

The conduct of the parties, the course of dealing, and trade usage are considered along with the contract terms in determining the parties' duties of performance. An assignment of a sales contract, unless otherwise agreed, includes the delegation of duties, and a general prohibition of the assignment of a contract bars only the delegation of duties. The assignor does not relieve himself of his liability for the performance of the contract by delegating his duties.

The basic duty of the seller is to deliver the goods called for by the contract, and the basic duty of the buyer is to accept and pay for the goods. Where the seller is to ship the goods, he must deliver conforming goods to a carrier and make a reasonable contract for their carriage. At delivery, the buyer generally has the right to inspect the goods before accepting and paying for them.

An acceptance of goods occurs when a buyer indicates to the seller, after the buyer has inspected the goods or has had an opportunity to inspect them, that he will keep the goods or when a buyer exercises acts of ownership over goods that are inconsistent with the seller's ownership. Acceptance of any part of a commercial unit is acceptance of the entire unit. The buyer must pay for accepted goods at the contract rate. If the buyer accepts nonconforming goods, he must, if he wishes to hold the seller liable, give the seller timely notice that the goods are nonconforming.

A buyer may revoke an acceptance if the nonconformity of the goods substantially impairs their value and was not discoverable or if the buyer relied on the seller's assurance of cure. Revocation of acceptance must be exercised before there is a substantial change in the goods. The buyer must act within a reasonable time and give the seller reasonable notice of his revocation.

If the contract is an installment contract, the buyer has the right to reject any nonconforming installment if the nonconformity substantially impairs the value of the installment and cannot be cured. The seller may cure the defect, but if the defect impairs the value of the whole contract, it is a breach of the whole contract.

If nonconforming goods are tendered, the buyer may reject all, accept all, or accept any commercial unit and reject the rest. Upon rejection, if the goods are in the buyer's possession or control, the buyer owes a duty to use reasonable care to protect them. He must hold the goods for a period sufficient to permit the seller to remove them; if the seller does not have a place of business or an agent in the market, the buyer must follow the seller's instructions as to disposition of the goods. If no instructions are given, the buyer must, if the goods are perishable or subject to speedy change in value, sell them for the seller's account. If the goods are not perishable, he may store or reship them or sell them for the seller's account. The buyer is entitled to reimbursement for his expenses plus a commission. If the buyer wrongfully rejects goods, he is liable to the seller for breach of contract.

If either party to a sales contract deems himself insecure, as tested by commercial standards, he may demand assurance before proceeding with performance. If a party repudiates a sales contract, the aggrieved party may wait or he may bring an action for breach of the contract. In the event of repudiation, the usual remedies for the breach of the sales contract are available to the aggrieved party. If the party who has repudiated a sales contract wishes to withdraw his repudiation, he may do so by giving the aggrieved party notice of his withdrawal before the aggrieved party has canceled the contract or materially changed his position in reliance on the repudiation.

A party to a sales contract is excused from performance if his performance, due to no fault on his part, becomes commercially impracticable. If the impracticability is as to means of transportation or means of payment, the affected party may resort to substitute means, if available. If the impracticability causes delay or ability to perform only partially, the seller must allocate performances among his buyers. A buyer may accept his allotment or cancel the contract.

## PROBLEM CASES

**1.** Baker was a buyer and distributor of popcorn. Ratzlaff was a farmer who grew popcorn. In 1973, Baker and Ratzlaff entered into a written contract. Ratzlaff agreed that in 1973 he would raise 380 acres of popcorn and sell the popcorn to Baker. Baker agreed to furnish the seed popcorn and to pay $4.75 per hundred pounds of popcorn. The popcorn was to be delivered to Baker as he ordered it, and Baker was to pay for the popcorn as it was delivered. At Baker's request, the first delivery was made on February 2 and the second on February 4. Ratzlaff did not ask Baker to pay, nor did Baker offer to pay, on either occasion. During that week, Ratzlaff and Baker had several phone conversations about further deliveries, but there was no discussion about payment. On February 11, Ratzlaff sent written notice to Baker that he was terminating the contract because Baker had not paid for the two deliveries. When Baker received the letter, he sent a check to pay for the two loads of popcorn that had been delivered. In the meantime, Ratzlaff had sold his remaining 1.6 million pounds of popcorn to another buyer at $8 per hundred pounds. Baker then sued Ratzlaff for breach of contract. Did Ratzlaff act in good faith in terminating the contract?

**2.** Umlas signed a contract to purchase a 1970 Oldsmobile from Acey Oldsmobile. The contract provided that Umlas would receive $650 for trading in his old car and allowed him to continue to drive it until his new car was delivered. The contract also provided that Acey could reappraise the used car when the new car was delivered. When Umlas brought his trade-in to the dealer to exchange it for his new car, an employee of Acey took the trade-in for a test drive. The employee told Umlas that it was worth $300 to $400. Acey told Umlas that it had been reappraised at $50. Umlas refused to go through with the sale and bought a car from another dealer. That dealer gave him $400 for trading in his old car. Umlas then sued Acey for breach of contract. Did Acey breach the contract by not acting in good faith in its reappraisal of the car?

**3.** Spada, an Oregon corporation, agreed to sell Belson, who operated a business in Chicago, two carloads of potatoes at "4.40 per sack, FOB Oregon shipping point." Spada had the potatoes put aboard the railroad cars; however, it did not have floor racks placed under the potatoes, as was customary during the winter months. As a result, there was no warm air circulating and the potatoes were frozen while in transit. Spada claims that its obligations ended with the delivery to the carrier and that the risk of loss was on Belson. What argument would you make for Belson?

**4.** In April, Reginald Bell contracted to sell potatoes to Red Ball Potato Company for fall delivery. The contract specified that the potatoes were to be "85% U.S. 1's." In Red Ball's dealings with Bell and other farmers, potatoes were delivered and paid for in truckload quantities. In the fall, Bell delivered several truckloads of potatoes. Samples of each load were taken for testing, and most of the loads were determined to be below 85 percent U.S. No 1. What options are open to Red Ball?

**5.** Bass and Sons was a retailer/wholesaler of hardware supplies. In October 1979, Bass received a number of wrench kits from H.P. Tool Company. The wrench kits were individually rolled up in vinyl-like pouches and packaged in sealed cartons. Upon receiving the goods, Bass, without opening the cartons, placed some of the goods in inventory and shipped some to its customers in the unopened cartons. In December, Bass began to receive complaints from its customers concerning the quality of the wrench kits. The wrenches were unpolished, though they were supposed to have a highly polished finish. Bass then advised H.P. Tool of the problems with the wrench kits. H.P. Tool sought to collect the full contract price from Bass, claiming that Bass had accepted the shipment. Should H.P. Tool be able to collect?

**6.** James Shelton, an experienced musician, operated the University Music Center. On Saturday, Barbara Farkas and her 22-year-old daughter, Penny, went to Shelton's store to look at violins. Penny had been studying violin in college for about nine months. They advised Shelton of the price range in which they were interested, and Penny told him that she was relying on his expertise. He selected a violin that was priced at \$368.90, including the case and sales tax. Shelton claimed that the instrument had originally been priced at \$465 but that he had discounted it because Mrs. Farkas was willing to take it on an "as is" basis. Mrs. Farkas and Penny alleged that Shelton had represented that the violin was "the best" and "a perfect violin for you" and that it was of high quality. Mrs. Farkas paid for it by check. On the following Monday, Penny took the violin to her college music teacher, who immediately told her that it had poor tone and a crack in the body and that it was not the right instrument for her. Mrs. Farkas telephoned Shelton and asked for a refund. He refused, saying that she had purchased and accepted the violin on an "as is" basis. Had Farkas "accepted" the violin so that it was too late for her to "reject" it?

**7.** The Davis for Men Shoe Store ordered 513 pairs of Banfi shoes. When the shoes arrived, in early summer of 1982, Davis notified Banfi that the shoes were nonconforming and that it was having extreme problems in fitting them. However, Davis placed the Banfi shoes in its inventory, offered the shoes for sale, and had sold approximately half of them by April 1983. At that time, Banfi filed suit against Davis for \$56,123 due on the shipment of shoes. Is Davis liable to Banfi?

**8.** Mulcahy purchased a new Oldsmobile from McDavid Oldsmobile and was issued a new-car warranty providing that the car and chassis, including all equipment and accessories, were warranted to be free from defects in material and workmanship under normal use and service. Within three months of his purchase of the car and after it had been driven approximately 3,500 miles, Mulcahy experienced some trouble with the battery. The battery had to be filled with water every time he filled the car with gasoline, and acid was leaking from the battery onto his driveway. The car had not been in an accident; the battery was well secured in the car; the battery never froze; and Mulcahy had it checked regularly. Although Mulcahy could not see a crack, he thought that the battery was cracked. Mulcahy took the car to McDavid Oldsmobile, which refused to replace the battery under the warranty. Mulcahy then left the car with McDavid and stopped making payments on the car. McDavid brought suit to recover the balance of the purchase price, and Mulcahy claimed that he had revoked acceptance of the car. What result should the court reach?

**9.** Bende, a seller of military supplies internationally, agreed to sell the government of Ghana 10,000 pairs of combat boots for $158,000. Bende contracted with Kiffe Products, a seller of camping and military supplies, to provide him with 10,000 pairs of boots "leather upper, lace-up front, black, with reinforced bottom sole, Korean made, but all Korean markings removed from boots, in neutral boxes." The boots were manufactured in Korea and shipped to the United States, where they were loaded on railroad cars for shipment to the East Coast. The train transporting the boots derailed near Omaha, Nebraska, and most of the boots were destroyed. When Bende sued Kiffe for failing to deliver the boots to it, Kiffe claimed that the derailment excused its performance under the contract. Has Kiffe stated a valid defense?

**10.** In March, Olwen Farms entered into a written contract whereby it agreed to sell Semo Grain Company, a grain dealer, 75,000 bushels of No. 1 yellow soybeans at $3.10 per bushel. Delivery of the soybeans by Olwen Farms was to be made at Semo Grain's elevator during the following January. Nothing in the agreement required Olwen Farms to grow the soybeans on any particular lands, and, for that matter, it was not obligated to grow the soybeans at all. From various farms that Olwen Farms either owned or rented, 19,885 bushels of soybeans were produced and harvested. These soybeans were sold by Olwen Farms to purchasers other than Semo Grain for prices in excess of $3.10 per bushel. Olwen Farms did not deliver any soybeans to Semo Grain. Semo Grain filed a suit in February, seeking to recover the difference between the contract price and the market price of soybeans as of January. Olwen Farms claimed that it was excused from performing the contract by reason of adverse weather conditions. Should Olwen Farms be excused from performance of its contract?

Chapter 34

# Remedies for Breach of Sales Contracts

## INTRODUCTION

Usually, both parties to a contract for the sale of goods perform the obligations that they assumed in the contract. Occasionally, however, one of the parties to a contract fails to perform his obligations. When this happens, the Uniform Commercial Code provides the injured party with a variety of remedies for breach of contract. This chapter will set forth and explain the remedies available to an injured party, as well as the Code's rules that govern buyer-seller agreements as to remedies, and the Code's statute of limitations. The *objective* of the Code remedies is to put the injured person in the *same position that he would have been in if the contract had been performed.* Under the Code, an injured party may not recover consequential or punitive damages unless such damages are specifically provided for in the Code or in another statute [1–106].[1]

**Agreements as to Remedies.** The buyer and seller may provide their own remedies

[1] The numbers in brackets refer to the sections of the Uniform Commercial Code.

in the contract, to be applied in the event that one of the parties fails to perform. They may also limit either the remedies that the law makes available or the damages that can be covered [2–719(1)]. If the parties agree on the amount of damages that will be paid to the injured party, this amount is known as **liquidated damages.** An agreement for liquidated damages is enforced if the *amount is reasonable* and if *actual damages* would be *difficult to prove* in the event of a breach of the contract. The amount is considered reasonable if it is not so large as to be a *penalty* or so small as to be *unconscionable* [2–718(1)].

For example, Carl Carpenter contracts to sell a display booth for $1,000 to Hank Hawker for Hawker to use at the state fair. Delivery is to be made to Hawker by September 1. If the booth is not delivered on time, Hawker will not be able to sell his wares at the fair. Carpenter and Hawker might agree that if delivery is not made by September 1, Carpenter will pay Hawker $750 as liquidated damages. The actual sales that Hawker might lose without a booth would be very hard to prove, so Hawker and Carpenter can provide some certainty through the liquidated damages agreement. Carpenter then knows what he will be liable for if he does not perform his obligation. Similarly, Hawker knows what he can recover if the booth is not delivered on time. The $750 amount is probably reasonable. If the amount were $500,000, it likely would be void as a penalty because it is way out of line with the damages that Hawker would reasonably be expected to sustain. And if the amount were too small, say $1, it might be considered unconscionable and therefore not enforceable. If a liquidated damages clause is not enforceable because it is a penalty or unconscionable, the injured party can recover the actual damages that he suffered.

Liability for **consequential damages** resulting from a breach of contract (such as lost profits or damage to property) may also be limited or excluded by agreement. The limitation or exclusion is not enforced if it would be unconscionable.

Any attempt to limit consequential damages for injury caused to a person by consumer goods is considered *prima facie unconscionable* [2–719(3)]. Suppose an automobile manufacturer makes a warranty as to the quality of an automobile that is purchased as a consumer good. It then tries to disclaim responsibility for any person injured if the car does not conform to the warranty and to limit its liability to replacing any defective parts. The disclaimer of consequential injuries in this case would be unconscionable and therefore would not be enforced. Exclusion of or limitation on consequential damages is permitted where the loss is commercial, as long as the exclusion or limitation is not unconscionable.

Effective limitation by a seller of its liability for consequential damages is illustrated by *Wille v. Southwestern Bell Telephone Co.*, which appears below.

The *Hartzell v. Justus Co., Inc.* case, which follows, illustrates how the Code applies to a situation where circumstances cause a limited remedy agreed to by the parties to fail in its essential purpose. When this happens, the limited remedy is not enforced and the general Code remedies are available to the injured party.

**Statute of Limitations.** The Code provides that a lawsuit for breach of a sales contract must be filed within *four years* after the breach occurs. The parties to a contract may shorten this period to one year, but they may not extend it for longer than four years [2–725]. Normally, a breach of warranty is considered to have occurred when the goods are delivered to the buyer. However, if the warranty covers future performance of goods (for example, a warranty on a tire for four years or 40,000 miles), then the breach occurs at the time the buyer should have discovered the defect in the product. If, for example, the buyer of the tire discovers the defect after driving 25,000 miles on the tire over a three-year period, he would have four years from that time to bring any lawsuit to remedy the breach.

The *Parzek v. New England Log Homes, Inc.* case, which appears below, provides an example of a warranty that extends to future performance.

## Hartzell v. Justus Co., Inc.

**693 F.2d 770 (8th Cir. 1982)**

Dr. Allan Hartzell purchased a log home construction kit manufactured by Justus Homes. Hartzell purchased the package for $38,622 from Del Carter, who was Justus Homes's dealer for the Sioux Falls area. He also hired Carter's construction company to build the house, which eventually cost about $150,000.

Hartzell was dissatisfied with the house in many respects. His chief complaints were that knotholes in the walls and ceilings leaked rain profusely and that the home was not weathertight because flashings were not included in the roofing materials and because the timbers were not kiln-dried and therefore shrank. He also complained that an undersized support beam, which eventually cracked, was included in the package. This defect resulted in floor cracks and in inside doors that would not close. Hartzell claimed that the structural defects were only partially remediable and that the fair market value of the house was reduced even after all practicable repairs had been made.

Hartzell brought suit against Justus Homes, alleging negligence and breach of implied and express warranties and seeking damages for loss in value and the cost of repairs. A jury awarded Hartzell a verdict of $34,794.67. Justus Homes appealed.

**Arnold, Circuit Judge.** Justus Homes contends the district court failed to adequately consider a limitation-of-remedies clause contained in its contract with Hartzell. Justus Homes relies on Clause 10c of the contract, which says that Justus will repair or replace defective materials, and Clause 10d, which states that this limited repair or replacement clause is the exclusive remedy available against Justus. These agreements, Justus asserts, are valid under the Uniform Commercial Code, § 2–719(1). Section 2–719(1) states:

> (1) Subject to the provisions of subsections (2) and (3) of this section and of § 2–718 on liquidation and limitation of damages,
>
> (a) The agreement may provide for remedies in addition to or in substitution for those provided in this chapter and may limit or alter the measure of damages recoverable under this chapter, as by limiting the buyer's remedies to return of the goods and repayment of the price or to repair and replacement of nonconforming goods or parts; and
>
> (b) Resort to a remedy as provided is optional unless the remedy is expressly agreed to be exclusive, in which case it is the sole remedy.

Subsection (1) of § 2–719 is qualified by subsection (2): "Where circumstances cause an exclusive or limited remedy to fail of its essential purpose, remedy may be had as provided in this title." The jury's verdict for Hartzell in an amount almost exactly equal to Hartzell's evidence of cost of repairs plus diminution in market value means it must have found that the structural defects were not entirely remediable. Such a finding necessarily means that the limited warranty failed of its essential purpose.

Two of our recent cases support this conclusion. In *Soo Line R.R. v. Fruehauf Corp.,* the defendant claimed, relying on a limitation-of-remedies clause similar to the one involved here, that the plaintiff's damages should be limited to the reasonable cost of repairing the railroad cars that plaintiff had bought from defendant. The jury verdict included, among other things, an award for the difference between the value of the cars as actually manufactured and what they would have been worth if they had measured up to the defendant's representations. This court affirmed the verdict for the larger amount. We held, construing the Minnesota UCC, which is identical to § 2–719 as adopted in South Dakota, that the limitation-of-remedies clause was ineffective because the remedy as thus limited failed of its essential purpose. The defendant, though called upon to make the necessary repairs, had refused to do so, and the repairs as performed by the plaintiff itself "did not fully restore the cars to totally acceptable operating conditions."

Here, Justus Homes attempted to help with the necessary repairs, which is more than Fruehauf did in the *Soo Line* case, but after the repairs had been completed, the house was still, according to the jury verdict, not what Justus had promised it would be. The purpose of a remedy is to give to a buyer what the seller promised him—that is, a house that did not leak. If repairs alone do not achieve that end, then to limit the buyer's remedy to repair would cause that remedy to fail of its essential purpose.

An analogous case is *Select Port, Inc. v. Babcock Swine, Inc.,* applying § 2–719 as adopted in Iowa. The defendant had promised to deliver to plaintiff certain extraordinary pigs known as Midwestern Gilts and Meatline Boars. Instead, only ordinary pigs were delivered. Plaintiff sued for breach of warranty, and defendant claimed that its damages, if any, should be limited to a return of the purchase price by an express clause to that effect in the contract. The district court held that the clause was unenforceable because it was unconscionable, see § 2–719(3), and because it failed of its essential purpose. We affirmed. "Having failed to deliver the highly-touted special pigs, defendants may not now assert a favorable clause to limit their liability."

So here, where the house sold was found by the jury to fall short of the seller's promises, and where repairs could not make it right, Justus Homes's liability cannot be limited to the cost of repairs. If the repairs had been adequate to restore the house to its promised condition, and if Dr. Hartzell had claimed additional consequential damages, for example, water damage to a rug from the leaky roof, the limitation-of-remedies clause would have been effective. But that is not this case.

The evidence in the record all demonstrates that the repair or replacement clause was a failure under the circumstances of this case. Some of the house's many problems simply could not be remedied by repair or replacement. The clause having failed of its essential purpose, that is, effective enjoyment of implied and express warranties, Dr. Hartzell was entitled, under UCC § 2–719(2), to any of the buyer's remedies provided by the Code. Among these remedies are consequential damages as provided in § 2–714 and § 2–715(2).

Judgment for Hartzell affirmed.

## Wille v. Southwestern Bell Telephone Co.

**549 P.2d 903 (Kan. Sup. Ct. 1976)**

Frank Wille operated a heating and air-conditioning sales and service business under the trade names Frank Wille Company and Frank Wille's Coleman Comfort Center, and for the 13 years prior to 1974 he had purchased some form of Yellow Pages listing for his business in the telephone directory published by Southwestern Bell Telephone Company for Wichita.

In February 1974, Wille signed a contract to list two of his business telephone numbers in the Yellow Pages directory to be published in July 1974. The new directory omitted one of the numbers. Upon learning of the omission, Wille began advertising his business on local television stations and in alternative forms of advertising, with total expenditures of between $4,000 and $5,000.

Wille was never billed nor did he pay for the omitted listing. The written contract between the parties was subject to 13 terms and conditions, which were set out on the back of the contract. The fourth paragraph of those conditions provided:

> The applicant agrees that the Telephone Company shall not be liable for errors in or omissions of the directory advertising beyond the amount paid for the directory advertising omitted, or in which errors occur, for the issue life of the directory involved.

Wille brought an action against Southwestern Bell to recover damages for breach of contract. The district court granted summary judgment in favor of Southwestern Bell. Wille appealed.

**Harmon, Chief Justice.** Wille contends that the exculpatory clause upon which Bell relies is contrary to public policy and should not be enforced. He asserts unconscionability of contract in two respects: The parties' unequal bargaining position and the form of the contract and the circumstances of its execution.

Although the UCC's application is primarily limited to contracts for the present or future sale of goods [2–102; 2–105], many courts have extended the statute by analogy into other areas of the law or have used the doctrine as an alternative basis for their holdings. The UCC neither defines the concept of unconscionability nor provides the elements or parameters of the doctrine.

The comment to 2–302 sheds some light on the drafters' intent. It provides in part:

> The basic test is whether, in light of the general commercial background and the commercial needs of the particular trade or case, the clauses involved are so one-sided as to be unconscionable under the circumstances existing at the time of the making of the contract. The principle is one of the prevention of oppression and unfair surprise and not of disturbance of allocation of risks because of superior bargaining power.

One commentator has elaborated on the two types of situations which the UCC is designed to deal with:

> One type of situation is that involving unfair surprise: where there has actually been no assent to the terms of the contract. Contracts involving unfair surprise are similar to contracts of adhesion.

Most often these contracts involve a party whose circumstances, perhaps his inexperience or ignorance, when compared with the circumstances of the other party, make his knowing assent to the fine print terms fictional. Courts have often found in these circumstances an absence of a meaningful bargain.

The other situation is that involving oppression: where, although there has been actual assent, the agreement, surrounding facts, and relative bargaining positions of the parties indicate the possibility of gross overreaching on the part of either party. Oppression and economic duress in a contract seem to be inseparably linked to an inequality of bargaining power. The economic position of the parties is such that one becomes vulnerable to a grossly unequal bargain.

The leading case on the question of the validity of a Limitation of Liability Clause in a contract for telephone directory advertising is *McTighe v. New England Tel. & Tel. Co.,* where Circuit Judge Medina, speaking for the Court of Appeals for the Second Circuit, said:

The inequality of bargaining power between the telephone company and the businessman desiring to advertise in the Yellow Pages of the directory is more apparent than real. It is not different from that which exists in any other case in which a potential seller is the only supplier of the particular article or service desired. There are many other modes of advertising to which the businessman may turn if the contract offered him by the telephone company is not attractive. We find in this record no basis for a conclusion that the application of the Limitation of Liability Clause could lead to a result so unreasonable as to shock the conscience. In the absence of most exceptional circumstances, which do not appear in this record, the insertion of a "Yellow Page" advertisement under the wrong classification heading will not produce a different result from that which would follow a complete omission of the advertisement from the directory. It would be virtually, if not completely, impossible to determine what portion of the business done by an advertiser is attributable to its use of "Yellow Page" advertising. There are many factors which enter into periodic fluctuations in the volume of business done by a seller of goods. The purpose of the Limitation of Liability Clause is to protect the telephone company from the danger of verdicts primarily speculative in amount. This is not an unreasonable objective. In this respect, the telephone company is not in a different position from the local newspaper, radio or television station, or other advertising media.

In *Steele v. J. I. Case Co.,* we recognized that liability for consequential damages may be limited or excluded contractually unless under all the surrounding facts and circumstances, the limitation or exclusion would be inequitable. Each case of this type must necessarily rest upon its own facts, but after examining the terms of the contract, the manner of its execution and the knowledge and experience of Wille, we think the contract was neither inequitable nor unconscionable so as to deny its enforcement.

Judgment in favor of the telephone company affirmed.

## Parzek v. New England Log Homes, Inc.

**460 N.Y.S.2d 698 (N.Y. Sup. Ct. 1983)**

Parzek purchased from New England Log Homes a log home kit consisting of hand-peeled logs, window frames, and doorframes. The brochure that Parzek had seen before buying the log home kit contained a statement that the logs were treated with a preservative "to protect the treated wood against decay, stain, termites, and other insects." Other statements indicated the maintenance-free nature of the logs, and there was a guarantee against any material and engineering defects.

The logs were delivered in May 1974 to the construction site, where they were stored in stacks covered with heavy tarpaulins. By fall of 1976, the walls were erected and the roof was on. In 1979, Parzek discovered 15 medium-sized blue metallic beetles on the interior walls of the home. He was assured by the dealer for New England Log Homes that the problem was not serious. The following April, however, Parzek observed hundreds of beetles and discovered larvae and "excavation channels" in the logs. When he contacted New England Log Homes, he was told that it did not guarantee that its logs were insect free. Parzek had the home treated by an exterminator and then brought suit against New England Log Homes. A jury awarded a verdict in favor of Parzek for $9,000.

**Per Curiam.** Relying upon § 2–725 of the Code, New England Log Homes contends that this action is untimely since it was commenced more than four years after the date of delivery. Section 2–725 (subd. 2) of the Code fixes the accrual date of a breach of warranty cause of action as the date when the breach was discovered or should have been discovered for warranties that explicitly extend to future performance. Here, the very nature of insect infestation, where the insects might not appear until several years after the infestation occurs, compels the conclusion that the warranty extended to future performance. New England Log Homes seeks to obscure the issue by arguing that it should not be held to have warranted the logs against infestation some 50 or 60 years after the sale. Here, however, the expert proof shows that the infestation occurred before delivery or within a relatively short time thereafter, and that the insects did not begin to appear until several years later. Under such circumstances, the extended accrual date for warranties of future performance [Uniform Commercial Code, § 2–725 (2)] is applicable.

Judgment for Parzek affirmed.

## SELLER'S REMEDIES

**Remedies Available to an Injured Seller.** A buyer may breach a contract in a number of ways. The most common are: (1) by wrongfully refusing to accept goods, (2) by wrongfully returning goods, (3) by failing to pay for goods when payment is due, and (4) by indicating an unwillingness to go ahead with the contract.

When a buyer breaches a contract, the seller has a number of remedies under the Code, including the right to:

1. *Cancel* the contract [2–703(f)].
2. *Withhold delivery* of undelivered goods [2–703(a)].
3. *Resell* the goods covered by the contract and *recover damages* from the buyer [2–706].
4. *Recover* from the buyer the *profit* that the seller would have made on the sale or the *damages* that the seller sustained [2–708].
5. *Recover* the *purchase price* of goods delivered to or accepted by the buyer [2–709].

In addition, a buyer may become insolvent and thus unable to pay the seller for goods already delivered or for goods that the seller is obligated to deliver. When a seller learns of a buyer's insolvency, the seller has a number of remedies, including the right to:

1. *Withhold delivery* of undelivered goods [2–703(a)].
2. *Recover goods* from a buyer upon the buyer's insolvency [2–702].
3. *Stop delivery* of goods that are in the

possession of a carrier or other bailee [2–705].

**Cancellation and Withholding of Delivery.** When a buyer breaches a contract, the seller has the right to *cancel* the contract and to *hold up* his own *performance* of the contract. The seller may then set aside any goods that were intended to fill his obligations under the contract [2–704].

If the seller is in the process of manufacturing the goods, he has two choices. He may complete manufacture of the goods, or he may stop manufacturing and sell the uncompleted goods for their scrap or salvage value. In choosing between these alternatives, the seller should select the alternative that will minimize the loss [2–704(2)]. Thus, a seller would be justified in completing the manufacture of goods that could be resold readily at the contract price. However, a seller would not be justified in completing specially manufactured goods that could not be sold to anyone other than the buyer who ordered them. The purpose of this rule is to permit the seller to follow a reasonable course of action to *mitigate* (minimize) the damages. In *Mott Equity Elevator v. Suihovec,* which follows, the seller, whose offer of delivery was refused by the buyer, was entitled to cancel the contract.

**Resale of Goods.** If the seller sets aside goods intended for the contract or completes the manufacture of such goods, he is not obligated to try to resell the goods to someone else. However, he may *resell* them and *recover damages.* The seller must make any resale in *good faith* and in a *commercially reasonable* manner. If the seller does so, he is entitled to recover from the buyer as damages the difference between the resale price and the price the buyer agreed to pay in the contract [2–706].

If the seller resells, he may also recover **incidental damages,** but the seller must give the buyer credit for any expenses that the seller saved because of the buyer's breach of contract. Incidental damages include storage charges and sales commissions paid when the goods were resold [2–710]. Expenses saved might be the cost of packaging the goods and/or shipping them to the buyer.

Recovery of damages, including incidental damages on resale of goods is illustrated by the *Cohn v. Fisher* case which follows.

If the buyer and seller have agreed as to the manner in which the resale is to be made, the courts will enforce the agreement unless it is found to be unconscionable [2–302]. If the parties have not entered into an agreement as to the resale of the goods, they may be resold at public or private sale, but in all events the resale must be made in good faith and in a commercially reasonable manner. The seller should make it clear that the goods he is selling are those related to the broken contract.

If the goods are resold at *private sale,* the seller must give the buyer reasonable notification of his intention to resell [2–706(3)]. If the resale is a *public sale,* such as an auction, the seller must give the buyer notice of the time and place of the sale unless the goods are perishable or threaten to decline in value rapidly. The sale must be made at a usual place or market for public sales if one is reasonably available; and if the goods are not within the view of those attending the sale, the notification of the sale must state the place where the goods are located and provide for reasonable inspection by prospective bidders. The seller may bid at a public sale [2–706(4)].

The purchaser at a public sale who buys in good faith takes free from any rights of the original buyer even though the seller has failed to conduct the sale in compliance with the rules set out in the Code [2–706(5)]. The seller is *not* accountable to the buyer for any profit that the seller makes on a resale [2–706(6)].

**Recovery of the Purchase Price.** In the normal performance of a contract, the seller delivers conforming goods (goods that meet the contract specifications) to the buyer. The buyer accepts the goods and pays for them. The seller is entitled to the purchase price of all goods accepted by the buyer. He is also entitled to the purchase price of all goods that conformed to the contract and were lost or damaged after the buyer assumed the risk for their loss [2–709]. For example, a contract calls for Frank, a farmer, to ship 1,000 dozen eggs to Sutton, a grocer, with shipment "FOB Frank's Farm." If the eggs are lost or damaged while on their way to Sutton, she is responsible for paying Frank for them. Risk of loss is discussed in Chapter 31.

In one other situation, the seller may recover the purchase or contract price from the buyer. This is where the seller has made an honest effort to resell the goods and was unsuccessful or where it is apparent that any such effort to resell would be unsuccessful. This might happen where the seller manufactured goods especially for the buyer and the goods are not usable by anyone else. Assume that Sarton's Supermarket sponsors a bowling team. Sarton's orders six green-and-red bowling shirts to be embroidered with "Sarton's Supermarket" on the back and the names of the team members on the pocket. After the shirts are completed, Sarton's wrongfully refuses to accept them. The manufacturer will be able to recover the agreed purchase price if it cannot sell the shirts to someone else.

If the seller sues the buyer for the contract price of the goods, he must hold the goods for the buyer. Then, the seller must turn the goods over to the buyer if the buyer pays for them. However, if resale becomes possible before the buyer pays for the goods, the seller may resell them. Then, the seller must give the buyer credit for the proceeds of the resale [2–709(2)].

**Damages for Rejection or Repudiation.** When the buyer refuses to accept goods that conform to the contract or repudiates the contract, the seller does not have to resell the goods. The seller has two other ways of determining the damages that the buyer is liable for because of the breach of contract: (1) the *difference* between the *contract price* and the *market price* at which the goods are currently selling and (2) the "*profit*" that the seller lost when the buyer did not go through with the contract [2–708].

The seller may recover as damages the difference between the contract price and the market price at the time and place the goods were to be delivered to the buyer. The seller may also recover any *incidental damages*, but must give the buyer credit for any expenses that the seller has saved [2–708(1)]. This measure of damages is most commonly sought by a seller when the market price of the goods dropped substantially between the time the contract was made and the time the buyer repudiated the contract.

For example, on January 1, Toy Maker, Inc. contracts with the Red Balloon Toy Shop to sell the shop 100,000 hula hoops at $1.50 each, with delivery to be made in Boston on June 1. By June 1, the hula hoop fad has passed and hula hoops are selling for $1 each in Boston. If Toy Shop repudiates the contract on June 1 and refuses to accept delivery of the 100,000 hula hoops, Toy Maker is entitled to the difference between the contract price of $150,000 and the June 1 market price in Boston of $100,000. Thus Toy Maker could recover $50,000 in damages plus any incidental expenses, but less any expenses saved by it in not having to ship the hula hoops to Toy Shop (such as packaging and transportation costs).

If getting the difference between the contract price and the market price would not put the seller in as good a financial position as the seller would have been in if the contract had been performed, the seller may choose an alternative measure of damages based on the *lost profit and overhead* that the seller would have made if the sale had gone through. The seller can recover this lost profit and overhead plus any *incidental expenses.* However, the seller must give the buyer credit for any expenses saved as a result of the buyer's breach of contract [2–708(2)].

Using the hula hoop example, assume that the direct labor and material cost to Toy Maker of making the hoops was 55 cents each. Toy Maker could recover as damages from Toy Shop the profit Toy Maker lost when Toy Shop defaulted on the contract. Toy Maker would be entitled to the difference between the contract price of $150,000 and its direct cost of $55,000. Thus, Toy Maker could recover $95,000 plus any incidental expenses and less any expenses saved.

**Seller's Remedies Where Buyer Is Insolvent.** If the seller has not agreed to extend credit to the buyer for the purchase price of goods, the buyer must make payment on delivery of the goods. If the seller tenders delivery of the goods, he may withhold delivery unless the agreed payment is made. Where the seller has agreed to extend credit to the buyer for the purchase price of the goods, but discovers before delivery that the buyer is *insolvent,* the seller may refuse delivery unless the buyer pays cash for the goods together with the unpaid balance for all goods previously delivered under the contract [2–702(1)].

At common law, a seller had the right to rescind a sales contract induced by fraud and to recover the goods unless they had been resold to a bona fide purchaser for value. Based on this general legal principle, the Code provides that where the seller discovers that the buyer has received goods while insolvent, the seller may *reclaim* the goods upon demand made within 10 days after their receipt. This right granted to the seller is based on constructive deceit on the part of the buyer. Receiving goods while insolvent is equivalent to a false representation of solvency. To protect his rights, all the seller is required to do is to make a demand within the 10-day period; he need not actually repossess the goods.

If the buyer has misrepresented his solvency to this particular seller in writing within three months before the delivery of the goods, the 10-day limitation on the seller's right to reclaim the goods does not apply. However, the seller's right to reclaim the goods is subject to the prior rights of purchasers in the ordinary course of the buyer's business, good faith purchasers for value, creditors with a perfected lien on the buyer's inventory [2–702(2) and (3)], and a trustee in bankruptcy. The relative rights of creditors to their debtor's collateral are discussed in Chapter 40.

**Seller's Right to Stop Delivery.** If the seller discovers that the buyer is insolvent, he has the *right to stop the delivery* of any goods that he has shipped to the buyer, regardless of the size of the shipment. If a buyer repudiates a sales contract or fails to make a payment due before delivery, the seller has the right to stop delivery of any large shipment of goods, such as a carload, a truckload, or a planeload [2–705].

To stop delivery, the seller must notify the carrier or other bailee in time for the bailee to prevent delivery of the goods. After receiving notice to stop delivery, the carrier or other bailee owes a duty to hold the goods and deliver them as directed by the seller. The seller is liable to the carrier or other bailee for expenses incurred or damages resulting from compliance with his order to stop delivery. If a nonnegotiable document of title has been issued for the goods, the carrier or other bailee does not have a duty to obey a stop-delivery order issued by any person other than the person who consigned the goods to him [2–705(3)].

**Liquidated Damages.** If the seller has justifiably withheld delivery of the goods because of the buyer's breach, the buyer is entitled to recover any money or goods he has delivered to the seller over and above the agreed amount of liquidated damages. If there is no such agreement, the seller will not be permitted to retain an amount in excess of $500 or 20 percent of the value of the total performance for which the buyer is obligated under the contract, whichever is smaller. This right of restitution is subject to the seller's right to recover damages under other provisions of the Code and to recover the amount of value of benefits received by the buyer directly or indirectly by reason of the contract [2–718].

## Cohn v. Fisher

**287 A.2d 222 (N.J. Super. Ct. 1972)**

Albert Cohn advertised a 30-foot sailboat for sale in the *New York Times.* Donald Fisher saw the ad, inspected the sailboat, and offered Cohn $4,650 for the boat. Cohn accepted the offer. Fisher gave Cohn a check for $2,535 as a deposit. He wrote on the check "Deposit on aux. sloop, D'Arc Wind, full amount $4,650." Fisher later refused to go through with the purchase and stopped payment on the deposit check. Cohn readvertised the boat and sold it for the highest offer he received, which was $3,000. Cohn then sued Fisher for breach of contract and asked for damages of $1,679.50. This represented the $1,650 difference between the contract price and the sales price plus $29.50 in incidental expenses in reselling the boat.

**Rosenberg, Judge.** The time and place for performance of the contract is not in dispute: both parties agree that final payment was to be made on May 25, 1968, at the boat yard where Cohn's sloop was stored. Section 2–507(1) requires tender of delivery as a condition to seller's right to payment according to the contract. It appears from the facts that Cohn complied with § 2–507(1) in tendering delivery, since he was ready, willing, and able to close the deal. Fisher's failure to rightfully reject under §§ 2–601 and 2–602 or to accept under § 2–606 constituted a breach of the contract.

Under § 2–706 the seller may resell the goods and recover from the defaulting buyer the difference between the contract price and the resale price, together with incidental damages allowed by § 2–710, but less any expense saved in consequence of the buyer's breach. The resale must be made in good faith and in a commercially reasonable manner with reasonable notification of the resale of the defaulting buyer. Incidental damages are additional expenses reasonably incurred by the aggrieved party by reason of the breach. They would include resale charges, storage charges, notice charges, and the like.

By letter of May 27, 1968, Cohn notified Fisher of his intention to resell the boat. Cohn then readvertised the boat in the *New York Times* and accepted the highest offer of $3,000 in early June. This court holds such a sale to have been conducted in good faith and in a commercially reasonable manner, which together with the fact of notice to Fisher, satisfies the requirements of § 2–706.

By reason of the foregoing, this court hereby grants Cohn's motion for summary judgment against Fisher for breach of contract and awards damages in the amount of $1,679.50 representing resale damages under § 2–706 of $1,650 and incidental damages under § 2–710 of $29.50.

Judgment for Cohn.

## Mott Equity Elevator v. Suihovec

**18 UCC Rep. 368 (N.D. Sup. Ct. 1975)**

On October 24, 1972, Mott Equity Elevator entered into a contract with Rudy Suihovec, a farmer, whereby Suihovec agreed to sell and deliver in March 4,000 bushels of spring wheat at $1.82 per bushel. Several times a week throughout March, Suihovec contacted Mott and asked when he could make delivery. Each time, he was told that the elevator was filled. Suihovec continued to inquire during April and May and was told that there was little or no space for his grain. Finally, in June, Suihovec sold and shipped his grain to another buyer for $2.20 per bushel. In mid-September, when the price of grain had risen to $4.40 a bushel, Mott called Suihovec and asked him to make delivery. He advised Mott that he was no longer obligated, because Mott had breached the contract. Mott then brought suit against Suihovec. The trial court awarded judgment to Suihovec.

**Vogel, Justice.** We agree with the trial judge's finding of unreasonable delay by Mott in making its demand for delivery in September, fully six months after the contract had expired.

The trial judge found that Mott failed to perform within a reasonable time after a tender of performance by the seller and after the time for performance had expired. The court further concluded that the general conduct of Mott was such as to justify the seller Suihovec in treating the contract as breached by Mott.

Mott strenuously argues that Suihovec was not entitled to resell his grain under Section 2–706, without giving reasonable notice of his intent to resell. The argument also is made that Section 2–309 imposes a duty on Suihovec to give reasonable notice to the other party that he was terminating the contract.

We find these arguments to be without merit. Before discussing these questions, it may be helpful to reiterate the remedies available to the seller following breach by the buyer. Under Section 2–703, the seller is entitled to, among other remedies, withhold delivery, resell and recover damages, recover damages for nonacceptance, or cancel. Suihovec pursued the remedy of cancellation, as was his right. He thereafter resold his grain to another buyer, as was his right. The parties have confused Suihovec's right to dispose of his grain as he wished under a canceled contract with the Code remedy allowing a seller to "resell and recover damages" under Section 2–703 and Section 2–706.

The seller's right to resell and recover damages is, of course, available to a seller in addition to his right to cancel; subsection 1–b of Section 2–719 creates a presumption that clauses prescribing remedies are cumulative rather than exclusive.

The only condition precedent to the seller's right to resell is a breach by the buyer within Section 2–703. The trial judge found that Suihovec had a right to pursue this remedy when he sold his grain directly to the Grain Terminal Association. We would agree that Suihovec did have such a right if it were necessary to apply this section to the seller's conduct in reselling his grain in this case. But the section does not apply. In a falling market Suihovec would probably have desired to resell and recover damages. To recover damages under this section he would be required to act in good faith, sell in a commercially reasonable manner, and give reasonable notice to the buyer of his intention to resell (if the sale was at private sale). Failure to act properly under this section merely deprives the seller of the measure of damages provided in subsection 1. In any event, the seller is not accountable to the buyer for any profit made on any resale under Section 2–706, where, as here, the resale occurred in a rising market and the contract had been canceled. In this case, involving a rising market, Suihovec suffered no damages and thus did not need to resort to this Code remedy.

We hold that the buyer breached the agreement in not accepting delivery within a reasonable time, giving rise to Suihovec's right to cancel under Section 2–703. "Cancellation" is defined in Section 2–106, as follows:

> "Cancellation" occurs when either party puts an end to the contract for breach by the other and its effect is the same as that of "termination" except that the cancelling party also retains any remedy for breach of the whole contract or any unperformed balance.

Mott makes the argument that Suihovec is not entitled to any "windfall" he might have received when he sold his grain in June to another buyer. Mott claims that Suihovec acted in "bad faith" by failing to notify Mott of his intention to resell his grain. From the record, we cannot find any evidence that Suihovec acted in bad faith when he trucked his wheat directly to the Grain Terminal Association and sold it for a slightly higher price than provided under the contract. There is no duty to notify of a resale where the contract is canceled. Suihovec appears to have made every effort to deliver his grain to Mott. In fact, testimony at trial revealed that he was desperate to deliver his grain to Mott. It must be remembered that the entire time Suihovec held the grain in storage on his farm, he suffered the risk of loss upon casualty to the grain. In fact, some of the contract grain had to be discarded due to insect damage.

Suihovec was not a seller out to take advantage of a rising market. He made arrangements to market his wheat immediately upon Mott's refusal in late May to accept delivery. When Suihovec sold the grain in June, the market price had risen to only $2.20 per bushel. The elevator, on the other hand, seeks to collect damages at the price of $4.40 per bushel, the market price in September 1973, when it contends Suihovec breached the contract.

We find no bad faith on the part of Suihovec.

Judgment for Suihovec affirmed.

## BUYER'S REMEDIES

**Buyer's Remedies in General.** A seller may breach a contract in a number of ways. The most common are: (1) failing to make an agreed delivery, (2) delivering goods that do not conform to the contract, and (3) indicating that he does not intend to fulfill the obligations under the contract.

A buyer whose seller breaks the contract is given a number of alternative remedies. These include:

1. *Buying other goods (covering)* and *recovering damages* from the seller based on any additional expense that the buyer incurs in obtaining the goods [2–712].
2. *Recovering damages* based on the *difference* between the *contract price* and the current *market price* of the goods [2–713].
3. *Recovering damages* for any nonconforming goods accepted by the buyer based on the *difference in value* between what the buyer got and what he should have gotten [2–714].
4. *Obtaining specific performance* of the contract where the goods are unique and cannot be obtained elsewhere [2–716].

In addition, the buyer can in some cases recover *consequential damages* (such as lost profits) and *incidental damages* (such as expenses incurred in buying substitute goods).

**Buyer's Right to Cover.** If the seller fails or refuses to deliver the goods called for in the contract, the buyer can purchase substitute goods; this is known as *"cover."* If the buyer does purchase substitute goods, the buyer can recover as damages from the seller the difference between the contract price and the cost of the substitute goods [2–712]. For example, Frank Farmer agrees to sell Ann's Cider Mill 1,000 bushels of apples at $5 a bushel. Farmer then refuses to deliver the apples. Cider Mill can purchase 1,000 bushels of similar apples, and if it has to pay $5.50 a bushel, it can recover the difference ($0.50 a bushel) between what it paid ($5.50) and the contract price ($5). Thus, Cider Mill could recover $500 from Farmer.

The buyer can also recover any incidental damages sustained, but must give the seller credit for any expenses saved. In addition, he may be able to obtain consequential damages. The buyer is not required to cover, however. If he does not cover, the other remedies under the Code are still available [2–712].

**Incidental Damages. Incidental damages** include expenses that the buyer incurs in receiving, inspecting, transporting, and storing goods shipped by the seller that do not conform to those called for in the contract. Incidental damages also include any reasonable expenses or charges that the buyer has to pay in obtaining substitute goods [2–715(1)].

**Consequential Damages.** In certain situations, an injured buyer is able to recover **consequential damages,** such as the buyer's lost profits caused by the seller's breach of contract. The buyer must be able to show that the seller knew or should have known at the time the contract was made that the buyer would suffer special damages if the seller did not perform his obligations. The buyer must also show that he could not have prevented the damage by obtaining substitute goods [2–715(2)].

Suppose Knitting Mill promises to deliver 1,000 yards of a special fabric to Dorsey by September 1. Knitting Mill knows that Dorsey wants to acquire the material to make garments suitable for the Christmas season. Knitting Mill also knows that in reliance on the contract with it, Dorsey will enter into contracts with department stores to deliver the finished garments by October 1. If Knitting Mill fails to deliver the fabric or delivers the fabric after September 1, it may be liable to Dorsey for any consequential damages that she sustains if she is unable to acquire the same material elsewhere in time to fulfill her October 1 contracts.

Consequential damages can also include an injury to a person or property caused by a breach of warranty. For example, an electric saw is defectively made. Hanson purchases the saw, and while he is using it, the blade comes off and severely cuts his arm. The injury to Hanson is consequential damage resulting from a nonconforming or defective product.

**Damages for Nondelivery.** If the seller fails or refuses to deliver the goods called for by the contract, the buyer has the option of recovering damages for the nondelivery. Thus, instead of covering, the buyer can get the *difference* between the *contract price* of the goods and their *market price* at the time he learns of the seller's breach. In addition, the buyer may recover any *incidental damages* and *consequential damages,* but must give the seller credit for any expenses saved [2–713].

Suppose Biddle agreed on June 1 to sell and deliver 1,500 bushels of wheat to a grain elevator on September 1 for $7 per bushel and then refused to deliver on September 1 because the market price was then $8 per bushel. The grain elevator could recover $1,500 damages from Biddle, plus incidental damages that could not have been prevented by cover.

The *Sun Maid Raisin Growers of California v. Victor Packing Co.* case, which follows, illustrates the application of the measure of damages for nondelivery. In this case, the market price of the goods at the time of delivery was significantly higher than the contract price, and the seller, who had gambled that the price would fall, had to pay substantial damages.

**Damages for Defective Goods.** If a buyer accepts defective goods and wants to hold the seller liable, the buyer must give the seller notice of the defect within a reasonable time after the buyer discovers the defect [2–607(3)]. Where goods are defective or not as warranted and the buyer gives the required notice, he can recover damages. The buyer is entitled to recover the *difference* between the *value of the goods received* and the *value the goods would have had* if they had been as warranted. He may also be entitled to *incidental* and *consequential damages* [2–714].

For example, Al's Auto Store sells Anders an automobile tire, warranting it to be four-ply construction. The tire goes flat when it is punctured by a nail, and Anders discovers that the tire is really only two-ply. If Anders gives the store prompt notice of the breach, she can keep the tire and recover from Al's the difference in value between a two-ply and a four-ply tire.

**Buyer's Right to Specific Performance.** Sometimes, the goods covered by a contract are unique and it is not possible for a buyer to obtain substitute goods. When this is the case, the buyer is entitled to **specific performance** of the contract.

Specific performance means that the buyer can require the seller to give the buyer the goods covered by the contract [2–716]. Thus, the buyer of an antique automobile such as a 1910 Ford might have a court order the seller to deliver the specified automobile to the buyer because it was one of a kind. On the other hand, the buyer of grain in a particular storage bin could not get specific performance if he could buy the same kind of grain elsewhere.

**Buyer and Seller Agreements as to Remedies.** As mentioned earlier in this chapter, the parties to a contract may provide remedies in addition to or as substitution for those expressly provided in the Code [2–719]. For example, the buyer's remedies may be limited by the contract to the return of the goods and the repayment of the price or to the replacement of nonconforming goods or parts. However, a court looks to see whether such a limitation was freely agreed to or whether it is unconscionable. In the latter case, the court does not enforce the limitation and the buyer has all the rights given to an injured buyer by the Code.

## Sun Maid Raisin Growers of California v. Victor Packing Co.

**194 Cal. Rptr. 612 (Cal. Ct. App. 1983)**

In November 1975, Victor Packing Company agreed to sell Sun Maid Raisin Growers 1,900 tons of raisins. The first 100 tons were sold at 39 cents per pound and the remainder at 40 cents per pound. No specific delivery date was agreed upon. Victor indicated to Sun Maid on August 10, 1976, that it would not complete performance, being unable to deliver the last 610 tons. Sun Maid was able to purchase 200 tons at 43 cents per pound. Because of heavy rains in September 1976, the new crop of raisins suffered extensive damage and the price of raisins increased dramatically.

Sun Maid brought suit against Victor to recover damages. The trial court awarded $307,339 in damages to Sun Maid. Victor appealed, claiming that the increase in the lost profits due to the disastrous rain damage was not foreseeable.

**Franson, Acting Presiding Judge.** The basic measure of damages for a seller's nondelivery or repudiation is the difference between the market price and the contract price.

In addition to the difference between the market price and the contract price, the buyer can recover incidental damages such as expenses of cover and consequential damages such as lost profits to the extent that they could not have been avoided by cover. The inability to cover after a prompt and reasonable effort to do so is a prerequisite to recovery of consequential damages. If the buyer is only able to cover in part, he is entitled to the net cost of cover (the difference between the cover price and the contract price plus expenses) together with any consequential damages but less expenses saved in consequence of the seller's breach.

Under § 2–715(2)(a), consequential damages include "any loss resulting from general or particular requirements and needs of which the seller at the time of contracting had reason to know and which could not reasonably be prevented by cover or otherwise." The "reason to know" language concerning the buyer's particular requirements and needs arises from *Hadley v. Baxendale.* The Code, however, has imposed an objective rather than a subjective standard in determining whether the seller should have anticipated the buyer's needs. Thus, actual knowledge by the seller of the buyer's requirements is not required. The only requirement under § 2–715(2)(a), is that the seller reasonably should have been expected to know of the buyer's exposure to loss.

Furthermore, comment 6 to § 2–715 provides that if the seller knows that the buyer is in the business of reselling the goods, the seller is charged with knowledge that the buyer will be selling the goods in anticipation of a profit. "Absent a contractual provision against consequential damages a seller in breach will therefore always be liable for the buyer's resulting loss of profit."

Finally, a buyer's failure to take any other steps by which the loss could reasonably have been prevented bars him from recovering consequential damages. This is merely a codification of the rule that the buyer must attempt to minimize damages.

In the present case, the evidence fully supports the finding that after Victor's breach of the contract on August 10, 1976, Sun Maid acted in good faith in a commercially reasonable manner and was able to cover by purchase only some 200 tons of substitute raisins at a cost of 43 cents per pound. There were no other natural Thompson seedless free tonnage raisins available for purchase in the market at or within a reasonable time after Victor's breach. Although the evidence indicates that Sun Maid actually was able to purchase an additional 410 tons of raisins after the September rainfall in its efforts to effect cover, these were badly damaged raisins which had to be reconditioned at a substantial cost to bring them up to market condition. According to Sun Maid, if the trial court had used the total cost of cover of the full 610 tons as the measure of damages rather than lost profits on resale, its damages would have totaled $377,720.

Although the trial court did not specify why it determined damages by calculating lost profits instead of the cost of cover, the court probably found that damages should be limited to the amount that would have put Sun Maid in "as good a position as if the other party had fully performed." Thus, Sun Maid was awarded the lesser of the actual cost of cover (treating the reconditioning of the 410 tons as a cost) and the loss of prospective profits.

In contending that the foreseeability requirements applies to the amount of the lost profits and not just to the fact of lost profits, Victor apparently acknowledges that it knew at the time of contracting that Sun Maid would be reselling the raisins to its customers in the domestic market. Victor has no alternative to this concession since it was an experienced packer and knew that Sun Maid marketed raisins year round in the domestic market. Furthermore, Victor must be presumed to have known that if it did not deliver the full quota of raisins provided under the contracts (1,800 tons) by the end of the crop year or before such reasonable time as thereafter might be agreed to, Sun Maid would be forced to go into the market to attempt to cover its then existing orders for sale of raisins. This is exactly what occurred.

Victor nonetheless contends it should not be liable for damages based on the extraordinarily high price of raisins in the fall of 1976 which was caused by the "disastrous" rains in September. These rains reportedly caused a 50 percent loss of the new crop which with the lack of a substantial carryover of 1975 raisins drove the market price from approximately $860 per packed weight ton to over $1,600 per packed weight ton.

Victor does not assert the doctrine of impossibility or impracticability of performance as a defense. [§ 2–615.] This is understandable since the nondelivery of raisins was not caused by the failure of a presupposed condition (continuance of the $860 per ton market price) but solely by Victor's failure to deliver the 610 tons of raisins during the 1975 crop year. This is where the trial court's findings of Victor's bad faith become pertinent. A reasonable inference may be drawn that from early spring Victor was gambling on the market price of raisins in deciding whether to perform its contracts with Sun Maid. If the price would fall below the contract price, Victor would buy raisins and deliver them to Sun Maid. If the market price went substantially above the contract price, Victor would sit tight. While we cannot read Victor's mind during the late spring and summer months, we can surmise that it speculated that the market price would remain below the contract price after the current crop year so that it could purchase new raisins for delivery to Sun Maid at the contract price. It threw the dice and lost.

> The possibility of "disastrous" rain damage to the 1976 raisin crop was clearly foreseeable to Victor. Such rains have occurred at sporadic intervals since raisins have been grown in the San Joaquin Valley. Raisin packers fully understand the great risk in contracting to sell raisins at a fixed price over a period of time extending into the next crop year. The market price may go up or down depending on consumer demand and the supply and quality of raisins. If the seller does not have sufficient inventory to fulfill his delivery obligations within the time initially required or as subsequently modified by the parties, he will have to go into the market to purchase raisins. The fact that he may be surprised by an extraordinary rise in the market price does not mean that the buyer's prospective profits on resale are unforeseeable as a matter of law.
>
> Judgment for Sun Maid affirmed.

## SUMMARY

The Code remedies for breach of contract are designed to put the injured party in the same position that he would have been in if the contract had been performed.

As a general rule, the courts will enforce an agreement of the parties relating to the damages to which the parties will be entitled, provided that the agreement is not void as an unconscionable contract or clause. A liquidated damages provision in a contract is enforceable if the amount is reasonable and the damages for the injury suffered by the injured party are not readily provable. The parties by agreement may provide for additional or supplemental damages, and they may limit or exclude consequential damages, except damages for injury to a person from consumer goods.

The statute of limitations on sales contracts is four years from the time the cause of action accrues. The parties may, by agreement, reduce the time limit to one year, but they cannot extend the time limit.

The seller is entitled to the purchase price of conforming goods delivered to and accepted by the buyer. The seller may also recover the purchase price of any conforming goods that were sent to the buyer and were lost or destroyed after the risk of loss had passed to the buyer. Also, if the goods have been identified to the contract and the buyer repudiates the sale, the seller is entitled to the purchase price of the goods that cannot, by a reasonable effort on the part of the seller, be resold for a fair price.

The seller is entitled to recover compensatory damages that were reasonably within the contemplation of the parties. The seller upon breach by the buyer is also entitled to incidental damages. If necessary to put the seller in the position he would have held had the buyer performed, the seller may be granted his lost profits, including overhead, as damages. The seller is not obligated to resell upon the buyer's refusal to accept goods, but if he does resell the goods in a commercially reasonable manner, he may recover as damages the difference between the sales price and the contract price.

Upon the buyer's insolvency, the seller may reclaim the goods if he makes the demand within 10 days after the buyer's receipt. If the buyer misrepresented his solvency in writing to the particular seller within the previous three months, the 10-day limitation does not apply. The seller may also, upon the buyer's insolvency, stop delivery of the goods by a carrier or other bailee. Delivery of large lots may be stopped upon the buyer's repudiation or failure to pay the amount due before delivery. Reasonable notice to stop delivery must be given to the carrier or other bailee.

As damages for nondelivery or repudiation on the seller's part, the buyer may recover the difference between the market price of the goods and the contract price plus incidental, and under some circumstances consequential, damages. If the buyer covers, the measure of his compensatory damages is the difference between the cost of the cover and the contract price. The buyer may be entitled to the remedy of specific performance if the goods that are the subject matter of the contract are unique or cannot be obtained by cover.

In the event that goods are defective and the buyer accepts them, he can, upon giving the seller notice of the breach, recover as damages the difference between the value of the goods received and what their value would have been if they had been conforming goods, plus incidental, and under some circumstances consequential, damages.

## PROBLEM CASES

**1.** Lobiano contracted with Property Protection, Inc. for the installation of a burglar alarm system. The contract provided in part:

> Alarm system equipment installed by Property Protection, Inc. is guaranteed against improper function due to manufacturing defects of workmanship for a period of 12 months. The installation of the above equipment carries a 90-day warranty. The liability of Property Protection, Inc. is limited to repair or replacement of security alarm equipment and does not include loss or damage to possessions, persons, or property.

As installed, the alarm system included a standby battery source of power in the event that the regular source of power failed.

During the 90-day warranty period, burglars broke into Lobiano's house and stole $35,815 worth of jewelry. First, they destroyed the electric meter so that there was no electric source to operate the system, and then they entered the house. The batteries in the standby system were dead, and thus the standby system failed to operate. Accordingly, no outside siren was activated and a telephone call that was supposed to be triggered was not made. Lobiano brought suit, claiming damage in the amount of her stolen jewelry because of the failure of the alarm system to work properly. Did the disclaimer effectively eliminate any liability on the alarm company's part for consequential damages?

**2.** Between August 29, 1974, and December 31, 1975, Outdoor Scenes, Inc., a nursery, sold and delivered 13 trees to Anthony Grace—and planted them at Grace's request. The agreed purchase price of $2,735 was never paid by Grace, and the nursery brought suit on August 29, 1980, to recover the moneys due. Grace claimed that the lawsuit was barred by the UCC's statute of limitations, while the nursery claimed that the six-year statute of limitations applicable to contracts for services was applicable. Is the nursery's lawsuit barred by the statute of limitations?

**3.** Dubrow, a widower, was engaged to be married. In October, he placed a large order with a furniture store for delivery the following January. The order included carpeting cut to special sizes for the prospective couple's new house and many pieces of furniture for various rooms in the house. One week later, Dubrow died. When the order was delivered, his daughter refused the furniture and carpeting. The furniture store then sued his estate to recover the full purchase price. It had not tried to resell the furniture and carpeting to anyone else. Under the circumstances, was the seller entitled to recover the purchase price of the goods?

**4.** Kohn ordered a custom-made suit from Meledandi Tailors. A few days later, before much work had been completed, Kohn told the tailors that he did not want the suit. They therefore stopped its manufacture and filed suit for the entire contract price. Is Kohn liable for the full purchase price?

**5.** Miles sold a dining room table and four chairs to Lyons for $100. She told Lyons that the table and chairs were hers, but in reality they belonged to her relatives. The value of the set at the time of the sale was $275. After the table and chairs were reclaimed by their rightful owners, Lyons instituted an action against Miles. What amount can he claim in damages?

**6.** Shreve Land Company contracted with Pac-Door to purchase 103 doors for a construction project in Louisiana. The price for the lot of doors was $11,483, with shipment to be made in a single delivery. Pac-Door shipped only 55 doors, with a value of $6,320. Shreve purchased the remaining 48 doors from another vendor at a cost of $13,581. Pac-Door then sued Shreve to recover the $6,320 due for the 55 doors. Is Shreve liable to Pac-Door?

**7.** In November, Sorenson Orchard Company contracted with Michigan Sugar Company for 800 bags of sugar to be used in processing frozen diced apples. Of the 800 bags, Sorenson returned 68 bags to Michigan Sugar because there was excessive "pan scale" in the bags, and the 68 bags were replaced by Michigan Sugar. Although Sorenson's inspection noticed some pan scale in the remaining 732 bags, Sorenson used the bags anyway. Sorenson completed packing the apples for its customers; the apples were put in cold storage; and Sorenson was paid for them. In the spring, Sorenson's customers began using the apples and rejected the batch after finding specks of pan scale in the apples. Over the next three years, Sorenson sold the frozen apples at a great loss. Michigan Sugar sued Sorenson to recover the contract price of the sugar, and Sorenson counterclaimed for breach of warranty, seeking as consequential damages the profits it had lost because of its customers' rejection of the frozen apples. Is Sorenson entitled to consequential damages?

**8.** The Carpels contracted with Saget Studios to take black-and-white photographs of their wedding for $110. Because of carelessness on the part of Saget Studios, the pictures were never delivered. The Carpels brought a lawsuit, claiming that they were entitled to consequential damages in excess of $10,000 because of the breach of contract. They contended that the damages should include the cost of restaging the wedding and photographing it, loss of sentimental value caused by Saget Studios' failure to perform in a timely manner, emotional distress caused by the failure to perform, and punitive damages. Should the Carpels be allowed to recover for these damages?

**9.** In 1972, Schweber contracted to purchase a certain black 1973 Rolls-Royce Corniche automobile from Rallye Motors. He made a $3,500 deposit on the car. Rallye later returned his deposit to him and told him that the car was not available. However, Schweber learned that the automobile was available to the dealer and was being sold to another customer. The dealer then offered to sell Schweber a similar car, but with a different interior design. Schweber brought a lawsuit against the dealer to prevent it from selling the Rolls Corniche to anyone else and to require that it be sold to him. Rallye Motors claimed that he could get only damages and not specific performance. Approximately 100 Rolls-Royce Corniches were being sold each year in the United States, but none of the others would have the specific features and detail of this one. Is the remedy of specific performance available to Schweber?

# PART IX

# COMMERCIAL PAPER

Chapter 35

# Negotiable Instruments

## INTRODUCTION

As commerce and trade developed, man moved beyond exclusive reliance on barter to the use of money and then to the use, as well, of substitutes for money. The term commercial paper encompasses a number of such substitutes that are in common usage today, including checks, promissory notes and certificates of deposit.

History discloses that every civilization that engaged to an appreciable extent in commerce used some form of commercial paper. Probably the oldest type of commercial paper used in the carrying on of trade is the promissory note. Archaeologists found a promissory note made payable to bearer that dated from about 2100 B.C. The merchants of Europe used commercial paper, which under the law merchant was negotiable, in the 13th and 14th centuries. Commercial paper does not appear to have been used in England until about A.D. 1600.

This chapter, and the three chapters that follow, outline and discuss the body of law that governs a number of types of commercial paper. Of particular interest are those kinds of commercial paper that have the attribute of negotiability—that is they generally can be readily transferred, and accepted, as a substitute for money. Chapter 35 discusses the nature and benefits of negotiable instruments and then outlines the requirements an instrument must meet to qualify as a negotiable instrument. The subsequent chapters discuss transfer and negotiation of instruments, the rights and liabilities of parties to negotiable instruments, and the rules applicable to checks.

## NATURE OF NEGOTIABLE INSTRUMENTS

When a person buys a television set and gives the merchant a check drawn on his checking account, that person is using a form of negotiable commercial paper. Similarly, a person who goes to a bank or a credit union to borrow money might sign a promissory note agreeing to pay the money back in 90 days. Again, a form of negotiable commercial paper is being used.

**Commercial paper** is basically a *contract for the payment of money.* It is commonly used as a substitute for money, and it can also be used as a means of extending credit. When a television set is bought by giving the merchant a check, the check is a substitute for money. Similarly, a credit union is willing to give a borrower money now in exchange for the borrower's promise to repay it later on certain terms.

**Uniform Commercial Code.** The law of commercial paper is covered in Article 3 (Commercial Paper) and Article 4 (Bank Deposits and Collections) of the Uniform Commercial Code. Other negotiable documents, such as investment securities and documents of title, are treated in other sections of the Code. Essentially, the Code makes no drastic changes in the basic rules governing the use of commercial paper that have been recognized for centuries, but it has adopted modern terminology and it has coordinated, clarified, and simplified the law.

**Commercial Paper.** There are two basic types of commercial paper: *promises to pay* money and *orders to pay* money. **Promissory notes** and **certificates of deposit** issued by banks are promises to pay someone money. **Drafts** and **checks** are orders to another person to pay money to a third person. A check is an order directed to a bank to pay money from a person's account to a third person.

**Negotiability.** Commercial paper that is **negotiable** or a **negotiable instrument** is a special kind of commercial paper. If commercial paper is negotiable, it can pass readily through our financial system and can be accepted in place of money. It has many advantages.

For example, Searle, the owner of a clothing store in New York, contracts with Amado, a swimsuit manufacturer in Los Angeles, for $10,000 worth of swimsuits. If negotiable instruments did not exist, Searle would have to send or carry $10,000 across the country, which would be both inconvenient and risky. If the money were stolen along the way, Searle would lose the $10,000 unless he could locate the thief. By using a check in which Searle orders his bank to pay $10,000 from his account to Amado, or to someone designated by Amado, Searle can make the payment in a far more convenient manner. He has sent only a single piece of paper to Amado. If the check is properly prepared and sent, sending the check is less risky than sending money. If the check is stolen along the way, Searle's bank may not pay it to anyone but Amado or someone authorized by Amado. And because the check gives Amado the right to either collect the $10,000 or transfer the right to collect it to someone else, the check is a practical substitute for cash to Amado as well as Searle.

In this chapter, and in the three chapters that follow, we will discuss the requirements that are necessary for a contract to qualify as a negotiable instrument. We will also explain the features that distinguish a negotiable instrument from a contract and that have led to the widespread use of negotiable instruments as a substitute for money.

## KINDS OF COMMERCIAL PAPER

**Promissory Notes.** The **promissory note** is the simplest form of commercial paper; it is simply a *promise to pay money.* A promissory note is a two-party instrument in which one person (known as the **maker**) makes an unconditional promise in writing to pay another person (the **payee**), or a person specified by that person, a sum of money either on demand or at some particular time in the future.

The promissory note is a credit instrument, and it is used in a wide variety of transactions in which credit is extended. For example, if a person purchases an automobile on credit, the dealer will probably have the person sign a promissory note for the unpaid balance of the purchase price. Similarly, if a person borrows money to purchase a house, the lender who makes the loan and takes a mortgage on the house will have the person sign a promissory note for the amount due on the loan. The note will probably state that it is secured by a mortgage. The terms of payment on the note should correspond with the terms of the sales contract for the purchase of the car or the house.

**Certificates of Deposit.** The **certificate of deposit** given by a bank or a savings and loan association when a deposit of money is made is a form of commercial paper and a type of note. Like the promissory note, the certificate of deposit is a promise to pay money. When a bank issues a certificate of deposit (CD), it acknowledges that it has received a deposit of a specific sum of money. The bank also agrees to pay the owner of the certificate the sum of money plus a stated rate of interest at some time in the future.

**Example of a Promissory Note**

$ 460.00 July 15 19 86

Sixty days after date I promise to pay to

the order of James Smith

Four hundred sixty and no/100 Dollars

at American National Bank, Chicago, Illinois 60606

Value received.

No. 143 Due 9/13/86 Henry Jenkins

Payee

Maker

**Example of a Certificate of Deposit**

CERTIFICATE OF DEPOSIT

BLOOMINGTON, IND. March 1 1986 No. 18866 71-227/712

THIS IS TO CERTIFY THAT Albert Wells HAS DEPOSITED IN

8 Fee Lane
STREET OR R.F.D.
Spencer, Indiana
CITY & STATE

ESTABLISHED 1871
CITIZENS FIRST NATIONAL BANK
OF BLOOMINGTON
BLOOMINGTON, IND.
47401

$1,000.00

One Thousand and no/100 Dollars

PAYABLE TO Albert Wells OR ORDER Six MONTHS

AFTER DATE WITH INTEREST THEREON AT THE RATE OF 9 PER CENT PER ANNUM FROM DATE ON THE RETURN OF THIS CERTIFICATE PROPERLY INDORSED. NO INTEREST WILL BE PAID UPON THIS CERTIFICATE AFTER ITS MATURITY. THE BANK IS PROHIBITED BY FEDERAL LAW FROM PAYING THIS DEPOSIT IN WHOLE OR IN PART BEFORE ITS MATURITY AND FROM PAYING INTEREST AFTER MATURITY. THE RATE OF INTEREST PAYABLE HEREUNDER IS SUBJECT TO CHANGE BY THE BANK TO SUCH EXTENT AS MAY BE NECESSARY TO COMPLY WITH REQUIREMENTS OF THE FEDERAL RESERVE BOARD MADE FROM TIME TO TIME PURSUANT TO THE FEDERAL RESERVE ACT. THE BANK RESERVES THE RIGHT TO REQUIRE THIRTY DAYS NOTICE OF WITHDRAWAL IN WRITING.

DUE August 31, 1986

Richard Roe
CASHIER

NOT SUBJECT TO CHECK

**Drafts.** A **draft** is a form of commercial paper that involves an *order to pay money* rather than a promise to pay money. The most common example of a draft is a check. A draft has three parties to it: one person (known as the **drawer**) orders a second person (the **drawee**) to pay a certain sum of money to a third person (the **payee**).

Drafts other than checks are used in a variety of commercial transactions. If Brown owes Ames money, Ames may draw a draft for the amount of the debt, naming Brown as drawee and himself or his bank as payee, and send the draft to Brown's bank for presentment and collection.

In freight shipments in which the terms are "cash on delivery," it is a common practice for the seller to ship the goods to the buyer on an "order bill of lading" consigned to himself at the place of delivery. The seller then indorses the bill of lading and attaches a draft naming the buyer as drawee. He then sends the bill of lading and the draft through banking channels to the buyer's bank. The draft is presented to the bank for payment, and when payment is made, the bill of lading is delivered to the buyer. Through this type of commercial transaction, the buyer gets the goods and the seller gets his money.

If credit is extended, the same procedure is followed, but a time draft—a draft payable at some future time—is used. In such a transaction, the buyer will "accept" the draft instead of paying it. To accept the draft, he writes his name across its face, thereby obligating himself to pay the amount of the draft when due.

**Checks.** A **check** is a *draft* on which the *drawee is always a bank* and that is *payable on demand.* It is the most widely used form of commercial paper. The issuer of a check is ordering the bank at which he maintains an account to pay a specified person, or someone designated by that person, a certain sum of money from the account. For example, Elizabeth Brown has a checking account at the National Bank of Washington. She goes to

**Example of a Draft**

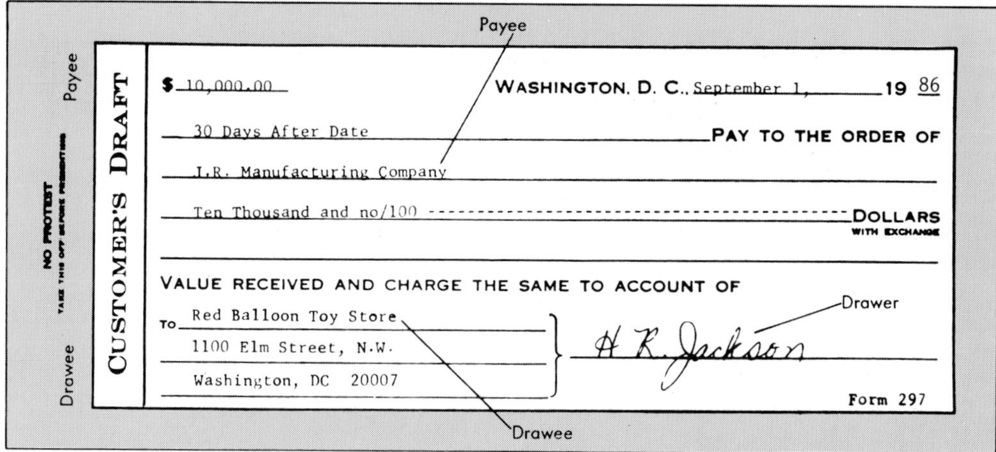
Payee
$ 10,000.00
WASHINGTON, D. C., September 1, 19 86
30 Days After Date
PAY TO THE ORDER OF
I.R. Manufacturing Company
Ten Thousand and no/100
DOLLARS WITH EXCHANGE
VALUE RECEIVED AND CHARGE THE SAME TO ACCOUNT OF
TO Red Balloon Toy Store
1100 Elm Street, N.W.
Washington, DC 20007
H. R. Jackson
Drawer
Form 297
Drawee
CUSTOMER'S DRAFT
NO PROTEST
Payee
Drawee

Sears and agrees to buy a washing machine priced at $359.95. If she writes a check to pay for it, she is the drawer of the check, the National Bank of Washington is the drawee, and Sears is the payee. By writing the check, Elizabeth is ordering her bank to pay $359.95 from her account to Sears or to Sears' order, that is, to whomever Sears asks the bank to pay the money.

## BENEFITS OF NEGOTIABLE INSTRUMENTS

**Rights of an Assignee of a Contract.** As we noted in Chapter 14, which discussed the assignment of contracts, the assignee of a contract can obtain no greater rights than the assignor had at the time of the assignment. For example, Farmer and Neam's Market enter into a contract that provides that Farmer

**Example of a Check**

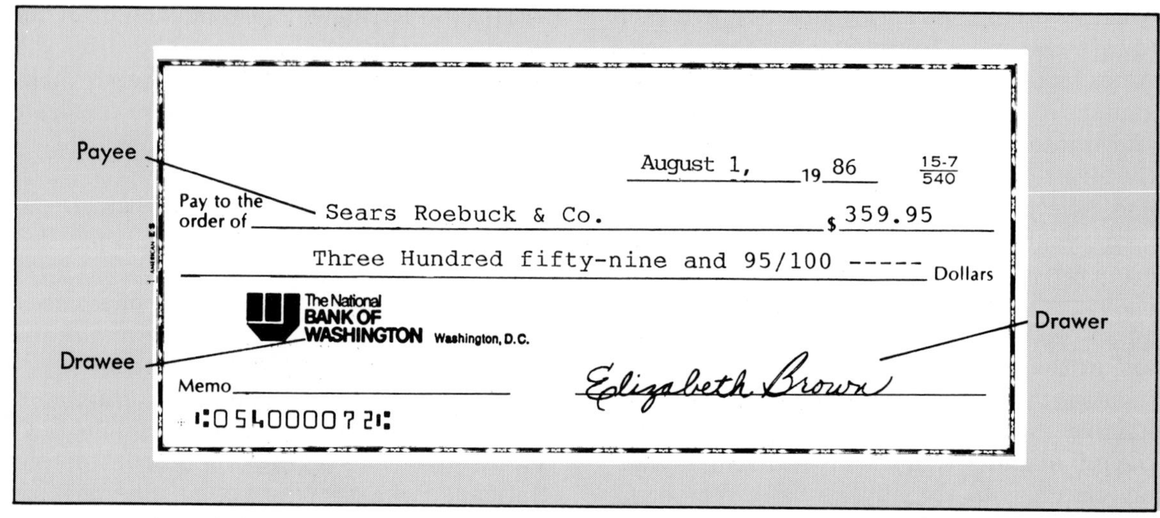

will sell Neam's a dozen crates of fresh eggs a week for a year and that Neam's will pay Farmer $4,000 at the end of the year. If at the end of the year Farmer assigns to Sanders his rights under the contract, including the right to collect the money from Neam's, then Sanders has whatever rights Farmer had at that time. If Farmer has delivered all the eggs to Neam's as he promised, then Farmer would be entitled to $4,000 and Sanders would obtain that right from him. However, if Farmer has not delivered all the eggs that he had promised to deliver, or if the eggs he delivered were not fresh, then Neam's might have a valid defense or reason to refuse to pay the full $4,000. In that case, Sanders would have only what rights Farmer had and would also be subject to the defense Neam's has against full payment.

Taking an assignment of a contract involves assuming certain risks. The assignee (Sanders) may not be aware of the nature and extent of any defenses that the party liable on the contract (Neam's) might have against the assignor (Farmer). If the assignee does not know for sure what rights he is getting, or what risks he is assuming, he may be reluctant to take an assignment of the contract.

**Rights of a Holder of a Negotiable Instrument.** The object of commercial paper (a contract for the payment of money) is to have it accepted readily as a substitute for money. For a person to accept it readily, the person must be able to take it free of many of the risks assumed by the assignee of a regular contract. Under the law of negotiable instruments, this is possible if two conditions are met: (1) the contract for the payment of money must be in the proper form so as to qualify as a **negotiable instrument;** and (2) the person who is acquiring the instrument must qualify as a **holder in due course.** Basically, a holder in due course is a person who has good title to the instrument, paid value for it, acquired it in good faith, and had no notice of any claims or defenses against it.

The proper form for a negotiable instrument will be discussed in the next section of this chapter. The requirements that a person must meet to qualify as a holder in due course will be discussed in Chapter 36.

A holder in due course of a negotiable instrument takes the instrument free of all "personal" defenses and claims to the instrument except those that concern its validity (these are known as "real" defenses). For example, a holder in due course of a note given in payment for goods does not have to worry if the buyer is claiming that the seller breached a warranty. However, if the maker of a note wrote it under duress (such as a threat of force) or was a minor, then even a holder in due course who acquires the note is subject to the "real" defenses of duress or lack of capacity. The person who holds the note could not obtain the payment from the maker but would have to try to recover from the person from whom he got the note.

The Federal Trade Commission has adopted a regulation that alters the holder in due course situation. This regulation is designed to allow a consumer who gives a negotiable instrument to use any defenses against payment of the instrument against even a holder in due course. Similarly, some states have enacted the Uniform Consumer Credit Code (UCCC), which produces a similar result. The rights of a holder in due course, as well as the FTC rule, will be discussed in more detail in the next chapter.

## FORMAL REQUIREMENTS FOR NEGOTIABILITY

**Basic Requirements.** An instrument, such as a check or a note, must meet certain formal requirements in order to be a "negotiable instrument." If the instrument does not meet these requirements, it is nonnegotiable; that is, it is treated as a simple contract and not as a negotiable instrument. A primary purpose for these formal requirements is to ensure the willingness of prospective purchasers of the instrument, particularly financial institutions such as banks, to accept the instrument as a substitute for money.

For an instrument to be negotiable, it must:

1. Be *in writing.*
2. Be *signed by the maker or drawer.*
3. Contain an *unconditional promise or order to pay a sum certain in money.*
4. Be *payable on demand or at a definite time.*
5. Be *payable to order or to bearer.*
6. *Not contain any other promise, order, obligation, or power unless* it is *authorized* by the Code [3–104].[1]

**Importance of Form.** Whether or not an instrument is drafted so that it satisfies these formal requirements is important for only one purpose, that is, for determining whether an instrument is negotiable or nonnegotiable. Negotiability should not be confused with validity or collectibility. If an instrument is *negotiable,* the *law of negotiable instruments* in the Code controls in determining the rights and liabilities of the parties to the instrument. If an instrument is *nonnegotiable,* the *general rules of contract law* control. The purpose of determining negotiability is to ascertain whether a possessor of the instrument can become a holder in due course.

An instrument that fills all of the formal requirements is a negotiable instrument even though it is void, voidable, unenforceable, or uncollectible. Negotiability is a matter of form and nothing else. Suppose a person gives an instrument in payment of a gambling debt in a state that has a statute declaring that any instrument or promise given in payment of a gambling debt is null and void. The instrument is a negotiable instrument if it is negotiable in form even though it is absolutely void. Also, an instrument that is negotiable in form is a negotiable instrument even though it is signed by a minor. The instrument is voidable at the option of the minor, but it is negotiable.

[1] The numbers in brackets refer to the sections of the Uniform Commercial Code.

## IN WRITING AND SIGNED

**Writing.** To be negotiable, an instrument must be *in writing* and must be *signed by the creator of the instrument, known as the maker or the drawer.* An instrument that is handwritten, typed, or printed is considered to be in writing [1–201(46)]. The writing does not have to be on any particular material; all that is required is that the instrument be in writing. A person could draw a negotiable instrument in pencil on a piece of wrapping paper. It would be poor business practice to do so, but the instrument would meet the statutory requirement that it be in writing.

**Signed.** An instrument has been *signed* if the maker or drawer has put a name or other symbol on it with *the intention of validating it* [3–401(2)]. Normally, the maker or drawer signs an instrument by writing his name on it; however, this is not required. A person or company may authorize an agent to sign instruments for it. A typed or rubber-stamped signature is sufficient if it was put on the instrument to validate it. A person who cannot write his name might make an *X* and have it witnessed by someone else. The *Littky & Mallon v. Michigan National Bank of Detroit* case, which follows, discusses the requirement that an instrument be signed by an authorized person.

## UNCONDITIONAL PROMISE OR ORDER

**Requirement of a Promise or Order.** If an instrument is promissory in nature, such as a note or a certificate of deposit, it must contain an *unconditional promise to pay* or else it cannot be negotiable. Merely acknowledging a debt is not sufficient. For example, indicating "I owe you $100" does not constitute a promise to pay. An IOU in this form is not a negotiable instrument.

If an instrument is an order to pay, such as a check or a draft, it must contain an *unconditional order.* A simple request to pay as a favor is not sufficient; however, a politely phrased demand can meet the requirement. The language "Pay to the order of ___________" is commonly used on checks. This satisfies the requirement that the check contain an order to pay. It should be noted that the order is the word *pay,* not the word *order.* The word *order* has another function—that of making the instrument payable "to order or to bearer."

**Promise or Order Must Be Unconditional.** An instrument is not negotiable unless the promise or order is *unconditional.* For example, a note that provides "I promise to pay to the order of Karl Adams $100 if he replaces the roof on my garage" is not negotiable, because it is payable on a condition.

To be negotiable, an instrument must be written so that a person can tell from reading the instrument alone what the obligations of the parties are. If a note contains the statement "Payment is subject to the terms of a mortgage dated November 20, 1986," it is not negotiable. To determine the rights of the parties on the note, another document—the mortgage—would have to be examined. However, the negotiability of a note would not be affected if the note contained this type of statement: "This note is secured by a mortgage dated August 30, 1986." In this case, the rights and duties of the parties to the note are not affected by the mortgage. It would not be necessary to examine the mortgage document to determine the rights of the parties to the note. The parties need only examine the instrument. This principle is illustrated in the *Holly Hill Acres, Ltd v. Charter Bank of Gainesville* case which follows.

The negotiability of an instrument is not affected by a statement of the consideration for which the instrument was given or by a statement of the transaction that gave rise to the instrument. For example, a negotiable instrument may contain a notation stating that it was given in payment of last month's rent or a statement that it was given in payment of the purchase price of goods. The statement does not affect the negotiability of the instrument.

A check may contain a notation as to the account to be debited without making the check nonnegotiable. For example, a check could contain the notation "payroll account" or "petty cash." Similarly, the account number that appears on personal checks does not make the instrument payable only out of a specific fund. On the other hand, if a check states that it is payable only out of a specific fund, the check is generally not negotiable. In this case, the check is conditioned on there being sufficient funds in the account. Thus, the check would not be unconditional and could not qualify as a negotiable instrument. This rule does not apply to instruments issued by a government or a governmental agency. It is permissible for the instruments of such bodies to contain a provision saying that the instruments are payable only out of a particular fund [3–105(1)(g)].

Note that a conditional indorsement does not destroy the negotiability of an otherwise negotiable instrument. Conditional indorsements are discussed in Chapter 36. Negotiability is determined at the time an instrument is written, and it is not affected by subsequent indorsements.

## SUM CERTAIN IN MONEY

**Sum Certain.** The promise or order in an instrument must be to pay a *sum certain in money.* The sum is certain if a person can compute from the information in the instrument the amount that is required to discharge—or pay off—the instrument at any given time. The Code permits an instrument to state different rates of interest before or after default. It also allows provisions for a discount or an addition if the note is paid early or if it is paid late. The key element is that a person can compute the amount that is due on the instrument at any given time. Thus, a provision for interest at "current bank rates" would not satisfy the requirement for a "sum certain."

Sometimes, notes contain a clause that provides for the payment of collection fees or attorney's fees in the event of a default on the note. Even though this would make the amount due on default uncertain until the collection or attorney's fees were determined, such a clause does not make the note nonnegotiable [3–106]. The amount can be determined at some time, and business practice justifies the inclusion of such a clause in the instrument.

**Payable in Money.** The amount specified in the instrument must be payable in money, which is a medium of exchange authorized or adopted by a government as part of its currency [1–201(24)]. If the person obligated to pay off an instrument can do something other than pay money, the instrument is not negotiable. For example, if a note reads "I promise to pay to the order of Sarah Smith, at my option, $20 or five bushels of apples, John Jones," the note is not negotiable.

## PAYABLE ON DEMAND OR AT A DEFINITE TIME

To be negotiable, an instrument must be payable either *on demand* or *at a specified time in the future.* This is so that the time when the instrument will be payable can be determined with some certainty. An instrument that is payable upon the happening of some uncertain event is not negotiable [3–109(2)]. Thus, a note payable "when my son graduates from college" is not negotiable, even though the son does graduate subsequently.

**Payable on Demand.** An instrument may state that it is payable "on demand." If no time for payment is stated in an instrument, the instrument is considered to be payable on demand [3–108]. For example, if the maker forgets to state when a note is payable, it is payable immediately at the request of the holder of the note. A check is considered to be payable on demand. However, a postdated check is treated as a "draft" and is not properly payable until the day it is dated. An instrument can be negotiable even though it is undated, postdated, or antedated [3–114].

**Payable at a Definite Time.** An instrument is payable at a definite time if: (1) it is payable on or before a stated date, such as "on July 1, 1988," or "on or before July 1, 1988"; (2) it is payable at a fixed time after a stated date, such as "30 days after date," provided that the instrument is dated; or (3) it is payable at a fixed time "after sight," which is in effect a provision that it will be paid at a fixed time after it is presented to the drawee for acceptance.

If an instrument that provides that it is payable "30 days after date" is not dated, then it is not payable at a fixed date and it is not negotiable; however, this defect may be cured if the holder of the instrument fills in the date before he negotiates it to someone else [3–115].

Under the Code, an instrument may contain a clause permitting the time for payment to be accelerated at the option of the maker. Similarly, an instrument may contain a clause allowing an extension of time at the option of the holder or allowing a maker or acceptor to extend payment to a further definite time. Or the due date of a note might be triggered by the happening of an event, such as the filing of a petition in bankruptcy against the maker. These kinds of clauses are allowed as long as the time for payment can be determined with certainty [3–109].

## PAYMENT TO ORDER OR BEARER

To be negotiable, an instrument must be *payable to order* or *to bearer.* A check that provides "Pay to the order of Sarah Smith" or "Pay to Sarah Smith or bearer" is negotiable; however, one that provides "Pay to Sarah Smith" is not. The words *to the order of* or *to bearer* show that the drawer of the check (or the maker of a note) intends to issue a negotiable instrument. The drawer or maker is not restricting payment of the instrument to just Sarah Smith but is willing to pay someone else designated by Sarah Smith. This is the essence of negotiability. The original payee of a check or a note can transfer the right to receive payment to someone else. By making the instrument payable "to the order of" or "to bearer," the drawer or maker is giving the payee the chance to negotiate the instrument to another person and to cut off certain defenses that the drawer or maker may have against payment of the instrument.

A check that is payable to the order of a specific person is known as **order paper.** Order paper can be negotiated or transferred only by indorsement. A check that is payable to bearer is known as **bearer paper.** A check made payable "to the order of cash" is considered to be payable to bearer and is also known as "bearer paper" [3–111]. Bearer paper can be negotiated or transferred without indorsement.

An instrument can be made payable to two or more payees. For example, a check could be drawn payable "to the order of John Jones and Henry Smith." Then, both John and Henry have to be involved in negotiating it or enforcing its payment. An instrument can also be made payable to alternative persons, for example, "to Susan Clark or Betsy Brown." In this case, either Clark or Brown could negotiate it or enforce its payment.

## SPECIAL TERMS

**Additional Terms.** Banks and other businesses sometimes use forms of commercial paper that have been drafted to meet their particular needs. These forms may include terms that do not affect the negotiability of an instrument. Thus, a note form may provide for a place of payment without affecting the instrument's negotiability. Similarly, insurance reimbursement checks frequently contain a clause on the back stating that the payee, by indorsing or cashing the check, acknowledges full payment of the claim. This clause does not affect the negotiability of the check [3–112(1)(f)].

A term authorizing the **confession of judgment** on the instrument when due does not affect the negotiability of the instrument [3–112(1)(d)]. However, some courts have held that a note is rendered nonnegotiable by a clause that authorizes confession of judgment and a demand for payment prior to the due date or the note. The *Federal Deposit Insurance Corp. v. Barnes* case, below, involves a note that authorized confession of judgment "with or without default." The court held that such a note was nonnegotiable.

**Ambiguous Terms.** Occasionally, a person may write or receive a check on which the amount written in figures differs from the amount written in words. Or a note may have conflicting terms or an ambiguous term. Where a conflict or an ambiguous term exists, there are general rules of interpretation that are applied to resolve the conflict or ambiguity. If there is a conflict between words and figures, the words control the figures, unless the words are ambiguous. Similarly, handwritten terms prevail over printed and typed terms, and typed terms prevail over printed terms [3–118]. The case below of *Yates v. Commercial Bank & Trust Co.,* involves a check on which there was a difference between the figures and the written words.

If a note provides for the payment of interest, but no interest rate is spelled out, then interest is payable at the judgment rate (the rate of interest imposed on court awards until they are paid by the losing party) at the place of payment.

## Littky & Mallon v. Michigan National Bank of Detroit

**287 N.W.2d 359 (Mich. Ct. App. 1980)**

Littky & Mallon maintained a corporate checking account at Manufacturer's National Bank. There were three authorized signers on the account: Louis Williams, Marvin Littky (the sole shareholder and president), and Jenny LaJoie (Littky's secretary). Louis Williams allowed another person to sign LaJoie's name to a Littky & Mallon check for $23,000 made payable in the name of Mary Ann McKay. A person identifying herself as McKay presented the check to Michigan National Bank, which paid her $23,000. The check was later dishonored by Manufacturer's National Bank (the drawee) because of an irregular drawer's signature. Michigan National Bank then sought to recover the $23,000 from Littky & Mallon. The trial court held for Littky & Mallon, and the bank appealed.

**Per Curiam.** The bank raises several issues on appeal. First, the bank argues that Littky & Mallon's name, imprinted at the top of the check in question, is a sufficient signature to bind Littky & Mallon. We note that the definition of the term "signature" in § 3–401(2) is broadly construed. However, we also note that pursuant to comment 39 following § 1–201, courts must use common sense and commercial experience in determining whether a mark constitutes a signature. We find that, based on both common sense and commercial experience, such a conclusion would be unreasonable where there was a written signature at the appropriate place on the check.

The bank next argues that the third party who actually signed the check in question had the authority to bind Littky & Mallon. The power to sign for another and thereby bind that party pursuant to § 3–403(1) may rest upon express, implied, or apparent authority. However, after thoroughly reviewing the testimony at trial and the stipulations of the parties, we find no evidence that such authority existed. While Mr. Williams may have had the authority to authorize a third person to sign his (Williams') name to the check, he did not have the authority to authorize such a third person to sign the name of another. Accordingly, this argument is without merit.

Judgment for Littky & Mallon affirmed.

---

## Holly Hill Acres, Ltd. v. Charter Bank of Gainesville

**314 So.2d 209 (Fla. Ct. App. 1975)**

On April 28, 1972, Holly Hill Acres, Ltd. executed a promissory note and mortgage and delivered them to Rogers and Blythe. The note contained the following stipulation:

> This note with interest is secured by a mortgage on real estate, of even date herewith, made by the maker hereof in favor of the said payee, and shall be construed and enforced according to the laws of the State of Florida. *The terms of said mortgage are by this reference made a part hereof.* (Emphasis supplied.)

Rogers and Blythe assigned the note to Charter Bank of Gainesville to secure payment of an obligation they owed to Charter Bank. When the Holly Hill note was not paid, Charter Bank brought suit to collect the note and foreclose the mortgage. Holly Hill asserted as a defense that fraud on the part of Rogers and Blythe induced the sale that gave rise to the note and mortgage. Charter Bank contended that it was a holder in due course of a negotiable instrument and thus not subject to the defense of fraud. The trial court awarded summary judgment to Charter Bank, and Holly Hill appealed.

**Scheb, Judge.** The note, having incorporated the terms of the purchase money mortgage, was not negotiable. The Bank was not a holder in due course; therefore Holly Hill was entitled to raise against the bank any defenses which could be raised between Holly Hill and Rogers and Blythe.

The note, incorporating by reference the terms of the mortgage, did not contain the unconditional promise to pay required by § 3–104(1)(b). Rather, the note falls within the scope of § 3–105(2)(a).

The Bank relies upon *Scott v. Taylor* as authority for the proposition that its note is negotiable. *Scott,* however, involved a note being secured by mortgage. Mention of a mortgage in a note is a common commercial practice, and such reference in itself does not impede the negotiability of the note. There is, however, a significant difference in a note stating that it is "secured by a mortgage" from one which provides, "the terms of said mortgage are by this reference made a part hereof." In the former instance the note merely refers to a separate agreement which does not impede its negotiability, while in the latter instance the note is rendered nonnegotiable. See §§ 3–105(2)(a); 3–119.

As a general rule the assignee of a mortgage securing a nonnegotiable note, even though a bona fide purchaser for value, takes subject to all defenses available as against the mortgagees.

Judgment reversed in favor of Holly Hill.

## Federal Deposit Insurance Corp. v. Barnes

**484 F. Supp. 1134 (E.D. Pa. 1980)**

On April 28, 1975, Barnes executed a promissory note in the amount of $64,835 to Centennial Bank, payable on demand. The note authorized the confession of judgment against him "with or without default." The note was assigned to the Federal Deposit Insurance Corporation (FDIC) when Centennial Bank went into receivership. The FDIC obtained a judgment against Barnes based on the confession of judgment clause. Barnes claimed to have a number of defenses against payment of the note and sought to open the judgment.

**Becker, District Judge.** Our threshold task is to determine whether to use the Uniform Commercial Code or the common law of assignment in analyzing the issues in this case. We readily conclude that the common law of assignment must be applied, for Barnes's note to the Centennial Bank is not a negotiable instrument. Under Pennsylvania law, the confession of judgment provision, which permits judgment to be entered either before or after default, renders the note nonnegotiable even though it is in form a demand note. Under Article 3 of the Uniform Commercial Code, an instrument which is otherwise negotiable is made nonnegotiable by a term authorizing the confession of judgment before payment is due. § 3–112(1)(d). Since the note is nonnegotiable, the substantive provisions of Article 3 are inapplicable and the rights of the parties are governed by common law contract principles.

Barnes's motion to open the judgment granted.

## Yates v. Commercial Bank & Trust Co.

**36 UCC Rep. 205 (Fla. Dist. Ct. 1983)**

Emmett McDonald, acting as the personal representative of the estate of Marion Cahill, wrote a check payable to himself, individually, on the estate checking account in the Commercial Bank & Trust Company. The instrument contained an obvious variance between the numbers and the written words that indicated the amount of the check. It said:

"Pay to the order of *Emmett E. McDonald $10075.00 Ten hundred seventy five....... Dollars."*

The bank paid the $10,075 sum stated by the numerals to McDonald who absconded with the funds. Yates, the successor representative, sued the bank on behalf of the estate to recover the $9,000 difference between that amount and the $1,075 which was written out. The trial court dismissed the complaint, and Yates appealed.

**Schwartz, Chief Judge.** It is clear that the complaint stated a cognizable claim against the bank. Section 3–118 provides:

> The following rules apply to every instrument: . . .
> (3) Words control figures except that if the words are ambiguous figures control.

Under this provision of the UCC, it was clearly improper for the bank to have paid the larger sum stated in numbers, rather than the smaller one unambiguously stated by McDonald's words. It is, therefore, prima facie liable to the estate for the excess.

Judgment reversed in favor of Yates.

## SUMMARY

Commercial paper is basically a contract for the payment of money. There are two types of commercial paper: promises to pay money and orders to pay money. Notes and certificates of deposit issued by banks are promises to pay someone a sum of money. Drafts and checks are orders to another person to pay a sum of money to a third person.

Commercial paper that is negotiable can pass readily through our financial system and be accepted in place of money. This gives it a number of advantages over a simple contract. Normally, the assignee of a contract can obtain no greater rights than his assignor had. However, a transferee of a negotiable instrument who qualifies as a holder in due course can obtain greater rights than his assignor had.

To qualify as a negotiable instrument, an instrument must (1) be in writing, (2) be signed by the maker or drawer, (3) contain an unconditional promise or order to pay a sum certain in money, (4) be payable on demand or at a definite time, (5) be payable to order or to bearer, and (6) not contain any other promise or obligation unless it is authorized by the Code. Since negotiability is merely a matter of form, an instrument that meets the formal requirements can be negotiable even though it is void, voidable, unenforceable, or uncollectible. If an instrument is negotiable, the law of negotiable instruments as set out in the Code controls in determining the rights and liabilities of the parties to the instrument. If an instrument is nonnegotiable, the general rules of contract law control.

Printed forms for commercial paper may contain certain clauses for business reasons that do not affect the negotiability of the instruments. If there are ambiguous terms in a negotiable instrument, the general rule of interpretation is that handwritten terms control typewritten and printed terms and that typewritten terms control printed terms. If there is a conflict between words and figures, the words control unless they are ambiguous, in which case the figures control.

## PROBLEM CASES

1. Is the following instrument a note, a check, or a draft? Why? If it is not a check, how would you have to change it to make it a check?

> To: *Arthur Adams* *January 1, 1987*
> TEN DAYS AFTER DATE PAY TO THE ORDER OF:
> *Bernie Brown*
> THE SUM OF: *Ten and no/100* DOLLARS
> SIGNED: *Carl Clark*

2. Is the following a negotiable instrument?

February 26, 1987
Subject to Approval of Title
Pay to the Order of Vernon Butterfield
$1,997.90.

The Culver Company
By A. M. Culver

3. An installment sales contract that would otherwise qualify as a negotiable instrument contains a clause stating that the holder of the contract can pay taxes, assessments, and insurance if the obligor does not and then recover what he pays from the obligor. Would this clause make the contract nonnegotiable?

4. Briggs signed a note as maker that contained a clause that permitted acceleration of the maturity date of the note in the event that the owner of the note deemed himself insecure and that authorized confession of judgment against the maker "if this note is not paid at any stated or accelerated maturity." Briggs contends that the note is nonnegotiable because of this clause. Is his contention correct?

5. Hotel Evans was the maker on a promissory note that contained a promise to pay $1,600 with "interest at bank rates." The holder of the note, A. Alport & Sons, brought a lawsuit to collect on the note. Hotel Evans claimed that the note was not negotiable, because it contained an indefinite interest rate. Was the promissory note that provided for "interest at bank rates" a negotiable instrument?

6. Sylvia signed a note dated May 25, 1986, obligating him to pay to Ferri or to her order $3,000 "within ten (10) years after date." Is this a negotiable instrument?

7. In 1964, S. Gentilotti wrote a check for $20,000 payable to the order of his son, Edward J. Gentilotti. He postdated the check November 4, 1984, which would be his son's 20th birthday. The father also wrote on the check that it should be paid from his estate if he died prior to November 4, 1984. The father then gave the check to Edward's mother for safekeeping. On May 31, 1972, the father died. The check was then presented for payment, but the bank refused to pay it. The mother and the son then brought a lawsuit against the executor of the father's estate to require payment. The executor claimed that the check was not a valid negotiable instrument because it had been postdated. Can a check be a negotiable instrument if it is postdated 20 years?

8. In 1955, Newman wrote two checks totaling $1,200 payable to Belle Epstein. There was a printed dateline on the checks that read "Detroit, Michigan __________ 195___," but Newman never filled it in. Newman claimed that over the next four years he paid Epstein all but $400 of the $1,200 he owed her. He also claimed that Epstein told him she had destroyed the checks. However, on April 17, 1964, the checks were cashed after having been indorsed in the name of Belle Epstein. Someone had written in the date "April 16, 1964," but the printed figures "__________ 195___" remained clearly visible. Newman objected to having his checking account charged with the two checks. Was the bank justified in paying the checks and charging them to Newman's account?

# Chapter 36

# Negotiation and Holder in Due Course

## INTRODUCTION

The preceding chapter discussed the nature and benefits of negotiable instruments and outlined the requirements an instrument must meet to qualify as a negotiable instrument and thus possess the qualities that allow it to be accepted as a substitute for money. This chapter focuses on negotiation—the process by which rights to a negotiable instrument are passed from one person to another. This commonly involves an indorsement and delivery of the instrument. This chapter also develops the requirements that a transferee must meet to qualify as a holder in due course and thus attain special rights under negotiable instruments law. These rights, which put a holder in due course in an enhanced position compared to an assignee of a contract, are discussed in some detail.

## NEGOTIATION

**Nature of Negotiation.** **Negotiation** is the transfer of an instrument in such a way that the person who receives it becomes a holder. A **holder** is a person who is in possession of an instrument (1) that was *issued* to him, (2) that has been *indorsed to him or to his order,* or (3) that is *payable to bearer* [1–201(20)].[1] For example, when an employee is given a paycheck payable to her by her employer, she is the holder of the check because the check was issued to her. When she writes her name on the back of the check and cashes it at the grocery store, she has negotiated the check to the grocery store, because the store is in possession of a check indorsed to it.

**Formal Requirements for Negotiation.** The formal requirements for negotiation are very simple. If an instrument is *payable to a specific payee,* it is called **order paper** and it can be negotiated only by delivery of the instrument after indorsement by the payee [3–202(1)].

For example, if Rachel Stern's employer gives her a check payable "to the order of Rachel Stern," then Stern can negotiate the check by indorsing her name on the back of the check and giving it to the person to whom she wants to transfer it. Note that the check is order paper, not because the word *order* appears on the check, but rather because it names a specific payee, Rachel Stern.

If an instrument is *payable to bearer or to cash,* it is called **bearer paper** and negotiating it is even simpler. A person who is given a check that is made payable "to the order of cash" can negotiate the check by giving it to the person to whom he wishes to transfer it. No indorsement is necessary to negotiate an instrument payable to bearer [3–202(1)]. However, the person who takes the instrument may ask for an indorsement for his protection. Indorsing the check signifies an agreement to be liable for its payment to that person if the drawee bank does not pay it when it is presented for payment. This liability will be discussed in the next chapter.

[1] The numbers in brackets refer to the sections of the Uniform Commercial Code.

**Nature of Indorsement.** An **indorsement** is made by adding the signature of the holder of the instrument to the instrument, usually on the back [3–202(2)]. The signature can be put there either by the holder or by someone who is authorized to sign on behalf of the holder. For example, a check payable to "H&H Meat Market" might be indorsed "H&H Meat Market by Jane Franklin, President" if Franklin is authorized to do this on behalf of the market.

If the back of an instrument is full of indorsements, further indorsements should be made on a paper attached firmly to the instrument. Such a paper is called an **allonge.**

**Wrong or Misspelled Name.** The indorser of an instrument should spell his name in the same way as it appears on the instrument. If the indorser's name is misspelled or wrong, then legally the indorsement can be made either in his name or in the name that is on the instrument. However, any person who pays the instrument or otherwise gives something of value for it may require the indorser to sign both names [3–203].

Suppose Joan Ash is issued a check payable to the order of "Joanne Ashe." She may indorse the check as either "Joan Ash" or "Joanne Ashe." However, if she takes the check to a bank to cash, the bank may require her to sign both "Joanne Ashe" and "Joan Ash."

The *Agaliotis v. Agaliotis* case, which follows, presents a situation where a check was accidentally made payable to the wrong person but indorsed by the person for whom it was intended.

**Indorsements by a Depository Bank.** When a customer deposits a check to his account with a bank and the customer forgets to indorse the check, the bank normally has the right to supply the customer's indorsement [4–205]. Instead of actually signing the customer's name to the check as the indorsement, the bank may just stamp on it that it was deposited by the customer or credited to his account. The only time the bank does not have the right to put the customer's indorsement on a check that the customer has deposited is when the drafter of the check specifically requires the payee's signature. Insurance and government checks commonly require the payee's signature.

**Transfer of Order Instrument.** If an order instrument is transferred without indorsement, the instrument has not been negotiated and the transferee cannot qualify as a holder. The transferee has the right to the unqualified indorsement of the transferor. Should the transferor refuse to indorse the instrument with an unqualified indorsement, the transferee would be entitled to a court order ordering the transferor to so indorse the instrument. The negotiation takes effect only when the indorsement is made, and until that time there is no presumption that the transferee is the owner.

## Agaliotis v. Agaliotis

**247 S.E.2d 28 (N.C. Ct. App. 1978)**

Louis Agaliotis took out a policy of insurance on his son, Robert. Louis paid all of the premiums on the policy, and under the terms of the policy he was entitled to any refunds on the premiums. The insurance company sent a refund check for $1,852 to Louis. By mistake, the check was made payable to "Robert L. Agaliotis." Louis indorsed the check "Robert L. Agaliotis" and cashed it. Robert then sued Louis to get the $1,852. The trial court held that Louis had wrongfully indorsed the check and awarded judgment to Robert. Louis appealed.

**ERWIN, JUDGE.** The findings of fact show, and it was not contradicted, that Louis Agaliotis was entitled to receive the proceeds of the insurance policy in question, that the insurance company intended to deliver the check to Louis and did so, and that only by administrative error was the check made payable to "Robert L. Agaliotis."

Thus, it appears to us that Robert's position is that Louis should be liable to him merely because of the administrative error and Louis's having indorsed the check "Robert L. Agaliotis." Section 3–203, "Wrong or misspelled name," provides in pertinent part:

> Where an instrument is made payable to a person under a misspelled name or one other than his own he may indorse in that name or his own or both.

Robert must show some basis, other than a mere misnomer, to recover of Louis; he has not done so. In fact, the trial court concluded that Robert was not entitled to the proceeds of the policy and yet granted summary judgment for him. In reality, Louis, not Robert, was the payee, and Louis did no more than indorse the check in a manner permitted under the Uniform Commercial Code.

Judgment reversed in favor of Louis Agaliotis.

## INDORSEMENTS

**Effects of an Indorsement.** There are two aspects to an indorsement. First, an indorsement is necessary in order to *negotiate* an instrument that is payable to the order of a specific payee. Thus, if a check is payable to the order of James Lee, Lee must indorse the check before it can be negotiated. The form of the indorsement that Lee uses will also affect future attempts to negotiate the instrument. For example, if Lee indorses the check "Pay to Sarah Hill," Hill must indorse it before it can be negotiated further.

Second, an indorsement generally makes a person *liable* on the instrument. By indorsing an instrument, a person makes a contractual promise to pay the instrument if the person primarily liable on it (for example, the "maker" of a note) does not pay it. The contractual liability of indorsers will be discussed in Chapter 37. In this chapter, the discussion will be limited to the effect of an indorsement on further negotiation of an instrument.

**Kinds of Indorsements.** There are four basic kinds of indorsements: (1) special, (2) blank, (3) restrictive, and (4) qualified.

**Special Indorsement.** A **special indorsement** contains the signature of the indorser along with words indicating to whom, or to whose order, the instrument is payable. For example, if a check drawn "Pay to the Order of Marcia Morse" is indorsed by Morse "Pay to the Order of Sam Smith, Marcia Morse" or "Pay to Sam Smith, Marcia Morse," it has been indorsed with a special indorsement (see accompanying figure). An instrument that is indorsed with a special indorsement remains or becomes **order paper.** It can be negotiated only with the indorsement of the person specified [3–204(1)]. In this example, Sam Smith must indorse the check before it can be negotiated to someone else.

**Example of a Special Indorsement**

Pay to Sam Smith
Marcia Morse

**Blank Indorsement.** If an indorser merely signs her name and does not specify to whom the instrument is payable, the instrument has been indorsed in **blank.** For example, if a check drawn "Pay to the Order of Natalie Owens" is indorsed "Natalie Owens," it has been indorsed in blank (see accompanying figure). An instrument indorsed in blank is payable to the bearer (the person in possession of it). This means that the check is **bearer paper.** As such, it can be negotiated by delivery alone and no further indorsement is necessary for negotiation [3–204(2)].

If Owens indorsed the check in blank and gave it to Karen Foley, Foley would have the right to convert the blank indorsement into a special indorsement [3–204(3)]. She could do this by writing the words "Pay to the Order of Karen Foley" above Owens' indorsement. Then, the check would have to be indorsed by Foley before it could be negotiated further.

Similarly, the payee of a bearer instrument can make the instrument an order instrument by a special indorsement. For example, Harold Fisher is the holder of a check made payable to "cash." If Fisher indorses the instrument on the back "Pay to Arlene Jones, Harold Fisher," it would be an order instrument and it would have to be indorsed by Arlene Jones before it could be negotiated further.

If a person takes a check indorsed in blank

to a bank and presents it for payment or for collection, the bank normally asks the person to indorse the check. The check does not need an indorsement to be negotiated, because the check indorsed in blank can be negotiated merely by delivering it to the bank cashier. The bank asks for the indorsement because it wants to make the person liable on the check if it is not paid when the bank sends it to the drawee bank for payment. The liability of indorsers will be discussed in the next chapter.

The *Westerly Hospital v. Higgins* case, which follows, illustrates how an instrument indorsed in blank can be negotiated merely by delivery, thus entitling the holder to enforce it against the maker.

Example of a Blank Indorsement

**Restrictive Indorsement.** A **restrictive indorsement** is one that *specifies the purpose of the indorsement or the use to be made of the instrument.* Among the more common types of restrictive indorsements are:

1. Indorsements for deposit—for example, "For deposit only" or "For deposit only to my account at the First Trust Company."

2. Indorsements for collection, which are commonly put on by banks involved in the collection process—for example, "Pay to any bank, banker, or trust company" or "For collection only."

3. Indorsements indicating that the indorsement is for the benefit or use of someone other than the person to whom it is payable—for example, "Pay to Arthur Attorney in trust for Mark Minor."

4. Indorsements purporting to prohibit further negotiation—for example, "Pay to Carl Clark only."

5. Conditional indorsements, which indicate that they are effective only if a certain condition is satisfied—for example, "Pay to Bernard Builder only if he completes construction of my house by November 1, 1986." A similar restriction by a maker or drawer would destroy the negotiability of the instrument; however, indorsers are permitted to so limit payment without affecting negotiability.

A restrictive indorsement (see accompanying figure) does not prevent further negotiation of an instrument [3–206(1)]. However, the person[2] who takes an instrument with a restrictive indorsement must pay or apply any money or other thing of value he gives for the instrument consistently with the indorsement. Suppose a person takes a check payable to "Arthur Attorney in trust for Mark Minor." The money for the check should be put in Mark Minor's trust account. A person would not be justified in taking the check in exchange for a television set that he knew Attorney was acquiring for his own—rather than Minor's—use.

Similarly, suppose Clark indorses a check payable to his order "for deposit" and deposits it in a bank in which Clark has a commercial account. The bank then credits Clark's account with the amount of the check. The bank is a holder for value to the extent that it allows Clark to draw on the credit for the check because the bank has applied the value it gave for the instrument consistently with the indorsement. However, if the transferee of a restrictively indorsed instrument does not

[2] Except an intermediary bank, which under § 3–206(2) is not affected by a restrictive indorsement of any person except its immediate transferor or the person presenting for payment.

make payment in accordance with the restrictive indorsement, the transferee is liable to the indorser for any loss that results from the failure to comply with the indorsement.

In *Brite Lite Lamps Corp. v. Manufacturers Hanover Trust Co.*, which follows, a depository bank was held liable to its customer when the bank failed to follow the customer's restrictive endorsement and to credit the customer's account; instead the bank had permitted the checks to be credited to another person's account.

**Example of a Restrictive Indorsement**

For Deposit Only to
My Account at the
First National Bank
Jane Frank

**Qualified Indorsement.** A **qualified indorsement** (see accompanying figure) is one in which the indorser *disclaims or limits* his liability to make the instrument good if the drawer or maker defaults on the instrument. Words such as "without recourse" are used to qualify an indorsement; they can be used with a special, a blank, or a restrictive indorsement and thus make it a qualified special, a qualified blank, or a qualified restrictive indorsement. The use of a qualified indorsement does not change the negotiable nature of the instrument. The effect is to limit the *contractual liability* of the indorser. This contractual liability will be discussed in detail in the next chapter.

**Example of a Qualified Indorsement**

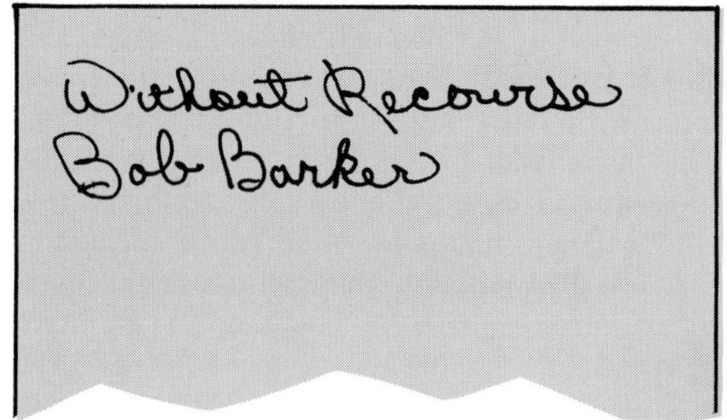


**Rescission of Indorsement.** Negotiation is effective to transfer an instrument even if the negotiation is made by a minor, a corporation exceeding its powers, or any other person without contractual capacity; or it is obtained by fraud, duress, or mistake of any kind; or it is part of an illegal transaction; or it is made in breach of duty. A negotiation made under the above circumstances is subject to **rescission** before the instrument has been negotiated to a transferee who can qualify as a holder in due course [3–207]. The situation in such instances is analogous to a sale of goods where the sale has been induced by fraud or misrepresentation. In such a case, the seller may rescind the sale and recover the goods, provided that the seller acts before the goods are resold to a bona fide purchaser for value.

## Westerly Hospital v. Higgins

### 256 A.2d 506 (R.I. Sup. Ct. 1969)

On July 13, 1967, Higgins executed a promissory note in the amount of $527.58 payable to the order of Westerly Hospital. The note, payable in 18 monthly installments of $29.31, was in consideration for services performed by the hospital in connection with the birth of Higgins' child. An agent of the hospital later indorsed the note in blank and negotiated it to the Industrial National Bank at a discount. The indorsement contained an express clause guaranteeing payment of the principal, interest, and late charges in the event of default by the maker.

Higgins made three payments, then failed to make any further payments. The provisions of the note made the entire balance immediately due. Industrial returned the note to the hospital pursuant to the indorsement guarantee. Industrial received payment from the hospital and negotiated the note to it by delivery.

The hospital then brought suit against Higgins on the note. Higgins contended, among other things, that Westerly was not the proper person to bring suit on the note. The trial court held for Westerly Hospital, and Higgins appealed.

**Roberts, Chief Justice.** In our opinion, the face of the instrument discloses as a matter of law that Westerly Hospital is the holder of the note in question and, therefore, a proper party to bring this action. The face of the instrument reveals that Westerly Hospital was the payee of the note made by Higgins and his wife as co-makers. It further discloses that an indorsement of guarantee was executed in blank by an authorized representative of Westerly Hospital. The note was then delivered to Industrial. The pertinent provisions of the Uniform Commercial Code provide that where, as in the instant case, there has been a blank indorsement, mere delivery is sufficient to constitute the transferee a holder thereof and is sufficient to make the transfer a valid negotiation. § 3–202; § 3–204. Thereafter, when Higgins defaulted, Industrial delivered the note to Westerly in return for the payment of the remaining amount of Higgins' obligation that had been guaranteed by Westerly Hospital.

Higgins argues that this delivery of the note back to Westerly was not sufficient to constitute a valid negotiation. It seems rather obvious that had the transfer of the note from Westerly Hospital to Industrial been other than in blank, this argument would have merit, it being true that an authorized signature of an agent of Industrial would be necessary to negotiate the instrument.

However, § 3–204(2) of the Uniform Commercial Code states, in pertinent part, that "An instrument payable to order and indorsed in blank becomes payable to bearer and may be negotiated by delivery alone until specially indorsed." Here Westerly Hospital as payee of the note caused its indorsement to appear thereon without specifying to whom or to whose order the instrument was payable. Instead, a blank indorsement, one specifying no particular indorsee, was made. The legal effect of such an indorsement and delivery was to authorize Industrial as the transferee and holder of the note to further negotiate the note without indorsement but by mere delivery alone. It is clear that any attempt on its part to achieve negotiation by indorsing the note to Westerly Hospital would have been mere surplusage.

In our opinion, then, the redelivery of the note in question by Industrial to Westerly Hospital accomplished a negotiation of the instrument, and the fact that a purported special indorsement to Westerly Hospital was not legally executed is of no consequence and does not affect Westerly Hospital's status as the holder of the note.

Judgment for Westerly Hospital affirmed.

## Brite Lite Lamps Corp. v. Manufacturers Hanover Trust Co.

**34 UCC Rep. 1221 (N.Y. Sup. Ct. 1982)**

In 1974, Brite Lite Lamps Corporation hired Lorraine Chirico as its office manager. Chirico's duties included depositing checks received by, and made payable to, Brite Lite by its customers into Brite Lite's corporate bank account at a Brooklyn, New York, branch of Manufacturers Hanover Trust Company. Prior to depositing the checks, Brite Lite stamped on each check the following restrictive indorsement: "Pay to the order of Manufacturers Hanover Trust Co., Brite Lite Lamps Corp. 0–00184."

Beginning in January 1975, Chirico embarked on a scheme to divert some of the checks to her own use. She did so by presenting the checks at Manufacturers Hanover, without further indorsement of any kind, for deposit into one of three individual checking accounts that she had opened at the same branch. Notwithstanding the corporate indorsement on each of the checks, the tellers at the bank accepted the checks for deposit in Chirico's personal accounts. The checks were never credited to Brite Lite's bank account in accordance with the indorsement. The scheme continued until January 1976.

Brite Lite recovered approximately $60,000 from Chirico. It then brought a lawsuit against Manufacturers Hanover for cashing the checks inconsistently with the indorsements.

**Adler, Judge.** A contractual relationship existed between the parties by virtue of Brite Lite being a depositor at the bank. Inherent in this relationship is the right of Brite Lite to deposit checks in its account by stamping a restrictive indorsement on the back of the checks in the manner described above [see §§ 3–205 and 3–206(3)]. These restrictive indorsements then impose an obligation on the bank that it "pay or apply" the proceeds of the checks "consistently with the indorsement" [§ 3–206(3)] by depositing the checks only in the account of Brite Lite as the restrictive indorser and named payee. The bank's "failure to do so" and its "failure to apply normal commercial standards with respect to any restrictions imposed by the indorsement" serve as a basis for liability against the bank.

The presence of a restriction imposes upon the depository bank an obligation not to accept that item other than in accord with the restriction. By disregarding the restriction, it not only subjects itself to liability for any losses resulting from its actions, but it also passes up what may well be the best opportunity to prevent the fraud. The presentation of a check in violation of a restrictive indorsement for deposit in the account of someone other than the restrictive indorser is an obvious warning sign, and the depository bank is required to investigate the situation rather than blindly accept the check.

Not only did the bank fail to follow the mandate of commercially reasonable behavior with respect to Brite Lite's account; it also violated its own banking procedures. The deposition testimony of an officer of the bank establishes beyond dispute that had its tellers complied with these bank procedures, none of the checks could have been misdeposited into Chirico's personal accounts. These procedures required a teller, before accepting a check for deposit, to inspect the indorsement on the check and verify that the indorsement corresponded to the name of the depositor on the deposit slip. Moreover, unless written authority to the contrary existed (and the bank concedes that it had no written authority from Brite Lite to deposit Brite Lite's checks into an account other than that of Brite Lite), a check presented for deposit which was payable to a corporation was required to be deposited to the account of that corporate payee. Finally, a check containing a restrictive indorsement must be deposited in accordance with the restriction, i.e., deposited in Brite Lite's account. If the check is presented for deposit into an account other than that of the corporate payee, the teller should not accept the deposit and should instead refer the transaction to an officer or tell the customer that it was the wrong deposit slip.

The bank has presented no evidence to negate or explain its uncontroverted failure to follow its own banking procedures or normal commercial standards or why its tellers ignored Brite Lite's restrictive indorsements and accepted the checks for deposit in other than Brite Lite's account in breach of the indorsement. The subject checks were patent on their face—i.e., on the front side they were payable to Brite Lite and on the back side they contained a restrictive indorsement (and no other indorsement) requiring that they be deposited only in Brite Lite's account. The checks were presented to the bank tellers in obvious violation of these restrictive indorsements—i.e., they were accompanied by a deposit slip depositing these checks in an account which was not Brite Lite's. There has been no indication that Chirico used any subterfuge in depositing these checks in her own accounts.

The bank is liable to Brite Lite for the proceeds of the various checks which the bank failed to deposit in Brite Lite's bank account as required by and in accordance with the restrictive indorsements placed on the checks.

Judgment for Brite Lite.

## HOLDER IN DUE COURSE

A person who qualifies as a **holder in due course** of a negotiable instrument gets special rights. Normally, the transferee of an instrument—like the assignee of a contract—receives only those rights in the instrument that the transferor had in the instrument. But a holder in due course can obtain better rights than his transferor had. A holder in due course takes a negotiable instrument free of all *personal defenses* and claims to the instrument except for so-called *real defenses,* which go to the validity of the instrument. The differences between personal and real defenses will be developed in more detail later in this chapter, but the following example illustrates the advantage that a holder in due course of a negotiable instrument may have.

Carl Carpenter contracts with Helen Homeowner to build her a garage for $4,500, payable on October 1, when the garage is expected to have been completed. Assume that Carpenter assigns his right to the $4,500 to First

National Bank in order to obtain money for materials. If the bank tries to collect the money from Homeowner on October 1, but Carpenter has not finished building the garage, then Homeowner may assert the fact that the garage is not complete as a defense to paying the bank. As assignee of a simple contract, the bank has only those rights that its assignor, Carpenter, has and is subject to all of the claims and defenses that Homeowner has against Carpenter.

Now assume that instead of simply signing a contract with Homeowner, Carpenter had Homeowner give him a negotiable promissory note in the amount of $4,500 payable to the order of Carpenter on October 1. Carpenter then negotiated the note to the bank. If the bank qualifies as a holder in due course, it would be entitled to collect the $4,500 from Homeowner on October 1, even through she might have a personal defense against payment of the note in that Carpenter had not completed the work on the garage. Homeowner cannot assert that personal defense against a holder in due course. She would have to pay the note to the bank and then independently seek to recover from Carpenter for breach of their agreement. The bank's improved position is due to its status as a holder in due course of a negotiable instrument. If the instrument in question was not negotiable, or if the bank could not qualify as a holder in due course, then it would be in the same position as the assignee of a simple contract and would be subject to the personal defense.

We turn now to a discussion of the requirements that must be met for the possessor of a negotiable instrument to qualify as a holder in due course.

**General Requirements.** In order to become a "holder in due course," a person who takes a negotiable instrument must be a **holder** and must take the instrument for *value,* in *good faith, without notice* that is *overdue* or has been *dishonored,* and *without notice* of any *defense* against it or *claim* to it [3–302]. If a person who takes a negotiable instrument does not meet these requirements, he is not a holder in due course and is in the same position as an assignee of a contract.

**Holder.** To be a **holder** of a negotiable instrument, a person must have *possession* of an instrument that has *all of the necessary indorsements* and is *delivered* to him. For example, if Teresa Gonzales is given a check by her grandmother that is made payable "to the order of Teresa Gonzales," Teresa is a holder of the check because it is made out to her. If Teresa indorses the check "Pay to the order of Ames Grocery, Teresa Gonzales" and gives it to Ames Grocery in payment for some groceries, then Ames Grocery is the holder of the check. Ames Grocery is a holder because it is in possession of a check that is indorsed to its order and delivered to it. If Ames Grocery indorses the check "Ames Grocery" and deposits it in its account at First National Bank, the bank becomes the holder. The bank is in possession of an instrument that is indorsed in blank and has been delivered to it.

It is important that all indorsements on the instrument at the time it is payable to the order of a specified payee are *authorized* indorsements. A *forged* indorsement is not an effective indorsement, and it prevents a person from becoming a holder.

For example, the U.S. government mails to Robert Washington an income tax refund check payable to him. Tom Turner steals the check from Washington's mailbox, signs (indorses) "Robert Washington" on the back of the check, and cashes it at a shoe store. The shoe store cannot be a holder of the check, because a necessary indorsement has been forged. The check has to be indorsed by Robert Washington for there to be a valid chain of indorsements and for any subsequent possessor to be a holder. Turner's signature is not effective for this purpose, because Washington did not authorize Turner to sign Washington's name to the check.

**Value.** To qualify as a holder in due course of an instrument, a person must give **value** for it. Value is different from simple consideration. Under the provisions of the Code, a holder takes an instrument for value if: (1) the agreed consideration has been performed, for example, if the instrument was given in exchange for a promise to deliver a refrigerator and the refrigerator has been delivered; (2) he acquires a security interest in, or a lien on, the instrument; (3) he takes the instrument in payment of (or as security for) an antecedent claim; (4) he gives a negotiable instrument for it; or (5) he makes an irrevocable commitment to a third person [3–303]. Thus, a person taking an instrument as a gift would not be able to qualify as a holder in due course.

A bank or any person who discounts an instrument in the regular course of trade has given value for it. Likewise, if a loan is made and an instrument is pledged as security for the repayment of the loan, the secured party has given value for the instrument to the extent of the amount of the loan. If Axe, who owes Bell a past-due debt, indorses and delivers to Bell, in payment of the debt or as security for its repayment, an instrument issued to Axe, Bell has given value for the instrument. If a bank allows its customer to draw against a check deposited for collection, it has given value to the extent of the credit drawn against. This is illustrated in the *Flagship Bank of Orlando* case which follows.

The purchaser of a limited interest in an instrument can be a holder in due course only to the extent of the interest purchased [3–302(4)]. For example, Arthur Wells agrees to purchase a note payable to the order of Helda Parks. The note is for the sum of $5,000. Wells pays Parks $1,000 on the negotiation of the note to him and agrees to pay the balance of $4,000 in 10 days. Before making the $4,000 payment, Wells learns that James Bell, the maker of the note, has a valid defense to it. Wells can be a holder in due course for only $1,000.

A person who has given all of the value for an instrument that he agreed to give can be a holder in due course for the full amount of the instrument even if the amount is less than the face amount. For example, if Hanks pays Parish $975 for a $1,000 note, Hanks can be a holder in due course for the entire $1,000.

**Good Faith.** To qualify as a holder in due course of a negotiable instrument, a person must take it in **good faith,** which means that the person must obtain it honestly [1–201(19)]. If a person obtains a check by trickery or with knowledge that it has been stolen, the person has not obtained the check in good faith and cannot be a holder in due course. A person who pays too little for an instrument, perhaps because he suspects that something may be wrong with the way it was obtained, may have trouble in meeting the good faith test. The high discount itself suggests that the purchase was not in good faith. For example, a finance company works closely with a door-to-door sales company that engages in shoddy practices, and it is aware of past consumer complaints against the sales company. If the finance company buys the consumers' notes from the sales company at a significant discount, it will not be able to meet the good faith test and qualify as a holder in due course of the notes.

The *Arcanum National Bank v. Hessler* case, below, illustrates the analysis a court goes through to ascertain whether "good faith" is present in a situation where the payee and a subsequent holder have had a close working relationship.

**Overdue and Dishonored.** In order to qualify as a holder in due course, a person must take a negotiable instrument before he has noticed that it is overdue or has been dishonored. The reason for this is that obligations are generally performed when they are due. If a negotiable instrument is not paid when it is due, this is considered to put the person taking it on notice that there may be defenses to its payment.

**Overdue Instruments.** If a negotiable instrument due on a certain date is not paid by that date, then it is overdue at the beginning of the next day after the due date. For example, if a promissory note dated January 1 is payable "30 days after date," it is due on January 31. If it is not paid by January 31, it is overdue beginning on February 1.

If a negotiable instrument is payable on demand, a person must acquire it within a reasonable time after it was issued. A reasonable time for presenting a check for payment is presumed to be 30 days [3–304(3)(c)]. Thus, a person who acquires a check 60 days after the date it is dated is probably taking it after it is overdue.

In determining when a demand note is overdue, business practices and the facts of the particular case must be considered. In a farming community, the normal period for loans to farmers may be six months. A demand note might be outstanding for six or seven months before it is considered overdue. On the other hand, a demand note issued in an industrial city where the normal period of such loans is 30 to 60 days would be considered overdue in a much shorter period of time.

**Dishonored Instruments.** To be a holder in due course, a person must not only take a negotiable instrument before he has notice that it is overdue but must also take it before it has been **dishonored.** A negotiable instrument has been dishonored when it has been *presented for payment* and payment has been *refused.*

For example, Susan Farley writes a check on her account at First National Bank that is payable "to the order of Sven Sorensen." Sorensen takes the check to First National Bank to cash it, but the bank refuses to pay it because Farley has insufficient funds in her account to cover it. The check has been dishonored. Sorensen then takes Farley's check to Harry's Hardware and uses it to pay for some paint. Harry's could not be a holder in due course of the check if Harry's is on notice that the check has been dishonored. It would have such notice if First National stamped the check "Payment Refused NSF" (not sufficient funds).

Similarly, suppose Carol Carson signs a 30-day note payable to Ace Appliance for $100 and gives the note to Ace as payment for a stereo set. When Ace asks Carson for payment, she refuses to pay because the stereo does not work properly. Ace then negotiates the note to First National Bank. If First National knows about Carson's refusal to pay, it cannot be a holder in due course.

**Notice of Defenses.** To qualify as a holder in due course, a person must also acquire a negotiable instrument without *notice* that there are any *defenses* or *adverse claims* to it. Notice of a possible defense might appear on the face of the instrument as it did in the *Arcanum National Bank* case, which follows, where a signature was accompanied by initials showing that it had been put there by someone other than the person whose name was signed.

**Incomplete Paper.** A person cannot be a holder in due course of a check (or other negotiable instrument) if some important or *material term* is blank. If a person is given a check that has been signed, but the space where the amount of the check is to be written has been left blank, then he cannot be a holder in due course of that check. The fact that a material term is blank puts the person on notice that the drawer may have a defense to its payment. To be material, the omitted term must be one that affects the legal obligations of the parties to the negotiable instrument. Material terms include the amount of the instrument and the name of the payee. If a negotiable instrument is completed after it was signed but before it is acquired, the person who acquires it can qualify as a holder in due course if he had no knowledge about any unauthorized completion.

For example, Fred Young writes a check payable to the order of Slidell's Shoes and leaves the amount blank. He gives the check to his friend Alice Termon, asks her to pick up a pair of shoes for him at Slidell's, and tells her to fill in the amount of the purchase. If Termon gives the incomplete check to Slidell, it cannot be enforced as is. If Slidell fills in the check for $49.95, the cost of the shoes, the check could be enforced as completed because the completion was authorized. However, if Slidell watched as Termon filled the blank in as $100 (and obtained the $50.05 difference in cash), Slidell could take the check as a holder in due course as long as he had no knowledge or notice that the completion was unauthorized. On the other hand, if Termon filled the amount in as $100 before she got to Slidell's, Slidell could be a holder in due course and enforce the check for $100. In the latter case, Young, who made the unauthorized completion possible, must bear the loss until he locates Termon.

**Irregular Paper.** If there is something apparently wrong with a negotiable instrument, such as an obvious alteration in the amount, then it is considered to be **irregular paper.** A person who takes an irregular instrument is considered to be on notice of any possible defenses to it. For example, Kevin Carlson writes a check for "one dollar" payable to Karen Held. Held inserts the word *hundred* in the amount, changes the figure "$1" to "$100," and gives the check to a druggist in exchange for a purchase of goods. If the alterations in the amount should be obvious to the druggist, perhaps because there are erasures, different handwritings, or different inks, then the druggist cannot be a holder in due course. The druggist would have taken irregular paper and would be considered to be on notice that there might be defenses to it. These defenses include Carlson's defense that he is liable for only $1 because that is the original amount of the check.

A person is put on notice if someone of his experience and training should, in the exercise of reasonable prudence, detect the irregularity. Any noticeable alteration makes an instrument irregular on its face, but a clever alteration does not. However, an alteration that might put a bank cashier on notice might not put on notice a person unaccustomed to handling negotiable instruments.

**Voidable Paper.** A person cannot qualify as a holder in due course of a negotiable instrument if he is aware that the obligation of a party to it is *voidable.* Thus, if a person knows that a signature on the instrument was obtained by fraud, misrepresentation, or duress, he cannot be a holder in due course. If he knows that the instrument has already been paid, he cannot become a holder in due course. Of course, the best way for the person who is liable on an instrument to be protected after he pays it is to mark it "paid" or "canceled."

**Negotiation by a Fiduciary.** A person may also be considered to be on notice of defenses if he is taking a negotiable instrument from a *fiduciary,* such as a trustee. If a negotiable instrument is payable to a person as a trustee or an attorney for someone, then any attempt by that person to negotiate it on his own behalf or for his use (or benefit) puts the person on notice that the beneficiary of the trust may have a claim [3–304(2)].

For example, a check is drawn "Pay to the order of Arthur Adams, Trustee for Mary Minor." Adams takes the check to Ace Appliance Store, indorses his name to it, and uses it to purchase a television set for himself. Ace Appliance cannot be a holder in due course, because it should know that the negotiation of the check is in violation of the fiduciary duty Adams owes to Mary Minor. Ace should know this because Adams is negotiating the check for his own benefit, not Minor's.

**Payee as Holder in Due Course.** A payee may be a holder in due course if he complies with all the requirements for a holder in due course [3–302(2)]. Ordinarily, a payee will have notice or knowledge of defenses to the instrument and will know whether it is overdue or has been dishonored; consequently, he could not qualify as a holder in due course. For example, Drew draws a check on First Bank as drawee, payable to the order of Parks, but leaves the amount blank. Drew delivers the check to Axe, his agent, and instructs Axe to fill in $300 as the amount. Axe, however, fills in $500 as the amount, and Parks gives Axe $500 for the check. Axe then gives Drew $300 and absconds with the extra $200. In such a case, Parks, as payee, is a holder in due course of the check since he has taken it for value, in good faith, and without notice of defenses.

Similarly, assume that Jarvis owes Fields $200. Jarvis agrees to sell Kirk a used television set for $200 that Jarvis assures Kirk is in working condition. In fact, the set is broken. Jarvis asks Kirk to make her check for $200 payable to Fields and then delivers the check to Fields in payment of the debt. Fields, as the payee, can be a holder in due course of the check if he is not aware of the misrepresentation that Jarvis made to Kirk in order to obtain the check.

**Shelter Provision.** When an instrument is transferred, the transferee obtains those rights that the transferor had. This means that any person who can trace his title to an instrument back to a holder in due course receives the same rights of a holder in due course even if he cannot meet the requirements himself. This is known as the *shelter* provision of the Code. For example, Archer makes a note payable to Bryant. Bryant negotiates the note to Carlyle, who qualifies as a holder in due course. Carlyle then negotiates the note to Darby, who cannot qualify as a holder in due course, because she knows the note is overdue. Since Darby can trace her title back to a holder in due course (Carlyle), Darby has the rights of a holder in due course when she seeks payment of the note from Archer.

There is, however, a limitation on the shelter provision. A transferee who has himself been a party to any fraud or illegality affecting the instrument, or who as a prior holder has notice of a claim to or defense against the instrument, cannot improve his position by taking from a later holder in due course [3–201(1)]. For example, Archer through fraudulent representations induces Bryant to execute a negotiable note payable to Archer and then negotiates the instrument to Carlyle, who takes as a holder in due course. If Archer thereafter takes the note for value from Carlyle, Archer cannot acquire Carlyle's rights as a holder in due course. Archer was a party to the fraud that induced the note, and the holder of an instrument cannot improve his position by negotiating the instrument and then reacquiring it.

## Flagship Bank of Orlando v. Central Florida Coach Lines, Inc.

### 33 UCC Rep. 613 (Pa. Ct. C.P. 1981)

On December 20, Central Florida Coach Lines issued two checks totaling $1,791.20 to Thomas York. York indorsed the checks and deposited them in his account at the Flagship Bank of Orlando. Sometime prior to December 31, Florida Coach instructed its bank, First Eastern Bank, to stop payment on both checks. When the checks were presented for payment in early January, First Eastern refused payment because of the stop payment order. In the interim, Flagship Bank had permitted York to draw checks against the deposit.

Flagship Bank then filed suit against Florida Coach to recover on the checks. The trial court awarded judgment to Flagship Bank, and Florida Coach appealed.

**Toole, Judge.** This case was tried by the Flagship Bank on the theory that it was a holder in due course of both checks and as such took them free of any personal defenses Florida Coach may have had against the depositor, Mr. York. Florida Coach contends that Flagship Bank is not a holder in due course because a stop order had been issued against the checks, and also because Flagship Bank permitted the depositor to withdraw funds before allowing appropriate clearance time for the checks. We are satisfied that the Bank is a holder in due course and entitled to the benefit of that statutory status.

A holder in due course is defined in the Uniform Commercial Code as follows:

> (1) A holder in due course is a holder who takes the instrument
> (a) for value; and
> (b) in good faith; and
> (c) without notice that it is overdue or has been dishonored or of any defense against or claim to it on the part of any person.

That Flagship Bank took the instruments in this case "for value" is established by the record. In making this determination, we are guided by the Uniform Commercial Code which provides:

> A holder takes the instrument for value
> (a) To the extent that the agreed consideration has been performed or that he acquires a security interest in or a lien on the instrument otherwise than by legal process;
> (b) when he takes the instrument in payment of or as security for an antecedent claim against any person whether or not the claim is due; or
> (c) when he gives a negotiable instrument for it or makes an irrevocable commitment to a third person.

In the instant case, checks were drawn, presented, and honored against the deposits posted to the account. Under these circumstances, we agree with the Bank that it would be deemed to have taken the instruments for value under either subsection (a) or (c).

We are also satisfied that the Bank took the instruments in good faith. Good faith, according to the Code, means "honesty in fact in the conduct or transaction concerned."

In the instant case, the record reveals that the Bank acted honestly in fact in the conduct or transaction concerned. Certainly there is nothing in the record to establish any willful dishonesty or actual knowledge on the part of this Bank which would require us to deny it "holder in due course" status.

Florida Coach also contends that the Bank did not act in good faith when it permitted the payee to withdraw from the account without awaiting collection. This same argument was presented and rejected in *Mellon Bank, N.A. v. Donegal Mutual Ins. Co.,* where the court stated:

> Payment by the collecting bank might be imprudent and is certainly a risk assumed by the depository-collecting bank as to the drawee, but it does not affect plaintiff's rights against defendant who by drawing the instrument and placing it in the stream of commerce has engaged to pay it to any holder.

The record also establishes that the Bank took the instruments without any notice of the stop payment order or of any defense or claim which Florida Coach may have had against the depositor. The Bank has therefore satisfied all of the statutory requirements necessary to qualify as a "holder in due course" of the instruments.

Judgment for Flagship Bank affirmed.

---

## Arcanum National Bank v. Hessler

**69 Ohio St. 2d 549 (Ohio Sup. Ct. 1982)**

Kenneth Hessler was in the business of raising hogs for the John Smith Grain Company. John Smith Grain Company would deliver hogs and feed to Hessler and require him to sign a promissory note payable to it to cover the cost of the hogs and feed. Without Hessler's knowledge or consent, John Smith Grain Company would then sell the note to the Arcanum National Bank, which would open a commercial loan account in Hessler's name. When the hogs were sold by John Smith Grain Company, a portion of the proceeds was applied to satisfy Hessler's note held by the bank. Hessler received a flat fee and a share of the net profits on each hog sold.

On January 4, 1977, Hessler signed a promissory note for $16,800 payable to John Smith Grain Company for hogs delivered on that date. On the advice of an officer of John Smith Grain Company, Hessler also signed his wife's name, Carla Hessler, to the note, placing his initials, K. H., after her name. John Smith Grain Company, as payee, assigned the note to the Arcanum National Bank. The pigs delivered on January 4 had previously been mortgaged by John Smith Grain Company. Early in 1977, the mortgagee took the pigs from Hessler's farm because John Smith Grain Company was in serious financial difficulty. The company later went into receivership. As a result, no funds were available to pay the bank for Hessler's note.

The bank sued Kenneth and Carla Hessler to collect the face amount of the note. The Hesslers claimed that they had a defense of want of consideration and should not be liable to the bank on the note. The trial court and the court of appeals held that the bank was a holder in due course and that the defense of want of consideration could not be asserted against it. Hessler appealed.

**KRUPANSKY, JUDGE.** The sole issue in this case is whether the bank is a holder in due course who takes the note free from Hessler's defense of want of consideration.

Hessler contends the bank has not established holder in due course status because the bank took the instrument with notice of a defense against it. We agree.

The requirement that the purchaser take the instrument without notice of a claim or defense in order to qualify as a holder in due course is explained, under the heading of "Notice to Purchaser," at § 3–304, which provides in relevant part:

> (A) The instrument is so incomplete, bears such visible evidence of forgery or alterations, or is otherwise so irregular as to call into question its validity, terms, or ownership or to create an ambiguity as to the party to pay.

Whether a transferee has taken an instrument with notice of a defense depends upon all the facts and circumstances of a particular situation and is generally a question of fact to be determined by the trier of fact.

Here the trial court, sitting as fact finder, weighed the evidence of the relationship between the bank and Hessler and reasoned: "The defect on the promissory note is that the signature of Carla Hessler was added by Kenneth Hessler and, since the Arcanum National Bank handled the Hesslers' personal finances, it should have noticed that there was a defect on the face of the instrument. . . . The note also bears the initials 'K. H.,' indicating that Kenneth Hessler has signed Carla Hessler's name." Accordingly, the trial court specifically found "this 'irregularity' does call into question the validity of the note, the terms of the note, the ownership of the note or create an ambiguity as to the party who is to pay the note." Thus, the trial court, while specifically finding the bank took the note with notice of a defense, nonetheless erroneously held the bank qualified as a holder in due course.

Hessler also contends, in essence, the bank failed in its burden of proving holder in due course status because it failed to establish it took the note in good faith as required under 3–302(1)(b).

"Good faith" is defined as "honesty in fact in the conduct or transaction concerned." Under the "close connectedness" doctrine, which was established by the Supreme Court of New Jersey in *Unico v. Owen,* a transferee does not take an instrument in good faith when the transferee is so closely connected with the transferor that the transferee may be charged with knowledge of an infirmity in the underlying transaction. The rationale for the close connectedness doctrine was enunciated in *Unico* as follows:

> In the field of negotiable instruments, good faith is a broad concept. The basic philosophy of the holder in due course status is to encourage free negotiability of commercial paper by removing certain anxieties of one who takes the paper as an innocent purchaser knowing no reason why the paper is not sound as its face would indicate. It would seem to follow, therefore, that the more the holder knows about the underlying transaction, and particularly the more he controls or participates or becomes involved in it, the less he fits the role of a good faith purchaser for value; the closer his relationship to the underlying agreement which is the source of the note, the less basis there is for giving him the tension-free rights considered necessary in a fast-moving, credit-extending world.

Soon after the decision in *Unico* was reached, the close connectedness doctrine was adopted by Ohio courts. *American Plan Corp. v. Woods* announced the following:

> A transferee of a negotiable note does not take in "good faith" and is not a holder in due course of a note given in the sale of consumer goods where the transferee is a finance company involved with the seller of the goods, and which has a pervasive knowledge of factors relating to the terms of the sale.

According to White and Summers, noted authorities on the Uniform Commercial Code, the following five factors are indicative of a close connection between the transferee and transferor:

(1) Drafting by the transferee of forms for the transferor; (2) approval or establishment or both of the transferor's procedures by the transferee (e.g., setting the interest rate, approval of a referral sales plan); (3) an independent check by the transferee on the credit of the debtor or some other direct contract between the transferee and the debtor; (4) heavy reliance by the transferor upon the transferee (e.g., transfer by the transferor of all or a substantial part of his paper to the transferee); and (5) common or connected ownership or management of the transferor and transferee.

An analysis of the above factors in relation to the facts of this case reveals an unusually close relationship between the bank (the transferee) and the John Smith Grain Company (the transferor-payee). The bank provided John Smith Grain Company with the forms used in the transaction and supplied the interest rate to be charged. At the time of the purchase of the first note, the bank ran an independent credit check on Hessler. There is evidence of a heavy reliance by John Smith Grain Company upon the bank insofar as it was customary for the grain company to transfer substantially all of its commercial paper to the bank. There was a common director of the bank and John Smith Grain Company.

The facts of this case clearly indicate such close connectedness between the bank and John Smith Grain Company as to impute knowledge by the bank of infirmities in the underlying transaction.

Judgment reversed in favor of Hessler.

## RIGHTS OF A HOLDER IN DUE COURSE

**Importance of Being a Holder in Due Course.** The preceding chapter showed that the advantage of negotiable instruments over other kinds of contracts is that they are accepted as substitutes for money. People are willing to accept negotiable instruments as substitutes for money because they can generally take them free of claims or defenses to payment between the original parties to the instruments. On the other hand, a person who takes an assignment of a simple contract receives only the same rights as the person had who assigned the contract.

There are two qualifications to the ability of a person who acquires a negotiable instrument to be free of claims or defenses between the original parties. First, the person who acquires the negotiable instrument must be a holder in due course. If not, he is subject to all of the claims or defenses to payment that any party to the instrument has. Second, the only claims or defenses that the holder in due course has to worry about are so-called **real defenses**—those that affect the *validity* of the instrument. For example, if the maker or drawer did not have legal capacity because she was a minor, the maker or drawer has a real defense. The holder in due course does not have to worry about so-called **personal defenses.**

**Personal Defenses.** The basic rule of negotiable instruments law is that a holder in due course of a negotiable instrument is not subject to any **personal** (or limited) **defenses** or claims that may exist between the original parties to the instrument [3–305]. Personal defenses include such things as breach of warranty, misrepresentation, fraud in the inducement of any underlying contract, and any failure of consideration.

The type of fraud that is a personal defense is known as **fraud in the inducement.** For example, an art dealer sells a lithograph to Cherne, telling her that it is a Picasso, and takes Cherne's check for $500 in payment. The art dealer knows that the lithograph is a forgery. The art dealer's fraudulent representation has induced Cherne to make the purchase and give her check. Because of this fraud, Cherne has a personal defense against having to honor her check to the art dealer. The distinction between fraud in the inducement and fraud in the essence is discussed in the *Standard Finance Co., Ltd. v. Ellis* case, which follows.

The following example illustrates the limited extent to which a maker or drawer can use personal defenses as a reason for not paying a negotiable instrument that he signed. Trent Tucker bought a used truck from Honest Harry's and gave Harry's a 60-day promissory note for $2,750 in payment for the truck. Honest Harry's "guaranteed" the truck to be in "good working condition," but in fact the truck had a cracked engine block. If Harry's tries to collect the $2,750 from Tucker, Tucker could claim breach of warranty as a reason for not paying Harry's the full $2,750 because Harry's is not a holder in due course. However, if Harry's negotiated the note to First National Bank and the bank was a holder in due course, the situation would be changed. If the bank tried to collect the $2,750 from Tucker, Tucker would have to pay the bank. Tucker's defense or claim of breach of warranty cannot be used as a reason for not paying a holder in due course. It is a personal defense and cannot be used against the bank, which qualifies as a holder in due course. Tucker must pay the bank the $2,750 and then pursue his breach of warranty claim against Harry's.

The rule that a holder in due course takes a negotiable instrument free of any personal defenses or claims to it has been modified to some extent, particularly in relation to instruments given by consumers. These modifications will be discussed in the next section of this chapter.

**Real Defenses.** There are some claims and defenses to payment of an instrument that go to the validity of the instrument. These claims and defenses are known as **real** (or universal) **defenses.** They can be used as reasons against payment of a negotiable instrument even if the person who requests payment is a holder in due course [3–305(2)].

Two common examples of real defenses are (1) incapacity of a person to execute a negotiable instrument and (2) duress or any other illegality that nullifies the obligation of a party liable to pay the instrument. If Mark Miller, age 17, signs a promissory note as maker, he can use his lack of capacity to contract as a defense against paying it even to a holder in due course. Similarly, if Harold points a gun at his grandmother and forces her to execute a promissory note, the grandmother can use duress as a defense against paying it even to a holder in due course.

Another example of real defense is **fraud in the essence.** This occurs where a person signs a negotiable instrument without knowing or having a reasonable chance to realize that it is a negotiable instrument. For example, Amy Jones is an illiterate person who lives alone. She signs a document that is actually a promissory note, but she is told that it is a grant of permission for a television set to be left in her house on a trial basis. Jones has a real defense against payment on the note. She does not have to pay the note to even a holder in due course. Fraud in the essence is distinguished from fraud in the inducement, discussed earlier, which is only a personal defense.

Discharge of the party liable in bankruptcy proceedings is also a real defense [3–305(2)]. The objective of our bankruptcy laws and other insolvency laws is to relieve the debtor from his debts and give him a new start. In general, the discharge features of these laws are broad enough to discharge the debtor of all his commercial obligations, including debts owing on negotiable instruments held by holders in due course.

Real defenses can be asserted even against a holder in due course of a negotiable instrument, because it is more desirable to protect people who have signed negotiable instruments in these situations than it is to protect persons who have taken negotiable instruments in the ordinary course of business.

The *Sea Air Support, Inc. v. Herrman* case, below, shows another situation in which a holder in due course is vulnerable to a defense. In this case it was a check issued in payment of a gambling debt that, under Nevada law, was void and unenforceable.

**Persons Not Holders in Due Course.** As you have learned, negotiable commercial paper is basically a contract to pay money. If the holder of such paper is not a holder in due course, his rights are no greater than the rights of any promisee or assignee of a simple contract. Such a holder takes the paper subject to all valid claims on the part of any person and subject to all defenses of any party that would be available in an action on a simple contract [3–306].

## Standard Finance Co., Ltd. v. Ellis

**657 P.2d 1056 (Hawaii Ct. App. 1983)**

On September 30, 1976, Betty Ellis and her husband, W. G. Ellis, executed and delivered a promissory note for $2,800 payable to Standard Finance Company. Nothing was paid on the note, and on May 15, 1980, Standard Finance brought a collection action against Betty Ellis. The trial court awarded a judgment of $5,413.35 against Ellis. She appealed, claiming that she had defenses against payment of misrepresentation, duress, and failure of consideration.

**TANAKA, JUSTICE.** Betty Ellis indicates that "shortly before" W. G. Ellis executed the note, he gave her "constant assurance" that her "signature was a formality and that he alone was liable and that the debt would be repaid without any participation by her." Thereafter, Betty Ellis accompanied W. G. Ellis to Standard Finance's office and executed the note.

Betty Ellis argues that W. G. Ellis' misrepresentation induced her to sign the note and since such misrepresentation dealt with its essential terms, her execution of the note was not a manifestation of her assent. Consequently, the note was void *ab initio* and unenforceable as to her.

The principles of law as to when misrepresentation prevents the formation of a contract and when it makes a contract voidable are set forth in *Restatement (Second) of Contracts.* Section 163 states:

> § 163. When a Misrepresentation Prevents Formation of a Contract
> If a misrepresentation as to the character or essential terms of a proposed contract induces conduct

that appears to be a manifestation of assent by one who neither knows nor has reasonable opportunity to know of the character or essential terms of the proposed contract, his conduct is not effective as a manifestation of assent.

Comment a to § 163 provides in part as follows:

> This Section involves an application of that principle where a misrepresentation goes to what is sometimes called the "factum" or the "execution" rather than merely the "inducement." If, because of a misrepresentation as to the character or essential terms of a proposed contract, a party does not know or have reasonable opportunity to know of its character or essential terms, then he neither knows nor has reason to know that the other party may infer from his conduct that he assents to that contract. In such a case there is no effective manifestation of assent and no contract at all.

Based on the facts in the record, we hold as a matter of law that the misrepresentation by W. G. Ellis was not a "fraud in the factum" or a "fraud in the execution" to render the note void at its inception.

A common illustration of "fraud in the factum" is that of the "maker who is tricked into signing a note in the belief that it is merely a receipt or some other document."

In the instant case, no representation was made to Betty Ellis that the note was anything other than a note. In fact, as indicated above, it is uncontradicted that Standard Finance's representative explained the "terms and conditions of the note" to Betty and W. G. Ellis prior to their execution of the note.

Comment 7 to § 3–305 further states that the defense of "fraud in the factum" is that of "excusable ignorance of the contents of the writing signed" and the party claiming such fraud "must also have had no reasonable opportunity to obtain knowledge." *Page v. Krekey* and *First National Bank of Odessa v. Fazzari,* both cited by Betty Ellis, are examples in this category of "fraud in the factum." In *Page,* an intoxicated, illiterate defendant, who could not read or write, was induced to sign a guaranty on a false representation that it was an application for a license. In *Fazzari,* a defendant who was unable to read or write English was induced to sign a note upon the misrepresentation that it was a statement of wages earned.

The record in this case fails to show any fact constituting "excusable ignorance" of the contents of the paper signed or "no reasonable opportunity to obtain knowledge" on the part of Betty Ellis.

In her answers to interrogatories, Betty Ellis states that she was "forced" to sign the note under duress. "Physical beatings" and "psychological pressure" on her by Ellis for at least three years prior to signing the note constituted the duress. She argues that her execution of the note which was compelled by duress was not a manifestation of her assent. Thus, the note is void and unenforceable.

The law concerning duress resulting in void or voidable contracts is discussed in *Restatement (Second) of Contracts.* Section 174 reads:

> § 174. When Duress by Physical Compulsion Prevents Formation of a Contract
> If conduct that appears to be a manifestation of assent by a party who does not intend to engage in that conduct is physically compelled by duress, the conduct is not effective as a manifestation of assent.

Comment a to § 174 provides in part:

> This Section involves an application of that principle to those relatively *rare situations in which actual physical force has been used* to compel a party to appear to assent to a contract. . . . The essence of this type of duress is that a party is compelled by physical force to do an act that he has no intention of doing. (Emphasis added.)

We hold that as a matter of law the facts in the record do not constitute the type of duress which renders the note void under § 174. Such duress involves the use of actual physical force to compel a person to sign a document. It may include the example given in Comment 6 to § 3–305 of an "instrument signed at the point of a gun" being void.

Here, the only evidence of duress is "physical beatings" and "psychological pressure" by W. G. Ellis on Betty Ellis over a course of three years prior to her signing of the note. Without more, such evidence does not constitute duress resulting in the voiding of the note. From such evidence it cannot reasonably be inferred that the physical beatings by W. G. Ellis directly resulted in Betty Ellis signing the note in question.

Finally, Betty Ellis claims that the entire amount of the loan of $2,800 went to Ellis and she received no part of it. Thus, there was lack or failure of consideration and summary judgment was improper. We cannot agree.

Standard Finance's check for $2,800 was made payable to "W. G. Ellis and Betty Ellis." The reverse side of the check bears the indorsement of "Betty Ellis." This was sufficient evidence of consideration for the transaction involved.

However, Betty Ellis states that she "never got the money or the use of it" and "it all went to my ex-husband and this was understood by Standard Finance." This fact does not constitute lack or failure of consideration. It is fundamental that consideration received by a co-maker on a note from the payee is sufficient consideration to bind the other co-maker.

Judgment for Standard Finance affirmed.

---

## Sea Air Support, Inc. v. Herrmann

**613 P.2d 413 (Nev. Sup. Ct. 1980)**

Ralph Herrmann wrote a check for $10,000 payable to Ormsby House, a hotel-casino located in Carson City, Nevada, and exchanged it for three counter checks he had written earlier that evening to acquire gaming chips. Ormsby House was unable to collect the proceeds from the check because Herrmann had insufficient funds in his account. The debt evidenced by the check was assigned to Sea Air Support, Inc., dba Automated Accounts Associates, for collection. Sea Air was also unsuccessful in its attempts to collect and filed a lawsuit against Herrmann to recover on the dishonored check. The trial court dismissed the lawsuit, and Sea Air appealed.

**Per Curiam.** The district judge dismissed the action on the ground that Sea Air's claim is barred by the Statute of Anne. Sea Air appeals the dismissal. We are asked to reconsider the long line of Nevada cases refusing to enforce gambling debts. We refuse to do so, and affirm the dismissal.

Nevada law incorporates the common law of gambling as altered by the Statute of 9 Anne, c14, § 1, absent conflicting statutory or constitutional provisions. The Statute provides that all notes drawn for the purpose of reimbursing or repaying any money knowingly lent or advanced for gaming are "utterly void, frustrate, and of none effect." Despite the fact that gambling, where licensed, is legal in Nevada, this court has long held that debts incurred, and checks drawn, for gambling purposes are void and unenforceable.

In this case, Herrmann's $10,000 check clearly was drawn for the purpose of repaying money knowingly advanced for gaming. The check is void and unenforceable in this state. If the law is to change, it must be done by legislative action.

Judgment for Herrmann affirmed.

## CHANGES IN THE HOLDER IN DUE COURSE RULE

**Consumer Disadvantages.** The rule that a holder in due course of a negotiable instrument is not subject to personal defenses between the original parties to it makes negotiable instruments a readily accepted substitute for money. This rule can also result in serious disadvantages to consumers. Consumers sometimes buy goods or services on credit and give the seller a negotiable instrument, such as a promissory note. They often do this without knowing the consequences of signing a negotiable instrument. If the goods or services are defective or not delivered, the consumer would like to withhold payment of the note until the seller corrects the problem or makes the delivery. Where the note is still held by the seller, the consumer can do this, because any defenses of breach of warranty or nonperformance are good against the seller.

However, the seller may have negotiated the note at a discount to a third party, such as a bank. If the bank qualifies as a holder in due course, the consumer must pay the note in full to the bank. The consumer's personal defenses are not valid against a holder in due course. The consumer must pay the holder in due course and then try to get her money back from the seller. This may be difficult if the seller cannot be found or will not accept responsibility. The consumer would be in a much stronger position if she could just withhold payment, even against the bank, until the goods or services are delivered or the performance is corrected.

**State Legislation.** Some state legislatures and state courts have limited the holder in due course doctrine, particularly as it relates to consumers. In 1968, the National Conference of Commissioners on Uniform State Laws promulgated a Uniform Consumer Credit Code, and various consumer organizations have developed model consumer acts. The Uniform Consumer Credit Code, which has been adopted by a relatively small number of states, virtually eliminates negotiable paper in consumer credit sales by prohibiting the seller from taking a negotiable instrument other than a check as evidence of the obligation of the buyer. Some states now require that instruments evidencing consumer indebtedness must carry the legend "consumer paper" and must state that instruments carrying the legend are not negotiable. Other states have enacted comprehensive measures that effectively abolish the holder in due course doctrine. The law at the state level is far from uniform, and the position of a consumer who has signed a negotiable instrument varies from state to state. The trend, though, is clearly toward limiting the holder in due course doctrine as it adversely affects consumers in consumer transactions.

**Federal Trade Commission Rules.** The Federal Trade Commission (FTC) has promulgated a regulation designed to protect consumers against the operation of the holder in due course rule. The FTC rule applies to persons who sell to, or who finance sales to, consumers on credit and have the consumer sign a note or an installment sales contract. The rule makes it an *unfair trade practice* for a seller, in the course of financing a consumer purchase of goods or services, to employ procedures that make the consumer's duty to pay independent of the seller's duty to fulfill his obligations.

The FTC regulation provides protection to the consumer in those situations where: (1) the buyer executes a sales contract that includes a promissory note; (2) the buyer signs an installment sales contract that includes a "waiver of defenses" clause; or (3) the seller arranges with a third-party lender for a direct loan to finance the buyer's purchase.

The FTC regulation deals with the first two situations by requiring that the following clause be included in bold type in any consumer credit contract to be signed by the consumer:

NOTICE: ANY HOLDER OF THIS CONSUMER CREDIT CONTRACT IS SUBJECT TO ALL CLAIMS AND DEFENSES WHICH THE DEBTOR COULD ASSERT AGAINST THE SELLER OF THE GOODS OR SERVICES OBTAINED PURSUANT HERETO OR WITH THE PROCEEDS HEREOF. RECOVERY HEREUNDER BY THE DEBTOR SHALL NOT EXCEED AMOUNTS PAID BY THE DEBTOR HEREUNDER.

Where the seller arranges for a direct loan to be made to finance a customer's purchase, the seller may not accept the proceeds of the loan unless the consumer credit contract between the buyer and the lender contains the following clause in bold type:

NOTICE: ANY HOLDER OF THIS CONSUMER CREDIT CONTRACT IS SUBJECT TO ALL CLAIMS AND DEFENSES WHICH THE DEBTOR COULD ASSERT AGAINST THE SELLER OF GOODS OR SERVICES OBTAINED WITH THE PROCEEDS HEREOF. RECOVERY HEREUNDER BY THE DEBTOR SHALL NOT EXCEED AMOUNTS PAID BY THE DEBTOR HEREUNDER.

The effect of the clause is to make a potential holder of the note or contract subject to all claims and defenses of the consumer. If the clause is not put in a note or contract where it is required, the consumer does not gain any rights that he would not otherwise have under state law. Thus, if the clause is omitted from the note or contract, the subsequent holder might qualify as a holder in due course. However, the FTC does have the right to seek a fine of as much as $10,000 for each violation against the seller (e.g., each note or contract that fails to contain the required clause). The *De La Fuente* case, which follows, illustrates a situation where the clause required by the FTC was included in a note and served to preserve the makers' rights against a subsequent holder of the note.

The court decisions, new state laws, and the FTC regulations modifying the holder in due course doctrine are an effort to balance the societal interests (1) in protecting the consumer and (2) in assuring the availability of credit along with the marketability of commercial paper.

## De La Fuente v. Home Savings Association

### 38 UCC Rep. 196 (Tex. Ct. App. 1984)

Pedro and Paula de la Fuente were visited by a representative of Aluminum Industries, Inc., who was seeking to sell them aluminum siding for their home. They agreed to purchase the siding and signed a number of documents, including a retail installment contract and a promissory note for $9,138.24. The contract granted Aluminum Industries, Inc. a first lien on the de la Fuentes' residence; this was in violation of the Texas Civil Code, which prohibited such provisions. The promissory note contained a notice in bold type as required by the Federal Trade Commission. It read in part:

NOTICE: ANY HOLDER OF THIS CONSUMER CREDIT CONTRACT IS SUBJECT TO ALL CLAIMS AND DEFENSES WHICH THE DEBTOR COULD ASSERT AGAINST THE SELLER OF GOODS OR SERVICES OBTAINED PURSUANT HERETO OR WITH THE PROCEEDS THEREOF

Aluminum Industries assigned the promissory note and first lien to Home Savings Association. Aluminum Industries subsequently went out of business. Home Savings brought suit against the de la Fuentes to collect the balance due on the note. The trial court held that Home Savings was a holder in due course and that the de la Fuentes could not assert any defenses against it that they had against Aluminum Industries. They appealed.

**KENNEDY, JUDGE.** We disagree that Home Savings was entitled to the protection of a holder in due course of a negotiable instrument because the holder in due course doctrine has been abolished in consumer credit transactions by FTC regulations, and this FTC Rule, subjecting the holder of the notice to the claims and defenses of the debtor, is in direct conflict with the doctrine of the holder in due course. The federal courts have stated, without so holding, that the effect of this FTC Rule is to abolish the holder in due course doctrine in consumer transactions.

The FTC, in its Statement of Basis and Purpose, specifically named the holder in due course doctrine as the evil addressed by its Holder in Due Course Rule. "A consumer's duty to pay for goods and services must not be separated from a seller's duty to perform as promised." The FTC intended the Rule to compel creditors to either absorb the costs of the seller misconduct or return the contracts to the sellers. The FTC "reached a determination that it constitutes an unfair and deceptive practice to use contractual boiler plate to separate a buyer's duty to pay from a seller's duty to perform." The effect of this Rule is to "give the courts the authority to examine the equities in an underlying sale, and it will prevent sellers from foreclosing judicial review of their conduct. Sellers and creditors will be responsible for seller misconduct." It was clearly the intention of the FTC Rule to have the holder of the paper bear the losses occasioned by the actions of the seller; therefore, the benefits of the holder in due course doctrine under § 3–302 are not available when the notice required by the FTC is placed on a consumer credit contract.

Judgment reversed in favor of the de la Fuentes.

## SUMMARY

Negotiation is the transfer of an instrument in such a way that the person who receives it becomes a holder. A holder is a person who is in possession of an instrument that was issued to him, that has been indorsed to him or to his order, or that is payable to bearer. An instrument payable to a specific payee is called order paper; it can be negotiated by delivery after indorsement by the payee. An instrument payable to bearer or to cash is called bearer paper; it can be negotiated simply by delivering it to the person to whom its possessor wishes to transfer it.

The holder of an instrument makes an indorsement by signing his name on the instrument or on a paper firmly affixed to it. When an instrument is transferred, the transferee acquires all of the rights that his transferor had in the instrument. The transferee for value of an unindorsed order instrument has the right, unless otherwise agreed, to have the unqualified indorsement of his transferor.

There are four basic kinds of indorsements: (1) special, (2) blank, (3) restrictive, and (4) qualified. The first three have an effect on the negotiation of the instrument; the last affects the liability of the indorser who qualifies his indorsement.

To qualify as a holder in due course, the holder must take the instrument for value, in good faith, and without notice that it is overdue or has been dishonored or of any defense against or claim to it on the part of any other person. A payee may be a holder in due course. One who purchases a limited interest in an instrument can be a holder in due course only to the extent of the interest purchased.

A holder in due course of negotiable commercial paper takes free from the personal defenses existing between the parties but takes subject to the real defenses. These include: minority and other incapacities available as a defense to a simple contract; duress or illegality of the transaction, which renders the obligation a nullity; fraud in the essence; discharge in insolvency proceedings; and discharges of which he has notice.

A holder who is not a holder in due course takes negotiable commercial paper subject to all of the defenses that would be available to a promisor on a simple contract to pay money.

The holder in due course doctrine as it relates to negotiable instruments signed by consumers has been abolished or modified by new state laws and court decisions. In addition, a regulation promulgated by the Federal Trade Commission renders the doctrine inapplicable in certain consumer credit transactions.

## PROBLEM CASES

1. A check was indorsed "Pay to the order of any bank, banker, or trust company. All prior indorsements guaranteed." What type of indorsement is this? What is the effect of this type of indorsement?

2. Davy Crockett Inn purchased a cashier's check payable to Investments Universal from the Bank of New Braunfels. Investments Universal was supposed to hold the check until it did certain work for Davy Crockett Inn. Without performing that work, however, it deposited the check, without indorsement, in its account at the Main Bank. The Main Bank credited the check to Investments Universal's account, stamped the check "credited to account of within named payee, absence of indorsement guaranteed," and sent it to the Bank of New Braunfels, where it was paid. Davy Crockett Inn brought suit against the banks claiming that the check had been improperly paid without Investments Universal's indorsement. Is Davy Crockett's contention correct?

**3.** A note payable to Petroleum Equipment Leasing Company is indorsed on the reverse side as follows:

> Pay to Equipment Leasing of California, its successors or assigns,
> Petroleum Equipment Leasing Company by Richard L. Burns, President

The note is then assigned, without further indorsement, by Equipment Leasing to Security Pacific National Bank as security for a loan. What kind of indorsement was put on the check by Petroleum Equipment? Is the bank a holder?

**4.** Program Aids accepted a number of drafts payable to Bean. The drafts were given as payment in Bean's sale of catalogs for physical training equipment to Program Aids. Bean negotiated the drafts to Bank, which took them as a holder in due course; Bank later negotiated the drafts back to Bean. Bean brought suit against Program Aids on the drafts. Program Aids sought to defend on the ground that Bean had breached the sales contract by improperly preparing the catalogs. Bean claims that he is not subject to the personal defense in this action, because he is a transferee from a holder in due course and therefore has the rights of a holder in due course. Is Bean's claim a valid one?

**5.** A cashier's check was issued payable to the "order of X." X specially indorsed the check "Pay to Simone Travel Bureau, Inc., X" and turned the check over to Y, an employee of the travel agency. Y signed his name above the special indorsement and delivered it to University Funding Corporation. University Funding then deposited the check to its account at Hamburg Savings Bank. X complained that the money had never been paid to the travel agency. Hamburg Bank refunded the money to X and then debited University Funding's account. University Funding complains that this is improper and that it was a holder in due course of the check. Was it?

**6.** Two notes were indorsed by the payee and negotiated to a bank as security for a loan before they were overdue. The indorser was a regular depositor of the bank, and the loan was made to enable him to purchase a business. The bank made no inquiry regarding the origin of the notes and had no knowledge of the fact that they had been given in payment for stock in an oil company that had never been delivered. Is the bank a holder in due course?

**7.** Mancen, agent for World Wide Distributors, Inc., called on the Normans and outlined "a program for direct advertising" to them. He represented to them that if they purchased a breakfront, he would pay them \$5 for each letter they wrote to a friend requesting an appointment for World Wide's agent to explain the details of a sound advertising program and \$20 for each sale that World Wide made to any such person. Each friend was to be given the same opportunity to supply names. Mancen persuaded the Normans to sign, without reading, a purchase agreement and an attached judgment note in blank. After the note was signed and taken from the Normans' home, it was filled in for \$1,079.40 and made payable to "H. Waldran T/A State Wide Products" at the office of Peoples National Fund. The note was purchased by Peoples on January 25, 1961, for \$831, and judgment was entered on the note on February 7, 1961. World Wide was nowhere to be found. Within approximately a year, its principals had operated first as Carpet Industries, then as State Wide, and finally as World Wide Distributors. Peoples had dealt with all three companies, and its officers had knowledge of the referral plan. The referral plan was a fraudulent scheme based on an operation similar to the chain letter racket. Peoples claims that even though World Wide may have been guilty of fraud, Peoples can collect on the note because it is a holder in due course. Is Peoples a holder in due course?

**8.** Factor Cab Corporation issued a series of notes drawn payable to "the order of Donald E. Richel as attorney for Francisco Silvestry." Twenty-one of the notes were indorsed by Richel and his wife and sold to Maber, Inc. In purchasing the notes, Maber made its check payable to Richel in his individual name, without qualification or restriction, in the amount of $5,796.24. In addition, it discharged by payment Richel's personal indebtedness to a bank in the amount of $3,903.75. Richel and his wife indorsed the notes as individuals. Can Maber be a holder in due course of the notes?

**9.** Panlick, the owner of an apartment building, entered into a written contract with Bucci, a paving contractor, whereby Bucci was to install asphalt paving on the parking lot of the building. The paving job was completed in May 1975, and the full price was to have been paid upon completion. However, Panlick gave Bucci a check for $6,500 and a promissory note for $7,593 with interest at 10 percent due six months from its date. When the note came due, Panlick refused to pay it. Bucci brought suit to collect the note, and Panlick claimed that there was a failure of consideration because the asphalt was defectively installed. Can Panlick assert this defense against Bucci?

**10.** Blackburn acquired an automobile from Vanella and gave him a check in payment for it. Vanella indorsed the check and took it to Marine Midland Bank, which gave him cash and credit in his account for the check. Blackburn found out that Vanella had misrepresented to him that the automobile was free of liens, and so he stopped payment on the check. Marine Midland sued Blackburn as drawer of the check. Even though Blackburn admitted that Marine Midland was a holder in due course, he claimed that he had a defense of fraud good against even a holder in due course. Is Blackburn correct?

# Chapter 37

# Liability of Parties

## INTRODUCTION

Thus far in the chapters in this section, the focus has been the nature of and requirements for negotiable instruments, as well as the rights that a party to an instrument can obtain and how to obtain them. There is another important aspect to negotiable instruments; namely, how a person becomes liable on a negotiable instrument and the nature of the liability incurred.

When a person signs a promissory note, he expects to be liable for paying the note on the day it is due. Similarly, when a person signs a check and mails it off to pay a bill, he expects that it will be paid by the drawee bank out of his checking account and that if there are not sufficient funds in the account to cover it, he will have to make it good out of other funds he has. The liability of the maker of a note and of the drawer of a check is commonly understood.

However, a person can become liable on a negotiable instrument in other ways. A person who indorses a paycheck is assuming liability on it; and a bank that cashes a check with a forged indorsement on it is liable for conversion of the check. This chapter and the following chapter will discuss the liabilities of the various parties to a negotiable instrument. The two chapters will also cover what happens when an instrument is not paid when it is supposed to be paid. For example, a check may not be paid if there are insufficient funds in the drawer's account or if the check has been forged. This chapter will also discuss the ways in which liability on an instrument can be discharged.

## LIABILITY IN GENERAL

Liability may be based on the fact that a person has signed a negotiable instrument or has authorized someone else to sign it. In that case, the liability depends on the capacity in which the person has signed the instrument. Liability can also be based on (1) certain warranties that are made when an instrument is transferred or presented for payment, (2) negligence, (3) improper payment, or (4) conversion.

## CONTRACTUAL LIABILITY

When a person signs a negotiable instrument, whether as maker, drawer, or indorser, or in some other capacity, he generally becomes *contractually liable* on the instrument. This contractual liability depends on the *capacity* in which the person signed the instrument. The terms of the contract of the parties to a negotiable instrument are not written out on the instrument; these terms are supplied by Article 3 of the Uniform Commercial Code (Commercial Paper). The terms of the contract are provided by law and are as much a part of the instrument as if they were written on it.

**Primary and Secondary Liability.** A party to a negotiable instrument may be either *primarily liable* or *secondarily liable* for payment of it. A person who is primarily liable has agreed to pay the negotiable instrument. For example, the maker of a promissory note is the person who is primarily liable on the note. A person who is secondarily liable is like a guarantor on a contract and is required to pay the negotiable instrument only if a person who is primarily liable defaults on that obligation. Guarantors are discussed in Chapter 39.

**Contract of a Maker.** The maker of a promissory note is primarily liable for payment of it. The maker has made an unconditional promise to pay a sum certain and is responsible for making good on that promise. The *contract of the maker* is to *pay the negotiable instrument according to its terms at the time he signs it* [3–143].[1] If the material terms of the note are not complete when the maker signs it, then the maker's contract is that he will pay the note as it is completed, provided that the terms filled in are as authorized.

**Contract of a Drawee.** At the time a check (or other draft) is written, *no party is primarily liable on it.* Usually, a check is paid by the drawee bank when it is presented for payment and no person becomes primarily liable. However, the drawee bank may be asked by the drawer or by a holder of the check to certify the check. The drawee bank certifies the check by signing its name to the check and thereby "accepting" liability as drawee. The drawee bank debits (takes the money out of) the drawer's account and holds the money to pay the check. If the drawee bank certifies the check, it becomes primarily (absolutely) liable for paying the check as it reads at the time it is certified [3–413].

A drawee has no liability on a check (or other draft) unless it certifies or accepts

[1] The numbers in brackets refer to the sections of the Uniform Commercial Code.

(agrees to be liable on) the check. However, a drawee bank that refuses to pay a check when it is presented for payment may be liable to the drawer for wrongfully refusing payment, if the drawer had sufficient funds in his checking account to cover it. This liability of a drawee bank will be discussed in the next chapter.

**Contract of a Drawer.** The *drawer's contract* is that *if the check (or draft) is dishonored* and *if the drawer is given notice of the dishonor, he will pay the amount of the check (or draft) to the holder or to any indorser who takes it back* [3–413(2)]. For example, Janis draws a check on her account at First National Bank payable to the order of Collbert. If First National does not pay the check when Collbert presents it for payment, then Janis is liable to Collbert on the basis of her drawer's contractual liability.

Because a drawer's liability on a draft or check is secondary, she may *disclaim* this liability by drawing it *without recourse* [3–413(2)].

**Contract of an Indorser.** A person who indorses a negotiable instrument is usually secondarily liable. Unless the indorsement is qualified, the *indorser agrees* that *if the instrument is not paid when presented for payment, then the indorser will make it good to the holder or to any later indorser who had to pay it* [3–414]. The indorser can avoid this liability only by putting a qualified indorsement, such as "without recourse," on the instrument when he indorses it.

Indorsers are liable to each other in the chronological order in which they indorse, from the last indorser back to the first. For example, Mark Maker gives a promissory note to Paul Payee. Payee indorses it and negotiates it to Fred First, who indorses it and negotiates it to Shirley Second. If Maker does not pay the note when Shirley takes it to him for payment, then Shirley can require Fred to pay it to her. Fred is secondarily liable on the basis of his indorsement. Fred, in turn, can require Payee to pay him because Payee also became secondarily liable when he indorsed it. Then, Payee is left to try to collect the note from Maker. Shirley could also have skipped over Fred and gone directly against Payee on his indorsement. Fred has no liability to Payee, however, because Fred indorsed after Payee indorsed the note.

**Contract of an Accommodation Party.** An **accommodation party** is a person who signs a negotiable instrument for the purpose of lending his credit to another party to the instrument. For example, a bank might be reluctant to lend money to and take a note from Paul because of Paul's shaky financial condition. However, the bank may be willing to lend money to Paul if he signs the note and has a relative or a friend also sign the note as an accommodation maker.

The contractual liability of an accommodation party depends on the capacity in which the party signs the instrument [3–415]. If Paul has his brother Sam sign a note as an accommodation maker, then Sam has the same contractual liability as a maker. Sam is primarily liable on the note. The bank may ask Sam to pay the note before asking Paul to pay. However, if Sam pays the note to the bank, he has the right to recover his payment from Paul—the person on whose behalf he signed.

Similarly, if a person signs a check as an accommodation indorser, his contractual liability is that of an indorser. If the accommodation indorser has to make good on that liability, he can collect in turn from the person on whose behalf he signed.

**Signing an Instrument.** No person is contractually liable on a negotiable instrument unless his signature appears on the instrument. A **signature** can be any name, word, or mark used in place of a written signature [3–401]. A negotiable instrument can be signed either by a person or by an authorized agent. As discussed above, the capacity in which a person signs an instrument will affect his liability on the instrument.

In determining the capacity in which a person has signed a negotiable instrument, the position of the signature is important. If a person signs a check in the lower right-hand corner, the presumption is that he signed it as the drawer. If a person signs a promissory note in the lower right-hand corner, the presumption is that he signed it as the maker. If the drawee named in a draft signs across the face of the instrument, it is a clear indication that he has "accepted" the draft; however, his signature on any part of the instrument, front or back, will be held to be an acceptance in the absence of credible evidence of an intent to sign in some other capacity. A signature on the back of an instrument is presumed to be an indorsement [3–402].

**Signature by an Authorized Agent.** A negotiable instrument can be signed by an authorized agent [3–403(1)]. If Sandra Smith authorized her attorney to sign checks as her agent, then she is liable on any checks properly signed by the attorney as her agent. All negotiable instruments signed by corporations have to be signed by an agent of the corporation who is authorized to sign negotiable instruments.

If an agent or a representative signs a negotiable instrument on behalf of someone else, the agent should clearly indicate that he is signing as the representative of someone else. For example, Kim Darby, the president of Swimwear, Inc., is authorized to sign negotiable instruments for the company. If Swimwear borrows money from the bank and is given a 90-day promissory note to sign, Darby should sign it either "Swimwear, Inc. by Kim Darby, President" or "Kim Darby, President, for Swimwear, Inc." Similarly, if Arthur Anderson, an attorney, is authorized to sign checks for Clara Carson, he should sign them "Clara Carson by Arthur Anderson, Agent." Otherwise, he risks being personally liable on them.

The agents or representatives who sign negotiable instruments are *personally liable* if they do not indicate that they are signing in a representative capacity and if they do not state the name of the person on whose behalf they are signing [3–403(2)]. Thus, if Kim Darby signed the promissory note merely "Kim Darby," she would be personally liable on the note. To protect herself and to ensure that the corporation will be the person liable, Darby should sign the name of the company and her title or office as well as her signature. In the *Schwartz v. Disneyland and Vista Records* case which follows, the president of a company was held personally liable on some notes he signed for the corporation because he failed to indicate that he was signing in a representative capacity.

If an authorized representative signs a negotiable instrument in his own name in a way that clearly indicates that he has signed in a representative capacity, but he fails to name the person represented, *parol evidence* is admissible, between the immediate parties to the instrument, to prove that they intended the principal to be liable and not the party who signed in the representative capacity. For example, if a negotiable instrument is signed "Axe, agent" and retained by the payee, who then sues Axe on the instrument, parol evidence would be admitted in a lawsuit to prove that the payee knew that Axe was acting as agent for Parks, his principal, and that the parties intended Parks to be bound rather than Axe. However, if this instrument had been negotiated to a holder in due course, Axe would be personally liable on the instrument and would be unable to use parol evidence to disprove his liability [3–403(2)].

Some state courts, albeit a minority, have declined to hold corporate officers personally liable on corporate checks they signed without indicating they were signing in a representative capacity. Typically, these courts have found that because the checks in question were imprinted with the corporation's name, the circumstances disclosed that the individuals signed as representatives. The *Valley National Bank v. Cook* case, which follows, is an example of a court that followed the minority rule.

If a negotiable instrument is signed in the name of an organization and the name of the organization is preceded or followed by the name and office of an authorized individual, the organization and not the officer who signed the instrument in a representative capacity will be bound [3–403(3)].

**Unauthorized Signature.** If a person's name is signed to a negotiable instrument without that person's authorization or approval, the person is not bound by the signature. For example, if Tom Thorne steals Ben Brown's checkbook and signs Brown's name to a check, Brown is not liable on the check, because Thorne was not authorized to sign Brown's name. Thorne is liable on the check, however, because he did sign it, even though he did not sign it in his own name. Thorne's forgery of Brown's signature operates as Thorne's signature [3–404].

## Schwartz v. Disneyland Vista Records

### 383 So. 2d 1117 (Fla. Ct. App. 1980)

American Music Industries, Inc. and Disneyland Vista Records had ongoing business dealings during 1975 and 1976. As of May 21, 1976, American owed Disneyland over $93,000. As evidence of that indebtedness, 10 promissory notes were issued, payable to Disneyland and signed by Irv Schwartz, the president of American Music. The notes contained no reference to American Music Industries, Inc., nor was there any indication that Schwartz signed in a representative capacity.

American paid four of the notes, then defaulted on the rest. Disneyland brought suit against Schwartz to recover on the remaining six promissory notes. Schwartz claimed that the notes had been prepared by Disneyland; that they did not correctly reflect the intent of the parties, because they did not name American as the maker; and that he signed the notes individually by mistake. The trial court ruled in favor of Disneyland, and Schwartz appealed.

**Downey, Judge.** Summary judgment against Schwartz was proper because his claim is controlled by § 3–403(2):

(2) An authorized representative who signs his own name to an instrument:
  (a) Is personally obligated if the instrument neither names the person represented nor shows that the representative signed in a representative capacity;
  (b) Except as otherwise established between the immediate parties, is personally obligated if the instrument names the person represented but does not show that the representative signed in a representative capacity.

The notes in question are payable to Disneyland and signed by Irv Schwartz. There is no indication that they are obligations of the corporation, American Music Industries, Inc., or that Irv Schwartz signed them in a representative capacity. Thus, under Section (2)(a), above, Irv Schwartz is liable on these notes as a matter of law.

The main thrust of Schwartz's defense is that he should be allowed to use parol evidence to show the parties intended the notes to be corporate obligations and that Schwartz's signing individually was a mistake. However, the evidence is not admissible to "disestablish" obligations such as the notes here involved. Paraphrased, the example used in the comment indicates the results that various signatures have upon the individual liability of an agent. If American Music Industries, Inc., is a principal and Irv Schwartz is its agent, a note might bear the following signatures affixed by the agent:

(a) American Music Industries, Inc.;
(b) Irv Schwartz;
(c) American Music Industries, Inc., by Irv Schwartz, agent;
(d) Irv Schwartz, Agent;
(e) American Music Industries, Inc., Irv Schwartz.

A signature in form (a) does not bind Irv Schwartz if authorized. A signature as in (b) personally obligates Irv Schwartz, and parol evidence is inadmissible under § 3–403(2)(a) to disestablish his obligation. The unambiguous way to make clear that Irv Schwartz is signing in his representative capacity without personal liability is to sign as in (c).

Judgment for Disneyland affirmed.

---

## Valley National Bank v. Cook

### 36 UCC Rep. 578 (Ariz. Ct. App. 1983)

J. M. Cook, then treasurer of Arizona Auto Auction, signed three corporate checks totaling $9,795 payable to Central Motors Company, which deposited them in its corporate account at Valley National Bank. Cook did not indicate on the check that she was signing as a representative of Arizona Auto Auction. When Valley National Bank sent the checks to the drawee bank, payment was refused because a stop payment order had been put on them. Valley National Bank charged back the checks to the account of Central Motors, but it was unable to recover the money from Central Motors.

Valley National Bank then brought suit against Arizona Auto Auction and J. M. Cook. The trial court held that the bank was a holder in due course, that Arizona Auto Auction was liable to the bank, and that J. M. Cook was not personally liable on the checks. The bank appealed the portion of the decision in favor of Cook.

**Corcoran, Presiding Judge.** The issue raised in this appeal is whether an individual who signs a check without indicating her representative capacity is personally liable on the obligation evidenced by the check when the check has the name of the corporate principal printed on it. We adopt the minority rule and hold that the individual is not personally liable.

The question of whether Cook signed in her individual or representative capacity is governed by § 3–403 of the Uniform Commercial Code as adopted in this state. It provides:

A. A signature may be made by an agent or other representative, and his authority to make it may be established as in other cases of representation. No particular form of appointment is necessary to establish such authority.

B. An authorized representative who signs his own name to an instrument:

1. Is personally obligated if the instrument neither names the person represented nor shows that the representative signed in a representative capacity;
2. Except as otherwise established between the immediate parties, is personally obligated if the instrument names the person represented but does not show that the representative signed in a representative capacity, or if the instrument does not name the person represented but does show that the representative signed in a representative capacity.

C. Except, as otherwise established the name of an organization preceded or followed by the name and office of an authorized individual is a signature made in a representative capacity.

The Bank argues that this section conclusively establishes Cook's personal liability on the checks. We do not agree. Admittedly, the checks fail to specifically show the office held by Cook. However, we do not find that this fact conclusively establishes liability since § 3–403(B)(2) imposes personal liability on an agent who signs his or her own name to an instrument only "if the instrument . . . does not show that the representative signed in a representative capacity." Thus, we must look to the entire instrument for evidence of the capacity of the signer.

The checks are boldly imprinted at the top "Arizona Auto Auction, Inc.," and also "Arizona Auto Auction, Inc." is imprinted above the signature line appearing at the lower right-hand corner. Under the imprinted name of Arizona Auto Auction appears the signature of Cook without any designation of office or capacity on each of the checks before us. Cook did not indorse the checks on the back. The record does not reflect that Cook made any personal guaranty of these checks or any other corporate obligation.

The Superior Court of Pennsylvania was confronted with a similar situation in *Pollin v. Mindy Mfg. Co., Inc.* There the court denied recovery by a third-party indorsee against one who affixed his signature to a payroll check directly beneath the printed corporate name without indicating his representative capacity. In *Pollin* the checks were boldly imprinted at the top with the corporate name, address, and appropriate check number. The printed name of the drawee bank appeared in the lower left-hand corner of the instrument, and the corporate name was imprinted in the lower right-hand corner. Directly beneath the corporate name were two blank lines. The officer had signed the top line without any designation of office or capacity. Pointing out that the Code imposes liability on the individual only when the instrument controverts any showing of representative capacity, the court considered the instrument in its entirety. The court in *Pollin* held that disclosure on the face of the instrument that the checks were payable from a special payroll account of the corporation over which the officer had no control as an individual negated any contention that the officer intended to make the instrument his own order to pay money to the payee.

In this case the checks clearly show the name of the corporation in two places and the money was payable from the account of Arizona Auto Auction, Inc., over which Cook as an individual had no control. Considering the instruments as a whole, we conclude under these circumstances that they sufficiently disclose that Cook signed them in a representative and not an individual capacity.

Judgment for Cook affirmed.

## CONTRACTUAL LIABILITY IN OPERATION

To bring the contractual liability of the various parties to a negotiable instrument into play, it is generally necessary that the instrument be *presented for payment.* In addition, to hold the parties that are secondarily liable on the instrument to their contractual liability, it is generally necessary that the instrument be *presented for payment* and *dishonored.*

**Presentment of a Note.** The maker of a note is primarily liable to pay it when it is due. Normally, the holder takes the note to the maker at the time it is due and asks the maker to pay it. Sometimes, the maker sends the payment to the holder at the due date. The party to whom **presentment** is made may, without dishonoring the instrument, require the exhibition of the instrument, reasonable identification of the person making presentment, and evidence of his authority to make it if he is making it for another person [3–505]. If the maker pays the note, he is entitled to have the note marked "paid" or "canceled" or to have it returned so that it can be destroyed.

If the maker does not pay a note when it is presented at its due date, the note has been **dishonored** [3–507(1)]. If the note is dishonored, the holder can seek payment from any persons who indorsed the note before the holder took it. The basis for going after the indorsers is that they are secondarily liable on it. To hold the indorsers to their contractual liability, the holder must give notice of the dishonor. The notice can be either written or oral [3–508].

For example, Susan Strong borrows $100 from Jack Jones and gives him a promissory note for $100 at 9 percent annual interest payable in 90 days. Jones indorses the note "Pay to the order of Ralph Smith" and negotiates the note to Ralph Smith. At the end of the 90 days, Smith takes the note to Strong and presents it for payment. If Strong pays Smith the $100 and accrued interest, she can have Smith mark it "paid" and give it back to her. If Strong does not pay the note to Smith when he presents it for payment, then the note has been dishonored. Smith should give notice of the dishonor to Jones and advise him that he intends to hold Jones secondarily liable on his indorsement. Smith is entitled to collect payment of the note from Jones. Jones, after making the note good to Smith, can try to collect the note from Strong on the ground that she defaulted on the contract she made as maker of the note. Of course, Smith could also sue Strong on the basis of her maker's liability.

**Presentment of a Check or a Draft.** A check or draft should be presented to the drawee. The presentment can be either for payment or for acceptance (certification) of the check or draft. *No one is primarily liable on a check or draft,* and the *drawee is not liable on a check or draft unless it accepts (certifies) it.* An acceptance of a draft is the drawee's signed commitment to honor the draft as presented. The acceptance must be written on the draft, and it may consist of the drawee's signature alone [3–410].

A drawer who writes a check is issuing an order to the drawee to pay a certain amount out of the drawer's account to the payee (or to someone authorized by the payee). This order is *not* an assignment of the funds in the drawer's account [3–409]. The drawee bank does not have an obligation to the payee to pay the check unless it has certified the check. However, the drawee bank usually does have a contractual obligation to the drawer to pay any properly payable checks for which funds are available in the drawer's account.

For example, Janet Payne has $100 in a checking account at First National Bank and writes a check for $10 drawn on First National and payable to Ralph Smith. The writing of the check is the issuance of an order by Payne to First National to pay $10 from her account to Smith or to whomever Smith requests it to be paid. First National owes no obligation to Smith to pay the $10 unless it has certified the check. However, if Smith presents the check for payment and First National refuses to pay it even though there are sufficient funds in Payne's account, then First National is liable to Payne for breaching its contractual obligation to her to pay items properly payable from existing funds in her account. The liability of a bank for wrongful dishonor of checks will be discussed in more detail in Chapter 38.

If the drawee bank does not pay or certify a check when it is properly presented for payment or acceptance (certification), the check has been **dishonored** [3–507]. The holder of the check can then proceed against either the drawer of the check or any indorsers on their secondary liability. To do so, the holder must give them **notice** of the dishonor [3–508].

Suppose Matthews draws a check for $100 on his account at a bank payable to the order of Williams. Williams indorses the check "Pay to the order of Clark, Williams" and negotiates it to Clark. When Clark takes the check to the bank, it refuses to pay the check because there are insufficient funds in Matthews's account to cover the check. The check has been presented and dishonored. Clark has two options. He can proceed against Williams on Williams's secondary liability as an indorser because by putting an unqualified indorsement on the check, Williams contracted to make the check good if it was not honored by the drawee. Or he can proceed against Matthews on Matthews's drawer's contractual liability because in drawing the check, Matthews promised to make it good to any holder if it was dishonored and he was given notice. Because Clark dealt with Williams, Clark is probably more likely to return the check to Williams for payment. Williams will then have to go against Matthews on Matthews's contractual liability as drawer.

**Time of Presentment.** If an instrument is payable at a definite time, it should be presented for payment on the due date. In the case of a demand instrument, a reasonable time for presentment for acceptance or payment is determined by the nature of the instrument, by trade or bank usage, and by the facts of the particular case. In a farming community, for example, a reasonable time to present a promissory note that is payable on demand may be six months or within a short time after the crops are sold, because it is expected that the payment will be made from the proceeds of the crops.

A reasonable time to present a check to hold the drawer liable is presumed to be 30 days [3–503]. Delay in presentment may be excused where, for example, the party is without notice that the instrument is due, or where the delay is caused by circumstances beyond his control and he operates with reasonable diligence [3–511].

**Effect of Unexcused Delay in Presentment.** If presentment of a negotiable instrument is delayed beyond the time it is due, and if there is no valid excuse for the delay, then the indorsers are *discharged from liability* on the instrument. Under certain circumstances, a drawer or maker can also be discharged of liability if the bank in which the funds to pay the note or draft were deposited becomes insolvent during the delay [3–502(1)].

To be able to hold an indorser of a check liable, the check should be presented for payment within seven days after the indorser signed it. If the holder of the check waits longer than that without a valid excuse, the indorsers are relieved of their secondary liability and the holder's only recourse is against the drawer. The holder must give the indorsers timely notice of any dishonor.

## WARRANTY LIABILITY

Whether or not a person signs a negotiable instrument, a person who transfers such an instrument or presents it for payment may incur liability on the basis of certain implied warranties. These warranties are of two types: (1) **transferor's warranties,** which are made by persons who *transfer* negotiable instruments; and (2) **presentment warranties,** which are made by persons who *present* negotiable instruments *for payment or acceptance (certification).*

**Transferor's Warranties.** A *person who transfers a negotiable instrument* to someone else and receives something of value in exchange makes five *warranties* to his transferee:

1. That the person has *good title* to the instrument or is *authorized to obtain payment* by someone who has good title.
2. That *all signatures* on the instrument are *genuine or authorized.*
3. That the instrument has *not been materially altered.*
4. That *no party* to the instrument has a *valid defense* against the person who is transferring it.
5. That the person transferring the instrument has *no knowledge of any insolvency proceedings* against the maker, drawer, or acceptor [3–417(2)].

If the transfer is by indorsement, the warranties are made to any subsequent holder who takes the instrument in good faith.

While contractual liability often furnishes a sufficient basis for suing a transferor when the party primarily liable does not pay, warranties are still important. First, they apply even when the transferor did not indorse. Second, unlike contractual liability, they do not depend on presentment, dishonor, and notice, but may be utilized before presentment has been made or after the time for giving notice has expired. Third, it may be easier to return the instrument to a transferor on the ground of breach of warranty than to prove one's status as a holder in due course against a maker or drawer.

**Rule of Finality of Payment.** A person who presents a negotiable instrument for payment or a check to be certified makes a different set of warranties. Normally, the person to whom a negotiable instrument is presented for payment does not pay it unless he either is obligated to do so or is entitled to credit or payment from someone else if he does pay. For example, a drawee bank does not normally pay a check unless there are funds in the drawer's account. And it should know whether the signature on the check is that of its customer—the drawer of the check. If a drawee bank pays the check to a holder in due course, it cannot later get the money back from the holder in due course if it discovers that there are insufficient funds in the drawer's account. Payment is usually *final* in favor of a holder in due course or a person who in good faith changed his position in reliance on the payment [3–418] unless one of the three presentment warranties is broken.

**Presentment Warranties.** The three *warranties* that are made by a *person who is presenting an instrument for payment* are:

1. That the presenter has *good title* to the instrument or is *authorized to obtain payment* by someone who has good title.
2. That the presenter has *no knowledge*

*that the signature of the maker or drawer is unauthorized.*

3. That the instrument has *not been materially altered* [3–417(1)].

A holder in due course who presents a note to a maker does not warrant that the signature of the maker is valid or that the note has not been materially altered. The maker should recognize whether the signature on the note is his signature and whether the note has been altered. Similarly, a holder in due course does not warrant to the drawer of a check that the drawer's signature is valid or that the check has not been materially altered, because the drawer should recognize his signature and whether the check has been altered.

The *Miller v. Federal Deposit Insurance Corp.* case, which follows, illustrates when a warranty of good title is made—as well as how it is breached when the presenter does not have a complete chain of indorsements.

**Operation of Warranties.** Following are some examples that show how the transferor's and presentment warranties shift the liability back to a wrongdoer or to the person who dealt immediately with a wrongdoer and thus was in the best position to avert the wrongdoing.

Arthur makes a promissory note for $100 payable to the order of Betts. Carlson steals the note from Betts, indorses her name on the back, and gives it to Davidson in exchange for a television set. Davidson negotiates the note for value to Earle, who presents the note to Arthur for payment. Assume that Arthur refuses to pay the note because he has been advised by Betts that it has been stolen. Earle can then proceed to recover the face amount of the note from Davidson on the grounds that as a transferor Davidson has warranted that he had good title to the note and that all signatures were genuine. Davidson, in turn, can proceed against Carlson on the same basis—if he can find Carlson. If he cannot, then Davidson must bear the loss caused by Carlson's wrongdoing. Davidson was in the best position to ascertain whether Carlson was the owner of the note and whether the indorsement of Betts was genuine. Of course, even though Arthur does not have to pay the note to Earle, Arthur remains liable for his underlying obligation to Betts.

Anderson draws a check for $10 on her checking account at First Bank payable to the order of Brown. Brown cleverly raises the check to $110, indorses it, and negotiates it to Carroll. Carroll then presents the check for payment to First Bank, which pays her $110 and charges Anderson's account for $110. Anderson then asks the bank to recredit her account for the altered check, and it does so. The bank can proceed against Carroll for breach of the presentment warranty that the instrument had not been materially altered, which she implied to the bank when she presented the check for payment. Carroll in turn can proceed against Brown for breach of his transferor's warranty that the check had not been materially altered—if she can find him.

Bates steals Albers' checkbook and forges Albers' signature to a check for $10 payable to "cash," which he uses to buy $10 worth of groceries from a grocer. The grocer presents the check to Albers' bank, which pays the amount of the check to the grocer and charges Albers' account. Albers then demands that the bank recredit his account. The bank can recover against the grocer only if the grocer knew that Albers' signature had been forged. Otherwise, the bank must look for Bates. The bank had the responsibility to recognize the true signature of its drawer, Albers, and not to pay the check that contained an unauthorized signature. The bank, however, may be able to resist recrediting Albers' account if it can show he was negligent. Negligence is discussed in the next section of this chapter.

## Miller v. Federal Deposit Insurance Corp.

**34 UCC Rep. 1640 (Ariz. Ct. App. 1982)**

Doris Strahl was the payee on a check in the amount of $3,000 drawn on Pacific First Federal Savings and Loan (drawee) by Puget Sound National Bank (drawer). Peter Miller, the owner of a service station, replaced the engine in a motor home owned by Strahl. His charge for the new engine was $2,500. Strahl gave him the $3,000 check without indorsing it, and he gave her $500 change. On March 22, 1979, Miller deposited the check in his business account at Southwestern Bank, which sent it for payment to Puget Sound National Bank. Puget Sound returned the check to Southwestern Bank on May 17, 1979, on the ground that the absence of an indorsement by the payee, Doris Strahl, constituted a breach by Southwestern Bank of the presentment warranty of good title. Southwestern in turn charged back Miller's account. Since Miller had written checks on his account in the interim, the charge-back resulted in his account being overdrawn. Miller brought suit against Southwestern Bank challenging the charge-back. The trial court found in favor of the bank, and Miller appealed.

**HOWARD, CHIEF JUDGE.** The purpose of the warranty of good title is to speed up the collection and transfer of checks and to take the burden off each bank to meticulously check the indorsement of each item transferred. "The theory is that the first bank in the chain has the duty to make certain all indorsements are valid; banks subsequently taking the paper have a right to rely on the forwarding bank." The warranty of good title involves a very limited inquiry: Does the instrument presented contain all necessary indorsements and are such indorsements genuine or otherwise deemed effective?

Was the indorsement of Doris Strahl necessary? UCC § 3–201(3) provides:

> Unless otherwise agreed any transfer for value of an instrument not then payable to the bearer gives the transferee the specifically enforceable right to have the unqualified indorsement of the transferor. Negotiation takes effect only when the indorsement is made and until that time there is no presumption that the transferee is the owner.

Since the check here was payable to order, the foregoing statute applies and the indorsement of Doris Strahl was necessary in order to negotiate it. We conclude that it was a necessary indorsement and that there was a breach of warranty of good title which allowed Puget Sound to revoke its settlement and which allowed Southwestern, in turn, to charge back the provisional credit it gave Miller.

Judgment in favor of Southwestern Bank affirmed.

## OTHER LIABILITY RULES

Normally, a check that has a forged indorsement of the payee may not be charged to the drawer's checking account. Similarly, a maker does not have to pay a note to the person who currently possesses the note if the payee's signature has been forged. And if a check or note has been materially altered, for example, if the amount has been raised, the drawer or maker is usually liable only for the instrument as it was originally written.

**Negligence.** A person can be so negligent in writing or signing a negotiable instrument that he in effect invites an alteration or an unauthorized signature on it. If a person has been negligent, he is not able to use the alteration or lack of authorization as a reason for not paying a holder in due course. A person is also not able to use the alteration or lack of authorization to claim that a payment was improperly made by a bank if the bank paid the item in good faith and in accordance with reasonable commercial standards [3–406].

For example, Diane Drawer makes out a check for $1 in such a way that someone could easily alter it to read $101. The check is so altered and is negotiated to Katherine Smith, who can qualify as a holder in due course. Smith will be able to collect $101 from Drawer. Drawer will not be able to claim alteration as a defense to paying it, because of her negligence in making the alteration possible. Drawer then has to find the person who "raised" her check and try to collect the $100 from him.

The *Leonard* case, which follows, vividly illustrates a drawer's carelessness in drawing a check so that it could be raised from $600 to $3600. The drawer then had to bear the loss caused by negligence.

**Impostor Rule.** The Code establishes special rules for negotiable instruments made payable to *impostors* and *fictitious persons.* An **impostor** is a *person who poses as someone else* and *convinces a drawer to make a check payable to the person being impersonated.* When this happens, the Code makes any indorsement in the name of the impersonated person effective [3– 405(1)(a)]. For example, suppose that Arthur steals Paulsen's automobile. Arthur finds the certificate of title in the automobile and then, representing himself to be Paulsen, sells the automobile to Berger Used Car Company. The car company draws its check payable to Paulsen for the agreed purchase price of the automobile and delivers the check to Arthur. Any person can negotiate the check by indorsing it in the name of Paulsen.

The rationale for the impostor rule is to put the responsibility for determining the true identity of the payee on the drawer of a check. The drawer is in a better position to do this than some later holder of the check, who may be entirely innocent. The impostor rule allows that later holder to have good title to the check by making the payee's signature valid even though it is a forgery. It forces the drawer to go after the wrongdoer who tricked him into signing the check.

The *Philadelphia Title Insurance Co.* case, which follows, illustrates the operation of the impostor rule. As you read the case, you might ask yourself what the title company should have done to protect itself.

**Fictitious Payee Rule.** A **fictitious payee** commonly arises in the following situation. A dishonest employee draws checks payable to someone who does not exist or to a person who does not do business with his employer. If the employee has the authority to do so, he may sign the check himself. If he does not have such authority, he presents the check to his employer for signature and represents that the employer owes money to the person to whom the check is made payable. The dishonest employee then takes the check, indorses it in the name of the payee, presents it for payment, and pockets the money. The employee may be in a position to cover up the wrongdoing by intercepting the canceled checks and/or juggling the company's books.

The Code allows any indorsement in the name of the fictitious payee to be effective as the payee's indorsement [3–405(1)(b) and (c)]. For example, Anderson, who is employed by Moore Corporation as an accountant in charge of accounts payable, prepares a false invoice naming Parks, Inc., a supplier of Moore Corporation, as having supplied Moore Corporation with goods, and draws a check payable to Parks, Inc. for the amount of the invoice. Anderson then presents the check to Temple, treasurer of Moore Corporation, together with other checks with invoices attached, all of which Temple signs and returns to Anderson for mailing. Anderson then withdraws the check payable to Parks, Inc. Anyone, including Anderson, can negotiate the check by indorsing it in the name of Parks, Inc.

The rationale for the fictitious payee rule is similar to that for the impostor rule. If someone has a dishonest employee or agent who is responsible for the forgery of some checks, the immediate loss of those checks should rest on the employer of the wrongdoer rather than on some other innocent party. In turn, the employer must locate the unfaithful employee or agent and try to recover from him.

**Conversion.** **Conversion** of an instrument is an *unauthorized assumption and exercise of ownership* over it. A negotiable instrument can be converted in a number of ways. For example, it might be presented for payment or acceptance, and the person to whom it is presented might refuse to pay, accept, or return it. An instrument is also converted if a person pays an instrument on a forged indorsement [3–419]. Thus, if a check that contains a forged indorsement is paid by a bank, the bank has converted the check by wrongfully paying it. The bank then becomes liable for the face amount of the check to the person whose indorsement was forged [3–419].

For example, Arthur Able draws a check for $50 on his account at First Bank, payable to the order of Bernard Barker. Carol Collins steals the check, forges Barker's indorsement on it, and cashes it at First Bank. First Bank has converted Barker's property, because it had no right to pay the check without Barker's valid indorsement. First Bank must pay Barker $50, and then it can try to locate Collins to get the $50 back from her. In the *O.K. Moving & Storage Co.* case, which follows, a bank was held liable for conversion because it paid checks containing forged payees' indorsements.

## Leonard v. National Bank of West Virginia

**145 S.E.2d 23 (W. Va. Sup. Ct. 1965)**

On August 3, 1961, J. P. Leonard made out a check for $600, signed it as drawer, and indorsed his signature on the back of the check. He did not date the check, nor did he fill in the payee's name. Leonard claimed that he gave the check to a man named Santo, to whom he owed $600, and that he indorsed the check on the back so that Santo could cash it "at the track." When the check was returned to Leonard by the

National Bank of West Virginia after it had charged the check to his account, "Thrity" [*sic*] had been written in front of "Six hundred," the name Martin Mattson had been entered as payee, and the indorsement of Martin Mattson appeared on the back of the check above Leonard's signature. Leonard then sued National Bank to have his account recredited for $3,600. The trial court found in favor of Leonard and the bank appealed.

**BERRY, JUSTICE.** The general rule with regard to altered or raised checks is that if a bank pays such checks it does so at its peril and can only debit the drawer's account for the amount of the check as originally drawn, but there is an exception in the case of altered or raised checks to the effect that if the altering or raising of the check is because of the carelessness of the maker or depositor, the bank cannot be held liable in such case.

It is clear from the evidence in this case and from the check, which was introduced into evidence as an exhibit, that the name of the payee was left blank, that the amount of the check opposite the dollar sign was left blank and a 1½-inch space to the left of the words "Six hundred" was left blank, and that Leonard's signature on the back of the check as an indorser left a blank space of one inch from the top of the check. As the check was drawn, the blank space for the payee's name could have been made to "cash," any amount could have been placed in the space for the figure opposite the dollar sign and more than enough room was left for words to be filled in before the words "Six hundred" in order to alter or raise this check, and all of such blank spaces were filled up in such manner that they could not easily arouse the suspicions of a careful person. It has been repeatedly held in such cases that the drawer is barred from recovery.

The check in question was drawn in such manner that it could be readily raised or altered and such changes could not be detected by the use of ordinary care. In fact, the carelessness of the drawing of the check in question would amount to gross negligence and Leonard would be estopped from any recovery if his were the only negligence involved, because such action on his part would amount to negligence as a matter of law.

However, it has been held that the negligence of a depositor in drawing a check which can be altered does not render him liable if the bank fails to exercise due care in paying such check, but if the drawer's carelessness is the proximate cause of the payment of such altered check on the part of the bank, the bank is not liable.

The negligence which Leonard endeavors to charge the bank with in connection with this transaction is almost entirely based on evidence introduced by Leonard to the effect that the bank was negligent in not having the person who presented the check to the bank for payment identified as the named payee and indorser on the check, Martin Mattson. There is no evidence in this case that the person who presented the check was not Martin Mattson, the named payee and also the person who indorsed the check above the indorsement of Leonard. It would therefore appear that the question as to whether the bank was guilty of negligence in not having Martin Mattson identified would be immaterial in this case when it was not proved that the signature was a forgery, and further the evidence indicated that the bank did perform some identification procedure in this instance.

Leonard also contends that the bank was negligent in not having the person who presented the check indorse it after the indorsement of J. P. Leonard. The signature in question speaks for itself, and the more than sufficient space for indorsement of a payee above the name of Leonard's signature on the back of the check would constitute negligence on the part of Leonard for having left such space above his indorsement, and the bank could not be charged with negligence in such instance. Leonard further stated that he indorsed the check on the back in order that it could be cashed at the track, which would clearly show his intention that the check could be cashed without difficulty, and the fact that he did indorse the check in blank and it was the last indorsement on the back thus made the check easily cashed without difficulty on the part of any person who presented it, because it made the check a bearer check payable on delivery.

The only other matter in which the bank could be charged with negligence in connection with the cashing of the check in question was the word evidently intended as "thirty" which appeared before the words "Six hundred" in a misspelled form as "Thrity." However, the writing is very similar to the words "Six hundred," which the jury found was in the handwriting of Leonard.

Judgment reversed in favor of National Bank of West Virginia.

---

## Philadelphia Title Insurance Co. v. Fidelity-Philadelphia Trust Co.

**212 A.2d 222 (Pa. Sup. Ct. 1965)**

Mrs. Jezemski was separated from her husband and decided to obtain some money from him by having a mortgage placed on some property that her husband held as administrator and heir of his mother's estate and taking the proceeds herself. She went to a lawyer, McAllister, with a gentleman whom she introduced as her husband, and they made out a bond and mortgage on her husband's land. Then, she went to a title insurance company, Philadelphia Title Insurance Company, which under Philadelphia custom took care of placing mortgages on property and paying the proceeds to the mortgagor. She told Philadelphia Title's representatives that her husband was too busy to come in that day but that her husband's signature on the mortgage had been witnessed by her lawyer. Philadelphia Title then placed a mortgage on the property and gave Mrs. Jezemski a check made payable to Edmund and Paula Jezemski and Edmund Jezemski as administrator for his mother's estate. Mrs. Jezemski then forged her husband's indorsement on the check and negotiated it to a bank. Eventually, the check was paid by Fidelity-Philadelphia Trust Company, the drawee, which then charged the check to Philadelphia Title's account.

Philadelphia Title brought a lawsuit against Fidelity-Philadelphia to have its account recredited. Philadelphia Title argued that one of the payees' signature had been forged, so that the check was not properly payable by Fidelity-Philadelphia. The trial court held for Fidelity-Philadelphia, and Philadelphia Title appealed.

**Cohen, Justice.** The parties do not dispute the proposition that as between payor bank (Fidelity-Philadelphia) and its customer, Philadelphia Title, ordinarily, the former must bear the loss occasioned by the forgery of a payee's indorsement (Edmund Jezemski) upon a check drawn by its customer and paid by it, § 3–414. The latter provides that "(1) Any unauthorized signature [Edmund Jezemski's] is wholly inoperative as that of the person whose name is signed unless he ratifies it or is precluded from denying it."

However, Fidelity-Philadelphia argues that this case falls within an exception to the above rule, making the forged indorsement of Edmund Jezemski's name effective so that Fidelity-Philadelphia was entitled to charge the account of its customer, the Philadelphia Title, which was the drawer of the check. The exception asserted by Fidelity-Philadelphia is found in § 3–405(1)(a), which provides:

> An indorsement by any person in the name of a named payee is effective if (a) an impostor by the use of the mails or otherwise has induced the maker or drawer to issue the instrument to him or his confederate in the name of the payee.

The lower court found and Philadelphia Title does not dispute that an impostor appeared before McAllister (attorney), impersonated Mr. Jezemski, and, in his presence, signed Mr. Jezemski's name to the deed, bond and mortgage; that Mrs. Jezemski was a confederate of the impostor; that the drawer, Philadelphia Title, issued the check to Mrs. Jezemski naming her and Mr. Jezemski as payees; and that some person other than Mr. Jezemski indorsed his name on the check.

Judgment for Fidelity-Philadelphia affirmed.

---

## O.K. Moving & Storage Co. v. Elgin National Bank

**363 So. 2d 160 (Fla. Dist. Ct. App. 1978)**

Raye Walker was a bookkeeper for O.K. Moving & Storage Company. She opened a checking account in her name at Elgin National Bank. She then took checks that were made payable to O.K. Moving & Storage, indorsed them "For Deposit Only, O.K. Moving & Storage Co., 80 Carson Drive, N.E., Fort Walton, Florida," and deposited them in her individual account at Elgin National Bank. In a period of one year, she deposited, and Elgin National Bank accepted for deposit to her account, checks totaling $19,356.01. When O.K. Moving & Storage discovered this, it sued Elgin National Bank for $19,356.01 for conversion of its checks. O.K. Moving & Storage claimed that the checks were improperly charged to its checking account, because the payee's indorsement had been forged. The trial court held that the bank was liable for only a portion of the checks deposited by Walker to her account. O.K. Moving & Storage appealed.

**MELVIN, JUDGE.** We note the finding of the trial court that there was no evidence that O.K. Moving & Storage had any contract of any nature with Elgin National Bank that would have induced the bank to open an account, accept the deposits, or deposit the same in the manner in which they were deposited. The issue here is whether the failure of O.K. Moving & Storage to discover that the checks that had been restrictively indorsed and had been wrongfully deposited into the account of its employee over a period of approximately 13 months constituted negligence that would limit O.K. Moving & Storage's recovery in its action against Elgin National Bank.

Elgin National Bank argues that the conversion of O.K. Moving & Storage's funds continued over such a long period of time that O.K. Moving & Storage should have discovered such embezzlement and its failure to discover constituted negligence that reduces the liability of the bank.

O.K. Moving & Storage committed no act that would cause Elgin National Bank to accept the restrictively indorsed instruments and deposit the same into the account of the O.K. Moving & Storage employee. Having committed no such act of inducement, there is no negligence on the part of O.K. Moving & Storage that proximately caused Elgin National Bank to conduct its operation as it did. In *Fargo National Bank v. Massey-Ferguson, Inc.* (8th Cir. 1968), the court held:

> "Negligence of the payee effective to bar recovery must be such as directly and *proximately* affects the conduct of the bank, contributing to and inducing its acceptance of the forged endorsement itself."

The court further held that the unbusinesslike manner in which the company conducted its affairs and lack of careful supervision over employees were facts too remote from the bank's acceptance of the forged indorsements to be the proximate cause of loss resulting from such indorsements.

Elgin National Bank leans upon the provision of Section 4–103(5), which in part provides:

> The measure of damages for failure to exercise ordinary care in handling an item is the amount of the item reduced by an amount which could not have been realized by the use of ordinary care.

Under the facts in this case, the provision of the statute quoted would have no application because of a complete absence of any act on the part of the payee to induce the bank to accept any one of the restrictively indorsed checks. In *Miami Beach First National Bank v. Edgerly,* the Florida Supreme Court held:

> It is the unconditional duty of the bank to pay the money only to the payee, or his order, and it is the responsibility of the bank solely to determine the genuineness of the indorsement and identity of the person presenting the check for payment.

Earlier, the same court held in *Lewis State Bank v. Raker:*

> A bank, paying a check upon the unauthorized indorsement of the payee and charging the amount thereof to the drawer's account, becomes liable to the payee for the amount of such check, unless the conduct of the payee excuses such payment, or prevents him from asserting such liability.

See also 49 ALR3d 843, Forgery by Debtor's Agent—Discharge, wherein the prevailing rule in the United States is stated to be:

> The right of the unpaid creditor to proceed directly against the collecting or drawee banks now appears to be clearly established. The drawee bank's payment of the check on a forged indorsement constitutes a conversion of the instrument as to the payee; and this view has been adopted by Uniform Commercial Code § 3–419(1)(c). Likewise, it is generally said that a bank which has obtained possession of a check upon an unauthorized or forged indorsement of the payee's signature, and has collected the amount of the check from the drawee, is liable for the proceeds to the payee or other owner, notwithstanding that the proceeds have been paid to the person from whom the check was obtained, and notwithstanding that the payee's signature was forged by his employee or agent, such cases taking the view that possession of the check on the forged or unauthorized indorsement is wrongful, and that when the money has been collected on the check, the bank can be held as for money had and received or in action for conversion.

Judgment reversed in favor of O.K. Moving & Storage for the total amount of checks accepted by Elgin National Bank, namely $19,356.01, together with interest.

## DISCHARGE OF NEGOTIABLE INSTRUMENTS

**Discharge of Liability.** Generally, all parties to a negotiable instrument are *discharged* (relieved from liability) when the person who is primarily liable on it pays the amount in full to a holder of the instrument. Any person is discharged of his liability to the extent that the person pays the holder of the instrument [3–603]. For example, Anderson makes a check for $75 payable to the order of Bruce. Bruce indorses the check "Pay to the order of Carroll, Bruce" and negotiates it to Carroll. Carroll takes the check to Anderson's bank, presents it for payment, and is paid $75 by the bank. The payment to Carroll discharges Bruce's secondary liability as indorser and Anderson's secondary liability as drawer.

A person is not discharged of liability if he pays someone who acquired the instrument by theft or from someone who had stolen it [3–603(1)(a)]. Also, if a negotiable instrument has been restrictively indorsed, the person who pays must comply with the restrictive indorsement in order to be discharged [3–603(1)(b)]. For example, Arthur makes a note of $100 payable to the order of Bryan. Bryan indorses the note "Pay to the order of my account no. 16154 at First Bank, Bryan." Bryan then gives the note to his employee, Clark, to take to the bank. Clark takes the note to Arthur, who pays Clark the $100. Clark then runs off with the money. Arthur is not discharged of his primary liability on the note because he did not make his payment consistent with the restrictive indorsement. In order to be discharged, Arthur has to pay the $100 into Bryan's account at First Bank.

**Discharge by Cancellation.** The holder of a negotiable instrument may discharge the liability of the parties to the instrument by *canceling* it. If the holder mutilates or destroys a negotiable instrument with the intent that it no longer evidence an obligation to pay money, it has been canceled [3–605]. For example, a grandfather lends $1,000 to his grandson for college expenses. The grandson gives his grandfather a promissory note for $1,000. If the grandfather later tears up the note with the intent that the grandson no longer owe him $1,000, the note has been canceled.

An accidental destruction or mutilation of a negotiable instrument is not a cancellation and does not discharge the parties to it. If an instrument is lost, accidentally mutilated, or destroyed, the holder can still enforce it. In such a case, the holder must prove that the instrument existed and that he was its holder when it was lost, mutilated, or destroyed.

**Discharge by Alteration.** Generally, a *fraudulent and material change* in a negotiable instrument discharges any party whose contract is changed [3–407(2)]. An alteration of an instrument is *material* if it *changes the contract of any of the parties to the instrument.* For example, if the amount due on a note is raised from $10 to $10,000, the contract of the maker has been changed. The maker promised to pay $10, but after the change has been made, he would be promising to pay much more. A change that does not affect the contract of one of the parties, such as dotting an *i* or correcting the grammar, is not material.

Assume that Anderson signs a promissory note for $100 payable to Bond. Bond indorses the note "Pay to the order of Connolly, Bond" and negotiates it to Connolly. Connolly changes the $100 to read $100,000. Connolly's change is unauthorized, fraudulent, and material. As a result, Anderson is discharged from her primary liability as maker of the note and Bond is discharged from her secondary liability as indorser. Neither of them has to pay Connolly. The contracts of both Anderson and Bond were changed because the amount that they had agreed to be liable for was altered.

The *Bluffestone* case, which follows, illustrates that a party will not be held responsible for an alteration to an instrument to which he did not consent.

There are exceptions to the general rule that a fraudulent and material alteration discharges parties whose contracts are changed. First, if in the above example Anderson was so negligent in writing the note that it could easily be altered, she cannot claim the alteration against a holder in due course of the note. Assume that Connolly indorsed the note "Connolly" and negotiated it to Davis, who qualifies as a holder in due course. If Davis was not aware of the alteration and it was not obvious, she could collect the $100,000 from Anderson. Anderson's only recourse would be to track down Connolly to try to get the difference between $100 and $100,000.

Second, a holder in due course who takes an instrument after it has been altered can enforce it for the original amount. When an incomplete instrument is completed after it leaves the drawer's or maker's hands, a holder in due course can enforce it as completed. For example, Swanson draws a check payable to Frank's Nursery, leaving the amount blank. He gives it to his gardener with instructions to purchase some fertilizer at Frank's and to fill in the purchase price of the fertilizer when it is known. The gardener fills in the check for $100 and gives it to Frank's in exchange for the fertilizer ($7.25) and the difference in cash ($92.75). The gardener then leaves town with the cash. If Frank's had no knowledge of the unauthorized completion, it could enforce the check for $100 against Swanson.

**Discharge by Impairment of Recourse.** If a party to an instrument has posted collateral to secure his performance and a holder surrenders the collateral without the consent of the parties who would benefit from the collateral, such parties are discharged [3–606].

## Bluffestone v. Abrahams

**27 UCC Rep. 1349 (Ariz. Ct. App. 1979)**

David Bluffestone lent money to Gary, Bert, and Lee Abrahams in connection with a car wash business that they operated together. When David died, his son-in-law, Alan Gilenko, came to help David's wife, Pearl, straighten out her financial affairs. He found a promissory note for $5,000 signed by Gary, Bert, and Lee Abrahams among David's possessions. At the time, the note did not have any provision for monthly payments or for attorney's fees. Gilenko added provisions for monthly payments and attorney's fees to the note. Bert and Lee Abrahams then re-signed the note with knowledge of the alterations. Gary did not sign the note again after the alterations had been made and did not have knowledge of them, but did make a subsequent $100 payment on the note.

When the Abrahams did not pay off the note, Pearl Bluffestone brought an action against Gary, Bert, and Lee to collect on the promissory note payable to her deceased husband. Gary Abrahams contended that he was not liable on the $5,000 note, because it had been materially altered without his consent or knowledge. The trial court awarded judgment to Bluffestone, and the Abrahams appealed.

**Howard, Judge.** The liability of Gary Abrahams on the $5,000 note presents a serious problem. The effect of the alteration of the $5,000 promissory note is governed by UCC § 3–407, which states:

A. Any alteration of an instrument is material which changes the contract of any party thereto in any respect, including any such change in:
1. The number or relations of the parties; or
2. An incomplete instrument, by completing it otherwise than as authorized; or
3. The writing as signed, by adding to it or by removing any part of it.

B. As against any person other than a subsequent holder in due course:
1. Alteration by the holder which is both fraudulent and material discharges any party whose contract is thereby changed unless that party assents or is precluded from asserting the defense;
2. No other alteration discharges any party and the instrument may be enforced according to its original tenor, or as to incomplete instruments according to the authority given.

Bluffestone contends that the evidence shows that the alterations were accomplished with Gary's knowledge and consent. She further contends that Gary's $100 payments on the note after alteration constituted a ratification of the alterations. We do not agree with either contention. Mr. Gilenko's answers to written interrogatories, admitted into evidence, show that after David's death, Gilenko had discussions with all of the Abrahams concerning the monies that were due and owing to David. As a result of these discussions Gilenko altered the $5,000 promissory note. Gilenko's answers to the interrogatories do not disclose what, if anything, was said to Gary Abrahams about the $5,000 note and its alterations. However, the record shows that Gilenko did completely discuss the alterations with Bert and Lee Abrahams and that the note was changed with the consent and approval of both.

A change made with the consent of the parties to the instrument does not avoid it, but will be binding on the consenting parties in its altered form. § 3–407(B)(1). Consent to the alteration of an instrument may be implied by the acts of the parties. In order to be binding, however, an implication of consent arising from the circumstances must be plain and unambiguous. We are unable to find anything in the evidence which indicates that Gary Abrahams expressly or impliedly consented to the alterations.

It is also the rule that by making payment of the principal or interest, with knowledge of an alteration, a party is held to ratify the instrument as altered. For this rule to be operable, mere payment is not enough; there must be a showing of payment with knowledge of the alteration. Direct evidence is not required, and the trier of fact may indulge all reasonable inferences from the facts shown by the evidence, or which unbiased and rational minds can properly deduce from the facts proved. The record does not show that the note either before or after alteration was ever in the possession of Gary. He did make a $100 payment on the note after the death of David, but $100 payments had been made on the note before it had been altered. We do not believe the evidence shows Gary made the payment with knowledge of the alteration.

Section 3–407(B)(1) requires that the alteration be both fraudulent and material. Fraud requires a dishonest and deceitful purpose to acquire more than one was entitled to under the note as signed by the maker rather than only a misguided purpose. We believe that the trial court, as the trier of fact, could legitimately have concluded that no fraud was shown, and that Gilenko was merely misguided in not obtaining Gary's consent when the $5,000 note was altered under a mistaken belief that Gary's consent was not necessary as long as the consent of the parties who were adding their names to the note, to wit, Gary's brother and father, had been obtained.

Because the note was a demand note, prior to its alteration, the trial court was correct in awarding Bluffestone the balance of the principal and interest on the note. However, since the note, prior to its alteration, contained no provision for attorney's fees, none should have been awarded as against Gary Abrahams.

The judgment is modified by striking the award of attorney's fees against Gary Abrahams.

Judgment for Bluffestone against the Abrahams affirmed, with modification.

## SUMMARY

Liability on a negotiable instrument may be based on (1) contract, (2) breach of warranty, (3) negligence, (4) improper payment, or (5) conversion. When a person signs a negotiable instrument, he generally becomes contractually liable on it. The terms of the contract of parties to a negotiable instrument are not written out on the instrument; they are supplied by Article 3 of the Code. Parties may be either primarily or secondarily liable. Makers of notes and acceptors of drafts and checks are primarily liable, while drawers of checks and drafts and indorsers of notes, checks and drafts are secondarily liable. An accommodation party is liable in the capacity in which he signed the instrument.

Under the Code, a person cannot be held contractually liable on a negotiable instrument unless his signature appears on the instrument. A person may use any name or symbol as his signature. A person who signs in a representative capacity should make it clear that he is signing as an agent, so that the principal rather than the agent will be liable.

Presentment for payment is necessary to hold parties liable on an instrument. Failure to present the instrument in a timely fashion discharges the indorsers from their contractual liability to make the instrument good. An instrument has been dishonored when it has been duly presented and acceptance or payment cannot be obtained within the prescribed time. When an instrument has been dishonored and required notices have been timely given, the holder has a right of recourse against the drawers and prior indorsers.

The transferor of an instrument warrants to his transferee that he has good title, that the signatures are genuine or authorized, that the instrument has not been materially altered, that no defenses of any party are good against him (if he qualifies his warranty, he warrants that he has no knowledge of defenses to the instrument), and that he has no knowledge of any insolvency proceedings against the maker, acceptor, or drawer of the instrument.

Any person who obtains payment or acceptance of an instrument warrants to a person who in good faith accepts or pays the instrument that he has good title to the instrument or is authorized to act for a person who has good title and that the instrument has not been materially altered. A holder in due course acting in good faith does not warrant to a maker or drawer the genuineness of the maker's or drawer's signature or that the instrument has not been altered.

A person who is negligent in writing or signing a negotiable instrument may be precluded from asserting an unauthorized signature or alteration as a reason for not paying a holder in due course. If a negotiable instrument is made payable to an impostor or a fictitious payee, any signature in the name of the payee is effective as an indorsement. A person who converts an instrument—that is, exercises unauthorized ownership over it—may be held liable to the real owner.

Liability of a party on an instrument may be discharged by payment, cancellation, material alteration, or impairment of recourse.

## PROBLEM CASES

1. Frederick Dowie was the president and sole stockholder of Fred Dowie Enterprises, Inc., a catering corporation. He obtained the opportunity to operate the concession stands at the Living History Farms during the pope's visit to Des Moines, Iowa. With high expectations, Dowie ordered 325,000 hot dog buns from Colonial Baking Company. Before the buns were delivered, he presented to Colonial Baking a postdated check in the amount of $28,640. This check showed the name of the corporation and its address in the upper left-hand corner. The signature on the check read "Frederick J. Dowie," and there were no other words of explanation. Unfortunately, only 300 buns were sold. Following a dispute over the ownership and responsibility for the remaining buns, Dowie stopped payment on the check. Colonial Baking then sued Dowie in his personal capacity as signer of the check. Is Dowie personally liable for the check?

2. Durbin bought some cattle through Woodrow, a livestock agent. In payment for the cattle, Durbin made three checks totaling $48,772 payable to Woodrow. When the checks were presented to the drawee bank for payment, the bank refused to pay the checks because Durbin did not have sufficient funds on deposit to cover the checks. The checks, marked "Drawn on Uncollected Funds," were returned unpaid to Woodrow by the drawee bank. Woodrow then brought suit against Durbin to collect the full amount of the checks. When these checks were dishonored by the drawee bank, did the payee have the right to hold the drawer of the checks liable for payment of them?

3. On February 1, 1972, a note in the amount of $18,000 payable 30 days from date to P. J. Panzeca was made by Klein Ventures, Ltd. and signed by Llobell in his capacity as president of Klein Ventures. The note, which was given to Panzeca in payment for labor and materials, was signed on the reverse side by Llobell personally. It was presented for payment, dishonored, and notice was given on March 2, 1972. Panzeca then brought suit against Llobell to recover the face amount of the note. Llobell claimed that he should not be liable, because his personal signature was given upon the oral representation of Panzeca that payment would be sought only from Klein Ventures and not from him personally. Is Llobell liable on the note?

4. Willard Cobb operated an insurance agency in Brattleboro, Vermont. He received a check in the amount of $13,750 issued by the Hartford Insurance Company and payable to R. A. McQuaide Milk Transport. The check was issued in payment of a property loss incurred by McQuaide under a policy issued by Hartford Insurance through Cobb's agency. Willard Cobb, without authorization from McQuaide, fraudulently indorsed McQuaide's name to the check and then added his own indorsement "For Deposit Only—Franklin County Trust Co., Willard D. Cobb." He gave the check to his brother Leon to deposit at Franklin County Trust in a new partnership account that they had opened in the name of "Econo Car Rental Center." The bank credited the partnership account with the money. Willard took the money from the account and left town. The bank had to pay Hartford Insurance back for the check that it had wrongfully paid to Willard and Leon rather than to McQuaide. Then, it sued Willard and Leon

Cobb to recover the money from them. Were Leon and Willard liable to the bank on the ground that they breached the warranty of good title?

**5.** Mrs. Johnson mailed a loan application to First National Bank in her husband's name and without his knowledge. The bank, having dealt with her husband before, approved the application and mailed a check in the amount requested to Mr. Johnson. Mrs. Johnson then indorsed the check in her husband's name and cashed it at Merchant's Bank. Merchant's Bank indorsed the check and presented it for payment. First National, having discovered the deception, refused to pay. Is First National liable on the check?

**6.** A construction company's superintendent wrote out several checks to the company's creditors and thereafter converted them to his own use by forging the indorsements of the creditors and cashing the checks at First National Bank. In an action by the construction company against First National for the value of the checks, is First National liable?

**7.** Temco kept its blank checks in an unlocked cabinet behind its bookkeeper's desk. It also kept a check Protectograph machine, which was used to print the amount on checks, in the bookkeeper's unlocked desk. On Friday night, a burglar broke into Temco's factory through a skylight, kicked open a locked door to its offices, and entered the bookkeeper's office. The burglar took 30 blank checks, used the Protectograph to make each check out for $186.34, and forged the name of Temco's bookkeeper, Lee Adams, who was authorized to sign checks for the company. The checks were made payable to either "Randall Lees" or "Anthony Hawes." The next day, Fred Meyer discovered that several identical checks had been cashed at its stores in the area that day. It contacted officials at Temco, who discovered the burglary and the loss of the checks. Temco refused to pay the checks on the ground that they were forgeries. Fred Meyer sued to collect on the checks, claiming that Temco's negligence had contributed to the forgeries. Was Temco barred from claiming that the signatures were unauthorized on the ground that it had been negligent in not keeping the checks and Protectograph in safekeeping?

**8.** Titan Corporation employed Dana as its bookkeeper. Without Titan's knowledge, Dana diverted large sums of money from it by appropriating its checks, making them payable to Titan's suppliers, forging the indorsements of the payees, and then depositing the checks in accounts of two corporations that Dana controlled. Dana's two corporations had their checking accounts in the same bank (Chase Manhattan) that Titan had its account; both used the same small branch bank, which had only two tellers, two clerks, an assistant manager, and a manager. The employees of the branch knew Dana and knew that he was employed by Titan. Because Titan had open accounts with its suppliers, Titan did not receive any complaints from those suppliers concerning nonpayment of invoices. Titan brought suit against Chase Manhattan, alleging that its negligence had made Titan's losses possible. Should the bank be held liable?

**9.** A check dated July 18 for $4,900 drawn on Bankers Trust Company was payable to the order of "Baiata Enterprises, Inc. & Small Business Administration, N.Y.C. & M. Spegal and Sons Oil Corp. & Tally Petroleum Corp. A.I.M.A." On July 18, the check was presented to the Chase Manhattan Bank by Rosario Baiata. At that time, the check bore indorsements in the names of all the payees. Chase gave Baiata $4,900, indorsed the check, and sent it to Bankers Trust which paid Chase for it. Later, it was discovered that the purported signature of "Arthur Dillon, Regional Director, SBA" on behalf of the SBA was a forgery. SBA's claim to the proceeds of the check was based on Baiata Enterprises' default on a loan that the SBA had made to it. Does the SBA have any claim against Chase Manhattan and/or Bankers Trust?

**10.** Nancy Ames purchased a 90-day, $10,000 certificate of deposit from the Great Southern Bank. When the certificate matured, Ames's bookkeeper, Suzanne Dealy, took the certificate to the bank to obtain payment. She surrendered the certificate, which had not been indorsed by Ames or anyone else, to the bank and was given $20,276.90 due on the CD. Dealy had acted on Ames's behalf in other transactions at the bank and was known to it. Ames brought suit against the bank, claiming that the bank was liable to her for conversion. Is the bank liable?

# Chapter 38

# Checks and Documents of Title

## INTRODUCTION

For most people, a checking account provides the majority of their contact with negotiable instruments. This chapter focuses on the relationship between the drawer with a checking account and the drawee bank. It addresses such common questions as: what happens if your bank refuses to pay a check even though you have sufficient funds in your account; does the bank have the right to create an overdraft in your account by paying an otherwise properly payable check; what are your rights and the bank's obligation if you stop payment on a check; what is the difference between a certified check and a cashier's check; and what are your responsibilities when you receive your monthly statement and cancelled checks? The second half of the chapter discusses the Code rules that apply to negotiable documents of title such as warehouse receipts and bills of lading.

## THE DRAWER-DRAWEE RELATIONSHIP

When a person deposits money in an account at the bank, he is a *creditor* of the bank and the bank becomes his *debtor*. If the deposit is made to a checking account, then the bank also becomes his *agent*. The obligations of the bank under banking law are set out in Article 4 of the Uniform Commercial Code (Bank Deposits and Collections). The bank as the person's agent owes a *duty* to him to follow his *reasonable instructions* concerning payments from his account.

**Bank's Duty to Pay.** When a bank receives a properly drawn and payable check on a person's account and there are sufficient funds to cover the check, the bank is under a *duty* to pay it. If the person has sufficient funds in the account and the bank refuses to pay (dishonors) the check, the bank is liable to him for damages caused by its wrongful dishonor. If the bank can show that it rejected the check by mistake, then the person can hold the bank liable only for any actual damages that he suffered. These damages can include both direct and consequential damages [4–402].[1]

For example, Donald Dodson writes a check for $1,500 to Ames Auto Sales in payment for a used car. At the time that Ames Auto presents the check for payment at Dodson's bank, First National Bank, Dodson has $1,800 in his account. However, a teller mistakenly refuses to pay the check and stamps it NSF (not sufficient funds). Ames Auto then goes to the local prosecutor and signs a complaint against Dodson for writing a bad check. As a result, Dodson is arrested. Dodson can recover from First National the damages that he sustained because his check was wrongfully dishonored, including the damages involved in his arrest, such as his attorney's fees.

**Bank's Right to Charge to Customer's Account.** The drawee bank has the right to charge any properly payable check to the account of the customer (drawer). The bank has this right even though payment of the check will create an overdraft in the account [4–401]. If an account is overdrawn, the customer owes the bank the amount of the overdraft and the bank may take that amount out of the next deposit that the customer makes. Alternatively, the bank might seek to collect the amount directly from the customer.

The bank does not owe a duty to its customer to pay any checks out of the account that are more than six months old. Such checks are called *stale checks*. However, the bank may in good faith pay a check that is more than six months old and charge it to the account of the customer (drawer) [4–404].

If the bank in good faith pays an altered check, it may charge the customer's account with the amount of the check as originally drawn. Also, if an incomplete check of a customer gets into circulation and is completed and presented to the drawee bank for payment, and the bank pays the check, the bank can charge the amount to the customer's account even though it knows that the check has been completed, unless it has notice that the completion was improper [4–401(2)].

**Stop Payment Order.** A **stop payment order** is a request made by the drawer of a check to the drawee bank asking it not to pay or certify the check. As the drawer's agent in the payment of checks, the drawee bank must follow the reasonable orders of the drawer as to payments made on the drawer's behalf. To be effective, a stop payment order must be received in time to give the drawee bank a *reasonable opportunity to act* on it. This means that the stop payment order must be given to the bank before it has paid or certified the check. The stop payment order must also come soon enough to give the bank time to

---

[1] The numbers in brackets refer to the sections of the Uniform Commercial Code.

instruct its tellers and other employees that they should not pay the check [4–403(1)].

An *oral stop payment order* can be given to the bank, but it is valid for only *14 days* unless it is confirmed in writing during that time. Banks normally require such written confirmation. A *written stop payment order* is valid for *six months* and can be extended for an additional six months by giving the bank instructions in writing to continue the order [4–403(2)].

Sometimes the information given the bank by the customer concerning the check on which payment is to be stopped is incorrect. For example, there may be an error in the payee's name, the amount of the check or the number of the check. The question then arises as to whether the customer has accorded the bank a reasonable opportunity to act on his request? The *FJS Electronics v. Fidelity Bank* case, which follows, involves such a problem.

**Bank's Liability for Payment after Stop Payment Order.** The drawee bank is liable to the drawer of a check that it pays while a stop payment order is in effect for any loss that the drawer suffers by reason of such payment. However, the drawer has the burden of establishing the amount of the loss. To show a loss, the drawer must establish that the drawee bank paid a person against whom the drawer had a valid defense to payment. To the extent that the drawer has such a defense, he has suffered a loss due to the drawee's failure to honor the stop payment order.

For example, Brown buys what is represented to be a new car from Foster Ford and gives Foster Ford his check for $7,280 drawn on First Bank. Brown then discovers that the car is in fact a used demonstrator model and calls First Bank, ordering it to stop payment on the check. If Foster Ford presents the check for payment the following day and First Bank pays the check despite the stop payment order, Brown can require the bank to recredit his account. Brown had a valid defense (misrepresentation) that he could have asserted against Foster Ford if it had sued him on the check. However, assume that Foster Ford negotiated the check to Smith and that Smith qualified as a holder in due course. Then, if the bank paid the check to Smith over the stop payment order, Brown would not be able to have his account recredited, because Brown would not be able to show that he sustained any loss. If the bank had refused to pay the check, so that Smith came against Brown on his drawer's liability, Brown's personal defense of misrepresentation could not be used as a reason for not paying Smith. Brown's only recourse would be to go directly against Foster Ford on his misrepresentation claim.

The bank may ask the customer to sign a form in which the bank tries to disclaim or limit its liability for the stop payment order. However, the bank is not permitted to disclaim its responsibility for its failure to act in good faith or to exercise ordinary care in paying a check over a stop payment order. Similarly, the bank cannot limit the measure of damages for such lack of good faith or failure to use ordinary care [4–103]. Such attempted disclaimers or limitations are not enforced by the courts.

If a bank pays a check after it has been given a stop payment order, it acquires all the rights of the person to whom it makes payment, including rights arising from the transaction on which the check was based [4–407]. In the above example involving Brown and Foster Ford, assume that Brown was able to have his account recredited because First Bank had paid the check to Foster Ford over his stop payment order. Then, the bank would have any rights that Brown had against Foster Ford for the misrepresentation.

If a person stops payment on a check and the bank honors the stop payment order, the person may still be liable to the holder of the check. Suppose Peters writes a check for $450 to Ace Auto Repair in payment for repairs to her automobile. While driving the car home, she concludes that the car was not properly repaired. She calls her bank and stops payment on the check. Ace Auto negotiated the check to Sam's Auto Parts, which took the check as a holder in due course. When Sam's takes the check to Peters' bank, payment is refused because of the stop payment order. Sam's then comes after Peters on her drawer's liability. All Peters has is a personal defense against payment, which is not good against a holder in due course. So, Peters must pay Sam's the $450 and pursue her claim separately against Ace. If Ace were still the holder of the check, however, the situation would be different. Peters' personal defense concerning the faulty work could be used against Ace to reduce or possibly cancel her obligation to pay the check.

**Certified Check.** Normally, a drawee bank is not obligated to certify a check. When a drawee bank does *certify* a check, it becomes *primarily liable for payment* of the check. At the time a check is certified, the bank usually debits the customer's account (takes the money out of the account) and sets the money aside in a special account at the bank. It also adds its signature to the check to show that it has accepted primary liability for paying it. The holder of a certified check looks to the drawee bank for payment.

If a check is certified by the drawee bank at the request of the drawer, the drawer remains secondarily liable on the check. However, if a check is certified by the drawee bank at the request of a holder of the check, then the drawer and any persons who have already indorsed the check are discharged of their liability on the check [3–411]. If the holder of a check chooses to have it certified, rather than seeking to have it paid at that time, the holder has made a conscious decision to look to the certifying bank for payment and is no longer relying on the drawer or the indorsers to make it good.

**Cashier's Check.** A **cashier's check** should be distinguished from a **certified check.** A check on which a bank is both the drawer and the drawee is a cashier's check. The bank is primarily liable on the cashier's check.

**Death or Incompetence of Customer.** Under the general principles of agency law, the death or incompetence of the principal terminates the agent's authority to act for the principal. However, slightly different rules apply to the authority of a bank to pay checks out of the account of a deceased or incompetent person. The bank has the right to pay the checks of an incompetent person until it has notice that a court has determined that the person is incompetent. Once the bank learns of this fact, it is no longer authorized to pay that person's checks.

Similarly, a bank has the right to pay the checks of a deceased customer until it has notice of the customer's death. Even if a bank knows of a customer's death, for a period of 10 days after the customer's death it can pay checks written by the customer prior to his death. However, the deceased person's heirs or other interested persons can order the bank to stop payment [4–405].

## FJS Electronics, Inc. v. Fidelity Bank

### 28 UCC Rep. 1462 (Pa. Ct. C.P. 1980)

On February 27, 1976, Multi-Tek issued Check No. 896 in the face amount of $1,844.98, drawn on Multi-Tek's account at Fidelity and made payable to Multilayer Computer Circuits. However, on March 9, 1976, Frank J. Suttill, Multi-Tek's president, telephoned Fidelity and placed a stop payment order. The order was received and simultaneously recorded by Roanna M. Sanders, Fidelity's employee. This recordation contained the following information: the name of the account, the account number, the check number, the date of the check, the date and hour that the stop payment order was received, and the amount of the check as $1,844.48. This recordation was essentially correct in all respects, except as to the amount of the check—there being a 50-cent difference between the face amount ($1,844.98) and the amount listed in the stop payment order ($1,844.48).

Subsequently, a confirmation notice bearing the date "03/09/76" was mailed by Fidelity to Multi-Tek. It contained, among other things, the following information:

PAYEE *MULTILATOR COMPUTER CIRCUITS*
AMOUNT $1,844.48
CK. NO. *896* DATE *02/27/76*

The instructions in this confirmation notice concluded with:

PLEASE ENSURE AMOUNT IS CORRECT.

This confirmation notice was signed by Suttill and returned to Fidelity.

Fidelity's computer was programmed to pull checks only if all of the digits on the stop payment order agreed with those on the check. As a result, Check No. 896 was honored by Fidelity and charged to Multi-Tek's account. Multi-Tek then brought suit against Fidelity to recover $1,844.98 on account of the check paid over the stop payment order.

**MARUTANI, JUDGE.** The Uniform Commercial Code, § 4–403(1), provides in pertinent part that:

> A customer may by order to his bank stop payment of any item payable for his account but the order must be received at such time and in such manner as to afford the bank a reasonable opportunity to act on it prior to any action by the bank with respect to the item.

In this case, there is no question that the transmittal of the stop-payment order was made timely; this leaves for resolution only whether such order was given "in such *manner* as to afford the bank a reasonable opportunity to act on it": UCC § 4–403(1); emphasis added. While the parties "may by agreement determine the standards by which [the bank's] responsibility is to be measured if such standards are not manifestly unreasonable," at the same time "no agreement can disclaim a bank's responsibility for its . . . failure to exercise ordinary care": UCC § 4–103(1).

The decisional law constituting § 4–403(1) appears to vary. Thus, in a recent decision of a trial court wherein the customer identified the check correctly as to the payee, the check number, and the date of issuance, but erred by 10 cents as to the amount of the check—$1,804.00 instead of the correct amount of $1,804.10—it was held that "the check was described with sufficient particularity and accuracy so that the bank should have known to give effect to the stop-payment order." However, where the customer provided the correct amount of the check but erred as to the date and name of the payee—one-day error in date, "Walter Morris Buick" instead of the correct name "Frank Morris Buick"—the Alabama Supreme Court held such to be insufficient notice.

In this case, as the parties by the stipulation agreed, "the Bank did not tell Mr. Suttill, nor did he request, information as to the procedure whereby the computer pulls checks on which stop payments have been issued." Under such circumstances, where the customer (Mr. Suttill) was called upon by the bank (Fidelity) to provide numerous data relating to the check in question, but the bank failed to emphasize to him that all such information may well be ineffective unless the *amount of the check* were *absolutely accurate,* we are constrained to be guided by the official comment to § 4–403 under "Purposes," which reads:

> 2. The position taken by this section is that stopping payment is a service which depositors expect and are entitled to receive from banks notwithstanding its difficulty, inconvenience and expense. The inevitable occasional losses through failure to stop should be borne by the banks as a cost of the business of banking.

Judgment for Multi-Tek.

## FORGED AND ALTERED CHECKS

**Bank's Right to Charge Account.** A check that has a forged signature of the drawer or payee is generally not properly chargeable to the customer's account. The bank is expected to be familiar with the authorized signature of its customer. It normally cannot charge the customer's account with checks on which the drawer's signature has been forged. Similarly, a check that was altered after the drawer made it out, for example, by increasing the amount of the check, is generally not properly chargeable to the customer's account. However, if the drawer is *negligent* and contributes to the forgery or alteration, he may be barred from claiming it as the reason that a particular check should not be charged to his account.

For example, Barton makes a check for $1 in a way that makes it possible for someone to easily alter it to read $101, and it is so altered. If a person who qualifies as a holder in due course takes the check, he can collect the $101 from Barton or her account if Barton's negligence contributed to the alteration. Similarly, if a company uses a mechanical checkwriter to write checks, it must use reasonable care to see that unauthorized persons do not have access to blank checks and to the checkwriter.

If a check has been obviously altered, the bank should note that fact and refuse to pay it when it is presented for payment. Occasionally, a check may have been so skillfully altered that the bank cannot detect the alteration. In that case, the bank is allowed to charge to the account the amount that the check was originally written for.

**Customer's Duty to Report Forgeries and Alterations.** The canceled checks drawn by a customer together with a statement of account are usually returned by the bank to the customer once a month. The customer, upon receiving the checks and statement, owes a duty to examine them to discover whether any signatures on the checks are forgeries or unauthorized or whether any of the checks have been altered [4–406(1)].

A customer who fails to examine the checks and statement within a reasonable time cannot hold the bank responsible for the payment of checks on which there are forgeries, unauthorized signings, or alterations if the bank can show that it suffered a loss because of the customer's failure [4–406(2)(a)]. For example, the bank might show that the forger absconded during that time.

A different rule applies if a series of unauthorized drawer's signatures or alterations are made by the same wrongdoer. The customer cannot hold the bank responsible for paying any such checks in good faith after the first check that had been altered or signed on behalf of the drawer without authority was available to the customer for a reasonable period not exceeding 14 calendar days and before the bank received notification from the customer of any such unauthorized signature or alteration [4–406(2)(b)].

Thus, checks forged or altered by the same person and presented to the bank more than 14 days after the first forged check was available to the customer are the customer's problem—not the bank's. The customer can hold the bank liable for such forgeries or alterations only if he can establish lack of due care on the part of the bank in paying any item [4–406(3)]. If the alterations were very obvious, the customer might show that the bank did not use due care. The amount of checks forged or altered by the same person and presented to the bank before and during the 14-day period after the statement first revealing such forgeries or alterations has been sent to the customer are the bank's responsibility and may not be recredited to the customer's account unless the bank can show that it suffered a loss because of the customer's failure to exercise reasonable care.

Suppose that Albers employs Farnum as an accountant and that over a period of three months Farnum forges Albers' signature to 10 checks and cashes them. One of the forged checks is included in the checks returned to Albers at the end of the first month. Within 14 calendar days after the return of these checks, Farnum forges two more checks and cashes them. Albers does not examine the returned checks until a lapse of three months after the checks that included the first forged check were returned to her. The bank would be responsible for the first forged check and for the two checks forged and cashed within the 14-day period after it sent the first statement and the canceled checks (unless the bank proves that it suffered a loss because of the customer's failure to examine the checks and notify it more promptly). It would not be liable for the seven forged checks cashed after the expiration of the 14-day period.

In any event, a customer must discover and report to the bank any *forgery of his signature*, any *unauthorized signature, or any alteration* within *one year* from the time the checks are made available to him. If the customer does not do so, he cannot require the bank to recredit his account for such checks. Similarly, a customer has *three years* from the time his checks are made available to discover and report any *unauthorized indorsement.* If the customer does not discover the unauthorized indorsement within three years, he cannot require the bank to recredit his account for the amount of the check [4–406(4)].

The *Winkie* case, which follows, illustrates the application of these rules to a situation where a business had a dishonest employee who forged the company's checks.

## Winkie, Inc. v. Heritage Bank of Whitefish Bay

**285 N.W.2d 899 (Wis. Ct. App. 1979)**

Winkie, Inc. maintained a checking account at the Heritage Bank of Whitefish Bay. Although several persons were authorized to sign Winkie, Inc. checks, W. J. Winkie, Jr., the company's president, was the only person who ever signed checks drawn on the Winkie, Inc. account.

Doris Britton, a secretarial employee of Winkie, Inc., recorded invoices for supplies and services rendered to the company and presented the invoices and checks drawn on the account in payment of the invoices to W. J. Winkie, Jr., for review of the invoices and execution of the checks. In the years 1965 to 1973, Britton forged the signature of W. J. Winkie, Jr., to hundreds of checks totaling $148,171.30 drawn on the Winkie, Inc. account. In addition to forging the signature of W. J. Winkie, Jr., Britton forged the indorsements of the payee on many of the checks.

None of the payees of the checks supplied the services or materials to Winkie, Inc. for which the forged checks were payment, and Winkie, Inc. neither intended payment nor received benefit of any kind by reason of the issuance of the checks. Britton directly or indirectly received all the proceeds of the forged checks.

In 1973, after approximately eight years of repeated forgeries, W. J. Winkie, Jr., discovered a forged check and immediately notified the bank. During the eight-year period, W. J. Winkie, Jr., did not personally examine the Winkie, Inc. checks or reconcile the bank statements of the account. Another Winkie, Inc. employee, not alleged to be involved in the systematic forgeries, was assigned those duties. Winkie, Inc. utilized the services of a certified public accountant, but those services did not expressly include bank statement reconciliation or an audit. Thus, the bank account examination and reconciliation were left to a single, unsupervised Winkie, Inc. employee.

Winkie, Inc. brought an action against the Heritage Bank to have its account recredited for the checks that had been forged by the Winkie employee and paid by the bank. The trial court held in favor of the Bank, and Winkie, Inc. appealed.

**Decker, Chief Judge.** The trial court found that Winkie, Inc. was negligent because of its obvious failure to examine the checks drawn on the bank account. In arriving at that conclusion, which was supported by overwhelming and virtually undisputed evidence, the trial court properly relied upon the duty expressed in *Wussow v. Badger State Bank,* that a depositor is obligated to "examine his checks and the statement and discover whether the balance stated was correct and whether any forgeries were included and report any discrepancies in balance and any forgeries to the bank at once." Our supreme court again indorsed the view that the "duty [to examine the bank checks and statement] is violated when [the depositor] neglects to do those things dictated by ordinary business customs and which, if done, would have prevented the wrongdoing."

The second dispositive finding by the trial court was that the Heritage Bank of Whitefish Bay was not negligent in paying the forged checks and charging them to the account of Winkie, Inc.

The last and most complex of the contentions of Winkie, Inc., that the bank was demonstrably negligent, is grounded upon the evidence that the bank, in posting the presented checks to the account of Winkie, Inc. failed to examine those checks to ascertain whether the checks were properly indorsed. The evidence establishes that one of the forged checks was paid by the bank, although there was no indorsement by the payee. Additionally, an employee of the bank testified that it was the bank's policy not to examine a check to ascertain the existence of a proper indorsement unless the check was for $1,000 or more.

There is a multifaceted significance to this contention and its relationship to the other issues that we have addressed. First, if Winkie, Inc. was not negligent in its failure to discover the forged checks, then the bank would bear the liability for paying the forged checks because it honored unauthorized payments from the depositor's account. That result is commanded by the common-law doctrine established in *Price v. Neal* and codified successively in the Negotiable Instruments Law and the Uniform Commercial Code. Second, if Winkie, Inc. was negligent, as determined by the trial court and confirmed by this court, such negligence does not bar its recovery from the bank if the latter was also negligent. Third, if Winkie, Inc. can recover because the bank is also negligent, the appropriate application of the "twin" statute of limitations is presented. Section 4–406(4) prescribes a one-year statute of limitations on recovery by a depositor from a bank for an improper charge against its account arising from the forgery of the drawer's signature and also prescribes a three-year statute of limitations on recovery from the bank by reason of its negligence in failing to discover forged indorsements.

We hold that Section 3–405(1)(b) controls this case. Because the forger of the checks, upon which the indorsements were forged, intended the payee to have no interest in the checks, an indorsement by any person was effective. Thus, the loss occurred not from the assumed negligence of the bank in failing to examine the checks for proper indorsements because *any* indorsement was effective. The negligence of Winkie, Inc. precludes its recovery from the bank, and Section 4–406(3) does not relieve Winkie, Inc. from the preclusion of Section 4–406(2). The three-year limitation provided by Section 4–406(4) is therefore inapplicable to Winkie, Inc.'s claim.

Judgment for Heritage Bank affirmed.

## ELECTRONIC BANKING

With the development of computer technology, many banks are encouraging their customers to transfer funds electronically by using computers rather than paper drafts and checks. A bank customer may use a specially coded card at terminals provided by the bank to make deposits to an account, to transfer money from one account (checking or savings) to another, to pay bills, or to withdraw cash from an account.

These new forms of transferring money have raised questions about the legal rules that will be applied to them, and the questions are only beginning to be resolved. In at least one court decision, *State of Illinois v. Continental Illinois National Bank,* which follows, the court held that a customer's withdrawal from a checking account by using a bank card at an electronic terminal should be treated in the same way as cashing a check.

**Electronic Funds Transfer Act.** The consumer who used electronic funds transfer systems (EFTs), the so-called cash machines or electronic tellers, in the early years often experienced problems in identifying and resolving mechanical errors resulting from malfunctioning EFTs. In response to these problems, Congress passed the Electronic Funds Transfer Act[2] in 1978 to provide "a basic framework, establishing the rights, liabilities, and responsibilities of participants in electronic funds transfer systems" and especially to provide "individual consumer rights."

There are four basic types of EFT systems: automated teller machines, point-of-sale terminals (which allow consumers to use their EFT cards like checks), preauthorized payments (e.g., automatic paycheck deposits or mortgage or utility payments), and telephone transfers (between accounts or to pay specific bills by phone).

Like the Truth in Lending Act and the Fair Credit Billing Act (FCBA) which are discussed in Chapter 46, the EFT Act requires disclosure of the terms and conditions of electronic fund transfers at the time the consumer contracts for the EFT service. Among the nine disclosures required are the following: the consumer's liability for unauthorized electronic fund transfers (those resulting from loss or theft), the nature of the EFT services under the consumer's account, any pertinent dollar or frequency limitations, any charges for the right to make EFTs, the consumer's right to stop payment of a preauthorized transfer, the financial institution's liability to the consumer for failure to make or stop payments, and the consumer's right to receive documentation of transfers both at the point or time of transfer and periodically. The act also requires 21 days' notice prior to the effective date of any change in the terms or conditions of the consumer's account that pertains to the required disclosures.

There are important differences between the EFT Act and the Fair Credit Billing Act (see Chapter 46). Under the EFT Act, the operators of EFT systems are given a maximum of 10 working days to investigate errors or provisionally recredit the consumer's account, whereas issuers of credit cards are given a maximum of 90 days under the FCBA. The liability of the consumer is different if an EFT card is lost or stolen than it is if a credit card is lost or stolen. Another important difference is that financial institutions cannot send consumers EFT cards that they did not request unless the cards are not valid for use; an "unsolicited" EFT card can be validated only at the consumer's request and only after the institution verifies that the consumer is the person whose name is on the card.

[2] Title 20 of the Financial Institutions Regulatory and Interest Rate Control Act of 1978, 15 U.S.C. § 1693 et seq.

## State of Illinois v. Continental Illinois National Bank

**536 F.2d 176 (7th Cir. 1976)**

Continental Illinois National Bank operated several so-called Customer Bank Communication Terminals (CBCTs). These unstaffed terminals were connected directly with the main office computer of Continental Illinois. Customers of the bank inserted a specially coded card into the terminal, entered an identification number, and then used keys on the transaction keyboard to indicate the type and amounts of the transactions that they wished to conduct. The customer might:

1. Withdraw cash (in the amount of $25 or any multiple thereof, up to $100) from their savings, checking, or credit card accounts.
2. Deposit checks or currency in a checking or savings account. At the time of the transaction, the customer was given a receipt at the CBCT indicating the amount and date of the deposit; until the deposit was received and verified at the main banking premises, it was not credited to his account and he could not draw on it.
3. Transfer funds between accounts: checking to savings, credit card to checking, or savings to checking.
4. Make payments on Continental Illinois installment loans or credit card charges.

When a transaction was completed, the customer received a receipt, and if he had withdrawn cash from his account, he received packets containing the cash. A copy of the receipt was retained in the machine, and the transaction was later verified by bank employees.

The Illinois banking commissioner brought an action against Continental Illinois to obtain a declaratory judgment that the unstaffed computer terminals that permitted customers using bank cards to withdraw cash, make deposits, transfer funds, or make payments constituted "branch banks." The U.S. district court held that the terminals amounted to branch banking, but it rejected the commissioner's contention that use of the machines to withdraw money from a customer's account constituted the "cashing of a check." The court of appeals reversed on this question, holding that this did constitute the cashing of a check.

**Per Curiam.** The district court here based its conclusion on the functions of CBCT as to the withdrawing of cash and the payment of installments on loans upon the provisions of the Uniform Commercial Code (UCC), in particular § 3–104(2), which declares a check to be a negotiable instrument drawn on a bank and payable on demand; a writing signed by the maker or drawer and containing an unconditional promise or order to pay a sum certain in money; with negotiability being the essential characteristic of a check. From this the district court concluded that a card inserted into the CBCT machine to secure money was not the cashing of a check within the meaning of the UCC or in the common understanding of check cashing. We cannot agree. This is exalting form over substance. The check is merely the means used by the bank to attain the desired objective, i.e., the payment of money to its customer. The card serves the same purpose as the check. It is an order on the bank. Any order to pay which is properly executed by a customer, whether it be check, card, or electronic device, must be recognized as a routine banking function when used as here. The relationship between the bank and its customer is the same. Indeed, the trial court here recognized this when it characterized a CBCT withdrawal as the "functional equivalent" of a written check. And Continental Bank gives the card transaction the same significance:

> The EFTS (Electronic Funds Transfer Systems) at issue in the present case are *extensions of* the principle of immediate access to customer accounts *in a manner dispensing with underlying paper such as checks.* (Emphasis added.)

Moreover, although the UCC defines a check as negotiable instrument, it also provides, § 3–104(3):

> As used in other Articles of this Act, and as the context may require, the term "check" may refer to instruments which are not negotiable within this Article as well as instruments which are so negotiable.

Just as a transfer of funds by cable or telegraph is in law a check, despite the nonnegotiability of the cable, the card here for the purpose of withdrawing cash is a check. What must be remembered is that the foundation of the relationship between the bank and its customer is the former's agreement to pay out the customer's money according to the latter's order. There are many ways in which an order may be given, and one way of late is by computer record. And the Ninth Circuit accepts the same concept that computer impulses constitute sufficient writing to meet the order test.

Judgment for Continental Illinois.

## DOCUMENTS OF TITLE

**Introduction.** Storing or shipping goods, giving a **warehouse receipt** or **bill of lading** representing the goods, and transferring such a receipt or bill of lading as representing the goods are practices of ancient origin. The warehouseman or the common carrier is a bailee of the goods, and he contracts to store or transport the goods and to deliver them to the owner or to act otherwise in accordance with the lawful directions of the owner. The warehouse receipt or the bill of lading may be either negotiable or nonnegotiable. To be negotiable, a warehouse receipt, bill of lading, or other document of title must provide that the goods are to be delivered to the bearer or to the order of a named person [7–104(1)]. The primary differences between the law of negotiable commercial paper and the law of negotiable documents of title are based on the differences between the obligation to pay money and the obligation to deliver specific goods.

The *Bishop v. Allied Van Lines, Inc.* case, which follows, illustrates the responsibility a warehouseman has to deliver the goods only as directed by the owner.

**Warehouse Receipts.** A warehouse receipt, to be valid, need not be in any particular form, but if it does not embody within its written or printed form each of the following, the warehouseman is liable for damages caused by the omission to a person injured as a result of it: (*a*) the location of the warehouse where the goods are stored; (*b*) the date of issue; (*c*) the consecutive number of the receipt; (*d*) whether the goods are to be delivered to the bearer or to the order of a named person; (*e*) the rate of storage and handling charges;[3] (*f*) a description of the goods or of the packages containing them; (*g*) the signature of the warehouseman or his agent; (*h*) whether the warehouseman is the owner of the goods, solely, jointly, or in common with others; and (*i*) a statement of the amount of the advances made and of the liabilities incurred for which the warehouseman claims a lien or security interest. Other terms may be inserted [7–202].

A warehouseman is liable to a purchaser for value in good faith of a warehouse receipt for nonreceipt or misdescription of goods. The receipt may conspicuously qualify the description by a statement such as "contents, condition and quantity unknown" [7–203].

Because a warehouseman is a bailee of the goods, he owes to the holder of the warehouse receipt the duties of a mutual benefit bailee and must exercise reasonable care [7–204]. The duties of a bailee are discussed in detail in Chapter 28. The warehouseman may terminate the relation by notification where, for

[3] Where goods are stored under a field warehouse arrangement, a statement of that fact is sufficient on a nonnegotiable receipt.

example, the goods are about to deteriorate or where they constitute a threat to other goods in the warehouse [7–206].

Unless the warehouse receipt provides otherwise, the warehouseman must keep separate the goods covered by each receipt; however, different lots of fungible goods, such as grain, may be mingled [7–207].

A warehouseman has a lien against the bailor on the goods covered by his receipt for his storage and other charges incurred in handling the goods [7–209]. The Code sets out a detailed procedure for enforcing this lien [7–210].

**Bills of Lading.** In many respects, the rights and liabilities of the parties to a negotiable bill of lading are the same as the rights and liabilities of the parties to a negotiable warehouse receipt. The contract of the issuer of a bill of lading is to transport goods, whereas the contract of the issuer of a warehouse receipt is to store goods. Like the issuer of a warehouse receipt, the issuer of a bill of lading is liable for nonreceipt or misdescription of the goods, but he may protect himself from liability where he does not know the contents of packages by marking the bill of lading "contents or condition of packages unknown" or similar language. Such terms are ineffective when the goods are loaded by an issuer who is a common carrier unless the goods are concealed by packages [7– 301].

A carrier who issues a bill of lading, or a warehouseman who issues a warehouse receipt, must exercise the same degree of care in relation to the goods as a reasonably careful person would exercise under like circumstances. In the *Joseph Reinfeld* case, which follows, a warehouseman was held liable for conversion of goods that disappeared, without sufficient explanation, while they were entrusted to him. Liability for damages not caused by the negligence of the carrier may be imposed on him by a special law or rule of law. Under tariff rules, a common carrier may limit his liability to a shipper's declaration of value, provided that the rates are dependent on value [7–309].

**Negotiation of Document of Title.** A negotiable document of title and a negotiable instrument are negotiated in substantially the same manner. If the document of title provides for the delivery of the goods to bearer, it may be negotiated by delivery. If it provides for delivery of the goods to the order of a named person, it must be indorsed by that person and delivered. If an order document of title is indorsed in blank, it may be negotiated by delivery unless it bears a special indorsement following the blank indorsement, in which event it must be indorsed by the special indorsee and delivered [7–501].

A person taking a negotiable document of title takes as a bona fide holder if he takes in good faith and in the regular course of business. The bona fide holder of a negotiable document of title has substantially the same advantages over a holder who is not a bona fide holder or over a holder of a nonnegotiable document of title as does a holder in due course of a negotiable instrument over a holder who is not a holder in due course or over a holder of a nonnegotiable instrument.

**Rights Acquired by Negotiation.** A person who acquires a negotiable document of title by due negotiation acquires (1) title to the document, (2) title to the goods, (3) the right to the goods delivered to the bailee after the issuance of the document, and (4) the direct obligation of the issuer to hold or deliver the goods according to the terms of the document [7–502(1)].

Under the broad general principle that a person cannot transfer title to goods he does not own, a thief or the owner of goods subject to a valid outstanding security interest cannot, by warehousing or shipping the goods on a negotiable document of title and then negotiating the document of title, transfer to the purchaser of the document of title a better title than he has [7–503].

**Warranties of Transferor of Document of Title.** The transferor of a negotiable document of title warrants to his immediate transferee, in addition to any warranty of goods, only that the document is genuine, that he has no knowledge of any facts that would impair its validity or worth, and that his negotiation or transfer is rightful and fully effective with respect to the title to the document and the goods it represents [7–507].

## Bishop v. Allied Van Lines, Inc.

**399 N.E.2d 698 (Ill. Ct. App. 1980)**

Estelle Smiley and her husband, R. V. Smiley, entered into an agreement with Allied Van Lines for the transfer and storage of household goods and were given a bill of lading. Afterward, the Smileys began divorce proceedings. Estelle Smiley then notified the agent for Allied not to deliver the household goods to either her or her husband without further instructions from her. The goods were delivered to R. V. Smiley after the notice had been given.

Estelle died, and Bishop, the executor of her estate, brought an action against Allied Van Lines, Inc. to recover damages for misdelivery of goods. The trial court dismissed the case for failure to state a cause of action, and Bishop appealed.

**Craven, Judge.** The trial judge stated that a bailee is required to deliver the goods to a person entered under the document upon payment of the bailee's lien. Person entitled under the document is defined in § 7–403 of the Code, subparagraph (4), as a holder in the case of a negotiable document or the person to whom delivery is to be made by the terms of or pursuant to written instructions under a nonnegotiable document. The bill of lading in question is conspicuously and expressly noted as nonnegotiable. Section 7–404 provides that a bailee in good faith and using reasonable commercial standards who delivers or otherwise disposes of the goods according to the terms of the document of title is not liable.

The Comments under that section state that delivery in the case of a nonnegotiable document is to the one to whom delivery is to be made under its terms or pursuant to written instructions under it. Such instructions would be a delivery order [§ 7–102(1)(d)]. Delivery order is a written order to deliver goods directed to a warehouseman, carrier, or other person who in the ordinary course of business issues warehouse receipts or bills of lading. No delivery orders were given at any time. Therefore, the person entitled under the document, this being a nonnegotiable document, must be the person to whom delivery is made by the terms of the nonnegotiable document.

Ordinarily in a bill of lading where no delivery orders are given, there is a blank space for the consignee and his or her address. Section 7–102(1)(b) defines "consignee" as the person named in a bill to whom or to whose order the bill promises delivery. The bill of lading in this case is no different. There is a blank space for a consignee, delivery address, city, and state. Also, there is a blank space at the bottom of the nonnegotiable bill of lading where the consignee is supposed to sign. The bill of lading in question had only blank spaces for this information. In other words, there was neither a consignee named nor any address given, nor was there a signature of any consignee. There was, then, no consignee at all, nor were any delivery orders given. The bill of lading, issued by Allied Van Lines, states that the shipper was Mr. and Mrs. R. V. Smiley, signed by R. V. Smiley.

Mrs. Smiley alleges in the complaint that she was the owner of the stored property and she was named as a joint shipper in the bill of lading. Mrs. R. V. Smiley would, then, be a joint bailor. A bailment is merely the delivery of goods for some purpose upon a contract, express or implied, and after the purpose has been fulfilled the goods are to be redelivered to the bailor, or otherwise dealt with according to his directions, or kept until reclaimed. Joint delivery by Mrs. Smiley and her then husband carries with it a presumption of joint title and a concession of a joint right of action.

Section 7–404 states that a bailee who in good faith, including observance of reasonable commercial standards, has received goods and delivered or disposed of them according to the terms of the document is not liable. Here it is alleged that the bailee had knowledge of an adverse claim between the bailors. On these pleadings, we hold that it cannot be said that the bailee acted in good faith. It cannot be said that the bailee observed reasonable commercial standards when the bailee delivered the bailed goods with knowledge of adverse claims between the bailors. Indeed, § 7–603 excuses the bailee from delivery until he had a reasonable time to ascertain the validity of adverse claims.

Judgment reversed in favor of the Estelle Smiley estate.

## Joseph H. Reinfeld, Inc. v. Griswold & Bateman Warehouse Co.

**458 A.2d 1341 (N.J. Super. Ct. 1983)**

Griswold and Bateman Warehouse Company stored 337 cases of Chivas Regal Scotch Whiskey for Joseph H. Reinfeld, Inc. in its bonded warehouse. A warehouse receipt was issued to Reinfeld that limited Griswold and Bateman's liability for negligence to 250 times the monthly storage rate, a total of $1,925. When Reinfeld sent its truck to pick up the whiskey, 40 cases were missing.

Reinfeld then brought suit seeking the wholesale market value of the whiskey, $6,417.60. Reinfeld presented evidence of the delivery of the whiskey, the demand for its return, and the failure of Griswold and Bateman to return it. Reinfeld claimed that the burden was on Griswold and Bateman to explain the disappearance of the whiskey. Griswold and Bateman admitted that it had been negligent, but sought to limit its liability to $1,925.

**Griffin, Judge.** Section 7–204(2) permits a warehouseman to limit his liability for negligent "loss or damage" to the bailed goods if stated in the storage agreement. The statute reads: "No such limitation is effective with respect to the warehouseman's liability for conversion to his own use." An inadvertent misdelivery is a conversion. Can a bailee simply refuse to explain a disappearance and then have his liability limited by § 7–204? If so, what will prevent a dishonest warehouseman from stealing the goods entrusted to his care and then saying, "I don't know what happened, but I admit my negligence." He would then pay only the amount limited by contract and pocket the difference.

A bailee who accepts responsibility for goods should have the burden of producing evidence as to the fate of those goods. To hold otherwise would place an impossible burden on the plaintiff. How is a plaintiff to present sufficient evidence of conversion when knowledge of the fate of the goods is available only to the defendant? This court holds that Reinfeld has presented a prima facie case of conversion, and the burden of going forward or producing evidence as to what happened to the whiskey shifts to Griswold and Bateman.

This court holds that to earn the protection of § 7–204(2), Griswold and Bateman must meet its burden of explaining the disappearance or be held liable for conversion. If Griswold and Bateman meet this burden, then the burden of proof that conversion or negligence exists shifts back to Reinfeld.

After the court's ruling Griswold and Bateman produced evidence of three possible explanations: United States Customs officials had been convicted of theft from the warehouse; some goods had been confiscated by the United States Customs Service; and there had been misdeliveries by warehouse employees.

This court finds that misdelivery was the most probable.

Misdelivery due to negligence is conversion. The *Restatement of Torts,* 2d § 234 provides:

> Conversion as Against Bailor by Misdelivery.
>
> A bailee, agent, or servant who makes an unauthorized delivery of a chattel is subject to liability for conversion to his bailor, principal, or master unless he delivers to one who is entitled to immediate possession of the chattel.

Comment "a" applies this section to bailees who make unauthorized delivery by "mistake or otherwise." Therefore, under the *Restatement,* mere misdelivery does constitute conversion.

Reinfeld's proof of delivery, demand and failure to return the goods raised a prima facie case of conversion. The evidence which Griswold and Bateman then produced not only failed to meet this case but established that there was a prior misdelivery. Griswold and Bateman fall within the exception to the limitation of liability contained in § 7–204(2) as the property was converted by misdelivery. Hence, Reinfeld is entitled to the market value of the whiskey, which is $6,417.60.

Judgment for Reinfeld.

## SUMMARY

The relation between a bank and a customer having a commercial account on which checks may be drawn is that of debtor and creditor and principal and agent. In drawing a check, the customer as principal authorizes the bank as agent to honor the check. The bank is under an obligation to pay all properly drawn checks, provided that the funds in the account are sufficient to cover the checks. A bank may pay a check even if doing so creates an overdraft. A bank does not owe a duty to pay stale checks—those that are over six months old—but it may do so in good faith.

The customer has the right to order the bank to stop payment on a check that has not been certified, and if the order to stop payment is received by the bank at such a time and in such form as to give it a reasonable opportunity to do so, the bank owes a duty to refuse payment on the check. If the bank pays a check in disregard of a valid stop payment order, it is liable to the drawer for any resulting loss.

A bank is not obligated to certify a check, but upon certification the bank becomes primarily liable on the check and, if the check has been certified at the request of the holder, the drawer and all prior indorsers are discharged.

A bank may pay checks drawn during a customer's lifetime or while the customer is competent and for a period of 10 days after the customer's death or until the bank learns of an adjudication of incompetence. A customer owes a duty to report to the bank, within a reasonable time after a statement of account and canceled checks have been made available, any unauthorized signatures and alterations. Forged drawer's signatures and alterations must in any event be reported within one year, and unauthorized indorsements within three years, or the drawer cannot require that his account be recredited.

Checks that have forged drawer's or payee's signatures and checks that have been materially altered are generally not properly chargeable to a customer's account. However, if the drawer is negligent and contributes to the forgery or alteration, he may be barred from claiming it as the reason that a particular item should not be charged to his account.

The warehouseman or common carrier is a bailee of goods, and he contracts to store or transport them. The warehouse receipt or bill of lading may be either negotiable or nonnegotiable. If the warehouse receipt issued by the warehouseman omits in its written or printed terms the information required under the provisions of the Code, the warehouseman is liable to a purchaser in good faith of a warehouse receipt for failure to describe the goods or for their misdescription. He owes to the holder of a warehouse receipt the duties of a mutual benefit bailee. The common carrier's liability on a negotiable bill of lading is the same in most respects as that of the issuer of a negotiable warehouse receipt. His liability may be increased by special law or rule.

The rules of law governing the negotiation of a negotiable document of title are the same in most respects as the rules of law governing the negotiation of negotiable commercial paper. In general, a holder by due negotiation of a negotiable document of title gets good title to the document and the goods and the contractual rights against the bailee. However, a thief or an owner of goods that are subject to a valid perfected security interest cannot, by warehousing or shipping the goods on a negotiable document of title and negotiating it, pass to the transferee greater rights in the goods than he has. A holder who transfers a negotiable document of title warrants to his immediate transferee that the document is genuine, that he has no knowledge of any facts that would impair its validity or worth, and that his transfer is rightful and fully effective.

## PROBLEM CASES

**1.** Michael Zappone was president of the MJZ Corporation, which owned a restaurant. In October 1979, the restaurant was sold and Zappone gave the new owners two signed but undated checks that were blank as to the amount. The checks were drawn on MJZ's corporate account at Gulfstream First Bank & Trust. On April 2, 1980, Zappone closed this account. Later in April, the two checks signed earlier were presented to the bank in the amounts of $6,998.22 and $11,000. Although the account had been closed, the bank honored the checks and looked to Zappone and the corporation for reimbursement. The bank said that it had a policy of continuing to honor checks for a period of 30 days after an account had been closed as a convenience to customers so that they could avoid "bounced" checks. Zappone and the corporation refused to pay the bank, claiming that it had no authority to honor the checks. Can the bank recover?

**2.** Atlantic Cement sold and delivered cement to Marshfield Sand and Gravel. It was paid by a check in the amount of $44,166 drawn on the South Shore Bank. When the check was presented for payment, payment was refused even though there were sufficient funds in Marshfield's account to pay the check. Atlantic Cement then brought suit against South Shore Bank for its refusal to pay the check. Is South Shore Bank liable to Atlantic Cement?

**3.** Eagle Masonry was hired by J. Wheeler Construction Corporation to do some masonry work. In partial payment for that work, Wheeler wrote a check to Eagle for $20,298. Eagle promptly cashed the check at Vail National Bank, where it had an account. Prior to cashing the check, Vail National called Wheeler's bank and was told that there were sufficient funds in Wheeler's account and that there was no stop payment order on the check. At the time, Eagle's checking account balance with Vail National was negligible. Two days later, Vail National presented the check for payment. Because Wheeler had since put a stop payment order on the check, it was dishonored and returned unpaid to Vail National. Vail National then brought suit against Wheeler for payment, claiming that it was a holder in due course. Should Vail National recover from Wheeler?

**4.** Cook issued a check payable to the order of Light. The next morning, before banking hours, Cook telephoned the bank, talked to the cashier, and ordered payment of the check stopped. The bank certified the check later in the day and subsequently paid it. When sued, the bank set up as a defense (*a*) that the stop payment order was not given during banking hours and (*b*) that the stop payment order was not in writing. Is either of these defenses good?

**5.** An employee of Lawrence Fashions Company forged 250 of the company's checks over a period extending from November 1965 to May 1968. Lawrence Fashions then filed an action against the bank to recover the amount paid on these instruments. Is the bank liable?

**6.** On December 6, 1970, Neo-Tech Systems filed a corporate resolution with Provident Bank that provided that all checks drawn on Neo-Tech's account in excess of $300 should bear the signature of both Richard Zielasko, president, and Robert Sherwood, treasurer. On November 24, 1971, Robert Sherwood resigned as treasurer of Neo-Tech, but no provision was made to replace him with some other party as signatory on the account with Provident Bank. Between November 24, 1971, and May 1973, numerous checks in excess of $300 were written on the Provident Bank account by Richard Zielasko. On September 4, 1973, Neo-Tech filed a lawsuit against Provident Bank seeking to recover the proceeds of checks in amounts exceeding $300 written between June 1, 1972, and April 18, 1973, drawn on its account and bearing only the signature of Richard Zielasko. Provident Bank contended that Neo-Tech was barred from recovering for any of the checks under section 4–406 of the Code because the first check with the unauthorized signature had been made available to Neo-Tech over a year prior to May 31, 1973, when Neo-Tech notified the bank of the lack of authorized signature problem. Is Provident Bank's contention correct?

**7.** Quantities of soybean oil for which nonnegotiable warehouse receipts were issued were delivered to Lawrence American Field Warehousing Corporation. National Dairy Products Corporation held warehouse receipts for some of the soybean oil. Upon presentation of the receipts, it was discovered that no soybean oil was in the storage tanks. No satisfactory explanation was given for the disappearance of the soybean oil—95,233,792 pounds. Either the soybean oil had been stolen, or the warehouse receipts had been issued without the receipt of soybean oil. National then sued Lawrence for failure to deliver the goods upon presentation of the warehouse receipts. Is Lawrence liable to National?

**8.** United Cargo Corporation issued a negotiable order bill of lading for four large packages consigned to Koreska in New York City. One of the printed terms of the bill of lading stated: "None of the terms of this bill of lading shall be deemed to have been waived by any person unless by express waiver signed by such person or his duly authorized agent." Upon arrival in New York, the goods were delivered by United to one of Koreska's customers, Park Whitney, supposedly because an agent of Koreska had orally advised United to make the delivery to Whitney. When United delivered the goods to Whitney, it did not obtain the negotiable order bill of lading. Koreska then sued United for the value of the goods delivered without taking up the negotiable order bill of lading. Is Koreska entitled to recover?

**9.** On January 14, 1975, Crawford sold two railroad carloads of bulk ammonium nitrate fertilizer to Cunningham and received two checks totaling $30,000 in payment for the fertilizer. On the same day, the goods were placed in the care and custody of the Missouri-Kansas-Texas Railroad for shipment to Cunningham's customer, the Eaton Agricultural Center in Indiana. The railroad issued two nonnegotiable bills of lading to cover the goods. On January 23, the checks were returned to Crawford by the bank because there were insufficient funds in Cunningham's account to cover them. The goods were in transit at the time, and Crawford instructed the railroad not to deliver them to the Eaton Agricultural Center, but rather to another place. The railroad complied with the instructions. The buyer from Cunningham then sued the railroad, contending that it had wrongfully breached its obligation to deliver the goods to Cunningham. Was the railroad correct in following Crawford's instructions?

**10.** Reed Farms stored 250 bales of cotton in a warehouse operated by Federal Compress & Warehouse Company. On October 21, 1972, a fire destroyed one section of the warehouse in which 7,000 bales of cotton, including 88 of the bales owned by Reed Farms, were stored. Because of the large number of bales lost, Federal was unable to notify all of the owners, including Reed, of the quantity of bales lost until November 22, 1972. Federal had the cotton insured for its value as of the date of destruction. The 88 bales belonging to Reed Farms were valued at $10,198.41 as of the date of the fire, and this amount was paid to Reed. The price of cotton was then increasing in value, however, and the 88 bales were worth $2,016.81 more on November 22, when Reed was notified of the loss. Reed then brought suit to recover the difference. Is Reed entitled to recover?

# PART X

# CREDIT

# Chapter 39 Credit and Secured Transactions

## INTRODUCTION

In the United States, a substantial portion of business transactions involve the extension of credit. The term **credit** has many meanings. In this chapter, it will be used to mean transactions in which goods are sold, services are rendered, or money is loaned in exchange for a promise to pay for them at some future date.

In some of these transactions a creditor is willing to rely on the debtor's promise to pay at a later time; in others the creditor wants some further assurance or security that the debtor will make good on his promise to pay. This chapter will discuss the differences between secured and unsecured credit and will detail various mechanisms that are available to the creditor who wants to obtain security. These mechanisms include obtaining liens or security interests in personal or real property, sureties, and guarantors. Security interests in real property, sureties and guarantors, and common law liens on personal property will be covered in this chapter, and the Code rules concerning security interests in personal property will be covered in Chapter 40. Chapter 41 will deal with bankruptcy law which may come into play when a debtor is unable to fulfill his obligation to pay his debts when they are due.

## CREDIT

**Unsecured Credit.** Many common transactions are based on *unsecured credit.* For example, a person may have a charge account at a department store or a Master Card account. If the person buys a sweater and charges it to his charge account or Master Card account, unsecured credit has been extended to him. He has received goods in return for his promise to pay for them later. Similarly, if a person goes to a dentist to have a tooth filled and the dentist sends him a bill payable by the end of the month, services have been rendered on the basis of unsecured credit. Consumers are not the only people who use unsecured credit. Many transactions between businesspeople utilize it. For example, a retailer buys merchandise or a manufacturer buys raw materials, promising to pay for the merchandise or materials within 30 days after receipt.

The "unsecured" credit transaction involves a maximum of risk to the creditor—the person who extends the credit. When goods are delivered, services are rendered, or money is loaned on unsecured credit, the creditor gives up all rights in the goods, services, or money. In return, the creditor gets a promise by the debtor to pay or to perform the promised act. If the debtor does not pay or keep the promise, the creditor's only course of action is to bring a lawsuit against the debtor and obtain a judgment. The creditor might then have the sheriff execute the judgment on any property owned by the debtor that is subject to execution. The creditor might also try to garnish the wages or other moneys to which the debtor is entitled. However, the debtor might be judgment-proof; that is, the debtor may not have any property subject to execution or may not have a steady job. Under these circumstances, execution or garnishment would be of little aid to the creditor in collecting the judgment.

A businessperson may obtain credit insurance to stabilize the credit risk of doing business on an unsecured credit basis. However, he passes the costs of the insurance to the business, or of the unsecured credit losses that the business sustains, on to the consumer. The consumer pays a higher price for goods or services purchased, or a higher interest rate on any money borrowed, from a business that has high credit losses.

**Secured Credit.** To minimize his credit risk, a creditor may contract for *security.* The creditor may require the debtor to convey to the creditor a **security interest** or **lien** on the debtor's property. Suppose a person borrows $1,000 from a credit union. The credit union might require him to put up his car as security for the loan or might ask that some other person agree to be liable if he defaults. For example, if a student who does not have a regular job goes to a bank to borrow money, the bank might ask that the student's father or mother cosign the note for the loan.

When the creditor has security for the credit he extends and the debtor defaults, the creditor can go against the security to collect the obligation. Assume that a person borrows $8,000 from a bank to buy a new car and that the bank takes a security interest (lien) on the car. If the person fails to make his monthly payments, the bank has the right to repossess the car and have it sold so that it can recover its money. Similarly, if the borrower's father cosigned for the car loan and the borrower defaults, the bank can sue the father to collect the balance due on the loan.

**Development of Security.** Various types of security devices have been developed as social and economic need for them arose. The rights and liabilities of the parties to a secured transaction depend on the nature of the security, that is, on whether the security pledged is the promise of another person to pay if the debtor does not or whether a security interest in goods, intangibles, or real estate is conveyed as security for the payment of a debt or obligation.

If personal credit is pledged, the other person may *guarantee the payment of the debt,* that is, become a **guarantor,** or the other person may *join the debtor in the debtor's promise to pay,* in which case the other person would become **surety** for the debt.

The oldest and simplest security device was the pledge. To have a pledge valid against third persons with an interest in the goods, such as subsequent purchasers or creditors, it was necessary that the property used as security be delivered to the pledgee or a pledge holder. Upon default by the pledger, the pledgee had the right to sell the property and apply the proceeds to the payment of the debt.

Situations arose in which it was desirable to leave the property used as security in the possession of the debtor. To accomplish this objective, the debtor would give the creditor a bill of sale to the property, thus passing title to the creditor. The bill of sale would provide that if the debtor performed his promise, the bill of sale would become null and void, thus revesting title to the property in the debtor. A secret lien on the goods was created by this device, and the early courts held that such a transaction was a fraud on third-party claimants and void as to them. An undisclosed or secret lien is unfair to creditors who might extend credit to the debtor on the strength of property that they see in the debtor's possession but that in fact is subject to the prior claim of another creditor. Statutes were enacted providing for the recording or filing of the bill of sale, which was later designated as a chattel mortgage. These statutes were not uniform in their provisions. Most of them set up formal requirements for the execution of the chattel mortgage and also stated the effect of recording or filing on the rights of third-party claimants.

To avoid the requirements for the execution and filing of the chattel mortgage, sellers of goods would sell the goods on a "conditional sales contract" under which the seller retained title to the goods until their purchase price had been paid in full. Upon default by the buyer, the seller could (*a*) repossess the goods or (*b*) pass title and recover a judgment for the unpaid balance of the purchase price. Abuses of this security device gave rise to some regulatory statutes. About one half of the states enacted statutes that provided that the conditional sales contract was void as to third parties unless it was filed or recorded.

No satisfactory device was developed whereby inventory could be used as security. The inherent difficulty is that inventory is intended to be sold and turned into cash and the creditor is interested in protecting his interest in the cash rather than in maintaining a lien on the sold goods. Field warehousing was used under the pledge, and an after-acquired property clause in a chattel mortgage on a stock of goods held for resale partially fulfilled this need. One of the devices used was the trust receipt. This short-term marketing security arrangement had its origin in the export-import trade. It was later used extensively as a means of financing retailers of consumer goods having a high unit value.

**Security Interests in Personal Property.** Chapter 40 will discuss how a creditor can obtain a security interest in the personal property or fixtures of a debtor. It will also explain the rights to the debtor's property of the creditor, the debtor, and other creditors of the debtor. These security interests are covered by Article 9 of the Uniform Commercial Code, which sets out a comprehensive scheme for regulating security interests in personal property and fixtures. The Code abolishes the old formal distinctions between different types of security devices used to create security interests in personal property.

**Security Interests in Real Property.** Three types of contractual security devices have been developed by which real estate may be used as security: (1) the real estate **mortgage,** (2) the **trust deed,** and (3) the **land contract.** In addition to these contract security devices, all of the states have enacted statutes granting the right to mechanic's liens on real estate. Security interests in real property are covered later in this chapter.

## LIENS ON PERSONAL PROPERTY

**Common Law Liens.** Under the common— or judge-made—law, artisans, innkeepers, and common carriers (such as airlines and trucking companies) were entitled to liens to secure the reasonable value of the services they performed. An artisan such as a furniture upholsterer or an auto mechanic uses his labor or materials to improve personal property that belongs to someone else. The improvement becomes part of the property and belongs to the owner of the property. Therefore, the artisan who made the improvement is given a lien on the property until he is paid. For example, the upholsterer who re-covers a sofa for a customer is entitled to a lien on the sofa.

The innkeeper and common carrier are in business to serve the public and are required by law to do so. Under the common law, the innkeeper, to secure payment for his reasonable charges for food and lodging, was allowed to claim a lien on the property that the guest brought to the hotel or inn. Similarly, the common carrier, such as a trucking company, was allowed to claim a lien on the goods carried for the *reasonable charges for the service.* The justification for such liens was that the innkeeper and common carrier were entitled to the protection of a lien because they were required by law to provide the service to anyone seeking it.

**Statutory Liens.** While common law liens are still generally recognized today, many states have incorporated this concept into statutes. Some of the state statutes have created additional liens, while others have modified the common law liens to some extent. The statutes commonly provide a procedure for foreclosing the lien. **Foreclosure** is the method by which a court authorizes the sale of the personal property subject to the lien so that the creditor can obtain the money to which he is entitled.

Carriers' liens and warehousemen's liens are provided for in Article 7, Documents of Title, of the Code. They are covered in Chapter 38.

**Characteristics of Liens.** The common law lien and most of the statutory liens are known as *possessory liens.* They give the artisan or other lienholder the *right to keep possession* of the debtor's property *until the reasonable charges for services have been paid.* For the lien to come into play, *possession* of the goods must have been *entrusted to the artisan.* Suppose a person takes a chair to an upholsterer to have it repaired. The upholsterer can keep possession of the chair until the person pays the reasonable value of the repair work. However, if the upholsterer comes to the person's home to make the repair, the upholsterer would not have a lien on the chair as the person did not give up possession of it.

The two essential elements of the lien are: (1) *possession by the improver or the provider of services* and (2) a *debt* created by the improvement or the provision of services concerning the goods. If the artisan or other lienholder gives up the goods voluntarily, he loses the lien. For example, if a person has a new engine put in his car and the mechanic gives the car back to him before he pays for the engine, the mechanic loses the lien on the car to secure the person's payment for the work and materials. However, if the debtor regains possession by fraud or another illegal act, the lien is not lost. Once the debt has been paid, the lien is terminated and the artisan or other lienholder no longer has the right to retain the goods. If the artisan keeps the goods after the debt has been paid, or keeps the goods without the right to a lien, he is liable for conversion or unlawful detention of goods.

The *Younger v. Plunkett* case, which follows, illustrates another important aspect of common law liens, namely that the work or service must have been performed at the request of the owner of the property. If the work or service is performed without the consent of the owner, no lien is created.

**Foreclosure of Lien.** The right of a lienholder to possess goods does not automatically give the lienholder the right to sell the goods or to claim ownership if his charges are not paid. Commonly, there is a procedure provided by statute for selling property once it has been held for a certain period of time. The lienholder is required to give notice to the debtor and to advertise the proposed sale by posting or publishing notices. If there is no statutory procedure, the lienholder must first bring a lawsuit against the debtor. After obtaining a judgment for his charges, the lienholder can have the sheriff seize the property and have it sold at a judicial sale.

## Younger v. Plunkett

**395 F. Supp. 702 (E.D. Pa. 1975)**

Thomas Younger was involved in a traffic accident when the car he was driving collided with another car. A police officer arrived at the scene, accompanied by a tow truck from the West End Towing Service. While Younger was talking to the police officer, West End towed Younger's car to its place of business. Younger claimed that this was done without his permission. West End did not dispute this and said that it had been ordered to tow the car by the police. Younger was told by West End that the bill for towing was $15 and that the storage charges were $53. Younger was arrested and convicted of criminal trespass when he tried to take his car without paying.

During May and June, John Shumate regularly parked his automobile on a vacant lot in downtown Philadelphia. At that time, no signs were posted prohibiting parking on the lot or indicating that vehicles parked there without authorization would be towed. On July 7, Shumate again left his car on the lot. When he returned two days later, the car was gone and the lot was posted with signs warning that parking was prohibited. Shumate learned that his car had been towed away by Ruffie's Towing Service and that the car was being held by Ruffie's at its place of business. Ruffie's refused to release the car until Shumate paid a towing fee of $44.50 plus storage charges of $4 per day. Shumate refused to pay the fee, and Ruffie's kept possession of the car.

Younger and Shumate brought lawsuits against Robert Plunkett and others, the owners of the two towing services, to recover possession of their automobiles.

**Higginbotham, District Judge.** Possessory liens are fundamentally consensual in nature and arise from some agreement, either express or implied, between the owner of goods and his bailee who renders some service with respect to those goods. At common law the right of a bailee to assert a lien meant the right to physically retain custody of the goods, even upon demand of the owner for their return, until the bailee was compensated for this service.

The consensual quality of the transaction which gave rise to possessory liens at early common law has been held an indispensable element of the common law possessory lien recognized by Pennsylvania courts, and this principle is nowhere more clearly stated than in *Meyers v. Bratespiece* (1896). In *Meyers,* Meyers contracted with one Abraham Harris to have cloth made into coats at 35 cents per coat. Harris then contracted with Bratespiece, without Meyers' knowledge or consent, to have the cloth made into coats at 50 cents per coat and thereafter absconded after collecting part of the money due from Meyers. After the coats were made, Bratespiece refused to deliver them to Meyers and claimed a possessory lien, and Meyers brought an action. The court held:

> We agree that Bratespiece had no lien for his labor on the goods of Meyers that he received from Harris, their bailee. There was no contractual relation between him and the owners.
>
> Whenever a workman or artisan, by his labor or skill, increases the value of personal property placed in his possession to be improved, he has a lien upon it for his proper charges until paid, but "in order to charge a chattel with this lien the labor for which the lien is claimed must have been done at the request of the owner, or under circumstances from which his assent can be reasonably implied. It does not extend to one not in privity with the owners." These appear to be well-settled principles relating to and governing the common law lien which Bratespiece claimed he had on Meyers' goods, but they very clearly demonstrate, we think that his claim was without any just or legal foundation. This principle has been followed by Pennsylvania courts without exception.

The power of the police to remove a disabled vehicle from a public way is not contested, but absent a statutory authorization, police are not thereby empowered to create a lien upon the vehicle in favor of a private towing company which is effective against the vehicle owner without his consent.

No exception to the assent requirement in the creation of possessory liens is recognized at common law under the circumstances alleged in the present case, and no such exception has been construed as arising by implication from the authority of a police officer to remove a disabled automobile from a public way or the right of a property owner to remove a vehicle left on his property without his consent. That is not to say that in some jurisdictions police officers and perhaps even property owners do not have such power, but it is one expressly granted by statute or ordinance. From the authorities my research has disclosed both in Pennsylvania and in other states, it is my conclusion that the Supreme Court of Pennsylvania if confronted with the state law question of whether these defendants have common law possessory liens on plaintiffs' automobiles would follow *Meyers v. Bratespiece,* and find that in the absence of plaintiffs' assent to the towing neither defendant is entitled to a possessory lien under common law principles.

Judgment for Younger and Shumate.

## SURETYSHIP AND GUARANTEE

**Sureties and Guarantors.** A **surety** is a person who is *liable for the payment of another person's debt* or for the *performance of another person's duty.* The surety joins with the person primarily liable in promising to make the payment or to perform the duty. For example, Kathleen, who is 17 years old, buys a used car on credit from Harry's Used Cars. She signs a promissory note, agreeing to pay $50 a month on the note until the note is paid in full. Harry's has Kathleen's father cosign the note; thus, her father is a surety. Similarly, the city of Chicago hires the B&B Construction Company to build a new sewage treatment plant. The city will probably require B&B to have a surety agree to be liable for B&B's performance of its contract. There are insurance companies that, for a fee, will agree to be a surety on the contract of a company such as B&B. If the person who is primarily liable (the **principal**) defaults, the surety is liable to pay or perform. Upon default, the creditor may ask the surety to pay even if he has not asked the principal debtor to pay. Then, the surety is entitled to be reimbursed by the principal.

A **guarantor** does not join in making a promise; rather, a guarantor *makes a separate promise* and *agrees to be liable upon the happening of a certain event.* For example, a father tells a merchant, "I will guarantee payment of my son Richard's debt to you if he does not pay it," or "If Richard becomes bankrupt, I will guarantee payment of his debt to you." A guarantor's promise must be made in writing to be enforceable under the statute of frauds.

The rights and liabilities of the surety and the guarantor are substantially the same. No distinction will be made between them in this chapter except where the distinction is of basic importance.

**Creation of Principal and Surety Relationship.** The relationship of principal and surety, or that of principal and guarantor, is created by contract. The basic rules of contract law apply in determining the existence and nature of the relationship as well as the rights and duties of the parties.

**Defenses of a Surety.** Suppose Jeffrey's father agrees to be a surety for Jeffrey on his purchase of a motorcycle. If the motorcycle was defectively made and Jeffrey refuses to make further payments on it, the dealer might try to collect the balance due from Jeffrey's father. As a surety, Jeffrey's father can use any defenses against the dealer that Jeffrey has if they go to the merits of the primary contract. Thus, if Jeffrey has a valid defense of breach of warranty against the dealer, his father can use it as a basis for not paying the dealer.

Other defenses that go to the merits include (1) lack or failure of consideration, (2) inducement of the contract by fraud or duress, and (3) breach of contract by the other party. Certain defenses of the principal cannot be used by the surety. These defenses include lack of capacity, such as minority or insanity, and bankruptcy. Thus, if Jeffrey is only 17 years old, the fact that he is a minor cannot be used by Jeffrey's father to defend against the dealer. This defense of Jeffrey's lack of capacity to contract does not go to the merits of the contract between Jeffrey and the dealer and cannot be used by Jeffrey's father.

A surety contracts to be responsible for the performance of the principal's obligation. If the principal and the creditor change that obligation by agreement, the surety is relieved of responsibility unless the surety agrees to the change. This is because the surety's obligation cannot be changed without his consent.

For example, Fredericks cosigns a note for his friend Kato, which she has given to Credit

Union to secure a loan. Suppose the note was originally for $500 and payable in 12 months with interest at 11 percent a year. Credit Union and Kato later agree that Kato will have 24 months to repay the note but that the interest will be 13 percent per year. Unless Fredericks consents to this change, he is discharged from his responsibility as surety. The obligation he agreed to assume was altered by the changes in the repayment period and the interest rate.

The most common kind of change affecting a surety is an extension of time to perform the contract. If the creditor merely allows the principal more time without the surety's consent, this does not relieve the surety of responsibility. The surety's consent is required only where there is an actual agreement between the creditor and the principal as to the extension of time. In addition, the courts usually make a distinction between accommodation sureties and compensated sureties. An *accommodation surety* is a person who acts as a surety without compensation, such as a friend who cosigns a note as a favor. A *compensated surety* is a person, usually a professional such as a bonding company, who is paid for serving as a surety.

The courts are more protective of accommodation sureties than of compensated sureties. Accommodation sureties are relieved of liability unless they consent to an extension of time. Compensated sureties, on the other hand, must show that they will be harmed by an extension of time before they are relieved of responsibility because of an extension without their consent. This principle is illustrated in the *Phoenix Assurance Co. v. City of Buckner* case which follows.

**Creditor's Duties to Surety.** The creditor is required to disclose any material facts about the risk involved to the surety. If he does not do so, the surety is relieved of liability. For example, a bank (creditor) knows that an employee, Arthur, has been guilty of criminal conduct in the past. If the bank applies to a bonding company to obtain a bond on Arthur, the bank must disclose this information about Arthur. Similarly, suppose the bank has an employee, Alison, covered by a bond and discovers that Alison is embezzling money. If the bank agrees to give Alison another chance but does not report her actions to the bonding company, the bonding company is relieved of responsibility for further wrongful acts by Alison.

If the principal posts security for the performance of an obligation, the creditor must not surrender the security without the consent of the surety. If the creditor does so, the surety is relieved of liability to the extent of the value surrendered.

**Subrogation and Contribution.** If the surety has to perform or pay the principal's obligation, then the surety acquires all of the rights that the creditor had against the principal. This is known as the surety's *right of subrogation.* For example, Amado cosigns a promissory note for $250 at the credit union for her friend Anders. Anders defaults on the note, and the credit union collects $250 from Amado on her suretyship obligation. Amado then gets the credit union's right against Anders, that is, the right to collect $250 from Anders.

Suppose several persons (Tom, Dick, and Harry) are cosureties of their friend Sam. When Sam defaults, Tom pays the whole obligation. Tom is entitled to collect one third from both Dick and Harry since he paid more than his prorated share. This is known as the cosurety's *right to contribution.*

## Phoenix Assurance Co. v. City of Buckner, Missouri

**305 F.2d 54 (8th Cir. 1962)**

On March 30, 1956, the city of Buckner entered into a contract with William Reser, doing business as Continental Construction Company. The contract called for the construction of a sewer system for the City at a cost of $97,036.85. By the terms of the contract, work was to commence at a date to be specified by the City in a written notice to proceed, delivered to the contractor, and was to be completed within 300 days thereafter; the contractor was to "pay the prevailing wage rates in the district pertaining to the trade" and to furnish a performance bond in an amount equal to the contract price, for the faithful carrying out of the contract and the payment of all persons performing labor or furnishing materials.

Reser procured the performance bond from the Phoenix Assurance Company by paying a premium of $870.37, in consideration of which Phoenix agreed to indemnify the City for any default by Reser in the performance of his contract. The bond contained the following provision:

> PROVIDED FURTHER, That the said Surety, for value received, hereby stipulates and agrees that no change, extension of time, alteration, or addition to the terms of the contract, or the work to be performed thereunder or in the specifications accompanying the same, shall in any wise affect its obligation on this bond, and it does hereby waive notice of any change, extension of time, alteration, or addition to the terms of the contract, or to the work, or to the specifications.

Prior to signing the contract with Reser, the City had applied to the federal Housing and Home Finance Agency for financial aid regarding the sewer project. Completion of the paperwork delayed HHFA approval until February 21, 1957, and the City notified Reser two days later to proceed with the work. Reser began the work in April, ran into a dispute with the union in September, and then "quit the job." The City gave notice of default, terminated the contract, and requested Phoenix to take over and complete the job, which it did not do. Instead, Phoenix brought suit against the City seeking to have the bond declared void. The trial court held for the city of Buckner, and Phoenix appealed.

**Sanborn, Circuit Judge.** Phoenix was a compensated surety. One who engages in the business of insurance for compensation may properly be held more rigidly to his obligation to indemnify the insured than one whose suretyship is an undertaking uncompensated or casual.

There is no merit in the contention of Phoenix that the performance bond was invalid because the City did not, at the time it contracted with Reser for the construction of the sewer system, have the funds on hand to complete the project. The City, in order to finance the project, had authorized the issuance of bonds, and had applied to the Housing and Home Finance Agency for their purchase. Neither Reser nor his surety could have had any illusions about how the project was to be financed or could have believed that it was to be an immediate "cash and carry" operation. Moreover, if the performance bond was invalid at the time of its execution, a return or tender back of the completely unearned premium would be a prerequisite to the maintenance of this action.

Phoenix contends that it was materially prejudiced by the long delay of the City in giving notice to Reser to proceed with the work—this because prices of material and labor had increased substantially in the interval, thus imposing upon Phoenix a greater risk than it was originally intended to bear—and that the provision in the bond that no change, extension of time, alteration, or addition to the terms of Reser's contract should affect the obligation of the surety is, for some reason not apparent to us, inapplicable under the facts of this case.

The general rule relative to extension of time is stated in 50 Am. Jur., Suretyship, § 322, as follows:

> In accordance with the rule that a surety company can be relieved from its obligation for suretyship only where a departure from the contract is shown to be a material variance, it is held that an extension of time will not relieve a surety company on a bond unless the extension exceeds the time limit in the bond for bringing suit thereon, or unless the surety company is thereby made to suffer material harm; and that there will be no presumption of injury unless injury is alleged and proved.

It was the obligation of Phoenix to protect the City from any default by Reser on the performance of his contract, and not the obligation of the City to protect Phoenix against loss on account of its assumption of a risk for which it was paid and which turned out badly because of Reser's lack of financial responsibility, and inability to complete his undertaking.

Judgment for the City of Buckner affirmed.

## SECURITY INTERESTS IN REAL PROPERTY

There are three basic contract devices for using real estate as security for an obligation: (1) the real estate **mortgage,** (2) the **deed of trust,** and (3) the **land contract.** In addition, the states have enacted statutes giving mechanics, such as carpenters and plumbers, and materialmen, such as lumberyards, a right to a lien on real property into which their labor or materials have been incorporated.

**Historical Developments of Mortgages.** A mortgage is a security interest in real property or a deed to real property that is given by the owner (the **mortgagor**) as security for a debt owed to the creditor (the **mortgagee**). The real estate mortgage was used as a form of security in England as early as the middle of the 12th century, but our present-day mortgage law developed from the common law mortgage of the 15th century. The common law mortgage was a deed that conveyed the land to the mortgagee, with the title to the land to return to the mortgagor upon payment of the debt secured by the mortgage. The mortgagee was given possession of the land during the term of the mortgage. If the mortgagor defaulted on the debt, the mortgagee's title to the land became absolute. The land was forfeited as a penalty, but the forfeiture did not discharge the debt. In addition to keeping the land, the mortgagee could sue on the debt, recover a judgment, and seek to collect the debt.

The early equity courts did not favor the imposition of penalties and would relieve mortgagors from such forfeitures, provided that the mortgagor's default was minor and was due to causes beyond his control. Gradually, the courts became more lenient in permitting redemptions and allowed the mortgagor to redeem (reclaim his property) if he tendered performance without unreasonable delay. Finally, the courts of equity recognized the mortgagor's right to redeem as an absolute right that would continue until the mortgagee asked the court of equity to decree that the mortgagor's right to redeem be foreclosed and cut off. Our present law regarding the foreclosure of mortgages developed from this practice.

Today, the mortgage is generally viewed as a lien on land rather than a conveyance of title to the land. There are still some states where the mortgagor goes through the process of giving the mortgagee some sort of legal title to the property. Even in these states, however, the mortgagee's title is minimal and the real ownership of the property remains in the mortgagor.

**Form, Execution, and Recording.** Because the real estate mortgage conveys an *interest in real property,* it must be executed with the same formality as a deed. Unless it is executed with the required formalities, it will not be eligible for recording in the local land records. Recordation of the mortgage does *not* affect its validity as between the mortgagor and the mortgagee. However, if it is not recorded, it will not be effective against subsequent purchasers of the property or creditors, including other mortgagees, who have no notice of the earlier mortgage. It is important to the mortgagee that the mortgage be recorded so that the world will be on notice of the mortgagee's interest in the property.

**Rights and Liabilities.** The owner (mortgagor) of property subject to a mortgage can sell the interest in the property without the consent of the mortgagee. However, the sale does not affect the mortgagee's interest in the property or the mortgagee's claim against the mortgagor.

For example, Eric Smith owns a lot on a lake. He wants to build a cottage on the land, so he borrows $35,000 from First National Bank. He signs a note for $35,000 and gives the bank a $35,000 mortgage on the land and cottage as security for his repayment of the loan. Several years later, Smith sells his land and cottage to Melinda Mason. The mortgage he gave First National might make the unpaid balance due on the mortgage payable on sale. If it does not, Smith can sell the property with the mortgage on it. If Mason agreed to assume the mortgage but defaults on making the mortgage payments, the bank can foreclose on the mortgage. If at the foreclosure sale the property does not bring enough money to cover the costs, interest, and balance due on the mortgage, First National is entitled to a deficiency judgment against Smith. However, some courts are reluctant to give deficiency judgments where real property is used as security for a debt. If on foreclosure the property sells for more than the debt, Mason is entitled to the surplus.

A purchaser of mortgaged property may buy it *subject to the mortgage* or may *assume the mortgage.* If she buys subject to the mortgage and there is a default and foreclosure, the purchaser is *not* personally liable for any deficiency. The property is liable for the mortgage debt and can be sold to satisfy it in case of default. If the buyer assumes the mortgage, then she becomes personally liable for the debt and for any deficiency on default and foreclosure.

The creditor (mortgagee) may assign his interest in the mortgaged property. To do this, the mortgagee must assign the mortgage as well as the debt for which the mortgage is security. In most jurisdictions, the negotiation of the note carries with it the right to the security and the holder of the note is entitled to the benefits of the mortgage.

**Foreclosure.** **Foreclosure** is the process by which any rights of the mortgagor or the current property owner are cut off. Foreclosure proceedings are regulated by statute in the state in which the property is located. In many states, two or more alternative methods of foreclosure are available to the mortgagee or his assignee. The methods in common use today are (1) **strict foreclosure,** (2) **action and sale,** and (3) **power of sale.**

A small number of states permit what is called "strict foreclosure." The creditor keeps the property in satisfaction of the debt, and the owner's rights are cut off. This means that the creditor has no right to a deficiency and the debtor has no right to any surplus. Strict foreclosure is normally limited to situations where the amount of the debt exceeds the value of the property.

Foreclosure by action and sale is permitted in all states, and it is the only method of foreclosure permitted in some states. Although the state statutes are not uniform, they are alike in their basic requirements. In a foreclosure by action and sale, suit is brought in a court having jurisdiction. Any party having a property interest that would be cut off by the foreclosure must be made a defendant, and if any such party has a defense, he must enter his appearance and set up his defense. After the case is tried, a judgment is entered and a sale of the property ordered. The proceeds of the sale are applied to the payment of the mortgage debt, and any surplus is paid over to the mortgagor. If there is a deficiency, a deficiency judgment is, as a general rule, entered against the mortgagor and such other persons as are liable on the debt. Deficiency judgments are generally not permitted where the property sold is the residence of the debtor.

The right to foreclose under a power of sale must be expressly conferred on the mortgagee by the terms of the mortgage. If the procedure for the exercise of the power is set out in the mortgage, that procedure must be followed. Several states have enacted statutes that set out the procedure to be followed in the exercise of a power of sale. No court action is required. As a general rule, notice of the default and sale must be given to the mortgagor. After the statutory period, the sale may be held. The sale must be advertised, and it must be at auction. The sale must be conducted fairly, and an effort must be made to sell the property at the highest price obtainable. The proceeds of the sale are applied to the payment of costs, interest, and the principal of the debt. Any surplus must be paid to the mortgagor. If there is a deficiency and the mortgagee wishes to recover a judgment for the deficiency, he must bring suit on the debt.

**Right of Redemption.** At common law and under existing statutes, the mortgagor or an assignee of the mortgagor has what is called an *equity of redemption* in the mortgaged real estate. This means that he has the absolute right to discharge the mortgage when due and to have title to the mortgaged property restored free and clear of the mortgage debt. Under the statutes of all states, the mortgagor or any party having an interest in the mortgaged property that will be cut off by the foreclosure may redeem the property after default and before the mortgagee forecloses the mortgage. In several states, the mortgagor or any other party in interest is given by statute what is known as a redemption period (usually six months or one year, beginning either after the foreclosure proceedings are started or after a foreclosure sale of the mortgaged property has been made) in which to pay the mortgaged debt, costs, and interest and to redeem the property.

As a general rule, if a party in interest wishes to redeem, he must, if the redemption period runs after the foreclosure sale, pay to the purchaser at the foreclosure sale the amount that the purchaser has paid plus interest up to the time of redemption. If the redemption period runs before the sale, the party in interest must pay the amount of the debt plus the costs and interest. The person who wishes to redeem from a mortgage foreclosure sale must redeem the entire mortgage interest; he cannot redeem a partial interest by paying a proportionate amount of the debt or by paying a proportionate amount of the price bid at the foreclosure sale.

**Deed of Trust.** There are three parties to a **deed of trust:** (1) the owner of the property who borrows the money (the **debtor**), (2) the **trustee** who holds legal title to the property put up as security, and (3) the lender who is the **beneficiary** of the trust. The purpose of the deed of trust is to make it easy for the security to be liquidated. However, most states treat the deed of trust like a mortgage in giving the borrower a relatively long period of time to redeem the property, thereby defeating this rationale for the arrangement.

In a deed of trust transaction, the borrower deeds to the trustee the property that is to be put up as security. The trust agreement usually gives the trustee the right to foreclose or sell the property if the debtor fails to make a required payment on the debt. Normally, the trustee does not sell the property until the lender notifies him that the borrower is in default and demands that the property be sold. The trustee must notify the debtor that he is in default and that the land will be sold. The trustee advertises the property for sale. After the statutory period, the trustee will sell the property at a public or private sale. The proceeds are applied to the costs of the foreclosure, interest, and debt. If there is a surplus, it is paid to the borrower. If there is a deficiency, the lender has to sue the borrower on the debt and recover a judgment.

**Land Contracts.** The **land contract** is a device for securing the balance due the seller on the purchase price of real estate. The buyer agrees to pay the purchase price over a period of time. The seller agrees to convey title to the property to the buyer when the full price is paid. Usually, the buyer takes possession of the property, pays the taxes, insures the property, and assumes the other obligations of an owner. However, the seller keeps legal title and does not turn over the deed until the purchase price is paid. If the buyer defaults, the seller usually has the right to declare a forfeiture and take over possession of the property. The buyer's rights to the property are cut off at that point. Most states give the buyer on a land contract a limited period of time to redeem his interest. Some states require the seller to go through a foreclosure proceeding. Generally, the procedure for declaring a forfeiture and recovering property sold on a land contract is simpler and less time consuming than foreclosure of a mortgage. In most states, the procedure in case of default is set out by statute. If the buyer, after default, voluntarily surrenders possession to the seller, no court procedure is necessary; the seller's title will become absolute, and the buyer's equity will be cut off. Purchases of farm property are commonly financed through the use of land contracts.

As can be seen in the following case, *Morris v. Weigle,* some courts have invoked the equitable doctrine against forfeitures and have required that the seller on a land contract must foreclose on the property in order to avoid injustice to a defaulting buyer.

## Morris v. Weigle

**383 N.E.2d 341 (Ind. Sup. Ct. 1978)**

In 1966, Wilford Morris agreed to purchase a farm for $57,000 from Charles and Ruth Weigle on a land sale contract. The down payment was $15,000, with $2,000 annual payments plus interest on the unpaid balance. The land sale contract included the following pertinent provisions: (1) annual payments were to be made each year on March 1; (2) time is of the essence; (3) improvements on the real estate were to be insured and kept in good repair; and (4) the Weigles, upon default and notice, could terminate the contract and keep the payments made as liquidated damages. When Morris fell behind in his payments, the Weigles repossessed the property and brought suit to declare a forfeiture of the payments that Morris had made. The trial court ruled in favor of the Weigles and the Court of Appeals affirmed. Morris appealed to the Indiana Supreme Court.

**Hunter, Justice.** At the time the Weigles repossessed the land, Morris had paid a total of $24,722.97 on the contract; of that amount, $16,922.97 was principal and $7,800.00 was interest. The trial court ruled, and the Court of Appeals affirmed, that the Weigles should retain the entire $24,722.97 as liquidated damages stemming from Morris's breach of contract. We disagree. Morris has paid 29.7 percent of the contract price. This is a substantial amount. His equity in the property mitigated against the enforcement of any forfeiture provision which might have appeared in the land contract. This Court discussed, in *Skendzel v. Marshall,* the fact that a land sale contract is akin to a mortgage and that, therefore, the remedy of foreclosure is more consonant with notions of fairness and justice. We outlined, in *Skendzel v. Marshall,* certain limited situations in which forfeiture would be justified:

> In the case of an abandoning, absconding vendee, forfeiture is a logical and equitable remedy. Forfeiture would also be appropriate where the vendee has paid a minimal amount on the contract at the time of default *and* seeks to retain possession while the vendor is paying taxes, insurance, and other upkeep in order to preserve the premises. Of course, in that latter situation, the vendee will have acquired very little, if any, equity in the property. However, a court of equity must *always* approach forfeitures with great caution, being forever aware of the possibility of inequitable dispossession of property and exorbitant monetary loss. We are persuaded that forfeiture may only be appropriate under circumstances in which it is found to be consonant with notions of fairness and justice under the law.

There was no showing that Morris intended to relinquish the property. The burden of proving abandonment was the Weigles' affirmative burden, and Mr. Weigle himself testified that until the point of repossession Morris maintained "custody and control" over the property. We note that until the Weigles repossessed the property, Morris had kept the real estate taxes and mortgage installments current. In fact, he tendered tax and mortgage payments after the Weigles had repossessed, but they were returned with the notation that payment had been received. The facts regarding late payments and the failure or inability of Morris to keep the property insured were conflicting; but, certainly, the evidence supported a finding that the contract had been breached.

Notwithstanding the breach, there was nothing in the record to suggest that foreclosure on the property would not have satisfactorily protected the interests of both parties. Although evidence was presented which showed that the market value of the house had decreased from $7,000 to $1,000 during the contract, the value of the entire real estate had not diminished at all. Therefore, the Weigles' security interest in the property was never endangered. Weigle testified that he *knew* that the property was worth more than the amount due under the contract. Morris was offered $65,000 for the property.

Properly applying the equitable principles outlined in *Skendzel v. Marshall,* it is obvious that this is neither a case of an abandoning or absconding vendee nor a case wherein a minimal amount has been paid and the security of the property has been endangered by the acts or omissions of the vendee. Forfeiture provisions in a land contract are not *per se* to be deemed unenforceable; but, under certain circumstances they may become unenforceable because of the equity underlying any contract. The court, in the exercise of its equitable powers, does not infringe upon the rights of citizens to freely contract, but the court does refuse, upon equitable grounds, to enforce the contract because of the actual circumstances at the time the court is called upon to enforce it. Foreclosure is the appropriate remedy, a remedy which is consonant with notions of fairness and justice under the law.

Judgment reversed in favor of Morris.

**Pivarnik, Justice, Dissenting.** I am in total disagreement with the majority opinion in that its effect is to set aside a legal contract entered into by the parties and to substitute contract provisions that were not contemplated or bargained for by any or all of the parties involved.

When parties enter into negotiations for the sale and purchase of real estate, there are generally two contract arrangements that can be chosen to effect this transfer. One of these is the mortgage arrangement, of course, which is most usually done through a professional banking or financial institution. The purchaser receives the legal title to the property and executes a note to the financial institution, together with a mortgage or pledge of the real estate for a payment of said purchase price. In the mortgage arrangement, the seller receives his full payment and no longer has an interest in the property. Foreclosure of the mortgage is the method of recovery for a mortgagor in the event that there is a default in the payment of the purchase price. This arrangement can also be entered into, of course, by individuals, but this is rarely done.

In the land contract arrangement, such as is presented by the present case, individuals who wish to enter into an agreement to buy and sell real estate contract between themselves as to the conditions of that sale and purchase. This method of contract is selected by the parties to meet the needs of their particular transaction. It has advantages to one or both of the parties because it presents terms as to down payment, interest rate, and other features of immediate transfer, different from a mortgage arrangement, which terms are more convenient or desirable for the parties at that particular time. The point I make is that mortgages and land contracts are two different types of contracts entered into by the parties openly, willingly, and to meet their own purposes. I see no need for a lengthy discussion here as to the differences in the two contract arrangements, as such differences are apparent, but I would simply state that appeals courts should honor contracts as they were made by the parties and enforce them regardless of where the chips may appear to fall from this perspective.

There is no denial by anyone, including the majority, that the contract in this case was breached by the purchasers. In *Skendzel v. Marshall,* this court found that a land sale contract is akin to a mortgage, and that therefore the remedy of foreclosure is more consonant with notions of fairness and justice. The problem with this view is that while a land sale contract may be akin to a mortgage, it is not a mortgage, and the remedy of foreclosure is not the remedy the parties agreed to. The standards set down in both *Skendzel* and in the majority in this case, for finding that forfeiture is appropriate, require the court to take the "mechanistic approach" and examine the facts and circumstances of the parties such as the amount paid on the contract, the amount due and owing, and the apparent gain or loss of one party or the other. Neither *Skendzel,* nor the majority in this case, holds that land sale contracts are illegal, unconscionable, or contrary to law. They merely find that in some cases they will be enforced and that in some cases they will not be. Because the trial court is invited to use its own judgment as to when it would be fair and just to enforce a contract, and when it would not be, parties entering into contracts, their attorneys advising them, and trial courts hearing the matters would have difficulty in knowing what the law is in any given case.

## MECHANIC'S AND MATERIALMAN'S LIENS

Each state has a statute that permits persons who contract to furnish labor or materials to improve real estate to claim a lien on the property until they are paid. There are many differences among states as to exactly who can claim such a lien and the requirements that must be met to do so.

**Rights of Subcontractors and Materialmen.** A general contractor is a person who has contracted with the owner to build, remodel, or improve real property. A subcontractor is a person who has contracted with the general contractor to perform a stipulated portion of the general contract. A materialman is a person who has contracted to furnish certain materials needed to perform a designated general contract.

Two distinct systems—the New York system and the Pennsylvania system—are followed by the states in allowing mechanic's liens on real estate to subcontractors and materialmen.

The New York system is based on the theory of subrogation, and the subcontractors or materialmen cannot recover more than is owed to the contractor at the time they file a lien or give notice of a lien to the owner. Under the Pennsylvania system, the subcontractors or materialmen have direct liens and are entitled to liens for the value of labor and materials furnished, irrespective of the amount due from the owner to the contractor. Under the New York system the general contractor's failure to perform his contract or his abandonment of the work has a direct effect on the lien rights of subcontractors and materialmen, whereas under the Pennsylvania system such breach or abandonment by the general contractor does not directly affect the lien rights of subcontractors and materialmen.

**Basis for Mechanic's or Materialman's Lien.** Some state statutes provide that no lien shall be claimed unless the contract for the improvement is in writing and embodies a statement of the materials to be furnished and a description of the land on which the improvement is to take place and of the work to be done. Other states permit the contract to be oral, but in no state is a licensee or volunteer entitled to a lien.

No lien can be claimed unless the work is done or the materials are furnished in the performance of a contract to improve specific real property. A sale of materials without reference to the improvement of specific real property does not entitle the person furnishing the materials to a lien on real property that is, in fact, improved by the use of the materials at some time after the sale.

Unless the state statute specifically includes submaterialmen, they are not entitled to a lien. For example, if a lumber dealer contracts to furnish the lumber for the erection of a specific building and orders from a sawmill a carload of lumber that is needed to fulfill the contract, the sawmill will not be entitled to a lien on the building in which the lumber is used unless the state statute expressly provides that submaterialmen are entitled to a lien.

At times, the question has arisen as to whether materials have been furnished. Some courts have held that the materialman must prove that the material furnished was actually incorporated into the structure. Under this ruling, if material delivered on the job is diverted by the general contractor or others and not incorporated into the structure, the materialman will not be entitled to a lien. Other courts have held that the materialman is entitled to a lien if he can provide proof that the material was delivered on the job under a contract to furnish the material.

The *Bowen v. Collins* case, below, discusses the requirement that a person claiming a materialman's lien must show that the materials were used in the building on which a lien is claimed.

**Requirements for Obtaining Lien.** The requirements for obtaining a mechanic's or materialman's lien must be complied with strictly. Although there is no uniformity in the statutes as to the requirements for obtaining a lien, the statutes generally require the *filing of a notice of lien* with a county official, such as the register of deeds or the county clerk, which notice sets forth the amount claimed, the name of the owner, the names of the contractor and the claimant, and a description of the property. Frequently, the notice of lien must be verified by an affidavit of the claimant. In some states, a copy of the notice must be served on the owner or posted on the property.

The notice of lien must be filed within a stipulated time. The time varies from 30 to 90 days, but the favored time is 60 days after the last work performed or after the last materials furnished. Some statutes distinguish between labor claims, materialmen's claims, and claims of general contractors as to time of filing. The lien, when filed, must be foreclosed within a specified time, which generally varies from six months to two years.

**Priorities and Foreclosure.** The provisions for priorities vary widely, but most of the statutes provide that a mechanic's lien has priority over all liens attaching after the first work is performed or after the first materials are furnished. This statutory provision creates a hidden lien on the property, in that a mechanic's lien, filed within the allotted period of time after completion of the work, attaches as of the time the first work is done or the first material is furnished, but no notice of lien need be filed during this period. And if no notice of lien is filed during this period, third persons would have no means of knowing of the existence of a lien. There are no priorities among lien claimants under the majority of the statutes.

The procedure followed in the foreclosure of a mechanic's lien on real estate follows closely the procedure followed in a court foreclosure of a real estate mortgage. The rights acquired by the filing of a lien and the extent of the property covered by the lien are set out in some of the mechanic's lien statutes. In general, the lien attaches only to the interest that the person has in the property that has been improved at the time the notice is filed. Some statutes provide that the lien attaches to the building and to the city lot on which the building stands, or if the improvement is to farm property, the lien attaches to a specified amount of land.

**Waiver of Lien.** The question often arises as to the effect of an express provision in a contract for the improvement of real estate that no lien shall attach to the property for the cost of the improvement. In some states, there is a statute requiring the recording or filing of the contract and making such a provision ineffective if the statute is not complied with. In some states, courts have held that such a provision is effective against everyone; in other states, courts have held that the provision is ineffective against everyone except the contractor; and in still other states, courts have held that such a provision is ineffective as to subcontractors, materialmen, and laborers. Whether the parties to the contract have notice of the waiver of lien provision plays an important part in several states in determining their right to a lien.

It is common practice that before a person who is having improvements made to his property makes final payment, he requires the contractor to sign an affidavit that all materialmen and subcontractors have been paid and to supply him with a release of lien signed by the subcontractors and materialmen.

## Bowen v. Collins

**217 S.E.2d (Ga. Ct. App. 1975)**

Bowen-Rogers Hardware Company was engaged in the business of furnishing materials for the construction of buildings. It delivered a quantity of materials to property owned by Ronald and Carol Collins. The materials were for the use of a contractor who was building a home for the Collinses as well as several other houses in the area. The hardware company was not paid for the materials by the contractor, and it sought to obtain a materialman's lien against the Collins' property. The Collinses claimed that even though the materials were delivered to their home, they were actually used to build other houses in the area. The trial court held that Bowen-Rogers Hardware was not entitled to a materialman's lien. Bowen-Rogers Hardware appealed.

**Evans, Judge.** Laws as to liens of mechanics and materialmen who supply labor or materials for the improvement of realty are in derogation of the common law and must be strictly construed; and one who claims a lien must bring himself clearly within the law. The burden was on Bowen-Rogers Hardware to prove that the materials furnished actually went into construction of the Collins' building, under a contract, and the value of same.

Since there was evidence here from which the jury could infer that much of the material charged against the Collins' job did not go into the construction of the Collins' dwelling, the court did not err in charging the jury that to obtain a lien, the supplies must be furnished for the purpose of improving the owner's property and that they were in fact used in such improvements. In *Schofield v. Stout,* it was held that such improvements must be attached to and become incorporated in the realty.

Where a materialman furnishes and delivers material to the owner's premises in reliance on the owner's representations that the material is intended to be used for the improvement of the property, the owner is estopped as between the parties to contend that the material was not in fact so used. But there was no estoppel of the owner under the facts here, and the above statement of law does not apply.

Bowen-Rogers Hardware proved the material was charged to the contractor but did not prove that all of same was delivered to the Collins' job. Materials were supplied to several other houses in the immediate area, and some of the materials were supposedly delivered to the job by the contractor's employees.

Judgment for Collins affirmed.

## SUMMARY

Credit is a transaction in which goods are sold and delivered, services are rendered, or money is loaned in exchange for the recipient's promise to pay at some future date. Unsecured credit is credit given on the recipient's unsupported promise to pay. Secured credit is credit supported by the grant of an interest in real or personal property or the supporting promise of a third person to whom the creditor can resort for payment if the debtor does not pay.

Artisans, innkeepers, and common carriers are entitled to common law liens for their reasonable charges. The common law lien is a possessory lien, and an artisan is not entitled to a lien unless possession of the property on which work is to be done is surrendered to him. The two essential elements of a common law lien are (1) a debt and (2) possession of the property by the creditor. Most states have enacted statutes defining the rights to liens on personal property. If the lienholder wishes to foreclose a common law lien, he must sue the debtor, obtain a judgment, have an execution issued on the judgment and levied on the goods, and have the goods sold at a sheriff's sale. In most states, a simplified foreclosure procedure has been provided for by statute.

A surety, in the broad sense, is a person who is liable for the payment of another person's debt. Technically, the surety joins with the principal in making the promise to the promisee, whereas the guarantor makes a collateral promise, promising to perform the principal's promise upon the happening of a condition precedent. The relationship of surety is created by contract, and the general rules of contract law apply in determining the existence of a contract and the rights and liabilities of the parties. As a general rule, any defense the principal has that goes to the merits of the case is available to the surety. Also, any agreement between the principal and the creditor that alters the risks involved in the primary contract will discharge the surety unless he consents to or ratifies the agreement or unless the rights against the surety are reserved. The creditor owes a duty to use reasonable care in his dealings and not to increase unnecessarily the burden of risk assumed by a surety. If a surety pays his principal's debt, the surety is entitled to all of the rights that the creditor had against the principal. If there are cosureties and one surety pays more than his share of his principal's debt, he is entitled to contribution from his cosureties.

There are three basic contract devices for using real estate as security for an obligation: (1) the real estate mortgage, (2) the deed of trust, and (3) the land contract.

A mortgage is a security interest in real property or a deed that is given by the owner (the mortgagor) as security for a debt owed to the creditor (the mortgagee). Because the real estate mortgage conveys an interest in real property, it must be executed with the same formality as a deed and it should be recorded to protect the mortgagee's interest in the property. The owner of property subject to a mortgage can sell the property without the mortgagee's consent, but the sale does not affect the mortgagee's interest in the property or his claim against the mortgagor. Foreclosure is the process by which any rights of the mortgagor or the current property owner are cut off. Foreclosure proceedings are regulated by state law and vary from state to state, but usually the mortgagor is given a period of time to redeem the property.

The deed of trust is a three-party transaction that is used in lieu of a mortgage in some states. The owner of the property, who is borrowing the money, conveys the property to a trustee. If the borrower defaults, the trustee, at the request of the lender, sells the property and pays the debt from the proceeds.

Where the owner of real property sells it on a land contract, he retains title to the property until the purchase price is paid in full. If the buyer defaults, the seller usually has the right to reclaim the property.

A mechanic's or materialman's lien is a statutory lien based on the improvement of one person's real estate by the addition of another person's labor or materials. To obtain a lien, the lien claimant must comply strictly with the statutory requirements as to the form, content, and time of giving notice of lien and any other statutory requirements. As a general rule, a mechanic's or materialman's lien dates from the time the first labor or materials are furnished and has priority over all subsequent liens. A lien is foreclosed in the same manner as that followed in a court foreclosure of a real estate mortgage. Under the provisions of some statutes, the right to a mechanic's or materialman's lien may be waived by the insertion of a waiver provision in a contract for the improvement of real estate.

## PROBLEM CASES

**1.** O'Brien owned a sailboat that Buxton, as sailing master, sailed for O'Brien. O'Brien did not pay Buxton for his services as sailing master, and Buxton, who had possession of the sailboat, claimed a common law lien on the sailboat for his services. Is Buxton entitled to a common law lien on the sailboat?

**2.** Mr. and Mrs. Marshall went to Beneficial Finance to borrow money but were deemed by Beneficial's office manager, Ruckett, to be bad credit risks. The Marshalls stated that their friend Garren would be willing to cosign a note for them if necessary. Ruckett advised Garren not to cosign, because the Marshalls were bad credit risks. This did not dissuade Garren from cosigning a note for $480, but it prompted him to ask Beneficial to take a lien or security interest in Marshall's custom-built Harley-Davidson motorcycle, then worth over $1,000. Beneficial took and perfected a security interest in the motorcycle. Marshall defaulted on the first payment. Beneficial gave notice of the default to Garren and advised him that it was looking to him for payment. Garren then discovered that Beneficial and Marshall had reached an agreement whereby Marshall would sell his motorcycle for $700; Marshall was to receive $345 immediately, which was to be applied to the loan, and he promised to pay the balance of the loan from his pocket. Marshall paid Beneficial $89.50 and left town without giving the proceeds of the sale to Beneficial. Because Beneficial was unable to get the proceeds from Marshall, it brought suit against Garren on his obligation as surety. When Beneficial released the security for the loan (the motorcycle) without Garren's consent, was Garren relieved of his obligation as surety for repayment of the loan?

3. Bayer was the general contractor on a Massachusetts State highway contract. He hired Deschenes as a subcontractor to do certain excavation work. Deschenes was to start the job by November 24, 1958, and to complete it on or before March 1, 1959. Deschenes was required to furnish a bond of $91,000 to assure his faithful performance of the subcontract, and he purchased such a bond from Aetna Insurance Company. Deschenes began the work on December 1, 1958, and quit on June 22, 1959, after completing only about half of the work. Bayer had made numerous efforts to get Deschenes to do the work and then completed the job himself when Deschenes walked off the job. Bayer then brought a lawsuit against Aetna on the bond, and Aetna claimed that it was discharged by the extension of time given to Deschenes. Should Bayer recover on the bond?

4. Philip and Edith Beh purchased some property from Alfred M. Gromer and his wife. Sometime earlier, the Gromers had borrowed money from City Mortgage. They had signed a note and had given City Mortgage a second deed of trust on the property. There was also a first deed of trust on the property at the time the Behs purchased it. In the contract of sale between the Behs and the Gromers, the Behs promised to "assume" the second deed of trust of approximately $5,000 at 6 percent interest. The Behs later defaulted on the first deed of trust. Foreclosure was held on the first deed of trust, but the proceeds of the sale left nothing for City Mortgage on its second deed of trust. City Mortgage then brought a lawsuit against the Behs to collect the balance due on the second deed of trust. When the Behs "assumed" the second deed of trust, did they become personally liable for it?

5. In October 1972, Verda Miller sold her 107-acre farm for $30,000 to Donald Kimball, who was acting on behalf of his own closely held corporation, American Wonderlands. Under the agreement, Miller retained title and Kimball was given possession pending full payment of all installments of the purchase price. The contract provided that Kimball was to pay all real estate taxes. If he did not pay them, Miller could discharge them and either add the amounts to the unpaid principal or demand immediate payment of the delinquencies plus interest. Miller also had the right to declare a forfeiture of the contract and regain possession if the terms of the agreement were not met. In 1975, Miller had to pay the real estate taxes on the property in the amount of $672.78. She demanded payment of this amount plus interest from Kimball. She also served a notice of forfeiture on him that he had 30 days to pay. Kimball paid the taxes but refused to pay interest of $10.48. Miller made continued demands on Kimball for two months, then filed notice of forfeiture with the county recorder in August 1975. She also advised Kimball of this. Was Miller justified in declaring a forfeiture and taking back possession of the land?

6. Brown hired a contractor to build a house for him. The contractor, in turn, hired a subcontractor, Electric Contracting Company, to do the electrical work. All of the electrical work was completed by March 10, except that a certain type of ground clamp required by a city ordinance was not then available. The city inspector permitted a different type of clamp to be installed at that time. On April 25, Electric Contracting replaced the clamp with a clamp of the required type. When Electric Contracting was not paid by the contractor, it filed a materialman's lien, on June 13, and then brought suit against Brown to recover for its work. Brown claimed that the lien was not enforceable, because it was not filed within 60 days of the time the work was completed as required by law. Should the court accept Brown's contention?

# Chapter 40

# Security Interests in Personal Property

## INTRODUCTION

Today, a large portion of our economy involves the extension of credit. In many credit transactions, the creditor takes a security interest (or lien) in personal property belonging to the debtor in order to protect his investment. The law covering security interests in personal property is contained in Article 9 of the Uniform Commercial Code. Article 9, entitled Secured Transactions, applies to situations that consumers and businesspeople commonly face, for example, the financing of an automobile, the purchase of a refrigerator on a time-payment plan, and the financing of business inventory.

If a creditor wants to obtain a security interest in the personal property of the debtor, he also wants to be sure that his interest will be superior to the claims of other creditors. To do so, the creditor must carefully comply with Article 9. In Part VIII, Sales, it was pointed out that businesspersons sometimes leave out necessary terms in a contract or insert vague terms to be worked out later. Such looseness is a luxury that is not permitted in secured transactions. If a debtor gets into financial difficulties and cannot meet his obligations, even a minor noncompliance with Article 9 may cause the creditor to lose his preferred claim to the personal property of the debtor. A creditor who loses his secured interest will be only a general creditor of the debtor if the debtor is declared bankrupt. As a general creditor in bankruptcy proceedings, he may have little chance of recovering the money owed by the debtor because of the relatively low priority of such claims. This will be covered in detail in Chapter 41.

Article 9 has not been adopted in exactly the same form in every state. The law of each state must be examined carefully to determine the procedure for obtaining a secured interest and the rights of creditors and debtors in that state. The general concepts are the same in each state, however, and these concepts will be the basis of our discussion in this chapter.

## SECURITY INTERESTS UNDER THE CODE

**Security Interests.** Basic to a discussion of secured consumer and commercial transactions is the term ***security interest.*** A security interest is an interest in personal property or fixtures that a creditor obtains to secure payment or performance of an obligation [1–201(37)].[1] For example, when a person borrows money from the bank to buy a new car, the bank takes a security interest (puts a lien) on the car until the loan is repaid. If the person defaults on the loan, the bank can repossess the car and have it sold to cover the unpaid balance. A security interest is a property interest in the collateral.

Although it is normal to think of various types of goods as collateral, the Code actually covers secured interests in a much broader grouping of personal property. The Code breaks down personal property into a number of different classifications that are of importance in determining how a creditor goes about getting an enforceable security interest in a particular type of collateral. These Code classifications are:

1. *Instruments.* This category includes checks, notes, drafts, stocks, bonds, and other investment securities [9–105].
2. *Documents of title.* This category includes bills of lading, dock warrants, dock receipts, and warehouse receipts.
3. *Accounts.* This category includes rights to payment for goods sold or leased or for services rendered that are not evidenced by instruments or chattel paper but are carried on open account. The category includes such rights to payment whether or not they have been earned by performance [9–106].
4. *Chattel paper.* This category includes written documents that evidence both an obligation to pay money and a security interest in specific goods [9–105]. A typical example of chattel paper is what is commonly known as a conditional sales contract. This is the type of contract that a consumer might sign when he buys a large appliance such as a refrigerator on a time-payment plan.
5. *General intangibles.* Among the items in this catchall category are patents, copyrights, literary royalty rights, franchises, and money [9–106].
6. *Goods.* Goods are divided into several classes; the same item of collateral may fall into different classes at different times, depending on its use.
   a. *Consumer goods.* These are goods used or bought for use primarily for

[1] The numbers in brackets refer to the sections of the Uniform Commercial Code. In 1972, a number of amendments to Article 9 were proposed by the National Conference of Commissioners on Uniform State Laws. The proposed amendments must be adopted by the state legislatures before they become law in any given state.

personal, family, or household purposes. They include automobiles, furniture, and appliances.

b. *Equipment.* This includes goods used or bought for use primarily in business, including farming and professions.

c. *Farm products.* These are crops, livestock, or supplies used or produced in farming operations as long as they are still in the possession of a debtor engaged in farming.

d. *Inventory.* This includes goods held for sale or lease or for use under contracts of service as well as raw materials, work in process, and materials used or consumed in a business.

e. *Fixtures.* These are goods so affixed to real property as to be considered a part of it [9–109].

It should be noted that an item such as a stove could in different situations be classified as inventory, equipment, and consumer goods. In the hands of the manufacturer or an appliance store, the stove is "inventory" goods. If it is being used in a restaurant, it is "equipment." In a home, it is classified as "consumer goods."

## ATTACHMENT OF THE SECURITY INTEREST

**Attachment.** A security interest is not legally enforceable against a debtor until it is attached to one or more particular items of the debtor's property. The *attachment* of the security interest takes place in a legal sense rather than in a physical sense. There are two basic requirements for a security interest to be attached to the goods of a debtor [9–203]. First, there must be an *agreement in which the debtor grants the creditor a security interest in particular property* (collateral) in which the debtor has an interest. Second, the creditor must give *something of value* to the debtor. The creditor must, for example, lend money or advance goods on credit to the debtor. Unless the debtor owes a debt to the creditor, there can be no security interest. The purpose of obtaining a security interest is to secure a debt.

**The Security Agreement.** The agreement in which a debtor grants a creditor a security interest in the debtor's property must generally be *in writing* and *signed by the debtor.* A written agreement is required in all cases except where the creditor has possession of the collateral [9–203]. Suppose Cole borrows $50 from Fox and gives Fox her wristwatch as a security for the loan. The agreement whereby Cole put up her watch as collateral does not have to be in writing to be enforceable. Because the creditor (Fox) is in possession of the collateral, an oral agreement is sufficient.

The security agreement must clearly describe the collateral so that it can readily be identified. For example, the year, make, and serial number of an automobile should be listed. The security agreement usually goes on to spell out the terms of the arrangement between the creditor and the debtor. Also, it normally contains a promise by the debtor to pay certain amounts of money in a certain way. It specifies what events, such as nonpayment by the buyer, will constitute a default. In addition, it may contain provisions that the creditor feels are necessary to protect his security interest. For example, the debtor may be required to keep the collateral insured, not to move it without the creditor's consent, or to periodically report sales of secured inventory goods.

The *American Restaurant Supply* case, which follows, provides an example of a creditor who neglected to provide a sufficient description of the collateral in the security

## SAMPLE SECURITY AGREEMENT

Mr. and Mrs.
Mrs.
BUYER Miss ______________________
ADDRESS ______________________
CITY ______________________ TEL. NO. __________
DELIVER TO: ______________________

| Account No. |
|---|
| Date |

## SECURITY AGREEMENT
## (NAME OF SELLER)

THIS AGREEMENT, executed between (name of Seller), as Secured Party ("Seller"), and Buyer named above, as Debtor ("Buyer"):

Seller agrees to sell and Buyer agrees to purchase, subject to the terms, conditions and agreements stated, the goods described below (the "Collateral"), Seller reserving and Buyer granting a purchase money security interest in the Collateral to secure the payment of the balance owed (Item 7) and all other present and future obligations of Buyer to Seller.

| DESCRIPTION OF COLLATERAL | | | | TERMS |
|---|---|---|---|---|
| Quantity | Article | Unit Price | Total | |
| | | | | (1) Cash Price |
| | | | | (2) Down Payment |
| | | | | Trade-in |
| | | | | |
| | | | | Unpaid Principal (3) Balance Owed |
| | | | | (4) Finance Charge |
| | | | | Time Balance |
| | | | | (5) Owed |
| | | | | (6) Sales Tax |
| | | | | (7) Balance Owed |

Buyer agrees to pay Seller, without relief from valuation and appraisement laws, the balance owed (Item 7) of $_____ in _____ successive weekly/monthly installments of $_____ each and a final installment of $_____, commencing on _________ ___, 19___, and continuing thereafter on the same day of each week/month, until paid, together with all delinquent charges, cost of repossession, collection, disposition, maintenance, and other like charges, allowed by law, and reasonable attorneys' fees.

This sale is made subject to the terms, conditions, and agreements stated above and on the reverse side hereof. Buyer hereby represents that the correct name and address of Buyer is as stated above, and that all statements made by Buyer as to financial condition and credit information are true.

Buyer acknowledges delivery by Seller to Buyer of a copy of this agreement.

Buyer warrants and represents that the Collateral will be kept at Buyer's address unless otherwise specified as follows: ______________________; and will be used or is purchased for use primarily for: (check one) family or household purposes ☐; business use ☐; farming operations ☐. The Collateral will not be affixed to real estate unless checked here ☐. If the Collateral is to be affixed to real estate, a description of the real estate is as follows: ______________________

______________________

______________________

and the name of the record owner is ______________________.

IN WITNESS WHEREOF, the parties have executed this agreement on this _____ day of ________, 19___.

BUYER'S SIGNATURE (NAME OF SELLER)

______________________ By ______________________

(as Debtor) (as Secured Party)

TERMS, CONDITIONS, AND AGREEMENTS

1. The security interest of Seller shall extend to all replacements, proceeds (including tort claims and insurance), and accessories, and shall continue until full performance by Buyer of all conditions and obligations.

2. Buyer shall maintain the Collateral in good repair, pay all taxes and other charges levied upon the Collateral when due, and shall defend the Collateral against any claims. Buyer shall not permit the Collateral to be removed from the place where kept without the prior written consent of Seller. Buyer shall give prompt written notice to Seller of any transfer, pledge, assignment, or any other process or action taken or pending, voluntary or involuntary, whereby a third party is to obtain or is attempting to obtain possession of or any interest in the Collateral. Seller shall have the right to inspect the Collateral at all reasonable times. At its option, but without obligation to Buyer and without relieving Buyer from any default, Seller may discharge any taxes, liens, or other encumbrances levied or placed upon the Collateral for which Buyer agrees to reimburse Seller upon demand.

3. If the Collateral is damaged or destroyed in any manner, the entire balance remaining unpaid under this agreement (the "Agreement Balance") shall immediately become due and payable and Buyer shall first apply any insurance or other receipts compensating for such loss to the Agreement Balance. Buyer shall fully insure the Collateral, for the benefit of both Seller and Buyer, against loss by fire, theft, and other casualties by comprehensive extended coverage insurance in an amount equal to the balance owed.

4. Buyer shall pay all amounts payable when due at the store of Seller from which this sale is made at or at Seller's principal office in ________________, Indiana, and upon default shall pay the maximum delinquent charges permitted by law. Upon prepayment of the Agreement Balance, Seller shall allow the minimum discount permitted by law.

5. Time is of the essence of this agreement. Buyer agrees that the following shall constitute an event of default under this Security Agreement: (a) the failure of Buyer to perform any condition or obligation contained; (b) when any statement, representation, or warranty made by Buyer shall be found to have been untrue in any material respect when made; or (c) if Seller in good faith believes that the prospect of payment or performance is impaired. Upon a default, Seller, at its option and without notice or demand to Buyer, shall be entitled to declare the Agreement Balance immediately due and payable, take immediate possession of the Collateral, and enter the premises at which the Collateral is located for such purpose or to render the Collateral unusable. Upon request, Buyer shall assemble and make the Collateral available to Seller at a place to be designated by Seller which is reasonably convenient to both parties. Upon repossession, Seller may retain or dispose of any or all of the Collateral in the manner prescribed by the Indiana Uniform Commercial Code and the proceeds of any such disposition shall be first applied in the following order: (a) to the reasonable expenses of retaking, holding, preparing for sale, selling, and the like; (b) to the reasonable attorneys' fees and legal expenses incurred by Seller; and (c) to the satisfaction of the indebtedness secured by this security interest. Buyer covenants to release and hold harmless Seller from any and all claims arising out of the repossession of the Collateral. No waiver of any default or any failure or delay to exercise any right or remedy by Seller shall operate as a waiver of any other default or of the same default in the future or as a waiver of any right or remedy with respect to the same or any other occurrence.

6. All rights and remedies of Seller specified in this agreement are cumulative and are in addition to, and shall not exclude, any rights and remedies Seller may have by law.

7. Seller shall not be liable for any damages, including special or consequential damages, for failure to deliver the Collateral or for any delay in delivery of the Collateral to Buyer.

8. Buyer agrees that Seller may carry this agreement, together with any other agreements and accounts, with Buyer in one account upon its records and unless otherwise instructed in writing by Buyer, any payment of less than all amounts then due on all agreements and accounts shall be applied to any accrued delinquent charges, cost of collection and maintenance, and to the balances owing under all agreements or accounts in such order as Seller in its discretion shall determine.

9. Buyer authorizes Seller to execute and file financing statements signed only by Seller covering the Collateral described.

10. Any notice required by this agreement shall be deemed sufficient when mailed to Seller (state Seller's address), or to Buyer at the address at which the Collateral is kept.

11. Buyer shall have the benefit of manufacturers' warranties, if any; however, Seller makes no express warranties (except a warranty of title) and no implied warranties, including any warranty of MERCHANTABILITY or FITNESS. Buyer agrees that there are no promises or agreements between the parties not contained in this agreement. Any modification or rescission of this agreement shall be ineffective unless in writing and signed by both Seller and Buyer.

12. ANY HOLDER OF THIS CONSUMER CREDIT CONTRACT IS SUBJECT TO ALL CLAIMS AND DEFENSES WHICH THE DEBTOR COULD ASSERT AGAINST THE SELLER OF GOODS OR SERVICES OBTAINED WITH THE PROCEEDS HEREOF. RECOVERY HEREUNDER BY THE DEBTOR SHALL NOT EXCEED AMOUNTS PAID BY THE DEBTOR HEREUNDER.

agreement and thus did not obtain an enforceable security interest.

**Future Advances.** A security agreement may provide that it covers advances of credit to be made at some time in the future [9–204(3)]. Such later extensions of credit are known as **future advances.** Future advances would be involved where, for example, a bank grants a business a line of credit for $100,000 but initially advances only $20,000. When the business draws further against its line of credit, it has received a future advance and the bank is considered to have given additional "value" at that time. The security interest that the creditor obtained earlier also covers these later advances of money.

**After-Acquired Property.** A security agreement may be drafted to grant a creditor a security interest in the **after-acquired property** of the debtor. After-acquired property is property that the debtor does not currently own or have rights in but that he may acquire in the future. However, the security interest does not attach until the debtor actually obtains some rights to the new property [9–204].[2] For example, Dan's Diner borrows $5,000 from the bank and gives it a security interest in all of its present restaurant equipment as well as all of the restaurant equipment that it may "hereafter acquire." If at the time Dan's owns only a stove, then the bank has a security interest only in the stove. However, if a month later Dan's buys a refrigerator, the bank's security interest would "attach" to the refrigerator when Dan's acquires some rights to it.

A security interest in after-acquired property may not have priority over certain other creditors if the debtor acquires his new property subject to what is known as a **purchase money security interest.** When the seller of goods retains a security interest in goods until they are paid for, or when money is loaned for the purpose of acquiring certain goods and the lender takes a security interest in those goods, the security interest is known as a "purchase money security interest." The rights of the holder of a purchase money security interest versus the rights of another creditor who filed earlier on after-acquired property of the debtor are discussed in detail later in this chapter in the section entitled "Priority Rules."

**Proceeds.** The creditor is commonly interested in having his security interest cover not only the collateral described in the agreement but also the **proceeds** on the disposal of the collateral by the debtor. For example, if a bank lends money to Dealer to enable Dealer to finance its inventory of new automobiles and the bank takes a security interest in the inventory, the bank wants its interest to continue in any cash proceeds obtained by Dealer when the automobiles are sold to customers. Under the 1972 amendments to Article 9, proceeds are automatically covered unless the security agreement specifically excludes them [9–203(3)].

**Assignment.** In the past, installment sales contracts and security agreements commonly included a provision that the buyer would not assert against the assignee of a sales contract any claims or defenses that the buyer had against the seller. Such clauses made it easier for a retailer to assign its installment sales contracts (security agreements) to a financial institution such as a bank. The bank knew that it could collect from the buyer without having to worry about any claims that the buyer had against the retailer, such as for breach of warranty. The waiver clauses were

[2] The Code imposes an additional requirement as to security interests in after-acquired consumer goods. Security interests do not attach to consumer goods other than accessions unless the consumer acquires them within 10 days after the secured party gave value [9–204(2)].

usually presented to the buyer on a take-it-or-leave-it basis.

Such clauses can operate to the disadvantage of the buyer. For example, Harriet Horn agrees to buy some storm windows from Ace Home Improvement Company. She signs an installment sales contract (security agreement) promising to pay $50 a month for 24 months and giving the company a security interest in the windows. The contract contains a waiver of defenses clause. Ace assigns the contract to First Bank and goes out of business. If the storm windows were of a poorer quality than was called for by the contract, Horn would have a claim of breach of warranty against Ace. She would not have to pay Ace the full amount if it tried to collect from her. Under these circumstances, however, Horn has to pay the full amount to the bank and can then try to collect from Ace for breach of warranty. Here, Horn might be out of luck.

Under the Uniform Commercial Code, an express or implied waiver of defenses is generally valid and enforceable by an assignee who takes his assignment for value, in good faith, and without notice of a claim or defense [9–206(1)]. There are two exceptions to this rule: (1) the waiver is not effective as to any type of defense that could be asserted against a holder in due course of a negotiable instrument; (2) the waiver is not effective if a statute or court decision establishes a different rule for buyers of consumer goods [9–206(1)].

Some states have enacted comprehensive legislation to abolish the waiver of defense clauses in consumer contracts, and others have limited their use. The Uniform Consumer Credit Code, which has been adopted by a number of states, gives the adopting states two alternatives regarding waiver of defense clauses: (1) Alternative A provides that an assignee of a consumer sales contract takes subject to all of the defenses that the buyer has against the seller arising out of the sale, regardless of whether the contract contains a waiver of defenses clause; and (2) Alternative B permits the enforcement of such clauses only by an assignee who is not related to the seller and who acquires the assignment of the contract in good faith and for value, gives the buyer notice of the assignment, and is not advised by the buyer in writing within three months that the buyer has any claims or defenses against the seller.

In addition, the Federal Trade Commission has promulgated a regulation (discussed in detail in Chapter 36) that applies to situations in which a buyer signs a waiver of defenses clause as part of an installment sales contract. The FTC regulation requires that a seller or financing agency insert in all consumer contracts and direct loan agreements a clause putting any holder of the contract on notice that the holder is subject to all of the claims and defenses that the buyer-debtor could assert against the seller of the goods or services covered by the contract.

## American Restaurant Supply Co. v. Wilson

**371 So.2d 489 (Fla. Dist. Ct. App. 1979)**

American Restaurant Supply Company sold restaurant equipment and supplies to Wilmark, Inc. and took a security interest in the equipment and supplies. The security agreement between American and Wilmark described the collateral as "Food service equipment and supplies delivered to San Marco Inn at St. Marks, Florida." Wilmark defaulted on its agreement, and American sought to enforce its security interest. Wilmark and its other creditors claimed that the description of the property pledged as security was not legally sufficient to enable the security interest to be enforced. The trial court ruled against American Restaurant Supply on the ground that the description of the property pledged as security was not sufficient. American Restaurant Supply appealed.

**MILLS, JUDGE.** A security interest cannot be enforced against the debtor or third parties unless the collateral is in the possession of the secured party or the security agreement contains a description of the collateral. Section 9–203(1). The description of collateral "is sufficient whether or not it is specific if it reasonably identifies what is described." Section 9–110. The Comment to § 9–110 of the Uniform Commercial Code states that the test of sufficiency of a description "is that the description do the job assigned to it—that it make possible the identification of the thing described."

Although § 9–110 sets forth the test for sufficiency of the description of collateral in both the security agreement and the financing statement, a description of collateral sufficient for a financing statement might not be sufficient in a security agreement. This is because the financing statement and the security agreement serve different purposes.

The purpose of the financing statement is merely to provide notice of a possible security interest in the collateral in question. Section 9–402 requires that the financing statement contain a description indicating the types of collateral in which the secured party may have a security interest. The description of collateral in a financing statement is sufficient if it reasonably informs third parties that an item in the possession of the debtor may be subject to a prior security interest, thus putting the parties on notice that further inquiry may be necessary.

The security agreement is the contract between the parties; it specifies what the security interest is. Because of its different function, greater particularity in the description of collateral is required in the security agreement than in the financing statement. A description of collateral in a security agreement is sufficient if the description makes possible the identification of the items in which a security interest is claimed.

The security agreement under consideration describes the collateral as: "Food service equipment and supplies delivered to San Marco Inn at St. Marks, Florida." Many courts have held that a description of collateral is sufficient when the agreement covers all of a certain type or types of assets. However, the agreement before us does not cover all of the food service equipment and supplies located at San Marco Inn or owned by the debtor. The agreement attempts to cover some food service equipment and supplies, but the description does not do its assigned job of making possible the identification of the equipment and supplies in which American claims a security interest.

We agree with the trial court that "the description of the property pledged as security in the security instrument was not legally sufficient" to enable the security interest to be enforced.

Judgment against American Restaurant Supply affirmed.

## PERFECTING THE SECURITY INTEREST

**Perfection.** Attachment of a security interest to collateral owned by the debtor gives the creditor rights vis-à-vis the debtor. However, a creditor is also concerned about making sure that he will have a better right to the collateral than any other creditor if the debtor defaults. In addition, a creditor may be concerned about protecting his interest in the collateral if the debtor sells it to someone else. The creditor gets protection against other creditors or purchasers of the collateral by *perfecting* his security interest. Perfection is not effective without an attachment of the security interest [9–303].

Under the Code, there are three main ways of perfecting a security interest:

1. By filing a *public notice* of the security interest.
2. By the creditor *taking possession* of the collateral.
3. In certain kinds of transaction, by mere *attachment* of the security interest *(automatic perfection).*

**Perfection by Public Filing.** The most common way of perfecting a security interest is to file a **financing statement** in the appropriate public office. The financing statement serves as *constructive notice* to the world that the creditor claims an interest in collateral that belongs to a certain named debtor. The financing statement usually consists of a multicopy form that is available from the office of the state secretary of state. (See accompanying figure.) However, the security agreement can be filed as the financing statement if it contains the required information and has been signed by the debtor.

To be sufficient, the financing statement must (1) contain the names of the debtor and of the secured party (the creditor), (2) be signed by the debtor, (3) give an address of the secured party from which additional information about the security interest can be obtained, (4) give a mailing address for the debtor, and (5) contain a statement of the types of collateral or a description of the collateral. If the financing statement covers goods that are to become fixtures, a description of the real estate must be included.

Each state specifies by statute where the financing statement has to be filed. In all states, a financing statement that covers fixtures must be filed in the office where a mortgage on real estate would be filed [9–401]. The secured party acquiring a security interest in property that is a fixture or is to become a fixture should, in order to obtain maximum security, double-file, that is, file the security interest as a fixture and as a nonfixture.

In regard to collateral other than fixtures, the state may require only central filing, usually in the office of the secretary of state. However, most states require the local filing of local transactions, such as transactions in which the collateral is equipment used in farming operations; farm products; accounts, contract rights, or general intangibles arising from or relating to the sale of farm products by a farmer; or consumer goods.

A financing statement is effective for a period of *five years* from the date of filing, and

UNIFORM COMMERCIAL CODE | STATE OF INDIANA FINANCING STATEMENT | FORM UCC-1

**INSTRUCTIONS**

1. Please type this form. Fold only along perforation for mailing.
2. Remove Secured Party and Debtor copies and send other three copies with interleaved carbon paper to the filing officer. Enclose filing fee of $1.00 (plus $ .50 if collateral is or to become a fixture).
3. When filing is to be with more than one office, Form UCC-2 may be placed over this set to avoid double typing.
4. If the space provided for any item(s) is inadequate, the item(s) may be continued on additional sheets, preferably 5"x 8" or sizes convenient to secured party in case of long schedules, indentures, etc. Only one sheet is required. Extra names of debtors may be continued below box "1" in space for description of property.
5. If the collateral is crops or goods which are or are to become fixtures, describe the goods and also the real estate with the name of the record owner if he is other than the debtor.
6. Persons filing a security agreement (as distinguished from a financing statement) are urged to complete this form with or without signature and send with security agreement.
7. If collateral is goods which are or are to become fixtures, use Form UCC-1a over this Form to avoid double typing, and enclose regular fee plus $ .50.
8. The filing officer will return the third page of this Form as an acknowledgment. Secured party at a later time may use third page as a Termination Statement by dating and signing the termination legend on that page.

This Financing Statement is presented to Filing Officer for filing pursuant to the UCC: | 3 Maturity Date (if any):

1 Debtor(s) (Last Name First) and Address(es) | 2 Secured Party(ies) and Address(es) | For Filing Officer (Date, Time, Number, and Filing Office)

4 This financing statement covers the following types (or items) of property (also describe realty where collateral is crops or fixtures):

Assignee of Secured Party

This statement is filed without the debtor's signature to perfect a security interest in collateral (check ☒ if so)

☐ under a security agreement signed by debtor authorizing secured party to file this statement, or

☐ already subject to a security interest in another jurisdiction when it was brought into this state, or

☐ which is proceeds of the following described original collateral which was perfected:

Check ☒ if covered: ☐ Proceeds of Collateral are also covered. ☐ Products of Collateral are also covered. No. of additional Sheets presented:

Filed with: ☐ Secretary of State ☐ Recorder of ____________ County

By: ____________ Signature(s) of Debtor(s)

By: ____________ Signature(s) of Secured Party(ies)

(1) Filing Officer Copy—Alphabetical
FORM UCC-1—INDIANA UNIFORM COMMERCIAL CODE

Approved by: Charles O. Hendricks
Secretary of State

it lapses then unless a **continuation statement** has been filed before that time. An exception is made for real estate mortgages, which are effective as fixture filings—they are effective until the mortgage is released or terminates [9–403].

A continuation statement may be filed within six months before and 60 days after a stated maturity date of five years or less; otherwise, it may be filed within six months before the five-year expiration date. The continuation statement must be signed by the secured party, identify the original statement by file number, and state that the original statement is still effective. Successive continuation statements may be filed [9–403(3)].

When the debtor completely fulfills all debts and obligations secured by a financing statement, he is entitled to a **termination statement** signed by the secured party or an assignee of record. Failure of the affected secured party to furnish a termination statement after proper demand subjects him to a fine of $100 plus damages for any loss caused to the debtor by such failure [9–404].

**Possession by Secured Party as Public Notice.** Public filing of a security interest is intended to put any interested members of the public on notice of the security interest. A potential creditor of the debtor or a potential buyer of the collateral can check the records to see whether anyone else claims an interest in the debtor's collateral. The same objective can be reached if the debtor gives up *possession* of the collateral to the creditor or to a third person who holds the collateral for the creditor. If a debtor does not have possession of collateral that he claims to own, then a potential creditor or debtor is on notice that someone else may claim an interest in it. Thus, a security interest is perfected by change of possession of collateral from the debtor to the creditor/secured party or his agent [9–302(1)(a)]. For example, Simpson borrows $50 from a pawnbroker and leaves his guitar as collateral for the loan. The pawnbroker's security interest in the guitar is perfected by virtue of his possession of the guitar.

Generally, possession by the secured party is the means for perfecting a security interest in instruments such as checks or notes.[3] Possession of the collateral by the secured party is an alternative means, and often the most satisfactory means, of perfecting a security interest in chattel paper, money, and negotiable documents of title. Possession is also a possible means for perfecting a security interest in inventory. This is sometimes done through the *field warehousing arrangement,* whereby part of the debtor's inventory is fenced off and withdrawals from it are permitted only on the approval of the secured party or his on-the-scene representative.

[3] Sections 9–304(4) and (5) permit a 21-day temporary perfection.

Possession by the secured party is usually not a practical means for perfecting a security interest in equipment, farm products, and consumer goods, and, of course, it is not possible at all with accounts or general intangibles.

The person to whom the collateral is delivered holds it as bailee, and he owes the duties of a bailee to the parties in interest [9–207].

**Perfection by Attachment.** Perfection by mere attachment of the security interest, sometimes known as *automatic perfection,* is the only form of perfection that occurs without the giving of public notice. It occurs automatically when all the requirements of attachment are complete. This form of perfection is limited to certain classes of collateral, and in addition it may be only a temporary perfection in some situations.[4]

A creditor who sells goods to a consumer on credit, or who lends money to enable a consumer to buy goods, can obtain limited perfection of a security interest merely by attaching the security interest to the goods. A creditor under these circumstances has what is called a *purchase money security interest in consumer goods.* For example, an appliance store sells a television set to Margaret Morse on a conditional sales contract (time-payment plan). The store does not have to file its purchase money security interest in the set. The security interest is considered perfected just by virtue of its attachment to the set in the hands of the consumer.

Perfection by attachment is not effective if the consumer goods are either fixtures or motor vehicles for which the state issues certificates of titles [9–302]. The special rules that

[4] Temporary perfection without filing or possession is automatically obtained for 21 days after attachment of the security interest in instruments and negotiable documents [9–304]. To get protection beyond the 21-day period, the secured party must perfect by filing or possession. During the 21-day period of temporary perfection, however, any holder in due course of commercial paper or any bona fide purchaser of a security or a negotiated document will prevail over the secured party relying on temporary perfection [9–309].

cover these kinds of collateral will be discussed below.

There is also a major limitation to the perfection by attachment principle. A retailer of consumer goods who relies on attachment of a security interest to perfect it prevails over other creditors of the debtor/buyer. However, the retailer does not prevail over someone who buys the collateral from the debtor if the buyer (1) has no knowledge of the security interest, (2) gives value for the goods, and (3) buys the goods for his personal, family, or household use [9–307(2)]. The retailer does not have priority over such a bona fide purchaser unless it filed its security interest.

For example, an appliance store sells a television set to Arthur for $750 on a conditional sales contract, reserving a security interest in the set until Arthur has paid for it. The store does not file a financing statement, but relies on attachment for perfection. Arthur later borrows money from a credit union and gives it a security interest in the television set. If Arthur defaults on his loans and the credit union tries to claim the set, the appliance store has a better claim to the set than does the credit union. The credit union then has the rights of an unsecured creditor against Arthur.

Now, suppose Arthur sells the television set for $500 to his neighbor Andrews. Andrews is not aware that Arthur still owes money on the set to the appliance store. Andrews buys it to use in her home. If Arthur defaults on his obligation to the store, it cannot recover the television set from Andrews. To be protected against such a purchaser from its debtor, the appliance store must file a financing statement rather than relying on attachment for perfection.

**Motor Vehicles.** If state law requires a *certificate of title for motor vehicles,* then a creditor who takes a security interest in a motor vehicle must have the security interest noted on the title [9–302]. Suppose a credit union lends Carlson money to buy a new car in a state that requires certificates of title for cars. The credit union cannot rely on attachment of its security interest in the car to perfect that interest; rather, it must have its security interest noted on the certificate of title.

This requirement protects the would-be buyer of the car or another creditor who might extend credit based on Carlson's ownership of the car. By checking the certificate of title to Carlson's car, a potential buyer or creditor would learn about the credit union's security interest in the car. If no security interest is noted on the certificate of title, the buyer can buy—or the creditor can extend credit—with confidence that there are no undisclosed security interests that would be effective against him.

**Fixtures.** The Code also provides special rules for perfecting security interests in consumer goods that will become fixtures by virtue of their attachment to or use with real property. A financing statement must be filed with the real estate records to perfect a security interest in fixtures [9–401(1)(a)]. Suppose a hardware store takes a security interest in some storm windows. Since the storm windows are likely to become fixtures through their use with the homeowner's home, the hardware store cannot rely merely on attachment to perfect its security interest. It must file a financing statement to perfect that interest.

This rule helps protect a person who is interested in buying the real property or a person who is considering lending money based on the real property. By checking the real estate records, the potential buyer or creditor would learn of the hardware store's security interest in the storm windows.

However, as the *Barnett Bank of Clearwater v. Rompon* case, which follows, illustrates, a check of the real estate records does not provide the prospective buyer with absolute protection. In this case a lien on a trailer affixed to the property was recorded on the title to the trailer and did not have to be filed with the real property records.

**Removal of Collateral.** Even where a creditor has a perfected security interest in collateral of his debtor, he needs to be concerned about the possibility that the debtor will remove the collateral from the state where the creditor has filed on it and take the collateral to another state where the creditor does not have his claim filed on the public record. Commonly, the security agreement between the creditor and the debtor provides where the collateral is to be kept and stipulates that it will not be moved unless the debtor gives notice to and/or obtains the permission of the creditor. There is, however, no absolute assurance that the debtor will be faithful to such an agreement.

Under the Code, a secured creditor who has perfected his security interest generally has *four months* after the collateral is brought into the new state to perfect his security interest in that state. If the creditor does not reperfect within the four months, his security interest becomes unperfected and he could lose the collateral to a person who purchases it, or takes an interest in it, after it has been removed [9–103(1)]. If the creditor has not perfected his security interest by the time the collateral is removed, or within the time period that the creditor has to perfect his security interest in the former location of the collateral, then his interest is unperfected and he does not obtain the advantage of the four-month grace period.

The Code rules that govern the removal of collateral covered by a state certificate of title—such as an automobile—are more complicated. If an automobile covered by a certificate of title issued in one state on which a security interest is noted is moved to another state, the perfected security interest is perfected for four months in the new state, or until the automobile is registered in the new state. If the original state did not require that security interests be noted on the title, and if a new title is used in the second state without notation of the security interest, then under certain circumstances a buyer of the automobile can take free of the original security interest. To qualify, the buyer must not be in the business of buying and selling automobiles and must (1) give value, (2) take delivery after issuance of the new title, and (3) buy without notice of the security interest [9–103(2)].[5]

[5] Other rules are set out in the Code for accounts, general intangibles, chattel paper, and mobile goods removed to other states [9–103(3) and (4)].

## Barnett Bank of Clearwater N.A. v. Rompon

**377 So.2d 981 (Fla. Ct. App. 1979)**

Rompon purchased a mobile home. The purchase was financed by the Barnett Bank, which perfected its security interest by notation on the title issued for the mobile home by the Florida Department of Highway Safety and Motor Vehicles. Rompon later moved the mobile home to a plot of land in Hillsborough County, removed the wheels and towing tongue, hooked up underground utilities, added a side porch, and otherwise firmly affixed the mobile home to the real estate. In all the years subsequent to the year of purchase, the mobile home was taxed as "real property."

In 1975, Langelier and Corbeil purchased at a sheriff's sale the land on which the mobile home was situated. They had searched the county records for evidence of encumbrances against the real property, but they had not searched the records of the Department of Highway Safety and Motor Vehicles. They had no actual notice of the bank's lien, and the mobile home bore no tags or other evidence that it was registered with the department. The first litigation—and the first appearance of the mobile home before the Florida court of appeals—involved the right of possession of the mobile home as between Rompon and Langelier and Corbeil. In that case, the trial court found—and the court of appeals affirmed—that under the facts the mobile home had become a fixture to real property and, as such, went to Langelier and Corbeil as purchasers of the real property. The bank then brought a lawsuit against Rompon, Langelier, and Corbeil to foreclose its lien. The trial court held against the bank on the ground that the mobile home was a fixture but that the bank had not properly perfected a security interest in a fixture. The bank appealed.

**OTT, JUDGE.** The court below found, under the facts, that the mobile home was a fixture to the real property and thus Barnett Bank's security interest in it should have been perfected pursuant to § 9–401(1)(b).

It may well be that the mobile home was so affixed to the land as to become a fixture, but that is not the determinative factor here. If a mobile home must be registered and titled as a motor vehicle under Florida law, then the provisions of § 9–302(2)(b) do not even apply.

There can be no doubt that a mobile home is classified as a motor vehicle under Florida law and must be registered with and titled by the Department. At the time Barnett Bank financed Rompon's purchase of the mobile home, it was registered and titled by the Department. Barnett Bank could only perfect its lien on it by filing notice thereof with the Department and having it noted on the certificate of title. Even when a mobile home is permanently affixed to land and taxed as real property, it still must have an RP license plate issued by the Department and attached to the rear of the mobile home in a conspicuous place.

At the time of financing the Rompon purchase of the mobile home, Barnett Bank perfected its security interest according to law. There is no requirement that the bank reperfect its security interest in the event that the mobile home subsequently becomes a fixture to real property. Under the provisions of Florida Statutes, Rompon's, Langelier's, and Corbeil's interest in the mobile home is subject to Barnett Bank's perfected security interest. A check of the records of the Department is required even though a mobile home has actually become a fixture to real property.

Judgment reversed in favor of Barnett Bank.

## PRIORITY RULES

**Importance of Determining Priority.** Because several creditors may claim a security interest in the same collateral of a debtor, the Code establishes a set of rules for determining which of the conflicting security interests has **priority.** Determining which creditor has priority, or the best claim, takes on particular importance in bankruptcy situations, where unless a creditor has a preferred secured interest in collateral that fully protects the obligation owed to him, the creditor may realize only a few cents on every dollar owed to him.

**General Priority Rules.** The *basic rule* established by the Code is that *when more than one security interest in the same collateral has been filed or otherwise perfected,* the *first security interest to be filed or perfected has priority* over any that are filed or perfected later. If only one security interest has been perfected, for example by filing, then that security interest has priority. However, *if none of the conflicting security interests has been perfected,* then the *first security interest* to *be attached to the collateral has priority* [9–312(5)].

Thus, if Bank A filed a financing statement covering Retailer's inventory on February 1, 1987, and Bank B filed a financing statement covering that same inventory on March 1, 1987, Bank A would have priority over Bank B even though Bank B might have made its loan and attached its security interest to the inventory before Bank A did so. However, if Bank A neglected to perfect its security interest by filing and Bank B did perfect, then Bank B, as the holder of the only perfected security interest in the inventory, would prevail.

If both of two creditors neglected to perfect their security interest, then the first security interest that attached would have priority. For example, if Bank Y has a security agreement, covering Dealer's equipment on June 1, 1987, and advances money to Dealer on that date, whereas Bank Z does not obtain a security agreement covering that equipment or advance money to Dealer until July 1, 1987, then Bank Y would have priority over Bank Z. In connection with the last situation, it is important to note that unperfected secured creditors do not enjoy a preferred position in bankruptcy proceedings, thus giving additional impetus to the desirability of filing or otherwise perfecting a security interest.

**Purchase Money Security Interests.** There are several very important exceptions to the general priority rules. First, a *perfected purchase money security interest in inventory has priority over a conflicting security interest in the same inventory if the purchase money security interest* is *perfected at the time the debtor receives possession of the inventory* and *if the purchase money secured party gives notification in writing* to the prior secured creditor *before* the debtor receives the inventory [9–312(3)].

Assume that Bank A takes and perfects a security interest in all present and after-acquired inventory of Debtor. Then, Debtor acquires some additional inventory from Wholesaler, who retains a security interest in the inventory until Debtor pays for it and who perfects this security interest. Wholesaler has a purchase money security interest in inventory goods and will have priority over the prior secured creditor (Bank A) if Wholesaler has perfected the security interest by the time the collateral reaches the Debtor and if Wholesaler sends notice of his purchase money security interest to Bank A before shipping the goods. Thus, to protect itself, Wholesaler must check the public records to see whether any of Debtor's creditors are claiming an interest in Debtor's inventory; when it discovers that some are claiming an interest, it should file its own security interest and give notice of it to the existing creditors.

As the *Westinghouse Credit Corp.* case, which follows, illustrates, the subsequent seller of inventory should not be too casual in his notification to the prior secured party or he will not obtain priority over that party.

Second, a *purchase money security interest* in *collateral other than inventory has priority over a conflicting security interest* in the same collateral *if* the *purchase money security interest is perfected at the time the debtor receives the collateral or within 10 days afterward* [9–312(4)].

Assume that Bank B takes and perfects a security interest in all the present and after-acquired equipment belonging to Debtor. Then, Supplier sells some equipment to Debtor, reserving a security interest in the equipment until it is paid for. If Supplier perfects the purchase money security interest by filing at the time Debtor obtains the collateral or within 10 days thereafter, it will have priority over Bank B because its purchase money security interest in noninventory collateral prevails over a prior perfected security interest if the purchase money security interest is perfected at the time Debtor takes possession or within 10 days afterward.

The preference given to purchase money security interests, provided that their holders comply with the statutory procedure in a timely manner, serves several ends. First, it prevents a single creditor from closing off all other sources of credit to a particular debtor and thus possibly preventing the debtor from obtaining additional inventory or equipment needed to maintain his business. The preference also makes it possible for a supplier of inventory or equipment to have first claim on it until it is paid for, at which time it may become subject to the after-acquired property clause of another creditor's security agreement. By requiring that the first perfected creditor be given notice of a purchase money security interest at the time the new inventory comes into the debtor's inventory, the Code serves to alert the first creditor to the fact that some of the inventory on which it may be relying for security is subject to a prior secured interest until it is paid for.

**Buyers in the Ordinary Course of Business.** Finally, a *buyer in the ordinary course of business* (other than a person buying farm products from a person engaged in farming operations) *takes free from a security interest created by his seller* even though the security interest is perfected and even though the buyer knows of its existence [9–307(1)]. For example, Bank loans money to Dealership to finance Dealership's inventory of new automobiles and takes a security interest in the inventory, which it perfects by filing. Then, Dealership sells an automobile out of inventory to Customer. Customer takes the automobile free of Bank's security interest even though Dealership may be in default on its loan agreement. As long as Customer is a buyer in the ordinary course of business, Customer is protected. The reasons for this rule are that Bank really expects to be paid from the proceeds of Dealership's automobile sales and that the rule is necessary to the smooth conduct of commerce. Customers would be very reluctant to buy goods if they could not be sure they were getting clear title to them from the merchants from whom they buy.

In the *First Dallas County Bank* case, below, a buyer of an automobile from a dealer obtained title free of a security interest previously given by the dealer to his creditor.

**Artisan's and Mechanic's Liens.** The Code also provides that *certain liens arising* by *operation of law* (such as artisans' liens) *have priority over a perfected security interest in the collateral* [9–310]. For example, Marshall takes her automobile, on which Credit Union has a perfected security interest, to Frank's Garage to have it repaired. Under common or statutory law, Frank's may have a lien on the car to secure payment for its repairwork that permits it to keep the car until it receives payment for it. If Marshall defaults on her loan to Credit Union, refuses to pay Frank's for the repairwork, and the car is sold to satisfy the liens, Frank's is entitled to its share of the proceeds before Credit Union gets anything.

**Fixtures.** A separate set of problems is raised when the collateral is goods that become fixtures by being so related to particular real estate that an interest in them arises under real estate law. Determining the priorities among a secured party with an interest in the fixtures, subsequent purchasers of the real estate, and those persons who have a secured interest—such as a mortgage—on the real property can involve both real estate law and the Code. However, the Code does set out a number of rules for determining when the holder of a perfected security interest in fixtures has priority over an encumbrancer or owner of the real estate. Some of the Code priority rules are as follows.

First, the holder of the secured interest in a fixture has priority if: (1) his interest is a *purchase money security interest* that was obtained prior to the time the goods become fixtures; (2) the security interest is perfected by "*fixture filing*" (that is, by filing in the recording office where a mortgage on the real estate would be filed[6] prior to, or within 10 days of, the time when the goods become fixtures) [9–313(4)(a)]; and (3) the debtor has a recorded interest in the real estate or is in possession of it. For example, Restaurant Supply sells Arnie's Diner a new gas stove on a conditional sales contract, reserving a security interest until the stove is paid for. The stove is to be installed in a restaurant where Arnold Schwab is in possession under a 10-year lease. Restaurant Supply can assure that its security interest in the stove will have priority over any claims to it by the owner of the restaurant and anyone holding a mortgage on it if: (1) it enters into a security agreement with Schwab before the stove is delivered to him; and (2) it perfects its security interest by fixture filing before the stove is hooked up by a plumber or within 10 days of that time.

Second, the secured party whose interest in fixtures is perfected will have priority where: (1) the fixtures are removable factory or office machines or readily removable replacements of domestic appliances that are consumer goods; and (2) the security interest was perfected before the goods became fixtures [9–313(4)(c)]. For example, Harriet Hurd's dishwasher breaks down and she contracts with Appliance Store to buy a new one on a time-payment plan. The mortgage on Hurd's house provides that it covers the real property along with all kitchen appliances, or their replacements. Appliance Store's security interest in the dishwasher will have priority over the interest of the holder of the mortgage if Appliance Store perfects its security interest before the new dishwasher is installed in Hurd's home. Perfection in consumer goods can, of course, be obtained merely by attaching the security interest through the signing of a valid security agreement.

Once a secured party has filed his security interest as a fixture filing, he will have priority over purchasers or encumbrancers whose interests are filed after that of the secured party [9–313(4)(b) and (d)].

Where the secured party has priority over all owners and encumbrancers of the real estate, he generally has the right on default to remove the collateral from the real estate. However, he must make reimbursement for the cost of any physical injury caused to the property by the removal [9–313(8)].

[6] 9–313(1)(b).

## Westinghouse Credit Corp. v. Steigerwald

**35 B.R. 254 (Bankr. E.D. Pa. 1983)**

Paul Steigerwald owned and operated a retail business under the name Staggs TV. In February 1977, Steigerwald entered into a security agreement with Westinghouse Credit Corporation (WCC) in which WCC agreed to finance his inventory. The security agreement provided that WCC was to have a security interest in all of his "present and future inventory." Financing statements covering the security interest were promptly filed.

Between 1978 and October 1981, Penn Appliance Distributors supplied inventory to Steigerwald. It retained a purchase money security interest in the inventory until it was paid for and perfected its interest by filing a financing statement. In February 1982, Steigerwald filed a voluntary petition in bankruptcy. One of the questions before the bankruptcy court was whether WCC or Penn Appliance had the priority interest in certain inventory that had been supplied to Steigerwald by Penn Appliance during 1981.

**TWARDOWSKI, BANKRUPTCY JUDGE.** The only factual dispute in this case is whether or not WCC timely "received notification" of the purchase money security interest within the meaning of § 9–312(c), which states:

(c) Purchase money security interests in inventory.—A purchase money security interest in inventory collateral has priority over a conflicting security interest in the same collateral if:

(1) the purchase money security interest is perfected at the time the debtor receives possession of the collateral;
(2) any secured party whose security interest is known to the holder of the purchase money security interest or who, prior to the date of the filing made by the holder of the purchase money security interest, had filed a financing statement covering the same items or type of inventory, has received notification of the purchase money security interest before the debtor receives possession of the collateral covered by the purchase money security interest; and
(3) such notification states that the person giving the notice has or expects to acquire a purchase money security interest in inventory of the debtor, describing such inventory by item or type.

Although Penn Appliance's purchase money security interest in the disputed inventory attached subsequent to WCC's security interest in the same inventory, Penn Appliance would still prevail if it can satisfy all of the requirements of the above-quoted § 9–312(c). WCC correctly concedes that Penn Appliance has satisfied the requirements of § 9–312(c)(1). However, WCC contends that it did not receive notification (or otherwise learn) of the purchase money security interest in question until January 1982, during the state legal proceedings involving WCC's seizure of the debtor's inventory and well after October 7, 1981, the last date upon which Penn Appliance furnished the debtor with inventory covered by the purchase money security interest. Thus, WCC argues that the requirements of § 9–312(c)(2) have not been met, thereby negating Penn Appliance's alleged security interest priority under § 9–312(c).

Penn Appliance submits, however, that WCC timely "received notification," within the meaning of § 9–312(c)(2), of the purchase money security interest as a result of a meeting in the summer of 1978 between the president and credit manager of Penn Appliance, on the one hand, and the Central Pennsylvania district manager for WCC and his superior, on the other hand. The president of Penn Appliance, Elmer A. Groene, Jr., and the WCC district manager, Ronald Ross, testified regarding this meeting at the hearing of this case. Both agreed that the meeting took place at the Penn Appliance offices in the summer of 1978 and that the purpose of the meeting was WCC's attempt to persuade Penn Appliance to finance the inventory of the dealers which it supplied through WCC. Mr. Groene testified that each dealer, including Staggs TV, which Penn Appliance supplied was discussed individually, along with whatever financing arrangements existed for the various dealers. He felt that WCC was thus made aware that Penn Appliance was supplying Staggs TV on a purchase money security interest basis.

Mr. Ross testified that he could not recall the specific discussion of any particular dealer, including Staggs TV. He further stated: "There were a number of accounts that were brought up. I'm sure Staggs was probably included." Mr. Ross also testified, regarding the meeting, that "no documentation was presented at all." Mr. Ross also testified that he did not learn of the purchase money security interest in question until January 1982, during the state legal proceedings involving WCC's seizure of the debtor's inventory.

We agree that the § 9–312(c)(2) notification need not be in writing. In the present case, however, Mr. Ross, according to his testimony, certainly did not come away from the meeting with any specific knowledge of the purchase money security interest in question.

We believe that the following statement from J. White and R. Summers, *Handbook of the Law under the Uniform Commercial Code,* is persuasive and very much relevant to the present case:

> Of course no sensible businessman would intentionally rely upon an oral notification; he will give written notification under 9–312(3). If our purchase money lender does not dot his "i's" and cross his "t's," but simply makes a phone call to the prior lender, what result? Neither 9–312(3) nor subsections 25 or 26 of 1–201 state that the notification must be in writing. However, the phrase in 9–312(3)(c) "such notification states" certainly presents the image of a written notification. We conclude that § 9–312(3) permits oral notification, but *we would expect a court to be slow to rely upon an uncorroborated statement of the purchase money lender.* (Emphasis added.)

In sum, we do not feel that the alleged "notification" at the meeting by Penn Appliance of the purchase money security interest was sufficiently clear or direct to constitute "notification" pursuant to § 9–312(c)(2). This alleged "notification" was also, of course, uncorroborated. Under these circumstances, it would likewise not be proper to charge WCC with the receipt of such alleged "notification" pursuant to § 9–312(c)(2). Therefore, we hold that the discussions during the meeting in the summer of 1978 do not constitute "notification" of the purchase money security interest in question under § 9–312(c)(2).

Judgment for WCC.

## First Dallas County Bank v. General Motors Acceptance Corp.

### 17 ABR 638 (Ala. Sup. Ct. 1983)

In April 1980, Julius Davis purchased a 1980 Pontiac for his personal use. Davis made a down payment and financed the balance with the proceeds of a loan from General Motors Acceptance Corporation (GMAC). A certificate of title was issued showing Davis as the owner and GMAC as first lienholder. Davis was to pay off the loan in 48 monthly installments, beginning on June 1, 1980.

Davis subsequently offered the car for sale through Davis Motor Company, a used-car business that he owned. The car was purchased on November 12, 1980, by Everette Smith. Smith made a small down payment and financed the balance of the purchase price with the proceeds of a loan obtained from the First Dallas County Bank. The loan agreement gave the bank a security interest in the automobile. Davis, an authorized title agent approved by the Alabama Department of Revenue, filled out the appropriate title applications and delivered a copy to the purchasers. In so doing, Davis failed to note the prior lien held by GMAC. Davis did not pay GMAC the balance due on his loan and thus did not obtain from GMAC the original certificate of title on the vehicle.

When GMAC discovered that Davis had sold the car, it brought a lawsuit against Smith and First Dallas County Bank seeking return of the car in which it claimed a security interest. The trial court ruled in favor of GMAC. The court of appeals reversed, holding that Smith was a buyer in the ordinary course of business and took the car free of GMAC's security interest. GMAC appealed to the Alabama Supreme Court.

**Torbert, Chief Justice.** The sole issue presented on this appeal is whether the Court of Civil Appeals erred in holding that Everette Smith and First Dallas County Bank were protected under § 9–307(1), thereby taking priority over GMAC's security interest in that vehicle.

First, GMAC argues that 9–307(1) is limited in its operation to "inventory and/or floor plan financing" arrangements. While these kinds of "financing" plans are typical of the situations contemplated by this section, we do not agree that the facts of this case fall outside its purview. That section provides:

> A buyer in ordinary course of business (subsection (9) of section 1–201) other than a person buying farm products from a person engaged in farming operations takes free of a security interest created by his seller even though the security interest is perfected and even though the buyer knows of its existence.

This section refers to the definitions section, § 1–201(9), which states

> "Buyer in ordinary course of business" means a person who in good faith and without knowledge that the sale to him is in violation of the ownership rights or security interest of a third party in the goods buys in ordinary course from a person in the business of selling goods of that kind but does not include a pawnbroker. "Buying" may be for cash or by exchange of other property or on secured or unsecured credit and includes receiving goods or documents of title under a preexisting contract for sale but does not include a transfer in bulk or as security for or in total or partial satisfaction of a money debt.

It is apparent that these sections apply to sales from inventory by a person who sells goods of that kind. We hold that the sale by Davis from his used car lot constituted a sale from inventory. Davis, owner of Davis Motor Company, was in the business of selling goods of this kind. Smith's purchase, evidenced by a bill of sale in the company's name, falls within the literal language of the section.

GMAC argues that the car was a consumer good when it was sold to Davis and that it remained a consumer good regardless of the actions taken by Davis. This is not the case. White and Summers deal directly with this kind of situation:

> Note well that 9–109 does not classify goods according to design or intrinsic nature but according to the use to which their owner puts them. It follows that as use changes, either because the owner finds some new task for the goods or because an owner sells the goods to another who uses it for another purpose, the classification of the goods will also change.

In this case it is clear that Davis, the debtor, found a new use for the goods when he sold the car from the used car lot. When the car was placed on the lot it became inventory and thus falls within § 9–307(1). Section 9–401(3) provides that the secured party's perfection will continue when the classification changes; however, perfection is not the issue here. There is no comparable provision making § 9–307(1) inapplicable in these cases. While the secured party is not required to police the collateral to maintain perfection, he must do so in order to avoid § 9–307(1).

It is clear that § 9–307(1) of the UCC was written to protect the consumer who purchases goods from a dealer by permitting the purchaser to take good title free of any security interest created by the seller.

> The rule reflects a belief that it would be impractical to expect buyers to search through the records of financing statements every time they purchased an item, even though they purchased in the ordinary course of their seller's business, and that it would likewise be unacceptable to put the risk of loss on the purchaser when the seller defaults on a loan supported by a security interest in the goods. The secured party is in a better position to look out for himself in this situation than is the buyer.

Thus, we hold that Smith is protected by Code § 9–307(1). When Smith purchased the car he took it free of GMAC's security interest. Thus, the security agreement between Smith and First Dallas County Bank is a valid one, and the Bank, in effect, receives the benefit of Smith's protection under § 9–307(1). The underlying policy of protecting both purchasers of collateral and secured parties is served by this approach. GMAC retains a security interest in the proceeds of the sale of the collateral received by Davis under Code § 9–203(2), and, in the event of the insolvency of this debtor, GMAC will remain a secured party as to those proceeds.

Judgment for Smith affirmed.

## DEFAULT AND FORECLOSURE

**Default.** Usually, the creditor and debtor state in their agreement what events constitute a *default* by the buyer. The Code does not define what constitutes default. Defining default is left to the parties' agreement, subject to the Code requirement that the parties act in good faith in doing so. If the debtor defaults, the secured creditor in a consumer goods transaction has several options: (1) forget the collateral, and sue the debtor on his note or promise to pay; (2) repossess the collateral, and use strict foreclosure (in some cases) to keep the collateral in satisfaction of the remaining debt; or (3) repossess and foreclose on the collateral, and then, depending on the circumstances, either sue for any deficiency or return the surplus to the debtor.

**Right to Possession.** The agreement between the creditor and the debtor may authorize the creditor to repossess the collateral in case of default. If the debtor does default, the creditor is entitled under the Code to possession of the collateral. If the creditor can obtain possession peaceably, he may do so. If the collateral is in the possession of the debtor and cannot be obtained without disturbing the peace, then the creditor must take court action to repossess the collateral [9–503]. See *Wade v. Ford Motor Credit Co.*, below, for a discussion of what constitutes repossession without breach of the peace.

If the collateral is intangible, such as accounts, chattel paper, instruments, or documents, and performance has been rendered to the debtor, the secured party may give notice and have payments made or performance rendered to him [9–502].

**Sale of the Collateral.** The secured party may dispose of the collateral by sale or lease or in any manner calculated to produce the greatest benefit to all parties concerned. However, the method of disposal must be *commercially reasonable* [9–504]. Notice of the time and place of a public sale must be given to the debtor, as must notice of a private sale. If the creditor decides to sell the collateral at a public sale, such as an auction, then the creditor must give the debtor notice of the time and place of the public sale. Similarly, if the creditor proposes to make a private sale of the collateral, notice must be given to the debtor. This gives the debtor a chance to object or to otherwise protect his interests [9–504]. The requirements a secured party must satisfy while selling the collateral are discussed in some detail in *Morrell Employees Credit Union v. Uselton,* which follows.

Until the collateral is actually disposed of by the creditor, the buyer has the *right to redeem* it. This means that the buyer can pay off the debt and recover the collateral from the creditor [9–506].

**Consumer Goods.** If the creditor has a security interest in consumer goods and the debtor has paid 60 percent or more of the purchase price or debt (and has not agreed in writing to a strict foreclosure), the creditor must sell the repossessed collateral. If less than 60 percent of the purchase price or debt has been paid, the creditor may propose to the debtor that the seller will keep the collateral in satisfaction of the debt. The consumer-debtor has 21 days to object in writing. If the consumer objects, the creditor must sell the collateral. Otherwise, the creditor may keep the collateral in satisfaction of the debt [9–505].

**Distribution of Proceeds.** The Code sets out the order in which any proceeds of sale of collateral by the creditor are to be distributed. First, any expenses of repossessing, storing, and selling the collateral, including reasonable attorney's fees, are paid. Second, the proceeds are used to satisfy the debt. Third, any junior liens are paid. Finally, if any proceeds remain, the debtor is entitled to them. If the proceeds are not sufficient to satisfy the debt, then the creditor is usually entitled to a *deficiency judgment.* This means that the debtor remains personally liable for any debt remaining after the sale of the collateral [9–504].

For example, suppose a loan company lends Christy $5,000 to purchase a car and takes a security interest. After making several payments and reducing the debt to $4,800,

Christy defaults. The loan company pays $50 to have the car repossessed and then has it sold at an auction, where it brings $4,500, thus incurring a sales commission of 10 percent ($450) and attorney's fees of $150. From the $4,500 proceeds, the repossession charges, sales commission, and attorney's fees, totaling $650, are paid first. The remaining $3,850 is applied to the $4,800 debt, leaving a balance due of $950. Christy remains liable to the loan company for the $950.

**Liability of Creditor.** A creditor who holds a security interest in collateral must be careful to comply with the provisions of Article 9 of the Code. If the creditor acts improperly in repossessing collateral or in its foreclosure and sale, he is liable to parties injured. Thus, a creditor can be liable to a debtor if he acts improperly in repossessing or selling collateral [9–507].

**Constitutional Requirements re Repossession.** In 1972, in *Fuentes v. Shevin,*[7] the U.S. Supreme Court held that state repossession statutes that authorize summary seizure of goods and chattels by state agents (such as a sheriff) upon an application by some private person who claims he is "lawfully entitled" to the property and posts a bond are unconstitutional because they deny the current possessor of the property an opportunity to be heard in court before the property is taken from him. The Court did not accept the argument that because the possessors of the property in question had signed conditional sales contracts that authorized the sellers to "take back" or "repossess" the property on default, they had waived their rights to a hearing. This decision raised some speculation that the provisions of the Code that permit secured parties to repossess collateral, in some cases without even judicial process, might be constitutionally defective.

Then, in 1974, in *Mitchell v. W. T. Grant,*[8] the Supreme Court limited the *Fuentes* holding to a requirement that where only property rights are involved, there must be some opportunity for a judicial hearing prior to any final determination of the rights of the parties claiming an interest in the property in question. This decision permits property to be seized by state officials, following the filing of an application and the posting of a bond, so long as the person from whom the property is seized has a later opportunity to assert in court his rights to the property.

The repossession provisions of the Code have been attacked in court as lacking in due process. However, the courts to date have upheld the Code repossession provisions as they relate to private repossession without judicial process.[9] Where judicial process is used, the procedures must conform to the standards laid down in *Fuentes* and *Mitchell.*

[7] 407 U.S. 67 (1972).

[8] 407 U.S. 600 (1974).

[9] See, e.g., *Gibbs v. Titelman,* 502 F.2d 1107 (3d Cir. 1974), and cases cited therein.

## Wade v. Ford Motor Credit Co.

**668 P.2d 183 (Kan. Ct. App. 1983)**

In August 1979, Norma Wade purchased a Ford Thunderbird automobile and gave Ford Motor Credit a security interest in it to secure her payment of the $7,000 balance of the purchase price. Wade fell behind on her monthly payments. Ford engaged the Kansas Recovery Bureau to repossess the car.

On February 10, 1980, an employee of the Recovery Bureau located the car in Wade's driveway, unlocked the door, got in, and started it. He then noticed a discrepancy between the serial number of the car and the number listed in his papers. He shut off the engine, got out, and locked the car. When Wade appeared at the door to her house, he advised her that he had been sent by Ford to repossess the car but would not do so until he had straightened out the serial number. She said that she had been making payments, that he was not going to take the car, and that she had a gun, which she would use. He suggested that Wade contact Ford to straighten out the problem. She called Ford and advised its representative that if she caught anybody on her property again trying to take her car, she would use her gun to "leave him laying right where I saw him."

Wade made several more payments, but Ford again contracted to have the car repossessed. At 2 A.M. on March 5, 1980, the employee of the Kansas Recovery Bureau successfully took the car from Wade's driveway. She said that she heard a car burning rubber, looked out of her window, and saw that her car was missing. There was no confrontation between Wade and the employee since he had safely left the area before she discovered that the car had been taken.

Wade then brought a lawsuit against Ford claiming that the car had been wrongfully repossessed. She sought actual and punitive damages, plus attorney's fees. Ford filed a counterclaim for the deficiency of $2,953.44 remaining after the car had been sold at public auction. The trial court found that Ford had breached the peace in repossessing the car and was liable to Wade for damages. It also found for Ford on its counterclaim. Ford appealed.

**SWINEHART, JUSTICE.** Ford contends that the trial court erred in finding that Ford breached the peace on March 10, 1980, when its agent repossessed Wade's car. The issue presented can be stated as follows: Does the repossession of a car, when there is no contact or confrontation between the repossessor and the debtor at the time and place of repossession, constitute a breach of the peace when there has been a prior threat of deadly violence if repossession is attempted? This particular set of facts has not been addressed by the courts before.

The trial court found that Ford had breached the peace in repossessing Wade's car. In its findings and conclusions made at the conclusion of the trial, the trial court emphasized Wade's lack of consent to the repossession and stated: "It's this court's view that the Legislature, when it permitted self-help repossession, it was meant to cover amicable situations where there was no dispute as there apparently was in this particular case." It appears that the trial court put a great deal of emphasis on Wade's lack of consent and the great potential for violence involved in the second repossession attempt.

Section 9–503 provides in part:

> Unless otherwise agreed a secured party has on default the right to take possession of the collateral. In taking possession a secured party may proceed without judicial process if this can be done without breach of the peace or may proceed by action.

The statutes do not define the term "breach of the peace." The courts are left with that job.

We find it is clear from a survey of the cases dealing with self-help repossession that the consent of the debtors to the repossession is not required. Section 9–112 even presupposes the lack of consent: "Upon default by a consumer, unless the consumer *voluntarily surrenders* possession." (Emphasis supplied.) The trial court's emphasis on the lack of consent by Wade in the present case and its view that "the Legislature, when it permitted self-help repossession, meant to cover amicable situations where there was no dispute" are not founded in case law. Repossession, without the consent of the debtor, absent more, does not constitute a breach of the peace by the creditor.

The trial court also emphasized the potential for violence brought on by Wade's threats made during the first repossession attempt. A breach of the peace may be caused by an act likely to produce violence. The facts presented in this case do not, however, rise to that level. A period of one month elapsed between the repossession attempts. During that period, Wade and Ford were in communication and two payments were made. We find the potential for violence was substantially reduced by the passage of time. Moreover, the actual repossession was such that in all likelihood no confrontation would materialize. In fact, Wade was totally unaware of the repossession until after the agent had successfully left the premises with the car. We therefore find that as a matter of law there was no breach of the peace in the repossession of Wade's car.

Judgment reversed in favor of Ford.

## Morrell Employees Credit Union v. Uselton

**28 UCC Rep. 269 (Tenn. Ct. App. 1979)**

On January 12, 1977, Uselton borrowed $6,315 from the Morrell Employees Credit Union to purchase a 1977 Ford LTD automobile. The loan was evidenced by a chattel mortgage under which Credit Union took a security interest in the automobile and Uselton agreed to repay in 36 consecutive monthly installments of $175.42 each, beginning January 31, 1977.

After making the first three payments, Uselton defaulted, leaving a principal balance of $5,788.77. The car was repossessed on June 20, 1977. In a letter entitled "Notice of Private Sale" and dated June 17, 1977, Phillip Donovan, general manager of Credit Union, gave written notice to Uselton by mail that the automobile would be sold at one or more private sales on or after July 7, 1977. On August 26, 1977, the automobile was sold to an individual for $5,400, which, when applied to the principal balance, left a deficiency of $388.77. To that amount, Credit Union added other charges, as follows:

| | |
|---|---|
| $ 388.77 | Balance owed on principal |
| 146.29 | Charges for repossession |
| 115.78 | Interest, 4/30/77–6/30/77 |
| 142.04 | Storage fees |
| 114.04 | Interest, 7/1/77–9/1/77 |
| $ 906.92 | Subtotal |
| 181.38 | 20% attorney's fees per contract |
| $1,088.30 | Total allegedly due under contract |

The sale was held at Credit Union on the property of John Morrell Company; only employees of the company had access to the property; and only members of Credit Union were permitted to bid. Notices of the proposed sale had been posted only on the property of John Morrell Company.

Credit Union brought suit against Uselton to recover the deficiency remaining on the installment contract after application of the proceeds of the sale. The trial court dismissed the complaint, and Credit Union appealed.

**EWELL, JUDGE.** If the sale held by Credit Union was a public sale, it was required to give Uselton reasonable notification of the time and place. If, on the other hand, it was a private sale, it was only required to give Uselton reasonable notification of the time after which a sale would be made. The notice given by Credit Union complied with the requirements for a private sale but not for a public sale. The court below held that the sale was a public sale, that the notice was insufficient and that Credit Union, therefore, could not recover. Credit Union insists that the sale was private and that adequate notice was given.

The sale described by Donovan had some aspects usually associated with a public sale and some aspects usually associated with a private sale. Since the terms "public sale" and "private sale" are not defined in the contract or the Uniform Commercial Code, we must look elsewhere to distinguish between the two. In the *Restatement of Security,* public sale is defined as, "one to which the public is invited by advertisement to appear and bid at auction for the goods to be sold." This definition conforms to established and generally accepted business practices, and applying thereto the facts of this case, we conclude that this could not have been a public sale. To so hold would necessitate the equating of "public" to "members of the Morrell Employees Credit Union," and we decline so to do. It follows, then, as between "public" and "private," this sale was "private," and the notice, therefore, was sufficient to comply with the Code.

The Code, however, demands more of Credit Union than adequate notice to Uselton. Specifically, every aspect of the sale, whether public or private and without regard to notice, including the method, manner, time, place, and terms thereof, must be commercially reasonable. See 9–504(3). The underlying consideration is to allow sufficient latitude to enable the secured party to sell in such manner as to get the best possible price for the goods. However, he must exercise due care and use reasonable efforts to obtain the best price to protect the debtor's interest. The disposition must be made in keeping with prevailing trade practices among reputable and responsible business and commercial enterprises engaged in the same or similar business.

The automobile was repossessed on June 20 but not sold until August 26. Credit Union offered no explanation for this delay of more than 60 days during which substantial storage charges and interest were accruing. The automobile was offered for sale to only members of the Morrell Employees Credit Union, and a bid from one not a member would have been rejected regardless of the amount thereof. The members were notified of the sale by the posting of four notices on the property of John Morrell Company. Credit Union did not prove the contents of the notice other than to show that it included a brief description of the automobile and gave notice that it would be sold. A copy of the notice was not forwarded to Uselton. One of the notices was posted in the cafeteria, but we are not advised as to where on the property the other notices were located. We do not know how long the notices were posted before the sale was held, and we do not know whether or not prior to the sale members were afforded an opportunity to examine the automobile. The sale was held on the property of John Morrell Company which was enclosed by a fence with a gate manned by a security guard who would grant admittance only to employees of John Morrell Company.

From the foregoing we conclude that Credit Union not only failed to prove that the sale was commercially reasonable but, to the contrary, presented evidence strongly suggesting that the sale was commercially unreasonable.

However, under 9–507(2) Credit Union could have overcome this handicap if it had proven (1) that the automobile was sold in the usual manner in any recognized market therefor, or (2) that the automobile was sold at the price current in such market at the time of sale, or (3) that the sale was in conformity with reasonable commercial practices among automobile dealers. The undisputed facts are such that comment on items (1) and (3) above is unnecessary. The proof demands that we address item (2).

Donovan testified that the sale price of $5,400 was deemed to be very good since it was more than the "book value" of the automobile at the time. The July 1977 issue of the South-Eastern edition of the *N.A.D.A. Official Used Car Guide* was admitted into evidence over the objection of Uselton's attorney, and Donovan pointed out that this particular vehicle was listed as having a value of $5,152. Donovan described the vehicle as "a basic Ford LTD for 1977 which did not have all of the possible accessories." This is the extent of the proof on the question of value. We are not advised as to the original purchase price, the optional accessories, the mileage at the time of sale or the general condition of the vehicle. There is no proof of any investigation made by Credit Union (other than that above noted) to determine value, and there is no proof of any other bids having been received. Based on this evidence we do not find that Credit Union has proven that the car sold "at the price current in the used car market at the time of sale." Therefore, under no theory can we hold that the sale was commercially reasonable.

Judgment for Uselton affirmed.

## BULK TRANSFERS

**Bulk Transfer Legislation.** Article 6 of the Uniform Commercial Code—Bulk Transfers—was enacted in order to prevent fraud on creditors. The bulk transfer law is intended to prevent the commercial fraud in which a merchant, owing debts, sells out his stock in trade for cash, pockets the proceeds, and then disappears, leaving his creditors unpaid. The bulk transfer law covers any transfer "in bulk," and not in the ordinary course of the transferor's business, of a major part of the materials, supplies, merchandise, or other inventory of an enterprise. A transfer of a substantial part of equipment is covered if the transfer is part of a bulk transfer of inventory. The enterprises subject to the bulk transfer law are those whose principal business is the sale of merchandise from stock, including retailers, wholesalers, and manufacturers [6–102].

The general plan of the bulk transfer law is to give creditors notice in advance of the transfer and to provide a plan for their protection. The seller is required to give the purchaser a schedule of the property to be transferred and a sworn list of the seller's creditors [6–104]. The purchaser is required to give the creditors on the list, and any other known creditors, notice of the pending transfer at least 10 days before he takes possession of the goods. In some states (New York, for example), the requirement is only that the creditors must receive notice of the proposed transfer; in other states (Pennsylvania, for example), the proceeds of the sale are distributed to the creditors [6–106].

The purchaser must make sure that the requirements of the bulk transfer law are met, or he is deemed to hold the goods in trust for the creditors of the seller. A creditor has only six months from the time the transfer took place to file suit to enforce his rights under the bulk transfer law; however, if the parties concealed the transfer, then the creditors have until six months after the transfer was discovered to bring suit [6–111]. The *Curtina International* case, which follows, provides an example of a purchaser's failure to comply with the bulk transfer law and illustrates the consequences of that noncompliance.

## In re Curtina International, Inc.
## Murdock v. Plymouth Enterprises, Inc.

**23 B.R. 969 (Bankr. S.D.N.Y. 1982)**

Curtina International was a corporation engaged in the business of importing and distributing confectionery products, mainly various varieties of wafers manufactured in Austria. From its inception in 1979, Curtina's business was not financially successful. By early 1981, Curtina was insolvent. Its largest unsecured creditor was one of its Austrian suppliers of wafers.

In February 1981, Curtina's president approached Plymouth Enterprises, a corporation engaged in the business of buying and selling closeouts (excess, old, or out-of-season inventory) from manufacturers and wholesalers at a fraction of their normal selling prices. He offered to sell Plymouth Curtina's line of wafers. In March, Plymouth agreed to purchase substantially all of Curtina's inventory of wafers at approximately $12 per case, for a total of about $66,000; the wafers usually sold for about $50 a case to retail stores. Plymouth's representative was not aware that wafers constituted Curtina's entire inventory. At no time did Plymouth ask Curtina for a list of its creditors, and Plymouth did not furnish notice of the sale to Curtina's creditors. It took Plymouth approximately nine months to resell the wafers.

Curtina was involuntarily thrown into bankruptcy in April 1981. Murdock, the trustee in bankruptcy, sought to avoid the sale of the wafers to Plymouth, contending that it was made in violation of the state bulk sales law.

**SCHWARTZBERG, BANKRUPTCY JUDGE.** Under Article 6 of the New York Uniform Commercial Code, referred to as the "Bulk Transfer Article," a creditor of a bulk transferor may look to § 6–104 and § 6–105 for purposes of avoiding a transfer that fails to comply with the notice requirements of the Bulk Transfer Article.

There is no question that Plymouth did not give the prescribed notice or otherwise comply with the Bulk Transfer Article. Plymouth maintains that the transaction in question was not a bulk transfer. A bulk transfer is defined under § 6–102(1) of the Uniform Commercial Code as:

> Any transfer in bulk and not in the ordinary course of the transferor's business of a major part of the materials, supplies, merchandise, or other inventory (Section 9–109) of an enterprise subject to this Article.

It is undisputed that Curtina sold all of its inventory of wafers to Plymouth. Therefore, in order to avoid Curtina's sale to Plymouth, the trustee must establish that the transfer was not in the ordinary course of Curtina's business. Consideration must therefore be given to the nature of Curtina's business and the manner in which it sold its merchandise. Evidence that Curtina had similar transactions in the past and that such transfers were common practice in the trade would be indicative that the questioned transfer occurred in the ordinary course of Curtina's business. Thus, the New York Court of Appeals in *Sternberg v. Rubenstein,* ruled that the sale of off-season shoes, the type of merchandise that was rendered "obsolete" by the passage of time, was exempt from the New York Bulk Sales Act. The New York Court of Appeals observed that the sale of obsolete inventory was an inevitable incident to the conduct of the transferor's business, provided that the sale did not constitute a discontinuance of a branch of business or a line of merchandise.

Other courts, interpreting a bulk sales provision similar to UCC § 6–102 have flatly rejected close-out sales as an excluded normal business practice. In *Jubas v. Sampsell,* a retail shoe store sold 25 percent of the number of pairs of shoes in its inventory, amounting to 15 percent in value, for one dollar per pair to another dealer, and then voluntarily filed a petition in bankruptcy. The one dollar per pair was the best offer obtainable. The trustee in bankruptcy was able to set aside the sale as violative of the California bulk sales law, despite the transferee's claim that "unloading" unmarketable shoes in that manner was a normal business practice. The court held that:

> The plain meaning of the statute is that when a storekeeper disposes of a substantial part of his stock in trade in bulk, and selling in bulk sales is not the usual and ordinary way in which he conducts his business from day to day, the sale falls within the statute.

The *Jubas* case was quoted with approval in *Danning v. Daylin,* where the court noted that the transferee's good faith and the absence of fraudulent intent are no defenses to a violation of the bulk sales law. The reason for such strict liability was to discourage a merchant who owes debts from selling out his stock in trade to anyone at any price, pocketing the proceeds, and disappearing without paying his creditors.

In the instant case, Plymouth has established that a close-out sale of the confectionery goods prior to total loss of shelf life is a common practice in the industry. However, there was no evidence that Curtina ever sold any portion of its line of wafers on a close-out basis since its inception in late 1979, and up to the time when it sold off all of its inventory in March of 1981. Moreover, the transfer to Plymouth resulted in the discontinuance of Curtina's entire business; it retained no other merchandise lines nor did it remain open as a going business.

Based upon the foregoing, it is held that the trustee has established, and Plymouth has failed to rebut, that Plymouth purchased Curtina's entire inventory of vanilla, raspberry, and orange wafers without complying with the notice provisions in § 6–104 and § 6–105 under Article 6 of the New York Uniform Commercial Code, referred to as the Bulk Transfer Article.

Article 6 of the New York Uniform Commercial Code imposes no specific remedy for failure to comply with the bulk sales law. Under § 6–104 and § 6–105 a noncomplying transfer is "ineffective" against creditors of the transferor. The Official Comment suggests that an objecting creditor may levy on or obtain possession of the merchandise but is silent as to money damages, especially where the merchandise has been resold by the transferee.

The New York cases interpreting the bulk sales law have held that a transfer in violation of the law obligates the transferee to account to the transferor's creditors for the value of the merchandise transferred.

In the instant case, it has been found that the reasonable equivalent value of the vanilla, raspberry, and orange wafers sold in bulk by Curtina to Plymouth was $66,766.32 at the time of the sale. Accordingly, Plymouth is liable to the Curtina estate and must account for this amount. However, Plymouth has paid the full purchase price to the debtor, and the funds appear to have been deposited by the debtor in its account with the European American Bank and Curtina's schedules reveal a sum of $44,639.49 on deposit in its account with the European American Bank at the time the involuntary petition was filed. In accounting for the value of the inventory, Plymouth is entitled to a credit for that portion of the proceeds from the sale that are traceable to the funds held by the trustee in bankruptcy.

Judgment for Murdock, the trustee in bankruptcy.

## SUMMARY

A security interest is an interest in personal property or fixtures that secures payment or performance of an obligation. The Code sets out rules for obtaining secured interests in instruments, documents of title, accounts, contract rights, chattel paper, general intangibles, and goods. Goods may be consumer goods, equipment, inventory, farm products, or fixtures. To obtain the maximum protection for his security interest, the creditor must attach and perfect that interest.

A security interest is not enforceable until it has been attached to the collateral. To effect this attachment, there must be an agreement between the debtor and the secured party that the security interest attach, that value must be given to the debtor, and that the debtor must have rights in the collateral. A security agreement may cover future advances to be made by the creditor to the debtor. A security agreement may also create a security interest in proceeds of the collateral and in after-acquired property of the debtor.

To protect his security interest against other creditors of the debtor and purchasers of the collateral, the secured party must perfect his security interest. Under the Code, there are three means of perfection: public filing of a financing statement; taking possession of the collateral; and, in some limited cases, mere attachment of the security interest.

A financing statement is filed at either the secretary of state's office or the local recorder's office, depending on the type of collateral that it secures. If no maturity date is stated, the filing is good for five years. It may be extended for additional five-year periods by filing a continuation statement. A debtor who has fulfilled his obligations is entitled to a termination statement, which removes the financing statement from the records.

The Code sets out a series of rules for determining the priority of conflicting claims of secured creditors to the same collateral. Where more than one security interest has been perfected, then the first security interest to be perfected has priority over any security interests that are perfected later or any that are unperfected. If none of the security interests have been perfected, then the first security interest to attach has priority. However, special rules provide that creditors who have purchase money security interests can prevail over prior secured creditors if they file. In addition, a buyer in the ordinary course of business takes free of a security interest created by his seller even though the security interest is perfected and the buyer knows about it.

A secured party holding a security interest in goods that may become fixtures must take special steps so that his claim is shown on the real estate records.

Within stated limitations, the parties may agree as to the rights of the secured party if the debtor defaults. Unless otherwise agreed, the secured party has the right to possess the collateral. If it is bulky or hard to remove, he may render it useless and sell it where it is located. He may sell the collateral at public or private sale, and he may buy the collateral, but he must act in good faith and the sale must be commercially reasonable. The proceeds of the sale are distributed as follows: expenses; reasonable attorney's fees; satisfaction of indebtedness; junior creditors, if any; and the balance to the debtor. Unless otherwise agreed, the seller is entitled to a deficiency judgment if the proceeds are not sufficient to cover the debt. If the security interest is in consumer goods, the secured party must sell if 60 percent of the debt has been paid. If less than 60 percent has been paid, the secured party may, upon appropriate notice, keep the collateral and cancel the debt.

The bulk transfer law is designed to prevent commercial fraud, and anyone who buys substantially all of the materials, supplies, inventory, or equipment of a business, must comply with it to make sure that he will take title free of claims from the seller's creditors.

## PROBLEM CASES

**1.** In August 1981, Agricultural Exports entered into a security agreement with Horizon Farms in which Horizon was granted a security interest in "all almond and/or prune crops now growing or to be grown" on Agricultural Exports' land. Several days later, a financing statement was filed that described the collateral as "All crops of prunes and almonds now growing on the real property." Does Horizon have a perfected security interest in crops grown after the 1981 crop year?

**2.** Robert and Billie Brown operated a paint and gift store. They borrowed $36,628.31 from the First National Bank of Dewey and gave the bank a security interest in "all goods, wares, merchandise, gifts, inventory, fixtures, and accounts receivable owned or thereafter acquired and used in the business." The security agreement also covered "all additions, accessions, and substitutions" to or for collateral and required the Browns to insure the collateral for the benefit of the bank. The bank perfected its security interest. The Browns obtained fire insurance but did not name the bank as a loss payee. The Browns' business was destroyed by fire, and the Browns received a $25,000 check from the insurance company for the loss of inventory. The bank then filed suit to obtain the check. Shortly thereafter, the Browns were adjudicated bankrupt. Does the bank have a perfected security interest in the insurance check?

**3.** Symons, a full-time insurance salesman, bought a set of drums and cymbals from Grinnel Brothers, Inc. A security agreement was executed between them but never filed. Symons purchased the drums to supplement his income by playing with a band. He had done this before, and his income from the two jobs was about equal. He also played several other instruments. Symons became bankrupt, and the trustee tried to acquire the drums as part of his bankruptcy estate. Grinnel Brothers tried to enforce the security agreement. What can Grinnel Brothers argue? Will it be successful?

**4.** The Bank of Pennsylvania acquired and perfected a nonpurchase money security interest in all of Perrotto Refrigeration's present and future inventory and accounts receivable and their proceeds. Subsequently, Perrotto purchased several ice machines for inventory from Appliance Buyers. Appliance Buyers took and perfected a security interest in the ice machines prior to their delivery to Perrotto and notified Bank of Pennsylvania that it was taking such a purchase money security interest. Perrotto has defaulted on its obligations to Appliance Buyers and to the bank. Between Appliance Buyers and the Bank of Pennsylvania, who has the priority interest in the ice machines?

**5.** On April 10, Benson purchased a new Ford Thunderbird automobile. She traded in her old automobile and financed the balance of $4,325 through the Magnavox Employees Credit Union, which took a security interest in the Thunderbird. In July, the Thunderbird was involved in two accidents and sustained major damage. It was taken to ACM for repairs that took seven months to make and resulted in charges of $2,139.54. Benson was unable to pay the charges, and ACM claimed a garageman's lien. Does Magnavox Credit Union's lien or ACM's lien have priority?

**6.** Kahn applied for a home improvement loan to construct an in-ground swimming pool. Union National Bank approved the loan, and construction was begun on Kahn's land. State Bank held a valid mortgage on this land. After the pool was completed, Union National gave Kahn the money with which he paid the contractor. Union National then perfected its interest by filing. State Bank later attempted to foreclose on its mortgage. Union National claimed the value of the pool. Is Union National entitled to recover the value of the pool?

**7.** A bank loaned money to Van Horn, a dealer in used cars, and took a security interest in a used Rolls-Royce owned by Van Horn. The bank did not file to perfect its security interest. Van Horn sold the Rolls-Royce to Larson, who bought the car without actual knowledge of the bank's interest. Van Horn defaulted on his loan obligation, and the bank tried to repossess the Rolls from Larson. Does the bank have the right to do so?

**8.** In October 1976, Henry purchased a combine from Trickey, paying $11,000 down against the $38,750 sales price. After complaining about repair problems on the combine and defaulting on his payments, Henry returned the combine to Trickey, who agreed to resell it. Trickey took possession prior to January 1, 1977. To sell the equipment, Trickey notified other dealers of the repossessed combine, but he did not advertise it or display it at auctions. The combine remained on Trickey's lot until it was sold through a dealer in September 1979 for $18,000. Until the sale, Trickey had had one offer for $13,000–$15,000, which he rejected. During the time that he had the combine, Trickey loaned its motor to one of his customers for a year to use during harvesting season. After the resale, Trickey brought suit seeking a deficiency judgment for the difference between the balance due on the purchase price and the amount to be received on the resale. Is Trickey entitled to a deficiency judgment?

**9.** C. W. Rutherford purchased a 1974 Cadillac from Big Three Motors, Inc. Rutherford fell behind in his payments to the dealer on the car. One day, while his wife, Christine, was driving the Cadillac on an interstate highway, two Big Three Motors employees driving a truck forced her off the road and blocked her direct access back to the highway. One of the employees then got into the car with Christine and rode with her to the Big Three Motors dealership. Christine locked the car, took the keys, and went into the office. When she left, she discovered that someone had taken the Cadillac from the spot where she had parked it. An employee of Big Three Motors told her that the car had been put "in storage" because C. W. Rutherford owed payments. She then took a taxi home. The Rutherfords brought suit against Big Three Motors seeking punitive damages for wrongful repossession. Do they have a valid claim?

# Chapter 41

# Bankruptcy

## INTRODUCTION

When an individual, a partnership, or a corporation is unable to pay debts to creditors, a number of problems can arise. Some creditors may demand security for past debts or start court actions on their claims in an effort to protect themselves. Such actions may adversely affect other creditors by depriving them of their fair share of the debtor's assets. In addition, quick depletion of the debtor's assets may effectively prevent the debtor who needs additional time to pay off his debts from having an opportunity to do so.

At the same time, creditors need to be protected against actions that, a debtor who is in financial difficulty might be tempted to take that would be to their detriment. For example, the debtor might run off with his remaining assets or might use them to pay certain favored creditors, leaving nothing for the other creditors. Finally, a means is needed by which a debtor can get a fresh start financially and not continue to be saddled with debts beyond his ability to pay. In this chapter the focus is on the body of law and procedure that have developed to deal with the competing interests that are present when a debtor is unable to pay his debts in a timely manner.

**The Bankruptcy Act.** The Bankruptcy Act is a federal law that provides an organized procedure under the supervision of a federal court for dealing with insolvent debtors. Debtors are considered insolvent if they are unable or fail to pay their debts as they become due. The power of Congress to enact bankruptcy legislation is provided in the Constitution. Through the years, there have been many amendments to the Bankruptcy Act. Congress completely revised it in 1978 and then passed significant amendments to it in 1984.

The Bankruptcy Act has several major purposes. One is to assure that the debtor's property is fairly distributed to the creditors and that some creditors do not obtain unfair advantage over the others. At the same time, the act is designed to protect all of the creditors against actions by the debtor that would unreasonably diminish the debtor's assets to which they are entitled. The act also provides the honest debtor with a measure of protection against the demands for payment by his creditors. Under some circumstances, the debtor will be given additional time to pay the creditors free of pressures that the creditors might otherwise exert. If the debtor makes a full and honest accounting of his assets and liabilities and deals fairly with the creditors, the debtor may have most, if not all, of the debts discharged so as to have a fresh start.

At one time, bankruptcy carried a strong stigma for the debtors who became involved in it. Today, this is less true. It is still desirable that a person conduct his financial affairs in a responsible manner. However, there is a greater understanding that such events as accidents, natural disasters, illness, divorce, and severe economic dislocations are often beyond the ability of individuals to control and may lead to financial difficulty and bankruptcy.

**Types of Bankruptcy Proceedings.** The Bankruptcy Act covers a number of types of bankruptcy proceedings. In this chapter, our focus will be on (1) liquidations, (2) reorganizations, and (3) consumer debt adjustments. The Bankruptcy Act also contains provisions regarding municipal bankruptcies, but these will not be covered in this chapter.

**Liquidations.** A liquidation proceeding, traditionally called *straight bankruptcy,* is brought under Chapter 7 of the Bankruptcy Act. The debtor must disclose all of the property he owns (the bankruptcy estate) and surrender it to the bankruptcy trustee. The trustee separates out certain property that the debtor is permitted to keep and then administers, liquidates, and distributes the remainder of the bankrupt debtor's estate. There is a mechanism for determining the relative rights of the creditors, for recovering any preferential payments made to creditors, and for disallowing any preferential liens obtained by creditors. If the bankrupt person has been honest in his business transactions and in the bankruptcy proceedings, he is usually given a discharge (relieved) of his debts.

**Reorganizations.** Chapter 11 of the Bankruptcy Act provides a proceeding whereby a debtor engaged in business can work out a plan to try to solve its financial problems under the supervision of a federal court. A *reorganization plan* is essentially a contract between a debtor and its creditors. The proceeding is intended for debtors, particularly businesses, whose financial problems may be solvable if they are given some time and guidance and if they are relieved of some pressure from creditors.

**Consumer Debt Adjustments.** Chapter 13 of the Bankruptcy Act sets out a special procedure for individuals with regular income who are in financial difficulty to develop a plan under court supervision to satisfy their creditors. Chapter 13 permits *compositions* (reductions) of debts and/or *extensions of time* to pay debts out of the debtor's future earnings.

## CHAPTER 7: LIQUIDATION PROCEEDINGS

**Petitions.** All bankruptcy proceedings, including liquidation proceedings, are begun by the filing of a *petition.* The petition may be either a voluntary petition filed by the debtor or an involuntary petition filed by a creditor or creditors of the debtor. A voluntary petition in bankruptcy may be filed by an individual, a partnership, or a corporation. However, municipal, railroad, insurance, and banking corporations and savings or building and loan associations are not permitted to file for straight bankruptcy proceedings. A person filing a voluntary petition need not be *insolvent*—that is, his debts need not be greater than his assets. However, the person must be able to allege that he has debts. The primary purpose for filing a voluntary petition is to obtain a discharge from some or all of the debts.

**Involuntary Petition.** An *involuntary petition* is a petition filed by creditors of a debtor. By filing it, they seek to have the debtor declared bankrupt and his assets distributed to the creditors. Involuntary petitions may be filed against many kinds of debtors. However, involuntary petitions in straight bankruptcy cannot be filed against (1) farmers; (2) ranchers; (3) nonprofit organizations; (4) municipal, railroad, insurance, and banking corporations; (5) credit unions; and (6) savings or building and loan associations. If a debtor has 12 or more creditors, an involuntary petition to declare him bankrupt must be signed by at least 3 creditors. If there are fewer than 12 creditors, then an involuntary petition can be filed by a single creditor. The creditor or creditors must have valid claims against the debtor that exceed by $5,000 or more the value of any security they hold. To be forced into involuntary bankruptcy, the debtor must be unable to pay his debts as they become due—or have had a custodian for his property appointed within the previous four months.

If an involuntary petition is filed against a debtor engaged in business, the debtor may be permitted to continue to operate the business. However, the court may appoint an interim trustee if this is necessary in order to preserve the bankruptcy estate or to prevent loss of the estate. A creditor who suspects that a debtor may dismantle its business or dispose of its assets at less than fair value may apply to the court for protection.

**Automatic Stay Provisions.** The filing of a bankruptcy petition operates as an *automatic stay* (holds in abeyance) various forms of creditor action against a debtor or his property. These actions include: (1) beginning or continuing judicial proceedings against the debtor; (2) actions to obtain possession of the debtor's property; (3) actions to create, perfect, or enforce a lien against the debtor's property; and (4) setoff of indebtedness owed to the debtor that arose before commencement of the bankruptcy proceeding. A court may give a creditor relief from the stay if the creditor can show that the stay does not give him "adequate protection" and jeopardizes his interest in certain property. The relief to the creditor might take the form of periodic cash payments or the granting of a replacement lien or an additional lien on property.

**The Bankruptcy Courts.** Bankruptcy cases and proceedings are filed in federal district courts. The district courts have the authority to refer the cases and proceedings to bankruptcy judges, who are considered to be units of the district court. If a dispute falls within what is known as a *core proceeding,* the bankruptcy judge can hear and determine the controversy. Core proceedings include a broad list of matters related to the administration of a bankruptcy estate. However, if a dispute is not a "core proceeding" but rather involves a state law claim, then the bankruptcy judge can only hear the case and prepare draft findings and conclusions for review by the district court judge. Certain kinds of proceedings that will have an effect on interstate commerce have to be heard by the district court judge if any party requests that this be done. Moreover, even the district courts are precluded from deciding certain state law claims that could not normally be brought in federal court, even if those claims are related to the bankruptcy matter. Bankruptcy judges are appointed by the president for terms of 14 years.

**Appointment of Trustee.** Once a bankruptcy petition has been filed, the first step is a court determination that relief should be ordered. If a voluntary petition is filed by the debtor or if the debtor does not contest an involuntary petition, this step is automatic. If the debtor contests an involuntary petition, then a trial is held on the question of whether the court should order relief. The court will order relief only if (1) the debtor is generally not paying his debts as they become due or (2) within four months of the filing of the petition a custodian was appointed or took possession of the debtor's property. The court also appoints an interim trustee pending election of a trustee by the creditors.

The bankrupt person is required to file a list of his assets, liabilities, and creditors and a statement of his financial affairs. Then, a meeting of the creditors is called by the court. The creditors may elect a creditors' committee and a **trustee** who, if approved by the judge, takes over administration of the bankrupt's estate. The trustee represents the creditors in handling the estate. At the meeting, the creditors have a chance to ask the debtor questions about his assets, liabilities, and financial difficulties. The questions commonly focus on whether the debtor has concealed or improperly disposed of assets.

**Duties of Trustee.** The trustee takes possession of the debtor's property and has it appraised. The debtor must also turn over his records to the trustee. For a time, the trustee may operate the debtor's business. The trustee sets aside the items of property that a debtor is permitted to keep under state exemption statutes or under federal law.

The trustee examines the claims that have been filed by various creditors and objects to those that are improper in any way. The trustee separates the unsecured property from the secured and otherwise exempt property. He also sells the bankrupt's nonexempt property as soon as is possible and consistent with the best interest of the creditors.

The trustee is required to keep an accurate account of all the property and money he receives and to promptly deposit moneys into the estate's accounts. At the final meeting of the creditors, the trustee presents a detailed statement of the administration of the bankruptcy estate.

**Exemptions.** Even in a liquidation proceeding, the bankrupt is generally not required to give up all of his property, but rather is permitted to *exempt* certain items of property. Under the new Bankruptcy Act, the debtor may choose to keep either (1) certain items or property that are exempted by state law or (2) certain items that are exempt under federal law—unless state law specifically forbids use of the federal exemptions. However, any such property that has been concealed or fraudulently transferred by the debtor may not be retained. A husband and wife who are involved in bankruptcy proceedings must both elect either the federal or the state exemptions; if they cannot agree, the federal exemptions are deemed elected.

The **exemptions** permit the bankrupt person to retain a minimum amount of the assets considered necessary to life and to his ability to continue to earn a living. They are part of the "fresh start" philosophy that is one of the purposes behind the Bankruptcy Act. The general effect of the federal exemptions is to make a minimum exemption available to debtors in all states. States that wish to be more generous to debtors can provide more liberal exemptions.

The specific items that are exempt under state statutes vary from state to state. Some states provide fairly liberal exemptions and, are considered "debtors' havens." Items that are commonly made exempt from sale to pay debts owed creditors include the family Bible, tools or books of the trade, life insurance policies, health aids (such as wheelchairs and, hearing aids), personal and household goods, and jewelry, furniture, and a motor vehicle worth up to a certain amount.

Eleven categories of property are exempt under the federal exemptions, which the debtor may elect in lieu of the state exemptions. The federal exemptions include: (1) the debtor's interest (not to exceed $7,500 in value) in real property or personal property that the debtor or a dependent of the debtor uses as a residence; (2) the debtor's interest (not to exceed $1,200 in value) in one motor vehicle; (3) the debtor's interest (not to exceed $200 in value as to any particular item) up to a total of $4,000 in household furnishings, household goods, wearing apparel, appliances, books, animals, crops, or musical instruments that are held primarily for the personal, family, or household use of the debtor or a dependent of the debtor; (4) the debtor's aggregate interest (not to exceed $500 in value) in jewelry held primarily for the personal, family, or household use of the debtor or a dependent of the debtor; (5) the debtor's aggregate interest (not to exceed $750 in value) in any implements, professional books, or tools of the trade; (6) life insurance contracts; (7) professionally prescribed health aids; (8) $400 in value of any other property of the debtor's choosing; and (9) social security, disability, alimony, and other benefits reasonably necessary for the support of the debtor or his dependents. The term *value* means "fair market value as of the date of the filing of the petition." In determining the debtor's interest in property, the amount of any liens against the property must be deducted. If the debtor does not use his full homestead exemption to exempt real property, he may use the remaining balance to exempt other property.

The *Perry* case, below, involves the application of a state exemption law to a fur coat owned by a debtor. In the following case, *In re Pockat,* the question presented is whether a tractor cab owned by a truck driver should be considered an exempt "tool" of his trade.

**Avoidance of Liens.** The debtor is also permitted to *void* certain liens against exempt properties that impair his exemptions. The liens that can be voided on this basis are judicial liens or nonpossessory, non–purchase money security interests in: (1) household furnishings, household goods, wearing apparel, appliances, books, animals, crops, musical instruments, or jewelry that are held primarily for the personal, family, or household use of the debtor or a dependent of the debtor; (2) implements, professional books, or tools of the trade of the debtor or a dependent of the debtor; and (3) professionally prescribed health aids for the debtor or a dependent of the debtor. Debtors are also permitted to *redeem* exempt personal property from secured creditors by paying them the value of the collateral. Then, the creditor is an unsecured creditor as to any remaining debt owed by the debtor.

**Claims.** If creditors wish to participate in the estate of a bankrupt debtor, they must file a *proof of claim* in the estate within a certain time (usually six months) after the first meeting of creditors. Only unsecured creditors are required to file proofs of claims; secured creditors do not have to do so. However, a secured creditor whose secured claim exceeds the value of the collateral is an unsecured creditor to the extent of the deficiency. A proof of claim must be filed to support the recovery of the deficiency.

The fact that a proof of claim is filed does not assure that a creditor can participate in the distribution of the assets of the bankruptcy estate. The claim must also be *allowed.* If the trustee has a valid defense to the claim, he can use the defense to disallow or reduce it. For example, if the claim is based on goods sold to the debtor and the seller breached a warranty, the trustee can assert the breach as a defense. All of the defenses that would have been available to the bankrupt person will be available to the trustee.

The trustee must also determine whether a creditor has a lien or secured interest to secure an allowable claim. If the debtor's property is subject to a secured claim of a creditor, that creditor has first claim to it. The property is available to satisfy claims of other creditors only to the extent that its value exceeds the amount of the debt secured.

**Priority Claims.** The Bankruptcy Act declares certain claims to have *priority* over other claims. These include: (1) expenses and fees incurred in administering the bankruptcy estate; (2) unsecured claims of up to $2,000 per individual for wages of employees earned within 90 days before the petition was filed; (3) contributions to employee benefit plans arising out of services performed within 180 days of the petition; (4) claims of up to $900 each by individuals for deposits made on goods or services for personal use that were not delivered or provided; and (5) taxes. These claims are paid after secured creditors realize on their security but before other unsecured claims are paid. Unsecured creditors frequently receive little or nothing on their claims. Secured claims, trustee's fees, and other priority claims often consume a large part of the bankruptcy estate.

Special rules are set out in the Bankruptcy Act for distribution of the property of a bankrupt stockbroker or commodities broker.

**Preferential Payments.** A major purpose of the Bankruptcy Act is to assure equal treatment for the creditors of an insolvent debtor. The act also seeks to prevent an insolvent debtor from distributing his assets to a few favored creditors to the detriment of the other creditors. The trustee has the right to recover for the benefit of the bankruptcy estate all **preferential payments** in excess of $600 made by the bankrupt person. A preferential payment is a payment made by an insolvent debtor within 90 days of the filing of the bankruptcy petition that enables the creditor receiving the payment to obtain a greater percentage of a preexisting debt than is obtained by other similar creditors of the debtor. It is irrelevant whether the creditor knew that the debtor was insolvent.

For example, Fredericks has $1,000 in cash and no other assets. He owes $650 to his friend Roberts, $1,500 to Credit Union, and $2,000 to Finance Company. If Fredericks pays $650 to Roberts and then files for bankruptcy, he has made a preferential payment to Roberts. Roberts has had his debt paid in full, whereas only $350 is left to satisfy the $3,500 owed to Credit Union and Finance Company. They stand to recover only 10 cents on each dollar that Fredericks owes them. The trustee has the right to get the $650 back from Roberts.

If the favored creditor is an "insider"—a relative of an individual debtor or an officer, director, or related party of a company—then a preferential payment made up to one year prior to the filing of the petition can be recovered.

**Preferential Liens.** **Preferential liens** are treated in a similar manner. A creditor might try to obtain an advantage over other creditors by obtaining a lien on the debtor's property to secure an existing debt. The creditor might seek to get the debtor's consent to a lien or to obtain a lien by legal process. Such a lien is considered preferential. It is invalid if it is obtained on property of an insolvent debtor within 90 days of the filing of a bankruptcy petition and if its purpose is to secure a preexisting debt. A preferential lien obtained by an insider within one year of the bankruptcy can be voided.

The provisions of the Bankruptcy Act that negate preferential payments and liens do not prevent a debtor from engaging in current business transactions. For example, George Grocer is insolvent. He is permitted to purchase and pay for new inventory, such as produce or meat, without the payment being considered preferential. His assets have not been reduced. He has simply traded money for goods to be sold in his business. Similarly, he could buy a new display counter and give the seller a security interest in the counter until he has paid for it. This is not a preferential lien. The seller of the counter has not gained an unfair advantage over other creditors, and Grocer's assets have not been reduced by the transaction. The unfair advantage comes where an existing creditor tries to take a lien or obtain a payment of more than his share of the debtor's assets. Then, the creditor has obtained a preference over other creditors and it will be disallowed.

The act also permits payments of accounts in the ordinary course of business. Such payments are not considered preferential.

**Fraudulent Transfers.** If a debtor *transfers property or incurs an obligation* with *intent to hinder, delay, or defraud creditors,* the transfer is *voidable* by the trustee. Transfers of property for less than reasonable value are similarly voidable. Suppose Kasper is in financial difficulty. She "sells" her $5,000 car to her mother for $100 so that her creditors cannot claim it. Kasper did not receive fair consideration for this transfer. The transfer could be declared void by a trustee if it was made within a year before the filing of a bankruptcy petition against Kasper. The provisions of law concerning **fraudulent transfers** are designed to prevent a debtor from concealing or disposing of his property in fraud of creditors. Such transfers may also subject the debtor to criminal penalties and prevent discharge of the debtor's unpaid liabilities.

The *Newman* case below illustrates the attempt of a debtor to put his assets beyond the reach of his creditors and the response of the trustee who was able to avoid the transfers as fraudulent.

## In re Perry

**6 B.R. 263 (W.D. Va. 1980)**

Lois Perry filed a voluntary petition pursuant to Chapter 7 of the Bankruptcy Act. Among the items of personal clothing that Perry listed as exempt from her creditors was a mink coat with a value of approximately $2,500. The trustee objected to the claimed exemption, contending that the mink coat was not "necessary" clothing.

The Code of Virginia, Section 34–26, provides in pertinent part that:

> In addition to the estate, not exceeding in value five thousand dollars, which every householder residing in this State shall be entitled to hold exempt, . . . of this title, he shall also be entitled to hold exempt from levy or distress the following articles or so much or so many thereof as he may have, to be selected by him or his agents:
>
> (1) The family Bible.
> (1a) Wedding and engagement rings.
> (2) Family pictures, schoolbooks and library for the use of the family.
> (3) A lot in a burial ground.
> (4) All necessary wearing apparel of the debtor and his family, all beds, bedsteads and bedding necessary for the use of such family, two dressers or two dressing tables, wardrobes, chifforobes or chests of drawers or a dresser and a dressing table, carpets, rugs, linoleum or other floor covering; and all stoves and appendages put up and kept for the use of the family not exceeding three.

**PEARSON, BANKRUPTCY JUDGE.** The Trustee lays claim to the coat as an asset, contending such item is not a "necessary" item of wearing apparel provided in § 34–26(4). The Debtor contends that the coat is a necessary item of wearing apparel and that the General Assembly did not place a value upon wearing apparel.

We first allude to the general rules of construction placed upon exemption statutes.

In 31 Am. Jur. 2nd, Exemptions § 8, the authority states with reference to strict or liberal construction the following:

> It is, therefore, the almost universal rule that they [exemption statutes] should receive a liberal construction in favor of those intended to be benefited and favorable to the object and purposes of the enactment . . . and where there is doubt as to whether certain property is exempt or not, the doubt should be resolved in favor of the exemption.

The statute here in question within its own provisions contains several instances of specific limitations prescribed by the Legislature. For example, a clothes dryer not to exceed $150.00 in value. Other specified items are listed as not to exceed "$50.00" or "$25.00." Additionally, an oysterman or fisherman's boat and tackle shall not exceed $1,500.00. Consequently, it would appear that the Legislature intended to fix a value upon items within the statutory scheme of the section itself. It should be noted likewise, that a most recent amendment increasing homestead exemptions from $3,000.00 to $5,000.00, in addition to those exempt items in § 34–26, made no change restricting the value of this section. Additionally, 1(a) was inserted giving exemption of wedding and engagement rings, without limitation.

The statutory language generally exempts "all necessary wearing apparel of the debtor and his family." The word "necessary" might appear to be a word of limitation requiring the fixing of a value upon the coat in question as a criterion in determining its exempt status. The practical effect of this construction would be to saddle upon a debtor the duty of defending such debtor's poor debtor exemptions from harassing court proceedings by creditors seeking to deprive an impoverished debtor of the exemption, the defense of which would be further impoverishing. That certainly is not the intent of the Legislature in setting apart property under § 34–26.

In the case of *Frazier v. Barnum,* the court there considered necessary wearing apparel in the nature of an expensive lace shawl of considerable value. In that case, the court ruled that the courts should not indulge in inquiries as to extravagance or bad taste of a debtor's wearing apparel in any consideration relating to its necessity. The court commented that good faith should be a factor. Where there is no question of a good faith claim that the coat is a reasonable necessary item of clothing, the value should not govern. The General Assembly could have fixed or set a limitation of one coat for each member of a family. It could have specified one coat of some inexpensive fabric. It has not chosen to do so. As herein mentioned, the Legislature most recently amended this statute providing the exemption of wedding and engagement rings without fixing any limitation. Indeed, it would be inappropriate to say that a diamond engagement ring of one carat is exempt but a diamond ring of more than one carat is not exempt within the legislative language of the statute.

For the reasons set forth, it is the considered judgment of the Court that the proper construction of § 34–26 warrants the granting of the exemption claimed.

Judgment for Perry.

## In re Pockat

### 6 B.R. 24 (W.D. Wis. 1980)

On March 9, 1979, Ronald Pockat borrowed money from Thorp Finance Corporation. He gave Thorp a security interest in an IHC tractor cab that he owned. At the time, Pockat was an over- the-road trucker who leased his cab and himself to various transport companies. He filed a voluntary petition in bankruptcy on November 15, 1979. After the petition was filed, Pockat sought to have the lien on the tractor voided on the ground that the tractor cab was a tool of the trade and thus exempt from creditors under the Bankruptcy Act.

**Frawley, Bankruptcy Judge.** The question herein involved is: Is the 1972 IHC Tractor, ID #259471Y033593, an implement or tool of trade of Ronald E. Pockat, as alleged in the complaint and claimed under the exemption of 11 U.S.C. § 522(d)(6)?

Counsel stated that it has been very difficult to find any case interpreting the items included in the term "implements, tools of trade of the debtor, or the trade of a dependent of the debtor." Counsel submitted that under the decisions of other states, law libraries of attorneys have been exempt under this terminology, as well as artists' pictures. The

Wisconsin Statutes and annotations are not enlightening in any way as to what is included under "tools of trade."

In *Cunningham v. Brictson,* the court said:

> This court has said over and over again that exemption laws must be liberally construed; that, in following out the constitutional mandate, the legislature must provide for the enactment of laws giving the debtor a reasonable amount of property to be held free from the claims of creditors; that such laws are founded on the soundest considerations of public policy, and are designed to stimulate individual freedom and manly citizenship.

Section 522(f)(2)(B) provides voiding the lien on implements, professional books or tools of the trade of the debtor or the trade of a dependent of the debtor. Certainly a debtor, in order to be an over-the-road trucker and continue in that field of trucking, would have to have the cab-tractor available to him to make his living as much as any printer would need his printing tools, or an electrician his electrical tools, or any other mechanic the tools used by him in making a living.

Thus, the cab-tractor is an implement or tool of the trade of Ronald E. Pockat.

Judgment for Pockat.

---

## In re Newman

**6 B.R. 798 (S.D.N.Y. 1980)**

On September 17, 1979, a jury verdict in favor of Chrysler Credit Corporation in the amount of $86,704 was rendered against Joseph Newman. Several days later, he assigned promissory notes due to him from the New Rochelle Manufacturing Corporation to his father-in-law, Andrew Charla. The notes were worth $93,337 at the time, but his father-in-law paid him only $54,500. On September 28, 1979, a corporation known as J.E.S. Equities, Inc. was formed. The sole officers and stockholders were Newman's children. On November 15, Newman transferred $40,000 in cash to the corporation in return for a promissory note from it. The note called for no payment of principal or interest until November 1982, at which time the note was to be paid off with interest at 7 percent over a period of nearly 37 years at the rate of $100 per month. On November 24, an involuntary petition in bankruptcy under Chapter 7 was filed against Newman. The trustee in bankruptcy then brought an action to recover the transfers of assets to Charla and J.E.S. Equities.

**Schwartzberg, Bankruptcy Judge.** The trustee seeks to avoid as fraudulent transfers the conveyances made by the debtor to Andrew Charla and J.E.S. Equities, Inc. Section 548(a) of the Bankruptcy Code states in part:

> (a) The trustee may avoid any transfer of an interest of the debtor in property, or any obligation incurred by the debtor, that was made or incurred on or within one year before the date of the filing of the petition, if the debtor—
>
> (1) made such transfer or incurred such obligation with actual intent to hinder, delay or defraud any entity to which the debtor was or became, on or after the date that such transfer occurred or such obligation was incurred, indebted; or

(2)(a) received less than a reasonable equivalent value in exchange for such transfer or obligation; and

(B)(i) was insolvent on the date that such transfer was made or such obligation was incurred, or became insolvent as a result of such transfer or obligation.

To prevail on the merits, the trustee will have to establish that the debtor's transfer of the property in which he had an interest was made within one year before the date of the filing of the petition and that the transfer was made with the actual intent to hinder, delay or defraud a creditor to whom the debtor became indebted on or after the date such transfer occurred, or that the debtor received less than a reasonably equivalent value in exchange for such transfer and that the debtor was insolvent on the date that such transfer was made or that the debtor became insolvent as a result of such transfer.

The debtor has admitted: (1) He had an interest in the New Rochelle notes transferred to Andrew Charla and the money transferred to J.E.S. Equities, Inc. (2) The transfers took place within one year before the date of the filing of the bankruptcy petition. (3) The debtor became indebted to the Chrysler Credit Corporation on September 19, 1979, a few days after the Charla transfer and about one month before the J.E.S. transfer, by virtue of the docketed judgment of $96,241.44. (4) On the date he transferred the New Rochelle notes to Charla, the present saleable value of his assets remaining after the transfer totaled less than the amount that was required to pay his probable liabilities on his existing debts as they became absolute and mature if it is assumed that the debts included the Chrysler debt in the amount of at least $86,704, i.e., the Charla transfer, in light of the Chrysler judgment, rendered the debtor insolvent within the meaning of 11 U.S.C. § 101(26)(A). (5) On the date he transferred $40,000 to J.E.S., the present saleable value of the debtor's assets remaining after the transfer totaled less than the amount that was required to pay his probable liability on his existing debts as they became absolute and mature, i.e., the debtor was insolvent when he made the J.E.S. transfer.

Therefore, the issues with respect to the merits of the trustee's action are whether the debtor transferred the notes and money with the actual intent to hinder, delay or defraud the Chrysler Credit Corporation, or alternatively, whether the debtor received less than a reasonably equivalent value in exchange for the property transferred.

A transaction prior to bankruptcy which results in the transfer of a debtor's property between members of a family does not ipso facto compel the conclusion that the transfer was fraudulent. However, "such transactions are generally subjected to close scrutiny when challenged by the trustee, and the relationship of the parties in conjunction with other circumstances often makes a trustee's case compelling notwithstanding the absence of direct evidence of fraud."

In this case, the debtor transferred notes worth $93,337 to his father-in-law, Andrew Charla, in exchange for $54,400 within six days after a jury rendered a verdict against the debtor in the amount of $86,704. It has been admitted by the debtor that this transfer rendered him insolvent in light of the verdict and subsequent judgment. In addition, within one month after the entry of the Chrysler judgment the debtor transferred $40,000 to J.E.S. Equities, Inc., a corporation incorporated approximately 10 days after entry of the judgment whose sole officers and shareholders are the debtor's children, for a $40,000 promissory note with a payout period of 36 years, 11 months which is not to commence until November 15, 1982.

The debtor transferred a note worth $93,337 with a final payment date of December 31, 1981, in exchange for $54,400. He also transferred $40,000 in exchange for a $40,000 note whose payments are not to commence until November 15, 1982, and whose payout period will last 36 years 11 months. It is evident that the trustee has made a clear showing of probable success on the issue of whether the debtor received less than a reasonably equivalent value for the transfer of the notes and money.

Judgment against Newman.

## DISCHARGE IN BANKRUPTCY

**Discharge.** A bankrupt person who has not been guilty of certain dishonest acts and has fulfilled his duties as a bankrupt is entitled to a **discharge in bankruptcy.** A discharge relieves the bankrupt person of further responsibility for dischargeable debts and gives him a fresh start. A person may file a written *waiver* of his right to a discharge. A corporation is not eligible for a discharge in bankruptcy. An individual may not be granted a discharge if he obtained one within the previous six years.

**Nondischargeable Debts.** Certain debts are not affected by the discharge of a bankrupt debtor. The Bankruptcy Act provides that a discharge in bankruptcy releases a debtor from all provable debts except those that: (1) are due as a tax or fine to the United States or any state or local unit of government; (2) result from liabilities for obtaining money by false pretenses or false representations; (3) are due for willful or malicious injury to a person or his property; (4) are due for alimony or child support; (5) were created by the debtor's larceny or embezzlement or by the debtor's fraud while acting in a fiduciary capacity; (6) are certain kinds of educational loans that became due within five years prior to the filing of the petition; or (7) were not scheduled in time for proof and allowance because the creditors holding the debts did not have notification of the proceeding even though the debtor was aware that he owed money to those creditors.

The 1984 amendments established several additional grounds for nondischargeability relating to debts incurred in contemplation of bankruptcy. Congress was concerned about debtors who ran up large expenditures on credit cards shortly before filing for bankruptcy relief. Cash advances in excess of $1,000 obtained by use of a credit card and a revolving line of credit at a credit union obtained within 20 days of filing a bankruptcy petition are presumed to be nondischargeable. Similarly, a debtor's purchase of more than $500 in *luxury goods* or *services* on credit from a single creditor within 40 days of filing a petition is presumed to be nondischargeable.

There is also an exception from dischargeability for debts reflected in a judgment arising out of a debtor's operation of a motor vehicle while legally intoxicated.

All of these nondischargeable debts are provable debts. The creditor who owns these claims can participate in the distribution of the bankrupt's estate. However, the creditor has an additional advantage: His right to recover the unpaid balance is not cut off by the bankrupt's discharge. All other provable debts are dischargeable; that is, the right to recover them is cut off by the bankrupt's discharge.

**Objections to Discharge.** After the bankrupt has paid all of the required fees, the court gives creditors and others a chance to file objections to the discharge of the bankrupt. Objections may be filed by the trustee, a creditor, or the U.S. attorney. If objections are filed, the court holds a hearing to listen to them. At the hearing, the court must determine whether the bankrupt person has committed any act that is a bar to discharge. If the bankrupt has not committed such an act, the court will grant the discharge. If the bankrupt has committed an act that is a bar to discharge, the discharge will be denied. The discharge will also be denied if the bankrupt fails to appear at the hearing on objections or if he refused earlier to submit to the questioning of the creditors.

**Acts That Bar Discharge.** Discharges in bankruptcy are intended for honest debtors. Therefore, there are a number of acts that will bar a debtor from being discharged. These acts include: (1) the unjustified falsifying, concealing, or destroying of records; (2) making false statements as to the debtor's financial condition in the course of obtaining credit or extensions of credit; (3) transferring, removing, or concealing property in order to hinder, delay, or defraud creditors; (4) failing to account satisfactorily for any assets; and (5) failing to obey court orders or to answer questions approved by the court.

**Reaffirmation Agreements.** Sometimes, creditors put pressure on debtors to *reaffirm* (agree to pay) debts that have been discharged in bankruptcy. When the 1978 amendments to the Bankruptcy Act were under consideration, some individuals urged Congress to prohibit such agreements. They argued that reaffirmation agreements were inconsistent with the fresh start philosophy of the Bankruptcy Act. Congress did not agree to a total prohibition; instead, it set up a rather elaborate procedure for a creditor to go through to get a debt reaffirmed. Essentially, the creditor must do so before the discharge is granted; the court must approve the reaffirmation; and the debtor must have 60 days after he agrees to a reaffirmation to rescind it. Court approval is not required for the reaffirmation of loans secured by real estate.

In the *Bryant* case, which follows below, the court was rigorous in reviewing and refusing to approve the proposed reaffirmation by a debtor of a loan on a luxury car.

A debtor may voluntarily pay any dischargeable obligation without entering into a reaffirmation agreement.

**Dismissal for Substantial Abuse.** As it considered the 1984 amendments to the Bankruptcy Act, Congress was concerned that too many individuals with an ability to pay their debts over time pursuant to a Chapter 13 plan were filing petitions to obtain Chapter 7 discharges of liability. The consumer finance industry urged that Congress should preclude Chapter 7 petitions where a debtor had the prospect of future disposable income to satisfy more than 50 percent of his prepetition unsecured debts. While Congress rejected this approach, it did authorize Bankruptcy Courts to dismiss cases that they determined were a *substantial abuse* of the bankruptcy process. This provision appears to cover situations where a debtor has acted in "bad faith" or where he has the present or future ability to pay a significant portion of his current debts.

## In re Conrad

**6 B.R. 151 (W.D. Ky. 1980)**

Paul George Conrad filed a voluntary petition in bankruptcy in October 1979, listing $37,354 in liabilities and $25 in assets. Conrad's obligations consisted of a loan executed in connection with a business venture, Double Dip Ice Cream Company; signature loans; revolving credit card accounts; and a student loan of $4,125.79 owed to the U.S. Department of Health, Education, and Welfare.

Conrad had used the GI Bill of Rights to study at five different colleges and had also obtained three federally guaranteed long-term, low-interest student loans. After receiving his bachelor's degree, he had been employed as a teacher. He was terminated as a full-time teacher in April 1979, and since that time he had been on call as a substitute teacher, for which he was paid $33 a day when he was called. He had not sought other full-time employment. He lived at home with his 75-year-old mother. He did not have a car of his own and used his mother's van. Several months after filing for bankruptcy, Conrad obtained a $5,000 loan, with his mother as a guarantor on the note. He used the proceeds only to make the monthly payments on the note. One of the issues in the bankruptcy proceedings was whether the student loan was dischargeable in bankruptcy.

**Deitz, Bankruptcy Judge.** Section 523(a) of the Bankruptcy Code provides that a bankruptcy discharge will not extend:

> (8) to a governmental unit, or a nonprofit institution of higher education, for an educational loan, unless . . . (B) excepting such debt from discharge under this paragraph will impose an undue hardship on the debtor.

Before examining the facts of the case before us, we will briefly review current decisions on the point. Even a cursory reading of them reveals the obvious—that each undue hardship case ultimately rests upon its own facts.

No undue hardship was found in *In re Kohn,* in which an unmarried 48-year-old man with no dependents, with income of $776 and expenses of $600 a month, on notice of impending unemployment, was required to repay a student loan. Judge Babbitt, unmoved by the anticipated joblessness, expressed the opinion, with which we agree, that "if temporary unemployment were the basis of discharge, bankrupts would be encouraged to become unemployed, seek an undue hardship discharge and then seek gainful employment."

Undue hardship was held to entitle the petitioner to a discharge of student debt in *In re Johnson.* The bankrupt was a young woman who was pregnant, being divorced, had recently been seriously injured in an automobile accident, and had been asked by her parents to move out of their home. She planned to rent a room, give birth to the child, and live on welfare.

With methodical precision, the *Johnson* court analyzed the elements to be considered in undue hardship cases. Without attempting to repeat that court's exhaustive treatment of the subject, we note that among the essential elements are present and predictable future income, both earned and unearned; marketable job skills and level of education attained; employment record and current employment status; health; sex; access to transportation; and number and age of dependents.

The claim of undue hardship in this case rests upon two asserted facts: (1) Conrad must support and provide for his elderly mother, and (2) he is unable to obtain employment because of his physical appearance.

Upon the first point, we have some question as to who is supporting whom. The mother, who gave birth to this healthy young man while in her 44th year, and who fancies a mode of transportation generally associated with drivers two generations her junior, may be a vital woman indeed. Although the record does not indicate the extent of her income or financial substance, it is at least clear that Union Trust Bank would not extend credit to the son without the mother's hand being put to the note.

Upon the second point, we must observe, with neither cynicism nor cruelty, that corpulence is a condition which may swiftly diminish with continued impecuniosity.

This unemployed former president of the Double Dip Ice Cream Company, having double-dipped the available federal subsidies to obtain a superior education, should consider some alternatives. Enlightened self-interest would seem to suggest the virtue of a vigorous and energetic search for a proper workshop in which to use those intellectual tools which have been well honed at federal expense. Productivity is preferable to living off the substance of the land. In order to stimulate some reflection upon such heretical theories of individual enterprise, it is hereby

Ordered that the indebtedness of Paul George Conrad to the Department of Health, Education and Welfare, United States of America, is not dischargeable in bankruptcy.

Judgment against Conrad.

## In re Bryant

**43 B.R. 189 (Bankr. E.D. Mich. 1984)**

Bryant filed a Chapter 7 petition on January 7, 1984. On March 8, she filed an application to reaffirm an indebtedness owed to General Motors Acceptance Corporation (GMAC) on her 1980 Cadillac automobile. Bryant was not married, and she supported two teenage daughters. She was not currently employed, and she collected $771 a month in unemployment benefits and $150 a month in rental income from her mother. Her monthly house payments were $259. The present value of the Cadillac was $9,175; she owed $7,956.37 on it, and her monthly payments were $345.93.

Bryant indicated that she wanted to keep the vehicle because it was reliable. GMAC admitted that Bryant had been, and continued to be, current in her payments. GMAC said that the car was in no danger of being repossessed but that, absent reaffirmation, it might decide to repossess it.

**Bernstein, Bankruptcy Judge.** This Court has been presented with a Chapter 7 debtor who is unemployed, has minor children for whom she is legally responsible, and has a very low income (which will most likely cease to exist within the year). She seeks to reaffirm a debt on an expensive luxury automobile accompanied by extremely high payments.

There has been no adequate showing that these car payments do not impose an undue hardship on her family, nor has there been any showing that reaffirmation, which could expose the debtor to a deficiency judgment sometime in the future, is in her best interest. In light of this debtor's present financial situation—which may indeed worsen—this Court has determined that the risk of the future loss of this car through repossession and the imposition of a deficiency judgment is too great a risk to allow her to take. The Court would hope that this creditor would not declare a default and seek to repossess this vehicle until the debtor has failed to make payments when due. Nevertheless, that risk is preferable to the situation in which she becomes unable to make those payments, loses the car and still remains indebted to GMAC for any deficiency. In enacting the Bankruptcy Code, Congress has placed the responsibility for the balancing of risks upon the Bankruptcy Court. These determinations are frequently difficult and are in opposition to the desires of both the creditor and the debtor, but they must be made.

Petition for reaffirmation denied.

## CHAPTER 11: REORGANIZATIONS

**Reorganization Proceedings.** Sometimes, creditors will benefit more from the continuation of a bankrupt debtor's business than from the liquidation of the debtor's property. Chapter 11 of the Bankruptcy Act provides a proceeding whereby the debtor's financial affairs can be *reorganized* rather than liquidated—under the supervision of the Bankruptcy Court. Chapter 11 proceedings are available to virtually all business enterprises, including individual proprietorships, partnerships, and corporations (except banks, savings and loan associations, insurance companies, commodities brokers, and stockbrokers). Petitions for reorganization proceedings can be filed voluntarily by the debtor or involuntarily by its creditors.

Once a petition for a reorganization proceeding is filed and relief is ordered, the court usually appoints (1) a committee of creditors holding unsecured claims, (2) a committee of equity security holders (shareholders), and (3) a trustee. The trustee may be given the responsibility for running the debtor's business. He is also usually responsible for developing a plan for handling the various claims of creditors and the various interests of persons (such as shareholders). The reorganization plan is essentially a contract between a debtor and its creditors. It may involve recapitalizing a debtor corporation and/or giving creditors some equity (shares) in the corporation in exchange for part or all of the debt owed to them. The plan must (1) divide the creditors into classes; (2) set forth how each creditor will be satisfied; (3) state which claims, or classes of claims, are impaired or adversely affected by the plan; and (4) provide the same treatment to each creditor in a particular class (unless the creditors in that class consent to different treatment).

The plan is then submitted to the creditors for approval. Approval generally requires that creditors holding two thirds in amount and one half in number of each class of claims impaired by the plan must accept it. Once approved, the plan goes before the court for confirmation. If the plan is confirmed, the debtor is responsible for carrying it out.

Collective bargaining contracts pose special problems. Prior to the 1984 amendments, there was concern that some companies would use Chapter 11 reorganizations as a vehicle for trying to avoid executed collective bargaining agreements. The 1984 amendments adopt a rigorous multistep process that must be complied with in determining whether a labor contract can be rejected or modified as part of a reorganization.

## CHAPTER 13: CONSUMER DEBT ADJUSTMENTS

**Relief for Individuals.** Chapter 13 (Adjustments of Debts for Individuals) of the Bankruptcy Act gives individuals who do not want to be declared bankrupt an opportunity to pay their debts in installments under the protection of a federal court. Under Chapter 13, the debtor has this opportunity free of such problems as garnishments and attachments of his property by creditors. Only individuals with regular incomes (including sole proprietors of businesses) who owe individually (or with their spouse) liquidated, unsecured debts of less than $100,000 and secured debts of less than $350,000 are eligible to file under Chapter 13. Under the pre-1978 Bankruptcy Act, Chapter 13 proceedings were known as "wage earner plans." The 1978 amendments expanded the coverage of these proceedings.

**Procedure.** Chapter 13 proceedings are initiated only by the *voluntary petition* of a debtor filed in the Bankruptcy Court. Creditors of the debtor may not file an involuntary petition for a Chapter 13 proceeding. The debtor in the petition states that he is insolvent or unable to pay his debts as they mature and that he desires to effect a composition or an extension, or both, out of future earnings or income. A *composition of debts* is an arrangement whereby the amount the person owes is reduced, whereas an *extension* provides the person a longer period of time in which to pay his debts. Commonly, the debtor files at the same time a list of his creditors as well as a list of his assets, liabilities, and executory contracts.

Following the filing of the petition, the court will call a meeting of creditors, at which time proofs of claims are received and allowed or disallowed. The debtor is examined, and he submits a plan of payment. The plan is submitted to the secured creditors for acceptance. If they accept the plan and if the court is satisfied that the plan is proposed in good faith, meets the legal requirements, and is in the interest of the creditors, the court will approve the plan. The court will then appoint a trustee to carry out the plan. The plan must provide for payments over a period of three years or less, unless the court approves a longer period (up to five years). The *Satterwhite* case, which follows, illustrates the scrutiny a bankruptcy judge may give a proposed plan.

No plan may be approved if the trustee or an unsecured creditor objects, unless the plan provides for the objecting creditor to be paid the present value of what he is owed *or* provides for the debtor to commit all of his projected disposable income for a three-year period to pay his creditors.

Under the 1984 amendments, a Chapter 13 debtor must begin making the installment payments proposed in his plan within 30 days after the plan is filed. The interim payments must continue to be made until the plan is confirmed or denied. If the plan is denied, the money, less any administrative expenses, is returned to the debtor by the trustee. The interim payments give the trustee an opportunity to observe the debtor's performance and to be in a better position to make a recommendation as to whether the plan should be approved.

Once approved, a plan may be subsequently modified on petition of a debtor or a creditor where there is a material change in the debtor's circumstances.

Suppose Curtis Brown has a monthly take-home pay of $700 and a few assets. He owes $1,500 to the credit union, borrowed for the purchase of furniture, that he is supposed to repay at $75 per month. He owes $1,800 to the finance company on the purchase of a used car that he is supposed to repay at $90 a month. He has also run up charges of $1,200 on a Master Charge account, primarily for emergency repairs to his car, that he must pay at $60 per month. His rent is $250 per month, and food and other living expenses run him another $300 per month.

Curtis was laid off from his job for a month and fell behind on his payments to his creditors. He then filed a Chapter 13 petition. In his plan, he might, for example, offer to repay the credit union $50 a month, the finance company $60 a month, and Master Charge $40 a month—with the payments spread over three years rather than the shorter time for which they are currently scheduled.

**Discharge.** When the debtor has completed his performance of the plan, the court will issue an order that discharges him from the debts covered by the plan. The debtor may also be discharged even though he did not complete his payments within the three years if the court is satisfied that the failure is due to circumstances for which the debtor cannot justly be held accountable. An active Chapter 13 proceeding *stays* (holds in abeyance) any straight bankruptcy proceedings and any actions by creditors to collect consumer debts. However, if the Chapter 13 proceeding is dismissed (for example, because the debtor fails to file an acceptable plan or defaults on an accepted plan), straight bankruptcy proceedings may proceed.

**Advantages of Chapter 13.** A debtor may choose to file under Chapter 13 to try to avoid the stigma of bankruptcy or to try to retain more of his property than is exempt from bankruptcy under state law. Chapter 13 can provide some financial discipline to a debtor as well as an opportunity to get his financial affairs back in good shape. It also gives him relief from the pressures of individual creditors so long as he makes the payments called for by the plan. The debtor's creditors may benefit by recovering a greater percentage of the debt owed to them than would be obtainable in straight bankruptcy.

## In re Satterwhite

**7 B.R. 39 (S.D. Tex. 1980)**

Roy Satterwhite filed a Chapter 13 petition. In his petition, Satterwhite listed his monthly take-home pay as $1,458 and his monthly expenses as $2,072.24, leaving a negative balance of $614.24. He claimed that all of his assets were exempt. He listed no secured debts and five unsecured debts totaling over $16,450. The largest of these debts was for a judgment against Satterwhite in the amount of $15,749.30 plus interest that stemmed from an action for assault brought against him by A. R. Regan.

Under his Chapter 13 plan, Satterwhite proposed to make a onetime payment of $1 to each creditor. Approval of the plan would have resulted in a payout to unsecured creditors of substantially less than 1 percent on their claims, which was more than they would have received under a liquidation distribution. The bankruptcy trustee objected to confirmation of the plan.

**SCHULTZ, BANKRUPTCY JUDGE.** The trustee's objection centers on Bankruptcy Code Section 1325(a)(3), which provides that confirmation will follow if "the plan has been proposed in good faith." The trustee argues that because the debtor, who is clearly unable to fund a reasonable plan, proposes a one (1%) percent payout on unsecured debts composed of essentially one judgment debt which is potentially nondischargeable under Chapter 7, the debtor's plan is not proposed in good faith. The trustee contends that because the debtor is incapable of meeting all the requirements of the Bankruptcy Code, the only purpose behind the plan is to obtain the liberal Chapter 13 discharge as a way of disposing of a potentially nondischargeable debt.

The debtor counters that Section 1325 contains no express minimum payout as a threshold condition to confirmation.

The Court believes that Congress restructured Chapter 13 to function as a device through which debtors would be encouraged to repay their debts over an extended period of time. Bankruptcy Code Section 109(e) limits relief to debtors with regular income. The Code defines this debtor as an individual with income sufficiently regular "to enable such individual to make *payments* under a plan." Bankruptcy Code Section 101(24) (emphasis added).

In this case, considering the debtor's monthly expenses exceed his income, a plan is tantamount to a liquidation via Chapter 13. Therefore, this Court must carefully scrutinize the debtor's total circumstances. The Court believes the debtor's plan to be directed more to the discharge of a nondischargeable debt to a major unsecured judgment creditor than to repayment of creditors. Chapter 13 may not be used as a substitute for Chapter 7 when the principal motive is to circumvent exceptions to discharge instead of meaningful payment of debts. To confirm a plan under such a scenario, in this Court's opinion, would make a mockery of Chapter 13.

Because the plan fails to satisfy the good faith requirement of Section 1325(a)(3), confirmation is denied.

Judgment against Satterwhite.

## SUMMARY

The Bankruptcy Act is a federal law that provides for an organized procedure for dealing with insolvent debtors under the supervision of a federal court. The act protects the rights of both creditors and debtors and also gives the debtor an opportunity to have most, if not all, of his debts discharged so that he will have a fresh start.

A liquidation proceeding under Chapter 7 can be initiated either by a voluntary petition of the debtor or by an involuntary petition filed by his creditors. After a determination that a debtor is entitled to relief, a meeting of creditors is held and a trustee in bankruptcy is elected or appointed. The trustee takes possession of all the assets of the bankrupt, collects all claims, sets aside the bankrupt's exemptions, liquidates the assets, and distributes the proceeds among the creditors.

If a creditor wishes to participate in the bankrupt's estate, he must usually file a proof of claim in the estate within six months of the first meeting of creditors. Certain debts are given priority by the provisions of the Bankruptcy Act.

A payment made to a creditor by an insolvent debtor within three months of the filing of a bankruptcy petition, which payment enables the creditor to realize a greater percentage of his claim than is realized by other creditors of the same class, is a preferential payment and may be recovered for the bankruptcy estate by the trustee. A preferential lien given by an insolvent debtor within three months of the filing of a bankruptcy petition, to secure a preexisting debt, is voidable by the trustee. Any transfer made or obligation incurred without consideration within one year before the filing of a bankruptcy petition is void as to creditors.

A bankrupt is granted a discharge unless he has been guilty of certain dishonest acts or has failed to fulfill his duties as a bankrupt. Corporations are not eligible to have their debts discharged, and an individual may not be granted a discharge if he has had one in the past six years. The grounds for denying a bankrupt's discharge are set out in the Bankruptcy Act. Certain kinds of debts are not dischargeable.

Under Chapter 11, business debtors can enter into reorganization proceedings under the supervision of the Bankruptcy Court to reorganize their financial affairs. A plan—which is essentially a contract between the debtor and the creditors—sets out how the various claims of the creditors will be met over a period of time.

Plans for individual debtors under Chapter 13 give them voluntary opportunities to effect a composition or an extension of their debts under the protection of a court and free of certain action by their creditors.

## PROBLEM CASES

**1.** On June 29, 1979, Gary Johnson filed a Chapter 13 bankruptcy petition. Shortly before filing the petition, Johnson, acting on the advice of his lawyer, sold an interest in real estate and used the proceeds to buy a life insurance policy with a face value of $31,460 and a cash value of $12,118. His wife was named as the beneficiary. He claimed that the policy was exempt under South Dakota law, which provides for an exemption of up to $20,000 for the proceeds of a policy of life insurance payable directly to the insured, his surviving spouse, or his family. A creditor objected to the exemption but made no showing of fraudulent intent on Johnson's part. Should the exemption be allowed?

**2.** On October 19, 1976, Wallace Tuttle, an attorney, and Peninsula Roofing entered into a retainer agreement for the performance of legal services at a stipulated hourly rate. In 1978 and 1979, Peninsula became delinquent in its payments for attorney's fees. The delinquencies reflected overall corporate financial problems that resulted in the permanent closing of Peninsula on July 25, 1979. On August 6, 1979, Peninsula received a check for $3,250 representing an account receivable due it. Peninsula turned the check over to Tuttle, who deposited it to his trust account, credited $1,946.96 against the past-due account, and created a trust fund from which payments for current services and disbursements would be made. On October 18, 1979, an involuntary petition was filed against Peninsula. The bankruptcy trustee sought to require Tuttle to turn the $3,250 back to him as a preferential payment. Should Tuttle be required to return the money he received?

**3.** In November 1979, Georgia Simmons became a motorcycle dealer in Riviera Beach under a franchise from Bombardier. Borg Warner financed her inventory through a floor plan agreement guaranteed by Bombardier that provided for the segregation of all sales proceeds in a separate trust account. Simmons received and sold 10 motorcycles before she closed her business in June 1980 and filed for bankruptcy on August 5, 1980. The promised trust fund was established, and the proceeds were properly deposited. However,

Simmons closed her other accounts and made all her disbursements from the trust account. In March, she sent the first payment to Borg Warner and Bombardier in the form of a check for $13,934 drawn on the trust account. The check bounced because there was only $11,500 in the account. Between March and June, Simmons spent the balance of the account, paying a variety of bills, including personal living expenses for herself, her husband, and an adult son. Borg Warner and Bombardier sought a money judgment against Simmons for $26,030 and assert that this claim is nondischargeable in the bankruptcy proceeding. Should the Bankruptcy Court grant the relief they seek?

**4.** While attending college, Barbara Barrington obtained a student loan from the New York State Higher Education Services Corporation. Barrington had had depressive illnesses all her life and was a third-generation depressive. Her grandmother was institutionalized, and her mother had been on medication for a long time. Barrington was discharged by Kodak because she could not face the problems and stress of her job. Since that time, she had stayed at home, slept a lot, and played with her dog. She made little or no effort to find other employment because of her depressed condition. She also filed for bankruptcy. In the bankruptcy proceeding, one of the questions was whether payment of her student loan would impose an undue hardship on Barrington and thus whether the loan was dischargeable. Should the student loan be discharged?

**5.** Barnhart had borrowed money from Credit Plan and was behind in her payments. She applied for a new loan, with which she intended to pay the existing loan and the interest on it. At the time the new loan was granted, the agent of Credit Plan prepared a financial statement that showed that Barnhart owed $837.50. In fact, she owed approximately $1,800. The agent was a schoolmate of Barnhart's and was familiar with her financial affairs. At the time the statement was prepared, Barnhart talked to the agent about her other debts. She signed the statement without reading it. Credit Plan filed objections to Barnhart's discharge on the ground that she had obtained credit on a materially false credit statement in writing. Should Barnhart be denied a discharge on this ground?

**6.** Tom Page was employed by Airo Supply Company as its only bookkeeper. Over a three-year period, he appropriated $14,775.77 of Airo Supply's money to his own use. Airo Supply discovered the embezzlement and obtained a civil judgment against Page for $14,775.77. Page then filed a voluntary petition in bankruptcy, and his discharge was granted. Page obtained new employment, and Airo Supply instituted proceedings to garnish his wages. Page defended on the ground that Airo Supply's judgment had been discharged in bankruptcy. Was Page's debt to Airo Supply discharged as part of his discharge in bankruptcy?

**7.** In 1980, John Barncastle filed a Chapter 13 plan proposing to pay all of his unsecured creditors 50 percent of their claims. These debts totaled less than $3,000, and Barncastle's assets exceeded $10,000. Barncastle attempted to claim as exempt under the Florida constitution the $12,000 equity in his residence, his equity in a 1978 Mercury Cougar, and his clothing. For entitlement to these exemptions, the Florida constitution required that the debtor be the "head of a family." Barncastle claimed to be the head of a family because his "fiancée," Jane Mower, and her child lived with him. However, he made no claim that he was morally or legally obligated to support them. Should this plan be confirmed?

**8.** On July 13, 1980, Robert Leal purchased a new 1980 Ford Bronco for $12,000. The down payment consisted of $1,000 borrowed from Fidelity Financial Services and two cars that were traded in. The remainder of the purchase price was financed by Ford Motor Credit Company, which took a first lien on the vehicle. Leal gave Fidelity a security interest in certain household goods and a second lien on the Bronco. Leal never made a payment to Fidelity. On August 1, 1980, Leal executed a Chapter 13 plan that, among other things, proposed to treat Fidelity as an unsecured creditor, valued the collateral held by Ford—the Bronco—at $8,600, and offered $1 per claim to Fidelity and 10 other holders of unsecured claims whose debts were scheduled at $18,447. Leal offered to repay Ford the full amount owed to it. Fidelity objected to the confirmation of the plan on the ground of lack of good faith. Should Fidelity's objection be sustained?

**9.** On December 8, 1971, Thomas Thompson filed a petition under Chapter 13 to pay his debts through a wage earner plan. After the notice to creditors, Ford Motor Credit Company, a secured creditor to which Thompson was indebted for payments on a 1970 Ford, filed a proof of claim and rejected the plan. The plan was confirmed over Ford's objections and provided for payments to Ford of $22.90 a week, equivalent to the same rate and adding up to the same total as in the original sales contract, and enjoined Ford from foreclosing on the automobile. In 1972, Thompson was injured at work and was able to work only part-time. He then fell behind in his payments to Ford, even though he was regularly submitting his disability checks to the trustee. Ford then filed a petition to reclaim the car, alleging that Thompson had failed to make the payments due on the car. Should Ford be permitted to have the plan disregarded so that it can foreclose its security interest on the car?

# PART XI

# REGULATION OF BUSINESS

# Chapter 42

# Business and the Constitution

## INTRODUCTION

Constitutions serve two general functions. They set up the structure of government, allocating power among its various branches and subdivisions. They also protect individual rights by limiting governmental power in certain areas. The U.S. Constitution performs both of these functions, but the way in which it does so has varied considerably over time. Many people like to think of the Constitution as an unchanging Fundamental Law. In fact, however, many of the Constitution's provisions have quite different meanings than they had when they were first enacted. Thus, constitutional law is much more *evolving* than static.

There are many reasons for the Constitution's flexibility and variability. For one thing, many of its key provisions are quite vague. Open-ended terms such as "due process of law" and "equal protection of the laws," for instance, invite diverse interpretations. Also, the historical information surrounding the enactment of constitutional provisions is sometimes sketchy, confused, or contradictory. Perhaps the most important reason for constitutional change, however, is the perceived need to adapt the Constitution to changing social conditions. The Supreme Court may not literally (as the old saying goes) "follow the election returns," but its decisions often reflect the social conditions in which it operates. For better or worse, "the Constitution" is somewhat relative to circumstances. In all likelihood, this reflects the general public's real wishes; many of the people who believe in a fixed Constitution, for instance, might be unhappy if they had to live under one.

In theory, constitutional change can be accomplished through the formal amendment process, but the Founders made this process fairly difficult to use, and amendments to the Constitution have been relatively infrequent as a result.[1] Thus, the Supreme Court has assumed the main role as constitutional amender. To invoke another old saying, the Constitution is largely what the Supreme Court says it is. The Supreme Court's ability to determine the Constitution's meaning gives it considerable political power, for it also has the ability to declare the actions of other governmental branches unconstitutional,[2] and how it exercises this ability will depend on how it chooses to read the Constitution's language. To a significant extent, therefore, the nine justices who sit on the U.S. Supreme Court are *policymakers*. (For this reason, the beliefs and values of the justices are of some importance in determining how the nation is governed, and this is why the nomination and confirmation of Supreme Court justices often involve much political controversy.) In deciding the business-related matters that are the main concern of this chapter, the justices are to a considerable degree *economic* policymakers.

However, the Supreme Court's (and other courts') power to shape the Constitution, while considerable, is not unlimited.[3] The language of the Constitution, for example, is not *completely* open-ended; some of its provisions, in fact, are quite clear. Also, past constitutional decisions do bind the courts to some degree. Moreover, the courts are dependent on the other branches of government—and, ultimately, on public belief in judicial integrity and fidelity to the rule of law—to make their decisions effective. Thus, judges are often wary of power struggles with other, more representative, governmental bodies. Courts that freely declare the actions of these bodies unconstitutional run the risk of eventually provoking such conflicts.

**The Coverage of This Chapter.** This chapter does not discuss constitutional law in its entirety. Instead, it provides a brief overview of selected constitutional provisions that are important to business. These provisions have one common feature: they all help define federal and state power to regulate the economy. In large part, the U.S. Constitution is concerned with limiting governmental power, and it does so in two general ways. First, it restricts *federal* legislative power by listing the powers that Congress can exercise.[4] It has long been understood that the power of Congress to legislate is limited to the **enumerated powers** specifically stated in the Constitution. To be constitutional, in other words, federal legislation must be based on one of these listed powers. Second, the U.S. Constitution limits *state and federal* power by placing certain **independent checks** in its path. These independent checks usually apply

[1] The recent history of the ERA suggests the difficulties confronted by those who would use the amendment process to make constitutional changes. But, as you will see later in the chapter, in the 1970s the Supreme Court began to read the Constitution's Equal Protection Clause as posing a significant obstacle to sex discrimination.

[2] This is the power of *judicial review,* which is briefly discussed at the beginning of Chapter 2.

[3] The limitations on the power of the courts discussed in Chapters 1 and 2 are relevant here.

[4] This includes types of law derived from federal legislation by delegation. See Chapter 1.

across-the-board to all the enumerated powers of Congress and to the various state legislative powers. In effect, they declare that, even if Congress or the states are otherwise empowered to act in a particular area, there are certain protected spheres into which their power cannot reach.

At the federal level, therefore, legislation must meet two general tests in order to be constitutional. It must be based on an enumerated power of Congress, and it must not collide with any of the independent checks. As you will see, for example, Congress has the power to regulate commerce among the states. By itself, this power would probably allow Congress to pass legislation declaring that certain racial minorities cannot cross state lines to buy or sell goods. But such a law, while arguably based on an enumerated power, would surely be unconstitutional. The reason is that it conflicts with an independent check: the *equal protection* guarantee discussed later in this chapter.

Over time, many of the listed powers of Congress have been read more and more broadly, with the result that the "enumerated powers" limitation has become less and less meaningful. This shift, which became firmly established by the end of the 1930s, can be seen as a response to the perceived need for greater federal regulation of the economy. This need began to be felt in the late 19th century and grew more intense during the Great Depression. Today, the main constitutional limitations on congressional legislative power are the independent checks. In general, these checks now place more significant limitations on government power when noneconomic "personal" rights are at issue than when economic regulation is challenged as unconstitutional. During the 1970s, however, certain independent checks that generally work to protect free economic activity (and business interests) assumed greater significance.

This chapter begins by discussing the most important state and federal powers to regulate economic matters. Next, the chapter examines certain independent checks—due process, equal protection, and the First Amendment—that apply to both the federal government and the states. The chapter concludes by discussing some independent checks that apply only to the states.

## STATE AND FEDERAL POWER TO REGULATE

**State Regulatory Power.** The U.S. Constitution does not specifically list the powers state legislatures may exercise, although *state* constitutions may do so. However, the U.S. Constitution does place certain independent checks in the path of state legislation. It also declares that certain powers (for example, creating currency and taxing imports) can be exercised only by Congress. In many other areas, though, Congress and the state legislatures have *concurrent powers;* within these areas, both can make law.[5] A very important state legislative power that operates concurrently with many congressional powers is the **police power.** The police power is a broad state power to regulate for the public health, safety, morals, and welfare.

**Federal Regulatory Power.** Article I, section 8 of the U.S. Constitution, the main source of the enumerated powers of Congress, states a number of business-related areas in which Congress can legislate. For example, it empowers Congress to coin and borrow money, regulate commerce with foreign nations, establish uniform laws regarding bankruptcies, create post offices, and regulate copyrights and patents. For our purposes, however, the most important congressional

[5] However, state law must give way when it expressly conflicts with federal law, and, as discussed later in the chapter, it may also be *preempted* by federal law.

powers contained in Article I, section 8 are the powers to regulate commerce among the states, to lay and collect taxes, and to spend for the general welfare. These three powers are by now quite extensive. They are the main constitutional bases for the wide-ranging role that the federal government plays today.

**The Commerce Power.** Article I, section 8 states that "Congress shall have power . . . To regulate Commerce . . . among the several States." The original reason for giving Congress this power to regulate *interstate commerce* was to limit the protectionist state restrictions on interstate trade that were common after the American Revolution, and thus to nationalize economic life. Over time, however, the **Commerce Clause** has come to have two major thrusts. First, in accordance with its original purpose, it presents an independent check on state regulation that unduly restricts interstate commerce. This aspect of the Commerce Clause is discussed later in the chapter. Our present concern is the second aspect of the Commerce Clause: its role as a source of congressional regulatory power.

Despite some language suggesting a broad reading of the Commerce Clause in the famous case of *Gibbons v. Ogden* (1824), the scope of congressional power under the clause was not a major concern for most of the 19th century. By today's standards, federal regulation of the economy was fairly infrequent and not too intrusive during this period. With the wave of federal regulation that began upon the passage of the Interstate Commerce Act in 1887 and the Sherman Act in 1890, however, the Supreme Court became increasingly preoccupied with defining the limits of the commerce power. For a time, the Court occasionally refused to read the clause broadly. An early example was *United States v. E. C. Knight Co.* (1895), where the application of the Sherman Act to a sugar refining monopoly was declared unconstitutional because refining was "manufacture," not "commerce." Increasingly, however, the Court began to expand the reach of the Commerce Clause, finding ever more extensive and intrusive forms of congressional regulation constitutional in the process. Since the early 1940s, the Commerce Clause has been an all-purpose federal police power applicable to all sorts of activities within a state's borders (*intrastate* matters).

The literal language of the Commerce Clause simply gives Congress the power to regulate commerce among the states. How, then, has the clause evolved into a generalized federal power to regulate for the public health, safety, morals, and welfare, and to reach most intrastate matters while doing so? Two interpretative techniques have been quite important in producing this result. First, the Supreme Court has established the power of Congress to regulate intrastate matters by reasoning that the power to regulate *interstate* commerce includes the ability to reach *intrastate* activities that have some impact on commerce among the states. In the *Shreveport Rate Cases* (1914), for example, the Supreme Court upheld the Interstate Commerce Commission's regulation of railroad rates within Texas (an *intrastate* matter outside the literal language of the Commerce Clause) because of the impact that these rates had on rail traffic between Texas and Louisiana (an *interstate* matter within the clause's language). The Court basically reasoned that the power to regulate rates within Texas was necessary for the full realization of Congress's undisputed power to regulate commerce between Texas and Louisiana. This "affecting commerce" argument is also illustrated by the *Wickard* case, which follows.

The second technique for advancing the reach of the Commerce Clause was to allow Congress to use the clause for noncommercial, "police power" ends. This occurred when the Court upheld federal legislation restricting the interstate movement of certain disfavored people or commodities. The Court upheld such legislation even though its purposes differed from the purposes originally underlying the Commerce Clause. For instance, Congress was allowed to attack sexual immorality, gambling, and food poisoning by limiting the interstate movement of prostitutes, lottery tickets, and impure food, respectively. For a time, this technique had its limits. In *Hammer v. Dagenhart* (1918), the Court struck down a federal statute banning the interstate shipment of goods manufactured by firms employing child labor. In 1941, however, it overruled *Hammer* while upholding Fair Labor Standards Act (FLSA) provisions prohibiting the interstate shipment of goods made by firms that violated the FLSA's minimum wage and maximum hours provisions.

Today, the Commerce Clause is effectively a federal police power with a very great intrastate reach.[6] The old distinction between "commerce" and "manufacture" has been abandoned. The commerce power now applies to intrastate activities having any appreciable effect on interstate commerce, whether direct or indirect. In our highly interdependent society, few activities do not affect interstate commerce. As a result, most behavior is within the Commerce Clause's reach. Also, the "affecting commerce" rationale is frequently used to support legislation whose purposes are clearly noncommercial. For example, the Supreme Court has upheld the application of the 1964 Civil Rights Act's "public accommodations" section to a family-owned restaurant in Birmingham, Alabama, because the restaurant's racial discrimination affected interstate commerce. It did so, the Court maintained, by reducing the restaurant's business, thus limiting its purchases of out-of-state meat, and by restricting the ability of blacks to travel among the states.

[6] In 1976, the Supreme Court established an independent check applicable only to the Commerce Clause when the Court held certain FLSA provisions inapplicable to state and local governments in *National League of Cities v. Usery*. It did so on grounds of state sovereignty. Later cases gave the doctrine established by *Usery* a limited reach. The Commerce Clause powers of Congress were blocked only when Congress regulated the *states themselves*, and then only when it intruded on *traditional* state functions in doing so. In early 1985, the Supreme Court overruled *Usery* in *Garcia v. San Antonio Metropolitan Transit Auth.*, 53 U.S.L.W. 4135 (1985).

## Wickard v. Filburn

### 317 U.S. 111 (U.S. Sup. Ct. 1942)

The Agricultural Adjustment Act of 1938 was passed by Congress in an effort to stabilize agricultural production and thus to give farmers reasonable minimum prices. The act empowered the secretary of agriculture to proclaim a yearly national acreage allotment for the coming wheat crop. This was apportioned among the states and their counties, and then among individual farms. Filburn was an Ohio farmer who raised a small acreage of winter wheat, some of which was sold but much of which was used on his farm. Filburn's permitted allotment for 1941 was 11.1 acres. However, he sowed and harvested 23 acres. For this, he was assessed a penalty of $117.11.

Filburn sued the secretary of agriculture (Wickard) for an injunction against enforcement of the penalty. A three-judge district court found in Filburn's favor, and the government appealed to the U.S. Supreme Court.

**Jackson, Justice.** It is urged that under the Commerce Clause Congress does not possess the power it has in this instance sought to exercise. The question would merit little consideration, except for the fact that this Act extends federal regulation to production not intended in any part for commerce but wholly for consumption on the farm. Filburn says that this is a regulation of production and consumption of wheat. Such activities are, he urges, beyond the reach of Congressional power under the Commerce Clause, since they are local in character, and their effects upon interstate commerce are at most "indirect." We believe that questions of the power of Congress are not to be decided by reference to any formula which would give controlling force to nomenclature such as "production" and "indirect," and foreclose consideration of the actual effects of the activity in question upon interstate commerce.

At the beginning Chief Justice Marshall described the federal commerce power with a breadth never yet exceeded in *Gibbons v. Ogden.* For nearly a century, however, decisions of this Court dealt rarely with questions of what Congress might do under the Clause, and almost entirely with the permissibility of state activity which discriminated against or burdened interstate commerce. During this period there was perhaps little occasion for the affirmative exercise of the commerce power, and the influence of the Clause on American life and law was a negative one, resulting almost wholly from its restraint upon the powers of the states. It was not until 1887, with the enactment of the Interstate Commerce Act, that the commerce power began to exert positive influence in American law and life. This was followed in 1890 by the Sherman Anti-Trust Act and, thereafter, by many others.

When it first dealt with this new legislation, the Court allowed but little scope to the power of Congress. However, other cases called forth broader interpretations of the Commerce Clause destined to supersede the earlier ones, and to bring about a return to the principles first enunciated by Chief Justice Marshall. It was soon demonstrated that the effects of many kinds of intrastate activity upon interstate commerce were such as to make them a proper subject of federal regulation. The relevance of economic effects in the application of the Commerce Clause has made the mechanical application of legal formulas no longer feasible. Whether the subject of the regulation in question was "production," "consumption," or "marketing" is, therefore, not material for deciding the question of federal power before us. That an activity is of local character may help in a doubtful case to determine whether Congress intended to reach it. But even if Filburn's activity be local and though it may not be regarded as commerce, it may still be reached by Congress if it exerts a substantial economic effect on interstate commerce, and this irrespective of whether such effect is what might at some earlier time have been defined as "direct" or "indirect."

The effect of consumption of home-grown wheat on interstate commerce is due to the fact that it constitutes the most variable factor in the disappearance of the wheat crop. Consumption on the farm where grown appears to vary in an amount greater than 20 percent of average production. That Filburn's own contribution to the demand for wheat may be trivial by itself is not enough to remove him from the scope of federal regulation where, as here, his contribution, taken together with that of many others similarly situated, is far from trivial.

The power to regulate commerce includes the power to regulate the prices at which commodities in that commerce are dealt in and practices affecting such prices. One of the primary purposes of the Act was to increase the market price of wheat, and to that end to limit the volume thereof that could affect the market. It can hardly be denied that a factor of such volume and variability as home-consumed wheat would have a substantial influence on price and market conditions. This may arise because such wheat overhangs the market and, if induced by rising prices, tends to flow into the market and check price increases. But if we assume that it is never marketed, it supplies a need of the man who grew it which would otherwise be reflected by purchases in the open market. Congress may properly have considered that wheat consumed on the farm where grown, if wholly outside the scheme of regulation, would have a substantial effect in defeating its purpose to stimulate trade therein at increased prices.

Judgment reversed in favor of Wickard.

**The Taxing Power.** Article I, section 8 of the Constitution also states that "Congress shall have Power To lay and collect Taxes, Duties, Imposts, and Excises." The main purpose behind this **taxing power,** of course, is to raise revenue.[7] But the taxing power can also serve as a regulatory device. This is often accomplished by imposing a heavy tax on a disfavored activity. "The power to tax," it has been observed, "is the power to destroy." Sometimes, the use of taxation to regulate may be held unconstitutional if the tax is deemed a "penalty." This happened in *Bailey v. Drexel Furniture Co.* (1922), where the Supreme Court struck down a 10 percent excise tax on employers of child labor. Since the 1930s, however, the Court has been very tolerant of congressional regulation-through-taxation in the relatively few cases presenting constitutional challenges to this practice. Today, the outer limits of the power are quite remote, and also poorly defined. However, a regulatory tax will almost certainly be constitutional if the purpose it advances could be furthered by one of the *other* powers of Congress. Because of the wide range of ends achievable through the commerce power, this may mean that the taxing power has few limits.

**The Spending Power.** If taxing power regulation uses a federal "club," congressional **spending power** regulation employs a federal "carrot." After stating the taxing power, Article I, section 8 empowers Congress to "pay the Debts and provide for the common Defense and general Welfare of the United States." This language is commonly read as giving Congress a broad ability to spend for the general welfare. By conditioning the receipt of federal money on the performance of certain conditions, Congress can use its spending power to advance specific regulatory ends. Conditional federal grants to the states, for instance, are quite common. Since 1937, congressional regulation based on the spending power has invariably been upheld. Like the taxing power, its range is quite wide and its outer limits rather unclear. The requirement that Congress spend only for the *general* welfare may block spending measures that benefit narrowly based interests, but the Supreme Court has tended to defer to congressional judgments on such questions.

**Eminent Domain.** The government's **eminent domain** power is its ability to condemn (or take) private property. The Fifth Amendment recognizes and restricts this power by stating that "private property [shall not] be taken for public use without just compensation." Thus, state[8] or federal exercises of the

[7] The Constitution imposes some restrictions on the types of taxes that may be used to raise revenue. Each state's dollar burden under a *direct* tax (mainly a tax imposed on property) must be proportional to that state's population. Because of the practical difficulties posed by this requirement, the Supreme Court has been reluctant to expand the list of direct taxes. For other taxes (called "indirect" taxes), the *rules* determining liability, amount due, and so forth must be uniform from state to state.

[8] The 5th Amendment applies only to the federal government, but its eminent domain requirements also apply to the states because these requirements have been "incorporated" within the 14th Amendment. The "incorporation" doctrine is discussed later in the chapter.

eminent domain power must be for a *public use* and the government must give the owner *just compensation* for the condemned property.

Before these requirements can come into play, however, there must be an actual *taking* by the government. This obviously occurs when formal condemnation procedures are used. In addition, some kinds of government regulation can so affect the value of property as to constitute a taking. There is no set formula for determining when this occurs. Among the factors considered are the overall economic impact of the regulation on the owner, how much the regulation interferes with investments based on the owner's legitimate expectations regarding the future use of the property, and the degree to which government physically invades the owner's property. Since otherwise the government's ability to regulate would be restricted by the "just compensation" requirement, most forms of regulation are not "takings." In particular, general social welfare measures applying to a wide range of properties are unlikely to be deemed takings; zoning is an example.

Once a taking has occurred, it will be unconstitutional unless it is for a "public use." The controversial *Midkoff* case, which follows, discusses this test; it seems to require only that the taking be *rationally related* to a *conceivable* public purpose.[9] The usual "just compensation" standard is the fair market value of the condemned property, or (where the taking only diminishes property values) the difference between the fair market value before the taking and the fair market value after the taking.

[9] This is a very lenient test resembling the "rational basis" test discussed later in the chapter.

## Hawaii Housing Authority v. Midkoff

**104 S. Ct. 2321 (U.S. Sup. Ct. 1984)**

Due to the continuing effects of the feudal land tenure system established by the Polynesian immigrants who originally settled the Hawaiian Islands, private landownership throughout the state of Hawaii had long been concentrated in relatively few hands. In the mid-1960s, 49 percent of Hawaii's land was owned by the state and federal governments and 47 percent was in the hands of only 72 private owners. These owners would typically lease portions of their holdings to, among others, residential tenants.

To change this situation, the Hawaii legislature enacted the Land Reform Act of 1967, which created a mechanism for condemning residential tracts and transferring ownership of the condemned land to the existing tenants. Under the complex condemnation scheme established by the act, the Hawaii Housing Authority (HHA) could condemn land after a public hearing to determine whether this would advance the act's public purposes and then sell the land to the residential tenants living on it. The HHA was required to pay the original owner the fair market value of the condemned land.

After the beginning of HHA proceedings against their land in 1977, Midkoff and others sued the HHA in federal district court, alleging that the act was unconstitutional and asking for an injunction against its enforcement. The district court entered a partial summary judgment in favor of the HHA, but the court of appeals reversed, holding that the condemnations allowed by the act were not for a "public use." The HHA appealed to the U.S. Supreme Court.

**O'CONNOR, JUSTICE.** The "public use" requirement is coterminous with the scope of a sovereign's police powers. There is, of course, a role for courts to play in reviewing a legislature's judgment of what constitutes a public use. But it is an extremely narrow one. The Court will not substitute its judgment for a legislature's judgment as to what constitutes a public use unless the use be palpably without reasonable foundation.

To be sure, the Court's cases have repeatedly stated that one person's property may not be taken for the benefit of another private person without a justifying public purpose, even though compensation be paid. But where the exercise of the eminent domain power is rationally related to a conceivable public purpose, the Court has never held a compensated taking to be proscribed by the Public Use Clause.

On this basis, we have no trouble concluding that the Hawaii Act is constitutional. The people of Hawaii have attempted to reduce the perceived social and economic evils of a land oligopoly traceable to their monarchs. The land oligopoly has created artificial deterrents to the normal functioning of the State's residential land market and forced thousands of individual homeowners to lease, rather than buy, the land underneath their homes. Regulating oligopoly and the evils associated with it is a classic exercise of a state's police powers.

Nor can we condemn as irrational the Act's approach to correcting the land oligopoly problem. It is a comprehensive and rational approach to identifying and correcting market failure. Of course, this Act, like any other, may not be successful in achieving its intended goals. But whether *in fact* the provision will accomplish its objectives is not the question: the [constitutional requirement] is satisfied if the state legislature *rationally could have believed* that the Act would promote its objective. When the legislature's purpose is legitimate and its means are not irrational, empirical debates over the wisdom of takings—no less than debates over the wisdom of other kinds of socioeconomic legislation—are not to be carried out in the federal courts.

The Court of Appeals read our "public use" cases as requiring that government possess and use property at some point during a taking. Since Hawaiian lessees retain possession of the property for private use throughout the condemnation process, the court found that the Act exacted takings for private use. The mere fact that property taken outright by eminent domain is transferred first to private beneficiaries does not condemn that taking as having only a private purpose. Government does not itself have to use property to legitimate the taking; it is only the taking's purpose, and not its mechanics, that must pass scrutiny under the Public Use Clause.

The Constitution forbids even a compensated taking of property when executed for no reason other than to confer a private benefit on a particular private party. But the Hawaii legislature enacted its Land Reform Act not to benefit a particular class of identifiable individuals but to attack certain perceived evils of concentrated property ownership in Hawaii—a legitimate public purpose. Use of the condemnation power to achieve this purpose is not irrational. Since we assume that the weighty demand of just compensation has been met, the requirements of the Fifth and Fourteenth Amendments have been satisfied.

Judgment reversed in favor of the HHA.

## INDEPENDENT CHECKS ON THE FEDERAL GOVERNMENT AND THE STATES

**Introduction.** The three most important business-related independent constitutional checks limiting both the federal government and the states are the **due process** and **equal protection** guarantees and the First Amendment's guarantee of **freedom of speech.** The 5th Amendment prevents the federal government from depriving any person "of life, liberty, or property, without due process of law," and the 14th Amendment does the same with respect to the states. The First Amendment applies only to the federal government. But, as part of the process of "incorporation" through which almost all Bill of Rights provisions have been made applicable to the states, the 1st Amendment's free speech guarantee has been included within the "liberty" protected by 14th Amendment due process. The 14th Amendment's statement that no state shall "deny to any person . . . the equal protection of the laws," on the other hand, has been made applicable to the federal government by incorporating it within the 5th Amendment's due process guarantee.

**Levels of Scrutiny.** Rarely, if ever, has the Supreme Court held that government action will *always* be unconstitutional if it restricts individual rights defined by the Constitution. Instead, it has recognized that in certain situations some governmental purposes must override individual rights claims. The First Amendment, for instance, states that "Congress shall make *no* law . . . abridging the freedom of speech." As Justice Oliver Wendell Holmes remarked long ago, however, this does not protect someone who falsely shouts "Fire!" in a crowded theater. How, then, do the courts weigh individual rights claims against the purposes served by the measures restricting those rights? Generally, they do so by holding such measures constitutional only when they serve sufficiently important purposes and are closely enough related to the furtherance of those purposes.

Certain individual rights protections are generally deemed more important than others. This means that more justification is needed to override some individual rights claims than is needed to defeat others. Thus, different *levels of judicial scrutiny* apply in different cases. The verbal tests used to describe these levels of scrutiny vary from situation to situation. In this chapter, we will refer to three basic levels of scrutiny, although this oversimplifies somewhat. These levels are: (1) the **rational basis** test (a minimal level of scrutiny), (2) **full strict scrutiny** (a very difficult test to meet), and (3) **intermediate scrutiny** (a fairly stringent test of constitutionality). These terms are most commonly used in equal protection cases. But, as the discussion below will indicate, similar tests appear in other areas of constitutional law. The aim of our three-level model is to give you a general idea of how closely the courts will scrutinize laws that restrict the different individual rights discussed in this section of the chapter.

Each of the tests mentioned above specifies two things: (1) how *important* a governmental purpose must be in order to defeat a particular individual rights claim and (2) how *effectively* a law challenged as unconstitutional must promote that purpose in order to be valid. A typical formulation of the rational basis test, for example, is that government action must have only a *reasonable* relation to the achievement of a *legitimate* governmental purpose to be constitutional. A court applying full strict scrutiny, on the other hand, might say that a challenged measure must be *necessary* to the fulfillment of a *compelling* governmental purpose. Intermediate scrutiny comes in many forms; an example is the requirement that a law discriminating on the basis of sex be *substantially* related to the furtherance of an *important* governmental purpose.

In applying tests like those just described, courts are not passively interpreting "the Constitution." Rather, it is the courts that decide, for example, what purposes are "important" and whether the challenged measure is "substantially related" to their furtherance. In cases where government regulation is alleged to deny economic rights, this means that the courts are to some extent economic policymakers.

**Government Action.** In theory, the Constitution's individual rights provisions only protect people against the actions of *governmental* bodies, state or federal.[10] *Private* denials of individual rights, while perhaps regulated by statute, are not supposed to be constitutional matters. This **governmental action** (or **state action**) requirement forces courts to distinguish between "governmental" behavior and "private" behavior. Making this distinction has presented immense problems.

Prior to World War II, state action determinations posed few difficulties, because the definition of state action was limited. At that time, the only actors restricted by constitutional checks were such formal organs of government as legislatures, administrative agencies, municipalities, courts, prosecutors, and state universities. After World War II, the range of activities considered to be government action increased considerably, with all sorts of traditionally "private" behavior being subjected to individual rights limitations. For example, private universities, a restaurant located in a parking garage, a railroad, a regulated monopoly transit company, low-income housing projects, and the American Stock Exchange have all been treated as "governmental" bodies in certain situations. The expansion of state action followed no consistent pattern, each case being decided on its own particular facts. Among the factors that led courts to find that the behavior of a seemingly private body constituted government action were: extensive government regulation, government financial aid, the private actor's monopoly status, and the existence of a "symbiotic" government-business partnership (as for instance in the defense industry).[11]

Two social factors probably assisted the expansion of government action. First, the rise of powerful private groups and the pervasive influence of activist government may have convinced some judges that the sharp public-private line underlying traditional state action doctrine was outmoded because the "public" and the "private" had become inextricably blurred. Second, the greater concern for racial equality and other personal rights that characterized American life after World War II produced a greater sensitivity to the ways in which traditionally private actors could deny those rights. This led judges to "constitutionalize" formally private behavior in order to protect the individual.

Due primarily to the changed composition of the Supreme Court, however, the reach of state action has been limited somewhat in the 1970s and 1980s. This cutback has not yet returned government action to its traditional definition. Nor has it appreciably reduced the confusion that has long existed in this area. Now, the Court is apt to say that, for state action to exist, a regular unit of government must be directly *responsible* for the be-

[10] However, the 13th Amendment, which bans slavery and involuntary servitude throughout the United States, does not have a state action requirement.

[11] Also worth mention here is the "public function" doctrine, which subjects certain private bodies to constitutional checks because of the practical resemblance of these bodies to the normal units of government. The classic public function case is *Marsh v. Alabama* (1946), where a "company town's" restriction of free expression was treated as government action because the town was in most respects indistinguishable from a normal municipality. By now, however, the public function doctrine is of very little significance. Today, it is limited to situations where a private entity exercises powers that have *traditionally* been *exclusively* reserved to the state. Police protection is one possible example.

havior alleged to have denied individual rights. The *Jackson* case below is an early and important example of the state action cutback.

## Jackson v. Metropolitan Edison Co.

**419 U.S. 345 (U.S. Sup. Ct. 1974)**

The Metropolitan Edison Company, a privately owned state-regulated electric utility, terminated Catherine Jackson's electrical service without notice or a hearing when she became delinquent in paying her electric bills. Jackson sued Metropolitan, seeking damages for the termination and an injunction requiring Metropolitan to continue providing electric power to her residence until she was given notice, a hearing, and an opportunity to pay any amounts found due. The basis of Jackson's claim was that Metropolitan's termination of service without notice or a hearing was state action violating the due process clause of the 14th Amendment. The district court granted Metropolitan's motion to dismiss on the ground that state action was not present; the court of appeals affirmed; and Jackson appealed to the U.S. Supreme Court.

**Rehnquist, Justice.** The Due Process Clause of the 14th Amendment provides "nor shall any State deprive any person of life, liberty or property, without due process of law." In 1883, this Court affirmed the essential dichotomy between deprivation by the state, subject to scrutiny under [constitutional] provisions, and private conduct, however discriminatory and wrongful, against which the 14th Amendment offers no shield. While the principle that private action is immune from the restrictions of the 14th Amendment is easily stated, the question whether particular conduct is "private," on the one hand, or "state action," on the other, frequently admits of no easy answer.

Here the action complained of was taken by a utility company which is privately owned and operated, but which is subject to extensive state regulation. The mere fact that a business is subject to state regulation does not by itself convert its action into that of the state for purposes of the 14th Amendment. Nor does the fact that the regulation is extensive and detailed, as in the case of most public utilities, do so. It may well be that acts of a heavily regulated utility with at least something of a governmentally protected monopoly will more readily be found to be "state" acts than will the acts of an entity lacking these characteristics. But the inquiry must be whether there is a sufficiently close nexus between the state and the challenged action of the regulated entity so that the action of the latter may be fairly treated as that of the state itself.

Jackson first argues that state action is present because of the monopoly status allegedly conferred upon Metropolitan by Pennsylvania. But this is not determinative in considering whether Metropolitan's termination of service was state action, because there was insufficient relationship between the challenged actions and Metropolitan's monopoly status.

Jackson next urges that state action is present because Metropolitan provides an essential public service, and hence performs a "public function." We have found state action present in the exercise by a private entity of powers traditionally exclusively reserved to the state. If we were dealing with the exercise of some power delegated by the state which is traditionally associated with sovereignty, such as eminent domain, our case would be quite a different one. But while the Pennsylvania statute imposes an obligation to furnish service on regulated utilities, it imposes no such obligation on the state. The Pennsylvania courts have rejected the contention that utility services are either state functions or municipal duties.

We also reject the notion that Metropolitan's termination is state action because the state has specifically authorized and approved the termination practice. Metropolitan filed with the Public Utilities Commission a general tariff—a provision of which states Metropolitan's right to terminate service for nonpayment. This provision has appeared in Metropolitan's previously filed tariffs for many years and has never been the subject of a hearing or other scrutiny by the Commission. Although the Commission did hold hearings on portions of Metropolitan's general tariff relating to a general rate increase, it never even considered the reinsertion of this provision in the newly filed general tariff.

We also find absent the symbiotic relationship presented in *Burton v. Wilmington Parking Authority* (1961). There, where a private lessee who practiced racial discrimination leased space for a restaurant from a state parking authority in a publicly owned building, the Court held that the state had so far insinuated itself into a position of interdependence with the restaurant that it was a joint participant in the enterprise. Metropolitan is a privately owned corporation and it does not lease its facilities from the state of Pennsylvania. It alone is responsible for the provision of power to its customers.

All of Jackson's arguments taken together show no more than that Metropolitan was a heavily regulated private utility, enjoying at least a partial monopoly in the providing of electrical service within its territory, and that it elected to terminate service in a manner which the Commission found permissible under state law. This is not sufficient to connect the state with Metropolitan's action so as to make the latter's conduct attributable to the state for purposes of the 14th Amendment.

Judgment for Metropolitan affirmed.

**Due Process.** The 5th and 14th Amendments require that the federal government and the states observe **due process** when they deprive a person of life, liberty, or property. The traditional idea of due process, called **procedural due process,** establishes the procedures that government must follow when it takes life, liberty, or property. Although the requirements of procedural due process vary from situation to situation, at their core is the idea that people are entitled to adequate notice of the action to be taken against them and to some sort of fair hearing before that action can occur. Some Supreme Court cases of the 1960s and 1970s adopted a fairly broad definition of the "liberty" and "property" interests whose taking triggers the due process requirement. For example, the Court held that due process must be observed in student disciplinary proceedings, the termination of welfare benefits, and the suspension of a driver's license. Later decisions, however, have somewhat restricted the meanings of liberty and property.

A procedural due process claim does not challenge rules of *substantive law*—the rules that set standards for individuals and groups as they act in society.[12] Instead, it attacks the *procedures* used by the governmental actors that enforce substantive rules. For example,

[12] On the distinction between substantive law and procedural law, see Chapter 1.

arguments against a hypothetical statute making pickpocketing a crime punishable by death go to the substance of the statute, while objections to a statute declaring that this penalty can be imposed without trial are procedural in nature.

Sometimes, however, the Due Process Clauses have been used to attack the substance of governmental action. For our purposes, the most important example of this **substantive due process** occurred in the late 19th and early 20th centuries, when probusiness courts influenced by laissez-faire economic ideas struck down various kinds of social legislation as denying due process. The technique for accomplishing this result was to read freedom of contract into the "liberty" protected by the 5th and 14th Amendments and to interpret "due process of law" as requiring that legislation denying freedom of contract have some reasonable relation to the achievement of a valid governmental purpose.[13] Many forms of social legislation (for example, wages and hours laws) violate freedom of contract by dictating terms of the employment relation in order to protect relatively powerless workers. Under this "economic" version of substantive due process, such measures had to satisfy the test described above. Quite often, probusiness courts resolved the resulting questions of "reasonableness" and "validity" in a manner hostile to social legislation.

Many statutes that were attacked on substantive due process grounds survived the challenge, but some did not. Not until 1937 was the doctrine of economic substantive due process definitively rejected by the Supreme Court. Today, substantive due process attacks on economic regulation have virtually no chance of success. But it is frequently said that substantive due process lives on as a device to protect "privacy" or "autonomy" rights of a personal nature. A possible example is the Supreme Court's 1973 decision striking down certain statutes that prohibited abortions.[14]

[13] This language resembles the lenient rational basis test described above, but it was sometimes read in such a way as to present significant obstacles to state legislation denying freedom of contract.

[14] For another application of the Constitutional right of privacy, see Chapter 50.

## Mennonite Board of Missions v. Adams

### 462 U.S. 791 (U.S. Sup. Ct. 1983)

Alfred Jean Moore purchased some real property located in Elkhart, Indiana from the Mennonite Board of Missions (MBM). The sale was on credit, and MBM took a mortgage on the property to secure payment of the $14,000 purchase price. Under the sales agreement, Moore was responsible for paying all property taxes. Unknown to MBM, however, she failed to do so. This eventually led Elkhart County to initiate proceedings for the sale of Moore's property in order to satisfy the tax debt. Under Indiana law at the time in question, the only forms of notice required to be given to holders of mortgage interests (mortgagees) in property destined for a tax sale were: (1) posted notice in the county courthouse and (2) published notice once each week for three consecutive weeks. The owner of the property, on the other hand, was entitled to notice by certified mail. Elkhart County complied with all of these requirements and eventually sold Moore's property to Richard Adams. Through no fault of its own, MBM did not learn of the tax deficiency or the sale until two years after the sale occurred. By then, the statutory period within which MBM could have redeemed the property had passed and Moore still owed MBM over $8,000.

Adams later sued in an Indiana trial court to quiet title to the property that he had purchased. In opposition to Adams's motion for summary judgment, MBM argued that it had not received constitutionally adequate notice of the tax sale and of its opportunity to redeem the property following the sale. The trial court found for Adams, and a state appellate court affirmed the judgment. MBM appealed to the U.S. Supreme Court.

**Marshall, Justice.** In *Mullane v. Central Hanover Bank & Trust Co.* (1950), this Court recognized that prior to an action which will affect an interest in life, liberty, or property protected by the Due Process Clause of the Fourteenth Amendment, a State must provide "notice reasonably calculated, under all circumstances, to apprise interested parties of the pendency of the action and afford them an opportunity to present their objections." Invoking this "elementary and fundamental requirement of due process," the Court held that published notice of an action to settle the accounts of a common trust fund was not sufficient to inform beneficiaries of the trust whose names and addresses were known. The Court explained that notice by publication was not reasonably calculated to provide actual notice of the pending proceeding and was therefore inadequate to inform those who could be notified by more effective means such as personal service or mailed notice.

This case is controlled by the analysis in *Mullane.* A mortgagee (e.g., MBM) possesses a substantial property interest that is significantly affected by a tax sale. Ultimately, the tax sale may result in the complete nullification of the mortgagee's interest, since the purchaser acquires title free of all liens and other encumbrances at the conclusion of the redemption period.

Since a mortgagee clearly has a legally protected property interest, he is entitled to notice reasonably calculated to apprise him of a pending tax sale. Unless the mortgagee is not reasonably identifiable, constructive notice alone does not satisfy the mandate of *Mullane.*

Neither notice by publication and posting, nor mailed notice to the property owner, are means such as one desirous of actually informing the mortgagee might reasonably adopt to accomplish it. Because they are designed primarily to attract prospective purchasers to the tax sale, publication and posting are unlikely to reach those who, although they have an interest in the property, do not make special efforts to keep abreast of such notices. Notice to the property owner also cannot be expected to lead to actual notice to the mortgagee. The County's use of these less reliable forms of notice is not reasonable where, as here, an inexpensive and efficient mechanism such as mail service is available.

Personal service or mailed notice is required even though sophisticated creditors have means at their disposal to discover whether property taxes have not been paid and whether tax sale proceedings are therefore likely to be initiated. A mortgage need not involve a complex commercial transaction among knowledgeable parties, and it may well be the least sophisticated creditor whose security interest is threatened by a tax sale. More importantly, a party's ability to safeguard its interests does not relieve the state of its constitutional obligation. Notice by mail or other means as certain to ensure actual notice is a minimum constitutional precondition to a proceeding which will adversely affect the liberty or property interests of *any* party, whether unlettered or well versed in commercial practice, if its name and address are reasonably ascertainable.

Judgment reversed in favor of MBM.

**Equal Protection.** The 14th Amendment and its **equal protection** guarantee were added to the Constitution after the Civil War. Some scholars argue that the Equal Protection Clause was originally intended to apply only to racial discrimination, but by the beginning of the 20th century it had become applicable to government discrimination of all sorts. The law inevitably classifies in various ways, benefiting or burdening some groups but not others. The equal protection guarantee sets the standards that such classifications must meet if they are to be constitutional.

The basic equal protection standard is the *rational basis* test described earlier in the chapter. This is the standard usually applied to economic regulation challenged as denying equal protection. As the following *Clover Leaf* case suggests, this test is rather lenient and it does not pose a significant obstacle to state and federal regulation of economic matters.

Laws that discriminate with respect to **fundamental rights** or involve **suspect classifications,** however, receive more rigorous scrutiny from the courts. For the most part, this is a development that began after World War II and greatly accelerated during the 1960s and 1970s. The list of rights regarded as "fundamental" for equal protection purposes is not completely clear, but it probably includes at least the following: voting, procreation, interstate travel, and certain criminal procedure protections. Laws creating unequal enjoyment of these rights receive something resembling the *full strict scrutiny* described above. In 1969, for instance, the Supreme Court struck down the District of Columbia's one-year residency requirement for receiving welfare benefits because that requirement unequally and impermissibly restricted the right of interstate travel.

The "suspect" bases of classification triggering more rigorous scrutiny are *race* (and national origin), *sex* (or gender),[15] *alienage* (status as an alien), and *illegitimacy*. Here, the level of scrutiny varies from category to category. Classifications disadvantaging racial or national minorities receive the strictest kind of strict scrutiny and will almost never be constitutional. However, the test controlling racial discrimination that *benefits* such minorities and disadvantages whites is unclear, although it seems that the Supreme Court treats such classifications more leniently. In 1978, for instance, the Court struck down an explicit racial quota giving minorities preferential admission to a state medical school, but it also stated that some consideration of race in the admissions process was permissible to promote student body diversity. In 1980, the Court upheld a federal public works provision requiring that 10 percent of each grant to a state or locality go to minority contractors or suppliers.

Although the verbal formulas vary from situation to situation, classifications based on gender, alienage, and illegitimacy generally receive some form of *intermediate scrutiny*.

[15] In *Frontiero v. Richardson* (1973), a majority of the Supreme Court declined the opportunity to formally declare sex a suspect classification. After 1976, however, the Court began to impose an "intermediate" standard of review in sex discrimination cases. In *Mississippi University for Women v. Hogan* (1982), for example, it stated that the burden of upholding a gender-based classification "is met only by showing at least that the classification serves important governmental objectives and that the discriminatory means employed are substantially related to the achievement of those objectives."

In the case of gender, the Supreme Court has explicitly stated that classifications disadvantaging men get the same degree of scrutiny as classifications disadvantaging women. This has not, however, prevented the Court from upholding both men-only draft registration and a state law making statutory rape a crime for men alone. In the case of alienage, the Court has refused to apply intermediate scrutiny to laws that bar aliens from public employment in occupations deemed sufficiently important for the proper functioning of government (for example, the state police and public school teaching).

## Minnesota v. Clover Leaf Creamery Co.

**449 U.S. 456 (U.S. Sup. Ct. 1981)**

In response to environmental concerns, the Minnesota legislature passed a statute banning the sale of milk in plastic nonrefillable, nonreusable containers but allowing the continued use of other nonreturnable, nonrefillable containers, such as paperboard cartons. The Clover Leaf Creamery Company and other dairy-related businesses sued to enjoin enforcement of the statute on the ground that it violated the Equal Protection Clause. The trial court and the Minnesota Supreme Court held for the plaintiffs, and the state appealed to the U.S Supreme Court.

**Brennan, Justice.** The standard of review applicable to this case is the familiar "rational basis" test. Moreover, the purposes of the Act cited by the legislature—promoting resource conservation, easing solid waste disposal problems, and conserving energy—are legitimate state purposes. Thus, the controversy in this case centers on the narrow issue whether the legislative classification between plastic and nonplastic nonreturnable milk containers is rationally related to achievement of the statutory purposes.

Clover Leaf produced impressive supporting evidence at trial to prove that the probable consequences of the ban on plastic nonreturnable milk containers will be to deplete natural resources, exacerbate solid waste disposal problems, and waste energy, because consumers unable to purchase milk in plastic containers will turn to paperboard milk cartons, allegedly a more environmentally harmful product. But states are not required to convince the courts of the correctness of their legislative judgments. Rather, those challenging the legislative judgment must convince the court that the facts on which the classification is apparently based could not reasonably be conceived to be true by the governmental decisionmaker.

The state identifies four reasons why the classification between plastic and nonplastic nonreturnables is rationally related to the articulated statutory purposes. If any one of the four substantiates the state's claim, we must reverse the Minnesota Supreme Court and sustain the Act.

First, the state argues that elimination of the popular milk jug will encourage the use of environmentally superior containers. Whether *in fact* the Act will promote more environmentally desirable milk packaging is not the question: the Equal Protection Clause is satisfied by our conclusion that the Minnesota legislature could *rationally have decided* that its ban on plastic nonreturnable milk jugs might foster greater use of environmentally desirable alternatives.

Second, the state argues that its ban on plastic nonreturnable milk containers will reduce the economic dislocation foreseen from the movement toward greater use of environmentally superior containers. The state notes that plastic nonreturnables have only recently been introduced on a wide scale in Minnesota, and that many Minnesota dairies were preparing to invest large amounts of capital in plastic container production. Moreover, the state explains, to ban both the plastic and the paperboard nonreturnable milk container at once would cause an enormous disruption in the milk industry because few dairies are now able to package their products in refillable bottles or plastic pouches. Thus, by banning the plastic container while continuing to permit the paperboard container, the state was able to prevent the industry from becoming reliant on the new container, while avoiding severe economic dislocation. The state legislature concluded that nonreturnable, nonrefillable milk containers pose environmental hazards, and decided to ban the most recent entry into the field. The fact that the legislature in effect "grandfathered" paperboard containers, at least temporarily, does not make the Act's ban on plastic nonreturnables arbitrary or irrational.

Third, the state argues that the Act will help to conserve energy. It points out that plastic milk jugs are made from plastic resin, an oil and natural gas derivative, whereas paperboard milk cartons are primarily composed of pulpwood, which is a renewable resource. The Minnesota Supreme Court concluded that production of plastic nonrefillables requires less energy than production of paper containers. The Court may be correct that the Act is not a sensible means of conserving energy. But we reiterate that it is up to legislatures, not courts, to decide on the wisdom and utility of legislation. Since the question clearly is at least debatable, the Court erred in substituting its judgment for that of the legislature.

Fourth, the state argues that the Act will ease the state's solid waste disposal problem. A reputable study before the Minnesota legislature indicated that plastic milk jugs occupy a greater volume in landfills than other nonreturnable milk containers. The Minnesota Supreme Court found that plastic milk jugs in fact take up less space in landfills and present fewer solid waste disposal problems than do paperboard containers. But its ruling on this point must be rejected for the same reason we rejected its ruling concerning energy conservation: it is not the function of the courts to substitute their evaluation of legislative facts for that of the legislature.

Judgment reversed in favor of Minnesota.

**Business and the First Amendment.** As noted earlier, the First Amendment's guarantee of free speech is not absolute. But freedom of speech is very highly protected and government action restricting speech receives something resembling full strict scrutiny. While the justifications for this high level of protection vary, perhaps the preeminent argument for free speech is the "marketplace" rationale. On this view, the free competition of ideas is the surest means of attaining truth and the "marketplace of ideas" best serves this end when restrictions on speech are kept to a minimum and all viewpoints can be considered. This chapter cannot consider all of the questions that the free speech guarantee has raised in the 20th century. Instead, it will consider two recent First Amendment doctrines affecting business. In each, the "marketplace" rationale figures prominently.

**Commercial Speech.** **Commercial speech** is expression proposing a commercial transaction; commercial advertising is the most common example of such expression. In 1942, the Supreme Court ruled that commercial speech was outside the First Amendment's protection, but in the 1970s the Court reversed its position. Now, restrictions on commercial speech receive what is basically an *intermediate* level of scrutiny that is less stringent than the review given laws restricting other forms of First Amendment speech. The *Youngs* case below discusses the applicable test in detail. As the case also states, the test does not apply to commercial speech that is false, deceptive, or misleading or that is related to illegal behavior; these forms of expression can be freely regulated. In addition, different First Amendment standards apply to laws that merely regulate the time, place, or manner (and not the *content*) of commercial speech.

The usual justification for protecting commercial speech is to promote informed consumer choice by removing barriers to the flow of commercial information. The Supreme Court's decisions striking down state restrictions on advertising by members of certain professions, decisions that arguably promoted price-fixing within these professions, seem consistent with this "marketplace" rationale. However, since the commercial speech doctrine gives constitutional backing to many of the advertising techniques that corporations use to generate demand for their offerings, the doctrine may ultimately work to the net benefit of business interests. This could happen if, for instance, government regulators ever decide to mount a serious attack on advertising that is not false or misleading but that attempts to manipulate consumers by appealing to irrational drives of all sorts.[16] In general, one's opinion about protecting commercial speech may depend on one's views about the impact of modern mass advertising and about the rationality with which consumers respond to it.

**Corporate Political Speech.** In *First National Bank of Boston v. Bellotti* (1978), the Supreme Court struck down a Massachusetts statute prohibiting corporate expenditures designed to influence the public's vote on matters not affecting the property or business of the corporation. The decision is generally regarded as establishing a corporation's First Amendment right to speak freely on political matters. Corporate political speech is entitled to *full* First Amendment protection, and not the lesser degree of protection accorded to commercial speech. (Note that, as the *Youngs* case suggests, the line between political speech and commercial speech is sometimes unclear.) The contours of this corporate political speech right have not been fully defined by the Supreme Court; the *Consolidated Edison* case below is the only major Supreme Court decision applying *Bellotti.*

The main policy argument for the *Bellotti* result was the "marketplace" reasoning discussed above. Corporate speech, the Court claimed, is just as vital to informed public debate as speech from other sources, and no one would argue that a state could silence noncorporate speakers. In other words, if the political marketplace of ideas functions best when all views are included, why arbitrarily restrict corporate participation? Critics of *Bellotti,* however, argue that the assets and communications skills possessed by large corporations will enable them to dominate the political "market" and that some limits on corporate speech may be necessary to ensure that the competition of ideas is tolerably fair and equal. As with commercial speech, one's opinion on this question may depend on one's views about the effectiveness of modern advertising and about the rationality with which the public approaches it.

[16] For a brief discussion of "commercial speech" challenges to the FTC's regulation of advertising, see Chapter 46.

## Bolger v. Youngs Drug Products Corp.

**463 U.S. 60 (U.S. Sup. Ct. 1983)**

Youngs Drug Products Corporation manufactures, sells, and distributes contraceptive devices (including prophylactics). It planned a marketing compaign involving the unsolicited mass mailing of advertising fliers and related materials to the general public. The mailings were to include: (1) fliers promoting a range of products obtainable in drugstores (including prophylactics); (2) fliers specifically promoting prophylactics; and (3) informational pamphlets discussing, among other things, the usefulness of prophylactics in preventing venereal disease and aiding family planning. After learning of Youngs' plans, the Postal Service warned Youngs that the mailings would violate a federal statute prohibiting the mailing of unsolicited advertisements for contraceptive devices.

Youngs sued in federal district court for an injunction barring enforcement of the statute against its mailings, arguing that such enforcement would violate the First Amendment. The district court decided in Youngs' favor, and the Postal Service appealed to the U.S. Supreme Court under a statute allowing direct appeals from decisions invalidating acts of Congress.

**MARSHALL, JUSTICE.** Our decisions have recognized the commonsense distinction between speech proposing a commercial transaction and other varieties of speech. Thus, we have held that the Constitution accords less protection to commercial speech than to other constitutionally safeguarded forms of expression. With respect to noncommercial speech, this Court has sustained content-based restrictions only in the most extraordinary circumstances. By contrast, in light of the greater potential for deception or confusion in the context of certain advertising messages, content-based restrictions on commercial speech may be permissible.

[Thus,] we must first determine the proper classification of the mailings at issue here. Most of Youngs' mailings fall within the core notion of commercial speech—speech which does no more than propose a commercial transaction. Youngs' informational pamphlets, however, cannot be characterized merely as proposals to engage in commercial transactions. The mere fact that these pamphlets are advertisements does not compel the conclusion that they are commercial speech. Similarly, the reference to a specific product does not by itself render the pamphlets commercial speech. Finally, the fact that Youngs has an economic motivation for mailing the pamphlets would clearly be insufficient by itself to turn the materials into commercial speech. The combination of all these characteristics, however, provides strong support for the conclusion that the informational pamphlets are properly characterized as commercial speech. The mailings constitute commercial speech notwithstanding the fact that they contain discussions of important public issues such as venereal disease and family planning.

We have adopted [the following] analysis for assessing the validity of restrictions on commercial speech. First, we determine whether the expression is constitutionally protected. For commercial speech to receive such protection, it at least must concern lawful activity and not be misleading. Second, we ask whether the governmental interest is substantial. If so, we must then determine whether the regulation directly advances the government interest asserted, and whether it is not more extensive than necessary to serve that interest. Applying this analysis, we conclude that the statute is unconstitutional as applied to mailings.

We turn first to the protection afforded by the First Amendment. The State may deal effectively with false, deceptive, or misleading sales techniques. In this case, however, the government has never claimed that Youngs' mailings fall into any of these categories. Youngs' commercial speech is therefore clearly protected by the First Amendment.

We must next determine whether the government's interest in prohibiting the mailing of unsolicited contraceptive advertisements is a substantial one. The government asserts that the statute: (1) shields recipients of mail from materials that they are likely to find offensive, and (2) aids parents' efforts to control the manner in which their children become informed about sensitive and important subjects such as birth control. The first of these interests carries little weight. At least where obscenity is not involved, we have consistently held that the fact that protected speech may be offensive to some does not justify its suppression. We have never held that the government can shut off the flow of mailings to protect those recipients who might potentially be offended. Recipients of objectionable mailings may effectively avoid bombardment of their sensibilities simply by averting their eyes.

The second interest asserted by the government—aiding parents' efforts to discuss birth control with their children—is undoubtedly substantial. As a means of effectuating this interest, however, this statute fails to withstand scrutiny. To begin, it provides only the most limited incremental support for the interest asserted. We can reasonably assume that parents already exercise substantial control over the disposition of mail once it enters their mailboxes. And parents must already cope with the multitude of external stimuli that color their children's perception of sensitive subjects. Under these circumstances, a ban on unsolicited advertisements serves only to assist those parents who desire to keep their children from confronting such mailings, who are otherwise unable to do so, and whose children have remained relatively free from such stimuli.

This marginal degree of protection is achieved by purging all mailboxes of unsolicited material that is entirely suitable for adults. A restriction of this scope is more extensive than the Constitution permits, for the government may not reduce the adult population to reading only what is fit for children. The level of discourse reaching a mailbox simply cannot be limited to that which would be suitable for a sandbox.

The justifications offered by the government are insufficient to warrant the sweeping prohibition on the mailing of unsolicited contraceptive advertisements. As applied to Youngs' mailings, the statute is unconstitutional.

Judgment for Youngs affirmed.

## Consolidated Edison Co. v. Public Service Commission

### 447 U.S. 530 (U.S. Sup. Ct. 1980)

The Consolidated Edison Company of New York, a regulated electric utility, placed written material favorable to nuclear power in the bills it sent to its customers. The New York State Public Service Commission then prohibited state utilities from using bill inserts to discuss controversial matters of public policy, including the desirability of nuclear power. Consolidated sought review of the Commission's order in the New York courts. It was successful in overturning the order at the trial court level, but the state's appellate courts decided in favor of the Commission. Consolidated then appealed to the U.S. Supreme Court.

**POWELL, JUSTICE.** The restriction on bill inserts cannot be upheld on the ground that Consolidated Edison is not entitled to freedom of speech. In *First National Bank of Boston v. Bellotti* (1978), we rejected the contention that a state may confine corporate speech to specified issues. That decision recognized that the inherent worth of the speech in terms of its capacity for informing the public does not depend upon the identity of its source, whether corporation, association, union, or individual. Because the state action limited protected speech, we concluded that the regulation could not stand absent a showing of a compelling state interest.

Freedom of speech is indispensable to the discovery and spread of political truth, and the best test of truth is the power of the thought to get itself accepted in the competition of the market. The First and Fourteenth Amendments remove governmental restraints from the arena of public discussion, putting the decision as to what views shall be voiced largely into the hands of each of us in the hope that use of such freedom will ultimately produce a more capable citizenry and a more perfect polity. The Commission has limited the means by which Consolidated Edison may participate in the public debate on the nuclear power question and other controversial issues of national interest and importance. Thus, the Commission's prohibition strikes at the heart of the freedom to speak.

The Commission's ban on bill inserts is not, of course, invalid merely because it imposes a limitation upon speech. The Commission's arguments require us to consider [two] theories that might justify the state action. We must determine whether the prohibition is a permissible subject-matter regulation, or a narrowly tailored means of serving a compelling state interest.

[First,] the Commission argues that its order is acceptable because it applies to all discussion of nuclear power, whether pro or con, in bill inserts. The prohibition, the Commission contends, is related to subject matter rather than to the views of a particular speaker. Because the regulation does not favor either side of a political controversy, the Commission asserts that it does not unconstitutionally suppress freedom of speech. The First Amendment's hostility to content-based regulation extends not only to restrictions on particular viewpoints, but also to prohibition of public discussion of an entire topic. To allow a government the choice of permissible subjects for public debate would be to allow that government control over the search for political truth.

[Secondly] where a government restricts the speech of a private person, the state action may be sustained only if the government can show that the regulation is a precisely drawn means of serving a compelling state interest. The Commission argues that its prohibition is necessary: (i) to avoid forcing Consolidated Edison's views on a captive audience, (ii) to allocate limited resources in the public interest, and (iii) to ensure that ratepayers do not subsidize the cost of the bill inserts.

Even if a short exposure to Consolidated Edison's views may offend the sensibilities of some consumers, the ability of government to shut off discourse solely to protect others from hearing it is dependent upon a showing that substantial privacy interests are being invaded in an essentially intolerable manner. Where a single speaker communicates to many listeners, the First Amendment does not permit the government to prohibit speech as intrusive unless the captive audience cannot avoid objectionable speech. Passengers on public transportation or residents of a neighborhood disturbed by the raucous broadcasts from a passing soundtruck may well be unable to escape an unwanted message. But customers of Consolidated Edison may escape exposure to objectionable material simply by transferring the bill insert from envelope to wastebasket.

The Commission contends that because a billing envelope can accommodate only a limited amount of information, political messages should not be allowed to take the place of inserts that promote energy conservation or safety, or that remind consumers of their legal rights. But the Commission has not shown that the presence of the bill inserts at issue would preclude the inclusion of other inserts that Consolidated Edison might be ordered lawfully to include in the billing envelope.

Finally, the Commission urges that its prohibition would prevent ratepayers from subsidizing the costs of policy-oriented bill inserts. But the Commission did not base its order on an inability to allocate costs between the shareholders of Consolidated Edison and the ratepayers. Rather, the Commission stated "that using bill inserts to proclaim a utility's viewpoint on controversial issues (even when the stockholder pays for it in full) is tantamount to taking advantage of a captive audience." Accordingly, there is no basis on this record to assume that the Commission could not exclude the cost of these bill inserts from the utility's rate base. Mere speculation of harm does not constitute a compelling state interest.

Judgment reversed in favor of Consolidated Edison.

## INDEPENDENT CHECKS APPLYING ONLY TO THE STATES

**The Contract Clause.** Article I, section 10 of the Constitution says: "No State shall . . . pass any . . . Law impairing the Obligation of Contracts." This **Contract Clause** limits the states' ability to change the terms of an *existing* contract (and thus the parties' performance obligations) by laws passed *after* the contract has been made. The original purpose behind the Contract Clause was to protect debt obligations owed to contract creditors by invalidating the many debtor relief statutes passed by the states after the Revolution. In the famous cases of *Fletcher v. Peck* (1810) and *Dartmouth College v. Woodward* (1819), however, the clause was held to embrace *governmental* contracts and grants (including corporate charters). Since the charter was the principal means for controlling corporations in the early 19th century, and since the Contract Clause blocked subsequent changes in its terms, these cases are said to have greatly assisted the rise of the corporation. Soon enough, however, Contract Clause doctrine changed to permit some charter amendments, and in any event the charter eventually became less important as a corporate control device.

The Contract Clause was probably the most important constitutional check on state regulation of the economy in the 19th century. Beginning in the latter part of that century, though, the clause gradually became subordinate to legislation based on the states' police powers. By the mid-20th century, most observers treated the clause as a constitutional dead letter. In 1977, however, the Supreme Court gave the Contract Clause new life when it decided *United States Trust Co. v. New Jersey.* In this case, the Court struck down New York's and New Jersey's 1974 repeal of terms protecting bondholders in a 1962 bistate agreement regarding the operation of the New York Port Authority. In the process, the Court announced a new, fairly strict, constitutional test governing situations where a state impairs *its own* contracts. The impairment, it said, must be "reasonable and necessary to serve an important public purpose." A year later, without articulating a clear constitutional standard, the Court struck down Minnesota's alteration of *private* pension contracts in *Allied Structural Steel Co. v. Spannaus.*

In the 1980s, the Court has seemingly moved back toward its pre-*U.S. Trust* position, at least so far as *private* contracts are concerned. The *Exxon* case, which follows, is an example. It is typical of the way in which the Supreme Court has treated state regulation affecting the obligations of private contracts in the 20th century. Where the state attempts to impair *its own* contracts, however, the *U.S. Trust* test stated above presumably still applies.

## Exxon Corporation v. Eagerton

**462 U.S. 176 (U.S. Sup. Ct. 1983)**

For years, the Exxon Corporation paid a severance tax on the oil and gas it drilled in Alabama. Under the sales contracts that Exxon made with purchasers of its oil and gas, it was able to pass on any tax increase to the purchasers. In 1979, Alabama raised the severance tax from 4 percent to 6 percent, and forbade producers of oil and gas from passing on the increase to purchasers.

Exxon and eight other oil and gas producers sued the Alabama commissioner of revenue in an Alabama trial court, seeking a ruling that the pass-on restriction was unconstitutional under the Contract Clause. The trial court found for Exxon, but the Alabama supreme court reversed. Exxon appealed to the U.S. Supreme Court.

**Marshall, Justice.** By barring Exxon from passing the tax increase through to its purchasers, the pass-through prohibition nullified the purchasers' contractual obligations to reimburse Exxon for any severance taxes.

While the prohibition thus affects contractual obligations, it does not follow that the prohibition constituted a "Law impairing the Obligations of Contracts" within the meaning of the Contract Clause. Although the language of the Clause is facially absolute, its prohibition must be accommodated to the inherent police power of the state to safeguard the vital interests of its people. If the law were otherwise, one would be able to obtain immunity from state regulation by making private contractual arrangements.

The Contract Clause does not deprive the states of their broad power to adopt general regulatory measures without being concerned that private contracts will be impaired, or even destroyed, as a result. Thus, a state prohibition law may be applied to contracts for the sale of beer that were valid when entered into, a law barring lotteries may be applied to lottery tickets that were valid when issued, and a workmen's compensation law may be applied to employers and employees operating under preexisting contracts of employment that made no provision for work-related injuries.

Like the laws upheld in these cases, the pass-through prohibition did not prescribe a rule limited in effect to contractual obligations or remedies, but instead imposed a generally applicable rule of conduct designed to advance a broad societal interest, protecting consumers from excessive prices. The prohibition applied to all oil and gas producers, regardless of whether they happened to be parties to sale contracts that contained a provision permitting them to pass tax increases through to their purchasers. The effect of the pass-through prohibition on existing contracts that did contain such a provision was incidental to its main effect of shielding consumers from the burden of the tax increase.

Because the pass-through prohibition imposed a generally applicable rule of conduct, it is sharply distinguishable from the measures struck down in *United States Trust Co. v. New Jersey* and *Allied Structural Steel Co. v. Spannaus. United States Trust* involved New York and New Jersey statutes whose sole effect was to repeal a covenant that the two states had entered into with the holders of bonds issued by The Port Authority of New York and New Jersey. Similarly, the statute at issue in *Allied Structural Steel* directly adjusted the rights and responsibilities of contracting parties. The statute required a private employer that had contracted with its employees to provide pension benefits to pay additional benefits, beyond those it had agreed to provide, if it terminated the pension plan or closed a Minnesota office. Since the statute applied only to employers that had entered into pension agreements, its sole effect was to alter contractual duties.

Judgment for the commissioner affirmed on the Contract Clause issue. Case returned to the Alabama Supreme Court for consideration of other questions.

**Burden on Interstate Commerce.** In addition to giving Congress the power to regulate interstate commerce, the Commerce Clause limits the ability of the states to hinder or burden such commerce.[17] This limitation is not expressly stated in the Constitution. Rather, it arises by implication from the Commerce Clause and reflects that clause's original purpose of blocking state protectionism and assuring the free flow of interstate trade.[18] The **burden-on-commerce** limitation operates independently of congressional legislation under the commerce power or any other federal power. If relevant federal regulation is present, the federal supremacy and preemption questions discussed in the next

[17] Also, Article I, section 8 gives Congress the power to regulate *foreign* commerce, and this indirectly limits the states' ability to regulate, tax, or burden such commerce. Here, the federal power is virtually supreme and the scope of permissible state action quite limited.

[18] The Commerce Clause also presents a similar obstacle to state *taxation* that restricts interstate commerce. In this very confused area of constitutional law, the tests differ somewhat from those stated in the next paragraph, but the general policy considerations are much the same.

section may also arise, either alone or alongside a burden-on-commerce claim.

Over time, different verbal tests have been used to determine when state regulation unduly burdens interstate commerce. Today, state regulation subject to a burden-on-commerce attack must first be *rationally related* to a *legitimate* state purpose. State regulation that survives this lenient scrutiny is then subjected to a *balancing* test. Only if the state's interest in its regulation outweighs the federal interest in the free flow of interstate trade will the state measure be constitutional. Although it does not distinguish them clearly, the *Kassel* case which follows apparently finds the state statute defective on both these grounds.

In balancing federal and state interests, the courts consider a wide range of factors. Obviously, they will assess the *importance* of the state interest and the *degree* to which it restricts the highly significant federal interest in promoting interstate commerce. State measures that *discriminate* against interstate commerce in favor of local economic interests are especially likely to be struck down. Here, the state's discriminatory purpose may not be immediately apparent. State farming or dairy interests, for example, often benefit from restrictions on the importation of out-of-state foodstuffs that are described as consumer protection measures. Courts also consider the *degree* to which the state regulatory scheme actually advances the purposes used to justify it. In doing so, they may ask whether there are other regulatory means less burdensome to interstate commerce but equally capable of advancing the state's purposes. Finally, as *Kassel* suggests, the courts are prone to strike down state regulations that pose obstacles to multistate business operations.

Recently, the Supreme Court has insulated state regulation from Commerce Clause attack when the state acts as a "market participant." In 1976, for instance, it upheld a Maryland statute under which the state would pay a "bounty" for used cars that had been converted to scrap, despite state documentation requirements that favored in-state scrap processors over out-of-state processors. In 1979, it upheld a South Dakota measure requiring that sales of cement from a state-owned plant be made only to state residents.

## Kassel v. Consolidated Freightways Corp.

**450 U.S. 662 (U.S. Sup. Ct. 1981)**

Consolidated Freightways Corporation is a large common carrier offering service in 48 states. At the time in question here, Consolidated mainly used two kinds of trucks. One consisted of a three-axle tractor pulling a 40-foot, two-axle trailer. This unit, commonly called a "single" or "semi," was 55 feet long. Consolidated also used a unit consisting of a two-axle tractor pulling a single-axle trailer, which in turn pulled a single-axle dolly and a second single-axle trailer. This combination, known as a "double" or "twin," was 65 feet long.

An Iowa statute restricted the length of the vehicles that could use its highways. Unlike all the other states in the West and Midwest, Iowa generally prohibited the use of 65-foot doubles within its borders. Instead, most truck combinations were limited to a length of 55 feet. However, doubles, mobile homes, trucks carrying vehicles such as tractors, and singles hauling livestock were permitted to be as long as 60 feet. Moreover, Iowa's statute permitted cities abutting the state line to pass ordinances adopting the length limitations of the adjoining state.

The Iowa statute posed obvious problems for Consolidated, and it sued the state in federal district court, alleging that the statute unconstitutionally burdened interstate commerce. Iowa defended the statute as a reasonable safety measure enacted pursuant to its police power. The district court found for Consolidated after a 14-day trial largely devoted to the safety question, and the court of appeals affirmed. Iowa appealed to the U.S. Supreme Court.

**POWELL, JUSTICE.** The Commerce Clause is a prolific source of national power and an equally prolific source of conflict with legislation of the states. The Clause permits Congress to legislate when it perceives that the national welfare is not furthered by the independent actions of the states. Also, the Clause is a limitation upon state power even without congressional implementation. The Clause requires that some aspects of trade generally must remain free from interference by the states. When a state ventures excessively into the regulation of these aspects of commerce, it trespasses upon national interests, and the courts will hold the state regulation invalid under the Clause alone.

The Commerce Clause does not, of course, invalidate all state restrictions on commerce. In the absence of conflicting legislation by Congress, there is a residuum of power in the state to make laws governing matters of local concern which nevertheless in some measure affect interstate commerce or even regulate it. The extent of permissible state regulation is not always easy to measure. It may be said with confidence, however, that a state's power to regulate commerce is never greater than in matters traditionally of local concern. For example, regulations that touch upon safety—especially highway safety—are those that the Court has been most reluctant to invalidate.

But the incantation of a purpose to promote the public health or safety does not insulate a state law from Commerce Clause attack. Regulations designed for that salutary purpose nevertheless may further the purpose so marginally, and interfere with commerce so substantially, as to be invalid under the Commerce Clause. We have declined to accept the state's contention that the inquiry under the Commerce Clause is ended without a weighing of the asserted safety purpose against the degree of interference with interstate commerce. This "weighing" by a court requires a sensitive consideration of the weight and nature of the state regulatory concern in light of the extent of the burden imposed on interstate commerce.

Applying these general principles, we conclude that the Iowa truck-length limitations unconstitutionally burden interstate commerce.

In *Raymond Motor Transportation, Inc. v. Rice* (1978), a Wisconsin statute that precluded the use of 65-foot doubles violated the Commerce Clause. This case is *Raymond* revisited. Here, as in *Raymond,* the state failed to present any persuasive evidence that 65-foot doubles are less safe than 55-foot singles. Moreover, Iowa's law is now out of step with the laws of all other midwestern and western states. Iowa thus substantially burdens the interstate flow of goods by truck. In the absence of congressional action to set uniform standards, some burdens associated with state safety regulations must be tolerated. But where, as here, the state's safety interest has been found to be illusory, and its regulations impair significantly the federal interest in efficient and safe interstate transportation, the state law cannot be harmonized with the Commerce Clause.

The District Court found that the twin is as safe as the semi. The record supports this finding. The evidence showed that the 65-foot double was at least the equal of the 55-

foot single in the ability to brake, turn, and maneuver. The double, because of its axle placement, produces less splash and spray in wet weather. And, because of its articulation in the middle, the double is less susceptible to dangerous "off tracking," and to wind. None of these findings is seriously disputed by Iowa. Indeed, the state points to only three ways in which the 55-foot single is even arguably superior: singles take less time to be passed and to clear intersections; they may back up for longer distances; and they are somewhat less likely to jackknife.

Consolidated, meanwhile, demonstrated that Iowa's law substantially burdens interstate commerce. Trucking companies that wish to use 65-foot doubles must route them around Iowa or detach the trailers of the doubles and ship them through separately. Alternatively, trucking companies must use the smaller 55-foot singles or 60-foot doubles permitted under Iowa law. Each of these options engenders inefficiency and added expense. The record shows that Iowa's law added about $12.6 million each year to the costs of trucking companies. Consolidated alone incurred about $2 million per year in increased costs.

Iowa's scheme has several exemptions that secure to Iowans many of the benefits of large trucks while shunting to neighboring states many of the costs associated with their use. First, singles hauling livestock or farm vehicles were permitted to be as long as 60 feet. This provision undoubtedly was helpful to local interests. Second, cities abutting other states were permitted to enact local ordinances adopting the larger length limitation of the neighboring state. This exemption offered the benefits of longer trucks to individuals and businesses in important border cities without burdening Iowa's highways with interstate through traffic. It is thus far from clear that Iowa was motivated primarily by a judgment that 65-foot doubles are less safe than 55-foot singles. Rather, Iowa seems to have hoped to limit the use of its highways by deflecting some through traffic. A state cannot constitutionally promote its own parochial interests by requiring safe vehicles to detour around it.

Judgment for Consolidated affirmed.

**Federal Preemption.** The constitutional principle of **federal supremacy** dictates that, where state law conflicts with valid federal law, the federal law is supreme. This obviously includes situations where there is a literal conflict between the state and federal measures and it is impossible to follow both simultaneously. But state law may also be required to give way even where it does not expressly conflict with federal law. In such cases, state law is said to be **preempted** by federal regulation.

Federal preemption cases usually present questions of statutory interpretation[19] that are decided on a case-by-case basis. As the *Silkwood* case below declares, preemption is mainly a matter of congressional *intent:* a more or less conscious legislative conclusion about the matter at issue. Thus, courts faced with preemption questions will examine the legislative history of the relevant federal act in an attempt to find specific statements about the role (if any) that state law was to play in a certain area. The history (or the statute itself) may contain explicit statements that state law is to be preempted within certain spheres or that it will be permitted to operate in certain areas. Courts usually give full effect to such statements. Also, courts sometimes infer an intent to preempt if the federal regu-

[19] See Chapter 1 for a discussion of statutory interpretation.

lation is *pervasive:* that is, if it regulates a subject in great breadth or in considerable detail.

Arguments based on congressional *purpose* also appear in preemption cases. Here, the courts' concern is whether the state measure is consistent with the *ends* underlying the federal law. Also, it has been suggested that courts are sometimes affected by "constitutional" concerns when they decide preemption cases. Thus, they may openly or covertly balance state and federal interests, or consider values such as the federal interest in free interstate trade that is central to burden-on-commerce cases. In fact, cases raising both preemption and burden-on-commerce issues are not uncommon. The former, however, are based on congressional regulation and the federal supremacy principle, while the latter are based on the Commerce Clause.

## Silkwood v. Kerr-McGee Corp.

**52 U.S.L.W. 4043 (U.S. Sup. Ct. 1984)**

Karen Silkwood was a laboratory analyst at an Oklahoma Kerr-McGee Corporation plant that fabricated plutonium fuel pins used in nuclear power plants. In November 1974, Silkwood and her apartment became contaminated by plutonium from the Kerr-McGee plant. After being sent to a scientific laboratory to determine the extent of her contamination, Silkwood returned to work on November 13, 1974. That night, she died in an automobile accident.

Bill Silkwood, Karen's father, brought a federal district court action against Kerr-McGee in his capacity as administrator of her estate. He sued to recover for the contamination injuries to Karen's person and property, basing the claim on Oklahoma tort law. The jury returned a verdict in favor of Silkwood, awarding $505,000 in actual damages and punitive damages of $10 million. The court of appeals reversed portions of the district court judgment, including the punitive damages award, finding the award to be preempted by federal law. Silkwood appealed the court of appeals' denial of punitive damages to the U.S. Supreme Court.

**White, Justice.** State law can be preempted in either of two general ways. If Congress evidences an intent to occupy a given field, any state law falling within that field is preempted. If Congress has not entirely displaced state regulation over the matter in question, state law is still preempted to the extent that it actually conflicts with federal law, that is, when it is impossible to comply with both state and federal law, or where the state law stands as an obstacle to the accomplishment of the full purposes and objectives of Congress.

In *Pacific Gas & Electric Company v. State Energy Resources Conservation & Development Commission* (1983), the statutory scheme and legislative history of the Atomic Energy Act convinced us that Congress intended that the federal government regulate the radiological safety aspects involved in the construction and operation of a nuclear plant. Thus, we concluded that the federal government has occupied the entire field of nuclear safety concerns, except for the limited powers expressly ceded to the states. Kerr-McGee argues that our ruling in *Pacific Gas & Electric* is dispositive of the issue in this case. Noting that regulation can be as effectively asserted through an award of damages as through some form of preventive relief, Kerr-McGee submits that because the state-authorized award of punitive damages in this case punishes and deters conduct related to radiation hazards, it falls within the prohibited field. However, a review of the legislative history, coupled with an examination of Congress's actions with respect to other portions of the Atomic Energy Act, convinces us that the preempted field does not extend as far as Kerr-McGee would have it.

Congress's decision to prohibit the states from regulating the safety aspects of nuclear development was premised on its belief that the Nuclear Regulatory Commission (NRC) was more qualified to determine what type of safety standards should be enacted in this complex area. If there were nothing more, this arguably would disallow resort to state law remedies by those suffering injuries from radiation in a nuclear plant. There is, however, ample evidence that Congress had no intention of forbidding the states from providing such remedies. Indeed, there is no indication that Congress even seriously considered precluding the use of such remedies either when it enacted the Atomic Energy Act in 1954 or when it amended it in 1959. This silence takes on added significance in light of Congress's failure to provide any federal remedy for persons injured by such conduct.

More importantly, the only congressional discussion concerning the relationship between the Atomic Energy Act and state tort remedies indicates that Congress assumed that such remedies would be available. In 1957 Congress passed the Price-Anderson Act. That Act established an indemnification scheme under which operators of licensed nuclear facilities could be required to obtain up to $60 million in private financial protection against [private] suits. The government would then provide indemnification for the next $500 million of liability, and the resulting $560 million would be the limit of liability for any one nuclear incident.

Although the Price-Anderson Act does not apply to the present situation, the discussion preceding its enactment and amendment indicates that Congress assumed that persons injured by nuclear accidents were free to utilize existing state tort law remedies. The belief that the NRC's exclusive authority to set safety standards did not foreclose the use of state tort remedies was reaffirmed when the Price-Anderson Act was amended in 1966. The 1966 amendment was designed to respond to concerns about the adequacy of state law remedies. It provided that in the event of an "extraordinary nuclear occurrence," licensees could be required to waive any issue of fault, any charitable or governmental immunity defense, and any statute of limitations defense of less than 10 years. The entire discussion surrounding the 1966 amendment was premised on the assumption that state remedies were available notwithstanding the NRC's exclusive regulatory authority. The Committee rejected a suggestion that it adopt a federal tort to replace existing state remedies, noting that such displacement of state remedies would engender great opposition. If other provisions of the Atomic Energy Act already precluded the states from providing remedies to their citizens, there would have been no need for such concerns.

No doubt there is tension between the conclusion that safety regulation is the exclusive concern of federal law and the conclusion that a state may nevertheless award damages based on its own law. But Congress [apparently] intended to stand by both concepts and to tolerate whatever tension there was between them. It may be that the award of damages based on the state law of negligence or strict liability is regulatory in the sense that a nuclear plant will be threatened with damages if it does not conform to state standards, but that consequence was something that Congress was quite willing to accept.

Kerr-McGee also contends that the award is preempted because it frustrates Congress's express desire to encourage widespread participation in the development and utilization of atomic energy for peaceful purposes. However, the provision cited by Kerr-McGee goes on to state that atomic energy should be developed and utilized only to the extent that it is consistent "with the health and safety of the public." Congress therefore disclaimed any interest in promoting the development and utilization of atomic energy by means that fail to provide adequate remedies for those who are injured by exposure to hazardous nuclear materials. Thus, the award of punitive damages in this case does not hinder the accomplishment of the purpose stated in the Atomic Energy Act.

Court of appeals judgment with respect to punitive damages reversed in favor of Silkwood. Case returned to court of appeals for proceedings consistent with Supreme Court's opinion.

## SUMMARY

The U.S. Constitution restricts congressional power to regulate the economy in two ways: by limiting Congress to the exercise of certain *enumerated powers* and by placing certain *independent checks* in the path of Congress when it exercises these enumerated powers. The Constitution does not impose an "enumerated powers" doctrine on the state legislatures. In fact, the most important state regulatory power, the *police power,* is a broad ability to regulate for the public welfare that has few inherent limits. The Constitution does, however, impose many independent checks on the states.

The most important business-related federal regulatory powers are the powers of Congress to control interstate commerce, tax, and spend for the general welfare. By now, there are few inherent limits on the exercise of these powers. Today, the *commerce power* is an all-purpose federal police power with a great intrastate reach. By taxing behavior that it deems undesirable, Congress can use the *taxing power* as a regulatory tool. By conditioning the receipt of federal money on the performance of chosen conditions, it does the same with the *spending power.* Today, both powers seem to have few effective limits.

The Constitution recognizes the state and federal *eminent domain* powers by stating that takings of private property require *just compensation* and can be exercised only for a *public purpose.* Various forms of government regulation can constitute "takings" that will trigger these two requirements. Today, the "public purpose" test seems to be quite easy to meet.

The most important business-related independent constitutional checks applying to both the federal government and the states are the *due process, equal protection,* and *free speech* guarantees. For these independent checks to operate, there must be *government action.* After World War II, the range of activities considered to be government action expanded to include many forms of behavior that are ordinarily regarded as private. Recently, the Supreme Court has restricted government action's reach somewhat, but the area is still marked by great confusion.

Due process can be *procedural* (setting standards of fairness that the government must follow as it enforces its laws) or *substantive* (assessing the wisdom of laws governing individual and group relations in society). Today, however, substantive due process is of little or no consequence where government regulates economic activity.

The basic equal protection standard, and the test applied to government regulation of economic matters, is the lenient *rational basis* requirement. However, discrimination with respect to certain *fundamental rights* attracts a high level of *strict scrutiny,* as does discrimination on the basis of race or national origin. Governmental classifications based on gender, alienage, and illegitimacy receive some *intermediate* degree of scrutiny.

When the government regulates *commercial speech,* the regulation will be subjected to an intermediate level of review that is less rigorous than the very strict standards used in most First Amendment cases. Corporate *political* speech, however, now receives full First Amendment protection.

There are three important business-related independent checks that apply only to the states. The *Contract Clause* prevents the states from impairing the obligations of existing contracts by measures passed after these contracts have come into existence. Included within the Contract Clause's definition of the term *contracts* are *governmental* contracts and grants. In the 20th century, the Contract Clause gradually became subordinate to the states' police powers, and by the mid-20th century it was of little importance. In the late-1970s, however, the Contract Clause underwent a revival, but recent cases cast some doubt on the significance of this.

In addition to serving as a source of congressional power to regulate, the Commerce Clause places an implied check on state laws that unduly *burden interstate commerce.* To be constitutional, state laws that restrict interstate commerce must be rationally related to a legitimate state end and must be backed by purposes capable of overriding the federal interest in free interstate trade.

Finally, state measures that do not directly conflict with federal law may still be *preempted* by federal regulation. Determining when this occurs is basically a matter of statutory interpretation.

## PROBLEM CASES

**1.** The Kraynak brothers owned a small coal mine in Pennsylvania. They did all of the work in the mine themselves and sold all of the coal they produced, about 10,000 tons annually, to Penntech Papers Company. Penntech was located in Pennsylvania, but its products were distributed nationwide. The Kraynaks claimed that they were exempt from the provisions of the Federal Coal Mine Health and Safety Act because of the intrastate nature of their operation. Were they?

**2.** Under the Airport and Airway Development and Revenue Act of 1970, Congress empowered the FAA to make grants to airports for improvements, under terms set by project grant agreements between the FAA and the airport. The FAA made an offer of funds to Walker Field, a public division of the state of Colorado. The offer was conditioned on an agreement by the city of Grand Junction and Mesa County that they would join as cosponsors of the project along with Walker Field. Walker Field accepted the FAA's offer, but the city and county refused to join as cosponsors. As a result, the FAA refused to forward the grant money that it had promised under the agreement. Walker Field sued the secretary of transportation, alleging that the grant condition imposed by the FAA was unconstitutional. Was the grant condition within Congress's authority under the spending power?

**3.** In May 1973, the board of supervisors of Bensalem Township granted final approval for a 557-unit condominium project to be constructed by Mark-Garner. In June 1973, the township amended its zoning ordinance to require lower density in housing developments. In 1976, the ordinance was again amended, and the number of units per acre further reduced. From 1973 to 1976, Mark-Garner proceeded with the construction of its project in reliance on the May 1973 approval. But in

1976, the township informed the developer that, because of the revised ordinance, only 200 units could be built, and denied further permits. Did this constitute a taking of property requiring compensation to Mark-Garner?

**4.** Willie and Mary Craft sued the Memphis Light, Gas, and Water Division, a municipal utility that was a division of the city of Memphis, for failing to afford them due process before terminating their utility service. Was there state action in this case?

**5.** A federal statute, which is intended to encourage the private development of nuclear power by placing a limit on liability, provides that in the event of a nuclear accident involving federally licensed nuclear power plants, the total liability of all such plants shall not exceed $560 million. In case of an accident causing greater damage, the statute provides that Congress "will take whatever action is deemed necessary and appropriate" to protect the public. The Carolina Environmental Group challenged the statute on due process grounds, claiming that the $560 million limitation was arbitrary and not rationally related to the potential losses. Is the statute unconstitutional under the Due Process Clause?

**6.** A New York City traffic regulation generally forbade the placing of advertising signs on vehicles. The asserted purpose of this regulation was to promote public safety by preventing distractions to drivers and pedestrians. However, the regulation allowed advertising signs to be posted on certain business delivery vehicles advertising products sold by the owners of the vehicles. The Railway Express Agency, which operated about 1,900 trucks in New York City and sold the space on the outer sides of these trucks for advertising, challenged the regulation as a denial of equal protection. What standard of equal protection review applies here? Under this standard, is the Railway Express Agency's challenge likely to be successful?

**7.** Oklahoma statutes set the age for drinking 3.2 beer at 21 for men and 18 for women. The asserted purpose behind the statutes (and the sex-based classification that they established) was traffic safety. The statutes were challenged as a denial of equal protection by male residents of Oklahoma. What level of scrutiny would this measure receive if *women* had been denied the right to drink 3.2 beer until they were 21 but men had been allowed to consume it at age 18? Should this standard change because the measure discriminates against *men?* Is the male challenge to the statute likely to be successful?

**8.** Virginia had a statute prohibiting licensed pharmacists from advertising the price of prescription drugs. The apparent purpose behind the statute was to protect the public by preventing price competition in the sale of prescription drugs, thus ensuring that the need to meet a competitor's price would not force pharmacists to dispense with full professional services in the compounding, handling, and dispensing of prescription drugs. What type of First Amendment speech is restricted by this statute? Is this speech entitled to full First Amendment protection? Will the statute survive a First Amendment challenge?

**9.** The New England Power Company operated several hydroelectric plants on the Connecticut River in New Hampshire. These plants were part of the New England Power Pool, an organization of utilities combining to service much of New England through a common electric grid. Using a 1903 New Hampshire statute that had not previously been employed for this purpose, the New Hampshire Public Utilities Commission prohibited New England Power from selling electricity produced by its hydroelectric plants outside the state of New Hampshire. The reason for this order was basically to limit the electrical costs borne by New Hampshire residents, since New Hampshire's alternative sources of electricity were more expensive than New England Power's hydro plants. What argument would you make for the unconstitutionality of the New Hampshire commission's order?

**10.** The Federal Aviation Act of 1958 gave the FAA broad authority to regulate the use of airspace, and the Noise Control Act of 1972 obligated the FAA and the EPA to develop a comprehensive scheme for federal control of the aircraft noise problem. In the performance of its duties under the Federal Aviation Act, the FAA must balance aircraft safety, efficiency, and the safety of persons on the ground. Any scheme for regulation of aircraft noise would have to reflect these concerns.

The city of Burbank, California, passed an ordinance making it illegal for jet aircraft to take off from the Hollywood-Burbank Airport between 11 P.M. of one day and 7 A.M. of the next. No federal statutory or regulatory provision specifically forbade the city's ordinance, nor was there any statement in the language or legislative history of any relevant federal act preempting localities from regulating aircraft takeoffs. Based on these facts, what is the best argument for the conclusion that the Burbank ordinance should be preempted by federal law? Assume that if the Burbank ordinance were constitutional, other municipalities could also regulate aircraft takeoffs.

# Chapter 43 The Protection of Creative Endeavor and Competitive Torts

## INTRODUCTION

Throughout this text, we have stressed the law's tendency to limit economic freedom in order to protect against abuses of that freedom. This chapter's discussion of copyright, patent, trademark, and trade secrets law and of certain commercial torts is a variation on this theme. These areas of the law contain certain restrictions on economic freedom whose main object is to preserve the benefits that economic freedom can bring. One advantage of free competition is the stimulus that it gives to creative or inventive endeavor. But if competition is so free that individuals cannot protect the fruits of such endeavor, this advantage may be lost. Similarly, a legal system that fails to prevent individuals and businesses from attacking or appropriating their competitors' business reputation, contractual relations, prospective business advantages, and trade secrets may also reduce the incentives to create and innovate.

Finally, many of the rules discussed in this chapter promote values that have little to do with free competition and its benefits. By putting some limits on the pursuit of private advantage, these rules make commercial and economic life more humane and civilized than would otherwise be the case.

## PATENTS

**Introduction.** An inventor who holds a patent has an exclusive (but temporary) federally granted right to make, use, and sell his invention. The purpose behind this grant of monopoly power is to encourage the creation and disclosure of inventions. People generally have less incentive to create and to make their creations public if others can freely appropriate and exploit their work. The obtaining of a patent can be viewed as an agreement between the inventor and the federal government. Under the terms of this agreement, the inventor gets a temporary monopoly on his invention in return for making the invention public by submitting information to the government. Due to this arrangement, society benefits from: (1) the availability of the invention and its possible transfer from the inventor to third parties, (2) the public's freedom to exploit the invention once the monopoly period ends, and (3) the possibility that third parties may develop the invention in ways that do not infringe the rights of the patent holder (**patentee**).

**What Is Patentable?** Any of the following may be the subject matter of a patent: (1) a *process* (described in the *Diamond* case below), (2) a *machine,* (3) a *manufacture* (or product), (4) a *composition of matter* (a combination of elements possessing qualities not found in the elements taken individually; for example, a new chemical compound), (5) an *improvement* of any of the above, (6) an *ornamental design* for a product, and (7) a *plant* produced by asexual reproduction. Naturally occurring things (for example, a new wild plant) and business methods (for example, a new accounting technique) are *not* patentable. Also, as the *Diamond* case relates, abstract ideas, scientific laws, and other mental concepts are not patentable, although their practical applications often will be.

Even though an invention fits within one of the above categories, it will not be patentable if it lacks novelty, is obvious, or fails to possess utility. One example of the *novelty* requirement is the doctrine of *anticipation,* which states that no patent should be issued where *before its creation* the invention has been: (1) known or in use in the United States, (2) patented in the United States or a foreign country, or (3) described in a printed publication in the United States or a foreign country. Another is the requirement that no patent should issue if more than one year before the *patent application* the invention was: (1) patented in the United States or a foreign country, (2) described in a printed publication in the United States or a foreign country, or (3) in public use or on sale in the United States. In addition, there can be no patent if at the time of its occurrence the "invention" would have been *obvious* to a person having ordinary skill in the area. Finally, except for design patents, there is a general requirement that the invention possess *utility,* or usefulness, in order to be patentable.

Two more obstacles to patentability deserve brief mention. There can be no patent if the party seeking it did not create the invention in question or if she abandoned the invention. *Creation* problems frequently arise where several people allegedly contributed to the invention. *Abandonment* can be by express statement (for example, publicly devoting an invention to mankind) or by implication from conduct (for example, delaying for an unreasonable length of time before applying for a patent).

**Obtaining a Patent.** Patent applications are handled by the Patent and Trademark Office of the Department of Commerce. The application must include a *specification* describing the invention with sufficient detail and clarity to enable any person skilled in the area to make and use it. One of the office's patent examiners will check the application for detail and clarity of description. She will also employ the office's huge fund of technical data and prior patent information to determine whether the invention meets the various tests for patentability. If the examiner initially rejects the application, the applicant may amend it. After one or more such exchanges, the examiner may approve the issuance of a patent. If not, the applicant may appeal to the Patent and Trademark Office's Board of Appeals and, if this proves unsuccessful, to the federal courts.

**Ownership and Transfer of Patent Rights.** Except for design patents, one who obtains a patent gets the exclusive right to make, use, and sell the patented invention for a 17-year period. Design patents are effective for 14 years. The patentee can assign all or part of his patent rights, thus transferring title to the rights assigned. He may also retain title and license all or some of his rights.

Usually, the party who created the invention will also be the patent holder. What happens, however, when the creator of the invention is an employee and her employer seeks rights in her invention? If the invention was developed by an employee *hired to do inventive or creative work,* she must use the invention solely for the employer's benefit and she must assign any patents she obtains to the employer. Also, regardless of the purpose for which the employee was hired, the *shop right* doctrine gives the employer a nonexclusive, royalty-free *license* to use the employee's invention if it was created on company time and through company facilities. However, if the employee was hired for purposes *other than invention or creation,* she will remain the owner of any patent and will have patent rights that are effective against third parties other than the employer.

**Patent Infringement.** A *direct* **patent infringement** occurs when a third party makes, uses, or sells a patented invention without the patentee's authorization. It is fairly easy to establish a direct infringement where the subject matter made, used, or sold is clearly within the language of a patent application approved by the Patent and Trademark Office. But courts will also find direct infringement where the subject matter made, used, or sold is *substantially equivalent* to the protected subject matter. This "doctrine of equivalents" is discussed in the *Kori* case below. Of course, it is possible to escape liability for direct infringement by "designing around" the patented invention.

Also, one who *actively induced* another's infringement of a patent is liable for that infringement if he knew that it would occur and acted with the intent that it occur. For example, a party might sell a patent infringer an instruction manual for using a patented machine with a conscious desire that the buyer infringe the patent on the machine. Finally, one who knowingly sells a component of a patented invention or something useful in employing a patented process may be liable for *contributory infringement* if the thing sold is a material part of the invention and is not a staple article of commerce. For instance, the manufacturer of patented convertible tops for automobiles may be able to recover against one who manufactures and sells replacement fabric for the convertible tops to automobile owners.

**Defenses.** An obvious defense to a patent infringement suit is that the subject matter of the alleged infringement simply does not fall within the scope of the patent. Also, as the *Kori* case suggests, the alleged infringer may defend by attacking the validity of the patent. Many patents granted by the Patent and Trademark Office are declared invalid when challenged in court. Usually, this is due to their failure to meet the tests of patentability.

Another patent infringement defense, *equitable estoppel,* arises where the patentee falsely represents or knowingly conceals material facts and this causes justifiable and detrimental reliance by the alleged patent infringer. In such a case, the patentee will be "estopped" (prevented) from asserting infringement against the relying party. For example, the patent holder might assure competitors that their manufacture, sale, or use does not violate the patent, and this may cause them to make substantial expenditures in reliance. Another form of equitable estoppel (called *laches*) occurs when the patent owner waits for an unreasonable length of time before asserting his rights under the patent.

Finally, in certain cases the defendant may be able to assert that the patentee has been guilty of *patent misuse.* This is behavior unjustifiably exploiting the patent monopoly. For example, the patent owner may require the purchaser of a license on his patent to buy his unpatented goods, or may tie the obtaining of a license on one of his patented inventions to the purchase of a license on another.[1] In such cases, one who refuses to accept the patentee's terms and later is sued for infringing the patent may be able to defend by arguing that the patent holder misused his monopoly position.

**Remedies.** If successful in an infringement suit, the patentee gets "damages adequate to compensate for the infringement" plus court costs and interest. The damages must not be less than a reasonable royalty for the use made of the invention by the infringer. Also, the court may in its discretion award damages of up to three times those actually found to exist. In addition, one who applies a patented *design* to any product sold or exposed for sale is liable to the patentee for profits realized thereby. Finally, injunctive relief is available to prevent violation of any right secured by the patent, and attorney's fees may be awarded in exceptional cases.

[1] Some forms of patent misuse may be antitrust violations. Various aspects of the interaction between patent law and antitrust law are discussed in Chapters 44 and 45.

## Diamond v. Diehr

**450 U.S. 175 (U.S. Sup. Ct. 1981)**

Diehr and Lutton attempted to obtain a patent covering a process for molding raw, uncured synthetic rubber into cured precision products. The process used a mold for shaping the uncured rubber under heat and pressure and then curing it in the mold so that it would retain its shape after the molding was completed. Previous efforts at curing and molding synthetic rubber had suffered from an inability to measure the temperature inside the molding press, and thus to determine a precise curing time. Diehr and Lutton's invention involved a process for constantly measuring the temperature inside the mold, feeding this information to a computer that constantly recalculated the curing time, and enabling the computer to signal the molding press to open at the correct instant.

The patent examiner rejected Diehr and Lutton's patent application because the portions of their process carried out by the computer involved an unpatentable computer program and the other portions of the process were conventional in nature. The Patent and Trademark Office Board of Appeals agreed with the examiner, but the Court of Customs and Patent Appeals reversed. The government (through Diamond as patent and trademark commissioner) appealed to the U.S. Supreme Court.

**Rehnquist, Justice.** A process has historically enjoyed patent protection. In defining the nature of a patentable process, this Court has stated:

> A process is a mode of treatment of certain materials to produce a given result. It is an act, or a series of acts, performed upon the subject matter to be transformed and reduced to a different state or thing. If new and useful, it is just as patentable as is a piece of machinery. The machinery pointed out as suitable to perform the process may or may not be new or patentable; whilst the process itself may be altogether new and produce an entirely new result. The process requires that certain things should be done with certain substances, and in a certain order; but the tools to be used in doing this may be of secondary consequence.

Recently, we repeated the above definition, adding: "Transformation and reduction of an article to a different state or thing is the clue to the patentability of a process claim that does not include particular machines." That Diehr and Lutton's claims involve the transformation of an article, raw uncured synthetic rubber, into a different state or thing cannot be disputed. Industrial processes such as this have historically been eligible to receive the protection of our patent laws.

Our conclusion is not altered by the fact that in several steps of the process a mathematical equation and a programmed digital computer are used. This Court has recognized limits to patentability and every discovery is not embraced within the statutory terms. Excluded from patent protection are laws of nature, physical phenomena and abstract ideas. Only last Term, we explained:

> A new mineral discovered in the earth or a new plant found in the wild is not patentable subject matter. Likewise, Einstein could not patent his celebrated law that $E=mc^2$; nor could Newton have patented the law of gravity. Such discoveries are "manifestations of . . . nature, free to all men and reserved exclusively to none."

Diehr and Lutton do not seek to patent a mathematical formula. Instead, they seek patent protection for a process of curing synthetic rubber. Their process employs a well-known mathematical equation, but they do not seek to preempt the use of that equation. They seek only to foreclose from others the use of that equation in conjunction with all the other steps in their process. Obviously, one does not need a computer to cure rubber, but if the computer use incorporated in the process patent significantly lessens the possibility of "overcuring" or "undercuring," the process as a whole does not thereby become unpatentable.

It is now a commonplace that an *application* of a law of nature or mathematical formula to a known structure or process may be deserving of patent protection. As Mr. Justice Stone explained four decades ago: "While a scientific truth, or the mathematical expression of it, is not a patentable invention, a novel and useful structure created with the aid of knowledge of scientific truth may be."

It may later be determined that the process is not deserving of patent protection because it fails to satisfy the statutory conditions of novelty or nonobviousness. A rejection on either of these grounds does not affect the determination that Diehr and Lutton's claims recited subject matter which was eligible for patent protection.

Judgment for Diehr and Lutton affirmed.

## Kori Corp. v. Wilco Marsh Buggies and Draglines, Inc.

**708 F.2d 151 (5th Cir. 1983)**

The discovery of oil beneath the marshes and swamps of the Gulf South called for a form of transportation capable of covering both wide-open treeless marshes and swamps laden with obstructions and tree stumps. Prior to 1974, the principal craft used for these purposes was an amphibian patented by Frank Reynolds in 1947. The Reynolds amphibian, however, could not carry heavy loads without frequent mishaps, and had difficulty in negotiating tree-filled swamps. In 1974, Huey J. Rivet patented an "Amphibious Marsh Craft" for hauling loads and laying pipeline in swamps. Rivet's craft could "walk" over stumps for extended periods while carrying heavy loads. The advantages of Rivet's model derived principally from: (1) placing plastic support blocks on the cleats to prevent pontoon puncturing, (2) spacing I-beams on pontoon bottoms for support, and (3) creating separate buoyant chambers by placing vertical bulkheads within the pontoons. Each of these techniques or devices had long been used in various applications, although they seemingly had never been employed together.

Robert J. Wilson worked for Rivet in 1974 as a contract welder, receiving detailed information on the design of Rivet's pontoon in the process. After finishing his work with Rivet, Wilson began building similar pontoons for Wilco Marsh Buggies and Draglines, Inc., a corporation formed and owned by his three sons. Later, Wilco bought a Rivet craft and one of the sons ordered copies of the Rivet patent. Then, Wilco began the production and sale of a marsh craft strikingly similar to the Rivet vehicle, especially to the model manufactured by the Kori Corporation, a licensee of Rivet.

Rivet, Kori, and another licensee sued Wilco and the Wilson brothers for patent infringement. A federal district court held that the patent was valid and that it had been infringed. Wilco and the Wilsons appealed.

**POLITZ, CIRCUIT JUDGE.** Wilco contends that the Rivet patent is invalid because: (1) it was anticipated in the prior art, and/or (2) its claims were obvious to one having ordinary skill in the relevant art. The Rivet patent, like all patents properly issued, is entitled to a presumption of validity. Wilco bears the burden of showing the invalidity of a patent regular on its face.

To be patentable, an invention must be novel. The defense of anticipation requires a showing of actual identity in the prior art. Indeed, unless all of the same elements or their equivalents are found in substantially the same situation where they do substantially the same work in the same way, there is no anticipation.

The District Court found that Wilco failed to establish the existence of any prior art which disclosed all or substantially all of the elements claimed under the Rivet patent. Although Wilco argues that prior public use involved vertical bulkheads, spaced I-beams, and support blocks, there is no suggestion that all three elements were found together in any previous unit. Further, many of the prior uses Wilco urges are in fact found in somewhat similar but distinct situations, such as airplane pontoons. While such uses offer a glimpse of what may have been apparent in the art, they do not provide a sufficient basis upon which to negate novelty.

Wilco also claims that the Rivet patent is invalid for obviousness. This defense prescribes that no valid patent will issue if the differences between the invention sought to be patented and the prior art are such that the invention "as a whole would have been obvious at the time the invention was made to a person having ordinary skill in the art to which said subject matter pertains."

Wilco again invites our attention to prior art devices which relate to elements of the Rivet invention. But "the linchpin is not whether the individual components of the patent were obvious at the time of the invention, but whether the aggregation produced a new or different result or achieved a synergistic effect." In judging obviousness, we thus look to the aggregate effect. The inquiry is nothing more than an instance of gestalt analysis: Is the whole greater than the sum of its parts?

Even though many elements in the Rivet patent can be separately found in the prior art, the combination is striking. No previous craft was capable of traveling safely for extended periods through stump-filled swamps. None could carry the heavy loads demanded by oil-related exploration and construction. The Rivet model made a quantum leap in transportation through the swamp. Other machines may have used two of the three modifications Rivet made, but two-out-of-three did not create a new buggy capable of matching the performance of the Rivet craft.

The final issue is whether Wilco's marsh buggy infringes the Rivet patent. Wilco suggests a number of modifications which, it is claimed, distinguish Wilco's product from Rivet's patent. These alterations may suffice to prevent literal infringement of some of the claims of the Rivet patent, but the doctrine of equivalents gives a patentee broad protection from minor deviations. Suffice it to say that a comparison of the two craft reveals substantial identity of means, operation, and result. The differences are cosmetic and trivial. The essence of both vehicles is the same: each relies on the Rivet improvements.

Judgment for Rivet, Kori, and the other licensee affirmed.

## COPYRIGHT

**Introduction.** Copyright law gives creative individuals certain exclusive rights regarding their intellectual endeavors, and thus enables them to prevent various uses of their work by others. These restrictive privileges benefit society by giving such individuals an incentive toward innovative activity. But copyright law also attempts to balance this purpose against the equally compelling public interest in the free movement of ideas, information, and commerce. Most copyrights and copyright issues are now governed by the federal Copyright Reform Act of 1976, which usually preempts state copyright law.

**Coverage.** The Copyright Reform Act covers a wide range of creative works, including books, periodicals, dramatic and musical compositions, works of art, motion pictures, sound recordings, lectures, and computer programs. In order to merit copyright protection, such works must be *fixed:* set out in any tangible medium of expression from which they can be perceived, reproduced, or communicated. They must also be *original* (the author's own work) and *creative* (a product of skill or judgment). Copyright protection does *not* extend to ideas, concepts, principles, discoveries, procedures, processes, systems, and methods of operation as such. However, it may protect the *form in which they are expressed.* Here, the line between protected and unprotected material is indistinct. The story line of a copyrighted play, for instance, is probably protected, but a very abstract statement of its theme probably is not. Finally, as the *ABC* case below states, there can be no copyright in facts as such.

**Formalities.** A copyright comes into existence upon the creation and fixing of a copyrightable work. For works created in 1978 and thereafter, it usually lasts for *the life of the author plus 50 years.* The copyright exists even though it is not registered with the Copyright Office of the Library of Congress. Registration, however, is often necessary before the owner of the copyright can begin a suit for copyright infringement (which is discussed below). The copyright may be invalidated if the owner fails to provide *notice* of the copyright once the work is published. Federal law authorizes various forms of notice for different kinds of copyrighted works. A book, for example, might include the term *Copyright,* the year of its first publication, and the name of the copyright owner in a location likely to give reasonable notice to readers. In addition to the possibility of losing copyright protection, an owner who fails to give notice may have difficulty mounting an infringement suit against a party who claims that her infringement was innocent because she relied on a copy of the work from which notice was absent.

**Ownership Rights.** Ownership of a copyright initially resides in the creator of the copyrighted work, but it may be transferred to another party. The owner has the exclusive rights to: (1) reproduce the copyrighted work, (2) prepare derivative works based on it (for example, a condensation or movie version of a novel), (3) distribute copies of the work by sale or otherwise, (4) perform the work publicly, and (5) display the work publicly. Each of these rights, or a portion of each, may be transferred individually without affecting ownership of the remaining rights. A transfer of copyright ownership usually requires a writing signed by the owner or his agent. The owner may also retain ownership while licensing the copyrighted work or a portion of it.

**Infringement.** Anyone violating any of the owner's exclusive rights may be liable for **copyright infringement.** Where the infringer makes, uses, or distributes a literal copy of the work, he will be liable unless a defense exists. Where the alleged infringement does not involve a literal copy of the work, the owner must show that the defendant had *access* to the copyrighted work and that there is *substantial similarity* between that work and the allegedly infringing work. Access can be proven circumstantially—for example, by wide circulation of the copyrighted work. Determining "substantial similarity" necessarily involves discretionary case-by-case judgments.

**Fair Use.** The main defense to a copyright infringement suit is the doctrine of **fair use.** This defense involves the weighing of several factors whose application will vary from case to case. These factors are: (1) the purpose and character of the use, (2) the nature of the copyrighted work, (3) the amount and substantiality of the portion used in relation to the copyrighted work as a whole, and (4) the effect of the use on the potential market for the copyrighted work or on its value. The use is more likely to be deemed "fair" where its purpose is educational or its effect is to promote knowledge than where neither is true and the infringer benefits commercially from the use. The chances for a successful fair use defense also rise when the copyrighted work and the allegedly infringing work are not in economic competition with each other. The *ABC* case elaborates on the fair use defense.

**Remedies.** The basic remedy available in a successful copyright infringement suit is an award of the owner's actual damages plus the profits received by the infringer. However, the plaintiff may elect to receive statutory damages not exceeding $50,000 in lieu of the basic remedy. Injunctive relief and awards of costs and attorney's fees are possible in certain cases. There are also criminal penalties for willful infringements involving the pursuit of commercial advantage.

## Iowa State University Research Foundation v. American Broadcasting Co.

**621 F.2d 57 (7th Cir. 1980)**

During the 1970–71 college term, James Doran and another Iowa State University student produced a 28-minute film entitled *Champion.* The film presented a short biography of a fellow student, Dan Gable, a wrestler who eventually won a gold medal at the 1972 Olympics. The film was financed jointly by the Iowa State University Research Foundation (Iowa State) and the Gable family. Iowa State obtained a valid statutory copyright to *Champion* and retained all rights to it. However, it did grant Doran the right to license the first television showing of the film, but only with the full knowledge and consent of the university. Prior to the summer of 1972, Doran attempted to sell the television rights to various networks, but met with no success.

In August 1972, Doran was employed by the American Broadcasting Company (ABC) as a temporary videotape operator in connection with its telecast of the 1972 Olympics. Toward the end of the month, with the Olympics fast approaching, Doran overheard some ABC producers discussing a filmed biography of Gable for the Olympic telecast. When Doran heard one of the producers complain that ABC's film crews had not provided enough film footage of Gable's biographical background, he informed the producer of the existence of *Champion.* At the producer's request, Doran gave him a copy of the film. ABC eventually televised its own videotape of portions of *Champion.* This was apparently done without the university's knowledge or consent.

Later, Iowa State sued ABC for infringement of its copyright to *Champion.* The district court held in favor of Iowa State, and ABC appealed.

**Kaufman, Circuit Judge.** Although ABC admitted virtually all allegations of copying, it raised the defense of fair use. The doctrine of fair use permits courts to avoid rigid application of the copyright statute when it would stifle the very creativity which that law is designed to foster. Resolution of a fair use claim depends on an examination of the facts in each case and cannot be determined by any arbitrary rules or fixed criteria. Four factors have traditionally been consulted in fair use cases: (1) the purpose and character of the use, (2) the nature of the copyrighted work, (3) the amount and substantiality of the material used in relation to the copyrighted work as a whole, and (4) the effect of the use on the copyright holder's potential market for the work. Resort to these factors in the case before us demonstrates that ABC's fair use defense must fail.

The network relies most heavily on the first factor—the purpose and character of its use. It claims that it was engaged in the laudable pursuit of disseminating the life history of an important public figure involved in an event of intense public interest. Thus, ABC asserts that the public benefit in the development of historical and biographical works suitable for mass distribution should impel us to the conclusion that it be free to use

*Champion* for this purpose. This argument proves too much. ABC possessed an unfettered right to use any factual information revealed in *Champion* for enlightening its audience, but it can claim no need to bodily appropriate Iowa State's expression of that information by utilizing portions of the actual film. The public interest in the free flow of information is assured by the law's refusal to recognize a valid copyright in facts. The fair use doctrine is not a license for corporate theft, empowering a court to ignore a copyright whenever the underlying work contains material of possible public importance. Indeed, we do not suppose that ABC would embrace its own defense theory if another litigant sought to apply it to the ABC evening news. Moreover, ABC's use of *Champion* was not motivated solely by its beneficence. While the fact that ABC sought to profit financially from its telecasts of the Olympics does not, standing alone, deprive ABC of the fair use defense, it is relevant that the film was used, at least in part, for commercial exploitation.

ABC also urges that the nature of the copyrighted work was essentially different from the network's Olympic broadcasts, characterizing *Champion* as an "educational" film with no significant television market. Nevertheless, the award of television rights to Doran suggests that Iowa State contemplated television exposure from the outset. Indeed, ABC's short vignettes on the lives of athletes in its 1972 Olympic coverage are essentially of the same genre as *Champion.*

In discussing the third fair use factor, ABC stresses that it used only 2½ minutes of a 28-minute film, suggesting that such limited copying is insignificant. But ABC actually broadcast approximately 8 percent of *Champion,* some of it on three separate occasions.

Finally, ABC asserts that there was no significant adverse effect on the market for *Champion* as a result of its broadcasts of the film. Nevertheless, ABC did foreclose a significant potential market to Iowa State—sale of its film for use on television in connection with the Olympics. In fact, because of its exclusive right to televise the games, ABC monopolized that market. When ABC telecast *Champion* without purchasing the film, it usurped an extremely significant market.

Judgment for Iowa State affirmed.

## TRADEMARKS.

**Introduction.** The main reason why trademark owners enjoy legal protection against users of their marks is to help purchasers identify favored products. This end would be defeated by a system of unrestricted competition that allowed anyone to use another's trademark at any time he desired. Such a system would also reduce the incentive for manufacturers to innovate and to strive for maximum product quality, since superior products are less likely to be purchased if consumers have difficulty in identifying their source.

**Protected Marks.** The Lanham Act,[2] which establishes federal protection for certain **marks,** defines a mark as any word, name, symbol, or device or any combination of these. In certain limited situations, however, federal trademark protection has been extended to cover colors, pictures, label and package designs, slogans, sounds, arrangements of numbers and/or letters (for example, 7-Eleven), and shapes of goods or their containers (for

[2] In addition, the owner of a trademark may enjoy legal protection under common law trademark doctrines, state trademark statutes, and the "palming off" rules discussed at the end of this chapter.

example, Coca-Cola bottles). The Lanham Act distinguishes four kinds of marks. **Trademarks** are used to identify and distinguish goods. **Service marks**—for example, Sanitone dry cleaning—are used to identify and distinguish services. **Certification marks** certify the quality, materials, or other aspects of goods and services, and are used by someone other than the owner of the mark. The Good Housekeeping Seal of Approval is an example. **Collective marks** are trademarks or service marks used by members of groups or organizations to identify themselves as the source of goods or services. Trade union and trade association marks fall into this category. Although all of these different marks receive federal protection, the discussion in this text mainly involves trademarks and service marks, using the terms *mark* or *trademark* to refer to both.

To merit Lanham Act protection, marks must be *distinctive.* Thus, as the *Toys* case below makes clear, *suggestive* or *fanciful* marks are protectible, while marks that are merely *generic* or *descriptive* usually receive no protection. However, descriptive marks will merit protection once they acquire a *secondary meaning.* This occurs when their identification with particular goods or services has become firmly established in the minds of a substantial number of buyers. Among the factors considered in "secondary meaning" determinations are the length of time that the mark has been used, the volume of sales associated with that use, and the nature of the advertising employing the mark. When applied to a package delivery service, for instance, the term *overnight* is usually just descriptive. But it may come to deserve protection as a trademark through long use by a single firm that has advertised it extensively and made many sales while doing so.

Regardless of their distinctiveness, however, some types of marks are specifically denied federal protection. Examples include marks that: (1) consist of the flags or other insignia of governments; (2) consist of the name, portrait, or signature of a living person; (3) are immoral, deceptive, or scandalous; or (4) are likely to cause confusion or deceive because they resemble a mark previously registered or used in the United States.

**Federal Registration.** The registration of trademarks is handled by the U.S. Patent and Trademark Office, which employs numerous trademark examiners to review applications for compliance with the above requirements. The examiner's decision to deny or grant the application can usually be contested either by the applicant or by a party who feels that he would be injured by registration of the mark. Such challenges may eventually find their way to the federal courts.

Once issued, a registered trademark may appear on the *Principal Register* or the *Supplemental Register* of the Patent and Trademark Office. The mark's inclusion in the Principal Register gives its owner several advantages. For example, placement on this register: (1) gives nationwide constructive notice of the owner's right to use the mark (thus eliminating the need to show that the defendant in an infringement suit had notice of the mark), (2) triggers Bureau of Customs protection against use of the mark by importers, and (3) makes the mark incontestable after five years (as described below). Certain otherwise valid marks may not be placed on the Principal Register. Examples include marks that: (1) are *deceptively misdescriptive* (for example, "Dura-Skin" plastic gloves), (2) are *geographically descriptive* (for example, "Nationwide" Life Insurance), or (3) are primarily a *surname* (because everyone should have the right to use his own name in connection with his business). However, such marks may be placed on the Principal Register if they have acquired a secondary meaning.

**Transfer of Rights.** Because of the purposes underlying trademark law, the transfer of trademark rights is more difficult than the transfer of copyright or patent interests. The owner of a trademark may license the use of the mark, but only if he controls the nature and quality of the goods or services that the licensee uses in connection with the mark. An uncontrolled "naked license" would allow the marketing of goods or services bearing the mark but lacking the qualities formerly associated with it, thus creating potential confusion for purchasers. Trademark rights may also be assigned or sold, but only along with the sale of the goodwill of the business originally using the mark.

**Losing Federal Trademark Protection.** Federal registration of a trademark lasts for 20 years, with the possibility of renewals for additional 20-year periods. However, trademark protection may be lost before the period expires. First, a third party may undertake a successful *cancellation proceeding* before the Patent and Trademark Office. If the mark is on the Principal Register, the proceeding must occur within five years of its issuance or the mark becomes *incontestable.* This means that a challenger's permissible reasons for attacking the mark become quite limited. However, there is no such time limitation for a mark that has been placed on the Supplemental Register. Second, trademark protection may also be lost if the Patent and Trademark Office cancels the registration as part of its "cleaning out" procedures. This will occur if the owner has failed to file an affidavit stating that the mark is in use (or justifying its nonuse) within six years of registration.

A third way in which the owner may lose trademark protection is by *abandonment.* This can occur through an express statement or agreement to abandon or through a failure to use the mark. Nonuse of the mark for two consecutive years creates a presumption of abandonment. Fourth, the owner may lose protection if the trademark acquires a *generic meaning* by coming to refer to a class of products or services rather than a particular product or service. This has happened to once-protected marks such as "aspirin" and "cellophane." In recent years, the manufacturer of Xerox copiers has sought to avoid a similar result by taking out national advertisements trying to induce people not to use the term *xerox* as a verb or as a synonym for copiers in general. Finally, *improperly licensing or assigning* trademark rights in the ways described above may also result in their loss.

**Trademark Infringement.** A trademark is infringed when, without the owner's consent, another party uses a substantially similar mark in connection with the advertisement or sale of goods or services, and this is likely to cause confusion, mistake, or deception regarding their origin. The *Toys* case discusses a number of the many factors that courts must sift and weigh when determining whether the use is likely to cause confusion, mistake, or deception.

**Remedies.** A trademark owner who wins an infringement suit can obtain an injunction against uses of the mark that are likely to cause confusion. In certain circumstances, the owner can also obtain money damages for provable injury resulting from the infringement and for profits realized by the defendant from the sale of infringing products or services.

## Toys "R" Us, Inc. v. Canarsie Kiddie Shop, Inc.

**559 F. Supp. 1189 (E.D.N.Y. 1983)**

Since 1960, Toys "R" Us, Inc. (Toys) had been engaged in the sale of children's clothing throughout the United States. It opened its first Brooklyn, New York store in 1975, and another in 1982. By 1977, it had at least seven stores in the New York City area. It also planned additional stores in that area. Since 1961, Toys had owned a registered trademark and a registered service mark, both in the name Toys "R" Us. It always aggressively marketed and advertised its products.

In 1977, Abe Pomeranc opened a children's clothing store in Brooklyn. He opened a second store in Brooklyn's Canarsie section in 1978, and eventually consolidated his whole business in that store. Pomeranc's stores were located within a 2-mile radius of one of Toys' stores. He was also considering opening a store about three blocks away from another of Toys' stores. Pomeranc's two stores did business under the name Kids 'r' Us. Pomeranc never registered this name as a trademark or service mark. Toys sued Pomeranc and his store in federal district court for trademark infringement.

**Glasser, District Judge.** Toys must establish that the defendant's use of the name Kids 'r' Us creates a likelihood of confusion. The pivotal inquiry is whether there is any likelihood that an appreciable number of ordinarily prudent purchasers are likely to be misled, or simply confused, as to the source of the goods in question. In assessing the likelihood of confusion, this court must consider:

1. *The Strength of the Senior User's Mark.* The term "strength" refers to the distinctiveness of the mark, or its tendency to identify goods as emanating from a particular source. A mark can fall into one of four general categories which, in order of ascending strength, are: (1) generic, (2) descriptive, (3) suggestive, and (4) arbitrary or fanciful. The strength of a mark is generally dependent both on its place upon the scale and on whether it has acquired secondary meaning.

A generic term refers to the genus of which the particular product is a species. A generic term is entitled to no trademark protection whatsoever, since any manufacturer or seller has the right to call a product by its name. A descriptive mark identifies a significant characteristic of the product, but is not the common name of the product. A mark is descriptive if it informs the purchasing public of the characteristics, quality, functions, uses, ingredients, components, or other properties of a product, or conveys comparable information about a service (for example, "exquisite" for wearing apparel). To achieve trademark protection, a descriptive term must have attained secondary meaning, that is, it must have become distinctive of the applicant's goods in commerce. A suggestive mark is one that requires imagination, thought, and perception to reach a conclusion as to the nature of the goods. These marks fall short of directly describing the qualities or functions of a particular product or service, but merely suggest such qualities (for example, "Dietene" for a dietary food supplement). If a term is suggestive, it is entitled to protection without proof of secondary meaning. Arbitrary or fanciful marks require no extended definition. They are marks which in no way describe or suggest the qualities of the product (for example, "Exxon").

The Toys "R" Us mark serves to describe the business of the plaintiff, and in this sense is merely descriptive. This descriptive quality, however, does require some imagination, thought, and perception on the part of the consumer, since Toys' mark, read quite literally, conveys the message "we are toys," rather than "we sell toys." Whether the leap of imagination required here is sufficient to render the mark suggestive rather than descriptive is a question with no clear-cut answer. Such an absolute categorization is not essential, however, since the defendants concede that through Toys' marketing and advertising efforts the Toys "R" Us mark has acquired secondary meaning in the minds of the public, at least in relation to its sale of toys. Such secondary meaning assures that the plaintiff's mark is entitled to protection even if it is merely descriptive.

2. *Degree of Similarity between the Two Marks.* Here, the key inquiry is not similarity per se, but rather whether a similarity exists which is likely to cause confusion. It must be determined whether the *impression* the infringing mark makes upon the consumer is such that he is likely to believe that the product is from the same source as the one he knows under the trademark.

Turning to the two marks, various similarities and differences are apparent. The patent similarity between the marks is that they both employ the phrase "R Us." Further, both employ the letter "R" in place of the word "are." The most glaring difference between the marks is that in one the phrase "R Us" is preceded by the word "Toys," while in the other it is preceded by the word "Kids." I find that, while the marks are clearly distinguishable when placed side by side, there are sufficiently strong similarities to create the possibility that some consumers might believe that the two marks emanated from the same source.

3. *Proximity of the Products.* Where the products in question are competitive, the likelihood of consumer confusion increases. Both plaintiff and defendant sell children's clothing, although clothing is not currently the major business of Toys. I do not find that any significant quality difference exists. Consequently, I find that the plaintiff and defendants currently are direct product competitors.

4. *The Likelihood that Plaintiff Will "Bridge the Gap."* "Bridging the gap" refers to two distinct possibilities: first, that the senior user presently intends to expand his sales efforts to compete directly with the junior user; second, that, while there is no present intention to bridge the gap, consumers will conclude that the parties are related companies. I find both possibilities present here. Plaintiff and defendants already are direct competitors. Toys has current plans to expand its sale of children's clothing and further bridge any gap that might still exist. Consumers seeing the Kids 'r' Us store and mark might assume that the defendants are in some manner an extension of Toys' business.

5. *Evidence of Actual Confusion.* Evidence of actual confusion is a strong indication that there is a likelihood of confusion. In the instant case, however, I find no evidence of actual confusion.

6. *Junior User's Good Faith.* The state of mind of the junior user is an important factor in striking the balance of the equities. Mr. Pomeranc asserted that he did not recall whether he was aware of Toys' mark when he chose to name his store in 1977. I do not find this testimony credible. In view of the proximity of the stores, the overlapping of their products, and the strong advertising and marketing effort conducted by Toys, it is difficult to believe that the defendants were unaware of the plaintiff's use of the Toys "R" Us mark.

7. *Quality of the Junior User's Product.* If the junior user's product is of low quality, the senior user's interest in avoiding any confusion is heightened. In the instant case, there is no suggestion that the defendants' products are inferior.

8. *Sophistication of the Purchasers.* Every product, because of the type of buyer that

it attracts, has its own threshold for confusion of the source of origin. The goods sold by plaintiff and defendants are moderately priced clothing articles, which are not major expenditures for most purchasers. Consumers of such goods do not exercise the same degree of care as when purchasing more expensive items. Further, it may be that consumers purchasing from the plaintiff and defendants are influenced by the desires of their children.

9. *Junior User's Goodwill.* A powerful equitable argument against finding infringement is created when the junior user develops goodwill in the mark. Here, the defendants have failed to demonstrate a significant development of goodwill in their mark. Defendants have not expended large sums advertising their store or promoting its name. Further, it appears that most of the defendants' customers are local "repeat shoppers." The defendants do not have a strong equitable interest in retaining the Kids 'r' Us mark.

*Conclusion on Likelihood of Confusion.* The determination whether a likelihood of confusion has been established here is difficult, for there are factors cutting both ways. However, I find that the defendants' use of the Kids 'r' Us mark does create a likelihood of confusion for an appreciable number of consumers.

The district court found Pomeranc and Kids 'r' Us liable for trademark infringement. It issued an injunction barring them from using the name Kids 'r' Us or any other imitation of Toys' mark and from doing any other act likely to induce the belief that their business was connected with Toys' business.

## TRADE SECRETS

By providing a civil remedy for the misappropriation of trade secrets, the law affords an alternative means for protecting creative inventions or other valuable information. The owner of such an invention or such information may "go public" and obtain monopoly patent rights. Or he may keep these matters secret and rely on trade secrets law to protect them. In either case, the law tries to stimulate innovation by giving inventive parties some assurance that their ideas will not be exploited by others. In doing so, the law again attempts to preserve the benefits of free competition by putting some limits on that competition.

**Definition of a Trade Secret.** A trade secret is any formula, process, device, or compilation of information used in business that gives its owner an advantage over competitors who are unaware of it or do not use it. Chemical formulas, techniques for making particular products, machines used in manufacturing, and customer lists, for example, can all be trade secrets. To be protectible, a trade secret must have some degree of originality, although it need not possess the novelty required for patentability.

Also, as its name suggests, a trade secret must be *secret.* Absolute secrecy is not required, but a substantial measure of secrecy must be present. Thus, a firm claiming a trade secret must usually show that only a few people were allowed access to it, that these people were required to sign a nondisclosure agreement, or that the secret was disclosed to people only on a confidential basis. Information that becomes public knowledge or becomes generally available in the trade cannot constitute a trade secret. Secrecy can be lost through independent discovery of the secret, the owner's advertising, the owner's acquisition of a patent on the secret, or product analysis by a third party.

**Improper Means.** To be liable for misappropriating a trade secret, the defendant must have obtained it by *improper means.* As the *Du Pont* case below suggests, there is little difficulty in meeting this requirement where the secret was obtained through theft, trespass, wiretapping, spying, bugging, bribery, or industrial espionage generally. There can also be liability if the secret was obtained through the breach of a confidential relationship. Where an employer is the owner of a trade secret, for example, an employee is generally bound not to use or disclose it either during his employment or thereafter.[3]

**Ownership and Transfer of Trade Secrets.** The owner's rights to a trade secret can be transferred by assignment (in which case the owner loses title) or by license (in which case the owner retains title). However, establishing the original ownership of a trade secret is sometimes a problem where an employee has developed a secret in the course of her employment. Courts will often hold the employer to be the owner where the employee was hired to do creative work related to the secret, the employee agreed not to divulge or use trade secrets, or other employees contributed to the development of the secret. Even where the employee becomes the owner of the secret, the employer may still obtain a royalty-free license to use the secret through the "shop right" doctrine discussed in the section on patents.

**Remedies.** A plaintiff who is successful in a suit for misappropriation of a trade secret may obtain damages and (where these are inadequate) injunctive relief. The courts have often disagreed regarding the measure of damages in trade secrets cases.

[3] This is a specific application of the agent's duty of loyalty, discussed in Chapter 16.

## E.I. du Pont de Nemours & Co. v. Christopher

**431 F.2d 1012 (5th Cir. 1970)**

Rolfe and Gary Christopher, two photographers, were hired by persons unknown to take aerial photographs of new construction at a plant that Du Pont was building. Du Pont claimed that the plant was being built to exploit a highly secret unpatented process for producing methanol, a process that gave Du Pont a competitive advantage over other producers. Du Pont sued the Christophers in federal district court for misappropriation of trade secrets. The Christophers' motion to dismiss and motion for summary judgment were denied. They obtained immediate appellate review of the district court's finding that Du Pont had stated a claim upon which relief could be granted.

**Goldberg, Circuit Judge.** The Christophers argue that they committed no actionable wrong because they conducted all of their activities in public airspace, violated no government aviation standard, did not breach any confidential relation, and did not engage in any fraudulent or illegal conduct. In short, the Christophers argue that for an appropriation of trade secrets to be wrongful there must be a trespass, other illegal conduct, or breach of a confidential relationship. We disagree.

We do not think that the Texas courts would limit the trade secret protection exclusively to these elements. On the contrary, the Texas Supreme Court has specifically adopted the rule found in section 757 of the *Restatement of Torts* (1939), which provides:

> One who discloses or uses another's trade secret, without a privilege to do so, is liable to the other if: (a) he discovered the secret by improper means, or (b) his disclosure or use constitutes a breach of confidence reposed in him by the other in disclosing the secret to him.

Thus, not limiting itself to specific wrongs, Texas adopted subsection (a) of the *Restatement,* which recognizes a cause of action for the discovery of a trade secret by any "improper" means.

Therefore, one may use his competitor's secret process if he discovers the process by reverse engineering applied to the finished product or if he discovers it by his own independent research; but one may not avoid these labors by taking the process without permission when [the owner] is taking reasonable precautions to maintain its secrecy.

We realize that industrial espionage of the sort here perpetrated has become a popular sport in some segments of our industrial community. However, our devotion to freewheeling industrial competition must not force us into accepting the law of the jungle as the standard of morality expected in our commercial relations. Our tolerance of the espionage game must cease when the protections required to prevent another's spying cost so much that the spirit of inventiveness is dampened. Commercial privacy must be protected from espionage which could not have been reasonably anticipated or prevented. We do not mean to imply, however, that everything not in plain view is within the protected vale, nor that all information obtained through every extra optical extension is forbidden. Indeed, for our industrial competition to remain healthy there must be breathing room for observing a competing industrialist. A competitor can and must shop his competition for pricing and examine their products for quality, components, and methods of manufacture.

Du Pont was in the midst of constructing a plant. During the period of construction, the trade secret was exposed to view from the air. To require Du Pont to put a roof over the unfinished plant to guard its secret would impose an enormous expense to prevent nothing more than a schoolboy's trick. We introduce here no new or radical ethic, since our ethos has never given moral sanction to piracy. The marketplace must not deviate far from our mores. "Improper" will always be a word of many nuances, determined by time, place, and circumstances. We therefore need not proclaim a catalogue of commercial improprieties. Clearly, however, one of its commandments does say: "Thou shall not appropriate a trade secret through deviousness under circumstances in which countervailing defenses are not reasonably available."

Judgment for Du Pont affirmed. Case returned to district court for proceedings on the merits.

## COMMERCIAL TORTS

In addition to the intentional torts discussed in Chapter 4, there are certain intentional torts that apply mainly to business or commercial activities, especially the activities of competitors. These torts illustrate once more the general theme of this chapter: that in order to preserve the benefits of economic freedom and maintain a modicum of commercial decency, restraints on economic freedom are often required.

**Injurious Falsehood.** **Injurious falsehood** involves the publication of false statements that disparage another's business, property, or title to property and thus harm another's economic interests. The two most common kinds of injurious falsehood are false statements disparaging another's *property rights* in land, things, or intangibles ("slander of title") and false statements disparaging the *quality* of another's land, things, or intangibles ("trade libel"). These two types of injurious falsehood cover all of the legally protected property interests that are capable of being sold. Examples include leases, mineral rights, trademarks, copyrights, and corporate stock. Injurious falsehood also covers false statements that harm another's economic interests and cause loss even though they do not disparage property as such. For example, one might falsely claim that the plaintiff's use of her property infringes a patent. The *Annbar* case, which follows, provides another example.

In all injurious falsehood cases, the plaintiff must prove the *falsity of the statement* and its *communication to a third party.* As the *Annbar* case suggests, the degree of fault required for liability is not completely clear.[4] It is often said that the general standard is one of "malice," but formulations of this differ. In any event, strict liability is no longer the standard in injurious falsehood cases. Also, there is probably no liability for false statements that are made negligently and in good faith.

A plaintiff seeking to recover for injurious falsehood must also prove that the false statement played a substantial part in causing him to suffer *special damages* (economic loss). These special damages can include: the expense of measures for counteracting the false statement (including litigation expenses), losses resulting from the breach of an existing contract by a third party, the loss of prospective business, and losses resulting from the diminished value of disparaged property. In cases involving the loss of prospective business, the plaintiff is usually required to show that some specific person(s) refused to buy because of the disparagement. But, as the *Annbar* case states, this rule is relaxed where the injurious falsehood is widely disseminated and it is reasonably certain that *some* lost business resulted. The special damages that the plaintiff is required to prove are usually his only remedy in injurious falsehood cases. Damages such as personal injury, emotional distress, and amounts that would have been earned by utilizing or investing the proceeds from lost business are generally not recoverable. Punitive damages and injunctive relief, however, are sometimes obtainable.

Injurious falsehood and defamation may overlap in some cases. If the false statement is limited to the plaintiff's business, property, or property rights, his only claim is for injurious falsehood. Statements impugning a businessperson's character or conduct, on the other hand, usually are only defamatory. Sometimes, however, both actions may be available. Suppose, for example, that the defendant falsely alleges that the plaintiff is a dishonest crook who routinely defrauds customers.

Defamation law's various absolute and conditional privileges[5] generally apply to injurious falsehood cases. Two additional privileges are also recognized in injurious falsehood cases: (1) a rival claimant may in good faith disparage another's property rights by asserting his own competing rights, and (2) one may make unfavorable comparisons between her own property and that of a competitor, even

[4] Further confusing the issue here is the likelihood that the constitutional "actual malice" standard for defamation cases involving public figures and public officials (knowledge of falsity or recklessness regarding truth or falsity) applies to injurious falsehood as well. On the actual malice standard, see Chapter 4.

[5] On these privileges, see Chapter 4.

if she does not believe her own to be superior. The second privilege is generally limited to "sales talk" asserting the superiority of one's own property. It does not cover specific unfavorable statements about the competitor's property.

## Annbar Associates v. American Express Co.

**565 S.W.2d 701 (Mo. Ct. App. 1978)**

Annbar Associates, a partnership, owned and operated the Muehlebach Hotel in Kansas City, Missouri. On May 9, 1972, Annbar and the American Express Company agreed that the hotel would honor American Express cards used by its guests. Annbar also contracted with American Express Reservations, Inc. (Reservations) for the latter to put the hotel on its computerized reservation system. Under this system, individuals could make reservations at member hotels through a toll-free telephone call to a Reservations facility. Annbar eventually canceled both agreements because of their expense; the cancellation became effective on May 23, 1973.

From the time of cancellation until October 1973, numerous telephone callers desiring to make reservations at the Muehlebach Hotel were told by Reservations employees that the hotel was "sold out," "booked," or "not available," when in fact the hotel was quite willing to receive guests. The errors occurred because the American Express computer consulted by Reservations employees when they received reservations requests displayed the words *not available* if the hotel in question had been removed from the system for any reason. Reservations employees were instructed to say, "I'm sorry—the hotel is not available," and to offer the caller accommodations at other hotels in the vicinity when these words appeared. The Reservations employee testifying on the company's procedures conceded that a caller might take this response to mean that the hotel had no rooms available.

Annbar sued Reservations for injurious falsehood, alleging that its false statements about the availability of rooms deprived Annbar of business from potential customers. After a jury verdict for Annbar, it was awarded $25,000 in actual damages and $100,000 in punitive damages. Reservations appealed.

**WELBORN, JUDGE.** The *Restatement (Second) of Torts* states the general principle of liability in this area as follows:

> One who publishes a false statement harmful to the interests of another is subject to liability for pecuniary loss resulting to the other if:
> (a) he intends for publication of the statement to result in harm to interests of the other having a pecuniary value, or either recognizes or should recognize that it is likely to do so, and
> (b) he knows that the statement is false or acts in reckless disregard of its truth or falsity.

Prosser describes the wrong of "injurious falsehood" as consisting of "the publication of matter derogatory to the plaintiff's . . . business in general, . . . of a kind calculated to prevent others from dealing with him." W. Prosser, *The Law of Torts* § 128, at 919–20 (4th ed. 1971).

Annbar's submission was upon a strict liability theory for publication of the false information. The *Restatement* originally adopted this theory of liability. However, the *Restatement*

*(Second)* has rejected strict liability in favor of the view expressed above. Prosser likewise rejects the strict liability theory.

Reservations' complaint that the jury instruction failed to require findings on essential elements of Annbar's case is valid. The tort of injurious falsehood involves, at least, legal malice. As Prosser expresses it:

> There is liability when the defendant acts for a spite motive, and out of a desire to do harm for its own sake; and equally so when he acts for the purpose of doing harm to the interests of the plaintiff in a manner in which he is not privileged so to interfere. There is also liability when the defendant knows that what he says is false, regardless of whether he has an ill motive or intends to affect the plaintiff at all. The deliberate liar must take the risk that his statement will prove to be economically damaging to others; and there is something like the "scienter" found in an action of deceit. Any of these three is sufficient to constitute "malice" and support the action. But in the absence of any of the three there is no liability, where the defendant has made his utterance in good faith, even though he may have been negligent in failing to ascertain the facts before he made it. *Prosser,* at 921–22.

Annbar produced no evidence of a spite motive. It produced no evidence of purposeful harm by Reservations. Therefore, Annbar was entitled to succeed only if Reservations knew that the "not available" response was false or acted in reckless disregard of the truth or falsity of this response. The trial court's instruction failed to submit any such issue to the jury.

Proof of pecuniary loss is an element of a claim for injurious falsehood. *Restatement (Second)* § 651 states: "This pecuniary loss may be established by: (a) proof of the conduct of specific persons, or (b) proof that the loss has resulted from the conduct of a number of persons whom it is impossible to identify." Comment (h) to this section states:

> Widely disseminated injurious falsehood may . . . cause serious and genuine pecuniary loss by affecting the conduct of a number of persons whom the plaintiff is unable to identify and so depriving him of a market that he would otherwise have found. When this can be shown with reasonable certainty, the rule requiring the identification of specific purchasers is relaxed and recovery is permitted for the loss of the market. As in analogous cases involving the loss of profits of an established business, . . . this may be proved by circumstantial evidence showing that the loss has in fact occurred, and eliminating other causes.

Annbar testified to two theories of damage. One [argued a] decrease of 12,830 room nights for the period in question below that for the comparable period for the preceding year, and computed the loss of profits on that basis at some $200,000. Evidence of damage on this theory is clearly too speculative to admit of a calculation on this ground.

Annbar's second theory was based upon the assumption that the Muehlebach lost 823 room nights, the total nights shown by the computer printout for which reservations had been requested or inquiries made of Reservations between June 1 and October 31, 1973. It computed a loss of profits for room rental of $16,297, being 90 percent of the anticipated room rental. It also figured what the profit would have been on food and beverage sales to the lost customers, based upon the percentage which such sales bore to room rentals for the year 1973 and the rate of profit shown for such operations. These computations produced a loss of $8,039 profit on food sales and $3,039 on beverages. This evidence sufficed to meet Annbar's burden in this case.

Judgment for Annbar reversed. Case remanded for a new trial.

**Interference with Contractual Relations.** In cases involving **intentional interference with contractual relations,** one party to a contract sues the defendant because the defendant's interference with the other party's performance of the contract has caused the plaintiff to lose the benefit of that performance.[6] The defendant can be liable where he causes the other party to breach the contract or where he otherwise prevents its performance. The "interference" can range from threats of violence, at one extreme, to mere persuasion, at the other. Liability exists only where the interference affects performance of an *existing* contract. This includes contracts that are voidable, terminable at the will of either party,[7] or subject to contract defenses. However, there is no liability for interference with void bargains or contracts to marry. To be liable, the defendant must have *intended* to cause the breach; this presupposes knowledge of the plaintiff's contract interest, or at least knowledge of facts from which that interest can be reasonably inferred. There is generally no liability for negligent contract interferences.

Even if these threshold requirements are met, the defendant will be liable only if his behavior was *improper* or *not privileged.* The *Landess* case below discusses some of the many factors that courts will weigh in making such determinations. Despite the flexible, case-by-case nature of "privilege" situations, a few generalizations about such situations are possible. Where the contract's performance was blocked by such clearly improper means as threats of physical violence, fraud, defamatory statements, bribery, harassment, and bad faith civil or criminal actions, the defendant will usually be liable. Liability is also likely where it can be shown that the interference was motivated solely by malice, spite, or a simple desire to meddle. In addition, one who interferes with the contracts of business competitors will usually be found liable. Here, the social interest in the security of established contract rights outweighs society's interest in free competition. But competitors are much less likely to incur liability where, as is still often true of employment contracts, the agreement interfered with is terminable at will.

Assuming that the means used are not improper, there is generally is no liability for impeding performance of a contract that is illegal or contrary to public policy. The same is true where the defendant acts in the public interest—for example, by informing a utility that a critical employee at a nuclear power plant is a habitual user of hallucinogenic drugs. It is also true where the defendant acts to protect a person for whose welfare she is responsible—for example, where a mother induces a private school to discharge a diseased student who could infect her children. Also, one who "interferes" by giving the breaching party truthful information or requested advice will usually escape liability.

Finally, a contract interference provoked by the defendant's good faith effort to protect her own legal interests will generally not create liability as long as the means used to advance those interests are appropriate. For example, if Smith contracts to sell Barnes property in which Isaac has a legitimate legal interest, Isaac will probably not be liable to Barnes if he threatens to sue Smith to protect his interest and this causes Smith to breach the sales contract. The result would be different, however, if the breach was caused by Isaac's threat to shoot Smith.

Damages for intentional interference with contractual relations include the value of the lost contract performance and compensatory

---

[6] Also, the defendant will be liable where his behavior frustrates the *plaintiff's* performance of the contract. Here, the plaintiff sues because his failure to perform has cost him the return performance of the other party to the contract.

[7] For a discussion of terminable at will employment contracts, see Chapter 47.

damages reasonably linked to the interference (including emotional distress and damage to reputation). In some cases, an injunction prohibiting further interferences may be obtained.

## Landess v. Borden, Inc.

### 667 F.2d 628 (7th Cir. 1981)

From 1976 to 1980, Edgar Landess collected milk from dairy farmers and delivered it to a Borden dairy. He operated under implied, terminable at will contracts with those dairy farmers. On February 1, 1980, Borden told Landess that it would no longer accept milk hauled by him. Borden also informed the dairy farmers of its new policy, telling them that it had arranged to have different haulers collect their milk, and expressly or impliedly stating that they had to employ those haulers if they wished to continue to sell to Borden. As a result, all of the farmers ceased using Landess's service.

Landess sued Borden for intentional interference with contractual relations. The federal district court granted Borden summary judgment, and Landess appealed.

**Bauer, Circuit Judge.** Wisconsin recognizes a tort of inducing termination of a contract terminable at will. By notifying the farmers that it would no longer accept milk delivered by Landess and by making other haulage services available, Borden did induce the farmers to terminate their contracts with Landess. Borden is liable for any harm caused by its interference unless its conduct was privileged. Factors to be considered in determining whether Borden's conduct was privileged include:

*The Nature of Borden's Conduct.* Under Wisconsin law, an individual inducing a third party to terminate a contract is liable for tortious interference only if he uses improper means, e.g., physical force or fraudulent misrepresentation, to induce termination. In this case, Borden's interference was not improper. Borden merely notified the farmers of its decision to stop accepting milk delivered by Landess and offered the farmers other haulage services if they desired to continue selling their milk to Borden.

*The Nature of Landess's Expectancy.* Wisconsin allows recovery for tortious interference with a terminable at will contract on the presumption that the contract is a subsisting relation, of value to the plaintiff, and presumably to continue in effect. If the facts do not give rise to a presumption that the contract will continue, there can be no tortious interference. Where the contract depends for its vitality on the continuance of a separate contract between the plaintiff and a third party, the presumption that the terminable at will contract will continue is rebutted upon proof that the other contract has been terminated. The implied contract between Landess and the farmers depended on Borden's willingness to accept Landess's services for its continued vitality. Therefore, Borden's decision to cease using Landess's haulage service "revolutionized" the contracts between Landess and the farmers. Under these circumstances, Landess had no protectible expectancy that the terminable at will contracts would continue indefinitely.

*The Relationships between Borden, Landess, and the Farmers.* The contractual relations between these three principals are intertwined. The farmers had an agreement with Landess, who agreed to haul their milk, and an equally valid arrangement with Borden, which agreed to purchase that milk. Similarly, Landess had the agreement with the farmers and an arrangement with Borden whereby Borden agreed to pay a portion of Landess's haulage fees. The vitality of Landess's relation with the farmers depended on the continuation of Landess's agreement with Borden and on the continuation of Borden's agreement with the farmers.

*The Interest Borden Sought to Advance.* By notifying the farmers of Borden's termination of Landess's services and the availability of a replacement haulage service, Borden sought to encourage the farmers to continue delivering their milk to Borden. Borden had a legitimate interest in continuing its business arrangement with the farmers.

*The Social Interests.* Reasonable men may differ about the appropriate balancing of social interests between protecting Landess's expectancy that his contracts with the farmers would continue and protecting Borden's freedom to deal with those with whom it chooses, but we believe that the social interest in preserving free competition ought to prevail. If Borden was dissatisfied with Landess's services, free market principles dictate that it should be permitted to terminate Landess's services while attempting to preserve its other valuable business arrangement with the farmers.

Summary judgment for Borden affirmed. The court also stated that Landess could not recover for interference with prospective advantage (discussed below), because the factors it considered applied to that claim as well.

**Interference with Prospective Advantage.** The rules and remedies for interference with prospective advantage parallel those for interference with contractual relations. The main difference is that the former tort covers interferences with *prospective* relations, not existing contracts. The future relations protected against interference are mainly contractual relations of a business or commercial sort. Liability for interference with them is based on intent, and plaintiffs usually cannot sue for negligent interferences.

With some modifications, the "privilege" factors weighed in interference with contract cases also apply to interference with prospective advantage. One difference, however, is that interference with prospective advantage can often be justified if the defendant is a competitor of the plaintiff and is acting to further his economic interests. Since *existing* contractual relations are not involved, courts generally emphasize the value of free competition and allow defendants to usurp their competitors' prospective business. Inducing a third party to break his existing contract by offering a better deal than that given by a competitor may result in liability, but attracting that party's future business by offering a lower price almost certainly will not.

## OTHER LIMITS ON COMPETITORS

In addition to the restrictions discussed in this chapter,[8] there are many other legal checks on the behavior in which competitors can engage. Some forms of competition may run afoul of state and federal regulatory schemes—most notably, antitrust law.[9] Also, the vaguely defined body of rules known as "unfair competition" law may block certain

[8] Another tort-based legal theory sometimes involving competitive misbehavior is the "right of publicity" discussed in Chapter 4.

[9] See Chapters 44 and 45.

competitive practices. The term *unfair competition* probably covers many forms of illegal behavior discussed earlier in this chapter. It also includes such behavior as bribery, sabotage, and the intimidation or harassment of a competitor's employees or customers. The tort of *palming off* or *passing off*, which has been rendered less important by federal trademark law, is one long-recognized example of unfair competition. This tort involves false representations that are likely to induce third parties to believe that the defendant's goods or services are those of the plaintiff. Such representations include imitations of the plaintiff's trademarks, trade names, packages, labels, containers, employee uniforms, and place of business.

## SUMMARY

This chapter discusses certain restrictions on free competition whose main object is preserving the benefits that free competition can produce. By protecting the works of creative persons against infringement, copyright law gives such persons an incentive to express their ideas in tangible form, and thus gives society the benefit of those ideas. Similarly, patent law promotes the creation and disclosure of new devices, products, processes, and designs by providing legal protection against infringing uses of such inventions.

The legal rules against misappropriation of trade secrets provide an alternative means for realizing these ends. Rather than "going public" by obtaining a patent or copyright, firms may instead try to preserve the secrecy of their information and rely on trade secrets law to maintain that secrecy. Again, the protection afforded by the law gives an incentive toward the utilization of creative advances that might otherwise remain unexploited. The Lanham Act's prohibitions against trademark infringement promote informed consumer choice by helping prevent confusion about the origin of favored products. They also provide an incentive toward innovation and superior quality by making it easier for consumers to identify products possessing those traits.

Many of the same considerations underlie the various commercial torts discussed in this chapter. An environment where injurious falsehoods, interferences with established contracts, and interferences with prospective business relations run rampant is an environment where creativity, inventiveness, and superior quality will probably receive less than their maximum reward.

## PROBLEM CASES

**1.** Ag Pro, Inc. patented a water flush system for removing cow manure from the floors of dairy barns. The system involved the release of water directly from tanks or pools onto the barn floor. Systems using water to clean animal wastes from barn floors had been known for centuries, and none of the 13 elements of Ag Pro's system were new. What differentiated Ag Pro's system from the prior systems was its abrupt release of the water directly from the tank or pool, causing a sheet of water to flow over the collected manure. The prior systems had involved high-pressure spot delivery of the water through pipes and hoses. Ag Pro's system was far more effective in removing wastes than its predecessors had been. Sakraida used Ag Pro's system without permission, and Ag Pro sued for patent infringement. Sakraida defended on the ground that Ag Pro's patent was invalid because its invention was obvious. Is Sakraida correct?

**2.** Britannica was a corporation engaged in the business of producing, acquiring, and licensing educational films. For 12 years, BOCES, a nonprofit corporation organized to provide educational services to more than 100 public schools, had been videotaping Britannica's copyrighted films, reproducing the tapes, and distributing them to various schools for classroom viewing. BOCES utilized equipment worth half a million dollars and employed between five and eight full-time employees to carry out this operation. The schools usually returned the tapes to BOCES for erasure after they had been shown to students. Upon learning of BOCES's copying activities, Britannica sued BOCES for copyright infringement. Can BOCES claim fair use as a defense?

**3.** Smith, doing business as Ta'Ron, Inc., advertised that its fragrance Second Chance was a duplicate of Chanel No. 5, at a fraction of the latter's price. The advertisements for Second Chance suggested that a "Blindfold Test" be used on "skeptical prospects," challenging them to detect any difference between a well-known fragrance and the Ta'Ron "duplicate." One suggested challenge was: "We dare you to try to detect any difference between Chanel #5 ($25) and Ta'Ron's Second Chance ($7)."

On an order blank printed as part of the advertisement, each Ta'Ron fragrance was listed, with the name of a well-known fragrance that it allegedly duplicated immediately beneath the listing. Below the Second Chance listing appeared "*(Chanel #5)." The asterisk referred to a statement at the bottom of the form, which stated: "Registered Trade Name of Original Fragrance House." Chanel, Inc. sued for trademark infringement. Can Chanel prevail?

**4.** The Piper Aircraft Corporation had long engaged in the business of manufacturing and selling aircraft. It had sold about 30,000 planes under the CUB label. It also produced a new SUPER CUB model. Piper registered both the CUB and SUPER CUB names as trademarks with the Patent and Trademark Office.

Wag-Aero, Inc. sold parts for out-of-production aircraft. In its brochures, advertising, and catalogs, it referred to its parts as CUB and SUPER CUB parts. Sometimes, Wag-Aero would add a small *y* after the names CUB and SUPER CUB. These parts were not manufactured by Piper, and Wag-Aero usually failed to state that Piper was not their manufacturer. Also, there was evidence that purchasers of Wag-Aero's parts were confused about their origin.

Piper sued Wag-Aero for trademark infringement. Will Wag-Aero's use of the small *y*, by itself, be a good defense? Is there evidence from which a court could infer that Wag-Aero's use of the names CUB and SUPER CUB was intentional? Overall, will Piper prevail in this case?

**5.** Hickory Specialties, Inc. manufactured "liquid smoke," which imparted smoke flavoring and color to meat products. Due to environmental and health problems associated with the traditional smoking process, the demand for liquid smoke had increased dramatically. Ledford had been employed by Hickory as supervisor of its bottling operation and later as its plant manager. In the latter capacity, he acquired a thorough working knowledge of Hickory's processes for manufacturing liquid smoke. Intending to put this knowledge to work, Ledford quit his job with Hickory and formed a new corporation for the manufacture of liquid smoke. Hickory sued Ledford for misappropriation of trade secrets. Evidence introduced at trial indicated that, although Hickory took some steps to assure the secrecy of its operations, these efforts were not sufficient to withstand a determined spying effort like Ledford's. If Ledford argues that Hickory's security efforts had to be reasonably capable of producing complete secrecy, will the argument be successful and prevent Hickory from recovering?

**6.** Frank and Frances Gardner sued Sailboat Key, Inc. to prevent it from constructing certain improvements pursuant to building permits issued by the city of Miami. Sailboat Key later sued the Gardners for injurious falsehood. It alleged that false statements contained in the Gardners' pleadings in the earlier case caused it to lose its interest in the land where the construction was to occur, because it could not obtain financing. The Gardners claimed that defamation law's absolute privilege for statements made in the course of judicial proceedings also applied to this injurious falsehood action, and thus protected them from liability. Are the Gardners correct?

**7.** The New York Yankees sought a temporary injunction restraining Pasquel, the president of the Mexican League, from inducing or attempting to induce Yankee players to repudiate their employment contracts with the Yankees and to play in Mexico. Pasquel argued that, because the players' contracts with the Yankees were terminable at will by either party and thus unenforceable, his interference with the Yankees' contractual relations was not wrongful. Is Pasquel correct in arguing that interference with a terminable at will contract can never be wrongful?

**8.** Carolina Overall Corporation and East Carolina Linen Supply were competitors in the industrial laundry business. East Carolina induced Lowe, a route salesman for Carolina Overall, to breach his employment contract and enter East Carolina's employ. Then, East Carolina, acting through Lowe and other agents, solicited the business of 14 Carolina Overall customers, inducing them to breach their laundry service contracts with Carolina Overall. Carolina Overall sued East Carolina for intentional interference with contractual relations. East Carolina defended by arguing that, as a competitor, it was privileged to interfere with Carolina Overall's contracts. Is this argument valid?

**9.** The Chrysler Corporation and the Fedders Corporation contracted for the sale of Chrysler's Airtemp Division to Fedders. As part of this contract, Chrysler agreed not to rehire any of its former Airtemp managerial employees if they refused employment with Fedders. The reason for this agreement was Fedders' desire to retain the skilled services of management-level employees so that the change in ownership would not disrupt the ongoing Airtemp business. Some Airtemp employees who refused employment with Fedders sued Fedders and Chrysler for intentional interference with prospective advantage. Assuming that there was interference, can Fedders successfully defend on the ground that it did not act for an improper purpose?

# Chapter 44

# Antitrust: The Sherman Act

## INTRODUCTION

After the Civil War, an important economic phenomenon emerged on the American scene: the growth of large industrial combines and trusts. Many of these large business entities acquired dominant positions in their industries by buying up smaller competitors or engaging in practices aimed at driving smaller competitors out of business. This behavior produced a public outcry for legislation to preserve competitive market structures and prevent the accumulation of great economic power in the hands of a few firms. The common law had long held that contracts unreasonably restraining trade were contrary to public policy, but all that the courts could do to police this rule was refuse to enforce such a contract if one of the parties objected to it. Legislation was therefore necessary to give the courts greater power to deal with this new social problem.

Congress responded by passing the Sherman Act in 1890 and later supplementing it with the Clayton Act, in 1914, and the Robinson-Patman Act, in 1936. In doing so, Congress adopted a public policy in favor of preserving and promoting free competition as the most efficient means of allocating social resources. The Supreme Court summarized the rationale for this faith in the positive effects of competition when it said:

> Basic to faith that a free economy best promotes the public weal is that goods must stand the cold test of competition; that the public, acting through the market's impersonal judgment, shall allocate the nation's resources and thus direct the course its economic development will take.[1]

The passage of the antitrust laws reflected a congressional assumption that competition was more likely to exist in an industrial structure characterized by a large number of competing firms than in concentrated industries dominated by a few large competitors. As Judge Learned Hand put it in the famous case of *United States v. Aluminum Company of America, Inc.:*

> Many people believe that possession of an unchallenged economic power deadens initiative, discourages thrift, and depresses energy; that immunity from competition is a narcotic, and rivalry is a stimulant, to industrial progress; that the spur of constant stress is necessary to counteract an inevitable disposition to let well enough alone.[2]

Despite this long-standing policy in favor of competitive market structures, the antitrust laws have not been very successful in halting the trend toward concentration in American industry. The market structure in many important industries today is highly *oligopolistic*—with the bulk of production accounted for by the output of a few dominant firms. Traditional antitrust concepts are often quite difficult to apply to the behavior of firms in such highly concentrated markets, and recent years have witnessed the emergence of new ideas that challenge many of the long-standing assumptions of traditional antitrust policy.

## THE ANTITRUST POLICY DEBATE

Antitrust enforcement necessarily reflects fundamental public policy judgments about the kinds of economic activity that should be allowed and about the industrial structure that is best suited to foster desirable economic activity. Since such judgments are vitally important to the future of the American economy, it is not surprising that antitrust policy is often the subject of vigorous public debate. In recent years, traditional antitrust values have faced a highly effective challenge from commentators and courts advocating the application of microeconomic theory to antitrust enforcement. As many of these new ideas originated among scholars associated with the University of Chicago, these new methods of antitrust analysis are commonly called "Chicago School" theories.

Chicago School advocates tend to view *economic efficiency* as the primary, if not the sole, goal of antitrust enforcement. They are far less concerned with the supposed effects of industrial concentration than are traditional antitrust thinkers. Even highly concentrated industries, they argue, may engage in significant forms of nonprice competition, such as competition in advertising, styling, and warranties. They also point out that concentration in a particular industry does not necessarily preclude *interindustry competition* among related industries. For example, a highly concentrated glass container industry may still face significant competition from the makers of metal, plastic, and fiberboard containers. Chicago School advocates are also quick to point out that many markets today are international in scope, so that highly concentrated domestic industries such as automobiles, steel, and electronics may nonetheless

[1] *Times-Picayune Co. v. United States,* 345 U.S. 594 (U.S. Sup. Ct. 1953).

[2] 148 F.2d 416 (2d Cir. 1945).

face effective foreign competition. In fact, they argue that the technological developments necessary for American industry to compete more effectively in international markets may require the great concentrations of capital that result from concentration in domestic industry.

From the Chicago School viewpoint, the traditional antitrust focus on the structure of industry has improperly emphasized protecting *competitors* rather than protecting *competition.* Chicago School theorists argue that the primary thrust of antitrust policy should involve *anticonspiracy* efforts rather than *anticoncentration* efforts. In addition, most of these theorists take a rather lenient view toward various vertically imposed restrictions on price and distribution that have been traditionally seen as undesirable, because they believe that such restrictions can promote efficiencies in distribution. Thus, they tend to view favorably attempts by manufacturers to control the prices at which their products are resold and to establish exclusive distribution systems for those products.

Traditional antitrust thinkers, however, contend that although economic efficiency is *an* important goal of antitrust enforcement, antitrust policy has historically embraced *political* as well as economic values. Concentrated economic power, they argue, is undesirable for a variety of noneconomic reasons. It can lead to antidemocratic concentrations of political power, and it can stimulate greater governmental intrusions into the economy in the same way that the activities of the trusts after the Civil War led to the passage of the antitrust laws. Lessening concentration, in their view, enhances individual freedom by reducing the barriers to entry that confront would-be competitors and by assuring a broader input into economic decisions that may have important social consequences. Judge Learned Hand summed up this way of looking at antitrust policy when he said in the *Alcoa* case:

> Great industrial consolidations are inherently undesirable, regardless of their economic results. Throughout the history of these statutes [sections 1 and 2 of the Sherman Act] it has been constantly assumed that one of their purposes was to perpetuate and preserve, for its own sake and in spite of possible cost, an organization of industry in small units which can effectively compete with each other.[3]

Chicago School ideas, however, have had a significant impact on the course of antitrust enforcement in recent years. The Supreme Court has given credence to Chicago School economic arguments in some cases, and many of President Reagan's appointees to the Justice Department and the Federal Trade Commission have expressed agreement with Chicago School policy views. If this trend continues, a large portion of existing antitrust law may be significantly revised in the years to come.

## JURISDICTION, PENALTIES, AND STANDING

**Jurisdiction.** The Sherman Act makes monopolization and agreements in restraint of trade illegal. However, since the federal government's power to regulate business originates in the Commerce Clause of the U.S. Constitution,[4] the federal antitrust laws apply only to behavior that has some significant impact on our *interstate* or *foreign* commerce. Given the interdependent nature of our national economy, it is generally fairly easy to demonstrate that a challenged activity either involves interstate commerce (the "in com-

[3] *United States v. Aluminum Co. of America, Inc.*, 148 F.2d 416 (2d Cir. 1945).

[4] The Commerce Clause is discussed in detail in Chapter 42.

merce" jurisdiction test) or has a substantial effect on interstate commerce (the "effect on commerce" jurisdiction test). As the *McClain* case, which follows, indicates, this may well be true even though the activity in question occurs solely within the borders of one state. Activities that are purely *intrastate* in their effects, however, are outside the scope of federal antitrust jurisdiction and must be challenged under state law.

The federal antitrust laws have also been extensively applied to activities affecting the international commerce of the United States. The activities of American firms operating outside our borders may be attacked under our antitrust laws if they have an intended effect on our foreign commerce. Likewise, foreign firms that are "continuously engaged" in our domestic commerce are subject to federal antitrust jurisdiction. Determining the full extent of the extraterritorial reach of our antitrust laws often involves courts in difficult questions of antitrust exemptions and immunities.[5] It also presents the troubling prospect that aggressive attempts to expand the reach of antitrust beyond our borders may produce a conflict between our antitrust policy and our foreign policy in general.

[5] These issues are discussed in detail in the next chapter.

## McClain v. Real Estate Board of New Orleans, Inc.

**444 U.S. 232 (U.S. Sup. Ct. 1980)**

McClain and others brought a private antitrust action under the Sherman Act against the Real Estate Board of New Orleans. They alleged price-fixing by means of fixed commission rates, fee splitting, and the suppression of market information useful to buyers. The trial court granted the Board's motion for dismissal on the ground that real estate brokerage activities were wholly local in nature and therefore lacked the effect on interstate commerce necessary to invoke the Sherman Act. McClain appealed.

**Burger, Chief Justice.** To establish the jurisdictional element of a Sherman Act violation it would be sufficient for McClain to demonstrate a substantial effect on interstate commerce generated by the Board's brokerage activity. McClain need not make a more particularized showing of an effect on interstate commerce caused by the alleged conspiracy to fix commission rates or by those other aspects of defendants' activity that are alleged to be unlawful.

It is clear that an appreciable amount of commerce is involved in the financing of residential property in the Greater New Orleans area and in the insuring of titles to such property. The presidents of two of the many lending institutions in the area stated in their deposition testimony that those institutions committed hundreds of millions of dollars to residential financing during the period covered by the complaint. The testimony further demonstrates that this appreciable commercial activity has occurred in interstate commerce. Funds were raised from out-of-state investors and from interbank loans obtained from interstate financial institutions. Multistate lending institutions took mortgages insured under federal programs which entailed interstate transfers of premiums and settlements. Mortgage obligations physically and constructively were traded as financial instruments in the interstate secondary mortgage market. Before making a mortgage loan in the Greater New Orleans area, lending institutions usually, if not always, required title insurance which was furnished by interstate corporations.

Brokerage activities necessarily affect both the frequency and the terms of residential sales transactions. Ultimately, whatever stimulates or retards the volume of residential sales, or has an impact on the purchase price, affects the demand for financing and title insurance, those two commercial activities that on this record are shown to have occurred in interstate commerce.

Judgment reversed in favor of McClain. Case remanded for trial.

**Penalties.** Violations of the Sherman Act may give rise to both criminal and civil liability. Individuals convicted of Sherman Act violations may receive a fine of up to $100,000 per violation and/or a term of imprisonment of up to three years. Corporations convicted of violating the Sherman Act may be fined up to $1 million per violation. Before an individual may be found criminally responsible under the Sherman Act, however, the government must prove both an *anticompetitive effect* flowing from the challenged activities and *criminal intent* on the part of the defendant. The level of criminal intent required for a violation is a "knowledge of [the act's] probable consequences" rather than a specific intent to violate the antitrust laws.[6] Civil violations of the antitrust laws, on the other hand, may be proven by evidence of either an unlawful purpose or an anticompetitive effect.

The federal courts have broad injunctive powers to remedy civil antitrust violations. They can order convicted defendants to *divest* themselves of the stock or assets of acquired companies, to *divorce* themselves from a functional level of their operations (e.g., they can order a manufacturer to sell its captive retail outlets), to refrain from particular conduct in the future, and to cancel existing contracts. In extreme cases, they can also enter a *dissolution* decree ordering a defendant to liquidate its assets and go out of business. Private individuals, as well as the Department of Justice (the arm of the federal government charged with enforcing the Sherman Act), may seek such injunctive relief from antitrust violations.

A significant percentage of the antitrust cases filed by the Department of Justice are settled out of court by the use of *nolo contendere* pleas in criminal cases and *consent decrees* in civil cases. Technically, a defendant who pleads nolo contendere has not admitted his guilt, although a sentencing court may elect to impose the same penalty that would be appropriate in the case of a guilty plea or a conviction. Consent decrees involve a defendant's consent to remedial measures aimed at remedying the competitive harm resulting from his actions. Both of these devices are often attractive to antitrust defendants, because neither a nolo plea nor a consent decree is admissible as proof of a violation of the Sherman Act in a later civil suit filed by a private plaintiff.

Section 4 of the Clayton Act gives private individuals a significant incentive to enforce the antitrust laws by providing that persons injured by violations of the Sherman Act or the Clayton Act may recover *treble damages* plus costs and attorney's fees from the defendant. This means that once antitrust plaintiffs

[6] *United States v. U.S. Gypsum Co.*, 438 U.S. 422 (U.S. Sup. Ct. 1978).

have proven the amount of their actual losses as a result of the challenged violation (lost profits, increased costs of doing business, etc.), this amount is tripled to compute the amount of their recovery. The potential for treble damage liability plainly presents a significant deterrent threat to potential antitrust violators. For example, a famous antitrust case against General Electric Company and several other electrical equipment manufacturers resulted in treble damage awards in excess of $200 million. Some Chicago School critics of antitrust have argued that treble damages should be available only for per se violations of the antitrust laws, with plaintiffs who prove "rule of reason" violations being restricted to a recovery of their actual damages. (Both per se and "rule of reason" violations are discussed later in this chapter.) Legislation to this effect has been introduced in Congress.

**Standing.** Private plaintiffs seeking to enforce the antitrust laws must first demonstrate that they have *standing* to sue. This means that they must show a *direct antitrust injury* as a result of the challenged behavior. An *antitrust injury* is one that results from the unlawful aspects of the challenged behavior and is of the type that Congress sought to prevent by enacting the antitrust laws. For example, in *Brunswick Corp. v. Pueblo Bowl-o-Mat, Inc.*,[7] the operator of a chain of bowling centers (Pueblo) challenged a bowling equipment manufacturer's (Brunswick) acquisition of a number of competing bowling centers that had defaulted on payments owed to the manufacturer for equipment purchases. The gist of Pueblo's complaint was that, but for Brunswick's acquisition of the failing businesses, they would have gone out of business and Pueblo's profits would have increased. The Supreme Court rejected Pueblo's claim, however, because Pueblo's claimed losses flowed from the fact that Brunswick had *preserved* competition by acquiring the failing centers. Allowing recovery for such losses would be contrary to the antitrust purpose of promoting competition.

Proof that an antitrust injury is *direct* is important because the Supreme Court, in *Illinois Brick Co. v. State of Illinois*,[8] held that *indirect purchasers* lack standing to sue for antitrust violations. In that case, the state of Illinois and several other governmental entities were denied the right to recover treble damages from concrete block suppliers who they alleged were guilty of illegally fixing the price of the block used in the construction of public buildings. The plaintiffs acknowledged that the builders who had been hired to construct the buildings in question had actually paid the inflated prices for the blocks, but argued that these illegal costs had probably been "passed on" to them in the form of higher prices for building construction. The Supreme Court refused to allow recovery, however, on the ground that granting standing to indirect purchasers would create a risk of "duplicative recoveries" by purchasers at various levels in a product's chain of distribution. The Court also said that affording standing to indirect purchasers would cause difficult problems of tracing competitive injuries through several levels of distribution and assessing the extent of an indirect purchaser's actual losses.

The Court's *Illinois Brick* decision has been widely criticized and has produced some unsuccessful congressional attempts to overturn the decision by corrective legislation. Some lower federal courts, however, have recognized exceptions to the "indirect purchaser" rule in cases where granting standing to indirect purchasers does not present the problems that concerned the Supreme Court in *Illinois Brick*. For example, cost-plus arrangements

[7] 429 U.S. 477 (U.S. Sup. Ct. 1977).

[8] 431 U.S. 720 (U.S. Sup. Ct. 1977).

as a result of which the entire increase in prices stemming from an antitrust violation is passed on down the chain of distribution have been treated as outside the scope of *Illinois Brick* because the indirect purchasers clearly suffered the entire overcharge and the intermediate purchasers suffered no loss.[9] Also, some courts have held that indirect purchasers are not barred from seeking injunctive relief for antitrust violations because only treble damage suits present problems of multiple recovery and speculative damages.[10]

## SECTION 1—RESTRAINTS OF TRADE

**Concerted Action.** Section 1 of the Sherman Act provides:

> Every contract, combination in the form of trust or otherwise, or conspiracy, in restraint of trade or commerce among the several states, or with foreign nations is declared to be illegal.

A *contract* is any agreement, express or implied, between two or more persons or business entities to restrain competition; a *combination* is a continuing partnership in restraint of trade; and a *conspiracy* occurs when two or more persons or business entities join for the purpose of restraining trade. From the language of the statute, it is apparent that Section 1 of the Sherman Act is aimed at *joint* or *concerted action* in restraint of trade. The statute expresses a basic public policy that requires persons or business entities to make important competitive decisions on their own, rather than in conjunction with competitors. Thus, *purely unilateral action* by a competitor will never amount to a violation of Section 1.

The concerted action requirement of Section 1 presents two major problems to antitrust enforcers. First, how separate must two business entities be before their joint activities will be subject to the Act's prohibitions? For example, it has long been held that a corporation cannot conspire with itself or its employees and that a corporation's employees cannot be guilty of a conspiracy in the absence of some independent party. But what about conspiracies among related corporate entities? In two earlier cases, the Supreme Court appeared to hold that a corporation could violate the Sherman Act by conspiring with a wholly owned subsidiary.[11] As the *Copperweld* case, which follows, indicates, however, the Court has recently repudiated the "intra-enterprise conspiracy doctrine" by holding, as a matter of law, that a parent company is incapable of conspiring with a wholly owned subsidiary in violation of the Sherman Act. Whether this new approach extends to corporate subsidiaries and affiliates that are not wholly owned remains to be seen.

A more difficult problem that constantly occurs in the enforcement of Section 1 concerns the circumstances in which a court will *infer* that an agreement or conspiracy to restrain trade exists in the absence of any *overt* agreement by the parties. Should parallel pricing behavior by several firms be enough, for example, to justify the inference that a price-fixing conspiracy exists? To date, the courts have consistently held that proof of pure "conscious parallelism," standing alone, is *not* enough to establish a violation of Section 1.[12] Instead, some other evidence must be presented to show that the defendants' actions were the product of an *agreement,* express or implied, rather than the results of independent business decisions. This makes it quite difficult to attack *oligopolies* (a few large firms

[9] *State of Illinois v. Borg, Inc.,* 553 F. Supp. 178 (N.D. Ill. 1982).

[10] *In re Beef Industry Antitrust Litigation,* 600 F.2d 1148 (5th Cir. 1979).

[11] *Kiefer-Stewart Co. v. Joseph E. Seagram & Sons, Inc.,* 340 U.S. 211 (U.S. Sup. Ct. 1951); *United States v. Yellow Cab Co.,* 332 U.S. 218 (U.S. Sup. Ct. 1947).

[12] *Theatre Enterprises v. Paramount Film Distributing Corp.,* 346 U.S. 537 (U.S. Sup. Ct. 1954).

that share one market) under Section 1, since such firms may independently elect to follow the pricing policies of the industry "price leader," rather than risk their large market shares by engaging in vigorous price competition.

## Copperweld Corp. v. Independence Tube Corp.

**52 U.S.L.W. 4821 (U.S. Sup. Ct. 1984)**

Copperweld Corporation purchased Regal Tube Company, a manufacturer of steel tubing, from Lear Siegler, Inc., in 1972. The sales agreement prohibited Lear Siegler and its subsidiaries from competing with Regal in the United States for five years. Copperweld then transferred Regal's assets to a newly formed, wholly owned Pennsylvania corporation, also named Regal Tube Company. The new subsidiary continued to conduct its manufacturing operations in Chicago, but shared Copperweld's corporate headquarters in Pittsburgh.

Shortly before Copperweld acquired Regal, David Grohne, an officer of Regal, accepted a job as a corporate officer of Lear Siegler. After the sale of Regal to Copperweld, and while continuing to serve as an officer of Lear Siegler, Grohne formed the Independence Tube Company to compete in the same market as Regal. Independence entered into an agreement with Yoder Company for the construction of a tubing mill required for Independence's operations.

When Copperweld and Regal learned of Grohne's plans, they consulted legal counsel and were told that, although Grohne was not bound by the sales agreement between Copperweld and Lear Siegler, it might be possible to enjoin his activities if it could be shown that he was using any technical information or trade secrets belonging to Regal. Copperweld then sent a letter to Yoder warning that it intended to take "any and all steps which are necessary to protect our rights under the terms of our purchase agreement and to protect the know-how, trade secrets, etc., which we purchased from Lear Siegler." Two days after receiving Copperweld's letter, Yoder canceled its agreement with Independence. Independence was able to get another company to build the mill, but its entry into the market was delayed by nine months as a result of Yoder's cancellation.

Independence filed suit against Copperweld, Regal, and Yoder, arguing that they had conspired to violate Section 1 of the Sherman Act. The jury agreed as to Copperweld and Regal, but found that Yoder was not party to the conspiracy. The Seventh Circuit Court of Appeals affirmed, and Copperweld appealed.

**Burger, Chief Justice.** The so-called "intra-enterprise conspiracy" doctrine provides that Section 1 liability is not foreclosed merely because a parent and its subsidiary are subject to common ownership. The doctrine derives from declarations in several of this Court's opinions. Copperweld and Regal, joined by the United States as *amicus curiae,* urge us to repudiate the intra-enterprise conspiracy doctrine. The central criticism is that the doctrine gives undue significance to the fact that a subsidiary is separately incorporated and thereby treats as the concerted activity of two entities what is really unilateral behavior flowing from decisions of a single enterprise.

The Sherman Act contains a "basic distinction between concerted and independent action." *Monsanto Co. v. Spray-Rite Service Corp.* (1984). The conduct of a single firm is governed by Section 2 alone and is unlawful only when it threatens actual monopolization. It is not enough that a single firm appears to "restrain trade" unreasonably, for even a vigorous competitor may leave that impression. For instance, an efficient firm may capture unsatisfied customers from an inefficient rival, whose own ability to compete may suffer as a result. This is the rule of the marketplace and is precisely the sort of competition that promotes the consumer interests that the Sherman Act aims to foster. In part because it is sometimes difficult to distinguish robust competition from conduct with long-run anticompetitive effects, Congress authorized Sherman Act scrutiny of single firms only when they pose a danger of monopolization. Judging unilateral conduct in this manner reduces the risk that the antitrust laws will dampen the competitive zeal of a single aggressive entrepreneur.

Section 1 of the Sherman Act, in contrast, reaches unreasonable restraints of trade effected by a "contract, combination . . . or conspiracy" between separate entities. It does not reach conduct that is "wholly unilateral." *Albrecht v. Herald Co.* (1968). Concerted activity subject to Section 1 is judged more sternly than unilateral activity under Section 2. Certain agreements, such as horizontal price fixing and market allocation, are thought so inherently anticompetitive that each is illegal *per se* without inquiry into the harm it has actually caused. Other combinations, such as mergers, joint ventures, and various vertical agreements, hold the promise of increasing a firm's efficiency and enabling it to compete more effectively. Accordingly, such combinations are judged under a rule of reason, an inquiry into market power and market structure designed to assess the combination's actual effect.

The reason Congress treated concerted behavior more strictly than unilateral behavior is readily appreciated. Concerted activity inherently is fraught with anticompetitive risk. It deprives the marketplace of the independent centers of decisionmaking that competition assumes and demands. In any conspiracy, two or more entities that previously pursued their own interests separately are combining to act as one for their common benefit. This not only reduces the diverse directions in which economic power is aimed but suddenly increases the economic power moving in one particular direction. Of course, such mergings of resources may well lead to efficiencies that benefit consumers, but their anticompetitive potential is sufficient to warrant scrutiny even in the absence of incipient monopoly.

The distinction between unilateral and concerted conduct is necessary for a proper understanding of the terms "contract, combination. . . or conspiracy" in Section 1. Nothing in the literal meaning of those terms excludes coordinated conduct among officers or employees of the *same* company. But it is perfectly plain that an internal "agreement" to implement a single, unitary firm's policies does not raise the antitrust dangers that Section 1 was designed to police. The officers of a single firm are not separate economic actors pursuing separate economic interests, so agreements among them do not suddenly bring together economic power that was previously pursuing divergent goals. Coordination within a firm is as likely to result from an effort to compete as from an effort to stifle competition. In the marketplace, such coordination may be necessary if a business enterprise is to compete effectively. For these reasons, officers or employees of the same firm do not provide the plurality of actors imperative for a Section 1 conspiracy.

There is also general agreement that Section 1 is not violated by the internally coordinated conduct of a corporation and one of its unincorporated divisions. Although this Court has not previously addressed the question, there can be little doubt that the operations of a corporate enterprise organized into divisions must be judged as the conduct of a single actor. The existence of an unincorporated division reflects no more than a firm's decision to adopt an organizational division of labor. A division within a corporate structure pursues the common interests of the whole rather than interests separate from those of the corporation itself; a business enterprise establishes divisions to further its own interests in the most efficient manner. Because coordination between a corporation and its division does not represent a sudden joining of two independent sources of economic power previously pursuing separate interests, it is not an activity that warrants Section 1 scrutiny.

For similar reasons, the coordinated activity of a parent and its wholly owned subsidiary must be viewed as that of a single enterprise for purposes of Section 1 of the Sherman Act. A parent and its wholly owned subsidiary have a complete unity of interest. Their objectives are common, not disparate; their general corporate actions are guided or determined not by two separate corporation consciousnesses, but one. They are not unlike a multiple team of horses drawing a vehicle under the control of a single driver. With or without a formal "agreement," the subsidiary acts for the benefit of the parent, its sole shareholder. If a parent and a wholly owned subsidiary do "agree" to a course of action, there is no sudden joining of economic resources that had previously served different interests, and there is no justification for Section 1 scrutiny.

The intra-enterprise conspiracy doctrine looks to the form of an entrepreneur's structure and ignores the reality. Antitrust liability should not depend on whether a corporate subunit is organized as an unincorporated division or a wholly owned subsidiary. A corporation has complete power to maintain a wholly owned subsidiary in either form. The economic, legal, or other considerations that lead corporate management to choose one structure over the other are not relevant to whether the enterprise's conduct seriously threatens competition. Rather, a corporation may adopt the subsidiary form of organization for valid management and related purposes. Separate incorporation may improve management, avoid special tax problems arising from multistate operations, or serve other legitimate interests. Especially in view of the increasing complexity of corporate operations, a business enterprise should be free to structure itself in ways that serve efficiency of control, economy of operations, and other factors dictated by business judgment without increasing its exposure to antitrust liability.

We hold that Copperweld and its wholly owned subsidiary Regal are incapable of conspiring with each other for purposes of Section 1 of the Sherman Act. To the extent that prior decisions of this Court are to the contrary, they are disapproved and overruled.

Judgment reversed in favor of Copperweld.

**Rule of Reason versus Per Se Analysis.** The statutory language of Section 1 condemns *every* contract, combination, and conspiracy in restraint of trade, but the Supreme Court has long held that the Sherman Act applies only to behavior that *unreasonably* restrains competition.[13] The Court has developed two fundamentally different approaches to analyzing behavior challenged under the act. It has concluded that some forms of behavior always have a negative effect on competition that can never be excused or justified. Such behavior is classed as per se illegal—conclusively presumed to violate the Act. Per se rules provide sure guidance to business and simplify otherwise lengthy antitrust litigation: once per se illegal behavior is proven, there are no justifications that a defendant

[13] *Standard Oil Co. of New Jersey v. United States,* 221 U.S. 1 (U.S. Sup. Ct. 1911).

may assert to avoid liability. Per se rules, however, are frequently criticized on the ground that they tend to oversimplify complex economic realities, and recent decisions indicate that the Court is moving away from per se rules in favor of rule of reason analysis for some kinds of economic activity. This trend is consistent with the Court's increased inclination to consider new economic theories that seek to justify behavior previously held to be illegal per se.

Behavior that is not classed as per se illegal is judged under the *rule of reason.* This requires a detailed inquiry into the actual competitive effects of the defendant's actions and includes consideration of any justifications that the defendant may advance. If the court concludes that the challenged activity had a significant anticompetitive effect that was not offset by any positive effect on competition or other social benefit (such as enhanced economic efficiency), the activity will be found to be in violation of Section 1. The following are some of the kinds of behavior that have been held to violate the Sherman Act.

**Price-Fixing.** An essential attribute of a free market is that the price of goods and services is determined by the free play of the impersonal forces of the marketplace. Attempts *by competitors* to interfere with market forces and control prices, called **horizontal price-fixing,** have long been held per se illegal under Section 1.[14] Price-fixing may take the form of direct agreements among competitors about the price at which they will sell or buy a particular product or service. It may also be accomplished by agreements on the quantity of goods that will be produced, offered for sale, or bought. In one famous case, an agreement by major oil refiners to purchase and store the excess production of small independent refiners was held to amount to price-fixing because the purpose of the agreement was to affect the market price for gasoline by artificially limiting the available supply.[15] Recently, some commentators have suggested that agreements to fix *maximum* prices should be treated under a rule of reason approach rather than under the harsher per se standard because, in some instances, such agreements may result in savings to consumers. However, the *Maricopa County* case, which follows, indicates that the Supreme Court is at present unwilling to deviate from its long-standing rule of per se illegality for any form of horizontal price-fixing.

Attempts by manufacturers to control the resale price of their products can also fall within the scope of Section 1. This kind of behavior, called **vertical price-fixing** or **resale price maintenance,** has long been held to be per se illegal.[16] Manufacturers can lawfully state a "suggested retail price" for their products, because such an action is purely unilateral in nature and does not involve the concerted action necessary for a violation of Section 1. However, any *agreement,* express or implied, between a manufacturer and its customers obligating the customers to resell at a price dictated by the manufacturer will be sufficient to trigger per se illegality.

The Section 1 emphasis on concerted action provides the basis for two indirect methods that some manufacturers may lawfully be able to use to control resale prices: *consignment sales* and *unilateral refusal to deal.* Consignments are agreements in which an owner of goods (the consignor) delivers them to another who is to act as the owner's agent in selling them (the consignee). Since the consignee is, in effect, the consignor's agent in selling the goods, and since the owners of

[14] *United States v. Trenton Potteries Co.,* 273 U.S. 392 (U.S. Sup. Ct. 1927).

[15] *United States v. Socony-Vacuum Oil Co.,* 310 U.S. 150 (U.S. Sup. Ct. 1940).

[16] *Dr. Miles Medical Co. v. John D. Park & Sons, Co.,* 220 U.S. 373 (U.S. Sup. Ct. 1911).

goods generally have the right to determine the price at which their goods are sold, one early Supreme Court case held that consignment sales were not covered by Section 1.[17] However, more recent cases have cast some doubt on the legality of resale price maintenance achieved by consignment dealing.[18] Consignment selling systems whose primary purpose is resale price maintenance may be held unlawful if they result in restraining price competition among a large number of consignees who would otherwise be in competition with one another. This is especially likely to be true in cases where the consignor has sufficient economic power over his consignees to permit him to refuse to deal with them on any basis other than a consignment. Finally, to have any hope of avoiding liability, the arrangement in question must be a true consignment: the consignor must retain title to the goods and bear the risk of loss of the goods while they are in the consignee's hands, and the consignee must have the right to return unsold goods.

In *United States v. Colgate & Co.*,[19] the Supreme Court held that a manufacturer could *unilaterally refuse to deal* with dealers who failed to follow its suggested resale prices. The idea behind this exception is that a single firm can deal or not deal with whomever it chooses without violating Section 1, because unilateral action, by definition, is not the concerted action prohibited by the Sherman Act. Subsequent cases, however, have narrowly construed the "Colgate doctrine." Manufacturers that enlist the aid of others (e.g., wholesalers or other dealers who are not price-cutting) to help enforce their pricing policies, or that engage in other joint action to further their policies, will probably be held to have violated Section 1.

Recent events have cast doubt on the long-term future of the rule of per se illegality for resale price maintenance agreements. Chicago School theorists argue that many of the same reasons that led the Supreme Court in the *Sylvania* case[20] to declare that vertically imposed nonprice restraints on distribution should be judged under the rule of reason are equally applicable to vertical price-fixing agreements. In particular, they argue that vertical restrictions limiting the maximum price at which a dealer can resell may prevent dealers with dominant market positions from exploiting consumers by price-gouging. However, the *Monsanto* case, which follows, seems to indicate that, for the moment, both the per se rule and the Colgate doctrine are alive and well.

[17] *United States v. General Electric Co.*, 272 U.S. 476 (U.S. Sup. Ct. 1926).

[18] *Simpson v. Union Oil Co. of California*, 377 U.S. 13 (U.S. Sup. Ct. 1964).

[19] 250 U.S. 300 (U.S. Sup. Ct. 1919).

[20] This case appears later in the chapter.

## Arizona v. Maricopa County Medical Society

**457 U.S. 332 (U.S. Sup. Ct. 1982)**

The Maricopa Foundation for Medical Care was a nonprofit organization established by the Maricopa County Medical Society to promote fee-for-service medicine. About 70 percent of the physicians in Maricopa County belonged to the Foundation. The Foundation's trustees set maximum fees that Foundation members could charge for medical services provided to policyholders of approved medical insurance plans. To obtain the

Foundation's approval, insurers had to agree to pay the fees of member physicians up to the prescribed maximum. Member physicians were free to charge less than the prescribed maximum, but had to agree not to seek additional payments in excess of the maximum from insured patients.

The Arizona attorney general filed suit for injunctive relief against the Maricopa County Medical Society and the Foundation, arguing that the fee agreement constituted per se illegal horizontal price-fixing. The district court denied the state's motion for a partial summary judgment, and the Ninth Circuit Court of Appeals affirmed on the ground that the per se rule was not applicable to the case.

**STEVENS, JUSTICE.** By 1927, the Court was able to state that "it has often been decided and always assumed that uniform price-fixing by those controlling in any substantial manner a trade or business in interstate commerce is prohibited by the Sherman Law." Thirteen years later, the Court could report that "for over 40 years this Court has consistently and without deviation adhered to the principle that price-fixing agreements are unlawful *per se* under the Sherman Act and that no showing of so-called competitive abuses or evils which those agreements were designed to eliminate or alleviate may be interposed as a defense." *United States v. Socony-Vacuum Oil Co.* (1940). In that case a glut in the spot market for gasoline had prompted the major oil refiners to engage in a concerted effort to purchase and store surplus gasoline in order to maintain stable prices. Absent the agreement, the companies argued, competition was cutthroat and self-defeating. The argument did not carry the day.

The application of the *per se* rule to maximum price-fixing agreements in *Kiefer-Stewart Co. v. Seagram & Sons* (1951), followed ineluctably from *Socony-Vacuum:*

> For such agreements, no less than those to fix minimum prices, cripple the freedom of traders and thereby restrain their ability to sell in accordance with their own judgment. We reaffirm what we said in *United States v. Socony-Vacuum Oil Co.:* "Under the Sherman Act a combination formed for the purpose and with the effect of raising, depressing, fixing, pegging, or stabilizing the price of a commodity in interstate or foreign commerce is illegal *per se.*"

Over the objection that maximum price-fixing agreements were not the "economic equivalent" of minimum price-fixing agreements, *Kiefer-Stewart* was reaffirmed in *Albrecht v. Herald Co.* (1968). *Kiefer-Stewart* and *Albrecht* place horizontal agreements to fix maximum prices on the same legal—even if not economic—footing as agreements to fix minimum or uniform prices. The *per se* rule "is grounded on faith in price competition as a market force [and not] on a policy of low selling prices at the price of eliminating competition." In this case the rule is violated by a price restraint that tends to provide the same economic rewards to all practitioners regardless of their skill, their experience, their training, or their willingness to employ innovative and difficult procedures in individual cases. Such a restraint also may discourage entry into the market and may deter experimentation and new developments by individual entrepreneurs. It may be a masquerade for an agreement to fix uniform prices, or it may in the future take on that character.

Nor does the fact that doctors—rather than nonprofessionals—are the parties to the price-fixing agreements support Maricopa's position. In *Goldfarb v. Virginia State Bar* (1975), we stated that the "public service aspect, and other features of the professions, may require that a particular practice, which could properly be viewed as a violation of the Sherman Act in another context, be treated differently." The price-fixing agreements in this case, however, are not premised on public service or ethical norms. Maricopa does not argue, as did the defendants in *Goldfarb,* that the quality of the professional service that its members provide is enhanced by the price restraint. Maricopa's claim for relief from the *per se* rule is simply that the doctors' agreement not to charge certain insureds more than a fixed price facilitates the successful marketing of an attractive insurance plan. But the claim that the price restraint will make it easier for customers to pay does not distinguish the medical profession from any other provider of goods or services.

Maricopa's principal argument is that the *per se* rule is inapplicable because its agreements are alleged to have procompetitive justifications. The argument indicates a misunderstanding of the *per se* concept. The anticompetitive potential inherent in all price-fixing agreements justifies their facial invalidation even if procompetitive justifications are offered for some. Those claims of enhanced competition are so unlikely to prove significant in any particular case that we adhere to the rule of law that is justified in its general application. Even when Maricopa is given every benefit of the doubt, the limited record in this case is not inconsistent with the presumption that Maricopa's agreements will not significantly enhance competition.

Judgment reversed in favor of Arizona.

## Monsanto Co. v. Spray-Rite Service Corp.

**52 U.S.L.W. 4341 (U.S. Sup. Ct. 1984)**

From 1957 to 1968, Spray-Rite Service Corporation, a wholesale distributor of agricultural chemicals, sold herbicides manufactured by Monsanto. By the late 1960s, Monsanto's sales amounted to approximately 15 percent of the corn herbicide market and 3 percent of the soybean herbicide market. Both markets were dominated by competitors of Monsanto that enjoyed far larger market shares. Spray-Rite was a family business whose owner and president, Donald Yapp, was also its sole salaried salesman. Spray-Rite was a discount operation, buying in large quantities (it was the 10th largest of Monsanto's 100 corn herbicide distributors) and selling at low margins.

In 1967, Monsanto announced that it would appoint distributors on a yearly basis and renew distributorships according to several new criteria. Among these criteria were: whether the distributor's primary activity was soliciting sales to retail dealers, whether it employed trained salesmen capable of educating their customers on the technical aspects of Monsanto's herbicides, and whether the distributor could be expected "to exploit fully" the market in its geographic area of primary responsibility. Shortly thereafter, Monsanto also introduced a number of incentive programs, such as making cash payments to distributors, sending salesmen to training classes, and providing free deliveries to customers within a distributor's area of primary responsibility.

In 1968, after receiving numerous complaints from other distributors about Spray-Rite's pricing policies, Monsanto refused to renew Spray-Rite's distributorship on the grounds that Spray-Rite had failed to hire trained salesmen and to promote sales to dealers adequately. Spray-Rite continued in business as a herbicide dealer until 1972. It later filed suit against Monsanto, arguing that Monsanto and some of its distributors had conspired to fix resale prices in violation of the Sherman Act and that Monsanto had terminated Spray-Rite's distributorship and adopted its compensation and shipping policies in furtherance of the conspiracy. The trial jury awarded Spray-Rite $10.5 million in treble damages. When the Seventh Circuit Court of Appeals affirmed the award, Monsanto appealed.

**POWELL, JUSTICE.** This Court has drawn two important distinctions that are at the center of this and any other distributor-termination case. First, there is the basic distinction between concerted and independent action—a distinction not always clearly drawn by parties and courts. Section 1 of the Sherman Act requires that there be a "contract, combination . . . or conspiracy" between the manufacturer and other distributors in order to establish a violation.

Independent action is not proscribed. A manufacturer of course generally has a right to deal, or refuse to deal, with whomever it likes, as long as it does so independently. *United States v. Colgate & Co.* (1919). Under *Colgate,* the manufacturer can announce its resale prices in advance and refuse to deal with those who fail to comply. And a distributor is free to acquiesce in the manufacturer's demand in order to avoid termination.

The second important distinction in distributor-termination cases is that between concerted action to set prices and concerted action on nonprice restrictions. The former have been *per se* illegal since the early years of national antitrust enforcement. The latter are judged under the rule of reason, which requires a weighing of the relevant circumstances of a case to decide whether a restrictive practice constitutes an unreasonable restraint on competition. See *Continental T.V., Inc. v. GTE Sylvania, Inc.* (1977).

While these distinctions in theory are reasonably clear, often they are difficult to apply in practice. In *Sylvania* we emphasized that the legality of arguably anticompetitive conduct should be judged primarily by its "market impact." But the economic effect of all of the conduct described above—unilateral and concerted vertical price-setting, agreements on price and nonprice restrictions—is in many, but not all, cases similar or identical.

Nevertheless, it is of considerable importance that independent action by the manufacturer, and concerted action on nonprice restrictions, be distinguished from price-fixing agreements, since under present law the latter are subject to *per se* treatment and treble damages. On a claim of concerted price-fixing, the antitrust plaintiff must present evidence sufficient to carry its burden of proving that there was such an agreement. If an inference of such an agreement may be drawn from highly ambiguous evidence, there is a considerable danger that the doctrines enunciated in *Sylvania* and *Colgate* will be seriously eroded.

The flaw in the evidentiary standard adopted by the Court of Appeals in this case is that it disregards this danger. Permitting an agreement to be inferred merely from the existence of complaints, or even from the fact that termination came about "in response to" complaints, could deter or penalize perfectly legitimate conduct. As Monsanto points out, complaints about price-cutters "are natural—and from the manufacturer's perspective, unavoidable—reactions by distributors to the activities of their rivals." Such complaints, particularly where the manufacturer has imposed a costly set of nonprice restrictions, "arise in the normal course of business and do not indicate illegal concerted action."

Moreover, distributors are an important source of information for manufacturers. In order to assure an efficient distribution system, manufacturers and distributors constantly must coordinate their activities to assure that their product will reach the consumer persuasively and efficiently. To bar a manufacturer from acting solely because the information upon which it acts orginated as a price complaint would create an irrational dislocation in the market.

In sum, "to permit the inference of concerted action on the basis of receiving complaints alone and thus to expose the defendant to treble damage liability would both inhibit management's exercise of independent business judgment and emasculate the terms of the statute." Thus, something more than evidence of complaints is needed. There must be evidence that tends to exclude the possibility that the manufacturer and nonterminated distributors were acting independently. As Judge Aldisert has written, the antitrust plaintiff should present direct or circumstantial evidence that reasonably tends to prove that the manufacturer and others "had a conscious commitment to a common scheme designed to achieve an unlawful objective."

Applying this standard to the facts of this case, we believe there was sufficient evidence for the jury reasonably to have concluded that Monsanto and some of its distributors were parties to an "agreement" or "conspiracy" to maintain resale prices and terminate price-cutters. In fact there was substantial *direct* evidence of agreements to maintain prices. There was testimony from a Monsanto district manager, for example, that Monsanto on at least two occasions in early 1969, about five months after Spray-Rite was terminated, approached price-cutting distributors and advised that if they did not maintain the suggested resale price, they would not receive adequate supplies of Monsanto's new corn herbicide.

When one of the distributors did not assent, this information was referred to the Monsanto regional office, and it complained to the distributor's parent company. There was evidence that the parent instructed its subsidiary to comply, and the distributor informed Monsanto that it would charge the suggested price. Evidence of this kind plainly is relevant and persuasive as to a meeting of minds.

An arguably more ambiguous example is a newsletter from one of the distributors to his dealer-customers. The newsletter is dated October 1, 1968, just four weeks before Spray-Rite was terminated. It was written after a meeting between the author and several Monsanto officials and discusses Monsanto's efforts to "get the market place in order." The newsletter reviews some of Monsanto's incentive and shipping policies, and then states that in addition "every effort will be made to maintain a minimum market price level." It is reasonable to interpret this newsletter as referring to an agreement or understanding that distributors and retailers would maintain prices, and Monsanto would not undercut those prices on the retail level and would terminate competitors who sold at prices below those of complying distributors; these were "the rules of the game."

If, as the courts below reasonably could have found, there was evidence of an agreement with one or more distributors to maintain prices, the remaining question is whether the termination of Spray-Rite was part of or pursuant to that agreement. It would be reasonable to find that it was, since it is necessary for competing distributors contemplating compliance with suggested prices to know that those who do not comply will be terminated. Moreover, there is some circumstantial evidence of such a link. Following the termination, there was a meeting between Spray-Rite's president and a Monsanto official. There was testimony that the first thing the official mentioned was the many complaints Monsanto had received about Spray-Rite's prices. In addition, there was reliable testimony that Monsanto never discussed with Spray-Rite prior to the termination the distributorship criteria that were the alleged basis for the action. By contrast, a former Monsanto salesman for Spray-Rite's area testified that Monsanto representatives on several occasions in 1965–1966 approached Spray-Rite, informed the distributor of complaints from other distributors—including one major and influential one—and requested that prices be maintained. Later that same year, Spray-Rite's president testified, Monsanto officials made explicit threats to terminate Spray-Rite unless it raised its prices.

Judgment for Spray-Rite affirmed.

**Division of Markets.** Any agreement among competing firms to divide up the available market by assigning one another certain exclusive territories or certain customers is a **horizontal division of markets** and illegal per se. Such agreements plainly represent agreements not to compete, and result in each firm being isolated from competition in the affected market.

*Vertically imposed* restraints on distribution also fall within the scope of the Sherman Act. A manufacturer has always had the power to *unilaterally* assign exclusive territories to its dealers or to limit the number of dealerships that it grants in a particular geographic area. However, manufacturers that require their dealers to *agree* not to sell outside their dealership territories or that place other restrictions on their dealers' right to resell their products (e.g., a prohibition against sales to unfranchised dealers inside the dealer's assigned territory) may run afoul of Section 1. In 1967, the Warren Court, in *United States v. Arnold, Schwinn & Co.*,[21] held that such **vertical restraints on distribution** were per se illegal when applied to goods that the manufacturer had sold to its dealers (consignment sales being treated under the rule of reason). The Burger Court disagreed, however, and in the *Sylvania* case, which follows, the Court abandoned the per se rule in favor of a rule of reason approach to most vertical restraints on distribution. In doing so, the Court accepted many Chicago School arguments concerning the potential economic efficiencies that could result from such restraints, which were alleged to offer a chance for increased *interbrand* competition (competition among the product lines of competing manufacturers) at the admitted cost of restraining *intrabrand* competition (competition among dealers in a particular manufacturer's product).

Subsequent decisions in this area have emphasized the importance of the market share of the manufacturer imposing vertical restraints on distribution in determining the legality of the restraints. Restraints imposed by manufacturers with large market shares are more likely to be found unlawful under the rule of reason because the resultant harm to intrabrand competition is unlikely to be offset by significant positive effects on interbrand competition.

[21] 338 U.S. 365 (U.S. Sup. Ct. 1967).

## United States v. Topco Associates, Inc.

### 405 U.S. 596 (U.S. Sup. Ct. 1972)

Topco Associates was a cooperative association created and controlled by 25 local and regional supermarket chains. Their purpose for forming Topco was to compete more effectively with national supermarket chains. Association members sold Topco brand products and were granted exclusive territories in their sale of Topco brand items. No member was allowed to expand into another member's territory without the consent of the other member. The government filed suit against Topco, arguing that the exclusive territory agreements violated the Sherman Act. Topco argued that the territorial divisions were necessary to maintain its private label program and enable it to compete with larger chains and that the association could not exist if the territorial divisions were nonexclusive. When the district court agreed with Topco and upheld the restrictions as reasonable and procompetitive, the government appealed.

**MARSHALL, JUSTICE.** On its face, Section 1 of the Sherman Act appears to bar any combination of entrepreneurs so long as it is "in restraint of trade." Theoretically, all manufacturers, distributors, merchants, sellers, and buyers could be considered as potential competitors of each other. Were Section 1 to be read in the narrowest possible way, any commercial contract could be deemed to violate it. The history underlying the formulation of the antitrust laws led this Court to conclude, however, that Congress did not intend to prohibit all contracts, nor even all contracts that might in some insignificant degree or attenuated sense restrain trade or competition. In lieu of the narrowest possible reading of Section 1, the Court adopted a "rule of reason" analysis for determining whether most business combinations or contracts violate the prohibitions of the Sherman Act. *Standard Oil Co. v. United States* (1911). An analysis of the reasonableness of particular restraints includes consideration of the facts peculiar to the business in which the restraint is applied, the nature of the restraint and its effects, and the history of the restraint and the reasons for its adoption.

While the Court has utilized the "rule of reason" in evaluating the legality of most restraints alleged to be violative of the Sherman Act, it has also developed the doctrine that certain business relationships are *per se* violations of the Act without regard to a consideration of their reasonableness.

It is only after considerable experience with certain business relationships that courts classify them as *per se* violations of the Sherman Act. One of the classic examples of a *per se* violation of Section 1 is an agreement between competitors at the same level of the market structure to allocate territories in order to minimize competition. Such concerted action is usually termed a "horizontal" restraint, in contradistinction to combinations of persons at different levels of the market structure, e.g., manufacturers and distributors, which are termed "vertical" restraints. This Court has reiterated time and time again that "horizontal territorial limitations . . . are naked restraints of trade with no purpose except stifling of competition." *White Motor Co. v. United States* (1963).

We think that it is clear that the restraint in this case is a horizontal one, and, therefore, a *per se* violation of Section 1. The District Court failed to make any determination as to whether there were *per se* horizontal territorial restraints in this case and simply applied a rule of reason in reaching its conclusions that the restraints were not illegal. In so doing, the District Court erred.

*United States v. Sealy* (1969) is, in fact, on all fours with this case. Sealy licensed manufacturers of mattresses and bedding to make and sell products using the Sealy trademark. Like Topco, Sealy was a corporation owned almost entirely by its licensees, who elected the Board of Directors and controlled the business. Just as in this case, Sealy agreed with the licensees not to license other manufacturers or sellers to sell Sealy brand products in a designated territory in exchange for the promise of the licensee who sold in that territory not to expand its sales beyond the area demarcated by Sealy. The Court held that this was a horizontal territorial restraint which was *per se* violative of the Sherman Act.

Whether or not we would decide this case the same way under the rule of reason used by the District Court is irrelevant to the issue before us. The fact is that courts are of limited utility in examining difficult economic problems. Our inability to weigh, in any meaningful sense, destruction of competition in one sector of the economy against promotion of competition in another sector is one important reason we have formulated *per se* rules. In applying these rigid rules, the Court has consistently rejected the notion that naked restraints of trade are to be tolerated because they are well-intended or because they are allegedly developed to increase competition.

Antitrust laws in general, and the Sherman Act in particular, are the Magna Charta of free enterprise. They are as important to the preservation of economic freedom and our free enterprise system as the Bill of Rights is to the protection of our fundamental personal freedoms. And the freedom guaranteed each and every business, no matter how small, is the freedom to compete—to assert with vigor, imagination, devotion, and ingenuity whatever economic muscle it can muster. Implicit in such freedom is the notion that it cannot be foreclosed with respect to one sector of the economy because certain private citizens or groups believe that such foreclosure might promote greater competition in a more important sector of the economy.

The District Court determined that by limiting the freedom of its individual members to compete with each other, Topco was doing a greater good by fostering competition between members and other large supermarket chains. But, the fallacy in this is that Topco has no authority under the Sherman Act to determine the respective values of competition in various sectors of the economy. On the contrary, the Sherman Act gives to each Topco member and to each prospective member the right to ascertain for itself whether or not competition with other supermarket chains is more desirable than competition in the sale of Topco brand products. Without territorial restrictions, Topco members may indeed "cut each other's throat." But, we have never found this possibility sufficient to warrant condoning horizontal restraints of trade.

There have been tremendous departures from the notion of a free enterprise system as it was originally conceived in this country. These departures have been the product of congressional action and the will of the people. If a decision is to be made to sacrifice competition in one portion of the economy for greater competition in another portion, this too is a decision which must be made by Congress and not by private forces or by the courts. Private forces are too keenly aware of their own interests in making such decisions and courts are ill-equipped and ill-situated for such decision-making. To analyze, interpret, and evaluate the myriad of competing interests and the endless data which would surely be brought to bear on such decisions, and to make the delicate judgment on the relative values to society of competitive areas of the economy, the judgment of the elected representatives of the people is required.

Judgment reversed in favor of the government.

## Continental T.V., Inc. v. GTE Sylvania, Inc.

**433 U.S. 36 (U.S. Sup. Ct. 1977)**

In the early 1950s, Sylvania's share of the national TV market had declined to about 1 percent. In an attempt to remedy this situation, Sylvania phased out all wholesalers and limited the number of retail franchises that it granted for a given area. Sylvania also required that each franchisee sell Sylvania products only from the sales location described in its franchise. This strategy apparently contributed to increasing sales by Sylvania, but it led to friction with some dealers when Sylvania shuffled sales location areas and refused to grant requests for expansion of some sales areas.

Continental, a Sylvania dealer, became unhappy when Sylvania franchised another dealer in part of Continental's market and then refused Continental's request for permission to expand into another market area. As the dispute developed, Sylvania reduced Continental's credit line. In response, Continental withheld all payments owed to the finance company that handled all credit arrangements between Sylvania and its retailers. Shortly thereafter, Sylvania terminated Continental's franchise and the finance company filed suit to recover payments due on merchandise purchased by Continental. Continental cross-claimed against Sylvania, arguing that Sylvania's location restriction was a per se violation of Section 1 of the Sherman Act. The trial jury agreed and awarded Continental $1.7 million in treble damages. The Ninth Circuit Court of Appeals reversed, holding that Sylvania's location restriction should be judged under the rule of reason because it presented less of a threat to competition than did the restrictions held per se illegal in the *Schwinn* case. Continental appealed.

**POWELL, JUSTICE.** Vertical restrictions reduce intrabrand competition by limiting the number of sellers of a particular product competing for the business of a given group of buyers. Location restrictions have this effect because of practical constraints on the effective marketing area of retail outlets. Although intrabrand competition may be reduced, the ability of retailers to exploit the resulting market may be limited both by the ability of consumers to travel to other franchised locations and, perhaps more importantly, to purchase the competing products of other manufacturers. None of these key variables, however, is affected by the form of the transaction by which a manufacturer conveys his products to the retailers.

Vertical restrictions promote interbrand competition by allowing the manufacturer to achieve certain efficiencies in the distribution of his products. These "redeeming virtues" are implicit in every decision sustaining vertical restrictions under the rule of reason. Economists have identified a number of ways in which manufacturers can use such restrictions to compete more effectively against other manufacturers. For example, new manufacturers and manufacturers entering new markets can use the restrictions in order to induce competent and aggressive retailers to make the kind of investment of capital and labor that is often required in the distribution of products unknown to the consumer. Established manufacturers can use them to induce retailers to engage in promotional activities or to provide service and repair facilities necessary to the efficient marketing of their products. Service and repair are vital for many products, such as automobiles and major household appliances. The availability and quality of such services affect a manufacturer's goodwill and the competitiveness of his product. Because of market imperfections such as the so-called free rider effect, these services might not be provided by retailers in a purely competitive situation, despite the fact that each retailer's benefit would be greater if all provided services than if none did.

Economists also have argued that manufacturers have an economic interest in maintaining as much intrabrand competition as is consistent with the efficient distribution of their products. Although the view that the manufacturer's interest necessarily corresponds with that of the public is not universally shared, even the leading critic of vertical restrictions concedes that *Schwinn's* distinction between sale and nonsale transactions is essentially unrelated to any relevant economic impact. Indeed, to the extent that the form of the transaction is related to interbrand benefits, the Court's distinction is inconsistent with its articulated concern for the ability of smaller firms to compete effectively with larger ones. Capital requirements and administrative expenses may prevent smaller firms from using the exception for nonsale transactions.

We revert to the standard articulated in *Northern Pac. R. Co.,* and reiterated in *White Motor,* for determining whether vertical restrictions must be "conclusively presumed to be unreasonable and therefore illegal without elaborate inquiry as to the precise harm they have caused or the business excuse for their use." Such restrictions, in varying forms, are widely used in our free market economy. As indicated above, there is substantial scholarly and judicial authority supporting their economic utility. There is relatively no showing in this case, either generally or with respect to Sylvania's agreements, that vertical restrictions have or are likely to have a "pernicious effect on competition" or that they "lack any redeeming virtue." Accordingly, we conclude that the *per se* rule stated in *Schwinn* must be overruled. In so holding we do not foreclose the possibility that particular applications of vertical restrictions might justify *per se* prohibition under *Northern Pac. R. Co.* But we do make clear that departure from the rule of reason standard must be based upon demonstrable economic effect rather than—as in *Schwinn*—upon formalistic line drawing.

In sum, we conclude that the appropriate decision is to return to the rule of reason that governed vertical restrictions prior to *Schwinn.* When competitive effects are shown to result from particular vertical restrictions they can be adequately policed under the rule of reason, the standard traditionally applied for the majority of anticompetitive practices challenged under Section 1 of the Act.

Judgment for Sylvania affirmed.

**Group Boycotts and Concerted Refusals to Deal.** While under the "Colgate doctrine" a single firm can lawfully refuse to deal with certain firms, it has long been said that agreements by two or more business entities to refuse to deal with others, or to deal with others only on certain terms and conditions, or to coerce suppliers or customers not to deal with one of their competitors, are *joint* restraints on trade and per se illegal under Section 1. For example, when a trade association of garment manufacturers agreed not to sell to retailers that sold clothing or fabrics with designs "pirated" from legitimate manufacturers, the agreement was held to be a per se violation of the Sherman Act.[22]

Recent antitrust developments, however, indicate that not all concerted refusals to deal will be subjected to per se analysis. Some lower federal courts have indicated that certain *vertical* boycotts involving parties at various levels of a product's chain of distribution will be judged under the rule of reason absent proof of a price-fixing intent. A manufacturer that terminates a distributor in response to complaints from other distributors that the terminated distributor was selling to customers outside its prescribed sales territory will have violated Section 1 only if the termination results in a significant harm to competition. On the other hand, a manufacturer that terminates a distributor as part of a resale price maintenance conspiracy is guilty of a per se violation of the Sherman Act (e.g., Monsanto's termination of Spray-Rite).

In addition, some recent cases have indicated that boycotts undertaken for *political purposes* may be protected by the First Amendment guarantees of freedom of speech and the right to petition the government for the redress of grievances. For example, when the state of Missouri sued the National Organization of Women (NOW) over NOW's boycott of states that had failed to ratify the Equal Rights Amendment, the U.S. Court of

[22] *Fashion Originators' Guild v. FTC,* 312 U.S. 457 (U.S. Sup. Ct. 1941).

Appeals for the Eighth Circuit ruled that NOW's activities were beyond the scope of the Sherman Act and were protected by the First Amendment.[23]

**Tying Agreements. Tying agreements** occur when a seller refuses to sell a buyer one product (the *tying product*) unless the buyer also agrees to purchase a different product (the *tied product*) from the seller. For example, a fertilizer manufacturer refuses to sell its dealers fertilizer (the tying product) unless they also agree to buy its line of pesticides (the tied product). The potential anticompetitive effect of a tying agreement is that the seller's competitors in the sale of the tied product may be foreclosed from competing with the seller for sales to customers that have entered into tying agreements with the seller. To the extent that tying agreements are coercively imposed, they also deprive buyers of the freedom to make independent decisions concerning their purchases of the tied product. The legality of tying agreements may be challenged under both Section 1 of the Sherman Act and Section 3 of the Clayton Act.[24]

It is often said that tying agreements are per se illegal under Section 1, but since a tying agreement must meet certain criteria before it will be subjected to per se analysis, and since evidence of certain justifications is sometimes considered in tying cases, the rule against tying agreements is, at best, a "soft" per se rule. Before a challenged agreement will be held to be an illegal tying agreement in violation of Section 1, it must be proven that: the agreement involves *two* separate and distinct items rather than integrated components of a larger product, service, or system of doing business; the tying product cannot be purchased unless the tied product is also purchased; the seller has sufficient economic power in the market for the tying product to appreciably restrain competition in the tied product market (e.g., a patent or a large market share); and a "not insubstantial" amount of commerce in the tied product is affected by the seller's tying agreements.[25]

The first two elements listed above have been particularly relevant in some recent cases involving alleged tying agreements among franchisors and their franchised dealers. For example, a recent suit by a McDonald's franchisee alleged that McDonald's violated Section 1 by requiring franchisees to lease their stores from McDonald's in order to acquire a McDonald's franchise. The Eighth Circuit Court of Appeals rejected the franchisee's claim, however, on the ground that no tying agreement was involved, because the franchise and the lease were integral components of a well-thought-out system of doing business.[26]

The lower federal courts have recognized two other possible justifications for true tying agreements. First, tying arrangements that are instrumental in launching a new competitor with an uncertain future may be lawful until the new business has established itself in the marketplace. The logic of this "new business" exception is obvious: if a tying agreement enables a fledgling firm to become a viable competitor, the ultimate net effect of the agreement on competition is a positive one. Also, some courts have recognized that, in some cases, tying agreements may be necessary to protect the reputation of the seller's product line (e.g., one of the seller's products will function properly only if used in conjunc-

[23] *Missouri v. National Organization of Women,* 620 F.2d 1301 (8th Cir. 1980).

[24] Section 3 of the Clayton Act applies, however, only when both the tying and the tied product are "commodities." Clayton Act standards for tying agreement legality are discussed in the next chapter.

[25] *U.S. Steel Corp. v. Fortner Enterprises, Inc.,* 429 U.S. 610 (U.S. Sup. Ct. 1977).

[26] *Principe v. McDonald's Corp.,* 631 F.2d 303 (4th Cir. 1980).

tion with another of its products). To successfully utilize this exception, however, the seller must convince the court that no viable means to protect its goodwill exist other than a tying arrangement.

Chicago School thinkers have long criticized the courts' approach to tying agreements because they do not believe that most tie-ins result in any significant economic harm. They argue that sellers that try to impose a tie-in in competitive markets gain no increased profits from the tie-in. This is so because instead of participating in a tying agreement, buyers may turn to substitutes for the tying product or may purchase the tying product from competing sellers. The net effect of a tie-in may therefore be that any increase in the seller's sales in the tied product will be offset by a loss in sales of the tying product. Only when the seller has substantial power in the tying product market does the potential arise that a tie-in may be used to increase the seller's power in the tied product market. However, even where the seller has such market power in the tying product, Chicago School thinkers argue that no harm to competition is likely to result if the seller faces strong competition in the tied product market. For these and other reasons, Chicago School thinkers favor a rule of reason approach to all tying agreements. While a majority of the Supreme Court has yet to accept these arguments, several current members of the Court appear to have done so. If other members of the Court are similarly persuaded in the future, a substantial change in the legal criteria applied to tying agreements will be the likely result.

**Reciprocal Dealing Agreements.** A **reciprocal dealing agreement** is one in which a buyer attempts to exploit its purchasing power by conditioning its purchases from its suppliers on reciprocal purchases by them of some product or service offered for sale by the buyer. For example, an oil company with a chain of wholly owned gas stations refuses to purchase the tires it sells in those stations from a tire manufacturer unless the tire manufacturer agrees to purchase from the oil company the petrochemicals used in the tire manufacturing process. Reciprocal dealing agreements are otherwise quite similar in motivation and effect to tying agreements, and the courts tend to treat them in a similar fashion. In seeking to impose the reciprocal dealing agreement on the tire manufacturer, the oil company is trying to gain a competitive advantage over its competitors in the petrochemical market. A court judging the legality of such an agreement would look at the dollar amount of petrochemical sales involved and at the oil company's economic power as a purchaser of tires.

**Exclusive Dealing Agreements. Exclusive dealing agreements** require the buyers of a particular product or service to purchase that product or service exclusively from a particular seller. For example, Standard Lawnmower Corporation requires its retail dealers to sell only Standard brand mowers. A common variation of an exclusive dealing agreement is the **requirements contract,** in which the buyer of a particular product agrees to purchase all of its requirements for that product from a particular supplier (e.g., a candy manufacturer agrees to buy all of its sugar requirements from one sugar refiner). Exclusive dealing contracts present a threat to competition similar to that involved in tying contracts: they can reduce interbrand competition by foreclosing a seller's competitors from the opportunity to compete for sales to its customers. Unlike tying contracts, however, exclusive dealing agreements can sometimes enhance efficiencies in distribution and stimulate interbrand competition. Exclusive dealing agreements reduce a manufacturer's sales costs and provide dealers with a secure source of supply. They may also encourage dealer efforts to more effectively market the manufacturer's products, since a dealer that sells only one product line has a greater stake in the success of that line than does a dealer that sells the products of several competing manufacturers.

Since many exclusive dealing agreements involve commodities, they may also be challenged under Section 3 of the Clayton Act. The legal tests applicable to exclusive dealing agreements under both Acts are identical. We will therefore defer discussion of them until the following chapter.

## Jefferson Parish Hospital Dist. No. 2 v. Hyde

### 52 U.S.L.W. 4385 (U.S. Sup. Ct. 1984)

In July 1977, Edwin G. Hyde, an anesthesiologist, applied for admission to the medical staff of East Jefferson Hospital in New Orleans. The credentials committee and the medical staff executive committee recommended approval, but the hospital board denied the application because the hospital was a party to a contract providing that all anesthesiological services required by the hospital's patients would be performed by Roux & Associates, a professional medical corporation. Hyde filed suit against the board, arguing that the contract violated Section 1 of the Sherman Act.

The district court ruled in favor of the board, finding that the anticompetitive effects of the contract were minimal and were outweighed by benefits in the form of improved patient care. It noted that there were at least 20 hospitals in the New Orleans metropolitan area and that about 70 percent of the patients residing in Jefferson Parish went to hospitals other than East Jefferson. It therefore concluded that East Jefferson lacked any significant market power and could not use the contract for anticompetitive ends. The Fifth Circuit Court of Appeals reversed, holding that the relevant market was the East Bank Jefferson Parish rather than the New Orleans metropolitan area. The Court therefore concluded that since 30 percent of the parish residents used East Jefferson and "patients tend to choose hospitals by location rather than price or quality," East Jefferson possessed sufficient market power to make the contract a per se illegal tying contract. The board appealed.

**Stevens, Justice.** It is far too late in the history of our antitrust jurisprudence to question the proposition that certain tying arrangements pose an unacceptable risk of stifling competition and therefore are unreasonable *per se.* The rule was first enunciated in *International Salt Co. v. United States* (1947), and has been endorsed by this Court many times since. The rule also reflects congressional policies underlying the antitrust laws. In enacting Section 3 of the Clayton Act, Congress expressed great concern about the anticompetitive character of tying arrangements. While this case does not arise under the Clayton Act, the congressional finding made therein concerning the competitive consequences of tying is illuminating, and must be respected.

It is clear, however, that every refusal to sell two products separately cannot be said to restrain competition. If each of the products may be purchased separately in a competitive market, one seller's decision to sell the two in a single package imposes no unreasonable restraint on either market, particularly if competing suppliers are free to sell either the entire package or its several parts. For example, we have written that "if one of a dozen food stores in a community were to refuse to sell flour unless the buyer also took sugar it would hardly tend to restrain competition if its competitors were ready and able to sell flour by itself." Buyers often find package sales attractive; a seller's decision to offer such packages can merely be an attempt to compete effectively—conduct that is entirely consistent with the Sherman Act.

Our cases have concluded that the essential characteristic of an invalid tying arrangement lies in the seller's exploitation of its control over the tying product to force the buyer into the purchase of a tied product that the buyer either did not want at all, or might have preferred to purchase elsewhere on different terms. When such "forcing" is present, competition on the merits in the market for the tied item is restrained and the Sherman Act is violated. Accordingly, we have condemned tying arrangements when the seller has some special ability—usually called "market power"—to force a purchaser to do something that he would not do in a competitive market.

*Per se* condemnation—condemnation without inquiry into actual market conditions—is only appropriate if the existence of forcing is probable. Thus, application of the *per se* rule focuses on the probability of anticompetitive consequences. Of course, as a threshold matter there must be a substantial potential for impact on competition in order to justify *per se* condemnation. If only a single purchaser were "forced" with respect to the purchase of a tied item, the resultant impact on competition would not be sufficient to warrant the concern of antitrust law. It is for this reason that we have refused to condemn tying arrangements unless a substantial volume of commerce is foreclosed thereby. Similarly, when a purchaser is "forced" to buy a product he would not have otherwise bought even from another seller in the tied product market, there can be no adverse impact on competition because no portion of the market which would otherwise have been available to other sellers has been foreclosed.

Once this threshold is surmounted, *per se* prohibition is appropriate if anticompetitive forcing is likely. For example, if the government has granted the seller a patent or similar monopoly over a product, it is fair to presume that the inability to buy the product elsewhere gives the seller market power. Any effort to enlarge the scope of the patent monopoly by using the market power it confers to restrain competition in the market for a second product will undermine competition on the merits in that second market. Thus, the sale or lease of a patented item on condition that the buyer make all his purchases of a separate tied product from the patentee is unlawful.

The same strict rule is appropriate in other situations in which the existence of market power is probable. When the seller's share of the market is high, or when the seller offers a unique product that competitors are not able to offer, the Court has held that the likelihood that market power exists and is being used to restrain competition in a separate market is sufficient to make *per se* condemnation appropriate.

When, however, the seller does not have either the degree or kind of market power that enables him to force customers to purchase a second, unwanted product in order to obtain the tying product, an antitrust violation can be established only by evidence of an unreasonable restraint on competition in the relevant market.

In sum, any inquiry into the validity of a tying arrangement must focus on the market or markets in which the two products are sold, for that is where the anticompetitive forcing has its impact. Thus, in this case our analysis of the tying issue must focus on the hospital's sale of services to its patients, rather than its contractual arrangements with the providers of anesthesiological services. In making that analysis, we must consider whether the hospital is selling two separate products that may be tied together, and, if so, whether it has used its market power to force its patients to accept the tying arrangement.

The hospital has provided its patients with a package that includes the range of facilities and services required for a variety of surgical operations. At East Jefferson Hospital the package includes the services of the anesthesiologist. The board argues that the package does not involve a tying arrangement at all—that they are merely providing a functionally integrated package of services. Therefore, the board contends that it is inappropriate to apply principles concerning tying arrangements to this case.

Our cases indicate, however, that the answer to the question whether one or two products are involved turns not on the functional relation between them, but rather on the character of the demand for the two items. Thus, in this case no tying arrangement can exist unless there is a sufficient demand for the purchase of anesthesiological services separate from hospital services to identify a distinct product market in which it is efficient to offer anesthesiological services separately from hospital services.

Unquestionably, the anesthesiological component of the package offered by the hospital could be provided separately and could be selected either by the individual patient or by one of the patient's doctors if the hospital did not insist on including anesthesiological services in the package it offers to its customers. As a matter of actual practice, anesthesiological services are billed separately from the hospital services petitioners provide. There was ample and uncontroverted testimony that patients or surgeons often request specific anesthesiologists to come to a hospital and provide anesthesia, and that the choice of an individual anesthesiologist separate from the choice of a hospital is particularly frequent in Hyde's specialty, obstetric anesthesiology. The record amply supports the conclusion that consumers differentiate between anesthesiological services and the other hospital services provided by the board.

Thus, the hospital's requirement that its patients obtain necessary anesthesiological services from Roux combined the purchase of two distinguishable services in a single transaction. Nevertheless, the fact that this case involves a required purchase of two services that would otherwise be purchased separately does not make the Roux contract illegal. As noted above, there is nothing inherently anticompetitive about packaged sales. Only if patients are forced to purchase Roux's services as a result of the hospital's market power would the arrangement have anticompetitive consequences. If no forcing is present, patients are free to enter a competing hospital and to use another anesthesiologist instead of Roux. The fact that the hospital's patients are required to purchase two separate items is only the beginning of the appropriate inquiry.

The question remains whether this arrangement involves the use of market power to force patients to buy services they would not otherwise purchase. Hyde's only basis for invoking the *per se* rule against tying and thereby avoiding analysis of actual market conditions is by relying on the preference of persons residing in Jefferson Parish to go to East Jefferson, the closest hospital. A preference of this kind, however, is not necessarily probative of significant market power.

Seventy percent of the patients residing in Jefferson Parish enter hospitals other than East Jefferson. Thus, East Jefferson's "dominance" over persons residing in Jefferson Parish is far from overwhelming. The fact that a substantial majority of the parish's residents elect not to enter East Jefferson means that the geographic data does not establish the kind of dominant market position that obviates the need for further inquiry into actual competitive conditions. The Court of Appeals acknowledged as much; it recognized that East Jefferson's market share alone was insufficient as a basis to infer market power, and buttressed its conclusion by relying on "market imperfections" that permit the hospital to charge noncompetitive prices for hospital services: the prevalence of third party payment for health care costs reduces price competition, and a lack of adequate information renders consumers unable to evaluate the quality of the medical care provided by competing hospitals. While these factors may generate "market power" in some abstract sense, they do not generate the kind of market power that justifies condemnation of tying.

Tying arrangements need only be condemned if they restrain competition on the merits by forcing purchases that would not otherwise be made. A lack of price or quality competition does not create this type of forcing. If consumers lack price consciousness, that fact will not force them to take an anesthesiologist whose services they do not want—their indifference to price will have no impact on their willingness or ability to go to another hospital where they can utilize the services of the anesthesiologist of their choice. Similarly, if consumers cannot evaluate the quality of anesthesiological services, it follows that they are indifferent between certified anesthesiologists even in the absence of a tying arrangement—such an arrangement cannot be said to have foreclosed a choice that would have otherwise been made "on the merits."

Thus, neither of the "market imperfections" relied upon by the Court of Appeals forces consumers to take anesthesiological services they would not select in the absence of a tie. It is safe to assume that every patient undergoing a surgical operation needs the services of an anesthesiologist; at least this record contains no evidence that the hospital "forced" any such services on unwilling patients. The record therefore does not provide a basis for applying the *per se* rule against tying to this arrangement.

In order to prevail in the absence of *per se* liability, Hyde has the burden of proving that the Roux contract violated the Sherman Act because it unreasonably restrained competition. That burden necessarily involves an inquiry into the actual effect of the exclusive contract on competition among anesthesiologists. This competition takes place in a market that has not been defined. The market is not necessarily the same as the market in which hospitals compete in offering services to patients; it may encompass competition among anesthesiologists for exclusive contracts such as the Roux contract and might be statewide or merely local. There is, however, insufficient evidence in this record to provide a basis for finding that the Roux contract, as it actually operates in the market, has unreasonably restrained competition.

Judgment reversed in favor of Jefferson Parish.

---

**Joint Ventures by Competitors.** A **joint venture** is a combined effort by two or more business entities for a limited purpose (e.g., a joint research venture). Because joint ventures may yield enhanced efficiencies by integrating the resources of more than one firm, they are commonly judged under the rule of reason. Under this approach, the courts tend to ask whether any restraints on competition that are incidental to the venture are necessary to accomplish its lawful objectives and, if so, whether these restraints are offset by the positive effects of the venture. Joint ventures whose primary purpose is illegal per se, however, have often been treated as per se illegal (e.g., two competing firms form a joint sales agency that is empowered to fix the price of their products).

Antitrust critics have long argued that the threat of antitrust prosecution seriously inhibits the formation of joint research and development ventures, with the result that American firms are placed at a competitive disadvantage in world markets. Such arguments have recently begun to enjoy more acceptance, given existing concerns about the performance of the American economy. As a result, Congress passed the National Cooperative Research Act in 1984. The Act applies to "joint research and development ventures" (JRDVs), which are broadly defined to include basic and applied research and joint activities in the licensing of technologies developed by such research. The Act requires the application of a "reasonableness" standard, instead of a per se rule, in judging a JRDV's legality. It also requires firms contemplating a JRDV to provide the Justice Department and the Federal Trade Commission with advance notice of their intent to do so, and it provides that only single (not treble) damages may be recovered for losses flowing from a JRDV that is ultimately found to be in violation of Section 1. In addition, the Act contains a novel provision that allows the parties to a challenged JRDV to recover attorney's fees from an unsuccessful challenger in certain circumstances.

## SECTION 2—MONOPOLIZATION

**Introduction.** Firms that acquire **monopoly power** in a given market have defeated the antitrust laws' objective of promoting competitive market structures. Monopolists, by definition, have the power to fix price unilaterally because they have no effective competition. Section 2 of the Sherman Act was designed to prevent the formation of monopoly power. It provides:

> Every person who shall monopolize, or attempt to monopolize, or combine or conspire with any other person to monopolize any part of trade or commerce among the several states, or with foreign nations shall be deemed guilty of a felony.

The language of Section 2 does not, however, outlaw monopolies: it outlaws the act of "monopolizing." You should also note that under Section 2 a *single firm* can be guilty of "monopolizing" or "attempting to monopolize" a part of trade or commerce. The proof of joint action required for violations of Section 1 is required only when two or more firms are charged with a conspiracy to monopolize under Section 2.

**Monopolization.** As the *Grinnell* case, which follows, indicates, **monopolization** is currently defined as "the willful acquisition or maintenance of monopoly power in a relevant market as opposed to growth as a consequence of superior product, business acumen, or historical accident." This means that to be guilty of monopolization a defendant must not only possess **monopoly power** but must also have demonstrated an **intent to monopolize.**

**Monopoly Power.** Monopoly power is usually defined for antitrust purposes as the power to *fix prices* or *exclude competitors* in a given market. Monopoly power is generally inferred from the fact that a firm has captured a predominant share of the relevant market. Although the exact percentage share necessary to support an inference of monopoly power remains unclear, and courts often look at other economic factors, such as the existence in the industry of barriers to the entry of new competitors, market shares in excess of 70 percent have historically justified an inference of monopoly power.

Before a court can determine a defendant's market share, it must first define the **relevant market.** This is a crucial part of Section 2 proceedings because a broad definition of the relevant market will normally result in a smaller market share for the defendant and a resulting reduction in the likelihood that the defendant will be found to possess monopoly power. There are two components to a relevant market determination: the relevant *geographic market* and the relevant *product market.*

The relevant geographic market is determined by economic realities prevailing in the industry: in what parts of the country can the defendant effectively compete with other firms in the sale of the product in question, and to whom may buyers turn for alternative sources of supply? Factors such as transportation costs may play a critical role in relevant market determinations. Thus, the relevant market for coal may be regional in nature, but the relevant market for transistors may be national in scope.

The relevant product market is composed of those products that are "reasonably interchangeable by consumers for the same purposes" (the *functional interchangeability* test). This test recognizes that a firm's ability to fix the price for its products is limited by the availability of competing products that buyers view as acceptable substitutes. In a famous antitrust case, for example, Du Pont was charged with monopolizing the national market for cellophane (it had a 75 percent share). The Supreme Court concluded, however, that the relevant market was all "flexible wrapping materials," including aluminum foil, waxed paper, and polyethylene, and that Du Pont's 20 percent share of that product market was far too small to amount to monopoly power.[27]

**Intent to Monopolize.** Proof of monopoly power standing alone, however, is never sufficient to prove a violation of Section 2. It must also be shown that the defendant had an intent to monopolize. Early cases under Section 2 required evidence that the defendant either acquired monopoly power by predatory or coercive means that themselves violated antitrust rules (e.g., price-fixing or discriminatory pricing) or abused monopoly power in some way after acquiring it (e.g., by price-gouging).[28] Contemporary courts look at how the defendant acquired monopoly power: if the defendant *intentionally acquired* it or *attempted to maintain it* after having acquired it, this is sufficient evidence of an intent to monopolize. Defendants that have monopoly power "thrust" upon them due to the superiority of their products or business decisions, or that hold monopoly power by virtue of a historical accident (e.g., the owner of a professional sports franchise in an area too small to support a competing franchise), will not be in violation of Section 2.

Purposeful acquisition or maintenance of monopoly power may be demonstrated in a variety of ways. Thus, in a famous monopolization case against Alcoa involving the American market for virgin aluminum ingot (Alcoa had a 90 percent market share), Alcoa was found guilty of purposefully maintaining its monopoly power by acquiring every new opportunity relating to the production or marketing of aluminum, thereby excluding potential competitors.[29] As the *Grinnell* case indicates, firms that acquire monopoly power by acquiring ownership or control of their competitors are very likely to be held to have demonstrated an intent to monopolize. Finally, some recent Section 2 cases have recognized a "leveraging" theory of monopolization, making it a violation of the Act for a firm with significant market power in one relevant market to use that power unfairly to acquire market power in another relevant market. In one recent case, for example, the sole sugar beet purchaser from beet growers in the state of Washington adopted a purchasing policy that discouraged growers from purchasing beet seeds from a would-be competitor in the sale of seeds. The Ninth Circuit Court of Appeals held that this could constitute monopo-

[27] *United States v. E. I. du Pont de Nemours & Co.*, 351 U.S. 377 (U.S. Sup. Ct. 1956).

[28] *Standard Oil Co. of New Jersey v. United States*, 221 U.S. 1 (U.S. Sup. Ct. 1911).

[29] *United States v. Aluminum Co. of America, Inc.*, 148 F.2d 416 (2d Cir. 1945).

lization if the evidence at trial indicated that no legitimate business justification motivated the policy.[30]

**Attempted Monopolization.** Firms that have not yet attained monopoly power may nonetheless be guilty of an *attempt to monopolize* in violation of Section 2 if they are dangerously close to acquiring monopoly power and are employing methods likely to result in monopoly power if left unchecked. In addition to proof of the probability that monopoly power will be acquired, attempt to monopolize cases, like monopolization cases, normally require proof of the relevant market. Unlike monopolization cases, attempt cases also require proof that the defendant possessed a specific intent to acquire monopoly power by anticompetitive means.

One controversial Section 2 issue that surfaces in many attempted monopolization cases concerns the role that *predatory pricing* can play in proving an intent to monopolize. The difficulty in predatory pricing cases is distinguishing between legitimate competitive behavior and illegitimate predatory conduct. Two noted antitrust authorities have suggested that pricing *below a firm's average variable cost* should be conclusively presumed to be illegal and that pricing above average variable cost should conclusively presumed to be lawful.[31] Some lower federal courts have adopted this test, while others have employed a variety of other standards.[32] The controversy is likely to continue until it is ultimately resolved by the Supreme Court.

**Conspiracy to Monopolize.** When two or more business entities *conspire to monopolize* a relevant market, this can amount to a violation of Section 2. This part of Section 2, however, largely overlaps Section 1, because it is difficult to conceive of a conspiracy to monopolize that would not also amount to a conspiracy in restraint of trade. The lower federal courts differ on the elements necessary to prove a conspiracy to monopolize. Some courts require proof of the relevant market, a specific intent to acquire monopoly power, and overt action in furtherance of the conspiracy in addition to proof of the existence of a conspiracy. Other courts do not require extensive proof of the relevant market, holding that proof that the defendants conspired to acquire control over prices in, or exclude competitors from, some significant area of commerce is sufficient to establish a violation.

[30] *Betaseed, Inc. v. U and I, Inc.*, 681 F.2d 1203 (9th Cir. 1982).

[31] Areeda & Turner, "Predatory Pricing and Related Practices under Section 2 of the Sherman Act," 88 *Harv. L. Rev.* 697 (1975).

[32] For example, the First Circuit Court of Appeals recently held that pricing above average total cost is presumptively lawful. *Barry Wright Corp. v. ITT Grinnell Corp.*, 724 F.2d 227 (1st Cir. 1983).

## United States v. Grinnell Corp.

### 384 U.S. 563 (U.S. Sup. Ct. 1966)

Grinnell manufactured plumbing supplies and fire sprinkler systems. It also owned 76 percent of the stock of ADT, 89 percent of the stock of AFA, and 100 percent of the stock of Holmes. ADT provided both burglary and fire protection services; Holmes provided burglary services alone; AFA supplied only fire protection service. Each offered a central station service under which hazard-detecting devices installed on the protected premises automatically transmitted an electrical signal to a central station. There were other forms of protective services. But the record indicated that subscribers to an accredited central station service (i.e., one approved by the insurance underwriters) received reductions in their insurance premiums that were substantially greater than the reductions received by the users of other kinds of protection services. In 1961, accredited companies in the central station service business grossed $65 million. ADT, Holmes, and AFA, all controlled by Grinnell, were the three largest companies in the business in terms of revenue, with about 87 percent of the business.

In 1907, Grinnell entered into a series of agreements with the other defendant companies that allocated the major cities and markets for central station alarm services in the United States. Each defendant agreed not to compete outside the market areas allocated.

Over the years, the defendants purchased the stock or assets of 30 companies engaged in the business of providing burglar or fire alarm services. After Grinnell acquired control of the other defendants, the latter continued in their attempts to acquire central station companies—offers being made to at least eight companies between the years 1955 and 1961, including four of the five largest nondefendant companies in the business. When the present suit was filed, each of those defendants had outstanding an offer to purchase one of the four largest nondefendant companies.

ADT over the years reduced its minimum basic rates to meet competition and renewed contracts at substantially increased rates in cities where it had a monopoly of accredited central station service. ADT threatened retaliation against firms that contemplated inaugurating central station service.

The government filed suit against Grinnell under Section 2 of the Sherman Act, asking that Grinnell be forced to divest itself of ADT, Holmes, and AFA and for other injunctive relief. The district court ruled in favor of the government, and Grinnell appealed.

**Douglas, Justice.** The offense of monopoly under Section 2 of the Sherman Act has two elements: (1) the possession of monopoly power in the relevant market and (2) the willful acquisition or maintenance of that power as distinguished from growth or development as a consequence of a superior product, business acumen, or historic accident. We shall see that this second ingredient presents no major problem here, as what was done in building the empire was done plainly and explicitly for a single purpose. In *United States v. E. I. du Pont de Nemours & Co.,* we defined monopoly power as "the power to control prices or exclude competition." The existence of such power ordinarily may be inferred from the predominant share of the market. In *American Tobacco Co. v. United States,* we said that "over two thirds of the entire domestic field of cigarettes, and over 80 percent of the field of comparable cigarettes" constituted "a substantial monopoly." In *United States v. Aluminum Co. of America,* 90 percent of the market constituted monopoly power. In the present case, 87 percent of the accredited central station service business leaves no doubt that the congeries of these defendants have monopoly power—power which, as our discussion of the record indicates, they did not hesitate to wield—if that business is the relevant market. The only remaining question therefore is, what is the relevant market?

In case of a product it may be of such a character that substitute products must also be considered, as customers may turn to them if there is a slight increase in the price of the main product. That is the teaching of the *Du Pont* case, that commodities reasonably interchangeable make up that "part" of trade or commerce which Section 2 protects against monopoly power.

The District Court treated the entire accredited central station service business as a single market and we think it was justified in so doing. Grinnell argues that the different central station services offered are so diverse that they cannot under *Du Pont* be lumped together to make up the relevant market. For example, burglar alarm services are not interchangeable with fire alarm services. It further urges that *Du Pont* requires that protective services other than those of the central station variety be included in the market definition.

But there is here a single use, i.e., the protection of property, through a central station that receives signals. It is that service, accredited, that is unique and that competes with all the other forms of property protection. We see no barrier to combining in a single market a number of different products or services where that combination reflects commercial realities. To repeat, there is here a single basic service—the protection of property through use of a central service station—that must be compared with all other forms of property protection.

There are, to be sure, substitutes for the accredited central station service. But none of them appears to operate on the same level as the central station service so as to meet the interchangeability test of the *Du Pont* case.

Grinnell earnestly urges that despite these differences, it faces competition from these other modes of protection. Grinnell seems to us seriously to overstate the degree of competition, but we recognize that (as the District Court found) it "does not have unfettered power to control the price of its services due to the fringe competition of other alarm or watchmen services." What Grinnell overlooks is that the high degree of differentiation between central station protection and the other forms means that for many customers, only central station protection will do.

As the District Court found, the relevant market for determining whether the defendants have monopoly power is not the several local areas which the individual stations serve, but the broader national market that reflects the reality of the way in which they built and conduct their business.

We have said enough about the great hold that the defendants have on this market. The percentage is so high as to justify the finding of monopoly. And, as the facts already related indicate, this monopoly was achieved in large part by unlawful and exclusionary practices. The restrictive agreements that pre-empted for each company a segment of the market where it was free of competition of the others were one device. Pricing practices that contained competitors were another. The acquisition by Grinnell of ADT, AFA, and Holmes were still another. Its control of the three other defendants eliminated any possibility of an outbreak of competition that might have occurred when the 1907 agreements terminated. By those acquisitions it perfected the monopoly power to exclude competitors and fix prices.

Judgment for the government affirmed.

## SUMMARY

The antitrust laws represent a congressional attempt to preserve competition as the most efficient means of allocating scarce social resources. Traditional antitrust policy placed significant emphasis on the structure of industry, believing that a fragmented market structure would foster competition. This and other long-standing premises of antitrust are being challenged today by critics espousing Chicago School economic ideas. Chicago

School thinkers tend to see economic efficiency as the primary goal of antitrust and are less concerned about industrial structure than are traditional antitrust thinkers.

The Sherman Act, passed in 1890, was the first of the federal antitrust laws. The Sherman Act is aimed at restraints of trade and monopolization of our interstate and foreign commerce. Economic activity that is solely intrastate in impact is outside the scope of the Sherman Act and must be regulated by state antitrust statutes. In today's interdependent economy, however, even economic activity carried on solely within the borders of one state is often found to have a significant enough impact on interstate commerce to justify federal antitrust jurisdiction.

The Sherman Act made restraints of trade and monopolization illegal, and also gave the federal courts broad injunctive powers to remedy antitrust violations. Individuals who violate the Sherman Act may be fined up to $100,000 per violation and imprisoned for up to three years. Corporate offenders may be fined up to $1 million per violation. Among the injunctive remedies that the federal courts may order in civil antitrust cases are divorcement, divestiture, and dissolution. The Clayton Act provides that private plaintiffs injured by antitrust violations may recover treble damages plus costs and attorney's fees from defendants that violate the antitrust laws. In order to recover treble damages, private plaintiffs must prove that they have suffered a direct antitrust injury.

Section 1 of the Sherman Act is aimed at joint or concerted action in restraint of trade. It outlaws contracts, combinations, and conspiracies in restraint of trade. Thus, a single firm cannot violate Section 1. This presents difficult enforcement problems because it raises difficult issues about how separate two business entities must be before they are capable of violating the Act and about the nature of the proof required to infer that parallel business behavior is the product of an illegal agreement to restrain trade rather than lawful unilateral action.

Two main methods of analysis are employed under Section 1. Activities that always have a negative effect on competition that can never be justified are classed as per se illegal and conclusively presumed to violate the act. All other activities are analyzed under the rule of reason, which means that the actual economic effects of the challenged activity must be examined to determine whether any negative effects on competition are offset by any positive effect on competition or by any other social benefit. In recent years, the Supreme Court has tended to move away from per se analysis in favor of affording rule of reason treatment to an increasing variety of economic activities.

Horizontal price-fixing and horizontal division of market schemes have long been held to be per se illegal and are likely to remain so. Vertical price-fixing (also called resale price maintenance) remains per se illegal, but Chicago School antitrust critics have argued that it should be treated under the rule of reason. Vertically imposed customer and market restrictions, once per se illegal, are now treated under the rule of reason, and many of the arguments used to justify this change in treatment have also been made on behalf of resale price maintenance.

Boycotts, or concerted refusals to deal, are normally said to be per se illegal. Recent cases, however, indicate that not all boycotts will be treated in this fashion. Some lower federal courts have applied the rule of reason standard to certain "vertical" boycotts, and "political" boycotts have been held to be constitutionally protected and thus outside the scope of the Sherman Act.

Tying agreements are often said to be per se illegal under Section 1, but because a tying arrangement must satisfy several tests to violate the act and because certain justifications may be advanced to legitimize some tying agreements, this is, at best, a "soft" per se rule.

Reciprocal dealing agreements are similar in many respects to tying agreements, and tend to be treated in a similar fashion by the courts. Exclusive dealing agreements can also violate the Sherman Act. Tying agreements, reciprocal dealing agreements, and exclusive dealing agreements can also be challenged under Section 3 of the Clayton Act if they involve commodities.

Joint ventures by competitors can also violate Section 1. Joint ventures tend to be scrutinized under the rule of reason unless their primary purpose is per se illegal. Some antitrust critics have charged that this potential illegality discourages joint venture activity and places American firms at a competitive disadvantage in the world marketplace. Legislation aimed at reducing the antitrust threat to joint ventures has recently been passed by Congress.

Section 2 of the Sherman Act prohibits monopolization, attempts to monopolize, and conspiracies to monopolize. A single firm can be guilty of monopolization or attempting to monopolize. To be guilty of monopolization, a firm must have monopoly power and an intent to monopolize. Monopoly power is normally inferred if the defendant has captured a predominant share of a relevant market. The relevant market determination, involving both the relevant product market and the relevant geographic market, is therefore a crucial part of any monopolization case. Intent to monopolize may be proven if it can be shown that a firm purposefully acquired or maintained monopoly power.

Attempted monopolization is demonstrated when a defendant is shown to be dangerously close to acquiring monopoly power and is employing methods that, if left unchecked, are likely to result in monopoly power. Attempt cases also require proof that the defendant has a specific intent to acquire monopoly power by anticompetitive means.

The conspiracy to monopolize portion of Section 2 is largely an overlap of the Section 1 prohibition of conspiracies in restraint of trade. The courts differ, however, on the elements required to prove a conspiracy to monopolize.

## PROBLEM CASES

**1.** Jona Goldschmidt, an Illinois attorney, placed an ad in a local newspaper that said, among other things, "Divorces, from $150 plus court costs." Shortly thereafter, he received a letter from the local state's attorney advising him that the ad violated an Illinois statute prohibiting advertising for the dissolution of marriage. Goldschmidt filed a suit against the state's attorney and an undetermined number of John Doe defendants, alleging a conspiracy in violation of Section 1 of the Sherman Act to prevent him from using local newspaper advertisements to solicit business. The trial court dismissed his claim without prejudice for failure to allege any connection between the defendants' actions and interstate commerce. Was the trial court's action correct?

**2.** National Bank of Canada filed suit under Section 1 of the Sherman Act seeking to enjoin Interbank Card Association, an American association licensing banks and other financial institutions to operate Master Charge businesses by issuing Master Charge credit cards, and Bank of Montreal, another Canadian bank, from carrying out their decision to terminate National Bank's Master Charge business. Should the Sherman Act apply to this case?

**3.** Beginning in early 1967, a group of beer wholesalers secretly agreed, in order to eliminate credit competition among themselves, that as of December they would sell to retailers only if payment were made in advance or upon delivery. Prior to the agreement, the wholesalers had extended credit without interest up to the limits of state law, had competed with one another with respect to trade credit, and had established credit terms for individual retailers that varied substantially. After entering into the agreement, the wholesalers uniformly refused to extend any credit at all. The retailers filed suit, arguing that the agreement to eliminate credit sales amounted to a per se illegal horizontal price-fixing agreement in violation of the Sherman Act. Were the retailers correct?

**4.** Two distributors filed suit against Pepperidge Farm, Inc., arguing that Pepperidge Farm's consignment agreements constituted per se illegal resale price maintenance agreements under Section 1 of the Sherman Act. Pepperidge dealt through independent distributors that had exclusive geographic territories and were forbidden to sell Pepperidge products outside their territories, but were allowed to distribute the products of other manufacturers inside their territories. Pepperidge had a dual system of accounts for its distributors: it directly billed chain stores of three or more retail stores, while the distributors billed all other customers. Pepperidge set wholesale prices on the direct billed accounts, but the distributors set wholesale prices on their own accounts and were free to solicit the directly billed customers as their own. Pepperidge retained title to, and risk of loss of, the goods until they reached retailers' shelves. It also paid applicable inventory and property taxes on the goods. Distributors did, however, have to absorb the cost of goods that went stale on their shelves. The trial court dismissed the distributors' claim. Was it correct in doing so?

**5.** Container Corporation of America and 17 other firms producing cardboard containers together accounted for approximately 90 percent of the market for cardboard containers in the southeastern United States. Each of these companies agreed to supply the others with price information about its most recent sales to identified customers. There was no express agreement among the companies to charge identical prices, and in some cases competitors had lowered their prices to get a specific order. In most cases, however, competitors receiving price information would quote a similar price. In the eight-year period covered by the government's complaint, several new competitors had entered the market and overall price levels had declined. The government filed a civil antitrust action against the companies, arguing that their customer information exchange was illegal horizontal price-fixing under Section 1 of the Sherman Act. Did the information exchange agreement amount to price-fixing?

**6.** Four major northeastern racetracks decided to adopt a "single tire rule" for the 1982 season, requiring drivers to use the Hoosier-brand Budget tire. M & H Tire Co., Inc., a rival racing tire manufacturer, sued Hoosier and the racetracks, arguing that the rule amounted to a per se illegal boycott in violation of the Sherman Act. The defendants argued that their actions were separate unilateral acts, but the evidence indicated that the rule was recommended by a committee of the New England Drivers and Owners Club (NEDOC) and agreed to by the promoters at a meeting with the NEDOC rules committee. The evidence also indicated that Hoosier had participated in the decision by submitting its tires for tests, agreeing to hold its retail prices at a specified level for the 1982 season, and agreeing to supply all of the tires needed. Finally, the evidence indicated that NEDOC's primary goal in adopting the rule was to prevent a rise in the price of racing tires over the 1982 season. Is M & H correct?

**7.** Between 1969 and 1978, North American Philips Corporation attempted to penetrate the U.S. small computer market, although its market share during this period never exceeded 5 percent. Philips's initial computer lines stored memory on magnetic ledger cards (mlc's). During the same period, Philips's products faced increasing competition from small computers using disk memories and cathode-ray tube (CRT) displays. Philips finally withdrew from the market in 1978. Philips also marketed mlc's manufactured by two German companies through Philips Business Systems, Inc., a subsidiary. In an attempt to expand its mlc sales, Philips allegedly denied service and warranty protection to computer owners who did not use its mlc's. General Business Systems (GBS), a Philips computer dealer, filed suit arguing that this action by Philips amounted to an illegal tying agreement in violation of the Sherman Act. Is GBS correct?

**8.** Baskin-Robbins Ice Cream Company (BRICO) distributed its ice cream through a dual distribution system. It established a system of exclusive area franchisors that were empowered to establish Baskin-Robbins franchised stores in their territories. BRICO acted as area franchisor in some territories; in others, it licensed independent manufacturers to manufacture and sell its ice cream products. A group of Baskin-Robbins franchisees filed a treble damage suit against BRICO, claiming that BRICO had unlawfully tied the sale of its ice cream products to the sale of its trademark by requiring them to sell only BRICO products purchased from the area franchisor in whose territory their stores were located. Have the franchisees demonstrated the existence of a tying agreement?

**9.** California Computer Products (CalComp) manufactured disk drives and controllers that were "plug compatible" with central processing units (CPUs) manufactured by IBM and others. CalComp's business strategy consisted of copying and, if possible, improving upon IBM designs and then underselling IBM to its own customers. CalComp sued IBM, arguing that it had monopolized or attempted to monopolize the market for disk products by cutting prices on existing IBM disk drives and controllers. The district court directed a verdict for IBM. Did IBM violate Section 2 of the Sherman Act?

**10.** Dimmitt Agri Industries, Inc. was a farmer's cooperative engaged in the production of cornstarch and corn syrup. Dimmitt filed suit against CPC International, Inc., the largest producer in the national corn wet milling market, alleging that CPC was guilty of monopolization and attempted monopolization by fixing unreasonably low prices in order to exclude competitors such as Dimmitt from the corn syrup and cornstarch markets. Dimmitt introduced into evidence confidential internal CPC documents that indicated an intent to gain control over prices in both markets by, among other things, lowering prices. However, Dimmitt's evidence also indicated that during the period in question CPC's market shares amounted to 25 percent of the national cornstarch market and 17 percent of the national corn syrup market. The trial jury found CPC guilty of monopolization but not guilty of attempted monopolization. Was the jury's verdict correct?

# Chapter 45

# The Clayton Act, the Robinson-Patman Act, and Antitrust Exemptions and Immunities

## INTRODUCTION

Despite the passage of the Sherman Act, the trend toward concentration in the American economy continued. Restrictive early judicial interpretations of Section 2 of the Act made it difficult to attack many monopolists, and critics argued for legislation that would "nip monopolies in the bud" before a full-blown restraint of trade or monopoly power was achieved. In 1914, Congress responded by passing the Clayton Act, which was designed to attack some of the specific practices that monopolists had historically employed to acquire monopoly power. The Clayton Act was intended to be a *preventive* measure. As a result, only a *probability* of a significant anticompetitive effect must be shown for most Clayton Act violations.

Because the Clayton Act deals only with probable harms to competition, there are no criminal penalties for violating its provisions. Private plaintiffs, however, can sue for treble damages or injunctive relief if they are injured, or threatened with injury, by a violation of the Act's provisions. The Justice Department and the Federal Trade Commission (FTC) share the responsibility for enforcing the Clayton Act, and both agencies have the power to seek injunctive relief to prevent or remedy violations of the Act. In addition, the FTC has the power to enforce the Act through the use of cease and desist orders (these are discussed in Chapter 46).

## CLAYTON ACT SECTION 3

Section 3 of the Clayton Act makes it unlawful for any person engaged in interstate commerce to *lease or sell commodities,* or to *fix a price* for commodities, on the *condition, agreement, or understanding* that the lessee or buyer of the commodities will not use or deal in the commodities of the lessor's or seller's competitors, where the effect of doing so *may be* to *substantially lessen competition* or *tend to create a monopoly* in any line of commerce. Section 3 is aimed primarily at two kinds of potentially anticompetitive behavior: *tying contracts* and *exclusive dealing contracts.* As you learned in the preceding chapter, both tying contracts and exclusive dealing contracts may also amount to restraints of trade in violation of Section 1 of the Sherman Act. The language of Section 3, however, imposes several limitations on its application to such agreements.

First, Section 3 applies only to those tying contracts and exclusive dealing contracts that involve *commodities.* Therefore, when such agreements involve services, real estate, or intangibles, they must be attacked under the Sherman Act. Also, Section 3 applies only when there has been a "lease" or "sale" of commodities, so it will not apply to true consignment agreements, because no "sale" or "lease" occurs in a consignment. Finally, although Section 3 speaks of sales on the "condition, agreement, or understanding" that the buyer or lessee will not deal in the commodities of the seller's or lessor's competitors, no formal agreement is required. Whenever a seller or lessor uses its economic power to prevent its customers from dealing with its competitors, this will be sufficient to satisfy the Clayton Act.

**Tying Agreements. Tying agreements** can plainly fall within the statutory language of Section 3. Any agreement that requires a buyer to purchase one product (the tied product) from a seller as a condition of purchasing another product from the same seller (the tying product) necessarily prevents the buyer from purchasing the tied product from the seller's competitors.

Only tying agreements that may "substantially lessen competition or tend to create a monopoly," however, will violate Section 3. The nature of the proof necessary to demonstrate such a probable anticompetitive effect is currently the subject of some disagreement among the lower federal courts. Over 30 years ago, the Supreme Court indicated that a tying agreement would violate the Clayton Act if the seller either had monopoly power over the tying product or restrained a substantial volume of commerce in the tied product.[1] Some lower federal courts today require essentially the same elements of proof for a Clayton Act violation that they require for a violation of the Sherman Act: proof that the challenged agreement involves two separate products, that sale of the tying product is "conditioned" on an accompanying sale of the tied product, that the seller has sufficient economic power in the market for the tying product to appreciably restrain competition in the tied product market, and that the seller's tying arrangements restrain a "not insubstantial" amount of commerce in the tied product market.[2] However, as the *Blackwell*

---

[1] *Times-Picayune Publ. Co. v. United States,* 345 U.S. 594 (U.S. Sup. Ct. 1953).

[2] For an example, see *Spartan Grain & Mill Co. v. Ayers,* 581 F.2d 419 (5th Cir. 1978).

case, which follows, indicates, other courts continue to apply a less demanding standard for Clayton Act tying liability, dispensing with proof of the seller's economic power in the market for the tying product as long as the seller's tying arrangements involve a "not insubstantial" amount of commerce in the tied product.

**Exclusive Dealing Arrangements.** In the last chapter, we discussed the nature of **exclusive dealing arrangements.** Such arrangements plainly fall under the language of Section 3 because buyers who agree to handle one seller's product exclusively, or to purchase all of their requirements for a particular commodity from one seller, are by definition agreeing not to purchase similar items from the seller's competitors. Once again, however, not all exclusive dealing agreements are illegal. Section 3 outlaws only those agreements that may "substantially lessen competition or tend to create a monopoly."

Exclusive dealing agreements were initially treated in much the same way as tying agreements. The courts looked at the dollar amount of commerce involved and declared agreements involving a "not insubstantial" amount of commerce illegal. For example, this "quantitative substantiality" test was employed by the U.S. Supreme Court in *Standard Oil Co. of California v. United States.*[3] Standard Oil of California was the largest refiner and supplier of gasoline in several western states, with roughly 14 percent of the retail market. Roughly half of these sales were made by retail outlets owned by Standard, and the other half were made by independent dealers who had entered into exclusive dealing contracts with Standard. Standard's six major competitors had entered into similar contracts with their own independent dealers. The Court recognized that exclusive dealing contracts, unlike tying agreements, could benefit both buyers and sellers,[4] but declared Standard's contracts illegal on the ground that nearly $58 million in commerce was involved.

The Court's decision in the *Standard Oil* case provoked considerable criticism, and in the *Tampa Electric* case, which follows, the Court applied a broader, "qualitative substantiality" test to gauge the legality of a long-term requirements contract for the sale of coal to an electric utility. In *Tampa,* the Court looked at the "area of effective competition," the total market for coal in the geographic region from which the utility could reasonably purchase its coal needs. The Court then determined the percentage of the total coal sales in this region that the challenged contract represented and, finding that percentage share to amount to less than 1 percent of total sales, upheld the agreement, although it represented more than $100 million in coal sales. *Tampa,* however, is distinguishable from *Standard Oil,* and the Court did not expressly overrule its earlier decision in the case against Standard. *Tampa,* unlike *Standard Oil,* involved parties with relatively equal bargaining power and an individual agreement rather than an industry-wide practice. In addition, there were obvious reasons why an electric utility such as Tampa Electric might want to "lock in" its coal costs by using a long-term requirements contract. Lower court opinions may be found employing both tests, and this situation is likely to continue until the Supreme Court clarifies its thinking on exclusive dealing contracts.

[3] 337 U.S. 293 (U.S. Sup. Ct. 1949).

[4] See the discussion of this point in the preceding chapter.

## Blackwell v. Power Test Corp.

**540 F. Supp. 802 (D.N.J. 1981)**

Robert Blackwell operated a gas station under a lease and franchise agreement with State Island Gasolines, Inc., a subsidiary of Power Test Petroleum Distributors. Blackwell's lease and franchise agreement required him to sell only Power Test gasoline products and provided for termination of the agreement in the event that Blackwell sold the products of others. In May 1980, Power Test's suppliers increased the price of the gasoline they sold to Power Test, and Power Test passed the price increase on to its franchised dealers. As a result of the pass-on, Blackwell was being forced to purchase gasoline at significantly higher prices than those being charged the distributors of major oil companies. After two purchases at these prices, Blackwell began buying gasoline from other sources. When Power Test moved to terminate his lease and franchise agreement, Blackwell filed suit for damages and injunctive relief on the ground that Power Test had violated Section 1 of the Sherman Act and Section 3 of the Clayton Act by tying the sale of gasoline products to his lease. Power Test moved for a summary judgment on Blackwell's claims.

**Meanor, District Judge.** In support of their motion for summary judgment with respect to the claimed violation of Section 3 of the Clayton Act, Power Test asserts that the Clayton Act is not applicable to this action. It is well established that a tie-in arrangement can be regarded as illegal under Section 3 of the Clayton Act and Section 1 of the Sherman Act. If the tying or tied products are goods, wares, or other commodities, the case falls within the ambit of the Clayton Act and the plaintiff need only show that a "substantial volume of commerce in the 'tied' product is restrained." *Times-Picayune Publishing Co. v. United States* (1952). If the tie does not involve a commodity but concerns land, services, or credit, which do not fit the Clayton Act's language, it is governed by the Sherman Act and the plaintiff is required to bear the additional burden of proving that the defendant's economic power with respect to the tying product is sufficient to produce an appreciable restraint.

In the instant action, Blackwell's specific allegations are that the "defendants have tied to a lease agreement a provision requiring plaintiff . . . to purchase all their gasoline requirements from defendants." Blackwell also alleged that "defendants have used their control over land in the form of gasoline sales outlets to coerce plaintiff . . . to purchase gasoline and other gasoline products only from defendants at fixed artificial prices higher than that in the open market." The lease agreement emphasized above is a real estate lease, not a lease of equipment. Even assuming that equipment was also leased, such equipment is affixed to the real property for a business purpose and thus partakes of the incidents of real property. Accordingly, the cause of action based on an alleged violation of the Clayton Act must be dismissed.

It is well established that to prove a *per se* illegal tie-in under the Sherman Act, Blackwell must establish three things. First, he must establish that the conduct in question was a tie-in: an agreement by a party to sell one product but only on the condition that the buyer also purchases a different (or tied) product. Second, he must establish that the seller has sufficient economic power with respect to the tying product to appreciably restrain free competition in the market for the tied product. And third, he must establish that a "not insubstantial" amount of interstate commerce is affected.

The first element of the alleged violation has been conceded by the defendants, *i.e.,* the existence of a tie-in. It is the second element upon which the dispute focuses.

Blackwell asserts that "an examination of the Form 10-K Annual Report filed by Power Test Corporation for the fiscal year ended January 31, 1980, reveals that the company is the largest independent (operating 455 gasoline outlets) and sixth largest gasoline marketing company in terms of share of market in the New York Metropolitan area." This argument, however, is misplaced. The focus must be on sufficiency of economic power in the tying product market, *i.e.,* ownership of real estate used as retail gasoline sales outlets, not Power Test's share of the retail sales market.

Power Test's Form 10-K reveals that "on January 31, 1980, the Company owned 173 gasoline stations and leased 184 additional gasoline stations. Approximately 90 percent of such leases expire subsequent to 1980. The Company in turn leased or subleased 351 of such gasoline stations to others." From this relatively small number of outlets, a mere 6 percent of the retail sales market in the Greater New York Metropolitan Area is controlled by Power Test. In addition to this obvious lack of market dominance or monopoly position, the tying product lacks the uniqueness recognized as critical by the Supreme Court. Furthermore, defendants do not possess "some advantage not shared by . . . competitors in the market for the tying product." *U.S. Steel Corp. v. Fortner Enterprises, Inc.* (U.S. Sup. Ct. 1977). Thus, it is clear that Power Test lacks the requisite market position essential for a violation of Section 1 of the Sherman Act.

Summary judgment granted for Power Test.

## Tampa Electric Co. v. Nashville Coal Co.

**365 U.S. 320 (U.S. Sup. Ct. 1961)**

Tampa Electric was a public utility serving an area of about 1,800 square miles in Florida. Tampa entered into a contract whereby it agreed to purchase all the coal requirements of its Gannon Station for a 20-year period from Nashville Coal Company. This purchase obligation also extended to any additional coal-using plants that Tampa might build at the Gannon Station during the life of the contract. A minimum price for the coal was set, with a cost-escalation clause. After Tampa had spent approximately $7.5 million in preparing to burn coal instead of oil, Nashville notified Tampa that it would not perform the contract because the contract violated Section 3 of the Clayton Act. Tampa filed suit for a declaratory judgment that the contract was lawful. The district court and the court of appeals ruled in favor of Nashville, and Tampa appealed to the Supreme Court.

**CLARK, JUSTICE.** Even though a contract is found to be an exclusive-dealing arrangement, it does not violate Section 3 unless the court believes it probable that performance of the contract will foreclose competition in a substantial share of the line of commerce affected. Following the guidelines of earlier decisions, certain considerations must be taken. *First,* the line of commerce, i.e., the type of goods, wares, or merchandise, etc., involved must be determined, where it is in controversy, on the basis of the facts peculiar to the case. *Second,* the area of effective competition in the known line of commerce must be charted by careful selection of the market area in which the seller operates, and to which the purchaser can practicably turn for supplies. In short, the threatened foreclosure of competition must be substantial in relation to the market affected.

To determine substantiality in a given case, it is necessary to weigh the probable effect of the contract on the relevant area of effective competition, taking into account the relative strength of the parties, the proportionate volume of commerce involved in relation to the total volume of commerce in the relevant market area, and the probable immediate and future effects which preemption of that share of the market might have on effective competition therein. It follows that a mere showing that the contract itself involves a substantial number of dollars is ordinarily of little consequence.

In applying these considerations to the facts of the case before us, it appears clear that both the Court of Appeals and the District Court have not given the required effect to a controlling factor in the case—the relevant competitive market area.

Neither the Court of Appeals nor the District Court considered in detail the question of the relevant market. They do seem, however, to have been satisfied with inquiring only as to competition within "Peninsular Florida." By far the bulk of the overwhelming tonnage marketed from the same producing area as serves Tampa is sold outside of Georgia and Florida, and the producers were "eager" to sell more coal in those States. While the relevant competitive market is not ordinarily susceptible to a "metes and bounds" definition, it is of course the area in which Nashville and the other 700 producers effectively compete. The record shows that, like Nashville, they sold bituminous coal "suitable for [Tampa's] requirements," mined in parts of Pennsylvania, Virginia, West Virginia, Kentucky, Tennessee, Alabama, Ohio and Illinois. It clearly appears that the proportionate volume of the total relevant coal product as to which the challenged contract preempted competition, less than 1 percent, is, conservatively speaking, quite insubstantial. A more accurate figure, even assuming preemption to the extent of the maximum anticipated total requirements, 2,250,000 tons a year, would be .77 percent.

The remaining determination, therefore, is whether the preemption of competition to the extent of the tonnage involved tends to substantially foreclose competition in the relevant coal market. We think not. There is here neither a seller with a dominant position in the market, nor myriad outlets with substantial sales volume, coupled with an industry-wide practice of relying upon exclusive contracts as in *Standard Oil,* nor a plainly restrictive tying arrangement. On the contrary, we seem to have only that type of contract which "may well be of economic advantage to buyers as well as to sellers." The 20-year period of the contract is singled out as the principal vice, but at least in the case of public utilities the assurance of a steady and ample supply of fuel is necessary in the public interest. Otherwise consumers are left unprotected against service failures owing to shutdowns; and increasingly unjustified costs might result in a more burdensome rate structure eventually to be reflected in the consumer's bill. In weighing the various factors, we have decided that in the competitive bituminous coal marketing area involved here the contract sued upon does not tend to foreclose a substantial volume of competition.

Judgment reversed in favor of Tampa.

## CLAYTON ACT SECTION 7

**Introduction.** Section 7 of the Clayton Act was designed to attack mergers—a term broadly used in this chapter to refer to the acquisition of one company by another. Our historical experience indicates that one of the ways in which monopolists acquired monopoly power was by acquiring control of their competitors. Section 7 prohibits any person engaged in commerce or in any activity affecting commerce from *acquiring* the *stock* or *assets* of any other such person where in *any line of commerce* or in any activity affecting commerce in *any section of the country* the effect *may* be to *substantially lessen competition* or *tend to create a monopoly.*

Section 7 is plainly an anticoncentration device, although, as the following text indicates, Section 7 has also been used to attack mergers that have had no direct effect on concentration in a particular industry. As such, its future evolution is in doubt, given the growing influence of Chicago School economic theories on antitrust enforcement and the more tolerant stance that those theories take toward merger activity. The Justice Department's recent merger guidelines (first announced in 1982 and amended in 1984) indicate a significant shift in the government's views about the proper role of Section 7 and, it is probably fair to say, signal a more permissive approach to merger activity. Of course, the guidelines only indicate the criteria that the department will employ in deciding whether to challenge particular mergers, and private enforcement of Section 7 is still possible. It remains to be seen how influential the department's thinking will be on the courts in those cases that ultimately go to trial.

Predictions concerning the ultimate judicial treatment that Section 7 will receive are complicated considerably by the fact that many of the important merger cases in recent years have been settled out of court. This leaves interested observers of antitrust policy with no definitive recent judicial statements about the courts' current thinking on many merger issues. Most of the available indications, however, point to significant revisions of merger policy in the years to come.

**Relevant Market Determination.** Regardless of the treatment that Section 7 ultimately receives in the courts, the determination of the **relevant market** affected by a merger is likely to remain a crucial component of any Section 7 case. Before a court can determine whether a particular merger will have the *probable* anticompetitive effect required by the Clayton Act, it must first determine the *line of commerce* (relevant product market) and the *section of the country* (relevant geographic market) that will probably be affected by the merger. In most cases, a broad relevant market definition adopted by the court means that the government or a private plaintiff will have greater difficulty in demonstrating a probable anticompetitive effect flowing from a challenged merger.

**Relevant Product Market.** "Line of commerce" determinations under the Clayton Act have traditionally employed *functional interchangeability* tests similar to those employed in relevant product market determinations under Section 2 of the Sherman Act. What products do the acquired and acquiring firms manufacture (assuming a merger between competitors), and what products are reasonably interchangeable by consumers to serve the same purposes? The new Justice Department merger guidelines indicate that the department will include in its relevant market determination those products that consumers view as "good substitutes at prevailing prices." The department also indicates that it will include any products that a significant percentage of current customers would shift to in the event of a "small, but significant and non-transitory increase in [the] price" of the products of the merged firms. Initially, the department stated that this meant a 5 percent increase in price sustained over a one-year period. More recently, the department, recognizing that the 5 percent figure might not be appropriate to all cases, given the wide disparity among the prevailing profit margins in many industries, has indicated that varying percentage figures may be employed, depending on the industry in question. By expanding the interchangeability standard in this fashion, the Justice Department has recognized that any price increases that result from a merger may be only temporarily sustainable because they may provoke further product substitution choices by consumers.

**Relevant Geographic Market.** In order to determine the probable anticompetitive effect of a particular merger on a "section of the country," the courts have traditionally asked where the effects of the merger will be "direct and immediate."[5] This means that the relevant geographic market may not be as broad as the markets in which the acquiring and acquired firms actually operate or, in the case of a merger between competitors, the markets in which they actually compete. The focus of the relevant market inquiry will be on those sections of the country in which competition is most likely to be injured by the merger. As a result, in a given case the relevant geographic market could be drawn as narrowly as one metropolitan area or as broadly as the nation as a whole. All that is necessary to satisfy this aspect of Section 7 is proof that the challenged merger might have a significant negative effect on competition in any economically significant geographic market.

The Justice Department's merger guidelines adopt a somewhat different approach to determining the relevant geographic market. They define the relevant geographic market as the geographic area in which a sole supplier of the product in question could profitably raise its price without causing outside suppliers to begin selling in the area. The department begins with the existing markets in which the parties to a merger compete, and then adds the markets of those suppliers that would enter the market in response to a "small, but significant and non-transitory increase in price." In most cases, this means a 5 percent price increase sustained over a one-year period, but different percentages may be employed to reflect the economic realities of particular industries.

**Horizontal Mergers.** The analytical approach employed to gauge a merger's probable effect on competition varies according to the nature of the merger in question. **Horizontal mergers,** mergers among firms competing in the same product and geographic markets, have traditionally been subjected to the most rigorous scrutiny because they clearly result in an increase in concentration in the relevant market. To determine the legality of such a merger, the courts look at the *market share* of the resulting firm. In *United States v. Philadelphia National Bank,*[6] the Supreme Court indicated that a horizontal merger producing a firm with an "undue percentage share" of the relevant market (30 percent in this case) and resulting in a "significant increase in concentration" of the firms in that market would be presumed illegal absent convincing evidence that the merger would not have an anticompetitive effect.

In the past, mergers involving firms with smaller market shares than those involved in the *Philadelphia National Bank* case were

[5] *United States v. Phillipsburg National Bank,* 399 U.S. 350 (U.S. Sup. Ct. 1970).

[6] 374 U.S. 321 (1963).

also frequently enjoined if other economic or historical factors pointed toward a probable anticompetitive effect. Some of the factors traditionally considered relevant by the courts have been: a trend toward concentration in the relevant market (a decreasing number of competing firms over time), the competitive position of the merging firms (Are the defendants dominant firms despite their relatively small market shares?), a past history of acquisitions by the acquiring firm (Are we dealing with a would-be "empire builder"?), and the nature of the acquired firm (Is it an aggressive, innovative competitor despite its small market share?).

Recent developments, however, indicate that the courts and federal antitrust enforcement agencies have become increasingly less willing to presume that anticompetitive effects will necessarily result from a merger that produces a firm with a relatively large market share. Instead, a more detailed inquiry will be made into the nature of the relevant market and of the merging firms to ascertain the likelihood of a probable harm to competition as a result of a challenged merger. The Justice Department merger guidelines indicate that, in assessing the probable effect of a merger, the department will focus on the existing concentration in the relevant market, the increase in concentration as a result of the proposed merger, and other non–market share factors.

To interpret market concentration data, the department uses a statistical device called the **Herfindahl-Hirschman Index** (HHI). The HHI is calculated by adding the squares of the individual market shares of the firms in the relevant market. So, a relevant market consisting of four firms, each controlling a 25 percent market share, would have an HHI of 2,500 ($25^2 + 25^2 + 25^2 + 25^2$). This approach emphasizes the presence of larger, and therefore more competitively significant, firms in the relevant market. For example, a market consisting of four firms with market shares of 40 percent, 30 percent, 20 percent, and 10 percent would have an HHI of 3,000. The increase in concentration resulting from a challenged merger is calculated by doubling the product of the market shares of the merging firms. For example, a merger between firms controlling market shares of 10 percent each would increase the HHI by 200 ($10 \times 10 \times 2$). The department has indicated that it is unlikely to challenge mergers in markets with a postmerger HHI under 1,000, more likely to challenge mergers in markets with a postmerger HHI of 1,000 to 1,800 if the change in the HHI as a result of the merger is over 100 points, and likely to challenge mergers in markets with a postmerger HHI of over 1,800 if the challenged merger will increase the HHI by more than 100 points.

The non–market share factors that the department will consider are more traditional. They include: the existence of barriers to the entry of new competitors into the relevant market, the prior conduct of the merging firms, and the probable future competitive strength of the acquired firm. The last factor is particularly important because both the courts and the Justice Department have acknowledged that a firm's current market share may not reflect its ability to compete in the future. For example, the courts have long recognized a "failing company" justification for some mergers. If the acquired firm is a failing company and no other purchasers are interested in acquiring it, its acquisition by a competitor may be lawful under Section 7. Similarly, if an acquired firm has financial problems that reflect some underlying structural weakness, or if it lacks new technologies that are necessary to compete effectively in the future, its current market share may overstate its future competitive importance.

Finally, given the greater weight that is currently being assigned to economic arguments in antitrust cases, two other merger justifications may be granted greater credence in the future. Some lower federal courts have recognized the idea that a merger between two "small companies" may be justifiable, despite the resulting statistical increase in concentration, if as a result of the merger they are able to compete more effectively with larger competitors. In a somewhat similar vein, some commentators have argued that mergers that result in enhanced economic efficiencies should sometimes be allowed despite the fact that they may have some anticompetitive impact. The courts have not been very receptive to efficiency arguments in the past, and the 1982 Justice Department guidelines rejected efficiency arguments on the ground that they were very difficult to prove. The 1984 amended guidelines, however, indicate that the department will consider efficiency claims supported by clear and convincing evidence in deciding whether to challenge a merger.

## United States v. General Dynamics Corp.

**415 U.S. 486 (U.S. Sup. Ct. 1974)**

Material Service Corporation was a producer of building materials and coal. All of its coal production, amounting to 15.1 percent of the Illinois market's production, was from deep-shaft mines. Material Service acquired effective control of United Electric's stock in 1959. United Electric, a coal producer with open-pit mines, had an 8.1 percent share of the Illinois market. General Dynamics subsequently acquired 100 percent of the Material Service stock. The government sued General Dynamics, as successor to Material Service, arguing that Material Service's acquisition of United Electric violated Section 7 of the Clayton Act. The district court ruled in favor of General Dynamics, and the government appealed.

**Stewart, Justice.** In prior decisions involving horizontal mergers between competitors, this Court has found prima facie violations of Section 7 of the Clayton Act from aggregate statistics of the sort relied on by the United States in this case. The effect of adopting this approach to a determination of a "substantial" lessening of competition is to allow the Government to rest its case on a showing of even small increases of market share or market concentration in those industries or markets where concentration is already great or has been recently increasing, since if concentration is already great, the importance of preventing even slight increases in concentration and so preserving the possibility of eventual deconcentration is correspondingly great.

While the statistical showing proffered by the Government in this case, the accuracy of which was not discredited by the District Court or contested by the respondents, would under this approach have sufficed to support a finding of "undue concentration" in the absence of other considerations, the question before us is whether the District Court was justified in finding that other pertinent factors affecting the coal industry and the business of the respondents mandated a conclusion that no substantial lessening of competition occurred or was threatened by the acquisition of United Electric. We are satisfied that the court's ultimate finding was not in error.

On the basis of more than three weeks of testimony and a voluminous record, the court discerned a number of clear and significant developments in the industry. First, it found that coal had become increasingly less able to compete with other sources of energy in many segments of the energy market. Following the War the industry entirely lost its largest single purchaser of coal—the railroads—and faced increasingly stiffer competition from oil and natural gas as sources of energy for industrial and residential uses.

Second, the court found that to a growing extent since 1954, the electric utility industry has become the mainstay of coal consumption. Third, and most significantly, the court found that to an increasing degree, nearly all coal sold to utilities is transferred under long-term requirements contracts, under which coal producers promise to meet utilities' coal consumption requirements for a fixed period of time, and at predetermined prices.

Because of these fundamental changes in the structure of the market for coal, the District Court was justified in viewing the statistics relied on by the Government as insufficient to sustain its case. Evidence of past production does not, as a matter of logic, necessarily give a proper picture of a company's future ability to compete. In most situations, of course, the unstated assumption is that a company that has maintained a certain share of a market in the recent past will be in a position to do so in the immediate future. In the coal market, as analyzed by the District Court, however, statistical evidence of coal *production* was of considerably less significance. In a market where the availability and price for coal are set by long-term contracts rather than immediate or short-term purchases and sales, reserves rather than past production are the best measure of a company's ability to compete.

The testimony and exhibits in the District Court revealed that United Electric's coal reserve prospects were "unpromising." United's relative position of strength in reserves was considerably weaker than its past and current ability to produce. United was found to be facing the future with relatively depleted resources at its disposal, and with the vast majority of those resources already committed under contracts allowing no further adjustment in price. In addition, the District Court found that "United Electric has neither the possibility of acquiring more [reserves] nor the ability to develop deep coal reserves," and thus was not in a position to increase its reserves to replace those already depleted or committed.

Viewed in terms of present and future reserve prospects— and thus in terms of probable future ability to compete—rather than in terms of past production, the District Court held that United Electric was a far less significant factor in the coal market than the Government contended or the production statistics seemed to indicate. While the company had been and remained a "highly profitable" and efficient producer of relatively large amounts of coal, its current and future power to compete for subsequent long-term contracts was severely limited by its scarce uncommitted resources. Irrespective of the company's size when viewed as a producer, its weakness as a competitor was properly analyzed by the District Court and fully substantiated that court's conclusion that its acquisition by Material Service would not "substantially lessen competition."

Judgment for General Dynamics affirmed.

---

**Vertical Mergers.** A **vertical merger** is a merger between firms that previously had, or could have had, a supplier-customer relationship. For example, a manufacturer may seek to vertically integrate its operations by acquiring a company that controls retail outlets that could sell the manufacturer's product line or by acquiring a company that produces a product that the manufacturer regularly uses in its production processes. Vertical mergers, unlike horizontal mergers, do not directly result in an increase in concentration. Nonetheless, they may harm competition in a variety of ways.

First, vertical mergers may *foreclose competitors* from a share of the relevant market. For example, if a major customer for a particular product acquires a captive supplier of that product, the competitors of the acquired firm will thereafter be foreclosed from competing with it for sales to the acquiring firm. Similarly, if a manufacturer acquires a captive retail outlet for its products, the manufacturer's competitors are foreclosed from competing for sales to that retail outlet. In the latter case, a vertical merger may also result in reduced competition at the retail level. For example, a shoe manufacturer acquires a chain of retail shoe stores that has a dominant share of the retail market in certain geographic areas and that has previously carried the brands of several competing manufacturers. If after the merger the retailer carries only the acquiring manufacturer's brands, competition among the acquiring manufacturer and its competitors will be reduced in the retail market for shoes.

Vertical mergers may also result in *increased barriers to entry* confronting new competitors. For example, if a major purchaser of a particular product acquires a captive supplier of that product, potential producers of the product may be discouraged from commencing production due to the contraction of the market for the product resulting from the merger.

Finally, some vertical mergers may *eliminate potential competition* in one of two ways. First, an acquiring firm may be perceived by existing competitors in the acquired firm's market as a likely potential entrant into that market. The threat of such a potential entrant "waiting in the wings" may serve to moderate the behavior of existing competitors because they fear that pursuing pricing policies that exploit their current market position might induce the potential entrant to enter the market. The acquiring firm's entry into the market by the acquisition of an existing competitor means the end of its moderating influence as a potential entrant. Second, a vertical merger may deprive the market of the potential benefits that would have resulted had the acquiring firm entered the market in a more procompetitive manner, by creating its own entrant into the market through a process of internal expansion or by making a "toehold" acquisition of a small existing competitor and subsequently building it into a more significant competitor.

Historically, courts seeking to determine the legality of vertical mergers have tended to look at the *share of the relevant market foreclosed to competition.* If a more than insignificant market share is foreclosed to competition, other economic and historical factors are considered. Factors that have been viewed as aggravating the anticompetitive potential of a vertical merger include: a trend toward concentration or vertical integration in the industry, a past history of vertical integration in the industry, a past history of vertical acquisitions by the acquiring company, and significant barriers to entry resulting from the merger. This approach to determining the legality of vertical mergers has been criticized by some commentators who argue that vertical integration can yield certain efficiencies of distribution and that vertical integration by merger may be more economically efficient than vertical integration by internal expansion. The Justice Department's 1984 amended merger guidelines indicate that the department will afford greater weight to efficiency arguments in cases involving vertical mergers than in cases involving horizontal mergers.

The guidelines also indicate that the department will apply the same criteria to all "nonhorizontal" mergers. Those criteria are discussed in the following section on conglomerate mergers.

**Conglomerate Mergers.** A **conglomerate merger** is a merger between two firms that are not in competition with each other (i.e., because they compete in different product or geographic markets) and that do not have a supplier-customer relationship. Conglomerate mergers come in two varieties: "market extension" mergers and "product extension" mergers. In a market extension merger, the acquiring firm expands into a new geographic market by purchasing an existing competitor in that market (e.g., a conglomerate that owns an East Coast grocery chain buys a West Coast grocery chain). In a product extension merger, the acquiring firm diversifies its operations by purchasing a company in a new product market (e.g., a conglomerate with interests in the aerospace and electronics industries purchases a chain of department stores). Considerable disagreement exists over the economic effects of conglomerate acquisitions. Although some conglomerate mergers have been attacked successfully under Section 7, there is general agreement that the Clayton Act is not well suited to dealing with conglomerate mergers. This realization has produced calls for specific legislation on the subject. Such legislation is probably desirable in the event that we ultimately conclude that conglomerate merger activity is a proper subject for regulation.

Three kinds of conglomerate mergers have been challenged with some degree of success under Section 7: mergers that involve *potential reciprocity,* mergers that *eliminate potential competition,* and mergers that give an acquired firm an *unfair advantage* over its competitors. A conglomerate merger may create a risk of potential reciprocity if the acquired firm produces a product that the acquiring firm's suppliers regularly purchase. Such suppliers, eager to continue their relationship with the acquiring firm, may thereafter purchase the acquired firm's products rather than those of its competitors.

A conglomerate merger, like some vertical mergers, may also result in the *elimination of potential competition.* If existing competitors perceive the acquiring company as a potential entrant in the acquired company's market, the acquiring company's entry by a conglomerate acquisition may result in the loss of the moderating influence that it had while "waiting in the wings." Also, when the acquiring company actually enters the new market by acquiring a well-established existing competitor rather than by starting a new competitor through internal expansion (a *de novo* entry) or by making a "toehold" acquisition, the market is deprived of the potential for increased competition flowing from the reduction in concentration that would have resulted had either of the latter strategies been employed. The most recent Supreme Court cases on point suggest, however, that a high degree of proof will be required before either potential competition argument will be accepted. Arguments that a conglomerate merger eliminated a *perceived potential entrant* must be accompanied by proof that existing competitors actually perceived the acquiring firm as a potential entrant.[7] Arguments that a conglomerate acquisition eliminated an *actual potential entrant,* depriving the market of the benefits of reduced concentration, must be accompanied by evidence that the acquiring firm had the ability to enter the market by internal expansion or a toehold acquisition and that doing so would

[7] *United States v. Falstaff Brewing Corp.,* 410 U.S. 526 (U.S. Sup. Ct. 1973).

have ultimately yielded a substantial reduction in concentration.[8]

Finally, when a large firm acquires a firm that already enjoys a significant position in its market, the acquired firm may gain an unfair advantage over its competitors through its ability to draw on the greater resources and expertise of its new owner. This may "entrench" the acquired firm in its market by deterring existing competitors from actively competing with it for market share and by producing barriers to entry to new competitors that may be reluctant to enter the market after the acquisition.

Virtually all of the important conglomerate merger cases of the last few years have been settled out of court. As a result, we do not have a clear indication of the Supreme Court's current thinking on conglomerate merger issues. The Justice Department merger guidelines indicate that the department may decline to employ many of the theories that have been used to challenge conglomerate mergers in the past. The guidelines indicate that the primary theories that the department will use to attack all nonhorizontal mergers are the elimination of perceived and actual potential competition theories. In employing these analytical tools, the department will also consider certain other economic factors. These include: the degree of concentration in the acquired firm's market (challenges are unlikely where the HHI is under 1,800), the existence of barriers to entry into the market and the presence or absence of other firms with a comparable ability to enter, and the market share of the acquired firm (challenges are unlikely where this is 5 percent or less, and likely where it is 20 percent or more). Whether or not the Supreme Court will accept this more restrictive view of the scope of Section 7 remains to be seen.

[8] *United States v. Marine Bancorporation, Inc.*, 418 U.S. 602 (U.S. Sup. Ct. 1974).

## Tenneco, Inc. v. FTC

### 689 F.2d 346 (2d Cir. 1982)

In 1975, Tenneco, Inc. was the 15th largest industrial corporation in America. Tenneco was a diversified corporation. Its Walker Manufacturing Division manufactured and distributed a wide variety of automotive parts, the most important of which were exhaust system parts. In 1975 and 1976, Walker was the nation's leading seller of exhaust system parts. Tenneco acquired control of Monroe Auto Equipment Company, a leading manufacturer of automotive shock absorbers. Monroe was the number two firm in the national market for replacement shock absorbers. Monroe and Gabriel, the industry leader, accounted for over 77 percent of replacement shock absorber sales in 1976. General Motors and Questor Corporation, the third and fourth largest firms, controlled another 15 percent of the market.

The replacement shock absorber market exhibited significant barriers to the entry of new competitors. Economies of scale in the industry dictated manufacturing plants of substantial size, and the nature of the industry required would-be entrants to acquire significant new technologies and marketing skills unique to the industry. The Federal Trade Commission (FTC) ordered Tenneco to divest itself of Monroe on the grounds that Tenneco's acquisition of Monroe violated Section 7 of the Clayton Act by eliminating both perceived and actual potential competition in the replacement shock absorber market. Tenneco appealed.

**MESKILL, CIRCUIT JUDGE.** The Supreme Court has described the theory of perceived potential competition, which it has approved for application to cases brought under Section 7 of the Clayton Act, as the principal focus of the potential competition doctrine. The Court has recognized that: "A market extension merger may be unlawful if the target market is substantially concentrated, if the acquiring firm has the characteristics, capabilities, and economic incentive to render it a perceived potential *de novo* entrant, and if the acquiring firm's presence on the fringe of the target market in fact tempered oligopolistic behavior on the part of existing participants in that market." *United States v. Marine Bancorporation, Inc.* (1974).

The actual potential competition theory, which has yet to receive sanction from the Supreme Court, would "proscribe a market extension merger solely on the ground that such a merger eliminates the prospect for long-term deconcentration of an oligopolistic market that in theory might result if the acquiring firm were forbidden to enter except through a *de novo* undertaking or through the acquisition of a small existing entrant."

We reject the Commission's finding that Tenneco was an actual potential entrant likely to increase competition in the market for replacement shock absorbers. The record strongly supports the conclusion that Tenneco was actively considering entry into the market and was pursuing all leads to that end at least since the late 1960s or early 1970s. Moreover, Tenneco clearly possessed adequate financial resources to make the large initial investment needed to attempt to penetrate the market. The record, however, is deficient in evidence that there were viable toehold options available to Tenneco or that Tenneco would have entered the market *de novo.*

The Commission conceded in its opinion that Tenneco never expressed any interest in entering the market for replacement shock absorbers "on a completely *de novo* basis." However, the Commission found that Tenneco had expressed interest in entering the market essentially *de novo,* building the required production facilities from scratch and acquiring the necessary technology via a license from an established foreign shock absorber producer. The Commission concluded that Tenneco would likely have done so absent its acquisition of Monroe.

The Commission's reasoning is flawed. It ignores Tenneco's decision not to enter the market during the 1960s and early 1970s, a period of high profitability for shock absorber manufacturers, because of anticipated inadequate earnings during early years. The record is devoid of evidentiary support for the Commission's assertion that in the period relevant to this case, when industry earnings were in decline, Tenneco would have been willing to suffer the "cost disadvantage" inherent in the building of an efficient scale plant that would remain underutilized "for a number of years."

The Commission's conclusion that Tenneco would likely have entered the replacement shock absorber market through toehold acquisition is similarly flawed. The Commission identified Armstrong Patents, Ltd. ("Armstrong"), a British shock absorber manufacturer, ("DeCarbon"), a French company, and Blackstone Manufacturing Corp. ("Blackstone"), a small United States producer of shock absorbers, as potential toeholds. However, the record reveals that Tenneco in fact negotiated unsuccessfully with Armstrong and DeCarbon. Armstrong management indicated that Tenneco would have to offer a 100 percent premium over the market price of its stock to generate its interest. Tenneco's negotiations with DeCarbon, which were conducted through an independent broker, were equally fruitless. DeCarbon had asked a selling price of 100 times its earnings.

As for Blackstone, the Commission itself described that company as "a small, struggling domestic firm burdened with aged equipment, a less than complete product line, declining market share and a mediocre reputation." Since 1974, Blackstone had unsuccessfully sought a buyer for its business, soliciting, among others, Midas International Corp., which operates a chain of muffler installation shops, and Questor. Nevertheless, the Commission remarkably concluded that Blackstone "would have served as a viable method of toehold entry, although this route would have been more difficult and less attractive than the acquisition of a substantial foreign firm."

We also conclude that the record contains inadequate evidence to support the Commission's conclusion that Tenneco's acquisition of Monroe violated section 7 by eliminating Tenneco as a perceived potential competitor in the market for replacement shock absorbers. There is abundant evidence that the oligopolists in the market for replacement shock absorbers perceived Tenneco as a potential entrant. Industry executives testified that they considered Tenneco one of very few manufacturers with both the incentive and the capability to enter the market. This perception was based on Tenneco's financial strength and on the compatibility of shock absorbers with exhaust system parts produced by Tenneco's Walker Division.

However, the analysis does not end here. The Commission's conclusion that the perception of Tenneco as a potential entrant actually tempered the conduct of oligopolists in the market must also be supported by substantial evidence. It is not.

Throughout this case, Tenneco has argued that in the years immediately preceding its acquisition of Monroe the market for replacement shock absorbers had become highly competitive. The Commission apparently agrees with this assessment. The rate of increase in advertised retail prices for shock absorbers fell significantly behind inflation, and so-called mass merchandisers such as Sears Roebuck replaced traditional wholesale distributors as the leading purchasers of replacement shock absorbers from manufacturers. Sears's retail prices for shock absorbers were frequently below the prices that manufacturers charged wholesale distributors, who were several levels above the retail customer in the traditional chain of distribution.

The advent of increased sales by mass merchandisers coincided with aggressive competition among shock absorber manufacturers. Manufacturers offered substantial discounts off their circulated price sheets to traditional wholesalers and implemented "stocklifting," a practice in which a manufacturer buys a wholesaler's inventory of a competing manufacturer's product and replaces it with his own product. Perhaps the most aggressive and certainly the most successful manufacturer was Maremont, which acquired Gabriel in 1962. At the time of the acquisition, Gabriel was, in the Commission's words, "in a downward trend," and ranked third in the industry with a market share of between 10 percent and 20 percent.

After the acquisition, Maremont undertook an aggressive campaign to improve its position. Since that time, Gabriel's market share has at least doubled and has possibly increased four-fold. Maremont today is the number one firm in the replacement shock absorber market.

While agreeing that competitive activity increased dramatically in the mid-1970's, the Commission stated:

> We disagree with [Tenneco] over the cause of that new competitive vigor. In brief, we find that the source of the improved economic performance lay in industry fears that Tenneco was likely to

attempt entry—an actual "edge effect"—rather than in the buyer power supposedly asserted by mass merchants against their suppliers.

The Commission's hypothesis depends almost entirely on inferences drawn from the activity of Maremont.

We have no doubt that direct evidence of an "edge effect" is not required to support a Commission finding of a section 7 violation. In this case, however, direct evidence concerning Tenneco's "edge effect" on Maremont was elicited by the Commission, though it does not support the Commission's conclusion. During the testimony of Byron Pond, Senior Vice-President and Director of Maremont, the following colloquy occurred:

Q [By Commission Counsel:] Did the presence of Walker, IPC or Midas and/or TRW as likely potential entrants into the shock absorber market, have any effect on Maremont's decisions, business decisions?

A [By Mr. Pond:] I don't think that we looked specifically at competitors on a periodic basis or potential competitors, in developing our strategy. I think we developed our strategy and approach to the business based on how we perceive it and how we perceived the opportunities.

Mr. Pond's testimony constitutes direct evidence that Tenneco had no direct effect on Maremont's business decisions or competitive activity. In the face of this contrary and unchallenged direct evidence, the substantiality of circumstantial evidence arguably suggesting an "edge effect" vanishes. Accordingly, we hold that the Commission's finding that Maremont's actions were probably taken in response to its desire to dissuade Tenneco from entering the market is unsupported by substantial evidence in the record.

FTC order set aside in favor of Tenneco.

## CLAYTON ACT SECTION 8

If the same people control theoretically competing corporations, an obvious potential exists for collusive anticompetitive conduct such as price-fixing or division of markets. Section 8 of the Clayton Act was designed to minimize the risks posed by such interlocks. Section 8 prohibits any person from serving as a director of two or more corporations (other than banks or common carriers) if either has "capital, surplus, and undivided profits aggregating more than $1,000,000" and the corporations are, or have been, competitors, "so that elimination of competition by agreement between them" would violate any of the antitrust laws.

Section 8 establishes a per se standard of liability in the sense that no harm to competition need be shown for an interlock to violate the statute. However, the statute's prohibition against interlocks is quite limited in scope: it prohibits only interlocking directorates. Nothing in the language of the statute prohibits one person from serving as an officer of two competing corporations, or as an officer of one competitor and a director of another.

Historically, government enforcement of Section 8 has been quite lax, though in recent years there have been some signs of growing government interest in the statute. The most recent Supreme Court case involving Section 8, however, resulted in a denial of the government bid for a more expansive interpretation of the statute. *BankAmerica Corp. v. United States*[9] grew out of a 1975 Justice Department attempt to police interlocking directorates between banks and insurance companies. Never

[9] 103 Sup. Ct. 2266 (U.S. Sup. Ct. 1983).

before had an interlock involving a bank been challenged under Section 8 because of the specific statutory language prohibiting interlocks between corporations "other than banks." Concerned about the increasing areas in which banks and a wide variety of other businesses were competing in rapidly changing financial markets, the Justice Department argued that the statutory exception should apply only when both of the companies at issue were banks. Had the department been successful, the consequences for the banking industry could have been significant, given the long history of interlocking directorates between banks and other business corporations. The Supreme Court, however, rejected the government's broad reading of the statute, holding that the "most natural reading" of the statute was that the interlocking corporations must all be corporations "other than banks."

Such signs of renewed government interest in Section 8 should produce significant concern in an era of conglomerate merger activity. Given the wide diversification that characterizes many large corporations, it should become increasingly easy to demonstrate some degree of competitive overlap among a substantial number of large, diversified corporations.

## THE ROBINSON-PATMAN ACT

**Background.** Section 2 of the Clayton Act originally prohibited *local and territorial price discrimination* by sellers, a practice frequently used by monopolists to destroy smaller competitors. A large company operating in a number of geographic markets would sell at or below cost in markets where it faced local competitors, making up its losses by selling at higher prices in areas where it faced no competition. Faced with such tactics, the smaller local competitors might eventually be driven out of business. Section 2 was aimed at such *primary level* (or "first line") price discrimination.

In the 1930s, Congress was confronted with complaints that large chain stores were using their buying power to induce manufacturers to sell to them at lower prices than those offered to their smaller, independent competitors. Chain stores were also able to receive other payments and services not available to their smaller competitors. Being able to purchase at lower prices and to obtain discriminatory payments and services arguably gave large firms a competitive advantage over their smaller competitors. Such price discrimination in sales to the competing customers of a particular seller is known as *secondary level* price discrimination.

In addition, the customers of a manufacturer's favored customer (e.g., a wholesaler that receives a "functional discount") may gain a competitive advantage over *their* competitors (e.g., other retailers purchasing directly from the manufacturer at a higher price) if the favored customer "passes on" all or a portion of its discount to them. This form of price discrimination is known as *tertiary level* (or "third line") price discrimination.

Congress responded to these problems by passing the Robinson-Patman Act in 1936. The Act amended Section 2 of the Clayton Act to outlaw secondary and tertiary level direct price discrimination and to prohibit indirect price discrimination in the form of discriminatory payments and services to a seller's customers. Since its enactment, the Robinson-Patman Act has been the subject of widespread dissatisfaction and criticism. Critics have long charged that in many cases the Act protects competitors at the expense of promoting competition. Governmental enforcement of the Act has been somewhat haphazard over the years, and current top officials in the Justice Department and the Federal Trade Commission have voiced significant disagreement with many of the Act's underlying policies and assumptions. This governmental stance, when combined with recent Supreme Court decisions making private enforcement of the Act more difficult, raises serious questions concerning the Act's future importance as a component of our antitrust laws.

**Jurisdiction.** The Robinson-Patman Act applies only to discriminatory acts that occur "in commerce." This test is narrower than the "affecting commerce" test employed under the Sherman Act. At least one of the discriminatory acts complained of must take place in interstate commerce. Thus, the Act probably would not apply if a Texas manufacturer discriminated in price in sales to two Texas customers. At least one lower federal court has indicated, however, that even wholly intrastate sales may be deemed "in the flow of commerce" if the nonfavored buyer bought the goods for resale to out-of-state customers.[10]

**Section 2(a).** Section 2(a) of the Robinson-Patman Act prohibits sellers from *discriminating in price* "between different purchasers of commodities of like grade or quality" where the effect of such discrimination may be "substantially to lessen competition or tend to create a monopoly in any line of commerce" or "to injure, destroy, or prevent competition with any person who either grants [primary level] or knowingly receives [secondary level] the benefit of such discrimination, or with the customers of either of them [tertiary level]."

**Price Discrimination.** To violate Section 2(a), a seller must have made two or more sales to different "purchasers" at different prices. Merely quoting a discriminatory price or refusing to sell except at a discriminatory price is not a violation of the statute, because no actual purchase is involved. For the same reason, price discrimination in lease or consignment transactions is also not covered by Section 2(a). Nor will actual sales at different prices to different purchasers necessarily be treated as discriminatory unless the sales were fairly close in time.

For purposes of deciding whether discriminatory prices have been charged to two or more purchasers, the degree of control that a parent corporation exercises over its subsidiaries can sometimes assume major importance. For example, a parent that sells a product directly to one customer at a low price may be found guilty of price discrimination if a wholesaler controlled by the parent contemporaneously sells the same product at a higher price to a competitor of the parent's customer. On the other hand, contemporaneous sales by a parent to a wholly owned subsidiary and to an independent competitor at different prices will not be treated as price discrimination, because no true "sale" has been made to the subsidiary.

Finally, Section 2(a) does not directly address the legality of "functional discounts": discounts granted to buyers at various levels in a product's chain of distribution because of differences in the functions that those buyers perform in the distribution system. The legality of such discounts depends on their competitive effect. Charging wholesale customers lower prices than retail customers will not violate the Act unless the lower wholesale prices are somehow "passed on" to retailers that are in competition with the seller's other retail customers.

**Commodities of Like Grade and Quality.** Section 2(a) applies only to price discrimination in the sale of "commodities." Price discrimination involving intangibles, real estate, or services must be challenged un-

[10] *L & L Oil Co. v. Murphy Oil Corp.*, 674 F.2d 1113 (5th Cir. 1982).

der the Sherman Act (as a restraint of trade or an attempt to monopolize) or under the FTC Act (as an unfair method of competition).[11] The essence of price discrimination is that two or more buyers are charged differing prices for the *same* commodity. Sales of commodities of varying grades or quality at varying prices, therefore, will not violate Section 2(a) so long as uniform prices are charged for commodities of equal quality. Some *physical difference* in the grade or quality of two products must be shown to justify a price differential between them. Differences solely in the brand name or label under which a product is sold (e.g., the seller's standard brand and a "house" brand sold to a large customer for resale under the customer's label) will not justify discriminatory pricing.

**Competitive Effect.** Only price discrimination that has a *probable* anticompetitive effect is prohibited by Section 2(a). Traditionally, the courts have required a higher degree of proof of likely competitive injury in cases involving primary level price discrimination (discrimination that may damage the seller's competitors) than in cases involving secondary or tertiary level discrimination (discrimination that threatens competition among the seller's customers or its customers' customers). To prove a primary level violation, it must be shown that the seller engaged in significant and sustained local price discrimination with the intent of "punishing" or "disciplining" a local competitor. Proof of "predatory pricing" is often offered as evidence of a seller's anticompetitive intent. As is the case with similar claims under Section 2 of the Sherman Act, however, the courts disagree on the proper test for predatory pricing.

In secondary or tertiary level cases, the courts tend to infer the existence of competitive injury from evidence of substantial price discrimination between competing purchasers over time. Several qualifications on this point are in order, however. Price discrimination for a short period of time ordinarily will not support an inference of competitive injury. Likewise, if the evidence indicates that nonfavored buyers could have purchased the same goods from other sellers at prices identical to those that the defendant seller charged its favored customers, no competitive injury will be inferred. Finally, as indicated by the *J. Truett Payne* case, which follows, buyers seeking treble damages for secondary or tertiary level harm must still prove that they suffered some actual damages as a result of a violation of the act.

[11] The FTC Act is discussed in the following chapter.

## J. Truett Payne Co. v. Chrysler Motors Corp.

**451 U.S. 557 (U.S. Sup. Ct. 1981)**

J. Truett Payne Company was one of four Chrysler-Plymouth dealers in the Birmingham, Alabama, area. Payne's business failed in 1974, and Payne filed a treble damage suit against Chrysler under the Robinson-Patman Act. Payne argued that Chrysler's sales incentive programs forced it to pay a higher price for cars than its competitors paid. Chrysler paid dealers a bonus for each car that they sold above a fixed sales target and also paid bonuses based on the number of cars that dealers bought in excess of a fixed quota. Payne argued that Chrysler set Payne's targets and quotas higher than those of its competitors, with the result that Payne received fewer bonuses than its competitors. Payne offered in evidence a statement by its salespeople that competitors were underselling Payne and market share data showing a 4 percent drop in sales between 1971 and 1972 but a 1 percent overall increase in sales between 1970 and 1973, the period of time at issue. Payne argued that it was entitled to "automatic damages" in the amount of the price discrimination once it had proven a violation of Section 2(a).

Chrysler argued that its sales incentive programs were not discriminatory and that the programs did not injure Payne or adversely affect competition. The jury awarded Payne $111,247.78 in damages, which the district court trebled. The court of appeals did not decide whether Chrysler's incentive programs violated Section 2(a). Instead, it reversed on the ground that Payne had failed to introduce substantial evidence of injury caused by the programs.

**Rehnquist, Justice.** Payne first contends that once it has proved a price discrimination in violation of Section 2(a) it is entitled at a minimum to so-called "automatic damages" in the amount of the price discrimination. Payne concedes that in order to recover damages it must establish cognizable injury attributable to an antitrust violation and some approximation of damage. It insists, however, that the jury should be permitted to infer the requisite injury and damage from a showing of a substantial price discrimination. Payne notes that this Court has consistently permitted such injury to be inferred in injunctive actions brought to enforce Section 2(a) and argues that private suits for damages under Section 4 should be treated no differently. We disagree.

By its terms Section 2(a) is a prophylactic statute which is violated merely upon a showing that "the effect of such discrimination *may* be substantially to lessen competition." As our cases have recognized, the statute does not "require that the discriminations must in fact have harmed competition." Section 4 of the Clayton Act, in contrast, is essentially a remedial statute. It provides treble damages to "any person who *shall be injured* in his business or property by reason of anything forbidden in the antitrust laws." To recover treble damages, then, a plaintiff must make some showing of actual injury attributable to something the antitrust laws were designed to prevent. It must prove more than a violation of Section 2(a), since such proof establishes only that injury *may* result.

Our decision here is virtually governed by our reasoning in *Brunswick Corp. v. Pueblo Bowl-O-Mat, Inc.* (1977). There we rejected the contention that the mere violation of Section 7 of the Clayton Act, which prohibits mergers which *may* substantially lessen competition, gives rise to a damage claim under Section 4. We explained that "to recover damages [under Section 4] respondents must prove more than that the petitioner violated Section 7, since such proof established only that injury may result." Likewise in this case, proof of a violation does not mean that a disfavored purchaser has been actually "injured" within the meaning of Section 4.

Payne next contends that even though it may not be entitled to "automatic damages" upon a showing of a violation of Section 2(a), it produced enough evidence of actual injury to survive a motion for a directed verdict. That evidence consisted primarily of the testimony of its owner, Mr. Payne, and an expert witness, a professor of economics. Payne testified that the price discrimination was one of the causes of the dealership going out of business. In support of that contention, he testified that his salesmen told him that the dealership lost sales to its competitors and that its market share of retail Chrysler-Plymouth sales in the Birmingham area was 24 percent in 1970, 27 percent in 1971, 23 percent in 1972, and 25 percent in 1973. Payne contended that it was proper to infer that the 4 percent drop in 1972 was a result of the incentive programs. He also testified that the discrimination caused him to "force" business so that he could meet his assigned quotas. That is, his desire to make a sale induced him to "overallow" on trade-ins, thus reducing his profits on his used car operation. Payne adduced evidence showing that his average gross profit on used car sales was below that of his competitors, though that same evidence revealed that his average gross profit on new sales was higher.

Neither Payne nor his expert witness offered documentary evidence as to the effect of the discrimination on retail prices. Although Payne asserted that his salesmen and customers told him that the dealership was being undersold, he admitted he did not know if his competitors did in fact pass on their lower costs to their customers. Payne's expert witness took a somewhat different position. He believed that the discrimination would ultimately cause retail prices to be held at an artifically high level since Payne's competitors would not reduce their retail prices as much as they would have done if Payne received an equal bonus from Chrysler. He also testified that Payne was harmed by the discrimination even if the favored purchasers did not lower their retail prices, since Payne in that case would make less money per car.

Even construed most favorably to Payne, the evidence of injury is weak. Payne nevertheless asks us to consider the sufficiency of its evidence in light of our traditional rule excusing antitrust plaintiffs from an unduly rigorous standard of proving antitrust injury. Our willingness to accept a degree of uncertainty in these cases rests in part on the difficulty of ascertaining business damages as compared, for example, to damages resulting from a personal injury or from condemnation of a parcel of land. The vagaries of the marketplace usually deny us sure knowledge of what a plaintiff's situation would have been in the absence of the defendant's antitrust violation. But our willingness also rests on the principle that it does not "come with very good grace" for the wrongdoer to insist upon specific and certain proof of the injury which it has itself inflicted.

Applying the foregoing principles to this case is not without difficulty. In the first place, it is a close question whether Payne's evidence would be sufficient to support a jury award even under our relaxed damage rules. In those cases where we have found sufficient evidence to permit a jury to infer antitrust injury and approximate the amount of damages, the evidence was more substantial than the evidence presented here.

But a more fundamental difficulty confronts us in this case. The cases relied upon by Payne all depend on greater or lesser part on the inequity of a wrongdoer defeating the recovery of damages against him by insisting upon a rigorous standard of proof. In this case, however, we cannot say with assurance that Chrysler is a "wrongdoer." Because the court below bypassed the issue of liability and went directly to the issue of damages, we simply do not have the benefit of its views as to whether Chrysler in fact violated Section 2(a). Absent such a finding, we decline to apply to this case the lenient damage rules of our previous cases. Had the court below found a violation, we could more confidently consider the adequacy of Payne's evidence.

Accordingly, we think the proper course is to remand the case so that the Court of Appeals may pass upon Chrysler's contention that the evidence adduced at trial was insufficient to support a finding of violation of the Robinson-Patman Act. We emphasize that even if there has been a violation of the Robinson-Patman Act, Payne is not excused from his burden of proving antitrust injury and damages. It is simply that once a violation has been established, that burden is to some extent lightened.

Judgment remanded for further proceedings.

**Defenses to Section 2(a) Liability.** There are three major statutory defenses to liability under Section 2(a): *cost justification, changing conditions,* and *meeting competition in good faith.*

**Cost Justification.** Section 2(a) specifically provides that price differentials that make only a "due allowance" for differences in the "cost of manufacture, sale, or delivery resulting from the differing methods or quantities" in which goods are sold or delivered to buyers are lawful. This defense recognizes the simple fact that it may be less costly for a seller to service some buyers than others. Sales to buyers that purchase in large quantities may in some cases be more cost effective than small-quantity sales to their competitors. Sellers are allowed to pass on such cost savings to their customers.

Utilizing this *cost justification* defense is quite difficult and expensive for sellers, however, because quantity discounts must be supported by *actual evidence* of cost savings. Sellers are allowed to average their costs and classify their customers into categories based on their average sales costs, but the customers included in any particular classification must be sufficiently similar to justify similar treatment.

**Changing Conditions.** Section 2(a) also specifically exempts price discriminations that reflect "changing conditions in the market for or the marketability of the goods." This defense has been narrowly confined to temporary situations caused by the physical nature of the goods (e.g., the deterioration of perishable goods or a declining market for seasonal goods). It also applies to forced judicial sales of the goods (e.g., during bankruptcy proceedings involving the seller) and to good faith sales by sellers that have decided to cease selling the goods in question.

**Meeting Competition.** Section 2(b) of the Robinson-Patman Act specifically states that price discrimination may be lawful if the discriminary lower price was charged "in good faith to meet an equally low price of a competitor." Such an exception is necessary to prevent the Act from stifling the very competition that it was designed to preserve. For example, suppose Sony Corporation has been selling a particular model of video recorder to its customers for $350 per unit. Sony then learns that General Electric is offering a comparable recorder to Acme Appliance Stores for $300 per unit. Acme, however, competes with Best Buy Video Stores, a Sony customer that has recently been charged the $350 price. Should Sony be forced to refrain from offering the lower competitive price to Acme for fear that if it does so, Best Buy will charge Sony with price discrimination? If so, competition between Sony and General Electric will plainly suffer.

Section 2(b) avoids this undesirable result by allowing sellers to charge a lower price to some customers if they have reasonable grounds for believing that the lower price is necessary to meet an equally low price offered by a competitor. However, this defense is subject to several significant qualifications. First, the lower price must be necessary to meet a lower price charged by a competitor of the *seller,* not to enable a customer of the seller to compete more effectively with that customer's competitors. Second, the seller may lawfully seek only to *meet, not beat,* its competitor's price. A seller may not, however, be held in violation of the Act for beating a competitor's price if it did so unknowingly in a good faith attempt to meet competition. Third, the seller may reduce its price only to meet competitors' prices for products of *similar quality.*

In addition, the courts have held that the discriminatory price must be a response to an individual competitive situation rather than the product of a seller's wholesale adoption of a competitor's discriminatory pricing system. However, the *Falls City* case, which follows, indicates that a seller's competitive response need not be on a "customer-by-customer" basis, so long as the lower price is offered only to those customers that the seller reasonably believes are being offered a lower price by its competitors. The *Falls City* case also clears up another point of contention about the "meeting competition" defense: sellers may meet competition "offensively" (i.e., to gain a new customer), as well as "defensively" (to keep an existing customer).

## Falls City Indus., Inc. v. Vanco Beverage, Inc.

**460 U.S. 428 (U.S. Sup. Ct. 1983)**

Falls City Industries, Inc., a Louisville, Kentucky, beer brewer, sold beer to wholesalers in Indiana, Kentucky, and nine other states. Vanco Beverage was Falls City's sole wholesale distributor in Vanderburgh County, Indiana. Dawson Springs was Falls City's only wholesale distributor in Henderson County, Kentucky, just across the state line from Vanderburgh County. From 1972 to 1978, Falls City followed the pricing patterns of larger brewers that sold beer in Indiana and Kentucky. Falls City sold beer to Dawson Springs and other Kentucky wholesalers at prices lower than those it charged to Vanco and other Indiana wholesalers. Vanco filed a Robinson-Patman suit against Falls City, arguing that Falls City's price discrimination violated the Act.

Indiana law required brewers to charge identical prices to all Indiana wholesalers, prohibited Indiana wholesalers from selling to out-of-state retailers, and required Indiana retailers to purchase beer only from Indiana wholesalers. The trial court held that Vanco had established a prima facie case of price discrimination. Even though Vanco and Dawson Springs did not compete for sales to the same retailers, the court found that they ultimately did compete for sales to consumers buying beer from retailers in the area, because many Indiana consumers went to Kentucky to buy cheaper beer there. The court agreed with Vanco's argument that Falls City's pricing policy prevented Vanco from competing effectively with Dawson Springs and resulted in lower sales to Indiana retailers.

Falls City argued that it was entitled to a "meeting competition" defense under Section 2(b) of the Robinson-Patman Act. The trial court disagreed on the ground that Falls City had raised its prices in Indiana more than it had raised its Kentucky prices, instead of lowering its price to meet a competitor's price. In addition, the court said that Falls City had charged a single price throughout each state, instead of adjusting prices on a customer-by-customer basis, and that this fact prevented the use of the "meeting competition" defense. The court of appeals affirmed the trial court's decision, and Falls City appealed.

**Blackmun, Justice.** When proved, the meeting-competition defense of Section 2(b) exonerates a seller from Robinson-Patman Act liability. This Court consistently has held that the meeting-competition defense "at least requires the seller, who has knowingly discriminated in price, to show the existence of facts which would lead a reasonable and prudent person to believe that the granting of a lower price would in fact meet the equally low price of a competitor." *United States v. United States Gypsum Co.* (1978). The seller must show that under the circumstances it was reasonable to believe that the quoted price or a lower one was available to the favored purchaser or purchasers from the seller's competitors. Neither the District Court nor the Court of Appeals addressed the question whether Falls City had shown information that would have led a reasonable and prudent person to believe that its lower Kentucky price would meet competitors' equally low prices there; indeed, no findings whatever were made regarding competitors' Kentucky prices, or the information available to Falls City about its competitors' Kentucky prices.

Instead, the Court of Appeals reasoned that Falls City had otherwise failed to show that its pricing "was a good faith effort" to meet competition. The Court of Appeals considered it sufficient to defeat the defense that the price difference "resulted from price increases in Indiana, not price decreases in Kentucky," and that the higher Indiana price was the result of Falls City's policy of following the Indiana prices of its larger competitors in order to enhance its profits. The Court of Appeals also suggested that Falls City's defense failed because it adopted a "general system of competition," rather than responding to "individual situations."

On its face, Section 2(b) requires more than a showing of facts that would have led a reasonable person to believe that a lower price was available to the favored purchaser from a competitor. The showing required is that the "lower price *was made* in good faith *to meet*" the competitor's low price. Thus, the defense requires that the seller offer the lower price in good faith *for the purpose* of meeting the competitor's price; that is, the lower price must actually have been a good faith response to that competing low price. In most situations, a showing of facts giving rise to a reasonable belief that equally low prices were available to the favored purchaser from a competitor will be sufficient to establish that the seller's lower price was offered in good faith to meet that price. In others, however, despite the availability from other sellers of a low price, it may be apparent that the defendant's low offer was not a good faith response.

Almost 20 years ago, the FTC set forth the standard that governs the requirement of a "good faith response."

> At the heart of Section 2(b) is the concept of "good faith." This is a flexible and pragmatic, not a technical or doctrinaire, concept. The standard of good faith is simply the standard of the prudent businessman responding fairly to what he reasonably believes is a situation of competitive necessity.

Whether this standard is met depends on "the facts and circumstances of the particular case, not abstract theories or remote conjectures." Although the District Court characterized the Indiana prices charged by Falls City and its competitors as "artificially high," there is no evidence that Falls City's lower prices in Kentucky were set as part of a plan to obtain artificially high profits in Indiana rather than in response to competitive conditions in Kentucky. Falls City did not adopt an illegal system of prices maintained by its competitors. The District Court found that Falls City's prices rose in Indiana in response to competitors' price increases there; it did not address the crucial question whether Falls City's Kentucky prices remained lower in response to competitors' prices in that State.

By its terms, the meeting-competition defense requires a seller to justify only its *lower* price. Thus, although the Sherman Act would provide a remedy if Falls City's higher Indiana price were set collusively, collusion is relevant to Vanco's Robinson-Patman Act claim only if it affected Falls City's lower Kentucky price. If Falls City set its lower price in good faith to meet an equally low price of a competitor, it did not violate the Robinson-Patman Act.

Moreover, the collusion argument founders on a complete lack of proof. Persistent, industry-wide price discrimination within a geographic market should certainly alert a court to a substantial possibility of collusion. Here, however, the persistent interstate price difference could well have been attributable, not to Falls City, but to extensive state regulation of the sale of beer. Indiana required each brewer to charge a single price for its beer throughout the State, and barred direct competition between Indiana and Kentucky distributors for sales to retailers. In these unusual circumstances, the prices charged to Vanco and other wholesalers in Vanderburgh County may have been influenced more by market conditions in distant Gary and Fort Wayne than by conditions in nearby Henderson County, Kentucky. Moreover, wholesalers in Henderson County competed directly, and attempted to price competitively, with wholesalers in neighboring Kentucky counties. A separate pricing structure might well have evolved in the two States without collusion, notwithstanding the existence of a common retail market along the border. Thus, the sustained price discrimination does not itself demonstrate that Falls City's Kentucky prices were not a good faith response to competitors' prices there.

The Court of Appeals explicitly relied on two other factors in rejecting Falls City's meeting-competition defense: the price discrimination was created by raising rather than lowering prices, and Falls City raised its prices in order to increase its profits. Neither of these factors is controlling. Nothing in Section 2(b) requires a seller to *lower* its price in order to meet competition. On the contrary, Section 2(b) requires the defendant to show only that its "lower price . . . was made in good faith to meet an equally low price of a competitor." A seller is required to justify a price difference by showing that it reasonably believed that an equally low price was available to the purchaser and that it offered the lower price for the reason; the seller is not required to show that the difference resulted from subtraction rather than addition.

Section 2(b) does not require a seller, meeting in good faith a competitor's lower price to certain customers, to forgo the profits that otherwise would be available in sales to its remaining customers. The very purpose of the defense is to permit a seller to treat different competitive situations differently. The prudent businessman responding fairly to what he believes in good faith is a situation of competitive necessity might well raise his prices to some customers to increase his profits, while meeting competitors' prices by keeping his prices to other customers low.

Vanco also contends that Falls City did not satisfy Section 2(b) because its price discrimination "was not a *defensive* response to competition." According to Vanco, the Robinson-Patman Act permits price discrimination only if its purpose is to retain a customer. We agree that a seller's response must be defensive, in the sense that the lower price must be calculated and offered in good faith to "meet not beat" the competitor's low price. Section 2(b), however, does not distinguish between one who meets a competitor's lower price to retain an old customer and one who meets a competitor's lower price in an attempt to gain new customers.

The Court of Appeals relied on *FTC v. A. E. Staley Co.* (1945) for the proposition that the meeting-competition defense "places emphasis on individual [competitive] situations, rather than upon a general system of competition," and "does not justify the maintenance of discriminatory pricing among classes of customers that results merely from the adoption of a competitor's discriminatory pricing structure." The Court of Appeals was apparently invoking the District Court's findings that Falls City set prices statewide rather than on a "customer to customer basis," and the District Court's conclusion that this practice disqualified Falls City from asserting the meeting-competition defense.

Section 2(b) specifically allows a "lower price . . . to any purchaser or purchasers" made in good faith to meet a competitor's equally low price. A single low price surely may be extended to numerous purchasers if the seller has a reasonable basis for believing that the competitor's lower price is available to them. A seller may have good reason to believe that a competitor or competitors are charging lower prices throughout a particular region. In such circumstances, customer-by-customer negotiations would be unlikely to result in prices different from those set according to information relating to competitors' territorial prices. A customer-by- customer requirement might also make meaningful price competition unrealistically expensive for smaller firms such as Falls City, which was attempting to compete with larger national breweries in 13 separate States.

In *Staley,* as in each of the later cases in which this Court has contrasted "general systems of competition" with "individual competitive situations," the seller's lower price was quoted not "*because* of lower prices by a competitor," but "*because* of a preconceived pricing scale which [was] operative regardless of variations in competitors' prices." In those cases, the contested lower prices were not truly "*responsive* to rivals' competitive prices," and therefore were not genuinely made to meet competitors' lower prices. Territorial pricing, however, can be a perfectly reasonable method—sometimes the most reasonable method—of responding to rivals' low prices. We choose not to read into Section 2(b) a restriction that would deny the meeting-competition defense to one whose areawide price is a well-tailored response to competitors' low prices.

Of course, a seller must limit its lower price to that group of customers reasonably believed to have the lower price available to it from competitors. A response that is not reasonably tailored to the competitive situation as known to the buyer, or one that is based on inadequate verification, would not meet the standard of good faith. Similarly, the response may continue only as long as the competitive circumstances justifying it, as reasonably known by the seller, persist. One choosing to price on a territorial basis, rather than on a customer-by-customer basis, must show that this decision was a genuine, reasonable response to prevailing competitive circumstances.

Falls City contends that it has established its meeting-competition defense as a matter of law. In the absence of further findings, we do not agree. The District Court and the Court of Appeals did not decide whether Falls City had shown facts that would have led a reasonable and prudent person to conclude that its lower price would meet the equally low price of its competitors in Kentucky throughout the period at issue in this suit. Nor did they apply the proper standards to the question whether Falls City's decision to set a single statewide price in Kentucky was a good faith, well-tailored response to the competitive circumstances prevailing there. The absence of allegations to the contrary is not controlling; the statute places the burden of establishing the defense on Falls City, not Vanco. There is evidence in the record that might support an inference that these requirements were met, but whether to draw that inference is a question for the trier of fact, not this Court.

Judgment remanded for further proceedings.

**Indirect Price Discrimination.** When Congress passed the Robinson-Patman Act, it recognized that a seller could also discriminate among competing buyers by making discriminatory payments to them or by furnishing them with services not available to their competitors. Three sections of the Act are designed to prevent such practices.

**False Brokerage.** Section 2(c) prohibits sellers from granting, and buyers from receiving, any "commission, brokerage, or other compensation, or any allowance or discount in lieu thereof, except for services rendered in connection with the sale or purchase of goods." This provision is designed to prevent large buyers, either directly or through subsidiary brokerage agents, from receiving phony commissions or brokerage payments from their suppliers. The courts and the FTC originally interpreted Section 2(c) as prohibiting any brokerage payments to a buyer or its agent, regardless of whether the buyer or agent had in fact provided services in connection with the sale that would otherwise have been performed by the seller or an independent broker. This narrow interpretation drew heavy criticism, however, because it operated to create a "closed shop" for independent brokers by denying large buyers any incentive to create their own brokerage services. This interpretation also made it difficult for small, independent retailers to create cooperative buying organizations and thereby to match more closely the buying power of their large competitors. More recent decisions have responded to these criticisms to allow payments for services actually performed by buyers and representing actual cost savings to sellers.

Section 2(c), unlike Section 2(a), establishes a per se standard of liability. No demonstration of probable anticompetitive effect is required for a violation, and neither the cost justification nor "meeting competition" defense is available in 2(c) cases.

**Discriminatory Payments and Services.** Sellers and their customers both benefit from merchandising activities that customers employ to promote the sellers' products. Section 2(d) prohibits sellers from making *discriminatory payments* to competing customers for such services as advertising and promotional activities, or such facilities as shelf space, that customers furnish in connection with the sale of the goods. Section 2(e) prohibits sellers from discriminating in the *services* that they provide to competing customers (e.g., providing favored customers with a display case or a demonstration kit).

A seller may lawfully provide such payments or services only if they are made available to all competing customers on *proportionately equal terms.* This means informing all customers of the availability of the payments or services and distributing them on some rational basis (e.g., the quantity of goods bought by the customer). The seller must also devise a flexible plan that enables its various classes of customers to participate in the program in an appropriate way.

Sections 2(d) and 2(e), like Section 2(c), create a per se liability standard. No proof of probable harm to competition is required for a violation, and no cost justification defense is available. However, the "meeting competition" defense provided by Section 2(b) is applicable to 2(d) and 2(e) actions.

**Buyer Inducement of Discrimination.** Section 2(f) of the Robinson-Patman Act makes it illegal for a buyer *knowingly to induce or receive* a discriminatory price in violation of Section 2(a). The logic of the section is that buyers that are successful in demanding discriminatory prices should be punished along with the sellers that acceded to their demands. To violate section 2(f), the buyer must know that the price it received was unjustifiably discriminatory (i.e., probably not cost justified or probably not made in response to changing conditions). Section 2(f) does not apply to buyer inducements of discriminatory payments or services prohibited by Sections 2(d) and 2(e). Such buyer actions may, however, be attacked as unfair methods of competition under Section 5 of the FTC Act.

A recent Supreme Court case, *Great Atlantic and Pacific Tea Co. v. FTC,*[12] further narrowed the effective reach of Section 2(f) by holding that buyers that knowingly receive a discriminatory price do not violate the act if their seller has a valid defense to the charge of violating Section 2(a). In that case, the seller had a "meeting competition in good faith" defense under Section 2(b). This fact was held to insulate the buyer from liability even though the buyer knew that the seller had beaten, rather than merely met, its competitors' price.

## ANTITRUST EXCEPTIONS AND EXEMPTIONS

**Introduction.** A wide variety of economic activities occur outside the reach of the antitrust laws, either because these activities have been specifically exempted by statute or because the courts have carved out nonstatutory exceptions designed to balance our antitrust policy against competing social policies. Critics have charged that a number of existing exemptions are no longer justifiable, and recent years have witnessed a judicial tendency to narrow the scope of many exemptions.

**Statutory Exemptions.** Sections 6 and 20 of the Clayton Act and the Norris-LaGuardia Act of 1932 provide that *labor unions* are not combinations or conspiracies in restraint of trade and exempt certain union activities, including boycotts and secondary picketing, from antitrust scrutiny. This statutory exemption does not, however, exempt union combinations with nonlabor groups aimed at restraining trade or creating a monopoly (e.g., a union agrees with employer A to call a strike at employer B's plants). In an attempt to accommodate the strong public policy in favor of collective bargaining, the courts have also created a limited nonstatutory exemption for legitimate agreements between unions and employers arising out of the collective bargaining context.

Section 6 of the Clayton Act and the Capper-Volstead Act exempt the formation and collective marketing activities of *agricultural cooperatives* from antitrust liability. This exemption, like many statutory antitrust exemptions, has been narrowly construed by the courts. Cooperatives including members that are not engaged in the production of agricultural commodities have been denied exempt status (e.g., a cooperative including retailers or wholesalers that do not also produce the commodity in question). Also, the exemption extends only to legitimate collective marketing activities; it does not legitimize coercive or predatory practices that are unnecessary to accomplish lawful cooperative goals (e.g., a boycott aimed at forcing nonmembers to adhere to prices established by the cooperative).

The Webb-Pomerene Act exempts the *joint export activities* of American companies, so long as those activities do not "artificially or intentionally enhance or depress prices within the United States." The purpose of the Act is to encourage export activity by domestic firms by allowing them to form combinations to compete more effectively with foreign cartels. Some critics have charged, however, that this exemption is no longer needed, because today there are far fewer foreign cartels and American firms often play a dominant role in foreign trade. Others question whether any group of American firms enjoying significant domestic market shares in the sale of a particular product could agree on an international marketing strategy (e.g., the amounts that they will export) without indirectly affecting domestic supplies and prices.

The McCarran-Ferguson Act exempts from federal antitrust scrutiny those aspects of the

[12] 440 U.S. 69 (U.S. Sup. Ct. 1979).

*business of insurance* that are subject to state regulation. The Act provides, however, that state law cannot legitimize any agreement to boycott, coerce, or intimidate others. Since the insurance industry is extensively regulated by the states, many practices in the industry are outside the reach of the federal antitrust laws. In recent years, however, the courts have tended to narrow the scope of this exemption by narrowly construing the meaning of the "business of insurance." For example, in *Union Labor Life Insurance Co. v. Pireno,*[13] the Supreme Court held that a "peer review system" in which an insurance company used a committee established by a state chiropractic association to review the reasonableness of particular chiropractors' charges was outside the scope of the insurance exemption. In order to qualify for exemption, the Court said that the challenged practice must have the effect of transferring or spreading policyholders' risk and be an integral part of the policy relationship between the insured and the insurer. Thus, only practices related to traditional functions of the insurance business such as underwriting and risk-spreading are likely to be exempt.

A large number of other *regulated industries* enjoy various degrees of antitrust immunity. The airline, banking, utility, railroad, shipping, and securities industries are regulated in the public interest. The regulatory agencies supervising these industries have frequently been given the power to approve industry practices such as rate-setting and mergers that would otherwise violate the antitrust laws. In recent years, there has been a distinct tendency to deregulate many regulated industries. If this trend continues, a greater portion of the economic activity in these industries will be subjected to antitrust scrutiny.

[13] 458 U.S. 119 (U.S. Sup. Ct. 1982).

## Connell Construction Co. v. Plumbers and Steamfitters Union

**421 U.S. 616 (U.S. Sup. Ct. 1975)**

The Dallas local of the Plumbers and Steamfitters Union was a party to a multiemployer collective bargaining agreement with the Mechanical Contractors Association of Dallas, a group of about 75 mechanical contractors. The agreement between the Union and the Association contained a "most favored nation clause," by which the Union agreed that if it granted a more favorable contract to any other contractor it would extend the same terms to all Association members. In an effort to organize subcontractors, the Union sought to get general contractors to agree to deal only with subcontractors that were parties to the Union's current collective bargaining agreement.

Connell Construction Company, a general building contractor that subcontracted all plumbing and mechanical work, refused to sign such an agreement. Instead, Connell indicated an intent to continue awarding subcontracts on a competitive bid basis, regardless of whether the subcontractor selected was a union or nonunion firm. Connell had no employees that the Union wished to represent, but in an effort to force Connell to sign the agreement, the Union picketed one of Connell's major construction sites. When several workers walked off the job and construction came to a halt, Connell signed the agreement under protest and filed suit against the Union for violating the Sherman Act. At the time of the trial, the Union had signed identical agreements with five other Dallas general contractors, and was selectively picketing those that, like Connell, had refused to sign. The trial court ruled in the Union's favor, and the Fifth Circuit Court of Appeals affirmed on the ground that the Union's actions were exempt from the federal antitrust laws. Connell appealed.

**POWELL, JUSTICE.** The basic source of organized labor's exemption from federal antitrust laws are Sections 6 and 20 of the Clayton Act and the Norris-LaGuardia Act. These statutes declare that labor unions are not combinations or conspiracies in restraint of trade, and exempt specific union activities, including secondary picketing and boycotts, from the operation of the antitrust laws. They do not exempt concerted action or agreements between unions and nonlabor parties. The court has recognized, however, that a proper accommodation between the congressional policy favoring collective bargaining under the National Labor Relations Act and the congressional policy favoring free competition in business markets requires that some union-employer agreements be accorded a limited nonstatutory exemption from antitrust sanctions.

The nonstatutory exemption has its source in the strong labor policy favoring the association of employees to eliminate competition over wages and working conditions. Union success in organizing workers and standardizing wages ultimately will affect price competition among employers, but the goals of federal labor law never could be achieved if this effect on business competition were held a violation of the antitrust laws. The Court therefore has acknowledged that labor policy requires tolerance for the lessening of business competition based on differences in wages and working conditions. Labor policy clearly does not require, however, that a union have the freedom to impose direct restraints on competition among those who employ its members. Thus, while the statutory exemption allows unions to accomplish some restraints by acting unilaterally, the nonstatutory exemption offers no similar protection when a union and a nonlabor party agree to restrain competition in a business market.

In this case, the Union used direct restraints on the business market to support its organizing campaign. The agreements with Connell and other general contractors indiscriminately excluded nonunion subcontractors from a portion of the market, even if their competitive advantages were not derived from substandard wages and working conditions but rather from more efficient operating methods. Curtailment of competition based on efficiency is neither a goal of federal labor policy nor a necessary effect of the elimination of competition among workers. Moreover, competition based on efficiency is a positive value that the antitrust laws strive to protect.

The multiemployer bargaining agreement between the Union and the Association, though not challenged in this suit, is relevant in determining the effect that the agreement between the Union and Connell would have on the business market. The "most favored nation" clause of the multiemployer agreement promised to eliminate competition between members of the Association and any other subcontractors that the Union might organize. By giving members of the Association a contractual right to insist on terms as favorable as those given any competitor, it guaranteed that the Union would make no agreements that would give an unaffiliated contractor a competitive advantage over members of the Association. Subcontractors in the Association thus stood to benefit from any extension of the Union's organization, but the method the Union chose also had the effect of sheltering them from outside competition in that portion of the market covered by subcontracting agreements between general contractors and the Union. In that portion of the market, the restriction on subcontracting would eliminate competition on all subjects covered by the multiemployer agreement, even on subjects unrelated to wages, hours and working conditions.

This record contains no evidence that the Union's goal was anything other than organizing as many subcontractors as possible. This goal was legal, even though a successful organizing campaign ultimately would reduce the competition that unionized employers face from nonunion firms. But the methods the Union chose are not immune from antitrust sanctions simply because the goal is legal. Here the Union, by agreement with several contractors, made nonunion subcontractors ineligible to compete for a portion of the available work. This kind of direct restraint on the business market has substantial anticompetitive effects, both actual and potential, that would not follow naturally from the elimination of competition over wages and working conditions. It contravenes antitrust policies to a degree not justified by congressional labor policy, and therefore cannot claim a nonstatutory exemption from the antitrust laws.

Judgment reversed in favor of Connell.

**State Action Exemption.** In *Parker v. Brown,*[14] the Supreme Court held that a California state agency's regulation of the production and price of raisins was a *state action* exempt from the federal antitrust laws. The "state action" exemption recognizes the states' right to regulate economic activity in the interest of their citizens. It also, however, may tempt state economic interests to seek "friendly" state regulation as a way of shielding anticompetitive activity from antitrust supervision. Recognizing this fact, the courts have placed several important limitations on the scope of the exemption.

First, the exemption extends only to governmental actions by a state or to actions compelled by a state acting in its sovereign capacity. Second, as the *Midcal* case, which follows, indicates, in order to qualify for immunity under this exemption the challenged activity must be "clearly articulated and affirmatively expressed as state policy" and "actively supervised" by the state. In other words, the price of antitrust immunity is real regulation by the state. Finally, the Supreme Court has recently held that the state action exemption does not confer immunity on the actions of municipalities.[15] This holding produced considerable concern that the threat of treble damage liability might inhibit legitimate regulatory action by municipal authorities. As a result, Congress passed the Local Government Antitrust Act of 1984. The Act eliminates damage actions against municipalities and their officers, agents, and employees for antitrust violations and makes injunctive relief the sole remedy in such cases. It does not, however, bar damage suits against private individuals who engage in anticompetitive conduct with local government agencies.

**The *Noerr-Pennington* Doctrine.** In the *Noerr* and *Pennington* cases,[16] the Supreme Court held that "the Sherman Act does not prohibit two or more persons from associating together in an attempt to persuade the legislature or the executive to take particular action with respect to a law that would produce a restraint or a monopoly." This exemption recognizes that the right to petition government

[14] 317 U.S. 341 (U.S. Sup. Ct. 1943).

[15] *Community Communications Co., Inc. v. City of Boulder,* 455 U.S. 40 (U.S. Sup. Ct. 1982).

[16] *Eastern R.R. President's Conference v. Noerr Motor Freight, Inc.,* 365 U.S. 127 (U.S. Sup. Ct. 1961); *United Mine Workers v. Pennington,* 381 U.S. 657 (U.S. Sup. Ct. 1965).

provided by the Bill of Rights takes precedence over the antitrust policy in favor of competition. The exemption does not, however, extend to "sham" activities that are attempts to interfere with the business activities of competitors rather than legitimate attempts to influence governmental action.[17]

**Patent Licensing.** There is a basic tension between the antitrust objective of promoting competition and the patent laws, which seek to promote innovation by granting a limited monopoly to those who develop new products or processes.[18] In the early case of *United States v. General Electric Company,*[19] the Supreme Court allowed General Electric to control the price at which other manufacturers sold light bulbs that they had manufactured under patent licensing agreements with General Electric. The Court recognized that an important part of holding a patent was the right to license others to manufacture the patented item. This right would be effectively negated if licensees were allowed to undercut the prices that patent holders charged for their own sales of patented products.

Patent holders cannot, however, lawfully control the price at which patented items are resold by distributors that purchase them from the patent holder. Nor can patent holders use their patents to impose tying agreements on their customers (e.g., by conditioning the sale of patented items on the purchase of nonpatented items) unless such agreements are otherwise lawful under the Sherman and Clayton Acts. Finally, firms that seek to monopolize an area of commerce by acquiring most, or all, of the patents related to that area of commerce may be guilty of violating Section 2 of the Sherman Act or Section 7 of the Clayton Act (since a patent has been held to be an "asset" within the meaning of Section 7).

**Foreign Commerce.** When foreign governments are involved in commercial activities affecting the domestic or international commerce of the United States, our antitrust policy may be at odds with our foreign policy. Congress and the courts have created a variety of antitrust exemptions aimed at reconciling this potential conflict. The Foreign Sovereign Immunities Act of 1976 (FSIA) provides that the governmental actions of foreign sovereigns and their agents are exempt from antitrust liability. The "commercial" activities of foreign sovereigns, however, are not included within this **sovereign immunity** exemption. Significant international controversy exists over the proper criteria for determining whether a particular governmental act is "commercial" in nature. Under the FSIA, the courts employ a "nature of the act" test, holding that a commercial activity is one that an individual might customarily carry on for a profit.

The **act of state doctrine** provides that an American court will not adjudicate a politically sensitive dispute that would require the court to judge the legality of a sovereign act by a foreign state. This doctrine reflects judicial deference to the primary role of the executive and legislative branches in the adoption and execution of our foreign policy. Like the doctrine of sovereign immunity, the act of state doctrine recognizes the importance of respecting the sovereignty of other nations. Unlike the doctrine of sovereign immunity, however, the act of state doctrine also reflects a fundamental attribute of our system of government: the principle of separation of powers.

Finally, the **sovereign compulsion doctrine** provides a defense to private parties that have been compelled by a foreign sovereign to commit acts within that sovereign's

---

[17] *California Motor Transport v. Trucking Unlimited,* 404 U.S. 508 (U.S. Sup. Ct. 1982).

[18] The patent laws were discussed in detail in Chapter 43.

[19] 272 U.S. 476 (U.S. Sup. Ct. 1926).

territory that would otherwise violate the antitrust laws due to their negative impact on our international commerce. To employ this defense successfully, a defendant must show that the challenged actions were the product of actual compulsion by a foreign sovereign, not mere encouragement or approval.

## California Retail Liquor Dealers Assoc. v. Midcal Aluminum, Inc.

**445 U.S. 97 (U.S. Sup. Ct. 1980)**

A California statute required all wine producers and wholesalers to file fair trade contracts or price schedules with the state. If a producer had not fixed prices through a fair trade contract, that producer's wholesalers had to post a resale price schedule and were prohibited from selling wine to any retailer at a price other than the price fixed in a price schedule or a fair trade contract. Midcal Aluminum, a wholesaler selling below the established prices, faced fines or license suspension or revocation. After being charged with selling wines for less than the prices set by posted resale price schedules and also for selling wines for which no fair trade contract or schedule had been filed, Midcal filed suit asking for an injunction against the state's wine-pricing scheme. The California court of appeal granted Midcal's request, holding that the pricing scheme violated the Sherman Act and rejecting the argument that the scheme was immune from liability under the state action doctrine.

**Powell, Justice.** California's system for wine pricing plainly constitutes resale price maintenance in violation of the Sherman Act. The wine producer holds the power to prevent price competition by dictating the price charged by wholesalers. As Mr. Justice Hughes pointed out in *Dr. Miles,* such vertical control destroys horizontal competition as effectively as if wholesalers "formed a combination and endeavored to establish the same restrictions by agreement with each other." Moreover, there can be no claim that the California program is simply intrastate regulation beyond the reach of the Sherman Act.

Thus, we must consider whether the State's involvement in the price-setting program is sufficient to establish antitrust immunity under *Parker v. Brown* (1943). That immunity for state regulatory programs is grounded in our federal structure. "In a dual system of government in which, under the Constitution, the states are sovereign, save only as Congress may constitutionally subtract from their authority, an unexpressed purpose to nullify a state's control over its officers and agents is not lightly to be attributed to Congress." In *Parker v. Brown,* this Court found in the Sherman Act no purpose to nullify state powers. Because the Act is directed against "individual and not state action," the Court concluded that state regulatory programs could not violate it.

Under the program challenged in *Parker,* the state Agricultural Prorate Advisory Commission authorized the organization of local cooperatives to develop marketing policies for the raisin crop. The Court emphasized that the Advisory Commission, which was appointed by the governor, had to approve cooperative policies following public hearings: "It is the state which has created the machinery for establishing the prorate program. It is the state, acting through the Commission, which adopts the program and enforces it."

In view of this extensive official oversight, the Court wrote, the Sherman Act did not apply. Without such oversight, the result could have been different. The Court expressly noted, "a state does not give immunity to those who violate the Sherman Act by authorizing them to violate it, or by declaring that their action is lawful."

Several recent decisions have applied *Parker's* analysis. In *Goldfarb v. Virginia State Bar* (1975), the Court concluded that fee schedules enforced by a state bar association were not mandated by ethical standards established by the State Supreme Court. The fee schedules therefore were not immune from antitrust attack. "It is not enough that . . . anticompetitive conduct is 'prompted' by state action: rather, anticompetitive conduct must be compelled by direction of the State acting as sovereign." Similarly, in *Cantor v. Detroit Edison Co.* (1976), a majority of the Court found that no antitrust immunity was conferred when a state agency passively accepted a public utility's tariff. In contrast, Arizona rules against lawyer advertising were held immune from Sherman Act challenge because they "reflect[ed] *a clear articulation* of the State's policy with regard to professional behavior" and were "*subject to pointed re-examination* by the policy-maker—the Arizona Supreme Court—in enforcement proceedings." *Bates v. State Bar of Arizona* (1977).

Only last Term, this Court found antitrust immunity for a California program requiring state approval of the location of new automobile dealerships. *New Motor Vehicle Bd. of California v. Orrin W. Fox Co.* (1978). That program provided that the State would hold a hearing if an automobile franchisee protested the establishment or relocation of a competing dealership. In view of the State's active role, the Court held, the program was not subject to the Sherman Act. The "clearly articulated and affirmatively expressed" goal of the state policy was to "displace unfettered business freedom in the matter of the establishment and relocation of automobile dealerships."

These decisions establish two standards for antitrust immunity under *Parker v. Brown.* First, the challenged restraint must be "one clearly articulated and affirmatively expressed as state policy"; second, the policy must be "actively supervised" by the State itself. The California system for wine pricing satisfies the first standard. The legislative policy is forthrightly stated and clear in its purpose to permit resale price maintenance. The program, however, does not meet the second requirement for *Parker* immunity. The State simply authorizes price-setting and enforces the prices established by private parties. The State neither establishes prices nor reviews the reasonableness of the price schedules; nor does it regulate the terms of fair trade contracts. The State does not monitor market conditions or engage in any "pointed reexamination" of the program. The national policy in favor of competition cannot be thwarted by casting such a gauzy cloak of state involvement over what is essentially a private price-fixing arrangement. As *Parker* teaches, "a state does not give immunity to those who violate the Sherman Act by authorizing them to violate it, or by deciding that their action is lawful."

Judgment for Midcal affirmed.

## SUMMARY

The Clayton Act was passed as a result of congressional disappointment at the Sherman Act's failure to halt the trend toward concentration in the American economy. The Clayton Act attempts to "nip monopolies in the bud" by outlawing specific practices that monopolists use to gain monopoly power.

Section 3 of the Clayton Act prohibits tying

and exclusive dealing agreements involving commodities if those agreements represent a probable threat to competition. Section 3 does not apply to tying or exclusive dealing agreements involving real estate, intangibles, or services. Such agreements must be challenged under the Sherman Act. Moreover, since Section 3 applies only if a sale or lease has occurred, refusals to deal and consignment dealing are also outside the scope of the act. Some courts require the same level of proof for tying illegality under the Clayton Act as they do under the Sherman Act. That is, it must be shown that: the challenged agreement involves two separate products; the sale of the tying product is conditioned on an accompanying sale of the tied product; the seller has sufficient economic power in the market for the tying product to appreciably restrain competition in the tied product market; and the seller's tying agreements foreclose competitors from a "not insubstantial" amount of commerce in the tied product market. Other courts do not require proof of the seller's market power in the tying product as long as the other three elements of tying liability are present.

There is similar confusion over the proper standard for judging the legality of exclusive dealing agreements. Courts tend to apply the same standards of legality to exclusive dealing agreements challenged under the Clayton Act as they do to those attacked under the Sherman Act. Two distinct approaches, however, have been used in exclusive dealing cases. Early Supreme Court cases employed a "quantitative substantiality" test, focusing on the annual dollar volume of the commerce foreclosed to the seller's competitors as a result of the challenged agreement. The most recent Supreme Court case, however, employed a "qualitative substantiality" approach, stressing the percentage share of the market foreclosed to competition and a variety of other economic factors.

Section 7 of the Clayton Act prohibits mergers and acquisitions that may substantially lessen competition or tend to create a monopoly in any line of commerce in any section of the country. The future of Section 7 is somewhat in doubt, as current merger guidelines announced by federal antitrust enforcers indicate a much more tolerant attitude toward merger activity and most important recent merger cases have been settled out of court. Legal analysis of mergers under Section 7 has traditionally varied depending on the nature of the challenged merger. Horizontal mergers (between competitors) involve the most immediate risk of harm to competition and consequently have been subjected to the most stringent standards. Traditional analysis looks at the market share of the merged firm, together with other economic and historical factors. Recent Justice Department merger guidelines indicate that the department uses a statistical device called the Herfindahl-Hirschman Index to gauge the current degree of concentration in the relevant market and the increase in concentration that would result from the challenged merger.

Vertical merger (supplier-customer) analysis, traditionally focused on the share of the relevant market foreclosed to competitors as a result of the challenged merger, although vertical mergers may also result in barriers to entry and an elimination of potential competition. Conglomerate mergers (those that are neither horizontal nor vertical) have traditionally been challenged on one or more of three theories: potential reciprocity, unfair advantage, or elimination of potential competition. The most recent Justice Department merger guidelines indicate, however, that the department will employ the same criteria to judge all "nonhorizontal" mergers and that these criteria emphasize an elimination of potential competition analysis.

Section 8 of the Clayton Act prohibits interlocking directorates between competing companies if either company has capital, surplus, or undivided profits in excess of $1 million. The enforcement of this section has historically been rather lax, but there are recent indications of renewed governmental interest in enforcing this part of the Act.

Section 2 of the original Clayton Act was designed to attack primary level price discrimination: localized price cuts by sellers designed to drive smaller rivals out of business. In 1936, Congress amended Section 2 by enacting the Robinson-Patman Act to attack price discrimination that resulted in secondary or tertiary level harms: price discrimination in sales to competing customers that results in a competitive advantage to a favored customer or to the customers of a favored customer. Section 2(a) of the Robinson-Patman Act prohibits direct price discrimination that results in a probability of competitive injury at any of these three levels. Price discrimination occurs when a seller makes relatively contemporaneous sales of products of like grade or quality at different prices to two or more customers. Price discrimination may in some cases be cost justified or justified by changing conditions affecting the marketability of the product in question. Section 2(b) of the act also provides a "meeting competition in good faith" defense that may excuse some discriminations in price. Section 2(f) makes it unlawful for a buyer knowingly to induce or receive a discriminatory price in violation of Section 2(a).

The Robinson-Patman Act also prohibits indirect price discrimination. Section 2(c) of the act prohibits false brokerage payments, and Sections 2(d) and 2(e) prohibit sellers from discriminating in promotional payments or services made to their customers unless such payments are made available to all customers on a proportionately equal basis.

A wide variety of economic activities occur outside the reach of the antitrust laws. Labor unions, agricultural cooperatives, exporters, and insurance companies and a number of other regulated industries enjoy partial statutory exemptions from antitrust liability. The courts have also created a number of antitrust exemptions designed to balance our antitrust policy against other important social policies. The "state action" exemption confers antitrust immunity to bona fide state regulatory activities and to private behavior pursuant to such activities. The *Noerr-Pennington* doctrine immunizes legitimate political action by competitors from antitrust scrutiny, even though such action may be aimed at anticompetitive ends. The "patent licensing" doctrine grants patent holders limited rights to exploit their patents by practices that would otherwise violate the antitrust laws. Finally, some activities by American firms in foreign countries and certain actions by foreign sovereigns may lie outside the reach of our antitrust laws due to three doctrines: sovereign immunity, act of state, and sovereign compulsion.

## PROBLEM CASES

**1.** Continental Cablevision, Inc. and Satellite Television and Associated Resources, Inc. (STAR) operated cable television systems in and around Richmond, Virginia. In 1978, Continental was concerned about the high cost of wiring multiple dwelling units (MDUs) for cable television and the accompanying risk of not receiving an adequate return on its investment. Accordingly, Continental offered apartment owners a choice: pay for the wiring themselves, or agree to give Continental exclusive pay television rights to their MDUs. The apartment owners chose to give Continental exclusive contracts. Continental abandoned the exclusivity provision in June 1980, after STAR was successful in delaying FCC proceedings necessary to Continental's profitability by complaining to the FCC about the exclusivity provision. Nonetheless, STAR filed suit against Continental in September 1980, arguing that Continental's exclusive dealing contracts violated Section 1 of the Sherman Act and Section 3 of the Clayton Act.

STAR admitted that potential customers perceived pay television to be reasonably interchangeable with the offerings of movie theaters, broadcast television, and videocassettes. STAR argued, however, that cable television was a "submarket," though it failed to offer any convincing evidence to support its claim. The trial court dismissed STAR's Clayton Act claim on the ground that pay television was a service, and therefore outside the scope of the Clayton Act. It also ruled for Continental on the Sherman Act claim, holding that since Continental's agreements affected only 8 percent of the potential pay television market in the metropolitan Richmond area, the harm to competition was insufficient to justify Sherman Act liability. Was the trial court correct?

**2.** Bob Maxfield, Inc. operated as an American Motors Corporation (AMC) dealer in Houston from March 1972 until May 1973, when AMC terminated Maxfield's franchise and took over the operation of the dealership. In the short time that Maxfield operated as an AMC dealer, it had numerous disputes with AMC. The most important of these disputes concerned the product mix in the line of cars that AMC sold Maxfield. During the period in question, AMC's small cars, the Gremlin and the Hornet, were so popular that demand exceeded AMC's production capacity, forcing AMC to ration the cars among its dealers. AMC's larger cars, the Ambassador and the Matador, were far less successful. After being terminated, Maxfield filed suit against AMC, alleging that AMC had forced Maxfield to buy the larger cars it did not want in order to get the smaller cars it needed.

The testimony at trial indicated that AMC representatives had repeatedly urged Maxfield to order the larger cars and had become angry on the occasions when Maxfield refused to do so. On one occasion, an AMC sales rep had ordered Ambassadors on Maxfield's behalf without its consent. Another AMC rep had talked Maxfield into taking big cars by promising to "move them away" if they did not sell—a promise that was later broken. The trial court, however, found no evidence of an actual requirement that Maxfield purchase large cars or face a cutoff of small cars. Instead, the trial court found that Maxfield's difficulties in receiving small cars were due to the nationwide shortage of those models. Assuming that the trial court's findings were accurate, was it correct in ruling in favor of AMC on Maxfield's Sherman and Clayton Act tying claims?

**3.** In 1961, Ford Motor Company bought Autolite, a manufacturer of spark plugs, in order to enter the profitable "aftermarket" for spark plugs sold as replacement parts. Ford and the other major automobile manufacturers had previously purchased "original equipment" spark plugs (those installed in new cars when they leave the factory) from independent producers such as Autolite and Champion at or below the producer's cost. The independents were willing to sell original equipment plugs so cheaply because they knew that aftermarket mechanics often replaced original equipment plugs with the same brand of spark plug. General Motors had previously moved into the spark plug market by developing its own AC division. Ford decided to do so by a vertical merger and acquired Autolite. Prior to acquiring Autolite, Ford had purchased 10 percent of the total spark plug output. The merger left Champion as the only major independent spark plug producer, and Champion's market share declined thereafter because Chrysler was the only major original equipment spark plug purchaser remaining in the market. The government filed a divestiture suit against

Ford, arguing that Ford's acquisition of Autolite violated Section 7 of the Clayton Act. Should Ford be ordered to divest itself of Autolite?

**4.** Procter & Gamble, a huge, diversified manufacturer of household products (detergents, soaps, cleansers, etc.), acquired Clorox, the leading manufacturer of household liquid bleach (48.8 percent of national sales). The household liquid bleach industry was highly concentrated, and Clorox had a distinct advantage over its competitors because it had plants distributed throughout the nation, allowing it to dominate sales in many parts of the country where it had no effective competition. Procter & Gamble, the nation's largest advertiser, decided to enter the household bleach market by acquiring Clorox rather than by entering independently. The FTC ordered divestiture, and Procter & Gamble appealed. Did Procter & Gamble's acquisition of Clorox violate Section 7?

**5.** Connecticut Bank, the fourth largest bank in Connecticut, and New Haven Bank, the eighth largest, initiated steps to consolidate their operations. Together, the two banks had just over 10 percent of the total bank deposits in the state. The areas served by the two banks overlapped slightly but were contiguous for the most part. The government brought suit to enjoin the consolidation as a violation of Section 7 of the Clayton Act. The trial court ruled that the state of Connecticut was the relevant market. Is this correct?

**6.** Metrix Warehouse, Inc. was a competitor of Mercedes-Benz North America (MBNA) in the sale of replacement parts to approximately 400 Mercedes-Benz dealers franchised by MBNA, the exclusive U.S. distributor of Mercedes-Benz automobiles. Metrix sued MBNA, arguing that MBNA had tied the sale of replacement parts to the sale of new cars in violation of the Sherman Act. MBNA counterclaimed, arguing that Metrix's incentive program violated Section 2(c) of the Robinson-Patman Act. Metrix's incentive program involved awarding points redeemable for cash or merchandise to the parts managers of Mercedes-Benz dealers. The value of the points amounted to approximately 3.5 percent of all the parts that a manager ordered from Metrix. The managers performed no services for Metrix other than placing their employers' parts orders with Metrix. Metrix mailed the payments to parts managers at their home addresses on a monthly basis, and between February 1974 and January 1980, Metrix had paid managers $119,980 in cash and $394,551 in cash and/or merchandise for the placement of approximately $13 million in spare parts orders with Metrix. The district court refused to grant MBNA's mo tion for summary judgment on the counterclaim, arguing that further inquiry into the competitive effects of Metrix's incentive program was necessary to determine whether the program resulted in the kind of harm to competition prohibited by Section 2(c). Was the district court's decision correct?

**7.** Double H Plastics, Inc. and Sunoco Products Company competed in the business of producing and selling small business machine cores—small spools that carry the paper used in adding machines, cash registers, and other business machines. Traditionally, the spools were made of paper, but since the mid-1970s various companies had offered plastic cores. The new plastic cores had captured 90 percent of the adding machine market, but were less successful in the cash register market. Double H was a pioneer in producing and marketing plastic cores, and by the late 1970s it had captured approximately 70 percent of the overall plastic core market. Sunoco was a major producer of paper cores. In 1980, after an unsuccessful attempt to buy Double H, Sunoco acquired its own equipment and began producing and selling plastic cores to compete in the adding machine market. Sunoco continued to sell paper cores for cash registers, and its major customer was NCR Corporation. NCR continued to buy paper cores from Sunoco, even though Double H offered to sell plastic cores for less. NCR's refusal to switch to plastic cores hurt Double H because many smaller cash register companies refused to switch to plastic cores until NCR, an industry leader, did so.

Double H filed suit against Sunoco, arguing that Sunoco had violated Section 2(a) of the Robinson-Patman Act by selling paper cores to NCR at prices substantially below those it charged its other cash register customers. The district court found that Sunoco had violated the Act, but ruled in Sunoco's favor on the grounds that Double H had failed to establish "actual injury" and damages. The district court based its finding that Sunoco had violated the Act on a Sunoco internal memorandum in which Sunoco's general manager stated that "the main account of cash register cores is NCR, and they have elected to stay with paper cores until the economics favor switching to plastics. The remainder of the marketplace is reluctant to switch until NCR makes the change." This statement, the court concluded, demonstrated a "predatory intent" on Sunoco's part. Was the district court's conclusion correct?

**8.** Murphy Oil Company was a manufacturer, refiner, and distributor of diesel fuel. L & L Oil Company supplied diesel fuel to inland and offshore oil drilling rigs. By January 1979, L & L was buying up to 80 percent of its fuel from Murphy. In March 1979, Murphy responded to an energy shortage by making severe reductions in its sales to L & L. Rather than following industry custom by reducing sales in proportion to a customer's prior purchases, Murphy drastically reduced sales to L & L while continuing to supply a high percentage of the needs of its other customers. Murphy justified this practice on the ground that L & L had "shopped around" when fuel was plentiful, whereas the other customers had remained loyal to Murphy. In addition, Murphy required L & L to pick up its fuel by truck instead of by barge, as it had done previously. Murphy charged L & L one-half cent more per gallon for fuel obtained by truck than it charged L & L's competitors, which continued to receive large quantities of fuel and thus were permitted to obtain fuel by barge. L & L incurred additional expenses because the cost of using trucks was higher than the cost of using barges. On April 11, 1979, Murphy terminated all sales to L & L. L & L was forced to buy fuel on the spot market at prices of up to 70 percent more than those charged by Murphy. As a result, L & L was forced to charge its customers higher prices to the point where it was ultimately unable to compete in its service area. L & L filed suit against Murphy, arguing that Murphy had violated Section 2(e) of the Robinson-Patman Act by forcing L & L to pick up its fuel by truck, whereas its competitors were permitted to take delivery by barge. L & L also argued that Murphy's refusal to deal with it violated Section 2(a) of the act. The district court dismissed both claims. Were the dismissals proper?

**9.** The International Association of Machinists and Aerospace Workers (IAM), a nonprofit labor union, filed suit against the Organization of Petroleum Exporting Countries (OPEC), arguing that OPEC's price-fixing activities violated American antitrust laws. The district court dismissed the IAM's claim on the ground that it lacked jurisdiction over the case because OPEC's actions were shielded by the doctrine of sovereign immunity. Was the sovereign immunity doctrine the proper basis for dismissing the IAM's claim?

**10.** Energy Conservation, Inc. (ECI), a solar energy company, filed suit against Heliodyne, Inc., a competitor, for an alleged violation of Section 2 of the Sherman Act. ECI alleged that Heliodyne had conspired with a law firm and several of the firm's clients (all of which were also named as defendants) to bring a sham suit against ECI in a California state court. ECI argued that the purpose of the suit was to generate adverse publicity about ECI, and thereby to cause ECI competitive harm. The defendants argued that their conduct was shielded by the *Noerr-Pennington* doctrine. The district court dismissed ECI's claim, but its grounds for doing so were unclear. It appeared that the court concluded either that a single lawsuit could never constitute a sham under *Noerr-Pennington* or that ECI's complaint lacked specificity. Was the dismissal proper?

# Chapter 46

# The Federal Trade Commission and Consumer Protection Laws

## INTRODUCTION

Throughout this book, we have stressed what should now be a familiar theme: how the rise of the large corporation and other private groups has created a perceived need for government intervention to protect individuals from the superior power that such organizations frequently possess. In few areas of the law has this been more true than in the area sometimes called "consumer law." As Chapter 32 demonstrated, the consumer's ability to recover civil damages for defective products has increased dramatically over the course of this century, especially during the 1960s and 1970s. But these decades also saw an increased level of consumer protection on a number of other legal fronts. Most of these involve *direct government regulation* of various matters relating to the consumer's purchase of goods and services.

This chapter examines the various forms of consumer protection regulation. It begins with a general discussion of America's major "consumer watchdog": the Federal Trade Commission (FTC). After describing how the FTC operates, the chapter focuses on its regulation of advertising. Then, following a brief look at selected provisions of the Magnuson-Moss Warranty Act, the chapter turns to a series of 1960s and 1970s measures regulating consumer credit arrangements. The chapter concludes with a brief survey of federal product safety regulation.

## THE FEDERAL TRADE COMMISSION

**The Commission and Its Functions.** The Federal Trade Commission (FTC) was organized in 1915, following passage of the Federal Trade Commission Act a year earlier. Like the Clayton Act, the FTC Act resulted from dissatisfaction with the Sherman Act's inability to curb anticompetitive practices and tendencies in the American economy. But over time the FTC's role has expanded beyond the regulation of private behavior that restricts free competition. Today, its announced mission is to keep the U.S. economy both free and *fair.* Thus, while still seeking to promote free competition, the FTC also seeks to control unfair and deceptive practices in the marketing and advertising of goods and services.

**The Commission.** The FTC is an independent federal agency, which means that it is not within the executive branch of the federal government and that it is less subject to political control than agencies that are executive departments. It is headed by five commissioners, no more than three of whom can be from one political party. The commissioners are appointed by the president and confirmed by the Senate, and they serve staggered seven-year terms. The president also designates one of the commissioners as chairman of the FTC. In 1984, the FTC had a Washington headquarters and 10 regional offices located in large cities throughout the United States.

**Functions of the FTC.** The FTC's general mission is to keep the U.S. economy from being stifled by monopoly and restraints on trade, or corrupted by unfair and deceptive practices. The FTC has specific statutory authority to enforce the Clayton and Robinson-Patman acts.[1] Its most important grant of authority, however, is Section 5 of the FTC Act, which empowers the FTC to prevent "unfair methods of competition" and "unfair or deceptive practices" in or affecting interstate commerce. Section 5's "unfair methods of competition" language includes any of the trade restraints declared illegal by the Sherman Act,[2] and may include anticompetitive behavior not covered by the Sherman, Clayton, and Robinson-Patman acts.

Section 5's "unfair or deceptive practices" language clearly establishes the FTC's ability to deal with business behavior affecting consumers. Perhaps the most important of the FTC's Section 5 consumer protection functions is the regulation of deceptive or unfair advertising. The FTC is also empowered to enforce a number of other federal acts. The most important of these are certain of the consumer protection and consumer credit statutes discussed in the last half of this chapter. To assist it in the enforcement of all the measures just mentioned, the FTC has broad investigative powers. It also engages in various kinds of economic fact-finding.

**The Changing Role of the FTC.** The FTC's influence on the conduct of business in the United States has waxed and waned over the past 20 years or so. During the 1970s, the Commission assumed an "activist" posture, vigorously attacking alleged antitrust violations and unfair trade practices affecting consumers, and attempting to define and enforce new, more stringent rules against such alleged business misbehavior. Not surprisingly, this effort generated opposition both in the

---

[1] The Clayton and Robinson-Patman Acts are discussed in Chapter 45.

[2] The Sherman Act is discussed in Chapter 44.

business community and in Congress. With the coming of the Reagan administration in 1980 and its appointment of several new FTC commissioners, the FTC's role changed considerably. Now, the Commission is significantly influenced by the Chicago School economic theories described in Chapter 44. Thus, it is more prone to stress the virtues of unregulated economic competition, and to make economic analysis the guide to its rulemaking, enforcement, and decision-making activities. The result of this shift in personnel and attitude, it is probably safe to say, has been a decline in the FTC's enforcement activities, and thus in the threat that the agency poses to business practices.

## FTC ENFORCEMENT PROCEDURES

**Voluntary Compliance.** The FTC has a wide array of legal devices for ensuring compliance with the statutes that it administers. It seeks to promote voluntary, cooperative behavior on the part of business by giving advisory opinions, issuing industry guides (also called trade practice rules), and promulgating trade regulation rules. An **advisory opinion** is the Commission's response to a private party's query about the legality of a proposed course of business conduct. The FTC is not required to furnish advisory opinions, and even if it does, it may reverse itself by rescinding such opinions when the public interest so requires. If the FTC does rescind an advisory opinion, it cannot proceed against the recipient of the opinion for actions taken in good faith reliance on the opinion without giving the recipient notice of the rescission and an opportunity to discontinue those actions.

**Industry guides** are FTC interpretations of the laws it administers. Their purpose is to encourage voluntary abandonment of unlawful practices by the members of an industry. To further this end, industry guides are written in lay language. Industry guides do not have the force of law, and the FTC cannot proceed against a private party merely because its behavior violated the language of an industry guide. Often, however, such behavior violates one of the statutes or other rules that the Commission does have power to enforce. Like industry guides, **trade regulation rules** are FTC interpretations of the statutes it enforces. Unlike industry guides, however, they are written in legalistic language and have the force of law. Thus, the FTC can proceed directly against practices forbidden by a trade regulation rule.

**FTC Adjudicative Proceedings.** The main way in which the FTC proceeds against violations of its statutes or trade regulation rules is by administrative action within the agency itself. The Commission gets evidence of possible violations from private parties, governmental bodies, and its own investigations. If, after further investigation and discussion, it decides to proceed against the possible offender (the *respondent*), it will enter a formal complaint. The case itself is heard in a public administrative hearing (called an "adjudicative proceeding") before an FTC administrative law judge. The proceeding resembles a regular court trial and is open to the public. The judge's initial decision becomes the FTC's decision after 30 days, unless the respondent appeals to the five commissioners or they decide to review it themselves. If the administrative law judge's decision is *against* the respondent and the commissioners do not overrule it, an FTC *order* (described below) is issued. The order usually becomes final after 60 days unless the respondent appeals to the appropriate federal court of appeals.

**Commission Orders.** The usual kind of order issued by the FTC against parties violating its statutes and trade regulation rules is called the **cease and desist order.** As its name suggests, this is basically a command to the respondent ordering it to cease its illegal behavior. However, the courts have often upheld FTC orders going beyond the mere command to cease and desist. For instance, the FTC may order the respondent to make affirmative disclosures, to divest itself of certain assets or stock, or to make restitution to injured parties. The civil penalty for failing to comply with a Commission order is up to $10,000 per violation. Where there is a continuing failure to obey a final order, each day that the violation continues is considered a separate violation.

**Consent Orders.** Many alleged violations are never adjudicated by the FTC, but instead are settled through a **consent order.** This is a negotiated agreement whereby the FTC typically promises not to proceed further against the respondent, in return for the respondent's promise to stop the challenged practices. A consent order does not require the respondent to admit any violation of the law. Failure to observe a consent order is punishable in the same fashion as violation of a formal Commission order.

**Other Enforcement Provisions.** A number of other enforcement devices are available to the FTC. Generally, they are less important than the devices already discussed, and their details are beyond the scope of this book. The FTC may obtain federal district court *injunctions* against private parties in a variety of situations. It may also obtain *civil penalties* in federal district court against, among others, those who knowingly violate a Commission order directed against *another party* that has engaged in *unfair or deceptive practices.* In certain circumstances, finally, the Commission may sue in a state or federal court to obtain *redress* for consumers or other parties injured by unfair or deceptive practices. Such redress may include the rescission or reformation of contracts, the refund of money, the payment of damages, or public notice of the unfair or deceptive practice.

## THE FTC AND THE ANTITRUST LAWS

As you have seen, the FTC has specific statutory authority to enforce the Clayton Act and the Robinson-Patman Act, and can sue for injunctive relief to enforce either act. Also, under the Hart-Scott-Rodino Antitrust Improvements Act of 1976, companies planning certain kinds of mergers are required to give *premerger notification* to the Commission and the Antitrust Division of the Justice Department, and to supply certain data to these bodies. The purpose of this requirement is to give the agencies time to analyze the merger, so that, if necessary, they may seek an injunction against it before it is consummated. Moreover, the "unfair methods of competition" language of Section 5 of the FTC Act includes all behavior made illegal by the Sherman Act.

In fact, Section 5 gives the FTC the power to attack anticompetitive practices not covered by other antitrust statutes. As the U.S. Supreme Court declared in 1972, the FTC "does not arrogate excessive power to itself if, in measuring a practice against the elusive . . . standard of fairness, it, like a court of equity, considers public values beyond simply those enshrined in the letter or encompassed in the spirit of the antitrust laws."[3] In the case from which this language came, for example, the Court held that the Sperry and Hutchinson Company's attempt to suppress trading stamp exchanges dealing in its Green Stamps was illegal under Section 5, even though that attempt violated neither the letter nor the spirit of the antitrust laws. Section 5 also enables the FTC to proceed against *potential* or *incipient* antitrust violations of all sorts.

For the most part, however, Section 5's application to anticompetitive behavior has been limited to the orthodox antitrust violations discussed in Chapters 44 and 45. When

[3] *FTC v. Sperry & Hutchinson Co.,* 405 U.S. 233 (1972).

the FTC proceeds against these and other kinds of anticompetitive behavior, it generally utilizes the enforcement devices discussed above.

## FTC REGULATION OF ADVERTISING

Section 5's "unfair or deceptive acts or practices" language, which was added to the FTC Act in 1938, gives the FTC extensive powers to regulate advertising. In doing so, the Commission has proceeded on a number of fronts.[4] It has often used its normal enforcement procedures to attack advertising that it regards as *deceptive,* and it has occasionally proceeded against advertising that it deems *unfair.* In addition, the FTC has issued a number of trade regulation rules and industry guides relating to advertising. Changes in the political climate and in the FTC's composition may have led the Commission to scale back its regulation of advertising in the 1980s.

**Deceptive Advertising.** The deceptiveness of advertising is a question of fact that the FTC decides on a case-by-case basis. Courts tend to defer to the Commission's decisions on this question. In order to introduce some predictability into this area, the FTC issued a policy statement regarding deceptive advertising on October 14, 1983,[5] and, as the *Cliffdale* case below indicates, the Commission seems inclined to follow the guidelines set by this statement. According to the policy statement, advertising violating Section 5 on grounds of deceptiveness must contain a *material* representation, omission, or practice that is *likely to mislead* a consumer acting *reasonably under the circumstances.* Two holdover FTC commissioners, however, dissented from this formulation, arguing that it changed prior law in ways not likely to benefit consumers.

**Representation, Omission, or Practice Likely to Mislead.** Often, advertisements expressly make false or misleading claims. Sometimes, too, false or misleading statements can be *implied* from the surrounding circumstances. In one case, for instance, the false conclusion that Listerine mouthwash could prevent and cure colds and sore throats was implied from the close conjunction of the following two advertising claims: (1) that Listerine "Kills Germs by Millions on Contact" and (2) that Listerine should be used for colds and sore throats. Also, advertisements can be deceptive if they omit significant facts or if they are misleading unless further information is supplied. For instance, an ad for clothing may fail to state that the clothing is made of flammable material. Finally, certain deceptive marketing *practices* may violate Section 5. In one such case, for example, encyclopedia salesmen gained entry to the homes of potential customers by posing as surveyors engaged in advertising research.

In all of these cases, the statement, omission, or practice must be *likely to mislead* a consumer. There is no requirement that there be *actual* deception. As the *Cliffdale* case suggests, it is unclear whether this formulation changes or weakens prior law. Of course, determining whether a particular ad or practice is "likely to mislead" requires that the FTC evaluate the accuracy of the claims that the seller has made.

**The "Reasonable Consumer" Test.** To be deceptive, the representation, omission, or practice must also be likely to mislead *reasonable consumers under the circumstances.* The purpose behind this requirement is to protect sellers from liability for every foolish, igno-

[4] The FTC also maintains an advertising substantiation program, which requires that firms making objective claims about their products have a "reasonable basis" for such claims. The Commission currently plans to implement this program by making nonpublic requests for substantiation to individual firms.

[5] 45 Antitrust and Trade Regulation Report (BNA) 689 (Oct. 27, 1983).

rant, or outlandish misconception that some consumer might entertain. As the Commission noted some years ago, advertising a pastry made in this country as "Danish Pastry" will not violate Section 5 just because "a few misguided souls believe . . . that all 'Danish Pastry' is made in Denmark."[6] When advertising is targeted to a specific audience, the Commission will look to its effect on a reasonable *member of that group.* Ads promising cancer cures, for example, will be judged by their effect on the "reasonable cancer patient," and not from the perspective of a healthy person. Also, Section 5 will usually not be violated by statements of opinion, sales talk, or "puffing"; statements about matters that consumers can easily evaluate for themselves; and statements regarding subjective matters (e.g., taste or smell). This is because such statements are unlikely to deceive reasonable consumers. As the concurring opinion in the *Cliffdale* case notes, however, the "reasonableness" standard may prevent the FTC from attacking some schemes aimed at the unsophisticated, naive, or gullible.

**Materiality.** Finally, the representation, omission, or practice must be *material.* Material information is information that is important to reasonable consumers and that is likely to affect their choice of a product or service. Examples of material information include statements or omissions regarding a product's cost, safety, effectiveness, performance, durability, quality, and warranty protection. In addition, express statements in advertisements are presumed to be material.

**Unfair Advertising.** Because Section 5 prohibits "unfair" as well as "deceptive" acts or practices, the FTC has occasionally proceeded against advertising that, while not necessarily deceptive in the senses just described, is felt to be objectionable for other reasons. Factors considered by the FTC when it makes "unfairness" determinations include: (1) whether the advertising offends public policy as defined by statutes, the common law, or other concepts of fairness; (2) whether the advertising is immoral or unethical; and (3) whether the advertising causes substantial injury to consumers. Also, disparities in resources, knowledge, or bargaining power between the seller and the consumer are factors that may influence the Commission in certain cases.

Sometimes, the FTC's efforts at regulating unfair advertising seem to have been guided by the perception that modern mass advertising can be very manipulative even when it is not deceptive. This was probably true of one of the FTC's most publicized recent efforts against allegedly unfair advertising: its unsuccessful late 1970s attempt to promulgate rules governing television advertising aimed at children (so-called kid-vid). Because the open-ended unfairness standard gives little guidance to sellers and expands the FTC's powers, it has been criticized, especially by the businesses subject to it. Perhaps for these reasons, the FTC has not aggressively pursued "unfair" advertising in the 1980s.

**Specific Rules and Guides.** The FTC has promulgated many trade regulation rules aimed at unfair or deceptive advertising and labeling of specific products and services. For example, it has issued rules on: the advertising and labeling of home insulation, the advertising of ophthalmic goods and services, ad and label claims regarding the length of extension ladders and the size of sleeping bags, funeral industry practices, and the use of the terms *leakproof* and *automatic* in battery and sewing machine ads and labels. The FTC has also published a large number of industry guides on particular subjects related

---

[6] *Heinz v. W. Kirchner,* 63 F.T.C. 1282, 1290 (1963).

to advertising. One example is its guide on endorsements by experts, celebrities, and others with the capacity to influence the public. Another is its guide telling sellers that they cannot "bait" buyers with ads offering goods or services at very low prices, and then "switch" them to higher-priced offerings once they reach the seller's premises. Such "bait and switch" advertising is usually a violation of Section 5.

**Remedies.** Several types of orders can result from a successful FTC adjudicative proceeding attacking deceptive or unfair advertising. An order simply telling the respondent to cease engaging in the deceptive or unfair behavior is one possibility. Another is the affirmative disclosure of information whose absence made the advertisement deceptive or unfair. Yet another is *corrective advertising.* This requires the seller's future advertisements to correct false impressions created by its past advertisements. Also, the order may sometimes extend beyond the product or service that was the subject of the advertisements attacked by the FTC, and include future advertisements for *other* products or services marketed by the seller. Such an "all products" order is most likely to be issued and upheld by the courts where: the violation is serious and deliberate, the violator has a past record of unfair or deceptive advertising practices, or the illegal advertising practice might readily be transferred to other products. In certain cases, finally, the FTC may seek the civil penalties or consumer redress noted earlier.

**First Amendment Considerations.** In the mid-1970s, the Supreme Court extended constitutional protection to commercial speech, including advertising. Commercial speech is not absolutely protected; rather, the free speech right is balanced against legitimate government interests in such a way that it receives an intermediate degree of constitutional protection.[7] Obviously, the various FTC orders discussed above restrict commercial speech, and they may be subject to First Amendment attack as a result. However, the purpose behind the protection of commercial speech—eliminating obstacles to the flow of consumer information in order to promote informed consumer choices—is not necessarily inconsistent with the FTC's mission of eliminating unfair and deceptive advertising. Thus, the constitutional protection given commercial speech does not apply to the regulation of false or deceptive advertising. But some FTC orders go beyond the simple prohibition of such advertising. In these cases, there must be a fairly close relationship between the FTC order and the transgressions that it seeks to correct. Thus, courts will occasionally modify or narrow the scope of a Commission order on First Amendment grounds. But rarely, if ever, will they strike down such an order in its entirety.

---

[7] See Chapter 42.

## *In re* Cliffdale Associates, Inc.

### 46 Antitrust & Trade Reg. Rep. (BNA) 703 (1984)

Cliffdale Associates marketed the Ball-Matic Gas Save Valve through mail-order advertisements. The Ball-Matic was an "air bleed" device designed to allow additional air to enter a car's engine and thus to improve gas mileage. Claiming that the company's advertising for the Ball-Matic was deceptive and unfair, the FTC instituted an adjudicative proceeding against Cliffdale. The administrative law judge (ALJ) held that Cliffdale's claims were unfair and deceptive under Section 5 and ordered that Cliffdale cease and desist from making such claims unless it had a reasonable basis for doing so. Cliffdale appealed to the full Commission.

**Opinion of the Commission.** At trial, the charge of *unfair* competition was not specifically addressed. The record does not contain sufficient evidence to support liability on this charge. Accordingly, we reverse those portions of the ALJ's decision that relate to unfair methods of competition. Deception was the standard under which the claims were actually tried, and this was the appropriate approach.

The ALJ concluded that "any advertising representation that has the tendency and capacity to mislead or deceive a prospective consumer is an unfair and deceptive practice." We find this approach inadequate to provide guidance on how a deception claim should be analyzed. Consistent with the Policy Statement on Deception, issued on October 14, 1983, the Commission will find an act or practice deceptive if, first, there is a representation, omission, or practice that, second, is likely to mislead consumers acting reasonably under the circumstances, and, third, the representation, omission, or practice is material.

The requirement that an act or practice be "likely to mislead" reflects the established principle that the Commission need not find *actual* deception to hold that a violation of section 5 has occurred. Similarly, the requirement that an act or practice be considered from the perspective of a "consumer acting reasonably in the circumstances" is not new. Virtually all representations can be misunderstood by some consumers. The third element is materiality. A material representation, omission, act, or practice involves information that is important to consumers and, hence, likely to affect their choice of, or conduct regarding, a product. Consumers are thus likely to suffer injury from a material misrepresentation.

The first step in analyzing whether a claim is deceptive is to determine what claim has been made. When the advertisement contains an express claim, the representation itself establishes its meaning. When the claim is implied, the Commission will often be able to determine the meaning through an examination of the representation, including an evaluation of the entire document, the juxtaposition of various phrases, the nature of the claim, and the nature of the transaction. In other situations, the Commission will require extrinsic evidence that reasonable consumers interpret the implied claims in a certain way. The evidence can consist of expert opinion, consumer testimony, copy tests, surveys, or any other reliable evidence of consumer interpretation.

1. *The Descriptive Claims.* Cliffdale's advertisements refer to the Ball-Matic as an "amazing automobile discovery" [and] as "the most significant automotive breakthrough in the

last ten years." These advertisements expressly claim that the Ball-Matic is an important, significant, and unique new invention. Further, Cliffdale expressly claimed that under normal driving conditions a typical driver could usually obtain a fuel economy improvement of 20 percent (or more). A consumer would be reasonable in expecting the average savings from the Ball-Matic to be within the stated range.

The Ball-Matic is a simple air-bleed device. Air-bleed devices have been around a long time, and are considered to be of little use by the automobile industry. The claim that the Ball-Matic was a new invention was expressly made. Having found such a claim to have been made, and that the claim is false, the Commission may infer that it is material. This claim was deceptive. The representation that the Ball-Matic would significantly improve fuel economy [is] false. The fuel savings do not approach those claimed by Cliffdale. Claims about enhanced fuel efficiency are clearly material to consumers, and were therefore deceptive.

2. *Representation that Competent Scientific Tests Prove the Fuel Economy Claims.* Some advertisements state that the Ball-Matic was tested and proven to yield up to a 20 percent increase in fuel economy. At trial, Cliffdale introduced a number of tests with varying evaluations of the Ball-Matic. The tests did not prove the fuel economy claims. First, none revealed improvement even close to that claimed. Moreover, the FTC counsel's expert witness testified that, given the basic theory of engineering and combustion, the Ball-Matic could never result in any significant improvement in fuel economy. The ALJ further noted a 1978 article in *Consumer Reports* magazine disclosing that there is no statistically significant effect on gasoline mileage from the use of air-bleed devices. The ALJ also noted an EPA test which gave similar results.

With respect to materiality, the performance of the Ball-Matic is difficult for consumers to evaluate for themselves. Accordingly, consumers will tend to rely more heavily on the scientific support claims made by Cliffdale. Clearly these false claims injured consumers by misleading them on a material point.

3. *Representations Based on Consumer Endorsements.* Numerous advertisements contained a black bordered box with statements by users about their fuel saving experiences. Consumers could reasonably interpret these advertisements as claiming that the Ball-Matic would produce significant fuel economy improvement, and that the testimonials were unrestrained and unbiased.

By printing the testimonials, Cliffdale implicitly made claims similar to those express claims already found to be false and deceptive. Thus, Cliffdale's use of the testimonials was, itself, deceptive. A good number of the testimonials were by business associates of the marketers of the product. Whenever there exists a connection between the endorser and the seller which might materially affect the weight or credibility of the endorsement, it should be disclosed. In a case such as this, where it is difficult for a consumer to evaluate the effectiveness of the product, the consumer is likely to rely more heavily on endorsements by other users, particularly if the consumer believes such endorsements are independent and unbiased.

Administrative law judge's decision for FTC affirmed by the Commission.

**Commissioner Pertschuk, Concurring in Part.** I concur in the finding that Cliffdale violated section 5. However, I disagree entirely with the legal analysis in the majority opinion. Cliffdale's misrepresentations were unambiguous and undoubtedly material. Normally, there would be little more to say. However, this is the first deception case since the announcement of the dubious Policy Statement on Deception of October 14, 1983. Apparently the new majority feels compelled to establish the Statement's legitimacy by jumping this case through the hoops of its analytical framework for deception cases. Under the guise of making the law more clear and understandable, the majority has actually raised the evidentiary threshold for deception cases. In this unusually simple case, the majority's approach does not affect the outcome. However, in other cases the harm from the majority's legal analysis will be palpable and painful.

The new deception analysis withdraws the protection of section 5 from consumers who do not act "reasonably." There is no support in the case law or academic literature for the proposition that deception cannot occur unless reasonable consumers are misled. In this case, it is clear that consumers would be "reasonable" in accepting the scientific-sounding, plausible-seeming explanations of Cliffdale. However, the majority offers no guidance [as to] how more difficult matters will be decided. How will the Commission judge the conduct of consumers who succumb to sales pitches for worthless or grossly over-valued investments? Do "reasonable" consumers buy diamonds or real estate, sight unseen, from total strangers? Is a consumer "acting reasonably" when he or she falls for a hard-sell telephone solicitation to buy "valuable" oil or gas leases from an unknown corporation?

The sad fact is that a small segment of our society makes its livelihood preying upon consumers who are very trusting and unsophisticated. Others specialize in weakening the defenses of especially vulnerable, but normally cautious, consumers. Through skillful exploitation of such common desires as the wish to get rich quick or to provide some measure of security for one's old age, professional con men can prompt conduct that many of their victims will readily admit—in hindsight—is patently unreasonable.

Consumers are better protected by the traditional test, which requires only that a substantial number of consumers could be misled. The traditional standard recognizes that sellers frequently design their promotional efforts to appeal to specific groups of consumers. In such cases, the Commission need only find that a substantial number of consumers in *the target group* could be misled, considering the sophistication of the persons in that group, their mental state, and their mental capabilities.

The third element of deception is materiality. Heretofore, any fact that is important to consumers has been considered material, regardless of whether consumer choices would actually turn on that fact. The majority opinion, however, suggests that a misrepresentation is not material unless it is likely to affect consumers' conduct and consumers thus are likely to suffer injury.

It is reasonable to assume that Cliffdale's misrepresentations caused consumers to buy the product and suffer monetary loss. However, what if this case had concerned misrepresentations about a product with many important performance and design features? If Cliffdale had made a false fuel efficiency claim for an automobile, would the FTC have been required to show that the claim would have tipped the scales for consumers in their weighing of the many features of automobiles? Such a requirement of proof would be exceedingly difficult, if not impossible, to meet. Indeed, it could preclude the Commission from challenging misrepresentations about complex products.

## THE MAGNUSON-MOSS WARRANTY ACT

**Introduction.** In the late 1960s and early 1970s, Congress conducted a number of investigations into consumer product warranties. It concluded that these warranties were often confusing, misleading, and frustrating to consumers. In response, Congress passed the Magnuson-Moss Warranty Act in 1975. One of the act's aims is to provide minimum warranty protection for consumers, and some of its provisions on that subject are discussed in Chapter 32. Here, we focus on Magnuson-Moss's rules requiring that consumer warranties contain certain information and that this information be made available to buyers before the sale.

The Magnuson-Moss Act generally applies to *written warranties* for *consumer products.* Nothing in the act requires a seller to give a written warranty, and the act does not cover sellers that fail to give a written warranty. The act defines a consumer product as personal property that is ordinarily used for personal, family, or household purposes. In addition, many Magnuson-Moss provisions apply only when a written warranty is given in connection with the sale of a consumer product to a *consumer.* For present purposes, a consumer is a buyer or transferee of a consumer product who does not use it either for resale or in his own business. Thus, for example, retailers purchasing inventory generally do not qualify as Magnuson-Moss consumers.

**Required Warranty Information.** The Magnuson-Moss Act and its regulations require the presentation of certain information in written warranties to consumers for consumer products costing more than \$15.[8] The presentation must be made in a simple, clear, and conspicuous fashion. The most important kinds of information that must be included are the following: (1) the persons who are protected by the warranty (but only if its coverage is limited to the original purchaser or is otherwise limited); (2) the products, parts, characteristics, components, or properties covered by the warranty; (3) what the warrantor will do in case of a product defect or other failure to conform to the warranty, including the items or services that the warrantor will pay for or provide; (4) the time the warranty begins (if different from the purchase date) and the duration of the warranty; and (5) a step-by-step explanation of the procedure that the consumer should follow to obtain the performance of warranty obligations, including detailed information on those who are authorized to perform these obligations.

The act also requires that the party giving the warranty disclose: (1) any limitations on the duration of implied warranties and (2) any attempt to limit consequential damages or other consumer remedies.[9] If the seller limits the duration of an implied warranty, the warranty must also include the following language: "Some states do not allow limitations on how long an implied warranty lasts, so the above limitation may not apply to you." If the seller attempts to limit the consumer's remedies, the following language must be included: "Some states do not allow the exclusion or limitation of incidental or consequential damages, so the above limitation or exclusion may not apply to you." Finally, all covered warranties must include the following statement: "This warranty gives you specific legal rights, and you may also have other rights which vary from state to state."

**Presale Availability of Warranty Information.** The regulations accompanying the

[8] For the rules in this section and the following section, the act itself states a \$5 figure. However, the regulations implementing the act state a \$15 figure. Note also that the dollar figure for triggering the Magnuson-Moss full and limited warranty provisions, discussed in Chapter 32, is *\$10.*

[9] Limitations on a warranty's duration and on a consumer's remedies are discussed in Chapter 32.

Magnuson-Moss Act also state very complex and detailed rules requiring that warranty terms be made available to the buyer before the sale. These rules generally govern sales of consumer products costing more than $15 to a consumer. They set out certain duties that must be met by "sellers" (most commonly, retailers) and by "warrantors" (most commonly, manufacturers) of such products. They also establish special rules for catalog, mail-order, and door-to-door sales of such products. Very briefly, these regulations require that:

1. *Sellers* must make the text of the warranty available for the prospective buyer's review prior to the sale, through one of several listed means.

2. *Sellers* must not unnecessarily remove or obscure any warranty disclosure materials provided by the warrantor, unless the sellers make the terms of the warranty available to the consumer through one of the listed means noted above.

3. *Catalog or mail-order sellers* must clearly and conspicuously disclose in their catalog or solicitation either the full text of the warranty or the address from which a free copy of the warranty can be obtained.

4. Before the conclusion of a *door-to-door sale,* the seller must have disclosed to the prospective buyer that the sales representative (the party dealing with the buyer) has copies of the warranty and that the buyer can inspect the warranty.

5. *Warrantors* must provide sellers with the warranty materials necessary for them to comply with the duties stated above and must provide catalog, mail-order, and door-to-door sellers with copies of the warranties that they need to meet their duties.

**Enforcement.** Any person's failure to comply with the above rules violates Section 5 of the FTC Act and can trigger the various FTC enforcement procedures discussed earlier in the chapter. Also, either the FTC or the attorney general may sue in federal district court to obtain injunctive relief against such violations. In addition, the FTC or the attorney general may request that the district court grant an injunction restraining any warrantor from making a *deceptive warranty* with respect to a consumer product. The act defines a "deceptive warranty" as one that: (1) contains false or fraudulent statements, (2) contains statements that would mislead a reasonably careful person, (3) omits information necessary to avoid misleading a reasonably careful person, or (4) uses such terms as *guaranty* or *warranty* but is so limited in scope as to deceive a reasonable person. The Magnuson-Moss Act also creates various civil actions for private parties; some of these are discussed in Chapter 32.

## CONSUMER CREDIT LAWS

In addition to being victimized by defective products, deceptive advertising, and inadequate disclosure of warranty terms, consumers may be victimized in the process of obtaining credit. Because of the widespread use of credit in consumer purchases, the federal government has enacted a variety of statutes and regulations governing consumer credit transactions. These laws are designed to help protect consumers from unfair treatment throughout the course of credit transactions.

**Truth in Lending Act.** The Truth in Lending Act (TILA) is one part of the Consumer Credit Protection Act of 1968.[10] The purposes of the TILA are to increase consumer knowledge and understanding of credit terms by compelling their *disclosure* and to give con-

[10] The Truth in Lending Act was significantly changed by the Truth in Lending Simplification and Reform Act of 1980, most of whose provisions apply only to transactions occurring on or after April 1, 1982. The discussion here will incorporate the 1980 amendments.

sumers more ability to shop for credit by commanding *uniform* disclosures. The TILA was enacted because creditors frequently failed to state credit information important to consumer borrowers, or stated it in ways that did not permit comparisons between creditors. Interest rate or finance charge formulas, for example, can be expressed in a variety of ways—many of them confusing to the average consumer either in isolation or when compared with other statements. The Truth in Lending Act is basically a *disclosure* provision; the act has little to say about the *content* of credit terms. State usury laws, however, may limit the interest rates that creditors can charge.

**Scope.** Generally, the Truth in Lending Act applies to *creditors* that extend *consumer credit* to a *debtor* in an amount *no greater than $25,000.* A "creditor" is a party that in the ordinary course of business regularly extends consumer credit, such as a bank, the issuer of a credit card, or a savings and loan association. The extension of credit need not be the creditor's primary business. Auto dealers and retail stores, for instance, are "creditors" if they regularly arrange or extend credit financing. To qualify as a creditor, the party in question must also either impose a finance charge, or by agreement require payment in more than four installments. "Consumer credit" is credit enabling the purchase of goods, services, or real estate used primarily for personal, family, or household purposes. Commercial, business, or agricultural purposes are not covered. The TILA "debtor" must be a *natural person;* the act does not protect business organizations. Finally, except for the real or dwelling property transactions discussed below, the amount financed must be $25,000 or less for the TILA to apply.

**Disclosure Provisions.** The disclosure provisions of the Truth in Lending Act and the regulation implementing them[11] are very long, detailed, and complex. Exactly what disclosures are necessary depends on whether the transaction is for *closed-end credit* or *open-end credit.* Closed-end credit (e.g., a car loan or a consumer loan from a finance company) is extended for a specific time period; and the total amount financed, number of payments, and due dates are all agreed upon at the time of the transaction. Open-end credit arrangements (e.g., VISA or a revolving charge account in a retail store) involve some plan that permits the creditor and the consumer to enter into a series of transactions and that allows the consumer the option of paying in variable installments or in full.

Examples of the disclosures necessary before the completion of a *closed-end* credit transaction include: (1) the total finance charge; (2) the annual percentage rate (APR); (3) the amount financed; (4) the total number of payments, their due dates, and the amount of each payment; (5) the total dollar value of all payments; (6) any late charges imposed for past-due payments; (7) any security interest taken by the creditor and the property that it covers; and (8) whether the consumer is entitled to a rebate for prepayment. For *open-end* credit, there are two kinds of required disclosures: (1) an initial statement made before the first transaction under the account and (2) a series of periodic statements, which usually must be made at each billing date. Among other things, the *initial statement* must disclose to the debtor: (1) the conditions under which a finance charge will be imposed, (2) the method of determining the balance on which the finance charge will be computed, (3) the elements of the finance charge (including such items as service charges), (4) an estimated APR, (5) when other charges will be imposed and the method for

[11] This is "Regulation Z," 12 C.F.R. § 226, which was promulgated by the Federal Reserve Board.

determining them, (6) when the creditor may acquire a security interest in the debtor's property, and (7) the minimum periodic payment required. The act requires an even lengthier list of disclosures on the *periodic statements* that the creditor must send to the consumer. Much of the information that you see on a monthly credit card statement, for example, is compelled by the TILA. For *all* credit transactions covered by the act, finally, the required disclosures must be made clearly, conspicuously, and in meaningful sequence.

**Real Estate Transactions.** As you have seen, credit transactions involving the sale of real estate (e.g., the purchase of a home) are subject to Truth in Lending. Here, the disclosure requirements differ slightly from those applied to other closed-end credit transactions. More importantly, the $25,000 maximum does *not* apply where the creditor takes a security interest in the debtor's real property or in personal property used as the debtor's principal dwelling (e.g., a mobile home). In such situations, the debtor may also have a *three-day rescission right.* This means that the debtor can cancel the transaction within three business days of either: (1) its completion or (2) the time the creditor has made all of the material disclosures required by the TILA. This cancellation right, however, *does not apply to first liens or mortgages on the property.* Thus, the ordinary home buyer will not have this rescission right. It applies only to the financing of such things as a major home repair where the home is already mortgaged and the creditor secures the loan with a subsequent lien on the home.

**Other TILA Provisions.** The Truth in Lending Act also has provisions dealing with *credit advertising.* For example, it prevents a creditor from "baiting" customers by advertising credit terms that it does not make generally available. In addition, the act requires that credit advertisers that use certain key terms in their advertisements state a variety of other terms as well. For instance, an advertisement using such terms as "$100 down payment," "8 percent interest," or "$99 per month" must state various *other* relevant terms (e.g., the APR) as well. The point of this "all or nothing" provision is to help the consumer put the advertised term in proper perspective.

Finally, the TILA has a few special rules relating to *credit cards.* The most important of these rules limits the cardholder's liability for unauthorized use of the card to a maximum of $50. The *Martin* case, which follows, defines "authorized" and "unauthorized" use.

**Enforcement.** A variety of federal agencies, including the FTC, enforce the TILA. In addition, the Justice Department may institute criminal actions against those who willfully and knowingly violate the act. Civil actions by private parties (including class actions) are also possible. Here, the recovery is usually the plaintiff's actual damages plus a statutory penalty.

## Martin v. American Express, Inc.

**361 So.2d 597 (Ala. Civ. App. 1979)**

In April 1975, Robert Martin gave his American Express credit card to E. L. McBride to use in McBride's business venture. Martin orally authorized McBride to charge up to $500 on the card. In June 1975, Martin received a statement from American Express declaring that the amount due on his account was approximately $5,300. Martin refused to pay this charge on the ground that he had not signed any of the credit card invoices. American Express then sued Martin in an Alabama trial court. There, Martin claimed that his liability for "unauthorized" use of the card was limited to $50 by the Truth in Lending Act. The trial court nonetheless found for American Express, and Martin appealed.

**Bradley, Judge.** The issue is whether the use of a credit card by a person who has received the card and permission to utilize it from the cardholder constitutes "unauthorized use" under the Truth in Lending Act. We hold that in instances where a cardholder, who is under no compulsion by fraud, duress, or otherwise, voluntarily permits the use of his credit card by another person, the cardholder has authorized the use of that card and is thereby responsible for any charges as a result of that use.

[The Act] limits a cardholder's liability to $50 for the "unauthorized use of a credit card." It defines "unauthorized use" as the "use of a credit card by a person other than the cardholder who does not have actual, implied, or apparent authority for such use, and from which the cardholder receives no benefit." Martin says he gave no authority for McBride to charge the large sum which eventually resulted in this suit. We cannot accept this contention. McBride was actually authorized by Martin to use the latter's card. And the authority to use it, if not actual, remained apparent even after McBride ignored Martin's directions by charging over $500. Consequently, Martin must be held responsible for any purchases made through the use of his card.

The TILA clearly indicates that protection is warranted where the card is obtained from the cardholder as a result of loss, theft, or wrongdoing. However, we are not persuaded that this protection is applicable where a cardholder voluntarily and knowingly allows another to use his card and that person subsequently misuses the card. Were we to adopt any other view, we would provide the unscrupulous and dishonest cardholder with the means to defraud the card issuer by allowing her friends to use the card and run up hundreds of dollars in charges, and then limit her liability to $50.

Judgment for American Express affirmed. (*Note:* Actual, implied, and apparent authority are explained in Chapter 17.)

**Consumer Leasing Act.** Individuals often lease (rather than purchase) consumer products such as cars, appliances, and televisions. As originally drafted, the Truth in Lending Act applied to only some of these consumer leases. In order to regulate such leases more effectively, Congress passed the Consumer Leasing Act in 1976. The act covers leases of personal property: (1) to natural persons (not organizations), (2) for consumer purposes, (3) for an amount not exceeding $25,000, and (4) for a period exceeding four months.

The act requires that the lessor make numerous written *disclosures* to the lessee before completion of the lease. Examples include: a description or identification of the leased property; the number, amount, and due dates of the lease payments; their total amount; any express warranties made by the lessor; and any security interest taken by the lessor. Like the TILA's "all or nothing" provision, the act also requires that lease *advertisements* include certain additional information if they *already* state: the amount of any payment, the number of required payments, the amount of the down payment, or that no down payment is required.

The Consumer Leasing Act has only one specific remedy provision. It makes creditors violating the act's disclosure requirements subject to the same civil suits that are permitted under the TILA. Also, the FTC enforces the act. The availability of the other TILA enforcement devices is uncertain.

**Fair Credit Reporting Act.** Credit bureaus and the reports they provide to various users can have a significant impact on an individual's ability to obtain credit, insurance, employment, and many of life's other goods. In addition, affected individuals are often unaware of the influence that credit reports have on such decisions. The Fair Credit Reporting Act (FCRA), which was enacted in 1970, gives individuals some protection against abuses in the process of disseminating information about personal creditworthiness.

**Duties of Consumer Reporting Agencies.** The FCRA imposes a number of duties on "consumer reporting agencies": agencies that regularly compile credit-related information on individuals for the purpose of furnishing credit reports to users. A consumer reporting agency must adopt "reasonable procedures" to:

1. Assure that users employ the information only for the following purposes: consumer credit sales, employment evaluations, the underwriting of insurance, the granting of a government license or other benefit, or any other business transaction where the user has a legitimate business need for the information.
2. Avoid including in a report "obsolete" information predating the report by more than a stated period, usually seven years. This duty does not apply to credit reports used in connection with: (*a*) credit transactions of $50,000 or more, (*b*) life insurance policies with a face amount of $50,000 or more, and (*c*) employment applications for jobs with a salary of $20,000 or more.
3. Assure the maximum possible accuracy regarding the information contained in credit reports.

However, the act does very little to limit the *types* of data that can be included in credit reports. In fact, all kinds of information regarding a person's character, reputation, personal traits, and mode of life are seemingly permitted. Also, as the *Thompson* case below states, the credit bureau is merely required to adopt *reasonable procedures* to assure compliance with the act's commands.

**Disclosure Duties on Users.** The Fair Credit Reporting Act also imposes certain disclosure duties on *users* of credit reports (mainly credit sellers, lenders, employers, and insurers). One of these duties applies to users that order an *investigative consumer report:* a credit report that includes information on a person's character, reputation, personal traits, or mode of living and that is based on interviews with neighbors, friends, associates, and the like. If a user procures such a report, it must disclose to the person affected that the report has been requested, that the report may contain information of the sort just described, and that the person has a right to obtain further disclosures about the user's investigation. If the person requests such disclosures within a reasonable time, the user must reveal the nature and scope of the investigation.

Another disclosure duty arises when, because of information contained in any credit report, a user: (1) rejects an applicant for consumer credit, insurance, or employment; or (2) charges a higher rate for credit or insurance. In these situations, the user must advise the affected individual that it relied on the credit report in making its decision and must also state the name and address of the consumer reporting agency that supplied the report. Again, however, the FCRA requires only that the user maintain *reasonable procedures* designed to assure that these duties are met.

**Disclosure and Correction of Credit Report Information.** After a request from a properly identified individual, a consumer reporting agency must disclose to that individual: (1) the nature and substance of all its information about the individual (except medical information), (2) the sources of this information (except for information used solely for "investigative" reports), and (3) the recipients of any credit reports that it has furnished within the past 6 months (10 months for employment-related reports). Then, a person disputing the completeness or accuracy of the agency's information can compel it to reinvestigate. If, after this investigation, the credit bureau finds the information to be inaccurate or unverifiable, it must delete the information from the person's file. An individual who is not satisfied with the agency's investigation may file a brief statement setting forth the nature of her dispute with the agency. If this is done, any subsequent credit report containing the disputed information must note that it is disputed and must provide either the individual's statement or a clear and accurate summary of it. Also, the agency may be required to notify certain prior recipients of deleted, unverifiable, or disputed information if the individual requests this. However, there is no duty to investigate or to include the consumer's version of the facts if the credit bureau has reason to believe that the individual's request is frivolous or irrelevant.

**Enforcement.** Violations of the Fair Credit Reporting Act are violations of Section 5 of the FTC Act, and the Commission may use its normal enforcement procedures in such cases. Other federal agencies may also enforce the FCRA in certain situations. The FCRA establishes criminal penalties for: (1) persons who knowingly and willfully obtain consumer information from a credit bureau under false pretenses and (2) credit bureau officers or employees who knowingly or willfully provide information to unauthorized persons. Violations of the FCRA may also trigger private suits for damages against consumer reporting agencies and users. If the violation is willful, the injured party can obtain his actual damages, attorney's fees, and court costs plus punitive damages. If the violation is only negligent, punitive damages are unavailable.

## Thompson v. San Antonio Retail Merchants Association

**682 F.2d 509 (5th Cir. 1982)**

The San Antonio Retail Merchants Association (SARMA) provided a computerized credit reporting service to local subscribers. Under SARMA's standard procedures, a subscriber seeking a particular individual's credit history would feed certain information identifying that individual from its own computer terminal into SARMA's central computer. When presented with this identifying information, SARMA's computer would search its records and display on the subscriber's terminal the credit history most clearly matching the information provided by the subscriber. SARMA's procedures did not establish any minimum number of "points of correspondence" between the information provided by the subscriber and the credit file that its computer disgorged. As a result, the decision whether to accept a particular credit file as actually representing the requested individual was almost completely within the discretion of the subscriber's terminal operator. Moreover, once the operator concluded that a particular file really did represent the credit history of a particular individual, he could add credit information to the file. SARMA's computer was programmed to accept such information automatically.

In November 1974, William Daniel Thompson, Jr. (Daniel) opened a credit account with Gordon's Jewelers in San Antonio. He subsequently ran up a delinquent account of $77.25 at Gordon's that was ultimately charged off as a bad debt. Gordon's voluntarily reported the bad debt to SARMA, which placed the information and a derogatory credit rating into a file numbered 5867114. Although Daniel had given his social security number to Gordon's, the SARMA file did not contain this number.

In early 1978, William Douglas Thompson III (Douglas) applied for credit with the Gulf Oil Corporation and Montgomery Ward. Shortly thereafter, Gulf's terminal operator mistakenly accepted file number 5867114 as applying to Douglas. In addition, the operator included the information from Douglas's credit application in this file. As a result, the file became a confused potpourri of information on both Thompsons. A short time after this, Ward's terminal operator ran a credit check on Douglas and received all of the data contained in file number 5867114. As a result, Ward's rejected Douglas's credit applications.

Still later, Gulf requested a "revision" of file number 5867114, a procedure that involved the rechecking of information contained in the file. Pursuant to this procedure, a SARMA employee called Gordon's to verify the information in the file. The proper social security number, however, was apparently never checked, and the file remained substantially unchanged. Thus, Gulf also rejected Douglas's credit application.

This situation continued until the middle of 1979, when Douglas finally discovered the error in SARMA's file. Previously, he had thought that the denials of credit had been due to his 1976 conviction for burglary. In June 1979, he went to SARMA in an attempt to purge the erroneous credit information. SARMA, however, did not notify Ward's of the corrections until October 16, 1979. By this time, Douglas had initiated a Fair Credit Reporting Act suit against SARMA. The federal district court found in Douglas's favor, awarding him $10,000 in damages plus $4,485 in attorney's fees. SARMA appealed.

**Per Curiam.** Under the Fair Credit Reporting Act, a consumer reporting agency is liable to any consumer for negligent failure to comply with any requirement imposed by the Act. The District Court determined that SARMA was liable for negligent failure to comply with section 1681e(b) of the Act, which provides: "When a consumer reporting agency prepares a consumer report, it shall follow reasonable procedures to assure maximum possible accuracy of information concerning the individual about whom the report relates." Section 1681e(b) does not impose strict liability for any inaccurate credit report, but only a duty of reasonable care in preparation of the report. That duty extends to updating procedures, because "preparation" of a consumer report should be viewed as a continuing process and the obligation to ensure accuracy arises with every addition of information. The standard of conduct by which the trier of fact must judge the adequacy of agency procedures is what a reasonably prudent person would do under the circumstances.

Applying the reasonable person standard, the District Court found two acts of negligence in SARMA's updating procedures. First, SARMA failed to exercise reasonable care in programming its computer to automatically capture information into a file without requiring any minimum number of "points of correspondence" between the consumer and the file, or having an adequate auditing procedure to foster accuracy. Second, SARMA failed to employ reasonable procedures designed to learn the disparity in social security numbers for the two Thompsons when it revised file number 5867114 at Gulf's request. This court can reverse the District Court on these findings of fact only if the judgment of the District Court is clearly erroneous. In light of the evidence, this court cannot conclude that the District Court was clearly erroneous in finding negligent violation of section 1681e(b).

The District Court's award of $10,000 in actual damages was based on humiliation and mental distress to Thompson. Even when there are no out-of-pocket expenses, humiliation and mental distress do constitute recoverable elements of damage under the Act. The amount of damages is a question of fact which may be reversed by this court only if the District Court's findings are clearly erroneous.

SARMA asserts that Thompson failed to prove any actual damages, or at best proved only minimal damages for humiliation and mental distress. There was evidence, however, that Thompson suffered humiliation and embarrassment from being denied credit. Thompson testified that the denial of credit hurt him deeply because of his mistaken belief that it resulted from his felony conviction:

> I was trying to build myself back up, trying to . . . get back on my feet again. I was working 60 hours a week and sometimes seventy. . . . I was going to school at night three nights a week, four nights a week, three hours a night, and [denial of credit] really hurt. It made me disgusted with myself . . . [I needed credit to] be able to obtain things that everybody else is able to obtain, to be able to buy clothes or set myself up where I can show my ability to be trusted. . . . Everything we had to do, we had to save up and pay cash for strictly.

The trial judge was entitled to conclude that the humiliation and mental distress were not minimal but substantial.

SARMA also asserts that Thompson was required to mitigate his damages by first exhausting alternative remedies. SARMA cites section 1681i of the Act, which sets forth a procedure for consumers to challenge the completeness or accuracy of any disputed information in the file. The Act, however, does not require that a consumer pursue the remedies provided in section 1681i before bringing suit.

Section 1681o also allows an award of attorney's fees. The District Court awarded

$4,485 in attorney's fees based on 41.5 hours of work at $90 per hour and other special fees. This court cannot say that the District Court clearly abused its discretion.

Judgment for Thompson affirmed.

**Equal Credit Opportunity Act.** Responding to studies showing sex discrimination in the granting of credit, Congress passed the Equal Credit Opportunity Act (ECOA) in 1974. Originally, the act prohibited credit discrimination on the basis of sex or marital status. In 1976, however, it was amended to include age, race, color, national origin, religion, and the obtaining of income from public assistance as additional forbidden grounds for credit decisions. The ECOA covers all entities that regularly extend, renew, or continue credit, as well as entities that regularly arrange these activities. Examples of covered entities include banks; savings and loan associations; credit card issuers; and many retailers, auto dealers, and realtors. The act usually preempts state laws that are inconsistent with its provisions; however, state laws that are *more* protective than the ECOA will not be preempted.

**ECOA Provisions.** The ECOA governs all phases of a credit transaction. As authorized by the act, the Federal Reserve Board has promulgated detailed regulations covering, among other things, the information that creditors may require in credit applications, the ways in which creditors can evaluate applications, and the permissible reasons for deciding whether to extend credit. To take just a few examples, the regulations prohibit the creditor from:

1. Requesting any information about the applicant's spouse or former spouse—unless the spouse will use the credit account, will be liable on it, or will be relied on for repayment in any of several ways.

2. Requesting the sex of the applicant, although such terms as "Ms.," "Miss," "Mr.," or "Mrs." may be requested if the application form makes their use optional.

3. Requesting the applicant's race, color, religion, or national origin, although requests regarding permanent residence and immigration status are permitted.

4. Evaluating credit applications by using assumptions or statistics assessing the likelihood that any group of persons will bear or raise children, or will have interrupted or reduced future income for that reason.

The *Miller* case below involves yet another Federal Reserve Board regulation. As the case suggests, the courts have disagreed on the treatment of creditor practices that appear neutral but may have a disproportionate impact on one or more of the groups protected by the ECOA. In such cases, some courts have required the plaintiff to demonstrate that the practice has a disparate impact on a protected class.[12] Finally, creditor behavior not specifically prohibited in the regulations may sometimes violate the ECOA.

The ECOA also requires the creditor to notify the applicant of the action taken on a credit application within 30 days of its receipt. If the action is unfavorable to the applicant, the applicant is entitled to a statement of reasons from the creditor. The ECOA and its accompanying regulations go into great detail when describing what the creditor must do to meet this requirement.

[12] This is similar to some of the methods of proof under Title VII of the 1964 Civil Rights Act. See Chapter 47.

**Enforcement.** The ECOA is enforced by several federal agencies, with overall enforcement resting in the hands of the FTC. Which agency will enforce the act depends on the type of creditor or credit involved. Civil actions by aggrieved private parties, including class actions, are also possible. In such cases, a successful plaintiff or plaintiffs can recover actual damages, attorney's fees, and court costs, and may also obtain injunctive relief where appropriate. Punitive damage recoveries are also possible; these are limited to $10,000 in individual actions and to $500,000 or 1 percent of the creditor's net worth, whichever is less, in class actions.

## Miller v. American Express Co.

**688 F.2d 1235 (9th Cir. 1982)**

Maurice Miller applied for and received an American Express (Amex) credit card in 1966. Later in 1966, his wife, Virginia, was granted a supplementary card. Maurice died in May 1979. Amex then canceled Mrs. Miller's credit card account. The termination had nothing to do with Virginia's creditworthiness or ability to pay. Instead, Amex acted pursuant to its general policy of automatically terminating the account of supplementary cardholders upon the death of the basic cardholder. Amex then invited Mrs. Miller to apply for a new card. She did so, and Amex approved the application. Nonetheless, Virginia sued Amex in federal district court under the Equal Credit Opportunity Act. She argued that Amex's practice of terminating supplementary cardholders upon the death of the basic cardholder violated the act. The district court granted Amex's motion for summary judgment, and Miller appealed.

**Boochever, Circuit Judge.** The ECOA makes it unlawful for any creditor to discriminate with respect to any credit transaction on the basis of marital status. It also authorizes the Board of Governors of the Federal Reserve System to prescribe regulations. Section 202.7(c)(1) [of these regulations] provides that a creditor shall not terminate the account of a person who is contractually liable on an existing open end account on the basis of a change in marital status in the absence of evidence of inability or unwillingness to pay. Under certain circumstances, a creditor may require a reapplication after a change in the applicant's marital status.

Mrs. Miller's Amex card was canceled after her marital status changed from married to widowed. Under the regulation, Amex could have asked her to reapply for credit, but instead it first terminated her card and then invited reapplication. There was no evidence that her widowhood rendered Mrs. Miller unable or unwilling to pay. Amex argues that there was no violation of the ECOA for two reasons: (1) that the regulation was beyond the scope of the Board's authority, and (2) that the termination did not constitute discrimination on the basis of marital status because it occurred pursuant to a policy of automatic cancellation of all supplementary cardholders whether they were widow, widower, sibling, or child of the basic cardholder.

We reject Amex's contention that the Board exceeded its authority in promulgating section 202.7(c)(1). Although the ECOA outlaws credit "discrimination," the meaning of that term must be defined with reference to the purposes of the Act. A definition of discrimination was deleted from the Act in order to leave broad flexibility in the Board to specify what conduct would be prohibited. The regulation is directly addressed to one of the evils that the ECOA was designed to prevent: loss of credit because of widowhood.

The ECOA was meant to protect women, among others, from arbitrary denial or termination of credit. We have held that there was credit "discrimination" within the meaning of the ECOA when a regulation promulgated under the ECOA was violated. No showing of any specific intent to discriminate was required. Not requiring proof of discriminatory intent is especially appropriate in analysis of ECOA violations because discrimination in credit transactions is more likely to be of the unintentional variety.

We also do not think that a statistical showing of an adverse impact on women is always necessary to the plaintiff's case. The ECOA's legislative history refers by analogy to the disparate treatment and adverse impact tests for discrimination under Title VII of the 1964 Civil Rights Act. Some district courts have treated the references to Title VII as if the ECOA plaintiff's case must always contain elements similar to those required under either the adverse impact or disparate treatment tests. These courts, like Amex here, relied on an incomplete reading of the Senate Report to the 1976 amendments. The Senate Report states that: "In determining the existence of discrimination, . . . courts or agencies are *free to look* at the effects of a creditor's practices as well as the creditor's motives or *conduct* in individual transactions." Read in full, the Senate Report allows but does not limit proof of credit discrimination to the two traditional Title VII tests for employment discrimination. It also expressly recognizes that a creditor's conduct may be considered to determine the existence of credit discrimination, quite apart from intent or from a statistical showing of adverse impact.

The conduct here was squarely within that prohibited by section 202.7(c)(1). Mrs. Miller's account was terminated in response to her husband's death and without reference to, or even inquiry regarding, her creditworthiness. Amex contends that its cancellation policy was necessary to protect it from non-creditworthy supplementary cardholders. The regulations, however, prohibit termination based on a spouse's death in the absence of evidence of inability or unwillingness to repay. The fact that the cancellation policy could also result in the termination of a supplemental cardholder who was not protected by the ECOA, such as a sibling or friend of the basic cardholder, does not change the essential fact that Mrs. Miller's account was terminated solely because of her husband's death.

Judgment reversed in favor of Mrs. Miller.

---

**Fair Credit Billing Act.** The Fair Credit Billing Act, effective in 1975, is mainly aimed at credit card issuers. Its most important provisions involve billing disputes. In order to trigger these provisions, the cardholder must give the issuer written notice of an alleged error in a billing statement within 60 days of the time that the statement is sent to the cardholder. Then, within two complete billing cycles or 90 days (whichever is less), the issuer must either: (1) correct the cardholder's account, or (2) send the cardholder a written statement justifying the statement's accuracy. Until the issuer takes either of these steps, it may not: (1) restrict or close the cardholder's account because of her failure to pay the disputed amount; (2) try to collect the disputed amount; and (3) report, or threaten to report, the cardholder's failure to pay the disputed amount to a third party (such as a consumer reporting agency).

Once the issuer has met the act's requirements, it must also give the cardholder at least 10 days to pay the disputed amount before making a report to a third party. When the cardholder continues to dispute the matter, the issuer can make a report to a third party only if it also tells the third party that the debt is disputed. In addition, the issuer must report the final resolution of the dispute to such a third party. Finally, an issuer that fails to comply with any of these rules forfeits its right to collect the disputed amount from the cardholder, but the amount forfeited cannot exceed $50. Thus, since the issuer may still be able to collect the balance on large disputed debts, the act's deterrent effect on issuers is doubtful.

The Fair Credit Billing Act also has other provisions relating to the credit card business. If the issuer guarantees that the cardholder can avoid finance charges by paying before a certain date, the issuer must mail the statement at least 14 days before the stated date. If the issuer fails to do so, it cannot collect any finance charge on transactions occurring within the billing period in question. In addition, the act forbids "tie-in" deals whereby a merchant must open an account with the issuer or procure any other service from it as a condition of participating in a credit card plan. Finally, the act puts some limits on depositary issuers such as banks when they try to use a customer's deposits to satisfy his credit card obligations.

**Fair Debt Collection Practices Act.** Public concern over various abusive, deceptive, and unfair practices by debt collectors led Congress to pass the Fair Debt Collection Practices Act (FDCPA) in 1977. Generally, the act covers only those that are in the business of collecting debts owed to *others;* creditors that collect their *own* debts usually are not included. Also, the debts in question must involve money, property, insurance, or services used for *consumer* purposes.

**Communication Rules.** Except where necessary to *locate* the consumer debtor, the FDCPA generally prevents debt collectors from contacting parties other than the debtor (e.g., the debtor's employer, relatives, or friends). The act also limits the collector's contacts with the debtor himself. Unless the debtor consents, for instance, the collector cannot contact him at unusual or inconvenient times or places, or at his place of employment if the employer forbids such contacts. Also, the collector cannot contact the debtor if it knows that the debtor is represented by an attorney, unless the attorney consents to such contact or fails to respond to the collector's communications. In addition, the collector must cease most communications with the debtor if the debtor gives the creditor written notification that he refuses to pay the debt or that he does not desire further communications from the collector.

The FDCPA also requires the collector to give the debtor certain information about the debt (including its amount and the creditor's name) within five days of the collector's first communication with the debtor. If the debtor disputes the debt in writing within 30 days after receiving this information, the collector must cease its collection efforts until it sends verification of the debt to the debtor.

**Specific Forbidden Practices.** The FDCPA also sets out lists of forbidden collector practices that amount to "harassment or abuse," "false or misleading misrepresentations," and "unfair practices." Threats of violence, obscene or abusive language, and repeated phone calls are examples of *harassment or abuse.* Among the listed *false or misleading misrepresentations* are statements that the debtor will be imprisoned for failure to pay, that the collector is affiliated with the government, or that misstate the amount of the debt. *Unfair practices* include: collecting from the debtor an amount exceeding the amount legally due, getting the debtor to accept a collect call before revealing the call's true purpose, and falsely or unjustifiably threatening to take the debtor's property. The *Rutyna* case below discusses other examples of harassment or abuse, false or misleading misrepresentations, and unfair practices.

**Enforcement.** Many of the states also regulate debt collection practices.[13] Collectors are not subject to state laws inconsistent with the FDCPA unless these laws afford the consumer *more* protection than does the federal act. The FTC is the principal enforcement agency for the FDCPA, although other agencies enforce it in certain cases. However, the FTC cannot promulgate trade regulation rules to enforce the act. The FDCPA also permits individual civil actions and class actions by the affected debtor or debtors. However, such suits will fail if the violation was an *unintentional bona fide error.* The *Rutyna* case provides one interpretation of this defense. If the suit is successful, the plaintiff(s) can recover their actual damages, "additional damages," court costs, and attorney's fees. The amount of additional damages cannot exceed $1,000 where the plaintiff is an individual. The limit is $500,000 or 1 percent of the collector's net worth (whichever is less) in class actions. Within these limits, the amount of additional damages is determined by such factors as the frequency, persistence, and nature of the violation.

[13] In addition, some collection agency tactics may subject the agency to liability for invasion of privacy. See Chapter 4.

## Rutyna v. Collection Accounts Terminal, Inc.

**478 F. Supp. 980 (N.D. Ill. 1979)**

Josephine Rutyna was a 60-year-old widow who suffered from high blood pressure and epilepsy. In late 1976 and early 1977, she incurred a debt for medical services. At the time, she believed that this debt had been paid by medicare or private health insurance. According to Rutyna, an agent of Collection Accounts Terminal, Inc. (Collection) telephoned her in July 1978, informing her that she still owed $56 in medical expenses. When she denied the existence of the debt, the voice on the telephone responded: "You owe it, you don't want to pay, so we're going to have to do something about it."

On August 10, 1978, Rutyna received a letter from Collection, which stated:

> You have shown that you are unwilling to work out a friendly settlement with us to clear the above debt. Our field investigator has now been instructed to make an investigation in your neighborhood and to personally call on your employer. The immediate payment of the full amount, or a personal visit to this office, will spare you this embarrassment.

The top of the letter stated the creditor's name and the amount of the alleged debt. The envelope containing the letter stated Collection's full name and its return address.

Rutyna claimed that she became very nervous, upset, and worried after receiving this letter. She was particularly concerned that Collection would embarrass her by informing her neighbors about the debt and about her medical problems. She sued Collection under the FDCPA in federal district court. Later, she moved for summary judgment.

**McMillen, District Judge.** *Harassment or Abuse.* The first sentence of FDCPA section 1692d provides: "A debt collector may not engage in any conduct the natural consequence of which is to harass, oppress, or abuse any person in connection with the collection of a debt." This section then lists six specifically prohibited types of conduct, without limiting the general application of the foregoing sentence. Mrs. Rutyna does not allege conduct which falls within one of the specific prohibitions contained in section 1692d, but we find that Collection's letter to her does violate this general standard.

Without doubt Collection's letter has the natural (and intended) consequence of harassing, oppressing, and abusing the recipient. The tone of the letter is one of intimidation, and was intended as such in order to effect a collection. The threat of an investigation and resulting embarrassment to the alleged debtor is clear and the actual effect on the recipient is irrelevant. The egregiousness of the violation is a factor to be considered in awarding statutory damages.

*Deception and Improper Threats.* FDCPA section 1692e bars a debt collector from using any "false, deceptive, or misleading representation or means in connection with the collection of any debt." Sixteen specific practices are listed in this provision, without limiting the application of this general standard. Section 1692e(5) bars a threat "to take any action that cannot legally be taken or that is not intended to be taken." Collection's letter threatened embarrassing contacts with Mrs. Rutyna's employer and neighbors. This constitutes a false representation of the actions that Collection could legally take. Section 1692c(b) prohibits communication by the debt collector with third parties (with certain limited exceptions not here relevant). Mrs. Rutyna's neighbors and employer could not legally be contacted by defendant in connection with this debt. The letter falsely represents to the contrary.

*Unfair Practice/Return Address.* The envelope received by Mrs. Rutyna bore a return address, which began "COLLECTION ACCOUNTS TERMINAL, INC." FDCPA section 1692f bars unfair or unconscionable means to collect or attempt to collect any debt. It specifically bars:

> Using any language or symbol, other than the debt collector's address, on any envelope when communicating with a consumer by use of the mails or by telegram, except that a debt collector may use his business name if such name does not indicate that he is in the debt collection business.

Collection's return address violated this provision, because its business name does indicate that it is in the debt collection business. The purpose of this provision is apparently to prevent embarrassment resulting from a conspicuous name on the envelope, indicating that the contents pertain to debt collection.

On the subject of the return address on the envelope, Collection cites section 1692k(c), which provides:

> A debt collector may not be held liable in any action brought under this subchapter if the debt collector shows by a preponderance of the evidence that the violation was not intentional and resulted from a bona fide error notwithstanding the maintenance of procedures reasonably adapted to avoid any such error.

Collection states that it was unaware that the return address could be considered a violation of any statute. However, the section does not immunize mistakes of law, even if properly proven (as this one is not). It is designed to protect the defendant who intended to prevent the conduct which constitutes a violation of this Act but who failed even though he maintained procedures reasonably adapted to avoid such an error. Collection obviously intended the conduct which violates the Act in respect to the return address, but it simply failed to acquaint itself with the pertinent law.

Rutyna's motion for summary judgment granted.

---

## REGULATION OF PRODUCT SAFETY AND OTHER MATTERS

Yet another facet of "consumer protection law" is federal regulation aimed at increasing product safety. As Chapter 32 discusses in detail, sellers and manufacturers of dangerously defective products will often be civilly liable to those injured by such products. Such civil recoveries, however, are at best an after-the-fact remedy for injuries caused by hazardous consumer products. And, for a variety of reasons discussed in Chapter 32, such recoveries are by no means assured. Thus, the law also seeks to promote product safety by *direct regulation* of dangerously defective products.

**Consumer Product Safety Act.** The large and growing number of injuries caused by defective consumer products led Congress to pass the Consumer Product Safety Act (CPSA) in 1972. In order to advance Congress's goal of promoting product safety, the act established the Consumer Product Safety Commission (CPSC), an independent regulatory agency composed of five presidentially appointed commissioners, each serving a seven-year term. The CPSC is the main federal agency concerned with product safety. Its authority is basically limited to *consumer products*. *Not* within the Commission's domain, however, are certain products regulated by other agencies, including motor vehicles and equipment, firearms, aircraft, boats, drugs, cosmetics, and food products.

The CPSC is empowered to issue *product safety standards*. These may: (1) involve the performance of consumer products or (2) require product warnings or instructions. A product safety standard should be issued only when the product in question presents an *unreasonable* risk of injury and the standard is *reasonably necessary* to prevent or reduce that risk. The Commission may also issue rules *banning* certain "hazardous" products. Such rules are permissible when, in addition to presenting an unreasonable risk of injury, the product is so dangerous that no feasible product safety standard would protect the public from the risks it poses.

In addition, the CPSC can bring suit in federal district court to eliminate the dangers presented by *imminently hazardous* consumer products. These are products that pose an immediate and unreasonable risk of death, serious illness, or severe personal injury. Finally, manufacturers, distributors, and retailers are required to notify the CPSC if they have reason to know that their products present a *substantial product hazard*. Such a hazard exists when the product creates a substantial risk of injury to the public, either because it violates a Commission safety rule or for other reasons. In such cases, the CPSC may, among other things, order the private party to give notice of the problem to those affected by it, repair or replace the product, or submit its own corrective action plan.

The CPSA provides a host of other remedies and enforcement devices in addition to those already discussed. The Commission and the U.S. attorney general may sue for *injunctive relief* or the *seizure* of products to enforce various provisions of the act. *Civil penalties* against those who knowingly violate various CPSA provisions and CPSC rules are also possible. *Criminal penalties* may be imposed on those who knowingly and willfully violate such provisions and rules after CPSC notification of their failure to comply. In addition, any *private party* may sue for an *injunction* to enforce any CPSC rule or order; but it must give notice to the CPSC, the attorney general, and the would-be defendant at least 30 days before the suit. No such suit may be brought, however, if at the time of the suit the Commission or the attorney general has begun a civil or criminal action against the alleged violation. Finally, those injured because of a knowing and willful violation of a CPSC rule or order may sue for *damages* if the amount in controversy exceeds $10,000.

**Other Federal Product Safety Legislation.** Innumerable other state and federal laws seek to ensure product safety or otherwise protect consumers. A detailed consideration of such measures is beyond the scope of this book, but often their titles provide some idea of their aims and scope. At the federal level, for example, we have the *Food, Drug, and Cosmetic Act;* the *Poison Prevention Packaging Act;* the *Flammable Fabrics Act;* the *National Highway Traffic and Motor Vehicle Safety Act;* the *Insecticide, Fungicide, and Rodenticide Act;* the *Federal Boat Safety Act;* the *Federal Meat Inspection Act;* the *Egg Products Inspection Act;* and the *Poultry Products Inspection Act,* among others. Also, the FTC enforces, or helps enforce, the following additional measures: the *Wool Products Labeling Act,* the *Fur Products Labeling Act,* the *Textile Products Identification Act,* the *Fair Packaging and Labeling Act,* and the *Hobby Protection Act.*

## SUMMARY

The Federal Trade Commission performs a number of functions. It has statutory authority to enforce the Clayton and Robinson-Patman acts, and it can also enforce the Sherman Act under the broad language of Section 5 of the FTC Act. In addition, Section 5 gives the FTC the ability to attack anticompetitive behavior that cannot be reached under other antitrust statutes. Perhaps the most important power granted the FTC by Section 5, however, is its ability to regulate advertising. Most of the FTC's activity in this area involves *deceptive* advertising, but occasionally the commission has proceeded against *unfair* advertising as well. Recently, the FTC stated that, for advertising to qualify as "deceptive" under Section 5, it must contain a *material* representation, omission, or practice that is *likely to mislead* a consumer who acts *reasonably under the circumstances.*

The FTC also has the authority to enforce a number of specific federal consumer protection measures. One of these is the *Magnuson-Moss Warranty Act,* which contains provisions requiring that written warranties for consumer products costing more than $15 and sold to a consumer: (1) contain certain information and (2) be made available to the buyer before the sale.

Most of the other consumer protection measures enforced by the FTC involve consumer credit transactions. Under the *Truth in Lending Act,* creditors are required to make a number of disclosures to consumer debtors where the amount financed is $25,000 or less. The act also regulates credit advertising. The *Consumer Leasing Act* applies similar disclosure and advertising requirements to *consumer leases.* The *Fair Credit Reporting Act* places a number of duties on "consumer reporting agencies" such as credit bureaus. In addition, it establishes procedures for affected individuals to dispute and correct erroneous information contained in an agency's files. The act also requires that *users* of information obtained from consumer reporting agencies make certain disclosures to those affected by the information. The *Equal Credit Opportunity Act* forbids credit decisions made on the bases of sex, marital status, age, race, color, national origin, religion, and the obtaining of income from public assistance.

The *Fair Credit Billing Act* establishes a number of requirements to which credit card issuers must conform. The most important of these requirements involves disputes over credit card billing. Finally, the *Fair Debt Collection Practices Act* regulates the behavior of debt collection agencies. The act puts limits on the ability of collectors to contact both the debtor and third parties. It also states lengthy lists of forbidden collector actions that amount to "harassment or abuse," "false or misleading misrepresentations," and "unfair practices."

The FTC uses a variety of means to enforce the various statutes discussed above. It tries to assure voluntary compliance with these statutes by issuing *advisory opinions* and *industry guides*. It also formulates *trade regulation rules:* rules that describe specific illegal practices and have the force of law. Violations of these rules, or of the statutes that the FTC enforces, may be attacked in an FTC *adjudicative proceeding*. This is an administrative hearing resembling a trial. If the administrative law judge concludes that there has been a violation of the statutes or rules that the FTC enforces, he will usually issue an order that the offending party *cease and desist* from its illegal behavior. In some situations, however, the FTC may avoid an adjudicative proceeding by obtaining a *consent order*. This is a negotiated agreement not to proceed further against a private party, in return for that party's promise to refrain from certain practices. Many of the measures enforced by the FTC are enforced in a number of other ways as well. Among the possibilities are: criminal proceedings, civil actions by private parties, and enforcement by other federal agencies.

In addition to providing civil recoveries for those injured by defective products, the law seeks to promote product safety by direct regulation. The most important federal agency seeking to advance this goal is the Consumer Product Safety Commission, which was established by the Consumer Product Safety Act. The CPSC issues *product safety standards* for consumer products that pose an unreasonable risk of injury, may *ban* products that are especially hazardous, and may sue to eliminate the dangers posed by "imminently hazardous" consumer products. In addition to the Consumer Product Safety Act, a number of other federal statutes regulate the safety of specific products.

## PROBLEM CASES

**1.** For a long time, advertisements for Listerine Antiseptic Mouthwash had claimed that Listerine was beneficial in the treatment of colds, cold symptoms, and sore throats. An FTC adjudicative proceeding concluded that these claims were false. Thus, the Commission ordered Warner-Lambert Company, the manufacturer of Listerine, to include the following statement in future Listerine advertisements: "Contrary to prior advertising, Listerine will not help prevent colds or sore throats or lessen their severity." Warner-Lambert argued that this order was invalid because it went beyond a command to simply cease and desist from illegal behavior. Is Warner-Lambert correct?

**2.** Patron Aviation, Inc., an aviation company, bought an airplane engine from L&M Aircraft. The engine was assembled and shipped to L&M by Teledyne Industries, Inc. L&M installed the engine in one of Patron's airplanes. The engine turned out to be defective, and Patron sued L&M and Teledyne. One of the issues presented by the case was whether the Magnuson-Moss Act was applicable. Does the Magnuson-Moss Act apply to this transaction?

**3.** Smith rented a television set from ABC Rental Systems. The rental agreement stated that the lease was a week-to-week arrangement and that it was terminable by either party at any time. The agreement stated the figures "$16.00/55.00" in a space provided for the rental rate. The $16 figure was the weekly rate, and the $55 figure was a reduced monthly rate available to a consumer who wished to pay monthly. Smith was never provided with any of the disclosures required by the Consumer Leasing Act. Does the Consumer Leasing Act apply to this transaction?

**4.** Carroll applied for an Exxon credit card. Because of a report from a credit reporting agency that supplied insufficient information regarding her credit history, the application was denied. Exxon wrote Carroll a letter informing her that her application had been denied, but did not state any reason for the denial and provided no other information. Carroll later asked Exxon to provide specific reasons for her denial. Exxon replied that the denial was based on her incomplete credit history, but it did not supply the name of the credit bureau from which it obtained its information. Did Exxon violate the Fair Credit Reporting Act?

**5.** Gardner and North was in the business of renovating, remodeling, and repairing homes. It extended credit to homeowners for whom it performed services. Although the company did not take a mortgage or other lien on a homeowner's property, state law gave home improvement contractors a contractor's or mechanic's lien on the customer's home at the time the work was performed. Would a homeowner be able to rescind an agreement with Gardner and North after completion of the agreement? If so, how quickly would the homeowner have to act? (Hint: the regulations accompanying the Truth in Lending Act define the term *security interest* to include "liens created by operation of law such as mechanic's, materialman's, artisan's, and similar liens.")

**6.** Jerry Markham and Marcia Harris were engaged to be married. Shortly after announcing their engagement, they began to look for a house. Soon, they signed an agreement to purchase a home. They then submitted a joint mortgage application to an agent of the Illinois Federal Savings and Loan Association. Illinois Federal's loan committee rejected the application, with this statement: "Separate income not sufficient for loan and job tenure." This basically meant that Illinois Federal refused to aggregate the incomes of an unmarried couple who applied for a joint mortgage. Did Illinois Federal violate the Equal Credit Opportunity Act?

**7.** John E. Koerner & Co., Inc. applied for a credit card account with the American Express Company. The application was for a "company account" designed for business customers. Koerner asked American Express to issue cards bearing the company's name to Louis Koerner and four other officers of the corporation. Mr. Koerner was required to sign a "company account" form, agreeing that he would be jointly and severally liable with the company for all charges incurred through use of the company card. American Express issued the cards requested by the company. Thereafter, the cards were used almost totally for business purposes, although Mr. Koerner occasionally used his card for personal expenses. Later, a dispute regarding charges appearing on the company account arose. Does the Fair Credit Billing Act apply to this dispute?

**8.** Ken Baker was indebted on his credit card accounts with the Shell Oil Company. Shell assigned Baker's accounts to the G. C. Services Corporation for collection. G. C. Services did not provide Baker with adequate information about the debt, as required by the Fair Debt Collection Practices Act, and it also violated the act by falsely representing that it intended to take legal action if the debt was not paid. G. C. Services argued that it had a "bona fide error" defense under the act because it acted under the advice of an attorney, who apparently had made legal errors. Will G. C. Services be successful in asserting this defense?

Chapter 47

## INTRODUCTION

This chapter discusses the most important legal rules that now govern the employment relationship. In order to provide some perspective on this swiftly changing area of the law, the chapter opens with a historical overview of American employment law. The overview illustrates the general themes that unite the many legal topics considered in the chapter.

**Early American Employment Law.** From colonial times until the middle of the 19th century, much of the American population was self-employed. For many Americans, therefore, the problems created by the modern employment relation simply did not arise. Due to the scarcity of heavy industry, those who *were* employed by others probably faced fewer on-the-job hazards than did workers in later periods. In addition, many of the common employment relations in existence at this time were quite paternalistic. To be an "employee" was often to occupy a status position whose rights and duties were determined by a tradition of employer authority, and not by free bargaining.

In the apprenticeship relations that were common in early America, for example, the master's duties were frequently compared to those of a parent, and the apprentice's to those of a son. The master was usually obligated to train his apprentices, to see to their religious and secular education, and to refrain from discharging them except for good cause. Indentured servants, who basically sold themselves to a master for a period of time, resembled temporary slaves. Although the law did impose certain duties of fair and humane treatment on the master, often the indentured servant could not marry without the master's consent and was denied the rights to vote or engage in trade. In the southern states, the law regulated and enforced the system of black slavery. Further reinforcing the employer's power during this period was the courts' tendency to declare that labor unions were illegal criminal conspiracies.

**The Period of Industrialization and Laissez-Faire.** By the end of the Civil War, self-employment was somewhat less common than it had been previously. In addition, the employment relation had lost much of its traditional paternalistic character. Two mid-19th century social developments help explain the changed nature of the employment relation. The first of these was the triumph of laissez-faire values in economic matters. This meant that many legal problems arising from the employment relation were resolved under the highly individualistic principles of 19th century contract law.[1] It also meant that the terms of employment increasingly came to be determined by free and impersonal bargaining between employer and employee.[2] Because the employee frequently dealt from a position of inferior power, however, these terms tended to favor the employer. Among the factors placing the employee in a weaker position were the rise of the large corporation, the emergence of a large labor pool increasingly composed of immigrants, and the periodic unemployment resulting from ups and downs in the business cycle.

The second social development influencing the employment relation was the ongoing industrialization of the U.S. economy. This increased the on-the-job hazards that workers had to face. Also, in order to ensure that industrialization continued, the law sought to protect infant manufacturing firms from potentially crippling liability and to maximize their freedom of action. This meant that the law often favored employers in legal confrontations with their employees. It generally did so through the highly individualistic contract doctrines that governed the employment relation.

**Employment at Will.** Perhaps the best example of 19th century contract law's influence on employment law is the doctrine of **employment at will.** This doctrine, whose current status is discussed at the end of the chapter, first clearly appeared around 1870. It states that either party can terminate a contract of employment that is not for a definite time period, and can do so at any time. This includes contracts for "steady," "regular," or "permanent" employment. The termination can be for good, bad, or no reason. The employment at will doctrine seems to derive from the 19th century view that parties should be bound only to contract terms on which they have clearly agreed, and that the courts should not imply contract terms. Thus, where employer and employee failed to agree on a definite term of employment, it was felt to be unfair to impose one. Since there was

[1] On 19th century contract law, see Chapter 6.

[2] Also, since employees are agents, the terms of the employment relation included (and continue to include) the duties that principals owe to agents and that agents owe to principals. On these duties, see Chapter 16.

no such term, either party could terminate at any time and for any reason. However, the employee could recover for work actually done.

The employment at will doctrine reflects laissez-faire values, since it maximizes the freedom of both employer and employee. The doctrine has given employers the flexibility to meet changing business conditions by freely discharging employees whose services are no longer needed. In the process, it has probably helped promote the development of the American economy. Where labor was mobile and job opportunities were abundant, the employment at will doctrine probably worked to the employee's advantage as well. In other situations, however, the doctrine's benefits were obtained at the cost of exposing discharged employees to the mercies of an uncertain economy.

**On-the-Job Injuries.** Contract principles also played a major role in determining liability when employees sued employers in negligence[3] for injuries suffered in on-the-job accidents. If the employment contract contained an express "assumption of risk" clause relieving the employer of liability for its negligence, the clause would ordinarily be upheld and the employee would be unable to recover. Much more common was the doctrine of *implied assumption of risk,* under which the employee was regarded as having assumed all the normal and customary risks of his employment simply by taking the job. One of these risks was the possibility of being injured by a coemployee's negligence. This gave rise to the *fellow-servant rule,* which stated that where an employee's injury resulted from the negligence of a coemployee (or fellow servant), the employer would not be liable. Finally, the traditional negligence rule that even a slight degree of contributory negligence is a complete defense also helped protect employers from liability in some cases.

These rules reflected the prevailing economic individualism by assuming that the worker was a strong, shrewd, self-reliant person capable of driving hard bargains with his employer and of protecting himself while on the job. Also, they obviously helped protect developing industries from liability, and thus may have aided the industrialization of the United States.

**The Rise of Organized Labor.** All of the developments just discussed—especially the growth in the size of corporate employers and the continuing workplace hazards accompanying industrialization—eventually generated worker unrest and spurred the rise of organized labor in the late 19th century. Underlying the rise of unions was the perception that the power of corporate groups could be countered only by creating new groups representing the interests of workers. By the 1860s, the old doctrine that trade unions are criminal conspiracies had fallen into disfavor, and union activity increased as a result. The increasing political influence of organized labor and the fact that more and more voters were becoming wage-dependent eventually affected the state legislatures. As a result, numerous laws protecting workers were passed in the late 19th and early 20th centuries. These included statutes outlawing "yellow dog" contracts (under which an employee would agree not to join or remain a member of a union), minimum wage and maximum hours legislation, laws regulating the employment of women and children, all sorts of factory safety measures, and the workers' compensation systems discussed later in the chapter.

The courts, however, tended to represent business interests during this period. Thus,

[3] On negligence law, and the defenses of assumption of risk and contributory negligence, see Chapter 5.

many of the measures just discussed were struck down on constitutional grounds.[4] Also, many courts were quick to issue temporary and permanent injunctions to restrain union picketing and boycotts and to help quell strikes. As the materials in this chapter demonstrate, however, the efforts of business to stem the rising tide of legislation protecting workers were unsuccessful in the long run.

**Employment Law Today.** As the 20th century progressed, the imbalance in inherent social power between the individual and her employer continued to grow. By now, relatively few people are self-employed and many people work for public, semipublic, and private organizations of great size and power. The rights, privileges, and duties attaching to particular positions within large organizations are determined less by free bargaining than by the needs of the employer. These rights, duties, and privileges remain relatively fixed no matter who occupies the positions. Consider, for example, the multitude of positions within large corporations, the many grades of government service, or the various ranks within the military. Finally, much sociological writing testifies to the way organizational affiliations determine the individual's economic prospects, social position, lifestyle, and even values. Also, at least until recently, the power of organized labor has grown considerably throughout the 20th century. While union membership obviously weakens the employer's control over the employee, it also makes the employee's terms of employment subject to bargaining between groups.

The importance of the employment relation to most individuals, their dependence on the employer, and the power that the employer exerts over them have inspired numerous efforts to protect the employee against abuses of employer power. Thus, despite his increasing subservience to the employer, the employee's legal, economic, and social position has steadily improved for most of the 20th century. Employers have come to assume paternalistic duties toward their employees, providing such fringe benefits as pensions, health insurance, and life insurance. More importantly, government (including the courts) has come to dictate more and more features of the employment relation by imposing duties of individual protection and fair treatment on employers and unions. This chapter provides many examples of this trend. The legal topics it discusses can be seen as a series of exceptions to the contract-based model of the employment relation that was dominant in the mid-19th century. That is, they can be viewed as yet another example of government intervention prompted by disparities in power between contracting parties.

## PROTECTION AGAINST ON-THE-JOB HAZARDS

The ongoing industrialization of the American economy has meant that employees have been increasingly subject to dangerous workplace conditions. Since the late 19th century, there have been innumerable state and federal efforts to protect workers against on-the-job injuries and their economic consequences. The two most important such measures are state **workers' compensation** systems (which seek to compensate injured employees), and the federal **Occupational Safety and Health Act** (which seeks to prevent such injuries by direct government regulation of workplace safety).

**Workers' Compensation.** As you have seen, 19th century law made it difficult for employees to sue their employers for on-the-

[4] The best example of this is the doctrine of economic substantive due process, discussed in Chapter 42.

job injuries. Making the injured employee's suit even more difficult was the need to *prove* negligent behavior on the employer's part. State workers' compensation statutes, which first began to appear at the beginning of the 20th century, were a response to this situation. Early in the development of workers' compensation, some state statutes covered only certain hazardous employments and some were declared unconstitutional. By the 1920s, however, the constitutional objections had largely faded and most states had enacted some kind of workers' compensation system. Today, all 50 states have such systems, and the systems usually cover both hazardous and nonhazardous employments.

**Basic Features.** The coverage of workers' compensation statutes varies from state to state. But where they apply, all workers' compensation systems have certain basic features in common. They allow the injured employee to recover on the basis of *strict liability,*[5] thus eliminating the need to prove the employer's negligence. They also *eliminate* the employer's traditional defenses of contributory negligence, assumption of risk, and the fellow-servant rule. In addition, they make workers' compensation the employee's *exclusive remedy* against the employer.

Workers' compensation is basically a social compromise. Because it is based on strict liability and eliminates the three traditional employer defenses, workers' compensation greatly increases the *probability* that the employee will recover. But the *amount* recovered under workers' compensation is generally set by statute at a figure lower than the amount obtainable in a successful negligence suit.

The fact that workers' compensation is the employee's sole remedy against the employer does not prevent employee suits against other parties. Product liability suits against third-party suppliers of machinery or raw materials for on-the-job injuries caused by their products are common today. Negligence suits against coemployees who caused the injury are also possible. In each situation, the law may require an employee obtaining a double recovery to indemnify the employer or the state agency administering the workers' compensation system, but the details are beyond the scope of this text.

[5] Strict liability is discussed in Chapter 5.

**The Work-Related Injury Requirement.** Another basic feature of workers' compensation is that the employee can recover only for *work-related* injuries. Interpretations of this requirement differ from state to state, but over time the courts have read it more broadly. The general test for "work-relatedness" is that the injury must: (1) arise out of the employment and (2) happen in the course of that employment.

The work-related injury requirement has generated many problems and a sizable amount of case law. Courts may conclude that the injury fails to "arise out of" the employment if it is not typical of the *type* of employment in question. For example, construction workers injured when an out-of-control city bus careens onto their worksite may not be covered by workers' compensation. Where a preexisting diseased condition is aggravated by the employment, however, courts are increasingly likely to treat the resulting injury as arising out of the employment. Employees injured off the employer's premises are generally not covered by workers' compensation, because such injuries are outside "the course of the employment." The common example is an injury suffered while traveling to or from work. But the employee may be covered where the off-the-premises injury occurred while she was performing employment-related duties. Injuries suffered during business trips or while running employment-related errands are examples.

Other problem situations presented by the work-related injury requirement include mental injuries arguably arising from the employment and injuries resulting from employee horseplay. Virtually all authorities, however, regard intentionally self-inflicted injuries as outside the scope of workers' compensation. Recovery for occupational diseases, on the other hand, is usually allowed today.

**Benefits.** As noted above, the amount of money that an injured employee obtains under workers' compensation is determined by state law. Although individual states may differ, the following four categories of damages are customary: (1) hospital and medical expenses, (2) disability benefits, (3) specified recoveries for the loss of certain bodily parts, and (4) death benefit payments to a deceased employee's survivors and/or dependents. Each type of damages is limited in innumerable ways by state statutes and regulations.

**Employers and Employees Covered.** The states usually exempt certain employments from workers' compensation. One common exemption is for firms employing fewer than a stated number of employees (often three). Domestic work and agricultural work are other examples of exempted employments. Some states make workers' compensation mandatory for covered employers. Others allow covered employers to elect whether or not to be subject to workers' compensation. Finally, workers' compensation coverage is limited to *employees* and does not include independent contractors.

**Administration and Funding.** Workers' compensation systems are usually administered by a state agency (often called an "industrial commission"). This agency adjudicates workers' compensation cases and administers the system's overall operation. The states assure funding for workers' compensation payments by compelling covered employers to: (1) purchase insurance, (2) self-insure (e.g., by maintaining a contingency fund), or (3) make payments into a state fund. In order to encourage workplace safety, states requiring the third alternative sometimes base the amount payable on the employer's past claims record.

**Cases outside Workers' Compensation.** Where for any reason the injured employee is not covered by workers' compensation, he can still proceed against the employer in negligence. In many such situations, courts or legislatures have eliminated the defenses of assumption of risk, contributory negligence, and the fellow-servant rule. The fellow-servant rule in particular is rarely, if ever, applied today. Also, some states have statutes applying strict liability to suits by injured employees.

**The Occupational Safety and Health Act.** While its costs may stimulate employers to provide safer working conditions, workers' compensation does not give workers direct protection against on-the-job hazards. Partly for this reason, some states have enacted workplace safety statutes of all sorts. Also, Congress has enacted health and safety legislation for certain hazardous industries. In addition, some employers have voluntarily developed safety programs. Despite all of these efforts, the overall U.S. workplace safety record was unimpressive in the middle of the 20th century. With the emergence of new technologies, chemicals, and materials, many of which posed little-known hazards, the prospects for future improvement were uncertain.

The first federal workplace health and safety statute of general application, the Occupational Safety and Health Act of 1970, was an effort to correct this situation. The act applies to all employers engaged in a business affecting interstate commerce. The act's "affecting commerce" language has been read so broadly as to include virtually all employers not specifically exempted from coverage. These exemptions include the U.S. government, the states and their political subdivisions, and certain industries regulated by other federal safety legislation. The act is administered by the Occupational Safety and Health Administration (OSHA) of the Department of Labor.

**General Standards.** The act requires employers to provide their employees with employment and a place of employment free from recognized hazards that are likely to cause death or serious physical harm. It also requires employers to comply with specific regulations promulgated by OSHA. These regulations are voluminous, covering all sorts of safety-related subjects. Frequently, they are also quite detailed. In response to criticisms by employers and others, OSHA has scaled back the scope and detail of its regulations, but these changes are only a matter of degree.

**Enforcement and Penalties.** OSHA is empowered to inspect places of employment for violations of the act and its regulations, although employers can insist that the agency obtain a search warrant before doing so. (Workers who notify OSHA of possible violations are protected against employer retaliation.) If an employer is found to be in violation of the act's general duty provision or any specific standard, OSHA will issue a citation. It must do so with reasonable promptness, and in no event more than six months after the violation. The citation becomes final after 15 workdays following its service on the employer, unless it is contested. Contested citations are reviewed by the Occupational Safety Health and Review Commission, a three-member body composed of presidential appointees. Further review by OSHA itself and the federal courts of appeals is possible in certain circumstances.

The main sanctions for violations of the act and the regulations are **civil penalties** imposed by OSHA. The agency *must* impose a penalty of up to $1,000 per violation when an employer has received a citation for a serious violation of the act or the regulations. OSHA *may* impose a penalty of up to $1,000 per violation when the employer has received a citation for a nonserious violation. A civil penalty not exceeding $10,000 per violation may be imposed on an employer who has committed willful or repeated violations. Where the employer fails to correct a violation for which a citation has been issued, OSHA may impose a civil penalty not exceeding $1,000 for each day that the violation continues. Any employer who commits a willful violation resulting in death to an employee will, upon conviction, be punished by a fine not exceeding $10,000, imprisonment for not more than six months, or both. Finally, the secretary of labor may seek injunctive relief when an employment hazard presents an imminent danger of death or physical harm that cannot be promptly eliminated by normal citation procedures.

**Record-Keeping, Reporting, and Notice.** The act and its accompanying regulations impose a number of record-keeping and reporting requirements on employers. For instance, employers must maintain accurate records of, and make periodic reports on, work-related deaths, illnesses, and injuries other than minor injuries. Employers must also maintain accurate records of employee exposures to certain toxic and harmful materials. Employees exposed to specified concentrations of such materials must receive prompt notification from the employer. Employers are also required to keep employees informed of their protections and obligations under the act and its regulations.

**The State Role.** When Congress enacted the Occupational Safety and Health Act, it did not intend to preempt state action in the field of workplace safety. In fact, the act encourages state regulation in this area. If a state desires to regulate an area controlled by OSHA standards, it must submit an appropriate plan to the secretary of labor. The secretary must approve the plan if, among other things, it sets standards at least as stringent as those imposed by federal law. The secretary must then monitor state enforcement of its plan, and has authority to reintroduce federal enforcement if the state substantially fails to comply with its plan. Many states have employed this procedure to regulate various aspects of worker safety.

## INCOME MAINTENANCE AND OLD-AGE PROTECTION

Under a system of complete laissez-faire, the employer's obligation to maintain the employee's income or otherwise contribute to his financial security would presumably end once the contract of employment ends. Today, however, employers play a major role in ensuring that their employees receive financial protection after termination of the employment relation. Sometimes, employers do this more or less voluntarily; the maintenance of employee pension plans is an example. More often, though, the law imposes these paternalistic duties on the employer.

**Unemployment Compensation.** The mass unemployment resulting from the Great Depression created political pressure for financial assistance to those who could not find work. The Federal Unemployment Tax Act of 1935 (FUTA) was a response to this pressure. The act imposes a federal unemployment tax on covered employers, but allows them to credit contributions to approved state unemployment programs against their federal tax bill. Since the tax burden on employers was much the same whether or not the states decided to protect the unemployed, FUTA reduced employer objections to funding state unemployment insurance and made it easier for the states to adopt such plans. By the late 1930s, all of the states had done so.

Thus, although FUTA provided the initial stimulus, unemployment compensation is basically administered by the states. Unemployment insurance plans vary somewhat from state to state, but usually are similar in certain general respects. In order to prevent payments to those who have not recently been employed, states often condition the receipt of benefits on the earning of a certain minimum income during a specified prior time period. Generally, those who have voluntarily quit work without good cause, have been fired for bad conduct, fail to actively seek suitable new work, or refuse such work are also ineligible for benefits. Benefit levels vary from state to state, as does the length of time that benefits can be received. If economic conditions so dictate, however, the maximum period may be extended. Many states have adopted *experience-rating provisions* in order to encourage employers to retain employees. These provisions reduce the unemployment tax burden on employers that have traditionally had lower unemployment in their work forces.

**Social Security.** The Federal Insurance Contributions Act (FICA) finances a system of old-age, survivors, disability, and medical and hospital insurance. FICA operates by imposing a flat percentage tax on all employee income below a certain base figure and by requiring the employer to pay a matching amount. Self-employed people pay a higher rate on a different wage base. (In both cases, the percentage and the wage base change frequently.) FICA covers a very wide range of employers and employees. Exceptions to its coverage include railroad workers (who have their own program) and federal employees covered by another retirement system. FICA revenues finance old-age benefits (what people usually call "social security"), payments to disabled workers and some of their dependents, survivors' benefits to certain members of a deceased worker's family, and health and medical care insurance for the elderly (medicare).

**Pension Plan Regulation.** Along with personal savings and social security payments, funds from pension plans are a significant source of postretirement income. In 1981, 44.3 percent of the civilian work force was covered by some kind of pension plan; and at the end of 1982, pension fund assets totaled $931.7 billion, with $573.4 billion of this total in the hands of private pension funds.[6] For a long time, the main federal law regulating private pension plans was the Internal Revenue Code, which did not concern itself with the details of pension plan operation. Partly for this reason, abuses and injustices were not uncommon. Examples include arbitrary plan terminations, arbitrary benefit reductions, and mismanagement of fund assets.

**ERISA.** The Employee Retirement Income Security Act of 1974 (ERISA) responded to these problems. The act is generally intended to protect employees from abuses in the operation of private pension plans and to protect the employee's expectation that pension benefits will be paid.[7] It does not require employers to establish or fund benefit plans, nor does it set benefit levels. In many ways, ERISA is a cautious regulatory response to the problems it addresses, for Congress did not wish to discourage the creation of pension plans by enacting overly stringent controls.

ERISA is a very long, complex, and detailed statute. Its main concern is to establish standards that pension plans must meet. Among these standards are: (1) fiduciary duties on pension fund managers; (2) record-keeping, reporting, and disclosure requirements; (3) eligibility provisions limiting the employer's ability to delay employee participation in the plan; (4) funding requirements designed to assure the availability of sufficient assets to pay benefits; and (5) plan termination insurance covering the contingency that the plan's assets will be insufficient to pay the required benefits. The Pension Benefit Guaranty Corporation, set up within the Labor Department, is the insurance agency established by the act.

Perhaps the most important feature of ERISA is its **vesting** requirements. Rights "vest" in a person when they become so fixed that they cannot be legally taken away. In the pension context, this occurs when the right to receive pension benefits upon retirement becomes nonforfeitable. Prior to ERISA, pension plans sometimes provided for late vesting of benefits from employer contributions to the plan. So far as such contributions were concerned, this made it possible for employers to avoid their obligations to employees who changed jobs or were fired prior to the vesting date.

ERISA requires the complete and immediate vesting of benefits attributable to *employee* contributions. The vesting of benefits attributable to *employer* contributions is governed by three statutory options, from which the employer must choose. First, the employer may formulate its plan so that an employee with 10 years of service has a nonforfeitable

[6] *1984 Statistical Abstract of the United States,* at 384. End-of-1983 figures of $1.15 trillion for public and private funds and $875 billion for private funds were stated by The Wall Street Journal, October 11, 1984, at 35.

[7] ERISA was amended by the Multiemployer Pension Plan Amendments Act of 1980. The act covers multiemployer pension plans (plans to which more than one unrelated employer contributes). Its main object is to protect against the problems peculiar to such plans—most importantly, the difficulties presented when contributing firms withdraw from the plan.

right to 100 percent of his accrued benefits. Second, the employer may provide that an employee completing at least five years of service has a nonforfeitable right to 25 percent of his accrued benefits. Then, an additional 5 percent of accrued benefits must vest for each of the next five years, followed by a 10 percent yearly increase for each of the five following years. Under this option, the employee's rights would be fully vested after 15 years. Third, under the "rule of 45," the employer may provide that an employee with five years of service have a vested right to 50 percent of his accrued benefits when the sum of his age and his years of service equals or exceeds 45. After that, the percentage of benefits vested must increase by 10 percent each year, so that vesting is complete after 10 years of service.

Under ERISA, plan participants and beneficiaries may enforce their rights under the terms of the plan, including the recovery of benefits. Along with the secretary of labor, they may also obtain equitable relief against violations of the act, and both legal and equitable relief against plan managers who breach their fiduciary duties. In addition, those who willfully violate the act's provisions can suffer criminal penalties.

## WAGES, HOURS, AND OTHER TERMS OF EMPLOYMENT

Under a laissez-faire, contract-based model of the employment relation, such basic terms as wages and hours worked would be determined by free bargaining. Yet for much of this century government has constantly intervened to set these terms of employment. The Fair Labor Standards Act provisions discussed below are just one example. Even where basic terms of employment are determined by bargaining, it is often a *labor union,* and not the individual, that has negotiated the terms. Moreover, government now subjects unions and their activities to extensive regulation.

**The Fair Labor Standards Act.** The most important provisions of the Fair Labor Standards Act of 1938 (FLSA) concern the regulation of **wages and hours.** Employees covered by the act are entitled to a specified minimum wage and to a "time and a half" rate for work in excess of 40 hours per week. The minimum wage became $3.35 per hour effective January 1, 1981, and had not been changed as of early 1985.

The coverage of the FLSA's wages and hours provisions is a complex matter. These provisions basically apply to employees who are: (1) engaged in interstate commerce or the production of goods for such commerce or (2) employed by an enterprise that is engaged in interstate commerce or the production of goods for such commerce. (Sometimes, enterprises falling within the second category must also exceed certain dollar figures for gross sales or gross volume of business done.) However, the FLSA exempts certain types of employees from its wages and hours standards. Perhaps most important are its exemptions for executive, administrative, professional, and outside sales employees. Also included in the FLSA's lengthy list of detailed exemptions are the employees of certain retail, service, or recreational establishments; certain employees engaged in fishing-related work; and certain agricultural employees. Due to a 1976 Supreme Court decision, state and local employees were once beyond the constitutional reach of the FLSA's wages and hours requirements, but the decision insulating such employees from the FLSA was overruled in early 1985.[8]

The FLSA also prohibits certain kinds of **child labor.** It forbids the use of "oppressive child labor" by any employer engaged in in-

[8] See Footnote 6, Chapter 42.

terstate commerce or in the production of goods for such commerce. It also forbids the interstate shipment of goods produced in an establishment where oppressive child labor takes place. The term *oppressive child labor* includes: (1) most employment of children below the age of 14, (2) employment of children aged 14–15 who do *not* work in one of a list of approved occupations set out by the Department of Labor, and (3) employment of children aged 16–17 who work in occupations declared particularly hazardous by the Labor Department (e.g., mining). Subject to conditions that vary with the age of the child, these provisions do not apply to agricultural employment. Also exempt from these provisions are children who work as actors or performers in radio, television, movie, and theatrical productions.

Private parties suing for violations of the FLSA's *wages and hours* provisions can recover the amount of the unpaid minimum wages or overtime, plus an additional equal amount as liquidated damages. Class actions are possible, but those included in the class must have filed a written consent with the court. In addition, the Labor Department may sue to recover the unpaid minimum wages or overtime owed to employees, along with the liquidated damages just described. In this case, the employee's right to sue terminates once the Labor Department begins its suit and the department will pay back the amounts it recovers to the injured employees. Employers violating the FLSA's *child labor* provisions are subject to civil penalties of up to $1,000 per violation. Finally, the Labor Department may sue for injunctive relief to enforce the FLSA's various provisions, and willful violations of those provisions subject employers to criminal liability.

**Labor Law.** American labor law is a very complex topic whose many details are beyond the scope of this text. However, no discussion of employment law is complete without some discussion of federal regulation of labor-management relations in the 20th century. The brief survey of labor law that follows illustrates many of the general themes discussed at the beginning of the chapter.

**Introduction.** Throughout the early part of the 20th century, the legal system often assisted employers seeking to check the growing power of labor. The employment at will doctrine enabled them to fire prounion employees, and employer blacklisting of such employees was not uncommon. Judicial injunctions and restraining orders, and the contempt citations that courts would issue upon their violation, continued to be useful in suppressing strikes and other union activities. Some union tactics were held to violate the antitrust laws. Yellow-dog contracts continued to be employed, and state legislation forbidding such contracts was sometimes declared unconstitutional. Despite all of these measures, however, the power of organized labor continued to grow. That power was cemented in the 1930s, when Congress explicitly recognized labor's rights to organize and to bargain collectively by passing the National Labor Relations Act. Later federal regulation of labor-management relations, which was mainly addressed to certain perceived abuses of union power, may have limited labor's power somewhat. But it has not seriously disturbed the position that labor achieved in the 1930s.

The rise of organized labor is a clear example of what has been called "countervailing power": the checking of organized group power by the creation of competing groups. It also underlines the degree to which organized groups, and not individuals acting as individuals, are the key units in American life today. By organizing to counter the influence of corporate groups over their working lives, workers have been able to achieve wages and working conditions that they would probably have been unable to obtain otherwise. In the process, however, they have become subordinate to another organized group—the union.

This section also illustrates a theme that pervades this text: the activist role played by government in the 20th century. In particular, the section emphasizes government's contemporary role as mediator between competing group interests. That role is quite important in the labor relations context, for one of labor law's main functions is to promote industrial peace and stability.

**The National Labor Relations Act.** In 1926, Congress passed the Railway Labor Act, which regulates labor relations in the railroad industry (and which was amended to include airlines in 1936). This was followed by the Norris-LaGuardia Act of 1932, which limited the circumstances in which federal courts could enjoin strikes and picketing in labor disputes. The act also prohibited federal court enforcement of yellow-dog contracts.

These two statutes, though, were only a prelude to the most important 20th century American labor statute, the National Labor Relations Act of 1935 (the NLRA or Wagner Act). The act gave employees the *right to organize* by enabling them to form, join, and assist labor organizations. It also allowed them to *bargain collectively* through representatives of their own choosing and to engage in other activities that would promote collective bargaining. In addition, the Wagner Act prohibited certain employer practices that were believed to discourage collective bargaining, and declared these to be *unfair labor practices.* Included in its list of unfair labor practices are:

1. Interfering with employees in the exercise of their rights to form, join, and assist labor unions.
2. Dominating or interfering with the formation or administration of any labor union, or giving financial or other support to a union.
3. Discriminating against employees in hiring, tenure, or any term of employment because of their union membership.
4. Discriminating against employees because they have filed charges or given testimony under the act.
5. Refusing to bargain collectively with any duly designated representative of the employees.

The NLRA also established the National Labor Relations Board (NLRB). The NLRB's main functions are: (1) to handle *representation cases* (which involve the process by which a union becomes the certified representative of the employees within a particular bargaining unit), and (2) to decide whether challenged employer or union activity constitutes an *unfair labor practice.*

**The Labor Management Relations Act.** The NLRA was amended by the Labor Management Relations Act (LMRA or Taft-Hartley Act) in 1947. The changes that the Taft-Hartley Act made reflected the more conservative political climate and the renewal of business power after World War II. Perhaps more importantly, they reflected public concern over frequent strikes, the perceived excessive power of union "bosses," and various unfair practices by unions. Thus, the Taft-Hartley Act declared that certain acts by *unions* were unfair labor practices. These include:

1. Restraining or coercing employees in the exercise of their guaranteed bargaining rights (in particular, their rights to refrain from joining a union or to engage in collective bargaining).
2. Causing an employer to discriminate

against an employee who is not a union member (unless the employee is not a member because of a failure to pay union dues).

3. Refusing to bargain collectively with the employer.
4. Conducting a secondary strike or a secondary boycott for a specified illegal purpose. (These are strikes or boycotts aimed at a third party with which the union has no real dispute. Their purpose is to coerce that party not to deal with an employer with which the union does have a dispute, and thus to gain some leverage over the employer.)
5. Requiring employees covered by union-shop contracts to pay excessive or discriminatory initiation fees or dues.
6. Featherbedding (forcing an employer to pay for work not actually performed).

The LMRA also established an 80-day "cooling off" period for strikes that the president finds likely to endanger national safety or health. In addition, it created a Federal Mediation and Conciliation Service to assist employers and unions in settling labor disputes.

**The Labor Management Reporting and Disclosure Act.** Congressional investigations during the 1950s uncovered considerable corruption in internal union affairs, and also revealed that the internal procedures of many unions were undemocratic. In response to these findings, Congress enacted the Labor Management Reporting and Disclosure Act (or Landrum-Griffin Act) in 1959. The act established a "bill of rights" for union members and attempted to make internal union affairs more democratic. It also amended the NLRA by adding to the LMRA's list of unfair labor practices by unions.

## EMPLOYMENT DISCRIMINATION—THE BASIC PROVISIONS

**Introduction.** If highly individualistic 19th century contract principles controlled the employment relation, no party to an employment contract could be bound to terms not of his choosing. So long as they did not violate any agreed-upon terms, for example, employers would be able to hire, fire, promote, and compensate on any basis they desired, no matter how arbitrary. An employer expressing this attitude might say: "It's a free country, it's *my* business, and I should be able to run it any way I want. If I don't feel like hiring some kinds of people, that's my concern. As for the people I do hire, no one is forcing them to stay. If they don't like the way I treat them, they can quit."

As the preceding discussion has illustrated, this attitude has become less influential over the course of the 20th century. Until the 1960s and 1970s, however, little was done to eliminate unfavorable employer decisions based on race, sex, age, and other personal attributes over which the individual has no control. When the tide finally turned, it did so with a vengeance. Today, employers are confronted with a mass of legal rules governing their treatment of women, racial minorities, older employees, and other groups. Changed social values—specifically, America's greater commitment to equal opportunity—are the most important explanation for this changed legal picture. But long-term structural shifts in the U.S. economy have played a role as well. Today, many employers are large organized groups whose employment decisions have great importance because of the number of people they employ and because the jobs they offer are quite important in determining the income, status, and life prospects of their employees. Discrimination by employers of this sort can have tremendous social consequences.

This section discusses the American legal system's basic employment discrimination provisions: the most important statutes, regulations, and executive orders utilized in the effort to eliminate such discrimination. The next section examines three fairly recent—and often controversial—problem areas that have arisen during this effort.

**The EEOC.** The Equal Employment Opportunity Commission (EEOC), established by the Civil Rights Act of 1964, is the single most important federal agency dealing with employment discrimination. The EEOC is a five-member, presidentially appointed independent agency with a sizable staff and numerous regional offices. It enforces Title VII of the 1964 Civil Rights Act, the Equal Pay Act, the Age Discrimination in Employment Act, and the portion of the Rehabilitation Act of 1973 dealing with discrimination against handicapped persons in the federal government.[9] The EEOC's functions include: (1) *enforcement* of the above statutes through lawsuits that it initiates or in which it intervenes, (2) *conciliation* of employment discrimination charges (by, for example, encouraging their negotiated settlement), (3) *investigation* of a wide range of discrimination-related matters (including the investigation of formal discrimination charges), and (4) *interpretation* of the statutes it enforces (through regulations and interpretative guidelines).

**The Equal Pay Act.** The Equal Pay Act of 1963 (EPA) basically forbids *sex* discrimination regarding *pay*. The EPA was passed as an amendment to the FLSA, and its coverage is very similar. Unlike the FLSA, however, the EPA covers executive, administrative, professional, and outside sales employees. It also reaches state and local government employees.

The act covers pay discrimination against men. But the typical EPA case involves an aggrieved woman who claims that she has received lower pay than that received by a male employee performing substantially equal work for the same employer. For the plaintiff to recover, her job and the job of the higher-paid male employee must involve *each* of the following: (1) equal effort, (2) equal skill, (3) equal responsibility, and (4) *similar* working conditions. "Effort" basically means physical or mental exertion. "Skill" refers to the experience, training, education, and ability required for the positions being compared. Here, the question is not whether the two employees actually possess equal skills but whether the *jobs require or utilize* substantially the same skills. "Responsibility" (or "accountability") involves such factors as the degree of higher level supervision each job requires and the practical consequences that flow from each job's duties. For instance, a retail sales position in which the employee is allowed to approve customer checks without higher level review will probably not be equal to a sales position in which the employee lacks this authority. "Working conditions" refers to such factors as temperature and weather conditions, fumes, ventilation, toxic conditions, and risk of injury. The *Grove* case below discusses a fairly common problem in this area: whether extra tasks performed by a male employee will make the two jobs unequal.

Once it has been established that the two jobs are substantially equal and that they are compensated unequally, the employer must prove one of the EPA's four defenses or it will lose the case. That is, the defendant must show that the pay disparity is based on: (1) seniority, (2) merit, (3) quality or quantity of production (e.g., a piecework system), or (4) any factor other than sex. As the *Grove* case emphasizes in the case of merit, the first three

[9] Employment discrimination within the federal government is beyond the scope of this text. Employment discrimination by state governments will be considered only to the extent that the provisions discussed below cover it.

defenses usually require the employer to show some organized, systematic, communicated rating system with predetermined criteria that apply equally to employees of each sex. Highly discretionary, subjective systems capable of serving as a cover for gender discrimination ordinarily will not suffice. The "any factor other than sex" defense is a catchall category that includes shift differentials, bonuses paid because the job is part of a training program, and perhaps differences in the profitability of the products or services on which the employees work. For this defense to exist, there must have been no prior discrimination regarding entry into the higher paid shift, the training program, or the higher profit job.

Since the Equal Pay Act is part of the FLSA, its remedies are very similar. The EPA's remedial scheme differs from the FLSA scheme described above in only two significant ways: (1) employee suits are for the amount of back pay lost because of the employer's discrimination (plus an equal amount as liquidated damages), not for unpaid minimum wages or overtime; and (2) the federal enforcement agency is the EEOC, not the Labor Department. Also, an employer violating the EPA cannot bring itself into compliance by reducing the wages of any employee (e.g., higher-paid male employees) or by transferring one sex out of a department into unequal work. Finally, unlike Title VII of the 1964 Civil Rights Act and the Age Discrimination in Employment Act, a private plaintiff under the EPA does not have to submit her complaint to the EEOC for evaluation and attempted conciliation.

## Grove v. Frostburg National Bank

**549 F. Supp. 922 (D. Md. 1982)**

Sheila Grove and David Klink were both hired as loan tellers by the Frostburg National Bank in 1967. Both were high school graduates at the time, and neither had had prior work experience, although Klink had attended a business school for two years. Each was paid the same yearly starting salary in 1967. Klink was drafted into the army in late 1967, and he returned to the bank in 1969. From that time until 1976, he basically performed a loan teller's duties, although he also took on a variety of miscellaneous tasks. Grove also basically performed loan teller duties during the period 1969–76. Throughout that period, Klink's yearly salary exceeded Grove's. Salary and raise determinations were made by David P. Willetts, the bank's vice president, who based these determinations primarily on his own observations of employees. Grove sued the bank in federal district court under the Equal Pay Act.

**Jones, District Judge.** The burden is on the plaintiff to make a prima facie showing, by a preponderance of the evidence, that the employer pays different wages to males and females for equal work requiring equal skill, effort, and responsibility under similar working conditions. Once that showing is made, the employer has the burden of showing, by a preponderance of the evidence, that the pay differential is justified under one of the four statutory exceptions. Only substantial equality of work need be proved; the jobs need not be identical. A wage differential is justified by extra tasks only if they create significant variations in skill, effort, and responsibility. If the purported extra tasks are not done; if females also have extra tasks of equal skill, effort, and responsibility; if females are not given the opportunity to do the extra tasks; or if the extra tasks only involve minimal time and are of peripheral importance, they do not justify a wage differential. Where some extra tasks are done but they require no skill, effort, or responsibility greater than the regular tasks performed by both males and females, they do not make a job unequal and justify higher wages.

Sheila Grove performed work substantially equal to that of David Klink from 1969 through September, 1976. Klink had some extra tasks from time to time. He set up the drive-in branch in 1970. He reviewed the safe deposit box rent records and noted some delinquencies and increases in 1971. After 1971, he arranged for drilling the boxes. Sometime in the 1970s, he began shredding paper.

Setting up the drive-in branch was a one-time task, involving taking supplies and equipment to the drive-in installation. To the extent that it involved any different skills or effort than the normal work of the loan tellers, they were largely physical. Moreover, no female loan teller had an opportunity to perform this task, because it was done at the request of Willetts. Although Klink's initiative in bringing the box rents up to date is commendable, the work did not consume a significant amount of time, as compared with his other duties. It was a one-time project. To the extent that he performed extra tasks thereafter in arranging for the drilling, no significant amount of time was involved. Shredding paper is a task involving less skill, effort, and responsibility than the regular work of loan tellers. It did not involve a significant amount of time, only occasional afternoons or Saturdays.

Grove has sustained her burden of demonstrating that her work as loan teller was substantially equal to that of Klink. Klink received a higher salary than Grove beginning in 1969 through September, 1976. The bank tried to justify Klink's higher salary on two grounds. It stated that Klink was paid a higher salary when he returned to the bank in 1969, which was perpetuated through yearly increases, as a reward for his patriotism in serving in the Army. The bank also claimed that Klink received higher pay because he was more responsible, conscientious, and harder-working: that is, on merit.

The bank has failed to show that Klink's 1969 salary was based on a factor other than sex. Even assuming that military service could be a proper reason for a wage differential, Klink was drafted into the service. No female worker could have been.

The bank has also failed to show that the wage differential was based on a legitimate merit system or other factor not based on sex. A merit system need not be in writing to be recognized; it must, however, be an organized and structured procedure with systematic evaluations under predetermined criteria. If it is not in writing, the employees must be aware of it. The system used by Willetts does not meet this test. It was not organized or structured; Willetts did not recall, for example, whether he had consulted with department supervisors at the end of each year concerning individual employees. A systematic evaluation, using predetermined criteria, was not made. Although Willetts cited a number of factors that influenced his pay decisions, these were not applied uniformly, and he eventually admitted that the primary criterion was his "gut feeling" about the employee. Finally, employees were not aware of the existence of any merit system.

Judgment for Grove.

**Title VII.** Title VII of the 1964 Civil Rights Act is the most comprehensive federal measure regulating employment discrimination. It prohibits discrimination based on *race, color, religion, sex, or national origin.* It does so for a wide range of employment decisions. These include hiring; firing; pay;[10] job assignment; access to training and apprenticeship programs; fringe benefits; and many other terms, conditions, and benefits of employment.

**Covered Entities.** Title VII covers all employers employing 15 or more employees and engaging in an industry affecting interstate commerce. The term *employer* includes individuals, partnerships, corporations, labor unions (with respect to their own employees), and state and local governments.[11] Also, referrals by employment agencies of *any* size are covered if the employer serviced by the agency has 15 or more employees. In addition, Title VII covers certain unions in their capacity as employee representative. Unions with 15 or more members are usually covered. Among those specifically exempted from Title VII's coverage are religious organizations (but only for discrimination based on religion), bona fide tax-exempt private clubs, and Indian tribes.

**Forms of Prohibited Discrimination.** Title VII's ban on race, color, religion, sex, and national origin discrimination has generated a mass of case law spelling out the coverage of these terms. *Race or color* discrimination, for instance, includes discrimination against blacks, other racial minorities, American Indians, and whites.[12] *National origin* discrimination is discrimination based on the country of one's ancestry or on one's possession of physical, cultural, or linguistic characteristics shared by people of a certain national origin. Employers who hire only U.S. citizens may violate Title VII if their policy has the purpose or effect of discriminating against national origin groups. This might happen if, for instance, such an employer is located in a region where aliens of a particular nationality are highly concentrated. Also, seemingly neutral employment criteria such as height or the ability to speak clear, unaccented English may disadvantage certain nationalities, and thus may violate Title VII if they are insufficiently related to the job for which they are imposed.

For Title VII purposes, the term *religion* includes almost any set of beliefs that are sincerely held and that, because they acknowledge a Supreme Being, a ritual, or a set of ethical tenets, have an effect on the believer's life similar to that produced by traditional religions. Title VII also covers discrimination based on religious observances or practices—for example, grooming, clothing, or the refusal to work on the Sabbath. But such discrimination will be justified if the employer demonstrates that it cannot reasonably accommodate the religious practice without undue hardship.

Title VII's ban on *sex* discrimination has probably posed the greatest interpretative problems. This is partly because the ban was added as a late amendment to Title VII in an apparent attempt to defeat the measure. Thus, there is very little legislative history on this provision of Title VII. Clearly, though, the provision is aimed at *gender* discrimination, and does not protect homosexuality or

[10] Thus, claims involving pay discrimination based on sex may proceed under both the EPA and Title VII. The Supreme Court has held that the EPA defenses (but not its "equal work" requirement) apply in Title VII suits of this kind.

[11] A 1972 amendment to Title VII covers employment discrimination in the federal government.

[12] So-called reverse discrimination is discussed in the next section of this chapter.

transsexuality as such. Just as clearly, Title VII's prohibition of sex discrimination applies to discrimination against either men or women. Also a 1978 amendment to Title VII forbids discrimination on the basis of pregnancy or childbirth. The amendment generally requires employers to treat pregnancy like any other condition similarly affecting working ability in their sick leave programs, medical benefit and disability plans, and other fringe benefits. In addition, employer-administered pension funds requiring women to make higher payments than men to obtain an equal lifetime annuity, or to accept a lower lifetime annuity for equal payments, violate Title VII despite the longer average life span of women. Finally, two other sex discrimination topics—sexual harassment and comparable worth—are discussed in the next section of this chapter.

**Proving Discrimination.** Where an employer has a policy expressly disfavoring one of Title VII's protected classes, plaintiffs have little difficulty in proving the existence of discrimination. But there are many other kinds of discrimination, both intentional and unintentional. In cases where there is no express discriminatory policy, employers often argue that the employment decision challenged by the plaintiff was made for nondiscriminatory reasons. When this happens, it is very difficult for the plaintiff to obtain direct proof of a discriminatory motive. Were such proof necessary, there would be very few successful Title VII suits. The rules for proving a Title VII violation, however, recognize these difficulties and ease the plaintiff's burden.

In certain Title VII suits called "disparate treatment" cases, the plaintiff alleges some *specific instance or instances of discriminatory treatment.* What the plaintiff will be required to prove in such cases varies with the type of employment decision made. In many *hiring* cases, for instance, it must be shown that: the plaintiff is within one of Title VII's five protected classes; he applied for, and was qualified to perform, a job for which the employer was seeking applicants; he was denied the job; and the employer continued to seek applicants after the rejection. A plaintiff who has met this burden of proof is said to have established a **prima facie case:** a case strong enough to require a counterargument from the defendant. Here, the defendant must allege legitimate, nondiscriminatory reasons for the refusal to hire or it will lose the lawsuit. If the defendant provides such reasons, it will prevail unless the plaintiff shows that the reasons are merely a pretext for a decision made with a discriminatory purpose.

A second common Title VII situation involves allegations that the employer has engaged in a pervasive *pattern or practice of discrimination.* Here, the most important type of proof is evidence showing that the percentage of protected group members (e.g., blacks) in the employer's work force is less than the protected group's percentage of some surrounding population (e.g., the local labor market). But the defendant may be able to rebut such statistical evidence in a variety of ways.

The third and fourth ways to prove a Title VII violation are related. The plaintiff may argue that the employer has adopted a *neutral rule that perpetuates the effects of past discrimination.* For example, suppose a labor union that has long excluded blacks finally abandons this practice, but retains a rule that new members must be related to, or recommended by, current members. Finally, the plaintiff may make a "disparate impact" argument, contending that the employer has adopted a *neutral rule with an adverse impact on a protected Title VII class.* Examples include testing, high school diploma, height, strength, and weight requirements—all of which can have a disproportionate impact on one or more of Title VII's protected groups. Once the needed proof has been provided in either of these two situations involving neutral rules, the employer must show that the rule is justified by *business necessity* in order to prevent the plaintiff from winning. However, the plaintiff may still triumph by showing that there are other selection methods that are less disadvantageous to the protected class, yet still capable of serving the employer's legitimate business needs.

The *Dothard* case at the end of the section illustrates this last method of proving a Title VII violation. The *Teamsters* case which precedes it discusses the second and third methods.

**Defenses.** Even if the plaintiff proves a violation of Title VII, the employer will still prevail if it can prove one of Title VII's various defenses. The three most important Title VII defenses are *merit, seniority,* and the *bona fide occupational qualification* (BFOQ) defense. Most of the situations presenting the merit defense involve testing. If the test has an adverse statistical impact on a protected class, it must be job-related or it will not protect the employer. The EEOC has promulgated guidelines for determining the job-relatedness of employment tests. Evaluation of these tests under the guidelines is a complex, technical matter drawing heavily on the work of educational and industrial psychologists.

Employer decisions resulting from the operation of a "bona fide seniority system" will not violate Title VII. For a seniority system to be "bona fide," it must be existing, formalized, and recognized, and it must treat all employees equally on its face. The *Teamsters* case discusses a major problem presented by the seniority defense: its application to a case where the plaintiff alleges that a seemingly neutral seniority system perpetuates the effects of past discrimination.[13]

[13] The *Stotts* case, which appears later in the chapter, presents another collision between seniority and the protection of racial minorities.

There are a few jobs whose effective performance may require the employer to discriminate on bases forbidden by Title VII. In such cases, the BFOQ defense may protect the employer from liability. The defense applies only to sex, religion, and national origin discrimination, and *not* to racial discrimination. In addition, it protects only *hiring* and *referral* decisions. Even where it can apply, the BFOQ defense is a very narrow one. Generally, the personal trait in question must be necessary for effective job performance. For example, the defense should be available to the employment of a female to model women's clothing, and the employment of a male actor to play a male character in a movie. The *Dothard* case involves another of the infrequent instances where the defense will be recognized. But the BFOQ defense is usually unavailable where the discrimination is based on stereotypes (e.g., that women are less aggressive than men) or on the preferences of coworkers or customers (e.g., the preference of airline travelers for stewardesses rather than stewards).

**Procedures.** The very complicated procedures that must be followed in Title VII suits are beyond the scope of this text. A few points, however, should be kept in mind. Private parties with a Title VII claim have no automatic right to sue. Instead, they must first file a charge with the EEOC or (in states with suitable fair employment laws and enforcement schemes) a state agency. The point of this requirement is to allow the EEOC or the state agency to investigate the claim, attempt conciliation if the claim has substance, or sue the employer itself. If the plaintiff files with a state agency and the state fails to act, the plaintiff can still file a charge with the EEOC. Even if the EEOC fails to act on the claim, the plaintiff may still mount his or her own suit. In such situations, the EEOC will issue a "right to sue letter" enabling the plaintiff to file suit.

**Remedies.** A wide range of remedies are possible once a private plaintiff or the EEOC wins a Title VII suit. Where the discrimination has caused lost wages, employees can obtain back pay accruing from a date two years prior to the filing of the charge. A successful private plaintiff is also very likely to recover attorney's fees. However, the courts are divided on the plaintiff's right to recover consequential damages for such things as emotional distress or loss of credit, and punitive damage recoveries are unlikely. Title VII also gives courts broad powers to fashion equitable remedies tailored to the case. This can include awards of retroactive seniority. Orders compelling the hiring or reinstatement of the plaintiff are also common. Various "affirmative action" orders—for example, injunctions compelling the active recruitment of minorities—are possible. This may include orders compelling quotalike preferences in employment and promotion, a very important topic discussed in the next section.

## Teamsters v. United States

**431 U.S. 234 (U.S. Sup. Ct. 1977)**

The United States brought an action against T.I.M.E.-D.C., a nationwide trucking concern, and the International Brotherhood of Teamsters for violations of Title VII. The government alleged that in hiring line drivers (intercity, over-the-road drivers), T.I.M.E.-D.C. had engaged in a pattern or practice of discriminating against blacks and other racial minorities. The government also alleged that T.I.M.E.-D.C. had engaged in a pattern or practice of giving minority members less desirable jobs as servicemen and local city drivers and then discriminating against them regarding transfers and promotions.

Despite eventual improvements in T.I.M.E.-D.C.'s employment practices, the government further alleged that the seniority system established by T.I.M.E.-D.C. and the Teamsters was discriminatory because it perpetuated the effects of T.I.M.E.-D.C.'s past discrimination. The seniority system established seniority for bidding for particular jobs and for layoff purposes on the basis of length of service in the bargaining unit. This meant that a city driver or serviceman who transferred to a line driver position had to forfeit all of the competitive seniority earned in his previous bargaining unit and go to the bottom of the roster for the line driver unit. Since blacks and other minorities had long been denied access to line driver positions, the government argued, the seniority system tended to perpetuate prior discrimination by discouraging transfers to line driver positions. In other words, minority members were required to forfeit competitive seniority earned in another job in order to get a line driver position. Thus, they would not be able to catch up to white drivers who never suffered from discrimination and were thereby deterred from taking line driver positions.

The district court and the court of appeals found for the government on all points and also rejected the defendants' attempt to use Title VII's seniority defense. T.I.M.E.-D.C. and the Teamsters appealed to the U.S. Supreme Court.

**Stewart, Justice.** The government's theory of discrimination was that the company regularly and purposefully treated Negroes and Spanish-named Americans less favorably than white persons. The disparity in treatment allegedly involved the refusal to recruit, hire, transfer, or promote minority group members on an equal basis with white people, particularly with respect to line driving positions. The government carried its burden of proof. As of March 31, 1971, the company had 6,472 employees. Of these, 314 (5 percent) were Negroes and 257 (4 percent) were Spanish-surnamed Americans. Of the 1,828 line drivers, however, there were only 8 (0.4 percent) Negroes and 5 (0.3 percent) Spanish-surnamed persons, and all of the Negroes had been hired after the litigation had commenced. With one exception, the company did not employ a Negro on a regular basis as a line driver until 1969. A great majority of the Negroes (83 percent) and Spanish-surnamed Americans (78 percent) who did work for the company held the lower-paying city operations and serviceman jobs, whereas only 39 percent of the nonminority employees held jobs in those categories. The government bolstered its statistical evidence with the testimony of individuals who recounted over 40 specific instances of discrimination.

The company's response is that statistics can never in and of themselves prove a pattern or practice of discrimination. But this was not a case in which the government relied on statistics alone. The individuals who testified about their personal experiences with the company brought the cold numbers convincingly to life. In any event, statistical analyses have served and will continue to serve an important role in cases in which the existence of discrimination is disputed. We caution only that statistics are not irrefutable; they come in infinite variety and may be rebutted.

The District Court and the Court of Appeals also found that the seniority system violated Title VII. The union, while acknowledging that the seniority system may perpetuate the effects of prior discrimination, asserts that the system is immunized from illegality by reason of [Title VII's seniority defense]. Because the company discriminated both before and after the enactment of Title VII, the seniority system is said to have operated to perpetuate the effects of both pre- and post-Act discrimination. Post-Act discriminatees, however, may obtain full "make whole" relief, including retroactive seniority, without attacking the legality of the seniority system as applied to them.

What remains for review is the judgment that the seniority system unlawfully perpetuated the effects of *pre-Act* discrimination. Congress proscribed not only overt discrimination but also practices that are fair in form but discriminatory in operation. Thus, a Title VII violation may be established by policies or practices that are neutral on their face and in intent but that nonetheless discriminate in effect against a particular group. One practice fair in form but discriminatory in operation is that which perpetuates the effects of prior discrimination. The seniority system in this case would seem to fall under this rationale. The heart of the system is its allocation of the choicest jobs, the greatest protection against layoffs, and other advantages to employees who have been line drivers for the longest time. Where, because of the employer's intentional discrimination, the line drivers with the longest tenure are white, the advantages of the seniority system flow disproportionately to them and away from Negro and Spanish-surnamed employees.

But the legislative history of Title VII demonstrates that Congress considered this very effect of seniority systems and extended a measure of immunity to them. The unmistakable purpose of [the seniority defense] was to make clear that the routine application of a bona fide seniority system would not be unlawful under Title VII. This was the intended result even where the employer's pre-Act discrimination resulted in whites having greater existing seniority rights than Negroes. Although a seniority system inevitably tends to perpetuate the effects of pre-Act discrimination in such cases, the congressional judgment was that Title VII should not outlaw the use of existing seniority lists and thereby destroy or water down the vested seniority rights of employees simply because their employer had engaged in discrimination prior to the Act.

The seniority system in this case is entirely bona fide. It applies equally to all races and ethnic groups. To the extent that it "locks" employees into non-line driver jobs, it does so for all. The placing of line drivers in a separate bargaining unit is rational, in accord with industry practice, and consistent with NLRB precedents. The system did not have its genesis in racial discrimination, and it was negotiated and has been maintained free from any illegal purpose. The single fact that the system extends no retroactive seniority to pre-Act discriminatees does not make it unlawful.

Judgment for the government affirmed in part and reversed in part.

## Dothard v. Rawlinson

**433 U.S. 321 (U.S. Sup. Ct. 1977)**

Dianne Rawlinson, a rejected female applicant for employment as a corrections counselor (prison guard) in the Alabama prison system, challenged three state rules restricting the employment prospects of herself and similarly situated women. The requirements were: (1) that all prison employees weigh at least 120 pounds, (2) that all such employees be at least 5 feet 2 inches in height, and (3) "Regulation 204," which set out explicit sex-based assignment policies restricting the employment of female correctional counselors in "contact positions" in maximum-security prisons. Contact positions required close physical proximity to inmates, and the duties of a correctional counselor made this largely a contact position. Alabama had separate prisons for men and women. The inmate quarters in its (largely male) maximum-security prisons were mainly large dormitories. In these prisons, sex offenders were not kept separate from the other convicts.

After getting a right to sue letter from the EEOC, Rawlinson entered a class action in federal district court, alleging that the three rules violated Title VII. The three-judge district court found in her favor on all points. The state appealed to the U.S. Supreme Court.

**Stewart, Justice.** The gist of the claim that the height and weight requirements discriminate against women does not involve an assertion of purposeful discriminatory motive. It is asserted, rather, that these facially neutral qualification standards work in fact disproportionately to exclude women from eligibility for employment. To establish a prima facie case of discrimination, a plaintiff need only show that the facially neutral standards select applicants for hire in a significantly discriminatory pattern. Once it is thus shown that the employment standards are discriminatory in effect, the employer must show that any given requirement has a manifest relation to the employment in question. If the employer proves that the challenged requirements are job-related, the plaintiff may show that other selection devices without a similar discriminatory effect would also serve the employer's legitimate interests.

Although women 14 years or older comprise 52.75 percent of the Alabama population and 36.89 percent of its labor force, they hold only 12.9 percent of its correctional counselor positions. The District Court found that the 5′2″ requirement would exclude 33.29 percent of the women in the United States between the ages of 18–79, while excluding only 1.28 percent of men between the same ages. The 120-pound weight restriction would exclude 22.29 percent of the women and 2.35 percent of the men in this age group.

When the height and weight restrictions are combined, Alabama's statutory standards would exclude 41.13 percent of the female population while excluding less than 1 percent of the male population.

We turn to the state's argument that it rebutted the prima facie case of discrimination by showing that the height and weight requirements are job-related. These requirements, they say, are related to strength, a sufficient but unspecified amount of which is essential to effective performance as a correctional counselor. However, the state produced no evidence correlating the requirements with the requisite amount of strength thought essential to good job performance. If the job-related quality that the state identifies is bona fide, its purpose could be achieved by adopting and validating a test that measures strength directly. Such a test, fairly administered, would satisfy Title VII because it would measure the person for the job and not the person in the abstract.

Thus, Title VII prohibits application of the height and weight requirements. Unlike the height and weight requirements, Regulation 204 explicitly discriminates on the basis of sex. In defense of this overt discrimination, the state relies on [Title VII's BFOQ defense]. The BFOQ exception was meant to be an extremely narrow exception to the general prohibition of discrimination on the basis of sex. In the particular factual circumstances of this case, however, we conclude that the District Court erred in rejecting the BFOQ exception.

The environment in Alabama's penitentiaries is a peculiarly inhospitable one for human beings of whatever sex. Because of inadequate staff and facilities, no attempt is made to classify or segregate inmates according to their offense or level of dangerousness. Consequently, the estimated 20 percent of the male prisoners who are sex offenders are scattered throughout the penitentiaries' dormitory facilities. In this environment of violence and disorganization, it would be an oversimplification to characterize Regulation 204 as an exercise in romantic paternalism. In the usual case, the argument that a particular job is too dangerous for women may be met by the rejoinder that it is the purpose of Title VII to allow the individual woman to make that choice for herself. More is at stake in this case, however.

The essence of a correctional counselor's job is to maintain prison security. A woman's relative ability to maintain order in a male, maximum security, unclassified penitentiary of the type Alabama now runs could be directly reduced by her womanhood. There is a basis for expecting that sex offenders who have criminally assaulted women in the past would be moved to do so again if access to women were established within the prison. There would also be a real risk that other inmates, deprived of a normal heterosexual environment, would assault women guards because they are women. The likelihood that inmates would assault a woman because she was a woman would pose a real threat not only to the victim of the assault but also to the basic control of the penitentiary and protection of its inmates and other security personnel.

Judgment for Rawlinson affirmed in part and reversed in part.

---

**Section 1981.** One provision of the Civil Rights Act of 1866 (Section 1981)[14] states: "All persons . . . shall have the same right . . . to make and enforce contracts . . . as is enjoyed by white persons." As its language indicates, Section 1981 is basically limited to racial discrimination. However, it has been applied to discrimination against people of

[14] 42 U.S.C. § 1981 (1982).

certain racially characterized national origins (e.g., Hispanics), and some courts have applied the section to discrimination against aliens. Since the employment relation is contractual, Section 1981 applies to it. The courts have read the section as forbidding discrimination in a wide range of employment contexts. All sorts of private and public employers (except the federal government) are covered.

Section 1981's coverage is obviously narrower than the coverage of Title VII. Where Section 1981 does apply, though, it gives employees substantive protections similar to those offered by Title VII. Also, Title VII's methods of proving discrimination apply in the Section 1981 context, as do most of its defenses. In addition, successful Section 1981 plaintiffs can usually obtain the many forms of equitable relief allowed under Title VII. In light of all these similarities, why should a private plaintiff bother to use Section 1981? First, plaintiffs can avoid Title VII's complex procedural and timing requirements by doing so. Second, the range of allowable cash damages (including back wages, compensatory damages, attorney's fees, and punitive damages) is probably greater in a Section 1981 suit than in a Title VII suit. For these reasons, plaintiffs often join a Section 1981 claim to their Title VII claim in cases covered by both statutes.

**The Age Discrimination in Employment Act.** The Age Discrimination in Employment Act (ADEA), passed in 1967, is intended to prohibit arbitrary age discrimination in employment and to ensure that older employees are evaluated on the basis of ability rather than age. The act protects those who are at least 40 but less than 70 years of age. People within this age group are protected against age discrimination in favor of both *younger* and *older* individuals.

**Coverage.** The entities covered by the ADEA include individuals, partnerships, labor organizations (as to their employees), and corporations. Each of these entities must: (1) be engaged in an industry affecting interstate commerce and (2) employ at least 20 persons. In addition, the act applies to state and local governments.[15] Referrals by an employment agency to a covered employer are within the ADEA's scope regardless of the agency's size. Moreover, the ADEA covers labor union practices affecting *union members;* usually, unions with at least 25 members are subject to the act.

Like Title VII, the ADEA protects covered individuals against discrimination in a wide range of employment contexts, including hiring, firing, pay, job assignment, and fringe benefits. The act also states that covered entities cannot publish employment-related notices or advertisements indicating any preference, limitation, or discrimination based on age. An employer, for example, usually may not run help-wanted ads stating that it wants "teenagers" or "students" for a particular job.

**Proving Age Discrimination.** Proof of age discrimination is easy where the employer uses an explicit age classification. In other situations, the various methods of proving a Title VII case probably apply in the ADEA context as well. As the *Massarsky* case below illustrates, Title VII proof rules apply where the plaintiff alleges that the defendant has engaged in a specific, isolated act of discrimination. Relatively few courts have considered whether the other Title VII proof techniques are available in the ADEA context. In *Massarsky,* the court did not have to decide whether the plaintiff could prove a Title VII violation by demonstrating that a neutral rule had a disparate impact. But

[15] The federal government is expressly excluded from the ADEA's list of covered entities. However, another section of the act sets out age discrimination standards that apply to certain sectors of the federal government.

it is likely that most courts would allow the plaintiff to employ such techniques in an appropriate case.

**Defenses.** Even if the plaintiff proves age discrimination, the defendant will still prevail if it establishes one of the ADEA's defenses. The act allows an employer to discharge or otherwise penalize an individual for *good cause.* It also allows an employer to observe the terms of a *bona fide seniority system.* To be bona fide, the system must be established, communicated, and applied with regularity, consistency, and neutrality. However, a 1978 amendment to the ADEA states that the seniority defense cannot be used to require or permit the involuntary retirement of anyone aged 40 through 69. In addition, the ADEA sometimes permits employers to use age criteria in *bona fide employee benefit plans,* such as retirement, pension, and insurance programs. However, such plans cannot be used to justify either a refusal to hire or the involuntary retirement of a person within the ADEA's protected age group. But there is one exception to the above protections against involuntary retirement. The act permits the compulsory retirement of executives or high policymakers who have reached the age of 65, if they are entitled to retirement benefits totaling at least $44,000 per year. Finally, the ADEA has a *bona fide occupational qualification* defense that resembles Title VII's BFOQ defense.

**Procedural Requirements.** The complex procedural requirements for an ADEA suit are beyond the scope of this text. Like Title VII, the ADEA requires that a private plaintiff file a charge with the EEOC and with an appropriate state agency (if one exists) before she can sue in her own right. The EEOC may also sue to enforce the ADEA. Although such suits often result from a charge filed by a private party, this filing is not necessary for an EEOC action. However, the EEOC must attempt conciliation before it can sue. A suit by the EEOC precludes private suits arising from the same alleged violation. For both government and private suits, the statute of limitations is three years from the date of an alleged *willful* violation and two years from the date of an alleged *nonwillful* violation.

**Remedies.** Remedies available after a successful ADEA suit include unpaid back wages resulting from the discrimination; an additional award of "liquidated damages" equaling these unpaid back wages (if the employer acted willfully); attorney's fees; and equitable relief, including hiring, reinstatement, and promotion. Most courts do not allow punitive damages and recoveries for pain, suffering, mental distress, and so forth.

## Massarsky v. General Motors Corp.

**706 F.2d 211 (3d Cir. 1983)**

William Massarsky was hired by General Motors in 1963 at the age of 40. Due to a division-wide force reduction caused by economic conditions, he was laid off in 1971. The layoff was pursuant to a company policy stating that, where ability, merit, and capacity were equal, those with the least time of service in a particular job classification would be the first to be released. When GM released Massarsky, it retained Joseph Biondo, aged 25, an employee with over two years less service than Massarsky. Biondo was a student in the General Motors Institute (GMI), a five-year work-study program allowing its 2,350 tuition-paying students to earn a college degree in engineering or management while working for GM. GM had an unpublicized company policy exempting GMI students from layoffs.

Massarsky sued GM in federal district court, alleging that his dismissal violated the ADEA. Following a judgment for GM, he appealed.

**ROSENN, CIRCUIT JUDGE.** The Supreme Court has said little about the elements of a cause of action under the ADEA. However, many courts have adapted to issues of age discrimination the principles applicable to cases arising under Title VII. A Title VII plaintiff may prosecute his claim under either of two distinct legal theories. First, he may allege that he is the victim of intentional discrimination, i.e., that his employer applied an expressly race-based or sex-based standard in its treatment of him (the "disparate treatment" theory). Alternatively, he may rely upon the "disparate impact" theory. This theory applies when the employer's adverse action resulted simply from application of facially neutral criteria that are alleged to have a disproportionate impact on members of the protected class and which cannot be justified by business necessity.

A plaintiff alleging *disparate treatment* bears the burden of persuading the jury that his treatment was caused by intentional discrimination. Because it often will be difficult to obtain direct evidence of the employer's motive, the Supreme Court has articulated rules of proof that give the plaintiff a presumption operating in his favor. This prima facie case is easily made out: a plaintiff alleging a discriminatory layoff need only show that he is a member of the protected class and that he was laid off from a job for which he was qualified while others not in the protected class were treated more favorably. The employer then bears the burden to dispel the prima facie showing by articulating some legitimate, non-discriminatory reason for its treatment of the employee. The plaintiff must then prove that the asserted reason was merely a pretext for unlawful discrimination.

Massarsky established a prima facie case by showing that he was within the protected age class and was laid off from his job even though he was qualified for that position. It is also undisputed that a person considerably younger in age and with less seniority was retained. General Motors countered by asserting that Massarsky's layoff was pursuant to a company policy to lay off the employee with the least service, except that under that policy GMI students were immune from layoff. Massarsky claims that immunizing GMI students from layoff was not a legitimate justification for the company's action because the company thereby extended favorable treatment to a class composed of young employees. But any disproportionate effect of the company's policy is irrelevant to a claim of disparate treatment so long as the personnel action was not motivated by any discriminatory animus. Massarsky had to show that the company's policy, though age-neutral on its face, was a mere pretext for unlawful discrimination.

The company adopted guidelines for use in reductions in salaried work force. The guidelines refer to "special considerations," among which was the following: "GMI students should not be laid off. A division has considerable investment in these students which should be protected." The GMI Institute is considerably more than a mere in-plant training program. The company policy was in place prior to Massarsky's discharge and was not a coverup for intentional discrimination.

Of course, where an employer's policy or practice is discriminatory on its face, it is unnecessary for the plaintiff to make a separate showing of intent to discriminate. But here General Motors' policy is not facially discriminatory because it is not expressed in terms of age. The employees who were insulated from layoff received this favorable treatment on the basis of their status as GMI students, not their age. We simply cannot infer that the company was using student status as a proxy for age merely because the GMI student population contained primarily younger individuals.

Massarsky also characterizes this case as one involving the alleged *disparate impact* of a facially neutral rule. He contends that General Motors' policy of insulating GMI students from layoff during a reduction in force, in conjunction with the policy of laying off the employee with the least seniority, operated to the detriment of members of the protected age group. This court has never ruled on whether a plaintiff can establish a violation of the Act by showing disparate impact alone. But even assuming, without deciding, that the disparate impact theory does apply, Massarsky is not entitled to any relief.

To establish a prima facie case under the disparate impact model, the plaintiff must show that the facially neutral employment practice had a significantly discriminatory impact. If that showing is made, the employer must then demonstrate that any given requirement has a manifest relationship to the employment in question. Even in such a case, however, the plaintiff may prevail if he shows that the employer was using the practice as a mere pretext for discrimination.

To establish his prima facie case of discriminatory impact, the plaintiff must show that the employer's selection process results in unfavorable treatment of a disproportionate number of members of the protected group. Because the ADEA only prohibits discrimination against those between the ages of 40 and 70, Massarsky had to show a disproportionate effect on individuals in that age group. He did show that the challenged employment practices had a pernicious effect on him. But he offered no evidence to show that other similarly situated employees were likewise affected. An adverse effect on a single employee, or even a few employees, is not sufficient to establish disparate impact.

We recognize that the GMI students may generally have been younger than the employees who were laid off in their place. But the ADEA is only implicated when a policy has a differential impact on those between 40 and 70 years of age. Even if all laid off employees were older than the GMI students, the Act would not be violated unless those age 40 to 70 were disproportionately represented among the laid off employees.

Judgment for General Motors affirmed.

**Federal Contractors.** Employers holding federal contracts are generally subject to the employment discrimination laws just described. In addition, they must comply with certain rules specifically addressed to federal contractors. These requirements are widely applicable because most large and many smaller businesses deal regularly with the federal government.

**Executive Order 11246.** Executive Order 11246, issued in 1965 and later amended, forbids race, national origin, religion, and sex discrimination by certain federal contractors. Enforcement and administration of the order have been delegated to the Office of Federal Contract Compliance Programs (OFCCP) of the Labor Department. The order requires each federal agency to insert an "equal opportunity clause" in its private-sector contracts if they exceed $10,000. Among other things, this clause requires that the contractor not discriminate on the grounds mentioned above and that it undertake affirmative action to prevent such discrimination. The clause also requires that the contractor obey the very long and detailed regulations promulgated by the secretary of labor under Executive Order 11246.[16] These regulations include requirements for employer affirmative action plans. Violations of the order or its regulations give rise to a variety of possible sanctions and remedies. These include injunctions, administrative orders, and (in extreme cases) cancellation of the contract or the barring of an employer from future government work.

**The Handicapped.** Section 503 of the Vocational Rehabilitation Act of 1973[17] requires employers with federal contracts exceeding $2,500 to take affirmative action to employ and advance qualified handicapped individuals. To implement this statute, the Labor Department requires that all covered federal contracts include a clause obligating the employer to refrain from discrimination against qualified handicapped people, to take affirmative action to assist them, and to comply with all applicable regulations. The many obligations that the act and its regulations impose on covered federal contractors are mainly enforced by the OFCCP; most courts have held that there is no private right of action under Section 503.

The act's definition of a "handicapped individual" is very broad. It includes those who: (1) have a physical or mental impairment that substantially limits one or more major life activities, (2) have a record of such an impairment, or (3) are regarded as having such an impairment. (The last two categories prevent discrimination against those who have formerly been misdiagnosed or who have recovered from previous impairments.) The covered physical or mental impairments include diseases such as epilepsy, cancer, and heart disorders; conditions such as amputation, blindness, and deafness; and mental problems such as retardation, emotional disorders, and learning diabilities. Recall, however, that the act protects only *qualified* handicapped individuals. This should exclude individuals whose handicaps prevent them from performing important aspects of their jobs.

**Other Prohibitions.** The Vietnam Era Veterans Readjustment Assistance Act of 1974 requires firms having federal contracts of at least $10,000 to take affirmative action to hire and promote: (1) qualified disabled veterans and (2) qualified veterans of the Vietnam era. Also, age discrimination by certain federal contractors is prohibited by executive order.

**Other Federal Antidiscrimination Laws.** A number of federal statutes forbid race, color, national origin, sex, and religion discrimination by various recipients of federal funding. Also, the Age Discrimination Act of 1975 prohibits age discrimination under any program or activity receiving federal financial assistance. Section 504 of the Vocational Rehabilitation Act forbids discrimination against the handicapped in programs receiving federal financial assistance. Its definition of a handicapped person is the same as that discussed above.

In addition to violating many of the measures discussed in this section, discrimination by a union against its members can violate the NLRA's duty of fair representation and constitute an unfair labor practice. Finally, veterans returning from military service are entitled to reemployment with their previous employer and to the pay, seniority, and other benefits that they would have received had not service intervened. They are also pro-

[16] For some time, the OFCCP has been promising new guidelines governing its enforcement activities under Executive Order 11246, but these had not been issued as of early 1985. Apparently, the agency is proceeding under informal guidelines that differ somewhat from the regulations currently on the books.

[17] Also, Section 501 of the act requires federal agencies to prepare and implement affirmative action programs for the handicapped.

tected from discharge without good cause for one year after resuming employment.

**State Antidiscrimination Laws.** Most of the states have statutes that parallel Title VII and the ADEA. Many have laws protecting the handicapped. Some of these statutes provide more extensive protection than their federal counterparts. In addition, some states prohibit forms of discrimination not barred by federal law. Examples include discrimination on the bases of marital status, physical appearance, sexual preference, and political affiliation.

## EMPLOYMENT DISCRIMINATION—CURRENT PROBLEM AREAS

As the effort to ensure equal employment opportunity has proceeded, it has assumed more and more controversial forms. This section discusses three employment discrimination problems of considerable current interest—reverse discrimination, sexual harassment, and comparable worth. These topics are discussed separately because today they are much-disputed problem areas where the law is in a state of flux. Also, they often extend across several of the provisions examined in the preceding section on employment discrimination.

**Reverse Discrimination.** Over the past 15 to 20 years, few questions have provoked more vehement public debate than has so-called reverse discrimination: the practice of explicitly preferring racial minorities[18] over whites when allocating scarce social benefits such as employment. Arguments in favor of such practices range from the allegation that whites as a group owe minority groups "reparations" for generations of past discrimination, to the pragmatic contention that minority preferences help buy a degree of social peace. Perhaps the most convincing argument for reverse discrimination in employment goes roughly as follows. "Due to the effects of past discrimination, racial minorities will not fare as well as whites even if the criteria for hiring and promotion are perfectly colorblind. Thus, through no fault of their own, minorities will be underrepresented in the better jobs, and racial preferences are necessary to correct this. In addition, since the performance of future generations is affected by the socioeconomic status of their parents, the effects of past discrimination will continue unless minorities are hired and promoted on a preferred basis. If this is done, they will eventually be able to compete on an equal basis with whites, and reverse discrimination will no longer be necessary."

Whatever the validity of these arguments, reverse racial discrimination involves undeniable costs. It contradicts traditional American ideas of equal opportunity, and it victimizes relatively innocent whites. Also, it may sometimes mean that less-qualified individuals occupy jobs whose proper performance is important to the public.

The courts have generally upheld minority employment preferences. Such preferences often take the following form: minorities are hired or promoted at some specified rate until a specified degree of minority representation in the employer's work force is reached. For example, an employer might be required to hire one minority member for each white until the minority percentage of its work force equals the minority percentage of the local work force. Preferences of this sort usually have risen in three legal contexts: (1) as a court-ordered equitable remedy for widespread violations of Title VII or Section 1981, (2) as part of a consent decree implementing the settlement of a Title VII or Section 1981 suit, or (3) as the result of OFCCP affirmative

[18] Some reverse discrimination plans involve preferences for women, but these plans are much less common than the minority preferences discussed here.

action requirements for federal contractors. The lower federal courts have repeatedly upheld each of these preferences against both constitutional and statutory attacks.[19] Sometimes, however, courts will say that minority preferences are permissible only where there has been severe long-term discrimination, that they cannot unduly restrict the employment opportunities of whites, that they can only be temporary, and that they cannot involve the hiring or promotion of unqualified workers.

Also, in the *Weber* case below the Supreme Court held that "voluntary" reverse racial discrimination by a private employer and a union did not violate Title VII. A bigger problem occurs when minority employment preferences collide with Title VII's strong protection of bona fide seniority systems. The *Stotts* case below illustrates one way in which this problem can arise. Some observers have argued that *Stotts* signals the eventual end of minority employment preferences; others see it as a decision that merely seeks to defend bona fide seniority systems.

[19] However, the *Stotts* case below may change this pattern. Also, the OFCCP's authority to impose minority preferences may soon be removed, and its willingness to do so is now doubtful in any event. On the constitutional treatment of reverse discrimination, finally, see Chapter 42.

## United Steelworkers v. Weber

**443 U.S. 193 (U.S. Sup. Ct. 1979)**

Under pressure from the OFCCP and fearing suits by minority members, the Kaiser Aluminum and Chemical Corporation reached a collective bargaining agreement with the United Steelworkers of America that created a new on-the-job craft training program at Kaiser's Gramercy, Louisiana, plant. The selection of trainees for the program was based on seniority, but at least 50 percent of the new trainees had to be black until the percentage of black skilled craft workers in the plant approximated the percentage of blacks in the local labor force.

Brian Weber was a rejected white applicant for the program who would have qualified had the racial preference not existed. He sued in federal district court, arguing that the program violated Title VII's ban on racial discrimination in employment. His suit was successful, and the court of appeals affirmed the district court. Kaiser and the union appealed to the U.S. Supreme Court.

**Brennan, Justice.** We emphasize the narrowness of our inquiry. Since the Kaiser-USWA plan does not involve state action, the case does not present an alleged violation of the Equal Protection Clause of the Constitution. Further, since the plan was adopted voluntarily, we are not concerned with what a court might order to remedy a past proven violation of Title VII. The only question before us is the narrow statutory issue whether Title VII *forbids* private employers and unions from voluntarily agreeing upon bona fide affirmative action plans that accord racial preferences in the manner and for the purpose provided in the Kaiser-USWA plan. That question was expressly left open in *McDonald v. Santa Fe Trail Transportation Co.* (1976), which held that Title VII protects whites as well as blacks from certain forms of racial discrimination.

Weber argues that Congress intended in Title VII to prohibit all race-conscious affirmative action plans. His argument rests upon a literal interpretation of sections 703(a) and (d) of the Act. Those sections make it unlawful to "discriminate . . . because of . . . race" in hiring and in the selection of apprentices for training programs. Since, the argument runs, Title VII forbids discrimination against whites as well as blacks, and since the plan operates to discriminate against white employees solely because they are white, the plan violates Title VII.

Weber's argument is not without force. But it overlooks the fact that the Kaiser-USWA plan is voluntarily adopted by private parties to eliminate traditional patterns of racial segregation. In this context, Weber's reliance upon a literal construction of sections 703(a) and (d) is misplaced. It is a familiar rule that a thing may be within the letter of the statute and yet not within the statute, because not within its spirit, nor within the intention of its makers. The prohibition against racial discrimination in Title VII must therefore be read against the background of the legislative history of Title VII and the historical context from which the Act arose. Examination of those sources makes clear that an interpretation of the sections that forbade all race-conscious affirmative action would bring about an end completely at variance with the purpose of the statute and must be rejected.

Congress's primary concern in enacting the prohibition against racial discrimination in Title VII was the plight of the Negro in our economy. Before 1964, blacks were largely relegated to unskilled and semi-skilled jobs. Because of automation the number of such jobs was rapidly decreasing. As a consequence, the relative position of the Negro was steadily worsening. Congress feared that the goal of the Civil Rights Act—the integration of blacks into American society—could not be achieved unless this trend were reversed. Accordingly, it was clear to Congress that the crux of the problem was to open employment opportunities for Negroes in occupations traditionally closed to them. It was to this problem that Title VII's prohibition against racial discrimination in employment was primarily addressed.

Given this legislative history, we cannot agree with Weber that Congress intended to prohibit the private sector from taking effective steps to accomplish the goal that Congress intended Title VII to achieve. It would be ironic indeed if a law triggered by a nation's concern over centuries of racial injustice and intended to improve the lot of those who had been excluded from the American dream for so long constituted the first legislative prohibition of all voluntary, private, race-conscious efforts to abolish traditional patterns of racial segregation and hierarchy.

We need not define in detail the line between permissible and impermissible affirmative action plans. It suffices to hold that the Kaiser-USWA plan falls on the permissible side of the line. The purposes of the plan mirror those of the statute. Both were designed to break down old patterns of racial segregation and hierarchy. The plan does not unnecessarily trammel the interests of the white employees [or] require the discharge of white workers and their replacement with new black hires. Nor does the plan create an absolute bar to the advancement of white employees; half of those trained in the program will be white. Moreover, the plan is a temporary measure; it is not intended to maintain racial balance, but simply to eliminate a manifest racial imbalance. Preferential selection of craft trainees will end as soon as the percentage of black skilled craft workers approximates the percentage of blacks in the local labor force.

Judgment reversed in favor of Kaiser and the union.

## Firefighters Local Union v. Stotts

**104 S. Ct. 2576 (U.S. Sup. Ct. 1984)**

In 1977, Carl Stotts, a black captain in the Memphis fire department, entered a class action suit in federal district court under Title VII and Section 1981. He alleged that the department and certain city officials were engaged in a pattern or practice of racial discrimination in hiring and promotion decisions. In 1980, the case was settled through a consent decree approved by the district court. The long-term goal of the consent decree was to increase minority representation in each fire department job classification to approximately the proportion of blacks in the local labor force. To achieve this end, the decree established an interim hiring goal of filling 50 percent of the department's annual job vacancies with qualified black applicants. The decree also stated that the department had to attempt to ensure that 20 percent of the promotions in each job classification be given to blacks. However, despite the presence of a bona fide seniority system in the fire department, the decree said nothing about awarding competitive seniority to blacks. Nor did it contain provisions dealing with layoffs or reductions in rank. The district court retained jurisdiction over the case for such further orders as might be necessary to effectuate the purposes of the decree.

In early May 1981, the city of Memphis announced that projected budget deficits required a reduction in nonessential government personnel, including firefighters. Layoffs were to be based on seniority, with the "last hired" being the "first fired." If implemented, the layoffs would have defeated the purposes to be served by the consent decree, since recently hired blacks would be the first discharged.

On May 4, 1981, Stotts requested that the district court enter an injunction prohibiting the city's discharge plan from interfering with the consent decree covering the fire department. At this point, his request was opposed by the local firefighters' union, which previously had not been a party to the case. On May 18, the court entered an injunction ordering the city not to apply its seniority-based layoff plan insofar as it would reduce the black percentage in certain fire department job classifications. To comply with the injunction, the city had to lay off white firefighters with more seniority than that of blacks who were retained. On appeal, the court of appeals upheld the injunction, and the city and the union then appealed to the U.S. Supreme Court.

**WHITE, JUSTICE.** The injunction does not enforce the agreement of the parties as reflected in the consent decree. If the injunction is to stand, it must be justified on some other basis. The Court of Appeals held that the injunction was still properly entered because the District Court had inherent authority to modify the decree when an economic crisis unexpectedly required layoffs which would undermine the affirmative action outlined in the decree. This was true, the court held, even though the modification conflicted with a bona fide seniority system adopted by the city. The Court of Appeals erred in reaching this conclusion.

Section 703(h) of Title VII provides that it is not an unlawful employment practice to apply different terms, conditions, or privileges of employment pursuant to a bona fide seniority system, provided that such differences are not the result of an intention to discriminate because of race. It is clear that the city had a seniority system, that its proposed layoff plan conformed to that system, and that in making the settlement the city had not agreed to award competitive seniority to any minority member whom the city later proposed to lay off. The District Court held that the city could not follow its seniority system in making its proposed layoffs because its proposal was discriminatory in effect. Section 703(h), however, permits the routine application of a seniority system absent proof of an intention to discriminate. Here, the layoff proposal was not adopted with the purpose or intent to discriminate on the basis of race.

[One argument] in support of the injunction was that it would be incongruous to hold that use of the preferred means of resolving an employment discrimination action [a consent decree] decreases the power of a court to order relief which vindicates the policies embodied within Title VII and section 1981. The Court of Appeals concluded that if the allegations in Stotts's original complaint had been proven, the District Court could have entered an order overriding the seniority provisions. Therefore, the court reasoned, the trial court has the authority to override the seniority provisions to effectuate the purpose of the 1980 decree.

This approach overstates the authority of the trial court to disregard a seniority system in fashioning a remedy after an employer has followed a pattern or practice having a discriminatory effect on black applicants or employees. If individual members of a plaintiff class demonstrate that they have been actual victims of the discriminatory practice, they may be given their rightful place on the seniority roster. However, mere membership in the disadvantaged class is insufficient to warrant a seniority award; each individual must prove that the discriminatory practice had an impact on him. Here, there was no finding that any of the blacks protected from layoff had been a victim of discrimination and no award of competitive seniority to any of them. Therefore, the Court of Appeals imposed on the parties as an adjunct of settlement something that could not have been ordered had the case gone to trial and the plaintiffs proved that a pattern or practice of discrimination existed.

Our ruling that a court can award competitive seniority only when the beneficiary has actually been a victim of illegal discrimination is consistent with the policy behind the remedies available in Title VII litigation. That policy, which is to provide make-whole relief only to those who have been actual victims of illegal discrimination, was repeatedly expressed by the sponsors of the Act during the congressional debates. Opponents of Title VII charged that if the bill were enacted, employers could be ordered to hire and promote persons in order to achieve a racially-balanced work force even though those persons had not been victims of illegal discrimination. Responding to these charges, Senator Humphrey explained the limits on a court's remedial powers as follows:

> No court order can require hiring, reinstatement, admission to membership, or back pay for anyone who was not fired, refused employment or advancement or admission to a union by an act of discrimination forbidden by this title. Contrary to the allegations of some opponents of this title, there is nothing in it that will give any power to any court to require firing of employees in order to meet a racial quota or to achieve a certain racial balance. That bugaboo has been brought up a dozen times, but it is nonexistent.

Similar assurances were provided by supporters of the bill throughout the legislative process.

Judgment reversed in favor of the city and the union.

**Sexual Harassment.** Sexual harassment, which became a recognized basis of Title VII recovery by the mid-to-late 1970s, is not nearly so controversial as the other two topics discussed in this section. But it is a developing area of the law whose coverage and details are still unclear, and it may come to have a significant effect on life in the workplace. Although not followed by all courts, the EEOC's 1980 Sexual Harassment Guidelines[20] help organize the law in this area. The guidelines first describe the kinds of behavior that may constitute sexual harassment: "unwelcome sexual advances, requests for sexual favors, and other verbal or physical conduct of a sexual nature." Then, the guidelines state that such conduct will violate Title VII when: (1) submission to it is explicitly or implicitly made a term or condition of employment; (2) an individual's submission to it or rejection of it is used as the basis for employment decisions affecting that individual; or (3) it has the purpose or effect of unreasonably interfering with an individual's work performance or of creating an intimidating, hostile, or offensive working environment.

The first two situations covered by the guidelines are closely related, and the *Henson* case below seems to blend them together. They generally involve some linkage between the employee's submission to sexually oriented behavior (or her refusal to submit) and decisions affecting her employment (whether favorable or unfavorable). This linkage usually must be present for the employee to recover under Title VII. Where an employee rejects a superior's advances without suffering any job-related disadvantages, for example, she may be unable to recover.

As the *Henson* case illustrates, however, no linkage between sexual conduct and employment decisions is needed in the third situation covered by the EEOC guidelines. Here, the EEOC and many courts take the position that some kinds of continued, pervasive sexually offensive behavior have such an effect on work performance or work enjoyment that they violate Title VII without anything more. The full range of activities covered by this kind of sexual harassment is unclear. Clearly, however, Title VII is violated where a female employee is subjected to a barrage of sex-related touchings, inquiries, comments, jokes, and abuse from her male co-employees. But the plaintiff may have trouble recovering if she instigated or contributed to the behavior in question.

Determining when the employer should be liable for employee sexual harassment is a significant problem. The EEOC guidelines make the employer *strictly* liable for the acts of its *supervisory* employees. This means that the employer will be liable where it had no actual knowledge or reason to know of its employees' behavior, or even where it expressly forbade sexual harassment by its employees. However, the employer will be liable for the acts of *nonsupervisory* employees only when it or its supervisory employees *knew or should have known* of those acts. Even if these tests are met, moreover, the employer will escape liability for the acts of *nonsupervisory* employees if it took immediate and appropriate corrective action to stop their behavior. The *Henson* case adopts the EEOC standard for certain kinds of sexual harassment, but not for others. Some other courts, however, are more lenient toward the employer.

Although virtually all sexual harassment cases involve female victims, a male can sue for sexual harassment in an appropriate case. The legal status of homosexually oriented sexual harassment is unclear. It resembles the behavior just discussed in many respects, but it does not involve *gender* discrimination. Another unresolved question is whether an em-

[20] 29 C.F.R. § 1604.11. The principles stated in the EEOC guidelines also apply to race, color, religious, and national origin discrimination.

ployee can sue the employer because *another* employee has gained an unfair advantage by freely giving sexual favors or submitting to sexual harassment.

## Henson v. City of Dundee

**682 F.2d 897 (11th Cir. 1982)**

Barbara Henson worked as a dispatcher in the Dundee, Florida, police department. According to Henson, Police Chief John Sellgren subjected her to numerous demeaning sexual inquiries and vulgarities during the time of her employment. In addition, she insisted, Sellgren repeatedly requested that she have sexual relations with him. Because she refused to do so, Henson continued, Sellgren prevented her from attending the local police academy. Henson eventually resigned after Sellgren suspended her for two days for violating a minor office policy that had not been enforced previously. Henson claimed that her resignation was involuntary, because she interpreted the suspension as a warning that she would be fired if she did not accede to Sellgren's sexual requests.

Henson sued the city of Dundee under Title VII in federal district court. The district judge dismissed her claim after she presented her evidence. Henson appealed.

**VANCE, CIRCUIT JUDGE.** *Sexual Harassment and Work Environment.* Henson contends that a plaintiff states a claim under Title VII by alleging that sexual harassment perpetrated or condoned by an employer has created a hostile or offensive work environment. She argues that the trial court erred by holding that a Title VII plaintiff must allege in addition some tangible job detriment as a result of working in such an environment. We agree that the creation of an offensive or hostile work environment due to sexual harassment can violate Title VII irrespective of tangible job detriment. Surely, a requirement that a man or woman run a gauntlet of sexual abuse in return for being allowed to work and make a living inflicts disparate treatment upon a member of one sex.

Of course, neither the courts nor the EEOC have suggested that every instance of such sexual harassment gives rise to a Title VII claim. To constitute harassment, the conduct must be unwelcome in the sense that the employee did not solicit or incite it, and in the sense that the employee regarded the conduct as undesirable or offensive. It must also be sufficiently pervasive to alter the conditions of employment and create an abusive working environment. Whether sexual harassment is sufficiently severe and persistent to seriously affect psychological well-being is determined with regard to the totality of the circumstances.

Where, as here, the plaintiff seeks to hold the employer responsible for the hostile environment created by the plaintiff's supervisor or co-worker, she must show that the employer knew or should have known of the harassment, and failed to take prompt remedial action. The employee can demonstrate that the employer knew of the harassment by showing that she complained to higher management, or by showing the pervasiveness of the harassment, which gives rise to the inference of knowledge or constructive knowledge.

In this case, Henson has made a prima facie showing of all elements necessary to establish a violation of Title VII. Dismissal of her claim was therefore erroneous.

*Constructive Discharge.* When an employee involuntarily resigns in order to escape intolerable and illegal employment requirements to which he or she is subjected because of race, color, religion, sex, or national origin, the employer has committed a constructive discharge in violation of Title VII. In this case, the judge disbelieved Henson's testimony that she resigned from the department because of sexual harassment, finding instead that she resigned because the man with whom she had been having an affair was forced to resign from the department. We cannot say that the finding of the district judge was clearly erroneous.

*Permission to Attend the Police Academy.* An employer may not require sexual consideration from an employee as a *quid pro quo* for job benefits. The acceptance or rejection of the harassment must be an express or implied condition to the receipt of a job benefit or the cause of a tangible job detriment in order to create liability under this theory of sexual harassment.

An employer is strictly liable for actions of its supervisors that amount to sexual harassment resulting in tangible job detriment to the subordinate employee. This holding requires differing treatment of *respondeat superior* claims in the two types of sexual harassment cases. In the classic *quid quo pro* case an employer is strictly liable for the conduct of its supervisors, while in the work environment case the plaintiff must prove that higher management knew or should have known of the sexual harassment. When a supervisor gratuitously insults an employee, he generally does so for his own reasons and by his own means. He thus acts outside the actual or apparent scope of the authority he possesses as a supervisor. His conduct cannot automatically be imputed to the employer. The typical case of *quid pro quo* harassment is fundamentally different. In such a case, the supervisor relies upon his apparent or actual authority to extort sexual consideration from the employee. Therein lies the *quid pro quo.* He acts within the scope of his actual or apparent authority to hire, fire, discipline, or promote. His conduct can fairly be imputed to the source of his authority.

In this case, Henson has alleged all the elements of a *quid pro quo* sexual harassment claim.

Judgment reversed in favor of Henson.

---

**Comparable Worth.** The topics discussed in this chapter are a series of exceptions to the laissez-faire, contract-based model of the employment relation that was dominant in the 19th century. None of them, however, depart from this model so radically as the new and highly controversial doctrine known as **comparable worth.** In general, this doctrine asserts that the compensation received for a particular job should reflect its inherent worth and that those holding jobs whose worth is comparable should get equal (or comparable) pay. The usual criterion for determining "worth" is the job's value to the organization (or to society), and *not* the value set by the market.

**The Argument for Comparable Worth.** Comparable worth is almost always regarded as a sex discrimination issue. Advocates of comparable worth argue that certain jobs largely held by women (e.g., secretarial and nursing positions) are systematically underpaid relative to their true worth, and should get the compensation given jobs of comparable real worth. These advocates usually begin their case by noting the continuing gap between the average wages paid male and female workers. Much of this difference, they maintain, is due to the clustering of women in certain jobs. This job segregation, in turn, reflects a long prior history of sex discrimination and gender stereotyping that has affected the attitudes of employers and of women themselves. These same factors, comparable worth advocates continue, explain why the jobs into which women are clustered suffer from low pay. Because of their stereotyped attitudes about women, employers consciously and unconsciously discriminate with respect to pay. Also, the lower expectations that many women bring to the working world lead them to accept this unequal treatment. Worse yet, pay disparities are exacerbated as the large numbers of women now seeking work concentrate on "female" jobs and thus drive down wages in these occupations. To correct this pattern of inequality, say proponents of comparable worth, such occupations should receive the same compensation as do other jobs of comparable worth.

How is the intrinsic social or organizational "worth" of different jobs to be determined? The usual method is to give different jobs point ratings in several variables resembling the Equal Pay Act criteria, add the ratings together to achieve a total point rating, and then compare the totals. Various jobs, for example, might be given a numerical score reflecting the skill, responsibility, effort, and working conditions that they involve. The total number of points received would indicate the worth of the position, thus providing a basis for determining which positions are underpaid.

**The Legal Status of Comparable Worth.** The legal status of the comparable worth idea is now quite uncertain. Comparable worth suits cannot be brought under the Equal Pay Act because the EPA covers only situations involving unequal pay for *equal* work. When the Supreme Court decided *County of Washington v. Gunther*[21] in 1981, however, it opened the door to possible comparable worth suits under Title VII. In that case, the Court held that only the EPA's *defenses,* and not its "equal work" limitation, apply to Title VII sex discrimination cases involving unequal pay. However, the Court emphasized that it was not deciding whether Title VII embraces comparable worth claims. As of early 1985, the few courts considering whether a comparable worth claim can be brought under Title VII were divided.

The comparable worth idea has probably had greater success in the state legislatures. As of late 1984, perhaps 15 states had adopted legislation requiring some kind of pay equity for jobs of "comparable character" or "comparable value." Almost all such statutes, however, have limited coverage and have been narrowly interpreted by the courts. Recently, many states have been considering broader and more stringent comparable worth provisions. Most of this proposed legislation is limited to public employers, but a few such measures cover private employers as well.

**Criticisms of Comparable Worth.** The comparable worth idea has attracted a number of criticisms. Some wonder whether the pay disparities it attacks can be attributed to "discrimination" without unduly stretching the word's meaning. Real employer discrimination, they add, is already forbidden by Title VII, the EPA, and many other laws. Others argue that, despite their appearance of scientific objectivity, quantitative "worth" ratings actually depend on subjective judgments. Who (if anyone) should be allowed to make such judgments? In fact, the critics continue, these decisions will probably be made

[21] 452 U.S. 161 (1981).

by unaccountable groups such as judges, bureaucrats, and management consulting firms, and not by groups directly responsive to the general public. This means that the power to upset established pay scales and make widespread wealth transfers will be exercised by relatively isolated elites. Even if all of these problems did not exist, the critics conclude, quantitative worth ratings would still fail to achieve their objectives, because they only measure "inputs" such as skill or effort, and not the job's actual contribution to the organization or to society.

Since it is plainly intended to replace the market as a means for determining pay scales, comparable worth has also attracted criticisms of an economic nature. Critics argue that its widespread implementation might make U.S. industry less competitive, promote the further exportation of jobs to other countries, and create labor shortages in certain occupations. They also contend that any full-blown comparable worth system would produce a nightmare of litigation whose main beneficiary would be the legal profession.

Finally, comparable worth would probably have mixed effects for women in general. For example, it would probably penalize both professional women and married women who do not work. While it would benefit women in traditionally "female" jobs, it would also reduce their incentive to leave such jobs.

## THE EROSION OF EMPLOYMENT AT WILL

The traditional **employment at will** doctrine, which allows either party to an employment contract for an indefinite term to terminate for any reason, has been eroded by many of the developments described in this chapter. For example, the NLRA forbids dismissal for union affiliation (and labor contracts typically bar termination without just cause), Title VII prohibits terminations based on certain personal traits, and the ADEA blocks firings on the basis of age. Over the past 10–15 years, courts have been carving out further exceptions to the doctrine. These exceptions can be grouped into three categories: (1) cases where the employee's dismissal contravenes public policy, (2) cases where the dismissal violates an implied contract term of good faith and fair dealing, and (3) cases where the dismissal contradicts express employer statements regarding termination policy. In states recognizing one or more of these exceptions, a terminated employee may be able to mount a suit for **unjust dismissal** or **wrongful discharge.**

By the early 1980s, at least half of the states recognized some exception to the employment at will doctrine. A few states have flatly refused to do so, but overall the number of states making exceptions has been steadily growing. However, as the cases below suggest, these courts often do not agree on the exceptions to be recognized, and sometimes treat similar fact situations under different exceptions. Also, as these cases make clear, such courts remain sensitive to a purpose traditionally served by employment at will: preserving employer flexibility to meet changing business conditions by eliminating superfluous employees.

**The Exceptions.** The *public policy* exception to the employment at will doctrine is the most common basis for a wrongful discharge suit. In such cases, the terminated employee argues that the discharge was wrongful because it violated public policy. To give the exception some precision and limit judicial discretion, many cases restrict "public policy" to the policies advanced by existing law. In these states, the ex-employee must show that he was fired for acts, or refusals to act, which are in harmony with the purposes behind state or federal statutes, constitutional provisions, or (perhaps) administrative regulations and common law rules. Examples include firings based on the employee's performing jury duty, filing a workers' compensation claim, refusing to participate in illegal price-fixing, refusing to commit perjury at a state hearing, "whistle blowing,"[22] refusing to date a foreman, insisting that the employer comply with state law, and refusing to take a polygraph test where such tests are forbidden by state law. Situations where the public policy exception was *not* recognized include discharges caused by objections to the marketing of an allegedly defective product and by a refusal to work on drug research that was felt to be medically unethical. Although the *Brockmeyer* case below disagrees, most courts recognizing the public policy exception regard the employee's claim as a tort action.

The employee's suit for breach of the *implied covenant of good faith and fair dealing* is a contract claim. Here, the employee argues that her discharge was unlawful because it was not made in good faith and thus violated this implied contract term. Relatively few courts have recognized this exception, and its scope is unclear. But, because it is so broadly worded, it can probably be used in many of the situations covered by the public policy exception.

The final exception to the employment at will doctrine involves situations where the employer's *failure to live up to its own express statements* is treated as a breach of the employment contract. In the few cases recognizing this exception, the employer's statements usually involved the reasons for which it would fire employees or the procedures that it would follow before doing so. Typically, such statements are made orally during hiring or employee orientation, or are written in company employee manuals and handbooks. This exception was rejected on the special facts of the *Gates* case below, but the court held that the obligation to follow the company handbook was part of the employer's *implied* duty of good faith and fair dealing.

**Remedies.** The question of remedies in a successful wrongful discharge suit has not been clearly resolved. The relief obtained will often depend on whether the plaintiff's suit is characterized as a contract action or as a tort action. Awards of lost back pay and (where appropriate) reinstatement should be available in either case. However, there may be a setoff for wages that were earned, or reasonably could have been earned in comparable employment, during the period after dismissal. Recoveries for mental pain and suffering and for punitive damages are most likely in tort cases.

**Other Theories.** Plaintiffs suing for wrongful discharge may also be able to employ some of the theories discussed earlier in this chapter. A wrongful discharge action, for example, might be coupled with a Title VII or ADEA claim. A discharged employee may be able to make other claims as well. Intentional infliction of emotional distress might be available where the employer's behavior was outrageous and the plaintiff suffered severe emotional distress. Fraud is a possibility where the employer has misrepresented its policies or the employee's prospects for continued employment. Derogatory statements about the employee could make the employer liable for defamation or invasion of privacy if communicated to third parties. (In defamation cases, however, truth is a defense and the employer may be able to assert a privilege.) Finally, job performance evaluations that fail to inform the employee that termination is possible unless performance improves may subject the employer to negligence liability.[23]

[22] "Whistle blowers" are employees who publicly disclose dangerous, illegal, or improper employer behavior. As of late 1984, five states had passed statutes protecting the employment rights of certain whistle blowers.

[23] *Chamberlin v. Bissel, Inc.*, 547 F. Supp. 1067 (W.D. Mich. 1982).

## Brockmeyer v. Dun & Bradstreet

**335 N.W.2d 834 (Wis. Sup. Ct. 1983)**

Charles Brockmeyer was Wisconsin district manager for Dun & Bradstreet's credit services division. His contract of employment was for an indefinite term. Despite good overall sales ability and income production, Brockmeyer's behavior while district manager was a continual source of concern to his superiors. In early 1980, Brockmeyer got into trouble for vacationing in Montana with his secretary when he was supposed to be working. At this time, Brockmeyer's superiors also learned that he had smoked marijuana in the presence of company personnel. After being called to a meeting with his supervisors, Brockmeyer admitted his various misdeeds, apologized, and promised to behave in the future. At the end of the meeting, he was told that he would be fired or reassigned if his conduct did not improve. It was also suggested to Brockmeyer that either he or his secretary find a job in another division of Dun & Bradstreet. After Brockmeyer was unable to find another position for the secretary, he was told to obtain her resignation, which he did.

Shortly thereafter, the secretary sued Dun & Bradstreet for sex discrimination. Brockmeyer was asked to submit a written report about the events leading to the secretary's resignation, but he refused, fearing that he would be made the scapegoat for the whole matter. He also indicated that, if called to testify, he would tell the truth about the situation. On May 27, 1980, Dun & Bradstreet settled the case with the secretary for $12,000. Three days later, Brockmeyer was fired.

Brockmeyer then sued Dun & Bradstreet for wrongful discharge. He was successful at the trial court level, but an appellate court reversed. Brockmeyer then appealed to the Wisconsin supreme court.

**Steinmetz, Justice.** Under English common law, an employment contract for an indefinite period was presumed to extend for one year unless there was reasonable cause to discharge. Early American courts followed this approach. In the late nineteenth century, apparently influenced by the laissez-faire climate of the industrial revolution, the American courts rejected the English rule and developed their own common law rule, the employment at will doctrine. The doctrine recognized that where an employment was for an indefinite term, an employer may discharge an employee for good cause, for no cause, or even for cause morally wrong, without thereby being guilty of legal wrong.

By the turn of the twentieth century, the at will doctrine was absolute. However, since the New Deal, government regulation in the workplace has increased dramatically as Congress and the state legislatures recognized the need to curb harsh applications and abuse of the rule. Statutory modification of the at will doctrine can be found in a variety of federal and state laws prohibiting certain forms of discrimination. Consistent with the philosophy of the statutory modifications, many state courts have recognized the need to protect workers who are wrongfully discharged under circumstances not covered by any legislation or whose job security is not safeguarded by a collective bargaining agreement or civil service regulations. The courts have accomplished this objective by modifying the at will doctrine. The courts have recognized both contract and tort actions under assorted legal theories. Two theories are often utilized by the courts.

The first, and the more expansive, of the two theories is an implied duty to terminate an employee only in good faith. We refuse to impose a duty to terminate in good faith into employment contracts. To do so would subject each discharge to judicial incursions into the amorphous concept of bad faith. Moreover, we feel it unnecessary and unwarranted for the courts to become arbiters of any termination that may have a tinge of bad faith attached. Imposing a good faith duty to terminate would unduly restrict an employer's discretion in managing the work force.

The second, and more popular, of the theories is the public policy exception. This theory allows the discharged employee to recover if the termination violates a well-established and important public policy. We have concluded that a narrow public policy exception should be adopted in Wisconsin. Accordingly, we hold that an employee has a cause of action for wrongful discharge when the discharge is contrary to a fundamental and well-defined public policy evidenced by existing law. The public policy must be evidenced by a constitutional or statutory provision. An employee cannot be fired for refusing to violate the constitution or a statute. Courts should proceed cautiously when making public policy determinations. No employer should be subject to suit merely because a discharged employee's conduct was praiseworthy or the public may have derived some benefit from it.

We believe that a narrowly circumscribed public policy exception properly balances the interests of employees, employers, and the public. Employee job security interests are safeguarded against employer actions that undermine fundamental policy preferences. Employers retain sufficient flexibility to make needed personnel decisions to adapt to changing economic conditions. Society also benefits from our holding in a number of ways. A more stable job market is achieved. Well-established public policies are advanced. Finally, the public is protected against frivolous lawsuits since courts will be able to screen cases where the discharged employee cannot allege a clear expression of public policy.

Whether the cause of action for wrongful discharge should be maintained in tort or contract or both needs to be resolved. Cases implying a contractual term of good faith dealing sound in contract. Most of the public policy exception cases are tort actions. The most significant distinction between the two causes of action is in the damages that may be recovered. In tort actions, the only limitations are those of proximate cause or public policy considerations. In contract actions, damages are limited by the concepts of foreseeability and mitigation. We believe that reinstatement and backpay are the most appropriate remedies for public policy exception wrongful discharges since the primary concern in these actions is to make the wronged employee whole. Therefore, we conclude that a contract action is most appropriate for wrongful discharges. This contract action is predicated on the breach of an implied provision that an employer will not discharge an employee for refusing to perform an act that violates a clear mandate of public policy.

Brockmeyer contends that Dun & Bradstreet's actions violated public policy as expressed in section 134.01 and section 134.03 of the Wisconsin Statutes. Section 134.01 prohibits willfully and maliciously injuring another in his reputation, trade, business, or profession. Section 134.03 prohibits the use of threats, intimidation, force, or coercion to keep a person from working. There is no evidence that Dun & Bradstreet engaged in any behavior of this sort. To hold that under the facts of this case Dun & Bradstreet violated the policies expressed in these sections would completely abolish the at will doctrine. While Dun & Bradstreet's discharge of Brockmeyer may have constituted bad faith, its actions did not contravene the policies of sections 134.01 and 134.03.

Brockmeyer next contends that he was asked to commit perjury in violation of section 946.31(1). The record is devoid of any evidence demonstrating that Dun & Bradstreet asked Brockmeyer to lie. Admittedly, an inference can be drawn that Dun & Bradstreet was concerned that Brockmeyer would tell the truth if asked to testify at proceedings concerning his former secretary's sex discrimination claim. This inference is a far cry from the allegation that Dun & Bradstreet wanted Brockmeyer to commit perjury. There is no clearly defined mandate of public policy against discharging an employee because his testimony may be contrary to an employer's interests. Such behavior may be indicative of bad faith, but is not contrary to established public policies.

Judgment for Dun & Bradstreet affirmed.

## Gates v. Life of Montana Insurance Co.

**683 P.2d 1063 (Mont. Sup. Ct. 1982)**

Marlene Gates began work as a cashier with Life of Montana Insurance Company in 1976 under a contract of indefinite duration. In 1978, Life of Montana issued an employee handbook, which stated that employees could be terminated without prior notice for dishonesty or the disclosure of confidential information. However, the handbook stated that notice would be given for terminations based on carelessness, incompetence, insubordination, irregular attendance, or continual tardiness. Gates had an evaluation meeting with her supervisor in May 1979. The supervisor testified that Gates was told that she was too slow, had a bad attitude, and was not getting along with her fellow employees. He admitted that he never told Gates that she would be fired if she failed to improve, but said that he did stress her need to improve. Gates claimed that she was told that her attitude was bad, but not that her work was substandard.

On October 19, 1979, Gates was called in to meet with her supervisor and given the option of resigning or being fired. She signed a letter of resignation at that time. According to Life of Montana, Gates was asked to resign because she was careless, incompetent, insubordinate, and excessively absent. However, it conceded that she was not guilty of dishonesty or the disclosure of confidential information. Arguing that the signing took place under duress when she was in a distraught condition, Gates later attempted to revoke her resignation. In the process, she claimed, she also tried to get back her resignation letter. Life of Montana later claimed that Gates did not appear distraught at the time of the signing and that later she only demanded a photocopy of the letter.

Gates was never reinstated. Eventually, she sued Life of Montana for wrongful discharge. The trial court granted Life of Montana's motion for summary judgment on all of Gates's claims, and she appealed.

**Haswell, Chief Justice.** All of Gates's theories for recovery depend upon an involuntary termination of employment. The employer maintains that she voluntarily resigned. Thus there is a threshold factual issue which should be submitted to a jury or factfinder.

For her first claim, Gates alleges that her termination was wrongful in that the employer breached the contractual terms of her employment as set forth in the employee handbook. There are factual disputes as to whether the conduct of the employer prior to Gates's termination constituted a prior warning and whether Gates was terminated for the causes stated in the company handbook. If the employer failed to follow the employee handbook, does this failure give rise to a claim for relief? The employee handbook was not distributed until about two years after Gates was hired. Its terms were not bargained for, and there was no meeting of the minds. The employee handbook was not part of Gates's employment contract at the time she was hired, nor could it have been a modification to her contract because there was no new and independent consideration for its terms. Therefore the handbook requirement of notice prior to termination is not enforceable as an express contract right.

Gates next contends that her employer owed her a duty to act in good faith with respect to her discharge. A general principle of good faith and fair dealing has been recognized in commercial transactions by the Uniform Commercial Code, and in insurance contracts. Recent decisions in other jurisdictions support the proposition that a covenant of good faith and fair dealing is implied in employment contracts. These cases emphasize the necessity of balancing the interests of the employer in controlling his work force with the interests of the employee in job security. An employer is entitled to serve its own legitimate business interests; an employer must have wide latitude in deciding whom it will employ in the face of the uncertainties of the business world; and an employer needs flexibility in the face of changing circumstances. Yet the employee is entitled to some protection from injustice.

Gates entered into an employment contract terminable at the will of either party at any time. The employer later promulgated a handbook establishing certain procedures with regard to terminations. The employer presumably sought to secure an orderly, cooperative, and loyal work force by establishing uniform policies. The employee, having faith that she would be treated fairly, then developed the peace of mind associated with job security. If the employer has failed to follow its own policies, the peace of mind of its employees is shattered and an injustice is done.

We hold that a covenant of good faith and fair dealing was implied in the employment contract of Gates. There remains a genuine issue of material fact which precludes a summary judgment, i.e., whether Life of Montana failed to afford Gates the process required, and, if so, whether Life of Montana thereby breached the covenant of good faith and fair dealing.

As to all other claims against the employer, however, summary judgment was properly entered. The trial court correctly concluded that Gates's claim in tort for wrongful discharge is unsupported by any showing of a violation of public policy.

Summary judgment for Life of Montana affirmed in part and reversed in part.

## SUMMARY

Nineteenth century employment law was largely based on highly individualistic contract law principles, and it tended to favor the stronger party—the employer—as a result. In the 20th century, the employer's power over the employee has generally increased, and the employment relationship has become even more important to the individual. Employment law, however, has become far more protective of the employee. In fact, modern employment law can be seen as a series of exceptions to the contract-based 19th century model of the employment relation.

Legal protection against on-the-job injuries is a major concern of employment law today. State *workers' compensation* systems provide injured employees with a strict liability recovery for injuries suffered during the course of their employment. The traditional employer defenses of assumption of risk, contributory negligence, and the fellow-servant rule do not apply. The injured employee's recovery, however, is often less than would have been obtained in a successful negligence suit. The law also seeks to protect the worker through direct regulation of workplace safety. The most important example is the federal *Occupational Safety and Health Act.*

The law also seeks to maintain the income of those who involuntarily lose their jobs through no fault of their own or who retire. State *unemployment compensation* systems, which were give a powerful boost by the Federal Unemployment Tax Act, protect the former group for limited time periods. The *Federal Insurance Contributions Act* finances a system of old-age, survivors, disability, and medical and hospital insurance. The *Employee Retirement Income Security Act* protects individuals from abuses in the operation of private pension plans.

The law further seeks to protect employees by regulating the terms and conditions of their employment. The *Fair Labor Standards Act* regulates wages and hours worked, and also forbids certain kinds of child labor. By recognizing the right of employees to bargain collectively through unions, *federal labor law* has powerfully (if indirectly) had a huge effect on the terms and conditions of employment. Federal labor law also protects employees by prohibiting certain unfair labor practices by both employers and unions.

Perhaps the best-known and most controversial aspect of employment law today is its protection against employment discrimination. The *Equal Pay Act* prohibits sex discrimination with respect to pay. *Title VII* of the 1964 Civil Rights Act, the single most important employment discrimination provision, forbids employment discrimination on the bases of race, color, national origin, sex, and religion. *Section 1981,* a post–Civil War antidiscrimination measure, provides quite similar protection against race or color discrimination. The Office of Federal Contract Compliance Programs applies antidiscrimination and affirmative action standards to *federal contractors.* The *Age Discrimination in Employment Act* protects those aged 40 through 69 against employer age discrimination. A host of other federal statutes prohibit employment discrimination against these groups and others (e.g., the handicapped). Many of these provisions apply only to federal contractors or recipients of federal funding.

For about a century, the doctrine of *employment at will* has been a centerpiece of American employment law. The doctrine states that either party to an employment contract for an indefinite term can terminate the contract at any time for any reason. The doctrine has been eroded by many of the legal rules described in this chapter. In recent years, courts have further eroded the doctrine by recognizing employee suits for *unjust dismissal* or *wrongful discharge.* They have done so under three theories: (1) that the dismissal is wrongful because it violates public policy (usually, a policy expressed by state or federal law), (2) that the dismissal is wrongful because it violates an implied term of good faith and fair dealing that courts read into the employment contract, or (3) that the dismissal violates employment terms that the employer has expressly agreed to (e.g., in an employment manual).

## PROBLEM CASES

**1.** Hardison, whose religious beliefs prevented him from working on Saturdays, worked in a TWA aircraft maintenance and overhaul base that operated 24 hours a day throughout the year. He was subject to a seniority system in a collective bargaining agreement under which employees with the most seniority had first choice for job and shift assignments. In his original job, Hardison had enough seniority to avoid having to work on Saturdays. However, problems began when, at his own request, he transferred to a job within the base where his seniority was relatively low. This meant that special arrangements were required to avoid forcing Hardison into Saturday work. TWA agreed to permit the union to seek a change of work assignments for Hardison, but the union was unwilling to violate its seniority system. TWA also rejected a proposal that Hardison work only four days a week, because this would impair critical functions in its operations. Finally, Hardison was discharged for refusing to work on Saturdays. He then sued TWA and the union for religious discrimination under Title VII. Was Hardison's suit successful?

**2.** Margaret Miller, a black woman, was an employee of the Bank of America. Her performance had been rated as "superior," and she had been given a raise in salary. Shortly thereafter, she was fired because she refused her supervisor's demand for sexual favors from, in his words, a "black chick." Miller then sued the bank for sex and race discrimination under Title VII. The bank defended on the ground that it had an established internal firm program forbidding sexual harassment. Would this defense succeed? Assume that the EEOC guidelines applied to this case. Suppose that the bank had tried to argue that it could not be liable for *racial* discrimination because there is no such thing as "racial harassment"? Would this argument work?

**3.** Joseph Donnell, a black General Motors employee, applied for admission into a company skilled trades apprenticeship program, but was rejected for failure to meet a requirement that applicants be high school graduates. This requirement caused 12.4 percent of black applicants and 12.7 percent of white applicants to be denied entry into the program. However, only 27.9 percent of black males over 14 in the relevant area had completed high school, while 49.1 percent of whites in the same age group had done so. Also, blacks were significantly underrepresented in the skilled trades and the skilled trades training program at the GM assembly plant in question. Only 3.3 percent of GM employees in the skilled trades and the skilled trades program were black; and only 0.3 percent of all GM's black employees were in the skilled trades, while 3.2 percent of its white employees were in such positions. Donnell sued GM under Title VII, arguing that the high school diploma was a neutral employment criterion with a disparate impact on blacks. Can Donnell prove a prima facie case of race discrimination under Title VII? Do *not* consider whether the requirement could be justified as a business necessity.

**4.** When the Westinghouse Corporation established a formal wage structure late in the 1930s, all job classifications were segregated by sex. At that time, the "female" jobs were generally lower paid than the "male" jobs. Later, men were employed in what had been women's jobs, and vice versa. In such cases, the pay scales for each job were the same no matter what the gender of the jobholder. In 1965, Westinghouse consolidated all of its job classifications, eliminating the former sex segregation. But the formerly female jobs were still generally lower paid than the formerly male jobs. Moreover, the vast majority of women were still employed in the formerly female jobs.

The International Union of Electrical Workers sued Westinghouse for sex discrimination under Title VII, arguing that Westinghouse's new system did not provide comparable pay for jobs of comparable worth. Westinghouse defended by arguing that the reach of Title VII is no greater than the reach of the Equal Pay Act. As a result, Westinghouse claimed, Title VII only forbade unequal pay for *equal* work. Will Westinghouse's argument succeed?

**5.** George Crosby, a 31-year-old male, was in an apprenticeship program of the United Brotherhood of Carpenters. The program required 8,000 hours of construction work and certain formal schooling to obtain the basic skills needed by a journeyman carpenter. The job of carpenter's apprentice required frequent bending, twisting, and heavy lifting. As an apprentice, Crosby had worked for several contractors over a 2½-year period and had accumulated over 3,600 hours in the program. He had suffered two back-related problems during this period. In 1976, the union referred Crosby to E. E. Black, Ltd., a construction contractor. Black required applicants to take a physical examination. Its physician took X-rays and detected a congenital abnormality in Crosby's back. He told Black that Crosby was a poor risk for a job involving heavy labor, and Black refused to hire Crosby. Crosby later obtained a different medical opinion, but Black still refused to hire him. Crosby then filed a complaint alleging a violation of the Rehabilitation Act of 1973. One argument for denying Crosby any recovery was that he failed to qualify as a "qualified handicapped individual," because, to be so regarded, an individual would have to have an impairment likely to affect his *employability generally*. Did Crosby have such an impairment? In any event, is this a proper definition of a qualified handicapped individual?

**6.** Blanche Strother was a cashier at Morrison's cafeteria. She worked until 9 P.M. each night. On each of three consecutive days, Strother observed two men in the cafeteria who were neither customers nor employees. On the third evening, she drove directly home following work, a 15- or 20-minute trip. When she got out of her car, one of the men she had observed in the cafeteria assaulted her and demanded the money or deposits from the cafeteria. Eventually, her purse was stolen. Strother brought a workers' compensation claim for her injuries, alleging that her injuries were work-related because her assailants thought that she was carrying the cafeteria's receipts. According to the discussion earlier in this chapter, are Strother's injuries likely to have either: (1) arisen out of her employment or (2) been sustained in the course of her employment?

**7.** Farah Manufacturing Company had a long-standing policy against employing aliens. Cecilia Espinoza, a lawfully admitted alien married to an American citizen, applied for employment as a seamstress at Farah. She was rejected, and sued Farah for discrimination on the basis of national origin in violation of Title VII. Did Farah's decision violate Title VII?

**8.** Robert M. Mau had worked for the Omaha National Bank for 28 years. At the time of his discharge, he was supervisor of the mail room. Mau was fired because of his failure to mail 300 pension checks issued from accounts administered by the bank's trust department. The would-be recipients of the checks had complained to the bank about their failure to receive them, but Mau assured his supervisor that the checks had been mailed. Mau was then ordered to conduct a personal search of the mail room, during which he found the checks in a desk drawer.

Mau sued the bank for wrongful discharge. First, he alleged that his termination violated public policy. Next, he argued that the bank had violated a contract of employment promising him a "career" guaranteed for life or until retirement at age 65. In support of the second claim, he introduced various company handbooks stating that certain fringe benefits (including retirement benefits) would be paid if he remained employed by the bank. Many of these handbooks were issued after Mau's employment by the bank, and one stated that "THIS BOOKLET IS NOT A CONTRACT." Will Mau's claims be successful?

**9.** Jack Gilbert and Bill Wade were employed as "resident mining engineers" or "mine surveyors" by the Old Ben Coal Corporation. Their duties were to drive wooden plugs into the roof of the mine, to report errors in the direction of operation of mining machines, and to prepare maps and reports. Neither they nor the employer kept records of the time they worked, although they estimated that they worked a weekly average of 48 to 50 hours. This problem is not specifically addressed in the text, but do you think that either an employee's or an employer's failure to keep records of hours worked will always prevent an employee from winning a claim for overtime pay under the FLSA?

**10.** James Arritt applied for employment as a police officer in Moundsville, West Virginia. His application was denied because he was 40 years of age and a West Virginia statute established an 18–35 age limit for applicants for original appointment to the police force of any city with a population of 10,000 or more. Arritt sued the city under the ADEA. The city defended on the ground that the ADEA does not apply to states and localities. Is the city correct?

# Chapter 48 Environmental Regulation

## INTRODUCTION

Today's business person must be concerned not only with com peting effectively against competitors but also with complying with a myriad of regulatory requirements. For many businesses, particularly those that manufacture goods or that generate wastes, the environmental laws and regulations loom large in terms of the requirements and costs they impose. They can have a significant effect on the way businesses have to be conducted as well as on their profitability. This area of the law has expanded dramatically over the last 15 years. This chapter will briefly discuss the development of environmental law and will outline the major federal statutes that have been enacted to control pollution of air, water, and land.

**Historical Perspective.** Historically, people assumed that the air, water, and land around them would absorb their waste products. In recent times, however, it has become clear that nature's capacity to assimilate people's wastes is not infinite. Burgeoning population, economic growth, affluence, and the products of our industrial society pose risks to human health and the environment.

Concern about the environment is not a recent phenomena. In medieval England, Parliament passed "smoke control" acts making it illegal to burn soft coal at certain times of the year. Where the owner or operator of a piece of property is using it in such a manner as to unreasonably interfere with another owner's (or the public's) health or enjoyment of his property, the courts have long entertained suits to abate the nuisance. Nuisance actions, which are discussed in Chapter 29, are frequently not ideal vehicles for dealing with widespread pollution problems. Rather than a hit-or-miss approach, a comprehensive across-the-board approach may be required. Realizing this, the federal government, as well as many state and local governments, had passed laws to abate air and water pollution by the late 1950s and 1960s. As the 1970s began, concern over the quality and future of the environment produced new laws and fresh public demands for action.

**The Environmental Protection Agency.** In 1970, the Environmental Protection Agency (EPA) was created to consolidate the federal government's environmental responsibilities. This was an explicit recognition that the problems of air and water pollution, solid waste disposal, water supply, and pesticides and radiation control were interrelated and required a coordinated approach. Congress passed comprehensive new legislation covering, among other things, air and water pollution, pesticides, ocean dumping, and waste disposal. Among the factors prompting these laws were: protection of human health, aesthetics, economic costs of continued pollution, and protection of natural systems.

The initial efforts were aimed at pollution problems that could largely be seen, smelled, or tasted. As control requirements have been put in place, implemented by industry and government, and progress has been noted in the form of cleaner air and water, attention has focused increasingly on problems that are somewhat less visible but even more threatening—the problems posed by toxic substances. These problems have come into more prominence as scientific research has disclosed the risks posed by some substances, as detection technology has enabled us to find the suspect substances in ever more minute quantities in the world around us, and as we do increased monitoring and testing.

**The National Environmental Policy Act.** The National Environmental Policy Act (NEPA) was signed into law on January 1, 1970. In addition to creating the Council of Environmental Quality in the Executive Office of the President, the act required that an **environmental impact statement** be prepared for every recommendation or report on legislation and for every *major federal action significantly affecting the quality of the environment.* The environmental impact statement must: (1) describe the environmental impact of the proposed action; (2) discuss impacts that cannot be avoided; (3) discuss the alternatives to the proposed action; (4) indicate differences between short- and long-term impacts; and (5) detail any irreversible commitments of resources. NEPA requires a federal agency to consider the environmental impact of a project before the project is undertaken. Other federal, state, and local agencies, as well as interested citizens, have an opportunity to comment on the environmental impact of the project before the agency can proceed. Where the process is not followed, citizens can and have gone to court to force compliance with NEPA. A number of states and local governments have passed their own environmental impact laws requiring NEPA-type statements for major public and private developments.

## AIR POLLUTION

**Background.** Fuel combustion, industrial processes, and solid waste disposal are the major contributors to air pollution. People's initial concern with air pollution related to that which they could see—visible or smoke pollution. In the 1880s, Chicago and Cincinnati enacted smoke control ordinances. As the technology became available to deal with smoke and particulate emissions, attention was given as well to other, less visible gases that could adversely affect human health and vegetation and that could lead to increased acidity of lakes, thus making them unsuitable for fish. The first federal legislation came in 1955, when Congress authorized $5 million each year for air pollution research. In 1963, the Clean Air Act was passed to provide assistance to the states and to deal with interstate air pollution; the act was amended in 1965 and 1967 to provide for, among other things, controls on pollution from automobiles. Comprehensive legislation enacted in 1970 provides the basis for our present approach to the air pollution control. In 1977, Congress made some modifications to the 1970 Clean Air Act and enacted provisions designed to prevent deterioration of the air in areas where its quality currently exceeds that required by federal law.

**Clean Air Act.** The Clean Air Act established a comprehensive approach for dealing with air pollution. EPA is required to set *national ambient air quality standards* for the major pollutants that have an adverse impact on human health—that is, to set the amount of a given pollutant that can be present in the air around us. The ambient air quality standards are to be set at two levels: (1) *primary standards,* which are designed to protect the public's health from harm; and (2) *secondary standards,* which are designed to protect vegetation, materials, climate, visibility, and economic values. Pursuant to this statutory mandate, EPA has set ambient air quality standards for carbon monoxide, nitrogen oxide, sulfur oxide, ozone, lead, and particulate matter.

The country is divided into air quality regions, and each region is required to have an *implementation plan* for meeting the national ambient air quality standards. This necessitates an inventory of the various sources of air pollution and their contribution to the total air pollution in the air quality region. The major emitters of pollutants are then required to reduce their emissions to a level that ensures the overall air quality will meet the national standards. The states have the responsibility for deciding which activities must be regulated or curtailed so that emissions will not exceed the national standards.

The Clean Air Act also requires EPA to regulate the emission of *toxic air pollutants.* Under this authority, EPA has set standards for asbestos, beryllium, mercury, vinyl chloride, benzene, and radionuclides and is investigating a number of other pollutants to see whether they require regulation.

The act requires that *new stationary sources,* such as factories and power plants install the *best available technology* for reducing air pollution. EPA is required to establish the standards to be met by new stationary sources and has done so for the major types of stationary sources of air pollution. The primary responsibility for enforcing the air quality standards lies with the states, but the federal government has the right to enforce the standards where the states fail to do so. The Clean Air Act also provides for suits by citizens to force industry or the government to fully comply with the act's provisions.

**Automobile Pollution.** The Clean Air Act provides specifically for air pollution controls on transportation sources such as automobiles. The major pollutants from automobiles are carbon monoxide, hydrocarbons, and nitrogen oxides. Carbon monoxide is a colorless, odorless gas that can dull mental performances and even cause death when inhaled in large quantities. Hydrocarbons, in the form of unburned fuel, are part of a category of air pollutants known as volatile organic compounds (VOCs). VOCs combine with nitrogen oxides under the influence of sunlight to become ozone. We sometimes know it as "smog."

The 1970 Clean Air Act required a reduction by 1975 of 90 percent in the amount of the carbon monoxide and hydrocarbons emitted by automobiles and by 1976 a 90 percent reduction in the amount of the nitrogen oxides emitted. Subsequently, Congress addressed the question of setting even more stringent limits on automobile emissions while at the same time requiring that the new automobiles get better gas mileage. The act also provides for the regulation and registration of fuel additives such as lead.

**Radiation Control.** In recent years, there has been concern with radioactivity, particularly radioactivity from nuclear-fueled power plants. Citizen concerns specifically related to nuclear plants include: possible release of radioactivity into the environment during normal operation of the nuclear reactor, possible accidents through human error or mechanical failure, and disposal of the radioactive wastes generated by the reactor. There is also concern that the discharge of heated water used to cool the reactor—thermal pollution—may cause damage to the environment.

Currently, the problems of reactor safety are under the jurisdiction of the Nuclear Regulatory Commission, which exercises licensing authority over nuclear power plants. The Environmental Protection Agency is responsible for setting standards for radioactivity in the overall environment and for dealing with the problem of disposal of some radioactive waste. The thermal pollution problem is handled by EPA pursuant to its water pollution control authorities. In addition, EPA has the responsibility for regulating emissions from a variety of other sources, such as uranium mill tailing piles and uranium mines.

## WATER POLLUTION

**Background.** History is replete with plagues and epidemics brought on by poor sanitation and polluted water. Indeed, preventing waterborne disease has through time been the major reason for combating water pollution. In the early 1970s, fishing and swimming were prohibited in many bodies of water, game fish could no longer survive in some waters where they had formerly thrived, and Lake Erie was becoming choked with algae and was considered to be dying. The nation recognized that water pollution could affect public health, recreation, commercial fishing, agriculture, water supplies, and aesthetics. During the 1970s, Congress enacted three major statutes to deal with protecting our water resources: the Clean Water Act; the Marine Protection, Research, and Sanctuaries Act; and the Safe Drinking Water Act.

**Early Federal Legislation.** Federal water pollution legislation dates back to the 19th century when Congress enacted the River and Harbor Act of 1886. In fact, this statute, recodified in the River and Harbor Act of 1899, furnished the legal basis for EPA's initial enforcement actions against polluters. The act provided that in order to deposit or discharge "refuse" into a navigable waterway, a discharge permit had to be obtained from the Army Corps of Engineers. Under some contemporary court decisions, even hot water discharged from nuclear power plants was considered "refuse." The permit system established pursuant to the "Refuse Act" was replaced in 1972 by a more comprehensive permit system administered by EPA.

The initial Federal Water Pollution Control Act (FWPCA) was passed in 1948. Amendments to the FWPCA in 1956, 1965, 1966, and 1970 increased the federal government's role in water pollution abatement and strengthened its enforcement powers. Gradually, the federal government paid a larger and larger share of the costs of building municipal sewage treatment plants; the federal share is now 55–75 percent, with the remainder being put up by state and local government.

**Clean Water Act.** The 1972 amendments to the FWPCA—known as the Clean Water Act—were as comprehensive in the water pollution field as the 1970 Clean Air Act was in the air pollution field. They proclaimed two general goals for this country: (1) to achieve wherever possible by July 1, 1983, water clean enough for swimming and other recreational uses and clean enough for the protection and propagation of fish, shellfish, and wildlife; and (2) by 1985 to have no discharges of pollutants into the nation's waters. The goals reflected a national frustration with the lack of progress in dealing with water pollution and a commitment to end such pollution. The new law set out a series of specific actions that federal, state, and local governments and industry were to take by certain dates and also provided strong enforcement provisions to back up the deadlines. In 1977, Congress enacted some modifications to the 1972 act that adjusted some of the deadlines and otherwise "fine-tuned" the act.

Under the Clean Water Act, the states have the primary responsibility for preventing, reducing, and eliminating water pollution, but the states have to do this within a national framework, with EPA empowered to move in if the states do not fulfill their responsibilities. The law set a number of deadlines to control water pollution from industrial sources. Industries discharging wastes into the nation's waterways were required to install the "best available" water pollution control technology and new sources of industrial pollution must use the "best available demonstrated control technology." In each instance, EPA is responsible for issuing guidelines as to the "best available" technologies. Industries that discharge their wastes into municipal systems are required to pretreat the wastes so that they will not interfere with the biological operation of the plant or pass through the plant without treatment.

The act continued and expanded the previously established system of setting *water quality standards* that define the uses of specific bodies of water—such as recreational, public water supply, propagation of fish and wildlife, and agricultural and industrial water supply. Then, the maximum daily loads of various kinds of pollutants are set so that the water will be suitable for the designated type of use. The act requires all *municipal and industrial dischargers* to obtain *permits* that spell out the amounts and types of pollutants that the permit holder will be allowed to discharge and any steps that it must take to reduce its present or anticipated discharge. Dischargers are also required to keep records, install and maintain monitoring equipment, and sample their discharges. Penalties for violating the law range from a minimum of $2,500 for a first offense up to $50,000 per day and two years in prison for subsequent violations.

Any citizen or group of citizens whose interests are adversely affected has the right to bring a court action against anyone violating an effluent standard or limitation or an order issued by EPA or a state. Citizens also have the right to take court action against EPA if it fails to carry out mandatory provisions of the law.

**Ocean Dumping.** The Marine Protection, Research, and Sanctuaries Act of 1972 set up a *permit system* regulating the dumping of all types of materials into ocean waters. EPA has the responsibility for designating disposal sites and for establishing the rules governing ocean disposal. This includes the responsibility for regulating the incineration of hazardous materials at sea.

**Drinking Water.** In 1974 Congress passed the Safe Drinking Water Act, which was designed to protect and enhance the quality of our drinking water. Under the act EPA sets *primary drinking water standards* which provide minimum levels of quality for water to be used for human consumption. The act also establishes a program governing the injection of wastes into wells. The primary responsibility for complying with the federally established standards lies with the states. Where the states fail to enforce the drinking water standards, the federal government has the right to enforce them.

## United States v. Reserve Mining Co.

**8 E.R.C. 1978 (D.C. Minn. 1976)**

The United States and a number of cities, states, and environmental groups brought a lawsuit against the Reserve Mining Company and others to halt the dumping of taconite tailings into Lake Superior. A series of trial and appellate court decisions resulted in a judgment that Reserve Mining's discharge of tailings violated state and federal law, constituted a health hazard, and should be enjoined. In this particular decision, the state of Minnesota sought an order imposing penalties against Reserve Mining for violation of the state pollution control laws.

**Devitt, Judge.** It has been established that Reserve has violated Minnesota's pollution control laws and regulations. Minnesota law authorizes a court to impose a fine of up to $10,000 per day for each violation of, *inter alia,* the laws and regulations violated by Reserve. Minnesota contends that Reserve should be fined for daily violations of these laws and regulations for almost a full year.

The daily dumping of approximately 67,000 tons of carcinogenic waste into Lake Superior polluting public water supplies in violation of its state discharge permits is, by far, Reserve's most serious offense.

In 1947 Reserve obtained from two state agencies, identical permits authorizing it to discharge tailings into Lake Superior. Subsection (d) of those permits prohibits discharges which

> result in any material clouding or discoloration of the water at the surface outside of [the specified discharge] zone nor shall such tailings be discharged so as to result in any material adverse effects on public water supplies.

The district court concluded that "the terms of the permits are being violated" because

> the discharge causes discoloration of the surface waters outside of the zone of discharge, causes an increase in turbidity, and adversely affects the public water supplies of several communities resulting in unlawful pollution of the lake.

The court of appeals agreed, stating that:

> The record shows that Reserve is discharging a substance into Lake Superior waters which under an acceptable but unproved medical theory may be considered as carcinogenic. This discharge gives rise to reasonable medical concern over the public health.

Clearly, these findings justify the conclusion that Reserve violated its discharge permits. The trial court has determined that Reserve was in violation of its state discharge permits every day during the May 20, 1973 to April 20, 1974 period.

Minnesota law requires Reserve to comply with the terms of its state permits or be subject to the penalties authorized by Minn. Stat. § 115.071. Therefore, because Reserve has violated its permits, the only remaining issue is the amount of the penalty.

In making this determination, the court is aware that, as a result of these discharges, Reserve is liable for the costs, expected to be approximately $6 million, of supplying clean water to the affected communities. In addition, the injunction resulting from this litigation will compel Reserve to either cease operations or expend substantial sums, estimated at over $300 million, to develop an alternative means of disposing of production wastes.

It is not disputed that Reserve, by supplying needed jobs and services, has revitalized the economy of northeastern Minnesota and, by adding to the supply of domestically produced raw iron, has contributed to the economy of the entire country. But similar contributions have been made by other corporations while complying with applicable pollution control laws and regulations.

It should be appreciated that Reserve did not set out to spoil the air and water or cause inconvenience to or apprehension among residents of the area. It launched its business venture with the encouragement, even the importuning, of all segments of government and society. But in this business venture, the record shows it returned very substantial profits to its corporate owner-parents, Republic and Armco. It is reasonable to conclude that some of those profits are attributable to operations made less costly by discharging tailings in Lake Superior rather than on land, as is done by its competitors. And, the record shows that Reserve, particularly through its Vice President Haley, frustrated the court in prompt resolution of the controversy by violation of court rules and orders and thus prolonged the status quo.

While the daily discharge of 67,000 tons of tailings into Lake Superior is shocking in these days of improved environmental awareness, those discharges were expressly authorized in 1947 by the State of Minnesota. Hindsight tells us that was a mistake, but the gravity of it has not yet been determined. The court of appeals held that Reserve's discharges have not yet been found to be harmful to the public health and that the danger is potential, not imminent. The court of appeals found that Reserve need not terminate its operations but directed that preventive and precautionary steps be taken. They have been taken. So while the record shows violations of the permits, it has not been shown, and in the view of the court of appeals it is not likely it can be shown, that the past violations have caused actual harm to the public health.

Upon consideration of all the factors and pursuant to authority of Minn. Stat. § 115.071, the court imposes a penalty of $2,500 per day for violations of the terms of Reserve's state discharge permits.

Penalty of $837,500 imposed against Reserve Mining.

## HAZARDOUS WASTE DISPOSAL

**Background.** Historically, concern about the environment focused on air and water pollution as well as the protection of natural resources and wildlife. Relatively little attention was paid to the disposal of wastes on land. When EPA was formed, much of the solid and hazardous waste generated was being disposed of in open dumps and landfills. While much of the waste we produce does not present significant health or environmental problems, some industrial, agricultural, and mining wastes, and even some household wastes, are hazardous and can present serious problems. Unless wastes are properly disposed of, they can cause air, water, and land pollution as well as contamination of the underground aquifers from which much of our drinking water is drawn. Once aquifers have been contaminated, it can take them a very long time to cleanse themselves of pollutants.

In the 1970s, the discovery of abandoned dump sites such as Love Canal in New York and the "Valley of the Drums" in Kentucky heightened public concern about the disposal of toxic and hazardous wastes. Congress has enacted several laws regulating the generation and disposal of hazardous waste: the Resource Conservation and Recovery Act is aimed at the proper management and disposal of wastes that are being generated currently, while the Comprehensive Environmental Response, Compensation, and Liability Act focuses on the cleanup of past disposal sites that threaten public health and the environment.

**The Resource Conservation and Recovery Act.** The Resource Conservation and Recovery Act (RCRA) was originally enacted in 1976 and significantly amended in 1984. It provides the federal government and the states with the authority to regulate facilities that *generate, treat, store, and dispose of hazardous waste.* Most of the wastes defined as hazardous are subject to a "cradle to the grave" tracking system and must be handled and disposed of in defined ways.

Under RCRA persons who generate, treat, store, or transport specified quantities of hazardous waste are required to obtain permits, to meet certain standards and follow specified procedures in the handling of the wastes, and to keep records. In addition, operators of land disposal facilities are required to meet financial responsibility requirements and to monitor groundwater quality.

EPA is required to determine whether certain kinds of wastes should be banned entirely from land disposal. In 1984 Congress directed that it also regulate underground product storage tanks, such as gasoline tanks, to prevent, and respond to, leaks from them that might contaminate underground water.

EPA sets minimum requirements for a state RCRA program and then delegates the responsibility for conducting the program to the states when they have the legal ability and interest to administer it. Until a state assumes partial or complete responsibility for an RCRA program, the federal government administers the program. Failure to comply with the hazardous waste regulations promulgated under RCRA can subject the violator to civil and criminal penalties. In the *Johnson & Towers* case, which follows, employees of a company that disposed of hazardous waste without a RCRA permit were held criminally liable.

**Superfund.** In 1980, Congress passed the Comprehensive Environmental Response Compensation and Liability Act (CERCLA), commonly known as "Superfund," to deal with the problem of *uncontrolled or abandoned hazardous waste sites.* Under the Superfund law, EPA was required to identify and assess the sites in the United States where hazardous wastes had been spilled, stored, or abandoned. Eventually, EPA expects to identify 22,000 such sites. The sites are ranked on the basis of the type, quantity, and toxicity of the wastes; the number of people potentially exposed to the wastes; the different ways (e.g., air or drinking water) in which they might be exposed; the risks to contamination of aquifers; and other factors. The sites with the highest ranking are placed on the National Priority List to receive priority federal and.or state attention for cleanup. These sites are subjected to a careful scientific and engineering study to determine the most appropriate cleanup plan. Once a site has been cleaned up, the state is responsible for managing it to prevent future environmental problems. EPA also has the authority to quickly initiate actions at hazardous waste sites—whether or not the site is on the priority list—to address imminent hazards, such as the risk of fire, explosion, or contamination of drinking water.

The cleanup activity is financed by a tax on chemicals and feedstocks. However, EPA has the authority to require that a site be cleaned up by those persons who were responsible for it, either as the owner or operator of the site, a transporter of wastes to the site, or the owner of wastes deposited at the site. Where EPA expends money to clean up a site, it has the legal authority to recover its costs from those who were responsible for the problem. The courts have held that such persons are "*jointly and severally* responsible for the cost of cleanup." The concept of joint liability is discussed in Chapter 5. The *Chem-Dyne* case, which follows, involves a challenge to the concept of joint and several liability by the contributors to a major hazardous waste site.

## United States v. Johnson & Towers, Inc.

**21 E.R.C. 1433 (3d Cir. 1984)**

Johnson & Towers, Inc. is in the business of overhauling large motor vehicles. It uses degreasers and other industrial chemicals that contain chemicals classified as "hazardous wastes" under the Resource Conservation and Recovery Act (RCRA), such as methylene chloride and tricholorethylene. For some period of time waste chemicals from cleaning operations were drained into a holding tank and, when the tank was full, pumped into a trench. The trench flowed from the plant property into Parker's Creek, a tributary of the Delaware River. Under RCRA, generators of such wastes must obtain a permit for disposal from the Environmental Protection Agency (EPA). EPA had neither issued, nor received an application for, a permit for the Johnson & Towers operations.

Over a three-day period, federal agents saw workers pump waste from the tank into the trench, and on the third day toxic chemicals flowed into the creek. The company and two of its employees, Jack Hopkins, a foreman, and Peter Angel, the service manager, were indicted for unlawfully disposing of hazardous wastes. The company pled guilty. The federal district court dismissed the criminal charges against the two individuals, holding that RCRA's criminal penalty provisions imposing fines and imprisonment did not apply to employees. The government appealed.

**SLOVITER, CIRCUIT JUDGE.** The single issue in this appeal is whether the individual defendants are subject to prosecution under RCRA's criminal provision (Section 6928 [d]) which applies to:

> any person who . . .
> (2) knowingly treats, stores, or disposes of any hazardous waste identified or listed under this subchapter either
> (A) without having obtained a permit under section 6925 of this title . . . or
> (B) in knowing violation of any material condition or requirement of such permit.

The permit provision in section 6925 requires "each person owning or operating a facility for the treatment, storage, or disposal of hazardous waste identified or listed under this subchapter to have a permit" from the EPA.

The parties offer contrary interpretations of section 6928(d). Defendants consider it an administrative enforcement mechanism, applying only to those who come within section 6925 and fail to comply; the government reads it as penalizing anyone who handles hazardous waste without a permit or in violation of a permit. Neither party has cited another case, nor have we found one, considering the application of this criminal provision to an individual other than an owner or operator.

Though the result may appear harsh, it is well established that criminal penalties attached to regulatory statutes intended to protect public health, in contrast to statutes based on common law crimes, are to be construed to effectuate the regulatory purpose.

Congress enacted RCRA in 1976 as a "cradle-to-grave" regulatory scheme for toxic materials, providing "nationwide protection against the dangers of improper hazardous waste disposal." RCRA was enacted to provide "a multifaceted approach toward solving the problems associated with the 3–4 billion tons of discarded materials generated each year, and the problems resulting from the anticipated 8 percent annual increase in the volume of such waste." The committee reports accompanying legislative consideration of RCRA contain numerous statements evincing the congressional view that improper disposal of toxic materials was a serious national problem.

The original statute made knowing disposal (but not treatment or storage) of such waste without a permit a misdemeanor. Amendments in 1978 and 1980 expanded the criminal provision to cover treatment and storage and made violation of section 6928 a felony. The fact that Congress amended the statute twice to broaden the scope of its substantive provisions and enhance the penalty is a strong indication of Congress' increasing concern about the seriousness of the prohibited conduct.

Although Congress' concern may have been directed primarily at owners and operators of generating facilities, since it imposed upon them in section 6925 the obligation to secure the necessary permit, Congress did not explicitly limit criminal liability for impermissible treatment, storage, or disposal to owners and operators. The House Committee's discussion of enforcement contains several references relevant only to owners and operators, but it says, in addition: "This section also provides for criminal penalties for the person who . . . disposes of any hazardous waste without a permit under this title." The "also" demonstrates that the reach of section 6928(d) is broader than that of the rest of the statute, particularly the administrative enforcement remedies. The acts that were made the subject of the criminal provision were distinguished in the House Report from the other conduct subject to administrative regulation because they were viewed as more serious offenses. As the Report explained, "the justification for the penalties section is to permit a broad variety of mechanisms so as to stop the illegal disposal of hazardous wastes."

We conclude that in RCRA, Congress endeavored to control hazards that, "in the circumstances of modern industrialism, are largely beyond self-protection." It would undercut the purposes of the legislation to limit the class of potential defendants to owners and operators when others also bear responsibility for handling regulated materials. The phrase, "without having obtained a permit *under section* 6925" (emphasis added) merely references the section under which the permit is required and exempts from prosecution under section 6928(d)(2)(A) anyone who has obtained a permit; we conclude that it has no other limiting effect. Therefore we reject the district court's construction limiting the substantive criminal provision by confining "any person" in section 6928 to owners or operators facilities that store, treat, or dispose of hazardous waste, as an unduly narrow view of both the statutory language and the congressional intent.

Case remanded to district court for trial.

## United States v. Chem-Dyne Corp.

**572 F. Supp 802 (S.D. Ohio 1983)**

The United States brought a lawsuit under the Comprehensive Environmental Response, Compensation, and Liability Act (CERCLA) against 24 defendants who had allegedly generated or transported some of the hazardous substances located at the Chem-Dyne treatment facility in Ohio. The government sought to be reimbursed for money that it had spent in cleaning up hazardous wastes at the facility and asserted that each defendant was jointly and severally liable for the entire cost of the cleanup. The defendants contested the claim that they were jointly and severally liable and moved for summary judgment in their favor on this issue.

**Rubin, Chief Judge.** CERCLA was enacted both to provide rapid responses to the nationwide threats posed by the 30,000–50,000 improperly managed hazardous waste sites in this country as well as to induce voluntary responses to those sites. The legislation established a $1.6 billion trust fund ("Superfund"), drawn from industry and federal appropriations, to finance the clean-up and containment efforts. The state or federal government may then pursue rapid recovery of the costs incurred from persons liable to reimburse the Superfund money expended. This recovery task may prove difficult when several companies used a site, when dumped chemicals react with others to form new or more toxic substances, or when records are unavailable. Nevertheless, those responsible for the problems caused by the hazardous wastes were intended to bear the costs and responsibilities for remedying the condition. The House sponsor, Representative Florio, commented at length:

> The liability provisions of this bill do not refer to the terms strict, joint and several liability, terms which were contained in the version of H.R. 7020 passed earlier by this body. The standard of liability in these amendments is intended to be . . . strict liability. . . . I have concluded that despite the absence of these specific terms, the strict liability standard already approved by this body is preserved. Issues of joint and several liability not resolved by this bill shall be governed by traditional and evolving principles of common law. The terms "joint and several" have been deleted with the intent that the liability of joint tortfeasors be determined under common or previous statutory law.

Typically, as in this case, there will be numerous hazardous substance generators or transporters who have disposed of wastes at a particular site. The term joint and several liability was deleted from the express language of the statute in order to avoid its universal application to inappropriate circumstances. An examination of the common law reveals that when two or more persons acting independently cause a distinct or single harm for which there is a reasonable basis for division according to the contribution of each, each is subject to liability only for the portion of the total harm that he has himself caused.

But where two or more persons cause a single and indivisible harm, each is subject to liability for the entire harm. *Restatement (Second) of Torts,* § 875. Furthermore, where the conduct of two or more persons liable under CERCIA has combined to violate the statute, and one or more of the defendants seek to limit their liability on the ground that the entire harm is capable of apportionment, the burden of proof as to apportionment is upon each defendant.

The question of whether the defendants are jointly or severally liable for the clean-up costs turns on a fairly complex factual determination. Read in the light most favorable to the United States, the following facts illustrate the nature of the problem. The Chem-Dyne facility contains a variety of hazardous waste from 289 generators or transporters, consisting of about 608,000 pounds of material. Some of the wastes have been commingled, but the identities of the sources of these wastes remain unascertained. The fact of the mixing of the wastes raises an issue as to the divisibility of the harm. Further, a dispute exists over which of the wastes have contaminated the groundwater, the degree of their migration, and the concomitant health hazard. Finally, the volume of waste of a particular generator is not an accurate predictor of the risk associated with the waste because the toxicity or migratory potential of a particular hazardous substance generally varies independently with the volume of the waste.

This case, as do most pollution cases, turns on the issue of whether the harm caused at Chem-Dyne is "divisible" or "indivisible." If the harm is divisible and if there is a reasonable basis for apportionment of damages, each defendant is liable only for the portion of harm he himself caused. In this situation, the burden of proof as to apportionment is upon each defendant. On the other hand, if the defendants caused an indivisible harm, each is subject to liability for the entire harm. The defendants have not carried their burden of demonstrating the divisibility of the harm and the degrees to which each defendant is responsible.

Defendants' motion for summary judgment is denied.

## REGULATION OF CHEMICALS

**Background.** More than 60,000 chemical substances are manufactured in the United States, and they are used in a wide variety of products. While these chemicals contribute much to the standard of living we enjoy, some of them are toxic or have the potential to cause cancer, birth defects, reproductive failures, and other health-related problems. These risks may be posed in the manufacturing process, during the use of a product, or as a result of the manner of disposal of the chemical or product. EPA has two statutory authorities that give it the ability to prevent or restrict the manufacture and use of new and existing chemicals to remove unreasonable risks to human health or the environment. These authorities are the Federal Insecticide, Fungicide, and Rodenticide Act and the Toxic Substances Control Act.

**Regulation of Agricultural Chemicals.** The vast increase in the American farmer's productivity over the past few decades has been in large measure attributable to the farmer's use of chemicals to kill the insects, pest, and weeds that have historically competed with the farmer for his crops. Some of the chemicals, such as pesticides and herbicides, were a mixed blessing. They enabled people to dramatically increase productivity and to conquer disease. On the other hand, dead fish and birds provided evidence that they were building up in the food chain and proving fatal to some species. And, unless such chemicals are carefully used and disposed of, they can present a danger to the applicator and to the consumer of food and water. Gradually, people realized the need to focus on the effects of using such chemicals.

EPA enforces the Federal Insecticide, Fungicide, and Rodenticide Act (FIFRA). This act gives EPA the authority to *register pesticides* before they can be sold, to provide for the certification of applicators of pesticides designated for "restrictive" use, to set limits on the amounts of pesticide residue permitted on crops that provide food for people or animals, and to register and inspect pesticide manufacturing establishments.

When the EPA administrator has reason to believe that continued use of a particular pesticide poses an "imminent hazard," he may suspend its registration and remove it from the market. When the administrator believes that there is a less than imminent hazard but that the environmental risks of continuing to use a pesticide outweigh its benefits, the administrator may initiate a cancellation of registration proceeding. This proceeding affords all interested persons—manufacturers, distributors, users, environmentalists, and scientists—an opportunity to present evidence on the proposed cancellation. Cancellation of the registration occurs when the administrator finds that the product will cause "unreasonable adverse effects on the environment."

Following this section of the text, the EPA Administrator's decision to cancel the use of DDT is excerpted.

**Toxic Substances Control Act.** The other major statute regulating chemical use focuses on other toxic substances—such as asbestos and PCBs—and on the new chemical compounds that are developed each year. The Toxic Substances Control Act, which was enacted in 1976, requires that chemicals be tested by manufacturers or processors to determine their effect on human health or the environment before the chemicals are introduced into commerce. The act also gives EPA the authority to regulate chemical substances or mixtures that present an *unreasonable risk of injury to health or the environment* and to take action against any such substances or mixtures that pose an imminent hazard. This legislation was enacted in response to the concern that thousands of new substances are released into the environment each year, sometimes without adequate consideration of their potential for harm, and that it is not until damage from a substance occurs that its manufacture or use is properly regulated. At the same time, a goal of the act is not to unduly impede, or create unnecessary economic barriers to, technological innovation.

## Consolidated DDT Hearings Opinion and Order of the Administrator

**37 Fed. Reg. 13,369 (1972)**

On January 15, 1971, the Environmental Protection Agency commenced a formal administrative review of all registrations for DDT products and uses pursuant to Section 4(c) of the Federal Insecticide, Fungicide, and Rodenticide Act. Thirty-one companies holding DDT registrations challenged EPA's cancellation of DDT use registrations. The U.S. Department of Agriculture intervened on the side of the registrants, and the Environmental Defense Fund intervened along with EPA to help present the case for cancellation.

After a lengthy public hearing, on April 25, 1972, the hearing examiner issued an opinion recommending to the EPA administrator that all "essential" uses of DDT be retained and that cancellation be lifted. The administrator took the opinion under advisement and received oral and written briefs both supporting and taking exception to the hearing officer's findings of fact and conclusions of law. The administrator then issued his opinion and order canceling virtually all uses of DDT as of December 31, 1972, except for its use on several minor crops and for disease control and other health-related uses.

**Ruckelshaus, Administrator.** This hearing represents the culmination of approximately three years of intensive administrative inquiry into the uses of DDT.

*Background.* DDT is the familiar abbreviation for the chemical (1,1,1,trichlorophenyl ethane), which was for many years the most widely used chemical pesticide in this country. DDT's insecticidal properties were originally discovered, apparently by accident, in 1939, and during World War II it was used extensively for typhus control. Since 1945, DDT has been used for general control of mosquitoes, boll-weevil infestation in cotton-growing areas, and a variety of other uses. Peak use of DDT occurred at the end of the 1950s, and present domestic use of DDT in various formulations has been estimated at 6,000 tons per year. According to Admission 7 of the record, approximately 86 percent or 10,-277,258 pounds of domestically used DDT is applied to cotton crops. The same admission indicates that 603,053 pounds and 937,901 pounds, or approximately 5 percent and 9 percent of the total formulated by 27 of the petitioners in these hearings, are used respectively on soybean and peanut crops. All other uses of the 11,996,196 pounds amount to 158,833 pounds of the total, or a little over 1 percent.

For the above uses it appears that DDT is sold in four different formulations: emulsifiable sprays; dust; wettable powder; and granular form.

Public concern over the widespread use of pesticides was stirred by Rachel Carson's book *Silent Spring,* and a natural outgrowth was the investigation of this popular and widely sprayed chemical. DDT, which for many years has been used with apparent safety, was, the critics alleged, a highly dangerous substance which killed beneficial insects, upset the natural ecological balance, and collected in the food chain, thus posing a hazard to man, and other forms of advanced aquatic and avian life.

*Application of Risk-Benefit to Crop Uses of DDT.* The Agency and the Environmental Defense Fund (EDF) have established that DDT is toxic to nontarget insects and animals, persistent, mobile, and transferable and that it builds up in the food chain. No label directions for use can completely prevent these hazards. In short, they have established at the very least the risk of the unknown. That risk is compounded where, as is the case with DDT, man and animals tend to accumulate and store the chemical. These facts alone constitute risks that are unjustified where apparently safer alternatives exist to achieve the same benefit. Where, however, there is a demonstrated laboratory relationship between the chemical and toxic effects in man or animals, this risk is, generally speaking, rendered even more unacceptable, if alternatives exist. In the case before us the risk to human health from using DDT cannot be discounted. While these risks might be acceptable were we forced to use DDT, they are not so trivial that we can be indifferent to assuming them unnecessarily.

The evidence of record showing storage in man and magnification in the food chain is a warning to the prudent that man may be exposing himself to a substance that may ultimately have a serious effect on his health.

As Judge Leventhal recently pointed out, cancer is a "sensitive and fright-laden" matter and as he noted earlier in his opinion, carcinogenic effects are "generally cumulative and irreversible when discovered." The possibility that DDT is a carcinogen is at present remote and unquantifiable; but if it is not a siren to panic, it is a semaphore which suggests that an identifiable public benefit is required to justify continued use of DDT. Where one chemical tests tumorigenic in a laboratory and one does not, and both accomplish the same risk, the latter is to be preferred, absent some extenuating circumstances.

The risks to the environment from continued use of DDT are more clearly established. There is no doubt that DDT runoff can cause contamination of waters, and given its propensity to volatilize and disperse during application, there is no assurance that curtailed usage on the order of 12 million pounds per year will not continue to affect widespread areas beyond the location of application. The agency staff established as well, the existence of acceptable substitutes for all crop uses of DDT except on onions and sweet potatoes in storage and green peppers.

Registrants attempted but failed to surmount the evidence of established risks and the existence of substitutes by arguing that the buildup of DDT in the environment and its migration to remote areas have resulted from past uses and misuses. There is, however, no persuasive evidence of record to show that the aggregate volume of use of DDT for all uses in question, given the method of application, will not result in continuing dispersal and buildup in the environment and thus add to or maintain the stress on the environment resulting from past use. The Department of Agriculture has, for its part, emphasized DDT's low acute toxicity in comparison to that of alternative chemicals and thus tried to make the risk and benefit equation balance out favorably for the continued use of DDT. While the acute toxicity of methyl parathion must, in the short run, be taken into account, it does not justify continued use of DDT on a long-term basis. Where a chemical can be safely used if label directions are followed, a producer cannot avoid the risk of his own negligence by exposing third parties and the environment to a long-term hazard.

All crop uses of DDT are canceled except for application to onions for control of cutworms, weevils on stored sweet potatoes, and sweet peppers.

## SUMMARY

In the 1970s many new environmental laws were passed. Older tools for protecting human health and welfare—such as the action to abate a nuisance—have to a large extent been supplanted by comprehensive legislation prescribing across-the-board measures to deal with the major kinds and sources of pollution. The National Environmental Policy Act was passed to require the federal government to take into account the environmental effects of the actions that it proposes to take.

The Clean Air Act of 1970, as amended in 1977, provides a comprehensive scheme for dealing with air pollution from mobile sources and stationary sources. The act sets out time schedules by which certain control measures must be instituted in order to reduce air pollution.

Water pollution has posed potential health problems for many years. Federal water pollution control legislation was first passed in 1948 and has been amended several times since then. The Clean Water Act of 1972 established a comprehensive framework for controlling water pollution. It provides for setting standards, issuing permits and constructing municipal waste water treatment systems with federal assistance.

The disposal of hazardous waste is regulated under the Resource Conservation and Recovery Act of 1976. The "Superfund" law, passed in 1980, provides a mechanism for identifying and cleaning up the most hazardous uncontrolled waste sites.

Use of agricultural chemicals in the last few decades has led to vast increases in productivity and at the same time has posed increased risks to the environment. The Federal Insecticide, Fungicide and Rodenticide Act gives EPA the responsibility to register pesticides before they can be sold, to restrict their use, to set limits on residues on food products, and to provide for the certification of applicators. Pesticides whose risks outweigh their benefits may have their registration canceled or suspended.

The development, use, storage, transportation, and disposal of toxic and other hazardous substances are regulated under the Toxic Substances Control Act.

## PROBLEM CASES

1. Washington, D.C.'s National Airport is owned by the federal government and operated by the Federal Aviation Administration. A group of citizens who lived and worked in the vicinity of National Airport were concerned about the congestion, noise, and air pollution accompanying the heavy use of National, while two other area airports, Dulles and Friendship, were substantially underutilized. In 1968, the FAA permitted the airlines servicing National to replace 727–100 model planes with the 727–200 model planes known as "stretch jets." The 727–200 is about 15–20 feet longer than the 727–100 and can carry 120 passengers, as opposed to the 98 carried by the 727–100. There is some evidence that the 727–200 is quieter and safer than the 727–100 and that it rarely, if ever, is loaded to a gross maximum weight greater than that of the 727–100. The group of citizens filed suit against the FAA, contending that the introduction of stretch jets required an environmental impact statement pursuant to NEPA. Should an impact statement be required?

2. As part of its iron ore processing operations at Silver Bay, Minnesota, Reserve discharges asbestos fibers into the air. Minnesota air pollution control regulations prohibit the operation of an emission source unless it has filtration equipment that will collect 99 percent, by weight, of the particulate matter discharged by the plant. The Reserve filtration equipment did not comply with this standard, thus resulting in levels of asbestos in the air

that were potentially harmful to public health. The state of Minnesota brought suit to enjoin the asbestos discharges as a public nuisance. Should an injunction be granted?

**3.** In 1970, Marshall Stacy bought for $40,000 a 240-acre farm with 40,000 Christmas trees on it. He cultivated and pruned the trees, and each year he cut a number of trees for sale in the Washington, D.C. metropolitan area. He noticed that the trees were not growing as fast as similar trees would normally grow and that many of the trees were discolored. He discovered that the cause of the retarded growth and damage was air pollution, primarily sulfur oxides in the emissions from a large power plant that was located about 22 miles away. Stacy brought suit against the power company, claiming as damages the difference between the value of the damaged trees and the value that they would have had if they had not been damaged. Should Stacy be able to recover?

**4.** In January 1969, crude oil began to escape under and near an oil drilling platform operated by the Union Oil Company in the Santa Barbara (California) channel. The crude oil was carried by winds and tides over the surface of the ocean and onto the adjacent coastlines, causing damages to property and to the ecology of the area, including the fishing potential. A group of commercial fishermen brought suit against Union Oil, claiming that they were entitled to compensation for the injury to commercial fishing attributable to its negligence. If the fishermen can show that Union Oil was negligent, should they be allowed to recover from it?

**5.** From 1939 to 1969, Barnes & Tucker Company operated a bituminous deep coal mine under approximately 6,600 acres in Cambria County, Pennsylvania, near the headwaters of the West Branch of the Susquehanna River. In July 1969, the mine was closed and sealed. Following the closure the mine became inundated with water, and in June 1970 substantial discharges of acid mine drainage were discovered coming from the mine and making their way into the river. The Pennsylvania Clean Streams Law, enacted in 1970, provides: "The discharge of sewage or industrial waste into the waters of this Commonwealth, which causes or contributes to pollution as herein defined or creates a danger of such pollution, is hereby declared not to be a reasonable or natural use of such waters, to be against public policy and to be a public nuisance." It further provides: "Any activity or condition declared by this act to be a nuisance, shall be abatable in the manner provided by law or equity for the abatement of nuisances." The Commonwealth brought suit against Barnes & Tucker to require it to abate or treat the acid mine drainage. Should the court require that the drainage be abated or treated?

**6.** Wilson owned a farm in Jefferson County, Virginia, on which cotton was grown. Three quarters of a mile away, the Elms Company owned land on which it grew rice. On a day when no wind was blowing, the Elms Company had its rice crop carefully dusted by an aviator who was a professional crop duster. He used 2–4–D, a powerful chemical manufactured by Chapman Chemical Company. The chemical is very damaging to any broad-leaved plant with which it has contact, but does no damage to grasses and plants that are not broad-leaved. The 2–4–D drifted and settled on the cotton on the Wilson farm, greatly reducing the yield of cotton. Wilson brought suit against Elm Company and Chapman Chemical Company to recover compensation for the damage. While Chapman warned users of the damage that the product would cause to broad-leaved plants, it had not done any tests to determine what dangers were posed by dusting 2–4–D by airplane, which it knew was a common way of applying agricultural chemicals. In fact, it recommended this method for applying 2–4–D. Users of agricultural chemicals, such as Elm Company, knew that these chemicals normally did not float more than 50–100 feet beyond the area where they were applied and were given no reason by Chapman to suspect otherwise as to 2–4–D. Should Elm and/or Chapman be liable to Wilson for the damage caused to her cotton crop?

# Chapter 49

# The Legal Environment for International Business

## INTRODUCTION

**Increasing Importance of International Transactions.** Since the end of World War II, transactions with people abroad have constituted a steadily increasing proportion of the business of U.S. firms. Many U.S. firms have come to realize that the world market for their products is many times the size of the domestic market. For a U.S. firm that has traditionally confined itself to the domestic market, the simplest way to exploit the world market is to continue to keep all of its manufacturing operations at home while seeking export customers abroad. Sometimes, however, a U.S. firm will find it more profitable to exploit the world market by having its product manufactured abroad, closer to where its potential foreign customers are located. Production abroad may permit the use of lower-priced labor and provide better access to raw materials as well as avoid the tariff and other trade barriers that exist for goods exported from the United States. A firm may arrange production abroad by *licensing* the technology associated with its product to an existing foreign company. The foreign company (the *licensee*) pays the U.S. firm (the *li-*

*censor*) a certain percentage of the revenues derived from selling the licensed product. Alternatively, the U.S. firm may decide to invest in its own production and sales facilities abroad.

**The International Legal Environment.** When a U.S. firm considers undertaking sales, licensing, or investment activities abroad, it faces a very different legal environment than when it considers undertaking any of these activities in the United States. International transactions, like their domestic counterparts, raise many legal questions about the rights of the parties vis-á-vis each other and about the kinds of business activities that are permissible. While some of the questions are similar to those raised by domestic transactions, others are special to international transactions because of the special features of the transactions themselves. The parties to international transactions are much less likely to know each other well because they are separated by great distances. It is more difficult to pursue remedies when multiple legal systems are involved. Currency exchanges are usually required. The answers to the legal questions raised by international transactions come from a mix of the laws of our own country, those of the other country or countries involved, and certain doctrines of international law. This chapter is intended to give a sense of the legal environment of international business by examining a few selected legal questions that frequently arise in connection with international sales, licensing, and investment.

## SALES ABROAD OF DOMESTICALLY MANUFACTURED PRODUCTS

The export of a product manufactured at home is the most common form of international transaction engaged in by U.S. firms. A firm may make direct sales to customers abroad, or it may appoint one or more distributors for a particular country or region that purchase the product from the U.S. firm and resell it to customers in their territory. These two methods of exploiting the world market can involve different legal problems.

**Direct Sales to Customers Abroad.** A *direct sale* to a customer abroad based simply on the customer's contractual promise to pay when the goods arrive frequently does not provide the seller with sufficient assurance of payment. The U.S. seller may not know its overseas customer well enough to determine the customer's financial condition or any tendency of the customer to refuse payment by quibbling over the conformity of the goods with the contract if the customer no longer wants the goods when they arrive. If payment is not forthcoming for either of these reasons, the seller will find it difficult and expensive to pursue its legal rights under the contract. Even if the seller feels assured that the buyer will pay for the goods upon arrival, the time required for shipping the goods will often mean that payment will not be received until months after shipment.

To solve these problems, the seller often insists on structuring the sale as a *documentary irrevocable letter of credit transaction.* The transaction usually has two parties in addition to the U.S. seller and its foreign customer: an *issuing bank* located in the customer's country, with which the customer typically has close banking relations, and a *confirming bank* located in the United States, which is well known to the seller. A **letter of credit** is an agreement by the issuing bank to pay a stated amount upon presentation to the issuing bank of a *bill of lading* covering the collection of goods identified in the letter together with any other documents called for in the letter. The **bill of lading** is a document issued by a carrier acknowledging that the seller has delivered particular goods to it, for example, eight tractors of a certain model, and entitling the holder to receive these goods at the place of destination. The letter of credit is issued by the issuing bank pursuant to an agreement between the buyer and the issuing bank. The confirmation of the letter of credit performs a function similar to that performed by the endorsement of a note; it constitutes a promise to the seller by the confirming bank to pay on the letter of credit in accordance with its terms. The confirmation is needed because the seller, unlike the confirming bank, may not know any more about the financial integrity of the issuing bank than it knows about that of the buyer.

The first stage in the transaction is a simple sales contract between the seller and the buyer that conditions shipment of the goods by the seller on the seller's prior receipt of a letter of credit and its confirmation. If everything works as planned, the seller delivers the goods to the carrier and is issued a bill of lading, which it presents to the confirming bank in return for payment. The confirming bank sends the bill of lading to the issuing bank for reimbursement. The issuing bank, which by that time will have received payment from the customer (unless the issuing bank and the buyer have entered into special credit arrangements between themselves), will deliver the bill of lading to the customer for use in obtaining the goods upon their arrival.

This arrangement solves the various problems confronting sellers in direct sales to customers abroad. The seller has a promise of immediate payment from an entity known by it to be financially solvent (the confirming bank). Since payment will have been made to the seller well before the goods arrive, if the customer no longer wants the goods upon arrival, it cannot claim that the goods are defective and refuse to accept delivery and pay for them, leaving the seller with the burden of suing. (If the goods are truly defective upon arrival, the customer can, of course, commence an action for damages against the seller based on the original sales contract between the seller and the customer.)

The letter of credit will typically bear the following legend:

> This credit is subject to the Uniform Customs and Practice for Documentary Credits (1974 Revision), International Chamber of Commerce Publication No. 290.

The Uniform Customs, which are essentially a codification of international practices that have developed with respect to letter of credit transactions over the last hundred years, are generally very protective of sellers' rights. If a seller were forced to sue a confirming bank for payment under a letter of credit bearing the above legend, a court in the state where the bank is located would look to the Uniform Customs for resolution of all issues covered by them, and to Article 5 of the Uniform Commercial Code for resolution of any remaining issues. The most important concept behind both the Uniform Customs and Article 5 is that the promises made by the issuing and confirming banks are *independent* of the underlying sales contract between the seller and the customer. The confirming bank's only responsibility is to make sure that the bill of lading covers the goods identified in the letter of credit and that any other documents that called for in the letter conform to its requirements. If so, the confirming bank is required to pay the seller. It is no defense that the customer has refused to pay the issuing bank or even, generally, that the customer claims to know that the goods are defective.

**Sales Abroad through a Distributor.** If a U.S. firm believes that there is a substantial market for its product in some area abroad, it may find that appointing a distributor located in that area (the "territory" of the distributorship) is a more effective and efficient way to exploit the market than selling directly to customers. A **distribution agreement** is a contract between the seller and the distributor that usually sets forth a wide range of terms and conditions. The interpretation and enforceability of most of these terms and conditions—such as price, method of payment, product warranties, guarantees of supply availability, and guarantees of minimum purchases—primarily involve contract law. To the extent that there is a difference between the contract law of the seller's jurisdiction and that of the distributor, courts in the United States and abroad will typically respect the choice of the parties as to which law applies if the parties, as is usual, have included a *choice of law* clause in the agreement.

Two possible provisions in an international distribution agreement can raise special problems. The first is an **exclusive dealing** or **requirements contract** provision, whereby the distributor promises not to distribute competing products of any other manufacturer. A seller often wants such a provision because it encourages the distributor to devote its full efforts to sales of the seller's product and not to sales of a competing product. The second is an **exclusive distributorship** provision, whereby the seller promises that it will not appoint another distributor in the same territory. Distributors frequently want such a provision in order to protect the efforts they make to build up a base of customers in the territory.

**Exclusive Dealing.** A U.S. seller's inclusion of an exclusive dealing provision in an international distribution agreement may, if the distributor represents a major outlet for products of the kind covered, raise serious problems under the U.S. antitrust laws even though all the sales will be abroad.[1] The objection under the U.S. laws is that such an arrangement could restrict the ability of other U.S. firms to export into the territory involved. In a comparable domestic transaction, where the distributor's territory was within the United States, such an agreement would under many circumstances violate Section 3 of the Clayton Act, but Section 3 applies only to sales of goods for use within the United States. Section 1 of the Sherman Act, however, applies to contracts in restraint of trade with foreign nations as well as among the several states. Exclusive dealing arrangements are among the types of activities that have been found to violate Section 1 of the Sherman Act if they fail the *rule of reason* test. Whether or not a particular exclusive dealing provision constitutes an unreasonable restraint of trade in violation of Section 1 would depend on such factors as the distributor's importance as an outlet for goods in the territory, the duration of the arrangement, the ability of the arrangement to reduce the costs of the seller or distributor, and the share of the market in the territory already commanded by the seller's product. (An exclusive dealing arrangement would be viewed more sympathetically if the seller were just entering the market and needed the arrangement to help it get a foothold.)

**Exclusive Distributorship.** A U.S. firm's appointment of an exclusive foreign distributor would not by itself normally raise problems under the U.S. antitrust laws, because the restraint involved neither affects competition within the United States nor denies any other U.S. seller access to a foreign market. It may, however, raise questions under the antitrust laws of the country or coun-

[1] The antitrust laws are discussed in detail in Chapters 44 and 45.

tries constituting the territory assigned to the foreign distributor because exclusive distributorships eliminate *intrabrand competition*—that is, competition among different distributors handling the same brand of the product. Most foreign countries have a less inclusive set of regulations concerning trade restraints than that of the United States. Since World War II, however, many of the developed Western nations have moved in the direction of the U.S. model. The most important development of this kind has been the establishment of the competition law of the European Economic Community (the Common Market), which includes all of our major European trading partners. The fundamental rules constituting the competition law are so basic to the scheme of the Common Market that they are set forth in the Treaty of Rome, which established it.

For example, paragraph 1 of Article 85 of the treaty prohibits

> all agreements . . . which may affect trade between member states and which have as their object or effect the prevention, restriction or distortion of competition within the common market.

Agreements prohibited by Article 85 are *void*, and fines may be imposed on parties entering into such agreements. Any exclusive distributorship for a territory covering more than one member state, if the market share of the seller's product and the volume of commerce are anything more than *de minimis* (inconsequential), is prohibited by paragraph 1 because it restricts competition among distributors of the product (intrabrand competition). Paragraph 3 of Article 85, however, provides that the Commission of the European Communities may declare the provisions of paragraph 1 to be inapplicable to any agreement

> which contributes to improving the production or distribution of goods or to promoting technical or economic progress, while allowing consumers a fair share of the resulting benefit, and which does not (a) impose . . . restrictions which are not indispensable to the attainment of these objectives; (b) afford [the parties] the possibility of eliminating competition in respect of a substantial part of the products in question.

Parties wishing to obtain such a declaration of inapplicability must "notify" the agreement to the Commission. The Commission would probably declare paragraph 1 inapplicable to an exclusive distributorship notified to it if the agreement provided for a relatively limited duration (less than five years) and involved the product of a U.S. firm not previously available in the Community in significant quantity. An exclusive distributorship in such a situation gives the distributor an incentive to make a vigorous introduction of the product into the Common Market and therefore enhances *interbrand competition* (competition among the products of competing manufacturers) more than it injures intrabrand competition. It should be noted that the probable result is the same as it would be under U.S. law in the case of a comparable domestic distributorship, but the basic scheme of regulation is quite different. The broad language of Section 1 of the Sherman Act could be interpreted to prohibit all exclusive distributorships, but the courts, applying the "rule of reason" test, have interpreted it more narrowly and made clear that an exclusive distributorship with the characteristics described above would not be illegal.[2] Paragraph 1 of Article 85, however, is interpreted as broadly as it reads and clearly prohibits such an exclusive distributorship. Exemption from the applicability of paragraph 1 is obtained only by application to the Commission, an administrative body with considerable discretion with respect to such matters.

If a distribution agreement is void under

---

[2] See the case of *Continental T.V., Inc. v. GTE Sylvania, Inc.* in Chapter 44.

the European Economic Community competition law, that fact renders irrelevant the status of the agreement under the laws of the nations covered by the territory. As the following case illustrates, the competition law gives private parties rights that can be adjudicated in national courts of member nations of the Common Market.

## Electric Massage Instruments

**CCH Common Mkt. Rptr. ¶ 8030 (Dist. Ct., Mannheim, West Germany 1965)**

An agreement between the German importer and its British supplier made the importer the sole distributor of certain electric massage appliances in France and the Federal Republic of Germany. On June 14, 1962, the German importer entered into an agreement with a French distributor making the latter the sole distributor of the appliances in France. Among other things, the French firm agreed to buy a certain minimum number of the devices per year from the German importer and to refrain from buying or distributing competing products. A provision of the agreement stated that it could not be terminated by either party before March 31, 1963. No notification of the agreement was filed with the EEC Commission.

Similar massage instruments appeared on the French market at considerably lower prices, and the French distributor stopped buying from the German importer in September 1962. On December 20, 1962, the distributor rejected the importer's demand for fulfillment of the agreement to purchase a certain number of devices. The German importer then sued for damages. The French distributor contended that the agreement violated Article 85, paragraph 1, of the Treaty of Rome, that it was null and void, and hence that it could not be the basis for a claim for damages.

THE DISTRICT COURT. The sole distributorship agreement entered into between the parties on June 14, 1962, meets the conditions set forth in paragraph 1 of Article 85 of the Treaty establishing the European Community.

The sole distributorship agreement restricts competition in the Common Market. It restricts participating enterprises in their freedom to deal. The plaintiff, located in Germany, is prevented from supplying other distributors in France with electric massage instruments, and the defendant, located in France, is prohibited from distributing the products of competitors.

This restriction of competition [in the market for electric massage instruments in EEC Member States] is perceptible. The restriction of competition need not affect the entire economy. The plaintiff's obligation to supply the defendant exclusively results in the defendant's having the distribution monopoly in the French market since the plaintiff, according to its pleadings, is the sole distributor in Germany and France. Electric massage instruments manufactured by other firms need not be considered here since, according to the circumstances in this case, they cannot be regarded as similar goods.

The restriction of competition resulting from the sole distributorship agreement is liable to affect trade between the Member States of the European Economic Community. According to the preventive intent of Treaty Article 85, the term "to affect" implies an artificial deflection of the inter-State flow of goods from its normal and natural course. Whatever the harmful or beneficial effect of this deflection may be is immaterial.

The fact that new products are usually introduced [into] markets via sole distributorship agreements, together with an exclusivity clause, does not prove that the flow of goods so channeled would take its normal, natural course and therefore would not affect trade between the Member States. Instead, the course taken by goods unhampered by such contractual regulation should be considered as normal and natural. Any restraints on competition, as in this case, imposed for reasons of technical marketing necessities probably could be taken into consideration in an exemption under Article 85, paragraph 3, of the treaty.

The sole distributorship agreement is not exempt from the prohibition of Treaty Article 85, paragraph 1. There can be no exemption by the EEC Commission under Article 85, paragraph 3, of the Treaty since the parties failed to notify their exclusive agreement. This notification could have been given after June 14, 1962, the day the agreement was entered into, and prior to December 20, 1962, the day the defendant permanently refused to fulfill its obligations, thus canceling the contract. The EEC Commission could at best have granted an exemption to take effect as of the date of notification.

Hence the sole distributorship agreement is invalid, i.e., void forever, and notification is no longer possible since both parties lost their mutual rights to demand fulfillment after the defendant's final refusal on December 20, 1962, to fulfill the agreement. Notification is possible only if it can have some bearing on the validity of an agreement for which notification is to be given. This was not the case here.

The consequences under civil law of the invalidity of the agreement are direct, according to Article 85, paragraph 2, without necessitating a constitutive or declaratory decision of the Commission, because Treaty Article 85 sets forth a genuine prohibition having direct effect.

The sole distributorship agreement is null and void in its entirety since those provisions that are void under cartel law cannot be taken out without rendering the entire agreement meaningless, in light of the parties' apparent intent. Without the plaintiff's obligation not to supply other distributors in France, the defendant would not have agreed to buy a certain number of items; and without the obligation to buy a certain number of items and not to carry competing products, the plaintiff would not have entrusted the defendant with the introduction of its products on the French market.

Judgment for the French distributor.

## LICENSING TECHNOLOGY TO MANUFACTURERS ABROAD

**Introduction.** As suggested in the introduction to this chapter, a U.S. firm can exploit the world market by *licensing* its technology to a foreign manufacturer. The technology may be embodied in the product (a *product* innovation), giving it superior features, or it may be used in the manufacture of the product (a *process* innovation), lowering the cost of production and permitting a more competitive price for the product.

Some of the technology that a firm develops is *patentable.*[3] If a firm acquires a valid patent in a particular country based on a process innovation, it can prohibit the use of the tech-

[3] Patent law is discussed in detail in Chapter 43.

nology in that country in the manufacture of any product. If the patent is based on a product innovation, sales in that country of the product, wherever manufactured, are prohibited as well. It is not difficult for a firm to acquire *parallel patents* in each of the major countries maintaining a patent system. Many such countries are parties to the International Convention for the Protection of Industrial Property Rights. This results in a certain degree of uniformity in their patent laws and in a recognition of the date of the first filing in any of the countries as the filing date for all. Once having established such a worldwide position, a U.S. firm can, in return for an agreement to pay royalties, license a manufacturer abroad to manufacture and, if a product innovation is involved, to sell the product within a particular territory.

Other technology may not be patented, either because it is not patentable or because a firm makes a business decision not to patent it. If the technology is a process innovation, the firm that developed it may still be able to control its use abroad by keeping it a secret. The firm can license the know-how to a particular manufacturer for use in a defined territory in return for promises to pay royalties and to keep the know-how confidential. Such an arrangement is more likely to be workable where considerable technical assistance from the licensor (in the form of plant design or employee skill training) is necessary in order to transfer the technology to the licensee.

**Antitrust Problems.** International licensing of technology, if done on an exclusive basis, sometimes gives rise to the same kinds of antitrust questions under the laws of the foreign country or countries constituting the territory as do exclusive distributorships. An exclusive license of a product innovation means that no one other than the licensee, not even the licensor, can manufacture or sell the product in the designated territory.

An exclusive license agreement limits competition among products using the same technology, a concept very similar to limitations on intrabrand competition. Such an agreement, like an exclusive distributorship, violates paragraph 1 of Article 85 of the Treaty of Rome and would be illegal and unenforceable unless the Commission of the European Communities granted an exemption under paragraph 3 of Article 85. The Commission would, however, probably find paragraph 1 inapplicable to an exclusive license of limited duration to manufacture and sell a product of a U.S. firm that is not being, and absent the exclusive license would not be expected to be, imported into the Common Market in significant quantities. The exclusivity feature would be regarded as a necessary incentive to get a manufacturer to introduce the product into the Common Market.

**Regulation of Technology Transfer.** Many countries, particularly in the developing parts of the world, regulate licensing agreements made with their nationals by requiring registration of all such agreements with a governmental agency that can approve or disapprove them. The rules governing approval tend to be quite complex and to permit the governmental agency considerable discretion. In a country such as Japan, the most prominent developed country with such a program, the primary goal of the program, which is administered by the Bank of Japan, appears to be to improve the ability of its manufacturers to obtain more favorable bargaining terms. Instead of having different Japanese manufacturers compete with one another to get a desirable piece of technology from a U.S. licensor, with the licensor awarding the license to the highest bidder, the governmental agency in effect tells the licensor that the large, prosperous Japanese market will not be available to it at all unless it agrees to accept considerably less favorable terms than would have resulted without the regulation.

The regulatory schemes in developing countries usually have other goals in addition to improving the bargaining power of their nationals. The agency administering the regulations may not want the country's scarce resources being used to pay royalties unless the licensed technology fits into the country's basic development plans. Technical training of local personnel may be required, and there may be a requirement that the technology be fully disclosed and become freely available to all nationals after a specified period of time (in Brazil, for example, the period for unpatented technology is customarily five years from the commencement of production, although extensions are sometimes granted). Conditions in a license agreement requiring the licensee to purchase machinery or raw materials exclusively from the licensor are frequently prohibited. Sometimes, the goal of the regulatory schemes is to make licensing so unattractive that the potential licensor will decide that it is more profitable to exploit the developing country's market by making a direct investment to set up a manufacturing facility in the country, the subject of the next section.

## INVESTMENT TO ESTABLISH A MANUFACTURING OPERATION ABROAD

**Introduction.** Before a U.S. firm decides to establish a manufacturing operation abroad, a wide variety of legal issues must be examined. Many of them are peculiar to the particular country that is being considered as the location of the facility. Labor laws may be very different from our own and may impose long-term obligations on the employer. Import license requirements and high tariffs may force the firm to use local sources of supplies and raw materials and to manufacture locally a certain percentage by value of the parts used in assembling the final product. Some countries, such as Mexico, generally prohibit foreigners from having a majority equity interest in any operation within their borders. The U.S. firm owns a 49 percent interest in the operation and must find one or more friendly local businesspersons to supply the other 51 percent of the necessary equity capital. Many of the manufacturing activities may require licenses from governmental authorities.

Two problems of a more general nature deserve particular attention: investment *repatriation* (bringing back to the United States earnings on the investment and, if the time ever arrives, the proceeds from the sale or liquidation of the operation) and *expropriation.*

**Repatriation of Earnings and Investment.** Many countries, particularly those in the developing world, have regulations concerning the conversion of their currency into a foreign currency, such as dollars, and the remittance of the funds so obtained to another country, such as the United States. When a U.S. firm wishes to *repatriate* some of the earnings from an operation in a country with such regulations by causing its subsidiary to pay a dividend, permission must be obtained from the currency exchange authorities. These authorities operate under rules that are intended to encourage foreign firms to reinvest their earnings in the country rather than bring them home. Some countries place an absolute limit, stated in terms of a set percentage of the amount that a firm has invested (the original amount and any reinvestment of retained earnings), on the amount of earnings that may be repatriated each year. Other countries place a substantial "income withholding tax" on repatriated earnings, which increases in percentage with the amount repatriated. If a U.S. firm wants to sell or liquidate its operations, all proceeds in excess of the original investment are usually considered dividends, and their repatriation may be either prohibited or taxed at a very high rate. The existence of such regulations in a country means that a U.S. firm should normally not consider a major investment in that country unless it is prepared to make a long-term commitment.

**Expropriation.** One of the biggest fears of a U.S. firm investing in a politically unstable country is *expropriation*—the taking of its facilities by the host government—without adequate compensation. If the property of a U.S. firm in a foreign country is taken by the host government and the U.S. firm does not receive adequate compensation after exhausting any legal remedies available to it in that country, the only legal option open to the firm is to try to find property that belongs to the host government and is located outside the country and to seek compensation from the proceeds of the sale of that property. This requires finding a legally recognized forum (a court of another nation or an international arbitral tribunal) that is willing to listen, establishing before the forum a claim that the taking without compensation has damaged the firm in violation of international law, and convincing the authority having jurisdiction over the host government's property that the property should be used to satisfy the claim. This is a very difficult course of action, and there is a high probability that the firm will be frustrated at some step and be left without compensation.

**Different Interpretations of International Law.** The first problem is that there is no consensus as to what kind of compensation international law requires in this kind of situation. The United States takes the position that international law requires adequate, effective, and prompt compensation anytime a foreign government takes property belonging to someone who is not a national of that country. Although this interpretation of applicable international law, which is consistent with the idea of due process under our Constitution, is shared by most of the developed Western nations, it is rejected by many of the developing countries and by the Communist countries. Some of these countries contend that international law only requires nondiscriminatory treatment of their nationals and nonnationals. Others recognize the principle that compensation is required, but assert that it may be delayed if immediate payment would frustrate what they view as vital state programs (as would almost always be the case where there is a social revolution that includes a program of massive expropriation).

**Finding a Forum.** The next problem is that it would be very difficult for a U.S. firm to persuade even a U.S. court (which clearly would adhere to the U.S. view of international law) to take and listen to such a claim, because of the **sovereign immunity** and **act of state** doctrines.[4] Although different, both are doctrines of judicial restraint that are intended, among other things, to prevent courts from making decisions that might lead to friction between a foreign country and our own. A court of another country is an even less likely forum because it will not be anxious to put itself in the middle of a dispute between a national of one foreign country and the government of another. No arbitral tribunal is available unless both parties consented at some point to use one. And even in a case where there was such a consent, the tribunal, while able to hear the case and render a decision, would not have the power to order the use of the host government's property to satisfy any claim that it might feel the U.S. firm established. That order would have to be sought separately from a court having juris-

[4] These doctrines are discussed in detail in Chapter 45.

diction over the property after a favorable decision of the tribunal.

**Other Remedies.** The best protection against the risk of expropriation is insurance. In order to encourage U.S. private investment in developing countries, the U.S. government established the Overseas Private Investment Corporation (OPIC), a government corporation that offers low-cost *expropriation insurance* for certain kinds of investment projects in designated countries. If an expropriation of an insured project occurs, the U.S. firm receives compensation from OPIC in return for assigning to OPIC the firm's claim against the host government. The program is available only for investments in countries that have signed executive agreements with the United States that recognize in advance the legitimacy of such assignments and provide for arbitration if any dispute does arise.

In the case of an uninsured expropriation, the U.S. government has a general policy of using measured diplomatic pressure to aid the U.S. firm involved, but the amount of pressure varies from administration to administration and from case to case. In many cases, this remedy, unlike the purely legal remedies described above, results in at least partial satisfaction of the firm's claim.

## SUMMARY

The legal environment for business transactions is frequently quite different abroad than in the United States. This is true whether the transactions are direct sales between a foreign customer and an American seller, sales through a foreign distributor, a transfer of technology to a foreign manufacturer, or the establishment by an American corporation of facilities within a foreign country.

Direct sales often involve documentary irrevocable letters of credit. After entering into a purchase contract, a foreign buyer arranges for the issuance of a letter of credit by an issuing bank. The confirmation of the letter of credit by a confirming bank is a promise to pay the seller by the confirming bank upon presentation by the seller of the documents required by the letter, including the bill of lading. The confirming bank sends the documents to the issuing bank for reimbursement, and the issuing bank passes the documents on to the buyer, thereby enabling the buyer to take delivery of the goods. The obligations of the confirming and issuing banks are contingent only on presentation of the proper documents and are independent of whether the seller has performed in accordance with the terms of the underlying sales contract.

International sales through distributors frequently involve an exclusive arrangement by which the seller agrees to give the distributor exclusive rights to distribute a product or line in a certain geographic area or the distributor agrees not to handle competing products. A U.S. manufacturer's appointment of an exclusive distributor abroad normally does not raise problems under American antitrust law, but it may under foreign law, especially within the Common Market under Article 85, paragraph 1, of the Treaty of Rome. Under paragraph 3 of Article 85, the Commission of the European Communities may, upon application of a party, declare paragraph 1 to be inapplicable. On the other hand, an agreement by a distributor not to handle competing products may constitute a violation of Section 1 of the Sherman Act even though all sales are abroad.

The exclusive licensing of technology to manufacturers abroad, whether that technology is protected by foreign patents or by secrecy, may also raise antitrust problems. In the Common Market, an exemption may be sought under paragraph 3 of Article 85.

Many countries, especially developing countries, require the registration of all licensing agreements with a governmental agency. Japan's goal in establishing such a requirement appears to be to gain favorable terms for Japanese firms by discouraging them from competing with one another in seeking a license. Developing countries seek to make the terms as advantageous as possible to their interests and to prevent their nationals from using scarce foreign exchange to make royalty payments on technology licenses not central to their plans for development.

American firms seeking to manufacture abroad face special problems. The most general problems are host country restraints on the repatriation of earnings and the possibility of expropriation by the host country of the American investment without compensation.

## PROBLEM CASES

**1.** R & M, a newsprint dealer located in New York City, entered into a sales contract with the *Times-Herald* (T-H) of Bermuda to make a 1,000-ton shipment of newsprint with a bursting strength of "11–12, 32 pounds" at a price of $75 per ton. The contract called for T-H to arrange for the issuance of a letter of credit confirmed by the National Park Bank of New York City in the amount of $75,000. The letter of credit was issued and confirmed. It stated that it was issued "to cover a shipment of 1,000 tons of newsprint 11–12, 32 lb. strength" and provided that payment to R & M would be made "upon presentation of the following documents: an invoice of R & M covering the goods and a bill of lading giving the holder control of the goods." Shortly before R & M made its shipment, T-H heard from some other publishers that R & M had been sending out paper with below-grade bursting strength. T-H requested National Park Bank not to pay on the letter of credit unless the two documents were accompanied by a certified report of an independent testing agency showing that the newsprint met the bursting strength requirements of the sales contract. R & M shipped the goods and presented the bank with its invoice (which purported to cover 1,000 tons of 11–12, 32 pound newsprint) and the bill of lading (acknowledging receipt by the carrier of 1,000 tons of newsprint). R & M refused to provide a test report. The bank refused to pay. R & M sued the bank on the letter of credit. Will it recover?

**2.** Minicomputer, Inc. (Mini), a U.S. manufacturer, started selling its tabletop computers in Europe several years ago and captured about 20 percent of the market, second only to Eurocomp S.A., a Belgian firm, which had 27 percent of the market. The computers of the two companies sold for approximately the same price. Mini felt that its product was at least equal to, and probably superior to, the Eurocomp product but that the Mini sales network was less effective. In order to rectify this situation, Mini entered into a 10-year distributorship arrangement with Continental, Europe's largest electronic products distributor. Mini agreed not to appoint any other distributor of its product in Europe, and Continental, in return, agreed not to distribute any competing model of tabletop computer. A year later Newcomp, Inc., a new U.S. manufacturer of tabletop computers with a growing share of the U.S. market, sued Mini, claiming that Newcomp's export sales to Europe were being hindered by the Mini-Continental arrangement. The suit claimed that the arrangement violated both Section 3 of the Clayton Act and Section 1 of the Sherman Act. Is the arrangement illegal?

**3.** Suppose that prior to any court decision in the suit discussed above, Newcomp and Mini reached a settlement by which Mini released Continental from its promise not to distribute any other brand of tabletop computer. Continental then gladly agreed with Newcomp to become a distributor of its promising new tabletop computer. Mini, fearing that Continental would curtail its efforts to sell Mini computers, appointed a second European distributor. Continental sued in a European court to block this action by Mini as a violation of their agreement. Suppose that neither Mini nor Continental had notified the agreement to the Commission of the European Communities. What would be the result of Continental's suit? If either of the parties had notified the agreement to the Commission, what would have been the likely outcome of the request for a declaration of the inapplicability of Article 85, paragraph 1, of the Treaty of Rome?

4. Amerco, a U.S. company has developed a low-cost method of producing plastic beverage bottles that it is employing in a number of plants in the United States. Because of high transportation costs relative to the value of the product, each plant must be located in close proximity to the beverage firm that utilizes the product. The process involves no patented technology, and its details are kept highly confidential by Amerco's management. Because of the success of the process in the United States, Amerco now wants to license it in other parts of the world, and it hopes to eventually include all the major countries of Europe and Latin America. Amerco is now negotiating a 12-year exclusive licensing agreement with its first potential foreign licensee, Britco, a United Kingdom firm. Britco is concerned that the details of the process remain confidential during the full 12-year period because the exclusivity feature of its license would be worthless if another British firm somehow obtained the details and used the process. Britco therefore requests agreement from Amerco that in any licensing arrangement Amerco makes with companies in other countries, the licensee will be required to keep the details secret for at least the 12-year period of Britco's license. Amerco is equally concerned about maintaining strict confidentiality during the next three or four years, but is less concerned about maintaining confidentiality thereafter because it expects to have perfected a new, even better process based on very different principles. Does Britco's request raise any problems for Amerco's licensing plans in other countries? Assuming that the exclusive licensing arrangement does not violate the United Kingdom's own antitrust laws, could it raise any problems under the Common Market antitrust laws?

5. Intelco owned subsidiaries in a number of developing countries that operated telephone systems. One of these systems, in the small Latin American country of Ecubia, was nationalized along with all of the other public utilities after a bloodless coup undertaken by a group of left-wing military officers. The government promised Intelco and the owners of the other public utilities (all Ecubians) that it would pay the full value of the property taken plus accrued interest in five years. The new government provided for such payment as part of its ambitious seven-year development plan. Intelco sued the government in an Ecubian court for immediate compensation, but the court ruled that the government's promise of payment in five years satisfied the requirements of Ecubian law.

Fortunately for Intelco, it had obtained OPIC expropriation insurance covering its investment when it built the Ecubian telephone system. Intelco assigned its claim to OPIC and received compensation in accordance with the insurance plan. The U.S. government on behalf of OPIC, its wholly owned corporation, undertook negotiations to obtain prompt compensation, and when these proved unsuccessful, it called for the formation of an international arbitral tribunal pursuant to the terms of the executive agreement signed 15 years ago by Ecubia and the United States in order to qualify investments in Ecubia for OPIC insurance. This executive agreement, like most other such OPIC program executive agreements, stated: "The arbitral tribunal shall base its decision exclusively on the applicable principles and rules of public international law." Can you predict the decision of the arbitral tribunal?

Chapter 50

# Computer Law

## INTRODUCTION

Our society has exploded into the computer age. Computers have become almost indispensable to businesses of all sizes, governments at all levels, and health, educational, religious, and charitable organizations of all kinds. Whereas the size and expense of early computers precluded their use by most segments of the population, technological advances that dramatically reduced the size and cost of computers have put them within the reach of even small businesses and ordinary consumers. They manage an almost limitless array of functions affecting our daily lives, from managing urban transportation to transferring funds and corporate shares electronically to planning household budgets. The capability of computers to process, store, and retrieve vast quantities of information makes possible greater organization, planning, conservation of human and material resources, and overall efficiency.

The benefits of this new technology are not gained without cost, however. In many instances, computer technology creates new risks of harm to which the law must respond. For example, as an increasing amount of information about people is collected, stored, and integrated, individual privacy is threatened. Unquestioning reliance on computer output that may be based on faulty or misleading data may result in a variety of wrongs, such as the reporting of derogatory credit information or the wrongful repossession of goods or the termination of utility services. Furthermore, the widespread use of computers creates a climate in which knowledgeable but dishonest individuals have the opportunity to use computer technology to accomplish criminal objectives.

The acquisition of computer systems and the marketing of computer products and services are also fraught with uncertainty and risk. Lawsuits seeking compensation from computer suppliers for losses caused by defective systems are now almost commonplace. In such cases, courts must adapt contract and product liability doctrines to computer transactions to determine who will bear the cost of malfunctions or defects in computer systems. Moreover, those who invest massive resources in the development and production of computer products are placed at risk by technology that makes it easy to copy computer equipment and programs. To respond to their need for legal protection against infringement and misappropriation, modifications in traditional law regarding the protection of intellectual property have been necessary.

Courts and legislatures are now engaged in adapting law to computer technology. Although this developing body of law may be termed "Computer Law," it is really not a distinct area of law. Rather, it is an integration of a host of traditional areas of law as they apply to the use of computers. Issues concerning computers cut across almost every area of law. Because of limitations of space and scope, this chapter will focus on a selection of some of the more prevalent legal issues relating to the use of computers: contract and product liability issues, computer crime, invasion of privacy, and protection of producers' rights in computer software.

## CONTRACTING FOR THE ACQUISITION OF COMPUTERS

**The Applicability of the Uniform Commercial Code.** In resolving contracts problems that arise regarding computers, one of the first issues encountered is whether the contract is governed by the Uniform Commercial Code or the common law of contracts. This determination has considerable significance. If the UCC applies, the Code's warranties, rules regarding disclaimers, statute of limitations, and other provisions apply.[1] If the common law of contracts applies, no implied warranties of quality will be applied, general disclaimers and exculpatory clauses[2] are more likely to be enforced, and other common law provisions such as non-UCC statutes of limitation will be applied.

As you learned in Chapter 6, section 2–103 of the UCC provides that Article 2 of the UCC applies to "transactions in goods." Goods are defined in section 2–105 as things that are *movable* at the time they are identified to the contract. Some sections of the Code (such as the warranty sections) speak in terms of the *sale* of goods. Thus, determining the applicable body of law requires a court to classify the transaction in question as a sale of goods. This classification is made more difficult by the differing nature of computer-related products and services and by the various ways in which those products or services are acquired.

A person may acquire computer **hardware** (the physical machinery components of the computer, such as the central processing unit,

---

[1] Specific provisions of Article 2 of the UCC are discussed in Chapters 31, 32, 33, and 34.

[2] Such clauses are discussed in Chapters 12 and 32.

keyboard, and printer) and **software** (the programs or set of instructions used with the hardware to accomplish a certain result). Software may be packaged for general uses (such as household accounting or word processing) or custom-designed by a software manufacturer or an independent consultant for a particular application. Software is often "licensed" rather than sold. The purported effect of such licenses is to permit the producer to retain title to the software while giving the customer the right to use it with strict restrictions on his ability to make copies of the program. (Software licenses will be discussed later in this chapter.) Hardware and software can be acquired together from the same source or separately from different suppliers. Some systems, marketed as "turnkey" systems, contain both hardware and software ready for use. Computer systems may be either purchased or leased from a manufacturer or other seller or a leasing company. In some transactions, a person who wishes to procure the services of a computer may contract for the performance of some service rather than buying or leasing a computer for his own use. For example, a person may contract with a *consultant* or a *service bureau* to process data using input that he supplies.

Obviously, some of the transactions described above are more readily characterized as the sale of goods than are others that are more service-oriented. It is clear that the sale of hardware is a sale of goods, just like the sale of any other manufactured product. The UCC has been held to apply to leases of hardware (and combinations of hardware and software), under the reasoning that such leases are analogous to sales and that they too constitute a "transaction" in goods.

The classification of software and the services of consultants and service bureaus is more difficult because these involve a blend of tangible goods and services. Computer programs are largely conceptual in nature, except for their tangible manifestation in tapes, disks, or punched cards. Custom-designed software is often the end result of the services of an independent consultant, and thus may be more readily characterized as a service rather than a sale of goods.

In determining the applicability of the UCC to these situations, a number of courts have asked whether the customer was bargaining primarily for goods or services. If the goods were the primary factor in the contract, and the services provided were incidental to the sale of goods, the Code will apply. If the reverse is true, and the tangible goods supplied were merely incidental to the services provided, the common law of contracts will apply. In determining the primary objective of the parties, a court might compare the relative cost of the goods and services aspects of the contract.

As a general rule, when software (even custom-designed software) is acquired along with hardware, the transaction will be considered a sale of goods. When packaged software is purchased, it too is likely to be considered a sale of goods. Although the question whether a license of software is a sale of goods has not yet been answered definitively, it is likely that a license of mass-produced and mass-marketed software sold over-the-counter will be considered to be a sale of goods for purposes of the UCC. However, when a customized program is provided as the end product of a consultant's services or when a service bureau supplies written printouts or reports, the transaction is more likely to be characterized as primarily a service, even though some tangible product is being supplied as an incident of the service. The *Triangle Underwriters* case, which follows, presents an analysis of the classification of custom-designed software purchased in combination with hardware. Note that the determination that software was "goods" had the effect of defeating the buyer's claim, since the four-year Code statute of limitations was held to apply instead of the longer statute of limitations that would have been applied had the software been considered services.

## Triangle Underwriters, Inc. v. Honeywell, Inc.

### 457 F. Supp. 765 (E.D.N.Y. 1978)

Honeywell, Inc. develops and sells computer systems. In 1970, Honeywell approached Triangle Underwriters, Inc. to sell or lease Honeywell's H–110 computer system to Triangle. The H–110 system is a package consisting of hardware, or the computer, printer, collator, and other equipment, and programming or software created for use in connection with the hardware. Honeywell supplies both standard programming aids of general application to its computers and "custom application software" designed specifically for the customer's individual needs. In March 1970, Honeywell submitted a formal proposal to Triangle regarding the installation of the H–110 system. The system was to be a turn-key system, with the software pre-prepared and the system ready for immediate functioning. The proposal set forth an implementation plan reciting the steps to be taken to make the system fully operational within 105 days of approval of the proposal. Honeywell employees were to install the system and train Triangle employees in its use, whereupon Triangle would take over complete supervision. The proposal contained no provision requiring Honeywell to update or amend the software after the Triangle employees assumed supervision. A printed lease form was executed in April 1970, and Honeywell began preparation of the custom application software.

In December 1970, Honeywell advised Triangle that the system was fully operational. Triangle then elected to purchase the hardware and entered into a contract to buy it. The system was installed in January 1971. The system failed to function effectively from the beginning. Various programs did not function as had been represented, and there were numerous errors in the system. Honeywell personnel attempted to correct the deficiencies in the programs, which according to the agreement should have been functioning properly at the time of installation. Honeywell personnel worked on these deficiencies until some time in 1972. In August 1975, Triangle brought suit against Honeywell on a variety of theories, including breach of express and implied warranties. Honeywell moved for a summary judgment, arguing that the suit was barred by the statute of limitations.

**Nickerson, District Judge.** Honeywell urges that the warranty counts are all barred by §2–725(1) of the U.C.C., which provides, "An action for breach of any contract for sale must be commenced within four years after the cause of action has accrued." This section applies to transactions in goods, and a cause of action accrues when the breach occurs. Honeywell contends that the essence of all the claims is that Honeywell breached a contract for the sale of goods, that the alleged breach occurred on the January 1971 date of installation, and that the action, brought on August 14, 1975, is therefore barred.

Triangle urges that the completed breach of contract did not occur until after Honeywell ceased in 1972 to correct the deficiencies in the programs. The date when the breach of contract occurred depends on what the agreement between the parties was. Triangle's claim from the inception has been that Honeywell undertook to deliver in January 1971 an entire system, including not only hardware but the programs or software to be used in the hardware. The system was to be a "turn-key" and ready to function immediately. A breach of that undertaking occurred in January 1971 when Honeywell allegedly delivered a defective system, and Triangle would have been entitled to bring suit forthwith.

Triangle contends that the system, which included the software, did not consist solely of "goods" within the definition of the U.C.C., and that what was sold was predominantly "services." If that were true, not the U.C.C. four year statute of limitations, but the longer six year period applicable on contracts generally would apply. This court must therefore consider the nature of this sale to determine how to characterize the transaction.

This court concludes that the H–110 computer system does not principally consist of services. The agreement with Honeywell did not contemplate that it would run a data processing service for Triangle but rather that Honeywell would develop a completed system and deliver it "turn-key" for Triangle to operate. After the installation and training period, Honeywell personnel were to withdraw, and Honeywell's major remaining obligation was to be maintenance. Although the ideas or concepts involved in the custom designed software remained Honeywell's intellectual property, Triangle was purchasing the product of those concepts. That product required efforts to produce, but it was a product nevertheless, and though intangible, is more readily characterized as goods than services. The system was subject to sale, and the services provided by Honeywell, design, installation, and maintenance, were incidental to that sale. Under these circumstances, the sale was subject to the U.C.C. statute of limitations.

Judgment for Honeywell.

---

**Contract Problems in Computer Transactions.** Almost any contract issue that arises in other transactions may arise in a transaction involving computers. Thus, the general principles that you have learned in earlier chapters regarding formation, performance, and third-party rights in contract law will be used to resolve contract problems involving computers. Computer transactions require great care on the part of the buyer, however. Although the cost of computer products and services has declined, a computer system is still a major investment for most buyers. A buyer's major concern is that the system meet his needs and perform as promised. Given the large investment involved in acquiring a computer system and the technical nature of the contract, people entering into contracts for the purchase or lease of computer products or services must take special care to define their needs and, if possible, to bargain for contractual protection.

Unfortunately, it is not always possible for a buyer or a lessee to negotiate favorable terms. Because of the relatively new and rapidly expanding nature of computer technology, computer-related products often do not have the same degree of reliability as other marketed products. Recognizing the potential for tremendous loss that can result from a computer system's failure, sellers of computer-related products attempt to place the risk of malfunction on the buyer through contract provisions that effectively limit or exclude seller liability. A buyer's ability to bargain for favorable terms is likely to be limited, particularly in the purchase of microcomputers and packaged software, which are usually accompanied by printed disclaimers about which the buyer (who is often a first-time user) has no opportunity to bargain. Thus, questions regarding the enforceability of contract clauses that limit or exclude liability are heightened in computer transactions.

**Unconscionability.** In circumstances in which the buyer lacks meaningful choice regarding the terms of the contract that he enters, terms that grant a powerful advantage to sellers of computer-related products are subject to claims or defenses of **unconscionability.** In Chapter 12, you learned that section 2–302 of the Uniform Commercial Code permits courts to refuse to enforce a term in a contract for the sale of goods that is found to be unconscionable. In cases governed by the common law of contracts, a number of courts have adopted the concept of unconscionability by analogy. Thus, the concept of unconscionability operates as a broad limitation on the enforceability of contract terms.

It is difficult to predict in advance whether a court will find a given clause to be unconscionable.[3] The mere fact that the contract term was advantageous to the seller is not sufficient. Courts will look for other facts indicating that the buyer's inferior bargaining power was being exploited or that the seller used unfair tactics in accomplishing the sale. Circumstances such as the length of the negotiation process, the buyer's opportunity to deliberate and have the contract reviewed by an adviser such as an attorney, and the experience and sophistication of the parties are all relevant to determining whether a given clause was unconscionable. A court is unlikely to find unconscionability in cases in which the buyer was a commercial enterprise, even when it is a first-time user of computer equipment, because commercial enterprises are presumed to be more knowledgeable and capable of protecting their own interests than are ordinary consumers.

**Box Top Licenses.** For various purposes, including attempting to prevent buyers of software from copying programs[4] and attempting to avoid liability under product liability doctrines, producers of software often market their products through licenses rather than outright sales. This device is intended to preserve the producer's title to the software and to limit the customer's right to make and sell copies of the program. Mass-marketed packaged software is often accompanied by a license agreement placed on the box inside a shrink-wrapped covering. Thus, such licenses have come to be called "box top licenses." They frequently state that the buyer's act of breaking the wrapping constitutes acceptance of the terms of the license. Licenses of this kind include such terms as restrictions on the user's ability to make copies of the program or to use the program on more than one computer. They also commonly contain nondisclosure agreements and restrictions on the use of the program by third parties. Furthermore, most of these licenses contain provisions that disclaim warranty protection and limit the remedies available to the buyer. The unilateral way in which the terms are imposed and the licensee's total inability to negotiate raise contract questions such as whether there was a "meeting of the minds" on the terms and whether the terms were unconscionable. Since many purchasers of packaged software accompanied by box top licenses are consumers and often first-time users, concern about unconscionability is increased. The enforceability of such clauses in box top licenses is still unsettled.

## PRODUCT LIABILITY AND THE COMPUTER

**Warranties of Quality.** If the computer transaction is deemed to be a sale of goods within the definition of the Uniform Commercial Code, UCC warranties of quality may apply. As you learned in Chapter 32, there are three such warranties: express warranties, implied warranties of merchantability and

[3] The factors that indicate unconscionability are discussed in Chapter 12.

[4] Protection of proprietary rights in software will be discussed later in this chapter. Patent, copyright, and trade secret protection are also discussed in Chapter 43.

implied warranties of fitness for a particular purpose.

Computer contracts sometimes contain formal, **express warranties** for a limited time. In some instances, however, an express warranty might be made even without the inclusion of formal language of warranty. Section 2–313 of the UCC provides that an express warranty is created by any affirmation of fact, description, or promise relating to the goods or a display of a sample or model of the goods that becomes part of the basis of the bargain. Thus, representations about the capacity, function, or nature of the system can be express warranties even if the seller did not intend to create an express warranty. A product demonstration may be considered a sample or model of goods, and thus might also constitute an express warranty. If the contract contains specifications or representations about the quality of the product, the seller's attempt to disclaim the express warranty will probably be ineffective. This is true because section 2–316 of the UCC provides that disclaimers or modifications of express warranties are ineffective if they are inconsistent with the language creating the warranty.

The **implied warranty of merchantability** will exist in any sale or lease of computer products deemed to be goods if the products are sold by a merchant, unless the warranty has been effectively disclaimed. This would mean that such a warranty would exist in a sale or lease by a manufacturer, retailer, leasing company, or other commercial enterprise engaged in the sale or lease of computer products, but not in a sale of a computer by someone who was not a merchant.

The **implied warranty of fitness for a particular purpose** applies when the seller has reason to know of the buyer's particular purpose and the sale is made under circumstances in which the seller has reason to know that the buyer is relying on him to select suitable goods. This warranty seems particularly appropriate in situations in which the seller sells a computer system specially manufactured or customized for a buyer's particular uses.

**Disclaimers of Warranty.** As a practical matter, a buyer's warranty protection is likely to be fairly limited. Almost all of the manufacturers that give express warranties limit the duration of the warranty, often to as short a period as 90 days. This may not be an adequate time for the user to determine whether the computer system works. While it is difficult to disclaim an express warranty, it is relatively easy to disclaim the implied warranties, provided that the seller follows the guidelines contained in section 2–316 of the UCC. Contractual language disclaiming the implied warranty of merchantability must mention the word *merchantability* and, if in writing, must be conspicuous. General language of disclaimer is sufficient to exclude the implied warranty of fitness for a particular purpose, provided that the disclaimer is in writing and conspicuous. Moreover, the phrase "as is," which is often used in printed disclaimers in the sale of packaged software, may exclude both implied warranties.[5]

**Limitation of Remedies.** A common clause included in contracts for the sale of computer products is one that excludes liability for consequential and incidental damages[6] and limits the remedies available to the buyer in case of the breach of a warranty.[7] In addition, such clauses usually provide that the buyer's *exclusive* remedy for breach of warranty is the repair or replacement of the system. The **limitation of remedies clause** is

[5] Other methods of disclaiming implied warranties are discussed in Chapter 32.

[6] You can read more about consequential and incidental damages in Chapters 15 and 34.

[7] See Chapter 34 for further discussion of the validity of contract provisions limiting the remedies available to a buyer.

a highly effective means of limiting the seller's potential exposure to liability. Suppose Jones buys a computer system for $20,000 under a contract that excludes consequential and incidental damages and contains a provision limiting remedies to repair or replacement. The system never works properly, causing losses of $10,000 for lost productivity and overtime pay for his employees. The application of the consequential damage exclusion and limited remedy clause would mean that Jones could not recover for the losses resulting from the system's failure and that he could not procure a substitute system and recover for the difference in cost. Instead, his compensation is limited to having the system repaired or replaced by the seller. Given the delay that this is likely to entail, the remedy is not very satisfactory from Jones's point of view.

Under section 2–719 of the UCC, contractual limitations of remedies are enforceable subject to two limitations. First, the exclusion of consequential damages is not enforceable if it is **unconscionable.** Such clauses are not likely to be found unconscionable, at least not in a commercial setting. Second, if the circumstances are such that the limited remedy *"fails of its essential purpose,"* the buyer will be able to take advantage of other remedies under the UCC.[8] A limited remedy would be considered to fail of its essential purpose if it leaves the buyer no meaningful remedy. For example, a remedy limited to repair of the product would fail of its essential purpose if the product could not be repaired, or if repair would cause unreasonable delay. In the *Chatlos* case, which follows, a court refused to enforce a limitation of remedies because the limited remedy failed of its essential purpose. In the absence of unconscionability or failure of essential purpose, then, a contract clause excluding consequential and incidental damages and limiting the remedies available to the buyer is enforceable.

**Merger Clauses.** Before investing in a computer system, a prospective buyer or lessee will seek information about the system from the seller. In the negotiation or marketing phase of the transaction, the seller is likely to make a number of representations to the buyer that could be considered warranties. If the parties later execute a written contract that does not contain the representations made at an earlier stage, the question may arise whether those representations are part of the contract. The parol evidence rule would operate to exclude from the contract evidence of prior statements if the contract is considered to be *fully integrated* (that is, if the written contract states the totality of the parties' agreement).[9] Most written computer contracts contain clauses that expressly state that the written contract is fully integrated. Such terms are called **merger** or **integration** clauses. Their effect is to exclude from the contract any presale representations or statements, and thus to limit the scope of the seller's responsibility. Merger clauses are generally enforceable.

**Tort Liability in the Sale of Computers.** Because of the obstacles to recovery for breach of contract or warranty, a number of frustrated computer buyers have turned to tort causes of action. Pursuing a tort remedy may hold more promise for the buyer because the warranty disclaimers and limitations of remedy that are so prevalent in computer contracts are, as a general rule, not effective to exclude tort liability.

**Fraud and Misrepresentation.** A buyer who has been induced to enter the contract

[8] The types of damages available for breach of a contract for the sale of goods are discussed in Chapter 34.

[9] The operation of the parol evidence rule is discussed in Chapter 13.

by the seller's misrepresentations of material fact may bring suit based on **fraud.** Fraud requires a false assertion of material fact that is justifiably relied on by the buyer. Note that it also requires that the seller have made the assertion with knowledge of its falsity and intent to deceive.[10] This may be difficult for the buyer to prove. There are, however, two related causes of action involving misrepresentation that do not require intent to deceive. These may be applicable to a computer transaction. The first is **negligent misrepresentation,** which is stated in section 552b of the *Restatement (Second) of Torts.* The buyer may establish negligent misrepresentation when he has been injured by his justifiable reliance on false information negligently supplied by one who supplies that information in the course of his business or employment. In addition, the buyer may bring an action for **innocent misrepresentation** (section 552c of the *Restatement (Second) of Torts*) if his injury results from justifiable reliance on a misstatement of material fact made by the seller in a sale, rental, or exchange transaction. The remedies for negligent misrepresentation and innocent misrepresentation are more limited than those available for fraud, however.

**Negligence.** A buyer injured by a defective computer system may have a cause of action in negligence. Establishing negligence may be difficult, however, particularly when the alleged negligence involves the design of a computer program. One problematic issue is that it is difficult to define the standard of care expected of computer designers and programmers. Some plaintiffs have attempted to press **malpractice** claims against computer designers and programmers who develop custom application software, arguing that such individuals are professionals who should be held to a standard of care higher than that of the reasonable person.[11] The few courts that have considered such claims have rejected them, however. At this time, there are no particular industry standards or licensing requirements for computer programmers. Courts have declined to characterize designers and programmers as professionals on the ground that computer programming, while requiring a high degree of skill, is primarily a mechanical task as distinguished from a task that involves the high degree of discretion exercised by such professionals as physicians and dentists. As computer technology becomes increasingly well established, designers and programmers may be subject to governmental regulation and better-defined standards of care. It remains to be seen, then, whether the tort of computer malpractice will be recognized.

**Strict Liability in Tort.** At present, the bulk of the litigation concerning defective computers involves *economic loss* rather than *personal injury* or *property damage.* Presumably, the strict liability analysis that you learned in Chapter 32 would apply to a case in which a buyer or user suffered personal injury or property damage as a result of a defect in computer *hardware.* In the more common situation, however, when a buyer suffers economic loss as a result of malfunction or defect in computer software, the application of strict liability in tort becomes more difficult.

One difficulty is determining whether software will be considered a "product" within the scope of strict liability. Another is that strict liability generally applies to personal injury and property damage rather than to economic loss. Thus, the application of strict liability in tort to the typical situation involving losses caused by defective software is questionable.

[10] The elements of fraud and the tort of deceit are discussed in Chapters 4 and 9.

[11] See Chapter 27 for a discussion of the standard of care applied to accountants and other professionals.

## Chatlos Systems, Inc. v. National Cash Register Corp.

**479 F. Supp. 738 (D.N.J. 1979)**

Chatlos Systems, Inc. designs and manufactures cable pressurization equipment for the telecommunications industry. In the spring of 1974, Chatlos became interested in purchasing a computer system. It contacted National Cash Register Corporation (NCR), which recommended that Chatlos acquire a computer known as the NCR 399 Magnetic Ledger Card System (399 MAG). After subsequent inquiry by Chatlos, however, NCR agreed to provide the 399/656 disk system, a computer using more advanced technology, as the appropriate model for Chatlos's needs. NCR represented that the system would provide six functions for Chatlos through the use of computer programs: accounts receivable, payroll, order entry, inventory deletion, state income tax, and cash receipts. NCR further stated that the system would resolve Chatlos's inventory problems, result in direct savings of labor costs, and be programmed by capable NCR personnel to be "up and running" (in full operation) within six months.

In July 1974, Chatlos signed a Systems Service Agreement for the system. The contract provided that the described equipment was warranted for "12 months after delivery against defects in material, workmanship and operational failure from ordinary use." It also provided that NCR's obligation was limited to correcting any error in any program that appeared within 60 days after the program was furnished, and expressly excluded liability for consequential or incidental damages. On July 24, 1974, Chatlos entered into a leasing agreement with a bank whereby Chatlos agreed to lease the system for $70,162.09, payable in 66 equal payments. (This is a common practice in the trade; the computer company sells the system to a bank, which in turn leases it to the "purchaser.") The hardware was delivered in December 1974. Chatlos understood that it would take slightly longer, that is, three months from the date of delivery, to have the system "up and running." It expected the system to be fully operational by March 1975.

An NCR employee began programming in January 1975, but by March only one of the functions—payroll—was in operation. One year later, the remaining functions were still not operative, despite repeated efforts by NCR to solve the problems. In August 1976, Chatlos experienced problems with the payroll function, the only function that the computer had been performing properly. Chatlos suffered substantial losses as a result of the failure of these functions, including such items as the cost of executive salaries for time devoted to working with NCR and lost profits caused by excesses and deficiencies in inventory. In September 1976, Chatlos asked to cancel the lease and have the computer removed from the premises. When NCR refused, Chatlos brought suit for damages on several theories, including breach of warranty.

**WHIPPLE, SENIOR DISTRICT JUDGE.** This transaction was for the "sale of goods" notwithstanding the incidental service aspects and the lease arrangement; therefore, Article 2 of the Uniform Commercial Code is the applicable law. Express written warranties were made by NCR in the contract where it specifically stated that NCR warranted the described equipment for 12 months. Furthermore, the July 24 Systems Service Agreement states, "NCR warrants that the services will be performed in a skillful and workmanlike manner." Though for services, this was part of the entire transaction for a sale of goods. Together with the written warranties, NCR made verbal warranties. All of these warranties were memorialized in the purchase order prepared by the bank. Since the written and verbal representations were obviously a basis of the bargain, it is clear that NCR created express warranties.

Under UCC section 2–315 an implied warranty of fitness for a particular purpose is created where a seller has reason to know of any particular purpose for which the goods are required and has reason to know that the buyer is relying on the seller's skill or judgment to select or furnish suitable goods. NCR recommended the 399/656 Disk System for Chatlos's express purpose. Furthermore, NCR was well aware that Chatlos was relying on NCR's skill and judgment. It is clear that NCR breached both express warranties and the implied warranty of fitness.

NCR maintains that an effective limitation on recovery of consequential damages appears in the System Services Agreement. These phrases clearly attempt to limit the purchaser's remedy to having any error corrected within 60 days after the appropriate programs are furnished. Since four of the six functions were never furnished, the attempted limitation falls squarely within UCC section 2–719, which provides that:

> Where circumstances cause an exclusive or limited remedy to fail of its essential purpose, remedy may be had as provided in this Act.

It is of the very essence of a sales contract that at least minimum adequate remedies be available. When the warrantor fails to correct the defect as promised within a reasonable time the limited, exclusive remedy fails of its purpose and is thus avoided. Because NCR never furnished four of the six promised functions, its attempted limitation of remedy failed of its essential purpose.

Judgment for Chatlos.

## COMPUTER CRIME

The use of computers to accomplish criminal objectives has become an increasing problem, which pretechnological criminal law is ill-equipped to resolve. As our society becomes increasingly dependent on computers to manage such functions as the transfer of funds and other valuables and the storage of personal records, new opportunities for crime have been created. Some of these "computer crimes" are crimes such as vandalism or theft of computer hardware and software in which the computer system itself is the target of the crime. Others involve the use of the computer as the instrumentality of crimes. Common examples are theft, embezzlement, espionage, blackmail, and fraud. A criminal with access to a bank's computer might, for example, cause funds to be transferred from other accounts into his own. An employee who has lawful access to his company's computer might use it for his own benefit without permission. Or, using telecommunications links, a criminal might infiltrate the computer system of a competitor to learn its trade secrets or to sabotage a competitor's operations by erasing valuable files.

Because of its technical nature, computer crime is often difficult to detect and to prosecute. Some victims, such as financial institutions, may be unwilling to report computer crime because they fear embarrassment or possible liability to customers. One of the biggest problems in punishing and deterring computer crime is that traditional criminal statutes frequently do not address the types of crime that can be committed through the use of computers.

Objectionable conduct may simply not be

forbidden by a jurisdiction's criminal law. For example, there may be no criminal law that covers computer "hackers" (people who infiltrate computer systems to "browse" through the files), even though such activity obviously involves an intrusion into private information. Moreover, the statutory prerequisites of traditional crimes may not address specific abuses of a computer. If the state statute regarding theft or larceny defines the crime as the theft of "property," a court may find it difficult to construe data stored in a computer as "property." A graphic example of the mismatch of statutory prerequisites for crimes and abuse of computers is presented in a New York case, *People v. Weg.*[12] In *Weg,* a computer programmer employed by New York City's Board of Education was charged with theft of services when he used the board's computer for his own benefit. The statute forbidding theft of services defined the crime as the intentional use of "business, commercial or industrial equipment of another person" under circumstances in which one knows that he is not entitled to such use. The court dismissed the charge against Weg, finding that the statutory elements of the crime were not satisfied, because the board's computer was used for a governmental purpose and was *not* "business, commercial, or industrial equipment" as required by the statute.

Obviously, the narrow interpretation of existing criminal laws increases the difficulty of prosecuting those who use computers to commit crimes. In contrast to the *Weg* case and others of its kind, a number of courts have interpreted existing statutes broadly to cover computer-assisted crime. The case of *United States v. Kelly,* which follows, exemplifies the latter approach. In light of the uncertainties that attend judicial interpretation of existing statutes, legislatures on both the state and federal level have become increasingly aware of the need to revise their criminal codes to specifically encompass the types of crimes that can be accomplished through the use of computers.

**State Computer Crime Laws.** A number of state legislatures have enacted or are considering revisions of their criminal codes to forbid specific abuses of computers. Michigan's computer crime statute,[13] enacted in 1980, provides a good example. The statute defines property broadly to include financial instruments, information, computer software and programs, and any tangible or intangible item of value. It forbids a wide range of criminal activity involving computers. For example, the statute makes it a crime to gain access to a computer system or network for the purpose of executing a scheme with the intent to defraud or for the purpose of obtaining money, property, or services. It further prohibits gaining access to, altering, damaging, or destroying a computer, computer system, software program, or data contained in a computer system. Furthermore, it specifically forbids the use of a computer, computer system, or computer network to commit a violation of a variety of other existing laws. A violation of the statute is a misdemeanor if the violation involves $100 or less, but a felony punishable by up to 10 years' imprisonment and/or a fine of up to $5,000 if it involves more than $100.

Such statutes may not make it easier for law enforcement officers to detect computer crime, but they do facilitate the conviction of those apprehended.

**Federal Computer Crime Legislation.** Computer-assisted crime on the federal level has been prosecuted with some success under existing federal statutes, primarily the statutes forbidding mail fraud, wire fraud, transportation of stolen property, and various theft or property offenses. *United States v. Kelly*

[12] 450 N.Y.S.2d 957 (Crim. Ct. N.Y. 1982).

[13] *Mich. Comp. L. Ann.* § 751.791–.797 (West Supp. 1984–85).

is an example of a prosecution of theft of computer time under the federal mail fraud statute. As is true of prosecutions on the state level, successful prosecution of such cases often depends on broad interpretation of the statutory prerequisites. Until recently, federal law did not specifically address the use of computer technology in crimes.

A number of bills relating to computer crime have been introduced in Congress in recent years. In 1984, Congress enacted the Counterfeit Access Device and Computer Fraud and Abuse Act of 1984. This law is more limited in scope than the Michigan statute discussed above. The act makes it a crime to "knowingly access" a computer: (1) to obtain restricted government information (information that requires protection against unauthorized disclosure for reasons of national defense or foreign relations, or data restricted under the Atomic Energy Act) with intent or reason to believe that such information is to be used to the injury of the United States or to the advantage of any foreign nation; (2) to obtain information contained in a financial record of a financial institution or a file of a consumer reporting agency on a consumer; or (3) to use, modify, destroy, or prevent the authorized use of a computer operated for or on behalf of the U.S. government or to disclose information contained in such a computer.

These prohibitions apply to persons who are not authorized to use the computer *and* to persons who are authorized to gain access to the computer but use the opportunity that such access provides to commit any of the three offenses described above. Substantial penalties are prescribed by the statute.

**Criminal Penalties for Violation of the Electronic Funds Transfer Act.** The Electronic Funds Transfer Act is a federal statute governing electronic funds transfer (EFT).[14] The best-known examples of EFT in use today are direct deposits of payroll and government benefit payments and "money machines" (or automated teller machines). The use of EFT is a highly efficient means of accomplishing the transfer of funds and, indeed, may operate to remove the opportunity for violent crimes against persons and property (such as the theft of a social security check). However, it also presents the opportunity for new types of theft accomplished through the use of such devices as counterfeit cards, stolen codes, wire interception, and alteration of data. Section 1693n of the EFT Act provides criminal penalties for violation of the act. For example, this section makes it a crime to use, sell, furnish, or transport in interstate commerce any counterfeit, fictitious, altered, forged, lost, stolen, or fraudulently obtained "debit instrument" (a card, code, or other device used to initiate an electronic fund transfer) to obtain money, goods, services, or anything else of value. Such violations of the EFT Act are punishable by up to 10 years imprisonment and/or a fine of up to $10,000.

[14] Electronic funds transfer is discussed in greater detail in Chapter 38.

**Need for Greater Security.** While state and federal law is evolving in the direction of providing more specific criminal statutes and more severe penalties to punish and deter criminal abuse of computers, it is obvious that steps need to be taken to improve computer security to prevent and detect instances of abuse. Although it is not feasible to create a completely crimeproof system, changes in hiring and operating procedures can help to reduce the opportunities for crime. For example, a number of companies have begun to restrict access to their computers to a greater extent and to screen applicants for computer-related jobs more carefully. To harness the immense power of computers, the development of programs and operations that police computer security must proceed hand in hand with current efforts to update criminal codes and law enforcement techniques.

## United States v. Kelly

### 507 F. Supp. 495 (E.D. Pa. 1981)

David Kelly and Matthew Palmer, Jr., were employed at Sperry Univac's applications development center, which develops and maintains programs to be used by Univac's customers. While employed at Univac, Kelly and Palmer developed a system for computerizing the generation of sheet music, which they called the "allegro" system. In developing the program, they used substantial amounts of computer time and storage capacity within the central processing unit of the applications development center. They also contracted with Broomall Industries to help them develop and promote the allegro system. After this agreement was formed, Kelly, Palmer, the president of Broomall, and another associate caused certain promotional materials to be mailed to five music publishers, inviting them to send representatives to an allegro demonstration. At no time did anyone from Univac give Kelly or Palmer authority to make such a use of the company's resources, nor did either Kelly or Palmer inform anyone at the company of their activities.

Eventually, Kelly and Palmer's use of Univac's resources was discovered by company personnel. Following an investigation by Univac security officials and the FBI, Kelly and Palmer were indicted on five counts of mail fraud and one count of conspiracy to commit mail fraud. In essence, the indictment alleged that by using their employer's computer time and storage facilities without authorization for the development of a private business venture, Kelly and Palmer defrauded Univac of their services as employees and used the U.S. mails in furtherance of their fraudulent scheme by causing the promotional materials to be mailed. After a trial by jury, both Kelly and Palmer were found guilty on all counts. They filed posttrial motions contending that the acts for which they were convicted did not constitute a "scheme or artifice to defraud" within the meaning of the mail fraud statute and that the mails were not used for the purpose of executing the scheme.

**Ditter, District Judge.** It is necessary to consider the general purpose and scope of the mail fraud statute. In pertinent part, 18 U.S.C. §1341 provides:

> Whoever, having devised or intending to devise any scheme or artifice to defraud . . . for the purpose of executing such scheme or artifice or attempting to do so, places in any post office or authorized depository for mail, any matter or thing whatever to be sent or delivered by the Post Office . . . or knowingly causes to be delivered by mail according to the direction thereon . . . shall be fined not more than $1,000.00 or imprisoned not more than five years or both.

The essential elements of mail fraud are (1) a scheme or artifice to defraud and (2) the use of the United States mails in execution of the scheme. The broad, amorphous statutory language has generally permitted the courts considerable latitude in determining what types of schemes come within the purview of the statute. The Supreme Court held that the perimeters of the term "scheme or artifice to defraud" are not limited to common law concepts of fraud or false pretenses and that the existence of such a scheme is not contingent upon a violation of state law. The mail fraud statute generally has been available to prosecute a scheme involving deception that employs the mails in its execution that is contrary to public policy and conflicts with accepted standards of moral uprightness, fundamental honesty, fair play and right dealing. It is clear that the propriety of Kelly and Palmer's convictions cannot be evaluated in a technical or mechanistic fashion. Rather, they must be considered in light of the broad language of the statute itself, the expansive interpretation which it has been accorded by the courts, and its general utility in meeting the multifarious types of schemes, complex or simple, which may be devised.

It is well established that a scheme which is directed at depriving an employer of the honest and faithful services of its employee or of its right to have its business conducted honestly may constitute a "scheme to defraud" within the meaning of the mail fraud statute. A review of the record shows more than ample evidence from which the jury could have determined that Kelly and Palmer took affirmative steps to conceal their unauthorized computer use from Univac. From this evidence, the jury could have inferred it was their intent to defraud Univac. The testimony was extensive and uncontradicted that Univac did not generally permit the use of its facilities to promote outside business ventures by its employees; that the use of its facilities for any purpose unrelated to business was permissible only when authorization was first obtained; that defendants had never sought or received authorization and that had they sought authorization for such activities it would have been denied. It is abundantly clear that Kelly and Palmer were aware of Univac's policy against the use of its facilities for personal business ventures. They nevertheless made extensive use of the Univac facilities in furtherance of their own pecuniary interests, took steps to conceal their activities and willfully failed to seek authorization for them. The evidence was more than sufficient to sustain the jury's determination that they acted with intent to defraud.

Kelly and Palmer contend that the mailing of the promotional materials was related only to their goal of ultimately making money from the completed allegro system. It did not, they assert, further the unauthorized use of Univac's computer facilities and therefore was unrelated to the execution of the fraudulent scheme. Kelly and Palmer posit an unduly restrictive interpretation of the perimeters of their scheme to defraud. Kelly and Palmer were charged with defrauding Univac by *using its resources for their own personal gain.* While they were utilizing Univac's facilities to develop the technological viability of the system, they were actively engaged in attempting to develop a market for the completed allegro program. Thus, the utilization of Univac's computer facilities cannot be viewed in isolation. The primary, if not exclusive, motivating factor in Kelly and Palmer's use of their employer's computer storage facility was their desire to market the completed allegro system at a substantial gain for themselves. Hence, their attempts to develop the technological capabilities of the system cannot be viewed as distinct from their attempts to sell it. Both activities were directed at a single goal—to derive financial gain from the marketing of the completed system. Indeed without this goal, the computer use was merely an academic exercise. The obvious purpose of the promotional material was to solicit potential sales for the completed allegro system. Viewed on this context, the mailings were directly related to the achievement of the fruits of Kelly and Palmer's scheme. I therefore conclude that the mailing in question was "for the purpose of executing" the scheme to defraud.

Judgment for the United States affirmed.

## PRIVACY AND THE COMPUTER

An increasing amount of information about each of us is constantly being entered and stored in computers. Every time you write a check, register for college courses, apply for a credit card or a student loan, donate money to a charitable organization, order a magazine subscription, claim benefits under a medical insurance or property insurance policy, or file a tax return, information about you is entered into a computer, where it can be stored and easily retrieved. Advances in computer technology make it possible to link separate data bases and unify files so as to aggregate large quantities of information about an individual. It may thus be possible for unknown observers to trace an individual's activities and associations and glean a "profile" of his character. While the efficient collection and retrieval of information helps to facilitate effective social and business planning, it also presents a threat to an individual's right of privacy, one aspect of which is the right of an individual to control the disclosure of *information* about himself.

Individuals are concerned, not only that they may lose the ability to control how much information is known about them, but also that they may lose the ability to control the *accuracy* of the information that is disclosed. The danger also exists that private information will be disclosed to persons or organizations that will use it for purposes very different from the purposes for which it was originally collected.

The **right of privacy** is protected to differing degrees by the Constitution, common law doctrines, and various legislation. The following discussion explores the framework of legal protection against computer-assisted invasions of privacy.

**Constitutional Protection of Privacy.** Although the U.S. Constitution does not specifically mention the right of privacy, courts have held that such a right is implied by other provisions of the Constitution and that certain areas of privacy (such as family and lifestyle issues and freedom of speech and association) are constitutionally protected from intrusion by the *government*. This does not mean, however, that it is unconstitutional for the government to collect and use data about individuals. The determination whether a given collection of data by the government is an unconstitutional invasion of privacy depends on the extent of governmental interest in collecting such data and on the uses and safeguards established for the protection of the data. In *Whalen v. Roe*,[15] the Supreme Court considered the constitutionality of a New York statute that required the collection of information regarding persons to whom certain legitimate but dangerous drugs were prescribed. This information was to be recorded in a centralized computer file by the state Health Department and retained for five years. The Court held that the statutory scheme did not constitute an unconstitutional invasion of privacy, because the state had a legitimate interest in recording the information in question and because adequate safeguards were established for protecting confidential information. Thus, the right to privacy against governmental intrusion is not an absolute right; its extent depends on a balancing of interests.

**The Application of Common Law Privacy Doctrines.** In Chapter 4, you learned about the common law tort of **invasion of privacy.** The two categories of this tort that are most likely to be applied to computer-assisted invasions of privacy are the *intrusion* theory and the *public disclosure of private facts* theory. The intrusion theory involves the physical invasion of privacy. Unauthorized intrusion

[15] 429 U.S. 589 (U.S. Sup. Ct. 1977).

into such private records as personal records kept on a home computer, medical records, or bank accounts might constitute such an invasion of privacy. The public disclosure theory involves making public a private fact about an individual that a reasonable person would consider offensive.

Although the tort cause of action for invasion of privacy might permit a person to obtain compensation for a given invasion, the existence of that remedy is not adequate to deter the problem created by the widespread collection of private information. Many such privacy invasions may be undetected or difficult to prove. Moreover, as was true in the criminal law context, it may be difficult for a plaintiff to satisfy the traditional elements of the tort. For example, one element of the public disclosure theory of invasion of privacy is that the private fact must be disclosed to "the public," or a large number of people. When information is transferred from one agency or business to another, a potential plaintiff may be unable to establish that the information was disclosed to a sufficiently large number of people to satisfy this element. In addition, the intrusion theory has traditionally involved an invasion into an individual's physical privacy or communications. It may be difficult for an individual to establish such an invasion when the nature of the invasion is an intrusion into such private information as bank records or medical records rather than an intrusion into his physical space or communications. Thus, to be an adequate remedy in a computer age, the tort of invasion of privacy must be updated to apply to typical computer-assisted invasions and disclosures.

**Statutory Protection of Privacy.** Mindful of the growing threat to individual privacy posed by the "information explosion," legislatures on both the federal and state level have enacted a number of statutes that serve to limit the circumstances under which certain types of private information can be obtained and used and, in some cases, to provide ways of challenging the accuracy of such information and remedies for the use of inaccurate information. While these state and federal privacy laws are not uniquely applicable to computer-assisted invasions of privacy, computers are generally used to collect, store, and transmit the private information involved.

Numerous federal statutes deal with protection of privacy in differing situations. For example, the Family Educational Rights and Privacy Act of 1974 limits access to educational records held by institutions of higher education. In addition, the Tax Reform Act of 1976 and various statutes dealing with alcohol and drug abuse treatment include provisions limiting the circumstances under which third persons may gain access to private information. The following discussion examines two of the most significant federal statutes regulating the disclosure of private information.

**Fair Credit Reporting Act of 1970.** The federal statute that is likely to have the most significant impact on ordinary consumers is the Fair Credit Reporting Act (FCRA) of 1970. Elaborate mechanisms involving the use of computers exist for investigating and evaluating the creditworthiness of consumers. Information about a person's credit rating or personal characteristics is amassed by consumer reporting agencies, and may be sought when that person applies for credit, insurance, employment, or certain licenses. If such information is disclosed to persons who have no legitimate interest in obtaining it or if the information given is erroneous, serious injury to the individual may result. Congress enacted the FCRA to provide procedural safeguards that ensure that consumer reporting agencies exercise care in providing accurate information and in respecting consumers' privacy. You can read about the specific provisions of the FCRA in Chapter 46.

Note that the new federal Counterfeit Access Device and Computer Fraud and Abuse Act, which was discussed earlier, makes it a crime to "access" or use a computer without authorization to obtain information contained in a file of a consumer reporting agency.

**The Right to Financial Privacy Act of 1978.** The Right to Financial Privacy Act applies to customers' financial records possessed by financial institutions, such as banks, savings banks, trust companies, consumer finance institutions, and savings and loan associations. It basically forbids a financial institution to give the *government* access to a customer's financial records or to any information contained in them unless the customer authorizes such disclosure or unless the government requests the disclosure pursuant to a valid subpoena, search warrant, or court order. It does not prohibit a financial institution from doing any act necessary to perfect a security interest, prove a claim, or collect a debt. Nor does it forbid a financial institution to notify the government that it has information that may be relevant to possible illegal activity. A customer must be notified that the federal government has requested access to financial records, and may generally contest such access. A financial institution or agency of the government that violates the provisions of the act may be held liable to the customer for at least $100 (regardless of the volume of the records involved), actual damages sustained by the customer, punitive damages in case of willful violation, and attorney's fees and costs. In addition, the Counterfeit Access Device and Computer Fraud and Abuse Act of 1984 provides that it is a crime to obtain information contained in a financial record of a financial institution through unauthorized access to or use of a computer.

**State Privacy Legislation.** A number of states have passed laws that protect different aspects of individual privacy, but these laws are by no means uniform. Some states have enacted statutes modeled on the Fair Credit Reporting Act and the Financial Privacy Act. As discussed previously in the computer crime section, a number of states have specifically declared that it is a crime to use a computer to gain access to private records.

## PROTECTION OF COMPUTER SOFTWARE

You learned in Chapter 43 (The Protection of Creative Endeavor and Competitive Torts) about the various mechanisms set up by our legal system to encourage and protect creativity and the competitive advantage that creativity affords. The inventor of a new machine or process may be able to obtain a legally protected monopoly in that invention by obtaining a **patent.** The author of a book obtains **copyright** protection for the expression represented in the book. Both of these devices are designed to encourage the production and disclosure of creative endeavors by giving their creators specified legal protection against infringement. Moreover, the law protects competitive advantage and encourages ethical behavior in the marketplace by protecting a business's **trade secrets.**

All of these protections are of special concern to companies engaged in the development and production of computer software. The development of computer software is a time-consuming and expensive endeavor. Yet the profits that a software supplier hopes to gain are imperiled by the relative ease with which software can be copied and distributed by users and improved upon by competitors.

As a result, the life cycle of computer software is short. To protect their enormous investment, software developers and distributors justifiably seek legal protection against infringement and misappropriation of their products through patent, copyright, and trade secrets law.

**Patent Protection of Software.** A patent on software would give the software producer the exclusive right to make, use, and sell the software for 17 years.[16] Such protection would extend to the concept embodied in the software, and not merely to the form in which it is expressed. A patent would protect the software producer from the danger that the software would be disclosed, copied, or independently created by a competitor. However, patent protection is not easy to obtain, and it is not yet clear that computer software is patentable. To be patentable, an invention (in the case of software, a process) must be useful, novel, and nonobvious.[17] Only a very small percentage of computer software stands a chance of satisfying the tests of novelty and nonobviousness. A large proportion of computer software merely permits the automation of tasks that can be done manually. Moreover, software mimics "mental processes," and mental processes are not in themselves patentable.

Moreover, mathematical formulas are not patentable, because they are considered to be laws of nature, and thus not novel. In view of the fact that processes involving computer software are often based on mathematical formulas or algorithms, a question existed whether such processes were proper subject matter for patents. The Supreme Court answered that question in the 1981 case of *Diamond v. Diehr.*[18] The invention in question in *Diamond* was a process for curing synthetic rubber that included in several of its steps the use of a mathematical formula and a programmed digital computer. The Court held that the subject matter of the inventionmet the statutory requirements for patentability, and did not become unpatentable simply because the invention used a mathematical formula or computer program. Note that the *Diamond* case did not hold that computer programs by themselves were patentable, but only that a program used in combination with an otherwise patentable process can be the subject of patent protection.

In addition to the great difficulty in satisfying the tests for patentability, obtaining a patent on computer software may be unfeasible because the process of obtaining a patent is a slow and expensive one. The time involved may delay the marketing of the software, which, given rapidly advancing technology, could be fatal to its ultimate success.

**Copyright Protection of Computer Software.** The Copyright Reform Act of 1976 gives individuals who create original works such as books, periodicals, or works of art certain exclusive rights in their creations.[19] In 1980, Congress amended the Copyright Act to include computer programs in the list of creative works that are the subject of copyright protection. Some doubt remained, however, as to whether a copyright existed in "object code" (program instructions written in a form that is machine-readable only and not intelligible to humans). The basic objection to copyright protection of object code is that, since humans cannot read it, it is not a "literary work." The *Apple Computer* case, which

[16] See Chapter 43 for more detailed discussion of patent protection.

[17] The requirements for patentability are discussed in Chapter 43.

[18] You can read this opinion in Chapter 43.

[19] The features of copyright law are discussed in detail in Chapter 43.

follows, is a highly influential case that rejects the distinction between programs readable by humans and programs that interact only with machines, and holds that copyright protection extends to object code.

A copyright comes into being the moment an original work is *fixed* in some *tangible medium of expression.* The protection gained through a copyright is not nearly as extensive as that gained by a patent, however. A copyright protects only the *expression* of an idea, whereas a patent protects the application of an idea. A copyright makes it illegal for a person to duplicate the exact expression or a substantially similar expression, but does not prevent a person from taking the basic idea of the program and accomplishing the same result through a different series of steps. Given that the basic value of computer programs lies in their *design,* copyright law provides limited protection to computer programs.

Moreover, another 1980 amendment to the Copyright Act permits persons who buy copyrighted software to make copies and adaptations of the software for their own use and for archival purposes. Under some circumstances, these copies can be transferred by the owner of the software. To avoid the application of this section, most software producers market software through **licenses** rather than sales.

Because of the limited protection offered by copyright law and the difficulty of obtaining patents, most software producers rely on the law of **trade secrets** to protect their proprietary rights.

**Trade Secret Protection of Software.** Protection of trade secrets is accorded by the common law of every state.[20] A **trade secret** is any formula, process, device, or compilation of information used in a business that gives its owner a competitive advantage over others who are not privy to the secret. To qualify for legal protection, the secret must have some degree of novelty (which generally means that it is *not commonly known in the trade*) and *commercial* or *economic* value (that is, it gives one a *competitive advantage*).

Trade secret protection is very broad. In contrast to copyright protection, trade secret protection covers not only the expression of an idea but the idea itself. Furthermore, in contrast to both patent and copyright protection, trade secret protection requires no registration, expensive and lengthy procedures, notice, or disclosure of the secret. Thus, computer software is an ideal subject for trade secret protection if the proper precautions are taken to preserve secrecy.

Since the essence of trade secret protection is to afford a business protection of secret information that gives it a competitive advantage, trade secret protection can be lost if the formula, information, or other secret is not closely guarded. While the information may be disclosed to some people (such as customers and employees), it must be clear that the business took steps to keep the information a secret. This can be shown by the fact that only a few people were allowed access to the secret, that the information was disclosed on a confidential basis, or that the persons to whom the secret was disclosed signed a nondisclosure agreement. Information that is disclosed to a large number of people without proper precautions or that becomes generally known in the trade cannot constitute a trade secret.

The preservation of secrecy is the most difficult aspect of maintaining trade secret protection for software. To preserve secrecy, it is necessary for a software producer to use great care in maintaining internal security and in disclosing secret information to customers only under confidential circumstances. It is common for a software producer to execute secrecy agreements with employees and to re-

[20] See Chapter 43 for a more complete discussion of trade secret law.

strict access to the secret. You can read about some of the means of maintaining internal security against misappropriation of trade secrets in the *J & K Computer Systems* case.

Furthermore, software licensing agreements are designed to preserve secrecy by restricting the licensee's disclosure of the program. They typically forbid the licensee to copy the program except for backup and archival purposes, require that the licensee and its employees sign confidentiality agreements, require that such employees use the program only in the scope of their jobs, and specify that the licensee use the program only in a single central processing unit.

There is some question whether mass-marketed software can be a secret, since these programs are distributed to so many people. The effectiveness of nondisclosure agreements in "box top licenses" to protect trade secrets is still uncertain.

Courts have also considered whether federal copyright law preempts (forecloses) state trade secret protection. Most of the courts that have dealt with this question have held that it does not and that trade secret protection and copyright protection can exist at the same time. A related issue is whether the placing of a copyright notice on a program forecloses the program's status as a trade secret, since it indicates the intent to disclose the secret. Again, the weight of authority is that copyright notice does not prevent trade secret protection for the program.

## Apple Computer, Inc. v. Franklin Computer Corp.

**714 F.2d 1240 (3d Cir. 1983)**

Apple Computer, Inc. is one of the leading manufacturers of microcomputers, related equipment, and computer programs. It has sold more that 400,000 Apple II computers. Franklin Computer Corporation is a much smaller manufacturer of computers. It manufactures and sells the ACE 100 personal computer, which was designed to be "Apple compatible," so that peripheral equipment and software developed for use with the Apple II could be used with the ACE 100.

In manufacturing the ACE 100, Franklin used 14 Apple operating programs. Apple brought suit against Franklin, claiming infringement of the copyrights it held in the 14 programs. The district court denied Apple's motion for a prelimary injunction because it doubted the copyrightability of Apple's programs. Apple appealed.

**SLOVITER, CIRCUIT JUDGE.** Like all computers, both the Apple II and the ACE 100 have a central processing unit (CPU), which is the integrated circuit that executes programs. In lay terms, the CPU does the work it is instructed to do. Those instructions are contained on computer programs. There are three levels of computer language in which computer programs may be written. High level language, such as BASIC or FORTRAN, uses English words and symbols, and is relatively easy to learn and understand. A somewhat lower level language is assembly language, which consists of alphanumeric labels. Statements in high level language and statements in assembly language are referred to as written in "source code." The third, or lowest level computer language, is machine language, a binary language using two symbols, 0 and 1. Statements in machine language are referred to as written in "object code." The CPU can only follow instructions written in object code. However, programs are usually written in source code, which is more intelligible to humans. Programs written in source code can be converted or translated by a "compiler" program into object code for use by the computer. Programs are generally distributed only in their object code version stored on a memory device.

A computer program can be stored or fixed on a variety of memory devices. Of particular relevance for this case is the ROM (Read Only Memory), an internal permanent memory device consisting of a semi-conductor chip which is incorporated into the circuitry of the computer. A program in object code is embedded on a ROM before it is incorporated in the computer.

Operating systems programs generally manage the internal functions of the computer or facilitate use of application programs. The 14 computer programs at issue in this suit are operating systems programs.

Franklin's principal defense is that the Apple operating system programs are not capable of copyright protection. In 1976, Congress enacted a new copyright law. Under the law, two primary requirements must be satisfied for a work to constitute copyrightable subject matter—it must be an "original work of authorship" and must be "fixed in a tangible medium of expression." The 1980 amendments added a definition of a computer program:

> A "computer program" is a set of statements or instructions to be used directly or indirectly in a computer in order to bring about a certain result.

The district court questioned whether copyright was to be limited to works designed to be read by a human reader. The suggestion that copyrightability depends on a communicative function to individuals stems from the early decision of *White-Smith Music Publishing Co. v. Apollo Co.,* which held a piano roll was not a copy of the musical composition because it was not in a form others, except for a very expert few, could perceive. However, it is clear from the language of the Act and its legislative history that it was intended to obliterate the distinctions engendered by *White-Smith.*

Under the statute, copyright extends to works in any tangible means of expression "from which they can be perceived, reproduced, or otherwise communicated, either directly or with the aid of a machine or device." Furthermore, the definition of computer program adopted by Congress is "sets of statements or instructions to be used *directly or indirectly* in a computer to bring about a certain result." As source code instructions must be translated into object code before the computer can act upon them, only instructions expressed in object code can be used "directly" by the computer. Thus, a computer program, whether in object code or source code, is a "literary work" and is protected from unauthorized copying, whether from its object or source code version. The statutory requirement of "fixation" is satisfied through the embodiment of the expression in the ROM device.

Franklin's position is that computer operating system programs, as distinguished from application programs, are not the proper subject of copyright regardless of the language or medium in which they are fixed. Franklin's attack on operating system programs seems inconsistent with its concession that application programs are an appropriate subject of copyright. Both types of programs instruct the computer to do something. Therefore, it should make no difference whether these instructions tell the computer to help prepare an income tax return (the task of an application program) or to translate a high level language from source code into its binary language object code form (the task of an operating system program such as "Applesoft"). There is no reason to afford any less copyright protection to the instructions in an operating system program than to the instructions in an application program. The mere fact that the operating system program may be etched on a ROM does not make the program either a machine, part of a machine, or its equivalent.

Since we believe that the district court's decision on the preliminary injunction was influenced by an erroneous view of the availability of copyright for operating system programs and unnecessary concerns about object code and ROMs, we must reverse the denial of the preliminary injunction and remand for reconsideration.

Reversed and remanded in favor of Apple.

## J & K Computer Systems, Inc. v. Parrish

**642 P.2d 722 (Utah Sup. Ct. 1982)**

J & K Computer Systems, Inc. was in the business of developing, marketing and installing computer software. Douglas Parrish began working for J & K as a computer programmer in March 1978. In August 1978, J & K required Parrish to sign an employment contract as a condition of continuing employment. One of the terms of the contract provided as follows:

> *Disclosure of Information:* The Employee recognizes and acknowledges that a list of the Employer's customers and the methods and programs used in conducting the Employer's business are valuable, special and unique assets of the Employer's business. The Employee will not, during or after the terms of employment, disclose methods or programs used in conducting the Employer's business or any part thereof to any person, firm, corporation, association, or other entity for any reason or purpose whatever.

In the months that followed, Parrish developed an open-item/balance forward accounts receivable program that would be usable on the IBM System 34. After the program was developed, Parrish installed it on behalf of J & K at the Arnold Machinery Company. He also contacted E. A. Miller and Sons Meat Packing Company about the possibility of installing the program.

In May 1979, J & K hired Parrish's brother-in-law, Chris Chlarson, as a trainee working under Parrish's supervision. Chlarson also signed an employment contract containing the nondisclosure agreement. Two months later, Parrish voluntarily left the employ of J & K and entered into a contract to provide Arnold Machinery with programming services. He also contracted with E. A. Miller for the installation of the accounts receivable program. Shortly thereafter, Chlarson left J & K and began working with Parrish; the two formed Dynamic Software Corporation. In July 1979, Parrish made an electronic copy of the accounts receivable program that J & K had installed at Arnold Machinery. This copy was made on a magnetic disk, which Parrish then gave to Chlarson. Chlarson took the disk to a computer workroom in the IBM building in Salt Lake City to work on the programs on the disk. While Chlarson was working with the disk, an employee of J & K saw one of J & K's programs displayed on the screen of the computer terminal and reported this to J & K. J & K filed suit against Parrish and Chlarson for misappropriation of a trade secret. The trial court awarded J & K damages and injunctive relief. Parrish and Chlarson appealed.

**Howe, Justice.** Parrish and Chlarson assail the judgment of the trial court, claiming that the accounts receivable programs were not confidential or trade secrets. There is no dispute that J & K regarded the programs which it developed and used in its business as proprietary. The employment contracts which Parrish and Chlarson signed specified that the computer programs were "valuable, special and unique assets" of J & K's business.

A trade secret includes any formula, patent, device, plan or compilation of information which is used in one's business and which gives him an opportunity to obtain an advantage over competitors who do not know it. It is a well recognized principle that our law will afford protection to the inventor of a special process or trade secret. The trial court could have reasonably determined that J & K's accounts receivable program was secret and worthy of protection by the law.

Parrish and Chlarson assert that the accounts receivable program was revealed to certain customers and therefore not protectable. The record, however, shows that J & K endeavored to keep its accounts receivable program secret. Its employees and customers were informed of the secret nature of the program. The program was marked with the following legend: "Program Products Proprietary To—J & K Computer Systems, Inc. Authorized Use by License Agreement Only." That a few of J & K's customers had access to the program does not prevent the program from being classified as a trade secret where J & K was attempting to keep the secret and the program is still unavailable to the computer trade as a whole.

Parrish and Chlarson argue that there is no basis to support the trial court's award of $7,500 to J & K as fair and equitable damages. The evidence, however, shows that J & K incurred costs of over $28,500 in developing the accounts receivable program and lost the Arnold Machinery Company as a customer because of the misappropriation of its program. There was evidence that J & K may have also lost E. A. Miller as a customer. Thus, considering J & K's loss of customers and the cost of developing its accounts receivable program, $7,500 does not appear to be an unreasonable assessment of damages.

Judgment for J & K affirmed.

## SUMMARY

The rapid proliferation of computers has produced a host of legal problems, some of which are not easily resolved by traditional legal doctrines. Courts and legislatures are engaged in adapting law to computer technology.

One question that arises at the outset of any contract case involving computer products is whether the Uniform Commercial Code applies to the contract. This requires the court to characterize the transaction as being primarily a contract for the sale of goods rather than a contract for services. Transactions in which the parties primarily bargained for the sale of goods are governed by the UCC, even though services incidental to the sale of goods may be provided. Thus, the sale of computer hardware and the sale of software in combination with the sale of computer hardware are considered to be contracts for the sale of goods. In all probability, the sale of mass-marketed software without hardware will be considered a sale of goods. Courts have held that *leases* of computers and computer-related products are governed by the UCC as well. If, however, the parties have bargained primarily for a service, the transaction will be governed by the common law of contracts, even if some tangible items incidental to the service are supplied. Thus, software individually designed and supplied by a computer consultant and the services of a computer service bureau will be governed by the common law of contracts.

Given the significant investment that a person who acquires a computer system makes, it is necessary that the contract for the sale or lease of the system be drafted and studied with special care. However, it is often impossible for a buyer to negotiate favorable terms that protect his right to compensation in case of defects or malfunction of the system. Computer products that are mass-marketed are accompanied by standard form contracts that limit the seller's responsibility to a great extent. Even in individually negotiated contracts, a seller may insist on the inclusion of clauses that limit liability. Terms that are unreasonably advantageous to the seller and are presented under circumstances in which the buyer has no meaningful choice but to agree may be attacked on the ground of *unconscionability.* However, it is unlikely that a court would hold liability-limiting terms to be unconscionable, at least in a situation involving a commercial buyer or lessee. The enforceability of such terms in "box top licenses" is still unsettled.

When a computer system proves to be defective, a buyer may seek a remedy under warranty law. There are three possible warranties that may apply: express warranty, implied warranty of merchantability, and implied warranty of fitness for a particular purpose. Warranty protection is likely to be strictly limited in the contract for sale of a computer, however. Sellers of computers often provide formal, express warranties for a very limited period of time in lieu of all implied warranties. In addition, such contracts usually contain disclaimers of implied warranties, provisions excluding consequential and incidental damages and limiting the remedies available for breach of warranty, and merger clauses to prevent the inclusion of precontract representations. So long as such contract provisions meet the requirements for disclaimers and limitations of remedies specified in the UCC, and so long as they are not unconscionable, they will be enforced.

An injured buyer may also attempt to proceed against the seller in a tort action, such as one based on fraud or misrepresentation. He may bring an action grounded on the products liability theories of negligence and strict liability in tort. At present, it appears that courts will reject a cause of action for malpractice against computer designers and programmers. When a person suffers *personal injuries or property damage* because of a defect in computer hardware, negligence and strict liability would seem to apply. However, it is still unclear whether a person who suffers solely *economic injury* would have a cause of action in strict liability; the question becomes even more complicated when the injury is caused by defective software, because the software may not be classified as a "product."

The increasing use of computers to accomplish the transfer of funds and the storage and analysis of important information has created new opportunities for highly lucrative criminal activity. Computer crime is difficult to detect and prosecute. The statutory elements of traditional crimes are often ill-suited to the types of activities involved in computer crimes. This has been a major problem in punishing and deterring computer crime. Although many courts have interpreted their criminal statutes broadly to encompass criminal activity accomplished through the use of computers, a strong trend now exists for legislatures to amend their criminal codes to specifically outlaw certain types of computer crimes. A number of states have enacted statutes that forbid a wide variety of computer crimes, such as theft of computer time, use of computers to accomplish fraud and theft, and use of computers to gain access to data contained in a computer system. In 1984, Congress enacted the Counterfeit Access Device and Computer Fraud and Abuse Act, which makes it a crime to gain access to or use a computer for several specified purposes.

The widespread use of computers to collect, store, and integrate information about people has led to well-founded concern about the loss of individual privacy. The concern is not only that an individual loses the right to control how much information is disclosed about him but also that he loses control over the *accuracy* of the information disclosed. The U.S. Constitution has been interpreted to protect individual privacy against unreasonable invasion by the government. In addition, the common law tort of invasion of privacy may provide a remedy to a person injured by such an invasion. Perhaps the most effective means of protecting privacy is provided by the host of statutes existing on both the state and federal level that guard against different types of invasion of privacy by the government and others. Although these laws are not uniquely applicable to computer-assisted invasions of privacy, they are intertwined with the use of computers because computers are commonly used to store and transmit information about an individual.

Another very important issue in computer law relates to the means by which a producer of computer products may obtain protection against infringement and misappropriation of its inventions, expressions, and trade secrets. This is a particular problem for producers of computer software. A producer of computer software may be able to obtain protection through patents, copyrights, and trade secret law. Because of the stringent nature of the requirements for patentability, however, only a very small percentage of computer software can qualify for a patent. The Supreme Court has not yet held that software, standing alone, can be patented, although it has held that software in combination with other patentable processes can be protected by a patent. Thus, patents are not a possible or feasible method of protection for most computer software. Computer software is copyrightable, regardless of whether it is expressed in a form readable only by machines or whether it is expressed in a language that humans can understand. Such a copyright protects only the *expression* of the ideas contained in the program, however, and not the ideas themselves.

Because of the difficulty in obtaining patents and the limited protection provided by copyright law, most software producers rely primarily on trade secrets law to protect their proprietary interests. To be a trade secret, a program must have some degree of novelty and usefulness, and the secrecy of the program must be closely guarded and disclosed only under confidential circumstances. Producers protect this secrecy in a variety of ways, such as by entering into nondisclosure agreements with employees and customers and by labeling their software as secret.

## PROBLEM CASES

**1.** M. Bryce & Associates marketed a management information systems (MIS) methodology called PRIDE, which it had developed at great expense. It informed its employees of the confidential nature of the program, and obtained their pledge to keep the program a secret. Harley-Davidson was engaged in revamping its MIS standards manual. In response to a request by Arthur Young & Company which was working with Harley-Davidson on this project, Bryce agreed to demonstrate the PRIDE system for Harley-Davidson. Before going into the details of PRIDE, Bryce required all of the participants to sign a nondisclosure form. Although only three of the five participants signed this form, Bryce continued the demonstration with the nonsigners present. Harley-Davidson opted not to purchase PRIDE, but to develop its own manual. When the manual was issued, Bryce filed suit against Harley-Davidson and its consultant for misappropriation of a trade secret, alleging that they had used the information disclosed in the PRIDE demonstration to appropriate and reproduce PRIDE without authorization. Harley-Davidson asserted that PRIDE was not a trade secret. Should PRIDE be considered a trade secret?

**2.** Office Systems contracted to buy computer hardware and software from Basic/Four. The contract provided for an express warranty against defects in materials, workmanship, and operating failure from ordinary use for 90 days from the date of installation. The contract specified that the express warranty was given in lieu of all other warranties. It also disclaimed all implied warranties and excluded consequential and incidental damages, limiting the available remedies to correction of defects without charge. The warranty period ended on January 6, 1976. Office Systems experienced problems with the system that began in October 1975 and persisted until February 1978. In June 1980, Office Systems filed suit against Basic/Four for damages for breach of warranty. Can Office Systems recover damages?

**3.** Garden State Food Distributors entered into a lease-purchase agreement with Sperry Univac to acquire a Sperry Univac BC/7 Computer System, which included hardware, software, and related services. The system was covered by a warranty, but the contract limited Garden State's remedies to the amount of money paid by Garden State for the products and services. Garden State made a down payment of $3,399 and rental and maintenance payments of $4,045.06. When the system failed to work, Garden State brought suit against Sperry Univac for damages for breach of warranty. Garden State argued that the contractual limitation of remedies was unenforceable because the exclusive remedy "failed of its essential purpose." Does the Uniform Commercial Code apply to this transaction? Is the limitation of remedies enforceable?

**4.** Wilson purchased a computer-assisted electrocardiographic system called MUSE from Marquette. Before the sale, Marquette orally represented that the system had a throughput capacity of 10,000 EKGs per month, that the system would not have "downtime" of more than 24 hours over two times per year, that the service given would be priority service, and that the equipment would operate in the environment of the Wilson office facility with the existing power facilities and temperature range. The system was accompanied by a written manual that did not contain any provisions relating to warranties. When the system was put into operation, a number of significant problems became evident. It would not operate in Wilson's office building environment, and it was capable of only 5,000 throughputs per month. Furthermore, the system was unreliable and experienced a number of breakdowns, many for more than 24 hours in duration. Wilson brought suit for breach of warranty. What warranties were created in this transaction?

**5.** Girard, a former agent of the Drug Enforcement Administration (DEA), and one James Bond discussed a proposed venture to smuggle a planeload of marijuana from Mexico into the United States. Girard told Bond that he had an inside source in the DEA and that for $500 per name he could secure reports from DEA files that would show whether any participant in the proposed operation was a government informant. Bond asked Girard to secure reports on four men. Girard's inside source, Lambert, procured the requested reports through a computer terminal located in his office. Because Bond was himself a government informant, Girard and Lambert's activities became known to the DEA, and the two were charged with and convicted of the federal statute outlawing the unauthorized sale of government property and the federal statute outlawing conspiracy to accomplish such a sale. Lambert and Girard appealed their convictions, arguing that the statutes applied only to the sale of tangible property or documents, and not to the sale of information. Should their convictions be overturned?

Chapter 51

# Business Ethics, Corporate Social Responsibility, and the Control and Governance of Corporations

## INTRODUCTION

Large modern American corporations have always been villains to some and heroes to others. For years, critics of corporations—and of business in general—have assailed corporations for maximizing profits to the alleged detriment of consumers, employees, communities, and the environment. Such critics have been quick to condemn corporations when they violate the many laws regulating their behavior. However, while almost everyone would agree that corporations should respect the minimum legal "rules of the game" discussed throughout this text, modern critics of the corporation often go further. They argue that business should adhere to a standard of ethical or socially responsible behavior higher than that imposed by the existing rules of law. That is, such critics want corporations to behave ethically and responsibly in their relations with consumers, employees, the communities in which they operate, and society generally. Thus, for example, they argue that corporations should make their products safer than the law requires, only terminate employees for good cause,[1] and not arbitrarily abandon communities that are economically dependent on them.

Arrayed against these modern critics of the corporation are those who argue that profit maximization should be the main goal of corporations and that the only ethical norms corporations should feel bound to follow are those embodied in society's laws. Since "ethical" corporations are unlikely to be consistent profit maximizers, defenders of profit maximization argue that the economic efficiencies it produces would be lost if corporations were to subordinate profit maximization to other social goals. By maximizing profits, they say, corporations ensure that scarce economic resources (e.g., iron ore, beef, or oil) will be allocated to the uses that society values most highly (e.g., automobiles, hamburgers, and gasoline). The end result is that society as a whole benefits because its total economic welfare is maximized.

**Chapter Organization.** This chapter considers the range of difficult issues posed by the claim that corporations should act responsibly and ethically. It opens by examining the argument that corporations should simply attempt to maximize profits while acting within the constraints of the law. Then, the chapter considers some difficulties with the view that the law can adequately control corporate misbehavior.[2] After this, it examines a question that is fundamental to the whole corporate social responsibility debate: Are large modern corporations really profit maximizers? Following this, the chapter considers the uncertainties inherent in the critics' claim that corporations should behave ethically. The chapter concludes by examining some "corporate governance" proposals whose usual aim is to produce responsible corporate behavior by changing the *internal structure* of corporations.

Our aim throughout this chapter is to present you with the most significant issues involved in the corporate social responsibility debate, not to resolve them. As you will quickly see, the corporate social responsibility question is exceedingly complex, and thus is not easily resolvable. The debate is likely to continue for as long as private corporations form the backbone of our economic system.

**Importance.** Why are the issues discussed in this chapter important to you? For one thing, your life is affected directly and indirectly by the decisions of corporate managers. Their decisions, for example, can influence the safety of the automobile you drive, your job security and working conditions, and the quality of the environment in which you live. Perhaps more importantly, these issues are likely to concern you if you become a corporate manager. In this case, *your* decisions may affect the health, physical security, livelihood, and lifestyle of employees, consumers, and a host of others.

## THE PROFIT-MAXIMIZATION CRITERION

**Allocational Efficiency.** As noted in Chapter 24, the primary stated objective of business corporations is to maximize profits.[3] This objective has been promoted by economists on the ground that it results in an *efficient allocation of society's scarce resources.* Firms that most efficiently use resources will generally be able to undersell their competitors and, due to the greater sales that should re-

[1] By now, some states come close to requiring this. See Chapter 47's discussion of the demise of the traditional employment at will doctrine.

[2] Although this chapter does not discuss the criminal law as such, the treatment of the criminal liability of corporations in Chapters 3 and 24 is relevant here.

[3] Although it is not presented in this way here, the goal of profit maximization is sometimes regarded as "ethical" corporate conduct.

sult, reap higher profits. As a result, they will often be able to outbid less efficient resource users. Hence, scarce resources will be allocated efficiently, that is, to the users and uses most highly valued by consumers and most capable of giving consumers a maximum return on their expenditures. If corporate managers choose to pursue goals other than profit maximization, resources will not be put to their most efficient uses and society's total wealth will be reduced by the resulting allocational inefficiencies.

To illustrate the last point, assume for the sake of argument that all the firms in the American steel industry spontaneously decide to observe pollution standards stricter than those now imposed by law. In addition, assume that they do so even though they know that their buyers may not be willing to buy "responsibly" produced steel or to pay more for such steel. Since socially responsible behavior of this sort costs money, the firms in question face a dilemma. They can attempt to pass on the increased costs to buyers in the form of higher prices, thus reducing the buyers' return per dollar spent and (possibly) their ability to purchase other goods and services. Or the firms can refuse to increase their prices and accept lower profits. In this case, dividends and employee salaries might have to be reduced and the firms' ability to bid for scarce resources such as iron ore might also suffer. The likely result is a flow of employees, investment funds, and resources away from the firms in question. This, in turn, may mean lower steel production and lower overall social wealth than would otherwise be the case. In either case, socially responsible corporate behavior involves undeniable social costs. The following excerpt from Milton Friedman's *Playboy* interview makes many of these points.

## *Playboy* Interview with Economist Milton Friedman



**PLAYBOY:** Quite apart from emission standards and effluent taxes, shouldn't corporate officials take action to stop pollution out of a sense of social responsibility?

**MILTON FRIEDMAN:** I wouldn't buy stock in a company that hired that kind of leadership. A corporate executive's responsibility is to make as much money for the shareholders as possible, as long as he operates within the rules of the game. When an executive decides to take action for reasons of social responsibility, he is taking money from someone else—from the shareholders, in the form of lower dividends; from the employees, in the form of lower wages; or from the consumer, in the form of higher prices. The responsibility of a corporate executive is to fulfill the terms of his contract. If he can't do that in good conscience, then he should quit his job and find another way to do good. He has the right to promote what he regards as desirable moral objectives only with his own money. If, on the other hand, the executives of U.S. Steel undertake to reduce pollution in Gary for the purpose of making the town attractive to employees and thus lowering labor costs, then they are doing the shareholders' bidding. And everyone benefits: The shareholders get higher dividends; the customer gets cheaper steel; the workers get more in return for their labor. That's the beauty of free enterprise.

**Criticisms of the Profit-Maximization Criterion.** In light of the arguments just made, why should anyone criticize profit maximization as the prime goal of corporate activity? Underlying most such criticisms is a simple claim: allocational efficiency is not society's only (or even its most important) goal, and sometimes this goal should be subordinated to other social concerns. Just as the pursuit of corporate social responsibility forces society to make material sacrifices, the uninhibited pursuit of allocational efficiency compels it to sacrifice other values.

Critics of the idea that corporations should be concerned solely with profit maximization usually stress that such an orientation can result in harm to employees, consumers, communities, the environment, and society as a whole. For example, corporations that leave a community when they find cheaper labor, favorable tax rates, and/or low-interest loans in another community may thereby enjoy increased profits, aid in the efficient allocation of scarce resources, and maximize total economic welfare. But this obviously is small consolation to the abandoned community, which may be left with little more than an empty factory shell. Even less likely to be consoled by these results are former employees who cannot find work or schoolchildren whose schools may be underfunded due to the erosion of the community's tax base.

Effects like these are worsened, critics continue, by the tremendous social and economic power that large corporations possess and by the inferior power available to those who are affected by corporate decisions. As suggested above, for instance, communities often vie for the benefits that a local business operation can bring and frequently have little power to influence corporate decisions to move to greener pastures. Nonunionized wage-earning employees generally do not engage in genuine bargaining regarding compensation and other terms and conditions of employment; instead, the employer's terms are offered on a take-it-or-leave-it basis. Similarly, consumers have no direct input in determining the products corporations produce, their features, or the prices at which they are sold. Even assuming that these disparities in power could be reduced or overcome, other difficulties confront those who might want to use free market mechanisms to influence corporate behavior in responsible directions. These are discussed in the following excerpt from Christopher Stone's book, *Where the Law Ends.*

## C. Stone, *Where the Law Ends*

**(New York: Harper & Row, 1975), pp. 88–92.** 

When one turns from the market as resource allocator to inspect its capacity to fulfill other societal desiderata, the case of the free-market man is even harder to support. One ought to be clear that those who have faith that profit orientation is an adequate guarantee of corporations realizing socially desirable consumer goals are implicitly assuming: (1) that the persons who are going to withdraw patronage know *the fact* that they are being "injured" (where injury refers to a whole range of possible grievances, from getting a worse deal than might be gotten elsewhere, to purchasing a product that is defective or below warranted standards, to getting something that produces actual physical injury); (2) that they know *where* to apply pressure of some sort; (3) that they are in a *position* to apply pressure of some sort; and (4) that their pressure will be *translated* into warranted changes in the institution's behavior. None of these assumptions is particularly well-founded.

As for the first, over a range of important cases the person who, under this model, should be shifting his patronage, does not even know that he is being "injured'" (in the broad sense referred to above). For example, from our vantage point in the present, we can look back on history and appreciate some of the dangers of smoking on a cigarette consumer's health, or of coal dust on a worker's lungs. It hardly strains the imagination to believe that we today, as consumers, employees, investors, and so forth, are being subjected by corporations to all sorts of injuries that we will learn about only in time. But we are not able to translate these general misgivings into market preference because we simply do not know enough about where dangers lie.

Second, that the individuals know *where* to apply pressure, is, in many instances also, too facile an assumption. Consider the case of the consumer disaffected by a certain product. If the free-market mechanism is working perfectly, he would be expected to withdraw his patronage from the management that produced that product, thereby "penalizing" those responsible for it and encouraging their rivals. But to do so, what exactly is he supposed to "boycott"? Consumers identify products by brand name, not usually by the producing company, of whose identity they are often ignorant. A dissatisfied Tide user who shifted from Tide to Dash, or to Duz—or to Bold, Oxydol, Cascade, Cheer, or Ivory Soap—would still, whether he knows it or not, be patronizing Procter & Gamble.

Even where the first two criteria are met—that is, the person being injured knows the fact that he is being injured and can discover against whom to apply pressure—he may still not be in a position in which he can apply pressure. This could come about for at least two major reasons.

First, the model presupposes the existence of some negotiating interface between the corporation and the person disaffected with it. Such a relationship is available for a worker who is a member of a union recognized by the corporation, and for a person who is directly a consumer of the corporation's products or services. But consider, for example, a person whose grievance is with an aluminum company that is showering his land with pollutants, or that is, in his estimate, exercising objectionable influences in Latin America. If, as is likely, he is not a direct purchaser of aluminum, what recourse does he have: to do a study of all the products he is contemplating buying that contain aluminum so as to determine the "parentage" of their aluminum components and know which of them to boycott?

Second, even if such a negotiating interface exists, the person dealing with the company may have no viable alternative source of supply or employment. The most obvious example is when the company with whose actions someone is concerned is a monopoly or near-monopoly. For example, there has been considerable concern recently over the low nutritional value of breakfast cereals, as well as some distaste expressed over the amount of rat hair and other extraneous matter that turn up in the boxes. But a disaffected consumer confronts a market in which 90 percent of the breakfast cereals are produced by four companies.

Finally, one ought to be chary, too, of the assumptions that even if economic pressure can be brought to bear on the "offending" corporation, the pressure will be smoothly translated into changes in the institution's behavior. The assumption rises and falls with one's belief that corporations are pure and simple profit maximizers. A company whose customers are being "turned off" for one reason or another may well, just as the model suggests, turn their patronage elsewhere. But this does not assure that the management will know why it lost sales, or, discovering the reason, that it will remedy the problem in the most desirable way possible.

There is a vivid example of this in a recent episode involving "snack packs," little cans of pudding with metal, tear-away lids, that had become a popular lunchbox item for schoolchildren. Unfortunately, not only were children cutting their fingers on the sharp, serrated edges, but they were regularly licking the custard from the snapped-off metal top, which Consumers Union found sharp enough to cut a chicken leg. Reports began to filter in of cuts. The surest remedy for this would presumably have been to replace the metal snap-off top with a plastic or screw-on variant. "It is easier to change the design of the can," one third-grade teacher wrote Consumers Union, "than it is to change the natural tendencies of a child." Well—that's what the third-grade teacher thought. What she overlooked is that for the company to change its top called for it to change its way of doing things—its own "natural tendencies." Instead of changing its tops, the company undertook an advertising campaign, distributing posters that told kiddies, in essence, to be careful. It took who knows how many complaints before the company finally gave in and promised to start using a safety lid or withdraw the product. The episode is not atypical. What those who put all their faith in the market fail to account for is one of the most fundamental principles of organizational theory: All large organizations seek to seal off or "buffer" their technical core from disruptive environmental influences (like the market—or the law). So far as possible their tendency is to fight rather than to switch.

**Rejoinders.** Defenders of the profit-maximization motive can make a number of rejoinders to the arguments just made. First, they can argue that, in most cases, the allocational efficiencies achieved by profit maximization simply outweigh the values sacrificed by that achievement. Critics of the corporation, of course, will make opposing moral arguments. Who is right? In many cases, your answer may depend on the particular "trade-off" in question. If, for instance, a small reduction in air pollution means big sacrifices in industrial productivity, you may have little trouble deciding that the environmental gains are not worth their material costs. But in other situations, fairly basic moral choices may be necessary. You may have to decide, for example, whether environmental protection is ultimately more important than economic growth, or vice versa. This text is not a treatise on ethics, and, in any event, it is doubtful whether such treatises would provide consistent answers to the questions we are posing. Despite the lack of authoritative guidance, however, moral questions of this sort are an inevitable part of human existence. And at some point in your life, you may be denied the luxury of refusing to decide.

**Market Forces and Corporate Responsibility.** Other defenders of profit maximization, however, could take a different approach. They could agree that other social values may sometimes outweigh allocational efficiency, or at least concede that the question is debatable. They would argue, however, that corporate managers need not concern themselves with questions of social responsibility, because market forces and free private activity will usually force them to behave in a responsible fashion.

As you have seen, Professor Stone is quite skeptical about this argument. But defenders of profit maximization might respond with the following illustrative hypothetical counterargument. What would consumers have to do to, for example, force a corporation to make a safer product or stop investing in South Africa? They would basically have to make their preferences known to management and to back up those preferences with a refusal to buy the corporation's products. It is often easy to obtain information about a corporation's products and activities. Getting a list of the products manufactured by a large corporation, for instance, is a fairly simple matter. Such lists are available from public records and from analysts following the manufacturer's securities. It is even easier for consumers to notify a corporation of their concerns and to make those concerns public. For example, letter-writing campaigns and boycotts can be organized, consumer interest groups can prepare press releases, and consumers who own stock in the corporation can make shareholder proposals. Such methods are often quite effective in getting the attention of corporate managers. And sometimes they succeed in changing corporate behavior, just as the consumers in Professor Stone's example finally succeeded in forcing the pudding manufacturer to change the tops on its pudding cans.

The central point, the profit maximizers' argument would continue, is that in a free society with a free economy people can organize to make their grievances felt. If a sufficient number do so, corporate behavior can be made more responsible without having managers abandon their basic profit maximization orientation and the social benefits it creates. If such efforts fail because they do not attract sufficient support, this suggests that the complaints were not valid in the first place. Or it may indicate that the consumers who did not "join up" expressly or implicitly decided that the costs of achieving success outweighed the benefits accruing from success. Who is Professor Stone to say that they are wrong?

The validity of arguments like the one just made will probably vary with the circumstances. However, there are a number of points that you should consider in evaluating it and in determining whether it effectively rebuts Professor Stone. First, note that the argument concedes a basic point made by critics of the corporation: in certain circumstances, some values may be more important than allocational efficiency. Also, does the argument assume an unwarranted degree of time, energy, concern, and sophistication on the part of consumers? Does it underestimate the difficulties involved in organizing to achieve collective purposes? Finally, does it underestimate the power of corporations to counter such activities?

## THE LAW AS A CORPORATE CONTROL DEVICE

**Introduction.** Whether or not the profit maximizers' final rejoinder is ultimately persuasive, it does lead to another argument for their position. The argument involves a factor that this chapter has largely ignored until now: *the law.* If irresponsible corporate behavior creates sufficient public dissatisfaction, the argument goes, that dissatisfaction will sooner or later find reflection in the law. Just as a free society permits individuals and groups to put moral and economic pressure on corporations, it also allows them to make their desires felt in the political arena. Plainly, such efforts are often successful; the table of contents to this text suggests as much. And while defenders of profit maximization may complain about particular forms of regulation, they always recognize that corporations have an obligation to obey the basic rules of the game established by the legal system. These rules, they say, state norms of behavior backed by a substantial social consensus.

The law's ability to deter socially irresponsible corporate actions depends heavily on the view that corporations are rational profit maximizers. The main way the law controls behavior is through the sanctions (e.g., imprisonment, fines, civil damages) it imposes on those who violate its rules. For deterrence to work effectively, those the law is to control must understand when its penalties will be imposed and must fear the costs those penalties create. Since corporations are assumed to be profit maximizers, it seems natural that they should fear the penalties the law imposes for misbehavior, which are largely financial. And if corporations are not *rational* actors with the ability to recognize monetary threats and respond accordingly, it is difficult to see how they could effectively maximize profits.

Unfortunately, the law's ability to control irresponsible corporate behavior, while significant, has its limits. The various (and somewhat conflicting) reasons for its relative ineffectiveness are discussed below. To the extent that these arguments are valid, the profit maximizers' case against modern critics of the corporation is weakened.

**Corporate Influence on the Content of the Law.** One problem with the idea that the law is an effective corporate control device stems from the fact that business has a significant voice in determining the content of the law. Thus, the law frequently tends to reflect *corporate* interests. As a result, corporations are sometimes free to engage in behavior that noncorporate segments of society would find unethical.

The political influence exerted by large corporations is a familiar subject. Because of their size, resources, and sophistication, they have (or can purchase) the ability to influence legislation through, for example, lobbying and contributions to business-oriented political action committees. Even if Congress or the state legislatures pass hostile regulatory legislation, corporations can sometimes blunt its impact. They may use their political influence to reduce the funding received by the agency enforcing the legislation. Over time, they may co-opt the agency by inducing it to take a probusiness view of its functions. One way this occurs is through the frequent exchange of personnel between the agency and the industry it is supposed to regulate in the public interest. And many political scientists have commented on the frequency with which an agency, the industry it regulates, and the congressional subcommittee controlling the agency form a mutually beneficial relationship that is relatively impervious to outside influence (the so-called Iron Triangle).

In evaluating this argument, however, you should note that by now critics of the corporation have also become adept at playing the political game, and on some occasions are able to counteract corporate political power. The influence of consumer groups is but one example.

**Conscious Lawbreaking.** Even where the legal rules do not reflect business interests, corporations may consciously decide that it makes sense to violate those rules. As rational actors with a desire to maximize profits, corporations may conclude that breaking the law poses acceptable risks if the benefits gained by doing so are great, the penalties for violation are relatively light, and/or the chances of being sued or prosecuted are low. Several other factors increase the likelihood that corporations will engage in conscious or semiconscious lawbreaking. The "let's take the risk" mentality may be reinforced when the law is (or is perceived to be) uncertain. Corporate or industry norms may regard a measure of illegal (or borderline) behavior as morally acceptable. This is especially likely to be true where corporate managers regard the relevant legal rules as misguided.

The tendency toward conscious lawbreaking could be reduced, many argue, by stiffer penalties and increased enforcement efforts. But corporate political influence may prevent either from occurring. As noted above, corporations sometimes try to blunt politically popular legislation by devoting their efforts to such less visible matters as agency funding.

State and federal prosecutors are usually either elected or politically appointed. And, more generally, the public is not always willing to fund increased enforcement efforts.

**Unknown Harms.** As Professor Stone argued in the excerpt quoted above, exclusive reliance on market forces to control corporate behavior rests on the assumption that consumers will always know when the environment is being degraded or their health is being threatened by the production or use of a particular product. Reliance on the *law* as a corporate control device involves a similar assumption: namely, that legislators and regulators will possess similar knowledge. Plainly, legal action to control socially harmful corporate behavior will not be forthcoming until the need for such action is apparent. Yet hardly a month goes by when we fail to learn that a product that we have used with perfect confidence for years has some newly discovered harmful side effects, or that some chemical commonly used in production processes poses risks to workers, consumers, or the environment.

In some such cases, after-the-fact legal action may simply be incapable of compensating for irreparable harms that have already occurred. Also, it is fairly obvious that corporate managers are often equally ignorant of the effects of their products or production processes. In some instances, however, corporate managers' intimate familiarity with their own products or production processes may make them aware of such dangers long before they are apparent to society in general. Such situations obviously confront corporate managers with a difficult ethical dilemma. Should they take no action until the dangers in question become apparent, hoping that any liability imposed on their corporation once discovery occurs will be manageable? Should they take immediate unilateral corrective action that puts their firm at a competitive disadvantage with competitors that fail to take similar corrective action? Or should they alert the public, so that the legal rules of the game are changed for all corporate players? Neither the law nor the market can effectively answer such questions.

**Are Corporations Always Rational Actors?** Another argument against the law's ability to control corporations conflicts somewhat with those just presented. Instead of basing the law's ineffectiveness on the conscious, rational activities of those firms, it contends that much of their irresponsible behavior results from an *inability to respond sensibly* to legal threats. As you saw above, the law's ability to affect business behavior depends on a clear perception of the penalties for illegal actions and a rational response to the resulting risk. To the extent that corporations fail these tests of clear perception and rational response, the law's ability to control them suffers.

Proponents of the view that corporations often act irrationally generally begin by noting that, as a rule, *people* are not especially perceptive and clearheaded. Everyone "blocks out" certain aspects of the external world, and the tendency to do so is especially noticeable when the excluded information is troubling. Thus, for example, corporate managers planning a highly profitable venture may discount potential legal problems that would render the venture less attractive. By combining the abilities of many people, though, organizations should be able to correct these individual deficiencies. But while this is often true, there are also certain features of organizational life that make perception and rational response *less* likely.

Social psychologists and students of organizational behavior, for instance, have long been aware of a phenomenon called *risky shift.* This means that a group of people who must reach a consensus on an acceptable level of risk often decide on a level of risk *higher* than the risk they would accept as individuals. Thus, the decisions made by a team of managers may create greater legal problems than the decisions made by an isolated manager. Also relevant here is the familiar phenomenon of *groupthink:* the tendency for members of a group to internalize the group's values and perceptions and to suppress critical thought. Thus, if our team of managers is planning a highly profitable venture to which the success of each team member is tied, each may minimize the venture's legal problems because these conflict with the group's goals.

Somewhat similar to groupthink is another familiar feature of organizational life: the tendency "for bad news not to get to the top." When subordinates know that top managers are strongly committed to a particular course of action, they may not report problems for fear of provoking their superiors' disapproval. Ideally, of course, managers should desire to be fully apprised of potential legal risks; but occasionally their response is to penalize the bearer of bad news instead. Finally, the complex organizational structures of modern corporations sometimes diminish their capacity for rational and effective responses to external legal problems. For example, the size and complexity of organizational structures worsen the tendency for "bad news" not to reach top managers. For the same reasons, it is sometimes difficult for top managers to ensure that their decisions are fully implemented at lower levels within the organization.

## ARE CORPORATIONS ALWAYS PROFIT MAXIMIZERS?

**Introduction.** Underlying the previous section's arguments against corporate rationality is a view of the corporation that does not square with the usual economists' picture of its operations. On the whole, economists see corporations as entities devoted to the rational pursuit of material gains (or profits). However, sociologists, organizational psychologists, and students of organizational behavior tend to see the corporation in a quite different light: as a bureaucratic organization that serves as a kind of community for its members and that pursues a variety of goals in the process. This disagreement has enormous implications for the issues discussed in this chapter. As you saw in the last section, the basic argument for the law's ability to control corporations was that its sanctions have a direct effect on profits. But if corporations pursue other goals besides profit maximization, the law's ability to deter undesirable behavior may suffer.[4] Even more importantly, if corporations do not always maximize profits, their ability to produce allocational efficiencies is reduced.[5] Neither implication, obviously, is very congenial to those who defend the corporation against its modern critics.

**The Arguments against Profit Maximization.** Those who argue that corporations pursue goals other than profit maximization usually focus on the large, modern "mature" corporation. They concede that smaller firms fighting for survival in competitive markets are primarily oriented toward profits. Established firms in oligopolistic industries, however, often face less severe competition,[6] and thus have the luxury of pursuing other aims.

[4] However, as noted in the next section, corporations that subordinate profit maximization to other goals might be less inclined to engage in socially irresponsible behavior.

[5] Of course, even corporations that embrace the goal of profit maximization may not be able to achieve that goal if they are not rational actors.

[6] Price competition in oligopolistic industries, for instance, is often minimal. Indeed, firms in such industries may engage in tacit price-fixing schemes, such as following industry price leaders, without running afoul of the antitrust laws. See Chapter 44.

Such goals include employee financial well-being, the creation of a congenial and stimulating internal environment, expansion, prestige, and innovation. These goals are not necessarily inconsistent with profit maximization; higher employee benefits, for instance, may produce greater profits by increasing employee satisfaction and job performance. But sometimes the pursuit of these goals can consume resources and human energy that might otherwise be devoted to profits. Thus, firms of this sort are said to seek only a *satisfactory* profit level: they "satisfice" (rather than maximize) profits. This generally means that such firms try to achieve only sufficient profits to satisfy shareholders. As a result, it is said, optimum allocational efficiencies are not achieved.

Another argument against profit maximization differs somewhat from the argument just presented. It concedes that corporations generally try to maximize profits, but argues that the profits sought are usually *short-term* profits. Such firms, in other words, sacrifice the future to the present and thus do not promote long-term allocational efficiency. The reward structures that exist in many corporations are said to further this tendency. For example, salary, bonus, and promotion decisions are frequently tied to year-end profitability; and top executives often have relatively brief terms of office. Thus, the interests of managers may not always be synonymous with the long-range interests of their corporate employers. In such cases, the corporation may be more inclined toward illegal or irresponsible behavior due to the short-term orientation of its managers. As noted in Chapter 3, the prospect of legal trouble "down the road" may not make much of an impression on such managers.

**Rejoinders.** The rejoinders to the arguments just made are generally economic in nature. Their general thrust is that profit satisficing and a short-term management orientation are not sound competitive strategies, and will ultimately create innumerable difficulties for firms that adopt these strategies. Hence, the rejoinder goes, most corporations do try to maximize profits, do achieve allocational efficiency in the process, and do respond to legal rules that threaten their profits.

One version of the rejoinder might go as follows. According to the efficient market hypothesis, all of the relevant information about a corporation's security is immediately reflected in the price of that security. This price represents the present value of future cash flows that an investor may expect from the security. Thus, if management makes short-run decisions that detrimentally affect the long-run profitability of the corporation, those decisions will be reflected immediately in the price of the security. This effect is even more obvious when management satisfices by trying to pay the dividends it thinks will satisfy shareholders. In either case, shareholders are likely to be dissatisfied if the actual value of their shares falls below the shares' potential maximum value. In other words, the only way to satisfice is to pursue profits with vigor. When shareholders become upset because they are not realizing the optimum return on their investment, they may well try to sell their shares (which further depresses prices). They may also try to oust the corporation's management. In addition, a corporation with securities selling below their maximum potential value is a target for a hostile takeover. And top corporate managers almost always lose their jobs after a hostile takeover.

Arguments of this sort are almost certainly true in extreme cases, and may apply in a number of other situations as well. But are they valid *in general*? In trying to answer this question, there are a number of points you should consider. Does the argument made above really boil down to the proposition that whatever corporations do is by definition efficient? Is the information necessary to make the efficient market hypothesis work always available? (In this connection, note that some studies have argued that not all market participants need be fully informed and rational for efficiency to result.) Do competitive conditions in the particular industry matter? Specifically, do firms in oligopolistic industries with managed prices generate sufficient revenue to keep shareholders content without maximizing profits? How good are large, established corporations at avoiding hostile takeover bids? Are all the various relevant parties (especially shareholders) really the rational economic actors that the argument assumes they are? Which are most and least likely to behave in this way?

## THE DILEMMAS OF "ETHICAL" CORPORATE BEHAVIOR

**Introduction.** By now, some readers of this chapter may have begun to entertain serious reservations about the arguments made by the profit maximizers. But are the critics who urge ethical corporate behavior on any stronger ground? This section takes a closer look at the "corporate social responsibility" position. It first considers the argument that the modern corporation is singularly equipped to assume a responsible role in American life. Then, it examines some more basic difficulties with the notion of ethical corporate behavior.

**The "Corporate Stewardship" Argument.** The previous section's suggestion that the modern mature corporation does not maximize profits has another implication for the concerns of this chapter. Once corporations are sufficiently secure to focus on other values besides profit maximization, the argument runs, they are free to behave in an ethical, responsible fashion. One proponent of this position has argued that modern corporate managers have come to resemble "a professional civil service far more than a group of property-owning and property-minded entrepreneurs."[7] But while this development is a *possible* implication of the hypothesis that corporations do not maximize profits, it is hardly a *necessary* implication of that hypothesis. As noted earlier, modern corporations may pursue such goals as maximum employee compensation, a pleasant work environment, size, and technological innovation. These goals are not exactly what critics of the corporation have in mind when they speak of ethical corporate behavior, and can obviously be pursued in quite irresponsible ways. Worse yet, the great size and power of the modern corporation, many argue, make it far less accountable to outside forces than are smaller, profit-oriented firms. If so, the incentives for irresponsible behavior may *increase* because firms can indulge in such behavior with relative impunity. Finally, some observers have argued that there is in fact no correlation between the abandonment of profit maximization and responsible corporate behavior.[8]

**What Is Ethical Corporate Behavior?** Suppose, however, that a corporation or some of its managers spontaneously decide to behave in an ethical fashion. What exactly does this entail? Many discussions of business ethics examine the various established ethical theories and attempt to apply them in the business context. Like the different varieties of natural law discussed in Chapter 1, these theories often conflict. Their respective merits have been debated for centuries, and the problems posed in this debate have remained as

[7] A. Berle, *Power without Property*, 118 (New York: Harcourt Brace, 1959).

[8] See E. Herman, *Corporate Control, Corporate Power*, 261–64 (Cambridge: Cambridge University Press, 1981).

intractable as they were when the debate began.

However, nothing we have just said should necessarily be read as endorsing the widespread view that moral questions are meaningless, that ethical statements are merely arbitrary, and that (in effect) "anything goes." Such conclusions do not logically follow from the fact that ethical disagreement exists. Moreover, moral questions are an inescapable part of human life, as Chapter 1's discussion of natural law emphasized, and at some point in your life you may be denied the luxury of refusing to decide such questions. But the preceding discussion should have made clear that there are numerous difficulties with the seemingly simple injunction that corporations should behave ethically and responsibly.

**The Problem of Ethical Diversity.** One possible escape from the philosophical problems just suggested is to base ethical corporate behavior on values that actually find wide acceptance today. However, corporations and managers adopting this course will immediately confront an unfortunate fact of modern American life: its bewildering array of conflicting ethical views. On some moral questions affecting the corporation, there is admittedly a general consensus. Almost everyone, for example, would agree that assassination and industrial sabotage are reprehensible means of dealing with competitors. But on many other questions, there is considerable disagreement. Some defenders of the corporation, for instance, feel that profit maximization *is* socially responsible corporate behavior, while critics of the corporation tend to see this as the basis for all the misdeeds that corporations commit. Even where there is widespread agreement on particular values, moreover, people disagree on the weight to be given each value when values are in conflict. Almost everyone, for example, affirms that material abundance and environmental protection are worthwhile goals, but there is often little consensus on the terms of the inevitable trade-offs that must be made between them.

For these reasons, a corporation foolish enough to allow individual managers to act on the basis of their own ethical views will almost certainly be plagued with inconsistent managerial decisions. The idea of socially responsible corporate behavior seems to require a real or imposed ethical homogeneity within the top ranks of the firm's management structure. Since, as discussed above, there are powerful forces tending to produce consensus within organizations, this homogeneity may not be impossible to achieve. But the basic question posed above still remains: Whose values should the ethical corporation try to advance? Among the innumerable possible responses to this question, we will discuss two commonly suggested sources of ethical guidance: industry codes and the values of the corporation's various constituencies.

**Corporate or Industry Codes of Ethical Conduct.** Many large corporations and several industries have adopted codes of conduct to guide executive decision making. For example, an industry code might define as unethical certain types of advertising or hiring practices and some corporate codes of conduct prohibit employees from accepting gifts from suppliers of the corporation.

There are two popular views of such codes. One view sees them as genuine attempts to foster ethical behavior within a corporation or an industry. The other view regards them as thinly disguised attempts to mislead the public into believing that business behaves ethically, to forestall legislation that would impose more severe constraints on business, or to limit competition under the veil of ethical standards. Since the capacity for identifying self-interest with morality is an obvious feature of human life, there may be occasions where the two views converge. On either view, however, there is no guarantee that the code in question will be ultimately right in a philosophical sense or that it will accurately reflect the values of society or of some relevant community.

**Constituency Values.** Today, it is widely recognized that the large modern corporation interacts with a number of important constituencies—for example, employees, unions, suppliers, customers, and the community in which it operates. Related to this perception is a view of corporate responsibility that resembles the "stewardship" notion discussed above. This is the view that the corporation should attempt to act in the best interests of all of its various constituencies. To the extent possible, for example, the corporation should treat its employees fairly, bargain honestly with unions, make its products as safe as possible, be a good citizen of the local community, and so forth.

The major problem with this conception of ethical corporate behavior is that the values (or interests) of these various constituencies may conflict. What is beneficial to one constituency, that is, may be harmful to another. For example, although one community will suffer when a corporation moves its plant to another community, the second community will generally benefit. How are corporate managers to balance such claims? Are they especially well equipped to do so?

## THE "CORPORATE GOVERNANCE" AGENDA

**Introduction.** In an apparent response to the many problems posed by the corporate social responsibility debate, corporate critics of the 1960s and 1970s made a number of proposals designed to affect the internal governance of corporations. Chapters 24 and 25 discuss some of these proposals, and the discussion in this chapter supplements Chapters 24 and 25. What unites such proposals is their essentially "procedural" nature. These proposals, that is, do not attempt to define ethical corporate behavior in detail. Instead, they try to generate more responsible corporate behavior by making the corporate decision-making process more sensitive to outside concerns. Although a few of the proposals have occasionally been adopted in modified form, public interest in them has diminished considerably since the 1970s. However, they may again become popular if the political winds shift. Below, we discuss three such recommendations—and the difficulties they present—in general terms.

**Greater Shareholder Power.** The traditional model of the corporation decrees that ultimate power resides with its shareholders, and despite the well-known separation of ownership and control that characterizes the modern large corporation, shareholders remain an important corporate constituency. Thus, some proposals for modifying internal corporate governance have advocated that shareholders be given a greater voice in shaping corporate policy. Specific recommendations along these lines include giving shareholders greater power to nominate directors and giving them the ability to adopt resolutions binding the directors.[9]

Of the various corporate governance proposals, granting greater power to shareholders probably has the least to recommend it. While it is arguable that corporate managers have abandoned the goal of profit maximization, the orientation of shareholders is almost always completely pecuniary. Shareholders, in other words, have a considerable interest in corporate profit maximization. While shareholders may sometimes lack the ability

[9] See Chapter 24.

or incentive to detect or respond to satisficing behavior by management, they are not likely to initiate or approve corporate actions avowedly hostile to profit maximization if confronted with an explicit choice. All of this is especially true, some say, of institutional investors such as pension funds, which own significant blocks of stock in many corporations. Thus, enhanced shareholder control could well lead to *greater* corporate irresponsibility.

Even if this very fundamental problem could somehow be surmounted, another difficulty with shareholder governance would remain. There is no guarantee that the values of "ethical" shareholders would be representative of the values of society as a whole. Fewer than 5 percent of all Americans own 60 percent of all the corporate shares held by individuals. Many of the shareholders within this group have sufficient wealth to isolate themselves from many of the socially undesirable effects of corporate actions. And there is little reason to think that institutional investors can effectively represent larger social concerns. Thus, a shareholder mandate to corporate executives is very unlikely to reflect broad social interests.

**Changing the Composition of the Board.** As discussed in Chapter 24, the corporation's directors theoretically have general responsibility for the management of the corporation. In large corporations, of course, this power is generally more theoretical than real, and actual power usually rests with management. Still, the formal legal powers of the board are considerable. Recognizing this, critics of the corporation have made innumerable recommendations for changing its composition to make management more responsible.[10] Some of the recommendations have been relatively modest: for example, creating nominating committees composed of outside directors,[11] requiring that there be more such directors and fewer insiders, and limiting the number of corporate boards on which one individual can serve. More extreme proposals include recommendations that constituencies of all sorts (e.g., labor, government, creditors, local communities, minorities, environmentalists) be represented, that certain directors be assigned special areas of concern (e.g., consumer protection, environmental affairs), and that special committees of the board be assigned similar functions.

From a social responsibility perspective, the basic problem with all such proposals is that they fail to confront the main reason for management's domination of the board: the limited time, information, and expertise that directors can bring to bear when considering corporate affairs. One solution to this problem is to give outside or constituency directors a full-time staff with the power to dig for information within the corporation. Doing so, however, effectively creates another—perhaps competing—layer of management within the corporate organizational structure. While this could curtail certain corporate misdeeds, it could also lessen the corporation's ability to innovate and respond to changing developments.

Another, more down-to-earth, set of problems with some of these proposals concerns the details of their implementation. Which constituencies deserve representation? How many directors should each constituency have? Within each constituency, what criteria should govern the choice of directors? For example, is it desirable or undesirable that they have business experience?

Finally, in addition to complicating the management structure, the implementation of these proposals might diminish the board's own cohesiveness and thus render it incapable of coherent action. Conflicts among constituency representatives or between insiders and outsiders are not unlikely. In fact, the addition of constituency directors might simply

---

[10] See Chapter 24.

[11] Outside and inside directors are defined in Chapter 24.

mean the intrusion of broader social conflicts into corporate boardrooms. The board, that is, could be divided by disputes among consumers who want lower prices, workers who want higher wages and job security, environmentalists who want polluters closed down, and communities that want to preserve jobs and their tax bases. This could render the board incapable of pushing management in responsible directions. As suggested earlier, it could also tend to check the corporation's ability to innovate and react to external stimuli.

**Changes in Management Structure.** As noted above, one of the great commonplaces about large 20th-century corporations is the so-called separation of ownership from control: the shift of power away from shareholders and directors to the corporation's managers. Once the full implications of this shift are grasped, some corporate reformers argue, it becomes evident that the best way to produce more responsible corporate behavior is to *make changes in the corporation's internal management structure.* The main proponent of this view, Professor Christopher Stone, has made a number of specific recommendations for such changes. They include the establishment of the following (each of which would probably have to be required by law): (1) certain specified offices within certain corporations (e.g., offices for environmental affairs, worker safety, and product safety); (2) requirements for holding certain corporate positions (e.g., certain educational requirements for safety engineers); (3) offices for ensuring that relevant external information is received by the corporation (e.g., data from auto repair shops for car manufacturers or data from doctors for drug companies); and (4) internal information-flow procedures for ensuring that relevant external information gets to the proper internal corporate departments (to guarantee, for instance, that bad news will get to the top). Stone and others have also recommended that corporations be required to make certain internal findings before undertaking various activities. For example, drug companies might be required to produce a document resembling an environmental impact statement before marketing a new product.

All of these proposed requirements are procedural in the sense that they do not dictate what decisions the corporation should make. Their general aim is to ensure that corporations have the means to anticipate problems before they arise so that timely responses to them are possible. Such requirements would probably do little to deter a strongly profit-oriented corporation from taking socially irresponsible actions. And it is entirely possible that the corporate personnel responsible for implementing these requirements will be influenced by a strong internal profit orientation or "frozen out" of the final decision-making process. In cases where irresponsible corporate behavior is less the product of profit-seeking than of failed perceptions, however, such proposals could have salutary results. But those results would probably be obtained only at the cost of further intraorganizational complexity, with a consequent reduction in the corporation's ability to make quick responses to changing business conditions.

## CONCLUSION

At this point, you are probably convinced of the truth of the assertion made at the beginning of the chapter that the corporate social responsibility issue is exceedingly complex. That complexity is undoubtedly a major factor in our failure as a society to resolve satisfactorily the many arguments that make up the corporate social responsibility debate. The complexity of the issue combined with the perceived failings of proposed "solutions" for resolving the debate probably assures the continued discussion of this issue for the foreseeable future.

As you have learned, many factors conspire to make markets less than perfect regulators of corporate behavior. Among other things, the relative ignorance and powerlessness of consumers, the relative isolation of some corporations from the discipline of the market, and the failure of some corporations to respond to market signals in a rational fashion indicate the necessity of some other control device.

As you have also learned, however, the efficacy of the formal mechanism of the law as a means for gaining sufficient control of corporations is highly problematic. As indicated in Chapter 3, significant difficulties exist in applying criminal sanctions to corporations and their employees. Many corporations may be unresponsive to profit threats aimed at them, and financial penalties may be passed on to consumers or borne by shareholders (and not by the managers who make corporate decisions). Attempts to impose liability on individual corporate managers pose difficult problems of proof due to the organizational nature of much corporate behavior, and imposing liability on individuals in the absence of personal moral culpability raises difficult moral questions. At the very least, reliance on the law as a major component of society's corporate control strategy requires the creation of new legal approaches to corporate control.[12] But even assuming that such new legal approaches are feasible, the law will always be an imperfect corporate control mechanism because corporations play a significant role in shaping legal rules. And the law, in any event, can only respond to dangers that are apparent to society as a whole. Finally, it is questionable whether the law could ever provide complete guidance for the resolution of every ethical issue that is likely to confront corporate managers.

[12] See the discussion of this point in Chapter 3.

These obvious shortcomings of both the law and markets are seen by some as ample justification for a third path: corporate conformity with ethical values that are neither enshrined in law nor demanded by the marketplace. The dilemma associated with such calls for ethical behavior is obvious: Whose ethics should prevail? Supporters of managerial profit maximization properly point out both management's legal duties to shareholders and shareholders' profit orientation. They note the diversity of both social and individual values, and they question whether ethical values that have not gained sufficient acceptance to be incorporated into legal rules should be considered proper guides for corporate behavior. This is particularly true when the pursuit of such values may result in a decline in economic efficiency that is detrimental to society as a whole.

Some critics of the corporation have proposed a wide variety of measures that, in effect, seek to change what corporations *are* by changing corporate structure. These proposals, ranging from giving shareholders more control over corporate directors to incorporating members of a corporation's constituencies into its board of directors, all suffer from a variety of flaws. Shareholders are primarily profit-oriented, and thus are unlikely to urge responsible behavior on the corporation. And the inclusion of constituency directors may simply result in the intrusion of broader social conflicts into corporate boardrooms, with a consequent reduction in corporate efficiency.

Finally, one may properly ask whether we as a society really *want* corporations to engage in the contentious and difficult task of resolving conflicting social claims. Legislatures were designed to perform this important social function, and, given the current structure of corporations, are better suited than corporations to do so. Until corporate critics are able to convince a social majority that other corporate forms are more likely to provide significant reductions in socially undesirable corporate behavior without reducing the manifold benefits that we all derive from the current system, the legislatures, along with the marketplace, are likely to remain the primary regulators of corporate conduct. Likewise, until corporate critics are able to construct an ethical system capable of earning the support of a broad social consensus, corporate managers seeking ethical guidance unavailable from either the law or the marketplace will have to rely on the ultimate guide available to all of us: individual conscience.

## PROBLEM CASES

**1.** You are a director of Will Dempsey, Incorporated, a business in the family entertainment field operating theme amusement parks and producing motion pictures. During its 50-year history, Will Dempsey, Inc. has produced only G-rated movies, which are suitable for all audiences. The corporation has refused to enter the lucrative teenage- and adult-movie market of PG- and R-rated movies, some of which espouse questionable moral values regarding criminal conduct, drugs, language, and sex. In each of the last five years, Will Dempsey's earnings have declined 10 percent. In an attempt to increase profitability, the president and the chairman of the board have proposed to the board of directors that Will Dempsey begin producing R-rated movies aimed at high school students. They have also proposed that these movies contain a mix of drug use and sexual promiscuity that will attract a large segment of the teenage moviegoing market. Their projections show that if Will Dempsey produces such movies, its profits will increase by 20 percent in each of the next three years. As a director of Will Dempsey, do you support the proposals of the president and the chairman of the board?

**2.** You are the general manager of a large retail department store in a large suburban shopping mall. Your assistant in charge of purchasing is Ann Granite, who has worked for the store for five years. Ann is the head of her household, supporting her husband and three children. In the last several months, Ann's work performance has been unsatisfactory. She has been absent about 10 percent of the time, and she has made several unprofitable purchasing decisions. You have spoken with Ann several times, but her performance has not improved. She says that it has been affected by her worries about her inability to pay all of her creditors. Ann is the highest-paid employee in the store, except for you. Her salary is higher than those of others with similar positions in other stores in the area. What do you do?

**3.** You are a director of Xeno Corporation, a manufacturer of ladies' garments. Xeno has a 9 percent share of the ladies' garment market, a market that is not dominated by any one manufacturer. Xeno's return on equity has averaged 17 percent the last five years. Xeno has a blouse factory in Tillman, Oklahoma. Due to high employee wages, unfavorable taxes, and a decreasing labor pool, the president of Xeno proposes to close the Tillman plant and move the operation to Kent, Ohio. Taxes are lower in Kent, the Kent labor pool is very large; and the city has promised Xeno a low-interest loan. Xeno is the largest employer in Tillman. If it closes the Tillman plant, unemployment there will reach 20 percent, and the city's tax revenues will fall by 15 percent. If it opens a plant in Kent, 1,000 new jobs will be created and Kent's annual tax revenues will be increased by $250,000. Xeno's profits will increase 1 percent during the first year after it moves its blouse operation to Kent. The president of Xeno has asked the board's approval to move the plant. What is your response to the president's request? What would your response be if the president proposed that the operations be moved to Taiwan?

**4.** You are a director of Jolly Charlie Tuna Corporation. Jolly Charlie has annual sales of $185,800,000 and annual profits of $24,350,000. Its business is catching tuna and canning the tuna for sale to consumers. Its fishing methods do not always permit its employees to determine whether they are catching tuna or dolphins, which often swim with tuna. The result is that many dolphins are killed. The Society to Protest Against the Murdering of Marine Mammals (SPAMMM) has discovered that Jolly Charlie has been killing dolphins and has asked it to change its fishing methods so that dolphins are not killed. If Jolly Charlie does not stop killing dolphins, SPAMMM will call a press conference on the matter and urge consumers to stop buying Jolly Charlie tuna. Making the requested change in fishing methods would cost Jolly Charlie $2,565,000 each year in increased labor costs. Jolly Charlie would have to absorb the increased cost or pass the cost on to consumers. If it passed the cost on to consumers, the price of each can of tuna would increase to 95 cents a can from the present price of 89 cents. Since Jolly Charlie's tuna now sells for the same price as other brands of tuna, Jolly Charlie expects its sales to fall by 10 percent if it increases the price of its tuna. The board is asked what it thinks the corporation should do. What is your solution?

**5.** During World War II, DDT, an insecticide, was used successfully to halt a typhus epidemic spread by lice and to control mosquitoes and flies. After World War II, it was used extensively to control agricultural and household pests. Today, DDT may not be used legally in the United States and most other countries. Although DDT has a rather low immediate toxicity to humans and other vertebrates, it becomes concentrated in fatty tissues of the body and may cause death months or years after it has been ingested. In addition, it degrades slowly, remaining toxic in the soil for years after its application. DDT has been blamed for the near extinction of bald eagles, whose population has increased greatly since DDT was banned.

While moving boxes in a warehouse, an employee of Eartho Chemical Corporation discovers 5,000 tons of DDT. Eartho stopped producing and selling DDT when it was banned in the United States and was unaware that it had any left in stock. The value of the DDT is about $10 million in countries in which its use is not banned. The president of Eartho wants to destroy the DDT. Some Eartho executives want to sell the DDT in countries that do not ban its use. You are a director of Eartho. The board has been asked what should be done with the DDT. What is your response?

**6.** Marigold Dairy Corporation sells milk products, including powdered milk formula for infants. Marigold has identified Japan as a country in which it hopes to increase its sales of powdered milk formula. Marigold's advertising department has developed an advertising scheme to convince mothers and expectant mothers that they should not breast-feed their babies but should use the Marigold formula instead. Doctors generally favor breast-feeding as beneficial to mothers (it helps the uterus return to normal size), to babies (it is nutritious, and it strengthens the bonds between the infant and the mother), and to families (it is inexpensive). Marigold's marketing plan stresses the good nutrition of its formula and the convenience to parents of using the formula, including not having to breast-feed. You are the vice president of marketing for Marigold. Do you approve this marketing plan? Would you approve the plan if the formula were to be sold to families in underdeveloped nations, such as Biafra?

**7.** Rammax Coal and Oil Corporation has been considering acquiring a new line of business that is compatible with its present businesses—coal mining, oil exploration, and oil refining. The treasurer proposes that Rammax enter the nuclear power plant construction field. The proposal is tentatively approved by the board of directors. When the expansion is announced, some Rammax shareholders object and submit a proposal to shareholders that the articles of incorporation be amended to prevent Rammax from "doing anything with nuclear energy until the problem of nuclear waste disposal has been solved." At a meeting of shareholders, only 2 percent of the outstanding shares vote in favor of the proposal. The losing shareholders vow to continue their fight to prevent Rammax from building nuclear power plants. Rammax's president is confident that an antinuclear proposal will never be approved by the shareholders. The yearly cost of dealing with the protesting shareholders is about $250,000. Rammax projects that building nuclear power plants will increase its annual earnings by $7 million in each of the first five years of this operation and by $82 million each year thereafter. As a director of Rammax, do you vote in favor of Rammax's entering the nuclear power plant construction business?

8. Batix Corporation manufactures batteries. In the manufacturing process, toxic waste is produced. Batix hired Tox-Mob Corporation to dispose of the waste. Tox-Mob charges $5,000 per day to do this job, which is half the amount that other companies charge. A year after Batix entered into its contract with Tox-Mob, you, as vice president of production, discover that Tox-Mob is not disposing of the toxic waste properly but is merely dumping it into the Missouri River. A corporation that knowingly has someone dispose of its toxic waste illegally is subject to a fine of $10,000 per day. However, there is only a 3 percent chance that the illegal dumping will be detected. Besides, no one else at Batix knows that Tox-Mob is illegally dumping the waste and no one anywhere knows that you know about the dumping. Hence, it would be difficult, if not impossible, to prove that Batix *knowingly* had someone dispose of its toxic waste illegally. What do you do?

# APPENDIXES

# Appendix Contents

# The Constitution of the United States

## PREAMBLE

We the People of the United States, in Order to form a more perfect Union, establish Justice, insure domestic Tranquility, provide for the common defence, promote the general Welfare, and secure the Blessings of Liberty to ourselves and our Posterity, do ordain and establish this Constitution for the United States of America.

## ARTICLE 1

Section 1. All legislative Powers herein granted shall be vested in a Congress of the United States, which shall consist of a Senate and House of Representatives.

Section 2. [1] The House of Representatives shall be composed of Members chosen every second Year by the People of the several States, and the Electors in each State shall have the Qualifications requisite for Electors of the most numerous Branch of the State Legislature.

[2] No Person shall be a Representative who shall not have attained to the Age of twenty five Years, and been seven Years a Citizen of the United States, and who shall not, when elected, be an Inhabitant of that State in which he shall be chosen.

[3] Representatives and direct Taxes shall be apportioned among the several States which may be included within this Union, according to their respective Numbers, which shall be determined by

adding to the whole Number of free Persons, including those bound to Service for a Term of Years, and excluding Indians not taxed, three fifths of all other Persons. The actual Enumeration shall be made within three Years after the first Meeting of the Congress of the United States, and within every subsequent Term of ten Years, in such Manner as they shall by Law direct. The Number of Representatives shall not exceed one for every thirty Thousand, but each State shall have at Least one Representative; and until such enumeration shall be made, the State of New Hampshire shall be entitled to chuse three, Massachusetts eight, Rhode Island and Providence Plantations one, Connecticut five, New York six, New Jersey four, Pennsylvania eight, Delaware one, Maryland six, Virginia ten, North Carolina five, South Carolina five, and Georgia three.

[4] When vacancies happen in the Representation from any State, the Executive Authority thereof shall issue Writs of Election to fill such Vacancies.

[5] The House of Representatives shall chuse their Speaker and other Officers; and shall have the sole Power of Impeachment.

Section 3. [1] The Senate of the United States shall be composed of two Senators from each State, chosen by the Legislature thereof, for six Years; and each Senator shall have one Vote.

[2] Immediately after they shall be assembled in Consequence of the first Election, they shall be divided as equally as may be into three Classes. The Seats of the Senators of the first Class shall be vacated at the Expiration of the Second Year, of the second Class at the Expiration of the fourth Year, and of the third Class at the Expiration of the sixth Year, so that one third may be chosen every second Year; and if Vacancies happen by Resignation, or otherwise, during the Recess of the Legislature of any State, the Executive thereof may make temporary Appointments until the next Meeting of the Legislature, which shall then fill such Vacancies.

[3] No Person shall be a Senator who shall not have attained to the Age of thirty Years, and been nine Years a Citizen of the United States, and who shall not, when elected, be an Inhabitant of that State for which he shall be chosen.

[4] The Vice President of the United States shall be President of the Senate, but shall have no Vote, unless they be equally divided.

[5] The Senate shall chuse their other Officers, and also a President pro tempore, in the Absence of the Vice President, or when he shall exercise the Office of President of the United States.

[6] The Senate shall have the sole Power to try all Impeachments. When sitting for that Purpose, they shall be on Oath or Affirmation. When the President of the United States is tried, the Chief Justice shall preside: And no Person shall be convicted without the Concurrence of two thirds of the Members present.

[7] Judgment in Cases of Impeachment shall not extend further than to removal from Office, and disqualification to hold and enjoy any Office of honor, Trust, or Profit under the United States: but the Party convicted shall nevertheless be liable and subject to Indictment, Trial, Judgment, and Punishment, according to Law.

Section 4. [1] The Times, Places and Manner of holding elections for Senators and Representatives, shall be prescribed in each State by the Legislature thereof; but the Congress may at any time by Law make or alter such Regulations, except as to the Places of chusing Senators.

[2] The Congress shall assemble at least once in every Year, and such Meeting shall be on the first Monday in December, unless they shall by Law appoint a different Day.

Section 5. [1] Each House shall be the Judge of the Elections, Returns, and Qualifications of its own Members, and a Majority of each shall constitute a Quorum to do Business; but a smaller Number may adjourn from day to day, and may be authorized to compel the Attendance of absent Members, in such Manner, and under such Penalties as each House may provide.

[2] Each House may determine the Rules of its Proceedings, punish its Members for disorderly Behavior, and, with the Concurrence of two thirds, expel a Member.

[3] Each House shall keep a Journal of its Proceedings, and from time to time publish the same, excepting such Parts as may in their Judgment require Secrecy; and the Yeas and Nays of the Members of either House on any question shall,

at the Desire of one fifth of those Present, be entered on the Journal.

[4] Neither House, during the Session of Congress, shall, without the Consent of the other, adjourn for more than three days, nor to any other Place than that in which the two Houses shall be sitting.

Section 6. [1] The Senators and Representatives shall receive a Compensation for their Services, to be ascertained by Law, and paid out of the Treasury of the United States. They shall in all Cases, except Treason, Felony and Breach of the Peace, be privileged from Arrest during their Attendance at the Session of their respective Houses, and in going to and returning from the same; and for any Speech or Debate in either House, they shall not be questioned in any other Place.

[2] No Senator or Representative shall, during the Time for which he was elected, be appointed to any civil Office under the Authority of the United States, which shall have been created, or the Emoluments whereof shall have been increased during such time; and no Person holding any Office under the United States, shall be a Member of either House during his Continuance in Office.

Section 7. [1] All Bills for raising Revenue shall originate in the House of Representatives; but the Senate may propose or concur with Amendments as on other Bills.

[2] Every Bill which shall have passed the House of Representatives and the Senate, shall, before it becomes a Law, be presented to the President of the United States; If he approve he shall sign it, but if not he shall return it, with his Objections to the House in which it shall have originated, who shall enter the Objections at large on their Journal, and proceed to reconsider it. If after such Reconsideration two thirds of that House shall agree to pass the Bill, it shall be sent together with the Objections, to the other House, by which it shall likewise be reconsidered, and if approved by two thirds of that House, it shall become a Law. But in all such Cases the Votes of both Houses shall be determined by yeas and Nays, and the Names of the Persons voting for and against the Bill shall be entered on the Journal of each House respectively. If any Bill shall not be returned by the President within ten Days (Sundays excepted) after it shall have been presented to him, the Same shall be a Law, in like Manner as if he had signed it, unless the Congress by their Adjournment prevent its Return in which Case it shall not be a Law.

[3] Every Order, Resolution, or Vote, to Which the Concurrence of the Senate and House of Representatives may be necessary (except on a question of Adjournment) shall be presented to the President of the United States; and before the Same shall take Effect, shall be approved by him, or being disapproved by him, shall be repassed by two thirds of the Senate and House of Representatives, according to the Rules and Limitations prescribed in the Case of a Bill.

Section 8. [1] The Congress shall have Power To lay and collect Taxes, Duties, Imposts and Excises, to pay the Debts and provide for the common Defence and general Welfare of the United States; but all Duties, Imposts and Excises shall be uniform throughout the United States;

[2] To borrow money on the credit of the United States;

[3] To regulate Commerce with foreign Nations, and among the several States, and with the Indian Tribes;

[4] To establish an uniform Rule of Naturalization, and uniform Laws on the subject of Bankruptcies throughout the United States;

[5] To coin Money, regulate the Value thereof, and of foreign Coin, and fix the Standard of Weights and Measures;

[6] To provide for the Punishment of counterfeiting the Securities and current Coin of the United States;

[7] To Establish Post Offices and Post Roads;

[8] To promote the Progress of Science and useful Arts, by securing for limited Times to Authors and Inventors the exclusive Right to their respective Writings and Discoveries;

[9] To constitute Tribunals inferior to the supreme Court;

[10] To define and punish Piracies and Felonies committed on the high Seas, and Offenses against the Law of Nations;

[11] To declare War, grant Letters of Marque

and Reprisal, and make Rules concerning Captures on Land and Water;

[12] To raise and support Armies, but no Appropriation of Money to that Use shall be for a longer Term than two Years;

[13] To provide and maintain a Navy;

[14] To make Rules for the Government and Regulation of the land and naval Forces;

[15] To provide for calling forth the Militia to execute the Laws of the Union, suppress Insurrections and repel Invasions;

[16] To provide for organizing, arming, and disciplining, the Militia, and for governing such Part of them as may be employed in the Service of the United States, reserving to the States respectively, the Appointment of the Officers, and the Authority of training the Militia according to the discipline prescribed by Congress;

[17] To exercise exclusive Legislation in all Cases whatsoever, over such District (not exceeding ten Miles square) as may, by Cession of particular States, and the Acceptance of Congress, become the Seat of the Government of the United States, and to exercise like Authority over all Places purchased by the Consent of the Legislature of the State in which the Same shall be, for the Erection of Forts, Magazines, Arsenals, dock-Yards and other needful Buildings;—And

[18] To make all Laws which shall be necessary and proper for carrying into Execution the foregoing Powers, and all other Powers vested by this Constitution in the Government of the United States, or in any Department or Officer thereof.

Section 9. [1] The Migration or Importation of Such Persons as any of the States now existing shall think proper to admit, shall not be prohibited by the Congress prior to the Year one thousand eight hundred and eight, but a Tax or duty may be imposed on such Importation, not exceeding ten dollars for each Person.

[2] The privilege of the Writ of Habeas Corpus shall not be suspended, unless when in Cases of Rebellion or Invasion the public Safety may require it.

[3] No Bill of Attainder or ex post facto Law shall be passed.

[4] No Capitation, or other direct, Tax shall be laid, unless in Proportion to the Census or Enumeration herein before directed to be taken.

[5] No Tax or Duty shall be laid on Articles exported from any State.

[6] No Preference shall be given by any Regulation of Commerce or Revenue to the Ports of one State over those of another: nor shall Vessels bound to, or from, one State be obliged to enter, clear, or pay Duties in another.

[7] No money shall be drawn from the Treasury, but in Consequence of Appropriations made by Law; and a regular Statement and Account of the Receipts and Expenditures of all public Money shall be published from time to time.

[8] No Title of Nobility shall be granted by the United States: And no Person holding any Office of Profit or Trust under them, shall, without the Consent of the Congress, accept of any present, Emolument, Office, or Title, of any kind whatever, from any King, Prince, or foreign State.

Section 10. [1] No State shall enter into any Treaty, Alliance, or Confederation; grant Letters of Marque and Reprisal; coin Money; emit Bills of Credit; make any Thing but gold and silver Coin a Tender in Payment of Debts; pass any Bill of Attainder, ex post facto Law, or Law impairing the Obligation of Contracts, or grant any Title of Nobility.

[2] No State shall, without the Consent of the Congress, lay any Imposts or Duties on Imports or Exports, except what may be absolutely necessary for executing it's inspection Laws: and the net Produce of all Duties and Imposts, laid by any State on Imports or Exports, shall be for the Use of the Treasury of the United States; and all such Laws shall be subject to the Revision and Control of the Congress.

[3] No State shall, without the Consent of Congress, lay any Duty of Tonnage, keep Troops, or Ships of War in time of Peace, enter into any Agreement or Compact with another State, or with a foreign Power, or engage in War, unless actually invaded, or in such imminent Danger as will not admit of delay.

## ARTICLE II

Section 1. [1] The executive Power shall be vested in a President of the United States of America. He shall hold his Office during the Term of four Years, and, together with the Vice President, chosen for the same Term, be elected, as follows:

[2] Each State shall appoint, in such Manner as the Legislature thereof may direct, a Number of Electors, equal to the whole Number of Senators and Representatives to which the State may be entitled in the Congress; but no Senator or Representative, or Person holding an Office of Trust or Profit under the United States, shall be appointed an Elector.

[3] The Electors shall meet in their respective States, and vote by Ballot for two Persons, of whom one at least shall not be an Inhabitant of the same State with themselves. And they shall make a List of all the Persons voted for, and of the Number of Votes for each; which List they shall sign and certify, and transmit sealed to the Seat of the Government of the United States, directed to the President of the Senate. The President of the Senate shall, in the Presence of the Senate and House of Representatives, open all the Certificates, and the Votes shall then be counted. The Person having the greatest Number of Votes shall be the President, if such Number be a Majority of the whole Number of Electors appointed; and if there be more than one who have such Majority, and have an equal Number of Votes, then the House of Representatives shall immediately chuse by Ballot one of them for President; and if no Person have a Majority, then from the five highest on the List the said House shall in like Manner chuse the President. But in chusing the President, the Votes shall be taken by States the Representation from each State having one Vote; A quorum for this Purpose shall consist of a Member of Members from two thirds of the States, and a Majority of all the States shall be necessary to a Choice. In every Case, after the Choice of the President, the Person having the greater Number of Votes of the Electors shall be the Vice President. But if there shall remain two or more who have equal Votes, the Senate shall chuse from them by Ballot the Vice President.

[4] The Congress may determine the Time of chusing the Electors, and the Day on which they shall give their Votes; which Day shall be the same throughout the United States.

[5] No person except a natural born Citizen, or a Citizen of the United States, at the time of the Adoption of this Constitution, shall be eligible to the Office of President; neither shall any Person be eligible to that Office who shall not have attained to the Age of thirty-five Years, and been fourteen Years a Resident within the United States.

[6] In case of the removal of the President from Office, or of his Death, Resignation or Inability to discharge the Powers and Duties of the said Office, the Same shall devolve on the Vice President, and the Congress may by Law provide for the Case of Removal, Death, Resignation or Inability, both of the President and Vice President, declaring what Officer shall then act as President, and such Officer shall act accordingly, until the Disability be removed, or a President shall be elected.

[7] The President shall, at stated Times, receive for his Services, a Compensation, which shall neither be increased nor diminished during the Period for which he shall have been elected, and he shall not receive within that Period any other Emolument from the United States, or any of them.

[8] Before he enter on the Execution of his Office, he shall take the following Oath or Affirmation: "I do solemnly swear (or affirm) that I will faithfully execute the Office of President of the United States, and will to the best of my Ability, preserve, protect and defend the Constitution of the United States."

Section 2. [1] The President shall be Commander in Chief of the Army and Navy of the United States, and of the militia of the several States, when called into the actual Service of the United States; he may require the Opinion, in writing, of the principal Officer in each of the Executive Departments, upon any Subject relating to the Duties of their respective Offices, and he shall have Power to grant Reprieves and Pardons for Offenses against the United States, except in Cases of Impeachment.

[2] He shall have Power, by and with the Advice and Consent of the Senate to make Treaties, provided two thirds of the Senators present concur; and he shall nominate, and by and with the Advice and Consent of the Senate, shall appoint Ambassadors, other public Ministers and Consuls, Judges of the supreme Court, and all other Officers of the United States, whose Appointments are not herein otherwise provided for, and which shall be established by Law; but the Congress may by Law vest

the Appointment of such inferior Officers, as they think proper, in the President alone, in the Courts of Law, or in the Heads of Departments.

[3] The President shall have Power to fill up all Vacancies that may happen during the Recess of the Senate, by granting Commissions which shall expire at the End of their next Session.

Section 3. He shall from time to time give to the Congress Information of the State of the Union, and recommend to their Consideration such Measures as he shall judge necessary and expedient; he may, on extraordinary Occasions, convene both Houses, or either of them, and in Case of Disagreement between them, with Respect to the Time of Adjournment, he may adjourn them to such Time as he shall think proper; he shall receive Ambassadors and other public Ministers; he shall take Care that the Laws be faithfully executed, and shall Commission all the Officers of the United States.

Section 4. The President, Vice President and all civil Officers of the United States, shall be removed from Office on Impeachment for, and Conviction of, Treason, Bribery, or other high Crimes and Misdemeanors.

## ARTICLE III

Section 1. The judicial Power of the United States, shall be vested in one supreme Court, and in such inferior Courts as the Congress may from time to time ordain and establish. The Judges, both of the supreme and inferior Courts, shall hold their Offices during good Behaviour, and shall, at stated Times, receive for their Services a Compensation, which shall not be diminished during their Continuance in Office.

Section 2. [1] The judicial Power shall extend to all Cases, in Law and Equity, arising under this Constitution, the Laws of the United States, and Treaties made, or which shall be made, under their Authority;—to all Cases affecting Ambassadors, other public Ministers and Consuls;—to all Cases of admiralty and maritime Jurisdiction;—to Controversies to which the United States shall be a Party;—to Controversies between two or more States;—between a State and Citizens of another State;—between Citizens of different States;—between Citizens of the same State claiming Lands under the Grants of different States, and between a State, or the Citizens thereof, and foreign States, Citizens or Subjects.

[2] In all Cases affecting Ambassadors, other public Ministers and Consuls, and those in which a State shall be a Party, the supreme Court shall have original Jurisdiction. In all the other Cases before mentioned, the supreme Court shall have appellate Jurisdiction, both as to Law and Fact, with such Exceptions, and under such Regulations as the Congress shall make.

[3] The trial of all Crimes, except in Cases of Impeachment, shall be by Jury; and such Trial shall be held in the State where the said Crimes shall have been committed; but when not committed within any State, the Trial shall be at such Place or Places as the Congress may by Law have directed.

Section 3. [1] Treason against the United States, shall consist only in levying War against them, or, in adhering to their Enemies, giving them Aid and Comfort. No Person shall be convicted of Treason unless on the Testimony of two Witnesses to the same overt Act, or on Confession in open Court.

[2] The Congress shall have Power to declare the Punishment of Treason, but no Attainder of Treason shall work Corruption of Blood, or Forfeiture except during the Life of the Person attainted.

## ARTICLE IV

Section 1. Full Faith and Credit shall be given in each State to the public Acts, Records, and judicial Proceedings of every other State. And the Congress may by general Laws prescribe the Manner in which such Acts, Records and Proceedings shall be proved, and the Effect thereof.

Section 2. [1] The Citizens of each State shall be entitled to all Privileges and Immunities of Citizens in the several States.

[2] A Person charged in any State with Treason, Felony, or other Crime, who shall flee from Justice, and be found in another State, shall on demand of the executive Authority of the State from which he fled, be delivered up, to be removed to the State having Jurisdiction of the Crime.

[3] No Person held to Service or Labour in one State, under the Laws thereof, escaping into another, shall, in Consequence of any Law or Regula-

tion therein, be discharged from such Service or Labour, but shall be delivered up on Claim of the Party to whom such Service or Labour may be due.

Section 3. [1] New States may be admitted by the Congress into this Union; but no new State shall be formed or erected within the Jurisdiction of any other State; nor any State be formed by the Junction of two or more States, or Parts of States, without the Consent of the Legislatures of the States concerned as well as of the Congress.

[2] The Congress shall have Power to dispose of and make all needful Rules and Regulations respecting the Territory or other Property belonging to the United States; and nothing in this Constitution shall be so construed as to Prejudice any Claims of the United States, or of any particular State.

Section 4. The United States shall guarantee to every State in this Union a Republican Form of Government, and shall protect each of them against Invasion; and on Application of the Legislature, or of the Executive (when the Legislature cannot be convened) against domestic Violence.

## ARTICLE V

The Congress, whenever two thirds of both Houses shall deem it necessary, shall propose Amendments to this Constitution, or, on the Application of the Legislatures of two thirds of the several States, shall call a Convention for proposing Amendments, which, in either case, shall be valid to all Intents and Purposes, as part of this Constitution, when ratified by the Legislatures of three fourths of the several States, or by Conventions in three fourths thereof, as the one or the other Mode of Ratification may be proposed by the Congress; Provided that no Amendment which may be made prior to the Year One thousand eight hundred and eight shall in any Manner affect the first and fourth Clauses in the Ninth Section of the first Article; and that no State, without its Consent, shall be deprived of its equal Suffrage in the Senate.

## ARTICLE VI

[1] All Debts contracted and Engagements entered into, before the Adoption of this Constitution shall be as valid against the United States under this Constitution, as under the Confederation.

[2] This Constitution, and the Laws of the United States which shall be made in Pursuance thereof; and all Treaties made, or which shall be made, under the Authority of the United States, shall be the supreme Law of the Land; and the Judges in every State shall be bound thereby, any Thing in the Constitution or Laws of any State to the Contrary notwithstanding.

[3] The Senators and Representatives before mentioned, and the Members of the several State Legislatures, and all executive and judicial Officers, both of the United States and of the several States, shall be bound by Oath or Affirmation, to support this Constitution; but no religious Test shall ever be required as a Qualification to any Office or public Trust under the United States.

## ARTICLE VII

The Ratification of the Conventions of nine States shall be sufficient for the Establishment of this Constitution between the States so ratifying the Same.

## AMENDMENTS

*Articles in addition to, and in amendment of, the Constitution of the United States of America, proposed by Congress, and ratified by the Legislatures of the several States pursuant to the Fifth Article of the original Constitution.*

### AMENDMENT I [1791]

Congress shall make no law respecting an establishment of religion, or prohibiting the free exercise thereof; or abridging the freedom of speech, or of the press; or the right of the people peaceably to assemble, and to petition the Government for a redress of grievances.

### AMENDMENT II [1791]

A well regulated Militia, being necessary to the security of a free State, the right of the people to keep and bear Arms, shall not be infringed.

## AMENDMENT III [1791]

No Soldier shall, in time of peace be quartered in any house, without the consent of the Owner, nor in time of war, but in a manner to be prescribed by law.

## AMENDMENT IV [1791]

The right of the people to be secure in their persons, houses, papers, and effects, against unreasonable searches and seizures, shall not be violated, and no Warrants shall issue, but upon probable cause, supported by Oath or affirmation, and particularly describing the place to be searched, and the persons or things to be seized.

## AMENDMENT V [1791]

No person shall be held to answer for a capital, or otherwise infamous crime, unless on a presentment or indictment of a Grand Jury, except in cases arising in the land or naval forces, or in the Militia, when in actual service in time of War or public danger; nor shall any person be subject for the same offence to be twice put in jeopardy of life or limb; nor shall be compelled in any criminal case to be a witness against himself, nor be deprived of life, liberty, or property, without due process of law; nor shall private property be taken for public use, without just compensation.

## AMENDMENT VI [1791]

In all criminal prosecutions, the accused shall enjoy the right to a speedy and public trial, by an impartial jury of the State and district wherein the crime shall have been committed, which district shall have been previously ascertained by law, and to be informed of the nature and cause of the accusation; to be confronted with the witnesses against him; to have compulsory process for obtaining witnesses in his favor, and to have the Assistance of Counsel for his defence.

## AMENDMENT VII [1791]

In Suits at common law, where the value in controversy shall exceed twenty dollars, the right of trial by jury shall be preserved, and no fact tried by jury, shall be otherwise re-examined in any Court of the United States, than according to the rules of common law.

## AMENDMENT VIII [1791]

Excessive bail shall not be required, nor excessive fines imposed, nor cruel and unusual punishments inflicted.

## AMENDMENT IX [1791]

The enumeration in the Constitution, of certain rights, shall not be construed to deny or disparage others retained by the people.

## AMENDMENT X [1791]

The powers not delegated to the United States by the Constitution, nor prohibited by it to the States, are reserved to the States respectively, or to the people.

## AMENDMENT XI [1798]

The Judicial power of the United States shall not be construed to extend to any suit in law or equity, commenced or prosecuted against one of the United States by Citizens of another State, or by Citizens or Subjects of any Foreign State.

## AMENDMENT XII [1804]

The Electors shall meet in their respective states and vote by ballot for President and Vice-President, one of whom, at least, shall not be an inhabitant of the same state with themselves; they shall name in their ballots the person voted for as President, and in distinct ballots the person voted for as Vice-President, and they shall make distinct lists of all persons voted for as President, and of all persons voted for as Vice-President, and of the number of votes for each, which lists they shall sign and certify, and transmit sealed to the seat of the government of the United States, directed to the President of the Senate;—The President of the Senate shall, in the presence of the Senate and House of Representatives, open all the certificates and the votes shall then be counted;—The person having the greatest number of votes for President, shall be the President, if such number be a majority of the whole number of Electors appointed; and if no person have such majority, then from the persons having the highest numbers not exceeding three on the list of those voted for as President, the House of Representatives shall choose immediately, by ballot, the President. But in choosing the President, the votes shall be taken by states, the representation from each state having one vote; a quorum for this purpose shall consist of a member or members from two-thirds of the states, and a majority of all states shall be necessary to a choice. And if the House of Representatives shall not choose a President whenever the right of choice shall devolve upon them before the fourth day of March next following, then the Vice-President shall act as President, as in the case of the death or other constitutional disability of the President.—The person having the greatest number of votes as Vice-President, shall be the Vice-President, if such number be a majority of the whole number of Electors appointed, and if no person have a majority, then from the two highest numbers on the list, the Senate shall choose the Vice-President; a quorum for the purpose shall consist of two-thirds of the whole number of Senators, and a majority of the whole number shall be necessary to a choice. But no person constitutionally ineligible to the office of President shall be eligible to that of Vice-President of the United States.

## AMENDMENT XIII [1865]

Section 1. Neither slavery nor involuntary servitude, except as a punishment for crime whereof the party shall have been duly convicted, shall exist within the United States, or any place subject to their jurisdiction.

Section 2. Congress shall have power to enforce this article by appropriate legislation.

## AMENDMENT XIV [1868]

Section 1. All persons born or naturalized in the United States, and subject to the jurisdiction thereof, are citizens of the United States and of the State wherein they reside. No State shall make or enforce any law which shall abridge the privileges or immunities of citizens of the United States; nor shall any State deprive any person of life, liberty, or property, without due process of law; nor deny to any person within its jurisdiction the equal protection of the laws.

Section 2. Representatives shall be apportioned among the several States according to their respective numbers, counting the whole number of persons in each State, excluding Indians not taxed. But when the right to vote at any election for the choice of electors for President and Vice President of the United States, Representatives in Congress, the Executive and Judicial officers of a State, or the members of the Legislature thereof, is denied to any of the male inhabitants of such State, being twenty-one years of age, and citizens of the United States, or in any way abridged, except for participation in rebellion, or other crime, the basis of representation therein shall be reduced in the proportion which the number of such male citizens shall bear to the whole number of male citizens twenty-one years of age in such State.

Section 3. No person shall be a Senator or Representative in Congress, or elector of President and Vice President, or hold any office, civil or military, under the United States, or under any State, who having previously taken an oath, as a member of Congress, or as an officer of the United States, or as a member of any State legislature, or as an executive or judicial officer of any State, to support the Constitution of the United States, shall have engaged in insurrection or rebellion against the same, or given aid or comfort to the enemies thereof. But Congress may by a vote of two-thirds of each House, remove such disability.

Section 4. The validity of the public debt of the United States, authorized by law, including debts incurred for payment of pensions and bounties for services in suppressing insurrection or rebellion, shall not be questioned. But neither the United States nor any State shall assume or pay any debt or obligation incurred in aid of insurrection or rebellion against the United States, or any claim for the loss or emancipation of any slave; but all such debts, obligations and claims shall be held illegal and void.

Section 5. The Congress shall have power to enforce, by appropriate legislation, the provisions of this article.

## AMENDMENT XV [1870]

Section 1. The right of citizens of the United States to vote shall not be denied or abridged by the United States or by any State on account of race, color, or previous condition of servitude.

Section 2. The Congress shall have power to enforce this article by appropriate legislation.

## AMENDMENT XVI [1913]

The Congress shall have power to lay and collect taxes on incomes, from whatever source derived, without apportionment among the several States, and without regard to any census or enumeration.

## AMENDMENT XVII [1913]

[1] The Senate of the United States shall be composed of two Senators from each State, elected by the people thereof, for six years; and each Senator shall have one vote. The electors in each State shall have the qualifications requisite for electors of the most numerous branch of the State legislatures.

[2] When vacancies happen in the representation of any State in the Senate, the executive authority of such State shall issue writs of election to fill such vacancies: *Provided,* That the legislature of any State may empower the executive thereof to make temporary appointments until the people fill the vacancies by election as the legislature may direct.

[3] This amendment shall not be so construed as to affect the election or term of any Senator chosen before it becomes valid as part of the Constitution.

## AMENDMENT XVIII [1919]

Section 1. After one year from the ratification of this article the manufacture, sale, or transportation of intoxicating liquors within, the importation thereof into, or the exportation thereof from the United States and all territory subject to the jurisdiction thereof for beverage purposes is hereby prohibited.

Section 2. The Congress and the several States shall have concurrent power to enforce this article by appropriate legislation.

Section 3. This article shall be inoperative unless it shall have been ratified as an amendment to the Constitution by the legislatures of the several States, as provided in the Constitution, within seven years from the date of the submission hereof to the States by the Congress.

## AMENDMENT XIX [1920]

[1] The right of citizens of the United States to vote shall not be denied or abridged by the United States or by any State on account of sex.

[2] Congress shall have power to enforce this article by appropriate legislation.

## AMENDMENT XX [1933]

Section 1. The terms of the President and Vice President shall end at noon on the 20th day of January, and the terms of Senators and Representatives at noon on the 3d day of January, of the years in which such terms would have ended if this article had not been ratified; and the terms of their successors shall then begin.

Section 2. The Congress shall assemble at least once in every year, and such meeting shall begin at noon on the 3d day of January, unless they shall by law appoint a different day.

Section 3. If, at the time fixed for the beginning of the term of the President, the President elect shall have died, the Vice President elect shall become President. If the President shall not have been chosen before the time fixed for the beginning of his term, or if the President elect shall have failed to qualify, then the Vice President elect shall act as President until a President shall have qualified; and the Congress may by law provide for the case wherein neither a President elect nor a Vice President elect shall have qualified, declaring who shall then act as President, or the manner in which one who is to act shall be selected, and such person shall act accordingly until a President or Vice President shall have qualified.

Section 4. The Congress may by law provide for the case of the death of any of the persons from whom the House of Representatives may choose a President whenever the right of choice shall have devolved upon them, and for the case of the death of any of the persons from whom the Senate may choose a Vice President whenever the right of choice shall have devolved upon them.

Section 5. Sections 1 and 2 shall take effect on the 15th day of October following the ratification of this article.

Section 6. This article shall be inoperative unless it shall have been ratified as an amendment to the Constitution by the legislatures of three-fourths of the several States within seven years from the date of its submission.

## AMENDMENT XXI [1933]

Section 1. The eighteenth article of amendment to the Constitution of the United States is hereby repealed.

Section 2. The transportation or importation into any State, Territory, or possession of the United States for delivery or use therein of intoxicating liquors, in violation of the laws thereof, is hereby prohibited.

Section 3. This article shall be inoperative unless it shall have been ratified as an amendment to the Constitution by conventions in the several States, as provided in the Constitution, within seven years from the date of the submission hereof to the States by the Congress.

## AMENDMENT XXII [1951]

Section 1. No person shall be elected to the office of the President more than twice, and no person who has held the office of President, or acted as President, for more than two years of a term to which some other person was elected President shall be elected to the office of President more than once. But this Article shall not apply to any person holding the office of President when this Article was proposed by the Congress, and shall not prevent any person who may be holding the office of President, or acting as President, during the term within which this Article becomes operative from holding the office of President or acting as President during the remainder of such term.

Section 2. This article shall be inoperative unless it shall have been ratified as an amendment to the Constitution by the legislatures of three-fourths of the several States within seven years from the date of its submission to the States by the Congress.

## AMENDMENT XXIII [1961]

Section 1. The District constituting the seat of Government of the United States shall appoint in such manner as the Congress may direct:

A number of electors of President and Vice President equal to the whole number of Senators and Representatives in Congress to which the District would be entitled if it were a State, but in no event more than the least populous state; they shall be in addition to those appointed by the states, but they shall be considered, for the purposes of the election of President and Vice President, to be electors appointed by a state; and they shall meet in the District and perform such duties as provided by the twelfth article of amendment.

Section 2. The Congress shall have power to enforce this article by appropriate legislation.

## AMENDMENT XXIV [1964]

Section 1. The right of citizens of the United States to vote in any primary or other election for President or Vice President, for electors for President or Vice President, or for Senator or Representative in Congress, shall not be denied or abridged by the United States, or any State by reason of failure to pay any poll tax or other tax.

Section 2. The Congress shall have power to enforce this article by appropriate legislation.

## AMENDMENT XXV [1967]

Section 1. In case of the removal of the President from office or of his death or resignation, the Vice President shall become President.

Section 2. Whenever there is a vacancy in the office of the Vice President, the President shall nominate a Vice President who shall take office upon confirmation by a majority vote of both Houses of Congress.

Section 3. Whenever the President transmits to the President pro tempore of the Senate and the Speaker of the House of Representatives his written declaration that he is unable to discharge the powers and duties of his office, and until he transmits to them a written declaration to the contrary, such powers and duties shall be discharged by the Vice President as Acting President.

Section 4. Whenever the Vice President and a majority of either the principal officers of the executive departments or of such other body as Congress may by law provide, transmit to the President pro tempore of the Senate and the Speaker of the House of Representatives their written declaration that the President is unable to discharge the powers and duties of his office, the Vice President shall immediately assume the powers and duties of the office as Acting President.

Thereafter, when the President transmits to the President pro tempore of the Senate and the Speaker of the House of Representatives his written declaration that no inability exists, he shall resume the powers and duties of his office unless the Vice President and a majority of either the principal officers of the executive department or of such other body as Congress may by law provide, transmit within four days to the President pro tempore of the Senate and the Speaker of the House of Representatives their written declaration and the President is unable to discharge the powers and duties of his office. Thereupon Congress shall decide the issue, assembling within forty-eight hours for that purpose if not in session. If the Congress, within twenty-one days after receipt of the latter written declaration, or, if Congress is not in session, within twenty-one days after Congress is required to assemble, determines by two-thirds vote of both Houses that the President is unable to discharge the powers and duties of his office, the Vice President shall continue to discharge the same as Acting President; otherwise, the President shall resume the powers and duties of his office.

## AMENDMENT XXVI [1971]

Section 1. The right of citizens of the United States, who are eighteen years of age or older, to vote shall not be denied or abridged by the United States or by any State on account of age.

Section 2. The Congress shall have power to enforce this article by appropriate legislation.

# Uniform Commercial Code (1978 Text)*

### Title

An Act

To be known as the Uniform Commercial Code, Relating to Certain Commercial Transactions in or regarding Personal Property and Contracts and other Documents concerning them, including Sales, Commercial Paper, Bank Deposits and Collections, Letters of Credit, Bulk Transfers, Warehouse Receipts, Bills of Lading, other Documents of Title, Investment Securities, and Secured Transactions, including certain Sales of Accounts, Chattel Paper, and Contract Rights; Providing for Public Notice to Third Parties in Certain Circumstances; Regulating Procedure, Evidence and Damages in Certain Court Actions Involving such Transactions, Contracts or Documents; to Make Uniform the Law with Respect Thereto; and Repealing Inconsistent Legislation.

## ARTICLE 1 GENERAL PROVISIONS

### Part 1 Short Title, Construction, Application and Subject Matter of the Act

**§ 1–101. Short Title**

This Act shall be known and may be cited as Uniform Commerical Code.

### § 1–102. Purposes; Rules of Construction; Variation by Agreement

(1) This Act shall be liberally construed and applied to promote its underlying purposes and policies.

(2) Underlying purposes and policies of this Act are

(a) to simplify, clarify and modernize the law governing commercial transactions;

(b) to permit the continued expansion of commercial practices through custom, usage and agreement of the parties;

(c) to make uniform the law among the various jurisdictions.

(3) The effect of provisions of this Act may be varied by agreement, except as otherwise provided in this Act and except that the obligations of good faith, diligence, reasonableness and care prescribed by this Act may not be disclaimed by agreement but the parties may by agreement determine the standards by which the performance of such obligations is to be measured if such standards are not manifestly unreasonable.

(4) The presence in certain provisions of this Act of the word "unless otherwise agreed" or words of similar import does not imply that the effect of other provisions may not be varied by agreement under subsection (3).

(5) In this Act unless the context otherwise requires

(a) words in the singular number include the plural, and in the plural include the singular;

(b) words of the masculine gender include the feminine and the neuter, and when the sense so indicates words of the neuter gender may refer to any gender.

### § 1–103. Supplementary General Principles of Law Applicable

Unless displaced by the particular provisions of this Act, the principles of law and equity, including the law merchant and the law relative to capacity to contract, principal and agent, estoppel, fraud, misrepresentation, duress, coercion, mistake, bankruptcy, or other validating or invalidating cause shall supplement its provisions.

### § 1–104. Construction Against Implicit Repeal

This Act being a general act intended as a unified coverage of its subject matter, no part of it shall be deemed to be impliedly repealed by subsequent legislation if such construction can reasonably be avoided.

### § 1–105. Territorial Application of the Act; Parties' Power to Choose Applicable Law

(1) Except as provided hereafter in this section, when a transaction bears a reasonable relation to this state and also to another state or nation the parties may agree that the law either of this state or of such other state or nation shall govern their rights and duties. Failing such agreement this Act applies to transactions bearing an appropriate relation to this state.

(2) Where one of the following provisions of this Act specifies the applicable law, that provision governs and a contrary agreement is effective only to the extent permitted by the law (including the conflict of laws rules) so specified:

Rights of creditors against sold goods. Section 2–402.

Applicability of the Article on Bank Deposits and Collections. Section 4–102.

Bulk transfers subject to the Article on Bulk Transfers. Section 6–102.

Applicability of the Article on Investment Securities. Section 8–106.

Perfection provisions of the Article on Secured Transactions. Section 9–103.

### § 1–106. Remedies to Be Liberally Administered

(1) The remedies provided by this Act shall be liberally administered to the end that the aggrieved party may be put in as good a position as if the other party had fully performed but neither consequential or special nor penal damages may be had except as specifically provided in this Act or by other rule of law.

(2) Any right or obligation declared by this Act is enforceable by action unless the provision declaring it specifies a different and limited effect.

### § 1–107. Waiver or Renunciation of Claim or Right After Breach

Any claim or right arising out of an alleged breach can be discharged in whole or in part without consideration by a written waiver or renunciation signed and delivered by the aggrieved party.

### § 1–108. Severability

If any provision or clause of this Act or application thereof to any person or circumstances is held invalid, such invalidity shall not affect otherprovisions or applications of the Act which can be given effect without the invalid provision or application, and to this end the provisions of this Act are declared to be severable.

### § 1–109. Section Captions

Section captions are parts of this Act.

## Part 2 General Definitions and Principles of Interpretation

### § 1–201. General Definitions

Subject to additional definitions contained in the subsequent Articles of this Act which are applicable to specific Articles or Parts thereof, and unless the context otherwise requires, in this Act:

(1) "Action" in the sense of a judicial proceeding includes recoupment, counterclaim, set-off, suit in equity and any other proceedings in which rights are determined.

(2) "Aggrieved party" means a party entitled to resort to a remedy.

(3) "Agreement" means the bargain of the parties in fact as found in their language or by implication from other circumstances including course of dealing or usage of trade or course of performance as provided in this Act (Sections 1–205 and 2–208). Whether an agreement has legal consequences is determined by the provisions of this Act, if applicable; otherwise by the law of contracts (Section 1–103). (Compare "Contract.")

(4) "Bank" means any person engaged in the business of banking.

(5) "Bearer" means the person in possession of an instrument, document of title, or certificated security payable to bearer or indorsed in blank.

(6) "Bill of lading" means a document evidencing the receipt of goods for shipment issued by a person engaged in the business of transporting or forwarding goods, and includes an airbill. "Airbill" means a document serving for air transportation as a bill of lading does for marine or rail transportation, and includes an air consignment note or air waybill.

(7) "Branch" includes a separately incorporated foreign branch of a bank.

(8) "Burden of establishing" a fact means the burden of persuading the triers of fact that the existence of the fact is more probable than its nonexistence.

(9) "Buyer in ordinary course of business" means a person who in good faith and without knowledge that the sale to him is in violation of the ownership rights or security interest of a third party in the goods buys in ordinary course from a person in the business of selling goods of that kind but does not include a pawnbroker. All persons who sell minerals or the like (including oil and gas) at wellhead or minehead shall be deemed to be persons in the business of selling goods of that kind. "Buying" may be for cash or by exchange of other property or on secured or unsecured credit and includes receiving goods or documents of title under a preexisting contract for sale but does not include a transfer in bulk or as security for or in total or partial satisfaction of a money debt.

(10) "Conspicuous": A term or clause is conspicuous when it is so written that a reasonable person against whom it is to operate ought to have noticed it. A printed heading in capitals (as: NON-NEGOTIABLE BILL OF LADING) is conspicuous. Language in the body of a form is "conspicuous" if it is in larger or other contrasting type or color. But in a telegram any stated term is "conspicuous." Whether a term or clause is "conspicuous" or not is for decision by the court.

(11) "Contract" means the total legal obligation which results from the parties' agreement as affected by this Act and any other applicable rules of law. (Compare "Agreement.")

(12) "Creditor" includes a general creditor, a secured creditor, a lien creditor and any representative of creditors, including an assignee for the benefit of creditors, a trustee in bankruptcy, a receiver in equity and an executor or administrator of an insolvent debtor's or assignor's estate.

(13) "Defendant" includes a person in the position of defendant in a cross-action or counterclaim.

(14) "Delivery" with respect to instruments, documents of title, chattel paper, or certificated securities means voluntary transfer of possession.

(15) "Document of title" includes bill of lading, dock warrant, dock receipt, warehouse receipt or order for the delivery of goods, and also any other document which in the regular course of business

or financing is treated as adequately evidencing that the person in possession of it is entitled to receive, hold and dispose of the document and the goods it covers. To be a document of title a document must purport to be issued by or addressed to a bailee and purport to cover goods in the bailee's possession which are either identified or are fungible portions of an identified mass.

(16) "Fault" means wrongful act, omission or breach.

(17) "Fungible" with respect to goods or securities means goods or securities of which any unit is, by nature or usage of trade, the equivalent of any other like unit. Goods which are not fungible shall be deemed fungible for the purposes of this Act to the extent that under a particular agreement or document unlike units are treated as equivalents.

(18) "Genuine" means free of forgery or counterfeiting.

(19) "Good faith" means honesty in fact in the conduct or transaction concerned.

(20) "Holder" means a person who is in possession of a document of title or an instrument or a certificated investment security drawn, issued, or indorsed to him or his order or to bearer or in blank.

(21) To "honor" is to pay or to accept and pay, or where a credit so engages to purchase or discount a draft complying with the terms of the credit.

(22) "Insolvency proceedings" includes any assignment for the benefit of creditors or other proceedings intended to liquidate or rehabilitate the estate of the person involved.

(23) A person is "insolvent" who either has ceased to pay his debts in the ordinary course of business or cannot pay his debts as they become due or is insolvent within the meaning of the federal bankruptcy law.

(24) "Money" means a medium of exchange authorized or adopted by a domestic or foreign government as a part of its currency.

(25) A person has "notice" of a fact when

(a) he has actual knowledge of it; or

(b) he has received a notice or notification of it; or

(c) from all the facts and circumstances known to him at the time in question he has reason to know that it exists.

A person "knows" or has "knowledge" of a fact when he has actual knowledge of it. "Discover" or "learn" or a word or phrase of similar import refers to knowledge rather than to reason to know. The time and circumstances under which a notice or notification may cease to be effective are not determined by this Act.

(26) A person "notifies" or "gives" a notice or notification to another by taking such steps as may be reasonably required to inform the other in ordinary course whether or not such other actually comes to know of it. A person "receives" a notice or notification when

(a) it comes to his attention; or

(b) it is duly delivered at the place of business through which the contract was made or at any other place held out by him as the place for receipt of such communications.

(27) Notice, knowledge or a notice or notification received by an organization is effective for a particular transaction from the time when it is brought to the attention of the individual conducting that transaction, and in any event from the time when it would have been brought to his attention if the organization had exercised due diligence. An organization exercises due diligence if it maintains reasonable routines for communicating significant information to the person conducting the transaction and there is reasonable complicance with the routines. Due diligence does not require an individual acting for the organization to communicate information unless such communication is part of his regular duties or unless he has reason to know of the transaction and that the transaction would be materially affected by the information.

(28) "Organization" includes a corporation, government or governmental subdivision or agency, business trust, estate, trust, partnership or association, two or more persons having a joint or common interest, or any other legal or commercial entity.

(29) "Party," as distinct from "third party," means a person who has engaged in a transaction or made an agreement within this Act.

(30) "Person" includes an individual or an organization (See Section 1–102).

(31) "Presumption" or "presumed" means that the trier of fact must find the existence of the fact presumed unless and until evidence is introduced

which would support a finding of its non-existence.

(32) "Purchase" includes taking by sale, discount, negotiation, mortgage, pledge, lien, issue or re-issue, gift or any other voluntary transaction creating an interest in property.

(33) "Purchaser" means a person who takes by purchase.

(34) "Remedy" means any remedial right to which an aggrieved party is entitled with or without resort to a tribunal.

(35) "Representative" includes an agent, an officer of a corporation or association, and a trustee, executor or administrator of an estate, or any other person empowered to act for another.

(36) "Rights" includes remedies.

(37) "Security interest" means an interest in personal property or fixtures which secures payment or performance of an obligation. The retention or reservation of title by a seller of goods notwithstanding shipment or delivery to the buyer (Section 2–401) is limited in effect to a reservation of a "security interest." The term also includes any interest of a buyer of accounts or chattel paper which is subject to Article 9. The special property interest of a buyer of goods on identification of such goods to a contract for sale under Section 2–401 is not a "security interest" but a buyer mayalso acquire a "security interest" by complying with Article 9. Unless a lease or consignment isintended as security, reservation of title thereunder is not a "security interest" but a consignment is in any event subject to the provisions on consignment sales (Section 2–326). Whether a lease is intended as security is to be determined by the facts of each case; however, (a) the inclusion of an option to purchase does not of itself make the lease one intended for security, and (b) an agreement that upon compliance with the terms of the lease the lessee shall become or has the option to become the owner of the property for no additional consideration or for a nominal consideration does make the lease one intended for security.

(38) "Send" in connection with any writing or notice means to deposit in the mail or deliver for transmission by any other usual means of communication with postage or cost of transmission provided for and properly addressed and in the case of an instrument to an address specified thereon or otherwise agreed, or if there be none to any address reasonable under the circumstances. The receipt of any writing or notice within the time at which it would have arrived if properly sent has the effect of a proper sending.

(39) "Signed" includes any symbol executed or adopted by a party with present intention to authenticate a writing.

(40) "Surety" includes guarantor.

(41) "Telegram" includes a message transmitted by radio, teletype, cable, any mechanical method of transmission, or the like.

(42) "Term" means that portion of an agreement which relates to a particular matter.

(43) "Unauthorized" signature or indorsement means one made without actual, implied or apparent authority and includes a forgery.

(44) "Value." Except as otherwise provided with respect to negotiable instruments and bank collections (Sections 3–303, 4–208 and 4–209) a person gives "value" for rights if he acquires them

(a) in return for a binding commitment to extend credit or for the extension of immediately available credit whether or not drawn upon and whether or not a chargeback is provided for in the event of difficulties in collection; or

(b) as security for or in total or partial satisfaction of a pre-existing claim; or

(c) by accepting delivery pursuant to a pre-existing contract for purchase; or

(d) generally, in return for any consideration sufficient to support a simple contract.

(45) "Warehouse receipt" means a receipt issued by a person engaged in the business of storing goods for hire.

(46) "Written" or "writing" includes printing, typewriting or any other intentional reduction to tangible form.

### § 1–202. Prima Facie Evidence by Third Party Documents

A document in due form purporting to be a bill of lading, policy or certificate of insurance, official weigher's or inspector's certificate, consular invoice, or any other document authorized or required by the contract to be issued by a third party shall be prima facie evidence of its own authenticity and genuineness and of the facts stated in the document by the third party.

### § 1–203. Obligation of Good Faith

Every contract or duty within this Act imposes an obligation of good faith in its performance or enforcement.

### § 1–204. Time; Reasonable Time; "Seasonably"

(1) Whenever this Act requires any action to be taken within a reasonable time, any time which is not mainfestly unreasonable may be fixed by agreement.
(2) What is a reasonable time for taking any action depends on the nature, purpose and circumstances of such action.
(3) An action is taken "seasonably" when it is taken at or within the time agreed or if no time is agreed at or within a reasonable time.

### § 1–205. Course of Dealing and Usage of Trade

(1) A course of dealing is a sequence of previous conduct between the parties to a particular transaction which is fairly to be regarded as establishing a common basis of understanding for interpreting their expressions and other conduct.
(2) A usage of trade is any practice or method of dealing having such regularity of observance in a place, vocation or trade as to justify an expectation that it will be observed with respect to the transaction in question. The existence and scope of such a usage are to be proved as facts. If it is established that such a usage is embodied in a written trade code or similar writing the interpretation of the writing is for the court.
(3) A course of dealing between parties and any usage of trade in the vocation or trade in which they are engaged or of which they are or should be aware given particular meaning to and supplement or qualify terms of an agreement.
(4) The express terms of an agreement and an applicable course of dealing or usage of trade shall be construed wherever reasonable as consistent with each other; but when such construction is unreasonable express terms control both course of dealing and usage of trade and course of dealing controls usage of trade.
(5) An applicable usage of trade in the place where any part of performance is to occur shall be used in interpreting the agreement as to that part of the performance.
(6) Evidence of a relevant usage of trade offered by one party is not admissible unless and until he has given the other party such notice as the court finds sufficient to prevent unfair surprise to the latter.

### § 1–206. Statute of Frauds for Kinds of Personal Property Not Otherwise Covered

(1) Except in the cases described in subsection (2) of this section a contract for the sale of personal property is not enforceable by way of action or defense beyond five thousand dollars in amount or value of remedy unless there is some writing which indicates that a contract for sale has been made between the parties at a defined or stated price, reasonably identifies the subject matter, and is signed by the party against whom enforcement is sought or by his authorized agent.
(2) Subsection (1) of this section does not apply to contracts for the sale of goods (Section 2–201) nor of securities (Section 8–319) nor to security agreements (Section 9–203).

### § 1–207. Performance or Acceptance Under Reservation of Rights

A party who with explicit reservation of rights performs or promises performance or assents to performance in a manner demanded or offered by the other party does not thereby prejudice the rights reserved. Such words as "without prejudice," "under protest" or the like are sufficient.

### § 1–208. Option to Accelerate at Will

A term providing that one party or his successor in interest may accelerate payment or performance or require collateral or additional collateral "at will" or "when he deems himself insecure" or in words of similar import shall be construed to mean that he shall have power to do so only if he is good faith believes that the prospect of payment or performance is impaired. The burden of establishing lack of good faith is on the party against whom the power had been exercised.

### § 1–209. Subordinated Obligations

An obligation may be issued as subordinated to payment of another obligation of the person obligated, or a creditor may subordinate his right to payment of an obligation by agreement with either the person obligated or another creditor of the person obligated. Such a subordination does not create a security interest as against either the common debtor or a subordinated creditor. This section shall be construed as declaring the law as it existed prior to the enactment of this section and not as modifying it.

**Note:** *The new section is proposed as an optional provision to make it clear that a subordination agreement does not create a security interest unless so intended.*

## ARTICLE 2 SALES

### Part 1 Short Title, General Construction and Subject Matter

#### § 2–101. Short Title

This Article shall be known and may be cited as Uniform Commercial Code—Sales.

#### § 2–102. Scope; Certain Security and Other Transactions Excluded From This Article

Unless the context otherwise requires, this Article applies to transactions in goods; it does not apply to any transaction which although in the form of an unconditional contract to sell or present sale is intended to operate only as a security transaction nor does this Article impair or repeal any statute regulating sales to consumers, farmers or other specified classes of buyers.

#### § 2–103. Definitions and Index of Definitions

(1) In this Article unless the context otherwise requires

(a) "Buyer" means a person who buys or contracts to buy goods.

(b) "Good faith" in the case of a merchant means honesty in fact and the observance of reasonable commercial standards of fair dealing in the trade.

(c) "Receipt" of goods means taking physical possession of them.

(d) "Seller" means a person who sells or contracts to sell goods.

(2) Other definitions applying to this Article or to specified Parts thereof, and the sections in which they appear are:

"Acceptance." Section 2–606.
"Banker's credit." Section 2–325.
"Between merchants." Section 2–104.
"Cancellation." Section 2–106(4).
"Commercial unit." Section 2–105.
"Confirmed credit." Section 2–325.
"Conforming to contract." Section 2–106.
"Contract for sale." Section 2–106.
"Cover." Section 2–712.
"Entrusting." Section 2–403.
"Financing agency." Section 2–104.
"Future goods." Section 2–105.
"Goods." Section 2–105.
"Identification." Section 2–501.
"Installment contract." Section 2–612.
"Letter of Credit." Section 2–325.
"Lot." Section 2–105.
"Merchant." Section 2–104.
"Overseas." Section 2–323.
"Person in position of seller." Section 2–707.
"Present sale." Section 2–106.
"Sale." Section 2–106.
"Sale on approval." Section 2–326.
"Sale or return." Section 2–326.
"Termination." Section 2–106.

(3) The following definitions in other Articles apply to this Article:

"Check." Section 3–104.
"Consignee." Section 7–102.
"Consignor." Section 7–102.
"Consumer goods." Section 9–109.
"Dishonor." Section 3–507.
"Draft." Section 3–104.

(4) In addition Article I contains general definitions and principles of construction and interpretation applicable throughout this Article.

#### § 2–104. Definitions: "Merchant"; "Between Merchants"; "Financing Agency"

(1) "Merchant" means a person who deals in goods of the kind or otherwise by his occupation holds himself out as having knowledge or skill peculiar to the practices or goods involved in the transaction or to whom such knowledge or skill may be attributed by his employment of an agent or broker or other intermediary who by his occupation holds himself out as having such knowledge or skill.

(2) "Financing agency" means a bank, finance company or other person who in the ordinary course of business makes advances against goods or documents of title or who by arrangement with either the seller or the buyer intervenes in ordinary course to make or collect payment due or claimed under the contract for sale, as by purchasing or paying the seller's draft or making advances against it or by merely taking it for collection whether or not documents of title accompany the draft. "Financing agency" includes also a bank or other person who similarly intervenes between persons who are in the position of seller and buyer in respect to the goods (Section 2–707).
(3) "Between merchants" means in any transaction with respect to which both parties are chargeable with the knowledge or skill of merchants.

### § 2–105. Definitions: Transferability; "Goods"; "Future" Goods; "Lot"; "Commercial Unit"

(1) "Goods" means all things (including specially manufactured goods) which are movable at the time of identification to the contract for sale other than the money in which the price is to be paid, investment securities (Article 8) and things in action. "Goods" also includes the unborn young of animals and growing crops and other identified things attached to realty as described in the section on goods to be severed from realty (Section 2–107).
(2) Goods must be both existing and identified before any interest in them can pass. Goods which are not both existing and identified are "future" goods. A purported present sale of future goods or of any interest therein operates as a contract to sell.
(3) There may be a sale of a part interest in existing identified goods.
(4) An undivided share in an identified bulk of fungible goods is sufficiently identified to be sold although the quantity of the bulk is not determined. Any agreed proportion of such a bulk or any quantity thereof agreed upon by number, weight or other measure may to the extent of the seller's interest in the bulk be sold to the buyer who then becomes an owner in common.
(5) "Lot" means a parcel or a single article which is the subject matter of a separate sale or delivery, whether or not it is sufficient to perform the contract.
(6) "Commercial unit" means such a unit of goods as by commercial usage is a single whole for purposes of sale and division of which materially impairs its character or value on the market or in use. A commercial unit may be a single article (as a machine) or a set of articles (as a suite of furniture or an assortment of sizes) or a quantity (as a bale, gross, or carload) or any other unit treated in use or in the relevant market as a single whole.

### § 2–106. Definitions: "Contract"; "Agreement"; "Contract for Sale"; "Sale"; "Present Sale"; "Conforming" to Contract; "Termination"; "Cancellation"

(1) In this Article unless the context otherwise requires "contract" and "agreement" are limited to those relating to the present or future sale of goods. "Contract for sale" includes both a present sale of goods and a contract to sell goods at a future time. A "sale" consists in the passingof title from the seller to the buyer for a price (Section 2–401). A "present sale" means a sale which is accomplished by the making of the contract.
(2) Goods or conduct including any part of a performance are "conforming" or conform to the contract when they are in accordance with the obligations under the contract.
(3) "Termination" occurs when either party pursuant to a power created by agreement or law puts an end to the contract otherwise than for its breach. On "termination" all obligations which are still executory on both sides are discharged but any right based on prior breach or performance survives.
(4) "Cancellation" occurs when either party puts an end to the contract for breach by the other and its effect is the same as that of "termination" except that the cancelling party also retains any remedy for breach of the whole contract or any unperformed balance.

### § 2–107. Goods to Be Severed From Realty: Recording

(1) A contract for the sale of minerals or the like (including oil and gas) or a structure or its materials to be removed from realty is a contract for the sale of goods within this Article if they are to be

severed by the seller but until severance a purported present sale thereof which is not effective as a transfer of an interest in land is effective only as a contract to sell.

(2) A contract for the sale apart from the land of growing crops or other things attached to realty and capable of severance without material harm thereto but not described in subsection (1) or of timber to be cut is a contract for the sale of goods within this Article whether the subject matter is to be severed by the buyer or by the seller even though it forms part of the realty at the time of contracting, and the parties can by identification effect a present sale before severance.

(3) The provisions of this section are subject to any third party rights provided by the law relating to realty records, and the contract for sale may be executed and recorded as a document transferring an interest in land and shall then constitute notice to third parties of the buyer's rights under the contract for sale.

## Part 2 Form, Formation and Readjustment of Contract

### § 2–201. Formal Requirements; Statute of Frauds

(1) Except as otherwise provided in this section a contract for the sale of goods for the price of $500 or more is not enforceable by way of action or defense unless there is some writing sufficient to indicate that a contract for sale has been made between the parties and signed by the party against whom enforcement is sought or by his authorized agent or broker. A writing is not insufficient because it omits or incorrectly states a term agreed upon but the contract is not enforceable under this paragraph beyond the quantity of goods shown in such writing.

(2) Between merchants if within a reasonable time a writing in confirmation of the contract and sufficient against the sender is received and the party receiving it has reason to know its contents, it satisfies the requirements of subsection (1) against such party unless written notice of objection to its contents is given within 10 days after it is received.

(3) A contract which does not satisfy the requirements of subsection (1) but which is valid in other respects is enforceable

(a) if the goods are to be specially manufactured for the buyer and are not suitable for sale to others in the ordinary course of the seller's business and the seller, before notice of repudiation is received and under circumstances which reasonably indicate that the goods are for the buyer, has made either a substantial beginning of their manufacture or commitments for their procurement; or

(b) if the party against whom enforcement is sought admits in his pleading, testimony or otherwise in court that a contract for sale was made, but the contract is not enforceable under this provision beyond the quantity of goods admitted; or

(c) with respect to goods for which payment has been made and accepted or which have been received and accepted (Sec. 2–606).

### § 2–202. Final Written Expression: Parol or Extrinsic Evidence

Terms with respect to which the confirmatory memoranda of the parties agree or which are otherwise set forth in a writing intended by the parties as a final expression of their agreement with respect to such terms as are included therein may not be contradicted by evidence of any prior agreement or of a contemporaneous oral agreement but may be explained or supplemented

(a) by course of dealing or usage of trade (Section 1–205) or by course of performance (Section 2–208); and

(b) by evidence of consistent additional terms unless the court finds the writing to have been intended also as a complete and exclusive statement of the terms of the agreement.

### § 2–203. Seals Inoperative

The affixing of a seal to a writing evidencing a contract for sale or an offer to buy or sell goods does not constitute the writing a sealed instrument and the law with respect to sealed instruments does not apply to such a contract or offer.

### § 2–204. Formation in General

(1) A contract for sale of goods may be made in any manner sufficient to show agreement, including conduct by both parties which recognizes the existence of such a contract.

(2) An agreement sufficient to constitute a contract for sale may be found even though the moment of its making is undetermined.
(3) Even though one or more terms are left open a contract for sale does not fail for indefiniteness if the parties have intended to make a contract and there is a reasonably certain basis for giving an appropriate remedy.

### § 2-205. Firm Offers

An offer by a merchant to buy or sell goods in a signed writing which by its terms give assurance that it will be held open is not revocable, for lack of consideration, during the time stated or if no time is stated for a reasonable time, but in no event may such period of irrevocability exceed three months; but any such term of assurance on a form supplied by the offeree must be separately signed by the offeror.

### § 2-206. Offer and Acceptance in Formation of Contract

(1) Unless otherwise unambiguously indicated by the language or circumstances
(a) an offer to make a contract shall be construed as inviting acceptance in any manner and by any medium reasonable in the circumstances;
(b) an order or other offer to buy goods for prompt or current shipment shall be construed as inviting acceptance either by a prompt promise to ship or by the prompt or current shipment of conforming or nonconforming goods, but such a shipment of non-conforming goods does not constitute an acceptance if the seller seasonably notifies the buyer that the shipment is offered only as an accommodation to the buyer.
(2) Where the beginning of a requested performance is a reasonable mode of acceptance an offeror who is not notified of acceptance within a reasonable time may treat the offer as having lapsed before acceptance.

### § 2-207. Additional Terms in Acceptance or Confirmation

(1) A definite and seasonable expression of acceptance or a written confirmation which is sent within a reasonable time operates as an acceptance even though it states terms additional to or different from those offered or agreed upon, unless acceptance is expressly made conditional on assent to the additional or different terms.
(2) The additional terms are to be construed as proposals for addition to the contract. Between merchants such terms become part of the contract unless:
(a) the offer expressly limits acceptance to the terms of the offer;
(b) they materially alter it; or
(c) notification of objection to them has already been given or is given within a reasonable time after notice of them is received.
(3) Conduct by both parties which recognizes the existence of a contract is sufficient to establish a contract for sale although the writings of the parties do not otherwise establish a contract. In such case the terms of the particular contract consist of those terms on which the writings of the parties agree, together with any supplementary terms incorporated under any other provisions of this Act.

### § 2-208. Course of Performance or Practical Construction

(1) Where the contract for sale involves repeated occasions for performance by either party with knowledge of the nature of the performance and opportunity for objection to it by the other, any course of performance accepted or acquiesced in without objection shall be relevant to determine the meaning of the agreement.
(2) The express terms of the agreement and any such course of performance, as well as any course of dealing and usage of trade, shall be construed whenever reasonable as consistent with each other; but when such construction is unreasonable, express terms shall control course of performance and course of performance shall control both course of dealing and usage of trade (Section 1-205).
(3) Subject to the provisions of the next section on modification and waiver, such course of performance shall be relevant to show a waiver or modification of any term inconsistent with such course of performance.

### § 2-209. Modification, Rescission and Waiver

(1) An agreement modifying a contract within this Article needs no consideration to be binding.
(2) A signed agreement which excludes modifica-

tion or rescission except by a signed writing cannot be otherwise modified or rescinded, but except as between merchants such a requirement on a form supplied by the merchant must be separately signed by the other party.

(3) The requirements of the statute of frauds section of this Article (Section 2–201) must be satisfied if the contract as modified is within its provisions.

(4) Although an attempt at modification or rescission does not satisfy the requirements of subsection (2) or (3) it can operate as a waiver.

(5) A party who has made a waiver affecting an executory portion of the contract may retract the waiver by reasonable notification received by the other party that strict performance will be required of any term waived, unless the retraction would be unjust in view of a material change of position in reliance on the waiver.

### § 2–210. Delegation of Performance; Assignment of Rights

(1) A party may perform his duty through a delegate unless otherwise agreed or unless the other party has a substantial interest in having his original promisor perform or control the acts required by the contract. No delegation of performance relieves the party delegating of any duty to perform or any liability for breach.

(2) Unless otherwise agreed all rights of either seller or buyer can be assigned except where the assignment would materially change the duty of the other party, or increase materially the burden or risk imposed on him by his contract, or impair materially his chance of obtaining return performance. A right to damages for breach of the whole contract or a right arising out of the assignor's due performance of his entire obligation can be assigned despite agreement otherwise.

(3) Unless the circumstances indicate the contrary a prohibition of assignment of "the contract" is to be construed as barring only the delegation to the assignee of the assignor's performance.

(4) An assignment of "the contract" or of "all my rights under the contract" or an assignment in similar general terms in an assignment of rights and unless the language or the circumstances (as in an assignment for security) indicate the contrary, it is a delegation of performance of the duties of the assignor and its acceptance by the assignee constitutes a promise by him to perform those duties. This promise is enforceable by either the assignor or the other party to the original contract.

(5) The other party may treat any assignment which delegates performance as creating reasonable grounds for insecurity and may without prejudice to his rights against the assignor demand assurances from the assignee (Section 2–609).

## Part 3 General Obligation and Construction of Contract

### § 2–301. General Obligations of Parties

The obligation of the seller is to transfer and deliver and that of the buyer is to accept and pay in accordance with the contract.

### § 2–302. Unconscionable Contract or Clause

(1) If the court as a matter of law finds the contract or any clause of the contract to have been unconscionable at the time it was made the court may refuse to enforce the contract, or it may enforce the remainder of the contract without the unconscionable clause, or it may so limit the application of any unconscionable clause as to avoid any unconscionable result.

(2) When it is claimed or appears to the court that the contract or any clause thereof may be unconscionable the parties shall be afforded a reasonable opportunity to present evidence as to its commercial setting, purpose and effect to aid the court in making the determination.

### § 2–303. Allocation or Division of Risks

Where this Article allocates a risk or a burden as between the parties "unless otherwise agreed," the agreement may not only shift the allocation but may also divide the risk or burden.

### § 2–304. Price Payable in Money, Goods, Realty, or Otherwise

(1) The price can be made payable in money or otherwise. If it is payable in whole or in part in goods each party is a seller of the goods which he is to transfer.

(2) Even though all or part of the price is payable in an interest in realty the transfer of the goods and the seller's obligations with reference to them

are subject to this Article, but not the transfer of the interest in realty or the transferor's obligations in connection therewith.

**§ 2–305. Open Price Term**

(1) The parties if they so intend can conclude a contract for sale even though the price is not settled. In such a case the price is a reasonable price at the time for delivery if

(a) nothing is said as to price; or

(b) the price is left to be agreed by the parties and they fail to agree; or

(c) the price is to be fixed in terms of some agreed market or other standard as set or recorded by a third person or agency and it is not so set or recorded.

(2) A price to be fixed by the seller or by the buyer means a price for him to fix in good faith.

(3) When a price left to be fixed otherwise than by agreement of the parties fails to be fixed through fault of one party the other may at his option treat the contract as cancelled or himself fix a reasonable price.

(4) Where, however, the parties intend not to be bound unless the price be fixed or agreed and it is not fixed or agreed there is no contract. In such a case the buyer must return any goods already received or if unable so to do must pay their reasonable value at the time of delivery and the seller must return any portion of the price paid on account.

**§ 2–306. Output, Requirements and Exclusive Dealings**

(1) A term which measures the quantity by the output of the seller or the requirements of the buyer means such actual output or requirements as may occur in good faith, except that no quantity unreasonably disproportionate to any stated estimate or in the absence of a stated estimate to any normal or otherwise comparable prior output or requirements may be tendered or demanded.

(2) A lawful agreement by either the seller or the buyer for exclusive dealing in the kind of goods concerned imposes unless otherwise agreed an obligation by the seller to use best efforts to supply the goods and by the buyer to use best efforts to promote the sale.

**§ 2–307. Delivery in Single Lot or Several Lots**

Unless otherwise agreed all goods called for by a contract for sale must be tendered in a single delivery and payment is due only on such tender but where the circumstances give either party the right to make or demand delivery in lots the price if it can be apportioned may be demanded for each lot.

**§ 2–308. Absence of Specified Place for Delivery**

Unless otherwise agreed

(a) the place for delivery of goods is the seller's place of business or if he has none his residence; but

(b) in a contract for sale of identified goods which to the knowledge of the parties at the time of contracting are in some other place, that place is the place for their delivery; and

(c) documents of title may be delivered through customary banking channels.

**§ 2–309. Absence of Specific Time Provisions; Notice of Termination**

(1) The time for shipment or delivery or any other action under a contract if not provided in this Article or agreed upon shall be a reasonable time.

(2) Where the contract provides for successive performances but is indefinite in duration it is valid for a reasonable time but unless otherwise agreed may be terminated at any time by either party.

(3) Termination of a contract by one party except on the happening of an agreed event requires that reasonable notification be received by the other party and an agreement dispensing with notification is invalid if its operation would be unconscionable.

**§ 2–310. Open Time for Payment or Running of Credit: Authority to Ship Under Reservation**

Unless otherwise agreed

(a) payment is due at the time and place at which the buyer is to receive the goods even though the place of shipment is the place of delivery; and

(b) if the seller is authorized to send the goods he may ship them under reservation, and may tender the documents of title, but the buyer may inspect the goods after their arrival before payment is due unless such inspection is inconsistent with the terms of the contract (Section 2–513); and

(c) if delivery is authorized and made by way of documents of title otherwise than by subsection (b) then payment is due at the time and place at which the buyer is to receive the documents regardless of where the goods are to be received; and

(d) where the seller is required or authorized to ship the goods on credit the credit period runs from the time of shipment but postdating the invoice or delaying its dispatch will correspondingly delay the starting of the credit period.

### § 2–311. Options and Cooperation Respecting Performance

(1) An agreement for sale which is otherwise sufficiently definite (subsection (3) of Section 2–204) to be a contract is not made invalid by the fact that it leaves particulars of performance to be specified by one of the parties. Any such specification must be made in good faith and within limits set by commercial reasonableness.

(2) Unless otherwise agreed specifications relating to assortment of the goods are at the buyer's option and except as otherwise provided in subsections (1) (c) and (3) of Section 2–319 specifications or arrangements relating to shipment are at the seller's option.

(3) Where such specification would materially affect the other party's performance but is not seasonably made or where one party's cooperation is necessary to the agreed performance of the other but is not seasonably forthcoming, the other party in addition to all other remedies

(a) is excused for any resulting delay in his own performance; and

(b) may also either proceed to perform in any reasonable manner or after the time for a material part of his own performance treat the failure to specify or to cooperate as a breach by failure to deliver or accept the goods.

### § 2–312. Warranty of Title and Against Infringement; Buyer's Obligation Against Infringement

(1) Subject to subsection (2) there is in a contract for sale a warranty by the seller that

(a) the title conveyed shall be good, and its transfer rightful; and

(b) the goods shall be delivered free from any security interest or other lien or encumbrance of which the buyer at the time of contracting has no knowledge.

(2) A warranty under subsection (1) will be excluded or modified only by specific language or by circumstances which give the buyer reason to know that the person selling does not claim title in himself or that he is purporting to sell only such right or title as he or a third person may have.

(3) Unless otherwise agreed a seller who is a merchant regularly dealing in goods of the kind warrants that the goods shall be delivered free of the rightful claim of any third person by way of infringement or the like but a buyer who furnishes specifications to the seller must hold the seller harmless against any such claim which arises out of compliance with the specifications.

### § 2–313. Express Warranties by Affirmation, Promise, Description, Sample

(1) Express warranties by the seller are created as follows:

(a) Any affirmation of fact or promise made by the seller to the buyer which relates to the goods and becomes part of the basis of the bargain creates an express warranty that the goods shall conform to the affirmation or promise.

(b) Any description of the goods which is made part of the basis of the bargain creates an express warranty that the goods shall conform to the description.

(c) Any sample or model which is made part of the basis of the bargain creates an express warranty that the whole of the goods shall conform to the sample or model.

(2) It is not necessary to the creation of an express warranty that the seller use formal words such as "warrant" or "guarantee" or that he have a specific intention to make a warranty, but an affirmation merely of the value of the goods or a statement purporting to be merely the seller's opinion or commendation of the goods does not create a warranty.

### § 2–314. Implied Warranty: Merchantability; Usage of Trade

(1) Unless excluded or modified (Section 2–316), a warranty that the goods shall be merchantable

is implied in a contract for their sale if the seller is a merchant with respect to goods of that kind. Under this section the serving for value of food or drink to be consumed either on the premises or elsewhere is a sale.

(2) Goods to be merchantable must be at least such as

(a) pass without objection in the trade under the contract description; and

(b) in the case of fungible goods, are of fair average quality within the description; and

(c) are fit for the ordinary purposes for which such goods are used; and

(d) run, within the variations permitted by the agreement, of even kind, quality and quantity within each unit and among all units involved; and

(e) are adequately contained, packaged, and labeled as the agreement may require; and

(f) conform to the promises or affirmations of fact made on the container or label if any.

(3) Unless excluded or modified (Section 2–316) other implied warranties may arise from course of dealing or usage of trade.

### § 2–315. Implied Warranty: Fitness for Particular Purpose

Where the seller at the time of contracting has reason to know any particular purpose for which the goods are required and that the buyer is relying on the seller's skill or judgment to select or furnish suitable goods, there is unless excluded or modified under the next section an implied warranty that the goods shall be fit for such purpose.

### § 2–316. Exclusion or Modification of Warranties

(1) Words or conduct relevant to the creation of an express warranty and words or conduct tending to negate or limit warranty shall be construed wherever reasonable as consistent with each other; but subject to the provisions of this Article on parol or extrinsic evidence (Section 2–202) negation or limitation is inoperative to the extent that such construction is unreasonable.

(2) Subject to subsection (3), to exclude or modify the implied warranty or merchantability or any part of it the language must mention merchantability and in case of a writing must be conspicuous, and to exclude or modify any implied warranty of fitness the exclusion must be by a writing and conspicuous. Language to exclude all implied warranties of fitness is sufficient if it states, for example, that "There are no warranties which extend beyond the description on the face hereof."

(3) Notwithstanding subsection (2)

(a) unless the circumstances indicate otherwise, all implied warranties are excluded by expressions like "as is," "with all faults" or other languages which in common understanding calls the buyer's attention to the exclusion of warranties and makes plain that there is no implied warranty; and

(b) when the buyer before entering into the contract has examined the goods or the sample or model as fully as he desired or has refused to examine the goods there is no implied warranty with regard to defects which an examination ought in the circumstances to have revealed to him; and

(c) an implied warranty can also be excluded or modified by course of dealing or course of performance or usage of trade.

(4) Remedies for breach of warranty can be limited in accordance with the provisions of this Article on liquidation or limitation of damages and on contractual modification of remedy (Sections 2–718 and 2–719).

### § 2–317. Cumulation and Conflict of Warranties Express or Implied

Warranties whether express or implied shall be construed as consistent with each other and as cumulative, but if such construction is unreasonable the intention of the parties shall determine which warranty is dominant. In ascertaining that intention the following rules apply:

(a) Exact or technical specifications displace an inconsistent sample or model or general language of description.

(b) A sample from an existing bulk displaces inconsistent general language of description.

(c) Express warranties displace inconsistent implied warranties other than an implied warranty of fitness for a particular purpose.

## § 2–318. Third Party Beneficiaries of Warranties Express or Implied

**Note:** *If this Act is introduced in the Congress of the Unites States this section should be omitted. (States to select one alternative.)*

### Alternative A

A seller's warranty whether express or implied extends to any natural person who is in the family or household of his buyer or who is a guest in his home if it is reasonable to expect that such person may use, consume or be affected by the goods and who is injured in person by breach of the warranty. A seller may not exclude or limit the operation of this section.

### Alternative B

A seller's warranty whether express or implied extends to any natural person who may reasonably be expected to use, consume or be affected by the goods and who is injured in person by breach of the warranty. A seller may not exclude or limit the operation of this section.

### Alternative C

A seller's warranty whether express or implied extends to any person who may reasonably be expected to use, consume or be affected by the goods and who is injured by breach of the warranty. A seller may not exclude or limit the operation of this section with respect to injury to the person of an individual to whom the warranty extends.

## § 2–319. F.O.B. AND F.A.S. Terms

(1) Unless otherwise agreed the term F.O.B. (which means "free on board") at a named place, even though used only in connection with the stated price, is a delivery term under which

(a) when the term is F.O.B. the place of shipment, the seller must at that place ship the goods in the manner provided in this Article (Section 2–504) and bear the expense and risk of putting them into the possession of the carrier; or

(b) when the term is F.O.B. the place of destination, the seller must at his own expense and risk transport the goods to that place and there tender delivery of them in the manner provided in this Article (Section 2–503);

(c) when under either (a) or (b) the term is also F.O.B. vessel, car or other vehicle, the seller must in addition at his own expense and risk load the goods on board. If the term is F.O.B. vessel the buyer must name the vessel and in an appropriate case the seller must comply with the provisions of this Article on the form of bill of lading (Section 2–323).

(2) Unless otherwise agreed the term F.A.S. vessel (which means "free alongside") at a named port, even though used only in connection with the stated price, is a delivery term under which the seller must

(a) at his own expense and risk deliver the goods alongside the vessel in the manner usual in that port or on a dock designated and provided by the buyer; and

(b) obtain and tender a receipt for the goods in exchange for which the carrier is under a duty to issue a bill of lading.

(3) Unless otherwise agreed in any case falling within subsection (1) (a) or (c) or subsection (2) the buyer must seasonably give any needed instructions for making delivery, including when the term is F.A.S. or F.O.B. the loading berth of the vessel and in an appropriate case its name and sailing date. The seller may treat the failure of needed instructions as a failure of cooperation under this Article (Section 2–311). He may also at his option move the goods in any reasonable manner preparatory to delivery or shipment.

(4) Under the term F.O.B. vessel or F.A.S. unless otherwise agreed the buyer must make payment against tender of the required documents and the seller may not tender nor the buyer demand delivery of the goods in substitution for the documents.

## § 2–320. C.I.F. AND C. & F. Terms

(1) The term C.I.F. means that the price includes in a lump sum the cost of the goods and the insurance and freight to the named destination. The term C. & F. or C.F. means that the price so includes cost and freight to the named destination.

(2) Unless otherwise agreed and even though used only in connection with the stated price and destination, the term C.I.F. destination or its equivalent requires the seller at his own expense and risk to

(a) put the goods into the possession of a carrier at the port for shipment and obtain a negotiable bill or bills of lading covering the entire transportation to the named destination; and

(b) load the goods and obtain a receipt from the carrier (which may be contained in the bill of lading) showing that the freight has been paid or provided for; and

(c) obtain a policy or certificate of insurance, including any war risk insurance, of a kind and on terms then current at the port of shipment in the usual amount, in the currency of the contract, shown to cover the same goods covered by the bill of lading and providing for payment of loss to the order of the buyer or for the account of whom it may concern; but the seller may add to the price the amount of the premium for any such war risk insurance; and

(d) prepare an invoice of the goods and procure any other documents required to effect shipment or to comply with the contract; and

(e) forward and tender with commerical promptness all the documents in due form and with any indorsement necessary to perfect the buyer's rights.

(3) Unless otherwise agreed the term C. & F. or its equivalent has the same effect and imposes upon the seller the same obligations and risks as a C.I.F. term except the obligation as to insurance.

(4) Under the term C.I.F. or C. & F. unless otherwise agreed the buyer must make payment against tender of the required documents and the seller may not tender nor the buyer demand delivery of the goods in substitution for the documents.

### § 2–321. C.I.F. or C. & F.: "Net Landed Weights"; "Payment on Arrival"; Warranty of Condition on Arrival

Under a contract containing a term C.I.F. or C. & F.

(1) Where the price is based on or is to be adjusted according to "net landed weights," "delivered weights," "out turn" quantity or quality or the like, unless otherwise agreed the seller must reasonably estimate the price. The payment due on tender of the documents called for by the contract is the amount so estimated, but after final adjustment of the price a settlement must be made with commercial promptness.

(2) An agreement described in subsection (1) or any warranty of quality or condition of the goods on arrival places upon the seller the risk of ordinary deterioration, shrinkage and the like in transportation but has no effect on the place or time of identification to the contract for sale or delivery or on the passing of the risk of loss.

(3) Unless otherwise agreed where the contract provides for payment on or after arrival of the goods the seller must before payment allow such preliminary inspection as is feasible; but if the goods are lost delivery of the documents and payment are due when the goods should have arrived.

### § 2–322. Delivery "Ex-Ship"

(1) Unless otherwise agreed a term for delivery of goods "ex-ship" (which means from the carrying vessel) or in equivalent language is not restricted to a particular ship and requires delivery from a ship which has reached a place at the named port of destination where goods of the kind are usually discharged.

(2) Under such a term unless otherwise agreed

(a) the seller must discharge all liens arising out of the carriage and furnish the buyer with a direction which puts the carrier under a duty to delivery the goods; and

(b) the risk of loss does not pass to the buyer until the goods leave the ship's tackle or are otherwise properly unloaded.

### § 2–323. Form of Bill of Lading Required in Overseas Shipment; "Overseas"

(1) Where the contract contemplates overseas shipment and contains a term C.I.F. or C. & F. or F.O.B. vessel, the seller unless otherwise agreed must obtain a negotiable bill of lading stating that the goods have been loaded on board or, in the case of a term C.I.F. or C. & F., received for shipment.

(2) Where in a case within subsection (1) a bill of lading has been issued in a set of parts, unless otherwise agreed if the documents are not to be sent from abroad the buyer may demand tender of the full set; otherwise only one part of the bill of lading need be tendered. Even if the agreement expressly requires a full set

(a) due tender of a single part is acceptable within the provisions of this Article on cure of improper delivery (subsection (1) of Section 2–508); and

(b) even though the full set is demanded, if the documents are sent from abroad the person tendering an incomplete set may nevertheless require payment upon furnishing an indemnity which the buyer in good faith deems adequate.

(3) A shipment by water or by air or a contract contemplating such shipment is "overseas" insofar as by usage of trade or agreement it is subject to the commercial, financing or shipping practices characteristic of international deep water commerce.

### § 2–324. "No Arrival, No Sale" Term

Under a term "no arrival, no sale" or terms of like meaning, unless otherwise agreed,

(a) the seller must properly ship conforming goods and if they arrive by any means he must tender them on arrival but he assumes no obligation that the goods will arrive unless he has caused the non-arrival; and

(b) where without fault of the seller the goods are in part lost or have so deteriorated as no longer to conform to the contract or arrive after the contract time, the buyer may proceed as if there had been casualty to identified goods (Section 2–613).

### § 2–325. "Letter of Credit" Term; "Confirmed Credit"

(1) Failure of the buyer seasonably to furnish an agreed letter of credit is a breach of the contract for sale.

(2) The delivery to seller of a proper letter of credit suspends the buyer's obligation to pay. If the letter of credit is dishonored, the seller may on seasonable notification to the buyer require payment directly from him.

(3) Unless otherwise agreed the term "letter of credit" or "banker's credit" in a contract for sale means an irrevocable credit issued by a financing agency of good repute and, where the shipment is overseas, of good international repute. The term "confirmed credit" means that the credit must also carry the direct obligation of such an agency which does business in the seller's financial market.

### § 2–326. Sale on Approval and Sale or Return; Consignment Sales and Rights of Creditors

(1) Unless otherwise agreed, if delivered goods may be returned by the buyer even though they conform to the contract, the transaction is

(a) a "sale on approval" if the goods are delivered primarily for use, and

(b) a "sale or return" if the goods are delivered primarily for resale.

(2) Except as provided in subsection (3), goods held on approval are not subject to the claims of the buyer's creditors until acceptance; goods held on sale or return are subject to such claims while in the buyer's possession.

(3) Where goods are delivered to a person for sale and such person maintains a place of business at which he deals in goods of the kind involved, under a name other than the name of the person making delivery, then with respect to claims of creditors of the person conducting the business the goods are deemed to be on sale or return. The provisions of this subsection are applicable even though an agreement purports to reserve title to the person making delivery until payment or resale or uses such words as "on consignment" or "on memorandum." However, this subsection is not applicable if the person making delivery

(a) complies with an applicable law providing for a consignor's interest or the like to be evidenced by a sign, or

(b) establishes that the person conducting the business is generally known by his creditors to be substantially engaged in selling the goods of others, or

(c) complies with the filing provisions of the Article on Secured Transactions (Article 9).

(4) Any "or return" term of a contract for sale is to be treated as a separate contract for sale within the statute of frauds section of this Article (Section 2–201) and as contradicting the sale aspect of the contract within the provisions of this Article or parol or extrinsic evidence (Section 2–202).

### § 2–327. Special Incidents of Sale on Approval and Sale or Return

(1) Under a sale on approval unless otherwise agreed

(a) although the goods are identified to the contract the risk of loss and the title do not pass to the buyer until acceptance; and

(b) use of the goods consistent with the purpose of trial is not acceptance but failure seasonably to notify the seller of election to return the goods is acceptance, and if the goods conform to the contract acceptance of any part is acceptance of the whole; and

(c) after due notification of election to return, the return is at the seller's risk and expense but a merchant buyer must follow any reasonable instructions.

(2) Under a sale or return unless otherwise agreed

(a) the option to return extends to the whole or any commercial unit of the goods while in substantially their original condition, but must be exercised seasonably; and

(b) the return is at the buyer's risk and expense.

### § 2–328. Sale by Auction

(1) In a sale by auction if goods are put up in lots each lot is the subject of a separate sale.

(2) A sale by auction is complete when the auctioneer so announces by the fall of the hammer or in other customary manner. Where a bid is made while the hammer is falling in acceptance of a prior bid the auctioneer may in his discretion reopen the bidding or declare the goods sold under the bid on which the hammer was falling.

(3) Such a sale is with reserve unless the goods are in explicit terms put up without reserve. In an auction with reserve the auctioneer may withdraw the goods at any time until he announces completion of the sale. In an auction without reserve, after the auctioneer calls for bids on an article or lot, that article or lot cannot be withdrawn unless no bid is made within a reasonable time. In either case a bidder may retract his bid until the auctioneer's announcement of completion of sale, but a bidder's retraction does not revive any previous bid.

(4) If the auctioneer knowingly receives a bid on the seller's behalf or the seller makes or procures such a bid, and notice has not been given that liberty for such bidding is reserved, the buyer may at his option avoid the sale or take the goods at the price of the last good faith bid prior to the completion of the sale. This subsection shall not apply to any bid at a forced sale.

## Part 4 Title, Creditors and Good Faith Purchasers

### § 2–401. Passing of Title; Reservation for Security; Limited Application of This Section

Each provision of this Article with regard to the rights, obligations and remedies of the seller, the buyer, purchasers or other third parties applies irrespective of title to the goods except where the provision refers to such title. Insofar as situations are not covered by the other provisions of this Article and matters concerning title become material the following rules apply:

(1) Title to goods cannot pass under a contract for sale prior to their identification to the contract (Section 2–501), and unless otherwise explicitly agreed the buyer acquires by their identification a special property as limited by this Act. Any retention or reservation by the seller of the title (property) in goods shipped or delivered to the buyer is limited in effect to a reservation of a security interest. Subject to these provisions and to the provisions of the Article on Secured Transactions (Article 9), title to goods passes from the seller to the buyer in any manner and on any conditions explicitly agreed on by the parties.

(2) Unless otherwise explicitly agreed title passes to the buyer at the time and place at which the seller completes his performance with reference to the physical delivery of the goods, despite any reservation of a security interest and even though a document of title is to be delivered at a different time or place; and in particular and despite any reservation of a security interest by the bill of lading

(a) if the contract requires or authorizes the seller to send the goods to the buyer but does not require him to deliver them at destination, title passes to the buyer at the time and place of shipment; but

(b) if the contract requires delivery at destination, title passes on tender there.

(3) Unless otherwise explicitly agreed where delivery is to be made without moving the goods,

(a) if the seller is to deliver a document of title, title passes at the time when and the place where he delivers such documents; or

(b) if the goods are at the time of contracting

already identified and no documents are to be delivered, title passes at the time and place of contracting.

(4) A rejection or other refusal by the buyer to receive or retain the goods, whether or not justified, or a justified revocation of acceptance revests title to the goods in the seller. Such revesting occurs by operation of law and is not a "sale."

### § 2–402. Rights of Seller's Creditors Against Sold Goods

(1) Except as provided in subsections (2) and (3), rights of unsecured creditors of the seller with respect to goods which have been identified to a contract for sale are subject to the buyer's rights to recover the goods under this Article (Sections 2–502 and 2–716).

(2) A creditor of the seller may treat a sale or an identification of goods to a contract for sale as void if as against him a retention of possession by the seller is fraudulent under any rule of law of the state where the goods are situated, except that retention of possession in good faith and current course of trade by a merchant-seller for a commercially reasonable time after a sale or identification is not fraudulent.

(3) Nothing in this Article shall be deemed to impair the rights of creditors of the seller

(a) under the provisions of the Article on Secured Transactions (Article 9); or

(b) where identification to the contract or delivery is made not in current course of trade but in satisfaction of or as security for a pre-existing claim for money, security or the like and is made under circumstances which under any rule of law of the state where the goods are situated would apart from this Article constitute the transaction a fraudulent transfer or voidable preference.

### § 2–403. Power to Transfer; Good Faith Purchase of Goods; "Entrusting"

(1) A purchaser of goods acquires all title which his transferor had or had power to transfer except that a purchaser of a limited interest acquires rights only to the extent of the interest purchased. A person with voidable title has power to transfer a good title to a good faith purchaser for value. When goods have been delivered under a transaction of purchase the purchaser has such power even though

(a) the transferor was deceived as to the identity of the purchaser, or

(b) the delivery was in exchange for a check which is later dishonored, or

(c) it was agreed that the transaction was to be a "cash sale," or

(d) the delivery was procured through fraud punishable as larcenous under the criminal law.

(2) Any entrusting of possession of goods to a merchant who deals in goods of that kind gives him power to transfer all rights of the entruster to a buyer in ordinary course of business.

(3) "Entrusting" includes any delivery and any acquiescence in retention of possession regardless of any condition expressed between the parties to the delivery or acquiescence and regardless of whether the procurement of the entrusting or the possessor's disposition of the goods have been such as to be larcenous under the criminal law.

(4) The rights of other purchasers of goods and of lien creditors are governed by the Articles on Secured Transactions (Article 9), Bulk Transfers (Article 6) and Documents of Title (Article 7).

## Part 5 Performance

### § 2–501. Insurable Interest in Goods; Manner of Identification of Goods

(1) The buyer obtains a special property and an insurable interest in goods by identification of existing goods as goods to which the contract refers even though the goods so identified are nonconforming and he has an option to return or reject them. Such identification can be made at any time and in any manner explicitly agreed to by the parties. In the absence of explicit agreement identification occurs

(a) when the contract is made if it is for the sale of goods already existing and identified;

(b) if the contract is for the sale of future goods other than those described in paragraph (c), when goods are shipped, marked or otherwise designated by the seller as goods to which the contract refers;

(c) when the crops are planted or otherwise become growing crops or the young are conceived if the contract is for the sale of unborn young to be born within twelve months after contracting or for the sale of crops to be harvested within twelve months or the next normal harvest season after contracting whichever is longer.

(2) The seller retains an insurable interest in goods so long as title to or any security interest in the goods remains in him and where the identification is by the seller alone he may until default or insolvency or notification to the buyer that the identification is final substitute other goods for those identified.

(3) Nothing in this section impairs any insurable interest recognized under any other statute or rule of law.

### § 2–502. Buyer's Right to Goods on Seller's Insolvency

(1) Subject to subsection (2) and even though the goods have not been shipped a buyer who has paid a part or all of the price of goods in which he has a special property under the provisions of the immediately preceding section may on making and keeping good a tender of any unpaid portion of their price recover them from the seller if the seller becomes insolvent within ten days after receipt of the first installment on their price.

(2) If the identification creating his special property has been made by the buyer he acquires the right to recover the goods only if they conform to the contract for sale.

### § 2–503. Manner of Seller's Tender of Delivery

(1) Tender of delivery requires that the seller put and hold conforming goods at the buyer's disposition and give the buyer any notification reasonably necessary to enable him to take delivery. The manner, time and place for tender are determined by the agreement and this Article, and in particular

(a) tender must be at a reasonable hour, and if it is of goods they must be kept available for the period reasonably necessary to enable the buyer to take possession; but

(b) unless otherwise agreed the buyer must furnish facilities reasonably suited to the receipt of the goods.

(2) Where the case is within the next section respecting shipment tender requires that the seller comply with its provisions.

(3) Where the seller is required to deliver at a particular destination tender requires that he comply with subsection (1) and also in any appropriate case tender documents as described in subsections (4) and (5) of this section.

(4) Where goods are in the possession of a bailee and are to be delivered without being moved

(a) tender requires that the seller either tender a negotiable document of title covering such goods or procure acknowledgement by the bailee of the buyer's right to possession of the goods; but

(b) tender to the buyer of a non-negotiable document of title or of a written direction to the bailee to deliver is sufficient tender unless the buyer seasonably objects, and receipt by the bailee of notification of the buyer's rights fixes those rights as against the bailee and all third persons; but risk of loss of the goods and of any failure by the bailee to honor the nonnegotiable document of title or to obey the direction remains on the seller until the buyer has had a reasonable time to present the document or direction, and a refusal by the bailee to honor the document or to obey the direction defeats the tender.

(5) Where the contract requires the seller to deliver documents

(a) he must tender all such documents in correct form, except as provided in this Article with respect to bills of lading in a set (subsection (2) of Section 2–323); and

(b) tender through customary banking channels is sufficient and dishonor of a draft accompanying the documents constitutes nonacceptance or rejection.

### § 2–504. Shipment by Seller

Where the seller is required or authorized to send the goods to the buyer and the contract does not require him to deliver them at a particular destination, then unless otherwise agreed he must

(a) put the goods in the possession of such a carrier and make such a contract for their transportation as may be reasonable having regard to the nature of the goods and other circumstances of the case; and

(b) obtain and promptly deliver or tender in due form any document necessary to enable the buyer to obtain possession of the goods or otherwise required by the agreement or by usage of trade; and

(c) promptly notify the buyer of the shipment. Failure to notify the buyer under paragraph (c) or to make a proper contract under paragraph (a) is a ground for rejection only if material delay or loss ensues.

### § 2–505. Seller's Shipment Under Reservation

(1) Where the seller has identified goods to the contract by or before shipment:

(a) his procurement of a negotiable bill of lading to his own order or otherwise reserves in him a security interest in the goods. His procurement of the bill to the order of a financing agency or of the buyer indicates in addition only the seller's expectation of transferring that interest to the person named.

(b) a non-negotiable bill of lading to himself or his nominee reserves possession of the goods as security but except in a case of conditional delivery (subsection (2) of Section 2–507) a non-negotiable bill of lading naming the buyer as consignee reserves no security interest even though the seller retains possession of the bill of lading.

(2) When shipment by the seller with reservation of a security interest is in violation of the contract for sale it constitutes an improper contract for transportation within the preceding section but impairs neither the rights given to the buyer by shipment and identification of the goods to the contract nor the seller's powers as a holder of a negotiable document.

### § 2–506. Rights of Financing Agency

(1) A financing agency by paying or purchasing for value a draft which relates to a shipment of goods acquires to the extent of the payment or purchase and in addition to its own rights under the draft and any document of title securing it any rights of the shipper in the goods including the right to stop delivery and the shipper's right to have the draft honored by the buyer.

(2) The right to reimbursement of a financing agency which has in good faith honored or purchased the draft under commitment to or authority from the buyer is not impaired by subsequent discovery of defects with reference to any relevant document which was apparently regular on its face.

### § 2–507. Effect of Seller's Tender; Delivery on Condition

(1) Tender of delivery is a condition to the buyer's duty to accept the goods and, unless otherwise agreed, to his duty to pay for them. Tender entitles the seller to acceptance of the goods and to payment according to the contract.

(2) Where payment is due and demanded on the delivery to the buyer of goods or documents of title, his right as against the seller to retain or dispose of them is conditional upon his making the payment due.

### § 2–508. Cure by Seller of Improper Tender or Delivery; Replacement

(1) Where any tender or delivery by the seller is rejected because non-conforming and the time for performance has not yet expired, the seller may seasonably notify the buyer of his intention to cure and may then within the contract time make a conforming delivery.

(2) Where the buyer rejects a non-conforming tender which the seller had reasonable grounds to believe would be acceptable with or without money allowance the seller may if he seasonably notifies the buyer have a further reasonable time to substitute a conforming tender.

### § 2–509. Risk of Loss in the Absence of Breach

(1) Where the contract requires or authorizes the seller to ship the goods by carrier

(a) if it does not require him to deliver them at a particular destination, the risk of loss passes to the buyer when the goods are duly delivered to the carrier even though the shipment is under reservation (Section 2–505); but

(b) if it does require him to deliver them at a particular destination and the goods are there duly tendered while in the possession of the carrier, the risk of loss passes to the buyer when the goods are there duly so tendered as to enable the buyer to take delivery.

(2) Where the goods are held by a bailee to be delivered without being moved, the risk of loss passes to the buyer

(a) on his receipt of a negotiable document of title covering the goods; or

(b) on acknowledgment by the bailee of the buyer's right to possession of the goods; or

(c) after his receipt of a non-negotiable document of title or other written direction to deliver, as provided in subsection (4) (b) of Section 2–503.

(3) In any case not within subsection (1) or (2), the risk of loss passes to the buyer on his receipt of the goods if the seller is a merchant; otherwise the risk passes to the buyer on tender of delivery.

(4) The provisions of this section are subject to contrary agreement of the parties and to the provisions of this Article on sale on approval (Section 2–327) and on effect of breach on risk of loss (Section 2–510).

### § 2–510. Effect of Breach on Risk of Loss

(1) Where a tender or delivery of goods so fails to conform to the contract as to give a right of rejection the risk of their loss remains on the seller until cure or acceptance.

(2) Where the buyer rightfully revokes acceptance he may to the extent of any deficiency in his effective insurance coverage treat the risk of loss as having rested on the seller from the beginning.

(3) Where the buyer as to conforming goods already identified to the contract for sale repudiates or is otherwise in breach before risk of their loss has passed to him, the seller may to the extent of any deficiency in his effective insurance coverage treat the risk of loss as resting on the buyer for a commercially reasonable time.

### § 2–511. Tender of Payment by Buyer; Payment by Check

(1) Unless otherwise agreed tender of payment is a condition to the seller's duty to tender and complete any delivery.

(2) Tender of payment is sufficient when made by any means or in any manner current in the ordinary course of business unless the seller demands payment in legal tender and gives any extension of time reasonably necessary to procure it.

(3) Subject to the provisions of this Act on the effect of an instrument on an obligation (Section 3–802), payment by check is conditional and is defeated as between the parties by dishonor of the check on due presentment.

### § 2–512. Payment by Buyer Before Inspection

(1) Where the contract requires payment before inspection non-conformity of the goods does not excuse the buyer from so making payment unless

(a) the non-conformity appears without inspection; or

(b) despite tender of the required documents the circumstances would justify injunction against honor under the provisions of this Act (Section 5–114).

(2) Payment pursuant to subsection (1) does not constitute an acceptance of goods or impair the buyer's right to inspect or any of his remedies.

### § 2–513. Buyer's Right to Inspection of Goods

(1) Unless otherwise agreed and subject to subsection (3), where goods are tendered or delivered or identified to the contract for sale, the buyer has a right before payment or acceptance to inspect them at any reasonable place and time and in any reasonable manner. When the seller is required or authorized to send the goods to the buyer, the inspection may be after their arrival.

(2) Expenses of inspection must be borne by the buyer but may be recovered from the seller if the goods do not conform and are rejected.

(3) Unless otherwise agreed and subject to the provisions of this Article on C.I.F. contracts (subsection (3) of Section 2–321), the buyer is not entitled to inspect the goods before payment of the price when the contract provides

(a) for delivery "C.O.D." or on other like terms; or

(b) for payment against documents of title, except where such payment is due only after the goods are to become available for inspection.

(4) A place or method of inspection fixed by the parties is presumed to be exclusive but unless otherwise expressly agreed it does not postpone identification or shift the place for delivery or for passing the risk of loss. If compliance becomes impossible, inspection shall be as provided in this section unless the place or method fixed was clearly intended as an indispensable condition failure of which avoids the contract.

### § 2–514. When Documents Deliverable on Acceptance; When on Payment

Unless otherwise agreed documents against which a draft is drawn are to be delivered to the drawee on acceptance of the draft if it is payable more than three days after presentment; otherwise, only on payment.

### § 2–515. Preserving Evidence of Goods in Dispute

In furtherance of the adjustment of any claim or dispute

(a) either party on reasonable notification to the other and for the purpose of ascertaining the facts and preserving evidence has the right to inspect, test and sample the goods including such of them as may be in the possession or control of the other; and

(b) the parties may agree to a third party inspection or survey to determine the conformity or condition of the goods and may agree that the findings shall be binding upon them in any subsequent litigation or adjustment.

## Part 6 Breach, Repudiation and Excuse

### § 2–601. Buyer's Rights on Improper Delivery

Subject to the provisions of this Article on breach in installment contracts (Section 2–612) and unless otherwise agreed under the sections on contractual limitations of remedy (Sections 2–718 and 2–719), if the goods or the tender of delivery fail in any respect to conform to the contract, the buyer may

(a) reject the whole; or

(b) accept the whole; or

(c) accept any commercial unit or units and reject the rest.

### § 2–602. Manner and Effect of Rightful Rejection

(1) Rejection of goods must be within a reasonable time after their delivery or tender. It is ineffective unless the buyer seasonably notifies the seller.

(2) Subject to the provisions of the two following sections on rejected goods (Sections 2–603 and 2–604),

(a) after rejection any exercise of ownership by the buyer with respect to any commercial unit is wrongful as against the seller; and

(b) if the buyer has before rejection taken physical possession of goods in which he does not have a security interest under the provisions of this Article (subsection (3) of Section 2–711), he is under a duty after rejection to hold them with reasonable care at the seller's disposition for a time sufficient to permit the seller to remove them; but

(c) the buyer has no further obligations with regard to goods rightfully rejected.

(3) The seller's rights with respect to goods wrongfully rejected are governed by the provisions of this Article on Seller's remedies in general (Section 2–703).

### § 2–603. Merchant Buyer's Duties as to Rightfully Rejected Goods

(1) Subject to any security interest in the buyer (subsection (3) of Section 2–711), when the seller has no agent or place of business at the market of rejection a merchant buyer is under a duty after rejection of goods in his possession or control to follow any reasonable instructions received from the seller with respect to the goods and in the absence of such instructions to make reasonable efforts to sell them for the seller's account if they are perishable or threaten to decline in value speedily. Instructions are not reasonable if on demand indemnity for expenses is not forthcoming.

(2) When the buyer sells goods under subsection (1), he is entitled to reimbursement from the seller or out of the proceeds for reasonable expenses of caring for and selling them, and if the expenses include no selling commission then to such commission as is usual in the trade or if there is none to a reasonable sum not exceeding ten per cent on the gross proceeds.

(3) In complying with this section the buyer is held only to good faith and good faith conduct hereunder is neither acceptance nor conversion nor the basis of an action for damages.

### § 2–604. Buyer's Options as to Salvage of Rightfully Rejected Goods

Subject to the provisions of the immediately preceding section on perishables if the seller gives no instructions within a reasonable time after notification of rejection the buyer may store the rejected goods for the seller's account or reship them to him or resell them for the seller's account with reimbursement as provided in the preceding section. Such action is not acceptance or conversion.

### § 2–605. Waiver of Buyer's Objections by Failure to Particularize

(1) The buyer's failure to state in connection with rejection a particular defect which is ascertainable

by reasonable inspection precludes him from relying on the unstated defect to justify rejection or to establish breach

(a) where the seller could have cured it if stated seasonably; or

(b) between merchants when the seller has after rejection made a request in writing for a full and final written statement of all defects on which the buyer proposes to rely.

(2) Payment against documents made without reservation of rights precludes recovery of the payment for defects apparent on the face of the documents.

### § 2–606. What Constitutes Acceptance of Goods

(1) Acceptance of goods occurs when the buyer

(a) after a reasonable opportunity to inspect the goods signifies to the seller that the goods are conforming or that he will take or retain them in spite of their non-conformity; or

(b) fails to make an effective rejection (subsection (1) of Section 2–602), but such acceptance does not occur until the buyer has had a reasonable opportunity to inspect them; or

(c) does any act inconsistent with the seller's ownership; but if such act is wrongful as against the seller it is an acceptance only if ratified by him.

(2) Acceptance of a part of any commercial unit is acceptance of that entire unit.

### § 2–607. Effect of Acceptance; Notice of Breach; Burden of Establishing Breach After Acceptance; Notice of Claim or Litigation to Person Answerable Over

(1) The buyer must pay at the contract rate for any goods accepted.

(2) Acceptance of goods by the buyer precludes rejection of the goods accepted and if made with knowledge of a non-conformity cannot be revoked because of it unless the acceptance was on the reasonable assumption that the non-conformity would be seasonably cured but acceptance does not of itself impair any other remedy provided by this Article for non-conformity.

(3) Where a tender has been accepted

(a) the buyer must within a reasonable time after he discovers or should have discovered any breach notify the seller of breach or be barred from any remedy; and

(b) if the claim is one for infringement or the like (subsection (3) of Section 2–312) and the buyer is sued as a result of such a breach he must so notify the seller within a reasonable time after he receives notice of the litigation or be barred from any remedy over for liability established by the litigation.

(4) The burden is on the buyer to establish any breach with respect to the goods accepted.

(5) Where the buyer is sued for breach of a warranty or other obligation for which his seller is answerable over

(a) he may give his seller written notice of the litigation. If the notice states that the seller may come in and defend and that if the seller does not do so he will be bound in any action against him by his buyer by any determination of fact common to the two litigations, then unless the seller after seasonable receipt of the notice does come in and defend he is so bound.

(b) if the claim is one for infringement or the like (subsection (3) of Section 2–312) the original seller may demand in writing that his buyer turn over to him control of the litigation including settlement or else be barred from any remedy over and if he also agrees to bear all expense and to satisfy any adverse judgment, then unless the buyer after seasonable receipt of the demand does turn over control the buyer is so barred.

(6) The provisions of subsections (3), (4) and (5) apply to any obligation of a buyer to hold the seller harmless against infringement or the like (subsection (3) of Section 2–312).

### § 2–608. Revocation of Acceptance in Whole or in Part

(1) The buyer may revoke his acceptance of a lot or commercial unit whose non-conformity substantially impairs its value to him if he has accepted it

(a) on the reasonable assumption that its non-conformity would be cured and it has not been seasonably cured; or

(b) without discovery of such non-conformity if his acceptance was reasonably induced either by the difficulty of discovery before acceptance or by the seller's assurances.

(2) Revocation of acceptance must occur within a reasonable time after the buyer discovers or should have discovered the ground for it and before

any substantial change in conditions of the goods which is not caused by their own defects. It is not effective until the buyer notifies the seller of it.

(3) A buyer who so revokes has the same rights and duties with regard to the goods involved as if he had rejected them.

### § 2–609. Right to Adequate Assurance of Performance

(1) A contract for sale imposes an obligation on each party that the other's expectation of receiving due performance will not be impaired. When reasonable grounds for insecurity arise with respect to the performance of either party the other may in writing demand adequate assurance of due performance and until he receives such assurance may if commercially reasonable suspend any performance of which he has not already received the agreed return.

(2) Between merchants the reasonableness of grounds for insecurity and the adequacy of any assurance offered shall be determined according to commercial standards.

(3) Acceptance of any improper delivery or payment does not prejudice the aggrieved party's right to demand adequate assurance of future performance.

(4) After receipt of a justified demand failure to provide within a reasonable time not exceeding thirty days such assurance of due performance as is adequate under the circumstances of the particular case is a repudiation of the contract.

### § 2–610. Anticipatory Repudiation

When either party repudiates the contract with respect to a performance not yet due the loss of which will substantially impair the value of the contract to the other, the aggrieved party may

(a) for a commercially reasonable time await performance by the repudiating party; or

(b) resort to any remedy for breach (Section 2–703 or Section 2–711), even though he has notified the repudiating party that he would await the latter's performance and has urged retraction; and

(c) in either case suspend his own performance or proceed in accordance with the provisions of this Article on the seller's right to identify goods to the contract notwithstanding breach or to salvage unfinished goods (Section 2–704).

### § 2–611. Retraction of Anticipatory Repudiation

(1) Until the repudiating party's next performance is due he can retract his repudiation unless the aggrieved party has since the repudiation cancelled or materially changed his position or otherwise indicated that he considers the repudiation final.

(2) Retraction may be by any method which clearly indicates to the aggrieved party that the repudiating party intends to perform, but must include any assurance justifiably demanded under the provisions of this Article (Section 2–609).

(3) Retraction reinstates the repudiating party's rights under the contract with due excuse and allowance to the aggrieved party for any delay occasioned by the repudiation.

### § 2–612. "Installment Contract"; Breach

(1) An "installment contract" is one which requires or authorizes the delivery of goods in separate lots to be separately accepted, even though the contract contains a clause "each delivery is a separate contract" or its equivalent.

(2) The buyer may reject any installment which is non-conforming if the non-conformity substantially impairs the value of that installment and cannot be cured or if the non-conformity is a defect in the required documents; but if the non-conformity does not fall within subsection (3) and the seller gives adequate assurance of its cure the buyer must accept that installment.

(3) Whenever non-conformity or default with respect to one or more installments substantially impairs the value of the whole contract there is a breach of the whole. But the aggrieved party reinstates the contract if he accepts a non-conforming installment without seasonably notifying of cancellation or if he brings an action with respect only to past installments or demands performance as to future installments.

### § 2–613. Casualty to Identified Goods

Where the contract requires for its performance goods identified when the contract is made, and the goods suffer casualty without fault of either party before the risk of loss passes to the buyer, or in a proper case under a "no arrival, no sale" term (Section 2–324) then

(a) if the loss is total the contract is avoided; and

(b) if the loss is partial or the goods have so deteriorated as no longer to conform to the contract the buyer may nevertheless demand inspection and at his option either treat the contract as avoided or accept the goods with due allowance from the contract price for the deterioration or the deficiency in quantity but without further right against the seller.

### § 2–614. Substituted Performance

(1) Where without fault of either party the agreed berthing, loading, or unloading facilities fail or an agreed type of carrier becomes unavailable or the agreed manner of delivery otherwise becomes commercially impracticable but a commercially reasonable substitute is available, such substitute performance must be tendered and accepted.

(2) If the agreed means or manner of payment fails because of domestic or foreign governmental regulation, the seller may withhold or stop delivery unless the buyer provides a means or manner of payment which is commercially a substantial equivalent. If delivery has already been taken, payment by the means or in the manner provided by the regulation discharges the buyer's obligation unless the regulation is discriminatory, oppressive or predatory.

### § 2–615. Excuse by Failure of Presupposed Conditions

Except so far as a seller may have assumed a greater obligation and subject to the preceding section on substituted performance:

(a) Delay in delivery or non-delivery in whole or in part by a seller who complies with paragraphs (b) and (c) is not a breach of his duty under a contract for sale if performance as agreed has been made impracticable by the occurrence of a contingency the nonoccurrence of which was a basic assumption on which the contract was made or by compliance in good faith with any applicable foreign or domestic governmental regulation or order whether or not it later proves to be invalid.

(b) Where the causes mentioned in paragraph (a) affect only a part of the seller's capacity to perform, he must allocate production and deliveries among his customers but may at his option include regular customers not then under contract as well as his own requirements for further manufacture. He may so allocate in any manner which is fair and reasonable.

(c) The seller must notify the buyer seasonably that there will be delay or non-delivery and, when allocation is required under paragraph (b), of the estimated quota thus made available for the buyer.

### § 2–616. Procedure on Notice Claiming Excuse

(1) Where the buyer receives notification of a material or indefinite delay or an allocation justified under the preceding section he may by written notification to the seller as to any delivery concerned, and where the prospective deficiency substantially impairs the value of the whole contract under the provisions of this Article relating to breach of installment contracts (Section 2–612), then also as to the whole,

(a) terminate and thereby discharge any unexecuted portion of the contract; or

(b) modify the contract by agreeing to take his available quota in substitution.

(2) If after receipt of such notification from the seller the buyer fails so to modify the contract within a reasonable time not exceeding thirty days the contract lapses with respect to any deliveries affected.

(3) The provisions of this section may not be negated by agreement except in so far as the seller has assumed a greater obligation under the preceding section.

## Part 7 Remedies

### § 2–701. Remedies for Breach of Collateral Contracts Not Impaired

Remedies for breach of any obligation or promise collateral or ancillary to a contract for sale are not impaired by the provisions of this Article.

### § 2–702. Seller's Remedies on Discovery of Buyer's Insolvency

(1) Where the seller discovers the buyer to be insolvent he may refuse delivery except for cash including payment for all goods theretofore delivered under the contract, and stop delivery under this Article (Section 2–705).

(2) Where the seller discovers that the buyer has received goods on credit while insolvent he may

reclaim the goods upon demand made within ten days after the receipt, but if misrepresentation of solvency has been made to the particular seller in writing within three months before delivery the ten day limitation does not apply. Except as provided in this subsection the seller may not base a right to reclaim goods on the buyer's fraudulent or innocent misrepresentation of solvency or of intent to pay.

(3) The seller's right to reclaim under subsection (2) is subject to the rights of a buyer in ordinary course or other good faith purchaser under this Article (Section 2–403). Successful reclamation of goods excludes all other remedies with respect to them.

### § 2–703. Seller's Remedies in General

Where the buyer wrongfully rejects or revokes acceptance of goods or fails to make a payment due on or before delivery or repudiates with respect to a part or the whole, then with respect to any goods directly affected and, if the breach is of the whole contract (Section 2–612), then also with respect to the whole undelivered balance, the aggrieved seller may

(a) withhold delivery of such goods;

(b) stop delivery by any bailee as hereafter provided (Section 2–705);

(c) proceed under the next section respecting goods still unidentified to the contract;

(d) resell and recover damages as hereafter provided (Section 2–706);

(e) recover damages for non-acceptance (Section 2–708) or in a proper case the price (Section 2–709);

(f) cancel.

### § 2–704. Seller's Right to Identify Goods to the Contract Notwithstanding Breach or to Salvage Unfinished Goods

(1) An aggrieved seller under the preceding section may

(a) identify to the contract conforming goods not already identified if at the time he learned of the breach they are in his possession or control;

(b) treat as the subject of resale goods which have demonstrably been intended for the particular contract even though those goods are unfinished.

(2) Where the goods are unfinished an aggrieved seller may in the exercise of reasonable commercial judgment for the purposes of avoiding loss and of effective realization either complete the manufacture and wholly identify the goods to the contract or cease manufacture and resell for scrap or salvage value or proceed in any other reasonable manner.

### § 2–705. Seller's Stoppage of Delivery in Transit or Otherwise

(1) The seller may stop delivery of goods in the possession of a carrier or other bailee when he discovers the buyer to be insolvent (Section 2–702) and may stop delivery of carload, truckload, planeload or larger shipments of express or freight when the buyer repudiates or fails to make a payment due before delivery or if for any other reason the seller has a right to withhold or reclaim the goods.

(2) As against such buyer the seller may stop delivery until

(a) receipt of the goods by the buyer; or

(b) acknowledgment to the buyer by any bailee of the goods except a carrier that the bailee holds the goods for the buyer; or

(c) such acknowledgment to the buyer by a carrier by reshipment or as warehouseman; or

(d) negotiation to the buyer of any negotiable document of title covering the goods.

(3) (a) To stop delivery the seller must so notify as to enable the bailee by reasonable diligence to prevent delivery of the goods.

(b) After such notification the bailee must hold and deliver the goods according to the directions of the seller but the seller is liable to the bailee for any ensuing charges or damages.

(c) If a negotiable document of title has been issued for goods the bailee is not obliged to obey a notification to stop until surrender of the document.

(d) A carrier who has issued a non-negotiable bill of lading is not obliged to obey a notification to stop received from a person other than the consignor.

### § 2–706. Seller's Resale Including Contract for Resale

(1) Under the conditions stated in Section 2–703 on seller's remedies, the seller may resell the goods

concerned or the undelivered balance thereof. Where the resale is made in good faith and in a commercially reasonable manner the seller may recover the difference between the resale price and the contract price together with any incidental damages allowed under the provisions of this Article (Section 2–710), but less expenses saved in consequence of the buyer's breach.

(2) Except as otherwise provided in subsection (3) or unless otherwise agreed resale may be at public or private sale including sale by way of one or more contracts to sell or of identification of an existing contract of the seller. Sale may be as a unit or in parcels and at any time and place and on any terms but every aspect of the sale including the method, manner, time, place and terms must be commercially reasonable. The resale must be reasonably identified as referring to the broken contract, but it is not necessary that the goods be in existence or that any or all of them have been identified to the contract before the breach.

(3) Where the resale is at private sale the seller must give the buyer reasonable notification of his intention to resell.

(4) Where the resale is at public sale

(a) only identified goods can be sold except where there is a recognized market for a public sale of futures in goods of the kind; and

(b) it must be made at a usual place or market for public sale if one is reasonably available and except in the case of goods which are perishable or threaten to decline in value speedily the seller must give the buyer reasonable notice of the time and place of the resale; and

(c) if the goods are not to be within the view of those attending the sale the notification of sale must state the place where the goods are located and provide for their reasonable inspection by prospective bidders; and

(d) the seller may buy

(5) A purchaser who buys in good faith at a resale takes the goods free of any rights of the original buyer even though the seller fails to comply with one or more of the requirements of this section.

(6) The seller is not accountable to the buyer for any profit made on any resale. A person in the position of a seller (Section 2–707) or a buyer who has rightfully rejected or justifiably revoked acceptance must account for any excess over the amount of his security interest, as hereinafter defined (subsection (3) of Section 2–711).

### § 2–707. "Person in the Position of a Seller"

(1) A "person in the position of a seller" includes as against a principal an agent who has paid or become responsible for the price of goods on behalf of his principal or anyone who otherwise holds a security interest or other right in goods similar to that of a seller.

(2) A person in the position of a seller may as provided in this Article withhold or stop delivery (Section 2–705) and resell (Section 2–706) and recover incidental damages (Section 2–710).

### § 2–708. Seller's Damages for Non-acceptance or Repudiation

(1) Subject to subsection (2) and to the provisions of this Article with respect to proof of market price (Section 2–723), the measure of damages for non-acceptance or repudiation by the buyer is the difference between the market price at the time and place for tender and the unpaid contract price together with any incidental damages provided in this Article (Section 2–710), but less expenses saved in consequence of the buyer's breach.

(2) If the measure of damages provided in subsection (1) is inadequate to put the seller in as good a position as performance would have done then the measure of damages is the profit (including reasonable overhead) which the seller would have made from full performance by the buyer, together with any incidental damages provided in this Article (Section 2–710), due allowance for costs reasonably incurred and due credit for payments or proceeds of resale.

### § 2–709. Action for the Price

(1) When the buyer fails to pay the price as it becomes due the seller may recover, together with any incidental damages under the next section, the price

(a) of goods accepted or of conforming goods lost or damaged within a commercially reasonable time after risk of their loss has passed to the buyer; and

(b) of goods identified to the contract if the seller is unable after reasonable effort to resell them at a reasonable price or the circumstances reasonably indicate that such effort will be unavailing.

(2) Where the seller sues for the price he must hold for the buyer any goods which have been identified to the contract and are still in his control except that if resale becomes possible he may resell them at any time prior to the collection of the judgment. The net proceeds of any such resale must be credited to the buyer and payment of the judgment entitles him to any goods not resold.

(3) After the buyer has wrongfully rejected or revoked acceptance of the goods or has failed to make a payment due or has repudiated (Section 2–610), a seller who is held not entitled to the price under this section shall nevertheless be awarded damages for non-acceptance under the preceding section.

### § 2–710. Seller's Incidental Damages

Incidental damages to an aggrieved seller include any commercially reasonable charges, expenses or commissions incurred in stopping delivery, in the transportation, care and custody of goods after the buyer's breach, in connection with return or resale of the goods or otherwise resulting from the breach.

### § 2–711. Buyer's Remedies in General; Buyer's Security Interest in Rejected Goods

(1) Where the seller fails to make delivery or repudiates or the buyer rightfully rejects or justifiably revokes acceptance then with respect to any goods involved, and with respect to the whole if the breach goes to the whole contract (Section 2–612), the buyer may cancel and whether or not he has done so may in addition to recovering so much of the price as has been paid

(a) "cover" and have damages under the next section as to all the goods affected whether or not they have been identified to the contract; or

(b) recover damages for non-delivery as provided in this Article (Section 2–713).

(2) Where the seller fails to deliver or repudiates the buyer may also

(a) if the goods have been identified recover them as provided in this Article (Section 2–502); or

(b) in a proper case obtain specific performance or replevy the goods as provided in this Article (Section 2–716).

(3) On rightful rejection or justifiable revocation of acceptance a buyer has a security interest in goods in his possession or control for any payments made on their price and any expenses reasonably incurred in their inspection, receipt, transportation, care and custody and may hold such goods and resell them in like manner as an aggrieved seller (Section 2–706).

### § 2–712. "Cover"; Buyer's Procurement of Substitute Goods

(1) After a breach within the preceding section the buyer may "cover" by making in good faith and without unreasonable delay any reasonable purchase of or contract to purchase goods in substitution for those due from the seller.

(2) The buyer may recover from the seller as damages the difference between the cost of cover and the contract price together with any incidental or consequential damages as hereinafter defined (Section 2–715), but less expenses saved in consequence of the seller's breach.

(3) Failure of the buyer to effect cover within this section does not bar him from any other remedy.

### § 2–713. Buyer's Damages for Non-Delivery or Repudiation

(1) Subject to the provisions of this Article with respect to proof of market price (Section 2–723), the measure of damages for non-delivery or repudiation by the seller is the difference between the market price at the time when the buyer learned of the breach and the contract price together with any incidental and consequential damages provided in this Article (Section 2–715), but less expenses saved in consequence of the seller's breach.

(2) Market price is to be determined as of the place for tender or, in cases of rejection after arrival or revocation of acceptance, as of the place of arrival.

### § 2–714. Buyer's Damages for Breach in Regard to Accepted Goods

(1) Where the buyer has accepted goods and given notification (subsection (3) of Section 2–607) he may recover as damages for any non-conformity of tender the loss resulting in the ordinary course of events from the seller's breach as determined in any manner which is reasonable.

(2) The measure of damages for breach of war-

ranty is the difference at the time and place of acceptance between the value of the goods accepted and the value they would have had if they had been as warranted, unless special circumstances show proximate damages of a different amount.
(3) In a proper case any incidental and consequential damages under the next section may also be recovered.

### § 2–715. Buyer's Incidental and Consequential Damages

(1) Incidental damages resulting from the seller's breach include expenses reasonably incurred in inspection, receipt, transportation and care and custody of goods rightfully rejected, any commercially reasonable charges, expenses or commissions in connection with effecting cover and any other reasonable expense incident to the delay or other breach.
(2) Consequential damages resulting from the seller's breach include

(a) any loss resulting from general or particular requirements and needs of which the seller at the time of contracting had reason to know and which could not reasonably be prevented by cover or otherwise; and

(b) injury to person or property proximately resulting from any breach of warranty.

### § 2–716. Buyer's Right to Specific Performance or Replevin

(1) Specific performance may be decreed where the goods are unique or in other proper circumstances.
(2) The decree for specific performance may include such terms and conditions as to payment of the price, damages, or other relief as the court may deem just.
(3) The buyer has a right of replevin for goods identified to the contract if after reasonable effort he is unable to effect cover for such goods or the circumstances reasonably indicate that such effort will be unavailing or if the goods have been shipped under reservation and satisfaction of the security interest in them has been made or tendered.

### § 2–717. Deduction of Damages From the Price

The buyer on notifying the seller of his intention to do so may deduct all or any part of the damages resulting from any breach of the contract from any part of the price still due under the same contract.

### § 2–718. Liquidation or Limitation of Damages; Deposits

(1) Damages for breach by either party may be liquidated in the agreement but only at an amount which is reasonable in the light of the anticipated or actual harm caused by the breach, the difficulties of proof of loss, and the inconvenience or nonfeasibility of otherwise obtaining an adequate remedy. A term fixing unreasonably large liquidated damages is void as a penalty.
(2) Where the seller justifiably withholds delivery of goods because of the buyer's breach, the buyer is entitled to restitution of any amount by which the sum of his payments exceeds

(a) the amount to which the seller is entitled by virtue of terms liquidating the seller's damages in accordance with subsection (1), or

(b) in the absence of such terms, twenty per cent of the value of the total performance for which the buyer is obligated under the contract or $500, whichever is smaller.

(3) The buyer's right to restitution under subsection (2) is subject to offset to the extent that the seller establishes

(a) a right to recover damages under the provisions of this Article other than subsection (1), and

(b) the amount or value of any benefits received by the buyer directly or indirectly by reason of the contract.

(4) Where a seller has received payment in goods their reasonable value or the proceeds of their resale shall be treated as payments for the purposes of subsection (2); but if the seller has notice of the buyer's breach before reselling goods received in part performance, his resale is subject to the conditions laid down in this Article on resale by an aggrieved seller (Section 2–706).

### § 2–719. Contractual Modification or Limitation of Remedy

(1) Subject to the provisions of subsections (2) and (3) of this section and of the preceding section on liquidation and limitation of damages,

(a) the agreement may provide for remedies in addition to or in substitution for those provided in this Article and may limit or alter the measure of damages recoverable under this Article, as by limiting the buyer's remedies to return of the goods and repayment of the price or to repair and replacement of non-conforming goods or parts; and

(b) resort to a remedy as provided is optional unless the remedy is expressly agreed to be exclusive, in which case it is the sole remedy.

(2) Where circumstances cause an exclusive or limited remedy to fail of its essential purpose, remedy may be had as provided in this Act.

(3) Consequential damages may be limited or excluded unless the limitation or exclusion is unconscionable. Limitation of consequential damages for injury to the person in the case of consumer goods is prima facie unconscionable but limitation of damages where the loss is commercial is not.

### § 2–720. Effect of "Cancellation" or "Rescission" on Claims for Antecedent Breach

Unless the contrary intention clearly appears, expressions of "cancellation" or "rescission" of the contract or the like shall not be construed as a renunciation or discharge of any claim in damages for an antecedent breach.

### § 2–721. Remedies for Fraud

Remedies for material misrepresentation or fraud include all remedies available under this Article for non-fraudulent breach. Neither rescission or a claim for rescission of the contract for sale nor rejection or return of the goods shall bar or be deemed inconsistent with a claim for damages or other remedy.

### § 2–722. Who Can Sue Third Parties for Injury to Goods

Where a third party so deals with goods which have been identified to a contract for sale as to cause actionable injury to a party to that contract

(a) a right of action against the third party is in either party to the contract for sale who has title to or a security interest or a special property or an insurable interest in the goods; and if the goods have been destroyed or converted a right of action is also in the party who either bore the risk of loss under the contract for sale or has since the injury assumed that risk as against the other;

(b) if at the time of the injury the party plaintiff did not bear the risk of loss as against the other party to the contract for sale and there is no arrangement between them for disposition of the recovery, his suit or settlement is, subject to his own interest, as a fiduciary for the other party to the contract;

(c) either party may with the consent of the other sue for the benefit of whom it may concern.

### § 2–723. Proof of Market Price: Time and Place

(1) If an action based on anticipatory repudiation comes to trial before the time for performance with respect to some or all of the goods, any damages based on market price (Section 2–708 or Section 2–713) shall be determined according to the price of such goods prevailing at the time when the aggrieved party learned of the repudiation.

(2) If evidence of a price prevailing at the times or places described in this Article is not readily available the price prevailing within any reasonable time before or after the time described or at any other place which in commercial judgment or under usage of trade would serve as a reasonable substitute for the one described may be used, making any proper allowance for the cost of transporting the goods to or from such other place.

(3) Evidence of a relevant price prevailing at a time or place other than the one described in this Article offered by one party is not admissible unless and until he has given the other party such notice as the court finds sufficient to prevent unfair surprise.

### § 2–724. Admissibility of Market Quotations

Whenever the prevailing price or value of any goods regularly bought and sold in any established commodity market is in issue, reports in official publications or trade journals or in newspapers or periodicals of general circulation published as the reports of such market shall be admissible in evidence. The circumstances of the preparation of such a report may be shown to affect its weight but not its admissibility.

### § 2–725. Statute of Limitations in Contracts for Sale

(1) An action for breach of any contract for sale must be commenced within four years after the cause of action has accrued. By the original agreement the parties may reduce the period of limi-

tation to not less than one year but may not extend it.

(2) A cause of action accrues when the breach occurs, regardless of the aggrieved party's lack of knowledge of the breach. A breach of warranty occurs when tender of delivery is made, except that where a warranty explicitly extends to future performance of the goods and discovery of the breach must await the time of such performance the cause of action accrues when the breach is or should have been discovered.

(3) Where an action commenced within the time limited by subsection (1) is so terminated as to leave available a remedy by another action for the same breach such other action may be commenced after the expiration of the time limited and within six months after the termination of the first action unless the termination resulted from voluntary discontinuance or from dismissal for failure or neglect to prosecute.

(4) This section does not alter the law on tolling of the statute of limitations nor does it apply to causes of action which have accrued before this Act becomes effective.

## ARTICLE 3 COMMERCIAL PAPER

### Part 1 Short Title, Form and Interpretation

#### § 3–101. Short Title

This Article shall be known and may be cited as Uniform Commercial Code—Commercial Paper.

#### § 3–102. Definitions and Index of Definitions

(1) In this Article unless the context otherwise requires

(a) "Issue" means the first delivery of an instrument to a holder or a remitter.

(b) An "order" is a direction to pay and must be more than an authorization or request. It must identify the person to pay with reasonable certainty. It may be addressed to one or more such persons jointly or in the alternative but not in succession.

(c) A "promise" is an undertaking to pay and must be more than an acknowledgment of an obligation.

(d) "Secondary party" means a drawer or endorser.

(e) "Instrument" means a negotiable instrument.

(2) Other definitions applying to this Article and the sections in which they appear are:

"Acceptance." Section 3–410.
"Accommodation party." Section 3–415.
"Alteration." Section 3–407.
"Certificate of deposit." Section 3–104.
"Certification." Section 3–411.
"Check." Section 3–104.
"Definite time." Section 3–109.
"Dishonor." Section 3–507.
"Draft." Section 3–104.
"Holder in due course." Section 3–302.
"Negotiation." Section 3–202.
"Note." Section 3–104.
"Notice of dishonor." Section 3–508.
"On demand." Section 3–108.
"Presentment." Section 3–504.
"Protest." Section 3–509.
"Restrictive Indorsement." Section 3–205.
"Signature." Section 3–401.

(3) The following definitions in other Articles apply to this Article:

"Account." Section 4–104.
"Banking Day." Section 4–104.
"Clearing house." Section 4–104.
"Collecting bank." Section 4–105.
"Customer." Section 4–104.
"Depositary Bank." Section 4–105.
"Documentary Draft." Section 4–104.
"Intermediary Bank." Section 4–105.
"Item." Section 4–104.
"Midnight deadline." Section 4–104.
"Payor bank." Section 4–105.

(4) In addition Article 1 contains general definitions and principles of construction and interpretation applicable throughout this Article.

#### § 3–103. Limitations on Scope of Article

(1) This Article does not apply to money, documents of title or investment securities.

(2) The provisions of this Article are subject to the provisions of the Article on Bank Deposits and Collections (Article 4) and Secured Transactions (Article 9).

### § 3–104. Form of Negotiable Instruments; "Draft"; "Check"; "Certificate of Deposit"; "Note"

(1) Any writing to be a negotiable instrument within this Article must

(a) be signed by the maker or drawer; and

(b) contain an unconditional promise or order to pay a sum certain in money and no other promise, order, obligation or power given by the maker or drawer except as authorized by this Article; and

(c) be payable on demand or at a definite time; and

(d) be payable to order or to bearer.

(2) A writing which complies with the requirements of this section is

(a) a "draft" ("bill of exchange") if it is an order;

(b) a "check" if it is a draft drawn on a bank and payable on demand;

(c) a "certificate of deposit" if it is an acknowledgment by a bank of receipt of money with an engagement to repay it;

(d) a "note" if it is a promise other than a certificate of deposit.

(3) As used in other Articles of this Act, and as the context may require, the terms "draft," "check," "certificate of deposit" and "note" may refer to instruments which are not negotiable within this Article as well as to instruments which are so negotiable.

### § 3–105. When Promise or Order Unconditional

(1) A promise or order otherwise unconditional is not made conditional by the fact that the instrument

(a) is subject to implied or constructive conditions; or

(b) states its consideration, whether performed or promised, or the transaction which gave rise to the instrument, or that the promise or order is made or the instrument matures in accordance with or "as per" such transaction; or

(c) refers to or states that it arises out of a separate agreement or refers to a separate agreement for rights as to repayment or acceleration; or

(d) states that it is drawn under a letter of credit; or

(e) states that it is secured, whether by mortgage, reservation of title or otherwise; or

(f) indicates a particular account to be debited or any other fund or source from which reimbursement is expected; or

(g) is limited to payment out of a particular fund or the proceeds of a particular source, if the instrument is issued by a government or governmental agency or unit; or

(h) is limited to payment out of the entire assets of a partnership, unincorporated association, trust or estate by or on behalf of which the instrument is issued.

(2) A promise or order is not unconditional if the instrument

(a) states that it is subject to or governed by any other agreement; or

(b) states that it is to be paid only out of a particular fund or source except as provided in this section. As amended 1962.

### § 3–106. Sum Certain

(1) The sum payable is a sum certain even though it is to be paid

(a) with stated interest or by stated installments; or

(b) with stated different rates of interest before and after default or a specified date; or

(c) with a stated discount or addition if paid before or after the date fixed for payment; or

(d) with exchange or less exchange, whether at a fixed rate or at the current rate; or

(e) with costs of collection or an attorney's fee or both upon default.

(2) Nothing in this section shall validate any term which is otherwise illegal.

### § 3–107. Money

(1) An instrument is payable in money if the medium of exchange in which it is payable is money at the time the instrument is made. An instrument payable in "currency" or "current funds" is payable in money.

(2) A promise or order to pay a sum stated in a foreign currency is for a sum certain in money and, unless a different medium of payment is specified in the instrument, may be satisfied by payment of that number of dollars which the stated foreign currency will purchase at the buying sight rate for that currency on the day on which the instrument is payable or, if payable on demand, on the day of demand. If such an instrument specifies a

foreign currency as the medium of payment the instrument is payable in that currency.

### § 3–108. Payable on Demand

Instruments payable on demand include those payable at sight or on presentation and those in which no time for payment is stated.

### § 3–109. Definite Time

(1) An instrument is payable at a definite time if by its terms it is payable

(a) on or before a stated date or at a fixed period after a stated date; or

(b) at a fixed period after sight; or

(c) at a definite time subject to any acceleration; or

(d) at a definite time subject to extension at the option of the holder, or to extension to a further definite time at the option of the maker or acceptor or automatically upon or after a specified act or event.

(2) An instrument which by its terms is otherwise payable only upon an act or event uncertain as to time of occurrence is not payable at a definite time even though the act or event has occurred.

### § 3–110. Payable to Order

(1) An instrument is payable to order when by its terms it is payable to the order or assigns of any person therein specified with reasonable certainty, or to him or his order, or when it is conspicuously designated on its face as "exchange" or the like and names a payee. It may be payable to the order of

(a) the maker or drawer; or

(b) the drawee; or

(c) a payee who is not maker, drawer or drawee; or

(d) two or more payees together or in the alternative; or

(e) an estate, trust or fund, in which case it is payable to the order of the representative of such estate, trust or fund or his successors; or

(f) an office, or an officer by his title as such in which case it is payable to the principal but the incumbent of the office or his successors may act as if he or they were the holder; or

(g) a partnership or unincorporated association, in which case it is payable to the partnership or association and may be indorsed or transferred by any person thereto authorized.

(2) An instrument not payable to order is not made so payable by such words as "payable upon return of this instrument properly indorsed."

(3) An instrument made payable both to order and to bearer is payable to order unless the bearer words are handwritten or typewritten.

### § 3–111. Payable to Bearer

An instrument is payable to bearer when by its terms it is payable to

(a) a bearer or the order of bearer; or

(b) a specified person or bearer; or

(c) "cash" or the order of "cash" or any other indication which does not purport to designate a specific payee.

### § 3–112. Terms and Omissions Not Affecting Negotiability

(1) The negotiability of an instrument is not affected by

(a) the omission of a statement of any consideration or of the place where the instrument is drawn or payable; or

(b) a statement that collateral has been given to secure obligations either on the instrument or otherwise of an obligor on the instrument or that in case of default on those obligations the holder may realize on or dispose of the collateral; or

(c) a promise or power to maintain or protect collateral or to give additional collateral; or

(d) a term authorizing a confession of judgment on the instrument if it is not paid when due; or

(e) a term purporting to waive the benefit of any law intended for the advantage or protection of any obligor; or

(f) a term in a draft providing that the payee by indorsing or cashing it acknowledges full satisfaction of an obligation of the drawer; or

(g) a statement in a draft drawn in a set of parts (Section 3–801) to the effect that the order is effective only if no other part has been honored.

(2) Nothing in this section shall validate any term which is otherwise illegal.

### § 3–113. Seal

An instrument otherwise negotiable is within this Article even though it is under a seal.

### § 3–114. Date, Antedating, Postdating

(1) The negotiability of an instrument is not affected by the fact that it is undated, antedated or postdated.

(2) Where an instrument is antedated or postdated the time when it is payable is determined by the stated date if the instrument is payable on demand or at a fixed period after date.

(3) Where the instrument or any signature thereon is dated, the date is presumed to be correct.

### § 3–115. Incomplete Instruments

(1) When a paper whose contents at the time of signing show that it is intended to become an instrument is signed while still incomplete in any necessary respect it cannot be enforced until completed, but when it is completed in accordance with authority given it is effective as completed.

(2) If the completion is unauthorized the rules as to material alteration apply (Section 3–407), even though the paper was not delivered by the maker or drawer; but the burden of establishing that any completion is unauthorized is on the party so asserting.

### § 3–116. Instruments Payable to Two or More Persons

An instrument payable to the order of two or more persons

(a) if in the alternative is payable to any one of them and may be negotiated, discharged or enforced by any of them who has possession of it;

(b) if not in the alternative is payable to all of them and may be negotiated, discharged or enforced only by all of them.

### § 3–117. Instruments Payable With Words of Description

An instrument made payable to a named person with the addition of words describing him

(a) as agent or officer of a specified person is payable to his principal but the agent or officer may act as if he were the holder;

(b) as any other fiduciary for a specified person or purpose is payable to the payee and may be negotiated, discharged or enforced by him;

(c) in any other manner is payable to the payee unconditionally and the additional words are without effect on subsequent parties.

### § 3–118. Ambiguous Terms and Rules of Construction

The following rules apply to every instrument:

(a) Where there is doubt whether the instrument is a draft or a note that holder may treat it as either. A draft drawn on the drawer is effective as a note.

(b) Handwritten terms control typewritten and printed terms, and typewritten control printed.

(c) Words control figures except that if the words are ambiguous figures control.

(d) Unless otherwise specified a provision for interest means interest at the judgment rate at the place of payment from the date of the instrument, or if it is undated from the date of issue.

(e) Unless the instrument otherwise specifies two or more persons who sign as maker, acceptor or drawer or indorser and as a part of the same transaction are jointly and severally liable even though the instrument contains such words as "I promise to pay."

(f) Unless otherwise specified consent to extension authorizes a single extension for not longer than the original period. A consent to extension, expressed in the instrument, is binding on secondary parties and accommodation makers. A holder may not exercise his option to extend an instrument over the objection of a maker or acceptor or other party who in accordance with Section 3–604 tenders full payment when the instrument is due.

### § 3–119. Other Writings Affecting Instrument

(1) As between the obligor and his immediate obligee or any transferee the terms of an instrument may be modified or affected by any other written agreement executed as a part of the same transaction, except that a holder in due course is not affected by any limitation of his rights arising out of the separate written agreement if he had no notice of the limitation when he took the instrument.

(2) A separate agreement does not affect the negotiability of an instrument.

### § 3–120. Instruments "Payable Through" Bank

An instrument which states that it is "payable through" a bank or the like designates that bank as a collecting bank to make presentment but does not of itself authorize the bank to pay the instrument.

### § 3–121. Instruments Payable at Bank

**Note:** *If this Act is introduced in the Congress of the United States this section should be omitted. (States to select either alternative.)*

#### Alternative A

A note or acceptance which states that it is payable at a bank is the equivalent of a draft drawn on the bank payable when it falls due out of any funds of the maker or acceptor in current account or otherwise available for such payment.

#### Alternative B

A note or acceptance which states that it is payable at a bank is not of itself an order or authorization to the bank to pay it.

### § 3–122. Accrual of Cause of Action

(1) A cause of action against a maker or an acceptor accrues

(a) in the case of a time instrument on the day after maturity;

(b) in the case of a demand instrument upon its date or, if no date is stated, on the date of issue.

(2) A cause of action against the obligor of a demand or time certificate of deposit accrues upon demand, but demand on a time certificate may not be made until on or after the date of maturity.

(3) A cause of action against a drawer of a draft or an indorser of any instrument accrues upon demand following dishonor of the instrument. Notice of dishonor is a demand.

(4) Unless an instrument provides otherwise, interest runs at the rate provided by law for a judgment

(a) in the case of a maker, acceptor or other primary obligor of a demand instrument, from the date of demand;

(b) in all other cases from the date of accrual of the cause of action.

## Part 2 Transfer and Negotiation

### § 3–201. Transfer: Right to Indorsement

(1) Transfer of an instrument vests in the transferee such rights as the transferor has therein, except that a transferee who has himself been a party to any fraud or illegality affecting the instrument or who as a prior holder had notice of a defense or claim against it cannot improve his position by taking from a later holder in due course.

(2) A transfer of a security interest in an instrument vests the foregoing rights in the transferee to the extent of the interest transferred.

(3) Unless otherwise agreed any transfer for value of an instrument not then payable to bearer gives the transferee the specifically enforceable right to have the unqualified indorsement of the transferor. Negotiation takes effect only when the indorsement is made and until that time there is no presumption that the transferee is the owner.

### § 3–202. Negotiation

(1) Negotiation is the transfer of an instrument in such form that the transferee becomes a holder. If the instrument is payable to order it is negotiated by delivery with any necessary indorsement; if payable to bearer it is negotiated by delivery.

(2) An indorsement must be written by or on behalf of the holder and on the instrument or on a paper so firmly affixed thereto as to become a part thereof.

(3) An indorsement is effective for negotiation only when it conveys the entire instrument or any unpaid residue. If it purports to be of less it operates only as a partial assignment.

(4) Words of assignment, condition, waiver, guaranty, limitation or disclaimer of liability and the like accompanying an indorsement do not affect its character as an indorsement.

### § 3–203. Wrong or Misspelled Name

Where an instrument is made payable to a person under a misspelled name or one other than his own he may indorse in that name or his own or both; but signature in both names may be required by a person paying or giving value for the instrument.

### § 3–204. Special Indorsement; Blank Indorsement

(1) A special indorsement specifies the person to whom or to whose order it makes the instrument payable. Any instrument specially indorsed becomes payable to the order of the special in-

dorsee and may be further negotiated by his indorsement.

(2) An indorsement in blank specifies no particular indorsee and may consist of a mere signature. An instrument payable to order and indorsed in blank becomes payable to bearer and may be negotiated by delivery alone until specially indorsed.

(3) The holder may convert a blank indorsement into a special indorsement by writing over the signature of the indorser in blank any contract consistent with the character of the indorsement.

### § 3–205. Restrictive Indorsements

An indorsement is restrictive which either

(a) is conditional; or

(b) purports to prohibit further transfer of the instrument; or

(c) includes the words "for collection," "for deposit," "pay any bank," or like terms signifying a purpose of deposit or collection; or

(d) otherwise states that it is for the benefit or use of the indorser or of another person.

### § 3–206. Effect of Restrictive Indorsement

(1) No restrictive indorsement prevents further transfer or negotiation of the instrument.

(2) An intermediary bank, or a payor bank which is not the depositary bank, is neither given notice nor otherwise affected by a restrictive indorsement of any person except the bank's immediate transferor or the person presenting for payment.

(3) Except for an intermediary bank, any transferee under an indorsement which is conditional or includes the words "for collection," "for deposit," "pay any bank," or like terms (subparagraphs (a) and (c) of Section 3–205) must pay or apply any value given by him for or on security of the instrument consistently with the indorsement and to the extent that he does so he becomes a holder for value. In addition such transferee is a holder in due course if he otherwise complies with the requirements of Section 3–302 on what constitutes a holder in due course.

(4) The first taker under an indorsement for the benefit of the indorser or another person (subparagraph (d) of Section 3–205) must pay or apply any value given by him for or on the security of the instrument consistently with the indorsement and to the extent that he does so he becomes a holder for value. In addition such taker is a holder in due course if he otherwise complies with the requirements of Section 3–302 on what constitutes a holder in due course. A later holder for value is neither given notice nor otherwise affected by such restrictive indorsement unless he has knowledge that a fiduciary or other person has negotiated the instrument in any transaction for his own benefit or otherwise in breach of duty (subsection (2) of Section 3–304).

### § 3–207. Negotiation Effective Although It May Be Rescinded

(1) Negotiation is effective to transfer the instrument although the negotiation is

(a) made by an infant, a corporation exceeding its powers, or any other person without capacity; or

(b) obtained by fraud, duress or mistake of any kind; or

(c) part of an illegal transaction; or

(d) made in breach of duty.

(2) Except as against a subsequent holder in due course such negotiation is in an appropriate case subject to rescission, the declaration of a constructive trust or any other remedy permitted by law.

### § 3–208. Reacquisition

Where an instrument is returned to or reacquired by a prior party he may cancel any indorsement which is not necessary to his title and reissue or further negotiate the instrument, but any intervening party is discharged as against the reacquiring party and subsequent holders not in due course and if his indorsement has been cancelled is discharged as against subsequent holders in due course as well.

## Part 3 Rights of a Holder

### § 3–301. Rights of a Holder

The holder of an instrument whether or not he is the owner may transfer or negotiate it and, except as otherwise provided in Section 3–603 on payment or satisfaction, discharge it or enforce payment in his own name.

### § 3–302. Holder in Due course

(1) A holder in due course is a holder who takes the instrument

(a) for value, and

(b) in good faith; and

(c) without notice that it is overdue or has been dishonored or of any defense against or claim to it on the part of any person.

(2) A payee may be a holder in due course.

(3) A holder does not become a holder in due course of an instrument:

(a) by purchase of it at judicial sale or by taking it under legal process; or

(b) by acquiring it in taking over an estate; or

(c) by purchasing it as part of a bulk transaction not in regular course of business of the transferor.

(4) A purchaser of a limited interest can be a holder in due course only to the extent of the interest purchased.

### § 3–303. Taking for Value

A holder takes the instrument for value

(a) to the extent that the agreed consideration has been performed or that he acquires a security interest in or a lien on the instrument otherwise than by legal process; or

(b) when he takes the instrument in payment of or as security for an antecedent claim against any person whether or not the claim is due; or

(c) when he gives a negotiable instrument for it or makes an irrevocable commitment to a third person.

### § 3–304. Notice to Purchaser

(1) The purchaser has notice of a claim or defense if

(a) the instrument is so incomplete, bears such visible evidence of forgery or alteration, or is otherwise so irregular as to call into question its validity, terms or ownership or to create an ambiguity as to the party to pay; or

(b) the purchaser has notice that the obligation of any party is voidable in whole or in part, or that all parties have been discharged.

(2) The purchaser has notice of a claim against the instrument when he has knowledge that a fiduciary has negotiated the instrument in payment of or as security for his own debt or in any transaction for his own benefit or otherwise in breach of duty.

(3) The purchaser has notice that an instrument is overdue if he has reason to know

(a) that any part of the principal amount is overdue or that there is an uncured default in payment of another instrument of the same series; or

(b) that acceleration of the instrument has been made; or

(c) that he is taking a demand instrument after demand has been made or more than a reasonable length of time after its issue. A reasonable time for a check drawn and payable within the states and territories of the United States and the District of Columbia is presumed to be thirty days.

(4) Knowledge of the following facts does not of itself give the purchaser notice of a defense or claim

(a) that the instrument is antedated or postdated;

(b) that it was issued or negotiated in return for an executory promise or accompanied by a separate agreement, unless the purchaser has notice that a defense or claim has arisen from the terms thereof;

(c) that any party has signed for accommodation;

(d) that an incomplete instrument has been completed, unless the purchaser has notice of any improper completion;

(e) that any person negotiating the instrument is or was a fiduciary;

(f) that there has been default in payment of interest on the instrument or in payment of any other instrument, except one of the same series.

(5) The filing or recording of a document does not of itself constitute notice within the provisions of this Article to a person who would otherwise be a holder in due course.

(6) To be effective notice must be received at such time and in such manner as to give a reasonable opportunity to act on it.

### § 3–305. Rights of a Holder in Due Course

To the extent that a holder is a holder in due course he takes the instrument free from

(1) all claims to it on the part of any person; and

(2) all defenses of any party to the instrument with whom the holder has not dealt except

(a) infancy, to the extent that it is a defense to a simple contract; and

(b) such other incapacity, or duress, or illegality

of the transaction, as renders the obligation of the party a nullity; and

(c) such misrepresentation as has induced the party to sign the instrument with neither knowledge nor reasonable opportunity to obtain knowledge of its character or its essential terms; and

(d) discharge in solvency proceedings; and

(e) any other discharge of which the holder has notice when he takes the instrument.

### § 3–306. Rights of One Not Holder in Due Course

Unless he has the rights of a holder in due course any person takes the instrument subject to

(a) all valid claims to it on the part of any person; and

(b) all defenses of any party which would be available in an action on a simple contract; and

(c) the defenses of want or failure of consideration, non-performance of any condition precedent, non-delivery, or delivery for a special purpose (Section 3–408); and

(d) the defense that he or a person through whom he holds the instrument acquired it by theft, or that payment or satisfaction to such holder would be inconsistent with the terms of a restrictive indorsement. The claim of any third person to the instrument is not otherwise available as a defense to any party liable thereon unless the third person himself defends the action for such party.

### § 3–307. Burden of Establishing Signatures, Defenses and Due Course

(1) Unless specifically denied in the pleadings each signature on an instrument is admitted. When the effectiveness of a signature is put in issue

(a) the burden of establishing it is on the party claiming under the signature; but

(b) the signature is presumed to be genuine or authorized except where the action is to enforce the obligation of a purported signer who had died or become incompetent before proof is required.

(2) When signatures are admitted or established, production of the instrument entitles a holder to recover on it unless the defendant establishes a defense.

(3) After it is shown that a defense exists a person claiming the rights of a holder in due course has the burden of establishing that he or some person under whom he claims is in all respects a holder in due course.

## Part 4 Liability of Parties

### § 3–401. Signature

(1) No person is liable on an instrument unless his signature appears thereon.

(2) A signature is made by use of any name, including any trade or assumed name, upon an instrument, or by any word or mark used in lieu of a written signature.

### § 3–402. Signature in Ambiguous Capacity

Unless the instrument clearly indicates that a signature is made in some other capacity it is an indorsement.

### § 3–403. Signature by Authorized Representative

(1) A signature may be made by an agent or other representative, and his authority to make it may be established as in other cases of representation. No particular form of appointment is necessary to establish such authority.

(2) An authorized representative who signs his own name to an instrument

(a) is personally obligated if the instrument neither names the person represented nor shows that the representatives signed in a representative capacity;

(b) except as otherwise established between the immediate parties, is personally obligated if the instrument names the person represented but does not show that the representative signed in a representative capacity, or if the instrument does not name the person represented but does show that the representative signed in a representative capacity.

(3) Except as otherwise established the name of an organization preceded or followed by the name and office of an authorized individual is a signature made in a representative capacity.

### § 3–404. Unauthorized Signatures

(1) Any unauthorized signature is wholly inoperative as that of the person whose name is signed unless he ratifies it or is precluded from denying it; but it operates as the signature of the unauthor-

ized signer in favor of any person who in good faith pays the instrument or takes it for value.
(2) Any unauthorized signature may be ratified for all purposes of this Article. Such ratification does not of itself affect any rights of the person ratifying against the actual signer.

### § 3–405. Impostors; Signature in Name of Payee

(1) An indorsement by any person in the name of a named payee is effective if
(a) an imposter by use of the mails or otherwise has induced the maker or drawer to issue the instrument to him or his confederate in the name of the payee; or
(b) a person signing as or on behalf of a maker or drawer intends the payee to have no interest in the instrument; or
(c) an agent or employee of the maker or drawer has supplied him with the name of the payee intending the latter to have no such interest.
(2) Nothing in this section shall affect the criminal or civil liability of the person so indorsing.

### § 3–406. Negligence Contributing to Alteration or Unauthorized Signature

Any person who by his negligence substantially contributes to a material alteration of the instrument or to the making of an unauthorized signature is precluded from asserting the alteration or lack of authority against a holder in due course or against a drawee or other payor who pays the instrument in good faith and in accordance with the reasonable commercial standards of the drawee's or payor's business.

### § 3–407. Alteration

(1) Any alteration of an instrument is material which changes the contract of any party thereto in any respect, including any such change in
(a) the number or relations of the parties; or
(b) an incomplete instrument, by completing it otherwise than as authorized; or
(c) the writing as signed, by adding to it or by removing any part of it.
(2) As against any person other than a subsequent holder in due course.
(a) alteration by the holder which is both fraudulent and material discharges any party whose contract is thereby changed unless that party assents or is precluded from asserting the defense.
(b) no other alteration discharges any part and the instrument may be enforced according to its original tenor, or as to incomplete instruments according to the authority given.
(3) A subsequent holder in due course may in all cases enforce the instrument according to its original tenor, and when an incomplete instrument has been completed, he may enforce it as completed.

### § 3–408. Consideration

Want or failure of consideration is a defense as against any person not having the rights of a holder in due course (Section 3–305), except that no consideration is necessary for an instrument or obligation thereon given in payment of or as security for an antecedent obligation of any kind. Nothing in this section shall be taken to displace any statute outside this Act under which a promise is enforceable notwithstanding lack or failure of consideration. Partial failure of consideration is a defense pro tanto whether or not the failure is in an ascertained or liquidated amount.

### § 3–409. Draft Not an Assignment

(1) A check or other draft does not of itself operate as an assignment of any funds in the hands of the drawee available for its payment, and the drawee is not liable on the instrument until he accepts it.
(2) Nothing in this section shall affect any liability in contract, tort or otherwise arising from any letter of credit or other obligation or representation which is not an acceptance.

### § 3–410. Definition and Operation of Acceptance

(1) Acceptance is the drawee's signed engagement to honor the draft as presented. It must be written on the draft, and may consist of his signature alone. It becomes operative when completed by delivery or notification.
(2) A draft may be accepted although it has not been signed by the drawer or is otherwise incomplete or is overdue or has been dishonored.
(3) Where the draft is payable at a fixed period after sight and the acceptor fails to date his acceptance the holder may complete it by supplying a date in good faith.

**§ 3–411. Certification of a Check**

(1) Certification of a check is acceptance. Where a holder procures certification the drawer and all prior indorsers are discharged.
(2) Unless otherwise agreed a bank has no obligation to certify a check.
(3) A bank may certify a check before returning it for lack of proper indorsement. If it does so the drawer is discharged.

**§ 3–412. Acceptance Varying Draft**

(1) Where the drawee's proffered acceptance in any manner varies the draft as presented the holder may refuse the acceptance and treat the draft as dishonored in which case the drawee is entitled to have his acceptance cancelled.
(2) The terms of the draft are not varied by an acceptance to pay at any particular bank or place in the United States, unless the acceptance states that the draft is to be paid only at such bank or place.
(3) Where the holder assents to an acceptance varying the terms of the draft each drawer and indorser who does not affirmatively assent is discharged.

**§ 3–413. Contract of Maker, Drawer and Acceptor**

(1) The maker or acceptor engages that he will pay the instrument according to its tenor at the time of his engagement or as completed pursuant to Section 3–115 on incomplete instruments.
(2) The drawer engages that upon dishonor of the draft and any necessary notice of dishonor or protest he will pay the amount of the draft to the holder or to any indorser who takes it up. The drawer may disclaim this liability by drawing without recourse.
(3) By making, drawing or accepting the party admits as against all subsequent parties including the drawee the existence of the payee and his then capacity to indorse.

**§ 3–414. Contract of Indorser; Order of Liability**

(1) Unless the indorsement otherwise specifies (as by such words as "without recourse") every indorser engages that upon dishonor and any necessary notice of dishonor and protest he will pay the instrument according to its tenor at the time of his indorsement to the holder or to any subsequent indorser who takes it up, even though the indorser who takes it up was not obligated to do so.
(2) Unless they otherwise agree indorsers are liable to one another in the order in which they indorse, which is presumed to be the order in which their signatures appear on the instrument.

**§ 3–415. Contract of Accommodation Party**

(1) An accommodation party is one who signs the instrument in any capacity for the purpose of lending his name to another party to it.
(2) When the instrument has been taken for value before it is due the accommodation party is liable in the capacity in which he has signed even though the taker knows of the accommodation.
(3) As against a holder in due course and without notice of the accommodation oral proof of the accommodation is not admissible to give the accommodation party the benefit of discharges dependent on his character as such. In other cases the accommodation character may be shown by oral proof.
(4) An indorsement which shows that it is not in the chain of title is notice of its accommodation character.
(5) An accommodation party is not liable to the party accommodated, and if he pays the instrument has a right of recourse on the instrument against such party.

**§ 3–416. Contract of Guarantor**

(1) "Payment guaranteed" or equivalent words added to a signature mean that the signer engages that if the instrument is not paid when due he will pay it according to its tenor without resort by the holder to any other party.
(2) "Collection guaranteed" or equivalent words added to a signature mean that the signer engages that if the instrument is not paid when due he will pay it according to its tenor, but only after the holder has reduced his claim against the maker or acceptor to judgment and execution has been returned unsatisfied, or after the maker or acceptor has become insolvent or it is otherwise apparent that it is useless to proceed against him.
(3) Words of guaranty which do not otherwise specify guarantee payment.

(4) No words of guaranty added to the signature of a sole maker or acceptor affect his liability on the instrument. Such words added to the signature of one of two or more makers or acceptors create a presumption that the signature is for the accommodation of the others.

(5) When words of guaranty are used presentment, notice of dishonor and protest are not necessary to charge the user.

(6) Any guaranty written on the instrument is enforcible notwithstanding any statute of frauds.

### § 3–417. Warranties on Presentment and Transfer

(1) Any person who obtains payment or acceptance and any prior transferor warrants to a person who in good faith pays or accepts that

(a) he has a good title to the instrument or is authorized to obtain payment or acceptance on behalf of one who has a good title; and

(b) he has no knowledge that the signature of the maker or drawer is unauthorized, except that this warranty is not given by a holder in due course acting in good faith

(i) to a maker with respect to the maker's own signature; or

(ii) to a drawer with respect to the drawer's own signature, whether or not the drawer is also the drawee; or

(iii) to an acceptor of a draft if the holder in due course took the draft after the acceptance or obtained the acceptance without knowledge that the drawer's signature was unauthorized; and

(c) the instrument has not been materially altered, except that this warranty is not given by a holder in due course acting in good faith

(i) to the maker of a note; or

(ii) to the drawer of a draft whether or not the drawer is also the drawee; or

(iii) to the acceptor of a draft with respect to an alteration made prior to the acceptance if the holder in due course took the draft after the acceptance, even though the acceptance provided "payable as originally drawn" or equivalent terms; or

(iv) to the acceptor of a draft with respect to an alteration made after the acceptance.

(2) Any person who transfers an instrument and receives consideration warrants to his transferee and if the transfer is by indorsement to any subsequent holder who takes the instrument in good faith that

(a) he has a good title to the instrument or is authorized to obtain payment or acceptance on behalf of one who has a good title and the transfer is otherwise rightful; and

(b) all signatures are genuine or authorized; and

(c) the instrument has not been materially altered; and

(d) no defense of any party is good against him; and

(e) he has no knowledge of any insolvency proceeding instituted with respect to the maker or acceptor or the drawer of an unaccepted instrument.

(3) By transferring "without recourse" the transferor limits the obligation stated in subsection (2) (d) to a warranty that he has no knowledge of such a defense.

(4) A selling agent or broker who does not disclose the fact that he is acting only as such gives the warranties provided in this section, but if he makes such disclosure warrants only his good faith and authority.

### § 3–418. Finality of Payment or Acceptance

Except for recovery of bank payments as provided in the Article on Bank Deposits and Collections (Article 4) and except for liability for breach of warranty on presentment under the preceding section, payment or acceptance of any instrument is final in favor of a holder in due course, or a person who has in good faith changed his position in reliance on the payment.

### § 3–419. Conversion of Instrument; Innocent Representative

(1) An instrument is converted when

(a) a drawee to whom it is delivered for acceptance refuses to return it on demand; or

(b) any person to whom it is delivered for payment refuses on demand either to pay or to return it; or

(c) it is paid on a forged indorsement.

(2) In an action against a drawee under subsection (1) the measure of the drawee's liability is the face amount of the instrument. In any other action under subsection (1) the measure of liability

is presumed to be the face amount of the instrument.

(3) Subject to the provisions of this Act concerning restrictive indorsements a representative, including a depositary or collecting bank, who has in good faith and in accordance with the reasonable commercial standards applicable to the business of such representative dealt with an instrument or its proceeds on behalf of one who was not the true owner is not liable in conversion or otherwise to the true owner beyond the amount of any proceeds remaining in his hands.

(4) An intermediary bank or payor bank which is not a depositary bank is not liable in conversion solely by reason of the fact that proceeds of an item indorsed restrictively (Sections 3–205 and 3–206) are not paid or applied consistently with the restrictive indorsement of an indorser other than its immediate transferor.

## Part 5 Presentment, Notice of Dishonor and Protest

### § 3–501. When Presentment, Notice of Dishonor, and Protest Necessary or Permissible

(1) Unless excused (Section 3–511) presentment is necessary to charge secondary parties as follows:

(a) presentment for acceptance is necessary to charge the drawer and indorsers of a draft where the draft so provides, or is payable elsewhere than at the residence or place of business of the drawee, or its date of payment depends upon such presentment. The holder may at his option present for acceptance any other draft payable at a stated date:

(b) presentment for payment is necessary to charge any indorser;

(c) in the case of any drawer, the acceptor of a draft payable at a bank or the maker of a note payable at a bank, presentment for payment is necessary, but failure to make presentment discharges such drawer, acceptor or maker only as stated in Section 3-502(1) (b).

(2) Unless excused (Section 3–511)

(a) notice of any dishonor is necessary to charge any indorser:

(b) in the case of any drawer, the acceptor of a draft payable at a bank or the maker of a note payable at a bank, notice of any dishonor is necessary, but failure to give such notice discharges such drawer, acceptor or maker only as stated in Section 3–502(1) (b).

(3) Unless excused (Section 3–511) protest of any dishonor is necessary to charge the drawer and indorsers of any draft which on its face appears to be drawn or payable outside of the states, territories, dependencies and possessions of the United States, the District of Columbia and the Commonwealth of Puerto Rico. The holder may at his option make protest of any dishonor of any other instrument and in the case of a foreign draft may on insolvency of the acceptor before maturity make protest for better security.

(4) Notwithstanding any provision of this section, neither presentment nor notice of dishonor nor protest is necessary to charge an indorser who has indorsed an instrument after maturity.

### § 3–502. Unexcused Delay; Discharge

(1) Where without excuse any necessary presentment or notice of dishonor is delayed beyond the time when it is due

(a) any indorser is discharged; and

(b) any drawer or the acceptor of a draft payable at a bank or the maker of a note payable at a bank who because the drawee or payor bank becomes insolvent during the delay is deprived of funds maintained with the drawee or payor bank to cover the instrument may discharge his liability by written assignment to the holder of his rights against the drawee or payor bank in respect of such funds, but such drawer, acceptor or maker is not otherwise discharged.

(2) Where without excuse a necessary protest is delayed beyond the time when it is due any drawer or indorser is discharged.

### § 3–503. Time of Presentment

(1) Unless a different time is expressed in the instrument the time for any presentment is determined as follows:

(a) where an instrument is payable at or a fixed period after a stated date any presentment for acceptance must be made on or before the date it is payable;

(b) where an instrument is payable after sight it must either be presented for acceptance or negotiated within a reasonable time after date or issue whichever is later;

(c) where an instrument shows the date on which it is payable presentment for payment is due on that date;

(d) where an instrument is accelerated presentment for payment is due within a reasonable time after the acceleration;

(e) with respect to the liability of any secondary party presentment for acceptance or payment of any other instrument is due within a reasonable time after such party becomes liable thereon.

(2) A reasonable time for presentment is determined by the nature of the instrument, any usage of banking or trade and the facts of the particular case. In the case of an uncertified check which is drawn and payable within the United States and which is not a draft drawn by a bank the following are presumed to be reasonable periods within which to present for payment or to initiate bank collection:

(a) with respect to the liability of the drawer, thirty days after date or issue whichever is later; and

(b) with respect to the liability of an indorser, seven days after his indorsement.

(3) Where any presentment is due on a day which is not a full business day for either the person making presentment or the party to pay or accept, presentment is due on the next following day which is a full business day for both parties.

(4) Presentment to be sufficient must be made at a reasonable hour, and if at a bank during its banking day.

### § 3–504. How Presentment Made

(1) Presentment is a demand for acceptance or payment made upon the maker, acceptor, drawee or other payor by or on behalf of the holder.

(2) Presentment may be made

(a) by mail, in which event the time of presentment is determined by the time of receipt of the mail; or

(b) through a clearing house; or

(c) at the place of acceptance or payment specified in the instrument or if there be none at the place of business or residence of the party to accept or pay. If neither the party to accept or pay nor anyone authorized to act for him is present or accessible at such place presentment is excused.

(3) It may be made

(a) to any one of two or more makers, acceptors, drawees or other payors; or

(b) to any person who has authority to make or refuse the acceptance or payment.

(4) A draft accepted or a note made payable at a bank in the United States must be presented at such bank.

(5) In the cases described in Section 4–210 presentment may be made in the manner and with the result stated in that section.

### § 3–505. Rights of Party to Whom Present Is Made

(1) The party to whom presentment is made may without dishonor require

(a) exhibition of the instrument; and

(b) reasonable identification of the person making presentment and evidence of his authority to make it if made for another; and

(c) that the instrument be produced for acceptance or payment at a place specified in it, or if there be none at any place reasonable in the circumstances; and

(d) a signed receipt on the instrument for any partial or full payment and its surrender upon full payment.

(2) Failure to comply with any such requirement invalidates the presentment but the person presenting has a reasonable time in which to comply and the time for acceptance or payment runs from the time of compliance.

### § 3–506. Time Allowed for Acceptance or Payment

(1) Acceptance may be deferred without dishonor until the close of the next business day following presentment. The holder may also in a good faith effort to obtain acceptance and without either dishonor of the instrument or discharge of secondary parties allow postponement of acceptance for an additional business day.

(2) Except as a longer time is allowed in the case of documentary drafts drawn under a letter of credit, and unless an earlier time is agreed to by the party to pay, payment of an instrument may be deferred without dishonor pending reasonable examination to determine whether it is properly payable, but payment must be made in any event before the close of business on the day of presentment.

### § 3–507. Dishonor; Holder's Right of Recourse; Term Allowing Re-Presentment

(1) An instrument is dishonored when

(a) a necessary or optional presentment is duly made and due acceptance or payment is refused or cannot be obtained within the prescribed time or in case of bank collections the instrument is seasonably returned by the midnight deadline (Section 4–301); or

(b) presentment is excused and the instrument is not duly accepted or paid.

(2) Subject to any necessary notice of dishonor and protest, the holder has upon dishonor an immediate right of recourse against the drawers and indorsers.

(3) Return of an instrument for lack of proper indorsement is not dishonor.

(4) A term in a draft or an indorsement thereof allowing a stated time for re-presentment in the event of any dishonor of the draft by nonacceptance if a time draft or by nonpayment if a sight draft gives the holder as against any secondary party bound by the term an option to waive the dishonor without affecting liability of the secondary party and he may present again up to the end of the stated time.

### § 3–508. Notice of Dishonor

(1) Notice of dishonor may be given to any person who may be liable on the instrument by or on behalf of the holder or any party who has himself received notice, or any other party who can be compelled to pay the instrument. In addition an agent or bank in whose hands the instrument is dishonored may give notice to his principal or customer or to another agent or bank from which the instrument was received.

(2) Any necessary notice must be given by a bank before its midnight deadline and by any other person before midnight of the third business day after dishonor or receipt of notice of dishonor.

(3) Notice may be given in any reasonable manner. It may be oral or written and in any terms which identify the instrument and state that it has been dishonored. A misdescription which does not mislead the party notified does not vitiate the notice. Sending the instrument bearing a stamp, ticket or writing stating that acceptance or payment has been refused or sending a notice of debit with respect to the instrument is sufficient.

(4) Written notice is given when sent although it is not received.

(5) Notice to one partner is notice to each although the firm has been dissolved.

(6) When any part is in insolvency proceedings instituted after the issue of the instrument notice may be given either to the party or to the representative of his estate.

(7) When any party is dead or incompetent notice may be sent to his last known address or given to his personal representative.

(8) Notice operates for the benefit of all parties who have rights on the instrument against the party notified.

### § 3–509. Protest; Noting for Protest

(1) A protest is a certificate of dishonor made under the hand and seal of a United States consul or vice consul or a notary public or other person authorized to certify dishonor by the law of the place where dishonor occurs. It may be made upon information satisfactory to such person.

(2) The protest must identify the instrument and certify either that due presentment has been made or the reason why it is excused and that the instrument has been dishonored by nonacceptance or nonpayment.

(3) The protest may also certify that notice of dishonor has been given to all parties or to specified parties.

(4) Subject to subsection (5) any necessary protest is due by the time that notice of dishonor is due.

(5) If, before protest is due, an instrument has been noted for protest by the officer to make protest, the protest may be made at any time thereafter as of the date of the noting.

### § 3–510. Evidence of Dishonor and Notice of Dishonor

The following are admissible as evidence and create a presumption of dishonor and of any notice of dishonor therein shown:

(a) a document regular in form as provided in the preceding section which purports to be a protest;

(b) the purported stamp or writing of the drawee, payor bank or presenting bank on the instrument of accompanying it stating that acceptance or payment has been refused for reasons consistent with dishonor;

(c) any book or record of the drawee, payor bank, or any collecting bank kept in the usual course of business which shows dishonor, even though there is no evidence of who made the entry.

### § 3–511. Waived or Excused Presentment, Protest or Notice of Dishonor or Delay Therein

(1) Delay in presentment, protest or notice of dishonor is excused when the party is without notice that it is due or when the delay is caused by circumstances beyond his control and he exercises reasonable diligence after the cause of the delay ceases to operate.

(2) Presentment or notice or protest as the case may be is entirely excused when

(a) the party to be charged has waived it expressly or by implication either before or after it is due; or

(b) such party has himself dishonored instrument or has countermanded payment or otherwise has no reason to expect or right to require that the instrument be accepted or paid; or

(c) by reasonable diligence the presentment or protest cannot be made or the notice given.

(3) Presentment is also entirely excused when

(a) the maker, acceptor, or drawee of any instrument except a documentary draft is dead or in insolvency proceedings instituted after the issue of the instrument; or

(b) acceptance or payment is refused but not for want of proper presentment.

(4) Where a draft has been dishonored by nonacceptance a later presentment for payment and any notice of dishonor and protest for nonpayment are excused unless in the meantime the instrument has been accepted.

(5) A waiver of protest is also a waiver of presentment and of notice of dishonor even though protest is not required.

(6) Where a waiver of presentment or notice or protest is embodied in the instrument itself it is binding upon all parties; but where it is written above the signature of an indorser it binds him only.

## Part 6 Discharge

### § 3–601. Discharge of Parties

(1) The extent of the discharge of any party from liability on an instrument is governed by the sections on

(a) payment or satisfaction (Section 3–603); or

(b) tender of payment (Section 3–604); or

(c) cancellation or renunciation (Section 3–605); or

(d) impairment of right of recourse or of collateral (Section 3–606); or

(e) reacquisition of the instrument by a prior party (Section 3–208); or

(f) fraudulent and material alteration (Section 3–407); or

(g) certification of a check (Section 3–411); or

(h) acceptance varying a draft (Section 3–412); or

(i) unexcused delay in presentment or notice of dishonor or protest (Section 3–502).

(2) Any party is also discharged from his liability on an instrument to another party by any other act or agreement with such party which would discharge his simple contract for the payment of money.

(3) The liability of all parties is discharged when any party who has himself no right of action or recourse on the instrument

(a) reacquires the instrument in his own right; or

(b) is discharged under any provision of this Article, except as otherwise provided with respect to discharge for impairment of recourse or of collateral (Section 3–606).

### § 3–602. Effect of Discharge Against Holder in Due Course

No discharge of any party provided by this Article is effective against a subsequent holder in due course unless he has notice thereof when he takes the instrument.

### § 3–603. Payment or Satisfaction

(1) The liability of any party is discharged to the extent of his payment or satisfaction to the holder even though it is made with knowledge of a claim of another person to the instrument unless prior to such payment or satisfaction the person making the claim either supplies indemnity deemed adequate by the party seeking the discharge or enjoins payment or satisfaction by order of a court of competent jurisdiction in an action in which the ad-

verse claimant and the holder are parties. This subsection does not, however, result in the discharge of the liability

(a) of a party who in bad faith pays or satisfies a holder who acquired the instrument by theft or who (unless having the rights of a holder in due course) holds through one who so acquired it; or

(b) of a party (other than an intermediary bank or aa payor bank which is not a depositary bank) who pays or satisfies the holder of an instrument which has been restrictively indorsed in a manner not consistent with the terms of such restrictive indorsement.

(2) Payment or satisfaction may be made with the consent of the holder by any person including a stranger to the instrument. Surrender of the instrument to such a person gives him the rights of a transferee (Section 3–201).

### § 3–604. Tender of Payment

(1) Any party making tender of full payment to a holder when or after it is due is discharged to the extent of all subsequent liability for interest, costs and attorney's fees.

(2) The holder's refusal of such tender wholly discharges any party who has a right of recourse against the party making the tender.

(3) Where the maker or acceptor of an instrument payable otherwise than on demand is able and ready to pay at every place of payment specified in the instrument when it is due, it is equivalent to tender.

### § 3–605. Cancellation and Renunciation

(1) The holder of an instrument may even without consideration discharge any party

(a) in any manner apparent on the face of the instrument or the indorsement, as by intentionally cancelling the instrument or the party's signature by destruction or mutilation, or by striking out the party's signature; or

(b) by renouncing his rights by a writing signed and delivered or by surrender of the instrument to the party to be discharged.

(2) Neither cancellation nor renunciation without surrender of the instrument affects the title thereto.

### § 3–606. Impairment of Recourse or of Collateral

(1) The holder discharges any party to the instrument to the extent that without such party's consent the holder

(a) without express reservation of rights releases or agrees not to sue any person against whom the party has to the knowledge of the holder a right of recourse or agrees to suspend the right to enforce against such person the instrument or collateral or otherwise discharges such person, except that failure or delay in effecting any required presentment, protest or notice of dishonor with respect to any such person does not discharge any party as to whom presentment, protest or notice of dishonor is effective or unnecessary; or

(b) unjustifiably impairs any collateral for the instrument given by or on behalf of the party or any person against whom he has a right of recourse.

(2) By express reservation of rights against a party with a right of recourse the holder preserves

(a) all his rights against such party as of the time when the instrument was originally due; and

(b) the right of the party to pay the instrument as of that time; and

(c) all rights of such party to recourse against others.

## Part 7 Advice of International Sight Draft

### § 3–701. Letter of Advice of International Sight Draft

(1) A "letter of advice" is a drawer's communication to the drawee that a described draft has been drawn.

(2) Unless otherwise agreed when a bank receives from another bank a letter of advice of an international sight draft the drawee bank may immediately debit the drawer's account and stop the running of interest pro tanto. Such a debit and any resulting credit to any account covering outstanding drafts leaves in the drawer full power to stop payment or otherwise dispose of the amount and creates no trust or interest in favor of the holder.

(3) Unless otherwise agreed and except where a draft is drawn under a credit issued by the drawee, the drawee of an international sight draft owes

the drawer no duty to pay an unadvised draft but if it does so and the draft is genuine, may appropriately debit the drawer's account.

## Part 8 Miscellaneous

### § 3–801. Drafts in a Set

(1) Where a draft is drawn in a set of parts, each of which is numbered and expressed to be an order only if no other part has been honored, the whole of the parts constitutes one draft but a taker of any part may become a holder in due course of the draft.

(2) Any person who negotiates, indorses or accepts a single part of a draft drawn in a set thereby becomes liable to any holder in due course of that part as if it were the whole set, but as between different holders in due course to whom different parts have been negotiated the holder whose title first accrues has all rights to the draft and its proceeds.

(3) As against the drawee the first presented part of a draft drawn in a set is the part entitled to payment, or if a time draft to acceptance and payment. Acceptance of any subsequently presented part renders the drawee liable thereon under subsection (2). With respect both to a holder and to the drawer payment of a subsequently presented part of a draft payable at sight has the same effect as payment of a check notwithstanding an effective stop order (Section 4–407).

(4) Except as otherwise provided in this section, where any part of a draft in a set is discharged by payment or otherwise the whole draft is discharged.

### § 3–802. Effect of Instrument on Obligation for Which It Is Given

(1) Unless otherwise agreed where an instrument is taken for an underlying obligation

(a) the obligation is pro tanto discharged if a bank is drawer, maker or acceptor of the instrument and there is no recourse on the instrument against the underlying obligor; and

(b) in any other case the obligation is suspended pro tanto until the instrument is due or if it is payable on demand until its presentment. If the instrument is dishonored action may be maintained on either the instrument or the obligation; discharge of the underlying obligor on the instrument also discharges him on the obligation.

(2) The taking in good faith of a check which is not postdated does not of itself so extend the time on the original obligation as to discharge a surety.

### § 3–803. Notice to Third Party

Where a defendant is sued for breach of an obligation for which a third person is answerable over under this Article he may give the third person written notice of the litigation, and the person notified may then give similar notice to any other person who is answerable over to him under this Article. If the notice states that the person notified may come in and defend and that if the person notified does not do so he will in any action against him by the person giving the notice be bound by any determination of fact common to the two litigations, then unless after seasonable receipt of the notice the person notified does come in and defend he is so bound.

### § 3–804. Lost, Destroyed or Stolen Instruments

The owner of an instrument which is lost, whether by destruction, theft or otherwise, may maintain an action in his own name and recover from any party liable thereon upon due proof of his ownership, the facts which prevent his production of the instrument and its terms. The court may require security indemnifying the defendant against loss by reason of further claims on the instrument.

### § 3–805. Instruments Not Payable to Order or to Bearer

This Article applies to any instrument whose terms do not preclude transfer and which is otherwise negotiable within this Article but which is not payable to order or to bearer, except that there can be no holder in due course of such an instrument.

# ARTICLE 4 BANK DEPOSITS AND COLLECTIONS

## Part 1 General Provisions and Definitions

### § 4–101. Short Title

This Article shall be known and may be cited as Uniform Commercial Code—Bank Deposits and Collections.

### § 4–102. Applicability

(1) To the extent that items within this Article are also within the scope of Articles 3 and 8, they are subject to the provisions of those Articles. In the event of conflict the provisions of this Article govern those of Article 3 but the provisions of Article 8 govern those of this Article.

(2) The liability of a bank for action or non-action with respect to any item handled by it for purposes of presentment, payment or collection is governed by the law of the place where the bank is located. In the case of action or non-action by or at a branch or separate office of a bank, its liability is governed by the law of the place where the branch or separate office is located.

### § 4–103. Variation by Agreement; Measure of Damages; Certain Action Constituting Ordinary Care

(1) The effect of the provisions of this Article may be varied by agreement except that no agreement can disclaim a bank's responsibility for its own lack of good faith or failure to exercise ordinary care or can limit the measure of damages for such lack of failure; but the parties may by agreement determine the standards by which such responsibility is to be measured if such standards are not manifestly unreasonable.

(2) Federal Reserve regulations and operating letters, clearing house rules, and the like, have the effect of agreements under subsection (1), whether or not specifically assented to by all parties interested in items handled.

(3) Action or non-action approved by this Article or pursuant to Federal Reserve regulations or operating letters constitutes the exercise of ordinary care and, in the absence of special instructions, action or non-action consistent with clearing house rules and the like or with a general banking usage not disapproved by this Article, prima facie constitutes the exercise of ordinary care.

(4) The specification or approval of certain procedures by this Article does not constitute disapproval of other procedures which may be reasonable under the circumstances.

(5) The measure of damages for failure to exercise ordinary care in handling an item is the amount of the item reduced by an amount which could not have been realized by the use of ordinary care, and where there is bad faith it includes other damages, if any, suffered by the party as a proximate consequence.

### § 4–104. Definitions and Index of Definitions

(1) In this Article unless the context otherwise requires

(a) "Account" means any account with a bank and includes a checking, time, interest or savings account;

(b) "Afternoon" means the period of a day between noon and midnight;

(c) "Banking day" means that part of any day on which a bank is open to the public for carrying on substantially all of its banking functions;

(d) "Clearing house" means any association of banks or other payor regularly clearing items;

(e) "Customer" means any person having an account with a bank or for whom a bank has agreed to collect items and includes a bank carrying an account with another bank;

(f) "Documentary draft" means any negotiable or non-negotiable draft with accompanying documents, securities or other papers to be delivered against honor of the draft;

(g) "Item" means any instrument for the payment of money even though it is not negotiable but does not include money;

(h) "Midnight deadline" with respect to a bank is midnight on its next banking day following the banking day on which it receives the relevant item or notice or from which the time for taking action commences to run, whichever is later;

(i) "Properly payable" includes the availability of funds for payment at the time of decision to pay or dishonor;

(j) "Settle" means to pay in cash, by clearing house settlement, in a charge or credit or by remittance, or otherwise as instructed. A settlement may be either provisional or final;

(k) "Suspends payments" with respect to a bank means that it has been closed by order of the supervisory authorities, that a public officer has been appointed to take it over or that it ceases or refuses to make payments in the ordinary course of business.

(2) Other definitions applying to this Article and the sections in which they appear are:

"Collecting bank." Section 4–105.
"Depositary bank." Section 4–105.
"Intermediary bank." Section 4–105.

"Payor bank." Section 4–105.
"Presenting bank." Section 4–105.
"Remitting bank." Section 4–105.

(3) The following definitions in other Articles apply to this Article:
"Acceptance." Section 3–410.
"Certificate of deposit." Section 3–104.
"Certification." Section 3–411.
"Check." Section 3–104.
"Draft." Section 3–104.
"Holder in due course." Section 3–302.
"Notice of dishonor." Section 3–508.
"Presentment." Section 3–504.
"Protest." Section 3–509.
"Secondary party." Section 3–102.

(4) In addition Article 1 contains general definitions and principles of construction and interpretation applicable throughout this Article.

### § 4–105. "Depository Bank"; "Intermediary Bank"; "Collecting Bank"; "Payor Bank"; "Presenting Bank"; "Remitting Bank"

In this Article unless the context otherwise requires:

(a) "Depositary bank" means the first bank to which an item is transferred for collection even though it is also the payor bank;

(b) "Payor bank" means a bank by which an item is payable as drawn or accepted;

(c) "Intermediary bank" means any bank to which an item is transferred in course of collection except the depositary or payor bank;

(d) "Collecting bank" means any bank handling the item for collection except the payor bank;

(e) "Presenting bank" means any bank presenting an item except a payor bank;

(f) "Remitting bank" means any payor or intermediary bank remitting for an item.

### § 4–106. Separate Office of a Bank

A branch or separate office of a bank [maintaining its own deposit ledgers] is a separate bank for the purpose of computing the time within which and determining the place at or to which action may be taken or notices or orders shall be given under this Article and under Article 3.

**Note:** *The brackets are to make it optional with the several states whether to require a branch to maintain its own deposit ledgers in order to be considered to be a separate bank for certain purposes under Article 4. In some states "maintaining its own deposit ledgers" is a satisfactory test. In others branch banking practices are such that this test would not be suitable.*

### § 4–107. Time of Receipt of Items

(1) For the purpose of allowing time to process items, prove balances and make the necessary entries on its books to determine its position for the day, a bank may fix an afternoon hour of 2 P.M. or later as a cut-off hour for the handling of money and items and the making of entries on its books.

(2) Any item or deposit of money received on any day after a cut-off hour so fixed or after the close of the banking day may be treated as being received at the opening of the next banking day.

### § 4–108. Delays

(1) Unless otherwise instructed, a collecting bank in a good faith effort to secure payment may, in the case of specific items and with or without the approval of any person involved, waive, modify or extend time limits imposed or permitted by this Act for a period not in excess of an additional banking day without discharge of secondary parties and without liability to its transferor or any prior party.

(2) Delay by a collecting bank or payor bank beyond time limits prescribed or permitted by this Act or by instructions is excused if caused by interruption of communication facilities, suspension of payments by another bank, war, emergency conditions or other circumstances beyond the control of the bank provided it exercises such diligence as the circumstances require.

### § 4–109. Process of Posting

The "process of posting" means the usual procedure followed by a payor bank in determining to pay an item and in recording the payment including one or more of the following or other steps as determined by the bank:

(a) verification of any signature;

(b) ascertaining that sufficient funds are available;

(c) affixing a "paid" or other stamp;

(d) entering a charge or entry to a customer's account;

(e) correcting or reversing an entry or erroneous action with respect to the item.

## Part 2 Collection of Items: Depositary and Collecting Banks

### § 4–201. Presumption and Duration of Agency Status of Collecting Banks and Provisional Status of Credits; Applicability of Article; Item Indorsed "Pay Any Bank"

(1) Unless a contrary intent clearly appears and prior to the time that a settlement given by a collecting bank for an item is or becomes final (subsection (3) of Section 4–211 and Sections 4–212 and 4–213) the bank is an agent or sub-agent of the owner of the item and any settlement given for the item is provisional. This provision applies regardless of the form of indorsement or lack of indorsement and even though credit given for the item is subject to immediate withdrawal as of right or is in fact withdrawn; but the continuance of ownership of an item by its owner and any rights of the owner to proceeds of the item are subject to rights of a collecting bank such as those resulting from outstanding advances on the item and valid rights of set-off. When an item is handled by banks for purposes of presentment, payment and collection, the relevant provisions of this Article apply even though action of parties clearly establishes that a particular bank has purchased the item and is the owner of it.

(2) After an item has been indorsed with the words "pay any bank" or the like, only a bank may acquire the rights of a holder

(a) until the item has been returned to the customer initiating collection; or

(b) until the item has been specially indorsed by a bank to a person who is not a bank.

### § 4–202. Responsibility for Collection; When Action Seasonable

(1) A collecting bank must use ordinary care in

(a) presenting an item or sending it for presentment; and

(b) sending notice of dishonor or non-payment or returning an item other than a documentary draft to the bank's transferor [or directly to the depositary bank under subsection (2) of Section 4–212] *(See note to Section 4–212)* after learning that the item has not been paid or accepted, as the case may be; and

(c) settling for an item when the bank receives final settlement; and

(d) making or providing for any necessary protest; and

(e) notifying its transferor of any loss or delay in transit within a reasonable time after discovery thereof.

(2) A collecting bank taking proper action before its midnight deadline following receipt of an item, notice or payment acts seasonably; taking proper action within a reasonably longer time may be seasonable but the bank has the burden of so establishing.

(3) Subject to subsection (1)(a), a bank is not liable for the insolvency, neglect, misconduct, mistake or default of another bank or person or for loss or destruction of an item in transit or in the possession of others.

### § 4–203. Effect of Instructions

Subject to the provisions of Article 3 concerning conversion of instruments (Section 3–419) and the provisions of both Article 3 and this Article concerning restrictive indorsements only a collecting bank's transferor can give instructions which affect the bank or constitute notice to it and a collecting bank is not liable to prior parties for any action taken pursuant to such instructions or in accordance with any agreement with its transferor.

### § 4–204. Methods of Sending and Presenting; Sending Direct to Payor Bank

(1) A collecting bank must send items by reasonably prompt method taking into consideration any relevant instructions, the nature of the item, the number of such items on hand, and the cost of collection involved and the method generally used by it or others to present such items.

(2) A collecting bank may send

(a) any item direct to the payor bank;

(b) any item to any non-bank payor if authorized by its transferor; and

(c) any item other than documentary drafts to any non-bank payor, if authorized by Federal Reserve regulation or operating letter, clearing house rule or the like.

(3) Presentment may be made by a presenting bank at a place where the payor bank has requested that presentment be made.

### § 4–205. Supplying Missing Indorsement; No Notice from Prior Indorsement

(1) A depositary bank which has taken an item for collection may supply any indorsement of the customer which is necessary to title unless the item contains the words "payee's indorsement required" or the like. In the absence of such a requirement a statement placed on the item by the depositary bank to the effect that the item was deposited by a customer or credited to his account is effective as the customer's indorsement.

(2) An intermeditary bank, or payor bank which is not a depositary bank, is neither given notice nor otherwise affected by a restrictive indorsement of any person except the bank's immediate transferor.

### § 4–206. Transfer Between Banks

Any agreed method which identifies the transferor bank is sufficient for the item's further transfer to another bank.

### § 4–207. Warranties of Customer and Collecting Bank on Transfer or Presentment of Items; Time for Claims

(1) Each customer or collecting bank who obtains payment or acceptance of an item and each prior customer and collecting bank warrants to the payor bank or other payor who in good faith pays or accepts the item that

(a) he has a good title to the item or is authorized to obtain payment or acceptance on behalf of one who has a good title; and

(b) he had no knowledge that the signature of the maker or drawer is unauthorized, except that this warranty is not given by any customer or collecting bank that is a holder in due course and acts in good faith

(i) to a maker with respect to the maker's own signature; or

(ii) to a drawer with respect to the drawer's own signature, whether or not the drawer is also the drawee; or

(iii) to an acceptor of an item if the holder in due course took the item after the acceptance or obtained the acceptance without knowledge that the drawer's signature was unauthorized; and

(c) the item has not been materially altered, except that this warranty is not given by any customer or collecting bank that is a holder in due course and acts in good faith

(i) to the maker of a note; or

(ii) to the drawer of a draft whether or not the drawer is also the drawee; or

(iii) to the acceptor of an item with respect to an alteration made prior to the acceptance if the holder in due course took the item after the acceptance, even though the acceptance provided "payable as originally drawn" or equivalent terms; or

(iv) to the acceptor of an item with respect to an alteration made after the acceptance.

(2) Each customer and collecting bank who transfers an item and receives a settlement or other consideration for it warrants to his transferee and to any subsequent collecting bank who takes the item in good faith that

(a) he has a good title to the item or is authorized to obtain payment or acceptance on behalf of one who has a good title and the transfer is otherwise rightful; and

(b) all signatures are genuine or authorized; and

(c) the item has not been materially altered; and

(d) no defense of any party is good against him; and

(e) he has no knowledge of any insolvency proceeding instituted with respect to the maker or acceptor or the drawer of an unaccepted item.

In addition each customer and collecting bank so transferring an item and receiving a settlement or other consideration engages that upon dishonor and any necessary notice of dishonor and protest he will take up the item.

(3) The warranties and the engagement to honor set forth in the two preceding subsections arise notwithstanding the absence of indorsement or words of guaranty or warranty in the transfer or

presentment and a collecting bank remains liable for their breach despite remittance to its transferor. Damages for breach of such warranties or engagement to honor shall not exceed the consideration received by the customer or collecting bank responsible plus finance charges and expenses related to the item, if any.

(4) Unless a claim for breach of warranty under this section is made within a reasonable time after the person claiming learns of the breach, the person liable is discharged to the extent of any loss caused by the delay in making claim.

### § 4–208. Security Interest of Collecting Bank in Items, Accompanying Documents and Proceeds

(1) A bank has a security interest in an item and any accompanying documents or the proceeds of either

(a) in case of an item deposited in an account to the extent to which credit given for the item has been withdrawn or applied;

(b) in case of an item for which it has given credit available for withdrawal as of right, to the extent of the credit given whether or not the credit is drawn upon and whether or not there is a right of charge-back; or

(c) if it makes an advance on or against the item.

(2) When credit which has been given for several items received at one time or pursuant to a single agreement is withdrawn or applied in part the security interest remains upon all the items, any accompanying documents or the proceeds of either. For the purpose of this section, credits first given are first withdrawn.

(3) Receipt by a collecting bank of a final settlement for an item is a realization on its security interest in the item, accompanying documents and proceeds. To the extent and so long as the bank does not receive final settlement for the item or give up possession of the item or accompanying documents for purposes other than collection, the security interest continues and is subject to the provisions of Article 9 except that

(a) no security agreement is necessary to make the security interest enforceable (subsection (1) (a) of Section 9–203); and

(b) no filing is required to perfect the security interest; and

(c) the security interest has priority over conflicting perfected security interests in the item, accompanying documents or proceeds.

### § 4–209. When Bank Gives Value for Purposes of Holder in Due Course

For purposes of determining its status as a holder in due course, the bank has given value to the extent that it has a security interest in an item provided that the bank otherwise complies with the requirements of Section 3–302 on what constitutes a holder in due course.

### § 4–210. Presentment by Notice of Item Not Payable by, through or at a Bank; Liability of Secondary Parties

(1) Unless otherwise instructed, a collecting bank may present an item not payable by, through or at a bank by sending to the party to accept or pay a written notice that the bank holds the item for acceptance or payment. The notice must be sent in time to be received on or before the day when presentment is due and the bank must meet any requirement of the party to accept or pay under Section 3–505 by the close of the bank's next banking day after it knows of the requirement.

(2) Where presentment is made by notice and neither honor nor request for compliance with a requirement under Section 3–505 is received by the close of business on the day after maturity or in the case of demand items by the close of business on the third banking day after notice was sent, the presenting bank may treat the item as dishonored and charge any secondary party by sending him notice of the facts.

### § 4–211. Media of Remittance; Provisional and Final Settlement in Remittance Cases

(1) A collecting bank may take in settlement of an item

(a) a check of the remitting bank or of another bank on any bank except the remitting bank; or

(b) a cashier's check or similar primary obligation of a remitting bank which is a member of or clears through a member of the same clearing house or group as the collecting bank; or

(c) appropriate authority to charge an account of the remitting bank or of another bank with the collecting bank; or

(d) if the item is drawn upon or payable by a person other than a bank, a cashier's check, certified check or other bank check or obligation.

(2) If before its midnight deadline the collecting bank properly dishonors a remittance check or authorization to charge on itself or presents or forwards for collection a remittance instrument of or on another bank which is of a kind approved by subsection (1) or has not been authorized by it, the collecting bank is not liable to prior parties in the event of the dishonor of such check, instrument or authorization.

(3) A settlement for an item by means of a remittance instrument or authorization to charge is or becomes a final settlement as to both the person making and the person receiving the settlement

(a) if the remittance instrument or authorization to charge is of a kind approved by subsection (1) or has not been authorized by the person receiving the settlement and in either case the person receiving the settlement acts seasonably before its midnight deadline in presenting, forwarding for collection or paying the instrument or authorization,—at the time the remittance instrument or authorization is finally paid by the payor by which it is payable;

(b) if the person receiving the settlement has authorized remittance by a non-bank check or obligation or by a cashier's check or similar primary obligation of or a check upon the payor or other remitting bank which is not of a kind approved by subsection (1) (b),—at the time of the receipt of such remittance check or obligation; or

(c) if in a case not covered by sub-paragraphs (a) or (b) the person receiving the settlement fails to seasonably present, forward for collection, pay or return a remittance instrument or authorization to it to charge before its midnight deadline,—at such midnight deadline.

### § 4–212. Right of Charge-Back or Refund

(1) If a collecting bank has made provisional settlement with its customer for an item and itself fails by reason of dishonor, suspension of payments by a bank or otherwise to receive a settlement for the item which is or becomes final, the bank may revoke the settlement given by it, charge back the amount of any credit given for the item to its customers' account or obtain refund from its customer whether or not it is able to return the items if by its midnight deadline or within a longer reasonable time after it learns the facts it returns the item or sends notification of the facts. These rights to revoke, charge-back and obtain refund terminate if and when a settlement for the item received by the bank is or becomes final (subsection (3) of Section 4–211 and subsections (2) and (3) of Section 4–213).

[(2) Within the time and manner prescribed by this section and Section 4–301, an intermediary or payor bank, as the case may be, may return an unpaid item directly to the depositary bank and may send for collection a draft on the depositary bank and obtain reimbursement. In such case, if the depositary bank has received provisional settlement for the item, it must reimburse the bank drawing the draft and any provisional credits for the item between banks shall become and remain final.]

**Note:** *Direct returns is recognized as an innovation that is not yet established bank practice, and therefore, Paragraph 2 has been bracketed. Some lawyers have doubts whether it should be included in legislation or left to development by agreement.*

(3) A depositary bank which is also the payor may charge-back the amount of an item to its customer's account or obtain refund in accordance with the section governing return of an item received by a payor bank for credit on its books (Section 4–301).

(4) The right to charge-back is not affected by

(a) prior use of the credit given for the item; or

(b) failure by any bank to exercise ordinary care with respect to the item but any bank so failing remains liable.

(5) A failure to charge-back or claim refund does not affect other rights of the bank against the customer or any other party.

(6) If credit is given in dollars as the equivalent of the value of an item payable in a foreign currency the dollar amount of any charge-back or refund shall be calculated on the basis of the buying sight rate for the foreign currency prevailing on

the day when the person entitled to the charge-back or refund learns that it will not receive payment in ordinary course.

### § 4–213. Final Payment of Item by Payor Bank; When Provisional Debits and Credits Become Final; When Certain Credits Become Available for Withdrawal

(1) An item is finally paid by a payor bank when the bank has done any of the following, whichever happens first:

(a) paid the item in cash; or

(b) settled for the item without reserving a right to revoke the settlement and without having such right under statute, clearing house rule or agreement; or

(c) completed the process of posting the item to the indicated account of the drawer, maker or other person to be charged therewith; or

(d) made a provisional settlement for the item and failed to revoke the settlement in the time and manner permitted by statute, clearing house rule or agreement.

Upon a final payment under subparagraphs (b), (c) or (d) the payor bank shall be accountable for the amount of the item.

(2) If provisional settlement for an item between the presenting and payor banks is made through a clearing house or by debits or credits in an account between them, then to the extent that provisional debits or credits for the item are entered in accounts between the presenting and payor banks or between the presenting and successive prior collecting banks seriatim, they become final upon final payment of the item by the payor bank.

(3) If a collecting bank receives a settlement for an item which is or becomes final (subsection (3) of Section 4–211, subsection (2) of Section 4–213) the bank is accountable to its customer for the amount of the item and any provisional credit given for the item in an account with its customer becomes final.

(4) Subject to any right of the bank to apply the credit to an obligation of the customer, credit given by a bank for an item in an account with its customer becomes available for withdrawal as of right

(a) in any case where the bank has received a provisional settlement for the item,—when such settlement becomes final and the bank has had a reasonable time to learn that the settlement is final.

(b) in any case where the bank is both a depositary bank and a payor bank and the item is finally paid,—at the opening of the bank's second banking day following receipt of the item.

(5) A deposit of money in a bank is final when made but, subject to any right of the bank to apply the deposit to an obligation of the customer, the deposit becomes available for withdrawal as of right at the opening of the bank's next banking day following receipt of the deposit.

### § 4–214. Insolvency and Preference

(1) Any item in or coming into the possession of a payor or collecting bank which suspends payment and which item is not finally paid shall be returned by the receiver, trustee or agent in charge of the closed bank to the presenting bank or the closed bank's customer.

(2) If a payor bank finally pays an item and suspends payments without making a settlement for the item with its customer or the presenting bank which settlement is or becomes final, the owner of the item has a preferred claim against the payor bank.

(3) If a payor bank gives or a collecting bank gives or receives a provisional settlement for an item and thereafter suspends payments, the suspension does not prevent or interfere with the settlement becoming final if such finality occurs automatically upon the lapse of certain time or the happening of certain events (subsection (3) of Section 4–211, subsections (1) (d), (2) and (3) of Section 4–213).

(4) If a collecting bank receives from subsequent parties settlement for an item which settlement is or becomes final and suspends payments without making a settlement for the item with its customer which is or becomes final, the owner of the item has a preferred claim against such collecting bank.

## Part 3 Collection of Items; Payor Banks

### § 4–301. Deferred Posting; Recovery of Payment by Return of Items; Time of Dishonor

(1) Where an authorized settlement for a demand item (other than a documentary draft) received by a payor bank otherwise than for immediate payment over the counter has been made before mid-

night of the banking day of receipt the payor bank may revoke the settlement and recover any payment if before it has made final payment (subsection (1) of Section 4–213) and before its midnight deadline it

(a) returns the item; or

(b) sends written notice of dishonor or nonpayment if the item is held for protest or is otherwise unavailable for return.

(2) If a demand item is received by a payor bank for credit on its books it may return such item or send notice of dishonor and may revoke any credit given or recover the amount thereof withdrawn by its customer, if it acts within the time limit and in the manner specified in the preceding subsection.

(3) Unless previous notice of dishonor has been sent an item is dishonored at the time when for purposes of dishonor it is returned or notice sent in accordance with this section.

(4) An item is returned:

(a) as to an item received through a clearing house, when it is delivered to the presenting or last collecting bank or to the clearing house or is sent or delivered in accordance with its rules; or

(b) in all other cases, when it is sent or delivered to the bank's customer or transferor or pursuant to his instructions.

### § 4–302. Payor Banks' Responsibility for Late Return of Item

In the absence of a valid defense such as breach of a presentment warranty (subsection (1) of Section 4–207), settlement effected or the like, if an item is presented on and received by a payor bank the bank is accountable for the amount of

(a) a demand item other than a documentary draft whether properly payable or not if the bank, in any case where it is not also the depositary bank, retains the item beyond midnight of the banking day of receipt without settling for it or, regardless of whether it is also the depositary bank, does not pay or return the item or send notice of dishonor until after its midnight deadline, or

(b) any other properly payable item unless within the time allowed for acceptance or payment of that item the bank either accepts or pays the item or returns it and accompanying documents.

### § 4–303. When Items Subject to Notice, Stop-Order, Legal Process or Setoff; Order in Which Items May Be Charged or Certified

(1) Any knowledge, notice or stop-order received by, legal process served upon or setoff exercised by a payor bank, whether or not effective under other rules of law to terminate, suspend or modify the bank's right or duty to pay an item or to charge its customer's account for the item, comes too late to so terminate, suspend or modify such right or duty if the knowledge, notice, stop-order or legal process is received or served and a reasonable time for the bank to act thereon expires or the setoff is exercised after the bank has done any of the following:

(a) accepted or certified the item;

(b) paid the item in cash;

(c) settled for the item without reserving a right to revoke the settlement and without having such right under statute, clearing house rule or agreement;

(d) completed the process of posting the item to the indicated account of the drawer, maker or other person to be charged therewith or otherwise has evidenced by examination of such indicated account and by action its decision to pay the item; or

(e) become accountable for the amount of the item under subsection (1) (d) of Section 4–213 and Section 4–302 dealing with the payor bank's responsibility for late return of items.

(2) Subject to the provisions of subsection (1) items may be accepted, paid, certified or charged to the indicated account of its customer in any order convenient to the bank.

## Part 4 Relationship Between Payor Bank and Its Customer

### § 4–401. When Bank May Charge Customer's Account

(1) As against its customer, a bank may charge against his account any item which is otherwise properly payable from that account even though the charge creates an overdraft.

(2) A bank which in good faith makes payment to a holder may charge the indicated account of its customer according to

(a) the original tenor of his altered item; or

(b) the tenor of his completed item, even though the bank knows the item has been completed unless the bank has notice that the completion was improper.

### § 4–402. Bank's Liability to Customer for Wrongful Dishonor

A payor bank is liable to its customer for damages proximately caused by the wrongful dishonor of an item. When the dishonor occurs through mistake liability is limited to actual damages proved. If so proximately caused and proved damages may include damages for an arrest or prosecution of the customer or other consequential damages. Whether any consequential damages are proximately caused by the wrongful dishonor is a question of fact to be determined in each case.

### § 4–403. Customer's Right to Stop Payment; Burden of Proof of Loss

(1) A customer may by order to his bank stop payment of any item payable for his account but the order must be received at such time and in such manner as to afford the bank a reasonable opportunity to act on it prior to any action by the bank with respect to the item described in Section 4–303.

(2) An oral order is binding upon the bank only for fourteen calendar days unless confirmed in writing within that period. A written order is effective for only six months unless renewed in writing.

(3) The burden of establishing the fact and amount of loss resulting from the payment of an item contrary to a binding stop payment order is on the customer.

### § 4–404. Bank Not Obligated to Pay Check More Than Six Months Old

A bank is under no obligation to a customer having a checking account to pay a check, other than a certified check, which is presented more than six months after its date, but it may charge its customer's account for a payment made thereafter in good faith.

### § 4–405. Death or Incompetence of Customer

(1) A payor or collecting bank's authority to accept, pay or collect an item or to account for proceeds of its collection if otherwise effective is not rendered ineffective by incompetence of a customer of either bank existing at the time the item is issued or its collection is undertaken if the bank does not know of an adjudication of incompetence. Neither death nor incompetence of a customer revokes such authority to accept, pay, collect or account until the bank knows of the fact of death or of an adjudication of incompetence and has reasonable opportunity to act on it.

(2) Even with knowledge a bank may for 10 days after the date of death pay or certify checks drawn on or prior to that date unless ordered to stop payment by a person claiming an interest in the account.

### § 4–406. Customer's Duty to Discover and Report Unauthorized Signature or Alteration

(1) When a bank sends to its customer a statement of account accompanied by items paid in good faith in support of the debit entries or holds the statement and items pursuant to a request or instructions of its customer or otherwise in a reasonable manner makes the statement and items available to the customer, the customer must exercise reasonable care and promptness to examine the statement and items to discover his unauthorized signature or any alteration on an item and must notify the bank promptly after discovery thereof.

(2) If the bank establishes that the customer failed with respect to an item to comply with the duties imposed on the customer by subsection (1) the customer is precluded from asserting against the bank

(a) his unauthorized signature or any alteration on the item if the bank also establishes that it suffered a loss by reason of such failure; and

(b) an unauthorized signature or alteration by the same wrongdoer or any other item paid in good faith by the bank after the first item and statement was available to the customer for a reasonable period not exceeding fourteen calendar days and before the bank receives notification from the customer of any such unauthorized signature or alteration.

(3) The preclusion under subsection (2) does not apply if the customer establishes lack of ordinary care on the part of the bank in paying the item(s).

(4) Without regard to care or lack of care of either the customer or the bank a customer who does not within one year from the time the statement and items are made available to the customer (subsection (1)) discover and report his unauthorized signature or any alteration on the face or back of the item or does not within 3 years from that time discover and report any unauthorized indorsement is precluded from asserting against the bank such unauthorized signature or indorsement or such alteration.
(5) If under this section a payor bank has a valid defense against a claim of a customer upon or resulting from payment of an item and waives or fails upon request to assert the defense the bank may not assert against any collecting bank or other prior party presenting or transferring the item a claim based upon the unauthorized signature or alteration giving rise to the customer's claim.

### § 4–407. Payor Bank's Right to Subrogation on Improper Payment

If a payor bank has paid an item over the stop payment order of the drawer or maker or otherwise under circumstances giving a basis for objection by the drawer or maker, to prevent unjust enrichment and only to the extent necessary to prevent loss to the bank by reason of its payment of the item, the payor bank shall be subrogated to the rights

(a) of any holder in due course on the item against the drawer or maker; and

(b) of the payee or any other holder of the item against the drawer or maker either on the item or under the transaction out of which the item arose; and

(c) of the drawer or maker against the payee or any other holder of the item with respect to the transaction out of which the item arose.

## Part 5 Collection of Documentary Drafts

### § 4–501. Handling of Documentary Drafts; Duty to Send for Presentment and to Notify Customer of Dishonor

A bank which takes a documentary draft for collection must present or send the draft and accompanying documents for presentment and upon learning that the draft has not been paid or accepted in due course must seasonably notify its customer of such fact even though it may have discounted or bought the draft or extended credit available for withdrawal as of right.

### § 4–502. Presentment of "On Arrival" Drafts

When a draft or the relevant instructions require presentment "on arrival," "when goods arrive" or the like, the collecting bank need not present until in its judgment a reasonable time for arrival of the goods has expired. Refusal to pay or accept because the goods have not arrived is not dishonor; the bank must notify its transferor of such refusal but need not present the draft again until it is instructed to do so or learns of the arrival of the goods.

### § 4–503. Responsibility of Presenting Bank for Documents and Goods; Report of Reasons for Dishonor; Referee in Case of Need

Unless otherwise instructed and except as provided in Article 5 a bank presenting a documentary draft

(a) must deliver the documents to the drawee on acceptance of the draft if it is payable more than three days after presentment; otherwise, only on payment; and

(b) upon dishonor, either in the case of presentment for acceptance or presentment for payment, may seek and follow instructions from any referee in case of need designated in the draft or if the presenting bank does not choose to utilize his services it must use diligence and good faith to ascertain the reason for dishonor, must notify its transferor of the dishonor and of the results of its effort to ascertain the reasons therefor and must request instructions.

But the presenting bank is under no obligation with respect to goods represented by the documents except to follow any reasonable instructions seasonably received; it has a right to reimbursement for any expense incurred in following instructions and to prepayment of or indemnity for such expenses.

### § 4–504. Privilege of Presenting Bank to Deal With Goods; Security Interest for Expenses

(1) A presenting bank which, following the dishonor of a documentary draft, has seasonably requested instructions but does not receive them

within a reasonable time may store, sell, or otherwise deal with the goods in any reasonable manner.
(2) For its reasonable expenses incurred by action under subsection (1) the presenting bank has a lien upon the goods or their proceeds, which may be foreclosed in the same manner as an unpaid seller's lien.

## ARTICLE 5 LETTERS OF CREDIT

### § 5–101. Short Title

This Article shall be known and may be cited as Uniform Commercial Code—Letters of Credit.

### § 5–102. Scope

(1) This Article applies

(a) to a credit issued by a bank if the credit requires a documentary draft or a documentary demand for payment; and

(b) to a credit issued by a person other than a bank if the credit requires that the draft or demand for payment be accompanied by a document of title; and

(c) to a credit issued by a bank or other person if the credit is not within subparagraphs (a) or (b) but conspicuously states that it is a letter of credit or is conspicuously so entitled.

(2) Unless the engagement meets the requirements of subsection (1), this Article does not apply to engagements to make advanced or to honor drafts or demands for payment, to authorities to pay or purchase, to guarantees or to general agreements.

(3) This Article deals with some but not all of the rules and concepts of letters of credit as such rules or concepts have developed prior to this act or may hereafter develop. The fact that this Article states a rule does not by itself require, imply or negate application of the same or a converse rule to a situation not provided for or to a person not specified by this Article.

### § 5–103. Definitions

(1) In this Article unless the context otherwise requires

(a) "Credit" or "letter of credit" means an engagement by a bank or other person made at the request of a customer and of a kind within the scope of this Article (Section 5–102) that the issuer will honor drafts or other demands for payment upon compliance with the conditions specified in the credit. A credit may be either revocable or irrevocable. The engagement may be either an agreement to honor or a statement that the bank or other person is authorized to honor.

(b) A "documentary draft" or a "documentary demand for payment" is one honor of which is conditioned upon the presentation of a document or documents. "Document" means any paper including document of title, security, invoice, certificate, notice of default and the like.

(c) An "issuer" is a bank or other person issuing a credit.

(d) A "beneficiary" of a credit is a person who is entitled under its terms to draw or demand payment.

(e) An "advising bank" is a bank which gives notification of the issuance of a credit by another bank.

(f) A "confirming bank" is a bank which engages either that it will itself honor a credit already issued by another bank or that such a credit will be honored by the issuer or a third bank.

(g) A "customer" is a buyer or other person who causes an issuer to issue a credit. The term also includes a bank which procures issuance or confirmation on behalf of that bank's customer.

(2) Other definitions applying to this Article and the sections in which they appear are:

"Notation of Credit." Section 5–108.
"Presenter." Section 5–112(3).

(3) Definitions in other Articles applying to this Article and the sections in which they appear are:

"Accept" or "Acceptance." Section 3–410.
"Contract for sale." Section 2–106.
"Draft." Section 3–104.
"Holder in due course." Section 3–302.
"Midnight deadline." Section 4–104.
"Security." Section 8–102.

(4) In addition, Article 1 contains general definitions and principles of construction and interpretation applicable throughout this Article.

### § 5–104. Formal Requirements; Signing

(1) Except as otherwise required in subsection (1) (c) of Section 5–102 on scope, no particular form of phrasing is required for a credit. A credit must

be in writing and signed by the issuer and a confirmation must be in writing and signed by the confirming bank. A modification of the terms of a credit or confirmation must be signed by the issuer or confirming bank.

(2) A telegram may be a sufficient signed writing if it identifies its sender by an authorized authentication. The authentication may be in code and the authorized naming of the issuer in an advance of credit is a sufficient signing.

### § 5–105. Consideration

No consideration is necessary to establish a credit or to enlarge or otherwise modify its terms.

### § 5–106. Time and Effect of Establishment of Credit

(1) Unless otherwise agreed a credit is established

(a) as regards the customer as soon as a letter of credit is sent to him or the letter of credit or an authorized written advice of its issuance is sent to the beneficiary; and

(b) as regards the beneficiary when he receives a letter of credit or an authorized written advice of its issuance.

(2) Unless otherwise agreed once an irrevocable credit is established as regards the customer it can be modified or revoked only with the consent of the customer and once it is established as regards the beneficiary it can be modified or revoked only with his consent.

(3) Unless otherwise agreed after a revocable credit is established it may be modified or revoked by the issuer without notice to or consent from the customer or beneficiary.

(4) Notwithstanding any modification or revocation of a revocable credit any person authorized to honor or negotiate under the terms of the original credit is entitled to reimbursement for or honor of any draft or demand for payment duly honored or negotiated before receipt of notice of the modification or revocation and the issuer in turn is entitled to reimbursement from its customer.

### § 5–107. Advice of Credit; Confirmation; Error in Statement of Terms

(1) Unless otherwise specified an advising bank by advising a credit issued by another bank does not assume any obligation to honor drafts drawn or demands for payment made under the credit but it does assume obligation for the accuracy of its own statement.

(2) A confirming bank by confirming a credit becomes directly obligated on the credit to the extent of its confirmation as though it were its issuer and acquires the rights of an issuer.

(3) Even though an advising bank incorrectly advises the terms of a credit it has been authorized to advise the credit is established as against the issuer to the extent of its original terms.

(4) Unless otherwise specified the customer bears as against the issuer all risks of transmissions and reasonable translation or interpretation of any message relating to a credit.

### § 5–108. "Notation Credit"; Exhaustion of Credit

(1) A credit which specifies that any person purchasing or paying drafts drawn or demands for payment made under it must note the amount of the draft or demand on the letter or advice of credit is a "notation credit."

(2) Under a notation credit

(a) a person paying the beneficiary or purchasing a draft or demand for payment from him acquires a right to honor only if the appropriate notation is made and by transferring or forwarding for honor the documents under the credit such a person warrants to the issuer that the notation has been made; and

(b) unless the credit or a signed statement that an appropriate notation has been made accompanies the draft or demand for payment the issuer may delay honor until evidence of notation has been procured which is satisfactory to it but its obligation and that of its customer continue for a reasonable time not exceeding thirty days to obtain such evidence.

(3) If the credit is not a notation credit

(a) the issuer may honor complying drafts or demands for payment presented to it in the order in which they are presented and is discharged pro tanto by honor of any such draft or demand;

(b) as between competing good faith purchasers of complying drafts or demands the person first purchasing has priority over a subsequent purchaser even though the later purchased draft or demand has been first honored.

### § 5–109. Issuer's Obligation to Its Customer

(1) An issuer's obligation to its customer includes good faith and observance of any general banking usage but unless otherwise agreed does not include liability or responsibility

(a) for performance of the underlying contract for sale or other transaction between the customer and the beneficary; or

(b) for any act or omission of any person other than itself or its own branch or for loss or destruction of a draft, demand or document in transit or in the possession of others; or

(c) based on knowledge or lack of knowledge of any usage of any particular trade.

(2) An issuer must examine documents with care so as to ascertain that on their face they appear to comply with the terms of the credit but unless otherwise agreed assumes no liability of responsibility for the genuineness, falsification or effect of any document which appears on such examination to be regular on its face.

(3) A non-bank issuer is not bound by any banking usage of which it has no knowlege.

### § 5–110. Availability of Credit in Portions; Presenter's Reservation of Lien or Claim

(1) Unless otherwise specified a credit may be used in portions in the discretion of the beneficiary.

(2) Unless otherwise specified a person by presenting a documentary draft or demand for payment under a credit relinquishes upon its honor all claims to the documents and a person by transferring such draft or demand or causing such presentment authorizes such relinquishment. An explicit reservation of claim makes the draft or demand non-complying.

### § 5–111. Warranties on Transfer and Presentment

(1) Unless otherwise agreed the beneficiary by transferring or presenting a documentary draft or demand for payment warrants to all interested parties that the necessary conditions of the credit have been complied with. This is in addition to any warranties arising under Articles 3, 4, 7 and 8.

(2) Unless otherwise agreed a negotiating, advising, confirming, collecting or issuing bank presenting or transferring a draft or demand for payment under a credit warrants only the matters warranted by a collecting bank under Article 4 and any such bank transferring a document warrants only the matters warranted by an intermediary under Articles 7 and 8.

### § 5–112. Time Allowed for Honor or Rejection; Withholding Honor or Rejection by Consent; "Presenter"

(1) A bank to which a documentary draft or demand for payment is presented under a credit may without dishonor of the draft, demand or credit

(a) defer honor until the close of the third banking day following receipt of the documents; and

(b) further defer honor if the presenter has expressly or impliedly consented thereto.

Failure to honor within the time here specified constitutes dishonor of the draft or demand and of the credit [except as otherwise provided in subsection (4) of Section 5–114 on conditional payment].

**Note:** *The bracketed language in the last sentence of subsection (1) should be included only if the optional provisions of Section 5–114(4) and (5) are included.*

(2) Upon dishonor the bank may unless otherwise instructed fulfill its duty to return the draft or demand and the documents by holding them at the disposal of the presenter and sending him an advice to that effect.

(3) "Presenter" means any person presenting a draft or demand for payment for honor under a credit even though that person is a confirming bank or other correspondent which is acting under an issuer's authorization

### § 5–113. Indemnities

(1) A bank seeking to obtain (whether for itself or another) honor, negotiation or reimbursement under a credit may give an indemnity to induce such honor, negotiation or reimbursement.

(2) An indemnity agreement inducing honor, negotiation or reimbursement

(a) unless otherwise explicitly agreed applies to defects in the documents but not in the goods; and

(b) unless a longer time is explicitly agreed expires at the end of ten business days following receipt of the documents by the ultimate customer unless notice of objection is sent before such expiration date. The ultimate customer may send notice of objection to the person from whom he received the documents and any bank receiving such notice is under a duty to send notice to its transferor before its midnight deadline.

### § 5–114. Issuer's Duty and Privilege to Honor; Right to Reimbursement

(1) An issuer must honor a draft or demand for payment which complies with the terms of the relevant credit regardless of whether the goods or documents conform to the underlying contract for sale or other contract between the customer and the beneficiary. The issuer is not excused from honor of such a draft or demand by reason of an additional general term that all documents must be satisfactory to the issuer, but an issuer may require that specified documents must be satisfactory to it.

(2) Unless otherwise agreed when documents appear on their face to comply with the terms of a credit but a required document does not in fact conform to the warranties made on negotiation or transfer of a document of title (Section 7–507) or of a certificated security (Section 8–306) or is forged or fraudulent or there is fraud in the transaction:

(a) the issuer must honor the draft or demand for payment if honor is demanded by a negotiating bank or other holder of the draft or demand which has taken the draft or demand under the credit and under circumstances which would make it a holder in due course (Section 3–302) and in an appropriate case would make it a person to whom a document of title has been duly negotiated (Section 7–502) or a bona fide purchaser of a certificated security (Section 8–302); and

(b) in all other cases as against its customer, an issuer acting in good faith may honor the draft or demand for payment despite notification from the customer of fraud, forgery or other defect not apparent on the face of the documents but a court of appropriate jurisdiction may enjoin such honor.

(3) Unless otherwise agreed an issuer which has duly honored a draft or demand for payment is entitled to immediate reimbursement of any payment made under the credit and to be put in effectively available funds not later than the day before maturity of any acceptance made under the credit.

[(4) When a credit provides for payment by the issuer on receipt of notice that the required documents are in the possession of a correspondent or other agent of the issuer

(a) any payment made on receipt of such notice is conditional; and

(b) the issuer may reject documents which do not comply with the credit if it does so within three banking days following its receipt of the documents; and

(c) in the event of such rejection, the issuer is entitled by charge back or otherwise to return of the payment made.]

[(5) In the case covered by subsection (4) failure to reject documents within the time specified in sub-paragraph (b) constitutes acceptance of the documents and makes the payment final in favor of the beneficiary.]

**Note:** *Subsections (4) and (5) are bracketed as optional. If they are included the bracketed language in that last sentence of Section 5–112(1) should also be included.*

### § 5–115. Remedy for Improper Dishonor or Anticipatory Repudiation

(1) When an issuer wrongfully dishonors a draft or demand for payment presented under a credit the person entitled to honor has with respect to any documents the rights of a person in the position of a seller (Section 2–707) and may recover from the issuer the face amount of the draft or demand together with incidental damages under Section 7–710 on seller's incidental damages and interest but less any amount realized by resale or other use or disposition of the subject matter of the transaction. In the event no resale or other utilization is made the documents, goods or other subject matter involved in the transaction must be turned over to the issuer on payment of judgment.

(2) When an issuer wrongfully cancels or otherwise repudiates a credit before presentment of a draft or demand for payment drawn under it the beneficiary has the rights of a seller after anticipatory repudiation by the buyer under Section 2–610 if he learns of the repudiation in time reasonably to avoid procurement of the required documents. Otherwise the beneficiary has an immediate right of action for wrongful dishonor.

### § 5–116. Transfer and Assignment

(1) The right to draw under a credit can be transferred or assigned only when the credit is expressly designated as transferable or assignable.

(2) Even though the credit specifically states that it is nontransferable or nonassignable the beneficiary may before performance of the conditions of the credit assign his right to proceeds. Such an assignment is an assignment of an account under Article 9 on Secured Transactions and is governed by that Article except that

(a) the assignment is ineffective until the letter of credit or advice of credit is delivered to the assignee which delivery constitutes perfection of the security interest under Article 9; and

(b) the issuer may honor drafts or demands for payment drawn under the credit until it receives a notification of the assignment signed by the beneficiary which reasonably identifies the credit involved in the assignment and contains a request to pay the assignee; and

(c) after what reasonably appears to be such a notification has been received the issuer may without dishonor refuse to accept or pay even to a person otherwise entitled to honor until the letter of credit or advice of credit is exhibited to the issuer.

(3) Except where the beneficiary has effectively assigned his right to draw or his right to proceeds, nothing in this section limits his right to transfer or negotiate drafts or demands drawn under the credit.

### § 5–117. Insolvency of Bank Holding Funds for Documentary Credit

(1) Where an issuer or an advising or confirming bank or a bank which has for a customer procured issuance of a credit by another bank becomes insolvent before final payment under the credit and the credit is one to which this Article is made applicable by paragraphs (a) or (b) of Section 5–102(1) on scope, the receipt or allocation of funds or collateral to secure or meet obligations under the credit shall have the following results:

(a) to the extent of any funds or collateral turned over after or before the insolvency as indemnity against or specifically for the purpose of payment of drafts or demands for payment drawn under the designated credit, the drafts or demands are entitled to payment in preference over depositors or other general creditors of the issuer or bank; and

(b) on expiration of the credit or surrender of the beneficiary's rights under it unused any person who has given such funds or collateral is similarly entitled to return thereof; and

(c) a charge to a general or current account with a bank if specifically consented to for the purpose of indemnity against or payment of drafts or demands for payment drawn under the designated credit falls under the same rules as if the funds had been drawn out in cash and then turned over with specific instructions.

(2) After honor or reimbursement under this section the customer or other person for whose account the insolvent bank has acted is entitled to receive the documents involved.

## ARTICLE 6 BULK TRANSFERS

### § 6–101. Short Title

This Article shall be known and may be cited as Uniform Commercial Code–Bulk Transfers.

### § 6–102. "Bulk Transfers"; Transfers of Equipment; Enterprises Subject to This Article; Bulk Transfers Subject to This Article

(1) A "bulk transfer" is any transfer in bulk and not in the ordinary course of the transferor's business of a major part of the materials, supplies, merchandise or other inventory (Section 9–109) of an enterprise subject to this Article.

(2) A transfer of a substantial part of the equipment (Section 9–109) of such an enterprise is a bulk transfer if it is made in connection with a bulk transfer of inventory, but not otherwise.

(3) The enterprises subject to this Article are all those whose principal business is the sale of merchandise from stock, including those who manufacture what they sell.

(4) Except as limited by the following section all bulk transfers of goods located within this state are subject to this Article.

### § 6–103. Transfers Excepted from This Article

The following transfers are not subject to this Article:

(1) Those made to give security for the performance of an obligation;
(2) General assignments for the benefit of all the creditors of the transferor, and subsequent transfers by the assignee thereunder;
(3) Transfers in settlement or realization of a lien or other security interests;
(4) Sales by executors, administrators, receivers, trustees in bankruptcy, or any public officer under judicial process;
(5) Sales made in the course of judicial or administrative proceedings for the dissolution or reorganization of a corporation and of which notice is sent to the creditors of the corporation pursuant to order of the court or administrative agency;
(6) Transfers to a person maintaining a known place of business in this State who becomes bound to pay the debts of the transferor in full and gives public notice of that fact, and who is solvent after becoming so bound;
(7) A transfer to a new business enterprise organized to take over and continue the business, if public notice of the transaction is given and the new enterprise assumes the debts of the transferor and he receives nothing from the transaction except an interest in the new enterprise junior to the claims of creditors;
(8) Transfers of property which is exempt from execution.
Public notice under subsection (6) or subsection (7) may be given by publishing once a week for two consecutive weeks in a newspaper of general circulation where the transferor had its principal place of business in this state an advertisement including the names and addresses of the transferor and transferee and the effective date of the transfer.

### § 6–104. Schedule of Property, List of Creditors

(1) Except as provided with respect to auction sales (Section 6–108), a bulk transfer subject to this Article is ineffective against any creditor of the transferor unless:

(a) The transferee requires the transferor to furnish a list of his existing creditors prepared as stated in this section; and

(b) The parties prepare a schedule of the property transferred sufficient to identify it; and

(c) The transferee preserves the list and schedule for six months next following the transfer and permits inspection of either or both and copying therefrom at all reasonable hours by any creditor of the transferor, or files the list and schedule in (a public office to be here identified).

(2) The list of creditors must be signed and sworn to or affirmed by the transferor or his agent. It must contain the names and business addresses of all creditors of the transferor, with the amounts when known, and also the names of all persons who are known to the transferor to assert claims against him even though such claims are disputed. If the transferor is the obligor of an outstanding issue of bonds, debentures or the like as to which there is an indenture trustee, the list of creditors need include only the name and address of the indenture trustee and the aggregate outstanding principal amount of the issue.
(3) Responsibility for the completeness and accuracy of the list of creditors rests on the transferor, and the transfer is not rendered ineffective by errors or omissions therein unless the transferee is shown to have had knowledge.

### § 6–105. Notice to Creditors

In addition to the requirements of the preceding section, any bulk transfer subject to this Article except one made by auction sale (Section 6–108) is ineffective against any creditor of the transferor unless at least ten days before he takes possession of the goods or pays for them, whichever happens first, the transferee gives notice of the transfer in the manner and to the persons hereafter provided (Section 6–107).

### § 6–106. Application of the Proceeds

In addition to the requirements of the two preceding sections:
(1) Upon every bulk transfer subject to this Article for which new consideration becomes payable except those made by sale at auction it is the duty of the transferee to assure that such consideration is applied so far as necessary to pay those debts of the transferor which are either shown on the list furnished by the transferor (Section 6–104) or filed in writing in the place stated in the notice (Section 6–107) within thirty days after the mailing of such notice. This duty of the transferee runs

to all the holders of such debts, and may be enforced by any of them for the benefit of all.
(2) If any of said debts are in dispute the necessary sum may be withheld from distribution until the dispute is settled or adjudicated.
(3) If the consideration payable is not enough to pay all of the said debts in full distribution shall be made pro rata.]

**Note:** *This section is bracketed to indicate division of opinion as to whether or not it is a wise provision, and to suggest that this is a point on which State enactments may differ without serious damage to the princple of uniformity.*

*In any State where this section is omitted, the following parts of sections, also bracketed in the text, should also be omitted, namely:*

*Section 6–107(2) (e).*
*6–108(3) (c).*
*6–109(2).*

*In any State where this section is enacted, these other provisions should be also.*

### Optional Subsection (4)

[(4) The transferee may within ten days after he takes possession of the goods pay the consideration into the (specify court) in the county where the transferor had its principal place of business in this state and thereafter may discharge his duty under this section by giving notice by registered or certified mail to all the persons to whom the duty runs that the consideration has been paid into that court and that they should file their claims there. On motion of any interested party, the court may order the distribution of the consideration to the persons entitled to it.]

**Note:** *Optional subsection (4) is recommended for those states which do not have a general statute providing for payment of money into court.*

## § 6–107. The Notice

(1) The notice to creditors (Section 6–105) shall state:

(a) that a bulk transfer is about to be made; and

(b) the names and business addresses of the transferor and transferee, and all other business names and addresses used by the transferor within three years last past so far as known to the transferee, and

(c) whether or not all the debts of the transferor are to be paid in full as they fall due as a result of the transaction, and if so, the address to which creditors should send their bills.

(2) If the debts of the transferor are not to be paid in full as they fall due or if the transferee is in doubt on that point then the notice shall state further:

(a) the location and general description of the property to be transferred and the estimated total of the transferor's debts;

(b) the address where the schedule of property and list of creditors (Section 6–104) may be inspected;

(c) whether the transfer is to pay existing debts and if so the amount of such debts and to whom owing;

(d) whether the transfer is for new consideration and if so the amount of such consideration and the time and place of payment; [and]

[(e) if for new consideration the time and place where creditors of the transferor are to file their claims.]

(3) The notice in any case shall be delivered personally or sent by registered or certified mail to all the persons shown on the list of creditors furnished by the transferor (Section 6–104) and to all other persons who are known to the transferee to hold or assert claims against the transferor.

**Note:** *The words in brackets are optional. See Note under Section 6–106.*

## § 6–108. Auction Sales; "Auctioneer"

(1) A bulk transfer is subject to this Article even though it is by sale at auction, but only in the manner and with the results stated in this section.

(2) The transferor shall furnish a list of his creditors and assist in the preparation of a schedule of the property to be sold, both prepared as before stated (Section 6–104).

(3) The person or persons other than the transferor who direct, control or are responsible for the auction are collectively called the "auctioneer." The auctioneer shall:

(a) receive and retain the list of creditors and prepare and retain the schedule of property for the period stated in this Article (Section 6–104);

(b) give notice of the auction personally or by

registered or certified mail at least ten days before it occurs to all persons shown on the list of creditors and to all other persons who are known to him to hold or assert claims against the transferor; [and]

[(c) assure that the net proceeds of the auction are applied as provided in this Article (Section 6–106).]

(4) Failure of the auctioneer to perform any of these duties does not affect the validity of the sale or the title of the purchasers, but if the auctioneer knows that the auction constitutes a bulk transfer such failure renders the auctioneer liable to the creditors of the transferor as a class for the sums owing to them from the transferor up to but not exceeding the net proceeds of the auction. If the auctioneer consists of several persons their liability is joint and several.

**Note:** *The words in brackets are optional. See Note under Section 6–106.*

### § 6–109. What Creditors Protected; [Credit for Payment to Particular Creditors]

(1) The creditors of the transferor mentioned in this Article are those holding claims based on transactions or events occurring before the bulk transfer, but creditors who become such after notice to creditors is given (Sections 6–105 and 6–107) are not entitled to notice.

[(2) Against the aggregate obligation imposed by the provisions of this Article concerning the application of the proceeds (Section 6–106 and subsection (3)(c) of 6–108) the transferee or auctioneer is entitled to credit for sums paid to particular creditors of the transferor, not exceeding the sums believed in good faith at the time of the payment to be properly payable to such creditors.]

**Note:** *The words in brackets are optional. See Note under Section 6–106.*

### § 6–110. Subsequent Transfers

When the title of a transferee to property is subject to a defect by reason of his non-compliance with the requirements of this Article, then:

(1) A purchaser of any of such property from such transferee who pays no value or who takes with notice of such non-compliance takes subject to such defect, but

(2) A purchaser for value in good faith and without such notice takes free of such defect.

### § 6–111. Limitation of Actions and Levies

No action under this Article shall be brought nor levy made more than six months after the date on which the transferee took possession of the goods unless the transfer has been concealed. If the transfer has been concealed, actions may be brought or levies made within six months after its discovery.

**Note:** *In any State where Section 6–106 is not enacted, the following parts of sections, also bracketed in the text, should also be omitted, namely:*

*Sec. 6–107(2)(e).*
*6–108(3)(c).*
*6–109(2).*

*In any State where Section 6–106 is enacted, these other provisions should be also.*

# ARTICLE 7 WAREHOUSE RECEIPTS, BILLS OF LADING AND OTHER DOCUMENTS OF TITLE

## Part 1 General

### § 7–101. Short Title

This Article shall be known and may be cited as Uniform Commercial Code—Documents of Title.

### § 7–102. Definitions and Index of Definitions

(1) In this Article, unless the context otherwise requires:

(a) "Bailee" means the person who by a warehouse receipt, bill of lading or other document of title acknowledges possession of goods and contracts to deliver them.

(b) "Consignee" means the person named in a bill to whom or to whose order the bill promises delivery.

(c) "Consignor" means the person named in a bill as the person from whom the goods have been received for shipment.

(d) "Delivery order" means a written order to deliver goods directed to a warehouseman, carrier or other person who in the ordinary course of business issues warehouse receipts or bills of lading.

(e) "Document" means document of title as defined in the general definitions in Article 1 (Section 1–201).

(f) "Goods" means all things which are treated as movable for the purposes of a contract of storage or transportation.

(g) "Issuer" means a bailee who issues a document except that in relation to an unaccepted delivery order it means the person who orders the possessor of goods to deliver. Issuer includes any person for whom an agent or employee purports to act in issuing a document if the agent or employee has real or apparent authority to issue documents, notwithstanding that the issuer received no goods or that the goods were misdescribed or that in any other respect the agent or employee violated his instructions.

(h) "Warehouseman" is a person engaged in the business of storing goods for hire.

(2) Other definitions applying to this Article or to specified Parts thereof, and the sections in which they appear are:

"Duly negotiate." Section 7–501.

"Person entitled under the document." Section 7–403(4).

(3) Definitions in other Articles applying to this Article and the sections in which they appear are:

"Contract for sale." Section 2–106.

"Overseas." Section 2–323.

"Receipt" of goods. Section 2–103.

(4) In addition Article 1 contains general definitions and principles of construction and interpretation applicable throughout this Article.

### § 7–103. Relation of Article to Treaty, Statute, Tariff, Classification or Regulation

To the extent that any treaty or statute of the United States, regulatory statute of this State or tariff, classification or regulation filed or issued pursuant thereto is applicable, the provisions of this Article are subject thereto.

### § 7–104. Negotiable and Non-Negotiable Warehouse Receipt, Bill of Lading or Other Document of Title

(1) A warehouse receipt, bill of lading or other document of title is negotiable

(a) if by its terms the goods are to be delivered to bearer or to the order of a named person; or

(b) where recognized in overseas trade, if it runs to a named person or assigns.

(2) Any other document is non-negotiable. A bill of lading in which it is stated that the goods are consigned to a named person is not made negotiable by a provision that the goods are to be delivered only against a written order signed by the same or another named person.

### § 7–105. Construction Against Negative Implication

The omission from either Part 2 or Part 3 of this Article of a provision corresponding to a provision made in the other Part does not imply that a corresponding rule of law is not applicable.

## Part 2 Warehouse Receipts: Special Provisions

### § 7–201. Who May Issue a Warehouse Receipt; Storage under Government Bond

(1) A warehouse receipt may be issued by any warehouseman.

(2) Where goods including distilled spirits and agricultural commodities are stored under a statute requiring a bond against withdrawal or a license for the issuance of recipts in the nature of warehouse receipts, a receipt issued for the goods has like effect as a warehouse receipt even though issued by a person who is the owner of the goods and is not a warehouseman.

### § 7–202. Form of Warehouse Receipt; Essential Terms; Optional Terms

(1) A warehouse receipt need not be in any particular form.

(2) Unless a warehouse receipt embodies within its written or printed terms each of the following, the warehouseman is liable for damages caused by the omission to a person injured thereby:

(a) the location of the warehouse where the goods are stored;

(b) the date of issue of the receipt;

(c) the consecutive number of the receipt;

(d) a statement whether the goods received will be delivered to the bearer, to a specified person, or to a specified person or his order;

(e) the rate of storage and handling charges, except that where goods are stored under a field warehousing arrangement a statement of that fact is sufficient on a non-negotiable receipt;

(f) a description of the goods or of the packages containing them;

(g) the signature of the warehouseman, which may be made by his authorized agent;

(h) if the receipt is issued for goods of which the warehouseman is owner, either solely or jointly or in common with others, the fact of such ownership; and

(i) a statement of the amount of advances made and of liabilities incurred for which the warehouseman claims a lien or security interest (Section 7–209). If the precise amount of such advances made or of such liabilities incurred is, at the time of the issue of the receipt, unknown to the warehouseman or to his agent who issues it, a statement of the fact that advances have been made or liabilities incurred and the purpose thereof is sufficient.

(3) A warehouseman may insert in his receipt any other terms which are not contrary to the provisions of this Act and do not impair his obligation of delivery (Section 7–403) or his duty of care (Section 7–204). Any contrary provisions shall be ineffective.

### § 7–203. Liability for Non-Receipt or Misdescription

A party to or purchaser for value in good faith of a document of title other than a bill of lading relying in either case upon the description therein of the goods may recover from the issuer damages caused by the non-receipt or misdescription of the goods, except to the extent that the document conspicuously indicates that the issuer does not know whether any part or all of the goods in fact were received or conform to the description, as where the description is in terms of marks or labels or kind, quantity or condition, or the receipt or description is qualified by "contents, condition and quality unknown," "said to contain" or the like, if such indication be true, or the party or purchaser otherwise has notice.

### § 7–204. Duty of Care; Contractual Limitation of Warehouseman's Liability

(1) A warehouseman is liable for damages for loss of or injury to the goods caused by his failure to exercise such care in regard to them as a reasonably careful man would exercise under like circumstances but unless otherwise agreed he is not liable for damages which could not have been avoided by the exercise of such care.

(2) Damages may be limited by a term in the warehouse receipt or storage agreement limiting the amount of liability in case of loss or damage, and setting forth a specific liability per article or item, or value per unit of weight, beyond which the warehouseman shall not be liable; provided, however, that such liability may on written request of the bailor at the time of signing such storage agreement or within a reasonable time after receipt of the warehouse receipt be increased on part or all of the goods thereunder, in which event increased rates may be charged based on such increased valuation, but that no such increase shall be permitted contrary to a lawful limitation of liability contained in the warehouseman's tariff, if any. No such limitation is effective with respect to the warehouseman's liability for conversion to his own use.

(3) Reasonable provisions as to the time and manner of presenting claims and instituting actions based on the bailment may be included in the warehouse receipt or tariff.

(4) This section does not impair or repeal . . .

**Note:** *Insert in subsection (4) a reference to any statue which imposes a higher responsibility upon the warehouseman or invalidates contractural limitations which would be permissible under this Article.*

### § 7–205. Title under Warehouse Receipt Defeated in Certain Cases

A buyer in the ordinary course of business of fungible goods sold and delivered by a warehouseman who is also in the business of buying and selling such goods takes free of any claim under a warehouse receipt even through it has been duly negotiated.

### § 7–206. Termination of Storage at Warehouseman's Option

(1) A warehouseman may on notifying the person on whose account the goods are held and any other person known to claim an interest in the goods require payment of any charges and removal of the goods from the warehouse at the termination of the period of storage fixed by the document, or, if no period is fixed, within a stated period not less than thirty days after the notification. If the

goods are not removed before the date specified in the notification, the warehouseman may sell them in accordance with the provisions of the section on enforcement of a warehouseman's lien (Section 7–210).

(2) If a warehouseman in good faith believes that the goods are about to deteriorate or decline in value to less than the amount of his lien within the time prescribed in subsection (1) for notification, advertisement and sale, the warehouseman may specify in the notification any reasonable shorter time for removal of the goods and in case the goods are not removed, may sell them at public sale held not less than one week after a single advertisement or posting.

(3) If as a result of a quality or condition of the goods of which the warehouseman had no notice at the time of deposit the goods are a hazard to other property or to the warehouse or to persons, the warehouseman may sell the goods at public or private sale without advertisement on reasonable notification to all persons known to claim an interest in the goods. If the warehouseman after a reasonable effort is unable to sell the goods he may dispose of them in any lawful manner and shall incur no liability by reason of such disposition.

(4) The warehouseman must deliver the goods to any person entitled to them under this Article upon due demand made at any time prior to sale or other disposition under this section.

(5) The warehouseman may satisfy his lien from the proceeds of any sale or disposition under this section but must hold the balance for delivery on the demand of any person to whom he would have been bound to deliver the goods.

## § 7–207. Goods Must Be Kept Separate; Fungible Goods

(1) Unless the warehouse receipt otherwise provides, a warehouseman must keep separate the goods covered by each receipt so as to permit at all times identication and delivery of those goods except that different lots of fungible goods may be commingled.

(2) Fungible goods so commingled are owned in common by the persons entitled thereto and the warehouseman is severally liable to each owner for that owner's share. Where because of overissue a mass of fungible goods in insufficient to meet all the receipts which the warehouseman has issued against it, the persons entitled include all holders to whom overissued receipts have been duly negotiated.

## § 7–208. Altered Warehouse Receipts

Where a blank in a negotiable warehouse receipt has been filled in without authority, a purchaser for value and without notice of the want of authority may treat the insertion as authorized. Any other unauthorized alteration leaves any receipt enforceable against the issuer according to its original tenor.

## § 7–209. Lien of Warehouseman

(1) A warehouseman has a lien against the bailor on the goods covered by a warehouse receipt or on the proceeds thereof in his possession for charges for storage or transportation (including demurrage and terminal charges), insurance, labor, or charges present or future in relation to the goods, and for expenses necessary for preservation of the goods or reasonably incurred in their sale pursuant to law. If the person on whose account the goods are held is liable for new charges or expenses in relation to other goods whenever deposited and it is stated in the receipt that a lien is claimed for charges and expenses in relation to other goods, the warehouseman also has a lien against him for such charges and expenses whether or not the other goods have been delivered by the warehouseman. But against a person to whom a negotiable warehouse receipt is duly negotiated a warehouseman's lien is limited to charges in an amount or at a rate specifed on the receipt or if no charges are so specified then to a reasonable charge for storage of the goods covered by the receipt subsequent to the date of receipt.

(2) The warehouseman may also reserve a security interest against the bailor for a maximum amount specified on the receipt for charges other than those specified in subsection (1), such as for money advanced and interest. Such a security interest is governed by the Article on Secured Transactions (Article 9).

(3) (a) A warehouseman's lien for charges and expenses under subsection (1) or a security interest under subsection (2) is also effective against any

person who so entrusted the bailor with possession of the goods that a pledge of them by him to a good faith purchaser for value would have been valid but is not effective against a person as to whom the document confers no right in the goods covered by it under Section 7–503.

(b) A warehouseman's lien on household goods for charges and expenses in relation to the goods under subsection (1) is also effective against all persons if the depositor was the legal possessor of the goods at the time of deposit. "Household goods" means furniture, furnishings, and personal effects used by the depositor in a dwelling.

(4) A warehouseman loses his lien on any goods which he voluntarily delivers or which he unjustifiably refuses to deliver.

### § 7–210. Enforcement of Warehouseman's Lien

(1) Except as provided in subseciton (2), a warehouseman's lien may be enforced by public or private sale of the goods in block or in parcels, at any time or place and on any terms which are commercially reasonable, after notifying all persons known to claim an interest in the goods. Such notification must include a statement of the amount due, the nature of the proposed sale and the time and place of any public sale. The fact that a better price could have been obtained by a sale at a different time or in a different method from that selected by the warehouseman is not of itself sufficient to establish that the sale was not made in a commercially reasonable manner. If the warehouseman either sells the goods in the usual manner in any recognized market therefor, or if he sells at the price current in such market at the time of his sale, or if he has otherwise sold in conformity with commercially reasonable practices among dealers in the type of goods sold, he has sold in a commercially reasonable manner. A sale of more goods than apparently necessary to be offered to insure satisfaction of the obligation is not commercially reasonable except in cases covered by the preceding sentence.

(2) A warehouseman's lien on goods other than goods stored by a merchant in the course of his business may be enforced only as follows:

(a) All persons known to claim an interest in the goods must be notified.

(b) The notification must be delivered in person or sent by registered or certified letter to the last known address of any person to be notified.

(c) The notification must include an itemized statement of the claim, a description of the goods subject to the lien, a demand for payment within a specified time or less than ten days after receipt of the notification, and a conspicuous statement that unless the claim is paid within that time the goods will be advertised for sale and sold by auction at a specified time and place.

(d) The sale must conform to the terms of the notification.

(e) The sale must be held at the nearest suitable place to that where the goods are held or stored.

(f) After the expiration of the time given in the notification, an advertisement of the sale must be published once a week for two weeks consecutively in a newspaper of general circulation where the sale is to be held. The advertisement must include a description of the goods, the name of the person on whose account they are being held, and the time and place of the sale. The sale must take place at least fifteen days after the first publication. If there is no newspaper of general circulation where the sale is to be held, the advertisement must be posted at least ten days before the sale in not less than six conspicuous places in the neighborhood of the proposed sale.

(3) Before any sale pursuant to this section any person claiming a right in the goods may pay the amount necessary to satisfy the lien and the reasonable expenses incurred under this section. In that event the goods must not be sold, but must be retained by the warehouseman subject to the terms of the receipt and this Article.

(4) The warehouseman may buy at any public sale pursuant to this section.

(5) A purchaser in good faith of goods sold to enforce a warehouseman's lien takes the goods free of any rights of persons against whom the lien was valid, despite noncompliance by the warehouseman with the requirements of this section.

(6) The warehouseman may satisfy his lien from the proceeds of any sale pursuant to this section but must hold the balance, if any, for delivery on demand to any person to whom he would have been bound to deliver the goods.

(7) The rights provided by this section shall be in addition to all other rights allowed by law to a creditor against his debtor.

(8) Where a lien is on goods stored by a merchant in the course of his business the lien may be enforced in accordance with either subsection (1) or (2).

(9) The warehouseman is liable for damages caused by failure to comply with the requirements for sale under this section and in case of willful violation is liable for conversion.

## Part 3 Bills of Lading: Special Provisions

### § 7–301. Liability for Non-Receipt or Misdescription; "Said to Contain"; "Shipper's Load and Count"; Improper Handling

(1) A consignee of a non-negotiable bill who has given value in good faith or a holder to whom a negotiable bill has been duly negotiated relying in either case upon the description therein of the goods, or upon the date therein shown, may recover from the issuer damages caused by the misdating of the bill or the non-receipt or misdescription of the goods, except to the extent that the document indicates that the issuer does not know whether any part or all of the goods in fact were received or conform to the description, as where the description is in terms of marks or labels or kind, quantity, or condition or the receipt or description is qualified by "contents or condition of contents of packages unknown," "said to contain." "shipper's weight, load and count" or the like, if such indication be true.

(2) When goods are loaded by an issuer who is a common carrier, the issuer must count the packages of goods if package freight and ascertain the kind and quantity if bulk freight. In such cases "shipper's weight, load and count" or other words indicating that the description was made by the shipper are ineffective except as to freight concealed by packages.

(3) When bulk freight is loaded by a shipper who makes available to the issuer adequate facilities for weighing such freight, an issuer who is a common carrier must ascertain the kind and quantity within a reasonable time after receiving the written request of the shipper to do so. In such cases "shipper's weight" or other words of like purport are ineffective.

(4) The issuer may be inserting in the bill the words "shipper's weight, load and count" or other words of like purport indicate that the goods were loaded by the shipper; and if such statement be true the issuer shall not be liable for damages caused by the improper loading. But their omission does not imply liability for such damages.

(5) The shipper shall be deemed to have guaranteed to the issuer the accuracy at the time of shipment of the description, marks, labels, number, kind, quantity, condition and weight, as furnished by him; and the shipper shall indemnify the issuer against damage caused by inaccuracies in such particulars. The right of the issuer to such indemnity shall in no way limit his responsibility and liability under the contract of carriage to any person other then the shipper.

### § 7–302. Through Bills of Lading and Similar Documents

(1) The issuer of a through bill of lading or other document embodying an undertaking to be performed in part by persons acting as its agents or by connecting carriers is liable to anyone entitled to recover on the document for any breach by such other persons or by a connecting carrier of its obligation under the document but to the extent that the bill covers an undertaking to be performed overseas or in territory not contiguous to the continental United States or an undertaking including matters other than transportation this liability may be varied by agreement of the parties.

(2) Where goods covered by a through bill of lading or other document embodying an undertaking to be performed in part by persons other than the issuer are received by any such person, he is subject with respect to his own performance while the goods are in his possession to the obligation of the issuer. His obligation is discharged by delivery of the goods to another such person pursuant to the document, and does not include liability for breach by any other such persons or by the issuer.

(3) The issuer of such through bill of lading or other document shall be entitled to recover from the connecting carrier or such other person in possession of the goods where the breach of the obligation under the document occurred, the amount it may be required to pay to anyone entitled to recover on the document therefor, as may be evidenced by any receipt, judgment, or transcript thereof, and the amount of any expense reasonably incurred by it in defending any acton brought by

anyone entitled to recover on the document therefor.

### § 7-303. Diversion; Reconsignment; Change of Instructions

(1) Unless the bill of lading otherwise provides, the carrier may deliver the goods to a person or destination other than that stated in the bill or may otherwise dispose of the goods on instructions from

(a) the holder of a negotiable bill; or

(b) the consignor on a non-negotiable bill notwithstanding contrary instructions from the consignee; or

(c) the consignee on a non-negotiable bill in the absence of contrary instructions from the consignor, if the goods have arrived at the billed destination or if the consignee is in possession of the bill; or

(d) the consignee on a non-negotiable bill if he is entitled as against the consignor to dispose of them.

(2) Unless such instructions are noted on a negotiable bill of lading, a person to whom the bill is duly negotiated can hold the bailee according to the original terms.

### § 7-304. Bills of Lading in a Set

(1) Except where customary in overseas transportation, a bill of lading must not be issued in a set of parts. The issuer is liable for damages caused by violation of this subsection.

(2) Where a bill of lading is lawfully drawn in a set of parts, each of which is numbered and expressed to be valid only if the goods have not been delivered against any other part, the whole of the parts constitute one bill.

(3) Where a bill of lading is lawfully issued in a set of parts and different parts are negotiated to different persons, the title of the holder to whom the first due negotiation is made prevails as to both the document and the goods even though any later holder may have received the goods from the carrier in good faith and discharged the carrier's obligation by surrender of his part.

(4) Any person who negotiates or transfers a single part of a bill of lading drawn in a set is liable to holders of that part as if it were the whole set.

(5) The bailee is obliged to deliver in accordance with Part 4 of this Article against the first presented part of a bill of lading lawfully drawn in a set. Such delivery discharges the bailee's obligation on the whole bill.

### § 7-305. Destination Bills

(1) Instead of issuing a bill of lading to the consignor at the place of shipment a carrier may at the request of the consignor procure the bill to be issued at destination or at any other place designated in the request.

(2) Upon request of anyone entitled as against the carrier to control the goods while in transit and on surrender of any outstanding bill of lading or other receipt covering such goods, the issuer may procure a substitute bill to be issued at any place designated in the request.

### § 7-306. Altered Bills of Lading

An unauthorized alteration or filling in of a blank in a bill of lading leaves the bill enforceable according to its original tenor.

### § 7-307. Lien of Carrier

(1) A carrier has a lien on the goods covered by a bill of lading for charges subsequent to the date of its receipt of the goods for storage or transportation (including demurrage and terminal charges) and for expenses necessary for preservation of the goods incident to their transportation or reasonably incurred in their sale pursuant to law. But against a purchaser for value of a negotiable bill of lading a carrier's lien is limited to charges stated in the bill or the applicable tariffs, or if no charges are stated then to a reasonable charge.

(2) A lien for charges and expenses under subsection (1) on goods which the carrier was required by law to receive for transportation is effective against the consignor or any person entitled to the goods unless the carrier had notice that the consignor lacked authority to subject the goods to such charges and expenses. Any other lien under subsection (1) is effective against the consignor and any person who permitted the bailor to have control or possession of the goods unless the carrier had notice that the bailor lacked such authority.

(3) A carrier loses his lien on any goods which he voluntarily delivers or which he unjustifiably refuses to deliver.

### § 7–308. Enforcement of Carrier's Lien

(1) A carrier's lien may be enforced by public or private sale of the goods, in block or in parcels, at any time or place and on any terms which are commercially reasonable, after notifying all persons known to claim an interest in the goods. Such notification must include a statement of the amount due, the nature of the proposed sale and the time and place of any public sale. The fact that a better price could have been obtained by a sale at a different time or in a different method from that selected by the carrier is not of itself sufficient to establish that the sale was not made in a commercially reasonable manner. If the carrier either sells the goods in the usual manner in any recognized market therefor or if he sells at the price current in such market at the time of his sale or if he has otherwise sold in conformity with commercially reasonable practices among dealers in the type of goods sold he has sold in a commercially reasonable manner. A sale of more goods than apparently necessary to be offered to ensure satisfaction of the obligation is not commercially reasonable except in cases covered by the preceding sentence.

(2) Before any sale pursuant to this section any person claiming a right in the goods may pay the amount necessary to satisfy the lien and the reasonable expenses incurred under this section. In that event the goods must not be sold, but must be retained by the carrier subject to the terms of the bill and this Article.

(3) The carrier may buy at any public sale pursuant to this section.

(4) A purchaser in good faith of goods sold to enforce a carrier's lien takes the goods free of any rights of persons against whom the lien was valid, despite noncompliance by the carrier with the requirements of this section.

(5) The carrier may satisfy his lien from the proceeds of any sale pursuant to this section but must hold the balance, if any, for delivery on demand to any person to whom he would have been bound to deliver the goods.

(6) The rights provided by this section shall be in addition to all other rights allowed by law to a creditor against his debtor.

(7) A carrier's lien may be enforced in accordance with either subsection (1) or the procedure set forth in subsection (2) of Section 7–210.

(8) The carrier is liable for damages caused by failure to comply with the requirements for sale under this section and in case of willful violation is liable for conversion.

### § 7–309. Duty of Care; Contractual Limitation of Carrier's Liability

(1) A carrier who issues a bill of lading whether negotiable or non-negotiable must exercise the degree of care in relation to the goods which a reasonably careful man would exercise under like circumstances. This subsection does not repeal or change any law or rule of law which imposes liability upon a common carrier for damages not caused by its negligence.

(2) Damages may be limited by a provision that the carrier's liability shall not exceed a value stated in the document if the carrier's rates are dependent upon value and the consignor by the carrier's tariff is afforded an opportunity to declare a higher value or a value as lawfully provided in the tariff, or where no tariff is filed he is otherwise advised of such opportunity; but no such limitation is effective with respect to the carrier's liability for conversion to its own use.

(3) Reasonable provisions as to the time and manner of presenting claims and instituting actions based on the shipment may be included in a bill of lading or tariff.

## Part 4 Warehouse Receipts and Bills of Lading: General Obligations

### § 7–401. Irregularities in Issue of Receipt or Bill or Conduct of Issuer

The obligations imposed by this Article on an issuer apply to a document of title regardless of the fact that

(a) the document may not comply with the requirements of this Article or of any other law or regulation regarding its issue, form or content; or

(b) the issuer may have violated laws regulating the conduct of his business; or

(c) the goods covered by the document were owned by the bailee at the time the document was issued; or

(d) the person issuing the document does not come within the definition of warehouseman if it purports to be a warehouse receipt.

### § 7–402. Duplicate Receipt or Bill; Overissue

Neither a duplicate nor any other document of title purporting to cover goods already represented by an outstanding document of the same issuer confers any right in the goods, except as provided in the case of bills in a set, overissue of documents for fungible goods and substitutes for lost, stolen or destroyed documents. But the issuer is liable for damages caused by his overissue or failure to identify a duplicate document as such by conspicuous notation on its face.

### § 7–403. Obligation of Warehouseman or Carrier to Deliver; Excuse

(1) The bailee must deliver the goods to a person entitled under the document who complies with subsections (2) and (3), unless and to the extent that the bailee establishes any of the following:

(a) delivery of the goods to a person whose receipt was rightful as against the claimant;

(b) damage to or delay, loss or destruction of the goods for which the bailee is not liable [, but the burden of establishing negligence in such cases is on the person entitled under the document];

**Note:** *The brackets in (1) (b) indicate that State enactments may differ on this point without serious damage to the principle of uniformity.*

(c) previous sale or other disposition of the goods in lawful enforcement of a lien or on warehouseman's lawful termination of storage;

(d) the exercise by a seller of his right to stop delivery pursuant to the provisions of the Article on Sales (Section 2–705);

(e) a diversion, reconsignment or other disposition pursuant to the provisions of this Article Section 7–303) or tariff regulating such right;

(f) release, satisfaction or any other fact affording a personal defense against the claimant;

(g) any other lawful excuse.

(2) A person claiming goods covered by a document of title must satisfy the bailee's lien where the bailee so requests or where the bailee is prohibited by law from delivering the goods until the charges are paid.

(3) Unless the person claiming is one against whom the document confers no right under Sec. 7–503(1), he must surrender for cancellation or notation of partial deliveries any outstanding negotiable document covering the goods, and the bailee must cancel the document or conspicuously note the partial delivery thereon or be liable to any person to whom the document is duly negotiated.

(4) "Person entitled under the document" means holder in the case of a negotiable document, or the person to whom delivery is to be made by the terms of or pursuant to written instructions under a non-negotiable document.

### § 7–404. No Liability for Good Faith Delivery Pursuant to Receipt or Bill

A bailee who in good faith including observance of reasonable commercial standards has received goods and delivered or otherwise disposed of them according to the terms of the document of title or pursuant to this Article is not liable therefor. This rule applies even though the person from whom he received the goods had no authority to procure the document or to dispose of the goods and even though the person to whom he delivered the goods had no authority to receive them.

## Part 5 Warehouse Receipts and Bills of Lading: Negotiation and Transfer

### § 7–501. Form of Negotiation and Requirements of "Due Negotiation"

(1) A negotiable document of title running to the order of a named person is negotiated by his indorsement and delivery. After his indorsement in blank or to bearer any person can negotiate it by delivery alone.

(2) (a) A negotiable document of title is also negotiated by delivery alone when by its original terms it runs to bearer.

(b) When a document running to the order of a named person is delivered to him the effect is the same as if the document had been negotiated.

(3) Negotiation of a negotiable document of title after it has been indorsed to a specified person requires indorsement by the special indorsee as well as delivery.

(4) A negotiable document of title is "duly negotiated" when it is negotiated in the manner stated in this section to a holder who purchases it in good faith without notice of any defense against or claim to it on the part of any person and for value, unless it is established that the negotiation is not in the

regular course of business or financing or involves receiving the document in settlement or payment of a money obligation.

(5) Indorsement of a non-negotiable document neither makes it negotiable nor adds to the transferee's rights.

(6) The naming in a negotiable bill of a person to be notified of the arrival of the goods does not limit the negotiability of the bill nor constitute notice to a purchaser thereof of any interest of such person in the goods.

### § 7–502. Rights Acquired by Due Negotiation

(1) Subject to the following section and to the provisions of Section 7–205 on fungible goods, a holder to whom a negotiable document of title has been duly negotiated acquires thereby:

(a) title to the document;

(b) title to the goods;

(c) all rights accruing under the law of agency or estoppel, including rights to goods delivered to the bailee after the document was issued; and

(d) the direct obligation of the issuer to hold or deliver the goods according to the terms of the document free of any defense or claim by him except those arising under the terms of the document or under this Article. In the case of a delivery order the bailee's obligation accrues only upon acceptance and the obligation acquired by the holder is that the issuer and any indorser will procure the acceptance of the bailee.

(2) Subject to the following section, title and rights so acquired are not defeated by any stoppage of the goods represented by the document or by surrender of such goods by the bailee, and are not impaired even though the negotiation or any prior negotiation constituted a breach of duty or even though any person has been deprived of possession of the document by misrepresentation, fraud, accident, mistake, duress, loss, theft or conversion, or even though a previous sale or other transfer of the goods or document has been made to a third person.

### § 7–503. Document of Title to Goods Defeated in Certain Cases

(1) A document of title confers no right in goods against a person who before issuance of the document had a legal interest or a perfected security interest in them and who neither

(a) delivered or entrusted them or any document of title covering them to the bailor or his nominee with actual or apparent authority to ship, store or sell or with power to obtain delivery under this Article (Section 7–403) or with power of disposition under this Act (Sections 2–403 and 9–307) or other statute or rule of law; nor

(b) acquiesced in the procurement by the bailor or his nominee of any document of title.

(2) Title to goods based upon an unaccepted delivery order is subject to the rights of anyone to whom a negotiable warehouse receipt or bill of lading covering the goods has been duly negotiated. Such a title may be defeated under the next section to the same extent as the rights of the issuer or a transferee from the issuer.

(3) Title to goods based upon a bill of lading issued to a freight forwarder is subject to the rights of anyone to whom a bill issued by the freight forwarder is duly negotiated; but delivery by the carrier in accordance with Part 4 of this Article pursuant to its own bill of lading discharges the carrier's obligation to deliver.

### § 7–504. Rights Acquired in the Absence of Due Negotiation; Effect of Diversion; Seller's Stoppage of Delivery

(1) A transferee of a document, whether negotiable or non-negotiable, to whom the document has been delivered but not duly negotiated, acquires the title and rights which his transferor had or had actual authority to convey.

(2) In the case of a non-negotiable document, until but not after the bailee receives notification of the transfer, the rights of the transferee may be defeated

(a) by those creditors of the transferor who could treat the sale as void under Section 2–402; or

(b) by a buyer from the transferor in ordinary course of business if the bailee has delivered the goods to the buyer or received notification of his rights; or

(c) as against the bailee by good faith dealings of the bailee with the transferor.

(3) A diversion or other change of shipping instructions by the consignor in a non-negotiable bill of lading which causes the bailee not to deliver to the consignee defeats the consignee's title to

the goods if they have been delivered to a buyer in ordinary course of business and in any event defeats the consignee's rights against the bailee.

(4) Delivery pursuant to a non-negotiable document may be stopped by a seller under Section 2–705, and subject to the requirement of due notification there provided. A bailee honoring the seller's instructions is entitled to be indemnified by the seller against any resulting loss or expense.

### § 7–505. Indorser Not a Guarantor for Other Parties

The indorsement of a document of title issued by a bailee does not make the indorser liable for any default by the bailee or by previous indorsers.

### § 7–506. Delivery without Indorsement: Right to Compel Indorsement

The transferee of a negotiable document of title has a specifically enforceable right to have his transferor supply any necessary indorsement but the transfer becomes a negotiation only as of the time the indorsement is supplied.

### § 7–507. Warranties on Negotiation or Transfer of Receipt or Bill

Where a person negotiates or transfers a document of title for value otherwise than as a mere intermediary under the next following section, then unless otherwise agreed he warrants to his immediate purchaser only in addition to any warranty made in selling the goods

(a) that the document is genuine; and

(b) that he has no knowledge of any fact which would impair its validity or worth; and

(c) that his negotiation or transfer is rightful and fully effective with respect to the title to the document and the goods it represents.

### § 7–508. Warranties of Collecting Bank as to Documents

A collecting bank or other intermediary known to be entrusted with documents on behalf of another or with collection of a draft or other claim against delivery of documents warrants by such delivery of the documents only its own good faith and authority. This rule applies even though the intermediary has purchased or made advances against the claim or draft to be collected.

## Part 6 Warehouse Receipts and Bills of Lading: Miscellaneous Provisions

### § 7–601. Lost and Missing Documents

(1) If a document has been lost, stolen or destroyed, a court may order delivery of the goods or issuance of a substitute document and the bailee may without liability to any person comply with such order. If the document was negotiable the claimant must post security approved by the court to indemnify any person who may suffer loss as a result of non-surrender of the document. If the document was not negotiable, such security may be required at the discretion of the court. The court may also in its discretion order payment of the bailee's reasonable costs and counsel fees.

(2) A bailee who without court order delivers goods to a person claiming under a missing negotiable document is liable to any person injured thereby, and if the delivery is not in good faith becomes liable for conversion. Delivery in good faith is not conversion if made in accordance with a filed classification or tariff or, where no classification or tariff is filed, if the claimant posts security with the bailee in an amount at least double the value of the goods at the time of posting to indemnify any person injured by the delivery who files a notice of claim within one year after the delivery.

### § 7–602. Attachment of Goods Covered by a Negotiable Document

Except where the document was originally issued upon delivery of the goods by a person who had no power to dispose of them, no lien attaches by virtue of any judicial process to goods in the possession of a bailee for which a negotiable document of title is outstanding unless the document be first surrendered to the bailee or its negotiation enjoined, and the bailee shall not be compelled to deliver the goods pursuant to process until the document is surrendered to him or impounded by the court. One who purchases the document for value without notice of the process or injunction takes free of the lien imposed by judicial process.

### § 7–603. Conflicting Claims; Interpleader

If more than one person claims title or possession of the goods, the bailee is excused from delivery until he has had a reasonable time to ascertain the validity of the adverse claims or to bring an action to compel all claimants to interplead and may compel such interpleader, either in defending an action for non-delivery of the goods, or by original action, whichever is appropriate.

## ARTICLE 8 INVESTMENT SECURITIES

### Part 1 Short Title and General Matters

#### § 8–101. Short Title

This Article shall be known and may be cited as Uniform Commercial Code—Investment Securities.

#### § 8–102. Definitions and Index of Definitions

(1) In this Article, unless the context otherwise requires:

(a) A "certificated security" is a share, participation, or other interest in property of or an enterprise of the issuer or an obligation of the issuer which is

(i) represented by an instrument issued in bearer or registered form;

(ii) of a type commonly dealt in on securities exchanges or markets or commonly recognized in any area in which it is issued or dealt in as a medium for investment; and

(iii) either one of a class or series or by its terms divisible into a class or series of shares, participations, interests, or obligations.

(b) An "uncertificated security" is a share, participation, or other interest in property or an enterprise of the issuer or an obligation of the issuer which is

(i) not represented by an instrument and the transfer of which is registered upon books maintained for that purpose by or on behalf of the issuer;

(ii) of a type commonly dealt in on securities exchanges or markets; and

(iii) either one of a class or series or by its terms divisible into a class or series of shares, participations, interests, or obligations,

(c) A "security" is either a certificated or an uncertificated security. If a security is certificated, the terms "security" and "certificated security" may mean either the intangible interest, the instrument representing that interest, or both, as the context requires. A writing that is a certificated security is governed by this Article and not by Article 3, even though it also meets the requirements of that Article. This Article does not apply to money. If a certificated security has been retained by or surrendered to the issuer or its transfer agent for reasons other than registration of transfer, other temporary purpose, payment, exchange, or acquisition by the issuer, that security shall be treated as an uncertificated security for purposes of this Article.

(d) A certificated security is in "registered form" if

(i) it specifies a person entitled to the security or the rights it represents; and

(ii) its transfer may be registered upon books maintained for that purpose by or on behalf of the issuer, or the security so states.

(e) A certificated security is in "bearer form" if it runs to bearer according to its terms and not by reason of any indorsement.

(2) A "subsequent purchaser" is a person who takes other than by original issue.

(3) A "clearing corporation" is a corporation registered as a "clearing agency" under the federal securities laws or a corporation:

(a) at least 90 percent of whose capital stock is held by or for one or more organizations, none of which, other than a national securities exchange or association, holds in excess of 20 percent of the capital stock of the corporation, and each of which is

(i) subject to supervision or regulation pursuant to the provisions of federal or state banking laws or state insurance laws,

(ii) a broker or dealer or investment company registered under the federal securities laws, or

(iii) a national securities exchange or association registered under the federal securities laws; and

(b) any remaining capital stock of which is held by individuals who have purchased it at or prior to the time of their taking office as directors of the corporation and who have purchased only so much of the capital stock as is necessary to permit them to qualify as directors.

(4) A "custodian bank" is a bank or trust company that is supervised and examined by state or

federal authority having supervision over banks and is acting as custodian for a clearing corporation.

(5) Other definitions applying to this Article or to specified Parts thereof and the sections in which they appear are:

"Adverse claim." Section 8–302.
"Bona fide purchaser." Section 8–302.
"Broker." Section 8–303.
"Debtor." Section 9–105.
"Financial intermediary." Section 8–313.
"Guarantee of the signature." Section 8–402.
"Initial transaction statement." Section 8–408.
"Instruction." Section 8–308.
"Intermediary bank." Section 4–105.
"Issuer." Section 8–201.
"Overissue." Section 8–104.
"Secured Party." Section 9–105.
"Security Agreement." Section 9–105.

(6) In addition, Article 1 contains general definitions and principles of construction and interpretation applicable throughout this Article.

### § 8–103. Issuer's Lien

A lien upon a security in favor of an issuer thereof is valid against a purchaser only if:

(a) the security is certificated and the right of the issuer to the lien is noted conspicuously thereon; or

(b) the security is uncertificated and a notation of the right of the issuer to the lien is contained in the initial transaction statement sent to the purchaser or, if his interest is transferred to him other then by registration of transfer, pledge, or release, the initial transaction statement sent to the registered owner or the registered pledgee.

### § 8–104. Effect of Overissue; "Overissue"

(1) The provisions of this Article which validate a security or compel its issue or reissue do not apply to the extent that validation, issue, or reissue would result in overissue; but if:

(a) an identical security which does not constitute an overissue is reasonably available for purchase, the person entitled to issue or validation may compel the issuer to purchase the security for him and either to deliver a certificated security or to register the transfer of an uncertificated security to him, against surrender of any certificated security he hold; or

(b) a security is not so available for purchase, the person entitled to issue or validation may recover from the issuer the price he or the last purchaser for value paid for it with interest from the date of his demand.

(2) "Overissue" means the issue of securities in excess of the amount the issuer has corporate power to issue.

### § 8–105. Certificated Securities Negotiable; Statements and Instructions Not Negotiable; Presumptions

(1) Certificated securities governed by this Article are negotiable instruments.

(2) Statements (Section 8–408), notices, or the like, sent by the issuer of uncertificated securities and instructions (Section 8–308) are neither negotiable instruments nor certificated securities.

(3) In any action on a security:

(a) unless specifically denied in the pleadings, each signature on a certificated security, in a necessary indorsement, on an initial transaction statement, or on an instruction, is admitted;

(b) if the effectiveness of a signature is put in issue, the burden of establishing it is on the party claiming under the signature, but the signature is presumed to be genuine or authorized;

(c) if signatures on a certificated security are admitted or established, production of the security entitles a holder to recover on it unless the defendant establishes a defense or a defect going to the validity of the security;

(d) if signatures on an initial transaction statement are admitted or established, the facts stated in the statement are presumed to be true as of the time of its issuance; and

(e) after it is shown that a defense or defect exists, the plaintiff has the burden of establishing that he or some person under whom he claims is a person against whom the defense or defect is ineffective (Section 8–202).

### § 8–106. Applicability

The law (including the conflict of laws rules) of the jurisdiction of organization of the issuer governs the validity of a security, the effectiveness of registration by the issuer, and the rights and duties of the issuer with respect to:

(a) registration of transfer of a certificated security;

(b) registration of transfer, pledge, or release of an uncertificated security; and

(c) sending of statements of uncertificated securities.

### § 8–107. Securities Transferable; Action for Price

(1) Unless otherwise agreed and subject to any applicable law or regulation respecting short sales, a person obligated to transfer securities may transfer any certificated security of the specified issue in bearer form or registered in the name of the transferee, or indorsed to him or in blank, or he may transfer an equivalent uncertificated security to the transferee or a person designated by the transferee.

(2) If the buyer fails to pay the price as it comes due under a contract of sale, the seller may recover the price of:

(a) certificated securities accepted by the buyer;

(b) uncertificated securities that have been transferred to the buyer or a person designated by the buyer; and

(c) other securities if efforts at their resale would be unduly burdensome or if there is no readily available market for their resale.

### § 8–108. Registration of Pledge and Release of Uncertificated Securities

A security interest in an uncertificated security may be evidenced by the registration of pledge to the secured party or a person designated by him. There can be no more than one registered pledge of an uncertificated security at any time. the registered owner of an uncertificated security is the person in whose name the security is registered, even if the security is subject to a registered pledge. The rights of a registered pledgee of an uncertificated security under this Article are terminated by the registration of release.

## Part 2 Issue–Issuer

### § 8–201. "Issuer"

(1) With respect to obligations on or defenses to a security, "issuer" includes a person who:

(a) places or authorizes the placing of his name on a certificated security (otherwise than as authenticating trustee, registrar, transfer agent, or the like) to evidence that it represents a share, participation, or other interest in his property or in an enterprise, or to evidence his duty to perform an obligation represented by the certificated security;

(b) creates shares, participations, or other interests in his property or in an enterprise or undertakes obligations, which shares, participations, interests, or obligations are uncertificated securities;

(c) directly or indirectly creates fractional interests in his rights or property, which fractional interests are represented by certificated securities; or

(d) becomes responsible for or in place of any other person described as an issuer in this section.

(2) With respect to obligations on or defenses to a security, a guarantor is an issuer to the extent of his guaranty, whether or not his obligation is noted on a certificated security or on statements of uncertificated securities sent pursuant to Section 8–408.

(3) With respect to registration of transfer, pledge, or release (Part 4 of this Article), "issuer" means a person on whose behalf transfer books are maintained.

### § 8–202. Issuer's Responsibility and Defenses; Notice of Defect or Defense

(1) Even against a purchaser for value and without notice, the terms of a security include:

(a) if the security is certificated, those stated on the security;

(b) if the security is uncertificated, those contained in the initial transaction statement sent to such purchaser, or, if his interest is transferred to him other than by registration of transfer, pledge, or release, the initial transaction statement sent to the registered owner or registered pledgee; and

(c) those made part of the security by reference, on the certificated security or in the initial transaction statement, to another instrument, indenture, or document or to a constitution, statute, ordinance, rule, regulation, order or the like, to the extent that the terms referred to do not conflict with the terms stated on the certificated security or contained in the statement. A reference under this paragraph does not of itself charge a purchaser for value with notice of a defect going to the valid-

ity of the security, even though the certificated security or statement expressly states that a person accepting it admits notice.
(2) A certificated security in the hands of a purchaser for value or an uncertificated security as to which an initial transaction statement has been sent to a purchaser for value, other than a security issued by a government or governmental agency or unit, even though issued with a defect going to its validity, is valid with respect to the purchaser if he is without notice of the particular defect unless the defect involves a violation of constitutional provisions, in which case the security is valid with respect to a subsequent purchaser for value and without notice of the defect. This subsection applies to an issuer that is a government or governmental agency or unit only if either there has been substantial compliance with the legal requirements governing the issue or the issuer has received a substantial consideration for the issue as a whole or for the particular security and a stated purpose of the issue is one for which the issuer has power to borrow money or issue the security.
(3) Except as provided in the case of certain unauthorized signatures (Section 8–205), lack of genuiness of a certificated security or an initial transaction statement is a complete defense, even against a purchaser for value and without notice.
(4) All other defenses of the issuer of a certificated or uncertificated security, including nondelivery and conditional delivery of a certificated security, are ineffective against a purchaser for value who has taken without notice of the particular defense.
(5) Nothing in this section shall be construed to affect the right of a party to a "when, as and if issued" or a "when distributed" contract to cancel the contract in the event of a material change in the character of the security that is the subject of the contract or in the plan or arrangement pursuant to which the security is to be issued or distributed.

### § 8–203. Staleness as Notice of Defects or Defenses

(1) After an act or event creating a right to immediate performance of the principal obligation represented by a certificated security or that sets a date on or after which the security is to be presented or surrendered for redemption or exchange, a purchaser is charged with notice of any defect in its issue or defense of the issuer if:
(a) the act or even is one requiring the payment of money, the delivery of certificated securities, the registration of transfer of uncertificated securities, or any of these on presentation or surrender of the certificated security, the funds or securities are available on the date set for payment or exchange, and he takes the security more than one year after that date; and
(b) the act or event is not covered by paragraph (a) and he takes the security more than 2 years after the date set for surrender or presentation or the date on which performance became due.
(2) A call that has been revoked is not within subsection (1).

### § 8–204. Effect of Issuer's Restrictions on Transfer

A restriction on transfer of a security imposed by the issuer, even if otherwise lawful, is ineffective against any person without actual knowledge of it unless:
(a) the security is certificated and the restriction is noted conspicuously thereon; or
(b) the security is uncertificated and a notation of the restriction is contained in the initial transaction statement sent to the person or, if his interest is transferred to him other than by registration of transfer, pledge, or release, the initial transaction statement sent to the registered owner or the registered pledgee.

### § 8–205. Effect of Unauthorized Signature on Certificated Security or Initial Transaction Statement

An unauthorized signature placed on a certificated security prior to or in the course of issue or placed on an initial transaction statement is ineffective, but the signature is effective in favor of a purchaser for value of the certificated security or a purchaser for value of an uncertificated security to whom the initial transaction statement has been sent, if the purchaser is without notice of the lack of authority and the signing has been done by:
(a) an authenticating trustee, registrar, transfer agent, or other person entrusted by the issuer with the signing of the security, of similar securities, or of initial transaction statements or the immediate preparation of signing of any of them; or

(b) an employee of the issuer, or of any of the foregoing, entrusted with responsible handling of the security or initial transaction statement.

### § 8-206. Completion or Alteration of Certificated Security or Initial Transaction Statement

(1) If a certificated security contains the signatures necessary to its issue or transfer but is incomplete in any other respect:

(a) any person may complete it by filling in the blanks as authorized; and

(b) even though the blanks are incorrectly filled in, the security as completed is enforceable by a purchaser who took it for value and without notice of the incorrectness.

(2) A complete certificated security that has been improperly altered, even though fraudulently, remains enforceable, but only according to its original terms.

(3) If an initial transaction statement contains the signatures necessary to its validity, but is incomplete in any other respect:

(a) any person may complete it by filling in the blanks as authorized; and

(b) even though the blanks are incorrectly filled in, the statement as completed is effective in favor of the person to whom it is sent if he purchased the security referred to therein for value and without notice of the incorrectness.

(4) A complete initial transaction statement that has been improperly altered, even though fraudulently, is effective in favor of a purchaser to whom it has been sent, but only according to its original terms.

### § 8-207. Rights and Duties of Issuer With Respect to Registered Owners and Registered Pledgees

(1) Prior to due presentment for registration of transfer of a certificated security in registered form, the issuer or indenture trustee may treat the registered owner as the person exclusively entitled to vote, to receive notifications, and otherwise to exercise all rights and powers of an owner.

(2) Subject to the provisions of subsections (3), (4), and (6), the issuer or indenture trustee may treat the registered owner of an uncertificated security as the person exclusively entitled to vote, to receive notifications, and otherwise to exercise all the rights and powers of an owner.

(3) The registered owner of an uncertificated security that is subject to a registered pledge is not entitled to registration of transfer prior to the due presentment to the issuer of a release instruction. The exercise of conversion rights with respect to a convertible uncertificated security is a transfer within the meaning of this section.

(4) Upon due presentment of a transfer instruction from the registered pledgee of an uncertificated security, the issuer shall:

(a) register the transfer of the security to the new owner free of pledge, if the instruction specifies a new owner (who may be the registered pledgee) and does not specify a pledgee;

(b) register the transfer of the security to the new owner subject to the interest of the existing pledgee, if the instruction specifies a new owner and the existing pledgee; or

(c) register the release of the security from the existing pledge and register the pledge of the security to the other pledgee, if the instruction specifies the existing owner and another pledgee.

(5) Continuity of perfection of a security interest is not broken by registration of transfer under subsection (4) (b) or by registration of release and pledge under subsection (4) (c), if the security interest is assigned.

(6) If an uncertificated security is subject to a registered pledge:

(a) any uncertificated securities issued in exchange for or distributed with respect to the pledged security shall be registered subject to the pledge;

(b) any certificated securities issued in exchange for or distributed with respect to the pledged security shall be delivered to the registered pledgee; and

(c) any money paid in exchange for or in redemption of part or all of the security shall be paid to the registered pledgee.

(7) Nothing in this Article shall be construed to affect the liability of the registered owner of a security for calls, assessments, or the like.

### § 8-208. Effect of Signature of Authenticating Trustee, Registrar, or Transfer Agent

(1) A person placing his signature upon a certificated security or an initial transaction statement

as authenticating trustee, registrar, transfer agent, or the like, warrants to a purchaser for value of the certificated security or a purchaser for value of an uncertificated security to whom the initial transaction statement has been sent, if the purchaser is without notice of the particular defect, that:

(a) the certificated security or initial transaction statement is genuine;

(b) his own participation in the issue or registration of the transfer, pledge, or release of the security is within his capacity and within the scope of the authority received by him from the issuer; and

(c) he has reasonable grounds to believe the security is in the form and within the amount the issuer is authorized to issue.

(2) Unless otherwise agreed, a person by so placing his signature does not assume responsibility for the validity of the security in other respects.

## Part 3 Transfer

### § 8–301. Rights Acquired by Purchaser

(1) Upon transfer of a security to a purchaser (Section 8–313), the purchaser acquires the rights in the security which his transferor had or had actual authority to convey unless the purchaser's rights are limited by Section 8–302(4).

(2) A transferee of a limited interest acquires rights only to the extent of the interest transferred. The creation or release of a security interest in a security is the transfer of a limited interest in that security.

### § 8–302. "Bona Fide Purchaser"; "Adverse Claim"; Title Acquired by Bona Fide Purchaser

(1) A "bona fide purchaser" is a purchaser for value in good faith and without notice of any adverse claim:

(a) who takes delivery of a certificated security in bearer form or in registered form, issued or indorsed to him or in blank;

(b) to whom the transfer, pledge, or release of an uncertificated security is registered on the books of the issuer; or

(c) to whom a security is transferred under the provisions of paragraph (c), (d) (i), or (g) of Section 8–313(1).

(2) "Adverse claim" includes a claim that a transfer was or would be wrongful or that a particular adverse person is the owner of or has an interest in the security.

(3) A bona fide purchaser in addition to acquiring the rights of a purchaser (Section 8–301) also acquires his interest in the security free of any adverse claim.

(4) Notwithstanding Section 8–301(1), the transferee of a particular certificated security who has been a party to any fraud or illegality affecting the security, or who as a prior holder of that certificated security had notice of an adverse claim, cannot improve his position by taking from a bona fide purchaser.

### § 8–303. "Broker"

"Broker" means a person engaged for all or part of his time in the business of buying and selling securities, who in the transaction concerned acts for, buys a security from, or sells a security to, a customer. Nothing in this Article determines the capacity in which a person acts for purposes of any other statute or rule to which the person is subject.

### § 8–304. Notice to Purchaser of Adverse Claims

(1) A purchaser (including a broker for the seller or buyer, but excluding an intermediary bank) of a certificated security is charged with notice of adverse claims if:

(a) the security, whether in bearer or registered form, has been indorsed "for collection" or "for surrender" or for some other purpose not involving transfer; or

(b) the security is in bearer form and has on it an unambiguous statement that it is the property of a person other than the transferor. The mere writing of a name on a security is not such a statement.

(2) A purchaser (including a broker for the seller or buyer, but excluding an intermediary bank) to whom the transfer, pledge, or release of an uncertificated security is registered is charged with notice of adverse claims as to which the issuer has a duty under Section 8–403(4) at the time of registration and which are noted in the initial transaction statement sent to the purchaser or, if his interest is transferred to him other than by registration

of transfer, pledge, or release, the initial transaction statement sent to the registered owner or the registered pledgee.

(3) The fact that the purchaser (including a broker for the seller or buyer) of a certificated or uncertificated security has notice that the security is held for a third person or is registered in the name of or indorsed by a fiduciary does not create a duty of inquiry into the rightfulness of the transfer or constitute constructive notice of adverse claims. However, if the purchaser (excluding an intermediary bank) has knowledge that the proceeds are being used or that the transaction is for the individual benefit of the fiduciary or otherwise in breach of duty, the purchaser is charged with notice of adverse claims.

### § 8–305. Staleness as Notice of Adverse Claims

An act or event that creates a right to immediate performance of the principal obligation represented by a certificated security or sets a date on or after which a certificated security is to be presented or surrendered for redemption or exchange does not itself constitute any notice of adverse claims except in the case of a transfer:

(a) after one year from any date set for presentment or surrender for redemption or exchange; or

(b) after 6 months from any date set for payment of money against presentation or surrender of the security if funds are available for payment on that date.

### § 8–306. Warranties on Presentment and Transfer of Certificated Securities; Warranties of Originators of Instructions

(1) A person who presents a certificated security for registration of transfer or for payment or exchange warrants to the issuer that he is entitled to the registration, payment, or exchange. But, a purchaser for value and without notice of adverse claims who receives a new, reissued, or re-registered certificated security on registration of transfer or receives an initial transaction statement confirming the registration of transfer of an equivalent uncertificated security to him warrants only that he has no knowledge of any unauthorized signature (Section 8–311) in a necessary indorsement.

(2) A person by transferring a certificated security to a purchaser for value warrants only that:

(a) his transfer is effective and rightful;

(b) the security is genuine and has not been materially altered; and

(c) he knows of no fact which might impair the validity of the security.

(3) If a certificated security is delivered by an intermediary known to be entrusted with delivery of the security on behalf of another or with collection of a draft or other claim against delivery, the intermediary by delivery warrants only his own good faith and authority, even though he has purchased or made advances against the claim to be collected against the delivery.

(4) A pledgee or other holder for security who redelivers a certificated security received, or after payment and on order of the debtor delivers that security to a third person, makes only the warranties of an intermediary under subsection (3).

(5) A person who originates an instruction warrants to the issuer that:

(a) he is an appropriate person to originate the instruction; and

(b) at the time the instruction is presented to the issuer he will be entitled to the registration of transfer, pledge, or release.

(6) A person who originates an instruction warrants to any person specially guaranteeing his signature (subsection 8–312(3)) that:

(a) he is an appropriate person to originate the instruction; and

(b) at the time the instruction is presented to the issuer

(i) he will be entitled to the registration of transfer, pledge, or release; and

(ii) the transfer, pledge, or release requested in the instruction will be registered by the issuer free from all liens, security interests, restrictions, and claims other than those specified in the instruction.

(7) A person who originates an instruction warrants to a purchaser for value and to any person guaranteeing the instruction (Section 8–312(6)) that:

(a) he is an appropriate person to originate the instruction;

(b) the uncertificated security referred to therein is valid; and

(c) at the time the instruction is presented to the issuer

(i) the transferor will be entitled to the registration of transfer, pledge, or release;

(ii) the transfer, pledge, or release requested in the instruction will be registered by the issuer free from all liens, security interests, restrictions, and claims other than those specified in the instruction; and

(iii) the requested transfer, pledge, or release will be rightful.

(8) If a secured party is the registered pledgee or the registered owner of an uncertificated security, a person who originates an instruction of release or transfer to the debtor or, after payment and on order of the debtor, a transfer instruction to a third person, warrants to the debtor or the third person only that he is an appropriate person to originate the instruction and, at the time the instruction is presented to the issuer, the transferor will be entitled to the registration of release or transfer. If a transfer instruction to a third person who is a purchaser for value is originated on order of the debtor, the debtor makes to the purchaser the warranties of paragraphs (b), (c) (ii) and (c) (iii) of subsection (7).

(9) A person who transfers an uncertificated security to a purchaser for value and does not originate an instruction in connection with the transfer warrants only that:

(a) his transfer is effective and rightful; and

(b) the uncertificated security is valid.

(10) A broker gives to his customer and to the issuer and a purchaser the applicable warranties provided in this section and has the rights and privileges of a purchaser under this section. The warranties of and in favor of the broker, acting as an agent are in addition to applicable warranties given by and in favor of his customer.

### § 8–307. Effect of Delivery Without Indorsement; Right to Compel Indorsement

If a certificated security in registered form has been delivered to a purchaser without a necessary indorsement he may become a bona fide purchaser only as of the time the indorsement is supplied; but against the transferor, the transfer is complete upon delivery and the purchaser has a specifically enforceable right to have any necessary indorsement supplied.

### § 8–308. Indorsements; Instructions

(1) An indorsement of a certificated security in registered form is made when an appropriate person signs on it or on a separate document an assignment or transfer of the security or a power to assign or transfer it or his signature is written without more upon the back of the security.

(2) An indorsement may be in blank or special. An indorsement in blank includes an indorsement to bearer. A special indorsement specifies to whom the security is to be transferred, or who has power to transfer it. A holder may convert a blank indorsement into a special indorsement.

(3) An indorsement purporting to be only of part of a certificated security representing units intended by the issuer to be separately transferable is effective to the extent of the indorsement.

(4) An "instruction" is an order to the issuer of an uncertificated security requesting that the transfer, pledge, or release from pledge of the uncertificated security specified therein be registered.

(5) An instruction originated by an appropriate person is:

(a) a writing signed by an appropriate person; or

(b) a communication to the issuer in any form agreed upon in a writing signed by the issuer and an appropriate person.

If an instruction has been originated by an appropriate person but is incomplete in any other respect, any person may complete it as authorized and the issuer may rely on it as completed even though it has been completed incorrectly.

(6) "An appropriate person" in subsection (1) means the person specified by the certificated security or by special indorsement to be entitled to the security.

(7) "An appropriate person" in subsection (5) means:

(a) for an instruction to transfer or pledge an uncertificated security which is then not subject to a registered pledge, the registered owner; or

(b) for an instruction to transfer or release an uncertificated security which is then subject to a registered pledge, the registered pledgee.

(8) In addition to the persons designated in sub-

sections (6) and (7), "an appropriate person" in subsections (1) and (5) includes:

(a) if the person designated is described as a fiduciary but is no longer serving in the described capacity, either that person or his successor;

(b) if the persons designated are described as more than one person as fiduciaries and one or more are no longer serving in the described capacity, the remaining fiduciary or fiduciaries, whether or not a successor has been appointed or qualified.

(c) if the person designated is an individual and is without capacity to act by virtue of death, incompetence, infancy, or otherwise, his executor, administrator, guardian, or like fiduciary;

(d) if the persons designated are described as more than one person as tenants by the entirety or with right of survivorship and by reason of death all cannot sign, the survivor or survivors;

(e) a person having power to sign under applicable law or controlling instrument; and

(f) to the extent that the person designated or any of the foregoing persons may act through an agent, his authorized agent.

(9) Unless otherwise agreed, the indorser of a certificated security by his indorsement or the originator of an instruction by his origination assumes no obligation that the security will be honored by the issuer but only the obligations provided in Section 8–306.

(10) Whether the person signing is appropriate is determined as of the date of signing and an indorsement made by or an instruction originated by him does not become unauthorized for the purposes of this Article by virtue of any subsequent change of circumstances.

(11) Failure of a fiduciary to comply with a controlling instrument or with the law of the state having jurisdiction of the fiduciary relationship, including any law requiring the fiduciary to obtain court approval of the transfer, pledge, or release, does not render his indorsement or an instruction originated by him unauthorized for the purposes of this Article.

### § 8–309. Effect of Indorsement Without Delivery

An indorsement of a certificated security, whether special or in blank, does not constitute a transfer until delivery of the certificated security on which it appears or, if the indorsement is on a separate document, until delivery of both the document and the certificated security.

### § 8–310. Indorsement of Certificated Security in Bearer Form

An indorsement of a certificated security in bearer form may give notice of adverse claims (Section 8–304) but does not otherwise affect any right to registration the holder possesses.

### § 8–311. Effect of Unauthorized Indorsement or Instruction

Unless the owner or pledgee has ratified an unauthorized indorsement or instruction or is otherwise precluded from asserting its ineffectiveness:

(a) he may assert its ineffectiveness against the issuer or any purchaser, other than a purchaser for value and without notice of adverse claims, who has in good faith received a new, reissued, or reregistered certificated security on registration of transfer or received an initial transaction statement confirming the registration of transfer, pledge, or release of an equivalent uncertificated security to him; and

(b) an issuer who registers the transfer of a certificated security upon the unauthorized indorsement or who registers the transfer, pledge, or release of an uncertificated security upon the unauthorized instruction is subject to liability for improper registration (Section 3–404).

### § 8–312. Effect of Guaranteeing Signature, Indorsement or Instruction

(1) Any person guaranteeing a signature of an indorser of a certificated security warrants that at the time of signing:

(a) the signature was genuine;

(b) the signer was an appropriate person to indorse (Section 8–308); and

(c) the signer had legal capacity to sign.

(2) Any person guaranteeing a signature of the originator of an instruction warrants that at the time of signing:

(a) the signature was genuine;

(b) the signer was an appropriate person to originate the instruction (Section 8–308) if the person specified in the instruction as the registered owner or registered pledgee of the uncertificated security was, in fact, the registered owner or registered pledgee of the security, as to which fact the signature guarantor makes no warranty;

(c) the signer had legal capacity to sign; and

(d) the taxpayer identification number, if any, appearing on the instruction as that of the registered owner or registered pledgee was the taxpayer identification number of the signer or of the owner or pledgee for whom the signer was acting.

(3) Any person specially guaranteeing the signature of the originator of an instruction makes not only the warranties of a signature guarantor (subsection (2)) but also warrants that at the time the instruction is presented to the issuer:

(a) the person specified in the instruction as the registered owner or registered pledgee of the uncertificated security will be the registered owner or registered pledgee; and

(b) the transfer, pledge, or release of the uncertificated security requested in the instruction will be registered by the issuer free from all liens, security interests, restrictions, and claims other than those specified in the instruction.

(4) The guarantor under subsections (1) and (2) or the special guarantor under subsection (3) does not otherwise warrant the rightfulness of the particular transfer, pledge, or release.

(5) Any person guaranteeing an indorsement of a certificated security makes not only the warranties of a signature guarantor under subsection (1) but also warrants the rightfulness of the particular transfer in all respects.

(6) Any person guaranteeing an instruction requesting the transfer, pledge, or release of an uncertificated security makes not only the warranties of a special signature guarantor under subsection (3) but also warrants the rightfulness of the particular transfer, pledge, or release in all respects.

(7) No issuer may require a special guarantee of signature (subsection (3)), a guarantee of indorsement (subsection (5)), or a guarantee of instruction (subsection (6)) as a condition to registration of transfer, pledge, or release.

(8) The foregoing warranties are made to any person taking or dealing with the security in reliance on the guarantee, and the guarantor is liable to the person for any loss resulting from breach of the warranties.

## § 8–313. When Transfer to Purchaser Occurs; Financial Intermediary as Bona Fide Purchaser; "Financial Intermediary"

(1) Transfer of a security or a limited interest (including a security interest) therein to a purchaser occurs only:

(a) at the time he or a person designated by him acquires possession of a certificated security;

(b) at the time the transfer, pledge, or release of an uncertificated security is registered to him or a person designated by him;

(c) at the time his financial intermediary acquires possession of a certificated security specially indorsed to or issued in the name of the purchaser;

(d) at the time a financial intermediary, not a clearing corporation, sends him confirmation of the purchase and also by book entry or otherwise identifies as belonging to the purchaser

(i) a specific certificated security in the financial intermediary's possession;

(ii) as quantity of securities that constitute or are part of a fungible bulk of certificated securities in the financial intermediary's possession or of uncertificated securities registered in the name of the financial intermediary; or

(iii) a quantity of securities that constitute or are part of a fungible bulk of securities shown on the account of the financial intermediary on the books of another financial intermediary;

(e) with respect to an identified certificated security to be delivered while still in the possession of a third person, not a financial intermediary, at the time that person acknowledges that he holds for the purchaser;

(f) with respect to a specific uncertificated security the pledge or transfer of which has been registered to a third person, not a financial intermediary, at the time that person acknowledges that he holds for the purchaser;

(g) at the time appropriate entries to the account of the purchaser or a person designated by him on the books of a clearing corporation are made under Section 8–320;

(h) with respect to the transfer of a security interest where the debtor has signed a security agreement containing a description of the security, at the time a written notification, which, in the case of the creation of the security interest, is signed by the debtor (which may be a copy of the security agreement) or which, in the case of the release or assignment of the security interest created pursuant to this paragraph, is signed by the secured party, is received by

(i) a financial intermediary on whose books the interest of the transferor in the security appears;

(ii) a third person, not a financial intermediary, in possession of the security, if it is certificated;

(iii) a third person, not a financial intermediary, who is the registered owner of the security, if it is uncertificated and not subject to a registered pledge; or

(iv) a third person, not a financial intermediary, who is the registered pledgee of the security, if it is uncertificated and subject to a registered pledge;

(i) with respect to the transfer of a security interest where the transferor has signed a security agreement containing a description of the security, at the time new value if given by the secured party; or

(j) with respect to the transfer of a security interest where the secured party is a financial intermediary and the security has already been transferred to the financial intermediary under paragraphs (a), (b), (c), (d), or (g), at the time the transferor has signed a security agreement containing a description of the security and value is given by the secured party.

(2) The purchaser is the owner of a security held for him by a financial intermediary, but cannot be a bona fide purchaser of a security so held except in the circumstances specified in paragraphs (c), (d) (i), and (g) of subsection (1). If a security so held is part of a fungible bulk, as in the circumstances specified in paragraphs (d) (ii) and (d) (iii) of subsection (1), the purchaser is the owner of a proportionate property interest in the fungible bulk.

(3) Notice of an adverse claim received by the financial intermediary or by the purchaser after the financial intermediary takes delivery of a certificated security as a holder for value or after the transfer, pledge, or release of an uncertificated security has been registered free of the claim to a financial intermediary who has given value is not effective either as to the financial intermediary or as to the purchaser. However, as between the financial intermediary and the purchaser the purchaser may demand transfer of an equivalent security as to which no notice of adverse claim has been received.

(4) A "financial intermediary" is a bank, broker, clearing corporation, or other person (or the nominee of any of them) which in the ordinary course of its business maintains security accounts for its customers and is acting in that capacity. A financial intermediary may have a security interest in securities held in account for its customer.

### § 8–314. Duty to Transfer, When Completed

(1) Unless otherwise agreed, if a sale of a security is made on an exchange or otherwise through brokers:

(a) the selling customer fulfills his duty to transfer at the time he:

(i) places a certificated security in the possession of the selling broker or a person designated by the broker;

(ii) causes an uncertificated security to be registered in the name of the selling broker or a person designated by the broker;

(iii) if requested, causes an acknowledgment to be made to the selling broker that a certificated or uncertificated security is held for the broker; or

(iv) places in the possession of the selling broker or of a person designated by the broker a transfer instruction for an uncertificated security, providing the issuer does not refuse to register the requested transfer if the instruction is presented to the issuer for registration within 30 days thereafter; and

(b) the selling broker, including a correspondent broker acting for a selling customer, fulfills his duty to transfer at the time he:

(i) places a certificated security in the possession of the buying broker or a person designated by the buying broker;

(ii) causes an uncertificated security to be registered in the name of the buying broker or a person designated by the buying broker;

(iii) places in the possession of the buying broker or of a person designated by the buying broker a transfer instruction for an uncertificated security, providing the issuer does not refuse to register the requested transfer if the instruction is presented to the issuer for registration within 30 days thereafter; or

(iv) effects clearance of the sale in accordance with the rules of the exchange on which the transaction took place.

(2) Except as provided in this section or unless otherwise agreed, a transferor's duty to transfer a security under a contract of purchase is not fulfilled until he:

(a) places a certificated security in form to be negotiated by the purchaser in the possession of the purchaser or of a person designated by the purchaser;

(b) causes an uncertificated security to be registered in the name of the purchaser or a person designated by the purchaser; or

(c) if the purchaser requests, causes an acknowledgment to be made to the purchaser that a certificated or uncertificated security is held for the purchaser.

(3) Unless made on an exchange, a sale to a broker purchasing for his own account is within subsection (2) and not within subsection (1).

### § 8–315. Action against Transferee Based upon Wrongful Transfer

(1) Any person against whom the transfer of a security is wrongful for any reason, including his incapacity, as against anyone except a bona fide purchaser, may:

(a) reclaim possession of the certificated security wrongfully transferred;

(b) obtain possession of any new certificated security representing all or part of the same rights;

(c) compel the origination of an instruction to transfer to him or a person designated by him an uncertificated security constituting all or part of the same rights; or

(d) have damages.

(2) If the transfer is wrongful because of an unauthorized indorsement of a certificated security, the owner may also reclaim or obtain possession of the security or a new certificated security, even from a bona fide purchaser, if the ineffectiveness of the purported indorsement can be asserted against him under the provisions of this Article on unauthorized indorsements (Section 8–311).

(3) The right to obtain or reclaim possession of a certificated security or to compel the origination of a transfer instruction may be specifically enforced and the transfer of a certificated or uncertificated security enjoined and a certificated security impounded pending the litigation.

### § 8–316. Purchaser's Right to Requisites for Registration of Transfer, Pledge, or Release on Books

Unless otherwise agreed, the transferor of a certificated security or the transferor, pledgor, or pledgee of an uncertificated security on due demand must supply his purchaser with any proof of his authority to transfer, pledge, or release or with any other requisite necessary to obtain registration of the transfer, pledge, or release of the security; but if the transfer, pledge, or release is not for value, a transferor, pledgor, or pledgee need not do so unless the purchaser furnishes the necessary expenses. Failure within a reasonable time to comply with a demand made gives the purchaser the right to reject or rescind the transfer, pledge, or release.

### § 8–317. Creditors' Rights

(1) Subject to the exceptions in subsections (3) and (4), no attachment or levy upon a certificated security or any share or other interest represented thereby which is outstanding is valid until the security is actually seized by the officer making the attachment or levy, but a certificated security which has been surrendered to the issuer may be reached by a creditor by legal process at the issuer's chief executive office in the United States.

(2) An uncertificated security registered in the name of the debtor may not be reached by a creditor except by legal process at the issuer's chief executive office in the United States.

(3) The interest of a debtor in a certificated security that is in the possession of a secured party not a financial intermediary or in an uncertificated security registered in the name of a secured party not a financial intermediary (or in the name of a nominee of the secured party) may be reached by a creditor by legal process upon the secured party.

(4) The interest of a debtor in a certificated security that is in the possession of or registered in the name of a financial intermediary or in an uncertificated security registered in the name of a financial intermediary may be reached by a creditor by legal process upon the financial intermediary on whose books the interest of the debtor appears.

(5) Unless otherwise provided by law, a creditor's lien upon the interest of a debtor in a security obtained pursuant to subsection (3) or (4) is not a restraint on the transfer of the security, free of the lien, to a third party for new value; but in the event of a transfer, the lien applies to the proceeds of the transfer in the hands of the secured party or financial intermediary, subject to any claims having priority.

(6) A creditor whose debtor is the owner of a security is entitled to aid from courts of appropriate jurisdiction, by injunction or otherwise, in reaching the security or in satisfying the claim by means allowed at law or in equity in regard to property that cannot readily be reached by ordinary legal process.

## § 8–318. No Conversion by Good Faith Conduct

An agent or bailee who in good faith (including observance of reasonable commercial standards if he is in the business of buying, selling, or otherwise dealing with securities) has received certificated securities and sold, pledged, or delivered them or has sold or caused the transfer or pledge of uncertificated securities over which he had control according to the instructions of his principal, is not liable for conversion or for participation in breach of fiduciary duty although the principal had no right so to deal with the securities.

## § 8–319. Statute of Frauds

A contract for the sale of securities is not enforceable by way of action or defense unless:

(a) there is some writing signed by the party against whom enforcement is sought or by his authorized agent or broker, sufficient to indicate that a contract has been made for sale of a stated quantity of described securities at a defined or stated price;

(b) delivery of a certificated security or transfer instruction has been accepted, or transfer of an uncertificated security has been registered and the transferee has failed to send written objection to the issuer within 10 days after receipt of the initial transaction statement confirming the registration, or payment has been made, but the contract is enforceable under this provision only to the extent of the delivery, registration, or payment;

(c) within a reasonable time a writing in confirmation of the sale or purchase and sufficient against the sender under paragraph (a) has been received by the party against whom enforcement is sought and he has failed to send written objection to its contents within 10 days after its receipt; or

(d) the party against whom enforcement is sought admits in his pleading, testimony, or otherwise in court that a contract was made for the sale of a stated quantity of described securities at a defined or stated price.

## § 8–320. Transfer or Pledge Within Central Depository System

(1) In addition to other methods, a transfer, pledge, or release of a security or any interest therein may be effected by the making of appropriate entries on the books of a clearing corporation reducing the account of the transferor, pledgor, or pledgee and increasing the account of the transferee, pledgee, or pledgor by the amount of the obligation or the number of shares or rights transferred, pledged, or released, if the security is shown on the account of a transferor, pledgor, or pledgee on the books of the clearing corporation; is subject to the control of the clearing corporation; and

(a) is certificated,

(i) is the custody of the clearing corporation, another clearing corporation, a custodian bank, or a nominee of any of them; and

(ii) is in bearer form or indorsed in blank by an appropriate person or registered in the name of the clearing corporation, a custodian bank, or a nominee of any of them; or

(b) if uncertificated, is registered in the name of the clearing corporation, another clearing corporation, a custodian bank, or a nominee of any of them.

(2) Under this section entries may be made with respect to like securities or interests therein as a part of a fungible bulk and may refer merely to a quantity of a particular security without reference to the name of the registered owner, certificate or bond number, or the like, and, in appropriate cases, may be on a net basis taking into account other transfers, pledges, or releases of the same security.

(3) A transfer under this section is effective (Section 8–313) and the purchaser acquires the rights

of the transferor (Section 8–301). A pledge or release under this section is the transfer of a limited interest. If a pledge or the creation of a security interest is intended, the security interest is perfected at the time when both value is given by the pledgee and the appropriate entries are made (Section 8–321). A transferee or pledgee under this section may be a bona fide purchaser (Section 8–302).

(4) A transfer or pledge under this section is not a registration of transfer under Part 4.

(5) That entries made on the books of the clearing corporation as provided in subsection (1) are not appropriate does not affect the validity or effect of the entries or the liabilities or obligations of the clearing corporation to any person adversely affected thereby.

### § 8–321. Enforceability, Attachment, Perfection and Termination of Security Interests

(1) A security interest in a security is enforceable and can attach only if it is transferred to the secured party or a person designated by him pursuant to a provision of Section 8–313(1).

(2) A security interest so transferred pursuant to agreement by a transferor who has rights in the security to a transferee who has given value is a perfected security interest, but a security interest that has been transferred solely under paragraph (i) of Section 8–313(1) becomes unperfected after 21 days unless, within that time, the requirements for transfer under any other provision of Section 8–313(1) are satisfied.

(3) A security interest in a security is subject to the provisions of Article 9, but:

(a) no filing is required to perfect the security interest; and

(b) no written security agreement signed by the debtor is necessary to make the security interest enforceable, except as provided in paragraph (h), (i), or (j) of Section 8–313(1). The secured party has the rights and duties provided under Section 9–207, to the extent they are applicable, whether or not the security is certificated, and, if certificated, whether or not it is in his possession.

(4) Unless otherwise agreed, a security interest in a security is terminated by transfer to the debtor or a person designated by him pursuant to a provision of Section 8–313(1). If a security is thus transferred, the security interest, if not terminated, becomes unperfected unless the security is certificated and is delivered to the debtor for the purpose of ultimate sale or exchange or presentation, collection, renewal, or registration of transfer. In that case, the security interest becomes unperfected after 21 days unless, within that time, the security (or securities for which it has been exchanged) is transferred to the secured party or a person designated by him pursuant to a provision of Section 8–313(1).

## Part 4 Registration

### § 8–401. Duty of Issuer to Register Transfer, Pledge, or Release

(1) If a certificated security in registered form is presented to the issuer with a request to register transfer or an instruction is presented to the issuer with a request to register transfer, pledge, or release, the issuer shall register the transfer, pledge, or release as requested if:

(a) the security is indorsed or the instruction was originated by the appropriate person or persons (Section 8–308);

(b) reasonable assurance is given that those indorsements or instructions are genuine and effective (Section 8–402);

(c) the issuer has no duty as to adverse claims or has discharged the duty (Section 8–403);

(d) any applicable law relating to the collection of taxes has been complied with; and

(e) the transfer, pledge, or release is in fact rightful or is to a bona fide purchaser.

(2) If an issuer is under a duty to register a transfer, pledge, or release of a security, the issuer is also liable to the person presenting a certificated security or an instruction for registration or his principal for loss resulting from any unreasonable delay in registration or from failure or refusal to register the transfer, pledge, or release.

### § 8–402. Assurance that Indorsements and Instructions Are Effective

(1) The issuer may require the following assurance that each necessary indorsement of a certificated security or each instruction (Section 8–308) is genuine and effective:

(a) in all cases, a guarantee of the signature (Section 8–312(1) or (2) of the person indorsing a certificated security or originating an instruction including, in the case of an instruction, a warranty of the taxpayer identification number or, in the absence thereof, other reasonable assurance of identity;

(b) if the indorsement is made or the instruction is originated by an agent, appropriate assurance of authority to sign;

(c) if the indorsement is made or the instruction is orginated by a fiduciary, appropriate evidence of appointment or incumbency;

(d) if there is more than one fiduciary, reasonable assurance that all who are required to sign have done so; and

(e) if the indorsement is made or the instruction is originated by a person not covered by any of the foregoing, assurance appropriate to the case corresponding as nearly as may be to the foregoing.

(2) A "guarantee of the signature" in subsection (1) means a guarantee signed by or on behalf of a person reasonably believed by the issuer to be responsible. The issuer may adopt standards with respect to responsibility if they are not manifestly unreasonable.

(3) "Appropriate evidence of appointment or incumbency" in subsection (1) means:

(a) in the case of a fiduciary appointed or qualified by a court, a certificate issued by or under the direction or supervision of that court or an officer thereof and dated within 60 days before the date of presentation for transfer, pledge, or release; or

(b) in any other case, a copy of a document showing the appointment or a certificate issued by or on behalf of a person reasonably believed by the issuer to be responsible or, in the absence of that document or certificate, other evidence reasonably deemed by the issuer to be appropriate. The issuer may adopt standards with respect to the evidence if they are not manifestly unreasonable. The issuer is not charged with notice of the contents of any document obtained pursuant to this paragraph (b) except to the extent that the contents relate directly to the appointment or incumbency.

(4) The issuer may elect to require reasonable assurance beyond that specified in this section, but if it does so and, for a purpose other than that specified in subsection (3)(b), both requires and obtains a copy of a will, trust, indenture, articles of co-partnership, bylaws, or other controlling instrument, it is charged with notice of all matters contained therein affecting the transfer, pledge, or release.

### § 8–403. Issuer's Duty as to Adverse Claims

(1) An issuer to whom a certificated security is presented for registration shall inquire into adverse claims if:

(a) a written notification of an adverse claim is received at a time and in a manner affording the issuer a reasonable opportunity to act on it prior to the issuance of a new, reissued, or re-registered certificated security, and the notification identifies the claimant, the registered owner, and the issue of which the security is a part, and provides an address for communications directed to the claimant; or

(b) the issuer is charged with notice of an adverse claim from a controlling instrument it has elected to require under Section 8–402(4).

(2) The issuer may discharge any duty of inquiry by any reasonable means, including notifying an adverse claimant by registered or certified mail at the address furnished by him or, if there be no such address, at his residence or regular place of business that the certificated security has been presented for registration of transfer by a named person, and that the transfer will be registered unless within 30 days from the date of mailing the notification, either:

(a) an appropriate restraining order, injunction, or other process issues from a court of competent jurisdiction; or

(b) there is filed with the issuer an indemnity bond, sufficient in the issuer's judgment to protect the issuer and any transfer agent, registrar, or other agent of the issuer involved from any loss it or they may suffer by complying with the adverse claim.

(3) Unless an issuer is charged with notice of an adverse claim from a controlling instrument which it has elected to require under Section 8–402(4) or receives notification of an adverse claim under subsection (1), if a certificated security presented for registration is indorsed by the appropriate per-

son or persons the issuer is under no duty to inquire into adverse claims. In particular:

(a) an issuer registering a certificated security in the name of a person who is a fiduciary or who is described as a fiduciary is not bound to inquire into the existence, extent, or correct description of the fiduciary relationship; and thereafter the issuer may assume without inquiry that the newly registered owner continues to be the fiduciary until the issuer receives written notice that the fiduciary is no longer acting as such with respect to the particular security;

(b) an issuer registering transfer on an indorsement by a fiduciary is not bound to inquire whether the transfer is made in compliance with a controlling instrument or with the law of the state having jurisdiction of the fiduciary relationship, including any law requiring the fiduciary to obtain court approval of the transfer; and

(c) the issuer is not charged with notice of the contents of any court or file or other recorded or unrecorded document even though the document is in its possession and even though the transfer is made on the indorsement of a fiduciary to the fiduciary himself or to his nominee.

(4) An issuer is under no duty as to adverse claims with respect to an uncertificated security except:

(a) claims embodied in a restraining order, injunction, or other legal process served upon the issuer if the process was served at a time and in a manner affording the issuer a reasonable opportunity to act on it in accordance with the requirements of subsection (5);

(b) claims of which the issuer has received a written notification from the registered owner or the registered pledgee if the notification was received at a time and in a manner affording the issuer a reasonable opportunity to act on it in accordance with the requirements of subsection (5);

(c) claims (including restrictions on transfer not imposed by the issuer) to which the registration of transfer to the present registered owner was subject and were so noted in the initial transaction statement sent to him; and

(d) claims as to which an issuer is charged with notice from a controlling instrument it has elected to require under Section 8–402(4).

(5) If the issuer of an uncertificated security is under a duty to an adverse claim, he discharges that duty by:

(a) including a notation of the claim in any statements sent with respect to the security under Sections 8–408 (3), (6), and (7); and

(b) refusing to register the transfer or pledge of the security unless the nature of the claim does not preclude transfer or pledge subject thereto.

(6) If the transfer of pledge of the security is registered subject to an adverse claim, a notation of the claim must be included in the initial transaction statement and all subsequent statements sent to the transferee and pledgee under Section 8–408.

(7) Notwithstanding subsections (4) and (5), if an uncertificated security was subject to a registered pledge at the time the issuer first came under a duty as to a particular adverse claim, the issuer has no duty as to that claim if transfer of the security is requested by the registered pledgee or an appropriate person acting for the registered pledgee unless:

(a) the claim was embodied in legal process which expressly provides otherwise;

(b) the claim was asserted in a written notification from the registered pledgee;

(c) the claim was one as to which the issuer was charged with notice from a controlling instrument it required under Section 8–402(4) in connection with the pledgee's request for transfer; or

(d) the transfer requested is to the registered owner.

### § 8–404. Liability and Non-Liability for Registration

(1) Except as provided in any law relating to the collection of taxes, the issuer in not liable to the owner, pledgee, or any other person suffering loss as a result of the registration of a transfer, pledge, or release of a security if:

(a) there were on or with a certificated security the necessary indorsements or the issuer had received an instruction originated by an appropriate person (Section 8–308); and

(b) the issuer had no duty as to adverse claims or has discharged the duty (Section 8–403).

(2) If an issuer had registered a transfer of a certificated security to a person not entitled to it, the issuer on demand shall deliver a like security to the true owner unless:

(a) the registration was pursuant to subsection (1);

(b) the owner is precluded from asserting any

claim for registering the transfer under Section 8–405(1); or

(c) the delivery would result in overissue, in which case the issuer's liability is governed by Section 8–104.

(3) If an issuer has improperly registered a transfer, pledge, or release of an uncertificated security, the issuer on demand from the injured party shall restore the records as to the injured party to the condition that would have obtained if the improper registration had not been made unless:

(a) the registration was pursuant to subsection (1); or

(b) the registration would result in overissue, in which case the issuer's liability is governed by Section 8–104.

### § 8–405. Lost, Destroyed, and Stolen Certificated Securities

(1) If a certificated security has been lost, apparently destroyed, or wrongfully taken, and the owner fails to notify the issuer of that fact within a reasonable time after he has notice of it and the issuer registers a transfer of the security before receiving notification, the owner is precluded from asserting against the issuer any claim for registering the transfer under Section 8–404 or any claim to a new security under this section.

(2) If the owner of a certificated security claims that the security has been lost, destroyed, or wrongfully taken, the issuer shall issue a new certificated security or, at the option of the issuer, an equivalent uncertificated security in place of the original security if the owner:

(a) so requests before the issuer has notice that the security has been acquired by a bona fide purchaser;

(b) files with the issuer a sufficient indemnity bond; and

(c) satisfies any other reasonable requirements imposed by the issuer.

(3) If, after the issue of a new certificated or uncertificated security, a bona fide purchaser of the original certificated security presents it for registration of transfer, the issuer shall register the transfer unless registration would result in overissue, in which event the issuer's liability is governed by Section 8–104. In addition to any rights on the indemnity bond, the issuer may recover the new certificated security from the person to whom it was issued or any person taking under him except a bona fide purchaser or may cancel the uncertificated security unless a bona fide purchaser or any person taking under a bona fide purchaser is then the registered owner or registered pledgee thereof.

### § 8–406. Duty of Authenticating Trustee, Transfer Agent, or Registrar

(1) If a person acts as authenticating trustee, transfer agent, registrar, or other agent for an issuer in the registration of transfers of its certificated securities or in the registration of transfers, pledges, and releases of its uncertificated securities, in the issue of new securities, or in the cancellation of surrendered securities:

(a) he is under a duty to the issuer to exercise good faith and due diligence in performing his functions; and

(b) with regard to the particular functions he performs, he has the same obligation to the holder or owner of a certificated security or to the owner or pledgee of an uncertificated security and has the same rights and privileges as the issuer has in regard to those functions.

(2) Notice to an authenticating trustee, transfer agent, registrar or other agent is notice to the issuer with respect to the functions performed by the agent.

### § 8–407. Exchangeability of Securities

(1) No issuer is subject to the requirements of this section unless it regularly maintains a system for issuing the class of securities involved under which both certificated and uncertificated securities are regularly issued to the category of owners, which includes the person in whose name the new security is to be registered.

(2) Upon surrender of a certificated security with all necessary indorsements and presentation of a written request by the person surrendering the security, the issuer, if he has no duty as to adverse claims or has discharged the duty (Section 8–403), shall issue to the person or a person designated by him an equivalent uncertificated security subject to all liens, restrictions, and claims that were noted on the certificated security.

(3) Upon receipt of a transfer instruction originated by an appropriate person who so requests, the issuer of an uncertificated security shall cancel the uncertificated security and issue an equivalent

certificated security on which must be noted conspicuously any liens and restrictions of the issuer and any adverse claims (as to which the issuer has a duty under Section 8–403(4) to which the uncertificated security was subject. The certificated security shall be registered in the name of and delivered to:

(a) the registered owner, if the uncertificated security was not subject to a registered pledge; or

(b) the registered pledgee, if the uncertificated security was subject to a registered pledge.

### § 8–408. Statements of Uncertificated Securities

(1) Within 2 business days after the transfer of an uncertificated security has been registered, the issuer shall send to the new registered owner and, if the security has been transferred subject to a registered pledge, to the registered pledgee a written statement containing:

(a) a description of the issue of which the uncertificated security is a part;

(b) the number of shares or units transferred;

(c) the name and address and any taxpayer identification number of the new registered owner and, if the security has been transferred subject to a registered pledge, the name and address and any taxpayer identification number of the registered pledgee;

(d) a notation of any liens and restrictions of the issuer and any adverse claims (as to which the issuer has a duty under Section 8–403(4)) to which the uncertificated security is or may be subject at the time of registration or a statement that there are none of those liens, restrictions, or adverse claims; and

(e) the date the transfer was registered.

(2) Within 2 business days after the pledge of an uncertificated security has been registered, the issuer shall send to the registered owner and the registered pledgee a written statement containing:

(a) a description of the issue of which the uncertificated security is a part;

(b) the number of shares or units pledged;

(c) the name and address and any taxpayer identification number of the registered owner and the registered pledgee;

(d) a notation of any liens and restrictions of the issuer and any adverse claims (as to which the issuer has a duty under Section 8–403(4)) to which the uncertificated security is or may be subject at the time of registration or a statement that there are none of those liens, restrictions, or adverse claims; and

(e) the date the pledge was registered.

(3) Within 2 business days after the release from pledge of an uncertificated security has been registered, the issuer shall send to the registered owner and the pledgee whose interest was released a written statement containing:

(a) a description of the issue of which the uncertificated security is a part;

(b) the number of shares or units released from pledge;

(c) the name and address and any taxpayer identification number of the registered owner and the pledgee whose interest was released;

(d) a notation of any liens and restrictions of the issuer and any adverse claims (as to which the issuer has a duty under Section 8–403(4)) to which the uncertificated security is or may be subject at the time of registration or a statement that there are none of those liens, restrictions, or adverse claims; and

(e) the date the release was registered.

(4) An "initial transaction statement" is the statement sent to:

(a) the new registered owner and, if applicable, to the registered pledgee pursuant to subsection (1);

(b) the registered pledgee pursuant to subsection (2); or

(c) the registered owner pursuant to subsection (3).

Each initial transaction statement shall be signed by or on behalf of the issuer and must be identified as "Initial Transaction Statement."

(5) Within 2 business days after the transfer of an uncertificated security has been registered, the issuer shall send to the former registered owner and the former registered pledgee, if any, a written statement containing:

(a) a description of the issue of which the uncertificated security is a part;

(b) the number of shares or units transferred;

(c) the name and address and any taxpayer

identification number of the former registered owner and of any former registered pledgee; and

(d) the date the transfer was registered.

(6) At periodic intervals no less frequent than annually and at any time upon the reasonable written request of the registered owner, the issuer shall send to the registered owner of each uncertificated security a dated written statement containing:

(a) a description of the issue of which the uncertificated security is a part;

(b) the name and address and any taxpayer identification number of the registered owner;

(c) the number of shares or units of the uncertificated security registered in the name of the registered owner on the date of the statement;

(d) the name and address and any taxpayer identification number of any registered pledgee and the number of shares of units subject to the pledge; and

(e) a notation of any liens and restrictions of the issuer and any adverse claims (as to which the issuer has a duty under Section 8–403(4)) to which the uncertificated security is or may be subject or a statement that there are none of those liens, restrictions, or adverse claims.

(7) At periodic intervals no less frequent than annually and at any time upon the reasonable written request of the registered pledgee, the issuer shall send to the registered pledgee of each uncertificated security a dated written statement containing:

(a) a description of the issue of which the uncertificated security is a part;

(b) the name and address and any taxpayer identification number of the registered owner;

(c) the name and address and any taxpayer identification number of the registered pledgee;

(d) the number of shares or units subject to the pledge; and

(e) a notation of any liens and restrictions of the issuer and any adverse claims (as to which the issuer has a duty under Section 8–403(4)) to which the uncertificated security is or may be subject or a statement that there are none of those liens, restrictions, or adverse claims.

(8) If the issuer sends the statements described in subsections (6) and (7) at periodic intervals no less frequent than quarterly, the issuer is not obliged to send additional statements upon request unless the owner or pledgee requesting them pays to the issuer the reasonable cost of furnishing them.

(9) Each statement sent pursuant to this section must bear a conspicuous legend reading substantially as follows: "This statement is merely a record of the rights of the addressee as of the time of its issuance. Delivery of this statement, of itself, confers no rights on the recipient. This statement is neither a negotiable instrument nor a security."

# ARTICLE 9 SECURED TRANSACTIONS; SALES OF ACCOUNTS AND CHATTEL PAPER

## Part 1 Short Title, Applicability and Definitions

### § 9–101. Short Title

This Article shall be known and may be cited as Uniform Commercial Code—Secured Transactions.

### § 9–102. Policy and Subject Matter of Article

(1) Except as otherwise provided in Section 9–104 on excluded transactions, this Article applies

(a) to any transaction (regardless of its form) which is intended to create a security interest in personal property or fixtures including goods, documents, instruments, general intangibles, chattel paper or accounts; and also

(b) to any sale of accounts or chattel paper.

(2) This Article applies to security interests created by contract including pledge, assignment, chattel mortgage, chattel trust, trust deed, factor's lien, equipment trust, conditional sale, trust receipt, other lien or title retention contract and lease or consignment intended as security. This Article does not apply to statutory liens except as provided in Section 9–310.

(3) The application of this Article to a security interest in a secured obligation is not affected by the fact that the obligation is itself secured by a transaction or interest to which this Article does not apply.

**Note:** *The adoption of this Article should be accompanied by the repeal of existing statutes dealing with conditional sales, trust receipts, factor's liens where the factor is given a non-possessory lien, chattel mortgages, crop mortgages, mortgages on railroad equipment, assignment of accounts and generally statutes regulating security interests in personal property.*

*Where the state has a retail installment selling act or small loan act, that legislation should be carefully examined to determine what changes in those acts are needed to conform them to this Article. This Article primarily sets out rules defining rights of a secured party against persons dealing with the debtor; it does not prescribe regulations and controls which may be necessary to curb abuses arising in the small loan business or in the financing of consumer purchases on credit. Accordingly there is no intention to repeal existing regulatory acts in those fields by enactment or re-enactment of Article 9. See Section 9–203(4) and the Note thereto.*

### § 9–103. Perfection of Security Interest in Multiple State Transactions

(1) Documents, instruments and ordinary goods.

(a) This subsection applies to documents and instruments and to goods other than those covered by a certificate of title described in subsection (2), mobile goods described in subsection (3), and minerals
described in subsection (5).

(b) Except as otherwise provided in this subsection, perfection and the effect of perfection or non-perfection of a security interest in collateral are governed by the law of the jurisdiction where the collateral is when the last event occurs on which is based the assertion that the security interest is perfected or unperfected.

(c) If the parties to a transaction creating a purchase money security interest in goods in one jurisdiction understand at the time that the security interest attaches that the goods will be kept in another jurisdiction, then the law of the other jurisdiction governs the perfection and the effect of perfection or non-perfection of the security interest from the time it attaches until thirty days after the debtor receives possession of the goods and thereafter if the goods are taken to the other jurisdiction before the end of the thirty-day period.

(d) When collateral is brought into and kept in this state while subject to a security interest perfected under the law of the jurisdiction from which the collateral was removed, the security interest remains perfected, but if action is required by Part 3 of this Article to perfect the security interest,

(i) if the action is not taken before the expiration of the period of perfection in the other jurisdiction or the end of four months after the collateral is brought into this state, whichever period first expires, the security interest becomes unperfected at the end of that period and is thereafter deemed to have been unperfected as against a person who became a purchaser after removal;

(ii) if the action is taken before the expiration of the period specified in subparagraph (i), the security interest continues perfected thereafter;

(iii) for the purpose of priority over a buyer of consumer goods (subsection (2) of Section 9–307), the period of the effectiveness of a filing in the jurisdiction from which the collateral is removed is governed by the rules with respect to perfection in subparagraphs (i) and (ii).

(2) Certificate of title.

(a) This subsection applies to goods covered by a certificate of title issued under a statute of this state or of another jurisdiction under the law of which indication of a security interest on the certificate is required as a condition of perfection.

(b) Except as otherwise provided in this subsection, perfection and the effect of perfection or non-perfection of the security interest are governed by the law (including the conflict of law rules) of the jurisdiction issuing the certificate until four months after the goods are removed from that jurisdiction and thereafter until the goods are registered in another jurisdiction, but in any event not beyond surrender of the certificate. After the expiration of that period, the goods are not covered by the certificate of title within the meaning of this section.

(c) Except with respect to the rights of a buyer described in the next paragraph, a security interest, perfected in another jurisdiction otherwise than by notation on a certificate of title, in goods brought into this state and thereafter covered by a certificate of title issued by this state is subject to the rules stated in paragraph (d) of subsection (1).

(d) If goods are brought into this state while a security interest therein is perfected in any manner under the law of the jurisdiction from which the goods are removed and a certificate of title is issued by this state and the certificate does not show that the goods are subject to the security interest or that they may be subject to security interests not shown on the certificate, the security interest is subordinate to the rights of a buyer of the goods who is not in the business of selling goods of that kind to the extent that he gives value and receives delivery of the goods after issuance of the certificate and without knowledge of the security interest.

(3) Accounts, general intangibles and mobile goods.

(a) This subsection applies to accounts (other than an account described in subsection (5) on minerals) and general intangibles (other than uncertificated securities) and to goods which are mobile and which are of a type normally used in more than one jurisdiction, such as motor vehicles, trailers, rolling stock, airplanes, shipping containers, road building and construction machinery and commercial harvesting machinery and the like, if the goods are equipment or are inventory leased or held for lease by the debtor to others, and are not covered by a certificate of title described in subsection (2).

(b) The law (including the conflict of laws rules) of the jurisdiction in which the debtor is located governs the perfection and the effect of perfection or non-perfection of the security interest.

(c) If, however, the debtor is located in a jurisdiction which is not a part of the United States, and which does not provide for perfection of the security interest by filing or recording in that jurisdiction, the law of the jurisdiction in the United States in which the debtor has its major executive office governs the perfection and the effect of perfection or non-perfection of the security interest through filing. In the alternative, if the debtor is located in a jurisdiction which is not a part of the United States or Canada and the collateral is accounts or general intangibles for money due or to become due, the security interest may be perfected by notification to the account debtor. As used in this paragraph, "United States" includes its territories and possessions and the Commonwealth of Puerto Rico.

(d) A debtor shall be deemed located at his place of business if he has one, at his chief executive office if he has more than one place of business, otherwise at his residence. If, however, the debtor is a foreign air carrier under the Federal Aviation Act of 1958, as amended, it shall be deemed located at the designated office of the agent upon whom service of process may be made on behalf of the foreign air carrier.

(e) A security interest perfected under the law of the jurisdiction of the location of the debtor is perfected until the expiration of four months after a change of the debtor's location to another jurisdiction, or until perfection would have ceased by the law of the first jurisdiction, whichever period first expires. Unless perfected in the new jurisdiction before the end of that period, it becomes unperfected thereafter and is deemed to have been unperfected as against a person who became a purchaser after the change.

(4) Chattel paper. The rules stated for goods in subsection (1) apply to a possessory security interest in chattel paper. The rules stated for accounts in subsection (3) apply to a non-possessory security interest in chattel paper, but the security interest may not be perfected by notification to the account debtor.

(5) Minerals. Perfection and the effect of perfection or non-perfection of a security interest which is created by a debtor who has an interest in minerals or the like (including oil and gas) before extraction and which attaches thereto as extracted, or which attaches to an account resulting from the sale thereof at the wellhead or minehead are governed by the law (including the conflict of laws rules) of the jurisdiction wherein the wellhead or minehead is located.

(6) Uncertificated securities. The law (including the conflict of laws rules) of the jurisdiction of organization of the issuer governs the perfection and the effect of perfection or non-perfection of a security interest in uncertificated securities.

### § 9–104. Transactions Excluded From Article

This Article does not apply

(a) to a security interest subject to any statute of the United States, to the extent that such statute governs the rights of parties to and third parties affected by transactions in particular types of property; or

(b) to a landlord's lien; or

(c) to a lien given by statute or other rule of law for services or materials except as provided in Section 9–310 on priority of such liens; or

(d) to a transfer of a claim for wages, salary or other compensation of an employee; or

(e) to a transfer by a government or governmental subdivision or agency; or

(f) to a sale of accounts or chattel paper as part of a sale of the business out of which they arose, or an assignment of accounts or chattel paper which is for the purpose of collection only, or a transfer of a right to payment under a contract to an assignee who is also to do the performance under the contract or a transfer of a single account to an assignee in whole or partial satisfaction of a preexisting indebtedness; or

(g) to a transfer of an interest in or claim in or under any policy of insurance, except as provided with respect to proceeds (Section 9–306) and priorities in proceeds (Section 9–312); or

(h) to a right represented by a judgment (other than a judgment taken on a right to payment which was collateral); or

(i) to any right of set-off; or

(j) except to the extent that provision is made for fixtures in Section 9–313, to the creation or transfer of an interest in or lien on real estate, including a lease or rents thereunder; or

(k) to a transfer in whole or in part of any claim arising out of tort; or

(l) to a transfer of an interest in any deposit account (subsection (1) of Section 9–105), except as provided with respect to proceeds (Section 9–306) and priorities in proceeds (Section 9–312).

### § 9–105. Definitions and Index of Definitions

(1) In this Article unless the context otherwise requires:

(a) "Account debtor" means the person who is obligated on an account, chattel paper or general intangible;

(b) "Chattel paper" means a writing or writings which evidence both a monetary obligation and a security interest in or a lease of specific goods, but a charter or other contract involving the use or hire of a vessel is not chattel paper. When a transaction is evidenced both by such a security agreement or a lease and by an instrument or a series of instruments, the group of writings taken together constitutes chattel paper;

(c) "Collateral" means the property subject to a security interest, and includes accounts and chattel paper which have been sold;

(d) "Debtor" means the person who owes payment or other performance of the obligation secured, whether or not he owns or has rights in the collateral, and includes the seller of accounts or chattel paper. Where the debtor and the owner of the collateral are not the same person, the term "debtor" means the owner of the collateral in any provision of the Article dealing with the collateral, the obligor in any provision dealing with the obligation, and may include both where the context so requires;

(e) "Deposit account" means a demand, time, savings, passbook or like account maintained with a bank, savings and loan association, credit union or like organization, other than an account evidenced by a certificate of deposit;

(f) "Document" means document of title as defined in the general definitions of Article 1 (Section 1–201), and a receipt of the kind described in subsection (2) of Section 7–201;

(g) "Encumbrance" includes real estate mortgages and other liens on real estate and all other rights in real estate that are not ownership interests;

(h) "Goods" includes all things which are movable at the time the security interest attaches or which are fixtures (Section 9–313), but does not include money, documents, instruments, accounts, chattel paper, general intangibles, or minerals or the like (including oil and gas) before extraction. "Goods" also includes standing timber which is to be cut and removed under a conveyance or contract for sale, the unborn young of animals, and growing crops;

(i) "Instrument" means a negotiable instrument (defined in Section 3–104), or a certificated security (defined in Section 8–102) or any other writing which evidences a right to the payment of money and is not itself a security agreement or lease and is of a type which is in ordinary course of business transferred by delivery with any necessary indorsement or assignment;

(j) "Mortgage" means a consensual interest created by a real estate mortgage, a trust deed on real estate, or the like;

(k) An advance is made "pursuant to commitment" if the secured party has bound himself to make it, whether or not a subsequent event of default or other event not within his control has relieved or may relieve him from his obligation;

(l) "Security agreement" means an agreement which creates or provides for a security interest;

(m) "Secured party" means a lender, seller or other person in whose favor there is a security interest, including a person to whom accounts or chattel paper have been sold. When the holders of obligations issued under an indenture of trust, equipment trust agreement or the like are represented by a trustee or other person, the representative is the secured party;

(n) "Transmitting utility" means any person primarily engaged in the railroad, street railway or trolley bus business, the electric or electronics communications transmission business, the transmission of goods by pipeline, or the transmission or the production and transmission of electricity, steam, gas or water, or the provision of sewer service.

(2) Other definitions applying to this Article and the sections in which they appear are:

"Account." Section 9–106.
"Attach." Section 9–203.
"Construction mortgage." Section 9–313 (1).
"Consumer goods." Section 9–109 (1).
"Equipment." Section 9–109 (2).
"Farm products." Section 9–109 (3).
"Fixture." Section 9–313 (1).
"Fixture filing." Section 9–313 (1).
"General intangibles." Section 9–106.
"Inventory." Section 9–109 (4).
"Lien creditor." Section 9–301 (3).
"Proceeds." Section 9–306 (1).
"Purchase money security interest." Section 9–107.
"United States." Section 9–103.

(3) The following definitions in other Articles apply to this Article:

"Check." Section 3–104.
"Contract for sale." Section 2–106.
"Holder in due course." Section 3–302.
"Note." Section 3–104.
"Sale." Section 2–106.

(4) In addition Article 1 contains general definitions and principles of construction and interpretation applicable throughout this Article.

### § 9–106. Definitions: "Account"; "General Intangibles"

"Account" means any right to payment for goods sold or leased or for services rendered which is not evidenced by an instrument or chattel paper, whether or not it has been earned by performance. "General intangibles" means any personal property (including things in action) other than goods, accounts, chattel paper, documents, instruments, and money. All rights to payment earned or unearned under a charter or other contract involving the use or hire of a vessel and all rights incident to the chart or contract are accounts.

### § 9–107. Definitions: "Purchase Money Security Interest"

A security interest is a "purchase money security interest" to the extent that it is

(a) taken or retained by the seller of the collateral to secure all or part of its price; or

(b) taken by a person who by making advances or incurring an obligation gives value to enable the debtor to acquire rights in or the use of collateral if such value is in fact so used.

### § 9–108. When After-Acquired Collateral Not Security for Antecedent Debt

Where a secured party makes an advance, incurs an obligation, releases a perfected security interest, or otherwise gives new value which is to be secured in whole or in part by after-acquired collateral shall be deemed to be taken for new value and not as security for an antecedent debt if the debtor acquires his rights in such collateral either in the ordinary course of his business or under a contract of purchase made pursuant to the security agreement within a reasonable time after new value is given.

### § 9–109. Classification of Goods; "Consumer Goods"; "Equipment"; "Farm Products"; "Inventory"

Goods are

(1) "consumer goods" if they are used or bought for use primarily for personal, family or household purposes;

(2) "equipment" if they are used or bought for use primarily in business (including farming or a profession) or by a debtor who is a non-profit orga-

nization or a governmental subdivision or agency or if the goods are not included in the definitions of inventory, farm products or consumer goods;
(3) "farm products" if they are crops or livestock or supplies used or produced in farming operations or if they are products of crops or livestock in their unmanufactured states (such as ginned cotton, wool-clip, maple syrup, milk and eggs), and if they are in the possession of a debtor engaged in raising, fattening, grazing or other farming operations. If goods are farm products they are neither equipment nor inventory;
(4) "inventory" if they are held by a person who holds them for sale or lease or to be furnished under contracts of service or if he has so furnished them, or if they are raw materials, work in process or materials used or consumed in a business. Inventory of a person is not to be classified as his equipment.

### § 9–110. Sufficiency of Description

For the purposes of this Article any description of personal property or real estate is sufficient whether or not it is specific if it reasonably identifies what is described.

### § 9–111. Applicability of Bulk Transfer Laws

The creation of a security interest is not a bulk transfer under Article 6 (see Section 6–103).

### § 9–112. Where Collateral Is Not Owned by Debtor

Unless otherwise agreed, when a secured party knows that collateral is owned by a person who is not the debtor, the owner of the collateral is entitled to receive from the secured party any surplus under Section 9–502(2) or under Section 9–504(1), and is not liable for the debt or for any deficiency after resale, and he has the same right as the debtor

(a) to receive statements under Section 9–208;

(b) to receive notice of and to object to a secured party's proposal to retain the collateral in satisfaction of the indebtedness under Section 9–505;

(c) to redeem the collateral under Section 9–506;

(d) to obtain injunctive or other relief under Section 9–507(1); and

(e) to recover losses caused to him under Section 9–208(2).

### § 9–113. Security Interests Arising under Article on Sales

A security interest arising solely under the Article on Sales (Article 2) is subject to the provisions of this Article except that to the extent that and so long as the debtor does not have or does not lawfully obtain possession of the goods

(a) no security agreement is necessary to make the security interest enforceable; and

(b) no filing is required to perfect the security interest; and

(c) the rights of the secured party on default by the debtor are governed by the Article on Sales (Article 2).

### § 9–114. Consignment

(1) A person who delivers goods under a consignment which is not a security interest and who would be required to file under this Article by paragraph (3) (c) of Section 2–326 has priority over a secured party who is or becomes a creditor of the consignee and who would have a perfected security interest in the goods if they were the property of the consignee, and also has priority with respect to identifiable cash proceeds received on or before delivery of the goods to a buyer, if

(a) the consignor complies with the filing provision of the Article on Sales with respect to consignments (paragraph (3) (c) of Section 2–326) before the consignee receives possession of the goods; and

(b) the consignor gives notification in writing to the holder of the security interest if the holder has filed a financing statement covering the same types of goods before the date of the filing made by the consignor; and

(c) the holder of the security interest receives the notification within five years before the consignee receives possession of the goods; and

(d) the notification states that the consignor expects to deliver goods on consignment to the consignee, describing the goods by item or type.

(2) In the case of a consignment which is not a security interest and in which the requirements of the preceding subsection have not been met, a person who delivers goods to another is subordinate to a person who would have a perfected security interest in the goods if they were the property of the debtor.

## Part 2 Validity of Security Agreement and Rights of Parties Thereto

### § 9–201. General Validity of Security Agreement

Except as otherwise provided by this Act a security agreement is effective according to its terms between the parties, against purchasers of the collateral and against creditors. Nothing in this Article validates any charge or practice illegal under any statute or regulation thereunder governing usury, small loans, retail installment sales, or the like, or extends the application of any such statute or regulation to any transaction not otherwise subject thereto.

### § 9–202. Title to Collateral Immaterial

Each provision of this Article with regard to rights, obligations and remedies applies whether title to collateral is in the secured party or in the debtor.

### § 9–203. Attachment and Enforceability of Security Interest; Proceeds; Formal Requisites

(1) Subject to the provisions of Section 4–208 on the security interest of a collecting bank, Section 8–321 on security interests in securities and Section 9–113 on a security interest arising under the Article on Sales, a security interest is not enforceable against the debtor or third parties with respect to the collateral and does not attach unless:

(a) the collateral is in the possession of the secured party pursuant to agreement, or the debtor has signed a security agreement which contains a description of the collateral and in addition, when the security interest covers crops growing or to be grown or timber to be cut, a description of the land concerned;

(b) value has been given; and

(c) the debtor has rights in the collateral.

(2) A security interest attaches when it becomes enforceable against the debtor with respect to the collateral. Attachment occurs as soon as all of the events specified in subsection (1) have taken place unless explicit agreement postpones the time of attaching.

(3) Unless otherwise agreed a security agreement gives the secured party the rights to proceeds provided by Section 9–306.

(4) A transaction, although subject to this Article, is also subject to . . . . . . . . . . . .*, and in the case of conflict between the provisions of this Article and any such statute, the provisions of such statute control. Failure to comply with any applicable statute has only the effect which is specified therein.

**Note:** *At * is subsection (4) insert reference to any local statute regulating small loans, retail installment sales and the like.*

*The foregoing subsection (4) is designed to make it clear that certain transactions, although subject to this Article, must also comply with other applicable legislation.*

*This Article is designed to regulate all the "security" aspects of transactions within its scope. There is, however, much regulatory legislation, particularly in the consumer field, which supplements this Article and should not be repealed by its enactment. Examples are small loan acts, retail installment selling acts and the like. Such acts may provide for licensing and rate regulation and may prescribe particular forms of contract. Such provisions should remain in force despite the enactment of this Article. On the other hand if a retail installment selling act contains provisions on filing, rights on default, etc., such provisions should be repealed as inconsistent with this Article except that inconsistent provisions as to deficiencies, penalties, etc., in the Uniform Consumer Credit Code and other recent related legislation should remain because those statutes were drafted after the substantial enactment of the Article and with the intention of modifying certain provisions of this Article as to consumer credit.*

### § 9–204. After-Acquired Property; Future Advances

(1) Except as provided in subsection (2), a security agreement may provide that any or all obligations covered by the security agreement are to be secured by after-acquired collateral.

(2) No security interest attaches under an after-acquired property clause to consumer goods other than accessions (Section 9–314) when given as additional security unless the debtor acquires rights in them within ten days after the secured party gives value.

(3) Obligations covered by a security agreement may include future advances or other value whether or not the advances or value are given pursuant to commitment (subsection (1) of Section 9–105).

### § 9–205. Use or Disposition of Collateral without Accounting Permissible

A security interest is not invalid or fraudulent against creditors by reason of liberty in the debtor to use, commingle or dispose of all or part of the collateral (including returned or repossessed goods) or to collect or compromise accounts or chattel paper, or to accept the return of goods or make repossessions, or to use, commingle or dispose of proceeds, or by reason of the failure of the secured party to require the debtor to account for proceeds or replace collateral. This section does not relax the requirements of possession where perfection of a security interest depends upon possession of the collateral by the secured party or by a bailee.

### § 9–206. Agreement Not to Assert Defenses against Assignee; Modification of Sales Warranties Where Security Agreement Exists

(1) Subject to any statute or decision which establishes a different rule for buyers or lessees of consumer goods, an agreement by a buyer or lessee that he will not assert against an assignee any claim or defense which he may have against the seller or lessor is enforceable by an assignee who takes his assignment for value, in good faith and without notice of a claim or defense, except as to defenses of a type which may be asserted against a holder in due course of a negotiable instrument under the Article on Commercial Paper (Article 3). A buyer who as part of one transaction signs both a negotiable instrument and a security agreement makes such an agreement.

(2) When a seller retains a purchase money security interest in goods the Article on Sales (Article 2) governs the sale and any disclaimer, limitation or modification of the seller's warranties.

### § 9–207. Rights and Duties When Collateral Is in Secured Party's Possession

(1) A secured party must use reasonable care in the custody and preservation of collateral in his possession. In the case of an instrument or chattel paper reasonable care includes taking necessary steps to preserve rights against prior parties unless otherwise agreed.

(2) Unless otherwise agreed, when collateral is in the secured party's possession

(a) reasonable expenses (including the cost of any insurance and payment of taxes or other charges) incurred in the custody, preservation, use or operation of the collateral are chargeable to the debtor and are secured by the collateral;

(b) the risk of accidental loss or damage is on the debtor to the extent of any deficiency in any effective insurance coverage;

(c) the secured party may hold as additional security any increase or profits (except money) received from the collateral, but money so received, unless remitted to the debtor, shall be applied in reduction of the secured obligation;

(d) the secured party must keep the collateral identifiable but fungible collateral may be commingled;

(e) the secured party may repledge the collateral upon terms which do not impair the debtor's right to redeem it.

(3) A secured party is liable for any loss caused by his failure to meet any obligation imposed by the preceding subsections but does not lose his security interest.

(4) A secured party may use or operate the collateral for the purpose of preserving the collateral or its value or pursuant to the order of a court of appropriate jurisdiction or, except in the case of consumer goods, in the manner and to the extent provided in the security agreement.

### § 9–208. Request for Statement of Account or List of Collateral

(1) A debtor may sign a statement indicating what he believes to be the aggregate amount of unpaid indebtedness as of a specified date and may send it to the secured party with a request that the statement be approved or corrected and returned to the debtor. When the security agreement or any other record kept by the secured party identifies the collateral a debtor may similarly request the secured party to approve or correct a list of the collateral.

(2) The secured party must comply with such a request within two weeks after receipt by sending a written correction or approval. If the secured party claims a security interest in all of a particular type of collateral owned by the debtor he may indicate that fact in his reply and need not approve

or correct an itemized list of such collateral. If the secured party without reasonable excuse fails to comply he is liable for any loss caused to the debtor thereby; and if the debtor has properly included in his request a good faith statement of the obligation or a list of the collateral or both the secured party may claim a security interest only as shown in the statement against persons misled by his failure to comply. If he no longer has an interest in the obligation or collateral at the time the request is received he must disclose the name and address of any successor in interest known to him and he is liable for any loss caused to the debtor as a result of failure to disclose. A successor in interest is not subject to this section until a request is received by him.
(3) A debtor is entitled to such a statement once every six months without charge. The secured party may require payment of a charge not exceeding $10 for each additional statement furnished.

## Part 3 Rights of Third Parties; Perfected and Unperfected Security Interests; Rules of Priority

### § 9–301. Persons Who Take Priority over Unperfected Security Interests; Rights of "Lien Creditor"

(1) Except as otherwise provided in subsection (2), an unperfected security interest is subordinate to the rights of

(a) persons entitled to priority under Section 9–312;

(b) a person who becomes a lien creditor before the security interest is perfected;

(c) in the case of goods, instruments, documents, and chattel paper, a person who is not a secured party and who is a transferee in bulk or other buyer not in ordinary course of business or is a buyer of farm products in ordinary course of business, to the extent that he gives value and receives delivery of the collateral without knowledge of the security interest and before it is perfected;

(d) in the case of accounts and general intangibles, a person who is not a secured party and who is a transferee to the extent that he gives value without knowledge of the security interest and before it is perfected.

(2) If the secured party files with respect to a purchase money security interest before or within ten days after the debtor receives possession of the collateral, he takes priority over the rights of a transferee in bulk or of a lien creditor which arise between the time the security interest attaches and the time of filing.

(3) A "lien creditor" means a creditor who has acquired a lien on the property involved by attachment, levy or the like and includes an assignee for benefit of creditors from the time of assignment, and a trustee in bankruptcy from the date of the filing of the petition or a receiver in equity from the time of appointment.

(4) A person who becomes a lien creditor while a security interest is perfected takes subject to the security interest only to the extent that it secures advances made before he becomes a lien creditor or within 45 days thereafter or made without knowledge of the lien or pursuant to a commitment entered into without knowledge of the lien.

### § 9–302. When Filing Is Required to Perfect Security Interest; Security Interests to Which Filing Provisions of This Article Do Not Apply

(1) A financing statement must be filed to perfect all security interests except the following:

(a) a security interest in collateral in possession of the secured party under Section 9–305;

(b) a security interest temporarily perfected in instruments or documents without delivery under Section 9–304 or in proceeds for a 10 day period under Section 9–306;

(c) a security interest created by an assignment of a beneficial interest in a trust or a decedent's estate;

(d) a purchase money security interest in consumer goods; but filing is required for a motor vehicle required to be registered; and fixture filing is required for priority over conflicting interests in fixtures to the extent provided in Section 9–313;

(e) an assignment of accounts which does not alone or in conjunction with other assignments to the same assignee transfer a significant part of the outstanding accounts of the assignor;

(f) a security interest of a collecting bank (Section 4–208) or in securities (Section 8–321) or arising under the Article on Sales (see Section 9–113) or covered in subsection (3) of this section;

(g) an assignment for the benefit of all the creditors of the transferor, and subsequent transfers by the assignee thereunder.

(2) If a secured party assigns a perfected security interest, no filing under this Article is required in order to continue the perfected status of the security interest against creditors of the transferees from the original debtor.

(3) The filing of a financing statement otherwise required by this Article is not necessary or effective to perfect a security interest in property subject to

(a) a statute or treaty of the United States which provides for a national or international registration or a national or international certificate of title or which specifies a place of filing different from that specified in this Article for filing of the security interest; or

(b) the following statutes of this state; [list any certificate of title statute covering automobiles, trailers, mobile homes, boats, farm tractors, or the like, and any central filing statute*.]; but during any period in which collateral is inventory held for sale by a person who is in the business of selling goods of that kind, the filing provisions of this Article (Part 4) apply to a security interest in that collateral created by him as debtor; or

(c) a certificate of title statute of another jurisdiction under the law of which indication of a security interest on the certificate is required as a condition of perfection (subsection (2) of Section 9–103).

(4) Compliance with a statute or treaty described in subsection (3) is equivalent to the filing of a financing statement under this Article, and a security interest in property subject to the statute or treaty can be perfected only by compliance therewith except as provided in Section 9–103 on multiple state transactions. Duration and renewal of perfection of a security interest perfected by compliance with the statute or treaty are governed by the provisions of the statute or treaty; in other respects the security interest is subject to this Article.

**Note:** *It is recommended that the provisions of certificate of title acts for perfection of security interests by notation on the certificates should be amended to exclude coverage of inventory held for sale.*

### § 9–303. When Security Interest Is Perfected; Continuity of Perfection

(1) A security interest is perfected when it has attached and when all of the applicable steps required for perfection have been taken. Such steps are specified in Sections 9–302, 9–304, 9–305 and 9–306. If such steps are taken before the security interest attaches, it is perfected at the time when it attaches.

(2) If a security interest is originally perfected in any way permitted under this Article and is subsequently perfected in some other way under this Article, without an intermediate period when it was unperfected, the security interest shall be deemed to be perfected continuously for the purposes of this Article.

### § 9–304. Perfection of Security Interest in Instruments, Documents, and Goods Covered by Documents; Perfection by Permissive Filing; Temporary Perfection Without Filing or Transfer of Possession

(1) A security interest in chattel paper or negotiable documents may be perfected by filing. A security interest in money or instruments (other than certificated securities or instruments which constitute part of chattel paper) can be perfected only by the secured party's taking possession, except as provided in subsections (4) and (5) of this section and subsections (2) and (3) of Section 9–306 on proceeds.

(2) During the period that goods are in the possession of the issuer of a negotiable document therefor, a security interest in the goods is perfected by perfecting a security interest in the document, and any security interest in the goods otherwise perfected during such period is subject thereto.

(3) A security interest in goods in the possession of a bailee other than one who has issued a negotiable document therefor is perfected by issuance of a document in the name of the secured party or by the bailee's receipt of notification of the se-

cured party's interest or by filing as to the goods.

(4) A security interest in instruments (other than certificated securities) or negotiable documents is perfected without filing or the taking of possession for a period of 21 days from the time it attaches to the extent that it arises from new value given under a written security agreement.

(5) A security interest remains perfected for a period of 21 days without filing where a secured party having a perfected security interest in an instrument (other than a certificated security), a negotiable document or goods in possession of a bailee other than one who has issued a negotiable document therefor

(a) makes available to the debtor the goods or documents representing the goods for the purpose of ultimate sale or exchange or for the purpose of loading, unloading, storing, shipping, transshipping, manufacturing, processing or otherwise dealing with them in a manner preliminary to their sale or exchange, but priority between conflicting security interests in the goods is subject to subsection (3) of Section 9–312; or

(b) delivers the instrument to the debtor for the purpose of ultimate sale or exchange or of presentation, collection, renewal or registration of transfer.

(6) After the 21 day period in subsections (4) and (5) perfection depends upon compliance with applicable provisions of this Article.

## § 9–305. When Possession by Secured Party Perfects Security Interest Without Filing

A security interest in letters of credit and advices of credit (subsection (2) (a) of Section 5–116), goods, instruments (other than certificated securities), money, negotiable documents, or chattel paper may be perfected by the secured party's taking possession of the collateral. If such collateral other than goods covered by a negotiable document is held by a bailee, the secured party is deemed to have possession from the time the bailee receives notification of the secured party's interest. A security interest is perfected by possession from the time possession is taken without a relation back and continues only so long as possession is retained, unless otherwise specified in this Article. The security interest may be otherwise perfected as provided in this Article before or after the period of possession by the secured party.

## § 9–306. "Proceeds"; Secured Party's Rights on Disposition of Collateral

(1) "Proceeds" includes whatever is received upon the sale, exchange, collection or other disposition of collateral or proceeds. Insurance payable by reason of loss or damage to the collateral is proceeds, except to the extent that it is payable to a person other than a party to the security agreement. Money, checks, deposit accounts, and the like are "cash proceeds." All other proceeds are "non-cash proceeds."

(2) Except where this Article otherwise provides, a security interest continues in collateral notwithstanding sale, exchange or other disposition thereof unless the disposition was authorized by the secured party in the security agreement or otherwise, and also continues in any identifiable proceeds including collections received by the debtor.

(3) The security interest in proceeds is a continuously perfected security interest if the interest in the original collateral was perfected but it ceases to be a perfected security interest and becomes unperfected ten days after receipt of the proceeds by the debtor unless

(a) a filed financing statement covers the original collateral and the proceeds are collateral in which a security interest may be perfected by filing in the office or offices where the financing statement has been filed and, if the proceeds are acquired with cash proceeds, the description of collateral in the financing statement indicates the types of property constituting the proceeds; or

(b) a filed financing statement covers the original collateral and the proceeds are identifiable cash proceeds; or

(c) the security interest in the proceeds is perfected before the expiration of the ten day period.

Except as provided in this section, a security interest in proceeds can be perfected only by the methods or under the circumstances permitted in this Article for original collateral of the same type.

(4) In the event of insolvency proceedings instituted by or against a debtor, a secured party with a perfected security interest in proceeds has a perfected security interest only in the following proceeds:

(a) in identifiable non-cash proceeds and in separate deposit accounts containing only proceeds;

(b) in identifiable cash proceeds in the form of money which is neither commingled with other money nor deposited in a deposit account prior to the insolvency proceedings;

(c) in identifiable cash proceeds in the form of checks and the like which are not deposited in a deposit account prior to the insolvency proceedings; and

(d) in all cash and deposit accounts of the debtor in which proceeds have been commingled with other funds, but the perfected security interest under this paragraph (d) is

(i) subject to any right to setoff; and

(ii) limited to an amount not greater than the amount of any cash proceeds received by the debtor within ten days before the institution of the insolvency proceedings less than sum of (I) the payments to the secured party on account of cash proceeds received by the debtor during such period and (II) the cash proceeds received by the debtor during such period to which the secured party is entitled under paragraphs (a) through (c) of this subsection (4).

(5) If a sale of goods results in an account or chattel paper which is transferred by the seller to a secured party, and if the goods are returned to or are repossessed by the seller or the secured party, the following rules determine priorities:

(a) If the goods were collateral at the time of sale, for an indebtedness of the seller which is still unpaid, the original security interest attaches again to the goods and continues as a perfected security interest if it was perfected at the time when the goods were sold. If the security interest was originally perfected by a filing which is still effective, nothing further is required to continue the perfected status; in any other case, the secured party must take possession of the returned or repossessed goods or must file.

(b) An unpaid transferee of the chattel paper has a security interest in the goods against the transferor. Such security interest is prior to a security interest asserted under paragraph (a) to the extent that the transferee of the chattel paper was entitled to priority under Section 9–308.

(c) An unpaid transferee of the account has a security interest in the goods against the transferor. Such security interest is subordinate to a security interest asserted under paragraph (a).

(d) A security interest of an unpaid transferee asserted under paragraph (b) or (c) must be perfected for protection against creditors of the transferor and purchasers of the returned or repossessed goods.

### § 9–307. Protection of Buyers of Goods

(1) A buyer in ordinary course of business (subsection (9) of Section 1–201) other than a person buying farm products from a person engaged in farming operations takes free of a security interest created by his seller even though the security interest is perfected and even though the buyer knows of its existence.

(2) In the case of consumer goods, a buyer takes free of a security interest even though perfected if he buys without knowledge of the security interest, for value and for his own personal, family or household purposes unless prior to the purchase the secured party has filed a financing statement covering such goods.

(3) A buyer other than a buyer in ordinary course of business (subsection (1) of this section) takes free of a security interest to the extent that it secures future advances made after the secured party acquires knowledge of the purchase, or more than 45 days after the purchase, whichever first occurs, unless made pursuant to a commitment entered into without knowledge of the purchase and before the expiration of the 45 day period.

### § 9–308. Purchase of Chattel Paper and Instruments

A purchaser of chattel paper or an instrument who gives new value and takes possession of it in the ordinary course of his business has priority over a security interest in the chattel paper or instrument

(a) which is perfected under Section 9–304 (permissive filing and temporary perfection) or under

Section 9–306 (perfection as to proceeds) if he acts without knowledge that the specific paper or instrument is subject to a security interest; or

(b) which is claimed merely as proceeds of inventory subject to a security interest (Section 9–306) even though he knows that the specific paper or instrument is subject to the security interest.

### § 9–309. Protection of Purchasers of Instruments, Documents and Securities

Nothing in this Article limits the rights of a holder in due course of a negotiable instrument (Section 3–302) or a holder to whom a negotiable document of title has been duly negotiated (Section 7–501) or a bona fide purchaser of a security (Section 8–302) and the holders or purchasers take priority over an earlier security interest even though perfected. Filing under this Article does not constitute notice of the security interest to such holders or purchasers.

### § 9–310. Priority of Certain Liens Arising by Operation of Law

When a person in the ordinary course of his business furnishes services or materials with respect to goods subject to a security interest, a lien upon goods in the possession of such person given by statute or rule of law for such materials or services takes priority over a perfected security interest unless the lien is statutory and the statute expressly provides otherwise.

### § 9–311. Alienability of Debtor's Rights: Judicial Process

The debtor's rights in collateral may be voluntarily or involuntarily transferred (by way of sale, creation of a security interest, attachment, levy, garnishment or other judicial process) notwithstanding a provision in the security agreement prohibiting any transfer or making the transfer constitute a default.

### § 9–312. Priorities among Conflicting Security Interests in the Same Collateral

(1) The rules of priority stated in other sections of this Part and in the following sections shall govern when applicable: Section 4–208 with respect to the security interests of collecting banks in items being collected, accompanying documents and proceeds; Section 9–103 on security interests related to other jurisdictions; Section 9–114 on consignments.

(2) A perfected security interest in crops for new value given to enable the debtor to produce the crops during the production season and given not more than three months before the crops become growing crops by planting or otherwise takes priority over an earlier perfected security interest to the extent that such earlier interest secures obligations due more than six months before the crops become growing crops by planting or otherwise, even though the person giving new value had knowledge of the earlier security interest.

(3) A perfected purchase money security interest in inventory has priority over a conflicting security interest in the same inventory and also has priority in identifiable cash proceeds received on or before the delivery of the inventory to a buyer if

(a) the purchase money security interest is perfected at the time the debtor receives possession of the inventory; and

(b) the purchase money secured party gives notification in writing to the holder of the conflicting security interest if the holder had filed a financing statement covering the same types of inventory (i) before the date of the filing made by the purchase money secured party, or (ii) before the beginning of the 21 day period where the purchase money security interest is temporarily perfected without filing or possession (subsection (5) of Section 9–304); and

(c) the holder of the conflicting security interest receives the notification within five years before the debtor receives possession of the inventory; and

(d) the notification states that the person giving the notice has or expects to acquire a purchase money security interest in inventory of the debtor, describing such inventory by item or type.

(4) A purchase money security interest in collateral other than inventory has priority over a conflicting security interest in the same collateral or its proceeds if the purchase money security interest is perfected at the time the debtor receives possession of the collateral or within ten days thereafter.

(5) In all cases not governed by other rules stated in this section (including cases of purchase money

security interests which do not qualify for the special priorities set forth in subsections (3) and (4) of this section), priority between conflicting security interests in the same collateral shall be determined according to the following rules:

(a) Conflicting security interests rank according to priority in time of filing or perfection. Priority dates from the time a filing is first made covering the collateral or the time the security interest is first perfected, whichever is earlier, provided that there is no period thereafter when there is neither filing nor perfection.

(b) So long as conflicting security interests are unperfected, the first to attach has priority.

(6) For the purposes of subsection (5) a date of filing or perfection as to collateral is also a date of filing or perfection as to proceeds.

(7) If future advances are made while a security interest is perfected by filing, the taking of possession, or under Section 8–321 on securities, the security interest has the same priority for the purposes of subsection (5) with respect to the future advances as it does with respect to the first advance. If a commitment is made before or while the security interest is so perfected, the security interest has the same priority with respect to advances made pursuant thereto. In other cases a perfected security interest has priority from the date the advance is made.

### § 9–313. Priority of Security Interests in Fixtures

(1) In this section and in the provisions of Part 4 of this Article referring to fixture filing, unless the context otherwise requires

(a) goods are "fixtures" when they become so related to particular real estate that an interest in them arises under real estate law

(b) a "fixture filing" is the filing in the office where a mortgage on the real estate would be filed or recorded of a financing statement covering goods which are or are to become fixtures and conforming to the requirements of subsection (5) of Section 9–402

(c) a mortgage is a "construction mortgage" to the extent that it secures an obligation incurred for the construction of an improvement on land including the acquisition cost of the land, if the recorded writing so indicates.

(2) A security interest under this Article may be created in goods which are fixtures or may continue in goods which become fixtures, but no security interest exists under this Article in ordinary building materials incorporated into an improvement on land.

(3) This Article does not prevent creation of an encumbrance upon fixtures pursuant to real estate law.

(4) A perfected security interest in fixtures has priority over the conflicting interest of an encumbrancer or owner of the real estate where

(a) the security interest is a purchase money security interest, the interest of the encumbrancer or owner arises before the goods become fixtures, the security interest is perfected by a fixture filing before the goods become fixtures or within ten days thereafter, and the debtor has an interest of record in the real estate or is in possession of the real estate; or

(b) the security interest is perfected by a fixture filing before the interest of the encumbrancer or owner is of record, the security interest has priority over any conflicting interest of a predecessor in title of the encumbrancer or owner, and the debtor has an interest of record in the real estate or is in possession of the real estate; or

(c) the fixtures are readily removable factory or office machines or readily removable replacements of domestic appliances which are consumer goods, and before the goods become fixtures the security interest is perfected by any method permitted by this Article; or

(d) the conflicting interest is a lien on the real estate obtained by legal or equitable proceedings after the security interest was perfected by any method permitted by this Article.

(5) A security interest in fixtures, whether or not perfected, has priority over the conflicting interest of an encumbrancer or owner of the real estate where

(a) the encumbrancer or owner has consented in writing to the security interest or has disclaimed an interest in the goods as fixtures; or

(b) the debtor has a right to remove the goods as against the encumbrancer or owner. If the debtor's right terminates, the priority of the security interest continues for a reasonable time.

(6) Notwithstanding paragraph (a) of subsection

(4) but otherwise subject to subsections (4) and (5), a security interest in fixtures is subordinate to a construction mortgage recorded before the goods become fixtures if the goods become fixtures before the completion of the construction. To the extent that it is given to refinance a construction mortgage, a mortgage has this priority to the same extent as the construction mortgage.

(7) In cases not within the preceding subsections, a security interest in fixtures is subordinate to the conflicting interest of an encumbrancer or owner of the related real estate who is not the debtor.

(8) When the secured party has priority over all owners and encumbrancers of the real estate, he may, on default, subject to the provisions of Part 5, remove his collateral from the real estate but he must reimburse any encumbrancer or owner of the real estate who is not the debtor and who has not otherwise agreed for the cost of repair of any physical injury, but not for any diminution in value of the real estate caused by the absence of the goods removed or by any necessity of replacing them. A person entitled to reimbursement may refuse permission to remove until the secured party gives adequate security for the performance of this obligation.

### § 9–314. Accessions

(1) A security interest in goods which attaches before they are installed in or affixed to other goods takes priority as to the goods installed or affixed (called in this section "accessions") over the claims of all persons to the whole except as stated in subsection (3) and subject to Section 9–315(1).

(2) A security interest which attaches to goods after they become part of a whole is valid against all persons subsequently acquiring interests in the whole except as stated in subsection (3) but is invalid against any person with an interest in the whole at the time the security interest attaches to the goods who has not in writing consented to the security interest or disclaimed an interest in the goods as part of the whole.

(3) The security interests described in subsections (1) and (2) do not take priority over

(a) a subsequent purchaser for value of any interest in the whole; or

(b) a creditor with a lien on the whole subsequently obtained by judicial proceedings; or

(c) a creditor with a prior perfected security interest in the whole to the extent that he makes subsequent advances

if the subsequent purchase is made, the lien by judicial proceedings obtained or the subsequent advance under the prior perfected security interest is made or contracted for without knowledge of the security interest and before it is perfected. A purchaser of the whole at a foreclosure sale other than the holder of a perfected security interest purchasing at his own foreclosure sale is a subsequent purchaser within this section.

(4) When under subsections (1) and (2) and (3) a secured party has an interest in accessions which has priority over the claims of all persons who have interests in the whole, he may on default subject to the provisions of Part 5 remove his collateral from the whole but he must reimburse any encumbrancer or owner of the whole who is not the debtor and who has not otherwise agreed for the cost of repair of any physical injury but not for any diminution in value of the whole caused by the absence of the goods removed or by any necessity for replacing them. A person entitled to reimbursement may refuse permission to remove until the secured party gives adequate security for the performance of this obligation.

### § 9–315. Priority When Goods Are Commingled or Processed

(1) If a security interest in goods was perfected and subsequently the goods or a part thereof have become part of a product or mass, the security interest continues in the product or mass if

(a) the goods are so manufactured, processed, assembled or commingled that their identity is lost in the product or mass; or

(b) a financing statement covering the original goods also covers the product into which the goods have been manufactured, processed or assembled.

In a case to which paragraph (b) applies, no separate security interest in that part of the original goods which have been manufactured, processed or assembled into the product may be claimed under Section 9–314.

(2) When under subsection (1) more than one security interest attaches to the product or mass, they rank equally according to the ratio that the cost of the goods to which each interest originally

attached bears to the cost of the total product or mass.

### § 9–316. Priority Subject to Subordination

Nothing in this Article prevents subordination by agreement by any person entitled to priority.

### § 9–317. Secured Party Not Obligated on Contract of Debtor

The mere existence of a security interest or authority given to the debtor to dispose of or use collateral does not impose contract or tort liability upon the secured part for the debtor's acts or omissions.

### § 9–318. Defenses against Assignee; Modification of Contract after Notification of Assignment; Term Prohibiting Assignment Ineffective; Identification and Proof of Assignment

(1) Unless an account debtor has made an enforceable agreement not to assert defenses or claims arising out of a sale as provided in Section 9–206 the rights of an assignee are subject to

(a) all the terms of the contract between the account debtor and assignor and any defense or claim arising therefrom; and

(b) any other defense or claim of the account debtor against the assignor which accrues before the account debtor receives notification of the assignment.

(2) So far as the right to payment or a part thereof under an assigned contract has not been fully earned by performance, and notwithstanding notification of the assignment, any modification of or substitution for the contract made in good faith and in accordance with reasonable commercial standards is effective against an assignee unless the account debtor has otherwise agreed but the assignee acquires corresponding rights under the modified or substituted contract. The assignment may provide that such modification or substitution is a breach by the assignor.

(3) The account debtor is authorized to pay the assignor until the account debtor receives notification that the amount due or to become due has been assigned and that payment is to be made to the assignee. A notification which does not reasonably identify the rights assigned is ineffective. If requested by the account debtor, the assignee must seasonably furnish reasonable proof that the assignment has been made and unless he does so the account debtor may pay the assignor.

(4) A term in any contract between an account debtor and an assignor is ineffective if it prohibits assignment of an account or prohibits creation of a security interest in a general intangible for money due or to become due or requires the account debtor's consent to such assignment or security interest.

## Part 4 Filing

### § 9–401. Place of Filing; Erroneous Filing; Removal of Collateral

*First Alternative Subsection (1)*

(1) The proper place to file in order to perfect a security interest is as follows:

(a) when the collateral is timber to be cut or is minerals or the like (including oil and gas) or accounts subject to subsection (5) of Section 9–103, or when the financing statement is filed as a fixture filing (Section 9–313) and the collateral is goods which are or are to become fixtures, then in the office where a mortgage on the real estate would be filed or recorded;

(b) in all other cases, in the office of the [Secretary of State].

*Second Alternative Subsection (1)*

(1) The proper place to file in order to perfect a security interest is as follows:

(a) when the collateral is equipment used in farming operations, or farm products, or accounts or general intangibles arising from or relating to the sale of farm products by a farmer, or consumer goods, then in the office of the . . . . . . . . in the county of the debt or's residence or if the debtor is not a resident of this state then in the office of the . . . . . . . . in the county of the debtor's residence or if the debtor is not a resident of this state then in the office of the . . . . . . . . in the county where the goods are kept, and in addition when the collateral is crops growing or to be grown in the office of the . . . . . . . . in the county where the land is located;

(b) when the collateral is timber to be cut or

is minerals or the like (including oil and gas) or accounts subject to subsection (5) of Section 9–103, or when the financing statement is filed as a fixture filing (Section 9–313) and the collateral is goods which are or are to become fixtures, then in the office where a mortgage on the real estate would be filed or recorded;

(c) in all other cases, in the office of the [Secretary of State].

*Third Alternative Subsection (1)*

(1) The proper place to file in order to perfect a security interest is as follows:

(a) when the collateral is equipment used in farming operations, or farm products, or accounts or general intangibles arising from or relating to the sale of farm products by a farmer, or consumer goods, then in the office of the . . . . . . in the county of the debtor's residence or if the debtor is not a resident of this state then in the office of the . . . . . . . . in the county where the goods are kept, and in addition when the collateral is crops growing or to be grown in the office of the . . . . . . in the county where the land is located;

(b) when the collateral is timber to be cut or is minerals or the like (including oil and gas) or accounts subject to subsection (5) of Section 9–103, or when the financing statement is filed as a fixture filing (Section 9–313) and the collateral is goods which are or are to become fixtures, then in the office where a mortgage on the real estate would be filed or recorded;

(c) in all other cases, in the office of the [Secretary of State] and in addition, if the debtor has a place of business in only one county of this state, also in the office of . . . . . . of such county, or, if the debtor has no place of business in this state, but resides in the state, also in the office of . . . . . . of the county in which he resides.

**Note:** *One of the three alternatives should be selected as subsection (1).*

(2) A filing which is made in good faith in an improper place or not in all of the places required by this section is nevertheless effective with regard to any collateral as to which the filing complied with the requirements of this Article and is also effective with regard to collateral covered by the financing statement against any person who has knowledge of the contents of such financing statement.

(3) A filing which is made in the proper place in this state continues effective even though the debtor's residence or place of business or the location of the collateral or its use, whichever controlled the original filing, is thereafter changed.

[(3) A filing which is made in the proper county continues effective for four months after a change to another county of the debtor's residence or place of business or the location of the collateral, whichever controlled the original filing. It becomes ineffective thereafter unless a copy of the financing statement signed by the secured party is filed in the new county within said period. The security interest may also be perfected in the new county after the expiration of the four-month period; in such case perfection dates from the time of perfection in the new county. A change in the use of the collateral does not impair the effectiveness of the original filing.]

(4) The rules stated in Section 9–103 determine whether filing is necessary in this state.

(5) Notwithstanding the preceding subsections, and subject to subsection (3) of Section 9–302, the proper place to file in order to perfect a security interest in collateral, including fixtures, of a transmitting utility is the office of the [Secretary of State]. This filing constitutes a fixture filing (Section 9–313) as to the collateral described therein which is or is to become fixtures.

(6) For the purposes of this section, the residence of an organization is its place of business if it has one or its chief executive office if it has more than one place of business.

**Note:** *Subsection (6) should be used only if the state chooses the Second or Third Alternative Subsection (1).*

### § 9–402. Formal Requisites of Financing Statement; Amendments; Mortgage as Financing Statement

(1) A financing statement is sufficient if it gives the names of the debtor and the secured party, is signed by the debtor, gives an address of the secured party from which information concerning the security interest may be obtained, gives a mail-

ing address of the debtor and contains a statement indicating the types, or describing the items, of collateral. A financing statement may be filed before a security agreement is made or a security interest otherwise attaches. When the financing statement covers crops growing or to be grown, the statement must also contain a description of the real estate concerned. When the financing statement covers timber to be cut or covers minerals or the like (including oil and gas) or accounts subject to subsection (5) of Section 9–103, or when the financing statement is filed as a fixture filing (Section 9–313) and the collateral is goods which are or are to become fixtures, the statement must also comply with subsection (5). A copy of the security agreement is sufficient as a financing statement if it contains the above information and is signed by the debtor. A carbon, photographic or other reproduction of a security agreement or a financing statement is sufficient as a financing statement if the security agreement so provides or if the original has been filed in this state.

(2) A financing statement which otherwise complies with subsection (1) is sufficient when it is signed by the secured party instead of the debtor if it is filed to perfect a security interest in

(a) collateral already subject to a security interest in another jurisdiction when it is brought into this state, or when the debtor's location is changed to this state. Such a financing statement must state that the collateral was brought into his state or that the debtor's location was changed to this state under such circumstances; or

(b) proceeds under Section 9–306 if the security interest in the original collateral was perfected. Such a financing statement must describe the original collateral; or

(c) collateral as to which the filing has lapsed; or

(d) collateral acquired after a change of name, identity or corporate structure of the debtor (subsection (7)).

(3) A form substantially as follows is sufficient to comply with subsection (1):

Name of debtor (or assignor) ..................
Address ..........................................
Name of secured party (or assignee) ...........
Address ..........................................

1. This financing statement covers the following types (or types) of property:
   (Describe) ................................
2. (If collateral is crops) The above described crops are growing or are to be grown on:
   (Describe Real Estate) ...................
3. (If applicable) The above goods are to become fixtures on:*
   (Describe Real Estate) ...................
   and this financing statement is to be filed [for record] in the real estate records. (If the debtor does not have an interest of record) The name of a record owner is ......................................
4. (If products of collateral are claimed) Products of the collateral are also covered.
   (Use whichever is applicable)

..........................................
Signature of Debtor (or Assignor)

..........................................
Signature of Secured Party (or Assignee)

(4) A financing statement may be amended by filing a writing signed by both the debtor and the secured party. An amendment does not extend the period of effectiveness of a financing statement. If any amendment adds collateral, it is effective as to the added collateral only from the filing date of the amendment. In this Article, unless the context otherwise requires, the term "financing statement" means the original financing statement and any amendments.

(5) A financing statement covering timber to be cut or covering minerals or the like (including oil and gas) or accounts subject to subsection (5) of Section 9–103, or a financing statement filed as a fixture filing (Section 9–313) where the debtor is not a transmitting utility, must show that it covers this type of collateral, must recite that it is to be filed [for record] in the real estate records, and the financing statement must contain a description of the real estate [sufficient if it were contained in a mortgage of the real estate to give constructive notice of the mortgage under the law of this state]. If the debtor does not have an interest of record in the real estate, the financing statement must show the name of a record owner.

(6) A mortgage is effective as a financing statement filed as a fixture filing from the date of its recording if

(a) the goods are described in the mortgage by item or type; and

(b) the goods are or are to become fixtures related to the real estate described in the mortgage; and

(c) the mortgage complies with the requirements for a financing statement in this section other than a recital that it is to be filed in the real estate records; and

(d) the mortgage is duly recorded.

No fee with reference to the financing statement is required other than the regular recording and satisfaction fees with respect to the mortgage.

(7) A financing statement sufficiently shows the name of the debtor if it gives the individual, partnership or corporate name of the debtor, whether or not it adds other trade names or names of partners. Where the debtor so changes his name or in the case of an organization its name, identity or corporate structure that a filed financing statement becomes seriously misleading, the filing is not effective to perfect a security interest in collateral acquired by the debtor more than four months after the change, unless a new appropriate financing statement is filed before the expiration of that time. A filed financing statement remains effective with respect to collateral transferred by the debtor even though the secured party knows of or consents to the transfer.

(8) A financing statement substantially complying with the requirements of this section is effective even though it contains minor errors which are not seriously misleading.

**Note:** *Language in brackets is optional.*

**Note:** *Where the state has any special recording system for real estate other than the usual grantor-grantee index (as, for instance, a tract system or a title registration or Torrens system) local adaptations of subsection (5) and Section 9–403(7) may be necessary. See Mass. Gen. Laws Chapter 106, Section 9–409.*

* *Where appropriate substitute either "The above timber is standing on . . ." or "The above minerals or the like (including oil and gas) or accounts will be financed at the wellhead or minehead of the well or mine located on . . . ."*

## § 9–403. What Constitutes Filing; Duration of Filing; Effect of Lapsed Filing; Duties of Filing Officer

(1) Presentation for filing of a financing statement and tender of the filing fee or acceptance of the statement by the filing officer constitutes filing under this Article.

(2) Except as provided in subsection (6) a filed financing statement is effective for a period of five years from the date of filing. The effectiveness of a filed financing statement lapses on the expiration of the five year period unless a continuation statement is filed prior to the lapse. If a security interest perfected by filing exists at the time insolvency proceedings are commenced by or against the debtor, the security interest remains perfected until termination of the insolvency proceedings and thereafter for a period of sixty days or until expiration of the five year period, whichever occurs later. Upon lapse the security interest becomes unperfected, unless it is perfected without filing. If the security interest becomes unperfected upon lapse, it is deemed to have been unperfected as against a person who became a purchaser or lien creditor before lapse.

(3) A continuation statement may be filed by the secured party within six months prior to the expiration of the five year period specified in subsection (2). Any such continuation statement must be signed by the secured party, identify the original statement by file number and state that the original statement is still effective. A continuation statement signed by a person other than the secured party of record must be accompanied by a separate written statement of assignment signed by the secured party of record and complying with subsection (2) of Section 9–405, including payment of the required fee. Upon timely filing of the continuation statement, the effectiveness of the original statement is continued for five years after the last date to which the filing was effective whereupon it lapses in the same manner as provided in subsection (2) unless another continuation statement is filed prior to such lapse. Succeeding continuation statements may be filed in the same manner to continue the effectiveness of the original statement. Unless a statute on disposition of public records provides otherwise, the filing officer may remove a lapsed statement from the files and destroy

it immediately if he has retained a microfilm or other photographic record, or in other cases after one year after the lapse. The filing officer shall so arrange matters by physical annexation of financing statements to continuation statements or other related filings, or by other means, that if he physically destroys the financing statements of a period more than five years past, those which have been continued by a continuation statement or which are still effective under subsection (6) shall be retained.

(4) Except as provided in subsection (7) a filing officer shall mark each statement with a file number and with the date and hour of filing and shall hold the statement or a microfilm or other photographic copy thereof for public inspection. In addition the filing officer shall index the statement according to the name of the debtor and shall note in the index the file number and the address of the debtor given in the statement.

(5) The uniform fee for filing and indexing and for stamping a copy furnished by the secured party to show the date and place of filing for an original financing statement or for a continuation statement shall be $. . . . . . . . . . if the statement is in the standard form prescribed by the [Secretary of State] and otherwise shall be $. . . . . . . . . . . , plus in each case, if the financing statement is subject to subsection (5) of Section 9–402, $. . . . . . . The uniform fee for each name more than one required to be indexed shall be $. . . . . . . . . The secured party may at his option show a trade name for any person and an extra uniform indexing fee of $. . . . . . . . . shall be paid with respect thereto.

(6) If the debtor is a transmitting utility (subsection (5) of Section 9–401) and a filed financing statement so states, it is effective until a termination statement is filed. A real estate mortgage which is effective as a fixture filing under subsection (6) of Section 9–402 remains effective as a fixure filing until the mortgage is released or satisfied of record or its effectiveness otherwise terminates as to the real estate.

(7) When a financing statement covers timber to be cut or covers minerals or the like (including oil and gas) or accounts subject to subsection (5) of Section 9–103, or is filed as a fixture filing, [it shall be filed for record and] the filing officer shall index it under the names of the debtor and any owner of record shown on the financing statement in the same fashion as if they were the mortgagors in a mortgage of the real estate described, and, to the extent that the law of this state provides for the indexing of mortgages under the name of the mortgagee, under the name of the secured party as if he were the mortgagee thereunder, or where indexing is by description in the same fashion as if the financing statement were a mortgage of the real estate described.

**Note:** *In states in which writings will not appear in the real estate records and indices unless actually recorded the bracketed language in subsection (7) should be used.*

### § 9–404. Termination Statement

(1) If a financing statement covering consumer goods is filed on or after . . . . . . . . . . . . . , then within one month or within ten days following written demand by the debtor after there is no outstanding secured obligation and no commitment to make advances, incur obligations or otherwise give value, the secured party must file with each filing officer with whom the financing statement was filed, a termination statement to the effect that he no longer claims a security interest under the financing statement, which shall be identified by file number. In other cases whenever there is no outstanding secured obligation and no commitment to make advances, incur obligations or otherwise give value, the secured party must on written demand by the debtor send the debtor, for each filing officer with whom the financing statement was filed, a termination statement to the effect that he no longer claims a security interest under the financing statement, which shall be identified by file number. A termination statement signed by a person other than the secured party of record must be accompanied by a separate written statement of assignment signed by the secured party of record complying with subsection (2) of Section 9–405, including payment of the required fee. If the affected secured party fails to file such a termination statement as required by this subsection, or to send such a termination statement within ten days after proper demand therefor, he shall be liable to the debtor for one hundred dollars, and in addition for any loss caused to the debtor by such failure.

(2) On presentation to the filing officer of such

a termination statement he must note it in the index. If he has received the termination statement in duplicate, he shall return one copy of the termination statement to the secured party stamped to show the time of receipt thereof. If the filing officer has a microfilm or other photographic record of the financing statement, and of any related continuation statement, statement of assignment and statement of release, he may remove the originals from the files at any time after receipt of the termination statement, or if he has no such record, he may remove them from the files at any time after one year after receipt of the termination statement.

(3) If the termination statement is in the standard form prescribed by the [Secretary of State], the uniform fee for filing and indexing the termination statement shall be $. . . . . . , and otherwise shall be $. . . . . . , plus in each case an additional fee of $. . . . . . for each name more than one against which the termination statement is required to be indexed.

**Note:** *The date to be inserted should be the effective date of the revised Article 9.*

### § 9–405. Assignment of Security Interest; Duties of Filing Officer; Fees

(1) A financing statement may disclose an assignment of a security interest in the collateral described in the financing statement by indication in the financing statement of the name and address of the assignee or by an assignment itself or a copy thereof on the face or back of the statement. On presentation to the filing officer of such a financing statement the filing officer shall mark the same as provided in Section 9–403(4). The uniform fee for filing, indexing and furnishing filing data for a financing statement so indicating an assignment shall be $. . . . . . if the statement is in the standard form prescribed by the [Secretary of State] and otherwise shall be $. . . . . . , plus in each case an additional fee of $. . . . . . for each name more than one against which the financing statement is required to be indexed.

(2) A secured party may assign of record all or part of his rights under a financing statement by the filing in the place where the original financing statement was filed of a separate written statement of assignment signed by the secured party of record and setting forth the name of the secured party of record and the debtor, the file number and the date of filing of the financing statement and the name and address of the assignee and containing a description of the collateral assigned. A copy of the assignment is sufficient as a separate statement if it complies with the preceding sentence. On presentation to the filing officer of such a separate statement, the filing officer shall mark such separate statement with the date and hour of the filing. He shall note the assignment on the index of the financing statement, or in the case of a fixture filing, or a filing covering timber to be cut, or covering minerals or the like (including oil and gas) or accounts subject to subsection (5) of Section 9–103, he shall index the assignment under the name of the assignor as grantor and, to the extent that the law of this state provides for indexing the assignment of a mortgage under the name of the assignee, he shall index the assignment of the financing statement under the name of the assignee. The uniform fee for filing, indexing and furnishing filing data about such a separate statement of assignment shall be $. . . . . . if the statement is in the standard form prescribed by the [Secretary of State] and otherwise shall be $. . . . . . , plus in each case an additional fee of $. . . . . . for each name more than one against which the statement of assignment is required to be indexed. Notwithstanding the provisions of this subsection, an assignment of record of a security interest in a fixture contained in a mortgage effective as a fixture filing (subsection (6) of Section 9–402) may be made only by an assignment of the mortgage in the manner provided by the law of this state other than this Act.

(3) After the disclosure or filing of an assignment under this section, the assignee is the secured party of record.

### § 9–406. Release of Collateral; Duties of Filing Officer; Fees

A secured party of record may by his signed statement release all or a part of any collateral described in a filed financing statement. The statement of release is sufficient if it contains a description of the collateral being released, the name and address of the debtor, the name and address of the secured party, and the file number of the financing statement. A statement of release signed by a person other than the secured party of record must be accompanied by a separate written statement of assignment signed by the secured party of record and complying with subsection (2) of Section 9–405, including payment of the required fee. Upon presentation of such a statement of release to the filing officer he shall mark the statement with the hour and date of filing and shall note the same upon the margin of the index of the filing of the financing statement. The uniform fee for filing and noting such a statement of release shall be $. . . . . . if the statement is in the standard form prescribed by the [Secretary of State] and otherwise shall be $. . . . . . , plus in each case an additional fee of $. . . . . . for each name more than one against which the statement of release is required to be indexed.

**[§ 9–407. Information from Filing Officer]**

[(1) If the person filing any financing statement, termination statement, statement of assignment, or statement of release, furnishes the filing officer a copy thereof, the filing officer shall upon request note upon the copy the file number and date and hour of the filing of the original and deliver or sent the copy to such person.]

[(2) Upon request of any person, the filing officer shall issue his certificate showing whether there is on file on the date and hour stated therein, any presently effective financing statement naming a particular debtor and any statement of assignment thereof and if there is, giving the date and hour of filing of each such statement and the names and addresses of each secured party therein. The uniform fee for such a certificate shall be $. . . . . . if the request for the certificate is in the standard form prescribed by the [Secretary of State] and otherwise shall be $. . . . . . Upon request the filing officer shall furnish a copy of any filed financing statement or statement of assignment for a uniform fee of $. . . . . . per page.]

**Note:** *This section is proposed as an optional provision to require filing officers to furnish certificates. Local law and practices should be consulted with regard to the advisability of adoption.*

**§ 9–408. Financing Statements Covering Consigned or Leased Goods**

A consignor or lessor of goods may file a financing statement using the terms "consignor," "consignee," "lessor," "lessee" or the like instead of the terms specified in Section 9–402. The provisions of this Part shall apply as appropriate to such a financing statement but its filing shall not of itself be a factor in determining whether or not the consignment or lease is intended as security (Section 1–201(37)). However, if it is determined for other reasons that the consignment or lease is so intended, a security interest of the consignor or lessor which attaches to the consigned or leased goods is perfected by such filing.

## Part 5 Default

**§ 9–501. Default; Procedure When Security Agreement Covers Both Real and Personal Property**

(1) When a debtor is in default under a security agreement, a secured party has the rights and remedies provided in this Part and except as limited by subsection (3) those provided in the security agreement. He may reduce his claim to judgment, foreclose or otherwise enforce the security interest by an available judicial procedure. If the collateral is documents the secured party may proceed either as to the documents or as to the goods covered thereby. A secured party in possession has the rights, remedies and duties provided in Section 9–207. The rights and remedies referred to in this subsection are cumulative.

(2) After default, the debtor has the rights and remedies provided in this Part, those provided in the security agreement and those provided in Section 9–207.

(3) To the extent that they give rights to the debtor and impose duties on the secured party, the rules stated in the subsections referred to below may not be waived or varied except as provided with respect to compulsory disposition of collateral (subsection (3) of Section 9–504 and Section 9–505) and with respect to redemption of collateral (Section 9–506) but the parties may be agreement determine the standards by which the fulfillment of these rights and duties is to be measured if such standards are not manifestly unreasonable:

(a) subsection (2) of Section 9–502 and subsection (2) of Section 9–504 insofar as they require accounting for surplus proceeds of collateral;

(b) subsection (3) of Section 9–504 and subsection (1) of Section 9–505 which deal with disposition of collateral;

(c) subsection (2) of Section 9–505 which deals with acceptance of collateral as discharge of obligation;

(d) section 9–506 which deals with redemption of collateral; and

(e) subsection (1) of Section 9–507 which deals with the secured party's liability for failure to comply with this Part.

(4) If the security agreement covers both real and personal property, the secured party may proceed under this Part as to the personal property or he may proceed as to both the real and the personal property in accordance with his rights and remedies in respect of the real property in which case the provisions of this Part do not apply.

(5) When a secured party has reduced his claim to judgment the lien of any levy which may be made upon his collateral by virtue of any execution based upon the judgment shall relate back to the date of the perfection of the security interest in such collateral. A judicial sale, pursuant to such execution, is a foreclosure of the security interest by judicial procedure within the meaning of this section, and the secured party may purchase at the sale and thereafter hold the collateral free of any other requirements of this Article.

### § 9–502. Collection Rights of Secured Party

(1) When so agreed and in any event on default the secured party is entitled to notify an account debtor or the obligor on an instrument to make payment to him whether or not the assignor was theretofore making collections on the collateral, and also to take control of any proceeds to which he is entitled under Section 9–306.

(2) A secured party who by agreement is entitled to charge back uncollected collateral or otherwise to full or limited recourse against the debtor and who undertakes to collect from the account debtors or obligors must proceed in a commercially reasonable manner and may deduct his reasonable expenses of realization from the collections. If the security agreement secures an indebtedness, the secured party must account to the debtor for any surplus, and unless otherwise agreed, the debtor is liable for any deficiency. But, if the underlying transaction was a sale of accounts or chattel paper, the debtor is entitled to any surplus or is liable for any deficiency only if the security agreement so provides.

### § 9–503. Secured Party's Right to Take Possession after Default

Unless otherwise agreed a secured party has on default the right to take possession of the collateral. In taking possession a secured party may proceed without judicial process if this can be done without breach of the peace or may proceed by action. If the security agreement so provides the secured party may require the debtor to assemble the collateral and make it available to the secured party at a place to be designated by the secured party which is reasonably convenient to both parties. Without removal a secured party may render equipment unusuable, and may dispose of collateral on the debtor's premises under Section 9–504.

### § 9–504. Secured Party's Right to Dispose of Collateral After Default; Effect of Disposition

(1) A secured party after default may sell, or lease otherwise dispose of any or all of the collateral in its then condition or following any commercially reasonable preparation or processing. Any sale of goods is subject to the Article on Sales (Article 2). The proceeds of disposition shall be applied in the order following to

(a) the reasonable expenses of retaking, holding, preparing for sale or lease, selling, leasing and the like and, to the extent provided for in the agreement and not prohibited by law, the reasonable attorney's fees and legal expenses incurred by the secured party;

(b) the satisfaction of indebtedness secured by the security interest under which the disposition is made;

(c) the satisfaction of indebtedness secured by any subordinate security interest in the collateral if written notification of demand therefor is received before distribution of the proceeds is completed. If requested by the secured party, the holder of a subordinate security interest must reasonably furnish reasonable proof of his interest, and unless he does so, the secured party need not comply with his demand.

(2) If the security interest secures an indebtedness, the secured party must account to the debtor for any surplus, and, unless otherwise agreed, the debtor is liable for any deficiency. But if the underlying transaction was a sale of accounts or chattel paper, the debtor is entitled to any surplus or is liable for any deficiency only if the security agreement so provides.

(3) Disposition of the collateral may be by public or private proceedings and may be made by way of one or more contracts. Sale or other disposition may be as a unit or in parcels and at any time and place and on any terms but every aspect of the disposition including the method, manner, time, place and terms must be commercially reasonable. Unless collateral is perishable or threatens to decline speedily in value or is of a type customarily sold on a recognized market, reasonable notification of the time and place of any public sale or reasonable notification of the time after which any private sale or other intended disposition is to be made shall be sent by the secured party to the debtor, if he has not signed after default a statement renouncing or modifying his right to notification of sale. In the case of consumer goods no other notification need be sent. In other cases notification shall be sent to any other secured party from whom the secured party has received (before sending his notification to the debtor or before the debtor's renunciation of his rights) written notice of a claim of an interest in the collateral. The secured party may buy at any public sale and if the collateral is of a type customarily sold in a recognized market or is of a type which is the subject of widely distributed standard price quotations he may buy at private sale.

(4) When collateral is disposed of by a secured party after default, the disposition transfers to a purchaser for value all of the debtor's rights therein, discharges the security interest under which it is made and any security interest or lien subordinate thereto. The purchaser takes free of all such rights and interests even though the secured party fails to comply with the requirements of this Part or of any judicial proceedings

(a) in the case of a public sale, if the purchaser has no knowledge of any defects in the sale and if he does not buy in collusion with the secured party, other bidders or the person conducting the sale; or

(b) in any other case, if the purchaser acts in good faith.

(5) A person who is liable to a secured party under a guaranty, indorsement, repurchase agreement or the like and who receives a transfer of collateral from the secured party or is subrogated to his rights has thereafter the rights and duties of the secured party. Such a transfer of collateral is not a sale or disposition of the collateral under this Article.

### § 9–505. Compulsory Disposition of Collateral; Acceptance of the Collateral as Discharge of Obligation

(1) If the debtor has paid sixty per cent of the cash price in the case of a purchase money security interest in consumer goods or sixty per cent of the loan in the case of another security interest in consumer goods, and has not signed after default a statement renouncing or modifying his rights under this Part a secured party who has taken possession of collateral must dispose of it under Section 9–504 and if he fails to do so within ninety days after he takes possession the debtor at his option may recover in conversion or under Section 9–507(1) on secured party's liability.

(2) In any other case involving consumer goods or any other collateral a secured party in possession may, after default, propose to retain the collateral in satisfaction of the obligation. Written notice of such proposal shall be sent to the debtor if he has not signed after default a statement renouncing or modifying his rights under this subsection. In the case of consumer goods no other notice need be given. In other cases notice shall be sent to any other secured party from whom the secured party has received (before sending his notice to the debtor or before the debtor's renunciation of his rights) written notice of a claim of an interest in the collateral. If the secured party receives objection in writing from a person entitled to receive notification within twenty-one days after the notice was sent, the secured party must dispose of the collateral under Section 9–504. In the absence of such written objection the secured party may retain the collateral in satisfaction of the debtor's obligation.

### § 9–506. Debtor's Right to Redeem Collateral

At any time before the secured party has disposed of collateral or entered into a contract for its disposition under Section 9–504 or before the obligation has been discharged under Section 9–505(2) the debtor or any other secured party may unless otherwise agreed in writing after default redeem the collateral by tendering fulfillment of all obligations secured by the collateral as well as the expenses reasonably incurred by the secured party in retaking, holding and preparing the collateral for disposition, in arranging for the sale, and to the extent provided in the agreement and not prohibited by law, his reasonable attorney's fees and legal expenses.

### § 9–507. Secured Party's Liability for Failure to Comply with This Part

(1) If it is established that the secured party is not proceeding in accordance with the provisions of this Part disposition may be ordered or restrained on appropriate terms and conditions. If the disposition has occurred the debtor or any person entitled to notification or whose security interest has been made known to the secured party prior to the disposition has a right to recover from the secured party any loss caused by a failure to comply with the provisions of this Part. If the collateral is consumer goods, the debtor has a right to recover in any event an amount not less than the credit service charge plus ten per cent of the principal amount of the debt or the time price differential plus 10 per cent of the cash price.

(2) The fact that a better price could have been obtained by a sale at a different time or in a different method from that selected by the secured party is not of itself sufficient to establish that the sale was not made in a commercially reasonable manner. If the secured party either sells the collateral in the usual manner in any recognized market therefor or if he sells at the price current in such market at the time of his sale or if he has otherwise sold in conformity with reasonable commercial practices among dealers in the type of property sold he has sold in a commercially reasonable manner. The principles stated in the two preceding sentences with respect to sales also apply as may be appropriate to other types of disposition. A disposition which has been approved in any judicial proceeding or by any bona fide creditors' committee or representative of creditors shall conclusively be deemed to be commercially reasonable, but this sentence does not indicate that any such approval must be obtained in any case nor does it indicate that any disposition not so approved is not commercially reasonable.

**Authors' note:** *Articles 10 and 11 have been omitted as unnecessary for the purposes of this text.*

## Part I Preliminary Provisions

### § 1. Name of Act

This act may be cited as Uniform Partnership Act.

### § 2. Definition of Terms

In this act, "Court" includes every court and judge having jurisdiction in the case.

"Business" includes every trade, occupation, or profession.

"Person" includes individuals, partnerships, corporations, and other associations.

"Bankrupt" includes bankrupt under the Federal Bankruptcy Act or insolvent under any state insolvent act.

"Conveyance" includes every assignment, lease, mortgage, or encumbrance.

"Real property" includes land and any interest or estate in land.

### § 3. Interpretation of Knowledge and Notice

(1) A person has "knowledge" of a fact within the meaning of this act not only when he has actual knowledge thereof, but also when he has knowledge of such other facts as in the circumstances shows bad faith.

(2) A person has "notice" of a fact within the

* Source: National Conference of Commissioners of Uniform State Laws. Reprinted with permission.

meaning of this act when the person who claims the benefit of the notice:

(a) States the fact to such person, or

(b) Delivers through the mail, or by other means of communication, a written statement of the fact to such person or to a proper person at his place of business or residence.

### § 4. Rules of Construction

(1) The rule that statutes in derogation of the common law are to be strictly construed shall have no application to this act.

(2) The law of estoppel shall apply under this act.

(3) The law of agency shall apply under this act.

(4) This act shall be so interpreted and construed as to effect its general purpose to make uniform the law of those states which enact it.

(5) This act shall not be construed so as to impair the obligations of any contract existing when the act goes into effect, nor to affect any action or proceedings begun or right accrued before this act takes effect.

### § 5. Rules for Cases Not Provided for in This Act

In any case not provided for in this act the rules of law and equity, including the law merchant, shall govern.

## Part II Nature of Partnership

### § 6. Partnership Defined

(1) A partnership is an association of two or more persons to carry on as co-owners a business for profit.

(2) But any association formed under any other statute of this state, or any statute adopted by authority, other than the authority of this state, is not a partnership under this act, unless such association would have been a partnership in this state prior to the adoption of this act; but this act shall apply to limited partnerships except in so far as the statutes relating to such partnerships are inconsistent herewith.

### § 7. Rules for Determining the Existence of a Partnership

In determining whether a partnership exists, these rules shall apply:

(1) Except as provided by section 16 persons who are not partners as to each other are not partners as to third persons.

(2) Joint tenancy, tenancy in common, tenancy by the entireties, joint property, common property, or part ownership does not of itself establish a partnership, whether such co-owners do or do not share any profits made by the use of the property.

(3) The sharing of gross returns does not of itself establish a partnership, whether or not the persons sharing them have a joint or common right or interest in any property from which the returns are derived.

(4) The receipt by a person of a share of the profits of a business is prima facie evidence that he is a partner in the business, but no such inference shall be drawn if such profits were received in payment:

(a) As a debt by installments or otherwise,

(b) As wages of an employee or rent to a landlord,

(c) As an annuity to a widow or representative of a deceased partner,

(d) As interest on a loan, though the amount of payment vary with the profits of the business,

(e) As the consideration for the sale of a goodwill of a business or other property by installments or otherwise.

### § 8. Partnership Property

(1) All property originally brought into the partnership stock or subsequently acquired by purchase or otherwise, on account of the partnership, is partnership property.

(2) Unless the contrary intention appears, property acquired with partnership funds is partnership property.

(3) Any estate in real property may be acquired in the partnership name. Title so acquired can be conveyed only in the partnership name.

(4) A conveyance to a partnership in the partnership name, though without words of inheritance, passes the entire estate of the grantor unless a contrary intent appears.

## Part III Relations of Partners to Persons Dealing with the Partnership

### § 9. Partner Agent of Partnership as to Partnership Business

(1) Every partner is an agent of the partnership for the purpose of its business, and the act of every

partner, including the execution in the partnership name of any instrument, for apparently carrying on in the usual way the business of the partnership of which he is a member binds the partnership, unless the partner so acting has in fact no authority to act for the partnership in the particular matter, and the person with whom he is dealing has knowledge of the fact that he has no such authority.

(2) An act of a partner which is not apparently for the carrying on of the business of the partnership in the usual way does not bind the partnership unless authorized by the other partners.

(3) Unless authorized by the other partners or unless they have abandoned the business, one or more but less than all the partners have no authority to:

(a) Assign the partnership property in trust for creditors or on the assignee's promise to pay the debts of the partnership,

(b) Dispose of the good-will of the business,

(c) Do any other act which would make it impossible to carry on the ordinary business of a partnership,

(d) Confess a judgment,

(e) Submit a partnership claim or liability to arbitration or reference.

(4) No act of a partner in contravention of a restriction on authority shall bind the partnership to persons having knowledge of the restriction.

### § 10. Conveyance of Real Property of the Partnership

(1) Where title to real property is in the partnership name, any partner may convey title to such property by a conveyance executed in the partnership name; but the partnership may recover such property unless the partner's act binds the partnership under the provisions of paragraph (1) of section 9, or unless such property has been conveyed by the grantee or a person claiming through such grantee to a holder for value without knowledge that the partner, in making the conveyance, has exceeded his authority.

(2) Where title to real property is in the name of the partnership, a conveyance executed by a partner, in his own name, passes the equitable interest of the partnership, provided the act is one within the authority of the partner under the provisions of paragraph (1) of section 9.

(3) Where title to real property is in the name of one or more but not all the partners, and the record does not disclose the right of partnership, the partners in whose name the title stands may convey title to such property, but the partnership may recover such property if the partners' act does not bind the partnership under the provisions of paragraph (1) of section 9, unless the purchaser or his assignee, is a holder for value, without knowledge.

(4) Where the title to real property is in the name of one or more or all the partners, or in a third person in trust for the partnership, a conveyance executed by a partner in the partnership name, or in his own name, passes the equitable interest of the partnership, provided the act is one within the authority of the partner under the provisions of paragraph (1) of section 9.

(5) Where the title to real property is in the names of all the partners a conveyance executed by all the partners passes all their rights in such property.

### § 11. Partnership Bound by Admission of Partner

An admission or representation made by any partner concerning partnership affairs within the scope of his authority as conferred by this act is evidence against the partnership.

### § 12. Partnership Charged with Knowledge of or Notice to Partner

Notice to any partner of any matter relating to partnership affairs, and the knowledge of the partner acting in the particular matter, acquired while a partner or then present to his mind, and the knowledge of any other partner who reasonably could and should have communicated it to the acting partner, operate as notice to or knowledge of the partnership, except in the case of a fraud on the partnership committed by or with the consent of that partner.

### § 13. Partnership Bound by Partner's Wrongful Act

Where, by any wrongful act or omission of any partner acting in the ordinary course of the business of the partnership or with the authority of his co-partners, loss or injury is caused to any person, not being a partner in the partnership, or any penalty is incurred, the partnership is liable therefor to the same extent as the partner so acting or omitting to act.

### § 14. Partnership Bound by Partner's Breach of Trust

The partnership is bound to make good the loss:

(a) Where one partner acting within the scope of his apparent authority receives money or property of a third person and misapplies it; and

(b) Where the partnership in the course of its business receives money or property of a third person and the money or property so received is misapplied by any partner while it is in the custody of the partnership.

### § 15. Nature of Partner's Liability

All partners are liable

(a) Jointly and severally for everything chargeable to the partnership under sections 13 and 14.

(b) Jointly for all other debts and obligations of the partnership; but any partner may enter into a separate obligation to perform a partnership contract.

### § 16. Partner by Estoppel

(1) When a person, by words spoken or written or by conduct, represents himself, or consents to another representing him to any one, as a partner in an existing partnership or with one or more persons not actual partners, he is liable to any such person to whom such representation has been made, who has, on the faith of such representation, given credit to the actual or apparent partnership, and if he has made such representation or consented to its being made in a public manner he is liable to such person, whether the representation has or has not been made or communicated to such person so giving credit by or with the knowledge of the apparent partner making the representation or consenting to its being made.

(a) When a partnership liability results, he is liable as though he were an actual member of the partnership.

(b) When no partnership liability results, he is liable jointly with the other persons, if any, so consenting to the contract or representation as to incur liability, otherwise separately.

(2) When a person has been thus represented to be a partner in an existing partnership, or with one or more persons not actual partners, he is an agent of the persons consenting to such representation to bind them to the same extent and in the same manner as though he were a partner in fact, with respect to persons who rely upon the representation. Where all the members of the existing partnership consent to the representation, a partnership act or obligation results; but in all other cases it is the joint act or obligation of the person acting and the persons consenting to the representation.

### § 17. Liability of Incoming Partner

A person admitted as a partner into an existing partnership is liable for all the obligations of the partnership arising before his admission as though he had been a partner when such obligations were incurred, except that this liability shall be satisfied only out of partnership property.

## Part IV Relations of Partners to One Another

### § 18. Rules Determining Rights and Duties of Partners

The rights and duties of the partners in relation to the partnership shall be determined, subject to any agreement between them, by the following rules:

(a) Each partner shall be repaid his contributions, whether by way of capital or advances to the partnership property and share equally in the profits and surplus remaining after all liabilities, including those to partners, are satisfied; and must contribute towards the losses, whether of capital or otherwise, sustained by the partnership according to his share in the profits.

(b) The partnership must indemnify every partner in respect of payments made and personal liabilities reasonably incurred by him in the ordinary and proper conduct of its business, or for the preservation of its business or property.

(c) A partner, who in aid of the partnership makes any payment or advance beyond the amount of capital which he agreed to contribute, shall be paid interest from the date of the payment or advance.

(d) A partner shall receive interest on the capital contributed by him only from the date when repayment should be made.

(e) All partners have equal rights in the management and conduct of the partnership business.

(f) No partner is entitled to remuneration for acting in the partnership business, except that a surviving partner is entitled to reasonable compensation for his services in winding up the partnership affairs.

(g) No person can become a member of a partnership without the consent of all the partners.

(h) Any difference arising as to ordinary matters connected with the partnership business may be decided by a majority of the partners; but no act in contravention of any agreement between the partners may be done rightfully without the consent of all the partners.

### § 19. Partnership Books

The partnership books shall be kept, subject to any agreement between the partners, at the principal place of business of the partnership, and every partner shall at all times have access to and may inspect and copy any of them.

### § 20. Duty of Partners to Render Information

Partners shall render on demand true and full information of all things affecting the partnership to any partner or the legal representative of any deceased partner or partner under legal disability.

### § 21. Partner Accountable as a Fiduciary

(1) Every partner must account to the partnership for any benefit, and hold as trustee for it any profits derived by him without the consent of the other partners from any transaction connected with the formation, conduct, or liquidation of the partnership or from any use by him of its property.

(2) This section applies also to the representatives of a deceased partner engaged in the liquidation of the affairs of the partnership as the personal representatives of the last surviving partner.

### § 22. Right to an Account

Any partner shall have the right to a formal account as to partnership affairs:

(a) If he is wrongfully excluded from the partnership business or possession of its property by his co-partners,

(b) If the right exists under the terms of any agreement,

(c) As provided by section 21,

(d) Whenever other circumstances render it just and reasonable.

### § 23. Continuation of Partnership Beyond Fixed Term

(1) When a partnership for a fixed term or particular undertaking is continued after the termination of such term or particular undertaking without any express agreement, the rights and duties of the partners remain the same as they were at such termination, so far as is consistent with a partnership at will.

(2) A continuation of the business by the partners or such of them as habitually acted therein during the term, without any settlement or liquidation of the partnership affairs, is prima facie evidence of a continuation of the partnership.

## Part V Property Rights of a Partner

### § 24. Extent of Property Rights of a Partner

The property rights of a partner are (1) his rights in specific partnership property, (2) his interest in the partnership, and (3) his right to participate in the management.

### § 25. Nature of a Partner's Right in Specific Partnership Property

(1) A partner is co-owner with his partners of specific partnership property holding as a tenant in partnership.

(2) The incidents of this tenancy are such that:

(a) A partner, subject to the provisions of this act and to any agreement between the partners, has an equal right with his partners to possess specific partnership property for partnership purposes; but he has no right to possess such property for any other purpose without the consent of his partners.

(b) A partner's right in specific partnership property is not assignable except in connection with the assignment of rights of all the partners in the same property.

(c) A partner's right in specific partnership property is not subject to attachment or execution, except on a claim against the partnership. When partnership property is attached for a partnership debt the partners, or any of them, or the representatives of a deceased partner, cannot claim any right under the homestead or exemption laws.

(d) On the death of a partner his right in specific partnership property vests in the surviving partner or partners, except where the deceased was the last surviving partner, when his right in such property vests in his legal representative. Such surviving partner or partners, or the legal representative of the last surviving partner, has no right to possess the partnership property for any but a partnership purpose.

(e) A partner's right in specific partnership property is not subject to dower, curtesy, or allowances to widows, heirs, or next of kin.

### § 26. Nature of Partner's Interest in the Partnership

A partner's interest in the partnership is his share of the profits and surplus, and the same is personal property.

### § 27. Assignment of Partner's Interest

(1) A conveyance by a partner of his interest in the partnership does not of itself dissolve the partnership, nor, as against the other partners in the absence of agreement, entitle the asignee, during the continuance of the partnership, to interfere in the management or administration of the partnership business or affairs, or to require any information or account of partnership transactions, or to inspect the partnership books; but it merely entitles the assignee to receive in accordance with his contract the profits to which the assigning partner would otherwise be entitled.

(2) In case of a dissolution of the partnership, the assignee is entitled to receive his assignor's interest and may require an account from the date only of the last account agreed to by all the partners.

### § 28. Partner's Interest Subject to Charging Order

(1) On due application to a competent court by any judgment creditor of a partner, the court would entered the judgment, order, or decree, or any other court, may charge the interest of the debtor partner with payment of the unsatisfied amount of such judgment debt with interest thereon; and may then or later appoint a receiver of his share of the profits, and of any other money due or to fall due to him in respect of the partnership, and make all other orders, directions, accounts and inquiries which the debtor partner might have made, or which the circumstances of the case may require.

(2) The interest charged may be redeemed at any time before foreclosure, or in case of a sale being directed by the court may be purchased without thereby causing a dissolution:

(a) With separate property, by any one or more of the partners, or

(b) With partnership property, by any one or more of the partners with the consent of all the partners whose interests are not so charged or sold.

(3) Nothing in this act shall be held to deprive a partner of his right, if any, under the exemption laws, as regards his interest in the partnership.

## Part VI Dissolution and Winding Up

### § 29. Dissolution Defined

The dissolution of a partnership is the change in the relation of the partners caused by any partner ceasing to be associated in the carrying on as distinguished from the winding up of the business.

### § 30. Partnership Not Terminated by Dissolution

On dissolution the partnership is not terminated, but continues until the winding up of partnership affairs is completed.

### § 31. Causes of Dissolution

Dissolution is caused:

(1) Without violation of the agreement between the partners,

(a) By the termination of the definite term or particular undertaking specified in the agreement,

(b) By the express will of any partner when no definite term or particular undertaking is specified,

(c) By the express will of all the partners who have not assigned their interests or suffered them to be charged for their separate debts, either before or after the termination of any specified term or particular undertaking,

(d) By the expulsion of any partner from the

business bona fide in accordance with such a power conferred by the agreement between the partners.
(2) In contravention of the agreement between the partners, where the circumstances do not permit a dissolution under any other provision of this section, by the express will of any partner at any time;
(3) By any event which makes it unlawful for the business of the partnership to be carried on or for the members to carry it on in partnership;
(4) By the death of any partner;
(5) By the bankruptcy of any partner or the partnership;
(6) By decree of court under section 32.

### § 32. Dissolution by Decree of Court

(1) On application by or for a partner the court shall decree a dissolution whenever;
(a) A partner has been declared a lunatic in any judicial proceeding or is shown to be of unsound mind,
(b) A partner becomes in any other way incapable of performing his part of the partnership contract,
(c) A partner has been guilty of such conduct as tends to affect prejudicially the carrying on of the business.
(d) A partner wilfully or persistently commits a breach of the partnership agreement, or otherwise so conducts himself in matters relating to the partnership business that it is not reasonably practicable to carry on the business in partnership with him,
(e) The business of the partnership can only be carried on at a loss,
(f) Other circumstances render a dissolution equitable.
(2) On the application of the purchaser of a partner's interest under sections 27 and 28:
(a) After the termination of the specified term or particular undertaking,
(b) At any time if the partnership was a partnership at will when the interest was assigned or when the charging order was issued.

### § 33. General Effect of Dissolution on Authority of Partner

Except so far as may be necessary to wind up partnership affairs or to complete transactions begun but not then finished, dissolution terminates all authority of any partner to act for the partnership,
(1) With respect to the partners,
(a) When the dissolution is not by the act, bankruptcy or death of a partner; or
(b) When the dissolution is by such act, bankruptcy or death of a partner, in cases where section 34 so requires.
(2) With respect to persons not partners, as declared in section 35.

### § 34. Right of Partner to Contribution from Co-partners after Dissolution

Where the dissolution is caused by the act, death or bankruptcy of a partner, each partner is liable to his co-partners for his share of any liability created by any partner acting for the partnership as if the partnership had not been dissolved unless
(a) The dissolution being by act of any partner, the partner acting for the partnership had knowledge of the dissolution, or
(b) The dissolution being by the death or bankruptcy of a partner, the partner acting for the partnership had knowledge or notice of the death or bankruptcy.

### § 35. Power of Partner to Bind Partnership to Third Persons after Dissolution

(1) After dissolution a partner can bind the partnership except as provided in Paragraph (3).
(a) By any act of appropriate for winding up partnership affairs or completing transactions unfinished at dissolution;
(b) By any transaction which would bind the partnership if dissolution had not taken place, provided the other party to the transaction
(i) Had extended credit to the partnership prior to dissolution and had no knowledge or notice of the dissolution; or
(ii) Though he had not so extended credit, had nevertheless known of the partnership prior to dissolution, and, having no knowledge or notice of dissolution, the fact of dissolution had not been advertised in a newspaper of general circulation in the place (or in each place if more than one) at which the partnership business was regularly carried on.
(2) The liability of a partner under Paragraph (1b) shall be satisfied out of partnership assets alone when such partner had been prior to dissolution

(a) Unknown as a partner to the person with whom the contract is made; and

(b) So far unknown and inactive in partnership affairs that the business reputation of the partnership could not be said to have been in any degree due to his connection with it.

(3) The partnership is in no case bound by any act of a partner after dissolution

(a) Where the partnership is dissolved because it is unlawful to carry on the business, unless the act is appropriate for winding up partnership affairs; or

(b) Where the partner has become bankrupt; or

(c) Where the partner has no authority to wind up partnership affairs; except by a transaction with one who

(i) Had extended credit to the partnership prior to dissolution and had no knowledge or notice of his want of authority; or

(ii) Had not extended credit to the partnership prior to dissolution, and, having no knowledge or notice of his want of authority, the fact of his want of authority has not been advertised in the manner provided for advertising the fact of dissolution in Paragraph (1b ii).

(4) Nothing in this section shall affect the liability under Section 16 of any person who after dissolution represents himself or consents to another representing him as a partner in a partnership engaged in carrying on business.

## § 36. Effect of Dissolution on Partner's Existing Liability

(1) The dissolution of the partnership does not of itself discharge the existing liability of any partner.

(2) A partner is discharged from any existing liability upon dissolution of the partnership by an agreement to that effect between himself, the partnership creditor and the person or partnership continuing the business; and such agreement may be inferred from the course of dealing between the creditor having knowledge of the dissolution and the person or partnership continuing the business.

(3) Where a person agrees to assume the existing obligations of a dissolved partnership, the partners whose obligations have been assumed shall be discharged from any liability to any creditor of the partnership who, knowing of the agreement, consents to a material alteration in the nature or time of payment of such obligations.

(4) The individual property of a deceased partner shall be liable for all obligations of the partnership incurred while he was a partner but subject to the prior payment of his separate debts.

## § 37. Right to Wind Up

Unless otherwise agreed the partners who have not wrongfully dissolved the partnership or the legal representative of the last surviving partner, not bankrupt, has the right to wind up the partnership affairs; provided, however, that any partner, his legal representative or his assignee, upon cause shown, may obtain winding up by the court.

## § 38. Rights of Partners to Application of Partnership Property

(1) When dissolution is caused in any way, except in contravention of the partnership agreement, each partner, as against his co-partners and all persons claiming through them in respect of their interests in the partnership, unless otherwise agreed, may have the partnership property applied to discharge its liabilities, and the surplus applied to pay in cash the net amount owing to the respective partners. But if dissolution is caused by expulsion of a partner, bona fide under the partnership agreement and if the expelled partner is discharged from all partnership liabilities, either by payment or agreement under section 36(2), he shall receive in cash only the net amount due him from the partnership.

(2) When dissolution is caused in contravention of the partnership agreement the rights of the partners shall be as follows:

(a) Each partner who has not caused dissolution wrongfully shall have,

(i) All the rights specified in paragraph (1) of this section, and

(ii) The right, as against each partner who has caused the dissolution wrongfully, to damages for breach of the agreement.

(b) The partners who have not caused the dissolution wrongfully, if they all desire to continue the business in the same name, either by themselves or jointly with others, may do so, during the agreed term for the partnership and for that purpose may possess the partnership property, provided they secure the payment by bond approved by the court, or pay to any partner who has caused the dissolution wrongfully, the value of his interest in the partnership at the dissolution, less any damages recoverable under clause (2a ii) of this section, and in like manner indemnify him against all present or future partnership liabilities.

(c) A partner who has caused the dissolution wrongfully shall have:

(i) If the business is not continued under the provisions of paragraph (2b) all the rights of a partner under paragraph (1), subject to clause (2a ii), of this section,

(ii) If the business is continued under paragraph (2b) of this section the right as against his co-partners and all claiming through them in respect of their interests in the partnership, to have the value of his interest in the partnership, less any damages caused to his co-partners by the dissolution, ascertained and paid to him in cash, or the payment secured by bond approved by the court, and to be released from all existing liabilities of the partnership; but in ascertaining the value of the partner's interest the value of the good-will of the business shall not be considered.

### § 39. Rights Where Partnership Is Dissolved for Fraud or Misrepresentation

Where a partnership contract is rescinded on the ground of the fraud or misrepresentation of one of the parties thereto, the party entitled to rescind is, without prejudice to any other right, entitled,

(a) To a lien on, or a right of retention of, the surplus of the partnership property after satisfying the partnership liabilities to third persons for any sum of money paid by him for the purchase of an interest in the partnership and for any capital or advances contributed by him; and

(b) To stand, after all liabilities to third persons have been satisfied, in the place of the creditors of the partnership for any payments made by him in respect of the partnership liabilities; and

(c) To be indemnified by the person guilty of the fraud or making the representation against all debts and liabilities of the partnership.

### § 40. Rules for Distribution

In settling accounts between the partners after dissolution, the following rules shall be observed, subject to any agreement to the contrary:

(a) The assets of the partnership are:

(i) The partnership property,

(ii) The contributions of the partners necessary for the payment of all the liabilities specified in clause (b) of this paragraph.

(b) The liabilities of the partnership shall rank in order of payment, as follows:

(i) Those owing to creditors other than partners,

(ii) Those owing to partners other than for capital and profits,

(iii) Those owing to partners in respect of capital,

(iv) Those owing to partners in respect of profits.

(c) The assets shall be applied in the order of their declaration in clause (a) of this paragraph to the satisfaction of the liabilities.

(d) The partners shall contribute, as provided by section 18 (a) the amount necessary to satisfy the liabilities; but if any, but not all, of the partners are insolvent, or, not being subject to process, refuse to contribute, the other partners shall contribute their share of the liabilities, and, in the relative proportions in which they share the profits, the additional amount necessary to pay the liabilities.

(e) An assignee for the benefit of creditors or any person appointed by the court shall have the right to enforce the contributions specified in clause (d) of this paragraph.

(f) Any partner or his legal representative shall have the right to enforce the contributions specified in clause (d) of this paragraph, to the extent of the amount which he has paid in excess of his share of the liability.

(g) The individual property of a deceased partner shall be liable for the contributions specified in clause (d) of this paragraph.

(h) When partnership property and the individual properties of the partners are in possession of a court for distribution, partnership creditors shall have priority on partnership property and separate creditors on individual property, saving the rights of lien or secured creditors as heretofore.

(i) Where a partner has become bankrupt or his estate is insolvent the claims against his separate property shall rank in the following order:

(i) Those owing to separate creditors,

(ii) Those owing to partnership creditors,

(iii) Those owing to partners by way of contribution.

### § 41. Liability of Persons Continuing the Business in Certain Cases

(1) When any new partner is admitted into an existing partnership, or when any partner retires and assigns (or the representative of the deceased partner assigns) his rights in partnership property to two or more of the partners, or to one or more of the partners and one or more third persons, if the business is continued without liquidation of the partnership affairs, creditors of the first or dissolved partnership are also creditors of the partnership so continuing the business.

(2) When all but one partner retire and assign (or the representative of a deceased partner assigns) their rights in partnership property to the remaining partner, who continues the business without liquidation of partnership affairs, either alone or with others, creditors of the dissolved partnership are also creditors of the person or partnership so continuing the business.

(3) When any partner retires or dies and the business of the dissolved partnership is continued as set forth in paragraphs (1) and (2) of this section, with the consent of the retired partners or the representative of the deceased partner, but without any assignment of his right in partnership property, rights of creditors of the dissolved partnership and of the creditors of the person or partnership continuing the business shall be as if such assignment has been made.

(4) When all the partners or their representatives assign their rights in partnership property to one or more third persons who promise to pay the debts and who continue the business of the dissolved partnership, creditors of the dissolved partnership are also creditors of the person or partnership continuing the business.

(5) When any partner wrongfully causes a dissolution and the remaining partners continue the business under the provisions of section 38(2b), either alone or with others, and without liquidation of the partnership affairs, creditors of the dissolved partnership are also creditors of the person or partnership continuing the business.

(6) When a partner is expelled and the remaining partners continue the business either alone or with others, without liquidation of the partnership affairs, creditors of the dissolved partnership are also creditors of the person or partnership continuing the business.

(7) The liability of a third person becoming a partner in the partnership continuing the business, under this section, to the creditors of the dissolved partnership shall be satisfied out of partnership property only.

(8) When the business of a partnership after dissolution is continued under any conditions set forth in this section the creditors of the dissolved partnership, as against the separate creditors of the retiring or deceased partner or the representative of the deceased partner, have a prior right to any claim of the retired partner or the representative of the deceased partner against the person or partnership continuing the business, on account of the retired or deceased partner's interest in the dissolved partnership or on account of any consideration promised for such interest or for his right in partnership property.

(9) Nothing in this section shall be held to modify any right of creditors to set aside any assignment on the ground of fraud.

(10) The use by the person or partnership continuing the business of the partnership name, or the name of a deceased partner as part thereof, shall not of itself make the individual property of the deceased partner liable for any debts contracted by such person or partnership.

### § 42. Rights of Retiring or Estate of Deceased Partner When the Business Is Continued

When any partner retires or dies, and the business is continued under any of the conditions set forth in section 41(1, 2, 3, 5, 6), or section 38(2b) without any settlement of accounts as between him or his estate and the person or partnership continuing the business, unless otherwise agreed, he or his legal representative as against such persons or partnership may have the value of his interest at the date of dissolution ascertained, and shall receive as an ordinary creditor an amount equal to the value of his interest in the dissolved partnership with interest, or, at his option or at the option of his legal representative, in lieu of interest, the profits attributable to the use of his right in the property of the dissolved partnership; provided that the creditors of the dissolved partnership as against the separate creditors, or the representative of the retired or deceased partner, shall have priority on any claim arising under this section, as provided by section 41(8) of this act.

### § 43. Accrual of Actions

The right to an account of his interest shall accrue to any partner, or his legal representative, as against the winding up partners or the surviving partners or the person or partnership continuing the business, at the date of dissolution, in the absence of any agreement to the contrary.

## Part VII Miscellaneous Provisions

### § 44. When Act Takes Effect

This act shall take effect on the . . . . . . . . . . day of . . . . . . . . . . one thousand nine hundred and . . . . . . . . . . . . . . .

### § 45. Legislation Repealed

All acts or parts of acts inconsistent with this act are hereby repealed.

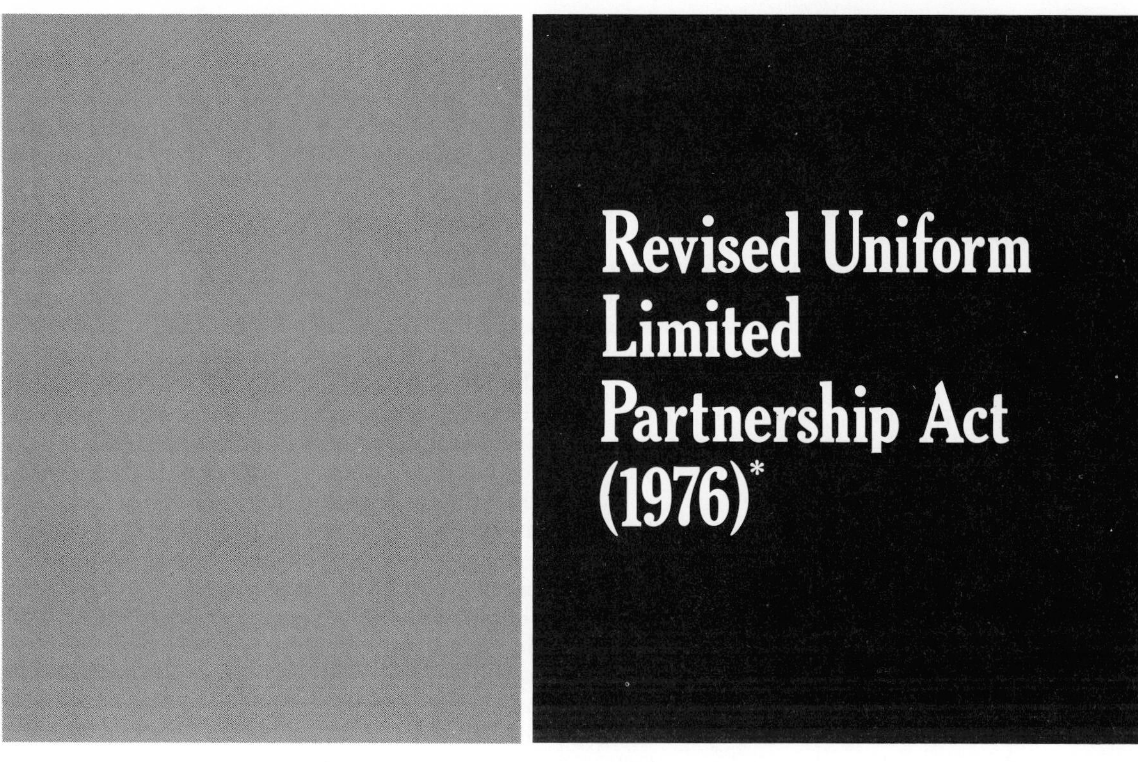


## ARTICLE 1 GENERAL PROVISIONS

### § 101. Definitions

As used in this Act, unless the context otherwise requires:

(1) "Certificate of limited partnership" means the certificate referred to in Section 201, and the certificate as amended.

(2) "Contribution" means any cash, property, services rendered, or a promissory note or other binding obligation to contribute cash or property or to perform services, which a partner contributes to a limited partnership in his capacity as a partner.

(3) "Event of withdrawal of a general partner" means an event that causes a person to cease to be a general partner as provided in Section 402.

(4) "Foreign limited partnership" means a partnership formed under the laws of any State other than this State and having as partners one or more general partners and one or more limited partners.

(5) "General partner" means a person who has been admitted to a limited partnership as a general partner in accordance with the partnership agreement and named in the certificate of limited partnership as a general partner.

(6) "Limited partner" means a person who has been admitted to a limited partnership as a limited partner in accordance with the partnership agree-

* Source: National Conference of Commissioners of Uniform State Laws. Reprinted with permission.

ment and named in the certificate of limited partnership as a limited partner.

(7) "Limited partnership" and "domestic limited partnership" mean a partnership formed by 2 or more persons under the laws of this State and having one or more general partners and one or more limited partners.

(8) "Partner" means a limited or general partner.

(9) "Partnership agreement" means any valid agreement, written or oral, of the partners as to the affairs of a limited partnership and the conduct of its business.

(10) "Partnership interest" means a partner's share of the profits and losses of a limited partnership and the right to receive distributions of partnership assets.

(11) "Person" means a natural person, partnership, limited partnership (domestic or foreign), trust, estate, association, or corporation.

(12) "State" means a state, territory, or possession of the United States, the District of Columbia, or the Commonwealth of Puerto Rico.

### § 102. Name

The name of each limited partnership as set forth in its certificate of limited partnership:

(1) shall contain without abbreviation the words "limited partnership";

(2) may not contain the name of a limited partner unless (i) it is also the name of a general partner or the corporate name of a corporate general partner, or (ii) the business of the limited partnership had been carried on under that name before the admission of that limited partner;

(3) may not contain any word or phrase indicating or implying that it is organized other than for a purpose stated in its certificate of limited partnership;

(4) may not be the same as, or deceptively similar to, the name of any corporation or limited partnership organized under the laws of this State or licensed or registered as a foreign corporation or limited partnership in this State; and

(5) may not contain the following words [here insert prohibited words].

### § 103. Reservation of Name

(a) The exclusive right to the use of a name may be reserved by:

(1) any person intending to organize a limited partnership under this Act and to adopt that name;

(2) any domestic limited partnership or any foreign limited partnership registered in this State which, in either case, intends to adopt that name;

(3) any foreign limited partnership intending to register in this State and adopt that name; and

(4) any person intending to organize a foreign limited partnership and intending to have it register in this State and adopt that name.

(b) The reservation shall be made by filing with the Secretary of State an application, executed by the applicant, to reserve a specified name. If the Secretary of State finds that the name is available for use by a domestic or foreign limited partnership, he shall reserve the name for the exclusive use of the applicant for a period of 120 days. Once having so reserved a name, the same applicant may not again reserve the same name until more than 60 days after the expiration of the last 120-day period for which that applicant reserved that name. The right to the exclusive use of a reserved name may be transferred to any other person by filing in the office of the Secretary of State a notice of the transfer, executed by the applicant for whom the name was reserved and specifying the name and address of the transferee.

### § 104. Specified Office and Agent

Each limited partnership shall continuously maintain in this State:

(1) an office, which may but need not be a place of its business in this State, at which shall be kept the records required by Section 105 to be maintained; and

(2) an agent for service of process on the limited partnership, which agent must be an individual resident of this State, a domestic corporation, or a foreign corporation authorized to do business in this State.

### § 105. Records to Be Kept

Each limited partnership shall keep at the office referred to in Section 104(1) the following: (1) a current list of the full name and last known business address of each partner set forth in alphabetical order, (2) a copy of the certificate of limited partnership and all certificates of amendment thereto, together with executed copies of any powers of attorney pursuant to which any certificate has been executed, (3) copies of the limited partnership's federal, state, and local income tax returns and reports, if any, for the 3 most recent years, and (4) copies of any then effective written partnership agreements and of any financial statements of the limited partnership for the 3 most recent years. Those records are subject to inspection and copying at the reasonable request, and at the expense, of any partner during ordinary business hours.

### § 106. Nature of Business

A limited partnership may carry on any business that a partnership without limited partners may carry on except [here designate prohibited activities].

### § 107. Business Transactions of Partner With the Partnership

Except as provided in the partnership agreement, a partner may lend money to and transact other business with the limited partnership and, subject to other applicable law, has the same rights and obligations with respect thereto as a person who is not a partner.

## ARTICLE 2. FORMATION; CERTIFICATE OF LIMITED PARTNERSHIP

### § 201. Certificate of Limited Partnership

(a) In order to form a limited partnership two or more persons must execute a certificate of limited partnership. The certificate shall be filed in the office of the Secretary of State and set forth:
(1) the name of the limited partnership;
(2) the general character of its business;
(3) the address of the office and the name and address of the agent for service of process required to be maintained by Section 104;
(4) the name and the business address of each partner (specifying separately the general partners and limited partners);
(5) the amount of cash and a description and statement of the agreed value of the other property or services contributed by each partner and which each partner has agreed to contribute in the future;
(6) the times at which or events on the happening of which any additional contributions agreed to be made by each partner are to be made;
(7) any power of a limited partner to grant the right to become a limited partner to an assignee of any part of his partnership interest, and the terms and conditions of the power;
(8) if agreed upon, the time at which or the events on the happening of which a partner may terminate his membership in the limited partnership and the amount of, or the method of determining the distribution to which he may be entitled respecting his partnership interest, and the terms and conditions of the termination and distribution;
(9) any right of a partner to receive distributions of property, including cash from the limited partnership;
(10) any right of a partner to receive, or of a general partner to make, distributions to a partner which include a return of all or any part of the partner's contribution;
(11) any time at which or events upon the happening of which the limited partnership is to be dissolved and its affairs wound up;
(12) any right of the remaining general partners to continue the business on the happening of an event of withdrawal of a general partner; and
(13) any other matters the partners determine to include therein.
(b) A limited partnership is formed at the time of the filing of the certificate of limited partnership in the office of the Secretary of State or at any later time specified in the certificate of limited partnership if, in either case, there has been substantial compliance with the requirements of this section.

### § 202. Amendment to Certificate

(a) A certificate of limited partnership is amended by filing a certificate of amendment thereto in the office of the Secretary of State. The certificate shall set forth:
(1) the name of the limited partnership;
(2) the date of filing of the certificate; and
(3) the amendment to the certificate.
(b) Within 30 days after the happening of any of the following events an amendment to a certificate of limited partnership reflecting the occurrence of the event or events shall be filed:

(1) a change in the amount or character of the contribution of any partner, or in any partner's obligation to make a contribution;
(2) the admission of a new partner;
(3) the withdrawal of a partner; or
(4) the continuation of the business under Section 801 after an event of withdrawal of a general partner.
(c) A general partner who becomes aware that any statement in a certificate of limited partnership was false when made or that any arrangements or other facts described have changed, making the certificate inaccurate in any respect, shall promptly amend the certificate, but an amendment to show a change of address of a limited partner need be filed only once every 12 months.
(d) A certificate of limited partnership may be amended at any time for any other proper purpose the general partners may determine.
(e) No person has any liability because an amendment to a certificate of limited partnership has not been filed to reflect the occurrence of any event referred to in subsection (b) of this Section if the amendment is filed within the 30-day period specified in subsection (b).

### § 203. Cancellation of Certificate

A certificate of limited partnership shall be cancelled upon the dissolution and the commencement of winding up of the partnership or at any other time there are no limited partners. A certificate of cancellation shall be filed in the office of the Secretary of State and set forth:
(1) the name of the limited partnership;
(2) the date of filing of its certificate of limited partnership;
(3) the reason for filing the certificate of cancellation;
(4) the effective date (which shall be a date certain) of cancellation if it is not to be effective upon the filing of the certificate; and
(5) any other information the general partners filing the certificate determine.

### § 204. Execution of Certificates

(a) Each certificate required by this Article to be filed in the office of the Secretary of State shall be executed in the following manner:
(1) an original certificate of limited partnership must be signed by all partners named therein;
(2) a certificate of amendment must be signed by at least one general partner and by each other partner designated in the certificate as a new partner or whose contribution is described as having been increased; and
(3) a certificate of cancellation must be signed by all general partners;
(b) Any person may sign a certificate by an attorney-in-fact, but a power of attorney to sign a certificate relating to the admission, or increased contribution, of a partner must specifically describe the admission or increase.
(c) The execution of a certificate by a general partner constitutes an affirmation under the penalties of perjury that the facts stated therein are true.

### § 205. Amendment or Cancellation by Judicial Act

If a person required by Section 204 to execute a certificate of amendment or cancellation fails or refuses to do so, any other partner, and any assignee of a partnership interest, who is adversely affected by the failure or refusal, may petition the [here designate the proper court] to direct the amendment or cancellation. If the court finds that the amendment or cancellation is proper and that any person so designated has failed or refused to execute the certificate, it shall order the Secretary of State to record an appropriate certificate of amendment or cancellation.

### § 206. Filing in Office of Secretary of State

(a) Two signed copies of the certificate of limited partnership and of any certificates of amendment or cancellation (or of any judicial decree of amendment or cancellation) shall be delivered to the Secretary of State. A person who executes a certificate as an agent or fiduciary need not exhibit evidence of his authority as a prerequisite to filing. Unless the Secretary of State finds that any certificate does not conform to law, upon receipt of all filing fees required by law he shall:
(1) endorse on each duplicate original the word "Filed" and the day, month, and year of the filing thereof;
(2) file one duplicate original in his office; and

(3) return the other duplicate original to the person who filed it or his representative.

(b) Upon the filing of a certificate of amendment (or judicial decree of amendment) in the office of the Secretary of State, the certificate of limited partnership shall be amended as set forth therein, and upon the effective date of a certificate of cancellation (or a judicial decree thereof), the certificate of limited partnership is cancelled.

### § 207. Liability for False Statement in Certificate

If any certificate of limited partnership or certificate of amendment or cancellation contains a false statement, one who suffers loss by reliance on the statement may recover damages for the loss from:

(1) any person who executes the certificate, or causes another to execute it on his behalf, and knew, and any general partner who knew or should have known, the statement to be false at the time the certificate was executed; and

(2) any general partner who thereafter knows or should have known that any arrangement or other fact described in the certificate has changed, making the statement inaccurate in any respect within a sufficient time before the statement was relied upon reasonably to have enabled that general partner to cancel or amend the certificate, or to file a petition for its cancellation or amendment under Section 205.

### § 208. Notice

The fact that a certificate of limited partnership is on file in the office of the Secretary of State is notice that the partnership is a limited partnership and the persons designated therein as limited partners are limited partners, but it is not notice of any other fact.

### § 209. Delivery of Certificates to Limited Partners

Upon the return by the Secretary of State pursuant to Section 206 of a certificate marked "Filed," the general partners shall promptly deliver or mail a copy of the certificate of limited partnership and each certificate to each limited partner unless the partnership agreement provides otherwise.

## ARTICLE 3. LIMITED PARTNERS

### § 301. Admission of Additional Limited Partners

(a) After the filing of a limited partnership's original certificate of limited partnership, a person may be admitted as an additional limited partner:

(1) in the case of a person acquiring a partnership interest directly from the limited partnership, upon the compliance with the partnership agreement or, if the partnership agreement does not so provide, upon the written consent of all partners; and

(2) in the case of an assignee of a partnership interest of a partner who has the power, as provided in Section 704, to grant the assignee the right to become a limited partner, upon the exercise of that power and compliance with any conditions limiting the grant or exercise of the power.

(b) In each case under subsection (a), the person acquiring the partnership interest becomes a limited partner only upon amendment of the certificate of limited partnership reflecting that fact.

### 302. Voting

Subject to Section 303, the partnership agreement may grant to all or a specified group of the limited partners the right to vote (on a per capita or other basis) upon any matter.

### § 303. Liability to Third Parties

(a) Except as provided in subsection (d), a limited partner is not liable for the obligations of a limited partnership unless he is also a general partner or, in addition to the exercise of his rights and powers as a limited partner, he takes part in the control of the business. However, if the limited partner's participation in the control of the business is not substantially the same as the exercise of the powers of a general partner, he is liable only to persons who transact business with the limited partnership with actual knowledge of his participation in control.

(b) A limited partner does not participate in the control of the business within the meaning of subsection (a) solely by doing one or more of the following:

(1) being a contractor for or an agent or employee of the limited partnership or of a general partner;
(2) consulting with and advising a general partner with respect to the business of the limited partnership;
(3) acting as surety for the limited partnership;
(4) approving or disapproving an amendment to the partnership agreement; or
(5) voting on one or more of the following matters:
(i) the dissolution and winding up of the limited partnership;
(ii) the sale, exchange, lease, mortgage, pledge, or other transfer of all or substantially all of the assets of the limited partnership other than in the ordinary course of its business;
(iii) the incurrence of indebtedness by the limited partnership other than in the ordinary course of its business;
(iv) a change in the nature of the business; or
(v) the removal of a general partner.
(c) The enumeration in subsection (b) does not mean that the possession or exercise of any other powers by a limited partner constitutes participation by him in the business of the limited partnership.
(d) A limited partner who knowingly permits his name to be used in the name of the limited partnership, except under circumstances permitted by Section 102(2)(i), is liable to creditors who extend credit to the limited partnership without actual knowledge that the limited partner is not a general partner.

### § 304. Person Erroneously Believing Himself Limited Partner

(a) Except as provided in subsection (b), a person who makes a contribution to a business enterprise and erroneously but in good faith believes that he has become a limited partner in the enterprise is not a general partner in the enterprise and is not bound by its obligations by reason of making the contribution, receiving distributions from the enterprise, or exercising any rights of a limited partner, if, on ascertaining the mistake, he:
(1) causes an appropriate certificate of limited partnership or a certificate of amendment to be executed and filed; or
(2) withdraws from future equity participation in the enterprise.
(b) A person who makes a contribution of the kind described in subsection (a) is liable as a general partner to any third party who transacts business with the enterprise (i) before the person withdraws and an appropriate certificate is filed to show withdrawal, or (ii) before an appropriate certificate is filed to show his status as a limited partner and, in the case of an amendment, after expiration of the 30-day period for filing an amendment relating to the person as a limited partner under Section 202, but in either case only if the third party actually believed in good faith that the person was a general partner at the time of the transaction.

### § 305. Information

Each limited partner has the right to:
(1) inspect and copy any of the partnership records required to be maintained by Section 105; and
(2) obtain from the general partners from time to time upon reasonable demand (i) true and full information regarding the state of the business and financial condition of the limited partnership, (ii) promptly after becoming available, a copy of the limited partnership's federal, state, and local income tax returns for each year, and (iii) other information regarding the affairs of the limited partnership as is just and reasonable.

## ARTICLE 4. GENERAL PARTNERS

### § 401. Admission of Additional General Partners

After the filing of a limited partnership's original certificate of limited partnership, additional general partners may be admitted only with the specific written consent of each partner.

### § 402. Events of Withdrawal

Except as approved by the specific written consent of all partners at the time, a person ceases to be a general partner of a limited partnership upon the happening of any of the following events:
(1) the general partner withdraws from the limited partnership as provided in Section 602;
(2) the general partner ceases to be a member of the limited partnership as provided in Section 702;
(3) the general partner is removed as a general partner in accordance with the partnership agreement;

(4) unless otherwise provided in the certificate of limited partnership, the general partner: (i) makes an assignment for the benefit of creditors; (ii) files a voluntary petition in bankruptcy; (iii) is adjudicated a bankrupt or insolvent; (iv) files a petition or answer seeking for himself any reorganization, arrangement, composition, readjustment, liquidation, dissolution, or similar relief under any statute, law, or regulation; (v) files an answer or other pleading admitting or failing to contest the material allegations of a petition filed against him in any proceeding of this nature; or (vi) seeks, consents to, or acquiesces in the appointment of a trustee, receiver, or liquidator of the general partner or of all or any substantial part of his properties;

(5) unless otherwise provided in the certificate of limited partnership, [120] days after the commencement of any proceeding against the general partner seeking reorganization, arrangement, composition, readjustment, liquidation, dissolution, or similar relief under any statute, law, or regulation, the proceeding has not been dismissed, or if within [90] days after the appointment without his consent or acquiescence of a trustee, receiver, or liquidator of the general partner or of all or any substantial part of his properties, the appointment is not vacated or stayed, or within [90] days after the expiration of any such stay, the appointment is not vacated;

(6) in the case of a general partner who is a natural person,

(i) his death; or

(ii) the entry by a court of competent jurisdiction adjudicating him incompetent to manage his person or his estate;

(7) in the case of a general partner who is acting as a general partner by virtue of being a trustee of a trust, the termination of the trust (but not merely the substitution of a new trustee);

(8) in the case of a general partner that is a separate partnership, the dissolution and commencement of winding up of the separate partnership;

(9) in the case of a general partner that is a corporation, the filing of a certificate of dissolution, or its equivalent, for the corporation or the revocation of its charter; or

(10) in the case of an estate, the distribution by the fiduciary of the estate's entire interest in the partnership.

### § 403. General Powers and Liabilities

(a) Except as provided in this Act or in the partnership agreement, a general partner of a limited partnership has the rights and powers and is subject to the restrictions of a partner in a partnership without limited partners.

(b) Except as provided in this Act, a general partner of a limited partnership has the liabilities of a partner in a partnership without limited partners to persons other than the partnership and the other partners. Except as provided in this Act or in the partnership agreement, a general partner of a limited partnership has the liabilities of a partner in a partnership without limited partners to the partnership and to the other partners.

### § 404. Contributions by a General Partner

A general partner of a limited partnership may make contributions to the partnership and share in the profits and losses of, and in distributions from, the limited partnership as a general partner. A general partner also may make contributions to and share in profits, losses, and distributions as a limited partner. A person who is both a general partner and a limited partner has the rights and powers, and is subject to the restrictions and liabilities, of a general partner and, except as provided in the partnership agreement, also has the powers, and is subject to the restrictions, of a limited partner to the extent of his participation in the partnership as a limited partner.

### § 405. Voting

The partnership agreement may grant to all or certain identified general partners the right to vote (on a per capita or any other basis), separately or with all or any class of the limited partners, on any matter.

## ARTICLE 5. FINANCE

### § 501. Form of Contribution

The contribution of a partner may be in cash, property, or services rendered, or a promissory note or other obligation to contribute cash or property or to perform services.

### § 502. Liability for Contributions

(a) Except as provided in the certificate of limited partnership, a partner is obligated to the limited partnership to perform any promise to contribute cash or property or to perform services, even if he is unable to perform because of death, disability or any other reason. If a partner does not make the required contribution of property or services, he is obligated at the option of the limited partnership to contribute cash equal to that portion of the value (as stated in the certificate of limited partnership) of the stated contribution that has not been made.

(b) Unless otherwise provided in the partnership agreement, the obligation of a partner to make a contribution or return money or other property paid or distributed in violation of this Act may be compromised only by consent of all the partners. Notwithstanding the compromise, a creditor of a limited partnership who extends credit, or whose claim arises, after the filing of the certificate of limited partnership or an amendment thereto which, in either case, reflects the obligation, and before the amendment or cancellation thereof to reflect the compromise, may enforce the original obligation.

### § 503. Sharing of Profits and Losses

The profits and losses of a limited partnership shall be allocated among the partners, and among classes of partners, in the manner provided in the partnership agreement. If the partnership agreement does not so provide, profits and losses shall be allocated on the basis of the value (as stated in the certificate of limited partnership) of the contributions made by each partner to the extent they have been received by the partnership and have not been returned.

### § 504. Sharing of Distributions

Distributions of cash or other assets of a limited partnership shall be allocated among the partners, and among classes of partners, in the manner provided in the partnership agreement. If the partnership agreement does not so provide, distributions shall be made on the basis of the value (as stated in the certificate of limited partnership) of the contributions made by each partner to the extent they have been received by the partnership and have not been returned.

## ARTICLE 6. DISTRIBUTIONS AND WITHDRAWAL

### § 601. Interim Distributions

Except as provided in this Article, a partner is entitled to receive distributions from a limited partnership before his withdrawal from the limited partnership and before the dissolution and winding up therof:

(1) to the extent and at the times or upon the happening of the events specified in the partnership agreement; and

(2) if any distribution constitutes a return of any part of his contribution under Section 608(c), to the extent and at the times or upon the happening of the events specified in the certificate of limited partnership.

### § 602. Withdrawl of General Partner

A general partner may withdraw from a limited partnership at any time by giving written notice to the other partners, but if the withdrawal violates the partnership agreement, the limited partnership may recover from the withdrawing general partner damages for breach of the partnership agreement and offset the damages against the amount otherwise distributable to him.

### § 603. Withdrawal of Limited Partner

A limited partner may withdraw from a limited partnership at the time or upon the happening of events specified in the certificate of limited partnership and in accordance with the partnership agreement. If the certificate does not specify the time or the events upon the happening of which a limited partner may withdraw or a definite time for the dissolution and winding up of the limited partnership, a limited partner may withdraw upon not less than 6 months' prior written notice to each general partner at his address on the books of the limited partnership at its office in this State.

### § 604. Distribution Upon Withdrawal

Except as provided in this Article, upon withdrawal any withdrawing partner is entitled to receive any distribution to which he is entitled under the partnership agreement and, if not otherwise provided in the agreement, he is entitled to receive, within a reasonable time after withdrawal, the fair value of his interest in the limited partnership as of the date of withdrawal based upon his right to share in distributions from the limited partnership.

### § 605. Distribution in Kind

Except as provided in the certificate of limited partnership, a partner, regardless of the nature of his contribution, has no right to demand and receive any distribution from a limited partnership in any form other than cash. Except as provided in the partnership agreement, a partner may not be compelled to accept a distribution of any asset in kind from a limited partnership to the extent that the percentage of the asset distributed to him exceeds a percentage of that asset which is equal to the percentage in which he shares in distributions from the limited partnership.

### § 606. Right to Distribution

At the time a partner becomes entitled to receive a distribution, he has the status of, and is entitled to all remedies available to, a creditor of the limited partnership with respect to the distribution.

### § 607. Limitations on Distribution

A partner may not receive a distribution from a limited partnership to the extent that, after giving effect to the distribution, all liabilities of the limited partnership, other than liabilities to partners on account of their partnership interests, exceed the fair value of the partnership assets.

### § 608. Liability Upon Return of Contribution

(a) If a partner has received the return of any part of his contribution without violation of the partnership agreement or this Act, he is liable to the limited partnership for a period of one year thereafter for the amount of the returned contribution, but only to the extent necessary to discharge the limited partnership's liabilities to creditors who extended credit to the limited partnership during the period the contribution was held by the partnership.

(b) If a partner has received the return of any part of his contribution in violation of the partnership agreement or this Act, he is liable to the limited partnership for a period of 6 years thereafter for the amount of the contribution wrongfully returned.

(c) A partner receives a return of his contribution to the extent that a distribution to him reduces his share of the fair value of the net assets of the limited partnership below the value (as set forth in the certificate of limited partnership) of his contribution which has not been distributed to him.

## ARTICLE 7. ASSIGNMENT OF PARTNERSHIP INTERESTS

### § 701. Nature of Partnership Interest

A partnership interest is personal property.

### § 702. Assignment of Partnership Interest

Except as provided in the partnership agreement, a partnership interest is assignable in whole or in part. An assignment of a partnership interest does not dissolve a limited partnership or entitle the assignee to become or to exercise any rights of a partner. An assignment entitles the assignee to receive, to the extent assigned, only the distribution to which the assignor would be entitled. Except as provided in the partnership agreement, a partner ceases to be a partner upon assignment of all his partnership interest.

### § 703. Rights of Creditor

On application to a court of competent jurisdiction by any judgment creditor of a partner, the court may charge the partnership interest of the partner with payment of the unsatisfied amount of the judgment with interest. To the extent so charged, the judgment creditor has only the rights of an assignee of the partnership interest. This Act does not deprive any partner of the benefit of any exemption laws applicable to his partnership interest.

### § 704. Right of Assignee to Become Limited Partner

(a) An assignee of a partnership interest, including an assignee of a general partner, may become

a limited partner if and to the extent that (1) the assignor gives the assignee that right in accordance with authority described in the certificate of limited partnership, or (2) all other partners consent.
(b) An assignee who has become a limited partner has, to the extent assigned, the rights and powers, and is subject to the restrictions and liabilities, of a limited partner under the partnership agreement and this Act. An assignee who becomes a limited partner also is liable for the obligations of his assignor to make and return contributions as provided in Article 6. However, the assignee is not obligated for liabilities unknown to the assignee at the time he became a limited partner and which could not be ascertained from the certificate of limited partnership.
(c) If an assignee of a partnership interest becomes a limited partner, the assignor is not released from his liability to the limited partnership under Section 207 and 502.

### § 705. Power of Estate of Deceased or Incompetent Partner

If a partner who is an individual dies or a court of competent jurisdiction adjudges him to be incompetent to manage his person or his property, the partner's executor, administrator, guardian, conservator, or other legal representative may exercise all of the partner's rights for the purpose of settling his estate or administering his property, including any power the partner had to give an assignee the right to become a limited partner. If a partner is a corporation, trust, or other entity and is dissolved or terminated, the powers of that partner may be exercised by its legal representative or successor.

## ARTICLE 8. DISSOLUTION

### § 801. Nonjudicial Dissolution

A limited partnership is dissolved and its affairs shall be wound up upon the happening of the first to occur of the following:
(1) at the time or upon the happening of events specified in the certificate of limited partnership;
(2) written consent of all partners;
(3) an event of withdrawal of a general partner unless at the time there is at least one other general partner and the certificate of limited partnership permits the business of the limited partnership to be carried on by the remaining general partner and that partner does so, but the limited partnership is not dissolved and is not required to be wound up by reason of any event of withdrawal if, within 90 days after the withdrawal, all partners agree in writing to continue the business of the limited partnership and to the appointment of one or more additional general partners if necessary or desired; or
(4) entry of a decree of judicial dissolution under Section 802.

### § 802. Judicial Dissolution

On application by or for a partner the [here designate the proper court] court may decree dissolution of a limited partnership whenever it is not reasonably practicable to carry on the business in conformity with the partnership agreement.

### § 803. Winding Up

Except as provided in the partnership agreement, the general partners who have not wrongfully dissolved a limited partnership or, if none, the limited partners, may wind up the limited partnership's affairs; but the [here designate the proper court] court may wind up the limited partnership's affairs upon application of any partner, his legal representative, or assignee.

### § 804. Distribution of Assets

Upon the winding up of a limited partnership, the assets shall be distributed as follows:
(1) to creditors, including partners who are creditors, to the extent otherwise permitted by law, in satisfaction of liabilities of the limited partnership other than liabilities for distributions to partners under Section 601 or 604;
(2) except as provided in the partnership agreement, to partners and former partners in satisfaction of liabilities for distributions under Section 601 or 604; and
(3) except as provided in the partnership agreement, to partners *first* for the return of their contributions and *secondly* respecting their partnership interests, in the proportions in which the partners share in distributions.

## ARTICLE 9. FOREIGN LIMITED PARTNERSHIPS

### § 901. Law Governing

Subject to the Constitution of this State, (1) the laws of the state under which a foreign limited partnership is organized govern its organization and internal affairs and the liability of its limited partners, and (2) a foreign limited partnership may not be denied registration by reason of any difference between those laws and the laws of this State.

### § 902. Registration

Before transacting business in this State, a foreign limited partnership shall register with the Secretary of State. In order to register, a foreign limited partnership shall submit to the Secretary of State, in duplicate, an application for registration as a foreign limited partnership, signed and sworn to by a general partner and setting forth:

(1) the name of the foreign limited partnership and, if different, the name under which it proposes to register and transact business in this State;

(2) the state and date of its formation;

(3) the general character of the business it proposes to transact in this State;

(4) the name and address of any agent for service of process on the foreign limited partnership whom the foreign limited partnership elects to appoint; the agent must be an individual resident of this State, a domestic corporation, or a foreign corporation having a place of business in, and authorized to do business in this State;

(5) a statement that the Secretary of State is appointed the agent of the foreign limited partnership for service of process if no agent has been appointed under paragraph (4) or, if appointed, the agent's authority has been revoked or if the agent cannot be found or served with the exercise of reasonable diligence;

(6) the address of the office required to be maintained in the State of its organization by the laws of that State or, if not so required, of the principal office of the foreign limited partnership; and

(7) If the certificate of limited partnership filed in the foreign limited partnership's state of organization is not required to include the names and business addresses of the partners, a list of the names and addresses.

### § 903. Issuance of Registration

(a) If the Secretary of State finds that an application for registration conforms to law and all requisite fees have been paid, he shall:

(1) endorse on the application the word "Filed", and the month, day, and year of the filing thereof;

(2) file in his office a duplicate original of the application; and

(3) issue a certificate of registration to transact business in this State.

(b) The certificate of registration, together with a duplicate original of the application, shall be returned to the person who filed the application or his representative.

### § 904. Name

A foreign limited partnership may register with the Secretary of State under any name (whether or not it is the name under which it is registered in its state of organization) that includes without abbreviation the words "limited partnership" and that could be registered by a domestic limited partnership.

### § 905. Changes and Amendments

If any statement in the application for registration of a foreign limited partnership was false when made or any arrangements or other facts described have changed, making the application inaccurate in any respect, the foreign limited partnership shall promptly file in the office of the Secretary of State a certificate, signed and sworn to by a general partner, correcting such statement.

### § 906. Cancellation of Registration

A foreign limited partnership may cancel its registration by filing with the Secretary of State a certificate of cancellation signed and sworn to by a general partner. A cancellation does not terminate the authority of the Secretary of State to accept service of process on the foreign limited partnership with respect to [claims for relief] [causes of action] arising out of the transactions of business in this State.

### § 907. Transaction of Business Without Registration

(a) A foreign limited partnership transacting business in this State may not maintain any action,

suit, or proceeding in any court of this State until it has registered in this State.
(b) The failure of a foreign limited partnership to register in this State does not impair the validity of any contract or act of the foreign limited partnership or prevent the foreign limited partnership from defending any action, suit, or proceeding in any court of this State.
(c) A limited partner of a foreign limited partnership is not liable as a general partner of the foreign limited partnership solely by reason of having transacted business in this State without registration.
(d) A foreign limited partnership, by transacting business in this State without registration, appoints the Secretary of State as its agent for service of process with respect to [claims for relief] [causes of action] arising out of the transaction of business in this State.

### § 908. Action by [Appropriate Official]

The [appropriate official] may bring an action to restrain a foreign limited partnership from transacting business in this State in violation of this Article.

## ARTICLE 10. DERIVATIVE ACTIONS

### § 1001. Right of Action

A limited partner may bring an action in the right of a limited partnership to recover a judgment in its favor if general partners with authority to do so have refused to bring the action or if an effort to cause those general partners to bring the action is not likely to succeed.

### § 1002. Proper Plaintiff

In a derivative action, the plaintiff must be a partner at the time of bringing the action and (1) at the time of the transaction of which he complains or (2) his status as a partner had devolved upon him by operation of law or pursuant to the terms of the partnership agreement from a person who was a partner at the time of the transaction.

### § 1003. Pleading

In a derivative action, the complaint shall set forth with particularity the effort of the plaintiff to secure initiation of the action by a general partner or the reasons for not making the effort.

### § 1004. Expenses

If a derivative action is successful, in whole or in part, or if anything is received by the plantiff as a result of a judgment, compromise, or settlement of an action or claim, the court may award the plaintiff reasonable expenses, including reasonable attorney's fees, and shall direct him to remit to the limited partnership the remainder of those proceeds received by him.

## ARTICLE 11. MISCELLANEOUS

### § 1101. Construction and Application

This Act shall be so applied and construed to effectuate its general purpose to make uniform the law with respect to the subject of this Act among states enacting it.

### § 1102. Short Title *(Text omitted.)*

### § 1103. Severability *(Text omitted.)*

### § 1104. Effective Date, Extended Effective Date and Repeal *(Text omitted.)*

### § 1105. Rules for Cases Not Provided for in This Act

In any case not provided for in this Act the provisions of the Uniform Partnership Act govern.

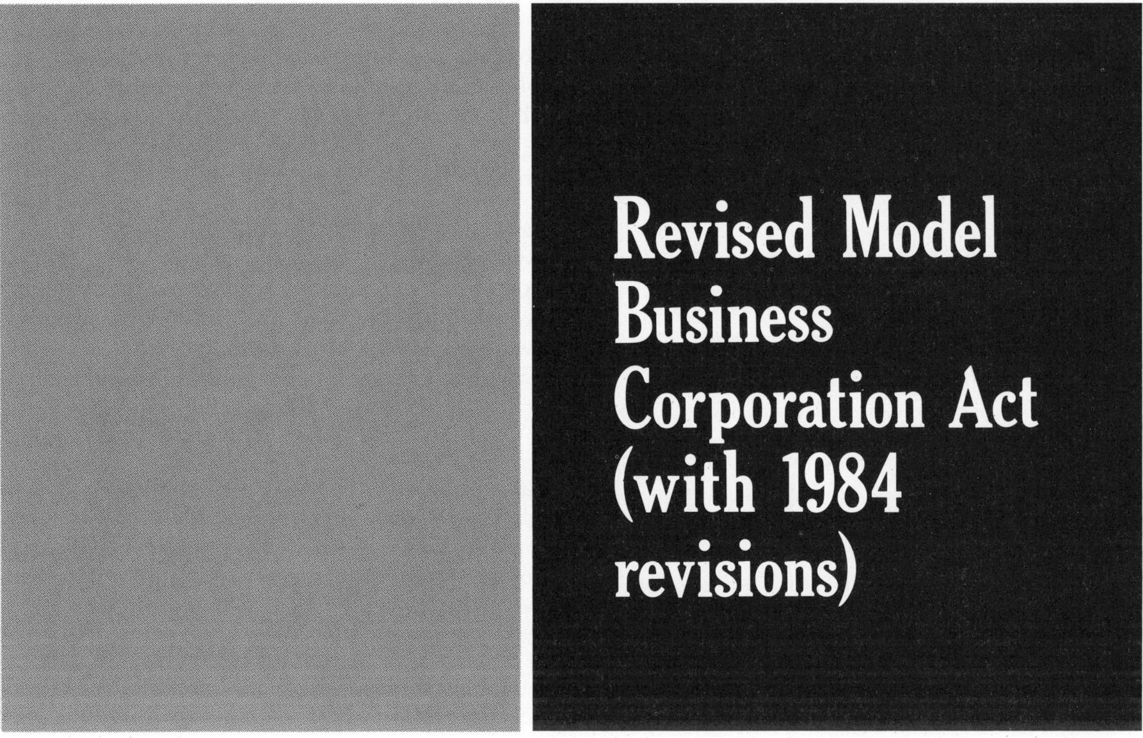


## CHAPTER 1. GENERAL PROVISIONS

### Subchapter A. Short Title and Reservation of Power

**§ 1.01. Short Title**

This Act shall be known and may be cited as the "[name of state] Business Corporation Act."

**§ 1.02. Reservation of Power to Amend or Repeal**

The [name of state legislature] has power to amend or repeal all or part of this Act at any time and all domestic and foreign corporations subject to this Act are governed by the amendment or repeal.

### Subchapter B. Filing Documents

**§ 1.20. Filing Requirements**

(a) A document must satisfy the requirements of this section, and of any other section that adds to or varies these requirements, to be entitled to filing by the secretary of state. *(Text of other subsections omitted.)*

**§ 1.21. Forms**

(a) The secretary of state may prescribe and furnish on request forms for: (1) an application for a certificate of existence, (2) a foreign corporation's application for a certificate of authority to transact business in this state, (3) a foreign corporation's application for a certificate of withdrawal, and (4) the annual report. If the secretary of state so requires, use of these forms is mandatory.

(b) The secretary of state may prescribe and furnish on request forms for other documents required or permitted to be filed by this Act but their use is not mandatory.

### § 1.22. Filing, Service, and Copying Fees *(Text omitted.)*

### § 1.23. Effective Time and Date of Document

(a) Except as provided in subsection (b) and section 1.24(c), a document accepted for filing is effective:

(1) at the time of filing on the date it is filed, as evidenced by the secretary of state's date and time endorsement on the original document; or

(2) at the time specified in the document as its effective time on the date it is filed. *(Text of other subsections omitted.)*

### § 1.24. Correcting Filed Document

(a) A domestic or foreign corporation may correct a document filed by the secretary of state if the document (1) contains an incorrect statement or (2) was defectively executed, attested, sealed, verified, or acknowledged. *(Text of other subsections omitted.)*

### § 1.25. Filing Duty of Secretary of State

(a) If a document delivered to the office of the secretary of state for filing satisfies the requirements of section 1.20, the secretary of state shall file it. *(Text of other subsections omitted.)*

### § 1.26. Appeal from Secretary of State's Refusal to File Document

(a) If the secretary of state refuses to file a document delivered to his office for filing, the domestic or foreign corporation may appeal the refusal to the [name or describe] court [of the county where the corporation's principal office (or, if none in this state, its registered office) is or will be located] [of ____ county]. The appeal is commenced by petitioning the court to compel filing the document and by attaching to the petition the document and the secretary of state's explanation of his refusal to file.

(b) The court may summarily order the secretary of state to file the document or take other action the court considers appropriate.

(c) The court's final decision may be appealed as in other civil proceedings.

### § 1.27. Evidentiary Effect of Copy of Filed Document

A certificate attached to a copy of a document filed by the secretary of state, bearing his signature (which may be in fascimile) and the seal of this state, is conclusive evidence that the original document is on file with the secretary of state.

### § 1.28. Certificate of Existence

(a) Anyone may apply to the secretary of state to furnish a certificate of existence for a domestic corporation or a certificate of authorization for a foreign corporation. *(Text of other subsections omitted.)*

### § 1.29. Penalty for Signing False Document

(a) A person commits an offense if he signs a document he knows is false in any material respect with intent that the document be delivered to the secretary of state for filing.

(b) An offense under this section is a [____] misdemeanor [punishable by a fine of not to exceed $____].

## Subchapter C. Secretary of State

### § 1.30. Powers

The secretary of state has the power reasonably necessary to perform the duties required of him by this Act. *(Text of other subsections omitted.)*

## Subchapter D. Definitions

### § 1.40. Act Definitions

In this Act:

(1) "Articles of incorporation" include amended and restated articles of incorporation and articles of merger.

(2) "Authorized shares" means the shares of all classes a domestic or foreign corporation is authorized to issue.

(3) "Conspicuous" means so written that a rea-

sonable person against whom the writing is to operate should have noticed it. For example, printing in italics or boldface or contrasting color, or typing in capitals or underlined, is conspicuous.

(4) "Corporation" or "domestic corporation" means a corporation for profit, which is not a foreign corporation, incorporated under or subject to the provisions of this Act.

(5) "Deliver" includes mail.

(6) "Distribution" means a direct or indirect transfer of money or other property (except its own shares) or incurrence of indebtedness by a corporation to or for the benefit of its shareholders in respect of any of its shares. A distribution may be in the form of a declaration or payment of a dividend; a purchase, redemption, or other acquisition of shares; a distribution of indebtedness; or otherwise.

(7) "Effective date of notice" is defined in section 1.41.

(8) "Employee" includes an officer but not a director. A director may accept duties that make him also an employee.

(9) "Entity" includes corporation and foreign corporation; not-for-profit corporation; profit and not-for-profit unincorporated association; business trust, estate, partnership, trust, and two or more persons having a joint or common economic interest; and state, United States, and foreign government.

(10) "Foreign corporation" means a corporation for profit incorporated under a law other than the law of this state.

(11) "Governmental subdivision" includes authority, county, district, and municipality.

(12) "Includes" denotes a partial definition.

(13) "Individual" includes the estate of an incompetent or deceased individual.

(14) "Means" denotes an exhaustive definition.

(15) "Notice" is defined in section 1.41.

(16) "Person" includes individual and entity.

(17) "Principal office" means the office (in or out of this state) so designated in the annual report where the principal executive offices of a domestic or foreign corporation are located.

(18) "Proceeding" includes civil suit and criminal, administrative, and investigatory action.

(19) "Record date" means the date established under chapter 6 or 7 on which a corporation determines the identity of its shareholders for purposes of this Act.

(20) "Secretary" means the corporate officer to whom the board of directors has delegated responsibility under section 8.40(c) for custody of the minutes of the meetings of the board of directors and of the shareholders and for authenticating records of the corporation.

(21) "Share" means the unit into which the proprietary interests in a corporation are divided.

(22) "Shareholder" means the person in whose name shares are registered in the records of a corporation or the beneficial owner of shares to the extent of the rights granted by a nominee certificate on file with a corporation.

(23) "State," when referring to a part of the United States, includes a state and commonwealth (and their agencies and governmental subdivisions) and a territory, and insular possession (and their agencies and governmental subdivisions) of the United States.

(24) "Subscriber" means a person who subscribes for shares in a corporation, whether before or after incorporation.

(25) "United States" includes district, authority, bureau, commission, department, and any other agency of the United States.

(26) "Voting group" means all shares of one or more classes or series that under the articles of incorporation or this Act are entitled to vote and be counted together collectively on a matter at a meeting of shareholders. All shares entitled by the articles of incorporation or this Act to vote generally on the matter are for that purpose a single voting group.

### § 1.41. Notice

(a) Notice under this Act shall be in writing unless oral notice is reasonable under the circumstances.

(b) Notice may be communicated in person; by telephone, telegraph, teletype, or other form of wire or wireless communication; or by mail or private carrier. If these forms of personal notice are impracticable, notice may be communicated by a newspaper of general circulation in the area where published; or by radio, television, or other form of public broadcast communication.

(c) Written notice by a domestic or foreign corporation to its shareholder, if in a comprehensible form, is effective when mailed, if mailed postpaid and correctly addressed to the shareholder's address shown in the corporation's current record of shareholders. *(Text of other subsections omitted.)*

### § 1.42. Number of Shareholders

(a) For purposes of this Act, the following identified as a shareholder in a corporation's current record of shareholders constitutes one shareholder:

(1) three or fewer coowners;

(2) a corporation, partnership, trust, estate, or other entity;

(3) the trustees, guardians, custodians, or other fiduciaries of a single trust, estate, or account.

(b) For purposes of this Act, shareholdings registered in substantially similar names constitute one shareholder if it is reasonable to believe that the names represent the same person.

## CHAPTER 2. INCORPORATION

### § 2.01. Incorporators

One or more persons may act as the incorporator or incorporators of a corporation by delivering articles of incorporation to the secretary of state for filing.

### § 2.02. Articles of Incorporation

(a) The articles of incorporation must set forth:

(1) a corporate name for the corporation that satisfies the requirements of section 4.01;

(2) the number of shares the corporation is authorized to issue;

(3) the street address of the corporation's initial registered office and the name of its initial registered agent at that office; and

(4) the name and address of each incorporator.

(b) The articles of incorporation may set forth:

(1) the names and addresses of the individuals who are to serve as the initial directors;

(2) provisions not inconsistent with law regarding:

(i) the purpose or purposes for which the corporation is organized;

(ii) managing the business and regulating the affairs of the corporation;

(iii) defining, limiting, and regulating the powers of the corporation, its board of directors, and shareholders;

(iv) a par value for authorized shares or classes of shares;

(v) the imposition of personal liability on shareholders for the debts of the corporation to a specified extent and upon specified conditions; and

(3) any provision that under this Act is required or permitted to be set forth in the bylaws.

(c) The articles of incorporation need not set forth any of the corporate powers enumerated in this Act.

### § 2.03. Incorporation

(a) Unless a delayed effective date is specified, the corporate existence begins when the articles of incorporation are filed.

(b) The secretary of state's filing of the articles of incorporation is conclusive proof that the incorporators satisfied all conditions precedent to incorporation except in a proceeding by the state to cancel or revoke the incorporation or involuntarily dissolve the corporation.

### § 2.04. Liability for Preincorporation Transactions

All persons purporting to act as or on behalf of a corporation, knowing there was no incorporation under this Act, are jointly and severally liable for all liabilities created while so acting.

### § 2.05. Organization of Corporation

(a) After incorporation:

(1) If initial directors are named in the articles of incorporation, the initial directors shall hold an organizational meeting, at the call of a majority of the directors, to complete the organization of the corporation by appointing officers, adopting bylaws, and carrying on any other business brought before the meeting;

(2) if initial directors are not named in the articles, the incorporator or incorporators shall hold

an organizational meeting at the call of a majority of the incorporators:

(i) to elect directors and complete the organization of the corporation; or

(ii) to elect a board of directors who shall complete the organization of the corporation.

(b) Action required or permitted by this Act to be taken by incorporators at an organizational meeting may be taken without a meeting if the action taken is evidenced by one or more written consents describing the action taken and signed by each incorporator.

(c) An organizational meeting may be held in or out of this state.

### § 2.06. Bylaws

(a) The incorporators or board of directors of a corporation shall adopt initial bylaws for the corporation.

(b) The bylaws of a corporation may contain any provision for managing the business and regulating the affairs of the corporation that is not inconsistent with law or the articles of incorporation.

### § 2.07. Emergency Bylaws

(a) Unless the articles of incorporation provide otherwise, the board of directors of a corporation may adopt bylaws to be effective only in an emergency defined in subsection (d). The emergency bylaws, which are subject to amendment or repeal by the shareholders, may make all provisions necessary for managing the corporation during the emergency, including:

(1) procedures for calling a meeting of the board of directors;

(2) quorum requirements for the meeting; and

(3) designation of additional or substitute directors.

(b) All provisions of the regular bylaws consistent with the emergency bylaws remain effective during the emergency. The emergency bylaws are not effective after the emergency ends.

(c) Corporate action taken in good faith in accordance with the emergency bylaws:

(1) binds the corporation; and

(2) may not be used to impose liability on a corporate director, officer, employee, or agent.

(d) An emergency exists for purposes of this section if a quorum of the corporation's directors cannot readily be assembled because of some catastrophic event.

## CHAPTER 3. PURPOSES AND POWERS

### § 3.01. Purposes

(a) Every corporation incorporated under this Act has the purpose of engaging in any lawful business unless a more limited purpose is set forth in the articles of incorporation.

(b) A corporation engaging in a business that is subject to regulation under another statute of this state may incorporate under this Act only if permitted by, and subject to all limitations of, the other statute.

### § 3.02. General Powers

Unless its articles of incorporation provide otherwise, every corporation has perpetual duration and succession in its corporate name and has the same powers as an individual to do all things necessary or convenient to carry out its business and affairs, including without limitation power:

(1) to sue and be sued, complain and defend in its corporate name;

(2) to have a corporate seal, which may be altered at will, and to use it, or a facsimile of it, by impressing or affixing it or in any other manner reproducing it;

(3) to make and amend bylaws, not inconsistent with its articles of incorporation or with the laws of this state, for managing the business and regulating the affairs of the corporation;

(4) to purchase, receive, lease, or otherwise acquire, and own, hold, improve, use, and otherwise deal with, real or personal property, or any legal or equitable interest in property, wherever located;

(5) to sell, convey, mortgage, pledge, lease, exchange, and otherwise dispose of all or any part of its property;

(6) to purchase, receive, subscribe for, or otherwise acquire; own, hold, vote, use, sell, mortgage, lend, pledge, or otherwise dispose of; and deal in and with shares or other interests in, or obligations of, any other entity;

(7) to make contracts and guarantees, incur liabilities, borrow money, issue its notes, bonds,

and other obligations, (which may be convertible into or include the option to purchase other securities of the corporation), and secure any of its obligations by mortgage or pledge of any of its property, franchises, or income;

(8) to lend money, invest and reinvest its funds, and receive and hold real and personal property as security for repayment;

(9) to be a promoter, partner, member, associate, or manager of any partnership, joint venture, trust, or other entity;

(10) to conduct its business, locate offices, and exercise the powers granted by this Act within or without this state;

(11) to elect directors and appoint officers, employees, and agents of the corporation, define their duties, fix their compensation, and lend them money and credit;

(12) to pay pensions and establish pension plans, pension trusts, profit sharing plans, share bonus plans, share option plans, and benefit or incentive plans for any or all of its current or former directors, officers, employees, and agents;

(13) to make donations for the public welfare or for charitable, scientific, or educational purposes;

(14) to transact any lawful business that will aid governmental policy;

(15) to make payments or donations, or do any other act, not inconsistent with law, that furthers the business and affairs of the corporation.

### § 3.03. Emergency Powers

(a) In anticipation of or during an emergency defined in subsection (d), the board of directors of a corporation may:

(1) modify lines of succession to accommodate the incapacity of any director, officer, employee, or agent; and

(2) relocate the principal office, designate alternative principal offices or regional offices, or authorize the officers to do so.

(b) During an emergency defined in subsection (d), unless emergency bylaws provide otherwise:

(1) notice of a meeting of the board of directors need be given only to those directors whom it is practicable to reach and may be given in any practicable manner, including by publication and radio; and

(2) one or more officers of the corporation present at a meeting of the board of directors may be deemed to be directors for the meeting, in order of rank and within the same rank in order of seniority, as necessary to achieve a quorum.

(c) Corporate action taken in good faith during an emergency under this section to further the ordinary business affairs of the corporation:

(1) binds the corporation; and

(2) may not be used to impose liability on a corporate director, officer, employee, or agent.

(d) An emergency exists for purposes of this section if a quorum of the corporation's directors cannot readily be assembled because of some catastrophic event.

### § 3.04. Ultra Vires

(a) Except as provided in subsection (b), the validity of corporate action may not be challenged on the ground that the corporation lacks or lacked power to act.

(b) A corporation's power to act may be challenged:

(1) in a proceeding by a shareholder against the corporation to enjoin the act;

(2) in a proceeding by the corporation, directly, derivatively, or through a receiver, trustee, or other legal representtive, against an incumbent or former director, officer, employee, or agent of the corporation; or

(3) in a proceeding by the Attorney General under section 14.30.

(c) In a shareholder's proceeding under subsection (b)(1) to enjoin an unauthorized corporate act, the court may enjoin or set aside the act, if equitable and if all affected persons are parties to the proceeding, and may award damages for loss (other than anticipated profits) suffered by the corporation or another party because of enjoining the unauthorized act.

## CHAPTER 4. NAME

### § 4.01. Corporate Name

(a) A corporate name:

(1) must contain the word "corporation," "incorporated," "company," or "limited," or the abbreviation "corp.," "inc.," "co.," or "ltd.", or words

or abbreviations of like import in another language; and

(2) may not contain language stating or implying that the corporation is organized for a purpose other than that permitted by section 3.01 and its articles of incorporation.

(b) Except as authorized by subsections (c) and (d), a corporate name must be distinguishable upon the records of the secretary of state from:

(1) the corporate name of a corporation incorporated or authorized to transact business in this state;

(2) a corporate name reserved or registered under section 4.02 or 4.03;

(3) the fictitious name adopted by a foreign corporation authorized to transact business in this state because its real name is unavailable; and

(4) the corporate name of a not-for-profit corporation incorporated or authorized to transact business in this state.

(c) A corporation may apply to the secretary of state for authorization to use a name that is not distinguishable upon his records from one or more of the names described in subsection (b). The secretary of state shall authorize use of the name applied for if:

(1) the other corporation consents to the use in writing and submits an undertaking in form satisfactory to the secretary of state to change its name to a name that is distinguishable upon the records of the secretary of state from the name of the applying corporation; or

(2) the applicant delivers to the secretary of state a certified copy of the final judgment of a court of competent jurisdiction establishing the applicant's right to use the name applied for in this state.

(d) A corporation may use the name (including the fictitious name) of another domestic or foreign corporation that is used in this state if the other corporation is incorporated or authorized to transact business in this state and the proposed user corporation:

(1) has merged with the other corporation;

(2) has been formed by reorganization of the other corporation; or

(3) has acquired all or substantially all of the assets, including the corporate name, of the other corporation.

(e) This Act does not control the use of fictitious names.

### § 4.02. Reserved Name

(a) A person may reserve the exclusive use of a corporate name, including a fictitious name for a foreign corporation whose corporate name is not available, by delivering an application to the secretary of state for filing. The application must set forth the name and address of the applicant and the name proposed to be reserved. If the secretary of state finds that the corporate name applied for is available, he shall reserve the name for the applicant's exclusive use for a nonrenewable 120-day period.

(b) The owner of a reserved corporate name may transfer the reservation to another person by delivering to the secretary of state a signed notice of the transfer that states the name and address of the transferee.

### § 4.03. Registered Name

(a) A foreign corporation may register its corporate name, or its corporate name with any addition required by section 15.06, if the name is distinguishable upon the records of the secretary of state from the corporate names that are not available under section 4.01(b)(3). *(Text of other subsections omitted.)*

## CHAPTER 5. OFFICE AND AGENT

### § 5.01. Registered Office and Registered Agent

Each corporation must continuously maintain in this state:

(1) a registered office that may be the same as any of its places of business; and

(2) a registered agent, who may be:

(i) an individual who resides in this state and whose business office is identical with the registered office;

(ii) a domestic corporation or not-for-profit domestic corporation whose business office is identical with the registered office; or

(iii) a foreign corporation or not-for-profit foreign corporation authorized to transact business in this state whose business office is identical with the registered office.

### § 5.02. Change of Registered Office or Registered Agent *(Text omitted.)*

### § 5.03. Resignation of Registered Agent *(Text omitted.)*

### § 5.04. Service on Corporation

(a) A corporation's registered agent is the corporation's agent for service of process, notice, or demand required or permitted by law to be served on the corporation.

(b) If a corporation has no registered agent, or the agent cannot with reasonable diligence be served, the corporation may be served by registered or certified mail, return receipt requested, addressed to the secretary of the corporation at its principal office. Service is perfected under this subsection at the earliest of:

(1) the date the corporation receives the mail;

(2) the date shown on the return receipt, if signed on behalf of the corporation; or

(3) five days after its deposit in the United States Mail, if mailed postpaid and correctly addressed.

(c) This section does not prescribe the only means, or necessarily the required means, of serving a corporation.

## CHAPTER 6. SHARES AND DISTRIBUTIONS

### Subchapter A. Shares

### § 6.01. Authorized Shares

(a) The articles of incorporation must prescribe the classes of shares and the number of shares of each class that the corporation is authorized to issue. If more than one class of shares is authorized, the articles of incorporation must prescribe a distinguishing designation for each class, and prior to the issuance of shares of a class the preferences, limitations, and relative rights of that class must be described in the articles of incorporation. All shares of a class must have preferences, limitations, and relative rights identical with those of other shares of the same class except to the extent otherwise permitted by section 6.02.

(b) The articles of incorporation must authorize (1) one or more classes of shares that together have unlimited voting rights, and (2) one or more classes of shares (which may be the same class or classes as those with voting rights) that together are entitled to receive the net assets of the corporation upon dissolution.

(c) The articles of incorporation may authorize one or more classes of shares that:

(1) have special, conditional, or limited voting rights, or no right to vote, except to the extent prohibited by this Act;

(2) are redeemable or convertible as specified in the articles of incorporation (i) at the option of the corporation, the shareholder, or another person or upon the occurrence of a designated event; (ii) for cash, indebtedness, securities, or other property; (iii) in a designated amount or in an amount determined in accordance with a designated formula or by reference to extrinsic data or events;

(3) entitle the holders to distributions calculated in any manner, including dividends that may be cumulative, noncumulative, or partially cumulative;

(4) have preference over any other class of shares with respect to distributions, including dividends and distributions upon the dissolution of the corporation.

(d) The description of the designations, preferences, limitations, and relative rights of share classes in subsection (c) is not exhaustive.

### § 6.02. Terms of Class or Series Determined by Board of Directors

(a) If the articles of incorporation so provide, the board of directors may determine, in whole or part, the preferences, limitations, and relative rights (within the limits set forth in section 6.01) of (1) any class of shares before the issuance of any shares of that class or (2) one or more series within a class before the issuance of any shares of that series.

(b) Each series of a class must be given a distinguishing designation.

(c) All shares of a series must have preferences, limitations, and relative rights identical with those of other shares of the same series and, except to the extent otherwise provided in the description of the series, of those of other series of the same class.

(d) Before issuing any shares of a class or series created under this section, the corporation must deliver to the secretary of state for filing articles of amendment, which are effective without shareholder action, that set forth:

(1) the name of the corporation;

(2) the text of the amendment determining the terms of the class or series of shares;

(3) the date it was adopted; and

(4) a statement that the amendment was duly adopted by the board of directors.

### § 6.03. Issued and Outstanding Shares

(a) A corporation may issue the number of shares of each class or series authorized by the articles of incorporation. Shares that are issued are outstanding shares until they are reacquired, redeemed, converted, or cancelled.

(b) The reacquisition, redemption, or conversion of outstanding shares is subject to the limitations of subsection (c) of this section and to section 6.40.

(c) At all times that shares of the corporation are outstanding, one or more shares that together have unlimited voting rights and one or more shares that together are entitled to receive the net assets of the corporation upon dissolution must be outstanding.

### § 6.04. Fractional Shares

(a) A corporation may:

(1) issue fractions of a share or pay in money the value of fractions of a share;

(2) arrange for disposition of fractional shares by the shareholders;

(3) issue scrip in registered or bearer form entitling the holder to receive a full share upon surrendering enough scrip to equal a full share.

(b) Each certificate representing scrip must be conspicuously labeled "scrip" and must contain the information required by section 6.25(b).

(c) The holder of a fractional share is entitled to exercise the rights of a shareholder, including the right to vote, to receive dividends, and to participate in the assets of the corporation upon liquidation. The holder of scrip is not entitled to any of these rights unless the scrip provides for them.

(d) The board of directors may authorize the issuance of scrip subject to any condition considered desirable, including:

(1) that the scrip will become void if not exchanged for full shares before a specified date; and

(2) that the shares for which the scrip is exchangeable may be sold and the proceeds paid to the scripholders.

## Subchapter B. Issuance of Shares

### § 6.20. Subscription for Shares Before Incorporation

(a) A subscription for shares entered into before incorporation is irrevocable for six months unless the subscription agreement provides a longer or shorter period or all the subscribers agree to revocation.

(b) The board of directors may determine the payment terms of subscriptions for shares that were entered into before incorporation, unless the subscription agreement specifies them. A call for payment by the board of directors must be uniform so far as practicable as to all shares of the same class or series, unless the subscription agreement specifies otherwise.

(c) Shares issued pursuant to subscriptions entered into before incorporation are fully paid and nonassessable when the corporation receives the consideration specified in the subscription agreement.

(d) If a subscriber defaults in payment of money or property under a subscription agreement entered into before incorporation, the corporation may collect the amount owed as any other debt. Alternatively, unless the subscription agreement provides otherwise, the corporation may rescind the agreement and may sell the shares if the debt remains unpaid more than 20 days after the corporation sends written demand for payment to the subscriber.

(e) A subscription agreement entered into after incorporation is a contract between the subscriber and the corporation subject to section 6.21.

### § 6.21. Issuance of Shares

(a) The powers granted in this section to the board of directors may be reserved to the shareholders by the articles of incorporation.

(b) The board of directors may authorize shares to be issued for consideration consisting of any tangible or intangible property or benefit to the corpo-

ration, including cash, promissory notes, services performed, contracts for services to be performed, or other securities of the corporation.
(c) Before the corporation issues shares, the board of directors must determine that the consideration received or to be received for shares to be issued is adequate. That determination by the board of directors is conclusive insofar as the adequacy of consideration for the issuance of shares relates to whether the shares are validly issued, fully paid, and nonassessable.
(d) When the corporation receives the consideration for which the board of directors authorized the issuance of shares, the shares issued therefor are fully paid and nonassessable.
(e) The corporation may place in escrow shares issued for a contract for future services or benefits or a promissory note, or make other arrangements to restrict the transfer of the shares, and may credit distributions in respect of the shares against their purchase price, until the services are performed, the note is paid, or the benefits received. If the services are not performed, the note is not paid, or the benefits are not received, the shares escrowed or restricted and the distributions credited may be cancelled in whole or part.

### § 6.22. Liability of Shareholders

(a) A purchaser from a corporation of its own shares is not liable to the corporation or its creditors with respect to the shares except to pay the consideration for which the shares were authorized to be issued (section 6.21) or specified in the subscription agreement (section 6.20).
(b) Unless otherwise provided in the articles of incorporation, a shareholder of a corporation is not personally liable for the acts or debts of the corporation except that he may become personally liable by reason of his own acts or conduct.

### § 6.23. Share Dividends

(a) Unless the articles of incorporation provide otherwise, shares may be issued pro rata and without consideration to the corporation's shareholders or to the shareholders of one or more classes or series. An issuance of shares under this subsection is a share dividend.
(b) Shares of one class or series may not be issued as a share dividend in respect of shares of another class or series unless (1) the articles of incorporation so authorize, (2) a majority of the votes entitled to be cast by the class or series to be issued approve the issue, or (3) there are no outstanding shares of the class or series to be issued.
(c) If the board of directors does not fix the record date for determining shareholders entitled to a share dividend, it is the date the board of directors authorizes the share dividend.

### § 6.24. Share Options

A corporation may issue rights, options, or warrants for the purchase of shares of the corporation. The board of directors shall determine the terms upon which the rights, options, or warrants are issued, their form and content, and the consideration for which the shares are to be issued.

### § 6.25. Form and Content of Certificates

(a) Shares may but need not be represented by certificates. Unless this Act or another statute expressly provides otherwise, the rights and obligations of shareholders are identical whether or not their shares are represented by certificates. *(Text of other subsections omitted.)*

### § 6.26. Shares without Certificates

(a) Unless the articles of incorporation or bylaws provide otherwise, the board of directors of a corporation may authorize the issue of some or all of the shares of any or all of its classes or series without certificates. The authorization does not affect shares already represented by certificates until they are surrendered to the corporation. *(Text of other subsection omitted.)*

### § 6.27. Restriction on Transfer of Shares and Other Securities

(a) The articles of incorporation, bylaws, an agreement among shareholders, or an agreement between shareholders and the corporation may impose restrictions on the transfer or registration of transfer of shares of the corporation. A restriction does not affect shares issued before the restriction was adopted unless the holders of the shares are parties to the restriction agreement or voted in favor of the restriction.
(b) A restriction on the transfer or registration of transfer of shares is valid and enforceable against the holder or a transferee of the holder if the restriction is authorized by this section and

its existence is noted conspicuously on the front or back of the certificate or is contained in the information statement required by section 6.26(b). Unless so noted, a restriction is not enforceable against a person without knowledge of the restriction.

(c) A restriction on the transfer or registration of transfer of shares is authorized:

(1) to maintain the corporation's status when it is dependent on the number or identity of its shareholders;

(2) to preserve exemptions under federal or state securities law;

(3) for any other reasonable purpose.

(d) A restriction on the transfer or registration of transfer of shares may:

(1) obligate the shareholder first to offer the corporation or other persons (separately, consecutively, or simultaneously) an opportunity to acquire the restricted shares;

(2) obligate the corporation or other persons (separately, consecutively, or simultaneously) to acquire the restricted shares;

(3) require the corporation, the holders of any class of its shares, or another person to approve the transfer of the restricted shares, if the requirement is not manifestly unreasonable;

(4) prohibit the transfer of the restricted shares to designated persons or classes of persons, if the prohibition is not manifestly unreasonable.

(e) For purposes of this section, "shares" includes a security convertible into or carrying a right to subscribe for or acquire shares.

### § 6.28. Expense of Issue

A corporation may pay the expenses of selling or underwriting its shares, and of organizing or reorganizing the corporation, from the consideration received for shares.

## Subchapter C. Subsequent Acquisition of Shares by Shareholders and Corporation

### § 6.30. Shareholders' Preemptive Rights

(a) The shareholders of a corporation do not have a preemptive right to acquire the corporation's unissued shares except to the extent the articles of incorporation so provide.

(b) A statement included in the articles of incorporation that "the corporation elects to have preemptive rights" (or words of similar import) means that the following principles apply except to the extent the articles of incorporation expressly provide otherwise:

(1) The shareholders of the corporation have a preemptive right, granted on uniform terms and conditions prescribed by the board of directors to provide a fair and reasonable opportunity to exercise the right, to acquire proportional amounts of the corporation's unissued shares upon the decision of the board of directors to issue them.

(2) A shareholder may waive his preemptive right. A waiver evidenced by a writing is irrevocable even though it is not supported by consideration.

(3) There is no preemptive right with respect to:

(i) shares issued as compensation to directors, officers, agents, or employees of the corporation, its subsidiaries or affiliates;

(ii) shares issued to satisfy conversion or option rights created to provide compensation to directors, officers, agents, or employees of the corporation, its subsidiaries or affiliates;

(iii) shares authorized in articles of incorporation that are issued within six months from the effective date of incorporation;

(iv) shares sold otherwise than for money.

(4) Holders of shares of any class without general voting rights but with preferential rights to distributions or assets have no preemptive rights with respect to shares of any class.

(5) Holders of shares of any class with general voting rights but without preferential rights to distributions or assets have no preemptive rights with respect to shares of any class with preferential rights to distributions or assets unless the shares with preferential rights are convertible into or carry a right to subscribe for or acquire shares without preferential rights.

(6) Shares subject to preemptive rights that are not acquired by shareholders may be issued to any person for a period of one year after being offered to shareholders at a consideration set by the board of directors that is not lower than the consideration set for the exercise of preemptive rights. An offer at a lower consideration or after the expiration

of one year is subject to the shareholders' preemptive rights.
(c) For purposes of this section, "shares" includes a security convertible into or carrying a right to subscribe for or acquire shares.

### § 6.31. Corporation's Acquisition of Its Own Shares

(a) A corporation may acquire its own shares and shares so acquired constitute authorized but unissued shares.
(b) If the articles of incorporation prohibit the reissue of acquired shares, the number of authorized shares is reduced by the number of shares acquired, effective upon amendment of the articles of incorporation.
(c) Articles of amendment may be adopted by the board of directors without shareholder action, shall be delivered to the secretary of state for filing, and shall set forth:
(1) the name of the corporation;
(2) the reduction in the number of authorized shares, itemized by class and series; and
(3) the total number of authorized shares, itemized by class and series, remaining after reduction of the shares.

## Subchapter D. Distributions

### § 6.40. Distributions to Shareholders

(a) A board of directors may authorize and the corporation may make distributions to its shareholders subject to restriction by the articles of incorporation and the limitation in subsection (c).
(b) If the board of directors does not fix the record date for determining shareholders entitled to a distribution (other than one involving a repurchase or reacquisition of shares), it is the date the board of directors authorizes the distribution.
(c) No distribution may be made if, after giving it effect:
(1) the corporation would not be able to pay its debts as they become due in the usual course of business; or
(2) the corporation's total assets would be less than the sum of its total liabilities plus (unless the articles of incorporation permit otherwise) the amount that would be needed, if the corporation were to be dissolved at the time of the distribution, to satisfy the preferential rights upon dissolution of shareholders whose preferential rights are superior to those receiving the distribution.
(d) The board of directors may base a determination that a distribution is not prohibited under subsection (c) either on financial statements prepared on the basis of accounting practices and principles that are reasonable in the circumstances or on a fair valuation or other method that is reasonable in the circumstances.
(e) The effect of a distribution under subsection (c) is measured:
(1) in the case of distribution by purchase, redemption, or other acquisition of the corporation's shares, as of the earlier of (i) the date money or other property is transferred or debt incurred by the corporation or (ii) the date the shareholder ceases to be a shareholder with respect to the acquired shares;
(2) in the case of any other distribution of indebtedness, as of the date the indebtedness is distributed;
(3) in all other cases, as of (i) the date the distribution is authorized if the payment occurs within 120 days after the date of authorization or (ii) the date the payment is made if it occurs more than 120 days after the date of authorization.
(f) A corporation's indebtedness to a shareholder incurred by reason of a distribution made in accordance with this section is at parity with the corporation's indebtedness to its general, unsecured creditors except to the extent subordinated by agreement.

# CHAPTER 7. SHAREHOLDERS

## Subchapter A. Meetings

### § 7.01. Annual Meeting

(a) A corporation shall hold annually at a time stated in or fixed in accordance with the bylaws a meeting of shareholders.
(b) Annual shareholders' meetings may be held in or out of this state at the place stated in or fixed in accordance with the bylaws. If no place is stated in or fixed in accordance with the bylaws, annual meetings shall be held at the corporation's principal office.
(c) The failure to hold an annual meeting at the time stated in or fixed in accordance with a corpo-

ration's bylaws does not affect the validity of any corporate action.

### § 7.02. Special Meeting

(a) A corporation shall hold a special meeting of shareholders:

(1) on call of its board of directors or the person or persons authorized to do so by the articles of incorporation or bylaws; or

(2) if the holders of at least 10 percent of all the votes entitled to be cast on any issue proposed to be considered at the proposed special meeting sign, date, and deliver to the corporation's secretary one or more written demands for the meeting describing the purpose or purposes for which it is to be held.

(b) If not otherwise fixed under sections 7.03 or 7.07, the record date for determining shareholders entitled to demand a special meeting is the date the first shareholder signs the demand.

(c) Special shareholders' meetings may be held in or out of this state at the place stated in or fixed in accordance with the bylaws. If no place is stated or fixed in accordance with the bylaws, special meetings shall be held at the corporation's principal office.

(d) Only business within the purpose or purposes described in the meeting notice required by section 7.05(c) may be conducted at a special shareholders' meeting.

### § 7.03. Court-Ordered Meeting

(a) The [name or describe] court of the county where a corporation's principal office (or, if none in this state, its registered office) is located may summarily order a meeting to be held:

(1) on application of any shareholder of the corporation entitled to participate in an annual meeting if an annual meeting was not held within the earlier of 6 months after the end of the corporation's fiscal year or 15 months after its last annual meeting; or

(2) on application of a shareholder who signed a demand for a special meeting valid under section 7.02 if:

(i) notice of the special meeting was not given within 30 days after the date the demand was delivered to the corporation's secretary; or

(ii) the special meeting was not held in accordance with the notice.

(b) The court may fix the time and place of the meeting, determine the shares entitled to participate in the meeting, specify a record date for determining shareholders entitled to notice of and to vote at the meeting, prescribe the form and content of the meeting notice, fix the quorum required for specific matters to be considered at the meeting (or direct that the votes represented at the meeting constitute a quorum for action on those matters), and enter other orders necessary to accomplish the purpose or purposes of the meeting.

### § 7.04. Action Without Meeting

(a) Action required or permitted by this Act to be taken at a shareholders' meeting may be taken without a meeting if the action is taken by all the shareholders entitled to vote on the action. The action must be evidenced by one or more written consents describing the action taken, signed by all the shareholders entitled to vote on the action, and delivered to the corporation for inclusion in the minutes or filing with the corporate records.

(b) If not otherwise determined under sections 7.03 or 7.07, the record date for determining shareholders entitled to take action without a meeting is the date the first shareholder signs the consent under subsection (a).

(c) A consent signed under this section has the effect of a meeting vote and may be described as such in any document.

(d) If this Act requires that notice of proposed action be given to nonvoting shareholders and the action is to be taken by unanimous consent of the voting shareholders, the corporation must give its nonvoting shareholders written notice of the proposed action at least 10 days before the action is taken. The notice must contain or be accompanied by the same material that, under this Act, would have been required to be sent to nonvoting shareholders in a notice of meeting at which the proposed action would have been submitted to the shareholders for action.

### § 7.05. Notice of Meeting

(a) A corporation shall notify shareholders of the date, time, and place of each annual and special shareholders' meeting no fewer than 10 nor more than 60 days before the meeting date. Unless this Act or the articles of incorporation require otherwise, the corporation is required to give notice only to shareholders entitled to vote at the meeting.

(b) Unless this Act or the articles of incorporation require otherwise, notice of an annual meeting need not include a description of the purpose or purposes for which the meeting is called.

(c) Notice of a special meeting must include a description of the purpose or purposes for which the meeting is called.

(d) If not otherwise fixed under sections 7.03 or 7.07, the record date for determining shareholders entitled to notice of and to vote at an annual or special shareholders' meeting is the close of business on the day before the first notice is delivered to shareholders.

(e) Unless the bylaws require otherwise, if an annual or special shareholders' meeting is adjourned to a different date, time, or place, notice need not be given of the new date, time, or place if the new date, time, or place is announced at the meeting before adjournment. If a new record date for the adjourned meeting is or must be fixed under section 7.07, however, notice of the adjourned meeting must be given under this section to persons who are shareholders as of the new record date.

### § 7.06. Waiver of Notice

(a) A shareholder may waive any notice required by this Act, the articles of incorporation, or bylaws before or after the date and time stated in the notice. The waiver must be in writing, be signed by the shareholder entitled to the notice, and be delivered to the corporation for inclusion in the minutes or filing with the corporate records.

(b) A shareholder's attendance at a meeting:

(1) waives objection to lack of notice or defective notice of the meeting, unless the shareholder at the beginning of the meeting objects to holding the meeting or transacting business at the meeting;

(2) waives objection to consideration of a particular matter at the meeting that is not within the purpose or purposes described in the meeting notice, unless the shareholder objects to considering the matter when it is presented.

### § 7.07. Record Date

(a) The bylaws may fix or provide the manner of fixing the record date for one or more voting groups in order to determine the shareholders entitled to notice of a shareholders' meeting, to demand a special meeting, to vote, or to take any other action. If the bylaws do not fix or provide for fixing a record date, the board of directors of the corporation may fix a future date as the record date.

(b) A record date fixed under this section may not be more than 70 days before the meeting or action requiring a determination of shareholders.

(c) A determination of shareholders entitled to notice of or to vote at a shareholders' meeting is effective for any adjournment of the meeting unless the board of directors fixes a new record date, which it must do if the meeting is adjourned to a date more than 120 days after the date fixed for the original meeting.

(d) If a court orders a meeting adjourned to a date more than 120 days after the date fixed for the original meeting, it may provide that the original record date continues in effect or it may fix a new record date.

## Subchapter B. Voting

### § 7.20. Shareholders' List for Meeting

(a) After fixing a record date for a meeting, a corporation shall prepare an alphabetical list of the names of all its shareholders who are entitled to notice of a shareholders' meeting. The list must be arranged by voting group (and within each voting group by class or series of shares) and show the address of and number of shares held by each shareholder.

(b) The shareholders' list must be available for inspection by any shareholder, beginning two business days after notice of the meeting is given for which the list was prepared and continuing through the meeting, at the corporation's principal office or at a place identified in the meeting notice in the city where the meeting will be held. A shareholder, his agent, or attorney is entitled on written demand to inspect and, subject to the requirements of section 16.02(c), to copy the list, during regular business hours and at his expense, during the period it is available for inspection.

(c) The corporation shall make the shareholders' list available at the meeting, and any shareholder, his agent, or attorney is entitled to inspect the list at any time during the meeting or any adjournment.

(d) If the corporation refuses to allow a shareholder, his agent, or attorney to inspect the shareholders' list before or at the meeting (or copy the list as permitted by subsection (b)), the [name or describe] court of the county where a corporation's principal office (or, if none in this state, its registered office) is located, on application of the shareholder, may summarily order the inspection or copying at the corporation's expense and may postpone the meeting for which the list was prepared until the inspection or copying is complete.
(e) Refusal or failure to prepare or make available the shareholders' list does not affect the validity of action taken at the meeting.

### § 7.21. Voting Entitlement of Shares

(a) Except as provided in subsections (b) and (c) or unless the articles of incorporation provide otherwise, each outstanding share, regardless of class, is entitled to one vote on each matter voted on at a shareholders' meeting. Only shares are entitled to vote.
(b) Absent special circumstances, the shares of a corporation are not entitled to vote if they are owned, directly or indirectly, by a second corporation, domestic or foreign, and the first corporation owns, directly or indirectly, a majority of the shares entitled to vote for directors of the second corporation.
(c) Subsection (b) does not limit the power of a corporation to vote any shares, including its own shares, held by it in a fiduciary capacity.
(d) Redeemable shares are not entitled to vote after notice of redemption is mailed to the holders and a sum sufficient to redeem the shares has been deposited with a bank, trust company, or other financial institution under an irrevocable obligation to pay the holders the redemption price on surrender of the shares.

### § 7.22. Proxies

(a) A shareholder may vote his shares in person or by proxy.
(b) A shareholder may appoint a proxy to vote or otherwise act for him by signing an appointment form, either personally or by his attorney-in-fact.
(c) An appointment of a proxy is effective when received by the secretary or other officer or agent authorized to tabulate votes. An appointment is valid for 11 months unless a longer period is expressly provided in the appointment form.
(d) An appointment of a proxy is revocable by the shareholder unless the appointment form conspicuously states that it is irrevocable and the appointment is coupled with an interest. Appointments coupled with an interest include the appointment of:
(1) a pledgee;
(2) a person who purchased or agreed to purchase the shares;
(3) a creditor of the corporation who extended it credit under terms requiring the appointment;
(4) an employee of the corporation whose employment contract requires the appointment; or
(5) a party to a voting agreement created under section 7.31.
(e) The death or incapacity of the shareholder appointing a proxy does not affect the right of the corporation to accept the proxy's authority unless notice of the death or incapacity is received by the secretary or other officer or agent authorized to tabulate votes before the proxy exercises his authority under the appointment.
(f) An appointment made irrevocable under subsection (d) is revoked when the interest with which it is coupled is extinguished.
(g) A transferee for value of shares subject to an irrevocable appointment may revoke the appointment if he did not know of its existence when he acquired the shares and the existence of the irrevocable appointment was not noted conspicuously on the certificate representing the shares or on the information statement for shares without certificates.
(h) Subject to section 7.24 and to any express limitation on the proxy's authority appearing on the face of the appointment form, a corporation is entitled to accept the proxy's vote or other action as that of the shareholder making the appointment.

### § 7.23. Shares Held by Nominees

(a) A corporation may establish a procedure by which the beneficial owner of shares that are registered in the name of a nominee is recognized by the corporation as the shareholder. The extent of this recognition may be determined in the procedure.

(b) The procedure may set forth:

(1) the types of nominees to which it applies;

(2) the rights or privileges that the corporation recognizes in a beneficial owner;

(3) the manner in which the procedure is selected by the nominee;

(4) the information that must be provided when the procedure is selected;

(5) the period for which selection of the procedure is effective; and

(6) other aspects of the rights and duties created.

## § 7.24. Corporation's Acceptance of Votes

(a) If the name signed on a vote, consent, waiver, or proxy appointment corresponds to the name of a shareholder, the corporation if acting in good faith is entitled to accept the vote, consent, waiver, or proxy appointment and give it effect as the act of the shareholder.

(b) If the name signed on a vote, consent, waiver, or proxy appointment does not correspond to the name of its shareholder, the corporation if acting in good faith is nevertheless entitled to accept the vote, consent, waiver, or proxy appointment and give it effect as the act of the shareholder if:

(1) the shareholder is an entity and the name signed purports to be that of an officer or agent of the entity;

(2) the name signed purports to be that of an administrator, executor, guardian, or conservator representing the shareholder and, if the corporation requests, evidence of fiduciary status acceptable to the corporation has been presented with respect to the vote, consent, waiver, or proxy appointment;

(3) the name signed purports to be that of a receiver or trustee in bankruptcy of the shareholder and, if the corporation requests, evidence of this status acceptable to the corporation has been presented with respect to the vote, consent, waiver, or proxy appointment;

(4) the name signed purports to be that of a pledgee, beneficial owner, or attorney-in-fact of the shareholder and, if the corporation requests, evidence acceptable to the corporation of the signatory's authority to sign for the shareholder has been presented with respect to the vote, consent, waiver, or proxy appointment;

(5) two or more persons are the shareholder as cotenants or fiduciaries and the name signed purports to be the name of at least one of the coowners and the person signing appears to be acting on behalf of all the coowners.

(c) The corporation is entitled to reject a vote, consent, waiver, or proxy appointment if the secretary or other officer or agent authorized to tabulate votes, acting in good faith, has reasonable basis for doubt about the validity of the signature on it or about the signatory's authority to sign for the shareholder.

(d) The corporation and its officer or agent who accepts or rejects a vote, consent, waiver, or proxy appointment in good faith and in accordance with the standards of this section are not liable in damages to the shareholder for the consequences of the acceptance or rejection.

(e) Corporate action based on the acceptance or rejection of a vote, consent, waiver, or proxy appointment under this section is valid unless a court of competent jurisdiction determines otherwise.

## § 7.25. Quorum and Voting Requirements for Voting Groups

(a) Shares entitled to vote as a separate voting group may take action on a matter at a meeting only if a quorum of those shares exists with respect to that matter. Unless the articles of incorporation or this Act provide otherwise, a majority of the votes entitled to be cast on the matter by the voting group constitutes a quorum of that voting group for action on that matter.

(b) Once a share is represented for any purpose at a meeting, it is deemed present for quorum purposes for the remainder of the meeting and for any adjournment of that meeting unless a new record date is or must be set for that adjourned meeting.

(c) If a quorum exists, action on a matter (other than the election of directors) by a voting group is approved if the votes cast within the voting group favoring the action exceed the votes cast opposing the action, unless the articles of incorporation or this Act require a greater number of affirmative votes.

(d) An amendment of articles of incorporation adding, changing, or deleting a quorum or voting requirement for a voting group greater than specified in subsection (b) or (c) is governed by section 7.27.

(e) The election of directors is governed by section 7.28.

### § 7.26. Action by Single and Multiple Voting Groups

(a) If the articles of incorporation or this Act provide for voting by a single voting group on a matter, action on that matter is taken when voted upon by that voting group as provided in section 7.25.

(b) If the articles of incorporation or this Act provide for voting by two or more voting groups on a matter, action on that matter is taken only when voted upon by each of those voting groups counted separately as provided in section 7.25. Action may be taken by one voting group on a matter even though no action is taken by another voting group entitled to vote on the matter.

### § 7.27. Greater Quorum or Voting Requirements

(a) The articles of incorporation may provide for a greater quorum or voting requirement for shareholders (or voting groups of shareholders) than is provided for by this Act.

(b) An amendment to the articles of incorporation that adds, changes, or deletes a greater quorum or voting requirement must meet the same quorum requirement and be adopted by the same vote and voting groups required to take action under the quorum and voting requirements then in effect or proposed to be adopted, whichever is greater.

### § 7.28. Voting for Directors; Cumulative Voting

(a) Unless otherwise provided in the articles of incorporation, directors are elected by a plurality of the votes cast by the shares entitled to vote in the election at a meeting at which a quorum is present.

(b) Shareholders do not have a right to cumulate their votes for directors unless the articles of incorporation so provide.

(c) A statement included in the articles of incorporation that "[all] [a designated voting group of] shareholders are entitled to cumulate their votes for directors" (or words of similar import) means that the shareholders designated are entitled to multiply the number of votes they are entitled to cast by the number of directors for whom they are entitled to vote and cast the product for a single candidate or distribute the product among two or more candidates.

(d) Shares otherwise entitled to vote cumulatively may not be voted cumulatively at a particular meeting unless:

(1) the meeting notice or proxy statement accompanying the notice states conspicuously that cumulative voting is authorized; or

(2) a shareholder who has the right to cumulate his votes gives notice to the corporation not less than 48 hours before the time set for the meeting of his intent to cumulate his votes during the meeting, and if one shareholder gives this notice all other shareholders in the same voting group participating in the election are entitled to cumulate their votes without giving further notice.

## Subchapter C. Voting Trusts and Agreements

### § 7.30. Voting Trusts

(a) One or more shareholders may create a voting trust, conferring on a trustee the right to vote or otherwise act for them, by signing an agreement setting out the provisions of the trust (which may include anything consistent with its purpose) and transferring their shares to the trustee. When a voting trust agreement is signed, the trustee shall prepare a list of the names and addresses of all owners of beneficial interests in the trust, together with the number and class of shares each transferred to the trust, and deliver copies of the list and agreement to the corporation's principal office.

(b) A voting trust becomes effective on the date the first shares subject to the trust are registered in the trustee's name. A voting trust is valid for not more than 10 years after its effective date unless extended under subsection (c).

(c) All or some of the parties to a voting trust may extend it for additional terms of not more than 10 years each by signing an extension agreement and obtaining the voting trustee's written consent to the extension. An extension is valid for 10 years from the date the first shareholder signs the extension agreement. The voting trustee must deliver copies of the extension agreement and list of beneficial owners to the corporation's principal office. An extension agreement binds only those parties signing it.

### § 7.31. Voting Agreements

(a) Two or more shareholders may provide for the manner in which they will vote their shares by signing an agreement for that purpose. A voting agreement created under this section is not subject to the provisions of section 7.30.
(b) A voting agreement created under this section is specifically enforceable.

## Subchapter D. Derivative Proceedings

### § 7.40. Procedure in Derivative Proceedings

(a) A person may not commence a proceeding in the right of a domestic or foreign corporation unless he was a shareholder of the corporation when the transaction complained of occurred or unless he became a shareholder through transfer by operation of law from one who was a shareholder at that time.
(b) A complaint in a proceeding brought in the right of a corporation must be verified and allege with particularity the demand made, if any, to obtain action by the board of directors and either that the demand was refused or ignored or why he did not make the demand. Whether or not a demand for action was made, if the corporation commences an investigation of the changes made in the demand or complaint, the court may stay any proceeding until the investigation is completed.
(c) A proceeding commenced under this section may not be discontinued or settled without the court's approval. If the court determines that a proposed discontinuance or settlement will substantially affect the interest of the corporation's shareholders or a class of shareholders, the court shall direct that notice be given the shareholders affected.
(d) On termination of the proceeding the court may require the plaintiff to pay any defendant's reasonable expenses (including counsel fees) incurred in defending the proceeding if it finds that the proceeding was commenced without reasonable cause.
(e) For purposes of this section, "shareholder" includes a beneficial owner whose shares are held in a voting trust or held by a nominee on his behalf.

# CHAPTER 8. DIRECTORS AND OFFICERS

## Subchapter A. Board of Directors

### § 8.01. Requirement for and Duties of Board of Directors

(a) Except as provided in subsection (c), each corporation must have a board of directors.
(b) All corporate powers shall be exercised by or under the authority of, and the business and affairs of the corporation managed under the direction of, its board of directors, subject to any limitation set forth in the articles of incorporation.
(c) A corporation having 50 or fewer shareholders may dispense with or limit the authority of a board of directors by describing in its articles of incorporation who will perform some or all of the duties of a board of directors.

### § 8.02. Qualifications of Directors

The articles of incorporation or bylaws may prescribe qualifications for directors. A director need not be a resident of this state or a shareholder of the corporation unless the articles of incorporation or bylaws so prescribe.

### § 8.03. Number and Election of Directors

(a) A board of directors must consist of one or more individuals, with the number specified in or fixed in accordance with the articles of incorporation or bylaws.
(b) If a board of directors has power to fix or change the number of directors, the board may increase or decrease by 30 percent or less the number of directors last approved by the shareholders, but only the shareholders may increase or decrease by more than 30 percent the number of directors last approved by the shareholders.
(c) The articles of incorporation or bylaws may establish a variable range for the size of the board of directors by fixing a minimum and maximum number of directors. If a variable range is established, the number of directors may be fixed or changed from time to time, within the minimum and maximum, by the shareholders or the board of directors. After shares are issued, only the shareholders may change the range for the size of the board or change from a fixed to a variable-range size board or vice versa.

(d) Directors are elected at the first annual shareholders' meeting and at each annual meeting thereafter unless their terms are staggered under section 8.06.

### § 8.04. Election of Directors by Certain Classes of Shareholders

If the articles of incorporation authorize dividing the shares into classes, the articles may also authorize the election of all or a specified number of directors by the holders of one or more authorized classes of shares. Each class (or classes) of shares entitled to elect one or more directors is a separate voting group for purposes of the election of directors.

### § 8.05. Terms of Directors Generally

(a) The terms of the initial directors of a corporation expire at the first shareholders' meeting at which directors are elected.
(b) The terms of all other directors expire at the next annual shareholders' meeting following their election unless their terms are staggered under section 8.06.
(c) A decrease in the number of directors does not shorten an incumbent director's term.
(d) The term of a director elected to fill a vacancy expires at the next shareholders' meeting at which directors are elected.
(e) Despite the expiration of a director's term, he continues to serve until his successor is elected and qualifies or until there is a decrease in the number of directors.

### § 8.06. Staggered Terms for Directors

If there are nine or more directors, the articles of incorporation may provide for staggering their terms by dividing the total number of directors into two or three groups, with each group containing one half or one-third of the total, as near as may be. In that event, the terms of directors in the first group expire at the first annual shareholders' meeting after their election, the terms of the second group expire at the second annual shareholders' meeting after their election, and the terms of the third group, if any, expire at the third annual shareholders' meeting after their election. At each annual shareholders' meeting held thereafter, directors shall be chosen for a term of two years or three years, as the case may be, to succeed those whose terms expire.

### § 8.07. Resignation of Directors

(a) A director may resign at any time by delivering written notice to the board of directors, its chairman, or to the corporation.
(b) A resignation is effective when the notice is delivered unless the notice specifies a later effective date.

### § 8.08. Removal of Directors by Shareholders

(a) The shareholders may remove one or more directors with or without cause unless the articles of incorporation provide that directors may be removed only for cause.
(b) If a director is elected by a voting group of shareholders, only the shareholders of that voting group may participate in the vote to remove him.
(c) If cumulative voting is authorized, a director may not be removed if the number of votes sufficient to elect him under cumulative voting is voted against his removal. If cumulative voting is not authorized, a director may be removed only if the number of votes cast to remove him exceeds the number of votes cast not to remove him.
(d) A director may be removed by the shareholders only at a meeting called for the purpose of removing him and the meeting notice must state that the purpose, or one of the purposes, of the meeting is removal of the director.

### § 8.09. Removal of Directors by Judicial Proceeding

(a) The [name or describe] court of the county where a corporation's principal office (or, if none in this state, its registered office) is located may remove a director of the corporation from office in a proceeding commenced either by the corporation or by its shareholders holding at least 10 percent of the outstanding shares of any class if the court finds that (1) the director engaged in fraudulent or dishonest conduct, or gross abuse of authority or discretion, with respect to the corporation and (2) removal is in the best interest of the corporation.
(b) The court that removes a director may bar the director from reelection for a period prescribed by the court.
(c) If shareholders commence a proceeding under

subsection (a), they shall make the corporation a party defendant.

### § 8.10. Vacancy on Board

(a) Unless the articles of incorporation provide otherwise, if a vacancy occurs on a board of directors, including a vacancy resulting from an increase in the number of directors:

(1) the shareholders may fill the vacancy;

(2) the board of directors may fill the vacancy; or

(3) if the directors remaining in office constitute fewer than a quorum of the board, they may fill the vacancy by the affirmative vote of a majority of all the directors remaining in office.

(b) If the vacant office was held by a director elected by a voting group of shareholders, only the holders of shares of that voting group are entitled to vote to fill the vacancy if it is filled by the shareholders.

(c) A vacancy that will occur at a specific later date (by reason of a resignation effective at a later date under section 8.07(b) or otherwise) may be filled before the vacancy occurs but the new director may not take office until the vacancy occurs.

### § 8.11. Compensation of Directors

Unless the articles of incorporation or bylaws provide otherwise, the board of directors may fix the compensation of directors.

## Subchapter B. Meetings and Action of the Board

### § 8.20. Meetings

(a) The board of directors may hold regular or special meetings in or out of this state.

(b) Unless the articles of incorporation or bylaws provide otherwise, the board of directors may permit any or all directors to participate in a regular or special meeting by, or conduct the meeting through the use of, any means of communication by which all directors participating may simultaneously hear each other during the meeting. A director participating in a meeting by this means is deemed to be present in person at the meeting.

### § 8.21. Action Without Meeting

(a) Unless the articles of incorporation or bylaws provide otherwise, action required or permitted by this Act to be taken at a board of directors' meeting may be taken without a meeting if the action is taken by all members of the board. The action must be evidenced by one or more written consents describing the action taken, signed by each director, and included in the minutes or filed with the corporate records reflecting the action taken.

(b) Action taken under this section is effective when the last director signs the consent, unless the consent specifies a different effective date.

(c) A consent signed under this section has the effect of a meeting vote and may be described as such in any document.

### § 8.22. Notice of Meeting

(a) Unless the articles of incorporation or bylaws provide otherwise, regular meetings of the board of directors may be held without notice of the date, time, place, or purpose of the meeting.

(b) Unless the articles of incorporation or bylaws provide for a longer or shorter period, special meetings of the board of directors must be preceded by at least two days' notice of the date, time, and place of the meeting. The notice need not describe the purpose of the special meeting unless required by the articles of incorporation or bylaws.

### § 8.23. Waiver of Notice

(a) A director may waive any notice required by this Act, the articles of incorporation, or bylaws before or after the date and time stated in the notice. Except as provided by subsection (b), the waiver must be in writing, signed by the director entitled to the notice, and filed with the minutes or corporate records.

(b) A director's attendance at or participation in a meeting waives any required notice to him of the meeting unless the director at the beginning of the meeting (or promptly upon his arrival) objects to holding the meeting or transacting business at the meeting and does not thereafter vote for or assent to action taken at the meeting.

### § 8.24. Quorum and Voting

(a) Unless the articles of incorporation or bylaws require a greater number, a quorum of a board of directors consists of:

(1) a majority of the fixed number of directors if the corporation has a fixed board size; or

(2) a majority of the number of directors prescribed, or if no number is prescribed the number in office immediately before the meeting begins, if the corporation has a variable-range size board.
(b) The articles of incorporation or bylaws may authorize a quorum of a board of directors to consist of no fewer than one-third of the fixed or prescribed number of directors determined under subsection (a).
(c) If a quorum is present when a vote is taken, the affirmative vote of a majority of directors present is the act of the board of directors unless the articles of incorporation or bylaws require the vote of a greater number of directors.
(d) A director who is present at a meeting of the board of directors or a committee of the board of directors when corporate action is taken is deemed to have assented to the action taken unless: (1) he objects at the beginning of the meeting (or promptly upon his arrival) to holding it or transacting business at the meeting; (2) his dissent or abstention from the action taken is entered in the minutes of the meeting; or (3) he delivers written notice of his dissent or abstention to the presiding officer of the meeting before its adjournment or to the corporation immediately after adjournment of the meeting. The right of dissent or abstention is not available to a director who votes in favor of the action taken.

### § 8.25. Committees

(a) Unless the articles of incorporation or bylaws provide otherwise, a board of directors may create one or more committees and appoint members of the board of directors to serve on them. Each committee may have two or more members, who serve at the pleasure of the board of directors.
(b) The creation of a committee and appointment of members to it must be approved by the greater of (1) a majority of all the directors in office when the action is taken or (2) the number of directors required by the articles of incorporation or bylaws to take action under section 8.24.
(c) Sections 8.20 through 8.24, which govern meetings, action without meetings, notice and waiver of notice, and quorum and voting requirements of the board of directors, apply to committees and their members as well.
(d) To the extent specified by the board of directors or in the articles of incorporation or bylaws, each committee may exercise the authority of the board of directors under section 8.01.
(e) A committee may not, however:
(1) authorize distributions;
(2) approve or propose to shareholders action that this Act requires to be approved by shareholders;
(3) fill vacancies on the board of directors or on any of its committees;
(4) amend articles of incorporation pursuant to section 10.02;
(5) adopt, amend, or repeal bylaws;
(6) approve a plan of merger not requiring shareholder approval;
(7) authorize or approve reacquisition of shares, except according to a formula or method prescribed by the board of directors; or
(8) authorize or approve the issuance or sale or contract for sale of shares, or determine the designation and relative rights, preferences, and limitations of a class or series of shares, except that the board of directors may authorize a committee (or a senior executive officer of the corporation) to do so within limits specifically prescribed by the board of directors.
(f) The creation of, delegation of authority to, or action by a committee does not alone constitute compliance by a director with the standards of conduct described in section 8.30.

## Subchapter C. Standards of Conduct

### § 8.30. General Standards for Directors

(a) A director shall discharge his duties as a director, including his duties as a member of a committee:
(1) in good faith;
(2) with the care an ordinarily prudent person in a like position would exercise under similar circumstances; and
(3) in a manner he reasonably believes to be in the best interests of the corporation.
(b) In discharging his duties a director is entitled to rely on information, opinions, reports, or statements, including financial statements and other financial data, if prepared or presented by:
(1) one or more officers or employees of the corporation whom the director reasonably believes to

be reliable and competent in the matters presented;

(2) legal counsel, public accountants, or other persons as to matters the director reasonably believes are within the person's professional or expert competence; or

(3) a committee of the board of directors of which he is not a member if the director reasonably believes the committee merits confidence.

(c) A director is not acting in good faith if he has knowledge concerning the matter in question that makes reliance otherwise permitted by subsection (b) unwarranted.

(d) A director is not liable for any action taken as a director, or any failure to take any action, if he performed the duties of his office in compliance with this section.

## § 8.31. Director Conflict of Interest

(a) A conflict of interest transaction is a transaction with the corporation in which a director of the corporation has a direct or indirect interest. A conflict of interest transaction is not voidable by the corporation solely because of the director's interest in the transaction if any one of the following is true:

(1) the material facts of the transaction and the director's interest were disclosed or known to the board of directors or a committee of the board of directors and the board of directors or committee authorized, approved, or ratified the transaction;

(2) the material facts of the transaction and the director's interest were disclosed or known to the shareholders entitled to vote and they authorized, approved, or ratified the transaction; or

(3) the transaction was fair to the corporation.

(b) For purposes of this section, a director of the corporation has an indirect interest in a transaction if (1) another entity in which he has a material financial interest or in which he is a general partner is a party to the transaction or (2) another entity of which he is a director, officer, or trustee is a party to the transaction and the transaction is or should be considered by the board of directors of the corporation.

(c) For purposes of subsection (a)(1), a conflict of interest transaction is authorized, approved, or ratified if it receives the affirmative vote of a majority of the directors on the board of directors (or on the committee) who have no direct or indirect interest in the transaction, but a transaction may not be authorized, approved, or ratified under this section by a single director. If a majority of the directors who have no direct or indirect interest in the transaction vote to authorize, approve, or ratify the transaction, a quorum is present for the purpose of taking action under this section. The presence of, or a vote cast by, a director with a direct or indirect interest in the transaction does not affect the validity of any action taken under subsection (a)(1) if the transaction is otherwise authorized, approved, or ratified as provided in that subsection.

(d) For purposes of subsection (a)(2), a conflict of interest transaction is authorized, approved, or ratified if it receives the vote of a majority of the shares entitled to be counted under this subsection. Shares owned by or voted under the control of a director who has a direct or indirect interest in the transaction, and shares owned by or voted under the control of an entity described in subsection (b)(1), may not be counted in a vote of shareholders to determine whether to authorize, approve, or ratify a conflict of interest transaction under subsection (a)(2). The vote of those shares, however, shall be counted in determining whether the transaction is approved under other sections of this Act. A majority of the shares, whether or not present, that are entitled to be counted in a vote on the transaction under this subsection constitutes a quorum for the purpose of taking action under this section.

## § 8.32. Loans to Directors

(a) Except as provided by subsection (c), a corporation may not lend money to or guarantee the obligation of a director of the corporation unless:

(1) the particular loan or guarantee is approved by a majority of the votes represented by the outstanding voting shares of all classes, voting as a single voting group, except the votes of shares owned by or voted under the control of the benefited director; or

(2) the corporation's board of directors determines that the loan or guarantee benefits the corporation and either approves the specific loan or guarantee or a general plan authorizing loans and guarantees.

(b) The fact that a loan or guarantee is made in

violation of this section does not affect the borrower's liability on the loan.

(c) This section does not apply to loans and guarantees authorized by statute regulating any special class of corporations.

### § 8.33. Liability for Unlawful Distributions

(a) Unless he complies with the applicable standards of conduct described in section 8.30, a director who votes for or assents to a distribution made in violation of this Act or the articles of incorporation is personally liable to the corporation for the amount of the distribution that exceeds what could have been distributed without violating this Act or the articles of incorporation.

(b) A director held liable for an unlawful distribution under subsection (a) is entitled to contribution:

(1) from every other director who voted for or assented to the distribution without complying with the applicable standards of conduct described in section 8.30; and

(2) from each shareholder for the amount the shareholder accepted knowing the distribution was made in violation of this Act or the articles of incorporation.

## Subchapter D. Officers

### § 8.40. Required Officers

(a) A corporation has the officers described in its bylaws or appointed by the board of directors in accordance with the bylaws.

(b) A duly appointed officer may appoint one or more officers or assistant officers if authorized by the bylaws or the board of directors.

(c) The bylaws or the board of directors shall delegate to one of the officers responsibility for preparing minutes of the directors' and shareholders' meetings and for authenticating records of the corporation.

(d) The same individual may simultaneously hold more than one office in a corporation.

### § 8.41. Duties of Officers

Each officer has the authority and shall perform the duties set forth in the bylaws or, to the extent consistent with the bylaws, the duties prescribed by the board of directors or by direction of an officer authorized by the board of directors to prescribe the duties of other officers.

### § 8.42. Standards of Conduct for Officers

(a) An officer with discretionary authority shall discharge his duties under that authority:

(1) in good faith;

(2) with the care an ordinarily prudent person in a like position would exercise under similar circumstances; and

(3) in a manner he reasonably believes to be in the best interests of the corporation.

(b) In discharging his duties an officer is entitled to rely on information, opinions, reports, or statements, including financial statements and other financial data, if prepared or presented by:

(1) one or more officers or employees of the corporation whom the officer reasonably believes to be reliable and competent in the matters presented; or

(2) legal counsel, public accountants, or other persons as to matters the officer reasonably believes are within the person's professional or expert competence.

(c) An officer is not acting in good faith if he has knowledge concerning the matter in question that makes reliance otherwise permitted by subsection (b) unwarranted.

(d) An officer is not liable for any action taken as an officer, or any failure to take any action, if he performed the duties of his office in compliance with this section.

### § 8.43. Resignation and Removal of Officers

(a) An officer may resign at any time by delivering notice to the corporation. A resignation is effective when the notice is delivered unless the notice specifies a later effective date. If a resignation is made effective at a later date and the corporation accepts the future effective date, its board of directors may fill the pending vacancy before the effective date if the board of directors provides that the successor does not take office until the effective date.

(b) A board of directors may remove any officer at any time with or without cause.

### § 8.44. Contract Rights of Officers

(a) The appointment of an officer does not itself create contract rights.

(b) An officer's removal does not affect the officer's contract rights, if any, with the corporation. An officer's resignation does not affect the corporation's contract rights, if any, with the officer.

## Subchapter E. Indemnification

### § 8.50. Subchapter Definitions

In this subchapter:

(1) "Corporation" includes any domestic or foreign predecessor entity of a corporation in a merger or other transaction in which the predecessor's existence ceased upon consummation of the transaction.

(2) "Director" means an individual who is or was a director of a corporation or an individual who, while a director of a corporation, is or was serving at the corporation's request as a director, officer, partner, trustee, employee, or agent of another foreign or domestic corporation, partnership, joint venture, trust, employee benefit plan, or other enterprise. A director is considered to be serving an employee benefit plan at the corporation's request if his duties to the corporation also impose duties on, or otherwise involve services by, him to the plan or to participants in or beneficiaries of the plan. "Director" includes, unless the context requires otherwise, the estate or personal representative of a director.

(3) "Expenses" include counsel fees.

(4) "Liability" means the obligation to pay a judgment, settlement, penalty, fine (including an excise tax assessed with respect to an employee benefit plan), or reasonable expenses incurred with respect to a proceeding.

(5) "Official capacity" means: (i) when used with respect to a director, the office of director in a corporation; and (ii) when used with respect to an individual other than a director, as contemplated in section 8.56, the office in a corporation held by the officer or the employment or agency relationship undertaken by the employee or agent on behalf of the corporation. "Official capacity" does not include service for any other foreign or domestic corporation or any partnership, joint venture, trust, employee benefit plan, or other enterprise.

(6) "Party" includes an individual who was, is, or is threatened to be made a named defendant or respondent in a proceeding.

(7) "Proceeding" means any threatened, pending, or completed action, suit, or proceeding, whether civil, criminal, administrative, or investigative and whether formal or informal.

### § 8.51. Authority to Indemnify

(a) Except as provided in subsection (d), a corporation may indemnify an individual made a party to a proceeding because he is or was a director against liability incurred in the proceeding if:

(1) he conducted himself in good faith; and

(2) he reasonably believed:

(i) in the case of conduct in his official capacity with the corporation, that his conduct was in its best interests; and

(ii) in all other cases, that his conduct was at least not opposed to its best interests; and

(3) in the case of any criminal proceeding, he had no reasonable cause to believe his conduct was unlawful.

(b) A director's conduct with respect to an employee benefit plan for a purpose he reasonably believed to be in the interests of the participants in and beneficiaries of the plan is conduct that satisfies the requirement of subsection (a)(2)(ii).

(c) The termination of a proceeding by judgment, order, settlement, conviction, or upon a plea of nolo contendere or its equivalent is not, of itself, determinative that the director did not meet the standard of conduct described in this section.

(d) A corporation may not indemnify a director under this section:

(1) in connection with a proceeding by or in the right of the corporation in which the director was adjudged liable to the corporation; or

(2) in connection with any other proceeding charging improper personal benefit to him, whether or not involving action in his official capacity, in which he was adjudged liable on the basis that personal benefit was improperly received by him.

(e) Indemnification permitted under this section in connection with a proceeding by or in the right of the corporation is limited to reasonable expenses incurred in connection with the proceeding.

### § 8.52. Mandatory Indemnification

Unless limited by its articles of incorporation, a corporation shall indemnify a director who was wholly successful, on the merits or otherwise, in the defense of any proceeding to which he was a party because he is or was a director of the corporation against reasonable expenses incurred by him in connection with the proceeding.

### § 8.53. Advance for Expenses

(a) A corporation may pay for or reimburse the reasonable expenses incurred by a director who is a party to a proceeding in advance of final disposition of the proceeding if:

(1) the director furnishes the corporation a written affirmation of his good faith belief that he has met the standard of conduct described in section 8.51;

(2) the director furnishes the corporation a written undertaking, executed personally or on his behalf, to repay the advance if it is ultimately determined that he did not meet the standard of conduct; and

(3) a determination is made that the facts then known to those making the determination would not preclude indemnification under this subchapter.

(b) The undertaking required by subsection (a)(2) must be an unlimited general obligation of the director but need not be secured and may be accepted without reference to financial ability to make repayment.

(c) Determinations and authorizations of payments under this section shall be made in the manner specified in section 8.55.

### § 8.54. Court-Ordered Indemnification

Unless a corporation's articles of incorporation provide otherwise, a director of the corporation who is a party to a proceeding may apply for indemnification to the court conducting the proceeding or to another court of competent jurisdiction. On receipt of an application, the court after giving any notice the court considers necessary may order indemnification if it determines:

(1) the director is entitled to mandatory indemnification under section 8.52, in which case the court shall also order the corporation to pay the director's reasonable expenses incurred to obtain court-ordered indemnification; or

(2) the director is fairly and reasonably entitled to indemnification in view of all the relevant circumstances, whether or not he met the standard of conduct set forth in section 8.51 or was adjudged liable as described in section 8.51(d), but if he was adjudged so liable his indemnification is limited to reasonable expenses incurred.

### § 8.55. Determination and Authorization of Indemnification

(a) A corporation may not indemnify a director under section 8.51 unless authorized in the specific case after a determination has been made that indemnification of the director is permissible in the circumstances because he has met the standard of conduct set forth in section 8.51.

(b) The determination shall be made:

(1) by the board of directors by majority vote of a quorum consisting of directors not at the time parties to the proceeding;

(2) if a quorum cannot be obtained under subdivision (1), by majority vote of a committee duly designated by the board of directors (in which designation directors who are parties may participate), consisting solely of two or more directors not at the time parties to the proceeding;

(3) by special legal counsel:

(i) selected by the board of directors or its committee in the manner prescribed in subdivision (1) or (2); or

(ii) if a quorum of the board of directors cannot be obtained under subdivision (1) and a committee cannot be designated under subdivision (2), selected by majority vote of the full board of directors (in which selection directors who are parties may participate); or

(4) by the shareholders, but shares owned by or voted under the control of directors who are at the time parties to the proceeding may not be voted on the determination.

(c) Authorization of indemnification and evaluation as to reasonableness of expenses shall be made in the same manner as the determination that indemnification is permissible, except that if the determination is made by special legal counsel, authorization of indemnification and evaluation as to reasonableness of expenses shall be made by those entitled under subsection (b)(3) to select counsel.

### § 8.56. Indemnification of Officers, Employees, and Agents

Unless a corporation's articles of incorporation provide otherwise:

(1) an officer of the corporation who is not a director is entitled to mandatory indemnification under section 8.52, and is entitled to apply for court-ordered indemnification under section 8.54, in each case to the same extent as a director;

(2) the corporation may indemnify and advance expenses under this subchapter to an officer, employee, or agent of the corporation who is not a director to the same extent as to a director; and

(3) a corporation may also indemnify and advance expenses to an officer, employee, or agent who is not a director to the extent, consistent with public policy, that may be provided by its articles of incorporation, bylaws, general or specific action of its board of directors, or contract.

### § 8.57. Insurance

A corporation may purchase and maintain insurance on behalf of an individual who is or was a director, officer, employee, or agent of the corporation, or who, while a director, officer, employee, or agent of the corporation, is or was serving at the request of the corporation as a director, officer, partner, trustee, employee, or agent of another foreign or domestic corporation, partnership, joint venture, trust, employee benefit plan, or other enterprise, against liability asserted against or incurred by him in that capacity or arising from his status as a director, officer, employee, or agent, whether or not the corporation would have power to indemnify him against the same liability under section 8.51 or 8.52.

### § 8.58. Application of Subchapter

(a) A provision treating a corporation's indemnification of or advance for expenses to directors that is contained in its articles of incorporation, bylaws, a resolution of its shareholders or board of directors, or in a contract or otherwise, is valid only if and to the extent the provision is consistent with this subchapter. If articles of incorporation limit indemnification or advance for expenses, indemnification and advance for expenses are valid only to the extent consistent with the articles.

(b) This subchapter does not limit a corporation's power to pay or reimburse expenses incurred by a director in connection with his appearance as a witness in a proceeding at a time when he has not been made a named defendant or respondent to the proceeding.

# CHAPTER 9. [Reserved]

# CHAPTER 10. AMENDMENT OF ARTICLES OF INCORPORATION AND BYLAWS

## Subchapter A. Amendment of Articles of Incorporation

### § 10.01. Authority to Amend

(a) A corporation may amend its articles of incorporation at any time to add or change a provision that is required or permitted in the articles of incorporation or to delete a provision not required in the articles of incorporation. Whether a provision is required or permitted in the articles of incorporation is determined as of the effective date of the amendment.

(b) A shareholder of the corporation does not have a vested property right resulting from any provision in the articles of incorporation, including provisions relating to management, control, capital structure, dividend entitlement, or purpose or duration of the corporation.

### § 10.02. Amendment by Board of Directors

Unless the articles of incorporation provide otherwise, a corporation's board of directors may adopt one or more amendments to the corporation's articles of incorporation without shareholder action:

(1) to extend the duration of the corporation if it was incorporated at a time when limited duration was required by law;

(2) to delete the names and addresses of the initial directors;

(3) to delete the name and address of the initial registered agent or registered office, if a statement of change is on file with the secretary of state;

(4) to change each issued and unissued authorized share of an outstanding class into a greater number of whole shares if the corporation has only shares of that class outstanding;

(5) to change the corporate name by substituting the word "corporation," "incorporated," "company," "limited," or the abbreviation "corp.," "inc.," "co.," or "ltd.," for a similar word or abbreviation in the name, or by adding, deleting, or changing a geographical attribution for the name; or

(6) to make any other change expressly permit-

ted by this Act to be made without shareholder action.

## § 10.03. Amendment by Board of Directors and Shareholders

(a) A corporation's board of directors may propose one or more amendments to the articles of incorporation for submission to the shareholders.

(b) For the amendment to be adopted:

(1) the board of directors must recommend the amendment to the shareholders unless the board of directors determines that because of conflict of interest or other special circumstances it should make no recommendation and communicates the basis for its determination to the shareholders with the amendment; and

(2) the shareholders entitled to vote on the amendment must approve the amendment as provided in subsection (e).

(c) The board of directors may condition its submission of the proposed amendment on any basis.

(d) The corporation shall notify each shareholder, whether or not entitled to vote, of the proposed shareholders' meeting in accordance with section 7.05. The notice of meeting must also state that the purpose, or one of the purposes, of the meeting is to consider the proposed amendment and contain or be accompanied by a copy or summary of the amendment.

(e) Unless this Act, the articles of incorporation, or the board of directors (acting pursuant to subsection (c)) require a greater vote or a vote by voting groups, the amendment to be adopted must be approved by:

(1) a majority of the votes entitled to be cast on the amendment by any voting group with respect to which the amendment would create dissenters' rights; and

(2) the votes required by sections 7.25 and 7.26 by every other voting group entitled to vote on the amendment.

## § 10.04. Voting on Amendments by Voting Groups

(a) The holders of the outstanding shares of a class are entitled to vote as a separate voting group (if shareholder voting is otherwise required by this Act) on a proposed amendment if the amendment would:

(1) increase or decrease the aggregate number of authorized shares of the class;

(2) effect an exchange or reclassification, of all or part of the shares of the class into shares of another class;

(3) effect an exchange or reclassification, or create the right of exchange, of all or part of the shares of another class into shares of the class;

(4) change the designation, rights, preferences, or limitations of all or part of the shares of the class;

(5) change the shares of all or part of the class into a different number of shares of the same class;

(6) create a new class of shares having rights or preferences with respect to distributions or to dissolution that are prior, superior, or substantially equal to the shares of the class;

(7) increase the rights, preferences, or number of authorized shares of any class that, after giving effect to the amendment, have rights or preferences with respect to distributions or to dissolution that are prior, superior, or substantially equal to the shares of the class;

(8) limit or deny an existing preemptive right of all or part of the shares of the class; or

(9) cancel or otherwise affect rights to distributions or dividends that have accumulated but not yet been declared on all or part of the shares of the class.

(b) If a proposed amendment would affect a series of a class of shares in one or more of the ways described in subsection (a), the shares of that series are entitled to vote as a separate voting group on the proposed amendment.

(c) If a proposed amendment that entitles two or more series of shares to vote as separate voting groups under this section would affect those two or more series in the same or a substantially similar way, the shares of all the series so affected must vote together as a single voting group on the proposed amendment.

(d) A class or series of shares is entitled to the voting rights granted by this section although the articles of incorporation provide that the shares are nonvoting shares.

## § 10.05. Amendment Before Issuance of Shares

If a corporation has not yet issued shares, its incorporators or board of directors may adopt one or more amendments to the corporation's articles of incorporation.

### § 10.06. Articles of Amendment

A corporation amending its articles of incorporation shall deliver to the secretary of state for filing articles of amendment setting forth:

(1) the name of the corporation;

(2) the text of each amendment adopted;

(3) if an amendment provides for an exchange, reclassification, or cancellation of issued shares, provisions for implementing the amendment if not contained in the amendment itself;

(4) the date of each amendment's adoption;

(5) if an amendment was adopted by the incorporators or board of directors without shareholder action, a statement to that effect and that shareholder action was not required;

(6) if an amendment was approved by the shareholders:

(i) the designation, number of outstanding shares, number of votes entitled to be cast by each voting group entitled to vote separately on the amendment, and number of votes of each voting group indisputably represented at the meeting;

(ii) either the total number of votes cast for and against the amendment by each voting group entitled to vote separately on the amendment or the total number of undisputed votes cast for the amendment by each voting group and a statement that the number cast for the amendment by each voting group was sufficient for approval by that voting group.

### § 10.07. Restated Articles of Incorporation

(a) A corporation's board of directors may restate its articles of incorporation at any time with or without shareholder action.

(b) The restatement may include one or more amendments to the articles. If the restatement includes an amendment requiring shareholder approval, it must be adopted as provided in section 10.03.

(c) If the board of directors submits a restatement for shareholder action, the corporation shall notify each shareholder, whether or not entitled to vote, of the proposed shareholders' meeting in accordance with section 7.05. The notice must also state that the purpose, or one of the purposes, of the meeting is to consider the proposed restatement and contain or be accompanied by a copy of the restatement that identifies any amendment or other change it would make in the articles.

(d) A corporation restating its articles of incorporation shall deliver to the secretary of state for filing articles of restatement setting forth the name of the corporation and the text of the restated articles of incorporation together with a certificate setting forth:

(1) whether the restatement contains an amendment to the articles requiring shareholder approval and, if it does not, that the board of directors adopted the restatement; or

(2) if the restatement contains an amendment to the articles requiring shareholder approval, the information required by section 10.06.

(e) Duly adopted restated articles of incorporation supersede the original articles of incorporation and all amendments to them.

(f) The secretary of state may certify restated articles of incorporation, as the articles of incorporation currently in effect, without including the certificate information required by subsection (d).

### § 10.08. Amendment Pursuant To Reorganization

(a) A corporation's articles of incorporation may be amended without action by the board of directors or shareholders to carry out a plan of reorganization ordered or decreed by a court of competent jurisdiction under federal statute if the articles of incorporation after amendment contain only provisions required or permitted by section 2.02.

(b) The individual or individuals designated by the court shall deliver to the secretary of state for filing articles of amendment setting forth:

(1) the name of the corporation;

(2) the text of each amendment approved by the court;

(3) the date of the court's order or decree approving the articles of amendment;

(4) the title of the reorganization proceeding in which the order or decree was entered; and

(5) a statement that the court had jurisdiction of the proceeding under federal statute.

(c) Shareholders of a corporation undergoing reorganization do not have dissenters' rights except as and to the extent provided in the reorganization plan.

(d) This section does not apply after entry of a final decree in the reorganization proceeding even though the court retains jurisdiction of the proceeding for limited purposes unrelated to consummation of the reorganization plan.

### § 10.09. Effect of Amendment

An amendment to articles of incorporation does not affect a cause of action existing against or in favor of the corporation, a proceeding to which the corporation is a party, or the existing rights of persons other than shareholders of the corporation. An amendment changing a corporation's name does not abate a proceeding brought by or against the corporation in its former name.

## Subchapter B. Amendment of Bylaws

### § 10.20. Amendment by Board of Directors or Shareholders

(a) A corporation's board of directors may amend or repeal the corporation's bylaws unless:

(1) the articles of incorporation or this Act reserve this power exclusively to the shareholders in whole or part; or

(2) the shareholders in amending or repealing a particular bylaw provide expressly that the board of directors may not amend or repeal that bylaw.

(b) A corporation's shareholders may amend or repeal the corporation's bylaws even though the bylaws may also be amended or repealed by its board of directors.

### § 10.21. Bylaw Increasing Quorum Or Voting Requirement For Shareholders

(a) If expressly authorized by the articles of incorporation, the shareholders may adopt or amend a bylaw that fixes a greater quorum or voting requirement for shareholders (or voting groups of shareholders) than is required by this Act. The adoption or amendment of a bylaw that adds, changes, or deletes a greater quorum or voting requirement for shareholders must meet the same quorum requirement and be adopted by the same vote and voting groups required to take action under the quorum and voting requirement then in effect or proposed to be adopted, whichever is greater.

(b) A bylaw that fixes a greater quorum or voting requirement for shareholders under subsection (a) may not be adopted, amended, or repealed by the board of directors.

### § 10.22 Bylaw Increasing Quorum or Voting Requirement for Directors

(a) A bylaw that fixes a greater quorum or voting requirement for the board of directors may be amended or repealed:

(1) if originally adopted by the shareholders, only by the shareholders;

(2) if originally adopted by the board of directors, either by the shareholders or by the board of directors.

(b) A bylaw adopted or amended by the shareholders that fixes a greater quorum or voting requirement for the board of directors may provide that it may be amended or repealed only by a specified vote of either the shareholders or the board of directors.

(c) Action by the board of directors under subsection (a)(2) to adopt or amend a bylaw that changes the quorum or voting requirement for the board of directors must meet the same quorum requirement and be adopted by the same vote required to take action under the quorum and voting requirement then in effect or proposed to be adopted, whichever is greater.

## CHAPTER 11. MERGER AND SHARE EXCHANGE

### § 11.01. Merger

(a) One or more corporations may merge into another corporation if the board of directors of each corporation adopts and its shareholders (if required by section 11.03) approve a plan of merger.

(b) The plan of merger must set forth:

(1) the name of each corporation planning to merge and the name of the surviving corporation into which each other corporation plans to merge;

(2) the terms and conditions of the merger; and

(3) the manner and basis of converting the shares of each corporation into shares, obligations, or other securities of the surviving or any other corporation or into cash or other property in whole or part.

(c) The plan of merger may set forth:

(1) amendments to the articles of incorporation of the surviving corporation; and

(2) other provisions relating to the merger.

## § 11.02. Share Exchange

(a) A corporation may acquire all of the outstanding shares of one or more classes or series of another corporation if the board of directors of each corporation adopts and its shareholders (if required by section 11.03) approve the exchange.

(b) The plan of exchange must set forth:

(1) the name of the corporation whose shares will be acquired and the name of the acquiring corporation;

(2) the terms and conditions of the exchange;

(3) the manner and basis of exchanging the shares to be acquired for shares, obligations, or other securities of the acquiring or any other corporation or for cash or other property in whole or part.

(c) The plan of exchange may set forth other provisions relating to the exchange.

(d) This section does not limit the power of a corporation to acquire all or part of the shares of one or more classes or series of another corporation through a voluntary exchange or otherwise.

## § 11.03. Action on Plan

(a) After adopting a plan of merger or share exchange, the board of directors of each corporation party to the merger, and the board of directors of the corporation whose shares will be acquired in the share exchange, shall submit the plan of merger (except as provided in subsection (g)) or share exchange for approval by its shareholders.

(b) For a plan of merger or share exchange to be approved:

(1) the board of directors must recommend the plan of merger or share exchange to the shareholders, unless the board of directors determines that because of conflict of interest or other special circumstances it should make no recommendation and communicates the basis for its determination to the shareholders with the plan; and

(2) the shareholders entitled to vote must approve the plan.

(c) The board of directors may condition its submission of the proposed merger or share exchange on any basis.

(d) The corporation shall notify each shareholder, whether or not entitled to vote, of the proposed shareholders' meeting in accordance with section 7.05. The notice must also state that the purpose, or one of the purposes, of the meeting is to consider the plan of merger or share exchange and contain or be accompanied by a copy or summary of the plan.

(e) Unless this Act, the articles of incorporation, or the board of directors (acting pursuant to subsection (c)) require a greater vote or a vote by voting groups, the plan of merger or share exchange to be authorized must be approved by each voting group entitled to vote separately on the plan by a majority of all the votes entitled to be cast on the plan by that voting group.

(f) Separate voting by voting groups is required:

(1) on a plan of merger if the plan contains a provision that, if contained in a proposed amendment to articles of incorporation, would require action by one or more separate voting groups on the proposed amendment under section 10.04;

(2) on a plan of share exchange by each class or series of shares included in the exchange, with each class or series constituting a separate voting group.

(g) Action by the shareholders of the surviving corporation on a plan of merger is not required if:

(1) the articles of incorporation of the surviving corporation will not differ (except for amendments enumerated in section 10.02) from its articles before the merger;

(2) each shareholder of the surviving corporation whose shares were outstanding immediately before the effective date of the merger will hold the same number of shares, with identical designations, preferences, limitations, and relative rights, immediately after;

(3) the number of voting shares outstanding immediately after the merger, plus the number of voting shares issuable as a result of the merger (either by the conversion of securities issued pursuant to the merger or the exercise of rights and warrants issued pursuant to the merger), will not exceed by more than 20 percent the total number of voting shares of the surviving corporation outstanding immediately before the merger; and

(4) the number of participating shares outstanding immediately after the merger, plus the number of participating shares issuable as a result of the merger (either by the conversion of securities issued pursuant to the merger or the exercise of rights and warrants issued pursuant to the merger), will not exceed by more than 20 percent the total number of participating shares outstanding immediately before the merger.

(h) As used in subsection (g):

(1) "Participating shares" means shares that entitle their holders to participate without limitation in distributions.

(2) "Voting shares" means shares that entitle their holders to vote unconditionally in elections of directors.

(i) After a merger or share exchange is authorized, and at any time before articles of merger or share exchange are filed, the planned merger or share exchange may be abandoned (subject to any contractual rights), without further shareholder action, in accordance with the procedure set forth in the plan of merger or share exchange or, if none is set forth, in the manner determined by the board of directors.

### § 11.04. Merger of Subsidiary

(a) A parent corporation owning at least 90 percent of the outstanding shares of each class of a subsidiary corporation may merge the subsidiary into itself without approval of the shareholders of the parent or subsidiary.

(b) The board of directors of the parent shall adopt a plan of merger that sets forth:

(1) the names of the parent and subsidiary; and

(2) the manner and basis of converting the shares of the subsidiary into shares, obligations, or other securities of the parent or any other corporation or into cash or other property in whole or part.

(c) The parent shall mail a copy or summary of the plan of merger to each shareholder of the subsidiary who does not waive the mailing requirement in writing.

(d) The parent may not deliver articles of merger to the secretary of state for filing until at least 30 days after the date it mailed a copy of the plan of merger to each shareholder of the subsidiary who did not waive the mailing requirement.

(e) Articles of merger under this section may not contain amendments to the articles of incorporation of the parent corporation (except for amendments enumerated in section 10.02).

### § 11.05. Articles of Merger or Share Exchange

(a) After a plan of merger or share exchange is approved by the shareholders, or adopted by the board of directors if shareholder approval is not required, the surviving or acquiring corporation shall deliver to the secretary of state for filing articles of merger or share exchange setting forth:

(1) the plan of merger or share exchange;

(2) if shareholder approval was not required, a statement to that effect;

(3) if approval of the shareholders of one or more corporations party to the merger or share exchange was required:

(i) the designation, number of outstanding shares, and number of votes entitled to be cast by each voting group entitled to vote separately on the plan as to each corporation; and

(ii) either the total number of votes cast for and against the plan by each voting group entitled to vote separately on the plan or the total number of undisputed votes cast for the plan separately by each voting group and a statement that the number cast for the plan by each voting group was sufficient for approval by that voting group.

(b) Unless a delayed effective date is specified, a merger or share exchange takes effect when the articles of merger or share exchange are filed.

### § 11.06. Effect of Merger or Share Exchange

(a) When a merger takes effect:

(1) every other corporation party to the merger merges into the surviving corporation and the separate existence of every corporation except the surviving corporation ceases;

(2) the title to all real estate and other property owned by each corporation party to the merger is vested in the surviving corporation without reversion or impairment;

(3) the surviving corporation has all liabilities of each corporation party to the merger;

(4) a proceeding pending against any corporation party to the merger may be continued as if the merger did not occur or the surviving corpora-

tion may be substituted in the proceeding for the corporation whose existence ceased;

(5) the articles of incorporation of the surviving corporation are amended to the extent provided in the plan of merger; and

(6) the shares of each corporation party to the merger that are to be converted into shares, obligations, or other securities of the surviving or any other corporation or into cash or other property are converted and the former holders of the shares are entitled only to the rights provided in the articles of merger or to their rights under chapter 13.

(b) When a share exchange takes effect, the shares of each acquired corporation are exchanged as provided in the plan, and the former holders of the shares are entitled only to the exchange rights provided in the articles of share exchange or to their rights under chapter 13.

### § 11.07. Merger or Share Exchange With Foreign Corporation

(a) One or more foreign corporations may merge or enter into a share exchange with one or more domestic corporations if:

(1) in a merger, the merger is permitted by the law of the state or country under whose law each foreign corporation is incorporated and each foreign corporation complies with that law in effecting the merger;

(2) in a share exchange, the corporation whose shares will be acquired is a domestic corporation, whether or not a share exchange is permitted by the law of the state or country under whose law the acquiring corporation is incorporated;

(3) the foreign corporation complies with section 11.05 if it is the surviving corporation of the merger or acquiring corporation of the share exchange; and

(4) each domestic corporation complies with the applicable provisions of sections 11.01 through 11.04 and, if it is the surviving corporation of the merger or acquiring corporation of the share exchange, with section 11.05.

(b) Upon the merger or share exchange taking effect, the surviving foreign corporation of a merger and the acquiring foreign corporation of a share exchange is deemed:

(1) to appoint the secretary of state as its agent for service of process in a proceeding to enforce any obligation or the rights of dissenting shareholders of each domestic corporation party to the merger or share exchange; and

(2) to agree that it will promptly pay to the dissenting shareholders of each domestic corporation party to the merger or share exchange the amount, if any, to which they are entitled under chapter 13.

(c) This section does not limit the power of a foreign corporation to acquire all or part of the shares of one or more classes or series of a domestic corporation through a voluntary exchange or otherwise.

## CHAPTER 12. SALE OF ASSETS

### § 12.01. Sale of Assets in Regular Course of Business and Mortgage of Assets

(a) A corporation may, on the terms and conditions and for the consideration determined by the board of directors:

(1) sell, lease, exchange, or otherwise dispose of all, or substantially all, of its property in the usual and regular course of business,

(2) mortgage, pledge, dedicate to the repayment of indebtedness (whether with or without recourse), or otherwise encumber any or all of its property whether or not in the usual and regular course of business, or

(3) transfer any or all of its property to a corporation all the shares of which are owned by the corporation.

(b) Unless the articles of incorporation require it, approval by the shareholders of a transaction described in subsection (a) is not required.

### § 12.02. Sale of Assets Other Than in Regular Course of Business

(a) A corporation may sell, lease, exchange, or otherwise dispose of all, or substantially all, of its property (with or without the good will), otherwise than in the usual and regular course of business, on the terms and conditions and for the consideration determined by the corporation's board of directors, if the board of directors proposes and its shareholders approve the proposed transaction.

(b) For a transaction to be authorized:

(1) the board of directors must recommend the proposed transaction to the shareholders unless

the board of directors determines that because of conflict of interest or other special circumstances it should make no recommendation and communicates the basis for its determination to the shareholders with the submission of the proposed transaction; and

(2) the shareholders entitled to vote must approve the transaction.

(c) The board of directors may condition its submission of the proposed transaction on any basis.

(d) The corporation shall notify each shareholder, whether or not entitled to vote, of the proposed shareholders' meeting in accordance with section 7.05. The notice must also state that the purpose, or one of the purposes, of the meeting is to consider the sale, lease, exchange, or other disposition of all, or substantially all, the property of the corporation and contain or be accompanied by a description of the transaction.

(e) Unless the articles of incorporation or the board of directors (acting pursuant to subsection (c)) require a greater vote or a vote by voting groups, the transaction to be authorized must be approved by a majority of all the votes entitled to be cast on the transaction.

(f) After a sale, lease, exchange, or other disposition of property is authorized, the transaction may be abandoned (subject to any contractual rights) without further shareholder action.

(g) A transaction that constitutes a distribution is governed by section 6.40 and not by this section.

## CHAPTER 13. DISSENTERS' RIGHTS

### Subchapter A. Right to Dissent and Obtain Payment for Shares

#### § 13.01. Definitions

In this chapter:

(1) "Corporation" means the issuer of the shares held by a dissenter before the corporate action, or the surviving or acquiring corporation by merger or share exchange of that issuer.

(2) "Dissenter" means a shareholder who is entitled to dissent from corporate action under section 13.02 and who exercises that right when and in the manner required by sections 13.20 through 13.28.

(3) "Fair value," with respect to a dissenter's shares, means the value of the shares immediately before the effectuation of the corporate action to which the dissenter objects, excluding any appreciation or depreciation in anticipation of the corporate action unless exclusion would be inequitable.

(4) "Interest" means interest from the effective date of the corporate action until the date of payment, at the average rate currently paid by the corporation on its principal bank loans or, if none, at a rate that is fair and equitable under all the circumstances.

(5) "Record shareholder" means the person in whose name shares are registered in the records of a corporation or the beneficial owner of shares to the extent of the rights granted by a nominee certificate on file with a corporation.

(6) "Beneficial shareholder" means the person who is a beneficial owner of shares held by a nominee as the record shareholder.

(7) "Shareholder" means the record shareholder or the beneficial shareholder.

#### § 13.02. Right to Dissent

(a) A shareholder is entitled to dissent from, and obtain payment of the fair value of his shares in the event of, any of the following corporate actions:

(1) consummation of a plan of merger to which the corporation is a party (i) if shareholder approval is required for the merger by section 11.03 or the articles of incorporation and the shareholder is entitled to vote on the merger or (ii) if the corporation is a subsidiary that is merged with its parent under section 11.04;

(2) consummation of a plan of share exchange to which the corporation is a party as the corporation whose shares will be acquired, if the shareholder is entitled to vote on the plan;

(3) consummation of a sale or exchange of all, or substantially all, of the property of the corporation other than in the usual and regular course of business, if the shareholder is entitled to vote on the sale or exchange, including a sale in dissolution, but not including a sale pursuant to court order or a sale for cash pursuant to a plan by which all or substantially all of the net proceeds of the sale will be distributed to the shareholders within one year after the date of sale;

(4) an amendment of the articles of incorpora-

tion that materially and adversely affects rights in respect of a dissenter's shares because it:
(i) alters or abolishes a preferential right of the shares;
(ii) creates, alters, or abolishes a right in respect of redemption, including a provision respecting a sinking fund for the redemption or repurchase, of the shares;
(iii) alters or abolishes a preemptive right of the holder of the shares to acquire shares or other securities;
(iv) excludes or limits the right of the shares to vote on any matter, or to cumulate votes, other than a limitation by dilution through issuance of shares or other securities with similar voting rights; or
(v) reduces the number of shares owned by the shareholder to a fraction of a share if the fractional share so created is to be acquired for cash under section 6.04; or

(5) any corporate action taken pursuant to a shareholder vote to the extent the articles of incorporation, bylaws, or a resolution of the board of directors provides that voting or nonvoting shareholders are entitled to dissent and obtain payment for their shares.

(b) A shareholder entitled to dissent and obtain payment for his shares under this chapter may not challenge the corporate action creating his entitlement unless the action is unlawful or fraudulent with respect to the shareholder or the corporation.

### § 13.03. Dissent by Nominees and Beneficial Owners *(Text omitted.)*

## Subchapter B. Procedure for Exercise of Dissenters' Rights

### § 13.20. Notice of Dissenters' Rights

(a) If proposed corporate action creating dissenters' rights under section 13.02 is submitted to a vote at a shareholders' meeting, the meeting notice must state that shareholders are or may be entitled to assert dissenters' rights under this chapter and be accompanied by a copy of this chapter.

(b) If corporate action creating dissenters' rights under section 13.02 is taken without a vote of shareholders, the corporation shall notify in writing all shareholders entitled to assert dissenters' rights that the action was taken and send them the dissenters' notice described in section 13.22.

### § 13.21. Notice of Intent to Demand Payment

(a) If proposed corporate action creating dissenters' rights under section 13.02 is submitted to a vote at a shareholders' meeting, a shareholder who wishes to assert dissenters' rights (1) must deliver to the corporation before the vote is taken written notice of his intent to demand payment for his shares if the proposed action is effectuated and (2) must not vote his shares in favor of the proposed action.

(b) A shareholder who does not satisfy the requirements of subsection (a) is not entitled to payment for his shares under this chapter.

### § 13.22. Dissenters' Notice

(a) If proposed corporate action creating dissenters' rights under section 13.02 is authorized at a shareholders' meeting, the corporation shall deliver a written dissenters' notice to all shareholders who satisfied the requirements of section 13.21.

(b) The dissenters' notice must be sent no later than 10 days after the corporate action was taken, and must:

(1) state where the payment demand must be sent and where and when certificates for certificated shares must be deposited;

(2) inform holders of uncertificated shares to what extent transfer of the shares will be restricted after the payment demand is received;

(3) supply a form for demanding payment that includes the date of the first announcement to news media or to shareholders of the terms of the proposed corporate action and requires that the person asserting dissenters' rights certify whether or not he acquired beneficial ownership of the shares before that date;

(4) set a date by which the corporation must receive the payment demand, which date may not be fewer than 30 nor more than 60 days after the date the subsection (a) notice is delivered; and

(5) be accompanied by a copy of this chapter.

### § 13.23. Duty to Demand Payment

(a) A shareholder sent a dissenters' notice described in section 13.22 must demand payment, certify whether he acquired beneficial ownership of the shares before the date required to be set forth in the dissenter's notice pursuant to section 13.22(b)(3), and deposit his certificates in accordance with the terms of the notice.

(b) The shareholder who demands payment and deposits his shares under section (a) retains all other rights of a shareholder until these rights are cancelled or modified by the taking of the proposed corporate action.

(c) A shareholder who does not demand payment or deposit his share certificates where required, each by the date set in the dissenters' notice, is not entitled to payment for his shares under this chapter.

### § 13.24. Share Restrictions

(a) The corporation may restrict the transfer of uncertificated shares from the date the demand for their payment is received until the proposed corporate action is taken or the restrictions released under section 13.26.

(b) The person for whom dissenters' rights are asserted as to uncertificated shares retains all other rights of a shareholder until these rights are cancelled or modified by the taking of the proposed corporate action.

### § 13.25. Payment

(a) Except as provided in section 13.27, as soon as the proposed corporate action is taken, or upon receipt of a payment demand, the corporation shall pay each dissenter who complied with section 13.23 the amount the corporation estimates to be the fair value of his shares, plus accrued interest.

(b) The payment must be accompanied by:

(1) the corporation's balance sheet as of the end of a fiscal year ending not more than 16 months before the date of payment, an income statement for that year, a statement of changes in shareholders' equity for that year, and the latest available interim financial statements, if any;

(2) a statement of the corporation's estimate of the fair value of the shares;

(3) an explanation of how the interest was calculated;

(4) a statement of the dissenter's right to demand payment under section 13.28; and

(5) a copy of this chapter.

### § 13.26. Failure to Take Action

(a) If the corporation does not take the proposed action within 60 days after the date set for demanding payment and depositing share certificates, the corporation shall return the deposited certificates and release the transfer restrictions imposed on uncertificated shares.

(b) If after returning deposited certificates and releasing transfer restrictions, the corporation takes the proposed action, it must send a new dissenters' notice under section 13.22 and repeat the payment demand procedure.

### § 13.27. After-Acquired Shares

(a) A corporation may elect to withhold payment required by section 13.25 from a dissenter unless he was the beneficial owner of the shares before the date set forth in the dissenters' notice as the date of the first announcement to news media or to shareholders of the terms of the proposed corporate action.

(b) To the extent the corporation elects to withhold payment under subsection (a), after taking the proposed corporate action, it shall estimate the fair value of the shares, plus accrued interest, and shall pay this amount to each dissenter who agrees to accept it in full satisfaction of his demand. The corporation shall send with its offer a statement of its estimate of the fair value of the shares, an explanation of how the interest was calculated, and a statement of the dissenter's right to demand payment under section 13.28.

### § 13.28. Procedure if Shareholder Dissatisfied with Payment or Offer

(a) A dissenter may notify the corporation in writing of his own estimate of the fair value of his shares and amount of interest due, and demand payment of his estimate (less any payment under section 13.25), or reject the corporation's offer under section 13.27 and demand payment of the fair value of his shares and interest due, if:

(1) the dissenter believes that the amount paid under section 13.25 or offered under section 13.27 is less than the fair value of his shares or that the interest due is incorrectly calculated;

(2) the corporation fails to make payment under section 13.25 within 60 days after the date set for demanding payment; or

(3) the corporation, having failed to take the proposed action, does not return the deposited certificates or release the transfer restrictions im-

posed on uncertificated shares within 60 days after the date set for demanding payment.
(b) A dissenter waives his right to demand payment under this section unless he notifies the corporation of his demand in writing under subsection (a) within 30 days after the corporation made or offered payment for his shares.

## Subchapter C. Judicial Appraisal of Shares

### § 13.30. Court Action

(a) If a demand for payment under section 13.28 remains unsettled, the corporation shall commence a proceeding within 60 days after receiving the payment demand and petition the court to determine the fair value of the shares and accrued interest. If the corporation does not commence the proceeding within the 60-day period, it shall pay each dissenter whose demand remains unsettled the amount demanded.
(b) The corporation shall commence the proceeding in the [name or describe] court of the county where a corporation's principal office (or, if none in this state, its registered office) is located. If the corporation is a foreign corporation without a registered office in this state, it shall commence the proceeding in the county in this state where the registered office of the domestic corporation merged with or whose shares were acquired by the foreign corporation was located.
(c) The corporation shall make all dissenters (whether or not residents of this state) whose demands remain unsettled parties to the proceeding as in an action against their shares and all parties must be served with a copy of the petition. Nonresidents may be served by registered or certified mail or by publication as provided by law.
(d) The jurisdiction of the court in which the proceeding is commenced under subsection (b) is plenary and exclusive. The court may appoint one or more persons as appraisers to receive evidence and recommend decision on the question of fair value. The appraisers have the powers described in the order appointing them, or in any amendment to it. The dissenters are entitled to the same discovery rights as parties in other civil proceedings.
(e) Each dissenter made a party to the proceeding is entitled to judgment (1) for the amount, if any, by which the court finds the fair value of his shares, plus interest, exceeds the amount paid by the corporation or (2) for the fair value, plus accrued interest, of his after-acquired shares for which the corporation elected to withhold payment under section 13.27.

### § 13.31. Court Costs and Counsel Fees

(a) The court in an appraisal proceeding commenced under section 13.30 shall determine all costs of the proceeding, including the reasonable compensation and expenses of appraisers appointed by the court. The court shall assess the costs against the corporation, except that the court may assess costs against all or some of the dissenters, in amounts the court finds equitable, to the extent the court finds the dissenters acted arbitrarily, vexatiously, or not in good faith in demanding payment under section 13.28.
(b) The court may also assess the fees and expenses of counsel and experts for the respective parties, in amounts the court finds equitable:
(1) against the corporation and in favor of any or all dissenters if the court finds the corporation did not substantially comply with the requirements of sections 13.20 through 13.28; or
(2) against either the corporation or a dissenter, in favor of any other party, if the court finds that the party against whom the fees and expenses are assessed acted arbitrarily, vexatiously, or not in good faith with respect to the rights provided by this chapter.
(c) If the court finds that the services of counsel for any dissenter were of substantial benefit to other dissenters similarly situated, and that the fees for those services should not be assessed against the corporation, the court may award to these counsel reasonable fees to be paid out of the amounts awarded the dissenters who were benefited.

# CHAPTER 14. DISSOLUTION

## Subchapter A. Voluntary Dissolution

### § 14.01. Dissolution by Incorporators or Initial Directors

A majority of the incorporators or initial directors of a corporation that has not issued shares or has not commenced business may dissolve the corporation by delivering to the secretary of state for filing articles of dissolution that set forth:

(1) the name of the corporation;

(2) the date of its incorporation;

(3) either (i) that none of the corporation's shares has been issued or (ii) that the corporation has not commenced business;

(4) that no debt of the corporation remains unpaid;

(5) that the net assets of the corporation remaining after winding up have been distributed to the shareholders, if shares were issued; and

(6) that a majority of the incorporators or initial directors authorized the dissolution.

### § 14.02. Dissolution by Board of Directors and Shareholders

(a) A corporation's board of directors may propose dissolution for submission to the shareholders.

(b) For a proposal to dissolve to be adopted:

(1) the board of directors must recommend dissolution to the shareholders unless the board of directors determines that because of conflict of interest or other special circumstances it should make no recommendation and communicates the basis for its determination to the shareholders; and

(2) the shareholders entitled to vote must approve the proposal to dissolve as provided in subsection (e).

(c) The board of directors may condition its submission of the proposal for dissolution on any basis.

(d) The corporation shall notify each shareholder, whether or not entitled to vote, of the proposed shareholders' meeting in accordance with section 7.05. The notice must also state that the purpose, or one of the purposes, of the meeting is to consider dissolving the corporation.

(e) Unless the articles of incorporation or the board of directors (acting pursuant to subsection (c)) require a greater vote or a vote by voting groups, the proposal to dissolve to be adopted must be approved by a majority of all the votes entitled to be cast on that proposal.

### § 14.03. Articles of Dissolution *(Text omitted.)*

### § 14.04. Revocation of Dissolution

(a) A corporation may revoke its dissolution within 120 days of its effective date. *(Text of other subsections omitted.)*

### § 14.05. Effect of Dissolution

(a) A dissolved corporation continues its corporate existence but may not carry on any business except that appropriate to wind up and liquidate its business and affairs, including:

(1) collecting its assets;

(2) disposing of its properties that will not be distributed in kind to its shareholders;

(3) discharging or making provision for discharging its liabilities;

(4) distributing its remaining property among its shareholders according to their interests; and

(5) doing every other act necessary to wind up and liquidate its business and affairs.

(b) Dissolution of a corporation does not:

(1) transfer title to the corporation's property;

(2) prevent transfer of its shares or securities, although the authorization to dissolve may provide for closing the corporation's share transfer records;

(3) subject its directors or officers to standards of conduct different from those prescribed in chapter 8;

(4) change quorum or voting requirements for its board of directors or shareholders; change provisions for selection, resignation, or removal of its directors or officers or both; or change provisions for amending its bylaws;

(5) prevent commencement of a proceeding by or against the corporation in its corporate name;

(6) abate or suspend a proceeding pending by or against the corporation on the effective date of dissolution; or

(7) terminate the authority of the registered agent of the corporation.

### § 14.06. Known Claims Against Dissolved Corporation

(a) A dissolved corporation may dispose of the known claims against it by following the procedure described in this section.

(b) The dissolved corporation shall notify its known claimants in writing of the dissolution at any time after its effective date. The written notice must:

(1) describe information that must be included in a claim;

(2) provide a mailing address where a claim may be sent;

(3) state the deadline, which may not be fewer than 120 days from the effective date of the written

notice, by which the dissolved corporation must receive the claim; and

(4) state that the claim will be barred if not received by the deadline.

(c) A claim against the dissolved corporation is barred:

(1) if a claimant who was given written notice under subsection (b) does not deliver the claim to the dissolved corporation by the deadline;

(2) if a claimant whose claim was rejected by the dissolved corporation does not commence a proceeding to enforce the claim within 90 days from the effective date of the rejection notice.

(d) For purposes of this section, "claim" does not include a contingent liability or a claim based on an event occurring after the effective date of dissolution.

### § 14.07. Unknown Claims Against Dissolved Corporation

(a) A dissolved corporation may also publish notice of its dissolution and request that persons with claims against the corporation present them in accordance with the notice.

(b) The notice must:

(1) be published one time in a newspaper of general circulation in the county where the dissolved corporation's principal office (or, if none in this state, its registered office) is or was last located;

(2) describe the information that must be included in a claim and provide a mailing address where the claim may be sent; and

(3) state that a claim against the corporation will be barred unless a proceeding to enforce the claim is commenced within five years after the publication of the notice.

(c) If the dissolved corporation publishes a newspaper notice in accordance with subsection (b), the claim of each of the following claimants is barred unless the claimant commences a proceeding to enforce the claim against the dissolved corporation within five years after the publication date of the newspaper notice:

(1) a claimant who did not receive written notice under section 14.06;

(2) a claimant whose claim was timely sent to the dissolved corporation but not acted on;

(3) a claimant whose claim is contingent or based on an event occurring after the effective date of dissolution.

(d) A claim may be enforced under this section:

(1) against the dissolved corporation, to the extent of its undistributed assets; or

(2) if the assets have been distributed in liquidation, against a shareholder of the dissolved corporation to the extent of his pro rata share of the claim or the corporate assets distributed to him in liquidation, whichever is less, but a shareholder's total liability for all claims under this section may not exceed the total amount of assets distributed to him.

## Subchapter B. Administrative Dissolution

### § 14.20. Grounds for Administrative Dissolution

The secretary of state may commence a proceeding under section 14.21 to administratively dissolve a corporation if:

(1) the corporation does not pay within 60 days after they are due any franchise taxes or penalties imposed by this Act or other law;

(2) the corporation does not deliver its annual report to the secretary of state within 60 days after it is due;

(3) the corporation is without a registered agent or registered office in this state for 60 days or more;

(4) the corporation does not notify the secretary of state within 60 days that its registered agent or registered office has been changed, that its registered agent has resigned, or that its registered office has been discontinued; or

(5) the corporation's period of duration stated in its articles of incorporation expires.

### § 14.21. Procedure for and Effect of Administrative Dissolution

(a) If the secretary of state determines that one or more grounds exist under section 14.20 for dissolving a corporation, he shall serve the corporation with written notice of his determination under section 5.04.

(b) If the corporation does not correct each ground for dissolution or demonstrate to the reasonable satisfaction of the secretary of state that each ground determined by the secretary of state does not exist within 60 days after service of the notice is perfected under section 5.04, the secretary of state shall administratively dissolve the corporation by signing a certificate of dissolution that recites the ground or grounds for dissolution and its effective date. The secretary of state shall file the original of the certificate and serve a copy on the corporation under section 5.04.

(c) A corporation administratively dissolved continues its corporate existence but may not carry on any business except that necessary to wind up and liquidate its business and affairs under section 14.05 and notify claimants under sections 14.06 and 14.07.

(d) The administrative dissolution of a corporation does not terminate the authority of its registered agent.

### § 14.22. Reinstatement Following Administrative Dissolution

(a) A corporation administratively dissolved under section 14.21 may apply to the secretary of state for reinstatement within two years after the effective date of dissolution. The application must:

(1) recite the name of the corporation and the effective date of its administrative dissolution;

(2) state that the ground or grounds for dissolution either did not exist or have been eliminated;

(3) state that the corporation's name satisfies the requirements of section 4.01; and

(4) contain a certificate from the [taxing authority] reciting that all taxes owed by the corporation have been paid.

(b) If the secretary of state determines that the application contains the information required by subsection (a) and that the information is correct, he shall cancel the certificate of dissolution and prepare a certificate of reinstatement that recites his determination and the effective date of reinstatement, file the original of the certificate, and serve a copy on the corporation under section 5.04.

(c) When the reinstatement is effective, it relates back to and takes effect as of the effective date of the administrative dissolution and the corporation resumes carrying on its business as if the administrative dissolution had never occurred.

### § 14.23. Appeal from Denial of Reinstatement

(a) If the secretary of state denies a corporation's application for reinstatement following administrative dissolution, he shall serve the corporation under section 5.04 with a written notice that explains the reason or reasons for denial.

(b) The corporation may appeal the denial of reinstatement to the [name or describe] court within 30 days after service of the notice of denial is perfected. The corporation appeals by petitioning the court to set aside the dissolution and attaching to the petition copies of the secretary of state's certificate of dissolution, the corporation's application for reinstatement, and the secretary of state's notice of denial.

(c) The court may summarily order the secretary of state to reinstate the dissolved corporation or may take other action the court considers appropriate.

(d) The court's final decision may be appealed as in other civil proceedings.

## Subchapter C. Judicial Dissolution

### § 14.30. Grounds for Judicial Dissolution

The [name or describe court or courts] may dissolve a corporation:

(1) in a proceeding by the attorney general if it is established that:

(i) the corporation obtained its articles of incorporation through fraud; or

(ii) the corporation has continued to exceed or abuse the authority conferred upon it by law;

(2) in a proceeding by a shareholder if it is established that:

(i) the directors are deadlocked in the management of the corporate affairs, the shareholders are unable to break the deadlock, and irreparable injury to the corporation is threatened or being suffered, or the business and affairs of the corporation can no longer be conducted to the advantage of the shareholders generally, because of the deadlock;

(ii) the directors or those in control of the corporation have acted, are acting, or will act in a manner that is illegal, oppressive, or fraudulent;

(iii) the shareholders are deadlocked in voting power and have failed, for a period that includes at least two consecutive annual meeting dates, to elect successors to directors whose terms have expired; or

(iv) the corporate assets are being misapplied or wasted;

(3) in a proceeding by a creditor if it is established that:
(i) the creditor's claim has been reduced to judgment, the execution on the judgment returned unsatisfied, and the corporation is insolvent; or
(ii) the corporation has admitted in writing that the creditor's claim is due and owing and the corporation is insolvent; or

(4) in a proceeding by the corporation to have its voluntary dissolution continued under court supervision.

### § 14.31. Procedure for Judicial Dissolution

(a) Venue for a proceeding by the attorney general to dissolve a corporation lies in [name the county or counties]. Venue for a proceeding brought by any other party named in section 14.30 lies in the county where a corporation's principal office (or, if none in this state, its registered office) is or was last located.
(b) It is not necessary to make shareholders parties to a proceeding to dissolve a corporation unless relief is sought against them individually.
(c) A court in a proceeding brought to dissolve a corporation may issue injunctions, appoint a receiver or custodian pendente lite with all powers and duties the court directs, take other action required to preserve the corporate assets wherever located, and carry on the business of the corporation until a full hearing can be held.

### § 14.32. Receivership or Custodianship

(a) A court in a judicial proceeding brought to dissolve a corporation may appoint one or more receivers to wind up and liquidate, or one or more custodians to manage, the business and affairs of the corporation. The court shall hold a hearing, after notifying all parties to the proceeding and any interested persons designated by the court, before appointing a receiver or custodian. The court appointing a receiver or custodian has exclusive jurisdiction over the corporation and all its property wherever located. *(Text of other subsections omitted.)*

### § 14.33. Decree of Dissolution

(a) If after a hearing the court determines that one or more grounds for judicial dissolution described in section 14.30 exist, it may enter a decree dissolving the corporation and specifying the effective date of the dissolution, and the clerk of the court shall deliver a certified copy of the decree to the secretary of state, who shall file it.
(b) After entering the decree of dissolution, the court shall direct the winding up and liquidation of the corporation's business and affairs in accordance with section 14.05 and the notification of claimants in accordance with sections 14.06 and 14.07.

## Subchapter D. Miscellaneous

### § 14.40. Deposit with State Treasurer

Assets of a dissolved corporation that should be transferred to a creditor, claimant, or shareholder of the corporation who cannot be found or who is not competent to receive them shall be reduced to cash and deposited with the state treasurer or other appropriate state official for safekeeping. When the creditor, claimant, or shareholder furnishes satisfactory proof of entitlement to the amount deposited, the state treasurer or other appropriate state official shall pay him or his representative that amount.

# CHAPTER 15. FOREIGN CORPORATIONS

## Subchapter A. Certificate of Authority

### § 15.01. Authority to Transact Business Required

(a) A foreign corporation may not transact business in this state until it obtains a certificate of authority from the secretary of state.
(b) The following activities, among others, do not constitute transacting business within the meaning of subsection (a):

(1) maintaining, defending, or settling any proceeding;

(2) holding meetings of the board of directors or shareholders or carrying on other activities concerning internal corporate affairs;

(3) maintaining bank accounts;

(4) maintaining offices or agencies for the trans-

fer, exchange, and registration of the corporation's own securities or maintaining trustees or depositaries with respect to those securities;

(5) selling through independent contractors;

(6) soliciting or obtaining orders, whether by mail or through employees or agents or otherwise, if the orders require acceptance outside this state before they become contracts;

(7) creating or acquiring indebtedness, mortgages, and security interests in real or personal property;

(8) securing or collecting debts or enforcing mortgages and security interests in property securing the debts;

(9) owning, without more, real or personal property;

(10) conducting an isolated transaction that is completed within 30 days and that is not one in the course of repeated transactions of a like nature;

(11) transacting business in interstate commerce.

(c) The list of activities in subsection (b) is not exhaustive.

### § 15.02. Consequences of Transacting Business Without Authority

(a) A foreign corporation transacting business in this state without a certificate of authority may not maintain a proceeding in any court in this state until it obtains a certificate of authority.

(b) The successor to a foreign corporation that transacted business in this state without a certificate of authority and the assignee of a cause of action arising out of that business may not maintain a proceeding based on that cause of action in any court in this state until the foreign corporation or its successor obtains a certificate of authority.

(c) A court may stay a proceeding commenced by a foreign corporation, its successor, or assignee until it determines whether the foreign corporation or its successor requires a certificate of authority. If it so determines, the court may further stay the proceeding until the foreign corporation or its successor obtains the certificate.

(d) A foreign corporation is liable for a civil penalty of $____ for each day, but not to exceed a total of $____ for each year, it transacts business in this state without a certificate of authority. The attorney general may collect all penalties due under this subsection.

(e) Notwithstanding subsections (a) and (b), the failure of a foreign corporation to obtain a certificate of authority does not impair the validity of its corporate acts or prevent it from defending any proceeding in this state.

### § 15.03. Application for Certificate of Authority

(a) A foreign corporation may apply for a certificate of authority to transact business in this state by delivering an application to the secretary of state for filing. The application must set forth:

(1) the name of the foreign corporation or, if its name is unavailable for use in this state, a corporate name that satisfies the requirements of section 15.06;

(2) the name of the state or country under whose law it is incorporated;

(3) its date of incorporation and period of duration;

(4) the street address of its principal office;

(5) the address of its registered office in this state and the name of its registered agent at that office; and

(6) the names and usual business addresses of its current directors and officers.

(b) The foreign corporation shall deliver with the completed application a certificate of existence (or a document of similar import) duly authenticated by the secretary of state or other official having custody of corporate records in the state or country under whose law it is incorporated.

### § 15.04 Amended Certificate of Authority

(a) A foreign corporation authorized to transact business in this state must obtain an amended certificate of authority from the secretary of state if it changes:

(1) its corporate name;

(2) the period of its duration; or

(3) the state or country of its incorporation.

(b) The requirements of section 15.03 for obtaining an original certificate of authority apply to obtaining an amended certificate under this section.

### § 15.05. Effect of Certificate of Authority

(a) A certificate of authority authorizes the foreign corporation to which it is issued to transact business in this state subject, however, to the right of the state to revoke the certificate as provided in this Act.
(b) A foreign corporation with a valid certificate of authority has the same but no greater rights and has the same but no greater privileges as, and except as otherwise provided by this Act is subject to the same duties, restrictions, penalties, and liabilities now or later imposed on, a domestic corporation of like character.
(c) This Act does not authorize this state to regulate the organization or internal affairs of a foreign corporation authorized to transact business in this state.

### § 15.06. Corporate Name of Foreign Corporation

(a) If the corporate name of a foreign corporation does not satisfy the requirements of section 4.01, the foreign corporation to obtain or maintain a certificate of authority to transact business in this state:

(1) may add the word "corporation," "incorporated," "company," or "limited," or the abbreviation "corp.," "inc.," "co.," or "ltd.," to its corporate name for use in this state; or

(2) may use a fictitious name to transact business in this state if its real name is unavailable and it delivers to the secretary of state for filing a copy of the resolution of its board of directors, certified by its secretary, adopting the fictitious name.

(b) Except as authorized by subsections (c) and (d), the corporate name (including a fictitious name) of a foreign corporation must be distinguishable upon the records of the secretary of state from:

(1) the corporate name of a corporation incorporated or authorized to transact business in this state;

(2) a corporate name reserved or registered under section 4.02 or 4.03;

(3) the fictitious name of another foreign corporation authorized to transact business in this state; and

(4) the corporate name of a not-for-profit corporation incorporated or authorized to transact business in this state.

### § 15.07. Registered Office and Registered Agent of Foreign Corporation

Each foreign corporation authorized to transact business in this state must continuously maintain in this state:

(1) a registered office that may be the same as any of its places of business; and

(2) a registered agent, who may be:

(i) an individual who resides in this state and whose business office is identical with the registered office;
(ii) a domestic corporation or not-for-profit domestic corporation whose business office is identical with the registered office; or
(iii) a foreign corporation or foreign not-for-profit corporation authorized to transact business in this state whose business office is identical with the registered office.

### § 15.08. Change of Registered Office or Registered Agent of Foreign Corporation *(Text omitted.)*

### § 15.09. Resignation of Registered Agent of Foreign Corporation *(Text omitted.)*

### § 15.10. Service on Foreign Corporation

(a) The registered agent of a foreign corporation authorized to transact business in this state is the corporation's agent for service of process, notice, or demand required or permitted by law to be served on the foreign corporation.
(b) A foreign corporation may be served by registered or certified mail, return receipt requested, addressed to the secretary of the foreign corporation at its principal office shown in its application for a certificate of authority or in its most recent annual report if the foreign corporation:

(1) has no registered agent or its registered agent cannot with reasonable diligence be served;

(2) has withdrawn from transacting business in this state under section 15.20; or

(3) has had its certificate of authority revoked under section 15.31.

## Subchapter B. Withdrawal

### § 15.20. Withdrawal of Foreign Corporation

(a) A foreign corporation authorized to transact business in this state may not withdraw from this state until it obtains a certificate of withdrawal from the secretary of state. *(Text of other subsections omitted.)*

## Subchapter C. Revocation of Certificate of Authority

### § 15.30. Grounds for Revocation

The secretary of state may commence a proceeding under section 15.31 to revoke the certificate of authority of a foreign corporation authorized to transact business in this state if:

(1) the foreign corporation does not deliver its annual report to the secretary of state within 60 days after it is due;

(2) the foreign corporation does not pay within 60 days after they are due any franchise taxes or penalties imposed by this Act or other law;

(3) the foreign corporation is without a registered agent or registered office in this state for 60 days or more;

(4) the foreign corporation does not inform the secretary of state under section 15.08 or 15.09 that its registered agent or registered office has changed, that its registered agent has resigned, or that its registered office has been discontinued within 60 days of the change, resignation, or discontinuance;

(5) an incorporator, director, officer, or agent of the foreign corporation signed a document he knew was false in any material respect with intent that the document be delivered to the secretary of state for filing;

(6) the secretary of state receives a duly authenticated certificate from the secretary of state or other official having custody of corporate records in the state or country under whose law the foreign corporation is incorporated stating that it has been dissolved or disappeared as the result of a merger.

### § 15.31. Procedure for and Effect of Revocation

(a) If the secretary of state determines that one or more grounds exist under section 15.30 for revocation of a certificate of authority, he shall serve the foreign corporation with written notice of his determination under section 15.10.

(b) If the foreign corporation does not correct each ground for revocation or demonstrate to the reasonable satisfaction of the secretary of state that each ground determined by the secretary of state does not exist within 60 days after service of the notice is perfected under section 15.10, the secretary of state may revoke the foreign corporation's certificate of authority by signing a certificate of revocation that recites the ground or grounds for revocation and its effective date. The secretary of state shall file the original of the certificate and serve a copy on the foreign corporation under section 15.10.

(c) The authority of a foreign corporation to transact business in this state ceases on the date shown on the certificate revoking its certificate of authority.

(d) The secretary of state's revocation of a foreign corporation's certificate of authority appoints the secretary of state the foreign corporation's agent for service of process in any proceeding based on a cause of action which arose during the time the foreign corporation was authorized to transact business in this state. Service of process on the secretary of state under this subsection is service on the foreign corporation. Upon receipt of process, the secretary of state shall mail a copy of the process to the secretary of the foreign corporation at its principal office shown in its most recent annual report or in any subsequent communication received from the corporation stating the current mailing address of its principal office, or, if none are on file, in its application for a certificate of authority.

(e) Revocation of a foreign corporation's certificate of authority does not terminate the authority of the registered agent of the corporation.

### § 15.32. Appeal from Revocation

(a) A foreign corporation may appeal the secretary of state's revocation of its certificate of authority to the [name or describe] court within 30 days after service of the certificate of revocation is perfected under section 15.10. The foreign corporation appeals by petitioning the court to set aside the revocation and attaching to the petition copies of

its certificate of authority and the secretary of state's certificate of revocation.
(b) The court may summarily order the secretary of state to reinstate the certificate of authority or may take any other action the court considers appropriate.
(c) The court's final decision may be appealed as in other civil proceedings.

## CHAPTER 16. RECORDS AND REPORTS

### Subchapter A. Records

#### § 16.01. Corporate Records

(a) A corporation shall keep as permanent records minutes of all meetings of its shareholders and board of directors, a record of all actions taken by a committee of the board of directors in place of the board of directors on behalf of the corporation.
(b) A corporation shall maintain appropriate accounting records.
(c) A corporation or its agent shall maintain a record of its shareholders, in a form that permits preparation of a list of the names and addresses of all shareholders, in alphabetical order by class of shares showing the number and class of shares held by each.
(d) A corporation shall maintain its records in written form or in another form capable of conversion into written form within a reasonable time.
(e) A corporation shall keep a copy of the following records at its principal office:

(1) its articles or restated articles of incorporation and all amendments to them currently in effect;

(2) its bylaws or restated bylaws and all amendments to them currently in effect;

(3) resolutions adopted by its board of directors creating one or more classes or series of shares, and fixing their relative rights, preferences, and limitations, if shares issued pursuant to those resolutions are outstanding;

(4) the minutes of all shareholders' meetings, and records of all action taken by shareholders without a meeting, for the past three years;

(5) all written communications to shareholders generally within the past three years, including the financial statements furnished for the past three years under section 16.20;

(6) a list of the names and business addresses of its current directors and officers; and

(7) its most recent annual report delivered to the secretary of state under section 16.22.

#### § 16.02. Inspection of Records by Shareholders

(a) Subject to section 16.03(c), a shareholder of a corporation is entitled to inspect and copy, during regular business hours at the corporation's principal office, any of the records of the corporation described in section 16.01(e) if he gives the corporation written notice of his demand at least five business days before the date on which he wishes to inspect and copy. *(Text of other subsections omitted.)*

#### § 16.03. Scope of Inspection Right

(a) A shareholder's agent or attorney has the same inspection and copying rights as the shareholder he represents.
(b) The right to copy records under section 16.02 includes, if reasonable, the right to receive copies made by photographic, xerographic, or other means.
(c) The corporation may impose a reasonable charge, covering the costs of labor and material, for copies of any documents provided to the shareholder. The charge may not exceed the estimated cost of production or reproduction of the records.
(d) The corporation may comply with a shareholder's demand to inspect the record of shareholder's under section 16.02(b)(3) by providing him with a list of its shareholders that was compiled no earlier than the date of the shareholder's demand.

#### § 16.04 Court-Ordered Inspection

(a) If a corporation does not allow a shareholder who complies with section 16.02(a) to inspect and copy any records required by that subsection to be available for inspection, the [name or describe court] of the county where the corporation's principal office (or, if none in this state, its registered office) is located may summarily order inspection and copying of the records demanded at the corporation's expense upon application of the shareholder.

(b) If a corporation does not within a reasonable time allow a shareholder to inspect and copy any other record, the shareholder who complies with section 16.02(b) and (c) may apply to the [name or describe court] in the county where the corporation's principal office (or, if none in this state, its registered office) is located for an order to permit inspection and copying of the records demanded. The court shall dispose of an application under this subsection on an expedited basis.

(c) If the court orders inspection and copying of the records demanded, it shall also order the corporation to pay the shareholder's costs (including reasonable counsel fees) incurred to obtain the order unless the corporation proves that it refused inspection in good faith because it had a reasonable basis for doubt about the right of the shareholder to inspect the records demanded.

(d) If the court orders inspection and copying of the records demanded, it may impose reasonable restrictions on the use or distribution of the records by the demanding shareholder.

## Subchapter B. Reports

### § 16.20. Financial Statements for Shareholders

(a) A corporation shall furnish its shareholders annual financial statements, which may be consolidated or combined statements of the corporation and one or more of its subsidiaries, as appropriate, that include a balance sheet as of the end of the fiscal year, an income statement for that year, and a statement of changes in shareholders' equity for the year unless that information appears elsewhere in the financial statements. If financial statements are prepared for the corporation on the basis of generally accepted accounting principles, the annual financial statements must also be prepared on that basis.

(b) If the annual financial statements are reported upon by a public accountant, his report must accompany them. If not, the statements must be accompanied by a statement of the president or the person responsible for the corporation's accounting records:

(1) stating his reasonable belief whether the statements were prepared on the basis of generally accepted accounting principles and, if not, describing the basis of preparation; and

(2) describing any respects in which the statements were not prepared on a basis of accounting consistent with the statements prepared for the preceding year.

(c) A corporation shall mail the annual financial statements to each shareholder within 120 days after the close of each fiscal year. Thereafter, on written request from a shareholder who was not mailed the statements, the corporation shall mail him the latest financial statements.

### § 16.21. Other Reports to Shareholders

(a) If a corporation indemnifies or advances expenses to a director under section 8.51, 8.52, 8.53, or 8.54 in connection with a proceeding by or in the right of the corporation, the corporation shall report the indemnification or advance in writing to the shareholders with or before the notice of the next shareholders' meeting.

### § 16.22. Annual Report for Secretary of State

(a) Each domestic corporation, and each foreign corporation authorized to transact business in this state, shall deliver to the secretary of state for filing an annual report that sets forth:

(1) the name of the corporation and the state or country under whose law it is incorporated;

(2) the address of its registered office and the name of its registered agent at that office in this state;

(3) the address of its principal office;

(4) the names and business addresses of its directors and principal officers;

(5) a brief description of the nature of its business;

(6) the total number of authorized shares, itemized by class and series, if any, within each class; and

(7) the total number of issued and outstanding shares, itemized by class and series, if any, within each class.

(b) Information in the annual report must be current as of the date the annual report is executed on behalf of the corporation.

(c) The first annual report must be delivered to the secretary of state between January 1 and April

1 of the year following the calendar year in which a domestic corporation was incorporated or a foreign corporation was authorized to transact business. Subsequent annual reports must be delivered to the secretary of state between January 1 and April 1 of the following calendar years.

(d) If an annual report does not contain the information required by this section, the secretary of state shall promptly notify the reporting domestic or foreign corporation in writing and return the report to it for correction. If the report is corrected to contain the information required by this section and delivered to the secretary of state within 30 days after the effective date of notice, it is deemed to be timely filed.

## CHAPTER 17. TRANSITION PROVISIONS

**§ 17.01. Application to Existing Domestic Corporations** ***(Text omitted.)***

**§ 17.02. Application to Qualified Foreign Corporations** ***(Text omitted.)***

**§ 17.03. Saving Provisions** ***(Text omitted.)***

**§ 17.04. Severability** ***(Text omitted.)***

**§ 17.05. Repeal** ***(Text omitted.)***

**§ 17.06. Effective Date** ***(Text omitted.)***

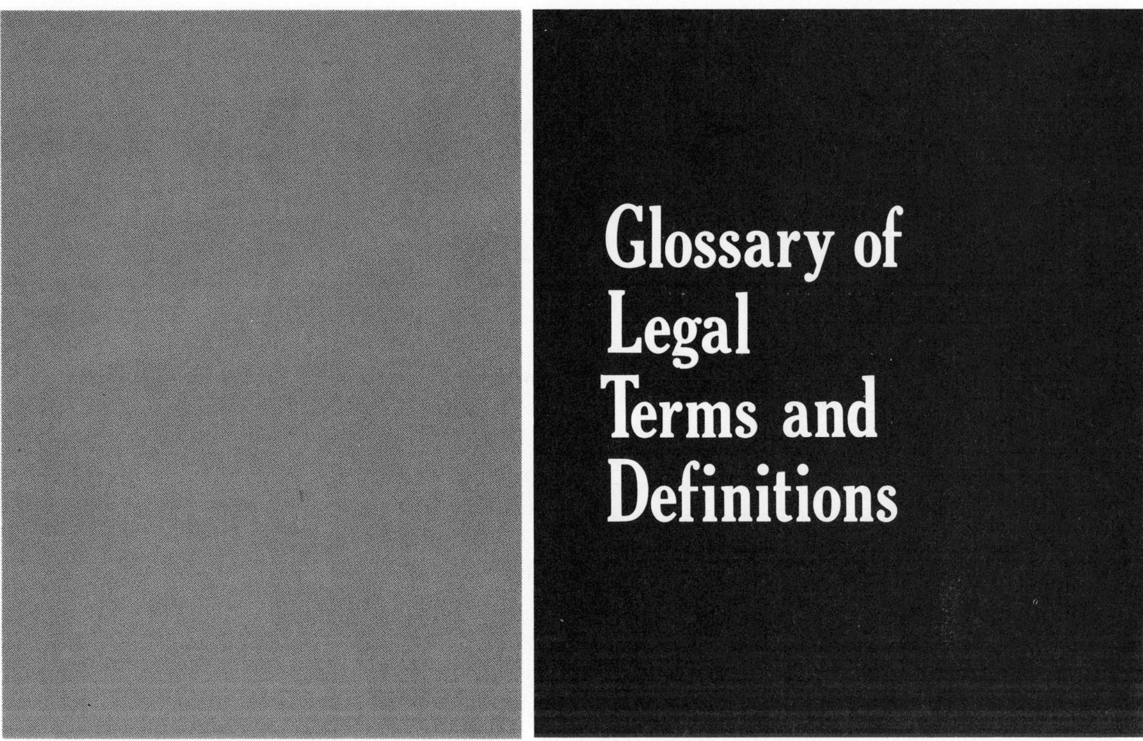

# Glossary of Legal Terms and Definitions

**abatement of nuisance.** Removal of a nuisance by court action.

**ab initio.** From the beginning. A contract which is void ab initio is void from its inception.

**absque injuria.** Without violation of a legal right.

**abstract of title.** A summary of the conveyances, transfers, and other facts relied on as evidence of title, together with all such facts appearing of record which may impair its validity. It should contain a brief but complete history of the title.

**abutting owners.** Those owners whose lands touch.

**acceleration.** The shortening of the time for the performance of a contract or the payment of a note by the operation of some provision in the contract or note itself.

**acceptance.** The actual or implied receipt and retention of that which is tendered or offered. The acceptance of an offer is the assent to an offer which is requisite to the formation of a contract. It is either express or evidenced by circumstances from which such assent may be implied.

**accession.** In its legal meaning it is generally used to signify the acquisition of property by its incorporation or union with other property.

**accommodation paper.** A negotiable instrument signed without consideration by a party as acceptor, drawer, or indorser for the purpose of enabling the payee to obtain credit.

**accord and satisfaction.** The adjustment of a disagreement as to what is due from one person to another, and the payment of the agreed amount.

**account stated.** An account which has been rendered by one to another and which purports to state the true balance due and which balance is either expressly or impliedly admitted to be due by the debtor.

**acknowledgment.** A form for authenticating instruments conveying property or otherwise conferring rights. It is a public declaration by the grantor that the act evidenced by the instrument is his act and deed. Also an admission or confirmation.

**acquit.** To set free or judicially to discharge from an accusation; to release from a debt, duty, obligation, charge or suspicion of guilt.

**act of God.** An occurrence resulting exclusively from natural forces which could not have been prevented or whose effects could not have been avoided by care or foresight.

**action ex contractu.** An action arising out of the breach of a contract.

**action ex delicto.** An action arising out of the violation of a duty or obligation created by positive law independent of contract. An action in tort.

**actionable.** Remedial by an action at law.

**ad litem.** During the pendency of the action or proceeding.

**adjudge.** To give judgment; to decide; to sentence.

**adjudicate.** To adjudge; to settle by judicial decree; to hear or try and determine, as a court.

**administrator.** A man appointed by a probate court to settle the estate of a deceased person. His duties are customarily defined by statute. If a woman is appointed she is called the administratrix.

**adverse possession.** Open and notorious possession of real property over a given length of time which denies ownership in any other claimant.

**advisement.** When a court takes a case under advisement it delays its decision until it has examined and considered the questions involved.

**affidavit.** A statement or declaration reduced to writing and sworn or affirmed to before an officer who has authority to administer an oath or affirmation.

**affirm.** To confirm a former judgment or order of a court. Also to declare solemnly instead of making a sworn statement.

**agent.** An agent is the substitute or representative of his principal and derives his authority from him.

**aggrieved.** One whose legal rights have been invaded by the act of another is said to be aggrieved. Also one whose pecuniary interest is directly affected by a judgment, or whose right of property may be divested thereby, is to be considered a party aggrieved.

**alienation.** The voluntary act or acts by which one person transfers his or her own property to another.

**aliquot.** Strictly, forming an exact proper divisor, but treated as meaning fractional when applied to trusts, etc.

**allegation.** A declaration, a formal averment or statement of a party to an action in a declaration or pleading of what the party intends to prove.

**allege.** To make a statement of fact; to plead.

**amortize.** In modern usage the word means to provide for the payment of a debt by creating a sinking fund or paying in installments.

**ancillary.** Auxiliary to. An ancillary receiver is a receiver who has been appointed in aid of, and in subordination to, the primary receiver.

**answer.** The pleading of a defendant in which he or she may deny any or all the facts set out in the plaintiff's declaration or complaint.

**anticipatory breach.** The doctrine of the law of contracts that when the promisor has repudiated the contract before the time of performance has arrived the promisee may sue forthwith.

**appearance.** The first act of the defendant in court.

**appellant.** A person who files an appeal.

**appellate jurisdiction.** Jurisdiction to revise or correct the work of a subordinate court.

**appellee.** A party against whom a cause is appealed from a lower court to a higher court, called the "respondent" in some jurisdictions.

**applicant.** A petitioner; one who files a petition or application.

**appurtenance.** An accessory; something that belongs to another thing; e.g., buildings are appurtenant to the land and a bar would be appurtenant to a tavern.

**arbitrate.** To submit some disputed matter to selected persons and to accept their decision or award as a substitute for the decision of a judicial tribunal.

**argument.** The discussion by counsel for the respective parties of their contentions on the law and the facts of the case being tried in order to aid the jury in arriving at a correct and just conclusion.

**assent.** To give or express one's concurrence or approval of something done. Assent does not include consent.

**assignable.** Capable of being lawfully assigned or transferred; transferable; negotiable. Also capable of being specified or pointed out as an assignable error.

**assignee.** A person to whom an assignment is made.

**assignment.** A transfer or setting over of property or some right or interest therein, from one person to another. In its ordinary application the word is limited to the transfer of choses in action, e.g., the assignment of a contract.

**assignor.** The maker of an assignment.

**assumpsit.** An action at common law to recover damages for breach of contract.

**attachment.** Taking property into the legal custody of an officer by virtue of the directions contained in a writ of attachment. A seizure under a writ of a debtor's property.

**attest.** To bear witness to; to affirm; to be true or genuine.

**attorney-in-fact.** A person who is authorized by his principal, either for some particular purpose, or to do a particular act, not of a legal character.

**authentication.** Such official attestation of a written instrument as will render it legally admissible in evidence.

**authority.** Judicial or legislative precedent; delegated power; warrant.

**averment.** A positive statement of fact made in a pleading.

**avoidable.** Capable of being nullified or made void.

**bad faith.** The term imports a person's actual intent to mislead or deceive another; an intent to take an unfair and unethical advantage of another.

**bailee.** The person to whom a bailment is made.

**bailment.** A delivery of personal property by one person to another in trust for a specific purpose, with a contract, express or implied, that the trust shall be faithfully executed and the property returned or duly accounted for when the special purpose is accomplished, or kept until the bailor reclaims it.

**bailor.** The maker of a bailment; one who delivers personal property to another to be held in bailment.

**bankruptcy.** The state of a person who is unable to pay his or her debts without respect to time; one whose liabilities exceed his or her assets.

**bar.** As a collective noun it is used to include those persons who are admitted to practice law, members of the bar. The court itself. A plea or peremptory exception of a defendant sufficient to destroy the plaintiff's action.

**barratry.** The habitual stirring up of quarrels and suits; a single act would not constitute the offense.

**bearer.** The designation of the bearer as the payee of a negotiable instrument signifies that the instrument is payable to the person who seems to be the holder.

**bench.** A court; the judges of a court; the seat

upon which the judges of a court are accustomed to sit while the court is in session.

**beneficiary.** The person for whose benefit an insurance policy, trust, will, or contract is established but not the promisee. In the case of a contract, the beneficiary is called a *third-party beneficiary.* A *donee beneficiary* is one who is not a party to a contract but who receives the promised performance as a gift. A *creditor beneficiary* is one who is not a party to a contract but receives the performance in discharge of a debt owed by the promisee to him.

**bequeath.** Commonly used to denote a testamentary gift of real estate; synonymous with "to devise."

**bid.** To make an offer at an auction or at a judicial sale. As a noun it means an offer.

**bilateral contract.** A contract in which the promise of one of the parties forms the consideration for the promise of the other; a contract formed by an offer requiring a reciprocal promise.

**bill of exchange.** An unconditional order in writing by one person to another, signed by the person giving it, requiring the person to whom it is addressed to pay on demand or at a fixed or determinable future time a sum certain in money to order or to bearer.

**bill or lading.** A written acknowledgment of the receipt of goods to be transported to a designated place and delivery to a named person or to his or her order.

**bill of sale.** A written agreement by which one person assigns or transfers interests or rights in personal property to another.

**binder.** Also called a binding slip—a brief memorandum or agreement issued by an insurer as a temporary policy for the convenience of all the parties, constituting a present insurance in the amount specified, to continue in force until the execution of a formal policy.

**"blue sky" laws.** A popular name for statutes regulating the sale of securities and intended to protect investors against fraudulent and visionary schemes.

**bona fide.** Good faith.

**bond.** A promise under seal to pay money.

**breaking bulk.** The division or separation of the contents of a package or container.

**brief.** A statement of a party's case; usually an abridgement of either the plaintiff's or defendant's case prepared by his or her attorneys for use of counsel on a trial at law. Also an abridgement of a reported case.

**broker.** An agent who bargains or carries on negotiations in behalf of the principal as an intermediary between the latter and third persons in transacting business relative to the acquisition of contractual rights, or to the sale or purchase of property the custody of which is not intrusted to him or her for the purpose of discharging the agency.

**bulk transfer.** The sale or transfer of a major part of the stock of goods of a merchant at one time and not in the ordinary course of business.

**burden of proof.** The necessity or obligation of affirmatively proving the fact or facts in dispute on an issue raised in a suit in court.

**bylaw.** A rule or law of a corporation for its government. It includes all self-made regulations of a corporation affecting its business and members which do not operate on third persons, or in any way affect their rights.

**call.** A notice of a meeting to be held by the stockholders or board of directors of a corporation. Also a demand for payment. In securities trading, a negotiable option contract granting the bearer the right to buy a certain quantity of a particular security at the agreed price on or before the agreed date.

**cancellation.** The act of crossing out a writing. The operation of destroying a written instrument.

**caption.** The heading or title of a document.

**carte blanche.** A signed blank instrument intended by the signer to be filled in and used by another person without restriction.

**case law.** The law extracted from decided cases.

**cashier's check.** A bill of exchange, drawn by a bank upon itself, and accepted by the act of issuance.

**cause of action.** A right of action at law arises from the existence of a primary right in the plaintiff, and an invasion of that right by some civil wrong on the part of the defendant, and that the facts which establish the existence of that right and that civil wrong constitute the cause of action.

**caveat emptor.** Let the buyer beware. This maxim expresses the general idea that the buyer purchases at his peril, and that there are no warranties, either express or implied, made by the seller.

**caveat venditor.** Let the seller beware. It is not accepted as a rule of law in the law of sales.

**certification.** The return of a writ; a formal attestation of a matter of fact; the appropriate marking of a certified check.

**certified check.** A check which has been "accepted" by the drawee bank and has been so marked or certified that it indicates such acceptance.

**cestui que trust.** The person for whose benefit property is held in trust by a trustee.

**champerty.** The purchase of an interest in a matter in dispute so as to take part in the litigation.

**chancellor.** A judge of a court of chancery.

**chancery.** Equity or a court of equity.

**charge.** To charge a jury is to instruct the jury as to the essential law of the case. The first step in the prosecution of a crime is to formally accuse the offender or charge him with the crime.

**charter.** An instrument or authority from the sovereign power bestowing the right or power to do business under the corporate form of organization. Also the organic law of a city or town, and representing a portion of the statute law of the state.

**chattel.** An article of tangible property other than land.

**chattel mortgage.** An instrument whereby the owner of chattels transfers the title to such property to another as security for the performance of an obligation subject to be defeated on the performance of the obligation. Under the U.C.C. called merely a security interest.

**chattel real.** Interests in real estate less than a freehold, such as an estate for years.

**check.** A written order on a bank or banker payable on demand to the person named or his order or bearer and drawn by virtue of credits due the drawer from the bank created by money deposited with the bank.

**chose in action.** A personal right not reduced to possession but recoverable by a suit at law.

**c.i.f.** An abbreviation for cost, freight, and insurance, used in mercantile transactions, especially in import transactions.

**citation.** A writ issued out of a court of competent jurisdiction, commanding the person therein named to appear on a day named to do something therein mentioned.

**citation of authorities.** The reference to legal authorities such as reported cases or treatises to support propositions advanced.

**civil action.** An action brought to enforce a civil right; in contrast to a criminal action.

**class action.** An action brought on behalf of the plaintiff and others similarly situated.

**close corporation.** A corporation in which directors and officers, rather than the shareholders, have the right to fill vacancies occurring in their ranks. Also used to refer to any corporation whose stock is not freely traded and whose shareholders are personally known to each other.

**c.o.d. "Cash on delivery."** When goods are delivered to a carrier for a cash on delivery shipment the carrier must not deliver without receiving payment of the amount due.

**code.** A system of law; a systematic and complete body of law.

**codicil.** Some addition to or qualification of one's last will and testament.

**cognovit.** To acknowledge an action. A cognovit note is a promissory note which contains an acknowledgement clause.

**collateral attack.** An attempt to impeach a decree, a judgment or other official act in a proceeding which has not been instituted for the express purpose of correcting or annulling or modifying the decree, judgment or official act.

**comaker.** A person who with another or others signs a negotiable instrument on its face and thereby becomes primarily liable for its payment.

**commercial law.** The law which relates to the rights of property and persons engaged in trade or commerce.

**commission merchant.** A person who sells goods in his own name at his own store, and on commission, from sample. Also one who buys and sells goods for a principal in his own name and without disclosing his principal.

**common carrier.** One who undertakes, for hire or reward, to transport the goods of such of the public as choose to employ him.

**compensatory damages.** See **damages.**

**complaint.** A form of legal process which usually consists of a formal allegation or charge against a party, made or presented to the appropriate court or officer. The technical name of a bill in equity by which the complainant sets out his cause of action.

**composition with creditors.** An agreement between creditors and their common debtor and between themselves whereby the creditors agree to accept the sum or security stipulated in full payment of their claims.

**concurrent.** Running with, simultaneously with. The word is used in different senses. In contracts concurrent conditions are conditions which must be performed simultaneously by the mutual acts required by each of the parties.

**condemn.** To appropriate land for public use. To adjudge a person guilty; to pass sentence upon a person convicted of a crime.

**condition.** A provision or clause in a contract which operates to suspend or rescind the principal obligation. A qualification or restriction annexed to a conveyance of lands, whereby it is provided that in the case a particular event does or does not happen, or in case the grantor or grantees do or omit to do a particular act, an estate shall commence, be enlarged or be defeated.

**condition precedent.** A condition which must happen before either party is bound by the principal obligation of a contract; e.g., one agrees to purchase goods if they are delivered before a stated day. Delivery before the stated day is a condition precedent to one's obligation to purchase.

**condition subsequent.** A condition which operates to relieve or discharge one from his obligation under a contract.

**conditional acceptance.** An acceptance of a bill of exchange containing some qualification limiting or altering the acceptor's liability on the bill.

**conditional sale.** The term is most frequently applied to a sale wherein the seller reserves the title to the goods, though the possession is delivered to the buyer, until the purchase price is paid in full.

**confession of judgment.** An entry of judgment upon the admission or confession of the debtor without the formality, time, or expense involved in an ordinary proceeding.

**conservator (of an insane person).** A person appointed by a court to take care of and oversee the person and estate of an idiot or other incompetent person.

**consignee.** A person to whom goods are consigned, shipped, or otherwise transmitted, either for sale or for safekeeping.

**consignment.** A bailment for sale. The consignee does not undertake the absolute obligation to sell or pay for the goods.

**consignor.** One who sends goods to another on consignment; a shipper or transmitter of goods.

**construe.** To read a statute or document for the purpose of ascertaining its meaning and effect but in doing so the law must be regarded.

**contempt.** Conduct in the presence of a legislative or judicial body tending to disturb its proceedings, or impair the respect due to its authority or a disobedience to the rules or orders of such a body which interferes with the due administration of law.

**contra.** Otherwise; disagreeing with; contrary to.

**contra bonos mores.** Contrary to good morals.

**contribution.** A payment made by each, or by any, of several having a common interest or liability of his share in the loss suffered, or in the money necessarily paid by one of the parties in behalf of the others.

**conversion.** Any distinct act of dominion wrongfully exerted over another's personal property in denial of or inconsistent with his rights therein. That tort which is committed by a person who deals with chattels not belonging to him in a manner which is inconsistent with the ownership of the lawful owner.

**conveyance.** In its common use it refers to a written instrument transferring the title to land or some interest therein from one person to another. It is sometimes applied to the transfer of the property in personalty.

**copartnership.** A partnership.

**corporation.** An artificial being, invisible, intangible and existing only in contemplation of law. It is exclusively the work of the law, and the best evidence of its existence is the grant of corporate powers by the commonwealth.

**corporeal.** Possessing physical substance; tangible; perceptible to the senses.

**counterclaim.** A claim which, if established, will defeat or in some way qualify a judgment to which the plaintiff is otherwise entitled.

**counteroffer.** A cross offer made by the offeree to the offeror.

**covenant.** The word is used in its popular sense as synonymous to contract. In its specific sense it ordinarily imparts an agreement reduced to writing, and executed by a sealing and delivery.

**covenantor.** A person who makes a covenant.

**coverture.** The condition of a married woman.

**credible.** As applied to a witness the word means competent.

**cross-action.** Cross-complaint; an independent action brought by a defendant against the plaintiff.

**culpable.** Blameworthy; denotes breach of legal duty but not criminal conduct.

**cumulative voting.** A method of voting by which an elector entitled to vote for several candidates for the same office may cast more than one vote for the same candidate, distributing among the candidates as he chooses a number of votes equal to the number of candidates to be elected.

**custody.** The bare control or care of a thing as distinguished from the possession of it.

**damages.** Indemnity to the person who suffers loss or harm from an injury; a sum recoverable as amends for a wrong. An adequate compensation for the loss suffered or the injury sustained.

**compensatory.** Damages that will compensate a party for direct losses due to an injury suffered.

**consequential.** Damages which are not produced without the concurrence of some other event attributable to the same origin or cause.

**liquidated.** Damages made certain by the prior agreement of the parties.

**nominal.** Damages which are recoverable where a legal right is to be vindicated against an invasion which has produced no actual present loss.

**special.** Actual damages that would not necessarily but because of special circumstances do in fact flow from an injury.

**date of issue.** As the term is applied to notes, bonds, etc., of a series, it usually means the arbitrary date fixed as the beginning of the term for which they run, without reference to the precise time when convenience or the state of the market may permit of their sale or delivery.

**d/b/a.** Doing business as; indicates the use of a trade name.

**deal.** To engage in transactions of any kind, to do business with.

**debenture.** A written acknowledgment of a debt; specifically an instrument under seal for the repayment of money lent.

**debtor.** A person who owes another anything, or who is under obligation, arising from express agreement, implication of law, or from the principles of natural justice, to render and pay a sum of money to another.

**deceit.** A tort involving intentional misrepresentation or cheating by means of some device.

**decision.** A decision is the judgment of a court, while the opinion represents merely the reasons for that judgment.

**declaration.** The pleadings by which a plaintiff in an action at law sets out his cause of action. An admission or statement subsequently used as evidence in the trial of an action.

**declaratory judgment.** One which expresses the opinion of a court on a question of law without ordering anything to be done.

**decree.** An order or sentence of a court of equity determining some right or adjudicating some matter affecting the merits of the cause.

**deed.** A writing, sealed and delivered by the parties; an instrument conveying real property.

**de facto.** In fact as distinguished from "de jure," by right.

**de jure.** By right; complying with the law in all respects.

**de minimis non curat lex.** The law is not concerned with trifles. The maxim has been applied to exclude the recovery of nominal damages where no unlawful intent or disturbance of a right of possession is shown, and where all possible damage is expressly disproved.

**de novo, trial.** Anew; over again; a second time. A trial de novo is a new trial in which the entire case is retried in all its detail.

**defalcation.** The word includes both embezzlement and misappropriation and is a broader term than either.

**default.** Fault; neglect; omission; the failure of a party to an action to appear when properly served with process; the failure to perform a duty or obligation; the failure of a person to pay money when due or when lawfully demanded.

**defeasible (of title to property).** Capable of being defeated. A title to property which is open to attack or which may be defeated by the performance of some act.

**defend.** To oppose a claim or action; to plead in defense of an action; to contest an action suit or proceeding.

**defendant.** A party sued in a personal action.

**defendant in error.** Any of the parties in whose favor a judgment was rendered which the losing party seeks to have reversed or modified by writ of error and whom he names as adverse parties.

**deficiency.** That part of a debt which a mortgage was made to secure, not realized by the liquidation of the mortgaged property. Something which is lacking.

**defraud.** To deprive another of a right by deception or artifice. To cheat; to wrong another by fraud.

**dehors.** Outside of; disconnected with; unrelated to.

**del credere agent.** An agent who guarantees his principal against the default of those with whom contracts are made.

**deliver.** To surrender property to another person.

**demand.** A claim; a legal obligation; a request to perform an alleged obligation; a written statement of a claim.

**demurrage.** A compensation for the delay of a vessel beyond the time allowed for loading, unloading, or sailing. It is also applied to the compensation for the similar delay of a railroad car.

**demurrer.** A motion to dismiss; an allegation in pleading to the effect that even if the facts alleged by the opposing party are true, they are insufficient to require an answer.

**dependent covenants.** Covenants made by two parties to a deed or agreement which are such that the thing covenanted or promised to be done on each part enters into the whole consideration for the covenant or promise on the part of the other, or such covenants as are concurrent, and to be performed at the same time. Neither party to such a covenant can maintain an action against the other without averring and proving performance on his part.

**deposition.** An affidavit; an oath; the written testimony of a witness given in the course of a judicial proceeding, either at law or in equity, in response to interrogatories either oral or written, and where an opportunity is given for cross-examination.

**deputy.** A person subordinate to a public officer whose business and object is to perform the duties of the principal.

**derivative action.** A suit by a shareholder to enforce a corporate cause of action.

**descent.** Hereditary succession. It is the title whereby a person on the death of an ancestor acquires the ancestor's estate by right of representation as heir at law.

**detinue.** A common-law action, now seldom used, which lies where a party claims the specific recovery of goods and chattels unlawfully detained from him.

**detriment.** A detriment is any act or forebearance by a promisee. A loss or harm suffered in person or property.

**dictum.** The opinion of a judge which does not embody the resolution or determination of the court and is made without argument, or full consideration of the point, and is not the professed deliberation of the judge himself.

**directed verdict.** A verdict which the jury returns as directed by the court. The court may thus withdraw the case from the jury whenever there is no competent, relevant and material evidence to support the issue.

**discharge in bankruptcy.** An order or decree rendered by a court in bankruptcy proceedings, the effect of which is to satisfy all debts provable against the estate of the brankrupt as of the time when the bankruptcy proceedings were initiated.

**discount.** A loan upon an evidence of debt, where the compensation for the use of the money until the maturity of the debt is deducted from the principal and retained by the lender at the time of making the loan.

**dismiss.** To order a cause, motion, or prosecution to be discontinued or quashed.

**diverse citizenship.** A term of frequent use in the interpretation of the federal constitutional provision for the jurisdiction of the federal courts which extends it to controversies between citizens of different states.

**divided court.** A court is so described when there has been a division of opinion between its members on a matter which has been submitted to it for decision.

**dividend.** A gain or profit. A fund which a corporation sets apart from its profits to be divided among its members.

**domain.** The ownership of land; immediate or absolute ownership. The public lands of a state are frequently termed the public domain.

**domicile.** A place where a person lives or has his home; in a strict legal sense, the place where he has his true, fixed, permanent home and principal establishment, and to which place he has whenever he is absent, the intention of returning.

**dominion (property).** The rights of dominion or property are those rights which a man may acquire in and to such external things as are unconnected with his body.

**donee.** A person to whom a gift is made.

**donor.** A person who makes a gift.

**dower.** The legal right or interest which his wife acquires by marriage in the real estate of her husband.

**draft.** A written order drawn upon one person by another, requesting him to pay money to a designated third person. A bill of exchange payable on demand.

**drawee.** A person upon whom a draft or bill of exchange is drawn by the drawer.

**drawer.** The maker of a draft or bill of exchange.

**due bill.** An acknowledgment of a debt in writing, not made payable to order.

**dummy.** One posing or represented as acting for himself, but in reality acting for another. A tool or "straw man" for the real parties in interest.

**duress.** Overpowering of the will of a person by force or fear.

**earnest.** Something given as part of the purchase price to bind the bargain.

**easement.** The right which one person has to use the land of another for a specific purpose.

**edict.** A command or prohibition promulgated by a sovereign and having the effect of law.

**effects.** As used in wills, the word is held equivalent to personal property. It denotes property in a more extensive sense than goods and includes all kinds of personal property but will be held not to include real property, unless the context discloses an intention on the part of the testator to dispose of his realty by the use of the word.

**e.g.** An abbreviation for "exempli gratia," meaning for or by the way of example.

**ejectment.** By statute in some states, it is an action to recover the immediate possession of real property. At common law, it was a purely possessory action, and as modified by statute, though based upon title, it is still essentially a possessory action.

**eleemosynary corporation.** A corporation created for a charitable purpose or for charitable purposes.

**emancipate.** To release; to set free. Where a father expressly or impliedly by his conduct waives his right generally to the services of his minor child, the child is said to be emancipated and he may sue on contracts made by him for his services.

**embezzlement.** A statutory offense consisting of the fraudulent conversion of another's personal property by one to whom it has been intrusted, with the intention of depriving the owner thereof, the gist of the offense being usually the violation of relations of fiduciary character.

**encumbrance.** An encumbrance on land is a right in a third person in the land to the diminution of the value of the land, though consistent with the passing of the fee by the deed of conveyance.

**endorsement.** See **indorsement.**

**entry.** Recordation; noting in a record; going upon land; taking actual possession of land.

**eo nominee.** By or in that name or designation.

**equity.** A system of justice that developed in England separate from the common-law courts. Few states in the United States still maintain separate equity courts though most apply equity principles and procedures when remedies derived from the equity courts are sought. A broader meaning denotes fairness and justice.

**error.** A mistake of law or fact; a mistake of the court in the trial of an action.

**escheat.** The revision of land to the state in the event there is no person competent to inherit it.

**estate.** Technically the word refers only to an interest in land.

**estate at will.** A lease of lands or tenements to be held at the will of the lessor. Such can be determined by either party.

**estate for a term.** An estate less than a freehold which is in fact a contract for the possession of land or tenements for some determinate period.

**estate for life.** An estate created by deed or grant conveying land or tenements to a person to hold for the term of his own life or for the life of any other person or for more lives than one.

**estate in fee simple.** An absolute inheritance, clear of any conditions, limitations or restrictions to particular heirs. It is the highest estate known to the law and necessarily implies absolute dominion over the land.

**estate per autre vie.** An estate which is to endure for the life of another person than the grantee, or for the lives of more than one, in either of which cases the grantee is called the tenant for life.

**estop.** To bar or stop.

**estoppel.** That state of affairs which arises when one is forbidden by law from alleging or denying a fact because of his previous action or inaction.

**et al.** An abbreviation for the Latin "et alius" meaning "and another" also of "et alii" meaning "an others."

**et ux.** An abbreviation for the Latin "et uxor" meaning "and his wife."

**eviction.** Originally, as applied to tenants, the word meant depriving the tenant of the possession of the demised premises, but technically, it is the disturbance of his possession, depriving him of the enjoyment of the premises demised or any portion thereof by title paramount or by entry and act of the landlord.

**evidence.** That which makes clear or ascertains the truth of the fact or point in issue either on the one side or the other; those rules of law whereby we determine what testimony is to be admitted and what rejected in each case and what is the weight to be given to the testimony admitted.

**exception.** An objection; a reservation; a contradiction.

**ex contractu.** From or out of a contract.

**ex delicto.** From or out of a wrongful act; tortious; tortiously.

**exculpatory clause.** A clause in a contract or trust instrument that excuses a party from some duty.

**executed.** When applied to written instruments the word is sometimes used as synonymous with the word "signed" and means no more than that, but more frequently it imports that everything has been done to complete the transaction; that is that the instrument has been signed, sealed, and delivered. An executed contract is one in which the object of the contract is performed.

**execution.** A remedy in the form of a writ or process afforded by law for the enforcement of a judgment. The final consummation of a contract of sale, including only those acts which are necessary to the full completion of an instrument, such as the signature of the seller, the affixing of his seal and its delivery to the buyer.

**executor.** A person who is designated in a will as one who is to administer the estate of the testator.

**executory.** Not yet executed; not yet fully performed, completed, fulfilled or carried out; to be performed wholly or in part.

**executrix.** Feminine of executor.

**exemption.** A release from some burden, duty or obligation; a grace; a favor; an immunity; taken out from under the general rule, not to be like others who are not exempt.

**exhibit.** A copy of a written instrument on which a pleading is founded, annexed to the pleading and by reference made a part of it. Any paper or thing offered in evidence and marked for identification.

**face value.** The nominal or par value of an instrument as expressed on its face; in the case of a bond this is the amount really due, including interest.

**factor.** An agent who is employed to sell goods for a principal, usually in his own name, and who is given possession of the goods.

**f.a.s.** An abbreviation for the expression "free alongside steamer."

**fee simple absolute.** Same as fee simple. See **estate in fee simple.**

**felony.** As a general rule all crimes punishable by death or by imprisonment in a state prison are felonies.

**feme covert.** A married woman.

**feme sole.** An unmarried woman.

**fiction.** An assumption made by the law that something is true which is or may be false.

**fiduciary.** One who holds goods in trust for another or one who holds a position of trust and confidence.

**fieri facias.** You cause to be made—an ordinary writ of execution whereby the officer is commanded to levy and sell and to "make," if he can, the amount of the judgment creditors demand.

**fixture.** A thing which was originally a personal chattel and which has been actually or constructively affixed to the soil itself or to some structure legally a part of the land.

**f.o.b.** An abbreviation of "free on board."

**forwarder.** A person who, having no interest in goods and no ownership or interest in the means of their carriage, undertakes, for hire, to forward them by a safe carrier to their destination.

**franchise.** A special privilege conferred by government upon individuals, and which does not belong to the citizens of a country generally, of common right. Also a contractual relationship establishing a means of marketing goods or services giving certain elements of control to the supplier (franchiser) in return for the right of the franchisee to use the supplier's tradename or trademark, usually in a specific marketing area.

**fungible goods.** Goods any unit of which is from its nature or by mercantile custom treated as the equivalent of any other unit.

**futures.** Contracts for the sale and future delivery of stocks or commodities, wherein either party may waive delivery, and receive or pay, as the case may be, the difference in market price at the time set for delivery.

**garnishee.** As a noun, the term signifies the person upon whom a garnishment is served, usually a debtor of the defendant in the action. Used as a verb, the word means to institute garnishment proceedings; to cause a garnishment to be levied on the garnishee.

**garnishment.** The term denotes a proceeding whereby property, money, or credits of a debtor in possession of another, the garnishee, are applied to the payment of the debts by means of process against the debtor and the garnishee. It is a statutory proceeding based upon contract relations, and can only be resorted to where it is authorized by statute.

**general issue.** A plea of the defendant amounting to a denial of every material allegation of fact in the plaintiff's complaint or declaration.

**going business.** An establishment which is still continuing to transact its ordinary business, though it may be insolvent.

**good faith.** An honest intention to abstain from taking an unfair advantage of another.

**grantee.** A person to whom a grant is made.

**grantor.** A person who makes a grant.

**gravamen.** Gist, essence; substance. The grievance complained of; the substantial cause of the action.

**guarantor.** A person who promises to answer for the debt, default or miscarriage of another.

**guaranty.** An undertaking by one person to be answerable for the payment of some debt, or the due performance of some contract or duty by another person, who remains liable to pay or perform the same.

**guardian.** A person (in some rare cases a corporation) to whom the law has entrusted the custody and control of the person, or estate, or both, of an infant, lunatic or incompetent person.

**habeas corpus.** Any of several common-law writs having as their object to bring a party before the court or judge. The only issue it presents is whether the prisoner is restrained of his liberty by due process.

**habendum.** The second part of a deed or conveyance following that part which names the grantee. It describes the estate conveyed and to what use. It is no longer essential and if included in a modern deed is a mere useless form.

**hearing.** The supporting of one's contentions by argument and if need be by proof. It is an absolute right and if denied to a contestant it would amount to the denial of one of his constitutional rights.

**hedging.** A market transaction in which a party buys a certain quantity of a given commodity at the price current on the date of the purchase and sells an equal quantity of the same commodity for future delivery for the purpose of getting protection against loss due to fluctuation in the market.

**heirs.** Those persons appointed by law to succeed to the real estate of a decedent, in case of intestacy.

**hereditaments.** A larger and more comprehensive word than either "land" or "tenements," and meaning anything capable of being inherited, whether it be real, personal, or mixed property.

**holder in due course.** A holder who has taken a negotiable instrument under the following conditions;

(1) That it is complete and regular on its face; (2) that he became the holder of it before it was overdue, and without notice that it had been previously dishonored, if such was the fact; (3) that he took it in good faith and for value; (4) that at the time it was negotiated to him he had no notice of any infirmity in the instrument or defect in the title of the person negotiating it.

**holding company.** A corporation whose purpose

or function is to own or otherwise hold the shares of other corporations either for investment or control.

**homestead.** In a legal sense the word means the real estate occupied as a home and also the right to have it exempt from levy and forced sale. It is the land, not exceeding the prescribed amount, upon which the dwelling house, or residence, or habitation, or abode of the owner thereof and his family resides, and includes the dwelling house as an indispensable part.

**illusory.** Deceiving or intending to deceive, as by false appearances; fallacious. An illusory promise is a promise which appears to be binding but which in fact does not bind the promisor.

**immunity.** A personal favor granted by law, contrary to the general rule.

**impanel.** To place the names of the jurors on a panel; to make a list of the names of those persons who have been selected for jury duty; to go through the process of selecting a jury which is to try a cause.

**implied warranty.** An implied warranty arises by operation of law and exists without any intention of the seller to create it. It is a conclusion or inference of law, pronounced by the court, on facts admitted or proved before the jury.

**in banc.** With all the judges of the court sitting.

**in camera.** In the judge's chambers; in private.

**in pari delicto.** Equally at fault in tort or crime; in equal fault or guilt.

**in personam.** Against the person.

**in re.** In the matter; in the transaction.

**in rem.** Against a thing and not against a person; concerning the condition or status of a thing.

**in statu quo.** In the existing state of things.

**in toto.** In the whole, altogether; wholly.

**in transitu.** On the journey. Goods are as a rule considered as in transitu while they are in the possession of a carrier, whether by land or water, until they arrive at the ultimate place of their destination and are delivered into the actual possession of the buyer, whether or not the carrier has been named or designated by the buyer.

**inalienable.** Incapable of being alienated, transferred, or conveyed; nontransferrable.

**incapacity.** In its legal meaning it applies to one's legal disability, such as infancy, want of authority, or other personal incapacity to alter legal relationship.

**inception.** Initial stage. The word does not refer to a state of actual existence but to a condition of things or circumstances from which the thing may develop; as the beginning of work on a building.

**inchoate.** Imperfect; incipient; not completely formed.

**indemnify.** To hold harmless against loss or damage.

**indemnity.** An obligation or duty resting on one person to make good any loss or damage another has incurred while acting at his request or for his benefit. By a contract of indemnity one may agree to save another from a legal consequence of the conduct of one of the parties or of some other person.

**indenture.** Indentures were deeds which originally were made in two parts formed by cutting or tearing a single sheet across the middle in a jagged or indented line, so that the two parts might be subsequently matched; and they were executed by both grantor and grantee. Later the indenting of the deed was discontinued, yet the term came to be applied to all deeds which were executed by both parties.

**independent contractor.** One who, exercising an independent employment, contracts to do a piece of work according to his or her own methods, and without being subject to the control of the employer except as to result. The legal effect is to insulate the employing party from liability for the misconduct of the independent contractor and his employees.

**indictment.** An accusation founded on legal testimony of a direct and positive character, and the concurring judgment of at least 12 of the grand jurors that upon the evidence presented to them the defendant is guilty.

**indorsement.** Writing on the back of an instrument; the contract whereby the holder of a bill or note transfers to another person his right to such instrument and incurs the liabilities incident to the transfer.

**infant.** See **minor.**

**information.** A written accusation of crime brought by a public prosecuting officer to a court without the intervention of a grand jury.

**injunction.** A restraining order issued by a court of equity; a prohibitory writ restraining a person from committing or doing an act, other than a criminal act, which appears to be against equity and conscience. There is also the mandatory injunction which commands an act to be done or undone and compels the performance of some affirmative act.

**insolvency.** The word has two distinct meanings. It may be used to denote the insufficiency of the entire property and assets of an individual to pay his or her debts, which is its general meaning and its meaning as used in the Bankruptcy Act; but in a more restricted sense, it expresses the inability of a party to pay his debts as they become due in the regular course of his business, and it is so used when traders and merchants are said to be insolvent.

**instrument.** In its broadest sense, the term includes formal or legal documents in writing, such as contracts, deeds, wills, bonds, leases, and mortgages. In the law of evidence it has still a wider meaning and includes not merely documents, but witnesses and things animate and inanimate which may be presented for inspection.

**insurable interest.** Any interest in property the owner of which interest derives a benefit from the existance of the property or would suffer a loss from its destruction. It is not necessary, to constitute an insurable interest, that the interest is such that the event insured against would necessarily subject the insured to loss; it is sufficient that it might do so.

**inter alia.** Among other things or matters.

**interlocutory.** Something not final but deciding only some subsidiary matter raised while a law suit is pending.

**interpleader.** An equitable remedy applicable where one fears injury from conflicting claims. Where a person does not know which of two or more persons claiming certain property held by him or her has a right to it, filing a bill of interpleader forces the claimants to litigate the title between themselves.

**inter se.** Among themselves.

**intervention.** A proceeding by which one not originally made a party to an action or suit is permitted, on his own application, to appear therein and join one of the original parties in maintaining his cause of action or defense, or to assert some cause of action against some or all of the parties to the proceeding as originally instituted.

**intestate.** A person who has died without leaving a valid will disposing of his or her property and estate.

**ipso facto.** By the fact itself; by the very fact; by the act itself.

**joint bank account.** A bank account of two persons so fixed that they shall be joint owners thereof during their mutual lives, and the survivor shall take the whole on the death of other.

**joint tenancy.** An estate held by two or more jointly, with an equal right in all to share in the enjoyments of the land during their lives. Four requisites must exist to constitute a joint tenancy, viz: the tenants must have one and the same interest; the interest must accrue by one and the same conveyance; they must commence at one and the same time; and the property must be held by one and the same undivided possession. If any one of these four elements is lacking, the estate will not be one of joint tenancy. An incident of joint tenancy is the right of survivorship.

**jointly.** Acting together or in concert or cooperating; holding in common or interdependently, not separately. Persons are "jointly bound" in a bond or note when both or all must be sued in one action for its enforcement, not either one at the election of the creditor.

**jointly and severally.** Persons who find themselves "jointly and severally" in a bond or note may all be sued together for its enforcement, or the creditor may select any one or more as the object of his suit.

**judgment.** The sentence of the law upon the record; the application of the law to the facts and pleadings. The last word in the judicial controversy; the final consideration and determination of a court of competent jurisdiction upon matters submitted to it in an action or proceeding.

**judgment lien.** The statutory lien upon the real property of a judgment debtor which is created by the judgment itself. At common law a judgment imposes no lien upon the real property of the judgment debtor, and to subject the property of the debtor to the judgment it was necessary to take out a writ called an elegit.

**judgment n.o.v. (judgment non obstante veredicto).** Judgment notwithstanding the verdict. Under certain circumstances the judge has the power to enter a judgment which is contrary to the verdict of the jury. Such a judgment is a judgment non obstante veredicto.

**jurisdiction.** The right to adjudicate concerning the subject matter in a given case. The modern tendency is to make the word include not only the power to hear and determine, but also the power to render the particular judgment in the particular case.

**jury.** A body of lay persons, selected by lot, or by some other fair and impartial means, to ascertain, under the guidance of the judge, the truth in questions of fact arising either in civil litigation or a criminal process.

**kite.** To secure the temporary use of money by issuing or negotiating worthless paper and then redeeming such paper with the proceeds of similar paper. The word is also used as a noun, meaning the worthless paper thus employed.

**laches.** The established doctrine of equity that, apart from any question of statutory limitation, its courts will discourage delay and sloth in the enforcement of rights. Equity demands conscience, good faith, and reasonable diligence.

**law merchant.** The custom of merchants, or lex mercatorio, which grew out of the necessity and convenience of business, and which, although different from the general rules of the common law, was engrafted into it and became a part of it. It was founded on the custom and usage of merchants.

**leading case.** A case often referred to by the courts and by counsel as having settled and determined a point of law.

**leading questions.** Those questions which suggest to the witness the answer desired, those which assume a fact to be proved which is not proved, or which, embodying a material fact, admit of an answer by a simple negative or affirmative.

**lease.** A contract for the possession and use of land on one side, and a recompense of rent or other income on the other, a conveyance to a person for life, or years, or at will in consideration of a return of rent or other recompense.

**legacy.** A bequest; a testamentary gift of personal property. Sometimes incorrectly applied to a testamentary gift of real property.

**legal.** According to the principles of law; according to the method required by statute; by means of judicial proceedings; not equitable.

**legitimacy.** A person's status embracing his right to inherit from his ancestors, to be inherited from, and to bear the name and enjoy the support of his father.

**letter of credit.** An instrument containing a request (general or special) to pay to the bearer or person named money, or sell him or her some commodity on credit or give something of value and look to the drawer of the letter for recompense.

**levy.** At common law a levy on goods consisted of an officer's entering the premises where they were and either leaving an assistant in charge of them or removing them after taking an inventory. Today courts differ as to what is a valid levy, but by the weight of authority there must be an actual or constructive seizure of the goods. In most states, a levy on land must be made by some unequivocal act of the officer indicating the intention of singling out certain real estate for the satisfaction of the debt.

**license.** A personal privilege to do some act or series of acts upon the land of another, without possessing any estate therein. A permit or authorization to do what, without a license, would be unlawful.

**lien.** In its most extensive meaning it is a charge upon property for the payment or discharge of a debt or duty; a qualified right; a proprietary interest which, in a given case, may be exercised over the property of another.

**life estate.** See **estate for life.**

**lis pendens.** A pending suit. As applied to the doctrine of lis pendens it is the jurisdiction, power, or control which courts acquire over property involved in a suit, pending the continuance of the action, and until its final judgment therein.

**listing contract.** A so-called contract whereby an owner of real property employs a broker to procure a purchaser without giving the broker an exclusive right to sell. Under such an agreement, it is generally held that the employment may be terminated by the owner at will, and that a sale of the property by the owner terminates the employment.

**litigant.** A party to a lawsuit.

**long arm statute.** A statute subjecting a foreign corporation to jurisdiction although it may have committed only a single act within the state.

**magistrate.** A word commonly applied to the lower judicial officers, such as justices of the peace, police judges, town recorders, and other local judicial functionaries. In a broader sense, a magistrate is a public civil officer invested with some part of the legislative, executive, or judicial power given by the Constitution. The President of the United States is the chief magistrate of the nation.

**maker.** A person who makes or executes an instrument, the signer of an instrument.

**mala fides.** Bad faith.

**malfeasance.** The doing of an act which a person ought not to do at all. It is to be distinguished from misfeasance, which is the improper doing of an act which a person might lawfully do.

**malum in se.** Evil in and of itself. An offense or act which is naturally evil as adjudged by the senses of a civilized community. Acts malum in se are usually criminal acts, but not necessarily so.

**malum prohibitum.** An act which is wrong because it is made so by statute.

**mandamus.** We command. It is a command issuing from a competent jurisdiction, in the name of the state or sovereign, directed to some inferior court, officer, corporation, or person, requiring the performance of a particular duty therein specified, which duty results from the official station of the party to whom it is directed, or from operation of law.

**margin.** A deposit by a buyer in stocks with a seller or a stockbroker, as security to cover fluctuations in the market in reference to stocks which the buyer has purchased, but for which he has not paid. Commodities are also traded on margin.

**marshals.** Ministerial officers belonging to the executive department of the federal government, who with their deputies have the same powers of executing the laws of the United States in each state as the sheriffs and their deputies in such state may have in executing the laws of that state.

**mechanic's lien.** A claim created by law for the purpose of securing a priority of payment of the price of value of work performed and materials furnished in erecting or repairing a building or other structure; as such it attaches to the land as well as to the buildings erected therein.

**mens rea.** A guilty mind, criminal intent.

**merchantable.** Of good quality and salable, but not necessarily the best. As applied to articles sold, the word requires that the article shall be such as is usually sold in the market, of medium quality and bringing the average price.

**minor.** A person who has not reached the age at which the law recognizes a general contractual capacity (called majority), formerly 21 years; recently changed to 18 in many states.

**misdemeanor.** Any crime which is punishable neither by death nor by imprisonment in a state prison.

**mistrial.** An invalid trial due to lack of jurisdiction, error in selection of jurors or some other fundamental requirement.

**mitigation of damages.** A reduction in the amount of damages due to extenuating circumstances.

**moiety.** One half.

**mortgage.** A conveyance of property to secure the performance of some obligation, the conveyance to be void on the due performance thereof.

**motive.** The cause or reason that induced a person to commit a crime.

**movables.** A word derived from the civil law and usually understood to signify the utensils which are to furnish or ornament a house, but it would seem to comprehend personal property generally.

**mutuality.** Reciprocal obligations of the parties required to make a contract binding on either party.

**necessaries.** With reference to a minor, the word includes whatever is reasonably necessary for his or her proper and suitable maintenance, in view of the income level and social position of the minor's family.

**negligence.** The word has been defined as the omission to do something which a reasonable man, guided by those considerations which ordinarily regulate human affairs, would do, or doing something which a prudent and reasonable man would not do.

**negotiable.** Capable of being transferred by indorsement or delivery so as to give the holder a right to sue in his or her own name and to avoid certain defenses against the payee.

**negotiable instrument.** An instrument which may be transferred or negotiated, so that the holder may maintain an action thereon in his own name.

**no arrival, no sale.** A sale of goods "to arrive" or "on arrival," per or ex a certain ship, has been construed to be a sale subject to a double condition precedent, namely, that the ship arrives in port and that when it arrives the goods are on board, and if either of these conditions fails, the contract becomes nugatory.

**nolo contendere.** A plea in a criminal action which has the same effect as a guilty plea except that it does not bind the defendant in a civil suit on the same wrong.

**nominal damages.** Damages which are recoverable where a legal right is to be vindicated against an invasion that has produced no actual present loss of any kind, or where there has been a breach of a contract and no actual damages whatever have been or can be shown, or where, under like conditions, there has been a breach of legal duty.

**non compos mentis.** Totally and positively incompetent. The term denotes a person entirely destitute or bereft of his memory or understanding.

**non obstante veredicto.** See **judgment non obstante veredicto.**

**nonfeasance.** In the law of agency, it is the total omission or failure of an agent to enter upon the performance of some distinct duty or undertaking which he or she has agreed with the principal to do.

**nonsuit.** A judgment given against a plaintiff who is unable to prove a case, or when the plaintiff refuses or neglects to proceedto trial.

**no-par value stock.** Stock of a corporation having no face or par value.

**noting protest.** The act of making a memorandum on a bill or note at the time of, and embracing the principal facts attending, its dishonor. The object is to have a record from which the instrument of protest may be written, so that a notary need not rely on his memory for the fact.

**novation.** A mutual agreement, between all parties concerned, for the discharge of a valid existing obligation by the substitution of a new valid obligation on the part of the debtor or another, or a like agreement for the discharge of a debtor to his creditor by the substitution of a new creditor.

**nudum pactum.** A naked promise, a promise for which there is no consideration.

**nuisance.** In legal parlance, the word extends to everything that endangers life or health, gives offense to the senses, violates the laws of decency, or obstructs the reasonable and comfortable use of property.

**oath.** Any form of attestation by which a person signifies that he is bound in conscience to perform an act faithfully and truthfully. It involves the idea of calling on God to witness what is averred as truth, and it is supposed to be accompanied with an invocation of His vengeance, or a renunciation of His favor, in the event of falsehood.

**obiter dictum.** That which is said in passing; a rule of law set forth in a court's opinion, but not necessary to decide the case.

**objection.** In the trial of a case it is the formal remonstrance made by counsel to something which has been said or done, in order to obtain the court's ruling thereon; and when the court has ruled, the alleged error is preserved by the objector's exception to the ruling, which exception is noted in the record.

**obligee.** A person to whom another is bound by a promise or other obligation; a promisee.

**obligor.** A person who is bound by a promise or other obligation; a promisor.

**offer.** A proposal by one person to another which is intended of itself to create legal relations on acceptance by the person to whom it is made.

**offeree.** A person to whom an offer is made.

**offeror.** A person who makes an offer.

**opinion.** The opinion of the court represents merely the reasons for its judgment, while the decision of the court is the judgment itself.

**option.** A contract whereby the owner of property agrees with another person that such person shall have the right to buy the property at a fixed price within a certain time. There are two independent elements in an option contract: First, the offer to sell, which does not become a contract until accepted; second, the completed contract to leave the offer open for a specified time.

**ordinance.** A legislative enactment of a county or an incorporated city or town.

**ostensible authority.** Such authority as a principal, either intentionally or by want of ordinary care, causes or allows a third person to believe the agent to possess.

**ostensible partners.** Members of a partnership whose names are made known and appear to the world as partners.

**overdraft.** The withdrawal from a bank by a depositor of money in excess of the amount of money he or she has on deposit there.

**overplus.** That which remains; a balance left over.

**owner's risk.** A term employed by common carriers in bills of lading and shipping receipts to signify that the carrier does not assume responsibility for the safety of the goods.

**par.** Par means equal, and par value means a value equal to the face of a bond or a stock certificate.

**parol.** Oral; verbal; by word of mouth; spoken as opposed to written.

**parties.** All persons who are interested in the subject matter of an action and who have a right to make defense, control the proceedings, examine and cross-examine witnesses, and appeal from the judgment.

**partition.** A proceeding the object of which is to enable those who own property as joint tenants or tenants in common, to put an end to the tenancy so as to vest in each a sole estate in specific property or an allotment of the lands and tenements. If a division of the estate is impracticable the estate ought to be sold, and the proceeds divided.

**partners.** Those persons who contribute property, money, or services to carry on a joint business for their common benefit, and who own and share the profits thereof in certain proportions; the members of a partnership.

**patent.** A patent for land is a conveyance of title to government lands by the government; a patent of an invention is the right of monopoly secured by statute to those who invent or discover new and useful devices and processes.

**pawn.** A pledge; a bailment of personal property as security for some debt or engagement, redeemable on certain terms, and with an implied power of sale on default.

**payee.** A person to whom a payment is made or is made payable.

**pecuniary.** Financial; pertaining or relating to money; capable of being estimated, computed, or measured by money value.

**pendente lite.** During the litigation.

**per curiam.** By the court; by the court as a whole.

**per se.** The expression means by or through itself; simply, as such; in its own relations.

**peremptory challenge.** A challenge to a proposed juror which a defendant in a criminal case may make as an absolute right, and which cannot be questioned by either opposing counsel or the court.

**performance.** As the word implies, it is such a thorough fulfillment of a duty as puts an end to obligations by leaving nothing to be done. The chief requisite of performance is that it shall be exact.

**perjury.** The willful and corrupt false swearing or affirming, after an oath lawfully administered, in the course of a judicial or quasi judicial proceeding as to some matter material to the issue or point in question.

**petition.** In equity pleading, a petition is in the nature of a pleading (at least when filed by a stranger to the suit) and forms a basis for independent action.

**plaintiff.** A person who brings a suit, action, bill, or complaint.

**plaintiff in error.** The unsuccessful party to the action who prosecutes a writ of error in a higher court.

**plea.** A plea is an answer to a declaration or complaint or any material allegation of fact therein which if untrue would defeat the action. In criminal procedure, a plea is the matter which the accused, on his arraignment, alleges in answer to the charge against him.

**pledge.** A pawn; a bailment of personal property as security for some debt or engagement, redeemable on certain terms, and with an implied power of sale on default.

**pledgee.** A person to whom personal property is pledged by a pledgor.

**pledgor.** A person who makes a pledge of personal property to a pledgee.

**positive law.** Laws actually and specifically enacted or adopted by proper authority for the government of a jural society as distinguished from principles of morality or laws of honor.

**possession.** Respecting real property, possession involves exclusive dominion and control such as owners of like property usually exercise over it. Manual control of personal property either as owner or as one having a qualified right in it.

**power of attorney.** A written authorization to an agent to perform specified acts on behalf of his or her principal. The writing by which the authority is evidenced is termed a letter of attorney and is dictated by the convenience and certainty of business.

**precedent.** A previous decision relied upon as authority.

**preference.** The act of a debtor in paying or securing one or more of his creditors in a manner more favorable to them than to other creditors or to the exclusion of such other creditors. In the absence of statute, a preference is perfectly good, but to be legal it must be bona fide, and not a mere subterfuge of the debtor to secure a future benefit to himself or to prevent the application of his property to his debts.

**prerogative.** A special power, privilege, or immunity, usually used in reference to an official or his office.

**presumption.** A term used to signify that which may be assumed without proof, or taken for granted. It is asserted as a self-evident result of human reason and experience.

**prima facie.** At first sight; a fact that is presumed to be true unless disproved by contrary evidence.

**privilege.** A right peculiar to an individual or body.

**privity.** A mutual or successive relationship as, for example, between the parties to a contract.

**pro rata.** According to the rate, proportion, or allowance.

**pro tanto.** For so much; to such an extent.

**probate.** A term used to include all matters of which probate courts have jurisdiction, which in many states are the estates of deceased persons and of persons under guardianship.

**process.** In law, generally the summons or notice of beginning of suit.

**proffer.** To offer for acceptance or to make a tender of.

**promisee.** The person to whom a promise is made.

**promisor.** A person who makes a promise to another; a person who promises.

**promissory estoppel.** An estoppel arising on account of a promise that the promissor should expect to and which does induce an action or forbearance of a substantial nature.

**promoters.** The persons who bring about the incorporation and organization of a corporation.

**prospectus.** An introductory proposal for a contract in which the representations may or may not form the basis of the contract actually made; it may contain promises which are to be treated as a sort of floating obligation to take effect when appropriated by persons to whom they are addressed, and amount to a contract when assented to by any person who invests his money on the faith of them.

**proximate cause.** That cause of an injury which, in natural and continuous sequence, unbroken by any efficient intervening cause, produces the injury, and without which the injury would not have occurred.

**qualified acceptance.** A conditional or modified acceptance. In order to create a contract an acceptance must accept the offer substantially as made; hence a qualified acceptance is no acceptance at all, is treated by the courts as a rejection of the offer made, and is in effect an offer by the offeree, which the offeror may, if he chooses, accept and thus create a contract.

**quantum meruit.** As much as is deserved. A part of a common law action in assumpsit for the value of services rendered.

**quash.** To vacate or make void.

**quasi contract.** An obligation arising not from an agreement between the parties but from the voluntary act of one of them or some relation between them which will be enforced by a court.

**quasi judicial.** Acts of public officers involving investigation of facts and drawing conclusions from them as a basis of official action.

**quiet title, action to.** An action to establish a claimant's title in land by requiring adverse claimants to come into court to prove their claim or to be barred from asserting it later.

**quitclaim deed.** A deed conveying only the right, title, and interest of the grantor in the property described, as distinguished from a deed conveying the property itself.

**quo warranto.** By what authority. The name of a writ (and also of the whole pleading) by which the government commences an action to recover an office or franchise from the person or corporation in possession of it.

**quorum.** That number of persons, shares represented, or officers who may lawfully transact the business of a meeting called for that purpose.

**ratification.** The adoption or affirmance by a person of a prior act that did not bind him.

**rebuttal.** Testimony addressed to evidence produced by the opposite party; rebutting evidence.

**receiver.** One appointed by a court to take charge of a business or the property of another during litigation to preserve it and/or to dispose of it as directed by the court.

**recognizance.** At common law, an obligation entered into before some court of record or magistrate duly authorized, with a condition to do some particular act, usually to appear and answer to a criminal accusation. Being taken in open court and entered upon the order book, it was valid without the signature or seal of any of the obligors.

**recorder.** A public officer of a town or county charged with the duty of keeping the record books required by law to be kept in his or her office and of receiving and causing to be copied in such books such instruments as by law are entitled to be recorded.

**redemption.** The buying back of one's property after it has been sold. The right to redeem property sold under an order or decree of court is purely a privilege conferred by, and does not exist independently of, statute.

**redress.** Remedy; indemnity; reparation.

**release.** The giving up or abandoning of a claim or right to a person against whom the claim exists or the rights is to be enforced or exercised. It is the discharge of a debt by the act of the party in distinction from an extinguishment which is a discharge by operation of law.

**remainderman.** One who is entitled to the remainder of the estate after a particular estate carved out of it has expired.

**remand.** An action of an appellate court returning a case to the trial court to take further action.

**remedy.** The appropriate legal form of relief by which a remediable right may be enforced.

**remittitur.** The certificate of reversal issued by an appellate court upon reversing the order or judgment appealed from.

**replevin.** A common-law action by which the owner recovers possession of his own goods.

**res.** The thing; the subject matter of a suit; the property involved in the litigation; a matter; property; the business; the affair; the transaction.

**res adjudicata.** A matter which has been adjudicated; that which is definitely settled by a judicial decision.

**rescind.** As the word is applied to contracts, to rescind in some cases means to terminate the contract as to future transactions, while in others it means to annul the contract from the beginning.

**residue.** All that portion of the estate of a testator of which no effectual disposition has been made by his will otherwise than in the residuary clause.

**respondent.** The defendant in an action; a party adverse to an appellant in an action which is appealed to a higher court. The person against whom a bill in equity was exhibited.

**restitution.** Indemnification.

**reversion.** The residue of a fee simple remaining in the grantor, to commence in possession after the determination of some particular estate granted out by him. The estate of a landlord during the existence of the outstanding leasehold estate.

**reversioner.** A person who is entitled to a reversion.

**right.** When we speak of a person having a right, we must necessarily refer to a civil right as distinguished from the elemental idea of a right absolute. We must have in mind a right given and protected by law, and a person's enjoyment thereof is regulated entirely by the law which creates it.

**riparian.** Pertaining to or situated on the bank of a river. The word has reference to the bank and not to the bed of the stream.

**sanction.** The penalty that will be incurred by a wrongdoer for the breach of law.

**satisfaction.** A performance of the terms of an accord. If such terms require a payment of a sum of money, then "satisfaction" means that such payment has been made.

**scienter.** In cases of fraud and deceit, the word means knowledge on the part of the person making the representations, at the time when they are made, that they are false. In an action for deceit it is generally held that scienter must be proved.

**seal.** At common law, a seal is an impression on wax or some other tenacious material, but in modern practice the letters "l.s." (locus sigilli) or the word "seal" enclosed in a scroll, either written, or printed, and acknowledged in the body of the instrument to be a seal, are often used as substitutes.

**security.** That which makes the enforcement of a promise more certain that the mere personal obligation of the debtor or promisor, whatever may be his possessions or financial standing. It may be a pledge of property or an additional personal obligation; but it means more than the mere promise of the debtor with property liable to general execution.

**security agreement.** An agreement which creates or provides a security interest or lien on personal property. A term used in the U.C.C. including a wide range of transactions in the nature of chattel mortgages, conditional sales, etc.

**seizin.** In a legal sense, the word means possession of premises with the intention of asserting a claim to a freehold estate therein; it is practically the same thing as ownership; it is a possession of a freehold estate, such as by the common law is created by livery of seizin.

**service.** As applied to a process of courts, the word ordinarily implies something in the nature of an act or proceeding adverse to the party served, or of a notice to him.

**setoff.** A setoff both at law and in equity is that right which exists between two parties, each of whom, under an independent contract, owes an ascertained amount to the other, to set off their respective debts by way of mutual deduction, so that, in any action brought for the larger debt, the residue only, after such deduction, shall be recovered.

**severable contract.** A contract which is not entire or indivisible. If the consideration is single, the contract is entire; but if it is expressly or by necessary implication apportioned, the contract is severable. The question is ordinarily determined by inquiring whether the contract embraces one or more subject matters, whether the obligation is due at the same time to the same person, and whether the consideration is entire or apportioned.

**share of stock.** The right which its owner has in the management, profits and ultimate assets of the corporation. The tangible property of a corporation and the shares of stock therein are separate and distinct kinds of property and belong to different owners, the first being the property of an artificial person—the corporation—the latter the property of the individual owner.

**shareholder.** It is generally held that one who holds shares on the books of the corporation is a shareholder and that one who merely holds a stock certificate is not. Shareholders may become such either by original subscription, by direct purchase from the corporation, or by subsequent transfer from the original holder.

**sight.** A term signifying the date of the acceptance or that of protest for the nonacceptance of a bill of exchange; for example, ten days after sight.

**sinking fund.** A fund accumulated by an issuer to redeem corporate securities.

**situs.** Location; local position; the place where a person or thing is, is his situs. Intangible property has no actual situs, but it may have a legal situs, and for the purpose of taxation its legal situs is at the place where it is owned and not at the place where it is owed.

**specific performance.** Performance of a contract precisely as agreed upon; the remedy that arose in equity law to compel the defendant to do what he agreed to do.

**stare decisis.** The doctrine or principle that the decisions of the court should stand as precedents for future guidance.

**stated capital.** Defined specifically in the Model Business Corporation Act; generally, the amount received by a corporation upon issuance of its shares except that assigned to capital surplus.

**status quo.** The existing state of things.

**stipulation.** An agreement between opposing counsel in a pending action, usually required to be made in open court and entered on the minutes of the court, or else to be in writing and filed in the action, ordinarily entered into for the purpose of avoiding delay, trouble, or expense in the conduct of the action.

**stockholder.** See **shareholder.**

**stoppage in transitu.** A right which the vendor of goods on credit has to recall them, or retake them, on the discovery of the insolvency of the vendee. It continues so long as the carrier remains in the possession and control of the goods or until there has been an actual or constructive delivery to the vendee, or some third person has acquired a bona fide right in them.

**sub judice.** Before a court.

**sub nom.** Under the name.

**subpoena.** A process the purpose of which is to

compel the attendance of a person whom it is desired to use as a witness.

**subrogation.** The substitution of one person in the place of another with reference to a lawful claim or right, frequently referred to as the doctrine of substitution. It is a device adopted or invented by equity to compel the ultimate discharge of a debt or obligation by the person who in good conscience ought to pay it.

**sui generis.** Of its own kind; peculiar to itself.

**summary judgment.** A decision of a trial court without hearing evidence.

**summary proceedings.** Proceedings, usually statutory, in the course of which many formalities are dispensed with. But such proceedings are not concluded without proper investigation of the facts, or without notice, or an opportunity to be heard by the person alleged to have committed the act, or whose property is sought to be affected.

**summons.** A writ or process issued and served upon a defendant in a civil action for the purpose of securing his appearance in the action.

**supra.** Above; above mentioned; in addition to.

**surety.** One who by accessory agreement called a contract of suretyship binds himself with another, called the principal, for the performance of an obligation in respect to which such other person is already bound and primarily liable for such performance.

**T/A.** Trading as, indicating the use of a trade name.

**tacking.** The adding together of successive periods of adverse possession of persons in privity with each other, in order to constitute one continuous adverse possession for the time required by the statute, to establish title.

**tangible.** Capable of being possessed or realized; readily apprehensible by the mind; real; substantial; evident.

**tenancy.** A tenancy exists when one has let real estate to another to hold of him as landlord. When duly created and the tenant put into possession, he is the owner of an estate for the time being, and has all the usual rights and remedies to defend his possession.

**tender.** An unconditional offer of payment, consisting in the actual production in money or legal tender of a sum not less than the amount due.

**tender offer.** An offer to security holders to acquire their securities in exchange for money or other securities.

**tenement.** A word commonly used in deeds which passes not only lands and other inheritances but also offices, rents, commons, and profits arising from lands. Usually it is applied exclusively to land, or what is ordinarily denominated real property.

**tenor.** The tenor of an instrument is an exact copy of the instrument. Under the rule that an indictment for forgery must set out in the instrument according to its "tenor," the word means an exact copy—that the instrument is set forth in the very words and figures.

**tenure.** The manner of holding or occupying lands or offices. The most common estate in land is tenure in "fee simple." With respect to offices tenure imports time, e.g., "tenure for life" or "during good behavior."

**testament.** A last will and testament is the disposition of one's property to take effect after death.

**testator.** A deceased person who died leaving a will.

**testatrix.** Feminine of testator.

**testimony.** In some contexts the word bears the same import as the word "evidence," but in most connections it has a much narrower meaning. Testimony is the words heard from the witness in court, and evidence is what the jury considers it worth.

**tort.** An injury or wrong committed, either with or without force, to the person or property of another. Such injury may arise by nonfeasance, or by the malfeasance or the misfeasance of the wrongdoer.

**tort-feasor.** A person who commits a tort; a wrongdoer.

**tortious.** Partaking of the nature of a tort; wrongful; injurious.

**trade fixtures.** Articles of personal property

which have been annexed to the freehold and which are necessary to the carrying on of a trade.

**transcript.** A copy of a writing.

**transferee.** A person to whom a transfer is made.

**transferor.** A person who makes a transfer.

**treasury shares.** Shares of stock of a corporation which have been issued as fully paid to shareholders and subsequently acquired by the corporation.

**treble damages.** Three times provable damages, as may be granted to private parties bringing an action under the antitrust laws.

**trespass.** Every unauthorized entry on another's property is a trespass and any person who makes such an entry is a trespasser. In its widest signification, trespass means any violation of law. In its most restricted sense, it signifies an injury intentionally inflicted by force either on the person or property of another.

**trial.** An examination before a competent tribunal, according to the law of the land, of the facts or law put in issue in a cause, for the purpose of determining such issue. When the court hears and determines any issue of fact or law for the purpose of determining the rights of the parties, it may be considered a trial.

**trover.** A common-law action for damages due to a conversion of personal property.

**trust.** A confidence reposed in one person, who is termed trustee, for the benefit of another, who is called the cestui que trust, respecting property, which is held by the trustee for the benefit of the cestui que trust. As the word is used in the law pertaining to unlawful combinations and monopolies, a trust in its original and typical form is a combination formed by an agreement among the shareholders in a number of competing corporations to transfer their shares to an unincorporated board of trustees, and to receive in exchange trust certificates in some agreed proportion to their shareholdings.

**trustee.** A person in whom property is vested in trust for another.

**trustee in bankruptcy.** The federal bankruptcy act defines the term as an officer, and he is an officer of the courts in a certain restricted sense, but not in any such sense as a receiver. He takes the legal title to the property of the bankrupt and in respect to suits stands in the same general position as a trustee of an express trust or an executor. His duties are fixed by statute. He is to collect and reduce to money the property of the estate of the bankrupt.

**ultra vires act.** An act of a corporation which is beyond the powers conferred upon the corporation.

**unilateral contract.** A contract formed by an offer or a promise on one side for an act to be done on the other, and a doing of the act by the other by way of acceptance of the offer or promise; that is, a contract wherein the only acceptance of the offer that is necessary is the performance of the act.

**unliquidated.** Undetermined in amount.

**usury.** The taking more than the law allows upon a loan or for forbearance of a debt. Illegal interest; interest in excess of the rate allowed by law.

**utter.** As applied to counterfeiting, to utter and publish is to declare or assert, directly or indirectly, by words or action, that the money or note is good. Thus to offer it in payment is an uttering or publishing.

**valid.** Effective; operative; not void; subsisting; sufficient in law.

**vendee.** A purchaser of property. The word is more commonly applied to a purchaser of real property, the word "buyer" being more commonly applied to the purchaser of personal property.

**vendor.** A person who sells property to a vendee. The words "vendor" and "vendee" are more commonly applied to the seller and purchaser of real estate, and the words "seller" and "buyer" are more commonly applied to the seller and purchaser of personal property.

**venire.** The name of a writ by which a jury is summoned.

**venue.** The word originally was employed to indicate the county from which the jurors were to come who were to try a case, but in modern times it refers to the county in which a case is to be tried.

**verdict.** The answer of a jury given to the court concerning the matters of fact committed to their trial and examination; it makes no precedent, and settles nothing but the present controversy to which it relates. It is the decision made by the jury and reported to the court, and as such it is an elemental entity which cannot be divided by the judge.

**verification.** The affidavit of a party annexed to his pleadings which states that the pleading is true of his own knowledge except as to matters which are therein stated on his information or belief, and as to those matters, that he believes it to be true. A sworn statement of the truth of the facts stated in the instrument verified.

**versus.** Against.

**vest.** To give an immediate fixed right of present or future enjoyment.

**void.** That which is entirely null. A void act is one which is not binding on either party, and which is not susceptible of ratification.

**voidable.** Capable of being made void; not utterly null, but annullable, and hence that may be either voided or confirmed.

**waive.** To throw away; to relinquish voluntarily, as a right which one may enforce, if he chooses.

**waiver.** The intentional relinquishment of a known right. It is a voluntary act and implies an election by the party to dispense with something of value, or to forego some advantage which he or she might have demanded and insisted on.

**warrant.** An order authorizing a payment of money by another person to a third person. Also an option to purchase a security. As a verb, the word means to defend; to guarantee; to enter into an obligation of warranty.

**warrant of arrest.** A legal process issued by competent authority, usually directed to regular officers of the law, but occasionally issued to private persons named in it, directing the arrest of a person or persons upon grounds stated therein.

**warranty.** In the sale of a commodity, an undertaking by the seller to answer for the defects therein is construed as a warranty. In a contract of insurance, as a general rule, any statement or description, or any undertaking on the part of the insured on the face of the policy or in another instrument properly incorporated in the policy, which relates to the risk, is a warranty.

**waste.** The material alteration, abuse, or destructive use of property by one in rightful possession of it which results in injury to one having an underlying interest in it.

**watered stock.** Stock issued by a corporation as fully paid up, when in fact it is not fully paid up.

**writ.** A commandment of a court given for the purpose of compelling a defendant to take certain action, usually directed to a sheriff or other officer to execute it.

**writ of certiorari.** An order of a court to an inferior court to forward the record of a case for reexamination by the superior court.

# CASE INDEX

## V



## W



## Y-Z

## SUBJECT INDEX

### A

## B



## C

## D



## E

## F

## Q-R



## S

## V



## W-Z



*This book has been set VideoComp in 10 and 9 point Century Schoolbook, leaded 2 points. Part and chapter numbers and titles are in Cheltenham Bold Condensed. Part and chapter numbers are 24 and 60 point, part titles are 36 point, and chapter titles are 30 point. The size of the type page is 37 by 48 picas.*